STATS™ 1993 Player Profiles

STATS, Inc.

STATS PUBLISHING

Published by STATS Publishing
A division of Sports Team Analysis & Tracking Systems, Inc.
Dr. Richard Cramer, Chairman • John Dewan, President

Cover by John Grimwade, New York, NY

First Edition: November, 1992

Printed in the United States of America

ISBN 0-9625581-9-2

This book is dedicated to Bill James.

He lit the way.

Acknowledgments

If the numbers you find in this book sometimes seem overwhelming, then so too does all the work that goes into producing them. That is because the STATS staff works at producing all these numbers each and every day of the baseball season. At the end of every day during the season, the STATS' staff works into the wee hours of the morning to crunch out all these and many more statistics, and that is no small task. Certainly we have some help from our computers but there is much more than number crunching that goes into producing these numbers. We need to coordinate a team of knowledgeable and trained reporters to cover the games. We need to continually check and recheck the accuracy and consistency of our information. We need our systems experts to develop and maintain the programs that tell the computers how to manage all that information. And, of course, we need a team of people who pull all that information into the readable format you find in this book. It is clear that this book is the product of everyone here at STATS, Inc.

Dr. Richard Cramer is the Chairman and founder of STATS, as well as the brains behind the computer system which manages all this information.

John Dewan, President and CEO, envisioned this book, developed its format and was responsible for making this first edition a reality.

Allan Spear along with Steve Moyer handled the overall administration of the book. This required lots of extra co-ordination to insure that the book was hot off the presses on November 1st. Steve Moyer also manages the reporter network.

Bob Mecca played a key role in developing the layout of the profiles and along with Rob McQuown programmed the computers to show us just what we wanted to know. Bob also manages the project of verifying the accuracy of our information.

Thanks to the rest of the STATS staff whose work every day during the baseball season made this book possible. They include:

Art Ashley, Vice President and manager of our programming staff and computer system.

Ross Schaufelberger who manages our fantasy operations, football operations and advertising among the many other projects in which he is involved.

Other baseball experts behind the scenes include Jules Aquino, Michael Canter,

Michael Coulter, Chuck Miller and Jim Musso. They are part of the knowledgeable staff that made sure the baseball operation ran smoothly. This included ensuring the timeliness and accuracy of over 2000 game accounts, running the fantasy leagues and developing new programs as part of our computer system, among many other jobs.

Alissa Hudson, Marge Morra, Suzette Neily and Deb Pokres keep the administrative side of the office running smoothly.

David Pinto brings STATS' information into your living room through his daily support of the ESPN broadcasts. Don Zminda's handiwork can be seen in other upcoming publications: **The Scouting Report: 1993** and **STATS Baseball Scoreboard: 1993**. Craig Wright continues to use his talents to oversee our Major League Operations.

This book is a tribute to these dedicated people who love the game of baseball.

— Sue Dewan, Vice-President

Table of Contents

Introduction

Welcome to the newest and biggest book from STATS, Inc!

Over the past few years, we have included a small sampling of these profiles in our annual Major League Handbooks. These generated a significant number of comments, so we decided to make a whole book of in-depth statistical information. We think you will find these statistical breakdowns as interesting as we do.

This is a reference book, pure and simple. We don't expect you to read it cover to cover, though some folks will. The purpose of this book is to put all the recently developed, newer statistics in one place. You can then find what you need on just about every player. Here are some of the statistics that are seeing the light of day in a comprehensive form for the first time:

For Pitchers:

Run Support
Pitches Thrown per Start
Groundball/Flyball Ratio
Effectiveness based on Days Rest
Pre- and Post-All Star Performance
Effectiveness based on Pitch Count
Holds and Save Opportunities
First Batter Efficiency
Performance at Pitch Counts

For Hitters:

Pitches per Plate Appearance
Groundball/Flyball Ratio
Performance vs. Groundball/Flyball Pitchers
Performance by Batting Position
Pre- and Post-All Star Performance
Performance at Pitch Counts

Of course, we're putting in all the other stats that have previously been in print, too.

Here's a few of the nuggets you might find here. Look at Dennis Eckersley. At home last season, he was a good reliever. On the road, he was almost totally unhittable, with an ERA under 1.00. Should Kirby Puckett be more patient at the plate? Well, maybe not. A quick check shows Kirby hit at a .440 clip when he swung at the first pitch last season.

Or, how about the very first page of this book. The first two Abbotts, Jim and Kyle, had records of 7-15 and 1-14 respectively. The most interesting stats that go along with those records are their run support numbers of 2.64 and 2.77 runs per nine innings pitched. Most teams average well over four runs a game. Those two run support stats explain the Abbotts' win-loss records far better than any other numbers on the page.

Take your time, peruse these pages, then astound your friends with your wealth of knowledge. Dissecting this book probably won't hurt your fantasy team either.

Don't forget to look at the glossary in the back. It will tell you what each number means.

Also, let us know what you think. We've got plenty more stats where these came from. If there's something you would like to see, drop us a line. Maybe next year we'll call the book the "1994 STATS and (your name here) Player Profiles."

— John Dewan

Jim Abbott — Angels

Pitches Left (groundball pitcher)

	ERA	W	L	Sv	G	GS	IP	BB	SO	Avg	H	2B	3B	HR	RBI	OBP	SLG	CG	ShO	Sup	QS	#P/S	SB	CS	GB	FB	G/F
1992 Season	2.77	7	15	0	29	29	211.0	68	130	.263	208	28	2	12	66	.323	.349	7	0	2.64	19	106	14	13	333	181	1.84
Career (1989-1992)	3.49	47	52	0	125	125	847.0	287	508	.268	866			55	310	.330	.365	20	4	4.01	78	102	70	39	1436	732	1.96

1992 Season

	ERA	W	L	Sv	G	GS	IP	H	HR	BB	SO		Avg	AB	H	2B	3B	HR	RBI	BB	SO	OBP	SLG
Home	3.32	2	8	0	13	13	95.0	107	6	28	56	vs. Left	.273	128	35	9	1	0	9	13	17	.343	.359
Away	2.33	5	7	0	16	16	116.0	101	6	40	74	vs. Right	.261	662	173	19	1	12	57	55	113	.320	.347
Day	2.11	1	3	0	7	7	47.0	40	3	8	32	Inning 1-6	.237	612	145	17	2	7	48	54	103	.300	.306
Night	2.96	6	12	0	22	22	164.0	168	9	60	98	Inning 7+	.354	178	63	11	0	5	18	14	27	.404	.500
Grass	3.19	5	13	0	24	24	172.0	177	11	58	98	None on	.263	452	119	16	1	5	5	41	75	.329	.336
Turf	0.92	2	2	0	5	5	39.0	31	1	10	32	Runners on	.263	338	89	12	1	7	61	27	55	.316	.367
April	1.80	1	3	0	5	5	35.0	35	0	9	23	Scoring Posn	.254	169	43	8	1	4	53	21	34	.333	.385
May	3.57	1	4	0	6	6	40.1	43	3	19	24	Close & Late	.363	91	33	5	0	3	11	8	12	.414	.516
June	3.49	2	2	0	5	5	38.2	44	2	11	24	None on/out	.300	210	63	8	1	3	3	13	30	.344	.390
July	2.70	0	2	0	3	3	20.0	20	1	3	17	vs. 1st Batr (relief)	.000	0	0	0	0	0	0	0	0	.000	.000
August	2.02	2	1	0	5	5	35.2	33	3	11	17	First Inning Pitched	.236	106	25	3	0	2	9	10	14	.308	.321
September/October	2.83	1	3	0	5	5	41.1	43	3	15	25	First 75 Pitches	.235	537	126	17	0	7	38	43	92	.293	.305
Starter	2.77	7	15	0	29	29	211.0	208	12	68	130	Pitch 76-90	.344	90	31	3	1	1	6	10	12	.416	.433
Reliever	0.00	0	0	0	0	0	0.0	0	0	0	0	Pitch 91-105	.293	75	22	5	1	1	14	10	12	.376	.427
0-3 Days Rest	0.00	0	0	0	0	0	0.0	0	0	0	0	Pitch 106+	.330	88	29	3	0	3	8	5	14	.366	.466
4 Days Rest	2.77	4	8	0	17	17	123.2	110	8	33	81	First Pitch	.344	122	42	4	0	4	10	2	0	.357	.475
5+ Days Rest	2.78	3	7	0	12	12	87.1	98	4	35	49	Ahead on Count	.170	359	61	10	1	0	23	0	121	.174	.203
Pre-All Star	2.96	4	11	0	19	19	134.0	133	6	42	88	Behind on Count	.335	176	59	9	0	4	18	34	0	.439	.455
Post-All Star	2.45	3	4	0	10	10	77.0	75	6	26	42	Two Strikes	.167	329	55	11	1	0	18	32	130	.245	.207

Career (1989-1992)

	ERA	W	L	Sv	G	GS	IP	H	HR	BB	SO		Avg	AB	H	2B	3B	HR	RBI	BB	SO	OBP	SLG
Home	3.78	19	27	0	62	62	421.2	455	31	129	241	vs. Left	.304	503	153	31	2	8	66	51	84	.368	.421
Away	3.20	28	25	0	63	63	425.1	411	24	158	267	vs. Right	.262	2723	713	94	9	47	244	236	424	.322	.355
Day	3.06	14	14	0	32	32	212.0	209	13	67	136	Inning 1-6	.261	2659	694	101	10	40	258	244	429	.324	.352
Night	3.63	33	38	0	93	93	635.0	657	42	220	372	Inning 7+	.303	567	172	24	1	15	52	43	79	.355	.429
Grass	3.47	38	41	0	104	104	706.0	715	49	233	422	None on	.270	1870	505	76	5	32	32	158	285	.331	.367
Turf	3.57	9	11	0	21	21	141.0	151	6	54	86	Runners on	.266	1356	361	49	6	23	278	129	223	.328	.362
April	3.96	2	10	0	16	16	100.0	115	4	35	57	Scoring Posn	.251	716	180	26	4	12	250	95	133	.333	.349
May	3.50	11	8	0	23	23	149.0	139	9	60	84	Close & Late	.312	285	89	5	1	7	33	24	34	.366	.411
June	3.94	8	7	0	21	21	144.0	145	11	51	86	None on/out	.280	843	236	36	3	16	16	61	116	.331	.387
July	2.58	8	8	0	19	19	136.0	134	7	26	91	vs. 1st Batr (relief)	.000	0	0	0	0	0	0	0	0	.000	.000
August	3.76	11	8	0	23	23	150.2	160	10	59	91	First Inning Pitched	.264	470	124	22	1	7	53	51	67	.339	.360
September/October	3.28	7	11	0	23	23	167.1	173	14	56	99	First 75 Pitches	.252	2271	572	81	6	35	202	208	367	.316	.339
Starter	3.49	47	52	0	125	125	847.0	866	55	287	508	Pitch 76-90	.308	428	132	18	2	8	46	37	57	.367	.416
Reliever	0.00	0	0	0	0	0	0.0	0	0	0	0	Pitch 91-105	.316	316	100	15	2	5	40	26	49	.368	.424
0-3 Days Rest	2.49	2	1	0	4	4	25.1	24	2	10	24	Pitch 106+	.294	211	62	11	1	7	22	16	35	.344	.455
4 Days Rest	3.41	27	28	0	72	72	493.2	503	30	151	301	First Pitch	.346	526	182	26	2	11	65	14	0	.362	.466
5+ Days Rest	3.68	18	23	0	49	49	328.0	339	23	126	183	Ahead on Count	.213	1474	314	39	4	19	113	1	445	.218	.284
Pre-All Star	3.63	24	29	0	68	68	446.2	455	26	157	275	Behind on Count	.320	678	217	37	3	17	85	162	0	.449	.459
Post-All Star	3.33	23	23	0	57	57	400.1	411	29	130	233	Two Strikes	.193	1386	268	35	3	15	94	109	508	.255	.255

Pitcher vs. Batter (career)

Pitches Best Vs.	Avg	AB	H	2B	3B	HR	RBI	BB	SO	OBP	SLG	Pitches Worst Vs.	Avg	AB	H	2B	3B	HR	RBI	BB	SO	OBP	SLG
Chris James	.000	15	0	0	0	0	0	0	3	.000	.000	Chris Hoiles	.750	8	6	0	0	0	1	2	0	.727	.750
Pat Tabler	.000	13	0	0	0	0	2	2	3	.133	.000	George Brett	.545	22	12	2	0	3	9	3	5	.600	1.045
Mike Huff	.000	13	0	0	0	0	0	1	2	.071	.000	Dave Henderson	.529	17	9	1	0	5	8	2	2	.550	1.471
Scott Fletcher	.045	22	1	0	0	0	0	1	1	.045	.045	Mike Devereaux	.526	19	10	2	0	1	2	3	2	.591	.789
Willie Wilson	.091	11	1	0	0	0	3	2	.083	.091		Alvin Davis	.500	8	4	2	0	0	7	5	1	.643	.750

Kyle Abbott — Phillies

Pitches Left

	ERA	W	L	Sv	G	GS	IP	BB	SO	Avg	H	2B	3B	HR	RBI	OBP	SLG	CG	ShO	Sup	QS	#P/S	SB	CS	GB	FB	G/F
1992 Season	5.13	1	14	0	31	19	133.1	45	88	.283	147	16	8	20	72	.338	.460	0	0	2.77	10	102	9	7	167	155	1.08
Career (1991-1992)	5.06	2	16	0	36	22	153.0	58	100	.285	169	20	8	22	81	.348	.457	0	0	2.82	12	101	10	9	193	177	1.09

1992 Season

	ERA	W	L	Sv	G	GS	IP	H	HR	BB	SO		Avg	AB	H	2B	3B	HR	RBI	BB	SO	OBP	SLG
Home	5.64	1	7	0	16	11	75.0	86	11	25	54	vs. Left	.326	129	42	2	1	3	17	8	28	.370	.426
Away	4.47	0	7	0	15	8	58.1	61	9	20	34	vs. Right	.269	391	105	14	7	17	55	37	60	.328	.471
Starter	4.62	1	14	0	19	19	117.0	124	14	39	73	Scoring Posn	.252	119	30	4	2	4	46	10	20	.299	.420
Reliever	8.82	0	0	0	12	0	16.1	23	6	6	15	Close & Late	.450	20	9	1	2	2	6	0	0	.450	1.000
0-3 Days Rest	1.50	0	1	0	1	1	6.0	8	1	1	3	None on/out	.280	132	37	7	1	4	4	9	23	.326	.439
4 Days Rest	5.25	0	10	0	12	12	73.2	77	10	26	43	First Pitch	.361	72	26	2	4	3	13	0	0	.361	.625
5+ Days Rest	3.86	1	3	0	6	6	37.1	39	4	12	27	Behind on Count	.358	123	44	8	2	9	22	22	0	.453	.675
Pre-All Star	5.15	0	11	0	13	13	80.1	82	11	29	53	Ahead on Count	.195	220	43	1	1	5	22	0	75	.194	.277
Post-All Star	5.09	1	3	0	18	6	53.0	65	9	16	35	Two Strikes	.206	257	53	6	2	3	88	6	24	.270	.296

Paul Abbott — Twins

Pitches Right (flyball pitcher)

	ERA	W	L	Sv	G	GS	IP	BB	SO	Avg	H	2B	3B	HR	RBI	OBP	SLG	GF	IR	IRS	Hld	SvOp	SB	CS	GB	FB	G/F
1992 Season	3.27	0	0	0	6	0	11.0	5	13	.279	12	2	1	1	7	.360	.442	5	7	3	0	0	2	0	15	8	1.88
Career (1990-1992)	5.03	3	6	0	28	10	93.0	69	81	.257	87	21	4	6	50	.382	.396	6	18	7	0	0	8	3	91	110	0.83

1992 Season

	ERA	W	L	Sv	G	GS	IP	H	HR	BB	SO		Avg	AB	H	2B	3B	HR	RBI	BB	SO	OBP	SLG
Home	2.57	0	0	0	3	0	7.0	7	0	3	7	vs. Left	.200	25	5	1	0	0	0	4	10	.310	.240
Away	4.50	0	0	0	3	0	4.0	5	1	2	6	vs. Right	.389	18	7	1	1	1	7	1	3	.429	.722

Shawn Abner — White Sox

Bats Right

	Avg	G	AB	R	H	2B	3B	HR	RBI	BB	SO	HBP	GDP	SB	CS	OBP	SLG	IBB	SH	SF	#Pit	#P/PA	GB	FB	G/F
1992 Season	.279	97	208	21	58	10	1	1	16	12	35	3	3	1	2	.323	.351	2	2	3	823	3.64	61	67	0.91
Last Five Years	.224	376	793	84	178	36	3	9	64	41	145	7	14	5	8	.267	.311	10	5	7	2943	3.47	258	255	1.01

1992 Season

	Avg	AB	H	2B	3B	HR	RBI	BB	SO	OBP	SLG		Avg	AB	H	2B	3B	HR	RBI	BB	SO	OBP	SLG
vs. Left	.254	122	31	6	0	1	9	8	20	.304	.328	Scoring Posn	.283	53	15	3	0	0	15	7	8	.349	.340
vs. Right	.314	86	27	4	1	0	7	4	15	.352	.384	Close & Late	.372	43	16	2	1	0	3	4	8	.429	.465
Home	.330	106	35	5	1	0	13	5	10	.365	.396	None on/out	.159	44	7	2	1	0	0	1	9	.213	.250
Away	.225	102	23	5	0	1	3	7	25	.279	.304	Batting #6	.272	103	28	4	0	1	8	5	22	.315	.340
First Pitch	.379	29	11	4	0	0	3	2	0	.406	.517	Batting #8	.207	58	12	3	0	0	5	5	7	.266	.259
Ahead on Count	.362	47	17	3	1	0	6	4	0	.404	.468	Other	.383	47	18	3	1	0	3	2	6	.412	.489
Behind on Count	.222	81	18	2	0	0	4	0	25	.229	.247	Pre-All Star	.300	70	21	4	0	0	4	4	8	.333	.357
Two Strikes	.189	95	18	2	0	1	4	6	35	.257	.242	Post-All Star	.268	138	37	6	1	1	12	8	27	.318	.348

Last Five Years

	Avg	AB	H	2B	3B	HR	RBI	BB	SO	OBP	SLG		Avg	AB	H	2B	3B	HR	RBI	BB	SO	OBP	SLG
vs. Left	.211	383	81	17	0	6	37	19	65	.253	.303	Scoring Posn	.243	185	45	12	0	4	59	19	37	.303	.373
vs. Right	.237	410	97	19	3	3	27	22	80	.279	.320	Close & Late	.262	149	39	6	2	1	12	8	34	.304	.349
Groundball	.243	239	58	16	0	4	27	15	46	.289	.360	None on/out	.210	210	44	7	2	2	2	8	33	.245	.290
Flyball	.198	192	38	2	0	2	15	8	31	.234	.240	Batting #6	.256	156	40	6	0	2	13	10	31	.308	.333
Home	.231	424	98	21	1	6	40	21	71	.273	.328	Batting #8	.210	334	70	18	1	2	27	22	59	.264	.287
Away	.217	369	80	15	2	3	24	20	74	.260	.293	Other	.224	303	68	12	2	5	24	9	55	.247	.327
Day	.226	246	56	10	1	2	18	10	47	.264	.301	April	.230	87	20	2	0	0	6	3	19	.258	.253
Night	.223	547	122	26	2	7	46	31	98	.268	.316	May	.182	137	25	7	1	3	8	11	23	.248	.314
Grass	.231	611	141	33	1	7	49	31	105	.272	.322	June	.219	128	28	3	0	2	10	5	21	.246	.289
Turf	.203	182	37	3	2	2	15	10	40	.247	.275	July	.279	111	31	4	1	2	11	6	24	.325	.387
First Pitch	.326	129	42	14	0	0	13	5	0	.353	.434	August	.228	184	42	12	1	2	22	6	32	.254	.337
Ahead on Count	.256	160	41	5	2	3	16	20	0	.337	.369	September/October	.219	146	32	8	0	0	7	10	26	.277	.274
Behind on Count	.189	296	56	13	0	2	21	2	91	.201	.253	Pre-All Star	.206	379	78	13	1	5	25	20	66	.247	.285
Two Strikes	.158	355	56	9	0	4	19	15	145	.199	.217	Post-All Star	.242	414	100	23	2	4	39	21	79	.284	.336

Batter vs. Pitcher (career)

Hits Best Against	Avg	AB	H	2B	3B	HR	RBI	BB	SO	OBP	SLG	Hits Worst Against	Avg	AB	H	2B	3B	HR	RBI	BB	SO	OBP	SLG
Joe Magrane	.333	12	4	1	0	0	2	0	2	.333	.417	Jimmy Key	.077	13	1	0	0	0	0	1	3	.143	.077
												Frank Viola	.125	16	2	0	0	0	0	1	2	.176	.125
												Jim Deshaies	.158	19	3	0	0	0	0	1	3	.200	.158
												Randy Johnson	.200	10	2	1	0	0	1	1	4	.385	.300

Jim Acker — Mariners

Pitches Right (groundball pitcher)

	ERA	W	L	Sv	G	GS	IP	BB	SO	Avg	H	2B	3B	HR	RBI	OBP	SLG	GF	IR	IRS	Hld	SvOp	SB	CS	GB	FB	G/F
1992 Season	5.28	0	0	0	17	0	30.2	12	11	.338	45	11	0	4	24	.388	.511	3	13	8	1	0	1	1	53	40	1.33
Last Five Years	3.90	9	20	4	224	5	378.2	124	226	.263	378	69	5	41	199	.322	.403	33	192	72	27	10	32	22	615	375	1.64

1992 Season

	ERA	W	L	Sv	G	GS	IP	H	HR	BB	SO		Avg	AB	H	2B	3B	HR	RBI	BB	SO	OBP	SLG
Home	3.31	0	0	0	9	0	16.1	21	2	5	7	vs. Left	.407	59	24	6	0	2	6	3	1	.435	.610
Away	7.53	0	0	0	8	0	14.1	24	2	7	4	vs. Right	.284	74	21	5	0	2	18	9	10	.353	.432

Last Five Years

	ERA	W	L	Sv	G	GS	IP	H	HR	BB	SO		Avg	AB	H	2B	3B	HR	RBI	BB	SO	OBP	SLG
Home	3.80	5	10	1	119	2	206.0	205	24	66	108	vs. Left	.299	633	189	37	3	14	68	65	54	.365	.433
Away	4.01	4	10	3	105	3	172.2	173	17	58	118	vs. Right	.234	806	189	32	2	27	131	59	172	.287	.380
Day	4.29	6	5	1	73	2	123.2	132	11	40	81	Inning 1-6	.260	512	133	24	3	17	84	49	82	.322	.418
Night	3.71	3	15	3	151	3	255.0	246	30	84	145	Inning 7+	.264	927	245	45	2	24	115	75	144	.322	.395
Grass	4.39	3	11	2	110	2	178.1	180	23	56	117	None on	.247	827	204	39	3	20	20	53	137	.296	.374
Turf	3.46	6	9	2	114	3	200.1	198	18	68	109	Runners on	.284	612	174	30	2	21	179	71	89	.354	.443
April	4.39	0	4	0	41	0	69.2	75	8	24	41	Scoring Posn	.274	383	105	19	1	16	163	59	60	.362	.454
May	2.62	2	3	0	44	2	75.2	55	7	27	37	Close & Late	.262	332	87	16	2	4	40	33	46	.332	.358
June	6.45	0	4	1	31	2	60.0	68	8	26	28	vs. 1st Batr (relief)	.258	353	91	17	1	10	10	21	51	.305	.397
July	3.04	2	1	0	30	0	50.1	46	5	11	41	vs. 1st Batr (relief)	.286	147	42	8	0	8	36	11	20	.338	.503
August	3.63	2	5	2	37	0	62.0	66	5	16	40	First Inning Pitched	.284	587	167	32	0	24	116	52	96	.344	.462
September/October	3.39	3	3	1	41	1	61.0	68	8	20	39	First 15 Pitches	.275	737	203	40	2	23	111	53	121	.325	.429

4

Last Five Years

	ERA	W	L	Sv	G	GS	IP	H	HR	BB	SO		Avg	AB	H	2B	3B	HR	RBI	BB	SO	OBP	SLG
Starter	6.39	1	3	0	5	5	25.1	22	6	17	10	Pitch 16-30	.244	446	109	17	2	8	48	39	69	.305	.345
Reliever	3.72	8	17	4	219	0	353.1	356	35	107	216	Pitch 31-45	.277	184	51	12	1	7	25	20	28	.346	.467
0 Days rest	3.25	1	4	2	44	0	74.2	70	7	17	46	Pitch 46+	.208	72	15	0	0	3	15	12	8	.321	.333
1 or 2 Days rest	3.78	3	6	1	101	0	154.2	162	18	44	94	First Pitch	.320	231	74	18	0	7	43	15	0	.366	.489
3+ Days rest	3.92	4	7	1	74	0	124.0	124	10	46	76	Ahead on Count	.183	573	105	11	2	11	42	1	187	.190	.267
Pre-All Star	4.03	3	11	1	124	4	221.1	209	23	80	121	Behind on Count	.353	363	128	23	1	18	82	64	0	.447	.570
Post-All Star	3.72	6	9	3	100	1	157.1	169	18	44	105	Two Strikes	.170	569	97	11	3	9	38	44	226	.234	.248

Pitcher vs. Batter (since 1984)

Pitches Best Vs.	Avg	AB	H	2B	3B	HR	RBI	BB	SO	OBP	SLG	Pitches Worst Vs.	Avg	AB	H	2B	3B	HR	RBI	BB	SO	OBP	SLG
Jim Gantner	.000	10	0	0	0	0	0	1	0	.091	.000	Alvin Davis	.700	10	7	2	0	1	3	3	0	.769	1.200
Walt Weiss	.000	8	0	0	0	0	1	3	0	.273	.000	Rafael Palmeiro	.600	10	6	1	0	0	0	3	1	.692	.700
Willie McGee	.083	12	1	0	0	1	1	0	3	.083	.167	Jose Canseco	.545	11	6	0	0	4	9	2	2	.615	1.636
Ozzie Guillen	.100	10	1	0	0	0	1	0	1	.091	.100	Robby Thompson	.500	8	4	1	0	2	5	3	0	.636	1.375
Willie Wilson	.182	11	2	0	0	0	1	0	1	.182	.182	Howard Johnson	.462	13	6	2	0	3	6	1	1	.500	1.308

Troy Afenir — Reds
Bats Right (flyball hitter)

	Avg	G	AB	R	H	2B	3B	HR	RBI	BB	SO	HBP	GDP	SB	CS	OBP	SLG	IBB	SH	SF	#Pit	#P/PA	GB	FB	G/F
1992 Season	.176	16	34	3	6	1	2	0	4	5	12	0	0	0	0	.282	.324	0	1	0	156	4.00	11	8	1.38
Last Five Years	.153	35	59	3	9	1	2	0	6	5	20	0	1	0	0	.215	.237	0	1	1	246	3.82	15	16	0.94

1992 Season

	Avg	AB	H	2B	3B	HR	RBI	BB	SO	OBP	SLG		Avg	AB	H	2B	3B	HR	RBI	BB	SO	OBP	SLG
vs. Left	.150	20	3	0	1	0	3	3	4	.261	.250	Scoring Posn	.154	13	2	1	0	0	3	2	3	.267	.231
vs. Right	.214	14	3	1	1	0	1	2	8	.313	.429	Close & Late	.000	3	0	0	0	0	0	1	1	.250	.000

Juan Agosto — Mariners
Pitches Left (groundball pitcher)

	ERA	W	L	Sv	G	GS	IP	BB	SO	Avg	H	2B	3B	HR	RBI	OBP	SLG	GF	IR	IRS	Hld	SvOp	SB	CS	GB	FB	G/F
1992 Season	6.12	2	4	0	39	1	50.0	12	25	.325	66	13	1	2	42	.365	.429	12	33	14	1	2	6	0	93	48	1.94
Last Five Years	3.89	30	22	11	339	1	403.0	152	188	.267	404	64	12	19	203	.338	.363	63	231	78	50	32	44	8	760	313	2.43

1992 Season

	ERA	W	L	Sv	G	GS	IP	H	HR	BB	SO		Avg	AB	H	2B	3B	HR	RBI	BB	SO	OBP	SLG
Home	9.72	2	2	0	21	0	25.0	46	2	7	12	vs. Left	.349	63	22	8	0	0	17	5	10	.414	.476
Away	2.52	0	2	0	18	1	25.0	20	0	5	13	vs. Right	.314	140	44	5	1	2	25	7	15	.342	.407
Starter	6.75	0	0	0	1	1	2.2	5	0	0	1	Scoring Posn	.397	68	27	7	0	1	39	5	8	.430	.544
Reliever	6.08	2	4	0	38	0	47.1	61	2	12	24	Close & Late	.311	45	14	3	0	0	11	6	7	.415	.378
0 Days rest	7.07	1	1	0	11	0	14.0	22	1	4	6	None on/out	.311	45	14	2	0	0	0	3	7	.354	.356
1 or 2 Days rest	8.18	0	2	0	11	0	11.0	18	0	6	4	First Pitch	.353	34	12	4	0	0	12	1	0	.361	.471
3+ Days rest	4.43	1	1	0	16	0	22.1	21	1	2	14	Behind on Count	.373	51	19	2	0	0	8	9	0	.460	.412
Pre-All Star	5.28	2	4	0	29	1	44.1	53	2	12	19	Ahead on Count	.268	82	22	5	1	1	16	0	20	.282	.390
Post-All Star	12.71	0	0	0	10	0	5.2	13	0	0	6	Two Strikes	.276	76	21	4	1	1	14	2	25	.304	.395

Last Five Years

	ERA	W	L	Sv	G	GS	IP	H	HR	BB	SO		Avg	AB	H	2B	3B	HR	RBI	BB	SO	OBP	SLG
Home	3.39	19	10	9	173	0	212.1	196	7	82	111	vs. Left	.231	485	112	21	3	2	66	42	87	.306	.299
Away	4.44	11	12	2	166	1	190.2	208	12	70	77	vs. Right	.285	1026	292	43	9	17	136	110	101	.354	.394
Day	3.93	8	8	3	93	1	116.2	129	6	36	52	Inning 1-6	.315	276	87	17	3	6	57	30	34	.381	.464
Night	3.87	22	14	8	246	0	286.1	275	13	116	136	Inning 7+	.257	1235	317	47	9	13	145	122	154	.329	.341
Grass	5.29	6	8	0	95	1	102.0	119	7	38	48	None on	.268	784	210	36	4	7	7	66	88	.328	.351
Turf	3.41	24	14	11	244	0	301.0	285	12	114	150	Runners on	.267	727	194	28	8	12	195	86	100	.349	.377
April	4.36	3	3	1	50	0	53.2	56	2	28	29	Scoring Posn	.285	445	127	19	6	5	176	74	63	.384	.389
May	3.00	8	3	1	63	0	87.0	77	3	17	36	Close & Late	.257	526	135	19	4	4	58	60	60	.338	.319
June	4.12	7	4	2	70	0	78.2	89	3	36	39	None on/out	.302	371	112	19	1	5	5	27	46	.353	.399
July	5.55	1	9	1	60	1	73.0	79	6	32	29	vs. 1st Batr (relief)	.277	300	83	16	3	3	38	26	39	.332	.380
August	2.93	5	3	3	47	0	55.1	62	2	13	38	First Inning Pitched	.261	1028	289	48	9	13	166	99	124	.347	.383
September/October	3.25	4	3	3	49	0	55.1	41	3	25	23	First 15 Pitches	.290	1006	292	48	10	12	150	95	114	.355	.394
Starter	6.75	0	0	0	1	1	2.2	5	0	0	1	Pitch 16-30	.225	383	86	14	2	4	39	44	46	.306	.303
Reliever	3.87	30	22	11	338	0	400.1	399	19	152	187	Pitch 31-45	.207	92	19	1	0	2	11	13	19	.321	.283
0 Days rest	3.13	13	9	2	126	0	146.2	145	7	46	68	Pitch 46+	.233	30	7	1	0	1	3	0	9	.233	.367
1 or 2 Days rest	4.35	12	9	9	128	0	147.0	151	8	66	69	First Pitch	.282	273	77	14	3	2	40	31	0	.366	.377
3+ Days rest	4.22	5	4	0	84	0	106.2	103	4	40	50	Ahead on Count	.213	606	129	17	5	6	61	0	159	.221	.267
Pre-All Star	3.98	19	13	5	205	0	248.2	255	12	89	114	Behind on Count	.339	375	127	25	3	7	55	84	0	.458	.477
Post-All Star	3.73	11	9	6	134	0	154.1	149	7	63	74	Two Strikes	.196	565	111	12	4	6	56	37	187	.252	.264

Pitcher vs. Batter (since 1984)

Pitches Best Vs.	Avg	AB	H	2B	3B	HR	RBI	BB	SO	OBP	SLG	Pitches Worst Vs.	Avg	AB	H	2B	3B	HR	RBI	BB	SO	OBP	SLG
Mike Scioscia	.056	18	1	0	0	0	0	0	2	.056	.056	Eric Davis	.556	9	5	0	0	1	2	2	3	.636	.889
Terry Pendleton	.083	12	1	0	0	0	0	1	0	.154	.083	Spike Owen	.545	11	6	2	1	1	3	0	0	.545	1.182
Eddie Murray	.125	16	2	0	0	0	1	3	1	.263	.125	Dave Justice	.385	13	5	0	0	1	5	1	1	.429	.615
Mark Grace	.143	14	2	0	0	0	2	0	1	.143	.143	Kal Daniels	.364	11	4	1	0	0	1	5	1	.611	.455
Brett Butler	.160	25	4	0	0	0	0	2	1	.222	.160	Howard Johnson	.357	14	5	1	0	1	6	2	3	.412	.643

5

Rick Aguilera — Twins · Pitches Right

	ERA	W	L	Sv	G	GS	IP	BB	SO	Avg	H	2B	3B	HR	RBI	OBP	SLG	GF	IR	IRS	Hld	SvOp	SB	CS	GB	FB	G/F
1992 Season	2.84	2	6	41	64	0	66.2	17	52	.238	60	8	0	7	32	.287	.353	61	40	7	0	48	5	0	75	82	0.91
Last Five Years	2.99	20	29	122	241	14	370.2	114	327	.230	318	56	7	25	156	.293	.336	175	136	34	2	149	31	7	405	402	1.01

1992 Season

	ERA	W	L	Sv	G	GS	IP	H	HR	BB	SO		Avg	AB	H	2B	3B	HR	RBI	BB	SO	OBP	SLG
Home	4.25	1	3	17	31	0	29.2	32	5	6	30	vs. Left	.248	129	32	1	0	3	17	11	29	.310	.326
Away	1.70	1	3	24	33	0	37.0	28	2	11	22	vs. Right	.228	123	28	7	0	4	15	6	23	.262	.382
Day	0.96	1	0	17	25	0	28.0	21	1	3	25	Inning 1-6	.000	0	0	0	0	0	0	0	0	.000	.000
Night	4.19	1	6	24	39	0	38.2	39	6	14	27	Inning 7+	.238	252	60	8	0	7	32	17	52	.287	.353
Grass	1.84	1	2	21	26	0	29.1	22	2	10	16	None on	.244	119	29	5	0	2	2	8	23	.291	.336
Turf	3.62	1	4	20	38	0	37.1	38	5	7	36	Runners on	.233	133	31	3	0	5	30	9	29	.283	.368
April	5.73	0	2	5	11	0	11.0	16	2	2	9	Scoring Posn	.212	85	18	1	0	5	30	8	17	.274	.400
May	2.63	0	2	9	12	0	13.2	13	0	3	9	Close & Late	.214	173	37	3	0	5	27	15	36	.275	.318
June	1.59	1	0	8	12	0	11.1	10	1	3	11	None on/out	.255	51	13	2	0	0	0	4	11	.309	.294
July	2.79	0	1	7	9	0	9.2	6	1	4	8	vs. 1st Batr (relief)	.200	60	12	2	0	1	6	4	15	.250	.283
August	4.00	0	1	5	9	0	9.0	5	2	3	5	First Inning Pitched	.240	225	54	6	0	7	29	15	49	.288	.360
September/October	0.75	1	0	7	11	0	12.0	10	1	2	10	First 15 Pitches	.238	193	46	6	0	5	18	10	41	.275	.347
Starter	0.00	0	0	0	0	0	0.0	0	0	0	0	Pitch 16-30	.200	55	11	1	0	1	8	6	11	.286	.273
Reliever	2.84	2	6	41	64	0	66.2	60	7	17	52	Pitch 31-45	.750	4	3	1	0	1	6	1	0	.800	1.750
0 Days rest	0.45	1	0	17	18	0	20.0	14	0	4	11	Pitch 46+	.000	0	0	0	0	0	0	0	0	.000	.000
1 or 2 Days rest	4.24	1	4	16	24	0	23.1	23	6	9	24	First Pitch	.261	23	6	1	0	0	2	3	0	.357	.304
3+ Days rest	3.47	0	2	8	22	0	23.1	23	1	4	17	Ahead on Count	.174	132	23	4	0	2	8	0	46	.174	.250
Pre-All Star	2.85	1	4	26	40	0	41.0	39	3	11	33	Behind on Count	.347	49	17	1	0	2	11	7	0	.429	.490
Post-All Star	2.81	1	2	15	24	0	25.2	21	4	6	19	Two Strikes	.146	130	19	2	0	1	8	7	52	.188	.185

Last Five Years

	ERA	W	L	Sv	G	GS	IP	H	HR	BB	SO		Avg	AB	H	2B	3B	HR	RBI	BB	SO	OBP	SLG
Home	2.87	12	11	59	125	7	185.1	151	15	52	177	vs. Left	.233	700	163	20	6	8	66	67	165	.301	.313
Away	3.11	8	18	63	116	7	185.1	167	10	62	150	vs. Right	.228	680	155	36	1	17	90	47	162	.284	.359
Day	2.61	10	8	37	91	5	148.0	124	9	47	125	Inning 1-6	.287	366	105	23	4	7	52	29	72	.343	.429
Night	3.23	10	21	85	150	9	222.2	194	16	67	202	Inning 7+	.210	1014	213	33	3	18	104	85	255	.275	.302
Grass	3.00	11	16	54	107	6	171.0	144	12	50	154	None on	.222	743	165	29	4	11	11	47	184	.274	.316
Turf	2.97	9	13	68	134	8	199.2	174	13	64	173	Runners on	.240	637	153	27	3	14	145	67	143	.314	.358
April	4.57	1	6	13	32	2	45.1	52	5	12	45	Scoring Posn	.233	386	90	15	1	12	131	56	95	.329	.370
May	1.39	4	4	28	44	0	64.2	46	1	19	67	Close & Late	.215	633	136	21	2	12	81	63	162	.286	.311
June	2.89	4	4	25	48	0	56.0	48	3	21	50	None on/out	.224	313	70	14	1	5	5	23	75	.285	.323
July	4.19	5	8	20	45	1	62.1	57	6	22	56	vs. 1st Batr (relief)	.196	204	40	10	0	2	19	19	51	.274	.275
August	3.41	4	4	17	33	6	66.0	61	6	17	51	First Inning Pitched	.222	689	153	26	4	15	84	60	171	.286	.337
September/October	2.12	5	3	19	39	5	76.1	54	4	23	58	First 15 Pitches	.227	701	159	29	4	12	71	61	174	.292	.331
Starter	4.00	3	7	0	14	14	87.2	94	7	20	63	Pitch 16-30	.225	325	73	7	0	5	40	29	89	.292	.292
Reliever	2.67	17	22	122	227	0	283.0	224	18	94	264	Pitch 31-45	.232	142	33	6	1	3	22	12	30	.297	.352
0 Days rest	3.58	6	6	34	49	0	50.1	48	4	21	41	Pitch 46+	.250	212	53	14	2	5	23	12	34	.293	.406
1 or 2 Days rest	2.75	6	12	56	94	0	121.0	96	11	37	117	First Pitch	.266	184	49	9	3	3	17	13	0	.322	.397
3+ Days rest	2.18	7	4	32	84	0	111.2	80	3	36	106	Ahead on Count	.168	697	117	21	2	11	59	1	294	.175	.251
Pre-All Star	3.02	9	16	75	143	9	196.2	173	10	67	183	Behind on Count	.352	253	89	14	0	7	43	49	0	.457	.490
Post-All Star	2.95	11	13	47	98	11	174.0	145	15	47	144	Two Strikes	.155	715	111	20	4	9	56	50	327	.213	.232

Pitcher vs. Batter (career)

Pitches Best Vs.	Avg	AB	H	2B	3B	HR	RBI	BB	SO	OBP	SLG	Pitches Worst Vs.	Avg	AB	H	2B	3B	HR	RBI	BB	SO	OBP	SLG
Lou Whitaker	.000	10	0	0	0	0	0	1	1	.091	.000	Jim Eisenreich	.583	12	7	1	1	0	0	0	1	.583	.833
Franklin Stubbs	.056	18	1	0	0	0	0	0	5	.056	.056	Kal Daniels	.571	14	8	2	0	0	1	2	3	.625	.714
Don Mattingly	.067	15	1	0	0	0	1	1	2	.125	.067	Tim Wallach	.423	26	11	4	0	0	10	4	5	.484	.577
Dave Henderson	.071	14	1	0	0	0	0	0	8	.071	.071	Lance Parrish	.385	13	5	2	0	1	5	1	4	.429	.769
Steve Lyons	.100	10	1	0	0	0	0	0	3	.182	.100	Sid Bream	.333	15	5	3	0	1	4	1	1	.353	.733

Scott Aldred — Tigers · Pitches Left (flyball pitcher)

	ERA	W	L	Sv	G	GS	IP	BB	SO	Avg	H	2B	3B	HR	RBI	OBP	SLG	CG	ShO	Sup	QS	#P/S	SB	CS	GB	FB	G/F
1992 Season	6.78	3	8	0	16	13	65.0	33	34	.307	80	17	1	12	44	.387	.517	0	0	5.12	3	81	7	4	79	84	0.94
Career (1990-1992)	5.80	6	14	0	31	27	136.2	73	76	.286	151	21	2	18	78	.373	.460	1	0	4.41	8	84	15	6	160	171	0.94

1992 Season

	ERA	W	L	Sv	G	GS	IP	H	HR	BB	SO		Avg	AB	H	2B	3B	HR	RBI	BB	SO	OBP	SLG
Home	6.14	1	3	0	7	6	29.1	34	6	16	15	vs. Left	.280	50	14	2	0	2	11	2	6	.308	.440
Away	7.32	2	5	0	9	7	35.2	46	6	17	19	vs. Right	.313	211	66	15	1	10	33	31	28	.403	.536
Starter	7.32	2	7	0	13	13	59.0	76	12	30	31	Scoring Posn	.246	65	16	2	0	4	31	16	9	.388	.462
Reliever	1.50	1	1	0	3	0	6.0	4	0	3	3	Close & Late	.429	7	3	1	0	0	1	4	1	.636	.571
0-3 Days Rest	0.00	0	0	0	0	0	0.0	0	0	0	0	None on/out	.323	62	20	7	1	1	1	10	8	.425	.516
4 Days Rest	7.57	0	5	0	7	7	35.2	43	9	13	21	First Pitch	.500	32	16	5	0	3	10	3	0	.526	.938
5+ Days Rest	6.94	2	2	0	6	6	23.1	33	3	17	10	Behind on Count	.293	75	22	6	0	2	7	14	0	.411	.453
Pre-All Star	6.99	2	6	0	12	12	56.2	70	12	27	30	Ahead on Count	.275	102	28	4	0	6	20	0	22	.272	.490
Post-All Star	5.40	1	2	0	4	1	8.1	10	0	6	4	Two Strikes	.239	117	28	4	0	1	5	18	34	.328	.419

Gerald Alexander — Rangers — Pitches Right (flyball pitcher)

	ERA	W	L	Sv	G	GS	IP	BB	SO	Avg	H	2B	3B	HR	RBI	OBP	SLG	GF	IR	IRS	Hld	SvOp	SB	CS	GB	FB	G/F
1992 Season	27.00	1	0	0	3	0	1.2	1	1	.500	5	1	0	1	5	.500	.900	0	1	0	0	0	0	0	5	3	1.67
Career (1990-1992)	5.79	6	3	0	36	11	98.0	54	59	.292	112	17	4	12	65	.380	.451	6	25	9	4	0	7	3	100	142	0.70

1992 Season

	ERA	W	L	Sv	G	GS	IP	H	HR	BB	SO		Avg	AB	H	2B	3B	HR	RBI	BB	SO	OBP	SLG
Home	0.00	1	0	0	2	0	1.0	1	0	0	1	vs. Left	.250	4	1	1	0	0	1	0	1	.200	.500
Away	67.50	0	0	0	1	0	0.2	4	1	1	0	vs. Right	.667	6	4	0	0	1	4	1	0	.714	1.167

Manny Alexander — Orioles — Bats Right (groundball hitter)

	Avg	G	AB	R	H	2B	3B	HR	RBI	BB	SO	HBP	GDP	SB	CS	OBP	SLG	IBB	SH	SF	#Pit	#P/PA	GB	FB	G/F
1992 Season	.200	4	5	1	1	0	0	0	0	0	3	0	0	0	0	.200	.200	0	0	0	22	4.40	2	0	0.00

1992 Season

	Avg	AB	H	2B	3B	HR	RBI	BB	SO	OBP	SLG		Avg	AB	H	2B	3B	HR	RBI	BB	SO	OBP	SLG
vs. Left	.000	0	0	0	0	0	0	0	0	.000	.000	Scoring Posn	.000	2	0	0	0	0	0	0	2	.000	.000
vs. Right	.200	5	1	0	0	0	0	0	3	.200	.200	Close & Late	.250	4	1	0	0	0	0	0	2	.250	.250

Luis Alicea — Cardinals — Bats Both

	Avg	G	AB	R	H	2B	3B	HR	RBI	BB	SO	HBP	GDP	SB	CS	OBP	SLG	IBB	SH	SF	#Pit	#P/PA	GB	FB	G/F
1992 Season	.245	85	265	26	65	9	11	2	32	27	40	4	5	2	5	.320	.385	1	2	4	1078	3.59	97	91	1.07
Career (1988-1992)	.224	234	630	51	141	22	15	3	56	60	91	6	17	3	7	.295	.321	5	6	6	2474	3.52	230	206	1.12

1992 Season

	Avg	AB	H	2B	3B	HR	RBI	BB	SO	OBP	SLG		Avg	AB	H	2B	3B	HR	RBI	BB	SO	OBP	SLG
vs. Left	.294	85	25	4	3	0	12	5	10	.340	.412	Scoring Posn	.225	71	16	3	3	0	25	7	13	.298	.352
vs. Right	.222	180	40	5	8	2	20	22	30	.311	.372	Close & Late	.206	63	13	1	1	1	6	9	12	.311	.302
Groundball	.214	117	25	4	4	0	12	9	16	.266	.316	None on/out	.203	59	12	2	1	0	0	6	8	.299	.271
Flyball	.386	44	17	2	3	1	9	7	6	.481	.636	Batting #7	.179	117	21	3	4	0	12	9	19	.246	.274
Home	.276	145	40	6	10	2	18	17	18	.361	.497	Batting #8	.310	87	27	3	5	1	13	13	9	.408	.494
Away	.208	120	25	3	1	0	14	10	22	.269	.250	Other	.279	61	17	3	2	1	7	5	12	.328	.443
Day	.311	74	23	3	5	2	12	9	12	.395	.568	April	.114	44	5	1	0	0	2	3	9	.163	.136
Night	.220	191	42	6	6	0	20	18	28	.290	.314	May	.349	63	22	2	6	1	12	6	5	.425	.619
Grass	.135	52	7	1	0	0	5	4	12	.193	.154	June	.000	0	0	0	0	0	0	0	0	.000	.000
Turf	.272	213	58	8	11	2	27	23	28	.350	.441	July	.294	34	10	1	1	0	2	3	6	.351	.382
First Pitch	.367	30	11	3	0	0	5	1	0	.382	.467	August	.213	75	16	3	3	0	4	11	12	.322	.333
Ahead on Count	.280	82	23	4	3	0	5	15	0	.388	.402	September/October	.245	49	12	2	1	1	12	4	8	.296	.388
Behind on Count	.195	77	15	3	1	1	11	0	22	.200	.299	Pre-All Star	.252	107	27	3	6	1	14	9	14	.320	.421
Two Strikes	.119	101	12	0	4	1	9	11	40	.219	.228	Post-All Star	.241	158	38	6	5	1	18	18	26	.320	.361

1992 By Position

Position	Avg	AB	H	2B	3B	HR	RBI	BB	SO	OBP	SLG	G	GS	Innings	PO	A	E	DP	Fld Pct	Rng Fctr	In Zone	Outs	Zone Rtg	MLB Zone
As 2b	.251	247	62	8	11	2	26	25	35	.326	.397	75	71	635.2	130	227	4	36	.989	5.05	252	230	.913	.892

Career (1988-1992)

	Avg	AB	H	2B	3B	HR	RBI	BB	SO	OBP	SLG		Avg	AB	H	2B	3B	HR	RBI	BB	SO	OBP	SLG
vs. Left	.212	193	41	7	3	0	17	12	24	.269	.280	Scoring Posn	.214	159	34	5	3	0	47	20	27	.303	.283
vs. Right	.229	437	100	15	12	3	39	48	67	.306	.339	Close & Late	.183	153	28	4	1	1	11	23	26	.296	.242
Groundball	.202	272	55	8	6	0	21	22	37	.262	.276	None on/out	.210	138	29	5	1	1		14	22	.292	.283
Flyball	.290	107	31	4	3	1	14	16	21	.391	.411	Batting #7	.210	233	49	7	5	1	24	18	38	.271	.296
Home	.246	317	78	12	13	3	30	35	41	.328	.394	Batting #8	.246	240	59	8	8	1	23	25	26	.321	.358
Away	.201	313	63	10	2	0	26	25	50	.261	.246	Other	.210	157	33	7	2	1	9	17	27	.290	.299
Day	.242	190	46	6	6	3	24	21	33	.326	.384	April	.134	67	9	1	1	0	5	7	13	.211	.179
Night	.216	440	95	16	9	0	32	39	58	.281	.293	May	.275	171	47	8	6	2	24	19	16	.354	.427
Grass	.189	169	32	6	0	0	14	18	29	.268	.225	June	.231	108	25	6	2	0	6	6	11	.276	.324
Turf	.236	461	109	16	15	3	42	42	62	.305	.356	July	.209	86	18	1	2	0	3	6	12	.261	.267
First Pitch	.318	85	27	5	0	0	11	2	0	.330	.376	August	.220	91	20	3	3	0	4	14	18	.330	.319
Ahead on Count	.239	184	44	10	6	0	12	37	0	.369	.359	September/October	.206	107	22	3	1	1	14	8	21	.265	.280
Behind on Count	.167	192	32	6	1	1	15	0	51	.168	.224	Pre-All Star	.227	365	83	15	9	2	35	33	40	.295	.334
Two Strikes	.148	243	36	4	5	2	18	19	91	.216	.230	Post-All Star	.219	265	58	7	6	1	21	27	51	.295	.302

Batter vs. Pitcher (career)

Hits Best Against	Avg	AB	H	2B	3B	HR	RBI	BB	SO	OBP	SLG	Hits Worst Against	Avg	AB	H	2B	3B	HR	RBI	BB	SO	OBP	SLG
Bobby Ojeda	.357	14	5	0	1	0	0	2	1	.438	.500	John Smoltz	.000	7	0	0	0	0	1	1	1	.273	.000
												Doug Drabek	.100	10	1	0	0	0	0	3	3	.308	.100
												Dennis Martinez	.182	11	2	1	0	0	0	0	0	.182	.273
												David Cone	.214	14	3	1	0	0	0	0	2	.214	.286

Andy Allanson — Brewers — Bats Right

	Avg	G	AB	R	H	2B	3B	HR	RBI	BB	SO	HBP	GDP	SB	CS	OBP	SLG	IBB	SH	SF	#Pit	#P/PA	GB	FB	G/F
1992 Season	.320	9	25	6	8	1	0	0	0	1	2	0	1	3	1	.346	.360	0	2	0	87	3.35	8	7	1.14
Last Five Years	.249	313	933	90	232	31	1	9	83	56	143	7	17	12	15	.294	.313	4	18	7	3543	3.53	321	280	1.15

1992 Season

	Avg	AB	H	2B	3B	HR	RBI	BB	SO	OBP	SLG		Avg	AB	H	2B	3B	HR	RBI	BB	SO	OBP	SLG
vs. Left	.143	7	1	0	0	0	0	0	1	.143	.143	Scoring Posn	.000	5	0	0	0	0	0	0	0	.000	.000
vs. Right	.389	18	7	1	0	0	0	1	1	.421	.444	Close & Late	.333	3	1	0	0	0	0	1	0	.500	.333

Last Five Years

	Avg	AB	H	2B	3B	HR	RBI	BB	SO	OBP	SLG		Avg	AB	H	2B	3B	HR	RBI	BB	SO	OBP	SLG
vs. Left	.253	320	81	15	1	0	21	16	50	.291	.306	Scoring Posn	.248	214	53	8	0	3	71	22	37	.320	.327
vs. Right	.246	613	151	16	0	9	62	40	93	.296	.316	Close & Late	.284	148	42	6	0	3	15	11	24	.333	.385
Groundball	.284	232	66	12	0	2	27	20	27	.346	.362	None on/out	.242	244	59	6	0	3	3	9	25	.269	.303
Flyball	.229	231	53	6	0	4	21	13	41	.275	.307	Batting #8	.248	569	141	17	1	4	39	32	91	.293	.302
Home	.246	447	110	12	0	5	47	32	66	.300	.306	Batting #9	.251	319	80	13	0	5	41	23	42	.299	.339
Away	.251	486	122	19	1	4	36	24	77	.289	.319	Other	.244	45	11	1	0	0	3	1	10	.277	.257
Day	.233	270	63	12	0	4	24	22	50	.293	.322	April	.231	160	37	9	0	1	14	6	21	.263	.306
Night	.255	663	169	19	1	5	59	34	93	.295	.309	May	.246	203	50	10	0	2	21	14	31	.297	.325
Grass	.249	794	198	27	0	9	77	47	123	.294	.317	June	.209	139	29	1	0	3	12	6	17	.255	.281
Turf	.245	139	34	4	1	0	6	9	20	.293	.288	July	.225	111	25	5	1	1	8	11	21	.294	.315
First Pitch	.266	143	38	4	0	1	15	1	0	.279	.315	August	.275	167	46	4	0	0	22	11	31	.317	.299
Ahead on Count	.314	207	65	14	0	3	26	31	0	.405	.425	September/October	.294	153	45	2	0	2	6	8	22	.333	.346
Behind on Count	.231	342	79	5	1	3	28	1	81	.238	.278	Pre-All Star	.238	564	134	24	1	6	52	31	77	.281	.316
Two Strikes	.175	395	69	8	0	1	21	23	142	.223	.203	Post-All Star	.266	369	98	7	0	3	31	25	66	.313	.309

Batter vs. Pitcher (career)

Hits Best Against	Avg	AB	H	2B	3B	HR	RBI	BB	SO	OBP	SLG	Hits Worst Against	Avg	AB	H	2B	3B	HR	RBI	BB	SO	OBP	SLG
Mike Flanagan	.600	10	6	0	0	0	2	1	0	.583	.600	Dave Stewart	.067	15	1	0	0	0	0	1	1	.125	.067
Chuck Crim	.500	12	6	2	0	0	4	0	2	.500	.667	Dennis Lamp	.071	14	1	1	0	0	0	0	3	.071	.143
Bob Welch	.455	11	5	0	0	1	2	0	2	.455	.727	Bobby Witt	.071	14	1	0	0	0	1	0	4	.071	.071
Jeff M. Robinson	.455	11	5	1	0	0	1	0		.500	.545	Jimmy Key	.167	24	4	1	0	0	0	0	3	.167	.208
Roger Clemens	.333	15	5	2	0	1	2	2	5	.412	.667	Bret Saberhagen	.174	23	4	0	0	0	1	0	2	.174	.174

Roberto Alomar — Blue Jays — Bats Both (groundball hitter)

	Avg	G	AB	R	H	2B	3B	HR	RBI	BB	SO	HBP	GDP	SB	CS	OBP	SLG	IBB	SH	SF	#Pit	#P/PA	GB	FB	G/F
1992 Season	.310	152	571	105	177	27	8	8	76	87	52	5	8	49	9	.405	.427	5	6	2	2641	3.97	249	144	1.73
Career (1988-1992)	.291	761	2962	439	862	146	31	39	302	292	369	15	55	192	50	.355	.401	18	60	20	12399	3.77	1210	767	1.58

1992 Season

	Avg	AB	H	2B	3B	HR	RBI	BB	SO	OBP	SLG		Avg	AB	H	2B	3B	HR	RBI	BB	SO	OBP	SLG
vs. Left	.308	156	48	5	0	5	23	25	17	.414	.436	Scoring Posn	.354	147	52	8	2	4	68	22	12	.439	.517
vs. Right	.311	415	129	22	8	3	53	62	35	.401	.424	Close & Late	.430	79	34	7	0	1	16	15	7	.526	.557
Groundball	.257	179	46	11	0	1	19	17	20	.325	.335	None on/out	.350	117	41	6	3	2	2	15	7	.424	.504
Flyball	.287	157	45	10	3	3	21	29	15	.402	.446	Batting #1	.455	11	5	0	0	1	4	2	1	.538	.727
Home	.354	268	95	14	5	5	49	42	22	.444	.500	Batting #2	.310	552	171	26	8	7	71	84	49	.404	.424
Away	.271	303	82	13	3	3	27	45	30	.369	.363	Other	.125	8	1	1	0	0	1	1	2	.222	.250
Day	.314	185	58	11	5	2	25	28	17	.404	.459	April	.382	89	34	3	0	3	19	9	9	.439	.517
Night	.308	386	119	16	3	6	51	59	35	.405	.412	May	.314	102	32	2	2	2	11	11	8	.391	.431
Grass	.269	238	64	11	3	2	19	31	24	.353	.366	June	.310	71	22	4	2	1	12	13	5	.424	.465
Turf	.339	333	113	16	5	6	57	56	28	.439	.471	July	.258	93	24	7	1	0	9	20	11	.395	.355
First Pitch	.431	65	28	3	2	2	10	4	0	.471	.631	August	.324	108	35	7	2	1	7	18	9	.421	.454
Ahead on Count	.366	134	49	8	0	4	21	44	0	.522	.515	September/October	.278	108	30	4	1	1	18	16	10	.370	.361
Behind on Count	.265	181	48	6	2	0	28	0	24	.276	.320	Pre-All Star	.323	300	97	13	5	6	45	41	27	.412	.460
Two Strikes	.250	248	62	11	4	2	32	40	52	.361	.351	Post-All Star	.295	271	80	14	3	2	31	46	25	.397	.391

1992 By Position

Position	Avg	AB	H	2B	3B	HR	RBI	BB	SO	OBP	SLG	G	GS	Innings	PO	A	E	DP	Fld Pct	Rng Fctr	In Zone	Outs	Zone Rtg	MLB Zone
As 2b	.309	567	175	27	7	7	72	85	52	.402	.418	150	149	1276.0	286	377	5	67	.993	4.68	420	374	.890	.892

Career (1988-1992)

	Avg	AB	H	2B	3B	HR	RBI	BB	SO	OBP	SLG		Avg	AB	H	2B	3B	HR	RBI	BB	SO	OBP	SLG
vs. Left	.264	924	244	46	6	21	104	91	147	.335	.395	Scoring Posn	.309	676	209	36	7	8	251	73	87	.370	.419
vs. Right	.303	2038	618	100	25	18	198	201	222	.365	.403	Close & Late	.300	477	143	23	3	5	55	62	70	.381	.392
Groundball	.278	993	276	60	6	5	84	90	127	.341	.366	None on/out	.304	678	206	40	7	16	16	67	74	.368	.454
Flyball	.293	709	208	31	8	12	69	76	95	.362	.410	Batting #1	.299	365	109	14	2	6	28	26	51	.346	.397
Home	.303	1444	438	64	20	23	180	152	170	.370	.423	Batting #2	.288	2274	655	108	25	31	234	232	280	.355	.398
Away	.279	1518	424	82	11	16	122	140	199	.341	.379	Other	.303	323	98	24	4	2	40	34	38	.367	.421
Day	.289	874	253	57	7	10	102	92	103	.357	.405	April	.290	379	110	16	1	5	39	30	46	.341	.377
Night	.292	2088	609	89	24	29	200	200	266	.355	.399	May	.293	546	160	21	6	11	59	47	61	.351	.414
Grass	.277	1771	490	75	12	17	164	151	229	.334	.361	June	.270	493	133	26	7	5	49	54	60	.344	.387
Turf	.312	1191	372	71	19	22	138	141	140	.386	.459	July	.285	477	136	25	5	1	41	49	60	.350	.365
First Pitch	.360	342	123	20	5	8	48	7	0	.370	.518	August	.290	551	160	30	8	7	47	58	88	.360	.412
Ahead on Count	.360	623	224	34	10	13	79	171	0	.496	.509	September/October	.316	516	163	25	4	10	67	54	54	.381	.438

8

Career (1988-1992)

	Avg	AB	H	2B	3B	HR	RBI	BB	SO	OBP	SLG		Avg	AB	H	2B	3B	HR	RBI	BB	SO	OBP	SLG
Behind on Count	.261	1067	279	40	7	11	113	2	203	.268	.343	Pre-All Star	.284	1569	446	78	16	22	159	143	187	.346	.396
Two Strikes	.219	1296	264	48	9	13	113	109	368	.283	.300	Post-All Star	.299	1393	416	68	15	17	143	149	182	.366	.406

Batter vs. Pitcher (career)

Hits Best Against	Avg	AB	H	2B	3B	HR	RBI	BB	SO	OBP	SLG	Hits Worst Against	Avg	AB	H	2B	3B	HR	RBI	BB	SO	OBP	SLG
Jack McDowell	.615	13	8	0	0	1	2	2	2	.667	.846	Charlie Hough	.063	16	1	0	0	0	2	2	1	.158	.063
Scott Sanderson	.500	16	8	2	1	0	2	2	3	.556	.750	Dan Plesac	.077	13	1	0	0	0	1	1	2	.143	.077
Neal Heaton	.400	20	8	3	0	2	4	2	4	.455	.850	Craig Lefferts	.091	11	1	0	0	0	0	0	3	.091	.091
Jeff Johnson	.400	15	6	0	0	2	5	0	3	.400	.800	Trevor Wilson	.091	11	1	0	0	0	0	0	0	.091	.091
Bob Welch	.385	13	5	1	0	1	1	3	0	.500	.692	Mike Mussina	.100	10	1	0	0	0	0	1	0	.182	.100

Sandy Alomar Jr — Indians   Bats Right

	Avg	G	AB	R	H	2B	3B	HR	RBI	BB	SO	HBP	GDP	SB	CS	OBP	SLG	IBB	SH	SF	#Pit	#P/PA	GB	FB	G/F
1992 Season	.251	89	299	22	75	16	0	2	26	13	32	5	7	3	3	.293	.324	3	3	0	1050	3.31	109	96	1.14
Career (1988-1992)	.262	280	948	93	248	52	2	12	105	49	106	11	22	7	8	.303	.359	7	10	7	3420	3.37	361	315	1.15

1992 Season

	Avg	AB	H	2B	3B	HR	RBI	BB	SO	OBP	SLG		Avg	AB	H	2B	3B	HR	RBI	BB	SO	OBP	SLG
vs. Left	.190	58	11	4	0	0	3	5	6	.277	.259	Scoring Posn	.231	65	15	2	0	1	24	3	9	.275	.308
vs. Right	.266	241	64	12	0	2	23	8	26	.298	.340	Close & Late	.266	64	17	2	0	0	7	2	8	.299	.297
Groundball	.333	69	23	2	0	0	4	3	6	.361	.362	None on/out	.318	66	21	5	0	0	0	3	8	.357	.394
Flyball	.190	84	16	5	0	1	6	3	11	.244	.286	Batting #7	.203	64	13	2	0	0	1	3	11	.239	.234
Home	.259	158	41	7	0	1	15	10	18	.304	.323	Batting #9	.286	161	46	10	0	1	18	5	12	.324	.366
Away	.241	141	34	9	0	1	11	3	14	.282	.326	Other	.216	74	16	4	0	1	7	5	9	.275	.311
Day	.219	73	16	2	0	0	4	5	8	.269	.247	April	.215	65	14	5	0	1	7	5	8	.271	.338
Night	.261	226	59	14	0	2	22	8	24	.301	.350	May	.205	39	8	3	0	0	4	1	6	.262	.282
Grass	.255	263	67	14	0	2	25	12	29	.297	.331	June	.240	75	18	1	0	1	6	2	8	.269	.293
Turf	.222	36	8	2	0	0	1	1	3	.263	.278	July	.324	74	24	4	0	0	8	2	4	.351	.378
First Pitch	.190	42	8	4	0	1	5	3	0	.277	.357	August	.239	46	11	3	0	0	1	3	6	.300	.304
Ahead on Count	.354	65	23	3	0	1	10	8	0	.425	.446	September/October	.000	0	0	0	0	0	0	0	0	.000	.000
Behind on Count	.246	114	28	7	0	0	5	0	23	.259	.307	Pre-All Star	.241	212	51	10	0	2	23	9	23	.284	.316
Two Strikes	.170	112	19	3	0	0	7	2	32	.205	.196	Post-All Star	.276	87	24	6	0	0	3	4	9	.315	.345

1992 By Position

Position	Avg	AB	H	2B	3B	HR	RBI	BB	SO	OBP	SLG	G	GS	Innings	PO	A	E	DP	Fld Pct	Rng Fctr	In Zone	Outs	Zone Rtg	MLB Zone
As c	.254	295	75	16	0	2	26	12	31	.295	.329	88	84	729.2	477	39	2	5	.996	---	---	---	---	---

Career (1988-1992)

	Avg	AB	H	2B	3B	HR	RBI	BB	SO	OBP	SLG		Avg	AB	H	2B	3B	HR	RBI	BB	SO	OBP	SLG
vs. Left	.288	222	64	10	0	2	22	18	23	.341	.360	Scoring Posn	.246	252	62	16	0	2	90	20	28	.304	.333
vs. Right	.253	726	184	42	2	10	83	31	83	.291	.358	Close & Late	.262	191	50	9	1	3	26	10	23	.300	.366
Groundball	.241	303	73	11	1	1	22	17	35	.286	.294	None on/out	.304	227	69	10	1	3		9	26	.342	.396
Flyball	.226	221	50	10	1	3	20	10	33	.270	.321	Batting #8	.283	332	94	20	0	6	47	21	34	.325	.398
Home	.275	472	130	24	0	7	51	31	50	.321	.371	Batting #9	.268	183	49	10	0	1	19	6	17	.306	.339
Away	.248	476	118	28	2	5	54	18	56	.285	.347	Other	.242	433	105	22	2	5	39	22	55	.286	.337
Day	.264	254	67	14	0	3	31	14	32	.310	.354	April	.242	178	43	11	0	2	20	9	26	.288	.337
Night	.261	694	181	38	2	9	74	35	74	.301	.360	May	.241	141	34	6	1	2	17	7	24	.285	.340
Grass	.271	797	216	44	2	10	86	44	82	.314	.369	June	.254	193	49	4	1	1	14	8	23	.286	.301
Turf	.212	151	32	8	0	2	19	5	24	.245	.305	July	.282	206	58	14	0	2	22	11	10	.326	.379
First Pitch	.230	148	34	9	0	5	23	5	0	.267	.392	August	.252	127	32	7	0	2	11	8	12	.299	.354
Ahead on Count	.358	193	69	11	2	2	26	33	0	.452	.466	September/October	.311	103	32	10	0	3	21	6	11	.348	.495
Behind on Count	.266	361	96	29	0	4	37	0	65	.273	.380	Pre-All Star	.262	581	152	28	2	5	58	29	77	.304	.343
Two Strikes	.193	379	73	14	0	3	32	9	105	.219	.253	Post-All Star	.262	367	96	24	0	7	47	20	29	.302	.384

Batter vs. Pitcher (career)

Hits Best Against	Avg	AB	H	2B	3B	HR	RBI	BB	SO	OBP	SLG	Hits Worst Against	Avg	AB	H	2B	3B	HR	RBI	BB	SO	OBP	SLG
Melido Perez	.455	11	5	2	0	0	4	0	0	.455	.636	Bob Milacki	.000	13	0	0	0	0	0	0	1	.000	.000
Mike Boddicker	.429	14	6	1	0	0	3	0	0	.429	.500	Randy Johnson	.000	9	0	0	0	0	0	4	1	.400	.000
Matt Young	.417	12	5	0	0	0	3	1	2	.462	.417	Todd Stottlemyre	.154	13	2	1	0	0	2	0	1	.154	.231
Greg Harris	.400	10	4	1	0	1	2	1	2	.455	.800	Jeff Montgomery	.182	11	2	0	0	0	1	0	4	.182	.182
Scott Sanderson	.313	16	5	1	0	1	2	0	3	.313	.625	Chuck Finley	.235	17	4	0	0	0	0	0	3	.235	.235

Moises Alou — Expos   Bats Right (flyball hitter)

	Avg	G	AB	R	H	2B	3B	HR	RBI	BB	SO	HBP	GDP	SB	CS	OBP	SLG	IBB	SH	SF	#Pit	#P/PA	GB	FB	G/F
1992 Season	.282	115	341	53	96	28	2	9	56	25	46	1	5	16	2	.328	.455	0	5	5	1319	3.55	108	118	0.92
Career (1990-1992)	.277	131	361	57	100	28	3	9	56	25	46	1	5	16	2	.321	.446	0	6	5	1371	3.50	117	123	0.95

1992 Season

	Avg	AB	H	2B	3B	HR	RBI	BB	SO	OBP	SLG		Avg	AB	H	2B	3B	HR	RBI	BB	SO	OBP	SLG
vs. Left	.294	136	40	11	0	2	14	7	13	.329	.419	Scoring Posn	.292	113	33	8	1	5	47	11	14	.346	.513
vs. Right	.273	205	56	17	2	7	42	18	33	.327	.478	Close & Late	.273	66	18	4	1	3	14	3	11	.300	.500
Groundball	.302	126	38	12	1	2	23	14	14	.368	.460	None on/out	.359	64	23	8	1	2	2	5	8	.406	.609

1992 Season

	Avg	AB	H	2B	3B	HR	RBI	BB	SO	OBP	SLG		Avg	AB	H	2B	3B	HR	RBI	BB	SO	OBP	SLG
Flyball	.247	85	21	6	1	4	18	3	16	.270	.482	Batting #3	.264	258	68	18	2	5	36	21	33	.316	.407
Home	.336	143	48	14	2	6	35	11	19	.376	.587	Batting #5	.280	25	7	2	0	2	10	0	4	.280	.600
Away	.242	198	48	14	0	3	21	14	27	.293	.359	Other	.362	58	21	8	0	2	10	4	9	.403	.603
Day	.336	113	38	13	0	3	16	8	13	.377	.531	April	.556	9	5	2	0	0	1	0	2	.556	.778
Night	.254	228	58	15	2	6	40	17	33	.304	.417	May	.275	51	14	4	1	1	4	6	7	.351	.451
Grass	.253	91	23	9	0	1	10	10	12	.320	.385	June	.316	79	25	6	1	3	22	6	8	.352	.532
Turf	.292	250	73	19	2	8	46	15	34	.331	.480	July	.250	44	11	5	0	0	5	2	7	.283	.364
First Pitch	.339	56	19	7	0	3	14	0	0	.328	.625	August	.227	88	20	6	0	2	8	8	14	.293	.364
Ahead on Count	.297	74	22	4	0	1	8	12	0	.391	.392	September/October	.300	70	21	5	0	3	16	3	8	.329	.500
Behind on Count	.258	120	31	9	1	2	16	0	22	.262	.400	Pre-All Star	.316	171	54	17	2	4	31	13	22	.358	.509
Two Strikes	.247	146	36	8	1	3	18	13	46	.311	.377	Post-All Star	.247	170	42	11	0	5	25	12	24	.297	.400

1992 By Position

Position	Avg	AB	H	2B	3B	HR	RBI	BB	SO	OBP	SLG	G	GS	Innings	PO	A	E	DP	Fld Pct	Rng Fctr	In Zone	Outs	Zone Rtg	MLB Zone
As Pinch Hitter	.467	15	7	3	0	0	1	0	3	.467	.667	16	0	---	---	---	---	---	---	---	---	---	---
As lf	.250	248	62	18	0	6	40	19	37	.300	.395	79	62	578.0	118	4	2	0	.984	1.90	131	119	.908	.809
As cf	.333	27	9	2	0	1	1	1	2	.357	.519	13	6	62.2	23	2	0	1	1.000	3.59	26	21	.808	.824
As rf	.353	51	18	5	2	2	14	5	4	.411	.647	15	12	107.2	28	0	2	0	.933	2.34	28	26	.929	.814

Wilson Alvarez — White Sox
Pitches Left

	ERA	W	L	Sv	G	GS	IP	BB	SO	Avg	H	2B	3B	HR	RBI	OBP	SLG	GF	IR	IRS	Hld	SvOp	SB	CS	GB	FB	G/F
1992 Season	5.20	5	3	1	34	9	100.1	65	66	.272	103	13	0	12	58	.381	.401	4	25	3	3	1	9	8	129	124	1.04
Career (1989-1992)	4.77	8	6	1	45	19	156.2	96	98	.261	153	20	1	23	79	.366	.416	4	25	3	3	1	9	12	200	190	1.05

1992 Season

	ERA	W	L	Sv	G	GS	IP	H	HR	BB	SO		Avg	AB	H	2B	3B	HR	RBI	BB	SO	OBP	SLG
Home	5.56	2	1	0	14	3	45.1	46	8	31	28	vs. Left	.225	89	20	6	0	0	11	19	19	.355	.292
Away	4.91	3	2	1	20	6	55.0	57	4	34	38	vs. Right	.286	290	83	7	0	12	47	46	47	.389	.434
Starter	5.55	3	1	0	9	9	48.2	47	9	29	32	Scoring Posn	.252	107	27	4	0	4	47	17	21	.354	.402
Reliever	4.88	2	2	1	25	0	51.2	56	3	36	34	Close & Late	.375	32	12	1	0	1	5	4	3	.474	.500
0 Days rest	9.00	0	1	0	3	0	5.0	7	0	3	3	None on/out	.242	91	22	3	0	2	2	12	14	.330	.341
1 or 2 Days rest	6.00	0	1	0	6	0	6.0	7	0	3	5	First Pitch	.154	39	6	2	0	0	3	2	0	.214	.205
3+ Days rest	4.20	2	0	1	16	0	40.2	42	3	30	26	Behind on Count	.371	97	36	8	0	3	17	34	0	.538	.546
Pre-All Star	4.24	2	3	1	18	4	51.0	48	4	33	28	Ahead on Count	.209	158	33	0	0	4	13	0	55	.217	.285
Post-All Star	6.20	3	0	0	16	5	49.1	55	8	32	38	Two Strikes	.178	174	31	0	0	17	29	66	0	.291	.178

Rich Amaral — Mariners
Bats Right

	Avg	G	AB	R	H	2B	3B	HR	RBI	BB	SO	HBP	GDP	SB	CS	OBP	SLG	IBB	SH	SF	#Pit	#P/PA	GB	FB	G/F
1992 Season	.240	35	100	9	24	3	0	1	7	5	16	0	4	4	2	.276	.300	0	4	0	388	3.70	37	29	1.28
Career (1991-1992)	.216	49	116	11	25	3	0	1	7	6	21	0	5	4	2	.260	.267	0	4	0	454	3.69	42	34	1.24

1992 Season

	Avg	AB	H	2B	3B	HR	RBI	BB	SO	OBP	SLG		Avg	AB	H	2B	3B	HR	RBI	BB	SO	OBP	SLG
vs. Left	.216	37	8	1	0	1	4	2	3	.256	.324	Scoring Posn	.240	25	6	1	0	1	7	0	2	.240	.400
vs. Right	.254	63	16	2	0	0	3	3	13	.288	.286	Close & Late	.214	14	3	1	0	0	1	0	3	.214	.286
Home	.222	45	10	1	0	0	1	3	7	.271	.244	None on/out	.235	17	4	0	0	0	0	2	5	.316	.235
Away	.255	55	14	2	0	1	6	2	9	.281	.345	Batting #2	.268	41	11	1	0	1	4	2	8	.302	.366
First Pitch	.318	22	7	0	0	0	2	0	0	.318	.318	Batting #9	.233	43	10	2	0	0	3	2	6	.267	.279
Ahead on Count	.190	21	4	0	0	1	3	3	0	.292	.333	Other	.188	16	3	0	0	0	0	1	2	.235	.188
Behind on Count	.300	30	9	1	0	1	4	0	9	.300	.433	Pre-All Star	.234	47	11	2	0	1	6	2	7	.265	.340
Two Strikes	.191	47	9	3	0	0	2	2	16	.224	.255	Post-All Star	.245	53	13	1	0	0	1	3	9	.286	.264

Ruben Amaro — Phillies
Bats Both

	Avg	G	AB	R	H	2B	3B	HR	RBI	BB	SO	HBP	GDP	SB	CS	OBP	SLG	IBB	SH	SF	#Pit	#P/PA	GB	FB	G/F
1992 Season	.219	126	374	43	82	15	6	7	34	37	54	9	11	11	5	.303	.348	1	4	2	1558	3.69	140	107	1.31
Career (1991-1992)	.219	136	397	43	87	16	6	7	36	40	57	9	12	11	5	.304	.343	2	4	2	1659	3.70	154	111	1.39

1992 Season

	Avg	AB	H	2B	3B	HR	RBI	BB	SO	OBP	SLG		Avg	AB	H	2B	3B	HR	RBI	BB	SO	OBP	SLG
vs. Left	.253	154	39	8	3	2	17	18	14	.343	.383	Scoring Posn	.155	84	13	3	2	0	24	12	15	.263	.238
vs. Right	.195	220	43	7	3	5	17	19	40	.275	.323	Close & Late	.197	66	13	2	0	1	3	9	14	.303	.273
Groundball	.211	180	38	11	3	5	16	15	30	.290	.389	None on/out	.269	108	29	6	3	2	2	10	13	.358	.435
Flyball	.274	73	20	2	1	1	7	8	8	.369	.370	Batting #1	.185	130	24	6	2	5	9	13	20	.284	.377
Home	.213	169	36	7	4	5	17	15	28	.291	.391	Batting #7	.224	85	19	4	3	2	14	6	14	.275	.412
Away	.224	205	46	8	2	2	17	22	26	.313	.312	Other	.245	159	39	5	1	0	11	18	20	.333	.289
Day	.195	123	24	2	2	3	11	12	20	.277	.317	April	.138	65	9	3	0	3	7	10	9	.273	.323
Night	.231	251	58	13	4	4	23	25	34	.316	.363	May	.239	46	11	2	0	0	5	6	9	.327	.283
Grass	.256	121	31	5	1	1	10	16	12	.355	.339	June	.203	74	15	3	1	1	7	11	13	.322	.311
Turf	.202	253	51	10	5	6	24	21	42	.278	.352	July	.232	56	13	0	1	1	3	3	6	.283	.321

1992 Season

	Avg	AB	H	2B	3B	HR	RBI	BB	SO	OBP	SLG		Avg	AB	H	2B	3B	HR	RBI	BB	SO	OBP	SLG
First Pitch	.269	67	18	2	2	1	6	1	0	.319	.403	August	.292	24	7	0	1	0	0	2	5	.346	.375
Ahead on Count	.310	71	22	8	1	3	9	19	0	.456	.577	September/October	.248	109	27	7	3	2	12	5	12	.300	.422
Behind on Count	.195	113	22	4	0	2	11	0	27	.214	.283	Pre-All Star	.203	236	48	8	2	5	22	30	35	.306	.318
Two Strikes	.161	161	26	2	1	3	15	17	54	.249	.242	Post-All Star	.246	138	34	7	4	2	12	7	19	.298	.399

1992 By Position

Position	Avg	AB	H	2B	3B	HR	RBI	BB	SO	OBP	SLG	G	GS	Innings	PO	A	E	DP	Fld Pct	Rng Fctr	In Zone	Outs	Zone Rtg	MLB Zone
As Pinch Hitter	.143	14	2	0	0	0	1	2	2	.250	.143	16	0	---	---	---	---	---	---	---	---	---	---	---
As lf	.288	80	23	3	2	1	13	7	11	.352	.413	27	18	188.0	66	1	0	0	1.000	3.21	73	64	.877	.809
As cf	.207	87	18	6	0	2	4	12	9	.337	.345	27	23	203.1	60	1	1	0	.984	2.70	70	58	.829	.824
As rf	.202	193	39	6	4	4	16	16	32	.270	.337	68	46	451.1	106	3	1	1	.991	2.17	122	104	.852	.814

Larry Andersen — Padres
Pitches Right (groundball pitcher)

	ERA	W	L	Sv	G	GS	IP	BB	SO	Avg	H	2B	3B	HR	RBI	OBP	SLG	GF	IR	IRS	Hld	SvOp	SB	CS	GB	FB	G/F
1992 Season	3.34	1	1	2	34	0	35.0	8	35	.202	26	2	0	2	17	.252	.264	13	17	7	8	2	7	1	45	25	1.80
Last Five Years	2.22	15	15	30	250	0	348.0	92	319	.225	289	31	6	9	137	.275	.279	61	183	69	45	44	50	9	480	290	1.66

1992 Season

	ERA	W	L	Sv	G	GS	IP	H	HR	BB	SO		Avg	AB	H	2B	3B	HR	RBI	BB	SO	OBP	SLG
Home	3.26	1	0	2	16	0	19.1	11	0	5	20	vs. Left	.203	69	14	2	0	1	9	8	17	.295	.275
Away	3.45	0	1	0	18	0	15.2	15	2	3	15	vs. Right	.200	60	12	0	0	1	8	0	18	.197	.250
Starter	0.00	0	0	0	0	0	0.0	0	0	0	0	Scoring Posn	.303	33	10	1	0	0	15	2	5	.333	.333
Reliever	3.34	1	1	2	34	0	35.0	26	2	8	35	Close & Late	.231	52	12	0	0	1	9	4	14	.298	.288
0 Days rest	0.00	1	0	0	6	0	5.1	4	0	0	3	None on/out	.152	33	5	1	0	0	0	4	9	.243	.182
1 or 2 Days rest	6.94	0	0	1	12	0	11.2	15	0	5	11	First Pitch	.250	8	2	0	0	0	2	0	0	.400	.250
3+ Days rest	2.00	0	1	1	16	0	18.0	7	2	3	21	Behind on Count	.111	18	2	0	0	0	4	0	0	.273	.111
Pre-All Star	4.34	0	0	1	18	0	18.2	19	0	5	19	Ahead on Count	.188	69	13	0	0	2	10	0	32	.186	.275
Post-All Star	2.20	1	1	1	16	0	16.1	7	2	3	16	Two Strikes	.187	75	14	1	0	2	9	2	35	.205	.280

Last Five Years

	ERA	W	L	Sv	G	GS	IP	H	HR	BB	SO		Avg	AB	H	2B	3B	HR	RBI	BB	SO	OBP	SLG
Home	1.57	11	5	15	138	0	189.0	152	2	41	190	vs. Left	.266	638	170	18	2	6	74	63	112	.332	.329
Away	3.00	4	10	15	112	0	159.0	137	7	51	129	vs. Right	.184	648	119	13	4	3	63	29	207	.216	.230
Day	2.40	5	3	10	64	0	97.1	85	3	26	88	Inning 1-6	.254	114	29	2	1	0	27	3	23	.267	.289
Night	2.15	10	12	20	186	0	250.2	204	6	66	231	Inning 7+	.222	1172	260	29	5	9	110	89	296	.276	.278
Grass	2.62	5	4	18	114	0	154.2	122	5	38	130	None on	.219	707	155	15	3	8	45	181	268	.283
Turf	1.91	10	11	12	136	0	193.1	167	4	54	189	Runners on	.231	579	134	16	3	1	129	47	138	.284	.275
April	1.61	4	1	2	35	0	44.2	39	0	15	25	Scoring Posn	.229	371	85	12	1	0	122	36	95	.288	.267
May	2.29	1	3	3	32	0	39.1	27	1	15	30	Close & Late	.233	615	143	14	2	5	72	52	144	.293	.286
June	1.92	4	2	4	51	0	75.0	68	3	14	73	None on/out	.223	300	67	5	1	2	26	78	.285	.267
July	3.63	3	4	8	43	0	62.0	56	2	18	61	vs. 1st Batr (relief)	.223	233	52	5	2	0	35	12	63	.261	.262
August	2.10	2	5	7	44	0	68.2	57	3	19	71	First Inning Pitched	.222	811	180	16	5	6	106	47	194	.262	.276
September/October	1.70	1	0	6	45	0	58.1	42	0	11	59	First 15 Pitches	.218	742	162	16	5	6	82	46	170	.264	.278
Starter	0.00	0	0	0	0	0	0.0	0	0	0	0	Pitch 16-30	.244	402	98	9	0	3	40	35	114	.300	.289
Reliever	2.22	15	15	30	250	0	348.0	289	9	92	319	Pitch 31-45	.197	122	24	5	1	0	10	9	31	.250	.254
0 Days rest	1.46	5	5	5	47	0	68.0	59	2	15	54	Pitch 46+	.250	20	5	1	0	0	5	2	4	.318	.300
1 or 2 Days rest	3.09	7	7	8	118	0	154.1	151	4	52	144	First Pitch	.250	124	31	5	2	1	17	19	0	.345	.347
3+ Days rest	1.58	3	3	17	85	0	125.2	79	3	25	121	Ahead on Count	.208	726	151	11	4	6	71	0	269	.208	.259
Pre-All Star	2.48	10	7	10	136	0	185.1	161	5	55	159	Behind on Count	.260	192	50	5	0	2	21	39	0	.383	.318
Post-All Star	1.94	5	8	20	114	0	162.2	128	4	37	160	Two Strikes	.178	723	129	11	3	5	62	34	319	.215	.223

Pitcher vs. Batter (since 1984)

Pitches Best Vs.	Avg	AB	H	2B	3B	HR	RBI	BB	SO	OBP	SLG	Pitches Worst Vs.	Avg	AB	H	2B	3B	HR	RBI	BB	SO	OBP	SLG
Mike Scioscia	.000	17	0	0	0	0	0	1	1	.056	.000	Wally Backman	.500	16	8	1	0	0	2	1	1	.529	.563
Benito Santiago	.077	13	1	0	0	0	2	1	3	.143	.077	Ozzie Smith	.467	15	7	1	0	0	5	6	1	.591	.533
Ryne Sandberg	.091	33	3	0	0	0	3	0	3	.088	.091	Mark Grace	.364	11	4	0	0	1	2	1	2	.417	.636
Lonnie Smith	.091	11	1	0	0	0	0	1	3	.167	.091	Gerald Perry	.357	14	5	2	0	1	3	0	0	.333	.714
Eddie Murray	.091	11	1	0	0	0	1	1	3	.167	.091	Dale Murphy	.346	26	9	1	0	3	8	1	6	.370	.731

Brady Anderson — Orioles
Bats Left

	Avg	G	AB	R	H	2B	3B	HR	RBI	BB	SO	HBP	GDP	SB	CS	OBP	SLG	IBB	SH	SF	#Pit	#P/PA	GB	FB	G/F
1992 Season	.271	159	623	100	169	28	10	21	80	98	98	9	2	53	16	.373	.449	14	10	9	2976	4.03	214	194	1.10
Career (1988-1992)	.238	549	1704	239	406	70	21	31	168	233	308	26	15	106	33	.336	.359	22	41	18	7960	4.02	562	523	1.07

1992 Season

	Avg	AB	H	2B	3B	HR	RBI	BB	SO	OBP	SLG		Avg	AB	H	2B	3B	HR	RBI	BB	SO	OBP	SLG
vs. Left	.226	190	43	8	2	5	26	31	35	.345	.368	Scoring Posn	.291	134	39	6	3	4	59	32	24	.406	.470
vs. Right	.291	433	126	20	8	16	54	67	63	.386	.485	Close & Late	.303	89	27	5	1	1	9	13	11	.390	.416
Groundball	.295	173	51	8	2	4	23	22	19	.382	.434	None on/out	.251	271	68	12	4	9	52	37	.424	
Flyball	.195	154	30	4	0	3	14	32	23	.339	.279	Batting #1	.272	622	169	28	10	21	80	98	98	.374	.450
Home	.262	313	82	14	2	15	46	48	54	.364	.463	Batting #9	.000	1	0	0	0	0	0	0	0	.000	.000

1992 Season

	Avg	AB	H	2B	3B	HR	RBI	BB	SO	OBP	SLG		Avg	AB	H	2B	3B	HR	RBI	BB	SO	OBP	SLG
Away	.281	310	87	14	8	6	34	50	44	.383	.435	Other	.000	0	0	0	0	0	0	0	0	.000	.000
Day	.286	185	53	8	7	5	19	26	28	.385	.486	April	.299	77	23	6	5	2	18	13	12	.417	.584
Night	.265	438	116	20	3	16	61	72	70	.369	.434	May	.287	115	33	8	0	7	19	11	15	.354	.539
Grass	.270	530	143	22	5	19	65	80	88	.368	.438	June	.266	109	29	4	1	4	11	15	16	.349	.431
Turf	.280	93	26	6	5	2	15	18	10	.402	.516	July	.288	111	32	3	0	2	13	16	15	.380	.369
First Pitch	.254	63	16	3	0	2	4	11	0	.373	.397	August	.273	99	27	2	3	3	11	28	13	.431	.444
Ahead on Count	.367	158	58	11	2	8	30	60	0	.539	.614	September/October	.223	112	25	5	1	3	8	15	27	.321	.366
Behind on Count	.222	194	43	6	1	4	15	0	45	.234	.325	Pre-All Star	.286	343	98	19	6	15	57	50	47	.381	.507
Two Strikes	.224	290	65	10	7	10	34	28	98	.301	.410	Post-All Star	.254	280	71	9	4	6	23	48	51	.365	.379

1992 By Position

Position	Avg	AB	H	2B	3B	HR	RBI	BB	SO	OBP	SLG	G	GS	Innings	PO	A	E	DP	Fld Pct	Rng Fctr	In Zone	Outs	Zone Rtg	MLB Zone
As If	.266	580	154	24	7	21	74	94	93	.372	.440	148	148	1330.0	359	10	7	4	.981	2.50	404	339	.839	.809

Career (1988-1992)

	Avg	AB	H	2B	3B	HR	RBI	BB	SO	OBP	SLG		Avg	AB	H	2B	3B	HR	RBI	BB	SO	OBP	SLG
vs. Left	.190	427	81	12	6	6	39	66	94	.309	.288	Scoring Posn	.267	363	97	13	6	7	134	74	69	.363	.394
vs. Right	.255	1277	325	58	15	25	129	167	214	.345	.382	Close & Late	.237	257	61	9	3	2	22	31	55	.324	.319
Groundball	.278	461	128	17	4	8	54	44	56	.346	.384	None on/out	.212	618	131	21	7	12	12	73	102	.303	.333
Flyball	.195	410	80	16	3	5	33	68	92	.316	.285	Batting #1	.252	1119	282	46	16	26	113	160	188	.352	.391
Home	.225	859	193	33	7	20	94	109	165	.321	.349	Batting #2	.200	325	65	19	2	5	37	41	60	.298	.317
Away	.252	845	213	37	14	11	74	124	143	.351	.368	Other	.227	260	59	5	3	0	18	32	60	.313	.269
Day	.267	484	129	20	12	6	46	59	84	.354	.407	April	.276	250	69	18	8	3	33	43	52	.396	.448
Night	.227	1220	277	50	9	23	122	174	224	.329	.339	May	.218	380	83	16	2	10	45	40	66	.300	.350
Grass	.234	1407	329	54	13	27	139	179	257	.327	.348	June	.230	209	48	9	1	5	17	34	35	.341	.354
Turf	.259	297	77	16	8	4	29	54	51	.377	.407	July	.295	224	66	8	3	4	24	36	31	.398	.411
First Pitch	.266	184	49	5	1	3	17	12	0	.310	.353	August	.202	307	62	4	3	6	27	48	54	.310	.293
Ahead on Count	.313	406	127	26	4	11	61	151	0	.498	.478	September/October	.234	334	78	15	4	3	22	32	70	.303	.329
Behind on Count	.193	528	102	16	7	7	33	3	155	.218	.290	Pre-All Star	.243	912	222	45	11	20	105	133	162	.349	.383
Two Strikes	.185	823	152	23	15	14	69	70	306	.258	.300	Post-All Star	.232	792	184	25	10	11	63	100	146	.320	.331

Batter vs. Pitcher (career)

Hits Best Against	Avg	AB	H	2B	3B	HR	RBI	BB	SO	OBP	SLG	Hits Worst Against	Avg	AB	H	2B	3B	HR	RBI	BB	SO	OBP	SLG
Walt Terrell	.563	16	9	1	0	0	1	2	1	.650	.625	Dave Stieb	.000	15	0	0	0	0	0	3	6	.167	.000
Kevin Tapani	.545	11	6	0	0	1	4	1	2	.583	.818	Nolan Ryan	.000	13	0	0	0	0	0	3	5	.188	.000
Mark Gubicza	.417	24	10	0	3	0	4	2	3	.462	.667	Floyd Bannister	.000	11	0	0	0	0	1	3	6	.200	.000
Scott Sanderson	.412	17	7	4	0	0	4	4	0	.524	.647	Rod Nichols	.000	11	0	0	0	0	0	0	4	.000	.000
Erik Hanson	.412	17	7	3	0	0	7	0	4	.389	.765	Curt Young	.083	12	1	0	0	0	0	0	1	.083	.083

Dave Anderson — Dodgers
Bats Right (groundball hitter)

	Avg	G	AB	R	H	2B	3B	HR	RBI	BB	SO	HBP	GDP	SB	CS	OBP	SLG	IBB	SH	SF	#Pit	#P/PA	GB	FB	G/F
1992 Season	.286	51	84	10	24	4	0	3	8	4	11	0	3	0	4	.311	.440	0	1	2	316	3.51	32	20	1.60
Last Five Years	.261	414	835	94	218	26	5	9	61	68	137	1	23	9	12	.316	.337	7	14	5	3189	3.51	353	192	1.84

1992 Season

	Avg	AB	H	2B	3B	HR	RBI	BB	SO	OBP	SLG		Avg	AB	H	2B	3B	HR	RBI	BB	SO	OBP	SLG
vs. Left	.250	64	16	4	0	2	7	4	7	.286	.406	Scoring Posn	.125	16	2	2	0	0	4	1	2	.158	.250
vs. Right	.400	20	8	0	0	1	1	0	4	.400	.550	Close & Late	.267	15	4	2	0	0	0	0	1	.267	.400

Last Five Years

	Avg	AB	H	2B	3B	HR	RBI	BB	SO	OBP	SLG		Avg	AB	H	2B	3B	HR	RBI	BB	SO	OBP	SLG
vs. Left	.240	383	92	13	1	4	28	34	55	.301	.311	Scoring Posn	.197	188	37	5	1	1	48	26	32	.291	.250
vs. Right	.279	452	126	13	4	5	33	34	82	.329	.358	Close & Late	.296	186	55	9	2	2	11	18	27	.354	.398
Groundball	.269	290	78	8	1	4	24	27	47	.331	.345	None on/out	.286	185	53	9	1	3		17	25	.347	.395
Flyball	.266	199	53	8	1	2	13	15	32	.317	.347	Batting #8	.244	418	102	11	3	4	31	41	73	.311	.313
Home	.247	409	101	11	3	4	35	37	66	.309	.318	Batting #9	.330	112	37	7	1	2	12	6	19	.364	.464
Away	.275	426	117	15	2	5	26	31	71	.323	.354	Other	.259	305	79	8	1	3	18	21	45	.305	.321
Day	.272	320	87	12	2	4	26	23	49	.320	.359	April	.308	52	16	2	0	1	3	5	10	.368	.404
Night	.254	515	131	14	3	5	35	45	88	.313	.322	May	.239	142	34	5	1	3	10	18	29	.299	.318
Grass	.259	588	152	16	3	5	46	49	103	.316	.321	June	.265	185	49	7	3	2	22	26	40	.355	.368
Turf	.267	247	66	10	2	4	15	19	34	.316	.372	July	.211	180	38	6	0	1	9	9	34	.249	.261
First Pitch	.323	133	43	7	2	1	6	2	0	.331	.429	August	.339	127	43	7	1	1	7	6	11	.366	.417
Ahead on Count	.309	191	59	8	1	4	23	36	0	.417	.424	September/October	.267	90	24	1	0	1	10	4	13	.298	.311
Behind on Count	.225	275	62	7	3	3	25	1	74	.229	.305	Pre-All Star	.257	499	128	16	4	6	42	53	88	.327	.341
Two Strikes	.199	332	66	7	1	1	21	28	137	.262	.235	Post-All Star	.268	336	90	10	1	3	19	15	49	.298	.330

Batter vs. Pitcher (since 1984)

Hits Best Against	Avg	AB	H	2B	3B	HR	RBI	BB	SO	OBP	SLG	Hits Worst Against	Avg	AB	H	2B	3B	HR	RBI	BB	SO	OBP	SLG
Roger McDowell	.545	11	6	0	0	0	0	3	1	.643	.545	Bruce Ruffin	.000	8	0	0	0	0	0	3	1	.273	.000
Joe Boever	.455	11	5	2	0	0	1	0	2	.455	.636	Craig Lefferts	.071	14	1	0	0	0	0	1	4	.133	.071
Frank Viola	.400	10	4	0	0	0	0	1	2	.455	.400	Don Robinson	.133	15	2	0	0	0	0	0	3	.133	.133
Sid Fernandez	.333	15	5	0	0	1	2	7	3	.545	.533	Doug Drabek	.167	12	2	0	0	0	0	0	3	.167	.167
Nolan Ryan	.318	22	7	1	1	0	0	3	5	.400	.455	Terry Mulholland	.200	15	3	0	0	0	0	0	2	.200	.200

Eric Anthony — Astros
Bats Left

	Avg	G	AB	R	H	2B	3B	HR	RBI	BB	SO	HBP	GDP	SB	CS	OBP	SLG	IBB	SH	SF	#Pit	#P/PA	GB	FB	G/F
1992 Season	.239	137	440	45	105	15	1	19	80	38	98	1	6	5	4	.298	.407	5	0	4	1792	3.71	159	124	1.28
Career (1989-1992)	.210	285	858	89	180	31	1	34	123	88	233	3	13	11	4	.282	.367	11	1	12	3643	3.79	292	237	1.23

1992 Season

	Avg	AB	H	2B	3B	HR	RBI	BB	SO	OBP	SLG		Avg	AB	H	2B	3B	HR	RBI	BB	SO	OBP	SLG
vs. Left	.212	156	33	6	0	5	28	12	44	.269	.346	Scoring Posn	.266	139	37	7	0	4	56	17	33	.338	.403
vs. Right	.254	284	72	9	1	14	52	26	54	.314	.440	Close & Late	.247	89	22	1	0	6	22	7	22	.299	.461
Groundball	.276	170	47	4	0	9	36	15	25	.335	.459	None on/out	.187	107	20	1	0	2	2	8	24	.243	.252
Flyball	.228	101	23	5	0	6	25	12	34	.310	.455	Batting #4	.258	190	49	8	0	9	39	16	38	.316	.442
Home	.261	207	54	8	1	9	36	14	46	.309	.440	Batting #5	.213	188	40	6	1	9	33	19	47	.282	.399
Away	.219	233	51	7	0	10	44	24	52	.288	.378	Other	.258	62	16	1	0	1	8	3	13	.292	.323
Day	.232	138	32	6	1	7	23	7	27	.264	.442	April	.167	12	2	0	0	0	0	1	3	.231	.167
Night	.242	302	73	9	0	12	57	31	71	.313	.391	May	.263	80	21	6	0	2	19	7	14	.318	.413
Grass	.218	142	31	3	0	8	28	14	30	.285	.408	June	.270	74	20	4	1	3	13	6	19	.325	.473
Turf	.248	298	74	12	1	11	52	24	68	.305	.406	July	.244	82	20	1	0	7	19	6	16	.292	.512
First Pitch	.283	60	17	4	0	3	16	4	0	.328	.500	August	.190	100	19	2	0	3	18	12	24	.277	.300
Ahead on Count	.296	81	24	2	0	4	18	16	0	.412	.469	September/October	.250	92	23	2	0	4	11	6	22	.296	.402
Behind on Count	.199	151	30	4	1	5	24	0	60	.200	.338	Pre-All Star	.249	201	50	10	1	9	41	17	43	.306	.443
Two Strikes	.158	222	35	4	0	4	28	18	98	.218	.230	Post-All Star	.230	239	55	5	0	10	39	21	55	.291	.377

1992 By Position

Position	Avg	AB	H	2B	3B	HR	RBI	BB	SO	OBP	SLG	G	GS	Innings	PO	A	E	DP	Fld Pct	Rng Fctr	In Zone	Outs	Zone Rtg	MLB Zone
As Pinch Hitter	.227	22	5	0	0	1	5	2	3	.292	.364	24	0	---	---	---	---	---	---	---	---	---	---	---
As rf	.237	417	99	15	1	18	75	36	95	.297	.408	113	110	900.1	172	6	5	0	.973	1.78	206	165	.801	.814

Career (1989-1992)

	Avg	AB	H	2B	3B	HR	RBI	BB	SO	OBP	SLG		Avg	AB	H	2B	3B	HR	RBI	BB	SO	OBP	SLG
vs. Left	.201	274	55	9	0	8	39	25	78	.269	.321	Scoring Posn	.224	228	51	13	0	6	83	32	63	.308	.360
vs. Right	.214	584	125	22	1	26	84	63	155	.288	.389	Close & Late	.244	164	40	4	0	8	28	18	47	.317	.415
Groundball	.228	285	65	10	0	11	48	27	68	.292	.379	None on/out	.178	214	38	2	0	5	5	22	51	.257	.257
Flyball	.179	207	37	6	0	11	35	26	63	.273	.367	Batting #5	.200	220	44	6	1	12	38	21	60	.267	.400
Home	.228	391	89	15	1	16	56	35	102	.292	.394	Batting #6	.184	239	44	11	0	2	18	31	71	.277	.255
Away	.195	467	91	16	0	18	67	53	131	.274	.345	Other	.231	399	92	14	0	20	67	36	102	.293	.416
Day	.199	251	50	12	1	10	35	20	65	.255	.375	April	.176	17	3	0	0	0	0	2	4	.263	.176
Night	.214	607	130	19	0	24	88	68	168	.293	.364	May	.253	154	39	9	0	6	27	18	38	.331	.429
Grass	.193	269	52	6	0	14	45	26	73	.261	.372	June	.210	210	44	10	1	7	25	21	65	.278	.367
Turf	.217	589	128	25	1	20	78	62	160	.292	.365	July	.182	176	32	6	0	8	28	13	51	.233	.352
First Pitch	.304	112	34	12	0	6	26	7	0	.339	.571	August	.182	121	22	3	0	4	20	15	29	.272	.306
Ahead on Count	.258	159	41	5	0	8	26	37	0	.396	.440	September/October	.222	180	40	3	0	9	23	19	46	.299	.389
Behind on Count	.164	298	49	7	1	9	37	2	131	.175	.285	Pre-All Star	.213	451	96	19	1	17	63	47	130	.285	.373
Two Strikes	.130	446	58	6	0	10	45	43	233	.206	.211	Post-All Star	.206	407	84	12	0	17	60	41	103	.278	.361

Batter vs. Pitcher (career)

Hits Best Against	Avg	AB	H	2B	3B	HR	RBI	BB	SO	OBP	SLG	Hits Worst Against	Avg	AB	H	2B	3B	HR	RBI	BB	SO	OBP	SLG
Jose DeLeon	.455	11	5	2	0	0	4	0	3	.455	.636	Trevor Wilson	.091	11	1	0	0	0	0	0	4	.091	.091
Mike Bielecki	.400	10	4	0	0	1	1	1	3	.455	.700	Don Robinson	.143	14	2	0	0	0	2	0	2	.133	.143
John Smoltz	.364	11	4	0	0	1	3	1	3	.417	.364	Doug Drabek	.154	13	2	0	0	0	1	0	2	.154	.154
Terry Mulholland	.353	17	6	1	0	0	3	1	2	.368	.412	Craig Lefferts	.182	11	2	0	0	0	1	0	2	.167	.273
												Tom Browning	.182	11	2	0	0	0	0	1	3	.250	.182

Kevin Appier — Royals
Pitches Right

	ERA	W	L	Sv	G	GS	IP	BB	SO	Avg	H	2B	3B	HR	RBI	OBP	SLG	CG	ShO	Sup	QS	#P/S	SB	CS	GB	FB	G/F
1992 Season	2.46	15	8	0	30	30	208.1	68	150	.217	167	37	6	10	53	.281	.319	3	0	4.02	23	106	18	9	245	243	1.01
Career (1989-1992)	3.10	41	30	0	102	90	623.1	195	445	.246	585	100	8	39	211	.304	.345	12	6	4.43	57	103	44	20	836	693	1.21

1992 Season

	ERA	W	L	Sv	G	GS	IP	H	HR	BB	SO		Avg	AB	H	2B	3B	HR	RBI	BB	SO	OBP	SLG
Home	2.60	8	5	0	15	15	104.0	83	4	31	82	vs. Left	.205	370	76	15	4	7	29	41	67	.283	.324
Away	2.33	7	3	0	15	15	104.1	84	6	37	68	vs. Right	.227	401	91	22	2	3	24	27	83	.278	.314
Day	1.96	5	0	0	6	6	41.1	35	2	20	29	Inning 1-6	.224	639	143	33	5	8	45	52	133	.283	.329
Night	2.59	10	8	0	24	24	167.0	132	8	48	121	Inning 7+	.182	132	24	4	1	2	8	16	17	.270	.273
Grass	2.14	5	2	0	12	12	84.0	62	4	33	57	None on/out	.242	442	107	23	6	5	5	42	74	.309	.355
Turf	2.68	10	6	0	18	18	124.1	105	6	35	93	Runners on	.182	329	60	14	0	5	48	26	76	.242	.271
April	1.27	2	0	0	5	5	35.1	18	1	12	23	Scoring Posn	.167	180	30	6	0	2	39	18	52	.243	.233
May	2.54	4	1	0	6	6	46.0	40	2	15	32	Close & Late	.110	91	10	2	0	2	7	13	12	.221	.198
June	3.24	4	0	0	5	5	33.1	32	2	7	22	None on/out	.258	198	51	10	4	2	2	19	32	.323	.379
July	1.55	4	0	0	6	6	46.1	35	0	11	33	1st Batr (relief)	.000	0	0	0	0	0	0	0	0	.000	.000
August	3.57	3	3	0	6	6	40.1	34	5	18	36	First Inning Pitched	.174	109	19	8	1	1	10	11	25	.252	.294
September/October	3.86	0	2	0	2	2	7.0	8	0	5	4	First 75 Pitches	.230	527	121	29	5	3	32	41	102	.286	.321
Starter	2.46	15	8	0	30	30	208.1	167	10	68	150	Pitch 76-90	.223	103	23	4	0	4	14	9	17	.286	.379

1992 Season

	ERA	W	L	Sv	G	GS	IP	H	HR	BB	SO		Avg	AB	H	2B	3B	HR	RBI	BB	SO	OBP	SLG
Reliever	0.00	0	0	0	0	0	0.0	0	0	0	0	Pitch 91-105	.160	81	13	2	1	3	6	11	18	.261	.321
0-3 Days Rest	0.00	0	0	0	0	0	0.0	0	0	0	0	Pitch 106+	.167	60	10	2	0	0	1	7	13	.254	.200
4 Days Rest	2.09	9	4	0	18	18	124.2	93	5	43	95	First Pitch	.272	103	28	8	1	1	9	4	0	.296	.398
5+ Days Rest	3.01	6	4	0	12	12	83.2	74	5	25	55	Ahead on Count	.164	365	60	13	3	3	13	0	121	.169	.241
Pre-All Star	2.33	10	3	0	19	19	135.0	108	5	42	95	Behind on Count	.328	180	59	14	2	5	17	35	0	.437	.511
Post-All Star	2.70	5	5	0	11	11	73.1	59	5	26	55	Two Strikes	.138	347	48	11	1	2	13	29	150	.208	.193

Career (1989-1992)

	ERA	W	L	Sv	G	GS	IP	H	HR	BB	SO		Avg	AB	H	2B	3B	HR	RBI	BB	SO	OBP	SLG
Home	2.91	21	15	0	47	42	290.2	260	14	81	217	vs. Left	.250	1128	282	50	6	25	119	119	179	.318	.371
Away	3.27	20	15	0	55	48	332.2	325	25	114	228	vs. Right	.243	1246	303	50	2	14	92	76	266	.290	.320
Day	2.51	12	7	0	27	24	154.0	153	10	64	107	Inning 1-6	.249	1968	491	83	6	35	181	158	381	.305	.351
Night	3.30	29	23	0	75	66	469.1	432	29	131	338	Inning 7+	.232	406	94	17	2	4	30	37	64	.300	.313
Grass	3.27	17	13	0	46	39	272.1	267	21	97	192	None on	.242	1377	333	54	7	20	20	117	255	.304	.335
Turf	2.97	24	17	0	56	51	351.0	318	18	98	253	Runners on	.253	997	252	46	1	19	191	78	190	.304	.358
April	2.44	1	5	0	11	9	59.0	50	4	21	40	Scoring Posn	.225	543	122	23	1	7	159	59	119	.295	.309
May	3.03	7	3	0	19	11	104.0	102	8	29	60	Close & Late	.185	232	43	5	1	3	18	19	39	.247	.254
June	4.03	7	8	0	22	20	127.1	128	12	42	83	None on/out	.244	607	148	29	4	9	9	52	109	.305	.349
July	2.86	11	2	0	18	18	126.0	110	2	32	101	vs. 1st Batr (relief)	.100	10	1	1	0	0	2	1	3	.167	.200
August	2.76	11	5	0	17	17	114.0	98	8	38	90	First Inning Pitched	.247	377	93	22	1	8	48	41	64	.315	.374
September/October	3.10	4	7	0	15	15	93.0	97	5	33	71	First 75 Pitches	.255	1700	434	81	6	26	156	134	315	.309	.356
Starter	3.04	41	29	0	90	90	598.2	551	36	185	422	Pitch 76-90	.223	282	63	7	0	8	25	26	56	.293	.333
Reliever	4.74	0	1	0	12	0	24.2	34	3	10	23	Pitch 91-105	.191	225	43	5	1	5	18	21	47	.260	.289
0-3 Days Rest	4.25	2	2	0	5	5	29.2	33	1	10	20	Pitch 106+	.269	167	45	7	1	0	12	14	27	.328	.323
4 Days Rest	2.60	22	14	0	47	47	318.1	274	18	106	230	First Pitch	.318	324	103	20	2	8	41	9	0	.333	.404
5+ Days Rest	3.45	17	13	0	38	38	250.2	244	17	69	172	Ahead on Count	.191	1107	211	33	3	11	63	0	382	.193	.256
Pre-All Star	3.38	20	17	0	59	47	336.0	322	24	107	219	Behind on Count	.326	521	170	30	3	12	57	96	0	.431	.464
Post-All Star	2.79	21	13	0	43	43	287.1	263	15	88	226	Two Strikes	.170	1076	183	30	1	9	67	90	445	.235	.225

Pitcher vs. Batter (career)

Pitches Best Vs.	Avg	AB	H	2B	3B	HR	RBI	BB	SO	OBP	SLG	Pitches Worst Vs.	Avg	AB	H	2B	3B	HR	RBI	BB	SO	OBP	SLG
Al Newman	.000	13	0	0	0	0	0	1	1	.071	.000	Leo Gomez	.500	14	7	1	0	1	2	2	3	.563	.786
Tino Martinez	.000	11	0	0	0	0	1	3	2	.214	.000	Greg Vaughn	.500	10	5	1	1	0	1	1	3	.615	.800
Mike Devereaux	.053	19	1	0	0	0	0	1	1	.053	.053	Gary DiSarcina	.500	10	5	1	0	1	4	2	0	.583	.900
Gary Gaetti	.077	13	1	0	0	0	0	0	6	.077	.077	Chili Davis	.364	11	4	0	0	3	6	1	2	.417	1.182
Bob Deer	.077	13	1	0	0	0	1	6	.143	.077	Kevin Reimer	.308	13	4	2	0	2	6	3	2	.412	.923

Luis Aquino — Royals

Pitches Right

	ERA	W	L	Sv	G	GS	IP	BB	SO	Avg	H	2B	3B	HR	RBI	OBP	SLG	CG	ShO	Sup	QS	#P/S	SB	CS	GB	FB	G/F
1992 Season	4.52	3	6	0	15	13	67.2	20	11	.303	81	14	0	5	29	.351	.412	0	0	2.53	3	73	1	3	108	84	1.29
Last Five Years	3.54	22	19	3	114	55	463.1	146	198	.266	473	88	7	28	197	.324	.370	5	3	4.23	24	86	22	17	655	599	1.09

1992 Season

	ERA	W	L	Sv	G	GS	IP	H	HR	BB	SO		Avg	AB	H	2B	3B	HR	RBI	BB	SO	OBP	SLG
Home	4.02	2	2	0	6	6	31.1	33	2	11	8	vs. Left	.314	118	37	7	0	2	12	8	3	.354	.424
Away	4.95	1	4	0	9	7	36.1	48	3	9	3	vs. Right	.295	149	44	7	0	3	17	12	8	.348	.403
Starter	4.08	3	5	0	13	13	64.0	74	4	18	10	Scoring Posn	.310	58	18	5	0	1	23	5	4	.348	.448
Reliever	12.27	0	1	0	2	0	3.2	7	1	2	1	Close & Late	.417	12	5	1	0	0	1	4	0	.563	.500
0-3 Days Rest	0.00	0	0	0	0	0	0.0	0	0	0	0	None on/out	.246	69	17	3	0	0	4	2	.297	.290
4 Days Rest	4.67	2	2	0	6	6	27.0	31	1	11	4	First Pitch	.361	36	13	2	0	0	4	1	0	.378	.417
5+ Days Rest	3.65	1	3	0	7	7	37.0	43	3	7	6	Behind on Count	.303	89	27	3	0	2	12	9	0	.370	.404
Pre-All Star	12.27	0	1	0	2	0	3.2	7	1	2	1	Ahead on Count	.232	99	23	5	0	1	8	0	10	.228	.313
Post-All Star	4.08	3	5	0	13	13	64.0	74	4	18	10	Two Strikes	.241	87	21	4	0	1	8	10	11	.313	.322

Last Five Years

	ERA	W	L	Sv	G	GS	IP	H	HR	BB	SO		Avg	AB	H	2B	3B	HR	RBI	BB	SO	OBP	SLG
Home	3.00	11	7	1	54	25	228.1	213	12	70	91	vs. Left	.279	847	236	46	6	11	92	83	98	.341	.386
Away	4.06	11	12	2	60	30	235.0	260	16	76	107	vs. Right	.254	932	237	42	1	17	105	63	100	.307	.356
Day	1.96	7	0	2	28	10	110.0	90	3	44	47	Inning 1-6	.275	1386	381	74	6	23	170	113	144	.332	.387
Night	4.02	15	19	1	86	45	353.1	383	25	102	151	Inning 7+	.234	393	92	14	1	5	27	33	54	.295	.313
Grass	3.63	9	8	2	46	23	188.1	202	11	56	98	None on	.257	1001	257	52	4	10	10	76	120	.312	.347
Turf	3.47	13	11	1	68	32	275.0	271	17	90	100	Runners on	.278	778	216	36	3	18	187	70	78	.338	.401
April	5.22	2	1	0	16	1	39.2	42	7	16	15	Scoring Posn	.259	432	112	20	2	8	160	49	49	.327	.370
May	3.35	2	1	0	19	2	48.1	45	1	15	30	Close & Late	.262	149	39	6	0	3	13	18	25	.341	.362
June	3.03	2	2	1	15	6	62.1	60	5	20	32	None on/out	.247	430	106	23	2	1	1	35	46	.306	.316
July	2.18	10	5	2	21	14	119.2	106	3	26	50	vs. 1st Batr (relief)	.275	51	14	5	0	0	14	5	8	.345	.373
August	3.97	3	5	0	19	19	106.2	117	8	40	44	First Inning Pitched	.278	428	119	18	2	7	72	43	55	.348	.379
September/October	4.57	3	5	0	24	13	86.2	103	4	29	27	First 75 Pitches	.270	1543	416	75	6	24	179	122	170	.326	.373
Starter	3.86	16	18	0	55	55	319.2	337	19	96	125	Pitch 76-90	.238	126	30	8	0	3	9	19	10	.340	.373
Reliever	2.82	6	1	3	59	0	143.2	136	6	48	73	Pitch 91-105	.293	75	22	5	1	1	9	4	9	.321	.427
0-3 Days Rest	3.83	3	2	0	6	6	40.0	40	3	13	15	Pitch 106+	.143	35	5	0	0	0	0	1	9	.167	.143
4 Days Rest	4.11	7	9	0	25	25	140.0	154	8	46	59	First Pitch	.325	277	90	15	2	5	51	13	0	.365	.448
5+ Days Rest	3.61	6	7	0	24	24	139.2	143	6	39	51	Ahead on Count	.213	734	156	25	3	9	64	0	164	.216	.292

14

Last Five Years

	ERA	W	L	Sv	G	GS	IP	H	HR	BB	SO		Avg	AB	H	2B	3B	HR	RBI	BB	SO	OBP	SLG
Pre-All Star	3.64	7	7	1	55	13	183.0	181	13	58	91	Behind on Count	.288	451	130	25	1	7	42	79	0	.395	.395
Post-All Star	3.47	15	12	2	59	42	280.1	292	15	88	107	Two Strikes	.202	677	137	27	2	7	58	54	198	.262	.279

Pitcher vs. Batter (career)

Pitches Best Vs.	Avg	AB	H	2B	3B	HR	RBI	BB	SO	OBP	SLG	Pitches Worst Vs.	Avg	AB	H	2B	3B	HR	RBI	BB	SO	OBP	SLG
Manuel Lee	.000	14	0	0	0	0	1	1	3	.067	.000	Frank Thomas	.545	11	6	1	0	3	6	2	0	.615	1.455
Alan Trammell	.059	17	1	0	0	0	0	1	0	.111	.059	Lance Johnson	.462	13	6	2	2	0	2	1	0	.500	.923
Paul Molitor	.071	14	1	0	0	0	0	0	3	.071	.071	Dan Pasqua	.400	15	6	1	0	2	3	1	2	.438	.867
Luis Rivera	.100	20	2	1	0	0	0	0	2	.100	.150	George Bell	.385	13	5	0	0	2	2	0	0	.467	.846
Brook Jacoby	.118	17	2	0	0	0	0	0	2	.118	.118	Chili Davis	.364	11	4	1	0	2	5	3	3	.467	1.000

Alex Arias — Cubs
Bats Right (groundball hitter)

	Avg	G	AB	R	H	2B	3B	HR	RBI	BB	SO	HBP	GDP	SB	CS	OBP	SLG	IBB	SH	SF	#Pit	#P/PA	GB	FB	G/F
1992 Season	.293	32	99	14	29	6	0	0	7	11	13	2	4	0	0	.375	.354	0	1	0	446	3.98	42	20	2.10

1992 Season

	Avg	AB	H	2B	3B	HR	RBI	BB	SO	OBP	SLG		Avg	AB	H	2B	3B	HR	RBI	BB	SO	OBP	SLG
vs. Left	.317	41	13	4	0	0	2	4	3	.378	.415	Scoring Posn	.286	21	6	1	0	0	6	2	0	.375	.333
vs. Right	.276	58	16	2	0	0	5	7	10	.373	.310	Close & Late	.333	15	5	0	0	0	0	3	5	.444	.333
Home	.236	55	13	3	0	0	5	3	8	.276	.291	None on/out	.350	20	7	1	0	0	0	5	3	.480	.400
Away	.364	44	16	3	0	0	2	8	5	.481	.432	Batting #2	.188	16	3	0	0	0	1	0	1	.188	.188
First Pitch	.200	10	2	0	0	0	1	0	0	.200	.200	Batting #8	.313	67	21	4	0	0	6	7	12	.395	.373
Ahead on Count	.375	24	9	2	0	0	3	4	0	.464	.458	Other	.313	16	5	2	0	0	0	4	0	.450	.438
Behind on Count	.237	38	9	2	0	0	4	0	8	.256	.289	Pre-All Star	.000	0	0	0	0	0	0	0	0	.000	.000
Two Strikes	.260	50	13	3	0	0	3	7	13	.362	.320	Post-All Star	.293	99	29	6	0	0	7	11	13	.375	.354

Jack Armstrong — Indians
Pitches Right

	ERA	W	L	Sv	G	GS	IP	BB	SO	Avg	H	2B	3B	HR	RBI	OBP	SLG	CG	ShO	Sup	QS	#P/S	SB	CS	GB	FB	G/F
1992 Season	4.64	6	15	0	35	23	166.2	67	114	.269	H 175	28	4	23	92	.337	.430	1	0	4.16	7	97	15	9	221	200	1.11
Career (1988-1992)	4.62	31	47	0	114	95	580.1	239	385	.264	588	107	16	70	295	.335	.421	4	1	4.40	41	89	62	26	727	720	1.01

1992 Season

	ERA	W	L	Sv	G	GS	IP	H	HR	BB	SO		Avg	AB	H	2B	3B	HR	RBI	BB	SO	OBP	SLG
Home	4.54	5	5	0	17	10	73.1	73	12	32	51	vs. Left	.274	277	76	10	2	10	42	39	39	.366	.433
Away	4.72	1	10	0	18	13	93.1	103	11	35	63	vs. Right	.265	377	100	18	2	13	50	28	75	.315	.427
Day	4.95	3	5	0	9	6	40.0	43	4	17	33	Inning 1-6	.263	556	146	26	2	21	85	58	93	.333	.430
Night	4.55	3	10	0	26	17	126.2	133	19	50	81	Inning 7+	.306	98	30	2	2	7	9	9	21	.364	.429
Grass	4.55	6	13	0	31	20	144.1	152	21	58	102	None on	.237	380	90	17	3	13	13	42	66	.316	.400
Turf	5.24	0	2	0	4	3	22.1	24	2	9	12	Runners on	.314	274	86	11	1	10	79	25	48	.367	.471
April	4.13	0	3	0	4	4	24.0	26	5	10	10	Scoring Posn	.303	155	47	6	1	5	66	20	26	.376	.452
May	5.34	1	3	0	6	6	32.0	39	3	15	19	Close & Late	.290	31	9	2	1	0	2	2	9	.333	.419
June	4.54	1	3	0	5	5	33.2	30	6	17	29	None on/out	.260	169	44	5	1	8	8	14	31	.321	.444
July	6.75	1	4	0	6	4	29.1	40	3	8	12	vs. 1st Batr (relief)	.273	11	3	0	0	1	2	1	5	.333	.545
August	3.48	2	1	0	6	2	20.2	15	3	7	15	First Inning Pitched	.272	136	37	7	0	4	29	20	22	.361	.412
September/October	3.00	1	1	0	8	2	27.0	26	3	10	29	First 75 Pitches	.257	502	129	24	2	17	67	57	88	.333	.414
Starter	5.44	3	15	0	23	23	135.2	159	21	57	87	Pitch 76-90	.268	82	22	2	0	3	15	6	17	.319	.402
Reliever	1.16	3	0	0	12	0	31.0	17	2	10	27	Pitch 91-105	.317	41	13	2	0	4	3	7	3	.364	.366
0-3 Days Rest	3.06	0	1	0	3	3	17.2	14	1	11	12	Pitch 106+	.414	29	12	0	2	3	6	1	2	.433	.862
4 Days Rest	5.62	0	6	0	9	9	57.2	73	8	19	42	First Pitch	.316	95	30	4	0	5	16	0	0	.316	.516
5+ Days Rest	5.97	3	8	0	11	11	60.1	72	12	27	33	Ahead on Count	.156	269	42	6	0	4	22	0	97	.164	.223
Pre-All Star	5.40	2	12	0	18	18	106.2	124	16	47	67	Behind on Count	.375	168	63	10	3	11	43	34	0	.475	.667
Post-All Star	3.30	4	3	0	17	5	60.0	52	7	20	47	Two Strikes	.164	262	43	7	0	3	10	33	114	.262	.225

Career (1988-1992)

	ERA	W	L	Sv	G	GS	IP	H	HR	BB	SO		Avg	AB	H	2B	3B	HR	RBI	BB	SO	OBP	SLG
Home	5.24	19	21	0	56	45	264.2	270	38	118	180	vs. Left	.274	1183	324	58	11	35	166	156	156	.358	.430
Away	4.11	12	26	0	58	50	315.2	318	32	121	205	vs. Right	.253	1045	264	49	5	35	129	83	229	.307	.410
Day	4.24	12	13	0	33	28	163.1	160	15	72	129	Inning 1-6	.264	1986	525	101	11	65	275	213	343	.335	.424
Night	4.77	19	34	0	81	67	417.0	428	55	167	256	Inning 7+	.260	242	63	6	5	5	20	26	42	.333	.388
Grass	4.49	12	22	0	54	41	270.2	284	39	108	173	None on	.240	1314	315	63	7	37	37	140	241	.316	.383
Turf	4.74	19	25	0	60	54	309.2	304	31	131	212	Runners on	.299	914	273	44	9	33	258	99	144	.361	.475
April	3.11	5	4	0	11	11	66.2	61	9	19	44	Scoring Posn	.288	535	154	24	6	19	218	71	92	.360	.462
May	3.66	8	7	0	20	19	123.0	111	7	51	72	Close & Late	.247	93	23	3	4	0	7	6	18	.300	.366
June	5.15	4	10	0	19	18	106.2	115	16	53	83	None on/out	.251	581	146	29	2	22	22	55	110	.320	.422
July	5.69	6	13	0	24	20	118.2	132	16	41	76	vs. 1st Batr (relief)	.222	18	4	1	0	1	2	1	7	.263	.444
August	6.43	6	10	0	14	10	56.0	61	10	32	30	First Inning Pitched	.285	438	125	18	2	15	88	60	73	.368	.438
September/October	4.03	5	7	0	26	17	109.1	108	12	43	80	First 75 Pitches	.257	1777	457	88	10	55	232	193	313	.330	.411
Starter	4.88	28	47	0	95	95	533.1	558	66	219	344	Pitch 76-90	.283	258	73	12	1	10	35	27	43	.351	.453
Reliever	1.72	3	0	0	19	0	47.0	30	4	20	41	Pitch 91-105	.269	130	35	6	2	1	15	15	21	.340	.369
0-3 Days Rest	3.86	1	2	0	7	7	35.0	23	4	18	27	Pitch 106+	.365	63	23	1	3	4	13	4	6	.406	.667
4 Days Rest	4.51	14	26	0	51	51	301.0	314	33	117	183	First Pitch	.342	363	124	26	1	18	65	11	0	.361	.573

Career (1988-1992)

	ERA	W	L	Sv	G	GS	IP	H	HR	BB	SO		Avg	AB	H	2B	3B	HR	RBI	BB	SO	OBP	SLG
5+ Days Rest	5.61	13	19	0	37	37	197.1	221	29	84	134	Ahead on Count	.183	916	168	27	4	19	86	0	325	.188	.284
Pre-All Star	4.30	21	26	0	60	58	351.1	349	40	137	236	Behind on Count	.324	555	180	27	8	23	100	120	0	.439	.526
Post-All Star	5.11	10	21	0	54	37	229.0	239	30	102	149	Two Strikes	.167	917	153	28	3	18	70	108	385	.256	.263

Pitcher vs. Batter (career)

Pitches Best Vs.	Avg	AB	H	2B	3B	HR	RBI	BB	SO	OBP	SLG	Pitches Worst Vs.	Avg	AB	H	2B	3B	HR	RBI	BB	SO	OBP	SLG
Mike Kingery	.000	12	0	0	0	0	0	1	1	.077	.000	Jay Bell	.545	11	6	0	1	0	1	2	1	.615	.727
Tim Raines	.063	16	1	0	0	0	1	1	2	.118	.063	Larry Walker	.417	12	5	1	0	1	4	1	1	.462	.750
Candy Maldonado	.111	9	1	0	0	0	2	4	.273	.111	Ron Gant	.389	18	7	0	0	3	5	1	3	.421	.889
Craig Biggio	.143	21	3	0	0	0	2	1	4	.182	.143	Dale Murphy	.375	16	6	1	0	2	6	1	2	.412	.813
Terry Pendleton	.190	21	4	0	0	0	0	0	3	.190	.190	Sid Bream	.353	17	6	1	0	2	9	3	1	.450	.765

Brad Arnsberg — Indians   Pitches Right

	ERA	W	L	Sv	G	GS	IP	BB	SO	Avg	H	2B	3B	HR	RBI	OBP	SLG	GF	IR	IRS	Hld	SvOp	SB	CS	GB	FB	G/F
1992 Season	11.81	0	0	0	8	0	10.2	11	5	.317	13	1	0	6	12	.481	.780	1	2	0	1	0	0	0	18	13	1.38
Last Five Years	4.12	8	3	6	86	1	131.0	71	83	.248	124	17	1	21	80	.348	.412	23	78	30	12	7	1	1	195	144	1.35

1992 Season

	ERA	W	L	Sv	G	GS	IP	H	HR	BB	SO		Avg	AB	H	2B	3B	HR	RBI	BB	SO	OBP	SLG
Home	10.80	0	0	0	4	0	3.1	3	1	9	2	vs. Left	.429	14	6	0	0	3	5	3	2	.529	1.071
Away	12.27	0	0	0	4	0	7.1	10	5	2	3	vs. Right	.259	27	7	1	0	3	7	8	3	.459	.630

Last Five Years

	ERA	W	L	Sv	G	GS	IP	H	HR	BB	SO		Avg	AB	H	2B	3B	HR	RBI	BB	SO	OBP	SLG
Home	4.20	6	0	2	46	0	70.2	69	11	40	48	vs. Left	.275	189	52	5	1	11	36	24	26	.361	.487
Away	4.03	2	3	4	40	1	60.1	55	10	31	35	vs. Right	.232	311	72	12	0	10	44	47	57	.340	.367
Day	3.60	4	2	0	19	1	35.0	30	5	19	20	Inning 1-6	.249	181	45	4	1	10	32	25	29	.344	.448
Night	4.31	4	1	6	67	0	96.0	94	16	52	63	Inning 7+	.248	319	79	13	0	11	48	46	54	.349	.392
Grass	3.97	7	3	6	77	1	120.0	112	18	66	76	None on	.237	270	64	14	1	7	7	42	45	.348	.374
Turf	5.73	1	0	0	9	0	11.0	12	3	5	7	Runners on	.261	230	60	3	0	14	73	29	38	.347	.457
April	6.29	0	0	1	17	0	34.1	32	10	19	20	Scoring Posn	.273	128	35	1	0	6	58	22	24	.381	.422
May	9.75	0	1	0	9	0	12.0	17	4	13	10	Close & Late	.247	146	36	7	0	2	15	26	25	.362	.336
June	1.06	2	1	0	12	0	17.0	12	1	6	11	None on/out	.200	115	23	4	1	6	6	18	21	.313	.409
July	2.25	2	0	3	14	0	16.0	12	1	12	14	vs. 1st Batr (relief)	.247	97	24	3	0	4	11	9	13	.353	.288
August	3.38	1	0	2	12	0	16.0	18	2	5	6	First Inning Pitched	.238	273	65	7	0	14	56	40	43	.343	.418
September/October	2.78	3	1	0	22	1	35.2	33	3	16	22	First 15 Pitches	.238	252	60	7	0	9	42	30	38	.328	.373
Starter	9.64	0	1	0	1	1	4.2	8	1	1	4	Pitch 16-30	.269	134	36	7	0	7	21	25	29	.384	.478
Reliever	3.92	8	2	6	85	0	126.1	116	20	70	82	Pitch 31-45	.234	64	15	2	0	2	8	9	9	.338	.359
0 Days rest	2.63	0	1	3	14	0	13.2	11	1	12	9	Pitch 46+	.260	50	13	1	1	3	9	7	7	.362	.500
1 or 2 Days rest	5.16	4	0	2	45	0	61.0	62	15	42	40	First Pitch	.393	56	22	3	0	1	7	1	0	.424	.500
3+ Days rest	2.79	4	1	1	26	0	51.2	43	4	16	33	Ahead on Count	.205	205	42	8	1	11	38	0	69	.210	.415
Pre-All Star	5.48	2	2	1	41	0	65.2	65	15	40	42	Behind on Count	.275	149	41	4	0	7	26	37	0	.422	.443
Post-All Star	2.76	6	1	5	45	1	65.1	59	6	31	41	Two Strikes	.184	212	39	5	1	9	30	33	83	.297	.344

Pitcher vs. Batter (career)

Pitches Best Vs.	Avg	AB	H	2B	3B	HR	RBI	BB	SO	OBP	SLG	Pitches Worst Vs.	Avg	AB	H	2B	3B	HR	RBI	BB	SO	OBP	SLG
												Bob Deer	.500	8	4	0	0	1	3	3	1	.636	.875

Andy Ashby — Phillies   Pitches Right (groundball pitcher)

	ERA	W	L	Sv	G	GS	IP	BB	SO	Avg	H	2B	3B	HR	RBI	OBP	SLG	CG	ShO	Sup	QS	#P/S	SB	CS	GB	FB	G/F
1992 Season	7.54	1	3	0	10	8	37.0	21	24	.290	42	7	2	6	26	.379	.490	0	0	5.59	2	72	4	2	57	35	1.63
Career (1991-1992)	6.72	2	8	0	18	16	79.0	40	50	.272	83	16	4	11	51	.359	.459	0	0	3.99	3	76	4	3	116	75	1.55

1992 Season

	ERA	W	L	Sv	G	GS	IP	H	HR	BB	SO		Avg	AB	H	2B	3B	HR	RBI	BB	SO	OBP	SLG
Home	6.00	1	1	0	5	4	21.0	17	3	10	14	vs. Left	.318	85	27	4	0	4	15	13	9	.406	.506
Away	9.56	0	2	0	5	4	16.0	25	3	11	10	vs. Right	.250	60	15	3	2	2	11	8	15	.338	.467

Billy Ashley — Dodgers   Bats Right (flyball hitter)

	Avg	G	AB	R	H	2B	3B	HR	RBI	BB	SO	HBP	GDP	SB	CS	OBP	SLG	IBB	SH	SF	#Pit	#P/PA	GB	FB	G/F
1992 Season	.221	29	95	6	21	5	0	2	6	5	34	0	2	0	0	.260	.337	0	0	0	387	3.87	24	25	0.96

1992 Season

	Avg	AB	H	2B	3B	HR	RBI	BB	SO	OBP	SLG		Avg	AB	H	2B	3B	HR	RBI	BB	SO	OBP	SLG
vs. Left	.333	30	10	2	0	2	4	1	6	.355	.600	Scoring Posn	.267	15	4	1	0	0	4	0	7	.267	.333
vs. Right	.169	65	11	3	0	0	2	4	28	.217	.215	Close & Late	.143	21	3	0	0	0	1	0	11	.143	.143
Home	.289	38	11	2	0	2	3	2	11	.325	.500	None on/out	.222	27	6	2	0	1	1	1	9	.250	.407
Away	.175	57	10	3	0	0	3	3	23	.217	.228	Batting #6	.130	46	6	2	0	1	1	0	22	.130	.239
First Pitch	.091	11	1	0	0	0	0	0	0	.091	.091	Batting #7	.302	43	13	2	0	1	5	5	11	.375	.419
Ahead on Count	.364	11	4	0	0	1	3	0	.500	.364	Other	.333	6	2	1	0	0	0	1	.333	.500
Behind on Count	.154	39	6	3	0	1	3	0	24	.154	.308	Pre-All Star	.000	0	0	0	0	0	0	0	0	.000	.000
Two Strikes	.190	58	11	4	0	2	2	34	.217	.259	Post-All Star	.221	95	21	5	0	2	6	5	34	.260	.337

16

Paul Assenmacher — Cubs — Pitches Left

	ERA	W	L	Sv	G	GS	IP	BB	SO	Avg	H	2B	3B	HR	RBI	OBP	SLG	GF	IR	IRS	Hld	SvOp	SB	CS	GB	FB	G/F
1992 Season	4.10	4	4	8	70	0	68.0	26	67	.271	72	18	1	6	39	.340	.414	23	62	13	20	13	9	2	84	69	1.22
Last Five Years	3.37	29	25	38	346	0	429.2	153	429	.246	393	66	8	33	198	.313	.359	75	312	97	65	71	35	19	501	404	1.24

1992 Season

	ERA	W	L	Sv	G	GS	IP	H	HR	BB	SO		Avg	AB	H	2B	3B	HR	RBI	BB	SO	OBP	SLG
Home	4.15	2	3	5	37	0	39.0	38	2	13	34	vs. Left	.220	91	20	5	0	3	11	9	28	.294	.374
Away	4.03	2	1	3	33	0	29.0	34	4	13	33	vs. Right	.297	175	52	13	1	3	28	17	39	.364	.434
Day	3.70	3	3	6	39	0	41.1	44	2	13	40	Inning 1-6	.286	14	4	3	0	0	4	1	3	.333	.500
Night	4.72	1	1	2	31	0	26.2	28	4	13	27	Inning 7+	.270	252	68	15	1	6	35	25	64	.340	.409
Grass	4.47	2	4	6	46	0	48.1	52	4	17	45	None on	.298	124	37	9	1	4	4	8	30	.341	.484
Turf	3.20	2	0	2	24	0	19.2	20	2	9	22	Runners on	.246	142	35	9	0	2	35	18	37	.339	.352
April	2.08	0	1	0	11	0	8.2	5	0	4	12	Scoring Posn	.213	94	20	7	0	2	35	15	25	.333	.351
May	1.50	1	0	2	9	0	12.0	9	1	3	9	Close & Late	.239	176	42	12	0	2	23	19	50	.322	.341
June	1.80	0	0	3	13	0	10.0	8	1	5	9	None on/out	.246	57	14	5	0	1	1	1	12	.259	.386
July	7.11	2	1	0	12	0	12.2	17	2	4	14	vs. 1st Batr (relief)	.143	63	9	3	0	2	7	6	20	.229	.286
August	2.70	0	0	2	8	0	10.0	12	2	4	10	First Inning Pitched	.243	206	50	15	1	4	31	24	52	.328	.383
September/October	7.36	1	2	1	17	0	14.2	21	0	6	13	First 15 Pitches	.242	190	46	14	1	6	28	18	49	.311	.421
Starter	0.00	0	0	0	0	0	0.0	0	0	0	0	Pitch 16-30	.333	72	24	4	0	0	11	7	18	.400	.389
Reliever	4.10	4	4	8	70	0	68.0	72	6	26	67	Pitch 31-45	.500	4	2	0	0	0	0	1	0	.600	.500
0 Days rest	3.71	3	1	3	20	0	17.0	16	1	7	18	Pitch 46+	.000	0	0	0	0	0	0	0	0	.000	.000
1 or 2 Days rest	5.14	1	3	4	36	0	35.0	40	3	16	33	First Pitch	.333	42	14	4	0	4	14	2	2	.364	.714
3+ Days rest	2.25	0	0	1	14	0	16.0	16	2	3	16	Ahead on Count	.222	135	30	8	1	0	15	0	57	.226	.296
Pre-All Star	2.87	2	2	5	39	0	37.2	32	3	14	40	Behind on Count	.372	43	16	3	0	1	7	16	0	.542	.512
Post-All Star	5.64	2	2	3	31	0	30.1	40	3	12	27	Two Strikes	.187	134	25	5	1	1	10	8	65	.236	.261

Last Five Years

	ERA	W	L	Sv	G	GS	IP	H	HR	BB	SO		Avg	AB	H	2B	3B	HR	RBI	BB	SO	OBP	SLG
Home	3.53	22	14	19	193	0	234.2	218	18	78	235	vs. Left	.223	524	117	19	2	7	68	37	159	.279	.307
Away	3.18	7	11	19	153	1	195.0	175	15	75	194	vs. Right	.257	1076	276	47	6	26	130	116	270	.328	.384
Day	3.14	17	7	22	168	0	218.0	202	17	79	224	Inning 1-6	.231	143	33	6	1	3	29	16	49	.306	.350
Night	3.61	12	18	16	178	1	211.2	191	16	74	205	Inning 7+	.247	1457	360	60	7	30	169	137	380	.313	.360
Grass	3.33	24	19	29	260	0	327.0	297	26	108	335	None on	.258	831	214	34	4	20	20	55	213	.304	.380
Turf	3.51	5	6	9	86	1	102.2	96	7	45	94	Runners on	.233	769	179	32	4	13	178	98	216	.322	.336
April	2.15	1	4	5	48	0	62.2	34	4	21	63	Scoring Posn	.233	484	113	21	1	7	156	84	138	.347	.324
May	2.83	4	4	4	63	0	76.1	68	5	24	69	Close & Late	.242	883	214	40	3	17	110	88	243	.313	.352
June	5.99	3	4	7	69	1	67.2	83	5	40	65	None on/out	.256	363	93	16	2	11	11	25	92	.304	.402
July	3.24	7	5	6	61	0	72.1	71	4	20	81	vs. 1st Batr (relief)	.202	258	52	5	1	11	41	28	73	.264	.357
August	1.95	6	1	7	45	0	69.1	49	9	20	71	First Inning Pitched	.251	891	224	41	4	22	137	105	224	.330	.380
September/October	3.98	8	7	9	60	0	81.1	88	6	28	80	First 15 Pitches	.253	954	241	41	4	22	134	102	236	.324	.373
Starter	36.00	0	0	0	1	1	1.0	4	1	2	1	Pitch 16-30	.244	500	122	23	4	7	49	36	145	.296	.348
Reliever	3.30	29	25	38	345	0	428.2	389	32	151	428	Pitch 31-45	.198	126	25	2	0	3	12	12	42	.264	.286
0 Days rest	4.39	11	13	11	108	0	125.0	128	10	51	123	Pitch 46+	.250	20	5	0	0	1	3	3	6	.348	.400
1 or 2 Days rest	3.19	10	10	15	151	0	183.2	163	14	66	178	First Pitch	.329	228	75	15	2	10	39	32	2	.411	.544
3+ Days rest	2.33	8	2	12	86	0	120.0	98	8	34	127	Ahead on Count	.182	847	154	31	4	9	74	0	378	.184	.260
Pre-All Star	3.69	11	14	16	204	1	232.0	211	16	92	220	Behind on Count	.350	266	93	11	2	9	56	78	0	.496	.508
Post-All Star	3.01	18	11	22	142	0	197.2	182	17	61	209	Two Strikes	.155	832	129	28	3	5	60	42	427	.197	.214

Pitcher vs. Batter (career)

Pitches Best Vs.	Avg	AB	H	2B	3B	HR	RBI	BB	SO	OBP	SLG	Pitches Worst Vs.	Avg	AB	H	2B	3B	HR	RBI	BB	SO	OBP	SLG
Milt Thompson	.063	16	1	1	0	0	1	1	2	.118	.125	Lenny Dykstra	.615	13	8	2	0	1	4	0	3	.571	1.000
Dave Martinez	.067	15	1	0	0	0	1	1	7	.125	.067	Robby Thompson	.545	11	6	2	0	0	3	0	1	.545	.727
Paul O'Neill	.071	14	1	0	0	0	1	1	7	.133	.071	Ray Lankford	.545	11	6	2	0	0	3	3	1	.643	.727
Keith Miller	.091	11	1	0	0	0	0	1	8	.167	.091	Jay Bell	.500	10	5	1	1	1	2	1	1	.545	1.100
Dave Hollins	.100	10	1	0	0	0	0	1		.250	.100	Kevin McReynolds	.474	19	9	3	0	1	6	2	3	.524	.789

Pedro Astacio — Dodgers — Pitches Right (groundball pitcher)

	ERA	W	L	Sv	G	GS	IP	BB	SO	Avg	H	2B	3B	HR	RBI	OBP	SLG	CG	ShO	Sup	QS	#P/S	SB	CS	GB	FB	G/F
1992 Season	1.98	5	5	0	11	11	82.0	20	43	.255	80	8	2	1	18	.302	.303	4	4	2.96	10	106	5	3	136	77	1.77

1992 Season

	ERA	W	L	Sv	G	GS	IP	H	HR	BB	SO		Avg	AB	H	2B	3B	HR	RBI	BB	SO	OBP	SLG
Home	1.68	3	3	0	6	6	48.1	47	1	10	22	vs. Left	.244	180	44	3	2	1	7	18	17	.315	.300
Away	2.41	2	2	0	5	5	33.2	33	0	10	21	vs. Right	.269	134	36	5	0	0	11	2	26	.283	.306
Starter	1.98	5	5	0	11	11	82.0	80	1	20	43	Scoring Posn	.225	71	16	1	0	0	15	7	11	.296	.239
Reliever	0.00	0	0	0	0	0	0.0	0	0	0	0	Close & Late	.348	23	8	1	0	1	2	1	2	.360	.522
0-3 Days Rest	0.00	0	0	0	0	0	0.0	0	0	0	0	None on/out	.197	76	15	1	0	1	1	9	12	.282	.250
4 Days Rest	2.33	2	4	0	6	6	46.1	52	1	8	19	First Pitch	.338	68	23	2	0	1	4	2	0	.352	.412
5+ Days Rest	1.51	3	1	0	5	5	35.2	28	0	12	24	Behind on Count	.275	51	14	3	0	0	5	14	0	.431	.333
Pre-All Star	1.69	1	1	0	2	2	16.0	12	1	6	12	Ahead on Count	.212	132	28	3	0	0	5	0	36	.222	.235
Post-All Star	2.05	4	4	0	9	9	66.0	68	0	14	31	Two Strikes	.201	134	27	3	1	0	6	4	43	.229	.239

Jim Austin — Brewers
Pitches Right (flyball pitcher)

	ERA	W	L	Sv	G	GS	IP	BB	SO	Avg	H	2B	3B	HR	RBI	OBP	SLG	GF	IR	IRS	Hld	SvOp	SB	CS	GB	FB	G/F
1992 Season	1.85	5	2	0	47	0	58.1	32	30	.191	38	9	0	2	16	.308	.266	12	43	13	9	1	2	4	48	85	0.56
Career (1991-1992)	2.69	5	2	0	52	0	67.0	43	33	.202	46	11	0	3	23	.338	.289	13	51	14	9	1	2	4	57	97	0.59

1992 Season

	ERA	W	L	Sv	G	GS	IP	H	HR	BB	SO		Avg	AB	H	2B	3B	HR	RBI	BB	SO	OBP	SLG
Home	1.11	2	1	0	25	0	32.1	21	1	14	19	vs. Left	.220	82	18	5	0	0	5	11	8	.316	.280
Away	2.77	3	1	0	22	0	26.0	17	1	18	11	vs. Right	.171	117	20	4	0	2	11	21	22	.302	.256
Starter	0.00	0	0	0	0	0	0.0	0	0	0	0	Scoring Posn	.180	61	11	4	0	1	15	11	10	.301	.295
Reliever	1.85	5	2	0	47	0	58.1	38	2	32	30	Close & Late	.176	51	9	3	0	0	7	11	9	.328	.235
0 Days rest	0.00	0	0	0	3	0	4.0	1	0	5	2	None on/out	.262	42	11	1	0	1	1	6	4	.380	.357
1 or 2 Days rest	1.57	2	2	0	21	0	23.0	16	0	11	14	First Pitch	.174	23	4	2	0	0	3	5	0	.310	.261
3+ Days rest	2.30	3	0	0	23	0	31.1	21	2	16	14	Behind on Count	.275	51	14	5	0	1	9	18	0	.464	.431
Pre-All Star	2.41	2	2	0	27	0	33.2	23	1	19	15	Ahead on Count	.108	83	9	0	0	0	2	0	27	.129	.108
Post-All Star	1.09	3	0	0	20	0	24.2	15	1	13	15	Two Strikes	.067	75	5	0	0	0	3	9	30	.176	.067

Steve Avery — Braves
Pitches Left

	ERA	W	L	Sv	G	GS	IP	BB	SO	Avg	H	2B	3B	HR	RBI	OBP	SLG	CG	ShO	Sup	QS	#P/S	SB	CS	GB	FB	G/F
1992 Season	3.20	11	11	0	35	35	233.2	71	129	.246	216	31	6	14	79	.300	.343	2	2	3.93	23	97	42	14	336	264	1.27
Career (1990-1992)	3.71	32	30	0	91	90	543.0	181	341	.254	526	69	13	42	226	.314	.371	6	4	4.41	46	93	83	33	792	589	1.34

1992 Season

	ERA	W	L	Sv	G	GS	IP	H	HR	BB	SO		Avg	AB	H	2B	3B	HR	RBI	BB	SO	OBP	SLG
Home	2.51	6	4	0	16	16	107.2	107	5	29	61	vs. Left	.258	155	40	5	0	3	18	20	38	.341	.348
Away	3.79	5	7	0	19	19	126.0	109	9	42	68	vs. Right	.243	723	176	26	6	11	61	51	91	.291	.342
Day	1.77	3	1	0	5	5	35.2	26	1	12	21	Inning 1-6	.234	743	174	25	6	13	64	58	118	.287	.336
Night	3.45	8	10	0	30	30	198.0	190	13	59	108	Inning 7+	.311	135	42	6	0	1	15	13	11	.369	.378
Grass	2.58	9	7	0	25	25	171.0	150	8	53	89	None on	.237	540	128	21	2	9	9	41	75	.291	.333
Turf	4.88	2	4	0	10	10	62.2	66	6	18	40	Runners on	.260	338	88	10	4	5	70	30	54	.314	.358
April	3.08	1	2	0	4	4	26.1	22	1	9	13	Scoring Posn	.231	199	46	7	1	2	60	24	36	.303	.307
May	3.22	2	3	0	7	7	44.2	43	3	22	29	Close & Late	.287	94	27	4	0	1	12	10	10	.352	.362
June	2.04	3	1	0	5	5	35.1	32	2	8	17	None on/out	.268	235	63	9	0	6	6	17	31	.317	.383
July	2.79	2	1	0	7	7	48.1	36	2	15	25	vs. 1st Batr (relief)	.000	0	0	0	0	0	0	0	0	.000	.000
August	4.72	2	2	0	6	6	40.0	51	1	11	19	First Inning Pitched	.260	131	34	3	0	3	14	13	21	.322	.351
September/October	3.23	1	2	0	6	6	39.0	32	5	6	26	First 75 Pitches	.240	650	156	21	6	12	57	50	106	.292	.346
Starter	3.20	11	11	0	35	35	233.2	216	14	71	129	Pitch 76-90	.240	125	30	4	0	1	8	7	14	.278	.296
Reliever	0.00	0	0	0	0	0	0.0	0	0	0	0	Pitch 91-105	.315	73	23	6	0	1	14	11	7	.395	.438
0-3 Days Rest	2.16	1	0	0	1	1	8.1	4	0	5	3	Pitch 106+	.233	30	7	0	0	0	0	3	2	.303	.233
4 Days Rest	3.19	9	8	0	27	27	186.1	167	12	55	98	First Pitch	.245	147	36	2	0	4	10	2	0	.253	.340
5+ Days Rest	3.46	1	3	0	7	7	39.0	45	2	11	28	Ahead on Count	.194	407	79	13	2	4	30	0	110	.193	.265
Pre-All Star	2.62	7	7	0	19	19	127.1	110	6	47	75	Behind on Count	.358	179	64	12	1	5	28	43	0	.473	.520
Post-All Star	3.89	4	4	0	16	16	106.1	106	8	24	54	Two Strikes	.174	386	67	8	2	4	26	26	129	.225	.244

Career (1990-1992)

	ERA	W	L	Sv	G	GS	IP	H	HR	BB	SO		Avg	AB	H	2B	3B	HR	RBI	BB	SO	OBP	SLG
Home	3.37	18	13	0	45	45	272.2	272	16	89	170	vs. Left	.226	380	86	10	3	6	40	37	90	.294	.316
Away	4.06	14	17	0	46	45	270.1	254	24	92	171	vs. Right	.261	1687	440	79	10	36	186	144	251	.318	.384
Day	4.44	9	8	0	23	22	127.2	131	15	39	82	Inning 1-6	.249	1784	445	77	12	37	192	158	307	.310	.368
Night	3.49	23	22	0	68	68	415.1	395	27	142	259	Inning 7+	.286	283	81	12	1	5	34	23	34	.341	.389
Grass	3.29	26	20	0	66	65	402.0	379	26	131	240	None on	.237	1237	293	56	7	21	21	106	192	.299	.344
Turf	4.91	6	10	0	25	25	141.0	147	16	50	101	Runners on	.281	830	233	33	6	21	205	75	149	.335	.411
April	2.98	3	3	0	8	8	48.1	39	3	18	25	Scoring Posn	.259	499	129	21	1	9	172	55	102	.323	.359
May	3.29	6	4	0	13	13	82.0	79	6	37	52	Close & Late	.258	163	42	5	1	1	20	15	20	.318	.319
June	3.86	5	5	0	14	14	81.2	88	6	29	47	None on/out	.265	543	144	28	4	12	12	46	84	.324	.398
July	3.35	6	5	0	19	19	121.0	99	7	42	64	vs. 1st Batr (relief)	.000	1	0	0	0	0	0	0	0	.000	.000
August	4.68	7	8	0	18	18	102.0	124	8	33	79	First Inning Pitched	.273	348	95	14	3	9	45	37	63	.339	.467
September/October	3.75	5	5	0	19	18	108.0	98	12	22	74	First 75 Pitches	.245	1567	384	69	13	32	164	132	282	.303	.367
Starter	3.68	32	29	0	90	90	541.0	521	42	181	341	Pitch 76-90	.277	260	72	8	0	6	27	23	33	.336	.377
Reliever	13.50	0	1	0	1	0	2.0	5	0	0	0	Pitch 91-105	.308	159	49	10	0	1	23	18	16	.374	.390
0-3 Days Rest	4.55	1	2	0	6	6	31.2	27	4	15	11	Pitch 106+	.259	81	21	2	0	3	12	8	10	.330	.395
4 Days Rest	3.42	25	18	0	63	63	395.0	368	32	124	247	First Pitch	.312	333	104	18	2	10	51	4	0	.320	.468
5+ Days Rest	4.33	6	9	0	21	21	114.1	126	6	42	83	Ahead on Count	.205	955	196	34	5	11	73	0	295	.206	.286
Pre-All Star	3.31	16	15	0	41	41	252.2	239	16	100	151	Behind on Count	.341	434	148	28	3	14	76	98	0	.457	.516
Post-All Star	4.06	16	15	0	50	49	290.1	287	26	81	190	Two Strikes	.180	941	169	26	4	9	59	79	341	.244	.244

Pitcher vs. Batter (career)

Pitches Best Vs.	Avg	AB	H	2B	3B	HR	RBI	BB	SO	OBP	SLG	Pitches Worst Vs.	Avg	AB	H	2B	3B	HR	RBI	BB	SO	OBP	SLG
Mike Scioscia	.000	11	0	0	0	0	1	1	1	.077	.000	Eric Yelding	.500	10	5	3	0	0	2	3	1	.615	.800
Gerald Perry	.000	11	0	0	0	0	0	2	1	.154	.000	Glenn Braggs	.464	28	13	2	1	4	11	2	2	.500	1.036
Gary Carter	.067	15	1	0	0	0	1	1	3	.125	.067	Jeff King	.455	11	5	3	0	1	6	1	3	.462	1.000
Luis Gonzalez	.071	14	1	1	0	0	0	0	1	.071	.143	Ryne Sandberg	.385	13	5	0	1	1	3	4	2	.529	.769
Luis Salazar	.083	12	1	0	0	0	0	2	1	.083	.083	Will Clark	.353	17	6	3	1	1	3	4	1	.389	.824

Bobby Ayala — Reds
Pitches Right (groundball pitcher)

	ERA	W	L	Sv	G	GS	IP	BB	SO	Avg	H	2B	3B	HR	RBI	OBP	SLG	CG	ShO	Sup	QS	#P/S	SB	CS	GB	FB	G/F
1992 Season	4.34	2	1	0	5	5	29.0	13	23	.297	33	10	0	1	12	.376	.414	0	0	4.66	3	87	2	3	53	18	2.94

1992 Season

	ERA	W	L	Sv	G	GS	IP	H	HR	BB	SO		Avg	AB	H	2B	3B	HR	RBI	BB	SO	OBP	SLG
Home	3.86	2	0	0	3	3	18.2	20	0	6	17	vs. Left	.286	63	18	6	0	0	7	8	14	.366	.381
Away	5.23	0	1	0	2	2	10.1	13	1	7	6	vs. Right	.313	48	15	4	0	1	5	5	9	.389	.458

Bob Ayrault — Phillies
Pitches Right (flyball pitcher)

	ERA	W	L	Sv	G	GS	IP	BB	SO	Avg	H	2B	3B	HR	RBI	OBP	SLG	GF	IR	IRS	Hld	SvOp	SB	CS	GB	FB	G/F
1992 Season	3.12	2	2	0	30	0	43.1	17	27	.209	32	9	2	0	20	.287	.294	7	16	8	0	0	3	0	45	50	0.90

1992 Season

	ERA	W	L	Sv	G	GS	IP	H	HR	BB	SO		Avg	AB	H	2B	3B	HR	RBI	BB	SO	OBP	SLG
Home	2.50	1	1	0	13	0	18.0	13	0	9	12	vs. Left	.253	79	20	4	1	0	10	7	13	.310	.329
Away	3.55	1	1	0	17	0	25.1	19	0	8	15	vs. Right	.162	74	12	5	1	0	10	10	14	.264	.257
Starter	0.00	0	0	0	0	0	0.0	0	0	0	0	Scoring Posn	.205	39	8	0	1	0	16	8	8	.320	.256
Reliever	3.12	2	2	0	30	0	43.1	32	0	17	27	Close & Late	.111	9	1	1	0	0	0	1	5	.200	.222
0 Days rest	0.00	0	0	0	3	0	3.1	3	0	2	2	None on/out	.250	36	9	2	0	0	0	3	5	.308	.306
1 or 2 Days rest	3.72	1	0	0	13	0	19.1	14	0	7	13	First Pitch	.120	25	3	1	0	0	1	1	0	.179	.160
3+ Days rest	3.05	1	2	0	14	0	20.2	15	0	8	12	Behind on Count	.281	32	9	2	0	0	4	9	0	.429	.344
Pre-All Star	3.97	0	1	0	14	0	22.2	18	0	8	15	Ahead on Count	.174	69	12	3	1	0	10	0	24	.171	.246
Post-All Star	2.18	2	1	0	16	0	20.2	14	0	9	12	Two Strikes	.209	67	14	5	0	0	8	7	27	.280	.284

Oscar Azocar — Padres
Bats Left

	Avg	G	AB	R	H	2B	3B	HR	RBI	BB	SO	HBP	GDP	SB	CS	OBP	SLG	IBB	SH	SF	#Pit	#P/PA	GB	FB	G/F
1992 Season	.190	99	168	15	32	6	0	0	8	9	12	0	3	1	0	.230	.226	1	4	1	541	3.04	66	57	1.16
Career (1990-1992)	.226	202	439	38	99	16	0	5	36	12	36	2	5	10	0	.248	.296	2	4	3	1307	2.87	178	141	1.26

1992 Season

	Avg	AB	H	2B	3B	HR	RBI	BB	SO	OBP	SLG		Avg	AB	H	2B	3B	HR	RBI	BB	SO	OBP	SLG
vs. Left	.400	5	2	1	0	0	0	0	0	.400	.600	Scoring Posn	.220	41	9	0	0	0	7	2	6	.250	.220
vs. Right	.184	163	30	5	0	0	8	9	12	.225	.215	Close & Late	.220	41	9	2	0	0	5	1	4	.233	.268
Home	.198	96	19	5	0	0	4	5	4	.238	.250	None on/out	.111	36	4	2	0	0	0	1	2	.135	.167
Away	.181	72	13	1	0	0	4	4	8	.221	.194	Batting #2	.156	64	10	2	0	0	1	3	3	.194	.188
First Pitch	.176	34	6	0	0	0	3	1	0	.194	.176	Batting #9	.180	50	9	1	0	0	5	2	5	.208	.200
Ahead on Count	.276	29	8	4	0	0	3	7	0	.417	.414	Pre-All Star	.221	86	19	3	0	0	5	5	8	.264	.256
Behind on Count	.172	64	11	1	0	0	0	0	11	.172	.188	Post-All Star	.159	82	13	3	0	0	3	4	4	.195	.195
Two Strikes	.150	60	9	0	0	0	0	1	12	.164	.150												

Wally Backman — Phillies
Bats Left (groundball hitter)

	Avg	G	AB	R	H	2B	3B	HR	RBI	BB	SO	HBP	GDP	SB	CS	OBP	SLG	IBB	SH	SF	#Pit	#P/PA	GB	FB	G/F
1992 Season	.271	42	48	6	13	1	0	0	6	6	9	0	3	1	0	.352	.292	1	1	0	249	4.61	28	3	9.33
Last Five Years	.270	426	1141	165	308	55	5	3	92	151	186	3	22	20	11	.354	.335	3	16	9	5009	3.84	524	203	2.58

1992 Season

	Avg	AB	H	2B	3B	HR	RBI	BB	SO	OBP	SLG		Avg	AB	H	2B	3B	HR	RBI	BB	SO	OBP	SLG
vs. Left	.000	1	0	0	0	0	0	0	1	.000	.000	Scoring Posn	.385	13	5	0	0	0	5	3	2	.500	.385
vs. Right	.277	47	13	1	0	0	6	6	8	.358	.298	Close & Late	.333	21	7	1	0	0	6	2	4	.391	.381

Last Five Years

	Avg	AB	H	2B	3B	HR	RBI	BB	SO	OBP	SLG		Avg	AB	H	2B	3B	HR	RBI	BB	SO	OBP	SLG
vs. Left	.223	148	33	5	1	0	15	19	26	.314	.270	Scoring Posn	.267	232	62	14	2	0	83	40	43	.363	.345
vs. Right	.277	993	275	50	4	3	77	132	160	.360	.344	Close & Late	.234	184	43	10	0	0	19	28	42	.332	.288
Groundball	.272	368	100	13	3	2	39	46	53	.354	.340	None on/out	.249	373	93	15	0	3	3	42	62	.325	.314
Flyball	.226	199	45	9	0	0	11	38	40	.347	.271	Batting #1	.280	475	133	26	3	3	39	55	71	.353	.366
Home	.291	547	159	33	3	0	46	77	89	.362	.362	Batting #2	.278	472	131	19	1	0	30	66	80	.366	.322
Away	.251	594	149	22	2	3	46	74	97	.332	.310	Other	.227	194	44	10	1	0	23	30	35	.329	.289
Day	.278	352	98	13	3	1	20	42	53	.355	.341	April	.284	190	54	6	2	0	16	17	30	.348	.337
Night	.266	789	210	42	2	2	72	109	133	.354	.332	May	.286	192	55	9	0	1	22	22	32	.358	.349
Grass	.301	479	144	23	1	3	40	55	78	.371	.372	June	.246	281	69	14	1	2	24	32	46	.320	.324
Turf	.248	662	164	32	4	0	52	96	108	.342	.308	July	.271	155	42	7	0	0	6	30	33	.385	.316
First Pitch	.448	116	52	11	1	1	17	1	0	.453	.586	August	.258	159	41	10	0	0	7	25	25	.362	.321
Ahead on Count	.333	309	103	18	2	0	27	89	0	.475	.405	September/October	.287	164	47	9	2	0	15	25	20	.377	.366
Behind on Count	.202	331	67	13	1	0	27	0	98	.207	.248	Pre-All Star	.269	743	200	32	3	3	67	86	128	.344	.332
Two Strikes	.190	520	99	18	2	1	39	59	166	.274	.238	Post-All Star	.271	398	108	23	2	0	25	65	58	.373	.339

Batter vs. Pitcher (since 1984)

Hits Best Against	Avg	AB	H	2B	3B	HR	RBI	BB	SO	OBP	SLG	Hits Worst Against	Avg	AB	H	2B	3B	HR	RBI	BB	SO	OBP	SLG
Doug Drabek	.500	18	9	0	0	0	0	1	4	.526	.500	Jeff Robinson	.077	13	1	0	0	0	1	0	1	.071	.077
Larry Andersen	.500	16	8	1	0	0	2	1	1	.529	.563	Craig Lefferts	.083	12	1	0	0	0	1	1	4	.154	.083
Ron Robinson	.455	11	5	0	1	0	0	1	2	.500	.636	Don Robinson	.100	20	2	0	0	0	0	1	5	.143	.100

Batter vs. Pitcher (since 1984)

Hits Best Against	Avg	AB	H	2B	3B	HR	RBI	BB	SO	OBP	SLG	Hits Worst Against	Avg	AB	H	2B	3B	HR	RBI	BB	SO	OBP	SLG
Shawn Boskie	.417	12	5	2	0	0	0	0	2	.417	.583	Mark Portugal	.100	10	1	0	0	0	0	1	0	.182	.100
Ramon Martinez	.357	14	5	3	0	0	4	3	2	.444	.571	Tim Belcher	.154	13	2	0	0	0	1	0	4	.143	.154

Carlos Baerga — Indians
Bats Both (groundball hitter)

	Avg	G	AB	R	H	2B	3B	HR	RBI	BB	SO	HBP	GDP	SB	CS	OBP	SLG	IBB	SH	SF	#Pit	#P/PA	GB	FB	G/F
1992 Season	.312	161	657	92	205	32	1	20	105	35	76	13	15	10	2	.354	.455	10	2	9	2373	3.32	295	175	1.69
Career (1990-1992)	.293	427	1562	218	457	77	5	38	221	99	207	23	31	13	6	.340	.421	17	7	17	5884	3.46	692	377	1.84

1992 Season

	Avg	AB	H	2B	3B	HR	RBI	BB	SO	OBP	SLG		Avg	AB	H	2B	3B	HR	RBI	BB	SO	OBP	SLG
vs. Left	.375	168	63	9	0	4	35	3	19	.387	.500	Scoring Posn	.308	182	56	5	0	5	81	17	17	.366	.418
vs. Right	.290	489	142	23	1	16	70	32	57	.343	.440	Close & Late	.317	126	40	9	0	2	13	8	12	.370	.437
Groundball	.309	165	51	9	0	4	27	9	16	.358	.436	None on/out	.272	114	31	6	0	4	4	5	16	.320	.430
Flyball	.311	193	60	11	0	7	30	7	26	.346	.477	Total	.312	657	205	32	1	20	105	35	76	.354	.455
Home	.353	329	116	17	0	9	50	18	36	.392	.486	Batting #3	.312	657	205	32	1	20	105	35	76	.354	.455
Away	.271	328	89	15	1	11	55	17	40	.318	.424	Other	.000	0	0	0	0	0	0	0	0	.000	.000
Day	.323	217	70	7	0	5	33	11	21	.365	.424	April	.304	92	28	3	0	2	10	3	8	.333	.402
Night	.307	440	135	25	1	15	72	24	55	.349	.470	May	.315	108	34	3	0	2	18	4	11	.353	.398
Grass	.323	557	180	25	0	18	89	31	65	.363	.465	June	.294	109	32	7	0	5	16	7	15	.333	.495
Turf	.250	100	25	7	1	2	16	4	11	.309	.400	July	.333	102	34	5	1	5	19	4	14	.369	.549
First Pitch	.293	75	22	2	0	2	16	10	0	.391	.400	August	.276	116	32	7	0	3	21	5	14	.326	.414
Ahead on Count	.372	164	61	13	1	8	27	13	0	.425	.610	September/October	.346	130	45	7	0	3	21	12	14	.401	.469
Behind on Count	.312	276	86	13	0	6	41	0	48	.319	.424	Pre-All Star	.323	350	113	15	0	12	53	16	40	.360	.469
Two Strikes	.258	264	68	13	0	4	34	12	76	.300	.352	Post-All Star	.300	307	92	17	1	8	52	19	36	.348	.440

1992 By Position

Position	Avg	AB	H	2B	3B	HR	RBI	BB	SO	OBP	SLG	G	GS	Innings	PO	A	E	DP	Fld Pct	Rng Fctr	In Zone	Outs	Zone Rtg	MLB Zone
As 2b	.313	654	205	32	1	20	105	35	75	.356	.457	160	160	1434.0	400	475	19	137	.979	5.49	495	471	.952	.892

Career (1990-1992)

	Avg	AB	H	2B	3B	HR	RBI	BB	SO	OBP	SLG		Avg	AB	H	2B	3B	HR	RBI	BB	SO	OBP	SLG
vs. Left	.326	432	141	21	0	8	71	12	55	.351	.431	Scoring Posn	.289	419	121	14	1	13	177	42	57	.353	.420
vs. Right	.280	1130	316	56	5	30	150	87	152	.337	.418	Close & Late	.270	293	79	19	0	5	35	23	46	.331	.386
Groundball	.275	461	127	25	3	6	63	31	71	.327	.382	None on/out	.279	308	86	16	0	7	7	20	34	.331	.399
Flyball	.290	369	107	16	1	12	50	28	56	.350	.436	Batting #3	.298	1210	360	60	3	28	169	64	159	.340	.421
Home	.319	778	248	40	3	14	110	47	89	.362	.432	Batting #5	.310	87	27	3	1	2	11	7	9	.371	.437
Away	.267	784	209	37	2	24	111	52	118	.319	.411	Other	.264	265	70	14	1	8	41	28	39	.332	.415
Day	.283	492	139	16	1	13	73	42	68	.346	.398	April	.268	183	49	4	1	5	18	10	17	.308	.383
Night	.297	1070	318	61	4	25	148	57	139	.338	.432	May	.290	269	78	8	1	5	41	17	26	.339	.383
Grass	.302	1323	400	64	4	36	196	83	163	.347	.438	June	.267	243	65	15	0	10	34	23	37	.332	.453
Turf	.238	239	57	13	1	2	25	16	44	.303	.326	July	.309	233	72	13	1	6	28	15	33	.354	.451
First Pitch	.325	191	62	8	0	4	30	15	0	.385	.429	August	.299	291	87	16	0	7	46	10	44	.335	.426
Ahead on Count	.358	380	136	28	4	14	71	53	0	.439	.563	September/October	.309	343	106	21	2	5	54	24	50	.359	.426
Behind on Count	.294	613	180	28	0	13	80	0	127	.303	.403	Pre-All Star	.285	772	220	31	2	24	106	56	92	.338	.424
Two Strikes	.235	648	152	27	1	12	68	29	207	.274	.335	Post-All Star	.300	790	237	46	3	14	115	43	115	.343	.419

Batter vs. Pitcher (career)

Hits Best Against	Avg	AB	H	2B	3B	HR	RBI	BB	SO	OBP	SLG	Hits Worst Against	Avg	AB	H	2B	3B	HR	RBI	BB	SO	OBP	SLG
Walt Terrell	.526	19	10	2	0	1	6	3	0	.591	.789	Dave Stieb	.000	9	0	0	0	0	0	2	0	.182	.000
Greg Hibbard	.500	22	11	0	0	2	7	2	2	.500	.773	David Wells	.067	15	1	1	0	0	2	1	2	.125	.133
Bob Welch	.474	19	9	3	0	1	3	0	1	.474	.789	Scott Erickson	.100	20	2	1	0	0	2	0	4	.100	.150
Mike Mussina	.455	11	5	4	0	0	2	0	0	.455	.818	Erik Hanson	.133	15	2	0	0	0	1	0	3	.235	.133
Bill Gullickson	.421	19	8	2	0	2	5	0	1	.400	.842	Storm Davis	.167	12	2	0	0	0	0	0	3	.167	.167

Kevin Baez — Mets
Bats Right

	Avg	G	AB	R	H	2B	3B	HR	RBI	BB	SO	HBP	GDP	SB	CS	OBP	SLG	IBB	SH	SF	#Pit	#P/PA	GB	FB	G/F
1992 Season	.154	6	13	0	2	0	0	0	0	0	0	0	1	0	0	.154	.154	0	0	0	38	2.92	6	5	1.20
Career (1990-1992)	.160	11	25	0	4	1	0	0	0	0	0	0	3	0	0	.160	.200	0	0	0	74	2.96	12	9	1.33

1992 Season

	Avg	AB	H	2B	3B	HR	RBI	BB	SO	OBP	SLG		Avg	AB	H	2B	3B	HR	RBI	BB	SO	OBP	SLG
vs. Left	.000	6	0	0	0	0	0	0	0	.000	.000	Scoring Posn	.000	0	0	0	0	0	0	0	0	.000	.000
vs. Right	.286	7	2	0	0	0	0	0	0	.286	.286	Close & Late	.000	1	0	0	0	0	0	0	0	.000	.000

Jeff Bagwell — Astros   Bats Right

	Avg	G	AB	R	H	2B	3B	HR	RBI	BB	SO	HBP	GDP	SB	CS	OBP	SLG	IBB	SH	SF	#Pit	#P/PA	GB	FB	G/F
1992 Season	.273	162	586	87	160	34	6	18	96	84	97	12	17	10	6	.368	.444	13	2	13	2665	3.83	197	188	1.05
Career (1991-1992)	.283	318	1140	166	323	60	10	33	178	159	213	25	29	17	10	.377	.440	18	3	20	5104	3.80	377	340	1.11

1992 Season

	Avg	AB	H	2B	3B	HR	RBI	BB	SO	OBP	SLG		Avg	AB	H	2B	3B	HR	RBI	BB	SO	OBP	SLG
vs. Left	.290	210	61	13	3	10	34	38	31	.394	.524	Scoring Posn	.266	177	47	6	2	5	78	39	34	.386	.407
vs. Right	.263	376	99	21	3	8	62	46	66	.354	.399	Close & Late	.354	99	35	6	1	8	28	25	13	.492	.677
Groundball	.263	232	61	14	3	8	42	27	37	.354	.453	None on/out	.301	136	41	11	1	5	5	20	23	.399	.507
Flyball	.257	136	35	5	0	4	22	23	24	.362	.382	Batting #3	.251	315	79	14	3	11	51	39	57	.340	.419
Home	.259	294	76	21	3	8	48	42	50	.355	.432	Batting #4	.299	264	79	20	3	7	43	45	39	.403	.477
Away	.288	292	84	13	3	10	48	42	47	.382	.455	Other	.286	7	2	0	0	0	2	0	1	.286	.286
Day	.306	160	49	9	1	6	27	22	25	.387	.488	April	.256	78	20	4	1	2	12	13	19	.370	.410
Night	.261	426	111	25	5	12	69	62	72	.361	.427	May	.210	105	22	5	0	4	19	11	20	.308	.371
Grass	.326	172	56	4	1	6	33	24	23	.407	.465	June	.289	97	28	5	0	3	13	17	13	.388	.433
Turf	.251	414	104	30	5	12	63	60	74	.352	.435	July	.239	88	21	4	3	3	14	12	18	.324	.455
First Pitch	.281	64	18	2	0	6	20	11	0	.385	.594	August	.248	105	26	7	2	1	16	16	13	.349	.381
Ahead on Count	.335	158	53	16	2	7	26	43	0	.481	.595	September/October	.381	113	43	9	0	5	22	15	14	.459	.593
Behind on Count	.227	185	42	12	1	3	22	0	46	.247	.351	Pre-All Star	.254	315	80	15	4	9	51	46	60	.356	.413
Two Strikes	.231	264	61	14	3	5	39	31	97	.315	.364	Post-All Star	.295	271	80	19	2	9	45	38	37	.383	.480

1992 By Position

Position	Avg	AB	H	2B	3B	HR	RBI	BB	SO	OBP	SLG	G	GS	Innings	PO	A	E	DP	Fld Pct	Rng Fctr	In Zone	Outs	Zone Rtg	MLB Zone
As 1b	.271	582	158	34	6	17	93	84	97	.368	.438	159	157	1401.1	1334	130	7	110	.995	---	321	276	860	843

Career (1991-1992)

	Avg	AB	H	2B	3B	HR	RBI	BB	SO	OBP	SLG		Avg	AB	H	2B	3B	HR	RBI	BB	SO	OBP	SLG
vs. Left	.305	416	127	23	3	17	71	71	68	.405	.498	Scoring Posn	.282	330	93	11	4	10	143	63	71	.392	.430
vs. Right	.271	724	196	37	7	16	107	88	145	.361	.407	Close & Late	.357	185	66	14	2	10	41	41	32	.467	.616
Groundball	.276	406	112	19	5	10	70	48	74	.368	.421	None on/out	.268	257	74	19	1	5	5	33	51	.382	.428
Flyball	.258	252	65	10	1	9	35	42	45	.367	.413	Batting #3	.277	593	164	28	6	20	100	77	102	.367	.445
Home	.276	568	157	36	5	14	83	78	102	.373	.431	Batting #4	.292	322	94	21	3	8	51	55	51	.403	.450
Away	.290	572	166	24	5	19	95	81	111	.382	.449	Other	.289	225	65	11	1	5	27	27	60	.366	.413
Day	.296	287	85	15	2	10	45	35	50	.373	.467	April	.255	137	35	7	1	4	20	22	36	.360	.409
Night	.279	853	238	45	8	23	133	124	163	.379	.431	May	.237	194	46	7	1	7	30	22	49	.330	.392
Grass	.303	330	100	6	3	12	63	52	63	.398	.448	June	.303	201	61	12	1	5	24	30	33	.391	.448
Turf	.275	810	223	54	7	21	115	107	150	.368	.437	July	.275	171	47	9	4	6	28	28	33	.377	.460
First Pitch	.338	142	48	9	1	9	35	15	0	.405	.606	August	.257	210	54	11	3	3	36	23	29	.364	.381
Ahead on Count	.347	285	99	21	4	12	45	68	0	.474	.575	September/October	.352	227	80	14	0	8	40	24	33	.428	.520
Behind on Count	.239	376	90	16	2	7	48	0	106	.260	.348	Pre-All Star	.275	589	162	29	7	17	87	84	131	.370	.435
Two Strikes	.226	523	118	24	4	11	74	77	213	.332	.350	Post-All Star	.292	551	161	31	3	16	91	75	82	.385	.446

Batter vs. Pitcher (career)

Hits Best Against	Avg	AB	H	2B	3B	HR	RBI	BB	SO	OBP	SLG	Hits Worst Against	Avg	AB	H	2B	3B	HR	RBI	BB	SO	OBP	SLG
Chris Nabholz	.583	12	7	2	0	0	1	1	2	.615	.750	Frank Castillo	.000	13	0	0	0	0	0	1	1	.071	.000
Norm Charlton	.500	8	4	1	0	1	2	3	1	.636	1.000	Tim Belcher	.067	15	1	1	0	0	0	3	4	.222	.133
Andy Benes	.471	17	8	3	0	1	1	5	2	.591	.824	Tom Candiotti	.091	11	1	0	0	0	0	2	3	.231	.091
Kevin Gross	.462	13	6	0	0	2	3	2	0	.500	.923	Sid Fernandez	.100	10	1	0	0	0	1	1	2	.167	.100
Randy Myers	.455	11	5	3	0	2	5	0	3	.455	1.273	Doug Drabek	.125	8	1	0	0	0	1	0	3	.273	.125

Scott Bailes — Angels   Pitches Left

	ERA	W	L	Sv	G	GS	IP	BB	SO	Avg	H	2B	3B	HR	RBI	OBP	SLG	GF	IR	IRS	Hld	SvOp	SB	CS	GB	FB	G/F
1992 Season	7.45	3	1	0	32	0	38.2	28	25	.351	59	7	0	7	41	.442	.518	10	28	12	4	0	4	1	64	48	1.33
Last Five Years	5.01	20	26	0	172	32	384.1	145	182	.275	411	60	7	49	235	.340	.423	30	147	55	22	4	33	8	605	459	1.32

1992 Season

	ERA	W	L	Sv	G	GS	IP	H	HR	BB	SO		Avg	AB	H	2B	3B	HR	RBI	BB	SO	OBP	SLG
Home	8.10	2	1	0	16	0	20.0	30	4	18	12	vs. Left	.360	50	18	3	0	0	10	6	7	.431	.420
Away	6.75	1	0	0	16	0	18.2	29	3	10	13	vs. Right	.347	118	41	4	0	7	31	22	18	.447	.559
Starter	0.00	0	0	0	0	0	0.0	0	0	0	0	Scoring Posn	.375	56	21	3	0	1	34	16	11	.500	.482
Reliever	7.45	3	1	0	32	0	38.2	59	7	28	25	Close & Late	.370	27	10	1	0	0	6	2	6	.414	.407
0 Days rest	14.73	1	0	0	4	0	3.2	7	0	4	4	None on/out	.306	36	11	1	0	2	2	0	3	.306	.500
1 or 2 Days rest	9.26	0	0	0	10	0	11.2	22	3	10	6	First Pitch	.464	28	13	2	0	2	8	4	0	.515	.750
3+ Days rest	5.40	2	1	0	18	0	23.1	30	4	14	15	Behind on Count	.348	46	16	4	0	1	18	14	0	.500	.500
Pre-All Star	7.99	3	0	0	19	0	23.2	30	4	19	15	Ahead on Count	.311	61	19	0	0	2	9	0	19	.317	.410
Post-All Star	6.60	0	1	0	13	0	15.0	29	3	9	10	Two Strikes	.258	62	16	0	0	3	12	10	25	.365	.403

Last Five Years

	ERA	W	L	Sv	G	GS	IP	H	HR	BB	SO		Avg	AB	H	2B	3B	HR	RBI	BB	SO	OBP	SLG
Home	4.55	16	11	0	79	17	200.0	198	24	67	91	vs. Left	.262	413	108	14	0	5	59	33	54	.323	.332
Away	5.52	4	15	0	93	15	184.1	213	25	78	91	vs. Right	.281	1080	303	46	7	44	176	112	128	.347	.458
Day	5.80	7	8	0	52	9	102.1	124	16	39	55	Inning 1-6	.271	912	247	40	4	29	151	84	89	.333	.419
Night	4.72	13	18	0	120	23	282.0	287	33	106	127	Inning 7+	.282	581	164	20	3	20	84	61	93	.352	.430
Grass	4.69	18	20	0	144	27	324.1	340	39	111	154	None on	.263	821	216	28	4	25	25	64	93	.323	.398

Last Five Years

	ERA	W	L	Sv	G	GS	IP	H	HR	BB	SO		Avg	AB	H	2B	3B	HR	RBI	BB	SO	OBP	SLG
Turf	6.75	2	6	0	28	5	60.0	71	10	34	28	Runners on	.290	672	195	32	3	24	210	81	89	.360	.454
April	3.48	4	4	0	24	4	62.0	57	1	33	28	Scoring Posn	.298	376	112	18	2	11	177	60	50	.382	.444
May	4.66	5	3	0	35	5	75.1	64	14	30	38	Close & Late	.284	176	50	4	0	5	27	18	29	.357	.392
June	4.77	6	5	0	38	9	100.0	106	13	33	44	None on/out	.284	370	105	19	0	12	12	24	40	.332	.432
July	7.71	2	6	0	21	11	70.0	103	17	18	23	vs. 1st Batr (relief)	.272	125	34	11	0	2	25	8	19	.314	.408
August	4.98	1	5	0	30	3	47.0	57	1	16	29	First Inning Pitched	.295	567	167	28	0	24	123	65	85	.366	.471
September/October	3.60	2	3	0	24	0	30.0	24	3	15	20	First 15 Pitches	.295	515	152	24	0	24	93	49	72	.355	.482
Starter	5.16	10	17	0	32	32	193.2	207	26	51	67	Pitch 16-30	.244	315	77	12	0	7	40	39	46	.336	.349
Reliever	4.86	10	9	0	140	0	190.2	204	23	94	115	Pitch 31-45	.278	216	60	8	3	2	25	30	28	.364	.370
0 Days rest	7.00	1	1	0	20	0	27.0	32	3	16	13	Pitch 46+	.273	447	122	16	4	16	77	27	36	.313	.434
1 or 2 Days rest	4.44	5	4	0	51	0	71.0	74	7	37	37	First Pitch	.316	288	91	16	1	12	40	12	0	.344	.503
3+ Days rest	4.56	4	4	0	69	0	92.2	98	13	41	65	Ahead on Count	.230	539	124	10	3	11	70	0	147	.236	.321
Pre-All Star	4.48	17	14	0	105	22	265.1	260	34	104	118	Behind on Count	.292	383	112	22	1	14	79	87	0	.421	.465
Post-All Star	6.20	3	12	0	67	10	119.0	151	15	41	64	Two Strikes	.208	539	112	8	3	14	70	46	182	.274	.312

Pitcher vs. Batter (career)

Pitches Best Vs.	Avg	AB	H	2B	3B	HR	RBI	BB	SO	OBP	SLG	Pitches Worst Vs.	Avg	AB	H	2B	3B	HR	RBI	BB	SO	OBP	SLG
Dick Schofield	.000	18	0	0	0	0	0	0	2	.000	.000	Pete Incaviglia	.643	14	9	2	0	4	8	1	0	.667	1.643
Jody Reed	.091	11	1	1	0	0	2	1	4	.167	.182	Kirby Puckett	.600	10	6	3	0	0	5	1	1	.636	.900
Darnell Coles	.100	10	1	1	0	0	1	1	0	.182	.200	Danny Tartabull	.500	18	9	1	0	3	7	2	0	.550	1.056
Ozzie Guillen	.118	17	2	0	0	0	1	0	2	.118	.118	Rickey Henderson	.500	10	5	1	1	0	1	7	2	.706	.800
B.J. Surhoff	.154	13	2	0	0	0	3	0	0	.154	.154	Brian Downing	.444	18	8	1	0	2	2	5	3	.565	.833

Mark Bailey — Giants   Bats Both (groundball hitter)

	Avg	G	AB	R	H	2B	3B	HR	RBI	BB	SO	HBP	GDP	SB	CS	OBP	SLG	IBB	SH	SF	#Pit	#P/PA	GB	FB	G/F
1992 Season	.154	13	26	0	4	1	0	0	1	3	7	0	0	0	0	.241	.192	0	0	0	120	4.14	11	7	1.57
Last Five Years	.143	26	56	2	8	1	0	1	4	8	15	0	1	0	1	.250	.214	0	0	0	258	4.03	23	14	1.64

1992 Season

	Avg	AB	H	2B	3B	HR	RBI	BB	SO	OBP	SLG		Avg	AB	H	2B	3B	HR	RBI	BB	SO	OBP	SLG
vs. Left	.000	3	0	0	0	0	0	0	1	.000	.000	Scoring Posn	.143	7	1	0	0	0	1	0	2	.143	.143
vs. Right	.174	23	4	1	0	0	3	6		.269	.217	Close & Late	.111	9	1	0	0	0	0	1	3	.200	.111

Harold Baines — Athletics   Bats Left (groundball hitter)

	Avg	G	AB	R	H	2B	3B	HR	RBI	BB	SO	HBP	GDP	SB	CS	OBP	SLG	IBB	SH	SF	#Pit	#P/PA	GB	FB	G/F
1992 Season	.253	140	478	58	121	18	0	16	76	59	61	0	11	1	3	.331	.391	6	0	6	1875	3.45	197	153	1.29
Last Five Years	.284	720	2485	314	705	126	4	81	384	338	396	3	76	1	10	.366	.435	65	0	29	10132	3.55	1005	603	1.67

1992 Season

	Avg	AB	H	2B	3B	HR	RBI	BB	SO	OBP	SLG		Avg	AB	H	2B	3B	HR	RBI	BB	SO	OBP	SLG
vs. Left	.245	53	13	0	0	1	8	5	16	.310	.302	Scoring Posn	.273	121	33	3	0	6	57	15	16	.338	.446
vs. Right	.254	425	108	18	0	15	68	54	45	.334	.402	Close & Late	.206	63	13	1	0	2	6	8	14	.296	.317
Groundball	.245	106	26	4	0	1	16	13	10	.320	.311	None on/out	.248	117	29	3	0	2	2	18	14	.348	.325
Flyball	.280	125	35	3	0	2	18	25	19	.395	.352	Batting #3	.228	101	23	4	0	3	19	12	17	.304	.356
Home	.277	231	64	8	0	10	46	26	28	.346	.442	Batting #4	.236	318	75	12	0	12	47	41	32	.320	.387
Away	.231	247	57	10	0	6	30	33	33	.318	.344	Other	.390	59	23	2	0	1	10	6	12	.439	.475
Day	.289	187	54	8	0	7	27	21	26	.359	.444	April	.194	72	14	3	0	1	5	6	15	.256	.278
Night	.230	291	67	10	0	9	49	38	35	.314	.357	May	.244	82	20	0	0	1	9	9	8	.309	.280
Grass	.259	398	103	16	0	15	70	51	48	.339	.412	June	.264	72	19	5	0	5	21	12	7	.365	.342
Turf	.225	80	18	2	0	1	6	8	13	.292	.288	July	.330	88	29	2	0	1	12	8	13	.385	.386
First Pitch	.356	104	37	6	0	6	20	4	0	.376	.587	August	.236	89	21	4	0	4	15	13	12	.333	.416
Ahead on Count	.293	123	36	8	0	5	24	31	0	.432	.480	September/October	.240	75	18	4	0	4	14	11	6	.330	.453
Behind on Count	.191	131	25	1	0	5	21	0	32	.187	.313	Pre-All Star	.248	262	65	10	0	8	40	29	35	.319	.378
Two Strikes	.193	171	33	4	0	2	21	24	61	.289	.251	Post-All Star	.259	216	56	8	0	8	36	30	26	.347	.407

1992 By Position

Position	Avg	AB	H	2B	3B	HR	RBI	BB	SO	OBP	SLG	G	GS	Innings	PO	A	E	DP	Fld Pct	Rng Fctr	In Zone	Outs	Zone Rtg	MLB Zone
As Designated Hitter	.237	410	97	16	0	15	69	50	58	.315	.385	116	110	---	---	---	---	---	---	---	---	---	---	---
As Pinch Hitter	.333	9	3	0	0	0	1	2	2	.455	.333	11	0	---	---	---	---	---	---	---	---	---	---	---
As rf	.362	47	17	1	0	1	5	5	2	.423	.447	17	13	100.0	19	0	1	0	.950	1.71	27	18	.667	.814

Last Five Years

	Avg	AB	H	2B	3B	HR	RBI	BB	SO	OBP	SLG		Avg	AB	H	2B	3B	HR	RBI	BB	SO	OBP	SLG
vs. Left	.262	573	150	29	0	14	92	61	121	.331	.386	Scoring Posn	.278	644	179	29	1	20	291	139	111	.392	.419
vs. Right	.290	1912	555	97	4	67	292	277	275	.377	.450	Close & Late	.272	371	101	20	1	15	53	67	67	.384	.453
Groundball	.314	673	211	38	2	13	101	88	94	.391	.434	None on/out	.272	541	147	29	0	18	18	59	87	.343	.425
Flyball	.263	558	147	32	0	16	90	103	108	.373	.407	Batting #3	.295	1161	342	72	2	35	178	149	192	.371	.450
Home	.260	1200	336	70	1	40	213	174	194	.366	.440	Batting #4	.263	877	231	39	1	33	146	134	109	.357	.423
Away	.287	1285	369	56	3	41	171	165	202	.366	.431	Other	.295	447	132	15	1	13	60	55	95	.372	.421
Day	.312	719	224	38	3	26	122	100	116	.390	.481	April	.249	361	90	19	1	8	45	45	65	.333	.374
Night	.272	1766	481	88	1	55	262	238	280	.357	.417	May	.300	416	125	18	0	13	64	61	57	.386	.438

Last Five Years

	Avg	AB	H	2B	3B	HR	RBI	BB	SO	OBP	SLG
Grass	.286	2072	592	107	2	72	339	293	327	.371	.444
Turf	.274	413	113	19	2	9	45	45	69	.343	.395
First Pitch	.364	511	186	26	1	23	89	28	0	.393	.554
Ahead on Count	.368	543	200	41	0	26	113	159	0	.506	.587
Behind on Count	.230	729	168	25	1	19	93	6	198	.236	.346
Two Strikes	.199	994	198	43	3	19	114	134	396	.293	.306

	Avg	AB	H	2B	3B	HR	RBI	BB	SO	OBP	SLG
June	.298	440	131	20	1	24	79	67	76	.388	.511
July	.327	394	129	25	1	11	66	53	66	.404	.480
August	.253	419	106	17	0	12	60	56	62	.338	.379
September/October	.273	455	124	27	1	13	70	56	70	.347	.422
Pre-All Star	.286	1349	386	70	2	50	215	187	223	.371	.452
Post-All Star	.281	1136	319	56	2	31	169	151	173	.361	.415

Batter vs. Pitcher (since 1984)

Hits Best Against	Avg	AB	H	2B	3B	HR	RBI	BB	SO	OBP	SLG
Eric Plunk	.556	9	5	0	0	0		4	2	.692	.556
Edwin Nunez	.545	11	6	2	0	2	7	1	2	.583	1.273
Ben McDonald	.462	13	6	1	0	2	5	2	1	.533	1.000
Bill Swift	.452	31	14	3	0	2	7	3	0	.486	.742
Nolan Ryan	.368	19	7	1	0	4	6	1	4	.400	1.053

Hits Worst Against	Avg	AB	H	2B	3B	HR	RBI	BB	SO	OBP	SLG
Mike Mussina	.000	10	0	0	0	0	0	1	3	.091	.000
Mark Leiter	.071	14	1	0	0	0	2	1	2	.133	.071
Joe Grahe	.077	13	1	0	0	0	2	3	1	.250	.077
Melido Perez	.100	30	3	0	0	0	3	4	6	.200	.100
Bud Black	.143	28	4	0	0	0	2	1	3	.161	.143

Jay Baller — Phillies Pitches Right

	ERA	W	L	Sv	G	GS	IP	BB	SO	Avg	H	2B	3B	HR	RBI	OBP	SLG	GF	IR	IRS	Hld	SvOp	SB	CS	GB	FB	G/F
1992 Season	8.18	0	0	0	8	0	11.0	10	9	.250	10	1	0	5	11	.392	.650	4	5	3	1	0	3	2	13	10	1.30
Last Five Years	9.45	0	1	0	11	0	13.1	12	10	.275	14	2	0	6	16	.415	.667	6	19	11	1	1	3	2	18	14	1.29

1992 Season

	ERA	W	L	Sv	G	GS	IP	H	HR	BB	SO		Avg	AB	H	2B	3B	HR	RBI	BB	SO	OBP	SLG
Home	22.50	0	0	0	2	0	2.0	3	2	3	1	vs. Left	.238	21	5	1	0	2	6	6	4	.407	.571
Away	5.00	0	0	0	6	0	9.0	7	3	7	8	vs. Right	.263	19	5	0	0	3	5	4	5	.375	.737

Scott Bankhead — Reds Pitches Right (flyball pitcher)

	ERA	W	L	Sv	G	GS	IP	BB	SO	Avg	H	2B	3B	HR	RBI	OBP	SLG	GF	IR	IRS	Hld	SvOp	SB	CS	GB	FB	G/F
1992 Season	2.93	10	4	1	54	0	70.2	29	53	.218	57	10	4	4	23	.301	.333	10	28	4	14	5	5	0	78	85	0.92
Last Five Years	3.60	34	27	1	129	67	489.2	158	333	.242	450	95	20	41	181	.302	.381	12	37	7	14	5	44	11	535	668	0.80

1992 Season

	ERA	W	L	Sv	G	GS	IP	H	HR	BB	SO		Avg	AB	H	2B	3B	HR	RBI	BB	SO	OBP	SLG
Home	3.19	6	0	0	29	0	36.2	33	2	13	25	vs. Left	.227	128	29	7	2	3	10	19	21	.327	.383
Away	2.65	4	4	1	25	0	34.0	24	2	16	28	vs. Right	.211	133	28	3	2	1	13	10	32	.275	.286
Starter	0.00	0	0	0	0	0	0.0	0	0	0	0	Scoring Posn	.174	69	12	3	1	1	18	13	17	.294	.290
Reliever	2.93	10	4	1	54	0	70.2	57	4	29	53	Close & Late	.244	119	29	6	0	3	10	16	19	.343	.370
0 Days rest	1.29	1	0	0	6	0	7.0	6	0	1	8	None on/out	.209	67	14	1	0	1	1	3	13	.264	.269
1 or 2 Days rest	3.41	4	2	1	24	0	29.0	24	2	12	15	First Pitch	.333	36	12	2	0	2	7	3	0	.385	.556
3+ Days rest	2.86	5	2	0	24	0	34.2	27	2	16	30	Behind on Count	.229	48	11	1	1	0	1	14	0	.397	.292
Pre-All Star	1.94	9	2	1	30	0	41.2	26	2	12	31	Ahead on Count	.143	126	18	3	2	0	8	0	45	.160	.198
Post-All Star	4.34	1	2	0	24	0	29.0	31	2	17	22	Two Strikes	.172	128	22	4	3	1	13	12	53	.255	.273

Last Five Years

	ERA	W	L	Sv	G	GS	IP	H	HR	BB	SO		Avg	AB	H	2B	3B	HR	RBI	BB	SO	OBP	SLG
Home	4.03	17	12	0	67	34	237.0	234	22	72	158	vs. Left	.248	925	229	57	8	19	86	85	157	.309	.388
Away	3.21	17	15	1	62	33	252.2	216	19	86	175	vs. Right	.237	934	221	38	12	22	95	73	176	.295	.374
Day	3.92	8	9	0	36	16	131.0	121	14	42	102	Inning 1-6	.242	1460	354	73	16	33	148	115	263	.298	.382
Night	3.49	26	18	1	93	51	358.2	329	27	116	231	Inning 7+	.241	399	96	22	4	8	33	43	70	.318	.376
Grass	3.00	13	10	1	43	26	192.0	164	16	60	133	None on	.229	1140	261	52	13	22		77	190	.281	.355
Turf	3.99	21	17	0	86	41	297.2	286	25	98	200	Runners on	.263	719	189	43	7	19	159	81	143	.333	.421
April	4.82	4	5	1	18	11	71.0	82	8	21	45	Scoring Posn	.243	411	100	24	5	9	128	64	89	.337	.392
May	3.75	5	6	0	21	12	74.1	71	7	27	57	Close & Late	.254	197	50	13	0	5	17	29	32	.355	.396
June	2.85	9	4	0	24	15	101.0	76	4	29	66	None on/out	.197	477	94	20	4	7	7	37	85	.259	.300
July	3.63	8	3	0	22	12	91.2	77	13	19	59	vs. 1st Batr (relief)	.196	56	11	1	0	0	2	4	11	.242	.214
August	4.01	3	7	0	23	11	85.1	90	5	34	65	First Inning Pitched	.240	463	111	20	5	10	57	45	96	.307	.369
September/October	2.71	5	2	0	21	6	66.1	54	4	28	41	First 15 Pitches	.259	406	105	17	5	10	43	30	69	.312	.399
Starter	3.73	23	22	0	67	67	401.0	377	35	124	275	Pitch 16-30	.173	323	56	13	2	9	33	44	70	.273	.310
Reliever	3.05	11	5	1	62	0	88.2	73	6	34	58	Pitch 31-45	.282	298	84	21	6	5	28	18	48	.323	.443
0 Days rest	1.29	1	0	0	6	0	7.0	6	0	1	8	Pitch 46+	.246	832	205	44	7	17	77	66	146	.302	.377
1 or 2 Days rest	3.41	4	2	1	24	0	29.0	24	2	12	15	First Pitch	.296	297	88	11	3	9	30	7	0	.310	.444
3+ Days rest	3.08	6	3	0	32	0	52.2	43	4	21	35	Ahead on Count	.197	801	158	35	3	8	50	0	274	.204	.278
Pre-All Star	3.51	23	16	1	72	42	282.1	256	21	83	192	Behind on Count	.282	380	107	31	7	11	48	72	0	.391	.487
Post-All Star	3.73	11	11	0	57	25	207.1	194	20	75	141	Two Strikes	.181	832	151	33	7	8	54	78	333	.255	.267

Pitcher vs. Batter (career)

Pitches Best Vs.	Avg	AB	H	2B	3B	HR	RBI	BB	SO	OBP	SLG
Kevin Seitzer	.000	11	0	0	0	0	0	2	2	.154	.000
Mickey Tettleton	.071	14	1	0	0	0	1	1	3	.125	.071
Rick Cerone	.091	11	1	0	0	0	0	0	3	.091	.091
Dick Schofield	.111	18	2	0	0	0	2	2	4	.190	.111
Tony Fernandez	.133	30	4	0	0	0	0	1	3	.161	.133

Pitches Worst Vs.	Avg	AB	H	2B	3B	HR	RBI	BB	SO	OBP	SLG
Mike Gallego	.600	10	6	2	0	0	1	2	1	.667	.800
Walt Weiss	.545	11	6	1	1	1	4	1	0	.583	1.091
George Bell	.448	29	13	4	0	5	7	0	2	.448	1.103
Rafael Palmeiro	.429	14	6	1	0	2	3	2	1	.500	.929
Matt Nokes	.417	12	5	1	0	2	7	0	2	.417	1.000

Willie Banks — Twins
Pitches Right

	ERA	W	L	Sv	G	GS	IP	BB	SO	Avg	H	2B	3B	HR	RBI	OBP	SLG	CG	ShO	Sup	QS	#P/S	SB	CS	GB	FB	G/F
1992 Season	5.70	4	4	0	16	12	71.0	37	37	.288	80	15	3	6	42	.370	.428	0	0	3.93	5	92	8	4	100	91	1.10
Career (1991-1992)	5.71	5	5	0	21	15	88.1	49	53	.288	101	17	3	7	53	.373	.413	0	0	4.18	6	89	10	4	125	105	1.19

1992 Season

	ERA	W	L	Sv	G	GS	IP	H	HR	BB	SO		Avg	AB	H	2B	3B	HR	RBI	BB	SO	OBP	SLG
Home	3.48	1	2	0	6	5	31.0	29	4	13	22	vs. Left	.293	140	41	7	1	3	17	16	22	.363	.421
Away	7.43	3	2	0	10	7	40.0	51	6	24	15	vs. Right	.283	138	39	8	2	3	25	21	15	.377	.435
Starter	4.43	4	4	0	12	12	65.0	66	5	29	33	Scoring Posn	.304	69	21	5	1	2	34	9	12	.361	.493
Reliever	19.50	0	0	0	4	0	6.0	14	1	8	4	Close & Late	.273	11	3	0	0	1	1	0	1	.273	.545
0-3 Days Rest	0.00	0	0	0	0	0	0.0	0	0	0	0	None on/out	.224	67	15	3	0	1	1	8	10	.307	.313
4 Days Rest	4.72	4	1	0	7	7	34.1	36	2	19	17	First Pitch	.452	31	14	2	0	3	8	0	0	.438	.806
5+ Days Rest	4.11	0	3	0	5	5	30.2	30	3	10	16	Behind on Count	.296	81	24	5	1	0	14	24	0	.453	.383
Pre-All Star	5.05	3	2	0	8	8	41.0	46	5	14	18	Ahead on Count	.243	107	26	4	2	1	10	0	27	.250	.346
Post-All Star	6.60	1	2	0	8	4	30.0	34	1	23	19	Two Strikes	.202	119	24	5	1	0	9	13	37	.287	.261

Floyd Bannister — Rangers
Pitches Left (flyball pitcher)

	ERA	W	L	Sv	G	GS	IP	BB	SO	Avg	H	2B	3B	HR	RBI	OBP	SLG	GF	IR	IRS	Hld	SvOp	SB	CS	GB	FB	G/F
1992 Season	6.32	1	1	0	36	0	37.0	21	30	.281	39	11	0	3	29	.371	.424	8	32	12	3	1	3	1	40	49	0.82
Last Five Years	4.60	17	15	0	97	45	326.2	117	194	.263	333	67	9	38	161	.327	.420	10	47	15	3	1	37	6	409	442	0.93

1992 Season

	ERA	W	L	Sv	G	GS	IP	H	HR	BB	SO		Avg	AB	H	2B	3B	HR	RBI	BB	SO	OBP	SLG
Home	5.70	1	0	0	18	0	23.2	22	1	16	25	vs. Left	.174	46	8	4	0	2	9	8	12	.288	.391
Away	7.43	0	1	0	18	0	13.1	17	2	5	5	vs. Right	.333	93	31	7	0	1	20	13	18	.414	.441
Starter	0.00	0	0	0	0	0	0.0	0	0	0	0	Scoring Posn	.218	55	12	3	0	2	27	11	15	.324	.382
Reliever	6.32	1	1	0	36	0	37.0	39	3	21	30	Close & Late	.368	19	7	0	0	0	4	4	3	.458	.368
0 Days rest	0.00	0	0	0	5	0	3.2	2	0	0	0	None on/out	.344	32	11	5	0	0	0	3	7	.417	.500
1 or 2 Days rest	9.00	0	0	0	16	0	17.0	19	0	14	11	First Pitch	.125	8	1	0	0	0	1	5	0	.462	.125
3+ Days rest	4.96	1	1	0	15	0	16.1	18	3	7	19	Behind on Count	.316	38	12	2	0	2	10	12	0	.462	.526
Pre-All Star	6.53	1	1	0	26	0	30.1	36	3	18	25	Ahead on Count	.188	64	12	5	0	0	6	0	23	.176	.266
Post-All Star	5.40	0	0	0	10	0	6.2	3	0	3	5	Two Strikes	.194	67	13	5	0	0	12	4	30	.237	.269

Last Five Years

	ERA	W	L	Sv	G	GS	IP	H	HR	BB	SO		Avg	AB	H	2B	3B	HR	RBI	BB	SO	OBP	SLG
Home	4.38	7	7	0	48	23	176.2	178	11	63	104	vs. Left	.237	270	64	18	0	5	29	23	48	.297	.359
Away	4.86	10	8	0	49	22	150.0	155	27	54	90	vs. Right	.270	996	269	49	9	33	132	94	146	.335	.437
Day	4.58	2	0	0	16	5	39.1	43	6	15	26	Inning 1-6	.258	1024	264	51	6	34	132	86	147	.317	.419
Night	4.60	15	15	0	81	39	287.1	290	32	102	168	Inning 7+	.285	242	69	16	3	4	29	31	47	.367	.426
Grass	4.45	9	5	0	61	15	141.2	135	16	64	95	None on	.258	748	193	37	4	23	23	59	113	.314	.410
Turf	4.72	8	10	0	36	30	185.0	198	22	53	99	Runners on	.270	518	140	30	5	15	138	58	81	.345	.434
April	3.69	6	1	0	24	11	85.1	76	6	30	44	Scoring Posn	.265	309	82	21	1	13	123	39	50	.344	.466
May	4.77	5	4	0	25	12	88.2	96	11	30	51	Close & Late	.315	54	17	0	1	0	5	10	6	.415	.352
June	7.01	2	3	0	15	7	43.2	56	8	23	23	None on/out	.269	324	87	17	1	8	8	25	49	.323	.401
July	5.85	0	2	0	17	4	32.1	34	6	12	15	vs. 1st Batr (relief)	.302	43	13	4	0	0	6	4	6	.353	.395
August	4.02	1	3	0	10	5	40.1	35	3	15	36	First Inning Pitched	.280	325	91	21	3	10	55	28	49	.337	.455
September/October	2.97	3	2	0	6	6	36.1	36	4	7	25	First 15 Pitches	.266	297	79	16	3	8	40	24	44	.321	.421
Starter	4.42	16	14	0	45	45	264.2	269	30	86	148	Pitch 16-30	.256	234	60	13	0	9	28	22	34	.320	.427
Reliever	5.37	1	1	0	52	0	62.0	64	8	31	46	Pitch 31-45	.250	204	51	6	2	7	21	9	26	.282	.402
0 Days rest	0.00	0	0	0	5	0	3.2	2	0	0	0	Pitch 46+	.269	531	143	32	4	14	72	62	90	.349	.424
1 or 2 Days rest	7.91	0	0	0	19	0	19.1	20	0	16	12	First Pitch	.324	179	58	7	2	8	27	8	0	.353	.520
3+ Days rest	4.62	1	1	0	28	0	39.0	42	8	15	34	Ahead on Count	.197	549	108	23	1	8	47	0	157	.200	.286
Pre-All Star	4.70	13	9	0	71	32	235.1	246	26	90	125	Behind on Count	.316	301	95	22	5	15	49	67	0	.438	.571
Post-All Star	4.34	4	6	0	26	13	91.1	87	12	27	69	Two Strikes	.183	535	98	21	0	4	51	42	194	.247	.273

Pitcher vs. Batter (since 1984)

Pitches Best Vs.	Avg	AB	H	2B	3B	HR	RBI	BB	SO	OBP	SLG	Pitches Worst Vs.	Avg	AB	H	2B	3B	HR	RBI	BB	SO	OBP	SLG
Mickey Tettleton	.000	11	0	0	0	0	1	1	3	.077	.000	Mike Pagliarulo	.600	10	6	1	0	2	6	1	0	.583	1.300
Brady Anderson	.000	11	0	0	0	0	1	3	6	.200	.000	Kelly Gruber	.417	12	5	1	0	2	7	0	2	.417	1.000
B.J. Surhoff	.000	10	0	0	0	0	1	0	0	.000	.000	Dave Winfield	.400	35	14	2	0	5	11	9	3	.523	.886
Mike Greenwell	.077	13	1	0	0	0	1	0	2	.077	.077	Julio Franco	.400	25	10	1	0	3	3	4	2	.483	.800
Mike Gallego	.077	13	1	0	0	0	0	1	4	.077	.077	Cory Snyder	.385	13	5	0	0	2	3	2	1	.467	.846

Bret Barberie — Expos
Bats Both

	Avg	G	AB	R	H	2B	3B	HR	RBI	BB	SO	HBP	GDP	SB	CS	OBP	SLG	IBB	SH	SF	#Pit	#P/PA	GB	FB	G/F
1992 Season	.232	111	285	26	66	11	0	1	24	47	62	8	4	9	5	.354	.281	3	1	2	1356	3.96	104	69	1.51
Career (1991-1992)	.271	168	421	42	114	23	2	3	42	67	84	10	8	9	5	.380	.356	5	2	5	2021	4.02	147	110	1.34

1992 Season

	Avg	AB	H	2B	3B	HR	RBI	BB	SO	OBP	SLG		Avg	AB	H	2B	3B	HR	RBI	BB	SO	OBP	SLG
vs. Left	.164	67	11	3	0	0	7	9	18	.288	.209	Scoring Posn	.227	75	17	4	0	0	23	13	18	.348	.280
vs. Right	.252	218	55	8	0	1	17	38	44	.374	.303	Close & Late	.226	62	14	4	0	0	7	7	17	.324	.290
Groundball	.289	128	37	7	0	0	9	25	28	.414	.344	None on/out	.253	79	20	4	0	1	1	4	13	.314	.342

1992 Season

	Avg	AB	H	2B	3B	HR	RBI	BB	SO	OBP	SLG		Avg	AB	H	2B	3B	HR	RBI	BB	SO	OBP	SLG
Flyball	.218	55	12	3	0	1	6	9	14	.343	.327	Batting #2	.254	118	30	6	0	0	5	19	20	.367	.305
Home	.288	132	38	4	0	0	15	26	23	.414	.318	Batting #7	.286	56	16	3	0	0	9	5	15	.359	.339
Away	.183	153	28	7	0	1	9	21	39	.300	.248	Other	.180	111	20	2	0	1	10	23	27	.338	.225
Day	.196	112	22	4	0	1	9	19	33	.323	.259	April	.229	70	16	4	0	0	1	14	18	.365	.286
Night	.254	173	44	7	0	0	15	28	29	.373	.295	May	.267	30	8	0	0	0	5	6	10	.405	.267
Grass	.194	93	18	3	0	1	6	10	27	.286	.258	June	.053	19	1	0	0	0	3	4	5	.240	.053
Turf	.250	192	48	8	0	0	18	37	35	.384	.292	July	.294	51	15	4	0	1	9	9	11	.419	.431
First Pitch	.324	34	11	1	0	1	2	3	0	.378	.441	August	.216	51	11	2	0	0	2	2	12	.286	.255
Ahead on Count	.318	66	21	5	0	0	5	21	0	.489	.394	September/October	.234	64	15	1	0	0	4	12	6	.351	.250
Behind on Count	.130	100	13	1	0	0	7	0	36	.171	.140	Pre-All Star	.214	154	33	6	0	1	14	28	42	.348	.273
Two Strikes	.129	139	18	3	0	0	10	24	62	.282	.151	Post-All Star	.252	131	33	5	0	0	10	19	20	.361	.290

1992 By Position

Position	Avg	AB	H	2B	3B	HR	RBI	BB	SO	OBP	SLG	G	GS	Innings	PO	A	E	DP	Fld Pct	Rng Fctr	In Zone	Outs	Zone Rtg	MLB Zone
As Pinch Hitter	.364	22	8	0	0	0	5	6	5	.500	.364	28	0	---	---	---	---	---	---	---	---	---	---	---
As 2b	.191	68	13	1	0	0	5	8	10	.282	.206	26	17	167.0	29	59	1	6	.989	4.74	62	60	.968	.892
As 3b	.232	194	45	10	0	1	14	32	47	.359	.299	63	57	508.2	37	126	12	10	.931	2.88	163	142	.871	.841

Jesse Barfield — Yankees   Bats Right

	Avg	G	AB	R	H	2B	3B	HR	RBI	BB	SO	HBP	GDP	SB	CS	OBP	SLG	IBB	SH	SF	#Pit	#P/PA	GB	FB	G/F
1992 Season	.137	30	95	8	13	2	0	2	7	9	27	0	5	1	1	.210	.221	2	0	1	414	3.94	30	27	1.11
Last Five Years	.233	553	1844	255	430	79	8	85	256	255	515	9	40	18	12	.327	.423	24	7	16	8811	4.15	538	534	1.01

1992 Season

	Avg	AB	H	2B	3B	HR	RBI	BB	SO	OBP	SLG		Avg	AB	H	2B	3B	HR	RBI	BB	SO	OBP	SLG
vs. Left	.152	33	5	0	0	1	2	6	7	.282	.242	Scoring Posn	.103	29	3	1	0	1	6	5	6	.229	.241
vs. Right	.129	62	8	2	0	1	5	3	20	.167	.210	Close & Late	.059	17	1	0	0	0	1	1	5	.105	.059
Home	.148	54	8	1	0	2	6	3	11	.190	.278	None on/out	.313	16	5	1	0	1	1	1	3	.353	.563
Away	.122	41	5	1	0	0	1	6	16	.234	.146	Batting #6	.077	26	2	0	0	0	0	4	7	.200	.077
First Pitch	.143	14	2	1	0	0	0	2	0	.250	.214	Batting #7	.132	53	7	2	0	0	2	2	15	.161	.170
Ahead on Count	.429	14	6	1	0	0	3	2	0	.471	.500	Other	.250	16	4	0	0	2	5	3	5	.368	.625
Behind on Count	.139	36	5	1	0	1	5	0	18	.139	.250	Pre-All Star	.137	95	13	2	0	2	7	9	27	.210	.221
Two Strikes	.071	56	4	0	0	2	4	5	27	.148	.179	Post-All Star	.000	0	0	0	0	0	0	0	0	.000	.000

Last Five Years

	Avg	AB	H	2B	3B	HR	RBI	BB	SO	OBP	SLG		Avg	AB	H	2B	3B	HR	RBI	BB	SO	OBP	SLG
vs. Left	.245	628	154	21	0	40	87	116	161	.365	.470	Scoring Posn	.218	459	100	22	3	20	168	93	138	.344	.410
vs. Right	.227	1216	276	58	8	45	169	139	354	.306	.399	Close & Late	.183	289	53	12	0	9	32	55	99	.315	.318
Groundball	.225	480	108	21	2	18	66	67	133	.318	.390	None on/out	.237	431	102	16	2	20	20	37	113	.297	.422
Flyball	.267	427	114	21	3	29	71	60	124	.358	.534	Batting #5	.234	612	143	28	1	29	91	101	187	.344	.425
Home	.230	920	212	42	5	44	132	119	248	.319	.430	Batting #6	.218	513	112	22	1	24	70	71	135	.314	.417
Away	.236	924	218	37	3	41	124	136	267	.334	.416	Other	.243	719	175	29	3	32	95	83	193	.321	.426
Day	.228	535	122	30	5	26	70	83	135	.334	.449	April	.213	328	70	14	2	14	46	36	94	.291	.396
Night	.235	1309	308	49	3	59	186	172	380	.324	.413	May	.206	321	66	10	1	17	47	47	97	.303	.402
Grass	.228	1331	303	54	3	61	184	190	382	.324	.410	June	.245	376	92	14	1	15	52	47	98	.330	.407
Turf	.248	513	127	25	5	24	72	65	133	.333	.456	July	.252	254	64	15	1	13	32	38	72	.350	.472
First Pitch	.326	181	59	10	1	16	50	10	0	.364	.657	August	.239	289	69	17	1	16	46	44	75	.340	.471
Ahead on Count	.339	361	129	21	4	22	66	132	0	.507	.588	September/October	.250	276	69	9	2	10	33	43	79	.355	.406
Behind on Count	.178	636	113	20	2	25	82	0	267	.180	.333	Pre-All Star	.225	1122	253	43	4	52	161	144	309	.313	.410
Two Strikes	.148	1053	156	34	1	32	99	107	514	.226	.274	Post-All Star	.245	722	177	36	4	33	97	111	206	.348	.443

Batter vs. Pitcher (since 1984)

Hits Best Against	Avg	AB	H	2B	3B	HR	RBI	BB	SO	OBP	SLG	Hits Worst Against	Avg	AB	H	2B	3B	HR	RBI	BB	SO	OBP	SLG
Steve Farr	.500	14	7	1	0	1	5	3	6	.588	.786	Nolan Ryan	.000	12	0	0	0	0	0	0	0	.000	.000
Bill Krueger	.455	22	10	1	0	2	5	4	4	.538	.864	Bob Welch	.000	11	0	0	0	0	0	2	3	.154	.000
Dan Plesac	.444	9	4	1	0	1	3	3	2	.583	.889	Mike Jackson	.000	11	0	0	0	0	0	1	5	.083	.000
Edwin Nunez	.389	18	7	0	0	3	6	2	5	.450	.889	Jose DeLeon	.083	12	1	0	0	0	1	1	7	.154	.083
Bryan Harvey	.333	9	3	0	0	2	4	1	4	.364	1.000	Kevin Tapani	.083	12	1	0	0	0	0	0	0	.083	.083

Brian Barnes — Expos   Pitches Left

	ERA	W	L	Sv	G	GS	IP	BB	SO	Avg	H	2B	3B	HR	RBI	OBP	SLG	CG	ShO	Sup	QS	#P/S	SB	CS	GB	FB	G/F
1992 Season	2.97	6	6	0	21	17	100.0	46	65	.213	77	15	0	9	29	.306	.329	0	0	3.78	7	85	14	7	114	110	1.04
Career (1990-1992)	3.66	12	15	0	53	48	288.0	137	205	.226	237	42	4	27	108	.319	.351	2	0	3.63	24	92	38	15	351	286	1.23

1992 Season

	ERA	W	L	Sv	G	GS	IP	H	HR	BB	SO		Avg	AB	H	2B	3B	HR	RBI	BB	SO	OBP	SLG
Home	2.47	4	3	0	11	9	58.1	41	4	25	42	vs. Left	.233	60	14	3	0	2	7	9	14	.347	.383
Away	3.67	2	3	0	10	8	41.2	36	5	21	23	vs. Right	.209	302	63	12	0	7	22	37	51	.297	.318
Starter	3.16	6	6	0	17	17	94.0	74	9	45	56	Scoring Posn	.195	77	15	3	0	3	20	14	20	.323	.351
Reliever	0.00	0	0	0	4	0	6.0	3	0	1	9	Close & Late	.100	10	1	0	0	0	0	1	3	.182	.100
0-3 Days Rest	0.00	0	0	0	0	0	0.0	0	0	0	0	None on/out	.200	100	20	4	0	2	2	10	18	.279	.300

1992 Season

	ERA	W	L	Sv	G	GS	IP	H	HR	BB	SO		Avg	AB	H	2B	3B	HR	RBI	BB	SO	OBP	SLG
4 Days Rest	2.32	4	2	0	9	9	50.1	43	5	26	27	First Pitch	.263	57	15	2	0	2	4	0	0	.259	.404
5+ Days Rest	4.12	2	4	0	8	8	43.2	31	4	19	29	Behind on Count	.321	84	27	7	0	4	12	27	0	.491	.548
Pre-All Star	2.42	1	2	0	5	4	26.0	23	2	14	12	Ahead on Count	.140	164	23	3	0	1	8	0	60	.140	.177
Post-All Star	3.16	5	4	0	16	13	74.0	54	7	32	53	Two Strikes	.103	156	16	2	0	3	9	19	65	.209	.173

Career (1990-1992)

	ERA	W	L	Sv	G	GS	IP	H	HR	BB	SO		Avg	AB	H	2B	3B	HR	RBI	BB	SO	OBP	SLG
Home	3.22	6	8	0	25	22	142.1	105	11	60	112	vs. Left	.238	185	44	9	2	7	23	31	35	.356	.422
Away	4.08	5	7	0	28	26	145.2	132	16	77	93	vs. Right	.224	863	193	33	2	20	85	106	170	.311	.336
Day	3.22	4	3	0	14	12	78.1	61	6	35	53	Inning 1-6	.230	943	217	36	4	27	102	129	181	.327	.363
Night	3.82	8	12	0	39	36	209.2	176	21	102	152	Inning 7+	.190	105	20	6	0	0	6	8	24	.248	.248
Grass	3.36	5	1	0	16	14	80.1	70	7	41	46	None on	.214	637	136	24	1	14	14	75	119	.302	.320
Turf	3.77	7	14	0	37	34	207.2	167	20	96	159	Runners on	.246	411	101	18	3	13	94	62	86	.344	.399
April	0.00	0	0	0	0	0	0.0	0	0	0	0	Scoring Posn	.228	237	54	9	1	7	75	32	59	.320	.363
May	8.38	0	2	0	4	4	19.1	23	2	11	14	Close & Late	.209	43	9	2	0	0	3	5	11	.292	.256
June	3.42	1	2	0	8	8	50.0	42	4	24	40	None on/out	.225	280	63	12	0	6	6	30	48	.307	.354
July	2.78	3	2	0	10	9	55.0	47	7	26	40	vs. 1st Batr (relief)	.200	5	1	0	0	0	0	0	2	.200	.200
August	3.24	3	4	0	12	11	66.2	47	7	30	41	First Inning Pitched	.156	179	28	8	0	2	11	28	40	.273	.235
September/October	3.62	5	5	0	19	16	97.0	78	7	46	70	First 75 Pitches	.224	835	187	33	3	23	86	103	162	.312	.353
Starter	3.74	12	15	0	48	48	281.1	233	27	136	196	Pitch 76-90	.237	118	28	4	1	3	16	19	27	.350	.364
Reliever	0.00	0	0	0	5	0	6.2	4	0	1	9	Pitch 91-105	.229	70	16	4	0	1	4	11	11	.341	.343
0-3 Days Rest	4.09	0	2	0	2	2	11.0	13	0	6	10	Pitch 106+	.240	25	6	1	0	0	2	4	5	.345	.280
4 Days Rest	3.26	6	6	0	25	25	148.1	117	16	71	94	First Pitch	.322	143	46	9	0	7	22	1	0	.329	.531
5+ Days Rest	4.28	6	7	0	21	21	122.0	103	11	59	92	Ahead on Count	.162	438	71	9	1	5	32	0	177	.166	.221
Pre-All Star	4.18	1	5	0	16	15	88.1	80	9	46	65	Behind on Count	.307	290	89	14	3	13	43	85	0	.467	.510
Post-All Star	3.43	11	10	0	37	33	199.2	157	18	91	140	Two Strikes	.138	463	64	10	0	6	29	51	205	.229	.199

Pitcher vs. Batter (career)

Pitches Best Vs.	Avg	AB	H	2B	3B	HR	RBI	BB	SO	OBP	SLG	Pitches Worst Vs.	Avg	AB	H	2B	3B	HR	RBI	BB	SO	OBP	SLG
Luis Salazar	.056	18	1	0	0	0	0	0	0	.056	.056	John Kruk	.400	15	6	2	0	1	5	2	2	.444	.733
Wes Chamberlain	.056	18	1	0	0	0	0	3	7	.190	.056	Charlie Hayes	.400	15	6	2	0	1	2	0	2	.400	.733
Chico Walker	.071	14	1	0	0	0	1	1	3	.133	.071	Ozzie Smith	.385	13	5	2	0	0	0	3	1	.500	.538
George Bell	.091	11	1	0	0	0	1	1	4	.167	.091	Dale Murphy	.375	16	6	2	0	0	1	7	1	.412	.688
Dickie Thon	.125	16	2	0	0	0	0	0	4	.125	.125	Barry Larkin	.333	9	3	0	0	1	3	4	0	.538	.667

Skeeter Barnes — Tigers
Bats Right (flyball hitter)

	Avg	G	AB	R	H	2B	3B	HR	RBI	BB	SO	HBP	GDP	SB	CS	OBP	SLG	IBB	SH	SF	#Pit	#P/PA	GB	FB	G/F
1992 Season	.273	95	165	27	45	8	1	3	25	10	18	2	4	3	1	.318	.388	1	2	2	614	3.43	51	59	0.86
Last Five Years	.278	175	327	56	91	21	3	8	42	19	42	2	5	13	9	.319	.434	2	4	3	1224	3.49	99	114	0.87

1992 Season

	Avg	AB	H	2B	3B	HR	RBI	BB	SO	OBP	SLG		Avg	AB	H	2B	3B	HR	RBI	BB	SO	OBP	SLG
vs. Left	.254	118	30	5	1	3	19	6	15	.294	.390	Scoring Posn	.366	41	15	0	1	2	21	3	3	.391	.561
vs. Right	.319	47	15	3	0	0	6	4	3	.377	.383	Close & Late	.259	27	7	2	0	0	4	1	3	.276	.333
Home	.296	81	24	6	1	3	17	4	10	.330	.506	None on/out	.220	41	9	1	0	0	0	1	5	.273	.244
Away	.250	84	21	2	0	0	8	6	8	.308	.274	Batting #7	.224	58	13	2	0	2	9	0	8	.237	.362
First Pitch	.190	21	4	0	0	0	2	1	0	.261	.190	Batting #8	.273	44	12	2	1	0	3	4	3	.347	.364
Ahead on Count	.404	47	19	4	1	1	11	4	0	.442	.596	Other	.317	63	20	4	0	1	13	6	7	.366	.429
Behind on Count	.250	56	14	1	0	1	6	0	12	.259	.321	Pre-All Star	.222	81	18	4	1	2	13	4	9	.264	.370
Two Strikes	.250	64	16	4	0	2	11	5	18	.310	.406	Post-All Star	.321	84	27	4	0	1	12	6	9	.370	.405

Tom Barrett — Red Sox
Bats Both (groundball hitter)

	Avg	G	AB	R	H	2B	3B	HR	RBI	BB	SO	HBP	GDP	SB	CS	OBP	SLG	IBB	SH	SF	#Pit	#P/PA	GB	FB	G/F
1992 Season	.000	4	3	1	0	0	0	0	0	2	0	0	0	0	0	.400	.000	0	1	0	24	4.80	1	2	0.50
Career (1988-1992)	.202	54	84	9	17	1	0	0	4	10	15	1	1	0	0	.295	.214	0	5	0	396	4.17	32	21	1.52

1992 Season

	Avg	AB	H	2B	3B	HR	RBI	BB	SO	OBP	SLG		Avg	AB	H	2B	3B	HR	RBI	BB	SO	OBP	SLG
vs. Left	.000	0	0	0	0	0	0	0	0	.000	.000	Scoring Posn	.000	0	0	0	0	0	0	0	0	.000	.000
vs. Right	.000	3	0	0	0	0	0	2	0	.400	.000	Close & Late	.000	2	0	0	0	0	0	0	0	.000	.000

Shawn Barton — Mariners
Pitches Left

	ERA	W	L	Sv	G	GS	IP	BB	SO	Avg	H	2B	3B	HR	RBI	OBP	SLG	GF	IR	IRS	Hld	SvOp	SB	CS	GB	FB	G/F
1992 Season	2.92	0	1	0	14	0	12.1	7	4	.238	11	2	1	1	6	.347	.405	2	19	4	0	1	0	3	15	10	1.50

1992 Season

	ERA	W	L	Sv	G	GS	IP	H	HR	BB	SO		Avg	AB	H	2B	3B	HR	RBI	BB	SO	OBP	SLG
Home	1.04	0	0	0	10	0	8.2	7	0	6	4	vs. Left	.389	18	7	2	1	0	4	1	1	.421	.611
Away	7.36	0	1	0	4	0	3.2	3	1	1	0	vs. Right	.125	24	3	0	0	1	2	6	3	.300	.250

Kevin Bass — Mets — Bats Both

	Avg	G	AB	R	H	2B	3B	HR	RBI	BB	SO	HBP	GDP	SB	CS	OBP	SLG	IBB	SH	SF	#Pit	#P/PA	GB	FB	G/F
1992 Season	.269	135	402	40	108	23	5	9	39	23	70	1	8	14	9	.308	.418	3	1	3	1591	3.71	149	103	1.45
Last Five Years	.261	564	1831	207	478	88	16	45	227	144	261	14	43	65	25	.318	.400	27	9	14	7096	3.54	745	525	1.42

1992 Season

	Avg	AB	H	2B	3B	HR	RBI	BB	SO	OBP	SLG		Avg	AB	H	2B	3B	HR	RBI	BB	SO	OBP	SLG
vs. Left	.222	144	32	13	1	4	17	3	22	.236	.410	Scoring Posn	.205	117	24	3	0	1	28	14	21	.284	.256
vs. Right	.295	258	76	10	4	5	22	20	48	.345	.422	Close & Late	.293	99	29	5	2	3	11	4	17	.317	.475
Groundball	.240	175	42	12	2	2	9	8	33	.277	.366	None on/out	.376	109	41	10	3	5	5	1	16	.387	.661
Flyball	.295	78	23	3	2	2	10	3	11	.313	.462	Batting #4	.218	101	22	7	1	2	9	6	22	.266	.366
Home	.292	216	63	16	2	7	25	12	41	.329	.481	Batting #5	.323	96	31	5	1	1	11	3	14	.343	.427
Away	.242	186	45	7	3	2	14	11	29	.283	.344	Other	.268	205	55	11	3	6	19	14	34	.312	.439
Day	.313	150	47	10	3	7	24	3	28	.331	.560	April	.316	38	12	2	1	1	6	4	11	.381	.500
Night	.242	252	61	13	2	2	15	20	42	.295	.333	May	.181	72	13	5	2	0	3	2	14	.211	.306
Grass	.282	298	84	18	2	8	32	16	55	.319	.436	June	.333	63	21	3	0	3	14	4	9	.368	.524
Turf	.231	104	24	5	3	1	7	7	15	.277	.365	July	.217	69	15	1	0	1	3	6	15	.280	.275
First Pitch	.237	38	9	1	0	0	6	3	0	.302	.263	August	.256	86	22	3	0	3	8	4	15	.286	.395
Ahead on Count	.327	110	36	9	1	3	18	8	0	.367	.509	September/October	.338	74	25	9	2	1	5	3	6	.364	.554
Behind on Count	.233	146	34	11	1	0	6	0	46	.233	.322	Pre-All Star	.261	222	58	11	3	5	26	11	42	.297	.405
Two Strikes	.234	175	41	10	3	3	9	12	70	.283	.377	Post-All Star	.278	180	50	12	2	4	13	12	28	.321	.433

1992 By Position

Position	Avg	AB	H	2B	3B	HR	RBI	BB	SO	OBP	SLG	G	GS	Innings	PO	A	E	DP	Fld Pct	Rng Fctr	In Zone	Outs	Zone Rtg	MLB Zone
As Pinch Hitter	.241	29	7	1	1	0	3	3	4	.303	.345	33	0	---	---	---	---	---	---	---	---	---	---	---
As lf	.290	272	79	20	4	7	26	15	46	.328	.471	84	68	603.2	137	1	2	0	.986	2.06	165	133	.806	.809
As rf	.218	101	22	2	0	2	10	5	20	.255	.297	34	22	227.2	55	1	1	0	.982	2.21	58	51	.879	.814

Last Five Years

	Avg	AB	H	2B	3B	HR	RBI	BB	SO	OBP	SLG		Avg	AB	H	2B	3B	HR	RBI	BB	SO	OBP	SLG
vs. Left	.265	623	165	46	2	23	95	28	80	.301	.456	Scoring Posn	.272	464	126	21	3	12	180	73	71	.362	.407
vs. Right	.259	1208	313	42	14	22	132	116	181	.326	.372	Close & Late	.265	359	95	10	4	10	54	34	50	.325	.398
Groundball	.257	686	176	32	8	15	82	62	93	.321	.392	None on/out	.267	434	116	21	6	10	10	17	55	.301	.412
Flyball	.255	400	102	19	3	10	55	24	54	.302	.393	Batting #5	.257	688	177	35	4	14	88	56	81	.317	.381
Home	.266	915	243	47	5	22	115	80	139	.325	.400	Batting #6	.278	360	100	20	4	10	42	32	54	.338	.439
Away	.257	916	235	41	11	23	112	64	122	.310	.401	Other	.257	783	201	33	8	21	97	56	126	.309	.400
Day	.244	590	144	22	6	17	80	38	102	.292	.388	April	.265	336	89	18	4	5	46	27	52	.320	.387
Night	.269	1241	334	66	10	28	147	106	159	.329	.406	May	.266	402	107	24	4	10	44	23	52	.309	.420
Grass	.252	982	247	40	8	28	121	77	163	.308	.396	June	.245	206	51	7	0	6	31	20	25	.322	.365
Turf	.272	849	231	48	7	17	106	67	98	.329	.425	July	.274	186	51	5	1	7	21	19	30	.340	.425
First Pitch	.279	233	65	12	0	5	34	13	0	.321	.395	August	.254	307	78	12	0	10	40	22	48	.305	.391
Ahead on Count	.321	505	162	30	4	17	75	62	0	.396	.497	September/October	.260	392	102	22	7	7	45	30	54	.321	.406
Behind on Count	.210	591	124	26	6	11	57	0	142	.215	.330	Pre-All Star	.261	1027	268	51	9	22	126	77	140	.316	.392
Two Strikes	.213	709	151	31	6	11	67	58	259	.275	.320	Post-All Star	.261	804	210	37	7	23	101	67	121	.320	.410

Batter vs. Pitcher (since 1984)

Hits Best Against	Avg	AB	H	2B	3B	HR	RBI	BB	SO	OBP	SLG	Hits Worst Against	Avg	AB	H	2B	3B	HR	RBI	BB	SO	OBP	SLG
Goose Gossage	.727	11	8	1	0	0	3	0	1	.727	.818	Norm Charlton	.056	18	1	1	0	0	0	0	5	.053	.111
Tim Crews	.667	9	6	0	1	0	1	4	0	.769	.889	Todd Worrell	.091	11	1	0	0	0	1	0	1	.091	.091
Mike Maddux	.600	10	6	1	1	0	2	2	1	.667	.900	Ramon Martinez	.100	10	1	0	0	0	0	1	3	.182	.100
Neal Heaton	.474	19	9	3	0	3	7	1	0	.500	1.105	Lee Smith	.111	18	2	0	0	0	1	0	4	.111	.111
Mitch Williams	.455	11	5	2	0	2	5	0	3	.455	1.182	Alejandro Pena	.111	18	2	0	0	0	1	1	4	.158	.111

Miguel Batista — Pirates — Pitches Right (groundball pitcher)

	ERA	W	L	Sv	G	GS	IP	BB	SO	Avg	H	2B	3B	HR	RBI	OBP	SLG	GF	IR	IRS	Hld	SvOp	SB	CS	GB	FB	G/F
1992 Season	9.00	0	0	0	1	0	2.0	3	1	.400	4	0	0	1	2	.538	.700	1	0	0	0	0	0	0	5	1	5.00

1992 Season

	ERA	W	L	Sv	G	GS	IP	H	HR	BB	SO		Avg	AB	H	2B	3B	HR	RBI	BB	SO	OBP	SLG
Home	0.00	0	0	0	0	0	0.0	0	0	0	0	vs. Left	.500	6	3	0	0	1	2	3	1	.667	1.000
Away	9.00	0	0	0	1	0	2.0	4	1	3	1	vs. Right	.250	4	1	0	0	0	0	0	0	.250	.250

Kim Batiste — Phillies — Bats Right (groundball hitter)

	Avg	G	AB	R	H	2B	3B	HR	RBI	BB	SO	HBP	GDP	SB	CS	OBP	SLG	IBB	SH	SF	#Pit	#P/PA	GB	FB	G/F
1992 Season	.206	44	136	9	28	4	0	1	10	4	18	0	7	0	0	.224	.257	1	2	3	464	3.24	63	38	1.66
Career (1991-1992)	.209	54	163	11	34	4	0	1	11	5	26	0	7	0	1	.228	.252	2	2	3	561	3.28	72	43	1.67

1992 Season

	Avg	AB	H	2B	3B	HR	RBI	BB	SO	OBP	SLG		Avg	AB	H	2B	3B	HR	RBI	BB	SO	OBP	SLG
vs. Left	.205	73	15	2	0	0	4	2	10	.224	.233	Scoring Posn	.176	34	6	0	0	0	8	2	4	.205	.176
vs. Right	.206	63	13	2	0	1	6	2	8	.224	.286	Close & Late	.292	24	7	1	0	0	3	2	6	.333	.333
Home	.214	56	12	4	0	0	2	3	8	.246	.286	None on/out	.188	32	6	1	0	0	0	0	5	.188	.219
Away	.200	80	16	0	0	1	8	1	10	.207	.238	Batting #7	.222	18	4	0	0	0	1	0	1	.222	.222

1992 Season

	Avg	AB	H	2B	3B	HR	RBI	BB	SO	OBP	SLG		Avg	AB	H	2B	3B	HR	RBI	BB	SO	OBP	SLG
First Pitch	.250	16	4	0	0	0	1	1	0	.278	.250	Batting #8	.207	116	24	4	0	1	9	4	16	.228	.267
Ahead on Count	.346	26	9	0	0	0	0	2	0	.393	.346	Other	.000	2	0	0	0	0	0	0	1	.000	.000
Behind on Count	.136	59	8	3	0	0	6	0	13	.131	.186	Pre-All Star	.206	136	28	4	0	1	10	4	18	.224	.257
Two Strikes	.140	57	8	3	0	0	6	1	18	.150	.193	Post-All Star	.000	0	0	0	0	0	0	0	0	.000	.000

Rod Beck — Giants   Pitches Right

	ERA	W	L	Sv	G	GS	IP	BB	SO	Avg	H	2B	3B	HR	RBI	OBP	SLG	GF	IR	IRS	Hld	SvOp	SB	CS	GB	FB	G/F
1992 Season	1.76	3	3	17	65	0	92.0	15	87	.190	62	8	1	4	25	.228	.257	42	41	9	4	23	2	4	99	82	1.21
Career (1991-1992)	2.49	4	4	18	96	0	144.1	28	125	.221	91	19	3	8	51	.263	.315	52	55	14	5	24	4	7	155	146	1.06

1992 Season

	ERA	W	L	Sv	G	GS	IP	H	HR	BB	SO		Avg	AB	H	2B	3B	HR	RBI	BB	SO	OBP	SLG
Home	2.06	2	3	9	31	0	43.2	35	1	4	43	vs. Left	.178	180	32	6	1	2	13	6	47	.212	.256
Away	1.49	1	0	8	34	0	48.1	27	3	11	44	vs. Right	.204	147	30	2	0	2	12	9	40	.248	.259
Day	1.80	0	0	8	27	0	35.0	21	1	4	40	Inning 1-6	.259	58	15	3	0	0	9	2	17	.302	.310
Night	1.74	3	3	9	38	0	57.0	41	3	11	47	Inning 7+	.175	269	47	5	1	4	16	13	70	.212	.245
Grass	1.66	2	3	15	46	0	65.0	50	2	7	62	None on	.195	190	37	3	1	4	4	9	50	.235	.284
Turf	2.00	1	0	2	19	0	27.0	12	2	8	25	Runners on	.182	137	25	5	0	0	21	6	37	.219	.219
April	0.00	0	0	1	8	0	17.0	8	0	3	16	Scoring Posn	.195	82	16	3	0	0	20	4	24	.236	.232
May	4.76	0	0	1	11	0	17.0	16	1	1	21	Close & Late	.193	187	36	5	1	2	14	10	47	.232	.262
June	2.19	0	2	2	9	0	12.1	11	1	3	9	None on/out	.195	77	15	1	0	2	2	4	17	.244	.286
July	2.35	1	1	5	12	0	15.1	13	1	2	22	vs. 1st Batr (relief)	.226	62	14	1	0	2	7	2	14	.246	.339
August	0.77	0	0	4	12	0	11.2	7	0	2	7	First Inning Pitched	.176	216	38	6	0	3	21	11	50	.221	.245
September/October	0.48	2	0	4	13	0	18.2	7	1	4	12	First 15 Pitches	.150	206	31	5	1	3	13	11	48	.196	.228
Starter	0.00	0	0	0	0	0	0.0	0	0	0	0	Pitch 16-30	.250	100	25	3	0	1	10	2	33	.272	.310
Reliever	1.76	3	3	17	65	0	92.0	62	4	15	87	Pitch 31-45	.286	21	6	0	0	0	2	2	6	.333	.286
0 Days rest	3.86	0	0	6	10	0	9.1	8	0	2	10	Pitch 46+	.000	0	0	0	0	0	0	0	0	.000	.000
1 or 2 Days rest	0.98	2	2	9	35	0	55.0	35	4	8	55	First Pitch	.234	47	11	2	1	0	1	2	0	.265	.319
3+ Days rest	2.60	1	1	2	20	0	27.2	19	0	5	22	Ahead on Count	.170	176	30	5	0	1	11	0	75	.174	.216
Pre-All Star	2.28	0	3	8	35	0	55.1	43	2	8	60	Behind on Count	.244	45	11	0	0	2	6	6	1	.340	.378
Post-All Star	0.98	3	0	9	30	0	36.2	19	2	7	27	Two Strikes	.139	173	24	4	0	0	10	7	86	.177	.162

Tim Belcher — Reds   Pitches Right

	ERA	W	L	Sv	G	GS	IP	BB	SO	Avg	H	2B	3B	HR	RBI	OBP	SLG	CG	ShO	Sup	QS	#P/S	SB	CS	GB	FB	G/F
1992 Season	3.91	15	14	0	35	34	227.2	80	149	.238	201	42	8	17	90	.303	.368	2	1	4.47	21	98	6	11	271	284	0.95
Last Five Years	3.22	61	50	5	167	148	999.2	334	759	.230	851	133	21	72	349	.295	.336	23	13	4.08	91	100	68	53	1154	1148	1.01

1992 Season

	ERA	W	L	Sv	G	GS	IP	H	HR	BB	SO		Avg	AB	H	2B	3B	HR	RBI	BB	SO	OBP	SLG
Home	3.43	11	7	0	19	18	126.0	104	10	47	88	vs. Left	.277	512	142	29	6	9	51	59	78	.350	.410
Away	4.51	4	7	0	16	16	101.2	97	7	33	61	vs. Right	.178	331	59	13	2	8	39	21	71	.228	.302
Day	3.20	4	4	0	11	10	70.1	60	3	25	45	Inning 1-6	.236	704	166	31	8	15	77	65	132	.298	.366
Night	4.23	11	10	0	24	24	157.1	141	14	55	104	Inning 7+	.252	139	35	11	0	2	13	15	17	.327	.374
Grass	3.84	3	4	0	11	11	72.2	58	4	21	43	None on	.205	523	107	22	4	11	11	46	94	.269	.325
Turf	3.95	12	10	0	24	23	155.0	143	13	59	106	Runners on	.294	320	94	20	4	6	79	34	55	.356	.438
April	4.98	1	3	0	5	5	34.1	32	1	8	30	Scoring Posn	.272	184	50	13	3	5	73	20	33	.329	.457
May	2.55	3	2	0	5	5	35.1	23	2	16	28	Close & Late	.302	86	26	7	0	2	11	9	10	.371	.453
June	3.02	3	1	0	6	6	41.2	34	4	17	20	None on/out	.216	227	49	12	3	8	8	19	36	.276	.401
July	3.92	2	3	0	7	6	41.1	44	4	18	19	vs. 1st Batr (relief)	.000	0	0	0	0	0	0	1	0	1.000	.000
August	5.20	2	3	0	6	6	36.1	38	2	13	21	First Inning Pitched	.302	129	39	7	2	2	24	21	26	.392	.434
September/October	3.96	4	2	0	6	6	38.2	30	4	8	31	First 75 Pitches	.238	617	147	27	8	11	62	60	119	.305	.361
Starter	3.85	15	13	0	34	34	226.2	199	16	78	149	Pitch 76-90	.232	125	29	8	0	6	20	9	16	.283	.440
Reliever	18.00	0	1	0	1	0	1.0	2	1	2	0	Pitch 91-105	.262	65	17	4	0	0	4	8	10	.342	.323
0-3 Days Rest	3.77	1	1	0	2	2	14.1	14	1	5	7	Pitch 106+	.222	36	8	3	0	0	4	3	4	.275	.306
4 Days Rest	3.52	10	7	0	23	23	156.0	127	10	49	103	First Pitch	.278	151	42	12	3	6	22	3	2	.291	.517
5+ Days Rest	4.79	4	5	0	9	9	56.1	58	5	24	39	Ahead on Count	.201	389	78	11	3	3	33	0	127	.203	.267
Pre-All Star	3.42	8	7	0	19	18	126.1	108	8	50	84	Behind on Count	.297	165	49	14	2	5	21	43	0	.438	.497
Post-All Star	4.53	7	7	0	16	16	101.1	93	9	30	65	Two Strikes	.180	367	66	9	2	4	30	34	147	.249	.248

Last Five Years

	ERA	W	L	Sv	G	GS	IP	H	HR	BB	SO		Avg	AB	H	2B	3B	HR	RBI	BB	SO	OBP	SLG
Home	2.77	40	21	2	81	72	524.0	436	36	153	409	vs. Left	.246	2068	508	81	12	33	173	212	399	.316	.344
Away	3.73	21	29	3	86	76	475.2	415	36	181	350	vs. Right	.211	1627	343	52	9	39	176	122	360	.268	.326
Day	3.51	16	15	1	57	47	307.1	287	18	109	222	Inning 1-6	.227	2971	673	100	19	61	291	268	630	.291	.335
Night	3.09	45	35	4	110	101	692.1	564	54	225	537	Inning 7+	.246	724	178	33	2	11	58	66	129	.311	.343
Grass	2.89	39	27	3	107	94	644.1	550	43	194	487	None on	.222	2264	506	77	9	44	44	178	455	.280	.321
Turf	3.82	22	23	2	60	54	355.1	301	29	140	272	Runners on	.245	1411	345	56	12	28	305	156	304	.319	.361
April	3.16	8	9	1	25	21	153.2	124	9	38	125	Scoring Posn	.243	774	188	34	9	17	271	96	183	.320	.376
May	3.48	12	9	0	26	26	168.0	144	12	65	131	Close & Late	.241	345	83	18	1	4	27	37	55	.312	.333
June	3.53	8	10	2	32	26	170.2	156	15	69	128	None on/out	.222	981	218	30	6	23	23	78	167	.282	.335
July	3.23	12	9	2	33	24	175.1	159	11	61	113	vs. 1st Batr (relief)	.188	16	3	0	0	0	1	3	6	.316	.188

Last Five Years

	ERA	W	L	Sv	G	GS	IP	H	HR	BB	SO		Avg	AB	H	2B	3B	HR	RBI	BB	SO	OBP	SLG
August	3.58	9	8	0	27	27	171.0	156	15	58	129	First Inning Pitched	.231	610	141	20	7	9	72	69	173	.310	.331
September/October	2.29	12	5	0	24	24	161.0	112	10	43	133	First 75 Pitches	.227	2638	598	91	17	50	236	232	588	.290	.331
Starter	3.20	59	47	0	148	148	962.0	818	67	321	719	Pitch 76-90	.263	460	121	23	2	16	65	40	64	.321	.426
Reliever	3.82	2	3	5	19	0	37.2	33	5	13	40	Pitch 91-105	.198	323	64	9	2	2	23	32	66	.272	.257
0-3 Days Rest	2.56	5	3	0	11	11	70.1	70	4	22	46	Pitch 105+	.248	274	68	10	0	4	25	30	41	.320	.328
4 Days Rest	3.08	35	24	0	86	86	569.2	462	39	179	450	First Pitch	.297	518	154	25	6	20	66	14	2	.320	.485
5+ Days Rest	3.55	19	20	0	51	51	322.0	286	24	120	223	Behind on Count	.190	1838	349	48	10	18	130	0	640	.194	.256
Pre-All Star	3.35	32	30	5	97	78	545.0	477	39	192	412	Ahead on Count	.277	653	181	26	3	21	96	163	0	.417	.423
Post-All Star	3.07	29	20	0	70	70	454.2	374	33	142	347	Two Strikes	.172	1828	314	42	8	22	120	157	755	.240	.240

Pitcher vs. Batter (career)

Pitches Best Vs.	Avg	AB	H	2B	3B	HR	RBI	BB	SO	OBP	SLG	Pitches Worst Vs.	Avg	AB	H	2B	3B	HR	RBI	BB	SO	OBP	SLG
Mitch Webster	.059	17	1	0	0	0	0	1	5	.111	.059	Delino DeShields	.556	9	5	0	0	0	2	3	1	.667	.556
Bip Roberts	.067	15	1	0	0	0	0	2	2	.176	.067	Ozzie Smith	.542	24	13	1	0	0	1	3	1	.593	.583
Jose Uribe	.095	21	2	0	0	0	0	0	4	.095	.095	Dave Magadan	.529	17	9	2	0	0	3	2	3	.579	.647
Tom Brunansky	.100	10	1	0	0	0	2	0	3	.091	.100	Vince Coleman	.500	22	11	0	1	0	1	3	5	.560	.591
Billy Hatcher	.107	28	3	1	0	0	1	1	4	.138	.143	Deion Sanders	.474	19	9	1	2	1	2	2		.524	.895

Stan Belinda — Pirates
Pitches Right (flyball pitcher)

	ERA	W	L	Sv	G	GS	IP	BB	SO	Avg	H	2B	3B	HR	RBI	OBP	SLG	GF	IR	IRS	Hld	SvOp	SB	CS	GB	FB	G/F
1992 Season	3.15	6	4	18	59	0	71.1	29	57	.223	58	13	2	8	41	.295	.381	42	28	18	0	24	12	2	66	101	0.65
Career (1989-1992)	3.50	16	14	42	182	0	218.1	95	193	.215	169	27	6	22	108	.300	.348	96	107	40	17	57	34	5	209	274	0.76

1992 Season

	ERA	W	L	Sv	G	GS	IP	H	HR	BB	SO		Avg	AB	H	2B	3B	HR	RBI	BB	SO	OBP	SLG
Home	1.89	2	1	8	27	0	33.1	27	2	11	27	vs. Left	.193	135	26	6	0	4	15	17	21	.277	.326
Away	4.26	4	3	10	32	0	38.0	31	6	18	30	vs. Right	.256	125	32	7	2	4	26	12	36	.314	.440
Starter	0.00	0	0	0	0	0	0.0	0	0	0	0	Scoring Posn	.241	79	19	4	1	6	36	11	14	.313	.544
Reliever	3.15	6	4	18	59	0	71.1	58	8	29	57	Close & Late	.224	196	44	9	1	6	29	23	42	.300	.372
0 Days rest	4.40	2	3	6	13	0	14.1	18	2	6	6	None on/out	.177	62	11	3	1	1	1	4	19	.227	.306
1 or 2 Days rest	2.35	2	1	6	24	0	30.2	20	3	15	28	First Pitch	.273	33	9	2	0	2	11	4	0	.325	.515
3+ Days rest	3.42	2	0	6	22	0	26.1	20	3	8	23	Behind on Count	.304	56	17	2	2	1	8	12	0	.414	.464
Pre-All Star	2.41	3	2	13	32	0	37.1	26	4	13	33	Ahead on Count	.177	130	23	8	0	3	16	0	51	.176	.308
Post-All Star	3.97	3	2	5	27	0	34.0	32	4	16	24	Two Strikes	.152	125	19	5	0	5	17	13	57	.230	.312

Career (1989-1992)

	ERA	W	L	Sv	G	GS	IP	H	HR	BB	SO		Avg	AB	H	2B	3B	HR	RBI	BB	SO	OBP	SLG
Home	3.10	5	5	23	86	0	107.1	91	6	40	93	vs. Left	.203	365	74	14	0	9	39	46	75	.293	.315
Away	3.89	11	9	19	96	0	111.0	78	16	55	100	vs. Right	.225	422	95	13	6	13	69	49	118	.305	.377
Day	5.03	3	5	14	48	0	59.0	56	8	33	50	Inning 1-6	.194	31	6	0	0	0	9	8	9	.333	.194
Night	2.94	13	9	28	134	0	159.1	113	14	62	143	Inning 7+	.216	756	163	27	6	22	99	87	184	.298	.354
Grass	4.42	4	5	7	47	0	53.0	39	10	28	44	None on	.189	439	83	13	4	9	9	48	121	.275	.298
Turf	3.21	12	9	35	135	0	165.1	130	12	67	149	Runners on	.247	348	86	14	2	13	99	47	72	.329	.411
April	3.24	1	1	7	12	0	16.2	7	1	7	18	Scoring Posn	.224	237	53	7	2	10	89	38	53	.321	.397
May	5.52	2	4	2	27	0	31.0	28	5	14	27	Close & Late	.211	487	103	20	4	12	67	60	114	.299	.343
June	1.01	3	2	9	34	0	35.2	22	0	15	36	None on/out	.182	181	33	7	2	5	5	17	55	.253	.326
July	4.09	2	3	8	35	0	44.0	32	9	24	36	vs. 1st Batr (relief)	.173	156	27	6	1	6	22	23	46	.275	.340
August	3.45	0	3	8	36	0	44.1	34	4	20	41	First Inning Pitched	.216	566	122	22	6	13	83	69	133	.299	.345
September/October	3.66	6	3	6	38	0	46.2	43	3	15	35	First 15 Pitches	.211	503	106	20	4	12	62	57	123	.291	.338
Starter	0.00	0	0	0	0	0	0.0	0	0	0	0	Pitch 16-30	.216	241	52	5	2	8	35	29	50	.299	.353
Reliever	3.50	16	14	42	182	0	218.1	169	22	95	193	Pitch 31-45	.256	43	11	2	0	2	11	9	11	.396	.442
0 Days rest	4.18	3	5	9	30	0	32.1	33	5	15	27	Pitch 46+	.000	0	0	0	0	0	0	0	0	.000	.000
1 or 2 Days rest	3.20	8	5	23	98	0	126.2	91	12	51	113	First Pitch	.297	91	27	7	0	3	23	10	0	.358	.473
3+ Days rest	3.79	5	4	10	54	0	59.1	45	5	29	53	Ahead on Count	.165	423	70	12	2	5	38	0	170	.170	.239
Pre-All Star	2.80	8	6	23	86	0	99.2	63	7	44	95	Behind on Count	.294	136	40	5	2	7	23	45	0	.465	.515
Post-All Star	4.10	8	8	19	96	0	118.2	106	15	51	98	Two Strikes	.154	426	66	8	3	10	41	39	193	.226	.257

Pitcher vs. Batter (career)

Pitches Best Vs.	Avg	AB	H	2B	3B	HR	RBI	BB	SO	OBP	SLG	Pitches Worst Vs.	Avg	AB	H	2B	3B	HR	RBI	BB	SO	OBP	SLG
Tim Wallach	.167	18	3	1	0	0	2	2	3	.250	.222	Andre Dawson	.417	12	5	0	0	4	10	0	1	.417	1.417
Andres Galarraga	.176	17	3	0	0	0	1	0	6	.176	.176	Ryne Sandberg	.417	12	5	0	0	1	3	1	1	.462	.667
Terry Pendleton	.182	11	2	0	0	1	3	0	3	.182	.455	Mark Grace	.333	9	3	1	0	0	1	5	0	.571	.444
Todd Zeile	.200	10	2	1	0	1	4	4	1	.429	.600												

Derek Bell — Blue Jays
Bats Right

	Avg	G	AB	R	H	2B	3B	HR	RBI	BB	SO	HBP	GDP	SB	CS	OBP	SLG	IBB	SH	SF	#Pit	#P/PA	GB	FB	G/F
1992 Season	.242	61	161	23	39	6	3	2	15	15	34	5	6	7	2	.324	.354	1	2	1	664	3.65	66	46	1.43
Career (1991-1992)	.228	79	189	28	43	6	3	2	16	21	39	6	6	10	4	.323	.323	1	2	2	801	3.69	78	53	1.47

1992 Season

	Avg	AB	H	2B	3B	HR	RBI	BB	SO	OBP	SLG		Avg	AB	H	2B	3B	HR	RBI	BB	SO	OBP	SLG
vs. Left	.255	47	12	3	1	2	6	3	9	.333	.489	Scoring Posn	.263	38	10	2	1	0	12	5	9	.356	.368

1992 Season

	Avg	AB	H	2B	3B	HR	RBI	BB	SO	OBP	SLG		Avg	AB	H	2B	3B	HR	RBI	BB	SO	OBP	SLG
vs. Right	.237	114	27	3	2	0	9	12	25	.320	.298	Close & Late	.286	21	6	0	0	1	2	3	3	.360	.429
Home	.167	84	14	1	2	2	5	8	18	.278	.298	None on/out	.289	45	13	2	1	1	1	3	6	.360	.444
Away	.325	77	25	5	1	0	10	7	16	.376	.416	Batting #1	.286	42	12	2	2	0	4	1	7	.333	.429
First Pitch	.360	25	9	1	0	1	4	1	0	.407	.520	Batting #7	.215	79	17	3	0	1	8	11	15	.323	.291
Ahead on Count	.289	38	11	2	1	1	5	8	0	.413	.474	Other	.250	40	10	1	1	1	3	3	12	.318	.400
Behind on Count	.180	61	11	3	0	0	3	0	19	.203	.230	Pre-All Star	.189	90	17	3	0	2	8	10	20	.282	.289
Two Strikes	.176	74	13	2	2	0	4	6	34	.235	.257	Post-All Star	.310	71	22	3	3	0	7	5	14	.380	.437

Eric Bell — Indians   Pitches Left

	ERA	W	L	Sv	G	GS	IP	BB	SO	Avg	H	2B	3B	HR	RBI	OBP	SLG	GF	IR	IRS	Hld	SvOp	SB	CS	GB	FB	G/F
1992 Season	7.63	0	2	0	7	1	15.1	9	10	.349	22	5	0	1	14	.432	.476	2	4	1	1	0	4	1	19	16	1.19
Last Five Years	3.78	4	2	0	17	1	33.1	14	17	.229	22	5	0	1	14	.319	.297	5	15	3	3	0	6	1	44	37	1.19

1992 Season

	ERA	W	L	Sv	G	GS	IP	H	HR	BB	SO		Avg	AB	H	2B	3B	HR	RBI	BB	SO	OBP	SLG
Home	6.75	0	2	0	4	1	13.1	16	1	8	9	vs. Left	.133	15	2	0	0	0	1	3	1	.316	.133
Away	13.50	0	0	0	3	0	2.0	6	0	1	1	vs. Right	.417	48	20	5	0	1	13	6	9	.473	.583

George Bell — White Sox   Bats Right (flyball hitter)

	Avg	G	AB	R	H	2B	3B	HR	RBI	BB	SO	HBP	GDP	SB	CS	OBP	SLG	IBB	SH	SF	#Pit	#P/PA	GB	FB	G/F
1992 Season	.255	155	627	74	160	27	0	25	112	31	97	6	29	5	2	.294	.418	8	0	6	2346	3.50	177	240	0.74
Last Five Years	.274	755	2974	370	815	147	7	113	485	162	365	18	92	18	15	.311	.442	29	0	48	11207	3.50	942	1136	0.83

1992 Season

	Avg	AB	H	2B	3B	HR	RBI	BB	SO	OBP	SLG		Avg	AB	H	2B	3B	HR	RBI	BB	SO	OBP	SLG
vs. Left	.310	142	44	8	0	7	28	10	17	.355	.514	Scoring Posn	.292	212	62	10	0	10	88	16	41	.339	.481
vs. Right	.239	485	116	19	0	18	84	21	80	.276	.390	Close & Late	.232	99	23	3	0	2	7	7	20	.283	.323
Groundball	.244	172	42	4	0	6	24	12	32	.301	.372	None on/out	.184	141	26	6	0	2	2	5	23	.223	.270
Flyball	.272	180	49	11	0	9	33	11	24	.314	.483	Batting #4	.257	436	112	20	0	20	85	22	68	.296	.440
Home	.261	326	85	11	0	16	63	14	54	.293	.442	Batting #5	.251	191	48	7	0	5	27	9	29	.291	.366
Away	.249	301	75	16	0	9	49	17	43	.295	.392	Other	.000	0	0	0	0	0	0	0	0	.000	.000
Day	.246	142	35	3	0	5	19	6	28	.288	.373	April	.356	73	26	2	0	4	13	1	9	.368	.548
Night	.258	485	125	24	0	20	93	25	69	.296	.431	May	.175	103	18	4	0	1	14	7	18	.234	.243
Grass	.258	531	137	19	0	24	103	30	84	.301	.429	June	.270	111	30	6	0	5	20	5	18	.302	.459
Turf	.240	96	23	8	0	1	9	1	13	.255	.354	July	.229	109	25	5	0	3	20	7	17	.286	.358
First Pitch	.295	61	18	3	0	3	17	6	0	.368	.492	August	.304	112	34	5	0	9	25	6	20	.339	.589
Ahead on Count	.342	152	52	9	0	10	37	17	0	.402	.599	September/October	.227	119	27	5	0	3	18	5	15	.262	.345
Behind on Count	.207	256	53	9	0	8	35	0	58	.215	.336	Pre-All Star	.266	335	89	15	0	13	65	17	50	.305	.427
Two Strikes	.192	276	53	7	0	5	33	8	97	.224	.272	Post-All Star	.243	292	71	12	0	12	47	14	47	.281	.408

1992 By Position

Position	Avg	AB	H	2B	3B	HR	RBI	BB	SO	OBP	SLG	G	GS	Innings	PO	A	E	DP	Fld Pct	Rng Fctr	In Zone	Outs	Zone Rtg	MLB Zone
As Designated Hitter	.247	570	141	23	0	22	98	26	90	.285	.404	140	140	---	---	---	---	---	---	---	---	---	---	---
As lf	.333	57	19	4	0	3	14	5	7	.381	.561	15	15	124.0	27	0	1	0	.964	1.96	30	26	.867	.809

Last Five Years

	Avg	AB	H	2B	3B	HR	RBI	BB	SO	OBP	SLG		Avg	AB	H	2B	3B	HR	RBI	BB	SO	OBP	SLG
vs. Left	.281	873	245	42	3	46	154	61	92	.325	.494	Scoring Posn	.289	859	248	42	2	34	374	64	123	.325	.461
vs. Right	.271	2101	570	105	4	67	331	101	273	.305	.421	Close & Late	.255	470	120	20	1	20	75	31	73	.300	.430
Groundball	.285	748	213	39	1	24	114	37	98	.319	.436	None on/out	.240	753	181	32	2	30	30	29	93	.270	.408
Flyball	.274	784	215	39	1	38	137	45	108	.312	.472	Batting #4	.269	2137	575	99	4	79	341	114	272	.305	.430
Home	.277	1473	408	72	5	53	243	78	180	.313	.441	Batting #5	.277	534	148	29	0	17	78	30	73	.319	.427
Away	.271	1501	407	75	2	60	242	84	185	.308	.444	Other	.304	303	92	19	3	17	66	18	20	.336	.554
Day	.263	969	255	49	3	36	147	57	127	.304	.431	April	.300	417	125	22	1	20	64	17	44	.328	.501
Night	.279	2005	560	98	4	77	338	105	238	.314	.447	May	.251	506	127	17	2	18	78	32	66	.297	.399
Grass	.269	1672	449	77	2	65	292	89	209	.304	.434	June	.282	536	151	30	0	22	100	33	77	.320	.461
Turf	.281	1302	366	70	5	48	193	73	156	.319	.453	July	.262	462	121	25	1	16	71	30	56	.311	.424
First Pitch	.315	295	93	17	0	14	64	12	0	.343	.515	August	.293	526	154	29	3	22	95	28	61	.324	.485
Ahead on Count	.298	751	224	42	1	40	145	94	0	.372	.517	September/October	.260	527	137	24	0	15	77	22	61	.288	.391
Behind on Count	.264	1178	311	55	3	38	178	3	213	.265	.413	Pre-All Star	.278	1628	453	82	3	66	274	94	201	.317	.454
Two Strikes	.220	1241	273	40	2	27	131	45	362	.251	.321	Post-All Star	.269	1346	362	65	4	47	211	68	164	.303	.428

Batter vs. Pitcher (since 1984)

Hits Best Against	Avg	AB	H	2B	3B	HR	RBI	BB	SO	OBP	SLG	Hits Worst Against	Avg	AB	H	2B	3B	HR	RBI	BB	SO	OBP	SLG
Neal Heaton	.462	26	12	4	0	4	10	0	0	.462	1.077	Paul Gibson	.000	11	0	0	0	0	1	2	2	.143	.000
Scott Bankhead	.448	29	13	4	0	5	7	0	2	.448	1.103	Rod Nichols	.083	12	1	0	0	0	0	0	0	.188	.167
Tom Browning	.364	11	4	0	0	3	4	2	2	.462	1.182	Jack McDowell	.091	11	1	0	0	0	1	0	2	.083	.091
John Habyan	.333	12	4	0	0	3	8	3	1	.467	1.083	Alan Mills	.091	11	1	0	0	0	0	0	1	.091	.091
Trevor Wilson	.333	9	3	1	0	2	4	2	0	.417	1.111	Brian Barnes	.091	11	1	0	0	0	1	1	4	.167	.091

Jay Bell — Pirates Bats Right

	Avg	G	AB	R	H	2B	3B	HR	RBI	BB	SO	HBP	GDP	SB	CS	OBP	SLG	IBB	SH	SF	#Pit	#P/PA	GB	FB	G/F
1992 Season	.264	159	632	87	167	36	6	9	55	55	103	4	12	7	5	.326	.383	0	19	2	2654	3.83	209	203	1.03
Last Five Years	.258	626	2305	332	595	114	25	36	222	212	411	13	53	36	22	.322	.376	1	99	15	9829	3.86	801	702	1.14

1992 Season

	Avg	AB	H	2B	3B	HR	RBI	BB	SO	OBP	SLG		Avg	AB	H	2B	3B	HR	RBI	BB	SO	OBP	SLG
vs. Left	.324	238	77	19	4	1	20	26	42	.396	.450	Scoring Posn	.333	120	40	10	1	1	41	13	17	.393	.458
vs. Right	.228	394	90	17	2	8	35	29	61	.282	.343	Close & Late	.278	115	32	4	3	2	11	10	15	.336	.417
Groundball	.228	228	52	8	3	2	12	15	39	.282	.316	None on/out	.237	135	32	6	1	3	3	7	15	.280	.363
Flyball	.310	145	45	12	1	4	17	14	29	.370	.490	Total	.264	632	167	36	6	9	55	55	103	.326	.383
Home	.278	302	84	19	3	5	27	33	49	.352	.411	Batting #2	.264	632	167	36	6	9	55	55	103	.326	.383
Away	.252	330	83	17	3	4	28	22	54	.301	.358	Other	.000	0	0	0	0	0	0	0	0	.000	.000
Day	.267	176	47	8	3	2	17	14	29	.321	.381	April	.236	72	17	2	0	0	5	14	7	.364	.264
Night	.263	456	120	28	3	7	38	41	74	.328	.384	May	.243	111	27	7	0	1	10	12	22	.317	.333
Grass	.271	166	45	11	2	3	18	10	28	.313	.416	June	.269	104	28	6	1	2	10	12	16	.347	.404
Turf	.262	466	122	25	4	6	37	45	75	.331	.371	July	.257	109	28	8	0	2	4	7	16	.302	.385
First Pitch	.279	68	19	8	1	5	12	0	0	.279	.647	August	.284	102	29	7	2	1	13	7	22	.336	.422
Ahead on Count	.295	132	39	8	2	4	13	37	0	.453	.477	September/October	.284	134	38	6	3	3	13	3	20	.304	.440
Behind on Count	.284	236	67	13	1	1	14	0	61	.290	.360	Pre-All Star	.260	335	87	19	1	3	26	40	50	.340	.349
Two Strikes	.216	305	66	12	3	0	22	18	103	.262	.275	Post-All Star	.269	297	80	17	5	6	29	15	53	.309	.421

1992 By Position

Position	Avg	AB	H	2B	3B	HR	RBI	BB	SO	OBP	SLG	G	GS	Innings	PO	A	E	DP	Fld Pct	Rng Fctr	In Zone	Outs	Zone Rtg	MLB Zone
As ss	.264	632	167	36	6	9	55	55	103	.326	.383	159	157	1411.1	268	527	22	94	.973	5.07	642	569	.886	.885

Last Five Years

	Avg	AB	H	2B	3B	HR	RBI	BB	SO	OBP	SLG		Avg	AB	H	2B	3B	HR	RBI	BB	SO	OBP	SLG
vs. Left	.295	830	245	50	15	10	81	99	128	.370	.428	Scoring Posn	.299	488	146	26	11	8	174	46	83	.353	.447
vs. Right	.237	1475	350	64	10	26	141	113	283	.294	.347	Close & Late	.267	359	96	13	7	5	39	37	66	.334	.384
Groundball	.256	813	208	41	9	8	67	68	128	.316	.358	None on/out	.255	431	110	17	5	10	10	44	78	.326	.387
Flyball	.231	515	119	22	5	11	53	48	121	.295	.357	Batting #2	.267	2006	535	105	23	33	192	188	342	.331	.391
Home	.263	1150	303	64	13	16	102	108	211	.328	.383	Batting #8	.157	153	24	4	1	1	14	11	30	.216	.216
Away	.253	1155	292	50	12	20	120	104	200	.316	.369	Other	.247	146	36	5	1	2	16	13	39	.306	.336
Day	.276	623	172	38	8	10	69	51	118	.334	.411	April	.195	302	59	8	2	2	25	35	53	.284	.255
Night	.251	1682	423	76	17	26	153	161	293	.318	.363	May	.270	355	96	23	2	7	40	37	67	.337	.406
Grass	.237	700	166	28	9	10	69	59	136	.297	.346	June	.272	327	89	15	7	5	31	32	64	.339	.407
Turf	.267	1605	429	86	16	26	153	153	275	.333	.389	July	.261	379	99	19	1	8	36	23	49	.302	.380
First Pitch	.307	287	88	20	6	5	39	1	0	.312	.470	August	.267	435	116	22	5	5	33	27	84	.312	.375
Ahead on Count	.309	456	141	25	7	11	53	133	0	.464	.467	September/October	.268	507	136	27	8	9	57	58	94	.347	.406
Behind on Count	.239	844	202	42	5	11	60	0	236	.241	.340	Pre-All Star	.248	1109	275	53	11	15	105	112	204	.317	.356
Two Strikes	.198	1107	219	41	10	12	83	77	411	.251	.285	Post-All Star	.268	1196	320	61	14	21	117	100	207	.327	.395

Batter vs. Pitcher (career)

Hits Best Against	Avg	AB	H	2B	3B	HR	RBI	BB	SO	OBP	SLG	Hits Worst Against	Avg	AB	H	2B	3B	HR	RBI	BB	SO	OBP	SLG
Mike Bielecki	.632	19	12	4	2	0	5	2	3	.667	1.053	Tommy Greene	.053	19	1	0	0	0	0	1	3	.100	.053
Jimmy Jones	.615	13	8	1	0	2	4	1	1	.643	1.154	John Smoltz	.077	26	2	0	0	0	1	1	6	.111	.077
Jack Armstrong	.545	11	6	0	1	0	1	2	1	.615	.727	Mike Maddux	.077	13	1	0	0	0	0	0	1	.077	.077
Paul Assenmacher	.500	10	5	1	1	1	2	1	1	.545	1.100	Greg W. Harris	.118	17	2	0	0	0	2	2	2	.200	.118
Randy Myers	.400	10	4	1	1	1	6	3	3	.538	1.000	Ramon Martinez	.133	15	2	0	0	0	4	1	6	.176	.133

Juan Bell — Phillies Bats Both

	Avg	G	AB	R	H	2B	3B	HR	RBI	BB	SO	HBP	GDP	SB	CS	OBP	SLG	IBB	SH	SF	#Pit	#P/PA	GB	FB	G/F
1992 Season	.204	46	147	12	30	3	1	1	8	18	29	1	1	5	0	.292	.259	5	0	2	622	3.70	51	46	1.11
Career (1989-1992)	.182	159	362	41	66	12	3	2	23	26	82	1	2	6	0	.237	.249	5	4	4	1439	3.66	127	97	1.31

1992 Season

	Avg	AB	H	2B	3B	HR	RBI	BB	SO	OBP	SLG		Avg	AB	H	2B	3B	HR	RBI	BB	SO	OBP	SLG
vs. Left	.194	62	12	2	0	1	3	7	13	.286	.226	Scoring Posn	.185	27	5	1	0	0	7	14	6	.455	.222
vs. Right	.212	85	18	1	1	0	5	11	16	.296	.282	Close & Late	.174	23	4	0	0	1	2	2	4	.240	.304
Home	.200	70	14	2	1	1	6	9	14	.296	.300	None on/out	.222	36	8	1	1	1	0	12		.222	.389
Away	.208	77	16	1	0	0	2	9	15	.287	.221	Batting #2	.250	4	1	0	0	0	0	0	2	.250	.250
First Pitch	.240	25	6	1	1	0	2	0	0	.345	.360	Batting #8	.209	139	29	3	1	1	8	17	25	.296	.266
Ahead on Count	.229	35	8	2	0	0	2	8	0	.364	.286	Other	.000	4	0	0	0	0	0	1	2	.200	.000
Behind on Count	.153	59	9	0	0	0	1	0	20	.153	.153	Pre-All Star	.000	0	0	0	0	0	0	0	0	.000	.000
Two Strikes	.154	78	12	0	0	1	3	7	29	.221	.192	Post-All Star	.204	147	30	3	1	1	8	18	29	.292	.259

Albert Belle — Indians   Bats Right

	Avg	G	AB	R	H	2B	3B	HR	RBI	BB	SO	HBP	GDP	SB	CS	OBP	SLG	IBB	SH	SF	#Pit	#P/PA	GB	FB	G/F
1992 Season	.260	153	585	81	152	23	1	34	112	52	128	4	18	8	2	.320	.477	5	1	8	2285	3.52	186	182	1.02
Career (1989-1992)	.260	347	1287	164	335	62	7	70	247	90	288	11	47	13	5	.311	.483	7	2	15	5022	3.58	435	383	1.14

1992 Season

	Avg	AB	H	2B	3B	HR	RBI	BB	SO	OBP	SLG		Avg	AB	H	2B	3B	HR	RBI	BB	SO	OBP	SLG
vs. Left	.254	138	35	10	0	8	27	12	33	.307	.500	Scoring Posn	.239	155	37	6	0	12	81	19	36	.319	.510
vs. Right	.262	447	117	13	1	26	85	40	95	.325	.470	Close & Late	.236	106	25	2	0	5	23	5	25	.267	.396
Groundball	.228	145	33	4	1	4	22	15	38	.299	.352	None on/out	.266	158	42	4	1	6	6	11	36	.314	.418
Flyball	.277	184	51	8	0	18	42	20	36	.346	.614	Total	.260	585	152	23	1	34	112	52	128	.320	.477
Home	.267	285	76	14	1	15	63	28	61	.331	.481	Batting #4	.260	585	152	23	1	34	112	52	128	.320	.477
Away	.253	300	76	9	0	19	49	24	67	.310	.473	Other	.000	0	0	0	0	0	0	0	0	.000	.000
Day	.246	191	47	14	0	6	31	19	44	.312	.414	April	.226	84	19	5	0	4	13	8	22	.298	.429
Night	.266	394	105	9	1	28	81	33	84	.325	.508	May	.322	90	29	3	1	7	21	11	22	.388	.611
Grass	.255	499	127	21	1	27	93	45	105	.315	.463	June	.243	103	25	2	0	6	14	7	18	.297	.437
Turf	.291	86	25	2	0	7	19	7	23	.351	.558	July	.242	91	22	3	0	3	16	3	19	.271	.374
First Pitch	.354	113	40	6	0	13	42	3	0	.364	.752	August	.253	95	24	4	0	6	19	11	24	.324	.484
Ahead on Count	.323	124	40	4	0	13	28	17	0	.403	.669	September/October	.270	122	33	6	0	8	29	12	23	.336	.516
Behind on Count	.242	182	44	8	1	3	21	0	58	.243	.346	Pre-All Star	.266	319	85	12	1	19	57	27	71	.324	.489
Two Strikes	.190	252	48	8	1	4	26	32	128	.282	.278	Post-All Star	.252	266	67	11	0	15	55	25	57	.316	.462

1992 By Position

Position	Avg	AB	H	2B	3B	HR	RBI	BB	SO	OBP	SLG	G	GS	Innings	PO	A	E	DP	Fld Pct	Rng Fctr	In Zone	Outs	Zone Rtg	MLB Zone
As Designated Hitter	.258	380	98	14	1	19	75	39	95	.326	.450	100	100	---	---	---	---	---	---	---	---	---	---	---
As lf	.265	204	54	9	0	15	37	13	33	.312	.529	52	52	423.2	94	1	3	0	.969	2.02	116	92	.793	.809

Career (1989-1992)

	Avg	AB	H	2B	3B	HR	RBI	BB	SO	OBP	SLG		Avg	AB	H	2B	3B	HR	RBI	BB	SO	OBP	SLG
vs. Left	.267	337	90	23	1	20	74	22	74	.307	.519	Scoring Posn	.283	346	98	24	2	21	175	32	83	.338	.546
vs. Right	.258	950	245	39	6	50	173	68	214	.312	.469	Close & Late	.225	213	48	5	1	8	44	15	59	.275	.371
Groundball	.237	358	85	11	1	10	50	30	88	.297	.358	None on/out	.268	321	86	13	3	15	15	22	67	.321	.467
Flyball	.277	318	88	19	2	26	66	24	66	.327	.594	Batting #4	.262	1003	263	50	3	56	195	77	224	.317	.486
Home	.257	649	167	35	2	27	125	45	144	.308	.442	Batting #6	.299	127	38	5	3	6	25	8	27	.341	.528
Away	.263	638	168	27	5	43	122	45	144	.314	.524	Other	.217	157	34	7	1	8	27	5	37	.242	.427
Day	.262	390	102	27	3	18	81	29	90	.316	.485	April	.238	160	38	7	0	9	25	12	42	.301	.450
Night	.260	897	233	35	4	52	166	61	198	.308	.482	May	.292	192	56	11	2	12	39	19	43	.355	.557
Grass	.256	1105	283	54	5	59	210	78	245	.306	.474	June	.231	134	31	4	0	7	19	7	25	.275	.418
Turf	.286	182	52	8	2	11	37	12	43	.338	.533	July	.268	231	62	8	2	13	49	13	47	.307	.489
First Pitch	.323	232	75	18	0	22	69	5	0	.339	.685	August	.250	284	71	13	1	16	51	18	69	.296	.472
Ahead on Count	.335	257	86	8	2	21	58	26	0	.392	.626	September/October	.269	286	77	19	2	13	64	21	62	.320	.486
Behind on Count	.252	412	104	18	4	16	55	0	150	.255	.432	Pre-All Star	.262	553	145	24	2	32	96	39	122	.314	.486
Two Strikes	.181	591	107	24	3	12	67	59	288	.257	.293	Post-All Star	.259	734	190	38	5	38	151	51	166	.308	.480

Batter vs. Pitcher (career)

Hits Best Against	Avg	AB	H	2B	3B	HR	RBI	BB	SO	OBP	SLG	Hits Worst Against	Avg	AB	H	2B	3B	HR	RBI	BB	SO	OBP	SLG
Todd Stottlemyre	.429	14	6	0	0	2	5	1	3	.467	.500	Jim Abbott	.083	12	1	0	0	0	0	1	3	.154	.083
Arthur Rhodes	.400	10	4	2	0	2	7	2	2	.500	1.200	Frank Viola	.091	11	1	1	0	0	1	0	3	.083	.182
Chuck Finley	.391	23	9	2	0	3	9	6	2	.517	.870	Kevin Tapani	.091	11	1	1	0	0	2	0	2	.286	.091
Danny Darwin	.385	13	5	1	0	2	5	0	3	.385	.923	Kevin Appier	.118	17	2	0	0	0	0	0	10	.118	.118
Greg Harris	.333	9	3	0	0	3	5	1	2	.364	1.333	Greg Hibbard	.167	18	3	0	0	0	0	0	1	.167	.167

Rafael Belliard — Braves   Bats Right (groundball hitter)

	Avg	G	AB	R	H	2B	3B	HR	RBI	BB	SO	HBP	GDP	SB	CS	OBP	SLG	IBB	SH	SF	#Pit	#P/PA	GB	FB	G/F
1992 Season	.211	144	285	20	60	6	1	0	14	14	43	3	6	0	1	.255	.239	4	13	0	867	2.87	150	51	2.94
Last Five Years	.223	529	1132	104	253	22	7	0	66	75	188	10	23	16	7	.278	.255	11	29	1	3900	3.20	543	217	2.50

1992 Season

	Avg	AB	H	2B	3B	HR	RBI	BB	SO	OBP	SLG		Avg	AB	H	2B	3B	HR	RBI	BB	SO	OBP	SLG
vs. Left	.197	61	12	0	0	0	3	1	13	.210	.197	Scoring Posn	.179	67	12	0	0	0	14	4	8	.225	.179
vs. Right	.214	224	48	6	1	0	11	13	30	.267	.250	Close & Late	.229	35	8	1	0	0	2	0	7	.229	.257
Groundball	.240	125	30	3	0	0	5	7	16	.286	.264	None on/out	.203	64	13	3	1	0	0	4	12	.261	.281
Flyball	.108	65	7	2	0	0	2	3	11	.147	.138	Batting #2	.263	19	5	0	0	0	0	0	1	.263	.263
Home	.200	125	25	2	0	0	5	8	12	.259	.216	Batting #8	.206	252	52	5	1	0	11	14	40	.257	.234
Away	.219	160	35	4	1	0	9	6	31	.251	.256	Other	.214	14	3	1	0	0	1	0	2	.214	.286
Day	.178	90	16	1	1	0	5	3	13	.204	.211	April	.255	55	14	1	0	0	1	4	8	.317	.273
Night	.226	195	44	5	0	0	9	11	30	.278	.251	May	.197	71	14	2	0	0	3	2	12	.219	.225
Grass	.194	206	40	3	0	0	10	11	32	.245	.209	June	.196	46	9	1	0	0	2	3	6	.260	.217
Turf	.253	79	20	3	1	0	4	3	11	.280	.316	July	.220	50	11	1	0	0	5	3	10	.264	.240
First Pitch	.282	85	24	3	0	0	10	4	0	.315	.318	August	.211	38	8	1	1	0	2	1	4	.250	.289
Ahead on Count	.207	29	6	1	0	0	0	9	0	.410	.241	September/October	.160	25	4	0	0	0	1	1	3	.192	.160
Behind on Count	.168	119	20	1	1	0	4	0	36	.175	.193	Pre-All Star	.215	191	41	5	0	0	8	10	31	.261	.241
Two Strikes	.148	115	17	0	1	0	3	1	43	.155	.165	Post-All Star	.202	94	19	1	1	0	6	4	12	.242	.234

1992 By Position

Position	Avg	AB	H	2B	3B	HR	RBI	BB	SO	OBP	SLG	G	GS	Innings	PO	A	E	DP	Fld Pct	Rng Fctr	In Zone	Outs	Zone Rtg	MLB Zone
As ss	.212	263	60	6	1	0	14	14	43	.257	.240	139	90	860.1	150	287	14	48	.969	4.57	339	296	.873	.885

Last Five Years

	Avg	AB	H	2B	3B	HR	RBI	BB	SO	OBP	SLG		Avg	AB	H	2B	3B	HR	RBI	BB	SO	OBP	SLG
vs. Left	.232	302	70	5	2	0	18	18	48	.277	.262	Scoring Posn	.244	258	63	6	3	0	64	21	37	.307	.291
vs. Right	.220	830	183	17	5	0	48	57	140	.278	.253	Close & Late	.241	141	34	1	1	0	4	8	27	.287	.262
Groundball	.223	421	94	5	1	0	25	22	60	.267	.240	None on/out	.180	261	47	5	2	0	20	52	.244	.215
Flyball	.186	247	46	4	0	0	10	17	44	.242	.202	Batting #2	.280	100	28	1	1	0	4	6	11	.321	.310
Home	.220	537	118	10	6	0	34	36	84	.274	.261	Batting #8	.217	981	213	19	6	0	57	64	168	.271	.249
Away	.227	595	135	12	1	0	32	39	104	.281	.250	Other	.235	51	12	2	0	0	5	5	9	.316	.275
Day	.230	343	79	8	3	0	22	27	51	.290	.271	April	.250	180	45	5	2	0	14	10	28	.297	.300
Night	.221	789	174	14	4	0	44	48	137	.272	.248	May	.247	215	53	6	1	0	16	13	36	.293	.284
Grass	.227	613	139	14	2	0	34	38	96	.277	.256	June	.220	232	51	2	0	0	10	16	33	.275	.228
Turf	.220	519	114	8	5	0	32	37	92	.278	.254	July	.205	200	41	4	3	0	14	11	33	.248	.255
First Pitch	.298	248	74	6	1	0	23	7	0	.318	.331	August	.190	168	32	1	1	0	7	13	32	.261	.208
Ahead on Count	.260	150	42	5	4	0	14	55	0	.481	.367	September/October	.226	137	31	4	0	0	5	12	26	.298	.255
Behind on Count	.175	479	84	8	2	0	21	0	138	.182	.200	Pre-All Star	.234	693	162	14	3	0	43	42	109	.282	.263
Two Strikes	.149	490	73	2	1	0	15	13	188	.179	.157	Post-All Star	.207	439	91	8	4	0	23	33	79	.270	.244

Batter vs. Pitcher (since 1984)

Hits Best Against	Avg	AB	H	2B	3B	HR	RBI	BB	SO	OBP	SLG	Hits Worst Against	Avg	AB	H	2B	3B	HR	RBI	BB	SO	OBP	SLG
Mike Bielecki	.417	12	5	1	0	0	2	1	2	.462	.500	Denny Cox	.077	13	1	0	0	0	0	2	3	.200	.077
Terry Mulholland	.417	12	5	1	1	0	2	1	1	.462	.667	Ramon Martinez	.077	13	1	0	0	0	0	1	2	.250	.077
												Jose Rijo	.091	11	1	0	0	0	0	1	1	.167	.091
												Andy Benes	.125	16	2	0	0	0	0	0	1	.222	.125
												Jimmy Jones	.143	14	2	0	0	0	0	0	1	.143	.143

Esteban Beltre — White Sox
Bats Right (groundball hitter)

	Avg	G	AB	R	H	2B	3B	HR	RBI	BB	SO	HBP	GDP	SB	CS	OBP	SLG	IBB	SH	SF	#Pit	#P/PA	GB	FB	G/F
1992 Season	.191	49	110	21	21	2	0	1	10	3	18	0	3	1	0	.211	.236	0	2	1	407	3.57	57	22	2.59
Career (1991-1992)	.190	57	116	21	22	2	0	1	10	4	19	0	3	2	0	.215	.233	0	2	1	422	3.49	62	22	2.82

1992 Season

	Avg	AB	H	2B	3B	HR	RBI	BB	SO	OBP	SLG		Avg	AB	H	2B	3B	HR	RBI	BB	SO	OBP	SLG
vs. Left	.235	51	12	1	0	1	5	1	7	.245	.314	Scoring Posn	.133	30	4	0	0	1	10	2	3	.182	.233
vs. Right	.153	59	9	1	0	0	5	2	11	.180	.169	Close & Late	.214	14	3	1	0	0	2	0	1	.214	.286
Home	.171	70	12	1	0	1	7	2	9	.192	.229	None on/out	.160	25	4	0	0	0	0	1	4	.192	.160
Away	.225	40	9	1	0	0	3	1	9	.244	.250	Batting #5	.000	2	0	0	0	0	0	0	2	.000	.000
First Pitch	.263	19	5	0	0	0	2	0	0	.263	.263	Batting #9	.181	105	19	2	0	1	10	3	16	.202	.229
Ahead on Count	.250	16	4	0	0	0	4	1	0	.278	.250	Other	.667	3	2	0	0	0	0	0	0	.667	.667
Behind on Count	.100	40	4	1	0	0	4	0	9	.098	.125	Pre-All Star	.294	17	5	0	0	0	0	0	1	.294	.294
Two Strikes	.120	50	6	1	0	0	1	2	18	.154	.140	Post-All Star	.172	93	16	2	0	1	10	3	17	.196	.226

Freddie Benavides — Reds
Bats Right (groundball hitter)

	Avg	G	AB	R	H	2B	3B	HR	RBI	BB	SO	HBP	GDP	SB	CS	OBP	SLG	IBB	SH	SF	#Pit	#P/PA	GB	FB	G/F
1992 Season	.231	74	173	14	40	10	1	1	17	10	34	1	3	0	1	.277	.318	4	2	0	632	3.43	66	39	1.69
Career (1991-1992)	.246	98	236	25	58	11	1	1	20	11	49	2	4	1	1	.284	.314	5	3	1	859	3.44	96	49	1.96

1992 Season

	Avg	AB	H	2B	3B	HR	RBI	BB	SO	OBP	SLG		Avg	AB	H	2B	3B	HR	RBI	BB	SO	OBP	SLG
vs. Left	.256	90	23	7	0	1	15	8	15	.323	.367	Scoring Posn	.255	51	13	3	0	0	14	6	8	.345	.314
vs. Right	.205	83	17	3	1	0	2	2	19	.224	.265	Close & Late	.276	29	8	4	0	0	8	4	4	.364	.414
Home	.227	75	17	5	0	1	7	3	14	.266	.333	None on/out	.158	38	6	1	1	0	0	1	6	.179	.237
Away	.235	98	23	5	1	0	10	7	20	.286	.306	Batting #3	.250	12	3	1	0	0	2	1	4	.308	.333
First Pitch	.250	36	9	1	0	0	3	4	0	.325	.278	Batting #8	.239	134	32	8	1	1	14	6	21	.277	.336
Ahead on Count	.378	37	14	3	1	0	7	5	0	.452	.514	Other	.185	27	5	1	0	0	1	3	9	.267	.222
Behind on Count	.143	56	8	4	0	0	2	0	21	.158	.214	Pre-All Star	.240	104	25	6	1	1	11	6	20	.288	.346
Two Strikes	.173	81	14	5	0	1	6	2	34	.202	.272	Post-All Star	.217	69	15	4	0	0	6	4	14	.260	.275

Andy Benes — Padres
Pitches Right (flyball pitcher)

	ERA	W	L	Sv	G	GS	IP	BB	SO	Avg	H	2B	3B	HR	RBI	OBP	SLG	CG	ShO	Sup	QS	#P/S	SB	CS	GB	FB	G/F
1992 Season	3.35	13	14	0	34	34	231.1	61	169	.264	230	39	6	14	84	.314	.371	2	2	3.03	23	102	20	11	263	249	1.06
Career (1989-1992)	3.33	44	39	0	109	108	713.1	220	542	.244	652	97	22	62	251	.302	.366	8	3	3.48	74	102	56	28	801	811	0.99

1992 Season

	ERA	W	L	Sv	G	GS	IP	H	HR	BB	SO		Avg	AB	H	2B	3B	HR	RBI	BB	SO	OBP	SLG
Home	3.55	7	6	0	17	17	116.2	126	8	25	84	vs. Left	.276	533	147	23	5	10	63	45	94	.333	.394
Away	3.14	6	8	0	17	17	114.2	104	6	36	85	vs. Right	.246	337	83	16	1	4	21	16	75	.283	.335
Day	2.34	6	1	0	10	10	73.0	58	4	13	62	Inning 1-6	.262	741	194	29	4	13	76	51	149	.311	.364
Night	3.81	7	13	0	24	24	158.1	172	10	48	107	Inning 7+	.279	129	36	10	2	1	8	10	20	.331	.411

1992 Season

	ERA	W	L	Sv	G	GS	IP	H	HR	BB	SO		Avg	AB	H	2B	3B	HR	RBI	BB	SO	OBP	SLG
Grass	3.64	10	9	0	25	25	165.2	176	11	43	121	None on	.257	514	132	20	4	8	8	34	97	.305	.358
Turf	2.60	3	5	0	9	9	65.2	54	3	18	48	Runners on	.275	356	98	19	2	6	76	27	72	.327	.390
April	3.97	2	2	0	5	5	34.0	35	2	6	29	Scoring Posn	.267	206	55	13	1	2	65	20	46	.329	.369
May	3.31	3	1	0	5	5	35.1	34	2	6	28	Close & Late	.284	74	21	5	1	1	4	7	13	.346	.419
June	3.40	1	2	0	6	6	42.1	49	2	12	25	None on/out	.299	234	70	9	2	5	5	12	40	.339	.419
July	3.48	2	4	0	6	6	41.1	42	2	13	30	vs. 1st Batr (relief)	.000	0	0	0	0	0	0	0	0	.000	.000
August	4.45	2	2	0	5	5	30.1	31	2	11	15	First Inning Pitched	.269	134	36	6	0	2	9	7	28	.310	.358
September/October	2.06	3	3	0	7	7	48.0	39	4	13	42	First 75 Pitches	.240	628	151	23	4	10	50	40	133	.289	.338
Starter	3.35	13	14	0	34	34	231.1	230	14	61	169	Pitch 76-90	.364	121	44	9	0	2	19	10	19	.414	.488
Reliever	0.00	0	0	0	0	0	0.0	0	0	0	0	Pitch 91-105	.309	81	25	2	2	1	10	8	11	.359	.420
0-3 Days Rest	0.00	0	0	0	0	0	0.0	0	0	0	0	Pitch 106+	.250	40	10	5	0	1	5	3	6	.311	.450
4 Days Rest	3.23	9	11	0	25	25	172.2	172	10	42	130	First Pitch	.331	154	51	6	0	4	14	6	0	.356	.448
5+ Days Rest	3.68	4	3	0	9	9	58.2	58	4	19	39	Behind on Count	.186	388	72	13	4	3	24	0	147	.190	.263
Pre-All Star	3.71	7	7	0	19	19	131.0	140	6	33	95	Ahead on Count	.321	156	50	9	0	4	25	28	0	.419	.455
Post-All Star	2.87	6	7	0	15	15	100.1	90	8	28	74	Two Strikes	.192	395	76	13	4	5	26	27	169	.246	.284

Career (1989-1992)

	ERA	W	L	Sv	G	GS	IP	H	HR	BB	SO		Avg	AB	H	2B	3B	HR	RBI	BB	SO	OBP	SLG
Home	3.79	22	17	0	55	54	356.0	354	34	115	291	vs. Left	.249	1569	391	55	16	36	154	140	294	.312	.373
Away	2.87	22	22	0	54	54	357.1	298	28	105	251	vs. Right	.236	1107	261	42	6	26	97	80	248	.288	.355
Day	2.78	15	7	0	32	32	210.2	186	19	60	183	Inning 1-6	.238	2307	550	81	18	52	217	189	477	.297	.393
Night	3.56	29	32	0	77	76	502.2	466	43	160	359	Inning 7+	.276	369	102	16	4	10	34	31	65	.333	.423
Grass	3.36	32	26	0	81	80	527.1	497	48	159	406	None on	.237	1638	388	54	16	40	40	125	325	.293	.363
Turf	3.19	12	13	0	28	28	186.0	155	14	61	136	Runners on	.254	1038	264	43	6	22	211	95	217	.315	.371
April	4.04	4	6	0	13	13	78.0	79	7	27	79	Scoring Posn	.233	580	135	24	5	8	177	60	132	.302	.333
May	3.65	8	7	0	17	17	116.0	104	12	33	82	Close & Late	.274	230	63	8	2	5	20	22	45	.336	.391
June	3.78	4	6	0	18	18	119.0	117	10	41	80	None on/out	.249	719	179	20	9	22	22	50	124	.301	.394
July	2.94	7	7	0	14	14	95.0	91	7	27	68	vs. 1st Batr (relief)	.000	1	0	0	0	0	0	0	0	.000	.000
August	3.75	12	5	0	21	20	129.2	106	12	45	85	First Inning Pitched	.212	397	84	13	1	7	29	40	92	.284	.302
September/October	2.41	12	8	0	26	26	175.2	155	14	47	148	First 75 Pitches	.227	1909	433	65	17	42	161	152	402	.285	.345
Starter	3.30	44	39	0	108	108	711.1	650	62	218	541	Pitch 76-90	.325	369	120	19	1	8	46	32	58	.380	.447
Reliever	13.50	0	0	0	1	0	2.0	2	0	2	1	Pitch 91-105	.252	246	62	5	4	7	29	22	52	.311	.390
0-3 Days Rest	7.20	1	1	0	2	2	10.0	15	0	4	7	Pitch 106+	.243	152	37	8	0	5	15	14	30	.308	.395
4 Days Rest	3.27	25	26	0	66	66	443.0	409	30	138	351	First Pitch	.309	392	121	16	3	9	41	12	0	.331	.434
5+ Days Rest	3.21	18	12	0	40	40	258.1	226	32	76	183	Ahead on Count	.184	1288	237	31	10	24	96	0	459	.187	.280
Pre-All Star	3.77	17	22	0	53	53	348.1	334	31	115	268	Behind on Count	.327	504	165	29	3	19	81	117	0	.452	.510
Post-All Star	2.91	27	17	0	56	55	365.0	318	31	105	274	Two Strikes	.172	1303	224	34	9	19	78	90	542	.227	.256

Pitcher vs. Batter (career)

Pitches Best Vs.	Avg	AB	H	2B	3B	HR	RBI	BB	SO	OBP	SLG	Pitches Worst Vs.	Avg	AB	H	2B	3B	HR	RBI	BB	SO	OBP	SLG
Chico Walker	.000	12	0	0	0	0	0	0	3	.000	.000	Jeff Bagwell	.471	17	8	3	0	1	1	5	2	.591	.824
Tom Foley	.071	14	1	0	0	0	2	2	1	.188	.071	Tommy Gregg	.438	16	7	3	0	0	4	4	5	.550	.625
Mike Felder	.071	14	1	0	0	0	0	2	3	.188	.071	Andy Van Slyke	.412	17	7	2	2	0	3	2	1	.474	.765
Steve Finley	.125	24	3	0	0	0	0	0	4	.125	.125	Barry Bonds	.385	13	5	0	0	3	12	4	0	.524	1.077
Rafael Belliard	.125	16	2	0	0	0	0	0	1	.222	.125	Kevin Mitchell	.350	20	7	2	0	4	6	2	5	.409	1.050

Mike Benjamin — Giants   Bats Right

	Avg	G	AB	R	H	2B	3B	HR	RBI	BB	SO	HBP	GDP	SB	CS	OBP	SLG	IBB	SH	SF	#Pit	#P/PA	GB	FB	G/F
1992 Season	.173	40	75	4	13	2	1	1	3	4	15	0	1	1	0	.215	.267	1	3	0	259	3.28	30	21	1.43
Career (1989-1992)	.160	130	243	29	39	8	2	5	14	14	52	2	4	5	0	.211	.272	4	6	2	857	3.28	86	79	1.09

1992 Season

	Avg	AB	H	2B	3B	HR	RBI	BB	SO	OBP	SLG		Avg	AB	H	2B	3B	HR	RBI	BB	SO	OBP	SLG
vs. Left	.250	36	9	1	1	1	3	3	4	.308	.417	Scoring Posn	.067	15	1	0	0	0	1	1	5	.125	.067
vs. Right	.103	39	4	1	0	0	0	1	11	.125	.128	Close & Late	.200	10	2	0	0	0	0	1	2	.273	.200

Todd Benzinger — Dodgers   Bats Both

	Avg	G	AB	R	H	2B	3B	HR	RBI	BB	SO	HBP	GDP	SB	CS	OBP	SLG	IBB	SH	SF	#Pit	#P/PA	GB	FB	G/F
1992 Season	.239	121	293	24	70	16	2	4	31	15	54	0	6	2	4	.272	.348	1	0	5	1103	3.52	108	95	1.14
Last Five Years	.251	649	2118	221	531	104	13	42	274	127	389	10	29	14	24	.293	.372	26	14	25	7885	3.46	745	657	1.13

1992 Season

	Avg	AB	H	2B	3B	HR	RBI	BB	SO	OBP	SLG		Avg	AB	H	2B	3B	HR	RBI	BB	SO	OBP	SLG
vs. Left	.270	126	34	5	1	1	16	3	12	.282	.349	Scoring Posn	.232	69	16	2	1	2	27	4	15	.256	.377
vs. Right	.216	167	36	11	1	3	15	12	42	.264	.347	Close & Late	.246	69	17	3	1	1	13	4	16	.280	.362
Groundball	.269	104	28	8	0	2	12	6	12	.304	.404	None on/out	.247	77	19	5	0	0	0	4	14	.284	.312
Flyball	.253	95	24	4	2	2	16	5	22	.287	.400	Batting #5	.227	132	30	6	1	2	16	8	27	.266	.333
Home	.238	143	34	9	1	1	8		24	.275	.336	Batting #6	.203	64	13	0	0	0	5	1	10	.203	.203
Away	.240	150	36	7	1	3	18	7	30	.269	.360	Other	.278	97	27	10	1	2	10	6	17	.317	.464
Day	.269	93	25	4	1	2	12	7	18	.311	.398	April	.200	40	8	4	0	0	2	1	10	.220	.300
Night	.225	200	45	12	1	2	19	8	36	.252	.325	May	.267	60	16	3	1	2	14	5	9	.309	.450

1992 Season

	Avg	AB	H	2B	3B	HR	RBI	BB	SO	OBP	SLG		Avg	AB	H	2B	3B	HR	RBI	BB	SO	OBP	SLG
Grass	.227	225	51	12	1	2	17	12	36	.261	.316	June	.234	77	18	5	0	0	4	2	16	.253	.299
Turf	.279	68	19	4	1	2	14	3	18	.306	.456	July	.241	58	14	3	0	0	4	4	9	.281	.293
First Pitch	.356	45	16	6	0	1	7	1	0	.362	.556	August	.184	38	7	1	0	0		2	8	.225	.211
Ahead on Count	.250	56	14	2	0	1	3	10	0	.358	.339	September/October	.350	20	7	0	1	2	5	1	2	.381	.750
Behind on Count	.171	111	19	6	1	0	9	0	30	.167	.243	Pre-All Star	.238	202	48	13	1	2	22	11	40	.272	.342
Two Strikes	.170	135	23	6	2	2	18	4	54	.191	.289	Post-All Star	.242	91	22	3	1	2	9	4	14	.271	.363

1992 By Position

Position	Avg	AB	H	2B	3B	HR	RBI	BB	SO	OBP	SLG	G	GS	Innings	PO	A	E	DP	Fld Pct	Rng Fctr	In Zone	Outs	Zone Rtg	MLB Zone
As Pinch Hitter	.271	48	13	4	0	2	8	3	11	.314	.479	51	0	---	---	---	---	---	---	---	---	---	---	---
As 1b	.221	68	15	7	0	0	4	2	14	.243	.324	42	13	174.0	177	17	0	17	1.000	---	41	37	.902	.843
As lf	.281	57	16	1	1	0	4	4	9	.317	.333	18	17	137.2	40	0	1	0	.976	2.62	43	39	.907	.809
As rf	.217	120	26	4	1	2	15	6	20	.248	.317	33	32	257.1	47	1	0	1	1.000	1.68	61	46	.754	.814

Last Five Years

	Avg	AB	H	2B	3B	HR	RBI	BB	SO	OBP	SLG		Avg	AB	H	2B	3B	HR	RBI	BB	SO	OBP	SLG
vs. Left	.254	775	197	33	2	12	85	37	82	.284	.348	Scoring Posn	.236	609	144	31	4	15	233	56	132	.295	.374
vs. Right	.249	1343	334	71	11	30	189	90	307	.298	.385	Close & Late	.226	371	84	11	5	8	55	34	71	.290	.348
Groundball	.271	687	186	38	4	19	104	38	110	.307	.413	None on/out	.269	501	135	21	2	4	4	29	85	.312	.343
Flyball	.255	534	136	31	7	12	76	36	98	.298	.406	Batting #5	.252	743	187	33	5	14	105	45	135	.293	.366
Home	.265	1059	281	67	8	19	135	64	167	.308	.398	Batting #6	.224	563	126	27	3	8	71	32	115	.268	.325
Away	.236	1059	250	37	5	23	139	63	222	.278	.346	Other	.268	812	218	44	5	20	98	50	139	.310	.409
Day	.247	667	165	31	4	10	75	49	126	.299	.351	April	.249	245	61	11	2	2	32	17	38	.290	.335
Night	.252	1451	366	73	9	32	199	78	263	.290	.381	May	.249	338	84	18	2	6	55	20	60	.283	.367
Grass	.251	996	250	52	3	23	125	63	187	.296	.379	June	.243	367	89	18	1	9	38	29	79	.302	.371
Turf	.250	1122	281	52	10	19	149	64	202	.290	.365	July	.269	387	104	20	1	10	48	21	67	.306	.403
First Pitch	.385	327	126	23	4	12	59	15	0	.411	.590	August	.235	417	98	21	4	10	56	15	80	.264	.376
Ahead on Count	.286	434	124	21	3	14	68	63	0	.378	.445	September/October	.261	364	95	16	3	5	45	25	65	.314	.363
Behind on Count	.207	786	163	34	3	7	74	1	229	.209	.285	Pre-All Star	.244	1062	259	51	5	19	134	73	198	.289	.355
Two Strikes	.171	920	157	27	5	11	90	41	389	.206	.247	Post-All Star	.258	1056	272	53	8	23	140	54	191	.297	.388

Batter vs. Pitcher (career)

Hits Best Against	Avg	AB	H	2B	3B	HR	RBI	BB	SO	OBP	SLG	Hits Worst Against	Avg	AB	H	2B	3B	HR	RBI	BB	SO	OBP	SLG
Derek Lilliquist	.688	16	11	0	0	0	0	1	1	.706	.688	Bob Tewksbury	.000	10	0	0	0	0	0	1	1	.091	.000
David Cone	.444	9	4	0	1	0	0	2	2	.545	.667	Greg W. Harris	.050	20	1	0	0	0	1	0	6	.050	.050
Mark Langston	.438	16	7	1	0	1	3	2	4	.500	.688	Kevin Gross	.100	10	1	0	0	0	2	0	1	.091	.100
Dennis Cook	.364	11	4	1	0	1	2	1	0	.417	.727	Terry Mulholland	.118	17	2	0	0	0	1	1	2	.167	.118
Walt Terrell	.353	17	6	1	0	4	9	1	4	.368	1.118	Dave Stewart	.154	13	2	0	0	0	2	0	4	.154	.154

Juan Berenguer — Royals

Pitches Right (flyball pitcher)

	ERA	W	L	Sv	G	GS	IP	BB	SO	Avg	H	2B	3B	HR	RBI	OBP	SLG	GF	IR	IRS	Hld	SvOp	SB	CS	GB	FB	G/F
1992 Season	5.42	4	5	1	47	2	78.0	36	45	.257	77	18	3	10	52	.337	.437	10	36	8	6	4	8	2	63	127	0.50
Last Five Years	3.73	29	20	23	260	3	448.2	222	367	.228	375	71	9	42	202	.321	.359	58	230	65	37	36	57	16	413	596	0.69

1992 Season

	ERA	W	L	Sv	G	GS	IP	H	HR	BB	SO		Avg	AB	H	2B	3B	HR	RBI	BB	SO	OBP	SLG
Home	6.07	3	4	0	23	1	40.0	42	4	15	23	vs. Left	.341	135	46	9	3	8	39	22	14	.430	.630
Away	4.74	1	1	1	24	1	38.0	35	6	21	22	vs. Right	.188	165	31	9	0	2	13	14	31	.257	.279
Starter	9.00	0	2	0	2	2	9.0	9	2	6	4	Scoring Posn	.250	104	26	5	0	4	40	17	15	.352	.413
Reliever	4.96	4	3	1	45	0	69.0	68	8	30	41	Close & Late	.292	65	19	4	0	4	18	9	5	.387	.538
0 Days rest	0.00	0	0	0	3	0	1.2	0	0	0	0	None on/out	.265	68	18	7	2	0	0	8	14	.342	.426
1 or 2 Days rest	5.40	1	2	1	21	0	31.2	32	3	15	18	First Pitch	.320	50	16	5	1	4	13	5	0	.393	.700
3+ Days rest	4.79	3	1	0	21	0	35.2	32	5	15	23	Behind on Count	.382	68	26	7	1	3	22	18	0	.511	.647
Pre-All Star	5.13	1	3	1	28	0	33.1	35	7	16	19	Ahead on Count	.149	134	20	4	1	3	12	0	38	.147	.261
Post-All Star	5.64	1	4	0	19	2	44.2	42	3	20	26	Two Strikes	.163	135	22	5	1	1	11	13	45	.235	.237

Last Five Years

	ERA	W	L	Sv	G	GS	IP	H	HR	BB	SO		Avg	AB	H	2B	3B	HR	RBI	BB	SO	OBP	SLG
Home	3.77	20	9	11	133	1	241.0	209	21	113	211	vs. Left	.269	750	202	38	6	25	112	121	145	.370	.436
Away	3.68	9	11	12	127	2	207.2	166	21	109	156	vs. Right	.194	893	173	33	3	17	90	101	222	.278	.295
Day	4.51	8	4	10	77	1	137.2	118	12	77	103	Inning 1-6	.238	454	108	19	2	12	77	63	88	.328	.368
Night	3.39	21	16	13	183	2	311.0	257	30	145	264	Inning 7+	.225	1189	267	52	7	30	125	159	279	.316	.356
Grass	4.38	8	11	17	122	1	183.0	155	20	88	141	None on	.231	856	198	44	5	18	18	116	191	.327	.357
Turf	3.29	21	9	6	138	2	265.2	220	22	134	226	Runners on	.225	787	177	27	4	24	184	106	176	.315	.361
April	3.82	4	3	1	40	0	70.2	57	7	43	65	Scoring Posn	.215	492	106	19	2	12	153	77	112	.315	.335
May	3.43	7	4	6	52	0	84.0	75	7	37	69	Close & Late	.217	512	111	22	3	14	62	66	113	.309	.354
June	2.93	8	4	8	51	0	83.0	62	9	44	69	None on/out	.225	359	83	25	4	1	1	55	86	.327	.322
July	3.11	5	2	4	44	0	72.1	56	6	30	57	vs. 1st Batr (relief)	.220	232	51	10	2	1	29	18	60	.272	.293
August	5.92	3	4	3			76.0	77	9	39	58	First Inning Pitched	.217	849	184	34	4	18	114	98	185	.299	.330
September/October	3.16	2	3	1	30	0	62.2	48	4	29	56	First 15 Pitches	.223	777	173	36	3	15	90	80	151	.298	.335
Starter	8.31	0	2	0	3	3	13.0	11	3	10	7	Pitch 16-30	.242	504	122	18	3	15	59	82	123	.348	.379
Reliever	3.59	29	18	23	257	0	435.2	364	39	212	360	Pitch 31-45	.206	252	52	11	2	6	28	33	72	.297	.337

35

Last Five Years

	ERA	W	L	Sv	G	GS	IP	H	HR	BB	SO		Avg	AB	H	2B	3B	HR	RBI	BB	SO	OBP	SLG
0 Days rest	1.55	3	1	6	31	0	46.1	30	0	25	38	Pitch 46+	.255	110	28	6	1	6	25	27	21	.401	.491
1 or 2 Days rest	3.33	16	11	11	130	0	218.2	187	18	103	181	First Pitch	.301	226	68	18	2	8	33	13	0	.340	.504
3+ Days rest	4.48	10	6	6	96	0	170.2	147	21	84	141	Ahead on Count	.162	786	127	19	2	8	55	0	301	.164	.221
Pre-All Star	3.58	21	11	16	156	0	256.1	223	26	133	216	Behind on Count	.330	321	106	28	3	16	72	118	0	.510	.586
Post-All Star	3.93	8	9	7	104	3	192.1	152	16	89	151	Two Strikes	.146	830	121	16	3	6	53	90	367	.231	.194

Pitcher vs. Batter (since 1984)

Pitches Best Vs.	Avg	AB	H	2B	3B	HR	RBI	BB	SO	OBP	SLG	Pitches Worst Vs.	Avg	AB	H	2B	3B	HR	RBI	BB	SO	OBP	SLG
Rob Deer	.000	12	0	0	0	0	0	1	5	.077	.000	Lou Whitaker	.625	8	5	0	0	2	5	6	1	.786	1.375
Devon White	.000	11	0	0	0	0	0	0	3	.000	.000	Willie Wilson	.524	21	11	1	0	1	6	2	0	.565	.714
Kelly Gruber	.000	9	0	0	0	0	1	3	2	.250	.000	B.J. Surhoff	.444	9	4	2	0	0	3	1		.583	.667
Dick Schofield	.056	18	1	0	0	0	0	2	9	.150	.056	George Brett	.429	14	6	0	1	1	6	2	3	.500	.786
Gary Pettis	.067	15	1	0	0	0	3	1	10	.125	.067	Daryl Boston	.400	10	4	0	0	2	4	1	2	.455	1.000

Dave Bergman — Tigers   Bats Left

	Avg	G	AB	R	H	2B	3B	HR	RBI	BB	SO	HBP	GDP	SB	CS	OBP	SLG	IBB	SH	SF	#Pit	#P/PA	GB	FB	G/F
1992 Season	.232	87	181	17	42	3	0	1	10	20	19	0	4	1	0	.305	.265	1	1	1	790	3.89	67	69	0.97
Last Five Years	.266	526	1254	136	333	50	3	22	137	170	154	2	25	6	8	.351	.363	11	8	11	5552	3.86	461	392	1.18

1992 Season

	Avg	AB	H	2B	3B	HR	RBI	BB	SO	OBP	SLG		Avg	AB	H	2B	3B	HR	RBI	BB	SO	OBP	SLG
vs. Left	.143	14	2	1	0	0	0	2	5	.250	.214	Scoring Posn	.167	42	7	1	0	0	9	6	4	.260	.190
vs. Right	.240	167	40	2	0	1	10	18	14	.310	.269	Close & Late	.192	26	5	0	0	1	2	4	4	.300	.308
Home	.204	93	19	1	0	1	4	8	10	.262	.247	None on/out	.351	37	13	0	0	0	0	3	4	.400	.351
Away	.261	88	23	2	0	6	6	12	9	.350	.284	Batting #6	.120	50	6	0	0	1	3	4	7	.182	.180
First Pitch	.318	22	7	1	0	0	4	0	0	.318	.364	Batting #7	.287	87	25	2	0	0	6	11	7	.367	.310
Ahead on Count	.146	41	6	0	0	0	1	12	0	.340	.146	Other	.250	44	11	1	0	0	1	5	5	.320	.273
Behind on Count	.235	51	12	1	0	1	3	0	8	.231	.314	Pre-All Star	.237	118	28	2	0	1	4	11	14	.300	.280
Two Strikes	.214	84	18	2	0	1	4	8	19	.277	.274	Post-All Star	.222	63	14	1	0	0	6	9	5	.315	.238

Last Five Years

	Avg	AB	H	2B	3B	HR	RBI	BB	SO	OBP	SLG		Avg	AB	H	2B	3B	HR	RBI	BB	SO	OBP	SLG
vs. Left	.185	124	23	7	0	0	12	10	34	.252	.242	Scoring Posn	.271	291	79	14	1	1	109	56	35	.379	.337
vs. Right	.274	1130	310	43	3	22	125	160	120	.362	.376	Close & Late	.218	220	48	6	0	3	22	31	35	.315	.286
Groundball	.240	358	86	14	0	3	32	56	36	.343	.304	None on/out	.242	277	67	10	0	6	6	31	30	.318	.343
Flyball	.248	282	70	9	1	7	33	35	43	.328	.362	Batting #6	.248	270	67	9	2	8	27	39	44	.342	.385
Home	.244	589	144	23	1	14	59	88	85	.340	.358	Batting #7	.293	270	79	10	0	1	33	38	32	.376	.341
Away	.284	665	189	27	2	8	78	82	69	.362	.367	Other	.252	714	187	31	1	13	77	93	78	.345	.363
Day	.280	446	125	20	1	6	52	67	60	.373	.370	April	.227	97	22	3	0	2	11	16	12	.336	.320
Night	.257	808	208	30	2	16	85	103	94	.339	.359	May	.240	175	42	4	0	1	10	20	26	.315	.280
Grass	.259	1073	278	42	1	19	115	144	130	.345	.353	June	.271	203	55	10	0	2	21	31	24	.360	.350
Turf	.304	181	55	8	2	3	22	26	24	.391	.420	July	.279	244	68	7	2	7	24	32	27	.361	.410
First Pitch	.342	161	55	10	1	3	26	2	0	.345	.472	August	.278	277	77	17	1	7	40	30	38	.347	.422
Ahead on Count	.278	288	80	10	0	9	40	88	0	.442	.406	September/October	.267	258	69	9	0	3	31	41	27	.370	.337
Behind on Count	.255	412	105	14	0	7	49	1	86	.256	.340	Pre-All Star	.255	572	146	19	0	9	55	80	72	.343	.336
Two Strikes	.209	575	120	16	1	5	44	75	154	.300	.266	Post-All Star	.274	682	187	31	3	13	82	90	82	.359	.386

Batter vs. Pitcher (since 1984)

Hits Best Against	Avg	AB	H	2B	3B	HR	RBI	BB	SO	OBP	SLG	Hits Worst Against	Avg	AB	H	2B	3B	HR	RBI	BB	SO	OBP	SLG
Dennis Lamp	.600	10	6	1	0	0	2	2	0	.667	.700	Tom Henke	.000	17	0	0	0	0	1	0	5	.000	.000
Storm Davis	.444	18	8	1	0	1	1	6	2	.583	.667	Jose Guzman	.000	10	0	0	0	0	0	1	1	.091	.000
Steve Farr	.429	14	6	0	0	2	4	1	2	.467	.857	Mike Mussina	.083	12	1	0	0	0	0	1	3	.154	.083
Jack McDowell	.357	14	5	2	0	1	3	0	0	.357	.714	Kevin Brown	.111	18	2	0	0	0	0	0	3	.111	.111
Bobby Thigpen	.308	13	4	0	0	2	3	1	1	.357	.769	Dennis Eckersley	.125	16	2	0	0	0	2	0	5	.125	.125

Geronimo Berroa — Reds   Bats Right (groundball hitter)

	Avg	G	AB	R	H	2B	3B	HR	RBI	BB	SO	HBP	GDP	SB	CS	OBP	SLG	IBB	SH	SF	#Pit	#P/PA	GB	FB	G/F
1992 Season	.267	13	15	2	4	1	0	0	0	2	1	1	1	0	1	.389	.333	0	0	0	66	3.67	7	4	1.75
Career (1989-1992)	.258	101	155	9	40	5	0	2	9	10	34	1	3	0	2	.307	.329	2	0	0	586	3.53	61	40	1.53

1992 Season

	Avg	AB	H	2B	3B	HR	RBI	BB	SO	OBP	SLG		Avg	AB	H	2B	3B	HR	RBI	BB	SO	OBP	SLG
vs. Left	.286	14	4	1	0	0	0	2	1	.412	.357	Scoring Posn	.000	3	0	0	0	0	0	1	0	.400	.000
vs. Right	.000	1	0	0	0	0	0	0	0	.000	.000	Close & Late	.200	5	1	0	0	0	0	0	1	.200	.200

Sean Berry — Expos
Bats Right (flyball hitter)

	Avg	G	AB	R	H	2B	3B	HR	RBI	BB	SO	HBP	GDP	SB	CS	OBP	SLG	IBB	SH	SF	#Pit	#P/PA	GB	FB	G/F
1992 Season	.333	24	57	5	19	1	0	1	4	1	11	0	0	1	2	1	.345	.404	0	0	0	213	3.67	21	16	1.31
Career (1990-1992)	.229	63	140	12	32	5	1	1	9	8	39	1	2	2	1	.275	.300	0	0	0	586	3.93	41	42	0.98

1992 Season

	Avg	AB	H	2B	3B	HR	RBI	BB	SO	OBP	SLG		Avg	AB	H	2B	3B	HR	RBI	BB	SO	OBP	SLG
vs. Left	.667	3	2	0	0	0	0	0	0	.667	.667	Scoring Posn	.286	14	4	0	0	0	2	1	4	.333	.286
vs. Right	.315	54	17	1	0	1	4	1	11	.327	.389	Close & Late	.429	14	6	0	0	0	0	0	4	.429	.429

Damon Berryhill — Braves
Bats Both

	Avg	G	AB	R	H	2B	3B	HR	RBI	BB	SO	HBP	GDP	SB	CS	OBP	SLG	IBB	SH	SF	#Pit	#P/PA	GB	FB	G/F
1992 Season	.228	101	307	21	70	16	1	10	43	17	67	1	4	0	2	.268	.384	4	0	3	1197	3.65	90	109	0.83
Last Five Years	.237	367	1163	96	276	59	2	28	145	66	233	4	33	3	4	.278	.364	15	7	13	4343	3.49	400	359	1.11

1992 Season

	Avg	AB	H	2B	3B	HR	RBI	BB	SO	OBP	SLG		Avg	AB	H	2B	3B	HR	RBI	BB	SO	OBP	SLG
vs. Left	.233	73	17	3	0	1	11	4		.269	.315	Scoring Posn	.273	88	24	8	0	3	35	9	23	.330	.466
vs. Right	.226	234	53	13	1	9	32	13	57	.268	.406	Close & Late	.228	57	13	3	1	1	5	3	14	.279	.368
Groundball	.266	154	41	8	0	6	29	7	31	.294	.435	None on/out	.295	61	18	2	0	3	3	3	9	.328	.475
Flyball	.167	66	11	3	0	2	5	7	18	.247	.303	Batting #6	.191	141	27	5	0	3	14	3	33	.208	.291
Home	.291	148	43	9	1	6	24	8	34	.325	.486	Batting #7	.267	131	35	10	1	4	23	10	24	.317	.450
Away	.170	159	27	7	0	4	19	9	33	.216	.289	Other	.229	35	8	1	0	3	6	4	10	.308	.514
Day	.186	86	16	4	0	2	11	8	25	.253	.302	April	.282	39	11	1	0	3	8	1	4	.300	.538
Night	.244	221	54	12	1	8	32	9	42	.275	.416	May	.172	64	11	1	0	3	8	2	17	.197	.328
Grass	.245	237	58	12	1	7	29	12	52	.283	.392	June	.300	40	12	4	0	0	7	3	11	.349	.400
Turf	.171	70	12	4	0	3	14	5	15	.221	.357	July	.140	43	6	3	0	0	2	5	12	.240	.209
First Pitch	.314	51	16	3	1	2	8	4	0	.364	.529	August	.240	50	12	3	0	3	7	2	8	.264	.480
Ahead on Count	.361	61	22	5	0	4	12	4	0	.394	.639	September/October	.254	71	18	4	1	1	11	4	15	.289	.380
Behind on Count	.184	114	21	5	0	2	12	0	34	.183	.281	Pre-All Star	.223	166	37	7	0	6	23	9	37	.263	.373
Two Strikes	.143	147	21	5	0	3	16	9	67	.195	.238	Post-All Star	.234	141	33	9	1	4	20	8	30	.275	.397

1992 By Position

Position	Avg	AB	H	2B	3B	HR	RBI	BB	SO	OBP	SLG	G	GS	Innings	PO	A	E	DP	Fld Pct	Rng Fctr	In Zone	Outs	Zone Rtg	MLB Zone
As Pinch Hitter	.250	16	4	0	0	1	2	4	6	.400	.438	20	0	---	---	---	---	---	---	---	---	---	---	---
As c	.227	291	66	16	1	9	41	13	61	.260	.381	84	75	661.0	427	30	1	6	.998	---	---	---	---	---

Last Five Years

	Avg	AB	H	2B	3B	HR	RBI	BB	SO	OBP	SLG		Avg	AB	H	2B	3B	HR	RBI	BB	SO	OBP	SLG
vs. Left	.248	310	77	12	0	6	39	13	38	.274	.345	Scoring Posn	.256	320	82	17	0	7	115	29	69	.309	.375
vs. Right	.233	853	199	47	2	22	106	53	195	.279	.370	Close & Late	.226	226	51	10	1	4	21	16	52	.279	.332
Groundball	.247	478	118	20	1	14	71	24	86	.280	.381	None on/out	.245	249	61	13	0	8	8	10	51	.277	.394
Flyball	.223	260	58	14	0	5	24	19	69	.277	.335	Batting #6	.242	466	113	23	0	10	46	21	96	.276	.356
Home	.271	583	158	36	2	17	86	34	122	.310	.427	Batting #7	.246	334	82	20	2	13	58	22	59	.289	.434
Away	.203	580	118	23	0	11	59	32	111	.245	.300	Other	.223	363	81	16	0	5	41	23	78	.270	.309
Day	.246	545	134	33	1	8	66	35	116	.287	.354	April	.200	85	17	3	0	4	10	5	17	.244	.376
Night	.230	618	142	26	1	20	79	31	117	.269	.372	May	.236	267	63	15	0	7	32	7	51	.254	.371
Grass	.248	807	200	42	2	21	109	45	165	.287	.383	June	.283	187	53	10	0	1	28	11	38	.319	.353
Turf	.213	356	76	17	0	7	36	21	68	.257	.320	July	.188	197	37	7	0	4	19	11	38	.237	.284
First Pitch	.320	219	70	20	1	4	30	7	0	.338	.475	August	.272	180	49	11	1	7	24	14	32	.325	.461
Ahead on Count	.318	211	67	11	0	9	37	18	0	.368	.498	September/October	.231	247	57	13	1	5	32	18	57	.280	.352
Behind on Count	.197	426	84	16	0	8	51	0	137	.200	.291	Pre-All Star	.243	593	144	29	0	13	76	27	114	.275	.358
Two Strikes	.154	530	87	16	1	12	58	34	233	.214	.266	Post-All Star	.232	570	132	30	2	15	69	39	119	.280	.370

Batter vs. Pitcher (career)

Hits Best Against	Avg	AB	H	2B	3B	HR	RBI	BB	SO	OBP	SLG	Hits Worst Against	Avg	AB	H	2B	3B	HR	RBI	BB	SO	OBP	SLG
Don Carman	.375	8	3	0	0	0	1	3	1	.545	.375	Orel Hershiser	.095	21	2	0	0	0	3	1	3	.136	.095
Tim Belcher	.353	17	6	2	0	1	1	1	3	.389	.647	Pete Smith	.100	10	1	1	0	0	1	1	3	.182	.200
Roger McDowell	.333	12	4	1	0	0	2	1	3	.467	.417	Sid Fernandez	.154	13	2	0	0	0	2	2	3	.267	.154
Bruce Ruffin	.333	12	4	0	0	1	1	1	3	.385	.583	Jose Rijo	.200	10	2	0	0	0	2	0	3	.182	.200
Kevin Gross	.313	16	5	2	0	0	6	0	3	.313	.438	Ron Darling	.211	19	4	1	0	0	4	0	3	.200	.263

Dante Bichette — Brewers
Bats Right

	Avg	G	AB	R	H	2B	3B	HR	RBI	BB	SO	HBP	GDP	SB	CS	OBP	SLG	IBB	SH	SF	#Pit	#P/PA	GB	FB	G/F
1992 Season	.287	112	387	37	111	27	2	5	41	16	74	3	13	18	7	.318	.406	3	2	3	1359	3.32	132	107	1.23
Career (1988-1992)	.254	424	1365	144	347	69	6	38	176	60	291	7	34	40	17	.286	.397	8	4	17	5096	3.52	468	398	1.18

1992 Season

	Avg	AB	H	2B	3B	HR	RBI	BB	SO	OBP	SLG		Avg	AB	H	2B	3B	HR	RBI	BB	SO	OBP	SLG
vs. Left	.286	119	34	8	2	2	23	9	27	.336	.437	Scoring Posn	.232	99	23	6	1	1	32	6	20	.269	.343
vs. Right	.287	268	77	19	0	3	18	7	47	.309	.392	Close & Late	.258	66	17	1	0	0	3	3	11	.290	.273
Groundball	.295	88	26	7	1	2	13	4	17	.323	.466	None on/out	.337	95	32	6	1	0	0	3	21	.364	.421
Flyball	.252	107	27	4	0	0	6	4	19	.274	.290	Batting #5	.248	109	27	4	0	0	5	4	25	.278	.284

1992 Season

	Avg	AB	H	2B	3B	HR	RBI	BB	SO	OBP	SLG		Avg	AB	H	2B	3B	HR	RBI	BB	SO	OBP	SLG
Home	.241	170	41	9	2	3	22	9	33	.280	.371	Batting #6	.320	122	39	12	1	2	15	6	19	.349	.484
Away	.323	217	70	18	0	2	19	7	41	.348	.433	Other	.288	156	45	11	1	3	21	6	30	.321	.429
Day	.336	149	50	10	1	4	21	7	29	.373	.497	April	.324	37	12	1	0	0	5	1	13	.342	.351
Night	.256	238	61	17	1	1	20	9	45	.283	.349	May	.308	91	28	5	0	1	5	6	15	.354	.396
Grass	.275	327	90	20	2	5	33	14	63	.308	.394	June	.338	77	26	10	2	3	19	3	10	.358	.636
Turf	.350	60	21	7	0	0	8	2	11	.371	.467	July	.333	48	16	2	0	1	5	0	8	.333	.438
First Pitch	.313	83	26	4	0	2	15	3	0	.333	.434	August	.230	74	17	7	0	0	5	4	17	.288	.324
Ahead on Count	.313	67	21	7	1	0	6	4	0	.370	.448	September/October	.200	60	12	2	0	0	2	2	11	.222	.233
Behind on Count	.233	150	35	7	1	0	12	0	49	.232	.293	Pre-All Star	.316	225	71	17	2	4	30	10	42	.345	.462
Two Strikes	.198	172	34	7	0	0	6	9	74	.236	.238	Post-All Star	.247	162	40	10	0	1	11	6	32	.281	.327

1992 By Position

Position	Avg	AB	H	2B	3B	HR	RBI	BB	SO	OBP	SLG	G	GS	Innings	PO	A	E	DP	Fld Pct	Rng Fctr	In Zone	Zone Outs	Zone Rtg	MLB Zone
As Pinch Hitter	.100	10	1	0	0	0	3	0	5	.091	.100	12	0	---	---	---	---	---	---	---	---	---	---	---
As rf	.294	371	109	27	2	5	38	15	68	.325	.418	101	93	846.0	186	6	2	3	.990	2.04	216	178	.824	.814

Career (1988–1992)

	Avg	AB	H	2B	3B	HR	RBI	BB	SO	OBP	SLG		Avg	AB	H	2B	3B	HR	RBI	BB	SO	OBP	SLG
vs. Left	.263	532	140	29	5	16	75	31	115	.302	.427	Scoring Posn	.233	344	80	15	3	11	136	21	84	.264	.390
vs. Right	.248	833	207	40	1	22	101	29	176	.275	.378	Close & Late	.271	247	67	6	2	6	38	10	58	.300	.385
Groundball	.278	345	96	21	2	9	55	15	60	.306	.429	None on/out	.271	314	85	16	2	7	7	12	71	.302	.401
Flyball	.255	325	83	15	1	8	43	10	73	.276	.382	Batting #6	.276	493	136	32	4	16	61	20	96	.303	.454
Home	.244	631	154	30	4	19	90	31	130	.280	.395	Batting #7	.216	348	75	12	1	13	59	14	78	.244	.368
Away	.263	734	193	39	2	19	86	29	161	.291	.399	Other	.260	524	136	25	1	9	56	26	117	.297	.363
Day	.276	428	118	21	2	16	61	24	93	.315	.446	April	.270	230	62	13	0	7	33	9	42	.296	.417
Night	.244	937	229	48	4	22	115	36	198	.272	.375	May	.252	322	81	16	1	10	39	16	71	.288	.401
Grass	.255	1147	292	55	6	34	152	50	240	.287	.402	June	.234	218	51	14	2	8	35	13	50	.275	.427
Turf	.252	218	55	14	0	4	24	10	51	.280	.372	July	.280	189	53	7	0	7	28	8	44	.305	.429
First Pitch	.310	216	67	9	1	8	43	6	0	.325	.472	August	.228	162	37	9	1	2	13	9	40	.286	.333
Ahead on Count	.348	224	78	20	3	11	40	20	1	.406	.612	September/October	.258	244	63	10	2	4	28	5	44	.268	.365
Behind on Count	.216	584	126	25	2	10	58	0	194	.215	.317	Pre-All Star	.254	824	209	45	3	26	118	39	178	.287	.410
Two Strikes	.164	653	107	19	0	8	52	33	290	.204	.230	Post-All Star	.255	541	138	24	3	12	58	21	113	.284	.377

Batter vs. Pitcher (career)

Hits Best Against	Avg	AB	H	2B	3B	HR	RBI	BB	SO	OBP	SLG	Hits Worst Against	Avg	AB	H	2B	3B	HR	RBI	BB	SO	OBP	SLG
Curt Young	.625	8	5	0	0	2	3	4	1	.750	1.375	Mike Moore	.000	9	0	0	0	0	0	2	2	.182	.000
Frank Viola	.429	14	6	3	0	1	4	0	1	.400	.857	Jimmy Key	.063	16	1	0	0	0	1	0	3	.059	.063
Roger Clemens	.412	17	7	1	0	0	1	0	6	.412	.471	Nolan Ryan	.071	14	1	0	0	0	0	0	6	.071	.071
Tom Bolton	.385	13	5	1	1	0	0	0	2	.385	.615	Todd Stottlemyre	.091	11	1	0	0	0	0	0	2	.091	.091
Bobby Witt	.357	14	5	1	0	0	2	0	5	.357	.429	Greg Swindell	.143	14	2	0	0	0	0	0	8	.143	.143

Mike Bielecki — Braves

Pitches Right

	ERA	W	L	Sv	G	GS	IP	BB	SO	Avg	H	2B	3B	HR	RBI	OBP	SLG	CG	ShO	Sup	QS	#P/S	SB	CS	GB	FB	G/F
1992 Season	2.57	2	4	0	19	14	80.2	27	62	.254	77	16	5	2	23	.315	.360	1	1	4.13	7	84	8	2	108	66	1.64
Last Five Years	3.86	43	35	1	148	106	683.0	250	420	.261	678	130	29	53	279	.326	.395	5	4	4.63	55	92	55	29	972	717	1.36

1992 Season

	ERA	W	L	Sv	G	GS	IP	H	HR	BB	SO		Avg	AB	H	2B	3B	HR	RBI	BB	SO	OBP	SLG
Home	2.54	1	2	0	10	7	39.0	37	1	14	32	vs. Left	.271	177	48	8	3	0	13	17	29	.335	.350
Away	2.59	1	2	0	9	7	41.2	40	1	13	30	vs. Right	.230	126	29	8	2	2	10	10	33	.288	.373
Starter	2.69	2	4	0	14	14	73.2	71	2	25	58	Scoring Posn	.250	72	18	3	1	0	18	7	15	.317	.319
Reliever	1.29	0	0	0	5	0	7.0	6	0	2	4	Close & Late	.111	18	2	0	0	0	0	1	5	.158	.111
0-3 Days Rest	3.60	0	1	0	1	1	5.0	8	0	3	5	None on/out	.260	77	20	3	0	0	0	7	18	.321	.299
4 Days Rest	2.41	2	1	0	7	7	33.2	34	1	9	24	First Pitch	.273	33	9	3	1	0	3	0	0	.273	.424
5+ Days Rest	2.83	0	2	0	6	6	35.0	29	1	13	29	Behind on Count	.377	69	26	5	2	6	13	0	0	.476	.551
Pre-All Star	2.64	2	4	0	17	13	75.0	73	2	26	56	Ahead on Count	.169	142	24	2	1	1	11	0	52	.172	.218
Post-All Star	1.59	0	0	0	2	1	5.2	4	0	1	6	Two Strikes	.184	136	25	5	1	0	7	14	62	.263	.235

Last Five Years

	ERA	W	L	Sv	G	GS	IP	H	HR	BB	SO		Avg	AB	H	2B	3B	HR	RBI	BB	SO	OBP	SLG
Home	3.79	21	20	0	70	55	347.0	332	32	120	226	vs. Left	.269	1448	389	72	14	30	143	162	215	.341	.400
Away	3.94	22	15	1	78	51	336.0	346	21	130	194	vs. Right	.252	1145	289	58	15	23	136	88	205	.306	.390
Day	4.24	21	18	1	71	51	335.2	338	31	128	205	Inning 1-6	.269	2166	582	115	25	45	237	205	335	.331	.407
Night	3.50	22	17	0	77	55	347.1	340	22	122	215	Inning 7+	.225	427	96	15	4	8	42	45	85	.300	.335
Grass	3.87	29	27	0	100	76	477.0	461	40	176	305	None on	.263	1517	399	79	16	35	35	124	235	.320	.405
Turf	3.84	14	8	1	48	30	206.0	217	13	74	115	Runners on	.259	1076	279	51	13	18	244	126	185	.334	.381
April	3.14	7	6	0	22	14	97.1	87	10	38	64	Scoring Posn	.264	617	163	29	8	8	211	97	103	.357	.376
May	3.03	9	4	0	27	19	121.2	118	5	50	76	Close & Late	.205	190	39	7	1	5	23	26	44	.303	.332
June	5.02	4	10	0	26	17	113.0	110	10	48	77	None on/out	.282	670	189	32	5	16	16	57	101	.341	.416
July	4.28	8	4	0	25	17	111.1	118	7	34	65	vs. 1st Batr (relief)	.205	39	8	4	1	1	3	10	0	.262	.436
August	4.22	8	3	0	23	22	130.0	129	16	43	76	First Inning Pitched	.268	537	144	29	8	14	81	73	84	.354	.430
September/October	3.36	7	8	1	25	17	109.2	107	5	37	62	First 75 Pitches	.267	2019	539	102	25	39	223	200	317	.332	.400

Last Five Years

	ERA	W	L	Sv	G	GS	IP	H	HR	BB	SO		Avg	AB	H	2B	3B	HR	RBI	BB	SO	OBP	SLG
Starter	3.93	38	32	0	106	106	613.0	612	51	218	373	Pitch 76-90	.242	297	72	18	1	8	36	21	43	.295	.391
Reliever	3.21	5	3	1	42	0	70.0	66	2	32	47	Pitch 91-105	.240	183	44	7	3	4	12	15	32	.302	.377
0-3 Days Rest	4.28	7	2	0	14	14	75.2	73	7	40	49	Pitch 106+	.245	94	23	3	0	2	8	14	28	.343	.340
4 Days Rest	4.14	21	21	0	60	60	345.1	365	33	110	208	First Pitch	.288	351	101	16	6	5	39	23	0	.327	.410
5+ Days Rest	3.42	10	9	0	32	32	192.0	174	11	68	116	Ahead on Count	.214	1104	236	36	9	13	100	2	361	.218	.298
Pre-All Star	3.92	23	22	0	82	57	370.0	368	29	150	245	Behind on Count	.310	654	203	46	12	21	81	131	0	.423	.514
Post-All Star	3.80	20	13	1	66	49	313.0	310	24	100	175	Two Strikes	.210	1126	236	37	9	18	95	95	420	.273	.306

Pitcher vs. Batter (career)

Pitches Best Vs.	Avg	AB	H	2B	3B	HR	RBI	BB	SO	OBP	SLG	Pitches Worst Vs.	Avg	AB	H	2B	3B	HR	RBI	BB	SO	OBP	SLG
Spike Owen	.000	22	0	0	0	0	0	1	5	.043	.000	Jay Bell	.632	19	12	4	2	0	5	2	3	.667	1.053
Glenn Davis	.000	16	0	0	0	0	1	2	3	.111	.000	Steve Finley	.571	14	8	1	2	1	2	1	1	.600	1.143
Barry Bonds	.063	32	2	1	0	0	2	6	8	.211	.094	Otis Nixon	.545	11	6	0	1	0	2	1	3	.583	.727
Alfredo Griffin	.083	12	1	1	0	0	0	0	0	.083	.167	Juan Samuel	.474	19	9	2	0	2	8	2	2	.478	.895
Todd Benzinger	.125	16	2	1	0	0	1	1	2	.176	.188	Kevin Mitchell	.333	15	5	1	2	2	6	0	1	.333	1.067

Craig Biggio — Astros

Bats Right

	Avg	G	AB	R	H	2B	3B	HR	RBI	BB	SO	HBP	GDP	SB	CS	OBP	SLG	IBB	SH	SF	#Pit	#P/PA	GB	FB	G/F
1992 Season	.277	162	613	96	170	32	3	6	39	94	95	7	5	38	15	.378	.369	9	5	2	2758	3.85	241	158	1.53
Career (1988-1992)	.274	645	2280	306	624	106	12	30	192	256	354	18	26	109	36	.350	.370	23	26	11	9328	3.64	872	615	1.42

1992 Season

	Avg	AB	H	2B	3B	HR	RBI	BB	SO	OBP	SLG		Avg	AB	H	2B	3B	HR	RBI	BB	SO	OBP	SLG
vs. Left	.275	218	60	10	1	3	14	50	22	.410	.372	Scoring Posn	.298	104	31	6	1	0	32	27	18	.440	.375
vs. Right	.278	395	110	22	2	3	25	44	73	.359	.367	Close & Late	.263	95	25	3	0	0	5	20	12	.402	.295
Groundball	.287	244	70	11	1	1	15	35	43	.377	.352	None on/out	.284	268	76	14	2	4	4	34	42	.370	.396
Flyball	.295	146	43	9	1	3	13	24	21	.399	.432	Batting #1	.276	602	166	32	3	6	39	93	94	.378	.369
Home	.281	303	85	19	2	3	17	48	44	.384	.386	Batting #9	.500	6	3	0	0	0	0	1	0	.571	.500
Away	.274	310	85	13	1	3	22	46	51	.373	.352	Other	.200	5	1	0	0	0	0	0	1	.200	.200
Day	.244	168	41	8	1	3	10	27	17	.355	.357	April	.313	83	26	5	1	1	2	9	13	.380	.434
Night	.290	445	129	24	2	3	29	67	78	.387	.373	May	.286	112	32	7	0	3	12	13	25	.357	.429
Grass	.255	188	48	5	0	1	10	23	25	.343	.298	June	.258	97	25	6	0	1	6	23	14	.402	.351
Turf	.287	425	122	27	3	5	29	71	70	.394	.400	July	.250	96	24	3	1	0	1	14	12	.357	.302
First Pitch	.301	73	22	4	0	2	4	8	0	.386	.438	August	.324	108	35	4	1	1	11	17	8	.430	.407
Ahead on Count	.235	81	19	7	1	1	9	62	0	.566	.392	September/October	.239	117	28	7	0	0	7	18	23	.346	.299
Behind on Count	.283	219	62	11	2	0	17	0	49	.287	.352	Pre-All Star	.284	334	95	20	2	5	20	49	59	.376	.401
Two Strikes	.239	305	73	8	2	1	14	24	95	.304	.289	Post-All Star	.269	279	75	12	1	1	19	45	36	.382	.330

1992 By Position

Position	Avg	AB	H	2B	3B	HR	RBI	BB	SO	OBP	SLG	G	GS	Innings	PO	A	E	DP	Fld Pct	Rng Fctr	In Zone	Outs	Zone Rtg	MLB Zone
As 2b	.278	612	170	32	3	6	39	93	95	.378	.369	161	157	1407.2	343	412	12	81	.984	4.83	506	426	.842	.892

Career (1988-1992)

	Avg	AB	H	2B	3B	HR	RBI	BB	SO	OBP	SLG		Avg	AB	H	2B	3B	HR	RBI	BB	SO	OBP	SLG
vs. Left	.259	783	203	31	4	9	55	114	87	.354	.344	Scoring Posn	.270	503	136	19	1	5	153	88	96	.376	.342
vs. Right	.281	1497	421	75	8	21	137	142	251	.348	.384	Close & Late	.256	410	105	18	2	5	43	49	63	.341	.346
Groundball	.286	786	225	40	3	6	70	93	111	.364	.368	None on/out	.257	638	164	34	7	13	13	67	82	.331	.393
Flyball	.260	531	138	22	1	10	49	62	96	.339	.362	Batting #1	.270	748	202	37	4	10	57	117	111	.372	.370
Home	.279	1131	316	62	9	12	94	131	172	.357	.382	Batting #2	.291	481	140	22	2	8	46	43	72	.350	.395
Away	.268	1149	308	44	3	18	98	125	166	.343	.359	Other	.268	1051	282	47	6	12	89	96	155	.333	.359
Day	.305	571	174	31	3	12	65	68	72	.384	.433	April	.302	248	75	9	1	4	15	28	43	.374	.395
Night	.263	1709	450	75	9	18	127	188	266	.339	.349	May	.296	378	112	21	1	5	40	38	66	.360	.397
Grass	.258	705	182	20	1	12	56	63	95	.322	.340	June	.265	392	104	17	0	7	30	53	52	.355	.362
Turf	.281	1575	442	86	11	18	136	193	243	.362	.383	July	.278	424	118	18	4	3	32	38	54	.346	.361
First Pitch	.317	303	96	18	0	7	27	18	0	.362	.446	August	.272	401	109	18	4	4	34	56	52	.364	.367
Ahead on Count	.317	420	133	27	4	9	52	160	0	.504	.464	September/October	.243	437	106	23	2	7	41	43	71	.314	.352
Behind on Count	.251	820	206	27	5	3	65	0	195	.256	.307	Pre-All Star	.280	1154	323	52	4	16	94	132	185	.355	.373
Two Strikes	.198	999	198	36	5	7	59	76	338	.260	.265	Post-All Star	.267	1126	301	54	8	14	98	124	153	.345	.367

Batter vs. Pitcher (career)

Hits Best Against	Avg	AB	H	2B	3B	HR	RBI	BB	SO	OBP	SLG	Hits Worst Against	Avg	AB	H	2B	3B	HR	RBI	BB	SO	OBP	SLG
Danny Jackson	.667	9	6	1	0	0	3	3	1	.750	.778	Kelly Downs	.000	11	0	0	0	0	1	0	2	.000	.000
John Wetteland	.556	9	5	0	0	2	5	2	3	.636	1.222	Curt Schilling	.000	10	0	0	0	0	0	1	2	.091	.000
Derek Lilliquist	.500	10	5	0	0	1	2	1	1	.545	.800	Neal Heaton	.071	14	1	0	0	0	0	0	0	.071	.071
Rich Rodriguez	.500	10	5	3	0	0	2	2	0	.583	.800	Randy Myers	.071	14	1	0	0	0	0	0	3	.071	.071
Les Lancaster	.417	12	5	0	1	1	2	0	1	.385	.833	Kevin Gross	.074	27	2	0	0	0	2	2	6	.138	.074

Dann Bilardello — Padres — Bats Right

	Avg	G	AB	R	H	2B	3B	HR	RBI	BB	SO	HBP	GDP	SB	CS	OBP	SLG	IBB	SH	SF	#Pit	#P/PA	GB	FB	G/F
1992 Season	.121	17	33	2	4	1	0	0	1	4	8	0	1	0	0	.216	.152	1	3	0	126	3.41	14	11	1.27
Last Five Years	.176	84	176	18	31	9	1	2	17	13	40	0	2	1	2	.233	.273	2	6	0	660	3.49	67	49	1.37

1992 Season

	Avg	AB	H	2B	3B	HR	RBI	BB	SO	OBP	SLG		Avg	AB	H	2B	3B	HR	RBI	BB	SO	OBP	SLG
vs. Left	.200	5	1	1	0	0	1	1	0	.333	.400	Scoring Posn	.000	9	0	0	0	0	0	1	4	.100	.000
vs. Right	.107	28	3	0	0	0	0	3	8	.194	.107	Close & Late	.400	5	2	0	0	0	0	1	1	.625	.400

Mike Birkbeck — Mets — Pitches Right (groundball pitcher)

	ERA	W	L	Sv	G	GS	IP	BB	SO	Avg	H	2B	3B	HR	RBI	OBP	SLG	CG	ShO	Sup	QS	#P/S	SB	CS	GB	FB	G/F
1992 Season	9.00	0	1	0	1	1	7.0	1	2	.387	12	3	0	3	6	.406	.774	0	0	5.14	0	114	1	0	14	6	2.33
Last Five Years	5.07	10	13	0	33	33	175.2	60	97	.296	210	32	5	17	90	.352	.427	1	0	5.28	10	83	15	5	325	155	2.10

1992 Season

	ERA	W	L	Sv	G	GS	IP	H	HR	BB	SO		Avg	AB	H	2B	3B	HR	RBI	BB	SO	OBP	SLG
Home	9.00	0	1	0	1	1	7.0	12	3	1	2	vs. Left	.407	27	11	3	0	3	6	0	2	.407	.852
Away	0.00	0	0	0	0	0	0.0	0	0	0	0	vs. Right	.250	4	1	0	0	0	0	0	1	.400	.250

Last Five Years

	ERA	W	L	Sv	G	GS	IP	H	HR	BB	SO		Avg	AB	H	2B	3B	HR	RBI	BB	SO	OBP	SLG
Home	5.22	6	7	0	18	18	91.1	113	8	36	47	vs. Left	.283	360	102	18	3	7	36	28	44	.333	.408
Away	4.91	4	6	0	15	15	84.1	97	9	24	50	vs. Right	.309	349	108	14	2	10	54	32	53	.371	.447
Day	4.75	2	4	0	7	7	36.0	41	1	12	20	Inning 1-6	.299	656	196	31	5	16	86	57	91	.355	.434
Night	5.16	8	9	0	26	26	139.2	169	16	48	77	Inning 7+	.264	53	14	1	0	1	4	3	6	.316	.340
Grass	5.05	9	10	0	26	26	139.0	161	16	50	77	None on	.295	400	118	17	2	11	11	23	53	.338	.430
Turf	5.15	1	3	0	7	7	36.2	49	1	10	20	Runners on	.298	309	92	15	3	6	79	37	44	.369	.424
April	5.16	2	4	0	6	6	29.2	34	3	19	19	Scoring Posn	.309	165	51	8	2	2	66	28	20	.402	.418
May	5.80	2	4	0	10	10	49.2	62	2	20	29	Close & Late	.250	12	3	0	0	0	1	1	2	.308	.250
June	9.00	0	1	0	1	1	5.0	8	0	3	2	None on/out	.291	182	53	11	1	2	2	9	17	.328	.396
July	1.89	3	0	0	5	5	33.1	32	1	5	19	vs. 1st Batr (relief)	.000	0	0	0	0	0	0	0	0	.000	.000
August	6.12	4	2	0	7	7	42.2	55	9	11	22	First Inning Pitched	.361	147	53	7	2	3	36	12	18	.414	.497
September/October	5.28	1	2	0	4	4	15.1	19	2	2	6	First 75 Pitches	.290	590	171	25	5	11	72	66	79	.343	.405
Starter	5.07	10	13	0	33	33	175.2	210	17	60	97	Pitch 76-90	.338	80	27	6	0	5	11	9	16	.404	.600
Reliever	0.00	0	0	0	0	0	0.0	0	0	0	0	Pitch 91-105	.286	35	10	0	0	0	4	5	2	.375	.286
0-3 Days Rest	0.00	0	0	0	0	0	0.0	0	0	0	0	Pitch 106+	.500	4	2	1	0	1	3	0	0	.500	1.500
4 Days Rest	5.37	7	7	0	22	22	114.0	140	14	37	69	First Pitch	.411	95	39	4	1	4	13	1	0	.414	.600
5+ Days Rest	4.52	3	6	0	11	11	61.2	70	3	23	28	Ahead on Count	.206	282	58	11	0	4	22	0	86	.211	.267
Pre-All Star	5.13	3	9	0	19	19	98.1	115	5	43	59	Behind on Count	.353	204	72	13	3	6	40	39	0	.453	.534
Post-All Star	5.00	7	4	0	14	14	77.1	95	12	17	38	Two Strikes	.193	275	53	10	0	4	24	20	97	.250	.273

Pitcher vs. Batter (career)

Pitches Best Vs.	Avg	AB	H	2B	3B	HR	RBI	BB	SO	OBP	SLG	Pitches Worst Vs.	Avg	AB	H	2B	3B	HR	RBI	BB	SO	OBP	SLG
Eddie Murray	.154	13	2	1	0	0	2	1	1	.200	.231	Kirby Puckett	.750	12	9	3	1	0	5	0	1	.750	1.167
Tony Fernandez	.167	12	2	1	0	0	1	0	1	.167	.250	Julio Franco	.500	12	6	1	1	1	1	3	1	.600	1.000
Willie Wilson	.182	22	4	0	0	0	2	4		.250	.182	Pete Incaviglia	.500	10	5	0	0	2	5	1	1	.500	1.100
Mel Hall	.200	15	3	1	0	0	1	0	2	.200	.267	Brook Jacoby	.467	15	7	2	0	1	3	2	1	.529	.800
Kevin Seitzer	.227	22	5	1	0	0	1	0	5	.227	.273	Joe Carter	.400	15	6	1	0	3	7	0	4	.353	1.067

Bud Black — Giants — Pitches Left

	ERA	W	L	Sv	G	GS	IP	BB	SO	Avg	H	2B	3B	HR	RBI	OBP	SLG	CG	ShO	Sup	QS	#P/S	SB	CS	GB	FB	G/F
1992 Season	3.97	10	12	0	28	28	177.0	59	82	.263	178	27	6	23	67	.321	.422	2	1	3.41	16	92	7	14	237	238	1.00
Last Five Years	3.82	51	54	1	160	132	901.1	277	443	.251	855	135	20	89	344	.308	.380	16	9	3.94	79	95	51	43	1292	1069	1.21

1992 Season

	ERA	W	L	Sv	G	GS	IP	H	HR	BB	SO		Avg	AB	H	2B	3B	HR	RBI	BB	SO	OBP	SLG
Home	2.91	8	5	0	16	16	111.1	104	13	32	58	vs. Left	.229	140	32	5	1	4	10	10	20	.281	.364
Away	5.76	2	7	0	12	12	65.2	74	10	27	24	vs. Right	.272	537	146	22	5	19	57	49	62	.332	.438
Day	2.62	7	2	0	11	11	75.2	71	9	18	39	Inning 1-6	.270	582	157	27	5	17	60	48	73	.324	.421
Night	4.97	3	10	0	17	17	101.1	107	14	41	43	Inning 7+	.221	95	21	0	1	6	7	11	9	.302	.432
Grass	3.36	9	8	0	22	22	142.0	135	14	45	68	None on	.274	430	118	18	4	15	15	29	49	.320	.440
Turf	6.43	1	4	0	6	6	35.0	43	9	14	14	Runners on	.243	247	60	9	2	8	52	30	33	.323	.393
April	0.00	0	0	0	0	0	0.0	0	0	0	0	Scoring Posn	.250	136	34	5	2	3	41	20	20	.342	.382
May	4.26	2	1	0	5	5	31.2	27	6	10	11	Close & Late	.214	42	9	0	1	3	4	5	3	.298	.476
June	3.48	2	1	0	5	5	31.0	34	0	12	16	None on/out	.263	186	49	7	0	4	4	11	19	.305	.366
July	1.59	5	1	0	6	6	45.1	34	3	10	20	vs. 1st Batr (relief)	.000	0	0	0	0	0	0	0	0	.000	.000
August	3.72	1	3	0	6	6	38.2	43	6	12	20	First Inning Pitched	.109	92	10	3	1	1	1	5	8	.155	.196
September/October	8.01	0	6	0	6	6	30.1	40	8	15	15	First 75 Pitches	.274	540	148	25	5	16	55	41	64	.325	.428
Starter	3.97	10	12	0	28	28	177.0	178	23	59	82	Pitch 76-90	.187	75	14	2	0	3	7	8	10	.262	.333
Reliever	0.00	0	0	0	0	0	0.0	0	0	0	0	Pitch 91-105	.311	45	14	0	1	3	4	3	7	.354	.556
0-3 Days Rest	0.00	0	0	0	0	0	0.0	0	0	0	0	Pitch 106+	.118	17	2	0	0	0	1	1	7	.375	.294
4 Days Rest	3.40	9	6	0	19	19	121.2	129	15	39	59	First Pitch	.342	114	39	7	1	4	17	9	0	.387	.526

1992 Season

	ERA	W	L	Sv	G	GS	IP	H	HR	BB	SO		Avg	AB	H	2B	3B	HR	RBI	BB	SO	OBP	SLG
5+ Days Rest	5.20	1	6	0	9	9	55.1	49	8	20	23	Ahead on Count	.219	256	56	9	2	4	14	0	69	.222	.316
Pre-All Star	3.00	7	2	0	13	13	87.0	80	8	25	41	Behind on Count	.279	172	48	9	1	6	18	20	0	.349	.448
Post-All Star	4.90	3	10	0	15	15	90.0	98	15	34	41	Two Strikes	.195	257	50	6	2	5	13	30	82	.279	.292

Last Five Years

	ERA	W	L	Sv	G	GS	IP	H	HR	BB	SO		Avg	AB	H	2B	3B	HR	RBI	BB	SO	OBP	SLG
Home	3.46	30	28	1	83	68	483.2	456	45	132	235	vs. Left	.234	649	152	17	1	20	72	56	77	.293	.356
Away	4.25	21	26	0	77	64	417.2	399	44	145	208	vs. Right	.255	2761	703	118	19	69	272	221	366	.311	.386
Day	3.14	18	13	1	51	41	281.1	265	26	83	156	Inning 1-6	.250	2789	697	123	16	70	288	225	348	.307	.381
Night	4.14	33	41	0	109	91	620.0	590	63	194	287	Inning 7+	.254	621	158	12	4	19	56	52	95	.313	.378
Grass	3.64	42	41	1	123	107	726.1	675	65	222	363	None on	.248	2147	532	84	11	52	52	133	270	.294	.370
Turf	4.58	9	13	0	37	25	175.0	180	24	55	80	Runners on	.256	1263	323	51	9	37	292	144	173	.330	.398
April	4.41	5	8	0	21	14	102.0	99	10	32	48	Scoring Posn	.237	701	166	28	7	18	242	88	104	.318	.374
May	2.70	12	7	0	33	22	176.2	139	15	55	82	Close & Late	.241	295	71	5	4	6	30	25	42	.302	.346
June	4.50	8	6	0	28	21	154.0	164	17	60	73	None on/out	.244	914	223	34	1	16	16	58	95	.289	.336
July	3.38	13	7	0	26	26	170.1	152	14	45	84	vs. 1st Batr (relief)	.200	10	2	0	0	0	2	1	2	.273	.200
August	4.91	5	13	0	24	24	132.0	150	14	41	71	First Inning Pitched	.227	525	119	23	3	12	50	32	65	.271	.350
September/October	3.63	8	13	1	28	25	166.1	151	14	19	44	85	First 75 Pitches	.255	2647	676	115	17	63	272	207	338	.310	.383
Starter	3.78	46	52	0	132	132	851.0	806	83	253	402	Pitch 76-90	.250	392	98	11	0	12	39	32	53	.309	.370
Reliever	4.65	5	2	1	28	0	50.1	49	6	24	41	Pitch 91-105	.242	244	59	7	3	10	22	14	37	.285	.418
0-3 Days Rest	4.70	1	3	0	4	4	23.0	23	1	3	11	Pitch 106+	.173	127	22	2	0	4	11	24	15	.305	.283
4 Days Rest	3.49	30	27	0	80	80	529.1	500	54	168	253	First Pitch	.283	576	163	30	5	13	73	16	0	.302	.420
5+ Days Rest	4.22	15	22	0	48	48	298.2	283	28	82	138	Ahead on Count	.214	1377	294	40	6	22	85	1	370	.218	.299
Pre-All Star	3.63	30	23	0	92	67	503.2	463	48	160	236	Behind on Count	.308	790	243	43	4	27	105	142	0	.410	.475
Post-All Star	4.07	21	31	1	68	65	397.2	392	41	117	207	Two Strikes	.192	1395	268	37	6	32	97	118	443	.258	.296

Pitcher vs. Batter (since 1984)

Pitches Best Vs.	Avg	AB	H	2B	3B	HR	RBI	BB	SO	OBP	SLG	Pitches Worst Vs.	Avg	AB	H	2B	3B	HR	RBI	BB	SO	OBP	SLG
Jose Lind	.000	14	0	0	0	0	0	0	1	.000	.000	Ruben Sierra	.667	21	14	4	0	2	7	1	0	.682	1.143
Dave Henderson	.000	13	0	0	0	0	1	0	0	.000	.000	Darrin Jackson	.545	11	6	2	0	1	2	0	1	.545	1.000
Kurt Stillwell	.000	12	0	0	0	0	0	0	5	.000	.000	Pete Incaviglia	.524	21	11	3	0	4	8	2	5	.565	1.238
B.J. Surhoff	.000	10	0	0	0	0	1	0	0	.000	.000	Tim Hulett	.500	20	10	3	0	2	5	2	2	.545	.950
Charlie Leibrandt	.071	14	1	0	0	0	0	0	4	.071	.071	Juan Samuel	.500	16	8	1	0	2	3	1	2	.556	.938

Willie Blair — Astros
Pitches Right

	ERA	W	L	Sv	G	GS	IP	BB	SO	Avg	H	2B	3B	HR	RBI	OBP	SLG	GF	IR	IRS	Hld	SvOp	SB	CS	GB	FB	G/F
1992 Season	4.00	5	7	0	29	8	78.2	25	48	.249	74	16	3	5	46	.309	.374	1	14	5	1	0	6	4	105	89	1.18
Career (1990-1992)	4.57	10	15	0	67	19	183.1	63	104	.277	198	39	7	16	105	.335	.418	10	42	15	2	1	12	7	251	216	1.16

1992 Season

	ERA	W	L	Sv	G	GS	IP	H	HR	BB	SO		Avg	AB	H	2B	3B	HR	RBI	BB	SO	OBP	SLG
Home	2.48	3	2	0	13	3	36.1	30	0	13	27	vs. Left	.250	156	39	8	1	1	17	16	25	.322	.333
Away	5.31	2	5	0	16	5	42.1	44	5	12	21	vs. Right	.248	141	35	8	2	4	29	9	23	.294	.404
Starter	5.40	1	5	0	8	8	38.1	44	2	14	26	Scoring Posn	.324	68	22	6	1	2	40	6	11	.364	.529
Reliever	2.68	4	2	0	21	0	40.1	30	3	11	22	Close & Late	.226	31	7	1	1	1	4	3	5	.294	.419
0 Days rest	4.91	0	1	0	2	0	3.2	2	2	2	2	None on/out	.182	77	14	3	0	2	2	6	9	.241	.299
1 or 2 Days rest	4.41	3	1	0	10	0	16.1	14	1	5	6	First Pitch	.400	40	16	4	1	0	8	2	0	.432	.550
3+ Days rest	0.89	1	0	0	9	0	20.1	14	0	4	14	Behind on Count	.273	66	18	6	0	2	16	17	0	.422	.455
Pre-All Star	4.26	1	4	0	6	4	25.1	31	1	8	16	Ahead on Count	.171	129	22	2	1	1	11	0	42	.174	.225
Post-All Star	3.88	4	3	0	23	4	53.1	43	4	17	32	Two Strikes	.178	135	24	3	2	0	10	6	48	.211	.230

Lance Blankenship — Athletics
Bats Right

	Avg	G	AB	R	H	2B	3B	HR	RBI	BB	SO	HBP	GDP	SB	CS	OBP	SLG	IBB	SH	SF	#Pit	#P/PA	GB	FB	G/F
1992 Season	.241	123	349	59	84	24	1	3	34	82	57	6	10	21	7	.393	.341	2	8	1	1835	4.19	130	108	1.20
Career (1988-1992)	.232	367	798	133	185	40	2	7	69	133	154	9	18	41	13	.346	.313	2	19	5	3833	4.06	271	237	1.14

1992 Season

	Avg	AB	H	2B	3B	HR	RBI	BB	SO	OBP	SLG		Avg	AB	H	2B	3B	HR	RBI	BB	SO	OBP	SLG
vs. Left	.247	89	22	9	0	0	5	30	11	.455	.348	Scoring Posn	.193	88	17	3	0	0	24	26	13	.390	.227
vs. Right	.238	260	62	15	1	3	29	52	46	.368	.338	Close & Late	.288	66	19	3	0	1	7	17	8	.440	.379
Groundball	.250	84	21	8	0	1	9	21	14	.402	.381	None on/out	.167	84	14	5	0	2	2	20	18	.327	.298
Flyball	.253	87	22	4	0	0	11	24	12	.414	.299	Batting #1	.221	77	17	5	1	0	9	21	12	.400	.312
Home	.257	167	43	13	1	1	19	49	24	.439	.365	Batting #9	.266	203	54	15	0	3	20	43	35	.400	.384
Away	.225	182	41	11	0	2	15	33	33	.346	.319	Other	.188	69	13	4	0	0	5	18	10	.364	.246
Day	.235	136	32	7	0	1	12	26	21	.366	.309	April	.250	72	18	3	0	1	8	11	11	.345	.333
Night	.244	213	52	17	1	2	22	56	36	.409	.362	May	.292	72	21	6	0	0	7	19	11	.440	.375
Grass	.248	307	76	22	1	2	33	77	50	.407	.345	June	.214	84	18	6	1	0	6	22	15	.383	.310
Turf	.190	42	8	2	0	1	1	5	7	.277	.310	July	.250	12	3	2	0	0	4	2	1	.400	.417
First Pitch	.208	24	5	0	0	0	2	0	.321	.208	August	.235	51	12	5	0	1	6	9	9	.371	.392
Ahead on Count	.337	98	33	9	0	1	12	38	0	.525	.459	September/October	.207	58	12	2	0	1	3	19	10	.418	.293
Behind on Count	.160	100	16	4	0	1	7	0	29	.176	.230	Pre-All Star	.250	240	60	17	1	2	25	54	38	.391	.342

1992 Season

	Avg	AB	H	2B	3B	HR	RBI	BB	SO	OBP	SLG		Avg	AB	H	2B	3B	HR	RBI	BB	SO	OBP	SLG
Two Strikes	.172	169	29	10	0	2	14	42	57	.343	.266	Post-All Star	.220	109	24	7	0	2	9	28	19	.397	.339

1992 By Position

Position	Avg	AB	H	2B	3B	HR	RBI	BB	SO	OBP	SLG	G	GS	Innings	PO	A	E	DP	Fld Pct	Rng Fctr	In Zone	Outs	Zone Rtg	MLB Zone
As 2b	.223	215	48	14	0	1	18	48	39	.371	.302	78	69	613.2	160	222	3	57	.992	5.60	250	224	.896	.892
As lf	.277	47	13	4	1	0	10	12	5	.424	.404	22	12	114.2	32	0	0	0	1.000	2.51	32	29	.906	.809
As cf	.257	35	9	5	0	1	3	8	5	.395	.486	16	11	108.2	29	0	1	0	.967	2.40	33	28	.848	.824
As rf	.206	34	7	0	0	0	1	7	6	.357	.206	20	10	101.0	29	1	1	0	.968	2.67	32	29	.906	.814

Career (1988-1992)

	Avg	AB	H	2B	3B	HR	RBI	BB	SO	OBP	SLG		Avg	AB	H	2B	3B	HR	RBI	BB	SO	OBP	SLG
vs. Left	.223	269	60	12	0	2	25	49	42	.348	.290	Scoring Posn	.191	204	39	4	0	0	51	36	38	.317	.211
vs. Right	.236	529	125	28	2	5	44	84	112	.345	.325	Close & Late	.224	125	28	6	0	1	7	26	25	.362	.296
Groundball	.249	225	56	14	0	2	20	42	45	.370	.338	None on/out	.198	187	37	7	1	3	3	33	38	.324	.294
Flyball	.251	187	47	8	0	2	24	29	33	.349	.326	Batting #1	.223	130	29	8	1	0	15	30	28	.374	.300
Home	.223	385	86	19	2	2	34	69	74	.347	.299	Batting #9	.239	310	74	18	0	4	24	53	53	.358	.335
Away	.240	413	99	21	0	5	35	64	80	.345	.327	Other	.229	358	82	14	1	3	30	50	73	.324	.299
Day	.217	337	73	13	1	2	21	50	69	.326	.279	April	.219	146	32	3	0	3	19	20	26	.310	.301
Night	.243	461	112	27	1	5	48	83	85	.361	.338	May	.250	136	34	9	0	0	10	30	25	.389	.316
Grass	.235	672	158	36	2	5	61	115	132	.352	.317	June	.210	195	41	12	1	2	13	25	44	.306	.313
Turf	.214	126	27	4	0	2	8	18	22	.315	.294	July	.218	87	19	4	0	0	8	13	17	.327	.264
First Pitch	.288	59	17	5	0	0	4	2	0	.344	.373	August	.238	80	19	6	0	1	8	13	14	.358	.350
Ahead on Count	.296	233	69	12	1	4	28	62	0	.445	.406	September/October	.260	154	40	6	1	1	11	32	26	.391	.331
Behind on Count	.180	244	44	7	0	1	14	0	79	.194	.221	Pre-All Star	.225	506	114	26	1	5	46	80	104	.334	.310
Two Strikes	.154	369	57	15	0	3	24	69	154	.280	.220	Post-All Star	.243	292	71	14	1	2	23	53	50	.365	.318

Batter vs. Pitcher (career)

Hits Best Against	Avg	AB	H	2B	3B	HR	RBI	BB	SO	OBP	SLG	Hits Worst Against	Avg	AB	H	2B	3B	HR	RBI	BB	SO	OBP	SLG
Frank Viola	.333	12	4	2	0	0	0	4	3	.500	.500	John Smiley	.000	9	0	0	0	0	0	0	0	.182	.000
Greg Cadaret	.333	6	2	0	0	0	1	5	0	.636	.333	Randy Johnson	.067	15	1	0	0	0	1	3	0	.222	.067
												Roger Clemens	.077	13	1	0	0	0	0	2	5	.200	.077
												Jaime Navarro	.158	19	3	1	0	0	1	2	2	.238	.211
												Mark Langston	.200	15	3	0	0	0	2	0	5	.200	.200

Jeff Blauser — Braves

Bats Right (flyball hitter)

	Avg	G	AB	R	H	2B	3B	HR	RBI	BB	SO	HBP	GDP	SB	CS	OBP	SLG	IBB	SH	SF	#Pit	#P/PA	GB	FB	G/F
1992 Season	.262	123	343	61	90	19	3	14	46	46	82	4	2	5	5	.354	.458	2	7	3	1622	4.10	93	107	0.87
Last Five Years	.264	527	1604	226	424	84	12	47	192	175	323	13	18	18	19	.339	.420	9	25	11	6901	3.83	493	523	0.94

1992 Season

	Avg	AB	H	2B	3B	HR	RBI	BB	SO	OBP	SLG		Avg	AB	H	2B	3B	HR	RBI	BB	SO	OBP	SLG
vs. Left	.303	142	43	11	1	9	24	25	30	.402	.585	Scoring Posn	.293	75	22	5	1	3	31	14	22	.398	.507
vs. Right	.234	201	47	8	2	5	22	21	52	.317	.368	Close & Late	.164	61	10	2	0	3	8	7	15	.271	.344
Groundball	.281	139	39	8	2	5	19	17	34	.370	.475	None on/out	.308	78	24	5	1	4	4	5	19	.349	.551
Flyball	.275	91	25	7	0	3	10	18	21	.391	.451	Batting #2	.302	199	60	14	2	9	26	31	40	.399	.528
Home	.284	162	46	9	2	5	19	22	36	.380	.457	Batting #7	.289	45	13	2	0	3	6	3	11	.340	.533
Away	.243	181	44	10	1	9	27	24	46	.330	.459	Other	.172	99	17	3	1	2	14	12	31	.265	.283
Day	.255	94	24	3	2	5	15	13	23	.357	.489	April	.180	50	9	1	1	1	6	2	16	.212	.300
Night	.265	249	66	16	1	9	31	33	59	.352	.446	May	.300	50	15	5	1	0	8	5	13	.368	.440
Grass	.278	248	69	14	3	11	33	32	57	.367	.492	June	.152	46	7	1	0	2	5	4	13	.231	.304
Turf	.221	95	21	5	0	3	13	14	25	.318	.368	July	.206	34	7	1	0	4	9	9	11	.372	.588
First Pitch	.273	33	9	4	0	1	5	1	0	.294	.485	August	.329	70	23	3	0	3	7	11	10	.415	.500
Ahead on Count	.413	63	26	7	2	6	15	27	0	.576	.873	September/October	.312	93	29	8	1	4	11	15	19	.418	.548
Behind on Count	.257	113	29	4	2	6	19	0	32	.274	.487	Pre-All Star	.222	162	36	7	2	7	26	16	46	.297	.420
Two Strikes	.188	181	34	5	1	6	18	18	82	.265	.326	Post-All Star	.298	181	54	12	1	7	20	30	36	.402	.492

1992 By Position

Position	Avg	AB	H	2B	3B	HR	RBI	BB	SO	OBP	SLG	G	GS	Innings	PO	A	E	DP	Fld Pct	Rng Fctr	In Zone	Outs	Zone Rtg	MLB Zone
As Pinch Hitter	.125	16	2	1	0	0	2	5	6	.364	.188	23	0	---	---	---	---	---	---	---	---	---	---	---
As 2b	.234	64	15	3	2	1	8	2	17	.269	.391	21	18	136.0	32	42	5	8	.937	4.90	48	43	.896	.892
As ss	.276	261	72	15	1	13	36	39	58	.370	.490	106	72	587.2	87	182	9	28	.968	4.12	221	192	.869	.885

Last Five Years

	Avg	AB	H	2B	3B	HR	RBI	BB	SO	OBP	SLG		Avg	AB	H	2B	3B	HR	RBI	BB	SO	OBP	SLG
vs. Left	.294	629	185	42	6	21	87	87	109	.378	.480	Scoring Posn	.287	345	99	22	4	8	136	58	76	.385	.443
vs. Right	.245	975	239	42	6	26	105	88	214	.314	.381	Close & Late	.222	311	69	12	3	12	38	25	75	.284	.395
Groundball	.291	561	163	33	4	12	63	53	90	.355	.428	None on/out	.281	385	108	24	2	14	14	23	65	.321	.462
Flyball	.234	432	101	25	5	13	46	46	101	.310	.405	Batting #2	.266	538	143	32	4	17	54	71	105	.354	.435
Home	.273	765	209	41	5	22	96	91	144	.355	.426	Batting #6	.249	358	89	13	3	12	49	40	70	.324	.402
Away	.256	839	215	43	7	25	96	84	179	.325	.414	Other	.271	708	192	39	5	18	89	64	148	.336	.417
Day	.253	392	99	12	4	12	47	43	87	.332	.395	April	.220	186	41	6	2	2	16	9	37	.256	.306
Night	.268	1212	325	72	8	35	145	132	236	.342	.427	May	.264	174	46	13	4	6	27	24	44	.356	.489

42

Last Five Years

	Avg	AB	H	2B	3B	HR	RBI	BB	SO	OBP	SLG		Avg	AB	H	2B	3B	HR	RBI	BB	SO	OBP	SLG
Grass	.260	1187	309	61	9	39	147	136	230	.340	.425	June	.273	269	79	20	2	7	40	26	55	.342	.429
Turf	.276	417	115	23	3	8	45	39	93	.337	.403	July	.245	265	65	11	1	9	35	37	55	.337	.396
First Pitch	.346	208	72	17	1	7	27	6	0	.369	.538	August	.281	303	85	13	0	10	31	37	52	.360	.422
Ahead on Count	.359	362	130	27	4	19	69	98	0	.494	.613	September/October	.279	387	108	21	3	13	43	40	80	.353	.450
Behind on Count	.219	544	119	28	5	12	46	1	172	.228	.355	Pre-All Star	.260	722	188	42	8	22	98	70	152	.328	.432
Two Strikes	.163	774	126	25	4	14	57	68	323	.232	.260	Post-All Star	.268	682	236	42	4	25	94	105	171	.348	.409

Batter vs. Pitcher (career)

Hits Best Against	Avg	AB	H	2B	3B	HR	RBI	BB	SO	OBP	SLG	Hits Worst Against	Avg	AB	H	2B	3B	HR	RBI	BB	SO	OBP	SLG
Bobby Ojeda	.500	18	9	2	0	0	4	2	1	.550	.611	Danny Darwin	.000	14	0	0	0	0	0	3	5	.176	.000
Mark Portugal	.462	13	6	0	0	3	5	1	2	.500	1.154	David Cone	.077	13	1	0	0	0	0	2	6	.200	.077
Danny Jackson	.381	21	8	0	1	1	4	3	3	.458	.619	Jose DeLeon	.091	11	1	0	0	0	0	1	2	.167	.091
Jeff Brantley	.364	11	4	1	0	1	3	1	1	.417	.727	Dennis Cook	.091	11	1	0	0	0	0	0	1	.091	.091
Rich Rodriguez	.364	11	4	3	0	0	1	2	0	.462	.636	Andy Benes	.136	22	3	0	0	0	1	1	4	.167	.136

Mike Blowers — Mariners

Bats Right (groundball hitter)

	Avg	G	AB	R	H	2B	3B	HR	RBI	BB	SO	HBP	GDP	SB	CS	OBP	SLG	IBB	SH	SF	#Pit	#P/PA	GB	FB	G/F
1992 Season	.192	31	73	7	14	3	0	1	2	6	20	1	0	3	0	.253	.274	0	1	0	302	3.82	31	15	2.07
Career (1989-1992)	.200	107	290	28	58	7	0	7	27	25	86	1	6	1	0	.266	.297	2	0	1	1221	3.86	102	59	1.73

1992 Season

	Avg	AB	H	2B	3B	HR	RBI	BB	SO	OBP	SLG		Avg	AB	H	2B	3B	HR	RBI	BB	SO	OBP	SLG
vs. Left	.130	23	3	1	0	0	0	2	6	.200	.174	Scoring Posn	.063	16	1	0	0	0	0	2	6	.167	.063
vs. Right	.220	50	11	2	0	1	2	4	14	.278	.320	Close & Late	.100	10	1	0	0	0	0	2	3	.250	.200

Bert Blyleven — Angels

Pitches Right

	ERA	W	L	Sv	G	GS	IP	BB	SO	Avg	H	2B	3B	HR	RBI	OBP	SLG	CG	ShO	Sup	QS	#P/S	SB	CS	GB	FB	G/F
1992 Season	4.74	8	12	0	25	24	133.0	29	70	.285	150	24	3	17	71	.326	.439	1	0	3.72	13	80	10	4	176	163	1.08
Last Five Years	4.35	43	41	0	114	113	715.1	149	415	.279	778	126	17	67	335	.321	.409	18	5	4.52	60	90	60	26	1003	836	1.20

1992 Season

	ERA	W	L	Sv	G	GS	IP	H	HR	BB	SO		Avg	AB	H	2B	3B	HR	RBI	BB	SO	OBP	SLG
Home	4.31	4	6	0	11	11	64.2	67	5	17	36	vs. Left	.261	253	66	10	2	6	26	17	38	.305	.387
Away	5.14	4	6	0	14	13	68.1	83	12	12	34	vs. Right	.308	273	84	14	1	11	45	12	32	.345	.487
Starter	4.77	8	12	0	24	24	132.0	149	17	29	70	Scoring Posn	.346	130	45	9	1	3	55	9	15	.379	.500
Reliever	0.00	0	0	0	1	0	1.0	1	0	0	0	Close & Late	.318	22	7	2	0	0	2	1	4	.348	.409
0-3 Days Rest	0.00	0	0	0	0	0	0.0	0	0	0	0	None on/out	.292	144	42	8	1	7	7	5	17	.315	.507
4 Days Rest	5.82	4	6	0	11	11	55.2	74	9	11	28	First Pitch	.398	83	33	6	0	4	15	2	0	.412	.614
5+ Days Rest	4.01	4	6	0	13	13	76.1	75	8	18	42	Behind on Count	.336	125	42	7	0	5	26	14	0	.392	.512
Pre-All Star	5.21	3	3	0	10	9	46.2	52	9	12	33	Ahead on Count	.196	230	45	3	2	1	14	0	58	.209	.239
Post-All Star	4.48	5	9	0	15	15	86.1	98	8	17	37	Two Strikes	.175	206	36	3	2	2	19	13	70	.230	.238

Last Five Years

	ERA	W	L	Sv	G	GS	IP	H	HR	BB	SO		Avg	AB	H	2B	3B	HR	RBI	BB	SO	OBP	SLG
Home	4.12	22	18	0	56	56	362.2	381	29	81	220	vs. Left	.281	1450	407	63	10	26	157	87	207	.324	.396
Away	4.59	21	23	0	58	57	352.2	397	38	68	195	vs. Right	.277	1337	371	63	7	39	178	62	208	.319	.423
Day	5.86	9	14	0	31	30	170.1	208	22	38	113	Inning 1-6	.280	2421	677	106	14	61	299	125	349	.321	.411
Night	3.88	34	27	0	83	83	545.0	570	45	111	302	Inning 7+	.276	366	101	20	3	6	36	24	66	.323	.396
Grass	4.14	28	25	0	77	76	481.0	528	46	91	254	None on	.265	1661	440	80	9	39	39	75	249	.304	.394
Turf	4.80	15	16	0	37	37	234.1	250	21	58	161	Runners on	.300	1126	338	46	8	28	296	74	166	.346	.430
April	5.31	4	5	0	14	14	83.0	95	14	17	52	Scoring Posn	.311	659	205	30	6	14	259	51	113	.358	.439
May	2.85	8	5	0	21	20	139.0	136	9	33	85	Close & Late	.272	136	37	4	1	2	14	11	29	.329	.360
June	3.78	12	4	0	22	22	143.0	148	12	25	97	None on/out	.280	726	203	33	3	18	18	26	90	.315	.408
July	6.61	5	11	0	23	23	126.2	166	18	29	63	vs. 1st Batr (relief)	.000	1	0	0	0	0	0	0	0	.000	.000
August	3.09	9	4	0	16	16	105.0	92	8	25	56	First Inning Pitched	.309	443	137	21	1	19	74	24	67	.349	.490
September/October	4.85	5	12	0	18	18	118.2	139	6	20	62	First 75 Pitches	.281	2231	628	97	11	54	267	120	320	.325	.407
Starter	4.36	43	41	0	113	113	714.1	777	67	149	415	Pitch 76-90	.244	308	75	16	1	6	26	11	50	.272	.360
Reliever	0.00	0	0	0	1	0	1.0	1	0	0	0	Pitch 91-105	.306	170	52	8	3	5	29	12	26	.353	.476
0-3 Days Rest	4.02	3	3	0	7	7	47.0	59	4	8	29	Pitch 106+	.295	78	23	5	2	2	13	6	19	.345	.487
4 Days Rest	4.42	26	24	0	65	65	413.2	444	34	86	256	First Pitch	.371	469	174	27	1	20	83	3	0	.379	.561
5+ Days Rest	4.33	14	14	0	41	41	253.2	274	29	55	130	Ahead on Count	.204	1227	250	26	3	12	83	0	359	.217	.259
Pre-All Star	4.01	25	17	0	65	64	410.1	439	39	82	259	Behind on Count	.334	643	215	47	6	17	107	80	0	.404	.505
Post-All Star	4.81	18	24	0	49	49	305.0	339	28	67	156	Two Strikes	.182	1101	200	24	5	9	69	66	415	.238	.237

Pitcher vs. Batter (since 1984)

Pitches Best Vs.	Avg	AB	H	2B	3B	HR	RBI	BB	SO	OBP	SLG	Pitches Worst Vs.	Avg	AB	H	2B	3B	HR	RBI	BB	SO	OBP	SLG
Don Slaught	.056	36	2	0	0	0	1	0	9	.056	.056	Eddie Murray	.432	37	16	1	0	6	8	4	4	.488	.946
Mike Pagliarulo	.065	31	2	0	0	0	1	2	5	.121	.065	Wally Joyner	.419	31	13	3	0	2	4	2	3	.455	.710
Greg Briley	.071	14	1	0	0	0	0	0	5	.071	.071	Mel Hall	.394	33	13	3	0	3	6	4	5	.447	.758
Tim Hulett	.083	12	1	0	0	0	1	0	2	.077	.083	Lance Parrish	.370	27	10	0	0	3	8	4	5	.452	.704
Bill Spiers	.083	12	1	0	0	0	0	0	5	.083	.083	Kent Hrbek	.333	30	10	1	0	1	4	7	1	.394	.800

Mike Boddicker — Royals
Pitches Right

	ERA	W	L	Sv	G	GS	IP	BB	SO	Avg	H	2B	3B	HR	RBI	OBP	SLG	GF	IR	IRS	Hld	SvOp	SB	CS	GB	FB	G/F
1992 Season	4.98	1	4	3	29	8	86.2	37	47	.270	92	22	2	5	53	.352	.390	8	16	10	1	3	13	2	137	92	1.49
Last Five Years	3.80	58	50	3	163	140	943.0	313	570	.265	956	179	22	70	374	.330	.384	9	19	10	2	3	84	41	1380	1011	1.36

1992 Season

	ERA	W	L	Sv	G	GS	IP	H	HR	BB	SO		Avg	AB	H	2B	3B	HR	RBI	BB	SO	OBP	SLG
Home	5.70	1	2	0	12	4	36.1	42	1	17	16	vs. Left	.292	168	49	6	2	2	25	16	16	.355	.387
Away	4.47	0	2	3	17	4	50.1	50	4	20	31	vs. Right	.249	173	43	16	0	3	28	21	31	.350	.393
Starter	6.69	0	4	0	8	8	39.0	48	2	16	18	Scoring Posn	.288	118	34	8	2	3	50	15	22	.379	.466
Reliever	3.59	1	0	3	21	0	47.2	44	3	21	29	Close & Late	.292	24	7	0	0	1	4	4	3	.379	.417
0 Days rest	0.00	0	0	0	0	0	0.0	0	0	0	0	None on/out	.333	78	26	8	0	0	0	10	8	.409	.436
1 or 2 Days rest	2.70	1	0	2	11	0	23.1	23	1	8	15	First Pitch	.362	47	17	3	0	1	10	3	0	.385	.489
3+ Days rest	4.44	0	0	1	10	0	24.1	21	2	13	14	Behind on Count	.322	87	28	11	2	1	20	22	0	.469	.529
Pre-All Star	4.37	0	4	3	23	6	70.0	72	2	30	38	Ahead on Count	.221	140	31	6	0	2	18	0	38	.232	.307
Post-All Star	7.56	1	0	0	6	2	16.2	20	3	7	9	Two Strikes	.185	146	27	6	0	2	17	12	47	.256	.267

Last Five Years

	ERA	W	L	Sv	G	GS	IP	H	HR	BB	SO		Avg	AB	H	2B	3B	HR	RBI	BB	SO	OBP	SLG
Home	3.87	33	29	0	82	72	493.0	526	29	143	299	vs. Left	.278	1892	526	93	16	36	206	158	202	.338	.401
Away	3.72	25	21	3	81	68	450.0	430	41	170	271	vs. Right	.250	1721	430	86	6	34	168	155	368	.322	.366
Day	4.12	17	15	2	49	41	253.1	272	22	99	156	Inning 1-6	.270	2994	808	163	19	58	337	264	466	.335	.395
Night	3.68	41	35	1	114	99	689.2	684	48	214	414	Inning 7+	.239	619	148	16	3	12	37	49	104	.309	.333
Grass	3.72	44	33	3	115	103	674.1	689	54	226	435	None on	.269	2072	558	110	14	39	39	165	327	.330	.392
Turf	3.99	14	17	0	48	37	268.2	267	16	87	135	Runners on	.258	1541	398	69	8	31	335	148	243	.330	.374
April	5.01	5	14	0	25	21	125.2	133	7	48	77	Scoring Posn	.240	881	211	38	6	14	287	97	160	.321	.344
May	4.06	9	8	1	28	22	161.2	152	15	59	103	Close & Late	.208	259	54	6	1	4	18	20	44	.275	.286
June	3.49	10	8	1	30	24	178.0	173	11	51	98	None on/out	.267	930	248	49	5	18	18	71	144	.327	.388
July	3.95	11	6	1	27	25	164.0	181	14	54	90	vs. 1st Batr (relief)	.286	21	6	2	0	0	5	2	3	.348	.381
August	2.93	11	9	0	26	23	166.0	171	15	49	108	First Inning Pitched	.235	515	121	28	4	12	61	44	75	.300	.375
September/October	3.66	12	5	0	27	25	147.2	146	8	52	94	First 15 Pitches	.257	560	144	35	4	9	44	44	68	.319	.382
Starter	3.81	56	50	0	140	140	893.1	911	67	291	541	Pitch 16-30	.270	555	150	27	3	15	69	61	95	.351	.411
Reliever	3.62	2	0	3	23	0	49.2	45	3	22	29	Pitch 31-45	.275	530	146	25	1	9	59	41	93	.332	.377
0 Days rest	0.00	0	0	0	0	0	0.0	0	0	0	0	Pitch 46+	.262	1968	516	92	14	37	202	167	314	.327	.380
1 or 2 Days rest	2.84	2	0	2	13	0	25.1	24	1	9	15	First Pitch	.338	520	176	31	1	16	71	13	0	.362	.494
3+ Days rest	4.44	0	0	1	10	0	24.1	21	2	13	14	Ahead on Count	.197	1486	293	53	7	14	115	0	480	.209	.271
Pre-All Star	4.06	28	33	3	93	75	526.0	513	38	175	315	Behind on Count	.322	918	296	51	11	24	121	146	0	.419	.480
Post-All Star	3.47	30	17	0	70	65	417.0	443	32	138	255	Two Strikes	.181	1517	275	62	5	12	104	154	570	.265	.252

Pitcher vs. Batter (since 1984)

Pitches Best Vs.	Avg	AB	H	2B	3B	HR	RBI	BB	SO	OBP	SLG	Pitches Worst Vs.	Avg	AB	H	2B	3B	HR	RBI	BB	SO	OBP	SLG
Jack Clark	.000	16	0	0	0	0	0	1	7	.059	.000	Darryl Hamilton	.545	11	6	1	1	0	1	1	0	.583	.818
Mike Felder	.067	15	1	0	0	0	1	1	0	.125	.067	Lance Johnson	.500	16	8	0	2	0	6	0	1	.500	.750
Steve Finley	.071	14	1	0	0	0	0	2	0	.188	.071	Jay Buhner	.500	12	6	4	0	1	3	3	3	.647	1.083
Jamie Quirk	.091	11	1	0	0	0	0	1	1	.167	.091	Fred McGriff	.480	25	12	2	0	2	3	1	3	.500	.800
Cecil Espy	.091	11	1	0	0	0	0	2	.091	.091	Geno Petralli	.444	36	16	4	0	2	3	4	5	.500	.722

Joe Boever — Astros
Pitches Right

	ERA	W	L	Sv	G	GS	IP	BB	SO	Avg	H	2B	3B	HR	RBI	OBP	SLG	GF	IR	IRS	Hld	SvOp	SB	CS	GB	FB	G/F
1992 Season	2.51	3	6	2	81	0	111.1	45	67	.248	103	13	2	3	41	.324	.310	26	61	10	7	6	7	5	145	127	1.14
Last Five Years	3.28	13	30	38	298	0	400.2	185	306	.242	360	59	7	26	179	.325	.343	87	168	43	21	58	44	18	468	462	1.01

1992 Season

	ERA	W	L	Sv	G	GS	IP	H	HR	BB	SO		Avg	AB	H	2B	3B	HR	RBI	BB	SO	OBP	SLG
Home	1.32	1	2	1	44	0	61.1	55	2	19	37	vs. Left	.242	186	45	7	2	1	20	28	30	.346	.317
Away	3.96	2	4	1	37	0	50.0	48	1	26	30	vs. Right	.252	230	58	6	0	2	21	17	37	.306	.304
Day	2.87	1	1	0	25	0	31.1	35	0	19	21	Inning 1-6	.208	125	26	1	0	1	12	12	25	.286	.240
Night	2.36	2	5	2	56	0	80.0	68	3	26	46	Inning 7+	.265	291	77	12	2	2	29	33	42	.340	.340
Grass	5.46	0	3	0	19	0	28.0	32	1	17	16	None on	.288	191	55	7	1	3	3	19	27	.355	.382
Turf	1.51	3	3	2	62	0	83.1	71	2	28	51	Runners on	.213	225	48	6	1	0	38	26	40	.298	.249
April	0.00	0	0	0	9	0	13.2	6	0	6	10	Scoring Posn	.226	133	30	5	1	0	38	21	26	.331	.278
May	3.09	1	1	1	20	0	23.1	22	0	10	11	Close & Late	.270	141	38	8	0	1	14	18	14	.352	.348
June	4.43	1	2	0	12	0	20.1	23	0	8	8	None on/out	.290	93	27	4	0	1	1	6	11	.340	.366
July	2.20	0	1	0	15	0	16.1	21	1	7	11	vs. 1st Batr (relief)	.205	73	15	0	0	2	5	3	10	.263	.288
August	2.87	1	2	0	11	0	15.2	11	1	6	11	First Inning Pitched	.224	254	57	7	0	2	24	27	41	.302	.276
September/October	1.64	0	0	1	14	0	22.0	20	1	8	16	First 15 Pitches	.225	258	58	4	0	3	16	23	34	.293	.275
Starter	0.00	0	0	0	0	0	0.0	0	0	0	0	Pitch 16-30	.277	130	36	7	2	0	17	20	29	.375	.362
Reliever	2.51	3	6	2	81	0	111.1	103	3	45	67	Pitch 31-45	.346	26	9	2	0	0	8	2	3	.393	.423
0 Days rest	3.82	0	2	2	26	0	30.2	32	0	13	19	Pitch 46+	.000	2	0	0	0	0	0	0	1	.000	.000
1 or 2 Days rest	1.83	2	3	0	45	0	69.0	62	3	28	39	First Pitch	.265	68	18	2	0	0	6	7	0	.338	.294
3+ Days rest	3.09	1	1	0	10	0	11.2	9	0	4	9	Ahead on Count	.187	187	35	4	0	0	14	0	56	.188	.209
Pre-All Star	2.77	2	4	1	47	0	65.0	62	0	26	32	Behind on Count	.263	80	21	3	1	2	8	24	0	.433	.400
Post-All Star	2.14	1	2	1	34	0	46.1	41	3	19	35	Two Strikes	.192	177	34	5	0	1	16	14	67	.254	.220

Last Five Years

	ERA	W	L	Sv	G	GS	IP	H	HR	BB	SO		Avg	AB	H	2B	3B	HR	RBI	BB	SO	OBP	SLG
Home	2.81	9	13	16	165	0	234.0	200	10	96	175	vs. Left	.230	749	172	25	5	8	87	115	154	.332	.308
Away	3.94	4	17	22	133	0	166.2	160	16	87	131	vs. Right	.254	741	188	34	2	18	92	70	152	.319	.378
Day	4.54	2	7	11	82	0	107.0	111	11	57	85	Inning 1-6	.230	213	49	5	1	5	31	22	45	.303	.333
Night	2.82	11	23	27	216	0	293.2	249	15	126	221	Inning 7+	.244	1277	311	54	6	21	148	163	261	.329	.345
Grass	3.69	7	16	18	135	0	180.2	165	14	84	141	None on	.253	770	195	28	3	20	20	79	155	.324	.375
Turf	2.95	6	14	20	163	0	220.0	195	12	101	165	Runners on	.229	720	165	31	4	6	159	106	151	.327	.308
April	2.70	2	3	5	37	0	56.2	42	4	29	48	Scoring Posn	.232	431	100	24	2	4	147	89	91	.359	.325
May	2.93	5	6	9	53	0	70.2	62	4	31	54	Close & Late	.239	670	160	30	2	12	71	100	139	.338	.343
June	5.46	1	4	6	47	0	64.1	67	5	46	50	None on/out	.243	341	83	12	2	9	9	29	61	.306	.370
July	1.86	2	2	9	49	0	58.0	48	1	24	33	vs. 1st Batr (relief)	.227	269	61	11	3	6	24	23	45	.293	.357
August	3.75	2	7	5	56	0	74.1	72	8	34	56	First Inning Pitched	.239	967	236	41	4	15	126	118	198	.320	.334
September/October	2.82	1	8	4	56	0	76.2	69	4	21	65	First 15 Pitches	.244	894	218	32	4	14	92	91	156	.313	.336
Starter	0.00	0	0	0	0	0	0.0	0	0	0	0	Pitch 16-30	.237	443	105	20	2	10	62	78	105	.352	.359
Reliever	3.28	13	30	38	298	0	400.2	360	26	185	306	Pitch 31-45	.234	128	30	7	1	2	23	13	39	.306	.352
0 Days rest	3.38	3	13	14	82	0	109.1	93	7	47	93	Pitch 46+	.280	25	7	0	0	0	2	3	6	.357	.280
1 or 2 Days rest	2.81	7	13	17	148	0	205.1	194	15	89	148	First Pitch	.314	207	65	14	0	2	32	27	0	.389	.411
3+ Days rest	4.29	3	4	7	68	0	86.0	73	4	49	65	Ahead on Count	.183	727	133	18	2	7	60	1	258	.185	.242
Pre-All Star	3.57	8	15	24	152	0	211.2	187	13	114	163	Behind on Count	.312	262	88	16	3	11	49	86	0	.469	.507
Post-All Star	2.95	5	15	14	146	0	189.0	173	13	71	143	Two Strikes	.166	736	122	18	1	8	65	69	306	.239	.226

Pitcher vs. Batter (career)

Pitches Best Vs.	Avg	AB	H	2B	3B	HR	RBI	BB	SO	OBP	SLG	Pitches Worst Vs.	Avg	AB	H	2B	3B	HR	RBI	BB	SO	OBP	SLG
Jose Uribe	.000	11	0	0	0	0	0	0	2	.000	.000	Eddie Murray	.556	9	5	1	0	1	6	3	0	.667	1.000
Robby Thompson	.056	18	1	0	0	0	2	5	4	.261	.056	Billy Hatcher	.538	13	7	2	0	1	3	2	0	.600	.923
Luis Salazar	.083	12	1	0	0	0	1	0	3	.077	.083	Felix Jose	.500	8	4	1	0	1	2	3	0	.636	1.000
Tom Foley	.091	11	1	0	0	0	0	1	5	.167	.091	Pedro Guerrero	.375	8	3	0	0	2	3	3	0	.545	1.125
Joe Oliver	.091	11	1	0	0	0	0	1	3	.167	.091	Hubie Brooks	.375	8	3	2	0	1	3	2	3	.455	1.000

Wade Boggs — Red Sox

Bats Left (groundball hitter)

	Avg	G	AB	R	H	2B	3B	HR	RBI	BB	SO	HBP	GDP	SB	CS	OBP	SLG	IBB	SH	SF	#Pit	#P/PA	GB	FB	G/F
1992 Season	.259	143	514	62	133	22	4	7	50	74	31	4	10	1	3	.353	.358	19	0	6	2277	3.81	241	128	1.88
Last Five Years	.319	753	2684	485	920	204	24	29	276	482	216	15	82	6	14	.415	.437	100	0	32	13905	4.07	1296	688	1.88

1992 Season

	Avg	AB	H	2B	3B	HR	RBI	BB	SO	OBP	SLG		Avg	AB	H	2B	3B	HR	RBI	BB	SO	OBP	SLG
vs. Left	.272	158	43	10	1	1	21	12	13	.326	.367	Scoring Posn	.311	106	33	6	0	2	44	35	7	.463	.425
vs. Right	.253	356	90	12	3	6	29	62	18	.364	.354	Close & Late	.322	90	29	8	0	0	10	16	8	.426	.411
Groundball	.235	136	32	5	0	1	16	13	9	.298	.294	None on/out	.254	142	36	6	1	1	1	12	6	.316	.331
Flyball	.292	144	42	7	3	4	13	20	12	.380	.465	Batting #1	.222	221	49	11	2	1	18	31	12	.315	.303
Home	.243	251	61	13	3	4	26	48	12	.366	.367	Batting #3	.287	289	83	11	2	6	32	40	19	.377	.401
Away	.274	263	72	9	1	3	24	26	19	.339	.350	Other	.250	4	1	0	0	0	0	3	0	.571	.250
Day	.259	193	50	5	0	1	12	31	11	.364	.301	April	.253	75	19	4	0	0	5	13	6	.360	.307
Night	.259	321	83	17	4	6	38	43	20	.346	.393	May	.291	86	25	7	0	3	10	13	3	.380	.477
Grass	.254	437	111	19	4	6	39	66	27	.353	.357	June	.242	95	23	3	1	3	9	17	4	.363	.389
Turf	.286	77	22	3	0	1	11	8	4	.353	.364	July	.304	79	24	2	0	0	8	9	3	.371	.380
First Pitch	.379	29	11	2	0	0	2	18	0	.625	.448	August	.198	96	19	3	1	1	11	12	4	.286	.281
Ahead on Count	.290	169	49	10	2	3	21	36	0	.415	.426	September/October	.277	83	23	3	0	0	7	10	11	.368	.313
Behind on Count	.242	157	38	7	0	2	15	1	16	.256	.325	Pre-All Star	.263	278	73	14	2	6	27	46	13	.366	.392
Two Strikes	.197	213	42	5	1	2	14	21	31	.273	.318	Post-All Star	.254	236	60	8	2	1	23	28	18	.337	.318

1992 By Position

Position	Avg	AB	H	2B	3B	HR	RBI	BB	SO	OBP	SLG	G	GS	Innings	PO	A	E	DP	Fld Pct	Rng Fctr	In Zone	Outs	Zone Rtg	MLB Zone
As Designated Hitter	.263	76	20	1	1	1	2	11	4	.352	.342	21	21	---	---	---	---	---	---	---	---	---	---	---
As 3b	.260	434	113	21	3	6	48	60	27	.352	.364	117	114	993.2	70	230	15	22	.952	2.72	294	255	.867	.841

Last Five Years

	Avg	AB	H	2B	3B	HR	RBI	BB	SO	OBP	SLG		Avg	AB	H	2B	3B	HR	RBI	BB	SO	OBP	SLG
vs. Left	.288	935	269	51	8	6	100	114	102	.367	.379	Scoring Posn	.326	576	188	38	4	5	232	197	51	.481	.432
vs. Right	.334	1949	651	153	16	23	176	368	114	.437	.464	Close & Late	.287	432	124	24	3	2	34	75	53	.394	.370
Groundball	.319	742	237	48	3	8	79	102	46	.400	.425	None on/out	.319	977	312	71	10	10	117	61		.394	.431
Flyball	.306	720	220	52	10	6	64	118	74	.403	.431	Batting #1	.320	1844	590	135	16	18	157	323	139	.420	.440
Home	.352	1397	492	137	13	19	152	280	105	.459	.510	Batting #3	.317	1030	326	69	8	11	117	155	76	.405	.431
Away	.288	1487	428	67	11	10	124	202	111	.371	.368	Other	.400	10	4	0	0	0	2	4	1	.571	.400
Day	.314	970	305	58	4	9	85	167	76	.415	.410	April	.296	385	114	27	0	4	35	78	35	.413	.397
Night	.321	1914	615	146	20	20	191	315	140	.415	.450	May	.315	457	144	35	7	7	49	87	37	.422	.468
Grass	.322	2420	779	180	21	27	235	417	185	.420	.447	June	.313	496	155	35	4	8	59	81	30	.409	.448
Turf	.304	464	141	24	3	2	41	65	31	.388	.381	July	.350	492	172	41	8	4	49	75	35	.430	.490
First Pitch	.395	129	51	13	0	0	15	53	0	.574	.496	August	.319	565	180	32	4	3	44	74	41	.399	.405
Ahead on Count	.384	800	307	76	9	15	97	242	0	.524	.558	September/October	.317	489	155	34	1	3	40	87	38	.421	.409
Behind on Count	.273	905	247	50	1	5	71	7	94	.281	.347	Pre-All Star	.316	1497	473	109	13	20	158	271	115	.419	.446
Two Strikes	.260	1362	354	68	8	8	94	162	216	.338	.339	Post-All Star	.322	1387	447	95	11	9	118	211	101	.411	.426

Hits Best Against	Avg	AB	H	2B	3B	HR	RBI	BB	SO	OBP	SLG	Hits Worst Against	Avg	AB	H	2B	3B	HR	RBI	BB	SO	OBP	SLG
Jose Rijo	.467	15	7	2	0	0	4	4	1	.579	.600	Bob Welch	.037	27	1	1	0	0	0	3	2	.133	.074
Mark Williamson	.467	15	7	1	0	1	3	2	1	.529	.733	Matt Young	.091	22	2	0	0	0	3	1	5	.130	.091
Walt Terrell	.433	60	26	8	1	2	8	4	2	.469	.700	Mike Mussina	.091	11	1	1	0	0	0	0	1	.091	.182
Jeff Russell	.385	13	5	2	0	1	1	4	1	.529	.769	Scott Sanderson	.125	24	3	1	0	0	0	1	2	.160	.167
Steve Olin	.364	11	4	0	0	2	4	2	1	.462	.909	Randy Johnson	.125	16	2	0	0	0	0	1	8	.176	.125

Brian Bohanon — Rangers   Pitches Left

	ERA	W	L	Sv	G	GS	IP	BB	SO	Avg	H	2B	3B	HR	RBI	OBP	SLG	GF	IR	IRS	Hld	SvOp	SB	CS	GB	FB	G/F
1992 Season	6.31	1	1	0	18	7	45.2	25	29	.297	57	7	2	7	38	.377	.464	3	17	8	0	0	0	3	69	55	1.25
Career (1990-1992)	5.74	5	7	0	40	24	141.0	66	78	.287	163	26	3	17	94	.361	.434	4	20	10	0	0	6	5	206	190	1.08

1992 Season

	ERA	W	L	Sv	G	GS	IP	H	HR	BB	SO		Avg	AB	H	2B	3B	HR	RBI	BB	SO	OBP	SLG
Home	4.94	1	1	0	8	4	27.1	27	3	15	16	vs. Left	.235	34	8	0	0	1	11	5	5	.325	.324
Away	8.35	0	0	0	10	3	18.1	30	4	10	13	vs. Right	.310	158	49	7	2	6	27	20	24	.389	.494

Tom Bolton — Reds   Pitches Left (groundball pitcher)

	ERA	W	L	Sv	G	GS	IP	BB	SO	Avg	H	2B	3B	HR	RBI	OBP	SLG	GF	IR	IRS	Hld	SvOp	SB	CS	GB	FB	G/F
1992 Season	4.54	4	5	0	37	9	75.1	37	50	.285	86	12	2	9	32	.369	.427	9	21	5	0	0	5	1	142	63	2.25
Last Five Years	4.57	23	26	1	115	48	352.2	159	209	.282	358	65	8	33	171	.356	.412	15	94	36	6	1	21	8	592	332	1.78

1992 Season

	ERA	W	L	Sv	G	GS	IP	H	HR	BB	SO		Avg	AB	H	2B	3B	HR	RBI	BB	SO	OBP	SLG
Home	4.98	2	3	0	19	5	47.0	50	6	22	31	vs. Left	.256	82	21	2	2	1	8	10	21	.344	.366
Away	3.81	2	2	0	18	4	28.1	36	3	15	19	vs. Right	.295	220	65	10	0	8	24	27	29	.378	.450
Starter	5.16	2	4	0	9	9	45.1	52	8	17	30	Scoring Posn	.214	84	18	2	0	2	22	16	19	.350	.310
Reliever	3.60	2	1	0	28	0	30.0	34	1	20	20	Close & Late	.275	40	11	2	0	0	2	8	6	.408	.325
0 Days rest	9.00	0	0	0	1	0	1.0	1	0	1	1	None on/out	.373	75	28	4	2	3	3	7	10	.427	.600
1 or 2 Days rest	2.45	1	0	0	11	0	11.0	13	1	6	9	First Pitch	.412	34	14	0	0	4	8	2	0	.444	.765
3+ Days rest	4.00	1	1	0	16	0	18.0	20	0	13	10	Behind on Count	.398	88	35	7	0	3	16	17	0	.495	.580
Pre-All Star	3.38	1	2	0	23	1	32.0	36	0	19	25	Ahead on Count	.197	122	24	2	2	1	5	0	42	.216	.270
Post-All Star	5.40	3	3	0	14	8	43.1	50	9	18	25	Two Strikes	.140	114	16	2	0	1	7	18	50	.269	.184

Last Five Years

	ERA	W	L	Sv	G	GS	IP	H	HR	BB	SO		Avg	AB	H	2B	3B	HR	RBI	BB	SO	OBP	SLG
Home	3.82	14	10	1	53	22	186.0	197	18	68	108	vs. Left	.255	330	84	16	3	4	41	29	57	.316	.358
Away	5.40	9	16	0	62	26	166.2	192	15	91	101	vs. Right	.290	1051	305	49	5	29	130	130	152	.369	.429
Day	4.64	7	11	1	37	16	116.1	140	9	39	72	Inning 1-6	.274	997	273	40	6	24	106	117	158	.351	.398
Night	4.53	16	15	0	78	32	236.1	249	24	120	137	Inning 7+	.302	384	116	25	2	9	45	42	51	.370	.448
Grass	4.47	19	21	1	89	37	273.2	310	25	118	164	None on	.270	762	206	32	4	16	16	78	114	.340	.386
Turf	4.90	4	5	0	26	11	79.0	79	8	41	45	Runners on	.296	619	183	33	4	17	155	81	95	.376	.444
April	3.00	2	1	0	5	2	21.0	21	0	6	10	Scoring Posn	.281	345	97	17	2	9	132	57	59	.375	.420
May	4.43	4	2	0	14	6	44.2	46	8	23	34	Close & Late	.362	130	47	8	0	3	15	17	15	.436	.492
June	5.80	2	4	0	17	6	40.1	60	4	20	23	None on/out	.285	351	100	15	3	10	10	33	51	.346	.430
July	2.56	6	6	0	29	9	88.0	90	7	38	48	vs. 1st Batr (relief)	.321	56	18	5	2	0	12	9	11	.409	.482
August	5.49	4	8	1	27	15	96.2	98	10	45	54	First Inning Pitched	.268	380	102	22	3	2	50	47	68	.352	.358
September/October	5.81	5	5	0	23	10	62.0	74	4	27	40	First 15 Pitches	.277	332	92	19	3	0	32	39	60	.356	.352
Starter	4.83	17	22	0	48	48	263.0	294	29	119	149	Pitch 16-30	.261	257	67	8	1	10	39	40	44	.361	.416
Reliever	3.81	6	4	1	67	0	89.2	95	4	40	60	Pitch 31-45	.300	217	65	9	1	6	28	23	28	.368	.433
0 Days rest	7.07	0	2	0	12	0	14.0	16	0	7	10	Pitch 46+	.287	575	165	29	3	17	72	57	77	.350	.437
1 or 2 Days rest	4.66	1	0	0	19	0	19.1	28	1	10	17	First Pitch	.346	179	62	9	0	11	35	6	0	.363	.581
3+ Days rest	2.72	5	2	1	36	0	56.1	51	3	23	33	Ahead on Count	.223	593	132	18	4	6	45	0	175	.226	.297
Pre-All Star	4.11	9	9	0	50	16	140.0	163	13	67	86	Behind on Count	.361	352	127	23	3	11	66	86	1	.481	.537
Post-All Star	4.87	14	17	1	65	32	212.2	226	20	92	123	Two Strikes	.200	560	112	16	1	7	41	66	208	.287	.270

Pitcher vs. Batter (career)

Pitches Best Vs.	Avg	AB	H	2B	3B	HR	RBI	BB	SO	OBP	SLG	Pitches Worst Vs.	Avg	AB	H	2B	3B	HR	RBI	BB	SO	OBP	SLG
Bill Pecota	.091	11	1	0	0	0	1	0	2	.091	.091	Julio Franco	.750	8	6	1	0	1	1	4	1	.833	1.250
Fred McGriff	.111	9	1	0	0	0	1	2	3	.273	.111	Alvin Davis	.545	11	6	2	0	1	3	2	2	.615	1.000
Wally Joyner	.111	9	1	0	0	0	0	2	0	.273	.111	Ivan Calderon	.417	12	5	1	0	2	4	0	1	.417	1.000
Donnie Hill	.182	11	2	0	0	0	0	1	0	.250	.182	Kent Hrbek	.375	8	3	1	0	0	0	4	1	.583	.500
Robin Ventura	.200	15	3	0	0	0	0	0	2	.200	.200	Mel Hall	.364	11	4	1	0	0	5	1	2	.417	.727

Barry Bonds — Pirates   Bats Left (flyball hitter)

	Avg	G	AB	R	H	2B	3B	HR	RBI	BB	SO	HBP	GDP	SB	CS	OBP	SLG	IBB	SH	SF	#Pit	#P/PA	GB	FB	G/F
1992 Season	.311	140	473	109	147	36	5	34	103	127	69	5	9	39	8	.456	.624	32	0	7	2352	3.84	139	189	0.74
Last Five Years	.285	747	2620	501	748	160	24	135	449	492	400	15	36	183	55	.397	.519	108	1	32	11856	3.75	830	960	0.86

1992 Season

	Avg	AB	H	2B	3B	HR	RBI	BB	SO	OBP	SLG		Avg	AB	H	2B	3B	HR	RBI	BB	SO	OBP	SLG
vs. Left	.311	222	69	19	3	13	44	55	35	.445	.599	Scoring Posn	.314	118	37	5	3	13	71	52	16	.508	.737

1992 Season

	Avg	AB	H	2B	3B	HR	RBI	BB	SO	OBP	SLG		Avg	AB	H	2B	3B	HR	RBI	BB	SO	OBP	SLG
vs. Right	.311	251	78	17	2	21	59	72	34	.465	.645	Close & Late	.253	91	23	4	2	3	10	34	17	.452	.440
Groundball	.317	142	45	13	1	8	22	40	15	.467	.592	None on/out	.318	129	41	13	1	6	6	25	21	.432	.574
Flyball	.303	109	33	10	1	10	26	35	24	.480	.688	Batting #4	.327	339	111	26	4	29	85	92	52	.468	.684
Home	.338	210	71	21	2	15	44	69	35	.498	.671	Batting #5	.273	132	36	10	1	5	18	35	15	.430	.477
Away	.289	263	76	15	3	19	59	58	34	.418	.586	Other	.000	2	0	0	0	0	0	0	2	.000	.000
Day	.305	131	40	7	2	10	32	40	21	.469	.618	April	.317	63	20	2	0	7	17	11	9	.434	.683
Night	.313	342	107	29	3	24	71	87	48	.451	.626	May	.297	101	30	9	0	6	23	20	9	.423	.564
Grass	.279	147	41	8	1	9	26	28	15	.393	.531	June	.244	41	10	1	1	2	3	16	8	.456	.463
Turf	.325	326	106	28	4	25	77	99	54	.482	.666	July	.313	83	26	9	3	5	19	19	14	.433	.675
First Pitch	.394	66	26	8	0	4	15	25	0	.553	.697	August	.253	83	21	5	0	3	14	28	14	.431	.422
Ahead on Count	.333	120	40	11	2	12	30	60	0	.558	.758	September/October	.392	102	40	10	1	11	27	33	15	.537	.833
Behind on Count	.240	129	31	6	1	5	17	0	29	.252	.419	Pre-All Star	.303	238	72	17	3	15	49	52	32	.434	.588
Two Strikes	.271	199	54	12	2	15	45	44	69	.403	.578	Post-All Star	.319	235	75	19	2	19	54	75	37	.476	.660

1992 By Position

Position	Avg	AB	H	2B	3B	HR	RBI	BB	SO	OBP	SLG	G	GS	Innings	PO	A	E	DP	Fld Pct	Rng Fctr	In Zone	Zone Outs	Zone Rtg	MLB Zone
As lf	.312	471	147	36	5	34	103	127	67	.457	.626	139	138	1240.2	310	4	3	0	.991	2.28	351	294	.838	.809

Last Five Years

	Avg	AB	H	2B	3B	HR	RBI	BB	SO	OBP	SLG		Avg	AB	H	2B	3B	HR	RBI	BB	SO	OBP	SLG
vs. Left	.294	1003	295	70	10	50	188	170	167	.397	.533	Scoring Posn	.313	594	186	35	7	35	308	194	86	.466	.572
vs. Right	.280	1617	453	90	14	85	261	322	233	.398	.511	Close & Late	.263	457	120	26	4	12	53	102	84	.394	.416
Groundball	.294	948	279	58	8	35	129	153	139	.392	.483	None on/out	.288	826	238	58	9	38	38	117	120	.380	.518
Flyball	.243	560	141	28	3	39	114	120	107	.371	.503	Batting #1	.269	1005	270	53	12	39	107	151	155	.364	.462
Home	.271	1246	338	65	10	62	202	246	201	.391	.489	Batting #5	.294	1224	360	79	8	64	251	240	183	.408	.529
Away	.298	1374	410	95	14	73	247	246	199	.403	.547	Other	.302	391	118	28	4	32	91	101	62	.443	.639
Day	.277	741	205	40	6	38	117	147	123	.393	.501	April	.264	375	99	27	4	21	55	34	68	.327	.525
Night	.289	1879	543	120	18	97	332	345	277	.399	.527	May	.283	466	132	23	5	26	86	62	69	.396	.521
Grass	.281	723	203	45	6	31	112	110	109	.372	.488	June	.297	401	119	30	4	15	53	88	55	.422	.504
Turf	.287	1897	545	115	18	104	337	382	291	.406	.531	July	.322	428	138	27	7	24	96	87	61	.431	.586
First Pitch	.317	378	120	30	3	25	81	59	0	.407	.611	August	.261	479	125	23	0	24	79	102	72	.388	.459
Ahead on Count	.333	723	241	44	9	58	159	243	0	.497	.660	September/October	.287	471	135	30	4	25	80	99	75	.407	.527
Behind on Count	.250	748	187	36	4	29	113	7	196	.260	.425	Pre-All Star	.264	1380	392	90	16	67	222	226	210	.385	.518
Two Strikes	.214	1077	231	59	6	33	140	171	399	.323	.372	Post-All Star	.287	1240	356	70	8	68	227	266	190	.410	.521

Batter vs. Pitcher (career)

Hits Best Against	Avg	AB	H	2B	3B	HR	RBI	BB	SO	OBP	SLG	Hits Worst Against	Avg	AB	H	2B	3B	HR	RBI	BB	SO	OBP	SLG
Marvin Freeman	.571	7	4	2	0	0	0	4	0	.727	.857	Jeff Brantley	.000	13	0	0	0	0	0	1	5	.071	.000
Tommy Greene	.538	13	7	1	0	3	9	4	3	.611	1.308	Ben Rivera	.000	7	0	0	0	0	1	2	0	.364	.000
Bill Gullickson	.467	15	7	3	1	1	4	2	0	.529	1.000	Chuck McElroy	.071	14	1	1	0	0	1	1	3	.125	.143
Bill Sampen	.429	7	3	0	0	2	4	4	1	.636	1.286	Kent Mercker	.091	11	1	0	0	0	0	0	4	.091	.091
Andy Benes	.385	13	5	0	0	3	12	4	0	.524	1.077	Charlie Leibrandt	.133	15	2	0	0	0	1	0	5	.133	.133

Ricky Bones — Brewers
Pitches Right

	ERA	W	L	Sv	G	GS	IP	BB	SO	Avg	H	2B	3B	HR	RBI	OBP	SLG	CG	ShO	Sup	QS	#P/S	SB	CS	GB	FB	G/F
1992 Season	4.57	9	10	0	31	28	163.1	48	65	.264	169	27	5	27	74	.321	.448	0	4	4.13	12	84	13	2	245	223	1.10
Career (1991-1992)	4.64	13	16	0	42	39	217.1	66	96	.265	226	34	6	30	104	.321	.424	0	4	4.89	17	84	16	3	342	268	1.28

1992 Season

	ERA	W	L	Sv	G	GS	IP	H	HR	BB	SO		Avg	AB	H	2B	3B	HR	RBI	BB	SO	OBP	SLG
Home	3.25	6	4	0	16	15	99.2	84	10	26	41	vs. Left	.268	302	81	13	3	9	22	21	22	.321	.421
Away	6.64	3	6	0	15	13	63.2	85	17	22	24	vs. Right	.260	339	88	14	2	18	52	27	43	.322	.472
Day	4.02	4	2	0	11	10	62.2	58	13	14	27	Inning 1-6	.269	576	155	24	5	25	69	43	58	.326	.458
Night	4.92	5	8	0	20	18	100.2	111	14	34	38	Inning 7+	.215	65	14	3	0	2	5	5	7	.282	.354
Grass	4.18	7	8	0	26	23	133.1	134	17	41	59	None on	.265	400	106	20	4	18	18	32	35	.329	.470
Turf	6.30	2	2	0	5	5	30.0	35	10	7	6	Runners on	.261	241	63	7	1	9	56	16	30	.309	.411
April	2.38	1	0	0	5	4	22.2	17	3	4	11	Scoring Posn	.221	122	27	2	1	3	43	13	19	.296	.328
May	5.34	0	2	0	5	5	28.2	25	5	9	14	Close & Late	.205	39	8	2	0	2	2	2	4	.244	.410
June	5.83	3	2	0	5	5	29.1	32	8	12	7	None on/out	.238	168	40	11	2	7	7	15	13	.316	.452
July	5.53	2	3	0	5	5	27.2	41	2	7	11	vs. 1st Batr (relief)	.000	1	0	0	0	0	1	1	1	.333	.000
August	3.56	1	2	0	6	4	30.1	29	6	8	13	First Inning Pitched	.221	113	25	4	0	4	11	12	13	.315	.363
September/October	4.38	2	1	0	5	5	24.2	25	3	8	9	First 75 Pitches	.264	527	139	22	5	24	63	40	55	.322	.461
Starter	4.76	9	10	0	28	28	155.0	161	26	46	60	Pitch 76-90	.243	74	18	3	0	2	9	6	6	.313	.365
Reliever	1.08	0	0	0	3	0	8.1	8	1	2	5	Pitch 91-105	.333	30	10	2	0	1	2	1	2	.355	.500
0-3 Days Rest	2.70	1	0	0	1	1	6.2	4	1	0	3	Pitch 106+	.200	10	2	0	0	0	0	1	2	.273	.200
4 Days Rest	5.56	3	7	0	15	15	79.1	94	11	30	32	First Pitch	.310	113	35	3	1	7	15	0	0	.313	.540
5+ Days Rest	4.04	5	3	0	12	12	69.0	63	14	16	25	Ahead on Count	.257	253	65	10	2	8	29	0	53	.276	.407
Pre-All Star	4.95	5	5	0	17	16	92.2	93	17	28	35	Behind on Count	.257	148	38	11	0	6	17	25	0	.362	.453
Post-All Star	4.08	4	5	0	14	12	70.2	76	10	20	30	Two Strikes	.233	240	56	9	3	8	23	23	65	.316	.396

Bobby Bonilla — Mets
Bats Both (flyball hitter)

	Avg	G	AB	R	H	2B	3B	HR	RBI	BB	SO	HBP	GDP	SB	CS	OBP	SLG	IBB	SH	SF	#Pit	#P/PA	GB	FB	G/F
1992 Season	.249	128	438	62	109	23	0	19	70	66	73	1	11	4	3	.348	.432	10	0	1	1781	3.52	136	155	0.88
Last Five Years	.279	767	2640	459	791	175	30	117	476	362	418	9	49	21	23	.357	.485	66	0	40	11541	3.55	951	1034	0.92

1992 Season

	Avg	AB	H	2B	3B	HR	RBI	BB	SO	OBP	SLG		Avg	AB	H	2B	3B	HR	RBI	BB	SO	OBP	SLG
vs. Left	.240	175	42	7	0	4	21	17	15	.307	.349	Scoring Posn	.256	117	30	6	0	5	51	23	18	.376	.436
vs. Right	.255	263	67	16	0	15	49	49	58	.373	.487	Close & Late	.270	74	20	3	0	6	15	16	15	.400	.554
Groundball	.230	165	38	7	0	5	22	31	28	.350	.364	None on/out	.273	99	27	5	0	7	7	13	14	.363	.535
Flyball	.302	96	29	6	0	5	15	13	18	.391	.521	Batting #3	.250	128	32	5	0	5	20	18	28	.342	.406
Home	.214	196	42	11	0	5	21	31	31	.325	.347	Batting #5	.261	238	62	13	0	14	43	33	36	.352	.492
Away	.277	242	67	12	0	14	49	35	42	.367	.500	Other	.208	72	15	5	0	0	7	15	9	.345	.278
Day	.203	148	30	9	0	5	19	13	22	.267	.365	April	.268	82	22	3	0	2	14	14	15	.375	.378
Night	.272	290	79	14	0	14	51	53	51	.386	.466	May	.233	90	21	3	0	3	15	17	13	.352	.367
Grass	.223	296	66	13	0	14	44	41	45	.319	.409	June	.292	89	26	11	0	3	14	17	18	.411	.517
Turf	.303	142	43	10	0	5	26	25	28	.407	.479	July	.263	80	21	4	0	4	11	7	15	.322	.463
First Pitch	.369	103	38	10	0	8	28	10	0	.425	.699	August	.196	51	10	1	0	6	14	3	3	.241	.569
Ahead on Count	.299	97	29	8	0	5	17	23	0	.433	.536	September/October	.196	46	9	1	0	1	2	8	9	.315	.283
Behind on Count	.186	118	22	4	0	2	9	0	33	.193	.271	Pre-All Star	.263	300	79	20	0	11	51	53	56	.375	.440
Two Strikes	.156	167	26	5	0	5	23	33	73	.294	.413	Post-All Star	.217	138	30	3	0	8	19	13	17	.285	.413

1992 By Position

Position	Avg	AB	H	2B	3B	HR	RBI	BB	SO	OBP	SLG	G	GS	Innings	PO	A	E	DP	Fld Pct	Rng Fctr	In Zone	Outs	Zone Rtg	MLB Zone
As rf	.247	417	103	22	0	19	67	64	70	.348	.436	121	121	988.0	238	7	2	1	.992	2.23	267	227	.850	.814

Last Five Years

	Avg	AB	H	2B	3B	HR	RBI	BB	SO	OBP	SLG		Avg	AB	H	2B	3B	HR	RBI	BB	SO	OBP	SLG
vs. Left	.259	1120	290	59	5	46	175	119	118	.327	.444	Scoring Posn	.285	776	221	49	7	30	345	170	122	.394	.482
vs. Right	.291	1720	501	116	25	71	301	243	300	.377	.512	Close & Late	.253	462	117	15	1	21	77	86	78	.369	.426
Groundball	.277	1045	289	62	10	31	167	114	147	.344	.444	None on/out	.295	756	223	48	11	34	34	57	100	.347	.522
Flyball	.279	613	171	34	9	32	100	95	84	.376	.520	Batting #4	.282	2464	694	156	30	98	412	309	353	.359	.489
Home	.266	1373	365	85	12	49	210	181	184	.350	.452	Batting #5	.261	238	62	13	0	14	43	33	36	.352	.492
Away	.290	1467	426	90	18	68	266	181	234	.364	.515	Other	.254	138	35	6	0	5	21	20	29	.348	.406
Day	.283	848	240	54	6	45	147	92	123	.353	.520	April	.299	425	127	25	2	20	82	40	60	.357	.508
Night	.277	1992	551	121	24	72	329	270	295	.359	.470	May	.297	478	142	29	5	23	86	67	86	.380	.523
Grass	.274	934	256	45	10	45	158	101	156	.343	.488	June	.253	467	118	35	6	15	66	66	71	.343	.450
Turf	.281	1906	535	130	20	72	318	261	262	.364	.483	July	.252	492	124	23	3	18	66	57	75	.328	.421
First Pitch	.352	568	200	52	11	22	115	36	0	.387	.599	August	.300	484	145	34	6	26	86	67	63	.382	.506
Ahead on Count	.353	691	244	54	7	37	140	151	0	.465	.612	September/October	.273	494	135	29	8	15	88	65	81	.353	.455
Behind on Count	.232	767	178	38	8	25	108	1	195	.233	.400	Pre-All Star	.279	1543	431	98	14	64	255	191	229	.356	.485
Two Strikes	.190	1143	217	48	7	39	151	160	418	.287	.346	Post-All Star	.278	1297	360	77	16	53	221	171	189	.359	.484

Batter vs. Pitcher (career)

Hits Best Against	Avg	AB	H	2B	3B	HR	RBI	BB	SO	OBP	SLG	Hits Worst Against	Avg	AB	H	2B	3B	HR	RBI	BB	SO	OBP	SLG
Les Lancaster	.571	7	4	1	0	0	1	7	2	.733	.714	Danny Darwin	.067	15	1	0	0	0	1	1	2	.125	.067
Shawn Boskie	.538	13	7	1	1	0	2	1	0	.625	.769	Tom Candiotti	.083	12	1	1	0	0	1	0	1	.083	.167
Pete Smith	.467	15	7	1	0	3	6	3	3	.526	1.133	Craig Lefferts	.087	23	2	0	0	0	3	0	4	.083	.087
John Dopson	.400	10	4	1	0	1	3	3	1	.538	.800	Todd Worrell	.091	11	1	1	0	0	0	0	6	.091	.182
Tom Browning	.390	41	16	4	1	8	17	1	2	.386	1.122	Jeff Brantley	.100	10	1	0	0	0	0	1	2	.182	.100

Bret Boone — Mariners
Bats Right (groundball hitter)

	Avg	G	AB	R	H	2B	3B	HR	RBI	BB	SO	HBP	GDP	SB	CS	OBP	SLG	IBB	SH	SF	#Pit	#P/PA	GB	FB	G/F
1992 Season	.194	33	129	15	25	4	0	4	15	4	34	1	4	1	1	.224	.318	0	1	0	513	3.83	46	28	1.64

1992 Season

	Avg	AB	H	2B	3B	HR	RBI	BB	SO	OBP	SLG		Avg	AB	H	2B	3B	HR	RBI	BB	SO	OBP	SLG
vs. Left	.150	40	6	1	0	0	1	2	12	.190	.175	Scoring Posn	.206	34	7	1	0	1	11	0	9	.206	.324
vs. Right	.213	89	19	3	0	4	14	2	22	.239	.382	Close & Late	.077	26	2	1	0	0	0	0	10	.077	.115
Home	.250	56	14	4	0	2	8	2	18	.276	.429	None on/out	.120	25	3	1	0	0	0	3	4	.214	.160
Away	.151	73	11	0	0	2	7	2	16	.184	.233	Batting #7	.222	45	10	0	0	2	7	1	11	.239	.356
First Pitch	.000	11	0	0	0	0	0	0	0	.000	.000	Batting #8	.176	34	6	1	0	0	3	2	9	.243	.206
Ahead on Count	.409	22	9	2	0	2	8	3	0	.480	.773	Other	.180	50	9	3	0	2	5	1	14	.196	.360
Behind on Count	.128	47	6	0	0	0	3	0	17	.146	.128	Pre-All Star	.000	0	0	0	0	0	0	0	0	.000	.000
Two Strikes	.151	73	11	2	0	2	5	1	34	.162	.260	Post-All Star	.194	129	25	4	0	4	15	4	34	.224	.318

Pedro Borbon — Braves
Pitches Left (groundball pitcher)

	ERA	W	L	Sv	G	GS	IP	BB	SO	Avg	H	2B	3B	HR	RBI	OBP	SLG	GF	IR	IRS	Hld	SvOp	SB	CS	GB	FB	G/F
1992 Season	6.75	0	1	0	2	0	1.1	1	1	.333	2	1	0	0	1	.429	.500	2	0	0	0	0	0	0	3	1	3.00

1992 Season

	ERA	W	L	Sv	G	GS	IP	H	HR	BB	SO		Avg	AB	H	2B	3B	HR	RBI	BB	SO	OBP	SLG
Home	6.75	0	1	0	2	0	1.1	2	0	1	1	vs. Left	.250	4	1	1	0	0	0	0	0	.250	.500

	ERA	W	L	Sv	G	GS	IP	H	HR	BB	SO		Avg	AB	H	2B	3B	HR	RBI	BB	SO	OBP	SLG
Away	0.00	0	0	0	0	0	0.0	0	0	0	0	vs. Right	.500	2	1	0	0	0	1	1	0	.667	.500

Pat Borders — Blue Jays
Bats Right

	Avg	G	AB	R	H	2B	3B	HR	RBI	BB	SO	HBP	GDP	SB	CS	OBP	SLG	IBB	SH	SF	#Pit	#P/PA	GB	FB	G/F
1992 Season	.242	138	480	47	116	26	2	13	53	33	75	2	11	1	1	.290	.385	3	1	5	1902	3.66	173	149	1.16
Career (1988-1992)	.258	518	1512	142	390	84	8	41	188	76	246	4	48	3	3	.293	.405	8	11	14	5552	3.46	549	451	1.22

1992 Season

	Avg	AB	H	2B	3B	HR	RBI	BB	SO	OBP	SLG		Avg	AB	H	2B	3B	HR	RBI	BB	SO	OBP	SLG
vs. Left	.233	120	28	8	0	0	9	18	14	.333	.300	Scoring Posn	.196	107	21	6	1	2	39	17	19	.300	.327
vs. Right	.244	360	88	18	2	13	44	15	61	.274	.414	Close & Late	.220	82	18	4	0	2	3	6	16	.281	.341
Groundball	.260	150	39	11	1	5	23	7	24	.292	.447	None on/out	.254	130	33	6	1	3	4	19	.276	.385
Flyball	.221	131	29	7	1	3	8	8	19	.266	.359	Batting #7	.208	72	15	4	0	2	7	8	15	.288	.347
Home	.242	231	56	13	1	7	27	16	30	.296	.398	Batting #8	.248	408	101	22	2	11	46	25	60	.291	.392
Away	.241	249	60	13	1	6	26	17	45	.285	.373	Other	.000	0	0	0	0	0	0	0	0	.000	.000
Day	.203	148	30	8	0	4	12	10	26	.253	.338	April	.300	70	21	5	0	3	8	9	13	.378	.500
Night	.259	332	86	18	2	9	41	23	49	.307	.407	May	.211	90	19	2	1	2	4	7	14	.268	.322
Grass	.231	195	45	9	1	6	22	14	38	.277	.379	June	.211	71	15	3	0	2	8	4	11	.250	.338
Turf	.249	285	71	17	1	7	31	19	37	.300	.389	July	.275	80	22	6	0	3	15	7	11	.330	.463
First Pitch	.316	79	25	3	0	3	7	3	0	.337	.468	August	.253	83	21	5	0	2	7	0	16	.259	.386
Ahead on Count	.248	113	28	5	1	5	19	14	0	.331	.442	September/October	.209	86	18	5	1	1	11	6	10	.261	.326
Behind on Count	.194	155	30	6	0	2	16	0	41	.191	.271	Pre-All Star	.235	260	61	12	1	7	21	24	44	.299	.369
Two Strikes	.207	208	43	10	1	3	17	16	75	.264	.308	Post-All Star	.250	220	55	14	1	6	32	9	31	.280	.405

1992 By Position

Position	Avg	AB	H	2B	3B	HR	RBI	BB	SO	OBP	SLG	G	GS	Innings	PO	A	E	DP	Fld Pct	Rng Fctr	In Zone	Zone Outs	Zone Rtg	MLB Zone
As c	.237	477	113	24	2	13	53	32	75	.285	.377	137	132	1160.2	784	88	8	7	.991	---	---	---	---	---

Career (1988-1992)

	Avg	AB	H	2B	3B	HR	RBI	BB	SO	OBP	SLG		Avg	AB	H	2B	3B	HR	RBI	BB	SO	OBP	SLG
vs. Left	.266	756	201	46	6	17	92	51	112	.311	.410	Scoring Posn	.241	361	87	19	3	8	136	35	58	.301	.377
vs. Right	.250	756	189	38	2	24	96	25	134	.273	.401	Close & Late	.257	288	74	15	1	7	34	15	59	.296	.389
Groundball	.265	400	106	20	2	10	52	16	69	.292	.400	None on/out	.281	363	102	20	2	13	13	11	52	.302	.455
Flyball	.248	363	90	25	2	12	40	20	69	.287	.427	Batting #7	.271	457	124	31	2	15	65	24	70	.307	.446
Home	.256	718	184	47	4	22	91	40	99	.296	.425	Batting #8	.257	599	154	32	2	18	75	38	91	.300	.407
Away	.259	794	206	37	4	19	97	36	147	.290	.388	Other	.246	456	112	21	4	8	48	14	85	.268	.362
Day	.225	484	109	27	2	14	50	19	91	.253	.376	April	.273	231	63	12	3	8	25	12	41	.308	.455
Night	.273	1028	281	57	6	27	138	57	155	.311	.419	May	.243	305	74	14	1	9	29	13	62	.273	.384
Grass	.264	625	165	28	3	15	79	32	115	.297	.390	June	.268	231	62	14	1	6	31	9	27	.296	.416
Turf	.254	887	225	56	5	26	109	44	131	.290	.416	July	.295	220	65	17	0	7	41	17	29	.346	.468
First Pitch	.325	265	86	14	3	9	29	5	0	.335	.502	August	.270	241	65	14	0	5	30	9	41	.294	.390
Ahead on Count	.306	357	110	23	4	19	79	41	0	.378	.555	September/October	.215	284	61	13	3	6	32	16	46	.255	.345
Behind on Count	.202	514	104	26	0	5	51	0	152	.203	.282	Pre-All Star	.254	841	214	44	5	24	93	43	144	.290	.404
Two Strikes	.191	619	118	29	1	5	40	28	245	.225	.265	Post-All Star	.262	671	176	40	3	17	95	33	102	.296	.407

Batter vs. Pitcher (career)

Hits Best Against	Avg	AB	H	2B	3B	HR	RBI	BB	SO	OBP	SLG	Hits Worst Against	Avg	AB	H	2B	3B	HR	RBI	BB	SO	OBP	SLG
Jeff Johnson	.500	10	5	0	0	0	3	2	0	.583	.500	Kirk McCaskill	.071	14	1	0	1	0	2	0	2	.071	.214
Bill Wegman	.455	11	5	1	0	1	2	0	4	.455	.818	Dan Plesac	.077	13	1	0	0	0	0	2	1	.200	.077
Greg Hibbard	.429	21	9	2	0	0	0	0	2	.429	.524	Bud Black	.125	16	2	0	0	0	0	0	3	.125	.125
Paul Gibson	.400	10	4	2	0	1	3	5	0	.563	.900	Jaime Navarro	.154	13	2	0	0	0	1	0	1	.154	.154
Kenny Rogers	.375	8	3	1	0	0	1	4	0	.583	.500	Frank Viola	.158	19	3	1	0	0	3	0	2	.158	.211

Mike Bordick — Athletics
Bats Right (groundball hitter)

	Avg	G	AB	R	H	2B	3B	HR	RBI	BB	SO	HBP	GDP	SB	CS	OBP	SLG	IBB	SH	SF	#Pit	#P/PA	GB	FB	G/F
1992 Season	.300	154	504	62	151	19	4	3	48	40	59	9	10	12	6	.358	.371	2	14	5	2129	3.82	217	142	1.53
Career (1990-1992)	.276	269	753	83	208	24	5	3	69	55	100	12	13	15	10	.333	.333	2	26	6	3150	3.81	324	199	1.63

1992 Season

	Avg	AB	H	2B	3B	HR	RBI	BB	SO	OBP	SLG		Avg	AB	H	2B	3B	HR	RBI	BB	SO	OBP	SLG
vs. Left	.336	131	44	5	2	1	15	12	12	.393	.427	Scoring Posn	.273	154	42	7	1	1	45	10	19	.320	.351
vs. Right	.287	373	107	14	2	2	33	28	47	.346	.351	Close & Late	.261	69	18	2	2	0	10	4	10	.308	.348
Groundball	.348	115	40	3	0	0	12	10	9	.398	.374	None on/out	.347	121	42	5	1	2	2	12	8	.410	.455
Flyball	.310	129	40	8	1	1	12	10	16	.371	.411	Batting #7	.265	68	18	1	0	0	2	5	9	.311	.279
Home	.296	240	71	7	4	3	25	19	30	.360	.396	Batting #8	.299	374	112	11	4	3	39	29	45	.357	.374
Away	.303	264	80	12	0	0	23	21	29	.357	.348	Other	.339	62	21	7	0	0	7	6	5	.414	.452
Day	.317	205	65	5	3	3	20	10	23	.359	.415	April	.355	76	27	2	0	0	10	5	9	.390	.382
Night	.288	299	86	14	1	0	28	30	36	.358	.341	May	.348	89	31	2	1	1	8	6	8	.385	.427
Grass	.282	422	119	12	4	3	39	29	53	.355	.338	June	.234	77	18	3	1	1	8	8	12	.314	.338
Turf	.390	82	32	7	0	0	9	11	6	.474	.476	July	.292	89	26	6	1	0	6	4	12	.337	.382
First Pitch	.523	44	23	2	0	0	8	1	0	.532	.568	August	.270	89	24	1	0	0	6	10	8	.358	.281

1992 Season

	Avg	AB	H	2B	3B	HR	RBI	BB	SO	OBP	SLG		Avg	AB	H	2B	3B	HR	RBI	BB	SO	OBP	SLG
Ahead on Count	.333	108	36	3	1	1	9	24	0	.459	.407	September/October	.298	84	25	5	1	1	10	7	10	.366	.417
Behind on Count	.241	174	42	8	3	0	14	0	40	.257	.322	Pre-All Star	.314	283	89	11	2	2	28	20	36	.362	.389
Two Strikes	.230	230	53	10	2	1	15	15	59	.287	.304	Post-All Star	.261	221	62	8	2	1	20	20	23	.355	.348

1992 By Position

Position	Avg	AB	H	2B	3B	HR	RBI	BB	SO	OBP	SLG	G	GS	Innings	PO	A	E	DP	Fld Pct	Rng Fctr	In Zone	Outs	Zone Rtg	MLB Zone
As 2b	.283	283	80	13	2	2	23	25	36	.354	.364	95	83	733.2	202	267	6	58	.987	5.75	306	264	.863	.892
As ss	.323	220	71	6	2	1	25	15	23	.366	.382	70	66	577.2	108	185	10	50	.967	4.56	215	206	.958	.885

Chris Bosio — Brewers   Pitches Right

	ERA	W	L	Sv	G	GS	IP	BB	SO	Avg	H	2B	3B	HR	RBI	OBP	SLG	CG	ShO	Sup	QS	#P/S	SB	CS	GB	FB	G/F
1992 Season	3.62	16	6	0	33	33	231.1	44	120	.254	223	38	3	21	88	.291	.376	4	2	5.21	22	94	12	7	328	266	1.23
Last Five Years	3.39	56	50	6	156	140	985.1	226	570	.254	956	144	17	80	367	.298	.365	30	7	4.55	82	95	60	22	1441	1042	1.38

1992 Season

	ERA	W	L	Sv	G	GS	IP	H	HR	BB	SO		Avg	AB	H	2B	3B	HR	RBI	BB	SO	OBP	SLG
Home	3.03	9	3	0	18	18	127.2	116	10	22	63	vs. Left	.273	421	115	19	2	10	39	24	40	.310	.399
Away	4.34	7	3	0	15	15	103.2	107	11	22	57	vs. Right	.236	457	108	19	1	11	49	20	80	.273	.354
Day	3.84	5	2	0	10	10	68.0	72	7	12	40	Inning 1-6	.250	719	180	29	3	19	78	40	99	.292	.378
Night	3.53	11	4	0	23	23	163.1	151	14	32	80	Inning 7+	.270	159	43	9	0	2	10	4	21	.287	.365
Grass	3.58	14	5	0	29	29	201.0	194	16	43	104	None on	.231	540	125	20	1	12	12	30	67	.273	.339
Turf	3.86	2	1	0	4	4	30.1	29	5	1	16	Runners on	.290	338	98	18	2	9	76	14	53	.319	.435
April	4.60	2	1	0	5	5	29.1	32	3	7	16	Scoring Posn	.247	174	43	9	1	6	65	8	27	.280	.414
May	6.23	1	2	0	6	6	39.0	48	5	14	24	Close & Late	.261	92	24	8	0	0	5	4	14	.289	.348
June	2.36	2	1	0	5	5	34.1	25	2	7	14	None on/out	.250	232	58	9	0	3	3	12	25	.287	.328
July	2.23	2	1	0	5	5	40.1	37	3	1	15	vs. 1st Batr (relief)	.000	0	0	0	0	0	0	0	0	.000	.000
August	3.77	4	0	0	6	6	43.0	40	3	10	27	First Inning Pitched	.223	121	27	5	0	2	11	9	18	.275	.314
September/October	2.78	4	1	0	6	6	45.1	41	5	5	24	First 75 Pitches	.251	674	169	26	3	15	67	36	92	.290	.365
Starter	3.62	16	6	0	33	33	231.1	223	21	44	120	Pitch 76-90	.257	105	27	8	0	5	14	5	16	.288	.476
Reliever	0.00	0	0	0	0	0	0.0	0	0	0	0	Pitch 91-105	.250	76	19	2	0	1	7	3	8	.288	.316
0-3 Days Rest	5.12	1	2	0	3	3	19.1	22	2	4	9	Pitch 106+	.348	23	8	2	0	0	0	0	4	.348	.435
4 Days Rest	3.46	11	3	0	21	21	150.2	139	12	33	78	First Pitch	.317	139	44	6	0	4	23	1	0	.329	.446
5+ Days Rest	3.52	4	1	0	9	9	61.1	62	7	7	33	Ahead on Count	.235	362	85	15	1	7	27	0	107	.236	.340
Pre-All Star	4.23	6	5	0	18	18	117.0	121	11	29	60	Behind on Count	.269	212	57	11	0	6	19	24	0	.345	.406
Post-All Star	2.99	10	1	0	15	15	114.1	102	10	15	60	Two Strikes	.196	337	66	14	0	5	24	19	120	.237	.282

Last Five Years

	ERA	W	L	Sv	G	GS	IP	H	HR	BB	SO		Avg	AB	H	2B	3B	HR	RBI	BB	SO	OBP	SLG
Home	3.21	30	25	3	81	73	524.1	517	39	117	306	vs. Left	.261	1977	516	74	10	41	193	123	231	.305	.371
Away	3.59	26	25	3	75	67	461.0	439	41	109	264	vs. Right	.246	1790	440	70	7	39	174	103	339	.290	.358
Day	2.95	18	15	3	52	47	330.0	294	28	81	207	Inning 1-6	.256	2987	765	113	14	72	312	176	481	.299	.376
Night	3.61	38	35	3	104	93	655.1	662	52	145	363	Inning 7+	.245	780	191	31	3	8	55	50	89	.292	.323
Grass	3.30	51	41	6	138	123	872.1	835	70	201	502	None on	.242	2280	551	78	11	46	46	127	337	.285	.346
Turf	4.06	5	9	0	18	17	113.0	121	10	25	68	Runners on	.272	1487	405	66	6	34	321	99	233	.318	.393
April	2.22	15	5	0	25	25	176.0	140	9	43	94	Scoring Posn	.250	801	200	31	4	17	271	64	136	.300	.362
May	3.81	8	15	0	31	31	212.2	232	25	39	125	Close & Late	.237	355	84	14	1	3	20	26	42	.288	.307
June	4.40	6	10	0	25	26	171.2	175	16	44	96	None on/out	.243	988	240	38	7	18	18	53	137	.283	.350
July	3.54	8	11	0	25	24	160.0	173	13	47	91	vs. 1st Batr (relief)	.063	16	1	0	0	0	0	0	4	.063	.063
August	3.07	9	5	1	22	18	137.2	131	7	31	86	First Inning Pitched	.215	568	122	20	0	9	46	39	102	.267	.298
September/October	3.09	10	4	5	27	16	125.1	105	10	22	78	First 75 Pitches	.255	2869	733	109	14	65	263	158	459	.296	.371
Starter	3.46	55	47	0	140	140	956.0	938	80	216	550	Pitch 76-90	.247	445	110	20	3	10	46	37	57	.307	.373
Reliever	1.23	1	3	6	16	0	29.1	18	0	10	20	Pitch 91-105	.247	292	72	7	0	4	29	19	33	.296	.312
0-3 Days Rest	4.00	2	5	0	9	9	63.0	65	10	13	39	Pitch 106+	.255	161	41	8	0	1	9	12	21	.314	.323
4 Days Rest	3.43	43	29	0	94	94	647.1	642	50	161	376	First Pitch	.300	656	197	23	3	18	84	4	0	.309	.427
5+ Days Rest	3.37	10	13	0	37	37	245.2	231	20	42	135	Ahead on Count	.215	1606	346	49	7	27	116	0	497	.218	.305
Pre-All Star	3.52	31	33	0	88	88	600.2	597	53	135	338	Behind on Count	.308	863	266	49	3	24	106	134	0	.400	.455
Post-All Star	3.18	25	17	6	68	52	384.2	359	27	91	232	Two Strikes	.182	1475	269	40	6	18	90	88	570	.229	.254

Pitcher vs. Batter (career)

Pitches Best Vs.	Avg	AB	H	2B	3B	HR	RBI	BB	SO	OBP	SLG	Pitches Worst Vs.	Avg	AB	H	2B	3B	HR	RBI	BB	SO	OBP	SLG
Dave Clark	.000	12	0	0	0	0	0	0	5	.000	.000	Ivan Rodriguez	.583	12	7	1	0	0	2	0	2	.583	.667
Willie Wilson	.045	22	1	0	0	0	2	0	6	.043	.045	Dion James	.500	20	10	3	0	0	3	2	1	.545	.650
Travis Fryman	.071	14	1	0	0	0	0	0	7	.071	.071	George Bell	.433	30	13	3	1	1	7	2	1	.500	.700
Tony Pena	.077	13	1	0	0	0	1	0	2	.077	.077	Carlos Baerga	.417	12	5	1	0	1	4	1	0	.462	.750
Roberto Kelly	.077	13	1	0	0	0	0	0	4	.077	.077	Kirk Gibson	.385	13	5	3	0	2	2	3	2	.500	.846

Shawn Boskie — Cubs — Pitches Right

	ERA	W	L	Sv	G	GS	IP	BB	SO	Avg	H	2B	3B	HR	RBI	OBP	SLG	CG	ShO	Sup	QS	#P/S	SB	CS	GB	FB	G/F
1992 Season	5.01	5	11	0	23	18	91.2	36	39	.284	96	25	0	14	50	.354	.482	0	0	3.34	5	74	2	1	114	126	0.90
Career (1990-1992)	4.69	14	26	0	66	53	318.1	119	150	.282	345	75	8	36	148	.347	.445	1	0	3.85	24	88	12	9	427	396	1.08

1992 Season

	ERA	W	L	Sv	G	GS	IP	H	HR	BB	SO		Avg	AB	H	2B	3B	HR	RBI	BB	SO	OBP	SLG
Home	5.40	3	3	0	12	8	40.0	42	8	16	15	vs. Left	.303	195	59	16	0	10	34	31	27	.392	.538
Away	4.70	2	8	0	11	10	51.2	54	6	20	24	vs. Right	.259	143	37	9	0	4	16	5	12	.296	.406
Starter	5.21	3	10	0	18	18	84.2	92	12	31	36	Scoring Posn	.303	66	20	4	0	2	30	12	8	.388	.455
Reliever	2.57	2	1	0	5	0	7.0	4	2	5	3	Close & Late	.176	17	3	1	0	2	2	5	1	.391	.588
0-3 Days Rest	10.57	1	1	0	2	2	7.2	10	4	3	6	None on/out	.309	94	29	6	0	5	5	7	10	.363	.532
4 Days Rest	5.84	1	2	0	5	5	24.2	26	1	10	11	First Pitch	.317	63	20	5	0	4	12	5	1	.352	.587
5+ Days Rest	4.13	1	7	0	11	11	52.1	56	7	18	19	Behind on Count	.353	68	24	7	0	5	15	16	0	.476	.676
Pre-All Star	3.95	5	5	0	15	13	68.1	62	7	24	32	Ahead on Count	.213	141	30	9	0	2	17	0	31	.231	.319
Post-All Star	8.10	0	6	0	8	5	23.1	34	7	12	7	Two Strikes	.203	148	30	8	0	2	16	15	38	.286	.297

Career (1990-1992)

	ERA	W	L	Sv	G	GS	IP	H	HR	BB	SO		Avg	AB	H	2B	3B	HR	RBI	BB	SO	OBP	SLG
Home	4.93	8	13	0	38	27	164.1	191	13	66	69	vs. Left	.301	700	211	49	8	22	93	95	77	.382	.489
Away	4.44	6	13	0	28	26	154.0	154	13	53	81	vs. Right	.257	522	134	26	0	14	55	24	73	.297	.387
Day	4.49	9	13	0	39	27	182.1	198	25	61	82	Inning 1-6	.260	1090	305	66	8	32	135	100	141	.341	.443
Night	4.96	5	13	0	27	26	136.0	147	11	58	68	Inning 7+	.303	132	40	9	0	4	13	19	9	.396	.462
Grass	5.25	9	20	0	49	37	217.2	256	18	92	95	None on	.281	713	200	49	4	20	20	63	101	.343	.445
Turf	3.49	5	6	0	17	16	100.2	89	8	27	55	Runners on	.285	509	145	26	4	16	128	56	49	.353	.446
April	3.28	5	2	0	8	7	46.2	40	5	16	24	Scoring Posn	.264	292	77	15	3	8	104	35	33	.332	.418
May	4.78	2	7	0	14	14	84.2	95	7	25	39	Close & Late	.263	76	20	5	0	3	8	14	7	.391	.447
June	4.98	3	6	0	15	13	68.2	71	4	29	37	None on/out	.309	317	98	25	4	11	11	30	40	.374	.517
July	4.05	2	5	0	10	10	60.0	66	6	21	24	vs. 1st Batr (relief)	.000	8	0	0	0	0	0	1	4	.385	.000
August	0.54	2	0	0	6	1	16.2	13	0	5	9	First Inning Pitched	.277	235	65	13	0	7	35	35	37	.368	.421
September/October	6.21	0	6	0	13	8	41.2	60	14	23	17	First 75 Pitches	.287	977	280	59	7	31	123	94	130	.350	.456
Starter	4.80	11	25	0	53	53	292.1	323	32	107	134	Pitch 76-90	.230	135	31	6	1	3	13	10	13	.286	.356
Reliever	3.46	3	1	0	13	0	26.0	22	4	12	16	Pitch 91-105	.300	80	24	7	0	2	10	11	5	.391	.463
0-3 Days Rest	5.95	3	3	0	7	7	39.1	48	4	8	11	Pitch 106+	.333	30	10	3	0	0	2	4	2	.412	.433
4 Days Rest	5.22	4	9	0	26	26	139.2	155	12	54	70	First Pitch	.365	189	69	14	1	10	36	11	1	.393	.608
5+ Days Rest	3.89	4	13	0	20	20	113.1	120	12	42	48	Ahead on Count	.222	510	113	28	3	8	51	0	131	.229	.335
Pre-All Star	4.51	11	17	0	41	38	221.2	233	18	82	109	Behind on Count	.326	282	92	20	3	10	35	65	0	.451	.525
Post-All Star	5.12	3	9	0	25	15	96.2	112	18	37	41	Two Strikes	.225	510	115	26	3	9	53	43	149	.286	.341

Pitcher vs. Batter (career)

Pitches Best Vs.	Avg	AB	H	2B	3B	HR	RBI	BB	SO	OBP	SLG	Pitches Worst Vs.	Avg	AB	H	2B	3B	HR	RBI	BB	SO	OBP	SLG
Pedro Guerrero	.000	10	0	0	0	0	0	1	2	.091	.000	Paul O'Neill	.600	10	6	1	0	2	2	2	1	.667	1.300
Dave Martinez	.087	23	2	0	0	0	0	3	3	.192	.087	Terry Pendleton	.545	11	6	4	0	1	1	1	1	.583	1.182
Alfredo Griffin	.091	11	1	0	0	0	0	0	0	.091	.091	Andy Van Slyke	.462	13	6	0	1	2	3	1	2	.467	1.077
Ken Caminiti	.091	11	1	0	0	0	0	0	1	.091	.091	Kal Daniels	.429	14	6	4	0	1	4	2	3	.471	.929
Spike Owen	.125	16	2	0	0	0	0	1	3	.176	.125	Eddie Murray	.400	15	6	2	0	0	5	3	1	.500	.933

Daryl Boston — Mets — Bats Left

	Avg	G	AB	R	H	2B	3B	HR	RBI	BB	SO	HBP	GDP	SB	CS	OBP	SLG	IBB	SH	SF	#Pit	#P/PA	GB	FB	G/F
1992 Season	.249	130	289		72	14	2	11	35	38	60	3	5	12	6	.338	.426	6	0	4	1301	3.90	87	101	0.86
Last Five Years	.254	593	1410	213	358	66	14	47	155	141	227	5	20	62	26	.322	.421	16	6	7	5926	3.79	474	454	1.04

1992 Season

	Avg	AB	H	2B	3B	HR	RBI	BB	SO	OBP	SLG		Avg	AB	H	2B	3B	HR	RBI	BB	SO	OBP	SLG
vs. Left	.319	47	15	3	0	1	4	5	9	.407	.447	Scoring Posn	.315	54	17	3	1	3	27	13	13	.431	.574
vs. Right	.236	242	57	11	2	10	31	33	51	.325	.421	Close & Late	.230	61	14	3	0	4	9	12	19	.373	.475
Groundball	.304	112	34	6	2	5	19	15	17	.385	.527	None on/out	.211	95	20	3	0	3	3	7	15	.265	.337
Flyball	.200	60	12	3	0	4	6	5	21	.279	.450	Batting #1	.296	98	29	4	2	5	17	12	19	.372	.531
Home	.229	140	32	5	1	5	17	16	32	.311	.386	Batting #3	.277	47	13	1	0	1	5	7	6	.357	.362
Away	.268	149	40	9	1	6	18	22	28	.364	.463	Other	.208	144	30	9	0	5	13	19	35	.309	.375
Day	.200	90	18	4	1	2	11	8	13	.267	.333	April	.250	40	10	1	1	1	4	6	9	.375	.400
Night	.271	199	54	10	1	9	24	30	47	.369	.467	May	.243	70	17	2	1	2	10	4	11	.284	.386
Grass	.256	223	57	7	2	10	29	24	43	.329	.439	June	.250	28	7	2	0	2	3	4	8	.333	.536
Turf	.227	66	15	7	0	1	6	14	17	.366	.379	July	.179	39	7	4	0	1	4	2	10	.214	.359
First Pitch	.290	31	9	1	0	0	2	5	0	.389	.323	August	.307	75	23	2	0	5	8	9	13	.388	.533
Ahead on Count	.290	69	20	6	0	6	13	20	0	.440	.638	September/October	.216	37	8	3	0	0	6	13	9	.404	.297
Behind on Count	.186	97	18	3	1	2	10	0	30	.200	.299	Pre-All Star	.236	157	37	7	2	6	19	15	33	.309	.420
Two Strikes	.157	134	21	4	0	2	10	13	60	.238	.231	Post-All Star	.265	132	35	7	0	5	16	23	27	.371	.432

1992 By Position

Position	Avg	AB	H	2B	3B	HR	RBI	BB	SO	OBP	SLG	G	GS	Innings	PO	A	E	DP	Fld Pct	Rng Fctr	In Zone	Outs	Zone Rtg	MLB Zone
As Pinch Hitter	.175	40	7	2	0	3	7	5	11	.261	.450	50	0	---	---	---	---	---	---	---	---	---	---	---
As lf	.241	187	45	7	2	5	21	24	39	.335	.380	66	51	472.2	95	5	1	1	.990	1.90	117	90	.769	.809
As cf	.324	37	12	3	0	1	4	6	7	.400	.486	16	8	92.1	23	0	0	0	1.000	2.24	28	22	.786	.824

1992 By Position

Position	Avg	AB	H	2B	3B	HR	RBI	BB	SO	OBP	SLG	G	GS	Innings	PO	A	E	DP	Fld Pct	Rng Fctr	In Zone	Outs	Zone Rtg	MLB Zone
As rf	.320	25	8	2	0	2	3	3	3	.393	.640	14	6	65.1	15	0	0	0	1.000	2.07	19	15	.789	.814

Last Five Years

	Avg	AB	H	2B	3B	HR	RBI	BB	SO	OBP	SLG		Avg	AB	H	2B	3B	HR	RBI	BB	SO	OBP	SLG
vs. Left	.238	193	46	10	2	2	17	12	45	.287	.342	Scoring Posn	.277	310	86	12	3	14	112	47	50	.369	.471
vs. Right	.256	1217	312	56	12	45	138	129	182	.328	.433	Close & Late	.242	256	62	16	4	6	23	35	53	.337	.406
Groundball	.293	437	128	20	7	13	63	37	56	.348	.460	None on/out	.269	402	108	20	5	15	15	37	63	.332	.455
Flyball	.216	301	65	11	0	11	24	34	68	.296	.362	Batting #1	.258	387	100	25	5	12	35	39	62	.326	.442
Home	.243	713	173	32	10	20	70	69	121	.310	.400	Batting #7	.290	321	93	13	1	10	50	41	49	.370	.430
Away	.265	697	185	34	4	27	85	72	106	.335	.442	Other	.235	702	165	28	8	25	70	61	116	.298	.405
Day	.244	439	107	22	3	13	52	44	63	.314	.396	April	.212	118	25	3	2	1	8	13	18	.299	.297
Night	.258	971	251	44	11	34	103	97	164	.327	.432	May	.239	213	51	10	3	9	27	15	25	.289	.441
Grass	.248	1111	275	49	12	39	125	105	173	.313	.419	June	.252	230	58	16	3	9	34	20	41	.316	.465
Turf	.278	299	83	17	2	8	30	36	54	.358	.428	July	.260	254	66	16	1	8	24	22	47	.318	.425
First Pitch	.355	169	60	7	2	7	27	6	0	.375	.544	August	.277	347	96	10	2	11	28	29	54	.332	.412
Ahead on Count	.297	353	105	24	1	20	53	79	0	.423	.541	September/October	.250	248	62	11	3	9	34	42	42	.356	.427
Behind on Count	.213	479	102	16	6	7	34	1	123	.217	.315	Pre-All Star	.247	645	159	36	8	25	78	57	100	.311	.443
Two Strikes	.178	657	117	23	6	10	39	48	227	.235	.277	Post-All Star	.260	765	199	30	6	22	77	84	127	.332	.401

Batter vs. Pitcher (career)

Hits Best Against	Avg	AB	H	2B	3B	HR	RBI	BB	SO	OBP	SLG	Hits Worst Against	Avg	AB	H	2B	3B	HR	RBI	BB	SO	OBP	SLG
Bryn Smith	.700	10	7	1	1	0	3	3	0	.769	1.000	Andy Benes	.071	14	1	0	0	1	1	0	5	.071	.286
Bob Walk	.545	11	6	1	0	2	9	3	0	.643	1.182	Jose Rijo	.063	12	1	0	0	0	0	2	4	.214	.063
Omar Olivares	.421	19	8	1	1	1	3	2	1	.455	.737	Ramon Martinez	.063	12	1	0	0	0	0	2	1	.214	.063
Juan Berenguer	.400	10	4	0	0	2	4	1	2	.455	1.000	Mike Moore	.067	23	2	0	0	2	0	0	6	.083	.174
Charlie Hough	.394	33	13	1	1	2	5	3	7	.444	.667	Tim Belcher	.100	10	1	0	0	0	0	1	2	.182	.100

Kent Bottenfield — Expos
Pitches Right

	ERA	W	L	Sv	G	GS	IP	BB	SO	Avg	H	2B	3B	HR	RBI	OBP	SLG	GF	IR	IRS	Hld	SvOp	SB	CS	GB	FB	G/F
1992 Season	2.23	1	2	1	10	4	32.1	11	14	.217	26	5	1	1	9	.284	.300	2	4	1	1	3	3	0	48	39	1.23

1992 Season

	ERA	W	L	Sv	G	GS	IP	H	HR	BB	SO		Avg	AB	H	2B	3B	HR	RBI	BB	SO	OBP	SLG
Home	3.68	0	1	0	5	2	14.2	14	1	3	11	vs. Left	.194	62	12	2	1	1	7	7	6	.271	.306
Away	1.02	1	1	1	5	2	17.2	12	0	8	3	vs. Right	.241	58	14	3	0	0	2	4	8	.297	.293

Denis Boucher — Indians
Pitches Left

	ERA	W	L	Sv	G	GS	IP	BB	SO	Avg	H	2B	3B	HR	RBI	OBP	SLG	CG	ShO	Sup	QS	#P/S	SB	CS	GB	FB	G/F
1992 Season	6.37	2	2	0	8	7	41.0	20	17	.302	48	5	1	9	28	.377	.516	0	0	6.80	3	93	0	1	53	64	0.83
Career (1991-1992)	6.18	3	9	0	20	19	99.0	44	46	.306	122	26	2	21	63	.376	.539	0	0	4.36	6	88	3	2	145	121	1.20

1992 Season

	ERA	W	L	Sv	G	GS	IP	H	HR	BB	SO		Avg	AB	H	2B	3B	HR	RBI	BB	SO	OBP	SLG
Home	12.71	0	1	0	3	3	11.1	23	4	6	3	vs. Left	.346	26	9	3	0	1	3	6	2	.469	.577
Away	3.94	2	1	0	5	4	29.2	25	5	14	14	vs. Right	.293	133	39	2	1	8	25	14	15	.358	.504

Rafael Bournigal — Dodgers
Bats Right

	Avg	G	AB	R	H	2B	3B	HR	RBI	BB	SO	HBP	GDP	SB	CS	OBP	SLG	IBB	SH	SF	#Pit	#P/PA	GB	FB	G/F
1992 Season	.150	10	20	1	3	1	0	0	0	1	2	1	0	0	0	.227	.200	0	0	0	58	2.64	10	7	1.43

1992 Season

	Avg	AB	H	2B	3B	HR	RBI	BB	SO	OBP	SLG		Avg	AB	H	2B	3B	HR	RBI	BB	SO	OBP	SLG
vs. Left	.125	8	1	0	0	0	0	1	2	.222	.125	Scoring Posn	.000	4	0	0	0	0	0	0	0	.000	.000
vs. Right	.167	12	2	1	0	0	0	0	0	.231	.250	Close & Late	.000	1	0	0	0	0	0	0	1	.500	.000

Ryan Bowen — Astros
Pitches Right (groundball pitcher)

	ERA	W	L	Sv	G	GS	IP	BB	SO	Avg	H	2B	3B	HR	RBI	OBP	SLG	CG	ShO	Sup	QS	#P/S	SB	CS	GB	FB	G/F
1992 Season	10.96	0	7	0	11	9	33.2	30	22	.333	48	9	1	8	35	.455	.576	0	0	3.21	0	70	5	3	63	34	1.85
Career (1991-1992)	7.01	6	11	0	25	22	105.1	66	71	.291	121	22	1	12	69	.389	.435	0	0	5.38	5	83	17	4	170	108	1.57

1992 Season

	ERA	W	L	Sv	G	GS	IP	H	HR	BB	SO		Avg	AB	H	2B	3B	HR	RBI	BB	SO	OBP	SLG
Home	9.43	0	4	0	6	5	21.0	27	6	16	12	vs. Left	.395	76	30	5	1	2	19	16	6	.511	.566
Away	13.50	0	3	0	5	4	12.2	21	2	14	10	vs. Right	.265	68	18	4	0	6	16	14	16	.390	.588

Scott Bradley — Mets

Bats Left (groundball hitter)

	Avg	G	AB	R	H	2B	3B	HR	RBI	BB	SO	HBP	GDP	SB	CS	OBP	SLG	IBB	SH	SF	#Pit	#P/PA	GB	FB	G/F
1992 Season	.333	7	6	1	2	0	0	0	1	2	1	0	0	0	0	.500	.333	0	0	0	32	4.00	3	0	0.00
Last Five Years	.245	397	1016	88	249	49	1	8	110	74	79	3	24	2	3	.294	.319	9	12	16	3338	3.01	496	269	1.84

1992 Season

	Avg	AB	H	2B	3B	HR	RBI	BB	SO	OBP	SLG		Avg	AB	H	2B	3B	HR	RBI	BB	SO	OBP	SLG
vs. Left	.000	0	0	0	0	0	0	0	0	.000	.000	Scoring Posn	.250	4	1	0	0	0	1	0	1	.250	.250
vs. Right	.333	6	2	0	0	0	1	2	1	.500	.333	Close & Late	.000	3	0	0	0	0	0	0	1	.000	.000

Last Five Years

	Avg	AB	H	2B	3B	HR	RBI	BB	SO	OBP	SLG		Avg	AB	H	2B	3B	HR	RBI	BB	SO	OBP	SLG
vs. Left	.156	96	15	2	0	0	12	7	10	.210	.177	Scoring Posn	.276	250	69	18	0	5	105	22	17	.321	.408
vs. Right	.254	920	234	47	1	8	98	67	69	.303	.334	Close & Late	.245	188	46	10	1	4	24	14	22	.298	.372
Groundball	.226	257	58	13	0	0	23	25	29	.295	.276	None on/out	.206	262	54	9	0	1		12	25	.244	.252
Flyball	.278	205	57	9	0	2	30	14	17	.321	.351	Batting #6	.308	182	56	13	0	3	21	11	12	.352	.429
Home	.248	500	124	28	1	5	56	38	40	.299	.338	Batting #8	.244	398	97	22	0	1	43	28	29	.289	.307
Away	.242	516	125	21	0	3	54	36	39	.289	.300	Other	.220	436	96	14	1	4	46	35	38	.275	.284
Day	.241	282	68	18	0	2	41	16	19	.277	.326	April	.299	97	29	7	1	0	21	5	8	.318	.392
Night	.247	734	181	31	1	6	69	58	60	.300	.316	May	.225	204	46	8	0	3	17	11	16	.266	.309
Grass	.251	402	101	19	0	3	47	25	31	.293	.321	June	.214	210	45	7	0	1	24	17	15	.270	.282
Turf	.241	614	148	30	1	5	63	49	48	.295	.318	July	.284	183	52	10	0	1	21	18	13	.348	.355
First Pitch	.289	249	72	10	0	5	31	6	0	.302	.390	August	.261	207	54	13	0	2	17	15	18	.311	.353
Ahead on Count	.271	262	71	14	1	4	35	49	0	.382	.344	September/October	.200	115	23	4	0	1	10	8	9	.248	.261
Behind on Count	.212	312	66	14	1	2	34	0	58	.210	.282	Pre-All Star	.241	557	134	24	1	4	66	39	40	.286	.309
Two Strikes	.185	281	52	10	0	1	19	17	79	.233	.231	Post-All Star	.251	459	115	25	0	4	44	35	39	.303	.331

Batter vs. Pitcher (career)

Hits Best Against	Avg	AB	H	2B	3B	HR	RBI	BB	SO	OBP	SLG	Hits Worst Against	Avg	AB	H	2B	3B	HR	RBI	BB	SO	OBP	SLG
Storm Davis	.412	17	7	1	0	0	1	1	0	.444	.471	Kevin Tapani	.059	17	1	0	0	0	0	0	0	.059	.059
Jeff Montgomery	.400	10	4	1	0	1	4	1	1	.455	.800	Duane Ward	.111	9	1	0	0	0	0	2	1	.273	.111
Tim Leary	.389	18	7	2	0	0	1	1	1	.421	.500	Kevin Brown	.111	9	1	0	0	3	1	0	1	.182	.111
Walt Terrell	.333	21	7	4	0	0	4	1	2	.348	.524	Bret Saberhagen	.136	22	3	0	0	0	0	1	0	.174	.136
Dave Stewart	.310	29	9	1	0	2	6	1	2	.323	.552	Jeff M. Robinson	.150	20	3	0	0	0	1	1	1	.190	.150

Glenn Braggs — Reds

Bats Right

	Avg	G	AB	R	H	2B	3B	HR	RBI	BB	SO	HBP	GDP	SB	CS	OBP	SLG	IBB	SH	SF	#Pit	#P/PA	GB	FB	G/F
1992 Season	.237	92	266	40	63	16	3	8	38	36	48	2	10	3	1	.330	.410	5	1	2	1119	3.66	89	86	1.03
Last Five Years	.256	502	1616	222	414	66	7	53	226	153	329	19	37	45	20	.324	.404	15	5	19	6643	3.68	594	456	1.30

1992 Season

	Avg	AB	H	2B	3B	HR	RBI	BB	SO	OBP	SLG		Avg	AB	H	2B	3B	HR	RBI	BB	SO	OBP	SLG
vs. Left	.248	145	36	7	2	5	24	21	24	.343	.428	Scoring Posn	.221	77	17	5	1	4	31	15	13	.347	.468
vs. Right	.223	121	27	9	1	3	14	15	24	.314	.388	Close & Late	.388	49	19	5	1	1	9	5	7	.446	.592
Groundball	.218	78	17	4	2	1	10	11	10	.322	.359	None on/out	.247	73	18	4	1	2	2	4	12	.286	.411
Flyball	.345	55	19	7	1	2	10	9	9	.438	.618	Batting #4	.203	59	12	3	0	1	8	10	14	.314	.305
Home	.239	117	28	7	2	4	19	19	22	.350	.436	Batting #5	.186	118	22	5	1	4	15	13	17	.271	.347
Away	.235	149	35	9	1	4	19	17	26	.314	.389	Other	.326	89	29	8	2	3	15	13	17	.417	.562
Day	.277	83	23	7	2	1	13	18	16	.406	.446	April	.212	33	7	1	0	0	3	3	6	.278	.242
Night	.219	183	40	9	1	7	25	18	32	.293	.393	May	.163	43	7	1	0	0	4	6	10	.280	.186
Grass	.313	80	25	7	1	2	12	8	13	.371	.500	June	.314	35	11	4	0	2	9	8	7	.442	.600
Turf	.204	186	38	9	2	6	26	28	35	.313	.371	July	.226	53	12	3	1	2	6	9	8	.333	.434
First Pitch	.360	25	9	2	1	1	5	3	0	.448	.640	August	.247	81	20	6	1	3	12	8	15	.319	.457
Ahead on Count	.333	66	22	5	1	4	11	29	0	.542	.621	September/October	.286	21	6	1	1	1	4	2	2	.348	.571
Behind on Count	.233	86	20	5	1	3	18	0	26	.230	.419	Pre-All Star	.200	125	25	6	0	2	17	20	26	.313	.296
Two Strikes	.175	120	21	5	0	3	13	4	48	.198	.292	Post-All Star	.270	141	38	10	3	6	21	16	22	.346	.511

1992 By Position

Position	Avg	AB	H	2B	3B	HR	RBI	BB	SO	OBP	SLG	G	GS	Innings	PO	A	E	DP	Fld Pct	Rng Fctr	In Zone	Outs	Zone Rtg	MLB Zone
As Pinch Hitter	.222	18	4	2	1	1	6	1	7	.263	.611	19	0	---	---	---	---	---	---	---	---	---	---	---
As lf	.237	173	41	11	1	5	22	21	28	.327	.399	56	44	401.2	65	2	1	0	.985	1.50	83	64	.771	.809
As rf	.240	75	18	3	1	2	10	14	13	.352	.387	29	24	191.2	37	1	5	0	.884	1.78	44	40	.909	.814

Last Five Years

	Avg	AB	H	2B	3B	HR	RBI	BB	SO	OBP	SLG		Avg	AB	H	2B	3B	HR	RBI	BB	SO	OBP	SLG
vs. Left	.276	645	178	27	3	27	105	80	111	.355	.453	Scoring Posn	.270	403	109	18	3	9	160	49	73	.345	.397
vs. Right	.243	971	236	39	4	26	121	73	218	.303	.372	Close & Late	.274	270	74	16	1	5	34	25	60	.347	.396
Groundball	.274	464	127	20	3	15	61	41	89	.342	.427	None on/out	.234	411	96	15	2	11	11	42	87	.309	.360
Flyball	.256	356	91	17	3	12	50	33	75	.322	.421	Batting #5	.236	556	131	22	2	20	80	50	108	.301	.390
Home	.250	816	204	33	6	31	125	80	172	.322	.419	Batting #6	.266	552	147	19	3	18	77	49	113	.331	.409
Away	.263	800	210	33	1	22	101	73	157	.327	.389	Other	.268	508	136	25	2	15	69	54	108	.343	.413
Day	.246	504	124	25	3	20	82	53	115	.325	.427	April	.239	247	59	9	1	8	37	26	55	.317	.381
Night	.261	1112	290	41	4	33	144	100	214	.324	.394	May	.243	367	89	11	1	16	56	34	76	.311	.409
Grass	.245	976	239	39	4	26	123	83	205	.308	.373	June	.276	341	94	14	2	11	46	28	77	.336	.425
Turf	.273	640	175	27	3	27	103	70	124	.349	.452	July	.254	240	61	13	1	5	29	28	43	.332	.379

Last Five Years																					
	Avg	AB	H	2B	3B	HR	RBI	BB	SO	OBP	SLG		Avg	AB	H	2B	3B	HR	RBI	BB	SO	OBP	SLG
First Pitch	.335	185	62	7	1	9	39	9	0	.376	.530	August	.253	297	75	15	1	7	40	21	52	.306	.380
Ahead on Count	.349	384	134	24	1	21	69	88	0	.472	.581	September/October	.290	124	36	4	1	6	18	16	26	.373	.484
Behind on Count	.213	526	112	22	3	14	67	0	170	.215	.346	Pre-All Star	.259	1025	265	39	4	37	146	97	218	.327	.413
Two Strikes	.154	726	112	19	1	10	64	52	327	.217	.225	Post-All Star	.252	591	149	27	3	16	80	56	111	.320	.389

Batter vs. Pitcher (career)																					
Hits Best Against	Avg	AB	H	2B	3B	HR	RBI	BB	SO	OBP	SLG	Hits Worst Against	Avg	AB	H	2B	3B	HR	RBI	BB	SO	OBP	SLG
Kirk McCaskill	.556	9	5	1	0	0	1	2	1	.636	.667	Dennis Rasmussen	.111	18	2	0	0	0	3	2	1	.200	.111
Steve Avery	.464	28	13	2	1	4	11	2	2	.500	1.036	Bert Blyleven	.154	13	2	0	0	0	2	0	2	.143	.154
Sid Fernandez	.400	10	4	1	1	0	3	2	3	.500	.700	Jose DeLeon	.154	13	2	0	0	0	1	1	5	.200	.154
Scott Bailes	.389	18	7	1	0	2	5	0	3	.350	.778	Terry Mulholland	.154	13	2	0	0	0	2	1	2	.188	.154
Bud Black	.364	22	8	4	0	1	5	2	3	.417	.682	Melido Perez	.182	11	2	0	0	0	1	1	2	.250	.182

Jeff Branson — Reds   Bats Left (groundball hitter)

	Avg	G	AB	R	H	2B	3B	HR	RBI	BB	SO	HBP	GDP	SB	CS	OBP	SLG	IBB	SH	SF	#Pit	#P/PA	GB	FB	G/F
1992 Season	.296	72	115	12	34	7	1	0	15	5	16	0	4	0	1	.322	.374	2	2	1	421	3.48	46	28	1.64

1992 Season

	Avg	AB	H	2B	3B	HR	RBI	BB	SO	OBP	SLG		Avg	AB	H	2B	3B	HR	RBI	BB	SO	OBP	SLG
vs. Left	.125	8	1	0	0	0	0	0	3	.125	.125	Scoring Posn	.308	39	12	5	0	0	15	2	6	.333	.436
vs. Right	.308	107	33	7	1	0	15	5	13	.336	.393	Close & Late	.367	30	11	2	0	0	6	1	6	.387	.433
Home	.308	52	16	3	1	0	9	2	5	.327	.404	None on/out	.318	22	7	1	0	0	0	2	1	.375	.364
Away	.286	63	18	4	0	0	6	3	11	.318	.349	Batting #6	.282	39	11	0	0	0	1	0	7	.275	.282
First Pitch	.346	26	9	1	0	0	0	2	0	.393	.385	Batting #9	.267	30	8	3	0	0	7	1	4	.290	.367
Ahead on Count	.263	19	5	3	0	0	5	2	0	.333	.421	Other	.326	46	15	4	1	0	7	4	5	.380	.457
Behind on Count	.231	39	9	3	0	0	4	0	8	.231	.308	Pre-All Star	.281	32	9	5	0	0	7	2	8	.314	.438
Two Strikes	.208	53	11	2	1	0	6	1	16	.218	.283	Post-All Star	.301	83	25	2	1	0	8	3	8	.326	.349

Cliff Brantley — Phillies   Pitches Right (groundball pitcher)

	ERA	W	L	Sv	G	GS	IP	BB	SO	Avg	H	2B	3B	HR	RBI	OBP	SLG	GF	IR	IRS	Hld	SvOp	SB	CS	GB	FB	G/F
1992 Season	4.60	2	6	0	28	9	76.1	58	32	.251	71	9	1	6	37	.382	.353	6	10	2	0	0	10	5	133	72	1.85
Career (1991-1992)	4.25	3	8	0	34	14	108.0	77	57	.244	97	13	2	6	48	.370	.332	6	13	3	0	0	16	7	176	95	1.85

1992 Season

	ERA	W	L	Sv	G	GS	IP	H	HR	BB	SO		Avg	AB	H	2B	3B	HR	RBI	BB	SO	OBP	SLG
Home	3.66	1	2	0	11	3	32.0	30	0	21	18	vs. Left	.301	153	46	5	1	3	25	32	13	.420	.405
Away	5.28	1	4	0	17	6	44.1	41	6	37	14	vs. Right	.192	130	25	4	0	3	12	26	19	.338	.292
Starter	5.05	2	4	0	9	9	46.1	46	5	37	16	Scoring Posn	.244	90	22	2	1	0	29	22	13	.388	.289
Reliever	3.90	0	2	0	19	0	30.0	25	1	21	16	Close & Late	.467	15	7	2	0	0	3	8	2	.652	.600
0 Days rest	1.69	0	0	0	4	0	5.1	3	1	4	4	None on/out	.261	69	18	3	0	2	2	10	3	.363	.391
1 or 2 Days rest	6.75	0	2	0	7	0	9.1	13	0	6	5	First Pitch	.250	32	8	0	0	0	2	3	0	.351	.250
3+ Days rest	2.93	0	0	0	8	0	15.1	9	0	11	7	Behind on Count	.307	88	27	3	0	2	14	39	0	.512	.409
Pre-All Star	5.01	2	5	0	15	6	46.2	49	2	37	20	Ahead on Count	.205	122	25	5	1	4	14	0	31	.218	.361
Post-All Star	3.94	0	1	0	13	3	29.2	22	4	21	12	Two Strikes	.183	120	22	5	1	3	13	16	32	.288	.317

Jeff Brantley — Giants   Pitches Right

	ERA	W	L	Sv	G	GS	IP	BB	SO	Avg	H	2B	3B	HR	RBI	OBP	SLG	GF	IR	IRS	Hld	SvOp	SB	CS	GB	FB	G/F
1992 Season	2.95	7	7	7	56	4	91.2	45	86	.207	67	12	0	8	40	.307	.319	32	32	11	3	9	4	1	76	105	0.72
Career (1988-1992)	2.94	24	14	42	246	6	391.2	173	308	.239	345	53	2	31	156	.324	.343	103	149	43	34	54	42	10	466	445	1.05

1992 Season

	ERA	W	L	Sv	G	GS	IP	H	HR	BB	SO		Avg	AB	H	2B	3B	HR	RBI	BB	SO	OBP	SLG
Home	2.30	4	3	3	30	2	47.0	31	3	21	42	vs. Left	.181	193	35	7	0	4	16	32	58	.300	.280
Away	3.63	3	4	4	26	2	44.2	36	5	24	44	vs. Right	.246	130	32	5	0	4	24	13	28	.320	.377
Starter	0.44	3	0	0	4	4	20.2	11	0	6	27	Scoring Posn	.217	92	20	5	0	3	33	16	24	.324	.370
Reliever	3.68	4	7	7	52	0	71.0	56	8	39	59	Close & Late	.252	111	28	4	0	3	21	20	27	.363	.369
0 Days rest	3.29	3	1	1	9	0	13.2	12	1	6	15	None on/out	.154	78	12	2	0	0	0	8	18	.233	.179
1 or 2 Days rest	4.17	1	4	5	26	0	36.2	29	3	23	25	First Pitch	.303	33	10	2	0	1	6	4	0	.400	.455
3+ Days rest	3.05	0	2	1	17	0	20.2	15	4	10	19	Behind on Count	.279	61	17	4	0	2	16	17	0	.430	.443
Pre-All Star	3.02	3	4	7	34	0	41.2	27	6	22	32	Ahead on Count	.147	170	25	4	0	3	8	0	79	.152	.224
Post-All Star	2.88	4	3	0	22	4	50.0	40	2	23	54	Two Strikes	.120	183	22	4	0	4	15	24	86	.221	.208

Career (1988-1992)

	ERA	W	L	Sv	G	GS	IP	H	HR	BB	SO		Avg	AB	H	2B	3B	HR	RBI	BB	SO	OBP	SLG
Home	2.58	14	6	19	112	4	181.2	155	12	77	149	vs. Left	.239	788	188	31	0	12	67	113	158	.334	.324
Away	3.26	10	8	23	134	2	210.0	190	19	96	159	vs. Right	.240	655	157	22	2	19	89	60	150	.312	.366
Day	2.55	13	4	14	99	3	155.1	139	11	72	122	Inning 1-6	.240	367	88	15	2	10	50	45	82	.325	.373
Night	3.20	11	10	28	147	3	236.1	206	20	101	186	Inning 7+	.239	1076	257	38	0	21	106	128	226	.324	.333
Grass	2.87	18	9	27	180	6	265.2	265	21	118	224	None on	.244	758	185	32	0	19	79	169	320	.320	.361
Turf	3.14	6	5	15	66	0	106.0	80	10	55	84	Runners on	.234	685	160	21	2	12	137	94	139	.328	.323
April	3.29	1	2	4	37	0	52.0	42	3	29	39	Scoring Posn	.209	430	90	11	0	9	127	68	102	.317	.298

Career (1988-1992)

	ERA	W	L	Sv	G	GS	IP	H	HR	BB	SO		Avg	AB	H	2B	3B	HR	RBI	BB	SO	OBP	SLG
May	1.44	2	2	11	45	0	62.1	46	3	27	43	Close & Late	.237	624	148	20	0	10	55	91	127	.337	.317
June	2.96	6	2	6	41	0	66.1	63	11	27	41	None on/out	.227	331	75	14	0	9	9	36	65	.306	.350
July	4.14	7	2	11	39	0	58.2	57	6	21	50	vs. 1st Batr (relief)	.212	208	44	8	1	5	23	23	42	.294	.332
August	2.73	4	4	6	47	1	79.0	71	4	43	63	First Inning Pitched	.227	825	187	23	1	19	101	107	187	.319	.326
September/October	3.19	4	2	4	37	5	73.1	66	4	26	72	First 15 Pitches	.236	709	167	25	1	16	77	83	147	.319	.341
Starter	3.00	3	2	0	6	6	30.0	22	1	12	33	Pitch 16-30	.244	480	117	16	1	9	42	60	100	.333	.338
Reliever	2.94	21	12	42	240	0	361.2	323	30	161	275	Pitch 31-45	.267	172	46	10	0	5	32	21	42	.349	.413
0 Days rest	3.28	6	2	10	43	0	60.1	56	6	19	52	Pitch 46+	.183	82	15	2	0	1	5	9	19	.264	.244
1 or 2 Days rest	2.96	10	7	23	129	0	201.0	181	16	97	147	First Pitch	.256	172	44	6	1	3	18	22	0	.343	.355
3+ Days rest	2.69	5	3	9	68	0	100.1	86	8	45	76	Ahead on Count	.194	716	139	23	0	8	46	2	261	.205	.260
Pre-All Star	2.55	13	6	25	136	0	201.1	168	18	88	142	Behind on Count	.299	274	82	12	1	13	48	74	0	.447	.493
Post-All Star	3.36	11	8	17	110	6	190.1	177	13	85	166	Two Strikes	.152	732	111	16	0	10	51	77	307	.239	.214

Pitcher vs. Batter (career)

Pitches Best Vs.	Avg	AB	H	2B	3B	HR	RBI	BB	SO	OBP	SLG	Pitches Worst Vs.	Avg	AB	H	2B	3B	HR	RBI	BB	SO	OBP	SLG
Barry Bonds	.000	13	0	0	0	0	0	1	5	.071	.000	Tony Gwynn	.647	17	11	1	0	0	1	3	0	.700	.706
Spike Owen	.083	12	1	0	0	0	0	2	2	.214	.083	Howard Johnson	.500	8	4	0	0	1	3	3	2	.583	.875
Barry Larkin	.083	12	1	0	0	0	0	0	1	.083	.083	John Kruk	.375	8	3	0	0	1	1	3	1	.545	.750
Bobby Bonilla	.100	10	1	0	0	0	0	1	2	.182	.100	Paul O'Neill	.364	11	4	0	0	2	6	6	1	.588	.909
Craig Biggio	.100	10	1	0	0	0	0	1	1	.182	.100	Ron Gant	.313	16	5	1	0	3	6	1	4	.353	.938

Sid Bream — Braves

Bats Left (flyball hitter)

	Avg	G	AB	R	H	2B	3B	HR	RBI	BB	SO	HBP	GDP	SB	CS	OBP	SLG	IBB	SH	SF	#Pit	#P/PA	GB	FB	G/F
1992 Season	.261	125	372	30	97	25	1	9	61	46	51	1	3	6	0	.340	.414	2	3	4	1483	3.51	125	118	1.06
Last Five Years	.262	530	1524	154	399	100	3	46	242	178	221	4	28	23	20	.336	.422	18	17	21	6176	3.58	519	534	0.97

1992 Season

	Avg	AB	H	2B	3B	HR	RBI	BB	SO	OBP	SLG		Avg	AB	H	2B	3B	HR	RBI	BB	SO	OBP	SLG
vs. Left	.242	33	8	4	0	1	7	1	5	.265	.455	Scoring Posn	.299	107	32	10	1	0	45	16	14	.383	.411
vs. Right	.263	339	89	21	1	9	54	45	46	.347	.410	Close & Late	.212	52	11	5	0	1	7	4	9	.263	.365
Groundball	.306	160	49	12	1	5	33	21	20	.383	.488	None on/out	.231	91	21	6	0	4	4	8	12	.293	.429
Flyball	.250	76	19	4	0	2	13	12	12	.352	.382	Batting #5	.248	282	70	18	1	6	43	34	40	.328	.383
Home	.264	178	47	11	0	4	32	26	20	.353	.393	Batting #6	.302	86	26	7	0	4	18	12	10	.384	.523
Away	.258	194	50	14	1	6	29	20	31	.329	.433	Other	.250	4	1	0	0	0	0	0	1	.250	.250
Day	.301	113	34	10	1	1	22	13	10	.378	.434	April	.176	51	9	3	0	0	2	9	9	.300	.235
Night	.243	259	63	15	0	9	39	33	41	.324	.405	May	.302	53	16	5	0	2	8	9	3	.413	.509
Grass	.254	276	70	17	1	7	45	36	39	.337	.399	June	.246	61	15	3	1	0	11	7	11	.319	.328
Turf	.281	96	27	8	0	3	16	10	12	.352	.458	July	.286	63	18	5	0	2	8	4	7	.324	.460
First Pitch	.269	67	18	2	0	2	10	2	0	.282	.388	August	.299	67	20	5	0	4	22	7	5	.355	.552
Ahead on Count	.277	101	28	8	0	1	16	26	0	.422	.386	September/October	.247	77	19	4	0	2	10	10	16	.333	.377
Behind on Count	.250	124	31	14	1	3	20	0	28	.254	.452	Pre-All Star	.250	188	47	12	1	2	21	26	26	.343	.356
Two Strikes	.197	137	27	10	1	4	26	19	51	.293	.372	Post-All Star	.272	184	50	13	0	8	40	20	25	.338	.473

1992 By Position

Position	Avg	AB	H	2B	3B	HR	RBI	BB	SO	OBP	SLG	G	GS	Innings	PO	A	E	DP	Fld Pct	Rng Fctr	In Zone	Outs	Zone Rtg	MLB Zone
As Pinch Hitter	.333	12	4	1	0	0	3	5	3	.529	.417	17	0	---	---	---	---	---	---	---	---	---	---	---
As 1b	.258	360	93	24	1	10	58	41	48	.333	.414	120	106	907.1	855	72	10	70	.989	---	138	119	.862	.843

Last Five Years

	Avg	AB	H	2B	3B	HR	RBI	BB	SO	OBP	SLG		Avg	AB	H	2B	3B	HR	RBI	BB	SO	OBP	SLG
vs. Left	.217	295	64	20	1	7	41	16	55	.257	.363	Scoring Posn	.284	437	124	28	1	11	182	71	64	.371	.428
vs. Right	.273	1229	335	80	2	39	201	162	166	.354	.436	Close & Late	.256	234	60	18	0	5	33	29	29	.331	.397
Groundball	.279	578	161	39	2	16	91	66	71	.352	.436	None on/out	.246	350	86	19	1	10	10	30	50	.305	.391
Flyball	.244	315	77	20	1	16	59	39	51	.323	.467	Batting #5	.257	719	185	52	1	17	112	79	96	.328	.403
Home	.260	708	184	52	1	21	117	79	98	.332	.425	Batting #6	.263	696	183	42	2	22	107	80	109	.336	.424
Away	.263	816	215	48	2	25	125	99	123	.340	.419	Other	.284	109	31	6	0	7	23	19	16	.389	.532
Day	.284	430	122	37	2	11	75	50	60	.357	.456	April	.247	243	60	22	0	4	21	28	38	.325	.387
Night	.253	1094	277	63	1	35	167	128	161	.324	.409	May	.260	273	71	17	0	11	52	38	44	.349	.443
Grass	.252	698	176	37	1	17	104	83	101	.327	.381	June	.325	246	80	18	2	8	45	17	29	.362	.512
Turf	.270	826	223	63	2	29	138	95	120	.344	.456	July	.244	205	50	9	0	7	33	26	32	.328	.390
First Pitch	.320	244	78	18	0	7	43	6	0	.333	.480	August	.288	257	74	21	0	7	51	31	30	.361	.451
Ahead on Count	.283	407	115	30	1	13	66	107	0	.429	.457	September/October	.213	300	64	13	1	9	40	38	48	.299	.353
Behind on Count	.226	468	106	36	1	13	75	1	115	.227	.391	Pre-All Star	.276	840	232	60	2	25	126	95	121	.347	.442
Two Strikes	.202	594	120	28	1	18	89	58	221	.269	.343	Post-All Star	.244	684	167	40	1	21	116	83	100	.323	.398

Batter vs. Pitcher (since 1984)

Hits Best Against	Avg	AB	H	2B	3B	HR	RBI	BB	SO	OBP	SLG	Hits Worst Against	Avg	AB	H	2B	3B	HR	RBI	BB	SO	OBP	SLG
Mike Maddux	.529	17	9	1	1	0	3	4	3	.619	.706	Tom Browning	.000	10	0	0	0	0	0	2	2	.167	.000
Shawn Boskie	.500	12	6	0	0	1	5	1	1	.500	.750	Sid Fernandez	.063	16	1	0	0	0	0	1	3	.118	.063
Bill Sampen	.500	10	5	0	0	1	3	0	2	.455	.800	Mark Gardner	.100	10	1	0	0	0	0	1	1	.308	.100
Randy Myers	.500	8	4	2	0	1	4	2	2	.500	1.125	Jim Deshaies	.133	15	2	0	0	0	1	0	2	.133	.133
Mark Davis	.400	10	4	1	0	2	8	1	0	.455	1.100	Paul Assenmacher	.143	14	2	0	0	0	0	0	4	.143	.143

George Brett — Royals
Bats Left

	Avg	G	AB	R	H	2B	3B	HR	RBI	BB	SO	HBP	GDP	SB	CS	OBP	SLG	IBB	SH	SF	#Pit	#P/PA	GB	FB	G/F
1992 Season	.285	152	592	55	169	35	5	7	61	35	69	6	15	8	6	.330	.397	6	0	4	2078	3.26	222	184	1.21
Last Five Years	.293	706	2687	371	786	188	20	67	392	290	305	12	85	47	15	.360	.452	59	1	35	10418	3.45	1053	847	1.24

1992 Season

	Avg	AB	H	2B	3B	HR	RBI	BB	SO	OBP	SLG		Avg	AB	H	2B	3B	HR	RBI	BB	SO	OBP	SLG
vs. Left	.277	184	51	11	1	0	20	7	24	.320	.348	Scoring Posn	.285	130	37	5	1	2	50	18	14	.370	.385
vs. Right	.289	408	118	24	4	7	41	28	45	.334	.419	Close & Late	.227	97	22	2	0	4	14	9	10	.294	.371
Groundball	.225	138	31	2	0	0	8	5	17	.260	.239	None on/out	.272	136	37	10	1	3	3	4	15	.298	.426
Flyball	.294	204	60	15	1	4	29	13	19	.341	.436	Batting #3	.305	305	93	13	2	3	35	14	41	.335	.390
Home	.288	312	90	19	3	1	35	16	27	.328	.378	Batting #5	.269	264	71	21	2	4	24	18	21	.325	.409
Away	.282	280	79	16	2	6	26	19	42	.331	.418	Other	.217	23	5	1	1	0	2	3	7	.308	.348
Day	.309	139	43	13	2	2	20	12	17	.362	.475	April	.197	66	13	5	0	2	6	8	7	.303	.364
Night	.278	453	126	22	3	5	41	23	52	.320	.373	May	.306	85	26	6	1	0	8	7	12	.366	.400
Grass	.280	218	61	12	2	5	21	14	33	.328	.422	June	.260	100	26	8	1	1	8	3	6	.288	.390
Turf	.289	374	108	23	3	2	40	21	36	.331	.382	July	.298	114	34	5	1	1	9	10	18	.360	.386
First Pitch	.299	117	35	6	0	1	8	5	0	.333	.376	August	.304	112	34	4	1	2	19	5	11	.328	.411
Ahead on Count	.315	143	45	13	1	5	24	17	0	.383	.524	September/October	.313	115	36	7	1	1	11	2	15	.325	.417
Behind on Count	.214	192	41	8	4	0	14	0	38	.224	.297	Pre-All Star	.264	303	80	22	3	4	27	22	30	.322	.396
Two Strikes	.254	213	54	11	3	0	17	13	69	.298	.333	Post-All Star	.308	289	89	13	2	3	34	13	39	.338	.398

1992 By Position

Position	Avg	AB	H	2B	3B	HR	RBI	BB	SO	OBP	SLG	G	GS	Innings	PO	A	E	DP	Fld Pct	Rng Fctr	In Zone	Outs	Zone Rtg	MLB Zone
As Designated Hitter	.282	521	147	26	4	7	53	30	62	.326	.388	132	131	---	---	---	---	---	---	---	---	---	---	---
As 1b	.339	56	19	7	1	0	7	5	7	.393	.500	15	15	133.0	137	12	2	9	.987	---	33	26	.788	.843

Last Five Years

	Avg	AB	H	2B	3B	HR	RBI	BB	SO	OBP	SLG		Avg	AB	H	2B	3B	HR	RBI	BB	SO	OBP	SLG
vs. Left	.275	903	248	56	6	19	132	81	111	.335	.413	Scoring Posn	.298	661	197	43	3	15	300	148	77	.412	.440
vs. Right	.302	1784	538	132	14	48	260	209	194	.372	.472	Close & Late	.254	422	107	24	2	10	55	64	53	.351	.391
Groundball	.306	653	200	45	1	0	83	76	69	.378	.438	None on/out	.280	539	151	41	2	15	37	59	328	.447
Flyball	.300	723	217	58	6	22	118	74	62	.365	.488	Batting #3	.293	2057	603	148	13	52	317	241	238	.364	.454
Home	.286	1362	390	86	14	23	197	146	124	.354	.421	Batting #5	.281	366	103	24	4	5	32	26	34	.333	.410
Away	.299	1325	396	102	6	44	195	144	181	.366	.485	Other	.303	264	80	16	3	10	43	23	33	.358	.500
Day	.314	685	215	57	4	25	122	68	78	.373	.518	April	.238	340	81	12	0	9	43	46	42	.327	.353
Night	.285	2002	571	131	16	42	270	222	227	.355	.430	May	.310	335	104	24	5	5	45	36	39	.378	.457
Grass	.296	1049	310	82	4	36	157	113	145	.364	.484	June	.267	435	116	39	1	8	58	42	43	.331	.416
Turf	.291	1638	476	106	16	31	235	177	160	.357	.432	July	.322	531	171	44	4	20	90	57	59	.388	.533
First Pitch	.339	487	165	42	2	12	82	26	0	.370	.507	August	.296	523	155	36	7	12	85	62	57	.366	.461
Ahead on Count	.322	667	215	50	7	26	109	151	0	.443	.535	September/October	.304	523	159	33	3	13	71	47	65	.360	.453
Behind on Count	.260	762	198	46	8	17	101	3	149	.262	.408	Pre-All Star	.275	1297	357	90	7	26	174	144	140	.347	.416
Two Strikes	.222	979	217	49	6	18	102	94	305	.290	.339	Post-All Star	.309	1390	429	98	13	41	218	146	155	.372	.486

Batter vs. Pitcher (since 1984)

Hits Best Against	Avg	AB	H	2B	3B	HR	RBI	BB	SO	OBP	SLG	Hits Worst Against	Avg	AB	H	2B	3B	HR	RBI	BB	SO	OBP	SLG
Todd Stottlemyre	.571	21	12	2	2	0	2	1	.609	.857	Scott Radinsky	.000	10	0	0	0	0	0	0	1	.167	.000
Jim Abbott	.545	22	12	2	0	3	9	3	5	.600	1.045	Bobby Thigpen	.067	15	1	0	0	0	1	2	0	.176	.067
Jose Rijo	.500	12	6	1	0	2	7	5	2	.647	1.083	Chuck Crim	.077	13	1	0	0	0	0	0	3	.143	.077
Edwin Nunez	.455	11	5	1	0	2	5	1	1	.500	1.091	Bud Black	.083	12	1	0	0	0	1	1	2	.154	.083
Jeff Russell	.400	15	6	0	0	3	9	5	2	.524	1.000	John Smiley	.091	11	1	0	0	0	0	0	1	.091	.091

Rod Brewer — Cardinals
Bats Left

	Avg	G	AB	R	H	2B	3B	HR	RBI	BB	SO	HBP	GDP	SB	CS	OBP	SLG	IBB	SH	SF	#Pit	#P/PA	GB	FB	G/F
1992 Season	.301	29	103	11	31	6	0	0	10	8	12	1	1	0	1	.354	.359	0	0	1	388	3.43	40	29	1.38
Career (1990-1992)	.270	62	141	15	38	7	0	0	13	8	21	1	2	0	1	.311	.319	0	0	1	507	3.36	53	39	1.36

1992 Season

	Avg	AB	H	2B	3B	HR	RBI	BB	SO	OBP	SLG		Avg	AB	H	2B	3B	HR	RBI	BB	SO	OBP	SLG
vs. Left	.292	24	7	2	0	0	2	0	3	.292	.375	Scoring Posn	.344	32	11	3	0	0	10	2	5	.371	.438
vs. Right	.304	79	24	4	0	0	8	8	9	.371	.354	Close & Late	.158	19	3	0	0	0	1	1	3	.238	.158
Home	.271	59	16	4	0	0	5	4	9	.323	.339	None on/out	.320	25	8	1	0	0	0	0	5	.320	.360
Away	.341	44	15	2	0	0	5	4	3	.396	.386	Batting #5	.383	47	18	2	0	0	7	2	7	.420	.426
First Pitch	.368	19	7	1	0	0	1	0	0	.381	.421	Batting #6	.231	52	12	3	0	0	3	5	5	.293	.288
Ahead on Count	.296	27	8	2	0	0	4	3	0	.367	.370	Other	.250	4	1	1	0	0	0	1	0	.400	.500
Behind on Count	.278	36	10	2	0	0	2	0	6	.278	.333	Pre-All Star	.000	0	0	0	0	0	0	0	0	.000	.000
Two Strikes	.231	39	9	3	0	0	4	5	12	.318	.308	Post-All Star	.301	103	31	6	0	0	10	8	12	.354	.359

Greg Briley — Mariners

Bats Left (groundball hitter)

	Avg	G	AB	R	H	2B	3B	HR	RBI	BB	SO	HBP	GDP	SB	CS	OBP	SLG	IBB	SH	SF	#Pit	#P/PA	GB	FB	G/F
1992 Season	.275	86	200	18	55	10	0	5	12	4	31	1	4	9	2	.290	.400	0	0	2	743	3.59	87	49	1.78
Career (1988-1992)	.260	478	1348	155	351	69	9	26	123	112	218	7	26	59	23	.317	.383	2	3	15	5463	3.69	552	353	1.56

1992 Season

	Avg	AB	H	2B	3B	HR	RBI	BB	SO	OBP	SLG		Avg	AB	H	2B	3B	HR	RBI	BB	SO	OBP	SLG
vs. Left	.000	5	0	0	0	0	0	0	0	.000	.000	Scoring Posn	.196	46	9	1	0	0	7	3	8	.235	.217
vs. Right	.282	195	55	10	0	5	12	4	31	.297	.410	Close & Late	.351	37	13	2	0	0	4	0	5	.368	.405
Home	.305	95	29	6	0	1	4	1	16	.316	.400	None on/out	.333	57	19	6	0	3	3	0	13	.345	.596
Away	.248	105	26	4	0	4	8	3	15	.266	.400	Batting #1	.274	84	23	5	0	3	6	2	17	.287	.440
First Pitch	.320	25	8	1	0	1	3	0	0	.308	.480	Batting #2	.262	42	11	2	0	1	3	2	5	.289	.381
Ahead on Count	.296	54	16	4	0	1	4	3	0	.339	.426	Other	.284	74	21	3	0	1	3	0	9	.293	.365
Behind on Count	.200	65	13	1	0	1	2	0	20	.200	.262	Pre-All Star	.244	135	33	5	0	3	8	2	22	.259	.348
Two Strikes	.172	87	15	3	0	1	3	1	31	.182	.241	Post-All Star	.338	65	22	5	0	2	4	2	9	.353	.508

Career (1988-1992)

	Avg	AB	H	2B	3B	HR	RBI	BB	SO	OBP	SLG		Avg	AB	H	2B	3B	HR	RBI	BB	SO	OBP	SLG
vs. Left	.246	134	33	6	2	1	19	11	31	.306	.343	Scoring Posn	.237	287	68	8	5	5	90	28	53	.291	.352
vs. Right	.262	1214	318	63	7	25	104	101	187	.318	.387	Close & Late	.272	235	64	13	3	2	21	11	49	.306	.379
Groundball	.259	382	99	19	2	6	35	33	56	.319	.366	None on/out	.254	319	81	15	1	6	6	20	50	.304	.364
Flyball	.271	292	79	19	3	7	29	22	41	.318	.428	Batting #2	.246	622	153	28	7	17	72	59	111	.311	.395
Home	.241	634	153	25	3	12	57	56	93	.302	.347	Batting #7	.252	250	63	14	1	0	15	17	32	.297	.316
Away	.277	714	198	44	6	14	66	56	125	.330	.415	Other	.284	476	135	27	1	9	36	36	75	.335	.401
Day	.247	364	90	13	2	8	32	24	63	.297	.360	April	.227	154	35	12	0	1	12	14	22	.294	.325
Night	.265	984	261	56	7	18	91	88	155	.324	.391	May	.263	236	62	10	0	4	23	12	35	.298	.356
Grass	.263	555	146	29	6	9	46	48	98	.322	.386	June	.239	247	59	12	1	6	21	13	51	.275	.368
Turf	.259	793	205	40	3	17	77	64	120	.314	.381	July	.296	199	59	10	3	7	28	23	29	.370	.482
First Pitch	.259	162	42	9	1	2	14	0	0	.262	.364	August	.250	252	63	13	3	5	21	25	44	.320	.385
Ahead on Count	.325	375	122	23	4	10	51	73	0	.433	.488	September/October	.281	260	73	12	2	3	18	25	37	.341	.377
Behind on Count	.233	451	105	20	2	6	29	1	128	.238	.339	Pre-All Star	.246	675	166	36	1	12	61	41	112	.289	.356
Two Strikes	.188	573	108	19	4	9	39	39	215	.241	.283	Post-All Star	.275	673	185	33	8	14	62	71	106	.344	.410

Batter vs. Pitcher (career)

Hits Best Against	Avg	AB	H	2B	3B	HR	RBI	BB	SO	OBP	SLG	Hits Worst Against	Avg	AB	H	2B	3B	HR	RBI	BB	SO	OBP	SLG
Jose Mesa	.636	11	7	2	0	0	0	0	0	.636	.818	Scott Sanderson	.000	20	0	0	0	0	0	0	3	.000	.000
Pete Harnisch	.529	17	9	4	0	1	4	2	0	.579	.941	Bert Blyleven	.071	14	1	0	0	0	0	0	5	.071	.071
Mike Boddicker	.414	29	12	2	0	0	3	2	2	.452	.483	Tim Leary	.091	22	2	1	0	0	0	2	1	.167	.136
Kirk McCaskill	.407	27	11	1	0	1	2	5	4	.500	.556	Bob Milacki	.091	11	1	1	0	0	0	0	4	.091	.182
Kevin Appier	.357	14	5	2	0	0	1	1	3	.400	.500	Bill Wegman	.143	14	2	0	0	0	0	0	4	.143	.143

Brad Brink — Phillies

Pitches Right

	ERA	W	L	Sv	G	GS	IP	BB	SO	Avg	H	2B	3B	HR	RBI	OBP	SLG	CG	ShO	Sup	QS	#P/S	SB	CS	GB	FB	G/F
1992 Season	4.14	0	4	0	8	7	41.1	13	16	.308	53	8	2	2	23	.360	.413	0	0	1.74	1	89	3	2	61	58	1.05

1992 Season

	ERA	W	L	Sv	G	GS	IP	H	HR	BB	SO		Avg	AB	H	2B	3B	HR	RBI	BB	SO	OBP	SLG
Home	4.70	0	3	0	4	4	23.0	32	2	6	9	vs. Left	.284	102	29	3	1	2	13	7	6	.330	.392
Away	3.44	0	1	0	4	3	18.1	21	0	7	7	vs. Right	.343	70	24	5	1	0	10	6	10	.403	.443

John Briscoe — Athletics

Pitches Right

	ERA	W	L	Sv	G	GS	IP	BB	SO	Avg	H	2B	3B	HR	RBI	OBP	SLG	CG	ShO	Sup	QS	#P/S	SB	CS	GB	FB	G/F
1992 Season	6.43	0	1	0	2	2	7.0	9	4	.400	12	2	0	0	5	.538	.467	0	0	3.86	0	69	0	1	11	8	1.38
Career (1991-1992)	6.86	0	1	0	13	2	21.0	19	13	.296	24	5	0	3	19	.426	.469	0	0	3.43	0	69	0	1	25	25	1.00

1992 Season

	ERA	W	L	Sv	G	GS	IP	H	HR	BB	SO		Avg	AB	H	2B	3B	HR	RBI	BB	SO	OBP	SLG
Home	7.36	0	0	0	1	1	3.2	6	0	5	1	vs. Left	.389	18	7	0	0	0	3	5	3	.522	.389
Away	5.40	0	1	0	1	1	3.1	6	0	4	3	vs. Right	.417	12	5	2	0	0	2	1	1	.563	.583

Bernardo Brito — Twins

Bats Right

	Avg	G	AB	R	H	2B	3B	HR	RBI	BB	SO	HBP	GDP	SB	CS	OBP	SLG	IBB	SH	SF	#Pit	#P/PA	GB	FB	G/F
1992 Season	.143	8	14	1	2	1	0	0	2	0	4	0	0	0	1	.133	.214	0	0	1	45	3.00	5	4	1.25

1992 Season

	Avg	AB	H	2B	3B	HR	RBI	BB	SO	OBP	SLG		Avg	AB	H	2B	3B	HR	RBI	BB	SO	OBP	SLG
vs. Left	.286	7	2	1	0	0	2	0	2	.250	.429	Scoring Posn	.250	4	1	1	0	0	2	0	1	.200	.500
vs. Right	.000	7	0	0	0	0	0	0	2	.000	.000	Close & Late	.333	6	2	1	0	0	1	0	3	.333	.500

Doug Brocail — Padres   Pitches Right

	ERA	W	L	Sv	G	GS	IP	BB	SO	Avg	H	2B	3B	HR	RBI	OBP	SLG	CG	ShO	Sup	QS	#P/S	SB	CS	GB	FB	G/F
1992 Season	6.43	0	0	0	3	3	14.0	5	15	.298	17	5	0	2	8	.355	.491	0	0	2.57	0	84	0	0	17	17	1.00

1992 Season

	ERA	W	L	Sv	G	GS	IP	H	HR	BB	SO		Avg	AB	H	2B	3B	HR	RBI	BB	SO	OBP	SLG
Home	0.00	0	0	0	0	0	0.0	0	0	0	0	vs. Left	.306	36	11	3	0	1	4	3	9	.359	.472
Away	6.43	0	0	0	3	3	14.0	17	2	5	15	vs. Right	.286	21	6	2	0	1	4	2	6	.348	.524

Rico Brogna — Tigers   Bats Left

	Avg	G	AB	R	H	2B	3B	HR	RBI	BB	SO	HBP	GDP	SB	CS	OBP	SLG	IBB	SH	SF	#Pit	#P/PA	GB	FB	G/F
1992 Season	.192	9	26	3	5	1	0	1	3	3	5	0	0	0	0	.276	.346	0	0	0	115	3.97	9	9	1.00

1992 Season

	Avg	AB	H	2B	3B	HR	RBI	BB	SO	OBP	SLG		Avg	AB	H	2B	3B	HR	RBI	BB	SO	OBP	SLG
vs. Left	.500	2	1	0	0	0	0	0	0	.500	.500	Scoring Posn	.125	8	1	0	0	0	1	1	2	.222	.125
vs. Right	.167	24	4	1	0	1	3	3	5	.259	.333	Close & Late	.000	1	0	0	0	0	0	0	1	.000	.000

Hubie Brooks — Angels   Bats Right

	Avg	G	AB	R	H	2B	3B	HR	RBI	BB	SO	HBP	GDP	SB	CS	OBP	SLG	IBB	SH	SF	#Pit	#P/PA	GB	FB	G/F
1992 Season	.216	82	306	28	66	13	0	8	36	12	46	1	10	3	0	.247	.337	3	0	1	1113	3.48	118	101	1.17
Last Five Years	.259	637	2361	267	611	117	5	78	337	163	432	15	66	21	23	.307	.412	26	0	27	9039	3.52	905	669	1.35

1992 Season

	Avg	AB	H	2B	3B	HR	RBI	BB	SO	OBP	SLG		Avg	AB	H	2B	3B	HR	RBI	BB	SO	OBP	SLG
vs. Left	.220	82	18	2	0	1	8	4	10	.256	.280	Scoring Posn	.218	78	17	3	0	2	26	6	14	.279	.333
vs. Right	.214	224	48	11	0	7	28	8	36	.244	.357	Close & Late	.250	56	14	1	0	2	6	4	9	.311	.375
Groundball	.139	72	10	2	0	0	5	2	10	.173	.167	None on/out	.172	87	15	4	0	2	2	2	7	.191	.287
Flyball	.239	92	22	3	0	3	16	4	15	.268	.370	Batting #4	.215	274	59	12	0	8	34	11	38	.247	.347
Home	.247	150	37	7	0	2	16	7	19	.280	.333	Batting #5	.313	16	5	1	0	0	1	0	5	.313	.375
Away	.186	156	29	6	0	6	20	5	27	.215	.340	Other	.125	16	2	0	0	0	1	1	3	.176	.375
Day	.203	79	16	4	0	1	7	2	7	.222	.291	April	.298	84	25	5	0	4	19	3	11	.318	.500
Night	.220	227	50	9	0	7	29	10	39	.255	.352	May	.165	91	15	2	0	2	7	3	11	.191	.253
Grass	.213	268	57	11	0	8	33	11	39	.246	.343	June	.164	55	9	3	0	1	4	3	13	.220	.273
Turf	.237	38	9	2	0	0	3	1	7	.256	.289	July	.000	0	0	0	0	0	0	0	0	.000	.000
First Pitch	.333	42	14	3	0	2	5	3	0	.370	.548	August	.000	0	0	0	0	0	0	0	0	.000	.000
Ahead on Count	.217	60	13	3	0	1	9	3	0	.254	.317	September/October	.224	76	17	3	0	1	6	3	11	.253	.303
Behind on Count	.179	123	22	4	0	1	9	0	35	.185	.236	Pre-All Star	.213	230	49	10	0	7	30	9	35	.245	.348
Two Strikes	.180	139	25	4	0	3	14	6	46	.219	.273	Post-All Star	.224	76	17	3	0	1	6	3	11	.253	.303

1992 By Position

Position	Avg	AB	H	2B	3B	HR	RBI	BB	SO	OBP	SLG	G	GS	Innings	PO	A	E	DP	Fld Pct	Rng Fctr	In Zone	Outs	Zone Rtg	MLB Zone
As Designated Hitter	.218	275	60	13	0	8	34	10	43	.247	.353	70	68	---	---	---	---	---	---	---	---	---	---	---

Last Five Years

	Avg	AB	H	2B	3B	HR	RBI	BB	SO	OBP	SLG		Avg	AB	H	2B	3B	HR	RBI	BB	SO	OBP	SLG
vs. Left	.264	738	195	42	1	26	111	67	117	.326	.438	Scoring Posn	.264	644	170	30	1	24	261	83	136	.341	.425
vs. Right	.256	1623	416	75	4	50	226	96	315	.299	.400	Close & Late	.268	421	113	16	1	17	65	31	90	.320	.432
Groundball	.266	867	231	44	3	19	118	69	139	.320	.390	None on/out	.261	591	154	36	0	20	20	20	88	.288	.423
Flyball	.274	530	145	23	2	18	80	34	100	.321	.426	Batting #4	.263	1111	292	59	1	40	153	81	188	.314	.426
Home	.259	1149	298	54	3	31	163	92	206	.314	.393	Batting #5	.255	748	191	38	2	23	113	50	146	.303	.404
Away	.258	1212	313	63	2	47	174	71	226	.302	.430	Other	.255	502	128	20	2	15	71	32	98	.300	.392
Day	.253	636	161	33	2	28	94	41	115	.302	.443	April	.262	390	102	18	1	17	63	20	66	.294	.444
Night	.261	1725	450	84	3	50	243	122	317	.309	.400	May	.240	496	119	17	2	12	58	22	95	.275	.355
Grass	.249	1260	314	52	3	42	184	83	228	.296	.395	June	.276	410	113	23	2	15	64	45	65	.347	.451
Turf	.270	1101	297	65	2	36	153	80	204	.321	.431	July	.224	375	84	15	0	11	52	26	69	.276	.352
First Pitch	.347	262	91	7	2	16	49	9	0	.366	.573	August	.276	323	89	21	0	10	37	22	67	.324	.433
Ahead on Count	.324	509	165	32	2	21	88	80	0	.417	.519	September/October	.283	367	104	23	0	13	63	28	70	.336	.452
Behind on Count	.237	988	234	48	1	21	122	1	294	.241	.351	Pre-All Star	.254	1419	361	63	4	47	205	96	249	.302	.405
Two Strikes	.192	1100	211	42	0	24	118	62	431	.237	.295	Post-All Star	.265	942	250	54	0	31	132	67	183	.315	.421

Batter vs. Pitcher (since 1984)

Hits Best Against	Avg	AB	H	2B	3B	HR	RBI	BB	SO	OBP	SLG	Hits Worst Against	Avg	AB	H	2B	3B	HR	RBI	BB	SO	OBP	SLG
Rick Honeycutt	.579	19	11	0	0	0	1	2	0	.619	.579	Randy Myers	.077	13	1	0	0	0	0	0	5	.077	.077
Pat Combs	.500	12	6	2	0	2	4	2	4	.571	1.167	Steve Avery	.091	11	1	0	0	0	1	1	2	.167	.091
Jeff Parrett	.500	10	5	2	0	0	6	0	0	.455	.700	Todd Worrell	.095	21	2	0	0	0	2	5	.174	.095
Joe Boever	.375	8	3	2	0	1	3	2	3	.455	1.000	Lee Smith	.118	17	2	1	0	0	0	7	.118	.176
Lance McCullers	.364	11	4	0	0	2	2	1	1	.417	.909	Ted Power	.143	28	4	0	0	0	1	1	4	.172	.143

58

Scott Brosius — Athletics — Bats Right (flyball hitter)

	Avg	G	AB	R	H	2B	3B	HR	RBI	BB	SO	HBP	GDP	SB	CS	OBP	SLG	IBB	SH	SF	#Pit	#P/PA	GB	FB	G/F
1992 Season	.218	38	87	13	19	2	0	4	13	3	13	2	0	3	0	.258	.379	1	0	1	338	3.63	30	35	0.86
Career (1991-1992)	.226	74	155	22	35	7	0	6	17	6	24	2	2	6	1	.262	.387	1	1	1	601	3.66	51	57	0.89

1992 Season

	Avg	AB	H	2B	3B	HR	RBI	BB	SO	OBP	SLG		Avg	AB	H	2B	3B	HR	RBI	BB	SO	OBP	SLG
vs. Left	.292	24	7	0	0	3	7	2	5	.346	.667	Scoring Posn	.261	23	6	0	0	1	9	3	3	.333	.391
vs. Right	.190	63	12	2	0	1	6	1	8	.224	.270	Close & Late	.059	17	1	0	0	0	2	2	6	.200	.059

Jarvis Brown — Twins — Bats Right

	Avg	G	AB	R	H	2B	3B	HR	RBI	BB	SO	HBP	GDP	SB	CS	OBP	SLG	IBB	SH	SF	#Pit	#P/PA	GB	FB	G/F
1992 Season	.067	35	15	8	1	0	0	0	0	2	4	1	0	2	2	.222	.067	0	0	0	72	4.00	3	6	0.50
Career (1991-1992)	.173	73	52	18	9	0	0	0	4	12	1	0	9	3	.246	.173	0	1	0	212	3.72	18	13	1.38

1992 Season

	Avg	AB	H	2B	3B	HR	RBI	BB	SO	OBP	SLG		Avg	AB	H	2B	3B	HR	RBI	BB	SO	OBP	SLG
vs. Left	.000	3	0	0	0	0	0		1	1	.250	.000	Scoring Posn	.000	3	0	0	0	0	0	2	1	.400	.000
vs. Right	.083	12	1	0	0	0	0		3	.214	.083	Close & Late	.000	4	0	0	0	0	0	0	2	.000	.000

Keith Brown — Reds — Pitches Right

	ERA	W	L	Sv	G	GS	IP	BB	SO	Avg	H	2B	3B	HR	RBI	OBP	SLG	CG	ShO	Sup	QS	#P/S	SB	CS	GB	FB	G/F
1992 Season	4.50	0	1	0	2	2	8.0	5	5	.313	10	3	0	2	5	.405	.594	0	0	5.63	0	71	0	0	10	10	1.00
Career (1988-1992)	3.40	2	2	0	25	5	47.2	18	23	.280	51	9	1	5	23	.345	.423	0	0	3.59	2	65	3	5	74	55	1.35

1992 Season

	ERA	W	L	Sv	G	GS	IP	H	HR	BB	SO		Avg	AB	H	2B	3B	HR	RBI	BB	SO	OBP	SLG
Home	8.10	0	1	0	1	1	3.1	5	1	1	1	vs. Left	.421	19	8	2	0	2	5	3	3	.500	.842
Away	1.93	0	0	0	1	1	4.2	5	1	4	4	vs. Right	.154	13	2	1	0	0	2	2		.267	.231

Kevin Brown — Rangers — Pitches Right (groundball pitcher)

	ERA	W	L	Sv	G	GS	IP	BB	SO	Avg	H	2B	3B	HR	RBI	OBP	SLG	CG	ShO	Sup	QS	#P/S	SB	CS	GB	FB	G/F
1992 Season	3.32	21	11	0	35	35	265.2	76	173	.260	262	40	1	11	104	.316	.335	11	1	4.74	23	107	7	12	495	205	2.41
Last Five Years	3.67	55	43	0	126	126	870.2	304	473	.261	870	144	7	53	351	.327	.357	25	3	4.91	81	103	29	34	1718	603	2.85

1992 Season

	ERA	W	L	Sv	G	GS	IP	H	HR	BB	SO		Avg	AB	H	2B	3B	HR	RBI	BB	SO	OBP	SLG
Home	2.71	11	4	0	16	16	123.0	118	4	27	89	vs. Left	.268	488	131	26	0	7	46	51	75	.339	.365
Away	3.85	10	7	0	19	19	142.2	144	7	49	84	vs. Right	.252	519	131	14	1	4	58	25	98	.294	.306
Day	5.53	1	4	0	6	6	42.1	52	4	18	21	Inning 1-6	.248	770	191	31	1	7	76	61	131	.309	.318
Night	2.90	20	7	0	29	29	223.1	210	7	58	152	Inning 7+	.300	237	71	9	0	4	28	15	42	.340	.388
Grass	3.19	15	10	0	27	27	203.0	199	9	57	138	None on	.240	574	138	21	1	4	4	39	98	.294	.301
Turf	3.73	6	1	0	8	8	62.2	63	2	19	35	Runners on	.286	433	124	19	0	7	100	37	75	.344	.379
April	3.08	4	1	0	5	5	38.0	32	0	11	25	Scoring Posn	.264	246	65	11	0	5	90	28	47	.335	.370
May	3.50	4	2	0	6	6	46.1	49	1	8	30	Close & Late	.323	133	43	5	0	1	19	9	18	.359	.383
June	3.20	4	1	0	6	6	45.0	37	1	18	32	None on/out	.278	259	72	11	1	0	0	12	42	.315	.328
July	4.03	2	3	0	5	5	38.0	39	4	9	21	vs. 1st Batr (relief)	.000	0	0	0	0	0	0	0	0	.000	.000
August	2.83	3	1	0	6	6	47.2	52	1	17	28	First Inning Pitched	.275	131	36	8	0	3	22	15	20	.354	.405
September/October	3.38	4	3	0	7	7	50.2	53	4	13	37	First 75 Pitches	.255	691	176	30	0	7	70	52	116	.314	.329
Starter	3.32	21	11	0	35	35	265.2	262	11	76	173	Pitch 76-90	.279	129	36	4	1	0	12	10	24	.324	.326
Reliever	0.00	0	0	0	0	0	0.0	0	0	0	0	Pitch 91-105	.227	110	25	5	0	1	9	8	17	.286	.300
0-3 Days Rest	0.00	0	0	0	0	0	0.0	0	0	0	0	Pitch 106+	.325	77	25	1	0	3	13	6	16	.365	.455
4 Days Rest	3.46	15	6	0	24	24	182.0	179	10	55	103	First Pitch	.311	164	51	12	0	2	22	2	0	.331	.421
5+ Days Rest	3.01	6	5	0	11	11	83.2	83	1	21	70	Ahead on Count	.197	452	89	13	1	1	26	0	153	.203	.237
Pre-All Star	3.01	14	4	0	19	19	146.2	131	3	41	98	Behind on Count	.345	235	81	12	0	6	46	49	0	.455	.472
Post-All Star	3.71	7	7	0	16	16	119.0	131	8	35	75	Two Strikes	.161	404	65	10	1	2	20	25	173	.217	.205

Last Five Years

	ERA	W	L	Sv	G	GS	IP	H	HR	BB	SO		Avg	AB	H	2B	3B	HR	RBI	BB	SO	OBP	SLG
Home	3.24	27	17	0	59	59	414.0	407	28	140	231	vs. Left	.260	1628	423	79	3	27	163	166	221	.328	.362
Away	4.06	28	26	0	67	67	456.2	463	25	164	242	vs. Right	.263	1700	447	65	4	26	188	138	252	.325	.352
Day	5.14	7	11	0	28	28	177.0	199	10	79	89	Inning 1-6	.257	2661	683	111	4	36	276	250	381	.325	.342
Night	3.30	48	32	0	98	98	693.2	671	43	225	384	Inning 7+	.280	667	187	33	3	17	75	54	92	.334	.415
Grass	3.62	45	36	0	102	102	708.2	703	44	250	387	None on	.255	1871	478	83	5	28	28	169	271	.322	.350
Turf	3.89	10	7	0	24	24	162.0	167	9	54	86	Runners on	.269	1457	392	61	2	25	323	135	202	.332	.365
April	3.81	11	3	0	17	17	113.1	103	6	44	60	Scoring Posn	.261	805	210	33	2	15	287	95	127	.336	.363
May	3.85	10	8	0	22	22	149.2	153	5	58	69	Close & Late	.302	381	115	19	3	12	52	38	44	.365	.462
June	2.72	13	7	0	23	23	175.2	136	6	53	94	None on/out	.256	845	216	38	3	8	8	69	121	.316	.336
July	3.69	6	10	0	22	22	161.0	156	17	52	91	vs. 1st Batr (relief)	.000	0	0	0	0	0	0	0	0	.000	.000
August	3.73	7	7	0	21	21	140.0	165	7	53	77	First Inning Pitched	.259	460	119	23	0	6	65	60	73	.348	.348
September/October	4.53	8	8	0	21	21	131.0	157	12	44	82	First 75 Pitches	.255	2315	591	98	3	29	232	213	335	.322	.338
Starter	3.67	55	43	0	126	126	870.2	870	53	304	473	Pitch 76-90	.271	431	117	17	3	10	47	37	57	.335	.394
Reliever	0.00	0	0	0	0	0	0.0	0	0	0	0	Pitch 91-105	.255	353	90	19	0	5	32	29	49	.316	.351

Last Five Years

	ERA	W	L	Sv	G	GS	IP	H	HR	BB	SO		Avg	AB	H	2B	3B	HR	RBI	BB	SO	OBP	SLG
0-3 Days Rest	1.84	0	1	0	2	2	14.2	9	0	7	6	Pitch 106+	.314	229	72	10	1	9	40	25	32	.375	.485
4 Days Rest	3.75	33	26	0	74	74	516.1	528	34	168	262	First Pitch	.312	539	168	33	2	9	72	11	0	.331	.430
5+ Days Rest	3.63	22	16	0	50	50	339.2	333	19	129	205	Ahead on Count	.208	1365	284	46	4	12	101	0	406	.217	.274
Pre-All Star	3.41	38	21	0	70	70	496.1	444	23	176	251	Behind on Count	.318	825	262	40	0	21	123	175	0	.436	.442
Post-All Star	4.02	17	22	0	56	56	374.1	426	30	128	222	Two Strikes	.182	1287	234	40	5	11	85	118	473	.258	.246

Pitcher vs. Batter (career)

Pitches Best Vs.	Avg	AB	H	2B	3B	HR	RBI	BB	SO	OBP	SLG	Pitches Worst Vs.	Avg	AB	H	2B	3B	HR	RBI	BB	SO	OBP	SLG
Ozzie Guillen	.000	22	0	0	0	0	0	0	1	.000	.000	John Olerud	.478	23	11	4	0	1	6	3	4	.538	.783
Franklin Stubbs	.091	11	1	0	0	0	0	0	2	.091	.091	Travis Fryman	.429	14	6	2	0	1	3	0	3	.500	.786
Carlton Fisk	.105	19	2	0	0	0	1	0	4	.105	.105	Dave Winfield	.417	24	10	0	0	4	7	4	3	.500	.917
Dave Bergman	.111	18	2	0	0	0	0	0	3	.111	.111	Joe Orsulak	.400	20	8	3	0	1	7	4	1	.500	.700
Gary Gaetti	.130	23	3	0	0	0	3	0	6	.125	.130	Kenny Lofton	.400	10	4	0	0	1	1	2	0	.500	.700

Kevin D. Brown — Mariners
Pitches Left (groundball pitcher)

	ERA	W	L	Sv	G	GS	IP	BB	SO	Avg	H	2B	3B	HR	RBI	OBP	SLG	GF	IR	IRS	Hld	SvOp	SB	CS	GB	FB	G/F
1992 Season	9.00	0	0	0	2	0	3.0	3	2	.333	4	1	1	1	4	.467	.833	0	2	2	0	0	0	0	5	4	1.25
Career (1990-1992)	4.82	3	5	0	24	13	89.2	45	44	.252	86	19	2	8	44	.341	.390	2	10	5	0	1	6	4	157	92	1.71

1992 Season

	ERA	W	L	Sv	G	GS	IP	H	HR	BB	SO		Avg	AB	H	2B	3B	HR	RBI	BB	SO	OBP	SLG
Home	9.00	0	0	0	2	0	3.0	4	1	3	2	vs. Left	.500	4	2	1	0	0	2	0	0	.500	.750
Away	0.00	0	0	0	0	0	0.0	0	0	0	0	vs. Right	.250	8	2	0	1	1	2	3	2	.455	.875

Jerry Browne — Athletics
Bats Both

	Avg	G	AB	R	H	2B	3B	HR	RBI	BB	SO	HBP	GDP	SB	CS	OBP	SLG	IBB	SH	SF	#Pit	#P/PA	GB	FB	G/F
1992 Season	.287	111	324	43	93	12	2	3	40	40	40	4	7	3	3	.366	.364	0	6	3	1439	3.85	122	97	1.26
Last Five Years	.270	584	1939	272	524	83	15	16	181	232	211	8	38	38	25	.346	.353	11	57	26	8204	3.72	795	573	1.39

1992 Season

	Avg	AB	H	2B	3B	HR	RBI	BB	SO	OBP	SLG		Avg	AB	H	2B	3B	HR	RBI	BB	SO	OBP	SLG
vs. Left	.184	49	9	1	0	0	5	3	6	.226	.204	Scoring Posn	.321	78	25	4	1	2	37	12	7	.392	.474
vs. Right	.305	275	84	11	2	3	35	37	34	.389	.393	Close & Late	.465	43	20	3	0	1	9	6	5	.529	.605
Groundball	.303	76	23	1	0	1	11	12	14	.411	.355	None on/out	.235	81	19	2	0	0	8	16	.311	.259
Flyball	.315	111	35	5	1	1	10	11	13	.381	.405	Batting #2	.310	158	49	8	1	3	21	26	19	.407	.430
Home	.281	146	41	5	0	1	17	18	20	.369	.384	Batting #7	.276	58	16	0	1	0	8	4	5	.323	.310
Away	.292	178	52	7	2	2	23	22	20	.364	.388	Other	.259	108	28	4	0	1	11	10	16	.325	.296
Day	.295	139	41	3	0	1	14	14	15	.367	.338	April	.222	9	2	0	0	0	0	1	0	.300	.222
Night	.281	185	52	9	2	2	26	26	25	.366	.384	May	.246	61	15	0	0	0	7	5	10	.309	.246
Grass	.274	277	76	7	2	3	34	37	36	.362	.347	June	.288	73	21	3	0	0	6	9	9	.373	.329
Turf	.362	47	17	5	0	0	6	3	4	.392	.468	July	.259	54	14	3	1	1	7	9	6	.369	.407
First Pitch	.276	29	8	1	0	0	7	0	0	.313	.310	August	.333	78	26	2	0	1	11	10	10	.411	.397
Ahead on Count	.349	83	29	6	0	1	10	30	0	.513	.458	September/October	.306	49	15	4	1	1	9	6	5	.362	.490
Behind on Count	.330	100	33	4	1	0	16	0	25	.337	.390	Pre-All Star	.271	181	49	6	1	1	19	22	24	.353	.331
Two Strikes	.246	138	34	2	1	1	14	10	40	.300	.297	Post-All Star	.308	143	44	6	1	2	21	18	16	.383	.406

1992 By Position

Position	Avg	AB	H	2B	3B	HR	RBI	BB	SO	OBP	SLG	G	GS	Innings	PO	A	E	DP	Fld Pct	Rng Fctr	In Zone	Outs	Zone Rtg	MLB Zone
As Pinch Hitter	.467	15	7	0	0	0	0	0	2	.467	.467	15	0	---	---	---	---	---	---	---	---	---	---	---
As 2b	.207	29	6	0	0	0	4	6	3	.361	.207	19	7	78.0	14	18	0	3	1.000	3.69	21	19	.905	.892
As 3b	.315	149	47	9	2	1	21	15	19	.375	.423	58	38	370.0	40	70	4	7	.965	2.68	85	76	.894	.841
As lf	.227	44	10	1	0	0	3	7	7	.346	.250	17	12	108.0	36	0	1	0	.973	3.00	40	35	.875	.809
As cf	.250	68	17	1	0	2	9	12	6	.354	.353	23	21	161.1	48	0	0	0	1.000	2.68	55	48	.873	.824

Last Five Years

	Avg	AB	H	2B	3B	HR	RBI	BB	SO	OBP	SLG		Avg	AB	H	2B	3B	HR	RBI	BB	SO	OBP	SLG
vs. Left	.268	511	137	22	6	2	47	54	46	.337	.346	Scoring Posn	.271	421	114	19	4	4	161	72	42	.361	.363
vs. Right	.271	1428	387	61	9	14	134	178	165	.350	.356	Close & Late	.311	322	100	12	4	3	35	47	39	.395	.398
Groundball	.287	488	140	21	2	5	49	65	54	.369	.369	None on/out	.245	588	144	25	7	4	4	61	73	.317	.332
Flyball	.270	515	139	17	5	5	47	61	64	.345	.351	Batting #1	.282	861	243	41	8	7	63	99	83	.355	.373
Home	.289	968	280	45	9	6	91	119	90	.368	.373	Batting #2	.262	718	188	33	2	8	82	97	86	.347	.347
Away	.251	971	244	38	6	10	90	113	121	.325	.334	Other	.258	360	93	9	5	1	36	36	40	.324	.319
Day	.268	631	169	20	4	3	55	73	62	.346	.326	April	.187	268	50	1	0	1	17	20	34	.239	.201
Night	.271	1308	355	63	11	13	126	159	149	.347	.366	May	.262	343	90	12	5	1	41	25	45	.310	.335
Grass	.274	1633	448	68	13	15	162	204	173	.353	.359	June	.288	364	105	15	2	3	26	48	25	.372	.365
Turf	.248	306	76	15	2	1	19	28	38	.309	.320	July	.286	297	85	17	4	3	21	45	29	.381	.401
First Pitch	.319	235	75	8	1	2	37	7	0	.335	.387	August	.338	299	101	13	2	6	38	39	32	.413	.455
Ahead on Count	.290	428	124	26	3	2	49	144	0	.460	.379	September/October	.253	368	93	25	2	2	38	55	46	.346	.348
Behind on Count	.244	643	157	29	2	5	60	0	128	.245	.319	Pre-All Star	.256	1074	275	34	11	7	92	114	114	.325	.328
Two Strikes	.219	807	177	25	7	3	52	76	211	.287	.279	Post-All Star	.288	865	249	49	4	9	89	118	97	.372	.385

60

Hits Best Against	Avg	AB	H	2B	3B	HR	RBI	BB	SO	OBP	SLG	Hits Worst Against	Avg	AB	H	2B	3B	HR	RBI	BB	SO	OBP	SLG
Chuck Crim	.636	11	7	1	0	1	1	1	1	.667	1.000	Greg Harris	.000	12	0	0	0	0	2	2	1	.133	.000
Scott Bankhead	.600	10	6	1	0	2	1	0	0	.636	.700	Chuck Finley	.050	20	1	1	0	0	1	0	1	.095	.100
Pete Harnisch	.538	13	7	2	0	1	4	1	1	.571	.923	Todd Stottlemyre	.077	13	1	0	0	0	0	1	1	.143	.077
Jeff M. Robinson	.444	9	4	1	0	0	1	3	1	.583	.556	Kirk McCaskill	.083	24	2	0	0	0	3	3	4	.185	.083
Tim Leary	.417	12	5	3	0	0	3	4	1	.529	.667	Tom Henke	.100	10	1	0	0	0	1	1	2	.182	.100

Tom Browning — Reds

Pitches Left (flyball pitcher)

	ERA	W	L	Sv	G	GS	IP	BB	SO	Avg	H	2B	3B	HR	RBI	OBP	SLG	CG	ShO	Sup	QS	#P/S	SB	CS	GB	FB	G/F
1992 Season	5.07	6	5	0	16	16	87.0	28	33	.311	108	28	7	6	45	.362	.484	0	0	5.38	7	81	11	1	112	124	0.90
Last Five Years	3.80	68	45	0	160	160	1045.1	264	489	.258	1030	201	25	129	435	.305	.417	17	5	4.60	93	90	70	36	1182	1557	0.76

1992 Season

	ERA	W	L	Sv	G	GS	IP	H	HR	BB	SO		Avg	AB	H	2B	3B	HR	RBI	BB	SO	OBP	SLG
Home	5.03	5	1	0	6	6	34.0	34	6	8	20	vs. Left	.325	83	27	7	1	1	20	8	8	.385	.470
Away	5.09	1	4	0	10	10	53.0	74	0	20	13	vs. Right	.307	264	81	21	6	5	25	20	25	.355	.489
Starter	5.07	6	5	0	16	16	87.0	108	6	28	33	Scoring Posn	.299	97	29	8	1	1	38	14	7	.379	.433
Reliever	0.00	0	0	0	0	0	0.0	0	0	0	0	Close & Late	.222	9	2	0	0	0	1	0	1	.222	.222
0-3 Days Rest	3.60	0	0	0	1	1	5.0	9	0	3	2	None on/out	.319	91	29	5	3	2	2	5	12	.354	.505
4 Days Rest	3.86	1	3	0	7	7	42.0	50	0	16	11	First Pitch	.298	57	17	5	0	1	5	7	0	.369	.439
5+ Days Rest	6.53	5	2	0	8	8	40.0	49	6	9	20	Behind on Count	.354	79	28	7	4	3	17	11	0	.429	.658
Pre-All Star	5.07	6	5	0	16	16	87.0	108	6	28	33	Ahead on Count	.302	149	45	13	2	1	18	0	28	.307	.436
Post-All Star	0.00	0	0	0	0	0	0.0	0	0	0	0	Two Strikes	.286	126	36	9	1	2	15	10	33	.343	.421

Last Five Years

	ERA	W	L	Sv	G	GS	IP	H	HR	BB	SO		Avg	AB	H	2B	3B	HR	RBI	BB	SO	OBP	SLG
Home	4.23	35	24	0	81	81	525.2	522	80	135	243	vs. Left	.254	744	189	42	5	24	100	70	138	.316	.421
Away	3.36	33	21	0	79	79	519.2	508	49	129	246	vs. Right	.259	3253	841	159	20	105	335	194	351	.302	.417
Day	3.75	20	18	0	50	50	314.1	335	33	95	146	Inning 1-6	.256	3392	868	167	23	107	379	235	421	.305	.413
Night	3.82	48	27	0	110	110	731.0	695	96	169	343	Inning 7+	.268	605	162	34	2	22	56	29	68	.302	.440
Grass	3.28	19	12	0	49	49	323.2	322	28	74	153	None on	.250	2503	626	108	13	86	86	148	305	.296	.407
Turf	4.03	49	33	0	111	111	721.2	708	101	190	336	Runners on	.270	1494	404	93	12	43	349	116	184	.319	.435
April	3.45	11	4	0	25	25	161.2	151	16	31	79	Scoring Posn	.271	756	205	50	7	14	274	93	102	.340	.411
May	4.08	9	14	0	28	28	176.1	176	25	53	79	Close & Late	.253	320	81	17	0	7	26	18	40	.293	.372
June	3.21	15	5	0	30	30	196.1	188	16	58	95	None on/out	.262	1084	284	45	7	40	40	50	117	.299	.422
July	3.78	10	8	0	26	26	173.2	172	27	34	76	vs. 1st Batr (relief)	.000	0	0	0	0	0	0	0	0	.000	.000
August	3.43	13	4	0	24	24	170.1	160	22	43	82	First Inning Pitched	.264	613	162	32	5	14	74	42	83	.309	.401
September/October	4.90	10	10	0	27	27	167.0	183	23	45	78	First 75 Pitches	.256	3203	820	153	21	100	342	208	395	.303	.411
Starter	3.80	68	45	0	160	160	1045.1	1030	129	264	489	Pitch 76-90	.267	494	132	29	3	15	54	27	54	.309	.429
Reliever	0.00	0	0	0	0	0	0.0	0	0	0	0	Pitch 91-105	.281	235	66	14	1	14	33	25	32	.346	.528
0-3 Days Rest	3.90	17	9	0	35	35	223.2	237	31	57	100	Pitch 106+	.185	65	12	5	0	0	6	4	8	.229	.262
4 Days Rest	3.53	37	22	0	87	87	576.2	545	68	146	262	First Pitch	.282	737	208	46	5	27	75	32	0	.313	.468
5+ Days Rest	4.33	14	14	0	38	38	245.0	248	30	61	127	Ahead on Count	.225	1801	406	76	6	47	169	1	428	.229	.353
Pre-All Star	3.63	39	25	0	93	93	593.0	574	64	157	275	Behind on Count	.292	782	228	42	12	29	113	131	0	.393	.487
Post-All Star	4.02	29	20	0	67	67	452.1	456	65	107	214	Two Strikes	.205	1563	320	50	4	38	134	100	488	.254	.315

Pitches Best Vs.	Avg	AB	H	2B	3B	HR	RBI	BB	SO	OBP	SLG	Pitches Worst Vs.	Avg	AB	H	2B	3B	HR	RBI	BB	SO	OBP	SLG
Sid Bream	.000	10	0	0	0	0	0	2	2	.167	.000	Willie Randolph	.533	15	8	1	0	1	3	3	0	.611	.800
Todd Zeile	.063	16	1	0	0	0	1	0	1	.059	.063	Spike Owen	.500	24	12	4	1	1	2	1	1	.520	.875
Otis Nixon	.067	30	2	0	0	0	4	3	2	.152	.067	Lance Parrish	.455	11	5	1	0	1	3	1	1	.500	.818
Milt Thompson	.071	14	1	0	0	0	0	1	3	.133	.071	Bobby Bonilla	.390	41	16	4	1	8	17	1	2	.366	1.122
Chico Walker	.077	13	1	0	0	0	0	0	1	.077	.077	George Bell	.364	11	4	0	0	3	4	2	2	.462	1.182

J.T. Bruett — Twins

Bats Left (groundball hitter)

	Avg	G	AB	R	H	2B	3B	HR	RBI	BB	SO	HBP	GDP	SB	CS	OBP	SLG	IBB	SH	SF	#Pit	#P/PA	GB	FB	G/F
1992 Season	.250	56	76	7	19	4	0	0	2	6	12	1	0	6	3	.313	.303	1	1	0	293	3.53	31	17	1.82

1992 Season

	Avg	AB	H	2B	3B	HR	RBI	BB	SO	OBP	SLG		Avg	AB	H	2B	3B	HR	RBI	BB	SO	OBP	SLG
vs. Left	.167	6	1	0	0	0	1	1	0	.286	.167	Scoring Posn	.000	9	0	0	0	0	1	2	1	.182	.000
vs. Right	.257	70	18	4	0	0	1	5	12	.316	.314	Close & Late	.231	13	3	0	0	0	0	2	2	.333	.231

Jacob Brumfield — Reds

Bats Right (flyball hitter)

	Avg	G	AB	R	H	2B	3B	HR	RBI	BB	SO	HBP	GDP	SB	CS	OBP	SLG	IBB	SH	SF	#Pit	#P/PA	GB	FB	G/F
1992 Season	.133	24	30	6	4	0	0	0	2	2	4	1	0	6	0	.212	.133	1	0	0	118	3.58	10	12	0.83

1992 Season

	Avg	AB	H	2B	3B	HR	RBI	BB	SO	OBP	SLG		Avg	AB	H	2B	3B	HR	RBI	BB	SO	OBP	SLG
vs. Left	.100	20	2	0	0	0	2	1	3	.182	.100	Scoring Posn	.200	5	1	0	0	0	2	2	1	.500	.200
vs. Right	.200	10	2	0	0	0	0	1	1	.273	.200	Close & Late	.125	8	1	0	0	0	1	1	1	.300	.125

Mike Brumley — Red Sox
Bats Both (groundball hitter)

	Avg	G	AB	R	H	2B	3B	HR	RBI	BB	SO	HBP	GDP	SB	CS	OBP	SLG	IBB	SH	SF	#Pit	#P/PA	GB	FB	G/F
1992 Season	.000	2	1	0	0	0	0	0	0	0	0	0	0	0	0	.000	.000	0	0	0		1.00	0	1	0.00
Last Five Years	.209	219	478	68	100	15	6	1	23	34	89	1	9	12	4	.263	.272	0	11	1	1797	3.50	190	109	1.74

1992 Season

	Avg	AB	H	2B	3B	HR	RBI	BB	SO	OBP	SLG		Avg	AB	H	2B	3B	HR	RBI	BB	SO	OBP	SLG
vs. Left	.000	0	0	0	0	0	0	0	0	.000	.000	Scoring Posn	.000	0	0	0	0	0	0	0	0	.000	.000
vs. Right	.000	1	0	0	0	0	0	0	0	.000	.000	Close & Late	.000	0	0	0	0	0	0	0	0	.000	.000

Last Five Years

	Avg	AB	H	2B	3B	HR	RBI	BB	SO	OBP	SLG		Avg	AB	H	2B	3B	HR	RBI	BB	SO	OBP	SLG
vs. Left	.246	142	35	5	1	1	8	6	25	.277	.317	Scoring Posn	.168	125	21	3	0	0	19	6	30	.205	.192
vs. Right	.193	336	65	10	5	0	15	28	64	.257	.253	Close & Late	.200	75	15	2	2	0	1	7	14	.268	.280
Groundball	.233	150	35	4	3	0	9	10	24	.281	.300	None on/out	.198	116	23	5	0	0	0	8	16	.256	.241
Flyball	.196	102	20	6	1	0	5	5	29	.234	.275	Batting #8	.176	34	6	0	1	1	5	3	4	.243	.324
Home	.214	238	51	10	3	1	15	13	42	.255	.294	Batting #9	.207	386	80	10	5	0	17	26	75	.258	.259
Away	.204	240	49	5	3	0	8	21	47	.270	.250	Other	.241	58	14	5	0	0	1	5	10	.302	.328
Day	.205	166	34	3	1	0	6	14	30	.267	.235	April	.152	46	7	1	1	0	3	4	2	.216	.217
Night	.212	312	66	12	5	1	17	20	59	.260	.292	May	.209	115	24	2	5	0	6	8	22	.260	.313
Grass	.209	335	70	11	2	1	19	25	65	.263	.263	June	.242	62	15	3	0	0	3	7	12	.329	.290
Turf	.210	143	30	4	4	0	4	9	24	.261	.294	July	.230	61	14	2	0	0	1	1	14	.242	.262
First Pitch	.226	93	21	1	2	1	5	0	0	.226	.312	August	.252	107	27	6	0	0	4	7	25	.298	.308
Ahead on Count	.295	112	33	8	1	0	7	20	0	.402	.384	September/October	.149	87	13	1	0	1	1	7	14	.213	.195
Behind on Count	.180	139	25	6	1	0	4	0	44	.186	.237	Pre-All Star	.203	232	47	6	6	0	12	19	37	.265	.280
Two Strikes	.147	204	30	4	2	0	7	14	89	.205	.186	Post-All Star	.215	246	53	9	0	1	11	15	52	.261	.264

Tom Brunansky — Red Sox
Bats Right (flyball hitter)

	Avg	G	AB	R	H	2B	3B	HR	RBI	BB	SO	HBP	GDP	SB	CS	OBP	SLG	IBB	SH	SF	#Pit	#P/PA	GB	FB	G/F
1992 Season	.266	138	458	47	122	31	3	15	74	66	96	0	11	2	5	.354	.445	2	2	7	2130	4.01	139	148	0.94
Last Five Years	.245	743	2563	308	629	134	16	90	387	326	483	13	61	30	34	.330	.416	20	3	35	11303	3.85	709	956	0.74

1992 Season

	Avg	AB	H	2B	3B	HR	RBI	BB	SO	OBP	SLG		Avg	AB	H	2B	3B	HR	RBI	BB	SO	OBP	SLG
vs. Left	.227	132	30	10	0	6	20	26	20	.354	.439	Scoring Posn	.270	115	31	11	1	4	58	20	27	.359	.487
vs. Right	.282	326	92	21	3	9	54	40	76	.354	.448	Close & Late	.289	90	26	6	1	4	23	17	22	.394	.511
Groundball	.333	117	39	8	1	4	24	22	22	.433	.521	None on/out	.223	121	27	2	2	4	4	12	21	.293	.372
Flyball	.266	128	34	8	1	4	15	20	33	.362	.438	Batting #4	.259	351	91	22	2	13	58	43	72	.337	.444
Home	.323	217	70	23	1	10	47	32	41	.405	.576	Batting #6	.350	40	14	2	1	1	8	9	9	.451	.525
Away	.216	241	52	8	2	5	27	34	55	.308	.328	Other	.254	67	17	7	0	1	8	14	15	.378	.403
Day	.252	159	40	8	0	6	26	16	34	.315	.415	April	.273	22	6	0	0	0	1	3	5	.346	.273
Night	.274	299	82	23	3	9	48	50	62	.374	.462	May	.259	58	15	2	0	2	11	15	14	.400	.397
Grass	.276	384	106	28	2	12	61	60	74	.370	.453	June	.286	84	24	12	1	0	6	3	15	.310	.452
Turf	.216	74	16	3	1	3	13	6	22	.268	.405	July	.276	98	27	6	2	8	32	12	20	.351	.622
First Pitch	.372	43	16	1	0	2	9	2	0	.383	.535	August	.289	97	28	5	0	4	13	21	18	.408	.464
Ahead on Count	.291	117	34	7	3	7	23	33	1	.444	.587	September/October	.222	99	22	6	0	1	11	12	24	.304	.313
Behind on Count	.245	139	34	9	0	3	16	0	44	.243	.374	Pre-All Star	.268	205	55	17	2	5	31	29	40	.353	.444
Two Strikes	.237	224	53	20	0	3	29	31	95	.328	.366	Post-All Star	.265	253	67	14	1	10	43	37	56	.355	.447

1992 By Position

Position	Avg	AB	H	2B	3B	HR	RBI	BB	SO	OBP	SLG	G	GS	Innings	PO	A	E	DP	Fld Pct	Rng Fctr	In Zone	Outs	Zone Rtg	MLB Zone
As Designated Hitter	.333	54	18	0	0	4	16	9	9	.415	.556	17	17	---	---	---	---	---	---	---	---	---	---	---
As Pinch Hitter	.286	7	2	0	0	0	2	5	1	.583	.286	12	0	---	---	---	---	---	---	---	---	---	---	---
As 1b	.282	71	20	6	0	0	7	10	11	.370	.366	28	18	164.2	184	10	2	20	.990	---	33	28	.848	.843
As rf	.252	326	82	25	3	11	49	42	75	.332	.448	92	89	784.1	189	6	4	2	.980	2.24	232	184	.793	.814

Last Five Years

	Avg	AB	H	2B	3B	HR	RBI	BB	SO	OBP	SLG		Avg	AB	H	2B	3B	HR	RBI	BB	SO	OBP	SLG
vs. Left	.255	865	221	49	4	32	131	115	119	.338	.432	Scoring Posn	.237	758	180	38	7	30	300	131	151	.340	.425
vs. Right	.240	1698	408	85	12	58	256	211	364	.325	.407	Close & Late	.231	437	101	29	2	10	59	75	97	.340	.375
Groundball	.260	838	218	44	1	26	129		148	.352	.408	None on/out	.231	636	147	35	4	15	15	62	117	.301	.369
Flyball	.243	614	149	33	3	25	96	72	121	.319	.406	Batting #4	.254	1230	312	64	10	48	195	161	234	.339	.439
Home	.270	1245	336	82	11	44	217	157	212	.350	.459	Batting #6	.251	717	180	44	5	27	121	80	134	.325	.439
Away	.222	1318	293	52	5	46	170	169	271	.311	.374	Other	.222	616	137	26	1	15	71	85	115	.316	.341
Day	.244	806	197	39	0	33	134	89	150	.319	.415	April	.221	281	62	11	1	11	39	39	46	.314	.384
Night	.246	1755	432	95	16	57	253	237	333	.334	.416	May	.260	446	116	20	0	18	91	69	75	.354	.426
Grass	.253	1477	373	77	7	63	238	197	269	.339	.442	June	.260	458	119	36	5	9	51	55	85	.342	.419
Turf	.236	1086	256	57	9	27	149	129	214	.316	.379	July	.225	467	105	20	4	20	79	60	105	.311	.413
First Pitch	.309	356	110	20	1	15	60	5	0	.317	.497	August	.269	465	125	23	5	18	68	56	90	.350	.456
Ahead on Count	.303	597	181	40	7	32	111	175	2	.457	.554	September/October	.229	446	102	24	1	14	59	47	82	.300	.381
Behind on Count	.216	792	171	39	7	18	105	6	233	.224	.351	Pre-All Star	.251	1346	338	77	7	46	213	184	243	.339	.421
Two Strikes	.194	1186	230	52	5	32	144	140	481	.281	.327	Post-All Star	.239	1217	291	57	9	44	174	142	240	.319	.409

Batter vs. Pitcher (since 1984)																				
Hits Best Against	Avg	AB	H	2B	3B	HR	RBI	BB	SO	OBP	SLG	Hits Worst Against	Avg	AB	H	2B	3B	HR	RBI	BB	SO	OBP	SLG
David Wells	.467	15	7	2	0	2	4	0	1	.467	1.000	Randy Johnson	.000	15	0	0	0	0	1	2	8	.111	.000
Mark Eichhorn	.438	16	7	3	0	1	8	3	1	.526	.813	Jose DeLeon	.000	8	0	0	0	0	1	2	5	.182	.000
Alex Fernandez	.400	15	6	0	1	2	6	0	3	.400	.933	Gene Nelson	.063	16	1	0	0	0	0	1	4	.118	.063
Duane Ward	.400	10	4	0	0	1	5	2	0	.500	.700	Sid Fernandez	.063	16	1	0	0	0	0	1	3	.118	.063
Kevin Gross	.385	13	5	0	2	1	3	3	3	.500	.923	Mike Henneman	.077	13	1	0	0	0	0	0	5	.077	.077

Steve Buechele — Cubs   Bats Right

	Avg	G	AB	R	H	2B	3B	HR	RBI	BB	SO	HBP	GDP	SB	CS	OBP	SLG	IBB	SH	SF	#Pit	#P/PA	GB	FB	G/F
1992 Season	.261	145	524	52	137	23	4	9	64	52	105	7	10	1	3	.334	.372	6	4	3	2293	3.91	172	150	1.15
Last Five Years	.248	698	2294	284	570	98	13	70	296	229	451	26	58	5	15	.323	.394	17	30	9	9876	3.86	776	667	1.16

1992 Season

	Avg	AB	H	2B	3B	HR	RBI	BB	SO	OBP	SLG		Avg	AB	H	2B	3B	HR	RBI	BB	SO	OBP	SLG
vs. Left	.304	207	63	17	1	5	26	21	33	.372	.469	Scoring Posn	.281	146	41	4	2	0	51	26	37	.390	.336
vs. Right	.233	317	74	6	3	4	38	31	72	.310	.309	Close & Late	.210	105	22	4	1	0	6	9	28	.291	.267
Groundball	.233	202	47	6	3	1	21	15	40	.291	.307	None on/out	.291	141	41	12	1	4	4	7	25	.333	.475
Flyball	.256	121	31	7	0	6	16	12	29	.341	.463	Batting #5	.275	160	44	9	2	1	14	10	27	.331	.375
Home	.246	276	68	9	3	4	32	27	56	.316	.344	Batting #6	.257	331	85	14	1	8	48	40	69	.340	.378
Away	.278	248	69	14	1	5	32	25	49	.355	.403	Other	.242	33	8	0	1	0	2	2	9	.286	.303
Day	.261	188	49	7	3	3	21	16	35	.325	.378	April	.236	72	17	4	1	2	15	6	14	.304	.403
Night	.262	336	88	16	1	6	43	36	70	.339	.369	May	.295	95	28	6	0	4	15	15	23	.393	.484
Grass	.266	218	58	14	3	2	27	18	46	.329	.385	June	.202	89	18	3	0	2	10	13	17	.301	.303
Turf	.258	306	79	9	1	7	37	34	59	.338	.363	July	.326	89	29	3	1	1	7	4	12	.355	.416
First Pitch	.200	40	8	2	1	0	3	4	0	.289	.300	August	.223	94	21	4	2	0	11	7	24	.295	.309
Ahead on Count	.346	107	37	7	2	1	18	32	0	.490	.477	September/October	.282	85	24	3	0	0	6	7	15	.351	.318
Behind on Count	.258	209	54	8	0	5	26	0	59	.271	.368	Pre-All Star	.255	294	75	15	1	8	43	34	62	.334	.395
Two Strikes	.193	274	53	8	0	3	21	16	105	.246	.255	Post-All Star	.270	230	62	8	3	1	21	18	43	.335	.343

1992 By Position

Position	Avg	AB	H	2B	3B	HR	RBI	BB	SO	OBP	SLG	G	GS	Innings	PO	A	E	DP	Fld Pct	Rng Fctr	In Zone	Outs	Zone Rtg	MLB Zone
As 3b	.261	522	136	23	4	9	63	52	104	.333	.372	143	140	1240.1	102	285	17	16	.958	2.81	365	299	.819	.841

Last Five Years

	Avg	AB	H	2B	3B	HR	RBI	BB	SO	OBP	SLG		Avg	AB	H	2B	3B	HR	RBI	BB	SO	OBP	SLG
vs. Left	.276	718	198	45	3	29	97	92	122	.361	.468	Scoring Posn	.261	609	159	31	6	13	217	81	129	.353	.396
vs. Right	.236	1576	372	53	10	41	199	137	329	.304	.360	Close & Late	.234	415	97	13	2	9	45	37	104	.305	.340
Groundball	.226	659	149	19	6	11	74	63	144	.303	.323	None on/out	.260	570	148	29	2	22	22	38	97	.309	.433
Flyball	.260	546	142	28	1	28	90	60	97	.338	.469	Batting #6	.245	605	148	24	3	17	91	60	122	.318	.379
Home	.251	1136	285	42	7	33	134	115	215	.326	.387	Batting #8	.244	794	194	29	2	21	95	76	160	.317	.365
Away	.246	1158	285	56	6	37	162	114	236	.319	.401	Other	.255	895	228	45	8	32	110	93	169	.331	.430
Day	.241	507	122	19	4	17	60	47	89	.313	.394	April	.257	296	76	13	2	13	43	32	60	.337	.446
Night	.251	1787	448	79	9	53	236	182	362	.325	.394	May	.292	366	107	21	1	16	50	38	74	.360	.486
Grass	.252	1640	414	73	10	50	209	158	310	.325	.401	June	.201	412	83	15	1	7	44	52	86	.296	.294
Turf	.239	654	156	25	3	20	87	71	141	.317	.378	July	.285	379	108	17	4	12	52	33	61	.346	.446
First Pitch	.280	257	72	10	3	9	45	7	0	.310	.447	August	.242	417	101	18	3	14	67	34	80	.309	.400
Ahead on Count	.323	468	151	32	4	26	80	133	0	.472	.575	September/October	.224	424	95	14	2	8	40	40	90	.299	.323
Behind on Count	.235	864	203	29	5	21	97	0	251	.244	.353	Pre-All Star	.251	1193	300	56	4	40	152	126	244	.328	.406
Two Strikes	.183	1151	211	31	3	19	91	85	451	.245	.265	Post-All Star	.245	1101	270	42	9	30	144	103	207	.317	.381

Batter vs. Pitcher (career)

Hits Best Against	Avg	AB	H	2B	3B	HR	RBI	BB	SO	OBP	SLG	Hits Worst Against	Avg	AB	H	2B	3B	HR	RBI	BB	SO	OBP	SLG
John Habyan	.500	10	5	1	0	0	2	1	2	.545	.600	Dave Schmidt	.000	15	0	0	0	0	0	2	4	.118	.000
Bret Saberhagen	.462	26	12	2	0	1	3	0	3	.462	.654	Duane Ward	.000	10	0	0	0	0	0	2	6	.167	.000
Tim Leary	.462	13	6	1	1	2	6	2	1	.533	1.154	Bill Wegman	.059	17	1	0	0	0	2	1	2	.111	.059
Todd Burns	.357	14	5	1	0	1	3	1	1	.400	.643	Mike Henneman	.059	17	1	0	0	0	2	1	6	.111	.059
Lee Guetterman	.353	17	6	2	1	2	6	2	1	.421	.941	Mark Eichhorn	.063	16	1	0	0	0	0	1	3	.118	.063

Jay Buhner — Mariners   Bats Right (flyball hitter)

	Avg	G	AB	R	H	2B	3B	HR	RBI	BB	SO	HBP	GDP	SB	CS	OBP	SLG	IBB	SH	SF	#Pit	#P/PA	GB	FB	G/F
1992 Season	.243	152	543	69	132	16	3	25	79	71	146	6	12	0	6	.333	.422	2	1	8	2388	3.80	153	187	0.82
Last Five Years	.246	483	1577	212	388	70	9	81	260	188	461	24	33	4	14	.332	.456	9	4	17	6984	3.87	435	497	0.88

1992 Season

	Avg	AB	H	2B	3B	HR	RBI	BB	SO	OBP	SLG		Avg	AB	H	2B	3B	HR	RBI	BB	SO	OBP	SLG
vs. Left	.230	148	34	4	0	10	25	21	38	.327	.459	Scoring Posn	.296	135	40	4	2	8	59	28	23	.405	.533
vs. Right	.248	395	98	12	3	15	54	50	108	.335	.408	Close & Late	.224	98	22	3	1	5	14	16	24	.330	.429
Groundball	.257	140	36	3	2	7	28	15	36	.329	.457	None on/out	.290	124	36	5	0	5	5	16	28	.371	.452
Flyball	.194	155	30	4	0	7	12	22	40	.306	.355	Batting #5	.242	244	59	11	0	10	30	39	64	.355	.410
Home	.259	263	68	12	3	9	39	38	72	.353	.430	Batting #6	.242	285	69	5	3	14	45	28	79	.306	.428
Away	.229	280	64	4	0	16	40	33	74	.313	.414	Other	.286	14	4	0	0	1	4	4	3	.444	.500
Day	.296	159	47	6	0	12	29	23	40	.383	.560	April	.227	66	15	2	0	1	5	12	16	.342	.303

63

1992 Season

	Avg	AB	H	2B	3B	HR	RBI	BB	SO	OBP	SLG		Avg	AB	H	2B	3B	HR	RBI	BB	SO	OBP	SLG
Night	.221	384	85	10	3	13	50	48	106	.311	.365	May	.235	85	20	0	0	4	17	16	19	.356	.376
Grass	.236	216	51	1	0	16	39	29	58	.328	.463	June	.192	104	20	2	1	4	12	3	30	.218	.346
Turf	.248	327	81	15	3	9	40	42	88	.336	.394	July	.312	93	29	2	1	8	19	13	26	.394	.613
First Pitch	.297	74	22	1	2	6	21	2	0	.316	.608	August	.243	103	25	4	1	4	15	17	32	.355	.417
Ahead on Count	.317	104	33	7	0	7	24	32	0	.471	.587	September/October	.250	92	23	6	0	4	11	10	23	.333	.446
Behind on Count	.222	198	44	5	0	7	23	0	79	.228	.354	Pre-All Star	.229	301	69	5	1	15	48	36	78	.309	.402
Two Strikes	.148	270	40	5	0	7	16	37	146	.254	.244	Post-All Star	.260	242	63	11	2	10	31	35	68	.361	.446

1992 By Position

Position	Avg	AB	H	2B	3B	HR	RBI	BB	SO	OBP	SLG	G	GS	Innings	PO	A	E	DP	Fld Pct	Rng Fctr	In Zone	Outs	Zone Rtg	MLB Zone
As rf	.241	539	130	16	2	24	74	71	146	.332	.412	150	149	1325.1	312	14	2	4	.994	2.21	367	287	.782	.814

Last Five Years

	Avg	AB	H	2B	3B	HR	RBI	BB	SO	OBP	SLG		Avg	AB	H	2B	3B	HR	RBI	BB	SO	OBP	SLG
vs. Left	.236	499	118	23	2	29	82	65	128	.330	.490	Scoring Posn	.271	398	108	18	6	19	173	64	107	.370	.490
vs. Right	.250	1078	270	47	7	52	178	123	333	.333	.452	Close & Late	.214	276	59	7	2	11	38	35	81	.300	.373
Groundball	.265	411	109	13	3	20	61	36	115	.332	.457	None on/out	.277	361	100	18	1	19	19	42	93	.356	.490
Flyball	.185	352	65	15	1	14	42	47	108	.290	.352	Batting #5	.251	426	107	23	0	18	57	46	119	.331	.432
Home	.241	773	186	37	5	40	126	102	234	.334	.457	Batting #6	.236	653	154	22	5	31	109	78	192	.323	.427
Away	.251	804	202	33	4	41	134	86	227	.330	.455	Other	.255	498	127	25	4	32	94	64	150	.346	.514
Day	.282	426	120	25	1	32	84	49	133	.360	.570	April	.229	118	27	5	1	5	12	20	36	.338	.415
Night	.233	1151	268	45	8	49	176	139	328	.322	.404	May	.237	131	31	1	1	6	28	23	32	.348	.397
Grass	.263	646	170	21	3	39	124	76	178	.347	.486	June	.223	350	78	11	2	20	71	29	104	.294	.437
Turf	.234	931	218	49	6	42	136	112	283	.322	.435	July	.265	211	56	7	1	17	35	22	61	.342	.550
First Pitch	.354	223	79	11	4	19	63	6	0	.374	.695	August	.276	370	102	27	4	18	64	47	116	.361	.516
Ahead on Count	.317	300	95	22	2	19	66	98	0	.484	.593	September/October	.237	397	94	19	0	15	50	47	112	.325	.398
Behind on Count	.215	536	115	21	2	21	73	2	230	.230	.379	Pre-All Star	.233	675	157	19	4	40	129	80	196	.318	.450
Two Strikes	.157	824	129	25	1	27	78	84	461	.240	.450	Post-All Star	.256	902	231	51	5	41	131	108	265	.343	.450

Batter vs. Pitcher (career)

Hits Best Against	Avg	AB	H	2B	3B	HR	RBI	BB	SO	OBP	SLG	Hits Worst Against	Avg	AB	H	2B	3B	HR	RBI	BB	SO	OBP	SLG
Mike Boddicker	.500	12	6	4	0	1	3	3	3	.647	1.083	David Wells	.000	11	0	0	0	0	0	1	2	.083	.000
Storm Davis	.500	12	6	1	0	1	4	2	2	.625	.833	Jeff Reardon	.000	10	0	0	0	0	0	1	2	.091	.000
Curt Young	.455	11	5	1	0	1	4	5	1	.588	.818	Bill Gullickson	.063	16	1	0	0	0	0	2	5	.167	.063
Ben McDonald	.455	11	5	0	0	2	4	1	1	.500	1.000	Mike Flanagan	.063	16	1	0	0	0	1	1	2	.118	.063
Bob Welch	.385	13	5	1	0	2	6	1	4	.400	.923	Roger Clemens	.067	15	1	0	0	0	1	1	6	.125	.067

Jim Bullinger — Cubs   Pitches Right

	ERA	W	L	Sv	G	GS	IP	BB	SO	Avg	H	2B	3B	HR	RBI	OBP	SLG	GF	IR	IRS	Hld	SvOp	SB	CS	GB	FB	G/F
1992 Season	4.66	2	8	7	39	9	85.0	54	36	.233	72	9	5	9	44	.350	.382	15	21	5	4	7	8	2	129	94	1.37

1992 Season

	ERA	W	L	Sv	G	GS	IP	H	HR	BB	SO		Avg	AB	H	2B	3B	HR	RBI	BB	SO	OBP	SLG
Home	3.48	2	6	4	21	6	54.1	43	4	31	23	vs. Left	.212	170	36	4	5	6	27	33	17	.343	.400
Away	6.75	0	2	3	18	3	30.2	29	5	23	13	vs. Right	.259	139	36	5	0	3	17	21	19	.360	.360
Starter	5.15	1	6	0	9	9	50.2	40	8	31	23	Scoring Posn	.270	74	20	4	2	3	35	21	7	.420	.500
Reliever	3.93	1	2	7	30	0	34.1	32	1	23	13	Close & Late	.200	90	18	1	2	1	9	17	13	.321	.289
0 Days rest	4.66	0	0	3	9	0	9.2	10	1	3	4	None on/out	.218	78	17	3	0	2	2	12	11	.330	.333
1 or 2 Days rest	1.42	0	1	4	13	0	12.2	10	0	9	7	First Pitch	.346	52	18	3	2	2	13	6	0	.407	.596
3+ Days rest	6.00	1	1	0	8	0	12.0	12	0	11	2	Behind on Count	.295	78	23	2	2	3	11	33	0	.504	.487
Pre-All Star	5.40	0	2	7	19	0	20.0	19	0	16	6	Ahead on Count	.170	112	19	3	1	3	15	0	28	.181	.295
Post-All Star	4.43	2	6	0	20	9	65.0	53	9	38	30	Two Strikes	.177	113	20	3	1	2	14	15	36	.280	.274

Eric Bullock — Expos   Bats Left (groundball hitter)

	Avg	G	AB	R	H	2B	3B	HR	RBI	BB	SO	HBP	GDP	SB	CS	OBP	SLG	IBB	SH	SF	#Pit	#P/PA	GB	FB	G/F
1992 Season	.000	8	5	0	0	0	0	0	0	1	0	0	0	0	0	.000	.000	0	0	0	33	6.60	3	1	3.00
Last Five Years	.220	107	100	10	22	4	0	1	9	12	17	0	1	3	7	1	.301	.290	0	0	1	435	3.85	46	25	1.84

1992 Season

	Avg	AB	H	2B	3B	HR	RBI	BB	SO	OBP	SLG		Avg	AB	H	2B	3B	HR	RBI	BB	SO	OBP	SLG
vs. Left	.000	0	0	0	0	0	0	0	0	.000	.000	Scoring Posn	.000	0	0	0	0	0	0	0	0	.000	.000
vs. Right	.000	5	0	0	0	0	0	0	1	.000	.000	Close & Late	.000	0	0	0	0	0	0	0	0	.000	.000

Dave Burba — Giants   Pitches Right

	ERA	W	L	Sv	G	GS	IP	BB	SO	Avg	H	2B	3B	HR	RBI	OBP	SLG	GF	IR	IRS	Hld	SvOp	SB	CS	GB	FB	G/F
1992 Season	4.97	2	7	0	23	11	70.2	31	47	.287	80	15	2	4	44	.358	.398	4	13	5	0	0	4	1	91	83	1.10
Career (1990-1992)	4.53	4	9	1	51	13	115.1	47	67	.272	122	22	4	10	61	.343	.406	17	24	9	0	1	6	2	156	142	1.10

1992 Season

	ERA	W	L	Sv	G	GS	IP	H	HR	BB	SO		Avg	AB	H	2B	3B	HR	RBI	BB	SO	OBP	SLG
Home	2.94	1	2	0	10	5	33.2	29	2	14	16	vs. Left	.318	151	48	11	1	1	18	12	18	.370	.424

1992 Season

	ERA	W	L	Sv	G	GS	IP	H	HR	BB	SO		Avg	AB	H	2B	3B	HR	RBI	BB	SO	OBP	SLG
Away	6.81	1	5	0	13	6	37.0	51	2	17	31	vs. Right	.250	128	32	4	1	3	26	19	29	.344	.367
Starter	5.16	1	6	0	11	11	45.1	55	3	21	22	Scoring Posn	.319	72	23	5	1	1	38	19	13	.448	.458
Reliever	4.62	1	1	0	12	0	25.1	25	1	10	25	Close & Late	.000	10	0	0	0	0	1	1	3	.083	.000
0 Days rest	0.00	0	0	0	0	0	0.0	0	0	0	0	None on/out	.294	68	20	3	0	2	2	4	10	.342	.426
1 or 2 Days rest	1.59	1	1	0	4	0	11.1	5	0	3	8	First Pitch	.455	44	20	5	0	1	8	2	0	.478	.636
3+ Days rest	7.07	0	0	0	8	0	14.0	20	1	7	17	Behind on Count	.306	72	22	5	0	2	12	16	0	.429	.458
Pre-All Star	5.40	2	6	0	15	7	51.2	59	4	23	33	Ahead on Count	.205	117	24	2	2	1	15	0	40	.210	.282
Post-All Star	3.79	0	1	0	8	4	19.0	21	0	8	14	Two Strikes	.224	116	26	2	1	1	13	13	47	.300	.284

Tim Burke — Yankees — Pitches Right (groundball pitcher)

	ERA	W	L	Sv	G	GS	IP	BB	SO	Avg	H	2B	3B	HR	RBI	OBP	SLG	GF	IR	IRS	Hld	SvOp	SB	CS	GB	FB	G/F
1992 Season	4.15	3	4	0	38	0	43.1	18	15	.299	52	14	1	3	27	.366	.443	19	21	6	5	2	5	1	84	43	1.95
Last Five Years	3.12	24	22	72	297	0	386.2	112	217	.255	371	61	8	30	184	.309	.369	85	211	73	22	106	40	6	608	391	1.55

1992 Season

	ERA	W	L	Sv	G	GS	IP	H	HR	BB	SO		Avg	AB	H	2B	3B	HR	RBI	BB	SO	OBP	SLG
Home	3.42	1	1	0	19	0	23.2	32	1	9	7	vs. Left	.218	78	17	3	1	0	2	6	8	.274	.282
Away	5.03	2	3	0	19	0	19.2	20	2	9	8	vs. Right	.365	96	35	11	0	3	25	12	7	.436	.573
Starter	0.00	0	0	0	0	0	0.0	0	0	0	0	Scoring Posn	.306	62	19	5	1	0	23	14	7	.429	.419
Reliever	4.15	3	4	0	38	0	43.1	52	3	18	15	Close & Late	.238	42	10	5	0	0	3	7	4	.347	.357
0 Days rest	3.38	0	1	0	4	0	5.1	9	0	1	3	None on/out	.425	40	17	4	0	2	2	1	3	.439	.675
1 or 2 Days rest	11.25	0	3	0	15	0	12.0	24	1	9	0	First Pitch	.270	37	10	0	0	2	6	0	0	.263	.432
3+ Days rest	1.04	3	0	0	19	0	26.0	19	2	8	12	Behind on Count	.357	28	10	4	0	0	6	10	0	.538	.500
Pre-All Star	3.90	2	3	0	23	0	27.2	34	2	9	10	Ahead on Count	.237	76	18	5	0	0	5	0	15	.237	.303
Post-All Star	4.60	1	1	0	15	0	15.2	18	1	9	5	Two Strikes	.247	73	18	7	0	0	8	8	15	.321	.342

Last Five Years

	ERA	W	L	Sv	G	GS	IP	H	HR	BB	SO		Avg	AB	H	2B	3B	HR	RBI	BB	SO	OBP	SLG
Home	3.03	15	7	30	144	0	199.0	194	19	56	109	vs. Left	.276	720	199	34	4	15	82	63	83	.332	.397
Away	3.21	9	15	42	153	0	187.2	177	11	56	108	vs. Right	.233	737	172	27	4	15	102	49	134	.286	.342
Day	2.83	6	9	25	93	0	124.0	107	12	33	86	Inning 1-6	.306	111	34	1	1	5	26	8	20	.355	.468
Night	3.26	18	13	47	204	0	262.2	264	18	79	131	Inning 7+	.250	1346	337	60	7	25	158	104	197	.305	.361
Grass	3.09	8	14	18	114	0	148.2	150	9	48	86	None on	.254	780	198	32	4	19	19	32	101	.286	.378
Turf	3.14	16	8	54	183	0	238.0	221	21	64	131	Runners on	.256	677	173	29	4	11	165	80	116	.333	.359
April	3.91	4	3	17	43	0	50.2	58	6	17	28	Scoring Posn	.265	431	114	21	2	7	151	69	77	.360	.371
May	4.16	5	4	15	59	0	71.1	75	7	21	45	Close & Late	.237	747	177	32	4	13	93	64	108	.299	.343
June	2.78	3	3	5	41	0	55.0	51	2	16	24	None on/out	.270	341	95	17	2	10	10	10	35	.299	.420
July	2.87	4	3	12	49	0	62.2	63	5	16	32	vs. 1st Batr (relief)	.286	273	78	16	2	6	28	16	37	.328	.425
August	3.20	2	6	11	55	0	76.0	76	4	23	39	First Inning Pitched	.263	966	254	43	4	17	140	72	143	.315	.369
September/October	1.90	6	3	12	50	0	71.0	48	6	19	49	First 15 Pitches	.272	952	259	42	5	20	116	66	121	.321	.390
Starter	0.00	0	0	0	0	0	0.0	0	0	0	0	Pitch 16-30	.225	414	93	14	3	10	59	31	79	.279	.345
Reliever	3.12	24	22	72	297	0	386.2	371	30	112	217	Pitch 31-45	.225	80	18	5	0	0	8	12	15	.326	.288
0 Days rest	2.36	7	3	27	70	0	91.1	83	7	20	62	Pitch 46+	.091	11	1	0	0	0	1	3	2	.266	.091
1 or 2 Days rest	3.72	10	13	29	141	0	176.2	180	14	62	84	First Pitch	.318	264	84	12	2	7	45	23	0	.370	.458
3+ Days rest	2.81	7	6	16	86	0	118.2	108	9	30	71	Ahead on Count	.210	670	141	21	4	7	62	0	183	.217	.285
Pre-All Star	3.68	12	11	39	154	0	190.2	195	16	57	113	Behind on Count	.298	275	82	13	1	10	40	50	0	.404	.462
Post-All Star	2.57	12	11	33	143	0	196.0	176	14	55	104	Two Strikes	.203	610	124	24	2	5	55	39	217	.254	.274

Pitcher vs. Batter (career)

Pitches Best Vs.	Avg	AB	H	2B	3B	HR	RBI	BB	SO	OBP	SLG	Pitches Worst Vs.	Avg	AB	H	2B	3B	HR	RBI	BB	SO	OBP	SLG
Charlie Hayes	.000	11	0	0	0	0	0	0	2	.000	.000	Glenn Davis	.556	18	10	3	0	2	7	1	1	.579	1.056
Mitch Webster	.000	10	0	0	0	0	0	1	3	.091	.091	Tim Teufel	.500	10	5	1	0	1	3	0	1	.455	.900
Candy Maldonado	.077	13	1	0	0	0	0	0	3	.077	.077	Pedro Guerrero	.429	21	9	1	0	2	5	2	2	.478	.762
Lenny Dykstra	.077	13	1	0	0	0	0	2	3	.200	.077	Jose Uribe	.429	14	6	2	0	1	4	1	0	.467	.786
Bobby Thompson	.118	17	2	0	0	0	0	0	5	.118	.118	Todd Zeile	.364	11	4	0	1	1	2	2	3	.462	.818

John Burkett — Giants — Pitches Right

	ERA	W	L	Sv	G	GS	IP	BB	SO	Avg	H	2B	3B	HR	RBI	OBP	SLG	CG	ShO	Sup	QS	#P/S	SB	CS	GB	FB	G/F
1992 Season	3.84	13	9	0	32	32	189.2	45	107	.264	194	34	7	13	83	.308	.382	3	1	4.70	15	86	17	7	272	206	1.32
Last Five Years	3.94	39	27	1	101	98	600.1	166	356	.266	618	98	11	50	262	.318	.383	8	2	4.84	51	90	52	30	904	643	1.41

1992 Season

	ERA	W	L	Sv	G	GS	IP	H	HR	BB	SO		Avg	AB	H	2B	3B	HR	RBI	BB	SO	OBP	SLG
Home	3.09	10	2	0	15	15	102.0	89	5	17	56	vs. Left	.296	466	138	26	6	11	58	27	56	.334	.448
Away	4.72	3	7	0	17	17	87.2	105	8	28	51	vs. Right	.208	269	56	8	1	2	25	18	51	.265	.268
Day	3.59	8	4	0	15	15	87.2	88	4	17	52	Inning 1-6	.260	653	170	28	7	11	73	39	98	.305	.375
Night	4.06	5	5	0	17	17	102.0	106	9	28	55	Inning 7+	.293	82	24	6	0	2	10	6	9	.333	.439
Grass	3.65	13	6	0	24	24	145.2	143	7	32	82	None on	.253	442	112	15	0	8	8	17	64	.284	.342
Turf	4.50	0	3	0	8	8	44.0	51	6	13	25	Runners on	.280	293	82	19	7	5	75	28	43	.343	.444
April	4.97	2	1	0	5	5	29.0	27	2	11	19	Scoring Posn	.304	168	51	12	5	3	66	20	30	.376	.488
May	2.43	3	0	0	5	5	33.1	28	3	4	21	Close & Late	.300	30	9	2	0	2	7	1	5	.303	.567

1992 Season

	ERA	W	L	Sv	G	GS	IP	H	HR	BB	SO		Avg	AB	H	2B	3B	HR	RBI	BB	SO	OBP	SLG
June	6.56	0	4	0	6	6	23.1	35	3	9	12	None on/out	.247	190	47	7	0	3	3	9	23	.285	.332
July	2.83	2	1	0	5	5	35.0	29	2	10	18	vs. 1st Batr (relief)	.000	0	0	0	0	0	0	0	0	.000	.000
August	2.75	4	1	0	5	5	36.0	33	1	4	13	First Inning Pitched	.256	125	32	5	1	3	14	8	26	.304	.384
September/October	4.64	2	2	0	6	6	33.0	42	2	7	24	First 75 Pitches	.266	605	161	30	7	9	66	35	92	.310	.383
Starter	3.84	13	9	0	32	32	189.2	194	13	45	107	Pitch 76-90	.296	81	24	3	0	3	12	6	11	.337	.444
Reliever	0.00	0	0	0	0	0	0.0	0	0	0	0	Pitch 91-105	.195	41	8	0	0	1	3	3	2	.250	.268
0-3 Days Rest	1.29	0	1	0	1	1	7.0	6	1	1	2	Pitch 106+	.125	8	1	1	0	0	2	1	2	.222	.250
4 Days Rest	3.79	9	5	0	19	19	116.1	113	9	22	71	First Pitch	.358	134	48	9	1	3	15	5	0	.379	.507
5+ Days Rest	4.21	4	3	0	12	12	66.1	75	3	22	34	Ahead on Count	.192	313	60	10	3	3	29	0	92	.195	.272
Pre-All Star	4.07	6	5	0	18	18	101.2	104	10	25	61	Behind on Count	.312	141	44	7	3	3	24	26	0	.426	.468
Post-All Star	3.58	7	4	0	14	14	88.0	90	3	20	46	Two Strikes	.184	305	56	7	2	6	26	14	107	.224	.279

Last Five Years

	ERA	W	L	Sv	G	GS	IP	H	HR	BB	SO		Avg	AB	H	2B	3B	HR	RBI	BB	SO	OBP	SLG
Home	3.54	22	10	0	48	48	315.1	293	27	75	195	vs. Left	.283	1387	392	70	8	35	171	102	191	.331	.420
Away	4.39	17	17	1	53	50	285.0	325	23	91	161	vs. Right	.242	933	226	28	3	15	91	64	165	.299	.327
Day	3.37	20	12	0	46	44	275.1	264	22	76	159	Inning 1-6	.268	2005	537	82	11	42	233	146	318	.321	.383
Night	4.43	19	15	1	55	54	325.0	354	28	90	197	Inning 7+	.257	315	81	16	0	8	29	20	38	.301	.384
Grass	3.64	30	19	1	74	71	450.0	444	36	118	267	Runners on	.279	976	272	52	8	19	231	83	142	.334	.407
Turf	4.85	9	8	0	27	27	150.1	174	14	48	89	Scoring Posn	.290	535	155	24	6	10	199	59	90	.354	.413
April	4.10	5	3	0	11	11	68.0	67	3	21	40	Close & Late	.273	143	39	6	0	5	20	10	17	.318	.420
May	3.59	6	2	0	17	17	102.2	104	9	32	62	None on/out	.278	601	167	24	1	14	14	34	83	.319	.391
June	3.45	5	6	0	18	17	104.1	95	10	35	61	vs. 1st Batr (relief)	.000	1	0	0	0	0	1	2	0	.667	.000
July	3.48	7	3	0	18	17	111.1	112	8	27	64	First Inning Pitched	.255	384	98	11	2	7	49	35	70	.325	.349
August	4.53	8	6	0	17	17	101.1	110	9	22	50	First 75 Pitches	.270	1818	490	77	11	38	212	127	286	.320	.387
September/October	4.55	8	7	1	20	19	112.2	130	11	29	79	Pitch 76-90	.281	263	74	12	0	8	34	24	36	.341	.418
Starter	3.97	39	27	0	98	98	595.2	616	50	164	355	Pitch 91-105	.242	157	38	6	0	3	10	8	21	.283	.338
Reliever	0.00	0	0	1	3	0	4.2	2	0	2	1	Pitch 106+	.195	82	16	3	0	1	6	7	13	.258	.268
0-3 Days Rest	4.10	6	5	0	18	18	112.0	113	10	37	73	First Pitch	.320	410	131	23	2	12	55	12	0	.343	.473
4 Days Rest	3.62	24	14	0	53	53	330.2	325	29	79	204	Ahead on Count	.193	975	188	23	5	13	69	0	310	.198	.267
5+ Days Rest	4.65	9	8	0	27	27	153.0	178	14	48	78	Behind on Count	.330	491	162	31	4	11	81	83	0	.426	.477
Pre-All Star	3.53	20	12	0	52	51	319.0	303	26	96	195	Two Strikes	.188	966	182	20	4	15	66	71	356	.249	.264
Post-All Star	4.41	19	15	1	49	47	261.1	315	24	70	161												

Pitcher vs. Batter (career)

Pitches Best Vs.	Avg	AB	H	2B	3B	HR	RBI	BB	SO	OBP	SLG	Pitches Worst Vs.	Avg	AB	H	2B	3B	HR	RBI	BB	SO	OBP	SLG
Orlando Merced	.056	18	1	0	0	0	1	1	4	.105	.056	Ryne Sandberg	.583	12	7	0	0	1	1	1	1	.615	.833
Pedro Guerrero	.067	15	1	0	0	0	1	2	2	.176	.067	Darren Daulton	.571	14	8	2	0	0	5	4	2	.600	.714
Kevin McReynolds	.083	12	1	0	0	0	0	0	0	.083	.083	John Kruk	.429	21	9	3	0	2	2	1	4	.455	.857
Joe Oliver	.083	12	1	0	0	0	0	3	0	.083	.083	Larry Walker	.412	17	7	0	0	3	7	0	1	.412	.941
Mariano Duncan	.100	20	2	0	0	0	5	0	0	.100	.100	Dave Hollins	.400	10	4	1	0	1	4	1	0	.417	.800

Ellis Burks — Red Sox

Bats Right

	Avg	G	AB	R	H	2B	3B	HR	RBI	BB	SO	HBP	GDP	SB	CS	OBP	SLG	IBB	SH	SF	#Pit	#P/PA	GB	FB	G/F
1992 Season	.255	66	235	35	60	8	3	8	30	25	48	1	5	5	2	.327	.417	2	0	2	1061	4.03	69	70	0.99
Last Five Years	.283	589	2236	346	633	130	25	73	328	210	352	16	46	66	38	.347	.462	11	10	17	9432	3.80	818	674	1.21

1992 Season

	Avg	AB	H	2B	3B	HR	RBI	BB	SO	OBP	SLG		Avg	AB	H	2B	3B	HR	RBI	BB	SO	OBP	SLG
vs. Left	.197	66	13	2	1	3	8	10	8	.299	.394	Scoring Posn	.200	65	13	5	0	2	20	11	14	.308	.369
vs. Right	.278	169	47	6	2	5	22	15	40	.339	.426	Close & Late	.240	50	12	1	0	2	8	4	15	.304	.380
Home	.231	108	25	5	2	4	18	12	21	.309	.426	None on/out	.217	60	13	0	1	1	1	4	19	.277	.300
Away	.276	127	35	3	1	4	12	13	27	.343	.409	Batting #4	.231	104	24	4	3	1	10	12	23	.305	.356
First Pitch	.261	23	6	1	1	0	3	2	0	.346	.391	Batting #6	.329	73	24	3	0	3	12	9	17	.410	.493
Ahead on Count	.311	61	19	3	2	4	13	11	0	.417	.623	Other	.207	58	12	1	0	4	8	4	8	.258	.431
Behind on Count	.213	80	17	1	0	2	4	0	21	.213	.300	Pre-All Star	.255	235	60	8	3	8	30	25	48	.327	.417
Two Strikes	.183	109	20	1	0	3	7	12	48	.262	.275	Post-All Star	.000	0	0	0	0	0	0	0	0	.000	.000

Last Five Years

	Avg	AB	H	2B	3B	HR	RBI	BB	SO	OBP	SLG		Avg	AB	H	2B	3B	HR	RBI	BB	SO	OBP	SLG
vs. Left	.282	634	179	38	6	20	91	75	82	.358	.456	Scoring Posn	.287	644	185	33	8	25	265	78	109	.358	.480
vs. Right	.283	1602	454	92	19	53	237	135	270	.342	.464	Close & Late	.259	352	91	20	5	9	42	43	76	.346	.420
Groundball	.286	576	165	30	7	13	76	46	98	.343	.431	None on/out	.272	518	141	25	7	20	20	45	71	.336	.463
Flyball	.289	561	162	42	5	18	83	49	86	.347	.478	Batting #3	.311	473	147	16	7	14	65	46	71	.376	.463
Home	.297	1087	323	75	12	36	167	105	159	.360	.488	Batting #5	.271	531	144	33	4	19	82	60	80	.348	.456
Away	.270	1149	310	55	13	37	161	105	193	.333	.437	Other	.278	1232	342	81	14	40	181	104	201	.334	.463
Day	.293	734	215	42	7	22	122	80	113	.367	.459	April	.263	350	92	22	4	7	40	47	64	.359	.409
Night	.278	1502	418	88	18	51	206	130	239	.336	.463	May	.288	445	128	26	8	13	56	40	69	.346	.470
Grass	.283	1886	533	108	19	62	276	178	297	.346	.459	June	.283	434	123	27	3	22	68	30	60	.328	.512
Turf	.286	350	100	22	6	11	52	32	55	.351	.477	July	.309	275	85	19	5	10	47	29	48	.380	.524
First Pitch	.327	245	80	21	3	6	39	5	0	.348	.510	August	.281	448	126	23	4	12	69	42	66	.342	.431
Ahead on Count	.313	544	170	27	9	28	104	114	0	.429	.550	September/October	.278	284	79	13	1	9	48	22	45	.333	.426
Behind on Count	.250	765	191	43	5	18	79	1	175	.255	.390	Pre-All Star	.282	1324	374	80	17	46	186	126	205	.346	.473

Last Five Years

	Avg	AB	H	2B	3B	HR	RBI	BB	SO	OBP	SLG		Avg	AB	H	2B	3B	HR	RBI	BB	SO	OBP	SLG
Two Strikes	.207	982	203	35	3	24	107	89	352	.275	.322	Post-All Star	.284	912	259	50	8	27	142	84	147	.347	.445

Batter vs. Pitcher (career)

Hits Best Against	Avg	AB	H	2B	3B	HR	RBI	BB	SO	OBP	SLG	Hits Worst Against	Avg	AB	H	2B	3B	HR	RBI	BB	SO	OBP	SLG
Erik Hanson	.545	22	12	1	0	2	4	1	3	.565	.864	Bill Krueger	.000	14	0	0	0	0	0	1	1	.067	.000
Bill Wegman	.500	16	8	1	0	1	5	4	2	.600	.750	Gregg Olson	.000	10	0	0	0	0	0	1	3	.091	.000
Jeff Russell	.450	20	9	2	0	2	6	2	3	.500	.850	Tim Leary	.071	14	1	0	0	0	0	1	5	.235	.071
Bud Black	.429	14	6	0	0	1	3	5	2	.579	.643	Jimmy Key	.080	25	2	1	0	0	1	1	3	.115	.120
Randy Johnson	.417	12	5	1	0	1	5	2	3	.500	.750	Jaime Navarro	.083	12	1	0	0	0	0	0	1	.083	.083

Todd Burns — Rangers
Pitches Right (flyball pitcher)

	ERA	W	L	Sv	G	GS	IP	BB	SO	Avg	H	2B	3B	HR	RBI	OBP	SLG	GF	IR	IRS	Hld	SvOp	SB	CS	GB	FB	G/F
1992 Season	3.84	3	5	1	35	10	103.0	32	55	.249	97	26	2	8	39	.309	.387	9	16	2	0	2	1	7	111	151	0.74
Career (1988-1992)	3.08	21	15	13	154	28	394.0	134	207	.236	344	70	10	29	147	.301	.358	23	96	28	19	18	11	20	461	521	0.88

1992 Season

	ERA	W	L	Sv	G	GS	IP	H	HR	BB	SO		Avg	AB	H	2B	3B	HR	RBI	BB	SO	OBP	SLG
Home	1.85	1	1	1	15	5	48.2	35	3	12	30	vs. Left	.235	166	39	8	1	2	9	15	20	.308	.331
Away	5.63	2	4	0	20	5	54.1	62	5	20	25	vs. Right	.259	224	58	18	1	6	30	17	35	.310	.429
Starter	3.20	2	4	0	10	10	64.2	56	3	17	37	Scoring Posn	.247	93	23	9	0	1	28	7	12	.288	.376
Reliever	4.93	1	1	1	25	0	38.1	41	5	15	18	Close & Late	.299	87	26	6	0	3	11	9	9	.364	.471
0 Days rest	4.76	0	0	1	5	0	5.2	4	1	5	2	None on/out	.257	101	26	7	1	3	3	7	17	.312	.436
1 or 2 Days rest	4.26	1	1	0	10	0	19.0	19	2	5	12	First Pitch	.255	51	13	3	0	0	2	1	0	.278	.314
3+ Days rest	5.93	0	0	0	10	0	13.2	18	2	5	4	Behind on Count	.327	107	35	11	2	4	18	16	0	.408	.579
Pre-All Star	3.49	2	2	0	11	7	56.2	48	6	17	33	Ahead on Count	.196	168	33	6	0	2	11	0	44	.211	.268
Post-All Star	4.27	1	3	1	24	3	46.1	49	2	15	22	Two Strikes	.173	162	28	6	0	3	10	15	55	.251	.265

Career (1988-1992)

	ERA	W	L	Sv	G	GS	IP	H	HR	BB	SO		Avg	AB	H	2B	3B	HR	RBI	BB	SO	OBP	SLG
Home	2.27	13	4	8	78	14	210.1	166	15	62	110	vs. Left	.226	668	151	28	8	10	45	69	80	.301	.337
Away	4.02	8	11	5	76	14	183.2	178	14	72	97	vs. Right	.245	788	193	42	2	19	102	65	127	.301	.376
Day	2.94	8	4	7	55	7	134.2	103	7	52	82	Inning 1-6	.240	801	192	41	7	16	86	67	119	.299	.368
Night	3.16	13	11	6	99	21	259.1	241	22	82	125	Inning 7+	.232	655	152	29	3	13	61	67	88	.303	.345
Grass	3.21	17	11	12	133	26	341.2	304	26	114	177	None on	.247	829	205	42	5	16	16	78	122	.315	.368
Turf	2.24	4	4	1	21	2	52.1	40	3	20	30	Runners on	.222	627	139	26	5	13	131	56	85	.283	.344
April	4.18	1	0	1	16	0	32.1	29	3	10	13	Scoring Posn	.238	332	79	17	2	6	109	42	47	.315	.355
May	1.52	4	0	2	17	2	41.1	30	1	7	24	Close & Late	.241	274	66	11	1	8	25	36	39	.328	.376
June	2.36	3	4	2	26	6	76.1	60	7	30	44	None on/out	.252	373	94	21	3	8	8	26	57	.304	.383
July	3.59	6	4	4	34	10	100.1	93	7	32	56	vs. 1st Batr (relief)	.327	107	35	8	1	3	14	14	20	.410	.505
August	3.90	4	2	1	28	5	62.1	56	3	29	34	First Inning Pitched	.269	506	136	25	4	13	83	57	92	.342	.411
September/October	2.88	3	5	3	33	5	81.1	76	8	26	35	First 15 Pitches	.279	470	131	24	3	12	68	49	76	.347	.419
Starter	3.06	11	6	0	28	28	185.0	163	13	50	93	Pitch 16-30	.205	322	66	13	3	4	24	34	46	.280	.301
Reliever	3.10	10	9	13	126	0	209.0	181	16	84	114	Pitch 31-45	.210	214	45	9	2	5	24	13	28	.261	.341
0 Days rest	4.41	0	1	3	11	0	16.1	13	3	11	11	Pitch 46+	.227	450	102	24	2	8	31	38	57	.286	.342
1 or 2 Days rest	3.33	4	6	4	50	0	81.0	66	6	31	51	First Pitch	.231	199	46	9	4	2	15	9	0	.265	.347
3+ Days rest	2.74	6	2	6	65	0	111.2	102	7	42	52	Ahead on Count	.198	621	123	18	2	8	41	0	165	.201	.272
Pre-All Star	2.73	9	6	7	74	12	191.1	153	13	61	105	Behind on Count	.307	371	114	28	3	13	57	73	0	.418	.504
Post-All Star	3.42	12	9	6	80	16	202.2	191	16	73	102	Two Strikes	.169	605	102	14	2	10	43	52	207	.235	.248

Pitcher vs. Batter (career)

Pitches Best Vs.	Avg	AB	H	2B	3B	HR	RBI	BB	SO	OBP	SLG	Pitches Worst Vs.	Avg	AB	H	2B	3B	HR	RBI	BB	SO	OBP	SLG
Rob Deer	.000	10	0	0	0	0	0	2	5	.167	.000	Gary Gaetti	.500	10	5	0	0	0	1	2	0	.583	.500
Mickey Tettleton	.000	10	0	0	0	0	0	1	5	.091	.000	Scott Fletcher	.444	9	4	2	0	0	2	2	1	.545	.667
Randy Milligan	.000	7	0	0	0	0	0	4	1	.364	.000	Joe Orsulak	.400	10	4	2	0	0	1	1	1	.455	.600
Cory Snyder	.091	11	1	0	0	0	0	0	2	.091	.091	Kirby Puckett	.400	10	4	2	0	1	1	2	2	.500	.900
Kevin Seitzer	.167	12	2	0	0	0	1	3	.231	.167		Cal Ripken	.375	16	6	1	0	2	4	0	2	.375	.813

Randy Bush — Twins
Bats Left (flyball hitter)

	Avg	G	AB	R	H	2B	3B	HR	RBI	BB	SO	HBP	GDP	SB	CS	OBP	SLG	IBB	SH	SF	#Pit	#P/PA	GB	FB	G/F
1992 Season	.214	100	182	14	39	8	1	2	22	11	37	2	5	1	1	.263	.302	3	0	3	708	3.58	56	60	0.93
Last Five Years	.258	543	1313	163	339	63	9	42	168	162	211	23	36	14	20	.347	.416	28	4	12	5375	3.56	420	457	0.92

1992 Season

	Avg	AB	H	2B	3B	HR	RBI	BB	SO	OBP	SLG		Avg	AB	H	2B	3B	HR	RBI	BB	SO	OBP	SLG
vs. Left	.000	8	0	0	0	0	0	0	4	.000	.000	Scoring Posn	.220	59	13	2	0	0	20	6	10	.279	.254
vs. Right	.224	174	39	8	1	2	22	11	33	.274	.316	Close & Late	.188	48	9	3	0	0	3	3	7	.235	.250
Home	.217	83	18	3	0	0	7	7	15	.286	.253	None on/out	.206	34	7	2	1	0	0	1	12	.229	.324
Away	.212	99	21	5	1	2	15	4	22	.243	.343	Batting #6	.220	41	9	2	0	1	6	1	4	.256	.341
First Pitch	.130	23	3	0	1	0	3	0		.231	.217	Batting #7	.214	42	9	1	1	0	4	4	9	.277	.286
Ahead on Count	.389	36	14	5	0	1	13	3	0	.415	.611	Other	.212	99	21	5	0	1	12	6	24	.259	.293
Behind on Count	.188	64	12	1	0	0	6	0	21	.200	.203	Pre-All Star	.233	90	21	5	0	1	15	8	15	.294	.322
Two Strikes	.155	84	13	2	0	1	4	5	37	.211	.214	Post-All Star	.196	92	18	3	1	1	7	3	22	.229	.283

67

Last Five Years

	Avg	AB	H	2B	3B	HR	RBI	BB	SO	OBP	SLG		Avg	AB	H	2B	3B	HR	RBI	BB	SO	OBP	SLG
vs. Left	.178	45	8	4	1	0	5	2	18	.220	.311	Scoring Posn	.258	333	86	17	2	11	125	79	58	.395	.420
vs. Right	.261	1268	331	59	4	42	163	160	193	.351	.420	Close & Late	.256	227	58	10	2	7	28	35	42	.362	.410
Groundball	.259	347	90	13	1	9	42	44	46	.350	.380	None on/out	.229	292	67	14	3	9	9	25	51	.299	.390
Flyball	.244	279	68	14	4	12	34	36	53	.334	.452	Batting #2	.271	291	79	12	0	9	38	27	41	.343	.405
Home	.255	611	156	32	5	22	82	90	102	.361	.432	Batting #6	.245	515	126	25	5	17	55	60	82	.332	.412
Away	.261	702	183	31	4	20	86	72	109	.335	.402	Other	.264	507	134	26	4	16	75	75	88	.364	.425
Day	.271	387	105	17	3	19	53	56	74	.379	.478	April	.224	165	37	8	1	5	20	20	24	.316	.376
Night	.253	926	234	46	6	23	115	106	137	.333	.390	May	.240	221	53	12	1	9	36	34	32	.340	.425
Grass	.259	532	138	25	3	16	69	61	81	.340	.406	June	.266	177	47	8	3	7	27	18	30	.351	.463
Turf	.257	781	201	38	6	26	99	101	130	.351	.421	July	.278	252	70	13	0	9	31	28	37	.355	.437
First Pitch	.314	185	58	13	2	6	30	10	0	.355	.503	August	.276	250	69	15	2	8	33	34	38	.374	.448
Ahead on Count	.311	338	105	21	2	16	61	73	0	.433	.527	September/October	.254	248	63	7	2	4	21	28	50	.336	.347
Behind on Count	.228	426	97	14	3	14	51	1	110	.245	.373	Pre-All Star	.243	639	155	31	5	23	89	78	102	.331	.415
Two Strikes	.184	516	95	11	1	13	47	70	211	.292	.285	Post-All Star	.273	674	184	32	4	19	79	84	109	.362	.417

Batter vs. Pitcher (since 1984)

Hits Best Against	Avg	AB	H	2B	3B	HR	RBI	BB	SO	OBP	SLG	Hits Worst Against	Avg	AB	H	2B	3B	HR	RBI	BB	SO	OBP	SLG
Bobby Thigpen	.667	9	6	2	0	1	6	3	0	.750	1.222	Storm Davis	.031	32	1	1	0	0	2	3	11	.114	.063
Tim Leary	.571	14	8	2	0	1	2	2	1	.625	.929	Mark Eichhorn	.056	18	1	1	0	0	2	0	3	.056	.111
Gene Nelson	.545	11	6	1	0	1	3	1	2	.583	.909	Mike Jackson	.100	10	1	0	0	0	0	2	2	.250	.100
Mike Morgan	.478	23	11	2	0	2	8	3	1	.538	.826	Tom Henke	.130	23	3	0	0	0	0	3	12	.231	.130
Mike Schooler	.385	13	5	0	0	2	7	1	2	.429	.846	Eric Plunk	.167	12	2	0	0	0	1	1	1	.231	.167

Mike Butcher — Angels

Pitches Right (flyball pitcher)

	ERA	W	L	Sv	G	GS	IP	BB	SO	Avg	H	2B	3B	HR	RBI	OBP	SLG	GF	IR	IRS	Hld	SvOp	SB	CS	GB	FB	G/F
1992 Season	3.25	2	2	0	19	0	27.2	13	24	.264	29	2	0	3	15	.352	.364	6	22	11	0	1	3	0	28	38	0.74

1992 Season

	ERA	W	L	Sv	G	GS	IP	H	HR	BB	SO		Avg	AB	H	2B	3B	HR	RBI	BB	SO	OBP	SLG
Home	1.72	0	1	0	8	0	15.2	17	0	6	11	vs. Left	.290	31	9	0	0	1	7	6	9	.421	.387
Away	5.25	2	1	0	11	0	12.0	12	3	7	13	vs. Right	.253	79	20	2	0	2	8	7	15	.322	.354

Brett Butler — Dodgers

Bats Left (groundball hitter)

	Avg	G	AB	R	H	2B	3B	HR	RBI	BB	SO	HBP	GDP	SB	CS	OBP	SLG	IBB	SH	SF	#Pit	#P/PA	GB	FB	G/F
1992 Season	.309	157	553	86	171	14	11	3	39	95	67	3	4	41	21	.413	.391	2	24	1	2743	4.21	230	98	2.35
Last Five Years	.297	789	2952	515	876	96	38	18	200	449	341	17	16	204	104	.391	.373	13	56	15	13891	4.05	1290	617	2.09

1992 Season

	Avg	AB	H	2B	3B	HR	RBI	BB	SO	OBP	SLG		Avg	AB	H	2B	3B	HR	RBI	BB	SO	OBP	SLG
vs. Left	.296	223	66	2	3	1	17	39	31	.402	.345	Scoring Posn	.262	126	33	5	3	0	34	17	19	.347	.349
vs. Right	.318	330	105	12	8	2	22	56	36	.420	.421	Close & Late	.348	92	32	3	0	0	1	18	17	.455	.380
Groundball	.286	196	56	3	2	0	10	30	22	.382	.321	None on/out	.288	184	53	2	3	2	2	34	24	.405	.364
Flyball	.340	159	54	4	5	1	9	28	23	.444	.447	Batting #1	.269	324	87	6	7	1	19	53	46	.374	.340
Home	.303	267	81	4	6	1	19	48	28	.411	.375	Batting #2	.362	224	81	8	4	2	20	40	20	.460	.460
Away	.315	286	90	10	5	2	20	47	39	.414	.406	Other	.600	5	3	0	0	0	0	2	1	.714	.600
Day	.277	166	46	6	1	1	10	29	27	.383	.343	April	.295	88	26	1	4	1	7	13	12	.386	.432
Night	.323	387	125	8	10	2	29	66	40	.425	.411	May	.238	84	20	1	0	0	2	10	17	.330	.250
Grass	.319	411	131	11	9	3	31	72	45	.421	.411	June	.271	96	26	4	3	0	9	19	11	.391	.375
Turf	.282	142	40	3	2	0	8	23	22	.389	.331	July	.442	95	42	3	2	1	12	22	9	.547	.547
First Pitch	.346	52	18	1	1	0	7	2	0	.364	.404	August	.299	97	29	3	2	1	7	15	11	.398	.402
Ahead on Count	.385	109	42	4	5	1	11	51	0	.581	.541	September/October	.301	93	28	2	0	0	2	16	7	.404	.323
Behind on Count	.307	199	61	3	2	0	10	0	35	.313	.342	Pre-All Star	.277	314	87	6	7	1	19	52	45	.382	.350
Two Strikes	.225	284	64	3	2	1	11	43	67	.331	.261	Post-All Star	.351	239	84	8	4	2	20	43	22	.452	.444

1992 By Position

Position	Avg	AB	H	2B	3B	HR	RBI	BB	SO	OBP	SLG	G	GS	Innings	PO	A	E	DP	Fld Pct	Rng Fctr	In Zone	Outs	Zone Rtg	MLB Zone
As cf	.309	550	170	14	11	3	39	94	66	.412	.391	155	152	1318.1	354	9	2	2	.995	2.48	411	345	.839	.824

Last Five Years

	Avg	AB	H	2B	3B	HR	RBI	BB	SO	OBP	SLG		Avg	AB	H	2B	3B	HR	RBI	BB	SO	OBP	SLG
vs. Left	.284	1114	316	23	13	4	84	180	160	.385	.338	Scoring Posn	.271	546	148	17	10	1	174	102	69	.381	.344
vs. Right	.305	1638	560	73	25	14	116	269	181	.394	.394	Close & Late	.291	478	139	14	3	3	39	78	76	.390	.351
Groundball	.286	1028	294	25	9	3	67	142	110	.376	.337	None on/out	.293	1257	368	41	15	10	10	181	130	.384	.373
Flyball	.298	681	203	22	10	6	41	106	61	.395	.386	Batting #1	.291	2715	790	88	34	16	180	405	320	.384	.384
Home	.310	1446	448	48	14	9	103	236	141	.407	.381	Batting #2	.362	224	81	8	4	2	20	40	20	.460	.460
Away	.284	1506	428	48	24	9	97	213	200	.375	.366	Other	.385	13	5	0	0	0	0	0	4	.529	.385
Day	.282	1048	296	34	6	9	79	155	134	.376	.352	April	.321	433	139	17	7	5	32	57	46	.399	.427
Night	.305	1904	580	62	32	9	121	294	207	.399	.385	May	.230	486	112	10	4	0	21	76	75	.339	.267
Grass	.306	2187	656	79	26	15	159	333	236	.398	.387	June	.299	482	144	15	5	3	36	82	53	.399	.369
Turf	.269	765	206	17	12	3	41	116	105	.371	.335	July	.327	502	164	13	9	3	50	78	50	.418	.406
First Pitch	.326	357	117	10	1	3	35	7	0	.344	.387	August	.307	515	158	18	6	5	40	80	62	.403	.394

Last Five Years

	Avg	AB	H	2B	3B	HR	RBI	BB	SO	OBP	SLG		Avg	AB	H	2B	3B	HR	RBI	BB	SO	OBP	SLG
Ahead on Count	.366	621	227	26	15	3	51	257	0	.549	.470	September/October	.298	534	159	23	7	2	21	76	55	.388	.378
Behind on Count	.272	916	249	29	11	0	52	1	166	.274	.328	Pre-All Star	.287	1558	447	43	17	10	107	244	187	.384	.356
Two Strikes	.243	1440	350	36	15	7	77	182	338	.329	.305	Post-All Star	.308	1394	429	53	21	8	93	205	154	.399	.393

Batter vs. Pitcher (since 1984)

Hits Best Against	Avg	AB	H	2B	3B	HR	RBI	BB	SO	OBP	SLG	Hits Worst Against	Avg	AB	H	2B	3B	HR	RBI	BB	SO	OBP	SLG
Dennis Lamp	.700	10	7	1	0	0	2	2	0	.750	.800	Al Osuna	.000	7	0	0	0	0	0	4	3	.364	.000
Paul Assenmacher	.600	10	6	0	0	0	1	1	2	.636	.600	Bill Wegman	.056	18	1	1	0	0	1	0	0	.056	.111
Craig Lefferts	.545	11	6	0	0	1	1	1	1	.583	.818	Bob Murphy	.083	12	1	0	0	0	2	3	4	.267	.083
Neal Heaton	.500	12	6	1	1	0	2	3	0	.600	.750	Bob McClure	.154	13	2	0	0	0	1	1	5	.200	.154
Chuck McElroy	.500	6	3	1	0	0	1	6	2	.750	.667	Tim Burke	.182	11	2	0	0	0	0	0	1	.182	.182

Francisco Cabrera — Braves — Bats Right

	Avg	G	AB	R	H	2B	3B	HR	RBI	BB	SO	HBP	GDP	SB	CS	OBP	SLG	IBB	SH	SF	#Pit	#P/PA	GB	FB	G/F
1992 Season	.300	12	10	2	3	0	0	2	3	1	1	0	0	0	0	.364	.900	0	0	0	41	3.73	2	7	0.29
Career (1989-1992)	.257	126	268	24	69	14	1	13	51	13	48	0	9	2	1	.290	.463	0	0	2	1009	3.57	97	91	1.07

1992 Season

	Avg	AB	H	2B	3B	HR	RBI	BB	SO	OBP	SLG		Avg	AB	H	2B	3B	HR	RBI	BB	SO	OBP	SLG
vs. Left	.222	9	2	0	0	2	3	1	1	.300	.889	Scoring Posn	.000	3	0	0	0	0	0	0	0	.000	.000
vs. Right	1.000	1	1	0	0	0	0	0	0	1.000	1.000	Close & Late	.286	7	2	0	0	1	1	1	1	.375	.714

Greg Cadaret — Yankees — Pitches Left

	ERA	W	L	Sv	G	GS	IP	BB	SO	Avg	H	2B	3B	HR	RBI	OBP	SLG	GF	IR	IRS	Hld	SvOp	SB	CS	GB	FB	G/F
1992 Season	4.25	4	8	1	46	11	103.2	74	73	.267	104	17	2	12	56	.385	.414	9	36	12	7	3	19	7	140	109	1.28
Last Five Years	3.86	27	25	10	272	35	538.1	290	402	.260	524	99	11	37	251	.353	.376	35	266	75	49	20	44	38	714	548	1.30

1992 Season

	ERA	W	L	Sv	G	GS	IP	H	HR	BB	SO		Avg	AB	H	2B	3B	HR	RBI	BB	SO	OBP	SLG
Home	3.29	4	3	0	27	6	65.2	61	5	44	47	vs. Left	.227	88	20	3	1	3	10	13	13	.340	.386
Away	5.92	0	5	1	19	5	38.0	43	7	30	26	vs. Right	.279	301	84	14	1	9	46	61	60	.397	.422
Starter	4.57	3	5	0	11	11	65.0	71	9	43	38	Scoring Posn	.218	133	29	4	1	4	46	32	32	.363	.353
Reliever	3.72	1	3	1	35	0	38.2	33	3	31	35	Close & Late	.320	50	16	5	0	1	8	17	11	.493	.480
0 Days rest	1.04	0	0	0	7	0	8.2	4	0	3	4	None on/out	.359	92	33	8	1	5	5	20	11	.473	.630
1 or 2 Days rest	5.82	1	2	0	13	0	17.0	19	2	18	15	First Pitch	.260	50	13	2	0	1	4	4	0	.315	.360
3+ Days rest	2.77	1	1	1	15	0	13.0	10	1	10	16	Behind on Count	.316	114	36	6	2	6	21	35	0	.470	.561
Pre-All Star	4.93	4	7	0	22	11	73.0	81	11	52	41	Ahead on Count	.203	138	28	6	0	2	17	0	56	.207	.290
Post-All Star	2.64	0	1	1	24	0	30.2	23	1	22	32	Two Strikes	.184	174	32	6	0	1	14	35	73	.324	.236

Last Five Years

	ERA	W	L	Sv	G	GS	IP	H	HR	BB	SO		Avg	AB	H	2B	3B	HR	RBI	BB	SO	OBP	SLG
Home	3.63	18	9	2	136	19	287.2	273	17	156	220	vs. Left	.236	554	131	23	1	7	61	68	100	.322	.319
Away	4.13	9	16	8	136	16	250.2	251	20	134	182	vs. Right	.269	1459	393	76	10	30	190	222	302	.364	.397
Day	4.13	14	11	6	100	15	213.1	215	16	117	171	Inning 1-6	.262	1120	293	55	5	27	160	150	214	.349	.392
Night	3.68	13	14	4	172	20	325.0	309	21	173	231	Inning 7+	.259	893	231	44	6	10	91	140	188	.358	.355
Grass	3.95	24	19	7	226	29	446.1	426	30	248	334	Runners on	.259	1029	266	55	4	20	203	148	378	.353	.378
Turf	3.42	3	6	3	46	6	92.0	98	7	42	68	Runners on	.262	984	258	44	7	17	231	154	199	.358	.373
April	3.98	4	5	0	35	7	74.2	65	4	42	61	Scoring Posn	.265	599	159	25	5	11	209	107	132	.368	.379
May	3.68	1	6	1	47	8	88.0	81	8	57	48	Close & Late	.252	397	100	18	4	3	41	68	91	.360	.340
June	3.65	4	3	0	49	2	86.1	89	7	45	60	None on/out	.255	467	119	29	1	11	11	68	90	.354	.392
July	3.94	6	4	3	45	5	89.0	92	7	34	56	vs. 1st Batr (relief)	.205	171	35	7	0	0	24	38	34	.348	.246
August	3.79	8	5	3	49	9	121.0	118	8	61	106	First Inning Pitched	.252	743	187	35	3	13	122	109	165	.346	.359
September/October	4.20	4	2	3	47	4	79.1	79	3	51	71	First 15 Pitches	.264	690	182	35	2	9	92	100	127	.356	.359
Starter	4.77	11	14	0	35	35	203.2	227	22	104	140	Pitch 16-30	.238	411	98	19	2	9	57	75	112	.354	.360
Reliever	3.31	16	11	10	237	0	334.2	297	15	186	262	Pitch 31-45	.214	276	59	9	1	3	22	42	55	.314	.286
0 Days rest	0.93	2	0	2	39	0	58.0	36	0	23	45	Pitch 46+	.291	636	185	36	6	16	80	73	108	.366	.442
1 or 2 Days rest	4.30	7	7	5	119	0	163.1	168	12	109	121	First Pitch	.323	235	76	13	2	5	35	12	0	.355	.460
3+ Days rest	3.10	7	4	3	79	0	113.1	93	3	54	96	Ahead on Count	.202	850	172	37	3	7	86	0	317	.204	.278
Pre-All Star	4.00	11	16	1	147	18	278.2	271	24	161	183	Behind on Count	.318	494	157	23	5	17	84	151	0	.472	.488
Post-All Star	3.71	16	9	9	125	17	259.2	253	13	129	219	Two Strikes	.184	962	181	41	4	8	84	125	402	.276	.259

Pitcher vs. Batter (career)

Pitches Best Vs.	Avg	AB	H	2B	3B	HR	RBI	BB	SO	OBP	SLG	Pitches Worst Vs.	Avg	AB	H	2B	3B	HR	RBI	BB	SO	OBP	SLG
Kent Hrbek	.059	17	1	0	0	0	2	3	3	.200	.059	Edgar Martinez	.778	9	7	4	0	0	1	2	0	.818	1.222
Devon White	.115	26	3	0	0	1	3	1	4	.148	.231	Gary Gaetti	.733	15	11	2	0	1	7	4	1	.750	1.067
Dante Bichette	.143	14	2	0	0	0	1	1	7	.200	.143	Dave Winfield	.545	11	6	2	0	0	3	3	1	.600	.727
Ozzie Guillen	.176	17	3	0	0	0	1	0	1	.176	.176	Tony Fernandez	.500	10	5	1	1	1	4	1	1	.500	1.100
Junior Felix	.182	11	2	0	0	0	0		4	.182	.182	Pete Incaviglia	.400	10	4	2	0	1	6	1	3	.455	.900

Ivan Calderon — Expos
Bats Right

	Avg	G	AB	R	H	2B	3B	HR	RBI	BB	SO	HBP	GDP	SB	CS	OBP	SLG	IBB	SH	SF	#Pit	#P/PA	GB	FB	G/F
1992 Season	.265	48	170	19	45	14	2	3	24	14	22	1	4	1	2	.323	.424	1	0	1	672	3.61	61	56	1.09
Last Five Years	.275	570	2133	296	586	128	16	64	295	195	325	8	63	75	39	.334	.440	21	3	28	8215	3.48	778	658	1.18

1992 Season

	Avg	AB	H	2B	3B	HR	RBI	BB	SO	OBP	SLG		Avg	AB	H	2B	3B	HR	RBI	BB	SO	OBP	SLG
vs. Left	.333	51	17	7	1	0	3	6	5	.414	.510	Scoring Posn	.209	43	9	3	0	0	17	4	4	.271	.279
vs. Right	.235	119	28	7	1	3	21	8	17	.281	.387	Close & Late	.241	29	7	1	1	1	4	1	4	.258	.448
Home	.257	101	26	8	1	2	15	6	13	.296	.416	None on/out	.273	33	9	3	0	1	1	2	4	.314	.455
Away	.275	69	19	6	1	1	9	8	9	.359	.435	Batting #3	.258	159	41	13	2	3	23	14	21	.322	.421
First Pitch	.370	27	10	2	0	1	3	1	0	.393	.556	Batting #5	.286	7	2	1	0	0	0	0	1	.286	.429
Ahead on Count	.294	34	10	3	1	0	8	8	0	.442	.441	Other	.500	4	2	0	0	0	1	0	0	.400	.500
Behind on Count	.160	50	8	4	1	0	5	0	14	.160	.280	Pre-All Star	.225	89	20	9	0	2	16	2	10	.239	.393
Two Strikes	.205	78	16	4	1	1	9	5	22	.253	.321	Post-All Star	.309	81	25	5	2	1	8	12	12	.404	.457

Last Five Years

	Avg	AB	H	2B	3B	HR	RBI	BB	SO	OBP	SLG		Avg	AB	H	2B	3B	HR	RBI	BB	SO	OBP	SLG
vs. Left	.314	703	221	50	8	26	100	78	85	.382	.519	Scoring Posn	.282	549	155	27	5	22	226	61	82	.339	.470
vs. Right	.255	1430	365	78	8	38	195	117	240	.309	.401	Close & Late	.279	348	97	23	1	9	41	40	65	.351	.428
Groundball	.291	561	163	31	5	12	71	52	84	.352	.428	None on/out	.273	458	125	33	2	16	16	41	65	.334	.459
Flyball	.254	496	126	31	2	19	70	45	79	.311	.440	Batting #3	.290	1314	381	87	10	31	179	129	178	.351	.442
Home	.271	1026	278	59	12	23	135	92	158	.329	.419	Batting #4	.230	564	130	26	4	26	82	50	110	.293	.429
Away	.278	1107	308	69	4	41	160	103	167	.338	.459	Other	.294	255	75	15	2	7	34	16	37	.332	.451
Day	.280	571	160	41	5	13	86	66	95	.354	.438	April	.235	361	85	21	0	15	64	38	68	.309	.418
Night	.273	1562	426	87	11	51	209	129	230	.326	.440	May	.299	402	120	26	2	14	62	39	62	.355	.478
Grass	.279	1428	398	86	13	41	200	120	211	.333	.443	June	.291	398	116	26	4	13	52	32	62	.340	.475
Turf	.267	705	188	42	3	23	95	75	114	.335	.433	July	.272	301	82	13	4	4	37	31	41	.339	.382
First Pitch	.306	428	131	23	4	15	63	11	0	.324	.484	August	.287	341	98	25	2	11	45	21	44	.329	.469
Ahead on Count	.346	462	160	36	5	17	86	96	0	.450	.556	September/October	.258	330	85	17	4	7	35	34	48	.328	.397
Behind on Count	.217	658	143	34	5	13	73	2	165	.222	.343	Pre-All Star	.273	1236	337	75	7	42	183	115	200	.331	.447
Two Strikes	.215	875	188	38	4	22	93	82	325	.261	.343	Post-All Star	.278	897	249	53	9	22	112	80	125	.337	.430

Batter vs. Pitcher (career)

Hits Best Against	Avg	AB	H	2B	3B	HR	RBI	BB	SO	OBP	SLG	Hits Worst Against	Avg	AB	H	2B	3B	HR	RBI	BB	SO	OBP	SLG
Mike Moore	.500	30	15	3	0	0	3	6	5	.583	.600	Jeff M. Robinson	.077	13	1	0	0	0	0	2	3	.200	.077
Walt Terrell	.455	11	5	0	0	1	2	0	1	.455	.727	Todd Stottlemyre	.077	13	1	1	0	0	0	0	4	.077	.154
Tom Bolton	.417	12	5	1	0	2	4	0	1	.417	1.000	Dave Schmidt	.091	11	1	0	0	0	1	0	4	.091	.091
Dennis Rasmussen	.400	15	6	0	0	3	6	2	3	.471	1.000	Juan Berenguer	.100	20	2	0	0	0	2	2	8	.182	.100
Mark Gubicza	.400	15	6	3	0	2	4	0	3	.400	1.000	Lee Smith	.100	10	1	0	0	0	0	1	3	.182	.100

Ken Caminiti — Astros
Bats Both

	Avg	G	AB	R	H	2B	3B	HR	RBI	BB	SO	HBP	GDP	SB	CS	OBP	SLG	IBB	SH	SF	#Pit	#P/PA	GB	FB	G/F
1992 Season	.294	135	506	68	149	31	2	13	62	44	68	9	14	10	4	.350	.441	13	2	4	1899	3.42	193	136	1.42
Last Five Years	.257	631	2269	261	589	114	10	41	272	194	361	9	57	27	14	.316	.370	36	11	17	8693	3.46	824	665	1.24

1992 Season

	Avg	AB	H	2B	3B	HR	RBI	BB	SO	OBP	SLG		Avg	AB	H	2B	3B	HR	RBI	BB	SO	OBP	SLG
vs. Left	.303	208	63	13	1	7	35	18	29	.357	.476	Scoring Posn	.250	136	34	8	0	4	45	23	20	.350	.397
vs. Right	.289	298	86	18	1	6	27	26	39	.345	.416	Close & Late	.283	92	26	7	0	2	11	17	16	.391	.424
Groundball	.276	199	55	11	0	5	20	16	22	.333	.407	None on/out	.341	126	43	8	1	3	3	5	13	.366	.492
Flyball	.274	117	32	10	1	4	20	16	19	.356	.479	Batting #3	.303	188	57	16	1	3	28	16	19	.356	.447
Home	.329	246	81	18	1	7	34	25	32	.389	.496	Batting #5	.257	206	53	9	1	5	18	21	29	.325	.383
Away	.262	260	68	13	1	6	28	19	36	.311	.388	Other	.348	112	39	6	0	5	16	7	20	.387	.536
Day	.282	156	44	5	2	0	9	14	25	.339	.340	April	.308	39	12	3	0	2	5	4	6	.372	.538
Night	.300	350	105	26	0	13	53	30	43	.354	.486	May	.243	37	9	2	0	0	1	6	5	.349	.297
Grass	.299	157	47	8	1	3	16	14	19	.355	.420	June	.349	109	38	9	0	3	18	11	13	.402	.514
Turf	.292	349	102	23	1	10	46	30	49	.347	.450	July	.313	96	30	4	1	2	11	6	7	.352	.438
First Pitch	.344	93	32	5	1	4	15	11	0	.411	.548	August	.275	109	30	8	1	3	14	9	17	.331	.450
Ahead on Count	.370	127	47	11	1	6	21	19	1	.452	.614	September/October	.259	116	30	5	0	3	13	8	20	.306	.379
Behind on Count	.212	151	32	7	0	2	12	0	37	.209	.298	Pre-All Star	.316	225	71	15	1	5	27	21	29	.371	.458
Two Strikes	.232	194	45	11	0	2	15	16	67	.289	.320	Post-All Star	.278	281	78	16	1	8	35	23	42	.332	.427

1992 By Position

Position	Avg	AB	H	2B	3B	HR	RBI	BB	SO	OBP	SLG	G	GS	Innings	PO	A	E	DP	Fld Pct	Rng Fctr	In Zone	Outs	Zone Rtg	MLB Zone
As 3b	.296	500	148	31	2	13	62	44	66	.352	.444	129	128	1140.2	103	208	11	19	.966	2.45	266	231	868	841

Last Five Years

	Avg	AB	H	2B	3B	HR	RBI	BB	SO	OBP	SLG		Avg	AB	H	2B	3B	HR	RBI	BB	SO	OBP	SLG
vs. Left	.287	869	249	48	5	23	127	59	118	.330	.433	Scoring Posn	.274	621	170	33	2	13	223	89	108	.357	.396
vs. Right	.239	1420	340	66	5	18	145	135	243	.307	.331	Close & Late	.254	422	107	13	3	8	41	37	90	.312	.355
Groundball	.256	796	204	36	4	16	90	66	117	.316	.372	None on/out	.282	547	154	35	3	8	8	29	82	.322	.400
Flyball	.251	510	128	30	4	15	67	51	87	.322	.414	Batting #5	.251	768	193	41	2	14	91	76	119	.321	.365
Home	.277	1153	319	70	5	21	147	100	187	.334	.401	Batting #6	.274	521	143	21	3	16	60	35	85	.320	.418
Away	.238	1136	270	44	5	20	125	94	174	.297	.338	Other	.253	1000	253	52	5	11	121	83	157	.310	.348

Last Five Years

	Avg	AB	H	2B	3B	HR	RBI	BB	SO	OBP	SLG		Avg	AB	H	2B	3B	HR	RBI	BB	SO	OBP	SLG
Day	.261	624	163	29	5	9	66	56	110	.321	.367	April	.275	265	73	15	0	5	28	20	44	.330	.389
Night	.256	1665	426	85	5	32	206	138	251	.314	.371	May	.255	337	86	10	2	6	36	31	40	.318	.350
Grass	.243	700	170	24	4	13	69	56	108	.299	.344	June	.254	398	101	21	1	7	48	33	65	.306	.364
Turf	.264	1589	419	90	6	28	203	138	253	.323	.381	July	.283	382	108	19	4	8	56	32	45	.340	.416
First Pitch	.315	409	129	23	1	8	56	25	0	.358	.435	August	.243	444	108	30	2	6	57	46	87	.315	.360
Ahead on Count	.310	539	167	32	4	15	79	94	1	.411	.468	September/October	.244	463	113	19	1	9	47	32	80	.294	.348
Behind on Count	.215	731	157	30	2	9	81	1	195	.217	.298	Pre-All Star	.261	1099	287	51	6	20	124	90	157	.317	.373
Two Strikes	.192	930	179	39	3	10	86	71	356	.250	.273	Post-All Star	.254	1190	302	63	4	21	148	104	204	.315	.366

Batter vs. Pitcher (career)

Hits Best Against	Avg	AB	H	2B	3B	HR	RBI	BB	SO	OBP	SLG	Hits Worst Against	Avg	AB	H	2B	3B	HR	RBI	BB	SO	OBP	SLG
Bobby Ojeda	.611	18	11	2	0	1	4	4	1	.682	.889	Chris Nabholz	.000	13	0	0	0	0	0	0	1	.000	.000
Mitch Williams	.500	10	5	0	0	1	3	3	2	.615	.800	Chris Hammond	.083	24	2	0	0	0	2	0	4	.083	.083
Danny Jackson	.455	11	5	1	0	1	2	0	1	.455	.818	Bill Landrum	.091	11	1	0	0	0	2	1	1	.167	.091
Alejandro Pena	.429	14	6	1	1	1	1	1	2	.467	.857	Shawn Boskie	.091	11	1	0	0	0	0	0	0	.091	.091
Mark Grant	.400	10	4	0	0	2	7	1	2	.455	1.000	Jay Howell	.125	16	2	0	0	0	0	0	6	.125	.125

Kevin Campbell — Athletics
Pitches Right (flyball pitcher)

	ERA	W	L	Sv	G	GS	IP	BB	SO	Avg	H	2B	3B	HR	RBI	OBP	SLG	GF	IR	IRS	Hld	SvOp	SB	CS	GB	FB	G/F
1992 Season	5.12	2	3	1	32	5	65.0	45	38	.267	66	12	1	4	29	.378	.372	6	22	3	4	1	2	5	77	87	0.89
Career (1991-1992)	4.50	3	3	1	46	5	88.0	59	54	.243	79	15	1	8	39	.359	.369	8	37	8	6	2	3	5	103	113	0.91

1992 Season

	ERA	W	L	Sv	G	GS	IP	H	HR	BB	SO		Avg	AB	H	2B	3B	HR	RBI	BB	SO	OBP	SLG
Home	3.11	1	1	0	17	3	37.2	31	2	20	24	vs. Left	.259	108	28	5	0	2	11	25	20	.396	.361
Away	7.90	1	2	1	15	2	27.1	35	2	25	14	vs. Right	.273	139	38	7	1	2	18	20	18	.363	.381
Starter	3.86	1	1	0	5	5	23.1	21	0	18	8	Scoring Posn	.275	69	19	5	0	0	23	18	12	.416	.348
Reliever	5.83	1	2	1	27	0	41.2	45	4	27	30	Close & Late	.192	26	5	1	0	0	1	7	5	.364	.231
0 Days rest	0.00	0	0	0	0	0	0.0	0	0	0	0	None on/out	.271	59	16	3	1	0	0	11	12	.386	.356
1 or 2 Days rest	8.22	0	0	0	8	0	15.1	17	2	13	13	First Pitch	.185	27	5	1	0	0	3	3	0	.258	.222
3+ Days rest	4.44	1	2	1	19	0	26.1	28	2	14	17	Behind on Count	.263	57	15	2	0	3	10	24	0	.481	.456
Pre-All Star	5.28	2	1	0	13	3	30.2	29	1	17	14	Ahead on Count	.257	109	28	8	0	0	14	0	31	.255	.330
Post-All Star	4.98	0	2	1	19	2	34.1	37	3	28	24	Two Strikes	.246	122	30	8	1	0	10	18	38	.340	.328

Mike Campbell — Rangers
Pitches Right (flyball pitcher)

	ERA	W	L	Sv	G	GS	IP	BB	SO	Avg	H	2B	3B	HR	RBI	OBP	SLG	GF	IR	IRS	Hld	SvOp	SB	CS	GB	FB	G/F
1992 Season	9.82	0	1	0	1	0	3.2	2	2	.231	3	1	0	1	4	.333	.538	0	1	0	0	0	1	0	4	4	1.00
Last Five Years	6.20	7	13	0	26	25	139.1	55	71	.282	159	36	2	23	87	.343	.476	0	1	0	0	0	22	3	167	213	0.78

1992 Season

	ERA	W	L	Sv	G	GS	IP	H	HR	BB	SO		Avg	AB	H	2B	3B	HR	RBI	BB	SO	OBP	SLG
Home	9.82	0	1	0	1	0	3.2	3	1	2	2	vs. Left	.286	7	2	1	0	1	3	1	1	.375	.857
Away	0.00	0	0	0	0	0	0.0	0	0	0	0	vs. Right	.167	6	1	0	0	0	1	1	1	.286	.167

Casey Candaele — Astros
Bats Both

	Avg	G	AB	R	H	2B	3B	HR	RBI	BB	SO	HBP	GDP	SB	CS	OBP	SLG	IBB	SH	SF	#Pit	#P/PA	GB	FB	G/F
1992 Season	.213	135	320	19	68	12	1	1	18	24	36	3	5	7	1	.269	.266	3	7	6	1193	3.38	128	97	1.32
Last Five Years	.243	473	1190	104	289	48	15	8	95	106	144	4	21	24	10	.305	.329	16	15	9	4504	3.44	472	321	1.47

1992 Season

	Avg	AB	H	2B	3B	HR	RBI	BB	SO	OBP	SLG		Avg	AB	H	2B	3B	HR	RBI	BB	SO	OBP	SLG
vs. Left	.266	128	34	7	0	1	9	12	11	.331	.344	Scoring Posn	.152	66	10	2	0	0	17	7	13	.225	.182
vs. Right	.177	192	34	5	1	0	9	12	25	.226	.214	Close & Late	.312	77	24	7	0	0	6	8	8	.368	.403
Groundball	.169	136	23	4	1	0	3	8	13	.214	.213	None on/out	.244	90	22	4	0	1	1	7	6	.313	.322
Flyball	.182	77	14	2	0	0	5	9	10	.258	.208	Batting #6	.172	116	20	3	0	1	4	5	13	.205	.224
Home	.195	159	31	6	1	1	9	15	15	.267	.264	Batting #8	.293	75	22	6	1	0	5	6	3	.345	.400
Away	.230	161	37	6	0	0	9	9	21	.272	.267	Other	.202	129	26	3	0	0	9	13	20	.279	.225
Day	.226	106	24	7	1	1	3	6	14	.272	.340	April	.200	55	11	0	0	1	3	1	8	.211	.255
Night	.206	214	44	5	0	0	15	18	22	.268	.229	May	.178	73	13	3	0	0	2	6	8	.241	.219
Grass	.229	105	24	3	0	0	7	2	15	.245	.257	June	.226	53	12	0	1	0	1	5	8	.305	.264
Turf	.205	215	44	9	1	1	11	22	21	.280	.270	July	.186	70	13	6	0	0	5	5	3	.241	.271
First Pitch	.300	50	15	3	0	0	4	3	0	.333	.360	August	.289	38	11	0	0	0	2	1	5	.300	.289
Ahead on Count	.214	70	15	4	1	0	7	15	0	.345	.300	September/October	.258	31	8	3	0	0	5	6	4	.385	.355
Behind on Count	.162	117	19	2	0	1	5	0	23	.174	.205	Pre-All Star	.180	206	37	4	1	1	8	13	26	.229	.223
Two Strikes	.159	126	20	2	0	1	6	6	36	.210	.198	Post-All Star	.272	114	31	8	0	0	10	11	10	.338	.342

1992 By Position

Position	Avg	AB	H	2B	3B	HR	RBI	BB	SO	OBP	SLG	G	GS	Innings	PO	A	E	DP	Fld Pct	Rng Fctr	In Zone	Outs	Zone Rtg	MLB Zone
As Pinch Hitter	.120	25	3	0	0	0	3	4	6	.226	.120	33	0	---	---	---	---	---	---	---	---	---	---	---
As 3b	.182	88	16	3	0	0	3	4	10	.215	.216	29	24	218.1	24	52	4	3	.950	3.13	66	55	.833	.841

1992 By Position

Position	Avg	AB	H	2B	3B	HR	RBI	BB	SO	OBP	SLG	G	GS	Innings	PO	A	E	DP	Fld Pct	Rng Fctr	In Zone	Outs	Zone Rtg	MLB Zone
As ss	.259	158	41	9	1	0	10	14	11	.326	.329	65	41	391.1	79	137	7	30	.969	4.97	167	152	.910	.885
As lf	.250	32	8	0	0	1	2	1	5	.273	.344	20	5	71.0	13	0	0	0	1.000	1.65	11	10	.909	.809

Last Five Years

	Avg	AB	H	2B	3B	HR	RBI	BB	SO	OBP	SLG		Avg	AB	H	2B	3B	HR	RBI	BB	SO	OBP	SLG
vs. Left	.286	475	136	23	4	4	36	44	43	.347	.377	Scoring Posn	.251	275	69	11	5	2	85	35	46	.330	.349
vs. Right	.214	715	153	25	11	4	59	62	101	.276	.297	Close & Late	.267	266	71	14	4	1	32	30	30	.339	.361
Groundball	.248	416	103	13	5	2	36	30	38	.298	.317	None on/out	.224	321	72	13	2	2	32	41	44	.299	.296
Flyball	.202	272	55	11	2	2	18	33	41	.285	.279	Batting #2	.249	233	58	7	4	1	18	15	29	.296	.326
Home	.249	595	148	25	12	3	57	65	72	.323	.346	Batting #8	.254	437	111	24	6	3	35	47	48	.325	.357
Away	.237	595	141	23	3	5	38	41	72	.286	.311	Other	.231	520	120	17	5	4	42	44	67	.291	.306
Day	.236	318	75	17	4	3	24	24	41	.291	.343	April	.213	154	35	6	3	2	14	13	22	.268	.323
Night	.245	872	214	31	11	5	71	82	103	.310	.323	May	.214	192	41	7	1	0	10	17	25	.278	.260
Grass	.256	348	89	12	1	4	29	21	43	.298	.330	June	.219	237	52	7	4	3	18	23	30	.290	.321
Turf	.238	842	200	36	14	4	66	85	101	.308	.321	July	.284	197	56	10	4	3	14	22	23	.354	.421
First Pitch	.301	193	58	12	0	0	17	9	0	.327	.363	August	.243	177	43	9	2	0	15	11	22	.286	.316
Ahead on Count	.250	256	64	11	6	5	32	67	0	.402	.396	September/October	.278	223	62	9	1	0	24	20	22	.340	.327
Behind on Count	.221	407	90	11	5	2	24	1	87	.225	.287	Pre-All Star	.214	655	140	22	8	7	49	56	86	.275	.304
Two Strikes	.201	478	96	9	7	1	29	25	144	.244	.255	Post-All Star	.279	535	149	26	7	1	46	50	58	.341	.359

Batter vs. Pitcher (career)

Hits Best Against	Avg	AB	H	2B	3B	HR	RBI	BB	SO	OBP	SLG	Hits Worst Against	Avg	AB	H	2B	3B	HR	RBI	BB	SO	OBP	SLG
Bob Patterson	.583	12	7	2	0	0	1	0	0	.583	.750	Bob Kipper	.000	10	0	0	0	0	0	2	1	.167	.000
Bobby Ojeda	.444	27	12	1	1	1	2	2	3	.483	.667	John Smoltz	.056	18	1	0	0	0	1	3	1	.190	.056
Ramon Martinez	.444	9	4	0	0	0	2	2	2	.545	.444	Sid Fernandez	.077	13	1	0	0	0	2	1	4	.125	.077
Brian Fisher	.375	8	3	2	0	0	0	3	0	.545	.625	Bob Walk	.083	12	1	0	0	0	0	1	0	.154	.083
John Burkett	.368	19	7	0	1	1	4	0	2	.429	.632	Mike Jackson	.100	10	1	0	0	0	0	1	1	.091	.100

John Candelaria — Dodgers

Pitches Left (flyball pitcher)

	ERA	W	L	Sv	G	GS	IP	BB	SO	Avg	H	2B	3B	HR	RBI	OBP	SLG	GF	IR	IRS	Hld	SvOp	SB	CS	GB	FB	G/F
1992 Season	2.84	2	5	5	50	0	25.1	13	23	.220	20	2	1	1	16	.311	.297	11	64	15	12	7	2	0	31	27	1.15
Last Five Years	3.74	26	24	13	203	33	361.0	83	296	.256	354	69	12	44	173	.295	.418	36	179	43	38	21	12	12	416	434	0.96

1992 Season

	ERA	W	L	Sv	G	GS	IP	H	HR	BB	SO		Avg	AB	H	2B	3B	HR	RBI	BB	SO	OBP	SLG
Home	2.92	1	3	2	23	0	12.1	8	0	6	12	vs. Left	.269	52	14	1	1	1	12	5	19	.328	.385
Away	2.77	1	2	3	27	0	13.0	12	1	7	11	vs. Right	.154	39	6	1	0	0	4	8	4	.292	.179
Starter	0.00	0	0	0	0	0	0.0	0	0	0	0	Scoring Posn	.243	37	9	0	1	1	16	8	14	.362	.378
Reliever	2.84	2	5	5	50	0	25.1	20	1	13	23	Close & Late	.230	74	17	1	1	0	10	10	21	.314	.270
0 Days rest	9.00	1	3	1	12	0	6.0	5	1	4	4	None on/out	.188	16	3	1	0	0	0	2	3	.278	.250
1 or 2 Days rest	0.00	0	0	2	18	0	6.2	7	0	5	6	First Pitch	.250	12	3	0	0	0	1	2	0	.357	.250
3+ Days rest	1.42	1	2	2	20	0	12.2	8	0	4	13	Behind on Count	.318	22	7	2	1	1	10	4	0	.407	.636
Pre-All Star	1.17	1	1	3	30	0	15.1	10	1	9	12	Ahead on Count	.125	40	5	0	0	0	2	0	21	.122	.125
Post-All Star	5.40	1	4	2	20	0	10.0	10	0	4	11	Two Strikes	.075	40	3	0	0	0	3	7	23	.208	.075

Last Five Years

	ERA	W	L	Sv	G	GS	IP	H	HR	BB	SO		Avg	AB	H	2B	3B	HR	RBI	BB	SO	OBP	SLG
Home	3.68	13	13	8	98	19	198.1	198	22	38	174	vs. Left	.190	336	64	7	3	6	37	22	114	.235	.283
Away	3.82	13	11	5	105	14	162.2	156	22	45	122	vs. Right	.277	1048	290	62	9	38	136	61	182	.315	.462
Day	2.96	9	2	4	55	11	109.1	99	9	23	85	Inning 1-6	.260	800	208	41	7	28	99	41	153	.296	.434
Night	4.08	17	22	9	148	22	251.2	255	35	60	211	Inning 7+	.250	584	146	28	5	16	74	42	143	.295	.397
Grass	3.86	17	19	6	135	25	244.2	233	31	61	218	None on	.258	817	211	49	4	26	26	29	154	.287	.424
Turf	3.48	9	5	7	68	8	116.1	121	13	22	78	Runners on	.252	567	143	20	8	18	147	54	142	.306	.411
April	3.31	6	4	2	32	10	98.0	88	15	17	75	Scoring Posn	.233	331	77	11	7	12	131	41	86	.299	.417
May	3.00	9	1	5	36	7	72.0	59	10	10	58	Close & Late	.241	319	77	15	4	6	47	30	90	.298	.370
June	3.31	4	5	2	34	4	51.2	49	3	13	37	None on/out	.262	355	93	16	1	11	11	6	68	.278	.406
July	3.25	6	4	2	35	6	61.0	48	7	14	60	vs. 1st Batr (relief)	.257	148	38	6	2	4	32	10	43	.294	.405
August	6.39	1	7	1	32	6	49.1	75	9	14	39	First Inning Pitched	.245	482	118	22	5	11	72	40	125	.297	.380
September/October	4.34	0	3	1	34	0	29.0	35	4	10	32	First 15 Pitches	.270	503	136	29	5	16	77	39	113	.318	.443
Starter	3.81	16	12	0	33	33	210.0	207	27	37	157	Pitch 16-30	.216	264	57	10	0	2	14	14	78	.252	.277
Reliever	3.64	10	12	13	170	0	151.0	147	17	46	139	Pitch 31-45	.268	164	44	7	2	8	27	10	26	.300	.482
0 Days rest	3.34	2	4	2	42	0	29.2	27	1	12	29	Pitch 46+	.258	453	117	23	5	18	55	20	79	.294	.450
1 or 2 Days rest	4.62	4	4	6	67	0	62.1	70	13	22	55	First Pitch	.317	167	53	9	2	8	26	10	0	.348	.539
3+ Days rest	2.75	4	4	5	61	0	59.0	50	3	12	55	Ahead on Count	.200	710	142	32	4	11	48	0	275	.199	.303
Pre-All Star	3.04	20	11	9	115	23	243.0	206	29	43	195	Behind on Count	.341	305	104	19	2	16	64	32	0	.401	.574
Post-All Star	5.19	6	13	4	88	10	118.0	148	15	40	101	Two Strikes	.172	656	113	24	2	11	47	41	296	.218	.265

Pitcher vs. Batter (since 1984)

Pitches Best Vs.	Avg	AB	H	2B	3B	HR	RBI	BB	SO	OBP	SLG	Pitches Worst Vs.	Avg	AB	H	2B	3B	HR	RBI	BB	SO	OBP	SLG
Al Newman	.083	12	1	0	0	0	1	0	1	.083	.083	Scott Fletcher	.579	19	11	2	1	0	1	3	0	.636	.789
Kirby Puckett	.091	22	2	1	0	0	4	4	6	.222	.136	Carlton Fisk	.417	12	5	0	0	3	9	3	1	.533	1.167
Dale Sveum	.091	11	1	0	0	0	0	2	3	.231	.091	Cal Ripken	.400	10	4	1	0	1	2	1	1	.455	.800

Pitcher vs. Batter (since 1984)

Pitches Best Vs.	Avg	AB	H	2B	3B	HR	RBI	BB	SO	OBP	SLG	Pitches Worst Vs.	Avg	AB	H	2B	3B	HR	RBI	BB	SO	OBP	SLG
Tony Gwynn	.154	13	2	0	0	0	0	0	1	.154	.154	Dave Valle	.400	10	4	2	0	1	3	1	0	.455	.900
Don Slaught	.182	11	2	0	0	0	0	0	3	.182	.182	Pedro Guerrero	.375	8	3	1	1	0	2	2	1	.455	.750

Tom Candiotti — Dodgers

	ERA	W	L	Sv	G	GS	IP	BB	SO	Avg	H	2B	3B	HR	RBI	OBP	SLG	CG	ShO	Sup	QS	#P/S	SB	CS	GB	FB	G/F
1992 Season	3.00	11	15	0	32	30	203.2	63	152	.237	177	35	4	13	70	.297	.347	6	2	3.23	19	104	30	5	274	199	1.38
Last Five Years	3.12	66	57	0	159	155	1066.1	299	708	.248	999	160	21	73	366	.302	.353	30	4	4.04	102	107	113	39	1530	1062	1.44

1992 Season

	ERA	W	L	Sv	G	GS	IP	H	HR	BB	SO		Avg	AB	H	2B	3B	HR	RBI	BB	SO	OBP	SLG
Home	2.33	6	6	0	13	12	89.0	80	3	17	65	vs. Left	.246	407	100	16	3	6	32	47	75	.322	.344
Away	3.53	5	9	0	19	18	114.2	97	10	46	87	vs. Right	.227	339	77	19	1	7	38	16	77	.266	.351
Day	4.53	4	5	0	10	9	55.2	58	4	17	42	Inning 1-6	.234	606	142	29	3	9	55	52	127	.296	.337
Night	2.43	7	10	0	22	21	148.0	119	9	46	110	Inning 7+	.250	140	35	6	1	4	15	11	25	.303	.393
Grass	3.11	7	12	0	23	21	144.2	125	12	37	107	None on	.260	457	119	26	4	7	7	29	90	.306	.381
Turf	2.75	4	3	0	9	9	59.0	52	1	26	45	Runners on	.201	289	58	9	0	6	63	34	62	.284	.294
April	3.62	3	0	0	4	4	32.1	28	4	8	31	Scoring Posn	.212	189	40	6	0	6	62	28	38	.311	.339
May	3.60	2	3	0	5	5	30.0	27	0	10	17	Close & Late	.255	102	26	4	0	3	12	9	20	.313	.382
June	2.11	1	3	0	7	6	42.2	36	3	12	28	None on/out	.303	201	61	16	3	4	4	10	43	.336	.473
July	2.92	2	3	0	6	5	37.0	27	5	13	35	vs. 1st Batr (relief)	.500	2	1	0	0	0	1	0	0	.500	.500
August	2.75	1	3	0	4	4	19.2	18	0	5	15	First Inning Pitched	.254	122	31	7	1	2	21	12	23	.324	.377
September/October	3.21	2	3	0	6	6	42.0	41	1	15	26	First 75 Pitches	.243	506	123	25	3	9	49	42	97	.301	.358
Starter	3.03	10	15	0	30	30	202.0	175	13	63	150	Pitch 76-90	.227	75	17	4	0	1	4	7	22	.289	.320
Reliever	0.00	1	0	0	2	0	1.2	2	0	0	2	Pitch 91-105	.244	78	19	4	0	2	6	5	17	.289	.372
0-3 Days Rest	4.50	0	2	0	3	3	20.0	18	5	4	13	Pitch 106+	.207	87	18	2	1	1	11	9	16	.286	.287
4 Days Rest	2.07	5	6	0	12	12	87.0	62	3	24	60	First Pitch	.234	77	18	5	0	2	9	5	0	.294	.377
5+ Days Rest	3.60	5	7	0	15	15	95.0	95	5	35	77	Ahead on Count	.206	344	71	15	1	4	26	0	121	.207	.291
Pre-All Star	3.05	7	8	0	19	17	121.0	104	10	33	92	Behind on Count	.310	158	49	9	1	4	21	29	0	.415	.456
Post-All Star	2.94	4	7	0	13	13	82.2	73	3	30	60	Two Strikes	.192	354	68	15	1	3	22	29	152	.253	.266

Last Five Years

	ERA	W	L	Sv	G	GS	IP	H	HR	BB	SO		Avg	AB	H	2B	3B	HR	RBI	BB	SO	OBP	SLG
Home	3.04	36	23	0	77	74	535.0	505	31	136	364	vs. Left	.254	2112	537	76	17	33	183	185	310	.314	.353
Away	3.20	30	34	0	82	81	531.1	494	42	163	344	vs. Right	.241	1914	462	84	4	40	183	114	398	.289	.352
Day	3.30	26	15	0	50	49	338.1	328	22	92	237	Inning 1-6	.247	3290	813	131	16	61	310	239	590	.300	.352
Night	3.04	40	42	0	109	106	728.0	671	51	207	471	Inning 7+	.253	736	186	29	5	12	56	60	118	.310	.355
Grass	3.22	52	46	0	123	119	827.0	779	62	211	541	None on	.252	2444	617	110	14	42	42	156	438	.301	.360
Turf	2.78	14	11	0	36	36	239.1	220	11	88	167	Runners on	.241	1582	382	50	7	31	324	143	270	.304	.341
April	2.96	14	2	0	20	20	149.0	138	13	42	119	Scoring Posn	.240	922	221	30	5	20	296	109	157	.317	.348
May	3.03	14	10	0	27	27	190.0	183	8	52	122	Close & Late	.245	392	96	16	2	5	30	39	65	.315	.334
June	3.53	8	17	0	30	29	193.2	194	18	58	123	None on/out	.244	1061	259	48	6	17	17	56	197	.283	.349
July	2.75	9	10	0	27	24	177.0	155	11	47	118	vs. 1st Batr (relief)	.250	4	1	0	0	0	1	0	1	.250	.250
August	2.79	11	7	0	25	25	164.2	141	12	47	115	First Inning Pitched	.266	617	164	28	4	10	73	53	111	.327	.373
September/October	3.56	10	11	0	30	30	192.0	188	11	53	111	First 75 Pitches	.247	2718	670	104	14	49	250	200	472	.301	.349
Starter	3.12	65	57	0	155	155	1058.1	990	72	296	699	Pitch 76-90	.249	489	122	19	1	10	35	30	88	.293	.354
Reliever	3.38	1	0	0	4	0	8.0	9	1	3	9	Pitch 91-105	.246	427	105	23	3	5	30	34	77	.302	.349
0-3 Days Rest	4.14	0	4	0	8	8	50.0	46	7	13	32	Pitch 106+	.260	392	102	14	3	9	51	35	71	.323	.380
4 Days Rest	3.07	41	32	0	89	89	628.1	577	44	170	407	First Pitch	.331	489	162	27	1	10	54	11	0	.348	.452
5+ Days Rest	3.08	24	21	0	58	58	380.0	367	21	113	260	Ahead on Count	.193	1753	339	53	7	19	115	1	568	.198	.264
Pre-All Star	3.21	38	32	0	86	83	583.1	561	45	168	405	Behind on Count	.311	929	289	55	5	28	122	149	0	.406	.471
Post-All Star	3.02	28	25	0	73	72	483.0	438	28	131	303	Two Strikes	.189	1843	348	58	11	23	123	138	706	.248	.270

Pitcher vs. Batter (since 1984)

Pitches Best Vs.	Avg	AB	H	2B	3B	HR	RBI	BB	SO	OBP	SLG	Pitches Worst Vs.	Avg	AB	H	2B	3B	HR	RBI	BB	SO	OBP	SLG
Jack Clark	.000	12	0	0	0	0	1	1	6	.071	.000	Alfredo Griffin	.700	10	7	1	0	0	0	1	1	.727	.800
Spike Owen	.034	29	1	0	0	0	0	2	2	.097	.034	George Bell	.529	34	18	6	0	2	8	3	4	.568	.882
Pat Tabler	.077	13	1	0	0	0	0	0	5	.077	.077	Rafael Palmeiro	.438	16	7	2	0	1	2	1	2	.471	.750
Edgar Martinez	.083	12	1	0	0	0	0	1	4	.154	.083	Mike Greenwell	.429	35	15	3	0	3	10	4	0	.487	.771
Bill Spiers	.100	20	2	0	0	0	3	1	5	.136	.100	Kirk Gibson	.412	17	7	1	2	1	4	2	1	.474	.882

John Cangelosi — Rangers

Bats Both (groundball hitter)

	Avg	G	AB	R	H	2B	3B	HR	RBI	BB	SO	HBP	GDP	SB	CS	OBP	SLG	IBB	SH	SF	#Pit	#P/PA	GB	FB	G/F
1992 Season	.188	73	85	12	16	2	0	1	6	18	16	0	0	6	5	.330	.247	0	3	0	449	4.36	33	20	1.65
Last Five Years	.219	318	439	61	96	12	3	1	24	81	64	5	3	33	19	.345	.267	2	9	2	2192	4.16	186	104	1.79

1992 Season

	Avg	AB	H	2B	3B	HR	RBI	BB	SO	OBP	SLG		Avg	AB	H	2B	3B	HR	RBI	BB	SO	OBP	SLG
vs. Left	.158	19	3	1	0	1	3	7	3	.385	.368	Scoring Posn	.222	18	4	0	0	1	6	4	3	.364	.389
vs. Right	.197	66	13	1	0	0	3	11	13	.312	.212	Close & Late	.231	13	3	1	0	0	1	3	2	.375	.308
Home	.189	37	7	1	0	0	2	7	6	.318	.216	None on/out	.167	30	5	1	0	0	0	6	7	.306	.200
Away	.188	48	9	1	0	1	4	11	10	.339	.271	Batting #1	.125	32	4	2	0	0	0	9	5	.317	.188

73

1992 Season

	Avg	AB	H	2B	3B	HR	RBI	BB	SO	OBP	SLG		Avg	AB	H	2B	3B	HR	RBI	BB	SO	OBP	SLG
First Pitch	.091	11	1	0	0	0	0	0	0	.091	.091	Batting #9	.185	27	5	0	0	0	0	6	5	.333	.185
Ahead on Count	.444	18	8	1	0	1	2	9	0	.630	.667	Other	.269	26	7	0	0	1	6	3	6	.345	.385
Behind on Count	.294	17	5	0	0	0	4	0	7	.294	.294	Pre-All Star	.195	82	16	2	0	1	6	18	15	.340	.256
Two Strikes	.091	44	4	0	0	0	4	9	16	.245	.091	Post-All Star	.000	3	0	0	0	0	0	0	1	.000	.000

Last Five Years

	Avg	AB	H	2B	3B	HR	RBI	BB	SO	OBP	SLG		Avg	AB	H	2B	3B	HR	RBI	BB	SO	OBP	SLG
vs. Left	.222	203	45	8	1	1	14	30	26	.332	.286	Scoring Posn	.237	76	18	2	0	1	24	17	14	.375	.303
vs. Right	.216	236	51	4	2	0	10	51	38	.356	.250	Close & Late	.229	144	33	5	1	0	4	28	28	.364	.278
Groundball	.200	150	30	6	1	0	11	36	20	.354	.253	None on/out	.183	202	37	6	3	0	0	28	31	.292	.243
Flyball	.257	113	29	1	2	0	8	20	15	.382	.301	Batting #1	.205	171	35	5	2	0	7	36	18	.351	.257
Home	.233	219	51	5	2	0	8	43	28	.364	.292	Batting #9	.175	143	25	3	1	0	1	15	23	.256	.210
Away	.205	220	45	3	1	1	16	38	36	.327	.241	Other	.288	125	36	4	0	1	16	30	23	.429	.344
Day	.237	131	31	4	1	0	10	27	20	.371	.282	April	.160	81	13	2	0	1	8	16	10	.313	.222
Night	.211	308	65	8	2	1	14	54	44	.334	.260	May	.208	72	15	2	0	0	1	15	16	.345	.236
Grass	.204	147	30	4	0	0	9	27	29	.331	.231	June	.225	80	18	2	1	0	4	18	13	.367	.275
Turf	.226	292	66	8	3	1	15	54	35	.352	.284	July	.196	51	10	0	0	0	3	12	4	.354	.196
First Pitch	.196	51	10	0	2	0	2	1	0	.222	.275	August	.225	89	20	2	1	0	2	11	13	.317	.270
Ahead on Count	.340	103	35	5	0	1	7	37	0	.514	.417	September/October	.303	66	20	4	1	0	6	9	8	.390	.394
Behind on Count	.175	114	20	4	0	0	8	1	37	.197	.211	Pre-All Star	.207	256	53	6	1	1	15	52	41	.345	.250
Two Strikes	.161	211	34	6	0	0	15	43	64	.306	.190	Post-All Star	.235	183	43	6	2	0	9	29	23	.346	.290

Batter vs. Pitcher (career)

Hits Best Against	Avg	AB	H	2B	3B	HR	RBI	BB	SO	OBP	SLG	Hits Worst Against	Avg	AB	H	2B	3B	HR	RBI	BB	SO	OBP	SLG
Bert Blyleven	.400	10	4	1	0	0	0	2	1	.500	.500	Sid Fernandez	.071	14	1	0	0	0	0	1	1	.133	.071
Jim Deshaies	.385	13	5	0	0	0	1	0	1	.385	.385	Jeff Parrett	.083	12	1	0	0	0	0	1	1	.154	.083
Dennis Martinez	.353	17	6	2	0	0	2	0	2	.353	.471	Bobby Ojeda	.091	11	1	0	0	0	0	0	2	.091	.091
Mike Flanagan	.333	12	4	0	1	1	2	0	2	.333	.750	Kirk McCaskill	.091	11	1	0	0	0	0	4	3	.333	.091
Jack Morris	.333	12	4	0	1	0	2	2	3	.429	.500	Charlie Hough	.100	10	1	0	0	0	2	3	0	.308	.100

Jose Canseco — Rangers
Bats Right (flyball hitter)

	Avg	G	AB	R	H	2B	3B	HR	RBI	BB	SO	HBP	GDP	SB	CS	OBP	SLG	IBB	SH	SF	#Pit	#P/PA	GB	FB	G/F
1992 Season	.244	119	439	74	107	15	0	26	87	63	128	6	16	6	7	.344	.456	2	0	4	2145	4.19	128	122	1.05
Last Five Years	.274	627	2329	432	639	104	4	166	491	314	635	32	60	97	42	.365	.536	32	1	27	10900	4.03	644	707	0.91

1992 Season

	Avg	AB	H	2B	3B	HR	RBI	BB	SO	OBP	SLG		Avg	AB	H	2B	3B	HR	RBI	BB	SO	OBP	SLG
vs. Left	.255	94	24	3	0	7	16	16	33	.372	.511	Scoring Posn	.274	146	40	3	0	7	63	17	40	.349	.438
vs. Right	.241	345	83	12	0	19	71	47	95	.336	.441	Close & Late	.286	70	20	2	0	6	19	10	19	.383	.571
Groundball	.257	101	26	3	0	7	28	12	30	.336	.495	None on/out	.295	78	23	4	0	7	7	9	18	.368	.615
Flyball	.242	132	32	4	0	7	33	17	36	.325	.432	Batting #3	.239	414	99	13	0	25	81	54	124	.331	.452
Home	.255	204	52	4	0	15	39	29	64	.351	.495	Batting #5	.381	21	8	2	0	1	6	9	3	.581	.619
Away	.234	235	55	11	0	11	48	34	64	.337	.421	Other	.000	4	0	0	0	0	0	0	1	.000	.000
Day	.278	158	44	6	0	12	37	22	43	.372	.544	April	.244	90	22	1	0	6	17	9	24	.310	.456
Night	.224	281	63	9	0	14	50	41	85	.328	.406	May	.213	75	16	1	0	4	12	8	17	.286	.387
Grass	.255	368	94	13	0	23	81	56	106	.358	.478	June	.298	84	25	3	0	8	19	9	21	.368	.619
Turf	.183	71	13	2	0	3	6	7	22	.266	.338	July	.176	34	6	2	0	1	3	5	7	.300	.324
First Pitch	.282	39	11	0	0	3	10	2	0	.349	.513	August	.253	83	21	4	0	3	21	17	35	.382	.410
Ahead on Count	.358	106	38	6	0	12	36	27	0	.489	.755	September/October	.233	73	17	4	0	4	15	15	24	.385	.452
Behind on Count	.214	140	30	6	0	7	18	0	54	.220	.407	Pre-All Star	.253	249	63	5	0	18	48	26	62	.323	.490
Two Strikes	.133	248	33	3	0	4	19	34	128	.241	.194	Post-All Star	.232	190	44	10	0	8	39	37	66	.369	.411

1992 By Position

Position	Avg	AB	H	2B	3B	HR	RBI	BB	SO	OBP	SLG	G	GS	Innings	PO	A	E	DP	Fld Pct	Rng Fctr	In Zone	Outs	Zone Rtg	MLB Zone
As Designated Hitter	.312	109	34	5	0	7	29	14	29	.392	.550	28	28	---	---	---	---	---	---	---	---	---	---	---
As rf	.223	327	73	10	0	19	58	49	98	.331	.428	90	88	766.2	195	5	3	3	.985	2.35	230	183	.796	.814

Last Five Years

	Avg	AB	H	2B	3B	HR	RBI	BB	SO	OBP	SLG		Avg	AB	H	2B	3B	HR	RBI	BB	SO	OBP	SLG
vs. Left	.282	553	156	28	1	44	112	80	158	.381	.575	Scoring Posn	.284	666	189	29	1	46	327	104	188	.373	.538
vs. Right	.272	1776	483	76	3	122	379	234	477	.359	.524	Close & Late	.249	366	91	17	0	23	83	46	100	.337	.484
Groundball	.262	661	173	28	2	35	132	80	175	.343	.469	None on/out	.276	434	120	19	1	33	33	56	106	.367	.553
Flyball	.281	548	154	23	1	41	110	71	149	.366	.551	Batting #3	.275	2204	606	97	4	157	465	298	606	.365	.536
Home	.276	1080	298	45	1	73	210	165	305	.376	.522	Batting #5	.264	53	14	3	0	3	10	12	14	.409	.491
Away	.273	1249	341	59	3	93	261	149	330	.354	.548	Other	.264	72	19	4	0	6	16	4	15	.299	.569
Day	.293	847	248	48	3	59	196	115	253	.384	.566	April	.271	314	85	9	0	23	66	61	82	.390	.519
Night	.264	1482	391	56	1	107	295	199	382	.353	.520	May	.273	381	104	12	0	25	77	53	100	.360	.501
Grass	.274	1931	529	82	3	131	398	269	519	.367	.523	June	.272	309	84	14	0	28	62	34	73	.356	.589
Turf	.276	398	110	22	1	35	93	45	116	.352	.601	July	.285	404	115	20	1	38	99	50	97	.368	.621
First Pitch	.363	204	74	9	1	23	60	10	0	.407	.755	August	.260	466	121	24	0	23	86	53	151	.340	.459
Ahead on Count	.373	499	186	28	3	59	169	149	0	.516	.796	September/October	.286	455	130	25	3	29	101	63	132	.377	.545
Behind on Count	.253	825	209	40	1	48	142	0	303	.259	.479	Pre-All Star	.274	1110	304	41	1	85	232	157	276	.368	.542

Last Five Years

	Avg	AB	H	2B	3B	HR	RBI	BB	SO	OBP	SLG	Post-All Star	Avg	AB	H	2B	3B	HR	RBI	BB	SO	OBP	SLG
Two Strikes	.189	1279	242	40	0	49	160	146	634	.275	.335	Post-All Star	.275	1219	335	63	3	81	259	157	359	.362	.531

Batter vs. Pitcher (career)

Hits Best Against	Avg	AB	H	2B	3B	HR	RBI	BB	SO	OBP	SLG	Hits Worst Against	Avg	AB	H	2B	3B	HR	RBI	BB	SO	OBP	SLG
Jim Acker	.545	11	6	0	0	4	9	2	2	.615	1.636	Duane Ward	.000	17	0	0	0	0	1	0	10	.000	.000
Dave Schmidt	.455	11	5	0	0	2	4	0	2	.455	1.000	Charles Nagy	.000	12	0	0	0	0	0	2	2	.143	.000
Terry Mathews	.400	10	4	1	0	2	5	2	1	.500	1.100	Mike Jackson	.000	11	0	0	0	0	0	2	3	.154	.000
Todd Stottlemyre	.375	24	9	0	0	7	14	3	6	.444	1.250	Greg Harris	.063	16	1	0	0	0	1	1	10	.118	.063
Bill Gullickson	.364	11	4	0	1	2	3	2	2	.462	1.091	Dennis Lamp	.077	13	1	0	0	0	2	1	2	.143	.077

Ozzie Canseco — Cardinals
Bats Right (flyball hitter)

	Avg	G	AB	R	H	2B	3B	HR	RBI	BB	SO	HBP	GDP	SB	CS	OBP	SLG	IBB	SH	SF	#Pit	#P/PA	GB	FB	G/F
1992 Season	.276	9	29	7	8	5	0	0	3	7	4	0	1	0	0	.417	.448	0	0	0	177	4.92	9	12	0.75
Career (1990-1992)	.208	18	48	8	10	6	0	0	4	8	14	0	1	0	0	.321	.333	0	0	0	259	4.63	13	14	0.93

1992 Season

	Avg	AB	H	2B	3B	HR	RBI	BB	SO	OBP	SLG		Avg	AB	H	2B	3B	HR	RBI	BB	SO	OBP	SLG
vs. Left	.375	8	3	2	0	0	1	3	0	.545	.625	Scoring Posn	.125	8	1	0	0	0	2	1	1	.222	.125
vs. Right	.238	21	5	3	0	0	2	4	4	.360	.381	Close & Late	.500	2	1	1	0	0	0	2	0	.750	1.000

Don Carman — Rangers
Pitches Left (flyball pitcher)

	ERA	W	L	Sv	G	GS	IP	BB	SO	Avg	H	2B	3B	HR	RBI	OBP	SLG	GF	IR	IRS	Hld	SvOp	SB	CS	GB	FB	G/F
1992 Season	7.71	0	0	0	2	0	2.1	0	2	.364	4	0	0	0	1	.364	.364	1	0	0	0	0	0	0	6	1	6.00
Last Five Years	4.65	21	33	2	174	53	475.2	213	272	.260	476	95	10	62	236	.338	.424	22	104	29	12	3	25	16	499	705	0.71

1992 Season

	ERA	W	L	Sv	G	GS	IP	H	HR	BB	SO		Avg	AB	H	2B	3B	HR	RBI	BB	SO	OBP	SLG
Home	7.71	0	0	0	2	0	2.1	4	0	0	2	vs. Left	.333	3	1	0	0	0	0	0	0	.333	.333
Away	0.00	0	0	0	0	0	0.0	0	0	0	0	vs. Right	.375	8	3	0	0	0	1	0	2	.375	.375

Last Five Years

	ERA	W	L	Sv	G	GS	IP	H	HR	BB	SO		Avg	AB	H	2B	3B	HR	RBI	BB	SO	OBP	SLG
Home	4.09	16	13	0	86	27	253.0	232	28	114	139	vs. Left	.237	410	97	15	1	19	60	36	60	.301	.417
Away	5.29	5	20	2	88	26	222.2	244	34	99	133	vs. Right	.266	1423	379	80	9	43	176	177	212	.348	.426
Day	4.79	7	8	1	53	14	142.2	140	15	87	78	Inning 1-6	.268	1360	364	74	9	52	200	158	211	.345	.450
Night	4.59	14	25	1	121	39	333.0	336	47	126	194	Inning 7+	.237	473	112	21	1	10	36	55	61	.318	.349
Grass	6.15	3	13	1	50	16	130.1	155	22	54	77	None on	.258	1064	275	67	5	40	40	90	160	.321	.444
Turf	4.09	18	20	1	124	37	345.1	321	40	159	195	Runners on	.261	769	201	28	5	22	196	123	112	.359	.397
April	3.60	4	5	0	23	10	75.0	70	14	31	40	Scoring Posn	.266	443	118	18	4	11	169	90	64	.380	.400
May	5.78	2	6	0	33	9	85.2	83	12	43	46	Close & Late	.202	173	35	2	1	2	12	24	21	.303	.260
June	4.50	4	5	1	41	6	84.0	83	11	38	40	None on/out	.271	472	128	31	2	22	22	38	63	.332	.485
July	3.94	5	2	0	31	8	77.2	73	8	28	47	vs. 1st Batr (relief)	.196	102	20	6	0	2	15	15	13	.292	.314
August	5.70	3	10	1	22	12	77.1	90	9	37	49	First Inning Pitched	.235	550	129	22	1	19	82	73	88	.328	.382
September/October	4.26	3	5	0	24	8	76.0	77	8	36	50	First 15 Pitches	.236	475	112	20	1	15	59	57	67	.323	.377
Starter	4.80	13	28	0	53	53	309.1	329	41	136	178	Pitch 16-30	.252	373	94	24	4	12	49	43	65	.331	.434
Reliever	4.38	8	5	2	121	0	166.1	147	21	77	94	Pitch 31-45	.231	268	62	12	0	11	25	32	45	.313	.399
0 Days rest	4.35	3	0	0	28	0	41.1	35	7	21	21	Pitch 46+	.290	717	208	39	5	24	103	81	95	.361	.459
1 or 2 Days rest	4.42	4	3	1	57	0	75.1	63	10	39	44	First Pitch	.308	253	78	19	1	9	46	16	0	.347	.498
3+ Days rest	4.35	1	2	1	36	0	49.2	49	4	17	29	Ahead on Count	.240	759	182	28	4	26	82	0	216	.247	.390
Pre-All Star	4.44	11	17	1	109	27	265.2	253	38	122	137	Behind on Count	.300	450	135	33	4	15	68	121	0	.445	.491
Post-All Star	4.93	10	16	1	65	26	210.0	223	24	91	135	Two Strikes	.207	821	170	32	4	21	73	75	272	.279	.333

Pitcher vs. Batter (since 1984)

Pitches Best Vs.	Avg	AB	H	2B	3B	HR	RBI	BB	SO	OBP	SLG	Pitches Worst Vs.	Avg	AB	H	2B	3B	HR	RBI	BB	SO	OBP	SLG
Otis Nixon	.000	14	0	0	0	0	0	1	1	.067	.000	Eric Davis	.615	13	8	1	0	5	10	4	1	.706	1.846
Alfredo Griffin	.063	16	1	0	0	0	2	2	1	.167	.063	Jose Lind	.500	22	11	2	1	1	4	2	2	.542	.818
Jim Lindeman	.083	12	1	0	0	0	0	2	2	.214	.083	Pedro Guerrero	.500	12	6	1	0	1	5	5	2	.611	.833
Tom Pagnozzi	.100	10	1	0	0	0	0	2	2	.250	.100	Ryne Sandberg	.444	18	8	1	1	2	5	4	3	.545	.944
Chris Sabo	.167	12	2	0	0	0	0	0	0	.167	.167	Andre Dawson	.400	25	10	2	1	4	6	2	5	.444	1.040

Cris Carpenter — Cardinals
Pitches Right (flyball pitcher)

	ERA	W	L	Sv	G	GS	IP	BB	SO	Avg	H	2B	3B	HR	RBI	OBP	SLG	GF	IR	IRS	Hld	SvOp	SB	CS	GB	FB	G/F
1992 Season	2.97	5	4	1	73	0	88.0	27	46	.220	69	13	2	10	45	.288	.371	21	64	19	7	8	11	3	104	114	0.91
Career (1988-1992)	3.66	21	15	1	180	13	277.2	84	158	.244	253	55	2	25	138	.301	.386	41	122	40	21	10	25	12	345	356	0.97

1992 Season

	ERA	W	L	Sv	G	GS	IP	H	HR	BB	SO		Avg	AB	H	2B	3B	HR	RBI	BB	SO	OBP	SLG
Home	3.59	1	1	1	33	0	42.2	31	5	10	21	vs. Left	.222	162	36	8	1	6	27	15	23	.287	.395
Away	2.38	4	3	0	40	0	45.1	38	5	17	25	vs. Right	.219	151	33	5	1	4	18	12	23	.290	.344
Day	3.44	2	3	0	18	0	18.1	18	3	5	11	Inning 1-6	.189	74	14	1	0	1	9	5	10	.238	.243
Night	2.84	3	1	1	55	0	69.2	51	7	22	35	Inning 7+	.230	239	55	12	2	9	36	22	36	.303	.410
Grass	0.83	2	1	0	19	0	21.2	16	2	7	13	None on	.214	159	34	7	1	7	7	12	25	.273	.403

1992 Season

	ERA	W	L	Sv	G	GS	IP	H	HR	BB	SO		Avg	AB	H	2B	3B	HR	RBI	BB	SO	OBP	SLG
Turf	3.66	3	3	1	54	0	66.1	53	8	20	33	Runners on	.227	154	35	6	1	3	38	15	21	.303	.338
April	2.25	1	1	0	12	0	12.0	10	2	2	7	Scoring Posn	.198	106	21	3	1	2	33	13	15	.290	.302
May	2.87	1	0	1	12	0	15.2	10	1	4	6	Close & Late	.256	121	31	10	1	6	21	14	20	.345	.504
June	2.70	1	1	0	13	0	16.2	12	1	7	9	None on/out	.182	66	12	1	0	2	2	5	9	.250	.288
July	4.30	0	2	0	11	0	14.2	12	4	2	9	vs. 1st Batr (relief)	.194	67	13	1	0	2	10	5	11	.250	.299
August	4.80	1	0	0	11	0	15.0	15	1	7	10	First Inning Pitched	.235	226	53	10	2	8	40	18	33	.296	.403
September/October	0.64	1	0	0	14	0	14.0	10	1	5	5	First 15 Pitches	.242	215	52	11	1	8	31	19	32	.307	.414
Starter	0.00	0	0	0	0	0	0.0	0	0	0	0	Pitch 16-30	.190	84	16	1	1	2	13	7	10	.266	.298
Reliever	2.97	5	4	1	73	0	88.0	69	10	27	46	Pitch 31-45	.071	14	1	1	0	0	1	1	4	.133	.143
0 Days rest	3.20	2	1	0	19	0	19.2	18	4	7	6	Pitch 46+	.000	0	0	0	0	0	0	0	0	.000	.000
1 or 2 Days rest	2.44	3	3	1	39	0	44.1	34	4	13	28	First Pitch	.167	48	8	0	0	3	8	7	0	.263	.354
3+ Days rest	3.75	0	0	0	15	0	24.0	17	2	7	12	Ahead on Count	.146	144	21	3	0	2	14	0	40	.162	.208
Pre-All Star	2.32	3	2	1	41	0	50.1	34	4	13	26	Behind on Count	.293	75	22	5	2	5	17	10	0	.376	.613
Post-All Star	3.82	2	2	0	32	0	37.2	35	4	13	20	Two Strikes	.154	136	21	5	0	2	16	10	46	.233	.235

Career (1988-1992)

	ERA	W	L	Sv	G	GS	IP	H	HR	BB	SO		Avg	AB	H	2B	3B	HR	RBI	BB	SO	OBP	SLG
Home	4.11	7	6	1	84	7	133.2	126	9	41	75	vs. Left	.261	524	137	34	4	11	71	51	69	.325	.405
Away	3.25	9	0	0	96	6	144.0	127	16	43	83	vs. Right	.225	515	116	21	5	14	67	33	89	.276	.367
Day	2.70	9	5	0	52	4	80.0	66	6	23	47	Inning 1-6	.264	451	119	21	5	6	65	29	61	.308	.373
Night	4.05	12	10	1	128	9	197.2	187	19	61	111	Inning 7+	.228	588	134	34	4	19	73	55	97	.296	.396
Grass	2.82	6	4	0	46	2	67.0	55	8	20	38	None on	.231	589	136	29	4	14	14	35	97	.276	.365
Turf	3.93	15	11	1	134	11	210.2	198	17	64	120	Runners on	.260	450	117	26	5	11	124	49	61	.331	.413
April	2.19	4	3	0	33	2	49.1	37	5	12	24	Scoring Posn	.232	302	70	16	5	5	106	44	43	.323	.368
May	3.53	6	3	1	40	5	74.0	62	2	19	42	Close & Late	.248	286	71	21	2	11	43	33	51	.328	.451
June	4.95	4	5	0	36	4	63.2	69	7	25	36	None on/out	.243	247	60	10	3	7	7	15	32	.292	.393
July	6.23	0	3	0	22	0	30.1	33	7	9	17	vs. 1st Batr (relief)	.253	150	38	6	1	5	26	13	24	.315	.407
August	3.42	4	0	0	24	0	26.1	22	1	11	22	First Inning Pitched	.243	563	137	31	7	16	94	47	100	.302	.409
September/October	1.59	3	1	0	25	2	34.0	30	3	8	17	First 15 Pitches	.254	520	132	32	7	16	80	43	91	.310	.435
Starter	4.10	3	5	0	13	13	74.2	86	4	16	36	Pitch 16-30	.182	258	47	7	1	4	28	23	34	.253	.264
Reliever	3.50	18	10	1	167	0	203.0	167	21	68	122	Pitch 31-45	.264	106	28	7	0	4	14	8	16	.313	.443
0 Days rest	1.71	8	1	0	40	0	42.0	27	4	9	19	Pitch 46+	.297	155	46	9	1	1	16	10	17	.343	.387
1 or 2 Days rest	4.41	8	9	1	96	0	112.1	104	13	43	72	First Pitch	.273	172	47	9	0	6	30	24	0	.355	.430
3+ Days rest	2.96	2	0	0	31	0	48.2	36	4	16	31	Ahead on Count	.179	486	87	18	4	4	44	0	138	.182	.257
Pre-All Star	3.60	14	11	1	118	11	197.2	176	14	58	109	Behind on Count	.310	229	71	17	3	11	44	33	0	.399	.555
Post-All Star	3.83	7	4	0	62	2	80.0	77	11	26	49	Two Strikes	.179	463	83	20	4	4	44	27	158	.229	.266

Pitcher vs. Batter (career)

Pitches Best Vs.	Avg	AB	H	2B	3B	HR	RBI	BB	SO	OBP	SLG	Pitches Worst Vs.	Avg	AB	H	2B	3B	HR	RBI	BB	SO	OBP	SLG
Barry Bonds	.000	8	0	0	0	0	0	3	3	.273	.000	Mark Grace	.583	12	7	1	0	0	1	1	0	.615	.667
Eric Davis	.091	11	1	0	0	0	0	0	2	.091	.091	Shawon Dunston	.500	12	6	1	1	0	4	0	2	.500	.750
Ricky Jordan	.100	10	1	0	0	0	0	1	0	.182	.100	Dwight Smith	.455	11	5	3	0	0	1	1	2	.500	.727
Andre Dawson	.154	13	2	0	0	0	0	1	0	.200	.154	Bobby Bonilla	.417	12	5	3	0	0	0	3	0	.533	.667
Dave Martinez	.182	11	2	0	0	0	0	0	1	.250	.182	Ron Gant	.400	10	4	2	0	1	0	0	1	.364	.900

Chuck Carr — Cardinals   Bats Both (groundball hitter)

	Avg	G	AB	R	H	2B	3B	HR	RBI	BB	SO	HBP	GDP	SB	CS	OBP	SLG	IBB	SH	SF	#Pit	#P/PA	GB	FB	G/F
1992 Season	.219	22	64	8	14	3	0	0	3	9	6	0	0	10	2	.315	.266	0	3	0	242	3.32	31	18	1.72
Career (1990-1992)	.208	38	77	9	16	3	0	0	4	9	10	0	0	12	2	.291	.247	0	3	0	294	3.42	34	22	1.55

1992 Season

	Avg	AB	H	2B	3B	HR	RBI	BB	SO	OBP	SLG		Avg	AB	H	2B	3B	HR	RBI	BB	SO	OBP	SLG
vs. Left	.250	24	6	1	0	0	0	1	3	.280	.292	Scoring Posn	.200	15	3	1	0	0	3	1	2	.250	.267
vs. Right	.200	40	8	2	0	0	3	8	3	.333	.250	Close & Late	.125	8	1	1	0	0	2	4	3	.417	.250

Mark Carreon — Tigers   Bats Right

	Avg	G	AB	R	H	2B	3B	HR	RBI	BB	SO	HBP	GDP	SB	CS	OBP	SLG	IBB	SH	SF	#Pit	#P/PA	GB	FB	G/F
1992 Season	.232	101	336	34	78	11	1	10	41	22	57	1	12	3	1	.278	.360	2	1	4	1376	3.79	99	125	0.79
Last Five Years	.258	364	920	107	237	37	1	31	105	63	130	6	28	8	5	.308	.401	4	2	5	3703	3.73	311	303	1.03

1992 Season

	Avg	AB	H	2B	3B	HR	RBI	BB	SO	OBP	SLG		Avg	AB	H	2B	3B	HR	RBI	BB	SO	OBP	SLG
vs. Left	.198	111	22	1	0	2	8	5	13	.235	.261	Scoring Posn	.200	90	18	3	0	2	29	7	13	.248	.300
vs. Right	.249	225	56	10	1	8	33	17	44	.299	.409	Close & Late	.267	45	12	0	0	1	5	2	5	.298	.333
Groundball	.278	90	25	5	1	1	8	1	8	.286	.389	None on/out	.242	66	16	2	1	2	2	7	11	.315	.394
Flyball	.176	108	19	1	0	4	9	8	29	.237	.296	Batting #6	.138	116	16	1	0	2	12	7	21	.192	.198
Home	.212	151	32	6	1	5	19	14	30	.278	.364	Batting #7	.264	87	23	3	0	4	7	9	20	.333	.437
Away	.249	185	46	5	0	5	22	8	27	.278	.357	Other	.293	133	39	7	1	4	22	6	16	.317	.451
Day	.235	136	32	4	1	4	15	3	18	.248	.368	April	.229	48	11	1	0	2	7	4	11	.288	.375
Night	.230	200	46	7	0	6	26	19	39	.297	.355	May	.274	95	26	4	1	4	16	7	19	.330	.463
Grass	.234	282	66	10	1	10	35	18	49	.279	.383	June	.250	20	5	0	0	0	0	0	5	.250	.250

1992 Season

	Avg	AB	H	2B	3B	HR	RBI	BB	SO	OBP	SLG		Avg	AB	H	2B	3B	HR	RBI	BB	SO	OBP	SLG
Turf	.222	54	12	1	0	0	6	4	8	.276	.241	July	.148	61	9	2	0	1	3	4	6	.200	.230
First Pitch	.250	40	10	1	0	1	6	2	0	.295	.350	August	.182	33	6	1	0	1	3	1	11	.200	.303
Ahead on Count	.223	94	21	4	1	4	15	10	0	.298	.415	September/October	.266	79	21	3	0	2	12	6	5	.307	.380
Behind on Count	.276	105	29	4	0	2	9	0	24	.271	.371	Pre-All Star	.250	188	47	6	1	7	25	15	35	.309	.404
Two Strikes	.253	146	37	5	0	4	13	10	57	.296	.370	Post-All Star	.209	148	31	5	0	3	16	7	22	.239	.304

1992 By Position

Position	Avg	AB	H	2B	3B	HR	RBI	BB	SO	OBP	SLG	G	GS	Innings	PO	A	E	DP	Fld Pct	Rng Fctr	In Zone	Outs	Zone Rtg	MLB Zone
As Designated Hitter	.227	44	10	2	0	1	3	3	8	.277	.341	13	13	---	---	---	---	---	---	---	---	---	---	---
As lf	.260	223	58	8	1	8	31	15	34	.306	.413	64	61	527.0	136	5	2	1	.986	2.41	162	136	.840	.809
As rf	.143	56	8	0	0	1	3	4	14	.197	.196	19	15	138.0	39	0	1	0	.975	2.54	44	35	.795	.814

Last Five Years

	Avg	AB	H	2B	3B	HR	RBI	BB	SO	OBP	SLG		Avg	AB	H	2B	3B	HR	RBI	BB	SO	OBP	SLG
vs. Left	.242	472	114	17	0	18	50	29	57	.289	.392	Scoring Posn	.236	259	61	10	0	4	72	18	40	.268	.320
vs. Right	.275	448	123	20	1	13	55	34	73	.326	.411	Close & Late	.272	184	50	4	0	10	21	11	31	.315	.457
Groundball	.301	272	82	16	1	5	32	15	24	.340	.423	None on/out	.261	203	53	9	1	12	12	13	30	.306	.493
Flyball	.200	240	48	6	0	9	18	15	53	.255	.338	Batting #6	.227	300	68	6	0	5	34	14	46	.264	.297
Home	.243	457	111	20	1	13	47	36	68	.304	.376	Batting #7	.295	156	46	4	0	7	17	18	28	.371	.455
Away	.272	463	126	17	0	18	58	27	62	.312	.425	Other	.265	464	123	27	1	19	54	31	56	.313	.450
Day	.254	339	86	14	1	12	39	19	49	.298	.407	April	.260	123	32	5	0	7	16	11	22	.326	.472
Night	.260	581	151	23	0	19	66	44	81	.314	.398	May	.255	161	41	8	1	7	22	10	31	.302	.447
Grass	.250	675	169	28	1	23	78	45	99	.301	.397	June	.259	139	36	3	0	5	12	7	19	.295	.388
Turf	.276	245	68	9	0	8	27	18	31	.327	.412	July	.204	157	32	8	0	5	20	16	20	.277	.350
First Pitch	.310	113	35	4	0	6	20	4	0	.342	.504	August	.219	137	30	3	0	2	8	4	21	.250	.285
Ahead on Count	.264	250	66	12	1	9	30	31	0	.352	.428	September/October	.325	203	66	10	0	5	27	15	17	.371	.448
Behind on Count	.250	288	72	12	0	7	21	0	59	.251	.365	Pre-All Star	.257	482	124	20	1	22	58	37		.313	.440
Two Strikes	.237	393	93	15	0	10	33	28	130	.287	.351	Post-All Star	.258	438	113	17	0	9	47	26	53	.302	.358

Batter vs. Pitcher (career)

Hits Best Against	Avg	AB	H	2B	3B	HR	RBI	BB	SO	OBP	SLG	Hits Worst Against	Avg	AB	H	2B	3B	HR	RBI	BB	SO	OBP	SLG
Neal Heaton	.636	11	7	0	0	2	5	0	0	.636	1.182	Scott Sanderson	.083	12	1	0	0	1	2	0	4	.083	.333
Mark Langston	.500	14	7	2	0	0	1	3	1	.588	.643	Tom Glavine	.083	12	1	0	0	0	0	0	1	.083	.083
Rheal Cormier	.417	12	5	0	0	1	3	0	0	.417	.667	Randy Myers	.091	11	1	0	0	0	0	0	4	.091	.091
Steve Avery	.385	13	5	3	0	0	1	0	0	.385	.615	Tom Browning	.154	13	2	1	0	0	0	0	0	.154	.231
Randy Tomlin	.364	11	4	0	0	1	1	1	0	.417	.636	Terry Mulholland	.214	14	3	0	0	0	1	0	1	.214	.214

Gary Carter — Expos

Bats Right (flyball hitter)

	Avg	G	AB	R	H	2B	3B	HR	RBI	BB	SO	HBP	GDP	SB	CS	OBP	SLG	IBB	SH	SF	#Pit	#P/PA	GB	FB	G/F
1992 Season	.218	95	285	24	62	18	1	5	29	33	37	2	4	0	4	.299	.340	4	1	4	1146	3.54	76	123	0.62
Last Five Years	.233	468	1385	123	323	66	3	33	143	126	161	17	30	3	9	.302	.357	9	3	15	5208	3.38	401	540	0.74

1992 Season

	Avg	AB	H	2B	3B	HR	RBI	BB	SO	OBP	SLG		Avg	AB	H	2B	3B	HR	RBI	BB	SO	OBP	SLG
vs. Left	.230	139	32	13	0	2	14	15	15	.301	.367	Scoring Posn	.205	73	15	6	0	0	19	16	13	.333	.288
vs. Right	.205	146	30	5	1	3	15	18	22	.298	.315	Close & Late	.213	47	10	1	0	0	3	3	9	.260	.234
Groundball	.257	113	29	7	1	2	12	12	11	.325	.389	None on/out	.161	62	10	3	1	1	1	6	11	.235	.290
Flyball	.123	65	8	3	0	0	3	10	14	.256	.169	Batting #6	.265	102	27	7	0	2	8	3	12	.287	.392
Home	.242	153	37	9	1	2	15	20	19	.335	.353	Batting #7	.218	87	19	2	1	2	9	11	7	.307	.333
Away	.189	132	25	9	0	3	14	13	19	.257	.326	Other	.167	96	16	9	0	1	12	19	18	.304	.292
Day	.263	95	25	8	0	3	8	14	13	.364	.442	April	.273	33	9	2	0	0	0	2	3	.314	.333
Night	.195	190	37	10	1	2	21	19	24	.266	.289	May	.250	68	17	5	0	3	10	9	13	.338	.456
Grass	.178	73	13	5	0	1	5	7	10	.250	.288	June	.207	58	12	4	0	0	3	5	8	.288	.276
Turf	.231	212	49	13	1	4	24	26	27	.316	.358	July	.151	53	8	0	0	0	2	4	3	.207	.151
First Pitch	.289	45	13	4	0	1	7	4	0	.360	.444	August	.175	40	7	1	1	2	7	9	4	.314	.400
Ahead on Count	.241	83	20	4	0	3	9	19	0	.379	.398	September/October	.273	33	9	6	0	0	7	4	6	.351	.455
Behind on Count	.213	89	19	5	1	3	14	0	19	.217	.393	Pre-All Star	.225	187	42	11	0	3	14	18	26	.298	.332
Two Strikes	.198	111	22	9	0	0	9	10	37	.266	.279	Post-All Star	.204	98	20	7	1	2	15	15	11	.302	.357

1992 By Position

Position	Avg	AB	H	2B	3B	HR	RBI	BB	SO	OBP	SLG	G	GS	Innings	PO	A	E	DP	Fld Pct	Rng Fctr	In Zone	Outs	Zone Rtg	MLB Zone
As Pinch Hitter	.200	10	2	1	0	0	1	1	2	.273	.300	11	0	---	---	---	---	---	---	---	---	---	---	---
As c	.222	270	60	17	1	5	28	30	35	.298	.348	85	79	665.0	482	50	6	3	.989	---	---	---	---	---

Last Five Years

	Avg	AB	H	2B	3B	HR	RBI	BB	SO	OBP	SLG		Avg	AB	H	2B	3B	HR	RBI	BB	SO	OBP	SLG
vs. Left	.236	647	153	36	1	15	64	63	62	.308	.365	Scoring Posn	.229	363	83	15	1	6	106	48	54	.317	.325
vs. Right	.230	738	170	30	2	18	79	63	99	.297	.350	Close & Late	.230	265	61	8	0	6	26	23	34	.293	.328
Groundball	.251	499	125	20	1	13	58	46	51	.314	.373	None on/out	.252	330	83	20	1	11	11	21	34	.302	.418
Flyball	.206	301	62	14	0	6	24	27	41	.282	.312	Batting #6	.236	729	172	28	2	16	71	46	84	.286	.346
Home	.228	710	162	27	1	17	77	55	89	.290	.341	Batting #7	.251	402	101	24	1	11	47	41	42	.327	.398
Away	.239	675	161	39	2	16	66	71	72	.314	.373	Other	.197	254	50	14	0	6	25	39	35	.306	.323

Last Five Years

	Avg	AB	H	2B	3B	HR	RBI	BB	SO	OBP	SLG
Day	.252	417	105	24	0	13	50	52	44	.335	.403
Night	.225	968	218	42	3	20	93	74	117	.287	.337
Grass	.239	856	205	37	1	25	95	68	98	.301	.373
Turf	.223	529	118	29	2	8	48	58	63	.304	.331
First Pitch	.291	258	75	16	1	5	34	5	0	.311	.419
Ahead on Count	.263	358	94	20	0	11	44	72	0	.388	.411
Behind on Count	.200	449	90	17	1	10	37	0	87	.211	.310
Two Strikes	.185	507	94	20	0	8	37	46	161	.263	.272

	Avg	AB	H	2B	3B	HR	RBI	BB	SO	OBP	SLG
April	.223	206	46	9	0	8	20	24	22	.308	.383
May	.221	249	55	13	1	7	31	30	32	.312	.365
June	.252	242	61	12	1	4	22	18	32	.312	.360
July	.244	234	57	10	0	5	23	15	23	.295	.350
August	.223	260	58	9	1	6	24	19	30	.276	.335
September/October	.237	194	46	13	0	3	23	20	22	.312	.351
Pre-All Star	.237	790	187	36	2	22	87	77	97	.311	.371
Post-All Star	.229	595	136	30	1	11	56	49	64	.290	.338

Batter vs. Pitcher (since 1984)

Hits Best Against	Avg	AB	H	2B	3B	HR	RBI	BB	SO	OBP	SLG
Joe Hesketh	.545	11	6	0	0	1	3	1	2	.538	.818
Kelly Downs	.500	8	4	2	0	0	1	3	1	.636	.750
Jeff Robinson	.476	21	10	0	1	3	5	0	3	.476	1.000
Greg Maddux	.429	14	6	3	0	1	5	0	1	.429	.857
Mark Grant	.364	11	4	2	0	1	4	0	5	.500	.818

Hits Worst Against	Avg	AB	H	2B	3B	HR	RBI	BB	SO	OBP	SLG
Steve Avery	.067	15	1	0	0	0	0	1	3	.125	.067
Dennis Martinez	.071	28	2	0	0	0	0	0	2	.071	.071
Pat Combs	.083	12	1	0	0	0	0	1	2	.154	.083
Danny Darwin	.091	11	1	0	0	0	1	0	1	.083	.091
Lee Smith	.105	19	2	0	0	0	0	0	6	.105	.105

Joe Carter — Blue Jays
Bats Right (flyball hitter)

	Avg	G	AB	R	H	2B	3B	HR	RBI	BB	SO	HBP	GDP	SB	CS	OBP	SLG	IBB	SH	SF	#Pit	#P/PA	GB	FB	G/F
1992 Season	.264	158	622	97	164	30	7	34	119	36	109	11	14	12	5	.309	.498	4	1	13	2562	3.76	146	266	0.55
Last Five Years	.256	801	3166	434	811	167	21	153	545	207	508	43	45	94	30	.307	.467	48	4	41	12444	3.60	862	1258	0.69

1992 Season

	Avg	AB	H	2B	3B	HR	RBI	BB	SO	OBP	SLG
vs. Left	.312	157	49	14	0	7	20	11	22	.355	.535
vs. Right	.247	465	115	16	7	27	99	25	87	.294	.486
Groundball	.247	182	45	10	1	10	29	13	32	.307	.478
Flyball	.260	181	47	9	3	7	28	8	32	.298	.459
Home	.259	301	78	15	3	21	65	17	53	.303	.538
Away	.268	321	86	15	4	13	54	19	56	.315	.461
Day	.258	194	50	10	1	12	40	10	41	.297	.505
Night	.266	428	114	20	6	22	79	26	68	.315	.495
Grass	.258	248	64	14	3	10	43	14	43	.301	.460
Turf	.267	374	100	16	4	24	76	22	66	.315	.524
First Pitch	.333	75	25	3	2	9	26	3	0	.358	.787
Ahead on Count	.387	124	48	13	1	8	34	19	0	.463	.702
Behind on Count	.196	250	49	9	1	11	34	0	55	.206	.372
Two Strikes	.173	295	51	8	3	12	35	14	109	.220	.342

	Avg	AB	H	2B	3B	HR	RBI	BB	SO	OBP	SLG
Scoring Posn	.279	179	50	4	6	10	83	17	37	.336	.536
Close & Late	.233	86	20	1	1	3	16	4	13	.269	.372
None on/out	.298	104	31	7	0	6	6	4	12	.336	.558
Batting #3	.264	621	164	30	7	34	119	36	109	.310	.499
Batting #5	.000	1	0	0	0	0	0	0	0	.000	.000
Other	.000	0	0	0	0	0	0	0	0	.000	.000
April	.256	90	23	6	0	2	11	2	18	.274	.389
May	.257	105	27	4	0	7	19	5	17	.316	.495
June	.330	106	35	4	3	8	23	6	22	.374	.651
July	.235	98	23	5	1	4	15	11	16	.319	.429
August	.241	112	27	8	1	8	26	9	20	.296	.545
September/October	.261	111	29	3	2	5	25	3	16	.275	.459
Pre-All Star	.274	340	93	16	4	19	63	18	64	.322	.512
Post-All Star	.252	282	71	14	3	15	56	18	45	.295	.482

1992 By Position

Position	Avg	AB	H	2B	3B	HR	RBI	BB	SO	OBP	SLG	G	GS	Innings	PO	A	E	DP	Fld Pct	Rng Fctr	In Zone	Outs	Zone Rtg	MLB Zone
As Designated Hitter	.229	96	22	2	0	5	15	6	17	.290	.406	24	24	---	---	---	---	---	---	---	---	---	---	---
As rf	.274	486	133	25	7	28	101	28	85	.317	.527	123	123	1043.2	246	10	8	2	.970	2.21	287	239	.833	.814

Last Five Years

	Avg	AB	H	2B	3B	HR	RBI	BB	SO	OBP	SLG
vs. Left	.269	867	233	50	2	39	131	61	127	.314	.466
vs. Right	.251	2299	578	117	19	114	414	146	381	.304	.468
Groundball	.252	882	222	48	3	36	136	63	142	.309	.435
Flyball	.255	753	192	51	10	32	122	55	120	.312	.477
Home	.258	1572	406	78	9	88	289	99	263	.309	.487
Away	.254	1594	405	89	12	65	256	108	245	.305	.447
Day	.242	973	235	49	5	43	159	57	166	.291	.435
Night	.263	2193	576	118	16	110	393	150	342	.314	.482
Grass	.248	2033	505	96	12	87	326	138	312	.301	.436
Turf	.270	1133	306	71	9	66	219	69	196	.318	.523
First Pitch	.347	386	134	30	4	31	96	18	0	.378	.687
Ahead on Count	.325	637	207	41	5	35	147	110	0	.421	.570
Behind on Count	.214	1274	272	57	4	50	180	6	300	.229	.382
Two Strikes	.192	1444	277	53	10	53	172	65	508	.232	.352

	Avg	AB	H	2B	3B	HR	RBI	BB	SO	OBP	SLG
Scoring Posn	.275	892	245	45	12	40	385	110	168	.352	.487
Close & Late	.209	517	108	17	4	18	78	39	96	.271	.362
None on/out	.261	639	167	35	3	33	33	66	77	.297	.480
Batting #3	.261	2027	530	107	15	104	342	127	324	.310	.483
Batting #4	.247	867	214	46	6	39	149	58	155	.301	.449
Other	.246	272	67	14	0	10	54	22	29	.302	.406
April	.280	422	118	25	0	17	73	23	66	.322	.460
May	.267	543	145	30	4	22	94	34	84	.317	.459
June	.258	523	135	31	4	35	97	33	99	.319	.512
July	.245	530	130	27	5	26	91	47	76	.310	.462
August	.251	566	142	31	2	31	104	35	89	.299	.477
September/October	.242	582	141	23	6	22	86	35	99	.287	.416
Pre-All Star	.265	1667	441	96	11	80	297	107	265	.316	.479
Post-All Star	.247	1499	370	71	10	73	248	100	243	.297	.454

Batter vs. Pitcher (since 1984)

Hits Best Against	Avg	AB	H	2B	3B	HR	RBI	BB	SO	OBP	SLG
Tim Leary	.588	17	10	2	0	4	7	0	2	.526	1.412
Bob Tewksbury	.455	11	5	0	0	2	3	1	0	.500	1.000
Bill Wegman	.415	41	17	4	2	5	10	2	4	.442	.976
Mike Birkbeck	.400	15	6	1	0	3	7	0	4	.353	1.067
Nolan Ryan	.357	14	5	3	1	1	4	2	4	.438	.929

Hits Worst Against	Avg	AB	H	2B	3B	HR	RBI	BB	SO	OBP	SLG
Todd Stottlemyre	.000	11	0	0	0	0	0	0	2	.000	.000
Jeff Russell	.067	15	1	0	0	0	1	0	4	.063	.067
Dennis Martinez	.077	13	1	0	0	0	0	1	2	.143	.077
Bobby Thigpen	.077	13	1	1	0	0	1	0	5	.077	.154
Bud Black	.111	18	2	0	0	0	0	0	6	.111	.111

Larry Carter — Giants
Pitches Right (flyball pitcher)

	ERA	W	L	Sv	G	GS	IP	BB	SO	Avg	H	2B	3B	HR	RBI	OBP	SLG	CG	ShO	Sup	QS	#P/S	SB	CS	GB	FB	G/F
1992 Season	4.64	1	5	0	6	6	33.0	18	21	.270	34	9	3	6	16	.359	.532	0	0	3.00	3	94	1	1	31	50	0.62

1992 Season

	ERA	W	L	Sv	G	GS	IP	H	HR	BB	SO		Avg	AB	H	2B	3B	HR	RBI	BB	SO	OBP	SLG
Home	5.06	0	1	0	1	1	5.1	7	1	2	2	vs. Left	.266	79	21	4	3	5	13	8	11	.330	.582
Away	4.55	1	4	0	5	5	27.2	27	5	16	19	vs. Right	.277	47	13	5	0	1	3	10	10	.404	.447

Larry Casian — Twins
Pitches Left

	ERA	W	L	Sv	G	GS	IP	BB	SO	Avg	H	2B	3B	HR	RBI	OBP	SLG	GF	IR	IRS	Hld	SvOp	SB	CS	GB	FB	G/F
1992 Season	2.70	1	0	0	6	0	6.2	1	2	.259	7	1	0	0	0	.286	.296	1	2	0	1	0	0	0	10	8	1.25
Career (1990-1992)	4.75	3	1	0	26	3	47.1	12	19	.319	61	17	0	6	22	.361	.503	6	18	1	3	0	0	0	71	54	1.31

1992 Season

	ERA	W	L	Sv	G	GS	IP	H	HR	BB	SO		Avg	AB	H	2B	3B	HR	RBI	BB	SO	OBP	SLG
Home	0.00	0	0	0	3	0	3.0	1	0	0	0	vs. Left	.083	12	1	0	0	0	0	0	2	.083	.083
Away	4.91	1	0	0	3	0	3.2	6	0	1	2	vs. Right	.400	15	6	1	0	0	0	1	0	.438	.467

Vinny Castilla — Braves
Bats Right (flyball hitter)

	Avg	G	AB	R	H	2B	3B	HR	RBI	BB	SO	HBP	GDP	SB	CS	OBP	SLG	IBB	SH	SF	#Pit	#P/PA	GB	FB	G/F
1992 Season	.250	9	16	1	4	1	0	0	1	1	4	1	0	0	0	.333	.313	1	0	0	50	2.78	3	6	0.50
Career (1991-1992)	.238	21	21	2	5	1	0	0	1	1	6	1	0	0	0	.304	.286	1	1	0	66	2.87	4	7	0.57

1992 Season

	Avg	AB	H	2B	3B	HR	RBI	BB	SO	OBP	SLG		Avg	AB	H	2B	3B	HR	RBI	BB	SO	OBP	SLG
vs. Left	.167	6	1	0	0	0	0	0	1	.167	.167	Scoring Posn	.500	4	2	1	0	0	1	1	1	.600	.750
vs. Right	.300	10	3	1	0	0	1	1	3	.417	.400	Close & Late	.250	4	1	0	0	0	0	0	0	.250	.250

Braulio Castillo — Phillies
Bats Right (groundball hitter)

	Avg	G	AB	R	H	2B	3B	HR	RBI	BB	SO	HBP	GDP	SB	CS	OBP	SLG	IBB	SH	SF	#Pit	#P/PA	GB	FB	G/F
1992 Season	.197	28	76	12	15	3	1	2	7	4	15	0	1	1	0	.238	.342	0	1	0	315	3.94	41	12	3.42
Career (1991-1992)	.188	56	128	15	24	6	1	2	9	5	30	0	2	2	1	.218	.297	0	1	0	515	3.87	57	25	2.28

1992 Season

	Avg	AB	H	2B	3B	HR	RBI	BB	SO	OBP	SLG		Avg	AB	H	2B	3B	HR	RBI	BB	SO	OBP	SLG
vs. Left	.182	33	6	0	1	1	4	0	5	.182	.333	Scoring Posn	.136	22	3	1	0	1	6	2	4	.208	.318
vs. Right	.209	43	9	3	0	1	3	4	10	.277	.349	Close & Late	.333	9	3	1	0	0	1	2	2	.455	.444

Frank Castillo — Cubs
Pitches Right

	ERA	W	L	Sv	G	GS	IP	BB	SO	Avg	H	2B	3B	HR	RBI	OBP	SLG	CG	ShO	Sup	QS	#P/S	SB	CS	GB	FB	G/F
1992 Season	3.46	10	11	0	33	33	205.1	63	135	.232	179	42	4	19	69	.294	.371	0	0	3.46	21	95	18	5	250	215	1.16
Career (1991-1992)	3.78	16	18	0	51	51	317.0	96	208	.239	286	65	6	24	113	.297	.364	4	0	3.66	29	94	25	13	402	329	1.22

1992 Season

	ERA	W	L	Sv	G	GS	IP	H	HR	BB	SO		Avg	AB	H	2B	3B	HR	RBI	BB	SO	OBP	SLG
Home	3.63	6	7	0	19	19	121.1	106	12	37	82	vs. Left	.228	451	103	21	1	11	43	49	74	.303	.353
Away	3.21	4	4	0	14	14	84.0	73	7	26	53	vs. Right	.238	319	76	21	3	8	26	14	61	.280	.398
Day	3.57	6	5	0	17	17	108.1	91	11	35	71	Inning 1-6	.220	685	151	37	4	16	59	52	125	.278	.356
Night	3.34	4	6	0	16	16	97.0	88	8	28	64	Inning 7+	.329	85	28	5	0	3	10	11	10	.414	.494
Grass	3.50	9	10	0	25	25	159.1	136	15	51	106	None on	.230	504	116	25	3	12	12	28	89	.276	.363
Turf	3.33	1	1	0	8	8	46.0	43	4	12	29	Runners on	.237	266	63	17	1	7	57	35	46	.325	.387
April	3.65	0	2	0	4	4	24.2	16	2	6	19	Scoring Posn	.229	144	33	8	1	3	47	32	23	.363	.361
May	2.01	3	2	0	5	5	31.1	26	2	9	24	Close & Late	.327	55	18	2	0	1	6	8	9	.406	.418
June	3.96	3	2	0	6	6	38.2	37	4	14	22	None on/out	.251	211	53	11	2	7	7	14	31	.304	.422
July	2.83	0	1	0	5	5	28.2	27	3	11	18	vs. 1st Batr (relief)	.000	0	0	0	0	0	0	0	0	.000	.000
August	4.35	2	3	0	6	6	39.1	31	5	12	18	First Inning Pitched	.197	122	24	2	0	0	4	9	26	.252	.213
September/October	3.59	2	1	0	7	7	42.2	42	3	11	34	First 75 Pitches	.222	589	131	31	3	14	48	44	107	.280	.357
Starter	3.46	10	11	0	33	33	205.1	179	19	63	135	Pitch 76-90	.194	103	20	5	1	2	11	8	16	.250	.320
Reliever	0.00	0	0	0	0	0	0.0	0	0	0	0	Pitch 91-105	.328	64	21	4	0	3	6	7	9	.411	.531
0-3 Days Rest	9.00	0	0	0	1	1	3.0	5	1	1	3	Pitch 106+	.500	14	7	2	0	0	4	4	3	.550	.643
4 Days Rest	3.63	8	8	0	22	22	141.1	125	14	45	91	First Pitch	.281	114	32	8	2	4	13	5	0	.314	.491
5+ Days Rest	2.80	2	3	0	10	10	61.0	49	4	17	41	Ahead on Count	.193	358	69	21	0	4	23	0	114	.196	.285
Pre-All Star	3.21	6	7	0	17	17	106.2	90	10	35	72	Behind on Count	.315	146	46	9	1	7	23	38	0	.454	.534
Post-All Star	3.74	4	4	0	16	16	98.2	89	9	28	63	Two Strikes	.166	367	61	16	1	4	20	20	135	.214	.248

79

Andujar Cedeno — Astros   Bats Right

	Avg	G	AB	R	H	2B	3B	HR	RBI	BB	SO	HBP	GDP	SB	CS	OBP	SLG	IBB	SH	SF	#Pit	#P/PA	GB	FB	G/F
1992 Season	.173	71	220	15	38	13	2	2	13	14	71	3	1	2	0	.232	.277	2	0	0	894	3.77	63	50	1.26
Career (1990-1992)	.207	145	479	42	99	26	4	11	49	23	150	4	4	6	3	.248	.347	3	1	2	1941	3.82	145	109	1.33

1992 Season

	Avg	AB	H	2B	3B	HR	RBI	BB	SO	OBP	SLG		Avg	AB	H	2B	3B	HR	RBI	BB	SO	OBP	SLG
vs. Left	.203	64	13	5	2	0	4	7	18	.282	.344	Scoring Posn	.115	52	6	3	0	0	9	7	18	.233	.173
vs. Right	.160	156	25	8	0	2	9	7	53	.211	.250	Close & Late	.188	32	6	2	0	1	2	3	8	.257	.344
Home	.188	128	24	10	1	2	8	13	41	.273	.328	None on/out	.212	52	11	2	0	0	2	19	.255	.250
Away	.152	92	14	3	1	0	5	1	30	.170	.207	Batting #7	.179	78	14	5	1	1	5	4	24	.220	.308
First Pitch	.162	37	6	2	1	0	3	2	0	.225	.270	Batting #8	.169	136	23	7	1	1	8	9	44	.236	.257
Ahead on Count	.083	24	2	0	0	0	3	4	0	.214	.083	Other	.167	6	1	1	0	0	1	3	.286	.333
Behind on Count	.149	87	13	5	1	0	2	0	37	.159	.230	Pre-All Star	.186	102	19	6	1	1	5	7	37	.252	.294
Two Strikes	.145	131	19	7	1	1	5	8	71	.206	.237	Post-All Star	.161	118	19	7	1	1	8	7	34	.214	.263

Rick Cerone — Expos   Bats Right

	Avg	G	AB	R	H	2B	3B	HR	RBI	BB	SO	HBP	GDP	SB	CS	OBP	SLG	IBB	SH	SF	#Pit	#P/PA	GB	FB	G/F
1992 Season	.270	33	63	10	17	4	0	1	7	3	5	1	0	1	2	.313	.381	0	1	0	207	3.09	21	28	0.75
Last Five Years	.267	358	989	99	264	52	2	12	109	92	114	7	29	2	3	.332	.360	3	7	7	3829	3.50	339	335	1.01

1992 Season

	Avg	AB	H	2B	3B	HR	RBI	BB	SO	OBP	SLG		Avg	AB	H	2B	3B	HR	RBI	BB	SO	OBP	SLG
vs. Left	.276	29	8	1	0	1	2	2	0	.323	.414	Scoring Posn	.316	19	6	1	0	0	6	1	2	.350	.368
vs. Right	.265	34	9	3	0	0	5	1	5	.306	.353	Close & Late	.143	14	2	0	0	0	1	0	3	.143	.143

Last Five Years

	Avg	AB	H	2B	3B	HR	RBI	BB	SO	OBP	SLG		Avg	AB	H	2B	3B	HR	RBI	BB	SO	OBP	SLG
vs. Left	.298	420	125	26	1	5	52	36	44	.351	.400	Scoring Posn	.267	240	64	14	1	0	85	39	32	.365	.333
vs. Right	.244	569	139	26	1	7	57	56	70	.317	.330	Close & Late	.221	163	36	9	0	2	15	16	16	.293	.313
Groundball	.248	282	70	15	0	3	27	22	30	.304	.333	None on/out	.279	247	69	16	0	3	3	22	27	.346	.381
Flyball	.263	232	61	13	1	5	26	23	27	.327	.392	Batting #7	.297	390	116	22	1	4	41	42	39	.369	.390
Home	.300	540	162	32	1	8	71	46	56	.354	.407	Batting #9	.230	282	65	11	1	5	42	31	39	.305	.330
Away	.227	449	102	20	1	4	38	46	58	.306	.303	Other	.262	317	83	19	0	3	26	19	36	.308	.350
Day	.288	330	95	19	0	3	36	27	37	.344	.373	April	.367	128	47	9	0	4	21	10	17	.408	.531
Night	.256	659	169	33	2	9	73	65	77	.325	.354	May	.284	194	55	10	0	3	17	25	24	.368	.381
Grass	.267	793	212	40	2	10	91	73	89	.329	.361	June	.280	186	52	10	1	0	21	22	16	.362	.344
Turf	.265	196	52	12	0	2	18	19	25	.342	.357	July	.250	168	42	8	0	1	22	11	18	.301	.315
First Pitch	.310	174	54	10	2	1	20	2	0	.322	.408	August	.250	192	48	9	0	2	17	16	22	.306	.328
Ahead on Count	.315	235	74	16	0	5	32	49	0	.431	.447	September/October	.165	121	20	6	1	2	11	8	17	.221	.281
Behind on Count	.252	301	76	15	0	3	37	1	48	.256	.332	Pre-All Star	.297	563	167	32	1	7	65	62	63	.370	.394
Two Strikes	.182	374	68	16	0	3	30	40	112	.262	.249	Post-All Star	.228	426	97	20	1	5	44	30	51	.278	.315

Batter vs. Pitcher (since 1984)

Hits Best Against	Avg	AB	H	2B	3B	HR	RBI	BB	SO	OBP	SLG	Hits Worst Against	Avg	AB	H	2B	3B	HR	RBI	BB	SO	OBP	SLG
Nolan Ryan	.467	15	7	2	0	2	4	1	1	.500	1.000	Scott Bankhead	.091	11	1	0	0	0	0	0	3	.091	.091
Tom Browning	.385	13	5	0	0	0	3	2	1	.467	.385	Mitch Williams	.100	10	1	0	0	0	3	2	1	.231	.100
Bruce Hurst	.375	16	6	1	0	0	2	0	2	.375	.438	Mark Langston	.120	25	3	1	0	0	1	3	7	.207	.160
Charlie Leibrandt	.370	27	10	1	0	1	3	3	3	.433	.519	Danny Jackson	.176	17	3	0	0	0	0	1	2	.222	.176
Jimmy Key	.333	12	4	3	0	0	1	1	3	.385	.583	Chuck Finley	.200	10	2	0	0	0	2	1	2	.333	.200

Wes Chamberlain — Phillies   Bats Right

	Avg	G	AB	R	H	2B	3B	HR	RBI	BB	SO	HBP	GDP	SB	CS	OBP	SLG	IBB	SH	SF	#Pit	#P/PA	GB	FB	G/F
1992 Season	.258	76	275	26	71	18	0	9	41	10	55	1	7	4	0	.285	.422	2	1	2	913	3.17	92	86	1.07
Career (1990-1992)	.250	195	704	86	176	37	3	24	95	42	137	3	15	17	4	.294	.413	2	2	2	2565	3.42	241	208	1.16

1992 Season

	Avg	AB	H	2B	3B	HR	RBI	BB	SO	OBP	SLG		Avg	AB	H	2B	3B	HR	RBI	BB	SO	OBP	SLG
vs. Left	.260	104	27	8	0	3	15	5	15	.291	.423	Scoring Posn	.250	76	19	3	0	2	31	5	14	.298	.368
vs. Right	.257	171	44	10	0	6	26	5	40	.281	.421	Close & Late	.229	48	11	2	0	1	5	2	12	.275	.333
Home	.278	144	40	10	0	3	19	5	29	.300	.410	None on/out	.273	66	18	5	0	3	3	1	16	.284	.485
Away	.237	131	31	8	0	6	22	5	26	.268	.435	Batting #5	.310	58	18	5	0	1	13	4	9	.355	.448
First Pitch	.340	47	16	6	0	3	11	2	0	.373	.660	Batting #6	.242	182	44	11	0	6	22	6	38	.268	.401
Ahead on Count	.360	50	18	6	0	4	10	6	0	.429	.720	Other	.257	35	9	2	0	2	6	0	8	.250	.486
Behind on Count	.232	125	29	6	0	2	17	0	31	.230	.328	Pre-All Star	.256	164	42	11	0	6	21	3	34	.272	.433
Two Strikes	.188	128	24	5	0	2	15	2	55	.200	.273	Post-All Star	.261	111	29	7	0	3	20	7	21	.303	.405

Career (1990-1992)

	Avg	AB	H	2B	3B	HR	RBI	BB	SO	OBP	SLG		Avg	AB	H	2B	3B	HR	RBI	BB	SO	OBP	SLG
vs. Left	.268	269	72	17	1	11	43	21	40	.322	.461	Scoring Posn	.251	179	45	7	1	9	70	17	35	.320	.453
vs. Right	.239	435	104	20	2	13	52	21	97	.277	.384	Close & Late	.229	131	30	6	0	2	13	7	27	.273	.321
Groundball	.241	294	71	14	3	9	37	14	51	.281	.401	None on/out	.245	143	35	7	1	4	4	6	28	.280	.392
Flyball	.282	124	35	6	0	7	20	11	33	.338	.500	Batting #3	.234	342	80	15	3	9	37	29	66	.298	.374
Home	.272	382	104	21	1	12	51	20	72	.309	.427	Batting #6	.259	193	50	11	0	9	32	8	40	.291	.456

Career (1990-1992)

	Avg	AB	H	2B	3B	HR	RBI	BB	SO	OBP	SLG
Away	.224	322	72	16	2	12	44	22	65	.277	.398
Day	.245	208	51	16	0	7	29	12	38	.285	.423
Night	.252	496	125	21	3	17	66	30	99	.298	.409
Grass	.235	183	43	10	0	7	25	7	36	.266	.404
Turf	.255	521	133	27	3	17	70	35	101	.304	.417
First Pitch	.321	137	44	11	0	7	24	2	0	.338	.555
Ahead on Count	.382	131	50	13	0	8	23	24	0	.477	.664
Behind on Count	.235	268	63	10	2	6	35	0	74	.237	.354
Two Strikes	.165	316	52	11	2	7	36	16	137	.205	.278

	Avg	AB	H	2B	3B	HR	RBI	BB	SO	OBP	SLG
Other	.272	169	46	11	0	6	26	5	31	.291	.444
April	.207	82	17	4	0	3	9	1	21	.226	.366
May	.167	12	2	1	0	0	0	0	5	.167	.250
June	.333	102	34	8	0	3	12	4	10	.361	.500
July	.268	164	44	11	0	5	28	3	30	.297	.427
August	.262	168	44	6	2	8	28	19	34	.337	.464
September/October	.199	176	35	7	1	5	18	11	37	.250	.335
Pre-All Star	.270	230	62	15	0	7	27	5	42	.290	.426
Post-All Star	.241	474	114	22	3	17	68	37	95	.296	.407

Batter vs. Pitcher (career)

Hits Best Against	Avg	AB	H	2B	3B	HR	RBI	BB	SO	OBP	SLG
Mike Bielecki	.385	13	5	1	1	0	2	0	0	.385	.615
Doug Drabek	.308	13	4	0	0	0	2	0	5	.308	.308
Frank Castillo	.308	13	4	1	0	0	2	0	3	.308	.385

Hits Worst Against	Avg	AB	H	2B	3B	HR	RBI	BB	SO	OBP	SLG
Brian Barnes	.056	18	1	0	0	0	0	3	7	.190	.056
Dennis Martinez	.118	17	2	0	1	0	0	1	2	.167	.235
Greg Maddux	.182	22	4	1	0	0	0	0	5	.182	.227
Chris Nabholz	.211	19	4	1	0	0	1	2	0	.286	.263
Mike Morgan	.235	17	4	2	0	0	0	0	3	.235	.353

Darrin Chapin — Phillies

Pitches Right

	ERA	W	L	Sv	G	GS	IP	BB	SO	Avg	H	2B	3B	HR	RBI	OBP	SLG	GF	IR	IRS	Hld	SvOp	SB	CS	GB	FB	G/F
1992 Season	9.00	0	0	0	1	0	2.0	0	1	.250	2	1	0	1	2	.250	.750	0	0	0	0	0	0	0	1	3	0.33
Career (1991-1992)	6.14	0	1	0	4	0	7.1	6	6	.185	5	3	0	1	4	.333	.407	2	1	0	0	0	1	0	8	8	1.00

1992 Season

	ERA	W	L	Sv	G	GS	IP	H	HR	BB	SO		Avg	AB	H	2B	3B	HR	RBI	BB	SO	OBP	SLG
Home	0.00	0	0	0	0	0	0.0	0	0	0	0	vs. Left	.000	4	0	0	0	0	0	0	0	1	.000	.000
Away	9.00	0	0	0	1	0	2.0	2	1	0	1	vs. Right	.500	4	2	1	0	1	2	0	0	.500	1.500

Norm Charlton — Reds

Pitches Left (groundball pitcher)

	ERA	W	L	Sv	G	GS	IP	BB	SO	Avg	H	2B	3B	HR	RBI	OBP	SLG	GF	IR	IRS	Hld	SvOp	SB	CS	GB	FB	G/F
1992 Season	2.99	4	2	26	64	0	81.1	26	90	.262	79	18	1	7	41	.323	.397	46	27	10	7	34	15	4	98	61	1.61
Career (1988-1992)	3.00	31	24	29	238	37	500.2	190	421	.234	429	73	10	34	190	.310	.340	69	91	32	27	42	56	22	677	444	1.52

1992 Season

	ERA	W	L	Sv	G	GS	IP	H	HR	BB	SO		Avg	AB	H	2B	3B	HR	RBI	BB	SO	OBP	SLG
Home	2.27	2	1	13	34	0	39.2	37	3	10	40	vs. Left	.296	71	21	4	1	2	10	6	11	.359	.465
Away	3.67	2	1	13	30	0	41.2	42	4	16	50	vs. Right	.251	231	58	14	0	5	31	20	79	.313	.377
Day	3.86	2	0	7	21	0	25.2	27	4	9	31	Inning 1-6	.000	2	0	0	0	0	0	0	0	.000	.000
Night	2.59	2	2	19	43	0	55.2	52	3	17	59	Inning 7+	.263	300	79	18	1	7	41	26	90	.325	.400
Grass	2.45	2	1	8	17	0	25.2	24	1	9	24	None on	.242	161	39	9	0	4	4	11	47	.299	.373
Turf	3.23	2	1	18	47	0	55.2	55	6	17	66	Runners on	.284	141	40	9	1	3	37	15	43	.350	.426
April	2.70	0	0	7	11	0	13.1	9	2	6	13	Scoring Posn	.274	95	26	6	1	3	36	13	34	.351	.453
May	2.30	1	0	4	13	0	15.2	18	2	3	21	Close & Late	.249	189	47	8	1	4	28	23	52	.333	.365
June	1.84	2	0	6	11	0	14.2	12	2	5	17	None on/out	.313	67	21	6	0	2	2	9	16	.395	.493
July	2.40	0	0	7	10	0	15.0	11	0	2	14	vs. 1st Batr (relief)	.321	56	18	6	0	3	8	7	10	.397	.589
August	5.87	0	1	1	13	0	15.1	20	1	7	18	First Inning Pitched	.243	222	54	16	0	4	32	17	71	.299	.369
September/October	2.45	1	1	1	6	0	7.1	9	0	3	7	First 15 Pitches	.257	191	49	13	0	3	21	12	57	.304	.372
Starter	0.00	0	0	0	0	0	0.0	0	0	0	0	Pitch 16-30	.277	101	28	5	1	3	18	11	31	.351	.436
Reliever	2.99	4	2	26	64	0	81.1	79	7	26	90	Pitch 31-45	.200	10	2	0	0	1	2	3	2	.385	.500
0 Days rest	0.00	1	0	8	14	0	16.1	8	0	4	15	Pitch 46+	.000	0	0	0	0	0	0	0	0	.000	.000
1 or 2 Days rest	4.34	2	2	12	35	0	47.2	55	4	17	54	First Pitch	.413	46	19	4	0	1	13	4	0	.471	.565
3+ Days rest	2.08	1	0	6	15	0	17.1	16	3	5	21	Ahead on Count	.169	142	24	4	1	0	14	0	72	.171	.211
Pre-All Star	2.56	3	0	21	40	0	52.2	47	6	15	61	Behind on Count	.404	57	23	7	0	4	8	11	0	.507	.737
Post-All Star	3.77	1	2	5	24	0	28.2	32	1	11	29	Two Strikes	.158	146	23	6	1	1	18	11	90	.217	.233

Career (1988-1992)

	ERA	W	L	Sv	G	GS	IP	H	HR	BB	SO		Avg	AB	H	2B	3B	HR	RBI	BB	SO	OBP	SLG
Home	3.13	13	11	15	116	19	239.0	210	20	92	182	vs. Left	.224	393	88	15	2	7	54	49	88	.325	.326
Away	2.89	18	13	14	122	18	261.2	219	14	98	239	vs. Right	.237	1440	341	58	8	27	136	141	333	.306	.344
Day	3.30	8	9	8	75	13	155.2	141	12	48	144	Inning 1-6	.245	834	204	32	3	19	94	92	138	.325	.359
Night	2.87	23	15	21	163	24	345.0	288	22	142	277	Inning 7+	.225	999	225	41	7	15	96	98	283	.298	.325
Grass	2.32	14	8	8	68	7	136.0	105	6	55	114	None on	.221	1062	235	41	7	19	19	102	247	.297	.327
Turf	3.26	17	16	21	170	30	364.2	324	28	135	307	Runners on	.252	771	194	32	3	15	171	88	174	.328	.359
April	2.57	2	2	7	32	4	63.0	45	3	30	61	Scoring Posn	.236	470	111	20	2	8	148	62	117	.320	.338
May	4.00	6	4	5	42	5	69.2	72	7	25	57	Close & Late	.229	547	125	23	4	10	60	61	153	.308	.340
June	3.34	7	0	7	38	2	62.0	54	4	20	52	None on/out	.248	463	115	24	3	9	9	46	96	.320	.371
July	2.62	3	6	7	34	4	68.2	55	4	20	52	vs. 1st Batr (relief)	.303	178	54	13	2	5	26	18	42	.369	.483
August	2.61	5	4	2	45	10	117.1	96	7	47	94	First Inning Pitched	.236	800	189	37	3	12	101	85	204	.314	.335
September/October	3.06	8	8	1	47	12	120.0	105	10	48	104	First 15 Pitches	.241	740	178	33	4	11	74	79	173	.320	.341
Starter	3.43	13	15	0	37	37	230.2	208	19	90	136	Pitch 16-30	.237	434	103	18	3	6	46	43	116	.308	.334
Reliever	2.63	18	9	29	201	0	270.0	221	15	100	285	Pitch 31-45	.181	210	38	6	1	5	16	20	54	.251	.290

Career (1988-1992)

	ERA	W	L	Sv	G	GS	IP	H	HR	BB	SO		Avg	AB	H	2B	3B	HR	RBI	BB	SO	OBP	SLG
0 Days rest	2.15	3	4	8	47	0	58.2	42	1	20	66	Pitch 46+	.245	449	110	16	2	12	54	48	78	.323	.370
1 or 2 Days rest	3.32	11	3	14	103	0	143.2	134	9	52	140	First Pitch	.326	307	100	19	2	3	48	16	0	.366	.430
3+ Days rest	1.60	4	2	7	51	0	67.2	45	5	28	79	Ahead on Count	.166	817	136	17	2	10	58	0	355	.171	.229
Pre-All Star	3.38	15	9	23	125	11	213.0	192	14	80	191	Behind on Count	.291	371	108	19	3	16	48	100	4	.447	.488
Post-All Star	2.72	16	15	6	113	26	287.2	237	20	140	230	Two Strikes	.144	800	115	19	2	6	53	73	421	.218	.195

Pitcher vs. Batter (career)

Pitches Best Vs.	Avg	AB	H	2B	3B	HR	RBI	BB	SO	OBP	SLG	Pitches Worst Vs.	Avg	AB	H	2B	3B	HR	RBI	BB	SO	OBP	SLG
Lenny Dykstra	.000	10	0	0	0	0	0	1	4	.091	.000	Terry Pendleton	.500	18	9	1	1	1	6	1	1	.526	.833
Tom Pagnozzi	.000	10	0	0	0	0	0	1	2	.091	.000	Jay Bell	.500	14	7	0	0	1	2	0	0	.500	.714
Ken Caminiti	.038	26	1	0	0	1	3	2	6	.107	.154	Jeff Bagwell	.500	8	4	1	0	1	2	3	1	.636	1.000
Kevin Bass	.056	18	1	1	0	0	1	0	5	.053	.111	Jose Oquendo	.417	12	5	1	0	1	3	3	0	.533	.750
Bobby Thompson	.091	11	1	0	0	0	0	1	4	.091	.091	Lonnie Smith	.412	17	7	1	1	2	3	2	4	.474	.941

Scott Chiamparino — Rangers   Pitches Right (groundball pitcher)

	ERA	W	L	Sv	G	GS	IP	BB	SO	Avg	H	2B	3B	HR	RBI	OBP	SLG	CG	ShO	Sup	QS	#P/S	SB	CS	GB	FB	G/F
1992 Season	3.55	0	4	0	4	4	25.1	5	13	.260	25	5	1	2	9	.294	.396	0	0	2.13	2	86	1	1	40	25	1.60
Career (1990-1992)	3.27	2	6	0	15	15	85.1	29	40	.265	87	14	2	4	31	.327	.357	0	0	3.80	8	86	5	4	147	85	1.73

1992 Season

	ERA	W	L	Sv	G	GS	IP	H	HR	BB	SO		Avg	AB	H	2B	3B	HR	RBI	BB	SO	OBP	SLG
Home	6.75	0	1	0	1	1	5.1	8	2	1	3	vs. Left	.310	42	13	2	1	1	3	4	6	.370	.476
Away	2.70	0	3	0	3	3	20.0	17	0	4	10	vs. Right	.222	54	12	3	0	1	6	1	7	.232	.333

Mike Christopher — Indians   Pitches Right (flyball pitcher)

	ERA	W	L	Sv	G	GS	IP	BB	SO	Avg	H	2B	3B	HR	RBI	OBP	SLG	GF	IR	IRS	Hld	SvOp	SB	CS	GB	FB	G/F
1992 Season	3.00	0	0	0	10	0	18.0	10	13	.254	17	4	2	2	9	.346	.463	4	13	4	1	0	2	2	20	24	0.83
Career (1991-1992)	2.45	0	0	0	13	0	22.0	13	15	.241	19	5	2	2	9	.344	.430	6	13	4	2	0	2	2	24	28	0.86

1992 Season

	ERA	W	L	Sv	G	GS	IP	H	HR	BB	SO		Avg	AB	H	2B	3B	HR	RBI	BB	SO	OBP	SLG
Home	4.91	0	0	0	3	0	7.1	8	2	4	4	vs. Left	.278	18	5	1	1	0	2	5	3	.435	.444
Away	1.69	0	0	0	7	0	10.2	9	0	6	9	vs. Right	.245	49	12	3	1	2	7	5	10	.309	.469

Archi Cianfrocco — Expos   Bats Right

	Avg	G	AB	R	H	2B	3B	HR	RBI	BB	SO	HBP	GDP	SB	CS	OBP	SLG	IBB	SH	SF	#Pit	#P/PA	GB	FB	G/F
1992 Season	.241	86	232	25	56	5	2	6	30	11	66	1	2	3	0	.276	.358	0	1	2	932	3.79	67	56	1.20

1992 Season

	Avg	AB	H	2B	3B	HR	RBI	BB	SO	OBP	SLG		Avg	AB	H	2B	3B	HR	RBI	BB	SO	OBP	SLG
vs. Left	.247	97	24	2	2	4	17	6	25	.286	.433	Scoring Posn	.230	61	14	0	1	1	22	4	22	.269	.311
vs. Right	.237	135	32	3	0	2	13	5	41	.270	.304	Close & Late	.356	45	16	1	1	0	5	3	14	.396	.422
Home	.198	96	19	0	1	3	16	7	28	.260	.313	None on/out	.264	53	14	2	0	1	1	1	11	.278	.358
Away	.272	136	37	5	1	3	14	4	38	.289	.390	Batting #6	.283	46	13	1	1	2	10	0	13	.298	.478
First Pitch	.423	26	11	3	0	0	1	0	0	.423	.538	Batting #7	.221	95	21	0	0	4	9	5	25	.260	.347
Ahead on Count	.267	30	8	0	0	1	6	6	0	.385	.367	Other	.242	91	22	4	1	0	11	6	28	.283	.308
Behind on Count	.178	90	16	1	1	2	6	0	38	.185	.278	Pre-All Star	.246	191	47	3	2	6	28	6	54	.270	.377
Two Strikes	.150	120	18	1	0	2	11	5	66	.184	.208	Post-All Star	.220	41	9	2	0	0	2	5	12	.304	.268

Dave Clark — Pirates   Bats Left (groundball hitter)

	Avg	G	AB	R	H	2B	3B	HR	RBI	BB	SO	HBP	GDP	SB	CS	OBP	SLG	IBB	SH	SF	#Pit	#P/PA	GB	FB	G/F
1992 Season	.212	23	33	3	7	0	0	2	7	6	8	0	0	0	0	.325	.394	0	0	1	158	3.95	15	8	1.88
Last Five Years	.252	283	623	58	157	20	3	18	75	62	140	0	19	7	5	.317	.380	8	1	5	2521	3.65	268	122	2.20

1992 Season

	Avg	AB	H	2B	3B	HR	RBI	BB	SO	OBP	SLG		Avg	AB	H	2B	3B	HR	RBI	BB	SO	OBP	SLG
vs. Left	.000	1	0	0	0	0	0	0	1	.000	.000	Scoring Posn	.100	10	1	0	0	1	6	3	6	.286	.400
vs. Right	.219	32	7	0	0	2	7	6	7	.333	.406	Close & Late	.250	12	3	0	0	1	4	3	4	.375	.500

Last Five Years

	Avg	AB	H	2B	3B	HR	RBI	BB	SO	OBP	SLG		Avg	AB	H	2B	3B	HR	RBI	BB	SO	OBP	SLG
vs. Left	.150	20	3	0	0	0	1	0	11	.143	.150	Scoring Posn	.230	161	37	5	1	2	55	30	44	.342	.311
vs. Right	.255	603	154	20	3	18	74	62	129	.323	.388	Close & Late	.225	160	36	2	1	4	20	16	41	.292	.325
Groundball	.278	169	47	5	0	6	29	16	33	.341	.414	None on/out	.229	153	35	4	0	7	7	11	32	.280	.392
Flyball	.292	171	50	5	1	9	26	21	38	.368	.491	Batting #5	.211	152	32	4	1	2	14	16	39	.286	.289
Home	.254	342	87	13	3	11	46	33	80	.318	.406	Batting #6	.250	132	33	4	0	5	10	12	25	.313	.394
Away	.249	281	70	7	0	7	29	29	60	.316	.349	Other	.271	339	92	12	2	11	51	34	76	.333	.416
Day	.275	265	73	12	2	10	39	28	58	.341	.449	April	.265	68	18	3	0	2	6	7	16	.333	.397
Night	.235	358	84	8	1	8	36	34	82	.299	.330	May	.173	104	18	0	0	5	11	12	23	.256	.317
Grass	.248	492	122	20	3	12	56	45	113	.309	.374	June	.228	136	31	5	2	2	18	17	29	.314	.338

	Avg	AB	H	2B	3B	HR	RBI	BB	SO	OBP	SLG		Avg	AB	H	2B	3B	HR	RBI	BB	SO	OBP	SLG
										Last Five Years													
Turf	.267	131	35	0	0	6	19	17	27	.347	.405	July	.346	78	27	6	0	3	12	7	18	.395	.538
First Pitch	.302	96	29	5	0	3	13	4	0	.324	.448	August	.236	110	26	2	1	3	13	6	32	.274	.355
Ahead on Count	.392	143	56	9	2	5	27	32	0	.500	.587	September/October	.291	127	37	4	0	3	15	13	22	.352	.394
Behind on Count	.187	198	37	3	1	3	15	0	69	.186	.258	Pre-All Star	.226	337	76	11	2	10	39	39	75	.304	.359
Two Strikes	.161	286	46	3	1	4	19	25	140	.228	.220	Post-All Star	.283	286	81	9	1	6	36	23	65	.333	.406

										Batter vs. Pitcher (career)													
Hits Best Against	Avg	AB	H	2B	3B	HR	RBI	BB	SO	OBP	SLG	Hits Worst Against	Avg	AB	H	2B	3B	HR	RBI	BB	SO	OBP	SLG
Mike Morgan	.364	11	4	0	0	1	3	0	2	.364	.636	Chris Bosio	.000	12	0	0	0	0	0	0	5	.000	.000
Mike Moore	.333	18	6	2	0	0	0	1	3	.368	.444	Dave Stewart	.059	17	1	1	0	0	1	0	4	.059	.118
												Bert Blyleven	.083	12	1	1	0	0	0	1	3	.154	.167
												Bobby Witt	.111	9	1	0	0	0	0	2	1	.273	.111
												Bob Tewksbury	.182	11	2	1	0	0	1	0	1	.182	.273

Jack Clark — Red Sox

Bats Right (flyball hitter)

	Avg	G	AB	R	H	2B	3B	HR	RBI	BB	SO	HBP	GDP	SB	CS	OBP	SLG	IBB	SH	SF	#Pit	#P/PA	GB	FB	G/F
1992 Season	.210		257		54	11	0	5	33	56	87	2	4	1	1	.350	.405	3	0	5	1358	4.24	71	68	1.04
Last Five Years	.244	628	2023	323	493	74	3	111	369	501	597	10	58	14	10	.393	.446	41	0	22	10606	4.15	556	560	0.99

											1992 Season									
	Avg	AB	H	2B	3B	HR	RBI	BB	SO	OBP	SLG		Avg	AB	H	2B	3B	HR	RBI	BB	SO	OBP	SLG
vs. Left	.295	95	28	6	0	2	14	30	27	.460	.421	Scoring Posn	.192	73	14	3	0	2	29	16	29	.319	.315
vs. Right	.160	162	26	5	0	3	19	26	60	.278	.247	Close & Late	.177	62	11	3	0	0	6	8	19	.268	.226
Groundball	.254	67	17	3	0	2	12	19	23	.425	.388	None on/out	.250	64	16	0	0	2	2	14	19	.385	.344
Flyball	.212	66	14	4	0	2	7	10	20	.325	.364	Batting #4	.226	93	21	3	0	3	17	21	31	.361	.355
Home	.259	116	30	6	0	0	10	27	32	.390	.310	Batting #5	.258	93	24	6	0	1	22	30	.400	.355
Away	.170	141	24	5	0	5	23	29	55	.316	.312	Other	.127	71	9	2	0	1	9	13	26	.267	.197
Day	.264	72	19	3	0	3	14	22	24	.433	.431	April	.125	48	6	1	0	0	1	7	18	.236	.146
Night	.189	185	35	8	0	2	19	34	63	.314	.265	May	.246	69	17	2	0	2	18	20	24	.402	.362
Grass	.205	229	47	11	0	3	24	49	78	.344	.293	June	.268	56	15	4	0	1	5	11	17	.386	.393
Turf	.250	28	7	0	0	2	9	7	9	.400	.464	July	.167	36	6	1	0	0	2	9	9	.333	.194
First Pitch	.357	28	10	1	0	2	9	2	0	.382	.607	August	.208	48	10	3	0	2	7	9	19	.345	.396
Ahead on Count	.386	44	17	5	0	1	9	31	0	.640	.568	September/October	.000	0	0	0	0	0	0	0	0	.000	.000
Behind on Count	.143	77	11	3	0	1	9	0	40	.154	.221	Pre-All Star	.214	196	42	8	0	3	24	44	64	.354	.301
Two Strikes	.123	155	19	4	0	1	12	23	87	.233	.168	Post-All Star	.197	61	12	3	0	2	9	12	23	.338	.344

									1992 By Position										
Position	Avg	AB	H	2B	3B	HR	RBI	BB	SO	OBP	SLG	G	GS	Innings	PO	A	E	DP	Fld Pct	Rng Fctr	In Zone	Zone Outs	MLB Zone Rtg
As Designated Hitter	.184	212	39	9	0	3	24	44	72	.323	.269	64	62	---	---	---	---	---	---	---	---	---	---
As 1b	.317	41	13	2	0	2	9	11	15	.462	.512	13	12	97.0	111	8	1	7	.992	---	23	19	.826 .843

											Last Five Years									
	Avg	AB	H	2B	3B	HR	RBI	BB	SO	OBP	SLG		Avg	AB	H	2B	3B	HR	RBI	BB	SO	OBP	SLG
vs. Left	.301	598	180	30	1	31	104	202	153	.474	.510	Scoring Posn	.249	579	144	21	0	35	260	197	180	.429	.466
vs. Right	.220	1425	313	44	2	80	265	299	444	.355	.422	Close & Late	.206	360	74	8	0	20	52	81	112	.349	.394
Groundball	.243	593	144	20	1	30	118	145	176	.391	.432	None on/out	.229	503	115	13	1	24	24	105	157	.365	.402
Flyball	.243	518	126	18	1	31	97	119	145	.386	.461	Batting #4	.249	1536	383	58	3	91	297	385	447	.398	.469
Home	.252	968	249	38	1	58	190	239	287	.395	.469	Batting #5	.261	268	70	13	0	12	41	60	77	.400	.444
Away	.236	1035	244	36	2	53	179	262	310	.391	.428	Other	.183	219	40	3	0	8	31	56	73	.349	.306
Day	.253	569	144	23	0	32	108	128	173	.391	.462	April	.220	277	61	5	0	15	48	72	105	.379	.401
Night	.240	1454	349	51	3	79	261	373	424	.393	.442	May	.225	338	76	13	0	11	52	97	110	.392	.361
Grass	.237	1661	393	61	1	90	283	399	500	.383	.437	June	.230	365	84	9	1	21	60	83	108	.374	.433
Turf	.276	362	100	13	2	21	86	102	97	.434	.497	July	.267	374	100	10	0	22	79	73	96	.384	.471
First Pitch	.354	243	86	16	0	15	54	14	0	.383	.605	August	.241	344	83	20	2	20	71	81	89	.390	.485
Ahead on Count	.371	348	129	21	1	30	101	230	0	.619	.695	September/October	.274	325	89	17	0	22	59	95	89	.438	.529
Behind on Count	.199	657	131	16	0	28	108	4	268	.207	.352	Pre-All Star	.228	1090	249	28	1	52	180	276	351	.382	.399
Two Strikes	.155	1130	175	27	1	43	140	245	595	.306	.295	Post-All Star	.262	933	244	46	2	59	189	225	246	.406	.505

											Batter vs. Pitcher (since 1984)									
Hits Best Against	Avg	AB	H	2B	3B	HR	RBI	BB	SO	OBP	SLG	Hits Worst Against	Avg	AB	H	2B	3B	HR	RBI	BB	SO	OBP	SLG
Bruce Ruffin	.556	9	5	0	0	1	4	6	3	.688	.889	Mike Boddicker	.000	16	0	0	0	0	0	1	7	.059	.000
Lee Smith	.500	14	7	0	2	1	7	4	0	.611	1.000	Bill Swift	.000	14	0	0	0	0	0	0	5	.000	.000
David Wells	.500	10	5	1	0	2	4	1	1	.545	1.200	Tom Candiotti	.000	12	0	0	0	0	1	1	6	.071	.000
Craig Lefferts	.455	11	5	1	0	4	9	4	2	.600	1.636	Scott Erickson	.000	10	0	0	0	0	0	1	3	.091	.000
Storm Davis	.400	10	4	1	0	2	5	4	1	.571	1.100	John Smiley	.000	9	0	0	0	0	0	2	4	.182	.000

Jerald Clark — Padres — Bats Right

	Avg	G	AB	R	H	2B	3B	HR	RBI	BB	SO	HBP	GDP	SB	CS	OBP	SLG	IBB	SH	SF	#Pit	#P/PA	GB	FB	G/F
1992 Season	.242	146	496	45	120	22	6	12	58	22	97	4	7	3	0	.278	.383	3	1	3	1789	3.41	151	148	1.02
Career (1988-1992)	.237	339	1022	88	242	45	7	28	126	61	224	10	20	5	2	.284	.377	5	2	8	3627	3.48	323	285	1.13

1992 Season

	Avg	AB	H	2B	3B	HR	RBI	BB	SO	OBP	SLG
vs. Left	.276	152	42	9	2	6	20	6	26	.306	.480
vs. Right	.227	344	78	13	4	6	38	16	71	.266	.340
Groundball	.272	202	55	10	3	3	22	10	34	.308	.396
Flyball	.231	104	24	3	1	4	15	2	27	.252	.394
Home	.255	247	63	9	3	9	34	11	40	.292	.425
Away	.229	249	57	13	3	3	24	11	57	.264	.341
Day	.250	148	37	6	0	4	15	6	26	.279	.372
Night	.239	348	83	16	6	8	43	16	71	.278	.388
Grass	.268	355	95	17	5	12	52	17	61	.302	.445
Turf	.177	141	25	5	1	0	6	5	36	.216	.227
First Pitch	.288	66	19	5	0	2	9	3	0	.314	.455
Ahead on Count	.291	103	30	7	2	3	15	5	0	.327	.485
Behind on Count	.197	208	41	8	2	2	14	0	65	.209	.284
Two Strikes	.144	222	32	7	2	2	15	14	97	.202	.221
Scoring Posn	.263	118	31	2	4	4	45	10	19	.323	.449
Close & Late	.211	95	20	3	1	3	17	4	18	.240	.358
None on/out	.268	127	34	7	0	2	2	5	23	.295	.370
Batting #6	.167	132	22	5	0	5	12	6	31	.203	.318
Batting #7	.277	282	78	15	6	6	38	13	51	.312	.436
Other	.244	82	20	2	0	1	8	3	15	.279	.305
April	.181	83	15	2	0	4	8	8	19	.261	.349
May	.187	91	17	3	0	0	4	3	18	.211	.220
June	.220	50	11	4	1	0	3	3	8	.273	.340
July	.376	85	32	6	2	3	17	7	14	.424	.600
August	.273	77	21	3	1	2	6	0	10	.291	.416
September/October	.218	110	24	4	2	3	20	1	28	.223	.373
Pre-All Star	.227	255	58	11	1	7	25	18	49	.282	.361
Post-All Star	.257	241	62	11	5	5	33	4	48	.274	.407

1992 By Position

Position	Avg	AB	H	2B	3B	HR	RBI	BB	SO	OBP	SLG	G	GS	Innings	PO	A	E	DP	Fld Pct	Rng Fctr	In Zone	Outs	Zone Rtg	MLB Zone
As Pinch Hitter	.222	9	2	0	0	0	1	0	1	.222	.222	10	0	---	---	---	---	---	---	---	---	---	---	---
As 1b	.400	15	6	1	0	0	1	2	2	.444	.467	11	4	50.0	59	0	0	1	1.000	---	3	3	1.000	.843
As lf	.226	398	90	17	4	11	45	19	80	.268	.372	115	107	958.0	241	9	3	2	.988	2.35	267	230	.861	.809
As rf	.310	71	22	4	2	1	11	0	14	.306	.465	22	18	167.0	40	4	0	1	1.000	2.21	42	40	.952	.814

Career (1988-1992)

	Avg	AB	H	2B	3B	HR	RBI	BB	SO	OBP	SLG
vs. Left	.223	355	79	13	3	12	36	19	76	.265	.377
vs. Right	.244	667	163	32	4	16	90	42	148	.295	.376
Groundball	.277	390	108	18	3	11	56	21	71	.316	.423
Flyball	.232	207	48	9	2	8	27	10	60	.276	.411
Home	.229	512	117	22	3	20	74	29	100	.275	.400
Away	.245	510	125	23	4	8	52	32	124	.293	.353
Day	.241	303	73	13	1	7	32	21	62	.292	.360
Night	.235	719	169	32	6	21	94	40	162	.281	.384
Grass	.247	746	184	34	6	26	109	43	162	.290	.413
Turf	.210	276	58	11	1	2	17	18	62	.268	.279
First Pitch	.346	156	54	11	1	5	31	5	0	.370	.526
Ahead on Count	.286	185	53	8	2	10	30	16	0	.345	.514
Behind on Count	.189	403	76	15	2	4	30	0	134	.198	.266
Two Strikes	.135	467	63	16	2	3	29	40	224	.211	.197
Scoring Posn	.242	248	60	7	4	8	95	15	45	.292	.399
Close & Late	.210	195	41	6	1	5	29	8	48	.243	.328
None on/out	.243	267	65	13	1	3	3	15	60	.286	.333
Batting #6	.224	304	68	13	1	9	32	16	75	.269	.362
Batting #7	.247	396	98	17	6	9	50	18	80	.285	.389
Other	.236	322	76	15	0	10	44	27	69	.297	.376
April	.224	165	37	5	0	7	21	17	37	.304	.382
May	.216	148	32	7	0	0	8	6	35	.250	.264
June	.261	142	37	10	1	5	20	15	19	.340	.451
July	.282	177	50	9	2	5	25	11	39	.324	.441
August	.237	152	36	6	1	3	12	5	27	.273	.349
September/October	.210	238	50	8	3	8	40	7	67	.232	.370
Pre-All Star	.249	511	127	25	1	16	61	43	102	.313	.395
Post-All Star	.225	511	115	20	6	12	65	18	122	.255	.358

Batter vs. Pitcher (career)

Hits Best Against	Avg	AB	H	2B	3B	HR	RBI	BB	SO	OBP	SLG
Orel Hershiser	.467	15	7	2	0	0	0	0	2	.467	.600
Mike Morgan	.389	18	7	2	0	1	3	0	2	.389	.667
Randy Tomlin	.385	13	5	1	0	1	2	0	0	.385	.692
Bud Black	.364	11	4	0	0	2	6	1	3	.417	.909
Bobby Ojeda	.353	17	6	0	1	2	5	1	4	.389	.824

Hits Worst Against	Avg	AB	H	2B	3B	HR	RBI	BB	SO	OBP	SLG
Danny Jackson	.000	13	0	0	0	0	0	0	4	.000	.000
Charlie Leibrandt	.000	11	0	0	0	0	0	0	1	.000	.000
John Smoltz	.000	11	0	0	0	0	0	0	1	.000	.000
Jose Rijo	.053	19	1	0	0	0	0	1	8	.100	.053
Frank Viola	.182	11	2	0	0	0	0	0	4	.182	.182

Mark Clark — Cardinals — Pitches Right

	ERA	W	L	Sv	G	GS	IP	BB	SO	Avg	H	2B	3B	HR	RBI	OBP	SLG	CG	ShO	Sup	QS	#P/S	SB	CS	GB	FB	G/F
1992 Season	4.45	3	10	0	20	20	113.1	36	44	.265	117	18	4	12	46	.318	.406	1	1	3.18	10	80	17	2	156	147	1.06
Career (1991-1992)	4.38	4	11	0	27	22	135.2	47	57	.258	134	20	4	15	55	.315	.398	1	1	3.78	11	81	22	3	184	179	1.03

1992 Season

	ERA	W	L	Sv	G	GS	IP	H	HR	BB	SO
Home	5.25	1	6	0	9	9	48.0	45	9	15	16
Away	3.86	2	4	0	11	11	65.1	72	3	21	28
Starter	4.45	3	10	0	20	20	113.1	117	12	36	44
Reliever	0.00	0	0	0	0	0	0.0	0	0	0	0
0-3 Days Rest	4.50	0	1	0	1	1	6.0	4	2	1	0
4 Days Rest	4.18	2	4	0	10	10	56.0	51	3	25	20
5+ Days Rest	4.73	1	5	0	9	9	51.1	62	7	10	24
Pre-All Star	2.79	2	3	0	8	8	51.2	42	5	14	18
Post-All Star	5.84	1	7	0	12	12	61.2	75	7	22	26

	Avg	AB	H	2B	3B	HR	RBI	BB	SO	OBP	SLG
vs. Left	.266	263	70	12	2	6	29	25	25	.326	.395
vs. Right	.264	178	47	6	2	6	17	11	19	.305	.421
Scoring Posn	.214	103	22	5	2	2	32	10	16	.274	.359
Close & Late	.333	21	7	2	1	0	3	0	1	.333	.524
None on/out	.263	114	30	7	0	3	3	7	11	.306	.404
First Pitch	.327	98	32	7	2	4	19	2	0	.337	.561
Behind on Count	.308	107	33	6	1	2	9	17	0	.397	.439
Ahead on Count	.196	163	32	2	1	3	12	0	38	.195	.276
Two Strikes	.199	161	32	2	1	4	12	17	44	.274	.298

Phil Clark — Tigers   Bats Right (groundball hitter)

	Avg	G	AB	R	H	2B	3B	HR	RBI	BB	SO	HBP	GDP	SB	CS	OBP	SLG	IBB	SH	SF	#Pit	#P/PA	GB	FB	G/F
1992 Season	.407	23	54	3	22	4	0	1	5	6	9	0	2	1	0	.467	.537	1	1	0	224	3.73	22	10	2.20

1992 Season

	Avg	AB	H	2B	3B	HR	RBI	BB	SO	OBP	SLG		Avg	AB	H	2B	3B	HR	RBI	BB	SO	OBP	SLG
vs. Left	.487	39	19	4	0	1	5	4	6	.535	.667	Scoring Posn	.455	11	5	0	0	0	3	2	2	.538	.455
vs. Right	.200	15	3	0	0	0	2	3		.294	.200	Close & Late	.333	12	4	0	0	1	2	2	.429	.333

Will Clark — Giants   Bats Left (flyball hitter)

	Avg	G	AB	R	H	2B	3B	HR	RBI	BB	SO	HBP	GDP	SB	CS	OBP	SLG	IBB	SH	SF	#Pit	#P/PA	GB	FB	G/F
1992 Season	.300	144	513	69	154	40	1	16	73	73	82	4	5	12	7	.384	.476	23	0	11	2111	3.51	152	169	0.90
Last Five Years	.302	767	2841	450	859	166	28	116	504	360	502	18	32	41	15	.379	.503	85	0	46	11747	3.60	858	919	0.93

1992 Season

	Avg	AB	H	2B	3B	HR	RBI	BB	SO	OBP	SLG		Avg	AB	H	2B	3B	HR	RBI	BB	SO	OBP	SLG
vs. Left	.307	205	63	12	0	2	30	21	31	.366	.395	Scoring Posn	.330	112	37	9	0	5	55	36	27	.459	.545
vs. Right	.295	308	91	28	1	14	43	52	51	.396	.529	Close & Late	.264	87	23	6	0	2	12	21	18	.404	.402
Groundball	.295	210	62	14	1	11	35	45	32	.416	.529	None on/out	.253	87	22	6	1	3	3	7	13	.323	.448
Flyball	.281	89	25	11	0	2	14	7	12	.330	.472	Batting #3	.299	511	153	40	1	15	70	73	82	.385	.470
Home	.337	270	91	26	1	11	44	42	39	.422	.563	Batting #5	.000	0	0	0	0	0	1	0	0	.000	.000
Away	.259	243	63	14	0	5	29	31	43	.342	.379	Other	.500	2	1	0	0	1	2	0	0	.500	2.000
Day	.288	212	61	20	1	4	19	34	38	.389	.448	April	.346	81	28	7	1	1	11	16	15	.444	.494
Night	.309	301	93	20	0	12	54	39	44	.381	.495	May	.287	94	27	5	0	3	11	16	17	.393	.436
Grass	.319	379	121	30	1	12	55	61	62	.409	.499	June	.324	71	23	5	0	4	11	10	7	.402	.563
Turf	.246	134	33	10	0	4	18	12	20	.311	.410	July	.283	92	26	8	0	3	16	8	18	.340	.467
First Pitch	.333	93	31	10	0	2	17	20	0	.437	.505	August	.260	96	25	8	0	3	16	14	13	.359	.438
Ahead on Count	.375	112	42	10	0	3	18	32	0	.507	.545	September/October	.316	79	25	7	0	2	8	9	12	.374	.481
Behind on Count	.261	161	42	8	0	3	15	0	41	.270	.366	Pre-All Star	.318	296	94	21	1	10	41	49	47	.411	.497
Two Strikes	.208	221	46	13	0	6	24	22	82	.285	.348	Post-All Star	.276	217	60	19	0	6	32	24	35	.347	.447

1992 By Position

Position	Avg	AB	H	2B	3B	HR	RBI	BB	SO	OBP	SLG	G	GS	Innings	PO	A	E	DP	Fld Pct	Rng Fctr	In Zone	Outs	Zone Rtg	MLB Zone
As 1b	.299	511	153	40	1	15	70	73	82	.385	.476	141	141	1229.2	1277	103	10	130	.993	---	238	197	828	843

Last Five Years

	Avg	AB	H	2B	3B	HR	RBI	BB	SO	OBP	SLG		Avg	AB	H	2B	3B	HR	RBI	BB	SO	OBP	SLG
vs. Left	.291	1087	316	52	12	35	207	95	189	.348	.457	Scoring Posn	.331	752	249	47	10	39	384	170	149	.435	.576
vs. Right	.310	1754	543	114	16	81	297	265	313	.397	.531	Close & Late	.274	457	125	23	5	17	89	75	100	.373	.457
Groundball	.305	994	303	55	7	36	169	143	183	.392	.483	None on/out	.282	525	148	24	6	20	20	44	82	.344	.465
Flyball	.299	646	193	39	4	33	113	68	109	.365	.525	Batting #3	.304	2818	856	166	28	115	500	355	494	.380	.505
Home	.306	1409	431	93	13	59	256	186	244	.382	.516	Batting #4	.091	11	1	0	0	0	1	0	3	.083	.091
Away	.299	1432	428	73	15	57	248	174	258	.376	.490	Other	.167	12	2	0	0	1	3	5	5	.389	.417
Day	.309	1110	343	79	15	48	199	164	198	.398	.537	April	.323	415	134	24	7	17	81	60	66	.407	.537
Night	.298	1731	516	87	13	68	305	196	304	.366	.481	May	.261	506	132	26	3	26	86	62	96	.343	.478
Grass	.306	2079	641	123	20	82	370	267	372	.384	.505	June	.327	443	145	20	6	23	100	65	67	.406	.555
Turf	.286	762	218	43	8	34	134	93	130	.364	.497	July	.301	479	144	27	3	16	78	54	97	.372	.470
First Pitch	.342	485	166	32	5	20	90	44	0	.395	.553	August	.309	518	160	40	4	19	88	56	92	.377	.512
Ahead on Count	.406	586	238	47	6	34	144	190	0	.542	.681	September/October	.300	448	144	29	5	15	71	63	84	.375	.475
Behind on Count	.246	934	230	36	8	28	135	2	264	.250	.392	Pre-All Star	.300	1522	456	76	18	73	293	213	261	.383	.517
Two Strikes	.213	1251	267	52	13	37	155	108	502	.277	.365	Post-All Star	.306	1319	403	90	10	43	211	147	241	.374	.487

Batter vs. Pitcher (career)

Hits Best Against	Avg	AB	H	2B	3B	HR	RBI	BB	SO	OBP	SLG	Hits Worst Against	Avg	AB	H	2B	3B	HR	RBI	BB	SO	OBP	SLG
Greg Mathews	.700	10	7	0	0	2	4	1	1	.727	1.300	Chris Nabholz	.000	12	0	0	0	0	0	1	0	.077	.000
Ron Robinson	.632	19	12	2	1	1	5	3	0	.682	1.000	Frank DiPino	.000	11	0	0	0	0	0	4	1	.267	.000
Todd Worrell	.600	10	6	2	0	1	3	3	2	.692	1.000	Mike Harkey	.000	11	0	0	0	0	0	1	3	.083	.000
Derek Lilliquist	.526	19	10	3	0	2	3	1	2	.550	1.000	Terry Mulholland	.071	28	2	1	0	1	4	0	7	.071	.214
Jimmy Jones	.444	18	8	2	1	2	7	4	2	.545	1.000	Norm Charlton	.105	19	2	0	0	0	0	2	5	.190	.105

Royce Clayton — Giants   Bats Right (groundball hitter)

	Avg	G	AB	R	H	2B	3B	HR	RBI	BB	SO	HBP	GDP	SB	CS	OBP	SLG	IBB	SH	SF	#Pit	#P/PA	GB	FB	G/F
1992 Season	.224	98	321	31	72	7	4	4	24	26	63	0	11	8	4	.281	.308	3	3	2	1339	3.84	144	71	2.03
Career (1991-1992)	.216	107	347	31	75	8	4	4	26	27	69	0	11	8	4	.271	.297	3	3	2	1431	3.81	152	79	1.92

1992 Season

	Avg	AB	H	2B	3B	HR	RBI	BB	SO	OBP	SLG		Avg	AB	H	2B	3B	HR	RBI	BB	SO	OBP	SLG
vs. Left	.250	96	24	4	2	0	4	11	21	.327	.333	Scoring Posn	.183	82	15	1	3	1	20	9	13	.258	.305
vs. Right	.213	225	48	3	2	4	20	15	42	.260	.298	Close & Late	.197	61	12	0	0	0	2	7	14	.279	.197
Groundball	.185	168	31	4	2	2	13	9	32	.225	.268	None on/out	.286	77	22	1	0	2	2	7	14	.345	.377
Flyball	.245	49	12	1	1	1	3	7	12	.333	.367	Batting #7	.224	58	13	3	0	1	5	5	19	.281	.328
Home	.250	172	43	3	2	3	15	15	23	.309	.343	Batting #8	.221	222	49	3	3	3	18	21	36	.287	.302
Away	.195	149	29	4	2	1	9	11	40	.248	.268	Other	.244	41	10	1	1	0	1	0	8	.244	.317

1992 Season

	Avg	AB	H	2B	3B	HR	RBI	BB	SO	OBP	SLG		Avg	AB	H	2B	3B	HR	RBI	BB	SO	OBP	SLG
Day	.220	132	29	2	2	2	12	13	17	.290	.311	April	.216	74	16	1	2	0	6	7	15	.280	.284
Night	.228	189	43	5	2	2	12	13	46	.275	.307	May	.207	58	12	4	0	2	8	6	12	.277	.379
Grass	.237	236	56	4	3	3	18	20	39	.296	.318	June	.191	47	9	1	1	1	2	4	9	.255	.319
Turf	.188	85	16	3	1	1	6	6	24	.239	.282	July	.000	0	0	0	0	0	0	0	0	.000	.000
First Pitch	.282	39	11	0	2	2	7	3	0	.326	.538	August	.314	35	11	0	0	0	3	4	3	.385	.314
Ahead on Count	.200	60	12	2	0	1	2	8	0	.294	.283	September/October	.224	107	24	1	1	1	5	5	24	.259	.280
Behind on Count	.169	124	21	2	1	1	6	0	36	.169	.226	Pre-All Star	.207	179	37	6	3	3	16	17	36	.273	.324
Two Strikes	.177	164	29	3	1	1	7	15	63	.246	.226	Post-All Star	.246	142	35	1	1	1	8	9	27	.291	.289

1992 By Position

Position	Avg	AB	H	2B	3B	HR	RBI	BB	SO	OBP	SLG	G	GS	Innings	PO	A	E	DP	Fld Pct	Rng Fctr	In Zone	Outs	Zone Rtg	MLB Zone
As ss	.225	320	72	7	4	4	24	26	62	.282	.309	94	91	787.2	142	256	11	52	.973	4.55	308	272	.883	.885

Roger Clemens — Red Sox Pitches Right

	ERA	W	L	Sv	G	GS	IP	BB	SO	Avg	H	2B	3B	HR	RBI	OBP	SLG	CG	ShO	Sup	QS	#P/S	SB	CS	GB	FB	G/F
1992 Season	2.41	18	11	0	32	32	246.2	62	208	.224	203	39	2	11	70	.279	.308	11	5	4.23	23	119	24	12	364	187	1.95
Last Five Years	2.62	92	50	0	168	168	1263.2	336	1179	.225	1047	187	25	70	364	.280	.320	53	24	4.51	124	117	100	68	1617	1120	1.44

1992 Season

	ERA	W	L	Sv	G	GS	IP	H	HR	BB	SO		Avg	AB	H	2B	3B	HR	RBI	BB	SO	OBP	SLG
Home	2.88	8	6	0	17	17	128.1	117	5	36	115	vs. Left	.226	447	101	15	1	6	27	30	98	.277	.304
Away	1.90	10	5	0	15	15	118.1	86	6	26	93	vs. Right	.222	460	102	24	1	5	43	32	110	.280	.311
Day	2.16	5	4	0	10	10	79.1	60	2	16	62	Inning 1-6	.221	688	152	30	2	7	52	48	163	.276	.301
Night	2.53	13	7	0	22	22	167.1	143	9	46	146	Inning 7+	.233	219	51	9	0	4	18	14	45	.288	.329
Grass	2.55	14	10	0	27	27	204.1	175	7	56	181	None on	.224	553	124	18	1	8	8	25	133	.268	.304
Turf	1.70	4	1	0	5	5	42.1	28	4	6	27	Runners on	.223	354	79	21	1	3	62	37	75	.295	.314
April	1.38	3	2	0	5	5	39.0	25	0	9	45	Scoring Posn	.201	209	42	12	0	0	52	26	49	.286	.258
May	1.76	5	1	0	6	6	51.0	33	2	8	35	Close & Late	.214	98	21	3	0	0	5	5	19	.274	.245
June	2.43	1	2	0	5	5	37.0	35	3	14	32	None on/out	.240	242	58	7	1	3	3	11	50	.281	.314
July	4.00	2	2	0	5	5	36.0	31	2	12	26	vs. 1st Batr (relief)	.000	0	0	0	0	0	0	0	0	.000	.000
August	1.90	5	1	0	6	6	47.1	40	4	8	40	First Inning Pitched	.252	119	30	6	1	0	10	11	29	.318	.319
September/October	3.47	2	3	0	5	5	36.1	39	0	11	30	First 75 Pitches	.228	545	124	22	1	5	35	36	129	.280	.299
Starter	2.41	18	11	0	32	32	246.2	203	11	62	208	Pitch 76-90	.190	126	24	5	1	0	5	6	26	.239	.246
Reliever	0.00	0	0	0	0	0	0.0	0	0	0	0	Pitch 91-105	.226	106	24	8	0	2	10	7	24	.278	.358
0-3 Days Rest	0.00	0	0	0	0	0	0.0	0	0	0	0	Pitch 106+	.238	130	31	4	0	4	20	13	29	.313	.362
4 Days Rest	2.47	14	7	0	22	22	164.0	138	10	46	145	Ahead on Count	.161	416	67	14	0	2	22	0	170	.167	.209
5+ Days Rest	2.29	4	4	0	10	10	82.2	65	1	16	63	Behind on Count	.319	182	58	12	1	4	19	21	0	.385	.462
Pre-All Star	2.31	9	6	0	18	18	140.0	109	5	37	120	Two Strikes	.142	451	64	14	0	2	19	37	208	.207	.186
Post-All Star	2.53	9	5	0	14	14	106.2	94	6	25	88												

Last Five Years

	ERA	W	L	Sv	G	GS	IP	H	HR	BB	SO		Avg	AB	H	2B	3B	HR	RBI	BB	SO	OBP	SLG
Home	2.77	42	24	0	82	82	610.1	537	35	165	590	vs. Left	.236	2462	582	107	13	31	186	197	558	.295	.328
Away	2.48	50	26	0	86	86	653.1	510	35	171	589	vs. Right	.211	2200	465	80	12	39	178	139	621	.263	.312
Day	1.98	32	12	0	55	55	423.2	322	14	98	385	Inning 1-6	.226	3607	816	150	20	55	307	254	907	.281	.325
Night	2.95	60	38	0	113	113	840.0	725	56	238	794	Inning 7+	.219	1055	231	37	5	15	57	82	272	.278	.306
Grass	2.77	77	45	0	144	144	1071.2	906	61	293	1036	None on	.224	2877	645	105	12	45	45	178	742	.274	.316
Turf	1.78	15	5	0	24	24	192.0	141	9	43	143	Runners on	.225	1785	402	82	13	25	319	158	437	.290	.328
April	1.73	18	4	0	26	26	203.1	134	8	44	213	Scoring Posn	.210	975	205	37	9	11	271	105	253	.285	.301
May	2.70	18	9	0	30	30	237.0	168	13	57	210	Close & Late	.195	560	109	22	3	5	30	52	151	.269	.271
June	2.86	13	11	0	27	27	195.1	197	12	55	181	None on/out	.225	1234	278	46	4	16	16	75	308	.274	.308
July	2.61	13	8	0	29	29	217.0	182	13	66	208	vs. 1st Batr (relief)	.000	0	0	0	0	0	0	0	0	.000	.000
August	2.91	17	8	0	30	30	216.1	192	14	62	198	First Inning Pitched	.252	635	160	29	6	8	61	53	157	.312	.354
September/October	2.91	13	10	0	26	26	194.2	174	10	52	169	First 75 Pitches	.230	2861	657	123	17	41	231	197	730	.284	.328
Starter	2.62	92	50	0	168	168	1263.2	1047	70	336	1179	Pitch 76-90	.195	606	118	20	3	10	41	42	138	.248	.287
Reliever	0.00	0	0	0	0	0	0.0	0	0	0	0	Pitch 91-105	.229	547	125	22	1	8	37	36	136	.279	.316
0-3 Days Rest	3.72	2	1	0	4	4	29.0	27	2	9	30	Pitch 106+	.227	648	147	22	4	11	55	61	175	.296	.324
4 Days Rest	2.73	68	37	0	124	124	926.1	789	58	259	877	First Pitch	.307	587	180	32	5	17	72	21	0	.337	.465
5+ Days Rest	2.19	22	12	0	40	40	308.1	231	10	68	272	Ahead on Count	.173	2308	399	74	7	23	138	0	967	.180	.274
Pre-All Star	2.52	53	26	0	93	93	707.2	567	40	177	674	Behind on Count	.295	823	243	45	8	16	94	155	0	.403	.428
Post-All Star	2.75	39	24	0	75	75	556.0	480	30	159	505	Two Strikes	.158	2463	389	76	7	19	126	159	1179	.212	.218

Pitcher vs. Batter (career)

Pitches Best Vs.	Avg	AB	H	2B	3B	HR	RBI	BB	SO	OBP	SLG	Pitches Worst Vs.	Avg	AB	H	2B	3B	HR	RBI	BB	SO	OBP	SLG
Ron Tingley	.000	11	0	0	0	0	0	0	5	.000	.000	Gary Sheffield	.533	15	8	1	0	0	2	1	1	.563	.600
Tim Teufel	.000	10	0	0	0	0	1	1	3	.083	.000	Alfredo Griffin	.474	19	9	3	0	0	2	1	3	.500	.632
Greg Vaughn	.056	18	1	0	0	0	0	0	10	.056	.056	Ken Griffey Jr	.407	27	11	5	0	1	5	5	3	.500	.704
Mike Devereaux	.071	14	1	0	0	0	1	0	3	.071	.071	Bill Spiers	.357	14	5	1	1	1	1	0	4	.357	.786
Cory Snyder	.087	23	2	0	0	0	0	0	12	.087	.087	Eddie Murray	.346	26	9	2	0	2	3	4	2	.433	.654

Pat Clements — Orioles
Pitches Left (groundball pitcher)

	ERA	W	L	Sv	G	GS	IP	BB	SO	Avg	H	2B	3B	HR	RBI	OBP	SLG	GF	IR	IRS	Hld	SvOp	SB	CS	GB	FB	G/F
1992 Season	2.98	4	1	0	50	0	48.1	23	20	.270	48	7	0	0	24	.364	.309	11	54	11	5	1	5	1	88	36	2.44
Last Five Years	3.73	9	2	0	100	2	123.0	58	55	.283	132	21	3	6	73	.363	.380	18	154	50	8	3	7	2	225	96	2.34

1992 Season

	ERA	W	L	Sv	G	GS	IP	H	HR	BB	SO		Avg	AB	H	2B	3B	HR	RBI	BB	SO	OBP	SLG
Home	1.34	2	0	0	31	0	33.2	21	0	16	11	vs. Left	.234	77	18	3	0	0	8	5	15	.298	.273
Away	6.75	2	1	0	19	0	14.2	27	0	7	9	vs. Right	.297	101	30	4	0	0	16	18	5	.410	.337
Starter	0.00	0	0	0	0	0	0.0	0	0	0	0	Scoring Posn	.274	62	17	3	0	0	23	12	5	.418	.323
Reliever	2.98	4	1	0	50	0	48.1	48	0	23	20	Close & Late	.194	36	7	0	0	0	4	4	6	.293	.194
0 Days rest	0.71	3	0	0	10	0	12.2	9	0	3	4	None on/out	.222	36	8	2	0	0	4	4	.300	.278
1 or 2 Days rest	3.15	1	0	0	23	0	20.0	15	0	11	10	First Pitch	.350	20	7	1	0	0	5	3	0	.462	.400
3+ Days rest	4.60	0	1	0	17	0	15.2	24	0	9	6	Ahead on Count	.282	51	15	4	0	0	5	10	0	.410	.373
Pre-All Star	2.49	2	1	0	28	0	25.1	26	0	12	11	Behind on Count	.282	78	22	2	0	0	10	0	19	.300	.308
Post-All Star	3.52	2	0	0	22	0	23.0	22	0	11	9	Two Strikes	.200	65	13	2	0	0	8	10	20	.316	.231

Dave Cochrane — Mariners
Bats Both

	Avg	G	AB	R	H	2B	3B	HR	RBI	BB	SO	HBP	GDP	SB	CS	OBP	SLG	IBB	SH	SF	#Pit	#P/PA	GB	FB	G/F
1992 Season	.250	65	152	10	38	5	0	2	12	34		1	3	1	0	.309	.322	0	2	0	676	4.10	44	44	1.00
Last Five Years	.241	199	452	39	109	22	1	7	41	35	107	3	4	1	3	.299	.341	0	3	1	1875	3.82	139	132	1.05

1992 Season

	Avg	AB	H	2B	3B	HR	RBI	BB	SO	OBP	SLG		Avg	AB	H	2B	3B	HR	RBI	BB	SO	OBP	SLG
vs. Left	.276	58	16	2	0	1	3	5	15	.333	.362	Scoring Posn	.194	31	6	0	0	0	9	1	11	.219	.194
vs. Right	.234	94	22	3	0	1	9	7	19	.294	.298	Close & Late	.265	34	9	0	0	0	5	5	9	.359	.265
Home	.190	63	12	1	0	0	4	4	17	.250	.206	None on/out	.282	39	11	4	0	0	0	4	6	.364	.385
Away	.292	89	26	4	0	2	8	8	17	.351	.404	Batting #6	.232	56	13	1	0	1	3	2	9	.271	.304
First Pitch	.240	25	6	0	0	1	2	0	0	.240	.360	Batting #7	.333	51	17	2	0	1	8	7	14	.414	.431
Ahead on Count	.438	32	14	3	0	0	4	0	.500	.531	Other	.178	45	8	2	0	0	1	3	11	.229	.222
Behind on Count	.243	37	9	2	0	1	6	0	14	.263	.378	Pre-All Star	.273	132	36	5	0	2	10	11	30	.333	.356
Two Strikes	.137	73	10	1	0	0	4	8	34	.232	.151	Post-All Star	.100	20	2	0	0	0	2	1	4	.143	.100

Last Five Years

	Avg	AB	H	2B	3B	HR	RBI	BB	SO	OBP	SLG		Avg	AB	H	2B	3B	HR	RBI	BB	SO	OBP	SLG
vs. Left	.239	134	32	8	0	1	15	10	15	.297	.321	Scoring Posn	.253	95	24	7	0	1	32	5	31	.294	.358
vs. Right	.242	318	77	14	1	6	26	25	82	.301	.349	Close & Late	.208	106	22	4	0	1	13	9	31	.282	.274
Groundball	.175	114	20	2	0	2	6	11	34	.260	.246	None on/out	.231	121	28	4	0	2	8	8	29	.290	.314
Flyball	.243	115	28	5	1	2	9	6	26	.281	.357	Batting #7	.266	143	38	8	0	4	17	16	38	.340	.406
Home	.241	216	52	11	1	4	25	22	60	.313	.356	Batting #8	.219	105	23	7	0	1	11	8	25	.274	.314
Away	.242	236	57	11	0	3	16	13	47	.287	.326	Other	.235	204	48	7	1	2	13	11	44	.283	.309
Day	.218	133	29	7	0	0	5	10	33	.278	.271	April	.348	23	8	3	0	0	2	5	.400	.478
Night	.251	319	80	15	1	7	36	25	74	.308	.370	May	.236	89	21	1	1	1	5	4	22	.284	.303
Grass	.281	167	47	9	0	2	13	10	27	.330	.371	June	.231	121	28	3	0	4	15	13	30	.306	.355
Turf	.218	285	62	13	1	5	28	25	80	.282	.323	July	.245	110	27	6	0	0	11	8	18	.294	.300
First Pitch	.247	81	20	4	1	2	8	0	0	.247	.395	August	.135	52	7	4	0	2	5	6	17	.224	.327
Ahead on Count	.363	91	33	8	0	2	8	11	0	.427	.516	September/October	.316	57	18	5	0	0	5	2	15	.350	.404
Behind on Count	.182	132	24	6	0	2	11	0	53	.194	.273	Pre-All Star	.257	276	71	9	1	5	24	25	63	.322	.351
Two Strikes	.178	219	39	7	0	1	16	24	107	.268	.224	Post-All Star	.216	176	38	13	0	2	17	10	44	.262	.324

Batter vs. Pitcher (career)

Hits Best Against	Avg	AB	H	2B	3B	HR	RBI	BB	SO	OBP	SLG	Hits Worst Against	Avg	AB	H	2B	3B	HR	RBI	BB	SO	OBP	SLG
Bill Gullickson	.316	19	6	2	0	0	0	0	2	.316	.421	Juan Guzman	.167	12	2	0	0	0	1	0	2	.167	.167
												Jimmy Key	.211	19	4	1	0	0	1	0	4	.211	.263

Craig Colbert — Giants
Bats Right (groundball hitter)

	Avg	G	AB	R	H	2B	3B	HR	RBI	BB	SO	HBP	GDP	SB	CS	OBP	SLG	IBB	SH	SF	#Pit	#P/PA	GB	FB	G/F
1992 Season	.230	49	126	10	29	5	2	1	16	9	22	0	8	1	0	.277	.325	0	2	2	447	3.26	49	31	1.58

1992 Season

	Avg	AB	H	2B	3B	HR	RBI	BB	SO	OBP	SLG		Avg	AB	H	2B	3B	HR	RBI	BB	SO	OBP	SLG
vs. Left	.232	56	13	2	1	1	10	3	3	.267	.357	Scoring Posn	.179	39	7	2	0	0	13	2	11	.209	.231
vs. Right	.229	70	16	3	1	0	6	6	19	.286	.300	Close & Late	.214	28	6	0	1	0	1	4	5	.313	.286
Home	.263	57	15	4	1	0	8	4	8	.302	.368	None on/out	.080	25	2	0	0	0	0	3	4	.179	.080
Away	.203	69	14	1	1	1	8	5	14	.257	.290	Batting #5	.235	17	4	0	0	0	1	4	2	.381	.235
First Pitch	.321	28	9	1	1	0	9	0	0	.310	.429	Batting #7	.284	74	21	5	2	1	12	3	11	.308	.446
Ahead on Count	.217	23	5	1	1	0	6	6	0	.379	.348	Other	.114	35	4	0	0	0	3	2	9	.158	.114
Behind on Count	.109	46	5	2	0	0	2	0	15	.109	.152	Pre-All Star	.161	31	5	1	0	0	3	3	8	.229	.194
Two Strikes	.196	51	10	3	0	0	4	3	22	.241	.255	Post-All Star	.253	95	24	4	2	1	13	6	14	.294	.368

Greg Colbrunn — Expos
Bats Right

	Avg	G	AB	R	H	2B	3B	HR	RBI	BB	SO	HBP	GDP	SB	CS	OBP	SLG	IBB	SH	SF	#Pit	#P/PA	GB	FB	G/F
1992 Season	.268	52	168	12	45	8	0	2	18	6	34	2	1	3	2	.294	.351	1	0	4	644	3.58	56	46	1.22

1992 Season

	Avg	AB	H	2B	3B	HR	RBI	BB	SO	OBP	SLG		Avg	AB	H	2B	3B	HR	RBI	BB	SO	OBP	SLG
vs. Left	.222	72	16	2	0	1	9	2	14	.237	.292	Scoring Posn	.238	42	10	2	0	0	15	4	9	.294	.286
vs. Right	.302	96	29	6	0	1	9	4	20	.337	.396	Close & Late	.292	24	7	1	0	0	0	1	4	.320	.333
Home	.287	87	25	5	0	1	8	3	14	.308	.379	None on/out	.306	49	15	2	0	1	1	1	11	.320	.408
Away	.247	81	20	3	0	1	10	3	20	.281	.321	Batting #5	.292	72	21	3	0	0	8	3	12	.329	.333
First Pitch	.250	20	5	0	0	0	2	1	0	.261	.250	Batting #7	.342	38	13	3	0	1	5	1	5	.341	.500
Ahead on Count	.353	34	12	4	0	1	6	4	0	.421	.559	Other	.190	58	11	2	0	1	5	2	17	.217	.276
Behind on Count	.286	77	22	3	0	1	5	0	20	.295	.364	Pre-All Star	.313	16	5	0	0	0	0	0	4	.313	.313
Two Strikes	.222	81	18	2	0		6	1	34	.241	.247	Post-All Star	.263	152	40	8	0	2	18	6	30	.293	.355

Alex Cole — Pirates
Bats Left (groundball hitter)

	Avg	G	AB	R	H	2B	3B	HR	RBI	BB	SO	HBP	GDP	SB	CS	OBP	SLG	IBB	SH	SF	#Pit	#P/PA	GB	FB	G/F
1992 Season	.255	105	302	44	77	4	7	0	15	28	67	1	4	16	6	.318	.315	1	1	2	1337	4.02	122	57	2.14
Career (1990-1992)	.263	290	916	145	259	26	14	0	49	114	152	3	14	83	32	.363	.342	3	5	4	4056	3.91	373	174	2.14

1992 Season

	Avg	AB	H	2B	3B	HR	RBI	BB	SO	OBP	SLG		Avg	AB	H	2B	3B	HR	RBI	BB	SO	OBP	SLG
vs. Left	.286	49	14	0	2	0	3	6	14	.368	.367	Scoring Posn	.218	55	12	1	2	0	14	8	15	.308	.309
vs. Right	.249	253	63	4	5	0	12	22	53	.308	.304	Close & Late	.217	60	13	2	1	0	5	7	17	.309	.283
Groundball	.242	95	23	2	3	0	2	9	27	.308	.326	None on/out	.219	114	25	2	1	0	0	12	20	.294	.254
Flyball	.239	67	16	0	0	0	4	7	15	.307	.239	Batting #1	.278	223	62	3	7	0	12	21	48	.341	.354
Home	.299	137	41	2	5	0	13	17	30	.378	.387	Batting #2	.239	46	11	1	0	0	2	4	7	.294	.261
Away	.218	165	36	2	2	0	2	11	37	.266	.255	Other	.121	33	4	0	0	0	1	3	12	.194	.121
Day	.253	83	21	0	0	0	4	6	21	.300	.253	April	.156	32	5	1	0	0	0	3	8	.229	.188
Night	.256	219	56	4	7	0	11	22	46	.325	.338	May	.234	47	11	0	0	0	5	5	10	.315	.234
Grass	.227	128	29	1	0	0	5	14	25	.303	.234	June	.235	17	4	0	0	0	0	2	3	.316	.235
Turf	.276	174	48	3	7	0	10	14	42	.330	.374	July	.279	68	19	0	4	0	5	7	18	.347	.397
First Pitch	.400	35	14	0	1	0	2	1	0	.432	.457	August	.356	59	21	2	1	0	1	5	12	.406	.424
Ahead on Count	.400	65	26	1	5	0	8	10	0	.474	.569	September/October	.215	79	17	1	2	0	4	6	16	.267	.278
Behind on Count	.190	79	15	1	1	0	2	0	31	.188	.228	Pre-All Star	.226	115	26	1	2	0	6	10	27	.291	.270
Two Strikes	.161	155	25	1	0	0	2	17	66	.244	.168	Post-All Star	.273	187	51	3	5	0	9	18	40	.335	.342

1992 By Position

Position	Avg	AB	H	2B	3B	HR	RBI	BB	SO	OBP	SLG	G	GS	Innings	PO	A	E	DP	Fld Pct	Rng Fctr	In Zone	Outs	Zone Rtg	MLB Zone
As Pinch Hitter	.133	30	4	1	0	0	1	2	10	.188	.167	32	0	---	---	---	---	---	---	---	---	---	---	---
As lf	.279	61	17	1	0	0	3	5	11	.343	.295	18	14	130.1	29	1	1	0	.968	2.07	36	29	.806	.809
As rf	.286	189	54	2	2	0	10	17	42	.343	.370	54	45	402.1	85	4	1	0	.989	1.99	96	80	.833	.814

Career (1990-1992)

	Avg	AB	H	2B	3B	HR	RBI	BB	SO	OBP	SLG		Avg	AB	H	2B	3B	HR	RBI	BB	SO	OBP	SLG
vs. Left	.313	163	51	5	4	0	15	30	32	.424	.393	Scoring Posn	.263	171	45	2	2	0	45	26	32	.356	.298
vs. Right	.276	753	208	21	10	0	34	84	120	.348	.331	Close & Late	.258	159	41	3	1	0	12	19	30	.344	.289
Groundball	.314	312	98	8	4	0	18	34	58	.383	.365	None on/out	.275	349	96	11	4	0	0	61	57	.383	.330
Flyball	.245	192	47	4	2	0	9	31	34	.351	.286	Batting #1	.289	823	238	25	14	0	45	106	132	.370	.354
Home	.298	440	131	13	8	0	36	68	80	.393	.364	Batting #2	.234	47	11	1	0	0	2	4	7	.288	.255
Away	.269	476	128	13	6	0	13	46	72	.333	.321	Other	.217	46	10	0	0	0	0	4	13	.294	.217
Day	.282	245	69	5	2	0	13	36	44	.371	.318	April	.259	85	22	4	1	0	2	7	15	.315	.329
Night	.283	671	190	21	12	0	36	78	108	.359	.350	May	.254	67	17	1	0	0	5	8	10	.338	.269
Grass	.279	652	182	18	6	0	35	88	102	.365	.325	June	.270	89	24	1	0	0	4	14	12	.371	.281
Turf	.292	264	77	8	8	0	14	26	50	.355	.383	July	.274	146	40	2	4	0	11	23	27	.373	.342
First Pitch	.394	132	52	4	2	0	7	3	0	.412	.455	August	.317	224	71	9	5	0	12	27	46	.393	.402
Ahead on Count	.358	212	76	6	9	0	20	52	0	.479	.472	September/October	.279	305	85	9	4	0	15	35	42	.351	.334
Behind on Count	.212	241	51	7	2	0	9	0	72	.213	.257	Pre-All Star	.264	276	73	6	3	0	14	34	46	.347	.308
Two Strikes	.183	410	75	8	2	0	11	59	151	.289	.212	Post-All Star	.291	640	186	20	11	0	35	80	106	.369	.356

Batter vs. Pitcher (career)

Hits Best Against	Avg	AB	H	2B	3B	HR	RBI	BB	SO	OBP	SLG	Hits Worst Against	Avg	AB	H	2B	3B	HR	RBI	BB	SO	OBP	SLG
Todd Stottlemyre	.636	11	7	1	0	0	0	0	1	.636	.727	Bill Wegman	.077	13	1	0	0	0	1	2	1	.200	.077
Scott Erickson	.571	14	8	0	0	0	0	1	0	.600	.571	Bobby Witt	.111	9	1	0	1	0	1	5	4	.429	.333
Walt Terrell	.438	16	7	0	0	0	2	3	3	.526	.438	Bill Gullickson	.167	12	2	2	0	0	0	0	1	.167	.333
Frank Castillo	.400	10	4	0	0	0	1	1	1	.455	.400												
Kevin Brown	.357	14	5	2	0	0	1	1	4	.400	.500												

Victor Cole — Pirates
Pitches Right

	ERA	W	L	Sv	G	GS	IP	BB	SO	Avg	H	2B	3B	HR	RBI	OBP	SLG	CG	ShO	Sup	QS	#P/S	SB	CS	GB	FB	G/F
1992 Season	5.48	0	2	0	8	4	23.0	14	12	.261	23	6	0	1	10	.359	.364	0	0	1.96	1	69	2	1	38	29	1.31

1992 Season

	ERA	W	L	Sv	G	GS	IP	H	HR	BB	SO		Avg	AB	H	2B	3B	HR	RBI	BB	SO	OBP	SLG
Home	5.65	0	1	0	5	2	14.1	12	0	10	7	vs. Left	.250	48	12	3	0	1	3	11	7	.390	.375
Away	5.19	0	1	0	3	2	8.2	11	1	4	5	vs. Right	.275	40	11	3	0	0	7	3	5	.318	.350

Vince Coleman — Mets
Bats Both (groundball hitter)

	Avg	G	AB	R	H	2B	3B	HR	RBI	BB	SO	HBP	GDP	SB	CS	OBP	SLG	IBB	SH	SF	#Pit	#P/PA	GB	FB	G/F
1992 Season	.275	71	229	37	63	11	1	2	21	27	41	2	1	24	9	.355	.358	3	2	1	967	3.73	93	49	1.90
Last Five Years	.267	565	2183	326	582	77	34	14	143	200	377	7	18	264	77	.329	.352	8	22	9	8774	3.66	902	473	1.91

1992 Season

	Avg	AB	H	2B	3B	HR	RBI	BB	SO	OBP	SLG		Avg	AB	H	2B	3B	HR	RBI	BB	SO	OBP	SLG
vs. Left	.283	60	17	4	1	1	9	7	11	.358	.433	Scoring Posn	.311	45	14	4	1	2	21	9	9	.418	.578
vs. Right	.272	169	46	7	0	1	12	20	30	.354	.331	Close & Late	.220	41	9	2	0	1	6	5	8	.304	.341
Home	.277	119	33	3	0	2	14	17	21	.370	.353	None on/out	.298	94	28	6	0	0		10	23	.377	.362
Away	.273	110	30	8	1	0	7	10	20	.339	.364	Batting #1	.274	223	61	11	1	2	21	27	40	.356	.359
First Pitch	.344	32	11	2	0	1	8	3	0	.389	.500	Batting #3	.000	3	0	0	0	0	0	0	1	.000	.000
Ahead on Count	.209	43	9	2	0	0	7	14	0	.404	.256	Other	.667	3	2	0	0	0	0	0	0	.667	.667
Behind on Count	.261	88	23	4	1	0	4	0	27	.278	.330	Pre-All Star	.316	114	36	6	0	2	13	13	15	.395	.421
Two Strikes	.241	108	26	4	1	1	4	10	41	.311	.324	Post-All Star	.235	115	27	5	1	0	8	14	26	.315	.296

Last Five Years

	Avg	AB	H	2B	3B	HR	RBI	BB	SO	OBP	SLG		Avg	AB	H	2B	3B	HR	RBI	BB	SO	OBP	SLG
vs. Left	.256	840	215	47	11	11	69	60	156	.306	.377	Scoring Posn	.248	444	110	20	9	4	130	49	81	.319	.360
vs. Right	.273	1343	367	30	23	3	74	140	221	.343	.337	Close & Late	.253	360	91	11	3	2	26	37	59	.325	.317
Groundball	.263	849	223	29	7	3	54	77	141	.325	.324	None on/out	.268	960	257	39	13	5		86	185	.331	.351
Flyball	.245	478	117	19	7	9	37	43	85	.307	.370	Batting #1	.269	2143	576	77	33	13	140	196	370	.331	.354
Home	.273	1088	297	41	19	10	86	109	178	.340	.373	Batting #9	.077	13	1	0	1	0	0	1	3	.143	.231
Away	.260	1095	285	36	15	4	57	91	199	.318	.332	Other	.185	27	5	0	0	1	3	3	4	.267	.296
Day	.264	655	173	16	10	7	45	53	119	.319	.351	April	.290	348	101	16	9	2	36	34	54	.353	.405
Night	.268	1528	409	61	24	7	98	147	258	.333	.353	May	.303	422	128	10	8	2	30	37	72	.360	.379
Grass	.248	781	194	18	4	4	43	83	146	.320	.297	June	.257	467	120	23	7	4	27	42	83	.320	.362
Turf	.277	1402	388	59	30	10	100	117	231	.334	.383	July	.236	292	69	7	2	2	15	32	52	.311	.295
First Pitch	.357	325	116	20	10	3	32	3	0	.363	.508	August	.277	408	113	13	6	3	33	38	58	.341	.360
Ahead on Count	.301	415	125	22	3	2	44	113	0	.449	.383	September/October	.207	246	51	8	2	1	12	17	58	.257	.268
Behind on Count	.224	789	177	24	10	1	36	2	229	.230	.284	Pre-All Star	.277	1315	364	50	24	8	88	123	219	.340	.370
Two Strikes	.203	1008	205	23	15	6	39	80	377	.264	.274	Post-All Star	.251	868	218	27	10	6	55	77	158	.313	.326

Batter vs. Pitcher (career)

Hits Best Against	Avg	AB	H	2B	3B	HR	RBI	BB	SO	OBP	SLG	Hits Worst Against	Avg	AB	H	2B	3B	HR	RBI	BB	SO	OBP	SLG
Pat Clements	.600	10	6	1	1	0	2	1	0	.636	.900	Randy Tomlin	.050	20	1	0	0	0	0	0	3	.050	.050
Jim Acker	.545	11	6	1	0	0	0	1	0	.583	.636	Pete Smith	.071	14	1	0	0	0	0	2	2	.188	.071
Barry Jones	.500	10	5	1	1	0	3	0	1	.545	.800	Dennis Rasmussen	.083	12	1	0	0	0	0	0	5	.083	.083
Mark Grant	.467	15	7	2	0	0	0	3	1	.556	.600	Trevor Wilson	.083	12	1	0	0	0	0	2	3	.214	.083
Jose Rijo	.417	12	5	0	2	0	1	3	4	.500	.750	Bob Welch	.095	21	2	0	0	0	1	1	9	.136	.095

Darnell Coles — Reds
Bats Right (flyball hitter)

	Avg	G	AB	R	H	2B	3B	HR	RBI	BB	SO	HBP	GDP	SB	CS	OBP	SLG	IBB	SH	SF	#Pit	#P/PA	GB	FB	G/F
1992 Season	.312	55	141	16	44	11	2	3	18	3	15	0	1	1	0	.322	.482	0	3	2	525	3.60	45	51	0.88
Last Five Years	.254	424	1311	145	333	62	8	31	167	83	183	14	27	10	11	.302	.384	4	8	17	5218	3.66	419	467	0.90

1992 Season

	Avg	AB	H	2B	3B	HR	RBI	BB	SO	OBP	SLG		Avg	AB	H	2B	3B	HR	RBI	BB	SO	OBP	SLG
vs. Left	.320	97	31	11	1	1	12	2	9	.330	.485	Scoring Posn	.357	28	10	3	0	1	16	0	3	.333	.571
vs. Right	.295	44	13	0	1	2	6	1	6	.304	.477	Close & Late	.333	27	9	1	1	0	3	0	3	.333	.444
Home	.250	60	15	4	1	1	7	0	7	.250	.400	None on/out	.257	35	9	1	0	1	1	0	2	.257	.371
Away	.358	81	29	7	1	2	11	3	8	.372	.543	Batting #5	.300	50	15	5	1	2	9	0	3	.294	.560
First Pitch	.391	23	9	1	0	0	1	0	0	.391	.435	Batting #7	.286	28	8	0	0	1	4	1	3	.310	.393
Ahead on Count	.323	31	10	2	1	1	3	1	0	.344	.548	Other	.333	63	21	6	1	0	5	2	9	.348	.460
Behind on Count	.268	41	11	5	0	0	6	0	8	.262	.390	Pre-All Star	.271	59	16	5	1	1	7	0	6	.267	.441
Two Strikes	.263	57	15	4	1	2	8	2	15	.288	.474	Post-All Star	.341	82	28	6	1	2	11	3	9	.360	.512

Last Five Years

	Avg	AB	H	2B	3B	HR	RBI	BB	SO	OBP	SLG		Avg	AB	H	2B	3B	HR	RBI	BB	SO	OBP	SLG
vs. Left	.265	517	137	32	4	13	69	39	65	.316	.418	Scoring Posn	.246	338	83	16	2	6	126	25	52	.294	.358
vs. Right	.247	794	196	30	4	18	98	44	118	.293	.363	Close & Late	.258	217	56	8	2	5	22	17	34	.317	.382
Groundball	.242	351	85	16	3	7	34	23	44	.291	.365	None on/out	.242	281	68	11	2	8		18	36	.290	.381
Flyball	.216	291	63	11	1	7	30	16	53	.260	.333	Batting #3	.280	232	65	11	1	9	36	18	30	.342	.453
Home	.261	635	166	30	4	18	86	46	77	.318	.406	Batting #5	.272	448	122	25	3	16	73	29	58	.316	.449
Away	.247	676	167	32	4	13	81	37	106	.286	.364	Other	.231	631	146	26	4	6	58	36	95	.276	.314

Last Five Years

	Avg	AB	H	2B	3B	HR	RBI	BB	SO	OBP	SLG		Avg	AB	H	2B	3B	HR	RBI	BB	SO	OBP	SLG
Day	.281	360	101	16	3	6	42	27	59	.331	.392	April	.241	162	39	8	1	3	23	9	18	.286	.358
Night	.244	951	232	46	5	25	125	56	124	.291	.382	May	.231	260	60	15	2	3	33	14	36	.277	.338
Grass	.243	547	133	18	2	10	60	28	90	.279	.338	June	.266	169	45	9	1	4	19	7	33	.269	.402
Turf	.262	764	200	44	6	21	107	55	93	.318	.418	July	.281	249	70	11	3	8	45	21	32	.338	.446
First Pitch	.345	165	57	12	1	3	23	1	0	.351	.485	August	.243	259	63	9	0	8	27	17	32	.294	.371
Ahead on Count	.289	318	92	16	2	9	53	48	0	.387	.437	September/October	.254	212	56	10	1	5	20	15	32	.320	.392
Behind on Count	.229	472	108	20	2	6	59	0	102	.237	.318	Pre-All Star	.245	666	163	36	5	12	87	38	96	.288	.368
Two Strikes	.189	577	109	20	3	10	45	32	183	.237	.402	Post-All Star	.264	645	170	26	3	19	80	45	85	.316	.402

Batter vs. Pitcher (since 1984)

Hits Best Against	Avg	AB	H	2B	3B	HR	RBI	BB	SO	OBP	SLG	Hits Worst Against	Avg	AB	H	2B	3B	HR	RBI	BB	SO	OBP	SLG
Jack Morris	.600	10	6	1	0	0	1	1	2	.636	.700	Dave Righetti	.000	4	0	0	0	0	0	2	4	.143	.000
Charlie Hough	.462	13	6	1	0	1	6	3	1	.529	.769	Doug Drabek	.000	11	0	0	0	0	0	0	2	.000	.000
Bill Wegman	.455	11	5	2	0	1	3	3	3	.571	.909	Jimmy Key	.077	26	2	0	0	0	1	2	2	.143	.077
Mike Moore	.444	9	4	0	1	3	9	2	0	.545	1.667	Dave Stieb	.077	13	1	0	0	0	2	1	1	.143	.077
Bobby Witt	.375	16	6	0	1	1	2	1	6	.412	.688	Bobby Thigpen	.143	14	2	0	0	0	0	1	0	.143	.143

Cris Colon — Rangers
Bats Both

	Avg	G	AB	R	H	2B	3B	HR	RBI	BB	SO	HBP	GDP	SB	CS	OBP	SLG	IBB	SH	SF	#Pit	#P/PA	GB	FB	G/F
1992 Season	.167	14	36	5	6	0	0	0	1	1	8	0	2	0	0	.189	.167	0	1	0	123	3.32	11	9	1.22

1992 Season

	Avg	AB	H	2B	3B	HR	RBI	BB	SO	OBP	SLG		Avg	AB	H	2B	3B	HR	RBI	BB	SO	OBP	SLG
vs. Left	.200	15	3	0	0	0	1	1	3	.250	.200	Scoring Posn	.125	8	1	0	0	0	1	0	2	.125	.125
vs. Right	.143	21	3	0	0	0	0	0	5	.143	.143	Close & Late	.000	2	0	0	0	0	0	0	0	.000	.000

Pat Combs — Phillies
Pitches Left

	ERA	W	L	Sv	G	GS	IP	BB	SO	Avg	H	2B	3B	HR	RBI	OBP	SLG	CG	ShO	Sup	QS	#P/S	SB	CS	GB	FB	G/F
1992 Season	7.71	1	1	0	4	4	18.2	12	12	.278	20	5	1	0	10	.376	.375	0	0	8.20	1	82	4	1	34	15	2.27
Career (1989-1992)	4.22	17	17	0	56	54	305.0	147	190	.257	299	61	6	21	131	.340	.373	5	3	4.93	26	91	30	14	452	304	1.49

1992 Season

	ERA	W	L	Sv	G	GS	IP	H	HR	BB	SO		Avg	AB	H	2B	3B	HR	RBI	BB	SO	OBP	SLG
Home	0.00	0	0	0	0	0	0.0	0	0	0	0	vs. Left	.250	12	3	0	1	0	1	3	2	.400	.417
Away	7.71	1	1	0	4	4	18.2	20	0	12	11	vs. Right	.283	60	17	5	0	0	9	9	9	.371	.367

Career (1989-1992)

	ERA	W	L	Sv	G	GS	IP	H	HR	BB	SO		Avg	AB	H	2B	3B	HR	RBI	BB	SO	OBP	SLG
Home	3.44	7	4	0	24	23	136.0	116	11	64	81	vs. Left	.245	204	50	5	2	6	24	31	38	.353	.377
Away	4.85	10	13	0	32	31	169.0	183	10	83	109	vs. Right	.259	961	249	56	4	15	107	116	154	.338	.373
Day	4.68	5	5	0	15	15	82.2	88	7	39	57	Inning 1-6	.266	1027	273	56	6	19	123	140	174	.354	.388
Night	4.05	12	12	0	41	39	222.1	211	14	108	133	Inning 7+	.188	138	26	5	0	2	8	7	16	.228	.268
Grass	5.86	2	10	0	17	17	81.1	102	8	39	52	None on	.249	630	157	30	5	6	6	83	92	.340	.341
Turf	3.62	15	7	0	39	37	223.2	197	13	108	138	Runners on	.265	535	142	31	1	15	125	64	98	.340	.411
April	5.35	2	3	0	8	8	35.1	34	5	22	23	Scoring Posn	.247	312	77	19	1	6	103	37	66	.319	.372
May	3.44	2	5	0	10	9	52.1	61	4	25	33	Close & Late	.160	75	12	1	0	1	2	4	11	.203	.213
June	4.57	3	4	0	13	12	69.0	61	5	44	41	None on/out	.259	278	72	12	3	1	1	51	39	.380	.335
July	6.13	2	3	0	7	7	39.2	46	2	21	27	vs. 1st Batr (relief)	.000	2	0	0	0	0	0	0	0	.000	.000
August	4.40	0	1	0	6	6	28.2	29	0	15	17	First Inning Pitched	.248	202	50	16	2	4	23	30	42	.343	.406
September/October	2.93	8	1	0	12	12	80.0	68	5	20	49	First 75 Pitches	.268	870	233	47	5	16	99	114	146	.353	.389
Starter	4.23	17	17	0	54	54	300.0	297	21	144	185	Pitch 76-90	.247	150	37	7	1	3	17	17	22	.325	.367
Reliever	3.60	0	0	0	2	0	5.0	2	0	3	5	Pitch 91-105	.190	105	20	4	0	1	7	11	20	.267	.257
0-3 Days Rest	6.43	0	0	0	1	1	7.0	11	1	3	3	Pitch 106+	.225	40	9	3	0	1	8	5	2	.311	.375
4 Days Rest	4.21	11	10	0	35	35	199.0	196	15	85	124	First Pitch	.358	162	58	15	1	5	22	7	0	.387	.556
5+ Days Rest	4.12	6	7	0	18	18	94.0	90	5	56	58	Ahead on Count	.182	488	89	15	3	7	50	0	160	.187	.268
Pre-All Star	4.76	7	14	0	34	32	170.1	171	15	101	106	Behind on Count	.322	298	96	16	0	7	35	87	0	.472	.446
Post-All Star	3.54	10	3	0	22	22	134.2	128	6	46	84	Two Strikes	.175	496	87	17	4	7	47	53	190	.256	.268

Pitcher vs. Batter (career)

Pitches Best Vs.	Avg	AB	H	2B	3B	HR	RBI	BB	SO	OBP	SLG	Pitches Worst Vs.	Avg	AB	H	2B	3B	HR	RBI	BB	SO	OBP	SLG
Gary Carter	.083	12	1	0	0	0	0	1	2	.154	.083	Hubie Brooks	.500	12	6	2	0	2	4	2	4	.571	1.167
Terry Pendleton	.091	11	1	0	0	0	0	0	1	.091	.091	Lonnie Smith	.500	8	4	1	0	0	3	3	2	.636	.625
Gregg Jefferies	.100	20	2	0	0	0	1	1	2	.143	.100	Ozzie Smith	.455	11	5	1	0	0	1	3	0	.571	.545
Kevin McReynolds	.105	19	2	0	0	0	1	2	1	.190	.105	Doug Dascenzo	.455	11	5	1	0	1	3	0	0	.455	.818
Ken Caminiti	.143	14	2	0	0	0	0	0	4	.143	.143	Andres Galarraga	.400	20	8	1	0	0	4	0	5	.400	.750

David Cone — Blue Jays — Pitches Right

	ERA	W	L	Sv	G	GS	IP	BB	SO	Avg	H	2B	3B	HR	RBI	OBP	SLG	CG	ShO	Sup	QS	#P/S	SB	CS	GB	FB	G/F
1992 Season	2.81	17	10	0	35	34	249.2	111	261	.219	201	30	9	15	81	.309	.321	7	5	4.43	24	119	49	10	242	258	0.94
Last Five Years	3.00	79	45	0	169	159	1145.0	403	1138	.223	943	149	38	79	373	.293	.332	33	15	4.70	109	112	154	54	1192	1178	1.01

1992 Season

	ERA	W	L	Sv	G	GS	IP	H	HR	BB	SO		Avg	AB	H	2B	3B	HR	RBI	BB	SO	OBP	SLG
Home	3.38	8	6	0	18	17	122.1	103	9	57	137	vs. Left	.230	505	116	17	4	10	48	72	123	.331	.339
Away	2.26	9	4	0	17	17	127.1	98	6	54	124	vs. Right	.207	411	85	13	5	5	33	39	138	.281	.299
Day	3.56	6	5	0	14	13	93.2	86	5	41	100	Inning 1-6	.213	733	156	25	7	12	70	87	221	.303	.315
Night	2.37	11	5	0	21	21	156.0	115	10	70	161	Inning 7+	.246	183	45	5	2	3	11	24	40	.333	.344
Grass	2.71	11	6	0	21	21	152.2	119	8	66	169	None on	.241	507	122	18	6	9		58	132	.326	.353
Turf	2.97	6	4	0	14	13	97.0	82	7	45	92	Runners on	.193	409	79	12	3	6	72	53	129	.289	.281
April	2.23	2	1	0	5	5	40.1	26	0	16	41	Scoring Posn	.181	238	43	9	1	4	65	37	74	.292	.277
May	2.55	3	2	0	6	6	42.1	33	3	18	42	Close & Late	.217	83	18	2	1	1	5	15	19	.337	.301
June	2.83	2	1	0	5	5	35.0	33	3	9	43	None on/out	.252	238	60	10	5	5	5	19	57	.313	.399
July	3.20	5	0	0	6	6	45.0	35	5	28	60	vs. 1st Batr (relief)	.000	1	0	0	0	0	0	0	0	.000	.000
August	4.65	1	4	0	6	6	40.2	42	1	18	33	First Inning Pitched	.177	124	22	3	0	2	8	15	38	.292	.250
September/October	1.55	4	2	0	7	6	46.1	32	3	22	42	First 75 Pitches	.222	572	127	20	5	7	47	64	180	.309	.311
Starter	2.83	17	10	0	34	34	247.2	198	15	111	259	Pitch 76-90	.210	105	22	5	1	3	20	11	20	.283	.362
Reliever	0.00	0	0	0	1	0	2.0	3	0	0	2	Pitch 91-105	.202	104	21	4	1	3	6	16	21	.314	.346
0-3 Days Rest	0.00	0	0	0	0	0	0.0	0	0	0	0	First Pitch	.322	118	38	8	1	5	14	4	0	.360	.534
4 Days Rest	2.82	9	7	0	21	21	150.0	124	11	63	167	Ahead on Count	.139	447	62	6	5	1	28	0	216	.151	.181
5+ Days Rest	2.86	8	3	0	13	13	97.2	74	4	48	92	Behind on Count	.339	180	61	7	3	5	24	62	0	.502	.494
Pre-All Star	2.56	9	4	0	19	19	140.2	109	9	58	154	Two Strikes	.132	492	65	8	5	3	28	45	261	.213	.187
Post-All Star	3.14	8	6	0	16	15	109.0	92	6	53	107												

Last Five Years

	ERA	W	L	Sv	G	GS	IP	H	HR	BB	SO		Avg	AB	H	2B	3B	HR	RBI	BB	SO	OBP	SLG
Home	2.99	39	22	0	81	78	577.0	471	42	190	591	vs. Left	.237	2400	568	103	26	45	206	259	530	.313	.358
Away	3.01	40	23	0	88	81	568.0	472	37	213	547	vs. Right	.205	1826	375	46	12	34	167	144	608	.266	.300
Day	3.55	25	17	0	57	52	363.0	323	27	117	356	Inning 1-6	.219	3344	733	120	29	60	311	330	942	.292	.326
Night	2.75	54	28	0	112	107	782.0	620	52	286	782	Inning 7+	.238	882	210	29	9	19	62	73	196	.296	.356
Grass	3.03	53	33	0	109	106	766.1	635	57	247	787	None on	.224	2543	569	95	22	44	44	223	669	.290	.330
Turf	2.95	26	12	0	60	53	378.2	308	22	156	351	Runners on	.222	1683	374	54	16	35	329	180	469	.297	.336
April	4.01	8	6	0	25	18	137.0	128	6	65	126	Scoring Posn	.201	992	199	29	9	22	264	139	308	.297	.315
May	2.53	13	7	0	26	25	177.2	142	12	52	172	Close & Late	.207	401	83	11	6	6	26	35	100	.269	.309
June	3.23	10	6	0	27	26	178.1	152	12	57	178	None on/out	.235	1120	263	39	13	26	26	83	274	.291	.363
July	3.06	16	4	0	28	28	203.0	157	26	76	210	vs. 1st Batr (relief)	.000	8	0	0	0	0	1	2	0	.200	.000
August	3.07	14	11	0	30	30	216.2	189	10	82	189	First Inning Pitched	.223	636	142	22	5	14	68	71	187	.311	.340
September/October	2.48	18	11	0	33	32	232.1	175	13	85	252	First 75 Pitches	.224	2721	609	99	24	47	241	269	769	.297	.330
Starter	3.00	77	45	0	159	159	1123.2	928	78	389	1117	Pitch 76-90	.225	502	113	21	6	11	54	45	125	.290	.357
Reliever	2.95	2	0	0	10	0	21.1	15	1	14	21	Pitch 91-105	.203	483	98	15	4	11	38	36	106	.260	.319
0-3 Days Rest	1.59	7	2	0	11	11	79.0	57	6	16	73	Pitch 106+	.237	520	123	14	4	10	40	53	138	.305	.337
4 Days Rest	3.24	35	28	0	82	82	577.0	493	46	212	593	First Pitch	.330	555	183	34	6	22	74	12	0	.345	.532
5+ Days Rest	2.94	35	15	0	66	66	467.2	378	26	161	451	Ahead on Count	.164	2112	347	49	19	16	120	1	960	.169	.228
Pre-All Star	3.16	37	20	0	88	79	569.1	480	39	209	549	Behind on Count	.317	747	237	34	10	23	95	201	0	.459	.482
Post-All Star	2.85	42	25	0	81	80	575.2	463	40	194	589	Two Strikes	.147	2240	329	49	16	17	118	187	1138	.216	.206

Pitcher vs. Batter (career)

Pitches Best Vs.	Avg	AB	H	2B	3B	HR	RBI	BB	SO	OBP	SLG	Pitches Worst Vs.	Avg	AB	H	2B	3B	HR	RBI	BB	SO	OBP	SLG
Chris James	.000	21	0	0	0	0	0	0	5	.000	.000	Deion Sanders	.600	10	6	0	0	1	1	1	1	.636	.900
Charlie Hayes	.053	19	1	1	0	0	1	0	7	.053	.105	Bret Barberie	.500	8	4	1	0	0	2	4	2	.714	.625
Jose Offerman	.059	17	1	0	0	0	0	0	6	.059	.059	Dwight Smith	.462	13	6	1	1	1	3	2	1	.533	.923
Rafael Ramirez	.067	15	1	0	0	0	0	1	1	.125	.067	Todd Benzinger	.444	9	4	0	1	0	0	2	1	.545	.667
Jeff Blauser	.077	13	1	0	0	0	0	2	6	.200	.077	John Morris	.435	23	10	1	0	1	1	6	0	.435	.783

Jeff Conine — Royals — Bats Right (flyball hitter)

	Avg	G	AB	R	H	2B	3B	HR	RBI	BB	SO	HBP	GDP	SB	CS	OBP	SLG	IBB	SH	SF	#Pit	#P/PA	GB	FB	G/F
1992 Season	.253	28	91	10	23	5	2	0	9	8	23	0	1	0	0	.313	.352	1	0	0	370	3.74	22	27	0.81
Career (1990-1992)	.252	37	111	13	28	7	2	0	11	10	28	0	2	0	0	.314	.351	1	0	0	435	3.60	26	34	0.76

1992 Season

	Avg	AB	H	2B	3B	HR	RBI	BB	SO	OBP	SLG		Avg	AB	H	2B	3B	HR	RBI	BB	SO	OBP	SLG
vs. Left	.304	23	7	1	0	0	3	5	5	.429	.348	Scoring Posn	.391	23	9	2	1	0	9	4	3	.481	.565
vs. Right	.235	68	16	4	2	0	6	3	18	.268	.353	Close & Late	.214	14	3	0	0	0	1	2		.267	.214

Dennis Cook — Indians — Pitches Left (flyball pitcher)

	ERA	W	L	Sv	G	GS	IP	BB	SO	Avg	H	2B	3B	HR	RBI	OBP	SLG	CG	ShO	Sup	QS	#P/S	SB	CS	GB	FB	G/F
1992 Season	3.82	5	7	0	32	25	158.0	50	96	.255	156	34	3	29	76	.312	.463	1	0	4.10	10	88	8	10	171	233	0.73
Career (1988-1992)	3.66	24	20	1	126	64	474.2	162	248	.248	442	83	9	68	216	.310	.418	6	3	4.23	28	89	32	24	558	674	0.83

1992 Season

	ERA	W	L	Sv	G	GS	IP	H	HR	BB	SO		Avg	AB	H	2B	3B	HR	RBI	BB	SO	OBP	SLG
Home	4.04	4	3	0	17	14	91.1	87	18	25	58	vs. Left	.235	98	23	3	1	4	12	3	10	.257	.408
Away	3.51	1	4	0	15	11	66.2	69	11	25	38	vs. Right	.259	513	133	31	2	25	64	47	86	.322	.474
Day	3.99	2	3	0	12	12	70.0	74	15	21	42	Inning 1-6	.264	553	146	34	2	26	71	41	86	.316	.474
Night	3.68	3	4	0	20	13	88.0	82	14	29	54	Inning 7+	.172	58	10	0	1	3	5	9	10	.284	.362
Grass	3.74	4	4	0	27	21	137.0	133	26	46	89	None on	.238	395	94	20	2	18	18	30	62	.293	.435
Turf	4.29	1	3	0	5	4	21.0	23	3	4	7	Runners on	.287	216	62	14	1	11	58	20	34	.346	.514
April	4.50	1	2	0	4	4	20.0	21	4	3	8	Scoring Posn	.256	129	33	6	0	5	41	13	17	.317	.419
May	7.31	0	2	0	6	4	16.0	24	5	5	7	Close & Late	.194	31	6	0	1	1	2	6	3	.324	.355
June	3.13	0	1	0	6	1	23.0	18	7	11	19	None on/out	.242	165	40	13	0	9	9	15	23	.306	.485
July	2.48	2	0	0	5	5	32.2	32	1	7	26	vs. 1st Batr (relief)	.429	7	3	0	0	0	1	0	1	.429	.429
August	4.85	2	1	0	5	5	29.2	28	6	12	17	First Inning Pitched	.258	132	34	6	0	10	24	7	27	.295	.530
September/October	2.70	0	1	0	6	6	36.2	33	6	12	19	First 75 Pitches	.263	505	133	29	2	28	66	36	79	.314	.495
Starter	3.91	5	6	0	25	25	138.0	141	24	42	77	Pitch 76-90	.268	56	15	4	0	0	7	7	9	.344	.339
Reliever	3.15	0	1	0	7	0	20.0	15	5	8	19	Pitch 91-105	.097	31	3	1	0	0	1	4	7	.200	.129
0-3 Days Rest	12.15	0	2	0	2	2	6.2	13	3	2	3	Pitch 106+	.263	19	5	0	1	1	2	3	1	.364	.526
4 Days Rest	3.57	2	2	0	12	12	63.0	59	10	23	30	First Pitch	.238	84	20	3	0	6	19	2	0	.258	.488
5+ Days Rest	3.42	3	2	0	11	11	68.1	69	11	17	44	Ahead on Count	.212	278	59	9	2	10	26	0	75	.214	.367
Pre-All Star	4.19	2	5	0	18	11	73.0	75	16	22	48	Behind on Count	.319	119	38	12	1	7	17	24	0	.434	.613
Post-All Star	3.49	3	2	0	14	14	85.0	81	13	28	48	Two Strikes	.212	274	56	12	2	9		24	96	.278	.369

Career (1988-1992)

	ERA	W	L	Sv	G	GS	IP	H	HR	BB	SO		Avg	AB	H	2B	3B	HR	RBI	BB	SO	OBP	SLG
Home	3.36	15	9	1	63	34	273.1	231	43	83	153	vs. Left	.253	328	83	14	3	12	47	29	42	.316	.424
Away	4.07	9	11	0	63	30	201.1	211	25	79	95	vs. Right	.246	1457	359	69	6	56	169	133	206	.308	.417
Day	3.19	10	7	0	45	26	186.1	173	27	59	105	Inning 1-6	.255	1493	380	76	8	60	192	131	216	.314	.437
Night	3.96	14	13	1	81	38	288.1	269	41	103	143	Inning 7+	.212	292	62	7	1	8	24	31	32	.285	.325
Grass	3.74	11	10	0	63	35	231.0	220	39	82	134	None on	.236	1155	273	51	5	43	43	78	163	.287	.401
Turf	3.58	13	10	1	63	29	243.2	222	29	80	114	Runners on	.268	630	169	32	4	25	173	84	85	.348	.451
April	2.28	4	2	0	8	7	47.1	36	5	9	14	Scoring Posn	.266	365	97	15	3	14	142	57	43	.352	.438
May	5.32	3	3	0	11	9	47.1	55	10	12	18	Close & Late	.269	119	32	1	1	3	13	18	12	.360	.370
June	3.35	3	3	0	20	9	83.1	73	12	36	55	None on/out	.223	471	105	27	1	17	17	37	61	.262	.393
July	2.88	6	3	1	31	11	100.0	89	10	29	61	vs. 1st Batr (relief)	.354	48	17	0	0	1	16	9	8	.426	.417
August	5.33	5	3	0	22	11	74.1	86	14	40	35	First Inning Pitched	.252	421	106	21	2	17	75	44	62	.318	.432
September/October	3.38	6	5	0	34	17	122.1	103	17	36	65	First 75 Pitches	.247	1487	367	70	8	58	185	129	202	.307	.422
Starter	3.85	20	18	0	64	64	371.1	360	58	118	196	Pitch 76-90	.314	153	48	8	0	5	19	19	21	.385	.464
Reliever	2.96	4	2	1	62	0	103.1	82	10	44	52	Pitch 91-105	.159	88	14	3	0	2	6	9	17	.235	.261
0-3 Days Rest	5.06	1	2	0	4	4	21.1	26	4	6	9	Pitch 106+	.228	57	13	2	1	3	6	5	8	.290	.456
4 Days Rest	3.48	9	9	0	30	30	176.1	160	28	60	86	First Pitch	.272	246	67	11	0	13	42	16	0	.323	.476
5+ Days Rest	4.09	10	7	0	30	30	171.2	174	26	52	101	Ahead on Count	.190	803	154	25	5	18	60	1	211	.190	.300
Pre-All Star	3.40	10	9	1	49	29	214.2	194	30	65	110	Behind on Count	.314	376	118	28	3	18	64	65	0	.437	.476
Post-All Star	3.88	14	11	0	77	35	260.0	248	38	97	135	Two Strikes	.194	778	151	29	5	20	64	60	248	.251	.321

Pitcher vs. Batter (career)

Pitches Best Vs.	Avg	AB	H	2B	3B	HR	RBI	BB	SO	OBP	SLG	Pitches Worst Vs.	Avg	AB	H	2B	3B	HR	RBI	BB	SO	OBP	SLG
Kevin McReynolds	.071	14	1	0	0	0	1	2	3	.188	.071	Mike Fitzgerald	.727	11	8	1	0	2	6	2	1	.769	1.364
Jeff Blauser	.091	11	1	0	0	0	0	0	1	.091	.091	Greg Litton	.615	13	8	1	0	1	2	0	0	.615	.923
Candy Maldonado	.111	9	1	0	0	0	0	2	3	.273	.111	Lonnie Smith	.412	17	7	1	0	3	6	0	1	.412	1.000
Will Clark	.167	18	3	1	0	0	2	0	5	.167	.222	Joe Carter	.364	11	4	1	0	1	1	4	0	.533	.727
Willie McGee	.182	11	2	0	0	0	0	1	0	.167	.182	Darryl Strawberry	.333	9	3	0	0	1	2	3	0	.500	.667

Steve Cooke — Pirates — Pitches Left

	ERA	W	L	Sv	G	GS	IP	BB	SO	Avg	H	2B	3B	HR	RBI	OBP	SLG	GF	IR	IRS	Hld	SvOp	SB	CS	GB	FB	G/F
1992 Season	3.52	2	0	1	11	0	23.0	4	10	.253	22	6	0	2	7	.286	.391	8	3	0	1	1	0	0	29	27	1.07

1992 Season

	ERA	W	L	Sv	G	GS	IP	H	HR	BB	SO		Avg	AB	H	2B	3B	HR	RBI	BB	SO	OBP	SLG
Home	1.32	1	0	0	4	0	13.2	12	0	3	6	vs. Left	.217	23	5	1	0	0	1	0	3	.217	.261
Away	6.75	1	0	1	7	0	9.1	10	2	1	4	vs. Right	.266	64	17	5	0	2	6	4	7	.309	.438

Scott Cooper — Red Sox — Bats Left

	Avg	G	AB	R	H	2B	3B	HR	RBI	BB	SO	HBP	GDP	SB	CS	OBP	SLG	IBB	SH	SF	#Pit	#P/PA	GB	FB	G/F
1992 Season	.276	123	337	34	93	21	0	5	33	37	33	0	5	1	1	.346	.383	0	2	2	1349	3.59	139	97	1.43
Career (1990-1992)	.292	139	373	40	109	25	2	5	40	39	36	0	5	1	1	.357	.410	0	2	2	1475	3.56	148	113	1.31

1992 Season

	Avg	AB	H	2B	3B	HR	RBI	BB	SO	OBP	SLG		Avg	AB	H	2B	3B	HR	RBI	BB	SO	OBP	SLG
vs. Left	.268	41	11	3	0	1	5	7	6	.375	.415	Scoring Posn	.278	72	20	2	0	0	28	10	12	.357	.306

1992 Season

	Avg	AB	H	2B	3B	HR	RBI	BB	SO	OBP	SLG		Avg	AB	H	2B	3B	HR	RBI	BB	SO	OBP	SLG
vs. Right	.277	296	82	18	0	4	28	30	27	.341	.378	Close & Late	.316	76	24	9	0	0	9	6	8	.366	.434
Groundball	.350	80	28	7	0	0	8	7	9	.402	.438	None on/out	.303	66	20	7	0	1	1	3	4	.333	.455
Flyball	.252	103	26	4	0	3	11	13	10	.333	.379	Batting #2	.358	67	24	4	0	2	8	7	6	.419	.507
Home	.290	155	45	6	0	2	10	15	17	.353	.368	Batting #7	.213	127	27	3	0	1	10	18	9	.308	.260
Away	.264	182	48	15	0	3	23	22	16	.340	.396	Other	.294	143	42	14	0	2	15	12	18	.346	.434
Day	.314	105	33	8	0	2	12	9	9	.365	.448	April	.100	10	1	0	0	0	2	2	2	.231	.100
Night	.259	232	60	13	0	3	21	28	24	.337	.353	May	.243	37	9	2	0	0	3	5	1	.333	.297
Grass	.277	292	81	16	0	5	29	30	28	.343	.384	June	.273	77	21	7	0	0	8	5	7	.313	.364
Turf	.267	45	12	5	0	0	4	7	5	.365	.378	July	.256	39	10	1	0	0	5	7	9	.370	.282
First Pitch	.283	53	15	4	0	0	4	0	0	.283	.358	August	.283	53	15	5	0	0	3	4	7	.333	.377
Ahead on Count	.392	97	38	10	0	3	15	20	0	.492	.588	September/October	.306	121	37	6	0	5	12	14	7	.378	.479
Behind on Count	.208	96	20	4	0	0	5	0	17	.206	.250	Pre-All Star	.253	150	38	9	0	0	18	16	17	.321	.313
Two Strikes	.192	120	23	2	0	2	12	17	33	.290	.258	Post-All Star	.294	187	55	12	0	5	15	21	16	.365	.439

1992 By Position

Position	Avg	AB	H	2B	3B	HR	RBI	BB	SO	OBP	SLG	G	GS	Innings	PO	A	E	DP	Fld Pct	Rng Fctr	In Zone	Outs	Zone Rtg	MLB Zone
As Pinch Hitter	.333	15	5	3	0	0	0	2	5	.412	.533	18	0	---	---	---	---	---	---	---	---	---	---	---
As 1b	.285	165	47	9	0	2	18	15	12	.344	.376	62	46	420.1	446	33	5	43	.990	---	86	76	.884	.843
As 3b	.263	152	40	9	0	3	14	20	14	.345	.382	47	39	375.0	26	102	4	5	.970	3.07	129	111	.860	.841

Joey Cora — White Sox   Bats Both (groundball hitter)

	Avg	G	AB	R	H	2B	3B	HR	RBI	BB	SO	HBP	GDP	SB	CS	OBP	SLG	IBB	SH	SF	#Pit	#P/PA	GB	FB	G/F
1992 Season	.246	68	122	27	30	7	1	0	9	22	13	4	2	10	3	.371	.320	1	2	3	573	3.79	49	30	1.63
Last Five Years	.252	231	469	81	118	13	4	0	30	49	43	9	4	30	12	.330	.296	2	10	6	1987	3.73	188	125	1.50

1992 Season

	Avg	AB	H	2B	3B	HR	RBI	BB	SO	OBP	SLG		Avg	AB	H	2B	3B	HR	RBI	BB	SO	OBP	SLG
vs. Left	.222	27	6	2	0	0	3	5	4	.353	.296	Scoring Posn	.208	24	5	1	0	0	9	7	4	.353	.250
vs. Right	.253	95	24	5	1	0	6	17	9	.376	.326	Close & Late	.143	28	4	1	0	0	0	4	4	.250	.179
Home	.174	46	8	2	0	0	3	7	4	.316	.217	None on/out	.286	42	12	4	1	0	0	6	3	.412	.429
Away	.289	76	22	5	1	0	6	15	9	.404	.382	Batting #1	.313	48	15	4	1	0	4	10	5	.443	.438
First Pitch	.192	26	5	1	0	0	5	1	0	.233	.231	Batting #2	.174	23	4	1	0	0	4	6	2	.364	.217
Ahead on Count	.467	15	7	2	0	0	1	12	0	.690	.600	Other	.216	51	11	2	0	0	1	6	6	.298	.255
Behind on Count	.105	38	4	2	0	0	1	0	6	.146	.158	Pre-All Star	.221	68	15	5	0	0	4	7	6	.313	.294
Two Strikes	.236	55	13	3	1	0	2	9	13	.364	.327	Post-All Star	.278	54	15	2	1	0	5	15	7	.437	.352

Last Five Years

	Avg	AB	H	2B	3B	HR	RBI	BB	SO	OBP	SLG		Avg	AB	H	2B	3B	HR	RBI	BB	SO	OBP	SLG
vs. Left	.281	114	32	2	0	0	5	12	13	.357	.298	Scoring Posn	.202	109	22	2	0	0	28	15	10	.290	.220
vs. Right	.242	355	86	11	4	0	25	37	30	.322	.296	Close & Late	.200	80	16	1	0	0	2	7	9	.278	.213
Groundball	.291	141	41	4	1	0	11	9	11	.338	.333	None on/out	.264	144	38	6	2	0	0	15	13	.350	.333
Flyball	.284	102	29	4	1	0	3	17	12	.407	.343	Batting #1	.271	96	26	6	1	0	4	14	9	.372	.354
Home	.280	218	61	7	2	0	16	22	15	.363	.330	Batting #8	.252	214	54	3	2	0	17	17	17	.309	.285
Away	.227	251	57	6	2	0	14	27	28	.302	.267	Other	.239	159	38	4	1	0	9	17	17	.332	.277
Day	.234	158	37	4	1	0	9	16	14	.315	.272	April	.207	29	6	1	0	0	1	3	1	.303	.241
Night	.260	311	81	9	3	0	21	33	29	.338	.309	May	.236	55	13	2	0	0	3	6	7	.323	.273
Grass	.258	384	99	12	4	0	24	44	35	.344	.310	June	.279	86	24	2	2	0	6	5	9	.337	.349
Turf	.224	85	19	1	0	0	6	5	8	.264	.235	July	.238	80	19	1	0	0	5	5	5	.295	.300
First Pitch	.247	73	18	1	1	0	7	1	0	.269	.288	August	.197	76	15	0	0	0	9	10	11	.284	.197
Ahead on Count	.320	100	32	3	2	0	9	23	0	.449	.390	September/October	.287	143	41	5	1	0	6	20	10	.378	.336
Behind on Count	.195	154	30	4	0	0	8	0	25	.217	.221	Pre-All Star	.260	181	47	7	2	0	10	14	18	.328	.320
Two Strikes	.225	200	45	6	1	0	8	24	43	.317	.265	Post-All Star	.247	288	71	6	2	0	20	35	25	.331	.281

Batter vs. Pitcher (career)

Hits Best Against	Avg	AB	H	2B	3B	HR	RBI	BB	SO	OBP	SLG	Hits Worst Against	Avg	AB	H	2B	3B	HR	RBI	BB	SO	OBP	SLG
												Bob Welch	.000	12	0	0	0	0	0	2	2	.143	.000
												Kelly Downs	.000	11	0	0	0	0	0	0	0	.000	.000
												John Smiley	.000	8	0	0	0	0	0	0	1	.333	.000

Wil Cordero — Expos   Bats Right (groundball hitter)

	Avg	G	AB	R	H	2B	3B	HR	RBI	BB	SO	HBP	GDP	SB	CS	OBP	SLG	IBB	SH	SF	#Pit	#P/PA	GB	FB	G/F
1992 Season	.302	45	126	17	38	4	1	2	8	9	31	1	2	0	0	.353	.397	0	1	0	570	4.19	48	23	2.09

1992 Season

	Avg	AB	H	2B	3B	HR	RBI	BB	SO	OBP	SLG		Avg	AB	H	2B	3B	HR	RBI	BB	SO	OBP	SLG
vs. Left	.471	34	16	1	0	0	2	3	4	.514	.500	Scoring Posn	.286	21	6	0	0	1	7	1	5	.348	.429
vs. Right	.239	92	22	3	1	2	6	6	27	.293	.359	Close & Late	.240	25	6	0	0	0	1	2	6	.296	.240
Home	.306	62	19	0	1	1	3	4	9	.348	.387	None on/out	.375	32	12	2	0	1	1	3	3	.429	.531
Away	.297	64	19	4	0	1	5	5	22	.357	.406	Batting #7	.243	37	9	2	0	0	1	3	11	.300	.297
First Pitch	.750	4	3	1	0	0	0	0	0	.750	1.000	Batting #8	.291	55	16	0	0	2	5	4	12	.350	.400
Ahead on Count	.455	33	15	2	0	1	3	4	0	.526	.606	Other	.382	34	13	2	1	0	2	2	8	.417	.500

1992 Season

	Avg	AB	H	2B	3B	HR	RBI	BB	SO	OBP	SLG		Avg	AB	H	2B	3B	HR	RBI	BB	SO	OBP	SLG
Behind on Count	.167	48	8	0	0	0	0	0	19	.167	.167	Pre-All Star	.000	0	0	0	0	0	0	0	0	.000	.000
Two Strikes	.127	63	8	1	0	0	0	5	31	.191	.143	Post-All Star	.302	126	38	4	1	2	8	9	31	.353	.397

Rheal Cormier — Cardinals — Pitches Left (groundball pitcher)

	ERA	W	L	Sv	G	GS	IP	BB	SO	Avg	H	2B	3B	HR	RBI	OBP	SLG	CG	ShO	Sup	QS	#P/S	SB	CS	GB	FB	G/F
1992 Season	3.68	10	10	0	31	30	186.0	33	117	.269	194	34	3	15	70	.305	.388	3	0	3.92	17	86	11	4	300	177	1.69
Career (1991-1992)	3.80	14	15	0	42	40	253.2	41	155	.272	268	50	4	20	97	.304	.391	5	0	3.69	22	87	12	7	392	261	1.50

1992 Season

	ERA	W	L	Sv	G	GS	IP	H	HR	BB	SO		Avg	AB	H	2B	3B	HR	RBI	BB	SO	OBP	SLG
Home	3.98	7	4	0	16	15	92.2	108	6	19	46	vs. Left	.288	132	38	10	1	1	12	5	25	.324	.402
Away	3.38	3	6	0	15	15	93.1	86	9	14	71	vs. Right	.265	588	156	24	2	14	58	28	92	.301	.384
Day	3.06	4	4	0	10	10	64.2	63	4	10	40	Inning 1-6	.268	624	167	29	3	14	63	27	103	.302	.391
Night	4.01	6	6	0	21	20	121.1	131	11	23	77	Inning 7+	.281	96	27	5	0	1	7	6	14	.324	.365
Grass	3.30	1	3	0	7	7	43.2	43	5	7	31	None on	.255	444	113	21	0	6	6	15	78	.284	.342
Turf	3.79	9	7	0	24	23	142.1	151	10	26	86	Runners on	.293	276	81	13	3	9	64	18	39	.338	.460
April	4.50	0	3	0	3	3	18.0	21	1	10	15	Scoring Posn	.252	159	40	8	1	5	54	14	28	.315	.409
May	7.80	0	2	0	6	6	30.0	38	4	6	16	Close & Late	.377	53	20	2	0	1	6	3	6	.411	.472
June	2.63	1	1	0	5	4	24.0	26	3	3	11	None on/out	.262	191	50	12	0	3	3	6	31	.288	.372
July	4.18	2	2	0	5	5	28.0	38	4	2	19	vs. 1st Batr (relief)	.000	1	0	0	0	0	0	0	0	.000	.000
August	1.91	2	2	0	6	6	42.1	30	1	8	22	First Inning Pitched	.241	116	28	6	1	1	10	6	19	.276	.336
September/October	2.47	5	0	0	6	6	43.2	41	2	4	34	First 75 Pitches	.270	589	159	27	3	13	59	27	95	.305	.392
Starter	3.70	10	10	0	30	30	185.0	193	15	33	117	Pitch 76-90	.241	79	19	2	0	1	5	2	15	.268	.304
Reliever	0.00	0	0	0	1	0	1.0	1	0	0	0	Pitch 91-105	.306	36	11	3	0	1	6	3	3	.359	.472
0-3 Days Rest	1.29	1	0	0	1	1	7.0	6	1	1	3	Pitch 106+	.313	16	5	2	0	0	1	0	4	.353	.438
4 Days Rest	2.82	5	4	0	15	15	99.0	91	7	15	60	First Pitch	.338	139	47	8	2	6	26	2	0	.352	.554
5+ Days Rest	5.01	4	6	0	14	14	79.0	96	7	17	54	Ahead on Count	.211	299	63	7	1	1	24	0	101	.220	.251
Pre-All Star	4.60	2	7	0	16	15	86.0	97	9	20	57	Behind on Count	.310	155	48	12	0	5	12	19	0	.383	.484
Post-All Star	2.88	8	3	0	15	15	100.0	97	6	13	60	Two Strikes	.203	276	56	7	1	2	24	12	117	.243	.257

Jim Corsi — Athletics — Pitches Right (groundball pitcher)

	ERA	W	L	Sv	G	GS	IP	BB	SO	Avg	H	2B	3B	HR	RBI	OBP	SLG	GF	IR	IRS	Hld	SvOp	SB	CS	GB	FB	G/F
1992 Season	1.43	4	2	0	32	0	44.0	18	19	.275	44	4	1	2	18	.344	.350	16	24	9	0	5	5	5	91	31	2.94
Career (1988-1992)	2.78	5	10	0	112	1	181.1	57	103	.250	166	18	3	11	77	.306	.335	31	63	22	10	3	19	9	331	128	2.59

1992 Season

	ERA	W	L	Sv	G	GS	IP	H	HR	BB	SO		Avg	AB	H	2B	3B	HR	RBI	BB	SO	OBP	SLG
Home	0.45	4	1	0	14	0	20.0	19	1	10	8	vs. Left	.357	70	25	3	0	1	8	6	8	.408	.443
Away	2.25	0	1	0	18	0	24.0	25	1	8	11	vs. Right	.211	90	19	1	1	1	10	12	11	.298	.278
Starter	0.00	0	0	0	0	0	0.0	0	0	0	0	Scoring Posn	.143	42	6	0	0	0	14	9	10	.283	.143
Reliever	1.43	4	2	0	32	0	44.0	44	2	18	19	Close & Late	.351	57	20	1	0	2	6	6	5	.413	.474
0 Days rest	1.35	0	0	0	4	0	6.2	5	1	5	3	None on/out	.375	40	15	1	0	2	2	3	1	.419	.550
1 or 2 Days rest	1.69	1	2	0	15	0	21.1	20	0	8	7	First Pitch	.286	21	6	0	0	0	4	2	0	.333	.286
3+ Days rest	1.13	3	0	0	13	0	16.0	19	1	5	9	Behind on Count	.364	55	20	2	0	1	5	5	0	.417	.455
Pre-All Star	4.32	1	1	0	5	0	8.1	9	0	2	2	Ahead on Count	.236	55	13	2	0	0	7	0	11	.232	.273
Post-All Star	0.76	3	1	0	27	0	35.2	35	2	16	17	Two Strikes	.203	59	12	2	0	1	8	11	19	.324	.288

Career (1988-1992)

	ERA	W	L	Sv	G	GS	IP	H	HR	BB	SO		Avg	AB	H	2B	3B	HR	RBI	BB	SO	OBP	SLG
Home	3.47	5	5	0	52	1	85.2	74	7	23	50	vs. Left	.265	310	82	9	1	6	29	26	43	.322	.358
Away	2.16	0	5	0	60	0	95.2	92	4	34	53	vs. Right	.237	355	84	9	2	5	48	31	60	.293	.315
Day	3.08	2	1	0	29	1	49.2	39	2	21	33	Inning 1-6	.257	222	57	8	0	4	35	21	35	.313	.347
Night	2.67	3	9	0	83	0	131.2	127	9	36	70	Inning 7+	.246	443	109	10	3	7	42	36	68	.302	.330
Grass	1.99	5	6	0	65	1	108.2	95	5	38	58	None on	.251	370	93	7	1	4	4	32	61	.313	.308
Turf	3.96	0	4	0	47	0	72.2	71	6	19	45	Runners on	.247	295	73	11	2	7	73	25	42	.298	.369
April	3.86	0	2	0	4	0	7.0	9	0	2	5	Scoring Posn	.264	159	42	6	1	2	58	19	27	.326	.352
May	4.20	0	1	0	10	0	15.0	15	3	5	11	Close & Late	.331	151	50	5	2	5	24	16	23	.395	.490
June	2.43	1	2	0	17	0	33.1	27	0	11	15	None on/out	.278	162	45	4	0	4	4	17	18	.346	.377
July	2.45	0	2	0	27	0	47.2	45	4	13	25	vs. 1st Batr (relief)	.230	100	23	3	0	0	8	9	12	.291	.260
August	4.19	2	2	0	25	1	38.2	41	3	13	26	First Inning Pitched	.264	386	102	10	1	4	50	35	60	.321	.326
September/October	1.36	2	1	0	29	0	39.2	29	1	3	26	First 15 Pitches	.273	355	97	10	1	4	45	30	51	.326	.341
Starter	10.80	0	0	0	1	1	5.0	7	0	2	1	Pitch 16-30	.246	191	47	4	2	4	17	18	33	.310	.351
Reliever	2.55	5	10	0	111	0	176.1	159	11	55	102	Pitch 31-45	.159	82	13	2	0	0	8	5	15	.207	.256
0 Days rest	2.33	1	0	0	10	0	19.1	17	1	8	11	Pitch 46+	.243	37	9	2	0	1	7	4	4	.310	.378
1 or 2 Days rest	2.57	1	5	0	46	0	77.0	67	4	22	40	First Pitch	.301	83	25	2	1	0	10	6	0	.344	.349
3+ Days rest	2.59	3	4	0	55	0	80.0	75	6	25	51	Ahead on Count	.221	267	59	10	1	4	30	0	71	.219	.311
Pre-All Star	3.13	1	6	0	41	0	74.2	70	6	21	34	Behind on Count	.288	156	45	5	0	4	24	27	0	.387	.397
Post-All Star	2.53	4	4	0	71	1	106.2	96	5	36	69	Two Strikes	.189	260	53	4	1	5	21	24	103	.252	.264

Tim Costo — Reds
Bats Right

	Avg	G	AB	R	H	2B	3B	HR	RBI	BB	SO	HBP	GDP	SB	CS	OBP	SLG	IBB	SH	SF	#Pit	#P/PA	GB	FB	G/F
1992 Season	.222	12	36	3	8	2	0	0	2	5	6	0	4	0	0	.310	.278	0	0	1	139	3.31	15	10	1.50

1992 Season

	Avg	AB	H	2B	3B	HR	RBI	BB	SO	OBP	SLG		Avg	AB	H	2B	3B	HR	RBI	BB	SO	OBP	SLG
vs. Left	.214	14	3	1	0	0	1	2	2	.294	.286	Scoring Posn	.200	5	1	0	0	0	2	2	1	.375	.200
vs. Right	.227	22	5	1	0	0	1	3	4	.320	.273	Close & Late	.500	4	2	0	0	0	0	0	0	.500	.500

Henry Cotto — Mariners
Bats Right

	Avg	G	AB	R	H	2B	3B	HR	RBI	BB	SO	HBP	GDP	SB	CS	OBP	SLG	IBB	SH	SF	#Pit	#P/PA	GB	FB	G/F
1992 Season	.259	108	294	42	76	11	1	5	27	14	49	1	2	23	2	.294	.354	3	3	1	1033	3.33	120	71	1.69
Last Five Years	.265	534	1507	211	400	60	9	32	149	81	225	12	34	97	15	.307	.381	8	15	8	5431	3.38	597	407	1.47

1992 Season

	Avg	AB	H	2B	3B	HR	RBI	BB	SO	OBP	SLG		Avg	AB	H	2B	3B	HR	RBI	BB	SO	OBP	SLG
vs. Left	.321	168	54	9	0	4	21	14	25	.375	.446	Scoring Posn	.297	64	19	2	1	1	22	8	10	.370	.406
vs. Right	.175	126	22	2	1	1	6	0	24	.175	.230	Close & Late	.216	51	11	1	1	1	5	2	8	.245	.333
Groundball	.215	65	14	2	0	0	4	2	17	.235	.246	None on/out	.198	96	19	3	0	1	1	4	17	.230	.260
Flyball	.271	107	29	6	0	2	12	5	17	.304	.383	Batting #1	.288	184	53	8	1	1	16	13	29	.337	.359
Home	.248	117	29	6	0	2	14	11	18	.315	.350	Batting #2	.136	44	6	1	0	0	2	1	9	.156	.159
Away	.266	177	47	5	1	3	13	3	31	.278	.356	Other	.258	66	17	2	0	4	9	0	11	.258	.470
Day	.232	99	23	3	1	2	10	3	21	.255	.343	April	.346	26	9	3	0	0	3	2	4	.393	.462
Night	.272	195	53	8	0	3	17	11	28	.313	.359	May	.243	37	9	1	0	3	7	3	8	.300	.514
Grass	.264	140	37	4	1	2	12	3	25	.280	.350	June	.261	46	12	1	0	1	4	3	7	.306	.348
Turf	.253	154	39	7	0	3	15	11	24	.305	.357	July	.218	55	12	2	0	0	1	1	4	.246	.255
First Pitch	.326	43	14	3	0	1	9	3	0	.370	.465	August	.327	55	18	2	0	0	8	4	13	.367	.364
Ahead on Count	.353	68	24	2	1	1	5	6	0	.408	.456	September/October	.213	75	16	2	1	1	4	1	13	.224	.307
Behind on Count	.165	115	19	1	0	3	8	0	29	.165	.252	Pre-All Star	.254	138	35	5	0	4	15	8	23	.295	.377
Two Strikes	.168	119	20	2	0	2	8	5	49	.202	.235	Post-All Star	.263	156	41	6	1	1	12	6	26	.293	.333

1992 By Position

Position	Avg	AB	H	2B	3B	HR	RBI	BB	SO	OBP	SLG	G	GS	Innings	PO	A	E	DP	Fld Pct	Rng Fctr	In Zone	Outs	Zone Rtg	MLB Zone
As Pinch Hitter	.500	18	9	1	0	1	5	1	1	.526	.722	22	0	---	---	---	---	---	---	---	---	---	---	---
As lf	.266	184	49	7	1	3	19	8	31	.295	.364	63	44	402.1	114	2	0	0	1.000	2.59	135	109	.807	.809
As cf	.200	65	13	3	0	1	3	5	13	.268	.292	30	15	162.1	50	0	0	0	1.000	2.77	58	48	.828	.824

Last Five Years

	Avg	AB	H	2B	3B	HR	RBI	BB	SO	OBP	SLG		Avg	AB	H	2B	3B	HR	RBI	BB	SO	OBP	SLG
vs. Left	.285	764	218	29	6	19	84	47	107	.328	.414	Scoring Posn	.260	334	87	6	4	6	104	32	47	.324	.356
vs. Right	.245	743	182	31	3	13	65	34	118	.284	.347	Close & Late	.224	250	56	4	2	5	21	15	44	.275	.316
Groundball	.285	330	94	14	2	6	34	21	53	.333	.394	None on/out	.263	396	104	17	1	10	10	19	57	.301	.386
Flyball	.253	384	97	21	0	7	39	23	63	.296	.362	Batting #1	.266	474	126	20	4	7	40	24	75	.302	.369
Home	.259	700	181	26	4	16	75	48	92	.313	.376	Batting #2	.250	631	158	25	3	9	60	38	96	.299	.342
Away	.271	807	219	34	5	16	74	33	133	.301	.385	Other	.289	402	116	15	2	16	49	19	54	.324	.455
Day	.269	416	112	19	4	9	39	16	76	.299	.399	April	.362	185	67	12	0	5	25	10	23	.394	.508
Night	.264	1091	288	41	5	23	110	65	149	.309	.374	May	.263	327	86	6	0	7	27	20	52	.307	.346
Grass	.289	603	174	25	4	12	59	28	95	.322	.403	June	.262	271	71	9	4	5	30	15	44	.305	.380
Turf	.250	904	226	35	4	20	90	53	130	.297	.366	July	.247	291	72	13	2	5	27	12	39	.285	.357
First Pitch	.342	237	81	15	1	5	33	5	0	.354	.477	August	.245	192	47	6	0	5	19	12	32	.291	.354
Ahead on Count	.360	358	129	18	4	13	48	40	0	.425	.542	September/October	.237	241	57	14	3	5	21	12	35	.278	.382
Behind on Count	.215	550	118	13	3	10	42	0	137	.219	.304	Pre-All Star	.276	901	249	29	4	19	92	48	134	.316	.381
Two Strikes	.171	614	105	15	2	6	35	33	224	.216	.231	Post-All Star	.249	606	151	31	5	13	57	33	91	.293	.381

Batter vs. Pitcher (career)

Hits Best Against	Avg	AB	H	2B	3B	HR	RBI	BB	SO	OBP	SLG	Hits Worst Against	Avg	AB	H	2B	3B	HR	RBI	BB	SO	OBP	SLG
Jack Morris	.500	16	8	2	0	1	1	0	2	.500	.813	Dave Stewart	.067	15	1	0	0	0	0	1	6	.125	.067
Rick Honeycutt	.444	9	4	0	0	1	2	1	1	.455	.778	Joe Hesketh	.077	13	1	1	0	0	0	0	2	.077	.154
Curt Young	.391	23	9	1	0	2	5	0	2	.391	.696	Mark Guthrie	.077	13	1	0	0	0	0	0	5	.077	.077
Greg Cadaret	.385	13	5	0	0	1	1	3	1	.500	.615	Bruce Hurst	.133	15	2	0	0	0	0	0	5	.133	.133
Chuck Crim	.308	13	4	1	0	1	1	0	2	.308	.692	Mark Langston	.152	33	5	0	0	0	0	1	7	.147	.152

Danny Cox — Pirates
Pitches Right

	ERA	W	L	Sv	G	GS	IP	BB	SO	Avg	H	2B	3B	HR	RBI	OBP	SLG	GF	IR	IRS	Hld	SvOp	SB	CS	GB	FB	G/F
1992 Season	4.60	5	3	3	25	7	62.2	27	48	.272	66	12	1	5	41	.341	.391	8	17	8	2	5	5	1	84	65	1.29
Last Five Years	4.37	12	17	3	61	37	251.0	91	141	.266	253	50	7	25	130	.328	.413	10	23	9	3	5	23	13	368	265	1.39

1992 Season

	ERA	W	L	Sv	G	GS	IP	H	HR	BB	SO		Avg	AB	H	2B	3B	HR	RBI	BB	SO	OBP	SLG
Home	3.89	3	2	2	15	4	37.0	37	3	16	28	vs. Left	.287	129	37	6	1	3	22	20	20	.377	.419
Away	5.61	2	1	1	10	3	25.2	29	2	11	20	vs. Right	.254	114	29	6	0	2	19	7	28	.295	.360
Starter	4.63	2	2	0	7	7	35.0	40	3	17	28	Scoring Posn	.314	70	22	4	1	1	33	12	15	.400	.443
Reliever	4.55	3	1	3	18	0	27.2	26	2	10	20	Close & Late	.222	54	12	4	0	0	7	6	9	.295	.296

1992 Season

	ERA	W	L	Sv	G	GS	IP	H	HR	BB	SO		Avg	AB	H	2B	3B	HR	RBI	BB	SO	OBP	SLG
0 Days rest	0.00	0	0	0	0	0	0.0	0	0	0	0	None on/out	.259	58	15	2	0	1	1	3	5	.295	.345
1 or 2 Days rest	3.20	3	1	2	12	0	19.2	15	1	8	15	First Pitch	.296	27	8	5	0	0	6	2	0	.333	.481
3+ Days rest	7.88	0	0	1	6	0	8.0	11	1	2	5	Behind on Count	.328	61	20	5	1	3	17	16	0	.468	.590
Pre-All Star	5.40	2	2	0	9	7	38.1	46	3	19	30	Ahead on Count	.225	111	25	0	0	1	7	0	42	.225	.252
Post-All Star	3.33	3	1	3	16	0	24.1	20	2	8	18	Two Strikes	.175	114	20	2	0	0	11	9	48	.236	.193

Last Five Years

	ERA	W	L	Sv	G	GS	IP	H	HR	BB	SO		Avg	AB	H	2B	3B	HR	RBI	BB	SO	OBP	SLG
Home	3.99	8	9	2	34	20	140.0	136	13	46	82	vs. Left	.302	494	149	32	5	15	81	61	49	.373	.478
Away	4.86	4	8	1	27	17	111.0	118	12	45	59	vs. Right	.228	456	104	18	2	10	49	30	92	.276	.342
Day	4.78	4	7	0	19	11	69.2	75	10	22	33	Inning 1-6	.265	777	206	41	6	21	104	75	111	.328	.414
Night	4.22	8	10	3	42	26	181.1	178	15	69	108	Inning 7+	.272	173	47	9	1	4	26	16	30	.328	.405
Grass	4.54	4	4	0	17	11	71.1	68	8	29	40	None on	.254	551	140	25	2	15	15	54	77	.321	.388
Turf	4.31	8	13	3	44	26	179.2	185	17	62	101	Runners on	.283	399	113	25	5	10	115	37	64	.337	.446
April	4.32	4	4	0	11	11	66.2	71	6	21	39	Scoring Posn	.275	251	69	14	4	6	102	28	41	.332	.434
May	4.86	1	2	0	8	6	33.1	34	3	17	22	Close & Late	.222	90	20	6	0	0	11	9	15	.284	.289
June	4.95	2	0	0	4	4	20.0	17	1	8	7	None on/out	.255	239	61	11	1	5	5	19	23	.310	.372
July	4.06	1	7	0	9	9	57.2	60	6	24	34	vs. 1st Batr (relief)	.227	22	5	0	0	1	9	0	2	.208	.364
August	4.98	2	3	1	11	7	43.1	49	6	10	18	First Inning Pitched	.258	217	56	13	2	5	41	22	32	.322	.406
September/October	3.30	2	1	2	18	0	30.0	22	3	11	21	First 15 Pitches	.262	191	50	11	2	5	26	19	26	.326	.419
Starter	4.44	9	16	0	37	37	211.0	219	21	78	115	Pitch 16-30	.253	194	49	11	2	4	28	15	31	.303	.392
Reliever	4.05	3	1	3	24	0	40.0	34	4	13	26	Pitch 31-45	.297	172	51	11	1	3	15	12	19	.341	.424
0 Days rest	0.00	0	0	0	0	0	0.0	0	0	0	0	Pitch 46+	.262	393	103	17	2	13	61	45	65	.335	.415
1 or 2 Days rest	2.82	3	1	2	14	0	22.1	16	1	8	16	First Pitch	.250	136	34	12	1	1	21	10	0	.293	.375
3+ Days rest	5.60	0	0	1	10	0	17.2	18	3	5	10	Ahead on Count	.214	401	86	17	0	2	24	0	117	.215	.272
Pre-All Star	4.56	7	9	0	26	24	140.0	141	12	53	79	Behind on Count	.361	227	82	10	5	14	54	45	0	.464	.634
Post-All Star	4.14	5	8	3	35	13	111.0	112	13	38	62	Two Strikes	.173	387	67	16	1	0	25	36	141	.243	.220

Pitcher vs. Batter (since 1984)

Pitches Best Vs.	Avg	AB	H	2B	3B	HR	RBI	BB	SO	OBP	SLG	Pitches Worst Vs.	Avg	AB	H	2B	3B	HR	RBI	BB	SO	OBP	SLG
Gary Redus	.000	14	0	0	0	0	0	0	2	.000	.000	Gerald Perry	.550	20	11	2	0	0	2	2	1	.591	.650
Rafael Belliard	.077	13	1	0	0	0	0	2	3	.200	.077	Denny Walling	.478	23	11	2	1	0	3	3	0	.500	.652
Kevin Bass	.120	25	3	0	0	1	1	2	3	.179	.120	Kal Daniels	.462	13	6	1	0	1	2	4	2	.588	.769
Mike LaValliere	.154	13	2	0	0	1	1	1	2	.214	.154	Matt D. Williams	.455	11	5	1	0	3	5	1	0	.500	1.364
Mariano Duncan	.154	13	2	0	0	0	0	2		.154	.154	Rafael Palmeiro	.364	11	4	2	0	1	2	1	1	.417	.818

Tim Crews — Dodgers

Pitches Right

	ERA	W	L	Sv	G	GS	IP	BB	SO	Avg	H	2B	3B	HR	RBI	OBP	SLG	GF	IR	IRS	Hld	SvOp	SB	CS	GB	FB	G/F
1992 Season	5.19	0	2	0	49	2	78.0	20	43	.310	95	10	3	6	49	.351	.422	13	37	9	1	1	12	6	116	91	1.27
Last Five Years	3.51	10	12	12	261	4	394.2	102	273	.271	414	68	13	32	192	.315	.395	48	197	70	17	22	46	20	577	415	1.39

1992 Season

	ERA	W	L	Sv	G	GS	IP	H	HR	BB	SO		Avg	AB	H	2B	3B	HR	RBI	BB	SO	OBP	SLG
Home	3.48	0	1	0	26	1	41.1	48	2	9	22	vs. Left	.331	151	50	7	3	3	25	14	16	.383	.477
Away	7.12	0	2	0	23	1	36.2	47	4	11	21	vs. Right	.290	155	45	3	0	3	24	6	27	.319	.368
Starter	3.00	0	1	0	2	2	12.0	14	1	1	3	Scoring Posn	.354	79	28	3	2	1	37	12	7	.417	.481
Reliever	5.59	0	2	0	47	0	66.0	81	5	19	40	Close & Late	.279	43	12	1	0	2	8	4	8	.354	.442
0 Days rest	8.10	0	1	0	8	0	10.0	19	1	5	8	None on/out	.274	73	20	3	0	0	0	0	12	.293	.315
1 or 2 Days rest	2.84	0	0	0	17	0	25.1	26	1	6	14	First Pitch	.321	56	18	2	0	3	13	8	0	.409	.518
3+ Days rest	7.04	0	1	0	22	0	30.2	36	3	8	18	Behind on Count	.295	61	18	3	0	2	11	4	0	.333	.443
Pre-All Star	4.96	0	1	0	30	1	45.1	54	1	15	24	Ahead on Count	.294	136	40	3	1	0	16	0	40	.293	.331
Post-All Star	5.51	0	2	0	19	1	32.2	41	5	5	19	Two Strikes	.306	134	41	4	1	1	16	8	43	.345	.373

Last Five Years

	ERA	W	L	Sv	G	GS	IP	H	HR	BB	SO		Avg	AB	H	2B	3B	HR	RBI	BB	SO	OBP	SLG
Home	3.56	6	6	6	132	2	202.1	228	16	46	131	vs. Left	.289	758	219	39	11	12	87	63	96	.341	.417
Away	3.46	4	6	6	129	2	192.1	186	16	56	142	vs. Right	.253	772	195	29	2	20	105	39	177	.289	.373
Day	3.40	6	3	6	81	3	127.0	144	7	41	79	Inning 1-6	.268	590	158	28	6	8	85	33	106	.302	.376
Night	3.56	4	9	6	180	1	267.2	270	25	61	194	Inning 7+	.272	940	256	40	7	24	107	69	167	.324	.406
Grass	3.28	8	8	9	198	4	299.0	308	25	72	193	None on	.262	881	231	37	6	12	12	22	161	.283	.359
Turf	4.23	2	4	3	63	0	95.2	106	7	30	80	Runners on	.282	649	183	31	7	20	180	80	112	.355	.444
April	3.62	0	0	2	35	0	49.2	59	5	15	42	Scoring Posn	.268	392	105	17	7	11	153	74	69	.373	.431
May	3.57	3	1	2	44	1	70.2	83	2	24	47	Close & Late	.258	333	86	14	3	8	46	29	59	.320	.390
June	3.65	2	2	5	46	0	66.2	72	3	17	41	None on/out	.242	372	90	19	3	1	1	4	66	.254	.317
July	3.46	1	4	2	48	1	78.0	81	9	17	49	vs. 1st Batr (relief)	.262	237	62	15	2	4	41	9	49	.287	.392
August	2.98	0	2	1	48	0	66.1	54	4	14	54	First Inning Pitched	.263	856	225	44	8	17	130	65	175	.313	.393
September/October	3.84	4	3	0	40	2	63.1	65	9	15	40	First 15 Pitches	.252	818	206	45	7	13	105	55	164	.297	.372
Starter	2.53	1	2	0	4	4	21.1	25	1	3	6	Pitch 16-30	.286	465	133	15	4	14	55	34	77	.336	.426
Reliever	3.57	9	10	12	257	0	373.1	389	31	99	267	Pitch 31-45	.294	177	52	4	2	4	26	11	25	.335	.407
0 Days rest	3.75	1	1	0	55	0	72.0	82	6	24	49	Pitch 46+	.329	70	23	4	0	1	6	2	7	.347	.429
1 or 2 Days rest	2.90	5	3	9	103	0	152.0	150	15	36	109	First Pitch	.308	211	65	12	0	8	34	39	0	.419	.479
3+ Days rest	4.16	3	4	2	99	0	149.1	158	10	39	109	Ahead on Count	.207	767	159	23	4	9	75	0	247	.206	.283
Pre-All Star	3.43	6	5	10	141	2	215.1	243	12	59	148	Behind on Count	.352	261	99	16	4	10	49	26	0	.401	.544

Last Five Years

	ERA	W	L	Sv	G	GS	IP	H	HR	BB	SO		Avg	AB	H	2B	3B	HR	RBI	BB	SO	OBP	SLG
Post-All Star	3.61	4	7	2	120	2	179.1	171	20	43	125	Two Strikes	.207	750	155	26	4	9	64	37	273	.243	.288

Pitcher vs. Batter (career)

Pitches Best Vs.	Avg	AB	H	2B	3B	HR	RBI	BB	SO	OBP	SLG	Pitches Worst Vs.	Avg	AB	H	2B	3B	HR	RBI	BB	SO	OBP	SLG
Jose Uribe	.000	12	0	0	0	0	0	0	3	.000	.000	Kevin Bass	.667	9	6	0	1	0	1	4	0	.769	.889
Jeff Blauser	.071	14	1	1	0	0	0	3	2	.235	.143	Delino DeShields	.636	11	7	3	0	0	2	1	2	.667	.909
Greg Olson	.077	13	1	0	0	0	0	1	2	.143	.077	Billy Doran	.600	10	6	2	0	0	1	1	0	.636	.800
Mariano Duncan	.091	11	1	0	0	0	0	0	6	.091	.091	Ozzie Smith	.545	11	6	2	0	1	4	0	1	.545	1.000
Tim Wallach	.125	16	2	1	0	0	0	1	4	.176	.188	Kevin Mitchell	.444	18	8	1	0	3	7	1	2	.474	.833

Chuck Crim — Angels
Pitches Right (groundball pitcher)

	ERA	W	L	Sv	G	GS	IP	H	HR	BB	SO	Avg	H	2B	3B	HR	RBI	OBP	SLG	GF	IR	IRS	Hld	SvOp	SB	CS	GB	FB	G/F
1992 Season	5.17	7	6	1	57	0	87.0	29	30	.293	100	15	1	11	65	.355	.440	16	55	23	8	3	7	5	151	96	1.57
Last Five Years	3.72	34	29	31	336	0	486.2	141	225	.272	512	70	9	45	261	.325	.391	70	352	123	71	49	37	13	826	506	1.63

1992 Season

	ERA	W	L	Sv	G	GS	IP	H	HR	BB	SO		Avg	AB	H	2B	3B	HR	RBI	BB	SO	OBP	SLG
Home	5.31	4	1	0	25	0	40.2	45	4	16	10	vs. Left	.241	137	33	5	0	2	21	9	8	.286	.321
Away	5.05	3	5	1	32	0	46.1	55	7	13	20	vs. Right	.328	204	67	10	1	9	44	20	22	.399	.520
Starter	0.00	0	0	0	0	0	0.0	0	0	0	0	Scoring Posn	.343	102	35	2	0	3	54	18	4	.437	.451
Reliever	5.17	7	6	1	57	0	87.0	100	11	29	30	Close & Late	.318	88	28	3	0	5	18	7	6	.375	.523
0 Days rest	13.50	0	2	0	6	0	6.2	17	6	1	0	None on/out	.284	81	23	6	0	5	5	3	5	.318	.543
1 or 2 Days rest	4.25	6	4	0	33	0	48.2	50	5	16	18	First Pitch	.269	52	14	1	0	1	6	4	0	.333	.346
3+ Days rest	4.83	1	0	1	18	0	31.2	33	0	12	12	Behind on Count	.362	94	34	8	0	1	25	15	0	.441	.479
Pre-All Star	6.08	2	2	0	29	0	50.1	60	4	19	21	Ahead on Count	.210	124	26	2	0	4	15	0	23	.231	.323
Post-All Star	3.93	5	4	1	28	0	36.2	40	7	10	9	Two Strikes	.260	131	34	3	1	6	23	10	30	.329	.435

Last Five Years

	ERA	W	L	Sv	G	GS	IP	H	HR	BB	SO		Avg	AB	H	2B	3B	HR	RBI	BB	SO	OBP	SLG
Home	3.78	18	13	17	172	0	250.0	261	22	62	109	vs. Left	.264	793	209	31	1	18	99	68	91	.322	.373
Away	3.65	16	16	14	164	0	236.2	251	23	79	116	vs. Right	.279	1086	303	39	8	27	162	73	134	.327	.404
Day	4.51	13	13	8	110	0	141.2	152	15	50	64	Inning 1-6	.277	285	79	8	0	12	67	18	34	.323	.432
Night	3.39	21	16	23	226	0	345.0	360	30	91	161	Inning 7+	.272	1594	433	62	9	33	194	123	191	.325	.384
Grass	3.61	28	25	26	284	0	409.1	431	35	117	181	None on	.258	1006	260	46	5	27	27	54	123	.300	.395
Turf	4.31	6	4	5	52	0	77.1	81	10	24	44	Runners on	.289	873	252	24	4	18	234	87	102	.352	.387
April	4.16	4	5	6	49	0	71.1	67	6	25	23	Scoring Posn	.292	531	155	14	4	14	221	74	60	.372	.412
May	4.29	6	5	3	61	0	77.2	87	5	23	41	Close & Late	.273	721	197	25	4	16	98	64	93	.332	.386
June	4.75	4	9	7	59	0	85.1	93	9	30	32	None on/out	.267	439	117	26	2	13	13	18	52	.298	.424
July	2.37	9	3	4	50	0	83.2	72	5	16	47	vs. 1st Batr (relief)	.286	308	88	12	2	11	64	17	48	.315	.445
August	3.65	7	3	6	57	0	86.1	95	13	22	40	First Inning Pitched	.283	1094	310	41	4	26	202	85	133	.334	.399
September/October	3.17	4	4	5	60	0	82.1	98	7	25	42	First 15 Pitches	.281	1096	308	40	5	26	173	70	126	.324	.403
Starter	0.00	0	0	0	0	0	0.0	0	0	0	0	Pitch 16-30	.260	524	136	22	3	10	62	50	55	.326	.370
Reliever	3.72	34	29	31	336	0	486.2	512	45	141	225	Pitch 31-45	.265	211	56	7	0	5	21	18	31	.328	.370
0 Days rest	4.65	9	6	9	77	0	102.2	129	15	27	50	Pitch 46+	.250	48	12	1	1	2	5	3	11	.308	.438
1 or 2 Days rest	3.36	19	18	18	179	0	270.2	270	23	84	115	First Pitch	.285	340	97	13	0	8	40	20	0	.327	.394
3+ Days rest	3.73	6	5	4	80	0	113.1	113	7	30	60	Ahead on Count	.223	766	171	19	4	10	86	1	192	.229	.298
Pre-All Star	4.15	18	19	16	184	0	264.2	272	21	84	118	Behind on Count	.321	445	143	27	1	15	81	65	0	.403	.488
Post-All Star	3.20	16	10	15	152	0	222.0	240	24	57	107	Two Strikes	.209	723	151	14	5	15	82	54	225	.269	.304

Pitcher vs. Batter (career)

Pitches Best Vs.	Avg	AB	H	2B	3B	HR	RBI	BB	SO	OBP	SLG	Pitches Worst Vs.	Avg	AB	H	2B	3B	HR	RBI	BB	SO	OBP	SLG
Cory Snyder	.063	16	1	0	0	0	0	0	5	.063	.063	Jerry Browne	.636	11	7	1	0	1	1	1	1	.667	1.000
Lou Whitaker	.067	15	1	0	0	0	0	1	0	.125	.067	Frank Thomas	.545	11	6	0	0	1	5	1	1	.583	.818
George Brett	.077	13	1	0	0	0	0	1	3	.143	.077	Cal Ripken	.529	17	9	1	0	1	6	1	1	.556	.765
Brian Harper	.091	11	1	0	0	0	2	0	0	.063	.091	Gary Gaetti	.438	16	7	2	0	1	4	2	1	.500	.750
Manuel Lee	.133	15	2	0	0	0	2	0	4	.133	.133	Fred McGriff	.333	9	3	1	0	1	2	2	1	.455	.778

Chris Cron — White Sox
Bats Right

	Avg	G	AB	R	H	2B	3B	HR	RBI	BB	SO	HBP	GDP	SB	CS	OBP	SLG	IBB	SH	SF	#Pit	#P/PA	GB	FB	G/F
1992 Season	.000	6	10	0	0	0	0	0	0	0	4	0	0	0	0	.000	.000	0	0	0	35	3.50	4	2	2.00
Career (1991-1992)	.080	12	25	0	2	0	0	0	0	2	9	0	0	0	0	.148	.080	0	0	0	108	4.00	7	7	1.00

1992 Season

	Avg	AB	H	2B	3B	HR	RBI	BB	SO	OBP	SLG		Avg	AB	H	2B	3B	HR	RBI	BB	SO	OBP	SLG
vs. Left	.000	6	0	0	0	0	0	0	3	.000	.000	Scoring Posn	.000	3	0	0	0	0	0	0	1	.000	.000
vs. Right	.000	4	0	0	0	0	0	0	1	.000	.000	Close & Late	.000	2	0	0	0	0	0	0	1	.000	.000

97

Chad Curtis — Angels
Bats Right (groundball hitter)

	Avg	G	AB	R	H	2B	3B	HR	RBI	BB	SO	HBP	GDP	SB	CS	OBP	SLG	IBB	SH	SF	#Pit	#P/PA	GB	FB	G/F
1992 Season	.259	139	441	59	114	16	2	10	46	51	71	6	10	43	18	.341	.372	2	5	4	1883	3.75	189	107	1.77

1992 Season

	Avg	AB	H	2B	3B	HR	RBI	BB	SO	OBP	SLG
vs. Left	.270	122	33	6	1	6	22	26	18	.393	.484
vs. Right	.254	319	81	10	1	4	24	25	53	.318	.329
Groundball	.220	109	24	1	0	0	6	12	18	.298	.229
Flyball	.287	136	39	5	1	5	22	15	28	.361	.449
Home	.264	201	53	6	1	5	20	24	32	.349	.378
Away	.254	240	61	10	1	5	26	27	39	.333	.367
Day	.216	111	24	2	0	3	11	16	15	.328	.315
Night	.273	330	90	14	2	7	35	35	56	.345	.391
Grass	.253	367	93	13	1	7	31	39	60	.329	.351
Turf	.284	74	21	3	1	3	15	12	11	.393	.473
First Pitch	.243	70	17	1	0	2	10	2	0	.276	.343
Ahead on Count	.360	86	31	4	1	5	17	21	0	.491	.605
Behind on Count	.226	164	37	6	0	1	8	0	44	.232	.280
Two Strikes	.232	224	52	5	1	3	16	28	71	.320	.304

	Avg	AB	H	2B	3B	HR	RBI	BB	SO	OBP	SLG
Scoring Posn	.226	106	24	3	1	4	38	10	17	.295	.387
Close & Late	.237	76	18	2	0	2	5	12	13	.348	.342
None on/out	.269	93	25	3	1	2	2	15	13	.382	.387
Batting #2	.265	170	45	4	1	3	14	18	25	.340	.353
Batting #5	.241	137	33	7	0	2	13	17	27	.329	.336
Other	.269	134	36	5	1	5	19	16	19	.353	.433
April	.333	27	9	2	1	0	4	4	3	.406	.481
May	.217	60	13	2	1	2	3	8	10	.309	.383
June	.280	82	23	2	0	2	14	8	11	.352	.378
July	.227	88	20	4	0	4	9	10	15	.320	.409
August	.224	85	19	2	0	1	7	13	18	.323	.282
September/October	.303	99	30	4	0	1	9	8	14	.366	.374
Pre-All Star	.257	206	53	9	2	6	26	24	31	.339	.408
Post-All Star	.260	235	61	7	0	4	20	27	40	.342	.340

1992 By Position

Position	Avg	AB	H	2B	3B	HR	RBI	BB	SO	OBP	SLG	G	GS	Innings	PO	A	E	DP	Fld Pct	Rng Fctr	In Zone	Outs	Zone Rtg	MLB Zone
As lf	.289	142	41	2	0	2	13	10	21	.338	.345	48	31	352.0	71	2	3	0	.961	1.87	86	67	.779	.809
As cf	.250	116	29	7	1	2	10	15	22	.343	.379	35	32	278.1	78	3	2	0	.976	2.62	92	74	.804	.824
As rf	.247	178	44	7	1	6	23	22	28	.337	.399	62	47	448.2	101	11	1	3	.991	2.25	121	94	.777	.814

Milt Cuyler — Tigers
Bats Both (groundball hitter)

	Avg	G	AB	R	H	2B	3B	HR	RBI	BB	SO	HBP	GDP	SB	CS	OBP	SLG	IBB	SH	SF	#Pit	#P/PA	GB	FB	G/F
1992 Season	.241	89	291	39	70	11	1	3	28	10	62	4	4	8	5	.275	.316	0	8	0	1122	3.68	102	58	1.76
Career (1990-1992)	.251	262	817	124	205	29	9	6	69	67	164	9	9	50	17	.314	.330	0	22	3	3327	3.71	315	151	2.09

1992 Season

	Avg	AB	H	2B	3B	HR	RBI	BB	SO	OBP	SLG
vs. Left	.291	86	25	2	0	2	8	3	11	.337	.384
vs. Right	.220	205	45	9	1	1	20	7	51	.249	.288
Groundball	.188	80	15	2	0	0	5	1	20	.207	.213
Flyball	.230	87	20	3	0	2	11	3	18	.264	.333
Home	.196	148	29	3	0	1	9	7	37	.252	.236
Away	.287	143	41	8	1	2	19	3	25	.301	.399
Day	.243	103	25	4	1	0	9	1	23	.257	.301
Night	.239	188	45	7	0	3	19	9	39	.285	.324
Grass	.229	249	57	9	1	2	21	9	56	.267	.297
Turf	.310	42	13	2	0	1	7	1	6	.326	.429
First Pitch	.295	44	13	2	0	1	8	0	0	.311	.409
Ahead on Count	.212	52	11	4	1	0	2	5	0	.281	.327
Behind on Count	.192	104	20	2	0	2	12	0	32	.208	.269
Two Strikes	.144	132	19	2	0	0	4	5	62	.181	.159

	Avg	AB	H	2B	3B	HR	RBI	BB	SO	OBP	SLG
Scoring Posn	.284	74	21	3	1	2	27	2	17	.312	.432
Close & Late	.162	37	6	2	0	0	0	1	11	.225	.216
None on/out	.254	63	16	3	0	0	3	3	17	.299	.302
Batting #1	.375	8	3	0	0	1	3	0	2	.375	.750
Batting #9	.237	283	67	11	1	2	25	10	60	.273	.304
Other	.000	0	0	0	0	0	0	0	0	.000	.000
April	.185	65	12	3	1	1	7	1	17	.197	.308
May	.254	71	18	1	0	1	8	1	12	.284	.310
June	.287	101	29	7	0	1	11	5	19	.333	.386
July	.204	54	11	0	0	0	2	3	14	.246	.204
August	.000	0	0	0	0	0	0	0	0	.000	.000
September/October	.000	0	0	0	0	0	0	0	0	.000	.000
Pre-All Star	.238	282	67	11	1	3	27	9	61	.271	.316
Post-All Star	.333	9	3	0	0	0	1	1	1	.400	.333

1992 By Position

Position	Avg	AB	H	2B	3B	HR	RBI	BB	SO	OBP	SLG	G	GS	Innings	PO	A	E	DP	Fld Pct	Rng Fctr	In Zone	Outs	Zone Rtg	MLB Zone
As cf	.242	289	70	11	1	3	28	9	62	.272	.316	88	84	733.2	233	4	4	1	.983	2.91	282	230	.816	.824

Career (1990-1992)

	Avg	AB	H	2B	3B	HR	RBI	BB	SO	OBP	SLG
vs. Left	.282	220	62	9	1	2	19	16	30	.340	.359
vs. Right	.240	597	143	20	8	4	50	51	134	.304	.320
Groundball	.213	258	55	8	3	0	23	21	57	.277	.267
Flyball	.275	182	50	10	1	4	18	15	30	.335	.407
Home	.224	388	87	10	3	2	26	43	74	.313	.281
Away	.275	429	118	19	6	4	43	24	90	.314	.375
Day	.267	243	65	11	3	2	32	18	51	.323	.362
Night	.244	574	140	18	6	4	37	49	113	.310	.317
Grass	.240	687	165	25	7	4	58	63	142	.310	.314
Turf	.308	130	40	4	2	2	11	4	22	.333	.415
First Pitch	.344	131	45	6	1	2	16	0	0	.346	.450
Ahead on Count	.275	182	50	12	5	1	13	39	0	.399	.412
Behind on Count	.218	248	54	6	4	2	25	0	76	.233	.298
Two Strikes	.158	348	55	6	2	0	15	28	164	.231	.187

	Avg	AB	H	2B	3B	HR	RBI	BB	SO	OBP	SLG
Scoring Posn	.234	197	46	8	4	3	65	15	49	.290	.360
Close & Late	.216	116	25	5	0	2	7	6	26	.278	.310
None on/out	.263	213	56	7	3	1	21	43		.338	.338
Batting #1	.242	165	40	6	2	1	8	17	37	.324	.321
Batting #9	.253	641	162	22	7	5	57	49	126	.311	.332
Other	.273	11	3	1	0	0	4	1	1	.308	.364
April	.200	105	21	4	1	1	7	3	23	.222	.286
May	.259	139	36	2	1	2	19	15	23	.338	.331
June	.260	181	47	8	2	3	15	8	32	.306	.376
July	.224	134	30	3	0	0	15	31		.300	.246
August	.224	107	24	6	2	0	14	25		.325	.318
September/October	.311	151	47	8	3	0	14	12	30	.364	.391
Pre-All Star	.240	492	118	15	4	6	44	29	100	.299	.323
Post-All Star	.268	325	87	14	5	0	25	38	64	.349	.342

Batter vs. Pitcher (career)

Hits Best Against	Avg	AB	H	2B	3B	HR	RBI	BB	SO	OBP	SLG
Mike Boddicker	.364	11	4	0	0	0	4	0	0	.462	.364
Jimmy Key	.364	11	4	1	0	0	0	0	2	.364	.455

Hits Worst Against	Avg	AB	H	2B	3B	HR	RBI	BB	SO	OBP	SLG
Tim Leary	.000	12	0	0	0	0	0	0	2	.000	.000
Chuck Finley	.000	10	0	0	0	0	0	2	3	.000	.000

Batter vs. Pitcher (career)

Hits Best Against	Avg	AB	H	2B	3B	HR	RBI	BB	SO	OBP	SLG	Hits Worst Against	Avg	AB	H	2B	3B	HR	RBI	BB	SO	OBP	SLG
Mike Moore	.333	12	4	2	0	0	4	1	3	.385	.500	Kevin Brown	.091	11	1	0	0	0	0	2	2	.231	.091
Charles Nagy	.333	12	4	0	1	0	0	0	3	.333	.500	Bill Wegman	.214	14	3	0	0	0	2	0	3	.214	.214
Jaime Navarro	.313	16	5	0	0	0	0	1	2	.353	.313	Scott Erickson	.222	9	2	0	0	0	0	3	0	.417	.222

Kal Daniels — Cubs
Bats Left (groundball hitter)

	Avg	G	AB	R	H	2B	3B	HR	RBI	BB	SO	HBP	GDP	SB	CS	OBP	SLG	IBB	SH	SF	#Pit	#P/PA	GB	FB	G/F
1992 Season	.241	83	212	21	51	11	0	6	25	22	54	2	10	0	2	.315	.377	0	0	2	931	3.91	79	47	1.68
Last Five Years	.271	545	1789	264	485	91	3	72	273	263	401	11	42	46	16	.371	.446	16	2	17	8301	3.95	698	425	1.64

1992 Season

	Avg	AB	H	2B	3B	HR	RBI	BB	SO	OBP	SLG		Avg	AB	H	2B	3B	HR	RBI	BB	SO	OBP	SLG
vs. Left	.231	65	15	4	0	1	9	4	19	.296	.338	Scoring Posn	.200	60	12	3	0	2	20	7	14	.275	.350
vs. Right	.245	147	36	7	0	5	16	18	35	.323	.395	Close & Late	.244	45	11	0	0	1	5	4	15	.300	.311
Home	.267	101	27	5	0	3	14	12	22	.339	.406	None on/out	.176	51	9	1	0	1	5	5	14	.250	.255
Away	.216	111	24	6	0	3	11	10	32	.293	.351	Batting #3	.240	100	24	5	0	2	8	9	28	.306	.350
First Pitch	.308	26	8	3	0	1	5	0	0	.308	.538	Batting #5	.238	42	10	2	0	3	8	5	10	.333	.500
Ahead on Count	.314	35	11	2	0	1	3	13	0	.500	.457	Other	.243	70	17	4	0	1	9	8	16	.316	.343
Behind on Count	.213	75	16	3	0	2	7	0	26	.231	.333	Pre-All Star	.250	120	30	5	0	4	14	16	33	.345	.392
Two Strikes	.193	114	22	4	0	3	11	9	54	.250	.307	Post-All Star	.228	92	21	6	0	2	11	6	21	.273	.359

Last Five Years

	Avg	AB	H	2B	3B	HR	RBI	BB	SO	OBP	SLG		Avg	AB	H	2B	3B	HR	RBI	BB	SO	OBP	SLG
vs. Left	.256	614	157	25	0	17	99	91	147	.353	.379	Scoring Posn	.283	463	131	24	2	24	209	109	112	.409	.499
vs. Right	.279	1175	328	66	3	55	174	192	254	.380	.481	Close & Late	.244	279	68	11	0	7	44	50	71	.353	.358
Groundball	.284	633	180	28	0	25	101	111	141	.393	.447	None on/out	.278	403	112	24	1	13	13	47	79	.359	.439
Flyball	.222	360	80	19	0	15	47	54	107	.325	.400	Batting #3	.288	962	277	44	1	45	159	164	213	.391	.476
Home	.283	870	246	45	1	41	145	140	189	.381	.478	Batting #5	.249	398	99	13	1	17	62	51	98	.334	.415
Away	.260	919	239	46	2	31	128	143	212	.362	.416	Other	.254	429	109	34	1	10	52	66	90	.359	.408
Day	.249	515	128	29	1	21	85	80	128	.352	.431	April	.254	287	73	18	0	8	44	57	53	.375	.401
Night	.280	1274	357	62	2	51	188	203	273	.379	.452	May	.292	318	93	18	1	12	47	36	75	.370	.469
Grass	.266	1040	277	49	2	43	172	160	243	.363	.441	June	.265	253	67	9	0	12	33	46	58	.376	.443
Turf	.278	749	208	42	1	29	101	123	158	.382	.453	July	.268	358	96	22	0	13	49	59	84	.371	.439
First Pitch	.389	234	91	15	0	16	53	3	0	.393	.658	August	.238	294	70	10	1	10	36	48	71	.343	.381
Ahead on Count	.334	380	127	26	0	24	72	156	0	.527	.592	September/October	.308	279	86	14	1	17	64	37	60	.392	.548
Behind on Count	.213	573	122	26	1	12	59	2	192	.222	.305	Pre-All Star	.270	973	263	54	1	36	139	162	217	.375	.439
Two Strikes	.193	911	176	33	3	21	103	115	401	.284	.305	Post-All Star	.272	816	222	37	2	36	134	121	184	.365	.455

Batter vs. Pitcher (career)

Hits Best Against	Avg	AB	H	2B	3B	HR	RBI	BB	SO	OBP	SLG	Hits Worst Against	Avg	AB	H	2B	3B	HR	RBI	BB	SO	OBP	SLG
Danny Darwin	.526	19	10	3	0	3	5	3	1	.565	1.158	Mark Davis	.000	13	0	0	0	0	0	2	4	.133	.000
Greg Maddux	.471	17	8	1	0	2	8	2	2	.526	.882	Bob Kipper	.059	17	1	0	0	0	0	0	5	.059	.059
Orel Hershiser	.429	28	12	1	0	4	6	6	6	.529	.893	Dennis Martinez	.091	33	3	0	0	1	1	3	10	.167	.182
Shawn Boskie	.429	14	6	4	0	1	4	2	3	.471	.929	Kelly Downs	.125	24	3	2	0	0	1	3	.160	.208
Mark Gardner	.333	12	4	0	1	2	6	3	3	.467	1.000	Bob Patterson	.182	11	2	0	0	0	2	0	2	.182	.182

Ron Darling — Athletics
Pitches Right

	ERA	W	L	Sv	G	GS	IP	BB	SO	Avg	H	2B	3B	HR	RBI	OBP	SLG	CG	ShO	Sup	QS	#P/S	SB	CS	GB	FB	G/F
1992 Season	3.66	15	10	0	33	33	206.1	72	99	.253	198	44	5	15	83	.318	.379	4	3	4.89	19	98	10	13	281	265	1.06
Last Five Years	3.76	61	57	0	165	150	984.2	317	641	.255	950	170	30	100	413	.315	.398	16	7	4.40	97	96	104	37	1264	1056	1.20

1992 Season

	ERA	W	L	Sv	G	GS	IP	H	HR	BB	SO		Avg	AB	H	2B	3B	HR	RBI	BB	SO	OBP	SLG
Home	3.57	8	6	0	16	16	106.0	85	7	36	49	vs. Left	.270	371	100	25	3	6	37	45	40	.348	.402
Away	3.77	7	4	0	17	17	100.1	113	8	36	50	vs. Right	.238	412	98	19	2	9	46	27	59	.290	.359
Day	2.90	8	4	0	14	14	93.0	72	8	32	48	Inning 1-6	.264	686	181	42	5	13	80	64	87	.328	.397
Night	4.29	7	6	0	19	19	113.1	126	7	40	51	Inning 7+	.175	97	17	2	0	2	3	8	12	.245	.258
Grass	3.66	14	10	0	29	29	182.0	175	14	61	91	None on	.239	469	112	24	3	10	10	38	66	.301	.367
Turf	3.70	1	0	0	4	4	24.1	23	1	11	8	Runners on	.274	314	86	20	2	5	73	34	33	.342	.398
April	4.80	1	1	0	5	5	30.0	33	3	12	17	Scoring Posn	.264	178	47	12	2	3	66	23	25	.343	.404
May	3.06	3	2	0	5	5	32.1	26	2	12	17	Close & Late	.136	44	6	0	0	0	0	5	8	.240	.136
June	5.74	3	2	0	5	5	26.2	29	1	8	10	None on/out	.244	205	50	6	2	4	4	16	30	.302	.351
July	2.93	2	3	0	6	6	40.0	35	4	15	17	vs. 1st Batr (relief)	.000	0	0	0	0	0	0	0	0	.000	.000
August	3.53	3	0	0	6	6	35.2	46	3	11	13	First Inning Pitched	.267	131	35	6	1	4	21	15	19	.347	.420
September/October	2.81	3	2	0	6	6	41.2	29	2	14	25	First 75 Pitches	.260	581	151	34	4	9	65	52	71	.322	.379
Starter	3.66	15	10	0	33	33	206.1	198	15	72	99	Pitch 76-90	.240	100	24	6	0	0	5	12	16	.321	.300
Reliever	0.00	0	0	0	0	0	0.0	0	0	0	0	Pitch 91-105	.271	70	19	3	1	5	11	6	8	.329	.557
0-3 Days Rest	4.50	0	1	0	1	1	6.0	8	2	2	2	Pitch 106+	.125	32	4	1	0	1	2	2	4	.200	.250
4 Days Rest	3.26	10	4	0	19	19	118.2	111	8	37	58	First Pitch	.322	118	38	11	0	1	18	3	0	.344	.441
5+ Days Rest	4.19	5	5	0	13	13	81.2	79	5	33	39	Ahead on Count	.171	293	50	9	2	3	24	0	84	.176	.246
Pre-All Star	4.37	8	7	0	18	18	107.0	104	9	39	51	Behind on Count	.332	220	73	16	1	7	28	31	0	.411	.509
Post-All Star	2.90	7	3	0	15	15	99.1	94	6	33	48	Two Strikes	.175	309	54	10	2	5	24	38	99	.267	.269

99

Last Five Years

	ERA	W	L	Sv	G	GS	IP	H	HR	BB	SO		Avg	AB	H	2B	3B	HR	RBI	BB	SO	OBP	SLG
Home	3.39	37	24	0	82	75	520.1	468	46	155	329	vs. Left	.262	1977	517	86	17	44	203	188	334	.325	.390
Away	4.17	24	33	0	83	75	464.1	482	54	162	312	vs. Right	.248	1745	433	82	13	56	209	129	307	.305	.406
Day	3.62	18	17	0	52	45	298.1	286	32	103	176	Inning 1-6	.259	3140	813	148	28	80	359	275	541	.320	.400
Night	3.82	43	40	0	113	105	686.1	664	68	214	465	Inning 7+	.235	582	137	22	2	20	53	42	100	.292	.383
Grass	3.70	51	41	0	125	115	768.0	727	83	234	512	None on	.247	2260	558	99	16	63	63	169	377	.304	.388
Turf	3.95	10	16	0	40	35	216.2	223	17	83	129	Runners on	.268	1462	392	71	14	37	349	148	264	.332	.412
April	3.67	6	9	0	22	21	127.2	126	13	46	82	Scoring Posn	.260	854	222	38	11	21	302	110	177	.336	.404
May	3.71	10	7	0	26	24	162.1	137	20	50	118	Close & Late	.212	250	53	8	2	4	18	23	45	.286	.308
June	4.34	11	8	0	27	24	153.1	162	10	45	82	None on/out	.248	987	245	32	6	24	24	54	173	.294	.366
July	3.86	10	13	0	29	27	177.1	179	23	59	122	vs. 1st Batr (relief)	.167	12	2	0	0	1	4	1	4	.200	.417
August	3.75	13	8	0	28	27	173.0	180	19	50	110	First Inning Pitched	.262	623	163	24	3	14	88	67	119	.334	.377
September/October	3.30	11	12	0	33	27	191.0	166	15	67	127	First 75 Pitches	.260	2821	733	129	26	67	316	241	476	.320	.395
Starter	3.75	60	55	0	150	150	955.1	923	96	307	618	Pitch 76-90	.256	461	118	26	2	16	47	42	85	.319	.425
Reliever	3.99	1	2	0	15	0	29.1	27	4	10	23	Pitch 91-105	.249	313	78	12	2	13	38	20	55	.293	.425
0-3 Days Rest	4.62	1	2	0	4	4	25.1	27	5	9	16	Pitch 106+	.165	127	21	3	0	4	12	14	25	.257	.283
4 Days Rest	4.00	35	32	0	90	90	569.1	566	55	195	373	First Pitch	.314	589	185	41	6	20	91	16	0	.334	.508
5+ Days Rest	3.29	24	21	0	56	56	360.2	326	36	103	229	Ahead on Count	.186	1566	291	40	5	19	114	0	550	.192	.254
Pre-All Star	3.92	31	27	0	84	77	495.2	476	49	160	318	Behind on Count	.331	922	305	55	12	43	149	153	0	.421	.556
Post-All Star	3.59	30	30	0	81	73	489.0	474	51	157	323	Two Strikes	.174	1573	273	44	5	23	101	148	641	.247	.252

Pitcher vs. Batter (since 1984)

Pitches Best Vs.	Avg	AB	H	2B	3B	HR	RBI	BB	SO	OBP	SLG	Pitches Worst Vs.	Avg	AB	H	2B	3B	HR	RBI	BB	SO	OBP	SLG
Brian McRae	.000	12	0	0	0	0	0	1	4	.000	.000	Lenny Dykstra	.500	10	5	2	0	1	2	1		.583	.700
Mark Grace	.042	24	1	1	0	2	4	1		.179	.083	Jeff King	.455	11	5	1	0	1	3	1	2	.500	.818
Dave Winfield	.083	12	1	0	0	0	1	2		.154	.083	Pedro Guerrero	.415	41	17	3	0	2	10	10	7	.519	.634
Gerald Young	.083	12	1	0	0	1	3			.154	.083	Greg Vaughn	.375	16	6	1	0	2	4	2	1	.444	.813
Joe Carter	.105	19	2	0	0	1	6			.150	.105	Jack Clark	.360	25	9	2	0	3	5	10		.484	.800

Danny Darwin — Red Sox
Pitches Right (flyball pitcher)

	ERA	W	L	Sv	G	GS	IP	BB	SO	Avg	H	2B	3B	HR	RBI	OBP	SLG	GF	IR	IRS	Hld	SvOp	SB	CS	GB	FB	G/F
1992 Season	3.96	9	9	3	51	15	161.1	53	124	.257	159	31	6	11	70	.319	.380	21	36	13	1	6	14	6	163	208	0.78
Last Five Years	3.37	42	36	15	223	64	706.0	180	508	.244	647	115	15	65	276	.295	.371	35	126	45	12	24	74	21	715	934	0.77

1992 Season

	ERA	W	L	Sv	G	GS	IP	H	HR	BB	SO		Avg	AB	H	2B	3B	HR	RBI	BB	SO	OBP	SLG
Home	4.26	6	4	1	24	7	76.0	86	4	23	62	vs. Left	.281	274	77	18	4	1	31	28	47	.345	.387
Away	3.69	3	5	2	27	8	85.1	73	7	30	62	vs. Right	.238	344	82	13	2	10	39	25	77	.297	.375
Day	2.01	3	1	1	19	5	67.0	44	1	16	55	Inning 1-6	.248	371	92	16	5	7	42	29	74	.301	.375
Night	5.34	6	8	2	32	10	94.1	115	10	37	69	Inning 7+	.271	247	67	15	1	4	28	24	50	.344	.389
Grass	3.65	9	8	3	43	13	145.2	138	10	41	117	None on	.246	338	83	18	1	6	6	27	73	.311	.358
Turf	6.89	0	1	0	8	2	15.2	21	1	12	7	Runners on	.271	280	76	13	5	5	64	26	51	.328	.407
April	2.45	1	0	1	7	0	18.1	17	0	3	19	Scoring Posn	.236	174	41	6	3	3	55	19	31	.303	.356
May	9.31	1	1	1	10	0	9.2	13	1	7	6	Close & Late	.250	144	36	7	0	3	16	15	33	.327	.361
June	5.49	2	3	1	14	0	19.2	23	4	14	6	None on/out	.268	153	41	8	0	4	4	9	29	.317	.399
July	4.24	1	1	0	8	3	23.1	19	0	10	15	vs. 1st Batr (relief)	.219	32	7	3	1	0	6	3	9	.286	.375
August	2.36	2	1	0	6	6	45.2	37	3	12	44	First Inning Pitched	.272	173	47	11	3	3	31	15	33	.330	.422
September/October	4.23	2	3	0	6	6	44.2	50	3	17	26	First 15 Pitches	.266	169	45	10	2	3	24	13	30	.321	.402
Starter	3.53	4	5	0	15	15	107.0	101	6	36	81	Pitch 16-30	.205	112	23	6	2	2	13	10	31	.270	.348
Reliever	4.80	5	4	3	36	0	54.1	58	5	17	43	Pitch 31-45	.364	77	28	9	0	3	10	9	14	.437	.597
0 Days rest	0.00	1	0	0	2	0	5.1	4	0	0	1	Pitch 46+	.242	260	63	6	2	3	23	21	49	.303	.315
1 or 2 Days rest	7.36	3	4	1	24	0	29.1	38	4	12	25	First Pitch	.319	94	30	5	1	4	16	7	0	.363	.521
3+ Days rest	2.29	1	0	2	10	0	19.2	16	1	5	17	Ahead on Count	.202	312	63	11	1	4	28	0	112	.209	.282
Pre-All Star	4.89	5	4	3	35	0	53.1	58	5	16	42	Behind on Count	.327	98	32	5	3	2	17	28	0	.477	.500
Post-All Star	3.50	4	5	0	16	15	108.0	101	6	37	82	Two Strikes	.177	293	52	11	0	1	21	18	124	.232	.225

Last Five Years

	ERA	W	L	Sv	G	GS	IP	H	HR	BB	SO		Avg	AB	H	2B	3B	HR	RBI	BB	SO	OBP	SLG
Home	3.24	23	15	7	117	32	363.1	342	24	91	276	vs. Left	.262	1403	367	72	11	24	134	105	245	.314	.380
Away	3.49	19	21	8	106	32	342.2	305	41	89	232	vs. Right	.223	1254	290	43	4	41	142	75	263	.273	.362
Day	3.32	12	12	3	68	22	230.1	208	25	60	177	Inning 1-6	.250	1607	402	77	12	42	179	101	293	.297	.391
Night	3.39	30	24	12	155	42	475.2	439	40	120	331	Inning 7+	.233	1050	245	38	3	23	97	79	215	.291	.341
Grass	3.89	21	24	7	99	35	342.1	338	40	83	259	None on	.242	1564	378	69	7	41	41	89	300	.289	.373
Turf	2.87	21	12	8	124	29	363.2	309	25	97	249	Runners on	.246	1093	269	46	8	24	235	91	208	.302	.369
April	3.21	6	3	1	33	7	95.1	85	7	21	73	Scoring Posn	.226	656	148	27	5	15	206	68	130	.293	.351
May	3.45	5	4	2	41	7	94.0	90	11	29	61	Close & Late	.215	503	108	16	1	9	42	47	104	.285	.304
June	4.86	8	12	5	49	12	129.2	145	20	31	90	None on/out	.260	672	175	31	3	18	18	31	125	.296	.396
July	2.77	9	4	4	35	12	123.1	98	7	30	95	vs. 1st Batr (relief)	.231	143	33	6	1	3	26	10	37	.282	.350
August	2.75	9	4	0	32	14	137.1	113	11	31	111	First Inning Pitched	.241	777	187	33	6	17	107	47	151	.285	.364
September/October	3.13	5	9	3	33	12	116.0	116	9	38	78	First 15 Pitches	.250	765	191	30	5	18	92	39	136	.287	.373
Starter	3.74	20	24	0	64	64	426.0	413	43	106	284	Pitch 16-30	.208	562	117	22	5	7	40	46	130	.269	.302
Reliever	2.80	22	12	15	159	0	260.0	234	22	74	224	Pitch 31-45	.280	361	101	21	1	12	44	26	74	.332	.443
0 Days rest	2.21	5	1	1	20	0	36.2	29	3	9	24	Pitch 46+	.246	969	238	42	4	28	100	69	168	.301	.384

Last Five Years

	ERA	W	L	Sv	G	GS	IP	H	HR	BB	SO
1 or 2 Days rest	3.39	12	9	9	99	0	162.0	148	14	44	128
3+ Days rest	1.86	5	2	5	40	0	81.1	57	5	21	72
Pre-All Star	3.91	22	21	8	136	31	361.2	360	43	89	257
Post-All Star	2.80	20	15	7	87	33	344.1	287	22	91	251

	Avg	AB	H	2B	3B	HR	RBI	BB	SO	OBP	SLG
First Pitch	.295	440	130	21	1	14	62	23	1	.332	.443
Ahead on Count	.191	1371	262	42	6	19	107	0	449	.195	.272
Behind on Count	.324	414	134	23	5	20	69	83	0	.436	.548
Two Strikes	.170	1262	214	44	5	15	90	72	506	.218	.248

Pitcher vs. Batter (since 1984)

Pitches Best Vs.	Avg	AB	H	2B	3B	HR	RBI	BB	SO	OBP	SLG
Jeff Blauser	.000	14	0	0	0	0	0	3	5	.176	.000
Curt Wilkerson	.000	10	0	0	0	0	0	1	1	.083	.000
Bobby Bonilla	.067	15	1	0	0	0	1	1	2	.125	.067
Gary Carter	.091	11	1	0	0	0	1	0	1	.083	.091
Otis Nixon	.091	11	1	1	0	0	0	1	3	.091	.091

Pitches Worst Vs.	Avg	AB	H	2B	3B	HR	RBI	BB	SO	OBP	SLG
Kal Daniels	.526	19	10	3	0	3	5	3	1	.565	1.158
Andre Dawson	.500	14	7	1	0	2	4	3	3	.556	1.000
Terry Steinbach	.500	10	5	0	0	3	4	1	2	.545	1.400
Brian Downing	.444	18	8	2	0	2	3	2	4	.545	.889
Jack Clark	.385	13	5	3	0	2	6	1	1	.400	1.077

Doug Dascenzo — Cubs   Bats Both (groundball hitter)

	Avg	G	AB	R	H	2B	3B	HR	RBI	BB	SO	HBP	GDP	SB	CS	OBP	SLG	IBB	SH	SF	#Pit	#P/PA	GB	FB	G/F
1992 Season	.255	139	376	37	96	13	4	0	20	27	32	0	3	6	8	.304	.311	2	4	2	1372	3.39	78	78	2.19
Career (1988-1992)	.240	443	1070	133	257	37	9	3	80	94	93	1	13	47	25	.301	.300	7	19	8	3910	3.33	480	257	1.87

1992 Season

	Avg	AB	H	2B	3B	HR	RBI	BB	SO	OBP	SLG
vs. Left	.243	169	41	7	1	0	10	8	7	.275	.296
vs. Right	.266	207	55	6	3	0	10	19	25	.326	.324
Groundball	.263	152	40	4	1	0	5	12	7	.315	.303
Flyball	.220	82	18	6	1	0	6	5	8	.261	.317
Home	.252	202	51	9	4	0	11	14	22	.301	.337
Away	.259	174	45	4	0	0	9	13	10	.307	.282
Day	.251	199	50	7	3	0	10	13	22	.297	.317
Night	.260	177	46	6	1	0	10	14	10	.311	.305
Grass	.250	272	68	10	4	0	12	18	25	.297	.316
Turf	.269	104	28	3	0	0	8	9	7	.322	.298
First Pitch	.345	84	29	4	0	0	2	2	0	.360	.393
Ahead on Count	.293	82	24	3	2	0	8	16	0	.404	.378
Behind on Count	.162	111	18	3	1	0	5	0	22	.162	.207
Two Strikes	.212	146	31	4	2	0	9	9	32	.256	.267

	Avg	AB	H	2B	3B	HR	RBI	BB	SO	OBP	SLG
Scoring Posn	.256	78	20	1	0	0	19	5	6	.294	.269
Close & Late	.259	81	21	1	0	0	3	7	6	.318	.272
None on/out	.221	131	29	6	1	0	0	8	15	.266	.282
Batting #1	.263	179	47	8	2	0	11	6	13	.285	.330
Batting #2	.202	89	18	2	1	0	4	5	6	.245	.247
Other	.287	108	31	3	1	0	5	16	13	.376	.333
April	.389	18	7	0	0	0	1	1	1	.421	.389
May	.160	25	4	0	0	0	1	1	4	.192	.160
June	.228	101	23	3	1	0	6	5	5	.262	.277
July	.268	71	19	3	1	0	3	12	10	.369	.338
August	.258	89	23	5	1	0	5	2	4	.275	.337
September/October	.278	72	20	2	1	0	4	6	8	.333	.333
Pre-All Star	.231	182	42	5	2	0	8	14	17	.284	.280
Post-All Star	.278	194	54	8	2	0	12	13	15	.322	.340

1992 By Position

Position	Avg	AB	H	2B	3B	HR	RBI	BB	SO	OBP	SLG	G	GS	Innings	PO	A	E	DP	Fld Pct	Rng Fctr	In Zone	Outs	Zone Rtg	MLB Zone
As Pinch Hitter	.429	21	9	0	0	0	2	3	2	.500	.429	26	0	---	---	---	---	---	---	---	---	---	---	---
As lf	.263	38	10	0	1	0	2	2	3	.300	.316	25	7	99.1	28	1	2	0	.935	2.63	32	28	.875	.809
As cf	.234	282	66	13	3	0	12	21	22	.285	.301	80	68	634.2	177	1	3	0	.983	2.52	201	177	.881	.824
As rf	.314	35	11	0	0	0	4	1	5	.333	.314	28	6	89.0	16	0	0	0	1.000	1.62	15	13	.867	.814

Career (1988-1992)

	Avg	AB	H	2B	3B	HR	RBI	BB	SO	OBP	SLG
vs. Left	.265	472	125	22	1	1	45	28	30	.305	.322
vs. Right	.221	598	132	15	8	2	35	66	63	.299	.283
Groundball	.269	413	111	15	3	1	30	30	30	.319	.327
Flyball	.185	259	48	12	1	0	18	23	25	.249	.239
Home	.248	561	139	21	7	1	41	48	50	.308	.316
Away	.232	509	118	16	2	2	39	46	43	.294	.283
Day	.237	558	132	21	4	1	40	46	58	.296	.294
Night	.244	512	125	16	5	2	40	48	35	.307	.307
Grass	.256	751	192	26	8	2	57	64	69	.315	.320
Turf	.204	319	65	11	1	1	23	30	24	.269	.254
First Pitch	.280	250	70	8	0	1	17	3	0	.287	.324
Ahead on Count	.271	229	62	6	3	1	23	56	0	.410	.336
Behind on Count	.182	324	59	12	2	0	18	1	61	.187	.221
Two Strikes	.204	393	80	14	5	1	28	32	93	.265	.272

	Avg	AB	H	2B	3B	HR	RBI	BB	SO	OBP	SLG
Scoring Posn	.234	235	55	4	0	0	71	23	18	.296	.251
Close & Late	.269	201	54	8	2	0	22	22	16	.339	.328
None on/out	.231	372	86	19	3	1	1	30	35	.290	.306
Batting #1	.255	631	161	24	4	2	47	50	47	.309	.315
Batting #8	.241	112	27	4	1	0	6	14	11	.320	.295
Other	.211	327	69	9	4	1	27	30	35	.280	.272
April	.261	69	18	2	0	1	8	8	4	.338	.333
May	.211	175	37	4	1	1	17	9	18	.250	.263
June	.233	210	49	9	2	0	12	17	18	.293	.295
July	.227	181	41	7	1	0	11	17	17	.291	.276
August	.273	172	47	10	3	0	11	12	12	.319	.366
September/October	.247	263	65	5	2	1	21	31	24	.327	.293
Pre-All Star	.231	532	123	19	4	2	41	45	49	.292	.293
Post-All Star	.249	538	134	18	5	1	39	49	44	.311	.307

Batter vs. Pitcher (career)

Hits Best Against	Avg	AB	H	2B	3B	HR	RBI	BB	SO	OBP	SLG
Frank Viola	.571	14	8	0	0	0	4	0	2	.571	.571
Pat Combs	.455	11	5	1	0	1	3	0	3	.455	.818
Dennis Rasmussen	.412	17	7	3	0	0	2	0	2	.412	.588
Ken Hill	.333	12	4	1	0	0	0	2	3	.429	.417
Rob Dibble	.333	9	3	0	1	0	3	2	1	.455	.556

Hits Worst Against	Avg	AB	H	2B	3B	HR	RBI	BB	SO	OBP	SLG
Jose Rijo	.000	13	0	0	0	0	0	1	3	.071	.000
Doug Drabek	.059	17	1	0	0	0	1	4	0	.238	.059
Bob Walk	.083	12	1	1	0	0	0	0	0	.167	.167
Jim Deshaies	.100	20	2	0	0	0	0	1	2	.143	.100
Ron Darling	.100	10	1	0	0	0	0	1	1	.182	.100

Jack Daugherty — Rangers

Bats Both

	Avg	G	AB	R	H	2B	3B	HR	RBI	BB	SO	HBP	GDP	SB	CS	OBP	SLG	IBB	SH	SF	#Pit	#P/PA	GB	FB	G/F
1992 Season	.205	59	127	13	26	9	0	0	9	16	21	1	3	2	1	.295	.276	1	0	2	544	3.73	51	33	1.55
Last Five Years	.261	294	687	72	179	36	6	8	77	65	114	4	10	5	2	.323	.365	2	6	11	2777	3.62	263	183	1.44

1992 Season

	Avg	AB	H	2B	3B	HR	RBI	BB	SO	OBP	SLG		Avg	AB	H	2B	3B	HR	RBI	BB	SO	OBP	SLG
vs. Left	.167	30	5	1	0	0	1	2	6	.212	.200	Scoring Posn	.226	31	7	2	0	0	9	3	8	.278	.290
vs. Right	.216	97	21	8	0	0	8	14	15	.319	.299	Close & Late	.207	29	6	3	0	0	3	6	4	.343	.310
Home	.230	61	14	3	0	0	3	9	7	.324	.279	None on/out	.214	28	6	2	0	0	0	8	2	.389	.286
Away	.182	66	12	6	0	0	6	7	14	.267	.273	Batting #1	.241	29	7	2	0	0	1	3	9	.313	.310
First Pitch	.278	18	5	3	0	0	0	1	0	.316	.444	Batting #2	.222	27	6	2	0	0	2	2	2	.267	.296
Ahead on Count	.323	31	10	3	0	0	5	8	0	.450	.419	Other	.183	71	13	5	0	0	6	11	10	.298	.254
Behind on Count	.073	41	3	1	0	0	3	0	14	.093	.098	Pre-All Star	.181	83	15	7	0	0	8	11	13	.278	.265
Two Strikes	.179	56	10	2	0	0	3	7	21	.277	.214	Post-All Star	.250	44	11	2	0	0	1	5	8	.327	.295

Last Five Years

	Avg	AB	H	2B	3B	HR	RBI	BB	SO	OBP	SLG		Avg	AB	H	2B	3B	HR	RBI	BB	SO	OBP	SLG
vs. Left	.250	160	40	6	2	1	16	15	37	.317	.331	Scoring Posn	.214	168	36	8	0	0	58	19	35	.285	.262
vs. Right	.264	527	139	30	4	7	61	50	77	.325	.376	Close & Late	.233	146	34	8	0	2	14	17	34	.310	.329
Groundball	.277	202	56	9	3	2	24	18	26	.336	.381	None on/out	.263	167	44	7	0	1	1	23	32	.353	.323
Flyball	.255	161	41	7	1	2	16	16	39	.320	.348	Batting #1	.192	120	23	4	2	1	9	7	22	.229	.283
Home	.274	350	96	16	4	6	37	34	53	.341	.394	Batting #2	.296	189	56	12	2	2	21	16	21	.349	.413
Away	.246	337	83	20	2	2	40	31	61	.305	.335	Other	.265	378	100	20	2	5	47	42	71	.340	.368
Day	.278	162	45	11	2	2	18	23	25	.361	.407	April	.151	73	11	2	0	0	5	9	13	.241	.178
Night	.255	525	134	25	4	6	59	42	89	.311	.352	May	.236	157	37	9	0	0	16	14	17	.294	.293
Grass	.263	567	149	29	4	7	61	58	92	.332	.365	June	.310	58	18	6	1	0	9	2	13	.339	.448
Turf	.250	120	30	7	2	1	16	7	22	.282	.367	July	.321	112	36	10	0	2	13	9	21	.369	.464
First Pitch	.304	125	38	8	1	2	12	1	0	.305	.432	August	.274	84	23	4	1	1	7	5	14	.319	.381
Ahead on Count	.352	165	58	15	2	2	29	36	0	.463	.503	September/October	.266	203	54	5	4	5	27	26	36	.349	.404
Behind on Count	.192	224	43	5	3	1	22	0	71	.195	.254	Pre-All Star	.257	331	85	22	1	2	35	28	46	.308	.347
Two Strikes	.196	280	55	9	2	1	20	28	113	.273	.254	Post-All Star	.264	356	94	14	5	6	42	39	68	.338	.382

Batter vs. Pitcher (career)

Hits Best Against	Avg	AB	H	2B	3B	HR	RBI	BB	SO	OBP	SLG	Hits Worst Against	Avg	AB	H	2B	3B	HR	RBI	BB	SO	OBP	SLG
Jack Morris	.462	13	6	2	0	0	3	2	1	.533	.615	Mike Moore	.200	10	2	1	0	1	1	1	1	.273	.600
Randy Johnson	.333	12	4	0	0	0	0	1	5	.385	.333	Erik Hanson	.200	10	2	0	1	0	1	1	2	.273	.400
												Mike Boddicker	.231	13	3	0	0	0	0	1	3	.286	.231

Darren Daulton — Phillies

Bats Left (flyball hitter)

	Avg	G	AB	R	H	2B	3B	HR	RBI	BB	SO	HBP	GDP	SB	CS	OBP	SLG	IBB	SH	SF	#Pit	#P/PA	GB	FB	G/F
1992 Season	.270	145	485	80	131	32	5	27	109	88	103	6	3	11	2	.385	.524	11	0	6	2246	3.84	132	172	0.77
Last Five Years	.238	566	1741	220	414	92	8	60	264	270	325	12	19	27	5	.341	.403	33	6	18	7785	3.81	563	588	0.96

1992 Season

	Avg	AB	H	2B	3B	HR	RBI	BB	SO	OBP	SLG		Avg	AB	H	2B	3B	HR	RBI	BB	SO	OBP	SLG
vs. Left	.257	202	52	16	0	11	40	30	45	.363	.500	Scoring Posn	.299	134	40	10	1	8	72	35	31	.432	.567
vs. Right	.279	283	79	16	5	16	69	58	58	.399	.541	Close & Late	.223	94	21	7	0	2	13	11	24	.318	.362
Groundball	.284	211	60	12	4	12	46	33	45	.379	.550	None on/out	.235	119	28	8	0	5	5	15	23	.336	.429
Flyball	.192	99	19	6	0	5	21	16	24	.302	.404	Batting #4	.254	130	33	11	1	5	24	22	27	.364	.469
Home	.319	229	73	17	4	17	63	46	51	.434	.651	Batting #5	.255	196	50	10	3	17	58	41	41	.384	.597
Away	.227	256	58	15	1	10	46	42	52	.339	.410	Other	.302	159	48	11	1	5	27	25	35	.402	.478
Day	.195	113	22	3	0	4	13	17	25	.303	.327	April	.227	66	15	4	2	1	16	12	18	.333	.394
Night	.293	372	109	29	5	23	96	71	78	.408	.583	May	.412	68	28	9	0	3	16	15	15	.524	.676
Grass	.208	144	30	8	0	5	26	19	24	.304	.368	June	.253	91	23	4	0	8	23	16	18	.361	.560
Turf	.296	341	101	24	5	22	83	69	79	.417	.589	July	.264	87	23	3	1	6	21	16	21	.383	.529
First Pitch	.365	52	19	6	2	1	13	9	0	.446	.615	August	.231	78	18	4	1	6	15	10	18	.333	.538
Ahead on Count	.355	121	43	8	1	10	43	43	0	.530	.686	September/October	.253	95	24	8	1	3	18	19	13	.383	.453
Behind on Count	.245	163	40	11	1	8	34	0	55	.247	.472	Pre-All Star	.269	271	73	18	2	13	59	49	63	.377	.494
Two Strikes	.194	222	43	11	1	11	34	36	103	.308	.410	Post-All Star	.271	214	58	14	3	14	50	39	40	.394	.561

1992 By Position

Position	Avg	AB	H	2B	3B	HR	RBI	BB	SO	OBP	SLG	G	GS	Innings	PO	A	E	DP	Fld Pct	Rng Fctr	In Zone	Zone Outs	Zone Rtg	MLB Zone
As c	.271	480	130	32	5	27	108	87	101	.385	.527	141	137	1200.2	760	69	11	8	.987	---	---	---	---	---

Last Five Years

	Avg	AB	H	2B	3B	HR	RBI	BB	SO	OBP	SLG		Avg	AB	H	2B	3B	HR	RBI	BB	SO	OBP	SLG
vs. Left	.228	487	111	28	1	15	67	72	109	.333	.382	Scoring Posn	.272	441	120	27	1	15	189	93	74	.389	.440
vs. Right	.242	1254	303	64	7	45	197	198	216	.344	.411	Close & Late	.223	349	78	13	0	7	48	33	89	.294	.321
Groundball	.278	643	179	38	5	24	105	91	108	.368	.465	None on/out	.207	405	84	22	0	12	12	49	74	.301	.351
Flyball	.184	370	68	17	0	11	56	53	72	.287	.319	Batting #6	.241	357	86	17	1	11	48	52	67	.337	.387
Home	.241	846	204	52	5	32	135	143	156	.351	.428	Batting #7	.221	452	100	22	2	14	60	60	89	.316	.372
Away	.235	895	210	40	3	28	129	127	169	.332	.380	Other	.245	932	228	53	5	35	156	158	169	.354	.425
Day	.224	441	99	19	0	14	56	59	90	.314	.363	April	.228	237	54	13	2	6	41	36	58	.331	.376
Night	.242	1300	315	73	8	46	208	211	235	.350	.417	May	.236	225	53	14	1	4	29	41	49	.353	.360

Last Five Years

	Avg	AB	H	2B	3B	HR	RBI	BB	SO	OBP	SLG		Avg	AB	H	2B	3B	HR	RBI	BB	SO	OBP	SLG
Grass	.239	489	117	20	1	15	71	65	100	.332	.376	June	.227	269	61	13	0	12	43	48	41	.339	.409
Turf	.237	1252	297	72	7	45	193	205	225	.345	.414	July	.227	379	86	16	2	16	56	56	63	.327	.406
First Pitch	.286	220	63	18	2	8	41	18	1	.344	.495	August	.238	366	87	18	1	16	50	49	68	.333	.423
Ahead on Count	.300	416	125	25	2	21	83	125	0	.460	.522	September/October	.275	265	73	18	2	6	45	40	46	.373	.426
Behind on Count	.200	569	114	24	1	15	75	1	166	.204	.325	Pre-All Star	.218	856	187	42	3	26	124	141	167	.327	.366
Two Strikes	.167	792	132	27	3	15	79	115	324	.274	.265	Post-All Star	.256	885	227	50	5	34	140	129	158	.355	.440

Batter vs. Pitcher (since 1984)

Hits Best Against	Avg	AB	H	2B	3B	HR	RBI	BB	SO	OBP	SLG	Hits Worst Against	Avg	AB	H	2B	3B	HR	RBI	BB	SO	OBP	SLG
John Burkett	.571	14	8	2	0	0	5	4	2	.600	.714	Bobby Ojeda	.000	11	0	0	0	0	0	0	5	.000	.000
Jimmy Jones	.455	11	5	1	0	0	3	2	3	.538	.545	Bob Patterson	.077	13	1	0	0	0	0	1	2	.143	.077
Rick Sutcliffe	.440	25	11	1	0	2	6	8	5	.559	.720	Pete Harnisch	.077	13	1	0	0	0	1	0	3	.077	.077
Jeff Robinson	.400	10	4	0	0	1	1	2	3	.500	.700	Craig Lefferts	.083	12	1	0	0	0	0	1	4	.154	.083
Tim Crews	.400	10	4	1	0	1	5	2	0	.500	.800	Kelly Downs	.083	12	1	0	0	0	0	1	2	.154	.083

Alvin Davis — Angels
Bats Left (flyball hitter)

	Avg	G	AB	R	H	2B	3B	HR	RBI	BB	SO	HBP	GDP	SB	CS	OBP	SLG	IBB	SH	SF	#Pit	#P/PA	GB	FB	G/F
1992 Season	.250	40	104	5	26	8	0	0	16	13	9	0	2	0	0	.331	.327	2	0	1	436	3.69	37	36	1.03
Last Five Years	.276	607	2036	258	561	98	3	68	317	350	257	14	48	1	7	.381	.427	49	0	31	9376	3.86	640	752	0.85

1992 Season

	Avg	AB	H	2B	3B	HR	RBI	BB	SO	OBP	SLG		Avg	AB	H	2B	3B	HR	RBI	BB	SO	OBP	SLG
vs. Left	.167	12	2	0	0	0	1	1	1	.231	.167	Scoring Posn	.391	23	9	3	0	0	14	7	2	.516	.522
vs. Right	.261	92	24	8	0	0	15	12	8	.343	.348	Close & Late	.563	16	9	2	0	0	4	0	1	.563	.688
Home	.304	46	14	5	0	0	4	9	2	.418	.413	None on/out	.120	25	3	1	0	0	0	2	2	.185	.160
Away	.207	58	12	3	0	0	12	4	7	.254	.259	Batting #4	.192	26	5	0	0	0	3	5	2	.313	.192
First Pitch	.538	13	7	0	0	0	6	1	0	.533	.538	Batting #5	.257	70	18	7	0	0	12	7	6	.325	.357
Ahead on Count	.206	34	7	3	0	0	4	8	0	.357	.294	Pre-All Star	.250	104	26	8	0	0	16	13	9	.331	.327
Behind on Count	.233	30	7	5	0	0	7	0	7	.233	.400	Post-All Star	.000	0	0	0	0	0	0	0	0	.000	.000
Two Strikes	.200	40	8	5	0	0	5	4	9	.273	.325												

Last Five Years

	Avg	AB	H	2B	3B	HR	RBI	BB	SO	OBP	SLG		Avg	AB	H	2B	3B	HR	RBI	BB	SO	OBP	SLG
vs. Left	.283	572	162	34	2	19	106	93	81	.386	.449	Scoring Posn	.302	493	149	27	2	13	230	141	56	.438	.444
vs. Right	.273	1464	399	64	1	49	211	257	176	.379	.418	Close & Late	.265	321	85	15	0	11	48	52	44	.366	.414
Groundball	.291	494	144	20	0	18	80	102	69	.409	.441	None on/out	.244	475	116	19	0	11	11	58	64	.331	.354
Flyball	.263	456	120	23	1	20	80	56		.372	.450	Batting #3	.296	889	263	47	2	31	130	164	96	.407	.458
Home	.294	1001	294	60	1	43	178	178	126	.399	.485	Batting #4	.278	569	158	22	0	20	94	117	67	.398	.422
Away	.258	1035	267	38	2	25	139	172	131	.363	.371	Other	.242	578	140	29	1	17	93	69	94	.319	.384
Day	.298	520	155	24	1	18	81	84	66	.393	.452	April	.287	321	92	19	0	7	49	59	32	.396	.411
Night	.268	1516	406	74	2	50	236	266	191	.376	.418	May	.301	372	112	15	1	17	68	46	47	.376	.484
Grass	.258	830	214	30	1	20	107	145	96	.366	.369	June	.243	342	83	14	1	8	39	58	45	.353	.360
Turf	.288	1206	347	68	2	48	210	205	161	.390	.467	July	.309	265	82	11	1	8	50	63	30	.434	.449
First Pitch	.313	163	51	9	0	7	32	18	0	.381	.497	August	.261	368	96	15	0	15	48	68	52	.372	.424
Ahead on Count	.320	641	205	34	1	35	134	214	0	.486	.540	September/October	.261	368	96	24	0	13	63	56	51	.364	.432
Behind on Count	.272	666	181	38	1	17	108	2	124	.276	.406	Pre-All Star	.275	1071	295	50	2	32	158	175	129	.376	.415
Two Strikes	.221	861	190	32	2	16	96	105	254	.290	.318	Post-All Star	.276	965	266	48	1	36	159	159	128	.385	.439

Batter vs. Pitcher (career)

Hits Best Against	Avg	AB	H	2B	3B	HR	RBI	BB	SO	OBP	SLG	Hits Worst Against	Avg	AB	H	2B	3B	HR	RBI	BB	SO	OBP	SLG
Jim Acker	.700	10	7	2	0	1	3	3	0	.769	1.200	Dennis Martinez	.000	13	0	0	0	0	0	2	2	.133	.000
Tom Bolton	.545	11	6	2	0	1	3	2	2	.615	1.000	Kevin Tapani	.091	22	2	0	0	0	1	1	4	.130	.091
Jim Abbott	.500	8	4	2	0	0	7	5	1	.643	.750	Jerry Don Gleaton	.091	11	1	0	0	0	1	1	3	.167	.091
Mark Williamson	.462	13	6	0	0	2	3	1	1	.500	.923	Bill Wegman	.107	28	3	0	0	0	3	1	1	.138	.107
Dennis Eckersley	.333	9	3	0	0	2	5	2	1	.455	1.000	Bob Milacki	.111	9	1	0	0	0	1	1	0	.182	.111

Chili Davis — Twins
Bats Both

	Avg	G	AB	R	H	2B	3B	HR	RBI	BB	SO	HBP	GDP	SB	CS	OBP	SLG	IBB	SH	SF	#Pit	#P/PA	GB	FB	G/F
1992 Season	.288	138	444	63	128	27	2	12	66	73	76	3	11	4	5	.386	.439	11	0	9	1981	3.74	169	123	1.37
Last Five Years	.274	716	2550	367	698	131	8	96	400	346	509	4	68	22	23	.357	.444	54	4	32	10783	3.68	946	692	1.37

1992 Season

	Avg	AB	H	2B	3B	HR	RBI	BB	SO	OBP	SLG		Avg	AB	H	2B	3B	HR	RBI	BB	SO	OBP	SLG
vs. Left	.256	121	31	5	0	4	22	13	25	.321	.397	Scoring Posn	.263	133	35	8	0	1	49	37	27	.409	.346
vs. Right	.300	323	97	22	2	8	44	60	51	.408	.455	Close & Late	.296	81	24	5	0	2	16	11	20	.372	.432
Groundball	.303	122	37	4	1	3	20	15	24	.371	.426	None on/out	.324	111	36	8	2	6	6	10	17	.380	.595
Flyball	.299	134	40	8	1	4	17	17	28	.377	.463	Batting #4	.282	206	58	7	0	7	31	37	39	.386	.417
Home	.273	245	67	18	2	6	40	38	42	.364	.437	Batting #5	.289	142	41	12	1	0	16	22	18	.386	.387
Away	.307	199	61	9	0	6	26	35	34	.412	.442	Other	.302	96	29	8	1	5	19	14	19	.384	.563
Day	.282	124	35	6	0	3	22	20	22	.377	.403	April	.246	65	16	2	1	0	4	12	12	.359	.308
Night	.291	320	93	21	2	9	44	53	54	.389	.453	May	.304	69	21	4	1	2	16	14	12	.409	.478
Grass	.274	146	40	6	0	3	18	26	22	.386	.377	June	.293	82	24	5	0	3	13	13	12	.389	.463

1992 Season

	Avg	AB	H	2B	3B	HR	RBI	BB	SO	OBP	SLG		Avg	AB	H	2B	3B	HR	RBI	BB	SO	OBP	SLG
Turf	.295	298	88	21	2	9	48	47	54	.385	.470	July	.292	89	26	6	0	2	14	10	13	.356	.427
First Pitch	.315	73	23	9	1	0	6	11	0	.405	.466	August	.258	89	23	7	0	1	6	13	17	.359	.371
Ahead on Count	.327	110	36	4	0	6	19	33	0	.469	.527	September/October	.360	50	18	3	0	4	13	11	10	.469	.660
Behind on Count	.227	128	29	4	0	5	24	0	33	.237	.375	Pre-All Star	.279	251	70	13	2	5	37	42	37	.377	.406
Two Strikes	.237	190	45	9	1	5	28	31	76	.342	.374	Post-All Star	.301	193	58	14	0	7	29	31	39	.397	.482

1992 By Position

Position	Avg	AB	H	2B	3B	HR	RBI	BB	SO	OBP	SLG	G	GS	Innings	PO	A	E	DP	Fld Pct	Rng Fctr	In Zone	Zone Outs	MLB Zone
As Designated Hitter	.280	428	120	25	2	11	60	72	73	.382	.425	125	115	---	---	---	---	---	---	---	---	---	---
As Pinch Hitter	.313	16	5	1	0	1	6	3	2	.400	.563	20	0	---	---	---	---	---	---	---	---	---	---

Last Five Years

	Avg	AB	H	2B	3B	HR	RBI	BB	SO	OBP	SLG		Avg	AB	H	2B	3B	HR	RBI	BB	SO	OBP	SLG
vs. Left	.256	840	215	37	3	35	137	90	178	.324	.432	Scoring Posn	.273	696	190	42	1	28	299	138	159	.380	.457
vs. Right	.282	1710	483	94	5	61	263	256	331	.373	.466	Close & Late	.254	397	101	21	0	11	53	65	94	.355	.390
Groundball	.297	622	185	32	5	21	114	72	110	.366	.466	None on/out	.275	597	164	36	2	26	26	58	107	.339	.472
Flyball	.259	641	166	30	2	28	94	72	153	.330	.443	Batting #4	.259	916	237	44	3	33	149	130	176	.347	.421
Home	.275	1293	355	65	6	47	199	182	252	.361	.443	Batting #5	.297	905	269	55	4	36	129	131	182	.385	.486
Away	.273	1257	343	66	2	49	201	164	257	.353	.446	Other	.263	729	192	32	1	27	122	85	151	.336	.421
Day	.262	656	172	29	2	22	114	92	136	.348	.413	April	.271	377	102	18	1	12	53	50	80	.354	.419
Night	.278	1894	526	102	6	74	286	254	373	.361	.455	May	.278	474	132	26	4	15	72	50	87	.343	.445
Grass	.262	1666	437	75	4	57	251	210	340	.342	.415	June	.259	455	118	19	0	25	79	59	85	.340	.466
Turf	.295	864	261	56	4	39	149	136	169	.386	.500	July	.281	391	110	21	0	19	72	56	74	.366	.481
First Pitch	.340	435	148	34	4	21	83	32	0	.381	.582	August	.276	461	128	29	1	14	71	65	99	.365	.436
Ahead on Count	.333	561	187	30	0	26	101	142	0	.463	.537	September/October	.276	392	108	18	2	11	53	66	84	.379	.416
Behind on Count	.228	829	189	28	3	27	120	1	249	.230	.367	Pre-All Star	.269	1451	391	69	5	57	223	180	273	.346	.442
Two Strikes	.193	1127	218	36	2	32	135	155	508	.295	.314	Post-All Star	.279	1099	307	62	3	39	177	166	236	.372	.446

Batter vs. Pitcher (since 1984)

Hits Best Against	Avg	AB	H	2B	3B	HR	RBI	BB	SO	OBP	SLG	Hits Worst Against	Avg	AB	H	2B	3B	HR	RBI	BB	SO	OBP	SLG
Mike Jackson	.667	9	6	0	0	0	2	5	0	.733	.667	Jeff Montgomery	.000	12	0	0	0	0	0	4	4	.250	.000
Jeff M. Robinson	.429	21	9	1	0	3	6	5	4	.538	.905	Jesse Orosco	.000	11	0	0	0	0	0	4	6	.267	.000
Bryn Smith	.429	14	6	1	0	2	3	1	2	.467	.929	Frank Viola	.100	20	2	0	0	0	3	2	9	.182	.100
Luis Aquino	.364	11	4	1	0	2	5	3	3	.467	1.000	Erik Hanson	.100	20	2	0	0	0	0	2	9	.182	.100
Kevin Appier	.364	11	4	0	0	3	6	1	2	.417	1.182	Ron Darling	.150	20	3	0	0	0	1	1	4	.182	.150

Doug Davis — Rangers   Bats Right (groundball hitter)

	Avg	G	AB	R	H	2B	3B	HR	RBI	BB	SO	HBP	GDP	SB	CS	OBP	SLG	IBB	SH	SF	#Pit	#P/PA	GB	FB	G/F
1992 Season	1.000	1	1	0	1	0	0	0	0	0	0	0	0	0	0	1.000	1.000	0	0	0	5	5.00	1	0	0.00
Career (1988-1992)	.077	7	13	1	1	0	0	0	0	0	3	1	0	1	0	.143	.077	0	0	0	38	2.71	5	2	2.50

1992 Season

	Avg	AB	H	2B	3B	HR	RBI	BB	SO	OBP	SLG		Avg	AB	H	2B	3B	HR	RBI	BB	SO	OBP	SLG
vs. Left	.000	0	0	0	0	0	0	0	0	.000	.000	Scoring Posn	.000	0	0	0	0	0	0	0	0	.000	.000
vs. Right	1.000	1	1	0	0	0	0	0	0	1.000	1.000	Close & Late	.000	0	0	0	0	0	0	0	0	.000	.000

Eric Davis — Dodgers   Bats Right

	Avg	G	AB	R	H	2B	3B	HR	RBI	BB	SO	HBP	GDP	SB	CS	OBP	SLG	IBB	SH	SF	#Pit	#P/PA	GB	FB	G/F
1992 Season	.228	76	267	21	61	8	1	5	32	36	71	3	8	19	1	.325	.322	2	0	2	1209	3.93	97	61	1.59
Last Five Years	.260	558	1939	299	505	76	8	100	345	277	345	14	45	110	16	.354	.463	35	0	21	8572	3.81	672	518	1.30

1992 Season

	Avg	AB	H	2B	3B	HR	RBI	BB	SO	OBP	SLG		Avg	AB	H	2B	3B	HR	RBI	BB	SO	OBP	SLG
vs. Left	.236	89	21	4	0	4	11	23	19	.393	.416	Scoring Posn	.275	80	22	2	0	1	26	16	16	.406	.338
vs. Right	.225	178	40	4	1	1	21	13	52	.286	.275	Close & Late	.200	45	9	1	0	0	6	5	6	.294	.222
Groundball	.255	102	26	3	0	2	11	10	24	.327	.343	None on/out	.232	56	13	0	0	3	3	4	15	.283	.393
Flyball	.232	56	13	3	1	0	6	8	17	.343	.321	Batting #4	.198	131	26	4	0	1	13	13	34	.269	.252
Home	.233	133	31	6	0	1	15	16	30	.316	.301	Batting #5	.310	84	26	4	1	4	16	15	27	.422	.524
Away	.224	134	30	2	1	4	17	20	41	.333	.343	Other	.173	52	9	0	0	0	3	8	10	.295	.173
Day	.174	92	16	2	1	0	8	10	26	.260	.217	April	.310	71	22	3	0	4	13	10	22	.398	.521
Night	.257	175	45	6	0	5	24	26	45	.358	.377	May	.167	42	7	3	0	0	3	6	14	.271	.238
Grass	.247	194	48	7	1	4	24	26	50	.342	.356	June	.209	43	9	1	0	0	5	4	11	.277	.233
Turf	.178	73	13	1	0	1	8	10	21	.277	.233	July	.217	83	18	1	1	1	10	12	18	.313	.289
First Pitch	.269	26	7	0	0	0	1	2	0	.321	.269	August	.222	18	4	0	0	0	1	2	6	.333	.222
Ahead on Count	.265	68	18	4	0	2	8	14	0	.390	.412	September/October	.100	10	1	0	0	0	0	2	0	.308	.100
Behind on Count	.202	84	17	2	0	0	7	0	32	.218	.226	Pre-All Star	.234	201	47	7	0	5	27	24	56	.316	.343
Two Strikes	.162	130	21	2	1	2	11	20	71	.286	.238	Post-All Star	.212	66	14	1	1	0	5	12	15	.350	.258

1992 By Position

Position	Avg	AB	H	2B	3B	HR	RBI	BB	SO	OBP	SLG	G	GS	Innings	PO	A	E	DP	Fld Pct	Rng Fctr	In Zone	Zone Outs	MLB Zone
As lf	.230	252	58	8	1	5	32	28	67	.312	.329	69	68	573.0	108	0	4	1	.964	1.70	126	106	.841	.809

Last Five Years

	Avg	AB	H	2B	3B	HR	RBI	BB	SO	OBP	SLG		Avg	AB	H	2B	3B	HR	RBI	BB	SO	OBP	SLG
vs. Left	.261	620	162	28	2	32	105	111	139	.374	.468	Scoring Posn	.262	543	153	31	3	26	237	124	131	.409	.494
vs. Right	.260	1319	343	48	6	68	240	166	364	.344	.460	Close & Late	.272	327	89	16	0	19	67	50	80	.371	.495
Groundball	.261	700	183	30	4	25	118	96	178	.354	.423	None on/out	.275	455	125	14	1	31	31	40	111	.336	.514
Flyball	.270	429	116	20	1	29	62	61	106	.363	.524	Batting #3	.251	470	118	12	1	25	70	67	126	.345	.440
Home	.254	882	224	32	2	48	171	151	230	.362	.458	Batting #4	.268	1281	343	57	6	66	239	185	315	.360	.476
Away	.266	1057	281	44	6	52	174	126	273	.347	.466	Other	.234	188	44	7	1	9	36	25	62	.329	.426
Day	.241	602	145	20	4	23	81	58	169	.312	.402	April	.236	314	74	13	1	13	45	52	89	.341	.408
Night	.269	1337	360	56	4	77	264	219	334	.371	.490	May	.240	271	65	14	0	13	48	38	75	.334	.435
Grass	.268	758	203	29	4	36	124	95	193	.354	.459	June	.286	322	92	7	2	24	70	43	60	.375	.543
Turf	.256	1181	302	47	4	64	221	182	310	.353	.465	July	.244	406	99	14	2	16	57	56	100	.338	.406
First Pitch	.370	257	95	17	1	21	62	15	0	.404	.689	August	.282	323	91	14	2	18	62	45	83	.368	.505
Ahead on Count	.348	454	158	24	2	35	114	130	1	.490	.641	September/October	.277	303	84	14	1	16	63	43	76	.366	.488
Behind on Count	.213	582	124	16	1	24	85	2	218	.220	.368	Pre-All Star	.246	1038	255	37	3	54	179	147	275	.341	.443
Two Strikes	.157	932	146	17	2	30	100	115	502	.252	.276	Post-All Star	.277	901	250	39	5	46	166	130	228	.369	.485

Batter vs. Pitcher (career)

Hits Best Against	Avg	AB	H	2B	3B	HR	RBI	BB	SO	OBP	SLG	Hits Worst Against	Avg	AB	H	2B	3B	HR	RBI	BB	SO	OBP	SLG
Don Carman	.615	13	8	1	0	5	10	4	1	.706	1.846	Todd Worrell	.000	12	0	0	0	0	0	3	2	.200	.000
John Smoltz	.556	18	10	2	0	4	6	2	2	.600	1.333	Lance McCullers	.000	9	0	0	0	0	0	2	4	.182	.000
Juan Agosto	.556	9	5	0	0	1	2	2	3	.636	.889	Nolan Ryan	.048	21	1	0	0	1	1	3	15	.167	.190
Frank DiPino	.455	11	5	2	0	1	5	5	2	.625	.909	Cris Carpenter	.091	11	1	0	0	0	0	0	2	.091	.091
Mark Grant	.450	20	9	1	0	4	9	5	4	.560	1.100	Larry Andersen	.136	22	3	1	0	0	1	1	7	.174	.182

Glenn Davis — Orioles   Bats Right (flyball hitter)

	Avg	G	AB	R	H	2B	3B	HR	RBI	BB	SO	HBP	GDP	SB	CS	OBP	SLG	IBB	SH	SF	#Pit	#P/PA	GB	FB	G/F
1992 Season	.276	106	398	46	110	15	2	13	48	37	65	2	12	1	0	.338	.422	2	1	4	1642	3.72	131	130	1.01
Last Five Years	.264	558	2043	284	540	91	8	109	328	221	348	33	39	21	8	.343	.477	56	1	21	8171	3.53	666	730	0.91

1992 Season

	Avg	AB	H	2B	3B	HR	RBI	BB	SO	OBP	SLG		Avg	AB	H	2B	3B	HR	RBI	BB	SO	OBP	SLG
vs. Left	.252	107	27	3	1	4	18	6	22	.287	.411	Scoring Posn	.253	99	25	5	1	1	31	10	18	.316	.354
vs. Right	.285	291	83	12	1	9	30	31	43	.356	.426	Close & Late	.185	54	10	1	0	2	3	8	10	.290	.315
Groundball	.269	108	29	3	1	3	15	8	17	.319	.398	None on/out	.298	104	31	4	0	4	4	10	15	.360	.452
Flyball	.363	91	33	5	0	5	18	14	16	.435	.582	Batting #4	.257	334	86	15	1	10	40	34	56	.326	.398
Home	.290	200	58	8	1	5	15	12	35	.330	.415	Batting #5	.404	47	19	0	0	4	3	6		.440	.532
Away	.263	198	52	7	1	8	33	25	30	.345	.429	Other	.294	17	5	0	1	1	4	0	3	.294	.588
Day	.248	101	25	4	2	1	8	10	17	.315	.356	April	.333	3	1	0	0	0	0	0	0	.333	.333
Night	.286	297	85	11	0	12	40	27	48	.345	.444	May	.255	51	13	1	1	3	9	3	9	.296	.490
Grass	.289	342	99	14	2	10	40	29	59	.346	.430	June	.237	59	14	1	0	2	5	4	11	.297	.356
Turf	.196	56	11	1	0	3	8	8	6	.292	.375	July	.380	79	30	3	0	3	14	13	9	.457	.532
First Pitch	.351	57	20	2	0	3	11	1	0	.356	.544	August	.232	99	23	6	1	2	8	10	16	.300	.374
Ahead on Count	.273	77	21	3	0	4	10	18	0	.402	.468	September/October	.271	107	29	4	0	3	12	7	20	.319	.393
Behind on Count	.287	136	39	6	1	2	18	0	37	.295	.390	Pre-All Star	.250	136	34	2	1	6	17	11	24	.309	.412
Two Strikes	.239	184	44	4	2	4	18	18	65	.309	.348	Post-All Star	.290	262	76	13	1	7	31	26	41	.353	.427

1992 By Position

Position	Avg	AB	H	2B	3B	HR	RBI	BB	SO	OBP	SLG	G	GS	Innings	PO	A	E	DP	Fld Pct	Rng Fctr	In Zone	Outs	Zone Rtg	MLB Zone
As Designated Hitter	.276	392	108	15	2	13	48	36	64	.336	.423	103	98	---	---	---	---	---	---	---	---	---	---	---

Last Five Years

	Avg	AB	H	2B	3B	HR	RBI	BB	SO	OBP	SLG		Avg	AB	H	2B	3B	HR	RBI	BB	SO	OBP	SLG
vs. Left	.254	590	150	25	1	41	104	75	80	.345	.508	Scoring Posn	.241	527	127	24	3	19	192	116	98	.372	.406
vs. Right	.268	1453	390	66	7	68	224	146	268	.341	.464	Close & Late	.251	358	90	15	1	15	47	48	72	.343	.425
Groundball	.266	700	186	24	4	31	100	76	101	.342	.444	None on/out	.257	584	150	24	1	28	28	35	96	.311	.445
Flyball	.291	444	129	23	3	29	89	60	84	.378	.552	Batting #4	.260	1928	501	88	6	103	310	215	325	.341	.472
Home	.284	1025	291	55	5	42	136	104	175	.356	.470	Batting #5	.359	78	28	2	1	3	6	5	14	.400	.526
Away	.245	1018	249	36	3	67	192	117	173	.329	.483	Other	.297	37	11	1	1	3	12	1	9	.316	.622
Day	.235	562	132	27	5	23	71	68	119	.327	.423	April	.299	278	83	14	0	24	59	33	58	.386	.608
Night	.275	1481	408	64	3	86	257	153	229	.348	.497	May	.245	363	89	15	1	16	65	29	61	.303	.424
Grass	.240	910	216	29	5	46	132	81	168	.309	.434	June	.214	332	71	7	2	21	49	32	62	.288	.437
Turf	.284	1133	322	62	3	63	196	140	180	.368	.511	July	.345	235	81	17	0	14	46	34	31	.426	.596
First Pitch	.332	304	101	16	1	26	69	12	0	.358	.648	August	.262	328	86	14	1	16	47	41	60	.346	.457
Ahead on Count	.299	395	118	18	1	30	80	109	0	.451	.577	September/October	.256	507	130	24	4	18	62	52	75	.338	.426
Behind on Count	.238	770	183	28	5	30	106	4	198	.255	.390	Pre-All Star	.250	1052	263	38	3	63	181	104	193	.325	.471
Two Strikes	.196	919	180	25	6	24	96	70	347	.262	.314	Post-All Star	.280	991	277	53	5	46	147	117	155	.361	.482

Batter vs. Pitcher (career)

Hits Best Against	Avg	AB	H	2B	3B	HR	RBI	BB	SO	OBP	SLG	Hits Worst Against	Avg	AB	H	2B	3B	HR	RBI	BB	SO	OBP	SLG
Tim Burke	.556	18	10	3	0	2	7	1	1	.579	1.056	Mike Bielecki	.000	16	0	0	0	0	1	2	3	.111	.000
Dennis Martinez	.481	27	13	0	0	6	12	3	2	.516	1.148	Lance McCullers	.050	20	1	0	0	0	1	2	6	.136	.050
Jeff Parrett	.455	11	5	2	0	2	4	4	3	.600	1.182	Jose Rijo	.083	24	2	1	0	0	1	0	4	.083	.125
Mike Dunne	.444	9	4	1	0	2	4	3	2	.583	1.222	Jose DeLeon	.091	11	1	0	0	0	0	0	5	.091	.091

Batter vs. Pitcher (career)

Hits Best Against	Avg	AB	H	2B	3B	HR	RBI	BB	SO	OBP	SLG	Hits Worst Against	Avg	AB	H	2B	3B	HR	RBI	BB	SO	OBP	SLG
Derek Lilliquist	.417	12	5	0	0	2	6	1	1	.462	.917	Dave Fleming	.091	11	1	0	0	0	0	0	1	.091	.091

Mark Davis — Braves
Pitches Left

	ERA	W	L	Sv	G	GS	IP	BB	SO	Avg	H	2B	3B	HR	RBI	OBP	SLG	GF	IR	IRS	Hld	SvOp	SB	CS	GB	FB	G/F
1992 Season	7.13	2	3	0	27	6	53.0	41	34	.300	64	15	1	9	45	.408	.507	11	14	5	0	0	8	1	69	67	1.03
Last Five Years	3.67	19	26	79	241	14	375.1	205	348	.233	326	59	6	32	198	.331	.353	47	239	66	13	94	34	5	460	369	1.25

1992 Season

	ERA	W	L	Sv	G	GS	IP	H	HR	BB	SO		Avg	AB	H	2B	3B	HR	RBI	BB	SO	OBP	SLG
Home	8.77	1	2	0	14	3	25.2	39	6	18	14	vs. Left	.305	59	18	3	0	1	9	6	8	.368	.407
Away	5.60	1	1	0	13	3	27.1	25	3	23	20	vs. Right	.299	154	46	12	1	8	36	35	26	.422	.545
Starter	10.27	1	3	0	6	6	23.2	34	5	20	7	Scoring Posn	.284	67	19	3	0	3	38	16	14	.404	.463
Reliever	4.60	1	0	0	21	0	29.1	30	4	21	27	Close & Late	.500	2	1	0	0	0	0	0	0	.500	.500
0 Days rest	0.00	0	0	0	0	0	0.0	0	0	0	0	None on/out	.318	44	14	2	1	2	2	11	6	.455	.545
1 or 2 Days rest	5.14	1	0	0	9	0	14.0	16	2	10	15	First Pitch	.370	27	10	4	0	2	8	2	0	.433	.741
3+ Days rest	4.11	0	0	0	12	0	15.1	14	2	11	12	Behind on Count	.339	62	21	3	1	4	16	23	0	.512	.613
Pre-All Star	7.18	1	3	0	13	6	36.1	42	6	15	19	Ahead on Count	.255	98	25	5	0	3	14	0	29	.248	.398
Post-All Star	7.02	1	0	0	14	0	16.2	22	3	13	15	Two Strikes	.213	94	20	4	0	2	14	16	34	.319	.319

Last Five Years

	ERA	W	L	Sv	G	GS	IP	H	HR	BB	SO		Avg	AB	H	2B	3B	HR	RBI	BB	SO	OBP	SLG
Home	3.37	13	6	40	118	7	187.0	161	12	101	175	vs. Left	.248	302	75	13	2	4	44	37	78	.340	.344
Away	3.97	6	20	39	123	7	188.1	165	20	104	173	vs. Right	.229	1096	251	46	4	28	154	168	270	.329	.355
Day	4.25	1	10	25	78	4	112.1	96	9	72	107	Inning 1-6	.246	341	84	18	2	11	57	71	60	.370	.408
Night	3.42	18	16	54	163	10	263.0	230	23	133	241	Inning 7+	.229	1057	242	41	4	21	141	134	288	.318	.335
Grass	2.87	11	14	58	144	6	229.0	185	21	105	218	None on	.230	682	157	30	2	15	15	81	168	.317	.346
Turf	4.92	8	12	21	97	8	146.1	141	11	100	130	Runners on	.236	716	169	29	4	17	183	124	180	.343	.359
April	4.15	1	3	18	37	3	60.2	54	7	30	65	Scoring Posn	.228	430	98	15	3	11	165	90	123	.353	.353
May	3.81	5	5	11	45	1	56.2	58	4	38	56	Close & Late	.233	460	107	12	2	8	62	61	123	.325	.320
June	4.66	3	9	12	47	1	56.0	52	5	34	58	None on/out	.215	297	64	8	1	8	8	39	78	.313	.330
July	5.36	2	3	8	27	3	42.0	42	7	30	26	vs. 1st Batr (relief)	.187	198	37	8	1	2	21	24	61	.281	.268
August	2.65	4	1	13	37	1	71.1	50	4	30	54	First Inning Pitched	.209	761	159	30	2	11	122	128	208	.323	.297
September/October	2.64	4	5	17	48	3	88.2	70	5	43	89	First 15 Pitches	.213	662	141	27	1	10	87	92	171	.311	.302
Starter	6.61	4	6	0	14	14	64.0	65	10	49	29	Pitch 16-30	.238	399	95	18	1	10	52	62	108	.340	.363
Reliever	3.06	15	20	79	227	0	311.1	261	22	156	319	Pitch 31-45	.235	170	40	5	2	3	22	30	36	.348	.341
0 Days rest	2.43	4	6	21	48	0	55.2	44	1	31	70	Pitch 46+	.299	167	50	9	2	9	37	21	33	.374	.539
1 or 2 Days rest	3.43	7	9	41	105	0	144.1	126	11	74	151	First Pitch	.309	162	50	12	1	5	24	15	4	.370	.488
3+ Days rest	2.91	4	5	17	74	0	111.1	91	10	51	98	Ahead on Count	.175	736	129	17	0	11	63	0	307	.178	.243
Pre-All Star	4.54	10	19	44	138	7	186.1	179	18	116	185	Behind on Count	.296	284	84	20	2	11	71	113	0	.491	.496
Post-All Star	2.81	9	7	35	103	7	189.0	147	14	89	163	Two Strikes	.155	718	111	13	2	9	67	77	344	.238	.216

Pitcher vs. Batter (since 1984)

Pitches Best Vs.	Avg	AB	H	2B	3B	HR	RBI	BB	SO	OBP	SLG	Pitches Worst Vs.	Avg	AB	H	2B	3B	HR	RBI	BB	SO	OBP	SLG
Kal Daniels	.000	13	0	0	0	0	0	2	4	.133	.000	Will Clark	.467	15	7	2	1	1	9	0	3	.467	.933
Tim Wallach	.000	11	0	0	0	0	0	1	5	.083	.000	Howard Johnson	.455	11	5	0	0	2	5	2	4	.538	1.000
Denny Walling	.091	11	1	0	0	0	0	0	3	.091	.091	Dickie Thon	.400	10	4	0	1	2	4	3	2	.538	1.200
Alfredo Griffin	.100	10	1	0	0	0	0	1	3	.182	.100	Sid Bream	.400	10	4	1	0	2	8	1	0	.455	1.100
Kevin McReynolds	.111	27	3	0	0	0	0	2	7	.172	.111	Dale Murphy	.393	28	11	0	0	4	10	6	4	.486	.821

Storm Davis — Orioles
Pitches Right

	ERA	W	L	Sv	G	GS	IP	BB	SO	Avg	H	2B	3B	HR	RBI	OBP	SLG	GF	IR	IRS	Hld	SvOp	SB	CS	GB	FB	G/F
1992 Season	3.43	7	3	4	48	2	89.1	36	53	.244	79	8	1	5	38	.320	.321	24	51	11	5	7	9	2	101	110	0.92
Last Five Years	4.21	52	36	6	184	95	686.2	275	386	.281	746	122	14	60	321	.347	.405	46	86	24	9	10	27	25	961	813	1.18

1992 Season

	ERA	W	L	Sv	G	GS	IP	H	HR	BB	SO		Avg	AB	H	2B	3B	HR	RBI	BB	SO	OBP	SLG
Home	2.85	5	1	1	25	0	47.1	39	3	19	22	vs. Left	.241	137	33	2	0	2	15	21	28	.338	.299
Away	4.07	2	2	3	23	2	42.0	40	2	17	31	vs. Right	.246	187	46	6	1	3	23	15	25	.306	.337
Starter	1.86	0	0	0	2	2	9.2	10	1	3	6	Scoring Posn	.267	90	24	2	1	2	34	15	13	.364	.378
Reliever	3.62	7	3	4	46	0	79.2	69	4	33	47	Close & Late	.221	113	25	1	0	2	11	13	19	.305	.283
0 Days rest	6.35	1	0	0	5	0	5.2	8	0	3	3	None on/out	.197	71	14	2	0	2	8	16	28	.278	.310
1 or 2 Days rest	1.40	6	1	3	23	0	51.1	35	1	17	30	First Pitch	.257	35	9	1	0	1	5	3	0	.300	.371
3+ Days rest	7.94	0	1	1	18	0	22.2	26	3	13	14	Behind on Count	.293	75	22	3	1	2	12	16	0	.413	.440
Pre-All Star	3.09	3	2	2	28	1	55.1	43	3	21	25	Ahead on Count	.239	142	34	3	0	2	17	0	43	.245	.303
Post-All Star	3.97	4	1	2	20	1	34.0	36	2	15	28	Two Strikes	.190	147	28	4	0	2	14	17	53	.279	.259

Last Five Years

	ERA	W	L	Sv	G	GS	IP	H	HR	BB	SO		Avg	AB	H	2B	3B	HR	RBI	BB	SO	OBP	SLG
Home	4.06	28	17	1	96	49	361.1	382	27	134	192	vs. Left	.279	1309	365	62	8	26	162	161	206	.355	.398
Away	4.37	24	19	5	88	46	325.1	364	33	142	194	vs. Right	.282	1350	381	60	6	34	159	115	178	.339	.411
Day	5.06	17	15	1	64	33	231.0	267	22	114	125	Inning 1-6	.281	2028	570	100	12	43	238	206	281	.346	.406
Night	3.77	35	21	5	120	62	455.2	479	38	162	261	Inning 7+	.279	631	176	22	2	17	83	68	105	.350	.401

Last Five Years

	ERA	W	L	Sv	G	GS	IP	H	HR	BB	SO		Avg	AB	H	2B	3B	HR	RBI	BB	SO	OBP	SLG
Grass	4.13	38	22	5	118	64	456.0	487	45	197	270	None on	.290	1447	420	78	9	34	34	133	208	.351	.427
Turf	4.37	14	14	1	66	31	230.2	259	15	79	116	Runners on	.269	1212	326	44	5	26	287	143	178	.342	.378
April	3.95	8	8	0	24	17	107.0	112	8	42	62	Scoring Posn	.274	671	184	29	4	13	254	99	98	.358	.387
May	5.40	4	9	0	29	19	116.2	140	10	61	62	Close & Late	.272	268	73	5	0	9	39	31	39	.347	.392
June	3.39	6	5	3	35	12	111.2	124	10	42	62	None on/out	.307	665	204	38	4	20	20	54	84	.361	.466
July	4.07	11	3	2	32	17	117.1	124	9	42	62	vs. 1st Batr (relief)	.239	71	17	2	0	3	13	14	9	.364	.394
August	3.57	15	6	1	37	19	148.2	155	11	59	79	First Inning Pitched	.306	671	205	27	4	13	102	79	96	.378	.416
September/October	5.27	8	5	0	27	11	85.1	109	10	40	52	First 15 Pitches	.302	587	177	25	2	13	56	58	74	.363	.417
Starter	4.11	44	29	0	95	95	540.1	588	47	215	300	Pitch 16-30	.255	518	132	23	3	8	71	59	84	.331	.357
Reliever	4.55	8	7	6	89	0	146.1	158	13	61	86	Pitch 31-45	.279	423	118	19	2	7	55	35	54	.333	.383
0 Days rest	6.88	1	4	0	14	0	17.0	20	1	11	8	Pitch 46+	.282	1131	319	55	7	32	139	124	174	.351	.428
1 or 2 Days rest	2.57	7	1	5	43	0	84.0	80	2	31	46	First Pitch	.319	373	119	24	1	10	48	14	0	.338	.469
3+ Days rest	7.35	0	2	1	32	0	45.1	58	10	19	32	Ahead on Count	.233	1135	264	49	2	11	106	0	313	.234	.308
Pre-All Star	4.22	20	23	3	96	53	371.1	391	33	148	210	Behind on Count	.312	618	193	31	5	24	99	137	0	.435	.495
Post-All Star	4.20	32	13	3	88	42	315.1	355	27	128	176	Two Strikes	.237	1160	275	45	6	15	107	125	386	.312	.325

Pitcher vs. Batter (since 1984)

Pitches Best Vs.	Avg	AB	H	2B	3B	HR	RBI	BB	SO	OBP	SLG	Pitches Worst Vs.	Avg	AB	H	2B	3B	HR	RBI	BB	SO	OBP	SLG
Dan Pasqua	.000	7	0	0	0	0	1	3	2	.273	.000	Jay Buhner	.500	12	6	1	0	1	4	2	2	.625	.833
Randy Bush	.031	32	1	1	0	0	2	3	11	.114	.063	Greg Gagne	.462	26	12	2	0	2	4	1	3	.481	.769
Pete Incaviglia	.056	18	1	0	0	0	0	3	5	.190	.056	Billy Ripken	.462	13	6	1	1	0	1	0		.500	.692
Al Newman	.083	12	1	0	0	0	0	0	0	.083	.083	Dave Bergman	.444	18	8	1	0	1	1	6	2	.583	.667
Dave Winfield	.158	19	3	0	0	0	2	0	2	.150	.158	Jack Clark	.400	10	4	1	0	2	5	4	1	.571	1.100

Andre Dawson — Cubs
Bats Right

	Avg	G	AB	R	H	2B	3B	HR	RBI	BB	SO	HBP	GDP	SB	CS	OBP	SLG	IBB	SH	SF	#Pit	#P/PA	GB	FB	G/F
1992 Season	.277	143	542	60	150	27	2	22	90	30	70	4	13	6	2	.316	.456	8	0	6	1953	3.36	200	162	1.23
Last Five Years	.264	714	2641	341	751	125	25	125	450	166	350	16	64	46	18	.327	.493	57	1	34	9483	3.32	970	857	1.13

1992 Season

	Avg	AB	H	2B	3B	HR	RBI	BB	SO	OBP	SLG		Avg	AB	H	2B	3B	HR	RBI	BB	SO	OBP	SLG
vs. Left	.287	195	56	12	1	7	35	10	24	.321	.467	Scoring Posn	.283	145	41	7	0	2	59	15	22	.341	.372
vs. Right	.271	347	94	15	1	15	55	20	46	.314	.450	Close & Late	.336	113	38	4	0	6	16	4	13	.364	.531
Groundball	.270	211	57	9	0	10	43	15	23	.314	.455	None on/out	.225	129	29	5	1	5	5	9	20	.286	.395
Flyball	.250	128	32	6	0	6	13	10	18	.302	.438	Batting #4	.274	446	122	25	2	17	69	26	55	.315	.453
Home	.306	252	77	16	2	13	48	20	34	.357	.540	Batting #5	.300	90	27	2	0	5	20	4	14	.330	.489
Away	.252	290	73	11	0	9	42	10	36	.279	.383	Other	.167	6	1	0	0	0	1	0	1	.167	.167
Day	.308	286	88	15	2	14	58	21	39	.356	.521	April	.254	59	15	3	0	3	12	1	11	.274	.458
Night	.242	256	62	12	0	8	32	9	31	.270	.383	May	.327	104	34	6	0	4	20	4	15	.345	.500
Grass	.310	365	113	21	2	18	70	26	46	.357	.526	June	.259	81	21	4	0	3	14	5	8	.303	.420
Turf	.209	177	37	6	0	4	20	4	24	.228	.311	July	.174	92	16	2	0	5	8	7	16	.232	.359
First Pitch	.326	95	31	5	1	5	18	9	0	.390	.558	August	.316	95	30	6	1	3	15	11	9	.393	.495
Ahead on Count	.270	100	27	5	0	7	22	16	0	.372	.530	September/October	.306	111	34	6	1	4	21	2	11	.322	.486
Behind on Count	.279	201	56	8	1	3	24	0	46	.279	.383	Pre-All Star	.277	289	80	15	0	13	51	15	43	.312	.464
Two Strikes	.245	233	57	9	1	6	26	5	70	.261	.369	Post-All Star	.277	253	70	12	2	9	39	15	27	.321	.447

1992 By Position

Position	Avg	AB	H	2B	3B	HR	RBI	BB	SO	OBP	SLG	G	GS	Innings	PO	A	E	DP	Fld Pct	Rng Fctr	In Zone	Outs	Zone Rtg	MLB Zone
As rf	.278	536	149	27	2	22	89	30	69	.318	.459	139	137	1182.1	222	11	2	4	.991	1.77	271	216	.797	.814

Last Five Years

	Avg	AB	H	2B	3B	HR	RBI	BB	SO	OBP	SLG		Avg	AB	H	2B	3B	HR	RBI	BB	SO	OBP	SLG
vs. Left	.295	872	257	45	7	43	151	56	105	.334	.510	Scoring Posn	.281	695	195	34	5	28	310	104	91	.364	.465
vs. Right	.279	1769	494	80	18	82	299	110	245	.323	.484	Close & Late	.281	477	134	16	1	21	66	40	72	.338	.451
Groundball	.261	962	251	38	11	37	144	47	126	.297	.439	None on/out	.254	653	166	27	6	30	30	27	98	.290	.452
Flyball	.288	605	174	34	3	38	104	44	85	.333	.542	Batting #4	.283	1791	506	86	16	83	300	115	228	.325	.487
Home	.296	1309	387	64	11	67	233	96	167	.344	.515	Batting #5	.280	472	132	18	5	24	89	27	72	.321	.492
Away	.273	1332	364	61	14	58	217	70	183	.309	.471	Other	.299	378	113	21	4	18	61	24	50	.341	.519
Day	.300	1421	426	66	17	72	260	103	182	.347	.522	April	.300	367	110	20	5	20	71	19	41	.333	.545
Night	.266	1220	325	59	8	53	190	63	168	.302	.458	May	.314	420	132	23	6	25	80	25	50	.352	.576
Grass	.288	1872	540	87	18	96	338	129	246	.333	.508	June	.272	426	116	22	1	15	60	31	55	.323	.434
Turf	.274	769	211	38	7	29	112	37	104	.309	.455	July	.281	423	119	18	2	18	70	33	62	.330	.461
First Pitch	.327	407	133	23	8	28	88	27	0	.364	.629	August	.259	490	127	18	7	19	74	29	70	.301	.441
Ahead on Count	.308	561	173	25	4	36	131	67	0	.384	.560	September/October	.285	515	147	24	4	28	95	29	72	.324	.511
Behind on Count	.259	1041	270	41	7	34	146	1	217	.260	.410	Pre-All Star	.296	1360	402	73	12	70	238	92	165	.340	.521
Two Strikes	.227	1100	250	38	7	35	130	44	350	.258	.370	Post-All Star	.272	1281	349	52	13	55	212	74	185	.312	.462

Batter vs. Pitcher (since 1984)

Hits Best Against	Avg	AB	H	2B	3B	HR	RBI	BB	SO	OBP	SLG	Hits Worst Against	Avg	AB	H	2B	3B	HR	RBI	BB	SO	OBP	SLG
Jesse Orosco	.600	10	6	1	0	1	3	1	1	.636	1.000	Bob Kipper	.000	14	0	0	0	0	0	2	3	.118	.000
Mark Grant	.571	21	12	2	1	3	9	1	0	.591	1.190	Dave Smith	.000	10	0	0	0	0	0	1	1	.091	.000
Danny Darwin	.500	14	7	1	0	2	4	3	3	.556	1.000	Danny Jackson	.071	14	1	0	0	0	0	0	3	.071	.071

Batter vs. Pitcher (since 1984)																					
Hits Best Against	Avg	AB	H	2B	3B	HR	RBI	BB	SO	OBP	SLG	Hits Worst Against	Avg	AB	H	2B	3B	HR	RBI	BB	SO	OBP	SLG
Stan Belinda	.417	12	5	0	0	4	10	0	1	.417	1.417	Pete Harnisch	.071	14	1	1	0	0	2	0	3	.063	.143
Don Carman	.400	25	10	2	1	4	6	2	5	.444	1.040	Jay Howell	.091	11	1	0	0	0	0	0	3	.091	.091

Steve Decker — Giants
Bats Right (flyball hitter)

	Avg	G	AB	R	H	2B	3B	HR	RBI	BB	SO	HBP	GDP	SB	CS	OBP	SLG	IBB	SH	SF	#Pit	#P/PA	GB	FB	G/F
1992 Season	.163	15	43	3	7	1	0	0	1	6	7	1	0	0	0	.280	.186	0	0	0	190	3.80	13	13	1.23
Career (1990-1992)	.215	109	330	19	71	10	1	8	33	23	61	4	8	0	1	.271	.324	1	3	4	1426	3.95	96	120	0.80

1992 Season

	Avg	AB	H	2B	3B	HR	RBI	BB	SO	OBP	SLG		Avg	AB	H	2B	3B	HR	RBI	BB	SO	OBP	SLG
vs. Left	.077	13	1	0	0	0	0	1	3	.143	.077	Scoring Posn	.250	8	2	0	0	0	1	3	2	.455	.250
vs. Right	.200	30	6	1	0	0	1	5	4	.333	.233	Close & Late	.143	7	1	0	0	0	1	3	2	.400	.143

Career (1990-1992)

	Avg	AB	H	2B	3B	HR	RBI	BB	SO	OBP	SLG		Avg	AB	H	2B	3B	HR	RBI	BB	SO	OBP	SLG
vs. Left	.230	122	28	3	1	4	15	4	16	.248	.369	Scoring Posn	.171	82	14	1	1	1	22	8	19	.234	.244
vs. Right	.207	208	43	7	0	4	18	19	45	.284	.298	Close & Late	.180	61	11	1	0	2	5	4	13	.231	.295
Groundball	.210	100	21	1	0	4	10	8	16	.279	.340	None on/out	.184	76	14	3	0	2	5	9	.244	.303	
Flyball	.173	75	13	1	0	3	9	6	15	.241	.307	Batting #7	.224	255	57	9	1	6	29	22	47	.289	.337
Home	.216	162	35	5	1	5	23	12	24	.275	.352	Batting #8	.114	35	4	0	0	0	0	0	7	.139	.114
Away	.214	168	36	5	0	3	10	11	37	.268	.296	Other	.250	40	10	1	0	2	4	1	7	.268	.425
Day	.242	120	29	5	1	2	18	12	25	.326	.350	April	.238	63	15	1	0	4	8	8	16	.319	.444
Night	.200	210	42	5	0	6	15	11	36	.238	.310	May	.145	55	8	2	0	1	5	1	9	.158	.236
Grass	.215	261	56	9	1	8	32	18	41	.268	.349	June	.255	51	13	3	0	0	5	2	11	.304	.314
Turf	.217	69	15	1	0	0	1	5	20	.286	.232	July	.240	25	6	1	0	0	2	3	3	.333	.280
First Pitch	.348	23	8	3	0	0	0	0	0	.333	.478	August	.000	0	0	0	0	0	0	0	0	.000	.000
Ahead on Count	.233	73	17	2	0	2	8	15	0	.360	.342	September/October	.213	136	29	3	1	3	13	9	22	.267	.316
Behind on Count	.256	121	31	4	0	3	14	1	35	.278	.364	Pre-All Star	.219	178	39	7	0	5	19	12	36	.270	.343
Two Strikes	.156	167	26	5	1	1	14	8	61	.198	.216	Post-All Star	.211	152	32	3	1	3	14	11	25	.273	.303

Rob Deer — Tigers
Bats Right (flyball hitter)

	Avg	G	AB	R	H	2B	3B	HR	RBI	BB	SO	HBP	GDP	SB	CS	OBP	SLG	IBB	SH	SF	#Pit	#P/PA	GB	FB	G/F
1992 Season	.247	110	393	66	97	20	1	32	64	51	131	3	8	4	2	.337	.547	1	0	1	1894	4.23	75	135	0.56
Last Five Years	.219	643	2239	330	491	91	6	133	347	315	764	18	23	20	21	.319	.444	17	0	13	10588	4.10	463	719	0.64

1992 Season

	Avg	AB	H	2B	3B	HR	RBI	BB	SO	OBP	SLG		Avg	AB	H	2B	3B	HR	RBI	BB	SO	OBP	SLG
vs. Left	.293	99	29	3	0	14	21	12	30	.369	.747	Scoring Posn	.212	99	21	6	0	5	32	19	42	.336	.424
vs. Right	.231	294	68	17	1	18	43	39	101	.326	.480	Close & Late	.262	65	17	4	0	5	9	6	22	.324	.554
Groundball	.286	98	28	7	0	7	16	12	33	.369	.571	None on/out	.327	98	32	6	0	11	11	11	26	.400	.724
Flyball	.217	129	28	6	0	10	17	13	44	.294	.496	Batting #6	.232	185	43	7	0	15	29	28	55	.336	.514
Home	.254	173	44	12	0	13	28	24	61	.352	.549	Batting #7	.236	127	30	7	1	9	18	8	43	.290	.520
Away	.241	220	53	8	1	19	36	27	70	.325	.545	Other	.296	81	24	6	0	8	17	15	33	.406	.667
Day	.233	129	30	6	1	12	25	22	47	.344	.574	April	.185	65	12	3	1	6	12	6	24	.254	.538
Night	.254	264	67	14	0	20	39	29	84	.333	.534	May	.244	86	21	4	0	9	14	13	33	.347	.605
Grass	.248	331	82	16	1	28	57	44	109	.341	.556	June	.188	80	15	2	0	6	12	11	23	.286	.438
Turf	.242	62	15	4	0	4	7	7	22	.314	.500	July	.500	10	5	0	0	2	2	0	2	.545	1.100
First Pitch	.394	33	13	2	0	4	7	0	0	.382	.818	August	.275	40	11	3	0	4	7	1	16	.293	.650
Ahead on Count	.390	82	32	3	0	13	24	24	0	.533	.902	September/October	.295	112	33	8	0	5	17	20	33	.406	.500
Behind on Count	.213	141	30	5	1	11	23	0	56	.218	.496	Pre-All Star	.208	231	48	9	1	21	38	30	80	.300	.528
Two Strikes	.147	224	33	10	1	9	18	27	131	.245	.321	Post-All Star	.302	162	49	11	0	11	26	21	51	.389	.574

1992 By Position

Position	Avg	AB	H	2B	3B	HR	RBI	BB	SO	OBP	SLG	G	GS	Innings	PO	A	E	DP	Fld Pct	Rng Fctr	In Zone	Outs	Zone Rtg	MLB Zone
As rf	.247	381	94	20	1	29	59	50	127	.338	.533	106	105	919.0	229	8	4	1	.983	2.32	272	229	.842	.814

Last Five Years

	Avg	AB	H	2B	3B	HR	RBI	BB	SO	OBP	SLG		Avg	AB	H	2B	3B	HR	RBI	BB	SO	OBP	SLG
vs. Left	.256	648	166	26	1	55	116	105	184	.360	.554	Scoring Posn	.229	584	134	22	0	37	219	112	203	.351	.457
vs. Right	.204	1591	325	65	5	78	231	210	580	.302	.398	Close & Late	.205	356	73	17	0	19	49	45	140	.302	.413
Groundball	.231	580	134	24	2	29	89	81	179	.327	.429	None on/out	.228	570	130	28	0	33	33	67	179	.313	.451
Flyball	.204	560	114	27	2	38	92	72	210	.298	.463	Batting #5	.237	497	118	27	1	29	78	56	161	.322	.471
Home	.218	1085	236	45	3	63	168	166	373	.329	.439	Batting #6	.192	699	134	17	1	47	100	104	241	.298	.421
Away	.221	1154	255	46	3	70	179	149	391	.309	.448	Other	.229	1043	239	47	4	57	169	155	362	.331	.446
Day	.215	734	158	34	1	45	121	114	246	.326	.448	April	.212	321	68	15	2	23	58	48	109	.321	.486
Night	.221	1505	333	57	5	88	226	201	518	.315	.441	May	.209	431	90	13	1	29	70	69	156	.320	.445
Grass	.223	1890	422	82	5	114	295	265	639	.323	.453	June	.210	447	94	16	0	30	76	55	143	.303	.447
Turf	.198	349	69	9	1	19	52	50	125	.297	.393	July	.231	294	68	13	1	17	37	36	100	.319	.456
First Pitch	.326	236	77	16	1	15	48	5	0	.344	.593	August	.230	357	82	17	2	22	58	49	127	.324	.473
Ahead on Count	.341	411	140	22	1	46	97	135	0	.509	.735	September/October	.229	389	89	17	0	12	47	58	129	.328	.365
Behind on Count	.173	780	135	16	3	46	113	1	357	.177	.378	Pre-All Star	.211	1293	273	47	3	85	212	184	440	.314	.449

108

Last Five Years

	Avg	AB	H	2B	3B	HR	RBI	BB	SO	OBP	SLG		Avg	AB	H	2B	3B	HR	RBI	BB	SO	OBP	SLG
Two Strikes	.137	1282	175	37	3	43	125	168	763	.238	.271	Post-All Star	.230	946	218	44	3	48	135	131	324	.325	.436

Batter vs. Pitcher (career)

Hits Best Against	Avg	AB	H	2B	3B	HR	RBI	BB	SO	OBP	SLG	Hits Worst Against	Avg	AB	H	2B	3B	HR	RBI	BB	SO	OBP	SLG
Bob Milacki	.500	14	7	2	1	1	4	2	2	.563	1.000	Erik Hanson	.000	16	0	0	0	0	0	0	9	.000	.000
Brad Arnsberg	.500	8	4	0	0	1	3	3	1	.636	.875	Nolan Ryan	.000	14	0	0	0	0	0	0	10	.000	.000
Lee Guetterman	.429	7	3	1	0	2	3	4	1	.636	1.429	Juan Berenguer	.000	12	0	0	0	0	0	1	5	.077	.000
Paul Gibson	.417	12	5	2	0	2	3	3	4	.533	1.083	Mike Jackson	.000	12	0	0	0	0	0	1	8	.077	.000
Donn Pall	.385	13	5	0	0	3	9	0	4	.385	1.077	Dan Plesac	.000	11	0	0	0	0	0	0	5	.000	.000

Jose DeLeon — Phillies
Pitches Right (flyball pitcher)

	ERA	W	L	Sv	G	GS	IP	BB	SO	Avg	H	2B	3B	HR	RBI	OBP	SLG	CG	ShO	Sup	QS	#P/S	SB	CS	GB	FB	G/F
1992 Season	4.37	2	8	0	32	18	117.1	48	79	.250	111	16	4	7	53	.322	.374	0	0	3.76	7	80	12	5	123	164	0.75
Last Five Years	3.58	43	58	0	162	148	932.2	361	770	.231	794	164	25	66	336	.305	.350	9	4	3.40	82	95	75	47	946	1146	0.83

1992 Season

	ERA	W	L	Sv	G	GS	IP	H	HR	BB	SO		Avg	AB	H	2B	3B	HR	RBI	BB	SO	OBP	SLG
Home	3.33	2	3	0	16	10	67.2	57	3	24	47	vs. Left	.282	245	69	12	4	5	33	26	38	.351	.424
Away	5.80	0	5	0	16	8	49.2	54	4	24	32	vs. Right	.211	199	42	14	0	2	20	22	41	.286	.312
Starter	4.50	2	8	0	18	18	96.0	95	7	36	64	Scoring Posn	.222	135	30	8	0	3	44	11	24	.270	.348
Reliever	3.80	0	0	0	14	0	21.1	16	0	12	15	Close & Late	.250	8	2	0	1	0	2	2	0	.417	.500
0-3 Days Rest	5.40	0	1	0	1	1	5.0	5	2	0	4	None on/out	.259	108	28	8	1	1	1	13	21	.339	.380
4 Days Rest	5.15	1	5	0	8	8	43.2	43	2	23	23	First Pitch	.387	75	29	7	0	2	12	1	0	.403	.560
5+ Days Rest	3.80	1	2	0	9	9	47.1	47	3	13	37	Behind on Count	.283	113	32	8	1	2	14	30	0	.425	.425
Pre-All Star	4.20	2	6	0	21	12	79.1	75	4	28	54	Ahead on Count	.174	184	32	8	3	0	13	0	68	.176	.250
Post-All Star	4.74	0	2	0	11	6	38.0	36	3	20	25	Two Strikes	.165	188	31	5	1	2	16	17	79	.233	.234

Last Five Years

	ERA	W	L	Sv	G	GS	IP	H	HR	BB	SO		Avg	AB	H	2B	3B	HR	RBI	BB	SO	OBP	SLG
Home	3.44	23	28	0	83	77	487.1	403	34	174	390	vs. Left	.259	1918	496	100	18	37	204	245	321	.342	.387
Away	3.74	20	30	0	79	71	445.1	391	32	187	380	vs. Right	.195	1525	298	64	7	29	132	116	449	.256	.304
Day	3.83	15	19	0	51	49	298.1	275	21	110	252	Inning 1-6	.228	2987	682	135	21	58	295	310	688	.302	.346
Night	3.46	28	39	0	111	99	634.1	519	45	251	518	Inning 7+	.246	456	112	29	4	8	41	51	82	.323	.379
Grass	3.36	11	19	0	45	40	262.1	231	14	93	227	None on	.218	2060	450	93	19	41	41	218	458	.298	.342
Turf	3.67	32	39	0	117	108	670.1	563	52	268	543	Runners on	.249	1383	344	71	6	25	295	143	312	.316	.363
April	3.19	9	7	0	24	24	143.2	108	14	56	111	Scoring Posn	.230	804	185	43	4	10	247	92	186	.304	.331
May	4.27	9	11	0	29	29	175.0	176	12	70	161	Close & Late	.230	222	51	12	3	3	19	26	46	.312	.351
June	3.62	6	12	0	31	25	164.0	145	10	63	143	None on/out	.224	893	200	45	5	17	17	105	198	.308	.343
July	3.48	7	13	0	30	23	160.1	144	8	60	121	vs. 1st Batr (relief)	.083	12	1	0	0	0	0	2	4	.214	.083
August	3.62	6	6	0	26	25	159.1	118	12	57	138	First Inning Pitched	.235	596	140	31	4	11	70	74	146	.322	.356
September/October	3.11	6	9	0	22	22	130.1	103	10	55	96	First 75 Pitches	.229	2596	595	124	20	45	241	260	566	.301	.344
Starter	3.57	43	58	0	148	148	911.1	778	66	349	755	Pitch 76-90	.222	414	92	13	2	12	44	45	88	.300	.350
Reliever	3.80	0	0	0	14	0	21.1	16	0	12	15	Pitch 91-105	.241	270	65	16	1	4	28	30	60	.316	.352
0-3 Days Rest	2.13	2	4	0	8	8	50.2	32	3	15	49	Pitch 106+	.258	163	42	11	2	5	23	26	36	.363	.442
4 Days Rest	3.71	33	31	0	91	91	579.2	483	40	221	473	First Pitch	.324	478	155	35	4	10	61	18	0	.357	.477
5+ Days Rest	3.56	8	23	0	49	49	281.0	263	23	113	233	Ahead on Count	.165	1648	272	52	12	13	113	1	679	.168	.235
Pre-All Star	3.78	24	34	0	93	84	521.2	468	37	205	450	Behind on Count	.317	751	238	59	9	29	109	206	0	.462	.535
Post-All Star	3.33	19	24	0	69	64	411.0	326	29	156	320	Two Strikes	.148	1654	244	40	10	18	106	136	770	.214	.216

Pitcher vs. Batter (since 1984)

Pitches Best Vs.	Avg	AB	H	2B	3B	HR	RBI	BB	SO	OBP	SLG	Pitches Worst Vs.	Avg	AB	H	2B	3B	HR	RBI	BB	SO	OBP	SLG
Danny Cox	.000	10	0	0	0	0	0	1	7	.091	.000	Terry Pendleton	.542	24	13	3	2	0	3	3	2	.593	.833
Tom Brunansky	.000	8	0	0	0	0	1	2	5	.182	.000	Kirby Puckett	.538	13	7	1	0	2	3	0	2	.538	1.077
Mike Fitzgerald	.067	15	1	0	0	2	1	1	5	.118	.067	John Kruk	.481	27	13	3	0	1	10	5	5	.563	.704
Willie Randolph	.071	14	1	0	0	0	0	1	5	.133	.071	Bip Roberts	.444	9	4	0	0	1	3	3	1	.538	.778
Glenn Davis	.091	11	1	0	0	0	0	0	5	.091	.091	Barry Bonds	.400	30	12	1	0	4	10	6	5	.500	.833

Rich DeLucia — Mariners
Pitches Right (flyball pitcher)

	ERA	W	L	Sv	G	GS	IP	BB	SO	Avg	H	2B	3B	HR	RBI	OBP	SLG	GF	IR	IRS	Hld	SvOp	SB	CS	GB	FB	G/F
1992 Season	5.49	3	6	1	30	11	83.2	35	66	.293	100	26	1	13	54	.361	.490	6	21	8	3	5	5	2	101	113	0.89
Career (1990-1992)	4.83	16	21	1	67	47	301.2	122	184	.266	306	65	6	46	155	.335	.452	6	21	8	3	5	9	12	327	444	0.74

1992 Season

	ERA	W	L	Sv	G	GS	IP	H	HR	BB	SO		Avg	AB	H	2B	3B	HR	RBI	BB	SO	OBP	SLG
Home	4.85	3	2	1	16	6	52.0	67	7	18	35	vs. Left	.316	152	48	12	0	4	19	17	20	.385	.474
Away	6.54	0	4	0	14	5	31.2	33	6	17	31	vs. Right	.275	189	52	14	1	9	35	18	46	.341	.503
Starter	6.62	3	6	0	11	11	50.1	70	9	19	37	Scoring Posn	.282	85	24	6	1	2	39	18	18	.406	.447
Reliever	3.78	0	0	1	19	0	33.1	30	4	16	29	Close & Late	.438	16	7	0	0	1	4	1	3	.471	.625
0 Days rest	1.17	0	0	0	2	0	7.2	6	1	2	6	None on/out	.261	88	23	3	0	3	3	1	14	.278	.398
1 or 2 Days rest	8.31	0	0	0	7	0	8.2	13	1	5	8	First Pitch	.286	42	12	4	0	2	6	1	0	.318	.524
3+ Days rest	2.65	0	0	1	10	0	17.0	11	3	9	15	Behind on Count	.385	78	30	8	0	7	17	20	0	.500	.756
Pre-All Star	6.05	3	5	0	14	10	55.0	74	7	21	39	Ahead on Count	.205	132	27	2	0	9	0	54		.205	.220

1992 Season

	ERA	W	L	Sv	G	GS	IP	H	HR	BB	SO		Avg	AB	H	2B	3B	HR	RBI	BB	SO	OBP	SLG
Post-All Star	4.40	0	1	1	16	1	28.2	26	6	14	27	Two Strikes	.214	168	36	9	0	3	17	14	66	.275	.321

Career (1990-1992)

	ERA	W	L	Sv	G	GS	IP	H	HR	BB	SO		Avg	AB	H	2B	3B	HR	RBI	BB	SO	OBP	SLG
Home	4.63	11	6	1	32	21	149.2	155	26	50	89	vs. Left	.292	542	158	27	5	16	63	76	60	.376	.448
Away	5.03	5	15	0	35	26	152.0	151	20	72	95	vs. Right	.243	610	148	38	1	30	92	46	124	.297	.456
Day	6.61	3	9	0	19	14	77.2	92	10	37	51	Inning 1-6	.260	968	252	54	6	32	130	109	153	.334	.428
Night	4.22	13	12	1	48	33	224.0	214	36	85	133	Inning 7+	.293	184	54	11	0	14	25	13	31	.338	.582
Grass	5.39	4	13	0	28	20	120.1	120	17	59	70	None on	.257	712	183	36	4	30	30	58	115	.315	.445
Turf	4.47	12	8	1	39	27	181.1	186	29	63	114	Runners on	.280	440	123	29	2	16	125	64	69	.365	.464
April	6.23	3	4	0	7	7	39.0	48	8	20	24	Scoring Posn	.267	236	63	13	1	8	104	46	42	.368	.432
May	5.95	3	1	0	9	6	39.1	49	5	16	28	Close & Late	.393	56	22	3	0	6	10	3	8	.424	.768
June	3.97	3	4	0	11	10	56.2	51	9	30	36	None on/out	.257	315	81	13	3	15	15	20	46	.304	.460
July	4.91	3	3	0	12	8	51.1	51	5	18	34	vs. 1st Batr (relief)	.200	15	3	1	0	0	4	4	5	.400	.267
August	3.62	2	2	0	7	5	32.1	30	7	6	14	First Inning Pitched	.291	244	71	15	1	8	54	39	54	.385	.459
September/October	4.66	2	7	1	21	11	83.0	77	12	32	48	First 15 Pitches	.299	177	53	14	0	5	17	27	35	.392	.463
Starter	5.02	15	21	0	47	47	263.2	274	41	104	150	Pitch 16-30	.238	189	45	8	1	7	38	24	32	.318	.402
Reliever	3.55	1	0	1	20	0	38.0	32	5	18	34	Pitch 31-45	.285	193	55	10	3	8	32	14	35	.336	.492
0 Days rest	1.17	0	0	0	2	0	7.2	6	1	2	6	Pitch 46+	.258	593	153	33	2	26	68	57	82	.322	.452
1 or 2 Days rest	8.31	0	0	0	7	0	8.2	13	0	5	8	First Pitch	.295	146	43	8	2	9	22	4	0	.314	.562
3+ Days rest	2.49	1	0	1	11	0	21.2	13	4	11	20	Ahead on Count	.221	458	101	17	0	9	44	1	144	.225	.317
Pre-All Star	5.15	10	10	0	31	26	150.1	161	22	73	99	Behind on Count	.299	268	80	15	1	18	43	66	0	.428	.563
Post-All Star	4.52	6	11	1	36	21	151.1	145	24	49	85	Two Strikes	.198	509	101	23	1	14	50	51	184	.271	.330

Pitcher vs. Batter (career)

Pitches Best Vs.	Avg	AB	H	2B	3B	HR	RBI	BB	SO	OBP	SLG	Pitches Worst Vs.	Avg	AB	H	2B	3B	HR	RBI	BB	SO	OBP	SLG
Carlton Fisk	.077	13	1	0	0	0	2	0	3	.077	.077	Dave Henderson	.417	12	5	1	0	2	4	0	0	.417	1.000
Mark McGwire	.118	17	2	1	0	0	0	1	3	.167	.176	Cecil Fielder	.400	10	4	0	0	3	11	2	1	.500	1.300
Robin Ventura	.133	15	2	0	0	1	2	2	2	.235	.333	Sam Horn	.375	8	3	0	0	1	2	5	2	.615	.750
Mike Devereaux	.143	14	2	1	0	0	0	1	2	.200	.214	Cal Ripken	.357	14	5	2	0	2	3	0	0	.357	.929
Devon White	.182	11	2	1	0	0	0	1	3	.250	.273	Jose Canseco	.333	15	5	1	0	3	3	1	3	.375	1.000

Rick Dempsey — Orioles   Bats Right (flyball hitter)

	Avg	G	AB	R	H	2B	3B	HR	RBI	BB	SO	HBP	GDP	SB	CS	OBP	SLG	IBB	SH	SF	#Pit	#P/PA	GB	FB	G/F
1992 Season	.111	8	9	2	1	0	0	0	0	2	1	0	1	0	0	.273	.111	0	0	0	27	2.45	3	3	1.00
Last Five Years	.214	286	602	71	129	30	0	17	82	103	131	1	25	3	2	.326	.349	4	2	9	2879	4.03	175	195	0.90

1992 Season

	Avg	AB	H	2B	3B	HR	RBI	BB	SO	OBP	SLG		Avg	AB	H	2B	3B	HR	RBI	BB	SO	OBP	SLG
vs. Left	.000	3	0	0	0	0	0	1	1	.250	.000	Scoring Posn	.000	2	0	0	0	0	0	1	0	.333	.000
vs. Right	.167	6	1	0	0	0	0	1	0	.286	.167	Close & Late	.167	6	1	0	0	0	0	1	0	.286	.167

Last Five Years

	Avg	AB	H	2B	3B	HR	RBI	BB	SO	OBP	SLG		Avg	AB	H	2B	3B	HR	RBI	BB	SO	OBP	SLG
vs. Left	.206	433	89	20	0	11	57	73	91	.317	.328	Scoring Posn	.295	156	46	9	0	5	64	35	25	.405	.449
vs. Right	.237	169	40	10	0	6	25	30	40	.348	.402	Close & Late	.210	143	30	3	0	5	18	23	30	.319	.336
Groundball	.263	209	55	13	0	5	32	40	37	.375	.397	None on/out	.199	141	28	3	0	8	8	18	31	.289	.390
Flyball	.164	165	27	5	0	4	18	24	50	.266	.267	Batting #7	.209	148	31	7	0	5	17	24	38	.314	.358
Home	.236	280	66	13	0	9	47	47	60	.339	.379	Batting #8	.237	241	57	10	0	8	33	47	42	.359	.378
Away	.196	322	63	17	0	8	35	56	71	.314	.323	Other	.192	213	41	13	0	4	32	32	51	.296	.310
Day	.206	189	39	17	0	5	21	30	50	.301	.376	April	.229	48	11	1	0	2	7	7	6	.327	.375
Night	.218	413	90	13	0	12	61	73	81	.333	.337	May	.228	92	21	6	0	4	15	15	19	.343	.424
Grass	.211	446	94	22	0	12	61	83	99	.330	.341	June	.182	110	20	6	0	3	10	15	32	.276	.318
Turf	.224	156	35	8	0	5	21	20	32	.324	.331	July	.223	121	27	7	0	2	20	19	26	.324	.331
First Pitch	.304	69	21	6	0	2	9	4	0	.342	.478	August	.262	107	28	7	0	3	16	22	19	.382	.411
Ahead on Count	.294	119	35	10	0	3	27	65	0	.529	.454	September/October	.177	124	22	3	0	3	14	25	29	.309	.274
Behind on Count	.176	193	34	6	0	4	22	1	62	.179	.269	Pre-All Star	.215	284	61	17	0	9	38	39	61	.309	.370
Two Strikes	.153	321	49	8	0	12	35	33	131	.230	.290	Post-All Star	.214	318	68	13	0	8	44	64	70	.340	.330

Batter vs. Pitcher (since 1984)

Hits Best Against	Avg	AB	H	2B	3B	HR	RBI	BB	SO	OBP	SLG	Hits Worst Against	Avg	AB	H	2B	3B	HR	RBI	BB	SO	OBP	SLG
Dave Righetti	.462	13	6	2	0	1	2	2	2	.533	.846	Matt Young	.000	8	0	0	0	0	0	5	1	.385	.000
Jimmy Key	.368	19	7	3	0	0	4	2	1	.429	.684	Zane Smith	.000	8	0	0	0	0	0	3	4	.273	.000
Charlie Leibrandt	.357	14	5	1	0	1	6	3	1	.471	.643	Kirk McCaskill	.000	8	0	0	0	0	0	4	3	.333	.000
Neal Heaton	.316	19	6	1	0	2	4	3	1	.409	.684	Danny Darwin	.100	20	2	0	0	0	0	1	4	.143	.100
Mike Moore	.316	19	6	0	0	2	3	4	1	.435	.632	Bruce Hurst	.100	20	2	0	0	1	1	3	5	.217	.100

Jim Deshaies — Padres
Pitches Left (flyball pitcher)

	ERA	W	L	Sv	G	GS	IP	BB	SO	Avg	H	2B	3B	HR	RBI	OBP	SLG	CG	ShO	Sup	QS	#P/S	SB	CS	GB	FB	G/F
1992 Season	3.28	4	7	0	15	15	96.0	33	46	.258	92	16	1	6	28	.321	.360	0	0	2.81	9	101	6	10	90	135	0.67
Last Five Years	3.54	42	55	0	142	142	899.0	340	543	.236	778	158	25	81	325	.307	.373	12	5	3.45	81	100	108	52	901	1259	0.72

1992 Season

	ERA	W	L	Sv	G	GS	IP	H	HR	BB	SO		Avg	AB	H	2B	3B	HR	RBI	BB	SO	OBP	SLG
Home	4.11	2	4	0	8	8	50.1	49	5	24	27	vs. Left	.356	59	21	3	0	1	4	11	10	.451	.458
Away	2.36	2	3	0	7	7	45.2	43	1	9	19	vs. Right	.239	297	71	13	1	5	24	22	36	.293	.340
Starter	3.28	4	7	0	15	15	96.0	92	6	33	46	Scoring Posn	.300	70	21	1	0	1	20	10	8	.378	.357
Reliever	0.00	0	0	0	0	0	0.0	0	0	0	0	Close & Late	.400	20	8	1	0	0	2	3	0	.478	.450
0-3 Days Rest	0.00	0	0	0	0	0	0.0	0	0	0	0	None on/out	.283	92	26	5	0	2		12	15	.365	.402
4 Days Rest	3.35	2	4	0	7	7	45.2	44	2	20	17	First Pitch	.318	44	14	2	0	0	4	2	0	.340	.364
5+ Days Rest	3.22	2	3	0	8	8	50.1	48	4	13	29	Behind on Count	.309	68	21	8	1	1	8	14	0	.422	.500
Pre-All Star	1.59	1	0	0	1	1	5.2	3	1	5	8	Ahead on Count	.210	162	34	5	0	1	7	0	36	.215	.259
Post-All Star	3.39	3	7	0	14	14	90.1	89	5	28	38	Two Strikes	.201	164	33	5	0	1	5	17	46	.276	.250

Last Five Years

	ERA	W	L	Sv	G	GS	IP	H	HR	BB	SO		Avg	AB	H	2B	3B	HR	RBI	BB	SO	OBP	SLG
Home	3.19	23	22	0	68	68	443.1	364	39	170	263	vs. Left	.261	527	148	29	5	12	58	85	86	.380	.423
Away	3.89	19	33	0	74	74	455.2	414	42	170	280	vs. Right	.227	2772	630	129	20	69	267	255	457	.292	.363
Day	3.37	11	13	0	37	37	238.0	204	19	80	160	Inning 1-6	.238	2658	680	142	21	73	301	303	486	.311	.379
Night	3.61	31	42	0	105	105	661.0	574	62	260	383	Inning 7+	.222	441	98	16	4	8	24	37	57	.260	.331
Grass	3.93	13	22	0	49	49	302.0	279	28	111	185	None on	.230	2018	464	90	13	52	52	193	316	.301	.365
Turf	3.35	29	33	0	93	93	597.0	499	53	229	358	Runners on	.245	1281	314	68	12	29	273	147	227	.317	.385
April	3.06	5	6	0	18	18	117.2	93	6	45	65	Scoring Posn	.236	724	171	35	6	18	234	111	153	.325	.376
May	3.89	9	6	0	22	22	141.0	120	11	60	62	Close & Late	.226	235	53	5	2	4	13	23	33	.293	.315
June	4.45	5	8	0	22	22	131.1	133	20	60	72	None on/out	.250	883	221	44	4	31	31	87	125	.320	.414
July	3.62	7	10	0	25	25	151.2	126	16	57	107	vs. 1st Batr (relief)	.000	0	0	0	0	0	0	0	0	.000	.000
August	3.74	7	15	0	28	28	183.0	162	15	69	125	First Inning Pitched	.259	529	137	29	3	12	67	64	80	.336	.393
September/October	2.63	9	10	0	27	27	174.1	144	13	49	112	First 75 Pitches	.236	2373	561	118	17	61	237	246	402	.309	.378
Starter	3.54	42	55	0	142	142	899.0	778	81	340	543	Pitch 76-90	.259	406	105	20	3	8	42	40	65	.320	.382
Reliever	0.00	0	0	0	0	0	0.0	0	0	0	0	Pitch 91-105	.202	302	61	11	2	7	31	28	47	.270	.321
0-3 Days Rest	0.00	0	0	0	0	0	0.0	0	0	0	0	Pitch 106+	.234	218	51	9	3	5	15	26	29	.312	.372
4 Days Rest	3.47	29	37	0	95	95	604.0	517	53	227	391	First Pitch	.299	521	156	37	5	13	63	18	0	.322	.464
5+ Days Rest	3.69	13	18	0	47	47	295.0	261	28	113	152	Ahead on Count	.205	1286	264	44	7	19	90	1	391	.209	.295
Pre-All Star	3.74	21	24	0	70	70	440.2	382	46	188	243	Behind on Count	.263	723	190	49	11	23	95	176	0	.405	.456
Post-All Star	3.36	21	31	0	72	72	458.1	396	35	152	300	Two Strikes	.172	1457	251	44	6	20	98	144	542	.247	.252

Pitcher vs. Batter (career)

Pitches Best Vs.	Avg	AB	H	2B	3B	HR	RBI	BB	SO	OBP	SLG	Pitches Worst Vs.	Avg	AB	H	2B	3B	HR	RBI	BB	SO	OBP	SLG
Luis Quinones	.053	19	1	0	0	0	0	1	4	.100	.053	Don Slaught	.583	12	7	3	0	0	3	3	1	.625	.833
Billy Hatcher	.067	15	1	0	0	0	0	1	1	.125	.067	Von Hayes	.533	15	8	2	0	0	3	6	2	.667	.667
Mike Sharperson	.105	19	2	0	0	0	0	1	1	.105	.105	Barry Larkin	.444	36	16	2	0	5	8	2	2	.474	.917
Charlie Hayes	.105	19	2	0	0	0	1	0	4	.100	.105	Randy Ready	.429	14	6	2	0	1	7	6	1	.571	.786
Tim Raines	.111	18	2	0	0	0	1	0	2	.105	.111	Lenny Dykstra	.429	7	3	0	1	0	1	4	0	.636	.714

Delino DeShields — Expos
Bats Left (groundball hitter)

	Avg	G	AB	R	H	2B	3B	HR	RBI	BB	SO	HBP	GDP	SB	CS	OBP	SLG	IBB	SH	SF	#Pit	#P/PA	GB	FB	G/F
1992 Season	.292	135	530	82	155	19	8	7	56	54	108	3	10	46	15	.359	.398	4	9	3	2371	4.02	217	112	1.94
Career (1990-1992)	.272	415	1592	234	433	62	18	21	152	215	355	9	26	144	60	.360	.373	9	18	10	7518	4.12	650	318	2.04

1992 Season

	Avg	AB	H	2B	3B	HR	RBI	BB	SO	OBP	SLG		Avg	AB	H	2B	3B	HR	RBI	BB	SO	OBP	SLG
vs. Left	.314	185	58	6	2	2	21	22	33	.389	.400	Scoring Posn	.304	115	35	5	1	2	47	19	28	.394	.417
vs. Right	.281	345	97	13	6	5	35	32	75	.343	.397	Close & Late	.293	82	24	4	1	2	19	9	22	.355	.439
Groundball	.299	204	61	4	4	5	24	24	38	.376	.431	None on/out	.288	191	55	2	2	3	3	12	32	.333	.366
Flyball	.232	125	29	3	3	0	7	8	31	.279	.304	Batting #1	.309	343	106	12	5	7	40	28	66	.366	.434
Home	.277	271	75	9	4	1	19	23	56	.338	.351	Batting #2	.274	175	48	7	3	0	15	22	38	.350	.349
Away	.309	259	80	10	4	6	37	31	52	.381	.448	Other	.083	12	1	0	0	0	1	4	4	.313	.083
Day	.329	155	51	6	2	2	18	21	34	.404	.432	April	.275	91	25	2	1	2	6	8	23	.337	.385
Night	.277	375	104	13	6	5	38	33	74	.340	.384	May	.244	86	21	4	0	0	7	10	22	.320	.291
Grass	.322	146	47	8	2	2	24	23	29	.409	.445	June	.330	100	33	4	4	0	9	15	19	.414	.450
Turf	.281	384	108	11	6	5	32	31	79	.339	.380	July	.376	117	44	5	1	3	13	12	20	.434	.513
First Pitch	.316	57	18	1	0	1	7	3	0	.355	.386	August	.280	93	26	3	1	2	20	7	14	.343	.398
Ahead on Count	.347	121	42	7	3	3	20	32	0	.487	.529	September/October	.140	43	6	1	1	0	1	2	10	.178	.209
Behind on Count	.265	155	41	7	3	1	12	0	51	.268	.368	Pre-All Star	.304	332	101	13	5	4	29	41	75	.379	.410
Two Strikes	.227	269	61	5	4	1	13	19	108	.324	.379	Post-All Star	.273	198	54	6	3	3	27	13	33	.324	.379

1992 By Position

Position	Avg	AB	H	2B	3B	HR	RBI	BB	SO	OBP	SLG	G	GS	Innings	PO	A	E	DP	Fld Pct	Rng Fctr	In Zone	Outs	Zone Rtg	MLB Zone
As 2b	.292	530	155	19	8	7	56	54	108	.359	.398	134	133	1183.1	253	360	15	71	.976	4.66	407	359	.882	.892

Career (1990-1992)

	Avg	AB	H	2B	3B	HR	RBI	BB	SO	OBP	SLG
vs. Left	.265	567	150	17	5	7	52	81	139	.360	.349
vs. Right	.276	1025	263	45	13	14	100	134	216	.360	.386
Groundball	.269	550	148	19	8	7	51	74	115	.358	.371
Flyball	.237	367	87	12	5	3	28	46	90	.323	.322
Home	.264	735	209	33	7	7	61	99	161	.372	.377
Away	.261	857	224	29	11	14	91	116	194	.350	.370
Day	.275	447	123	19	2	4	45	60	111	.359	.353
Night	.271	1145	310	43	16	17	107	155	244	.360	.381
Grass	.253	459	116	15	6	7	49	64	110	.342	.357
Turf	.280	1133	317	47	12	14	103	151	245	.367	.380
First Pitch	.323	167	54	7	0	3	19	4	0	.349	.419
Ahead on Count	.374	385	144	22	10	11	64	107	0	.508	.569
Behind on Count	.218	431	94	16	4	3	28	1	154	.224	.295
Two Strikes	.190	802	152	19	5	1	37	101	355	.281	.349

	Avg	AB	H	2B	3B	HR	RBI	BB	SO	OBP	SLG
Scoring Posn	.280	329	92	21	4	3	127	64	76	.387	.395
Close & Late	.253	269	73	11	3	3	36	41	74	.345	.343
None on/out	.277	603	167	14	7	10	10	60	116	.347	.373
Batting #1	.276	1203	332	47	15	20	114	163	257	.365	.390
Batting #2	.273	304	83	12	3	0	25	37	67	.347	.332
Other	.212	85	18	3	0	1	13	15	31	.340	.282
April	.295	234	69	10	3	4	16	30	51	.376	.415
May	.236	276	65	10	2	5	20	47	66	.348	.341
June	.304	260	79	10	6	2	28	45	63	.406	.412
July	.313	268	84	13	1	3	24	33	46	.389	.403
August	.278	302	84	12	4	4	39	32	53	.354	.384
September/October	.206	252	52	7	2	3	25	28	76	.286	.286
Pre-All Star	.283	844	239	33	11	13	71	133	199	.381	.395
Post-All Star	.259	748	194	29	7	8	81	82	156	.335	.349

Batter vs. Pitcher (career)

Hits Best Against	Avg	AB	H	2B	3B	HR	RBI	BB	SO	OBP	SLG
Tim Crews	.636	11	7	3	0	0	2	1	2	.667	.909
Tim Belcher	.556	9	5	0	0	0	2	3	1	.667	.556
Rheal Cormier	.500	10	5	0	0	1	3	3	3	.615	.800
Anthony Young	.417	12	5	1	2	0	2	0	1	.417	.833
Curt Schilling	.400	15	6	0	0	2	6	1	2	.438	.800

Hits Worst Against	Avg	AB	H	2B	3B	HR	RBI	BB	SO	OBP	SLG
Trevor Wilson	.067	15	1	0	0	0	0	2	4	.176	.067
Wally Whitehurst	.091	11	1	0	1	0	1	0	3	.091	.273
Tom Browning	.118	17	2	0	0	0	1	1	4	.167	.118
Bryn Smith	.167	18	3	0	0	0	0	0	5	.167	.167
Mike Hartley	.167	12	2	0	0	0	0	0	0	.167	.167

Mike Devereaux — Orioles   Bats Right

	Avg	G	AB	R	H	2B	3B	HR	RBI	BB	SO	HBP	GDP	SB	CS	OBP	SLG	IBB	SH	SF	#Pit	#P/PA	GB	FB	G/F
1992 Season	.276	156	653	76	180	29	11	24	107	44	94	4	14	10	8	.321	.464	1	0	9	2782	3.92	221	242	0.91
Last Five Years	.259	565	2062	265	535	89	25	63	263	157	327		44	61	41	.312	.419	3	13	20	8626	3.84	725	690	1.05

1992 Season

	Avg	AB	H	2B	3B	HR	RBI	BB	SO	OBP	SLG
vs. Left	.351	168	59	9	2	9	29	10	24	.383	.589
vs. Right	.249	485	121	20	9	15	78	34	70	.300	.421
Groundball	.264	174	46	8	1	5	29	14	28	.314	.408
Flyball	.249	173	43	7	2	6	25	12	34	.298	.416
Home	.257	334	86	12	7	14	54	21	43	.301	.461
Away	.295	319	94	17	4	10	53	23	51	.342	.467
Day	.193	187	36	6	2	3	15	16	31	.261	.294
Night	.309	466	144	23	9	21	92	28	63	.346	.532
Grass	.270	549	148	23	10	22	90	36	82	.314	.468
Turf	.308	104	32	6	1	2	17	8	12	.360	.442
First Pitch	.250	40	10	2	0	3	8	1	0	.279	.525
Ahead on Count	.322	171	55	10	3	9	30	22	0	.393	.573
Behind on Count	.266	222	59	11	4	4	40	0	41	.271	.405
Two Strikes	.254	319	81	12	4	11	50	21	94	.301	.420

	Avg	AB	H	2B	3B	HR	RBI	BB	SO	OBP	SLG
Scoring Posn	.285	179	51	12	3	7	86	13	27	.322	.503
Close & Late	.214	98	21	1	1	6	21	6	22	.259	.429
None on/out	.265	113	30	4	3	6	6	11	15	.331	.513
Batting #2	.281	416	117	19	10	16	80	28	51	.322	.490
Batting #3	.307	127	39	3	1	5	17	6	23	.346	.465
Other	.218	110	24	7	0	3	10	10	20	.289	.364
April	.278	79	22	3	1	4	10	6	14	.329	.494
May	.219	105	23	7	1	4	17	11	12	.294	.419
June	.345	119	41	6	3	4	22	6	13	.373	.546
July	.246	118	29	3	4	3	14	7	21	.287	.415
August	.292	113	33	5	1	6	27	11	12	.352	.513
September/October	.269	119	32	5	1	3	17	3	22	.293	.403
Pre-All Star	.281	356	100	18	6	13	54	24	46	.325	.475
Post-All Star	.269	297	80	11	5	11	53	20	48	.317	.451

1992 By Position

Position	Avg	AB	H	2B	3B	HR	RBI	BB	SO	OBP	SLG	G	GS	Innings	PO	A	E	DP	Fld Pct	Rng Fctr	In Zone	Outs	Zone Rtg	MLB Zone
As cf	.275	652	179	29	11	24	107	44	94	.320	.463	155	155	1396.0	431	5	5	3	.989	2.81	497	423	.851	.824

Last Five Years

	Avg	AB	H	2B	3B	HR	RBI	BB	SO	OBP	SLG
vs. Left	.284	708	201	33	10	25	85	56	98	.335	.465
vs. Right	.247	1354	334	56	15	38	178	101	229	.299	.394
Groundball	.262	535	140	27	6	16	74	57	77	.331	.424
Flyball	.237	455	108	24	5	13	56	32	89	.289	.398
Home	.248	1002	248	39	13	34	131	81	156	.303	.414
Away	.271	1060	287	50	12	29	132	76	171	.319	.423
Day	.249	558	139	24	4	13	52	39	91	.299	.376
Night	.263	1504	396	65	21	50	211	118	236	.316	.434
Grass	.256	1724	442	70	23	58	222	134	261	.310	.425
Turf	.275	338	93	19	2	5	41	23	46	.322	.468
First Pitch	.264	174	46	8	1	7	30	2	0	.271	.443
Ahead on Count	.318	491	156	26	6	23	76	83	0	.414	.536
Behind on Count	.224	729	163	35	10	12	80	0	179	.227	.346
Two Strikes	.214	1009	216	31	14	19	88	72	327	.267	.329

	Avg	AB	H	2B	3B	HR	RBI	BB	SO	OBP	SLG
Scoring Posn	.258	493	127	26	9	17	203	41	74	.306	.450
Close & Late	.246	337	83	6	2	13	46	25	63	.296	.392
None on/out	.250	561	140	25	6	17	17	46	90	.309	.406
Batting #1	.261	792	207	37	11	20	73	67	141	.320	.412
Batting #2	.268	568	152	23	11	20	103	37	72	.306	.452
Other	.251	702	176	29	3	23	87	53	114	.304	.399
April	.227	216	49	9	2	7	21	21	30	.297	.384
May	.271	280	76	20	2	9	36	22	41	.322	.454
June	.270	363	98	13	7	10	45	28	50	.319	.427
July	.262	373	105	12	6	12	49	30	63	.333	.442
August	.245	392	96	15	5	12	57	34	61	.307	.401
September/October	.253	438	111	20	3	13	55	22	82	.290	.402
Pre-All Star	.260	979	255	45	12	29	115	77	140	.313	.420
Post-All Star	.259	1083	280	44	13	34	146	80	187	.310	.417

Batter vs. Pitcher (career)

Hits Best Against	Avg	AB	H	2B	3B	HR	RBI	BB	SO	OBP	SLG
Jim Abbott	.526	19	10	2	0	1	2	2	0	.591	.789
Bill Krueger	.476	21	10	1	0	2	2	0	2	.476	.810
Dave Fleming	.455	11	5	1	0	1	5	1	0	.500	.818
Kirk McCaskill	.409	22	9	3	0	2	4	2	1	.458	.818

Hits Worst Against	Avg	AB	H	2B	3B	HR	RBI	BB	SO	OBP	SLG
Kevin Appier	.053	19	1	0	0	0	0	0	1	.053	.053
Roger Clemens	.071	14	1	0	0	0	0	0	3	.071	.071
Tom Henke	.077	13	1	0	0	0	0	1	6	.143	.077
Bret Saberhagen	.077	13	1	0	0	0	1	0	3	.077	.077

Hits Best Against	Avg	AB	H	2B	3B	HR	RBI	BB	SO	OBP	SLG	Hits Worst Against	Avg	AB	H	2B	3B	HR	RBI	BB	SO	OBP	SLG
Jeff Johnson	.364	11	4	0	1	1	4	1	1	.417	.818	Bobby Witt	.091	11	1	0	0	0	0	0	1	.091	.091

Mark Dewey — Mets   Pitches Right (groundball pitcher)

	ERA	W	L	Sv	G	GS	IP	BB	SO	Avg	H	2B	3B	HR	RBI	OBP	SLG	GF	IR	IRS	Hld	SvOp	SB	CS	GB	FB	G/F
1992 Season	4.32	1	0	0	20	0	33.1	10	24	.280	37	5	0	2	17	.331	.364	6	14	5	1	0	1	3	59	28	2.11
Career (1990-1992)	3.70	2	1	0	34	0	56.0	15	35	.272	59	8	2	3	25	.319	.369	11	18	6	2	1	3	4	95	49	1.94

1992 Season

	ERA	W	L	Sv	G	GS	IP	H	HR	BB	SO		Avg	AB	H	2B	3B	HR	RBI	BB	SO	OBP	SLG
Home	0.69	0	0	0	8	0	13.0	12	1	4	6	vs. Left	.254	67	17	1	0	0	2	5	6	.306	.269
Away	6.64	1	0	0	12	0	20.1	25	1	6	18	vs. Right	.308	65	20	4	0	2	15	5	18	.357	.462
Starter	0.00	0	0	0	0	0	0.0	0	0	0	0	Scoring Posn	.316	38	12	3	0	1	15	3	6	.366	.474
Reliever	4.32	1	0	0	20	0	33.1	37	2	10	24	Close & Late	.280	25	7	1	0	0	2	3	7	.357	.320
0 Days rest	12.46	0	0	0	2	0	4.1	9	0	2	3	None on/out	.258	31	8	1	0	0	0	2	6	.303	.290
1 or 2 Days rest	8.31	1	0	0	7	0	8.2	18	1	2	11	First Pitch	.478	23	11	3	0	0	4	2	0	.520	.609
3+ Days rest	0.89	0	0	0	11	0	20.1	10	1	6	10	Behind on Count	.222	27	6	0	0	1	3	0	.300	.222
Pre-All Star	6.52	0	0	0	5	0	9.2	11	1	3	2	Ahead on Count	.213	61	13	1	0	1	5	0	21	.213	.279
Post-All Star	3.42	1	0	0	15	0	23.2	26	1	7	22	Two Strikes	.226	62	14	2	0	1	6	5	24	.284	.306

Alex Diaz — Brewers   Bats Both (flyball hitter)

	Avg	G	AB	R	H	2B	3B	HR	RBI	BB	SO	HBP	GDP	SB	CS	OBP	SLG	IBB	SH	SF	#Pit	#P/PA	GB	FB	G/F
1992 Season	.111	22	9	5	1	0	0	0	1	0	0	0	0	3	2	.111	.111	0	0	0	22	2.44	2	6	0.33

1992 Season

	Avg	AB	H	2B	3B	HR	RBI	BB	SO	OBP	SLG		Avg	AB	H	2B	3B	HR	RBI	BB	SO	OBP	SLG
vs. Left	.000	1	0	0	0	0	0	0	0	.000	.000	Scoring Posn	.333	3	1	0	0	0	1	0	0	.333	.333
vs. Right	.125	8	1	0	0	0	1	0	0	.125	.125	Close & Late	.000	1	0	0	0	0	0	0	0	.000	.000

Mario Diaz — Rangers   Bats Right

	Avg	G	AB	R	H	2B	3B	HR	RBI	BB	SO	HBP	GDP	SB	CS	OBP	SLG	IBB	SH	SF	#Pit	#P/PA	GB	FB	G/F
1992 Season	.226	19	31	2	7	1	0	0	1	1	2	0	2	0	1	.250	.258	1	1	0	87	2.72	15	10	1.50
Last Five Years	.236	211	381	41	90	14	0	2	40	26	35	0	12	0	2	.283	.289	1	10	3	1358	3.31	158	116	1.36

1992 Season

	Avg	AB	H	2B	3B	HR	RBI	BB	SO	OBP	SLG		Avg	AB	H	2B	3B	HR	RBI	BB	SO	OBP	SLG
vs. Left	.222	18	4	0	0	0	1	0	1	.222	.222	Scoring Posn	.000	8	0	0	0	0	1	1	0	.111	.000
vs. Right	.231	13	3	1	0	0	1	1	1	.286	.308	Close & Late	.500	2	1	0	0	0	0	0	0	.667	.500

Last Five Years

	Avg	AB	H	2B	3B	HR	RBI	BB	SO	OBP	SLG		Avg	AB	H	2B	3B	HR	RBI	BB	SO	OBP	SLG
vs. Left	.229	179	41	7	0	0	17	14	15	.284	.268	Scoring Posn	.248	101	25	2	0	0	34	8	4	.295	.267
vs. Right	.243	202	49	7	0	2	23	12	20	.282	.307	Close & Late	.344	64	22	2	0	0	5	3	9	.368	.375
Groundball	.330	88	29	5	0	1	11	7	9	.375	.420	None on/out	.188	85	16	4	0	0	8	12	.258	.235
Flyball	.207	82	17	4	0	1	7	5	8	.250	.293	Batting #8	.209	110	23	6	0	0	6	6	8	.248	.264
Home	.215	172	37	7	0	1	14	14	14	.271	.273	Batting #9	.255	196	50	7	0	1	23	13	22	.300	.301
Away	.254	209	53	7	0	1	26	12	21	.293	.301	Other	.227	75	17	1	0	1	11	7	5	.289	.280
Day	.235	81	19	6	0	1	11	4	5	.264	.346	April	.171	35	6	0	0	1	4	2	1	.216	.257
Night	.237	300	71	8	0	1	29	22	30	.288	.273	May	.276	58	16	4	0	1	11	5	2	.333	.397
Grass	.271	240	65	9	0	2	34	20	23	.323	.333	June	.317	41	13	1	0	0	2	5	3	.391	.341
Turf	.177	141	25	5	0	0	6	6	12	.211	.213	July	.276	76	21	4	0	0	12	3	10	.296	.329
First Pitch	.324	74	24	4	0	1	12	1	0	.333	.419	August	.188	96	18	3	0	0	7	3	14	.212	.219
Ahead on Count	.244	82	20	2	0	0	13	18	0	.373	.268	September/October	.213	75	16	2	0	0	4	8	5	.286	.240
Behind on Count	.206	136	28	5	0	0	11	0	26	.203	.243	Pre-All Star	.296	152	45	6	0	2	23	12	7	.345	.375
Two Strikes	.174	144	25	2	0	0	9	7	35	.211	.188	Post-All Star	.197	229	45	8	0	0	17	14	28	.241	.231

Rob Dibble — Reds   Pitches Right

	ERA	W	L	Sv	G	GS	IP	BB	SO	Avg	H	2B	3B	HR	RBI	OBP	SLG	GF	IR	IRS	Hld	SvOp	SB	CS	GB	FB	G/F
1992 Season	3.07	3	5	25	63	0	70.1	31	110	.193	48	5	2	3	34	.285	.265	49	41	10	4	30	8	2	53	54	0.98
Career (1988-1992)	2.35	25	19	69	309	0	409.0	150	570	.195	282	49	8	17	151	.270	.275	135	218	52	51	92	73	15	383	321	1.19

1992 Season

	ERA	W	L	Sv	G	GS	IP	H	HR	BB	SO		Avg	AB	H	2B	3B	HR	RBI	BB	SO	OBP	SLG
Home	1.47	2	1	16	32	0	36.2	19	0	11	67	vs. Left	.180	128	23	2	1	2	17	22	64	.298	.258
Away	4.81	1	4	9	31	0	33.2	29	3	20	43	vs. Right	.207	121	25	3	1	1	17	9	46	.271	.273
Day	3.80	1	2	6	17	0	21.1	19	1	9	38	Inning 1-6	.000	0	0	0	0	0	0	0	0	.000	.000
Night	2.76	2	3	19	46	0	49.0	29	2	22	72	Inning 7+	.193	249	48	5	2	3	34	31	110	.285	.265
Grass	4.64	0	2	7	20	0	21.1	19	2	13	22	None on	.151	126	19	2	1	1	1	17	61	.252	.206
Turf	2.39	3	3	18	43	0	49.0	29	1	18	88	Runners on	.236	123	29	3	1	2	33	14	49	.319	.325
April	0.00	0	0	2	6	0	5.0	1	0	4	3	Scoring Posn	.211	90	19	1	1	2	32	11	37	.298	.311
May	5.54	0	2	4	12	0	13.0	13	0	7	20	Close & Late	.178	163	29	0	2	3	26	17	79	.261	.258

1992 Season

	ERA	W	L	Sv	G	GS	IP	H	HR	BB	SO		Avg	AB	H	2B	3B	HR	RBI	BB	SO	OBP	SLG
June	4.91	0	1	5	12	0	14.2	12	0	8	22	None on/out	.113	53	6	0	0	1	1	7	27	.217	.170
July	1.46	1	1	2	9	0	12.1	9	1	4	19	vs. 1st Batr (relief)	.167	54	9	1	0	2	7	7	25	.258	.296
August	3.38	1	1	4	13	0	13.1	4	2	5	22	First Inning Pitched	.196	204	40	4	2	3	32	27	85	.291	.279
September/October	0.75	1	0	8	11	0	12.0	9	0	3	24	First 15 Pitches	.175	171	30	3	1	2	13	21	73	.268	.240
Starter	0.00	0	0	0	0	0	0.0	0	0	0	0	Pitch 16-30	.227	66	15	1	1	1	19	8	32	.316	.318
Reliever	3.07	3	5	25	63	0	70.1	48	3	31	110	Pitch 31-45	.250	12	3	1	0	0	2	2	5	.357	.333
0 Days rest	3.86	1	2	7	14	0	16.1	14	0	8	26	Pitch 46+	.000	0	0	0	0	0	0	0	0	.000	.000
1 or 2 Days rest	3.46	1	3	14	35	0	39.0	25	3	18	60	First Pitch	.433	30	13	1	0	3	10	2	1	.486	.767
3+ Days rest	1.20	1	0	4	14	0	15.0	9	0	5	24	Ahead on Count	.123	154	19	2	0	0	11	0	91	.123	.136
Pre-All Star	4.46	0	4	12	33	0	36.1	30	1	21	47	Behind on Count	.333	21	7	0	1	0	7	15	0	.595	.429
Post-All Star	1.59	3	1	13	30	0	34.0	18	2	10	63	Two Strikes	.099	161	16	3	0	0	13	14	109	.171	.118

Career (1988-1992)

	ERA	W	L	Sv	G	GS	IP	H	HR	BB	SO		Avg	AB	H	2B	3B	HR	RBI	BB	SO	OBP	SLG
Home	2.32	12	9	40	154	0	201.2	141	8	79	285	vs. Left	.191	739	141	28	4	7	70	99	309	.285	.268
Away	2.39	13	10	29	155	0	207.1	141	9	71	285	vs. Right	.199	710	141	21	4	10	81	51	261	.254	.282
Day	2.45	9	4	16	83	0	117.1	77	6	48	161	Inning 1-6	.196	138	27	6	2	1	13	18	45	.284	.290
Night	2.31	16	15	53	226	0	291.2	205	11	102	409	Inning 7+	.195	1311	255	43	6	16	138	132	525	.269	.273
Grass	2.71	6	7	15	95	0	129.1	95	6	42	169	None on	.187	769	144	24	5	8	8	74	322	.261	.263
Turf	2.19	19	12	54	214	0	279.2	187	11	108	401	Runners on	.203	680	138	25	3	9	143	76	248	.280	.288
April	1.80	4	0	11	39	0	45.0	34	0	18	65	Scoring Posn	.183	496	91	17	1	7	135	58	192	.263	.264
May	2.41	3	3	13	46	0	56.0	39	1	24	90	Close & Late	.218	806	176	27	4	13	106	79	318	.268	.310
June	2.31	3	5	17	56	0	74.0	41	4	29	109	None on/out	.193	321	62	13	1	4	4	31	128	.266	.277
July	3.05	3	3	4	46	0	65.0	49	5	30	70	vs. 1st Batr (relief)	.200	275	55	8	1	6	31	25	113	.265	.302
August	2.40	7	5	10	62	0	93.2	66	5	31	134	First Inning Pitched	.197	961	193	31	7	15	126	100	389	.270	.288
September/October	2.03	5	3	14	60	0	75.1	53	2	18	102	First 15 Pitches	.205	879	180	28	6	14	96	82	339	.273	.298
Starter	0.00	0	0	0	0	0	0.0	0	0	0	0	Pitch 16-30	.175	458	80	14	1	3	41	54	181	.263	.229
Reliever	2.35	25	19	69	309	0	409.0	282	17	150	570	Pitch 31-45	.178	107	19	6	1	0	13	14	49	.268	.252
0 Days rest	2.77	4	5	19	70	0	81.1	64	3	33	114	Pitch 46+	.600	5	3	1	0	0	1	0	1	.600	.800
1 or 2 Days rest	2.07	17	13	35	170	0	235.0	146	9	82	337	First Pitch	.408	152	62	9	2	6	33	20	1	.481	.612
3+ Days rest	2.72	4	1	15	69	0	92.2	72	5	35	119	Ahead on Count	.138	878	121	24	2	5	65	2	494	.140	.187
Pre-All Star	2.28	11	9	43	158	0	197.0	130	8	81	286	Behind on Count	.286	199	57	10	2	3	25	64	0	.455	.402
Post-All Star	2.42	14	10	26	151	0	212.0	152	9	69	284	Two Strikes	.114	881	100	24	0	0	56	64	569	.172	.148

Pitcher vs. Batter (career)

Pitches Best Vs.	Avg	AB	H	2B	3B	HR	RBI	BB	SO	OBP	SLG	Pitches Worst Vs.	Avg	AB	H	2B	3B	HR	RBI	BB	SO	OBP	SLG
Darryl Strawberry	.000	10	0	0	0	0	0	2	6	.167	.000	Pedro Guerrero	.455	11	5	1	0	2	7	2	0	.467	.545
Kevin Elster	.000	8	0	0	0	0	1	2	5	.182	.000	Ozzie Smith	.455	11	5	0	0	0	1	1	1	.500	.455
Matt D. Williams	.071	14	1	0	0	0	0	0	9	.071	.071	Willie McGee	.455	11	5	0	0	0	1	2	2	.538	.455
Ricky Jordan	.083	12	1	1	0	0	1	0	3	.083	.167	Juan Samuel	.400	10	4	1	0	1	7	0	4	.364	.800
Dale Murphy	.150	20	3	0	0	0	2	0	11	.150	.150	Doug Dascenzo	.333	9	3	0	1	0	3	2	2	.455	.556

Frank DiPino — Cardinals

Pitches Left (groundball pitcher)

	ERA	W	L	Sv	G	GS	IP	BB	SO	Avg	H	2B	3B	HR	RBI	OBP	SLG	GF	IR	IRS	Hld	SvOp	SB	CS	GB	FB	G/F
1992 Season	1.64	0	0	0	9	0	11.0	3	8	.220	9	2	0	0	4	.273	.268	3	3	2	1	0	0	0	13	13	1.00
Last Five Years	3.89	16	5	9	201	0	270.2	86	170	.267	276	52	8	20	161	.319	.391	27	224	79	20	16	13	11	423	262	1.61

1992 Season

	ERA	W	L	Sv	G	GS	IP	H	HR	BB	SO		Avg	AB	H	2B	3B	HR	RBI	BB	SO	OBP	SLG
Home	3.60	0	0	0	4	0	5.0	5	0	2	1	vs. Left	.188	16	3	1	0	0	3	1	5	.235	.250
Away	0.00	0	0	0	5	0	6.0	4	0	1	7	vs. Right	.240	25	6	1	0	0	1	2	3	.296	.280

Last Five Years

	ERA	W	L	Sv	G	GS	IP	H	HR	BB	SO		Avg	AB	H	2B	3B	HR	RBI	BB	SO	OBP	SLG
Home	3.08	9	3	5	105	0	140.1	125	10	45	87	vs. Left	.231	403	93	16	2	2	51	26	79	.273	.295
Away	4.76	7	2	4	96	0	130.1	151	10	41	83	vs. Right	.290	630	183	36	6	18	110	60	91	.348	.452
Day	3.86	6	1	5	85	0	109.2	111	8	33	72	Inning 1-6	.291	382	111	27	3	7	78	28	60	.334	.432
Night	3.91	10	4	4	116	0	161.0	165	12	53	98	Inning 7+	.253	651	165	25	5	13	83	58	110	.310	.367
Grass	3.67	7	2	4	84	0	112.2	111	8	29	75	None on	.252	539	136	21	3	7	7	39	89	.303	.341
Turf	4.04	9	3	5	117	0	158.0	165	12	57	95	Runners on	.283	494	140	31	5	13	154	47	81	.336	.445
April	2.41	0	0	1	23	0	33.2	34	3	3	14	Scoring Posn	.296	301	89	17	3	6	131	39	45	.358	.432
May	4.36	3	1	2	36	0	43.1	46	6	14	26	Close & Late	.262	191	50	5	1	5	33	21	36	.329	.377
June	5.16	4	3	0	35	0	45.1	47	5	20	30	None on/out	.249	237	59	10	2	4	4	11	31	.282	.359
July	3.00	3	0	2	27	0	42.0	43	2	11	27	vs. 1st Batr (relief)	.236	178	42	10	4	3	38	11	30	.266	.388
August	4.65	3	1	3	34	0	40.2	39	1	14	26	First Inning Pitched	.261	613	160	28	8	13	124	59	106	.319	.396
September/October	3.56	3	0	1	46	0	65.2	67	3	24	47	First 15 Pitches	.264	595	157	24	7	13	107	53	87	.319	.393
Starter	0.00	0	0	0	0	0	0.0	0	0	0	0	Pitch 16-30	.266	301	80	20	1	7	39	21	63	.310	.409
Reliever	3.89	16	5	9	201	0	270.2	276	20	86	170	Pitch 31-45	.314	105	33	7	0	0	11	11	13	.379	.381
0 Days rest	5.37	2	3	2	45	0	55.1	66	5	20	29	Pitch 46+	.188	32	6	1	0	0	4	1	7	.206	.219
1 or 2 Days rest	3.70	4	1	4	101	0	141.0	141	9	48	85	First Pitch	.352	162	57	15	1	3	29	24	0	.429	.512
3+ Days rest	3.15	4	1	3	55	0	74.1	69	6	18	56	Ahead on Count	.224	460	103	22	6	4	65	0	145	.221	.324
Pre-All Star	4.09	9	4	3	105	0	141.0	154	15	42	79	Behind on Count	.304	214	65	9	0	9	36	34	0	.398	.472
Post-All Star	3.68	7	1	6	96	0	129.2	122	5	44	91	Two Strikes	.210	452	95	19	4	4	57	28	170	.253	.296

Pitcher vs. Batter (since 1984)

Pitches Best Vs.	Avg	AB	H	2B	3B	HR	RBI	BB	SO	OBP	SLG	Pitches Worst Vs.	Avg	AB	H	2B	3B	HR	RBI	BB	SO	OBP	SLG
Will Clark	.000	11	0	0	0	0	0	4	1	.267	.000	Candy Maldonado	.615	13	8	0	0	1	5	1	2	.643	.846
Tony Gwynn	.056	18	1	0	0	0	2	1	2	.100	.056	Paul O'Neill	.500	10	5	2	1	0	4	2	3	.583	.900
Ken Oberkfell	.067	15	1	0	0	0	3	1	2	.118	.067	Eric Davis	.455	11	5	2	0	1	5	5	2	.625	.909
Tim Wallach	.077	13	1	0	0	0		2	5	.200	.077	Tim Raines	.417	12	5	1	0	1	4	3	0	.533	.750
John Kruk	.111	18	2	0	0	0	1	0	9	.111	.111	Howard Johnson	.350	20	7	0	0	4	6	4	5	.458	.950

Gary DiSarcina — Angels
Bats Right (groundball hitter)

	Avg	G	AB	R	H	2B	3B	HR	RBI	BB	SO	HBP	GDP	SB	CS	OBP	SLG	IBB	SH	SF	#Pit	#P/PA	GB	FB	G/F
1992 Season	.247	157	518	48	128	19	0	3	42	20	50	7	15	9	7	.283	.301	0	5	3	1727	3.15	220	136	1.62
Career (1989-1992)	.234	195	632	61	148	22	1	3	45	26	64	9	18	10	7	.273	.286	0	8	3	2126	3.17	277	160	1.73

1992 Season

	Avg	AB	H	2B	3B	HR	RBI	BB	SO	OBP	SLG		Avg	AB	H	2B	3B	HR	RBI	BB	SO	OBP	SLG
vs. Left	.228	114	26	4	0	0	4	5	12	.264	.263	Scoring Posn	.229	118	27	4	0	0	36	7	14	.282	.263
vs. Right	.252	404	102	15	0	3	38	15	38	.288	.312	Close & Late	.132	91	12	1	0	1	7	6	12	.194	.176
Groundball	.258	132	34	6	0	0	8	5	13	.293	.303	None on/out	.301	123	37	6	0	0		4	10	.328	.350
Flyball	.191	152	29	2	0	1	9	8	19	.245	.224	Batting #7	.256	90	23	3	0	0	9	1	7	.277	.289
Home	.235	251	59	9	0	2	25	9	21	.269	.295	Batting #9	.242	356	86	13	0	3	30	18	33	.286	.303
Away	.258	267	69	10	0	1	17	11	29	.296	.307	Other	.264	72	19	3	0	0	3	1	10	.274	.306
Day	.243	144	35	6	0	2	12	9	14	.292	.326	April	.306	62	19	3	0	0	3	6	9	.371	.355
Night	.249	374	93	13	0	1	30	11	36	.279	.291	May	.250	80	20	2	0	0	5	5	6	.299	.275
Grass	.241	435	105	14	0	2	35	18	40	.279	.287	June	.235	85	20	4	0	2	7	2	4	.270	.353
Turf	.277	83	23	5	0	1	7	2	10	.302	.373	July	.214	84	18	2	0	0	7	4	8	.250	.238
First Pitch	.327	104	34	8	0	1	9	0	0	.336	.433	August	.243	103	25	4	0	1	15	1	9	.262	.311
Ahead on Count	.262	107	28	6	0	2	9	7	0	.313	.374	September/October	.250	104	26	4	0	0	5	2	14	.271	.288
Behind on Count	.190	205	39	3	0	0	13	0	37	.193	.205	Pre-All Star	.246	260	64	10	0	2	16	14	24	.293	.308
Two Strikes	.168	179	30	3	0	0	14	13	50	.230	.184	Post-All Star	.248	258	64	9	0	1	26	6	26	.272	.295

1992 By Position

Position	Avg	AB	H	2B	3B	HR	RBI	BB	SO	OBP	SLG	G	GS	Innings	PO	A	E	DP	Fld Pct	Rng Fctr	In Zone	Outs	Zone Rtg	MLB Zone
As ss	.248	517	128	19	0	3	42	20	50	.283	.302	157	155	1376.1	250	485	25	110	.967	4.81	544	516	.949	.885

Benny Distefano — Astros
Bats Left

	Avg	G	AB	R	H	2B	3B	HR	RBI	BB	SO	HBP	GDP	SB	CS	OBP	SLG	IBB	SH	SF	#Pit	#P/PA	GB	FB	G/F
1992 Season	.233	52	60	4	14	0	2	0	7	5	14	1	1	0	0	.303	.300	1	0	0	222	3.36	17	16	1.06
Last Five Years	.255	164	243	22	62	11	3	3	28	25	48	4	8	1	0	.333	.362	5	2	1	955	3.50	81	70	1.16

1992 Season

	Avg	AB	H	2B	3B	HR	RBI	BB	SO	OBP	SLG		Avg	AB	H	2B	3B	HR	RBI	BB	SO	OBP	SLG
vs. Left	.000	2	0	0	0	0	0	0	1	.000	.000	Scoring Posn	.238	21	5	0	1	0	7	1	7	.273	.333
vs. Right	.241	58	14	0	2	0	7	5	13	.313	.310	Close & Late	.192	26	5	0	0	1	5	1	5	.222	.269

John Doherty — Tigers
Pitches Right (groundball pitcher)

	ERA	W	L	Sv	G	GS	IP	BB	SO	Avg	H	2B	3B	HR	RBI	OBP	SLG	GF	IR	IRS	Hld	SvOp	SB	CS	GB	FB	G/F
1992 Season	3.88	7	4	3	47	11	116.0	25	37	.287	131	13	1	4	51	.328	.346	9	33	11	10	4	4	4	248	82	3.02

1992 Season

	ERA	W	L	Sv	G	GS	IP	H	HR	BB	SO		Avg	AB	H	2B	3B	HR	RBI	BB	SO	OBP	SLG
Home	3.83	5	1	1	25	5	56.1	65	4	15	21	vs. Left	.240	200	48	6	0	1	26	8	17	.267	.285
Away	3.92	2	3	2	22	6	59.2	66	0	10	16	vs. Right	.323	257	83	7	1	3	25	17	20	.374	.393
Starter	3.67	5	2	0	11	11	61.1	77	2	10	16	Scoring Posn	.284	116	33	3	0	1	44	11	7	.346	.336
Reliever	4.12	2	2	3	36	0	54.2	54	2	15	21	Close & Late	.390	59	23	1	0	1	7	4	5	.429	.458
0 Days rest	4.50	0	0	0	3	0	2.0	3	0	1	1	None on/out	.273	110	30	3	1	0		3	11	.298	.318
1 or 2 Days rest	5.87	1	2	2	23	0	30.2	35	1	9	12	First Pitch	.290	69	20	0	0	2	15	3	0	.338	.377
3+ Days rest	1.64	1	0	1	10	0	22.0	16	1	5	8	Behind on Count	.271	118	32	3	1	1	8	11	0	.333	.339
Pre-All Star	4.25	2	1	2	28	0	42.1	44	2	12	14	Ahead on Count	.307	179	55	7	0	1	20	0	32	.308	.363
Post-All Star	3.67	5	3	1	19	11	73.2	87	2	13	23	Two Strikes	.269	156	42	7	0	1	14	11	37	.322	.333

Chris Donnels — Mets
Bats Left (groundball hitter)

	Avg	G	AB	R	H	2B	3B	HR	RBI	BB	SO	HBP	GDP	SB	CS	OBP	SLG	IBB	SH	SF	#Pit	#P/PA	GB	FB	G/F
1992 Season	.174	45	121	8	21	4	0	0	6	17	25	0	1	1	0	.275	.207	0	1	0	549	3.98	54	26	2.08
Career (1991-1992)	.195	82	210	15	41	6	0	0	11	31	44	0	1	2	1	.299	.224	1	2	0	944	3.92	84	47	1.79

1992 Season

	Avg	AB	H	2B	3B	HR	RBI	BB	SO	OBP	SLG		Avg	AB	H	2B	3B	HR	RBI	BB	SO	OBP	SLG
vs. Left	.167	24	4	1	0	0	1	2	8	.231	.208	Scoring Posn	.222	18	4	0	0	0	4	7	3	.440	.222
vs. Right	.175	97	17	3	0	0	5	15	17	.286	.206	Close & Late	.227	22	5	2	0	0	1	4	4	.346	.318
Home	.138	65	9	2	0	0		4	16	.188	.169	None on/out	.042	24	1	1	0	0	0	5	7	.207	.083
Away	.214	56	12	2	0	0	2	13	9	.362	.250	Batting #2	.167	54	9	2	0	0	2	6	14	.250	.204

	Avg	AB	H	2B	3B	HR	RBI	BB	SO	OBP	SLG		Avg	AB	H	2B	3B	HR	RBI	BB	SO	OBP	SLG
First Pitch	.267	15	4	1	0	0	2	0	0	.267	.333	Batting #7	.154	26	4	1	0	0	2	4	4	.267	.192
Ahead on Count	.242	33	8	2	0	0	3	9	0	.405	.303	Other	.195	41	8	1	0	0	2	7	7	.313	.220
Behind on Count	.150	40	6	1	0	0	3	0	7	.150	.175	Pre-All Star	.000	6	0	0	0	0	0	2	1	.250	.000
Two Strikes	.105	57	6	0	0	0	0	8	25	.215	.105	Post-All Star	.183	115	21	4	0	0	6	15	24	.277	.217

John Dopson — Red Sox — Pitches Right (groundball pitcher)

	ERA	W	L	Sv	G	GS	IP	BB	SO	Avg	H	2B	3B	HR	RBI	OBP	SLG	CG	ShO	Sup	QS	#P/S	SB	CS	GB	FB	G/F
1992 Season	4.08	7	11	0	25	25	141.1	38	55	.287	159	30	1	17	62	.334	.437	0	0	4.01	11	82	17	7	267	119	2.24
Last Five Years	3.65	22	30	0	85	83	498.0	175	260	.257	490	75	8	48	197	.319	.380	3	0	3.87	46	87	80	19	921	411	2.24

1992 Season

	ERA	W	L	Sv	G	GS	IP	H	HR	BB	SO		Avg	AB	H	2B	3B	HR	RBI	BB	SO	OBP	SLG
Home	2.69	5	5	0	14	14	83.2	91	6	16	31	vs. Left	.276	257	71	12	1	5	23	18	17	.324	.389
Away	6.09	2	6	0	11	11	57.2	68	11	22	24	vs. Right	.296	297	88	18	0	12	39	20	38	.343	.478
Starter	4.08	7	11	0	25	25	141.1	159	17	38	55	Scoring Posn	.273	132	36	8	0	2	40	8	13	.315	.379
Reliever	0.00	0	0	0	0	0	0.0	0	0	0	0	Close & Late	.444	36	16	4	0	2	7	4	1	.500	.722
0-3 Days Rest	1.42	0	0	0	1	1	6.1	7	1	2	4	None on/out	.264	140	37	10	1	2	2	15	15	.335	.393
4 Days Rest	5.63	2	6	0	12	12	64.0	86	12	22	28	First Pitch	.329	79	26	4	0	2	11	2	0	.346	.456
5+ Days Rest	2.92	5	5	0	12	12	71.0	66	4	14	23	Behind on Count	.351	131	46	9	0	4	18	17	0	.428	.511
Pre-All Star	3.39	6	4	0	11	11	69.0	72	8	15	20	Ahead on Count	.214	234	50	7	0	8	21	0	49	.214	.346
Post-All Star	4.73	1	7	0	14	14	72.1	87	9	23	35	Two Strikes	.187	209	39	4	1	5	15	19	55	.254	.287

Last Five Years

	ERA	W	L	Sv	G	GS	IP	H	HR	BB	SO		Avg	AB	H	2B	3B	HR	RBI	BB	SO	OBP	SLG
Home	3.28	12	16	0	48	47	288.1	287	25	100	148	vs. Left	.257	935	240	29	4	18	82	95	110	.323	.354
Away	4.16	10	14	0	37	36	209.2	203	23	75	112	vs. Right	.257	973	250	46	4	30	115	80	150	.316	.405
Day	3.24	10	5	0	27	25	147.1	145	15	55	66	Inning 1-6	.244	1680	410	58	5	41	171	161	242	.310	.358
Night	3.82	12	25	0	58	58	350.2	345	33	120	194	Inning 7+	.351	228	80	17	3	7	26	14	18	.388	.544
Grass	3.92	18	18	0	59	58	332.2	331	34	122	164	None on	.261	1121	293	41	5	30	30	109	168	.328	.387
Turf	3.10	4	12	0	26	25	165.1	159	14	53	96	Runners on	.250	787	197	34	3	18	167	66	92	.306	.370
April	1.94	2	1	0	8	7	46.1	29	1	18	35	Scoring Posn	.244	459	112	21	2	8	142	46	60	.308	.351
May	3.71	5	6	0	13	13	80.0	74	8	28	35	Close & Late	.324	102	33	7	1	3	14	6	8	.358	.500
June	4.08	6	6	0	18	18	106.0	109	14	36	51	None on/out	.252	493	124	19	3	11	11	54	74	.325	.369
July	2.97	4	2	0	15	15	91.0	106	6	26	45	vs. 1st Batr (relief)	.000	1	0	0	0	0	0	1	1	.500	.000
August	4.00	1	6	0	14	14	81.0	82	9	38	41	First Inning Pitched	.246	317	78	11	1	7	32	34	45	.315	.353
September/October	4.32	4	9	0	17	16	93.2	90	10	29	53	First 75 Pitches	.243	1537	374	52	5	36	153	138	216	.305	.354
Starter	3.65	21	30	0	83	83	491.1	484	48	173	256	Pitch 76-90	.299	214	64	13	0	7	25	26	29	.373	.458
Reliever	4.05	1	0	0	2	0	6.2	6	0	2	4	Pitch 91-105	.317	123	39	7	3	4	14	10	11	.375	.520
0-3 Days Rest	1.86	1	1	0	3	3	19.1	15	2	3	14	Pitch 106+	.382	34	13	3	0	1	5	1	4	.400	.559
4 Days Rest	3.74	15	15	0	45	45	269.2	274	34	107	148	First Pitch	.307	306	94	7	2	11	38	4	0	.314	.451
5+ Days Rest	3.69	5	14	0	35	35	202.1	195	12	63	94	Ahead on Count	.189	818	155	23	1	12	63	0	226	.190	.264
Pre-All Star	3.50	16	14	0	45	44	270.1	265	26	91	136	Behind on Count	.333	451	150	25	2	17	58	97	0	.448	.510
Post-All Star	3.83	6	16	0	40	39	227.2	225	22	84	124	Two Strikes	.175	756	132	16	2	11	54	73	260	.249	.247

Pitcher vs. Batter (career)

Pitches Best Vs.	Avg	AB	H	2B	3B	HR	RBI	BB	SO	OBP	SLG	Pitches Worst Vs.	Avg	AB	H	2B	3B	HR	RBI	BB	SO	OBP	SLG
Mickey Tettleton	.000	10	0	0	0	0	0	1	2	.091	.000	Bobby Bonilla	.400	10	4	1	0	1	3	3	1	.538	.800
Rafael Palmeiro	.067	15	1	1	0	0	0	1	2	.125	.133	Mel Hall	.333	15	5	0	0	2	5	2	3	.412	.733
Steve Sax	.087	23	2	0	0	0	0	3	1	.192	.087	Juan Samuel	.333	12	4	0	2	1	3	0	1	.333	.917
Roberto Kelly	.100	10	1	0	0	0	0	1	0	.182	.100	Andy Van Slyke	.333	12	4	1	0	1	2	1	3	.385	.667
Wally Joyner	.167	12	2	0	0	0	0	0	1	.167	.167	Kirk Gibson	.333	9	3	1	0	1	1	2	0	.455	.778

Billy Doran — Reds — Bats Both

	Avg	G	AB	R	H	2B	3B	HR	RBI	BB	SO	HBP	GDP	SB	CS	OBP	SLG	IBB	SH	SF	#Pit	#P/PA	GB	FB	G/F
1992 Season	.235	132	387	48	91	16	2	8	47	64	40	0	11	7	4	.342	.349	9	3	2	1654	3.65	130	146	0.89
Last Five Years	.254	643	2138	289	543	100	9	36	230	313	260	3	33	74	24	.348	.360	17	11	15	9034	3.66	799	690	1.16

1992 Season

	Avg	AB	H	2B	3B	HR	RBI	BB	SO	OBP	SLG		Avg	AB	H	2B	3B	HR	RBI	BB	SO	OBP	SLG
vs. Left	.200	125	25	5	0	2	11	30	13	.353	.288	Scoring Posn	.210	105	22	4	0	2	38	31	15	.384	.305
vs. Right	.252	262	66	11	2	6	36	34	27	.337	.378	Close & Late	.235	68	16	4	0	2	17	14	12	.361	.382
Groundball	.237	139	33	3	0	3	13	18	14	.323	.324	None on/out	.274	73	20	1	0	2	2	10	10	.361	.370
Flyball	.247	85	21	5	0	3	14	15	13	.356	.412	Batting #6	.221	122	27	6	1	2	16	13	13	.294	.336
Home	.223	197	44	6	0	6	25	34	18	.338	.345	Batting #7	.193	114	22	7	0	1	10	22	13	.324	.281
Away	.247	190	47	10	2	2	22	30	22	.347	.353	Other	.278	151	42	3	1	5	21	29	14	.392	.411
Day	.246	126	31	9	2	2	16	17	12	.336	.397	April	.200	65	13	2	0	1	10	9	7	.289	.277
Night	.230	261	60	7	0	6	31	47	28	.345	.326	May	.278	79	22	6	1	4	13	11	10	.367	.532
Grass	.250	104	26	5	1	1	9	14	9	.333	.346	June	.240	50	12	2	0	0	4	7	5	.333	.280
Turf	.230	283	65	11	1	7	38	50	31	.345	.350	July	.215	65	14	4	0	2	7	6	7	.282	.369
First Pitch	.232	69	16	4	0	1	7	7	0	.299	.333	August	.154	65	10	0	0	1	8	19	7	.345	.200
Ahead on Count	.365	85	31	2	0	5	26	34	0	.542	.565	September/October	.317	63	20	2	1	0	5	12	4	.427	.381

1992 Season

	Avg	AB	H	2B	3B	HR	RBI	BB	SO	OBP	SLG		Avg	AB	H	2B	3B	HR	RBI	BB	SO	OBP	SLG
Behind on Count	.197	122	24	6	1	1	10	0	21	.197	.287	Pre-All Star	.234	214	50	13	1	5	28	29	28	.322	.374
Two Strikes	.170	165	28	6	2	2	8	24	40	.275	.267	Post-All Star	.237	173	41	3	1	3	19	35	12	.365	.318

1992 By Position

Position	Avg	AB	H	2B	3B	HR	RBI	BB	SO	OBP	SLG	G	GS	Innings	PO	A	E	DP	Fld Pct	Rng Fctr	In Zone	Outs	Zone Rtg	MLB Zone
As Pinch Hitter	.071	14	1	0	0	0	1	2	2	.188	.071	16	0	---	---	---	---	---	---	---	---	---	---	---
As 1b	.213	61	13	2	1	2	9	10	9	.319	.377	25	15	149.0	136	8	0	5	1.000	---	23	20	.870	.843
As 2b	.247	312	77	14	1	6	37	52	29	.353	.356	104	91	792.0	170	242	5	55	.988	4.68	285	241	.846	.892

Last Five Years

	Avg	AB	H	2B	3B	HR	RBI	BB	SO	OBP	SLG		Avg	AB	H	2B	3B	HR	RBI	BB	SO	OBP	SLG
vs. Left	.244	643	157	32	3	12	61	122	70	.364	.359	Scoring Posn	.254	515	131	21	2	9	185	103	66	.370	.355
vs. Right	.258	1495	366	68	6	24	169	191	190	.341	.360	Close & Late	.216	371	80	11	1	7	44	66	58	.332	.307
Groundball	.238	777	185	34	2	10	81	101	86	.325	.326	None on/out	.264	473	125	22	1	11	11	67	64	.356	.385
Flyball	.251	483	121	24	1	12	61	76	69	.351	.379	Batting #2	.259	572	148	32	3	11	49	109	75	.375	.383
Home	.268	1044	280	51	6	18	122	165	117	.366	.380	Batting #3	.238	677	161	26	1	11	92	79	80	.318	.328
Away	.240	1094	263	49	3	18	108	148	143	.330	.340	Other	.263	889	234	42	5	14	89	125	105	.352	.369
Day	.267	640	171	42	3	10	77	72	81	.340	.389	April	.249	342	85	20	1	3	41	45	37	.334	.339
Night	.248	1498	372	58	6	26	153	241	179	.351	.347	May	.279	312	87	15	2	7	46	40	36	.360	.407
Grass	.258	654	169	31	2	11	69	87	78	.344	.362	June	.285	400	114	16	1	9	52	61	45	.378	.398
Turf	.252	1484	374	69	7	25	161	226	182	.350	.358	July	.237	396	94	14	1	11	46	49	63	.321	.361
First Pitch	.307	348	107	22	1	5	38	9	0	.323	.420	August	.208	399	83	18	3	4	26	76	54	.333	.298
Ahead on Count	.319	564	180	30	3	16	84	193	0	.490	.468	September/October	.277	289	80	17	1	2	19	42	25	.367	.363
Behind on Count	.201	636	128	22	2	7	53	0	128	.202	.275	Pre-All Star	.264	1161	307	55	4	20	149	158	142	.351	.370
Two Strikes	.177	824	146	37	3	10	67	103	259	.268	.266	Post-All Star	.242	977	236	45	5	16	81	155	118	.344	.347

Batter vs. Pitcher (since 1984)

Hits Best Against	Avg	AB	H	2B	3B	HR	RBI	BB	SO	OBP	SLG	Hits Worst Against	Avg	AB	H	2B	3B	HR	RBI	BB	SO	OBP	SLG
Tim Crews	.600	10	6	2	0	0	1	1	0	.636	.800	Jose Rijo	.056	18	1	0	0	0	0	3	5	.190	.056
Don Carman	.500	14	7	1	0	0	2	5	0	.632	.571	Rob Murphy	.077	13	1	0	0	0	2	3	0	.250	.077
Mike Maddux	.400	15	6	2	0	1	2	4	2	.526	.733	Greg Harris	.091	11	1	0	0	0	0	0	2	.091	.091
John Wetteland	.400	10	4	0	0	1	5	2	1	.500	.700	Norm Charlton	.100	10	1	0	0	0	0	1	3	.182	.100
Mark Grant	.308	13	4	0	1	1	3	3	2	.438	.692	Mike Dunne	.100	10	1	0	0	0	0	1	3	.182	.100

Brian Downing — Rangers   Bats Right

	Avg	G	AB	R	H	2B	3B	HR	RBI	BB	SO	HBP	GDP	SB	CS	OBP	SLG	IBB	SH	SF	#Pit	#P/PA	GB	FB	G/F
1992 Season	.278	107	320	53	89	18	0	10	39	62	58	8	7	1	0	.407	.428	2	0	1	1728	4.42	109	99	1.10
Last Five Years	.270	603	2085	315	563	96	8	80	262	307	323	42	43	5	7	.372	.439	19	6	17	10333	4.22	723	691	1.05

1992 Season

	Avg	AB	H	2B	3B	HR	RBI	BB	SO	OBP	SLG		Avg	AB	H	2B	3B	HR	RBI	BB	SO	OBP	SLG
vs. Left	.281	121	34	8	0	3	14	30	30	.429	.421	Scoring Posn	.211	76	16	3	0	2	28	18	22	.378	.329
vs. Right	.276	199	55	10	0	7	25	32	28	.392	.432	Close & Late	.184	49	9	3	0	1	4	7	12	.322	.306
Groundball	.295	88	26	4	0	4	17	11	19	.392	.477	None on/out	.296	115	34	7	0	4	4	19	14	.400	.461
Flyball	.286	77	22	6	0	3	7	15	15	.409	.481	Batting #1	.292	202	59	10	0	7	27	37	30	.414	.446
Home	.307	163	50	12	0	4	16	32	30	.430	.454	Batting #5	.222	45	10	2	0	0	0	7	9	.340	.267
Away	.248	157	39	6	0	6	23	30	28	.382	.401	Other	.274	73	20	6	0	3	12	18	19	.426	.479
Day	.328	61	20	4	0	4	19	5	10	.423	.590	April	.256	39	10	1	0	2	5	14	6	.482	.436
Night	.266	259	69	14	0	6	20	57	48	.403	.390	May	.286	49	14	1	0	2	5	12	5	.435	.429
Grass	.293	273	80	17	0	9	35	49	48	.412	.454	June	.232	56	13	4	0	1	5	10	12	.358	.357
Turf	.191	47	9	1	0	1	4	13	10	.377	.277	July	.276	58	16	4	0	3	11	8	14	.373	.500
First Pitch	.300	10	3	2	0	0	4	2	0	.462	.500	August	.319	72	23	3	0	2	10	12	11	.424	.444
Ahead on Count	.246	65	16	1	0	5	9	36	0	.520	.492	September/October	.283	46	13	5	0	0	3	6	10	.370	.391
Behind on Count	.262	103	27	3	0	2	11	0	28	.274	.350	Pre-All Star	.253	162	41	6	0	7	18	39	27	.415	.420
Two Strikes	.262	183	48	11	0	3	21	24	58	.362	.372	Post-All Star	.304	158	48	12	0	3	21	23	31	.397	.437

1992 By Position

Position	Avg	AB	H	2B	3B	HR	RBI	BB	SO	OBP	SLG	G	GS	Innings	PO	A	E	DP	Fld Pct	Rng Fctr	In Zone	Outs	Zone Rtg	MLB Zone
As Designated Hitter	.285	309	88	18	0	10	38	60	52	.411	.440	93	90	---	---	---	---	---	---	---	---	---	---	---
As Pinch Hitter	.000	12	0	0	0	0	1	2	7	.200	.000	15	0	---	---	---	---	---	---	---	---	---	---	---

Last Five Years

	Avg	AB	H	2B	3B	HR	RBI	BB	SO	OBP	SLG		Avg	AB	H	2B	3B	HR	RBI	BB	SO	OBP	SLG
vs. Left	.282	741	209	34	1	33	78	144	118	.409	.464	Scoring Posn	.249	481	120	18	3	10	171	102	92	.381	.362
vs. Right	.263	1344	354	62	7	47	184	163	205	.351	.425	Close & Late	.271	369	100	14	1	16	57	45	58	.362	.444
Groundball	.333	478	159	18	1	22	83	65	65	.419	.513	None on/out	.262	669	175	34	1	26	26	78	95	.346	.441
Flyball	.243	518	126	24	3	23	64	88	91	.362	.434	Batting #1	.282	1029	290	45	5	43	125	142	156	.379	.461
Home	.277	1018	282	48	4	44	124	147		.383	.462	Batting #5	.262	385	101	20	1	14	43	51	62	.351	.429
Away	.263	1067	281	48	4	36	138	146	176	.362	.417	Other	.256	671	172	31	2	23	94	114	105	.372	.411
Day	.253	487	123	20	3	17	71	63	68	.353	.411	April	.249	241	60	7	0	8	28	48	32	.391	.378
Night	.275	1598	440	76	5	63	191	244	255	.378	.447	May	.307	348	107	12	3	17	42	46	46	.400	.506
Grass	.270	1776	479	81	8	72	224	255	274	.369	.446	June	.250	348	87	25	1	8	36	46	58	.348	.397

Last Five Years

	Avg	AB	H	2B	3B	HR	RBI	BB	SO	OBP	SLG		Avg	AB	H	2B	3B	HR	RBI	BB	SO	OBP	SLG
Turf	.272	309	84	15	0	8	38	52	49	.387	.398	July	.279	394	110	15	2	19	54	66	60	.387	.472
First Pitch	.349	106	37	10	0	6	21	8	0	.402	.613	August	.272	345	94	16	0	14	57	48	56	.366	.441
Ahead on Count	.337	430	145	20	2	26	72	184	0	.541	.574	September/October	.257	409	105	21	2	14	45	53	70	.347	.421
Behind on Count	.245	701	172	21	3	20	76	3	145	.267	.369	Pre-All Star	.271	1050	285	47	4	41	123	159	155	.380	.441
Two Strikes	.218	1118	244	46	4	26	100	110	336	.299	.336	Post-All Star	.269	1035	278	49	4	39	139	148	168	.364	.437

Batter vs. Pitcher (since 1984)

Hits Best Against	Avg	AB	H	2B	3B	HR	RBI	BB	SO	OBP	SLG	Hits Worst Against	Avg	AB	H	2B	3B	HR	RBI	BB	SO	OBP	SLG
Charlie Leibrandt	.512	41	21	4	0	3	10	7	6	.583	.829	Bobby Ojeda	.000	10	0	0	0	0	1	3	0	.214	.000
Jeff M. Robinson	.500	8	4	0	0	1	1	5	1	.692	.875	Jaime Navarro	.071	14	1	1	0	0	1	1	1	.133	.143
Danny Darwin	.444	18	8	2	0	2	3	2	4	.545	.889	Kevin Tapani	.083	12	1	1	0	0	1	0	1	.077	.167
Scott Bailes	.444	18	8	1	0	2	2	5	3	.565	.833	Tom Gordon	.091	11	1	0	0	0	0	1	3	.167	.091
Bill Krueger	.375	24	9	0	0	4	8	5	3	.483	.875	Tom Henke	.111	18	2	0	0	0	2	0	8	.100	.111

Kelly Downs — Athletics   Pitches Right

	ERA	W	L	Sv	G	GS	IP	BB	SO	Avg	H	2B	3B	HR	RBI	OBP	SLG	CG	ShO	Sup	QS	#P/S	SB	CS	GB	FB	G/F
1992 Season	3.37	6	7	0	37	20	144.1	70	71	.254	137	23	2	8	54	.343	.348	0	0	2.87	7	86	17	8	181	193	0.94
Last Five Years	3.73	36	30	0	140	81	569.2	216	331	.241	514	107	7	40	236	.313	.354	6	3	4.52	39	83	51	20	798	660	1.21

1992 Season

	ERA	W	L	Sv	G	GS	IP	H	HR	BB	SO		Avg	AB	H	2B	3B	HR	RBI	BB	SO	OBP	SLG
Home	3.23	4	2	0	16	8	64.0	50	2	31	36	vs. Left	.274	263	72	12	2	1	24	36	25	.359	.346
Away	3.47	2	5	0	21	12	80.1	87	6	39	35	vs. Right	.235	277	65	11	0	7	30	34	46	.329	.350
Starter	3.65	4	7	0	20	20	106.0	103	8	56	41	Scoring Posn	.176	136	24	3	0	2	43	27	22	.310	.243
Reliever	2.58	2	0	0	17	0	38.1	34	0	14	30	Close & Late	.289	38	11	1	0	0	5	5	6	.372	.316
0-3 Days Rest	0.00	0	0	0	0	0	0.0	0	0	0	0	None on/out	.243	140	34	5	0	1	1	14	11	.321	.300
4 Days Rest	3.36	2	4	0	13	13	69.2	67	5	41	29	First Pitch	.172	93	16	4	0	0	7	3	0	.202	.215
5+ Days Rest	4.21	2	3	0	7	7	36.1	36	3	15	12	Behind on Count	.355	124	44	9	0	14	36	0	0	.497	.524
Pre-All Star	3.58	1	3	0	21	9	70.1	78	4	26	36	Ahead on Count	.216	218	47	6	2	1	17	0	57	.232	.275
Post-All Star	3.16	5	4	0	16	11	74.0	59	4	44	35	Two Strikes	.223	224	50	6	2	1	22	31	71	.324	.281

Last Five Years

	ERA	W	L	Sv	G	GS	IP	H	HR	BB	SO		Avg	AB	H	2B	3B	HR	RBI	BB	SO	OBP	SLG
Home	3.29	22	9	0	67	40	287.1	227	15	107	173	vs. Left	.248	1130	280	58	6	17	126	115	136	.316	.355
Away	4.18	14	21	0	73	41	282.1	287	25	109	158	vs. Right	.234	1001	234	49	1	23	110	101	195	.309	.354
Day	3.51	14	7	0	53	27	210.1	170	14	68	115	Inning 1-6	.249	1738	432	86	6	34	202	178	267	.321	.364
Night	3.86	22	23	0	87	54	359.1	344	26	148	216	Inning 7+	.209	393	82	21	1	6	34	38	64	.277	.313
Grass	3.36	32	19	0	100	61	433.1	368	25	167	240	None on	.237	1240	294	56	3	20	20	109	196	.303	.335
Turf	4.89	4	11	0	40	20	136.1	146	15	49	91	Runners on	.247	891	220	51	4	20	216	107	135	.325	.380
April	3.39	3	7	0	17	17	101.0	83	3	35	55	Scoring Posn	.229	512	117	23	3	10	183	78	84	.323	.344
May	4.63	4	6	0	20	15	81.2	86	8	40	53	Close & Late	.200	180	36	5	0	1	14	21	26	.283	.244
June	3.78	6	3	0	21	7	64.1	56	5	19	36	None on/out	.241	551	133	23	0	10	10	47	69	.307	.338
July	2.55	10	3	0	20	12	86.1	73	4	25	63	vs. 1st Batr (relief)	.268	56	15	4	0	2	9	2	11	.288	.464
August	3.84	7	6	0	32	17	122.0	117	13	56	63	First Inning Pitched	.263	518	136	33	1	11	79	58	88	.339	.394
September/October	4.17	6	5	0	30	13	112.1	97	7	41	61	First 75 Pitches	.244	1824	445	90	7	38	208	174	288	.312	.363
Starter	3.80	27	30	0	81	81	461.2	428	31	175	256	Pitch 76-90	.223	179	40	10	0	1	17	24	30	.310	.296
Reliever	3.42	9	0	0	59	0	108.0	86	9	41	75	Pitch 91-105	.189	95	18	5	0	0	3	12	13	.287	.242
0-3 Days Rest	3.86	4	1	0	7	7	42.0	39	3	10	29	Pitch 106+	.333	33	11	2	0	1	6	6	0	.436	.485
4 Days Rest	3.79	14	14	0	43	43	242.1	227	17	100	128	First Pitch	.266	402	107	22	2	7	55	22	2	.303	.383
5+ Days Rest	3.81	9	15	0	31	31	177.1	162	11	65	99	Ahead on Count	.180	885	159	35	2	9	70	0	268	.187	.254
Pre-All Star	3.69	15	17	0	64	43	275.1	253	16	100	158	Behind on Count	.318	465	148	30	2	18	69	103	0	.439	.508
Post-All Star	3.76	21	13	0	76	38	294.1	261	24	116	173	Two Strikes	.172	837	144	30	2	6	67	91	329	.257	.234

Pitcher vs. Batter (career)

Pitches Best Vs.	Avg	AB	H	2B	3B	HR	RBI	BB	SO	OBP	SLG	Pitches Worst Vs.	Avg	AB	H	2B	3B	HR	RBI	BB	SO	OBP	SLG
Joey Cora	.000	11	0	0	0	0	0	0	0	.000	.000	Chris Sabo	.545	11	6	3	0	1	3	1	0	.583	1.091
Craig Biggio	.000	11	0	0	0	0	1	0	2	.000	.000	Pedro Guerrero	.500	22	11	2	0	1	4	2	2	.577	.727
Alfredo Griffin	.077	26	2	1	0	0	0	0	2	.077	.115	Gary Carter	.500	8	4	2	0	0	1	3	1	.636	.750
Willie McGee	.083	12	1	0	0	0	1	0	2	.063	.083	Mike LaValliere	.478	23	11	3	0	0	3	5	1	.571	.609
Darren Daulton	.083	12	1	0	0	0	0	1	2	.154	.083	Andres Galarraga	.440	25	11	2	0	3	6	1	5	.462	.880

D.J. Dozier — Mets   Bats Right

	Avg	G	AB	R	H	2B	3B	HR	RBI	BB	SO	HBP	GDP	SB	CS	OBP	SLG	IBB	SH	SF	#Pit	#P/PA	GB	FB	G/F
1992 Season	.191	25	47	4	9	2	0	0	2	4	19	0	1	4	0	.264	.234	0	1	1	188	3.55	13	10	1.30

1992 Season

	Avg	AB	H	2B	3B	HR	RBI	BB	SO	OBP	SLG		Avg	AB	H	2B	3B	HR	RBI	BB	SO	OBP	SLG
vs. Left	.167	30	5	0	0	0	2	4	11	.278	.167	Scoring Posn	.286	7	2	0	0	0	2	1	1	.400	.286
vs. Right	.235	17	4	2	0	0	0	0	8	.235	.353	Close & Late	.286	7	2	0	0	0	0	0	3	.286	.286

Doug Drabek — Pirates

	ERA	W	L	Sv	G	GS	IP	BB	SO	Avg	H	2B	3B	HR	RBI	OBP	SLG	CG	ShO	Sup	QS	#P/S	SB	CS	GB	FB	G/F
1992 Season	2.77	15	11	0	34	34	256.2	54	177	.231	218	35	4	17	75	.274	.330	10	4	3.93	25	108	18	14	403	221	1.82
Last Five Years	2.89	81	50	0	170	168	1186.1	291	700	.241	1062	173	22	90	368	.290	.352	35	15	4.50	118	101	102	57	1742	1195	1.46

1992 Season

	ERA	W	L	Sv	G	GS	IP	H	HR	BB	SO		Avg	AB	H	2B	3B	HR	RBI	BB	SO	OBP	SLG
Home	2.44	8	3	0	14	14	110.2	92	3	27	87	vs. Left	.261	548	143	21	3	11	47	42	90	.314	.370
Away	3.02	7	8	0	20	20	146.0	126	14	27	90	vs. Right	.189	397	75	14	1	6	28	12	87	.217	.275
Day	2.68	2	2	0	5	5	40.1	29	3	10	19	Inning 1-6	.235	744	175	28	3	17	68	39	144	.277	.349
Night	2.79	13	9	0	29	29	216.1	189	14	44	158	Inning 7+	.214	201	43	7	1	0	7	15	33	.266	.259
Grass	4.35	1	6	0	9	9	60.0	58	11	16	34	None on	.240	605	145	24	2	11	11	26	113	.271	.340
Turf	2.29	14	5	0	25	25	196.2	160	6	38	143	Runners on	.215	340	73	11	2	6	64	28	64	.280	.312
April	2.75	3	2	0	5	5	36.0	29	2	9	21	Scoring Posn	.177	192	34	4	0	4	56	24	40	.269	.260
May	3.19	0	2	0	6	6	42.1	36	6	5	35	Close & Late	.214	131	28	6	0	0	6	11	20	.272	.260
June	3.02	3	2	0	6	6	44.2	37	2	10	38	None on/out	.233	257	60	9	1	3	3	9	54	.259	.311
July	1.76	2	2	0	5	5	41.0	35	2	8	21	vs. 1st Batr (relief)	.000	0	0	0	0	0	0	0	0	.000	.000
August	2.98	2	2	0	6	6	45.1	42	5	13	31	First Inning Pitched	.300	140	42	10	1	6	19	3	30	.324	.514
September/October	2.85	5	1	0	6	6	47.1	39	0	9	31	First 75 Pitches	.240	649	156	24	2	13	55	30	123	.277	.344
Starter	2.77	15	11	0	34	34	256.2	218	17	54	177	Pitch 76-90	.193	109	21	3	1	3	11	9	23	.258	.321
Reliever	0.00	0	0	0	0	0	0.0	0	0	0	0	Pitch 91-105	.225	111	25	2	1	1	3	6	17	.263	.288
0-3 Days Rest	0.00	0	0	0	0	0	0.0	0	0	0	0	Pitch 106+	.211	76	16	6	0	0	6	3	14	.289	.289
4 Days Rest	2.32	9	6	0	21	21	163.0	132	7	33	112	First Pitch	.276	123	34	5	3	2	11	7	0	.321	.415
5+ Days Rest	3.56	6	5	0	13	13	93.2	86	10	21	65	Ahead on Count	.165	448	74	11	1	5	22	0	156	.172	.228
Pre-All Star	2.76	7	7	0	19	19	140.0	117	10	28	101	Behind on Count	.317	205	65	14	0	5	23	21	0	.378	.459
Post-All Star	2.78	8	4	0	15	15	116.2	101	7	26	76	Two Strikes	.156	435	68	9	1	7	26	26	177	.208	.230

Last Five Years

	ERA	W	L	Sv	G	GS	IP	H	HR	BB	SO		Avg	AB	H	2B	3B	HR	RBI	BB	SO	OBP	SLG
Home	2.55	43	22	0	82	81	601.0	514	45	141	384	vs. Left	.257	2480	637	111	11	42	206	191	321	.309	.361
Away	3.24	38	28	0	88	87	585.1	548	45	150	316	vs. Right	.221	1919	425	62	11	48	162	100	379	.264	.340
Day	2.65	24	10	0	46	44	309.0	264	22	72	167	Inning 1-6	.241	3604	868	141	20	75	315	230	581	.288	.353
Night	2.97	57	40	0	124	124	877.1	798	68	219	533	Inning 7+	.244	795	194	32	2	15	53	61	119	.297	.346
Grass	4.38	17	21	0	48	47	297.2	307	31	88	150	None on	.241	2769	666	109	14	59	59	164	466	.284	.354
Turf	2.39	64	29	0	122	121	888.2	755	59	203	550	Runners on	.243	1630	396	64	8	31	309	127	234	.299	.349
April	2.96	12	10	0	25	25	167.0	148	12	45	83	Scoring Posn	.219	936	205	32	4	18	272	98	148	.290	.319
May	3.03	9	10	0	27	27	190.0	165	18	49	108	Close & Late	.218	472	103	16	0	6	25	43	76	.284	.290
June	3.34	9	8	0	28	28	186.0	180	17	55	117	None on/out	.253	1185	300	49	6	23	23	62	194	.290	.363
July	2.96	18	6	0	28	28	203.2	178	18	58	124	vs. 1st Batr (relief)	.000	1	0	0	0	0	0	1	0	.500	.000
August	2.42	16	8	0	31	30	219.2	196	18	43	150	First Inning Pitched	.245	642	157	31	2	14	62	41	91	.292	.364
September/October	2.74	17	8	0	31	30	220.0	195	7	41	139	First 75 Pitches	.239	3216	770	122	16	61	251	191	510	.284	.344
Starter	2.89	80	50	0	168	168	1182.1	1057	90	290	698	Pitch 76-90	.242	538	130	24	5	14	57	48	85	.307	.383
Reliever	2.25	1	0	0	2	0	4.0	5	0	1	2	Pitch 91-105	.250	412	103	11	1	10	37	27	63	.296	.354
0-3 Days Rest	1.59	1	1	0	2	2	17.0	17	1	2	10	Pitch 106+	.253	233	59	16	0	5	23	25	42	.321	.386
4 Days Rest	2.78	53	32	0	110	110	771.2	689	49	181	457	First Pitch	.313	667	209	37	5	19	74	20	0	.337	.469
5+ Days Rest	3.18	26	17	0	56	56	393.2	351	40	107	230	Ahead on Count	.192	1977	380	59	4	26	109	1	606	.199	.266
Pre-All Star	3.02	36	30	0	90	90	616.2	557	50	165	352	Behind on Count	.279	965	269	44	7	28	108	144	1	.370	.426
Post-All Star	2.75	45	20	0	80	78	569.2	505	40	126	348	Two Strikes	.174	1904	331	55	5	27	103	125	699	.226	.251

Pitcher vs. Batter (career)

Pitches Best Vs.	Avg	AB	H	2B	3B	HR	RBI	BB	SO	OBP	SLG	Pitches Worst Vs.	Avg	AB	H	2B	3B	HR	RBI	BB	SO	OBP	SLG
Darnell Coles	.000	11	0	0	0	0	0	0	2	.000	.000	Tony Gwynn	.429	35	15	6	1	0	2	1	2	.444	.657
Curt Wilkerson	.000	11	0	0	0	0	0	0	4	.000	.000	Glenn Davis	.407	27	11	2	0	1	2	2	3	.448	.593
Kirt Manwaring	.000	11	0	0	0	0	0	1	3	.083	.000	Steve Sax	.400	10	4	0	0	1	3	1	0	.455	.700
Lenny Harris	.048	21	1	0	0	0	1	1	1	.091	.048	Kevin Elster	.370	27	10	1	1	2	7	4	4	.452	.704
Ricky Jordan	.059	17	1	1	0	0	0	0	8	.059	.118	Eric Davis	.333	27	9	2	1	2	5	3	8	.400	.704

Brian Drahman — White Sox

	ERA	W	L	Sv	G	GS	IP	BB	SO	Avg	H	2B	3B	HR	RBI	OBP	SLG	GF	IR	IRS	Hld	SvOp	SB	CS	GB	FB	G/F
1992 Season	2.57	0	0	0	5	0	7.0	2	1	.222	6	1	0	0	3	.276	.259	2	1	1	2	0	1	0	8	11	0.73
Career (1991-1992)	3.11	3	2	0	33	0	37.2	15	19	.199	27	4	1	0	23	.276	.331	10	37	11	4	2	1	1	50	46	1.09

1992 Season

	ERA	W	L	Sv	G	GS	IP	H	HR	BB	SO		Avg	AB	H	2B	3B	HR	RBI	BB	SO	OBP	SLG
Home	6.75	0	0	0	2	0	2.2	4	0	1	0	vs. Left	.083	12	1	1	0	0	2	0	0	.083	.167
Away	0.00	0	0	0	3	0	4.1	2	0	1	1	vs. Right	.333	15	5	0	0	0	1	2	1	.412	.333

Rob Ducey — Angels
Bats Left (flyball hitter)

	Avg	G	AB	R	H	2B	3B	HR	RBI	BB	SO	HBP	GDP	SB	CS	OBP	SLG	IBB	SH	SF	#Pit	#P/PA	GB	FB	G/F
1992 Season	.188	54	80	7	15	4	0	0	2	5	22	0	1	2	4	.233	.238	0	0	1	321	3.73	16	29	0.55
Last Five Years	.242	180	331	42	80	19	3	1	26	32	95	1	5	8	6	.307	.326				1468	3.99	85	89	0.96

1992 Season

	Avg	AB	H	2B	3B	HR	RBI	BB	SO	OBP	SLG		Avg	AB	H	2B	3B	HR	RBI	BB	SO	OBP	SLG
vs. Left	.111	9	1	1	0	0	0	1	5	.200	.222	Scoring Posn	.000	15	0	0	0	0	2	3	6	.158	.000
vs. Right	.197	71	14	3	0	0	2	4	17	.237	.239	Close & Late	.267	15	4	1	0	0	1	1	6	.313	.333

Mariano Duncan — Phillies
Bats Right (groundball hitter)

	Avg	G	AB	R	H	2B	3B	HR	RBI	BB	SO	HBP	GDP	SB	CS	OBP	SLG	IBB	SH	SF	#Pit	#P/PA	GB	FB	G/F
1992 Season	.267	142	574	71	153	40	3	8	50	17	108	5	15	23	3	.292	.389	0	5	4	2192	3.65	247	140	1.76
Last Five Years	.273	461	1600	216	436	84	20	33	166	61	443	17	28	50	19	.304	.412	4	16	11	5846	3.46	646	410	1.58

1992 Season

	Avg	AB	H	2B	3B	HR	RBI	BB	SO	OBP	SLG		Avg	AB	H	2B	3B	HR	RBI	BB	SO	OBP	SLG
vs. Left	.286	231	66	14	1	4	19	6	42	.308	.407	Scoring Posn	.246	122	30	8	1	4	44	3	27	.262	.426
vs. Right	.254	343	87	26	2	4	31	11	66	.281	.376	Close & Late	.267	90	24	4	0	1	8	3	18	.302	.344
Groundball	.257	249	64	16	1	4	22	9	44	.287	.378	None on/out	.321	112	36	9	2	1	1	3	18	.339	.464
Flyball	.280	132	37	11	1	2	14	6	27	.319	.424	Batting #2	.236	416	98	27	3	7	36	13	81	.263	.365
Home	.243	276	67	19	1	3	18	12	56	.277	.351	Batting #6	.319	72	23	6	0	1	5	0	14	.324	.444
Away	.289	298	86	21	2	5	32	5	52	.305	.423	Other	.372	86	32	7	0	0	9	4	13	.402	.453
Day	.344	151	52	11	1	4	16	4	29	.361	.510	April	.311	90	28	10	0	0	8	1	17	.344	.422
Night	.239	423	101	29	2	4	34	13	79	.267	.345	May	.236	110	26	6	1	2	12	1	22	.241	.364
Grass	.304	158	48	15	1	3	15	2	32	.317	.468	June	.307	114	35	7	1	2	14	4	17	.336	.439
Turf	.252	416	105	25	2	5	35	15	76	.282	.358	July	.238	105	25	6	0	2	4	6	22	.277	.352
First Pitch	.221	68	15	4	0	2	9	0	0	.221	.368	August	.226	84	19	5	1	1	9	4	13	.258	.345
Ahead on Count	.297	118	35	9	2	2	9	8	0	.344	.458	September/October	.282	71	20	6	0	1	3	1	17	.292	.408
Behind on Count	.263	228	60	13	1	4	17	0	61	.267	.382	Pre-All Star	.280	368	103	26	2	6	37	7	69	.300	.410
Two Strikes	.220	273	60	15	0	2	21	9	108	.247	.297	Post-All Star	.243	206	50	14	1	2	13	10	39	.276	.350

1992 By Position

Position	Avg	AB	H	2B	3B	HR	RBI	BB	SO	OBP	SLG	G	GS	Innings	PO	A	E	DP	Fld Pct	Rng Fctr	In Zone	Outs	Zone Rtg	MLB Zone
As 2b	.299	197	59	13	3	2	21	8	30	.335	.426	52	50	420.2	94	126	7	27	.969	4.71	157	133	.847	.892
As ss	.270	111	30	3	0	2	5	6	28	.311	.351	42	26	231.0	37	80	5	15	.959	4.56	105	87	.829	.885
As lf	.235	251	59	23	0	4	23	2	46	.243	.375	65	58	514.0	123	1	3	0	.976	2.17	136	116	.853	.809

Last Five Years

	Avg	AB	H	2B	3B	HR	RBI	BB	SO	OBP	SLG		Avg	AB	H	2B	3B	HR	RBI	BB	SO	OBP	SLG
vs. Left	.327	658	215	45	9	15	79	26	103	.356	.491	Scoring Posn	.278	360	100	18	6	8	131	12	70	.302	.428
vs. Right	.235	942	221	39	11	18	87	35	180	.268	.357	Close & Late	.258	264	68	8	1	2	26	11	58	.295	.318
Groundball	.276	617	170	41	5	5	54	21	102	.301	.382	None on/out	.273	374	102	20	6	8	8	16	61	.310	.422
Flyball	.260	362	94	18	7	10	43	15	69	.295	.431	Batting #2	.265	702	186	40	6	16	70	27	122	.294	.407
Home	.274	803	220	43	9	20	84	34	140	.307	.425	Batting #7	.248	274	68	14	4	4	30	8	40	.278	.372
Away	.271	797	216	41	11	13	82	27	143	.301	.399	Other	.292	624	182	30	10	13	66	26	121	.327	.434
Day	.282	433	122	18	10	10	48	20	72	.317	.439	April	.313	195	61	17	1	5	24	9	34	.358	.487
Night	.269	1167	314	66	10	23	118	41	211	.300	.402	May	.243	288	70	12	5	2	28	7	46	.264	.340
Grass	.269	483	130	30	8	7	53	15	95	.301	.408	June	.266	271	72	14	3	5	25	9	42	.302	.395
Turf	.274	1117	306	54	12	26	113	46	188	.306	.414	July	.257	241	62	13	2	4	16	9	49	.285	.378
First Pitch	.307	231	71	10	4	5	36	0	0	.308	.450	August	.308	289	89	13	6	8	39	15	46	.343	.478
Ahead on Count	.349	312	109	22	10	11	41	32	0	.413	.590	September/October	.259	316	82	15	3	9	34	12	66	.287	.411
Behind on Count	.237	624	148	27	5	16	57	0	176	.246	.373	Pre-All Star	.269	834	224	46	9	15	85	26	137	.300	.399
Two Strikes	.200	709	142	26	4	10	60	27	283	.235	.291	Post-All Star	.277	766	212	38	11	18	81	35	146	.309	.426

Batter vs. Pitcher (career)

Hits Best Against	Avg	AB	H	2B	3B	HR	RBI	BB	SO	OBP	SLG	Hits Worst Against	Avg	AB	H	2B	3B	HR	RBI	BB	SO	OBP	SLG
Lee Smith	.500	14	7	0	2	0	3	0	1	.500	.786	Rick Sutcliffe	.000	14	0	0	0	0	0	0	4	.000	.000
Bruce Ruffin	.500	14	7	1	1	1	8	1	3	.533	.929	Jim Gott	.077	13	1	0	0	0	1	1	2	.133	.077
Mark Portugal	.400	10	4	1	0	1	1	1	1	.455	.800	Tim Crews	.091	11	1	0	0	0	0	0	6	.091	.091
Derek Lilliquist	.400	10	4	1	0	1	2	1	1	.455	.800	John Smoltz	.091	11	1	0	0	0	1	1	1	.167	.091
Bob Kipper	.389	18	7	2	0	2	3	2	3	.450	.833	John Burkett	.100	20	2	0	0	0	0	0	5	.100	.100

Mike Dunne — White Sox
Pitches Right (groundball pitcher)

	ERA	W	L	Sv	G	GS	IP	BB	SO	Avg	H	2B	3B	HR	RBI	OBP	SLG	GF	IR	IRS	Hld	SvOp	SB	CS	GB	FB	G/F
1992 Season	4.26	2	0	0	4	1	12.2	6	6	.255	12	1	0	0	6	.352	.277	0	0	0	1	1	0	0	22	13	1.69
Last Five Years	4.63	12	24	0	62	53	311.0	157	133	.272	328	53	4	27	149	.357	.390	0	7	1	1	1	37	9	521	331	1.57

1992 Season

	ERA	W	L	Sv	G	GS	IP	H	HR	BB	SO		Avg	AB	H	2B	3B	HR	RBI	BB	SO	OBP	SLG
Home	3.60	0	0	0	1	1	5.0	3	0	3	3	vs. Left	.222	27	6	0	0	0	2	1	3	.250	.222
Away	4.70	2	0	0	3	0	7.2	9	0	3	3	vs. Right	.300	20	6	1	0	0	4	5	3	.462	.350

Last Five Years

	ERA	W	L	Sv	G	GS	IP	H	HR	BB	SO		Avg	AB	H	2B	3B	HR	RBI	BB	SO	OBP	SLG
Home	3.89	8	12	0	33	31	187.1	179	20	88	80	vs. Left	.261	615	173	31	4	8	71	96	41	.376	.384
Away	5.75	4	12	0	29	22	123.2	149	7	69	53	vs. Right	.262	591	155	22	0	19	78	61	92	.336	.396
Day	4.52	2	5	0	17	13	79.2	73	8	45	29	Inning 1-6	.273	1061	295	49	3	24	135	136	117	.355	.390
Night	4.67	10	19	0	45	40	231.1	255	19	112	104	Inning 7+	.264	125	33	4	1	3	14	21	16	.369	.384
Grass	5.86	2	5	0	25	20	101.1	119	9	58	50	Runners on	.284	553	157	25	1	10	132	73	55	.366	.387
Turf	4.03	10	13	0	37	33	209.2	209	18	99	83	Scoring Posn	.273	337	92	17	0	6	121	57	38	.372	.377
April	6.10	2	2	0	6	6	31.0	43	2	13	14	Close & Late	.255	47	12	2	0	1	6	13	6	.410	.362
May	5.43	3	6	0	12	11	58.0	76	8	26	29	None on/out	.254	303	77	15	0	9	9	35	37	.335	.393
June	4.07	2	5	0	11	9	55.1	44	6	40	22	vs. 1st Batr (relief)	.571	7	4	1	0	1	2	1	0	.556	1.143
July	4.44	1	4	0	10	9	52.2	44	3	29	18												
August	3.91	1	6	0	13	11	71.1	76	6	26	37	First Inning Pitched	.291	230	67	10	1	6	45	44	26	.398	.422
September/October	4.64	3	1	0	10	7	42.2	45	2	23	13	First 15 Pitches	.293	198	58	10	1	4	20	31	19	.387	.414
Starter	4.70	10	24	0	53	53	293.0	313	25	153	123	Pitch 16-30	.250	200	50	5	0	6	34	30	22	.343	.365
Reliever	3.50	2	0	0	9	0	18.0	15	2	4	10	Pitch 31-45	.264	216	57	11	0	2	22	21	18	.335	.343
0 Days rest	0.00	0	0	0	0	0	0.0	0	0	0	0	Pitch 46+	.275	592	163	27	3	15	73	75	74	.359	.407
1 or 2 Days rest	0.00	0	0	0	2	0	3.1	3	0	0	0	First Pitch	.332	211	70	17	0	4	33	3	0	.339	.469
3+ Days rest	4.30	2	0	0	7	0	14.2	12	2	4	10	Ahead on Count	.238	480	114	18	0	10	51	0	112	.242	.338
Pre-All Star	5.02	8	14	0	32	29	159.2	175	16	93	71	Behind on Count	.298	322	96	11	1	8	45	96	0	.459	.413
Post-All Star	4.22	4	10	0	30	24	151.1	153	11	64	62	Two Strikes	.220	468	103	17	0	8	45	58	132	.308	.308

Pitcher vs. Batter (career)

Pitches Best Vs.	Avg	AB	H	2B	3B	HR	RBI	BB	SO	OBP	SLG	Pitches Worst Vs.	Avg	AB	H	2B	3B	HR	RBI	BB	SO	OBP	SLG
Lance Parrish	.071	14	1	0	0	0	0	5	3	.316	.071	Dave Martinez	.500	16	8	0	2	0	0	1	1	.529	.750
Jeff Reed	.091	11	1	0	0	0	0	0	0	.091	.091	Mitch Webster	.444	27	12	0	1	3	6	2	4	.483	.852
Billy Doran	.100	10	1	0	0	0	0	1	1	.182	.100	Glenn Davis	.444	9	4	1	0	2	4	3	2	.583	1.222
Chris James	.118	17	2	0	0	0	4	1	2	.167	.118	Von Hayes	.412	17	7	1	0	1	3	7	3	.583	.647
Tony Pena	.154	13	2	0	0	0	3	1	2	.154	.154	Kal Daniels	.333	9	3	3	0	0	0	4	0	.538	.667

Shawon Dunston — Cubs   Bats Right

	Avg	G	AB	R	H	2B	3B	HR	RBI	BB	SO	HBP	GDP	SB	CS	OBP	SLG	IBB	SH	SF	#Pit	#P/PA	GB	FB	G/F
1992 Season	.315	18	73	8	23	3	1	0	2	3	13	0	0	2	3	.342	.384	0	0	0	288	3.79	17	18	0.94
Last Five Years	.263	599	2156	261	568	90	28	47	234	87	358	10	31	97	34	.292	.397	29	18	23	7438	3.27	745	661	1.13

1992 Season

	Avg	AB	H	2B	3B	HR	RBI	BB	SO	OBP	SLG		Avg	AB	H	2B	3B	HR	RBI	BB	SO	OBP	SLG
vs. Left	.417	24	10	0	0	0	0	0	4	.417	.417	Scoring Posn	.100	10	1	0	0	0	1	0	3	.100	.100
vs. Right	.265	49	13	3	1	0	2	3	9	.308	.367	Close & Late	.286	14	4	0	0	0	0	0	2	.286	.286

Last Five Years

	Avg	AB	H	2B	3B	HR	RBI	BB	SO	OBP	SLG		Avg	AB	H	2B	3B	HR	RBI	BB	SO	OBP	SLG
vs. Left	.274	712	195	27	12	20	83	27	96	.298	.430	Scoring Posn	.258	504	130	16	10	13	184	38	88	.301	.407
vs. Right	.258	1444	373	63	16	27	151	60	262	.289	.380	Close & Late	.281	398	112	14	4	6	46	17	70	.315	.382
Groundball	.275	737	203	36	13	10	73	28	102	.301	.400	None on/out	.273	590	161	26	6	11	11	23	97	.305	.393
Flyball	.247	507	125	22	6	15	63	20	97	.277	.402	Batting #7	.268	877	235	37	13	23	92	36	138	.293	.418
Home	.282	1021	288	45	13	22	113	42	167	.313	.416	Batting #8	.269	687	185	30	8	16	87	34	126	.308	.406
Away	.247	1135	280	45	15	25	121	45	191	.273	.379	Other	.250	592	148	23	7	8	55	17	94	.273	.353
Day	.279	1147	320	54	11	27	128	47	197	.308	.416	April	.255	333	85	12	3	9	29	18	52	.291	.390
Night	.246	1009	248	36	17	20	106	40	161	.274	.375	May	.269	368	99	17	3	10	41	16	63	.303	.413
Grass	.272	1494	407	65	17	36	167	59	259	.301	.411	June	.277	368	102	19	5	11	60	10	67	.299	.446
Turf	.243	662	161	25	11	11	67	28	99	.272	.364	July	.254	358	91	12	4	7	34	18	60	.288	.369
First Pitch	.334	332	111	22	3	10	52	18	0	.368	.509	August	.295	386	114	18	9	5	42	14	66	.318	.427
Ahead on Count	.291	368	107	11	8	13	48	51	0	.373	.470	September/October	.224	343	77	12	4	5	28	11	50	.250	.327
Behind on Count	.231	914	211	30	10	16	72	0	259	.232	.338	Pre-All Star	.265	1191	316	53	11	34	144	49	206	.295	.414
Two Strikes	.195	916	179	28	9	12	68	12	358	.207	.285	Post-All Star	.261	965	252	37	17	13	90	38	152	.288	.375

Batter vs. Pitcher (career)

Hits Best Against	Avg	AB	H	2B	3B	HR	RBI	BB	SO	OBP	SLG	Hits Worst Against	Avg	AB	H	2B	3B	HR	RBI	BB	SO	OBP	SLG
Cris Carpenter	.500	12	6	1	1	0	4	0	2	.500	.750	Nolan Ryan	.080	25	2	0	0	0	1	1	12	.115	.080
John Burkett	.364	11	4	0	0	1	2	0	1	.364	.636	Steve Avery	.083	12	1	0	0	0	0	1	4	.154	.083
Mike Maddux	.333	18	6	3	0	1	2	2	6	.400	.667	Ken Hill	.125	16	2	0	0	0	1	0	5	.125	.125
Mike Morgan	.333	15	5	2	0	1	2	2	1	.412	.667	Todd Worrell	.133	15	2	0	0	0	2	0	4	.133	.133
Craig Lefferts	.333	15	5	0	0	2	5	0	3	.333	.733	Tom Glavine	.150	20	3	0	0	0	0	4		.150	.150

Lenny Dykstra — Phillies   Bats Left

	Avg	G	AB	R	H	2B	3B	HR	RBI	BB	SO	HBP	GDP	SB	CS	OBP	SLG	IBB	SH	SF	#Pit	#P/PA	GB	FB	G/F
1992 Season	.301	85	345	53	104	18	0	6	39	40	32	3	1	30	5	.375	.406	4	0	4	1473	3.76	139	96	1.45
Last Five Years	.286	569	2121	330	606	117	15	33	176	256	196	17	17	147	34	.365	.402	22	9	14	8699	3.61	787	644	1.22

1992 Season

	Avg	AB	H	2B	3B	HR	RBI	BB	SO	OBP	SLG		Avg	AB	H	2B	3B	HR	RBI	BB	SO	OBP	SLG
vs. Left	.322	146	47	7	0	4	23	16	15	.389	.452	Scoring Posn	.368	68	25	5	0	1	31	12	6	.440	.485

1992 Season

	Avg	AB	H	2B	3B	HR	RBI	BB	SO	OBP	SLG		Avg	AB	H	2B	3B	HR	RBI	BB	SO	OBP	SLG
vs. Right	.286	199	57	11	0	2	16	24	17	.364	.372	Close & Late	.414	58	24	3	0	1	15	4	5	.446	.517
Groundball	.288	153	44	6	0	3	12	9	9	.331	.386	None on/out	.260	150	39	6	0	2	2	16	17	.339	.340
Flyball	.240	75	18	3	0	2	10	13	14	.348	.360	Total	.301	345	104	18	0	6	39	40	32	.375	.406
Home	.306	196	60	8	0	5	27	26	18	.385	.423	Batting #1	.301	345	104	18	0	6	39	40	32	.375	.406
Away	.295	149	44	10	0	1	12	14	14	.361	.383	Other	.000	0	0	0	0	0	0	0	0	.000	.000
Day	.291	86	25	5	0	1	11	8	7	.371	.384	April	.172	29	5	2	0	0	2	3	3	.273	.241
Night	.305	259	79	13	0	5	28	32	25	.376	.413	May	.277	101	28	4	0	3	16	13	10	.362	.406
Grass	.236	55	13	4	0	0	3	4	4	.300	.309	June	.314	102	32	7	0	0	10	10	8	.374	.382
Turf	.314	290	91	14	0	6	36	36	28	.389	.424	July	.379	58	22	3	0	2	8	9	5	.456	.534
First Pitch	.235	51	12	3	0	1	5	3	0	.278	.353	August	.309	55	17	2	0	1	3	5	6	.367	.400
Ahead on Count	.333	87	29	2	0	3	9	26	0	.491	.460	September/October	.000	0	0	0	0	0	0	0	0	.000	.000
Behind on Count	.277	94	26	3	0	0	10	0	17	.276	.309	Pre-All Star	.280	232	65	13	0	3	28	26	21	.356	.375
Two Strikes	.299	144	43	8	0	1	17	11	32	.348	.375	Post-All Star	.345	113	39	5	0	3	11	14	11	.414	.469

1992 By Position

Position	Avg	AB	H	2B	3B	HR	RBI	BB	SO	OBP	SLG	G	GS	Innings	PO	A	E	DP	Fld Pct	Rng Fctr	In Zone	Outs	Zone Rtg	MLB Zone
As cf	.301	345	104	18	0	6	39	40	32	.375	.406	85	85	750.2	252	6	3	4	.989	3.09	303	249	822	824

Last Five Years

	Avg	AB	H	2B	3B	HR	RBI	BB	SO	OBP	SLG		Avg	AB	H	2B	3B	HR	RBI	BB	SO	OBP	SLG
vs. Left	.282	667	188	26	8	8	58	83	81	.364	.381	Scoring Posn	.303	366	111	20	3	2	130	79	42	.418	.391
vs. Right	.287	1454	418	91	7	25	118	173	165	.365	.411	None on/out	.256	917	235	43	9	18	18	105	83	.338	.382
Groundball	.260	789	205	36	7	8	55	83	77	.333	.354	Batting #1	.285	2061	587	112	14	32	170	243	187	.363	.399
Flyball	.299	451	135	34	1	11	52	68	51	.390	.452	Batting #9	.381	21	8	3	0	0	2	5	2	.481	.524
Home	.294	1029	303	52	6	22	83	145	92	.383	.421	Other	.282	39	11	2	1	1	4	8	7	.400	.462
Away	.277	1092	303	65	9	11	93	111	104	.348	.384	April	.315	270	85	24	4	6	29	36	20	.401	.500
Day	.277	632	175	40	2	13	57	75	59	.358	.408	May	.302	367	111	20	1	5	34	46	36	.383	.403
Night	.289	1489	431	77	13	20	119	181	137	.366	.399	June	.321	383	123	22	2	5	31	46	28	.394	.428
Grass	.256	788	202	43	6	10	65	84	79	.331	.364	July	.296	395	117	20	3	3	25	56	37	.387	.380
Turf	.303	1333	404	74	9	23	111	172	117	.385	.424	August	.252	457	115	26	5	8	32	40	47	.315	.383
First Pitch	.295	376	111	25	2	8	50	5	0	.304	.436	September/October	.221	249	55	5	1	6	25	32	28	.309	.321
Ahead on Count	.324	513	166	29	7	12	42	144	0	.474	.478	Pre-All Star	.306	1106	338	71	7	16	100	143	89	.388	.426
Behind on Count	.250	619	155	27	6	2	38	1	107	.256	.323	Post-All Star	.254	1015	268	46	8	17	76	113	107	.340	.375
Two Strikes	.224	834	187	33	4	7	51	94	196	.306	.299												

Batter vs. Pitcher (career)

Hits Best Against	Avg	AB	H	2B	3B	HR	RBI	BB	SO	OBP	SLG	Hits Worst Against	Avg	AB	H	2B	3B	HR	RBI	BB	SO	OBP	SLG
Paul Assenmacher	.615	13	8	2	0	1	4	0	3	.571	1.000	Norm Charlton	.000	10	0	0	0	0	0	1	4	.091	.000
Ken Hill	.600	20	12	2	0	1	1	4	0	.667	.850	Tim Burke	.077	13	1	0	0	0	0	2	3	.200	.077
Ron Darling	.500	10	5	2	0	0	1	2	1	.583	.700	Joe Magrane	.087	23	2	0	0	0	0	1	1	.125	.087
Jim Deshaies	.429	7	3	0	1	0	1	4	0	.636	.714	Greg W. Harris	.118	17	2	0	0	0	0	1	2	.167	.118
Mark Grant	.400	10	4	2	0	1	1	1	1	.455	.900	John Franco	.133	15	2	0	0	0	0	1	0	.133	.133

Damion Easley — Angels

Bats Right

	Avg	G	AB	R	H	2B	3B	HR	RBI	BB	SO	HBP	GDP	SB	CS	OBP	SLG	IBB	SH	SF	#Pit	#P/PA	GB	FB	G/F
1992 Season	.258	47	151	14	39	5	0	1	12	8	26	3	2	9	5	.307	.311	0	2	1	605	3.71	54	44	1.23

1992 Season

	Avg	AB	H	2B	3B	HR	RBI	BB	SO	OBP	SLG		Avg	AB	H	2B	3B	HR	RBI	BB	SO	OBP	SLG
vs. Left	.278	36	10	1	0	0	3	2	6	.316	.306	Scoring Posn	.265	34	9	0	0	1	12	2	6	.316	.353
vs. Right	.252	115	29	4	0	1	9	6	20	.304	.313	Close & Late	.235	34	8	0	0	1	4	1	7	.257	.324
Home	.269	67	18	2	0	1	6	4	11	.329	.343	None on/out	.306	49	15	5	0	0	4	8	.370	.408	
Away	.250	84	21	3	0	0	6	4	15	.289	.286	Batting #1	.242	33	8	0	0	0	1	2	10	.286	.242
First Pitch	.333	21	7	1	0	0	1	0	0	.333	.381	Batting #9	.351	37	13	2	0	0	3	2	4	.390	.405
Ahead on Count	.447	38	17	2	0	1	7	5	0	.533	.579	Other	.222	81	18	3	0	1	8	4	12	.276	.296
Behind on Count	.140	50	7	0	0	0	3	0	16	.137	.140	Pre-All Star	.000	0	0	0	0	0	0	0	0	.000	.000
Two Strikes	.159	69	11	2	0	0	1	3	26	.205	.188	Post-All Star	.258	151	39	5	0	1	12	8	26	.307	.311

Dennis Eckersley — Athletics

Pitches Right (flyball pitcher)

	ERA	W	L	Sv	IP	BB	SO	Avg	H	2B	3B	HR	RBI	OBP	SLG	GF	Hld	SvOp	SB	CS	GB	FB	G/F
1992 Season	1.91	7	1	51	80.0	11	93	.211	62	11	1	5	18	.242	.306	65	31	2	0	54	9	63	93	0.68
Last Five Years	1.90	24	9	220	359.2	38	378	.190	247	36	4	28	110	.214	.288	185	197	47	2	247	24	5	315	412	0.76

1992 Season

	ERA	W	L	Sv	G	GS	IP	H	HR	BB	SO		Avg	AB	H	2B	3B	HR	RBI	BB	SO	OBP	SLG
Home	2.76	7	0	21	35	0	42.1	37	4	8	55	vs. Left	.262	149	39	7	0	3	11	8	33	.299	.369
Away	0.96	0	1	30	34	0	37.2	25	1	3	38	vs. Right	.159	145	23	4	1	2	7	3	60	.181	.241
Day	1.99	3	0	16	22	0	22.2	21	0	3	32	Inning 1-6	.000	0	0	0	0	0	0	0	0	.000	.000
Night	1.88	4	1	35	47	0	57.1	41	5	8	61	Inning 7+	.211	294	62	11	1	5	18	11	93	.242	.306
Grass	2.06	7	1	41	57	0	65.2	54	5	10	78	None on	.235	162	38	6	1	4	4	4	52	.257	.358
Turf	1.26	0	0	10	12	0	14.1	8	0	1	15	Runners on	.182	132	24	5	0	1	14	7	41	.223	.242

122

1992 Season

	ERA	W	L	Sv	G	GS	IP	H	HR	BB	SO		Avg	AB	H	2B	3B	HR	RBI	BB	SO	OBP	SLG
April	0.82	1	0	8	10	0	11.0	7	0	1	13	Scoring Posn	.158	76	12	3	0	1	14	7	28	.229	.237
May	0.79	0	0	10	10	0	11.1	8	1	0	17	Close & Late	.172	227	39	7	1	1	12	8	75	.200	.225
June	3.31	1	0	9	13	0	16.1	17	1	3	16	None on/out	.215	65	14	3	0	1	1		20	.227	.308
July	0.87	1	0	6	9	0	10.1	6	1	1	11	vs. 1st Batr (relief)	.179	67	12	2	1	1	1	2	20	.203	.284
August	3.21	3	1	9	13	0	14.0	13	0	4	13	First Inning Pitched	.219	242	53	10	1	3	15	7	74	.241	.306
September/October	1.59	1	0	9	14	0	17.0	11	2	2	23	First 15 Pitches	.226	226	51	10	1	5	12	5	68	.246	.345
Starter	0.00	0	0	0	0	0	0.0	0	0	0	0	Pitch 16-30	.156	64	10	1	0	0	6	6	23	.229	.172
Reliever	1.91	7	1	51	69	0	80.0	62	5	11	93	Pitch 31-45	.250	4	1	0	0	0	0	0	2	.250	.250
0 Days rest	2.38	1	0	18	21	0	22.2	17	1	1	25	Pitch 46+	.000	0	0	0	0	0	0	0	0	.000	.000
1 or 2 Days rest	1.93	4	1	20	30	0	37.1	27	3	8	42	First Pitch	.333	30	10	2	0	1	1	5	0	.429	.500
3+ Days rest	1.35	2	0	13	18	0	20.0	18	1	2	26	Ahead on Count	.167	198	33	6	1	3	9	0	87	.171	.253
Pre-All Star	1.67	2	0	30	37	0	43.0	35	2	5	50	Behind on Count	.346	26	9	3	0	1	5	4	0	.433	.577
Post-All Star	2.19	5	1	21	32	0	37.0	27	3	6	43	Two Strikes	.157	185	29	3	0	3	10	2	93	.166	.222

Last Five Years

	ERA	W	L	Sv	G	GS	IP	H	HR	BB	SO		Avg	AB	H	2B	3B	HR	RBI	BB	SO	OBP	SLG
Home	2.02	20	4	102	158	0	187.0	124	15	26	212	vs. Left	.215	642	138	19	1	13	57	22	136	.242	.308
Away	1.77	4	5	118	152	0	172.2	123	13	12	166	vs. Right	.166	658	109	17	3	15	53	16	242	.186	.269
Day	1.97	11	4	83	126	0	146.1	103	10	23	161	Inning 1-6	.000	0	0	0	0	0	0	0	0	.000	.000
Night	1.86	13	5	137	184	0	213.1	144	18	15	217	Inning 7+	.190	1300	247	36	4	28	110	38	378	.214	.288
Grass	1.87	23	7	181	262	0	302.2	205	24	33	321	Runners on	.193	784	151	23	4	14		14	233	.211	.286
Turf	2.05	1	2	39	48	0	57.0	42	4	5	57	Runners on	.186	516	96	13	0	14	96	24	145	.219	.293
April	0.85	3	1	39	46	0	52.2	29	2	3	49	Scoring Posn	.189	291	55	10	0	8	83	20	87	.235	.306
May	2.05	3	1	37	50	0	57.0	45	5	2	68	Close & Late	.175	753	132	21	3	14	71	25	231	.203	.267
June	1.71	2	1	34	44	0	52.2	42	3	9	47	None on/out	.197	300	59	10	1	5	5		85	.207	.287
July	2.47	1	3	30	47	0	54.2	34	8	6	64	vs. 1st Batr (relief)	.192	302	58	10	1	5	24	5	85	.206	.281
August	2.07	7	1	42	58	0	65.1	50	3	9	65	First Inning Pitched	.183	1031	191	28	3	21	85	27	203	.205	.277
September/October	2.09	8	2	38	65	0	77.1	47	7	9	85	First 15 Pitches	.195	955	186	29	3	21	73	24	263	.215	.297
Starter	0.00	0	0	0	0	0	0.0	0	0	0	0	Pitch 16-30	.170	311	53	6	0	6	30	11	103	.201	.248
Reliever	1.90	24	9	220	310	0	359.2	247	28	38	378	Pitch 31-45	.235	34	8	1	1	1	7	3	12	.297	.412
0 Days rest	1.20	5	0	66	78	0	82.2	56	3	9	85	Pitch 46+	.000	0	0	0	0	0	0	0	0	.000	.000
1 or 2 Days rest	2.54	13	7	93	134	0	159.2	119	17	18	170	First Pitch	.314	159	50	6	0	3	11	10	0	.355	.409
3+ Days rest	1.53	6	2	61	98	0	117.1	72	8	11	123	Ahead on Count	.151	842	127	20	3	16	48	0	340	.153	.239
Pre-All Star	1.51	8	3	118	152	0	179.0	127	11	16	178	Behind on Count	.298	114	34	7	1	5	23	11	0	.354	.509
Post-All Star	2.29	16	6	102	158	0	180.2	120	17	22	200	Two Strikes	.124	788	98	12	2	10	36	16	378	.143	.183

Pitcher vs. Batter (since 1984)

Pitches Best Vs.	Avg	AB	H	2B	3B	HR	RBI	BB	SO	OBP	SLG	Pitches Worst Vs.	Avg	AB	H	2B	3B	HR	RBI	BB	SO	OBP	SLG
Lance Parrish	.000	12	0	0	0	0	0	0	5	.000	.000	Jim Eisenreich	.500	10	5	2	0	0	1	1	3	.545	.700
Kirby Puckett	.063	16	1	0	0	0	1	0	4	.059	.063	Tim Raines	.421	19	8	2	0	0	2	1	2	.450	.526
Pat Tabler	.077	13	1	0	0	0	0	1	4	.143	.077	Tom Brunansky	.364	11	4	2	0	1	3	0	2	.364	.818
Mickey Tettleton	.077	13	1	0	0	0	0	0	4	.077	.077	Gene Larkin	.357	14	5	3	0	0	1	0	0	.357	.571
Dave Bergman	.125	16	2	0	0	0	2	0	5	.125	.125	Alvin Davis	.333	9	3	0	0	2	5	2	1	.455	1.000

Tom Edens — Twins

Pitches Right (groundball pitcher)

	ERA	W	L	Sv	G	GS	IP	BB	SO	Avg	H	2B	3B	HR	RBI	OBP	SLG	GF	IR	IRS	Hld	SvOp	SB	CS	GB	FB	G/F
1992 Season	2.83	6	3	3	52	0	76.1	36	57	.236	65	8	3	1	26	.329	.298	14	47	11	11	5	15	5	100	64	1.56
Last Five Years	3.77	12	10	5	95	12	198.1	79	116	.251	188	28	6	11	82	.326	.349	23	74	19	13	7	26	12	298	185	1.61

1992 Season

	ERA	W	L	Sv	G	GS	IP	H	HR	BB	SO		Avg	AB	H	2B	3B	HR	RBI	BB	SO	OBP	SLG
Home	3.80	5	1	2	26	0	42.2	37	1	23	39	vs. Left	.248	109	27	1	2	0	12	7	29	.299	.294
Away	1.60	1	2	1	26	0	33.2	28	0	13	18	vs. Right	.229	166	38	7	1	1	14	29	28	.347	.301
Starter	0.00	0	0	0	0	0	0.0	0	0	0	0	Scoring Posn	.239	88	21	3	1	0	24	16	20	.356	.295
Reliever	2.83	6	3	3	52	0	76.1	65	1	36	57	Close & Late	.211	109	23	3	0	1	6	14	24	.306	.266
0 Days rest	4.91	1	0	0	6	0	7.1	10	0	7	5	None on/out	.273	66	18	3	1	1	1	6	13	.333	.394
1 or 2 Days rest	3.50	1	2	3	29	0	23.2	38	0	20	31	First Pitch	.205	39	8	1	0	0	2	1	0	.225	.231
3+ Days rest	1.07	4	0	0	17	0	25.1	17	1	9	21	Behind on Count	.230	61	14	3	1	0	5	20	0	.427	.311
Pre-All Star	1.17	5	0	2	28	0	46.0	31	0	18	32	Ahead on Count	.197	117	23	2	1	0	12	0	43	.203	.231
Post-All Star	5.34	1	3	1	24	0	30.1	34	1	18	25	Two Strikes	.213	141	30	3	1	1	13	15	56	.293	.270

Mark Eichhorn — Blue Jays

Pitches Right (groundball pitcher)

	ERA	W	L	Sv	G	GS	IP	BB	SO	Avg	H	2B	3B	HR	RBI	OBP	SLG	GF	IR	IRS	Hld	SvOp	SB	CS	GB	FB	G/F
1992 Season	3.08	4	4	2	65	0	87.2	25	61	.255	86	11	4	3	43	.306	.338	26	44	19	5	6	6	2	152	60	2.53
Last Five Years	3.26	14	20	17	277	0	389.0	107	256	.268	396	66	9	16	206	.321	.357	89	343	112	44	29	28	13	659	305	2.16

1992 Season

	ERA	W	L	Sv	G	GS	IP	H	HR	BB	SO		Avg	AB	H	2B	3B	HR	RBI	BB	SO	OBP	SLG
Home	3.79	3	0	2	30	0	40.1	46	2	8	32	vs. Left	.341	129	44	4	2	2	20	14	25	.400	.450
Away	2.47	1	4	0	35	0	47.1	40	1	17	29	vs. Right	.202	208	42	7	2	1	23	11	36	.246	.269
Day	2.92	3	3	0	25	0	37.0	44	2	9	20	Inning 1-6	.298	47	14	1	1	1	17	2	11	.302	.426

1992 Season

	ERA	W	L	Sv	G	GS	IP	H	HR	BB	SO
Night	3.20	1	1	2	40	0	50.2	42	1	16	41
Grass	3.03	3	3	2	49	0	65.1	59	2	20	45
Turf	3.22	1	1	0	16	0	22.1	27	1	5	16
April	2.76	0	0	0	11	0	16.1	16	1	3	6
May	2.00	1	3	0	12	0	18.0	14	1	6	14
June	0.96	0	0	1	8	0	9.1	9	0	0	4
July	3.46	1	1	1	11	0	13.0	12	0	9	18
August	4.79	2	0	0	14	0	20.2	23	0	6	11
September/October	3.48	0	0	0	9	0	10.1	12	1	1	8
Starter	0.00	0	0	0	0	0	0.0	0	0	0	0
Reliever	3.08	4	4	2	65	0	87.2	86	3	25	61
0 Days rest	1.35	2	0	0	11	0	13.1	11	0	4	9
1 or 2 Days rest	4.35	2	3	1	37	0	49.2	55	2	18	31
3+ Days rest	1.46	0	1	1	17	0	24.2	20	1	3	21
Pre-All Star	2.13	1	4	1	36	0	50.2	45	2	16	34
Post-All Star	4.38	3	0	1	29	0	37.0	41	1	9	27

	Avg	AB	H	2B	3B	HR	RBI	BB	SO	OBP	SLG
Inning 7+	.248	290	72	10	3	2	26	23	50	.307	.324
None on	.236	182	43	4	2	2	2	7	28	.268	.313
Runners on	.277	155	43	7	2	1	41	18	33	.346	.368
Scoring Posn	.255	106	27	4	1	1	40	18	24	.349	.340
Close & Late	.309	136	42	5	1	2	15	14	27	.377	.404
None on/out	.244	78	19	4	1	1	1	3	14	.280	.359
vs. 1st Batr (relief)	.288	59	17	4	0	1	12	5	13	.338	.407
First Inning Pitched	.243	214	52	5	3	2	32	12	44	.283	.322
First 15 Pitches	.245	216	53	5	4	2	28	13	38	.291	.333
Pitch 16-30	.253	99	25	4	0	1	9	10	19	.315	.323
Pitch 31-45	.368	19	7	1	0	0	5	1	4	.400	.421
Pitch 46+	.333	3	1	1	0	0	1	0	0	.500	.667
First Pitch	.291	55	16	2	2	0	10	6	0	.354	.400
Ahead on Count	.187	150	28	3	0	1	8	0	52	.187	.227
Behind on Count	.297	74	22	3	0	1	14	13	0	.398	.378
Two Strikes	.162	130	21	1	0	1	9	6	61	.197	.200

Last Five Years

	ERA	W	L	Sv	G	GS	IP	H	HR	BB	SO
Home	3.43	8	10	6	135	0	194.1	203	8	51	126
Away	3.10	6	10	11	142	0	194.2	193	8	56	130
Day	3.07	5	9	4	91	0	140.2	152	6	38	92
Night	3.37	9	11	13	186	0	248.1	244	10	69	164
Grass	3.22	9	18	12	205	0	276.2	275	12	68	188
Turf	3.36	5	2	5	72	0	112.1	121	4	39	68
April	3.01	0	4	4	41	0	71.2	65	1	19	42
May	2.08	1	7	5	44	0	69.1	65	4	17	42
June	1.80	3	1	6	55	0	65.0	69	2	9	44
July	4.73	4	3	1	47	0	66.2	79	2	24	54
August	4.55	4	3	1	47	0	63.1	64	3	23	43
September/October	3.57	2	2	0	43	0	53.0	54	4	15	31
Starter	0.00	0	0	0	0	0	0.0	0	0	0	0
Reliever	3.26	14	20	17	277	0	389.0	396	16	107	256
0 Days rest	3.65	4	4	5	62	0	74.0	78	2	25	50
1 or 2 Days rest	3.30	6	11	9	137	0	193.2	196	8	55	139
3+ Days rest	2.97	4	5	3	78	0	121.1	122	6	27	67
Pre-All Star	2.73	4	14	15	158	0	234.1	234	9	59	147
Post-All Star	4.07	10	6	2	119	0	154.2	162	7	48	109

	Avg	AB	H	2B	3B	HR	RBI	BB	SO	OBP	SLG
vs. Left	.305	656	200	31	5	7	90	50	97	.356	.399
vs. Right	.238	823	196	35	4	9	116	57	159	.293	.323
Inning 1-6	.304	247	75	11	2	4	59	21	40	.358	.413
Inning 7+	.261	1232	321	55	7	12	147	86	216	.313	.346
None on	.260	730	190	31	3	7	7	38	111	.301	.340
Runners on	.275	749	206	35	6	9	199	69	145	.339	.374
Scoring Posn	.259	526	136	23	2	8	190	54	110	.327	.356
Close & Late	.262	546	143	27	2	5	68	49	103	.327	.346
None on/out	.266	319	85	21	1	3	3	15	48	.308	.367
vs. 1st Batr (relief)	.282	259	73	18	0	5	46	14	50	.322	.409
First Inning Pitched	.261	914	239	39	5	13	156	61	173	.312	.358
First 15 Pitches	.265	893	237	38	6	10	130	52	148	.311	.355
Pitch 16-30	.237	426	101	19	1	5	42	42	83	.306	.322
Pitch 31-45	.372	121	45	6	2	0	27	8	19	.415	.455
Pitch 46+	.333	39	13	3	0	1	7	5	6	.422	.487
First Pitch	.265	196	52	11	2	2	24	15	0	.317	.372
Ahead on Count	.224	686	154	21	4	6	84	0	222	.229	.293
Behind on Count	.297	330	98	18	0	2	52	56	0	.406	.370
Two Strikes	.193	611	118	14	4	9	70	36	256	.240	.273

Pitcher vs. Batter (since 1984)

Pitches Best Vs.	Avg	AB	H	2B	3B	HR	RBI	BB	SO	OBP	SLG
Cecil Fielder	.000	12	0	0	0	0	1	0	5	.000	.000
Brook Jacoby	.050	20	1	0	0	0	1	1	3	.095	.050
Randy Bush	.056	18	1	1	0	0	2	0	3	.056	.111
Steve Buechele	.063	16	1	0	0	0	0	1	3	.118	.063
Rob Deer	.118	17	2	0	0	0	0	0	10	.118	.118

Pitches Worst Vs.	Avg	AB	H	2B	3B	HR	RBI	BB	SO	OBP	SLG
Dave Valle	.455	11	5	2	0	0	3	1	0	.500	.636
Jim Eisenreich	.444	9	4	1	0	0	0	2	0	.545	.556
Tom Brunansky	.438	16	7	3	0	1	8	3	1	.526	.813
Mark McGwire	.438	16	7	0	0	1	5	1	3	.471	.625
Mickey Tettleton	.364	11	4	0	0	4	5	2	5	.429	1.455

Dave Eiland — Padres

Pitches Right (groundball pitcher)

	ERA	W	L	Sv	G	GS	IP	BB	SO	Avg	H	2B	3B	HR	RBI	OBP	SLG	CG	ShO	Sup	QS	#P/S	SB	CS	GB	FB	G/F
1992 Season	5.67	0	2	0	7	7	27.0	5	10	.287	33	8	2	1	17	.317	.417	0	0	5.00	1	60	4	0	67	17	3.94
Career (1988-1992)	5.24	5	11	0	39	34	177.0	50	62	.296	206	42	10	24	105	.346	.485	0	0	4.93	9	72	15	5	333	180	1.85

1992 Season

	ERA	W	L	Sv	G	GS	IP	H	HR	BB	SO
Home	6.32	0	1	0	5	5	15.2	22	1	3	8
Away	4.76	0	1	0	2	2	11.1	11	0	2	2

	Avg	AB	H	2B	3B	HR	RBI	BB	SO	OBP	SLG
vs. Left	.364	66	24	6	2	1	12	2	4	.382	.561
vs. Right	.184	49	9	2	0	0	5	3	6	.231	.224

Career (1988-1992)

	ERA	W	L	Sv	G	GS	IP	H	HR	BB	SO
Home	5.56	4	5	0	23	21	100.1	118	16	28	42
Away	4.81	1	6	0	16	13	76.2	92	8	22	20
Day	8.48	2	3	0	11	8	40.1	65	8	10	6
Night	4.28	3	8	0	28	26	136.2	145	16	40	56
Grass	5.48	5	10	0	37	32	164.1	197	24	47	60
Turf	2.13	0	1	0	2	2	12.2	13	0	3	2
April	3.99	1	2	0	8	8	38.1	38	3	9	13
May	8.02	0	3	0	6	6	21.1	35	2	9	5
June	3.62	1	1	0	4	4	27.1	23	2	11	8
July	7.88	0	2	0	4	4	16.0	26	3	4	6
August	8.10	0	2	0	7	5	26.2	39	9	11	12
September/October	3.42	3	1	0	10	7	47.1	49	5	6	18
Starter	5.18	5	11	0	34	34	166.2	193	19	47	60

	Avg	AB	H	2B	3B	HR	RBI	BB	SO	OBP	SLG
vs. Left	.305	390	119	23	8	14	54	28	22	.352	.513
vs. Right	.284	320	91	19	2	10	51	22	40	.339	.450
Inning 1-6	.301	652	196	40	9	21	101	48	57	.353	.486
Inning 7+	.241	58	14	2	1	3	4	2	5	.267	.466
None on	.279	419	117	22	2	15	15	30	36	.332	.449
Runners on	.320	291	93	20	8	9	90	20	26	.366	.536
Scoring Posn	.333	168	56	14	4	2	66	14	18	.381	.500
Close & Late	.267	15	4	1	1	0	1	0	1	.267	.467
None on/out	.289	190	55	14	1	7	7	11	16	.335	.484
vs. 1st Batr (relief)	.400	5	2	0	0	2	4	0	0	.400	1.600
First Inning Pitched	.276	156	43	8	3	8	24	18	13	.354	.519
First 75 Pitches	.297	634	188	38	7	23	98	47	54	.349	.487
Pitch 76-90	.286	56	16	3	2	0	6	2	7	.310	.411

Career (1988-1992)

	ERA	W	L	Sv	G	GS	IP	H	HR	BB	SO		Avg	AB	H	2B	3B	HR	RBI	BB	SO	OBP	SLG
Reliever	6.10	0	0	0	5	0	10.1	17	5	3	2	Pitch 91-105	.235	17	4	1	0	1	1	1	1	.278	.471
0-3 Days Rest	0.00	0	0	0	0	0	0.0	0	0	0	0	Pitch 106+	.667	3	2	0	1	0	0	0	0	.667	1.333
4 Days Rest	4.93	3	4	0	15	15	69.1	85	6	18	21	First Pitch	.386	101	39	11	0	8	22	2	0	.400	.733
5+ Days Rest	5.36	2	7	0	19	19	97.1	106	13	29	39	Ahead on Count	.303	330	100	21	3	8	47	1	51	.314	.458
Pre-All Star	5.00	2	7	0	21	21	99.0	113	8	32	29	Behind on Count	.252	159	40	6	3	7	24	33	0	.378	.459
Post-All Star	5.54	3	4	0	18	13	78.0	97	16	18	33	Two Strikes	.275	269	74	11	3	6	30	14	61	.322	.405

Jim Eisenreich — Royals

Bats Left

	Avg	G	AB	R	H	2B	3B	HR	RBI	BB	SO	HBP	GDP	SB	CS	OBP	SLG	IBB	SH	SF	#Pit	#P/PA	GB	FB	G/F
1992 Season	.269	113	353	31	95	13	3	2	28	24	36	0	6	11	6	.313	.340	4	0	3	1275	3.36	144	98	1.47
Last Five Years	.279	606	1901	229	530	105	21	19	204	129	197	2	34	64	34	.322	.386	17	10	21	6699	3.26	823	556	1.48

1992 Season

	Avg	AB	H	2B	3B	HR	RBI	BB	SO	OBP	SLG		Avg	AB	H	2B	3B	HR	RBI	BB	SO	OBP	SLG
vs. Left	.240	75	18	4	1	0	7	5	15	.284	.320	Scoring Posn	.196	97	19	4	0	0	25	9	14	.257	.237
vs. Right	.277	278	77	9	2	2	21	19	21	.321	.345	Close & Late	.278	79	22	4	1	1	5	7	11	.330	.392
Groundball	.244	82	20	5	1	0	9	6	6	.295	.329	None on/out	.376	85	32	5	1	1	1	10	9	.442	.494
Flyball	.250	120	30	3	0	0	6	9	21	.300	.275	Batting #6	.277	130	36	6	1	0	8	8	13	.314	.338
Home	.244	160	39	2	3	1	13	14	15	.301	.313	Batting #7	.217	69	15	2	1	1	6	5	10	.270	.319
Away	.290	193	56	11	0	1	15	10	21	.324	.363	Other	.286	154	44	5	1	1	14	11	13	.331	.351
Day	.287	94	27	3	0	1	10	7	7	.333	.351	April	.188	32	6	0	0	1	3	5	7	.289	.281
Night	.263	259	68	10	3	1	18	17	29	.306	.336	May	.292	65	19	5	0	1	9	7	7	.351	.415
Grass	.316	158	50	10	0	1	14	9	17	.353	.399	June	.278	72	20	4	0	0	4	3	7	.307	.333
Turf	.231	195	45	3	3	1	14	15	19	.282	.292	July	.286	77	22	2	2	0	7	2	5	.304	.364
First Pitch	.306	72	22	4	2	1	5	3	0	.329	.458	August	.138	29	4	0	0	0	2	3	1	.219	.138
Ahead on Count	.320	103	33	5	1	0	11	13	0	.397	.388	September/October	.308	78	24	2	1	0	3	4	9	.341	.359
Behind on Count	.255	102	26	4	0	0	11	0	19	.252	.294	Pre-All Star	.279	219	61	11	2	2	20	15	24	.321	.374
Two Strikes	.210	124	26	2	0	1	5	9	36	.263	.250	Post-All Star	.254	134	34	2	1	0	8	9	12	.301	.284

1992 By Position

Position	Avg	AB	H	2B	3B	HR	RBI	BB	SO	OBP	SLG	G	GS	Innings	PO	A	E	DP	Fld Pct	Rng Fctr	In Zone	Outs	Zone Rtg	MLB Zone
As Pinch Hitter	.370	27	10	1	0	0	4	2	1	.400	.407	30	0	---	---	---	---	---	---	---	---	---	---	---
As lf	.304	79	24	2	1	0	3	5	9	.345	.354	48	21	195.0	48	0	0	0	1.000	2.22	57	44	.772	.809
As rf	.236	212	50	6	2	2	18	13	21	.278	.311	66	53	499.0	125	1	1	1	.992	2.27	132	116	.879	.814

Last Five Years

	Avg	AB	H	2B	3B	HR	RBI	BB	SO	OBP	SLG		Avg	AB	H	2B	3B	HR	RBI	BB	SO	OBP	SLG
vs. Left	.281	462	130	21	4	4	58	24	62	.315	.370	Scoring Posn	.261	513	134	24	5	6	183	50	59	.316	.363
vs. Right	.278	1439	400	84	17	15	146	105	135	.324	.391	Close & Late	.265	343	91	15	7	5	30	27	49	.316	.394
Groundball	.289	544	157	29	6	1	52	35	42	.329	.369	None on/out	.305	505	154	42	4	6	6	31	54	.345	.440
Flyball	.269	483	130	32	7	8	55	37	73	.317	.414	Batting #5	.280	731	205	48	11	10	91	40	79	.315	.417
Home	.275	916	252	45	16	9	109	70	81	.323	.389	Batting #6	.270	400	108	18	1	2	31	33	41	.323	.335
Away	.282	985	278	60	5	10	95	59	116	.321	.384	Other	.282	770	217	39	9	7	82	56	77	.326	.383
Day	.317	537	170	37	8	6	74	36	44	.356	.449	April	.271	266	72	16	3	4	32	12	39	.297	.398
Night	.264	1364	360	68	13	13	130	93	153	.309	.361	May	.288	351	101	24	3	2	39	30	42	.343	.390
Grass	.289	767	222	48	3	5	66	47	94	.329	.379	June	.268	362	97	16	1	2	28	30	29	.320	.334
Turf	.272	1134	308	57	18	14	138	82	103	.317	.391	July	.271	303	82	19	7	0	28	22	24	.319	.380
First Pitch	.319	405	129	32	6	6	46	9	0	.330	.472	August	.328	250	82	14	3	6	38	16	20	.366	.480
Ahead on Count	.317	498	158	27	9	5	77	67	0	.393	.438	September/October	.260	369	96	16	4	5	39	19	43	.294	.366
Behind on Count	.241	536	129	22	5	3	49	1	99	.239	.317	Pre-All Star	.274	1104	302	63	11	8	108	79	120	.319	.372
Two Strikes	.229	617	141	24	4	4	41	49	197	.285	.300	Post-All Star	.286	797	228	42	10	11	96	50	77	.326	.405

Batter vs. Pitcher (since 1984)

Hits Best Against	Avg	AB	H	2B	3B	HR	RBI	BB	SO	OBP	SLG	Hits Worst Against	Avg	AB	H	2B	3B	HR	RBI	BB	SO	OBP	SLG
Rick Aguilera	.583	12	7	1	1	0	0	0	1	.583	.833	David Wells	.091	11	1	0	0	0	0	0	0	.091	.091
Lee Guetterman	.545	11	6	2	0	0	2	0	2	.615	.727	Mike Mussina	.091	11	1	1	0	0	0	0	1	.091	.182
Dennis Eckersley	.500	10	5	2	0	0	1	1	3	.545	.700	Bert Blyleven	.097	31	3	0	0	0	1	1	4	.121	.097
Mark Eichhorn	.444	9	4	1	0	0	0	2	0	.545	.556	Nolan Ryan	.105	19	2	0	0	0	1	3	5	.217	.105
Mike Boddicker	.429	21	9	4	0	1	3	0	3	.429	.762	Mark Williamson	.188	16	3	0	0	0	1	0	1	.176	.188

Cal Eldred — Brewers — Pitches Right (flyball pitcher)

	ERA	W	L	Sv	G	GS	IP	BB	SO	Avg	H	2B	3B	HR	RBI	OBP	SLG	CG	ShO	Sup	QS	#P/S	SB	CS	GB	FB	G/F
1992 Season	1.79	11	2	0	14	14	100.1	23	62	.207	76	10	3	4	14	.258	.283	2	1	6.55	12	112	8	4	114	142	0.80
Career (1991-1992)	2.17	13	2	0	17	17	116.1	29	72	.221	96	11	3	6	21	.273	.302	2	1	6.19	13	108	11	5	132	167	0.79

1992 Season

	ERA	W	L	Sv	G	GS	IP	H	HR	BB	SO		Avg	AB	H	2B	3B	HR	RBI	BB	SO	OBP	SLG
Home	0.76	7	0	0	8	8	59.0	40	2	16	30	vs. Left	.188	154	29	2	0	2	4	11	21	.251	.240
Away	3.27	4	2	0	6	6	41.1	36	2	7	32	vs. Right	.221	213	47	8	3	2	10	12	41	.262	.315
Starter	1.79	11	2	0	14	14	100.1	76	4	23	62	Scoring Posn	.104	67	7	0	0	0	7	2	18	.130	.104
Reliever	0.00	0	0	0	0	0	0.0	0	0	0	0	Close & Late	.208	48	10	1	2	0	3	1	12	.240	.313
0-3 Days Rest	0.00	0	0	0	0	0	0.0	0	0	0	0	None on/out	.250	100	25	0	1	2	2	7	16	.299	.330
4 Days Rest	2.59	4	2	0	7	7	48.2	42	2	11	28	First Pitch	.176	34	6	0	0	2	2	0	0	.200	.353
5+ Days Rest	1.05	7	0	0	7	7	51.2	34	2	12	34	Behind on Count	.215	93	20	2	1	2	5	13	0	.311	.323
Pre-All Star	0.00	0	0	0	0	0	0.0	0	0	0	0	Ahead on Count	.192	151	29	3	1	0	4	0	47	.197	.225
Post-All Star	1.79	11	2	0	14	14	100.1	76	4	23	62	Two Strikes	.166	181	30	3	1	0	5	10	62	.214	.193

Kevin Elster — Mets — Bats Right (flyball hitter)

	Avg	G	AB	R	H	2B	3B	HR	RBI	BB	SO	HBP	GDP	SB	CS	OBP	SLG	IBB	SH	SF	#Pit	#P/PA	GB	FB	G/F
1992 Season	.222	6	18	0	4	0	0	0	0	0	2	0	1	0	0	.222	.222	0	0	0	61	3.39	7	8	0.88
Last Five Years	.224	513	1544	162	346	72	6	34	173	139	233	7	27	10	6	.288	.345	31	14	18	6082	3.56	513	534	0.96

1992 Season

	Avg	AB	H	2B	3B	HR	RBI	BB	SO	OBP	SLG		Avg	AB	H	2B	3B	HR	RBI	BB	SO	OBP	SLG
vs. Left	.167	6	1	0	0	0	0	0	0	.167	.167	Scoring Posn	.000	4	0	0	0	0	0	0	2	.000	.000
vs. Right	.250	12	3	0	0	0	0	0	2	.250	.250	Close & Late	.000	2	0	0	0	0	0	0	0	.000	.000

Last Five Years

	Avg	AB	H	2B	3B	HR	RBI	BB	SO	OBP	SLG		Avg	AB	H	2B	3B	HR	RBI	BB	SO	OBP	SLG
vs. Left	.253	588	149	30	1	8	47	56	63	.317	.349	Scoring Posn	.249	381	95	18	3	8	135	62	71	.342	.375
vs. Right	.206	956	197	42	5	26	126	83	170	.270	.342	Close & Late	.177	248	44	8	0	4	18	27	41	.256	.258
Groundball	.259	567	147	23	3	14	68	42	80	.311	.384	None on/out	.214	360	77	10	2	10	10	23	49	.267	.336
Flyball	.194	309	60	21	0	6	26		57	.263	.320	Batting #7	.256	219	56	10	0	4	23	22	28	.318	.356
Home	.221	784	173	37	2	16	88	64	122	.281	.334	Batting #8	.214	1145	245	55	5	25	125	96	173	.276	.336
Away	.226	760	173	35	4	18	85	75	111	.295	.355	Other	.250	180	45	7	1	5	25	21	32	.325	.383
Day	.198	510	101	22	2	12	62	39	84	.255	.320	April	.216	250	54	10	3	5	27	21	38	.275	.340
Night	.237	1034	245	50	4	22	111	100	169	.304	.357	May	.220	268	59	7	0	7	29	32	43	.302	.325
Grass	.228	1071	244	54	3	23	127	87	157	.286	.348	June	.216	296	64	23	0	5	42	23	49	.274	.345
Turf	.216	473	102	18	3	11	46	52	76	.294	.336	July	.218	271	59	13	1	7	33	17	43	.269	.351
First Pitch	.254	228	58	13	1	9	31	1	0	.290	.439	August	.259	228	59	9	0	5	21	21	32	.319	.364
Ahead on Count	.271	354	96	22	3	9	59	86	0	.414	.427	September/October	.221	231	51	10	2	5	21	25	28	.296	.346
Behind on Count	.209	536	112	26	1	9	56	3	126	.216	.315	Pre-All Star	.214	911	195	43	4	19	106	81	151	.278	.333
Two Strikes	.171	667	114	20	0	11	49	36	233	.213	.250	Post-All Star	.239	633	151	29	2	15	67	58	82	.302	.362

Batter vs. Pitcher (career)

Hits Best Against	Avg	AB	H	2B	3B	HR	RBI	BB	SO	OBP	SLG	Hits Worst Against	Avg	AB	H	2B	3B	HR	RBI	BB	SO	OBP	SLG
Juan Agosto	.455	11	5	0	0	0	2	1	0	.500	.455	Rob Dibble	.000	8	0	0	0	0	1	2	5	.182	.000
Bruce Hurst	.421	19	8	2	0	1	2	2		.476	.526	Jim Deshaies	.063	16	1	0	0	0	2	4		.167	.063
Steve Avery	.417	12	5	2	0	3	0	0		.417	.583	Mark Portugal	.083	12	1	0	0	0	1	0	1	.077	.083
Joe Magrane	.385	13	5	2	0	0	1	1	0	.429	.538	Pete Smith	.091	11	1	1	0	0	0	0	7	.091	.182
Doug Drabek	.370	27		1	1	2	7	4	4	.452	.704	Charlie Leibrandt	.125	16	2	1	0	0	0	0		.125	.188

Alan Embree — Indians — Pitches Left

	ERA	W	L	Sv	G	GS	IP	BB	SO	Avg	H	2B	3B	HR	RBI	OBP	SLG	CG	ShO	Sup	QS	#P/S	SB	CS	GB	FB	G/F
1992 Season	7.00	0	2	0	4	4	18.0	8	12	.271	19	5	0	3	11	.346	.471	0	0	3.50	0	76	3	0	28	19	1.47

1992 Season

	ERA	W	L	Sv	G	GS	IP	H	HR	BB	SO		Avg	AB	H	2B	3B	HR	RBI	BB	SO	OBP	SLG
Home	7.20	0	1	0	2	2	10.0	13	2	5	10	vs. Left	.100	10	1	0	0	0	0	2	2	.308	.100
Away	6.75	0	1	0	2	2	8.0	6	1	3	2	vs. Right	.300	60	18	5	0	3	11	6	10	.353	.533

Scott Erickson — Twins — Pitches Right (groundball pitcher)

	ERA	W	L	Sv	G	GS	IP	BB	SO	Avg	H	2B	3B	HR	RBI	OBP	SLG	CG	ShO	Sup	QS	#P/S	SB	CS	GB	FB	G/F
1992 Season	3.40	13	12	0	32	32	212.0	83	101	.252	197	29	5	18	78	.328	.371	5	3	4.37	18	97	23	7	391	159	2.46
Career (1990-1992)	3.20	41	24	0	83	81	529.0	205	262	.251	494	84	12	40	194	.326	.367	11	6	5.05	50	94	33	20	971	427	2.27

1992 Season

	ERA	W	L	Sv	G	GS	IP	H	HR	BB	SO		Avg	AB	H	2B	3B	HR	RBI	BB	SO	OBP	SLG
Home	3.43	8	6	0	18	18	123.1	123	7	36	57	vs. Left	.241	410	99	10	4	7	39	41	41	.311	.337
Away	3.35	5	6	0	14	14	88.2	74	11	47	44	vs. Right	.264	371	98	19	1	11	39	42	60	.345	.410
Day	2.45	9	5	0	16	16	110.0	96	4	41	55	Inning 1-6	.248	654	162	24	3	13	66	68	79	.323	.353
Night	4.41	4	7	0	16	16	102.0	101	14	42	46	Inning 7+	.276	127	35	5	2	5	12	15	22	.352	.465
Grass	2.81	5	5	0	12	12	77.0	64	7	43	37	None on	.263	445	117	18	4	11	11	49	50	.345	.396

1992 Season

	ERA	W	L	Sv	G	GS	IP	H	HR	BB	SO		Avg	AB	H	2B	3B	HR	RBI	BB	SO	OBP	SLG
Turf	3.73	8	7	0	20	20	135.0	133	11	40	64	Runners on	.238	336	80	11	1	7	67	34	51	.304	.339
April	5.10	0	3	0	5	5	30.0	27	2	13	9	Scoring Posn	.223	184	41	2	1	6	62	23	30	.299	.342
May	4.82	3	1	0	5	5	28.0	32	3	10	18	Close & Late	.308	91	28	3	2	3	9	9	14	.370	.484
June	3.52	3	1	0	5	5	30.2	33	4	14	12	None on/out	.275	204	56	12	1	6	6	19	16	.345	.431
July	2.25	1	2	0	5	5	36.0	27	4	13	17	vs. 1st Batr (relief)	.000	0	0	0	0	0	0	0	0	.000	.000
August	2.76	2	3	0	6	6	42.1	33	3	20	21	First Inning Pitched	.256	117	30	5	1	5	14	14	10	.331	.444
September/October	2.80	4	2	0	6	6	45.0	45	2	13	24	First 75 Pitches	.250	596	149	19	2	14	60	60	68	.322	.359
Starter	3.40	13	12	0	32	32	212.0	197	18	83	101	Pitch 76-90	.270	89	24	5	2	2	9	11	15	.359	.438
Reliever	0.00	0	0	0	0	0	0.0	0	0	0	0	Pitch 91-105	.237	59	14	3	0	1	7	7	12	.318	.339
0-3 Days Rest	9.00	0	0	0	1	1	5.0	9	2	1	2	Pitch 106+	.270	37	10	2	1	1	2	5	6	.357	.459
4 Days Rest	3.59	10	6	0	19	19	123.0	121	14	49	63	First Pitch	.361	122	44	4	2	7	28	2	0	.377	.598
5+ Days Rest	2.79	3	6	0	12	12	84.0	67	2	33	36	Ahead on Count	.201	288	58	11	1	3	16	0	81	.208	.278
Pre-All Star	4.16	6	6	0	17	17	101.2	104	11	42	44	Behind on Count	.263	243	64	6	2	5	25	45	0	.378	.366
Post-All Star	2.69	7	6	0	15	15	110.1	93	7	41	57	Two Strikes	.179	273	49	8	1	3	12	36	101	.280	.249

Career (1990-1992)

	ERA	W	L	Sv	G	GS	IP	H	HR	BB	SO		Avg	AB	H	2B	3B	HR	RBI	BB	SO	OBP	SLG
Home	3.47	25	11	0	46	45	298.2	303	22	89	152	vs. Left	.264	1051	277	45	7	19	104	113	97	.336	.374
Away	2.85	16	13	0	37	36	230.1	191	18	116	110	vs. Right	.237	914	217	39	5	21	90	92	165	.314	.360
Day	2.73	19	9	0	35	35	233.2	212	9	81	113	Inning 1-6	.248	1656	411	71	9	27	159	169	225	.322	.351
Night	3.57	22	15	0	48	46	295.1	282	31	124	149	Inning 7+	.269	309	83	13	3	13	35	36	37	.346	.456
Grass	2.33	15	8	0	29	28	185.1	145	12	95	86	None on	.257	1122	288	53	6	23	23	124	152	.337	.376
Turf	3.67	26	16	0	54	53	343.2	349	28	110	176	Runners on	.244	843	206	31	6	17	171	81	110	.310	.356
April	3.54	2	5	0	9	9	61.0	56	3	25	24	Scoring Posn	.229	449	103	12	4	9	147	58	71	.309	.334
May	2.66	8	1	0	11	11	74.1	67	6	23	47	Close & Late	.273	172	47	7	3	5	18	16	22	.335	.436
June	2.75	9	3	0	13	13	88.1	79	6	33	51	None on/out	.256	507	130	28	1	14	14	53	65	.334	.398
July	3.54	4	3	0	15	13	84.0	87	11	37	35	vs. 1st Batr (relief)	1.000	1	1	0	0	0	0	1	0	1.000	1.000
August	4.81	5	8	0	16	16	88.0	99	7	36	40	First Inning Pitched	.255	306	78	14	1	7	32	33	40	.325	.376
September/October	2.36	13	4	0	19	19	133.1	106	7	51	65	First 75 Pitches	.254	1481	376	60	7	28	148	150	198	.326	.361
Starter	3.16	41	24	0	81	81	523.1	486	38	199	261	Pitch 76-90	.255	231	59	13	3	6	25	29	32	.343	.416
Reliever	6.35	0	0	0	2	0	5.2	6	2	6	1	Pitch 91-105	.221	154	34	5	1	3	14	10	20	.273	.325
0-3 Days Rest	4.09	0	1	0	2	2	11.0	13	2	4	6	Pitch 106+	.253	99	25	6	1	3	7	16	12	.357	.424
4 Days Rest	3.32	27	14	0	49	49	312.0	295	23	125	162	First Pitch	.319	317	101	14	2	11	54	5	0	.331	.479
5+ Days Rest	2.88	14	9	0	30	30	200.1	178	13	70	93	Ahead on Count	.196	740	145	33	3	8	42	0	212	.206	.261
Pre-All Star	2.98	19	10	0	36	36	241.2	222	17	89	131	Behind on Count	.285	578	165	21	4	15	64	119	0	.407	.413
Post-All Star	3.38	22	14	0	47	45	287.1	272	23	111	131	Two Strikes	.172	698	120	29	3	6	35	81	262	.246	.248

Pitcher vs. Batter (career)

Pitches Best Vs.	Avg	AB	H	2B	3B	HR	RBI	BB	SO	OBP	SLG	Pitches Worst Vs.	Avg	AB	H	2B	3B	HR	RBI	BB	SO	OBP	SLG
Kevin Seitzer	.000	12	0	0	0	0	1	0	0	.000	.000	Alex Cole	.571	14	8	0	0	0	0	1	0	.600	.571
Jack Clark	.000	10	0	0	0	0	0	1	3	.091	.000	Ken Griffey Jr	.526	19	10	3	0	1	3	0	0	.591	.684
Mike Greenwell	.063	16	1	0	0	0	0	0	1	.063	.063	Mark McGwire	.444	18	8	2	0	3	7	3	3	.524	1.056
Carlos Baerga	.100	20	2	1	0	0	2	0	4	.100	.150	Greg Vaughn	.444	9	4	0	0	1	1	2	3	.545	.778
B.J. Surhoff	.100	10	1	0	0	0	0	1	0	.182	.100	Dan Pasqua	.400	15	6	1	0	3	5	0	3	.400	1.067

Cecil Espy — Pirates   Bats Both (groundball hitter)

	Avg	G	AB	R	H	2B	3B	HR	RBI	BB	SO	HBP	GDP	SB	CS	OBP	SLG	IBB	SH	SF	#Pit	#P/PA	GB	FB	G/F
1992 Season	.258	112	194	21	50	7	3	1	20	15	40	0	3	6	3	.310	.340	2	1	5	801	3.81	88	42	2.10
Last Five Years	.246	472	1169	149	287	40	16	7	102	88	259	3	8	99	38	.298	.325	5	20	8	4737	3.74	436	263	1.66

1992 Season

	Avg	AB	H	2B	3B	HR	RBI	BB	SO	OBP	SLG		Avg	AB	H	2B	3B	HR	RBI	BB	SO	OBP	SLG
vs. Left	.210	62	13	2	0	1	4	7	6	.290	.290	Scoring Posn	.268	56	15	3	1	0	18	5	15	.323	.357
vs. Right	.280	132	37	5	3	0	16	8	34	.319	.364	Close & Late	.154	65	10	2	1	0	4	8	17	.247	.215
Home	.278	97	27	2	2	0	12	8	23	.333	.340	None on/out	.240	50	12	1	2	0	0	5	6	.309	.340
Away	.237	97	23	5	1	1	8	7	17	.286	.340	Batting #1	.260	77	20	3	0	0	5	8	14	.326	.299
First Pitch	.296	27	8	2	0	0	6	2	0	.345	.370	Batting #9	.260	50	13	1	2	0	9	5	14	.327	.360
Ahead on Count	.367	30	11	0	0	0	4	5	0	.457	.367	Other	.254	67	17	3	1	1	6	2	12	.275	.373
Behind on Count	.280	75	21	3	2	1	9	0	23	.276	.413	Pre-All Star	.270	141	38	5	2	1	17	9	26	.311	.355
Two Strikes	.188	101	19	3	3	1	8	8	40	.245	.307	Post-All Star	.226	53	12	2	1	0	3	6	14	.305	.302

Last Five Years

	Avg	AB	H	2B	3B	HR	RBI	BB	SO	OBP	SLG		Avg	AB	H	2B	3B	HR	RBI	BB	SO	OBP	SLG
vs. Left	.245	257	63	9	1	5	25	20	48	.297	.346	Scoring Posn	.263	278	73	10	3	3	95	18	64	.299	.353
vs. Right	.246	912	224	31	15	2	77	68	211	.298	.319	Close & Late	.204	226	46	5	1	1	19	31	51	.296	.248
Groundball	.252	321	81	9	3	2	29	25	66	.306	.318	None on/out	.242	384	93	12	10	2	2	32	78	.302	.341
Flyball	.223	318	71	8	4	2	27	29	72	.290	.292	Batting #1	.238	676	161	17	10	3	42	49	138	.290	.306
Home	.272	569	155	18	12	5	57	55	125	.313	.373	Batting #9	.227	132	30	5	3	0	15	16	41	.309	.311
Away	.220	600	132	22	4	2	45	53	134	.285	.280	Other	.266	361	96	18	3	4	45	23	80	.310	.366
Day	.218	262	57	7	5	1	18	19	69	.272	.294	April	.280	161	45	6	5	0	15	7	33	.310	.379
Night	.254	907	230	33	11	6	84	69	190	.306	.334	May	.227	176	40	6	1	0	7	14	36	.284	.273
Grass	.250	779	195	23	12	4	60	54	170	.300	.326	June	.251	219	55	6	0	4	24	18	50	.304	.333

Last Five Years

	Avg	AB	H	2B	3B	HR	RBI	BB	SO	OBP	SLG		Avg	AB	H	2B	3B	HR	RBI	BB	SO	OBP	SLG
Turf	.236	390	92	17	4	3	42	34	89	.295	.323	July	.211	180	38	5	3	1	16	12	45	.268	.289
First Pitch	.339	180	61	9	1	3	28	3	0	.344	.450	August	.238	210	50	6	3	2	19	15	47	.296	.324
Ahead on Count	.301	173	52	9	4	0	18	54	0	.463	.399	September/October	.265	223	59	11	4	0	21	22	48	.329	.350
Behind on Count	.203	448	91	11	7	3	37	1	161	.208	.279	Pre-All Star	.242	632	153	20	7	5	51	45	134	.292	.320
Two Strikes	.166	584	97	10	5	2	29	30	259	.207	.211	Post-All Star	.250	537	134	20	9	2	51	43	125	.305	.331

Batter vs. Pitcher (since 1984)

Hits Best Against	Avg	AB	H	2B	3B	HR	RBI	BB	SO	OBP	SLG	Hits Worst Against	Avg	AB	H	2B	3B	HR	RBI	BB	SO	OBP	SLG
Roger Clemens	.421	19	8	1	0	0	2	1	5	.450	.474	Mike Moore	.071	14	1	1	0	0	1	2	5	.188	.143
Scott Bankhead	.316	19	6	1	0	0	1	1	4	.350	.368	Mike Boddicker	.091	11	1	0	0	0	0	0	2	.091	.091
												Jack Morris	.154	13	2	1	0	0	1	2	5	.250	.231
												Todd Burns	.154	13	2	2	0	0	0	0	4	.154	.308
												Dave Stewart	.206	24	5	1	0	0	3	0	8	.206	.250

Paul Faries — Padres   Bats Right (groundball hitter)

	Avg	G	AB	R	H	2B	3B	HR	RBI	BB	SO	HBP	GDP	SB	CS	OBP	SLG	IBB	SH	SF	#Pit	#P/PA	GB	FB	G/F
1992 Season	.455	10	11	3	5	1	0	0	1	1	2	0	0	0	0	.500	.545	0	0	0	41	3.42	3	3	1.00
Career (1990-1992)	.197	81	178	20	35	5	1	0	10	19	30	2	5	3	2	.280	.236	0	6	1	735	3.68	78	38	2.05

1992 Season

	Avg	AB	H	2B	3B	HR	RBI	BB	SO	OBP	SLG		Avg	AB	H	2B	3B	HR	RBI	BB	SO	OBP	SLG
vs. Left	.500	6	3	1	0	0	1	0	1	.500	.667	Scoring Posn	.500	2	1	0	0	0	1	1	0	.667	.500
vs. Right	.400	5	2	0	0	0	0	1	1	.500	.400	Close & Late	.500	4	2	1	0	0	1	0	0	.500	.750

Monty Fariss — Rangers   Bats Right

	Avg	G	AB	R	H	2B	3B	HR	RBI	BB	SO	HBP	GDP	SB	CS	OBP	SLG	IBB	SH	SF	#Pit	#P/PA	GB	FB	G/F
1992 Season	.217	67	166	13	36	7	1	3	21	17	51	2	3	0	2	.297	.325	0	2	0	721	3.90	50	39	1.28
Career (1991-1992)	.223	86	197	19	44	8	1	4	27	24	62	2	3	0	2	.314	.335	0	2	0	879	3.94	60	45	1.33

1992 Season

	Avg	AB	H	2B	3B	HR	RBI	BB	SO	OBP	SLG		Avg	AB	H	2B	3B	HR	RBI	BB	SO	OBP	SLG
vs. Left	.187	75	14	1	0	2	11	8	30	.274	.280	Scoring Posn	.213	47	10	2	1	0	14	6	14	.315	.298
vs. Right	.242	91	22	6	1	1	10	9	21	.317	.363	Close & Late	.273	33	9	2	1	1	3	3	12	.333	.485
Home	.243	74	18	3	0	0	9	8	22	.317	.284	None on/out	.229	35	8	0	0	0	0	3	11	.289	.229
Away	.196	92	18	4	1	3	12	9	29	.282	.359	Batting #6	.250	32	8	1	0	1	4	5	6	.351	.375
First Pitch	.250	16	4	0	0	0	3	0	0	.250	.250	Batting #8	.156	32	5	1	0	1	3	3	11	.229	.281
Ahead on Count	.316	38	12	2	0	1	8	9	0	.447	.447	Other	.225	102	23	5	1	1	14	9	34	.301	.324
Behind on Count	.210	62	13	2	1	1	8	0	30	.234	.323	Pre-All Star	.233	30	7	0	0	1	6	7	12	.395	.333
Two Strikes	.096	83	8	1	1	2	6	8	51	.194	.205	Post-All Star	.213	136	29	7	1	2	15	10	39	.272	.324

Steve Farr — Yankees   Pitches Right

	ERA	W	L	Sv	G	GS	IP	BB	SO	Avg	H	2B	3B	HR	RBI	OBP	SLG	GF	IR	IRS	Hld	SvOp	SB	CS	GB	FB	G/F
1992 Season	1.56	2	2	30	50	0	52.0	19	37	.186	34	4	0	2	16	.267	.240	42	18	8	0	36	7	0	57	62	0.92
Last Five Years	2.42	27	23	92	280	9	395.0	139	319	.233	339	63	6	22	151	.305	.330	110	200	67	15	115	22	13	479	420	1.14

1992 Season

	ERA	W	L	Sv	G	GS	IP	H	HR	BB	SO		Avg	AB	H	2B	3B	HR	RBI	BB	SO	OBP	SLG
Home	1.86	1	1	18	27	0	29.0	17	1	12	17	vs. Left	.217	83	18	0	0	1	6	15	14	.347	.253
Away	1.17	1	1	12	23	0	23.0	17	1	7	20	vs. Right	.160	100	16	4	0	1	10	4	23	.190	.230
Starter	0.00	0	0	0	0	0	0.0	0	0	0	0	Scoring Posn	.200	35	7	1	0	1	15	8	3	.333	.314
Reliever	1.56	2	2	30	50	0	52.0	34	2	19	37	Close & Late	.184	125	23	3	0	2	15	15	26	.268	.256
0 Days rest	2.70	1	0	6	7	0	6.2	5	0	4	4	None on/out	.208	48	10	1	0	1	1	2	6	.255	.292
1 or 2 Days rest	2.13	0	2	14	24	0	25.1	17	2	9	18	First Pitch	.286	21	6	1	0	0	5	0	0	.304	.333
3+ Days rest	0.45	1	0	10	19	0	20.0	12	0	6	15	Behind on Count	.222	27	6	2	0	0	2	10	0	.421	.296
Pre-All Star	1.78	0	1	12	25	0	25.1	19	1	7	21	Ahead on Count	.140	93	13	1	0	1	4	0	28	.149	.183
Post-All Star	1.35	2	1	18	25	0	26.2	15	1	12	16	Two Strikes	.143	98	14	1	0	1	7	9	37	.222	.184

Last Five Years

	ERA	W	L	Sv	G	GS	IP	H	HR	BB	SO		Avg	AB	H	2B	3B	HR	RBI	BB	SO	OBP	SLG
Home	1.97	19	8	56	147	5	210.1	162	6	61	169	vs. Left	.249	683	170	31	3	7	61	80	132	.334	.334
Away	2.92	8	15	36	133	4	184.2	177	16	78	150	vs. Right	.219	772	169	32	3	15	90	59	187	.278	.326
Day	2.87	7	10	21	72	3	119.0	105	6	46	97	Inning 1-6	.219	283	62	10	1	3	21	26	67	.290	.293
Night	2.22	20	13	71	208	6	276.0	234	16	93	222	Inning 7+	.236	1172	277	53	5	19	130	113	252	.308	.339
Grass	2.72	9	15	58	157	3	205.1	179	17	78	167	None on	.249	796	198	43	5	11	11	56	169	.304	.357
Turf	2.09	18	8	34	123	6	189.2	166	5	61	152	Runners on	.214	659	141	20	1	11	140	83	150	.306	.297
April	3.38	1	3	10	36	0	48.0	43	4	20	46	Scoring Posn	.198	400	79	13	1	7	128	60	103	.307	.288
May	1.51	5	3	12	53	0	71.1	55	3	26	65	Close & Late	.240	542	130	20	1	9	76	61	123	.320	.330
June	2.23	3	3	20	52	3	68.2	52	3	20	57	None on/out	.257	343	88	24	2	5	5	24	68	.311	.382
July	2.54	6	4	14	43	1	56.2	52	5	24	45	vs. 1st Batr (relief)	.222	243	54	10	0	4	23	24	53	.297	.313
August	3.11	4	5	17	50	1	72.1	68	3	21	48	First Inning Pitched	.218	919	200	37	4	11	108	93	203	.294	.298
September/October	2.08	8	5	19	46	5	78.0	71	4	28	58	First 15 Pitches	.229	802	184	36	2	10	81	71	177	.300	.317

Last Five Years

	ERA	W	L	Sv	G	GS	IP	H	HR	BB	SO		Avg	AB	H	2B	3B	HR	RBI	BB	SO	OBP	SLG
Starter	1.32	7	1	0	9	9	54.2	47	2	16	38	Pitch 16-30	.230	361	83	12	2	7	41	45	82	.314	.332
Reliever	2.59	20	22	92	271	0	340.1	292	20	123	281	Pitch 31-45	.250	160	40	10	1	2	16	8	37	.292	.363
0 Days rest	3.45	5	4	23	47	0	47.0	58	4	13	30	Pitch 46+	.242	132	32	5	1	3	13	15	23	.324	.364
1 or 2 Days rest	2.64	9	13	42	131	0	173.2	144	12	76	145	First Pitch	.305	187	57	8	2	2	29	15	0	.357	.401
3+ Days rest	2.18	6	5	27	93	0	119.2	90	4	34	106	Ahead on Count	.180	767	138	24	4	10	59	3	262	.194	.261
Pre-All Star	2.13	10	9	49	154	4	207.0	161	11	72	184	Behind on Count	.307	231	71	15	0	6	33	60	0	.447	.450
Post-All Star	2.73	17	14	43	126	5	188.0	178	14	67	135	Two Strikes	.167	768	128	24	4	8	59	63	319	.237	.240

Pitcher vs. Batter (career)

Pitches Best Vs.	Avg	AB	H	2B	3B	HR	RBI	BB	SO	OBP	SLG	Pitches Worst Vs.	Avg	AB	H	2B	3B	HR	RBI	BB	SO	OBP	SLG
Mickey Tettleton	.071	14	1	0	0	0	0	2	9	.188	.071	Ruben Sierra	.500	18	9	1	0	1	3	2	6	.550	.722
Kelly Gruber	.077	13	1	0	0	0	0	0	3	.077	.077	Jesse Barfield	.500	14	7	1	0	1	5	3	6	.588	.786
Jody Reed	.091	11	1	0	0	0	0	1	1	.167	.091	Dave Bergman	.429	14	6	0	0	2	4	1	2	.467	.857
Dick Schofield	.100	20	2	0	0	0	1	3	6	.208	.100	Don Mattingly	.400	15	6	1	0	2	4	2	0	.471	.867
Dave Winfield	.143	21	3	0	0	0	1	1	2	.182	.143	Pete Incaviglia	.308	13	4	1	0	2	3	1	7	.357	.846

Jeff Fassero — Expos
Pitches Left (groundball pitcher)

	ERA	W	L	Sv	G	GS	IP	BB	SO	Avg	H	2B	3B	HR	RBI	OBP	SLG	GF	IR	IRS	Hld	SvOp	SB	CS	GB	FB	G/F
1992 Season	2.84	8	7	1	70	0	85.2	34	63	.249	81	12	5	1	32	.322	.326	22	51	13	12	7	12	2	156	55	2.84
Career (1991-1992)	2.68	10	12	9	121	0	141.0	51	105	.229	120	19	7	2	52	.300	.303	52	89	23	19	18	15	3	241	103	2.34

1992 Season

	ERA	W	L	Sv	G	GS	IP	H	HR	BB	SO		Avg	AB	H	2B	3B	HR	RBI	BB	SO	OBP	SLG
Home	4.05	6	3	0	38	0	40.0	43	1	21	26	vs. Left	.269	93	25	2	1	1	12	6	24	.320	.344
Away	1.77	2	4	1	32	0	45.2	38	0	13	37	vs. Right	.241	232	56	10	4	0	20	28	39	.323	.319
Day	3.92	2	1	0	19	0	20.2	25	0	6	12	Inning 1-6	.267	30	8	3	0	0	7	4	5	.371	.367
Night	2.49	6	6	1	51	0	65.0	56	1	28	51	Inning 7+	.247	295	73	9	5	1	25	30	58	.317	.322
Grass	3.00	0	2	0	13	0	18.0	19	0	5	12	None on	.237	169	40	8	2	0	0	13	31	.295	.308
Turf	2.79	8	5	1	57	0	67.2	62	1	29	51	Runners on	.263	156	41	4	3	1	32	21	32	.350	.346
April	3.63	0	1	0	11	0	17.1	14	0	8	9	Scoring Posn	.233	103	24	3	1	1	29	17	24	.341	.311
May	2.93	2	1	0	12	0	15.1	11	1	6	14	Close & Late	.236	157	37	6	2	1	16	17	27	.311	.318
June	1.72	1	2	1	11	0	15.2	11	0	6	11	None in/out	.244	78	19	3	2	0	0	6	14	.298	.333
July	5.40	1	1	0	11	0	11.2	18	0	6	11	vs. 1st Batr (relief)	.161	62	10	1	0	0	3	7	12	.243	.177
August	0.00	1	0	0	11	0	12.1	14	0	3	11	First Inning Pitched	.255	220	56	9	2	1	25	23	41	.325	.327
September/October	3.38	3	2	0	14	0	13.1	13	0	5	8	First 15 Pitches	.269	208	56	8	2	1	22	22	41	.336	.341
Starter	0.00	0	0	0	0	0	0.0	0	0	0	0	Pitch 16-30	.242	91	22	4	2	0	8	9	15	.324	.330
Reliever	2.84	8	7	1	70	0	85.2	81	1	34	63	Pitch 31-45	.130	23	3	0	1	0	2	2	6	.200	.217
0 Days rest	4.61	4	4	0	20	0	27.1	25	0	14	18	Pitch 46+	.000	3	0	0	0	0	0	1	1	.250	.000
1 or 2 Days rest	1.96	3	3	0	33	0	36.2	37	1	15	25	First Pitch	.241	54	13	1	0	0	7	5	0	.317	.296
3+ Days rest	2.08	1	0	1	17	0	21.2	19	0	5	20	Ahead on Count	.221	149	33	6	3	0	12	0	54	.221	.302
Pre-All Star	3.25	3	5	1	39	0	52.2	45	1	22	36	Behind on Count	.274	62	17	2	1	0	6	15	0	.410	.339
Post-All Star	2.18	5	2	0	31	0	33.0	36	0	12	27	Two Strikes	.227	154	35	5	1	0	10	14	63	.290	.273

Mike Felder — Giants
Bats Both (groundball hitter)

	Avg	G	AB	R	H	2B	3B	HR	RBI	BB	SO	HBP	GDP	SB	CS	OBP	SLG	IBB	SH	SF	#Pit	#P/PA	GB	FB	G/F
1992 Season	.286	145	322	44	92	13	3	4	23	21	29	2	3	14	4	.330	.382	1	3	3	1269	3.65	127	99	1.28
Last Five Years	.260	565	1303	197	339	42	14	10	96	96	126	4	10	89	26	.311	.337	5	25	8	5123	3.63	562	345	1.63

1992 Season

	Avg	AB	H	2B	3B	HR	RBI	BB	SO	OBP	SLG		Avg	AB	H	2B	3B	HR	RBI	BB	SO	OBP	SLG
vs. Left	.307	88	27	5	0	1	6	5	7	.340	.398	Scoring Posn	.259	54	14	3	2	1	19	5	6	.306	.444
vs. Right	.278	234	65	8	3	3	17	16	22	.327	.376	Close & Late	.289	90	26	3	1	1	9	8	9	.350	.378
Groundball	.293	150	44	4	1	1	9	8	14	.327	.353	None in/out	.316	117	37	4	0	2	2	8	10	.365	.402
Flyball	.393	56	22	1	2	7	2	2	.424	.661	Batting #1	.282	213	60	12	1	4	15	14	22	.328	.404
Home	.262	164	43	7	1	1	7	7	16	.299	.335	Batting #9	.294	51	15	0	0	0	0	4	4	.345	.294
Away	.310	158	49	6	2	3	16	14	13	.362	.430	Other	.293	58	17	1	2	0	8	3	3	.328	.379
Day	.240	146	35	4	1	3	14	9	16	.287	.342	April	.333	36	12	0	0	0	1	1	3	.351	.333
Night	.324	176	57	9	2	1	9	12	13	.366	.415	May	.314	51	16	1	3	1	12	4	5	.351	.510
Grass	.268	239	64	7	2	1	11	14	24	.313	.326	June	.185	54	10	3	0	0	1	5	7	.254	.241
Turf	.337	83	28	6	1	3	12	7	5	.380	.542	July	.250	52	13	3	0	1	2	3	6	.291	.365
First Pitch	.303	33	10	1	1	3	7	1	0	.361	.667	August	.333	63	21	3	0	2	4	3	2	.373	.476
Ahead on Count	.250	56	14	3	0	1	7	15	0	.403	.357	September/October	.303	66	20	3	0	0	3	5	6	.356	.348
Behind on Count	.269	119	32	6	0	1	9	0	17	.264	.345	Pre-All Star	.260	173	45	6	3	1	14	11	20	.301	.347
Two Strikes	.250	148	37	5	0	2	5	29	.273	.284	Post-All Star	.315	149	47	7	0	3	9	10	9	.364	.423

1992 By Position

Position	Avg	AB	H	2B	3B	HR	RBI	BB	SO	OBP	SLG	G	GS	Innings	PO	A	E	DP	Fld Pct	Rng Fctr	In Zone	Outs	Zone Rtg	MLB Zone
As Pinch Hitter	.224	49	11	0	1	0	5	4	3	.273	.265	55	0	---	---	---	---	---	---	---	---	---	---	---
As lf	.279	86	24	3	1	0	2	3	4	.303	.337	53	13	214.2	49	1	0	0	1.000	2.10	54	47	.870	.809
As cf	.296	179	53	9	1	4	15	14	22	.352	.425	58	44	376.1	106	1	1	0	.991	2.56	124	105	.847	.824

129

1992 By Position

Position	Avg	AB	H	2B	3B	HR	RBI	BB	SO	OBP	SLG	G	GS	Innings	PO	A	E	DP	Fld Pct	Rng Fctr	In Zone	Outs	Zone Rtg	MLB Zone
As rf	.400	5	2	0	0	0	1	0	0	.400	.400	11	0	22.0	4	0	0	0	1.000	1.64	5	4	.800	.814

Last Five Years

	Avg	AB	H	2B	3B	HR	RBI	BB	SO	OBP	SLG		Avg	AB	H	2B	3B	HR	RBI	BB	SO	OBP	SLG
vs. Left	.268	399	107	14	3	4	31	27	35	.312	.348	Scoring Posn	.245	273	67	11	4	2	83	29	26	.310	.337
vs. Right	.257	904	232	28	11	6	65	69	91	.311	.332	Close & Late	.234	273	64	8	3	3	30	32	33	.316	.319
Groundball	.272	438	119	10	5	1	32	29	40	.315	.324	None on/out	.267	460	123	17	1	6	6	30	43	.315	.348
Flyball	.263	278	73	15	3	6	27	20	27	.313	.403	Batting #1	.268	720	193	26	10	8	46	52	72	.317	.365
Home	.240	616	148	17	6	3	36	41	60	.289	.302	Batting #8	.243	202	49	8	1		17	16	24	.293	.297
Away	.278	687	191	25	8	7	60	55	66	.331	.368	Other	.255	381	97	8	4	1	33	26	30	.309	.304
Day	.227	488	111	10	4	6	36	38	53	.285	.301	April	.310	100	31	1	0	0	4	8	11	.358	.320
Night	.280	815	228	32	10	4	60	58	73	.327	.358	May	.264	239	63	5	8	1	26	13	27	.301	.368
Grass	.252	1029	259	27	10	7	69	70	105	.300	.318	June	.248	282	70	11	1	0	13	26	23	.314	.294
Turf	.292	274	80	15	4	3	27	26	21	.353	.409	July	.244	217	53	9	1	3	17	15	18	.293	.336
First Pitch	.340	147	50	8	2	4	19	4	0	.366	.503	August	.256	211	54	7	2	4	18	11	18	.293	.365
Ahead on Count	.286	283	81	9	3	4	36	64	0	.416	.382	September/October	.268	254	68	8	2	2	18	23	29	.329	.339
Behind on Count	.236	462	109	16	5	2	34	0	68	.237	.305	Pre-All Star	.258	686	177	23	9	1	45	51	69	.310	.322
Two Strikes	.195	586	114	11	4	1	23	28	125	.231	.232	Post-All Star	.263	617	162	19	5	9	51	45	57	.313	.353

Batter vs. Pitcher (career)

Hits Best Against	Avg	AB	H	2B	3B	HR	RBI	BB	SO	OBP	SLG	Hits Worst Against	Avg	AB	H	2B	3B	HR	RBI	BB	SO	OBP	SLG
Tom Candiotti	.429	14	6	0	0	0	1	0	0	.429	.429	Paul Gibson	.000	14	0	0	0	0	0	1	3	.067	.000
Juan Berenguer	.400	10	4	0	0	0	1	0	1	.455	.400	Mike Boddicker	.067	15	1	0	0	0	1	1	0	.125	.067
John Smoltz	.389	18	7	1	1	0	2	1	2	.476	.556	Andy Benes	.071	14	1	0	0	0	0	2	3	.188	.071
Frank Tanana	.364	11	4	0	1	0	1	1	0	.385	.545	Walt Terrell	.077	13	1	0	0	0	0	1	2	.143	.077
Terry Mulholland	.333	12	4	1	0	1	1	0	2	.333	.667	Lee Guetterman	.091	11	1	0	0	0	0	0	0	.091	.091

Junior Felix — Angels

Bats Both (groundball hitter)

	Avg	G	AB	R	H	2B	3B	HR	RBI	BB	SO	HBP	GDP	SB	CS	OBP	SLG	IBB	SH	SF	#Pit	#P/PA	GB	FB	G/F
1992 Season	.246	139	509	63	125	22	5	9	72	33	128	2	9	8	8	.289	.361	5	5	9	2051	3.71	204	114	1.79
Career (1989-1992)	.259	442	1617	230	419	69	22	35	209	122	363	10	23	46	33	.312	.394	7	7	19	6395	3.62	624	361	1.73

1992 Season

	Avg	AB	H	2B	3B	HR	RBI	BB	SO	OBP	SLG		Avg	AB	H	2B	3B	HR	RBI	BB	SO	OBP	SLG
vs. Left	.271	118	32	7	1	3	18	3	30	.285	.424	Scoring Posn	.262	141	37	2	3	2	59	14	38	.315	.362
vs. Right	.238	391	93	15	4	6	54	30	98	.291	.343	Close & Late	.185	81	15	1	0	1	3	5	25	.233	.235
Groundball	.280	125	35	4	2	1	21	10	26	.329	.368	None on/out	.223	103	23	6	0	3	3	7	30	.273	.369
Flyball	.225	160	36	3	2	4	23	12	50	.280	.344	Batting #2	.267	75	20	2	1	2	14	3	16	.291	.400
Home	.247	251	62	8	2	5	32	16	60	.292	.355	Batting #3	.238	361	86	16	3	6	51	26	91	.289	.349
Away	.244	258	63	14	3	4	40	17	68	.287	.368	Other	.260	73	19	4	1	1	7	4	21	.288	.384
Day	.256	164	42	7	3	5	31	10	39	.299	.427	April	.291	86	25	2	1	3	20	4	19	.319	.442
Night	.241	345	83	15	2	4	41	23	89	.285	.330	May	.282	71	20	5	0	2	11	2	17	.293	.437
Grass	.244	427	104	15	5	9	61	29	110	.290	.365	June	.239	71	17	3	0	0	6	3	15	.263	.282
Turf	.256	82	21	7	0	0	11	4	18	.287	.341	July	.196	92	18	4	2	1	14	11	19	.286	.315
First Pitch	.320	75	24	3	0	5	15	3	0	.350	.560	August	.250	116	29	4	1	2	15	7	32	.290	.353
Ahead on Count	.339	109	37	10	0	1	19	19	0	.434	.459	September/October	.219	73	16	4	1	1	6	6	26	.280	.342
Behind on Count	.175	177	31	7	1	2	21	0	75	.175	.260	Pre-All Star	.264	265	70	13	2	5	43	14	60	.296	.385
Two Strikes	.151	245	37	4	3	1	23	12	128	.189	.204	Post-All Star	.225	244	55	9	3	4	29	19	68	.283	.336

1992 By Position

Position	Avg	AB	H	2B	3B	HR	RBI	BB	SO	OBP	SLG	G	GS	Innings	PO	A	E	DP	Fld Pct	Rng Fctr	In Zone	Outs	Zone Rtg	MLB Zone
As cf	.244	467	114	20	4	9	66	31	116	.289	.362	125	122	1076.2	334	9	6	3	.983	2.87	387	329	.850	.824

Career (1989-1992)

	Avg	AB	H	2B	3B	HR	RBI	BB	SO	OBP	SLG		Avg	AB	H	2B	3B	HR	RBI	BB	SO	OBP	SLG
vs. Left	.233	454	106	22	5	14	64	33	127	.286	.396	Scoring Posn	.264	416	110	15	5	8	168	37	96	.319	.382
vs. Right	.269	1163	313	47	17	21	145	89	256	.322	.393	Close & Late	.200	250	50	5	2	7	23	16	74	.252	.320
Groundball	.294	418	123	14	9	9	62	28	77	.336	.435	None on/out	.288	441	127	20	8	12	12	34	113	.340	.451
Flyball	.216	403	87	14	4	9	48	32	122	.280	.337	Batting #1	.262	507	133	20	10	9	61	40	112	.316	.394
Home	.255	791	202	27	15	18	88	66	172	.315	.396	Batting #3	.245	383	94	16	3	7	53	28	95	.297	.358
Away	.263	826	217	42	7	17	121	56	211	.308	.392	Other	.264	727	192	33	9	19	95	54	176	.317	.413
Day	.269	509	137	23	7	14	80	32	110	.314	.424	April	.282	220	62	10	4	7	47	17	47	.343	.459
Night	.255	1108	282	46	15	21	129	90	273	.310	.380	May	.283	322	91	14	4	10	36	23	76	.328	.444
Grass	.264	958	253	38	9	22	132	66	236	.310	.391	June	.280	314	88	16	2	5	44	27	72	.333	.392
Turf	.252	659	166	31	13	13	77	56	147	.314	.398	July	.225	222	50	9	5	4	26	21	51	.294	.365
First Pitch	.369	252	93	12	2	14	49	5	0	.389	.599	August	.222	275	61	10	3	4	26	16	73	.266	.324
Ahead on Count	.366	358	131	29	8	9	70	73	0	.467	.567	September/October	.254	264	67	10	4	5	30	18	64	.301	.379
Behind on Count	.193	543	105	16	4	7	53	0	215	.199	.276	Pre-All Star	.274	955	262	44	12	25	143	74	222	.327	.424
Two Strikes	.150	759	114	17	7	6	50	45	382	.200	.215	Post-All Star	.237	662	157	25	10	10	66	48	161	.290	.350

Hits Best Against	Avg	AB	H	2B	3B	HR	RBI	BB	SO	OBP	SLG	Hits Worst Against	Avg	AB	H	2B	3B	HR	RBI	BB	SO	OBP	SLG
Kirk McCaskill	.556	9	5	0	0	1	2	2	0	.636	.889	Bill Krueger	.000	16	0	0	0	0	0	0	7	.000	.000
Dennis Lamp	.455	11	5	1	1	1	4	0	1	.455	1.000	Alex Fernandez	.063	16	1	0	0	0	0	0	6	.063	.063
Charlie Hough	.444	9	4	2	0	1	3	1		.583	1.000	Bret Saberhagen	.083	12	1	0	0	0	1	2	5	.214	.083
Frank Tanana	.400	15	6	3	0	1	1	3	2	.500	.800	Todd Stottlemyre	.091	11	1	0	0	0	1	1	3	.154	.091
Bob Milacki	.364	11	4	2	1	0	1	0	0	.364	.727	Jaime Navarro	.118	17	2	0	0	0	0	2	5	.211	.118

Felix Fermin — Indians   Bats Right (groundball hitter)

	Avg	G	AB	R	H	2B	3B	HR	RBI	BB	SO	HBP	GDP	SB	CS	OBP	SLG	IBB	SH	SF	#Pit	#P/PA	GB	FB	G/F
1992 Season	.270	79	215	27	58	7	2	0	13	18	10	1	7	0	0	.326	.321	1	9	2	769	3.26	117	46	2.54
Last Five Years	.255	555	1624	163	414	42	9	1	107	119	96	11	54	17	12	.308	.294	2	68	12	5758	3.26	881	302	2.92

1992 Season

	Avg	AB	H	2B	3B	HR	RBI	BB	SO	OBP	SLG		Avg	AB	H	2B	3B	HR	RBI	BB	SO	OBP	SLG
vs. Left	.333	42	14	1	0	0	4	8	3	.440	.357	Scoring Posn	.286	49	14	1	0	0	13	8	2	.373	.306
vs. Right	.254	173	44	6	2	0	9	10	7	.296	.312	Close & Late	.216	37	8	1	0	0	1	4	4	.310	.243
Home	.294	102	30	3	2	0	7	9	6	.351	.363	None on/out	.271	48	13	1	0	0	0	3	4	.314	.292
Away	.248	113	28	4	0	0	6	9	4	.304	.283	Batting #2	.250	112	28	4	1	0	6	10	6	.309	.304
First Pitch	.324	37	12	0	0	0	1	0	0	.359	.324	Batting #9	.167	54	9	0	0	0	3	1	1	.193	.167
Ahead on Count	.208	53	11	2	0	0	3	11	0	.344	.245	Other	.429	49	21	3	1	0	4	7	3	.500	.531
Behind on Count	.333	72	24	4	1	0	5	0	5	.333	.417	Pre-All Star	.275	91	25	2	1	0	7	2	3	.295	.319
Two Strikes	.194	67	13	1	1	0	3	6	10	.257	.239	Post-All Star	.266	124	33	5	1	0	6	16	7	.348	.323

Last Five Years

	Avg	AB	H	2B	3B	HR	RBI	BB	SO	OBP	SLG		Avg	AB	H	2B	3B	HR	RBI	BB	SO	OBP	SLG
vs. Left	.271	457	124	10	2	0	36	46	20	.337	.302	Scoring Posn	.239	393	94	10	2	0	102	36	26	.303	.275
vs. Right	.249	1167	290	32	7	1	71	73	76	.296	.290	Close & Late	.238	231	55	5	0	0	10	19	16	.304	.260
Groundball	.248	499	124	9	4	1	28	30	28	.296	.289	None on/out	.265	396	105	6	2	1	1	28	22	.315	.298
Flyball	.244	332	81	11	3	0	30	38	19	.326	.295	Batting #2	.240	442	106	12	4	0	27	39	28	.307	.285
Home	.268	795	213	28	7	1	62	62	46	.323	.325	Batting #9	.251	900	226	26	2	1	68	59	46	.297	.288
Away	.242	829	201	14	2	0	45	57	50	.294	.264	Other	.291	282	82	4	3	0	12	21	22	.345	.326
Day	.266	507	135	10	1	1	29	36	39	.317	.296	April	.214	154	33	1	1	1	13	13	8	.274	.253
Night	.250	1117	279	32	8	0	78	83	57	.304	.293	May	.254	264	67	8	2	0	17	16	16	.299	.299
Grass	.250	1319	330	36	6	1	87	96	72	.303	.289	June	.249	305	76	8	0	0	12	18	16	.292	.275
Turf	.275	305	84	6	3	0	20	23	24	.328	.315	July	.241	299	72	7	2	0	20	18	17	.285	.278
First Pitch	.291	344	100	10	1	0	18	2	0	.296	.326	August	.285	260	74	10	1	0	28	18	13	.332	.331
Ahead on Count	.239	305	73	7	3	0	21	77	0	.392	.282	September/October	.269	342	92	8	3	0	17	36	26	.344	.310
Behind on Count	.240	579	139	17	4	0	36	0	69	.248	.283	Pre-All Star	.246	805	198	18	4	1	47	49	43	.290	.282
Two Strikes	.224	568	127	11	2	1	31	40	96	.280	.261	Post-All Star	.264	819	216	24	5	0	60	70	53	.325	.305

Batter vs. Pitcher (career)

Hits Best Against	Avg	AB	H	2B	3B	HR	RBI	BB	SO	OBP	SLG	Hits Worst Against	Avg	AB	H	2B	3B	HR	RBI	BB	SO	OBP	SLG
Mark Guthrie	.909	11	10	1	0	0	3	0	1	.909	1.000	Jeff M. Robinson	.000	9	0	0	0	0	0	2	0	.182	.000
Terry Leach	.636	11	7	3	0	0	1	0	0	.636	.909	Charlie Hough	.067	15	1	1	0	0	0	1	1	.125	.133
Bobby Witt	.611	18	11	2	0	0	5	4	0	.682	.722	Nolan Ryan	.077	13	1	0	0	0	1	1	1	.143	.077
Bill Gullickson	.500	12	6	1	0	0	1	0	0	.500	.583	Melido Perez	.077	13	1	0	0	0	1	0	0	.071	.077
Randy Johnson	.368	19	7	2	0	0	1	6	3	.520	.474	Bert Blyleven	.091	11	1	0	0	0	0	1	0	.167	.091

Alex Fernandez — White Sox   Pitches Right

	ERA	W	L	Sv	G	GS	IP	BB	SO	Avg	H	2B	3B	HR	RBI	OBP	SLG	CG	ShO	Sup	QS	#P/S	SB	CS	GB	FB	G/F
1992 Season	4.27	8	11	0	29	29	187.2	50	95	.270	199	30	3	21	87	.322	.405	4	2	4.17	14	101	15	4	236	258	0.91
Career (1990-1992)	4.28	22	29	0	76	74	467.0	172	301	.265	474	73	11	43	206	.331	.390	9	2	3.91	41	102	31	19	581	569	1.02

1992 Season

	ERA	W	L	Sv	G	GS	IP	H	HR	BB	SO		Avg	AB	H	2B	3B	HR	RBI	BB	SO	OBP	SLG
Home	4.39	4	7	0	17	17	110.2	110	12	35	50	vs. Left	.251	351	88	16	2	9	49	19	45	.295	.385
Away	4.09	4	4	0	12	12	77.0	89	9	15	45	vs. Right	.288	385	111	14	1	12	38	31	50	.346	.423
Day	6.04	0	1	0	5	5	28.1	38	2	10	20	Inning 1-6	.273	609	166	26	3	17	80	46	80	.330	.409
Night	3.95	8	10	0	24	24	159.1	161	19	40	75	Inning 7+	.260	127	33	4	0	4	7	4	15	.282	.386
Grass	4.53	6	11	0	25	25	157.0	168	19	46	77	None on	.257	439	113	18	1	16	16	23	59	.300	.412
Turf	2.93	2	0	0	4	4	30.2	31	2	4	18	Runners on	.290	297	86	12	2	5	71	27	36	.352	.394
April	4.44	1	2	0	4	4	24.1	28	3	10	15	Scoring Posn	.266	177	47	6	0	3	63	19	25	.340	.350
May	3.19	1	3	0	5	5	36.2	31	2	12	20	Close & Late	.263	76	20	0	0	3	5	1	11	.273	.382
June	5.23	1	2	0	5	5	32.2	34	1	10	17	None on/out	.238	189	45	8	1	5	5	11	22	.291	.370
July	3.86	1	0	0	3	3	21.0	21	3	5	12	vs. 1st Batr (relief)	.000	0	0	0	0	0	0	0	0	.000	.000
August	5.10	2	1	0	6	6	30.0	39	3	4	11	First Inning Pitched	.296	125	37	6	1	1	17	9	22	.343	.384
September/October	3.98	2	3	0	6	6	43.0	46	9	9	20	First 75 Pitches	.267	505	135	20	3	12	60	40	62	.328	.390
Starter	4.27	8	11	0	29	29	187.2	199	21	50	95	Pitch 76-90	.292	89	26	5	0	3	9	4	12	.326	.449
Reliever	0.00	0	0	0	0	0	0.0	0	0	0	0	Pitch 91-105	.225	80	18	3	0	2	10	3	11	.253	.338
0-3 Days Rest	0.00	0	0	0	0	0	0.0	0	0	0	0	Pitch 106+	.323	62	20	2	0	4	8	3	10	.354	.548
4 Days Rest	3.66	6	5	0	17	17	118.0	116	8	24	57	First Pitch	.322	90	29	2	1	4	14	1	0	.340	.500
5+ Days Rest	5.30	2	6	0	12	12	69.2	83	13	26	38	Ahead on Count	.228	312	71	15	1	6	23	0	76	.240	.340

1992 Season

	ERA	W	L	Sv	G	GS	IP	H	HR	BB	SO		Avg	AB	H	2B	3B	HR	RBI	BB	SO	OBP	SLG
Pre-All Star	4.23	3	7	0	14	14	93.2	93	6	32	52	Behind on Count	.286	175	50	11	0	8	30	28	0	.380	.486
Post-All Star	4.31	5	4	0	15	15	94.0	106	15	18	43	Two Strikes	.231	308	71	11	2	5	22	21	95	.283	.328

Career (1990-1992)

	ERA	W	L	Sv	G	GS	IP	H	HR	BB	SO		Avg	AB	H	2B	3B	HR	RBI	BB	SO	OBP	SLG
Home	4.35	11	15	0	38	36	234.0	219	19	82	137	vs. Left	.256	857	219	42	4	16	93	78	138	.319	.370
Away	4.21	11	14	0	38	38	233.0	255	24	90	164	vs. Right	.273	934	255	31	7	27	113	94	163	.342	.408
Day	5.40	3	7	0	16	16	91.2	105	7	34	70	Inning 1-6	.272	1523	414	67	10	34	189	153	258	.341	.396
Night	4.00	19	22	0	60	58	375.1	369	36	138	231	Inning 7+	.224	268	60	6	1	9	17	19	43	.274	.354
Grass	4.51	17	28	0	65	63	391.0	396	38	143	252	None on	.247	1041	257	40	7	28	28	91	173	.312	.379
Turf	3.08	5	1	0	11	11	76.0	78	5	29	49	Runners on	.289	750	217	33	4	15	178	81	128	.356	.404
April	6.29	3	4	0	9	9	44.1	55	6	26	35	Scoring Posn	.273	403	110	16	1	8	156	54	72	.353	.377
May	3.92	1	5	0	10	10	66.2	58	5	31	43	Close & Late	.224	156	35	1	0	4	10	10	27	.271	.308
June	4.96	3	5	0	11	11	69.0	68	3	23	46	None on/out	.251	454	114	18	3	9	9	45	67	.325	.363
July	3.99	2	0	0	9	8	49.2	50	7	12	26	vs. 1st Batr (relief)	.000	2	0	0	0	0	0	0	0	.000	.000
August	4.83	5	7	0	18	18	104.1	118	6	29	65	First Inning Pitched	.254	299	76	12	2	4	32	28	67	.317	.348
September/October	3.11	8	8	0	19	19	133.0	125	16	51	86	First 75 Pitches	.272	1235	336	58	11	26	148	119	208	.339	.400
Starter	4.30	22	29	0	74	74	464.1	473	43	171	299	Pitch 76-90	.244	225	55	5	0	6	21	20	34	.305	.347
Reliever	0.00	0	0	0	2	0	2.2	1	0	1	2	Pitch 91-105	.286	185	53	7	0	5	21	18	32	.350	.405
0-3 Days Rest	4.91	0	1	0	2	2	11.0	13	1	5	10	Pitch 106+	.205	146	30	3	0	6	16	15	27	.278	.349
4 Days Rest	4.59	17	18	0	49	49	302.0	316	25	112	187	First Pitch	.369	236	87	12	2	8	37	1	0	.372	.538
5+ Days Rest	3.69	5	10	0	23	23	151.1	144	17	54	102	Ahead on Count	.215	806	173	28	4	11	56	0	250	.223	.300
Pre-All Star	4.89	7	14	0	32	31	191.1	192	15	83	128	Behind on Count	.269	391	113	23	3	13	58	82	0	.407	.463
Post-All Star	3.85	15	15	0	44	43	275.2	282	28	89	173	Two Strikes	.195	605	157	18	5	12	62	89	301	.279	.275

Pitcher vs. Batter (career)

Pitches Best Vs.	Avg	AB	H	2B	3B	HR	RBI	BB	SO	OBP	SLG	Pitches Worst Vs.	Avg	AB	H	2B	3B	HR	RBI	BB	SO	OBP	SLG
Franklin Stubbs	.000	11	0	0	0	0	0	0	7	.000	.000	Carney Lansford	.500	8	4	1	0	0	0	4	1	.667	.625
Jeff Huson	.000	9	0	0	0	0	1	3	1	.231	.000	Joe Orsulak	.467	15	7	1	2	0	2	0	0	.467	.800
Junior Felix	.063	16	1	0	0	0	0	6		.063	.063	Tom Brunansky	.400	15	6	0	1	2	6	0	3	.400	.933
Jose Canseco	.071	14	1	0	0	0	2	2	9	.176	.071	Jay Buhner	.400	15	6	2	0	1	3	2	3	.471	.733
Gary Pettis	.091	11	1	0	0	0	1	1	3	.167	.091	Travis Fryman	.375	16	6	2	1	1	2	1	2	.412	.813

Sid Fernandez — Mets   Pitches Left (flyball pitcher)

	ERA	W	L	Sv	G	GS	IP	BB	SO	Avg	H	2B	3B	HR	RBI	OBP	SLG	CG	ShO	Sup	QS	#P/S	SB	CS	GB	FB	G/F
1992 Season	2.73	14	11	0	32	32	214.2	67	193	.210	162	37	9	12	60	.273	.328	5	2	4.40	26	107	17	9	155	310	0.50
Last Five Years	2.98	50	43	0	136	133	844.1	288	792	.201	612	115	29	70	265	.272	.327	14	6	4.46	88	100	87	26	615	1146	0.54

1992 Season

	ERA	W	L	Sv	G	GS	IP	H	HR	BB	SO		Avg	AB	H	2B	3B	HR	RBI	BB	SO	OBP	SLG
Home	2.17	7	4	0	14	14	99.1	68	5	26	101	vs. Left	.188	149	28	6	5	0	12	16	45	.272	.295
Away	3.20	7	7	0	18	18	115.1	94	7	41	92	vs. Right	.215	622	134	31	4	12	48	51	148	.273	.336
Day	2.35	3	2	0	8	8	53.2	37	5	18	58	Inning 1-6	.204	653	133	31	8	10	54	60	179	.270	.322
Night	2.85	11	9	0	24	24	161.0	125	7	49	135	Inning 7+	.246	118	29	6	1	2	6	7	14	.294	.364
Grass	2.60	11	6	0	20	20	138.1	105	9	38	127	None on	.208	514	107	24	6	9	9	31	131	.257	.331
Turf	2.95	3	5	0	12	12	76.1	57	4	29	66	Runners on	.214	257	55	13	3	3	51	36	62	.302	.323
April	5.54	1	2	0	5	5	26.0	20	3	13	39	Scoring Posn	.192	146	28	8	0	1	43	22	40	.279	.267
May	1.89	2	3	0	5	5	33.1	22	4	6	31	Close & Late	.316	57	18	3	0	1	4	5	8	.381	.421
June	2.38	3	2	0	6	6	41.2	34	4	10	37	None on/out	.212	217	46	8	3	5	5	12	51	.253	.346
July	2.08	3	1	0	5	5	34.2	19	0	11	31	vs. 1st Batr (relief)	.000	0	0	0	0	0	0	0	0	.000	.000
August	3.63	2	1	0	6	6	39.2	39	0	15	24	First Inning Pitched	.244	119	29	5	3	2	15	16	36	.328	.387
September/October	1.60	3	2	0	5	5	39.1	28	1	12	31	First 75 Pitches	.203	502	102	25	7	7	42	49	146	.274	.323
Starter	2.73	14	11	0	32	32	214.2	162	12	67	193	Pitch 76-90	.194	108	21	4	1	2	9	9	23	.252	.306
Reliever	0.00	0	0	0	0	0	0.0	0	0	0	0	Pitch 91-105	.273	88	24	2	1	3	7	3	18	.301	.420
0-3 Days Rest	0.00	0	0	0	0	0	0.0	0	0	0	0	Pitch 106+	.205	73	15	6	0	0	2	6	6	.266	.288
4 Days Rest	2.75	9	7	0	20	20	134.1	111	9	39	119	First Pitch	.279	86	24	8	2	1	10	4	0	.316	.453
5+ Days Rest	2.69	5	4	0	12	12	80.1	51	3	28	74	Ahead on Count	.167	443	74	14	2	3	23	0	166	.167	.228
Pre-All Star	3.19	7	8	0	18	18	113.0	83	11	36	115	Behind on Count	.295	129	38	8	4	7	16	29	0	.421	.581
Post-All Star	2.21	7	3	0	14	14	101.2	79	1	31	78	Two Strikes	.147	441	65	13	1	3	18	34	193	.208	.202

Last Five Years

	ERA	W	L	Sv	G	GS	IP	H	HR	BB	SO		Avg	AB	H	2B	3B	HR	RBI	BB	SO	OBP	SLG
Home	2.29	31	16	0	67	67	451.0	282	33	144	458	vs. Left	.218	504	110	21	7	7	49	51	155	.295	.329
Away	3.78	19	27	0	69	66	393.1	330	37	144	334	vs. Right	.198	2539	502	94	22	63	216	237	637	.268	.327
Day	3.18	12	13	0	41	41	249.1	190	24	89	263	Inning 1-6	.195	2624	511	94	26	58	238	254	713	.268	.317
Night	2.90	38	30	0	95	92	595.0	422	46	199	529	Inning 7+	.241	419	101	21	3	12	27	34	79	.303	.391
Grass	2.74	37	26	0	92	91	594.0	413	53	185	581	None on	.195	1977	385	73	17	39	39	171	560	.263	.308
Turf	3.56	13	17	0	44	42	250.1	199	17	103	211	Runners on	.213	1066	227	42	12	31	226	117	232	.289	.362
April	4.58	5	3	0	18	16	92.1	67	8	49	83	Scoring Posn	.203	556	113	22	4	14	178	74	141	.289	.333
May	2.65	7	10	0	21	20	125.2	100	13	37	114	Close & Late	.293	164	48	9	1	4	13	11	34	.341	.433
June	3.14	8	5	0	21	21	129.0	98	16	46	122	None on/out	.207	839	174	25	8	22	22	60	224	.263	.335
July	2.56	10	7	0	24	24	151.0	98	10	51	153	vs. 1st Batr (relief)	.500	2	1	0	0	0	0	0	0	.667	.500
August	2.83	9	8	0	30	30	194.1	148	15	52	170	First Inning Pitched	.206	490	101	19	6	14	53	60	127	.295	.355

Last Five Years

	ERA	W	L	Sv	G	GS	IP	H	HR	BB	SO		Avg	AB	H	2B	3B	HR	RBI	BB	SO	OBP	SLG
September/October	2.76	11	8	0	22	22	152.0	101	8	53	150	First 75 Pitches	.192	2132	409	76	20	44	183	210	604	.267	.308
Starter	2.98	50	43	0	133	133	838.1	608	69	267	788	Pitch 76-90	.197	395	78	16	5	13	41	34	83	.260	.362
Reliever	3.00	0	0	0	3	0	6.0	4	1	1	4	Pitch 91-105	.242	297	72	10	2	9	25	22	65	.298	.380
0-3 Days Rest	2.12	1	0	0	3	3	17.0	12	1	4	17	Pitch 106+	.242	219	53	13	2	4	16	22	40	.311	.374
4 Days Rest	2.74	34	22	0	78	78	509.1	357	43	163	469	First Pitch	.289	360	104	29	5	10	46	11	0	.315	.481
5+ Days Rest	3.43	15	21	0	52	52	312.0	239	25	120	302	Ahead on Count	.152	1616	245	44	13	21	95	0	674	.156	.234
Pre-All Star	3.22	24	21	0	67	64	393.2	288	40	148	360	Behind on Count	.274	551	151	26	8	26	75	141	4	.420	.492
Post-All Star	2.78	26	22	0	69	69	450.2	324	30	140	432	Two Strikes	.134	1666	224	37	10	18	81	135	792	.203	.201

Pitcher vs. Batter (since 1984)

Pitches Best Vs.	Avg	AB	H	2B	3B	HR	RBI	BB	SO	OBP	SLG	Pitches Worst Vs.	Avg	AB	H	2B	3B	HR	RBI	BB	SO	OBP	SLG
Luis Rivera	.000	12	0	0	0	0	0	2	3	.143	.000	Mariano Duncan	.405	42	17	6	2	0	5	3	5	.458	.643
Jim Lindeman	.000	10	0	0	0	0	1	1	3	.091	.000	Mike Fitzgerald	.400	15	6	2	0	2	7	3	2	.500	.933
Ron Gant	.000	10	0	0	0	0	1	2	5	.154	.000	Glenn Braggs	.400	10	4	1	1	0	3	2	3	.500	.700
Tom Brunansky	.063	16	1	0	0	0	0	1	3	.118	.063	Lance Parrish	.389	18	7	1	0	2	4	3	4	.476	.778
Sid Bream	.063	16	1	0	0	0		1	3	.118	.063	Dave Anderson	.333	15	5	0	0	1	2	1	3	.545	.533

Tony Fernandez — Padres

Bats Both (groundball hitter)

	Avg	G	AB	R	H	2B	3B	HR	RBI	BB	SO	HBP	GDP	SB	CS	OBP	SLG	IBB	SH	SF	#Pit	#P/PA	GB	FB	G/F
1992 Season	.275	155	622	84	171	32	4	4	37	56	62	4	5	20	20	.337	.359	4	9	3	2413	3.52	250	158	1.58
Last Five Years	.274	755	3036	389	831	152	39	28	275	256	322	18	51	106	53	.331	.377	12	23	24	11842	3.55	1230	819	1.50

1992 Season

	Avg	AB	H	2B	3B	HR	RBI	BB	SO	OBP	SLG		Avg	AB	H	2B	3B	HR	RBI	BB	SO	OBP	SLG
vs. Left	.280	207	58	9	0	1	18	22	12	.349	.338	Scoring Posn	.273	99	27	3	0	1	34	12	11	.353	.333
vs. Right	.272	415	113	23	4	3	19	34	50	.331	.369	Close & Late	.320	103	33	4	1	0	6	10	10	.377	.379
Groundball	.285	256	73	17	2	2	15	18	22	.333	.391	None on/out	.274	277	76	16	4	1	1	19	22	.326	.372
Flyball	.252	127	32	5	0	0	7	11	14	.314	.291	Batting #1	.274	620	170	32	4	4	37	55	62	.336	.358
Home	.282	301	85	16	1	3	19	34	35	.355	.372	Batting #6	.500	2	1	0	0	0	0	1	0	.667	.500
Away	.268	321	86	16	3	1	18	22	27	.320	.346	Other	.000	0	0	0	0	0	0	0	0	.000	.000
Day	.243	189	46	6	0	1	13	19	24	.318	.291	April	.314	86	27	3	0	1	6	5	9	.352	.384
Night	.289	433	125	26	4	3	24	37	38	.346	.388	May	.327	107	35	7	1	1	12	8	12	.381	.439
Grass	.269	461	124	25	4	4	28	48	49	.339	.367	June	.277	101	28	4	2	0	5	15	13	.378	.356
Turf	.292	161	47	7	0	0	9	8	13	.331	.335	July	.183	104	19	6	0	0	3	7	9	.234	.240
First Pitch	.325	123	40	7	2	1	6	3	0	.341	.439	August	.258	93	24	4	1	0	5	10	5	.327	.323
Ahead on Count	.353	150	53	11	1	2	10	30	0	.456	.480	September/October	.290	131	38	8	0	2	6	11	14	.345	.397
Behind on Count	.278	180	50	8	0	1	12	0	30	.290	.339	Pre-All Star	.297	340	101	18	3	2	25	32	37	.362	.385
Two Strikes	.220	241	53	9	0	1	17	23	62	.295	.270	Post-All Star	.248	282	70	14	1	2	12	24	25	.306	.326

1992 By Position

Position	Avg	AB	H	2B	3B	HR	RBI	BB	SO	OBP	SLG	G	GS	Innings	PO	A	E	DP	Fld Pct	Rng Fctr	In Zone	Outs	Zone Rtg	MLB Zone
As ss	.275	622	171	32	4	4	37	56	62	.337	.359	155	155	1348.1	241	403	11	65	.983	4.30	489	421	.861	.885

Last Five Years

	Avg	AB	H	2B	3B	HR	RBI	BB	SO	OBP	SLG		Avg	AB	H	2B	3B	HR	RBI	BB	SO	OBP	SLG
vs. Left	.266	997	265	40	7	9	86	94	83	.328	.347	Scoring Posn	.301	631	190	37	10	7	238	67	71	.365	.425
vs. Right	.278	2039	566	112	32	19	189	162	239	.333	.392	Close & Late	.308	441	136	16	6	2	35	41	34	.368	.385
Groundball	.271	883	239	42	11	6	65	71	85	.326	.364	None on/out	.260	938	244	42	11	7	7	73	94	.318	.351
Flyball	.274	669	183	37	11	6	68	55	65	.330	.389	Batting #1	.271	1533	416	81	12	12	126	125	161	.329	.363
Home	.282	1485	419	79	23	11	139	139	163	.344	.389	Batting #2	.271	1182	320	58	20	12	107	107	135	.331	.384
Away	.266	1551	412	73	16	17	136	117	159	.319	.366	Other	.296	321	95	13	7	4	42	24	26	.346	.417
Day	.268	920	247	44	8	11	79	78	111	.328	.370	April	.278	353	98	9	3	4	41	22	51	.326	.354
Night	.276	2116	584	108	31	17	196	178	211	.333	.380	May	.265	558	148	31	5	6	47	52	66	.328	.371
Grass	.272	1604	436	77	16	19	134	144	180	.333	.375	June	.292	538	157	30	8	3	46	59	56	.363	.394
Turf	.276	1432	395	75	23	9	141	112	142	.330	.379	July	.221	489	108	23	6	5	35	35	51	.271	.323
First Pitch	.343	545	187	33	10	4	52	4	0	.348	.462	August	.277	537	149	26	11	3	51	41	48	.330	.384
Ahead on Count	.308	790	243	44	20	9	80	137	0	.405	.448	September/October	.305	561	171	33	6	7	55	47	50	.360	.422
Behind on Count	.246	931	229	42	8	8	79	0	172	.253	.334	Pre-All Star	.273	1626	444	78	18	15	146	148	187	.336	.384
Two Strikes	.219	1197	262	45	3	10	93	109	322	.289	.287	Post-All Star	.274	1410	387	74	21	13	129	108	135	.326	.384

Batter vs. Pitcher (since 1984)

Hits Best Against	Avg	AB	H	2B	3B	HR	RBI	BB	SO	OBP	SLG	Hits Worst Against	Avg	AB	H	2B	3B	HR	RBI	BB	SO	OBP	SLG
Jeff M. Robinson	.500	18	9	3	0	1	3	3	1	.571	.833	Chris Nabholz	.000	12	0	0	0	0	0	1	1	.077	.000
Greg Cadaret	.500	10	5	1	1	0	4	1	1	.500	1.100	Bobby Thigpen	.000	10	0	0	0	0	0	1	1	.091	.000
Curt Schilling	.500	10	5	2	1	0	2	2	3	.583	.900	Dwight Gooden	.118	17	2	0	0	0	0	1	4	.167	.118
Kirk McCaskill	.429	42	18	2	0	3	8	2	1	.455	.690	Scott Bankhead	.133	30	4	0	0	0	0	1	3	.161	.133
Paul Gibson	.421	19	8	2	2	1	8	6	2	.560	.895	Danny Darwin	.167	12	2	0	0	0	0	0	2	.167	.167

Mike Fetters — Brewers

Pitches Right (groundball pitcher)

	ERA	W	L	Sv	G	GS	IP	BB	SO	Avg	H	2B	3B	HR	RBI	OBP	SLG	GF	IR	IRS	Hld	SvOp	SB	CS	GB	FB	G/F
1992 Season	1.87	5	1	2	50	0	62.2	24	43	.185	38	8	0	3	26	.290	.268	11	58	18	8	5	4	3	92	44	2.09
Career (1989-1992)	3.58	8	7	3	96	6	178.1	73	106	.261	173	21	1	17	95	.344	.373	29	93	32	9	7	16	10	303	129	2.35

1992 Season

	ERA	W	L	Sv	G	GS	IP	H	HR	BB	SO
Home	0.63	2	0	1	26	0	28.2	14	0	12	18
Away	2.91	3	1	1	24	0	34.0	24	3	12	25
Starter	0.00	0	0	0	0	0	0.0	0	0	0	0
Reliever	1.87	5	1	2	50	0	62.2	38	3	24	43
0 Days rest	8.68	2	0	0	6	0	9.1	10	3	3	8
1 or 2 Days rest	1.26	2	1	2	22	0	28.2	15	0	7	20
3+ Days rest	0.00	1	0	0	22	0	24.2	13	0	14	15
Pre-All Star	0.84	4	1	1	22	0	32.1	16	1	8	22
Post-All Star	2.97	1	0	1	28	0	30.1	22	2	16	21

	Avg	AB	H	2B	3B	HR	RBI	BB	SO	OBP	SLG
vs. Left	.225	71	16	3	0	1	8	15	9	.360	.310
vs. Right	.164	134	22	5	0	2	18	9	34	.250	.246
Scoring Posn	.224	67	15	4	0	1	24	10	15	.333	.328
Close & Late	.146	89	13	1	0	1	12	15	22	.294	.191
None on/out	.209	43	9	1	0	0	0	5	8	.306	.233
First Pitch	.154	26	4	2	0	0	3	0		.185	.231
Behind on Count	.283	46	13	3	0	1	12	18	0	.478	.413
Ahead on Count	.149	94	14	2	0	2	8	0	37	.175	.234
Two Strikes	.098	92	9	2	0	0	6		43	.170	.185

Cecil Fielder — Tigers

Bats Right (flyball hitter)

	Avg	G	AB	R	H	2B	3B	HR	RBI	BB	SO	HBP	GDP	SB	CS	OBP	SLG	IBB	SH	SF	#Pit	#P/PA	GB	FB	G/F
1992 Season	.244	155	594	80	145	22	0	35	124	73	151	2	14	0	0	.325	.458	8	0	7	2594	3.84	160	181	0.88
Last Five Years	.258	550	1965	310	507	78	2	139	412	255	537	14	52	0	2	.345	.512	31	0	17	8799	3.91	522	602	0.87

1992 Season

	Avg	AB	H	2B	3B	HR	RBI	BB	SO	OBP	SLG
vs. Left	.231	134	31	5	0	9	31	24	45	.352	.470
vs. Right	.248	460	114	17	0	26	93	49	106	.317	.454
Groundball	.227	150	34	4	0	7	27	15	42	.299	.393
Flyball	.215	200	43	4	0	9	33	24	54	.298	.370
Home	.257	296	76	15	0	18	68	36	66	.339	.490
Away	.232	298	69	7	0	17	56	37	85	.312	.426
Day	.259	201	52	5	0	16	51	22	50	.327	.522
Night	.237	393	93	17	0	19	73	51	101	.324	.425
Grass	.253	513	130	18	0	34	114	64	121	.336	.487
Turf	.185	81	15	4	0	1	10	9	30	.261	.272
First Pitch	.386	70	27	5	0	10	34	7	0	.436	.886
Ahead on Count	.339	127	43	7	0	10	32	34	0	.475	.630
Behind on Count	.204	211	43	4	0	5	25	0	80	.204	.294
Two Strikes	.152	302	46	4	0	10	38	33	151	.237	.265

	Avg	AB	H	2B	3B	HR	RBI	BB	SO	OBP	SLG
Scoring Posn	.264	182	48	7	0	10	82	26	41	.344	.467
Close & Late	.349	83	29	1	0	5	20	7	18	.396	.542
None on/out	.273	165	45	6	0	12	12	19	42	.348	.527
Batting #3	.250	4	1	0	0	1	2	2	1	.500	1.000
Batting #4	.244	590	144	22	0	34	122	71	150	.324	.464
Other	.000	0	0	0	0	0	0	0	0	.000	.000
April	.231	78	18	2	0	7	20	7	13	.287	.526
May	.213	75	16	8	0	1	13	9	23	.294	.360
June	.265	113	30	4	0	8	32	16	32	.359	.513
July	.224	107	24	2	0	6	21	12	32	.303	.411
August	.260	104	27	3	0	7	22	11	28	.328	.490
September/October	.256	117	30	3	0	6	16	18	23	.356	.436
Pre-All Star	.244	312	76	14	0	18	75	39	81	.326	.462
Post-All Star	.245	282	69	8	0	17	49	34	70	.325	.454

1992 By Position

Position	Avg	AB	H	2B	3B	HR	RBI	BB	SO	OBP	SLG	G	GS	Innings	PO	A	E	DP	Fld Pct	Rng Fctr	In Zone	Outs	Zone Rtg	MLB Zone
As Designated Hitter	.234	167	39	5	0	7	30	21	51	.317	.389	43	43	---	---	---	---	---	---	---	---	---	---	---
As 1b	.248	427	106	17	0	28	94	52	100	.329	.485	114	112	954.1	957	89	10	98	.991	---	188	164	.872	.843

Last Five Years

	Avg	AB	H	2B	3B	HR	RBI	BB	SO	OBP	SLG
vs. Left	.287	616	177	30	1	56	137	99	167	.389	.612
vs. Right	.245	1349	330	48	1	83	275	156	370	.324	.466
Groundball	.255	557	142	17	0	29	89	58	144	.331	.442
Flyball	.224	495	111	14	1	39	112	73	156	.323	.493
Home	.258	951	245	41	0	76	213	132	241	.350	.540
Away	.258	1014	262	37	2	63	199	123	296	.339	.485
Day	.229	621	142	17	0	50	143	78	166	.316	.498
Night	.272	1344	365	61	2	89	269	177	371	.358	.504
Grass	.261	1592	415	61	0	115	342	221	424	.353	.517
Turf	.247	373	92	17	1	24	70	34	113	.308	.491
First Pitch	.382	249	95	18	0	23	76	17	0	.420	.731
Ahead on Count	.361	386	148	30	0	47	125	111	0	.518	.822
Behind on Count	.210	648	136	17	0	32	102	1	254	.216	.384
Two Strikes	.168	1023	172	19	1	45	134	118	535	.256	.321

	Avg	AB	H	2B	3B	HR	RBI	BB	SO	OBP	SLG
Scoring Posn	.271	550	149	23	2	36	260	107	152	.385	.516
Close & Late	.258	298	77	6	0	11	52	42	86	.353	.389
None on/out	.264	527	139	19	0	41	41	44	141	.323	.533
Batting #3	.197	117	23	2	0	8	19	11	43	.275	.419
Batting #4	.261	1641	426	65	1	114	351	224	433	.351	.510
Other	.271	207	56	11	1	17	42	20	61	.335	.580
April	.238	248	59	7	0	18	59	24	55	.312	.484
May	.277	303	84	24	0	20	56	44	90	.369	.554
June	.283	350	99	12	0	28	93	48	98	.370	.557
July	.259	343	89	11	1	27	71	40	98	.338	.534
August	.244	352	86	18	1	23	73	50	103	.340	.497
September/October	.244	369	90	6	0	23	60	49	93	.333	.447
Pre-All Star	.269	1021	275	44	0	74	234	129	279	.353	.530
Post-All Star	.246	944	232	34	2	65	178	126	258	.336	.493

Batter vs. Pitcher (career)

Hits Best Against	Avg	AB	H	2B	3B	HR	RBI	BB	SO	OBP	SLG
Mike Jeffcoat	.600	10	6	0	0	2	6	3	1	.692	1.200
Rich DeLucia	.400	10	4	0	0	3	11	2	1	.500	1.300
Jack Morris	.375	16	6	1	0	3	7	1	3	.412	1.000
Dennis Lamp	.364	11	4	1	0	2	2	1	2	.417	1.000
Matt Young	.308	13	4	0	0	3	10	4	4	.471	1.000

Hits Worst Against	Avg	AB	H	2B	3B	HR	RBI	BB	SO	OBP	SLG
Mark Eichhorn	.000	12	0	0	0	0	1	0	5	.000	.000
Juan Guzman	.000	8	0	0	0	0	1	3	3	.250	.000
Roger Clemens	.048	21	1	0	0	0	1	2	11	.130	.048
Gene Nelson	.050	20	1	0	0	0	1	0	5	.095	.050
Dennis Eckersley	.091	11	1	0	0	0	2	1	7	.167	.091

Bien Figueroa — Cardinals
Bats Right (groundball hitter)

	Avg	G	AB	R	H	2B	3B	HR	RBI	BB	SO	HBP	GDP	SB	CS	OBP	SLG	IBB	SH	SF	#Pit	#P/PA	GB	FB	G/F
1992 Season	.182	12	11	1	2	1	0	0	4	1	2	0	0	0	0	.250	.273	0	0	0	39	3.25	4	2	2.00

1992 Season

	Avg	AB	H	2B	3B	HR	RBI	BB	SO	OBP	SLG		Avg	AB	H	2B	3B	HR	RBI	BB	SO	OBP	SLG
vs. Left	.000	1	0	0	0	0	0	0	0	.000	.000	Scoring Posn	.143	7	1	1	0	0	4	0	2	.143	.286
vs. Right	.200	10	2	1	0	0	4	1	2	.273	.300	Close & Late	.000	2	0	0	0	0	0	0	0	.000	.000

Tom Filer — Mets
Pitches Right (groundball pitcher)

	ERA	W	L	Sv	G	GS	IP	BB	SO	Avg	H	2B	3B	HR	RBI	OBP	SLG	GF	IR	IRS	Hld	SvOp	SB	CS	GB	FB	G/F
1992 Season	2.05	0	1	0	9	1	22.0	6	9	.222	18	3	1	2	5	.276	.358	1	8	1	0	0	3	1	34	26	1.31
Last Five Years	4.09	14	15	0	48	34	218.0	71	76	.273	226	31	8	18	82	.331	.394	2	13	1	2	0	16	7	395	213	1.85

1992 Season

	ERA	W	L	Sv	G	GS	IP	H	HR	BB	SO		Avg	AB	H	2B	3B	HR	RBI	BB	SO	OBP	SLG
Home	2.25	0	0	0	4	1	16.0	13	2	6	6	vs. Left	.150	40	6	0	1	1	2	3	3	.209	.275
Away	1.50	0	1	0	5	0	6.0	5	0	0	3	vs. Right	.293	41	12	3	0	1	3	3	6	.341	.439

Last Five Years

	ERA	W	L	Sv	G	GS	IP	H	HR	BB	SO		Avg	AB	H	2B	3B	HR	RBI	BB	SO	OBP	SLG
Home	3.62	7	9	0	22	15	99.1	103	9	33	41	vs. Left	.249	421	105	13	6	9	41	45	30	.325	.373
Away	4.47	7	6	0	26	19	118.2	123	9	38	35	vs. Right	.297	408	121	18	2	9	41	26	46	.338	.417
Day	5.21	3	5	0	12	8	48.1	52	2	19	16	Inning 1-6	.273	722	197	29	8	17	80	66	64	.334	.406
Night	3.77	11	10	0	36	26	169.2	174	16	52	60	Inning 7+	.271	107	29	2	0	1	2	5	12	.310	.318
Grass	3.97	12	13	0	40	29	188.0	193	15	62	65	None on	.269	498	134	19	8	5	5	35	50	.320	.369
Turf	4.80	2	2	0	8	5	30.0	33	3	9	11	Runners on	.278	331	92	12	0	13	77	36	26	.347	.432
April	1.29	2	1	0	4	2	14.0	8	0	5	7	Scoring Posn	.243	173	42	6	0	10	68	22	14	.324	.451
May	5.19	2	2	0	5	4	26.0	28	2	9	6	Close & Late	.444	18	8	1	0	0	0	2	4	.500	.500
June	4.34	2	2	0	5	5	29.0	38	1	8	7	None on/out	.300	217	65	9	3	3	3	14	18	.342	.410
July	3.71	3	3	0	14	7	53.1	47	7	20	29	vs. 1st Batr (relief)	.286	14	4	0	0	1	2	0	3	.286	.500
August	4.17	3	6	0	14	10	69.0	71	5	20	22	First Inning Pitched	.295	176	52	7	3	5	25	15	17	.347	.455
September/October	4.72	2	1	0	6	6	26.2	34	3	9	5	First 15 Pitches	.267	165	44	6	2	4	18	11	15	.311	.400
Starter	4.11	14	12	0	34	34	197.0	206	16	66	67	Pitch 16-30	.253	146	37	3	2	1	7	11	17	.308	.322
Reliever	3.86	0	3	0	14	0	21.0	20	2	5	9	Pitch 31-45	.284	141	40	7	0	6	18	11	12	.336	.461
0 Days rest	0.00	0	0	0	1	0	1.0	1	0	0	0	Pitch 46+	.279	377	105	15	4	7	39	36	32	.347	.395
1 or 2 Days rest	8.10	0	2	0	4	0	3.1	5	0	0	3	First Pitch	.295	129	38	4	0	2	7	5	0	.321	.372
3+ Days rest	3.24	0	1	0	9	0	16.2	14	2	5	6	Ahead on Count	.237	337	80	11	3	6	31	0	63	.240	.341
Pre-All Star	3.89	7	6	0	18	14	90.1	92	6	27	33	Behind on Count	.327	220	72	10	2	6	27	36	0	.418	.473
Post-All Star	4.23	7	9	0	30	20	127.2	134	12	44	43	Two Strikes	.208	293	61	7	3	4	20	30	76	.284	.294

Pitcher vs. Batter (since 1984)

Pitches Best Vs.	Avg	AB	H	2B	3B	HR	RBI	BB	SO	OBP	SLG	Pitches Worst Vs.	Avg	AB	H	2B	3B	HR	RBI	BB	SO	OBP	SLG
Cal Ripken	.000	12	0	0	0	0	2	2	3	.133	.000	Dave Henderson	.500	8	4	1	0	0	2	3	2	.636	.625
Mike Greenwell	.167	12	2	0	0	0	0	1	1	.231	.167	Wade Boggs	.364	11	4	1	0	1	2	0	.429	.455
Fred McGriff	.222	9	2	1	0	0	2	1	.364	.333											

Chuck Finley — Angels
Pitches Left

	ERA	W	L	Sv	G	GS	IP	BB	SO	Avg	H	2B	3B	HR	RBI	OBP	SLG	CG	ShO	Sup	QS	#P/S	SB	CS	GB	FB	G/F
1992 Season	3.96	7	12	0	31	31	204.1	98	124	.278	212	34	3	24	88	.359	.425	4	1	3.74	17	109	21	18	271	245	1.11
Last Five Years	3.36	68	54	0	157	157	1061.2	444	739	.252	989	171	19	92	376	.329	.376	26	6	4.43	98	107	86	71	1367	1172	1.17

1992 Season

	ERA	W	L	Sv	G	GS	IP	H	HR	BB	SO		Avg	AB	H	2B	3B	HR	RBI	BB	SO	OBP	SLG
Home	3.93	3	5	0	16	16	105.1	110	9	48	70	vs. Left	.402	87	35	5	1	1	9	6	9	.441	.517
Away	4.00	4	7	0	15	15	99.0	102	15	50	54	vs. Right	.262	675	177	29	2	23	79	92	115	.349	.413
Day	5.04	1	3	0	11	11	64.1	76	11	36	37	Inning 1-6	.278	650	181	30	3	22	80	88	108	.363	.435
Night	3.47	6	9	0	20	20	140.0	136	13	62	87	Inning 7+	.277	112	31	4	0	2	8	10	16	.333	.366
Grass	3.97	5	11	0	27	27	176.2	187	20	85	111	None on	.304	415	126	24	2	14	14	63	69	.399	.472
Turf	3.90	2	1	0	4	4	27.2	25	4	13	13	Runners on	.248	347	86	10	1	10	74	35	55	.309	.369
April	5.00	1	1	0	2	2	9.0	7	5	5	6	Scoring Posn	.224	196	44	4	1	5	62	24	38	.296	.332
May	6.12	0	3	0	6	6	32.1	45	8	17	21	Close & Late	.242	62	15	2	0	2	6	7	12	.314	.371
June	5.35	1	4	0	6	6	37.0	48	3	16	18	None on/out	.305	190	58	11	2	6	6	29	34	.403	.479
July	3.67	1	1	0	5	5	34.1	33	3	18	18	vs. 1st Batr (relief)	.000	0	0	0	0	0	0	0	0	.000	.000
August	2.87	1	2	0	6	6	47.0	41	4	26	34	First Inning Pitched	.288	118	34	5	1	5	15	16	17	.368	.475
September/October	2.42	1	0	0	6	6	44.2	38	1	16	27	First 75 Pitches	.283	505	143	23	3	18	61	74	79	.372	.448
Starter	3.96	7	12	0	31	31	204.1	212	24	98	124	Pitch 76-90	.270	100	27	3	0	2	12	12	16	.351	.360
Reliever	0.00	0	0	0	0	0	0.0	0	0	0	0	Pitch 91-105	.250	84	21	4	0	3	8	7	16	.304	.405
0-3 Days Rest	0.00	0	0	0	0	0	0.0	0	0	0	0	Pitch 106+	.288	73	21	4	0	1	7	5	13	.329	.384
4 Days Rest	3.95	4	5	0	21	21	141.1	149	12	65	81	First Pitch	.260	104	27	4	0	7	21	1	0	.257	.500
5+ Days Rest	4.00	3	7	0	10	10	63.0	63	12	33	43	Ahead on Count	.250	320	80	10	1	5	19	0	95	.253	.334
Pre-All Star	5.44	2	9	0	16	16	92.2	113	18	47	51	Behind on Count	.344	180	62	12	0	8	26	58	0	.502	.544
Post-All Star	2.74	5	3	0	15	15	111.2	99	6	51	73	Two Strikes	.222	351	78	10	2	7	29	39	124	.301	.322

Last Five Years

	ERA	W	L	Sv	G	GS	IP	H	HR	SO		Avg	AB	H	2B	3B	HR	RBI	BB	SO	OBP	SLG
Home	2.95	36	27	0	81	81	570.2	516	49	215	422	vs. Left	.272	551	150	23	1	6	37	59	80	.346	.350
Away	3.83	32	27	0	76	76	491.0	473	43	229	317	vs. Right	.249	3373	839	148	18	86	339	385	659	.326	.380
Day	3.67	17	16	0	43	43	281.2	273	28	123	195	Inning 1-6	.249	3207	798	138	18	72	319	360	622	.326	.370
Night	3.24	51	38	0	114	114	780.0	716	64	321	544	Inning 7+	.266	717	191	33	1	20	57	84	117	.345	.399
Grass	3.41	53	50	0	134	134	903.2	855	81	378	662	None on	.258	2309	595	101	10	61	61	268	425	.338	.389
Turf	3.08	15	4	0	23	23	158.0	134	11	66	77	Runners on	.244	1615	394	70	9	31	315	176	314	.317	.356
April	2.53	13	7	0	20	20	135.0	103	9	49	83	Scoring Posn	.240	858	206	37	6	14	270	117	182	.322	.346
May	3.95	13	9	0	27	27	173.0	181	16	72	125	Close & Late	.260	435	113	20	1	11	37	49	81	.335	.386
June	3.75	11	13	0	30	30	197.0	192	19	77	153	None on/out	.248	1040	258	41	6	22	22	101	175	.319	.363
July	3.60	11	5	0	25	25	177.1	171	16	68	125	vs. 1st Batr (relief)	.000	0	0	0	0	0	0	0	0	.000	.000
August	3.28	10	10	0	26	26	178.1	163	19	78	117	First Inning Pitched	.251	573	144	21	5	12	66	66	98	.330	.368
September/October	2.87	10	10	0	29	29	201.0	179	13	100	136	First 75 Pitches	.255	2605	665	112	16	62	266	294	489	.331	.382
Starter	3.36	68	54	0	157	157	1061.2	989	92	444	739	Pitch 76-90	.239	498	119	23	2	13	45	55	88	.319	.371
Reliever	0.00	0	0	0	0	0	0.0	0	0	0	0	Pitch 91-105	.248	423	105	19	1	6	29	38	89	.310	.340
0-3 Days Rest	6.51	3	1	0	5	5	27.2	23	4	17	17	Pitch 106+	.251	398	100	17	0	11	36	57	73	.346	.377
4 Days Rest	3.10	34	28	0	93	93	644.2	606	51	270	452	Ahead on Count	.193	1734	335	49	5	25	104	1	620	.199	.270
5+ Days Rest	3.56	27	25	0	59	59	389.1	360	37	157	270	Behind on Count	.307	902	277	52	3	28	106	247	0	.454	.465
Pre-All Star	3.51	40	31	0	84	84	555.2	517	49	222	397	Two Strikes	.179	1810	324	51	7	31	119	189	739	.260	.266
Post-All Star	3.18	28	23	0	73	73	506.0	472	43	222	342												

Pitcher vs. Batter (career)

Pitches Best Vs.	Avg	AB	H	2B	3B	HR	RBI	BB	SO	OBP	SLG	Pitches Worst Vs.	Avg	AB	H	2B	3B	HR	RBI	BB	SO	OBP	SLG
Greg Vaughn	.000	14	0	0	0	0	0	0	7	.000	.000	Mark Whiten	.500	16	8	3	1	0	1	2	3	.556	.813
Terry Shumpert	.000	14	0	0	0	0	0	0	1	.000	.000	Shane Mack	.464	28	13	5	1	1	1	5	5	.545	.821
Milt Cuyler	.000	10	0	0	0	0	2	0	3	.000	.000	Candy Maldonado	.444	18	8	2	0	2	6	2	3	.500	.889
Jerry Browne	.050	20	1	1	0	0	0	1	0	.095	.100	Dean Palmer	.400	10	4	2	0	1	1	1	2	.455	.900
Steve Lyons	.083	12	1	0	0	0	0		5	.083	.083	Albert Belle	.391	23	9	2	0	3	9	5	2	.517	.870

Steve Finley — Astros   Bats Left (groundball hitter)

	Avg	G	AB	R	H	2B	3B	HR	RBI	BB	SO	HBP	GDP	SB	CS	OBP	SLG	IBB	SH	SF	#Pit	#P/PA	GB	FB	G/F
1992 Season	.292	162	607	84	177	29	13	5	55	58	63	3	10	44	9	.355	.407	6	16	2	2427	3.62	270	145	1.86
Career (1989-1992)	.276	544	1884	249	520	78	29	18	171	147	211	8	29	117	39	.329	.377	15	42	15	7359	3.58	814	465	1.75

1992 Season

	Avg	AB	H	2B	3B	HR	RBI	BB	SO	OBP	SLG		Avg	AB	H	2B	3B	HR	RBI	BB	SO	OBP	SLG
vs. Left	.279	226	63	8	5	1	19	17	31	.336	.372	Scoring Posn	.277	141	39	3	5	0	40	18	17	.354	.369
vs. Right	.299	381	114	21	8	4	36	41	32	.366	.428	Close & Late	.314	102	32	5	0	2	12	11	8	.377	.422
Groundball	.305	233	71	9	7	2	20	23	23	.367	.429	None on/out	.236	110	26	4	1	0	0	9	11	.294	.291
Flyball	.302	149	45	9	4	1	14	10	13	.346	.436	Batting #1	.300	20	6	0	0	0	1	1	3	.333	.300
Home	.303	294	89	11	7	5	31	35	34	.381	.439	Batting #2	.295	580	171	29	13	5	53	56	59	.359	.416
Away	.281	313	88	18	6	0	24	23	29	.329	.377	Other	.000	7	0	0	0	0	1	1	1	.125	.000
Day	.268	179	48	7	4	0	13	18	19	.335	.352	April	.279	86	24	4	2	1	7	4	15	.311	.407
Night	.301	428	129	22	9	5	42	40	44	.364	.430	May	.297	118	35	8	3	1	7	7	11	.341	.441
Grass	.280	186	52	12	1	0	11	13	20	.325	.355	June	.269	104	28	5	5	0	10	11	7	.339	.413
Turf	.297	421	125	17	12	5	44	45	43	.368	.430	July	.250	92	23	1	1	0	4	8	9	.310	.283
First Pitch	.300	70	21	2	1	0	9	5	0	.359	.357	August	.281	89	25	6	0	0	13	16	9	.396	.348
Ahead on Count	.358	134	48	9	3	3	17	37	0	.497	.537	September/October	.356	118	42	5	2	3	14	12	12	.415	.508
Behind on Count	.232	224	52	9	4	3	16	0	39	.235	.348	Pre-All Star	.281	342	96	18	10	2	26	26	37	.333	.409
Two Strikes	.259	255	66	10	7	2	23	17	63	.307	.376	Post-All Star	.306	265	81	11	3	3	29	32	26	.383	.404

1992 By Position

Position	Avg	AB	H	2B	3B	HR	RBI	BB	SO	OBP	SLG	G	GS	Innings	PO	A	E	DP	Fld Pct	Rng Fctr	In Zone	Outs	Zone Rtg	MLB Zone
As cf	.293	605	177	29	13	5	54	57	63	.355	.408	160	153	1352.1	417	8	3	3	.993	2.83	478	401	.839	.824

Career (1989-1992)

	Avg	AB	H	2B	3B	HR	RBI	BB	SO	OBP	SLG		Avg	AB	H	2B	3B	HR	RBI	BB	SO	OBP	SLG
vs. Left	.244	562	137	17	6	4	50	32	78	.287	.317	Scoring Posn	.277	404	112	12	9	5	144	47	57	.344	.389
vs. Right	.290	1322	383	61	23	14	121	115	133	.346	.402	Close & Late	.260	289	81	10	0	3	33	25	36	.334	.346
Groundball	.290	603	175	18	12	5	50	52	58	.346	.385	None on/out	.276	503	139	23	8	3	3	33	60	.322	.372
Flyball	.278	414	115	21	4	6	43	29	47	.322	.391	Batting #1	.286	651	186	28	10	9	58	39	79	.325	.401
Home	.265	955	253	39	18	6	75	76	121	.320	.362	Batting #2	.275	1102	303	44	18	9	98	95	112	.334	.372
Away	.287	929	267	39	11	12	96	71	90	.338	.392	Other	.237	131	31	6	1	0	15	13	20	.304	.298
Day	.262	488	128	23	5	3	35	43	43	.322	.348	April	.255	231	59	8	5	2	20	18	31	.308	.359
Night	.281	1396	392	55	24	15	136	104	168	.331	.387	May	.274	339	93	21	7	4	29	24	38	.321	.413
Grass	.274	957	262	42	8	8	84	64	115	.319	.359	June	.261	329	86	15	5	3	28	31	27	.329	.365
Turf	.278	927	258	36	21	10	87	83	96	.339	.395	July	.292	291	85	7	4	2	22	20	34	.341	.364
First Pitch	.337	243	82	6	4	2	39	9	0	.339	.420	August	.282	280	79	14	3	1	33	28	31	.347	.364
Ahead on Count	.344	392	135	25	9	5	46	95	0	.471	.492	September/October	.285	414	118	13	5	6	39	26	50	.325	.384
Behind on Count	.229	682	156	25	9	8	44	2	133	.234	.327	Pre-All Star	.268	989	265	46	17	10	88	81	111	.324	.379
Two Strikes	.218	804	175	28	12	6	52	42	211	.259	.305	Post-All Star	.285	895	255	32	12	8	83	66	100	.334	.374

Batter vs. Pitcher (career)																								
Hits Best Against	Avg	AB	H	2B	3B	HR	RBI	BB	SO	OBP	SLG	Hits Worst Against	Avg	AB	H	2B	3B	HR	RBI	BB	SO	OBP	SLG
Mike Bielecki	.571	14	8	1	2	1	2	1	1	.600	1.143	Greg Swindell	.048	21	1	1	0	0	0	1	4	.091	.095
Jeff M. Robinson	.455	11	5	0	2	0	2	1	0	.500	.818	Bob Welch	.063	16	1	0	0	0	0	1	0	.118	.063
Orel Hershiser	.450	20	9	0	1	1	1	3	2	.522	.700	Mike Boddicker	.071	14	1	0	0	0	0	2	0	.188	.071
Jack Morris	.400	10	4	0	1	0	0	3	2	.538	.600	Bret Saberhagen	.091	11	1	1	0	0	0	0	1	.091	.182
Roger McDowell	.375	8	3	0	2	0	1	2	0	.455	.875	Andy Benes	.125	24	3	0	0	0	0	4		.125	.125

Steve Fireovid — Rangers   Pitches Right (groundball pitcher)

	ERA	W	L	Sv	G	GS	IP	BB	SO	Avg	H	2B	3B	HR	RBI	OBP	SLG	GF	IR	IRS	Hld	SvOp	SB	CS	GB	FB	G/F
1992 Season	4.05	1	0	0	3	0	6.2	4	0	.370	10	1	1	0	6	.452	.481	0	3	1	0	0	0	2	15	2	7.50

1992 Season

	ERA	W	L	Sv	G	GS	IP	H	HR	BB	SO		Avg	AB	H	2B	3B	HR	RBI	BB	SO	OBP	SLG
Home	0.00	0	0	0	1	0	3.1	4	0	2	0	vs. Left	.300	10	3	1	0	0	1	3	0	.462	.400
Away	8.10	1	0	0	2	0	3.1	6	0	2	0	vs. Right	.412	17	7	0	1	0	5	1	0	.444	.529

Brian Fisher — Mariners   Pitches Right (flyball pitcher)

	ERA	W	L	Sv	G	GS	IP	BB	SO	Avg	H	2B	3B	HR	RBI	OBP	SLG	CG	ShO	Sup	QS	#P/S	SB	CS	GB	FB	G/F
1992 Season	4.53	4	3	1	22	14	91.1	47	26	.234	80	20	0	9	39	.326	.371	0	0	5.22	8	89	6	3	91	160	0.57
Last Five Years	4.85	12	16	3	68	39	259.2	114	101	.269	271	62	7	25	128	.343	.419	1		4.68	15	88	40	7	329	380	0.87

1992 Season

	ERA	W	L	Sv	G	GS	IP	H	HR	BB	SO		Avg	AB	H	2B	3B	HR	RBI	BB	SO	OBP	SLG
Home	6.34	2	2	0	11	8	44.0	51	6	32	13	vs. Left	.234	167	39	7	0	2	13	32	9	.351	.311
Away	2.85	2	1	1	11	6	47.1	29	3	15	13	vs. Right	.234	175	41	13	0	7	26	15	17	.298	.429
Starter	4.59	4	3	0	14	14	80.1	74	9	40	20	Scoring Posn	.195	77	15	6	0	4	31	12	7	.293	.429
Reliever	4.09	0	0	1	8	0	11.0	6	0	7	6	Close & Late	.231	39	9	2	0	0	4	12	2	.412	.282
0-3 Days Rest	6.00	1	1	0	3	3	15.0	22	1	8	0	None on/out	.191	89	17	2	0	1		8	5	.258	.247
4 Days Rest	4.27	3	0	0	8	8	46.1	40	6	20	12	First Pitch	.288	52	15	3	0	2	5	2	0	.315	.462
5+ Days Rest	4.26	0	2	0	3	3	19.0	12	2	12	8	Behind on Count	.299	87	26	10	0	4	19	25	0	.447	.552
Pre-All Star	5.40	0	0	0	3	0	5.0	4	0	2	2	Ahead on Count	.186	145	27	5	0	2	10	0	21	.186	.262
Post-All Star	4.48	4	3	1	19	14	86.1	76	9	45	24	Two Strikes	.172	128	22	4	0	3	12	20	26	.284	.273

Last Five Years

	ERA	W	L	Sv	G	GS	IP	H	HR	BB	SO		Avg	AB	H	2B	3B	HR	RBI	BB	SO	OBP	SLG
Home	4.78	7	9	0	34	22	143.0	163	14	70	62	vs. Left	.315	496	156	30	6	12	64	78	39	.402	.472
Away	4.94	5	7	3	34	17	116.2	108	11	44	39	vs. Right	.225	511	115	32	1	13	63	36	62	.282	.368
Day	4.56	1	3	2	20	10	71.0	66	6	34	31	Inning 1-6	.270	814	220	49	5	24	105	84	83	.340	.431
Night	4.96	11	13	1	48	29	188.2	205	19	80	70	Inning 7+	.264	193	51	13	2	1	22	30	18	.357	.368
Grass	3.77	1	3	2	18	9	62.0	49	7	23	22	None on	.270	582	157	31	4	13	13	49	51	.328	.404
Turf	5.19	11	13	1	50	30	197.2	222	18	91	79	Runners on	.268	425	114	31	3	12	114	65	50	.363	.440
April	2.78	3	1	0	8	5	32.1	36	1	8	12	Scoring Posn	.241	270	65	21	1	5	93	43	35	.340	.381
May	4.56	1	1	1	7	4	25.2	29	1	13	17	Close & Late	.229	83	19	7	0	0	7	18	8	.363	.313
June	8.68	0	7	0	8	8	37.1	54	9	18	13	None on/out	.273	260	71	13	1	5	5	17	22	.318	.388
July	3.28	3	2	0	13	6	49.1	43	2	24	19	vs. 1st Batr (relief)	.259	27	7	2	0	0	4	1	2	.276	.333
August	5.55	2	3	0	17	9	60.0	63	8	25	23	First Inning Pitched	.301	259	78	19	2	7	43	28	29	.368	.471
September/October	4.25	3	2	2	15	7	55.0	46	4	26	17	First 75 Pitches	.272	831	226	52	6	22	107	92	90	.345	.428
Starter	5.24	10	15	0	39	39	211.1	230	24	95	80	Pitch 76-90	.215	93	20	3	1	2	10	9	7	.282	.333
Reliever	3.17	2	1	3	29	0	48.1	41	1	19	21	Pitch 91-105	.286	42	12	5	0	1	9	8	3	.392	.476
0-3 Days Rest	7.71	1	2	0	5	5	21.0	35	1	10	3	Pitch 106+	.317	41	13	2	0	0	2	5	1	.391	.366
4 Days Rest	5.01	6	6	0	19	19	111.1	115	15	47	39	First Pitch	.317	142	45	11	1	6	17	6	0	.340	.535
5+ Days Rest	4.90	3	7	0	15	15	79.0	80	8	38	38	Ahead on Count	.218	450	98	20	1	7	47	0	85	.222	.313
Pre-All Star	5.55	4	9	1	27	18	105.1	127	11	44	47	Behind on Count	.343	233	80	20	4	10	44	63	0	.475	.592
Post-All Star	4.37	8	7	2	41	21	154.1	144	14	70	54	Two Strikes	.212	416	88	15	2	6	43	45	99	.292	.300

Pitcher vs. Batter (career)																								
Pitches Best Vs.	Avg	AB	H	2B	3B	HR	RBI	BB	SO	OBP	SLG	Pitches Worst Vs.	Avg	AB	H	2B	3B	HR	RBI	BB	SO	OBP	SLG
Billy Hatcher	.000	10	0	0	0	0	1	2	2	.167	.000	Paul Molitor	.538	13	7	4	0	0	3	2	1	.600	.846
Ryne Sandberg	.118	17	2	0	0	0	0	1	3	.167	.118	Dale Murphy	.500	12	6	1	1	2	5	3	3	.600	1.250
Gary Gaetti	.167	12	2	0	0	1	0	0	0	.167	.167	Darryl Strawberry	.500	10	5	1	0	2	5	2	3	.583	1.200
Brook Jacoby	.182	11	2	0	0	0	0	1	5	.250	.182	Howard Johnson	.500	8	4	0	0	2	2	4	0	.667	1.250
Rafael Palmeiro	.200	20	4	1	0	0	1	0	1	.200	.250	Ruben Sierra	.333	6	2	0	0	1			5	.636	.833

Carlton Fisk — White Sox   Bats Right (flyball hitter)

	Avg	G	AB	R	H	2B	3B	HR	RBI	BB	SO	HBP	GDP	SB	CS	OBP	SLG	IBB	SH	SF	#Pit	#P/PA	GB	FB	G/F
1992 Season	.229	62	188	12	43	4	1	3	21	23	38	1	2	3	0	.313	.309	5	0	2	869	4.06	53	68	0.78
Last Five Years	.268	512	1728	203	463	83	4	71	278	189	297	23	54	12	4	.346	.444	34	1	12	7178	3.68	553	582	0.95

1992 Season

	Avg	AB	H	2B	3B	HR	RBI	BB	SO	OBP	SLG		Avg	AB	H	2B	3B	HR	RBI	BB	SO	OBP	SLG
vs. Left	.204	49	10	0	0	0		9	10	.328	.204	Scoring Posn	.213	47	10	2	1	0	17	9	10	.328	.298
vs. Right	.237	139	33	4	1	3	21	14	28	.308	.345	Close & Late	.333	33	11	2	0	0	7	7	6	.450	.394

1992 Season

	Avg	AB	H	2B	3B	HR	RBI	BB	SO	OBP	SLG		Avg	AB	H	2B	3B	HR	RBI	BB	SO	OBP	SLG
Home	.228	79	18	2	0	2	7	13	13	.340	.329	None on/out	.174	46	8	0	0	2	2	5	13	.255	.304
Away	.229	109	25	2	1	1	14	10	25	.292	.294	Batting #6	.250	56	14	1	0	1	5	9	10	.348	.321
First Pitch	.154	13	2	1	0	1	2	4	0	.353	.462	Batting #8	.227	88	20	2	1	2	14	11	20	.317	.341
Ahead on Count	.111	27	3	0	0	0	5	9	0	.324	.111	Other	.205	44	9	1	0	0	2	3	8	.255	.227
Behind on Count	.216	74	16	2	0	1	8	0	23	.224	.284	Pre-All Star	.209	67	14	0	0	0	4	6	17	.274	.209
Two Strikes	.208	106	22	2	1	1	9	10	38	.276	.274	Post-All Star	.240	121	29	4	1	3	17	17	21	.333	.364

Last Five Years

	Avg	AB	H	2B	3B	HR	RBI	BB	SO	OBP	SLG		Avg	AB	H	2B	3B	HR	RBI	BB	SO	OBP	SLG
vs. Left	.261	584	164	29	2	28	103	71	80	.360	.481	Scoring Posn	.261	487	127	22	2	14	192	76	84	.363	.400
vs. Right	.261	1144	299	54	2	43	175	118	217	.339	.425	Close & Late	.269	320	86	21	0	15	64	39	69	.352	.475
Groundball	.276	478	132	27	0	7	61	42	78	.341	.377	None on/out	.276	388	107	21	1	18	18	35	70	.343	.474
Flyball	.289	388	112	15	1	24	77	47	67	.368	.518	Batting #4	.256	546	140	29	1	24	91	56	89	.334	.445
Home	.277	824	228	46	1	29	137	105	126	.362	.441	Batting #5	.290	614	178	29	1	26	98	67	103	.363	.467
Away	.260	904	235	37	3	42	141	84	171	.331	.447	Other	.255	568	145	25	2	21	89	66	105	.339	.417
Day	.238	311	74	14	0	12	42	36	52	.316	.399	April	.307	199	61	11	0	7	25	15	30	.364	.467
Night	.275	1417	389	69	4	59	236	153	245	.352	.454	May	.243	189	46	8	0	7	29	26	39	.342	.397
Grass	.271	1445	392	70	4	55	227	161	239	.350	.439	June	.266	271	72	9	1	9	39	29	52	.339	.406
Turf	.251	283	71	13	0	16	51	28	58	.326	.466	July	.270	281	76	17	1	10	46	24	40	.328	.445
First Pitch	.384	198	76	18	0	15	43	12	0	.420	.702	August	.286	392	112	21	2	20	73	43	61	.360	.503
Ahead on Count	.309	375	116	25	1	22	83	102	0	.459	.557	September/October	.242	396	96	17	0	18	66	52	75	.341	.422
Behind on Count	.239	640	153	25	0	18	87	0	174	.253	.363	Pre-All Star	.272	747	203	34	1	27	109	76	139	.344	.428
Two Strikes	.194	789	153	22	3	15	76	61	297	.258	.286	Post-All Star	.265	981	260	49	3	44	169	113	158	.347	.456

Batter vs. Pitcher (since 1984)

Hits Best Against	Avg	AB	H	2B	3B	HR	RBI	BB	SO	OBP	SLG	Hits Worst Against	Avg	AB	H	2B	3B	HR	RBI	BB	SO	OBP	SLG
Greg Swindell	.478	23	11	1	0	4	9	1	3	.500	1.043	Curt Young	.069	29	2	0	0	0	1	1	4	.097	.069
Eric Plunk	.462	13	6	0	0	2	6	2	2	.533	.923	Rich DeLucia	.077	13	1	0	0	0	2	0	3	.077	.077
Pete Harnisch	.429	7	3	1	0	1	2	4	1	.636	1.000	Jose Rijo	.100	10	1	0	0	0	0	1	2	.182	.100
John Candelaria	.417	12	5	0	0	3	9	3	1	.533	1.167	Kevin Brown	.105	19	2	0	0	0	1	0	4	.105	.105
Tom Gordon	.385	13	5	1	0	2	4	3	3	.500	.923	Jose Guzman	.154	13	2	0	0	0	1	0	4	.143	.154

Mike Fitzgerald — Angels

Bats Right

	Avg	G	AB	R	H	2B	3B	HR	RBI	BB	SO	HBP	GDP	SB	CS	OBP	SLG	IBB	SH	SF	#Pit	#P/PA	GB	FB	G/F
1992 Season	.212	95	189	19	40	2	0	6	17	22	34	0	4	2	2	.294	.317	0	3	0	803	3.81	62	63	0.98
Last Five Years	.233	440	1145	122	267	49	6	31	151	158	212	4	26	19	11	.326	.368	9	15	10	5030	3.82	382	369	1.04

1992 Season

	Avg	AB	H	2B	3B	HR	RBI	BB	SO	OBP	SLG		Avg	AB	H	2B	3B	HR	RBI	BB	SO	OBP	SLG
vs. Left	.304	69	21	2	0	3	12	10	13	.392	.464	Scoring Posn	.255	47	12	0	0	0	9	6	6	.340	.255
vs. Right	.158	120	19	0	0	3	5	12	21	.235	.233	Close & Late	.175	40	7	0	0	1	2	4	9	.250	.250
Home	.207	92	19	0	0	3	7	11	17	.291	.304	None on/out	.164	55	9	0	0	3	3	5	13	.233	.327
Away	.216	97	21	2	0	3	10	11	17	.296	.330	Batting #7	.281	32	9	0	0	3	8	4	2	.361	.464
First Pitch	.355	31	11	1	0	1	2	0	0	.355	.484	Batting #8	.220	109	24	2	0	2	6	16	23	.320	.294
Ahead on Count	.268	41	11	1	0	2	5	10	0	.412	.439	Other	.146	48	7	0	0	1	3	2	9	.180	.208
Behind on Count	.145	62	9	1	0	0	3	0	21	.145	.161	Pre-All Star	.191	110	21	1	0	4	9	13	19	.276	.309
Two Strikes	.157	89	14	1	0	0	3	9	12	34	.257	.258	Post-All Star	.241	79	19	1	0	2	8	9	15	.318	.329

Last Five Years

	Avg	AB	H	2B	3B	HR	RBI	BB	SO	OBP	SLG		Avg	AB	H	2B	3B	HR	RBI	BB	SO	OBP	SLG
vs. Left	.252	461	116	15	4	13	70	71	74	.348	.386	Scoring Posn	.255	321	82	16	2	7	112	54	60	.355	.383
vs. Right	.221	684	151	34	2	18	81	87	138	.310	.355	Close & Late	.237	287	68	13	1	4	37	35	47	.318	.331
Groundball	.220	414	91	13	2	11	48	52	80	.309	.341	None on/out	.195	266	52	8	2	8	8	41	52	.305	.331
Flyball	.250	284	71	13	3	7	42	39	55	.341	.391	Batting #6	.210	224	47	9	2	4	23	30	34	.302	.321
Home	.234	529	124	24	4	12	65	66	94	.321	.363	Batting #7	.242	612	148	36	4	16	79	79	110	.329	.392
Away	.232	616	143	25	2	19	86	92	118	.330	.372	Other	.233	309	72	4	0	11	49	49	68	.336	.353
Day	.258	356	92	24	2	10	51	53	66	.356	.421	April	.208	106	22	2	0	3	9	24	13	.354	.311
Night	.222	789	175	25	4	21	100	105	146	.312	.343	May	.242	190	46	11	0	6	24	27	35	.341	.395
Grass	.232	435	101	16	0	14	53	58	79	.319	.366	June	.216	194	42	12	3	3	26	30	41	.322	.356
Turf	.234	710	166	33	6	17	98	100	133	.330	.369	July	.237	236	56	8	2	8	34	20	47	.297	.390
First Pitch	.313	179	56	13	1	4	30	6	0	.335	.464	August	.195	200	39	3	0	4	20	28	36	.289	.270
Ahead on Count	.322	267	86	17	2	11	44	75	0	.468	.524	September/October	.283	219	62	13	1	7	38	29	40	.365	.447
Behind on Count	.202	346	70	9	1	9	38	1	109	.204	.312	Pre-All Star	.228	567	129	29	4	13	70	90	100	.335	.362
Two Strikes	.151	523	79	7	3	9	39	75	211	.225	.228	Post-All Star	.239	578	138	20	2	18	81	68	112	.317	.374

Batter vs. Pitcher (since 1984)

Hits Best Against	Avg	AB	H	2B	3B	HR	RBI	BB	SO	OBP	SLG	Hits Worst Against	Avg	AB	H	2B	3B	HR	RBI	BB	SO	OBP	SLG
Dennis Cook	.727	11	8	1	0	2	6	2	1	.769	1.364	Ron Robinson	.000	11	0	0	0	0	0	2	2	.154	.000
Paul Assenmacher	.556	9	5	0	0	0	1	2	3	.636	.556	Bobby Ojeda	.050	20	1	0	0	0	0	3	4	.174	.050
Sid Fernandez	.400	15	6	2	0	2	7	3	2	.500	.933	Rick Honeycutt	.063	16	1	0	0	0	0	2	6	.167	.063
Kevin Gross	.364	11	4	1	0	1	3	1	1	.417	.727	Jose DeLeon	.067	15	1	0	0	0	2	1	5	.118	.067
Mike Bielecki	.308	13	4	0	0	2	4	1	5	.357	.769	Dennis Rasmussen	.083	12	1	0	0	0	0	1	3	.154	.083

John Flaherty — Red Sox
Bats Right

	Avg	G	AB	R	H	2B	3B	HR	RBI	BB	SO	HBP	GDP	SB	CS	OBP	SLG	IBB	SH	SF	#Pit	#P/PA	GB	FB	G/F
1992 Season	.197	35	66	3	13	2	0	0	2	3	7	0	0	0	0	.229	.227	0	1	1	254	3.63	25	19	1.32

1992 Season

	Avg	AB	H	2B	3B	HR	RBI	BB	SO	OBP	SLG		Avg	AB	H	2B	3B	HR	RBI	BB	SO	OBP	SLG
vs. Left	.200	20	4	1	0	0	0	1	0	.238	.250	Scoring Posn	.125	16	2	0	0	0	2	2	1	.211	.125
vs. Right	.196	46	9	1	0	0	2	2	7	.224	.217	Close & Late	.300	10	3	0	0	0	0	0	0	.300	.300

Mike Flanagan — Orioles
Pitches Left

	ERA	W	L	Sv	G	GS	IP	BB	SO	Avg	H	2B	3B	HR	RBI	OBP	SLG	GF	IR	IRS	Hld	SvOp	SB	CS	GB	FB	G/F
1992 Season	8.05	0	0	0	42	0	34.2	23	17	.338	50	6	1	3	36	.438	.453	15	36	10	10	0	2	0	58	37	1.57
Last Five Years	4.06	25	32	3	175	70	536.0	183	223	.276	568	110	10	45	235	.338	.405	39	83	22	24	5	42	19	856	573	1.49

1992 Season

	ERA	W	L	Sv	G	GS	IP	H	HR	BB	SO		Avg	AB	H	2B	3B	HR	RBI	BB	SO	OBP	SLG
Home	7.71	0	0	0	16	0	14.0	26	1	8	8	vs. Left	.274	62	17	0	0	0	6	10	11	.378	.274
Away	8.27	0	0	0	26	0	20.2	24	2	15	9	vs. Right	.384	86	33	6	1	3	30	13	6	.481	.581
Starter	0.00	0	0	0	0	0	0.0	0	0	0	0	Scoring Posn	.365	63	23	3	1	2	33	8	11	.432	.540
Reliever	8.05	0	0	0	42	0	34.2	50	3	23	17	Close & Late	.421	19	8	1	0	1	7	4	5	.500	.632
0 Days rest	8.44	0	0	0	8	0	5.1	4	0	8	3	None on/out	.261	23	6	0	0	0	6	1		.452	.261
1 or 2 Days rest	14.09	0	0	0	14	0	7.2	17	2	6	4	First Pitch	.476	21	10	2	0	0	9	1	0	.500	.571
3+ Days rest	5.82	0	0	0	20	0	21.2	29	1	9	10	Behind on Count	.326	43	14	2	1	0	7	10	0	.453	.419
Pre-All Star	8.72	0	0	0	30	0	21.2	31	2	18	13	Ahead on Count	.322	59	19	1	0	3	17	0	15	.344	.492
Post-All Star	6.92	0	0	0	12	0	13.0	19	1	5	4	Two Strikes	.275	51	14	0	0	0	3	12	17	.433	.451

Last Five Years

	ERA	W	L	Sv	G	GS	IP	H	HR	BB	SO		Avg	AB	H	2B	3B	HR	RBI	BB	SO	OBP	SLG
Home	3.87	13	16	0	84	35	267.2	300	25	79	120	vs. Left	.229	411	94	13	0	6	43	34	62	.291	.304
Away	4.26	12	16	3	91	35	268.1	268	20	104	103	vs. Right	.288	1648	474	97	10	39	192	149	161	.350	.430
Day	4.19	5	14	0	58	23	167.2	183	15	70	77	Inning 1-6	.281	1488	418	88	9	36	180	130	143	.340	.425
Night	4.01	20	18	3	117	47	368.1	385	30	113	146	Inning 7+	.263	571	150	22	1	9	55	53	80	.332	.352
Grass	4.71	7	16	2	115	25	240.2	257	22	91	119	None on	.283	1129	320	61	5	33	112	115		.352	.434
Turf	3.53	18	16	1	60	45	295.1	311	23	92	104	Runners on	.267	930	248	49	5	12	202	71	108	.321	.369
April	3.21	5	3	0	31	14	103.2	96	4	42	40	Scoring Posn	.276	478	132	22	4	8	178	47	63	.339	.389
May	6.00	5	10	1	36	14	84.0	110	11	30	39	Close & Late	.252	230	58	8	0	5	28	26	34	.332	.352
June	3.70	4	3	0	27	10	90.0	88	3	36	38	None on/out	.306	523	160	31	4	22	22	44	46	.363	.507
July	2.93	6	3	0	33	12	107.2	94	9	26	34	vs. 1st Batr (relief)	.283	92	26	0	0	4	15	9	16	.352	.413
August	4.87	3	8	1	26	10	77.2	105	9	21	37	First Inning Pitched	.282	577	163	26	2	10	93	59	74	.355	.386
September/October	4.32	2	5	1	22	10	73.0	75	9	28	35	First 15 Pitches	.287	574	165	28	1	13	66	47	71	.347	.408
Starter	4.20	23	26	0	70	70	407.0	441	38	136	153	Pitch 16-30	.270	389	105	23	3	9	56	36	48	.331	.414
Reliever	3.63	2	6	3	105	0	129.0	127	7	47	70	Pitch 31-45	.272	327	89	16	4	4	42	20	24	.317	.382
0 Days rest	5.95	0	3	0	20	0	19.2	16	1	13	16	Pitch 46+	.272	769	209	43	2	19	71	80	80	.343	.407
1 or 2 Days rest	2.32	2	1	2	48	0	66.0	61	4	15	34	First Pitch	.323	310	100	24	1	9	48	6	0	.344	.494
3+ Days rest	4.57	0	2	1	37	0	43.1	50	2	19	20	Ahead on Count	.235	818	192	32	3	13	79	0	195	.235	.329
Pre-All Star	4.23	15	17	1	104	42	308.2	327	22	114	130	Behind on Count	.300	586	176	31	4	15	75	101	0	.405	.444
Post-All Star	3.84	10	15	2	71	28	227.1	241	23	69	93	Two Strikes	.226	758	171	26	4	12	66	75	223	.297	.318

Pitcher vs. Batter (since 1984)

Pitches Best Vs.	Avg	AB	H	2B	3B	HR	RBI	BB	SO	OBP	SLG	Pitches Worst Vs.	Avg	AB	H	2B	3B	HR	RBI	BB	SO	OBP	SLG
Jay Buhner	.063	16	1	0	0	0	1	1	2	.118	.063	Andy Allanson	.600	10	6	0	0	0	2	1	0	.583	.600
Devon White	.071	14	1	0	0	0	1	1	1	.071	.143	Robin Yount	.543	35	19	4	1	2	8	3	0	.579	.886
Rafael Palmeiro	.071	14	1	0	0	0	0	1	1	.133	.071	Steve Sax	.500	16	8	1	0	2	4	1	0	.529	.938
Ellis Burks	.083	12	1	1	0	0	1	0	1	.083	.167	Dan Gladden	.435	23	10	4	0	1	3	3	2	.500	.739
Lance Johnson	.154	13	2	0	0	0	1	0	2	.154	.154	Brian Downing	.379	29	11	3	0	3	7	4	1	.455	.793

Dave Fleming — Mariners
Pitches Left

	ERA	W	L	Sv	G	GS	IP	BB	SO	Avg	H	2B	3B	HR	RBI	OBP	SLG	CG	ShO	Sup	QS	#P/S	SB	CS	GB	FB	G/F
1992 Season	3.39	17	10	0	33	33	228.1	60	112	.257	225	53	4	13	81	.306	.371	7	4	4.34	22	105	18	14	322	275	1.17
Career (1991-1992)	3.62	18	10	0	42	36	246.0	63	123	.258	244	59	5	16	94	.309	.382	7	4	4.28	22	102	19	15	350	294	1.19

1992 Season

	ERA	W	L	Sv	G	GS	IP	H	HR	BB	SO		Avg	AB	H	2B	3B	HR	RBI	BB	SO	OBP	SLG
Home	3.53	7	5	0	15	15	112.1	108	9	29	56	vs. Left	.248	141	35	8	1	2	12	11	24	.307	.362
Away	3.26	10	5	0	18	18	116.0	117	4	31	56	vs. Right	.258	736	190	45	3	11	69	49	88	.306	.372
Day	5.64	2	5	0	9	9	52.2	72	5	16	29	Inning 1-6	.249	699	174	41	2	9	70	51	91	.303	.352
Night	2.72	15	5	0	24	24	175.2	153	8	44	83	Inning 7+	.287	178	51	12	2	4	11	9	21	.321	.444
Grass	3.49	8	3	0	14	14	85.0	89	4	22	42	None on	.266	516	137	32	3	8	8	31	61	.310	.386
Turf	3.33	9	7	0	19	19	143.1	136	9	38	70	Runners on	.244	361	88	21	1	5	73	29	51	.302	.349
April	6.53	2	1	0	4	4	20.2	25	2	9	15	Scoring Posn	.232	211	49	11	1	1	59	16	26	.290	.308
May	1.87	5	0	0	6	6	43.1	38	1	20	16	Close & Late	.256	78	20	4	1	2	5	6	10	.310	.410
June	3.23	3	2	0	6	6	39.0	40	1	10	20	None on/out	.278	227	63	15	1	4	4	14	27	.322	.405
July	2.50	2	1	0	5	5	39.2	33	4	3	16	vs. 1st Batr (relief)	.000	0	0	0	0	0	0	0	0	.000	.000
August	3.00	3	2	0	6	6	48.0	41	5	8	27	First Inning Pitched	.269	130	35	5	1	2	14	10	20	.336	.369

1992 Season

	ERA	W	L	Sv	G	GS	IP	H	HR	BB	SO		Avg	AB	H	2B	3B	HR	RBI	BB	SO	OBP	SLG
September/October	5.02	2	4	0	6	6	37.2	48	0	10	18	First 75 Pitches	.250	585	146	38	2	6	57	44	79	.306	.352
Starter	3.39	17	10	0	33	33	228.1	225	13	60	112	Pitch 76-90	.289	121	35	5	0	3	11	7	12	.326	.405
Reliever	0.00	0	0	0	0	0	0.0	0	0	0	0	Pitch 91-105	.268	97	26	5	1	2	7	4	11	.297	.402
0-3 Days Rest	33.75	0	0	0	1	1	1.1	6	0	1	1	Pitch 106+	.243	74	18	5	1	2	6	5	10	.291	.419
4 Days Rest	3.25	10	6	0	21	21	144.0	149	9	43	72	First Pitch	.300	120	36	10	2	1	15	3	0	.317	.442
5+ Days Rest	3.14	7	4	0	11	11	83.0	70	4	16	39	Ahead on Count	.215	331	71	9	0	3	17	0	85	.221	.269
Pre-All Star	3.20	11	3	0	18	18	118.0	113	6	41	56	Behind on Count	.276	232	64	21	1	5	31	34	0	.367	.440
Post-All Star	3.59	6	7	0	15	15	110.1	112	7	19	56	Two Strikes	.201	349	70	12	1	6	19	23	112	.255	.292

Darrin Fletcher — Expos   Bats Left

	Avg	G	AB	R	H	2B	3B	HR	RBI	BB	SO	HBP	GDP	SB	CS	OBP	SLG	IBB	SH	SF	#Pit	#P/PA	GB	FB	G/F
1992 Season	.243	83	222	13	54	10	2	2	26	14	28	2	8	0	2	.289	.333	3	2	4	893	3.69	75	80	0.94
Career (1989-1992)	.237	145	369	22	92	19	2	4	41	21	49	2	10	0	3	.276	.326	3	3	4	1517	3.65	134	127	1.06

1992 Season

	Avg	AB	H	2B	3B	HR	RBI	BB	SO	OBP	SLG		Avg	AB	H	2B	3B	HR	RBI	BB	SO	OBP	SLG
vs. Left	.286	14	4	1	0	0	1	3	3	.412	.357	Scoring Posn	.224	58	13	3	0	0	21	8	10	.310	.276
vs. Right	.240	208	50	9	2	2	25	11	25	.280	.332	Close & Late	.163	43	7	3	0	0	1	2	11	.196	.233
Home	.224	85	19	4	1	0	10	5	10	.258	.294	None on/out	.379	58	22	3	0	1	1	1	4	.390	.483
Away	.255	137	35	6	1	2	16	9	18	.309	.358	Batting #5	.306	72	22	3	1	0	11	6	7	.350	.375
First Pitch	.226	31	7	0	0	0	2	2	0	.265	.226	Batting #7	.243	74	18	2	0	2	10	5	7	.296	.351
Ahead on Count	.280	50	14	5	2	0	7	10	0	.400	.460	Other	.184	76	14	5	1	0	5	3	14	.222	.276
Behind on Count	.200	80	16	2	1	1	11	0	15	.207	.288	Pre-All Star	.212	99	21	2	0	1	10	6	13	.269	.263
Two Strikes	.228	101	23	4	0	1	12	2	28	.252	.297	Post-All Star	.268	123	33	8	2	1	16	8	15	.306	.390

Scott Fletcher — Brewers   Bats Right

	Avg	G	AB	R	H	2B	3B	HR	RBI	BB	SO	HBP	GDP	SB	CS	OBP	SLG	IBB	SH	SF	#Pit	#P/PA	GB	FB	G/F
1992 Season	.275	123	386	53	106	18	3	3	51	30	33	7	4	17	10	.335	.360	1	6	4	1399	3.28	155	112	1.38
Last Five Years	.254	646	2204	257	560	90	13	9	225	218	216	28	42	28	21	.326	.319	6	49	22	8705	3.52	923	632	1.46

1992 Season

	Avg	AB	H	2B	3B	HR	RBI	BB	SO	OBP	SLG		Avg	AB	H	2B	3B	HR	RBI	BB	SO	OBP	SLG
vs. Left	.308	104	32	5	1	0	13	7	10	.360	.375	Scoring Posn	.336	107	36	5	0	2	47	12	10	.409	.439
vs. Right	.262	282	74	13	2	3	38	23	23	.326	.355	Close & Late	.286	63	18	3	0	1	14	6	4	.352	.381
Groundball	.344	90	31	1	1	1	14	9	9	.413	.411	None on/out	.255	94	24	6	0	1	1	6	8	.300	.351
Flyball	.325	117	38	9	0	0	14	9	10	.380	.402	Batting #8	.283	60	17	5	0	0	3	5	5	.348	.367
Home	.314	175	55	11	1	2	26	16	15	.379	.423	Batting #9	.277	307	85	12	3	3	45	25	26	.339	.365
Away	.242	211	51	7	2	1	25	14	18	.297	.308	Other	.211	19	4	1	0	0	3	0	2	.211	.263
Day	.284	109	31	6	2	0	10	10	6	.350	.376	April	.344	32	11	1	1	0	3	3	3	.400	.438
Night	.271	277	75	12	1	3	41	20	27	.329	.354	May	.298	47	14	1	1	1	7	3	3	.333	.426
Grass	.277	332	92	16	3	3	42	25	30	.332	.370	June	.307	75	23	4	0	0	9	9	6	.388	.360
Turf	.259	54	14	2	0	0	9	5	3	.349	.296	July	.211	71	15	5	1	1	9	5	6	.263	.352
First Pitch	.353	68	24	3	1	2	13	0	0	.389	.515	August	.306	85	26	5	0	0	14	7	6	.368	.365
Ahead on Count	.344	93	32	8	1	0	13	19	0	.452	.452	September/October	.224	76	17	2	0	1	9	3	9	.282	.289
Behind on Count	.248	137	34	3	1	1	20	1	20	.250	.307	Pre-All Star	.289	187	54	7	3	1	19	18	15	.353	.374
Two Strikes	.174	132	23	3	1	0	11	11	33	.236	.212	Post-All Star	.261	199	52	11	0	2	32	12	18	.318	.347

1992 By Position

Position	Avg	AB	H	2B	3B	HR	RBI	BB	SO	OBP	SLG	G	GS	Innings	PO	A	E	DP	Fld Pct	Rng Fctr	In Zone	Outs	Zone Rtg	MLB Zone
As 2b	.263	323	85	15	2	3	44	27	26	.331	.350	106	99	855.1	206	319	4	70	.992	5.52	350	319	.911	.892
As ss	.362	58	21	3	1	0	7	3	6	.387	.448	22	16	159.0	29	64	5	14	.949	5.26	71	68	.958	.885

Last Five Years

	Avg	AB	H	2B	3B	HR	RBI	BB	SO	OBP	SLG		Avg	AB	H	2B	3B	HR	RBI	BB	SO	OBP	SLG
vs. Left	.285	705	201	31	4	1	57	71	61	.355	.345	Scoring Posn	.282	577	163	29	4	4	209	65	60	.354	.367
vs. Right	.239	1499	359	59	9	8	168	147	155	.312	.307	Close & Late	.241	369	89	10	2	2	43	42	42	.327	.295
Groundball	.261	551	144	13	4	4	59	46	51	.324	.318	None on/out	.211	494	104	17	1	2	2	47	53	.283	.261
Flyball	.275	570	157	32	3	3	69	47	56	.337	.358	Batting #2	.252	1103	278	42	6	1	92	141	100	.341	.304
Home	.263	1077	283	47	5	3	112	105	101	.332	.324	Batting #8	.237	431	102	23	2	1	32	27	56	.283	.306
Away	.246	1127	277	43	8	6	113	113	115	.320	.314	Other	.269	670	180	25	5	7	101	50	60	.327	.332
Day	.260	542	141	21	5	1	50	63	40	.336	.323	April	.241	294	71	10	3	1	31	43	32	.341	.306
Night	.252	1662	419	69	8	8	175	155	176	.323	.318	May	.259	421	109	14	4	2	36	38	45	.318	.325
Grass	.253	1853	468	76	8	9	181	189	181	.327	.317	June	.262	385	101	22	1	1	35	46	33	.349	.332
Turf	.262	351	92	14	5	0	44	29	35	.322	.330	July	.254	323	82	14	1	2	33	24	28	.306	.322
First Pitch	.311	305	95	14	3	3	39	0	1	.326	.407	August	.271	414	112	17	1	0	47	40	35	.342	.316
Ahead on Count	.302	590	178	35	6	2	82	138	0	.434	.392	September/October	.232	367	85	13	3	3	43	27	43	.297	.308
Behind on Count	.228	712	162	29	2	4	69	1	130	.231	.291	Pre-All Star	.253	1216	308	51	9	4	106	137	120	.332	.320
Two Strikes	.183	845	155	21	4	3	52	76	215	.256	.228	Post-All Star	.255	988	252	39	4	5	119	81	96	.319	.318

Hits Best Against	Avg	AB	H	2B	3B	HR	RBI	BB	SO	OBP	SLG	Hits Worst Against	Avg	AB	H	2B	3B	HR	RBI	BB	SO	OBP	SLG
John Candelaria	.579	19	11	2	1	0	1	3	0	.636	.789	Jim Abbott	.045	22	1	0	0	0	1	0	1	.045	.045
Scott Sanderson	.550	20	11	1	0	2	7	0	1	.550	.900	Todd Stottlemyre	.056	18	1	0	0	0	1	2	2	.150	.056
Tom Edens	.500	10	5	0	0	0	2	1	0	.545	.500	Bill Krueger	.083	12	1	1	0	0	0	1	1	.154	.167
Todd Burns	.444	9	4	2	0	0	2	2	1	.545	.667	Bob Milacki	.100	10	1	0	0	0	1	1	0	.167	.100
David Wells	.417	12	5	2	0	0	3	2	0	.563	.583	Rick Aguilera	.154	13	2	0	0	0	1	0	2	.154	.154

Tom Foley — Expos   Bats Left

	Avg	G	AB	R	H	2B	3B	HR	RBI	BB	SO	HBP	GDP	SB	CS	OBP	SLG	IBB	SH	SF	#Pit	#P/PA	GB	FB	G/F
1992 Season	.174	72	115	7	20	3	1	0	5	8	21	1	6	3	0	.230	.217	2	3	2	446	3.54	43	34	1.26
Last Five Years	.230	480	1199	97	276	56	8	12	114	109	175	6	27	9	11	.295	.320	22	9	13	4594	3.46	414	393	1.05

1992 Season

	Avg	AB	H	2B	3B	HR	RBI	BB	SO	OBP	SLG		Avg	AB	H	2B	3B	HR	RBI	BB	SO	OBP	SLG
vs. Left	.158	19	3	0	0	0	1	1	5	.190	.158	Scoring Posn	.167	24	4	0	0	0	5	4	3	.267	.167
vs. Right	.177	96	17	3	1	0	4	7	16	.238	.229	Close & Late	.120	25	3	0	0	0	0	1	8	.154	.120
Home	.172	64	11	2	1	0	2	2	9	.194	.234	None on/out	.296	27	8	0	1	0	0	1	6	.321	.370
Away	.176	51	9	1	0	0	3	6	12	.271	.196	Batting #8	.157	89	14	3	1	0	5	6	14	.214	.213
First Pitch	.160	25	4	1	0	0	1	2	0	.214	.200	Batting #9	.182	11	2	0	0	0	0	1	2	.250	.182
Ahead on Count	.263	19	5	1	0	0	3	1	0	.286	.316	Other	.267	15	4	0	0	0	0	1	5	.313	.267
Behind on Count	.211	38	8	1	0	0	1	0	11	.231	.237	Pre-All Star	.179	78	14	2	0	0	4	7	13	.253	.205
Two Strikes	.125	48	6	1	1	0	0	6	21	.236	.188	Post-All Star	.162	37	6	1	1	0	1	1	8	.179	.243

Last Five Years

	Avg	AB	H	2B	3B	HR	RBI	BB	SO	OBP	SLG		Avg	AB	H	2B	3B	HR	RBI	BB	SO	OBP	SLG
vs. Left	.200	100	20	3	1	0	7	3	22	.224	.250	Scoring Posn	.260	304	79	15	4	4	103	46	44	.348	.375
vs. Right	.233	1099	256	53	7	12	107	106	153	.301	.327	Close & Late	.227	269	61	14	2	2	24	27	56	.299	.316
Groundball	.235	485	114	22	2	6	48	35	55	.291	.326	None on/out	.239	272	65	12	3	2	2	13	34	.279	.327
Flyball	.166	253	42	9	0	2	25	27	57	.242	.225	Batting #6	.265	340	90	24	2	5	36	34	35	.332	.391
Home	.220	624	137	32	4	7	52	49	92	.277	.317	Batting #8	.220	322	71	13	3	0	28	29	54	.281	.280
Away	.242	575	139	24	4	5	62	60	83	.314	.323	Other	.214	537	115	19	3	7	50	46	86	.279	.300
Day	.240	341	82	12	4	5	35	26	42	.295	.343	April	.214	131	28	5	0	2	19	9	19	.259	.298
Night	.226	858	194	44	4	7	79	83	133	.294	.311	May	.224	232	52	13	3	0	18	19	37	.283	.306
Grass	.257	307	79	12	2	4	25	29	41	.322	.349	June	.241	216	52	11	2	1	24	30	30	.329	.324
Turf	.221	892	197	44	6	8	89	80	134	.285	.311	July	.257	210	54	13	2	4	18	19	34	.328	.395
First Pitch	.269	219	59	13	1	5	26	6	0	.264	.406	August	.204	201	41	5	1	4	21	17	26	.264	.299
Ahead on Count	.298	242	72	14	5	3	29	67	0	.449	.434	September/October	.234	209	49	9	0	1	14	15	29	.288	.292
Behind on Count	.201	422	85	17	1	2	27	3	95	.207	.261	Pre-All Star	.244	665	162	34	6	7	75	65	93	.309	.344
Two Strikes	.161	504	81	15	2	1	32	26	175	.202	.204	Post-All Star	.213	534	114	22	2	5	39	44	82	.276	.290

Batter vs. Pitcher (since 1984)

Hits Best Against	Avg	AB	H	2B	3B	HR	RBI	BB	SO	OBP	SLG	Hits Worst Against	Avg	AB	H	2B	3B	HR	RBI	BB	SO	OBP	SLG
Brian Fisher	.524	21	11	2	1	1	2	1	1	.545	.857	Jose Rijo	.000	13	0	0	0	0	1	0	3	.000	.000
Les Lancaster	.385	13	5	1	0	1	3	1	2	.400	.692	Andy Benes	.071	14	1	0	0	0	2	2	1	.188	.071
Jeff Robinson	.353	17	6	1	1	1	4	1	1	.350	.706	Omar Olivares	.083	12	1	0	0	0	0	1	1	.083	.083
Ron Darling	.348	46	16	1	0	2	9	3	4	.388	.500	Joe Boever	.091	11	1	0	0	0	0	1	5	.167	.091
Bill Gullickson	.333	21	7	2	1	0	2	2	2	.391	.524	Jimmy Jones	.125	16	2	1	0	0	2	0	2	.118	.188

Tim Fortugno — Angels   Pitches Left (flyball pitcher)

	ERA	W	L	Sv	G	GS	IP	BB	SO	Avg	H	2B	3B	HR	RBI	OBP	SLG	GF	IR	IRS	Hld	SvOp	SB	CS	GB	FB	G/F
1992 Season	5.18	1	1	1	14	5	41.2	19	31	.236	37	4	0	5	22	.316	.357	5	5	3	0	1	5	2	36	66	0.55

1992 Season

	ERA	W	L	Sv	G	GS	IP	H	HR	BB	SO		Avg	AB	H	2B	3B	HR	RBI	BB	SO	OBP	SLG
Home	5.85	1	0	0	10	4	32.1	31	5	16	23	vs. Left	.286	28	8	0	0	1	6	4	6	.364	.393
Away	2.89	0	1	1	4	0	9.1	6	0	3	8	vs. Right	.225	129	29	4	0	4	16	15	25	.306	.349

Tony Fossas — Red Sox   Pitches Left (groundball pitcher)

	ERA	W	L	Sv	G	GS	IP	BB	SO	Avg	H	2B	3B	HR	RBI	OBP	SLG	GF	IR	IRS	Hld	SvOp	SB	CS	GB	FB	G/F
1992 Season	2.43	1	2	2	60	0	29.2	14	19	.279	31	10	1	1	24	.365	.414	17	70	20	14	3	4	2	42	29	1.45
Career (1988-1992)	3.84	8	9	4	212	0	182.2	76	114	.274	192	35	5	12	124	.347	.389	44	230	74	53	10	13	6	306	144	2.13

1992 Season

	ERA	W	L	Sv	G	GS	IP	H	HR	BB	SO		Avg	AB	H	2B	3B	HR	RBI	BB	SO	OBP	SLG
Home	1.40	1	2	1	35	0	19.1	14	0	7	11	vs. Left	.214	56	12	6	0	0	9	3	16	.254	.321
Away	4.35	0	0	1	25	0	10.1	17	1	7	8	vs. Right	.345	55	19	4	1	1	15	11	3	.463	.509
Day	3.12	0	2	1	18	0	8.2	9	0	4	5	Inning 1-6	.000	0	0	0	0	0	0	0	0	.000	.000
Night	2.14	1	0	1	42	0	21.0	22	1	10	14	Inning 7+	.279	111	31	10	1	1	24	14	19	.365	.414
Grass	1.78	1	2	2	53	0	25.1	24	1	12	18	None on	.256	39	10	3	0	1	1	7	5	.383	.410
Turf	6.23	0	0	0	7	0	4.1	7	0	2	1	Runners on	.292	72	21	7	1	0	23	7	14	.354	.417
April	6.75	0	1	0	5	0	1.1	1	0	0	1	Scoring Posn	.296	54	16	6	1	0	23	6	12	.367	.444
May	6.75	0	1	0	7	0	4.0	7	0	0	0	Close & Late	.295	44	13	2	0	0	9	3	7	.354	.341

1992 Season

	ERA	W	L	Sv	G	GS	IP	H	HR	BB	SO		Avg	AB	H	2B	3B	HR	RBI	BB	SO	OBP	SLG
June	2.84	0	0	1	11	0	6.1	5	1	4	6	None on/out	.200	20	4	2	0	0	0	3	2	.304	.300
July	0.00	1	0	0	14	0	6.1	4	0	3	7	vs. 1st Batr (relief)	.245	53	13	5	0	0	13	4	11	.310	.340
August	3.60	0	1	0	13	0	5.0	8	0	3	2	First Inning Pitched	.280	107	30	9	1	1	24	13	19	.364	.411
September/October	0.00	0	0	1	10	0	6.2	6	0	4	3	First 15 Pitches	.299	97	29	9	1	1	24	10	14	.370	.443
Starter	0.00	0	0	0	0	0	0.0	0	0	0	0	Pitch 16-30	.143	14	2	1	0	0	0	4	5	.333	.214
Reliever	2.43	1	2	2	60	0	29.2	31	1	14	19	Pitch 31-45	.000	0	0	0	0	0	0	0	0	.000	.000
0 Days rest	2.77	1	0	0	24	0	13.0	14	0	4	9	Pitch 46+	.000	0	0	0	0	0	0	0	0	.000	.000
1 or 2 Days rest	3.38	0	2	2	14	0	5.1	7	1	2	5	First Pitch	.235	17	4	2	0	0	4	3	0	.350	.353
3+ Days rest	1.59	0	0	0	22	0	11.1	10	0	8	5	Ahead on Count	.200	40	8	1	0	0	7	0	16	.220	.225
Pre-All Star	3.95	1	1	1	27	0	13.2	14	1	7	10	Behind on Count	.345	29	10	4	1	0	9	5	0	.441	.552
Post-All Star	1.13	0	1	1	33	0	16.0	17	0	7	9	Two Strikes	.200	45	9	2	0	0	7	6	19	.308	.244

Career (1988-1992)

	ERA	W	L	Sv	G	GS	IP	H	HR	BB	SO		Avg	AB	H	2B	3B	HR	RBI	BB	SO	OBP	SLG
Home	2.89	4	2	3	109	0	99.2	95	5	38	66	vs. Left	.210	267	56	9	0	4		23	70	.279	.288
Away	4.99	4	7	1	103	0	83.0	97	7	38	48	vs. Right	.313	434	136	26	5	8	83	53	44	.388	.452
Day	3.48	2	4	2	68	0	72.1	79	3	32	42	Inning 1-6	.260	123	32	8	0	1	24	13	22	.328	.350
Night	4.08	6	5	2	144	0	110.1	113	9	44	72	Inning 7+	.277	578	160	27	5	11	100	63	92	.351	.398
Grass	3.63	7	7	4	181	0	156.1	159	11	67	99	None on	.257	292	75	14	4	5	5	28	41	.330	.384
Turf	5.13	1	2	0	31	0	26.1	33	1	9	15	Runners on	.266	409	117	21	1	7	119	48	73	.359	.394
April	6.35	1	4	0	21	0	17.0	19	2	8	10	Scoring Posn	.279	280	78	15	1	4	113	41	51	.368	.382
May	4.50	0	1	0	34	0	28.0	32	3	11	7	Close & Late	.253	166	42	9	2	2	34	24	29	.356	.367
June	2.63	2	0	1	38	0	37.2	36	4	13	32	None on/out	.221	136	30	4	2	1		16	25	.307	.301
July	4.41	2	1	0	42	0	32.2	36	2	18	24	vs. 1st Batr (relief)	.211	185	39	8	0	0	35	14	40	.275	.254
August	4.78	3	3	1	38	0	32.0	37	1	12	24	First Inning Pitched	.271	531	144	28	4	8	105	55	93	.342	.384
September/October	2.04	0	0	2	39	0	35.1	32	0	14	17	First 15 Pitches	.272	523	142	26	4	7	92	50	88	.339	.377
Starter	0.00	0	0	0	0	0	0.0	0	0	0	0	Pitch 16-30	.264	144	38	9	1	3	25	22	20	.361	.403
Reliever	3.84	8	9	4	212	0	182.2	192	12	76	114	Pitch 31-45	.409	22	9	0	0	2	6	3	3	.480	.682
0 Days rest	2.54	3	2	2	70	0	63.2	56	2	25	40	Pitch 46+	.250	12	3	0	0	0	1	1	3	.308	.250
1 or 2 Days rest	5.04	3	4	2	80	0	69.2	85	8	21	44	First Pitch	.369	122	45	6	1	3	31	18	0	.447	.508
3+ Days rest	3.83	2	3	0	62	0	49.1	51	2	30	30	Ahead on Count	.169	290	49	7	1	4	34	0	106	.176	.241
Pre-All Star	3.81	4	5	1	102	0	89.2	95	9	36	56	Behind on Count	.359	170	61	16	2	2	41	32	0	.466	.512
Post-All Star	3.87	4	4	3	110	0	93.0	97	3	40	58	Two Strikes	.165	266	44	7	2	6	35	26	114	.245	.274

Pitcher vs. Batter (career)

Pitches Best Vs.	Avg	AB	H	2B	3B	HR	RBI	BB	SO	OBP	SLG	Pitches Worst Vs.	Avg	AB	H	2B	3B	HR	RBI	BB	SO	OBP	SLG
Ken Griffey Jr	.091	11	1	0	0	0	1	1	3	.167	.091												
Kent Hrbek	.111	9	1	0	0	0	1	2	3	.273	.111												

Steve Foster — Reds   Pitches Right

	ERA	W	L	Sv	G	GS	IP	BB	SO	Avg	H	2B	3B	HR	RBI	OBP	SLG	GF	IR	IRS	Hld	SvOp	SB	CS	GB	FB	G/F
1992 Season	2.88	1	1	2	31	0	50.0	13	34	.275	52	8	3	4	19	.319	.413	7	23	7	4	3	1	1	74	46	1.61
Career (1991-1992)	2.67	1	1	2	42	0	64.0	17	45	.248	59	9	3	5	22	.296	.374	12	26	7	4	3	1	1	93	62	1.50

1992 Season

	ERA	W	L	Sv	G	GS	IP	H	HR	BB	SO		Avg	AB	H	2B	3B	HR	RBI	BB	SO	OBP	SLG
Home	0.40	0	0	1	15	0	22.1	18	1	3	13	vs. Left	.300	90	27	3	2	2	9	5	10	.333	.444
Away	4.88	1	1	1	16	0	27.2	34	3	10	21	vs. Right	.253	99	25	5	1	2	10	8	24	.306	.384
Starter	13.50	0	1	0	1	1	3.1	7	1	1	2	Scoring Posn	.200	50	10	1	1	1	16	4	10	.250	.320
Reliever	2.12	1	0	2	30	0	46.2	45	3	12	32	Close & Late	.174	46	8	0	0	0	0	6	10	.269	.174
0 Days rest	0.00	0	0	0	5	0	4.2	3	0	2	3	None on/out	.333	45	15	1	1	1	1	2	5	.362	.467
1 or 2 Days rest	1.11	1	0	1	14	0	24.1	20	2	5	15	First Pitch	.318	22	7	2	1	1	1	1	0	.348	.636
3+ Days rest	4.08	0	0	1	11	0	17.2	22	1	5	14	Behind on Count	.364	33	12	2	1	0	6	6	0	.462	.485
Pre-All Star	5.25	1	0	0	5	0	12.0	18	0	7	8	Ahead on Count	.222	99	22	3	1	1	6	0	31	.218	.303
Post-All Star	2.13	0	1	2	26	1	38.0	34	4	6	26	Two Strikes	.235	85	20	4	0	1	6	6	34	.283	.318

Eric Fox — Athletics   Bats Both (flyball hitter)

	Avg	G	AB	R	H	2B	3B	HR	RBI	BB	SO	HBP	GDP	SB	CS	OBP	SLG	IBB	SH	SF	#Pit	#P/PA	GB	FB	G/F
1992 Season	.238	51	143	24	34	5	2	3	13	13	29	0	1	3	4	.299	.364	0	6	1	617	3.93	43	44	0.98

1992 Season

	Avg	AB	H	2B	3B	HR	RBI	BB	SO	OBP	SLG		Avg	AB	H	2B	3B	HR	RBI	BB	SO	OBP	SLG
vs. Left	.227	22	5	1	0	0	1	2	6	.292	.273	Scoring Posn	.205	44	9	1	1	1	10	5	13	.280	.341
vs. Right	.240	121	29	4	2	3	12	11	23	.301	.380	Close & Late	.091	22	2	1	0	1	3	1	8	.130	.273
Home	.250	76	19	4	1	0	3	7	14	.313	.329	None on/out	.222	45	10	4	0	1	1	3	6	.271	.378
Away	.224	67	15	1	1	3	10	6	15	.284	.403	Batting #1	.317	63	20	5	2	2	11	4	10	.353	.556
First Pitch	.125	8	1	0	0	0	0	0	0	.125	.125	Batting #2	.175	40	7	0	0	0	0	2	8	.214	.175
Ahead on Count	.429	28	12	1	2	0	4	8	0	.536	.607	Other	.175	40	7	0	0	1	2	7	11	.298	.250
Behind on Count	.155	58	9	1	0	1	1	0	13	.155	.224	Pre-All Star	.143	14	2	0	0	0	3	1	4	.188	.357
Two Strikes	.158	76	12	2	0	0	2	5	29	.210	.184	Post-All Star	.248	129	32	5	2	3	10	12	25	.312	.364

John Franco — Mets
Pitches Left (groundball pitcher)

	ERA	W	L	Sv	G	GS	IP	BB	SO	Avg	H	2B	3B	HR	RBI	OBP	SLG	GF	IR	IRS	Hld	SvOp	SB	CS	GB	FB	G/F
1992 Season	1.64	6	2	15	31	0	33.0	11	20	.209	24	6	1	1	10	.273	.304	30	12	5	1	17	2	3	55	22	2.50
Last Five Years	2.40	26	28	149	268	0	322.2	113	227	.239	268	36	5	13	121	.303	.310	126	135	40	3	172	15	13	563	216	2.61

1992 Season

	ERA	W	L	Sv	G	GS	IP	H	HR	BB	SO		Avg	AB	H	2B	3B	HR	RBI	BB	SO	OBP	SLG
Home	0.92	4	1	8	17	0	19.2	13	0	3	8	vs. Left	.250	28	7	1	0	0	3	7	6	.389	.286
Away	2.70	2	1	7	14	0	13.1	11	1	8	12	vs. Right	.195	87	17	5	1	1	7	4	14	.228	.310
Starter	0.00	0	0	0	0	0	0.0	0	0	0	0	Scoring Posn	.192	26	5	0	0	0	7	7	4	.343	.192
Reliever	1.64	6	2	15	31	0	33.0	24	1	11	20	Close & Late	.220	91	20	5	1	0	9	9	14	.284	.297
0 Days rest	4.15	0	2	5	8	0	8.2	11	0	3	7	None on/out	.207	29	6	2	0	0	0	3	.207	.276
1 or 2 Days rest	0.00	3	0	2	8	0	8.0	4	0	3	3	First Pitch	.462	13	6	2	1	0	3	1	0	.467	.769
3+ Days rest	1.10	3	0	8	15	0	16.1	9	1	5	10	Behind on Count	.172	29	5	2	0	0	1	7	0	.333	.241
Pre-All Star	1.44	6	1	11	22	0	25.0	17	0	7	16	Ahead on Count	.167	48	8	1	0	0	3	0	17	.167	.188
Post-All Star	2.25	0	1	4	9	0	8.0	7	1	4	4	Two Strikes	.173	52	9	1	0	0	4	3	20	.214	.192

Last Five Years

	ERA	W	L	Sv	G	GS	IP	H	HR	BB	SO		Avg	AB	H	2B	3B	HR	RBI	BB	SO	OBP	SLG
Home	2.41	17	13	80	143	0	172.0	154	3	53	118	vs. Left	.230	239	55	9	2	1	26	24	47	.301	.297
Away	2.39	9	15	69	125	0	150.2	134	10	60	109	vs. Right	.241	965	233	27	3	12	94	89	180	.304	.313
Day	2.80	12	10	44	92	0	119.0	109	6	50	98	Inning 1-6	.500	4	2	0	0	0	2	0	1	.500	.500
Night	2.17	14	18	105	176	0	203.2	179	7	63	129	Inning 7+	.238	1200	286	36	5	13	118	113	226	.303	.309
Grass	2.08	12	11	76	138	0	160.0	148	8	54	118	None on	.237	617	146	16	1	7	46	116	.290	.300
Turf	2.71	14	17	73	130	0	162.2	140	5	59	109	Runners on	.242	587	142	20	4	6	113	67	111	.317	.320
April	0.91	2	2	26	39	0	49.2	21	0	13	32	Scoring Posn	.235	341	80	13	2	4	103	51	65	.330	.320
May	1.51	5	5	21	39	0	53.2	44	2	20	34	Close & Late	.235	765	180	20	4	9	85	72	142	.300	.307
June	3.25	7	8	22	50	0	55.1	66	1	21	41	None on/out	.236	275	65	9	0	3	14	45	.273	.302
July	2.41	2	3	32	44	0	52.1	45	5	15	38	vs. 1st Batr (relief)	.217	249	54	10	0	0	13	15	39	.259	.257
August	1.45	6	4	26	54	0	62.0	53	3	21	42	First Inning Pitched	.233	924	215	29	5	6	89	81	181	.292	.294
September/October	5.07	4	6	22	42	0	49.2	59	2	23	40	First 15 Pitches	.226	810	183	23	5	7	60	62	146	.279	.293
Starter	0.00	0	0	0	0	0	0.0	0	0	0	0	Pitch 16-30	.265	328	87	11	0	5	45	39	71	.343	.345
Reliever	2.40	26	28	149	268	0	322.2	268	13	113	227	Pitch 31-45	.281	64	18	2	0	1	16	12	9	.395	.359
0 Days rest	2.92	6	6	32	53	0	61.2	63	3	24	50	Pitch 46+	.000	2	0	0	0	0	0	0	1	.000	.000
1 or 2 Days rest	1.61	11	11	74	127	0	150.2	114	3	55	104	First Pitch	.341	164	56	7	1	3	24	14	0	.389	.451
3+ Days rest	3.18	9	11	43	88	0	110.1	111	7	34	73	Ahead on Count	.181	531	96	9	1	2	31	0	191	.180	.213
Pre-All Star	1.84	15	14	83	145	0	176.0	143	4	61	124	Behind on Count	.274	277	76	13	3	5	40	56	0	.396	.397
Post-All Star	3.07	11	14	66	123	0	146.2	145	9	52	103	Two Strikes	.177	564	100	8	1	3	38	43	227	.234	.231

Pitcher vs. Batter (career)

Pitches Best Vs.	Avg	AB	H	2B	3B	HR	RBI	BB	SO	OBP	SLG	Pitches Worst Vs.	Avg	AB	H	2B	3B	HR	RBI	BB	SO	OBP	SLG
Tom Pagnozzi	.000	12	0	0	0	0	0	2	5	.143	.000	Mariano Duncan	.500	16	8	1	0	0	0	2	4	.556	.563
Mike Scioscia	.071	14	1	0	0	0	1	2	.133	.071	Terry Pendleton	.500	14	7	1	0	0	2	1	1	.533	.571
Jose Lind	.083	12	1	0	0	0	0	0	1	.083	.083	Todd Zeile	.417	12	5	0	0	1	1	1	3	.462	.667
Ken Oberkfell	.118	17	2	0	0	0	1	1	1	.167	.118	Kevin McReynolds	.385	13	5	1	0	1	4	2	1	.467	.692
Lenny Dykstra	.133	15	2	0	0	0	0	4	.133	.133	Kevin Mitchell	.333	12	4	0	0	1	1	5	2	.529	.583

Julio Franco — Rangers
Bats Right (groundball hitter)

	Avg	G	AB	R	H	2B	3B	HR	RBI	BB	SO	HBP	GDP	SB	CS	OBP	SLG	IBB	SH	SF	#Pit	#P/PA	GB	FB	G/F
1992 Season	.234	35	107	19	25	7	0	2	8	15	17	0	3	1	1	.328	.355	2	1	0	479	3.93	57	18	3.17
Last Five Years	.310	640	2439	391	757	115	15	51	301	264	319	8	72	114	34	.382	.433	28	4	14	10301	3.75	1081	556	1.94

1992 Season

	Avg	AB	H	2B	3B	HR	RBI	BB	SO	OBP	SLG		Avg	AB	H	2B	3B	HR	RBI	BB	SO	OBP	SLG
vs. Left	.333	39	13	3	0	1	3	5	8	.409	.487	Scoring Posn	.136	22	3	0	0	1	6	9	5	.387	.273
vs. Right	.176	68	12	4	0	1	5	10	9	.282	.279	Close & Late	.125	16	2	0	0	0	1	6	4	.364	.125
Home	.313	64	20	6	0	2	7	9	12	.397	.500	None on/out	.293	41	12	6	0	0	0	3	6	.341	.439
Away	.116	43	5	1	0	0	1	6	5	.224	.140	Batting #1	.266	64	17	6	0	1	5	7	7	.338	.406
First Pitch	.125	8	1	0	0	0	0	1	0	.222	.125	Batting #5	.214	14	3	0	0	0	0	4	2	.389	.214
Ahead on Count	.333	30	10	3	0	0	3	8	0	.474	.433	Other	.172	29	5	1	0	1	3	4	8	.273	.310
Behind on Count	.179	39	7	2	0	1	3	0	11	.179	.308	Pre-All Star	.234	107	25	7	0	2	8	15	17	.328	.355
Two Strikes	.212	52	11	2	0	2	4	6	17	.293	.365	Post-All Star	.000	0	0	0	0	0	0	0	0	.000	.000

Last Five Years

	Avg	AB	H	2B	3B	HR	RBI	BB	SO	OBP	SLG		Avg	AB	H	2B	3B	HR	RBI	BB	SO	OBP	SLG
vs. Left	.330	667	220	43	7	22	91	91	82	.408	.514	Scoring Posn	.320	566	181	29	5	12	238	106	91	.422	.452
vs. Right	.303	1772	537	72	8	29	210	193	237	.372	.402	Close & Late	.325	382	124	16	1	9	47	48	54	.400	.442
Groundball	.297	680	202	30	4	14	87	81	80	.372	.415	None on/out	.293	666	195	29	3	14	14	54	83	.347	.406
Flyball	.305	587	179	33	4	14	75	70	78	.379	.446	Batting #1	.284	676	192	25	6	11	50	61	82	.342	.388
Home	.343	1214	416	68	9	25	153	147	154	.412	.475	Batting #5	.306	758	232	39	5	16	104	86	102	.375	.434
Away	.278	1225	341	47	6	26	148	137	165	.352	.390	Other	.331	1005	333	51	4	24	147	137	135	.413	.462
Day	.289	499	144	22	5	7	63	62	66	.371	.395	April	.254	334	85	12	0	7	46	29	41	.315	.353
Night	.316	1940	613	93	10	44	238	222	253	.385	.442	May	.336	426	143	25	4	13	64	50	66	.406	.505
Grass	.320	2027	648	100	12	43	252	241	266	.392	.444	June	.315	492	155	23	4	14	61	57	74	.384	.463
Turf	.265	412	109	15	3	8	49	43	53	.336	.374	July	.321	399	128	21	1	4	49	46	42	.392	.409

Last Five Years

	Avg	AB	H	2B	3B	HR	RBI	BB	SO	OBP	SLG
First Pitch	.357	224	80	6	2	5	21	10	0	.381	.469
Ahead on Count	.376	647	243	39	5	18	104	179	0	.508	.535
Behind on Count	.258	855	221	41	4	10	87	1	163	.262	.351
Two Strikes	.249	1092	272	45	7	22	115	88	318	.307	.364

	Avg	AB	H	2B	3B	HR	RBI	BB	SO	OBP	SLG
August	.311	389	121	14	2	6	45	48	45	.385	.404
September/October	.313	399	125	20	4	7	36	54	51	.396	.436
Pre-All Star	.305	1375	420	63	8	35	181	149	195	.373	.439
Post-All Star	.317	1064	337	52	7	16	120	135	124	.394	.424

Batter vs. Pitcher (since 1984)

Hits Best Against	Avg	AB	H	2B	3B	HR	RBI	BB	SO	OBP	SLG
Tom Bolton	.750	8	6	1	0	1	1	4	1	.833	1.250
Bobby Thigpen	.636	11	7	2	0	1	1	0	1	.636	1.091
Scott Sanderson	.500	14	7	0	0	2	4	3	0	.588	.929
Mike Birkbeck	.500	12	6	1	1	1	1	3	1	.600	1.000
Jerry Don Gleaton	.500	10	5	1	0	1	3	1	1	.500	.900

Hits Worst Against	Avg	AB	H	2B	3B	HR	RBI	BB	SO	OBP	SLG
Tom Henke	.118	17	2	0	0	0	1	1	2	.167	.118
Scott Erickson	.118	17	2	0	0	0	0	2	4	.211	.118
Scott Bankhead	.136	22	3	0	0	0	1	1	2	.174	.136
Chuck Crim	.143	21	3	0	0	0	3	2	1	.217	.143
Bert Blyleven	.171	35	6	0	0	0	1	2	4	.216	.171

Marvin Freeman — Braves　　　　Pitches Right (groundball pitcher)

	ERA	W	L	Sv	G	GS	IP	BB	SO	Avg	H	2B	3B	HR	RBI	OBP	SLG	GF	IR	IRS	Hld	SvOp	SB	CS	GB	FB	G/F
1992 Season	3.22	7	5	3	58	0	64.1	29	41	.251	61	9	1	7	41	.332	.383	15	42	20	16	6	7	5	120	47	2.55
Last Five Years	4.14	11	10	5	129	15	215.0	107	150	.242	196	29	4	16	112	.336	.347	26	80	29	26	8	28	13	369	174	2.12

1992 Season

	ERA	W	L	Sv	G	GS	IP	H	HR	BB	SO
Home	2.50	4	3	1	28	0	36.0	30	4	13	28
Away	4.13	3	2	2	30	0	28.1	31	3	16	13
Starter	0.00	0	0	0	0	0	0.0	0	0	0	0
Reliever	3.22	7	5	3	58	0	64.1	61	7	29	41
0 Days rest	2.81	2	2	1	14	0	16.0	12	1	8	10
1 or 2 Days rest	2.83	3	2	2	30	0	28.2	28	1	15	20
3+ Days rest	4.12	2	1	0	14	0	19.2	21	5	6	11
Pre-All Star	3.21	2	3	2	29	0	33.2	33	4	14	22
Post-All Star	3.23	5	2	1	29	0	30.2	28	3	15	19

	Avg	AB	H	2B	3B	HR	RBI	BB	SO	OBP	SLG
vs. Left	.246	114	28	1	0	5	17	16	13	.336	.386
vs. Right	.256	129	33	8	1	2	24	13	28	.329	.380
Scoring Posn	.224	85	19	2	1	0	32	13	19	.330	.271
Close & Late	.227	119	27	5	0	3	15	15	22	.313	.345
None on/out	.254	59	15	0	0	5	5	4	7	.302	.508
First Pitch	.361	36	13	2	0	2	10	5	0	.439	.583
Behind on Count	.300	50	15	2	0	2	10	19	0	.500	.460
Ahead on Count	.216	116	25	5	1	0	15	0	38	.214	.276
Two Strikes	.175	103	18	4	0	0	10	5	41	.211	.214

Last Five Years

	ERA	W	L	Sv	G	GS	IP	H	HR	BB	SO
Home	3.57	5	5	3	67	7	113.1	94	7	51	81
Away	4.78	6	5	2	62	8	101.2	102	9	56	69
Day	4.95	3	1	1	37	5	63.2	59	6	25	43
Night	3.81	8	9	4	92	10	151.1	137	10	82	107
Grass	2.88	8	5	3	86	5	137.2	111	11	48	90
Turf	6.40	3	5	2	43	10	77.1	85	5	59	60
April	3.32	2	1	0	14	1	19.0	15	1	16	11
May	4.08	0	1	3	23	0	28.2	30	2	11	22
June	4.31	0	2	0	16	3	31.1	30	5	9	19
July	3.96	2	2	1	27	0	36.1	31	3	12	30
August	5.53	2	2	1	25	5	42.1	43	2	27	28
September/October	3.45	5	2	0	24	6	57.1	47	3	32	40
Starter	6.25	2	4	0	15	15	67.2	72	5	51	46
Reliever	3.18	9	6	5	114	0	147.1	124	11	56	104
0 Days rest	2.03	2	2	1	21	0	26.2	20	1	10	19
1 or 2 Days rest	2.64	5	2	4	58	0	75.0	61	4	28	56
3+ Days rest	4.73	2	2	0	35	0	45.2	43	6	18	29
Pre-All Star	3.76	2	5	3	63	4	93.1	87	9	39	60
Post-All Star	4.44	9	5	2	66	11	121.2	109	7	68	90

	Avg	AB	H	2B	3B	HR	RBI	BB	SO	OBP	SLG
vs. Left	.268	400	107	14	3	8	57	70	52	.378	.378
vs. Right	.218	409	89	15	1	8	55	37	98	.293	.318
Inning 1-6	.260	457	119	19	4	8	69	70	84	.366	.372
Inning 7+	.219	352	77	10	0	8	43	37	66	.295	.315
None on	.228	438	100	16	1	10	10	56	75	.320	.338
Runners on	.259	371	96	13	3	6	102	51	75	.355	.358
Scoring Posn	.259	239	62	10	3	2	92	39	48	.373	.351
Close & Late	.219	178	39	7	0	3	20	22	36	.305	.309
None on/out	.222	198	44	3	0	6	6	21	31	.300	.328
vs. 1st Batr (relief)	.219	105	23	1	0	1	14	7	17	.272	.257
First Inning Pitched	.223	421	94	12	3	5	64	43	62	.304	.302
First 15 Pitches	.222	396	88	11	1	5	47	40	69	.300	.293
Pitch 16-30	.249	221	55	9	2	7	35	27	49	.336	.403
Pitch 31-45	.254	63	16	0	1	1	6	15	13	.397	.333
Pitch 46+	.287	129	37	9	0	3	24	25	19	.408	.426
First Pitch	.322	121	39	9	0	3	25	8	1	.362	.471
Ahead on Count	.180	378	68	10	2	4	36	0	128	.190	.249
Behind on Count	.287	178	51	5	2	5	34	72	0	.498	.421
Two Strikes	.174	357	62	9	1	3	27	27	149	.235	.230

Pitcher vs. Batter (career)

Pitches Best Vs.	Avg	AB	H	2B	3B	HR	RBI	BB	SO	OBP	SLG
Barry Larkin	.000	13	0	0	0	0	1	0	0	.000	.000
Robby Thompson	.091	11	1	0	0	0	1	0	2	.167	.182
Mark Grace	.154	13	2	0	0	0	1	0	1	.154	.154
Jose Lind	.182	11	2	0	0	0	1	1	2	.250	.182
Howard Johnson	.200	10	2	1	0	0	0	1	0	.273	.300

Pitches Worst Vs.	Avg	AB	H	2B	3B	HR	RBI	BB	SO	OBP	SLG
Barry Bonds	.571	7	4	2	0	0	0	4	0	.727	.857
Gary Carter	.364	11	4	1	0	0	1	0	2	.364	.455
Doug Dascenzo	.333	9	3	0	0	0	0	2	1	.455	.333

Steve Frey — Angels　　　　Pitches Left

	ERA	W	L	Sv	G	GS	IP	BB	SO	Avg	H	2B	3B	HR	RBI	OBP	SLG	GF	IR	IRS	Hld	SvOp	SB	CS	GB	FB	G/F
1992 Season	3.57	4	2	4	51	0	45.1	22	24	.238	39	4	0	6	17	.330	.372	20	50	5	4	5	3	3	56	67	0.84
Career (1989-1992)	3.67	15	7	14	153	0	162.0	85	89	.256	155	23	1	17	72	.348	.381	46	102	23	14	16	14	7	209	208	1.00

1992 Season

	ERA	W	L	Sv	G	GS	IP	H	HR	BB	SO
Home	3.00	2	1	2	24	0	21.0	21	3	4	10
Away	4.07	2	1	2	27	0	24.1	18	3	18	14
Starter	0.00	0	0	0	0	0	0.0	0	0	0	0
Reliever	3.57	4	2	4	51	0	45.1	39	6	22	24
0 Days rest	6.00	0	0	2	6	0	6.0	6	2	1	5

	Avg	AB	H	2B	3B	HR	RBI	BB	SO	OBP	SLG
vs. Left	.189	53	10	0	0	5	8	5	9	.271	.472
vs. Right	.261	111	29	4	0	1	9	17	15	.356	.324
Scoring Posn	.127	55	7	0	0	1	10	9	8	.250	.182
Close & Late	.234	77	18	3	0	1	5	15	12	.351	.312
None on/out	.294	34	10	0	0	1	1	3	4	.368	.382

1992 Season

	ERA	W	L	Sv	G	GS	IP	H	HR	BB	SO
1 or 2 Days rest	1.21	3	1	1	26	0	22.1	16	2	13	10
3+ Days rest	5.82	1	1	1	19	0	17.0	17	2	8	9
Pre-All Star	1.44	3	1	1	29	0	31.1	22	1	17	20
Post-All Star	8.36	1	1	3	22	0	14.0	17	5	5	4

	Avg	AB	H	2B	3B	HR	RBI	BB	SO	OBP	SLG
First Pitch	.211	19	4	0	0	1	1	3	0	.318	.368
Behind on Count	.353	51	18	2	0	2	5	10	0	.452	.510
Ahead on Count	.196	56	11	1	0	2	7	0	17	.203	.321
Two Strikes	.159	69	11	1	0	3	10	9	24	.259	.304

Career (1989-1992)

	ERA	W	L	Sv	G	GS	IP	H	HR	BB	SO
Home	2.74	7	2	9	76	0	75.2	70	6	33	42
Away	4.48	8	5	5	77	0	86.1	85	11	52	47
Day	3.63	7	2	7	55	0	57.0	61	7	26	35
Night	3.69	8	5	7	98	0	105.0	94	10	59	54
Grass	4.84	4	5	6	69	0	67.0	66	10	38	30
Turf	2.84	11	2	8	84	0	95.0	89	7	47	59
April	3.09	2	1	4	27	0	32.0	22	4	15	17
May	3.13	2	1	0	35	0	37.1	33	2	20	24
June	3.05	3	1	2	19	0	20.2	21	1	10	12
July	3.86	4	1	0	27	0	23.1	27	3	15	12
August	7.17	2	3	3	21	0	21.1	32	6	12	7
September/October	2.63	2	0	5	24	0	27.1	21	1	13	17
Starter	0.00	0	0	0	0	0	0.0	0	0	0	0
Reliever	3.67	15	7	14	153	0	162.0	155	17	85	89
0 Days rest	2.13	1	0	4	23	0	25.1	19	3	9	12
1 or 2 Days rest	2.74	8	5	8	67	0	69.0	52	8	40	35
3+ Days rest	5.19	6	2	2	63	0	67.2	84	6	36	42
Pre-All Star	3.10	8	3	6	90	0	98.2	87	7	55	58
Post-All Star	4.55	7	4	8	63	0	63.1	71	10	30	31

	Avg	AB	H	2B	3B	HR	RBI	BB	SO	OBP	SLG
vs. Left	.254	197	50	7	0	8	33	26	42	.344	.411
vs. Right	.257	409	105	16	1	9	39	59	47	.349	.367
Inning 1-6	.320	103	33	5	1	3	23	13	13	.407	.476
Inning 7+	.243	503	122	18	0	14	49	72	76	.336	.362
None on	.236	297	70	11	1	11	11	45	47	.344	.391
Runners on	.275	309	85	12	0	6	61	40	42	.351	.372
Scoring Posn	.230	183	42	5	0	2	51	32	26	.333	.290
Close & Late	.232	271	63	9	0	6	19	44	37	.336	.332
None on/out	.252	139	35	3	1	5	5	16	20	.342	.396
vs. 1st Batr (relief)	.290	131	38	6	0	5	21	16	19	.368	.450
First Inning Pitched	.257	443	114	19	0	13	58	60	67	.346	.388
First 15 Pitches	.264	386	102	16	0	14	50	51	55	.351	.415
Pitch 16-30	.228	171	39	6	1	1	16	29	27	.338	.292
Pitch 31-45	.350	40	14	1	0	2	8	5	4	.422	.525
Pitch 46+	.000	9	0	0	0	0	0	0	3	.000	.000
First Pitch	.267	90	24	3	0	3	13	13	0	.352	.400
Ahead on Count	.215	223	48	10	0	4	20	0	67	.222	.314
Behind on Count	.320	150	48	7	1	6	22	30	0	.455	.500
Two Strikes	.199	256	51	10	0	3	25	33	88	.295	.309

Pitcher vs. Batter (career)

Pitches Best Vs.	Avg	AB	H	2B	3B	HR	RBI	BB	SO	OBP	SLG

Pitches Worst Vs.	Avg	AB	H	2B	3B	HR	RBI	BB	SO	OBP	SLG
Barry Bonds	.500	12	6	1	0	1	6	1	1	.538	.833

Todd Frohwirth — Orioles
Pitches Right (groundball pitcher)

	ERA	W	L	Sv	G	GS	IP	BB	SO	Avg	H	2B	3B	HR	RBI	OBP	SLG	GF	IR	IRS	Hld	SvOp	SB	CS	GB	FB	G/F
1992 Season	2.46	4	3	4	65	0	106.0	41	58	.247	97	15	0	4	52	.323	.316	23	64	26	15	7	11	2	194	88	2.20
Last Five Years	2.82	13	9	7	178	0	278.0	105	186	.232	236	40	6	12	134	.307	.319	33	180	62	32	14	31	9	498	194	2.57

1992 Season

	ERA	W	L	Sv	G	GS	IP	H	HR	BB	SO
Home	1.84	2	1	2	33	0	58.2	52	3	15	26
Away	3.23	2	2	2	32	0	47.1	45	1	26	32
Day	4.97	1	1	0	21	0	29.0	34	2	17	22
Night	1.52	3	2	4	44	0	77.0	63	2	24	36
Grass	2.56	4	3	4	54	0	84.1	83	4	32	35
Turf	2.08	0	0	0	11	0	21.2	14	0	9	23
April	2.08	1	0	1	6	0	8.2	3	0	4	11
May	2.30	0	0	1	12	0	15.2	20	0	5	7
June	1.74	1	0	0	12	0	20.2	24	1	6	9
July	3.86	1	2	1	13	0	25.2	19	2	10	12
August	0.83	1	0	0	13	0	21.2	18	1	11	15
September/October	3.95	0	1	1	9	0	13.2	13	0	5	4
Starter	0.00	0	0	0	0	0	0.0	0	0	0	0
Reliever	2.46	4	3	4	65	0	106.0	97	4	41	58
0 Days rest	2.70	1	1	0	14	0	30.0	27	0	11	14
1 or 2 Days rest	1.35	1	0	3	34	0	46.2	39	2	17	28
3+ Days rest	3.99	2	2	1	17	0	29.1	31	2	13	16
Pre-All Star	1.74	2	0	3	36	0	62.0	54	1	20	36
Post-All Star	3.48	2	3	1	29	0	44.0	43	3	21	22

	Avg	AB	H	2B	3B	HR	RBI	BB	SO	OBP	SLG
vs. Left	.246	142	35	3	0	1	15	19	15	.341	.289
vs. Right	.248	250	62	12	0	3	37	22	43	.311	.332
Inning 1-6	.221	68	15	4	0	1	10	2	8	.239	.324
Inning 7+	.253	324	82	11	0	3	42	39	50	.339	.315
None on	.228	189	43	5	0	2	2	21	23	.311	.286
Runners on	.266	203	54	10	0	2	50	20	35	.333	.345
Scoring Posn	.272	136	37	5	0	2	46	14	29	.342	.353
Close & Late	.226	155	35	6	0	1	25	22	29	.326	.284
None on/out	.222	81	18	1	0	1	1	10	9	.323	.272
vs. 1st Batr (relief)	.300	60	18	3	0	1	15	4	11	.344	.400
First Inning Pitched	.293	208	61	8	0	3	42	20	34	.359	.375
First 15 Pitches	.292	202	59	8	0	2	37	20	30	.357	.361
Pitch 16-30	.193	109	21	5	0	2	10	12	18	.279	.294
Pitch 31-45	.230	61	14	2	0	0	4	6	8	.309	.262
Pitch 46+	.150	20	3	0	0	0	1	3	2	.261	.150
First Pitch	.214	56	12	4	0	1	10	4	0	.262	.339
Ahead on Count	.221	181	40	6	0	1	25	0	48	.230	.271
Behind on Count	.296	81	24	3	0	2	11	21	1	.447	.407
Two Strikes	.180	161	29	4	0	1	13	16	57	.263	.211

Last Five Years

	ERA	W	L	Sv	G	GS	IP	H	HR	BB	SO
Home	2.57	7	2	3	91	0	154.0	125	8	41	102
Away	3.12	6	7	4	87	0	124.0	111	4	64	84
Day	4.66	4	3	2	49	0	73.1	76	4	38	52
Night	2.15	9	6	5	129	0	204.2	160	7	67	134
Grass	2.61	9	6	7	110	0	179.0	158	6	65	108
Turf	3.18	4	3	0	68	0	99.0	76	6	40	78
April	3.98	1	2	1	22	0	20.1	14	1	17	18
May	4.63	0	0	1	21	0	23.1	29	2	11	18
June	1.75	4	2	0	30	0	51.1	49	2	22	33
July	3.34	3	3	2	35	0	64.2	55	3	16	37
August	2.44	3	0	1	38	0	62.2	49	3	23	44
September/October	2.43	2	2	2	32	0	55.2	40	1	16	36
Starter	0.00	0	0	0	0	0	0.0	0	0	0	0

	Avg	AB	H	2B	3B	HR	RBI	BB	SO	OBP	SLG
vs. Left	.269	391	105	18	4	4	56	56	49	.364	.366
vs. Right	.210	625	131	22	2	8	78	49	137	.270	.290
Inning 1-6	.225	262	59	12	1	3	43	21	48	.282	.313
Inning 7+	.235	754	177	28	5	9	91	84	138	.316	.321
None on	.218	542	118	18	3	6	6	42	103	.278	.295
Runners on	.249	474	118	22	3	6	128	63	83	.339	.346
Scoring Posn	.256	324	83	14	2	6	123	52	65	.362	.367
Close & Late	.216	328	71	8	2	2	40	43	67	.310	.287
None on/out	.203	227	46	5	3	1	1	18	45	.270	.264
vs. 1st Batr (relief)	.242	157	38	5	2	2	31	16	26	.314	.338
First Inning Pitched	.255	546	139	19	3	8	102	63	95	.335	.350
First 15 Pitches	.243	535	130	18	3	7	87	54	91	.314	.327
Pitch 16-30	.235	281	66	15	2	4	27	29	51	.311	.345

Last Five Years

	ERA	W	L	Sv	G	GS	IP	H	HR	BB	SO		Avg	AB	H	2B	3B	HR	RBI	BB	SO	OBP	SLG
Reliever	2.82	13	9	7	178	0	278.0	236	12	105	186	Pitch 31-45	.214	145	31	4	1	1	15	13	28	.268	.276
0 Days rest	2.62	3	3	1	44	0	65.1	59	1	24	38	Pitch 46+	.164	55	9	3	0	0	5	9	16	.281	.218
1 or 2 Days rest	2.17	8	1	4	83	0	132.2	105	4	46	95	First Pitch	.266	158	42	9	2	4	28	11	0	.314	.424
3+ Days rest	4.05	2	5	2	51	0	80.0	72	7	35	53	Ahead on Count	.161	459	74	11	2	3	50	0	156	.166	.214
Pre-All Star	2.88	5	5	3	85	0	118.2	107	6	57	83	Behind on Count	.314	226	71	11	1	3	33	58	1	.458	.412
Post-All Star	2.77	8	4	4	93	0	159.1	129	6	48	103	Two Strikes	.152	433	66	9	1	3	34	36	185	.222	.199

Pitcher vs. Batter (career)

Pitches Best Vs.	Avg	AB	H	2B	3B	HR	RBI	BB	SO	OBP	SLG	Pitches Worst Vs.	Avg	AB	H	2B	3B	HR	RBI	BB	SO	OBP	SLG
Kirby Puckett	.000	13	0	0	0	0	0	0	4	.000	.000												

Jeff Frye — Rangers
Bats Right (groundball hitter)

	Avg	G	AB	R	H	2B	3B	HR	RBI	BB	SO	HBP	GDP	SB	CS	OBP	SLG	IBB	SH	SF	#Pit	#P/PA	GB	FB	G/F
1992 Season	.256	67	199	24	51	9	1	1	12	16	21	3	2	1	3	.320	.327	0	11	1	917	4.19	84	55	1.53

1992 Season

	Avg	AB	H	2B	3B	HR	RBI	BB	SO	OBP	SLG		Avg	AB	H	2B	3B	HR	RBI	BB	SO	OBP	SLG
vs. Left	.309	68	21	5	0	1	6	5	10	.356	.426	Scoring Posn	.175	40	7	1	0	0	8	3	4	.227	.200
vs. Right	.229	131	30	4	1	0	6	11	17	.301	.275	Close & Late	.269	26	7	2	0	0	3	1	2	.321	.346
Home	.260	104	27	5	1	0	5	7	13	.310	.327	None on/out	.194	62	12	2	0	1	1	9	15	.306	.274
Away	.253	95	24	4	0	1	7	9	14	.330	.326	Batting #1	.254	67	17	5	1	1	6	5	10	.311	.403
First Pitch	.714	7	5	2	0	0	2	0	0	.750	1.000	Batting #9	.274	73	20	4	0	0	2	6	12	.338	.329
Ahead on Count	.317	41	13	2	0	0	3	14	0	.491	.366	Other	.237	59	14	0	0	0	4	5	5	.308	.237
Behind on Count	.241	83	20	2	0	0	4	0	18	.241	.265	Pre-All Star	.294	17	5	1	1	0	2	1	3	.316	.471
Two Strikes	.175	114	20	5	0	0	2	2	27	.203	.219	Post-All Star	.253	182	46	8	0	1	10	15	24	.320	.313

Travis Fryman — Tigers
Bats Right (flyball hitter)

	Avg	G	AB	R	H	2B	3B	HR	RBI	BB	SO	HBP	GDP	SB	CS	OBP	SLG	IBB	SH	SF	#Pit	#P/PA	GB	FB	G/F
1992 Season	.266	161	659	87	175	31	4	20	96	45	144	6	13	8	4	.316	.416	1	5	6	2744	3.83	182	194	0.94
Career (1990-1992)	.268	376	1448	184	388	78	8	50	214	102	344	10	29	23	12	.318	.436	1	12	12	6042	3.84	379	427	0.89

1992 Season

	Avg	AB	H	2B	3B	HR	RBI	BB	SO	OBP	SLG		Avg	AB	H	2B	3B	HR	RBI	BB	SO	OBP	SLG
vs. Left	.285	158	45	7	1	7	31	12	30	.337	.475	Scoring Posn	.268	194	52	11	2	3	72	13	54	.312	.392
vs. Right	.259	501	130	24	3	13	65	33	114	.309	.397	Close & Late	.200	85	17	4	0	4	13	8	26	.271	.388
Groundball	.259	166	43	6	2	3	24	8	29	.298	.373	None on/out	.275	109	30	6	1	4	4	4	18	.301	.459
Flyball	.257	218	56	9	0	9	35	13	45	.302	.422	Batting #3	.252	531	134	26	4	14	76	34	120	.300	.395
Home	.232	319	74	9	2	9	40	22	70	.289	.357	Batting #8	.270	37	10	0	0	2	3	2	10	.325	.432
Away	.297	340	101	22	2	11	56	23	74	.341	.471	Other	.341	91	31	5	0	4	17	9	14	.400	.527
Day	.265	219	58	9	3	5	28	15	48	.312	.402	April	.308	78	24	1	0	3	7	5	11	.357	.436
Night	.266	440	117	22	1	15	68	30	96	.317	.423	May	.259	112	29	5	0	5	18	9	30	.311	.438
Grass	.271	558	151	22	3	19	78	39	115	.322	.423	June	.309	123	38	10	2	4	25	3	23	.331	.520
Turf	.238	101	24	9	1	1	18	6	29	.282	.376	July	.261	111	29	7	0	3	16	7	27	.308	.405
First Pitch	.319	91	29	3	0	4	20	1	0	.326	.484	August	.265	117	31	4	1	3	14	8	23	.312	.393
Ahead on Count	.374	155	58	11	0	10	35	17	0	.440	.639	September/October	.203	118	24	4	1	2	16	13	30	.289	.305
Behind on Count	.206	204	42	7	3	3	25	1	71	.215	.314	Pre-All Star	.291	361	105	19	2	13	57	20	76	.332	.463
Two Strikes	.168	316	53	9	1	4	25	27	144	.232	.241	Post-All Star	.235	298	70	12	2	7	39	25	68	.296	.359

1992 By Position

Position	Avg	AB	H	2B	3B	HR	RBI	BB	SO	OBP	SLG	G	GS	Innings	PO	A	E	DP	Fld Pct	Rng Fctr	In Zone	Outs	Zone Rtg	MLB Zone
As 3b	.310	100	31	4	0	6	16	8	19	.361	.530	27	27	220.0	15	46	2	4	.968	2.50	62	49	.790	.841
As ss	.258	559	144	27	4	14	80	37	125	.308	.395	137	134	1202.2	205	443	20	88	.970	4.85	498	458	.920	.885

Career (1990-1992)

	Avg	AB	H	2B	3B	HR	RBI	BB	SO	OBP	SLG		Avg	AB	H	2B	3B	HR	RBI	BB	SO	OBP	SLG
vs. Left	.296	398	118	23	3	17	66	31	89	.350	.497	Scoring Posn	.270	404	109	29	3	8	153	28	106	.313	.416
vs. Right	.257	1050	270	55	5	33	148	71	255	.306	.413	Close & Late	.234	197	46	10	1	7	29	15	55	.288	.401
Groundball	.278	421	117	23	2	9	61	20	91	.315	.406	None on/out	.290	262	76	17	3	9	9	16	55	.331	.481
Flyball	.258	384	99	19	0	16	58	29	87	.315	.432	Batting #3	.255	596	152	29	4	18	82	40	141	.306	.408
Home	.243	688	167	27	5	22	90	56	172	.304	.392	Batting #6	.263	205	54	11	1	8	28	14	44	.314	.444
Away	.291	760	221	51	3	28	124	46	172	.331	.476	Other	.281	647	182	38	3	24	104	48	159	.331	.461
Day	.269	464	125	22	4	14	61	36	112	.321	.425	April	.257	140	36	2	1	5	17	12	22	.318	.393
Night	.267	984	263	56	4	36	153	66	232	.317	.442	May	.254	197	50	10	0	8	37	15	51	.302	.426
Grass	.273	1235	337	62	7	43	173	86	288	.322	.439	June	.279	226	63	16	2	7	36	10	53	.313	.460
Turf	.239	213	51	16	1	7	41	16	56	.296	.423	July	.267	255	68	17	1	12	38	18	67	.315	.482
First Pitch	.333	201	67	9	2	12	41	1	0	.333	.577	August	.285	312	89	15	2	9	35	21	76	.333	.433
Ahead on Count	.386	293	113	29	1	17	62	44	0	.469	.666	September/October	.258	318	82	18	2	9	51	26	75	.319	.412
Behind on Count	.228	496	113	21	3	15	62	1	166	.236	.373	Pre-All Star	.264	647	171	32	3	23	102	42	150	.310	.430
Two Strikes	.165	726	120	23	2	11	73	57	344	.227	.248	Post-All Star	.271	801	217	46	5	27	112	60	194	.324	.442

Gary Gaetti — Angels
Bats Right

	Avg	G	AB	R	H	2B	3B	HR	RBI	BB	SO	HBP	GDP	SB	CS	OBP	SLG	IBB	SH	SF	#Pit	#P/PA	GB	FB	G/F
1992 Season	.226	130	456	41	103	13	2	12	48	21	79	6	9	3	1	.267	.342	4	0	3	1593	3.28	152	157	0.97
Last Five Years	.250	699	2585	269	645	102	14	93	362	151	456	25	66	27	13	.294	.408	18	5	31	9465	3.39	863	854	1.01

1992 Season

	Avg	AB	H	2B	3B	HR	RBI	BB	SO	OBP	SLG		Avg	AB	H	2B	3B	HR	RBI	BB	SO	OBP	SLG
vs. Left	.250	124	31	6	0	5	15	8	13	.299	.419	Scoring Posn	.250	112	28	3	1	3	35	10	24	.315	.375
vs. Right	.217	332	72	7	2	7	33	13	66	.256	.313	Close & Late	.230	87	20	4	1	1	10	4	9	.261	.333
Groundball	.226	115	26	2	1	2	16	6	19	.274	.313	None on/out	.196	107	21	4	0	2	2	2	14	.232	.290
Flyball	.201	134	27	2	1	5	14	7	25	.243	.343	Batting #4	.185	151	28	1	1	6	19	5	25	.220	.325
Home	.260	231	60	7	1	8	30	7	40	.289	.403	Batting #6	.205	127	26	6	1	1	7	7	27	.257	.291
Away	.191	225	43	6	1	4	18	14	39	.246	.280	Other	.275	178	49	6	1	5	22	9	27	.314	.393
Day	.217	129	28	1	2	4	26	4	21	.239	.349	April	.212	66	14	2	1	2	5	4	15	.264	.364
Night	.229	327	75	12	0	8	22	17	58	.278	.339	May	.250	92	23	5	0	1	6	5	12	.289	.337
Grass	.235	378	89	12	1	10	41	17	66	.273	.352	June	.220	82	18	0	0	2	8	4	15	.273	.293
Turf	.179	78	14	1	1	2	7	4	13	.244	.295	July	.274	73	20	3	0	2	15	3	11	.295	.397
First Pitch	.224	98	22	1	0	1	6	3	0	.252	.265	August	.136	66	9	1	1	1	3	4	15	.208	.227
Ahead on Count	.295	88	26	4	2	3	21	9	0	.364	.489	September/October	.247	77	19	2	0	4	11	1	11	.266	.429
Behind on Count	.223	157	35	6	1	3	15	0	45	.233	.331	Pre-All Star	.226	266	60	7	1	5	22	14	49	.270	.316
Two Strikes	.165	176	29	6	0	2	6	9	79	.221	.233	Post-All Star	.226	190	43	6	1	7	26	7	30	.264	.379

1992 By Position

Position	Avg	AB	H	2B	3B	HR	RBI	BB	SO	OBP	SLG	G	GS	Innings	PO	A	E	DP	Fld Pct	Rng Fctr	In Zone	Outs	Zone Rtg	MLB Zone
As Designated Hitter	.230	61	14	1	0	3	4	3	15	.277	.393	17	17	---	---	---	---	---	---	---	---	---	---	---
As 1b	.216	153	33	5	1	3	19	6	21	.258	.320	44	40	368.2	371	32	5	36	.988	---	80	66	.825	.843
As 3b	.230	235	54	7	1	5	22	12	42	.271	.332	67	63	563.1	51	163	17	16	.926	3.42	209	184	.880	.841

Last Five Years

	Avg	AB	H	2B	3B	HR	RBI	BB	SO	OBP	SLG		Avg	AB	H	2B	3B	HR	RBI	BB	SO	OBP	SLG
vs. Left	.252	730	184	32	2	28	109	59	104	.306	.416	Scoring Posn	.266	668	178	24	3	31	277	68	135	.327	.451
vs. Right	.249	1855	461	70	12	65	253	92	352	.288	.404	Close & Late	.233	408	95	13	2	19	66	20	59	.266	.414
Groundball	.241	685	165	20	5	22	105	42	119	.291	.381	None on/out	.247	660	163	28	2	29	29	23	96	.280	.427
Flyball	.239	594	142	20	4	27	93	45	104	.294	.423	Batting #4	.238	752	179	22	5	33	124	48	129	.284	.412
Home	.262	1265	332	45	7	46	183	74	223	.307	.418	Batting #5	.249	1190	296	54	7	42	163	68	210	.293	.412
Away	.237	1320	313	57	7	47	179	77	233	.281	.398	Other	.264	643	170	26	2	18	75	35	117	.307	.395
Day	.261	736	192	25	2	32	133	34	133	.296	.431	April	.255	368	94	15	3	14	48	24	78	.302	.427
Night	.245	1849	453	77	12	61	229	117	323	.293	.399	May	.258	511	132	26	3	18	82	24	78	.291	.427
Grass	.249	1475	367	57	5	57	198	89	269	.295	.410	June	.270	478	129	15	1	21	67	30	78	.319	.437
Turf	.250	1110	278	45	9	36	164	62	187	.293	.405	July	.262	446	117	21	1	17	74	30	81	.310	.428
First Pitch	.325	508	165	25	1	18	72	9	0	.340	.484	August	.206	412	85	12	4	14	40	25	78	.256	.357
Ahead on Count	.310	487	151	24	5	26	103	76	0	.402	.540	September/October	.238	370	88	13	2	9	51	18	63	.281	.357
Behind on Count	.223	927	207	34	7	26	126	2	257	.229	.359	Pre-All Star	.263	1508	396	60	8	57	214	86	268	.305	.426
Two Strikes	.176	1098	193	29	6	27	103	62	226	.226	.287	Post-All Star	.231	1077	249	42	6	36	148	65	188	.279	.382

Greg Gagne — Twins
Bats Right

	Avg	G	AB	R	H	2B	3B	HR	RBI	BB	SO	HBP	GDP	SB	CS	OBP	SLG	IBB	SH	SF	#Pit	#P/PA	GB	FB	G/F
1992 Season	.246	146	439	53	108	23	0	7	39	19	83	2	11	6	7	.280	.346	0	12	1	1690	3.67	150	124	1.21
Last Five Years	.251	721	2156	282	541	117	19	45	215	113	421	15	54	51	35	.291	.385	2	43	14	8213	3.57	707	672	1.05

1992 Season

	Avg	AB	H	2B	3B	HR	RBI	BB	SO	OBP	SLG		Avg	AB	H	2B	3B	HR	RBI	BB	SO	OBP	SLG
vs. Left	.181	105	19	4	0	1	6	6	20	.225	.248	Scoring Posn	.280	100	28	6	0	2	31	6	18	.324	.400
vs. Right	.266	334	89	19	0	6	33	13	63	.297	.377	Close & Late	.267	75	20	2	0	1	4	3	15	.295	.333
Groundball	.276	116	32	7	0	0	6	6	19	.311	.336	None on/out	.238	105	25	6	0	1	1	4	25	.266	.324
Flyball	.221	113	25	7	0	2	9	2	33	.241	.336	Batting #8	.283	53	15	3	0	2	6	1	11	.296	.453
Home	.228	219	50	12	0	1	18	10	48	.265	.297	Batting #9	.233	347	81	16	0	4	31	18	67	.274	.314

147

1992 Season

	Avg	AB	H	2B	3B	HR	RBI	BB	SO	OBP	SLG		Avg	AB	H	2B	3B	HR	RBI	BB	SO	OBP	SLG
Away	.264	220	58	11	0	6	21	9	35	.294	.395	Other	.308	39	12	4	0	1	2	0	5	.308	.487
Day	.264	144	38	9	0	1	10	5	31	.287	.347	April	.274	62	17	2	0	1	4	3	6	.318	.355
Night	.237	295	70	14	0	6	29	14	52	.277	.346	May	.313	83	26	5	0	1	10	6	10	.360	.410
Grass	.274	164	45	7	0	4	16	7	30	.306	.390	June	.190	79	15	4	0	3	10	3	13	.220	.354
Turf	.229	275	63	16	0	3	23	12	53	.264	.320	July	.227	75	17	2	0	0	4	2	22	.244	.253
First Pitch	.313	67	21	5	0	2	6	0	0	.324	.478	August	.259	81	21	8	0	2	10	4	15	.302	.432
Ahead on Count	.250	88	22	3	0	0	4	12	0	.340	.284	September/October	.203	59	12	2	0	0	1	1	17	.217	.237
Behind on Count	.189	159	30	8	0	2	10	0	49	.189	.277	Pre-All Star	.253	257	65	13	0	5	26	12	38	.288	.362
Two Strikes	.201	209	42	10	0	3	17	7	83	.229	.292	Post-All Star	.236	182	43	10	0	2	13	7	45	.268	.324

1992 By Position

Position	Avg	AB	H	2B	3B	HR	RBI	BB	SO	OBP	SLG	G	GS	Innings	PO	A	E	DP	Fld Pct	Rng Fctr	In Zone	Outs	Zone Rtg	MLB Zone
As ss	.247	438	108	23	0	7	39	19	83	.280	.347	141	131	1146.1	207	438	18	82	.973	5.06	507	451	.890	.885

Last Five Years

	Avg	AB	H	2B	3B	HR	RBI	BB	SO	OBP	SLG		Avg	AB	H	2B	3B	HR	RBI	BB	SO	OBP	SLG
vs. Left	.272	628	171	41	12	13	60	43	115	.322	.438	Scoring Posn	.227	532	121	23	6	9	162	44	117	.267	.344
vs. Right	.242	1528	370	76	7	32	155	70	306	.278	.364	Close & Late	.257	296	76	12	4	4	21	14	63	.293	.365
Groundball	.264	588	155	35	5	9	57	31	83	.305	.386	None on/out	.277	501	139	30	7	12	12	17	89	.301	.437
Flyball	.236	474	112	25	7	12	42	25	130	.280	.395	Batting #8	.234	547	128	32	7	10	49	40	114	.292	.373
Home	.251	1038	261	62	10	17	109	61	198	.297	.380	Batting #9	.255	1310	334	68	8	28	140	59	249	.288	.383
Away	.250	1118	280	55	9	28	106	52	223	.285	.391	Other	.264	299	79	17	4	7	26	14	58	.302	.418
Day	.249	646	161	38	6	14	63	31	136	.286	.392	April	.269	305	82	17	2	7	26	25	59	.330	.407
Night	.252	1510	380	79	13	31	152	82	285	.293	.383	May	.258	396	102	20	5	9	43	23	77	.300	.402
Grass	.260	873	227	45	6	23	80	42	167	.295	.404	June	.230	404	93	22	6	10	48	20	76	.270	.389
Turf	.245	1283	314	72	13	22	135	71	254	.289	.373	July	.236	369	87	16	0	6	31	14	71	.267	.328
First Pitch	.302	361	109	31	4	7	37	0	0	.304	.468	August	.280	378	106	28	4	7	40	20	68	.319	.431
Ahead on Count	.283	441	125	24	5	12	53	78	0	.389	.442	September/October	.234	304	71	14	2	6	27	11	70	.262	.352
Behind on Count	.205	794	163	30	3	17	58	0	270	.210	.315	Pre-All Star	.249	1227	305	65	13	27	127	72	234	.294	.389
Two Strikes	.184	988	182	39	6	15	77	33	421	.215	.281	Post-All Star	.254	929	236	52	8	18	88	41	187	.288	.381

Batter vs. Pitcher (since 1984)

Hits Best Against	Avg	AB	H	2B	3B	HR	RBI	BB	SO	OBP	SLG	Hits Worst Against	Avg	AB	H	2B	3B	HR	RBI	BB	SO	OBP	SLG
Charles Nagy	.529	17	9	3	0	0	1	0	2	.529	.706	Bob Welch	.063	16	1	0	0	0	0	2	5	.167	.063
Storm Davis	.462	26	12	2	0	2	4	1	3	.481	.769	Dave Schmidt	.077	13	1	0	0	0	1	0	2	.071	.077
Bill Krueger	.444	18	8	3	0	1	3	0	3	.444	.778	Mike Morgan	.077	13	1	1	0	0	0	0	0	.077	.154
Greg Hibbard	.438	16	7	3	0	1	2	0	0	.438	.813	Jeff Montgomery	.100	10	1	0	0	0	0	1	1	.182	.100
Jose DeLeon	.385	13	5	2	0	1	2	0	3	.385	.769	David Wells	.118	17	2	0	0	0	0	2	4	.211	.118

Andres Galarraga — Cardinals

Bats Right (groundball hitter)

	Avg	G	AB	R	H	2B	3B	HR	RBI	BB	SO	HBP	GDP	SB	CS	OBP	SLG	IBB	SH	SF	#Pit	#P/PA	GB	FB	G/F
1992 Season	.243	95	325	38	79	14	2	10	39	11	69	8	8	5	4	.282	.391	0	0	3	1162	3.35	123	91	1.35
Last Five Years	.260	666	2460	312	640	128	13	91	336	161	635	37	52	45	20	.314	.434	32	0	14	9642	3.61	902	554	1.63

1992 Season

	Avg	AB	H	2B	3B	HR	RBI	BB	SO	OBP	SLG		Avg	AB	H	2B	3B	HR	RBI	BB	SO	OBP	SLG
vs. Left	.320	125	40	7	1	6	19	5	23	.348	.536	Scoring Posn	.191	94	18	3	1	1	27	8	26	.269	.277
vs. Right	.195	200	39	7	1	4	20	6	46	.242	.300	Close & Late	.236	72	17	4	0	2	9	2	16	.263	.375
Groundball	.212	132	28	4	1	3	10	5	27	.252	.326	None on/out	.296	81	24	6	1	4	4	1	14	.321	.543
Flyball	.313	64	20	5	0	3	14	1	14	.353	.531	Batting #4	.237	118	28	9	0	4	13	5	23	.295	.415
Home	.264	159	42	6	1	4	16	3	36	.298	.390	Batting #5	.260	96	25	1	0	4	17	6	23	.311	.396
Away	.223	166	37	8	1	6	23	8	33	.268	.392	Other	.234	111	26	4	2	2	9	0	23	.241	.360
Day	.202	84	17	5	0	3	7	3	20	.239	.369	April	.167	6	1	0	0	0	1	0	1	.286	.167
Night	.257	241	62	9	2	7	32	8	49	.297	.398	May	.206	34	7	0	0	0	2	1	9	.250	.206
Grass	.221	77	17	3	1	4	10	3	17	.259	.442	June	.177	79	14	4	1	0	3	1	20	.217	.253
Turf	.250	248	62	11	1	6	29	8	52	.289	.375	July	.300	90	27	4	1	5	12	4	13	.344	.533
First Pitch	.298	57	17	4	0	1	8	0	0	.305	.421	August	.245	98	24	6	0	3	17	3	20	.269	.398
Ahead on Count	.328	61	20	2	0	5	13	5	0	.386	.607	September/October	.333	18	6	0	0	2	4	2	6	.381	.667
Behind on Count	.236	127	30	5	2	3	12	0	40	.254	.378	Pre-All Star	.186	156	29	6	1	2	10	3	36	.230	.276
Two Strikes	.107	149	16	4	1	3	11	6	69	.158	.208	Post-All Star	.296	169	50	8	1	8	29	8	33	.330	.497

1992 By Position

Position	Avg	AB	H	2B	3B	HR	RBI	BB	SO	OBP	SLG	G	GS	Innings	PO	A	E	DP	Fld Pct	Rng Fctr	In Zone	Outs	Zone Rtg	MLB Zone
As 1b	.248	319	79	14	2	10	39	11	66	.287	.398	90	83	754.1	778	62	8	72	.991	---	170	139	.818	.843

Last Five Years

	Avg	AB	H	2B	3B	HR	RBI	BB	SO	OBP	SLG		Avg	AB	H	2B	3B	HR	RBI	BB	SO	OBP	SLG
vs. Left	.279	817	228	49	3	42	137	54	207	.325	.501	Scoring Posn	.236	664	157	26	6	20	230	79	194	.322	.384
vs. Right	.251	1643	412	79	10	49	199	107	428	.308	.400	Close & Late	.247	502	124	25	1	19	67	41	138	.310	.414
Groundball	.259	945	245	57	6	28	107	63	209	.313	.421	None on/out	.266	531	141	36	2	16		26	132	.310	.431
Flyball	.245	550	135	29	1	26	82	38	180	.303	.444	Batting #3	.266	926	246	48	6	38	141	71	259	.326	.454
Home	.266	1179	314	73	11	40	173	80	304	.322	.449	Batting #5	.263	539	142	27	4	22	65	36	132	.319	.451

Last Five Years

	Avg	AB	H	2B	3B	HR	RBI	BB	SO	OBP	SLG		Avg	AB	H	2B	3B	HR	RBI	BB	SO	OBP	SLG
Away	.254	1281	326	55	2	51	163	81	331	.306	.420	Other	.253	995	252	53	3	31	130	54	244	.298	.406
Day	.249	684	170	36	4	28	84	62	192	.317	.436	April	.257	303	78	17	0	10	39	26	79	.333	.413
Night	.265	1776	470	92	9	63	252	99	443	.312	.433	May	.278	406	113	21	2	16	57	18	100	.316	.458
Grass	.250	647	162	26	1	28	83	38	183	.296	.423	June	.262	397	104	26	2	13	51	27	100	.320	.436
Turf	.264	1813	478	102	12	63	253	123	452	.320	.437	July	.269	454	122	25	4	18	62	35	114	.327	.460
First Pitch	.340	335	114	27	2	12	47	14	0	.376	.540	August	.228	479	109	16	1	15	54	27	128	.277	.359
Ahead on Count	.347	525	182	37	1	36	119	55	0	.413	.627	September/October	.271	421	114	23	4	19	73	28	114	.317	.480
Behind on Count	.223	875	195	38	5	22	88	0	340	.232	.353	Pre-All Star	.272	1254	341	75	4	45	168	85	315	.328	.446
Two Strikes	.161	1177	189	38	6	25	98	78	632	.219	.267	Post-All Star	.248	1206	299	53	9	46	168	76	320	.298	.421

Batter vs. Pitcher (career)

Hits Best Against	Avg	AB	H	2B	3B	HR	RBI	BB	SO	OBP	SLG	Hits Worst Against	Avg	AB	H	2B	3B	HR	RBI	BB	SO	OBP	SLG
Dennis Rasmussen	.500	10	5	1	0	2	4	2	1	.583	1.200	Ron Robinson	.000	15	0	0	0	0	0	1	6	.063	.000
Danny Darwin	.455	22	10	4	0	1	3	1	2	.458	.773	Bob Tewksbury	.000	13	0	0	0	0	0	0	2	.000	.000
Kelly Downs	.440	25	11	2	0	3	6	1	5	.462	.660	Wally Whitehurst	.083	12	1	0	0	0	0	0	2	.214	.083
Craig Lefferts	.348	23	8	1	0	4	9	0	4	.348	.913	Randy Tomlin	.083	12	1	0	0	0	0	0	4	.083	.083
Randy Myers	.333	15	5	0	0	2	7	4	5	.474	.733	Jeff Innis	.143	14	2	0	0	0	0	0	2	.143	.143

Dave Gallagher — Mets   Bats Right

	Avg	G	AB	R	H	2B	3B	HR	RBI	BB	SO	HBP	GDP	SB	CS	OBP	SLG	IBB	SH	SF	#Pit	#P/PA	GB	FB	G/F
1992 Season	.240	98	175	20	42	11	1	1	13	13	8	1	7	4	5	.307	.331	0	3	7	728	3.60	66	59	1.12
Last Five Years	.275	518	1519	197	418	69	7	8	135	125	190	6	33	17	21	.330	.346	4	42	12	6328	3.81	575	461	1.25

1992 Season

	Avg	AB	H	2B	3B	HR	RBI	BB	SO	OBP	SLG		Avg	AB	H	2B	3B	HR	RBI	BB	SO	OBP	SLG
vs. Left	.262	103	27	5	1	0	13	13	8	.333	.330	Scoring Posn	.196	46	9	2	0	0	18	7	4	.267	.239
vs. Right	.208	72	15	6	0	1	8	6	8	.268	.333	Close & Late	.176	51	9	5	0	0	3	4	3	.250	.275
Home	.237	93	22	6	0	1	13	12	8	.309	.333	None on/out	.175	40	7	0	0	1	1	4	2	.250	.250
Away	.244	82	20	5	1	0	8	7	8	.304	.329	Batting #2	.273	44	12	5	0	0	3	5	6	.340	.386
First Pitch	.310	29	9	2	0	0	4	0	0	.281	.379	Batting #6	.167	42	7	3	0	0	7	5	4	.240	.238
Ahead on Count	.333	39	13	1	1	1	7	7	0	.417	.487	Other	.258	89	23	3	1	1	11	9	6	.324	.348
Behind on Count	.148	54	8	3	0	0	5	0	13	.145	.204	Pre-All Star	.208	77	16	6	0	1	11	7	4	.261	.325
Two Strikes	.154	65	10	5	0	0	8	12	16	.278	.231	Post-All Star	.265	98	26	5	1	0	10	12	12	.342	.337

Last Five Years

	Avg	AB	H	2B	3B	HR	RBI	BB	SO	OBP	SLG		Avg	AB	H	2B	3B	HR	RBI	BB	SO	OBP	SLG
vs. Left	.274	669	183	27	5	1	59	57	72	.329	.333	Scoring Posn	.265	359	95	14	1	1	120	44	53	.335	.318
vs. Right	.276	850	235	42	2	7	76	68	118	.331	.355	Close & Late	.221	276	61	14	0	1	20	24	26	.285	.283
Groundball	.297	361	113	23	0	3	35	31	45	.349	.381	None on/out	.285	473	135	24	1	3	3	34	53	.333	.359
Flyball	.266	319	85	12	2	2	29	33	37	.333	.335	Batting #1	.272	669	182	25	2	2	47	47	83	.320	.324
Home	.271	737	200	34	3	3	64	66	79	.330	.338	Batting #2	.289	357	103	22	1	2	33	42	46	.362	.373
Away	.279	782	218	35	4	5	71	59	111	.331	.353	Other	.270	493	133	22	4	4	55	36	61	.322	.355
Day	.271	421	114	20	2	4	31	40	42	.330	.356	April	.286	147	42	6	1	1	23	17	10	.351	.361
Night	.277	1098	304	49	5	4	104	85	148	.330	.342	May	.301	183	55	4	1	1	12	21	22	.373	.350
Grass	.281	1239	348	57	5	7	115	113	148	.340	.352	June	.277	282	78	13	1	3	21	19	36	.322	.362
Turf	.250	280	70	12	2	1	20	12	42	.284	.318	July	.287	272	78	12	1	1	20	20	42	.341	.349
First Pitch	.321	165	53	7	1	1	19	0	0	.316	.394	August	.240	342	82	15	2	0	31	16	49	.275	.295
Ahead on Count	.308	377	116	19	4	3	43	68	0	.411	.403	September/October	.283	293	83	19	1	2	28	32	31	.353	.375
Behind on Count	.259	459	119	24	1	2	43	0	108	.262	.329	Pre-All Star	.281	694	195	30	3	5	60	64	80	.340	.354
Two Strikes	.237	670	159	25	1	2	50	56	190	.237	.297	Post-All Star	.270	825	223	39	4	3	75	61	110	.322	.338

Batter vs. Pitcher (career)

Hits Best Against	Avg	AB	H	2B	3B	HR	RBI	BB	SO	OBP	SLG	Hits Worst Against	Avg	AB	H	2B	3B	HR	RBI	BB	SO	OBP	SLG
Danny Jackson	.545	11	6	2	0	0	1	1	1	.583	.727	Chris Bosio	.091	11	1	1	0	0	1	1	2	.167	.182
Scott Bankhead	.462	13	6	0	1	0	3	1	0	.500	.615	Roger Clemens	.100	10	1	0	0	0	0	1	4	.182	.100
Mike Flanagan	.455	11	5	1	0	0	3	0	2	.455	.545	Jack Morris	.125	16	2	0	0	0	1	0	2	.125	.125
Bob Milacki	.455	11	5	0	0	0	1	2	2	.538	.455	David Wells	.154	13	2	0	0	0	0	0	1	.154	.154
Bert Blyleven	.412	17	7	0	0	0	2	0	1	.412	.529	Jaime Navarro	.182	11	2	0	0	0	0	0	1	.182	.182

Mike Gallego — Yankees   Bats Right

	Avg	G	AB	R	H	2B	3B	HR	RBI	BB	SO	HBP	GDP	SB	CS	OBP	SLG	IBB	SH	SF	#Pit	#P/PA	GB	FB	G/F
1992 Season	.254	53	173	24	44	7	1	3	14	20	22	4	5	0	1	.343	.358	0	3	1	714	3.61	58	64	0.91
Last Five Years	.233	614	1678	210	391	57	9	23	147	191	252	20	42	20	23	.317	.319	3	46	9	7077	3.73	627	488	1.28

1992 Season

	Avg	AB	H	2B	3B	HR	RBI	BB	SO	OBP	SLG		Avg	AB	H	2B	3B	HR	RBI	BB	SO	OBP	SLG
vs. Left	.237	38	9	2	1	0	4	10	3	.396	.342	Scoring Posn	.242	33	8	3	0	0	9	6	5	.366	.333
vs. Right	.259	135	35	5	0	3	10	10	19	.327	.363	Close & Late	.410	39	16	4	0	1	3	1	6	.425	.590
Home	.221	77	17	4	1	1	8	6	11	.291	.338	None on/out	.231	52	12	0	0	2	2	6	4	.322	.346
Away	.281	96	27	3	0	2	6	14	11	.384	.375	Batting #1	.245	53	13	3	0	1	7	4	4	.344	.358
First Pitch	.188	32	6	1	0	0	2	0	0	.235	.219	Batting #9	.261	115	30	4	1	2	7	10	18	.333	.365
Ahead on Count	.209	43	9	2	0	1	2	11	0	.370	.326	Other	.200	5	1	0	0	0	0	3	0	.500	.200

1992 Season

	Avg	AB	H	2B	3B	HR	RBI	BB	SO	OBP	SLG		Avg	AB	H	2B	3B	HR	RBI	BB	SO	OBP	SLG
Behind on Count	.246	57	14	2	1	0	5	0	13	.254	.316	Pre-All Star	.252	131	33	5	1	3	12	16	15	.349	.374
Two Strikes	.254	67	17	4	1	2	9	9	22	.354	.433	Post-All Star	.262	42	11	2	0	0	2	4	7	.326	.310

Last Five Years

	Avg	AB	H	2B	3B	HR	RBI	BB	SO	OBP	SLG		Avg	AB	H	2B	3B	HR	RBI	BB	SO	OBP	SLG
vs. Left	.246	516	127	24	2	7	44	67	71	.334	.341	Scoring Posn	.232	362	84	13	3	2	115	44	51	.326	.301
vs. Right	.227	1162	264	33	7	16	103	124	181	.310	.309	Close & Late	.258	252	65	9	2	4	21	25	43	.330	.357
Groundball	.236	488	115	19	3	2	39	44	67	.314	.299	None on/out	.213	451	96	14	1	12	12	58	92	.304	.328
Flyball	.218	362	79	15	0	10	36	58	57	.327	.343	Batting #8	.251	529	133	23	3	13	49	56	92	.327	.380
Home	.244	814	199	26	7	12	72	105	107	.334	.338	Batting #9	.225	983	221	26	6	9	84	110	136	.310	.291
Away	.222	864	192	31	2	11	75	86	145	.301	.301	Other	.223	166	37	8	0	1	14	25	24	.326	.289
Day	.228	601	137	18	4	8	56	80	96	.324	.311	April	.256	180	46	8	1	1	15	27	25	.351	.328
Night	.236	1077	254	39	5	15	91	111	156	.313	.323	May	.229	306	70	14	3	5	39	36	46	.318	.343
Grass	.235	1397	328	47	8	18	120	159	200	.319	.319	June	.231	338	78	6	1	4	22	33	51	.301	.290
Turf	.224	261	63	10	1	5	27	32	52	.309	.320	July	.231	334	77	14	2	6	34	31	47	.306	.338
First Pitch	.276	283	78	11	2	4	23	2	0	.293	.371	August	.239	209	50	7	1	4	20	27	21	.335	.340
Ahead on Count	.273	425	116	16	3	5	28	96	0	.408	.360	September/October	.225	311	70	8	1	3	17	37	62	.314	.286
Behind on Count	.157	523	82	12	2	3	36	0	145	.165	.205	Pre-All Star	.236	937	221	30	6	13	87	104	137	.317	.322
Two Strikes	.175	707	124	17	3	11	60	93	252	.275	.314	Post-All Star	.229	741	170	27	3	10	60	87	115	.318	.314

Batter vs. Pitcher (career)

Hits Best Against	Avg	AB	H	2B	3B	HR	RBI	BB	SO	OBP	SLG	Hits Worst Against	Avg	AB	H	2B	3B	HR	RBI	BB	SO	OBP	SLG
Scott Bankhead	.600	10	6	2	0	0	1	2	1	.667	.800	Bill Krueger	.000	9	0	0	0	0	0	2	2	.182	.000
Jimmy Key	.400	25	10	1	0	0	3	1	4	.467	.440	Mark Gubicza	.059	17	1	0	0	0	0	3	3	.200	.059
Charlie Leibrandt	.385	26	10	4	0	0	3	1	2	.407	.538	Erik Hanson	.067	15	1	0	0	0	0	2	5	.176	.067
Chris Bosio	.382	34	13	1	1	1	4	1	4	.400	.559	Bob Milacki	.071	14	1	0	0	0	0	0	1	.071	.071
Jim Abbott	.353	17	6	1	0	1	6	1	3	.389	.588	Floyd Bannister	.077	13	1	0	0	0	0	0	4	.077	.077

Ron Gant — Braves

Bats Right (flyball hitter)

	Avg	G	AB	R	H	2B	3B	HR	RBI	BB	SO	HBP	GDP	SB	CS	OBP	SLG	IBB	SH	SF	#Pit	#P/PA	GB	FB	G/F
1992 Season	.259	153	544	74	141	22	6	17	80	45	101	7	10	32	10	.321	.415	5	0	6	2236	3.71	187	175	1.07
Last Five Years	.259	680	2503	393	648	127	23	109	354	232	472	17	31	127	57	.323	.459	17	5	21	10396	3.75	772	890	0.87

1992 Season

	Avg	AB	H	2B	3B	HR	RBI	BB	SO	OBP	SLG		Avg	AB	H	2B	3B	HR	RBI	BB	SO	OBP	SLG
vs. Left	.254	177	45	7	3	5	32	17	32	.322	.412	Scoring Posn	.257	152	39	6	2	3	63	22	24	.343	.382
vs. Right	.262	367	96	15	3	12	48	28	69	.320	.417	Close & Late	.259	85	22	5	0	1	6	9	14	.333	.353
Groundball	.266	233	62	12	3	8	31	18	38	.329	.446	None on/out	.310	126	39	7	0	5	5	3	20	.331	.484
Flyball	.231	147	34	5	1	7	26	16	30	.306	.422	Batting #3	.304	214	65	13	1	6	31	22	34	.376	.458
Home	.276	257	71	12	3	10	45	19	44	.336	.463	Batting #4	.200	150	30	4	2	5	25	10	35	.261	.353
Away	.244	287	70	10	3	7	35	26	57	.307	.373	Other	.256	180	46	5	3	6	24	13	32	.303	.417
Day	.220	141	31	4	2	6	17	20	35	.329	.404	April	.273	77	21	3	0	5	19	10	21	.367	.506
Night	.273	403	110	18	4	11	63	25	66	.317	.419	May	.291	110	32	8	2	2	18	13	16	.371	.455
Grass	.261	398	104	16	3	13	57	30	70	.320	.415	June	.269	93	25	5	1	3	9	5	12	.324	.441
Turf	.253	146	37	6	3	4	23	15	31	.323	.418	July	.221	95	21	2	1	1	7	1	18	.232	.295
First Pitch	.301	73	22	3	1	4	14	3	0	.350	.534	August	.203	69	14	2	1	1	9	11	20	.309	.304
Ahead on Count	.359	117	42	9	2	6	26	30	0	.490	.624	September/October	.280	100	28	2	1	5	18	5	14	.311	.470
Behind on Count	.214	187	40	7	2	5	23	0	41	.218	.364	Pre-All Star	.273	319	87	16	3	10	48	28	56	.341	.436
Two Strikes	.199	266	53	7	2	4	28	12	101	.241	.286	Post-All Star	.240	225	54	6	3	7	32	17	45	.291	.387

1992 By Position

Position	Avg	AB	H	2B	3B	HR	RBI	BB	SO	OBP	SLG	G	GS	Innings	PO	A	E	DP	Fld Pct	Rng Fctr	In Zone	Outs	Zone Rtg	MLB Zone
As Pinch Hitter	.222	9	2	0	0	0	2	1	3	.300	.222	10	0	...	...	...	...	...	...	...	...	...	...
As lf	.253	471	119	21	4	14	63	36	89	.313	.403	138	120	1096.2	236	3	4	0	.984	1.96	267	229	.858	.809
As cf	.313	64	20	1	2	3	15	8	9	.373	.531	23	17	141.1	40	2	0	1	1.000	2.67	47	41	.872	.824

Last Five Years

	Avg	AB	H	2B	3B	HR	RBI	BB	SO	OBP	SLG		Avg	AB	H	2B	3B	HR	RBI	BB	SO	OBP	SLG
vs. Left	.264	817	216	52	7	35	127	94	134	.340	.474	Scoring Posn	.251	629	158	38	5	15	232	82	113	.330	.399
vs. Right	.256	1686	432	75	16	74	227	138	338	.315	.451	Close & Late	.215	396	85	16	2	11	50	42	81	.292	.348
Groundball	.264	865	228	40	5	34	115	76	136	.326	.439	None on/out	.295	668	197	36	4	42	42	44	107	.342	.549
Flyball	.233	621	145	32	5	31	84	73	129	.315	.451	Batting #1	.269	643	173	36	5	30	68	48	115	.322	.481
Home	.268	1205	323	58	14	58	184	113	217	.335	.484	Batting #3	.279	798	223	45	5	34	116	80	126	.347	.476
Away	.250	1298	325	69	9	51	170	119	255	.313	.435	Other	.237	1062	252	46	13	45	170	104	231	.306	.432
Day	.241	607	146	23	3	25	83	71	137	.327	.412	April	.191	272	52	13	2	9	33	32	64	.280	.353
Night	.265	1896	502	104	20	84	271	161	335	.322	.474	May	.260	488	127	26	3	23	77	34	95	.308	.467
Grass	.258	1819	470	80	17	82	260	169	342	.324	.456	June	.272	430	117	23	7	20	57	31	72	.326	.498
Turf	.250	684	178	47	6	27	94	63	130	.321	.465	July	.272	427	116	22	4	17	58	30	79	.320	.461
First Pitch	.338	355	120	25	5	22	76	10	0	.359	.623	August	.256	398	102	20	4	17	53	50	77	.343	.455
Ahead on Count	.346	558	193	45	6	39	116	139	0	.475	.624	September/October	.275	488	134	23	3	23	76	55	85	.348	.475
Behind on Count	.221	801	177	37	8	25	85	0	215	.223	.381	Pre-All Star	.255	1326	338	69	14	57	186	101	258	.310	.457
Two Strikes	.183	1205	221	37	7	32	109	79	472	.236	.305	Post-All Star	.263	1177	310	58	9	52	168	131	214	.338	.460

Batter vs. Pitcher (career)

Hits Best Against	Avg	AB	H	2B	3B	HR	RBI	BB	SO	OBP	SLG	Hits Worst Against	Avg	AB	H	2B	3B	HR	RBI	BB	SO	OBP	SLG
Omar Olivares	.600	10	6	2	0	2	3	3	1	.692	1.400	Alejandro Pena	.000	11	0	0	0	0	0	0	3	.000	.000
Cris Carpenter	.400	10	4	2	0	1	4	0	0	.364	.900	Sid Fernandez	.000	10	0	0	0	0	0	2	5	.154	.000
Jack Armstrong	.389	18	7	0	0	3	5	1	3	.421	.889	Anthony Young	.000	8	0	0	0	0	0	3	2	.273	.000
Joe Magrane	.364	11	4	1	0	2	2	0	0	.364	1.000	Scott Scudder	.000	7	0	0	0	0	0	4	2	.364	.000
Jeff Brantley	.313	16	5	1	0	3	6	1	4	.353	.938	Jim Gott	.133	15	2	0	0	0	2	3	3	.235	.133

Jim Gantner — Brewers
Bats Left (groundball hitter)

	Avg	G	AB	R	H	2B	3B	HR	RBI	BB	SO	HBP	GDP	SB	CS	OBP	SLG	IBB	SH	SF	#Pit	#P/PA	GB	FB	G/F
1992 Season	.246	101	256	22	63	12	1	1	18	12	17	0	9	6	2	.278	.313	2	3	2	845	3.13	103	80	1.29
Last Five Years	.272	600	2053	239	558	93	15	3	171	123	153	18	51	68	25	.317	.336	10	40	13	7000	3.17	932	536	1.74

1992 Season

	Avg	AB	H	2B	3B	HR	RBI	BB	SO	OBP	SLG		Avg	AB	H	2B	3B	HR	RBI	BB	SO	OBP	SLG
vs. Left	.206	34	7	1	0	0	5	5	0	.300	.235	Scoring Posn	.242	62	15	4	1	0	15	4	4	.279	.339
vs. Right	.252	222	56	11	1	1	13	7	17	.274	.324	Close & Late	.226	53	12	2	1	1	2	6	4	.305	.358
Home	.243	136	33	6	0	1	10	7	8	.278	.309	None on/out	.241	58	14	2	0	1	1	4	5	.290	.328
Away	.250	120	30	6	1	0	8	5	9	.278	.317	Batting #8	.245	98	24	1	1	0	6	7	9	.292	.276
First Pitch	.233	60	14	3	1	1	6	2	0	.254	.367	Batting #9	.246	122	30	9	0	0	8	3	5	.262	.320
Ahead on Count	.274	62	17	3	0	0	8	3	0	.303	.323	Other	.250	36	9	2	0	1	4	2	3	.289	.389
Behind on Count	.216	88	19	3	0	0	1	0	10	.216	.250	Pre-All Star	.231	182	42	7	1	0	10	10	14	.268	.280
Two Strikes	.221	86	19	4	0	0	2	7	17	.280	.267	Post-All Star	.284	74	21	5	0	1	8	2	3	.303	.392

Last Five Years

	Avg	AB	H	2B	3B	HR	RBI	BB	SO	OBP	SLG		Avg	AB	H	2B	3B	HR	RBI	BB	SO	OBP	SLG
vs. Left	.273	520	142	19	1	0	49	37	28	.326	.313	Scoring Posn	.256	477	122	22	7	0	161	46	52	.321	.331
vs. Right	.271	1533	416	74	14	3	122	86	125	.313	.344	Close & Late	.276	337	93	22	1	2	33	26	24	.328	.365
Groundball	.301	509	153	23	2	1	45	30	33	.342	.360	None on/out	.307	495	152	21	3	2	29	31	352	.374	
Flyball	.249	450	112	22	4	1	40	33	45	.306	.322	Batting #2	.290	611	177	41	6	1	54	32	46	.329	.381
Home	.270	1012	273	49	3	2	82	69	78	.320	.330	Batting #8	.262	511	134	14	4	0	37	29	49	.303	.305
Away	.274	1041	285	44	12	1	89	54	75	.314	.342	Other	.265	931	247	38	5	2	80	62	58	.316	.323
Day	.271	594	161	31	6	0	49	40	38	.321	.343	April	.243	222	54	8	2	0	20	15	21	.295	.297
Night	.272	1459	397	62	9	3	122	83	115	.315	.333	May	.274	365	100	20	0	0	26	18	26	.314	.329
Grass	.271	1757	476	74	12	3	133	116	134	.319	.332	June	.250	328	82	15	1	0	27	22	26	.301	.302
Turf	.277	296	82	19	3	0	38	7	19	.304	.361	July	.276	399	110	17	3	0	39	27	33	.326	.333
First Pitch	.307	456	140	21	4	2	35	8	0	.321	.384	August	.294	402	118	15	6	1	35	14	25	.319	.368
Ahead on Count	.302	536	162	32	5	1	60	66	0	.377	.386	September/October	.279	337	94	18	3	2	24	27	22	.337	.368
Behind on Count	.210	647	136	17	4	0	34	0	88	.220	.249	Pre-All Star	.263	1057	278	47	5	0	91	63	86	.309	.317
Two Strikes	.196	644	126	18	1	0	48	48	153	.260	.227	Post-All Star	.281	996	280	46	10	3	80	60	67	.325	.356

Batter vs. Pitcher (since 1984)

Hits Best Against	Avg	AB	H	2B	3B	HR	RBI	BB	SO	OBP	SLG	Hits Worst Against	Avg	AB	H	2B	3B	HR	RBI	BB	SO	OBP	SLG
Charles Nagy	.545	11	6	1	0	0	0	0	1	.545	.636	Bobby Thigpen	.000	11	0	0	0	0	0	1	1	.083	.000
Greg Cadaret	.467	15	7	2	0	0	3	2	1	.529	.600	Jim Acker	.000	10	0	0	0	0	0	1	0	.091	.000
Bill Swift	.444	18	8	3	0	0	2	2	2	.500	.611	Ben McDonald	.083	12	1	1	0	0	0	1	1	.154	.167
Jose Guzman	.423	26	11	4	0	0	3	1	0	.444	.577	Frank Tanana	.130	23	3	0	0	0	1	1	1	.167	.130
Doug Jones	.412	17	7	2	0	0	2	1	1	.444	.529	Dennis Rasmussen	.154	13	2	0	0	0	0	0	1	.154	.154

Carlos Garcia — Pirates
Bats Right

	Avg	G	AB	R	H	2B	3B	HR	RBI	BB	SO	HBP	GDP	SB	CS	OBP	SLG	IBB	SH	SF	#Pit	#P/PA	GB	FB	G/F
1992 Season	.205	22	39	4	8	1	0	0	4	0	9	0	1	0	0	.195	.231	0	1	2	130	3.17	13	11	1.18
Career (1990-1992)	.239	38	67	7	16	1	2	0	5	1	19	0	2	0	0	.243	.313	0	1	2	237	3.39	19	15	1.27

1992 Season

	Avg	AB	H	2B	3B	HR	RBI	BB	SO	OBP	SLG		Avg	AB	H	2B	3B	HR	RBI	BB	SO	OBP	SLG
vs. Left	.000	8	0	0	0	0	1	0	1	.000	.000	Scoring Posn	.125	8	1	0	0	0	4	0	1	.100	.125
vs. Right	.258	31	8	1	0	0	3	0	8	.250	.290	Close & Late	.000	2	0	0	0	0	1	0	0	.000	.000

Mike Gardiner — Red Sox
Pitches Right

	ERA	W	L	Sv	G	GS	IP	BB	SO	Avg	H	2B	3B	HR	RBI	OBP	SLG	CG	ShO	Sup	QS	#P/S	SB	CS	GB	FB	G/F
1992 Season	4.75	4	10	0	28	18	130.2	58	79	.253	126	15	6	12	64	.330	.380	0	0	3.24	7	94	3	2	176	146	1.21
Career (1990-1992)	5.07	13	22	0	55	43	273.1	110	176	.270	268	44	10	31	141	.338	.417	0	0	4.91	15	92	14	8	378	313	1.21

1992 Season

	ERA	W	L	Sv	G	GS	IP	H	HR	BB	SO		Avg	AB	H	2B	3B	HR	RBI	BB	SO	OBP	SLG
Home	4.41	2	1	0	10	7	51.0	50	2	25	26	vs. Left	.258	221	57	8	5	3	23	23	38	.327	.380
Away	4.97	2	9	0	18	11	79.2	76	10	33	53	vs. Right	.249	277	69	7	1	9	41	35	41	.333	.379
Starter	4.82	2	8	0	18	18	102.2	101	9	44	64	Scoring Posn	.278	115	32	3	3	2	45	21	22	.380	.409
Reliever	4.50	2	2	0	10	0	28.0	25	3	14	15	Close & Late	.290	31	9	1	0	0	3	5	9	.405	.323
0-3 Days Rest	2.70	0	0	0	1	1	6.2	5	0	1	5	None on/out	.210	124	26	3	0	3	3	15	23	.295	.306
4 Days Rest	5.23	0	4	0	8	8	43.0	48	6	17	21	First Pitch	.269	67	18	0	1	0	10	2	0	.296	.299
5+ Days Rest	4.75	2	4	0	9	9	53.0	48	3	26	38	Behind on Count	.222	99	22	1	1	0	4	29	0	.400	.253

1992 Season

	ERA	W	L	Sv	G	GS	IP	H	HR	BB	SO		Avg	AB	H	2B	3B	HR	RBI	BB	SO	OBP	SLG
Pre-All Star	4.90	3	9	0	17	14	93.2	93	8	42	60	Ahead on Count	.232	220	51	9	3	5	22	0	63	.231	.368
Post-All Star	4.38	1	1	0	11	4	37.0	33	4	16	19	Two Strikes	.200	230	46	7	2	6	22	27	79	.283	.326

Jeff Gardner — Padres

Bats Left

	Avg	G	AB	R	H	2B	3B	HR	RBI	BB	SO	HBP	GDP	SB	CS	OBP	SLG	IBB	SH	SF	#Pit	#P/PA	GB	FB	G/F
1992 Season	.105	15	19	0	2	0	0	0	0	1	8	0	0	0	0	.150	.105	0	0	0	84	4.20	7	2	3.50
Career (1991-1992)	.143	28	56	3	8	0	0	0	1	5	14	0	0	0	0	.210	.143	0	0	1	247	3.98	17	17	1.00

1992 Season

	Avg	AB	H	2B	3B	HR	RBI	BB	SO	OBP	SLG		Avg	AB	H	2B	3B	HR	RBI	BB	SO	OBP	SLG
vs. Left	.000	2	0	0	0	0	0	0	1	.000	.000	Scoring Posn	.000	3	0	0	0	0	0	1	1	.250	.000
vs. Right	.118	17	2	0	0	0	1	1	7	.167	.118	Close & Late	.200	5	1	0	0	0	0	0	1	.200	.200

Mark Gardner — Expos

Pitches Right (flyball pitcher)

	ERA	W	L	Sv	G	GS	IP	BB	SO	Avg	H	2B	3B	HR	RBI	OBP	SLG	CG	ShO	Sup	QS	#P/S	SB	CS	GB	FB	G/F
1992 Season	4.36	12	10	0	33	30	179.2	60	132	.259	179	36	3	15	79	.324	.386	0	0	4.36	17	97	29	11	205	226	0.91
Career (1989-1992)	3.96	28	33	0	94	87	527.0	207	395	.241	473	81	11	47	217	.319	.366	3	3	3.74	51	96	64	35	604	624	0.97

1992 Season

	ERA	W	L	Sv	G	GS	IP	H	HR	BB	SO		Avg	AB	H	2B	3B	HR	RBI	BB	SO	OBP	SLG
Home	4.80	6	5	0	19	18	105.0	104	8	32	89	vs. Left	.272	397	108	23	3	7	49	31	62	.330	.398
Away	3.74	6	5	0	14	12	74.2	75	7	28	43	vs. Right	.242	293	71	13	0	8	30	29	70	.316	.369
Day	3.88	4	5	0	11	11	65.0	71	4	17	52	Inning 1-6	.248	612	152	34	0	11	69	51	117	.313	.358
Night	4.63	8	5	0	22	19	114.2	108	11	43	80	Inning 7+	.346	78	27	2	3	4	10	9	15	.409	.603
Grass	2.45	4	2	0	7	6	40.1	34	4	15	22	None on	.250	408	102	20	2	11	11	29	71	.306	.390
Turf	4.91	8	8	0	26	24	139.1	145	11	45	110	Runners on	.273	282	77	16	1	4	68	31	61	.348	.379
April	3.48	2	1	0	5	5	31.0	27	2	14	25	Scoring Posn	.264	178	47	8	1	3	60	26	43	.361	.371
May	3.64	1	3	0	5	5	29.2	29	2	12	28	Close & Late	.286	49	14	0	2	1	4	8	11	.386	.429
June	4.34	3	2	0	5	5	29.0	29	3	10	18	None on/out	.260	177	46	8	2	7	7	17	28	.335	.446
July	3.12	4	2	0	6	6	40.1	39	5	8	28	vs. 1st Batr (relief)	.000	2	0	0	0	0	1	0	0	.000	.000
August	5.93	1	1	0	5	5	27.1	25	2	10	18	First Inning Pitched	.299	134	40	9	0	2	25	16	22	.396	.410
September/October	6.85	1	1	0	7	4	22.1	30	1	6	15	First 75 Pitches	.260	515	134	29	0	11	61	40	103	.321	.381
Starter	4.26	11	10	0	30	30	175.1	171	15	60	131	Pitch 76-90	.207	82	17	5	2	0	8	10	15	.290	.317
Reliever	8.31	1	0	0	3	0	4.1	8	0	0	1	Pitch 91-105	.313	64	20	1	1	4	9	7	6	.380	.547
0-3 Days Rest	0.00	0	0	0	0	0	0.0	0	0	0	0	Pitch 106+	.276	29	8	1	0	0	1	3	8	.344	.310
4 Days Rest	3.17	10	2	0	17	17	105.0	92	9	38	82	First Pitch	.289	83	24	3	0	2	8	1	0	.299	.398
5+ Days Rest	5.89	1	8	0	13	13	70.1	79	6	22	49	Ahead on Count	.211	337	71	13	2	5	29	0	100	.223	.306
Pre-All Star	3.61	8	7	0	18	18	109.2	104	10	40	83	Behind on Count	.347	144	50	13	1	5	27	26	0	.445	.556
Post-All Star	5.53	4	3	0	15	12	70.0	75	5	20	49	Two Strikes	.174	344	60	9	2	6	27	33	132	.253	.265

Career (1989-1992)

	ERA	W	L	Sv	G	GS	IP	H	HR	BB	SO		Avg	AB	H	2B	3B	HR	RBI	BB	SO	OBP	SLG
Home	3.26	15	15	0	46	42	259.2	223	16	93	220	vs. Left	.242	1162	281	48	10	26	126	138	209	.324	.367
Away	4.65	13	20	0	48	45	267.1	250	31	114	175	vs. Right	.241	797	192	33	1	21	91	69	186	.312	.364
Day	4.70	7	17	0	32	32	176.1	188	23	69	142	Inning 1-6	.237	1714	407	72	7	41	197	181	346	.316	.359
Night	3.59	21	16	0	62	55	350.2	285	24	138	253	Inning 7+	.269	245	66	9	4	6	20	26	49	.338	.412
Grass	4.92	7	12	0	28	27	155.1	157	22	65	110	None on	.214	1203	258	44	5	27	27	111	246	.286	.327
Turf	3.56	21	21	0	66	60	371.2	316	25	142	285	Runners on	.284	756	215	37	6	20	190	96	149	.369	.429
April	3.40	2	3	0	8	7	42.1	39	3	19	33	Scoring Posn	.270	459	124	20	4	12	160	71	102	.371	.410
May	3.23	3	6	0	18	16	97.2	90	7	35	86	Close & Late	.274	146	40	3	3	3	12	20	32	.361	.397
June	3.98	8	6	0	16	16	95.0	90	10	38	55	None on/out	.233	515	120	20	3	13	13	47	99	.303	.359
July	2.04	8	6	0	17	17	123.2	82	7	40	97	vs. 1st Batr (relief)	.000	6	0	0	0	0	1	0	0	.000	.000
August	4.75	5	5	0	16	16	89.0	88	6	35	65	First Inning Pitched	.280	361	101	17	0	8	58	49	67	.372	.393
September/October	7.26	2	7	0	19	15	79.1	84	14	40	59	First 75 Pitches	.239	1441	344	62	4	34	165	148	302	.317	.358
Starter	3.96	27	32	0	87	87	516.1	463	47	206	391	Pitch 76-90	.219	260	57	9	4	7	27	30	48	.299	.365
Reliever	4.22	1	1	0	7	0	10.2	10	0	1	4	Pitch 91-105	.295	176	52	7	3	5	19	14	23	.347	.455
0-3 Days Rest	7.88	0	2	0	2	2	8.0	11	3	4	7	Pitch 106+	.244	82	20	3	0	1	6	15	22	.361	.317
4 Days Rest	3.25	18	14	0	51	51	318.0	260	29	128	245	First Pitch	.278	245	68	7	2	5	21	7	0	.312	.384
5+ Days Rest	4.96	9	16	0	34	34	190.1	192	15	74	139	Ahead on Count	.195	912	178	26	6	14	79	0	309	.201	.283
Pre-All Star	3.23	17	17	0	48	45	278.2	251	23	109	204	Behind on Count	.295	434	128	31	1	16	66	114	0	.444	.482
Post-All Star	4.78	11	16	0	46	42	248.1	222	24	98	191	Two Strikes	.169	934	158	27	7	14	76	86	395	.243	.258

Pitcher vs. Batter (career)

Pitches Best Vs.	Avg	AB	H	2B	3B	HR	RBI	BB	SO	OBP	SLG	Pitches Worst Vs.	Avg	AB	H	2B	3B	HR	RBI	BB	SO	OBP	SLG
Curt Wilkerson	.091	11	1	0	0	0	0	1	3	.167	.091	Pedro Guerrero	.500	14	7	0	0	2	2	2	1	.563	.929
Jose Oquendo	.091	11	1	0	0	1	2	2	2	.214	.091	Dwight Smith	.429	14	6	1	1	1	3	2	2	.471	.857
Sid Bream	.100	10	1	0	0	0	1	1	1	.308	.100	Felix Jose	.357	14	5	1	0	2	4	3	4	.471	.857
Eric Yelding	.154	13	2	0	0	0	0	0	4	.154	.154	Andre Dawson	.348	23	8	4	0	3	10	0	5	.348	.913
Gary Varsho	.167	12	2	0	0	0	0	0	1	.167	.167	Kal Daniels	.333	12	4	0	1	2	6	3	3	.467	1.000

Rich Gedman — Cardinals   Bats Left

	Avg	G	AB	R	H	2B	3B	HR	RBI	BB	SO	HBP	GDP	SB	CS	OBP	SLG	IBB	SH	SF	#Pit	#P/PA	GB	FB	G/F
1992 Season	.219	41	105	5	23	4	0	1	8	11	22	0	0	0	0	.291	.286	1	0	1	427	3.65	39	27	1.44
Last Five Years	.206	325	877	76	181	35	0	18	81	76	163	4	19	0	2	.270	.308	10	14	10	3447	3.56	335	247	1.36

1992 Season

	Avg	AB	H	2B	3B	HR	RBI	BB	SO	OBP	SLG		Avg	AB	H	2B	3B	HR	RBI	BB	SO	OBP	SLG
vs. Left	.000	11	0	0	0	0	0	1	4	.083	.000	Scoring Posn	.222	27	6	2	0	0	7	6	4	.353	.296
vs. Right	.245	94	23	4	0	1	8	10	18	.314	.319	Close & Late	.111	27	3	0	0	0	0	2	4	.172	.111
Home	.219	64	14	2	0	1	5	9	13	.311	.297	None on/out	.160	25	4	1	0	1	1	1	5	.192	.320
Away	.220	41	9	2	0	0	3	2	9	.256	.268	Batting #7	.200	20	4	0	0	0	1	4	6	.333	.200
First Pitch	.267	15	4	2	0	0	2	1	0	.313	.400	Batting #8	.232	82	19	4	0	1	7	7	16	.289	.317
Ahead on Count	.318	22	7	0	0	1	1	8	0	.500	.455	Other	.000	3	0	0	0	0	0	0	0	.000	.000
Behind on Count	.175	40	7	1	0	0	3	0	12	.171	.200	Pre-All Star	.118	51	6	2	0	0	1	2	14	.151	.157
Two Strikes	.167	48	8	2	0	0	3	3	22	.216	.208	Post-All Star	.315	54	17	2	0	1	7	9	8	.406	.407

Last Five Years

	Avg	AB	H	2B	3B	HR	RBI	BB	SO	OBP	SLG		Avg	AB	H	2B	3B	HR	RBI	BB	SO	OBP	SLG
vs. Left	.192	104	20	7	0	1	15	9	24	.267	.288	Scoring Posn	.181	215	39	10	0	3	58	28	42	.265	.270
vs. Right	.208	773	161	28	0	17	66	67	139	.270	.310	Close & Late	.175	154	27	6	0	3	12	15	27	.246	.273
Groundball	.232	224	52	12	0	3	18	13	31	.272	.326	None on/out	.197	223	44	8	0	7	7	13	43	.248	.327
Flyball	.155	219	34	4	0	6	19	18	54	.221	.256	Batting #8	.215	423	91	19	0	7	41	38	78	.261	.310
Home	.215	409	88	15	0	9	46	49	67	.300	.318	Batting #9	.211	242	51	12	0	6	24	19	41	.270	.335
Away	.199	468	93	20	0	9	35	27	96	.242	.299	Other	.184	212	39	4	0	5	16	19	44	.248	.274
Day	.208	317	66	12	0	7	32	36	62	.287	.312	April	.126	103	13	3	0	3	9	6	24	.184	.243
Night	.205	560	115	23	0	11	49	40	101	.260	.305	May	.200	110	22	2	0	0	8	12	22	.274	.218
Grass	.221	574	127	26	0	13	55	44	95	.279	.334	June	.211	175	37	9	0	5	14	24	33	.310	.349
Turf	.178	303	54	9	0	5	26	32	68	.253	.257	July	.195	159	31	5	0	2	14	12	23	.247	.264
First Pitch	.179	151	27	6	0	4	17	1	0	.188	.298	August	.255	141	36	7	0	5	21	11	24	.307	.411
Ahead on Count	.250	156	39	5	0	3	11	41	0	.403	.340	September/October	.222	189	42	9	0	3	15	11	37	.267	.317
Behind on Count	.188	345	65	13	0	6	29	1	96	.189	.278	Pre-All Star	.184	461	85	17	0	8	33	45	89	.258	.273
Two Strikes	.176	392	69	12	0	6	29	30	163	.216	.257	Post-All Star	.231	416	96	18	0	10	48	31	74	.283	.346

Batter vs. Pitcher (since 1984)

Hits Best Against	Avg	AB	H	2B	3B	HR	RBI	BB	SO	OBP	SLG	Hits Worst Against	Avg	AB	H	2B	3B	HR	RBI	BB	SO	OBP	SLG
Bill Swift	.600	15	9	2	0	0	2	2	1	.647	.733	Dennis Martinez	.000	15	0	0	0	0	0	1	2	.063	.000
Storm Davis	.500	18	9	1	0	0	1	1	3	.526	.556	Mark Portugal	.000	8	0	0	0	0	0	3	2	.273	.000
Walt Terrell	.421	19	8	1	0	0	3	5	0	.542	.474	Dave Schmidt	.056	18	1	0	0	0	0	1	6	.143	.056
Gene Nelson	.333	12	4	0	0	2	3	0	1	.333	.917	Pete Harnisch	.083	12	1	0	0	0	1	0	2	.083	.083
Frank Tanana	.316	19	6	0	0	2	6	1	5	.350	.632	Neal Heaton	.091	11	1	0	0	0	1	0	3	.167	.091

Kirk Gibson — Pirates   Bats Left

	Avg	G	AB	R	H	2B	3B	HR	RBI	BB	SO	HBP	GDP	SB	CS	OBP	SLG	IBB	SH	SF	#Pit	#P/PA	GB	FB	G/F
1992 Season	.196	16	56	6	11	0	0	2	5	3	12	0	1	3	1	.237	.304	0	1	0	235	3.98	24	12	2.00
Last Five Years	.254	458	1628	287	413	73	9	60	202	219	355	18	27	90	14	.346	.420	22	5	13	7242	3.86	518	496	1.04

1992 Season

	Avg	AB	H	2B	3B	HR	RBI	BB	SO	OBP	SLG		Avg	AB	H	2B	3B	HR	RBI	BB	SO	OBP	SLG
vs. Left	.000	7	0	0	0	0	0	0	2	.000	.000	Scoring Posn	.143	7	1	0	0	1	4	1	0	.250	.571
vs. Right	.224	49	11	0	0	2	5	3	10	.269	.347	Close & Late	.125	8	1	0	0	0	0	1	3	.222	.125

Last Five Years

	Avg	AB	H	2B	3B	HR	RBI	BB	SO	OBP	SLG		Avg	AB	H	2B	3B	HR	RBI	BB	SO	OBP	SLG
vs. Left	.230	540	124	21	4	20	74	55	137	.311	.394	Scoring Posn	.242	347	84	18	3	11	126	78	81	.378	.406
vs. Right	.266	1088	269	52	5	40	128	164	218	.363	.433	Close & Late	.244	271	66	13	4	7	39	41	62	.349	.399
Groundball	.248	561	139	22	4	20	68	83	109	.349	.408	None on/out	.267	363	97	17	4	13	13	29	74	.333	.444
Flyball	.275	345	95	17	1	16	49	51	84	.367	.470	Batting #2	.267	535	143	32	5	15	62	71	102	.360	.430
Home	.257	803	206	28	9	24	97	106	169	.347	.403	Batting #3	.266	783	208	38	2	34	109	99	182	.351	.450
Away	.251	825	207	45	0	36	105	113	186	.346	.436	Other	.200	310	62	3	2	11	31	49	71	.310	.329
Day	.223	497	111	21	2	21	60	60	104	.312	.400	April	.247	239	59	7	1	12	35	27	58	.332	.435
Night	.267	1131	302	52	7	39	142	159	251	.361	.429	May	.277	224	62	14	2	9	24	26	42	.353	.478
Grass	.265	990	262	44	3	44	130	131	222	.356	.448	June	.231	364	84	13	2	18	54	52	80	.326	.426
Turf	.237	638	151	29	6	16	72	88	133	.332	.376	July	.282	319	90	18	1	7	35	35	43	.366	.411
First Pitch	.370	211	78	15	3	13	39	7	1	.390	.654	August	.286	280	80	13	3	12	39	44	67	.386	.482
Ahead on Count	.333	360	120	24	4	21	69	100	0	.478	.597	September/October	.188	202	38	8	0	2	15	35	65	.321	.257
Behind on Count	.209	578	121	16	1	15	54	0	181	.264	.318	Pre-All Star	.252	916	231	38	5	40	127	115	194	.338	.436
Two Strikes	.158	778	123	20	1	16	53	106	354	.248	.248	Post-All Star	.256	712	182	35	4	20	75	104	161	.357	.400

Batter vs. Pitcher (since 1984)

Hits Best Against	Avg	AB	H	2B	3B	HR	RBI	BB	SO	OBP	SLG	Hits Worst Against	Avg	AB	H	2B	3B	HR	RBI	BB	SO	OBP	SLG
Kirk McCaskill	.526	19	10	2	0	4	6	7	4	.654	1.263	Tim Leary	.071	14	1	0	0	0	0	1	3	.133	.071
Charlie Leibrandt	.500	12	6	2	0	1	3	0	1	.500	.917	Jose Rijo	.063	36	3	1	0	0	2	6	13	.209	.111
Eric Plunk	.500	10	5	0	0	3	5	3	3	.615	1.400	Jimmy Key	.083	24	2	0	0	0	0	6	9	.214	.083
Tom Candiotti	.412	17	7	1	2	1	4	2	1	.474	.882	John Burkett	.091	11	1	0	0	0	0	2	4	.231	.091
Scott Bankhead	.364	11	4	0	0	2	5	2	2	.462	.909	Bret Saberhagen	.125	32	4	0	0	0	0	2	16	.176	.125

Paul Gibson — Mets

Pitches Left

	ERA	W	L	Sv	G	GS	IP	BB	SO	Avg	H	2B	3B	HR	RBI	OBP	SLG	GF	IR	IRS	Hld	SvOp	SB	CS	GB	FB	G/F
1992 Season	5.23	0	1	0	43	1	62.0	25	49	.287	70	17	3	7	40	.352	.467	12	20	11	5	0	7	3	84	70	1.20
Career (1988-1992)	4.06	18	22	11	257	15	479.1	208	284	.269	493	95	13	44	249	.344	.407	57	241	81	27	23	42	21	606	587	1.03

1992 Season

	ERA	W	L	Sv	G	GS	IP	H	HR	BB	SO		Avg	AB	H	2B	3B	HR	RBI	BB	SO	OBP	SLG
Home	3.26	0	0	0	20	0	30.1	28	1	4	28	vs. Left	.338	71	24	4	2	3	10	10	12	.420	.577
Away	7.11	0	1	0	23	1	31.2	42	6	21	21	vs. Right	.266	173	46	13	1	4	30	15	37	.323	.422
Starter	3.86	0	0	0	1	1	4.2	6	0	1	1	Scoring Posn	.314	70	22	4	1	1	27	10	13	.395	.443
Reliever	5.34	0	0	0	42	0	57.1	64	7	24	48	Close & Late	.314	35	11	2	0	1	3	3	8	.368	.457
0 Days rest	6.75	0	0	0	7	0	6.2	8	0	3	8	None on/out	.321	56	18	3	1	2	2	8	5	.406	.518
1 or 2 Days rest	6.05	0	0	0	17	0	19.1	28	2	10	12	First Pitch	.263	19	5	1	1	0	5	0	0	.263	.421
3+ Days rest	4.60	0	0	0	18	0	31.1	28	5	11	28	Behind on Count	.333	54	18	5	0	1	10	11	0	.446	.481
Pre-All Star	4.76	0	0	0	32	0	39.2	44	6	15	35	Ahead on Count	.238	126	30	6	2	3	16	0	44	.236	.389
Post-All Star	6.04	0	1	0	11	1	22.1	26	1	10	14	Two Strikes	.217	120	26	6	1	3	14	14	49	.296	.358

Career (1988-1992)

	ERA	W	L	Sv	G	GS	IP	H	HR	BB	SO		Avg	AB	H	2B	3B	HR	RBI	BB	SO	OBP	SLG
Home	3.18	12	8	6	125	7	257.1	234	14	102	174	vs. Left	.264	546	155	21	5	17	92	54	63	.345	.434
Away	5.07	6	14	5	132	8	222.0	259	30	106	110	vs. Right	.263	1287	338	74	8	27	157	154	221	.344	.395
Day	3.81	6	5	3	77	5	146.1	158	9	58	86	Inning 1-6	.269	854	230	53	2	20	127	94	126	.343	.406
Night	4.16	12	17	8	180	10	333.0	335	35	150	198	Inning 7+	.269	979	263	42	11	24	122	114	158	.346	.408
Grass	3.69	17	17	7	198	14	390.0	394	32	152	231	None on	.273	941	257	52	4	23	23	98	155	.345	.410
Turf	5.64	1	5	4	59	1	89.1	99	12	56	53	Runners on	.265	892	236	43	9	21	226	110	129	.343	.404
April	3.81	4	2	1	35	1	56.2	62	5	28	36	Scoring Posn	.260	527	137	22	5	10	190	93	77	.362	.378
May	3.61	3	5	5	53	5	109.2	102	9	48	73	Close & Late	.272	393	107	13	3	13	45	37	60	.334	.420
June	4.28	3	4	1	43	1	75.2	82	4	29	46	None on/out	.286	419	120	28	2	11	11	47	65	.364	.442
July	3.87	2	2	1	39	6	95.1	86	9	41	50	vs. 1st Batr (relief)	.305	213	65	14	4	3	43	19	31	.354	.451
August	5.03	2	8	1	45	1	73.1	92	11	29	38	First Inning Pitched	.282	793	224	45	6	22	145	102	125	.362	.438
September/October	3.93	4	1	2	42	1	68.2	69	6	33	41	First 15 Pitches	.276	722	199	43	5	17	113	84	106	.348	.420
Starter	4.45	2	5	0	15	15	89.0	95	7	33	45	Pitch 16-30	.242	455	110	16	3	13	58	59	92	.334	.376
Reliever	3.97	16	17	11	242	0	390.1	398	37	175	239	Pitch 31-45	.275	284	78	12	3	6	27	27	45	.335	.401
0 Days rest	5.04	2	2	1	50	0	64.1	81	7	31	39	Pitch 46+	.285	372	106	24	2	8	51	38	41	.356	.425
1 or 2 Days rest	3.78	7	6	9	108	0	173.2	167	13	86	108	First Pitch	.316	244	77	13	3	7	46	28	0	.387	.480
3+ Days rest	3.72	7	9	1	84	0	152.1	150	17	58	92	Ahead on Count	.219	852	187	34	5	16	73	1	248	.225	.323
Pre-All Star	3.92	10	12	8	144	9	266.0	270	22	117	171	Behind on Count	.319	398	127	30	4	9	69	101	0	.453	.482
Post-All Star	4.22	8	10	3	113	6	213.1	223	22	91	113	Two Strikes	.205	836	171	34	2	14	77	77	284	.275	.300

Pitcher vs. Batter (career)

Pitches Best Vs.	Avg	AB	H	2B	3B	HR	RBI	BB	SO	OBP	SLG	Pitches Worst Vs.	Avg	AB	H	2B	3B	HR	RBI	BB	SO	OBP	SLG
Mike Felder	.000	14	0	0	0	0	0	1	3	.067	.000	Ken Griffey Jr	.583	12	7	2	0	1	1	2	0	.643	1.000
George Bell	.000	11	0	0	0	0	1	2	2	.143	.000	Tony Fernandez	.421	19	8	2	2	1	8	6	2	.560	.895
Brian Downing	.083	12	1	0	0	0	2	2		.214	.083	Rob Deer	.417	12	5	2	0	2	3	3	4	.533	1.083
Devon White	.083	12	1	0	0	1	1	3		.154	.167	Pat Borders	.400	10	4	2	0	1	3	5	0	.563	.900
Kelly Gruber	.118	17	2	0	0	0	1	1		.167	.118	Alvin Davis	.385	13	5	2	0	1	3	0	0	.385	.769

Bernard Gilkey — Cardinals

Bats Right

	Avg	G	AB	R	H	2B	3B	HR	RBI	BB	SO	HBP	GDP	SB	CS	OBP	SLG	IBB	SH	SF	#Pit	#P/PA	GB	FB	G/F
1992 Season	.302	131	384	56	116	19	4	7	43	39	52	1	5	18	12	.364	.427	1	3	4	1456	3.40	147	125	1.18
Career (1990-1992)	.270	230	716	95	193	31	8	13	66	86	90	2	20	38	21	.347	.390	1	4	6	2639	3.50	279	229	1.22

1992 Season

	Avg	AB	H	2B	3B	HR	RBI	BB	SO	OBP	SLG		Avg	AB	H	2B	3B	HR	RBI	BB	SO	OBP	SLG
vs. Left	.352	176	62	7	2	2	20	16	18	.402	.449	Scoring Posn	.359	78	28	3	3	2	35	14	9	.438	.551
vs. Right	.260	208	54	12	2	5	23	23	34	.333	.409	Close & Late	.309	94	29	5	0	3	11	10	14	.371	.457
Groundball	.310	168	52	8	1	2	16	12	22	.350	.405	None on/out	.276	123	34	8	1	2	2	6	17	.310	.407
Flyball	.364	66	24	5	2	1	5	10	12	.447	.545	Batting #1	.233	193	45	9	2	3	20	24	27	.320	.347
Home	.296	196	58	11	2	3	20	14	24	.338	.418	Batting #6	.380	92	35	7	1	3	10	5	12	.412	.576
Away	.309	188	58	8	2	4	23	25	28	.391	.436	Other	.364	99	36	3	1	1	13	10	13	.411	.444
Day	.298	94	28	6	1	2	10	9	13	.362	.447	April	.298	47	14	3	0	0	2	3	9	.340	.362
Night	.303	290	88	13	3	5	33	30	39	.365	.421	May	.294	34	10	1	1	0	4	3	5	.351	.382
Grass	.295	95	28	4	2	1	11	14	17	.391	.411	June	.383	47	18	3	1	0	6	5	9	.434	.489
Turf	.304	289	88	15	2	6	32	25	35	.355	.433	July	.260	77	20	3	1	1	10	8	12	.326	.364
First Pitch	.410	83	34	3	0	1	11	1	0	.412	.482	August	.230	100	23	5	0	3	12	13	13	.319	.370
Ahead on Count	.324	102	33	8	0	5	19	20	0	.431	.549	September/October	.392	79	31	4	1	3	9	7	4	.438	.582
Behind on Count	.227	110	25	6	2	3	11	0	28	.227	.400	Pre-All Star	.313	150	47	8	2	0	13	12	27	.362	.393
Two Strikes	.185	130	24	4	2	1	9	18	52	.285	.269	Post-All Star	.295	234	69	11	2	7	30	27	25	.366	.449

1992 By Position

Position	Avg	AB	H	2B	3B	HR	RBI	BB	SO	OBP	SLG	G	GS	Innings	PO	A	E	DP	Fld Pct	Rng Fctr	In Zone	Outs	Zone Rtg	MLB Zone
As Pinch Hitter	.200	20	4	0	0	0	2	4	5	.320	.200	25	0	---	---	---	---	---	---	---	---	---	---	---
As lf	.310	361	112	19	4	7	41	33	47	.367	.443	110	85	814.0	216	8	5	3	.978	2.48	232	208	.897	.809

Career (1990-1992)

	Avg	AB	H	2B	3B	HR	RBI	BB	SO	OBP	SLG		Avg	AB	H	2B	3B	HR	RBI	BB	SO	OBP	SLG
vs. Left	.281	342	96	14	4	4	29	40	35	.356	.380	Scoring Posn	.295	149	44	7	4	2	52	35	24	.416	.436
vs. Right	.259	374	97	17	4	9	37	46	55	.339	.398	Close & Late	.295	139	41	8	0	4	16	21	19	.383	.439
Groundball	.276	272	75	12	2	3	23	25	32	.332	.368	None on/out	.271	229	62	12	2	6	6	17	23	.324	.419
Flyball	.263	133	35	6	3	3	9	26	21	.384	.421	Batting #1	.233	399	93	16	6	5	31	51	47	.322	.341
Home	.251	378	95	16	4	5	31	39	41	.321	.354	Batting #6	.315	130	41	8	1	5	14	8	16	.355	.508
Away	.290	338	98	15	4	8	35	47	49	.375	.429	Other	.316	187	59	7	1	3	21	27	27	.394	.412
Day	.267	202	54	10	1	5	19	18	25	.327	.401	April	.274	124	34	4	1	1	7	15	20	.353	.347
Night	.270	514	139	21	7	8	47	68	65	.354	.385	May	.229	105	24	4	1	2	9	18	12	.341	.343
Grass	.269	142	41	5	2	4	18	21	25	.382	.437	June	.321	84	27	3	2	0	8	7	12	.370	.405
Turf	.265	574	152	26	6	9	48	65	65	.338	.378	July	.228	127	29	4	1	1	13	14	21	.306	.299
First Pitch	.352	145	51	8	0	2	17	1	0	.354	.448	August	.205	127	26	6	0	3	14	15	16	.289	.323
Ahead on Count	.312	199	62	10	3	9	29	45	0	.437	.528	September/October	.356	149	53	10	3	6	15	17	9	.418	.584
Behind on Count	.211	204	43	8	2	5	13	0	46	.211	.341	Pre-All Star	.269	335	90	12	4	3	25	41	48	.347	.355
Two Strikes	.154	246	38	6	3	2	13	40	90	.276	.228	Post-All Star	.270	381	103	19	4	10	41	45	42	.346	.420

Batter vs. Pitcher (career)

Hits Best Against	Avg	AB	H	2B	3B	HR	RBI	BB	SO	OBP	SLG	Hits Worst Against	Avg	AB	H	2B	3B	HR	RBI	BB	SO	OBP	SLG
Chris Hammond	.778	9	7	2	0	0	2	2	0	.818	1.000	Randy Tomlin	.125	24	3	1	0	0	1	2	4	.192	.167
Terry Mulholland	.526	19	10	1	2	0	2	1	0	.550	.789	Jim Deshaies	.125	8	1	0	0	0	0	3	0	.364	.125
Charlie Leibrandt	.500	14	7	1	0	0	3	2	0	.563	.571	John Smiley	.154	13	2	1	0	0	0	1	2	.214	.231
Jim Bullinger	.500	8	4	0	0	0	0	1	1	.636	.500	Bruce Hurst	.167	12	2	0	0	0	1	1	1	.214	.167
Craig Lefferts	.455	11	5	0	0	0	2	1	1	.500	.636	Doug Drabek	.200	20	4	2	0	0	0	0	2	.200	.300

Joe Girardi — Cubs
Bats Right (groundball hitter)

	Avg	G	AB	R	H	2B	3B	HR	RBI	BB	SO	HBP	GDP	SB	CS	OBP	SLG	IBB	SH	SF	#Pit	#P/PA	GB	FB	G/F
1992 Season	.270	91	270	19	73	3	1	1	12	19	38	1	8	0	2	.320	.300	3	0	1	981	3.37	127	56	2.27
Career (1989-1992)	.262	304	893	73	234	39	3	3	70	53	120	6	25	10	6	.306	.323	20	6	6	2886	3.01	407	215	1.89

1992 Season

	Avg	AB	H	2B	3B	HR	RBI	BB	SO	OBP	SLG		Avg	AB	H	2B	3B	HR	RBI	BB	SO	OBP	SLG
vs. Left	.299	137	41	2	1	0	5	9	16	.342	.328	Scoring Posn	.235	51	12	2	0	0	11	6	8	.310	.275
vs. Right	.241	133	32	1	0	1	7	10	22	.297	.271	Close & Late	.258	62	16	0	0	0	3	4	5	.303	.258
Home	.305	128	39	1	1	1	7	9	21	.350	.352	None on/out	.283	60	17	0	0	0	0	4	5	.328	.283
Away	.239	142	34	2	0	0	5	10	17	.292	.254	Batting #6	.414	29	12	0	0	0	1	1	3	.433	.414
First Pitch	.352	54	19	2	0	1	5	3	0	.379	.444	Batting #7	.241	195	47	3	1	1	11	14	26	.294	.282
Ahead on Count	.333	54	18	0	1	0	2	11	0	.446	.370	Other	.304	46	14	0	1	0	0	4	9	.360	.304
Behind on Count	.237	93	22	1	1	0	3	0	20	.245	.269	Pre-All Star	.274	164	45	1	0	1	9	17	25	.344	.299
Two Strikes	.230	113	26	1	0	0	4	5	38	.263	.239	Post-All Star	.264	106	28	1	1	0	3	2	13	.278	.302

Career (1989-1992)

	Avg	AB	H	2B	3B	HR	RBI	BB	SO	OBP	SLG		Avg	AB	H	2B	3B	HR	RBI	BB	SO	OBP	SLG
vs. Left	.292	363	106	23	2	1	33	19	38	.325	.375	Scoring Posn	.266	203	54	10	0	1	63	27	35	.346	.330
vs. Right	.242	530	128	16	1	2	37	34	82	.293	.287	Close & Late	.285	165	47	5	1	0	9	7	26	.314	.327
Groundball	.275	338	93	12	1	1	29	12	44	.311	.325	None on/out	.252	222	56	9	0	1	1	8	29	.288	.305
Flyball	.243	222	54	13	2	0	14	11	42	.278	.320	Batting #7	.242	219	53	3	1	1	17	14	31	.289	.279
Home	.274	441	121	15	2	2	46	29	60	.320	.331	Batting #8	.266	617	164	36	2	2	52	38	79	.311	.340
Away	.250	452	113	24	1	1	24	24	60	.292	.314	Other	.298	57	17	0	0	0	1	1	10	.310	.298
Day	.264	474	125	21	1	2	45	28	62	.305	.325	April	.262	141	37	3	0	0	7	3	17	.289	.284
Night	.260	419	109	18	2	1	25	25	58	.307	.320	May	.260	146	38	6	1	1	15	18	21	.343	.336
Grass	.266	616	164	21	2	3	56	41	79	.314	.321	June	.280	143	40	6	1	2	11	4	22	.304	.378
Turf	.253	277	70	18	1	0	14	12	41	.287	.325	July	.298	124	37	6	0	0	11	6	7	.323	.347
First Pitch	.290	214	62	14	1	2	23	8	0	.311	.393	August	.235	200	47	10	1	0	14	14	26	.285	.295
Ahead on Count	.317	161	51	7	1	0	8	21	0	.396	.373	September/October	.252	139	35	8	0	0	12	8	27	.297	.309
Behind on Count	.232	327	76	11	1	1	22	1	80	.245	.281	Pre-All Star	.268	466	125	18	2	3	35	28	61	.315	.335
Two Strikes	.186	334	62	7	0	0	21	14	120	.224	.207	Post-All Star	.255	427	109	21	1	0	35	25	59	.296	.309

Batter vs. Pitcher (career)

Hits Best Against	Avg	AB	H	2B	3B	HR	RBI	BB	SO	OBP	SLG	Hits Worst Against	Avg	AB	H	2B	3B	HR	RBI	BB	SO	OBP	SLG
Bruce Ruffin	.500	12	6	2	0	1	4	1	2	.538	.917	Bob Tewksbury	.063	16	1	0	0	0	0	0	1	.167	.063
Mark Portugal	.471	17	8	2	0	0	3	1	0	.471	.588	Bud Black	.100	10	1	0	0	0	1	1	1	.182	.100
Jose Rijo	.455	11	5	1	0	1	2	1	1	.500	.818	Jose DeLeon	.130	23	3	2	0	0	1	3	11	.231	.217
Trevor Wilson	.364	11	4	1	0	0	0	0	1	.364	.455	Tom Glavine	.167	12	2	0	0	0	0	2	2	.286	.167
Terry Mulholland	.333	12	4	1	0	0	3	2	1	.429	.417	Frank Viola	.188	16	3	0	0	0	2	0	2	.188	.188

Dan Gladden — Tigers
Bats Right

	Avg	G	AB	R	H	2B	3B	HR	RBI	BB	SO	HBP	GDP	SB	CS	OBP	SLG	IBB	SH	SF	#Pit	#P/PA	GB	FB	G/F
1992 Season	.254	113	417	57	106	20	1	7	42	30	64	2	10	4	2	.304	.357	0	5	5	1626	3.58	120	137	0.88
Last Five Years	.269	637	2449	346	658	116	25	37	242	161	318	22	55	95	35	.317	.382	10	18	25	9401	3.54	875	789	1.11

1992 Season

	Avg	AB	H	2B	3B	HR	RBI	BB	SO	OBP	SLG		Avg	AB	H	2B	3B	HR	RBI	BB	SO	OBP	SLG
vs. Left	.282	124	35	8	1	4	18	12	17	.341	.460	Scoring Posn	.263	114	30	4	1	4	38	6	14	.288	.421

1992 Season

	Avg	AB	H	2B	3B	HR	RBI	BB	SO	OBP	SLG		Avg	AB	H	2B	3B	HR	RBI	BB	SO	OBP	SLG
vs. Right	.242	293	71	12	0	3	24	18	47	.288	.314	Close & Late	.338	65	22	4	0	1	8	6	5	.389	.446
Groundball	.272	103	28	6	1	3	15	8	22	.321	.437	None on/out	.231	108	25	8	0	1	1	10	15	.303	.333
Flyball	.221	131	29	7	0	1	9	9	23	.268	.298	Batting #2	.265	147	39	9	1	3	17	13	23	.325	.401
Home	.226	177	40	9	1	3	18	17	26	.291	.339	Batting #6	.270	148	40	5	0	3	17	12	27	.319	.365
Away	.275	240	66	11	0	4	24	13	38	.314	.371	Other	.221	122	27	6	0	1	8	5	14	.258	.295
Day	.257	136	35	5	0	1	8	12	27	.327	.316	April	.188	85	16	1	1	2	9	6	8	.242	.294
Night	.253	281	71	15	1	6	34	18	37	.293	.377	May	.480	25	12	4	0	1	5	0	2	.500	.760
Grass	.234	354	83	17	1	4	27	27	53	.286	.322	June	.350	60	21	4	0	0	3	6	7	.412	.417
Turf	.365	63	23	3	0	3	15	3	11	.400	.556	July	.213	75	16	4	0	0	6	6	14	.268	.267
First Pitch	.306	72	22	5	0	1	13	0	0	.293	.417	August	.280	93	26	3	0	4	15	7	17	.324	.441
Ahead on Count	.347	98	34	6	0	2	9	21	0	.467	.469	September/October	.190	79	15	4	0	0	4	5	16	.235	.241
Behind on Count	.228	123	28	5	1	4	14	0	36	.224	.382	Pre-All Star	.272	195	53	10	1	3	18	13	23	.321	.379
Two Strikes	.153	170	26	5	0	2	8	9	64	.198	.218	Post-All Star	.239	222	53	10	0	4	24	17	41	.289	.338

1992 By Position

Position	Avg	AB	H	2B	3B	HR	RBI	BB	SO	OBP	SLG	G	GS	Innings	PO	A	E	DP	Fld Pct	Rng Fctr	In Zone	Outs	Zone Rtg	MLB Zone
As lf	.258	341	88	14	1	7	35	26	53	.309	.367	95	85	754.2	202	9	3	2	.986	2.52	234	199	.850	.809
As cf	.183	60	11	3	0	0	4	3	11	.219	.233	17	13	121.2	24	0	0	0	1.000	1.78	29	25	.862	.824

Last Five Years

	Avg	AB	H	2B	3B	HR	RBI	BB	SO	OBP	SLG		Avg	AB	H	2B	3B	HR	RBI	BB	SO	OBP	SLG
vs. Left	.288	719	207	37	8	16	84	60	79	.342	.428	Scoring Posn	.273	556	152	28	7	9	198	40	75	.343	.397
vs. Right	.261	1730	451	79	17	21	158	101	239	.306	.362	Close & Late	.268	355	95	22	3	6	49	32	46	.333	.397
Groundball	.310	654	203	38	12	7	76	46	68	.359	.437	None on/out	.266	868	231	40	6	17	17	55	105	.319	.385
Flyball	.248	569	141	25	4	12	52	38	80	.295	.369	Batting #1	.268	1740	467	82	20	24	171	111	214	.316	.380
Home	.284	1206	342	60	15	17	118	90	140	.336	.400	Batting #2	.295	363	107	17	2	8	38	20	48	.334	.419
Away	.254	1243	316	56	10	20	124	71	178	.298	.364	Other	.243	346	84	17	3	5	33	30	56	.302	.353
Day	.252	678	171	32	2	11	53	54	89	.314	.354	April	.255	380	97	22	1	7	40	23	30	.308	.374
Night	.275	1771	487	84	23	26	189	107	229	.318	.392	May	.300	444	133	30	6	8	47	23	64	.335	.448
Grass	.245	1125	276	52	5	16	105	72	157	.293	.343	June	.283	420	119	16	4	6	36	36	51	.343	.383
Turf	.289	1324	382	64	20	21	137	89	161	.337	.415	July	.263	289	76	17	2	1	35	23	43	.317	.346
First Pitch	.332	413	137	25	3	5	50	3	0	.337	.443	August	.252	469	118	13	5	10	58	26	59	.295	.365
Ahead on Count	.325	621	202	38	12	16	79	95	0	.415	.502	September/October	.257	447	115	18	7	5	28	30	71	.302	.362
Behind on Count	.203	764	155	23	11	11	72	0	183	.212	.305	Pre-All Star	.275	1322	363	70	11	21	129	86	162	.323	.392
Two Strikes	.194	985	191	32	4	11	59	57	318	.243	.268	Post-All Star	.262	1127	295	46	14	16	113	75	156	.309	.370

Batter vs. Pitcher (since 1984)

Hits Best Against	Avg	AB	H	2B	3B	HR	RBI	BB	SO	OBP	SLG	Hits Worst Against	Avg	AB	H	2B	3B	HR	RBI	BB	SO	OBP	SLG
Ted Power	.545	11	6	2	0	1	5	3	0	.643	1.000	Lee Guetterman	.071	14	1	0	0	0	0	0	2	.071	.071
Jaime Navarro	.533	15	8	2	0	0	2	0	1	.533	.667	Juan Guzman	.091	11	1	0	0	0	0	0	4	.091	.091
Mike Flanagan	.435	23	10	4	0	1	3	3	2	.500	.739	Bill Swift	.118	17	2	0	0	0	1	1	2	.167	.118
Joe Hesketh	.429	14	6	3	0	0	0	1	0	.467	.643	Jeff Russell	.133	30	4	0	0	0	2	0	8	.129	.133
Curt Young	.348	23	8	2	0	2	4	4	5	.444	.696	Dennis Eckersley	.143	14	2	0	0	0	0	0	5	.143	.143

Tom Glavine — Braves

Pitches Left

	ERA	W	L	Sv	G	GS	IP	BB	SO	Avg	H	2B	3B	HR	RBI	OBP	SLG	CG	ShO	Sup	QS	#P/S	SB	CS	GB	FB	G/F
1992 Season	2.76	20	8	0	33	33	225.0	70	129	.235	197	37	4	6	70	.293	.310	7	5	5.32	21	100	13	10	318	218	1.46
Last Five Years	3.51	71	56	0	163	163	1067.1	320	624	.249	1003	174	21	73	398	.305	.357	24	10	4.69	99	97	79	51	1585	1119	1.42

1992 Season

	ERA	W	L	Sv	G	GS	IP	H	HR	BB	SO		Avg	AB	H	2B	3B	HR	RBI	BB	SO	OBP	SLG
Home	2.31	13	4	0	20	20	140.0	124	2	37	72	vs. Left	.273	176	48	7	1	1	17	23	32	.353	.341
Away	3.49	7	4	0	13	13	85.0	73	4	33	57	vs. Right	.225	663	149	30	3	5	53	47	97	.277	.302
Day	3.82	5	4	0	11	11	66.0	70	4	25	38	Inning 1-6	.239	686	164	30	4	6	62	62	107	.301	.321
Night	2.32	15	4	0	22	22	159.0	127	2	45	91	Inning 7+	.216	153	33	7	0	0	8	8	22	.259	.261
Grass	2.69	14	6	0	24	24	164.0	151	5	45	90	None on	.228	496	113	21	2	4	4	40	81	.287	.302
Turf	2.95	6	2	0	9	9	61.0	46	1	25	39	Runners on	.245	343	84	16	2	2	66	30	48	.303	.321
April	2.48	3	1	0	5	5	36.1	31	2	5	30	Scoring Posn	.256	172	44	7	2	2	63	24	27	.340	.355
May	3.51	4	2	0	6	6	41.0	40	0	13	18	Close & Late	.224	107	24	6	0	0	7	5	19	.259	.280
June	2.49	4	0	0	6	6	47.0	31	1	17	23	None on/out	.225	209	47	11	0	1	1	20	40	.296	.292
July	1.42	5	0	0	5	5	38.0	31	1	12	21	vs. 1st Batr (relief)	.000	0	0	0	0	0	0	0	0	.000	.000
August	4.01	3	2	0	6	6	33.2	37	1	12	22	First Inning Pitched	.305	128	39	10	0	1	19	12	18	.357	.406
September/October	2.79	1	3	0	5	5	29.0	25	1	11	15	First 75 Pitches	.241	606	146	30	3	4	54	56	92	.303	.320
Starter	2.76	20	8	0	33	33	225.0	197	6	70	129	Pitch 76-90	.204	113	23	2	1	2	6	5	19	.237	.292
Reliever	0.00	0	0	0	0	0	0.0	0	0	0	0	Pitch 91-105	.247	73	18	3	0	0	7	5	11	.304	.288
0-3 Days Rest	0.00	0	0	0	1	1	5.0	1	0	0	4	Pitch 106+	.213	47	10	2	0	0	3	4	7	.275	.255
4 Days Rest	2.95	16	5	0	23	23	158.2	142	4	52	83	Ahead on Count	.175	348	61	11	1	2	16	0	108	.179	.230
5+ Days Rest	2.49	4	3	0	9	9	61.1	54	2	18	42	Behind on Count	.346	188	65	11	2	3	36	40	0	.459	.473
Pre-All Star	2.57	13	3	0	19	19	140.1	116	3	37	78	Two Strikes	.164	365	60	12	2	1	18	26	129	.223	.216
Post-All Star	3.08	7	5	0	14	14	84.2	81	3	33	51												

	ERA	W	L	Sv	G	GS	IP	H	HR	BB	SO		Avg	AB	H	2B	3B	HR	RBI	BB	SO	OBP	SLG
Home	3.58	36	27	0	81	81	530.2	513	47	144	290	vs. Left	.252	731	184	25	5	10	64	83	144	.329	.341
Away	3.44	35	29	0	82	82	536.2	490	26	176	334	vs. Right	.249	3294	819	149	16	63	334	237	480	.299	.361
Day	4.50	17	18	0	47	47	278.0	299	21	100	171	Inning 1-6	.248	3347	829	141	18	56	340	283	537	.306	.351
Night	3.16	54	38	0	116	116	789.1	704	52	220	453	Inning 7+	.257	678	174	33	3	17	58	37	87	.297	.389
Grass	3.52	51	38	0	115	115	751.2	730	59	206	427	None on	.238	2472	589	101	9	52	52	144	394	.283	.350
Turf	3.48	20	18	0	48	48	315.2	273	14	114	197	Runners on	.267	1553	414	73	12	21	346	176	230	.338	.370
April	2.95	9	8	0	22	22	152.1	136	11	31	92	Scoring Posn	.266	847	225	40	7	12	311	142	136	.364	.372
May	3.47	15	7	0	29	29	181.2	160	13	63	109	Close & Late	.264	356	94	21	2	5	32	22	48	.305	.376
June	3.81	13	10	0	29	29	193.2	194	15	53	118	None on/out	.244	1061	259	51	5	17	17	59	156	.288	.350
July	3.13	11	6	0	25	25	172.1	160	15	46	103	vs. 1st Batr (relief)	.000	0	0	0	0	0	0	0	0	.000	.000
August	4.15	11	16	0	31	31	188.2	196	10	62	103	First Inning Pitched	.285	635	181	32	8	8	92	63	105	.347	.398
September/October	3.38	12	9	0	27	27	178.2	157	9	65	99	First 75 Pitches	.245	2946	721	133	17	50	286	240	472	.302	.352
Starter	3.51	71	56	0	163	163	1067.1	1003	73	320	624	Pitch 76-90	.240	542	130	19	2	10	47	34	66	.283	.338
Reliever	0.00	0	0	0	0	0	0.0	0	0	0	0	Pitch 91-105	.289	356	103	15	1	9	49	28	60	.343	.413
0-3 Days Rest	4.45	2	5	0	10	10	58.2	62	3	14	35	Pitch 106+	.271	181	49	7	1	4	16	18	26	.337	.387
4 Days Rest	3.48	50	35	0	104	104	680.1	634	39	220	401	First Pitch	.291	619	180	41	1	7	58	20	0	.311	.394
5+ Days Rest	3.40	19	16	0	49	49	328.1	307	31	86	188	Ahead on Count	.199	1713	341	53	9	29	124	0	531	.204	.291
Pre-All Star	3.31	41	26	0	88	88	584.1	541	41	158	351	Behind on Count	.320	943	302	53	6	24	134	175	0	.424	.466
Post-All Star	3.75	30	30	0	75	75	483.0	462	32	162	273	Two Strikes	.183	1696	310	45	10	26	124	125	624	.243	.267

Pitcher vs. Batter (career)

Pitches Best Vs.	Avg	AB	H	2B	3B	HR	RBI	BB	SO	OBP	SLG	Pitches Worst Vs.	Avg	AB	H	2B	3B	HR	RBI	BB	SO	OBP	SLG
Stan Javier	.000	12	0	0	0	0	0	3	2	.200	.000	Pedro Guerrero	.455	22	10	3	0	2	6	0	2	.455	.864
Paul O'Neill	.050	20	1	0	0	0	0		7	.050	.050	Robby Thompson	.441	34	15	7	1	1	3	3	5	.486	.794
Mark Parent	.050	20	1	0	0	0	0		2	.050	.050	Gregg Jefferies	.429	14	6	1	0	1	2	0	2	.429	.714
Mark Carreon	.083	12	1	0	0	0	0		1	.083	.083	Lloyd McClendon	.407	27	11	0	0	2	7	6	4	.515	.630
Don Slaught	.111	18	2	0	0	0	1	1	0	.158	.111	Tim Wallach	.386	44	17	4	1	5	11	5	2	.449	.864

Jerry Don Gleaton — Pirates

Pitches Left

	ERA	W	L	Sv	G	GS	IP	BB	SO	Avg	H	2B	3B	HR	RBI	OBP	SLG	GF	IR	IRS	Hld	SvOp	SB	CS	GB	FB	G/F
1992 Season	4.26	1	0	0	23	0	31.2	19	18	.283	34	6	0	4	13	.379	.433	6	13	2	2	2	3	3	52	36	1.44
Last Five Years	3.72	5	9	18	184	0	242.0	106	159	.252	223	35	5	18	114	.332	.363	56	223	50	24	25	16	17	320	236	1.36

1992 Season

	ERA	W	L	Sv	G	GS	IP	H	HR	BB	SO		Avg	AB	H	2B	3B	HR	RBI	BB	SO	OBP	SLG
Home	3.12	1	0	0	10	0	17.1	17	1	10	12	vs. Left	.286	42	12	2	0	1	3	7	7	.388	.405
Away	5.65	0	0	0	13	0	14.1	17	3	9	6	vs. Right	.282	78	22	4	0	3	10	12	11	.374	.449
Starter	0.00	0	0	0	0	0	0.0	0	0	0	0	Scoring Posn	.222	27	6	2	0	0	8	11	6	.436	.296
Reliever	4.26	1	0	0	23	0	31.2	34	4	19	18	Close & Late	.091	11	1	0	0	0	0	4	2	.333	.091
0 Days rest	0.00	0	0	0	3	0	2.2	1	0	3	6	None on/out	.179	28	5	0	0	0		3	6	.258	.179
1 or 2 Days rest	5.50	1	0	0	10	0	18.0	19	4	6	9	First Pitch	.250	16	4	0	0	0		3	0	.368	.250
3+ Days rest	3.27	0	0	0	10	0	11.0	14	0	10	9	Behind on Count	.412	34	14	3	0	3	8	6	0	.500	.765
Pre-All Star	4.40	1	0	0	22	0	30.2	34	4	17	18	Ahead on Count	.277	47	13	3	0	0	3	0	16	.277	.340
Post-All Star	0.00	0	0	0	1	0	1.0	0	0	0	2	Two Strikes	.255	51	13	3	0	0	2	10	18	.371	.314

Last Five Years

	ERA	W	L	Sv	G	GS	IP	H	HR	BB	SO		Avg	AB	H	2B	3B	HR	RBI	BB	SO	OBP	SLG
Home	3.65	4	4	8	88	0	120.2	95	6	50	81	vs. Left	.258	275	71	8	3	4	40	22	51	.318	.353
Away	3.76	1	5	10	96	0	121.1	128	12	56	78	vs. Right	.249	611	152	27	2	14	74	84	108	.338	.368
Day	4.55	1	2	6	51	0	65.1	59	5	21	42	Inning 1-6	.257	206	53	9	1	0	26	23	34	.328	.311
Night	3.41	4	7	12	133	0	176.2	164	13	85	117	Inning 7+	.250	680	170	26	4	18	86	83	125	.333	.379
Grass	3.60	4	6	13	111	0	152.2	129	12	64	105	None on	.275	436	120	18	3	10	10	45	72	.346	.399
Turf	3.93	1	3	5	73	0	89.1	94	6	42	54	Runners on	.229	450	103	17	2	8	104	61	87	.319	.329
April	6.75	1	1	1	22	0	21.1	24	2	9	12	Scoring Posn	.219	269	59	9	1	4	90	45	51	.328	.305
May	3.22	1	1	2	31	0	44.2	40	4	25	28	Close & Late	.258	225	58	6	2	6	32	34	44	.359	.382
June	3.25	3	1	2	34	0	52.2	46	4	22	32	None on/out	.247	190	47	3	1	3	3	20	36	.325	.321
July	2.87	0	1	3	26	0	37.2	29	0	22	25	vs. 1st Batr (relief)	.209	158	33	2	1	2	26	19	22	.291	.272
August	4.36	0	3	5	33	0	53.2	54	6	14	38	First Inning Pitched	.237	511	121	17	4	6	72	60	88	.320	.321
September/October	3.09	0	2	5	36	0	32.0	30	2	14	24	First 15 Pitches	.239	472	113	14	3	6	57	52	73	.317	.333
Starter	0.00	0	0	0	0	0	0.0	0	0	0	0	Pitch 16-30	.268	272	73	15	1	4	34	35	57	.350	.375
Reliever	3.72	5	9	18	184	0	242.0	223	18	106	159	Pitch 31-45	.280	100	28	5	1	5	18	15	22	.373	.500
0 Days rest	2.96	1	4	5	37	0	51.2	35	4	27	36	Pitch 46+	.214	42	9	1	0	1	5	4	7	.277	.310
1 or 2 Days rest	4.08	3	2	7	74	0	99.1	92	12	38	59	First Pitch	.325	114	37	5	1	2	18	11	0	.384	.439
3+ Days rest	3.76	1	3	6	73	0	91.0	96	2	41	64	Ahead on Count	.210	396	83	8	3	4	35	0	130	.214	.275
Pre-All Star	3.69	5	3	6	94	0	134.0	124	10	65	80	Behind on Count	.290	193	56	12	1	6	42	51	0	.434	.456
Post-All Star	3.75	0	6	12	90	0	108.0	99	8	41	79	Two Strikes	.199	413	82	10	3	6	36	44	159	.279	.281

Pitcher vs. Batter (since 1984)

Pitches Best Vs.	Avg	AB	H	2B	3B	HR	RBI	BB	SO	OBP	SLG	Pitches Worst Vs.	Avg	AB	H	2B	3B	HR	RBI	BB	SO	OBP	SLG
Alvin Davis	.091	11	1	0	0	0	1	1	3	.167	.091	Julio Franco	.500	10	5	1	0	1	3	1	1	.500	.900
Devon White	.091	11	1	0	0	0	0	0	1	.091	.091	Ozzie Guillen	.455	11	5	0	0	0	3	0	1	.455	.455
Greg Gagne	.200	10	2	0	0	0	0	1	3	.273	.200	Wade Boggs	.400	10	4	1	0	0	6	1	1	.417	.500
Brian Downing	.222	9	2	0	0	1	1	2	2	.364	.556	Ruben Sierra	.385	13	5	2	0	1	3	2	1	.467	.769

Pitches Best Vs.	Avg	AB	H	2B	3B	HR	RBI	BB	SO	OBP	SLG	Pitches Worst Vs.	Avg	AB	H	2B	3B	HR	RBI	BB	SO	OBP	SLG
												Pete O'Brien	.308	13	4	0	0	1	5	2	3	.400	.538

Jerry Goff — Expos
Bats Left

	Avg	G	AB	R	H	2B	3B	HR	RBI	BB	SO	HBP	GDP	SB	CS	OBP	SLG	IBB	SH	SF	#Pit	#P/PA	GB	FB	G/F
1992 Season	.000	3	3	0	0	0	0	0	0	0	3	0	0	0	0	.000	.000	0	0	0	12	4.00	0	0	0.00
Career (1990-1992)	.221	55	122	14	27	1	0	3	7	21	39	0	0	0	2	.336	.303	4	1	0	562	3.93	30	30	1.00

1992 Season

	Avg	AB	H	2B	3B	HR	RBI	BB	SO	OBP	SLG		Avg	AB	H	2B	3B	HR	RBI	BB	SO	OBP	SLG
vs. Left	.000	0	0	0	0	0	0	0	0	.000	.000	Scoring Posn	.000	0	0	0	0	0	0	0	0	.000	.000
vs. Right	.000	3	0	0	0	0	0	0	3	.000	.000	Close & Late	.000	2	0	0	0	0	0	0	2	.000	.000

Leo Gomez — Orioles
Bats Right (flyball hitter)

	Avg	G	AB	R	H	2B	3B	HR	RBI	BB	SO	HBP	GDP	SB	CS	OBP	SLG	IBB	SH	SF	#Pit	#P/PA	GB	FB	G/F
1992 Season	.265	137	468	62	124	24	0	17	64	63	78	8	14	2	3	.356	.425	4	5	8	2199	4.02	116	199	0.58
Career (1990-1992)	.249	267	898	105	224	41	2	33	110	111	167	10	27	3	4	.334	.410	4	11	15	4182	4.04	230	366	0.63

1992 Season

	Avg	AB	H	2B	3B	HR	RBI	BB	SO	OBP	SLG		Avg	AB	H	2B	3B	HR	RBI	BB	SO	OBP	SLG
vs. Left	.250	104	26	7	0	4	17	23	17	.391	.433	Scoring Posn	.225	120	27	5	0	5	47	18	22	.318	.392
vs. Right	.269	364	98	17	0	13	47	40	61	.345	.423	Close & Late	.221	68	15	4	0	4	10	8	14	.299	.456
Groundball	.308	143	44	7	0	6	18	13	19	.379	.483	None on/out	.284	95	27	3	0	2	2	10	16	.364	.379
Flyball	.196	107	21	5	0	3	16	20	20	.328	.327	Batting #6	.286	84	24	5	0	5	13	13	13	.392	.524
Home	.261	226	59	10	0	6	25	32	34	.358	.385	Batting #7	.243	284	69	14	0	10	44	46	52	.352	.398
Away	.269	242	65	14	0	11	39	31	44	.355	.463	Other	.310	100	31	5	0	2	7	4	13	.336	.420
Day	.259	143	37	5	0	6	19	14	20	.321	.420	April	.258	66	17	5	0	7	10	6	.351	.333
Night	.268	325	87	19	0	11	45	49	58	.371	.428	May	.342	76	26	5	0	4	12	8	19	.398	.566
Grass	.265	381	101	18	0	15	55	48	58	.352	.430	June	.278	79	22	3	0	1	8	14	9	.394	.354
Turf	.264	87	23	6	0	2	9	15	20	.375	.402	July	.239	92	22	5	0	5	18	11	21	.333	.457
First Pitch	.208	48	10	1	0	1	5	4	0	.286	.292	August	.238	84	20	3	0	6	12	15	17	.373	.488
Ahead on Count	.312	109	34	10	0	3	15	29	0	.455	.486	September/October	.239	71	17	3	0	1	7	5	6	.282	.324
Behind on Count	.289	135	39	4	0	7	15	0	27	.299	.474	Pre-All Star	.288	257	74	16	0	6	30	37	42	.379	.420
Two Strikes	.182	214	39	8	0	6	24	30	78	.283	.304	Post-All Star	.237	211	50	8	0	11	34	26	36	.329	.431

1992 By Position

Position	Avg	AB	H	2B	3B	HR	RBI	BB	SO	OBP	SLG	G	GS	Innings	PO	A	E	DP	Fld Pct	Rng Fctr	In Zone	Outs	Zone Rtg	MLB Zone
As 3b	.265	468	124	24	0	17	64	63	78	.356	.425	137	136	1221.2	106	244	18	19	.951	2.58	322	262	.814	.841

Career (1990-1992)

	Avg	AB	H	2B	3B	HR	RBI	BB	SO	OBP	SLG		Avg	AB	H	2B	3B	HR	RBI	BB	SO	OBP	SLG
vs. Left	.237	236	56	11	0	10	33	37	38	.338	.411	Scoring Posn	.211	209	44	7	0	7	73	43	300	.344
vs. Right	.254	662	168	30	2	23	77	74	129	.332	.409	Close & Late	.207	145	30	6	0	7	17	16	34	.262	.393
Groundball	.259	270	70	12	0	9	30	26	42	.332	.404	None on/out	.228	197	45	6	1	6	6	21	42	.312	.360
Flyball	.188	186	35	7	0	6	23	27	45	.291	.323	Batting #6	.267	116	31	7	0	7	19	19	21	.379	.509
Home	.247	449	111	22	2	13	48	58	74	.335	.392	Batting #7	.240	576	138	26	2	21	74	72	117	.324	.401
Away	.252	449	113	19	0	20	62	53	93	.333	.428	Other	.267	206	55	8	0	5	17	20	29	.335	.379
Day	.253	245	62	10	0	9	29	24	43	.318	.404	April	.265	102	27	7	0	0	7	15	13	.356	.333
Night	.248	653	162	31	2	24	81	87	124	.339	.412	May	.306	85	26	5	0	4	12	8	23	.361	.506
Grass	.249	754	188	35	2	28	93	90	134	.330	.412	June	.268	149	40	5	1	4	20	27	21	.389	.396
Turf	.250	144	36	6	0	5	17	21	33	.351	.396	July	.216	190	41	12	0	8	29	20	38	.294	.405
First Pitch	.240	104	25	3	1	3	10	4	0	.289	.375	August	.225	169	38	5	1	12	25	22	35	.323	.479
Ahead on Count	.294	194	57	13	0	6	27	48	0	.428	.454	September/October	.256	203	52	7	0	5	17	19	37	.314	.365
Behind on Count	.265	260	69	10	1	14	34	0	56	.268	.473	Pre-All Star	.274	398	109	24	1	10	46	58	69	.369	.415
Two Strikes	.185	438	81	18	1	11	42	59	166	.280	.306	Post-All Star	.230	500	115	17	1	23	64	53	98	.305	.406

Batter vs. Pitcher (career)

Hits Best Against	Avg	AB	H	2B	3B	HR	RBI	BB	SO	OBP	SLG	Hits Worst Against	Avg	AB	H	2B	3B	HR	RBI	BB	SO	OBP	SLG
Kevin Appier	.500	14	7	1	0	1	2	2	3	.563	.786	Charlie Hough	.083	12	1	0	0	0	0	3	0	.267	.083
Erik Hanson	.500	10	5	0	0	0	2	3	3	.583	.500	Mark Leiter	.100	10	1	0	0	0	0	1	5	.182	.100
Alex Fernandez	.400	10	4	1	0	0	3	1	2	.455	.500	Todd Stottlemyre	.133	15	2	0	0	1	1	0	2	.133	.333
Mike Gardiner	.400	10	4	1	0	1	2	3	3	.538	.800	Charles Nagy	.154	13	2	0	0	0	0	0	3	.154	.154
Jack Morris	.375	16	6	2	0	1	3	3	3	.474	.688	Jim Abbott	.222	9	2	0	0	0	0	0	2	.417	.222

Rene Gonzales — Angels
Bats Right (groundball hitter)

	Avg	G	AB	R	H	2B	3B	HR	RBI	BB	SO	HBP	GDP	SB	CS	OBP	SLG	IBB	SH	SF	#Pit	#P/PA	GB	FB	G/F
1992 Season	.277	104	329	47	91	17	1	7	38	41	46	4	17	7	4	.363	.398	1	5	1	1372	3.66	128	84	1.52
Last Five Years	.234	405	953	105	223	33	2	12	82	90	144	11	36	15	9	.306	.311	1	28	5	3827	3.61	394	243	1.62

1992 Season

	Avg	AB	H	2B	3B	HR	RBI	BB	SO	OBP	SLG		Avg	AB	H	2B	3B	HR	RBI	BB	SO	OBP	SLG
vs. Left	.268	71	19	3	0	3	11	10	11	.369	.437	Scoring Posn	.323	65	21	2	1	3	33	15	9	.444	.523

1992 Season

	Avg	AB	H	2B	3B	HR	RBI	BB	SO	OBP	SLG		Avg	AB	H	2B	3B	HR	RBI	BB	SO	OBP	SLG
vs. Right	.279	258	72	14	1	4	27	31	35	.361	.388	Close & Late	.192	52	10	1	0	1	6	12	9	.354	.269
Groundball	.278	79	22	4	0	1	5	11	9	.367	.367	None on/out	.325	80	26	5	0	1	1	7	14	.393	.425
Flyball	.298	94	28	2	1	3	17	12	8	.394	.436	Batting #5	.243	74	18	4	0	0	9	7	7	.329	.297
Home	.298	168	50	12	0	6	24	22	22	.380	.476	Batting #6	.283	159	45	9	1	2	14	25	26	.384	.390
Away	.255	161	41	5	1	1	14	19	24	.344	.317	Other	.292	96	28	4	0	5	15	9	13	.352	.490
Day	.264	106	28	9	0	2	13	14	14	.350	.406	April	.304	23	7	2	0	3	6	8	3	.484	.783
Night	.283	223	63	8	1	5	25	27	32	.369	.395	May	.271	85	23	2	1	3	13	8	14	.333	.424
Grass	.298	272	81	15	1	7	35	36	36	.383	.438	June	.245	94	23	8	0	1	10	9	11	.324	.362
Turf	.175	57	10	2	0	0	3	5	10	.266	.211	July	.270	89	24	3	0	0	6	13	12	.359	.303
First Pitch	.304	56	17	2	0	1	6	1	0	.316	.393	August	.368	38	14	2	0	0	3	3	6	.442	.421
Ahead on Count	.254	67	17	4	0	2	9	17	0	.405	.403	September/October	.000	0	0	0	0	0	0	0	0	.000	.000
Behind on Count	.265	113	30	5	0	3	11	0	33	.288	.389	Pre-All Star	.253	241	61	12	1	7	32	29	35	.338	.398
Two Strikes	.235	136	32	5	1	3	12	23	46	.356	.353	Post-All Star	.341	88	30	5	0	0	6	12	11	.427	.398

1992 By Position

Position	Avg	AB	H	2B	3B	HR	RBI	BB	SO	OBP	SLG	G	GS	Innings	PO	A	E	DP	Fld Pct	Rng Fctr	In Zone	Outs	Zone Rtg	MLB Zone
As 1b	.273	22	6	2	0	1	2	4	4	.385	.500	13	6	63.0	75	9	0	8	1.000	---	19	16	.842	.843
As 2b	.256	129	33	5	1	4	17	12	18	.319	.403	42	36	322.1	78	91	1	28	.994	4.72	105	88	.838	.892
As 3b	.305	164	50	9	0	2	17	23	19	.401	.396	53	51	445.0	32	112	7	9	.954	2.91	141	115	.816	.841

Last Five Years

	Avg	AB	H	2B	3B	HR	RBI	BB	SO	OBP	SLG		Avg	AB	H	2B	3B	HR	RBI	BB	SO	OBP	SLG
vs. Left	.253	261	66	9	1	4	28	38	42	.353	.341	Scoring Posn	.244	201	49	8	2	3	70	31	34	.346	.348
vs. Right	.227	692	157	24	1	8	54	52	102	.287	.299	Close & Late	.250	156	39	4	0	2	11	18	27	.331	.314
Groundball	.233	275	64	10	0	3	19	29	32	.305	.302	None on/out	.252	226	57	8	0	3	3	17	40	.310	.327
Flyball	.258	240	62	6	1	5	32	21	37	.328	.354	Batting #8	.253	229	58	7	0	4	23	14	28	.300	.336
Home	.248	448	111	22	0	9	40	49	67	.327	.357	Batting #9	.210	395	83	11	1	4	28	35	66	.281	.273
Away	.222	505	112	11	2	3	42	41	77	.286	.269	Other	.249	329	82	15	1	4	31	41	50	.339	.337
Day	.213	301	64	14	1	4	33	28	45	.287	.306	April	.216	102	22	3	0	4	12	15	19	.319	.363
Night	.244	652	159	19	1	8	49	62	99	.314	.313	May	.265	200	53	5	1	5	28	19	26	.336	.375
Grass	.244	733	179	28	2	10	68	70	107	.312	.329	June	.215	205	44	13	0	2	17	19	28	.269	.307
Turf	.200	220	44	5	0	2	14	20	37	.286	.250	July	.265	151	40	6	0	1	8	19	22	.345	.325
First Pitch	.295	146	43	5	0	1	10	1	0	.299	.349	August	.228	206	47	4	1	0	16	11	34	.273	.257
Ahead on Count	.232	194	45	10	1	5	20	46	0	.384	.371	September/October	.191	89	17	2	0	0	1	7	15	.265	.213
Behind on Count	.212	345	73	8	0	3	25	0	91	.224	.261	Pre-All Star	.237	566	134	22	1	12	62	57	83	.313	.343
Two Strikes	.188	409	77	8	1	4	28	43	144	.273	.242	Post-All Star	.230	387	89	11	1	0	20	33	61	.296	.264

Batter vs. Pitcher (career)

Hits Best Against	Avg	AB	H	2B	3B	HR	RBI	BB	SO	OBP	SLG	Hits Worst Against	Avg	AB	H	2B	3B	HR	RBI	BB	SO	OBP	SLG
Randy Johnson	.500	10	5	0	0	1	2	3	2	.706	.800	Bob Welch	.000	11	0	0	0	0	0	0	3	.000	.000
Jack McDowell	.364	11	4	2	0	0	3	0	3	.364	.545	Frank Tanana	.063	16	1	0	0	0	0	2	4	.167	.063
Mark Langston	.357	14	5	0	1	0	3	2	3	.438	.500	Jack Morris	.091	11	1	0	0	0	1	0	4	.091	.091
Scott Sanderson	.333	12	4	0	0	0	0	0	3	.333	.333	Roger Clemens	.125	16	2	0	0	0	0	0	3	.125	.125
Nolan Ryan	.308	13	4	1	0	0	2	1	2	.438	.385	Mike Moore	.150	20	3	0	0	0	0	1	1	.190	.200

Jose Gonzalez — Angels

Bats Right

	Avg	G	AB	R	H	2B	3B	HR	RBI	BB	SO	HBP	GDP	SB	CS	OBP	SLG	IBB	SH	SF	#Pit	#P/PA	GB	FB	G/F
1992 Season	.182	33	55	4	10	2	0	0	2	7	20	0	2	0	1	.270	.218	1	1	1	256	4.06	18	9	2.00
Last Five Years	.212	362	556	72	118	21	6	7	35	51	152	2	7	23	5	.279	.309	7	5	4	2389	3.90	176	144	1.22

1992 Season

	Avg	AB	H	2B	3B	HR	RBI	BB	SO	OBP	SLG		Avg	AB	H	2B	3B	HR	RBI	BB	SO	OBP	SLG
vs. Left	.196	46	9	2	0	0	1	6	14	.288	.239	Scoring Posn	.182	11	2	0	0	0	2	2	5	.286	.182
vs. Right	.111	9	1	0	0	0	1	1	6	.182	.111	Close & Late	.333	12	4	0	0	0	1	3	4	.467	.333

Last Five Years

	Avg	AB	H	2B	3B	HR	RBI	BB	SO	OBP	SLG		Avg	AB	H	2B	3B	HR	RBI	BB	SO	OBP	SLG
vs. Left	.214	332	71	12	4	2	18	28	78	.277	.292	Scoring Posn	.186	113	21	3	1	1	26	14	40	.267	.257
vs. Right	.210	224	47	9	2	5	17	23	74	.282	.335	Close & Late	.229	109	25	2	2	1	5	13	37	.311	.312
Groundball	.257	183	47	6	2	2	12	10	49	.297	.344	None on/out	.226	159	36	8	1	1	1	11	33	.281	.308
Flyball	.187	139	26	3	2	0	7	12	36	.250	.237	Batting #7	.194	93	18	2	1	0	5	7	23	.255	.237
Home	.214	252	54	9	2	5	20	25	71	.287	.325	Batting #8	.233	103	24	6	0	3	10	13	30	.325	.379
Away	.211	304	64	12	4	2	15	26	81	.272	.296	Other	.211	360	76	13	5	4	20	31	99	.272	.308
Day	.244	176	43	9	4	3	10	23	43	.335	.358	April	.167	12	2	0	0	0	0	1	4	.231	.167
Night	.197	380	75	13	2	4	25	28	109	.252	.274	May	.210	62	13	2	3	1	4	3	17	.246	.387
Grass	.206	399	82	16	3	6	27	42	109	.283	.306	June	.264	106	28	2	1	0	5	14	25	.344	.302
Turf	.229	157	36	5	3	1	8	9	43	.268	.318	July	.175	126	22	5	0	2	9	6	31	.211	.262
First Pitch	.313	67	21	5	1	3	9	6	0	.373	.552	August	.235	119	28	6	1	3	10	10	27	.298	.378
Ahead on Count	.280	107	30	8	2	2	13	16	0	.365	.449	September/October	.191	131	25	6	1	1	6	17	48	.269	.275
Behind on Count	.160	200	32	2	2	0	7	0	84	.164	.190	Pre-All Star	.237	228	54	9	4	2	14	23	58	.304	.338
Two Strikes	.131	282	37	5	2	2	9	28	152	.210	.184	Post-All Star	.195	328	64	12	2	5	21	28	94	.261	.290

Batter vs. Pitcher (career)

Hits Best Against	Avg	AB	H	2B	3B	HR	RBI	BB	SO	OBP	SLG	Hits Worst Against	Avg	AB	H	2B	3B	HR	RBI	BB	SO	OBP	SLG
Dennis Rasmussen	.333	15	5	0	0	0	1	5	1	.500	.333	Frank Viola	.083	12	1	0	0	0	0	1	4	.154	.083
Tom Glavine	.318	22	7	2	0	3	0	0	3	.304	.409	Tom Browning	.118	17	2	0	0	0	0	1	3	.167	.118
												John Smiley	.143	14	2	0	0	0	1	2	3	.250	.143
												Joe Magrane	.167	12	2	0	1	0	0	0	1	.167	.333
												Don Carman	.182	11	2	0	0	0	0	0	1	.182	.182

Juan Gonzalez — Rangers   Bats Right (flyball hitter)

	Avg	G	AB	R	H	2B	3B	HR	RBI	BB	SO	HBP	GDP	SB	CS	OBP	SLG	IBB	SH	SF	#Pit	#P/PA	GB	FB	G/F
1992 Season	.260	155	584	77	152	24	2	43	109	35	143	5	16	0	1	.304	.529	1	0	8	2325	3.68	167	198	0.84
Career (1989-1992)	.259	346	1279	172	331	68	4	75	230	85	296	12	32	4	6	.308	.494	8	2	12	5038	3.63	376	444	0.85

1992 Season

	Avg	AB	H	2B	3B	HR	RBI	BB	SO	OBP	SLG		Avg	AB	H	2B	3B	HR	RBI	BB	SO	OBP	SLG
vs. Left	.253	158	40	6	0	8	28	12	43	.302	.443	Scoring Posn	.254	177	45	7	0	10	69	10	46	.282	.463
vs. Right	.263	426	112	18	2	35	81	23	100	.304	.561	Close & Late	.258	93	24	5	0	6	12	9	29	.327	.505
Groundball	.311	135	42	6	0	15	27	9	29	.358	.689	None on/out	.238	122	29	5	1	7	7	4	30	.279	.467
Flyball	.226	168	38	7	0	13	37	14	50	.290	.500	Batting #4	.257	218	56	9	0	18	38	15	53	.316	.546
Home	.265	294	78	18	2	19	50	15	83	.305	.534	Batting #5	.245	216	53	10	0	13	40	7	51	.268	.472
Away	.255	290	74	6	0	24	59	20	60	.303	.524	Other	.287	150	43	5	2	12	31	13	39	.335	.587
Day	.293	99	29	5	0	8	23	6	21	.336	.586	April	.267	90	24	3	0	4	15	5	17	.299	.433
Night	.254	485	123	19	2	35	86	29	122	.297	.518	May	.252	103	26	5	1	3	10	5	21	.284	.408
Grass	.256	493	126	21	2	36	87	29	125	.298	.525	June	.292	96	28	2	1	11	24	10	31	.352	.677
Turf	.286	91	26	3	0	7	22	6	18	.337	.549	July	.232	95	22	3	0	8	21	1	24	.248	.516
First Pitch	.451	51	23	1	0	8	15	1	0	.491	.941	August	.260	104	27	6	0	12	25	11	28	.330	.663
Ahead on Count	.344	131	45	10	1	13	39	24	0	.439	.733	September/October	.260	96	25	5	0	5	14	3	22	.304	.469
Behind on Count	.193	243	47	8	1	10	28	0	86	.193	.358	Pre-All Star	.267	326	87	12	2	19	57	20	77	.308	.491
Two Strikes	.163	288	47	6	1	12	28	10	143	.189	.316	Post-All Star	.252	258	65	12	0	24	52	15	66	.299	.578

1992 By Position

Position	Avg	AB	H	2B	3B	HR	RBI	BB	SO	OBP	SLG	G	GS	Innings	PO	A	E	DP	Fld Pct	Rng Fctr	In Zone	Outs	Zone Rtg	MLB Zone
As lf	.294	102	30	3	0	7	19	6	26	.336	.529	31	26	229.0	68	3	2	0	.973	2.79	80	67	.838	.809
As cf	.257	459	118	21	2	34	86	28	110	.301	.534	123	117	1023.1	309	6	8	1	.975	2.77	361	299	.828	.824

Career (1989-1992)

	Avg	AB	H	2B	3B	HR	RBI	BB	SO	OBP	SLG		Avg	AB	H	2B	3B	HR	RBI	BB	SO	OBP	SLG
vs. Left	.266	353	94	16	0	18	60	31	84	.322	.465	Scoring Posn	.257	385	99	15	1	17	147	36	96	.317	.434
vs. Right	.256	926	237	52	4	57	170	54	212	.303	.505	Close & Late	.236	212	50	11	0	14	34	18	55	.307	.486
Groundball	.308	344	106	19	0	24	68	20	73	.349	.573	None on/out	.230	270	62	16	1	12	12	12	58	.270	.430
Flyball	.235	319	75	17	1	22	73	20	85	.284	.502	Batting #4	.240	300	72	13	0	20	47	19	77	.294	.483
Home	.264	640	169	38	3	30	103	38	164	.312	.473	Batting #5	.276	453	125	25	1	28	91	24	102	.314	.521
Away	.254	639	162	30	1	45	127	47	132	.305	.515	Other	.255	526	134	30	3	27	92	42	117	.311	.477
Day	.282	206	58	12	1	13	46	13	45	.335	.539	April	.288	104	30	5	0	5	20	6	21	.321	.481
Night	.254	1073	273	56	3	62	184	72	251	.303	.486	May	.290	207	60	16	1	8	38	18	41	.346	.493
Grass	.262	1055	276	54	3	63	186	70	248	.310	.498	June	.273	198	54	5	1	15	41	23	51	.344	.535
Turf	.246	224	55	14	1	12	44	15	48	.299	.478	July	.243	185	45	9	0	15	41	8	51	.281	.535
First Pitch	.331	121	40	6	0	11	24	7	0	.396	.653	August	.279	233	65	13	1	21	49	14	54	.321	.614
Ahead on Count	.357	283	101	24	1	27	75	44	0	.443	.735	September/October	.219	352	77	20	1	11	41	16	78	.266	.375
Behind on Count	.226	521	118	23	1	23	80	0	169	.225	.407	Pre-All Star	.282	570	161	30	2	31	111	50	127	.340	.505
Two Strikes	.177	617	109	22	3	17	65	34	296	.218	.305	Post-All Star	.240	709	170	38	2	44	119	35	169	.282	.485

Batter vs. Pitcher (career)

Hits Best Against	Avg	AB	H	2B	3B	HR	RBI	BB	SO	OBP	SLG	Hits Worst Against	Avg	AB	H	2B	3B	HR	RBI	BB	SO	OBP	SLG
Jim Abbott	.588	17	10	0	0	1	4	0	3	.588	.765	Mike Moore	.050	20	1	1	0	0	0	0	6	.050	.100
Charles Nagy	.455	11	5	0	0	1	2	1	4	.500	.727	Chris Bosio	.067	15	1	0	0	0	0	1	5	.125	.067
Tom Gordon	.438	16	7	2	2	1	3	0	2	.438	1.000	Bill Krueger	.091	11	1	0	0	0	0	3	2	.286	.091
Mike Mussina	.357	14	5	0	0	3	5	0	4	.357	1.000	Jimmy Key	.125	16	2	1	0	0	0	0	3	.125	.188
Charlie Hough	.333	12	4	1	0	2	4	1	2	.385	.917	Mark Leiter	.143	14	2	0	0	0	3	1	3	.200	.143

Luis Gonzalez — Astros   Bats Left

	Avg	G	AB	R	H	2B	3B	HR	RBI	BB	SO	HBP	GDP	SB	CS	OBP	SLG	IBB	SH	SF	#Pit	#P/PA	GB	FB	G/F
1992 Season	.243	122	387	40	94	19	3	10	55	24	52	2	6	7	7	.289	.385	3	1	2	1450	3.49	134	126	1.06
Career (1990-1992)	.247	271	881	92	218	49	12	23	124	66	158	10	15	17	14	.305	.409	8	2	6	3406	3.54	282	280	1.01

1992 Season

	Avg	AB	H	2B	3B	HR	RBI	BB	SO	OBP	SLG		Avg	AB	H	2B	3B	HR	RBI	BB	SO	OBP	SLG
vs. Left	.350	80	28	6	2	1	13	7	11	.404	.513	Scoring Posn	.250	108	27	4	0	4	45	10	15	.314	.398
vs. Right	.215	307	66	13	1	9	42	17	41	.258	.352	Close & Late	.310	71	22	3	1	3	15	6	12	.364	.507
Groundball	.188	154	29	4	1	4	19	9	16	.233	.305	None on/out	.288	80	23	6	1	4	4	5	12	.329	.538
Flyball	.307	88	27	8	2	5	16	10	14	.384	.614	Batting #3	.217	120	26	5	0	3	19	5	15	.246	.333
Home	.206	204	42	10	1	4	25	14	35	.255	.324	Batting #6	.284	109	31	4	3	4	17	10	10	.345	.486
Away	.284	183	52	9	2	6	30	10	17	.328	.454	Other	.234	158	37	10	0	3	19	9	27	.282	.354

160

1992 Season

	Avg	AB	H	2B	3B	HR	RBI	BB	SO	OBP	SLG		Avg	AB	H	2B	3B	HR	RBI	BB	SO	OBP	SLG
Day	.232	112	26	5	2	2	12	6	16	.271	.366	April	.120	50	6	2	0	1	4	4	11	.196	.220
Night	.247	275	68	14	1	8	43	18	36	.296	.393	May	.200	45	9	2	0	0	2	1	7	.217	.244
Grass	.278	126	35	5	2	3	19	5	14	.316	.421	June	.319	69	22	4	0	5	19	5	7	.365	.594
Turf	.226	261	59	14	1	7	36	19	38	.277	.368	July	.237	38	9	2	2	0	2	6	7	.341	.395
First Pitch	.319	69	22	3	1	2	9	3	0	.355	.478	August	.337	83	28	2	1	2	13	3	6	.360	.458
Ahead on Count	.330	100	33	7	0	2	20	12	0	.402	.460	September/October	.196	102	20	7	0	2	15	5	14	.239	.324
Behind on Count	.219	114	25	7	0	2	14	0	28	.219	.333	Pre-All Star	.234	192	45	9	2	6	26	16	29	.295	.396
Two Strikes	.164	146	24	4	1	5	18	9	52	.213	.308	Post-All Star	.251	195	49	10	1	4	29	8	23	.283	.374

1992 By Position

Position	Avg	AB	H	2B	3B	HR	RBI	BB	SO	OBP	SLG	G	GS	Innings	PO	A	E	DP	Fld Pct	Rng Fctr	In Zone	Outs	Zone Rtg	MLB Zone
As Pinch Hitter	.294	17	5	1	0	1	7	3	3	.400	.529	20	0	---	---	---	---	---	---	---	---	---	---	---
As lf	.241	370	89	18	3	9	48	21	49	.284	.378	111	96	859.1	259	5	2	1	.992	2.76	266	234	.880	.809

Career (1990-1992)

	Avg	AB	H	2B	3B	HR	RBI	BB	SO	OBP	SLG		Avg	AB	H	2B	3B	HR	RBI	BB	SO	OBP	SLG
vs. Left	.241	203	49	13	3	2	26	19	42	.314	.365	Scoring Posn	.260	246	64	13	2	7	95	29	56	.338	.415
vs. Right	.249	678	169	36	9	21	98	47	116	.303	.422	Close & Late	.294	153	45	8	2	3	24	14	28	.363	.431
Groundball	.233	300	70	11	4	9	42	17	43	.277	.387	None on/out	.250	176	44	10	2	8	8	12	27	.302	.466
Flyball	.282	202	57	13	4	11	35	21	43	.361	.550	Batting #3	.198	192	38	7	2	5	25	7	30	.228	.333
Home	.242	438	106	26	7	8	57	36	78	.302	.388	Batting #4	.221	340	75	20	3	11	48	26	76	.283	.394
Away	.253	443	112	23	5	15	67	30	80	.308	.429	Other	.301	349	105	22	7	7	51	33	52	.367	.464
Day	.239	230	55	11	2	7	26	19	37	.303	.396	April	.135	111	15	5	1	1	7	8	30	.205	.225
Night	.250	651	163	38	10	16	98	47	121	.306	.413	May	.259	139	36	10	3	6	25	6	25	.286	.504
Grass	.258	263	73	11	3	9	44	17	50	.306	.413	June	.266	154	41	11	1	6	24	16	22	.343	.468
Turf	.242	598	145	38	9	14	80	49	108	.305	.406	July	.262	122	32	5	3	3	18	14	23	.345	.426
First Pitch	.314	156	49	8	2	7	25	5	0	.347	.526	August	.296	159	47	5	3	4	24	8	27	.339	.440
Ahead on Count	.309	207	64	12	3	6	34	25	0	.385	.483	September/October	.240	196	47	13	1	3	26	14	31	.292	.362
Behind on Count	.205	292	60	12	4	5	37	2	92	.217	.325	Pre-All Star	.233	454	106	28	7	14	64	41	84	.300	.419
Two Strikes	.180	362	65	16	4	7	38	34	158	.255	.304	Post-All Star	.262	427	112	21	5	9	60	25	74	.311	.398

Batter vs. Pitcher (career)

Hits Best Against	Avg	AB	H	2B	3B	HR	RBI	BB	SO	OBP	SLG	Hits Worst Against	Avg	AB	H	2B	3B	HR	RBI	BB	SO	OBP	SLG
Mike Bielecki	.500	10	5	0	1	0	2	1	1	.545	.700	Ken Hill	.071	14	1	0	1	0	2	1	4	.133	.214
Doug Drabek	.462	13	6	1	0	0	1	1	2	.467	.538	Steve Avery	.071	14	1	0	0	0	0	0	3	.071	.143
Greg Maddux	.409	22	9	2	0	3	9	2	3	.458	.909	Kevin Gross	.077	13	1	0	1	0	1	0	3	.077	.231
Tim Belcher	.357	14	5	2	0	1	3	1	2	.400	.714	Bryn Smith	.083	12	1	0	0	0	1	0	3	.063	.083
Jose Deleon	.333	12	4	0	0	2	3	0	2	.333	.833	Tom Candiotti	.143	14	2	0	0	0	0	0	2	.143	.143

Dwight Gooden — Mets

Pitches Right (groundball pitcher)

	ERA	W	L	Sv	G	GS	IP	BB	SO	Avg	H	2B	3B	HR	RBI	OBP	SLG	CG	ShO	Sup	QS	#P/S	SB	CS	GB	FB	G/F
1992 Season	3.67	10	13	0	31	31	206.0	70	145	.255	197	43	7	11	86	.317	.371	3	0	3.58	21	102	22	11	306	188	1.63
Last Five Years	3.48	69	40	1	145	143	995.1	300	794	.251	946	165	25	50	377	.308	.348	18	5	5.27	95	105	201	60	1512	770	1.96

1992 Season

	ERA	W	L	Sv	G	GS	IP	H	HR	BB	SO		Avg	AB	H	2B	3B	HR	RBI	BB	SO	OBP	SLG
Home	4.25	7	5	0	15	15	97.1	95	6	34	63	vs. Left	.267	450	120	22	1	9	45	48	63	.337	.380
Away	3.15	3	8	0	16	16	108.2	102	5	36	82	vs. Right	.238	323	77	21	6	2	41	22	82	.288	.359
Day	3.53	3	4	0	10	10	66.1	59	7	27	42	Inning 1-6	.253	664	168	39	6	7	74	64	131	.318	.361
Night	3.74	7	9	0	21	21	139.2	138	9	43	103	Inning 7+	.266	109	29	4	1	4	12	6	14	.308	.431
Grass	3.88	9	9	0	22	22	144.0	143	8	49	92	None on	.248	439	109	25	4	6	6	41	89	.315	.364
Turf	3.19	1	4	0	9	9	62.0	54	3	21	53	Runners on	.263	334	88	18	3	5	80	29	56	.318	.380
April	3.16	2	1	0	4	4	25.2	20	0	12	17	Scoring Posn	.237	207	49	9	0	2	65	22	40	.304	.309
May	4.10	2	4	0	6	6	37.1	40	3	15	30	Close & Late	.229	70	16	1	0	2	8	4	9	.267	.329
June	3.95	1	2	0	6	6	41.0	36	1	16	28	None on/out	.302	202	61	15	0	3	3	12	40	.344	.421
July	4.08	1	2	0	3	3	17.2	17	1	6	13	vs. 1st Batr (relief)	.000	0	0	0	0	0	0	0	0	.000	.000
August	4.60	2	2	0	5	5	29.1	35	3	11	22	First Inning Pitched	.265	113	30	8	0	1	15	13	21	.333	.363
September/October	2.78	2	2	0	7	7	55.0	49	3	10	35	First 75 Pitches	.252	543	137	33	6	6	59	50	107	.314	.368
Starter	3.67	10	13	0	31	31	206.0	197	11	70	145	Pitch 76-90	.252	103	26	4	0	1	9	9	22	.313	.320
Reliever	0.00	0	0	0	0	0	0.0	0	0	0	0	Pitch 91-105	.270	89	24	5	1	2	13	6	9	.313	.416
0-3 Days Rest	0.00	0	0	0	0	0	0.0	0	0	0	0	Pitch 106+	.263	38	10	1	0	2	5	5	7	.364	.447
4 Days Rest	3.19	9	6	0	22	22	155.0	138	7	46	111	First Pitch	.312	109	34	10	1	2	10	7	0	.350	.477
5+ Days Rest	5.12	1	7	0	9	9	51.0	59	4	24	34	Ahead on Count	.198	369	73	16	6	4	32	0	124	.201	.306
Pre-All Star	3.81	6	8	0	18	18	118.0	108	5	47	86	Behind on Count	.340	156	53	11	0	3	25	28	0	.441	.468
Post-All Star	3.48	4	5	0	13	13	88.0	89	6	23	59	Two Strikes	.189	370	70	15	5	5	36	35	145	.261	.297

Last Five Years

	ERA	W	L	Sv	G	GS	IP	H	HR	BB	SO		Avg	AB	H	2B	3B	HR	RBI	BB	SO	OBP	SLG
Home	3.28	39	16	0	72	72	512.2	459	27	149	421	vs. Left	.245	2106	516	92	11	26	195	199	419	.310	.336
Away	3.69	30	24	1	73	71	482.2	487	23	151	373	vs. Right	.259	1661	430	73	14	24	182	101	375	.305	.363
Day	3.75	23	14	0	49	48	326.1	320	16	104	260	Inning 1-6	.249	3113	775	144	21	40	316	256	671	.308	.347
Night	3.35	46	26	0	96	95	669.0	626	34	196	534	Inning 7+	.261	654	171	21	4	10	61	44	123	.306	.352

Last Five Years

	ERA	W	L	Sv	G	GS	IP	H	HR	BB	SO
Grass	3.27	57	22	1	103	102	726.2	672	37	217	574
Turf	4.05	12	18	0	42	41	268.2	274	13	83	220
April	2.88	15	4	0	24	24	165.2	128	7	55	148
May	3.78	11	12	0	30	30	209.2	214	12	66	170
June	4.23	12	9	0	28	28	191.2	186	12	61	138
July	2.58	12	4	0	19	19	132.1	119	5	36	104
August	4.25	9	5	0	22	22	139.2	150	8	48	109
September/October	2.88	10	8	1	22	20	156.1	147	6	34	125
Starter	3.50	69	40	0	143	143	988.1	941	50	298	788
Reliever	1.29	0	0	1	2	0	7.0	5	0	2	6
0-3 Days Rest	12.46	0	1	0	1	1	4.1	9	1	2	5
4 Days Rest	3.38	49	21	0	97	97	682.0	634	33	196	537
5+ Days Rest	3.64	20	18	0	45	45	302.0	298	16	100	246
Pre-All Star	3.64	42	28	0	89	89	614.0	570	35	193	495
Post-All Star	3.23	27	12	1	56	54	381.1	376	15	107	299

	Avg	AB	H	2B	3B	HR	RBI	BB	SO	OBP	SLG
None on	.248	2168	538	96	15	25	25	178	446	.309	.341
Runners on	.255	1599	408	69	10	25	352	122	348	.307	.358
Scoring Posn	.250	1014	253	42	5	14	314	98	247	.312	.342
Close & Late	.236	318	75	5	0	6	33	22	62	.284	.308
None on/out	.264	961	254	53	5	13	13	72	181	.319	.370
vs. 1st Batr (relief)	.500	2	1	0	0	0	0	0	0	.500	.500
First Inning Pitched	.229	537	123	26	5	5	52	47	115	.294	.324
First 75 Pitches	.249	2631	655	126	21	33	248	203	555	.305	.350
Pitch 76-90	.274	475	130	18	1	8	53	41	100	.332	.366
Pitch 91-105	.221	399	88	14	2	5	41	29	81	.271	.303
Pitch 106+	.279	262	73	7	1	4	35	27	58	.344	.359
First Pitch	.311	614	191	29	7	13	82	15	0	.329	.445
Ahead on Count	.204	1750	357	63	13	12	129	0	673	.209	.275
Behind on Count	.318	735	234	42	5	16	100	124	0	.416	.454
Two Strikes	.178	1767	314	62	10	13	130	161	793	.249	.246

Pitcher vs. Batter (career)

Pitches Best Vs.	Avg	AB	H	2B	3B	HR	RBI	BB	SO	OBP	SLG
Chico Walker	.063	16	1	0	0	0	0	1	1	.118	.063
Gary Redus	.067	15	1	1	0	0	1	1	5	.118	.133
Jose Oquendo	.077	26	2	0	0	0	0	1	3	.111	.077
Tony Fernandez	.118	17	2	0	0	0	0	1	4	.167	.118
Tony Pena	.128	39	5	0	1	0	3	0	14	.128	.179

Pitches Worst Vs.	Avg	AB	H	2B	3B	HR	RBI	BB	SO	OBP	SLG
Tom Pagnozzi	.565	23	13	2	0	0	4	0	1	.565	.652
Randy Ready	.500	12	6	1	1	0	0	1	2	.538	.750
Ray Lankford	.421	19	8	1	0	1	4	4	3	.522	.632
Chris Sabo	.400	20	8	3	1	0	2	2	2	.455	.650
Lloyd McClendon	.333	9	3	0	0	0	1	2	0	.455	.667

Tom Goodwin — Dodgers
Bats Left

	Avg	G	AB	R	H	2B	3B	HR	RBI	BB	SO	HBP	GDP	SB	CS	OBP	SLG	IBB	SH	SF	#Pit	#P/PA	GB	FB	G/F
1992 Season	.233	57	73	15	17	1	1	0	3	6	10	0	0	7	3	.291	.274	0	0	0	278	3.52	25	16	1.56
Career (1991-1992)	.225	73	80	18	18	1	1	0	3	6	10	0	0	8	4	.279	.263	0	0	0	303	3.52	27	21	1.29

1992 Season

	Avg	AB	H	2B	3B	HR	RBI	BB	SO	OBP	SLG
vs. Left	.250	8	2	0	0	0	0	0	1	.250	.250
vs. Right	.231	65	15	1	1	0	3	6	9	.296	.277

	Avg	AB	H	2B	3B	HR	RBI	BB	SO	OBP	SLG
Scoring Posn	.150	20	3	1	0	0	3	1	2	.190	.200
Close & Late	.150	20	3	1	0	0	1	2	3	.227	.200

Tom Gordon — Royals
Pitches Right

	ERA	W	L	Sv	G	GS	IP	BB	SO	Avg	H	2B	3B	HR	RBI	OBP	SLG	GF	IR	IRS	Hld	SvOp	SB	CS	GB	FB	G/F
1992 Season	4.59	6	10	0	40	11	117.2	55	98	.258	116	23	2	9	63	.340	.379	13	19	5	0	2	5	7	164	119	1.38
Career (1988-1992)	3.93	44	46	2	171	75	649.2	334	611	.238	575	91	21	53	288	.331	.358	24	71	27	9	13	34	29	829	626	1.32

1992 Season

	ERA	W	L	Sv	G	GS	IP	H	HR	BB	SO
Home	3.36	5	4	0	22	5	59.0	54	2	28	44
Away	5.83	1	6	0	18	6	58.2	62	7	27	54
Starter	6.08	0	5	0	11	11	50.1	60	4	27	35
Reliever	3.48	6	5	0	29	0	67.1	56	5	28	63
0 Days rest	0.00	0	0	0	0	0	0.0	0	0	0	0
1 or 2 Days rest	3.89	4	2	0	16	0	37.0	39	3	13	35
3+ Days rest	2.97	2	3	0	13	0	30.1	17	2	15	28
Pre-All Star	5.23	2	9	0	22	9	74.0	80	8	28	52
Post-All Star	3.50	4	1	0	18	2	43.2	36	1	27	46

	Avg	AB	H	2B	3B	HR	RBI	BB	SO	OBP	SLG
vs. Left	.287	202	58	10	1	3	27	22	45	.352	.391
vs. Right	.235	247	58	13	1	6	36	33	53	.331	.368
Scoring Posn	.289	128	37	5	1	1	48	15	24	.353	.367
Close & Late	.316	57	18	6	0	2	10	8	18	.418	.526
None on/out	.208	106	22	2	1	2	2	14	23	.306	.302
First Pitch	.308	52	16	0	0	1	8	3	0	.351	.365
Behind on Count	.310	100	31	6	0	3	18	35	0	.478	.460
Ahead on Count	.220	200	44	10	1	2	22	0	72	.227	.310
Two Strikes	.152	224	34	8	2	2	18	17	98	.211	.232

Career (1988-1992)

	ERA	W	L	Sv	G	GS	IP	H	HR	BB	SO
Home	3.56	25	23	1	90	39	349.1	297	19	166	319
Away	4.36	19	23	1	81	36	300.1	278	34	168	292
Day	3.23	13	15	0	45	21	181.0	161	16	77	171
Night	4.21	31	31	2	126	54	468.2	414	37	257	440
Grass	4.96	10	18	1	59	26	208.2	214	29	117	205
Turf	3.45	34	28	1	112	49	441.0	361	24	217	406
April	2.52	6	4	0	23	9	89.1	76	7	33	97
May	4.27	5	9	0	27	15	109.2	88	8	60	90
June	4.38	8	6	0	27	10	88.1	84	9	50	91
July	4.32	7	10	0	27	12	110.1	107	11	67	102
August	2.45	13	5	1	25	13	128.1	98	9	48	123
September/October	5.53	5	12	0	42	16	123.2	122	9	76	108
Starter	4.36	24	32	0	75	75	441.2	425	41	232	383
Reliever	3.03	20	14	2	96	0	208.0	150	12	102	228
0 Days rest	1.71	2	1	0	10	0	21.0	11	1	6	28
1 or 2 Days rest	3.49	9	6	1	44	0	90.1	79	7	46	93
3+ Days rest	2.89	9	7	1	42	0	96.2	60	4	50	107
Pre-All Star	3.92	21	24	1	87	37	323.1	280	27	167	312

	Avg	AB	H	2B	3B	HR	RBI	BB	SO	OBP	SLG
vs. Left	.248	1204	299	42	10	17	130	169	274	.340	.342
vs. Right	.227	1217	276	49	11	36	158	165	337	.322	.374
Inning 1-6	.244	1653	404	63	18	39	211	236	391	.339	.375
Inning 7+	.223	768	171	28	3	14	77	98	220	.314	.322
None on	.238	1333	317	53	12	33	33	176	334	.328	.370
Runners on	.237	1088	258	38	9	20	255	158	277	.334	.344
Scoring Posn	.252	642	162	27	8	13	231	94	170	.346	.380
Close & Late	.246	370	91	15	2	5	38	50	111	.342	.338
None on/out	.231	593	137	20	6	15	15	74	151	.318	.361
vs. 1st Batr (relief)	.165	79	13	5	1	0	13	15	21	.305	.253
First Inning Pitched	.209	583	122	23	4	7	87	98	176	.322	.298
First 15 Pitches	.201	478	96	19	4	6	49	75	130	.309	.295
Pitch 16-30	.224	495	111	13	2	10	63	78	150	.331	.319
Pitch 31-45	.272	382	104	16	2	4	52	62	101	.376	.356
Pitch 46+	.248	1066	264	43	13	33	124	119	230	.324	.405
First Pitch	.334	305	102	11	4	9	63	12	0	.360	.485
Ahead on Count	.181	1166	211	31	7	18	85	0	486	.185	.266
Behind on Count	.306	500	153	28	5	16	84	219	0	.514	.478

Career (1988-1992)

	ERA	W	L	Sv	G	GS	IP	H	HR	BB	SO		Avg	AB	H	2B	3B	HR	RBI	BB	SO	OBP	SLG
Post-All Star	3.94	23	22	1	84	38	326.1	295	26	167	299	Two Strikes	.145	1214	176	29	7	15	70	103	611	.214	.217

Pitcher vs. Batter (career)

Pitches Best Vs.	Avg	AB	H	2B	3B	HR	RBI	BB	SO	OBP	SLG	Pitches Worst Vs.	Avg	AB	H	2B	3B	HR	RBI	BB	SO	OBP	SLG
Roberto Kelly	.000	13	0	0	0	0	1	0	6	.000	.000	Ozzie Guillen	.615	13	8	1	0	0	3	1	0	.643	.692
Dave Henderson	.000	12	0	0	0	0	0	1	9	.077	.000	Alan Trammell	.455	11	5	0	0	2	3	1	1	.571	1.000
Robin Ventura	.000	12	0	0	0	0	0	2	4	.143	.000	Kevin Reimer	.444	9	4	2	0	1	2	2	4	.545	1.000
Dave Valle	.000	10	0	0	0	0	0	2	6	.167	.000	Juan Gonzalez	.438	16	7	2	2	1	3	0	2	.438	1.000
Mel Hall	.071	14	1	0	0	0	1	0	5	.067	.071	Carlton Fisk	.385	13	5	1	0	2	4	3	3	.500	.923

Goose Gossage — Athletics
Pitches Right

	ERA	W	L	Sv	G	GS	IP	BB	SO	Avg	H	2B	3B	HR	RBI	OBP	SLG	GF	IR	IRS	Hld	SvOp	SB	CS	GB	FB	G/F
1992 Season	2.84	0	2	0	30	0	38.0	19	26	.230	32	2	0	5	14	.327	.353	13	13	2	5	1	4	2	44	51	0.86
Last Five Years	3.40	11	9	19	162	0	180.0	80	114	.245	161	27	3	14	97	.332	.359	29	136	50	15	35	19	13	222	214	1.04

1992 Season

	ERA	W	L	Sv	G	GS	IP	H	HR	BB	SO		Avg	AB	H	2B	3B	HR	RBI	BB	SO	OBP	SLG
Home	3.10	0	0	0	15	0	20.1	18	4	12	17	vs. Left	.286	56	16	1	0	1	2	7	8	.365	.357
Away	2.55	0	2	0	15	0	17.2	14	1	7	9	vs. Right	.193	83	16	1	0	4	12	12	18	.303	.349
Starter	0.00	0	0	0	0	0	0.0	0	0	0	0	Scoring Posn	.229	35	8	0	0	1	10	5	7	.310	.314
Reliever	2.84	0	2	0	30	0	38.0	32	5	19	26	Close & Late	.224	58	13	1	0	4	8	13	14	.370	.448
0 Days rest	3.86	0	0	0	5	0	7.0	7	2	1	4	None on/out	.355	31	11	2	0	2	2	5	4	.474	.613
1 or 2 Days rest	1.69	0	1	0	11	0	16.0	11	2	7	9	First Pitch	.450	20	9	1	0	0	1	3	0	.542	.500
3+ Days rest	3.60	0	1	0	14	0	15.0	14	1	11	13	Behind on Count	.276	29	8	0	0	4	8	9	0	.436	.690
Pre-All Star	2.80	0	2	0	28	0	35.1	29	4	18	24	Ahead on Count	.169	65	11	1	0	0	3	0	24	.179	.185
Post-All Star	3.38	0	0	0	2	0	2.2	3	1	1	2	Two Strikes	.143	63	9	1	0	1	2	7	26	.236	.206

Last Five Years

	ERA	W	L	Sv	G	GS	IP	H	HR	BB	SO		Avg	AB	H	2B	3B	HR	RBI	BB	SO	OBP	SLG
Home	2.77	5	4	11	75	0	81.1	76	8	31	58	vs. Left	.254	284	72	14	2	3	32	40	40	.344	.349
Away	3.92	6	5	8	87	0	98.2	85	6	49	56	vs. Right	.238	374	89	13	1	11	65	40	74	.324	.366
Day	3.98	3	4	7	54	0	61.0	65	4	22	42	Inning 1-6	.356	45	16	3	1	1	17	8	5	.444	.533
Night	3.10	8	5	12	108	0	119.0	96	10	58	72	Inning 7+	.237	613	145	24	2	13	80	72	109	.324	.346
Grass	2.91	8	6	14	136.0	0	136.0	116	12	56	94	None on	.234	321	75	15	1	6	6	37	58	.324	.343
Turf	4.91	3	3	5	41	0	44.0	45	2	24	20	Runners on	.255	337	86	12	2	8	91	43	56	.340	.374
April	2.00	3	2	2	29	0	36.0	24	3	20	25	Scoring Posn	.273	198	54	6	1	4	81	36	32	.384	.374
May	3.06	2	0	6	34	0	35.1	27	3	19	33	Close & Late	.246	224	55	10	0	7	45	39	47	.370	.384
June	3.40	2	2	4	32	0	39.2	37	2	14	20	None on/out	.287	136	39	4	0	4	17	24	.382	.426
July	4.41	0	2	3	29	0	32.2	34	4	16	19	vs. 1st Batr (relief)	.278	115	32	6	0	5	19	10	25	.362	.461
August	7.13	1	1	3	18	0	17.2	21	2	5	9	First Inning Pitched	.264	398	105	19	3	10	70	42	72	.344	.402
September/October	1.45	3	2	1	20	0	18.2	18	0	6	8	First 15 Pitches	.277	451	125	22	3	12	77	53	75	.362	.419
Starter	0.00	0	0	0	0	0	0.0	0	0	0	0	Pitch 16-30	.190	179	34	5	0	2	18	22	34	.278	.251
Reliever	3.40	11	9	19	162	0	180.0	161	14	80	114	Pitch 31-45	.077	26	2	0	0	0	2	5	5	.226	.077
0 Days rest	5.56	3	1	2	21	0	22.2	23	3	10	10	Pitch 46+	.000	2	0	0	0	0	0	0	0	.000	.000
1 or 2 Days rest	3.34	6	4	12	80	0	89.0	79	8	40	61	First Pitch	.323	96	31	2	0	3	16	8	0	.381	.438
3+ Days rest	2.77	2	4	5	61	0	68.1	59	3	30	43	Ahead on Count	.203	306	62	10	0	2	28	0	106	.208	.255
Pre-All Star	2.91	7	5	12	102	0	120.2	96	8	57	86	Behind on Count	.276	145	40	10	2	7	36	40	0	.434	.517
Post-All Star	4.40	4	4	7	60	0	59.1	65	6	23	28	Two Strikes	.179	291	52	9	0	1	23	32	114	.267	.220

Pitcher vs. Batter (since 1984)

Pitches Best Vs.	Avg	AB	H	2B	3B	HR	RBI	BB	SO	OBP	SLG	Pitches Worst Vs.	Avg	AB	H	2B	3B	HR	RBI	BB	SO	OBP	SLG
Denny Walling	.000	10	0	0	0	0	0	1	0	.091	.000	Kevin Bass	.727	11	8	1	0	0	3	0	1	.727	.818
Franklin Stubbs	.000	10	0	0	0	0	0	2	5	.167	.000	Andy Van Slyke	.545	11	6	0	0	1	4	0	1	.545	.818
Gerald Perry	.100	10	1	0	0	0	2	0	2	.091	.100	Mike Fitzgerald	.500	10	5	0	0	0	1	1	0	.545	.500
Dale Murphy	.130	23	3	0	0	1	6	0	6	.130	.261	Lenny Dykstra	.417	12	5	0	1	0	3	0	0	.417	.583
Chili Davis	.182	11	2	0	0	0	1	1	4	.250	.182	Hubie Brooks	.400	15	6	0	0	1	4	0	5	.400	.600

Jim Gott — Dodgers
Pitches Right (groundball pitcher)

	ERA	W	L	Sv	G	GS	IP	BB	SO	Avg	H	2B	3B	HR	RBI	OBP	SLG	GF	IR	IRS	Hld	SvOp	SB	CS	GB	FB	G/F
1992 Season	2.45	3	3	6	68	0	88.0	41	75	.225	72	6	1	4	26	.314	.288	28	38	12	11	7	6	5	135	53	2.55
Last Five Years	2.93	16	17	45	241	0	304.0	130	269	.236	263	30	6	23	111	.316	.335	76	153	45	22	57	19	10	425	256	1.66

1992 Season

	ERA	W	L	Sv	G	GS	IP	H	HR	BB	SO		Avg	AB	H	2B	3B	HR	RBI	BB	SO	OBP	SLG
Home	1.79	1	1	2	31	0	40.1	33	1	15	39	vs. Left	.264	148	39	4	1	3	17	28	39	.382	.365
Away	3.02	2	2	4	37	0	47.2	39	3	26	36	vs. Right	.192	172	33	2	0	1	9	13	36	.249	.221
Day	2.00	0	0	2	19	0	27.0	26	2	13	18	Inning 1-6	.222	36	8	0	0	2	4	5	.300	.306
Night	2.66	3	3	4	49	0	61.0	46	2	28	57	Inning 7+	.225	284	64	6	1	3	24	37	70	.316	.306
Grass	2.22	2	1	5	51	0	69.0	53	3	31	58	None on	.250	160	40	4	0	3	3	18	39	.326	.331
Turf	3.32	1	2	1	17	0	19.0	19	1	10	17	Runners on	.200	160	32	2	1	1	23	23	36	.303	.244
April	1.32	0	1	2	13	0	13.2	13	0	4	12	Scoring Posn	.185	92	17	1	1	0	20	20	21	.327	.217
May	2.70	0	0	0	7	0	10.0	6	0	4	12	Close & Late	.200	165	33	4	1	3	16	25	41	.309	.291

163

1992 Season

	ERA	W	L	Sv	G	GS	IP	H	HR	BB	SO
June	1.80	1	1	0	14	0	20.0	15	1	10	16
July	2.12	0	0	2	13	0	17.0	14	1	7	14
August	0.90	1	0	2	14	0	20.0	10	1	10	14
September/October	11.05	1	1	0	7	0	7.1	14	1	6	7
Starter	0.00	0	0	0	0	0	0.0	0	0	0	0
Reliever	2.45	3	3	6	68	0	88.0	72	4	41	75
0 Days rest	1.53	1	0	2	15	0	17.2	12	1	10	13
1 or 2 Days rest	2.55	2	3	3	40	0	53.0	41	2	22	49
3+ Days rest	3.12	0	0	1	13	0	17.1	19	1	9	13
Pre-All Star	1.94	1	2	3	39	0	51.0	39	2	21	47
Post-All Star	3.16	2	1	3	29	0	37.0	33	2	20	28

	Avg	AB	H	2B	3B	HR	RBI	BB	SO	OBP	SLG
None on/out	.333	75	25	4	0	3	11		14	.419	.507
vs. 1st Batr (relief)	.295	61	18	3	0	1	4	7	10	.368	.393
First Inning Pitched	.235	217	51	5	1	1	22	32	51	.332	.281
First 15 Pitches	.238	206	49	5	1	1	20	30	47	.333	.286
Pitch 16-30	.220	100	22	1	0	3	6	10	26	.297	.320
Pitch 31-45	.000	10	0	0	0	0	0	1	2	.091	.000
Pitch 46+	.250	4	1	0	0	0	0	0	0	.250	.250
First Pitch	.154	39	6	1	0	1	4	12	0	.346	.256
Ahead on Count	.198	172	34	1	0	2	11	0	66	.198	.238
Behind on Count	.271	59	16	1	0	1	5	15	0	.427	.339
Two Strikes	.194	170	33	1	0	2	10	14	75	.255	.235

Last Five Years

	ERA	W	L	Sv	G	GS	IP	H	HR	BB	SO
Home	2.30	8	6	21	117	0	152.1	107	9	69	143
Away	3.56	8	11	24	124	0	151.2	156	14	61	126
Day	3.05	4	3	13	63	0	82.2	86	8	40	70
Night	2.89	12	14	32	178	0	221.1	177	15	90	199
Grass	2.92	7	11	15	142	0	185.0	161	13	93	156
Turf	2.95	9	6	30	99	0	119.0	102	10	37	113
April	2.23	1	1	5	29	0	36.1	28	2	12	31
May	2.35	1	1	4	29	0	38.1	31	1	15	36
June	3.93	4	6	3	44	0	50.1	51	6	31	48
July	1.90	1	2	10	43	0	52.0	43	2	22	37
August	2.48	6	3	13	50	0	72.2	48	9	28	62
September/October	4.47	3	4	10	46	0	54.1	62	3	22	55
Starter	0.00	0	0	0	0	0	0.0	0	0	0	0
Reliever	2.93	16	17	45	241	0	304.0	263	23	130	269
0 Days rest	2.10	5	1	15	62	0	73.0	49	7	35	63
1 or 2 Days rest	2.84	6	12	23	120	0	152.1	140	9	53	139
3+ Days rest	3.89	5	4	7	59	0	78.2	74	7	42	67
Pre-All Star	2.83	6	10	15	118	0	143.0	125	10	68	129
Post-All Star	3.02	10	7	30	123	0	161.0	138	13	62	140

	Avg	AB	H	2B	3B	HR	RBI	BB	SO	OBP	SLG
vs. Left	.241	553	133	15	5	12	50	78	130	.335	.351
vs. Right	.231	562	130	15	1	11	61	52	139	.296	.320
Inning 1-6	.185	108	20	1	0	4	10	16	25	.286	.306
Inning 7+	.241	1007	243	29	6	19	101	114	244	.319	.339
None on	.234	623	146	17	2	14	53		150	.296	.335
Runners on	.238	492	117	13	4	9	97	77	119	.338	.335
Scoring Posn	.206	311	64	5	4	4	83	62	80	.332	.286
Close & Late	.241	453	109	13	3	10	58	64	112	.337	.349
None on/out	.272	265	72	12	0	7	7	29	56	.346	.396
vs. 1st Batr (relief)	.270	215	58	9	0	3	23	21	44	.332	.353
First Inning Pitched	.235	786	185	22	5	15	92	102	195	.323	.333
First 15 Pitches	.247	726	179	25	3	14	78	81	171	.321	.347
Pitch 16-30	.207	324	67	4	2	7	26	45	88	.305	.296
Pitch 31-45	.273	55	15	1	1	2	7	4	9	.322	.436
Pitch 46+	.200	10	2	0	0	0	0	0	1	.200	.200
First Pitch	.279	136	38	5	2	3	20	25	0	.390	.412
Ahead on Count	.168	565	95	6	2	7	31	0	242	.169	.223
Behind on Count	.352	233	82	15	0	7	35	51	0	.466	.506
Two Strikes	.153	554	85	5	3	6	24	54	269	.230	.206

Pitcher vs. Batter (since 1984)

Pitches Best Vs.	Avg	AB	H	2B	3B	HR	RBI	BB	SO	OBP	SLG
Kevin Mitchell	.000	10	0	0	0	0	0	1	2	.091	.000
Casey Candaele	.071	14	1	0	0	0	0	3	2	.235	.071
Darryl Strawberry	.077	13	1	0	0	0	1	3	5	.250	.077
Mariano Duncan	.077	13	1	0	0	0	1	1	2	.133	.077
Ozzie Smith	.154	13	2	0	0	0	1	0	1	.143	.154

Pitches Worst Vs.	Avg	AB	H	2B	3B	HR	RBI	BB	SO	OBP	SLG
Rafael Ramirez	.529	17	9	2	0	0	1	0	0	.529	.647
Mark Grace	.500	10	5	1	0	0	0	1	0	.545	.600
Juan Samuel	.455	11	5	1	0	1	3	0	2	.455	.818
Vince Coleman	.455	11	5	0	1	0	1	0	2	.455	.636
Eric Davis	.357	14	5	0	0	2	4	3	5	.471	.929

Mauro Gozzo — Twins
Pitches Right (groundball pitcher)

	ERA	W	L	Sv	G	GS	IP	BB	SO	Avg	H	2B	3B	HR	RBI	OBP	SLG	GF	IR	IRS	Hld	SvOp	SB	CS	GB	FB	G/F
1992 Season	27.00	0	0	0	2	0	1.2	0	1	.583	7	2	0	2	6	.583	1.250	0	1	1	0	0	0	0	2	3	0.67
Career (1989-1992)	7.02	4	1	0	15	5	41.0	18	16	.323	53	16	1	3	27	.387	.488	1	4	2	1	1	2	0	73	39	1.87

1992 Season

	ERA	W	L	Sv	G	GS	IP	H	HR	BB	SO		Avg	AB	H	2B	3B	HR	RBI	BB	SO	OBP	SLG
Home	45.00	0	0	0	1	0	1.0	5	2	0	1	vs. Left	.667	6	4	1	0	1	3	0	0	.667	1.333
Away	0.00	0	0	0	1	0	0.2	2	0	0	0	vs. Right	.500	6	3	1	0	1	3	0	1	.500	1.167

Mark Grace — Cubs
Bats Left (groundball hitter)

	Avg	G	AB	R	H	2B	3B	HR	RBI	BB	SO	HBP	GDP	SB	CS	OBP	SLG	IBB	SH	SF	#Pit	#P/PA	GB	FB	G/F
1992 Season	.307	158	603	72	185	37	5	9	79	72	36	4	14	6	1	.380	.430	8	2	8	2385	3.47	234	180	1.30
Career (1988-1992)	.299	751	2807	370	840	146	18	46	355	341	228	12	54	41	21	.374	.414	38	10	30	10962	3.44	1160	750	1.55

1992 Season

	Avg	AB	H	2B	3B	HR	RBI	BB	SO	OBP	SLG
vs. Left	.280	225	63	11	1	3	29	17	19	.329	.378
vs. Right	.323	378	122	26	4	6	50	55	17	.409	.460
Groundball	.345	232	80	20	2	2	40	25	10	.409	.474
Flyball	.285	151	43	10	1	2	17	22	9	.371	.404
Home	.281	285	80	17	0	5	40	45	18	.373	.393
Away	.330	318	105	20	5	4	39	27	18	.387	.462
Day	.296	314	93	19	3	8	45	45	18	.381	.452
Night	.318	289	92	18	2	1	34	27	18	.379	.405
Grass	.287	418	120	22	3	6	54	56	31	.369	.397
Turf	.351	185	65	15	2	3	25	16	5	.407	.503
First Pitch	.327	104	34	5	0	2	18	7	0	.360	.433
Ahead on Count	.353	170	60	15	3	3	21	41	0	.474	.529

	Avg	AB	H	2B	3B	HR	RBI	BB	SO	OBP	SLG
Scoring Posn	.326	138	45	14	1	1	65	24	13	.413	.464
Close & Late	.343	108	37	1	1	2	18	16	6	.430	.426
None on/out	.248	117	29	6	1	3	16	7	3	.338	.393
Batting #3	.292	428	125	27	4	7	54	47	31	.361	.423
Batting #5	.396	101	40	7	0	2	11	14	2	.470	.525
Other	.270	74	20	3	1	0	14	11	3	.365	.338
April	.224	67	15	4	1	2	8	15	1	.366	.403
May	.324	105	34	7	3	2	20	19	8	.423	.505
June	.404	94	38	6	0	0	9	9	2	.457	.468
July	.277	94	26	5	1	1	9	13	7	.373	.383
August	.281	121	34	4	0	4	16	9	9	.333	.413
September/October	.311	122	38	11	0	0	17	8	8	.341	.402

1992 Season

	Avg	AB	H	2B	3B	HR	RBI	BB	SO	OBP	SLG		Avg	AB	H	2B	3B	HR	RBI	BB	SO	OBP	SLG
Behind on Count	.263	179	47	13	3	0	20	0	18	.269	.369	Pre-All Star	.313	310	97	18	4	5	42	50	17	.409	.445
Two Strikes	.263	194	51	7	2	3	22	25	36	.351	.366	Post-All Star	.300	293	88	19	1	4	37	22	19	.348	.413

1992 By Position

Position	Avg	AB	H	2B	3B	HR	RBI	BB	SO	OBP	SLG	G	GS	Innings	PO	A	E	DP	Fld Pct	Rng Fctr	In Zone	Outs	Zone Rtg	MLB Zone
As 1b	.307	602	185	37	5	9	79	72	36	.380	.430	157	157	1414.0	1578	141	4	120	.998	---	347	309	.890	.843

Career (1988-1992)

	Avg	AB	H	2B	3B	HR	RBI	BB	SO	OBP	SLG		Avg	AB	H	2B	3B	HR	RBI	BB	SO	OBP	SLG
vs. Left	.281	968	272	45	9	15	129	99	113	.348	.393	Scoring Posn	.299	712	213	41	7	8	296	127	60	.395	.410
vs. Right	.309	1839	568	103	9	31	226	242	115	.387	.425	Close & Late	.309	466	144	15	2	7	58	78	34	.410	.395
Groundball	.306	1003	307	56	6	12	133	122	64	.379	.410	None on/out	.295	584	172	26	2	14	14	51	47	.352	.418
Flyball	.285	681	194	35	4	9	76	81	65	.361	.388	Batting #2	.294	425	125	18	5	6	36	45	34	.361	.402
Home	.306	1423	436	75	5	22	186	194	107	.388	.413	Batting #3	.294	1545	454	90	7	26	208	173	132	.364	.412
Away	.292	1384	404	73	13	24	169	147	121	.359	.415	Other	.312	637	261	40	6	14	111	123	62	.399	.424
Day	.301	1522	458	80	8	29	199	205	123	.383	.421	April	.271	284	77	16	2	5	35	50	17	.381	.394
Night	.297	1285	382	68	10	17	156	136	105	.363	.405	May	.299	518	155	27	4	8	64	52	48	.363	.413
Grass	.300	2014	605	103	10	30	254	247	169	.375	.406	June	.317	426	135	19	4	3	48	52	30	.389	.401
Turf	.296	793	235	45	8	16	101	94	59	.372	.434	July	.289	463	134	27	2	10	56	60	32	.370	.421
First Pitch	.331	583	193	29	6	10	88	22	0	.354	.453	August	.319	567	181	27	4	15	80	58	54	.382	.460
Ahead on Count	.332	756	251	50	6	14	114	198	0	.467	.470	September/October	.288	549	158	32	2	5	72	69	47	.364	.381
Behind on Count	.284	782	222	41	8	11	92	1	106	.284	.399	Pre-All Star	.297	1387	412	71	11	21	169	174	109	.374	.410
Two Strikes	.243	949	231	40	5	16	92	115	228	.324	.347	Post-All Star	.301	1420	428	77	7	25	186	167	119	.374	.418

Batter vs. Pitcher (career)

Hits Best Against	Avg	AB	H	2B	3B	HR	RBI	BB	SO	OBP	SLG	Hits Worst Against	Avg	AB	H	2B	3B	HR	RBI	BB	SO	OBP	SLG
Cris Carpenter	.583	12	7	1	0	0	1	1	0	.615	.667	Vince Palacios	.000	8	0	0	0	0	0	3	1	.273	.000
Joe Boever	.556	9	5	1	0	0	4	4	1	.692	.667	Ron Darling	.042	24	1	1	0	0	2	4	1	.179	.083
Craig Lefferts	.500	10	5	2	0	0	1	3	0	.615	.700	Mitch Williams	.083	12	1	0	0	0	0	0	2	.083	.083
Mike Maddux	.474	19	9	1	0	1	5	2	2	.524	.684	Jimmy Jones	.083	12	1	0	0	0	1	2	0	.294	.083
Randy Myers	.429	14	6	0	2	1	6	1	3	.467	.929	Juan Agosto	.143	14	2	0	0	0	2	0	1	.143	.143

Joe Grahe — Angels   Pitches Right (groundball pitcher)

	ERA	W	L	Sv	G	GS	IP	BB	SO	Avg	H	2B	3B	HR	RBI	OBP	SLG	GF	IR	IRS	Hld	SvOp	SB	CS	GB	FB	G/F
1992 Season	3.52	5	6	21	46	7	94.2	39	39	.246	85	12	0	5	37	.329	.324	31	18	3	1	24	7	5	175	77	2.27
Career (1990-1992)	4.27	11	17	21	72	25	211.0	95	104	.271	220	44	5	10	104	.354	.374	33	25	6	2	24	19	11	378	180	2.10

1992 Season

	ERA	W	L	Sv	G	GS	IP	H	HR	BB	SO		Avg	AB	H	2B	3B	HR	RBI	BB	SO	OBP	SLG
Home	3.94	2	4	14	24	3	45.2	40	4	22	17	vs. Left	.287	157	45	5	0	1	14	16	16	.365	.338
Away	3.12	3	2	7	22	4	49.0	45	1	17	22	vs. Right	.212	189	40	7	0	4	23	23	23	.300	.312
Starter	5.90	2	3	0	7	7	39.2	45	3	22	17	Scoring Posn	.247	89	22	4	0	2	32	14	14	.355	.360
Reliever	1.80	3	3	21	39	0	55.0	40	2	17	22	Close & Late	.200	150	30	3	0	2	19	15	15	.294	.260
0 Days rest	2.16	0	1	6	7	0	8.1	6	0	8	3	None on/out	.220	82	18	4	0	0	0	11	10	.319	.268
1 or 2 Days rest	1.13	2	1	11	19	0	32.0	21	2	8	13	First Pitch	.286	49	14	2	0	1	8	1	0	.314	.388
3+ Days rest	3.07	1	1	4	13	0	14.2	13	0	1	6	Behind on Count	.272	81	22	2	0	1	8	23	0	.434	.333
Pre-All Star	4.40	2	3	4	17	7	57.1	55	4	24	30	Ahead on Count	.201	154	31	2	0	2	16	0	35	.217	.253
Post-All Star	2.17	3	3	17	29	0	37.1	30	1	15	9	Two Strikes	.206	141	29	5	0	2	13	15	39	.290	.284

Mark Grant — Mariners   Pitches Right

	ERA	W	L	Sv	G	GS	IP	BB	SO	Avg	H	2B	3B	HR	RBI	OBP	SLG	GF	IR	IRS	Hld	SvOp	SB	CS	GB	FB	G/F
1992 Season	3.89	2	4	0	23	10	81.0	22	42	.311	100	22	1	6	31	.357	.441	4	7	1	2	0	4	2	106	100	1.06
Last Five Years	3.87	14	17	5	165	22	386.1	127	241	.279	410	81	7	40	189	.337	.425	25	112	50	8	10	27	16	551	410	1.34

1992 Season

	ERA	W	L	Sv	G	GS	IP	H	HR	BB	SO		Avg	AB	H	2B	3B	HR	RBI	BB	SO	OBP	SLG
Home	3.29	1	3	0	12	4	38.1	52	2	7	24	vs. Left	.336	149	50	9	0	3	13	11	17	.385	.456
Away	4.43	1	1	0	11	6	42.2	48	4	15	18	vs. Right	.289	173	50	13	1	3	18	11	25	.333	.428
Starter	4.60	2	4	0	10	10	58.2	80	4	18	27	Scoring Posn	.225	80	18	5	0	1	20	7	6	.284	.325
Reliever	2.01	0	0	0	13	0	22.1	20	2	4	15	Close & Late	.522	23	12	1	0	2	3	0	4	.522	.826
0 Days rest	0.00	0	0	0	0	0	0.0	0	0	0	0	None on/out	.353	85	30	6	0	1	1	4	14	.389	.459
1 or 2 Days rest	3.12	0	0	0	4	0	8.2	7	2	3	7	First Pitch	.278	54	15	4	0	2	6	2	0	.304	.463
3+ Days rest	1.32	0	0	0	9	0	13.2	13	0	1	8	Behind on Count	.344	96	33	7	1	1	11	14	0	.429	.469
Pre-All Star	3.91	0	1	0	7	3	23.0	25	3	9	12	Ahead on Count	.269	119	32	7	0	1	10	0	35	.275	.353
Post-All Star	3.88	2	3	0	16	7	58.0	75	3	13	30	Two Strikes	.273	121	33	6	0	1	6	6	42	.313	.347

Last Five Years

	ERA	W	L	Sv	G	GS	IP	H	HR	BB	SO		Avg	AB	H	2B	3B	HR	RBI	BB	SO	OBP	SLG
Home	4.53	6	8	4	84	10	179.0	195	26	66	122	vs. Left	.263	729	206	41	5	14	81	68	112	.344	.410
Away	3.30	8	9	1	81	12	207.1	215	14	61	119	vs. Right	.275	741	204	40	2	26	108	59	129	.330	.440
Day	3.63	3	5	2	54	8	151.1	149	18	47	93	Inning 1-6	.267	854	245	45	4	28	132	76	130	.345	.447
Night	4.02	11	12	3	111	14	235.0	261	22	80	148	Inning 7+	.268	616	165	36	3	12	57	51	111	.326	.394

Last Five Years

	ERA	W	L	Sv	G	GS	IP	H	HR	BB	SO		Avg	AB	H	2B	3B	HR	RBI	BB	SO	OBP	SLG
Grass	4.19	9	10	5	116	15	264.1	265	34	99	166	None on	.280	811	227	45	3	20	20	62	142	.334	.417
Turf	3.17	5	7	0	49	7	122.0	145	6	28	75	Runners on	.278	659	183	36	4	20	169	65	99	.341	.436
April	5.56	0	3	0	20	3	43.2	47	9	17	27	Scoring Posn	.245	379	93	21	2	8	134	53	65	.330	.375
May	2.37	3	2	0	19	5	57.0	48	3	23	36	Close & Late	.309	188	58	9	0	7	24	23	33	.393	.468
June	4.26	1	3	0	27	3	57.0	61	9	19	41	None on/out	.302	367	111	20	1	8	8	22	60	.347	.428
July	3.98	4	4	0	33	6	81.1	95	7	30	41	vs. 1st Batr (relief)	.238	130	31	7	1	4	24	8	21	.282	.400
August	4.41	3	4	2	31	4	69.1	83	7	23	42	First Inning Pitched	.288	591	170	37	5	20	108	48	105	.338	.469
September/October	3.12	3	1	3	35	1	78.0	76	5	15	54	First 15 Pitches	.288	563	162	36	5	19	82	44	86	.337	.471
Starter	4.60	3	9	0	22	22	125.1	145	16	49	70	Pitch 16-30	.278	407	113	19	0	10	51	26	77	.324	.398
Reliever	3.52	11	8	5	143	0	261.0	265	24	78	171	Pitch 31-45	.268	205	55	16	2	4	26	24	35	.346	.424
0 Days rest	3.37	2	1	1	18	0	34.2	37	2	12	27	Pitch 46+	.271	295	80	10	0	7	30	31	43	.348	.376
1 or 2 Days rest	4.86	3	5	4	65	0	111.0	123	15	40	72	First Pitch	.290	255	74	19	3	6	28	21	0	.343	.459
3+ Days rest	2.26	6	2	0	60	0	115.1	105	7	26	72	Ahead on Count	.225	610	137	24	3	8	62	0	198	.230	.313
Pre-All Star	3.72	6	9	0	78	14	196.0	193	23	76	125	Behind on Count	.340	338	115	20	1	14	55	61	0	.439	.530
Post-All Star	4.02	8	8	5	87	8	190.1	217	17	51	116	Two Strikes	.210	596	125	24	1	8	54	45	241	.268	.294

Pitcher vs. Batter (career)

Pitches Best Vs.	Avg	AB	H	2B	3B	HR	RBI	BB	SO	OBP	SLG	Pitches Worst Vs.	Avg	AB	H	2B	3B	HR	RBI	BB	SO	OBP	SLG
Jack Clark	.000	9	0	0	0	0	0	1	0	.250	.000	Andre Dawson	.571	21	12	2	1	3	9	1	0	.591	1.190
Rafael Ramirez	.083	12	1	0	0	0	2	0	1	.077	.083	Eddie Murray	.500	8	4	0	0	2	6	3	0	.636	1.250
Ozzie Smith	.105	19	2	0	0	0	2	3	2	.227	.105	Eric Davis	.450	20	9	1	0	4	9	5	4	.560	1.100
Matt D. Williams	.167	12	2	0	0	0	1	0	4	.154	.167	Kevin Mitchell	.421	19	8	2	0	3	6	2	4	.476	1.000
Hubie Brooks	.182	11	2	0	0	0	2	0	1	.182	.182	Ken Caminiti	.400	10	4	0	0	2	7	1	2	.455	1.000

Craig Grebeck — White Sox

Bats Right (flyball hitter)

	Avg	G	AB	R	H	2B	3B	HR	RBI	BB	SO	HBP	GDP	SB	CS	OBP	SLG	IBB	SH	SF	#Pit	#P/PA	GB	FB	G/F
1992 Season	.268	88	287	24	77	21	2	3	35	30	34	3	5	0	3	.341	.387	0	10	3	1261	3.90	86	103	0.83
Career (1990-1992)	.254	254	630	68	160	40	6	10	75	76	98	6	10	1	6	.337	.384	0	17	7	2794	3.89	178	228	0.78

1992 Season

	Avg	AB	H	2B	3B	HR	RBI	BB	SO	OBP	SLG		Avg	AB	H	2B	3B	HR	RBI	BB	SO	OBP	SLG
vs. Left	.291	86	25	8	0	0	9	6	8	.344	.384	Scoring Posn	.265	68	18	7	0	0	27	7	13	.338	.368
vs. Right	.259	201	52	13	2	3	26	24	26	.339	.388	Close & Late	.200	60	12	2	0	0	6	5	7	.258	.233
Groundball	.255	94	24	5	1	0	10	6	11	.294	.330	None on/out	.260	77	20	4	0	1	1	6	8	.313	.351
Flyball	.325	77	25	5	0	3	15	12	8	.422	.506	Batting #8	.315	54	17	4	1	1	5	2	8	.333	.481
Home	.269	134	36	11	1	2	23	18	13	.357	.410	Batting #9	.259	162	42	12	1	2	26	24	18	.361	.383
Away	.268	153	41	10	1	1	12	12	21	.325	.366	Other	.254	71	18	5	0	0	4	4	8	.293	.324
Day	.222	72	16	4	1	0	11	9	4	.298	.306	April	.217	23	5	2	0	1	6	2	2	.280	.435
Night	.284	215	61	17	1	3	24	21	30	.356	.414	May	.257	74	19	6	0	0	8	11	7	.356	.338
Grass	.289	246	71	18	2	3	32	26	29	.360	.415	June	.266	94	25	7	1	1	7	8	12	.320	.394
Turf	.146	41	6	3	0	0	3	4	5	.222	.220	July	.308	91	28	6	1	1	14	8	12	.373	.429
First Pitch	.333	39	13	4	0	0	9	0	0	.325	.436	August	.000	5	0	0	0	0	0	1	1	.167	.000
Ahead on Count	.313	64	20	8	0	3	16	18	0	.465	.578	September/October	.000	0	0	0	0	0	0	0	0	.000	.000
Behind on Count	.277	94	26	8	0	1	9	0	18	.292	.394	Pre-All Star	.263	240	63	18	2	2	25	23	29	.327	.379
Two Strikes	.152	125	19	4	1	0	4	12	34	.232	.200	Post-All Star	.298	47	14	3	0	1	10	7	5	.404	.426

1992 By Position

Position	Avg	AB	H	2B	3B	HR	RBI	BB	SO	OBP	SLG	G	GS	Innings	PO	A	E	DP	Fld Pct	Rng Fctr	In Zone	Outs	Zone Rtg	MLB Zone
As ss	.272	272	74	19	2	3	35	28	32	.343	.390	85	82	728.2	110	276	8	45	.980	4.77	329	308	.936	.885

Career (1990-1992)

	Avg	AB	H	2B	3B	HR	RBI	BB	SO	OBP	SLG		Avg	AB	H	2B	3B	HR	RBI	BB	SO	OBP	SLG
vs. Left	.253	289	73	19	3	5	34	32	48	.326	.391	Scoring Posn	.253	150	38	13	0	2	57	23	28	.350	.380
vs. Right	.255	341	87	21	3	5	41	44	50	.345	.378	Close & Late	.220	118	26	5	1	1	14	13	15	.299	.305
Groundball	.275	193	53	9	1	1	16	27	33	.333	.347	None on/out	.241	170	41	7	1	3	3	15	31	.303	.347
Flyball	.266	154	41	8	2	6	26	23	30	.365	.416	Batting #8	.236	178	42	9	1	3	15	17	32	.307	.348
Home	.260	300	78	19	2	6	41	39	45	.343	.397	Batting #9	.244	197	48	13	2	3	28	25	28	.335	.376
Away	.248	330	82	21	4	4	34	37	53	.331	.373	Other	.275	255	70	18	3	4	32	34	38	.358	.416
Day	.269	167	45	9	1	1	22	20	20	.340	.353	April	.220	41	9	2	0	2	8	4	5	.283	.415
Night	.248	463	115	31	5	9	53	56	78	.335	.395	May	.238	126	30	8	0	0	13	12	16	.307	.302
Grass	.268	512	137	35	5	9	69	62	80	.349	.408	June	.233	159	37	11	1	3	12	13	23	.289	.371
Turf	.195	118	23	5	1	1	6	14	18	.280	.280	July	.308	120	37	7	2	3	18	12	16	.375	.475
First Pitch	.320	97	31	8	1	3	23	0	0	.324	.515	August	.261	88	23	5	2	1	13	11	16	.350	.398
Ahead on Count	.286	140	40	14	1	6	26	46	0	.466	.529	September/October	.250	96	24	7	1	1	11	24	22	.405	.375
Behind on Count	.234	197	46	14	1	1	15	0	55	.239	.330	Pre-All Star	.237	388	92	24	3	5	37	34	55	.298	.353
Two Strikes	.151	279	42	7	1	1	14	30	98	.234	.194	Post-All Star	.281	242	68	16	3	5	38	42	43	.392	.434

Batter vs. Pitcher (career)

Hits Best Against	Avg	AB	H	2B	3B	HR	RBI	BB	SO	OBP	SLG	Hits Worst Against	Avg	AB	H	2B	3B	HR	RBI	BB	SO	OBP	SLG
Matt Young	.571	14	8	1	0	0	2	1	4	.600	.643	Randy Johnson	.000	13	0	0	0	0	0	2	4	.235	.000
Frank Tanana	.353	17	6	1	0	0	2	2	2	.421	.412	Erik Hanson	.091	11	1	0	0	0	0	1	2	.167	.091
David Wells	.333	12	4	1	0	1	0	0	2	.333	.667	Jim Abbott	.235	17	4	1	0	0	0	3	1	.350	.294

Gary Green — Reds
Bats Right

	Avg	G	AB	R	H	2B	3B	HR	RBI	BB	SO	HBP	GDP	SB	CS	OBP	SLG	IBB	SH	SF	#Pit	#P/PA	GB	FB	G/F
1992 Season	.333	8	12	3	4	1	0	0	0	0	2	0	0	0	0	.333	.417	0	0	0	35	2.92	7	3	2.33
Last Five Years	.224	93	147	17	33	8	0	0	9	8	27	0	2	1	2	.263	.279	0	6	1	562	3.60	52	42	1.24

1992 Season

	Avg	AB	H	2B	3B	HR	RBI	BB	SO	OBP	SLG		Avg	AB	H	2B	3B	HR	RBI	BB	SO	OBP	SLG
vs. Left	.333	6	2	0	0	0	0	0	0	.333	.333	Scoring Posn	.500	2	1	0	0	0	0	0	0	.500	.500
vs. Right	.333	6	2	1	0	0	0	0	2	.333	.500	Close & Late	.250	8	2	1	0	0	0	0	2	.250	.375

Tommy Greene — Phillies
Pitches Right (flyball pitcher)

	ERA	W	L	Sv	G	GS	IP	BB	SO	Avg	H	2B	3B	HR	RBI	OBP	SLG	CG	ShO	Sup	QS	#P/S	SB	CS	GB	FB	G/F
1992 Season	5.32	3	3	0	13	12	64.1	34	39	.291	75	14	2	5	31	.371	.419	0	0	6.16	6	94	13	1	90	85	1.06
Career (1989-1992)	4.04	20	15	0	68	52	349.2	132	231	.246	324	63	8	37	152	.314	.391	4	3	4.43	28	97	34	16	425	451	0.94

1992 Season

	ERA	W	L	Sv	G	GS	IP	H	HR	BB	SO		Avg	AB	H	2B	3B	HR	RBI	BB	SO	OBP	SLG
Home	3.26	2	0	0	5	5	30.1	32	1	14	20	vs. Left	.370	127	47	8	2	2	15	21	16	.459	.512
Away	7.15	1	3	0	8	7	34.0	43	4	20	19	vs. Right	.214	131	28	6	0	3	16	13	23	.281	.328
Starter	5.26	3	3	0	12	12	63.1	74	5	32	38	Scoring Posn	.268	71	19	4	1	2	25	10	12	.349	.437
Reliever	9.00	0	0	0	1	0	1.0	1	0	2	1	Close & Late	.667	3	2	0	0	0	1	0	0	.667	.667
0-3 Days Rest	0.00	0	0	0	0	0	0.0	0	0	0	0	None on/out	.323	62	20	4	1	0	0	6	11	.382	.419
4 Days Rest	6.30	1	3	0	8	8	40.0	49	4	23	21	First Pitch	.270	37	10	3	0	1	6	1	0	.289	.432
5+ Days Rest	3.47	2	0	0	4	4	23.1	25	1	9	17	Behind on Count	.383	47	18	5	1	0	6	21	0	.574	.532
Pre-All Star	6.32	2	1	0	6	6	31.1	34	3	22	23	Ahead on Count	.217	115	25	4	0	3	10	0	36	.217	.330
Post-All Star	4.36	1	2	0	7	6	33.0	41	2	12	16	Two Strikes	.203	123	25	4	1	4	15	12	39	.274	.350

Career (1989-1992)

	ERA	W	L	Sv	G	GS	IP	H	HR	BB	SO		Avg	AB	H	2B	3B	HR	RBI	BB	SO	OBP	SLG
Home	3.42	11	6	0	34	27	181.1	161	16	66	131	vs. Left	.264	736	209	40	7	22	91	90	116	.360	.447
Away	4.70	9	9	0	34	25	168.1	163	21	66	100	vs. Right	.199	579	115	23	1	15	61	42	115	.253	.320
Day	4.54	6	5	0	16	13	83.1	66	13	41	65	Inning 1-6	.252	1136	286	55	7	34	138	115	199	.319	.402
Night	3.89	14	10	0	52	39	266.1	258	24	91	166	Inning 7+	.212	179	38	8	1	3	14	17	32	.279	.318
Grass	5.20	4	3	0	19	13	81.1	79	13	36	46	None on	.236	795	188	33	2	24	24	77	156	.306	.374
Turf	3.69	16	12	0	49	39	268.1	245	24	96	185	Runners on	.262	520	136	30	6	13	128	55	75	.325	.417
April	5.94	2	1	0	13	5	50.0	51	4	28	26	Scoring Posn	.270	285	77	17	4	6	104	35	49	.334	.421
May	1.24	4	0	0	7	4	36.1	17	0	15	33	Close & Late	.219	73	16	3	0	1	6	7	18	.288	.301
June	3.86	2	1	0	9	8	51.1	50	8	15	37	None on/out	.228	337	77	14	1	7	7	34	66	.301	.318
July	4.00	2	3	0	6	6	36.0	32	5	15	24	vs. 1st Batr (relief)	.214	14	3	0	0	0	3	0	1	.200	.214
August	4.71	2	4	0	9	9	49.2	52	7	19	34	First Inning Pitched	.230	239	55	12	2	5	38	34	42	.320	.360
September/October	3.92	8	6	0	24	20	126.1	122	13	40	77	First 75 Pitches	.249	968	241	53	7	26	117	102	165	.320	.399
Starter	3.93	19	15	0	52	52	314.0	289	34	115	216	Pitch 76-90	.263	156	41	4	0	6	18	16	31	.328	.404
Reliever	5.05	1	0	0	16	0	35.2	35	3	17	15	Pitch 91-105	.209	115	24	2	1	4	9	8	24	.258	.348
0-3 Days Rest	0.75	1	0	0	2	2	12.0	8	1	7	6	Pitch 106+	.237	76	18	4	0	1	8	6	11	.286	.329
4 Days Rest	4.44	10	13	0	33	33	202.2	196	23	70	138	First Pitch	.256	195	50	11	1	5	22	5	0	.272	.400
5+ Days Rest	3.26	8	2	0	17	17	99.1	85	10	38	72	Ahead on Count	.184	599	110	17	1	6	37	0	206	.185	.245
Pre-All Star	4.13	8	4	0	31	19	148.1	131	14	61	102	Behind on Count	.360	275	99	26	4	16	62	75	0	.490	.658
Post-All Star	3.98	12	11	0	37	33	201.1	193	23	71	129	Two Strikes	.173	636	110	18	3	13	46	52	231	.237	.269

Pitcher vs. Batter (career)

Pitches Best Vs.	Avg	AB	H	2B	3B	HR	RBI	BB	SO	OBP	SLG	Pitches Worst Vs.	Avg	AB	H	2B	3B	HR	RBI	BB	SO	OBP	SLG
Jose Lind	.000	13	0	0	0	0	1	1	1	.067	.000	Felix Jose	.571	14	8	4	1	0	4	2	2	.556	1.000
Jay Bell	.053	19	1	0	0	0	1	3	3	.100	.053	Barry Bonds	.538	13	7	1	0	3	9	4	1	.611	1.308
Ivan Calderon	.067	15	1	1	0	0	1	2	3	.176	.133	Bobby Bonilla	.467	15	7	3	0	0	2	5	1	.600	.667
Will Clark	.100	10	1	0	0	0	0	2	0	.250	.100	Ray Lankford	.389	18	7	2	1	2	5	1	2	.421	.944
Milt Thompson	.133	15	2	1	0	0	1	0	1	.133	.200	Paul O'Neill	.357	14	5	0	0	2	6	0	3	.357	.786

Willie Greene — Reds
Bats Left (flyball hitter)

	Avg	G	AB	R	H	2B	3B	HR	RBI	BB	SO	HBP	GDP	SB	CS	OBP	SLG	IBB	SH	SF	#Pit	#P/PA	GB	FB	G/F
1992 Season	.269	29	93	10	25	5	2	2	13	10	23	0	1	0	2	.337	.430	0	0	1	361	3.47	26	29	0.90

1992 Season

	Avg	AB	H	2B	3B	HR	RBI	BB	SO	OBP	SLG		Avg	AB	H	2B	3B	HR	RBI	BB	SO	OBP	SLG
vs. Left	.250	28	7	0	1	0	4	2	7	.290	.321	Scoring Posn	.421	19	8	2	1	0	8	3	5	.478	.632
vs. Right	.277	65	18	5	1	2	9	8	16	.356	.477	Close & Late	.417	12	5	0	1	0	3	1	4	.462	.583
Home	.271	59	16	2	0	2	6	7	16	.548	.407	None on/out	.150	20	3	0	0	0	0	4	6	.292	.150
Away	.265	34	9	3	2	0	7	3	7	.316	.471	Batting #2	.256	43	11	2	1	0	7	5	4	.327	.349
First Pitch	.182	22	4	1	0	1	2	0	0	.182	.364	Batting #5	.111	18	2	0	1	0	1	1	5	.158	.222
Ahead on Count	.556	18	10	3	0	1	3	5	0	.652	.889	Other	.375	32	12	3	0	2	5	4	14	.444	.656
Behind on Count	.276	29	8	0	2	0	5	0	11	.276	.414	Pre-All Star	.000	0	0	0	0	0	0	0	0	.000	.000
Two Strikes	.158	38	6	1	1	0	3	5	23	.256	.211	Post-All Star	.269	93	25	5	2	2	13	10	23	.337	.430

167

Mike Greenwell — Red Sox   Bats Left

	Avg	G	AB	R	H	2B	3B	HR	RBI	BB	SO	HBP	GDP	SB	CS	OBP	SLG	IBB	SH	SF	#Pit	#P/PA	GB	FB	G/F
1992 Season	.233	49	180	16	42	2	0	2	18	18	19	2	8	2	3	.307	.278	1	0	2	696	3.45	81	48	1.69
Last Five Years	.302	658	2502	336	756	133	20	61	388	269	179	21	70	54	28	.372	.444	52	1	23	9046	3.21	1049	788	1.33

1992 Season

	Avg	AB	H	2B	3B	HR	RBI	BB	SO	OBP	SLG		Avg	AB	H	2B	3B	HR	RBI	BB	SO	OBP	SLG
vs. Left	.224	58	13	1	0	0	5	6	8	.308	.241	Scoring Posn	.176	51	9	0	0	0	13	5	6	.241	.176
vs. Right	.238	122	29	1	0	2	13	12	11	.307	.295	Close & Late	.395	38	15	0	0	0	4	4	4	.452	.395
Home	.229	83	19	0	0	0	8	10	8	.313	.229	None on/out	.258	31	8	0	0	0	0	3	4	.324	.258
Away	.237	97	23	2	0	2	10	8	11	.302	.320	Batting #2	.267	75	20	2	0	1	10	7	9	.325	.333
First Pitch	.194	36	7	0	0	0	1	0		.216	.194	Batting #3	.180	50	9	0	0	0	2	6	6	.276	.180
Ahead on Count	.257	35	9	0	0	2	7	11	0	.426	.429	Other	.236	55	13	0	0	1	6	5	4	.311	.291
Behind on Count	.222	54	12	0	0	0	7	0	11	.236	.222	Pre-All Star	.233	180	42	2	0	2	18	18	19	.307	.278
Two Strikes	.221	68	15	2	0	0	5	6	19	.293	.250	Post-All Star	.000	0	0	0	0	0	0	0	0	.000	.000

Last Five Years

	Avg	AB	H	2B	3B	HR	RBI	BB	SO	OBP	SLG		Avg	AB	H	2B	3B	HR	RBI	BB	SO	OBP	SLG
vs. Left	.281	827	232	37	4	13	113	46	70	.324	.382	Scoring Posn	.282	733	207	34	7	13	309	114	57	.373	.401
vs. Right	.313	1675	524	96	16	48	275	223	109	.394	.475	Close & Late	.286	364	104	15	4	5	40	48	33	.373	.390
Groundball	.299	648	194	27	3	11	101	62	47	.365	.401	None on/out	.294	564	166	35	5	14	14	38	32	.341	.449
Flyball	.285	592	169	33	3	20	91	63	37	.357	.453	Batting #4	.310	1056	327	64	8	30	192	116	78	.377	.471
Home	.312	1235	385	61	10	29	211	142	84	.383	.467	Batting #5	.314	892	280	50	8	22	144	88	53	.379	.462
Away	.293	1267	371	48	10	32	177	127	95	.360	.422	Other	.269	554	149	19	4	9	52	65	48	.349	.366
Day	.315	819	258	57	3	19	134	93	57	.389	.462	April	.274	358	98	13	2	10	41	50	32	.375	.405
Night	.296	1683	498	76	17	42	254	176	122	.363	.436	May	.279	437	122	18	2	9	63	59	36	.365	.391
Grass	.307	2120	651	122	15	51	336	234	143	.378	.451	June	.326	500	163	24	2	12	90	39	33	.377	.454
Turf	.275	382	105	11	5	10	52	35	36	.337	.408	July	.310	406	126	21	4	12	56	41	25	.372	.470
First Pitch	.316	544	172	26	1	16	90	20	0	.339	.456	August	.323	390	126	28	4	8	71	37	24	.378	.477
Ahead on Count	.345	669	231	46	11	30	123	146	0	.463	.581	September/October	.294	411	121	29	6	10	67	43	29	.363	.467
Behind on Count	.278	770	214	35	5	13	114	3	99	.288	.387	Pre-All Star	.298	1433	427	61	7	35	217	161	109	.372	.424
Two Strikes	.239	787	188	30	5	8	92	87	179	.319	.320	Post-All Star	.308	1069	329	72	13	26	171	108	70	.371	.472

Batter vs. Pitcher (career)

Hits Best Against	Avg	AB	H	2B	3B	HR	RBI	BB	SO	OBP	SLG	Hits Worst Against	Avg	AB	H	2B	3B	HR	RBI	BB	SO	OBP	SLG
Bill Krueger	.625	16	10	1	1	0	3	0	1	.625	.813	Scott Erickson	.063	16	1	0	0	0	0	0	1	.063	.063
Jeff Russell	.615	13	8	1	0	2	11	2	2	.667	1.154	Kenny Rogers	.067	15	1	0	0	0	0	3		.067	.133
Lee Guetterman	.533	15	8	0	1	1	4	2	2	.588	.867	Floyd Bannister	.077	13	1	0	0	0	1	0	2	.077	.077
Bill Wegman	.529	17	9	2	0	1	4	5	0	.636	.824	Bryan Harvey	.091	11	1	0	0	0	1	0	2	.083	.091
Dave Schmidt	.500	16	8	0	0	3	6	1	0	.529	1.063	Russ Swan	.091	11	1	0	0	0	0	3		.154	.091

Tommy Gregg — Braves   Bats Left

	Avg	G	AB	R	H	2B	3B	HR	RBI	BB	SO	HBP	GDP	SB	CS	OBP	SLG	IBB	SH	SF	#Pit	#P/PA	GB	FB	G/F
1992 Season	.263	18	19		5	0	0	1	1	1	7	0	1	1	0	.300	.421	0	0	0	70	3.50	5	4	1.25
Last Five Years	.245	341	685	61	168	33	2	14	67	54	121	2	10	10	10	.301	.361	9	3	3	2659	3.57	254	210	1.21

1992 Season

	Avg	AB	H	2B	3B	HR	RBI	BB	SO	OBP	SLG		Avg	AB	H	2B	3B	HR	RBI	BB	SO	OBP	SLG
vs. Left	.000	4	0	0	0	0	0	0	3	.000	.000	Scoring Posn	.000	2	0	0	0	0	0	0	0	.000	.000
vs. Right	.333	15	5	0	0	1	1	1	4	.375	.533	Close & Late	.200	5	1	0	0	1	1	1	2	.333	.800

Last Five Years

	Avg	AB	H	2B	3B	HR	RBI	BB	SO	OBP	SLG		Avg	AB	H	2B	3B	HR	RBI	BB	SO	OBP	SLG
vs. Left	.174	92	16	1	0	0	2	9	31	.248	.185	Scoring Posn	.232	164	38	5	1	5	54	22	30	.321	.366
vs. Right	.256	593	152	32	2	14	65	45	90	.309	.388	Close & Late	.210	143	30	6	0	4	15	14	36	.260	.336
Groundball	.248	222	55	5	1	4	24	14	39	.297	.333	None on/out	.214	145	31	7	1	2	2	5	28	.240	.317
Flyball	.225	169	38	9	0	4	13	22	35	.314	.349	Batting #5	.218	188	41	10	1	1	16	14	34	.271	.298
Home	.247	344	85	17	1	6	39	22	53	.293	.355	Batting #6	.260	123	32	7	0	3	12	8	20	.303	.390
Away	.243	341	83	16	1	8	28	32	68	.309	.367	Other	.254	374	95	16	1	10	39	32	67	.315	.382
Day	.325	154	50	15	1	2	17	16	23	.386	.474	April	.258	66	17	5	0	1	8	6	13	.315	.379
Night	.222	531	118	18	1	12	50	38	98	.276	.328	May	.083	24	2	1	0	1	1	5	3	.267	.250
Grass	.247	518	128	22	2	11	55	34	87	.294	.361	June	.236	148	35	6	0	0	9	12	17	.298	.277
Turf	.240	167	40	11	0	3	12	20	34	.323	.399	July	.236	123	29	2	1	5	17	8	24	.280	.390
First Pitch	.376	101	38	6	0	4	16	4	0	.402	.554	August	.274	157	43	11	1	4	15	8	30	.309	.433
Ahead on Count	.324	136	44	14	0	8	23	23	0	.419	.603	September/October	.251	167	42	8	0	3	17	15	34	.311	.353
Behind on Count	.191	262	50	5	1	4	21	0	72	.194	.263	Pre-All Star	.234	265	62	14	0	4	23	24	34	.301	.332
Two Strikes	.161	316	51	7	2	1	18	24	121	.220	.206	Post-All Star	.252	420	106	19	2	10	44	30	87	.301	.379

Batter vs. Pitcher (career)

Hits Best Against	Avg	AB	H	2B	3B	HR	RBI	BB	SO	OBP	SLG	Hits Worst Against	Avg	AB	H	2B	3B	HR	RBI	BB	SO	OBP	SLG
Andy Benes	.438	16	7	3	0	0	0	4	5	.550	.625	Ron Darling	.071	14	1	0	0	1	3	1	4	.133	.286
Mike Morgan	.364	22	8	1	0	0	1	0	1	.364	.409	Scott Scudder	.077	13	1	0	0	0	1	3		.143	.077
Ramon Martinez	.350	20	7	2	0	1	1	1	3	.381	.600	David Cone	.091	11	1	1	0	0	0	2	2	.231	.182
Jose Rijo	.333	12	4	2	0	0	1	0	1	.333	.500	Tim Belcher	.176	17	3	0	0	0	1	2	1	.263	.176
												Doug Drabek	.211	19	4	1	0	0	0	2	2	.286	.263

Ken Griffey Jr — Mariners
Bats Left

	Avg	G	AB	R	H	2B	3B	HR	RBI	BB	SO	HBP	GDP	SB	CS	OBP	SLG	IBB	SH	SF	#Pit	#P/PA	GB	FB	G/F
1992 Season	.308	142	565	83	174	39	4	27	103	44	67	5	14	10	5	.361	.535	15	0	3	2103	3.41	209	181	1.15
Career (1989-1992)	.301	578	2165	311	652	132	12	87	344	222	313	10	40	60	29	.366	.494	56	5	20	8503	3.52	776	639	1.21

1992 Season

	Avg	AB	H	2B	3B	HR	RBI	BB	SO	OBP	SLG		Avg	AB	H	2B	3B	HR	RBI	BB	SO	OBP	SLG
vs. Left	.358	173	62	10	0	12	35	11	23	.413	.624	Scoring Posn	.333	150	50	11	1	10	76	25	16	.428	.620
vs. Right	.286	392	112	29	4	15	68	33	44	.339	.495	Close & Late	.333	81	27	5	0	3	12	15	10	.443	.506
Groundball	.357	154	55	13	1	5	25	12	12	.407	.552	None on/out	.284	116	33	7	1	5	5	9	12	.336	.491
Flyball	.252	163	41	8	0	11	34	14	21	.317	.503	Batting #3	.302	533	161	39	4	26	99	41	62	.356	.537
Home	.314	277	87	22	2	16	51	22	25	.369	.581	Batting #4	.440	25	11	0	0	1	4	3	4	.500	.560
Away	.302	288	87	17	2	11	52	22	42	.354	.490	Other	.286	7	2	0	0	0	0	0	1	.286	.286
Day	.355	152	54	9	1	4	25	19	20	.437	.507	April	.256	78	20	4	0	2	12	8	7	.322	.385
Night	.291	413	120	30	3	23	78	25	47	.332	.545	May	.340	100	34	9	0	7	19	4	14	.368	.640
Grass	.310	226	70	14	2	9	43	20	31	.368	.509	June	.250	48	12	3	0	5	13	6	8	.345	.625
Turf	.307	339	104	25	2	18	60	24	36	.357	.552	July	.325	117	38	9	1	4	17	6	15	.360	.521
First Pitch	.367	109	40	4	2	9	29	13	0	.432	.688	August	.324	108	35	8	1	6	21	13	11	.402	.583
Ahead on Count	.367	128	47	16	0	4	18	19	0	.449	.586	September/October	.307	114	35	6	2	3	21	7	12	.352	.474
Behind on Count	.306	193	59	14	1	6	28	0	33	.311	.482	Pre-All Star	.285	277	79	18	0	15	50	20	33	.336	.513
Two Strikes	.202	223	45	8	2	8	34	14	67	.254	.363	Post-All Star	.330	288	95	21	4	12	53	24	34	.386	.556

1992 By Position

Position	Avg	AB	H	2B	3B	HR	RBI	BB	SO	OBP	SLG	G	GS	Innings	PO	A	E	DP	Fld Pct	Rng Fctr	In Zone	Outs	Zone Rtg	MLB Zone
As cf	.310	549	170	38	4	25	100	44	64	.364	.530	137	136	1187.0	358	8	1	4	.997	2.78	419	345	.823	.824

Career (1989-1992)

	Avg	AB	H	2B	3B	HR	RBI	BB	SO	OBP	SLG		Avg	AB	H	2B	3B	HR	RBI	BB	SO	OBP	SLG
vs. Left	.305	669	204	40	1	25	95	57	129	.364	.480	Scoring Posn	.319	562	179	37	3	21	247	104	102	.416	.507
vs. Right	.299	1496	448	92	11	62	249	165	184	.367	.500	Close & Late	.264	329	87	14	2	11	45	50	73	.362	.419
Groundball	.327	562	184	39	4	17	86	60	64	.392	.502	None on/out	.271	446	121	18	4	18	18	26	50	.313	.451
Flyball	.303	501	152	30	1	26	88	48	78	.363	.523	Batting #3	.309	1413	436	97	9	57	242	143	189	.372	.511
Home	.311	1082	336	75	6	50	187	116	141	.377	.530	Batting #5	.290	458	133	25	2	18	60	48	60	.357	.472
Away	.292	1083	316	57	6	37	157	106	172	.354	.458	Other	.282	294	83	10	1	12	42	31	64	.350	.446
Day	.319	570	182	31	4	24	89	59	95	.383	.514	April	.316	310	98	14	1	12	44	30	44	.373	.484
Night	.295	1595	470	101	8	63	255	163	218	.360	.487	May	.311	386	120	25	1	22	61	37	58	.370	.552
Grass	.296	840	249	41	5	30	131	86	130	.361	.464	June	.262	324	85	22	0	10	43	44	48	.350	.423
Turf	.304	1325	403	91	7	57	213	136	183	.369	.512	July	.332	364	121	26	2	14	64	33	53	.386	.530
First Pitch	.383	347	133	21	3	24	87	35	0	.439	.669	August	.314	369	116	27	3	17	59	39	52	.381	.542
Ahead on Count	.363	474	172	34	0	22	84	115	0	.484	.574	September/October	.272	412	112	16	5	12	73	39	58	.337	.427
Behind on Count	.270	748	202	48	4	21	94	4	176	.274	.429	Pre-All Star	.296	1140	337	66	2	49	164	121	171	.362	.486
Two Strikes	.216	927	200	41	5	26	105	63	312	.266	.355	Post-All Star	.307	1025	315	66	10	38	180	101	142	.370	.502

Batter vs. Pitcher (career)

Hits Best Against	Avg	AB	H	2B	3B	HR	RBI	BB	SO	OBP	SLG	Hits Worst Against	Avg	AB	H	2B	3B	HR	RBI	BB	SO	OBP	SLG
Bob Milacki	.667	9	6	1	0	0	3	2	0	.727	.778	Greg Hibbard	.077	13	1	0	0	0	1	0	2	.188	.077
Paul Gibson	.583	12	7	2	0	1	1	2	0	.643	1.000	Bret Saberhagen	.083	12	1	0	0	0	2	3	.214	.083
Shawn Hillegas	.500	10	5	1	1	1	3	2	0	.583	1.100	Tony Fossas	.091	11	1	0	0	0	1	1	3	.167	.091
David Wells	.444	18	8	2	0	2	4	0	4	.500	.889	Bob Welch	.154	26	4	0	0	1	3	3	.241	.154
Charles Nagy	.412	17	7	2	2	2	5	3	4	.500	1.000	Mike Boddicker	.154	26	4	0	0	0	2	5	.207	.154

Alfredo Griffin — Blue Jays
Bats Both

	Avg	G	AB	R	H	2B	3B	HR	RBI	BB	SO	HBP	GDP	SB	CS	OBP	SLG	IBB	SH	SF	#Pit	#P/PA	GB	FB	G/F
1992 Season	.233	63	150	21	35	7	0	0	10	9	19	0	3	3	1	.273	.280	0	3	2	544	3.38	61	39	1.56
Last Five Years	.227	544	1783	174	405	59	10	2	128	113	220	5	21	31	20	.273	.275	25	38	13	6203	3.24	710	499	1.42

1992 Season

	Avg	AB	H	2B	3B	HR	RBI	BB	SO	OBP	SLG		Avg	AB	H	2B	3B	HR	RBI	BB	SO	OBP	SLG
vs. Left	.310	29	9	1	0	0	2	4	3	.394	.345	Scoring Posn	.303	33	10	0	0	0	10	4	6	.359	.303
vs. Right	.215	121	26	6	0	0	8	5	16	.242	.264	Close & Late	.273	22	6	3	0	0	1	0	4	.273	.409
Home	.214	70	15	4	0	0	5	6	6	.269	.271	None on/out	.211	38	8	1	0	0	0	4	5	.286	.237
Away	.250	80	20	3	0	0	5	3	13	.277	.288	Batting #2	.143	14	2	1	0	0	0	0	4	.143	.214
First Pitch	.267	30	8	3	0	0	4	0	0	.250	.367	Batting #9	.230	126	29	5	0	0	7	7	14	.269	.270
Ahead on Count	.250	24	6	2	0	0	0	5	0	.379	.333	Other	.400	10	4	1	0	0	3	2	1	.462	.500
Behind on Count	.213	61	13	1	0	0	3	0	12	.213	.230	Pre-All Star	.143	35	5	0	0	0	3	1	3	.158	.143
Two Strikes	.177	62	11	2	0	2	4	4	19	.227	.227	Post-All Star	.261	115	30	7	0	0	7	8	16	.309	.322

Last Five Years

	Avg	AB	H	2B	3B	HR	RBI	BB	SO	OBP	SLG		Avg	AB	H	2B	3B	HR	RBI	BB	SO	OBP	SLG
vs. Left	.243	613	149	13	4	1	45	49	85	.299	.262	Scoring Posn	.243	416	101	12	6	0	125	41	59	.305	.300
vs. Right	.219	1170	256	46	6	1	83	64	135	.264	.271	Close & Late	.241	299	72	8	1	1	18	16	46	.284	.264
Groundball	.262	610	160	23	2	0	42	26	59	.292	.307	None on/out	.196	505	99	14	3	1	1	33	66	.247	.242
Flyball	.199	386	77	9	3	1	30	31	62	.260	.246	Batting #1	.227	344	78	13	1	0	20	23	42	.274	.270
Home	.219	854	187	27	2	0	52	58	100	.268	.255	Batting #8	.231	1107	256	32	7	2	81	71	143	.278	.278
Away	.235	929	218	32	8	2	76	55	120	.279	.293	Other	.214	332	71	14	2	0	27	19	35	.255	.268

169

Last Five Years

	Avg	AB	H	2B	3B	HR	RBI	BB	SO	OBP	SLG		Avg	AB	H	2B	3B	HR	RBI	BB	SO	OBP	SLG
Day	.216	536	116	20	3	1	42	30	64	.260	.271	April	.220	304	67	18	3	0	26	14	31	.253	.299
Night	.232	1247	289	39	7	1	86	83	156	.279	.277	May	.217	217	47	4	2	0	21	19	24	.262	.253
Grass	.223	1254	280	41	5	0	83	78	165	.269	.264	June	.261	303	79	8	2	1	21	14	47	.292	.310
Turf	.235	529	125	18	5	2	45	35	55	.283	.301	July	.227	255	58	9	1	0	17	18	26	.279	.271
First Pitch	.311	373	116	21	1	2	37	7	1	.318	.389	August	.218	317	69	9	0	1	17	22	36	.268	.256
Ahead on Count	.240	325	78	13	2	0	29	51	0	.341	.292	September/October	.220	387	85	11	2	0	26	26	56	.269	.258
Behind on Count	.203	700	142	18	6	0	53	0	134	.206	.246	Pre-All Star	.231	904	209	33	7	1	75	54	111	.274	.287
Two Strikes	.155	685	106	14	3	0	32	41	217	.206	.184	Post-All Star	.223	879	196	26	3	1	53	59	109	.273	.263

Batter vs. Pitcher (since 1984)

Hits Best Against	Avg	AB	H	2B	3B	HR	RBI	BB	SO	OBP	SLG	Hits Worst Against	Avg	AB	H	2B	3B	HR	RBI	BB	SO	OBP	SLG
Tom Candiotti	.700	10	7	1	0	0	0	1	1	.727	.800	Don Carman	.063	16	1	0	0	0	2	2	1	.167	.063
Matt Young	.545	11	6	0	1	0	0	0	1	.545	.727	Kelly Downs	.077	26	2	1	0	0	0	0	2	.077	.115
Bud Black	.500	20	10	2	1	0	0	0	2	.500	.700	Scott Scudder	.083	12	1	0	0	0	1	1	0	.143	.083
Roger Clemens	.474	19	9	3	0	0	2	1	3	.500	.632	Shawn Boskie	.091	11	1	0	0	0	0	0	0	.091	.091
Mike Boddicker	.455	33	15	4	0	0	5	2	2	.486	.576	Don Robinson	.095	21	2	0	0	0	2	1	1	.136	.095

Marquis Grissom — Expos
Bats Right

	Avg	G	AB	R	H	2B	3B	HR	RBI	BB	SO	HBP	GDP	SB	CS	OBP	SLG	IBB	SH	SF	#Pit	#P/PA	GB	FB	G/F
1992 Season	.276	159	653	99	180	39	6	14	66	42	81	5	12	78	13	.322	.418	6	3	4	2398	3.41	270	190	1.42
Career (1989-1992)	.268	431	1573	230	422	78	17	24	136	115	231	6	24	177	32	.320	.385	8	12	5	6087	3.58	653	437	1.49

1992 Season

	Avg	AB	H	2B	3B	HR	RBI	BB	SO	OBP	SLG		Avg	AB	H	2B	3B	HR	RBI	BB	SO	OBP	SLG
vs. Left	.269	212	57	14	4	6	24	17	26	.325	.458	Scoring Posn	.292	154	45	12	0	3	50	19	17	.369	.429
vs. Right	.279	441	123	25	2	8	42	25	55	.321	.399	Close & Late	.229	109	25	3	1	2	10	9	8	.288	.330
Groundball	.277	271	75	19	3	3	22	15	27	.321	.402	None on/out	.302	179	54	11	2	5	5	7	26	.332	.469
Flyball	.254	138	35	6	0	4	14	14	18	.320	.384	Batting #1	.297	320	95	20	4	6	30	22	38	.343	.441
Home	.266	316	84	24	2	8	31	17	38	.309	.430	Batting #2	.255	208	53	13	1	3	19	10	25	.296	.370
Away	.285	337	96	15	4	6	35	25	43	.335	.407	Other	.256	125	32	6	1	5	17	10	18	.314	.440
Day	.271	199	54	7	2	5	21	13	30	.321	.402	April	.277	94	26	5	1	3	12	8	8	.333	.447
Night	.278	454	126	32	4	9	45	29	51	.323	.425	May	.261	92	24	3	1	2	8	4	19	.299	.380
Grass	.281	171	48	10	2	1	18	10	27	.324	.380	June	.311	103	32	10	1	0	11	14	11	.395	.427
Turf	.274	482	132	29	4	13	48	32	54	.322	.432	July	.252	123	31	5	1	2	15	4	16	.277	.358
First Pitch	.363	91	33	10	0	5	14	5	0	.402	.637	August	.264	110	29	7	1	4	9	8	16	.311	.455
Ahead on Count	.280	168	47	10	0	5	21	26	0	.372	.429	September/October	.290	131	38	9	1	3	11	4	11	.321	.443
Behind on Count	.248	234	58	14	3	3	24	0	49	.259	.372	Pre-All Star	.273	355	97	20	3	5	37	28	47	.327	.389
Two Strikes	.206	262	54	11	4	3	18	11	81	.241	.313	Post-All Star	.279	298	83	19	3	9	29	14	34	.316	.453

1992 By Position

Position	Avg	AB	H	2B	3B	HR	RBI	BB	SO	OBP	SLG	G	GS	Innings	PO	A	E	DP	Fld Pct	Rng Fctr	In Zone	Outs	Zone Rtg	MLB Zone
As cf	.276	652	180	39	6	14	66	42	81	.323	.419	157	156	1402.1	402	7	7	2	.983	2.62	444	384	.865	.824

Career (1989-1992)

	Avg	AB	H	2B	3B	HR	RBI	BB	SO	OBP	SLG		Avg	AB	H	2B	3B	HR	RBI	BB	SO	OBP	SLG
vs. Left	.266	638	170	37	7	11	59	58	94	.328	.398	Scoring Posn	.281	370	104	20	1	7	109	43	60	.355	.397
vs. Right	.270	935	252	41	10	13	77	57	137	.314	.376	Close & Late	.227	299	68	7	2	6	32	24	47	.285	.324
Groundball	.278	593	165	26	6	6	44	40	66	.327	.373	None on/out	.276	409	113	21	6	9	9	31	65	.329	.423
Flyball	.232	357	83	12	2	6	28	32	65	.294	.328	Batting #1	.277	481	133	27	9	6	35	32	66	.322	.407
Home	.269	732	197	38	7	13	67	55	111	.322	.393	Batting #2	.270	770	208	40	6	10	63	56	118	.322	.377
Away	.268	841	225	40	10	11	69	60	120	.317	.378	Other	.252	322	81	11	2	8	38	27	47	.310	.373
Day	.247	453	112	16	4	10	46	35	86	.303	.366	April	.251	203	51	15	1	4	23	16	29	.306	.394
Night	.277	1120	310	62	13	14	90	80	145	.326	.393	May	.280	286	80	10	2	6	21	19	46	.327	.392
Grass	.260	438	114	14	5	3	32	26	68	.304	.336	June	.292	219	64	14	2	0	19	24	29	.363	.374
Turf	.271	1135	308	64	12	21	104	89	163	.325	.404	July	.240	271	65	8	4	3	28	17	43	.288	.332
First Pitch	.305	197	60	12	3	8	26	5	0	.325	.518	August	.247	243	60	14	5	6	20	15	33	.290	.420
Ahead on Count	.299	401	120	27	3	6	37	72	0	.404	.426	September/October	.291	351	102	17	3	5	25	24	51	.339	.399
Behind on Count	.252	544	137	29	6	4	42	0	126	.257	.349	Pre-All Star	.268	810	217	42	6	10	69	66	122	.323	.372
Two Strikes	.216	677	146	26	8	6	43	36	231	.257	.304	Post-All Star	.269	763	205	36	11	14	67	49	109	.315	.400

Batter vs. Pitcher (career)

Hits Best Against	Avg	AB	H	2B	3B	HR	RBI	BB	SO	OBP	SLG	Hits Worst Against	Avg	AB	H	2B	3B	HR	RBI	BB	SO	OBP	SLG
Curt Schilling	.688	16	11	2	0	1	5	0	1	.688	1.000	Mitch Williams	.000	16	1	0	0	0	0	2	1	.154	.000
Bruce Hurst	.480	25	12	0	0	1	4	3	3	.536	.600	Mike Hartley	.100	10	1	0	0	0	0	2	3	.250	.100
Bruce Ruffin	.444	9	4	2	0	0	0	2	2	.545	.667	Bobby Ojeda	.136	22	3	0	0	0	1	1	2	.174	.136
Bob Walk	.421	19	8	1	1	1	1	1	1	.450	.737	Kelly Downs	.154	13	2	0	0	0	0	0	3	.154	.154
Trevor Wilson	.353	17	6	1	0	2	3	2	1	.421	.765	Roger McDowell	.182	11	2	0	0	0	1	0	2	.182	.182

Buddy Groom — Tigers

	ERA	W	L	Sv	G	GS	IP	BB	SO	Avg	H	2B	3B	HR	RBI	OBP	SLG	CG	ShO	Sup	QS	#P/S	SB	CS	GB	FB	G/F
1992 Season	5.82	0	5	1	12	7	38.2	22	15	.320	48	10	2	4	24	.402	.493	0	0	4.19	2	79	0	2	63	31	2.03

1992 Season

	ERA	W	L	Sv	G	GS	IP	H	HR	BB	SO		Avg	AB	H	2B	3B	HR	RBI	BB	SO	OBP	SLG
Home	6.63	0	3	0	6	4	19.0	32	2	10	8	vs. Left	.355	31	11	0	1	0	5	5	5	.432	.419
Away	5.03	0	2	1	6	3	19.2	16	2	12	7	vs. Right	.311	119	37	10	1	4	19	17	10	.394	.513

Kevin Gross — Dodgers

	ERA	W	L	Sv	G	GS	IP	BB	SO	Avg	H	2B	3B	HR	RBI	OBP	SLG	CG	ShO	Sup	QS	#P/S	SB	CS	GB	FB	G/F
1992 Season	3.17	8	13	0	34	30	204.2	77	158	.241	182	30	5	11	71	.311	.337	4	3	3.52	21	98	18	9	296	177	1.67
Last Five Years	3.87	50	62	3	175	130	916.2	369	684	.252	873	141	23	68	368	.326	.365	15	8	3.90	75	101	137	47	1192	959	1.24

1992 Season

	ERA	W	L	Sv	G	GS	IP	H	HR	BB	SO		Avg	AB	H	2B	3B	HR	RBI	BB	SO	OBP	SLG
Home	3.35	5	9	0	16	16	113.0	95	4	35	91	vs. Left	.276	409	113	23	4	5	48	52	75	.356	.389
Away	2.95	3	4	0	18	14	91.2	87	7	42	67	vs. Right	.199	347	69	7	1	6	23	25	83	.255	.277
Day	2.25	3	3	0	9	7	52.0	43	3	23	40	Inning 1-6	.237	629	149	26	5	9	63	65	134	.308	.337
Night	3.48	5	10	0	25	23	152.2	139	8	54	118	Inning 7+	.260	127	33	4	0	2	8	12	24	.329	.339
Grass	3.41	6	10	0	26	23	155.2	143	7	61	122	None on	.240	437	105	18	1	6	6	44	101	.313	.327
Turf	2.39	2	3	0	8	7	49.0	39	4	16	36	Runners on	.241	319	77	12	4	5	65	33	57	.309	.351
April	4.01	0	3	0	4	4	24.2	33	0	4	17	Scoring Posn	.227	181	41	5	3	3	56	24	38	.308	.337
May	1.65	3	1	0	7	4	32.2	19	1	10	42	Close & Late	.270	100	27	4	0	1	6	8	20	.330	.340
June	5.76	0	4	0	5	5	29.2	30	5	11	21	None on/out	.269	193	52	9	1	3	3	23	43	.350	.373
July	2.79	2	2	0	6	6	38.2	38	1	12	24	vs. 1st Batr (relief)	.667	3	2	0	0	0	0	1	0	.750	.667
August	3.21	1	3	0	6	5	33.2	23	2	15	24	First Inning Pitched	.270	115	31	7	0	2	17	20	18	.370	.383
September/October	2.38	2	0	0	6	6	45.1	39	2	15	30	First 75 Pitches	.250	572	143	24	4	9	57	58	119	.318	.353
Starter	3.18	8	13	0	30	30	200.2	176	11	70	155	Pitch 76-90	.191	89	17	3	1	1	8	10	20	.280	.281
Reliever	2.25	0	0	0	4	0	4.0	6	0	7	3	Pitch 91-105	.250	64	16	2	0	1	4	7	11	.324	.328
0-3 Days Rest	1.69	1	1	0	2	2	16.0	7	1	3	17	Pitch 106+	.194	31	6	1	0	0	2	2	8	.242	.226
4 Days Rest	3.09	4	7	0	14	14	102.0	84	4	37	71	First Pitch	.298	131	39	8	0	5	18	6	0	.324	.473
5+ Days Rest	3.59	3	5	0	14	14	82.2	85	6	30	67	Ahead on Count	.172	348	60	8	3	2	28	0	139	.173	.230
Pre-All Star	3.67	5	9	0	19	16	108.0	103	7	39	94	Behind on Count	.301	153	46	9	1	3	11	39	0	.446	.431
Post-All Star	2.61	3	4	0	15	14	96.2	79	4	38	64	Two Strikes	.163	344	56	10	4	0	24	32	158	.234	.215

Last Five Years

	ERA	W	L	Sv	G	GS	IP	H	HR	BB	SO		Avg	AB	H	2B	3B	HR	RBI	BB	SO	OBP	SLG
Home	3.71	27	27	1	81	63	451.1	408	28	171	347	vs. Left	.271	1920	520	93	17	38	228	261	352	.358	.396
Away	4.02	23	35	2	94	67	465.1	465	40	198	337	vs. Right	.228	1547	353	48	6	30	140	108	332	.284	.325
Day	3.38	13	15	0	45	31	234.0	213	12	82	170	Inning 1-6	.246	2769	682	117	21	51	301	301	563	.322	.359
Night	4.03	37	47	3	130	99	682.2	660	56	287	514	Inning 7+	.274	698	191	24	2	17	67	68	121	.343	.387
Grass	3.78	22	30	3	87	54	404.1	394	28	159	303	None on	.247	2022	499	76	9	45	45	184	412	.314	.360
Turf	3.93	28	32	0	88	76	512.1	479	40	210	381	Runners on	.259	1445	374	65	14	23	323	185	272	.342	.371
April	3.52	7	10	0	23	22	135.1	139	9	55	110	Scoring Posn	.246	883	217	37	11	16	296	137	193	.343	.367
May	3.16	15	6	0	30	24	179.2	152	11	60	147	Close & Late	.276	340	94	12	0	7	33	27	73	.335	.374
June	4.62	8	12	2	29	22	157.2	159	12	59	108	None on/out	.274	899	246	38	6	24	24	81	174	.337	.409
July	3.64	7	11	0	28	19	136.0	120	10	71	102	vs. 1st Batr (relief)	.350	40	14	3	0	2	4	5	8	.422	.575
August	4.53	6	13	0	34	22	153.0	147	15	62	109	First Inning Pitched	.255	623	159	26	6	9	79	92	124	.352	.360
September/October	3.77	7	10	0	31	21	155.0	156	11	62	108	First 75 Pitches	.251	2546	638	102	15	47	258	259	521	.322	.358
Starter	4.00	43	56	0	130	130	832.2	784	62	336	612	Pitch 76-90	.270	404	109	21	6	13	66	56	73	.361	.448
Reliever	2.57	7	6	3	45	0	84.0	89	6	33	72	Pitch 91-105	.240	304	73	7	2	4	18	26	52	.303	.316
0-3 Days Rest	3.76	5	5	0	10	10	64.2	50	6	28	50	Pitch 106+	.249	213	53	11	0	4	26	28	38	.340	.357
4 Days Rest	4.06	25	32	0	74	74	483.0	450	38	195	365	First Pitch	.320	541	173	32	3	16	80	24	0	.353	.479
5+ Days Rest	3.95	13	19	0	46	46	285.0	284	18	113	197	Ahead on Count	.180	1541	277	43	9	11	112	0	568	.184	.241
Pre-All Star	3.80	32	32	3	91	74	516.1	494	35	197	394	Behind on Count	.339	737	250	40	7	29	110	195	0	.477	.531
Post-All Star	3.96	18	30	0	84	56	400.1	379	33	172	290	Two Strikes	.163	1574	257	45	10	11	108	149	683	.238	.226

Pitcher vs. Batter (since 1984)

Pitches Best Vs.	Avg	AB	H	2B	3B	HR	RBI	BB	SO	OBP	SLG	Pitches Worst Vs.	Avg	AB	H	2B	3B	HR	RBI	BB	SO	OBP	SLG
Bob Melvin	.000	10	0	0	0	0	0	1	4	.091	.000	Dave Justice	.600	10	6	0	0	2	5	2	2	.571	1.200
Craig Biggio	.074	27	2	0	0	0	2	2	6	.138	.074	Jeff Bagwell	.462	13	6	0	0	2	3	2	0	.500	.923
Mark Bailey	.077	13	1	0	0	0	0	2	6	.200	.077	Rafael Palmeiro	.429	14	6	2	1	1	5	3	0	.529	.929
Todd Benzinger	.100	10	1	0	0	0	2	0	1	.091	.100	Tom Brunansky	.385	13	5	0	2	1	3	3	3	.500	.923
Orlando Merced	.100	10	1	0	0	0	1	1	1	.182	.100	Von Hayes	.364	11	4	0	1	1	3	4	1	.533	1.091

Kip Gross — Dodgers

	ERA	W	L	Sv	G	GS	IP	BB	SO	Avg	H	2B	3B	HR	RBI	OBP	SLG	GF	IR	IRS	Hld	SvOp	SB	CS	GB	FB	G/F
1992 Season	4.18	1	1	0	16	1	23.2	10	14	.323	32	5	1	1	11	.385	.424	7	9	1	0	2	1	44	15	2.93
Career (1990-1992)	3.66	7	5	0	50	10	115.2	52	57	.289	131	17	2	9	55	.360	.394	15	24	11	3	0	11	5	200	108	1.85

1992 Season

	ERA	W	L	Sv	G	GS	IP	H	HR	BB	SO		Avg	AB	H	2B	3B	HR	RBI	BB	SO	OBP	SLG
Home	5.00	1	1	0	5	1	9.0	13	0	3	6	vs. Left	.326	46	15	3	1	0	5	7	8	.415	.435

1992 Season

	ERA	W	L	Sv	G	GS	IP	H	HR	BB	SO		Avg	AB	H	2B	3B	HR	RBI	BB	SO	OBP	SLG
Away	3.68	0	0	11	0	14.2	19	1	7	8	vs. Right	.321	53	17	2	0	1	6	3	6	.357	.415

Jeff Grotewold — Phillies   Bats Left (groundball hitter)

	Avg	G	AB	R	H	2B	3B	HR	RBI	BB	SO	HBP	GDP	SB	CS	OBP	SLG	IBB	SH	SF	#Pit	#P/PA	GB	FB	G/F
1992 Season	.200	72	65	7	13	2	0	3	5	9	16	1	4	0	0	.307	.369	0	0	0	327	4.36	26	15	1.73

1992 Season

	Avg	AB	H	2B	3B	HR	RBI	BB	SO	OBP	SLG		Avg	AB	H	2B	3B	HR	RBI	BB	SO	OBP	SLG
vs. Left	.200	10	2	0	0	1	1	2	4	.333	.500	Scoring Posn	.182	11	2	0	0	0	1	3	4	.400	.182
vs. Right	.200	55	11	2	0	2	4	7	12	.302	.345	Close & Late	.200	25	5	0	0	3	4	2	9	.259	.560

Kelly Gruber — Blue Jays   Bats Right

	Avg	G	AB	R	H	2B	3B	HR	RBI	BB	SO	HBP	GDP	SB	CS	OBP	SLG	IBB	SH	SF	#Pit	#P/PA	GB	FB	G/F
1992 Season	.229	120	446	42	102	16	3	11	43	26	72	4	14	7	7	.275	.352	3	1	4	1613	3.36	150	161	0.93
Last Five Years	.267	676	2581	350	688	127	20	96	380	173	388	28	67	66	26	.316	.443	11	10	31	9378	3.33	942	841	1.12

1992 Season

	Avg	AB	H	2B	3B	HR	RBI	BB	SO	OBP	SLG		Avg	AB	H	2B	3B	HR	RBI	BB	SO	OBP	SLG
vs. Left	.243	107	26	5	1	3	10	7	20	.291	.393	Scoring Posn	.239	113	27	5	0	3	30	6	22	.274	.363
vs. Right	.224	339	76	11	2	8	33	19	52	.270	.339	Close & Late	.236	72	17	4	1	1	8	4	14	.276	.361
Groundball	.270	141	38	6	0	5	19	9	17	.312	.418	None on/out	.221	104	23	4	1	1	1	2	16	.243	.308
Flyball	.210	124	26	4	2	2	9	6	24	.246	.323	Batting #5	.227	220	50	11	2	7	24	12	34	.269	.391
Home	.242	211	51	8	3	7	28	11	39	.284	.408	Batting #7	.238	147	35	3	0	2	14	9	26	.280	.299
Away	.217	235	51	8	0	4	15	15	33	.267	.302	Other	.215	79	17	2	1	2	5	5	12	.281	.342
Day	.192	130	25	5	2	1	10	11	24	.257	.285	April	.246	69	17	6	1	3	10	4	10	.284	.493
Night	.244	316	77	11	1	10	33	15	48	.283	.380	May	.250	96	24	4	1	5	13	6	16	.298	.469
Grass	.234	188	44	7	0	4	15	13	23	.286	.335	June	.192	73	14	1	0	0	4	2	9	.213	.205
Turf	.225	258	58	9	3	7	28	13	49	.266	.364	July	.250	24	6	0	0	1	3	2	5	.321	.375
First Pitch	.235	81	19	2	0	0	4	2	0	.267	.259	August	.195	77	15	1	1	0	1	5	14	.262	.234
Ahead on Count	.237	93	22	5	1	3	15	15	0	.339	.409	September/October	.243	107	26	4	0	2	12	7	18	.287	.336
Behind on Count	.233	159	37	3	0	6	16	0	39	.241	.365	Pre-All Star	.231	238	55	11	2	8	27	12	35	.269	.395
Two Strikes	.177	181	32	7	2	4	15	9	72	.219	.304	Post-All Star	.226	208	47	5	1	3	16	14	37	.282	.303

1992 By Position

Position	Avg	AB	H	2B	3B	HR	RBI	BB	SO	OBP	SLG	G	GS	Innings	PO	A	E	DP	Fld Pct	Rng Fctr	In Zone	Outs	Zone Rtg	MLB Zone
As 3b	.229	445	102	16	3	11	43	26	72	.276	.353	120	118	1021.2	104	214	17	11	.949	2.80	275	234	.851	.841

Last Five Years

	Avg	AB	H	2B	3B	HR	RBI	BB	SO	OBP	SLG		Avg	AB	H	2B	3B	HR	RBI	BB	SO	OBP	SLG
vs. Left	.280	738	207	40	8	27	108	50	109	.323	.466	Scoring Posn	.288	688	198	39	10	27	287	56	98	.337	.491
vs. Right	.261	1843	481	87	12	69	272	123	279	.313	.434	Close & Late	.271	410	111	19	3	13	75	25	68	.315	.427
Groundball	.255	689	176	33	3	18	113	52	85	.315	.390	None on/out	.249	566	141	22	4	16	16	26	78	.289	.387
Flyball	.272	635	173	31	11	30	99	45	105	.321	.498	Batting #3	.273	1028	281	56	8	46	169	73	149	.323	.478
Home	.274	1309	359	56	12	51	191	77	205	.318	.452	Batting #5	.256	438	112	23	2	16	57	23	69	.295	.427
Away	.259	1272	329	71	8	45	189	96	183	.314	.433	Other	.265	1115	295	48	10	34	154	77	170	.318	.417
Day	.258	810	209	41	7	30	125	55	127	.309	.437	April	.299	364	109	19	4	19	68	25	64	.348	.530
Night	.270	1771	479	86	13	66	255	118	261	.319	.446	May	.273	403	110	25	3	15	62	37	64	.336	.462
Grass	.263	1039	273	65	7	41	166	81	141	.320	.457	June	.289	464	134	23	3	20	69	30	59	.339	.481
Turf	.269	1542	415	62	13	55	214	92	247	.314	.433	July	.243	395	96	15	0	14	47	20	58	.286	.367
First Pitch	.305	512	156	30	2	20	62	7	0	.321	.488	August	.219	434	95	21	3	6	39	21	64	.259	.323
Ahead on Count	.307	499	153	35	7	26	106	83	0	.403	.561	September/October	.276	521	144	24	7	22	95	40	79	.327	.476
Behind on Count	.242	952	230	32	6	33	131	1	234	.246	.392	Pre-All Star	.282	1331	376	71	10	54	205	96	196	.335	.473
Two Strikes	.186	1061	201	35	7	26	124	81	387	.219	.303	Post-All Star	.250	1250	312	56	10	42	175	77	192	.296	.411

Batter vs. Pitcher (career)

Hits Best Against	Avg	AB	H	2B	3B	HR	RBI	BB	SO	OBP	SLG	Hits Worst Against	Avg	AB	H	2B	3B	HR	RBI	BB	SO	OBP	SLG
Jeff Reardon	.500	12	6	2	0	1	2	2	1	.571	.917	Steve Farr	.077	13	1	0	0	0	0	0	3	.077	.077
Jeff Russell	.429	14	6	1	0	2	6	0	0	.400	.929	Jose Guzman	.077	13	1	0	0	0	0	0	4	.077	.077
Floyd Bannister	.417	12	5	1	0	2	7	0	2	.417	1.000	Mark Langston	.080	25	2	0	0	0	0	1	10	.115	.080
Charles Nagy	.400	20	8	3	0	2	6	2	2	.455	.850	Tim Leary	.083	12	1	0	0	0	1	1	3	.154	.083
Jeff M. Robinson	.400	10	4	1	0	1	4	1	2	.417	.800	Nolan Ryan	.091	22	2	0	0	0	0	1	6	.130	.091

Mark Gubicza — Royals   Pitches Right (groundball pitcher)

	ERA	W	L	Sv	G	GS	IP	BB	SO	Avg	H	2B	3B	HR	RBI	OBP	SLG	CG	ShO	Sup	QS	#P/S	SB	CS	GB	FB	G/F
1992 Season	3.72	7	6	0	18	18	111.1	36	81	.259	110	19	3	8	44	.316	.374	2	1	3.88	8	96	4	4	157	110	1.43
Last Five Years	3.59	55	44	0	131	131	863.0	262	597	.262	868	145	21	44	329	.318	.358	20	7	4.40	70	101	65	27	1454	679	2.14

1992 Season

	ERA	W	L	Sv	G	GS	IP	H	HR	BB	SO		Avg	AB	H	2B	3B	HR	RBI	BB	SO	OBP	SLG
Home	2.88	5	2	0	10	10	68.2	64	2	19	38	vs. Left	.228	215	49	10	2	5	22	18	39	.285	.363
Away	5.06	2	4	0	8	8	42.2	46	6	17	43	vs. Right	.290	210	61	9	1	3	22	18	42	.348	.386

1992 Season

	ERA	W	L	Sv	G	GS	IP	H	HR	BB	SO
Starter	3.72	7	6	0	18	18	111.1	110	8	36	81
Reliever	0.00	0	0	0	0	0	0.0	0	0	0	0
0-3 Days Rest	0.00	0	0	0	0	0	0.0	0	0	0	0
4 Days Rest	2.77	5	2	0	11	11	68.1	62	4	22	46
5+ Days Rest	5.23	2	4	0	7	7	43.0	48	4	14	35
Pre-All Star	3.72	7	6	0	18	18	111.1	110	8	36	81
Post-All Star	0.00	0	0	0	0	0	0.0	0	0	0	0

	Avg	AB	H	2B	3B	HR	RBI	BB	SO	OBP	SLG
Scoring Posn	.305	95	29	3	3	2	37	14	17	.384	.463
Close & Late	.250	40	10	1	0	2	7	7	4	.354	.425
None on/out	.221	113	25	6	0	4	4	5	25	.254	.381
First Pitch	.302	63	19	1	0	4	13	3	0	.319	.508
Behind on Count	.366	93	34	8	0	2	10	19	0	.473	.516
Ahead on Count	.211	180	38	5	2	1	13	0	58	.211	.278
Two Strikes	.215	191	41	5	3	2	17	14	81	.268	.304

Last Five Years

	ERA	W	L	Sv	G	GS	IP	H	HR	BB	SO
Home	3.56	28	21	0	69	69	455.2	454	15	134	297
Away	3.62	27	23	0	62	62	407.1	414	29	128	300
Day	3.79	16	13	0	38	38	254.0	260	10	87	178
Night	3.50	39	31	0	93	93	609.0	608	34	175	419
Grass	3.54	18	17	0	47	47	310.1	310	22	97	228
Turf	3.62	37	27	0	84	84	552.2	558	22	165	369
April	3.77	6	8	0	19	19	121.2	126	2	51	70
May	3.58	12	12	0	29	29	203.2	203	9	61	128
June	3.10	15	7	0	27	27	183.0	184	11	50	135
July	3.97	5	5	0	19	19	115.2	122	13	36	77
August	3.05	10	5	0	19	19	129.2	116	2	33	100
September/October	4.45	7	7	0	18	18	109.1	117	7	31	87
Starter	3.59	55	44	0	131	131	863.0	868	44	262	597
Reliever	0.00	0	0	0	0	0	0.0	0	0	0	0
0-3 Days Rest	3.59	3	4	0	11	11	67.2	69	3	23	38
4 Days Rest	3.47	35	28	0	83	83	557.1	542	24	172	392
5+ Days Rest	3.86	17	12	0	37	37	238.0	257	17	67	167
Pre-All Star	3.42	35	29	0	83	83	555.1	562	25	171	368
Post-All Star	3.89	20	15	0	48	48	307.2	306	19	91	229

	Avg	AB	H	2B	3B	HR	RBI	BB	SO	OBP	SLG
vs. Left	.260	1667	434	73	10	22	151	155	267	.326	.356
vs. Right	.264	1645	434	72	11	22	177	107	330	.310	.361
Inning 1-6	.265	2739	726	122	14	36	282	222	490	.322	.359
Inning 7+	.248	573	142	23	7	8	46	40	107	.297	.354
None on	.258	1895	489	86	13	25	25	151	349	.316	.357
Runners on	.267	1417	379	59	8	19	303	111	248	.320	.361
Scoring Posn	.252	813	205	33	6	13	275	80	162	.315	.355
Close & Late	.238	294	70	15	2	4	23	27	55	.303	.344
vs. 1st Batr (relief)	.000	0	0	0	0	0	0	0	0	.000	.000
First Inning Pitched	.259	491	127	16	0	5	46	38	88	.317	.322
First 75 Pitches	.263	2365	622	106	11	28	216	178	411	.317	.353
Pitch 76-90	.279	394	110	12	7	6	50	30	80	.330	.391
Pitch 91-105	.262	286	75	14	2	4	34	35	52	.345	.367
Pitch 106+	.228	267	61	13	1	6	29	19	54	.283	.352
First Pitch	.311	540	168	32	5	12	91	17	0	.327	.456
Ahead on Count	.187	1305	244	40	9	8	91	0	485	.194	.250
Behind on Count	.366	815	298	53	4	16	99	134	0	.453	.499
Two Strikes	.174	1386	241	37	8	9	78	111	597	.240	.232

Pitcher vs. Batter (career)

Pitches Best Vs.	Avg	AB	H	2B	3B	HR	RBI	BB	SO	OBP	SLG
Dick Schofield	.000	27	0	0	0	0	0	1	5	.036	.000
Stan Javier	.000	11	0	0	0	0	0	1	1	.000	.000
Geno Petralli	.053	19	1	0	0	0	0	2	6	.136	.053
Mark McLemore	.083	12	1	0	0	0	1	0	1	.083	.083
Al Newman	.095	21	2	0	0	0	0		4	.136	.095

Pitches Worst Vs.	Avg	AB	H	2B	3B	HR	RBI	BB	SO	OBP	SLG
Fred McGriff	.500	20	10	3	0	4	4	3	3	.565	1.250
Edgar Martinez	.500	12	6	2	0	1	3	1	1	.538	.917
Dion James	.417	12	5	1	0	1	3	2	1	.500	.750
Randy Milligan	.417	12	5	1	1	2	7	1	4	.462	1.167
Ivan Calderon	.400	15	6	3	0	2	4	0	3	.400	1.000

Juan Guerrero — Astros   Bats Right

	Avg	G	AB	R	H	2B	3B	HR	RBI	BB	SO	HBP	GDP	SB	CS	OBP	SLG	IBB	SH	SF	#Pit	#P/PA	GB	FB	G/F
1992 Season	.200	79	125	8	25	4	2	1	14	10	32	1	0	1	0	.261	.288	2	1	2	524	3.80	36	32	1.13

1992 Season

	Avg	AB	H	2B	3B	HR	RBI	BB	SO	OBP	SLG
vs. Left	.197	61	12	3	0	0	8	8	14	.286	.246
vs. Right	.203	64	13	1	2	1	6	2	18	.235	.328
Home	.222	45	10	1	2	1	5	8	17	.340	.400
Away	.188	80	15	3	0	0	9	2	15	.212	.289
First Pitch	.250	8	2	1	1	0	2		0	.400	.625
Ahead on Count	.300	30	9	2	0	1	5	3	0	.353	.467
Behind on Count	.167	54	9	1	0	0	4	0	21	.179	.185
Two Strikes	.111	63	7	0	1	0	3	5	32	.176	.143

	Avg	AB	H	2B	3B	HR	RBI	BB	SO	OBP	SLG
Scoring Posn	.125	40	5	0	0	0	9	5	12	.213	.125
Close & Late	.233	30	7	0	0	1	4	4	6	.314	.333
None on/out	.074	27	2	0	1	0	0	2	6	.167	.148
Batting #7	.211	38	8	1	1	0	3	1	13	.225	.289
Batting #8	.212	33	7	2	1	0	6	2	3	.270	.333
Other	.185	54	10	1	0	1	5	7	16	.279	.259
Pre-All Star	.167	60	10	2	2	0	7	5	17	.231	.267
Post-All Star	.231	65	15	2	0	1	7	5	15	.288	.308

Pedro Guerrero — Cardinals   Bats Right

	Avg	G	AB	R	H	2B	3B	HR	RBI	BB	SO	HBP	GDP	SB	CS	OBP	SLG	IBB	SH	SF	#Pit	#P/PA	GB	FB	G/F
1992 Season	.219	43	146	10	32	6	1	1	16	11	25	0	4	2	2	.270	.295	3	0	2	545	3.43	57	47	1.21
Last Five Years	.284	559	2005	193	569	105	6	49	348	217	284	11	52	13	6	.351	.415	41	0	39	8015	3.53	735	653	1.13

1992 Season

	Avg	AB	H	2B	3B	HR	RBI	BB	SO	OBP	SLG
vs. Left	.211	38	8	1	0	1	2	4	6	.286	.316
vs. Right	.222	108	24	5	1	0	14	7	19	.265	.287
Home	.254	71	18	3	0	1	13	8	13	.325	.338
Away	.187	75	14	3	1	0	3	3	12	.215	.253
First Pitch	.250	32	8	3	0	0	6	2	0	.278	.344
Ahead on Count	.200	25	5	1	1	1	4	7	0	.375	.440
Behind on Count	.128	47	6	1	0	1	3	0	12	.128	.213
Two Strikes	.197	66	13	1	0	0	4	2	25	.221	.212

	Avg	AB	H	2B	3B	HR	RBI	BB	SO	OBP	SLG
Scoring Posn	.170	53	9	2	0	0	14	6	15	.246	.208
Close & Late	.240	25	6	0	0	0	2	4	5	.323	.240
None on/out	.282	39	11	2	1	0	0	2	6	.317	.385
Batting #4	.195	87	17	5	1	1	8	4	18	.226	.310
Batting #5	.269	52	14	1	0	0	8	5	6	.333	.288
Other	.143	7	1	0	0	0	0	2	1	.333	.143
Pre-All Star	.221	145	32	6	1	1	16	11	25	.272	.297
Post-All Star	.000	1	0	0	0	0	0	0	0	.000	.000

Last Five Years

	Avg	AB	H	2B	3B	HR	RBI	BB	SO	OBP	SLG
vs. Left	.281	709	199	43	2	16	103	88	105	.357	.415

	Avg	AB	H	2B	3B	HR	RBI	BB	SO	OBP	SLG
Scoring Posn	.326	622	203	43	2	15	298	108	87	.408	.474

Last Five Years

	Avg	AB	H	2B	3B	HR	RBI	BB	SO	OBP	SLG		Avg	AB	H	2B	3B	HR	RBI	BB	SO	OBP	SLG
vs. Right	.285	1296	370	62	4	33	245	129	179	.347	.416	Close & Late	.263	304	80	12	0	5	53	45	42	.354	.352
Groundball	.284	716	203	26	0	15	106	85	94	.359	.385	None on/out	.261	505	132	23	2	10	10	31	72	.304	.374
Flyball	.276	445	123	27	1	16	98	50	72	.343	.449	Batting #3	.297	340	101	19	2	15	74	46	52	.376	.497
Home	.286	1021	292	61	2	21	196	115	155	.353	.411	Batting #4	.282	1594	450	85	4	34	262	162	224	.346	.405
Away	.262	984	277	44	4	28	152	102	129	.349	.420	Other	.254	71	18	1	0	0	12	9	8	.333	.268
Day	.285	600	171	31	2	16	101	69	84	.357	.423	April	.289	377	109	18	0	13	74	43	49	.361	.440
Night	.283	1405	398	74	4	33	247	148	200	.348	.412	May	.284	395	112	24	3	6	64	37	49	.340	.405
Grass	.298	650	194	26	3	21	108	63	86	.359	.445	June	.279	326	91	16	2	3	49	38	44	.349	.368
Turf	.277	1355	375	79	3	28	240	154	198	.347	.401	July	.294	221	65	16	0	8	42	21	30	.353	.475
First Pitch	.371	361	134	25	2	12	86	15	0	.389	.551	August	.289	308	89	12	1	8	49	36	50	.361	.412
Ahead on Count	.347	475	165	36	2	19	118	119	0	.470	.552	September/October	.272	378	103	19	0	11	70	42	62	.344	.410
Behind on Count	.246	646	159	26	1	13	85	2	150	.248	.350	Pre-All Star	.283	1188	336	62	5	26	205	122	155	.346	.409
Two Strikes	.201	840	169	24	2	9	87	63	284	.257	.267	Post-All Star	.285	817	233	43	1	23	143	95	129	.357	.425

Batter vs. Pitcher (since 1984)

Hits Best Against	Avg	AB	H	2B	3B	HR	RBI	BB	SO	OBP	SLG	Hits Worst Against	Avg	AB	H	2B	3B	HR	RBI	BB	SO	OBP	SLG
Dennis Rasmussen	.733	15	11	2	0	0	4	0	0	.733	.867	Dave Smith	.000	10	0	0	0	0	0	3	1	.231	.000
Mark Gardner	.500	14	7	0	0	2	2	2	1	.563	.929	Shawn Boskie	.000	10	0	0	0	0	0	1	2	.091	.000
Don Carman	.500	12	6	1	0	1	5	5	2	.611	.833	Orel Hershiser	.063	16	1	0	0	0	0	0	2	.063	.063
Tom Glavine	.455	22	10	3	0	2	6	0	2	.455	.864	John Burkett	.067	15	1	0	0	0	1	2	2	.176	.067
Joe Boever	.375	8	3	0	0	2	3	3	0	.545	1.125	Pete Smith	.118	17	2	0	0	0	3	0	1	.111	.118

Lee Guetterman — Mets
Pitches Left (groundball pitcher)

	ERA	W	L	Sv	G	GS	IP	BB	SO	Avg	H	2B	3B	HR	RBI	OBP	SLG	GF	IR	IRS	Hld	SvOp	SB	CS	GB	FB	G/F
1992 Season	7.09	4	5	2	58	0	66.0	27	20	.335	92	16	2	10	54	.390	.516	22	32	10	9	3	5	1	133	65	2.05
Last Five Years	3.96	24	23	23	276	2	390.2	118	169	.274	410	64	11	30	197	.327	.392	80	226	64	44	33	22	9	741	337	2.20

1992 Season

	ERA	W	L	Sv	G	GS	IP	H	HR	BB	SO		Avg	AB	H	2B	3B	HR	RBI	BB	SO	OBP	SLG
Home	8.41	3	4	1	27	0	35.1	54	5	17	11	vs. Left	.278	90	25	4	0	1	9	10	6	.353	.356
Away	5.58	1	1	1	31	0	30.2	38	5	10	9	vs. Right	.362	185	67	12	2	9	45	17	14	.408	.595
Starter	0.00	0	0	0	0	0	0.0	0	0	0	0	Scoring Posn	.338	80	27	9	1	3	43	16	7	.426	.588
Reliever	7.09	4	5	2	58	0	66.0	92	10	27	20	Close & Late	.324	111	36	4	0	7	21	12	11	.381	.550
0 Days rest	5.95	2	1	1	16	0	19.2	26	2	7	7	None on/out	.270	63	17	4	0	2	1		2	.292	.429
1 or 2 Days rest	8.49	1	3	1	23	0	23.1	39	6	11	6	First Pitch	.422	45	19	3	0	2	10	5	0	.471	.622
3+ Days rest	6.65	1	1	0	19	0	23.0	27	2	9	7	Behind on Count	.369	65	24	4	2	3	14	11	0	.455	.631
Pre-All Star	6.69	2	1	1	30	0	40.1	53	6	18	11	Ahead on Count	.304	115	35	6	0	3	22	0	18	.305	.435
Post-All Star	7.71	2	4	1	28	0	25.2	39	4	9	9	Two Strikes	.298	104	31	7	0	1	19	11	20	.359	.394

Last Five Years

	ERA	W	L	Sv	G	GS	IP	H	HR	BB	SO		Avg	AB	H	2B	3B	HR	RBI	BB	SO	OBP	SLG
Home	4.15	18	11	14	146	1	227.2	238	17	67	104	vs. Left	.239	439	105	16	3	5	43	40	61	.307	.323
Away	3.70	6	12	9	130	1	163.0	172	13	51	65	vs. Right	.289	1055	305	48	8	25	154	78	108	.335	.421
Day	3.07	10	6	6	85	0	114.1	112	9	35	39	Inning 1-6	.274	230	63	11	1	5	36	24	38	.340	.396
Night	4.33	14	17	17	191	2	276.1	298	21	83	130	Inning 7+	.275	1264	347	53	10	25	161	94	131	.324	.392
Grass	3.85	22	19	20	237	2	339.0	353	23	104	150	None on	.284	775	220	33	4	15	15	39	86	.322	.395
Turf	4.70	2	4	3	39	0	51.2	57	7	14	19	Runners on	.264	719	190	31	7	15	182	79	83	.332	.389
April	3.36	1	1	3	34	0	56.1	58	5	17	30	Scoring Posn	.250	440	110	19	5	12	168	62	58	.334	.398
May	2.59	3	2	7	44	0	59.0	48	4	19	21	Close & Late	.277	552	153	16	4	19	81	44	57	.331	.424
June	3.61	5	2	2	48	0	62.1	72	1	16	24	None on/out	.294	337	99	15	0	7	7	9	34	.316	.401
July	4.45	5	6	4	43	0	60.2	67	9	20	21	vs. 1st Batr (relief)	.227	247	56	10	2	2	34	18	31	.275	.308
August	5.38	4	5	4	58	1	80.1	92	6	25	38	First Inning Pitched	.259	884	229	29	9	17	129	70	96	.312	.370
September/October	3.88	6	7	3	49	1	72.0	73	5	21	35	First 15 Pitches	.267	847	226	29	7	18	106	63	85	.316	.381
Starter	9.45	0	2	0	2	2	6.2	13	1	4	3	Pitch 16-30	.294	436	128	23	2	8	57	29	53	.338	.411
Reliever	3.87	24	21	23	274	0	364.0	397	29	114	166	Pitch 31-45	.224	143	32	8	2	2	19	16	22	.300	.350
0 Days rest	3.18	8	3	7	70	0	90.2	91	7	21	37	Pitch 46+	.353	68	24	4	0	2	15	10	9	.436	.500
1 or 2 Days rest	3.25	8	9	11	122	0	177.1	164	13	57	80	First Pitch	.313	211	66	10	0	5	33	21	0	.371	.431
3+ Days rest	5.35	8	8	5	82	0	116.0	142	9	36	49	Ahead on Count	.218	618	135	21	4	6	59	1	148	.222	.294
Pre-All Star	3.16	11	6	16	143	0	205.0	204	14	58	88	Behind on Count	.332	385	128	18	4	15	65	51	0	.408	.517
Post-All Star	4.85	13	17	7	133	2	185.2	206	16	60	81	Two Strikes	.203	572	116	19	4	1	50	45	169	.262	.255

Pitcher vs. Batter (career)

Pitches Best Vs.	Avg	AB	H	2B	3B	HR	RBI	BB	SO	OBP	SLG	Pitches Worst Vs.	Avg	AB	H	2B	3B	HR	RBI	BB	SO	OBP	SLG
Gary Pettis	.000	11	0	0	0	0	0	0	2	.000	.000	Dave Winfield	.900	10	9	0	1	1	4	1	0	.909	1.400
Dan Gladden	.071	14	1	0	0	0	0	0	2	.071	.071	Jim Eisenreich	.545	11	6	2	0	0	0	2	0	.615	.727
Mike Felder	.091	11	1	0	0	0	0	0	0	.091	.091	Mike Greenwell	.533	15	8	0	1	1	4	2	2	.588	.867
Ellis Burks	.133	15	2	0	0	0	0	0	2	.133	.133	Rob Deer	.429	7	3	1	0	2	3	4	1	.536	1.429
B.J. Surhoff	.154	13	2	0	0	0	1	0	1	.143	.154	Steve Buechele	.353	17	6	2	1	2	6	2	1	.421	.941

Ozzie Guillen — White Sox — Bats Left (groundball hitter)

	Avg	G	AB	R	H	2B	3B	HR	RBI	BB	SO	HBP	GDP	SB	CS	OBP	SLG	IBB	SH	SF	#Pit	#P/PA	GB	FB	G/F
1992 Season	.200	12	40	5	8	4	0	0	7	1	5	0	1	1	0	.214	.300	0	1	1	109	2.60	8	17	0.47
Last Five Years	.265	637	2243	239	594	81	22	5	207	78	168	3	36	96	62	.288	.327	15	50	19	6940	2.96	1010	617	1.64

1992 Season

	Avg	AB	H	2B	3B	HR	RBI	BB	SO	OBP	SLG		Avg	AB	H	2B	3B	HR	RBI	BB	SO	OBP	SLG
vs. Left	.158	19	3	3	0	0	1	0	3	.158	.316	Scoring Posn	.400	15	6	2	0	0	7	0	2	.375	.533
vs. Right	.238	21	5	1	0	0	6	1	2	.261	.286	Close & Late	.000	8	0	0	0	0	0	1	0	.111	.000

Last Five Years

	Avg	AB	H	2B	3B	HR	RBI	BB	SO	OBP	SLG		Avg	AB	H	2B	3B	HR	RBI	BB	SO	OBP	SLG
vs. Left	.248	766	190	22	3	1	70	16	73	.262	.289	Scoring Posn	.292	559	163	27	9	3	197	30	31	.319	.388
vs. Right	.274	1477	404	59	19	4	137	62	95	.301	.347	Close & Late	.276	438	121	19	4	1	48	25	35	.315	.345
Groundball	.263	598	157	20	3	2	61	19	38	.283	.281	None on/out	.234	552	129	22	2	0	0	18	52	.258	.261
Flyball	.273	516	141	17	6	1	41	18	41	.297	.335	Batting #8	.280	493	138	12	4	0	38	22	36	.310	.320
Home	.264	1063	286	37	14	2	104	39	85	.288	.330	Batting #9	.273	1257	343	55	12	5	143	37	87	.291	.348
Away	.266	1160	308	44	8	3	103	39	83	.289	.325	Other	.229	493	113	14	6	0	26	19	45	.258	.282
Day	.276	601	166	22	7	1	56	25	48	.305	.341	April	.238	349	83	13	3	0	28	12	31	.260	.292
Night	.261	1642	428	59	15	4	151	53	120	.282	.322	May	.297	417	124	16	4	0	25	17	33	.323	.355
Grass	.258	1912	494	69	19	5	174	65	145	.281	.322	June	.265	385	102	13	3	0	38	5	27	.273	.314
Turf	.302	331	100	12	3	0	33	13	23	.328	.356	July	.280	354	99	9	4	0	39	11	27	.304	.328
First Pitch	.281	570	160	25	4	3	70	3	0	.281	.354	August	.246	374	92	17	4	3	40	14	19	.270	.337
Ahead on Count	.293	345	101	15	3	1	41	45	0	.372	.362	September/October	.258	364	94	13	4	2	37	19	31	.294	.332
Behind on Count	.251	853	214	26	7	1	71	0	120	.250	.301	Pre-All Star	.266	1246	332	44	10	0	98	37	101	.286	.318
Two Strikes	.222	772	171	24	8	0	50	21	168	.243	.273	Post-All Star	.263	997	262	37	12	5	109	41	67	.291	.339

Batter vs. Pitcher (career)

Hits Best Against	Avg	AB	H	2B	3B	HR	RBI	BB	SO	OBP	SLG	Hits Worst Against	Avg	AB	H	2B	3B	HR	RBI	BB	SO	OBP	SLG
Tom Gordon	.615	13	8	1	0	0	3	1	0	.643	.692	Kevin Brown	.000	22	0	0	0	0	0	0	1	.000	.000
Danny Jackson	.526	19	10	0	0	0	2	0	2	.526	.526	Matt Young	.000	17	0	0	0	0	0	0	5	.000	.000
Mike Flanagan	.500	22	11	1	0	1	3	0	2	.500	.682	Kenny Rogers	.071	14	1	0	0	0	2	0	0	.071	.071
Lee Guetterman	.500	16	8	1	0	0	6	0	1	.471	.563	Rick Honeycutt	.095	21	2	0	0	0	1	0	2	.095	.095
Rod Nichols	.462	13	6	1	0	0	1	1	1	.500	.538	Jim Acker	.100	10	1	0	0	0	0	1	0	.091	.100

Bill Gullickson — Tigers — Pitches Right

	ERA	W	L	Sv	G	GS	IP	BB	SO	Avg	H	2B	3B	HR	RBI	OBP	SLG	CG	ShO	Sup	QS	#P/S	SB	CS	GB	FB	G/F
1992 Season	4.34	14	13	0	34	34	221.2	50	64	.267	228	38	5	35	98	.305	.447	4	1	5.32	17	89	20	8	276	318	0.87
Last Five Years	4.03	44	36	0	101	101	641.1	155	228	.281	705	126	21	84	290	.321	.441	10	2	5.00	53	88	58	25	897	841	1.07

1992 Season

	ERA	W	L	Sv	G	GS	IP	H	HR	BB	SO		Avg	AB	H	2B	3B	HR	RBI	BB	SO	OBP	SLG
Home	4.28	6	9	0	18	18	130.1	137	24	25	32	vs. Left	.280	414	116	18	4	18	52	28	21	.322	.473
Away	4.43	8	4	0	16	16	91.1	91	11	25	32	vs. Right	.255	439	112	20	1	17	46	22	43	.288	.421
Day	4.72	3	6	0	12	12	74.1	81	13	17	16	Inning 1-6	.264	701	185	33	4	29	83	39	57	.299	.447
Night	4.15	11	7	0	22	22	147.1	147	22	33	48	Inning 7+	.283	152	43	5	1	6	15	11	7	.329	.447
Grass	4.30	11	11	0	27	27	184.1	192	30	40	53	None on	.280	540	151	28	3	19	19	30	41	.318	.448
Turf	4.58	3	2	0	7	7	37.1	36	5	10	11	Runners on	.246	313	77	10	2	16	79	20	23	.284	.444
April	3.94	3	2	0	5	5	32.0	32	7	7	12	Scoring Posn	.265	162	43	7	1	6	56	17	10	.319	.432
May	2.09	3	1	0	6	6	43.0	37	2	5	13	Close & Late	.308	78	24	2	0	4	9	6	2	.353	.487
June	3.81	3	1	0	5	5	28.1	25	2	10	13	None on/out	.296	230	68	13	3	8	8	16	20	.341	.483
July	4.89	2	3	0	6	6	42.1	40	7	9	7	vs. 1st Batr (relief)	.000	0	0	0	0	0	0	0	0	.000	.000
August	3.92	3	1	0	6	6	41.1	42	4	8	8	First Inning Pitched	.279	129	36	5	2	7	21	6	8	.307	.512
September/October	7.79	0	5	0	6	6	34.2	52	13	11	11	First 75 Pitches	.267	652	174	30	4	28	76	34	47	.300	.454
Starter	4.34	14	13	0	34	34	221.2	228	35	50	64	Pitch 76-90	.252	103	26	6	1	3	10	10	10	.316	.417
Reliever	0.00	0	0	0	0	0	0.0	0	0	0	0	Pitch 91-105	.288	73	21	1	0	3	8	5	5	.312	.425
0-3 Days Rest	0.00	0	0	0	0	0	0.0	0	0	0	0	Pitch 106+	.280	25	7	1	0	1	4	3	2	.357	.440
4 Days Rest	4.54	8	6	0	21	21	140.2	152	20	31	34	First Pitch	.239	142	34	5	1	7	17	2	0	.245	.437
5+ Days Rest	4.00	6	5	0	13	13	81.0	76	15	19	30	Ahead on Count	.253	324	82	12	1	6	31	0	56	.252	.352
Pre-All Star	3.36	9	6	0	19	19	126.0	116	14	27	40	Behind on Count	.269	234	63	15	2	14	29	37	0	.366	.530
Post-All Star	5.64	5	7	0	15	15	95.2	112	21	23	24	Two Strikes	.252	274	69	14	0	6	24	11	64	.280	.369

Last Five Years

	ERA	W	L	Sv	G	GS	IP	H	HR	BB	SO		Avg	AB	H	2B	3B	HR	RBI	BB	SO	OBP	SLG
Home	4.37	24	20	0	54	54	348.1	387	53	79	124	vs. Left	.291	1369	398	73	11	45	161	96	86	.336	.459
Away	3.62	20	16	0	47	47	293.0	318	25	76	104	vs. Right	.269	1143	307	53	10	33	129	59	142	.302	.419
Day	4.11	11	12	0	34	34	214.2	245	28	56	72	Inning 1-6	.275	2131	587	111	18	63	247	126	202	.314	.433
Night	3.99	33	24	0	67	67	426.2	460	50	99	156	Inning 7+	.310	381	118	15	3	15	43	29	26	.357	.483
Grass	4.12	27	21	0	61	61	402.1	435	54	94	140	None on	.283	1522	431	81	11	46	46	80	146	.322	.442
Turf	3.88	17	15	0	40	40	239.0	270	24	61	88	Runners on	.277	990	274	45	10	32	244	75	82	.320	.439
April	4.28	9	6	0	12	12	72.1	75	9	17	28	Scoring Posn	.279	535	149	24	3	16	195	63	49	.340	.424
May	3.48	8	5	0	18	18	113.2	127	7	25	40	Close & Late	.319	182	58	7	1	7	24	15	16	.370	.484
June	2.94	9	6	0	17	17	119.1	119	9	31	52	None on/out	.276	663	183	31	5	19	19	35	67	.314	.424
July	5.42	7	7	0	17	17	104.2	128	18	25	28	vs. 1st Batr (relief)	.000	0	0	0	0	0	0	0	0	.000	.000
August	3.57	8	6	0	18	18	113.1	114	14	25	36	First Inning Pitched	.301	395	119	19	7	11	60	26	31	.343	.514

Last Five Years

	ERA	W	L	Sv	G	GS	IP	H	HR	BB	SO		Avg	AB	H	2B	3B	HR	RBI	BB	SO	OBP	SLG
September/October	4.66	6	9	0	19	19	123.0	142	21	32	44	First 75 Pitches	.271	1985	538	102	17	60	220	114	184	.309	.430
Starter	4.03	44	36	0	101	101	641.1	705	78	155	228	Pitch 76-90	.299	304	91	18	3	7	34	21	26	.344	.447
Reliever	0.00	0	0	0	0	0	0.0	0	0	0	0	Pitch 91-105	.358	159	57	4	1	8	26	16	12	.415	.547
0-3 Days Rest	1.23	2	0	0	2	2	14.2	15	1	0	7	Pitch 106+	.297	64	19	2	0	3	10	4	6	.338	.469
4 Days Rest	4.01	28	24	0	70	70	453.1	510	49	108	150	First Pitch	.269	427	115	22	3	15	53	23	0	.305	.440
5+ Days Rest	4.31	14	12	0	29	29	173.1	180	28	47	71	Ahead on Count	.261	1001	261	44	7	20	114	0	203	.260	.379
Pre-All Star	3.60	25	16	0	53	53	340.0	368	29	85	129	Behind on Count	.298	651	194	38	9	28	69	93	0	.383	.513
Post-All Star	4.51	19	20	0	48	48	301.1	337	49	70	99	Two Strikes	.250	864	216	44	4	17	90	39	228	.281	.369

Pitcher vs. Batter (since 1984)

Pitches Best Vs.	Avg	AB	H	2B	3B	HR	RBI	BB	SO	OBP	SLG	Pitches Worst Vs.	Avg	AB	H	2B	3B	HR	RBI	BB	SO	OBP	SLG
Manuel Lee	.000	13	0	0	0	0	0	2	1	.133	.000	Don Mattingly	.533	15	8	2	0	1	5	1	0	.563	.867
Jay Buhner	.063	16	1	0	0	0	0	2	5	.167	.063	Barry Bonds	.467	15	7	3	1	1	4	2	0	.529	1.000
Dann Bilardello	.067	15	1	0	0	0	0	0	3	.067	.067	Roberto Kelly	.455	11	5	1	0	2	7	1	3	.462	1.091
B.J. Surhoff	.077	13	1	0	0	0	1	1	0	.133	.077	Darryl Strawberry	.433	30	13	3	0	4	10	6	5	.500	.933
Jeff Treadway	.167	12	2	0	0	0	1	0	0	.167	.167	Jose Canseco	.364	11	4	0	1	2	3	2	2	.462	1.091

Eric Gunderson — Mariners   Pitches Left (flyball pitcher)

	ERA	W	L	Sv	G	GS	IP	BB	SO	Avg	H	2B	3B	HR	RBI	OBP	SLG	GF	IR	IRS	Hld	SvOp	SB	CS	GB	FB	G/F
1992 Season	8.68	2	1	0	9	0	9.1	5	2	.324	12	3	0	1	11	.400	.486	4	5	1	0	0	1	3	8	20	0.40
Career (1990-1992)	6.40	3	3	1	18	4	32.1	17	18	.309	42	8	0	3	30	.385	.434	6	10	4	0	1	3	5	41	46	0.89

1992 Season

	ERA	W	L	Sv	G	GS	IP	H	HR	BB	SO		Avg	AB	H	2B	3B	HR	RBI	BB	SO	OBP	SLG
Home	9.72	2	1	0	6	0	8.1	12	1	3	1	vs. Left	.385	13	5	1	0	0	2	0	1	.357	.462
Away	0.00	0	0	0	3	0	1.0	0	0	2	1	vs. Right	.292	24	7	2	0	1	9	5	1	.419	.500

Mark Guthrie — Twins   Pitches Left

	ERA	W	L	Sv	G	GS	IP	BB	SO	Avg	H	2B	3B	HR	RBI	OBP	SLG	GF	IR	IRS	Hld	SvOp	SB	CS	GB	FB	G/F
1992 Season	2.88	2	3	5	54	0	75.0	23	76	.215	59	6	1	7	23	.274	.321	15	57	9	19	7	6	2	107	61	1.75
Career (1989-1992)	3.86	18	21	7	132	41	375.0	124	287	.274	395	64	7	33	154	.331	.397	28	75	19	24	9	37	25	520	377	1.38

1992 Season

	ERA	W	L	Sv	G	GS	IP	H	HR	BB	SO		Avg	AB	H	2B	3B	HR	RBI	BB	SO	OBP	SLG
Home	2.02	2	0	3	25	0	35.2	26	2	13	39	vs. Left	.205	88	18	3	1	0	6	5	22	.242	.261
Away	3.66	0	3	2	29	0	39.1	33	5	10	37	vs. Right	.220	186	41	3	0	7	17	18	54	.289	.349
Starter	0.00	0	0	0	0	0	0.0	0	0	0	0	Scoring Posn	.157	83	13	1	0	1	16	13	26	.265	.205
Reliever	2.88	2	3	5	54	0	75.0	59	7	23	76	Close & Late	.208	96	20	3	1	1	9	10	32	.280	.292
0 Days rest	1.69	0	1	0	5	0	5.1	2	0	1	6	None on/out	.323	62	20	1	0	0	0	4	13	.364	.371
1 or 2 Days rest	2.03	1	1	4	30	0	44.1	31	2	14	44	First Pitch	.185	27	5	1	1	1	5	7	0	.353	.407
3+ Days rest	4.62	1	1	1	19	0	25.1	26	5	8	26	Behind on Count	.255	51	13	1	0	2	9	12	1	.385	.392
Pre-All Star	3.45	1	2	2	30	0	47.0	39	5	17	46	Ahead on Count	.167	144	24	2	0	1	4	0	63	.167	.201
Post-All Star	1.93	1	1	3	24	0	28.0	20	2	6	30	Two Strikes	.157	134	21	2	0	1	2	4	75	.181	.194

Career (1989-1992)

	ERA	W	L	Sv	G	GS	IP	H	HR	BB	SO		Avg	AB	H	2B	3B	HR	RBI	BB	SO	OBP	SLG
Home	3.96	7	9	4	62	21	181.2	190	17	58	160	vs. Left	.297	317	94	11	1	9	34	17	54	.330	.404
Away	3.77	11	12	3	70	20	193.1	205	16	66	127	vs. Right	.268	1123	301	53	6	26	120	107	233	.331	.395
Day	2.53	7	5	3	45	10	117.1	104	9	34	89	Inning 1-6	.282	978	276	42	5	25	114	80	170	.336	.412
Night	4.47	11	16	4	87	31	257.2	291	24	90	198	Inning 7+	.258	462	119	22	2	8	40	44	117	.322	.366
Grass	3.15	10	6	3	50	14	143.0	144	8	42	94	None on	.294	805	237	43	3	18	18	68	149	.350	.422
Turf	4.31	8	15	4	82	27	232.0	251	25	82	193	Runners on	.249	635	158	21	4	15	136	56	138	.307	.365
April	6.75	0	2	0	14	3	21.1	27	5	12	17	Scoring Posn	.247	360	89	12	1	6	110	43	89	.323	.336
May	3.14	7	1	1	17	7	66.0	61	4	25	55	Close & Late	.285	221	63	13	2	5	24	20	55	.346	.430
June	7.62	1	5	0	16	8	41.1	63	8	20	30	None on/out	.301	362	109	19	3	6	6	25	69	.346	.420
July	1.97	3	2	3	26	4	64.0	61	2	14	54	vs. 1st Batr (relief)	.250	84	21	4	0	1	13	5	19	.289	.333
August	3.95	3	5	1	27	8	82.0	97	9	29	63	First Inning Pitched	.235	421	99	18	2	12	52	42	102	.300	.373
September/October	3.32	4	6	2	32	11	100.1	96	5	24	68	First 15 Pitches	.255	384	98	17	2	10	39	34	82	.312	.388
Starter	4.60	13	17	0	41	41	236.2	274	21	77	158	Pitch 16-30	.276	304	84	13	1	11	38	32	76	.343	.434
Reliever	2.60	5	4	7	91	0	138.1	121	12	47	129	Pitch 31-45	.279	219	61	8	1	3	25	11	35	.312	.365
0 Days rest	1.23	0	1	1	6	0	7.1	3	0	1	9	Pitch 46+	.285	533	152	26	3	9	52	47	94	.345	.396
1 or 2 Days rest	2.57	1	1	4	44	0	63.0	54	5	22	60	First Pitch	.302	189	57	15	2	3	25	10	0	.337	.450
3+ Days rest	2.78	4	2	2	41	0	68.0	64	7	24	60	Ahead on Count	.203	651	132	19	0	9	47	0	242	.203	.273
Pre-All Star	4.66	8	9	2	55	18	145.0	162	18	62	116	Behind on Count	.396	321	127	17	4	12	62	61	1	.487	.586
Post-All Star	3.37	10	12	5	77	23	230.0	233	15	62	171	Two Strikes	.198	666	132	24	0	9	42	52	286	.256	.275

Pitcher vs. Batter (career)

Pitches Best Vs.	Avg	AB	H	2B	3B	HR	RBI	BB	SO	OBP	SLG	Pitches Worst Vs.	Avg	AB	H	2B	3B	HR	RBI	BB	SO	OBP	SLG
Greg Vaughn	.000	11	0	0	0	0	0	1	3	.083	.000	Felix Fermin	.909	11	10	1	0	0	3	0	1	.909	1.000
Manuel Lee	.071	14	1	0	0	0	0	1	4	.133	.071	Glenallen Hill	.583	12	7	2	0	1	4	0	3	.583	1.000
Tony Phillips	.077	13	1	0	0	0	1	3	4	.235	.077	Danny Tartabull	.545	11	6	0	0	2	5	6	2	.706	1.091
Henry Cotto	.077	13	1	0	0	0	0	0	5	.077	.077	Ken Griffey Jr	.500	14	7	0	0	1	2	2	1	.563	.714

Pitcher vs. Batter (career)

Pitches Best Vs.	Avg	AB	H	2B	3B	HR	RBI	BB	SO	OBP	SLG	Pitches Worst Vs.	Avg	AB	H	2B	3B	HR	RBI	BB	SO	OBP	SLG
Paul Molitor	.143	14	2	0	0	0	1	0	3	.143	.143	Alvin Davis	.400	10	4	1	0	1	1	2	1	.500	.800

Johnny Guzman — Athletics
Pitches Left (groundball pitcher)

	ERA	W	L	Sv	G	GS	IP	BB	SO	Avg	H	2B	3B	HR	RBI	OBP	SLG	GF	IR	IRS	Hld	SvOp	SB	CS	GB	FB	G/F
1992 Season	12.00	0	0	0	2	0	3.0	0	0	.471	8	2	0	0	4	.500	.588	2	0	0	0	0	0	0	10	3	3.33
Career (1991-1992)	10.13	1	0	0	7	0	8.0	2	3	.487	19	6	0	0	9	.524	.641	3	7	2	0	0	0	0	19	5	3.80

1992 Season

	ERA	W	L	Sv	G	GS	IP	H	HR	BB	SO		Avg	AB	H	2B	3B	HR	RBI	BB	SO	OBP	SLG
Home	12.00	0	0	0	2	0	3.0	8	0	0	0	vs. Left	.400	5	2	0	0	0	1	0	0	.400	.400
Away	0.00	0	0	0	0	0	0.0	0	0	0	0	vs. Right	.500	12	6	2	0	0	3	0	0	.538	.667

Jose Guzman — Rangers
Pitches Right

	ERA	W	L	Sv	G	GS	IP	BB	SO	Avg	H	2B	3B	HR	RBI	OBP	SLG	CG	ShO	Sup	QS	#P/S	SB	CS	GB	FB	G/F
1992 Season	3.66	16	11	0	33	33	224.0	73	179	.268	229	52	4	17	86	.327	.399	5	0	5.46	21	105	16	15	282	219	1.29
Last Five Years	3.51	40	31	0	88	88	600.1	239	461	.247	561	119	8	47	209	.321	.369	16	3	4.86	57	105	51	35	820	593	1.38

1992 Season

	ERA	W	L	Sv	G	GS	IP	H	HR	BB	SO		Avg	AB	H	2B	3B	HR	RBI	BB	SO	OBP	SLG
Home	4.28	6	7	0	15	15	103.0	113	12	31	79	vs. Left	.278	399	111	32	1	6	44	29	65	.323	.409
Away	3.12	10	4	0	18	18	121.0	116	5	42	100	vs. Right	.260	454	118	20	3	11	42	44	114	.330	.390
Day	3.98	3	1	0	6	6	43.0	47	0	16	42	Inning 1-6	.266	706	188	49	4	14	74	65	147	.329	.407
Night	3.58	13	10	0	27	27	181.0	182	17	57	137	Inning 7+	.279	147	41	3	0	3	12	8	32	.316	.361
Grass	3.90	12	11	0	28	28	189.1	201	17	65	145	None on	.282	493	139	33	2	15	15	47	107	.346	.448
Turf	2.34	4	0	0	5	5	34.2	28	0	8	34	Runners on	.250	360	90	19	2	2	71	26	72	.301	.331
April	2.43	2	2	0	5	5	33.1	26	1	11	22	Scoring Posn	.245	208	51	11	2	1	64	18	41	.302	.332
May	3.89	2	1	0	6	6	41.2	45	1	12	32	Close & Late	.313	80	25	1	0	0	8	4	14	.345	.325
June	5.70	3	2	0	5	5	30.0	39	5	9	20	None on/out	.268	220	59	21	1	6	6	19	35	.326	.455
July	4.65	1	3	0	5	5	31.0	37	2	14	27	vs. 1st Batr (relief)	.000	0	0	0	0	0	0	0	0	.000	.000
August	2.36	4	2	0	6	6	45.2	41	6	9	43	First Inning Pitched	.256	125	32	11	2	2	11	10	28	.309	.424
September/October	3.61	4	1	0	6	6	42.1	41	2	18	35	First 75 Pitches	.258	574	148	43	4	10	57	59	111	.327	.399
Starter	3.66	16	11	0	33	33	224.0	229	17	73	179	Pitch 76-90	.313	128	40	6	0	4	18	3	22	.328	.453
Reliever	0.00	0	0	0	0	0	0.0	0	0	0	0	Pitch 91-105	.352	91	32	0	0	3	6	7	27	.400	.451
0-3 Days Rest	0.00	0	0	0	0	0	0.0	0	0	0	0	Pitch 106+	.150	60	9	3	0	0	5	4	19	.203	.200
4 Days Rest	2.91	12	3	0	21	21	148.2	147	7	50	114	First Pitch	.345	145	50	9	1	3	15	0	0	.347	.483
5+ Days Rest	5.14	4	8	0	12	12	75.1	82	10	23	65	Ahead on Count	.175	349	61	13	1	4	20	0	148	.176	.252
Pre-All Star	3.93	7	7	0	18	18	119.0	127	8	35	89	Behind on Count	.332	202	67	14	1	7	29	36	0	.430	.515
Post-All Star	3.34	9	4	0	15	15	105.0	102	9	38	90	Two Strikes	.171	368	63	18	1	1	23	37	179	.247	.234

Last Five Years

	ERA	W	L	Sv	G	GS	IP	H	HR	BB	SO		Avg	AB	H	2B	3B	HR	RBI	BB	SO	OBP	SLG
Home	3.72	17	17	0	40	40	278.1	263	30	99	211	vs. Left	.243	1057	257	61	3	20	105	117	184	.318	.363
Away	3.33	23	14	0	48	48	322.0	298	17	140	250	vs. Right	.251	1211	304	58	5	27	104	122	277	.323	.374
Day	2.72	6	2	0	14	14	96.0	85	2	51	79	Inning 1-6	.246	1862	458	104	7	37	181	205	382	.323	.369
Night	3.66	34	29	0	74	74	504.1	476	45	188	382	Inning 7+	.254	406	103	15	1	10	28	34	79	.311	.369
Grass	3.40	34	26	0	73	73	500.1	464	43	190	377	None on	.255	1321	337	72	4	33	33	138	282	.328	.391
Turf	4.05	6	5	0	15	15	100.0	97	4	49	84	Runners on	.237	947	224	47	4	14	176	101	179	.311	.339
April	1.93	5	3	0	9	9	65.1	44	7	14	49	Scoring Posn	.212	529	112	25	4	4	147	75	107	.306	.297
May	3.74	4	4	0	14	14	98.2	98	5	48	75	Close & Late	.261	211	55	8	0	4	16	19	39	.322	.355
June	4.44	8	7	0	17	17	117.2	115	17	50	87	None on/out	.262	587	154	40	2	14	14	52	105	.327	.409
July	3.36	6	5	0	16	16	104.1	105	8	48	77	vs. 1st Batr (relief)	.000	0	0	0	0	0	0	0	0	.000	.000
August	3.40	9	5	0	17	17	108.2	112	9	31	89	First Inning Pitched	.228	325	74	19	3	8	28	34	72	.299	.378
September/October	3.49	8	6	0	15	15	105.2	87	6	48	84	First 75 Pitches	.239	1535	367	84	6	24	130	169	308	.316	.349
Starter	3.51	40	31	0	88	88	600.1	561	47	239	461	Pitch 76-90	.286	308	88	18	1	15	50	22	54	.335	.497
Reliever	0.00	0	0	0	0	0	0.0	0	0	0	0	Pitch 91-105	.283	240	68	9	1	6	19	27	52	.356	.404
0-3 Days Rest	4.22	1	1	0	2	2	10.2	14	0	5	9	Pitch 106+	.205	185	38	8	0	2	10	21	47	.286	.281
4 Days Rest	3.22	26	12	0	51	51	352.2	329	28	149	267	First Pitch	.297	360	107	23	2	6	39	3	0	.306	.422
5+ Days Rest	3.91	13	18	0	35	35	237.0	218	19	85	185	Ahead on Count	.179	972	174	33	2	12	59	0	391	.180	.254
Pre-All Star	3.47	20	16	0	45	45	316.1	285	28	124	241	Behind on Count	.312	513	160	32	3	21	67	127	0	.448	.509
Post-All Star	3.55	20	15	0	43	43	284.0	276	19	115	220	Two Strikes	.163	984	160	34	2	7	53	109	461	.248	.223

Pitcher vs. Batter (career)

Pitches Best Vs.	Avg	AB	H	2B	3B	HR	RBI	BB	SO	OBP	SLG	Pitches Worst Vs.	Avg	AB	H	2B	3B	HR	RBI	BB	SO	OBP	SLG
Dave Bergman	.000	10	0	0	0	0	0	1	1	.091	.000	Pat Listach	.545	11	6	1	0	0	2	1	1	.583	.636
Dan Pasqua	.000	10	0	0	0	0	0	2	2	.167	.000	Brook Jacoby	.464	28	13	2	0	2	4	2	3	.500	.750
Darryl Hamilton	.059	17	1	0	0	0	1	0	1	.059	.059	Danny Tartabull	.375	40	15	2	1	3	7	4	11	.432	.700
Kelly Gruber	.077	13	1	0	0	0	0	0	4	.077	.077	Kent Hrbek	.344	32	11	3	0	3	6	6	4	.447	.719
Tony Pena	.083	12	1	0	0	0	0	0	1	.083	.083	Brian Downing	.318	22	7	2	0	2	4	5	4	.444	.682

177

Juan Guzman — Blue Jays
Pitches Right

	ERA	W	L	Sv	G	GS	IP	BB	SO	Avg	H	2B	3B	HR	RBI	OBP	SLG	CG	ShO	Sup	QS	#P/S	SB	CS	GB	FB	G/F
1992 Season	2.64	16	5	0	28	28	180.2	72	165	.207	135	24	1	6	48	.286	.275	1	0	4.88	20	106	27	8	183	188	0.97
Career (1991-1992)	2.79	26	8	0	51	51	319.1	138	288	.203	233	37	3	12	93	.269	.272	2	0	5.35	33	103	38	14	348	331	1.05

1992 Season

	ERA	W	L	Sv	G	GS	IP	H	HR	BB	SO		Avg	AB	H	2B	3B	HR	RBI	BB	SO	OBP	SLG
Home	2.89	7	2	0	13	13	84.0	67	2	30	75	vs. Left	.214	323	69	7	0	1	16	34	58	.288	.245
Away	2.42	9	3	0	15	15	96.2	68	4	42	90	vs. Right	.201	329	66	17	1	5	32	38	107	.284	.304
Day	3.07	4	3	0	11	11	67.1	54	4	31	68	Inning 1-6	.215	564	121	20	1	6	43	59	150	.289	.285
Night	2.38	12	2	0	17	17	113.1	81	2	41	97	Inning 7+	.159	88	14	4	0	0	5	13	15	.267	.205
Grass	2.11	7	2	0	12	12	76.2	52	3	35	69	None on	.204	393	80	14	0	3	3	41	105	.280	.262
Turf	3.03	9	3	0	16	16	104.0	83	3	37	96	Runners on	.212	259	55	10	1	3	45	31	60	.294	.293
April	1.82	3	0	0	5	5	34.2	23	1	17	39	Scoring Posn	.199	156	31	5	1	2	39	24	40	.301	.282
May	1.95	3	0	0	5	5	37.0	23	1	12	26	Close & Late	.122	41	5	0	0	0	2	7	9	.250	.122
June	2.65	4	1	0	5	5	34.0	24	1	10	31	None on/out	.217	175	38	6	0	2	2	12	40	.267	.286
July	1.71	2	1	0	5	5	31.2	22	1	11	37	vs. 1st Batr (relief)	.000	0	0	0	0	0	0	0	0	.000	.000
August	6.48	1	0	0	2	2	8.1	8	1	5	7	First Inning Pitched	.194	98	19	3	0	0	5	18	31	.316	.224
September/October	4.11	4	2	0	6	6	35.0	35	1	17	25	First 75 Pitches	.208	451	94	16	0	6	36	51	111	.289	.284
Starter	2.64	16	5	0	28	28	180.2	135	6	72	165	Pitch 76-90	.264	87	23	4	1	0	8	2	24	.278	.333
Reliever	0.00	0	0	0	0	0	0.0	0	0	0	0	Pitch 91-105	.087	69	6	0	0	0	1	8	18	.182	.087
0-3 Days Rest	3.86	1	0	0	1	1	7.0	7	0	2	1	Pitch 106+	.267	45	12	4	0	0	3	11	12	.411	.356
4 Days Rest	3.61	5	3	0	11	11	67.1	60	2	28	70	First Pitch	.289	83	24	3	1	0	6	2	0	.306	.349
5+ Days Rest	1.95	10	2	0	16	16	106.1	68	4	42	94	Ahead on Count	.151	305	46	6	0	3	12	0	132	.151	.200
Pre-All Star	2.11	11	2	0	18	18	127.2	85	4	44	122	Behind on Count	.302	129	39	10	0	1	15	30	0	.432	.403
Post-All Star	3.91	5	3	0	10	10	53.0	50	2	28	43	Two Strikes	.131	343	45	6	0	3	15	0	165	.222	.175

Chris Gwynn — Royals
Bats Left

	Avg	G	AB	R	H	2B	3B	HR	RBI	BB	SO	HBP	GDP	SB	CS	OBP	SLG	IBB	SH	SF	#Pit	#P/PA	GB	FB	G/F
1992 Season	.286	34	84	10	24	3	2	1	7	3	10	0	1	0	0	.303	.405	0	1	2	313	3.52	42	16	2.63
Last Five Years	.264	273	443	56	117	14	5	11	58	23	72	1	9	2	1	.296	.393	3	4	9	1671	3.51	169	133	1.27

1992 Season

	Avg	AB	H	2B	3B	HR	RBI	BB	SO	OBP	SLG		Avg	AB	H	2B	3B	HR	RBI	BB	SO	OBP	SLG
vs. Left	.250	8	2	0	1	1	2	0	2	.250	.875	Scoring Posn	.143	21	3	0	0	1	7	0	2	.130	.286
vs. Right	.289	76	22	3	1	0	5	3	8	.309	.355	Close & Late	.158	19	3	0	1	0	2	1	2	.190	.263

Last Five Years

	Avg	AB	H	2B	3B	HR	RBI	BB	SO	OBP	SLG		Avg	AB	H	2B	3B	HR	RBI	BB	SO	OBP	SLG
vs. Left	.176	51	9	1	1	1	5	3	12	.222	.294	Scoring Posn	.259	108	28	3	0	5	48	10	20	.305	.426
vs. Right	.276	392	108	13	4	10	53	20	60	.306	.406	Close & Late	.213	108	23	4	4	2	16	6	13	.248	.380
Groundball	.283	127	36	7	2	0	17	7	24	.314	.370	None on/out	.227	110	25	2	2	2	3	18	.248	.336
Flyball	.184	114	21	3	1	3	11	5	17	.221	.307	Batting #3	.275	80	22	4	0	4	16	4	16	.299	.475
Home	.280	186	52	4	2	3	16	8	29	.307	.371	Batting #9	.229	109	25	2	2	3	15	3	17	.252	.367
Away	.253	257	65	10	3	8	42	15	43	.289	.409	Other	.276	254	70	8	3	4	27	16	39	.314	.378
Day	.350	140	49	5	2	2	16	9	23	.382	.457	April	.293	41	12	1	0	0	5	3	7	.341	.317
Night	.224	303	68	9	3	9	42	14	49	.256	.363	May	.273	132	36	7	2	1	15	9	22	.315	.379
Grass	.285	295	84	5	3	8	33	18	50	.324	.403	June	.259	81	21	2	2	3	10	4	13	.287	.444
Turf	.223	148	33	9	2	3	25	5	22	.241	.372	July	.228	79	18	3	0	3	14	5	13	.264	.380
First Pitch	.389	72	28	4	2	1	6	1	0	.392	.542	August	.277	47	13	1	0	3	10	0	9	.286	.489
Ahead on Count	.400	95	38	4	0	7	27	9	0	.435	.663	September/October	.270	63	17	0	1	1	4	2	8	.288	.349
Behind on Count	.209	172	36	5	2	5	23	0	48	.213	.349	Pre-All Star	.275	269	74	10	4	4	32	16	45	.311	.387
Two Strikes	.141	198	28	3	3	1	9	11	72	.190	.202	Post-All Star	.247	174	43	4	1	7	26	7	27	.273	.402

Batter vs. Pitcher (career)

Hits Best Against	Avg	AB	H	2B	3B	HR	RBI	BB	SO	OBP	SLG	Hits Worst Against	Avg	AB	H	2B	3B	HR	RBI	BB	SO	OBP	SLG
John Smoltz	.357	14	5	1	0	0	1	1	2	.400	.429	Bryn Smith	.214	14	3	0	0	0	0	0	2	.214	.214

Tony Gwynn — Padres
Bats Left (groundball hitter)

	Avg	G	AB	R	H	2B	3B	HR	RBI	BB	SO	HBP	GDP	SB	CS	OBP	SLG	IBB	SH	SF	#Pit	#P/PA	GB	FB	G/F
1992 Season	.317	128	520	77	165	27	3	6	41	46	16	0	13	3	6	.371	.415	12	0	3	1791	3.15	230	138	1.67
Last Five Years	.319	694	2748	371	876	132	36	25	307	231	128	2	60	94	49	.369	.420	69	22	21	10122	3.37	1327	613	2.16

1992 Season

	Avg	AB	H	2B	3B	HR	RBI	BB	SO	OBP	SLG		Avg	AB	H	2B	3B	HR	RBI	BB	SO	OBP	SLG
vs. Left	.327	205	67	8	1	3	16	14	5	.368	.424	Scoring Posn	.322	90	29	9	2	1	32	22	6	.443	.500
vs. Right	.311	315	98	19	2	3	25	32	11	.372	.413	Close & Late	.360	75	27	4	1	2	8	11	1	.437	.520
Groundball	.360	203	73	12	1	2	19	20	5	.417	.458	None on/out	.358	95	34	5	1	0	5	1	.390	.432
Flyball	.257	109	28	6	2	2	10	7	5	.299	.404	Batting #2	.318	519	165	27	3	6	41	46	16	.371	.416
Home	.306	229	70	8	0	4	15	25	11	.371	.393	Batting #8	.000	1	0	0	0	0	0	0	0	.000	.000
Away	.326	291	95	19	3	2	26	21	5	.371	.433	Other	.000	0	0	0	0	0	0	0	0	.000	.000
Day	.280	161	45	5	3	1	10	14	8	.335	.366	April	.347	98	34	6	1	0	4	8	4	.393	.429
Night	.334	359	120	22	0	5	31	32	8	.387	.437	May	.389	90	35	6	1	4	19	10	0	.446	.611
Grass	.290	372	108	15	0	5	23	32	15	.344	.371	June	.252	107	27	3	0	2	7	15	3	.341	.336

1992 Season

	Avg	AB	H	2B	3B	HR	RBI	BB	SO	OBP	SLG		Avg	AB	H	2B	3B	HR	RBI	BB	SO	OBP	SLG
Turf	.385	148	57	12	3	1	18	14	1	.438	.527	July	.261	88	23	3	1	0	4	8	4	.323	.318
First Pitch	.463	80	37	10	1	0	13	12	0	.527	.613	August	.333	99	33	6	0	0	5	4	4	.359	.394
Ahead on Count	.252	119	30	5	1	0	8	25	0	.379	.311	September/October	.342	38	13	3	0	0	2	1	1	.359	.421
Behind on Count	.330	194	64	10	1	2	11	0	9	.330	.423	Pre-All Star	.321	327	105	16	2	6	30	36	9	.385	.437
Two Strikes	.291	158	46	4	1	2	11	9	16	.327	.367	Post-All Star	.311	193	60	11	1	0	11	10	7	.345	.378

1992 By Position

Position	Avg	AB	H	2B	3B	HR	RBI	BB	SO	OBP	SLG	G	GS	Innings	PO	A	E	DP	Fld Pct	Rng Fctr	In Zone	Outs	Zone Rtg	MLB Zone
As rf	.318	519	165	27	3	6	41	46	16	.371	.416	127	127	1127.2	270	9	5	3	.982	2.23	301	258	.857	.814

Last Five Years

	Avg	AB	H	2B	3B	HR	RBI	BB	SO	OBP	SLG		Avg	AB	H	2B	3B	HR	RBI	BB	SO	OBP	SLG
vs. Left	.303	1048	318	34	10	8	111	65	55	.343	.378	Scoring Posn	.339	617	209	40	12	5	261	120	35	.434	.467
vs. Right	.328	1700	558	98	26	19	196	166	73	.385	.446	Close & Late	.332	458	152	18	3	4	48	45	22	.389	.410
Groundball	.339	995	337	50	14	5	119	81	48	.387	.432	None on/out	.306	546	167	14	7	6	6	25	21	.337	.390
Flyball	.287	589	169	27	7	9	62	49	27	.340	.402	Batting #2	.316	696	220	35	4	9	54	57	28	.366	.417
Home	.312	1309	409	58	15	13	132	126	63	.370	.409	Batting #3	.321	1933	621	94	30	15	247	168	95	.373	.424
Away	.325	1439	467	74	21	12	175	105	65	.368	.430	Other	.294	119	35	3	2	1	6	6	7	.328	.378
Day	.299	814	243	32	13	4	77	65	42	.348	.385	April	.325	434	141	21	7	4	35	35	20	.373	.433
Night	.327	1934	633	100	23	21	230	166	86	.378	.435	May	.333	457	152	30	9	7	64	37	15	.382	.484
Grass	.309	1994	617	89	23	17	197	185	93	.366	.403	June	.322	537	173	23	5	6	64	56	27	.382	.417
Turf	.344	754	259	43	13	8	110	46	35	.378	.467	July	.296	497	147	18	7	5	45	38	28	.345	.390
First Pitch	.381	344	131	23	3	2	42	32	0	.429	.483	August	.339	525	178	26	4	3	60	41	29	.385	.421
Ahead on Count	.322	701	226	31	12	10	94	116	0	.414	.444	September/October	.285	298	85	14	4	0	39	24	9	.335	.359
Behind on Count	.312	909	284	54	8	11	107	3	66	.313	.426	Pre-All Star	.327	1579	516	78	23	17	176	139	71	.379	.438
Two Strikes	.278	902	251	30	10	7	91	55	128	.319	.357	Post-All Star	.308	1169	360	54	13	8	131	92	57	.357	.397

Batter vs. Pitcher (since 1984)

Hits Best Against	Avg	AB	H	2B	3B	HR	RBI	BB	SO	OBP	SLG	Hits Worst Against	Avg	AB	H	2B	3B	HR	RBI	BB	SO	OBP	SLG
Jeff Brantley	.647	17	11	1	0	0	1	3	0	.700	.706	Omar Olivares	.000	10	0	0	0	0	0	1	0	.091	.000
Jeff Robinson	.483	29	14	2	2	0	3	2	0	.516	.690	Pete Schourek	.000	10	0	0	0	0	0	1	0	.091	.000
Mark Gardner	.471	17	8	0	2	0	3	1	0	.500	.706	Frank DiPino	.056	18	1	0	0	0	0	2	1	.100	.056
Don Carman	.467	30	14	4	0	1	4	2	0	.500	.700	Tom Candiotti	.091	11	1	0	0	0	1	1	1	.154	.091
John Smoltz	.465	43	20	2	2	2	9	1	1	.477	.744	John Candelaria	.154	13	2	0	0	0	0	0	1	.154	.154

Dave Haas — Tigers
Pitches Right

	ERA	W	L	Sv	G	GS	IP	BB	SO	Avg	H	2B	3B	HR	RBI	OBP	SLG	CG	ShO	Sup	QS	#P/S	SB	CS	GB	FB	G/F
1992 Season	3.94	5	3	0	12	11	61.2	16	29	.276	68	9	1	8	29	.323	.419	1	1	6.28	6	80	1	1	91	79	1.15
Career (1991-1992)	4.35	6	3	0	23	11	72.1	28	35	.272	76	10	1	9	37	.341	.412	1	1	6.72	6	80	1	2	108	85	1.27

1992 Season

	ERA	W	L	Sv	G	GS	IP	H	HR	BB	SO		Avg	AB	H	2B	3B	HR	RBI	BB	SO	OBP	SLG
Home	4.65	2	1	0	6	6	31.0	35	4	10	13	vs. Left	.284	116	33	4	0	3	9	9	12	.336	.397
Away	3.23	3	2	0	6	5	30.2	33	4	6	16	vs. Right	.269	130	35	5	1	5	20	7	17	.312	.438
Starter	4.01	5	3	0	11	11	60.2	68	8	16	28	Scoring Posn	.267	60	16	2	1	1	20	2	9	.290	.383
Reliever	0.00	0	0	0	1	0	1.0	0	0	0	1	Close & Late	.000	3	0	0	0	0	0	0	1	.250	.000
0-3 Days Rest	0.00	0	0	0	0	0	0.0	0	0	0	0	None on/out	.328	64	21	3	0	3	3	4	8	.368	.516
4 Days Rest	4.06	3	2	0	7	7	37.2	45	4	7	17	First Pitch	.341	41	14	0	0	2	4	1	0	.372	.488
5+ Days Rest	3.91	2	1	0	4	4	23.0	23	4	9	11	Behind on Count	.309	55	17	6	0	2	8	11	0	.424	.527
Pre-All Star	0.00	0	0	0	0	0	0.0	0	0	0	0	Ahead on Count	.205	112	23	1	1	3	10	0	28	.205	.313
Post-All Star	3.94	5	3	0	12	11	61.2	68	8	16	29	Two Strikes	.222	99	22	1	0	4	12	4	29	.252	.354

John Habyan — Yankees
Pitches Right (groundball pitcher)

	ERA	W	L	Sv	G	GS	IP	BB	SO	Avg	H	2B	3B	HR	RBI	OBP	SLG	GF	IR	IRS	Hld	SvOp	SB	CS	GB	FB	G/F
1992 Season	3.84	5	6	7	56	0	72.2	21	44	.295	84	13	2	6	42	.344	.418	20	36	17	16	12	5	0	116	72	1.61
Last Five Years	3.05	10	8	9	135	0	186.0	47	122	.268	189	40	6	10	92	.316	.384	37	118	43	36	17	11	2	295	159	1.86

1992 Season

	ERA	W	L	Sv	G	GS	IP	H	HR	BB	SO		Avg	AB	H	2B	3B	HR	RBI	BB	SO	OBP	SLG
Home	4.17	5	3	3	28	0	36.2	55	3	10	19	vs. Left	.339	118	40	7	0	2	15	10	10	.388	.449
Away	3.50	3	4	3	28	0	36.0	29	3	11	25	vs. Right	.263	167	44	6	2	4	27	11	34	.313	.395
Starter	0.00	0	0	0	0	0	0.0	0	0	0	0	Scoring Posn	.286	84	24	7	2	3	38	12	9	.370	.524
Reliever	3.84	5	6	7	56	0	72.2	84	6	21	44	Close & Late	.296	189	56	6	1	4	29	13	30	.343	.402
0 Days rest	8.59	1	1	1	8	0	7.1	13	0	5	5	None on/out	.338	65	22	0	0	2	2	6	6	.394	.431
1 or 2 Days rest	3.60	2	3	5	27	0	35.0	39	4	10	23	First Pitch	.292	48	14	1	0	0	4	3	0	.333	.313
3+ Days rest	2.97	2	2	1	21	0	30.1	32	2	6	16	Behind on Count	.382	76	29	4	2	4	19	14	0	.473	.645
Pre-All Star	1.81	3	3	6	36	0	49.2	42	1	13	29	Ahead on Count	.234	124	29	6	0	1	12	0	37	.246	.306
Post-All Star	8.22	2	3	1	20	0	23.0	42	5	8	15	Two Strikes	.188	117	22	6	0	2	13	4	44	.226	.291

Last Five Years

	ERA	W	L	Sv	G	GS	IP	H	HR	BB	SO		Avg	AB	H	2B	3B	HR	RBI	BB	SO	OBP	SLG
Home	2.75	8	3	5	65	0	91.2	99	3	23	57	vs. Left	.302	281	85	18	2	3	37	18	29	.341	.413

179

Last Five Years

	ERA	W	L	Sv	G	GS	IP	H	HR	BB	SO
Away	3.34	2	5	4	70	0	94.1	90	7	24	65
Day	4.35	4	4	4	39	0	51.2	62	2	11	36
Night	2.55	6	4	5	96	0	134.1	127	8	36	86
Grass	2.87	10	6	8	116	0	160.0	157	9	42	98
Turf	4.15	0	2	1	19	0	26.0	32	1	5	24
April	1.11	1	1	1	17	0	24.1	22	0	7	19
May	2.29	4	1	1	25	0	39.1	32	1	11	20
June	3.47	2	2	0	22	0	23.1	23	2	3	16
July	2.88	1	2	6	25	0	40.2	43	2	10	26
August	5.55	2	0	1	21	0	24.1	31	3	8	22
September/October	3.44	2	0	1	25	0	34.0	38	2	8	19
Starter	0.00	0	0	0	0	0	0.0	0	0	0	0
Reliever	3.05	10	8	9	135	0	186.0	189	10	47	122
0 Days rest	4.40	2	1	1	25	0	28.2	35	2	9	22
1 or 2 Days rest	3.28	4	4	6	60	0	82.1	85	6	20	55
3+ Days rest	2.28	4	3	2	50	0	75.0	69	2	18	45
Pre-All Star	2.38	8	5	7	76	0	109.2	103	4	25	67
Post-All Star	4.01	2	3	2	59	0	76.1	86	6	22	55

	Avg	AB	H	2B	3B	HR	RBI	BB	SO	OBP	SLG
vs. Right	.245	424	104	22	4	7	55	29	93	.299	.366
Inning 1-6	.234	171	40	11	0	3	24	14	23	.298	.351
Inning 7+	.279	534	149	29	6	7	68	33	99	.322	.395
None on	.258	365	94	12	1	5	5	19	70	.300	.337
Runners on	.279	340	95	28	5	5	87	28	52	.332	.435
Scoring Posn	.277	213	59	18	5	5	81	25	34	.350	.479
Close & Late	.276	340	94	10	4	5	45	24	63	.327	.374
None on/out	.263	156	41	3	1	2	2	10	22	.307	.333
vs. 1st Batr (relief)	.268	123	33	7	2	2	21	10	20	.328	.407
First 15 Pitches	.257	447	115	27	5	5	56	31	81	.306	.374
Pitch 16-30	.299	177	53	11	1	4	25	15	30	.359	.441
Pitch 31-45	.231	65	15	2	0	1	10	0	9	.235	.308
Pitch 46+	.375	16	6	0	0	1	0	1	2	.412	.375
First Pitch	.287	115	33	4	0	0	11	5	0	.325	.322
Ahead on Count	.205	327	67	17	1	3	33	0	103	.209	.291
Behind on Count	.386	171	66	15	4	6	35	28	0	.468	.626
Two Strikes	.161	299	48	14	0	4	29	14	122	.203	.247

Pitcher vs. Batter (career)

Pitches Best Vs.	Avg	AB	H	2B	3B	HR	RBI	BB	SO	OBP	SLG
Lou Whitaker	.083	12	1	0	0	0	0	3	0	.267	.083
Paul Molitor	.083	12	1	0	0	0	0	1	4	.154	.083
Rob Deer	.083	12	1	0	0	0	0	1	4	.154	.083
Tony Phillips	.091	11	1	0	0	0	0	0	1	.091	.091
Ruben Sierra	.167	12	2	0	0	0	2	0	3	.154	.167

Pitches Worst Vs.	Avg	AB	H	2B	3B	HR	RBI	BB	SO	OBP	SLG
Dave Winfield	.600	10	6	3	0	0	3	2	1	.667	.900
Steve Buechele	.500	10	5	1	0	0	2	1	2	.545	.600
Scott Fletcher	.400	10	4	1	0	0	1	2	1	.500	.500
George Bell	.333	12	4	0	0	3	8	3	1	.467	1.083
Joe Carter	.333	12	4	0	1	2	4	0	4	.333	1.000

Mel Hall — Yankees   Bats Left

	Avg	G	AB	R	H	2B	3B	HR	RBI	BB	SO	HBP	GDP	SB	CS	OBP	SLG	IBB	SH	SF	#Pit	#P/PA	GB	FB	G/F
1992 Season	.280	152	583	67	163	36	3	15	81	29	53	1	12	4	2	.310	.429	4	0	9	2142	3.44	227	196	1.16
Last Five Years	.274	669	2311	298	634	123	11	69	336	110	226	9	42	11	6	.305	.427	28	3	34	8102	3.29	883	805	1.10

1992 Season

	Avg	AB	H	2B	3B	HR	RBI	BB	SO	OBP	SLG
vs. Left	.257	179	46	8	1	2	18	8	23	.284	.346
vs. Right	.290	404	117	28	2	13	63	21	30	.322	.465
Groundball	.281	153	43	9	0	2	19	5	20	.300	.379
Flyball	.277	159	44	12	1	2	22	11	14	.322	.403
Home	.246	285	70	12	0	7	35	19	19	.292	.361
Away	.312	298	93	24	3	8	46	10	34	.328	.493
Day	.317	183	58	12	2	6	33	8	15	.344	.503
Night	.263	400	105	24	1	9	48	21	38	.295	.395
Grass	.273	495	135	29	0	13	68	27	41	.308	.410
Turf	.318	88	28	7	3	2	13	2	12	.326	.534
First Pitch	.333	90	30	8	0	3	15	2	0	.351	.522
Ahead on Count	.315	181	57	12	1	8	37	17	0	.365	.525
Behind on Count	.251	183	46	11	2	4	20	0	33	.247	.399
Two Strikes	.224	210	47	11	1	0	15	10	53	.256	.286

	Avg	AB	H	2B	3B	HR	RBI	BB	SO	OBP	SLG
Scoring Posn	.309	149	46	6	2	2	62	11	20	.341	.416
Close & Late	.284	116	33	12	1	1	14	3	12	.295	.431
None on/out	.256	125	32	11	0	7	7	4	11	.279	.512
Batting #4	.254	260	66	18	2	7	36	8	26	.273	.419
Batting #5	.288	139	40	6	1	2	23	9	15	.329	.388
Other	.310	184	57	12	0	6	22	12	12	.348	.473
April	.275	80	22	6	0	5	18	2	6	.286	.538
May	.241	112	27	10	1	1	14	4	14	.269	.375
June	.269	108	29	9	0	5	13	4	10	.287	.491
July	.330	88	29	4	0	2	12	9	5	.388	.443
August	.295	105	31	2	1	1	11	5	8	.327	.362
September/October	.278	90	25	5	1	1	13	5	10	.313	.389
Pre-All Star	.263	339	89	27	1	12	52	17	31	.294	.454
Post-All Star	.303	244	74	9	2	3	29	12	22	.333	.393

1992 By Position

Position	Avg	AB	H	2B	3B	HR	RBI	BB	SO	OBP	SLG	G	GS	Innings	PO	A	E	DP	Fld Pct	Rng Fctr	In Zone	Outs	Zone Rtg	MLB Zone
As Designated Hitter	.238	42	10	2	0	0	2	2	5	.273	.286	12	9	---	---	---	---	---	---	---	---	---	---	---
As Pinch Hitter	.333	12	4	0	0	0	4	0	2	.333	.333	13	0	---	---	---	---	---	---	---	---	---	---	---
As lf	.281	395	111	30	2	15	61	19	35	.310	.481	99	96	860.0	218	9	2	1	.991	2.38	247	209	.846	.809
As rf	.279	136	38	4	1	0	15	8	12	.317	.324	37	34	302.0	63	1	1	1	.985	1.91	75	60	.800	.814

Last Five Years

	Avg	AB	H	2B	3B	HR	RBI	BB	SO	OBP	SLG
vs. Left	.241	514	124	18	2	10	66	26	57	.278	.342
vs. Right	.284	1797	510	105	9	59	270	84	169	.312	.451
Groundball	.266	612	163	33	2	18	95	5	59	.307	.415
Flyball	.270	559	151	33	1	14	76	27	59	.301	.408
Home	.271	1168	317	53	7	37	173	65	97	.307	.424
Away	.277	1143	317	70	4	32	163	45	129	.302	.430
Day	.276	753	208	41	5	22	123	41	67	.311	.432
Night	.273	1558	426	82	6	47	213	69	159	.302	.424
Grass	.270	1964	536	98	8	61	289	93	179	.300	.420
Turf	.300	327	98	25	3	8	47	17	47	.332	.468
First Pitch	.319	476	152	28	2	19	93	11	0	.329	.506
Ahead on Count	.324	598	194	39	2	30	117	57	0	.378	.547
Behind on Count	.243	749	182	33	7	16	85	1	134	.244	.370
Two Strikes	.204	825	168	33	3	12	71	37	226	.238	.295

	Avg	AB	H	2B	3B	HR	RBI	BB	SO	OBP	SLG
Scoring Posn	.276	616	170	34	6	13	258	52	63	.318	.414
Close & Late	.269	383	103	25	2	13	55	21	45	.303	.446
None on/out	.244	545	133	30	1	17	17	13	56	.262	.396
Batting #4	.272	1167	317	63	6	36	170	47	117	.297	.428
Batting #5	.282	699	197	35	5	24	109	33	68	.310	.449
Other	.270	445	120	25	0	9	57	30	41	.316	.387
April	.269	264	71	19	2	8	44	9	28	.290	.447
May	.249	361	90	26	1	10	50	12	36	.273	.410
June	.299	441	132	25	0	19	69	26	41	.334	.485
July	.326	387	126	21	2	12	66	20	43	.355	.483
August	.272	482	131	21	3	9	63	27	47	.309	.384
September/October	.223	376	84	11	3	11	44	16	31	.253	.356
Pre-All Star	.279	1217	340	77	5	43	191	59	124	.309	.457
Post-All Star	.269	1094	294	46	6	26	145	51	102	.300	.393

Hits Best Against	Avg	AB	H	2B	3B	HR	RBI	BB	SO	OBP	SLG	Hits Worst Against	Avg	AB	H	2B	3B	HR	RBI	BB	SO	OBP	SLG
Todd Stottlemyre	.500	42	21	5	0	1	5	2	2	.523	.690	Bill Krueger	.000	15	0	0	0	0	0	0	3	.000	.000
Bobby Thigpen	.500	14	7	0	0	2	3	0	0	.500	.929	Tom Henke	.000	14	0	0	0	0	0	1	5	.067	.000
Erik Hanson	.400	20	8	4	0	1	6	0	5	.400	.750	Mark Langston	.000	11	0	0	0	0	0	0	4	.000	.000
Bert Blyleven	.394	33	13	3	0	3	6	4	5	.447	.758	Tom Gordon	.071	14	1	0	0	0	1	0	5	.067	.071
David Wells	.333	12	4	1	0	2	3	4	4	.333	.917	Bryan Harvey	.083	12	1	1	0	0	0	0	4	.083	.167

Darryl Hamilton — Brewers

Bats Left (groundball hitter)

	Avg	G	AB	R	H	2B	3B	HR	RBI	BB	SO	HBP	GDP	SB	CS	OBP	SLG	IBB	SH	SF	#Pit	#P/PA	GB	FB	G/F
1992 Season	.298	128	470	67	140	19	7	5	62	45	42	1	10	41	14	.356	.400	0	4	7	2059	3.94	209	100	2.09
Career (1988-1992)	.292	383	1134	172	331	43	13	8	148	99	101	2	23	74	26	.347	.374	2	14	11	4721	3.79	507	247	2.05

1992 Season

	Avg	AB	H	2B	3B	HR	RBI	BB	SO	OBP	SLG		Avg	AB	H	2B	3B	HR	RBI	BB	SO	OBP	SLG
vs. Left	.247	89	22	3	1	0	13	10	9	.323	.303	Scoring Posn	.294	136	40	3	1	1	56	19	11	.368	.353
vs. Right	.310	381	118	16	6	5	49	35	33	.363	.423	Close & Late	.362	69	25	4	2	1	8	8	5	.423	.522
Groundball	.256	121	31	2	1	0	22	6	11	.287	.289	None on/out	.280	93	26	7	2	0	0	3	10	.302	.398
Flyball	.346	130	45	6	1	4	19	17	8	.417	.500	Batting #2	.293	266	78	9	4	3	39	23	20	.349	.391
Home	.288	233	67	11	4	1	30	26	19	.356	.382	Batting #6	.301	83	25	6	1	2	10	5	11	.333	.470
Away	.308	237	73	8	3	4	32	19	23	.355	.418	Other	.306	121	37	4	2	0	13	17	11	.383	.372
Day	.228	145	33	4	2	2	20	16	10	.302	.324	April	.227	66	15	1	1	1	11	7	8	.297	.318
Night	.329	325	107	15	5	3	42	29	32	.380	.434	May	.235	34	8	2	0	1	3	2	5	.278	.382
Grass	.287	387	111	18	4	3	48	36	35	.344	.377	June	.372	86	32	3	2	0	11	10	5	.433	.453
Turf	.349	83	29	1	3	2	14	9	7	.409	.506	July	.298	94	28	8	1	1	9	7	13	.337	.436
First Pitch	.333	39	13	1	2	1	6	0	0	.341	.538	August	.267	75	20	5	1	0	16	9	2	.337	.360
Ahead on Count	.280	107	30	7	1	2	14	30	0	.438	.421	September/October	.322	115	37	0	2	2	12	10	9	.381	.409
Behind on Count	.268	168	45	8	2	0	14	0	21	.265	.339	Pre-All Star	.305	226	69	9	3	2	29	23	23	.364	.398
Two Strikes	.245	204	50	7	3	2	31	15	42	.291	.338	Post-All Star	.291	244	71	10	4	3	33	22	19	.348	.402

1992 By Position

Position	Avg	AB	H	2B	3B	HR	RBI	BB	SO	OBP	SLG	G	GS	Innings	PO	A	E	DP	Fld Pct	Rng Fctr	In Zone	Outs	Zone Rtg	MLB Zone
As lf	.269	104	28	2	0	0	3	9	10	.330	.288	30	26	231.0	49	2	0	0	1.000	1.99	59	47	.797	.809
As cf	.234	94	22	2	2	1	19	10	11	.308	.330	32	23	226.0	79	0	0	0	1.000	3.15	88	78	.886	.824
As rf	.331	269	89	15	5	4	38	24	20	.379	.468	74	69	599.0	151	8	0	1	1.000	2.39	168	140	.833	.814

Career (1988-1992)

	Avg	AB	H	2B	3B	HR	RBI	BB	SO	OBP	SLG		Avg	AB	H	2B	3B	HR	RBI	BB	SO	OBP	SLG
vs. Left	.228	215	49	8	2	0	25	18	24	.291	.284	Scoring Posn	.319	313	100	10	4	3	139	29	26	.367	.406
vs. Right	.307	919	282	35	11	8	123	81	77	.360	.395	Close & Late	.353	170	60	7	2	1	22	22	19	.425	.435
Groundball	.274	317	87	6	1	1	47	25	25	.327	.309	None on/out	.260	250	65	13	2	1	1	16	23	.305	.340
Flyball	.294	252	74	13	2	4	40	22	17	.346	.409	Batting #2	.307	384	118	15	6	3	58	31	28	.358	.401
Home	.296	534	158	24	8	3	66	55	48	.360	.388	Batting #6	.292	202	59	8	3	2	24	15	20	.338	.391
Away	.288	600	173	19	5	5	82	44	53	.334	.362	Other	.281	548	154	20	4	3	66	53	53	.342	.349
Day	.269	350	94	11	4	3	47	32	22	.331	.349	April	.228	101	23	2	1	1	13	14	12	.319	.297
Night	.302	784	237	32	9	5	101	67	79	.354	.385	May	.240	75	18	3	0	1	7	4	6	.278	.320
Grass	.284	932	265	38	9	6	121	79	86	.338	.364	June	.337	181	61	9	2	0	26	13	14	.379	.409
Turf	.327	202	66	5	4	2	27	20	15	.386	.421	July	.273	278	76	16	3	3	32	25	33	.330	.385
First Pitch	.364	107	39	5	3	2	15	2	0	.378	.523	August	.309	246	76	10	3	1	38	19	14	.354	.386
Ahead on Count	.298	252	75	10	1	2	31	66	0	.445	.369	September/October	.304	253	77	3	4	2	32	24	22	.366	.372
Behind on Count	.246	402	99	14	2	1	44	0	51	.243	.299	Pre-All Star	.289	450	130	20	3	3	58	39	42	.343	.367
Two Strikes	.234	475	111	17	5	4	61	31	101	.277	.320	Post-All Star	.294	684	201	23	10	5	90	60	59	.349	.393

Batter vs. Pitcher (career)

Hits Best Against	Avg	AB	H	2B	3B	HR	RBI	BB	SO	OBP	SLG	Hits Worst Against	Avg	AB	H	2B	3B	HR	RBI	BB	SO	OBP	SLG
Kevin Appier	.600	10	6	0	0	0	1	1	1	.636	.600	Jeff Montgomery	.000	11	0	0	0	0	0	1	0	.083	.000
Mike Boddicker	.545	11	6	1	1	0	1	0	1	.583	.818	Jose Guzman	.059	17	1	0	0	0	1	0	1	.059	.059
Bill Gullickson	.400	10	4	1	0	1	3	2	0	.500	.800	Ron Darling	.125	16	2	0	0	0	2	2	3	.222	.125
Bret Saberhagen	.364	11	4	1	0	1	4	1	5	.417	.727	Jimmy Key	.143	14	2	0	0	0	1	0	1	.200	.143
Jack Armstrong	.364	11	4	1	0	1	4	1	1	.417	.636	Roger Clemens	.176	17	3	0	0	0	3	0	5	.167	.176

Chris Hammond — Reds

Pitches Left (groundball pitcher)

	ERA	W	L	Sv	G	GS	IP	BB	SO	Avg	H	2B	3B	HR	RBI	OBP	SLG	CG	ShO	Sup	QS	#P/S	SB	CS	GB	FB	G/F
1992 Season	4.21	7	10	0	28	26	147.1	55	79	.266	149	20	8	13	62	.333	.399	0	0	3.85	13	82	7	4	248	143	1.73
Career (1990-1992)	4.25	14	19	0	51	47	258.1	115	133	.261	254	40	10	19	111	.341	.382	0	0	3.59	23	81	16	8	438	251	1.75

1992 Season

	ERA	W	L	Sv	G	GS	IP	H	HR	BB	SO		Avg	AB	H	2B	3B	HR	RBI	BB	SO	OBP	SLG
Home	3.92	5	4	0	15	14	82.2	79	7	31	42	vs. Left	.291	117	34	4	3	5	17	12	20	.356	.504
Away	4.59	2	6	0	13	12	64.2	70	6	24	37	vs. Right	.259	444	115	16	5	8	45	43	59	.327	.372
Starter	4.24	7	10	0	26	26	144.1	147	13	54	77	Scoring Posn	.292	106	31	3	2	4	42	22	19	.409	.472
Reliever	3.00	0	0	0	2	0	3.0	2	0	1	2	Close & Late	.375	24	9	2	1	0	1	5	3	.483	.542
0-3 Days Rest	0.00	0	0	0	0	0	0.0	0	0	0	0	None on/out	.227	150	34	5	3	2	2	8	17	.270	.340

1992 Season

	ERA	W	L	Sv	G	GS	IP	H	HR	BB	SO		Avg	AB	H	2B	3B	HR	RBI	BB	SO	OBP	SLG
4 Days Rest	4.09	5	7	0	15	15	81.1	79	8	23	44	First Pitch	.366	82	30	5	0	2	9	5	0	.404	.500
5+ Days Rest	4.43	2	3	0	11	11	63.0	68	5	31	33	Behind on Count	.270	159	43	7	2	5	24	32	0	.393	.434
Pre-All Star	3.71	5	5	0	16	15	89.2	81	6	37	46	Ahead on Count	.226	217	49	4	5	5	22	0	65	.232	.359
Post-All Star	4.99	2	5	0	12	11	57.2	68	7	18	33	Two Strikes	.191	225	43	4	4	4	18	18	79	.256	.298

Chris Haney — Royals   Pitches Left

	ERA	W	L	Sv	G	GS	IP	BB	SO	Avg	H	2B	3B	HR	RBI	OBP	SLG	CG	ShO	Sup	QS	#P/S	SB	CS	GB	FB	G/F
1992 Season	4.61	4	6	0	16	13	80.0	26	54	.248	75	21	3	11	42	.310	.446	2	2	3.94	5	83	9	4	101	109	0.93
Career (1991-1992)	4.32	7	13	0	32	29	164.2	69	105	.264	169	41	5	17	83	.338	.424	2	2	3.72	11	88	17	10	234	201	1.16

1992 Season

	ERA	W	L	Sv	G	GS	IP	H	HR	BB	SO		Avg	AB	H	2B	3B	HR	RBI	BB	SO	OBP	SLG
Home	5.91	2	4	0	9	8	42.2	45	6	11	26	vs. Left	.258	66	17	5	2	2	12	1	16	.290	.485
Away	3.13	2	2	0	7	5	37.1	30	5	15	28	vs. Right	.245	237	58	16	1	9	30	25	38	.315	.435
Starter	4.46	4	6	0	13	13	72.2	68	10	23	45	Scoring Posn	.234	64	15	5	1	2	30	8	14	.304	.438
Reliever	6.14	0	0	0	3	0	7.1	7	1	3	9	Close & Late	.167	6	1	0	0	1	1	1	2	.286	.667
0-3 Days Rest	15.75	0	1	0	1	1	4.0	8	1	1	0	None on/out	.263	76	20	2	0	3	3	8	12	.341	.408
4 Days Rest	4.66	1	3	0	5	5	29.0	30	3	11	20	First Pitch	.081	37	3	0	0	2	5	1	0	.100	.243
5+ Days Rest	3.18	3	2	0	7	7	39.2	30	6	11	25	Behind on Count	.351	74	26	11	0	2	14	19	0	.479	.581
Pre-All Star	5.45	2	3	0	9	6	38.0	40	6	10	27	Ahead on Count	.207	140	29	7	2	2	11	0	46	.217	.329
Post-All Star	3.86	2	3	0	7	7	42.0	35	5	16	27	Two Strikes	.175	137	24	5	2	5	13	6	54	.214	.350

Todd Haney — Expos   Bats Right (flyball hitter)

	Avg	G	AB	R	H	2B	3B	HR	RBI	BB	SO	HBP	GDP	SB	CS	OBP	SLG	IBB	SH	SF	#Pit	#P/PA	GB	FB	G/F
1992 Season	.300	7	10	0	3	1	0	0	1	0	0	0	1	0	0	.300	.400	0	1	0	42	4.20	2	5	0.40

1992 Season

	Avg	AB	H	2B	3B	HR	RBI	BB	SO	OBP	SLG		Avg	AB	H	2B	3B	HR	RBI	BB	SO	OBP	SLG
vs. Left	.286	7	2	0	0	0	1	0	0	.286	.286	Scoring Posn	.333	3	1	0	0	0	1	0	0	.333	.333
vs. Right	.333	3	1	1	0	0	0	0	0	.333	.667	Close & Late	.000	0	0	0	0	0	0	0	0	.000	.000

Dave Hansen — Dodgers   Bats Left

	Avg	G	AB	R	H	2B	3B	HR	RBI	BB	SO	HBP	GDP	SB	CS	OBP	SLG	IBB	SH	SF	#Pit	#P/PA	GB	FB	G/F
1992 Season	.214	132	341	30	73	11	0	6	22	34	49	1	7	0	2	.286	.299	3	0	2	1413	3.74	133	98	1.36
Career (1990-1992)	.220	190	404	33	89	15	0	7	28	36	64	1	9	1	2	.284	.309	3	0	2	1683	3.80	154	116	1.33

1992 Season

	Avg	AB	H	2B	3B	HR	RBI	BB	SO	OBP	SLG		Avg	AB	H	2B	3B	HR	RBI	BB	SO	OBP	SLG
vs. Left	.196	46	9	2	0	0	1	4	8	.255	.239	Scoring Posn	.157	70	11	2	0	0	13	10	15	.256	.186
vs. Right	.217	295	64	9	0	6	21	30	41	.291	.308	Close & Late	.145	69	10	1	0	0	3	6	16	.211	.159
Groundball	.203	118	24	2	0	1	5	12	12	.277	.246	None on/out	.238	101	24	3	0	3	3	6	11	.280	.356
Flyball	.253	91	23	7	0	3	8	12	17	.346	.429	Batting #7	.292	113	33	6	0	4	8	12	18	.365	.451
Home	.231	182	42	4	0	1	10	16	22	.295	.269	Batting #8	.158	114	18	2	0	1	7	7	16	.203	.202
Away	.195	159	31	7	0	5	12	18	27	.275	.333	Other	.193	114	22	3	0	1	7	15	15	.287	.246
Day	.205	117	24	4	0	2	12	12	19	.275	.291	April	.147	34	5	1	0	1	3	2	4	.194	.265
Night	.219	224	49	7	0	4	10	22	30	.291	.304	May	.250	48	12	3	0	2	4	9	4	.368	.438
Grass	.218	252	55	7	0	3	17	23	33	.284	.282	June	.171	41	7	2	0	1	2	6	6	.277	.293
Turf	.202	89	18	4	0	3	5	11	16	.290	.348	July	.271	70	19	2	0	1	7	2	10	.288	.343
First Pitch	.220	59	13	1	0	0	4	3	0	.270	.237	August	.192	73	14	1	0	0	5	8	10	.277	.205
Ahead on Count	.230	74	17	4	0	3	8	18	0	.376	.405	September/October	.213	75	16	2	0	1	1	7	15	.280	.280
Behind on Count	.170	106	18	4	0	2	6	0	22	.168	.264	Pre-All Star	.233	159	37	7	0	4	13	18	18	.311	.352
Two Strikes	.190	158	30	3	0	2	7	13	49	.250	.247	Post-All Star	.198	182	36	4	0	2	9	16	31	.264	.253

1992 By Position

Position	Avg	AB	H	2B	3B	HR	RBI	BB	SO	OBP	SLG	G	GS	Innings	PO	A	E	DP	Fld Pct	Rng Fctr	In Zone	Outs	Zone Rtg	MLB Zone
As Pinch Hitter	.200	25	5	1	0	1	2	4	7	.310	.360	32	0	---	---	---	---	---	---	---	---	---	---
As 3b	.215	316	68	10	0	5	20	30	42	.284	.294	108	98	832.1	61	183	8	14	.968	2.64	229	196	.856	.841

Erik Hanson — Mariners   Pitches Right (groundball pitcher)

	ERA	W	L	Sv	G	GS	IP	BB	SO	Avg	H	2B	3B	HR	RBI	OBP	SLG	CG	ShO	Sup	QS	#P/S	SB	CS	GB	FB	G/F
1992 Season	4.82	8	17	0	31	30	186.2	57	112	.287	209	34	4	14	99	.341	.402	6	1	3.91	15	94	15	4	338	154	2.19
Career (1988-1992)	3.76	45	42	0	114	113	752.1	225	577	.256	734	131	17	56	294	.312	.373	14	3	4.51	69	103	49	31	1079	694	1.55

1992 Season

	ERA	W	L	Sv	G	GS	IP	H	HR	BB	SO		Avg	AB	H	2B	3B	HR	RBI	BB	SO	OBP	SLG
Home	4.78	6	6	0	15	15	90.1	104	8	28	56	vs. Left	.241	365	88	11	3	5	45	26	56	.291	.329
Away	4.86	2	11	0	16	15	96.1	105	6	29	56	vs. Right	.333	363	121	23	1	9	54	31	56	.390	.477
Day	3.99	4	3	0	10	9	49.2	57	0	18	25	Inning 1-6	.292	613	179	29	4	11	90	48	93	.346	.406
Night	5.12	4	14	0	21	21	137.0	152	14	39	87	Inning 7+	.261	115	30	5	0	3	9	9	19	.312	.383

1992 Season

	ERA	W	L	Sv	G	GS	IP	H	HR	BB	SO		Avg	AB	H	2B	3B	HR	RBI	BB	SO	OBP	SLG
Grass	4.55	2	9	0	14	13	83.0	86	5	25	50	None on	.260	438	114	15	2	7	7	26	69	.305	.352
Turf	5.04	6	8	0	17	17	103.2	123	9	32	62	Runners on	.328	290	95	19	2	7	92	31	43	.391	.479
April	5.04	1	3	0	5	5	30.1	33	4	9	17	Scoring Posn	.372	148	55	10	2	5	83	20	28	.436	.568
May	4.74	1	4	0	6	6	38.0	41	4	14	27	Close & Late	.283	53	15	3	0	2	6	4	11	.333	.453
June	2.80	3	3	0	6	6	45.0	45	3	13	25	None on/out	.280	193	54	9	0	5	5	9	24	.315	.404
July	3.70	3	3	0	6	5	41.1	37	2	9	25	vs. 1st Batr (relief)	.000	1	0	0	0	0	0	0	0	.000	.000
August	15.92	0	2	0	4	4	13.0	28	1	5	4	First Inning Pitched	.261	119	31	6	1	1	13	7	14	.308	.353
September/October	4.26	0	2	0	4	4	19.0	25	0	7	14	First 75 Pitches	.288	532	153	26	2	10	75	45	83	.346	.400
Starter	4.85	7	17	0	30	30	183.2	207	14	57	111	Pitch 76-90	.289	97	28	5	1	1	14	6	10	.327	.392
Reliever	3.00	1	0	0	1	0	3.0	2	0	0	1	Pitch 91-105	.338	65	22	3	1	3	9	5	11	.389	.554
0-3 Days Rest	1.35	1	0	0	2	2	13.1	9	0	6	11	Pitch 106+	.176	34	6	0	0	0	1	1	8	.200	.176
4 Days Rest	4.69	5	10	0	18	18	119.0	129	7	28	77	First Pitch	.302	126	38	7	1	2	11	0	0	.310	.421
5+ Days Rest	6.14	1	7	0	10	10	51.1	69	7	23	23	Ahead on Count	.163	239	39	7	0	1	18	0	92	.165	.205
Pre-All Star	3.96	7	11	0	20	19	131.2	135	12	40	79	Behind on Count	.417	206	86	17	1	9	46	36	0	.500	.641
Post-All Star	6.87	1	6	0	11	11	55.0	74	2	17	33	Two Strikes	.165	278	46	6	1	2	29	21	112	.224	.216

Career (1988-1992)

	ERA	W	L	Sv	G	GS	IP	H	HR	BB	SO		Avg	AB	H	2B	3B	HR	RBI	BB	SO	OBP	SLG
Home	4.11	22	21	0	57	57	369.2	388	34	101	291	vs. Left	.232	1481	343	66	10	23	148	107	305	.284	.336
Away	3.41	23	21	0	57	56	382.2	346	22	124	286	vs. Right	.283	1381	391	65	7	33	146	118	272	.342	.412
Day	3.75	10	11	0	30	29	180.0	185	15	61	125	Inning 1-6	.262	2369	620	112	14	50	260	186	462	.317	.384
Night	3.76	36	31	0	84	84	572.1	549	41	164	452	Inning 7+	.231	493	114	19	3	6	34	39	115	.286	.318
Grass	3.28	18	16	0	46	45	307.1	265	18	103	240	None on	.242	1757	425	68	9	34	34	119	361	.293	.349
Turf	4.09	27	26	0	68	68	445.0	469	38	122	337	Runners on	.260	1105	309	63	8	22	260	106	216	.341	.412
April	3.41	7	6	0	19	19	121.1	115	8	43	97	Scoring Posn	.265	592	157	31	8	12	223	70	131	.338	.405
May	4.75	7	10	0	20	20	119.1	134	11	44	92	Close & Late	.232	237	55	10	2	3	21	19	55	.288	.329
June	3.70	7	7	0	14	14	99.2	97	10	32	72	None on/out	.224	758	170	32	3	14	14	45	152	.270	.330
July	3.69	8	7	0	17	16	114.2	106	8	29	84	vs. 1st Batr (relief)	.000	1	0	0	0	0	0	0	0	.000	.000
August	4.71	3	5	0	17	17	109.0	112	8	29	79	First Inning Pitched	.257	436	112	26	1	9	40	33	70	.311	.383
September/October	2.87	13	7	0	27	27	186.1	170	11	48	153	First 75 Pitches	.265	2015	534	100	9	43	218	157	386	.320	.388
Starter	3.76	44	42	0	113	113	749.1	732	56	225	576	Pitch 76-90	.255	353	90	14	6	5	38	29	62	.310	.371
Reliever	3.00	1	0	0	1	0	3.0	2	0	0	1	Pitch 91-105	.216	278	60	7	1	7	21	20	82	.272	.324
0-3 Days Rest	1.35	1	0	0	2	2	13.1	9	0	6	11	Pitch 106+	.231	216	50	10	1	1	17	19	47	.293	.301
4 Days Rest	4.01	25	24	0	64	64	426.2	428	33	128	322	First Pitch	.311	437	136	25	4	14	45	7	0	.327	.483
5+ Days Rest	3.52	18	18	0	47	47	309.1	295	23	91	243	Ahead on Count	.169	1093	185	29	7	10	74	0	483	.173	.236
Pre-All Star	3.95	24	25	0	59	58	376.0	379	32	128	287	Behind on Count	.352	741	261	55	3	23	110	100	0	.427	.528
Post-All Star	3.56	21	17	0	55	55	376.1	355	24	97	290	Two Strikes	.163	1280	209	32	7	13	94	118	576	.236	.230

Pitcher vs. Batter (career)

Pitches Best Vs.	Avg	AB	H	2B	3B	HR	RBI	BB	SO	OBP	SLG	Pitches Worst Vs.	Avg	AB	H	2B	3B	HR	RBI	BB	SO	OBP	SLG
Sam Horn	.000	21	0	0	0	0	0	2	8	.087	.000	Kevin Seitzer	.600	15	9	2	0	0	2	6	2	.714	.733
Rob Deer	.000	16	0	0	0	0	0	0	9	.000	.000	Brian Harper	.583	12	7	1	0	1	3	1	1	.615	.917
Mickey Tettleton	.000	13	0	0	0	0	0	3	8	.188	.000	Ellis Burks	.545	22	12	1	0	1	2	4	3	.565	.864
Travis Fryman	.063	16	1	0	0	0	0	0	6	.063	.063	Frank Thomas	.533	15	8	1	0	1	2	6	3	.667	.800
Randy Velarde	.091	11	1	0	0	0	0	0	3	.091	.091	Rickey Henderson	.389	18	7	2	0	2	3	4	4	.478	.833

Shawn Hare — Tigers   Bats Left

	Avg	G	AB	R	H	2B	3B	HR	RBI	BB	SO	HBP	GDP	SB	CS	OBP	SLG	IBB	SH	SF	#Pit	#P/PA	GB	FB	G/F
1992 Season	.115	15	26	0	3	1	0	0	5	2	4	0	0	0	0	.172	.154	0	0	1	125	4.31	11	8	1.38
Career (1991-1992)	.089	24	45	0	4	2	0	0	5	4	5	0	0	0	3	.160	.133	0	0	1	210	4.20	21	15	1.40

1992 Season

	Avg	AB	H	2B	3B	HR	RBI	BB	SO	OBP	SLG		Avg	AB	H	2B	3B	HR	RBI	BB	SO	OBP	SLG
vs. Left	.000	1	0	0	0	0	0	0	1	.000	.000	Scoring Posn	.333	9	3	1	0	0	5	1	2	.364	.444
vs. Right	.120	25	3	1	0	0	5	2	3	.179	.160	Close & Late	.333	6	2	1	0	0	3	0	2	.333	.500

Mike Harkey — Cubs   Pitches Right

	ERA	W	L	Sv	G	GS	IP	BB	SO	Avg	H	2B	3B	HR	RBI	OBP	SLG	CG	ShO	Sup	QS	#P/S	SB	CS	GB	FB	G/F
1992 Season	1.89	4	0	0	7	7	38.0	15	21	.243	34	6	3	4	13	.316	.414	0	0	7.11	3	84	3	3	52	46	1.13
Career (1988-1992)	3.12	16	11	0	43	43	265.0	95	148	.240	241	46	11	21	96	.310	.371	2	1	4.69	27	95	16	14	406	286	1.42

1992 Season

	ERA	W	L	Sv	G	GS	IP	H	HR	BB	SO		Avg	AB	H	2B	3B	HR	RBI	BB	SO	OBP	SLG
Home	1.96	2	0	0	3	3	18.1	18	2	7	8	vs. Left	.233	86	20	2	3	3	8	9	12	.302	.430
Away	1.83	2	0	0	4	4	19.2	16	2	8	13	vs. Right	.259	54	14	4	0	1	5	6	9	.339	.389

Career (1988-1992)

	ERA	W	L	Sv	G	GS	IP	H	HR	BB	SO		Avg	AB	H	2B	3B	HR	RBI	BB	SO	OBP	SLG
Home	2.65	7	4	0	20	20	135.2	132	10	44	71	vs. Left	.242	594	144	29	6	11	53	58	84	.310	.367
Away	3.62	9	7	0	23	23	129.1	109	11	51	77	vs. Right	.237	409	97	17	5	10	43	37	64	.311	.377
Day	2.84	12	6	0	29	29	190.0	165	12	57	104	Inning 1-6	.241	883	213	40	9	18	84	84	140	.312	.368
Night	3.84	4	5	0	14	14	75.0	76	9	38	44	Inning 7+	.233	120	28	6	2	3	12	11	8	.296	.392

Career (1988-1992)

	ERA	W	L	Sv	G	GS	IP	H	HR	BB	SO		Avg	AB	H	2B	3B	HR	RBI	BB	SO	OBP	SLG
Grass	2.70	12	5	0	28	28	186.1	164	17	56	99	None on	.248	613	152	31	7	17	17	41	92	.300	.405
Turf	4.12	4	6	0	15	15	78.2	77	4	39	49	Runners on	.228	390	89	15	4	4	79	54	56	.325	.318
April	4.00	2	3	0	7	7	36.0	30	4	13	26	Scoring Posn	.210	229	48	10	2	1	69	42	35	.331	.284
May	5.35	3	0	0	6	6	33.2	43	5	13	20	Close & Late	.250	76	19	3	2	2	9	10	4	.337	.421
June	2.79	0	2	0	4	4	29.0	23	2	9	14	None on/out	.231	264	61	11	4	8	8	18	43	.293	.394
July	3.28	5	2	0	8	8	46.2	48	3	15	26	vs. 1st Batr (relief)	.000	0	0	0	0	0	0	0	0	.000	.000
August	2.33	6	1	0	11	11	73.1	57	7	23	38	First Inning Pitched	.287	171	49	7	1	2	21	9	18	.333	.374
September/October	2.14	0	3	0	7	7	46.1	40	0	22	24	First 75 Pitches	.230	765	176	32	8	13	67	67	122	.297	.344
Starter	3.12	16	11	0	43	43	265.0	241	21	95	148	Pitch 76-90	.296	115	34	9	1	5	14	13	18	.374	.522
Reliever	0.00	0	0	0	0	0	0.0	0	0	0	0	Pitch 91-105	.270	74	20	3	2	2	11	9	3	.349	.446
0-3 Days Rest	4.67	3	2	0	5	5	27.0	28	0	9	15	Pitch 106+	.224	49	11	2	0	1	4	6	5	.309	.327
4 Days Rest	2.64	8	5	0	23	23	153.2	125	15	54	86	First Pitch	.229	144	33	5	2	5	14	8	0	.273	.396
5+ Days Rest	3.52	5	4	0	15	15	84.1	88	6	32	47	Ahead on Count	.214	444	95	17	5	4	24	0	134	.224	.302
Pre-All Star	4.02	6	5	0	18	18	105.1	103	12	37	62	Behind on Count	.289	242	70	10	4	8	35	57	0	.423	.463
Post-All Star	2.54	10	6	0	25	25	159.2	138	9	58	86	Two Strikes	.199	433	86	16	4	4	26	30	148	.256	.282

Pitcher vs. Batter (career)

Pitches Best Vs.	Avg	AB	H	2B	3B	HR	RBI	BB	SO	OBP	SLG	Pitches Worst Vs.	Avg	AB	H	2B	3B	HR	RBI	BB	SO	OBP	SLG
Will Clark	.000	11	0	0	0	0	0	1	3	.083	.000	Matt D. Williams	.545	11	6	0	0	2	4	0	1	.545	1.091
Andres Galarraga	.100	10	1	0	1	0	1	1	2	.182	.300	Paul O'Neill	.500	10	5	0	0	2	4	3	0	.615	1.100
Tim Wallach	.182	11	2	0	1	0	0	2	1	.306	.364	Barry Larkin	.455	11	5	0	0	0	2	1	1	.571	.455
Pedro Guerrero	.200	15	3	0	0	0	0	4	1	.368	.200	Milt Thompson	.400	10	4	0	0	0	1	5	0	.571	.400
Terry Pendleton	.222	9	2	1	0	0	1	3	1	.417	.333	Jose Oquendo	.364	11	4	0	0	0	1	5	0	.529	.364

Pete Harnisch — Astros   Pitches Right (flyball pitcher)

	ERA	W	L	Sv	G	GS	IP	BB	SO	Avg	H	2B	3B	HR	RBI	OBP	SLG	CG	ShO	Sup	QS	#P/S	SB	CS	GB	FB	G/F
1992 Season	3.70	9	10	0	34	34	206.2	64	164	.234	182	37	8	18	85	.294	.371	0	0	4.27	15	95	27	6	216	250	0.86
Career (1988-1992)	3.73	37	41	0	118	117	728.1	306	538	.237	650	123	20	60	272	.315	.363	9	2	4.31	64	102	88	22	798	891	0.90

1992 Season

	ERA	W	L	Sv	G	GS	IP	H	HR	BB	SO		Avg	AB	H	2B	3B	HR	RBI	BB	SO	OBP	SLG
Home	2.75	7	4	0	21	21	137.2	106	7	38	107	vs. Left	.234	466	109	17	7	10	52	41	78	.300	.365
Away	5.61	2	6	0	13	13	69.0	76	11	26	57	vs. Right	.233	313	73	20	1	8	33	23	86	.285	.380
Day	4.07	1	4	0	9	9	48.2	44	6	17	47	Inning 1-6	.226	695	157	31	8	15	74	58	148	.289	.358
Night	3.59	8	6	0	25	25	158.0	138	12	47	117	Inning 7+	.298	84	25	6	0	3	11	6	16	.341	.476
Grass	4.35	2	4	0	9	9	49.2	51	2	20	38	None on	.217	484	105	18	6	10	10	36	107	.277	.341
Turf	3.50	7	6	0	25	25	157.0	131	10	44	126	Runners on	.261	295	77	19	2	8	75	28	57	.322	.420
April	2.41	1	3	0	5	5	33.2	28	2	8	23	Scoring Posn	.269	171	46	14	1	4	65	22	36	.343	.433
May	5.50	1	2	0	6	6	36.0	32	5	11	30	Close & Late	.245	53	13	5	0	1	4	4	13	.293	.396
June	4.04	1	2	0	6	6	35.2	32	6	16	24	None on/out	.232	211	49	6	1	3	3	9	47	.264	.313
July	3.00	1	1	0	5	5	30.0	25	1	11	22	vs. 1st Batr (relief)	.000	0	0	0	0	0	0	0	0	.000	.000
August	4.26	1	1	0	5	5	25.1	27	2	6	27	First Inning Pitched	.246	130	32	7	1	3	17	13	23	.313	.385
September/October	3.13	4	1	0	7	7	46.0	38	2	12	38	First 75 Pitches	.220	590	130	28	6	11	58	44	129	.278	.344
Starter	3.70	9	10	0	34	34	206.2	182	18	64	164	Pitch 76-90	.241	108	26	5	1	2	12	13	18	.322	.361
Reliever	0.00	0	0	0	0	0	0.0	0	0	0	0	Pitch 91-105	.333	63	21	3	1	4	12	4	13	.368	.603
0-3 Days Rest	3.60	0	1	0	1	1	5.0	7	2	1	3	Pitch 106+	.278	18	5	1	0	1	3	3	4	.381	.500
4 Days Rest	3.92	6	6	0	21	21	126.1	116	14	43	94	First Pitch	.273	110	30	9	1	1	14	3	0	.298	.400
5+ Days Rest	3.35	3	3	0	12	12	75.1	59	2	20	67	Ahead on Count	.184	375	69	14	1	7	32	0	144	.187	.283
Pre-All Star	3.76	3	7	0	19	19	117.1	101	13	40	89	Behind on Count	.327	150	49	10	1	8	23	27	0	.430	.567
Post-All Star	3.63	6	3	0	15	15	89.1	81	5	24	75	Two Strikes	.155	381	59	10	3	4	26	34	164	.227	.228

Career (1988-1992)

	ERA	W	L	Sv	G	GS	IP	H	HR	BB	SO		Avg	AB	H	2B	3B	HR	RBI	BB	SO	OBP	SLG
Home	3.14	24	15	0	59	58	380.2	307	25	124	298	vs. Left	.251	1555	391	74	16	33	155	184	259	.334	.383
Away	4.37	13	26	0	59	59	347.2	343	35	182	240	vs. Right	.219	1183	259	49	4	27	117	122	279	.291	.336
Day	4.04	7	8	0	26	26	153.2	144	17	72	122	Inning 1-6	.235	2392	563	105	16	51	238	264	478	.313	.357
Night	3.65	30	33	0	92	91	574.2	506	43	234	416	Inning 7+	.251	346	87	18	4	9	34	42	60	.332	.405
Grass	3.82	21	23	0	60	59	358.0	329	34	178	259	None on	.228	1605	366	64	14	36	36	171	320	.307	.353
Turf	3.65	16	18	0	58	58	370.1	321	26	128	279	Runners on	.251	1133	284	59	6	24	236	135	218	.327	.377
April	2.62	4	4	0	15	15	92.2	74	6	45	63	Scoring Posn	.230	649	149	34	3	13	203	105	136	.338	.351
May	4.12	6	7	0	18	18	115.2	100	8	41	73	Close & Late	.204	206	42	7	3	4	14	28	39	.297	.325
June	3.20	5	7	0	17	17	109.2	90	13	46	84	None on/out	.235	716	168	32	4	15	15	70	135	.307	.353
July	4.52	5	6	0	21	20	125.1	124	13	50	83	vs. 1st Batr (relief)	.000	1	0	0	0	0	0	0	1	.000	.000
August	3.48	6	10	0	24	24	150.0	140	12	72	127	First Inning Pitched	.236	440	104	19	2	5	46	59	86	.322	.323
September/October	4.13	11	7	0	23	23	135.0	122	8	52	108	First 75 Pitches	.231	1923	445	87	10	37	185	206	390	.308	.345
Starter	3.73	37	41	0	117	117	728.0	650	60	306	537	Pitch 76-90	.254	351	89	17	5	10	38	41	58	.330	.416
Reliever	0.00	0	0	0	1	0	0.1	0	0	0	1	Pitch 91-105	.251	259	65	10	3	8	26	27	60	.324	.405
0-3 Days Rest	3.20	3	2	0	6	6	39.1	34	3	17	26	Pitch 106+	.249	205	51	9	2	5	23	32	30	.349	.385
4 Days Rest	3.78	21	24	0	66	66	414.2	390	33	179	279	First Pitch	.284	380	108	27	2	8	48	11	0	.307	.429
5+ Days Rest	3.74	13	15	0	45	45	274.0	226	24	110	232	Ahead on Count	.201	1379	277	45	8	18	102	1	469	.204	.284
Pre-All Star	3.41	15	21	0	56	56	353.1	301	30	144	243	Behind on Count	.284	500	142	28	3	24	70	161	0	.456	.496
Post-All Star	4.03	22	20	0	62	61	375.0	349	30	162	295	Two Strikes	.182	1366	248	45	11	17	90	133	538	.257	.268

Pitcher vs. Batter (career)

Pitches Best Vs.	Avg	AB	H	2B	3B	HR	RBI	BB	SO	OBP	SLG	Pitches Worst Vs.	Avg	AB	H	2B	3B	HR	RBI	BB	SO	OBP	SLG
Ruben Sierra	.067	15	1	0	0	0	1	1	3	.118	.067	Kent Hrbek	.556	9	5	2	0	2	7	2	0	.636	1.444
Darren Daulton	.077	13	1	0	0	0	1	0	3	.077	.077	Jerry Browne	.538	13	7	2	0	1	4	1	1	.571	.923
Joe Oliver	.077	13	1	0	0	0	0	0	3	.077	.077	Greg Briley	.529	17	9	4	0	1	4	2	0	.579	.941
Rich Gedman	.083	12	1	0	0	0	1	0	2	.083	.083	Eddie Murray	.500	14	7	2	0	1	3	1	1	.533	.857
Mitch Webster	.091	11	1	0	0	0	0	0	3	.091	.091	Carlton Fisk	.429	7	3	1	0	1	2	4	1	.636	1.000

Brian Harper — Twins   Bats Right

	Avg	G	AB	R	H	2B	3B	HR	RBI	BB	SO	HBP	GDP	SB	CS	OBP	SLG	IBB	SH	SF	#Pit	#P/PA	GB	FB	G/F
1992 Season	.307	140	502	58	154	25	0	9	73	26	22	7	15	0	1	.343	.410	7	1	10	1865	3.42	187	185	1.01
Last Five Years	.307	583	1973	231	606	130	5	36	273	82	99	29	72	6	12	.340	.433	16	9	25	6754	3.20	762	673	1.13

1992 Season

	Avg	AB	H	2B	3B	HR	RBI	BB	SO	OBP	SLG		Avg	AB	H	2B	3B	HR	RBI	BB	SO	OBP	SLG
vs. Left	.275	109	30	6	0	1	13	13	6	.339	.358	Scoring Posn	.286	147	42	5	0	1	61	13	8	.339	.340
vs. Right	.316	393	124	19	0	8	60	13	16	.344	.425	Close & Late	.298	84	25	2	0	1	9	8	3	.365	.357
Groundball	.348	132	46	8	0	2	20	10	6	.393	.455	None on/out	.337	98	33	5	0	4	4	6	2	.387	.510
Flyball	.288	153	44	4	0	2	19	5	7	.319	.353	Batting #5	.281	221	62	11	0	2	29	12	8	.319	.357
Home	.324	241	78	10	0	3	31	15	11	.361	.402	Batting #6	.336	271	91	14	0	7	43	14	13	.372	.465
Away	.291	261	76	15	0	6	42	11	11	.326	.418	Other	.100	10	1	0	0	0	1	0	1	.091	.100
Day	.333	141	47	12	0	3	26	7	7	.366	.482	April	.279	68	19	2	0	1	7	4	1	.315	.353
Night	.296	361	107	13	0	6	47	19	15	.334	.382	May	.325	80	26	7	0	0	17	4	4	.364	.413
Grass	.318	192	61	11	0	4	36	10	10	.352	.438	June	.330	94	31	5	0	3	13	4	4	.354	.479
Turf	.300	310	93	14	0	5	37	16	12	.337	.394	July	.306	85	26	6	0	0	10	4	4	.337	.376
First Pitch	.242	62	15	1	0	1	6	7	0	.342	.306	August	.284	95	27	2	0	3	14	4	4	.310	.400
Ahead on Count	.356	118	42	6	0	3	25	14	0	.415	.483	September/October	.313	80	25	3	0	2	12	6	5	.376	.425
Behind on Count	.261	180	47	7	0	1	20	0	13	.269	.317	Pre-All Star	.301	276	83	15	0	4	42	14	12	.334	.399
Two Strikes	.289	204	59	12	0	1	28	6	22	.289	.363	Post-All Star	.314	226	71	0	0	5	31	12	10	.354	.425

1992 By Position

Position	Avg	AB	H	2B	3B	HR	RBI	BB	SO	OBP	SLG	G	GS	Innings	PO	A	E	DP	Fld Pct	Rng Fctr	In Zone	Outs	Zone Rtg	MLB Zone
As c	.308	487	150	24	0	9	72	24	22	.343	.413	133	128	1114.0	744	58	13	8	.984	---	---	---	---	---

Last Five Years

	Avg	AB	H	2B	3B	HR	RBI	BB	SO	OBP	SLG		Avg	AB	H	2B	3B	HR	RBI	BB	SO	OBP	SLG
vs. Left	.304	573	174	43	2	11	73	36	32	.345	.443	Scoring Posn	.303	548	166	33	1	9	226	38	30	.347	.416
vs. Right	.309	1400	432	87	3	25	200	46	67	.338	.429	Close & Late	.311	309	96	10	1	9	52	15	11	.345	.437
Groundball	.336	547	184	41	2	8	79	21	28	.364	.463	None on/out	.313	435	136	32	0	10	10	14	11	.343	.455
Flyball	.271	469	127	16	0	9	69	15	22	.300	.362	Batting #5	.302	635	192	46	2	8	81	22	30	.331	.419
Home	.311	951	296	60	4	12	126	45	51	.344	.421	Batting #6	.309	768	237	42	2	16	115	30	38	.338	.431
Away	.303	1022	310	70	1	24	147	37	48	.336	.444	Other	.311	570	177	42	1	12	77	30	31	.351	.451
Day	.318	519	165	39	1	11	85	22	31	.353	.461	April	.298	208	62	13	0	6	32	12	7	.348	.447
Night	.303	1454	441	91	4	25	188	60	68	.335	.423	May	.313	291	91	25	0	6	59	11	15	.339	.460
Grass	.297	765	227	51	0	19	118	32	40	.330	.438	June	.314	344	108	20	1	4	37	15	21	.351	.413
Turf	.314	1208	379	79	5	17	155	50	59	.346	.430	July	.328	363	119	25	0	4	45	14	13	.352	.430
First Pitch	.357	314	112	27	0	6	47	12	0	.386	.500	August	.303	409	124	25	3	10	61	9	20	.322	.452
Ahead on Count	.360	478	172	44	2	12	84	50	0	.416	.536	September/October	.285	358	102	22	1	6	39	21	23	.332	.402
Behind on Count	.276	735	203	40	1	8	95	0	56	.287	.366	Pre-All Star	.315	962	303	65	1	19	146	44	49	.351	.444
Two Strikes	.262	684	179	34	2	5	72	20	99	.296	.339	Post-All Star	.300	1011	303	65	4	17	127	38	50	.329	.422

Batter vs. Pitcher (since 1984)

Hits Best Against	Avg	AB	H	2B	3B	HR	RBI	BB	SO	OBP	SLG	Hits Worst Against	Avg	AB	H	2B	3B	HR	RBI	BB	SO	OBP	SLG
Erik Hanson	.583	12	7	1	0	1	3	1	1	.615	.917	David Wells	.083	12	1	0	0	0	1	0	1	.077	.083
Dan Plesac	.545	11	6	0	0	3	8	1	0	.583	1.364	Chuck Crim	.091	11	1	0	0	0	2	0	0	.083	.091
Bob Welch	.414	29	12	2	0	2	6	3	4	.469	.690	Melido Perez	.100	20	2	0	0	1	4	0	0	.100	.250
Edwin Nunez	.400	10	4	1	0	1	3	2	1	.500	.800	Bert Blyleven	.100	10	1	0	0	0	2	1	0	.154	.100
Mike Jeffcoat	.400	10	4	0	0	1	4	1	0	.455	.700	Rod Nichols	.182	11	2	0	0	0	0	0	0	.182	.182

Donald Harris — Rangers   Bats Right

	Avg	G	AB	R	H	2B	3B	HR	RBI	BB	SO	HBP	GDP	SB	CS	OBP	SLG	IBB	SH	SF	#Pit	#P/PA	GB	FB	G/F
1992 Season	.182	24	33	3	6	1	0	0	1	0	15	0	0	0	0	.182	.182	0	0	0	108	3.27	8	5	1.60
Career (1991-1992)	.220	42	41	7	9	1	0	1	3	1	18	0	0	0	2	.238	.317	0	0	0	146	3.48	8	8	1.00

1992 Season

	Avg	AB	H	2B	3B	HR	RBI	BB	SO	OBP	SLG		Avg	AB	H	2B	3B	HR	RBI	BB	SO	OBP	SLG
vs. Left	.278	18	5	1	0	0	1	0	10	.278	.333	Scoring Posn	.125	8	1	0	0	0	1	0	3	.125	.125
vs. Right	.067	15	1	0	0	0	0	0	5	.067	.067	Close & Late	.125	8	1	0	0	0	0	0	4	.125	.125

Gene Harris — Padres
Pitches Right (groundball pitcher)

	ERA	W	L	Sv	G	GS	IP	BB	SO	Avg	H	2B	3B	HR	RBI	OBP	SLG	GF	IR	IRS	Hld	SvOp	SB	CS	GB	FB	G/F
1992 Season	4.15	0	2	0	22	1	30.1	15	25	.207	23	3	0	3	11	.307	.315	4	11	1	2	0	4	0	47	26	1.81
Career (1989-1992)	5.00	3	9	2	76	7	135.0	80	99	.260	132	27	4	13	77	.360	.406	19	49	12	5	5	15	3	201	124	1.62

1992 Season

	ERA	W	L	Sv	G	GS	IP	H	HR	BB	SO		Avg	AB	H	2B	3B	HR	RBI	BB	SO	OBP	SLG
Home	5.40	0	0	0	7	1	11.2	11	0	5	7	vs. Left	.135	52	7	2	0	0	3	7	10	.250	.173
Away	3.38	0	2	0	15	0	18.2	12	3	10	18	vs. Right	.271	59	16	1	0	3	8	8	15	.358	.441
Starter	9.82	0	0	0	1	1	3.2	6	0	1	3	Scoring Posn	.167	36	6	1	0	1	9	4	5	.250	.278
Reliever	3.38	0	2	0	21	0	26.2	17	3	14	22	Close & Late	.207	29	6	0	0	0	1	4	7	.324	.207
0 Days rest	0.00	0	0	0	2	0	3.2	1	0	1	1	None on/out	.286	28	8	2	0	0	2	6	.333	.357
1 or 2 Days rest	1.86	0	1	0	8	0	9.2	6	0	5	8	First Pitch	.160	25	4	0	0	0	2	0	0	.160	.160
3+ Days rest	5.40	0	1	0	11	0	13.1	10	3	8	13	Behind on Count	.444	18	8	1	0	2	5	9	0	.630	.833
Pre-All Star	5.85	0	1	0	15	1	20.0	18	3	9	15	Ahead on Count	.192	52	10	1	0	1	3	0	20	.208	.269
Post-All Star	0.87	0	1	0	7	0	10.1	5	0	6	10	Two Strikes	.145	55	8	1	0	1	2	6	25	.242	.218

Greg Harris — Red Sox
Pitches Right (groundball pitcher)

	ERA	W	L	Sv	G	GS	IP	BB	SO	Avg	H	2B	3B	HR	RBI	OBP	SLG	GF	IR	IRS	Hld	SvOp	SB	CS	GB	FB	G/F
1992 Season	2.51	4	9	4	70	2	107.2	60	73	.215	82	11	4	6	40	.324	.312	22	73	18	19	10	3	6	137	102	1.34
Last Five Years	3.36	36	40	8	282	54	675.1	316	464	.237	590	107	14	47	272	.325	.348	40	210	71	36	19	41	29	959	632	1.52

1992 Season

	ERA	W	L	Sv	G	GS	IP	H	HR	BB	SO		Avg	AB	H	2B	3B	HR	RBI	BB	SO	OBP	SLG
Home	2.79	3	1	3	40	1	58.0	40	5	35	49	vs. Left	.211	142	30	5	1	2	14	25	27	.335	.303
Away	2.17	1	8	1	30	1	49.2	42	1	25	24	vs. Right	.217	240	52	6	3	4	26	35	46	.317	.317
Day	3.43	3	4	2	28	0	39.1	24	2	25	29	Inning 1-6	.200	80	16	3	1	1	9	13	19	.305	.300
Night	1.98	1	5	2	42	2	68.1	58	4	35	44	Inning 7+	.219	302	66	8	3	5	31	47	54	.329	.315
Grass	2.60	4	5	4	59	2	93.1	71	5	54	65	None on	.212	193	41	5	1	4	4	27	42	.315	.311
Turf	1.88	0	4	0	11	0	14.1	11	1	6	8	Runners on	.217	189	41	6	3	2	36	33	31	.332	.312
April	1.84	1	1	0	7	0	14.2	8	1	8	18	Scoring Posn	.193	119	23	4	3	1	34	25	20	.331	.303
May	0.98	1	2	0	12	0	18.1	10	0	6	10	Close & Late	.207	164	34	3	1	2	12	28	29	.330	.274
June	1.62	0	0	0	16	0	16.2	9	0	13	10	None on/out	.226	84	19	1	0	1	1	14	16	.350	.274
July	2.25	0	3	1	15	1	20.0	15	1	13	10	vs. 1st Batr (relief)	.172	58	10	2	1	0	8	8	7	.279	.241
August	5.48	1	1	2	10	1	21.1	28	3	8	16	First Inning Pitched	.220	205	45	8	2	3	32	36	34	.339	.322
September/October	2.16	1	2	1	10	0	16.2	12	1	12	9	First 15 Pitches	.197	178	35	8	2	2	25	28	23	.311	.298
Starter	1.38	0	1	0	2	2	13.0	8	1	7	6	Pitch 16-30	.284	102	29	1	2	2	11	19	30	.395	.392
Reliever	2.66	4	8	4	68	0	94.2	74	5	53	67	Pitch 31-45	.212	52	11	1	0	1	2	6	11	.293	.288
0 Days rest	2.91	1	0	1	21	0	21.2	15	1	20	14	Pitch 46+	.140	50	7	1	0	1	2	7	9	.246	.220
1 or 2 Days rest	1.98	2	6	2	33	0	54.2	40	3	19	40	First Pitch	.255	47	12	2	0	0	6	7	0	.375	.298
3+ Days rest	4.42	1	3	1	14	0	18.1	19	1	14	13	Ahead on Count	.172	180	31	3	2	2	10	0	61	.180	.244
Pre-All Star	1.52	2	4	1	40	1	59.1	32	2	32	43	Behind on Count	.250	80	20	3	1	2	15	26	1	.422	.388
Post-All Star	3.72	2	5	3	30	1	48.1	50	4	28	30	Two Strikes	.171	187	32	5	2	2	10	27	72	.276	.251

Last Five Years

	ERA	W	L	Sv	G	GS	IP	H	HR	BB	SO		Avg	AB	H	2B	3B	HR	RBI	BB	SO	OBP	SLG
Home	3.59	18	19	7	141	24	326.0	291	28	164	243	vs. Left	.225	1157	260	50	7	17	118	156	200	.319	.324
Away	3.14	18	21	1	141	30	349.1	299	19	152	221	vs. Right	.248	1330	330	57	7	30	154	160	264	.330	.369
Day	3.11	17	8	3	87	15	191.0	150	10	103	147	Inning 1-6	.244	1363	333	68	7	24	150	153	259	.320	.357
Night	3.46	19	32	5	195	39	484.1	440	37	213	317	Inning 7+	.229	1124	257	39	7	23	122	163	205	.331	.337
Grass	3.55	28	23	6	177	44	451.1	402	33	204	311	None on	.230	1386	319	62	8	32	32	157	262	.314	.356
Turf	2.97	8	17	2	105	10	224.0	188	14	112	153	Runners on	.246	1101	271	45	6	15	240	159	202	.339	.339
April	2.63	5	3	0	28	5	72.0	50	6	35	54	Scoring Posn	.236	640	151	23	5	8	213	122	125	.353	.325
May	3.70	4	9	1	50	10	114.1	105	5	48	66	Close & Late	.221	498	110	12	4	6	40	71	91	.323	.274
June	3.08	8	4	1	55	11	125.2	101	5	61	86	None on/out	.226	605	137	26	4	17	17	70	106	.317	.367
July	3.16	5	10	2	51	11	134.0	125	9	54	82	vs. 1st Batr (relief)	.215	163	35	6	2	4	25	17	28	.295	.350
August	2.73	10	4	2	49	10	131.2	103	12	53	108	First Inning Pitched	.220	773	170	28	4	16	100	108	147	.319	.329
September/October	4.96	4	10	2	49	7	97.2	106	10	65	68	First 15 Pitches	.223	821	183	32	5	19	102	108	136	.319	.343
Starter	4.13	19	21	0	54	54	318.0	308	24	130	213	Pitch 16-30	.252	592	149	24	4	14	61	84	145	.345	.377
Reliever	2.67	17	19	8	228	0	357.1	282	23	186	251	Pitch 31-45	.207	362	75	10	1	1	21	29	70	.264	.249
0 Days rest	2.70	4	1	3	65	0	83.1	59	5	57	56	Pitch 46+	.257	712	183	41	4	13	88	95	113	.346	.381
1 or 2 Days rest	2.64	5	10	3	100	0	170.2	137	13	70	115	First Pitch	.255	345	88	11	0	5	40	34	0	.329	.330
3+ Days rest	2.70	8	8	2	63	0	103.1	86	5	59	80	Ahead on Count	.190	1111	211	40	5	14	83	1	398	.198	.273
Pre-All Star	3.20	18	17	3	148	29	340.2	281	18	155	224	Behind on Count	.299	596	178	35	7	19	98	160	1	.443	.477
Post-All Star	3.52	18	23	5	134	25	334.2	309	24	161	240	Two Strikes	.178	1138	202	44	5	14	86	121	463	.259	.262

Pitcher vs. Batter (since 1984)

Pitches Best Vs.	Avg	AB	H	2B	3B	HR	RBI	BB	SO	OBP	SLG	Pitches Worst Vs.	Avg	AB	H	2B	3B	HR	RBI	BB	SO	OBP	SLG
Jerry Browne	.000	12	0	0	0	0	2	2	1	.133	.000	George Bell	.450	20	9	2	0	2	7	1	2	.476	.850
Jose Canseco	.063	16	1	0	0	0	1	1	10	.118	.063	Gary Sheffield	.444	9	4	1	0	1	3	2	0	.545	.889
Gene Larkin	.077	13	1	0	0	0	1	2	1	.143	.077	Dan Pasqua	.400	10	4	2	0	1	2	2	2	.500	.800
Frank Thomas	.077	13	1	0	0	0	1	2	4	.188	.077	Rance Mulliniks	.364	11	4	1	1	1	4	2	1	.533	.909
Billy Doran	.091	11	1	0	0	0	0	2	1	.091	.091	Albert Belle	.333	9	3	0	0	3	5	1	2	.364	1.333

Greg W. Harris — Padres

Pitches Right

	ERA	W	L	Sv	G	GS	IP	BB	SO	Avg	H	2B	3B	HR	RBI	OBP	SLG	CG	ShO	Sup	QS	#P/S	SB	CS	GB	FB	G/F
1992 Season	4.12	4	8	0	20	20	118.0	35	66	.252	113	18	1	13	55	.307	.384	1	0	4.35	8	85	18	5	165	128	1.29
Career (1988-1992)	2.74	31	30	15	172	49	521.1	166	379	.229	440	67	5	43	181	.291	.336	5	2	3.45	31	92	49	20	695	506	1.37

1992 Season

	ERA	W	L	Sv	G	GS	IP	H	HR	BB	SO		Avg	AB	H	2B	3B	HR	RBI	BB	SO	OBP	SLG
Home	3.36	2	3	0	9	9	61.2	54	6	15	37	vs. Left	.279	287	80	10	1	11	40	23	34	.330	.436
Away	4.95	2	5	0	11	11	56.1	59	7	20	29	vs. Right	.205	161	33	8	0	2	15	12	32	.267	.292
Starter	4.12	4	8	0	20	20	118.0	113	13	35	66	Scoring Posn	.270	100	27	1	0	5	45	16	12	.372	.430
Reliever	0.00	0	0	0	0	0	0.0	0	0	0	0	Close & Late	.200	30	6	0	0	1	2	2	2	.250	.300
0-3 Days Rest	0.00	0	0	0	0	0	0.0	0	0	0	0	None on/out	.289	121	35	7	0	4	4	5	22	.317	.446
4 Days Rest	3.11	3	4	0	10	10	66.2	58	6	23	39	First Pitch	.309	81	25	3	0	4	16	1	0	.310	.494
5+ Days Rest	5.44	1	4	0	10	10	51.1	55	7	12	27	Behind on Count	.353	102	36	5	1	7	20	21	0	.463	.627
Pre-All Star	4.05	2	4	0	12	12	66.2	65	10	23	40	Ahead on Count	.183	191	35	6	0	1	14	0	58	.191	.230
Post-All Star	4.21	2	4	0	8	8	51.1	48	3	12	26	Two Strikes	.196	184	36	5	0	2	14	13	66	.251	.255

Career (1988-1992)

	ERA	W	L	Sv	G	GS	IP	H	HR	BB	SO		Avg	AB	H	2B	3B	HR	RBI	BB	SO	OBP	SLG
Home	2.35	18	13	4	80	25	260.1	214	21	80	201	vs. Left	.249	1142	284	40	3	27	112	97	197	.307	.360
Away	3.14	13	17	11	92	24	261.0	226	22	86	178	vs. Right	.200	781	156	27	2	16	69	69	182	.268	.301
Day	3.11	14	10	4	54	17	173.2	136	8	68	119	Inning 1-6	.248	1092	271	41	2	31	113	80	208	.300	.375
Night	2.56	17	20	11	118	32	347.2	304	35	98	260	Inning 7+	.203	831	169	26	3	12	68	86	171	.280	.285
Grass	2.30	24	19	10	123	35	379.1	308	27	115	280	None on	.228	1193	272	47	1	27	27	72	240	.275	.337
Turf	3.93	7	11	5	49	14	142.0	132	16	51	99	Runners on	.230	730	168	20	4	16	154	94	139	.316	.334
April	1.79	4	2	0	21	8	70.1	53	6	12	46	Scoring Posn	.211	421	89	11	2	8	132	74	93	.324	.304
May	3.89	3	5	6	30	6	71.2	63	11	33	62	Close & Late	.198	499	99	15	1	4	41	63	110	.289	.257
June	2.66	3	3	1	25	1	40.2	31	2	23	35	None on/out	.218	496	108	24	0	10	10	30	102	.265	.327
July	3.91	2	8	1	25	8	76.0	72	7	25	49	vs. 1st Batr (relief)	.218	110	24	6	1	2	16	8	27	.270	.345
August	2.68	7	5	2	30	12	107.1	92	6	32	77	First Inning Pitched	.231	590	136	20	3	10	67	59	128	.300	.325
September/October	2.14	12	7	5	41	14	155.1	129	11	41	110	First 75 Pitches	.227	1632	371	58	4	31	148	141	326	.290	.325
Starter	3.12	17	17	0	49	49	311.1	280	33	87	215	Pitch 76-90	.252	147	37	3	0	9	21	11	22	.304	.456
Reliever	2.19	14	13	15	123	0	210.0	160	10	79	164	Pitch 91-105	.258	89	23	5	1	1	7	11	20	.340	.371
0-3 Days Rest	1.32	2	1	0	4	4	27.1	21	2	11	22	Pitch 106+	.164	55	9	1	0	2	5	3	11	.207	.291
4 Days Rest	2.85	18	8	0	25	25	164.0	144	16	45	112	First Pitch	.294	323	95	12	0	12	46	21	0	.333	.443
5+ Days Rest	3.90	5	8	0	20	20	120.0	115	15	31	81	Ahead on Count	.159	857	136	20	2	6	51	3	322	.166	.208
Pre-All Star	2.85	10	11	8	84	16	198.2	162	20	72	148	Behind on Count	.300	423	127	22	3	21	57	87	0	.419	.515
Post-All Star	2.68	21	19	7	88	33	322.2	278	23	94	231	Two Strikes	.167	858	143	21	2	7	51	55	379	.219	.220

Pitcher vs. Batter (career)

Pitches Best Vs.	Avg	AB	H	2B	3B	HR	RBI	BB	SO	OBP	SLG	Pitches Worst Vs.	Avg	AB	H	2B	3B	HR	RBI	BB	SO	OBP	SLG
Matt D. Williams	.000	14	0	0	0	0	0	0	3	.000	.000	Larry Walker	.643	14	9	1	0	3	5	2	1	.688	1.357
Andujar Cedeno	.000	11	0	0	0	0	1	2	.063	.000	Paul O'Neill	.440	25	11	1	0	2	4	2	3	.481	.720
Todd Benzinger	.050	20	1	0	0	0	1	0	6	.050	.050	Gary Carter	.417	12	5	1	0	1	1	1	2	.462	.750
Gerald Young	.071	14	1	0	0	0	0	0	1	.071	.071	Jeff Bagwell	.375	8	3	0	0	1	2	3	1	.615	.750
Dave Justice	.091	11	1	0	0	0	0	0	2	.091	.091	Darryl Strawberry	.360	25	9	1	0	3	8	5	3	.452	.760

Lenny Harris — Dodgers

Bats Left (groundball hitter)

	Avg	G	AB	R	H	2B	3B	HR	RBI	BB	SO	HBP	GDP	SB	CS	OBP	SLG	IBB	SH	SF	#Pit	#P/PA	GB	FB	G/F
1992 Season	.271	135	347	28	94	11	0	0	30	24	24	1	10	19	7	.318	.303	3	6	2	1227	3.28	189	73	2.59
Career (1988-1992)	.279	548	1585	191	443	54	6	8	131	115	124	9	49	64	30	.330	.336	10	23	7	5521	3.22	812	348	2.33

1992 Season

	Avg	AB	H	2B	3B	HR	RBI	BB	SO	OBP	SLG		Avg	AB	H	2B	3B	HR	RBI	BB	SO	OBP	SLG
vs. Left	.139	36	5	0	0	0	0	3	6	.205	.139	Scoring Posn	.298	84	25	10	0	0	30	5	5	.330	.417
vs. Right	.286	311	89	11	0	0	30	21	18	.331	.322	Close & Late	.283	60	17	0	0	0	5	7	3	.358	.283
Groundball	.312	138	43	6	0	0	15	5	9	.336	.355	None on/out	.217	69	15	0	0	0	1	4		.229	.217
Flyball	.228	92	21	0	0	4	9	6	.301	.250	Batting #2	.305	151	46	3	0	0	9	11	10	.350	.325
Home	.266	177	47	5	0	0	15	11	13	.307	.294	Batting #3	.274	117	32	6	0	0	17	6	7	.312	.325
Away	.276	170	47	6	0	0	15	13	11	.330	.312	Other	.203	79	16	2	0	0	4	7	7	.267	.228
Day	.286	119	34	3	0	0	12	12	9	.348	.311	April	.340	53	18	0	0	0	3	4	2	.386	.340
Night	.263	228	60	8	0	0	18	12	15	.302	.298	May	.232	56	13	2	0	0	1	5	7	.295	.268
Grass	.280	268	75	6	0	0	22	18	18	.323	.302	June	.306	62	19	4	0	0	9	3	5	.338	.371
Turf	.241	79	19	5	0	0	8	6	6	.302	.304	July	.238	63	15	1	0	0	2	0	3	.238	.254
First Pitch	.353	68	24	4	0	0	11	2	0	.371	.412	August	.269	52	14	3	0	0	5	5	3	.345	.327
Ahead on Count	.253	83	21	4	0	0	9	15	0	.360	.301	September/October	.246	61	15	1	0	0	10	7	4	.314	.262
Behind on Count	.264	106	28	1	0	0	6	0	15	.271	.264	Pre-All Star	.274	208	57	6	0	0	14	12	15	.314	.303
Two Strikes	.256	121	31	2	0	0	5	7	24	.302	.273	Post-All Star	.266	139	37	5	0	0	16	12	9	.325	.302

1992 By Position

Position	Avg	AB	H	2B	3B	HR	RBI	BB	SO	OBP	SLG	G	GS	Innings	PO	A	E	DP	Fld Pct	Rng Fctr	In Zone	Outs	Zone Rtg	MLB Zone
As Pinch Hitter	.207	29	6	0	0	0	2	3	4	.281	.207	33	0	---	---	---	---	---	---	---	---	---	---	---
As 2b	.297	222	66	8	0	0	16	14	15	.339	.333	81	65	541.0	161	205	14	40	.963	6.09	237	206	.869	.892
As 3b	.239	46	11	0	0	0	4	2	3	.271	.239	33	10	127.1	12	26	5	5	.884	2.69	38	34	.895	.841

187

1992 By Position

Position	Avg	AB	H	2B	3B	HR	RBI	BB	SO	OBP	SLG	G	GS	Innings	PO	A	E	DP	Fld Pct	Rng Fctr	In Zone	Outs	Zone Rtg	MLB Zone
As ss	.250	16	4	0	0	0	3	2	0	.333	.250	10	2	37.2	6	16	6	4	.786	5.26	23	14	.609	.885

Career (1988-1992)

	Avg	AB	H	2B	3B	HR	RBI	BB	SO	OBP	SLG		Avg	AB	H	2B	3B	HR	RBI	BB	SO	OBP	SLG
vs. Left	.216	236	51	2	1	1	18	16	28	.282	.246	Scoring Posn	.279	333	93	12	3	3	116	26	33	.325	.360
vs. Right	.291	1349	392	52	5	7	113	99	96	.339	.352	Close & Late	.269	253	68	6	0	0	17	27	25	.345	.292
Groundball	.278	554	154	18	1	2	52	23	43	.308	.325	None on/out	.273	436	119	9	2	1	1	26	26	.315	.310
Flyball	.292	346	101	15	1	1	27	33	31	.360	.350	Batting #1	.291	430	125	19	3	2	29	26	34	.333	.363
Home	.273	788	215	25	3	2	59	54	61	.322	.320	Batting #2	.296	378	112	12	0	2	31	37	29	.360	.344
Away	.286	797	228	29	3	6	72	61	63	.339	.353	Other	.265	777	206	23	3	4	71	52	61	.315	.318
Day	.273	483	132	13	2	4	45	44	47	.336	.333	April	.277	148	41	0	1	0	11	10	6	.321	.291
Night	.282	1102	311	41	4	4	86	71	77	.328	.338	May	.303	231	70	10	2	0	14	23	27	.369	.364
Grass	.279	1093	305	34	5	6	93	76	86	.326	.336	June	.281	317	89	11	1	3	28	16	26	.317	.350
Turf	.280	492	138	20	1	2	38	39	38	.340	.337	July	.241	274	66	11	1	1	20	15	17	.288	.299
First Pitch	.337	350	118	13	2	4	45	4	0	.345	.420	August	.284	264	75	11	0	1	22	18	18	.332	.337
Ahead on Count	.295	356	105	18	2	0	33	70	0	.411	.357	September/October	.291	351	102	11	1	3	36	33	30	.351	.353
Behind on Count	.252	460	121	14	1	2	30	2	66	.260	.298	Pre-All Star	.274	803	220	22	4	4	59	52	63	.319	.326
Two Strikes	.242	533	129	10	0	3	31	39	124	.296	.278	Post-All Star	.285	782	223	32	2	4	72	63	61	.341	.347

Batter vs. Pitcher (career)

Hits Best Against	Avg	AB	H	2B	3B	HR	RBI	BB	SO	OBP	SLG	Hits Worst Against	Avg	AB	H	2B	3B	HR	RBI	BB	SO	OBP	SLG
Joe Boever	.556	9	5	2	0	0	1	2	0	.636	.778	Doug Drabek	.048	21	1	0	0	0	0	1	1	.091	.048
Randy Myers	.400	10	4	0	0	0	0	2	3	.500	.400	Scott Scudder	.100	10	1	0	0	0	0	2	1	.250	.100
Mark Gardner	.381	21	8	1	0	1	1	1	0	.409	.571	Darryl Kile	.143	14	2	0	0	0	1	3	1	.294	.143
Mark Portugal	.375	24	9	0	0	1	5	2	4	.423	.500	Dennis Martinez	.192	26	5	0	0	0	0	0	3	.192	.192
Jimmy Jones	.357	14	5	2	0	0	3	2	1	.412	.500	Frank Castillo	.200	10	2	0	0	0	1	0	1	.182	.200

Mike Hartley — Phillies

Pitches Right (flyball pitcher)

	ERA	W	L	Sv	G	GS	IP	BB	SO	Avg	H	2B	3B	HR	RBI	OBP	SLG	GF	IR	IRS	Hld	SvOp	SB	CS	GB	FB	G/F
1992 Season	3.44	7	6	0	46	0	55.0	23	53	.255	54	12	2	5	26	.332	.401	15	17	7	8	4	8	2	60	59	1.02
Career (1989-1992)	3.50	17	11	3	141	6	223.2	100	196	.225	188	31	7	23	100	.315	.362	39	67	25	16	11	35	4	232	257	0.90

1992 Season

	ERA	W	L	Sv	G	GS	IP	H	HR	BB	SO		Avg	AB	H	2B	3B	HR	RBI	BB	SO	OBP	SLG
Home	3.65	3	2	0	22	0	24.2	25	2	9	32	vs. Left	.252	107	27	6	0	0	9	13	23	.331	.308
Away	3.26	4	4	0	24	0	30.1	29	3	14	21	vs. Right	.257	105	27	6	2	5	17	10	30	.333	.495
Starter	0.00	0	0	0	0	0	0.0	0	0	0	0	Scoring Posn	.218	78	17	5	2	2	23	11	25	.319	.410
Reliever	3.44	7	6	0	46	0	55.0	54	5	23	53	Close & Late	.231	104	24	3	1	2	12	16	27	.344	.337
0 Days rest	5.59	2	2	0	9	0	9.2	11	2	6	6	None on/out	.373	51	19	6	0	2	2	4	4	.418	.608
1 or 2 Days rest	3.05	1	3	0	18	0	20.2	22	1	6	22	First Pitch	.211	38	8	1	0	0	4	6	0	.318	.237
3+ Days rest	2.92	6	1	0	19	0	24.2	21	2	11	25	Behind on Count	.310	42	13	2	0	3	7	13	0	.473	.571
Pre-All Star	2.42	4	4	0	20	0	26.0	24	2	10	24	Ahead on Count	.196	97	19	5	2	2	12	0	44	.202	.351
Post-All Star	4.34	3	2	0	26	0	29.0	30	3	13	29	Two Strikes	.202	104	21	1	2	2	12	4	53	.236	.327

Career (1989-1992)

	ERA	W	L	Sv	G	GS	IP	H	HR	BB	SO		Avg	AB	H	2B	3B	HR	RBI	BB	SO	OBP	SLG
Home	2.90	10	3	1	71	3	115.0	91	11	44	114	vs. Left	.228	429	98	14	5	7	37	62	89	.328	.333
Away	4.14	7	8	2	70	3	108.2	97	12	56	82	vs. Right	.222	405	90	17	2	16	63	38	107	.300	.393
Day	3.52	5	4	1	43	1	64.0	58	7	31	54	Inning 1-6	.218	307	67	8	3	9	42	32	63	.300	.352
Night	3.49	12	7	2	98	5	159.2	130	16	69	142	Inning 7+	.230	527	121	23	4	14	58	68	133	.323	.368
Grass	3.09	10	7	2	72	5	131.0	99	12	62	108	None on	.222	465	103	15	2	11	11	52	107	.308	.333
Turf	4.08	7	4	1	69	1	92.2	89	11	38	88	Runners on	.230	369	85	16	5	12	89	48	89	.323	.398
April	2.50	0	0	0	13	0	18.0	11	3	6	19	Scoring Posn	.211	247	52	12	4	8	79	39	66	.322	.389
May	3.47	1	0	1	27	0	36.1	36	4	22	32	Close & Late	.237	190	45	8	2	3	25	32	43	.358	.347
June	4.14	5	2	1	24	0	37.0	38	3	19	34	None on/out	.232	203	47	9	1	4	4	19	41	.307	.345
July	4.54	2	3	0	26	0	35.2	32	4	19	41	vs. 1st Batr (relief)	.233	120	28	11	0	3	15	12	28	.306	.400
August	3.14	6	2	1	24	3	48.2	34	3	21	32	First Inning Pitched	.240	466	112	22	4	14	72	55	112	.326	.395
September/October	3.00	3	4	0	27	3	48.0	37	6	13	38	First 15 Pitches	.243	415	101	20	4	12	49	43	92	.318	.398
Starter	2.52	3	2	0	6	6	35.2	21	2	12	23	Pitch 16-30	.225	227	51	8	2	5	31	35	69	.341	.344
Reliever	3.69	14	9	3	135	0	188.0	167	21	88	173	Pitch 31-45	.198	111	22	1	0	6	15	9	21	.258	.342
0 Days rest	3.46	2	2	1	29	0	41.2	35	5	26	31	Pitch 46+	.173	81	14	2	1	1	5	13	14	.295	.259
1 or 2 Days rest	4.06	3	5	1	58	0	75.1	75	9	33	66	First Pitch	.276	123	34	5	0	3	15	14	0	.364	.390
3+ Days rest	3.42	9	2	1	48	0	71.0	57	7	29	76	Ahead on Count	.184	407	75	13	4	9	47	0	159	.194	.302
Pre-All Star	3.51	7	5	2	75	0	107.2	98	12	57	101	Behind on Count	.288	160	46	6	2	10	25	52	0	.463	.538
Post-All Star	3.49	10	6	1	66	6	116.0	90	11	43	95	Two Strikes	.151	430	65	10	3	7	43	34	196	.221	.237

Pitcher vs. Batter (career)

Pitches Best Vs.	Avg	AB	H	2B	3B	HR	RBI	BB	SO	OBP	SLG	Pitches Worst Vs.	Avg	AB	H	2B	3B	HR	RBI	BB	SO	OBP	SLG
Marquis Grissom	.100	10	1	0	0	0	0	2	3	.250	.100	Gregg Jefferies	.364	11	4	0	0	0	0	2	1	.462	.364
Delino DeShields	.167	12	2	0	0	0	0	0	4	.167	.167	Spike Owen	.333	9	3	1	0	0	3	1	2	.364	.444
Andres Galarraga	.200	10	2	0	0	1	2	2	2	.333	.500	Ron Gant	.333	9	3	1	1	0	4	2	2	.455	.667

188

Jeff Hartsock — Cubs
Pitches Right

	ERA	W	L	Sv	G	GS	IP	BB	SO	Avg	H	2B	3B	HR	RBI	OBP	SLG	GF	IR	IRS	Hld	SvOp	SB	CS	GB	FB	G/F
1992 Season	6.75	0	0	0	4	0	9.1	4	6	.375	15	1	0	2	12	.422	.550	0	6	5	0	0	1	2	16	12	1.33

1992 Season

	ERA	W	L	Sv	G	GS	IP	H	HR	BB	SO		Avg	AB	H	2B	3B	HR	RBI	BB	SO	OBP	SLG
Home	5.14	0	0	0	2	0	7.0	10	1	3	4	vs. Left	.348	23	8	1	0	0	5	4	4	.429	.391
Away	11.57	0	0	0	2	0	2.1	5	1	1	2	vs. Right	.412	17	7	0	0	2	7	0	2	.412	.765

Bryan Harvey — Angels
Pitches Right

	ERA	W	L	Sv	G	GS	IP	BB	SO	Avg	H	2B	3B	HR	RBI	OBP	SLG	GF	IR	IRS	Hld	SvOp	SB	CS	GB	FB	G/F
1992 Season	2.83	0	4	13	25	0	28.2	11	34	.208	22	2	0	4	12	.275	.340	22	9	2	0	16	2	0	34	27	1.26
Last Five Years	2.53	16	20	126	247	0	302.2	124	362	.196	213	27	3	24	117	.276	.292	132	160	40	2	154	34	5	300	286	1.05

1992 Season

	ERA	W	L	Sv	G	GS	IP	H	HR	BB	SO		Avg	AB	H	2B	3B	HR	RBI	BB	SO	OBP	SLG
Home	3.07	0	3	6	12	0	14.2	13	3	5	16	vs. Left	.172	58	10	1	0	2	7	4	18	.222	.293
Away	2.57	0	1	7	13	0	14.0	9	1	6	18	vs. Right	.250	48	12	1	0	2	5	7	16	.333	.396
Starter	0.00	0	0	0	0	0	0.0	0	0	0	0	Scoring Posn	.083	36	3	0	0	0	8	4	14	.163	.083
Reliever	2.83	0	4	13	25	0	28.2	22	4	11	34	Close & Late	.222	81	18	1	0	2	10	8	27	.283	.309
0 Days rest	2.08	0	0	4	4	0	4.1	4	1	0	7	None on/out	.238	21	5	1	0	1	1	3	5	.333	.429
1 or 2 Days rest	2.16	0	3	7	13	0	16.2	11	1	8	22	First Pitch	.143	14	2	0	0	1	1	1	0	.200	.357
3+ Days rest	4.70	0	1	2	8	0	7.2	7	2	3	5	Behind on Count	.500	14	7	1	0	3	5	2	0	.529	1.214
Pre-All Star	2.83	0	4	13	25	0	28.2	22	4	11	34	Ahead on Count	.138	65	9	1	0	0	5	0	33	.134	.154
Post-All Star	0.00	0	0	0	0	0	0.0	0	0	0	0	Two Strikes	.150	60	9	1	0	0	4	8	34	.243	.167

Last Five Years

	ERA	W	L	Sv	G	GS	IP	H	HR	BB	SO		Avg	AB	H	2B	3B	HR	RBI	BB	SO	OBP	SLG
Home	2.65	10	10	60	126	0	163.0	125	15	64	185	vs. Left	.173	571	99	16	2	12	65	69	202	.260	.271
Away	2.38	6	10	66	121	0	139.2	88	9	60	177	vs. Right	.220	518	114	11	1	12	52	55	160	.294	.315
Day	2.09	3	3	32	60	0	77.1	59	7	28	95	Inning 1-6	.250	12	3	0	0	0	1	0	3	.231	.250
Night	2.68	13	17	94	187	0	225.1	154	17	96	267	Inning 7+	.195	1077	210	27	3	24	116	124	359	.276	.292
Grass	2.68	13	17	109	215	0	265.0	182	21	110	317	None on	.208	552	115	11	0	17	17	44	179	.268	.321
Turf	1.43	3	3	17	32	0	37.2	31	3	14	45	Runners on	.182	537	98	16	3	7	100	80	183	.283	.263
April	1.61	3	2	16	37	0	44.2	29	3	19	53	Scoring Posn	.158	342	54	9	3	6	96	66	125	.286	.254
May	2.66	3	5	21	49	0	67.2	51	5	23	68	Close & Late	.198	626	124	16	1	15	80	73	219	.279	.299
June	2.12	0	3	24	44	0	51.0	33	2	25	65	None on/out	.208	226	47	8	0	7	7	22	67	.281	.336
July	3.80	6	5	15	36	0	45.0	40	5	19	48	vs. 1st Batr (relief)	.235	217	51	9	0	7	25	27	68	.318	.373
August	0.75	2	1	21	35	0	48.0	24	3	13	71	First Inning Pitched	.190	811	154	19	2	17	95	103	260	.279	.281
September/October	4.27	2	4	29	46	0	46.1	36	6	25	57	First 15 Pitches	.199	703	140	14	1	19	71	72	218	.272	.303
Starter	0.00	0	0	0	0	0	0.0	0	0	0	0	Pitch 16-30	.188	319	60	10	1	5	32	42	120	.281	.273
Reliever	2.53	16	20	126	247	0	302.2	213	24	124	362	Pitch 31-45	.190	63	12	2	1	0	13	9	23	.264	.254
0 Days rest	0.79	3	0	35	43	0	45.1	24	2	12	37	Pitch 46+	.250	4	1	1	0	0	1	1	1	.333	.500
1 or 2 Days rest	3.40	8	15	60	112	0	143.0	113	10	70	192	First Pitch	.236	110	26	4	0	3	10	14	0	.320	.355
3+ Days rest	2.13	5	5	31	92	0	114.1	76	12	42	133	Ahead on Count	.148	637	94	11	1	6	42	0	320	.146	.196
Pre-All Star	2.29	8	10	67	141	0	177.0	126	10	72	200	Behind on Count	.316	552	50	7	1	10	46	56	0	.486	.563
Post-All Star	2.86	8	10	59	106	0	125.2	87	14	52	162	Two Strikes	.133	645	86	11	1	5	42	54	362	.199	.175

Pitcher vs. Batter (career)

Pitches Best Vs.	Avg	AB	H	2B	3B	HR	RBI	BB	SO	OBP	SLG	Pitches Worst Vs.	Avg	AB	H	2B	3B	HR	RBI	BB	SO	OBP	SLG
Kent Hrbek	.000	10	0	0	0	0	0	1	3	.091	.000	Jesse Barfield	.333	9	3	0	0	2	4	1	4	.364	1.000
Mel Hall	.083	12	1	0	0	0	0	0	4	.063	.167												
Mike Greenwell	.091	11	1	0	0	0	1	0	2	.083	.091												
Carlton Fisk	.100	10	1	0	0	0	0	2	5	.250	.100												
Kirby Puckett	.100	10	1	0	0	0	0	1	4	.182	.100												

Bill Haselman — Mariners
Bats Right (groundball hitter)

	Avg	G	AB	R	H	2B	3B	HR	RBI	BB	SO	HBP	GDP	SB	CS	OBP	SLG	IBB	SH	SF	#Pit	#P/PA	GB	FB	G/F
1992 Season	.263	8	19	1	5	0	0	0	0	0	7	0	1	0	0	.263	.263	0	0	0	64	3.37	6	4	1.50
Career (1990-1992)	.219	15	32	1	7	0	0	0	3	0	12	0	1	0	0	.242	.219	0	0	0	123	3.73	11	6	1.83

1992 Season

	Avg	AB	H	2B	3B	HR	RBI	BB	SO	OBP	SLG		Avg	AB	H	2B	3B	HR	RBI	BB	SO	OBP	SLG
vs. Left	.429	7	3	0	0	0	0	0	0	.429	.429	Scoring Posn	.333	3	1	0	0	0	0	0	2	.333	.333
vs. Right	.167	12	2	0	0	0	0	0	7	.167	.167	Close & Late	.500	2	1	0	0	0	0	0	1	.500	.500

Billy Hatcher — Red Sox · Bats Right

	Avg	G	AB	R	H	2B	3B	HR	RBI	BB	SO	HBP	GDP	SB	CS	OBP	SLG	IBB	SH	SF	#Pit	#P/PA	GB	FB	G/F
1992 Season	.249	118	409	47	102	19	2	3	33	22	52	3	11	4	8	.290	.328	1	6	4	1460	3.33	173	100	1.73
Last Five Years	.258	675	2366	298	610	116	17	23	202	148	267	26	34	101	47	.306	.350	16	22	20	8542	3.34	994	666	1.49

1992 Season

	Avg	AB	H	2B	3B	HR	RBI	BB	SO	OBP	SLG		Avg	AB	H	2B	3B	HR	RBI	BB	SO	OBP	SLG
vs. Left	.241	141	34	6	1	2	7	7	15	.275	.340	Scoring Posn	.252	103	26	5	0	0	27	4	10	.270	.301
vs. Right	.254	268	68	13	1	1	26	15	37	.298	.321	Close & Late	.321	81	26	4	0	1	8	3	10	.341	.407
Groundball	.268	112	30	4	0	0	13	7	13	.306	.304	None on/out	.250	116	29	4	0	2	2	9	14	.315	.336
Flyball	.248	105	26	7	2	1	9	6	15	.298	.381	Batting #1	.208	207	43	9	1	1	11	10	27	.250	.275
Home	.272	191	52	12	0	1	17	14	18	.327	.351	Batting #2	.262	145	38	9	1	2	18	7	21	.297	.379
Away	.229	218	50	7	2	2	16	8	34	.257	.307	Other	.368	57	21	1	0	0	4	5	4	.413	.386
Day	.240	121	29	7	0	1	11	5	8	.266	.322	April	.293	41	12	1	0	1	4	1	6	.302	.390
Night	.253	288	73	12	2	2	22	17	44	.300	.330	May	.267	15	4	0	0	0	1	1	4	.313	.267
Grass	.259	313	81	15	2	3	30	19	36	.305	.348	June	.313	32	10	2	0	1	4	3	1	.361	.469
Turf	.219	96	21	4	0	0	3	3	16	.240	.260	July	.287	87	25	7	0	0	6	6	8	.330	.368
First Pitch	.215	65	14	1	1	0	6	1	0	.224	.262	August	.276	105	29	5	1	1	12	8	16	.333	.371
Ahead on Count	.185	81	15	5	0	0	6	17	0	.323	.247	September/October	.171	129	22	4	1	0	6	3	17	.200	.217
Behind on Count	.263	171	45	9	1	1	10	0	41	.272	.345	Pre-All Star	.297	111	33	5	0	2	12	6	12	.325	.396
Two Strikes	.217	157	34	5	1	2	8	4	52	.239	.299	Post-All Star	.232	298	69	14	2	1	21	16	40	.277	.302

1992 By Position

Position	Avg	AB	H	2B	3B	HR	RBI	BB	SO	OBP	SLG	G	GS	Innings	PO	A	E	DP	Fld Pct	Rng Fctr	In Zone	Outs	Zone Rtg	MLB Zone
As Pinch Hitter	.238	21	5	0	0	0	1	2	3	.304	.238	22	0	---	---	---	---	---	---	---	---	---	---	---
As lf	.253	336	85	15	2	3	30	15	43	.288	.336	86	82	701.2	145	5	5	0	.968	1.92	190	144	.758	.809
As cf	.231	52	12	4	0	0	2	5	6	.298	.308	13	12	106.1	29	0	1	0	.967	2.45	35	28	.800	.824

Last Five Years

	Avg	AB	H	2B	3B	HR	RBI	BB	SO	OBP	SLG		Avg	AB	H	2B	3B	HR	RBI	BB	SO	OBP	SLG
vs. Left	.263	854	225	38	6	10	66	53	87	.306	.357	Scoring Posn	.261	559	146	25	4	3	170	52	72	.319	.336
vs. Right	.255	1512	385	78	11	13	136	95	180	.307	.347	Close & Late	.280	415	116	19	4	3	40	27	61	.329	.366
Groundball	.264	825	218	28	8	7	71	52	78	.309	.343	None on/out	.251	697	175	37	4	8	8	43	84	.304	.350
Flyball	.238	534	127	30	4	4	43	33	72	.289	.331	Batting #1	.237	916	217	49	6	7	61	58	105	.289	.326
Home	.255	1147	293	64	10	8	93	87	124	.312	.350	Batting #2	.276	771	213	36	8	9	76	49	85	.324	.379
Away	.260	1219	317	52	7	15	109	61	143	.300	.351	Other	.265	679	180	31	3	7	65	41	77	.309	.351
Day	.241	627	151	37	3	10	65	49	60	.303	.357	April	.258	326	84	10	3	4	33	17	45	.297	.344
Night	.264	1739	459	79	14	13	137	99	207	.308	.348	May	.286	360	103	16	2	2	27	19	40	.332	.358
Grass	.256	894	229	39	6	11	77	51	104	.299	.350	June	.280	432	121	28	7	6	42	29	48	.328	.419
Turf	.259	1472	381	77	11	12	125	97	163	.311	.351	July	.260	415	108	22	0	2	32	33	52	.315	.328
First Pitch	.289	440	127	16	2	2	39	7	0	.300	.348	August	.231	412	95	24	2	6	33	26	44	.283	.342
Ahead on Count	.275	509	140	29	4	9	53	88	0	.385	.401	September/October	.235	421	99	16	3	3	35	24	37	.282	.309
Behind on Count	.228	864	197	42	7	6	62	2	171	.238	.314	Pre-All Star	.275	1248	343	60	12	13	114	78	147	.322	.373
Two Strikes	.201	914	184	37	6	6	61	45	267	.244	.275	Post-All Star	.239	1118	267	56	5	10	88	70	120	.288	.325

Batter vs. Pitcher (career)

Hits Best Against	Avg	AB	H	2B	3B	HR	RBI	BB	SO	OBP	SLG	Hits Worst Against	Avg	AB	H	2B	3B	HR	RBI	BB	SO	OBP	SLG
Bill Landrum	.600	15	9	0	0	2	4	1	0	.625	.867	Brian Fisher	.000	10	0	0	0	0	1	2	2	.167	.000
Joe Boever	.538	13	7	2	0	1	3	2	0	.600	.923	Dennis Martinez	.063	16	1	0	0	0	0	1	1	.118	.063
Alejandro Pena	.474	19	9	4	0	1	5	0	5	.474	.842	Jim Deshaies	.067	15	1	0	0	0	0	1	1	.125	.067
Ted Power	.474	19	9	1	0	1	2	0	1	.474	.684	Joe Magrane	.100	30	3	0	0	0	0	1	4	.129	.100
Bill Gullickson	.440	25	11	0	1	2	3	0	3	.440	.640	Kelly Downs	.136	22	3	0	0	0	1	0	1	.136	.136

Hilly Hathaway — Angels · Pitches Left

	ERA	W	L	Sv	G	GS	IP	BB	SO	Avg	H	2B	3B	HR	RBI	OBP	SLG	CG	ShO	Sup	QS	#P/S	SB	CS	GB	FB	G/F
1992 Season	7.94	0	0	0	2	1	5.2	3	1	.333	8	1	0	1	5	.393	.500	0	0	6.35	0	70	0	0	11	10	1.10

1992 Season

	ERA	W	L	Sv	G	GS	IP	H	HR	BB	SO		Avg	AB	H	2B	3B	HR	RBI	BB	SO	OBP	SLG
Home	7.94	0	0	0	2	1	5.2	8	1	3	1	vs. Left	.500	4	2	0	0	1	1	1	0	.600	1.250
Away	0.00	0	0	0	0	0	0.0	0	0	0	0	vs. Right	.300	20	6	1	0	0	4	2	1	.348	.350

Charlie Hayes — Yankees · Bats Right

	Avg	G	AB	R	H	2B	3B	HR	RBI	BB	SO	HBP	GDP	SB	CS	OBP	SLG	IBB	SH	SF	#Pit	#P/PA	GB	FB	G/F
1992 Season	.257	142	509	52	131	19	2	18	66	28	100	3	12	3	5	.297	.409	0	3	6	2025	3.71	162	170	0.95
Career (1988-1992)	.250	530	1845	168	461	77	4	48	219	83	319	6	43	13	13	.282	.374	7	7	16	6849	3.51	663	569	1.17

1992 Season

	Avg	AB	H	2B	3B	HR	RBI	BB	SO	OBP	SLG		Avg	AB	H	2B	3B	HR	RBI	BB	SO	OBP	SLG
vs. Left	.213	150	32	3	0	6	18	9	23	.262	.353	Scoring Posn	.259	108	28	4	0	2	41	10	22	.317	.352
vs. Right	.276	359	99	16	2	12	48	19	77	.312	.432	Close & Late	.242	91	22	4	0	3	7	3	23	.271	.385
Groundball	.234	145	34	4	1	4	12	8	31	.277	.359	None on/out	.261	138	36	4	2	7	7	7	24	.297	.471
Flyball	.283	138	39	4	0	6	23	8	28	.320	.442	Batting #7	.216	134	29	4	1	5	18	7	29	.262	.373

1992 Season

	Avg	AB	H	2B	3B	HR	RBI	BB	SO	OBP	SLG		Avg	AB	H	2B	3B	HR	RBI	BB	SO	OBP	SLG
Home	.220	245	54	9	1	7	30	14	44	.267	.351	Batting #8	.275	363	100	14	1	12	46	21	68	.314	.419
Away	.292	264	77	10	1	11	36	14	56	.325	.462	Other	.167	12	2	1	0	1	2	0	3	.167	.500
Day	.278	162	45	6	1	4	16	8	35	.314	.401	April	.325	77	25	2	0	1	9	0	9	.329	.390
Night	.248	347	86	13	1	14	50	20	65	.288	.412	May	.247	97	24	5	0	5	12	5	18	.282	.454
Grass	.249	422	105	13	2	17	61	23	84	.289	.410	June	.244	90	22	3	1	3	11	9	22	.310	.400
Turf	.299	87	26	6	0	1	5	5	16	.337	.402	July	.155	84	13	2	0	2	10	2	25	.189	.250
First Pitch	.341	91	31	2	0	6	16	0	0	.344	.560	August	.274	106	29	4	1	4	13	9	16	.328	.443
Ahead on Count	.337	92	31	4	2	5	15	13	0	.411	.587	September/October	.327	55	18	3	0	3	11	3	10	.362	.545
Behind on Count	.220	164	36	8	0	2	17	0	45	.229	.305	Pre-All Star	.252	301	76	10	1	10	36	16	58	.293	.392
Two Strikes	.168	250	42	8	0	3	23	15	100	.216	.236	Post-All Star	.264	208	55	9	1	8	30	12	42	.302	.433

1992 By Position

Position	Avg	AB	H	2B	3B	HR	RBI	BB	SO	OBP	SLG	G	GS	Innings	PO	A	E	DP	Fld Pct	Rng Fctr	In Zone	Outs	Zone Rtg	MLB Zone
As 3b	.259	498	129	19	2	17	64	27	98	.298	.408	139	137	1211.2	95	251	13	31	.964	2.57	325	274	.843	.841

Career (1988-1992)

	Avg	AB	H	2B	3B	HR	RBI	BB	SO	OBP	SLG		Avg	AB	H	2B	3B	HR	RBI	BB	SO	OBP	SLG
vs. Left	.257	649	167	34	0	16	76	28	97	.289	.384	Scoring Posn	.243	445	108	18	1	10	161	24	80	.277	.355
vs. Right	.246	1196	294	43	4	32	143	55	222	.278	.369	Close & Late	.264	341	90	15	1	11	36	14	69	.294	.411
Groundball	.252	628	158	21	3	10	58	34	105	.290	.342	None on/out	.258	450	116	20	2	18	18	16	89	.283	.431
Flyball	.232	439	102	12	0	15	55	16	85	.258	.362	Batting #6	.256	668	171	37	2	14	74	29	107	.287	.380
Home	.239	936	224	43	3	19	114	43	160	.273	.353	Batting #8	.275	484	133	17	1	15	57	29	88	.313	.407
Away	.261	909	237	34	1	29	105	40	159	.292	.396	Other	.227	693	157	23	1	19	88	25	124	.254	.345
Day	.247	523	129	24	3	14	58	22	98	.277	.384	April	.269	219	59	8	0	4	26	6	33	.291	.361
Night	.251	1322	332	53	1	34	161	61	221	.284	.370	May	.239	285	68	11	1	10	26	16	51	.278	.389
Grass	.247	772	191	28	2	28	96	39	139	.283	.398	June	.261	268	70	11	1	6	29	15	53	.300	.377
Turf	.252	1073	270	49	2	20	123	44	180	.281	.357	July	.211	313	66	11	0	10	44	16	62	.250	.342
First Pitch	.311	366	114	18	0	11	43	4	0	.323	.451	August	.258	430	111	25	1	11	48	13	62	.280	.398
Ahead on Count	.303	320	97	14	2	13	45	31	0	.358	.481	September/October	.264	330	87	11	1	7	42	17	58	.299	.367
Behind on Count	.215	646	139	26	0	10	69	0	164	.218	.302	Pre-All Star	.247	885	219	33	2	22	94	43	160	.283	.364
Two Strikes	.186	846	157	31	1	13	85	45	319	.201	.271	Post-All Star	.252	960	242	44	2	26	125	40	159	.281	.383

Batter vs. Pitcher (career)

Hits Best Against	Avg	AB	H	2B	3B	HR	RBI	BB	SO	OBP	SLG	Hits Worst Against	Avg	AB	H	2B	3B	HR	RBI	BB	SO	OBP	SLG
Randy Tomlin	.600	10	6	1	0	0	1	1	1	.636	.700	Tim Burke	.000	11	0	0	0	0	0	0	2	.000	.000
Rick Reed	.556	18	10	1	0	2	6	0	3	.556	.944	Randy Johnson	.000	9	0	0	0	0	2	0	2	.167	.000
Kevin Gross	.462	13	6	1	0	1	2	1	0	.500	.769	David Cone	.053	19	1	1	0	0	1	0	7	.053	.105
Mike Morgan	.455	11	5	1	1	0	0	0	0	.455	.727	Greg Maddux	.087	23	2	0	0	0	0	0	3	.087	.087
Walt Terrell	.444	9	4	0	1	1	1	2	1	.545	1.000	Bill Landrum	.091	11	1	0	0	0	0	0	2	.091	.091

Von Hayes — Angels

Bats Left

	Avg	G	AB	R	H	2B	3B	HR	RBI	BB	SO	HBP	GDP	SB	CS	OBP	SLG	IBB	SH	SF	#Pit	#P/PA	GB	FB	G/F
1992 Season	.225	94	307	35	69	17	1	4	29	37	54	0	9	11	6	.305	.326	4	3	3	1377	3.97	116	77	1.51
Last Five Years	.252	558	1965	264	495	101	9	53	246	305	339	12	35	84	31	.351	.393	40	4	30	9012	3.90	682	585	1.17

1992 Season

	Avg	AB	H	2B	3B	HR	RBI	BB	SO	OBP	SLG		Avg	AB	H	2B	3B	HR	RBI	BB	SO	OBP	SLG
vs. Left	.119	42	5	1	0	0	4	5	11	.208	.143	Scoring Posn	.153	72	11	4	1	3	26	14	10	.281	.361
vs. Right	.242	265	64	16	1	4	25	32	43	.321	.355	Close & Late	.217	46	10	2	0	2	9	6	8	.302	.391
Groundball	.286	84	24	10	0	0	11	8	8	.348	.405	None on/out	.203	79	16	6	0	0	0	6	13	.259	.278
Flyball	.233	86	20	3	0	0	2	7	20	.287	.267	Batting #3	.239	109	26	5	1	2	12	17	19	.339	.358
Home	.241	162	39	9	1	2	22	19	28	.315	.346	Batting #4	.172	87	15	4	0	1	10	4	18	.209	.253
Away	.207	145	30	8	0	2	7	18	26	.294	.303	Other	.252	111	28	8	0	1	7	16	17	.341	.351
Day	.262	84	22	4	0	1	7	9	11	.333	.345	April	.273	55	15	4	0	2	8	8	8	.365	.455
Night	.211	223	47	13	1	3	22	28	43	.295	.318	May	.239	67	16	5	1	1	3	8	13	.320	.388
Grass	.217	276	60	15	1	4	27	34	45	.300	.322	June	.262	65	17	3	0	0	4	11	15	.359	.308
Turf	.290	31	9	2	0	0	2	3	9	.353	.355	July	.205	78	16	3	0	1	13	5	12	.253	.282
First Pitch	.303	33	10	4	0	1	10	3	0	.342	.515	August	.119	42	5	2	0	0	1	5	11	.208	.167
Ahead on Count	.296	81	24	4	1	2	7	18	0	.424	.444	September/October	.000	0	0	0	0	0	0	0	0	.000	.000
Behind on Count	.226	93	21	4	1	2	8	0	21	.223	.355	Pre-All Star	.243	218	53	13	1	3	17	31	37	.335	.353
Two Strikes	.148	142	21	5	0	1	11	17	54	.238	.204	Post-All Star	.180	89	16	4	0	1	12	6	17	.229	.258

1992 By Position

Position	Avg	AB	H	2B	3B	HR	RBI	BB	SO	OBP	SLG	G	GS	Innings	PO	A	E	DP	Fld Pct	Rng Fctr	In Zone	Outs	Zone Rtg	MLB Zone
As rf	.211	275	58	14	1	4	27	36	50	.300	.313	85	79	681.2	169	1	3	0	.983	2.24	191	161	.843	.814

Last Five Years

	Avg	AB	H	2B	3B	HR	RBI	BB	SO	OBP	SLG		Avg	AB	H	2B	3B	HR	RBI	BB	SO	OBP	SLG
vs. Left	.229	620	142	23	3	16	84	84	123	.324	.353	Scoring Posn	.233	493	115	26	5	13	186	103	69	.350	.385
vs. Right	.262	1345	353	78	6	37	162	221	216	.364	.412	Close & Late	.240	325	78	14	1	10	38	66	59	.369	.382
Groundball	.259	664	172	33	5	17	92	87	114	.349	.401	None on/out	.242	446	108	29	1	12	12	58	84	.335	.392
Flyball	.235	459	108	21	1	13	47	74	68	.340	.370	Batting #3	.254	1024	260	44	7	33	138	174	173	.361	.407

Last Five Years

	Avg	AB	H	2B	3B	HR	RBI	BB	SO	OBP	SLG		Avg	AB	H	2B	3B	HR	RBI	BB	SO	OBP	SLG
Home	.244	896	219	44	6	29	119	151	154	.351	.404	Batting #5	.238	265	63	14	0	10	34	41	49	.345	.404
Away	.258	1069	276	57	3	24	127	154	185	.352	.384	Other	.254	676	172	43	2	10	74	90	117	.338	.368
Day	.297	539	160	40	1	18	83	91	79	.393	.475	April	.282	333	94	23	1	11	53	64	58	.396	.456
Night	.235	1426	335	61	8	35	163	214	260	.335	.363	May	.265	434	115	25	3	12	49	63	71	.356	.419
Grass	.264	774	204	39	1	17	101	102	132	.348	.382	June	.233	377	88	21	4	6	47	65	64	.344	.358
Turf	.244	1191	291	62	8	36	145	203	207	.353	.401	July	.255	282	72	9	0	5	33	35	46	.334	.340
First Pitch	.342	243	83	19	2	14	58	15	0	.374	.609	August	.215	251	54	13	1	12	32	38	44	.319	.418
Ahead on Count	.326	475	156	32	1	21	73	164	0	.493	.533	September/October	.250	288	72	10	0	7	32	40	56	.343	.358
Behind on Count	.218	616	134	24	1	10	60	2	154	.221	.306	Pre-All Star	.261	1247	325	73	8	30	156	203	210	.362	.404
Two Strikes	.177	943	167	36	5	9	72	111	339	.264	.255	Post-All Star	.237	718	170	28	1	23	90	102	129	.332	.375

Batter vs. Pitcher (since 1984)

Hits Best Against	Avg	AB	H	2B	3B	HR	RBI	BB	SO	OBP	SLG	Hits Worst Against	Avg	AB	H	2B	3B	HR	RBI	BB	SO	OBP	SLG
Scott Ruskin	.545	11	6	1	0	1	2	1	3	.583	.909	Dave Smith	.000	13	0	0	0	0	0	0	3	.000	.000
Jim Deshaies	.533	15	8	2	0	0	3	6	2	.667	.667	Mike Morgan	.000	11	0	0	0	0	0	0	2	.000	.000
Rick Sutcliffe	.443	61	27	9	1	5	13	9	8	.514	.869	Rick Reed	.059	17	1	0	0	0	0	2	4	.158	.059
Bob Walk	.405	42	17	4	0	3	12	10	3	.519	.714	Walt Terrell	.095	21	2	0	0	0	0	3	3	.208	.095
Kevin Gross	.364	11	4	0	1	2	3	4	1	.533	1.091	Bobby Ojeda	.147	34	5	0	0	0	2	2	5	.189	.147

Neal Heaton — Brewers
Pitches Left

	ERA	W	L	Sv	G	GS	IP	BB	SO	Avg	H	2B	3B	HR	RBI	OBP	SLG	GF	IR	IRS	Hld	SvOp	SB	CS	GB	FB	G/F
1992 Season	4.07	3	1	0	32	0	42.0	23	31	.269	43	6	0	5	21	.358	.400	9	22	7	8	2	9	0	52	45	1.16
Last Five Years	3.81	27	30	2	178	54	501.1	180	243	.258	483	91	11	54	208	.326	.405	16	53	15	16	7	50	22	704	611	1.15

1992 Season

	ERA	W	L	Sv	G	GS	IP	H	HR	BB	SO		Avg	AB	H	2B	3B	HR	RBI	BB	SO	OBP	SLG
Home	5.23	2	0	0	16	0	20.2	23	2	11	16	vs. Left	.222	54	12	1	0	1	5	7	11	.313	.296
Away	2.95	1	1	0	16	0	21.1	20	3	12	15	vs. Right	.292	106	31	5	0	4	16	16	20	.382	.453
Starter	0.00	0	0	0	0	0	0.0	0	0	0	0	Scoring Posn	.256	43	11	1	0	0	14	5	10	.314	.279
Reliever	4.07	3	1	0	32	0	42.0	43	5	23	31	Close & Late	.233	73	17	4	0	1	6	10	16	.333	.329
0 Days rest	2.25	1	0	0	6	0	8.0	9	1	6	3	None on/out	.211	38	8	2	0	1	4	9	.286	.342
1 or 2 Days rest	5.52	1	0	0	11	0	14.2	16	2	7	13	First Pitch	.269	26	7	1	0	1	3	1	0	.310	.423
3+ Days rest	3.72	1	1	0	15	0	19.1	18	2	10	15	Behind on Count	.438	32	14	1	0	2	7	14	0	.596	.656
Pre-All Star	4.17	3	1	0	30	0	41.0	42	5	22	29	Ahead on Count	.240	75	18	4	0	2	9	0	27	.240	.373
Post-All Star	0.00	0	0	0	2	0	1.0	1	0	1	2	Two Strikes	.164	67	11	2	0	1	8	8	31	.253	.239

Last Five Years

	ERA	W	L	Sv	G	GS	IP	H	HR	BB	SO		Avg	AB	H	2B	3B	HR	RBI	BB	SO	OBP	SLG
Home	3.68	12	15	0	85	27	244.1	237	22	98	121	vs. Left	.246	435	107	17	1	11	41	36	73	.307	.366
Away	3.92	15	15	2	93	27	257.0	246	32	82	122	vs. Right	.262	1435	376	74	10	43	167	144	170	.331	.417
Day	3.66	6	9	0	49	16	142.2	145	15	57	60	Inning 1-6	.258	1335	344	70	11	40	161	129	178	.326	.416
Night	3.86	21	21	1	129	38	358.2	338	39	123	183	Inning 7+	.260	535	139	21	0	14	47	51	65	.326	.378
Grass	4.57	5	12	1	53	14	136.0	138	18	48	65	None on	.255	1119	285	56	6	39	99	95	136	.319	.420
Turf	3.52	22	18	1	125	40	365.1	345	36	132	178	Runners on	.264	751	198	35	5	15	169	85	107	.336	.383
April	3.49	6	4	0	23	9	77.1	65	8	31	34	Scoring Posn	.247	461	114	20	2	8	145	61	69	.332	.351
May	4.20	6	7	0	35	17	133.0	126	15	43	50	Close & Late	.275	244	67	14	0	5	24	29	35	.356	.393
June	4.75	5	5	0	36	10	89.0	104	16	32	40	None on/out	.262	496	130	25	2	20	20	38	54	.318	.442
July	4.08	3	6	2	32	5	70.2	70	8	31	36	vs. 1st Batr (relief)	.263	118	31	3	0	2	8	3	12	.285	.339
August	2.71	3	7	0	31	6	73.0	64	2	30	40	First Inning Pitched	.252	620	156	25	3	14	75	67	96	.326	.369
September/October	2.93	4	1	0	21	7	58.0	54	5	13	43	First 15 Pitches	.258	590	152	28	2	12	49	57	73	.325	.373
Starter	3.97	18	22	0	54	54	308.1	302	39	105	129	Pitch 16-30	.225	440	99	22	5	10	50	40	76	.298	.366
Reliever	3.54	9	8	2	124	0	193.0	181	15	75	114	Pitch 31-45	.272	268	73	9	0	8	31	31	35	.348	.396
0 Days rest	1.40	2	1	0	17	0	25.2	21	1	8	8	Pitch 46+	.278	572	159	32	4	24	78	52	59	.338	.474
1 or 2 Days rest	4.90	2	3	1	48	0	75.1	78	8	33	46	First Pitch	.304	342	104	18	3	12	42	17	0	.337	.480
3+ Days rest	3.03	5	4	1	59	0	92.0	82	6	34	60	Ahead on Count	.211	769	162	27	2	17	74	0	211	.218	.317
Pre-All Star	4.13	17	18	2	107	37	324.2	324	42	119	136	Behind on Count	.303	435	132	31	4	14	53	102	0	.434	.490
Post-All Star	3.21	10	12	0	71	17	176.2	159	12	61	107	Two Strikes	.181	708	128	22	0	12	66	61	242	.250	.263

Pitcher vs. Batter (since 1984)

Pitches Best Vs.	Avg	AB	H	2B	3B	HR	RBI	BB	SO	OBP	SLG	Pitches Worst Vs.	Avg	AB	H	2B	3B	HR	RBI	BB	SO	OBP	SLG
Craig Biggio	.071	14	1	0	0	0	0	0	0	.071	.071	Mark Carreon	.636	11	7	0	0	2	5	0	0	.636	1.182
Rich Gedman	.091	11	1	0	0	0	1	1	3	.167	.091	Kevin Bass	.474	19	9	3	0	3	7	1	0	.500	1.105
Lonnie Smith	.111	18	2	0	0	0	1	2	2	.200	.111	George Bell	.462	26	12	4	0	4	10	0	0	.462	1.077
Dave Henderson	.118	17	2	0	0	0	3	2	4	.200	.118	Barry Bonds	.400	10	4	2	0	1	2	1	1	.455	.900
Luis Salazar	.143	21	3	0	0	0	2	0	3	.136	.143	Darryl Strawberry	.316	19	6	1	0	4	8	1	2	.350	1.000

192

Bert Heffernan — Mariners
Bats Left (groundball hitter)

	Avg	G	AB	R	H	2B	3B	HR	RBI	BB	SO	HBP	GDP	SB	CS	OBP	SLG	IBB	SH	SF	#Pit	#P/PA	GB	FB	G/F
1992 Season	.091	8	11	0	1	1	0	0	1	0	1	0	1	0	0	.091	.182	0	0	0	38	3.45	6	2	3.00

1992 Season

	Avg	AB	H	2B	3B	HR	RBI	BB	SO	OBP	SLG		Avg	AB	H	2B	3B	HR	RBI	BB	SO	OBP	SLG
vs. Left	.000	0	0	0	0	0	0	0	0	.000	.000	Scoring Posn	.000	2	0	0	0	0	1	0	1	.000	.000
vs. Right	.091	11	1	1	0	0	1	0	1	.091	.182	Close & Late	.000	4	0	0	0	0	1	0	1	.000	.000

Scott Hemond — White Sox
Bats Right

	Avg	G	AB	R	H	2B	3B	HR	RBI	BB	SO	HBP	GDP	SB	CS	OBP	SLG	IBB	SH	SF	#Pit	#P/PA	GB	FB	G/F
1992 Season	.225	25	40	8	9	2	0	0	2	4	13	0	2	1	0	.289	.275	0	0	1	175	3.89	11	9	1.22
Career (1989-1992)	.211	59	76	14	16	2	0	0	3	5	25	0	2	2	2	.256	.237	0	0	1	313	3.82	20	19	1.05

1992 Season

	Avg	AB	H	2B	3B	HR	RBI	BB	SO	OBP	SLG		Avg	AB	H	2B	3B	HR	RBI	BB	SO	OBP	SLG
vs. Left	.200	20	4	1	0	0	2	2	7	.261	.250	Scoring Posn	.111	9	1	0	0	0	2	1	4	.182	.111
vs. Right	.250	20	5	1	0	0	2	6	.318	.300	Close & Late	.250	8	2	0	0	0	0	0	4	.250	.250

Dave Henderson — Athletics
Bats Right (flyball hitter)

	Avg	G	AB	R	H	2B	3B	HR	RBI	BB	SO	HBP	GDP	SB	CS	OBP	SLG	IBB	SH	SF	#Pit	#P/PA	GB	FB	G/F
1992 Season	.143	20	63	9	9	1	0	0	2	16		0	0	0	0	.169	.159	0	0	0	215	3.31	11	28	0.39
Last Five Years	.271	595	2171	329	588	124	4	84	324	201	457	12	40	19	16	.334	.448	6	8	17	9150	3.81	607	723	0.84

1992 Season

	Avg	AB	H	2B	3B	HR	RBI	BB	SO	OBP	SLG		Avg	AB	H	2B	3B	HR	RBI	BB	SO	OBP	SLG
vs. Left	.208	24	5	1	0	0	2	0	8	.208	.250	Scoring Posn	.095	21	2	1	0	0	2	1	6	.136	.143
vs. Right	.103	39	4	0	0	0	2	8	.146	.103	Close & Late	.200	10	2	0	0	0	0	1	1	.273	.200

Last Five Years

	Avg	AB	H	2B	3B	HR	RBI	BB	SO	OBP	SLG		Avg	AB	H	2B	3B	HR	RBI	BB	SO	OBP	SLG
vs. Left	.318	619	197	43	1	30	96	56	100	.376	.536	Scoring Posn	.278	582	162	33	2	14	221	65	146	.344	.414
vs. Right	.252	1552	391	81	3	54	228	145	357	.317	.412	Close & Late	.263	335	88	13	1	12	42	25	71	.313	.415
Groundball	.286	615	176	38	1	20	91	52	111	.342	.449	None on/out	.293	461	135	31	0	22	22	29	79	.340	.503
Flyball	.281	499	140	23	1	25	78	48	103	.348	.481	Batting #2	.272	998	271	58	2	44	158	87	201	.333	.466
Home	.276	1078	298	53	1	48	164	94	231	.335	.461	Batting #5	.252	477	120	24	0	18	66	48	99	.322	.415
Away	.265	1093	290	71	3	36	160	107	226	.332	.435	Other	.283	696	197	42	2	22	100	66	157	.342	.444
Day	.261	800	225	47	2	37	135	74	167	.340	.464	April	.308	266	82	15	2	16	46	37	54	.390	.560
Night	.265	1371	363	77	2	47	189	127	290	.330	.427	May	.275	385	106	24	1	15	63	26	72	.325	.460
Grass	.279	1849	515	100	4	75	280	171	386	.341	.459	June	.255	372	95	22	1	18	58	39	78	.329	.465
Turf	.227	322	73	24	0	9	44	30	71	.293	.385	July	.268	400	107	21	0	14	47	34	63	.326	.395
First Pitch	.359	276	99	23	0	14	46	3	0	.372	.594	August	.280	393	110	26	0	15	58	29	76	.331	.461
Ahead on Count	.375	453	170	37	3	37	119	126	1	.510	.715	September/October	.248	355	88	16	0	10	52	36	94	.315	.377
Behind on Count	.216	772	167	35	1	17	88	0	247	.220	.330	Pre-All Star	.267	1142	305	66	4	50	178	117	232	.337	.463
Two Strikes	.187	1085	203	43	1	25	110	70	454	.237	.298	Post-All Star	.275	1029	283	58	0	34	146	84	225	.330	.431

Batter vs. Pitcher (since 1984)

Hits Best Against	Avg	AB	H	2B	3B	HR	RBI	BB	SO	OBP	SLG	Hits Worst Against	Avg	AB	H	2B	3B	HR	RBI	BB	SO	OBP	SLG
Bill Swift	.615	13	8	1	0	0	2	1	0	.600	.692	Bud Black	.000	13	0	0	0	0	1	0	0	.000	.000
Jim Abbott	.529	17	9	1	0	5	8	2	2	.550	1.471	Tom Gordon	.000	12	0	0	0	0	1	1	9	.077	.000
Tom Filer	.500	8	4	1	0	0	2	3	2	.636	.625	Dave Righetti	.000	10	0	0	0	0	1	0	0	.000	.000
Jack McDowell	.417	12	5	3	0	0	2	2	1	.500	.667	Rick Aguilera	.071	14	1	0	0	0	0	0	8	.071	.071
Rich DeLucia	.417	12	5	1	0	2	4	0	0	.417	1.000	Eric King	.100	20	2	0	0	0	2	0	6	.100	.100

Rickey Henderson — Athletics
Bats Right

	Avg	G	AB	R	H	2B	3B	HR	RBI	BB	SO	HBP	GDP	SB	CS	OBP	SLG	IBB	SH	SF	#Pit	#P/PA	GB	FB	G/F
1992 Season	.283	117	396	77	112	18	3	15	46	95	56	6	5	48	11	.426	.457	5	0	3	2261	4.52	124	156	0.79
Last Five Years	.291	677	2450	532	714	124	12	79	271	498	311	23	39	341	66	.413	.449	20	4	18	12721	4.26	876	791	1.11

1992 Season

	Avg	AB	H	2B	3B	HR	RBI	BB	SO	OBP	SLG		Avg	AB	H	2B	3B	HR	RBI	BB	SO	OBP	SLG
vs. Left	.267	105	28	5	1	5	13	24	17	.403	.476	Scoring Posn	.258	89	23	2	1	2	28	30	15	.448	.371
vs. Right	.289	291	84	13	2	10	33	71	39	.434	.450	Close & Late	.280	50	14	2	1	2	13	19	6	.472	.480
Groundball	.356	90	32	6	1	2	13	15	10	.458	.511	None on/out	.303	178	54	12	2	8	8	30	25	.407	.528
Flyball	.305	105	32	5	0	5	12	28	19	.455	.495	Batting #1	.283	392	111	18	3	15	46	94	55	.426	.459
Home	.295	200	59	8	1	10	27	52	22	.441	.495	Batting #9	.000	2	0	0	0	0	0	0	0	.000	.000
Away	.270	196	53	10	2	5	19	43	34	.410	.418	Other	.500	2	1	0	0	0	0	1	1	.667	.500
Day	.255	149	38	8	1	4	16	40	23	.417	.403	April	.228	79	18	3	0	3	11	20	21	.384	.380
Night	.300	247	74	10	2	11	30	55	33	.432	.490	May	.338	77	26	5	0	3	8	19	8	.474	.519
Grass	.303	340	103	17	3	14	42	82	41	.440	.494	June	.256	39	10	2	0	1	3	9	4	.396	.385
Turf	.161	56	9	1	0	1	4	13	15	.342	.232	July	.276	29	8	1	1	1	3	5	1	.382	.483
First Pitch	.267	15	4	1	0	1	1	4	0	.421	.533	August	.309	94	29	4	0	4	15	22	11	.451	.479
Ahead on Count	.358	109	39	6	1	9	22	59	1	.587	.679	September/October	.269	78	21	3	2	3	6	20	11	.420	.474

193

1992 Season

	Avg	AB	H	2B	3B	HR	RBI	BB	SO	OBP	SLG		Avg	AB	H	2B	3B	HR	RBI	BB	SO	OBP	SLG
Behind on Count	.239	92	22	6	1	0	9	0	18	.247	.326	Pre-All Star	.277	195	54	10	0	7	22	48	33	.422	.436
Two Strikes	.235	226	53	8	2	3	17	33	55	.335	.327	Post-All Star	.289	201	58	8	3	8	24	47	23	.430	.478

1992 By Position

Position	Avg	AB	H	2B	3B	HR	RBI	BB	SO	OBP	SLG	G	GS	Innings	PO	A	E	DP	Fld Pct	Rng Fctr	In Zone	Outs	Zone Rtg	MLB Zone
As If	.291	374	109	18	3	15	45	90	52	.434	.476	108	105	883.1	229	8	4	1	.983	2.41	258	218	.845	.809

Last Five Years

	Avg	AB	H	2B	3B	HR	RBI	BB	SO	OBP	SLG		Avg	AB	H	2B	3B	HR	RBI	BB	SO	OBP	SLG
vs. Left	.307	687	211	40	3	27	74	140	81	.426	.492	Scoring Posn	.255	482	123	16	2	16	186	154	74	.432	.396
vs. Right	.285	1763	503	84	9	52	197	358	230	.408	.432	Close & Late	.302	331	100	12	3	13	65	85	46	.442	.474
Groundball	.304	701	213	36	7	21	77	126	81	.414	.465	None on/out	.301	1034	311	60	6	37	37	180	121	.406	.478
Flyball	.299	552	165	25	2	23	70	111	80	.417	.476	Batting #1	.292	2433	710	124	12	79	270	493	305	.413	.450
Home	.292	1177	344	59	6	35	131	252	133	.419	.442	Batting #9	.143	7	1	0	0	0	1	1	3	.250	.143
Away	.291	1273	370	65	6	44	140	246	178	.406	.455	Other	.300	10	3	0	0	0	0	4	3	.500	.300
Day	.289	802	232	42	3	29	101	169	108	.413	.458	April	.303	353	107	25	2	10	41	60	47	.402	.470
Night	.292	1648	482	82	9	50	170	329	203	.413	.444	May	.287	446	128	23	1	14	48	103	53	.423	.437
Grass	.287	2051	589	101	10	65	221	420	260	.410	.441	June	.297	330	98	12	2	9	38	86	35	.443	.427
Turf	.313	399	125	23	2	14	50	78	51	.427	.486	July	.317	404	128	21	3	16	50	69	50	.420	.502
First Pitch	.275	160	44	8	0	7	28	13	0	.324	.456	August	.278	453	126	19	0	15	49	85	57	.396	.419
Ahead on Count	.343	688	236	48	4	47	113	308	1	.546	.629	September/October	.274	464	127	24	4	15	45	95	69	.401	.440
Behind on Count	.266	666	178	28	5	13	58	3	136	.275	.382	Pre-All Star	.297	1252	372	67	5	40	146	269	156	.421	.454
Two Strikes	.248	1252	311	49	5	14	86	177	310	.346	.329	Post-All Star	.285	1198	342	57	7	39	125	229	155	.404	.442

Batter vs. Pitcher (since 1984)

Hits Best Against	Avg	AB	H	2B	3B	HR	RBI	BB	SO	OBP	SLG	Hits Worst Against	Avg	AB	H	2B	3B	HR	RBI	BB	SO	OBP	SLG
Rick Sutcliffe	.667	6	4	0	0	1	3	5	2	.182	1.167	Charles Nagy	.000	9	0	0	0	0	2	2	1	.182	.000
Ben McDonald	.500	16	8	2	0	2	3	5	1	.619	1.000	Scott Kamieniecki	.000	9	0	0	0	0	0	3	2	.250	.000
Scott Bailes	.500	10	5	1	1	0	1	7	2	.706	.800	Julio Valera	.091	11	1	0	0	0	0	1	3	.167	.091
Mark Portugal	.500	8	4	1	0	1	3	2	0	.545	1.000	John Smiley	.100	10	1	0	0	0	0	1	1	.182	.100
Todd Stottlemyre	.364	11	4	0	0	2	2	7	2	.611	.909	Mike Campbell	.100	10	1	0	0	0	1	1	0	.182	.100

Tom Henke — Blue Jays   Pitches Right (flyball pitcher)

	ERA	W	L	Sv	G	GS	IP	BB	SO	Avg	H	2B	3B	HR	RBI	OBP	SLG	GF	IR	IRS	Hld	SvOp	SB	CS	GB	FB	G/F
1992 Season	2.26	3	2	34	57	0	55.2	22	46	.197	40	9	0	5	19	.272	.315	50	7	2	4	37	2	1	51	75	0.68
Last Five Years	2.29	17	15	143	283	0	337.2	101	356	.209	257	52	6	28	127	.270	.330	151	192	58	10	163	18	5	321	375	0.86

1992 Season

	ERA	W	L	Sv	G	GS	IP	H	HR	BB	SO		Avg	AB	H	2B	3B	HR	RBI	BB	SO	OBP	SLG
Home	2.48	2	0	19	29	0	29.0	18	4	10	20	vs. Left	.190	105	20	4	0	2	13	14	23	.279	.286
Away	2.03	1	2	15	28	0	26.2	22	1	12	26	vs. Right	.204	98	20	5	0	3	6	8	23	.264	.347
Starter	0.00	0	0	0	0	0	0.0	0	0	0	0	Scoring Posn	.226	53	12	2	0	2	16	8	10	.313	.377
Reliever	2.26	3	2	34	57	0	55.2	40	5	22	46	Close & Late	.222	126	28	7	0	4	14	8	32	.265	.373
0 Days rest	3.68	0	1	3	8	0	7.1	8	1	4	6	None on/out	.208	53	11	3	0	2	2	3	11	.250	.377
1 or 2 Days rest	1.27	1	0	22	28	0	28.1	19	3	6	21	First Pitch	.324	34	11	1	0	2	4	1	0	.333	.529
3+ Days rest	3.15	2	1	9	21	0	20.0	13	1	12	19	Behind on Count	.175	40	7	1	0	2	5	12	0	.358	.350
Pre-All Star	1.67	3	1	15	28	0	27.0	16	3	12	22	Ahead on Count	.186	97	18	4	0	1	8	0	41	.186	.258
Post-All Star	2.83	0	1	19	29	0	28.2	24	2	10	24	Two Strikes	.144	90	13	3	0	1	7	9	46	.222	.211

Last Five Years

	ERA	W	L	Sv	G	GS	IP	H	HR	BB	SO
Home	2.43	12	2	67	137	0	159.0	120	19	49	176
Away	2.17	5	13	76	146	0	178.2	137	9	52	180
Day	2.41	2	4	36	85	0	97.0	80	8	40	89
Night	2.24	15	11	107	198	0	240.2	177	20	61	267
Grass	2.27	5	11	56	113	0	139.0	109	9	44	145
Turf	2.31	12	4	87	170	0	196.2	148	19	57	211
April	3.03	2	4	13	36	0	35.2	36	5	14	33
May	2.72	3	2	17	42	0	53.0	35	6	20	50
June	1.27	3	0	28	50	0	56.2	34	1	16	55
July	2.59	2	4	29	52	0	62.2	46	4	17	65
August	2.19	2	2	31	53	0	70.0	54	7	12	85
September/October	2.26	5	3	25	50	0	59.2	52	5	22	68
Starter	0.00	0	0	0	0	0	0.0	0	0	0	0
Reliever	2.29	17	15	143	283	0	337.2	257	28	101	356
0 Days rest	2.44	3	4	32	55	0	55.1	48	8	17	72
1 or 2 Days rest	2.11	8	7	77	137	0	162.0	118	12	40	167
3+ Days rest	2.47	6	5	34	93	0	120.1	91	8	44	117
Pre-All Star	2.09	9	6	68	147	0	167.2	113	14	54	158
Post-All Star	2.49	8	9	75	136	0	170.0	144	14	47	198

	Avg	AB	H	2B	3B	HR	RBI	BB	SO	OBP	SLG
vs. Left	.209	621	130	24	3	14	72	61	171	.278	.325
vs. Right	.209	608	127	28	3	14	55	40	185	.261	.334
Inning 1-6	.214	14	3	2	0	0	2	2	5	.313	.357
Inning 7+	.209	1215	254	50	6	28	125	99	351	.270	.329
None on	.214	705	151	34	3	13	43	43	204	.261	.326
Runners on	.202	524	106	18	3	15	114	58	152	.281	.334
Scoring Posn	.211	332	70	13	3	9	100	44	96	.298	.349
Close & Late	.212	623	132	25	4	19	90	43	191	.262	.356
None on/out	.231	299	69	14	2	6	6	13	78	.265	.351
vs. 1st Batr (relief)	.236	267	63	10	1	9	30	11	65	.270	.382
First Inning Pitched	.203	955	194	40	5	22	101	75	270	.261	.325
First 15 Pitches	.206	840	173	38	4	20	80	60	231	.259	.332
Pitch 16-30	.213	287	61	8	2	6	33	25	93	.275	.317
Pitch 31-45	.214	84	18	5	0	2	11	14	25	.340	.345
Pitch 46+	.278	18	5	1	0	0	3	2	7	.350	.333
First Pitch	.313	176	55	11	1	7	22	0	0	.348	.506
Ahead on Count	.167	684	114	23	2	8	52	0	314	.169	.241
Behind on Count	.264	163	43	10	1	7	22	48	0	.432	.466
Two Strikes	.146	694	101	21	3	7	47	44	356	.196	.211

Pitcher vs. Batter (since 1984)

Pitches Best Vs.	Avg	AB	H	2B	3B	HR	RBI	BB	SO	OBP	SLG	Pitches Worst Vs.	Avg	AB	H	2B	3B	HR	RBI	BB	SO	OBP	SLG
Dave Bergman	.000	17	0	0	0	0	1	0	5	.000	.000	Jody Reed	.556	9	5	1	0	0	1	2	0	.636	.667
Mel Hall	.000	14	0	0	0	0	0	1	5	.067	.000	Mike Greenwell	.417	12	5	1	0	1	6	1	3	.462	.750
Dick Schofield	.000	11	0	0	0	0	0	1	4	.083	.000	Ruben Sierra	.417	12	5	1	0	1	3	0	5	.417	.750
Lou Whitaker	.074	27	2	0	0	0	0	1	6	.107	.074	Don Mattingly	.368	19	7	1	0	2	5	2	4	.429	.737
Brian Downing	.111	18	2	0	0	0	2	0	8	.100	.111	Wally Joyner	.357	14	5	1	0	1	2		4	.438	.643

Mike Henneman — Tigers
Pitches Right (groundball pitcher)

	ERA	W	L	Sv	G	GS	IP	BB	SO	Avg	H	2B	3B	HR	RBI	OBP	SLG	GF	IR	IRS	Hld	SvOp	SB	CS	GB	FB	G/F
1992 Season	3.96	2	6	24	60	0	77.1	20	58	.256	75	11	2	6	35	.299	.369	53	13	4	0	28	2	1	121	66	1.83
Last Five Years	3.07	40	24	97	314	0	437.1	162	296	.247	402	65	7	23	181	.316	.338	156	268	71	14	121	20	7	628	410	1.53

1992 Season

	ERA	W	L	Sv	G	GS	IP	H	HR	BB	SO		Avg	AB	H	2B	3B	HR	RBI	BB	SO	OBP	SLG
Home	3.19	1	4	14	33	0	42.1	40	4	9	34	vs. Left	.278	144	40	8	1	2	18	9	22	.314	.389
Away	4.89	1	2	10	27	0	35.0	35	2	11	24	vs. Right	.235	149	35	3	1	4	17	11	36	.284	.349
Day	1.37	1	1	6	18	0	26.1	20	0	6	20	Inning 1-6	.000	0	0	0	0	0	0	0	0	.000	.000
Night	5.29	1	5	18	42	0	51.0	55	6	14	38	Inning 7+	.256	293	75	11	2	6	35	20	58	.299	.369
Grass	4.01	2	5	20	51	0	67.1	65	6	18	52	None on	.256	168	43	5	1	4	4	7	32	.286	.369
Turf	3.60	0	1	4	9	0	10.0	10	0	2	6	Runners on	.256	125	32	6	1	2	31	13	26	.315	.368
April	6.23	0	0	2	8	0	8.2	10	0	4	9	Scoring Posn	.292	65	19	2	0	2	30	11	18	.370	.415
May	3.55	0	2	6	11	0	12.2	14	1	4	11	Close & Late	.269	171	46	9	1	4	26	13	36	.312	.404
June	2.60	0	1	4	12	0	17.1	10	2	4	11	None on/out	.229	70	16	0	1	0	0	3	14	.260	.257
July	7.36	0	2	5	10	0	11.0	15	1	3	6	vs. 1st Batr (relief)	.263	57	15	0	0	0	0	3	16	.300	.263
August	2.45	1	1	5	11	0	14.2	12	1	2	10	First Inning Pitched	.271	214	58	7	1	4	27	14	44	.310	.369
September/October	3.46	1	0	2	8	0	13.0	14	1	3	11	First 15 Pitches	.266	218	58	7	2	4	24	14	40	.305	.372
Starter	0.00	0	0	0	0	0	0.0	0	0	0	0	Pitch 16-30	.242	62	15	4	0	2	10	5	16	.294	.403
Reliever	3.96	2	6	24	60	0	77.1	75	6	20	58	Pitch 31-45	.167	12	2	0	0	0	1	0	2	.167	.167
0 Days rest	3.32	0	1	7	18	0	21.2	25	1	5	15	Pitch 46+	.000	1	0	0	0	0	0	1	0	.500	.000
1 or 2 Days rest	3.60	1	3	12	20	0	25.0	21	2	5	15	First Pitch	.286	49	14	2	0	1	8	10	0	.400	.388
3+ Days rest	4.70	1	2	5	22	0	30.2	29	3	10	28	Ahead on Count	.205	151	31	7	1	1	9	0	56	.204	.285
Pre-All Star	3.66	0	5	16	37	0	46.2	41	4	13	37	Behind on Count	.358	53	19	1	0	3	16	6	0	.403	.547
Post-All Star	4.40	2	1	8	23	0	30.2	34	2	7	21	Two Strikes	.164	140	23	4	2	2	7	4	58	.186	.264

Last Five Years

	ERA	W	L	Sv	G	GS	IP	H	HR	BB	SO		Avg	AB	H	2B	3B	HR	RBI	BB	SO	OBP	SLG
Home	2.96	28	10	51	171	0	234.0	201	14	74	175	vs. Left	.262	711	186	38	3	5	66	92	105	.346	.345
Away	3.19	12	14	46	143	0	203.1	201	9	88	121	vs. Right	.235	918	216	27	4	18	115	70	191	.292	.332
Day	3.42	11	9	31	99	0	142.0	141	8	58	80	Inning 1-6	.375	40	15	3	0	0	13	6	8	.447	.450
Night	2.90	29	15	66	215	0	295.1	261	15	104	216	Inning 7+	.244	1589	387	62	7	23	168	156	288	.312	.335
Grass	2.99	38	19	81	271	0	381.2	354	21	138	266	None on	.245	864	212	30	3	10	10	60	156	.298	.322
Turf	3.56	2	5	16	43	0	55.2	48	2	24	30	Runners on	.248	765	190	35	4	13	171	102	140	.334	.356
April	2.63	2	1	19	45	0	54.2	43	0	20	36	Scoring Posn	.224	460	103	20	3	6	152	82	99	.331	.320
May	3.52	7	8	17	49	0	69.0	63	3	29	36	Close & Late	.250	872	218	34	2	13	98	101	168	.327	.338
June	2.67	7	3	19	59	0	84.1	68	6	35	64	None on/out	.236	373	88	10	3	2	2	20	61	.277	.295
July	5.45	10	7	13	57	0	74.1	80	6	38	54	vs. 1st Batr (relief)	.242	281	68	8	0	4	27	26	54	.306	.313
August	2.09	7	3	15	52	0	77.2	79	5	24	53	First Inning Pitched	.245	1049	257	41	3	12	128	99	192	.310	.324
September/October	2.09	7	2	14	52	0	77.1	69	3	16	53	First 15 Pitches	.236	994	235	35	3	12	99	86	183	.296	.314
Starter	0.00	0	0	0	0	0	0.0	0	0	0	0	Pitch 16-30	.270	485	131	25	3	9	59	57	84	.353	.390
Reliever	3.07	40	24	97	314	0	437.1	402	23	162	296	Pitch 31-45	.228	123	28	4	0	1	20	15	23	.309	.285
0 Days rest	1.51	10	4	29	80	0	95.1	78	3	32	64	Pitch 46+	.296	27	8	1	1	1	3	4	6	.387	.519
1 or 2 Days rest	3.35	24	14	44	149	0	225.2	226	11	80	155	First Pitch	.283	223	63	9	2	3	29	46	0	.404	.381
3+ Days rest	3.79	6	6	24	85	0	116.1	98	9	50	77	Ahead on Count	.213	809	172	25	2	12	74	0	258	.217	.293
Pre-All Star	3.10	18	16	61	173	0	238.1	203	13	98	155	Behind on Count	.260	315	82	13	1	5	51	65	0	.381	.356
Post-All Star	3.03	22	8	36	141	0	199.0	199	10	64	141	Two Strikes	.193	788	152	27	3	8	50	50	295	.245	.265

Pitcher vs. Batter (career)

Pitches Best Vs.	Avg	AB	H	2B	3B	HR	RBI	BB	SO	OBP	SLG	Pitches Worst Vs.	Avg	AB	H	2B	3B	HR	RBI	BB	SO	OBP	SLG
Fred McGriff	.000	16	0	0	0	0	1	1	4	.059	.000	Harold Reynolds	.615	13	8	2	1	1	5	2	1	.667	1.154
Carney Lansford	.000	11	0	0	0	0	0	0	0	.000	.000	Luis Polonia	.600	10	6	0	0	0	2	1	0	.636	.600
Don Slaught	.000	10	0	0	0	0	1		3	.091	.000	Kirby Puckett	.500	10	5	2	0	0	1	4	1	.600	.700
Tom Brunansky	.077	13	1	0	0	0	0	0	0	.077	.077	B.J. Surhoff	.400	10	4	2	1	0	1	1	1	.455	.800
Pete Incaviglia	.077	13	1	0	0	0	1	0	3	.071	.077	Paul Molitor	.385	13	5	2	0	2	7	0	2	.357	1.000

Butch Henry — Astros
Pitches Left

	ERA	W	L	Sv	G	GS	IP	BB	SO	Avg	H	2B	3B	HR	RBI	OBP	SLG	CG	ShO	Sup	QS	#P/S	SB	CS	GB	FB	G/F
1992 Season	4.02	6	9	0	28	28	165.2	41	96	.285	185	38	5	16	69	.325	.433	2	1	3.37	10	87	10	7	241	183	1.32

1992 Season

	ERA	W	L	Sv	G	GS	IP	H	HR	BB	SO		Avg	AB	H	2B	3B	HR	RBI	BB	SO	OBP	SLG
Home	3.27	3	3	0	14	14	88.0	91	7	19	51	vs. Left	.298	141	42	10	0	2	13	12	14	.351	.411
Away	4.87	3	6	0	14	14	77.2	94	9	22	45	vs. Right	.281	508	143	28	5	14	56	29	82	.318	.439

1992 Season

	ERA	W	L	Sv	G	GS	IP	H	HR	BB	SO
Day	2.45	5	1	0	10	10	69.2	68	4	11	49
Night	5.16	1	8	0	18	18	96.0	117	12	30	47
Grass	4.50	1	3	0	7	7	38.0	45	3	14	23
Turf	3.88	5	6	0	21	21	127.2	140	13	27	73
April	4.37	0	2	0	4	4	22.2	28	2	9	14
May	5.24	1	2	0	6	6	34.1	40	3	6	16
June	5.32	1	2	0	5	5	23.2	26	1	12	14
July	3.03	1	1	0	6	6	38.2	42	3	8	25
August	3.29	2	2	0	6	6	41.0	46	6	6	25
September/October	1.69	1	0	0	1	1	5.1	3	1	0	2
Starter	4.02	6	9	0	28	28	165.2	185	16	41	96
Reliever	0.00	0	0	0	0	0	0.0	0	0	0	0
0-3 Days Rest	0.00	0	0	0	0	0	0.0	0	0	0	0
4 Days Rest	3.65	3	6	0	16	16	91.1	100	8	26	51
5+ Days Rest	4.48	3	3	0	12	12	74.1	85	8	15	45
Pre-All Star	4.58	3	6	0	18	18	98.1	115	7	32	58
Post-All Star	3.21	3	3	0	10	10	67.1	70	9	9	38

	Avg	AB	H	2B	3B	HR	RBI	BB	SO	OBP	SLG
Inning 1-6	.282	568	160	33	5	15	64	38	84	.325	.437
Inning 7+	.309	81	25	5	0	1	5	3	12	.329	.407
None on	.303	393	119	26	3	9	9	20	61	.338	.453
Runners on	.258	256	66	12	2	7	60	21	35	.306	.402
Scoring Posn	.248	129	32	4	0	4	48	18	16	.325	.372
Close & Late	.262	42	11	3	0	1	2	1	6	.273	.405
None on/out	.259	170	44	11	2	3	3	10	26	.300	.400
vs. 1st Batr (relief)	.000	0	0	0	0	0	0	0	0	.000	.000
First Inning Pitched	.271	107	29	4	0	0	9	7	13	.316	.308
First 75 Pitches	.272	515	140	26	4	13	54	33	77	.314	.414
Pitch 76-90	.347	75	26	5	1	2	10	5	10	.383	.520
Pitch 91-105	.317	41	13	7	0	0	2	2	6	.349	.488
Pitch 106+	.333	18	6	0	0	1	3	1	3	.368	.500
First Pitch	.295	112	33	7	2	2	10	7	0	.336	.446
Ahead on Count	.184	310	57	11	1	1	21	0	89	.183	.235
Behind on Count	.434	122	53	12	1	5	19	24	0	.517	.672
Two Strikes	.191	282	54	10	1	4	17	10	96	.218	.277

Doug Henry — Brewers

Pitches Right (flyball pitcher)

	ERA	W	L	Sv	G	GS	IP	BB	SO	Avg	H	2B	3B	HR	RBI	OBP	SLG	GF	IR	IRS	Hld	SvOp	SB	CS	GB	FB	G/F
1992 Season	4.02	1	4	29	68	0	65.0	24	52	.256	64	14	2	6	40	.319	.400	56	26	9	1	33	4	3	72	70	1.03
Career (1991-1992)	2.94	3	5	44	100	0	101.0	38	80	.216	80	20	2	7	47	.266	.338	81	44	12	4	49	4	4	102	115	0.89

1992 Season

	ERA	W	L	Sv	G	GS	IP	H	HR	BB	SO
Home	2.72	0	1	19	37	0	36.1	30	3	10	28
Away	5.65	1	3	10	31	0	28.2	34	3	14	24
Day	1.59	0	0	12	23	0	22.2	14	0	8	11
Night	5.31	1	4	17	45	0	42.1	50	6	16	41
Grass	2.89	1	4	26	58	0	56.0	48	4	18	46
Turf	11.00	0	0	3	10	0	9.0	16	2	6	6
April	5.63	0	0	4	8	0	8.0	14	0	3	4
May	2.31	1	1	3	12	0	11.2	6	1	6	8
June	0.66	0	0	6	12	0	13.2	6	1	4	13
July	4.35	0	0	7	12	0	10.1	12	1	4	10
August	10.22	0	1	5	13	0	12.1	18	4	5	9
September/October	1.00	0	2	4	11	0	9.0	8	0	2	8
Starter	0.00	0	0	0	0	0	0.0	0	0	0	0
Reliever	4.02	1	4	29	68	0	65.0	64	6	24	52
0 Days rest	2.49	1	0	13	21	0	21.2	17	1	9	12
1 or 2 Days rest	2.74	0	4	12	25	0	23.0	19	1	7	15
3+ Days rest	7.08	0	0	4	22	0	20.1	28	4	8	25
Pre-All Star	2.82	1	1	16	37	0	38.1	31	2	15	29
Post-All Star	5.74	0	3	13	31	0	26.2	33	4	9	23

	Avg	AB	H	2B	3B	HR	RBI	BB	SO	OBP	SLG
vs. Left	.208	106	22	4	0	1	12	16	17	.306	.274
vs. Right	.292	144	42	10	2	5	28	8	35	.329	.493
Inning 1-6	.000	0	0	0	0	0	0	0	0	.000	.000
Inning 7+	.256	250	64	14	2	6	40	24	52	.319	.400
None on	.213	155	33	8	0	2	2	6	34	.242	.303
Runners on	.326	95	31	6	2	4	38	18	18	.426	.558
Scoring Posn	.386	57	22	4	1	4	35	14	9	.493	.702
Close & Late	.248	141	35	8	1	1	22	16	32	.321	.340
None on/out	.197	61	12	3	0	1	1	4	13	.246	.295
vs. 1st Batr (relief)	.233	60	14	5	0	1	8	8	11	.324	.367
First Inning Pitched	.259	220	57	12	1	6	37	22	45	.324	.405
First 15 Pitches	.262	191	50	12	0	4	24	17	38	.319	.387
Pitch 16-30	.240	50	12	1	1	2	14	5	11	.309	.420
Pitch 31-45	.400	5	2	1	1	0	2	2	2	.571	1.000
Pitch 46+	.000	4	0	0	0	0	0	0	1	.000	.000
First Pitch	.273	33	9	0	1	0	5	4	0	.333	.333
Ahead on Count	.202	119	24	6	0	1	11	0	45	.202	.277
Behind on Count	.393	56	22	5	1	4	17	8	0	.469	.732
Two Strikes	.183	131	24	5	0	1	11	12	52	.252	.221

Dwayne Henry — Reds

Pitches Right (flyball pitcher)

	ERA	W	L	Sv	G	GS	IP	BB	SO	Avg	H	2B	3B	HR	RBI	OBP	SLG	GF	IR	IRS	Hld	SvOp	SB	CS	GB	FB	G/F
1992 Season	3.33	3	3	0	60	0	83.2	44	72	.199	59	14	4	4	32	.301	.313	11	37	14	6	2	6	2	75	106	0.71
Last Five Years	4.02	8	10	4	169	0	212.2	122	183	.230	178	36	6	17	118	.337	.358	50	118	54	11	9	19	9	212	265	0.80

1992 Season

	ERA	W	L	Sv	G	GS	IP	H	HR	BB	SO
Home	2.47	2	1	0	31	0	43.2	28	2	21	46
Away	4.28	1	2	0	29	0	40.0	31	2	23	26
Day	1.74	1	1	0	18	0	20.2	13	0	14	15
Night	3.86	2	2	0	42	0	63.0	46	4	30	57
Grass	5.40	0	1	0	19	0	25.0	22	2	14	18
Turf	2.45	3	2	0	41	0	58.2	37	2	30	54
April	2.40	0	0	0	10	0	15.0	8	1	7	10
May	2.81	1	1	0	9	0	16.0	9	0	10	8
June	3.55	0	1	0	10	0	12.2	8	2	5	9
July	3.75	1	0	0	9	0	12.0	12	0	6	7
August	4.15	1	1	0	12	0	13.0	12	0	7	21
September/October	3.60	0	0	0	10	0	15.0	10	1	9	17
Starter	0.00	0	0	0	0	0	0.0	0	0	0	0
Reliever	3.33	3	3	0	60	0	83.2	59	4	44	72
0 Days rest	4.66	0	0	0	14	0	19.1	19	0	10	16
1 or 2 Days rest	3.26	2	3	0	27	0	38.2	24	2	20	37
3+ Days rest	2.45	1	0	0	19	0	25.2	16	2	14	19
Pre-All Star	3.19	1	2	0	31	0	48.0	31	3	22	30

	Avg	AB	H	2B	3B	HR	RBI	BB	SO	OBP	SLG
vs. Left	.208	130	27	9	3	3	15	24	29	.335	.392
vs. Right	.192	167	32	5	1	1	17	20	43	.274	.251
Inning 1-6	.128	78	10	2	0	2	8	14	22	.269	.231
Inning 7+	.224	219	49	12	4	2	24	30	50	.313	.342
None on	.174	167	29	7	2	2	2	27	38	.289	.275
Runners on	.231	130	30	7	2	2	30	17	34	.318	.362
Scoring Posn	.253	75	19	4	1	1	25	13	22	.352	.373
Close & Late	.151	73	11	4	1	0	4	12	19	.267	.233
None on/out	.169	71	12	2	1	2	2	11	8	.280	.310
vs. 1st Batr (relief)	.188	48	9	3	0	1	8	10	5	.322	.313
First Inning Pitched	.156	173	27	5	1	1	16	26	48	.264	.214
First 15 Pitches	.186	167	31	6	1	1	15	23	39	.281	.251
Pitch 16-30	.200	95	19	6	2	2	8	19	24	.333	.368
Pitch 31-45	.265	34	9	2	1	1	9	2	9	.316	.471
Pitch 46+	.000	1	0	0	0	0	0	0	0	.000	.000
First Pitch	.316	38	12	5	0	0	7	5	0	.386	.447
Ahead on Count	.163	160	26	3	1	3	13	0	57	.168	.250
Behind on Count	.213	47	10	3	2	0	5	18	0	.431	.362

1992 Season

	ERA	W	L	Sv	G	GS	IP	H	HR	BB	SO		Avg	AB	H	2B	3B	HR	RBI	BB	SO	OBP	SLG
Post-All Star	3.53	2	1	0	29	0	35.2	28	1	22	42	Two Strikes	128	164	21	2	1	4	16	21	72	230	226

Last Five Years

	ERA	W	L	Sv	G	GS	IP	H	HR	BB	SO		Avg	AB	H	2B	3B	HR	RBI	BB	SO	OBP	SLG
Home	3.78	6	3	2	88	0	116.2	92	10	64	110	vs. Left	.236	369	87	20	5	9	60	68	82	.356	.390
Away	4.31	2	7	2	81	0	96.0	86	7	58	73	vs. Right	.225	405	91	16	1	8	58	54	101	.318	.328
Day	4.56	1	3	2	47	0	51.1	51	2	29	41	Inning 1-6	.219	169	37	8	1	4	33	26	40	.326	.349
Night	3.85	7	7	2	122	0	161.1	127	15	93	142	Inning 7+	.233	605	141	28	5	13	85	96	143	.339	.360
Grass	4.68	2	5	1	78	0	92.1	82	8	50	81	None on	.191	423	81	15	3	10	10	60	111	.293	.312
Turf	3.52	6	5	3	91	0	120.1	96	9	72	102	Runners on	.276	351	97	21	3	7	108	62	72	.386	.413
April	2.43	2	0	2	25	0	33.1	19	2	15	20	Scoring Posn	.281	231	65	16	2	3	96	51	53	.410	.407
May	4.91	2	2	0	28	0	36.2	32	4	30	25	Close & Late	.254	248	63	12	1	6	43	40	60	.357	.383
June	6.26	0	1	0	21	0	23.0	25	2	13	16	None on/out	.212	184	39	6	1	7	7	22	38	.296	.370
July	2.35	2	0	0	22	0	30.2	22	1	16	30	vs. 1st Batr (relief)	.250	144	36	8	0	5	32	23	25	.351	.410
August	3.79	2	4	0	30	0	40.1	39	2	21	36	First Inning Pitched	.237	506	120	22	3	13	91	86	119	.348	.370
September/October	4.62	0	3	2	43	0	48.2	41	6	27	56	First 15 Pitches	.248	451	112	20	2	14	75	65	96	.344	.395
Starter	0.00	0	0	0	0	0	0.0	0	0	0	0	Pitch 16-30	.206	243	50	13	3	2	31	47	69	.332	.309
Reliever	4.02	8	10	4	169	0	212.2	178	17	122	183	Pitch 31-45	.200	75	15	3	1	1	12	8	18	.299	.307
0 Days rest	4.71	1	3	1	40	0	49.2	49	4	30	43	Pitch 46+	.200	5	1	0	0	0	0	2	0	.429	.200
1 or 2 Days rest	3.93	4	5	2	69	0	84.2	63	8	56	76	First Pitch	.326	92	30	7	0	1	13	12	0	.400	.435
3+ Days rest	3.66	3	2	1	60	0	78.1	66	5	36	64	Ahead on Count	.164	372	61	8	3	6	35	0	149	.168	.250
Pre-All Star	4.44	4	3	2	76	0	97.1	82	8	58	64	Behind on Count	.346	153	53	12	2	8	43	58	0	.530	.608
Post-All Star	3.67	4	7	2	93	0	115.1	96	9	64	119	Two Strikes	.132	410	54	6	3	7	40	52	183	.232	.212

Pitcher vs. Batter (career)

Pitches Best Vs.	Avg	AB	H	2B	3B	HR	RBI	BB	SO	OBP	SLG	Pitches Worst Vs.	Avg	AB	H	2B	3B	HR	RBI	BB	SO	OBP	SLG
Mike Scioscia	.200	10	2	1	0	1	2	1	2	.385	.600	Eddie Murray	.455	11	5	1	0	1	3	2	0	.538	.818

Pat Hentgen — Blue Jays — Pitches Right (flyball pitcher)

	ERA	W	L	Sv	G	GS	IP	BB	SO	Avg	H	2B	3B	HR	RBI	OBP	SLG	GF	IR	IRS	Hld	SvOp	SB	CS	GB	FB	G/F
1992 Season	5.36	5	2	0	28	2	50.1	32	39	.254	49	11	1	7	23	.357	.430	10	10	1	1	1	5	0	50	73	0.68
Career (1991-1992)	4.99	5	2	0	31	3	57.2	35	42	.249	54	13	1	8	25	.355	.429	11	10	1	1	1	6	0	56	86	0.65

1992 Season

	ERA	W	L	Sv	G	GS	IP	H	HR	BB	SO		Avg	AB	H	2B	3B	HR	RBI	BB	SO	OBP	SLG
Home	4.91	3	1	0	15	2	29.1	29	2	19	23	vs. Left	.253	87	22	5	1	1	6	19	13	.383	.368
Away	6.00	2	1	0	13	0	21.0	20	5	13	16	vs. Right	.255	106	27	6	0	6	17	13	26	.333	.481
Starter	5.63	0	1	0	2	2	8.0	10	0	7	4	Scoring Posn	.160	50	8	3	0	0	13	14	8	.333	.220
Reliever	5.31	5	1	0	26	0	42.1	39	7	25	35	Close & Late	.222	27	6	1	1	1	4	6	7	.343	.444
0 Days rest	9.00	0	0	0	2	0	3.0	4	2	0	1	None on/out	.234	47	11	4	0	1	1	7	10	.333	.383
1 or 2 Days rest	1.00	2	0	0	11	0	18.0	9	1	8	20	First Pitch	.222	18	4	2	0	1	4	4	0	.364	.500
3+ Days rest	8.44	3	1	0	13	0	21.1	26	4	17	14	Behind on Count	.410	39	16	3	0	5	9	14	0	.556	.872
Pre-All Star	4.54	5	1	0	20	2	37.2	38	4	21	28	Ahead on Count	.239	92	22	5	1	0	7	0	32	.239	.315
Post-All Star	7.82	0	1	0	8	0	12.2	11	3	11	11	Two Strikes	.173	104	18	4	0	0	5	14	39	.271	.212

Gil Heredia — Expos — Pitches Right (groundball pitcher)

	ERA	W	L	Sv	G	GS	IP	BB	SO	Avg	H	2B	3B	HR	RBI	OBP	SLG	GF	IR	IRS	Hld	SvOp	SB	CS	GB	FB	G/F
1992 Season	4.23	2	3	0	20	5	44.2	20	22	.270	44	8	0	4	25	.351	.393	4	13	7	1	0	5	3	80	34	2.35
Career (1991-1992)	4.06	2	5	0	27	9	77.2	27	35	.254	71	11	1	8	38	.320	.387	5	13	7	1	0	7	5	139	65	2.14

1992 Season

	ERA	W	L	Sv	G	GS	IP	H	HR	BB	SO		Avg	AB	H	2B	3B	HR	RBI	BB	SO	OBP	SLG
Home	4.79	1	2	0	10	2	20.2	18	2	8	11	vs. Left	.310	87	27	4	0	1	18	11	13	.384	.391
Away	3.75	1	1	0	10	3	24.0	26	2	12	11	vs. Right	.224	76	17	4	0	3	7	9	9	.314	.395
Starter	6.10	0	3	0	5	5	20.2	23	1	11	7	Scoring Posn	.421	38	16	3	0	1	22	8	3	.511	.579
Reliever	2.63	2	0	0	15	0	24.0	21	3	9	15	Close & Late	.133	15	2	0	0	0	0	0	2	.133	.133
0 Days rest	0.00	0	0	0	0	0	0.0	0	0	0	0	None on/out	.178	45	8	2	0	2	2	3	10	.229	.356
1 or 2 Days rest	2.25	1	0	0	5	0	8.0	8	1	1	7	First Pitch	.370	27	10	1	0	0	1	1	0	.393	.407
3+ Days rest	2.81	1	0	0	10	0	16.0	13	2	8	8	Behind on Count	.317	41	13	3	0	1	16	13	0	.473	.463
Pre-All Star	5.40	2	3	0	13	4	30.0	32	3	16	15	Ahead on Count	.215	65	14	1	0	3	7	0	19	.227	.369
Post-All Star	1.84	0	0	0	7	1	14.2	12	1	4	7	Two Strikes	.167	66	11	2	0	2	4	6	22	.236	.288

Carlos Hernandez — Dodgers — Bats Right

	Avg	G	AB	R	H	2B	3B	HR	RBI	BB	SO	HBP	GDP	SB	CS	OBP	SLG	IBB	SH	SF	#Pit	#P/PA	GB	FB	G/F
1992 Season	.260	69	173	11	45	4	0	3	17	11	21	4	8	0	1	.316	.335	1	0	2	602	3.17	64	48	1.33
Career (1990-1992)	.251	94	207	14	52	6	0	3	19	11	28	5	10	1	1	.301	.324	1	0	3	717	3.17	79	57	1.39

1992 Season

	Avg	AB	H	2B	3B	HR	RBI	BB	SO	OBP	SLG		Avg	AB	H	2B	3B	HR	RBI	BB	SO	OBP	SLG
vs. Left	.287	108	31	3	0	3	9	7	9	.336	.398	Scoring Posn	.243	37	9	1	0	1	14	3	3	.333	.351
vs. Right	.215	65	14	1	0	0	8	4	12	.284	.231	Close & Late	.243	37	9	0	0	0	2	1	3	.263	.243

1992 Season

	Avg	AB	H	2B	3B	HR	RBI	BB	SO	OBP	SLG		Avg	AB	H	2B	3B	HR	RBI	BB	SO	OBP	SLG
Home	.264	87	23	3	0	1	8	10	11	.353	.333	None on/out	.244	41	10	1	0	0	0	3	4	.295	.268
Away	.256	86	22	1	0	2	9	1	10	.273	.337	Batting #7	.282	131	37	3	0	2	12	10	17	.349	.351
First Pitch	.345	29	10	0	0	1	3	1	0	.355	.448	Batting #8	.318	22	7	1	0	1	4	0	4	.304	.500
Ahead on Count	.256	43	11	1	0	1	5	7	0	.360	.349	Other	.050	20	1	0	0	0	1	1	0	.095	.050
Behind on Count	.267	60	16	3	0	0	5	0	11	.297	.317	Pre-All Star	.248	101	25	2	0	0	6	7	12	.316	.267
Two Strikes	.153	59	9	1	0	0	3	3	21	.231	.169	Post-All Star	.278	72	20	2	0	3	11	4	9	.316	.431

Cesar Hernandez — Reds   Bats Right

	Avg	G	AB	R	H	2B	3B	HR	RBI	BB	SO	HBP	GDP	SB	CS	OBP	SLG	IBB	SH	SF	#Pit	#P/PA	GB	FB	G/F
1992 Season	.275	34	51	6	14	4	0	0	4	0	10	0	1	3	1	.275	.353	0	0	0	196	3.84	16	12	1.33

1992 Season

	Avg	AB	H	2B	3B	HR	RBI	BB	SO	OBP	SLG		Avg	AB	H	2B	3B	HR	RBI	BB	SO	OBP	SLG
vs. Left	.342	38	13	4	0	0	2	0	6	.342	.447	Scoring Posn	.231	13	3	1	0	0	4	0	4	.231	.308
vs. Right	.077	13	1	0	0	0	2	0	4	.077	.077	Close & Late	.385	13	5	2	0	0	2	0	2	.385	.538

Jeremy Hernandez — Padres   Pitches Right (groundball pitcher)

	ERA	W	L	Sv	G	GS	IP	BB	SO	Avg	H	2B	3B	HR	RBI	OBP	SLG	GF	IR	IRS	Hld	SvOp	SB	CS	GB	FB	G/F
1992 Season	4.17	1	4	1	26	0	36.2	11	25	.291	39	3	1	4	15	.338	.418	11	14	2	3	2	3	1	57	32	1.78
Career (1991-1992)	3.00	1	4	3	35	0	51.0	16	34	.254	47	5	1	4	17	.309	.357	18	17	3	4	4	3	1	85	41	2.07

1992 Season

	ERA	W	L	Sv	G	GS	IP	H	HR	BB	SO		Avg	AB	H	2B	3B	HR	RBI	BB	SO	OBP	SLG
Home	4.38	0	3	0	17	0	24.2	29	2	9	16	vs. Left	.294	68	20	1	0	3	10	8	13	.350	.441
Away	3.75	1	1	1	9	0	12.0	10	2	2	9	vs. Right	.288	66	19	2	1	1	5	3	12	.324	.394
Starter	0.00	0	0	0	0	0	0.0	0	0	0	0	Scoring Posn	.250	32	8	0	0	0	10	7	7	.356	.250
Reliever	4.17	1	4	1	26	0	36.2	39	4	11	25	Close & Late	.327	55	18	1	0	1	5	5	7	.377	.400
0 Days rest	2.84	0	1	0	8	0	12.2	13	1	4	7	None on/out	.324	34	11	3	0	0	0	1	4	.343	.412
1 or 2 Days rest	4.72	0	3	1	10	0	13.1	15	2	5	8	First Pitch	.345	29	10	1	0	1	5	3	0	.406	.483
3+ Days rest	5.06	1	0	0	8	0	10.2	11	1	2	10	Behind on Count	.478	23	11	1	1	2	5	6	0	.531	.870
Pre-All Star	4.95	0	1	0	12	0	20.0	22	2	7	14	Ahead on Count	.174	69	12	1	0	0	2	0	24	.181	.188
Post-All Star	3.24	1	3	1	14	0	16.2	17	2	4	11	Two Strikes	.186	59	11	1	0	0	3	2	25	.222	.254

Jose Hernandez — Indians   Bats Right (groundball hitter)

	Avg	G	AB	R	H	2B	3B	HR	RBI	BB	SO	HBP	GDP	SB	CS	OBP	SLG	IBB	SH	SF	#Pit	#P/PA	GB	FB	G/F
1992 Season	.000	3	4	0	0	0	0	0	0	0	2	0	0	0	0	.000	.000	0	0	0	18	4.50	0	1	0.00
Career (1991-1992)	.176	48	102	8	18	2	1	0	4	3	33	0	0	0	1	.200	.216	0	6	0	404	3.85	37	17	2.18

1992 Season

	Avg	AB	H	2B	3B	HR	RBI	BB	SO	OBP	SLG		Avg	AB	H	2B	3B	HR	RBI	BB	SO	OBP	SLG
vs. Left	.000	0	0	0	0	0	0	0	0	.000	.000	Scoring Posn	.000	1	0	0	0	0	0	0	0	.000	.000
vs. Right	.000	4	0	0	0	0	0	0	2	.000	.000	Close & Late	.000	2	0	0	0	0	0	0	0	.000	.000

Roberto Hernandez — White Sox   Pitches Right

	ERA	W	L	Sv	G	GS	IP	BB	SO	Avg	H	2B	3B	HR	RBI	OBP	SLG	GF	IR	IRS	Hld	SvOp	SB	CS	GB	FB	G/F
1992 Season	1.65	7	3	12	43	0	71.0	20	68	.180	45	11	0	4	24	.249	.272	27	38	13	6	16	4	4	66	72	0.92
Career (1991-1992)	2.72	8	3	12	52	3	86.0	27	74	.202	63	15	0	5	36	.272	.298	28	41	16	6	16	6	4	93	89	1.04

1992 Season

	ERA	W	L	Sv	G	GS	IP	H	HR	BB	SO		Avg	AB	H	2B	3B	HR	RBI	BB	SO	OBP	SLG
Home	0.44	5	1	6	23	0	40.2	23	0	7	42	vs. Left	.187	107	20	7	0	1	13	11	36	.264	.280
Away	3.26	2	2	6	20	0	30.1	22	4	13	26	vs. Right	.175	143	25	4	0	3	11	9	32	.237	.266
Starter	0.00	0	0	0	0	0	0.0	0	0	0	0	Scoring Posn	.172	64	11	2	0	1	20	6	11	.263	.250
Reliever	1.65	7	3	12	43	0	71.0	45	4	20	68	Close & Late	.191	162	31	9	0	2	19	13	39	.265	.284
0 Days rest	0.87	1	1	3	6	0	10.1	5	0	5	11	None on/out	.167	60	10	1	0	0	3	5	17	.231	.333
1 or 2 Days rest	1.87	4	1	6	22	0	33.2	28	2	6	31	First Pitch	.207	29	6	1	0	1	4	1	0	.273	.345
3+ Days rest	1.67	2	1	3	15	0	27.0	12	2	9	26	Behind on Count	.250	40	10	3	0	2	7	9	0	.388	.475
Pre-All Star	2.45	2	1	1	15	0	22.0	12	1	13	19	Ahead on Count	.153	144	22	6	0	1	13	0	58	.162	.215
Post-All Star	1.29	5	2	11	28	0	49.0	33	3	7	49	Two Strikes	.155	142	22	6	0	1	9	10	68	.209	.218

Xavier Hernandez — Astros   Pitches Right (groundball pitcher)

	ERA	W	L	Sv	G	GS	IP	BB	SO	Avg	H	2B	3B	HR	RBI	OBP	SLG	GF	IR	IRS	Hld	SvOp	SB	CS	GB	FB	G/F
1992 Season	2.11	9	1	7	77	0	111.0	42	96	.200	81	11	2	5	35	.279	.275	25	48	12	8	10	10	4	144	103	1.40
Career (1989-1992)	3.58	14	9	10	150	7	259.0	106	182	.237	232	38	3	21	111	.314	.346	43	92	26	15	17	26	9	391	244	1.60

1992 Season

	ERA	W	L	Sv	G	GS	IP	H	HR	BB	SO		Avg	AB	H	2B	3B	HR	RBI	BB	SO	OBP	SLG
Home	1.83	6	1	5	35	0	59.0	44	2	14	50	vs. Left	.211	209	44	7	2	2	13	29	51	.310	.292
Away	2.42	3	0	2	42	0	52.0	37	3	28	46	vs. Right	.190	195	37	4	0	3	22	13	45	.245	.256

1992 Season

	ERA	W	L	Sv	G	GS	IP	H	HR	BB	SO		Avg	AB	H	2B	3B	HR	RBI	BB	SO	OBP	SLG
Day	3.41	3	1	1	23	0	29.0	19	3	12	24	Inning 1-6	.243	107	26	1	1	1	12	13	24	.331	.299
Night	1.65	6	0	6	54	0	82.0	62	2	30	72	Inning 7+	.185	297	55	10	1	4	23	29	72	.261	.266
Grass	2.64	3	0	1	25	0	30.2	22	2	16	30	None on	.196	224	44	8	0	0	0	20	46	.265	.232
Turf	1.90	6	1	6	52	0	80.1	59	3	26	66	Runners on	.206	180	37	3	2	5	35	22	50	.296	.328
April	0.00	2	0	0	7	0	13.1	7	0	7	13	Scoring Posn	.160	106	17	0	1	2	27	19	31	.283	.236
May	4.08	1	0	0	14	0	17.2	14	2	5	10	Close & Late	.207	150	31	6	1	1	11	17	34	.294	.280
June	2.25	2	0	3	15	0	24.0	21	1	8	23	None on/out	.191	89	17	3	0	0	0	8	16	.258	.225
July	1.23	1	1	1	12	0	14.2	11	0	4	7	vs. 1st Batr (relief)	.222	72	16	0	0	0	8	4	13	.260	.222
August	2.33	2	0	0	16	0	19.1	12	1	12	26	First Inning Pitched	.217	254	55	7	1	5	31	28	56	.297	.311
September/October	2.05	1	0	3	13	0	22.0	16	1	6	17	First 15 Pitches	.213	263	56	7	1	3	23	22	54	.277	.281
Starter	0.00	0	0	0	0	0	0.0	0	0	0	0	Pitch 16-30	.179	112	20	3	0	2	10	18	33	.298	.259
Reliever	2.11	9	1	7	77	0	111.0	81	5	42	96	Pitch 31-45	.192	26	5	1	1	0	2	2	9	.250	.308
0 Days rest	3.89	4	0	4	24	0	34.2	32	2	16	31	Pitch 46+	.000	3	0	0	0	0	0	0	0	.000	.000
1 or 2 Days rest	1.38	4	1	3	36	0	52.1	34	2	17	43	First Pitch	.280	75	21	2	1	2	12	5	0	.333	.413
3+ Days rest	1.13	1	0	0	17	0	24.0	15	1	9	22	Ahead on Count	.144	180	26	3	0	2	15	0	87	.153	.194
Pre-All Star	2.09	5	0	4	41	0	60.1	45	3	21	48	Behind on Count	.232	95	22	4	1	1	7	24	0	.383	.326
Post-All Star	2.13	4	1	3	36	0	50.2	36	2	21	48	Two Strikes	.122	172	21	2	0	2	10	13	96	.187	.169

Career (1989-1992)

	ERA	W	L	Sv	G	GS	IP	H	HR	BB	SO		Avg	AB	H	2B	3B	HR	RBI	BB	SO	OBP	SLG
Home	2.40	9	4	6	69	3	127.1	94	6	37	89	vs. Left	.241	490	118	18	3	7	50	72	89	.340	.333
Away	4.72	5	5	4	81	4	131.2	138	15	69	93	vs. Right	.233	489	114	20	0	14	61	34	93	.286	.360
Day	3.80	4	3	1	37	1	66.1	56	9	29	50	Inning 1-6	.235	421	99	19	1	11	52	52	73	.320	.363
Night	3.50	10	6	9	113	6	192.2	176	12	77	132	Inning 7+	.238	558	133	19	2	10	59	54	109	.309	.333
Grass	4.10	4	3	3	51	2	83.1	84	10	44	62	None on	.233	527	123	23	0	9	9	53	92	.308	.328
Turf	3.33	10	6	7	99	5	175.2	148	11	62	120	Runners on	.241	452	109	15	3	12	102	53	90	.320	.367
April	1.44	2	1	0	18	1	31.1	20	0	13	21	Scoring Posn	.210	271	57	6	2	7	88	44	56	.316	.325
May	7.56	1	4	0	26	4	50.0	61	11	20	30	Close & Late	.229	223	51	7	1	1	20	26	49	.312	.283
June	2.79	3	1	3	27	1	61.1	58	3	28	39	None on/out	.229	223	51	12	0	4	4	23	39	.301	.336
July	5.81	1	1	1	20	0	31.0	32	5	12	15	vs. 1st Batr (relief)	.237	131	31	2	0	2	20	9	23	.280	.298
August	2.05	2	0	0			30.2	22	1	12	33	First Inning Pitched	.222	491	109	12	1	13	65	58	100	.304	.330
September/October	1.65	5	2	6	37	1	54.2	39	1	21	44	First 15 Pitches	.224	495	111	11	1	10	49	48	94	.297	.311
Starter	6.00	0	6	0	7	7	36.0	37	5	25	24	Pitch 16-30	.249	273	68	16	1	7	35	33	52	.331	.392
Reliever	3.19	14	3	10	143	0	223.0	195	16	81	158	Pitch 31-45	.263	114	30	7	1	2	16	11	21	.333	.395
0 Days rest	3.30	4	1	5	32	0	43.2	38	2	22	35	Pitch 46+	.237	97	23	4	0	2	11	14	15	.330	.340
1 or 2 Days rest	2.34	7	2	5	64	0	92.1	74	3	34	74	First Pitch	.290	186	54	6	2	4	26	17	0	.357	.409
3+ Days rest	4.03	3	0	0	47	0	87.0	83	11	25	49	Ahead on Count	.185	428	79	15	0	8	46	0	167	.190	.276
Pre-All Star	4.59	6	6	4	80	6	155.0	154	18	69	95	Behind on Count	.273	220	60	8	1	7	23	59	0	.423	.414
Post-All Star	2.06	8	3	6	70	1	104.0	78	3	37	87	Two Strikes	.157	395	62	11	0	5	32	30	182	.219	.223

Pitcher vs. Batter (career)

Pitches Best Vs.	Avg	AB	H	2B	3B	HR	RBI	BB	SO	OBP	SLG	Pitches Worst Vs.	Avg	AB	H	2B	3B	HR	RBI	BB	SO	OBP	SLG
Brett Butler	.100	10	1	1	0	0	0	5	1	.400	.400	Will Clark	.400	10	4	0	0	0	1	2	0	.500	.400
Paul O'Neill	.133	15	2	0	0	0	2	4	3	.316	.133	Matt D. Williams	.364	11	4	1	0	1	3	0	2	.364	.727
Bip Roberts	.154	13	2	0	0	0	0	1	4	.214	.154	Barry Larkin	.357	14	5	0	0	0	1	1	1	.400	.357
Hal Morris	.182	11	2	1	0	0	1	2	1	.308	.273	Lenny Harris	.333	12	4	1	0	0	2	1	1	.385	.417
Chris Sabo	.188	16	3	1	0	0	1	0	1	.188	.250												

Orel Hershiser — Dodgers

Pitches Right (groundball pitcher)

	ERA	W	L	Sv	G	GS	IP	BB	SO	Avg	H	2B	3B	HR	RBI	OBP	SLG	CG	ShO	Sup	QS	#P/S	SB	CS	GB	FB	G/F
1992 Season	3.67	10	15	0	33	33	210.2	69	130	.257	209	42	3	15	79	.320	.372	1	0	3.29	19	91	13	7	366	191	1.92
Last Five Years	2.83	56	41	1	128	125	871.2	255	575	.239	781	133	13	46	260	.297	.330	24	12	3.99	88	96	48	28	1500	712	2.11

1992 Season

	ERA	W	L	Sv	G	GS	IP	H	HR	BB	SO		Avg	AB	H	2B	3B	HR	RBI	BB	SO	OBP	SLG
Home	2.75	7	5	0	17	17	118.0	111	7	31	70	vs. Left	.286	455	130	21	3	11	45	56	60	.366	.418
Away	4.86	3	10	0	16	16	92.2	98	8	38	60	vs. Right	.221	357	79	21	0	4	34	13	70	.257	.314
Day	4.20	2	6	0	10	10	64.1	77	3	19	36	Inning 1-6	.258	724	187	39	3	13	74	60	120	.319	.374
Night	3.44	8	9	0	23	23	146.1	132	12	50	94	Inning 7+	.250	88	22	3	0	2	5	9	10	.327	.352
Grass	3.30	10	8	0	25	25	163.2	157	11	50	98	None on	.256	469	120	25	3	12	12	32	78	.310	.399
Turf	4.98	0	7	0	8	8	47.0	52	4	19	32	Runners on	.259	343	89	17	0	3	67	37	52	.332	.335
April	4.13	2	2	0	5	5	32.2	26	2	11	22	Scoring Posn	.234	205	48	9	0	1	58	29	41	.329	.293
May	2.89	2	1	0	5	5	28.0	26	2	12	18	Close & Late	.262	61	16	2	0	2	5	6	8	.338	.393
June	2.78	2	2	0	5	5	35.2	26	2	12	16	None on/out	.278	212	59	12	2	6	6	15	36	.326	.439
July	5.19	1	4	0	6	6	34.2	54	3	9	19	vs. 1st Batr (relief)	.000	0	0	0	0	0	0	0	0	.000	.000
August	3.67	2	2	0	6	6	41.2	39	2	15	22	First Inning Pitched	.288	132	38	7	0	1	15	11	16	.353	.364
September/October	3.32	1	4	0	6	6	38.0	38	4	10	36	First 75 Pitches	.261	647	169	38	3	12	67	50	109	.319	.385
Starter	3.67	10	15	0	33	33	210.2	209	15	69	130	Pitch 76-90	.194	103	20	2	0	2	8	11	14	.272	.272
Reliever	0.00	0	0	0	0	0	0.0	0	0	0	0	Pitch 91-105	.333	51	17	1	0	1	4	6	4	.407	.412
0-3 Days Rest	0.00	0	0	0	0	0	0.0	0	0	0	0	Pitch 106+	.273	11	3	1	0	0	0	2	3	.385	.364
4 Days Rest	3.23	7	7	0	18	18	119.2	121	7	32	75	First Pitch	.268	153	41	3	0	6	12	12	0	.333	.405
5+ Days Rest	4.25	3	8	0	15	15	91.0	88	8	37	55	Ahead on Count	.232	341	79	18	1	3	34	0	112	.241	.317

1992 Season

	ERA	W	L	Sv	G	GS	IP	H	HR	BB	SO		Avg	AB	H	2B	3B	HR	RBI	BB	SO	OBP	SLG
Pre-All Star	3.43	7	7	0	18	18	115.1	109	7	39	70	Behind on Count	.287	178	51	11	1	6	21	38	0	.408	.461
Post-All Star	3.97	3	8	0	15	15	95.1	100	8	30	60	Two Strikes	.188	320	60	14	0	2	27	19	130	.241	.250

Last Five Years

	ERA	W	L	Sv	G	GS	IP	H	HR	BB	SO		Avg	AB	H	2B	3B	HR	RBI	BB	SO	OBP	SLG
Home	2.75	31	21	0	65	65	451.1	407	24	125	281	vs. Left	.255	1764	449	71	12	32	154	182	247	.325	.363
Away	2.91	25	20	1	63	60	420.1	374	22	130	294	vs. Right	.222	1498	332	62	1	14	106	73	328	.263	.292
Day	2.87	18	12	1	40	38	273.0	258	10	65	161	Inning 1-6	.240	2695	648	109	11	40	227	199	485	.295	.334
Night	2.81	38	29	0	88	87	598.2	523	36	190	414	Inning 7+	.235	567	133	24	2	6	33	56	90	.305	.316
Grass	2.81	44	30	1	97	95	657.2	589	34	185	429	None on	.246	1947	478	80	9	32	32	115	330	.291	.345
Turf	2.90	12	11	0	31	30	214.0	192	12	70	146	Runners on	.230	1315	303	53	4	14	228	144	245	.305	.309
April	2.80	11	5	0	19	19	135.0	104	4	37	91	Scoring Posn	.213	732	156	30	3	10	209	111	168	.316	.303
May	3.14	8	6	1	18	17	117.1	111	10	38	81	Close & Late	.233	335	78	14	1	5	26	36	54	.310	.325
June	2.59	11	7	0	23	22	163.1	142	11	55	110	None on/out	.264	864	228	35	4	17	17	43	147	.302	.373
July	3.77	8	7	0	23	22	140.2	145	7	43	81	vs. 1st Batr (relief)	.000	3	0	0	0	0	0	0	0	.000	.000
August	3.35	9	7	0	23	23	153.1	148	9	42	100	First Inning Pitched	.274	500	137	26	0	5	46	35	73	.325	.356
September/October	1.56	9	9	0	22	22	162.0	131	5	40	112	First 75 Pitches	.242	2502	606	101	11	38	196	174	442	.295	.337
Starter	2.85	56	41	0	125	125	861.2	775	46	252	563	Pitch 76-90	.227	396	90	17	0	3	35	39	75	.295	.293
Reliever	0.90	0	0	0	3	0	10.0	6	0	3	12	Pitch 91-105	.225	222	50	7	1	2	15	24	32	.299	.293
0-3 Days Rest	3.25	4	2	0	6	6	44.1	43	4	13	23	Pitch 106+	.246	142	35	8	1	3	14	18	26	.337	.380
4 Days Rest	2.62	32	20	0	70	70	491.2	446	22	121	315	First Pitch	.274	574	157	20	2	13	60	32	0	.315	.383
5+ Days Rest	3.15	20	19	0	49	49	325.2	286	20	118	225	Ahead on Count	.188	1406	264	47	5	12	80	0	507	.192	.254
Pre-All Star	2.99	33	21	1	68	65	461.0	418	29	141	314	Behind on Count	.298	728	217	42	3	18	90	145	0	.416	.438
Post-All Star	2.65	23	20	0	60	60	410.2	363	17	114	261	Two Strikes	.163	1326	216	37	4	11	65	78	573	.213	.222

Pitcher vs. Batter (since 1984)

Pitches Best Vs.	Avg	AB	H	2B	3B	HR	RBI	BB	SO	OBP	SLG	Pitches Worst Vs.	Avg	AB	H	2B	3B	HR	RBI	BB	SO	OBP	SLG
Spike Owen	.000	13	0	0	0	0	0	2	2	.133	.000	Craig Biggio	.465	43	20	7	0	0	2	1	6	.477	.628
Junior Ortiz	.000	11	0	0	0	0	1	0	0	.000	.000	Steve Finley	.450	20	9	0	1	1	1	3	2	.522	.700
Randy Ready	.000	11	0	0	0	0	0	1	1	.083	.000	Kal Daniels	.429	28	12	1	0	4	6	6	8	.529	.893
Pedro Guerrero	.063	16	1	0	0	0	0	0	2	.063	.063	Deion Sanders	.375	16	6	0	1	1	1	1	2	.412	.688
Kirt Manwaring	.083	12	1	0	0	0	0	0	1	.083	.083	Bobby Bonilla	.306	36	11	3	0	4	10	4	3	.375	.722

Joe Hesketh — Red Sox

Pitches Left (groundball pitcher)

	ERA	W	L	Sv	G	GS	IP	BB	SO	Avg	H	2B	3B	HR	RBI	OBP	SLG	CG	ShO	Sup	QS	#P/S	SB	CS	GB	FB	G/F
1992 Season	4.36	8	9	1	30	25	148.2	58	104	.276	162	39	2	15	69	.339	.425	1	0	5.02	11	87	17	4	225	144	1.56
Last Five Years	3.95	31	26	18	217	44	482.2	197	366	.266	490	109	10	47	223	.335	.412	1	0	5.00	22	89	41	17	680	452	1.50

1992 Season

	ERA	W	L	Sv	G	GS	IP	H	HR	BB	SO		Avg	AB	H	2B	3B	HR	RBI	BB	SO	OBP	SLG
Home	4.50	4	4	0	14	12	66.0	81	5	31	43	vs. Left	.255	98	25	5	0	2	13	4	20	.288	.367
Away	4.25	4	5	1	16	13	82.2	81	10	27	61	vs. Right	.280	490	137	34	2	13	56	54	84	.349	.437
Starter	4.29	7	9	0	25	25	138.1	152	13	50	99	Scoring Posn	.262	141	37	6	0	3	51	19	31	.337	.369
Reliever	5.23	1	0	1	5	0	10.1	10	2	8	5	Close & Late	.259	27	7	3	0	1	2	3	4	.333	.481
0-3 Days Rest	3.60	1	0	0	1	1	5.0	7	1	2	5	None on/out	.280	157	44	13	0	8	8	10	27	.323	.516
4 Days Rest	4.78	2	7	0	12	12	64.0	68	4	25	46	First Pitch	.356	90	32	7	0	2	14	5	0	.389	.500
5+ Days Rest	3.89	4	2	0	12	12	69.1	77	8	23	48	Behind on Count	.367	147	54	13	1	6	26	32	0	.473	.592
Pre-All Star	3.82	4	6	0	16	16	96.2	95	8	34	68	Ahead on Count	.202	238	48	12	1	6	24	0	88	.202	.336
Post-All Star	5.37	4	3	1	14	9	52.0	67	7	24	36	Two Strikes	.181	243	44	13	0	5	16	21	104	.244	.296

Last Five Years

	ERA	W	L	Sv	G	GS	IP	H	HR	BB	SO		Avg	AB	H	2B	3B	HR	RBI	BB	SO	OBP	SLG
Home	3.96	15	11	8	109	20	231.2	246	22	104	183	vs. Left	.249	393	98	19	1	9	60	47	94	.330	.372
Away	3.94	16	15	10	108	24	251.0	244	25	93	183	vs. Right	.270	1450	392	90	9	38	163	150	272	.337	.423
Day	3.49	12	8	2	73	17	180.2	180	16	64	134	Inning 1-6	.271	1104	299	67	6	35	130	96	209	.327	.438
Night	4.23	19	18	16	144	27	302.0	310	31	133	232	Inning 7+	.258	739	191	42	4	12	93	101	157	.346	.375
Grass	3.93	19	18	6	113	36	320.2	332	31	129	231	None on	.279	1020	285	65	5	29	29	94	188	.342	.438
Turf	4.00	12	8	12	104	8	162.0	158	16	68	135	Runners on	.249	823	205	44	5	18	194	103	178	.327	.380
April	3.89	4	0	1	22	3	39.1	40	1	21	25	Scoring Posn	.235	486	114	22	1	12	170	80	119	.333	.358
May	4.34	5	4	2	43	5	85.0	84	6	39	67	Close & Late	.235	281	66	12	2	6	39	39	60	.330	.356
June	4.72	2	5	6	44	7	82.0	82	12	43	66	None on/out	.273	462	126	30	3	14	14	38	87	.329	.442
July	3.97	7	6	3	40	9	88.1	95	10	27	63	vs. 1st Batr (relief)	.230	152	35	10	1	3	26	16	34	.298	.368
August	4.53	6	5	3	35	10	89.1	106	11	30	66	First Inning Pitched	.254	688	175	35	1	12	100	81	149	.330	.360
September/October	2.46	7	5	3	33	10	98.2	83	7	37	79	First 75 Pitches	.265	1658	440	98	9	44	206	164	338	.330	.415
Starter	3.79	17	15	0	44	44	259.0	272	27	80	183	Pitch 76-90	.281	114	32	5	0	2	10	18	21	.379	.377
Reliever	4.14	14	11	18	173	0	223.2	218	20	117	183	Pitch 91-105	.246	61	15	5	1	1	7	12	5	.370	.410
0-3 Days Rest	8.16	1	2	0	3	3	14.1	23	5	6	11	Pitch 106+	.300	10	3	1	0	0	0	3	2	.462	.400
4 Days Rest	3.50	7	10	0	23	23	136.1	139	9	41	97	First Pitch	.304	276	84	16	2	7	46	19	0	.346	.453
5+ Days Rest	3.57	9	3	0	18	18	108.1	110	13	33	75	Ahead on Count	.200	816	163	38	3	11	78	0	310	.200	.294
Pre-All Star	4.42	13	12	11	122	17	234.1	233	23	115	176	Behind on Count	.375	411	154	39	3	19	69	99	0	.491	.623
Post-All Star	3.52	18	14	7	95	27	248.1	257	24	82	190	Two Strikes	.174	806	140	33	3	10	53	79	366	.246	.259

Pitcher vs. Batter (career)

Pitches Best Vs.	Avg	AB	H	2B	3B	HR	RBI	BB	SO	OBP	SLG	Pitches Worst Vs.	Avg	AB	H	2B	3B	HR	RBI	BB	SO	OBP	SLG
Rob Deer	.000	9	0	0	0	0	0	3	3	.250	.000	Kevin Mitchell	.600	15	9	2	0	1	3	2	2	.647	.933
Don Mattingly	.071	14	1	0	0	0	3	1	2	.118	.071	Shane Mack	.571	14	8	1	0	2	5	1	1	.600	1.071
Henry Cotto	.077	13	1	1	0	0	0	0	2	.077	.154	Mickey Tettleton	.462	13	6	2	0	2	3	2	3	.533	1.077
Lance Parrish	.083	12	1	0	0	0	0	1	4	.154	.083	Kent Hrbek	.455	11	5	2	0	1	4	2	3	.538	.909
Chris James	.091	11	1	0	0	0	0	0	2	.091	.091	Travis Fryman	.364	11	4	0	1	2	4	1	4	.500	1.091

Greg Hibbard — White Sox

Pitches Left (groundball pitcher)

	ERA	W	L	Sv	G	GS	IP	BB	SO	Avg	H	2B	3B	HR	RBI	OBP	SLG	CG	ShO	Sup	QS	#P/S	SB	CS	GB	FB	G/F
1992 Season	4.40	10	7	1	31	28	176.0	57	69	.277	187	25	5	17	82	.337	.404	0	0	3.94	16	86	9	6	329	133	2.47
Career (1989-1992)	3.78	41	34	1	119	113	718.1	210	287	.266	266	112	18	56	266	.320	.382	10	4	4.23	56	90	35	28	1237	687	1.80

1992 Season

	ERA	W	L	Sv	G	GS	IP	H	HR	BB	SO		Avg	AB	H	2B	3B	HR	RBI	BB	SO	OBP	SLG
Home	3.44	7	3	1	15	14	96.2	89	11	29	39	vs. Left	.224	85	19	1	0	1	7	6	15	.302	.271
Away	5.56	3	4	0	16	14	79.1	98	6	28	30	vs. Right	.285	590	168	24	5	16	75	51	54	.342	.424
Day	5.87	4	1	0	7	7	38.1	36	4	16	11	Inning 1-6	.274	577	158	22	5	15	76	49	58	.333	.407
Night	3.99	6	6	1	24	21	137.2	151	13	41	58	Inning 7+	.296	98	29	3	0	2	6	8	11	.358	.388
Grass	4.35	9	5	1	26	24	153.0	158	16	49	63	None on	.261	399	104	11	2	12	12	35	47	.325	.388
Turf	4.70	1	2	0	5	4	23.0	29	1	8	6	Runners on	.301	276	83	14	3	5	70	22	22	.354	.428
April	2.83	4	0	0	4	4	28.2	23	2	9	7	Scoring Posn	.271	144	39	9	2	2	61	14	12	.339	.403
May	5.45	1	3	0	7	6	36.1	46	7	16	15	Close & Late	.300	70	21	3	0	2	6	6	8	.367	.429
June	4.42	1	1	0	6	6	36.2	40	4	6	12	None on/out	.237	177	42	5	1	6	6	15	21	.301	.379
July	5.14	1	1	0	5	5	28.0	23	2	15	16	vs. 1st Batr (relief)	.000	3	0	0	0	0	0	0	0	.000	.000
August	3.21	2	1	1	5	4	28.0	26	1	8	11	First Inning Pitched	.248	113	28	2	0	2	12	11	16	.317	.319
September/October	5.40	1	1	0	4	3	18.1	29	1	3	8	First 75 Pitches	.272	559	152	19	4	14	66	44	55	.327	.395
Starter	4.55	10	7	0	28	28	170.0	183	17	56	66	Pitch 76-90	.274	73	20	2	0	3	7	7	9	.341	.425
Reliever	0.00	0	0	1	3	0	6.0	4	0	1	3	Pitch 91-105	.389	36	14	3	1	0	8	6	4	.488	.528
0-3 Days Rest	6.75	0	1	0	1	1	6.2	10	0	3	5	Pitch 106+	.143	7	1	1	0	0	1	0	1	.250	.286
4 Days Rest	5.09	4	2	0	15	15	88.1	94	10	35	41	First Pitch	.241	112	27	4	0	0	12	2	0	.250	.277
5+ Days Rest	3.72	6	4	0	12	12	75.0	79	7	18	24	Ahead on Count	.238	286	68	6	2	3	23	0	58	.244	.304
Pre-All Star	4.20	7	4	0	19	18	115.2	118	13	38	41	Behind on Count	.360	150	54	6	2	10	28	32	0	.478	.627
Post-All Star	4.77	3	3	1	12	10	60.1	69	4	19	28	Two Strikes	.241	249	60	6	2	2	12	23	69	.315	.305

Career (1989-1992)

	ERA	W	L	Sv	G	GS	IP	H	HR	BB	SO		Avg	AB	H	2B	3B	HR	RBI	BB	SO	OBP	SLG
Home	3.19	23	16	1	60	58	378.1	349	28	114	146	vs. Left	.245	364	89	13	1	6	41	26	46	.303	.335
Away	4.45	18	18	0	59	55	340.0	378	28	96	141	vs. Right	.269	2369	638	99	17	50	245	184	241	.322	.389
Day	4.45	11	7	0	29	29	176.0	172	19	50	81	Inning 1-6	.268	2346	628	100	18	48	267	184	249	.321	.387
Night	3.57	30	27	1	90	84	542.1	555	37	160	206	Inning 7+	.256	387	99	12	0	8	19	26	38	.310	.349
Grass	3.56	36	27	1	100	95	616.0	603	47	179	245	None on	.254	1651	420	57	8	34	34	127	180	.311	.360
Turf	5.10	5	7	0	19	18	102.1	124	9	31	42	Runners on	.284	1082	307	55	10	22	252	83	107	.333	.414
April	2.36	8	1	0	11	11	76.1	59	4	26	31	Scoring Posn	.282	561	158	36	8	10	217	51	54	.337	.428
May	3.93	4	8	0	20	19	123.2	126	13	40	48	Close & Late	.260	250	65	11	0	4	13	18	25	.319	.352
June	4.01	6	7	0	22	22	139.0	156	17	31	52	None on/out	.239	732	175	25	5	16	16	49	70	.289	.352
July	4.44	6	4	0	21	21	121.2	121	12	38	56	vs. 1st Batr (relief)	.000	6	0	0	0	0	0	0	0	.000	.000
August	3.82	8	9	1	22	21	129.2	132	5	42	47	First Inning Pitched	.227	437	99	13	2	8	41	38	63	.292	.320
September/October	3.59	9	5	0	23	19	128.0	133	5	33	53	First 75 Pitches	.267	2153	575	86	15	43	232	163	221	.319	.381
Starter	3.86	40	34	0	113	113	701.2	715	56	209	278	Pitch 76-90	.266	334	89	13	2	8	29	23	41	.318	.389
Reliever	0.54	1	0	1	6	0	16.2	12	0	1	9	Pitch 91-105	.259	174	45	11	1	4	18	18	20	.332	.402
0-3 Days Rest	1.77	2	1	0	5	5	35.2	29	1	9	18	Pitch 106+	.250	72	18	2	0	1	7	6	5	.325	.319
4 Days Rest	4.13	24	15	0	63	63	398.1	404	38	123	159	First Pitch	.291	444	129	14	3	6	45	3	0	.300	.376
5+ Days Rest	3.73	14	18	0	45	45	267.2	282	17	77	101	Ahead on Count	.211	1077	227	22	8	16	90	0	243	.214	.291
Pre-All Star	3.52	20	18	0	60	59	383.1	379	36	109	152	Behind on Count	.330	706	233	48	4	25	96	131	0	.434	.516
Post-All Star	4.08	21	16	1	59	54	335.0	348	20	101	135	Two Strikes	.203	1025	208	26	8	13	73	76	287	.262	.282

Pitcher vs. Batter (career)

Pitches Best Vs.	Avg	AB	H	2B	3B	HR	RBI	BB	SO	OBP	SLG	Pitches Worst Vs.	Avg	AB	H	2B	3B	HR	RBI	BB	SO	OBP	SLG
Lee Stevens	.000	11	0	0	0	0	2	1	2	.083	.000	Carlos Baerga	.500	22	11	0	0	2	7	2	2	.500	.773
Randy Velarde	.063	16	1	1	0	0	2	0	2	.063	.125	Lance Parrish	.500	18	9	0	0	2	3	2	1	.550	.833
Ken Griffey Jr	.077	13	1	0	0	0	1	0	2	.188	.077	Mickey Tettleton	.500	16	8	3	0	2	4	1	3	.529	1.063
Pete O'Brien	.083	12	1	0	0	0	0	0	3	.083	.063	Greg Gagne	.438	16	7	3	0	1	2	0	0	.438	.813
Luis Sojo	.091	11	1	0	0	0	1	0	1	.091	.091	Mike Macfarlane	.333	9	3	1	0	0	2	3	2	.455	1.000

Bryan Hickerson — Giants

Pitches Left (flyball pitcher)

	ERA	W	L	Sv	G	GS	IP	BB	SO	Avg	H	2B	3B	HR	RBI	OBP	SLG	GF	IR	IRS	Hld	SvOp	SB	CS	GB	FB	G/F
1992 Season	3.09	5	3	0	61	1	87.1	21	68	.236	74	19	1	7	35	.282	.369	8	39	11	8	5	1	6	96	103	0.93
Career (1991-1992)	3.28	7	5	0	78	7	137.1	38	111	.250	127	30	1	10	51	.301	.373	12	45	11	9	5	7	10	149	154	0.97

1992 Season

	ERA	W	L	Sv	G	GS	IP	H	HR	BB	SO		Avg	AB	H	2B	3B	HR	RBI	BB	SO	OBP	SLG
Home	3.95	2	3	0	28	0	41.0	37	5	6	33	vs. Left	.235	102	24	5	1	1	8	6	15	.273	.333

	ERA	W	L	Sv	G	GS	IP	H	HR	BB	SO		Avg	AB	H	2B	3B	HR	RBI	BB	SO	OBP	SLG
Away	2.33	3	0	0	33	1	46.1	37	2	15	35	vs. Right	.236	212	50	14	0	6	27	15	53	.286	.387
Day	4.15	1	1	0	22	0	34.2	29	3	6	27	Inning 1-6	.252	115	29	6	1	3	15	7	21	.296	.400
Night	2.39	4	2	0	39	1	52.2	45	4	15	41	Inning 7+	.226	199	45	13	0	4	20	14	47	.273	.352
Grass	3.30	3	3	0	43	1	62.2	57	6	11	48	None on	.217	189	41	14	1	2	2	14	47	.275	.333
Turf	2.55	2	0	0	18	0	24.2	17	1	10	20	Runners on	.264	125	33	5	0	5	33	7	21	.292	.424
April	0.93	1	1	0	10	0	9.2	7	1	3	10	Scoring Posn	.250	72	18	3	0	3	28	4	10	.272	.417
May	3.45	1	0	0	11	0	15.2	14	1	4	12	Close & Late	.241	116	28	7	0	3	15	12	26	.305	.379
June	4.26	0	0	0	9	0	12.2	11	1	4	11	None on/out	.188	80	15	5	0	0	0	3	16	.217	.250
July	2.04	2	0	0	10	0	17.2	12	2	1	12	vs. 1st Batr (relief)	.113	53	6	1	0	0	6	2	10	.136	.132
August	4.50	1	2	0	11	0	14.0	12	1	5	9	First Inning Pitched	.232	190	44	10	0	6	25	13	41	.278	.379
September/October	3.06	0	0	0	10	1	17.2	18	1	4	14	First 15 Pitches	.195	195	38	8	0	5	20	13	39	.243	.313
Starter	0.00	0	0	0	1	1	4.0	4	0	1	3	Pitch 16-30	.295	88	26	9	0	2	11	6	24	.340	.466
Reliever	3.24	5	3	0	60	0	83.1	70	7	20	65	Pitch 31-45	.346	26	9	2	1	0	4	2	4	.393	.500
0 Days rest	1.11	2	0	0	12	0	24.1	10	1	2	27	Pitch 46+	.200	5	1	0	0	0	0	0	1	.200	.200
1 or 2 Days rest	3.63	3	2	0	29	0	39.2	39	2	11	25	First Pitch	.292	48	14	5	0	2	7	2	0	.314	.521
3+ Days rest	5.12	1	0	0	19	0	19.1	21	4	7	13	Ahead on Count	.194	155	30	6	1	1	13	0	64	.195	.265
Pre-All Star	2.51	3	1	0	33	0	46.2	38	3	11	38	Behind on Count	.242	66	16	5	0	1	9	13	0	.363	.364
Post-All Star	3.76	2	2	0	28	1	40.2	36	4	10	30	Two Strikes	.219	155	34	6	1	2	14	6	68	.250	.310

Donnie Hill — Twins   Bats Both

	Avg	G	AB	R	H	2B	3B	HR	RBI	BB	SO	HBP	GDP	SB	CS	OBP	SLG	IBB	SH	SF	#Pit	#P/PA	GB	FB	G/F
1992 Season	.294	25	51	7	15	3	0	0	2	5	6	1	0	0	0	.368	.353	0	2	0	217	3.81	17	14	1.21
Last Five Years	.247	287	833	96	206	35	4	6	74	90	86	9	14	5	3	.320	.321	3	14	7	3640	3.91	318	260	1.22

1992 Season

	Avg	AB	H	2B	3B	HR	RBI	BB	SO	OBP	SLG		Avg	AB	H	2B	3B	HR	RBI	BB	SO	OBP	SLG
vs. Left	.000	2	0	0	0	0	0	0	1	.000	.000	Scoring Posn	.167	12	2	0	0	0	2	2	3	.286	.167
vs. Right	.306	49	15	3	0	0	2	5	5	.382	.367	Close & Late	.250	8	2	1	0	0	0	1	2	.333	.375

Last Five Years

	Avg	AB	H	2B	3B	HR	RBI	BB	SO	OBP	SLG		Avg	AB	H	2B	3B	HR	RBI	BB	SO	OBP	SLG
vs. Left	.219	196	43	12	1	2	21	33	30	.329	.321	Scoring Posn	.246	203	50	9	2	2	67	35	27	.347	.340
vs. Right	.256	637	163	23	3	4	53	57	56	.317	.320	Close & Late	.243	144	35	4	1	1	14	21	15	.339	.306
Groundball	.253	198	50	10	0	0	20	23	18	.332	.303	None on/out	.269	175	47	7	1	1	17	20		.333	.337
Flyball	.233	210	49	7	2	2	20	22	27	.301	.314	Batting #2	.251	279	70	14	2	1	21	27	22	.318	.326
Home	.233	378	88	15	1	2	30	47	38	.315	.294	Batting #9	.242	182	44	7	0	1	21	20	24	.309	.297
Away	.259	455	118	20	3	4	44	43	48	.323	.343	Other	.247	372	92	14	2	4	32	43	40	.326	.328
Day	.263	259	68	9	1	2	25	23	24	.323	.328	April	.280	118	33	5	1	0	15	14	15	.351	.339
Night	.240	574	138	26	3	4	49	67	62	.318	.317	May	.241	162	39	7	1	2	15	19	17	.328	.333
Grass	.245	687	168	25	2	3	53	74	68	.317	.300	June	.243	173	42	11	0	0	14	22	14	.327	.306
Turf	.260	146	38	10	2	3	21	16	18	.333	.418	July	.246	142	35	3	1	1	14	14	18	.310	.303
First Pitch	.297	91	27	3	1	1	11	1	0	.312	.385	August	.250	160	36	7	0	2	7	13	13	.283	.306
Ahead on Count	.317	208	66	15	0	2	19	47	0	.440	.418	September/October	.269	78	21	2	1	1	9	8	9	.330	.359
Behind on Count	.263	251	66	8	1	1	19	0	41	.264	.315	Pre-All Star	.246	495	122	25	2	2	46	57	56	.325	.317
Two Strikes	.197	375	74	12	2	1	30	41	85	.248	.248	Post-All Star	.249	338	84	10	2	4	28	33	30	.312	.325

Batter vs. Pitcher (since 1984)

Hits Best Against	Avg	AB	H	2B	3B	HR	RBI	BB	SO	OBP	SLG	Hits Worst Against	Avg	AB	H	2B	3B	HR	RBI	BB	SO	OBP	SLG
Bud Black	.444	18	8	1	0	1	4	4	2	.545	.667	Greg Swindell	.071	14	1	0	0	0	0	0	3	.071	.071
Juan Berenguer	.417	12	5	2	1	0	4	1	0	.462	.750	Jose Guzman	.100	10	1	1	0	0	0	1	2	.182	.200
Bobby Witt	.400	10	4	0	0	0	1	5	2	.600	.400	Bruce Hurst	.130	23	3	1	0	0	0	1	3	.167	.174
Rick Honeycutt	.333	12	4	1	0	1	2	0	0	.333	.667	Mark Langston	.152	33	5	0	0	1	3	0	5	.147	.242
Jimmy Key	.333	12	4	1	0	1	1	0	0	.333	.667	Roger Clemens	.167	24	4	1	0	0	2	0	4	.167	.208

Glenallen Hill — Indians   Bats Right

	Avg	G	AB	R	H	2B	3B	HR	RBI	BB	SO	HBP	GDP	SB	CS	OBP	SLG	IBB	SH	SF	#Pit	#P/PA	GB	FB	G/F
1992 Season	.241	102	369	38	89	16	1	18	49	20	73	4	11	9	6	.287	.436	0	0	1	1332	3.38	118	121	0.98
Career (1989-1992)	.245	277	902	118	221	35	6	39	113	64	201	4	23	25	14	.297	.427	0	1	4	3417	3.51	292	283	1.03

1992 Season

	Avg	AB	H	2B	3B	HR	RBI	BB	SO	OBP	SLG		Avg	AB	H	2B	3B	HR	RBI	BB	SO	OBP	SLG
vs. Left	.267	105	28	7	0	7	18	7	14	.319	.533	Scoring Posn	.244	86	21	6	0	3	31	7	21	.298	.419
vs. Right	.231	264	61	9	1	11	31	13	59	.274	.398	Close & Late	.200	80	16	1	0	7	13	4	26	.256	.475
Groundball	.370	100	37	6	0	6	20	6	16	.413	.610	None on/out	.267	75	20	2	0	7	7	4	15	.329	.573
Flyball	.181	105	19	4	0	5	13	5	29	.225	.362	Batting #2	.229	118	27	6	1	3	11	2	27	.248	.373
Home	.257	179	46	9	0	7	24	12	31	.311	.425	Batting #6	.252	131	33	7	0	7	18	8	24	.300	.466
Away	.226	190	43	7	1	11	25	8	42	.264	.447	Other	.242	120	29	3	0	8	20	10	22	.308	.467
Day	.222	108	24	7	0	1	7	8	26	.282	.315	April	.214	56	12	2	0	1	4	0	15	.228	.304
Night	.249	261	65	9	1	17	42	12	47	.289	.487	May	.222	18	4	2	0	0	1	1	4	.263	.333
Grass	.235	311	73	12	1	13	39	18	62	.284	.405	June	.280	75	21	3	1	5	12	3	12	.325	.547
Turf	.276	58	16	4	0	5	10	2	11	.300	.603	July	.297	74	22	4	0	3	7	4	11	.342	.473

1992 Season

	Avg	AB	H	2B	3B	HR	RBI	BB	SO	OBP	SLG
First Pitch	.357	70	25	4	0	3	9	0	0	.375	.543
Ahead on Count	.309	94	29	4	0	8	19	9	0	.365	.606
Behind on Count	.141	135	19	2	0	3	11	0	48	.153	.222
Two Strikes	.143	154	22	5	1	2	9	11	73	.205	.227

	Avg	AB	H	2B	3B	HR	RBI	BB	SO	OBP	SLG
August	.191	89	17	4	0	3	13	8	14	.258	.337
September/October	.228	57	13	1	0	6	12	4	17	.274	.561
Pre-All Star	.256	172	44	8	1	8	21	7	37	.297	.453
Post-All Star	.228	197	45	8	0	10	28	13	36	.278	.421

1992 By Position

Position	Avg	AB	H	2B	3B	HR	RBI	BB	SO	OBP	SLG	G	GS	Innings	PO	A	E	DP	Fld Pct	Rng Fctr	In Zone	Outs	Zone Rtg	MLB Zone
As Designated Hitter	.209	134	28	4	1	5	12	3	31	.237	.366	34	32	---	---	---	---	---	---	---	---	---	---	---
As Pinch Hitter	.111	9	1	0	0	0	2	1	4	.200	.111	10	0	---	---	---	---	---	---	---	---	---	---	---
As lf	.266	192	51	10	0	11	29	12	32	.314	.490	50	50	460.0	108	5	6	2	.950	2.21	132	104	.788	.809

Career (1989-1992)

	Avg	AB	H	2B	3B	HR	RBI	BB	SO	OBP	SLG
vs. Left	.253	375	95	19	4	17	47	31	75	.312	.461
vs. Right	.239	527	126	16	2	22	66	33	126	.286	.402
Groundball	.303	234	71	13	1	7	34	22	43	.365	.457
Flyball	.186	210	39	4	1	11	27	13	62	.236	.371
Home	.260	447	116	23	1	18	54	31	86	.310	.436
Away	.231	455	105	12	5	21	59	33	115	.283	.418
Day	.237	278	66	16	1	9	30	19	69	.288	.399
Night	.248	624	155	19	5	30	83	45	132	.301	.439
Grass	.244	587	143	17	4	23	74	40	134	.294	.404
Turf	.248	315	78	18	2	16	39	24	67	.301	.470
First Pitch	.349	166	58	10	1	5	19	0	0	.357	.512
Ahead on Count	.319	188	60	7	0	11	30	29	0	.406	.532
Behind on Count	.155	317	49	5	2	11	28	0	114	.160	.287
Two Strikes	.144	402	58	9	2	11	36	35	201	.214	.259

	Avg	AB	H	2B	3B	HR	RBI	BB	SO	OBP	SLG
Scoring Posn	.260	204	53	9	2	7	74	21	49	.323	.426
Close & Late	.205	161	33	3	0	7	14	9	45	.256	.354
None on/out	.254	228	58	10	2	12	57	17	50	.315	.474
Batting #6	.223	229	51	10	3	9	27	15	53	.272	.410
Batting #7	.243	185	45	4	1	10	27	16	43	.307	.438
Other	.256	488	125	21	2	20	59	33	105	.304	.430
April	.277	119	33	6	0	4	11	6	22	.313	.429
May	.150	120	18	4	2	4	14	7	37	.197	.317
June	.291	148	43	8	1	7	21	11	23	.348	.500
July	.295	156	46	6	0	9	21	13	30	.351	.506
August	.217	235	51	10	3	8	26	20	53	.278	.387
September/October	.242	124	30	1	0	7	18	7	36	.280	.419
Pre-All Star	.251	426	107	20	3	19	53	27	89	.299	.446
Post-All Star	.239	476	114	15	3	20	60	37	112	.295	.410

Batter vs. Pitcher (career)

Hits Best Against	Avg	AB	H	2B	3B	HR	RBI	BB	SO	OBP	SLG
Mark Guthrie	.583	12	7	2	0	1	4	0	3	.583	1.000
Kirk McCaskill	.500	8	4	0	0	0	2	5	1	.692	.500
Greg Hibbard	.381	21	8	2	2	0	3	3	2	.500	.667
Jack Morris	.375	16	6	2	0	1	3	2	3	.444	.500
Joe Hesketh	.333	12	4	1	0	1	2	0	0	.333	.667

Hits Worst Against	Avg	AB	H	2B	3B	HR	RBI	BB	SO	OBP	SLG
Bret Saberhagen	.063	16	1	0	0	0	0	0	7	.063	.063
Matt Young	.100	10	1	0	0	0	0	1	2	.182	.100
Randy Johnson	.143	14	2	0	0	1	2	3	4	.294	.357
Mark Langston	.188	16	3	0	0	1	3	0	6	.188	.375
Greg Swindell	.200	15	3	0	1	0	1	0	4	.294	.333

Ken Hill — Expos

Pitches Right (groundball pitcher)

	ERA	W	L	Sv	G	GS	IP	BB	SO	Avg	H	2B	3B	HR	RBI	OBP	SLG	CG	ShO	Sup	QS	#P/S	SB	CS	GB	FB	G/F
1992 Season	2.68	16	9	0	33	33	218.0	75	150	.230	187	36	5	13	67	.297	.335	3	3	4.50	24	95	30	8	331	194	1.71
Career (1988-1992)	3.61	39	41	0	117	111	688.2	260	447	.240	615	110	22	44	261	.316	.352	6	4	4.00	69	92	78	32	1032	665	1.55

1992 Season

	ERA	W	L	Sv	G	GS	IP	H	HR	BB	SO
Home	3.15	6	6	0	15	15	94.1	91	4	39	62
Away	2.33	10	3	0	18	18	123.2	96	9	36	88
Day	2.07	5	4	0	12	12	82.2	60	3	27	56
Night	3.06	11	5	0	21	21	135.1	127	10	48	94
Grass	2.14	4	2	0	8	8	54.2	38	3	16	42
Turf	2.87	12	7	0	25	25	163.1	149	10	59	108
April	1.42	2	2	0	5	5	38.0	30	1	8	20
May	3.81	2	0	0	5	5	28.1	26	2	15	17
June	2.92	4	2	0	6	6	37.0	31	2	13	22
July	3.41	4	0	0	5	5	31.2	25	5	14	30
August	2.28	2	3	0	6	6	43.1	40	1	12	30
September/October	2.72	2	2	0	6	6	39.2	35	2	13	31
Starter	2.68	16	9	0	33	33	218.0	187	13	75	150
Reliever	0.00	0	0	0	0	0	0.0	0	0	0	0
0-3 Days Rest	0.00	0	0	0	0	0	0.0	0	0	0	0
4 Days Rest	2.53	8	7	0	21	21	142.1	129	8	43	100
5+ Days Rest	2.97	8	2	0	12	12	75.2	58	5	32	50
Pre-All Star	2.59	9	4	0	18	18	118.0	96	8	41	73
Post-All Star	2.79	7	5	0	15	15	100.0	91	5	34	77

	Avg	AB	H	2B	3B	HR	RBI	BB	SO	OBP	SLG
vs. Left	.222	469	104	19	4	6	32	50	80	.298	.318
vs. Right	.242	343	83	17	1	7	35	25	70	.295	.359
Inning 1-6	.232	695	161	34	5	8	58	61	127	.296	.329
Inning 7+	.222	117	26	2	0	5	9	14	23	.303	.368
None on	.244	463	113	27	3	8		43	88	.312	.367
Runners on	.212	349	74	9	2	5	59	32	62	.276	.292
Scoring Posn	.199	226	45	5	1	3	53	28	40	.284	.270
Close & Late	.258	62	16	0	0	4	8	8	13	.338	.452
None on/out	.227	211	48	11	1	2		14	41	.279	.318
vs. 1st Batr (relief)	.000	0	0	0	0	0	0	0	0	.000	.000
First Inning Pitched	.258	128	33	8	0	3	20	21	33	.360	.391
First 75 Pitches	.228	623	142	30	4	7	51	55	119	.293	.323
Pitch 76-90	.274	113	31	3	1	5	11	10	15	.331	.451
Pitch 91-105	.232	56	13	3	0	1	5	6	13	.306	.339
Pitch 106+	.050	20	1	0	0	0	0	4	3	.208	.050
First Pitch	.315	143	45	7	0	3	12	3	0	.331	.427
Ahead on Count	.145	385	56	7	2	7	28	0	135	.149	.229
Behind on Count	.327	159	52	16	2	3	18	36	0	.451	.509
Two Strikes	.121	356	43	10	1	5	20	36	150	.203	.197

Career (1988-1992)

	ERA	W	L	Sv	G	GS	IP	H	HR	BB	SO
Home	3.69	16	17	0	52	51	307.0	280	12	130	186
Away	3.54	23	24	0	65	60	381.2	335	32	150	261
Day	2.98	15	15	0	42	42	266.0	227	16	95	176
Night	4.00	24	26	0	75	69	422.2	388	28	185	271
Grass	3.07	12	10	0	33	30	196.2	159	15	65	134
Turf	3.82	27	31	0	86	81	492.0	456	29	215	313
April	2.79	5	4	0	15	12	64.0	76	4	28	40

	Avg	AB	H	2B	3B	HR	RBI	BB	SO	OBP	SLG
vs. Left	.244	1443	352	54	14	21	133	178	230	.327	.344
vs. Right	.235	1119	263	56	8	23	128	102	217	.302	.361
Inning 1-6	.237	2244	531	103	18	34	230	246	396	.313	.344
Inning 7+	.264	318	84	7	4	10	31	34	51	.340	.406
None on	.236	1472	347	64	10	27		161	256	.316	.348
Runners on	.246	1090	268	46	12	17	234	119	191	.317	.357
Scoring Posn	.242	636	154	25	6	12	208	93	121	.332	.357

Career (1988-1992)

	ERA	W	L	Sv	G	GS	IP	H	HR	BB	SO
May	3.14	6	4	0	17	17	109.0	92	9	43	77
June	3.36	8	5	0	17	17	101.2	93	5	45	64
July	4.19	8	5	0	18	18	107.1	90	8	49	75
August	3.93	6	10	0	19	19	110.0	104	7	45	75
September/October	3.87	6	13	0	31	28	176.2	160	11	70	116
Starter	3.51	39	41	0	111	111	676.0	596	43	273	442
Reliever	8.53	0	0	0	6	0	12.2	19	1	7	5
0-3 Days Rest	4.00	2	1	0	6	6	36.0	43	3	13	24
4 Days Rest	3.38	20	25	0	63	63	394.0	352	25	151	262
5+ Days Rest	3.66	17	15	0	42	42	246.0	201	15	109	156
Pre-All Star	3.22	22	13	0	55	52	329.2	289	23	131	206
Post-All Star	3.96	17	28	0	62	59	359.0	326	21	149	241

	Avg	AB	H	2B	3B	HR	RBI	BB	SO	OBP	SLG
Close & Late	.307	176	54	4	3	7	25	22	31	.368	.483
None on/out	.238	652	155	25	5	15	15	74	102	.322	.360
vs. 1st Batr (relief)	.200	5	1	0	0	0	0	1	0	.333	.200
First Inning Pitched	.241	432	104	21	3	9	61	70	84	.346	.386
First 75 Pitches	.235	1998	469	89	15	30	201	217	350	.311	.339
Pitch 76-90	.278	317	88	13	4	9	39	33	50	.342	.429
Pitch 91-105	.244	180	44	7	3	4	18	17	36	.323	.383
Pitch 106+	.209	67	14	1	0	1	3	13	11	.338	.269
First Pitch	.315	419	132	24	1	8	51	8	0	.331	.434
Behind on Count	.176	1145	201	24	10	15	89	1	390	.180	.253
Ahead on Count	.316	550	174	42	7	14	84	160	0	.467	.485
Two Strikes	.159	1125	179	33	8	16	83	110	447	.236	.245

Pitcher vs. Batter (career)

Pitches Best Vs.	Avg	AB	H	2B	3B	HR	RBI	BB	SO	OBP	SLG
Terry Pendleton	.000	14	0	0	0	0	0	2	0	.000	.000
Dale Murphy	.000	12	0	0	0	0	1	1	3	.077	.000
Ruben Amaro	.000	10	0	0	0	0	0	1		.167	.000
Steve Buechele	.091	11	1	0	0	0	0	4		.091	.091
Bobby Thompson	.091	11	1	0	0	0	0	1		.091	.091

Pitches Worst Vs.	Avg	AB	H	2B	3B	HR	RBI	BB	SO	OBP	SLG
Tim Raines	.714	14	10	3	1	0	4	7	1	.810	1.071
Lenny Dykstra	.600	20	12	2	0	1	1	4	0	.667	.850
Otis Nixon	.600	15	9	1	0	0	0	4	1	.684	.667
Lonnie Smith	.545	11	6	3	0	0	2	3	0	.643	.818
Fred McGriff	.333	15	5	0	0	3	7	5	1	.500	.933

Milt Hill — Reds
Pitches Right

	ERA	W	L	Sv	G	GS	IP	BB	SO	Avg	H	2B	3B	HR	RBI	OBP	SLG	GF	IR	IRS	Hld	SvOp	SB	CS	GB	FB	G/F
1992 Season	3.15	0	0	1	14	0	20.0	5	10	.211	15	3	1	1	8	.269	.324	5	7	1	1	1	1	0	33	21	1.57
Career (1991-1992)	3.54	1	1	1	36	0	53.1	13	30	.264	51	11	2	2	24	.308	.373	13	26	7	1	2	5	4	75	59	1.27

1992 Season

	ERA	W	L	Sv	G	GS	IP	H	HR	BB	SO		Avg	AB	H	2B	3B	HR	RBI	BB	SO	OBP	SLG
Home	0.73	0	0	1	8	0	12.1	6	0	4	4	vs. Left	.040	25	1	0	0	0	1	5	4	.200	.040
Away	7.04	0	0	0	6	0	7.2	9	1	1	6	vs. Right	.304	46	14	3	1	1	7	0	6	.313	.478

Shawn Hillegas — Athletics
Pitches Right (flyball pitcher)

	ERA	W	L	Sv	G	GS	IP	BB	SO	Avg	H	2B	3B	HR	RBI	OBP	SLG	GF	IR	IRS	Hld	SvOp	SB	CS	GB	FB	G/F
1992 Season	5.23	1	8	0	26	9	86.0	37	49	.303	104	19	4	13	52	.368	.496	6	14	2	0	0	16	6	127	105	1.21
Last Five Years	4.40	17	29	10	151	41	396.2	174	252	.258	391	67	13	41	197	.335	.401	40	102	36	13	12	33	20	489	524	0.93

1992 Season

	ERA	W	L	Sv	G	GS	IP	H	HR	BB	SO		Avg	AB	H	2B	3B	HR	RBI	BB	SO	OBP	SLG
Home	4.08	0	2	0	14	4	46.1	49	6	17	34	vs. Left	.358	165	59	8	3	4	23	21	21	.428	.515
Away	6.58	1	6	0	12	5	39.2	55	7	20	15	vs. Right	.253	178	45	11	1	9	29	16	28	.311	.478
Starter	5.98	1	5	0	9	9	49.2	65	6	21	27	Scoring Posn	.297	91	27	2	1	3	39	14	17	.380	.440
Reliever	4.21	0	3	0	17	0	36.1	39	7	16	22	Close & Late	.292	24	7	0	0	1	1	0	3	.292	.417
0 Days rest	2.70	0	2	0	2	0	3.1	3	1	0	2	None on/out	.235	85	20	4	1		4	6	9	.286	.447
1 or 2 Days rest	2.08	0	0	0	3	0	8.2	7	1	2	8	First Pitch	.341	41	14	3	1	2	7	2	0	.364	.610
3+ Days rest	5.18	0	1	0	12	0	24.1	29	5	14	12	Behind on Count	.438	80	35	5	0	8	22	15	0	.526	.800
Pre-All Star	4.02	0	3	0	14	2	40.1	44	7	16	24	Ahead on Count	.255	149	38	7	1	3	15	0	35	.252	.376
Post-All Star	6.31	1	5	0	12	7	45.2	60	6	21	25	Two Strikes	.229	157	36	6	3	0	15	20	49	.313	.306

Last Five Years

	ERA	W	L	Sv	G	GS	IP	H	HR	BB	SO		Avg	AB	H	2B	3B	HR	RBI	BB	SO	OBP	SLG
Home	3.82	11	12	6	82	19	217.0	193	18	92	152	vs. Left	.284	739	210	31	6	15	91	102	109	.370	.403
Away	5.11	6	17	4	69	22	179.2	198	23	82	100	vs. Right	.234	774	181	36	7	26	106	72	143	.301	.399
Day	5.14	4	8	1	46	12	112.0	117	11	47	69	Inning 1-6	.261	950	248	47	10	29	139	103	153	.334	.423
Night	4.11	13	21	9	105	29	284.2	274	30	127	183	Inning 7+	.254	563	143	20	3	12	58	71	99	.337	.364
Grass	4.05	14	22	8	127	32	331.1	312	31	141	210	None on	.250	856	214	31	10	24	88		137	.322	.394
Turf	6.20	3	7	2	24	9	65.1	79	10	33	42	Runners on	.269	657	177	36	3	17	173	86	115	.351	.411
April	4.13	0	3	0	8	5	32.2	30	3	16	19	Scoring Posn	.258	387	100	20	2	12	156	62	73	.352	.413
May	5.88	1	4	4	22	5	52.0	60	7	23	37	Close & Late	.268	272	73	11	1	6	33	41	45	.358	.382
June	3.14	6	4	2	25	2	63.0	54	7	31	44	None on/out	.231	376	87	13	4	14	14	31	61	.292	.399
July	4.44	5	8	2	38	11	99.1	101	10	40	55	vs. 1st Batr (relief)	.221	86	19	5	1	2	16	21	18	.373	.372
August	6.17	1	6	1	28	6	58.1	73	7	30	43	First Inning Pitched	.239	456	109	16	9	13	89	73	84	.341	.399
September/October	3.35	4	4	1	30	12	91.1	73	7	34	54	First 15 Pitches	.240	413	99	16	8	11	63	62	66	.338	.397
Starter	4.84	9	18	0	41	41	223.0	241	23	86	122	Pitch 16-30	.243	337	82	14	2	6	41	40	68	.320	.350
Reliever	3.83	8	11	10	110	0	173.2	150	18	88	130	Pitch 31-45	.248	242	60	12	1	5	30	22	42	.312	.368
0 Days rest	4.82	2	2	2	13	0	18.2	17	3	10	12	Pitch 46+	.288	521	150	25	2	19	63	50	76	.353	.453
1 or 2 Days rest	3.65	5	6	3	52	0	81.1	67	8	42	59	First Pitch	.343	210	72	13	1	6	36	9	0	.369	.500
3+ Days rest	3.79	1	3	3	45	0	73.2	66	7	36	59	Ahead on Count	.215	701	151	21	4	10	66	1	199	.223	.300
Pre-All Star	4.04	8	15	7	68	16	187.1	181	20	84	122	Behind on Count	.340	324	110	15	5	21	66	80	0	.465	.611
Post-All Star	4.73	9	14	3	83	25	209.1	210	21	90	130	Two Strikes	.184	707	130	21	6	7	60	85	252	.274	.260

Pitcher vs. Batter (career)

Pitches Best Vs.	Avg	AB	H	2B	3B	HR	RBI	BB	SO	OBP	SLG	Pitches Worst Vs.	Avg	AB	H	2B	3B	HR	RBI	BB	SO	OBP	SLG
Dave Valle	.063	12	1	0	0	1	2	1	3	.154	.333	Roberto Kelly	.545	11	6	3	0	2	0	2	.545	.818
Glenn Davis	.100	10	1	0	0	0	1	1	1	.182	.100	Ken Griffey Jr	.500	10	5	1	1	1	3	2	0	.583	1.100
Billy Hatcher	.154	13	2	1	0	0	0	0	2	.154	.231	Kevin Bass	.455	11	5	1	0	1	3	1	2	.500	.818
Brian Downing	.167	12	2	1	0	0	1	1	2	.231	.250	Don Mattingly	.444	9	4	0	0	2	4	1	0	.455	1.111
Wade Boggs	.182	11	2	0	0	1	2	1		.308	.182	Robin Yount	.429	14	6	1	0	2	4	0	1	.429	.929

Eric Hillman — Mets — Pitches Left (groundball pitcher)

	ERA	W	L	Sv	G	GS	IP	BB	SO	Avg	H	2B	3B	HR	RBI	OBP	SLG	CG	ShO	Sup	QS	#P/S	SB	CS	GB	FB	G/F
1992 Season	5.33	2	2	0	11	8	52.1	10	16	.318	67	10	1	9	29	.353	.502	0	0	4.64	3	78	4	5	105	50	2.10

1992 Season

	ERA	W	L	Sv	G	GS	IP	H	HR	BB	SO		Avg	AB	H	2B	3B	HR	RBI	BB	SO	OBP	SLG
Home	3.99	1	1	0	5	4	29.1	36	6	1	11	vs. Left	.297	37	11	2	0	0	0	2	6	.350	.351
Away	7.04	1	1	0	6	4	23.0	31	3	9	5	vs. Right	.322	174	56	8	1	9	29	8	10	.353	.534
Starter	5.32	2	2	0	8	8	45.2	57	8	8	13	Scoring Posn	.326	43	14	2	0	2	21	4	4	.375	.512
Reliever	5.40	0	0	0	3	0	6.2	10	1	2	3	Close & Late	.200	10	2	0	0	0	0	0	3	.273	.200
0-3 Days Rest	0.00	0	0	0	0	0	0.0	0	0	0	0	None on/out	.400	55	22	4	1	2	2	0	3	.421	.618
4 Days Rest	8.37	0	2	0	5	5	23.2	37	8	6	7	First Pitch	.270	37	10	1	0	1	7	1	0	.308	.378
5+ Days Rest	2.05	2	0	0	3	3	22.0	20	0	2	6	Behind on Count	.432	44	19	1	1	3	6	8	0	.519	.705
Pre-All Star	9.00	0	0	0	2	0	3.0	7	1	2	1	Ahead on Count	.313	99	31	7	0	3	13	0	15	.320	.475
Post-All Star	5.11	2	2	0	9	8	49.1	60	8	8	15	Two Strikes	.263	80	21	3	0	4	10	1	16	.277	.450

Sterling Hitchcock — Yankees — Pitches Left (flyball pitcher)

	ERA	W	L	Sv	G	GS	IP	BB	SO	Avg	H	2B	3B	HR	RBI	OBP	SLG	CG	ShO	Sup	QS	#P/S	SB	CS	GB	FB	G/F
1992 Season	8.31	0	2	0	3	3	13.0	6	6	.377	23	5	0	2	12	.441	.557	0	0	5.54	1	89	1	1	18	23	0.78

1992 Season

	ERA	W	L	Sv	G	GS	IP	H	HR	BB	SO		Avg	AB	H	2B	3B	HR	RBI	BB	SO	OBP	SLG
Home	8.31	0	2	0	3	3	13.0	23	2	6	6	vs. Left	.333	6	2	2	0	0	1	1	1	.500	.667
Away	0.00	0	0	0	0	0	0.0	0	0	0	0	vs. Right	.382	55	21	3	0	2	11	5	5	.433	.545

Chris Hoiles — Orioles — Bats Right (flyball hitter)

	Avg	G	AB	R	H	2B	3B	HR	RBI	BB	SO	HBP	GDP	SB	CS	OBP	SLG	IBB	SH	SF	#Pit	#P/PA	GB	FB	G/F
1992 Season	.274	96	310	49	85	10	1	20	40	55	60	2	8	0	2	.384	.506	2	1	3	1499	4.05	81	122	0.66
Career (1989-1992)	.250	232	723	92	181	29	1	32	78	90	136	3	19	0	4	.334	.426	4	1	4	3209	3.91	198	279	0.71

1992 Season

	Avg	AB	H	2B	3B	HR	RBI	BB	SO	OBP	SLG		Avg	AB	H	2B	3B	HR	RBI	BB	SO	OBP	SLG
vs. Left	.288	80	23	0	0	4	5	16	7	.406	.438	Scoring Posn	.205	73	15	3	0	3	23	16	20	.337	.370
vs. Right	.270	230	62	10	1	16	35	39	53	.376	.530	Close & Late	.205	44	9	1	0	3	8	3	13	.250	.432
Groundball	.365	74	27	1	0	9	16	17	19	.489	.743	None on/out	.295	78	23	2	1	8		9	12	.368	.654
Flyball	.223	94	21	2	0	3	8	11	18	.299	.340	Batting #7	.305	82	25	2	0	3	6	12	11	.402	.439
Home	.274	164	45	6	0	8	20	24	28	.368	.457	Batting #8	.324	111	36	7	0	7	19	15	24	.398	.577
Away	.274	146	40	4	1	12	20	31	32	.400	.562	Other	.205	117	24	1	1	10	15	28	25	.359	.482
Day	.270	89	24	3	0	9	12	13	22	.359	.607	April	.328	64	21	4	0	5	11	10	12	.413	.625
Night	.276	221	61	7	1	11	28	42	38	.393	.466	May	.265	83	22	2	1	5	11	22	13	.419	.494
Grass	.285	263	75	8	1	19	36	46	50	.392	.540	June	.239	46	11	0	0	4	6	9	10	.368	.500
Turf	.213	47	10	2	0	1	4	9	10	.339	.319	July	.000	0	0	0	0	0	0	0	0	.000	.000
First Pitch	.343	35	12	3	0	1	5	1	0	.361	.514	August	.244	41	10	1	0	1	4	6	7	.340	.341
Ahead on Count	.373	67	25	2	1	8	16	26	0	.543	.791	September/October	.276	76	21	3	0	5	8	8	18	.349	.513
Behind on Count	.209	91	19	2	0	6	7	0	27	.226	.429	Pre-All Star	.280	193	54	6	1	14	28	41	35	.405	.539
Two Strikes	.159	145	23	2	0		14	28	60	.297	.338	Post-All Star	.265	117	31	4	0	6	12	14	25	.346	.453

1992 By Position

Position	Avg	AB	H	2B	3B	HR	RBI	BB	SO	OBP	SLG	G	GS	Innings	PO	A	E	DP	Fld Pct	Rng Fctr	In Zone	Zone Outs	Zone Rtg	MLB Zone
As c	.275	306	84	10	1	20	40	55	58	.385	.510	95	93	817.1	500	32	3	7	.994	---	---	---	---	---

Career (1989-1992)

	Avg	AB	H	2B	3B	HR	RBI	BB	SO	OBP	SLG		Avg	AB	H	2B	3B	HR	RBI	BB	SO	OBP	SLG
vs. Left	.242	231	56	6	0	10	13	29	30	.326	.398	Scoring Posn	.210	157	33	7	0	5	49	29	39	.326	.350
vs. Right	.254	492	125	23	1	22	65	61	106	.338	.439	Close & Late	.203	118	24	1	0	9	22	12	30	.275	.441
Groundball	.315	200	63	9	0	15	38	27	39	.397	.585	None on/out	.253	182	46	7	1	13		18	32	.320	.516
Flyball	.186	161	30	3	0	4	10	18	38	.265	.280	Batting #6	.214	112	24	3	0	6	10	25	26	.358	.402
Home	.252	353	89	15	0	14	35	44	60	.338	.414	Batting #8	.264	416	110	22	0	15	42	36	83	.323	.425
Away	.249	370	92	14	1	18	43	46	76	.331	.438	Other	.241	195	47	4	1	11	26	29	27	.342	.441
Day	.225	178	40	6	0	11	24	19	39	.296	.444	April	.257	101	26	5	0	5	11	12	21	.339	.455
Night	.259	545	141	23	1	21	54	71	97	.346	.439	May	.263	133	35	4	1	7	15	33	22	.407	.466
Grass	.250	603	151	22	1	30	64	77	112	.336	.439	June	.223	121	27	4	0	6	16	15	22	.312	.405
Turf	.250	120	30	7	0	2	14	13	24	.323	.358	July	.307	75	23	4	0	3	10	3	12	.333	.480
First Pitch	.302	96	29	6	0	4	13	1	0	.309	.490	August	.230	135	31	6	0	3	11	10	26	.283	.341

Career (1989-1992)																						
	Avg	AB	H	2B	3B	HR	RBI	BB	SO	OBP	SLG		Avg	AB	H	2B	3B	HR	RBI	BB	SO	OBP	SLG
Ahead on Count	.352	165	58	10	1	13	30	43	0	.481	.661	September/October	.247	158	39	6	0	8	15	17	31	.322	.437
Behind on Count	.196	225	44	6	0	8	18	1	71	.210	.329	Pre-All Star	.246	378	93	14	1	19	44	62	68	.353	.439
Two Strikes	.160	331	53	5	0	10	22	46	136	.266	.269	Post-All Star	.255	345	88	15	0	13	34	28	68	.312	.412

Batter vs. Pitcher (career)																						
Hits Best Against	Avg	AB	H	2B	3B	HR	RBI	BB	SO	OBP	SLG	Hits Worst Against	Avg	AB	H	2B	3B	HR	RBI	BB	SO	OBP	SLG
Jim Abbott	.750	8	6	0	0	0	1	2	0	.727	.750	Jack Morris	.091	11	1	0	0	0	0	1	3	.167	.091
Erik Hanson	.400	10	4	2	0	0	1	4	1	.571	.600	Joe Slusarski	.167	12	2	1	0	0	0	1	1	.231	.250
Chuck Finley	.364	11	4	0	0	1	1	0	1	.364	.636	Jimmy Key	.200	10	2	1	0	0	0	2	1	.333	.300
Alex Fernandez	.333	9	3	0	0	0	0	2	1	.455	.333	Greg Harris	.231	13	3	1	0	0	0	2	6	.333	.308
												Jaime Navarro	.231	13	3	1	0	0	0	0	2	.231	.308

Dave Hollins — Phillies   Bats Both

	Avg	G	AB	R	H	2B	3B	HR	RBI	BB	SO	HBP	GDP	SB	CS	OBP	SLG	IBB	SH	SF	#Pit	#P/PA	GB	FB	G/F
1992 Season	.270	156	586	104	158	28	4	27	93	76	110	19	8	9	6	.369	.469	8	0	7	2635	3.85	204	182	1.12
Career (1990-1992)	.263	284	851	136	224	38	6	38	129	103	164	23	11	10	7	.356	.456	8	0	7	3740	3.80	284	271	1.05

1992 Season

	Avg	AB	H	2B	3B	HR	RBI	BB	SO	OBP	SLG		Avg	AB	H	2B	3B	HR	RBI	BB	SO	OBP	SLG
vs. Left	.322	245	79	16	3	17	45	23	44	.391	.620	Scoring Posn	.262	164	43	8	0	4	55	33	29	.393	.384
vs. Right	.232	341	79	12	1	10	48	53	66	.355	.361	Close & Late	.237	97	23	3	1	4	16	8	23	.333	.412
Groundball	.262	263	69	10	1	10	45	31	51	.361	.422	None on/out	.226	115	26	6	0	1	1	10	22	.305	.304
Flyball	.238	130	31	7	2	6	19	20	34	.351	.462	Batting #3	.274	463	127	24	4	20	73	61	91	.376	.473
Home	.265	291	77	19	2	14	48	46	54	.384	.488	Batting #5	.185	81	15	1	0	3	7	9	13	.283	.309
Away	.275	295	81	9	2	13	45	30	56	.354	.451	Other	.381	42	16	3	0	4	13	6	6	.460	.738
Day	.270	159	43	6	2	11	35	20	37	.372	.541	April	.228	79	18	2	0	3	16	12	16	.371	.367
Night	.269	427	115	22	2	16	58	56	73	.368	.443	May	.289	90	26	7	1	3	11	16	16	.409	.489
Grass	.270	152	41	5	1	8	27	13	36	.345	.474	June	.278	108	30	3	1	4	11	11	19	.342	.435
Turf	.270	434	117	23	3	19	66	63	74	.377	.468	July	.264	106	28	6	2	4	19	9	23	.350	.472
First Pitch	.288	73	21	6	1	4	12	4	0	.358	.562	August	.253	95	24	4	0	6	14	14	19	.351	.484
Ahead on Count	.346	136	47	11	1	7	23	43	0	.500	.596	September/October	.296	108	32	6	0	7	22	14	17	.394	.546
Behind on Count	.295	210	62	8	2	12	41	0	55	.324	.524	Pre-All Star	.256	324	83	13	3	11	42	41	62	.359	.417
Two Strikes	.199	272	54	5	0	11	38	29	110	.300	.338	Post-All Star	.286	262	75	15	1	16	51	35	48	.382	.534

1992 By Position

Position	Avg	AB	H	2B	3B	HR	RBI	BB	SO	OBP	SLG	G	GS	Innings	PO	A	E	DP	Fld Pct	Rng Fctr	In Zone	Outs	Zone Rtg	MLB Zone
As 3b	.270	586	158	28	4	27	93	76	110	.369	.469	156	156	1367.2	120	253	18	22	.954	2.45	346	290	.838	.841

Jessie Hollins — Cubs   Pitches Right

	ERA	W	L	Sv	G	GS	IP	BB	SO	Avg	H	2B	3B	HR	RBI	OBP	SLG	GF	IR	IRS	Hld	SvOp	SB	CS	GB	FB	G/F
1992 Season	13.50	0	0	0	4	0	4.2	5	0	.400	8	1	0	1	8	.481	.600	3	2	1	0	0	0	0	9	8	1.13

1992 Season

	ERA	W	L	Sv	G	GS	IP	H	HR	BB	SO		Avg	AB	H	2B	3B	HR	RBI	BB	SO	OBP	SLG
Home	16.88	0	0	0	3	0	2.2	5	0	4	0	vs. Left	.333	9	3	0	0	0	1	2	0	.455	.333
Away	9.00	0	0	0	1	0	2.0	3	1	1	0	vs. Right	.455	11	5	1	0	1	7	3	0	.500	.818

Darren Holmes — Brewers   Pitches Right

	ERA	W	L	Sv	G	GS	IP	BB	SO	Avg	H	2B	3B	HR	RBI	OBP	SLG	GF	IR	IRS	Hld	SvOp	SB	CS	GB	FB	G/F
1992 Season	2.55	4	4	6	41	0	42.1	11	31	.224	36	6	2	1	11	.284	.308	25	35	6	2	8	4	1	56	40	1.40
Career (1990-1992)	4.10	5	9	9	95	0	136.0	49	109	.267	140	24	3	8	68	.330	.370	35	81	23	5	14	9	6	188	145	1.30

1992 Season

	ERA	W	L	Sv	G	GS	IP	H	HR	BB	SO		Avg	AB	H	2B	3B	HR	RBI	BB	SO	OBP	SLG
Home	3.26	3	2	3	20	0	19.1	17	0	3	13	vs. Left	.224	67	15	4	0	0	5	5	11	.278	.284
Away	1.96	1	2	3	21	0	23.0	18	1	8	18	vs. Right	.225	89	20	2	2	1	6	6	20	.289	.326
Starter	0.00	0	0	0	0	0	0.0	0	0	0	0	Scoring Posn	.140	50	7	1	0	0	9	7	11	.259	.160
Reliever	2.55	4	4	6	41	0	42.1	35	1	11	31	Close & Late	.238	80	19	2	2	0	5	10	19	.322	.313
0 Days rest	3.18	1	3	1	10	0	11.1	11	0	6	10	None on/out	.333	33	11	2	1	1	1	2	4	.371	.545
1 or 2 Days rest	3.29	2	1	2	14	0	13.2	10	1	4	12	First Pitch	.370	27	10	1	1	0	3	3	0	.433	.481
3+ Days rest	1.56	1	0	3	17	0	17.1	14	0	1	9	Behind on Count	.296	27	8	2	1	1	3	5	0	.406	.556
Pre-All Star	3.32	2	3	1	20	0	19.0	19	1	7	18	Ahead on Count	.167	78	13	1	0	0	3	0	27	.188	.179
Post-All Star	1.93	2	1	5	21	0	23.1	16	0	4	13	Two Strikes	.151	73	11	3	0	0	2	3	31	.195	.192

Rick Honeycutt — Athletics
Pitches Left (groundball pitcher)

	ERA	W	L	Sv	G	GS	IP	BB	SO	Avg	H	2B	3B	HR	RBI	OBP	SLG	GF	IR	IRS	Hld	SvOp	SB	CS	GB	FB	G/F
1992 Season	3.69	1	4	3	54	0	39.0	10	32	.272	41	5	2	2	26	.327	.371	7	48	14	18	7	4	1	54	34	1.59
Last Five Years	3.07	10	14	29	279	0	296.1	103	195	.235	254	39	6	18	127	.303	.332	27	208	52	102	46	14	8	479	252	1.90

1992 Season

	ERA	W	L	Sv	G	GS	IP	H	HR	BB	SO		Avg	AB	H	2B	3B	HR	RBI	BB	SO	OBP	SLG
Home	3.06	1	2	2	27	0	17.2	14	0	5	13	vs. Left	.258	62	16	2	0	1	9	3	13	.313	.339
Away	4.22	0	2	1	27	0	21.1	27	2	5	19	vs. Right	.281	89	25	3	2	1	17	7	19	.337	.393
Starter	0.00	0	0	0	0	0	0.0	0	0	0	0	Scoring Posn	.255	51	13	3	0	1	24	7	12	.350	.373
Reliever	3.69	1	4	3	54	0	39.0	41	2	10	32	Close & Late	.261	88	23	3	1	2	17	5	18	.305	.386
0 Days rest	0.84	0	2	2	13	0	10.2	8	1	2	7	None on/out	.192	26	5	0	1	0	0	2	9	.276	.269
1 or 2 Days rest	5.40	0	1	1	22	0	15.0	20	1	5	9	First Pitch	.333	21	7	2	0	0	3	3	0	.417	.429
3+ Days rest	4.05	1	1	0	19	0	13.1	13	0	3	16	Behind on Count	.429	35	15	2	0	1	10	5	0	.488	.571
Pre-All Star	2.92	1	2	1	33	0	24.2	22	2	5	20	Ahead on Count	.191	68	13	1	2	1	7	0	28	.214	.309
Post-All Star	5.02	0	2	2	21	0	14.1	19	0	5	12	Two Strikes	.176	68	12	1	2	1	7	2	32	.233	.294

Last Five Years

	ERA	W	L	Sv	G	GS	IP	H	HR	BB	SO		Avg	AB	H	2B	3B	HR	RBI	BB	SO	OBP	SLG
Home	2.40	5	7	16	137	0	142.2	109	6	43	95	vs. Left	.198	389	77	11	1	7	40	33	78	.266	.285
Away	3.69	5	7	13	142	0	153.2	145	12	60	100	vs. Right	.255	693	177	28	5	11	87	70	117	.324	.358
Day	2.35	4	5	11	104	0	122.1	98	11	41	89	Inning 1-6	.258	93	24	3	1	3	26	6	13	.308	.409
Night	3.57	6	9	18	175	0	174.0	156	7	62	106	Inning 7+	.233	989	230	36	5	15	101	97	182	.303	.325
Grass	2.82	9	11	24	234	0	249.1	200	16	87	166	None on	.237	541	128	13	4	8	8	47	96	.304	.320
Turf	4.40	1	3	5	45	0	47.0	54	2	16	29	Runners on	.233	541	126	26	2	10	119	56	99	.303	.344
April	2.08	1	2	5	35	0	47.2	34	3	14	37	Scoring Posn	.227	291	66	9	1	6	107	43	59	.319	.326
May	2.87	3	1	6	40	0	37.2	31	2	12	27	Close & Late	.201	518	104	16	3	6	51	57	99	.280	.278
June	3.25	1	2	5	43	0	55.1	46	5	8	36	None on/out	.249	237	59	9	3	5	5	12	49	.288	.376
July	4.22	3	4	4	58	0	59.2	58	3	27	38	vs. 1st Batr (relief)	.188	250	47	7	2	4	25	14	50	.234	.280
August	3.06	2	3	6	54	0	50.0	43	2	20	33	First Inning Pitched	.234	757	177	27	4	12	94	63	142	.296	.328
September/October	2.54	0	2	3	49	0	46.0	42	3	22	24	First 15 Pitches	.243	753	183	27	4	14	92	57	130	.300	.345
Starter	0.00	0	0	0	0	0	0.0	0	0	0	0	Pitch 16-30	.181	238	43	8	0	2	19	37	48	.292	.239
Reliever	3.07	10	14	29	279	0	296.1	254	18	103	195	Pitch 31-45	.366	71	26	3	2	2	15	7	11	.413	.549
0 Days rest	2.62	2	3	11	56	0	55.0	42	4	17	32	Pitch 46+	.100	20	2	1	0	0	2	1	6	.174	.150
1 or 2 Days rest	3.15	6	8	13	135	0	154.1	141	7	54	96	First Pitch	.269	160	43	9	0	2	15	10	0	.310	.363
3+ Days rest	3.21	2	3	5	88	0	87.0	71	7	32	67	Ahead on Count	.180	494	89	13	4	4	33	0	165	.192	.247
Pre-All Star	3.10	5	8	18	137	0	165.1	133	12	41	121	Behind on Count	.350	214	75	12	1	7	51	51	0	.464	.514
Post-All Star	3.02	5	6	11	142	0	131.0	121	6	62	74	Two Strikes	.158	469	74	8	4	4	30	42	195	.238	.232

Pitcher vs. Batter (since 1984)

Pitches Best Vs.	Avg	AB	H	2B	3B	HR	RBI	BB	SO	OBP	SLG	Pitches Worst Vs.	Avg	AB	H	2B	3B	HR	RBI	BB	SO	OBP	SLG
Lou Whitaker	.000	12	0	0	0	0	0	3	2	.200	.000	Hubie Brooks	.579	19	11	0	0	0	1	2	0	.619	.579
Fred McGriff	.000	12	0	0	0	0	1	0	5	.000	.000	Kevin Mitchell	.538	13	7	2	0	2	3	0	0	.538	1.154
Manuel Lee	.000	11	0	0	0	0	0	2	2	.154	.000	Jack Clark	.500	12	6	0	0	1	3	7	1	.684	.750
Bip Roberts	.000	11	0	0	0	0	0	1	2	.083	.000	Kevin McReynolds	.469	32	15	2	0	1	5	3	3	.514	.625
Ozzie Guillen	.095	21	2	0	0	0	1	0	2	.095	.095	Henry Cotto	.444	9	4	0	0	1	2	1	1	.455	.778

Sam Horn — Orioles
Bats Left (flyball hitter)

	Avg	G	AB	R	H	2B	3B	HR	RBI	BB	SO	HBP	GDP	SB	CS	OBP	SLG	IBB	SH	SF	#Pit	#P/PA	GB	FB	G/F
1992 Season	.235	63	162	13	38	10	1	5	19	20	60	1	8	0	1	.324	.401	2	0	1	740	4.00	38	38	1.00
Last Five Years	.226	320	840	93	190	41	1	44	137	113	257	4	31	0	5	.319	.435	11	0	5	3746	3.89	229	241	0.95

1992 Season

	Avg	AB	H	2B	3B	HR	RBI	BB	SO	OBP	SLG		Avg	AB	H	2B	3B	HR	RBI	BB	SO	OBP	SLG
vs. Left	.000	2	0	0	0	0	0	1	1	.500	.000	Scoring Posn	.171	41	7	3	0	0	10	6	12	.271	.244
vs. Right	.238	160	38	10	1	5	19	20	59	.320	.406	Close & Late	.042	24	1	0	0	0	1	5	11	.233	.042
Home	.235	85	20	2	1	2	9	12	30	.337	.353	None on/out	.262	42	11	2	1	3	3	4	19	.326	.571
Away	.234	77	18	8	0	3	10	9	30	.310	.455	Batting #4	.244	135	33	9	1	5	16	16	49	.327	.437
First Pitch	.192	26	5	2	0	2	4	1	0	.222	.500	Batting #9	.125	8	1	0	0	0	1	3	5	.364	.125
Ahead on Count	.417	24	10	1	0	3	6	9	0	.576	.833	Other	.211	19	4	1	0	0	2	2	6	.286	.263
Behind on Count	.200	50	10	1	1	1	4	0	26	.196	.320	Pre-All Star	.255	137	35	10	1	5	18	18	52	.346	.453
Two Strikes	.170	94	16	6	1	0	6	11	60	.255	.255	Post-All Star	.120	25	3	0	0	0	1	3	8	.207	.120

Last Five Years

	Avg	AB	H	2B	3B	HR	RBI	BB	SO	OBP	SLG		Avg	AB	H	2B	3B	HR	RBI	BB	SO	OBP	SLG
vs. Left	.087	46	4	0	0	1	1	3	19	.160	.152	Scoring Posn	.232	228	53	14	0	13	91	38	68	.338	.465
vs. Right	.234	794	186	41	1	43	136	110	238	.328	.451	Close & Late	.213	141	30	6	0	5	27	20	46	.317	.362
Groundball	.246	252	62	11	0	14	41	37	67	.344	.456	None on/out	.209	211	44	8	1	11	11	16	66	.264	.412
Flyball	.259	174	45	12	1	10	31	25	59	.353	.511	Batting #4	.232	466	108	31	1	21	69	54	137	.314	.438
Home	.230	434	100	18	1	24	67	68	133	.337	.442	Batting #6	.211	161	34	2	0	11	29	23	55	.306	.420
Away	.222	406	90	23	0	20	70	45	124	.300	.426	Other	.225	213	48	8	0	12	39	36	65	.339	.432
Day	.215	256	55	10	1	13	42	31	77	.304	.414	April	.239	159	38	5	0	6	30	25	57	.341	.384
Night	.231	584	135	31	0	31	95	82	180	.325	.443	May	.189	185	35	6	1	8	22	21	61	.275	.362
Grass	.227	715	162	34	1	39	117	96	222	.319	.441	June	.268	123	33	14	0	6	17	21	35	.379	.528

Last Five Years

	Avg	AB	H	2B	3B	HR	RBI	BB	SO	OBP	SLG		Avg	AB	H	2B	3B	HR	RBI	BB	SO	OBP	SLG
Turf	.224	125	28	7	0	5	20	17	35	.322	.400	July	.224	125	28	4	0	10	23	20	38	.327	.496
First Pitch	.258	128	33	7	0	9	25	5	0	.286	.523	August	.170	106	18	4	0	3	9	16	22	.279	.292
Ahead on Count	.348	141	49	12	0	15	37	56	0	.525	.752	September/October	.268	142	38	8	0	11	36	10	44	.320	.556
Behind on Count	.196	280	55	8	1	13	44	1	124	.201	.371	Pre-All Star	.230	513	118	26	1	25	80	70	168	.325	.431
Two Strikes	.145	447	65	15	1	13	47	51	257	.235	.271	Post-All Star	.220	327	72	15	0	19	57	43	89	.310	.440

Batter vs. Pitcher (career)

Hits Best Against	Avg	AB	H	2B	3B	HR	RBI	BB	SO	OBP	SLG	Hits Worst Against	Avg	AB	H	2B	3B	HR	RBI	BB	SO	OBP	SLG
Bill Wegman	.500	16	8	2	0	2	4	2	0	.556	1.000	Erik Hanson	.000	21	0	0	0	0	0	2	8	.087	.000
Bret Saberhagen	.421	19	8	1	0	4	9	0	7	.421	1.105	Bobby Witt	.000	10	0	0	0	0	1	2	7	.154	.000
Rich DeLucia	.375	8	3	0	0	1	2	5	2	.615	.750	Mike Gardiner	.000	10	0	0	0	0	0	2	2	.167	.000
Bill Gullickson	.353	17	6	2	0	2	3	1	5	.389	.824	Bert Blyleven	.077	13	1	1	0	0	0	0	4	.077	.154
Eric King	.333	9	3	0	0	2	4	2	1	.455	1.000	Alex Fernandez	.100	10	1	0	0	0	0	1	3	.182	.100

Vince Horsman — Athletics   Pitches Left

	ERA	W	L	Sv	G	GS	IP	BB	SO	Avg	H	2B	3B	HR	RBI	OBP	SLG	GF	IR	IRS	Hld	SvOp	SB	CS	GB	FB	G/F
1992 Season	2.49	2	1	1	58	0	43.1	21	18	.252	39	4	0	3	17	.339	.335	9	48	11	10	2	0	2	63	50	1.26
Career (1991-1992)	2.28	2	1	1	62	0	47.1	24	20	.246	41	4	0	3	19	.339	.323	11	54	13	11	2	0	2	66	54	1.22

1992 Season

	ERA	W	L	Sv	G	GS	IP	H	HR	BB	SO		Avg	AB	H	2B	3B	HR	RBI	BB	SO	OBP	SLG
Home	3.25	0	1	0	37	0	27.2	23	3	13	10	vs. Left	.203	74	15	0	0	1	11	11	9	.302	.243
Away	1.15	2	0	1	21	0	15.2	16	0	8	8	vs. Right	.296	81	24	4	0	2	6	10	9	.374	.420
Starter	0.00	0	0	0	0	0	0.0	0	0	0	0	Scoring Posn	.217	46	10	0	0	2	16	7	8	.315	.348
Reliever	2.49	2	1	1	58	0	43.1	39	3	21	18	Close & Late	.138	29	4	0	0	0	2	5	5	.257	.138
0 Days rest	2.70	2	1	0	15	0	6.2	9	1	4	2	None on/out	.344	32	11	1	0	1	1	2	2	.382	.469
1 or 2 Days rest	2.53	0	0	1	23	0	21.1	16	2	10	11	First Pitch	.200	15	3	0	0	0	0	3	0	.333	.200
3+ Days rest	2.35	0	0	0	20	0	15.1	14	0	7	5	Behind on Count	.213	47	10	1	0	1	4	10	0	.345	.298
Pre-All Star	2.25	2	0	1	33	0	28.0	28	3	10	13	Ahead on Count	.240	50	12	1	0	1	6	0	10	.240	.320
Post-All Star	2.93	0	1	0	25	0	15.1	11	0	11	5	Two Strikes	.186	59	11	1	0	2	9	8	18	.284	.305

Steve Hosey — Giants   Bats Right

	Avg	G	AB	R	H	2B	3B	HR	RBI	BB	SO	HBP	GDP	SB	CS	OBP	SLG	IBB	SH	SF	#Pit	#P/PA	GB	FB	G/F
1992 Season	.250	21	56	6	14	1	0	1	6	0	15	0	1	1	1	.241	.321	0	0	2	238	4.10	17	15	1.13

1992 Season

	Avg	AB	H	2B	3B	HR	RBI	BB	SO	OBP	SLG		Avg	AB	H	2B	3B	HR	RBI	BB	SO	OBP	SLG
vs. Left	.276	29	8	0	0	1	3	0	8	.267	.379	Scoring Posn	.286	14	4	1	0	0	5	0	3	.250	.357
vs. Right	.222	27	6	1	0	0	3	0	7	.214	.259	Close & Late	.091	11	1	0	0	0	0	0	0	.091	.091

Charlie Hough — White Sox   Pitches Right

	ERA	W	L	Sv	G	GS	IP	BB	SO	Avg	H	2B	3B	HR	RBI	OBP	SLG	CG	ShO	Sup	QS	#P/S	SB	CS	GB	FB	G/F
1992 Season	3.93	7	12	0	27	27	176.1	66	76	.239	160	25	4	19	74	.311	.373	4	0	3.73	15	102	17	3	236	224	1.05
Last Five Years	3.90	53	63	0	154	152	1028.1	500	565	.233	887	141	22	112	433	.326	.370	28	2	4.05	83	108	117	39	1402	1246	1.13

1992 Season

	ERA	W	L	Sv	G	GS	IP	H	HR	BB	SO		Avg	AB	H	2B	3B	HR	RBI	BB	SO	OBP	SLG
Home	3.49	6	4	0	15	15	100.2	91	8	30	40	vs. Left	.236	267	63	10	0	7	22	26	25	.304	.352
Away	4.52	1	8	0	12	12	75.2	69	11	36	36	vs. Right	.241	403	97	15	4	12	52	40	51	.316	.387
Day	3.45	1	1	0	7	7	44.1	32	6	14	18	Inning 1-6	.232	548	127	18	4	13	56	56	64	.306	.350
Night	4.09	6	11	0	20	20	132.0	128	13	52	58	Inning 7+	.270	122	33	7	0	6	18	10	12	.333	.475
Grass	3.94	7	8	0	21	21	141.2	132	15	47	60	Runners on	.224	410	92	18	0	11	11	36	48	.295	.349
Turf	3.89	0	4	0	6	6	34.2	28	4	19	16	Scoring Posn	.262	260	68	7	4	8	63	30	28	.336	.412
April	6.43	0	1	0	2	2	14.0	20	2	3	4	Close & Late	.266	64	17	4	0	3	9	7	6	.351	.469
May	3.38	1	1	0	5	5	26.2	17	3	14	7	None on/out	.203	177	36	9	0	2		9	23	.246	.288
June	2.31	3	2	0	5	5	39.0	24	3	17	17	vs. 1st Batr (relief)	.000	0	0	0	0	0	0	0	0	.000	.000
July	3.18	0	3	0	5	5	39.2	30	4	18	16	First Inning Pitched	.265	102	27	3	1	1	18	22	14	.391	.343
August	6.23	2	4	0	6	6	34.2	46	5	9	20	First 75 Pitches	.234	441	103	14	3	10	48	48	53	.313	.347
September/October	3.63	1	1	0	4	4	22.1	23	2	5	12	Pitch 76-90	.286	91	26	7	0	2	7	7	5	.333	.429
Starter	3.93	7	12	0	27	27	176.1	160	19	66	76	Pitch 91-105	.152	66	10	2	0	0	3	6	11	.233	.182
Reliever	0.00	0	0	0	0	0	0.0	0	0	0	0	Pitch 106+	.292	72	21	2	1	7	16	5	7	.346	.639
0-3 Days Rest	0.00	0	0	0	0	0	0.0	0	0	0	0	First Pitch	.264	91	24	5	0	3	7	1	0	.289	.418
4 Days Rest	3.81	3	8	0	16	16	104.0	90	11	44	55	Ahead on Count	.221	276	61	8	3	6	30	0	60	.226	.337
5+ Days Rest	4.11	4	4	0	11	11	72.1	70	8	22	21	Behind on Count	.252	163	41	7	0	7	23	43	0	.405	.423
Pre-All Star	3.29	4	5	0	14	14	95.2	72	10	42	36	Two Strikes	.215	279	60	7	3	6	28	22	76	.275	.326
Post-All Star	4.69	3	7	0	13	13	80.2	88	9	24	40												

Last Five Years

	ERA	W	L	Sv	G	GS	IP	H	HR	BB	SO		Avg	AB	H	2B	3B	HR	RBI	BB	SO	OBP	SLG
Home	3.90	30	31	0	75	75	509.2	452	58	227	274	vs. Left	.233	1757	410	64	10	40	180	234	249	.325	.349
Away	3.90	23	32	0	79	77	518.2	435	54	273	291	vs. Right	.233	2047	477	77	12	72	253	266	316	.327	.388

Last Five Years

	ERA	W	L	Sv	G	GS	IP	H	HR	BB	SO		Avg	AB	H	2B	3B	HR	RBI	BB	SO	OBP	SLG
Day	3.48	13	12	0	38	36	253.1	195	23	120	147	Inning 1-6	.232	3091	718	118	18	89	369	416	467	.327	.368
Night	4.04	40	51	0	116	116	775.0	692	89	380	418	Inning 7+	.237	713	169	23	4	23	64	84	98	.321	.377
Grass	3.84	48	47	0	125	123	841.2	720	94	406	465	None on	.228	2294	522	94	7	74	74	272	348	.316	.371
Turf	4.19	5	16	0	29	29	186.2	167	18	94	100	Runners on	.242	1510	365	47	15	38	359	228	217	.341	.368
April	3.97	6	8	0	19	18	124.2	106	16	65	76	Scoring Posn	.230	844	194	24	8	17	304	165	139	.347	.338
May	4.87	8	10	0	26	25	153.1	149	15	84	80	Close & Late	.250	344	86	13	1	12	35	55	51	.356	.398
June	2.97	15	9	0	29	29	221.1	155	29	98	127	None on/out	.226	1011	228	42	4	29	29	101	133	.302	.361
July	3.82	2	16	0	25	25	172.0	145	22	88	90	vs. 1st Batr (relief)	.000	2	0	0	0	0	0	0	1	.000	.000
August	4.63	12	11	0	28	28	179.0	174	17	93	101	First Inning Pitched	.232	560	130	24	2	13	84	100	105	.352	.352
September/October	3.54	10	9	0	27	27	178.0	158	13	72	91	First 75 Pitches	.236	2518	593	98	15	73	307	321	399	.326	.373
Starter	3.89	53	63	0	152	152	1022.2	883	112	495	560	Pitch 76-90	.240	488	117	21	2	11	40	58	60	.323	.359
Reliever	6.35	0	0	0	2	0	5.2	4	0	5	5	Pitch 91-105	.203	379	77	8	2	6	31	66	41	.323	.282
0-3 Days Rest	3.12	3	3	0	6	6	43.1	37	5	18	24	Pitch 106+	.239	419	100	14	3	22	55	55	65	.333	.444
4 Days Rest	3.73	31	35	0	84	84	559.2	469	57	283	335	First Pitch	.286	504	144	22	0	12	64	4	0	.303	.401
5+ Days Rest	4.18	19	25	0	62	62	419.2	377	50	194	201	Ahead on Count	.184	1590	292	44	11	32	142	0	446	.188	.286
Pre-All Star	3.90	29	33	0	82	80	552.0	450	68	279	313	Behind on Count	.292	918	268	49	6	44	132	309	0	.470	.502
Post-All Star	3.91	24	30	0	72	72	476.1	437	44	221	252	Two Strikes	.178	1615	288	41	8	32	146	185	564	.266	.273

Pitcher vs. Batter (since 1984)

Pitches Best Vs.	Avg	AB	H	2B	3B	HR	RBI	BB	SO	OBP	SLG	Pitches Worst Vs.	Avg	AB	H	2B	3B	HR	RBI	BB	SO	OBP	SLG
Roberto Alomar	.063	16	1	0	0	0	2	2	1	.158	.063	Cecil Fielder	.545	11	6	3	0	0	4	2	1	.571	.818
Felix Fermin	.067	15	1	1	0	0	0	1	1	.125	.133	Darnell Coles	.462	13	6	1	0	1	6	3	1	.529	.769
Don Slaught	.091	11	1	0	0	0	0	1	2	.167	.091	Junior Felix	.444	9	4	2	0	1	1	3	1	.583	1.000
Luis Polonia	.115	26	3	0	0	0	1	1	2	.148	.115	Rob Deer	.429	14	6	0	0	2	9	3	3	.529	.857
Gary Pettis	.143	28	4	1	0	0	1	0	7	.143	.179	Juan Gonzalez	.333	12	4	1	0	2	4	1	2	.385	.917

Dave Howard — Royals
Bats Both

	Avg	G	AB	R	H	2B	3B	HR	RBI	BB	SO	HBP	GDP	SB	CS	OBP	SLG	IBB	SH	SF	#Pit	#P/PA	GB	FB	G/F
1992 Season	.224	74	219	19	49	6	2	1	18	15	43	0	3	3	4	.271	.283	0	8	2	859	3.64	72	61	1.18
Career (1991-1992)	.220	168	455	39	100	13	2	2	35	31	88	1	4	6	6	.269	.270	0	17	4	1811	3.69	154	124	1.24

1992 Season

	Avg	AB	H	2B	3B	HR	RBI	BB	SO	OBP	SLG		Avg	AB	H	2B	3B	HR	RBI	BB	SO	OBP	SLG
vs. Left	.208	72	15	2	1	0	2	2	15	.230	.264	Scoring Posn	.245	53	13	0	0	1	17	5	8	.300	.302
vs. Right	.231	147	34	4	1	1	16	13	28	.290	.293	Close & Late	.243	37	9	3	0	1	4	3	7	.300	.405
Home	.238	122	29	3	1	1	14	10	27	.293	.303	None on/out	.250	56	14	1	2	0	0	3	12	.288	.339
Away	.206	97	20	3	1	0	4	5	16	.243	.258	Batting #8	.146	48	7	0	0	1	6	5	10	.226	.208
First Pitch	.213	47	10	0	0	0	6	0	0	.208	.213	Batting #9	.247	170	42	6	2	0	12	10	32	.286	.306
Ahead on Count	.333	36	12	2	1	1	5	7	0	.432	.528	Other	.000	1	0	0	0	0	0	0	1	.000	.000
Behind on Count	.147	68	10	1	0	0	3	0	25	.145	.162	Pre-All Star	.077	26	2	0	0	0	3	3	6	.172	.077
Two Strikes	.168	101	17	2	1	0	2	8	43	.229	.208	Post-All Star	.244	193	47	6	2	1	15	12	37	.285	.311

Thomas Howard — Indians
Bats Both (groundball hitter)

	Avg	G	AB	R	H	2B	3B	HR	RBI	BB	SO	HBP	GDP	SB	CS	OBP	SLG	IBB	SH	SF	#Pit	#P/PA	GB	FB	G/F
1992 Season	.277	122	361	37	100	15	2	2	32	17	60	0	4	15	8	.308	.346	1	11	2	1334	3.51	148	80	1.85
Career (1990-1992)	.265	248	686	71	182	29	5	6	54	41	128	1	9	25	16	.306	.348	5	14	3	2596	3.55	278	142	1.96

1992 Season

	Avg	AB	H	2B	3B	HR	RBI	BB	SO	OBP	SLG		Avg	AB	H	2B	3B	HR	RBI	BB	SO	OBP	SLG
vs. Left	.288	104	30	3	0	2	11	6	21	.327	.375	Scoring Posn	.306	85	26	2	0	0	27	5	16	.337	.329
vs. Right	.272	257	70	12	2	0	21	11	39	.300	.335	Close & Late	.280	75	21	4	0	1	9	3	9	.304	.373
Groundball	.360	75	27	2	2	0	12	3	3	.385	.440	None on/out	.261	88	23	4	0	0	0	5	16	.301	.307
Flyball	.260	96	25	5	0	0	6	4	20	.287	.313	Batting #1	.244	90	22	4	1	1	7	4	15	.277	.344
Home	.271	181	49	5	2	1	18	9	31	.304	.337	Batting #2	.296	233	69	11	1	1	24	9	40	.320	.365
Away	.283	180	51	10	0	1	14	8	29	.312	.356	Other	.237	38	9	0	0	0	1	4	5	.310	.237
Day	.280	125	35	6	0	1	8	8	16	.323	.352	April	.353	51	18	2	0	0	2	3	7	.389	.392
Night	.275	236	65	9	2	1	24	9	44	.300	.343	May	.246	65	16	2	1	0	4	0	11	.242	.308
Grass	.277	310	86	13	2	1	28	17	50	.313	.342	June	.274	73	20	4	0	0	7	4	8	.308	.329
Turf	.275	51	14	2	0	1	4	0	10	.275	.373	July	.286	35	10	0	0	1	5	3	7	.342	.371
First Pitch	.462	65	30	6	1	2	11	1	0	.463	.677	August	.333	78	26	4	1	0	9	3	14	.358	.410
Ahead on Count	.323	65	21	1	1	0	4	7	0	.389	.369	September/October	.169	59	10	3	0	1	5	4	13	.222	.271
Behind on Count	.193	135	26	3	0	0	12	0	38	.191	.215	Pre-All Star	.284	201	57	8	1	0	14	10	27	.315	.333
Two Strikes	.164	159	26	0	0	0	10	8	60	.199	.176	Post-All Star	.269	160	43	7	1	2	18	7	33	.299	.363

1992 By Position

Position	Avg	AB	H	2B	3B	HR	RBI	BB	SO	OBP	SLG	G	GS	Innings	PO	A	E	DP	Fld Pct	Rng Fctr	In Zone	Outs	Zone Rtg	MLB Zone
As Pinch Hitter	.318	22	7	1	0	0	2	0	3	.318	.364	24	0	---	---	---	---	---	---	---	---	---	---	---
As lf	.293	198	58	8	1	1	22	10	35	.325	.359	68	46	453.0	115	3	2	0	.983	2.34	119	106	.891	.809
As cf	.221	86	19	3	1	1	6	4	15	.256	.314	22	18	177.2	44	1	0	0	1.000	2.28	53	44	.830	.824
As rf	.327	49	16	3	0	0	2	3	7	.358	.388	13	12	106.0	26	0	0	0	1.000	2.29	31	25	.806	.814

Career (1990-1992)

	Avg	AB	H	2B	3B	HR	RBI	BB	SO	OBP	SLG		Avg	AB	H	2B	3B	HR	RBI	BB	SO	OBP	SLG
vs. Left	.277	148	41	3	1	3	13	11	32	.327	.372	Scoring Posn	.279	165	46	5	0	2	46	16	42	.337	.345
vs. Right	.262	538	141	26	4	3	41	30	96	.301	.342	Close & Late	.238	147	35	6	0	2	16	7	24	.271	.320
Groundball	.299	201	60	5	4	1	24	13	24	.344	.378	None on/out	.237	186	44	9	1	0	0	9	33	.272	.296
Flyball	.238	164	39	8	1	2	9	7	34	.267	.335	Batting #1	.259	205	53	11	2	1	10	10	36	.293	.346
Home	.268	343	92	9	3	5	32	20	66	.310	.356	Batting #2	.295	254	75	12	1	1	24	10	45	.320	.362
Away	.262	343	90	20	2	1	22	21	62	.303	.341	Other	.238	227	54	6	2	4	20	21	47	.304	.335
Day	.279	222	62	10	1	3	14	15	31	.328	.374	April	.346	52	18	2	0	0	2	3	7	.382	.385
Night	.259	464	120	19	4	3	40	26	97	.296	.336	May	.234	107	25	3	2	0	6	3	21	.250	.299
Grass	.269	542	146	22	4	5	46	31	99	.309	.352	June	.285	151	43	7	1	1	13	11	15	.335	.364
Turf	.250	144	36	7	1	1	8	10	29	.297	.333	July	.258	128	33	4	0	1	5	11	30	.317	.313
First Pitch	.470	115	54	8	1	3	16	1	0	.488	.635	August	.282	124	35	7	1	1	14	4	24	.305	.379
Ahead on Count	.302	126	38	6	1	2	12	12	0	.362	.413	September/October	.226	124	28	6	1	3	14	9	31	.278	.363
Behind on Count	.204	270	55	7	1	2	22	0	77	.205	.259	Pre-All Star	.273	355	97	12	3	1	22	22	53	.315	.332
Two Strikes	.160	312	50	6	1	0	15	23	128	.217	.186	Post-All Star	.257	331	85	17	2	5	32	19	75	.297	.366

Batter vs. Pitcher (career)

Hits Best Against	Avg	AB	H	2B	3B	HR	RBI	BB	SO	OBP	SLG	Hits Worst Against	Avg	AB	H	2B	3B	HR	RBI	BB	SO	OBP	SLG
Les Lancaster	.545	11	6	4	0	1	3	0	2	.545	1.182	Dwight Gooden	.200	10	2	0	0	0	0	1	3	.273	.200
John Smiley	.417	12	5	1	0	1	3	0	4	.417	.750												
Bob Tewksbury	.333	12	4	1	0	0	1	1	1	.385	.417												

Steve Howe — Yankees   Pitches Left (groundball pitcher)

	ERA	W	L	Sv	G	GS	IP	BB	SO	Avg	H	2B	3B	HR	RBI	OBP	SLG	GF	IR	IRS	Hld	SvOp	SB	CS	GB	FB	G/F
1992 Season	2.45	3	0	6	20	0	22.0	3	12	.122	9	0	0	1	7	.154	.162	10	24	5	5	7	0	0	36	21	1.71
Last Five Years	1.92	6	1	9	57	0	70.1	10	46	.192	48	8	0	2	18	.230	.248	20	67	16	12	10	1	0	104	67	1.55

1992 Season

	ERA	W	L	Sv	G	GS	IP	H	HR	BB	SO		Avg	AB	H	2B	3B	HR	RBI	BB	SO	OBP	SLG
Home	3.14	1	0	4	12	0	14.1	7	1	1	6	vs. Left	.200	20	4	0	0	0	2	0	0	.200	.200
Away	1.17	2	0	2	8	0	7.2	2	0	2	6	vs. Right	.093	54	5	0	0	1	5	3	12	.138	.148
Starter	0.00	0	0	0	0	0	0.0	0	0	0	0	Scoring Posn	.250	16	4	0	0	0	5	2	2	.316	.250
Reliever	2.45	3	0	6	20	0	22.0	9	1	3	12	Close & Late	.141	64	9	0	0	1	7	3	11	.176	.188
0 Days rest	1.17	0	0	2	5	0	7.2	2	1	0	6	None on/out	.000	16	0	0	0	0	0	0	0	.000	.000
1 or 2 Days rest	5.68	1	0	2	8	0	6.1	5	0	1	3	First Pitch	.231	13	3	0	0	0	0	1	0	.286	.231
3+ Days rest	1.13	2	0	2	7	0	8.0	2	0	2	3	Behind on Count	.077	13	1	0	0	0	2	1	0	.143	.077
Pre-All Star	2.45	3	0	6	20	0	22.0	9	1	3	12	Ahead on Count	.081	37	3	0	0	0	3	0	12	.079	.081
Post-All Star	0.00	0	0	0	0	0	0.0	0	0	0	0	Two Strikes	.061	33	2	0	0	0	2	1	12	.086	.061

Jay Howell — Dodgers   Pitches Right

	ERA	W	L	Sv	G	GS	IP	BB	SO	Avg	H	2B	3B	HR	RBI	OBP	SLG	GF	IR	IRS	Hld	SvOp	SB	CS	GB	FB	G/F
1992 Season	1.54	1	3	4	41	0	46.2	18	36	.230	41	3	0	2	14	.303	.281	26	18	7	5	6	7	1	61	51	1.20
Last Five Years	2.07	22	19	85	236	0	308.1	92	260	.216	243	37	5	14	102	.279	.296	96	127	46	10	107	30	6	347	336	1.03

1992 Season

	ERA	W	L	Sv	G	GS	IP	H	HR	BB	SO		Avg	AB	H	2B	3B	HR	RBI	BB	SO	OBP	SLG
Home	1.57	1	2	0	19	0	23.0	19	0	8	19	vs. Left	.242	91	22	2	0	2	7	8	19	.310	.330
Away	1.52	0	1	4	22	0	23.2	22	2	10	17	vs. Right	.218	87	19	1	0	0	7	10	17	.296	.230
Starter	0.00	0	0	0	0	0	0.0	0	0	0	0	Scoring Posn	.233	43	10	0	0	0	12	8	9	.346	.233
Reliever	1.54	1	3	4	41	0	46.2	41	2	18	36	Close & Late	.295	88	26	2	0	0	10	10	20	.370	.318
0 Days rest	1.35	1	0	1	6	0	6.2	4	0	1	6	None on/out	.250	44	11	1	0	1	1	2	9	.283	.341
1 or 2 Days rest	1.61	0	2	2	19	0	22.1	22	1	12	17	First Pitch	.292	24	7	1	0	0	2	3	0	.370	.333
3+ Days rest	1.53	0	1	1	16	0	17.2	15	1	5	13	Behind on Count	.281	32	9	1	0	0	0	7	0	.410	.313
Pre-All Star	1.29	0	0	0	18	0	21.0	15	0	11	16	Ahead on Count	.200	90	18	1	0	1	6	0	34	.209	.244
Post-All Star	1.75	1	3	4	23	0	25.2	26	2	7	20	Two Strikes	.205	88	18	1	0	2	6	8	36	.271	.284

Last Five Years

	ERA	W	L	Sv	G	GS	IP	H	HR	BB	SO		Avg	AB	H	2B	3B	HR	RBI	BB	SO	OBP	SLG
Home	1.98	15	10	40	118	0	163.1	122	5	43	144	vs. Left	.208	621	129	22	3	8	58	54	150	.275	.291
Away	2.17	7	9	45	118	0	145.0	121	9	49	116	vs. Right	.227	502	114	15	2	6	44	38	110	.284	.301
Day	1.40	4	5	31	76	0	96.2	69	4	27	80	Inning 1-6	.111	9	1	0	0	0	1	2	1	.273	.111
Night	2.38	18	14	54	160	0	211.2	174	10	65	180	Inning 7+	.217	1114	242	37	5	14	101	90	259	.279	.297
Grass	2.03	18	12	66	176	0	230.2	180	7	65	205	None on	.210	639	134	23	1	11	11	36	143	.262	.300
Turf	2.20	4	7	19	60	0	77.2	63	7	27	55	Runners on	.225	484	109	14	4	3	91	54	117	.301	.289
April	1.65	3	3	5	23	0	32.2	28	0	11	26	Scoring Posn	.227	308	70	7	4	2	86	38	77	.309	.295
May	2.50	2	5	17	39	0	50.1	46	2	19	36	Close & Late	.228	654	149	17	4	8	67	62	148	.300	.303
June	1.76	4	3	15	50	0	66.2	48	3	20	59	None on/out	.243	276	67	9	1	8	8	13	58	.282	.317
July	1.43	3	1	15	38	0	50.1	36	2	14	44	vs. 1st Batr (relief)	.235	217	51	8	1	6	20	16	50	.294	.364
August	1.86	5	6	19	51	0	67.2	49	4	15	57	First Inning Pitched	.210	777	163	25	4	10	81	63	174	.273	.291
September/October	3.54	5	1	14	35	0	40.2	36	3	13	39	First 15 Pitches	.219	734	161	24	3	12	69	53	154	.277	.309
Starter	0.00	0	0	0	0	0	0.0	0	0	0	0	Pitch 16-30	.209	330	69	10	2	2	30	35	90	.285	.270
Reliever	2.07	22	19	85	236	0	308.1	243	14	92	260	Pitch 31-45	.228	57	13	3	0	0	3	4	14	.266	.281

Last Five Years

	ERA	W	L	Sv	G	GS	IP	H	HR	BB	SO		Avg	AB	H	2B	3B	HR	RBI	BB	SO	OBP	SLG
0 Days rest	2.51	7	6	18	48	0	57.1	43	2	16	49	Pitch 46+	.000	2	0	0	0	0	0	0	0	.000	.000
1 or 2 Days rest	1.64	9	6	38	101	0	137.1	108	5	42	122	First Pitch	.297	165	49	8	1	2	26	14	3	.348	.394
3+ Days rest	2.38	6	7	29	87	0	113.2	92	7	34	89	Ahead on Count	.183	562	103	13	2	4	32	0	225	.193	.235
Pre-All Star	2.02	9	11	38	122	0	160.2	135	5	53	131	Behind on Count	.254	201	51	9	2	6	24	43	0	.385	.408
Post-All Star	2.13	13	8	47	114	0	147.2	108	9	39	129	Two Strikes	.164	567	93	11	2	4	31	34	257	.213	.212

Pitcher vs. Batter (since 1984)

Pitches Best Vs.	Avg	AB	H	2B	3B	HR	RBI	BB	SO	OBP	SLG	Pitches Worst Vs.	Avg	AB	H	2B	3B	HR	RBI	BB	SO	OBP	SLG
Andre Dawson	.091	11	1	0	0	0	0	0	2	.091	.091	Paul O'Neill	.727	11	8	2	1	2	10	2	1	.769	1.636
Tom Brunansky	.100	10	1	0	0	0	1	1	1	.182	.100	Mike Pagliarulo	.385	13	5	2	0	0	3	1	3	.429	.538
Robby Thompson	.125	16	2	0	0	0	2	0	9	.125	.125	Matt D. Williams	.385	13	5	3	0	0	2	0	4	.385	.615
Ken Caminiti	.125	16	2	0	0	0	0	0	6	.125	.125	Brian Downing	.357	14	5	0	0	2	4	1	0	.400	.786
Cal Ripken	.143	14	2	0	0	0	1	0	2	.143	.143	Dale Murphy	.308	13	4	1	0	1	2	1	3	.357	.615

Pat Howell — Mets   Bats Both (groundball hitter)

	Avg	G	AB	R	H	2B	3B	HR	RBI	BB	SO	HBP	GDP	SB	CS	OBP	SLG	IBB	SH	SF	#Pit	#P/PA	GB	FB	G/F
1992 Season	.187	31	75	9	14	1	0	0	1	2	15	1	0	4	2	.218	.200	0	1	0	254	3.26	32	11	2.91

1992 Season

	Avg	AB	H	2B	3B	HR	RBI	BB	SO	OBP	SLG		Avg	AB	H	2B	3B	HR	RBI	BB	SO	OBP	SLG
vs. Left	.219	32	7	1	0	0	1	1	9	.242	.250	Scoring Posn	.083	12	1	0	0	0	1	1	3	.214	.083
vs. Right	.163	43	7	0	0	0	1	6		.200	.163	Close & Late	.143	7	1	0	0	0	0	2		.143	.143

Dann Howitt — Mariners   Bats Left

	Avg	G	AB	R	H	2B	3B	HR	RBI	BB	SO	HBP	GDP	SB	CS	OBP	SLG	IBB	SH	SF	#Pit	#P/PA	GB	FB	G/F
1992 Season	.188	35	85	7	16	4	1	2	10	8	9	0	6	1	1	.250	.329	1	1	3	367	3.82	35	31	1.13
Career (1989-1992)	.171	73	152	15	26	5	2	3	14	12	35	0	7	1	1	.226	.289	1	1	4	640	3.81	54	46	1.17

1992 Season

	Avg	AB	H	2B	3B	HR	RBI	BB	SO	OBP	SLG		Avg	AB	H	2B	3B	HR	RBI	BB	SO	OBP	SLG
vs. Left	.000	7	0	0	0	0	0	1	2	.125	.000	Scoring Posn	.143	21	3	1	0	1	8	1	3	.160	.333
vs. Right	.205	78	16	4	1	2	10	7	7	.261	.359	Close & Late	.222	9	2	0	0	0	1	1		.273	.222

Peter Hoy — Red Sox   Pitches Right (groundball pitcher)

	ERA	W	L	Sv	G	GS	IP	BB	SO	Avg	H	2B	3B	HR	RBI	OBP	SLG	GF	IR	IRS	Hld	SvOp	SB	CS	GB	FB	G/F
1992 Season	7.36	0	0	0	5	0	3.2	2	2	.471	8	2	0	0	5	.526	.588	2	4	3	1	1	2	0	6	3	2.00

1992 Season

	ERA	W	L	Sv	G	GS	IP	H	HR	BB	SO		Avg	AB	H	2B	3B	HR	RBI	BB	SO	OBP	SLG
Home	54.00	0	0	0	2	0	0.1	4	0	0	1	vs. Left	.600	5	3	2	0	0	3	2	0	.714	1.000
Away	2.70	0	0	0	3	0	3.1	4	0	2	1	vs. Right	.417	12	5	0	0	0	2	0	2	.417	.417

Kent Hrbek — Twins   Bats Left

	Avg	G	AB	R	H	2B	3B	HR	RBI	BB	SO	HBP	GDP	SB	CS	OBP	SLG	IBB	SH	SF	#Pit	#P/PA	GB	FB	G/F
1992 Season	.244	112	394	52	96	20	0	15	58	71	56	0	13	5	2	.357	.409	9	2	3	1671	3.57	156	120	1.30
Last Five Years	.282	639	2233	319	629	114	1	107	386	327	238	8	61	17	11	.372	.477	32	10	24	8886	3.43	869	748	1.16

1992 Season

	Avg	AB	H	2B	3B	HR	RBI	BB	SO	OBP	SLG		Avg	AB	H	2B	3B	HR	RBI	BB	SO	OBP	SLG
vs. Left	.265	83	22	5	0	1	9	7	14	.319	.361	Scoring Posn	.210	124	26	7	0	3	42	36	16	.380	.339
vs. Right	.238	311	74	15	0	14	49	64	42	.366	.421	Close & Late	.250	64	16	4	0	1	8	11	7	.355	.359
Groundball	.250	104	26	5	0	1	14	13	11	.331	.327	None on/out	.227	88	20	5	0	7	7	12	15	.320	.523
Flyball	.280	107	30	7	0	2	14	21	16	.398	.402	Batting #4	.248	286	71	13	0	13	46	54	38	.364	.430
Home	.259	193	50	10	0	10	29	31	29	.358	.466	Batting #7	.313	48	15	5	0	2	6	8	7	.411	.542
Away	.229	201	46	10	0	5	29	40	27	.355	.353	Other	.167	60	10	2	0	0	6	9	11	.275	.200
Day	.217	129	28	5	0	3	15	22	15	.329	.326	April	.389	18	7	3	0	1	4	3	4	.476	.722
Night	.257	265	68	15	0	12	43	49	41	.370	.449	May	.271	85	23	6	0	2	11	21	6	.411	.412
Grass	.226	155	35	8	0	2	21	33	22	.360	.316	June	.311	90	28	5	0	7	20	16	12	.411	.600
Turf	.255	239	61	12	0	13	37	38	34	.355	.469	July	.204	93	19	4	0	1	11	12	17	.295	.280
First Pitch	.271	85	23	5	0	2	8	8	0	.333	.400	August	.167	90	15	1	0	4	11	15	15	.283	.311
Ahead on Count	.315	108	34	5	0	8	21	36	0	.479	.583	September/October	.222	18	4	1	0	0	1	4	2	.364	.278
Behind on Count	.230	100	23	5	0	3	17	0	24	.228	.370	Pre-All Star	.294	231	68	15	0	10	41	47	28	.411	.489
Two Strikes	.148	149	22	6	0	2	15	27	56	.277	.294	Post-All Star	.172	163	28	5	0	5	17	24	28	.277	.294

1992 By Position

Position	Avg	AB	H	2B	3B	HR	RBI	BB	SO	OBP	SLG	G	GS	Innings	PO	A	E	DP	Fld Pct	Rng Fctr	In Zone	Zone Outs	Zone Rtg	MLB Zone
As 1b	.242	368	89	19	0	15	56	64	51	.352	.416	104	102	903.1	954	67	3	76	.997	---	161	145	.901	.843

Last Five Years

	Avg	AB	H	2B	3B	HR	RBI	BB	SO	OBP	SLG		Avg	AB	H	2B	3B	HR	RBI	BB	SO	OBP	SLG
vs. Left	.271	579	157	26	0	17	94	75	80	.355	.404	Scoring Posn	.262	618	162	31	0	27	273	136	80	.365	.443
vs. Right	.285	1654	472	88	1	90	292	252	158	.378	.503	Close & Late	.316	326	103	16	0	17	56	48	37	.399	.521
Groundball	.275	578	159	24	0	22	92	88	66	.370	.431	None on/out	.268	555	149	31	0	27	27	66	63	.348	.470
Flyball	.337	502	169	40	0	27	94	77	52	.422	.578	Batting #4	.287	1581	453	80	0	82	292	240	157	.378	.493
Home	.290	1120	325	62	0	59	223	164	113	.378	.504	Batting #6	.237	215	51	12	0	4	29	25	24	.314	.349
Away	.273	1113	304	52	1	48	163	163	125	.366	.451	Other	.286	437	125	22	1	21	65	62	57	.379	.485
Day	.275	640	176	32	0	26	101	87	63	.361	.447	April	.271	273	74	19	0	14	56	38	29	.362	.495
Night	.284	1593	453	82	1	81	285	240	175	.376	.490	May	.288	389	112	18	1	20	60	66	32	.390	.494
Grass	.276	842	232	42	0	39	131	128	92	.372	.464	June	.294	344	101	23	0	12	53	56	38	.401	.465
Turf	.285	1391	397	72	1	68	255	199	146	.372	.485	July	.273	443	121	20	0	24	74	65	48	.368	.481
First Pitch	.338	535	181	32	0	32	104	14	0	.353	.578	August	.282	476	134	21	0	26	90	57	62	.352	.489
Ahead on Count	.299	598	179	35	1	35	121	169	0	.451	.537	September/October	.282	306	87	13	0	11	53	45	29	.372	.432
Behind on Count	.247	600	148	20	0	22	93	2	121	.250	.390	Pre-All Star	.288	1142	329	66	1	55	194	184	116	.386	.492
Two Strikes	.217	750	163	30	0	16	85	133	238	.335	.321	Post-All Star	.275	1091	300	48	0	52	192	143	122	.357	.462

Batter vs. Pitcher (since 1984)

Hits Best Against	Avg	AB	H	2B	3B	HR	RBI	BB	SO	OBP	SLG	Hits Worst Against	Avg	AB	H	2B	3B	HR	RBI	BB	SO	OBP	SLG
Pete Harnisch	.556	9	5	2	0	2	7	2	0	.636	1.444	Bryan Harvey	.000	10	0	0	0	0	0	1	3	.091	.000
Dennis Martinez	.545	11	6	2	0	1	3	1	0	.583	1.000	Dan Plesac	.000	8	0	0	0	0	2	1	1	.091	.000
Doug Jones	.500	14	7	2	0	2	5	1	1	.533	1.071	Greg Cadaret	.059	17	1	0	0	0	2	3	3	.200	.059
Joe Hesketh	.455	11	5	2	0	1	4	2	3	.538	.909	Charles Nagy	.067	15	1	0	0	0	0	2	4	.176	.067
Jeff M. Robinson	.423	26	11	2	0	5	9	6	4	.531	1.077	Jimmy Key	.143	21	3	0	0	0	2	0	7	.143	.143

Rex Hudler — Cardinals
Bats Right

	Avg	G	AB	R	H	2B	3B	HR	RBI	BB	SO	HBP	GDP	SB	CS	OBP	SLG	IBB	SH	SF	#Pit	#P/PA	GB	FB	G/F
1992 Season	.245	61	98	17	24	4	0	3	5	2	23	1	0	2	6	.265	.378	0	1	1	371	3.64	33	28	1.18
Last Five Years	.257	424	896	128	230	46	6	21	69	40	141	4	8	76	35	.290	.392	10	6	6	3380	3.57	324	258	1.26

1992 Season

	Avg	AB	H	2B	3B	HR	RBI	BB	SO	OBP	SLG		Avg	AB	H	2B	3B	HR	RBI	BB	SO	OBP	SLG
vs. Left	.346	52	18	4	0	2	3	1	10	.358	.538	Scoring Posn	.238	21	5	0	0	0	2	1	4	.261	.238
vs. Right	.130	46	6	0	0	1	2	1	13	.163	.196	Close & Late	.265	34	9	1	0	2	2	0	10	.265	.471
Home	.213	47	10	2	0	2	2	1	10	.229	.383	None on/out	.222	36	8	1	0	0	0	1	5	.263	.250
Away	.275	51	14	2	0	1	3	1	13	.296	.373	Batting #7	.233	30	7	0	0	1	2	1	6	.258	.333
First Pitch	.364	11	4	1	0	0	0	0	0	.364	.455	Batting #9	.267	30	8	2	0	2	2	0	5	.267	.533
Ahead on Count	.389	18	7	0	0	2	4	2	0	.429	.722	Other	.237	38	9	2	0	0	1	1	12	.268	.289
Behind on Count	.167	36	6	0	0	0	0	0	11	.189	.167	Pre-All Star	.200	60	12	2	0	2	3	1	12	.226	.333
Two Strikes	.091	44	4	0	0	0	0	0	23	.091	.091	Post-All Star	.316	38	12	2	0	1	2	1	11	.325	.447

Last Five Years

	Avg	AB	H	2B	3B	HR	RBI	BB	SO	OBP	SLG		Avg	AB	H	2B	3B	HR	RBI	BB	SO	OBP	SLG
vs. Left	.264	564	149	29	4	15	46	27	82	.297	.410	Scoring Posn	.227	203	46	11	3	2	46	19	31	.288	.340
vs. Right	.244	332	81	17	2	6	23	13	59	.276	.361	Close & Late	.228	206	47	5	1	8	14	5	44	.244	.379
Groundball	.255	337	86	18	2	7	24	18	58	.294	.383	None on/out	.233	270	63	11	2	6	6	8	40	.261	.356
Flyball	.234	218	51	12	0	7	20	8	30	.262	.385	Batting #1	.250	168	42	8	1	2	9	8	22	.285	.345
Home	.251	422	106	24	3	9	34	22	67	.291	.386	Batting #8	.265	155	41	11	1	4	9	12	26	.315	.426
Away	.262	474	124	22	3	12	35	18	74	.289	.397	Other	.257	573	147	27	4	15	51	20	93	.284	.396
Day	.265	264	70	15	2	7	28	13	46	.295	.417	April	.250	80	20	5	0	1	2	2	14	.268	.350
Night	.253	632	160	31	4	14	41	27	95	.287	.381	May	.283	92	26	2	1	3	12	5	11	.316	.424
Grass	.237	232	55	9	0	5	19	12	33	.274	.341	June	.250	116	29	7	1	2	7	8	18	.304	.379
Turf	.264	664	175	37	6	16	50	28	108	.295	.410	July	.240	208	50	11	1	3	12	12	33	.285	.346
First Pitch	.348	115	40	8	0	3	9	2	0	.364	.496	August	.307	218	67	14	3	8	22	7	36	.330	.509
Ahead on Count	.391	161	63	13	3	6	23	27	0	.479	.621	September/October	.209	182	38	7	0	4	14	6	29	.233	.313
Behind on Count	.212	387	82	14	3	4	20	1	88	.214	.295	Pre-All Star	.247	348	86	16	3	7	25	19	52	.289	.371
Two Strikes	.163	424	69	11	1	8	24	4	141	.171	.250	Post-All Star	.263	548	144	30	3	14	44	21	89	.290	.405

Batter vs. Pitcher (career)

Hits Best Against	Avg	AB	H	2B	3B	HR	RBI	BB	SO	OBP	SLG	Hits Worst Against	Avg	AB	H	2B	3B	HR	RBI	BB	SO	OBP	SLG
Bruce Hurst	.429	21	9	1	0	0	1	1	2	.455	.476	Mitch Williams	.091	11	1	0	0	0	0	0	3	.091	.091
Joe Magrane	.429	14	6	3	0	2	6	1	2	.438	1.071	Randy Tomlin	.154	13	2	0	1	0	1	0	3	.154	.308
Chris Nabholz	.429	14	6	2	0	2	2	2	2	.500	1.000	Terry Mulholland	.174	23	4	0	0	0	0	0	2	.174	.174
Jim Deshaies	.400	20	8	2	0	1	4	0	1	.400	.650	Randy Myers	.188	16	3	0	0	0	0	0	2	.188	.188
Bruce Ruffin	.375	16	6	2	1	0	0	1	5	.375	.625	Bobby Ojeda	.194	31	6	0	0	0	1	1	6	.219	.194

Mike Huff — White Sox
Bats Right

	Avg	G	AB	R	H	2B	3B	HR	RBI	BB	SO	HBP	GDP	SB	CS	OBP	SLG	IBB	SH	SF	#Pit	#P/PA	GB	FB	G/F
1992 Season	.209	60	115	13	24	5	0	0	8	10	24	1	2	1	2	.273	.252	1	2	2	472	3.69	43	20	2.15
Career (1989-1992)	.235	174	383	59	90	16	2	4	35	50	78	8	9	15	7	.333	.319	3	9	4	1771	3.98	136	96	1.42

1992 Season

	Avg	AB	H	2B	3B	HR	RBI	BB	SO	OBP	SLG		Avg	AB	H	2B	3B	HR	RBI	BB	SO	OBP	SLG
vs. Left	.213	89	19	5	0	0	8	9	16	.280	.270	Scoring Posn	.250	24	6	2	0	0	8	3	5	.310	.333

1992 Season

	Avg	AB	H	2B	3B	HR	RBI	BB	SO	OBP	SLG		Avg	AB	H	2B	3B	HR	RBI	BB	SO	OBP	SLG
vs. Right	.192	26	5	0	0	0	0	1	8	.250	.192	Close & Late	.241	29	7	0	0	0	1	1	7	.290	.241
Home	.164	61	10	2	0	0	4	4	15	.221	.197	None on/out	.241	29	7	2	0	0	0	1	3	.290	.310
Away	.259	54	14	3	0	0	4	6	9	.333	.315	Batting #2	.043	23	1	0	0	0	1	2	7	.154	.043
First Pitch	.267	15	4	2	0	0	2	0	0	.250	.400	Batting #6	.283	53	15	3	0	0	4	5	7	.339	.340
Ahead on Count	.233	30	7	2	0	0	2	6	0	.361	.300	Other	.205	39	8	2	0	0	3	3	10	.256	.256
Behind on Count	.094	32	3	0	0	0	0	0	14	.121	.094	Pre-All Star	.243	74	18	3	0	0	6	7	14	.301	.284
Two Strikes	.118	51	6	0	0	0	0	4	24	.196	.118	Post-All Star	.146	41	6	2	0	0	2	3	10	.222	.195

Career (1989-1992)

	Avg	AB	H	2B	3B	HR	RBI	BB	SO	OBP	SLG		Avg	AB	H	2B	3B	HR	RBI	BB	SO	OBP	SLG
vs. Left	.228	228	52	10	1	4	18	26	39	.314	.333	Scoring Posn	.273	88	24	4	1	0	31	14	18	.358	.341
vs. Right	.245	155	38	6	1	0	17	24	39	.359	.297	Close & Late	.269	78	21	3	1	0	6	6	18	.337	.333
Groundball	.205	117	24	2	1	0	10	17	18	.326	.239	None on/out	.259	112	29	6	1	2	2	18	18	.371	.384
Flyball	.205	78	16	3	0	1	7	10	21	.300	.282	Batting #1	.231	169	39	6	1	2	9	26	29	.340	.314
Home	.232	190	44	9	2	1	15	23	41	.330	.316	Batting #6	.284	74	21	3	0	0	5	6	14	.341	.324
Away	.238	193	46	7	0	3	20	27	37	.335	.321	Other	.214	140	30	7	1	2	21	18	35	.319	.321
Day	.178	118	21	3	1	0	4	19	29	.302	.220	April	.244	45	11	2	1	0	3	8	7	.358	.333
Night	.260	265	69	13	1	4	31	31	49	.346	.362	May	.257	101	26	6	0	0	9	17	26	.376	.317
Grass	.242	306	74	13	2	2	29	40	65	.338	.317	June	.229	70	16	1	0	2	4	7	10	.299	.329
Turf	.208	77	16	3	0	2	6	10	13	.311	.325	July	.136	22	3	1	0	0	3	3	6	.231	.182
First Pitch	.381	16	6	2	1	0	4	1	0	.386	.476	August	.286	63	18	3	1	2	12	7	11	.375	.460
Ahead on Count	.244	78	19	5	1	0	9	29	0	.449	.333	September/October	.195	82	16	3	0	0	4	8	18	.283	.232
Behind on Count	.208	130	27	5	0	0	9	1	38	.248	.246	Pre-All Star	.241	220	53	9	1	2	16	32	44	.344	.318
Two Strikes	.172	198	34	7	0	4	13	19	78	.262	.268	Post-All Star	.227	163	37	7	1	2	19	18	34	.317	.319

Batter vs. Pitcher (career)

Hits Best Against	Avg	AB	H	2B	3B	HR	RBI	BB	SO	OBP	SLG	Hits Worst Against	Avg	AB	H	2B	3B	HR	RBI	BB	SO	OBP	SLG
Chuck Finley	.333	9	3	1	0	0	0	4	2	.538	.444	Jim Abbott	.000	13	0	0	0	0	0	1	2	.071	.000
												Frank Tanana	.077	13	1	0	0	0	0	1	2	.143	.077
												David Wells	.091	11	1	0	0	0	1	1	1	.154	.091
												Jimmy Key	.188	16	3	2	0	0	0	0	1	.188	.313

Tim Hulett — Orioles
Bats Right (flyball hitter)

	Avg	G	AB	R	H	2B	3B	HR	RBI	BB	SO	HBP	GDP	SB	CS	OBP	SLG	IBB	SH	SF	#Pit	#P/PA	GB	FB	G/F
1992 Season	.289	57	142	11	41	7	2	2	21	10	31	1	7	0	1	.340	.408	1	0	0	606	3.96	32	47	0.68
Last Five Years	.249	222	598	68	149	28	3	15	73	48	138	1	15	1	2	.307	.381	1	3	1	2614	4.03	170	185	0.92

1992 Season

	Avg	AB	H	2B	3B	HR	RBI	BB	SO	OBP	SLG		Avg	AB	H	2B	3B	HR	RBI	BB	SO	OBP	SLG
vs. Left	.294	68	20	4	0	2	9	5	13	.342	.441	Scoring Posn	.417	36	15	3	1	1	19	3	8	.462	.639
vs. Right	.284	74	21	3	2	0	12	5	18	.338	.378	Close & Late	.371	35	13	1	1	0	3	2	7	.405	.457
Home	.371	70	26	4	2	1	15	8	12	.443	.529	None on/out	.257	35	9	1	1	1	1	1	7	.278	.429
Away	.208	72	15	3	0	1	6	2	19	.230	.292	Batting #6	.171	41	7	1	0	2	7	3	8	.227	.341
First Pitch	.250	12	3	0	0	0	1	0		.357	.250	Batting #8	.406	32	13	1	1	0	6	3	8	.472	.500
Ahead on Count	.318	44	14	3	0	0	7	5	0	.388	.386	Other	.304	69	21	5	1	0	8	4	15	.342	.406
Behind on Count	.286	49	14	4	0	2	10	0	16	.286	.490	Pre-All Star	.289	83	24	5	1	1	14	7	16	.352	.410
Two Strikes	.174	69	12	2	0	2	7	4	31	.219	.290	Post-All Star	.288	59	17	2	1	1	7	3	15	.323	.407

Last Five Years

	Avg	AB	H	2B	3B	HR	RBI	BB	SO	OBP	SLG		Avg	AB	H	2B	3B	HR	RBI	BB	SO	OBP	SLG
vs. Left	.218	238	52	9	1	8	33	17	51	.273	.366	Scoring Posn	.295	149	44	9	2	3	58	12	38	.346	.443
vs. Right	.269	360	97	19	2	7	40	31	87	.328	.392	Close & Late	.268	112	30	3	1	4	12	7	22	.311	.420
Groundball	.284	148	42	8	0	3	15	8	26	.321	.399	None on/out	.224	134	30	4	1	5	5	5	33	.252	.381
Flyball	.282	163	46	7	2	6	26	13	49	.335	.460	Batting #2	.221	136	30	6	0	2	9	11	30	.284	.309
Home	.280	250	70	12	2	6	31	24	59	.344	.416	Batting #7	.260	131	34	10	1	2	16	6	33	.292	.397
Away	.227	348	79	16	1	9	42	24	79	.279	.356	Other	.257	331	85	12	2	11	48	31	75	.321	.405
Day	.247	158	39	10	2	3	19	10	44	.296	.392	April	.225	40	9	1	0	1	4	3	11	.279	.325
Night	.250	440	110	18	1	12	54	38	94	.310	.377	May	.292	89	26	6	1	4	15	7	17	.351	.517
Grass	.266	497	132	20	3	13	62	41	112	.322	.396	June	.252	127	32	3	0	2	10	11	26	.317	.323
Turf	.168	101	17	8	0	2	11	7	26	.229	.307	July	.167	78	13	2	1	2	10	8	19	.244	.295
First Pitch	.245	49	12	1	0	3	6	1	0	.288	.449	August	.274	113	31	6	0	2	15	10	30	.333	.381
Ahead on Count	.281	153	43	10	1	2	16	27	0	.389	.399	September/October	.252	151	38	10	1	4	19	9	35	.292	.411
Behind on Count	.249	197	49	9	0	5	30	0	61	.247	.371	Pre-All Star	.255	286	73	11	2	8	34	23	59	.315	.392
Two Strikes	.205	308	63	13	0	8	37	20	138	.253	.325	Post-All Star	.244	312	76	17	1	7	39	25	79	.299	.372

Batter vs. Pitcher (since 1984)

Hits Best Against	Avg	AB	H	2B	3B	HR	RBI	BB	SO	OBP	SLG	Hits Worst Against	Avg	AB	H	2B	3B	HR	RBI	BB	SO	OBP	SLG
Bud Black	.500	20	10	3	0	2	5	2	2	.545	.950	Bert Blyleven	.063	12	1	0	0	0	1	0	2	.077	.063
Jack McDowell	.500	10	5	2	0	0	4	1	2	.545	.700	Walt Terrell	.063	12	1	0	0	0	2	2	3	.214	.063
Neal Heaton	.368	19	7	1	2	1	4	2	1	.429	.789	Mike Flanagan	.167	12	2	0	0	0	1	0	0	.154	.167
Jose Rijo	.364	11	4	3	0	0	1	0	2	.364	.636	Bruce Hurst	.188	16	3	0	0	0	0	2	3	.278	.188
Bill Krueger	.333	24	8	3	1	1	5	1	2	.360	.667	John Candelaria	.200	15	3	0	0	0	4	0	3	.200	.200

David Hulse — Rangers

Bats Left (groundball hitter)

	Avg	G	AB	R	H	2B	3B	HR	RBI	BB	SO	HBP	GDP	SB	CS	OBP	SLG	IBB	SH	SF	#Pit	#P/PA	GB	FB	G/F
1992 Season	.304	32	92	14	28	4	0	0	2	3	18	0	0	3	1	.326	.348	0	2	0	322	3.39	36	13	2.77

1992 Season

	Avg	AB	H	2B	3B	HR	RBI	BB	SO	OBP	SLG		Avg	AB	H	2B	3B	HR	RBI	BB	SO	OBP	SLG
vs. Left	.286	21	6	1	0	0	1	1	5	.318	.333	Scoring Posn	.077	13	1	0	0	0	2	1	5	.143	.077
vs. Right	.310	71	22	3	0	0	1	2	13	.329	.352	Close & Late	.214	14	3	1	0	0	0	0	4	.214	.286

Mike Humphreys — Yankees

Bats Right (flyball hitter)

	Avg	G	AB	R	H	2B	3B	HR	RBI	BB	SO	HBP	GDP	SB	CS	OBP	SLG	IBB	SH	SF	#Pit	#P/PA	GB	FB	G/F
1992 Season	.100	4	10	0	1	0	0	0	0	0	1	0	2	0	0	.100	.100	0	0	0	35	3.50	5	4	1.25
Career (1991-1992)	.180	29	50	9	9	0	0	0	3	9	8	0	2	2	0	.305	.180	0	0	0	248	4.20	13	23	0.57

1992 Season

	Avg	AB	H	2B	3B	HR	RBI	BB	SO	OBP	SLG		Avg	AB	H	2B	3B	HR	RBI	BB	SO	OBP	SLG
vs. Left	.000	6	0	0	0	0	0	0	0	.000	.000	Scoring Posn	.000	2	0	0	0	0	0	0	0	.000	.000
vs. Right	.250	4	1	0	0	0	0	0	1	.250	.250	Close & Late	.000	3	0	0	0	0	0	0	0	.000	.000

Todd Hundley — Mets

Bats Both

	Avg	G	AB	R	H	2B	3B	HR	RBI	BB	SO	HBP	GDP	SB	CS	OBP	SLG	IBB	SH	SF	#Pit	#P/PA	GB	FB	G/F
1992 Season	.209	123	358	32	75	17	0	7	32	19	76	4	8	3	0	.256	.316	4	7	2	1400	3.66	119	106	1.12
Career (1990-1992)	.200	180	485	45	97	23	1	8	41	31	108	5	12	3	0	.254	.301	4	9	3	1920	3.66	162	143	1.13

1992 Season

	Avg	AB	H	2B	3B	HR	RBI	BB	SO	OBP	SLG		Avg	AB	H	2B	3B	HR	RBI	BB	SO	OBP	SLG
vs. Left	.177	113	20	3	0	4	10	4	32	.217	.310	Scoring Posn	.157	83	13	3	0	2	26	10	20	.258	.265
vs. Right	.224	245	55	14	0	3	22	15	44	.274	.318	Close & Late	.250	76	19	5	0	0	3	4	19	.305	.316
Groundball	.206	155	32	9	0	1	9	8	39	.247	.284	None on/out	.214	98	21	5	0	2	2	3	19	.238	.327
Flyball	.206	68	14	3	0	4	8	2	10	.239	.426	Batting #7	.185	135	25	4	0	1	9	8	33	.229	.237
Home	.221	181	40	8	0	2	16	11	38	.272	.298	Batting #8	.254	142	36	11	0	5	20	8	20	.312	.437
Away	.198	177	35	9	0	5	16	8	38	.239	.333	Other	.173	81	14	2	0	1	3	3	23	.200	.235
Day	.235	98	23	4	0	3	7	7	24	.286	.367	April	.150	40	6	0	0	2	2	3	10	.227	.300
Night	.200	260	52	13	0	4	25	12	52	.245	.296	May	.193	57	11	2	0	1	5	7	12	.303	.281
Grass	.220	254	56	14	0	3	20	16	53	.274	.311	June	.203	59	12	5	0	3	13	1	10	.217	.441
Turf	.183	104	19	3	0	4	12	3	23	.211	.327	July	.245	49	12	3	0	1	2	2	10	.275	.367
First Pitch	.254	59	15	5	0	0	6	4	0	.302	.339	August	.210	62	13	4	0	0	1	3	17	.258	.274
Ahead on Count	.257	74	19	5	0	1	10	10	0	.337	.365	September/October	.231	91	21	3	0	0	9	3	17	.250	.264
Behind on Count	.144	132	19	2	0	3	11	0	45	.163	.227	Pre-All Star	.186	177	33	9	0	6	20	12	38	.250	.339
Two Strikes	.165	176	29	6	0	6	13	6	76	.201	.301	Post-All Star	.232	181	42	8	0	1	12	7	38	.262	.293

1992 By Position

Position	Avg	AB	H	2B	3B	HR	RBI	BB	SO	OBP	SLG	G	GS	Innings	PO	A	E	DP	Fld Pct	Rng Fctr	In Zone	Outs	Zone Rtg	MLB Zone
As c	.211	351	74	16	0	7	31	19	74	.258	.316	121	98	892.1	701	47	3	2	.996	---	---	---	---	---

Brian Hunter — Braves

Bats Right (flyball hitter)

	Avg	G	AB	R	H	2B	3B	HR	RBI	BB	SO	HBP	GDP	SB	CS	OBP	SLG	IBB	SH	SF	#Pit	#P/PA	GB	FB	G/F
1992 Season	.239	102	238	34	57	13	2	14	41	21	50	0	2	1	2	.292	.487	3	1	8	961	3.67	48	101	0.48
Career (1991-1992)	.246	199	509	66	125	29	3	26	91	38	98	1	8	1	4	.294	.468	3	1	10	2019	3.62	134	196	0.68

1992 Season

	Avg	AB	H	2B	3B	HR	RBI	BB	SO	OBP	SLG		Avg	AB	H	2B	3B	HR	RBI	BB	SO	OBP	SLG
vs. Left	.271	155	42	10	1	12	32	16	23	.326	.581	Scoring Posn	.196	56	11	5	0	1	23	5	13	.232	.339
vs. Right	.181	83	15	3	1	2	9	5	27	.225	.313	Close & Late	.146	41	6	2	0	4	9	6	13	.245	.488
Home	.290	107	31	5	1	9	23	15	24	.362	.607	None on/out	.186	59	11	3	0	4	4	7	15	.273	.441
Away	.198	131	26	8	1	5	18	6	26	.229	.389	Batting #5	.254	59	15	2	0	3	10	9	14	.338	.441
First Pitch	.350	40	14	3	0	6	13	3	0	.370	.875	Batting #6	.212	151	32	7	1	9	24	11	28	.257	.450
Ahead on Count	.348	46	16	4	0	6	13	11	0	.466	.826	Other	.357	28	10	4	1	2	7	1	8	.379	.786
Behind on Count	.235	85	20	5	1	0	8	0	30	.227	.318	Pre-All Star	.225	142	32	7	2	8	25	8	28	.255	.472
Two Strikes	.153	124	19	4	1	2	12	7	50	.194	.250	Post-All Star	.260	96	25	6	0	6	16	13	22	.345	.510

Bruce Hurst — Padres

Pitches Left

	ERA	W	L	Sv	G	GS	IP	BB	SO	Avg	H	2B	3B	HR	RBI	OBP	SLG	CG	ShO	Sup	QS	#P/S	SB	CS	GB	FB	G/F
1992 Season	3.85	14	9	0	32	32	217.1	51	131	.267	223	31	3	22	85	.308	.390	6	4	3.81	22	96	18	10	314	206	1.52
Last Five Years	3.31	73	43	0	162	161	1124.0	304	779	.247	1048	175	11	97	390	.297	.363	36	11	4.42	109	100	77	41	1562	1058	1.48

1992 Season

	ERA	W	L	Sv	G	GS	IP	H	HR	BB	SO		Avg	AB	H	2B	3B	HR	RBI	BB	SO	OBP	SLG
Home	4.38	5	4	0	15	15	100.2	99	15	26	65	vs. Left	.305	151	46	3	1	8	22	10	26	.348	.497
Away	3.39	9	5	0	17	17	116.2	124	7	25	66	vs. Right	.259	684	177	28	2	14	63	41	105	.299	.367
Day	3.40	3	2	0	7	7	50.1	52	4	10	33	Inning 1-6	.269	691	186	24	3	18	76	45	112	.312	.391

1992 Season

	ERA	W	L	Sv	G	GS	IP	H	HR	BB	SO		Avg	AB	H	2B	3B	HR	RBI	BB	SO	OBP	SLG
Night	3.99	11	7	0	25	25	167.0	171	18	41	98	Inning 7+	.257	144	37	7	0	4	9	6	19	.287	.389
Grass	3.48	11	5	0	23	23	160.1	154	17	37	99	None on	.259	510	132	14	0	13	13	39	82	.311	.363
Turf	4.89	3	4	0	9	9	57.0	69	5	14	32	Runners on	.280	325	91	17	3	9	72	12	49	.302	.434
April	4.83	1	2	0	5	5	31.2	34	4	10	24	Scoring Posn	.270	174	47	8	1	4	48	7	26	.292	.345
May	2.84	3	2	0	6	6	44.1	40	4	13	27	Close & Late	.297	74	22	4	0	2	7	3	4	.325	.432
June	1.93	4	1	0	6	6	46.2	39	3	7	35	None on/out	.250	220	55	5	0	8	8	13	38	.292	.382
July	4.32	3	1	0	6	6	41.2	48	5	12	24	vs. 1st Batr (relief)	.000	0	0	0	0	0	0	0	0	.000	.000
August	4.91	2	1	0	5	5	29.1	30	3	6	10	First Inning Pitched	.258	120	31	5	1	3	15	9	22	.308	.392
September/October	6.08	1	2	0	4	4	23.2	32	3	3	11	First 75 Pitches	.273	620	169	24	3	16	66	37	95	.312	.398
Starter	3.85	14	9	0	32	32	217.1	223	22	51	131	Pitch 76-90	.264	106	28	4	0	2	11	8	18	.316	.358
Reliever	0.00	0	0	0	0	0	0.0	0	0	0	0	Pitch 91-105	.257	74	19	2	0	3	6	4	11	.295	.405
0-3 Days Rest	0.00	0	0	0	0	0	0.0	0	0	0	0	Pitch 106+	.200	35	7	1	0	1	2	2	7	.243	.314
4 Days Rest	3.54	10	4	0	20	20	140.0	137	11	35	86	First Pitch	.295	146	43	6	1	1	11	3	0	.309	.370
5+ Days Rest	4.42	4	5	0	12	12	77.1	86	11	16	45	Ahead on Count	.234	397	93	10	1	10	33	0	115	.234	.340
Pre-All Star	3.25	8	5	0	19	19	135.2	128	15	35	98	Behind on Count	.323	158	51	8	1	7	24	31	0	.429	.519
Post-All Star	4.85	6	4	0	13	13	81.2	95	7	16	33	Two Strikes	.195	354	69	10	1	8	26	17	131	.231	.297

Last Five Years

	ERA	W	L	Sv	G	GS	IP	H	HR	BB	SO		Avg	AB	H	2B	3B	HR	RBI	BB	SO	OBP	SLG
Home	3.20	41	20	0	87	87	618.2	539	58	177	473	vs. Left	.258	743	192	29	3	20	86	63	147	.316	.386
Away	3.44	32	23	0	75	74	505.1	509	39	127	306	vs. Right	.245	3495	856	147	7	304	241	632	.293	.358
Day	3.25	18	9	0	42	41	299.1	287	21	85	216	Inning 1-6	.249	3450	858	144	9	78	328	249	666	.299	.363
Night	3.33	55	34	0	120	120	824.2	761	76	219	563	Inning 7+	.241	788	190	32	2	19	62	55	113	.291	.359
Grass	3.18	60	27	0	123	122	874.2	781	78	242	616	Runners on	.241	2582	622	92	4	63	63	189	504	.293	.353
Turf	3.75	13	16	0	39	39	249.1	267	19	62	163	Scoring Posn	.257	1656	426	84	7	34	327	115	275	.304	.378
April	3.58	10	6	0	23	23	163.1	139	17	43	130	Scoring Posn	.260	882	229	43	2	18	274	73	153	.312	.374
May	3.57	13	10	0	29	29	204.1	200	19	61	146	Close & Late	.258	391	101	12	2	9	36	28	52	.309	.368
June	3.31	13	8	0	29	29	204.0	201	21	52	140	None on/out	.227	1106	251	43	3	31	31	88	207	.285	.355
July	3.88	13	7	0	27	27	178.2	180	18	52	120	vs. 1st Batr (relief)	.000	1	0	0	0	0	0	0	1	.000	.000
August	2.96	15	4	0	27	27	191.2	170	12	52	118	First Inning Pitched	.241	606	146	26	1	9	59	52	132	.299	.332
September/October	2.57	9	8	0	27	26	182.0	158	10	44	125	First 75 Pitches	.245	3010	738	124	9	64	267	217	560	.296	.356
Starter	3.30	73	43	0	161	161	1123.0	1046	97	304	778	Pitch 76-90	.260	561	146	25	0	18	61	39	100	.308	.401
Reliever	9.00	0	0	0	1	0	1.0	2	0	0	1	Pitch 91-105	.252	429	108	16	2	7	36	26	64	.295	.347
0-3 Days Rest	2.93	3	1	0	4	4	27.2	24	1	8	18	Pitch 106+	.235	238	56	11	0	8	26	22	35	.302	.382
4 Days Rest	3.16	48	27	0	104	104	728.0	657	51	205	504	First Pitch	.311	673	209	30	2	15	72	14	0	.324	.428
5+ Days Rest	3.60	22	15	0	53	53	367.1	365	45	91	256	Ahead on Count	.207	2066	427	64	2	36	148	0	681	.208	.292
Pre-All Star	3.62	38	27	0	90	90	625.2	602	66	173	454	Behind on Count	.302	821	248	43	5	31	106	173	0	.423	.480
Post-All Star	2.91	35	16	0	72	71	498.1	446	31	131	325	Two Strikes	.174	1892	330	57	2	34	125	115	779	.223	.261

Pitcher vs. Batter (since 1984)

Pitches Best Vs.	Avg	AB	H	2B	3B	HR	RBI	BB	SO	OBP	SLG	Pitches Worst Vs.	Avg	AB	H	2B	3B	HR	RBI	BB	SO	OBP	SLG
Stan Javier	.118	17	2	0	0	0	0	1	2	.167	.118	Kirby Puckett	.577	26	15	1	0	1	5	3	4	.621	.731
Darryl Strawberry	.125	24	3	0	0	0	1	1	3	.160	.125	Dave Hollins	.500	14	7	1	0	2	5	4	3	.611	1.000
Kent Hrbek	.125	16	2	1	0	0	0	0	4	.125	.188	Barry Bonds	.462	26	12	3	0	3	4	8	4	.588	.923
Ruben Sierra	.130	23	3	0	0	0	0	0	7	.130	.130	Lance Parrish	.385	13	5	0	0	3	7	3	4	.500	1.077
Henry Cotto	.133	15	2	0	0	0	0	0	5	.133	.133	Kevin Mitchell	.333	21	7	1	0	5	8	5	2	.462	1.095

Jon Hurst — Expos
Pitches Right (flyball pitcher)

	ERA	W	L	Sv	G	GS	IP	BB	SO	Avg	H	2B	3B	HR	RBI	OBP	SLG	CG	ShO	Sup	QS	#P/S	SB	CS	GB	FB	G/F
1992 Season	5.51	1	1	0	3	3	16.1	7	4	.281	18	3	1	1	7	.361	.406	0	0	3.31	1	90		3	22	26	0.85

1992 Season

	ERA	W	L	Sv	G	GS	IP	H	HR	BB	SO		Avg	AB	H	2B	3B	HR	RBI	BB	SO	OBP	SLG
Home	10.38	0	0	0	1	1	4.1	8	0	0	2	vs. Left	.325	40	13	2	1	1	6	5	2	.400	.500
Away	3.75	1	1	0	2	2	12.0	10	1	7	2	vs. Right	.208	24	5	1	0	0	1	2	2	.296	.250

Jeff Huson — Rangers
Bats Left

	Avg	G	AB	R	H	2B	3B	HR	RBI	BB	SO	HBP	GDP	SB	CS	OBP	SLG	IBB	SH	SF	#Pit	#P/PA	GB	FB	G/F
1992 Season	.261	123	318	49	83	14	3	4	24	41	43	1	7	18	6	.342	.362	2	8	6	1417	3.87	117	96	1.22
Career (1988-1992)	.237	439	1098	150	260	41	8	6	83	136	134	3	29	43	14	.320	.305	7	27	10	4765	3.82	437	307	1.42

1992 Season

	Avg	AB	H	2B	3B	HR	RBI	BB	SO	OBP	SLG		Avg	AB	H	2B	3B	HR	RBI	BB	SO	OBP	SLG
vs. Left	.281	32	9	2	0	1	3	4	10	.361	.438	Scoring Posn	.172	64	11	5	1	0	18	11	15	.280	.281
vs. Right	.259	286	74	12	3	3	21	37	33	.339	.353	Close & Late	.148	54	8	2	1	0	1	7	12	.258	.222
Groundball	.243	74	18	4	1	0	3	7	7	.313	.324	None on/out	.261	88	23	3	0	1	1	14	12	.363	.330
Flyball	.192	78	15	1	1	0	3	13	13	.304	.231	Batting #1	.226	106	24	3	1	0	5	8	18	.276	.274
Home	.255	149	38	6	1	0	12	16	21	.325	.309	Batting #8	.297	74	22	5	2	1	6	14	9	.409	.459
Away	.266	169	45	8	2	4	12	25	22	.355	.408	Other	.268	138	37	6	0	3	13	19	16	.352	.377
Day	.234	77	18	4	0	1	3	11	16	.330	.325	April	.281	57	16	2	1	0	2	3	9	.317	.351
Night	.270	241	65	10	3	3	21	30	27	.345	.373	May	.220	82	18	6	1	1	5	8	9	.297	.354

215

1992 Season

	Avg	AB	H	2B	3B	HR	RBI	BB	SO	OBP	SLG		Avg	AB	H	2B	3B	HR	RBI	BB	SO	OBP	SLG
Grass	.279	262	73	13	2	3	21	28	35	.345	.378	June	.326	43	14	1	0	0	1	9	6	.434	.349
Turf	.179	56	10	1	1	1	3	13	8	.329	.286	July	.313	48	15	2	1	2	7	9	8	.407	.521
First Pitch	.341	41	14	3	1	1	5	2	0	.364	.537	August	.228	79	18	3	0	1	8	12	11	.323	.304
Ahead on Count	.342	79	27	7	0	1	6	21	0	.480	.468	September/October	.222	9	2	0	0	0	0	1	0	.200	.222
Behind on Count	.225	102	23	0	1	2	6	0	17	.221	.304	Pre-All Star	.262	195	51	10	2	1	9	28	26	.354	.349
Two Strikes	.197	147	29	4	1	2	12	18	43	.278	.279	Post-All Star	.260	123	32	4	1	3	15	13	17	.321	.382

1992 By Position

Position	Avg	AB	H	2B	3B	HR	RBI	BB	SO	OBP	SLG	G	GS	Innings	PO	A	E	DP	Fld Pct	Rng Fctr	In Zone	Outs	Zone Rtg	MLB Zone
As Pinch Hitter	.083	12	1	0	0	0	0	0	3	.083	.083	12	0	---	---	---	---	---	---	---	---	---	---	---
As 2b	.254	122	31	6	0	2	7	16	19	.343	.352	47	32	313.2	69	83	0	22	1.000	4.36	86	86	1.000	.892
As ss	.279	183	51	8	3	2	17	25	21	.357	.388	82	56	507.0	109	167	9	45	.968	4.90	215	179	.833	.885

Career (1988-1992)

	Avg	AB	H	2B	3B	HR	RBI	BB	SO	OBP	SLG		Avg	AB	H	2B	3B	HR	RBI	BB	SO	OBP	SLG
vs. Left	.210	124	26	4	0	1	8	13	26	.288	.266	Scoring Posn	.218	243	53	8	3	1	70	39	38	.320	.288
vs. Right	.240	974	234	37	8	5	75	123	112	.324	.310	Close & Late	.227	176	40	3	1	0	8	26	24	.328	.256
Groundball	.209	339	71	11	5	0	16	33	34	.280	.271	None on/out	.236	314	74	17	0	1	1	41	42	.326	.299
Flyball	.251	235	59	8	1	0	20	30	36	.337	.294	Batting #1	.209	349	73	8	3	0	22	32	49	.276	.249
Home	.221	548	121	19	4	1	40	67	78	.307	.276	Batting #9	.256	356	91	13	2	4	35	46	47	.339	.337
Away	.253	550	139	22	4	5	43	69	60	.333	.335	Other	.244	393	96	20	3	2	26	58	42	.340	.326
Day	.245	241	59	10	0	1	18	32	28	.335	.299	April	.269	134	36	4	2	0	13	15	21	.338	.328
Night	.235	857	201	31	8	5	65	103	110	.316	.307	May	.235	213	50	16	2	1	10	26	27	.322	.343
Grass	.248	852	211	32	7	5	73	101	114	.327	.319	June	.267	176	47	4	2	1	12	25	21	.356	.330
Turf	.199	246	49	9	1	0	10	35	24	.297	.256	July	.250	204	51	8	2	3	18	25	25	.330	.353
First Pitch	.276	134	37	4	2	1	16	4	0	.269	.358	August	.212	198	42	6	0	1	16	26	27	.301	.258
Ahead on Count	.284	268	76	15	1	1	20	72	0	.436	.358	September/October	.197	173	34	3	0	0	14	19	17	.275	.214
Behind on Count	.201	353	71	9	3	3	18	1	68	.207	.269	Pre-All Star	.248	577	143	26	6	2	37	77	76	.337	.324
Two Strikes	.177	479	85	13	4	3	30	57	130	.254	.240	Post-All Star	.225	521	117	15	2	4	46	59	62	.301	.284

Batter vs. Pitcher (career)

Hits Best Against	Avg	AB	H	2B	3B	HR	RBI	BB	SO	OBP	SLG	Hits Worst Against	Avg	AB	H	2B	3B	HR	RBI	BB	SO	OBP	SLG
Jack McDowell	.381	21	8	2	0	0	2	2	3	.435	.476	Todd Stottlemyre	.000	9	0	0	0	0	0	2	1	.182	.000
Jaime Navarro	.375	16	6	0	2	0	3	2	1	.444	.625	Alex Fernandez	.000	9	0	0	0	0	0	3	1	.231	.000
Rick Sutcliffe	.357	14	5	1	0	2	2	1		.438	.571	Kevin Tapani	.056	18	1	1	0	0	1	0	2	.056	.111
Tom Gordon	.333	15	5	1	1	0	3	1	3	.375	.533	Dave Stewart	.091	11	1	0	0	0	0	0	0	.091	.091
Storm Davis	.333	9	3	1	0	0	1	2	2	.455	.444	Bob Welch	.100	10	1	0	0	0	0	1	1	.182	.100

Pete Incaviglia — Astros   Bats Right

	Avg	G	AB	R	H	2B	3B	HR	RBI	BB	SO	HBP	GDP	SB	CS	OBP	SLG	IBB	SH	SF	#Pit	#P/PA	GB	FB	G/F
1992 Season	.266	113	349	31	93	22	1	11	44	25	99	3	6	2	2	.319	.430	2	0	2	1412	3.73	93	105	0.89
Last Five Years	.239	612	2086	235	499	107	9	89	302	177	626	26	48	17	20	.305	.427	10	1	15	8507	3.69	621	543	1.14

1992 Season

	Avg	AB	H	2B	3B	HR	RBI	BB	SO	OBP	SLG		Avg	AB	H	2B	3B	HR	RBI	BB	SO	OBP	SLG
vs. Left	.282	170	48	13	1	7	27	16	50	.344	.494	Scoring Posn	.196	92	18	6	0	1	25	11	36	.290	.293
vs. Right	.251	179	45	9	0	4	17	9	49	.295	.369	Close & Late	.277	65	18	5	0	2	7	7	21	.347	.446
Groundball	.243	136	33	6	1	2	14	10	35	.299	.346	None on/out	.266	79	21	6	1	2	2	3	13	.301	.443
Flyball	.274	84	23	4	0	4	10	3	31	.303	.464	Batting #5	.270	126	34	7	1	4	13	7	38	.324	.437
Home	.296	189	56	15	0	6	26	9	60	.338	.471	Batting #6	.248	133	33	10	0	5	21	15	30	.320	.436
Away	.231	160	37	7	1	5	18	16	39	.298	.381	Other	.289	90	26	5	0	2	10	3	31	.312	.411
Day	.284	95	27	3	1	6	20	9	27	.343	.526	April	.250	72	18	4	0	1	7	0	26	.270	.347
Night	.260	254	66	19	0	5	24	16	72	.310	.394	May	.267	75	20	3	0	1	8	6	19	.317	.347
Grass	.250	80	20	5	0	0	3	6	22	.302	.313	June	.281	64	18	5	0	4	11	6	23	.343	.547
Turf	.271	269	73	17	1	11	41	19	77	.324	.465	July	.323	65	21	7	0	3	9	6	13	.380	.569
First Pitch	.364	55	20	4	0	5	10	2	0	.379	.709	August	.214	42	9	1	0	1	3	2	8	.244	.310
Ahead on Count	.362	69	25	6	0	0	6	8	0	.430	.449	September/October	.226	31	7	2	1	1	1	6	5	.351	.452
Behind on Count	.187	134	25	8	0	2	13	0	57	.193	.291	Pre-All Star	.283	223	63	14	0	7	29	14	70	.329	.439
Two Strikes	.166	175	29	8	1	3	18	15	99	.236	.274	Post-All Star	.238	126	30	8	1	4	15	11	29	.302	.413

1992 By Position

Position	Avg	AB	H	2B	3B	HR	RBI	BB	SO	OBP	SLG	G	GS	Innings	PO	A	E	DP	Fld Pct	Rng Fctr	In Zone	Outs	Zone Rtg	MLB Zone
As Pinch Hitter	.222	18	4	0	0	1	3	1	9	.263	.389	20	0	---	---	---	---	---	---	---	---	---	---	---
As lf	.253	170	43	13	0	6	25	18	39	.325	.435	57	49	401.0	115	3	3	1	.975	2.65	116	106	.914	.809
As rf	.286	161	46	9	1	4	16	6	51	.320	.420	74		351.0	5	3	0		.963	2.03	92	73	.793	.814

Last Five Years

	Avg	AB	H	2B	3B	HR	RBI	BB	SO	OBP	SLG		Avg	AB	H	2B	3B	HR	RBI	BB	SO	OBP	SLG
vs. Left	.244	710	173	40	4	30	99	66	198	.313	.438	Scoring Posn	.225	569	128	33	1	18	197	60	182	.302	.381
vs. Right	.237	1376	326	67	5	59	203	111	428	.300	.422	Close & Late	.211	370	78	22	1	11	49	29	120	.269	.365
Groundball	.252	600	151	25	6	25	104	48	158	.314	.438	None on/out	.236	471	111	27	3	24	24	38	130	.300	.459
Flyball	.224	522	117	27	1	21	58	46	191	.293	.400	Batting #5	.240	470	113	22	2	20	70	42	143	.312	.423

Last Five Years

	Avg	AB	H	2B	3B	HR	RBI	BB	SO	OBP	SLG		Avg	AB	H	2B	3B	HR	RBI	BB	SO	OBP	SLG
Home	.250	1023	256	53	3	52	167	98	312	.321	.460	Batting #6	.233	750	175	40	2	38	121	63	214	.296	.444
Away	.229	1063	243	54	6	37	135	79	314	.289	.395	Other	.244	866	211	45	3	31	111	72	269	.308	.415
Day	.207	463	96	14	1	17	59	53	151	.296	.352	April	.230	343	79	16	1	13	46	22	118	.264	.397
Night	.248	1623	403	93	8	72	243	124	475	.307	.449	May	.240	417	100	25	1	19	66	37	121	.310	.441
Grass	.240	1544	370	78	7	70	224	140	465	.308	.435	June	.251	334	84	18	2	11	42	23	93	.306	.416
Turf	.238	542	129	29	2	19	78	37	161	.296	.404	July	.270	352	95	22	2	22	67	30	101	.327	.531
First Pitch	.334	329	110	23	2	25	71	2	0	.334	.644	August	.201	334	67	9	1	11	36	32	111	.281	.332
Ahead on Count	.338	385	130	30	1	24	82	88	0	.465	.606	September/October	.242	306	74	17	2	13	45	33	82	.320	.438
Behind on Count	.183	731	134	30	1	20	81	2	333	.196	.309	Pre-All Star	.245	1174	288	66	5	49	169	90	352	.306	.435
Two Strikes	.139	1061	148	39	4	23	94	83	626	.211	.249	Post-All Star	.231	912	211	41	4	40	133	87	274	.303	.417

Batter vs. Pitcher (career)

Hits Best Against	Avg	AB	H	2B	3B	HR	RBI	BB	SO	OBP	SLG	Hits Worst Against	Avg	AB	H	2B	3B	HR	RBI	BB	SO	OBP	SLG
Scott Bailes	.643	14	9	2	0	4	8	1	0	.667	1.643	Bob Welch	.056	18	1	0	0	0	0	1	7	.105	.056
Bud Black	.524	21	11	3	0	4	8	2	5	.565	1.238	Greg Swindell	.061	33	2	0	0	0	1	3	16	.139	.061
Mike Birkbeck	.500	10	5	0	0	2	5	1	1	.500	1.100	Dan Plesac	.063	16	1	0	0	0	2	1	4	.118	.063
Bob Milacki	.462	13	6	3	0	3	8	2	3	.533	1.385	Jeff Reardon	.077	13	1	1	0	0	2	0	6	.077	.154
Dave Righetti	.400	10	4	2	0	2	6	3	3	.538	1.200	Mike Henneman	.077	13	1	0	0	0	1	0	3	.071	.077

Jeff Innis — Mets

Pitches Right (groundball pitcher)

	ERA	W	L	Sv	G	GS	IP	BB	SO	Avg	H	2B	3B	HR	RBI	OBP	SLG	GF	IR	IRS	Hld	SvOp	SB	CS	GB	FB	G/F
1992 Season	2.86	6	9	1	76	0	88.0	36	39	.266	85	11	3	4	35	.348	.357	28	50	15	16	4	8	5	176	61	2.89
Last Five Years	2.72	8	16	2	204	0	257.2	79	128	.242	227	32	6	12	100	.303	.328	69	145	43	23	9	34	10	507	166	3.05

1992 Season

	ERA	W	L	Sv	G	GS	IP	H	HR	BB	SO		Avg	AB	H	2B	3B	HR	RBI	BB	SO	OBP	SLG
Home	2.81	3	5	1	41	0	48.0	46	2	19	24	vs. Left	.289	159	46	8	1	2	23	28	16	.399	.390
Away	2.93	3	4	0	35	0	40.0	39	2	17	15	vs. Right	.244	160	39	3	2	2	12	8	23	.291	.325
Day	3.18	0	4	0	20	0	22.2	27	2	7	12	Inning 1-6	.286	14	4	0	0	0	3	2	2	.375	.286
Night	2.76	6	5	1	56	0	65.1	58	2	29	27	Inning 7+	.266	305	81	11	3	4	32	34	37	.347	.361
Grass	2.80	4	5	1	55	0	61.0	60	3	24	28	None on	.264	174	46	5	2	2	2	14	22	.323	.351
Turf	3.00	2	4	0	21	0	27.0	25	1	12	11	Runners on	.269	145	39	6	1	2	33	22	17	.375	.366
April	2.61	3	1	0	10	0	10.1	11	1	3	10	Scoring Posn	.240	96	23	3	1	1	30	18	13	.364	.323
May	3.21	1	0	0	11	0	14.0	14	1	8	3	Close & Late	.313	182	57	10	3	2	25	22	19	.399	.434
June	3.32	0	3	0	16	0	19.0	22	0	6	11	None on/out	.282	78	22	3	0	2	2	6	9	.333	.397
July	3.06	1	3	1	14	0	17.2	15	1	6	6	vs. 1st Batr (relief)	.250	68	17	1	0	2	9	5	9	.307	.353
August	0.73	0	1	0	12	0	12.1	5	0	2	4	First Inning Pitched	.249	229	57	9	1	3	27	18	32	.311	.336
September/October	3.68	1	1	0	13	0	14.2	18	1	11	5	First 15 Pitches	.251	215	54	8	1	4	26	17	26	.317	.353
Starter	0.00	0	0	0	0	0	0.0	0	0	0	0	Pitch 16-30	.330	88	29	3	2	0	8	14	10	.422	.409
Reliever	2.86	6	9	1	76	0	88.0	85	4	36	39	Pitch 31-45	.133	15	2	0	0	0	1	5	3	.364	.133
0 Days rest	2.70	1	3	0	26	0	30.0	36	2	10	11	Pitch 46+	.000	1	0	0	0	0	0	0	0	.000	.000
1 or 2 Days rest	3.16	2	4	1	36	0	42.2	38	1	19	18	First Pitch	.280	50	14	0	1	1	7	4	0	.351	.380
3+ Days rest	2.35	3	2	0	14	0	15.1	11	1	7	10	Ahead on Count	.209	134	28	6	0	0	10	0	33	.213	.254
Pre-All Star	2.82	5	5	1	44	0	54.1	55	3	20	28	Behind on Count	.318	85	27	3	1	2	10	20	0	.463	.447
Post-All Star	2.94	1	4	0	32	0	33.2	30	1	16	11	Two Strikes	.192	125	24	4	1	0	9	12	38	.261	.240

Last Five Years

	ERA	W	L	Sv	G	GS	IP	H	HR	BB	SO		Avg	AB	H	2B	3B	HR	RBI	BB	SO	OBP	SLG
Home	2.41	5	10	2	108	0	138.1	110	7	40	74	vs. Left	.281	399	112	21	2	7	53	47	41	.358	.396
Away	3.09	3	6	0	96	0	119.1	117	5	39	54	vs. Right	.214	538	115	11	4	5	47	32	87	.259	.277
Day	2.89	2	7	0	68	0	84.0	78	5	25	46	Inning 1-6	.199	166	33	6	1	1	20	13	23	.253	.265
Night	2.64	6	9	2	136	0	173.2	149	7	54	82	Inning 7+	.252	771	194	26	5	11	80	66	105	.313	.341
Grass	2.68	6	11	2	148	0	184.2	156	11	55	94	None on	.244	521	127	16	4	10	10	28	75	.285	.347
Turf	2.84	2	5	0	56	0	73.0	71	1	24	34	Runners on	.240	416	100	16	2	2	90	51	53	.323	.303
April	4.44	3	4	0	21	0	24.1	25	3	9	20	Scoring Posn	.215	274	59	7	2	1	85	43	40	.315	.266
May	2.00	1	0	0	23	0	27.0	20	2	9	10	Close & Late	.290	338	98	16	4	5	44	37	44	.366	.405
June	2.18	2	3	0	43	0	53.2	49	0	15	31	None on/out	.271	221	60	6	1	4	4	16	36	.315	.362
July	3.03	1	5	1	43	0	65.1	56	3	17	30	vs. 1st Batr (relief)	.237	186	44	4	1	4	26	14	32	.291	.333
August	3.03	0	1	0	38	0	38.2	37	2	12	20	First Inning Pitched	.218	611	133	19	2	8	68	47	90	.276	.295
September/October	2.22	1	3	0	36	0	48.2	40	2	17	17	First 15 Pitches	.229	611	140	23	3	9	62	41	87	.281	.321
Starter	0.00	0	0	0	0	0	0.0	0	0	0	0	Pitch 16-30	.268	265	71	8	3	3	29	28	34	.337	.355
Reliever	2.72	8	16	2	204	0	257.2	227	12	79	128	Pitch 31-45	.268	56	15	1	0	0	9	10	7	.371	.286
0 Days rest	3.06	2	4	0	62	0	73.0	77	2	26	38	Pitch 46+	.200	5	1	0	0	0	0	0	0	.200	.200
1 or 2 Days rest	2.88	3	6	2	84	0	112.2	105	3	35	52	First Pitch	.315	146	46	5	1	2	21	9	0	.354	.404
3+ Days rest	2.13	3	6	0	58	0	72.0	45	7	18	38	Ahead on Count	.196	404	79	12	1	3	32	0	115	.197	.252
Pre-All Star	2.66	7	9	2	102	0	128.1	113	8	38	71	Behind on Count	.275	247	68	10	3	5	30	42	0	.386	.401
Post-All Star	2.78	1	7	0	102	0	129.1	114	4	41	57	Two Strikes	.167	359	60	8	1	3	24	27	127	.226	.220

Pitcher vs. Batter (career)

Pitches Best Vs.	Avg	AB	H	2B	3B	HR	RBI	BB	SO	OBP	SLG	Pitches Worst Vs.	Avg	AB	H	2B	3B	HR	RBI	BB	SO	OBP	SLG
Matt D. Williams	.100	10	1	0	0	0	0	1	2	.182	.100	Tim Wallach	.313	16	5	1	0	0	4	0	6	.313	.375
Andres Galarraga	.143	14	2	0	0	0	0	0	2	.143	.143												
Jose Lind	.200	10	2	0	0	0	1	1	0	.273	.200												

Pitcher vs. Batter (career)																				
Pitches Best Vs.	Avg	AB	H	2B	3B	HR	RBI	BB	SO	OBP	SLG	Pitches Worst Vs.	Avg	AB	H	2B	3B	HR	RBI	BB	SO	OBP	SLG
Ryne Sandberg	.222	18	4	0	0	0	0	1	1	.263	.222										
Mark Grace	.222	9	2	0	0	0	3	2	0	.333	.222										

Daryl Irvine — Red Sox

Pitches Right (groundball pitcher)

	ERA	W	L	Sv	G	GS	IP	BB	SO	Avg	H	2B	3B	HR	RBI	OBP	SLG	GF	IR	IRS	Hld	SvOp	SB	CS	GB	FB	G/F
1992 Season	6.11	3	4	0	21	0	28.0	14	10	.287	31	4	1	1	15	.370	.370	8	28	12	2	3	0	1	57	22	2.59
Career (1990-1992)	5.68	4	5	0	41	0	63.1	33	27	.287	71	14	2	3	44	.372	.397	19	53	24	2	3	1	1	120	49	2.45

1992 Season

	ERA	W	L	Sv	G	GS	IP	H	HR	BB	SO		Avg	AB	H	2B	3B	HR	RBI	BB	SO	OBP	SLG
Home	2.08	3	1	0	12	0	17.1	17	0	6	9	vs. Left	.244	45	11	2	1	0	3	8	2	.370	.333
Away	12.66	0	3	0	9	0	10.2	14	1	8	1	vs. Right	.317	63	20	2	0	1	12	6	8	.370	.397
Starter	0.00	0	0	0	0	0	0.0	0	0	0	0	Scoring Posn	.280	25	7	0	0	0	13	10	4	.475	.280
Reliever	6.11	3	4	0	21	0	28.0	31	1	14	10	Close & Late	.347	49	17	1	0	0	6	6	2	.439	.367
0 Days rest	0.00	0	0	0	1	0	2.0	2	0	1	2	None on/out	.240	25	6	1	0	1	1	0	3	.240	.400
1 or 2 Days rest	7.41	2	2	0	13	0	17.0	23	1	7	5	First Pitch	.267	15	4	1	0	0	2	2	0	.389	.333
3+ Days rest	5.00	1	2	0	7	0	9.0	6	0	6	3	Behind on Count	.394	33	13	3	1	0	7	7	0	.488	.545
Pre-All Star	0.00	1	0	0	5	0	8.1	6	0	2	4	Ahead on Count	.189	37	7	0	0	1	3	0	6	.179	.270
Post-All Star	8.69	2	4	0	16	0	19.2	25	1	12	6	Two Strikes	.114	35	4	0	0	1	4	5	10	.214	.200

Danny Jackson — Pirates

Pitches Left (groundball pitcher)

	ERA	W	L	Sv	G	GS	IP	BB	SO	Avg	H	2B	3B	HR	RBI	OBP	SLG	CG	ShO	Sup	QS	#P/S	SB	CS	GB	FB	G/F
1992 Season	3.84	8	13	0	34	34	201.1	77	97	.272	211	39	6	6	80	.337	.361	0	0	3.84	19	88	21	13	343	186	1.84
Last Five Years	3.96	44	43	0	128	124	765.2	293	435	.257	747	128	18	48	324	.325	.363	16	6	4.64	64	91	61	32	1318	630	2.09

1992 Season

	ERA	W	L	Sv	G	GS	IP	H	HR	BB	SO		Avg	AB	H	2B	3B	HR	RBI	BB	SO	OBP	SLG
Home	2.85	6	4	0	18	18	116.2	116	1	44	54	vs. Left	.246	118	29	2	0	2	14	16	20	.333	.314
Away	5.21	2	9	0	16	16	84.2	95	5	33	43	vs. Right	.277	657	182	37	6	4	66	61	77	.338	.370
Day	3.65	4	6	0	14	14	81.1	87	3	29	43	Inning 1-6	.265	712	189	38	6	5	76	74	87	.334	.357
Night	3.97	4	7	0	20	20	120.0	124	3	48	54	Inning 7+	.349	63	22	1	0	1	4	3	10	.379	.413
Grass	3.28	2	8	0	16	16	96.0	86	5	39	41	None on	.272	405	110	20	6	4	4	42	48	.346	.380
Turf	4.36	6	5	0	18	18	105.1	125	1	38	56	Runners on	.273	370	101	19	0	2	76	35	49	.328	.341
April	6.39	0	4	0	5	5	25.1	36	0	10	12	Scoring Posn	.278	216	60	14	0	0	69	22	31	.331	.343
May	3.86	0	3	0	6	6	35.0	35	2	16	18	Close & Late	.419	43	18	0	0	1	4	2	6	.444	.488
June	3.54	4	1	0	6	6	40.2	36	1	17	19	None on/out	.297	192	57	11	3	3	3	23	22	.381	.432
July	1.91	1	2	0	5	5	33.0	25	3	12	12	vs. 1st Batr (relief)	.000	0	0	0	0	0	0	0	0	.000	.000
August	4.85	1	1	0	5	5	26.0	28	0	10	18	First Inning Pitched	.256	125	32	5	1	1	17	22	17	.364	.336
September/October	3.48	2	2	0	7	7	41.1	51	0	12	18	First 75 Pitches	.250	627	157	30	4	5	61	70	82	.326	.335
Starter	3.84	8	13	0	34	34	201.1	211	6	77	97	Pitch 76-90	.378	82	31	7	2	0	12	7	6	.422	.512
Reliever	0.00	0	0	0	0	0	0.0	0	0	0	0	Pitch 91-105	.327	49	16	1	0	1	5	0	8	.320	.408
0-3 Days Rest	7.50	0	0	0	1	1	6.0	11	0	2	2	Pitch 106+	.412	17	7	1	0	0	2	0	1	.412	.471
4 Days Rest	3.73	7	8	0	23	23	137.2	144	6	56	63	First Pitch	.281	128	36	7	0	1	10	5	0	.306	.359
5+ Days Rest	3.75	1	5	0	10	10	57.2	56	1	19	32	Ahead on Count	.227	321	73	17	1	3	31	0	86	.229	.315
Pre-All Star	4.22	4	9	0	19	19	113.0	117	5	48	51	Behind on Count	.345	177	61	10	3	2	23	43	0	.471	.469
Post-All Star	3.36	4	4	0	15	15	88.1	94	1	29	46	Two Strikes	.207	280	58	12	1	1	24	29	97	.283	.268

Last Five Years

	ERA	W	L	Sv	G	GS	IP	H	HR	BB	SO		Avg	AB	H	2B	3B	HR	RBI	BB	SO	OBP	SLG
Home	3.67	23	17	0	66	63	404.1	384	27	153	216	vs. Left	.257	467	120	15	4	6	54	54	89	.333	.345
Away	4.28	21	26	0	62	61	361.1	363	21	140	219	vs. Right	.257	2438	627	113	14	42	270	239	346	.323	.367
Day	4.29	13	17	0	46	45	255.2	268	14	106	132	Inning 1-6	.257	2508	644	113	16	38	290	266	365	.328	.360
Night	3.79	31	26	0	82	79	510.0	479	31	187	303	Inning 7+	.259	397	103	15	2	10	34	27	70	.305	.383
Grass	4.09	16	20	0	55	53	325.2	327	24	130	189	None on	.241	1666	401	72	14	23	23	155	254	.307	.342
Turf	3.87	28	23	0	73	71	440.0	420	24	163	246	Runners on	.279	1239	346	56	4	25	301	138	181	.348	.391
April	5.38	4	11	0	21	21	113.2	125	11	57	55	Scoring Posn	.279	750	209	37	2	13	268	89	114	.348	.385
May	3.97	4	8	0	19	19	113.1	103	4	45	62	Close & Late	.268	209	56	7	2	7	22	11	36	.303	.421
June	4.32	12	6	0	24	24	152.0	155	6	63	95	None on/out	.251	729	183	29	5	11	11	87	109	.333	.350
July	2.00	9	5	0	18	18	126.0	95	9	44	72	vs. 1st Batr (relief)	.667	3	2	0	0	0	1	1	0	.750	.667
August	3.98	8	4	0	21	20	122.0	111	7	41	71	First Inning Pitched	.260	480	125	22	3	12	71	75	78	.360	.394
September/October	4.15	7	9	0	25	22	138.2	133	11	43	80	First 75 Pitches	.256	2246	576	106	14	32	247	245	332	.329	.359
Starter	3.93	44	43	0	124	124	760.0	736	48	289	431	Pitch 76-90	.259	317	82	8	2	6	39	26	47	.316	.353
Reliever	7.94	0	0	0	4	0	5.2	11	0	4	4	Pitch 91-105	.247	239	59	8	0	5	22	12	41	.280	.343
0-3 Days Rest	3.33	10	5	0	18	18	119.0	115	5	45	70	Pitch 106+	.291	103	30	6	2	5	16	10	15	.354	.534
4 Days Rest	3.82	25	23	0	69	69	436.1	405	26	166	245	First Pitch	.295	495	146	25	0	7	53	20	0	.322	.388
5+ Days Rest	4.53	9	15	0	37	37	204.2	216	15	78	116	Ahead on Count	.204	1271	259	38	8	17	120	0	372	.205	.286
Pre-All Star	4.24	24	26	0	71	71	425.0	414	25	182	236	Behind on Count	.333	643	214	38	7	16	95	170	0	.471	.488
Post-All Star	3.62	20	17	0	57	53	340.2	333	23	111	199	Two Strikes	.179	1137	204	30	5	11	93	103	435	.249	.244

Pitcher vs. Batter (since 1984)

Pitches Best Vs.	Avg	AB	H	2B	3B	HR	RBI	BB	SO	OBP	SLG	Pitches Worst Vs.	Avg	AB	H	2B	3B	HR	RBI	BB	SO	OBP	SLG
Gary Redus	.000	18	0	0	0	0	1	4	2	.182	.000	Craig Biggio	.667	9	6	1	0	0	3	3	1	.750	.778
Jerald Clark	.000	13	0	0	0	0	0	4	4	.000	.000	Darrin Jackson	.500	18	9	1	0	2	4	3	3	.571	.889
Mark Lemke	.000	11	0	0	0	0	0	2	0	.154	.000	Felix Jose	.500	12	6	5	0	0	4	0	1	.500	.917
Andre Dawson	.071	14	1	0	0	0	0	3	.071	.071	Kent Hrbek	.450	20	9	5	0	1	4	2	4	.500	.850	
Kevin McReynolds	.091	22	2	0	0	0	1	2	5	.167	.091	Rob Deer	.364	11	4	0	0	2	7	4	4	.500	.909

Darrin Jackson — Padres
Bats Right

	Avg	G	AB	R	H	2B	3B	HR	RBI	BB	SO	HBP	GDP	SB	CS	OBP	SLG	IBB	SH	SF	#Pit	#P/PA	GB	FB	G/F
1992 Season	.249	155	587	72	146	23	5	17	70	26	106	4	21	14	3	.283	.392	4	6	5	2150	3.46	174	196	0.89
Last Five Years	.251	505	1417	179	356	56	9	51	168	76	258	7	32	27	11	.290	.411	13	12	12	5236	3.46	449	449	1.00

1992 Season

	Avg	AB	H	2B	3B	HR	RBI	BB	SO	OBP	SLG		Avg	AB	H	2B	3B	HR	RBI	BB	SO	OBP	SLG
vs. Left	.202	188	38	6	4	7	19	9	33	.242	.388	Scoring Posn	.301	136	41	8	2	6	57	12	22	.355	.522
vs. Right	.271	399	108	17	1	10	51	17	73	.302	.393	Close & Late	.283	92	26	3	1	6	16	8	21	.340	.533
Groundball	.250	224	56	9	1	8	30	8	37	.276	.406	None on/out	.273	154	42	6	2	5	5	4	30	.291	.435
Flyball	.238	130	31	8	1	4	13	6	24	.284	.408	Batting #5	.259	255	66	13	2	6	35	8	47	.281	.396
Home	.288	299	86	13	3	11	45	11	50	.313	.462	Batting #6	.262	145	38	6	2	5	18	7	27	.306	.434
Away	.208	288	60	10	2	6	25	15	56	.252	.319	Other	.225	187	42	4	1	6	17	11	32	.268	.353
Day	.236	165	39	12	0	6	22	10	36	.283	.418	April	.220	82	18	3	1	4	12	6	15	.278	.427
Night	.254	422	107	11	5	11	48	16	70	.283	.382	May	.270	100	27	4	0	3	13	2	18	.284	.400
Grass	.278	446	124	19	5	15	57	19	73	.309	.462	June	.301	93	28	5	2	2	11	6	13	.347	.462
Turf	.156	141	22	4	0	2	13	7	33	.200	.227	July	.263	99	26	3	2	3	11	3	18	.284	.424
First Pitch	.209	91	19	5	1	2	8	3	0	.242	.352	August	.237	93	22	4	0	3	16	5	16	.280	.376
Ahead on Count	.257	109	28	5	0	7	22	16	0	.349	.495	September/October	.208	120	25	4	0	2	7	4	26	.236	.292
Behind on Count	.264	227	60	8	3	7	25	0	63	.267	.419	Pre-All Star	.273	319	87	13	3	10	41	15	52	.308	.426
Two Strikes	.188	260	49	5	1	3	17	8	106	.217	.250	Post-All Star	.220	268	59	10	2	7	29	11	54	.254	.351

1992 By Position

Position	Avg	AB	H	2B	3B	HR	RBI	BB	SO	OBP	SLG	G	GS	Innings	PO	A	E	DP	Fld Pct	Rng Fctr	In Zone	Outs	Zone Rtg	MLB Zone
As cf	.250	579	145	22	5	17	70	26	106	.285	.394	152	150	1338.1	425	18	2	7	.996	2.98	468	411	.878	.824

Last Five Years

	Avg	AB	H	2B	3B	HR	RBI	BB	SO	OBP	SLG		Avg	AB	H	2B	3B	HR	RBI	BB	SO	OBP	SLG
vs. Left	.250	612	153	26	6	27	79	36	95	.293	.444	Scoring Posn	.257	342	88	18	2	12	123	34	60	.323	.427
vs. Right	.252	805	203	30	3	24	89	38	163	.289	.386	Close & Late	.230	244	56	6	1	10	31	18	55	.282	.385
Groundball	.252	511	129	18	2	20	65	29	94	.290	.413	None on/out	.286	385	110	19	2	18	18	13	70	.309	.486
Flyball	.231	320	74	16	1	16	35	18	62	.280	.438	Batting #5	.245	282	69	13	2	6	35	10	52	.270	.369
Home	.270	682	184	26	5	28	89	33	115	.306	.446	Batting #6	.269	249	67	12	2	8	32	12	45	.311	.430
Away	.234	735	172	30	4	23	79	43	143	.276	.380	Other	.248	886	220	31	5	37	101	54	161	.291	.420
Day	.256	497	127	28	4	19	62	28	91	.295	.443	April	.246	134	33	6	1	6	18	9	26	.295	.440
Night	.249	920	229	28	5	32	106	48	167	.288	.395	May	.229	258	59	10	0	6	21	15	49	.271	.337
Grass	.267	1058	282	39	7	44	133	54	183	.304	.441	June	.290	200	58	8	5	7	27	11	29	.324	.485
Turf	.206	359	74	17	2	7	35	22	75	.251	.323	July	.260	177	46	6	2	7	22	7	23	.292	.435
First Pitch	.253	233	59	13	1	8	26	7	0	.276	.451	August	.232	233	54	9	1	9	33	12	50	.271	.395
Ahead on Count	.321	262	84	15	1	17	48	39	0	.406	.580	September/October	.255	415	106	17	0	16	47	22	81	.294	.412
Behind on Count	.221	552	122	17	5	15	48	1	161	.226	.351	Pre-All Star	.256	661	169	25	6	22	75	37	112	.295	.411
Two Strikes	.180	643	116	12	2	16	46	29	258	.219	.280	Post-All Star	.247	756	187	31	3	29	93	39	146	.287	.411

Batter vs. Pitcher (career)

Hits Best Against	Avg	AB	H	2B	3B	HR	RBI	BB	SO	OBP	SLG	Hits Worst Against	Avg	AB	H	2B	3B	HR	RBI	BB	SO	OBP	SLG
Bud Black	.545	11	6	2	0	1	2	0	1	.545	1.000	Randy Tomlin	.000	11	0	0	0	0	0	1	2	.083	.000
Danny Jackson	.500	18	9	1	0	2	4	3	3	.571	.889	Ramon Martinez	.059	17	1	0	0	0	1	0	2	.059	.059
Roger McDowell	.500	12	6	2	0	0	1	1	2	.538	.667	Terry Mulholland	.087	23	2	0	1	0	3	1	5	.125	.174
John Smoltz	.400	20	8	3	0	1	4	0	4	.400	.700	Jim Deshaies	.143	14	2	0	0	0	4	4	.333	.143	
Joe Magrane	.389	18	7	3	0	1	3	1	1	.421	.722	Tim Belcher	.167	24	4	1	0	0	1	10	.259	.208	

Mike Jackson — Giants
Pitches Right (flyball pitcher)

	ERA	W	L	Sv	G	GS	IP	BB	SO	Avg	H	2B	3B	HR	RBI	OBP	SLG	GF	IR	IRS	Hld	SvOp	SB	CS	GB	FB	G/F
1992 Season	3.73	6	6	2	67	0	82.0	33	80	.252	76	14	3	7	34	.331	.387	24	28	8	9	3	6	3	97	85	1.14
Last Five Years	3.41	28	31	30	329	0	446.2	208	393	.222	359	67	6	38	226	.315	.341	87	329	107	50	58	46	12	478	508	0.94

1992 Season

	ERA	W	L	Sv	G	GS	IP	H	HR	BB	SO		Avg	AB	H	2B	3B	HR	RBI	BB	SO	OBP	SLG
Home	3.15	3	0	1	30	0	40.0	30	1	16	39	vs. Left	.265	162	43	11	1	3	14	24	33	.363	.401
Away	4.29	3	1	1	37	0	42.0	46	6	17	41	vs. Right	.236	140	33	3	2	4	20	9	47	.291	.371
Day	2.67	2	1	1	27	0	33.2	21	3	14	31	Inning 1-6	.286	49	14	4	2	1	11	5	11	.379	.510
Night	4.17	4	5	1	40	0	40.1	55	4	19	49	Inning 7+	.245	253	62	10	1	6	23	28	69	.330	.364
Grass	3.98	5	3	1	48	0	61.0	55	5	25	54	None on	.231	182	42	5	2	6	6	9	50	.275	.379
Turf	3.00	1	3	1	19	0	21.0	21	2	8	26	Runners on	.283	120	34	9	1	1	28	24	30	.405	.400
April	2.63	0	1	0	10	0	13.2	10	2	3	14	Scoring Posn	.225	71	16	4	0	0	22	21	17	.400	.282

219

1992 Season

	ERA	W	L	Sv	G	GS	IP	H	HR	BB	SO		Avg	AB	H	2B	3B	HR	RBI	BB	SO	OBP	SLG
May	2.81	1	0	2	11	0	16.0	14	1	3	14	Close & Late	.240	150	36	5	1	5	12	11	46	.309	.387
June	2.77	2	1	0	10	0	13.0	12	1	7	9	None on/out	.224	76	17	2	1	2	2	5	23	.272	.355
July	2.70	2	1	0	11	0	13.1	9	1	5	22	vs. 1st Batr (relief)	.197	61	12	0	1	2	5	5	19	.269	.328
August	4.15	0	2	0	13	0	13.0	9	1	9	13	First Inning Pitched	.260	219	57	11	2	5	27	28	57	.352	.397
September/October	7.62	1	1	0	12	0	13.0	22	1	6	8	First 15 Pitches	.266	188	50	9	2	5	21	23	48	.352	.415
Starter	0.00	0	0	0	0	0	0.0	0	0	0	0	Pitch 16-30	.208	101	21	5	0	2	10	9	31	.279	.317
Reliever	3.73	6	6	2	67	0	82.0	76	7	33	80	Pitch 31-45	.385	13	5	0	1	0	3	1	1	.429	.538
0 Days rest	2.25	1	1	0	11	0	12.0	9	2	6	12	Pitch 46+	.000	0	0	0	0	0	0	0	0	.000	.000
1 or 2 Days rest	3.67	3	4	1	38	0	49.0	44	5	19	49	First Pitch	.265	34	9	1	0	1	3	7	0	.386	.382
3+ Days rest	4.71	2	1	1	18	0	21.0	23	0	8	19	Ahead on Count	.208	149	31	5	1	1	10	0	64	.219	.275
Pre-All Star	2.54	4	2	2	36	0	49.2	40	5	15	49	Behind on Count	.352	54	19	2	2	2	6	18	1	.514	.574
Post-All Star	5.57	2	4	0	31	0	32.1	36	2	18	31	Two Strikes	.173	162	28	5	1	1	10	8	79	.221	.235

Last Five Years

	ERA	W	L	Sv	G	GS	IP	H	HR	BB	SO		Avg	AB	H	2B	3B	HR	RBI	BB	SO	OBP	SLG
Home	3.41	16	11	11	161	0	226.2	173	21	96	200	vs. Left	.250	704	176	40	3	20	104	113	114	.354	.401
Away	3.40	12	20	19	168	0	220.0	186	17	112	193	vs. Right	.200	913	183	27	3	18	122	95	279	.283	.296
Day	3.23	6	7	6	93	0	119.2	77	9	61	97	Inning 1-6	.261	165	43	10	2	4	42	28	41	.365	.418
Night	3.47	22	24	24	236	0	327.0	282	29	147	296	Inning 7+	.218	1452	316	57	4	34	184	180	352	.309	.333
Grass	3.45	13	13	15	148	0	198.0	162	15	101	177	None on	.216	850	184	27	3	26	26	76	201	.288	.347
Turf	3.37	15	18	15	181	0	248.2	197	23	107	216	Runners on	.228	767	175	40	3	12	200	132	192	.342	.335
April	3.48	2	5	3	43	0	67.1	60	4	20	50	Scoring Posn	.228	499	114	28	0	7	182	111	124	.365	.327
May	2.73	7	2	7	55	0	82.1	60	10	27	71	Close & Late	.226	748	169	28	4	16	115	101	190	.324	.338
June	3.02	6	4	12	53	0	80.1	54	8	37	71	None on/out	.243	367	89	10	2	12	12	30	80	.303	.379
July	4.56	7	6	1	59	0	71.0	66	5	40	72	vs. 1st Batr (relief)	.213	277	59	9	1	5	50	36	79	.303	.307
August	2.36	4	7	4	65	0	80.0	49	5	47	67	First Inning Pitched	.228	1043	238	41	5	21	172	132	253	.319	.337
September/October	4.66	2	7	3	54	0	65.2	70	5	37	62	First 15 Pitches	.235	961	226	39	3	22	150	113	219	.320	.351
Starter	0.00	0	0	0	0	0	0.0	0	0	0	0	Pitch 16-30	.195	507	99	24	2	12	54	64	136	.290	.321
Reliever	3.41	28	31	30	329	0	446.2	359	38	208	393	Pitch 31-45	.217	120	26	4	1	3	16	24	31	.349	.342
0 Days rest	5.36	6	13	7	67	0	80.2	70	11	47	68	Pitch 46+	.276	29	8	0	0	1	6	7	7	.421	.379
1 or 2 Days rest	2.75	14	13	17	168	0	242.0	182	16	107	212	First Pitch	.302	225	68	12	1	9	50	34	0	.397	.484
3+ Days rest	3.41	8	5	6	94	0	124.0	107	11	54	113	Ahead on Count	.155	793	123	19	1	9	61	0	332	.166	.216
Pre-All Star	3.08	17	13	23	171	0	257.0	198	26	93	230	Behind on Count	.312	301	94	17	2	11	59	106	1	.490	.492
Post-All Star	3.84	11	18	7	158	0	189.2	161	12	115	163	Two Strikes	.146	821	120	21	3	8	72	68	392	.215	.208

Pitcher vs. Batter (career)

Pitches Best Vs.	Avg	AB	H	2B	3B	HR	RBI	BB	SO	OBP	SLG	Pitches Worst Vs.	Avg	AB	H	2B	3B	HR	RBI	BB	SO	OBP	SLG
Paul Molitor	.000	12	0	0	0	0	0	1	4	.077	.000	Rafael Palmeiro	.778	9	7	1	0	2	3	2	1	.818	1.556
Rob Deer	.000	12	0	0	0	0	0	1	8	.077	.000	Chili Davis	.667	9	6	0	0	0	2	5	0	.733	.667
Jesse Barfield	.000	11	0	0	0	0	0	1	5	.083	.000	Dave Martinez	.571	7	4	0	0	0	1	3	1	.636	.571
Jose Canseco	.000	11	0	0	0	0	0	2	3	.154	.000	Candy Maldonado	.455	11	5	1	0	2	6	0	3	.455	1.091
Cory Snyder	.000	10	0	0	0	0	0	2	5	.167	.000	Ellis Burks	.308	13	4	0	0	2	4	2	2	.400	.769

Brook Jacoby — Indians

Bats Right

	Avg	G	AB	R	H	2B	3B	HR	RBI	BB	SO	HBP	GDP	SB	CS	OBP	SLG	IBB	SH	SF	#Pit	#P/PA	GB	FB	G/F
1992 Season	.261	120	291	30	76	7	0	4	36	28	54	1	13	0	3	.324	.326	2	3	4	1125	3.47	89	96	0.93
Last Five Years	.260	696	2334	243	606	103	10	44	268	228	357	10	73	7	16	.325	.369	16	5	25	8605	3.31	818	741	1.10

1992 Season

	Avg	AB	H	2B	3B	HR	RBI	BB	SO	OBP	SLG		Avg	AB	H	2B	3B	HR	RBI	BB	SO	OBP	SLG
vs. Left	.258	97	25	3	0	2	11	8	17	.311	.351	Scoring Posn	.306	72	22	2	0	1	33	14	18	.400	.375
vs. Right	.263	194	51	4	0	2	25	20	37	.330	.314	Close & Late	.320	50	16	1	0	1	8	7	13	.397	.400
Groundball	.266	79	21	1	0	2	13	6	13	.314	.354	None on/out	.286	63	18	1	0	1	1	4	8	.328	.349
Flyball	.205	83	17	3	0	0	6	10	18	.292	.241	Batting #7	.239	176	42	3	0	3	19	15	32	.299	.307
Home	.310	126	39	5	0	3	22	12	22	.362	.421	Batting #8	.280	93	26	2	0	1	12	11	18	.352	.333
Away	.224	165	37	2	0	1	14	16	32	.295	.255	Other	.364	22	8	2	0	0	5	2	4	.400	.455
Day	.188	96	18	1	0	1	12	10	22	.266	.229	April	.245	49	12	1	0	1	10	2	9	.269	.327
Night	.297	195	58	6	0	3	24	18	32	.353	.374	May	.310	71	22	2	0	0	10	9	15	.390	.338
Grass	.274	241	66	6	0	4	31	23	43	.335	.349	June	.232	56	13	2	0	2	5	7	7	.313	.375
Turf	.200	50	10	1	0	0	5	5	11	.273	.220	July	.281	32	9	0	0	0	1	1	5	.303	.281
First Pitch	.283	53	15	0	0	0	3	1	0	.286	.283	August	.246	57	14	2	0	1	6	5	9	.306	.333
Ahead on Count	.413	63	26	3	0	1	15	12	0	.507	.508	September/October	.231	26	6	0	0	0	4	4	9	.323	.231
Behind on Count	.225	102	23	1	0	2	13	0	24	.223	.294	Pre-All Star	.280	182	51	5	0	3	26	19	32	.346	.357
Two Strikes	.157	121	19	3	0	3	9	15	54	.254	.256	Post-All Star	.229	109	25	2	0	1	10	9	22	.286	.275

1992 By Position

Position	Avg	AB	H	2B	3B	HR	RBI	BB	SO	OBP	SLG	G	GS	Innings	PO	A	E	DP	Fld Pct	Rng Fctr	In Zone	Outs	Zone Rtg	MLB Zone
As Pinch Hitter	.556	9	5	1	0	0	3	1	2	.600	.667	10	0	---	---	---	---	---	---	---	---	---	---	---
As 1b	.235	17	4	1	0	0	2	2	7	.300	.294	10	5	51.0	45	2	0	7	1.000	---	5	3	.600	.843
As 3b	.253	265	67	5	0	4	31	25	45	.316	.317	111	77	731.1	46	175	10	17	.957	2.72	217	188	.866	.841

Last Five Years

	Avg	AB	H	2B	3B	HR	RBI	BB	SO	OBP	SLG		Avg	AB	H	2B	3B	HR	RBI	BB	SO	OBP	SLG
vs. Left	.275	652	179	26	3	15	70	61	88	.337	.396	Scoring Posn	.257	544	140	19	1	7	209	93	104	.356	.335
vs. Right	.254	1682	427	75	7	29	198	167	269	.320	.359	Close & Late	.234	394	92	14	0	8	42	37	71	.301	.330
Groundball	.271	649	176	27	4	8	85	67	83	.339	.362	None on/out	.251	553	139	24	0	11	11	47	79	.311	.354
Flyball	.257	571	147	31	0	13	80	62	106	.331	.380	Batting #6	.264	1014	268	45	6	21	127	94	139	.328	.383
Home	.261	1089	264	50	7	25	148	123	146	.335	.388	Batting #7	.259	698	181	25	2	14	77	80	120	.333	.361
Away	.259	1245	322	53	3	19	120	105	211	.316	.352	Other	.252	622	157	33	2	9	64	54	98	.311	.355
Day	.227	713	162	27	3	7	76	57	123	.286	.303	April	.286	322	92	19	3	6	38	26	55	.337	.419
Night	.274	1621	444	76	7	37	192	171	234	.342	.398	May	.258	426	110	13	2	15	50	43	81	.326	.404
Grass	.268	1950	523	93	9	40	243	196	281	.334	.387	June	.267	431	115	18	1	11	42	46	55	.335	.390
Turf	.216	364	83	10	1	4	25	32	76	.278	.279	July	.275	324	89	10	0	3	45	28	44	.333	.333
First Pitch	.299	528	158	35	4	7	54	5	0	.306	.420	August	.243	449	109	24	1	6	46	50	56	.320	.341
Ahead on Count	.335	555	186	26	3	22	97	121	0	.452	.512	September/October	.238	382	91	19	3	3	47	35	66	.301	.327
Behind on Count	.201	692	139	17	4	9	72	1	187	.206	.276	Pre-All Star	.271	1253	340	53	6	33	143	122	201	.335	.402
Two Strikes	.166	824	137	27	1	9	59	99	356	.256	.234	Post-All Star	.246	1081	266	50	4	11	125	106	156	.313	.330

Batter vs. Pitcher (since 1984)

Hits Best Against	Avg	AB	H	2B	3B	HR	RBI	BB	SO	OBP	SLG	Hits Worst Against	Avg	AB	H	2B	3B	HR	RBI	BB	SO	OBP	SLG
Mike Birkbeck	.467	15	7	2	0	1	3	2	2	.529	.800	Mark Eichhorn	.050	20	1	0	0	0	1	1	3	.095	.050
Jose Guzman	.464	28	13	2	0	2	4	2	3	.500	.750	David Wells	.053	19	1	0	0	0	0	2	7	.143	.053
Dennis Lamp	.444	27	12	2	0	3	11	0	2	.444	.852	Dan Plesac	.071	14	1	0	0	0	1	0	4	.067	.071
Edwin Nunez	.417	12	5	3	1	0	2	2	3	.467	.833	Bill Swift	.118	17	2	0	0	0	5	0	0	.111	.118
Scott Bankhead	.333	9	3	2	0	1	2	2	1	.455	.889	Luis Aquino	.118	17	2	0	0	0	0	0	2	.118	.118

John Jaha — Brewers   Bats Right

	Avg	G	AB	R	H	2B	3B	HR	RBI	BB	SO	HBP	GDP	SB	CS	OBP	SLG	IBB	SH	SF	#Pit	#P/PA	GB	FB	G/F
1992 Season	.226	47	133	17	30	3	1	2	10	12	30	2	1	10	0	.291	.308	1	1	4	560	3.71	48	37	1.30

1992 Season

	Avg	AB	H	2B	3B	HR	RBI	BB	SO	OBP	SLG		Avg	AB	H	2B	3B	HR	RBI	BB	SO	OBP	SLG
vs. Left	.174	46	8	1	0	1	5	6	10	.268	.261	Scoring Posn	.222	27	6	1	0	0	8	7	7	.359	.259
vs. Right	.253	87	22	2	1	1	5	6	20	.305	.333	Close & Late	.316	19	6	0	0	0	1	2	5	.409	.316
Home	.218	87	19	3	1	1	5	4	24	.260	.310	None on/out	.212	33	7	0	1	1	1	2	7	.257	.364
Away	.239	46	11	0	0	1	5	8	6	.345	.304	Batting #6	.303	33	10	1	0	1	5	6	8	.390	.424
First Pitch	.278	18	5	1	0	1	3	1	0	.333	.500	Batting #7	.211	71	15	1	1	1	2	5	13	.278	.296
Ahead on Count	.222	27	6	1	1	0	1	9	0	.421	.333	Other	.172	29	5	1	0	0	3	1	9	.194	.207
Behind on Count	.167	54	9	0	0	1	2	0	19	.167	.222	Pre-All Star	.357	14	5	0	0	0	1	0	2	.333	.357
Two Strikes	.188	69	13	1	0	1	4	2	30	.211	.246	Post-All Star	.210	119	25	3	1	2	9	12	28	.287	.303

Chris James — Giants   Bats Right

	Avg	G	AB	R	H	2B	3B	HR	RBI	BB	SO	HBP	GDP	SB	CS	OBP	SLG	IBB	SH	SF	#Pit	#P/PA	GB	FB	G/F
1992 Season	.242	111	248	25	60	10	4	5	32	14	45	2	2	2	3	.285	.375	2	0	3	932	3.49	90	79	1.14
Last Five Years	.255	648	2261	230	576	99	13	54	274	120	318	14	56	21	16	.294	.382	12	9	16	8182	3.39	895	672	1.33

1992 Season

	Avg	AB	H	2B	3B	HR	RBI	BB	SO	OBP	SLG		Avg	AB	H	2B	3B	HR	RBI	BB	SO	OBP	SLG
vs. Left	.302	116	35	7	1	2	13	5	18	.333	.431	Scoring Posn	.258	66	17	2	2	0	23	6	16	.316	.348
vs. Right	.189	132	25	3	3	3	19	9	27	.243	.326	Close & Late	.244	41	10	2	0	1	2	4	10	.319	.366
Home	.213	127	27	5	3	3	19	5	26	.239	.370	None on/out	.154	52	8	0	1	1	1	2	8	.185	.250
Away	.273	121	33	5	1	2	13	9	19	.331	.380	Batting #4	.213	127	27	6	1	2	15	5	23	.246	.323
First Pitch	.432	37	16	0	1	2	5	2	0	.462	.649	Batting #6	.296	54	16	3	1	0	7	5	8	.355	.389
Ahead on Count	.313	64	20	2	2	3	10	5	0	.362	.547	Other	.254	67	17	1	2	3	10	4	14	.296	.463
Behind on Count	.149	87	13	3	0	0	10	0	23	.165	.184	Pre-All Star	.221	104	23	5	2	3	12	11	23	.297	.394
Two Strikes	.140	100	14	3	1	0	11	7	45	.200	.190	Post-All Star	.257	144	37	5	2	2	20	3	22	.275	.361

Last Five Years

	Avg	AB	H	2B	3B	HR	RBI	BB	SO	OBP	SLG		Avg	AB	H	2B	3B	HR	RBI	BB	SO	OBP	SLG
vs. Left	.266	734	195	31	4	22	101	46	100	.309	.409	Scoring Posn	.255	620	158	22	4	12	214	47	96	.303	.361
vs. Right	.250	1527	381	68	9	32	173	74	218	.287	.369	Close & Late	.236	382	90	15	0	6	32	26	65	.287	.322
Groundball	.260	796	207	38	6	17	104	43	100	.302	.381	None on/out	.230	509	117	19	2	15	15	24	69	.270	.363
Flyball	.255	482	123	26	3	16	58	33	67	.304	.421	Batting #3	.274	343	94	13	4	5	54	14	47	.300	.379
Home	.268	1090	292	50	7	27	147	59	135	.308	.401	Batting #5	.273	874	239	39	5	28	108	53	113	.317	.426
Away	.243	1171	284	49	6	27	127	61	183	.282	.364	Other	.233	1044	243	47	4	21	112	53	158	.274	.346
Day	.266	655	174	39	6	17	96	35	107	.306	.421	April	.229	292	67	9	0	5	32	14	48	.267	.353
Night	.250	1606	402	60	7	37	178	85	211	.290	.366	May	.238	374	89	14	1	9	46	22	56	.284	.353
Grass	.264	1417	374	56	11	32	183	75	200	.302	.387	June	.263	407	107	22	3	9	50	24	59	.306	.398
Turf	.239	844	202	43	2	22	91	45	118	.281	.373	July	.256	438	112	20	4	12	48	23	57	.297	.402
First Pitch	.302	315	95	15	3	13	42	5	0	.313	.492	August	.303	400	121	22	1	12	51	18	52	.333	.453
Ahead on Count	.329	569	187	35	4	24	110	70	0	.402	.531	September/October	.229	350	80	12	4	7	47	19	46	.269	.346
Behind on Count	.232	841	195	29	5	10	78	3	190	.236	.314	Pre-All Star	.246	1207	297	49	6	26	141	68	181	.289	.361
Two Strikes	.177	905	160	22	6	10	72	43	318	.218	.248	Post-All Star	.265	1054	279	50	7	28	133	52	137	.301	.405

Batter vs. Pitcher (career)

Hits Best Against	Avg	AB	H	2B	3B	HR	RBI	BB	SO	OBP	SLG	Hits Worst Against	Avg	AB	H	2B	3B	HR	RBI	BB	SO	OBP	SLG
Les Lancaster	.538	13	7	0	0	2	6	1	1	.571	1.000	David Cone	.000	21	0	0	0	0	1	0	5	.000	.000
Kevin Appier	.500	14	7	0	0	1	2	0	1	.500	.714	Jim Abbott	.000	15	0	0	0	0	0	0	3	.000	.000
Barry Jones	.500	10	5	1	1	0	2	1	1	.545	.800	Charlie Leibrandt	.000	12	0	0	0	0	0	1	2	.077	.000
Neal Heaton	.450	20	9	2	0	2	5	1	1	.476	.850	Jose Rijo	.091	11	1	1	0	0	0	0	2	.091	.182
Zane Smith	.400	15	6	1	0	2	4	1	2	.438	.867	Joe Hesketh	.091	11	1	0	0	0	0	0	2	.091	.091

Dion James — Yankees

Bats Left (groundball hitter)

	Avg	G	AB	R	H	2B	3B	HR	RBI	BB	SO	HBP	GDP	SB	CS	OBP	SLG	IBB	SH	SF	#Pit	#P/PA	GB	FB	G/F
1992 Season	.262	67	145	24	38	8	0	3	17	22	15	1	3	1	0	.359	.379				610	3.59	61	42	1.45
Last Five Years	.271	420	1194	139	324	58	7	12	109	156	146	4	30	17	19	.356	.362	14	10	6	4856	3.57	519	299	1.74

1992 Season

	Avg	AB	H	2B	3B	HR	RBI	BB	SO	OBP	SLG		Avg	AB	H	2B	3B	HR	RBI	BB	SO	OBP	SLG
vs. Left	.214	14	3	0	0	1	4	4	2	.421	.429	Scoring Posn	.256	43	11	1	0	2	15	6	5	.333	.419
vs. Right	.267	131	35	8	0	2	13	18	13	.351	.374	Close & Late	.167	30	5	0	0	0	1	2	4	.219	.167
Home	.315	54	17	3	0	2	10	7	8	.391	.481	None on/out	.194	31	6	2	0	0	0	4	1	.286	.258
Away	.231	91	21	5	0	1	7	15	7	.340	.319	Batting #1	.211	38	8	1	0	0	1	8	3	.348	.237
First Pitch	.300	20	6	0	0	1	3	0	0	.318	.450	Batting #2	.357	42	15	4	0	2	9	3	4	.404	.595
Ahead on Count	.276	58	16	6	0	1	7	10	0	.382	.431	Other	.231	65	15	3	0	1	7	11	8	.338	.323
Behind on Count	.162	37	6	1	0	0	1	0	10	.162	.189	Pre-All Star	.209	86	18	6	0	2	9	14	8	.317	.349
Two Strikes	.205	44	9	2	0	0	3	12	15	.368	.250	Post-All Star	.339	59	20	2	0	1	8	8	7	.420	.424

Last Five Years

	Avg	AB	H	2B	3B	HR	RBI	BB	SO	OBP	SLG		Avg	AB	H	2B	3B	HR	RBI	BB	SO	OBP	SLG
vs. Left	.173	110	19	5	1	1	8	17	16	.289	.264	Scoring Posn	.258	260	67	7	2	2	87	54	32	.378	.323
vs. Right	.281	1084	305	53	6	11	101	139	130	.363	.372	Close & Late	.215	219	47	6	2	1	12	36	36	.324	.274
Groundball	.266	406	108	19	3	5	45	61	44	.364	.365	None on/out	.255	290	74	11	2	1	1	29	35	.325	.317
Flyball	.242	244	59	10	2	2	19	36	27	.339	.324	Batting #2	.302	232	70	13	1	4	23	26	16	.374	.418
Home	.262	565	148	31	4	4	52	78	75	.352	.352	Batting #3	.305	351	107	19	3	4	45	42	44	.378	.410
Away	.280	629	176	27	3	8	57	78	71	.359	.370	Other	.241	611	147	26	3	4	41	88	86	.337	.313
Day	.291	351	102	14	4	6	40	46	39	.374	.405	April	.231	147	34	5	1	0	8	22	14	.329	.279
Night	.263	843	222	44	3	6	69	110	107	.348	.344	May	.278	230	64	15	1	2	20	36	30	.379	.365
Grass	.265	936	248	41	7	8	79	119	118	.349	.349	June	.256	219	56	12	2	2	18	29	31	.341	.356
Turf	.295	258	76	17	0	4	30	37	28	.380	.407	July	.301	216	65	12	2	5	27	31	22	.390	.444
First Pitch	.323	192	62	6	2	1	22	5	0	.342	.391	August	.268	239	64	10	0	2	18	20	31	.323	.335
Ahead on Count	.321	336	108	21	1	5	46	96	0	.469	.435	September/October	.287	143	41	4	1	2	18	18	18	.368	.371
Behind on Count	.217	387	84	16	2	3	22	0	85	.221	.292	Pre-All Star	.260	658	171	35	4	5	54	91	78	.350	.348
Two Strikes	.197	457	90	19	2	3	23	51	145	.280	.267	Post-All Star	.285	536	153	23	3	7	55	65	68	.363	.379

Batter vs. Pitcher (since 1984)

Hits Best Against	Avg	AB	H	2B	3B	HR	RBI	BB	SO	OBP	SLG	Hits Worst Against	Avg	AB	H	2B	3B	HR	RBI	BB	SO	OBP	SLG
Todd Stottlemyre	.636	11	7	1	0	0	1	4	0	.733	.727	Nolan Ryan	.050	20	1	0	0	0	0	2	4	.136	.050
Ted Power	.500	12	6	2	0	0	3	3	1	.600	.667	Lance McCullers	.100	10	1	0	0	0	0	2	3	.250	.100
Bob Walk	.455	22	10	6	0	0	4	3	1	.520	.727	Bryn Smith	.105	19	2	1	0	0	0	1	5	.150	.158
Mark Gubicza	.417	12	5	1	0	1	3	2	1	.500	.750	Mike Dunne	.182	11	2	0	0	0	3	1	1	.250	.182
Greg Maddux	.333	12	4	1	1	1	5	2	2	.429	.833	Orel Hershiser	.188	32	6	0	0	0	0	1	5	.235	.188

Stan Javier — Phillies

Bats Both (groundball hitter)

	Avg	G	AB	R	H	2B	3B	HR	RBI	BB	SO	HBP	GDP	SB	CS	OBP	SLG	IBB	SH	SF	#Pit	#P/PA	GB	FB	G/F
1992 Season	.249	130	334	42	83	17	1	1	29	37	54	3	4	18	3	.327	.314	2	3	2	1427	3.80	145	70	2.07
Last Five Years	.256	611	1526	214	390	56	16	8	130	156	246	6	33	72	14	.325	.329	6	22	11	6380	3.76	674	317	2.13

1992 Season

	Avg	AB	H	2B	3B	HR	RBI	BB	SO	OBP	SLG		Avg	AB	H	2B	3B	HR	RBI	BB	SO	OBP	SLG
vs. Left	.219	146	32	8	1	0	5	12	22	.283	.288	Scoring Posn	.278	79	22	5	0	1	27	11	12	.359	.380
vs. Right	.271	188	51	9	0	1	24	25	32	.359	.335	Close & Late	.156	64	10	2	0	0	5	7	13	.243	.188
Groundball	.222	126	28	4	1	0	8	12	24	.293	.270	None on/out	.219	96	21	2	1	0	0	15	15	.324	.260
Flyball	.200	75	15	5	0	1	12	8	16	.286	.307	Batting #1	.228	167	38	5	1	0	11	21	23	.314	.269
Home	.273	150	41	11	0	1	16	14	22	.337	.367	Batting #2	.256	43	11	2	0	0	1	6	8	.360	.302
Away	.228	184	42	6	1	0	13	23	32	.319	.272	Other	.274	124	34	10	0	1	17	10	23	.333	.379
Day	.213	94	20	3	1	0	4	11	15	.302	.266	April	.190	21	4	0	0	0	2	1	2	.227	.190
Night	.263	240	63	14	0	1	25	26	39	.337	.333	May	.188	16	3	0	0	1	3	2	5	.316	.375
Grass	.211	123	26	3	0	1	9	14	16	.295	.260	June	.150	20	3	3	0	0	0	3	4	.261	.300
Turf	.270	211	57	14	1	0	20	23	38	.346	.346	July	.263	80	21	3	0	0	6	12	12	.372	.300
First Pitch	.294	51	15	1	0	1	7	2	0	.315	.373	August	.283	92	26	6	0	0	9	8	14	.340	.348
Ahead on Count	.291	55	16	4	0	0	7	25	0	.513	.364	September/October	.248	105	26	5	1	0	9	11	17	.314	.314
Behind on Count	.200	110	22	6	0	0	7	0	28	.214	.255	Pre-All Star	.219	105	23	3	0	1	7	14	18	.322	.276
Two Strikes	.211	161	34	8	1	0	9	10	54	.262	.273	Post-All Star	.262	229	60	14	1	0	22	23	36	.329	.332

222

1992 By Position

Position	Avg	AB	H	2B	3B	HR	RBI	BB	SO	OBP	SLG	G	GS	Innings	PO	A	E	DP	Fld Pct	Rng Fctr	In Zone	Outs	Zone Rtg	MLB Zone
As Pinch Hitter	.233	30	7	2	0	1	4	2	5	.281	.400	33	0	---	---	---	---	---	---	---	---	---	---	---
As lf	.241	112	27	7	0	0	13	10	20	.315	.304	42	29	272.2	78	2	0	0	1.000	2.64	92	77	.837	.809
As cf	.249	185	46	7	1	0	11	23	28	.332	.297	51	46	398.0	148	5	3	1	.981	3.46	171	144	.842	.824
As rf	.429	7	3	1	0	0	1	2	1	.556	.571	12	0	23.1	3	0	0	0	1.000	1.16	4	3	.750	.814

Last Five Years

	Avg	AB	H	2B	3B	HR	RBI	BB	SO	OBP	SLG		Avg	AB	H	2B	3B	HR	RBI	BB	SO	OBP	SLG
vs. Left	.254	532	135	16	7	3	39	47	82	.316	.327	Scoring Posn	.253	363	92	13	5	1	117	54	56	.344	.325
vs. Right	.257	994	255	40	9	5	91	109	166	.329	.330	Close & Late	.224	312	70	11	3	2	32	38	60	.307	.298
Groundball	.273	451	123	18	9	0	36	41	59	.334	.353	None on/out	.265	374	99	15	4	3	38	62		.333	.350
Flyball	.213	342	73	13	5	3	33	35	69	.287	.307	Batting #1	.279	359	100	12	4	2	25	47	52	.361	.351
Home	.256	708	181	26	4	3	61	81	108	.331	.316	Batting #2	.263	388	102	9	5	1	24	42	59	.338	.320
Away	.256	818	209	30	12	5	69	75	140	.319	.340	Other	.241	779	188	35	7	5	81	67	137	.301	.323
Day	.232	560	130	14	5	3	41	63	96	.311	.291	April	.264	182	48	9	3	1	16	16	25	.320	.363
Night	.269	966	260	42	11	5	89	93	152	.333	.351	May	.238	248	59	4	6	1	31	26	43	.312	.315
Grass	.240	1072	257	32	9	6	90	118	173	.315	.303	June	.285	316	90	18	3	3	26	27	43	.341	.389
Turf	.293	454	133	24	7	2	40	38	75	.349	.390	July	.247	275	68	5	2	1	17	27	52	.319	.291
First Pitch	.289	228	66	4	2	1	21	3	0	.295	.338	August	.230	226	52	10	1	0	19	26	44	.308	.283
Ahead on Count	.295	302	89	15	5	2	22	91	0	.457	.397	September/October	.262	279	73	10	1	2	21	34	41	.341	.326
Behind on Count	.237	515	122	20	4	3	40	0	129	.239	.309	Pre-All Star	.263	876	230	32	13	6	78	86	132	.329	.349
Two Strikes	.210	708	149	26	8	2	58	58	248	.271	.278	Post-All Star	.246	650	160	24	3	2	52	70	116	.320	.302

Batter vs. Pitcher (career)

Hits Best Against	Avg	AB	H	2B	3B	HR	RBI	BB	SO	OBP	SLG	Hits Worst Against	Avg	AB	H	2B	3B	HR	RBI	BB	SO	OBP	SLG
Eric King	.500	12	6	0	1	0	0	1	1	.538	.667	Tom Glavine	.000	12	0	0	0	0	0	3	2	.200	.000
Rheal Cormier	.417	12	5	0	0	0	1	0	2	.417	.417	Mark Gubicza	.000	11	0	0	0	0	0	0	1	.000	.000
Danny Jackson	.389	18	7	2	0	0	2	2	2	.450	.500	Frank Tanana	.095	21	2	1	0	0	4	0	5	.095	.143
Trevor Wilson	.333	12	4	1	0	0	1	0	0	.385	.417	Bruce Hurst	.118	17	2	0	0	0	0	1	2	.167	.118
Dennis Rasmussen	.333	9	3	0	0	1	1	4	1	.538	.667	John Smoltz	.133	15	2	0	0	0	1	0	2	.133	.133

Mike Jeffcoat — Rangers

Pitches Left

	ERA	W	L	Sv	G	GS	IP	BB	SO	Avg	H	2B	3B	HR	RBI	OBP	SLG	CG	ShO	Sup	QS	#P/S	SB	CS	GB	FB	G/F
1992 Season	7.32	0	1	0	6	3	19.2	5	6	.350	28	6	2	2	15	.379	.550	0	0	3.66	1	65	0	1	25	32	0.78
Last Five Years	4.54	19	18	6	147	39	350.2	96	176	.296	412	73	16	30	176	.343	.436	3	2	4.70	19	85	7	13	516	419	1.23

1992 Season

	ERA	W	L	Sv	G	GS	IP	H	HR	BB	SO		Avg	AB	H	2B	3B	HR	RBI	BB	SO	OBP	SLG
Home	6.23	0	0	0	3	2	8.2	12	1	3	4	vs. Left	.350	20	7	0	0	0	2	1	2	.364	.350
Away	8.18	0	1	0	3	1	11.0	16	1	2	2	vs. Right	.350	60	21	6	2	2	13	4	4	.385	.617

Last Five Years

	ERA	W	L	Sv	G	GS	IP	H	HR	BB	SO		Avg	AB	H	2B	3B	HR	RBI	BB	SO	OBP	SLG
Home	3.76	12	3	4	75	20	179.2	204	11	50	100	vs. Left	.262	344	97	13	4	4	43	16	49	.317	.378
Away	5.37	7	15	2	72	19	171.0	208	19	46	76	vs. Right	.300	1049	315	60	12	26	133	80	127	.352	.455
Day	4.27	1	3	0	28	7	59.0	76	7	12	33	Inning 1-6	.302	873	264	50	11	20	121	62	100	.352	.454
Night	4.60	18	15	6	119	32	291.2	336	23	84	143	Inning 7+	.285	520	148	23	5	10	55	34	76	.330	.406
Grass	4.36	17	14	5	122	32	284.2	335	25	82	143	None on	.286	795	227	39	8	12	49	116		.332	.400
Turf	5.32	2	4	1	25	7	66.0	77	5	14	33	Runners on	.309	598	185	34	8	18	164	47	60	.358	.483
April	5.67	1	2	2	19	2	27.0	33	2	9	14	Scoring Posn	.324	315	102	18	4	10	136	30	27	.372	.502
May	4.22	0	3	1	30	4	59.2	71	5	16	22	Close & Late	.299	221	66	13	2	4	24	16	38	.345	.430
June	4.67	8	3	0	26	13	94.1	109	7	27	44	None on/out	.304	359	109	18	5	6	6	20	51	.347	.432
July	6.18	3	5	1	17	7	43.2	60	5	15	23	vs. 1st Batr (relief)	.320	97	31	4	2	4	21	8	11	.374	.526
August	3.60	4	3	0	21	7	60.0	68	5	14	34	First Inning Pitched	.304	483	147	23	7	13	85	42	61	.364	.462
September/October	3.95	3	2	2	34	6	66.0	71	6	15	39	First 75 Pitches	.292	1199	350	59	14	26	149	84	147	.341	.430
Starter	4.83	12	14	0	39	39	218.0	264	18	59	99	Pitch 76-90	.319	113	36	10	1	3	18	6	17	.347	.504
Reliever	4.07	7	4	6	108	0	132.2	148	12	37	77	Pitch 91-105	.375	48	18	1	0	1	8	5	8	.444	.458
0-3 Days Rest	5.40	0	1	0	1	0	6.2	10	2	1	2	Pitch 106+	.242	33	8	3	1	0	1	1	4	.257	.394
4 Days Rest	3.61	7	4	0	21	21	127.0	144	8	29	67	First Pitch	.295	193	57	8	1	5	24	5	0	.324	.425
5+ Days Rest	6.62	5	9	0	17	17	84.1	110	8	29	30	Ahead on Count	.258	593	153	27	5	7	63	0	153	.266	.356
Pre-All Star	4.50	10	9	4	79	21	196.0	225	15	57	57	Behind on Count	.331	338	112	17	6	10	53	50	0	.413	.506
Post-All Star	4.60	9	9	2	68	18	154.2	187	15	39	89	Two Strikes	.237	565	134	25	4	8	52	41	176	.295	.338

Pitcher vs. Batter (since 1984)

Pitches Best Vs.	Avg	AB	H	2B	3B	HR	RBI	BB	SO	OBP	SLG	Pitches Worst Vs.	Avg	AB	H	2B	3B	HR	RBI	BB	SO	OBP	SLG
Dick Schofield	.077	13	1	0	0	0	0	0	0	.200	.077	Cecil Fielder	.600	10	6	0	0	2	6	3	1	.692	1.200
Mike Macfarlane	.083	12	1	1	0	0	3	0	3	.063	.167	Kirby Puckett	.500	12	6	1	2	1	5	0	2	.500	1.167
Lou Whitaker	.143	14	2	1	0	0	3	1	3	.188	.214	Brian Downing	.444	18	8	3	0	1	1	2	3	.500	.778
Jim Gantner	.158	19	3	0	0	0	1	1	2	.190	.158	Carlton Fisk	.417	12	5	1	1	1	5	2	1	.467	.917
Ozzie Guillen	.167	12	2	0	0	0	0	0	0	.167	.167	Brian Harper	.400	10	4	0	0	1	1	0	1	.455	.700

223

Gregg Jefferies — Royals   Bats Both

	Avg	G	AB	R	H	2B	3B	HR	RBI	BB	SO	HBP	GDP	SB	CS	OBP	SLG	IBB	SH	SF	#Pit	#P/PA	GB	FB	G/F
1992 Season	.285	152	604	66	172	36	3	10	75	43	29	1	24	19	9	.329	.404	4	0	9	2263	3.44	258	190	1.36
Last Five Years	.277	611	2311	312	641	131	12	52	278	183	163	13	66	82	23	.331	.412	16	3	22	8852	3.50	896	751	1.19

1992 Season

	Avg	AB	H	2B	3B	HR	RBI	BB	SO	OBP	SLG		Avg	AB	H	2B	3B	HR	RBI	BB	SO	OBP	SLG
vs. Left	.257	179	46	10	0	3	12	7	11	.282	.363	Scoring Posn	.253	154	39	1	2	3	61	15	7	.303	.344
vs. Right	.296	425	126	26	3	7	63	36	18	.348	.421	Close & Late	.282	110	31	5	0	1	14	9	4	.333	.355
Groundball	.242	153	37	11	1	2	18	6	7	.267	.366	None on/out	.303	145	44	9	1	3	3	8	6	.344	.441
Flyball	.326	215	70	18	0	3	23	18	11	.377	.451	Batting #2	.307	228	70	16	0	5	31	18	12	.349	.443
Home	.289	280	81	15	3	3	37	26	12	.346	.396	Batting #3	.251	171	43	11	0	3	17	6	9	.277	.368
Away	.281	324	91	21	0	7	38	17	17	.313	.410	Other	.288	205	59	9	3	2	27	19	8	.346	.390
Day	.318	151	48	12	1	4	16	9	5	.360	.490	April	.203	79	16	8	0	0	5	8	5	.270	.304
Night	.274	453	124	24	2	6	59	34	24	.319	.375	May	.286	119	34	8	0	1	12	3	6	.303	.378
Grass	.273	264	72	14	0	6	32	12	10	.301	.394	June	.329	76	25	5	0	3	15	5	2	.361	.513
Turf	.294	340	100	22	3	4	43	31	19	.349	.412	July	.333	117	39	6	1	3	16	8	8	.370	.479
First Pitch	.315	73	23	7	0	1	7	4	0	.359	.452	August	.326	92	30	5	1	1	12	13	2	.411	.435
Ahead on Count	.256	180	46	8	0	4	19	32	0	.361	.367	September/October	.231	121	28	4	1	2	15	6	6	.264	.331
Behind on Count	.320	181	58	11	3	2	31	0	14	.314	.448	Pre-All Star	.274	329	90	21	0	5	36	19	18	.310	.383
Two Strikes	.246	195	48	12	1	0	20	8	29	.275	.318	Post-All Star	.298	275	82	15	3	5	39	24	11	.351	.429

1992 By Position

Position	Avg	AB	H	2B	3B	HR	RBI	BB	SO	OBP	SLG	G	GS	Innings	PO	A	E	DP	Fld Pct	Rng Fctr	In Zone	Outs	Zone Rtg	MLB Zone
As 3b	.284	598	170	36	3	10	75	41	29	.327	.405	146	146	1288.1	96	302	26	23	.939	2.78	410	342	.834	.841

Last Five Years

	Avg	AB	H	2B	3B	HR	RBI	BB	SO	OBP	SLG		Avg	AB	H	2B	3B	HR	RBI	BB	SO	OBP	SLG
vs. Left	.269	785	211	47	4	18	89	45	58	.311	.408	Scoring Posn	.270	563	152	27	5	8	211	62	45	.333	.378
vs. Right	.282	1526	430	84	8	34	189	138	105	.341	.414	Close & Late	.262	389	102	15	0	5	42	34	26	.324	.339
Groundball	.281	741	208	40	5	18	86	51	54	.330	.421	None on/out	.284	553	157	33	2	18	18	43	35	.336	.448
Flyball	.273	567	155	33	2	9	56	50	41	.332	.386	Batting #1	.302	526	159	30	3	18	59	41	34	.354	.473
Home	.300	1139	342	73	8	27	141	111	74	.363	.450	Batting #3	.274	829	227	44	4	18	105	59	49	.322	.402
Away	.255	1172	299	58	4	25	137	72	89	.298	.375	Other	.267	956	255	57	5	16	114	83	80	.326	.387
Day	.289	748	216	46	4	14	85	53	52	.339	.417	April	.208	274	57	22	0	1	25	26	25	.282	.299
Night	.272	1563	425	85	8	38	193	130	111	.327	.409	May	.288	351	101	26	0	7	42	11	26	.310	.422
Grass	.289	1509	436	92	5	36	173	115	99	.340	.428	June	.305	361	110	21	1	12	53	34	18	.365	.468
Turf	.256	802	205	39	7	16	105	68	64	.314	.382	July	.291	371	108	18	4	11	57	32	27	.347	.450
First Pitch	.271	277	75	17	1	6	38	13	0	.305	.404	August	.287	401	115	21	4	5	41	31	29	.340	.397
Ahead on Count	.295	640	189	42	2	16	88	133	0	.413	.442	September/October	.271	553	150	23	3	16	60	49	38	.328	.410
Behind on Count	.278	759	211	40	7	14	94	1	95	.283	.404	Pre-All Star	.272	1092	297	71	1	22	133	81	61	.324	.399
Two Strikes	.244	851	208	44	4	11	80	35	163	.277	.344	Post-All Star	.282	1219	344	60	11	30	145	102	82	.337	.423

Batter vs. Pitcher (career)

Hits Best Against	Avg	AB	H	2B	3B	HR	RBI	BB	SO	OBP	SLG	Hits Worst Against	Avg	AB	H	2B	3B	HR	RBI	BB	SO	OBP	SLG
Jose Mesa	.615	13	8	2	0	1	0	0	0	.615	1.000	Bryn Smith	.059	17	1	0	0	0	0	0	1	.059	.059
Dave Stewart	.556	9	5	1	0	1	1	2	1	.636	1.000	John Smoltz	.059	17	1	0	0	0	0	1	1	.111	.118
Randy Kramer	.455	11	5	0	0	1	2	0	0	.455	.727	Bill Landrum	.083	12	1	1	0	0	0	0	3	.083	.167
Ted Power	.417	12	5	1	0	2	4	1	0	.462	1.000	Jack McDowell	.091	11	1	0	0	0	0	1	0	.167	.091
Mark Portugal	.389	18	7	1	0	2	2	1	2	.421	.778	Pat Combs	.100	20	2	1	0	0	0	1	2	.143	.100

Reggie Jefferson — Indians   Bats Both (groundball hitter)

	Avg	G	AB	R	H	2B	3B	HR	RBI	BB	SO	HBP	GDP	SB	CS	OBP	SLG	IBB	SH	SF	#Pit	#P/PA	GB	FB	G/F
1992 Season	.337	24	89	8	30	6	2	1	6	1	17	1	2	0	0	.352	.483	0	0	0	309	3.40	34	16	2.13
Career (1991-1992)	.259	55	197	19	51	9	2	4	19	3	41	1	2	0	0	.279	.386	0	0	1	719	3.52	76	45	1.69

1992 Season

	Avg	AB	H	2B	3B	HR	RBI	BB	SO	OBP	SLG		Avg	AB	H	2B	3B	HR	RBI	BB	SO	OBP	SLG
vs. Left	.263	19	5	1	1	1	3	1	7	.300	.579	Scoring Posn	.313	16	5	1	1	0	5	1	4	.389	.500
vs. Right	.357	70	25	5	1	0	3	0	10	.366	.457	Close & Late	.500	16	8	2	0	0	2	0	2	.529	.625

Shawn Jeter — White Sox   Bats Left (flyball hitter)

	Avg	G	AB	R	H	2B	3B	HR	RBI	BB	SO	HBP	GDP	SB	CS	OBP	SLG	IBB	SH	SF	#Pit	#P/PA	GB	FB	G/F
1992 Season	.111	13	18	1	2	0	0	0	0	0	7	0	0	0	0	.111	.111	0	0	0	65	3.61	4	5	0.80

1992 Season

	Avg	AB	H	2B	3B	HR	RBI	BB	SO	OBP	SLG		Avg	AB	H	2B	3B	HR	RBI	BB	SO	OBP	SLG
vs. Left	.000	4	0	0	0	0	0	0	1	.000	.000	Scoring Posn	.000	3	0	0	0	0	0	0	1	.000	.000
vs. Right	.143	14	2	0	0	0	0	0	6	.143	.143	Close & Late	.000	2	0	0	0	0	0	0	1	.000	.000

Howard Johnson — Mets
Bats Both (flyball hitter)

	Avg	G	AB	R	H	2B	3B	HR	RBI	BB	SO	HBP	GDP	SB	CS	OBP	SLG	IBB	SH	SF	#Pit	#P/PA	GB	FB	G/F
1992 Season	.223	100	350	48	78	19	0	7	43	55	79	2	7	22	5	.329	.337	5	0	3	1619	3.95	86	125	0.69
Last Five Years	.251	711	2570	434	646	152	11	126	419	365	529	7	28	150	44	.341	.468	62	2	41	11077	3.71	599	995	0.60

1992 Season

	Avg	AB	H	2B	3B	HR	RBI	BB	SO	OBP	SLG		Avg	AB	H	2B	3B	HR	RBI	BB	SO	OBP	SLG
vs. Left	.227	132	30	8	0	4	21	23	30	.340	.379	Scoring Posn	.242	95	23	8	0	1	35	23	20	.380	.358
vs. Right	.220	218	48	11	0	3	22	32	49	.323	.312	Close & Late	.245	49	12	3	0	1	8	14	16	.415	.367
Groundball	.189	148	28	9	0	3	20	20	29	.292	.311	None on/out	.256	78	20	3	0	1	8	27	.326	.333
Flyball	.206	63	13	1	0	2	6	10	12	.315	.317	Batting #3	.221	140	31	6	0	0	10	17	27	.306	.264
Home	.189	164	31	8	0	2	16	25	41	.293	.274	Batting #4	.204	93	19	7	0	3	14	11	26	.299	.376
Away	.253	186	47	11	0	5	27	30	38	.361	.392	Other	.239	117	28	6	0	4	19	27	26	.377	.393
Day	.252	111	28	8	0	4	21	13	25	.339	.432	April	.203	79	16	6	0	3	14	9	19	.297	.392
Night	.209	239	50	11	0	3	22	42	54	.325	.293	May	.200	85	17	4	0	1	11	21	21	.352	.282
Grass	.195	231	45	11	0	2	22	37	55	.304	.268	June	.261	92	24	6	0	3	9	13	21	.352	.424
Turf	.277	119	33	8	0	5	21	18	24	.379	.471	July	.233	86	20	2	0	0	9	12	15	.327	.256
First Pitch	.233	43	10	3	0	0	9	4	0	.286	.302	August	.125	8	1	1	0	0	0	0	3	.125	.250
Ahead on Count	.276	87	24	7	0	4	15	28	1	.452	.494	September/October	.000	0	0	0	0	0	0	0	0	.000	.000
Behind on Count	.232	99	23	6	0	1	11	0	31	.248	.323	Pre-All Star	.228	298	68	17	0	7	37	48	68	.336	.356
Two Strikes	.189	164	31	8	0	2	16	23	78	.287	.274	Post-All Star	.192	52	10	2	0	0	6	7	11	.288	.231

1992 By Position

Position	Avg	AB	H	2B	3B	HR	RBI	BB	SO	OBP	SLG	G	GS	Innings	PO	A	E	DP	Fld Pct	Rng Fctr	In Zone	Outs	Zone Rtg	MLB Zone
As If	.216	51	11	1	0	0	5	8	9	.322	.235	16	13	124.0	25	1	1	0	.963	1.89	27	24	.889	.809
As cf	.224	294	66	18	0	7	38	47	69	.332	.357	84	82	713.0	181	3	3	0	.984	2.32	218	174	.798	.824

Last Five Years

	Avg	AB	H	2B	3B	HR	RBI	BB	SO	OBP	SLG		Avg	AB	H	2B	3B	HR	RBI	BB	SO	OBP	SLG
vs. Left	.233	906	211	46	2	37	126	134	216	.326	.411	Scoring Posn	.266	638	170	46	0	27	287	148	140	.385	.466
vs. Right	.261	1664	435	106	9	91	293	231	313	.348	.500	Close & Late	.252	421	106	22	2	22	75	76	107	.364	.470
Groundball	.262	928	243	53	6	42	159	115	183	.340	.468	None on/out	.292	643	188	36	3	46	59	124	.355	.572
Flyball	.237	497	118	29	1	27	85	83	106	.346	.463	Batting #3	.272	813	221	50	2	41	138	101	164	.348	.490
Home	.244	1232	301	61	6	64	202	171	253	.332	.459	Batting #5	.237	490	116	22	4	27	89	77	96	.333	.463
Away	.258	1338	345	91	5	64	217	194	276	.349	.477	Other	.244	1267	309	80	5	60	192	187	269	.340	.457
Day	.265	868	230	56	1	48	162	113	166	.346	.498	April	.231	338	78	16	0	18	61	47	74	.323	.438
Night	.244	1702	416	96	10	80	257	252	363	.339	.454	May	.245	470	115	24	2	23	72	73	95	.342	.451
Grass	.252	1799	453	101	8	89	287	250	358	.340	.465	June	.263	487	128	35	4	30	87	58	94	.337	.536
Turf	.250	771	193	51	3	39	132	115	171	.344	.470	July	.254	452	115	28	1	17	66	83	81	.365	.434
First Pitch	.339	354	120	30	3	21	92	21	0	.369	.619	August	.260	404	105	23	2	20	60	52	77	.344	.475
Ahead on Count	.300	616	185	46	3	38	126	190	1	.460	.570	September/October	.251	419	105	26	2	20	73	52	108	.331	.465
Behind on Count	.219	794	174	47	1	26	95	3	245	.222	.379	Pre-All Star	.253	1449	366	85	6	77	247	203	287	.340	.479
Two Strikes	.169	1147	194	41	3	43	126	124	527	.248	.323	Post-All Star	.250	1121	280	67	5	51	172	162	242	.343	.455

Batter vs. Pitcher (since 1984)

Hits Best Against	Avg	AB	H	2B	3B	HR	RBI	BB	SO	OBP	SLG	Hits Worst Against	Avg	AB	H	2B	3B	HR	RBI	BB	SO	OBP	SLG
Scott Scudder	.833	6	5	3	0	2	6	4	0	.818	2.333	Kelly Downs	.063	16	1	0	0	0	1	3	2	.211	.063
Todd Worrell	.556	9	5	0	0	4	8	6	1	.733	1.889	Chris Nabholz	.100	10	1	0	0	0	1	3	.167	.100
Brian Fisher	.500	8	4	0	0	2	2	4	0	.667	1.250	John Smiley	.103	39	4	1	0	0	1	1	11	.125	.128
Jim Acker	.462	13	6	2	0	3	6	1	1	.500	1.308	Bob Welch	.133	15	2	0	0	0	1	1	5	.188	.133
Mark Davis	.455	11	5	0	0	2	5	2	4	.538	1.000	Alejandro Pena	.154	13	2	0	0	0	0	1	4	.154	.154

Jeff Johnson — Yankees
Pitches Left (groundball pitcher)

	ERA	W	L	Sv	G	GS	IP	BB	SO	Avg	H	2B	3B	HR	RBI	OBP	SLG	CG	ShO	Sup	QS	#P/S	SB	CS	GB	FB	G/F
1992 Season	6.66	2	3	0	13	8	52.2	23	14	.329	71	17	2	4	39	.395	.481	0	0	4.27	3	82	4	2	92	64	1.44
Career (1991-1992)	6.15	8	14	0	36	31	179.2	56	76	.312	227	38	7	19	116	.365	.462	0	0	4.21	12	85	22	6	319	197	1.62

1992 Season

	ERA	W	L	Sv	G	GS	IP	H	HR	BB	SO		Avg	AB	H	2B	3B	HR	RBI	BB	SO	OBP	SLG
Home	6.46	1	2	0	6	4	30.2	38	1	11	12	vs. Left	.308	39	12	3	1	1	8	3	4	.364	.513
Away	6.95	1	1	0	7	4	22.0	33	3	12	2	vs. Right	.333	177	59	14	1	3	31	20	10	.402	.475
Starter	6.69	2	3	0	8	8	40.1	54	4	19	10	Scoring Posn	.400	60	24	5	0	4	36	6	7	.449	.683
Reliever	6.57	0	0	0	5	0	12.1	17	0	4	4	Close & Late	.714	7	5	1	0	0	1	0	0	.714	.857
0-3 Days Rest	0.00	0	0	0	0	0	0.0	0	0	0	0	None on/out	.367	49	18	4	0	0	0	7	3	.456	.449
4 Days Rest	8.74	2	2	0	5	5	22.2	37	2	9	4	First Pitch	.375	40	15	4	0	1	5	0	0	.375	.550
5+ Days Rest	4.08	0	1	0	3	3	17.2	17	2	10	6	Behind on Count	.517	60	31	8	2	1	18	14	0	.600	.767
Pre-All Star	6.43	2	3	0	11	8	49.0	65	4	22	12	Ahead on Count	.217	69	15	2	0	1	8	0	12	.239	.290
Post-All Star	9.82	0	0	0	2	0	3.2	6	0	1	2	Two Strikes	.205	73	15	4	0	1	11	9	14	.306	.301

Lance Johnson — White Sox
Bats Left (groundball hitter)

	Avg	G	AB	R	H	2B	3B	HR	RBI	BB	SO	HBP	GDP	SB	CS	OBP	SLG	IBB	SH	SF	#Pit	#P/PA	GB	FB	G/F
1992 Season	.279	157	567	67	158	15	12	3	47	34	33	1	20	41	14	.318	.363		4	5	1860	3.06	293	128	2.29
Last Five Years	.275	551	2000	254	550	59	37	4	169	116	171	3	47	125	52	.314	.348	8	22	12	6696	3.14	996	398	2.50

1992 Season

	Avg	AB	H	2B	3B	HR	RBI	BB	SO	OBP	SLG		Avg	AB	H	2B	3B	HR	RBI	BB	SO	OBP	SLG
vs. Left	.266	158	42	3	2	0	14	8	15	.302	.310	Scoring Posn	.275	142	39	6	5	0	43	14	7	.333	.387
vs. Right	.284	409	116	12	10	3	33	26	18	.324	.384	Close & Late	.223	94	21	1	0	0	5	8	8	.286	.234
Groundball	.266	154	41	1	4	0	12	10	10	.315	.325	None on/out	.288	132	38	0	4	2	2	4	6	.309	.394
Flyball	.283	166	47	2	3	1	10	10	7	.320	.349	Batting #7	.282	284	80	8	8	2	26	22	13	.333	.387
Home	.263	274	72	7	4	2	25	20	12	.312	.339	Batting #8	.275	200	55	4	2	1	15	8	16	.301	.330
Away	.294	293	86	8	8	1	22	14	21	.324	.386	Other	.277	83	23	3	2	0	6	4	4	.303	.361
Day	.312	138	43	4	3	0	5	12	7	.367	.384	April	.296	71	21	1	1	0	4	1	4	.306	.338
Night	.268	429	115	11	9	3	42	22	26	.302	.357	May	.205	83	17	1	0	1	4	4	10	.239	.253
Grass	.277	481	133	8	9	3	36	31	28	.319	.349	June	.302	96	29	5	2	0	7	7	7	.343	.396
Turf	.291	86	25	7	3	0	11	3	5	.311	.442	July	.352	108	38	0	3	0	11	4	6	.377	.407
First Pitch	.257	148	38	3	4	0	12	2	0	.266	.331	August	.250	96	24	1	2	2	9	10	3	.321	.365
Ahead on Count	.297	138	41	2	4	1	13	25	0	.402	.391	September/October	.257	113	29	7	4	0	12	8	3	.303	.389
Behind on Count	.240	146	35	5	1	1	16	0	25	.238	.308	Pre-All Star	.261	299	78	7	4	1	20	14	26	.291	.321
Two Strikes	.214	173	37	4	4	0	5	7	33	.243	.283	Post-All Star	.299	268	80	8	8	2	27	20	7	.347	.410

1992 By Position

Position	Avg	AB	H	2B	3B	HR	RBI	BB	SO	OBP	SLG	G	GS	Innings	PO	A	E	DP	Fld Pct	Rng Fctr	In Zone	Outs	Zone Rtg	MLB Zone
As cf	.278	564	157	15	12	3	47	34	33	.318	.363	157	151	1364.0	433	11	6	4	.987	2.93	478	409	856	824

Last Five Years

	Avg	AB	H	2B	3B	HR	RBI	BB	SO	OBP	SLG		Avg	AB	H	2B	3B	HR	RBI	BB	SO	OBP	SLG
vs. Left	.267	558	149	11	7	0	47	32	70	.307	.312	Scoring Posn	.281	466	131	15	11	1	160	38	35	.331	.367
vs. Right	.278	1442	401	48	30	4	122	84	101	.317	.361	Close & Late	.231	342	79	6	5	0	26	25	40	.284	.278
Groundball	.271	568	154	11	10	0	45	33	52	.312	.326	None on/out	.270	545	147	17	11	2	28	39	8	.305	.352
Flyball	.289	461	133	17	12	2	46	27	38	.326	.390	Batting #1	.238	526	125	20	5	1	37	35	49	.285	.300
Home	.267	972	260	27	18	2	80	60	75	.308	.338	Batting #7	.276	492	136	11	14	2	36	35	28	.325	.368
Away	.282	1028	290	32	19	2	89	56	96	.319	.356	Other	.294	982	289	28	18	1	96	46	94	.324	.363
Day	.280	543	152	16	10	0	41	35	54	.322	.346	April	.240	262	63	7	2	0	16	10	27	.268	.282
Night	.273	1457	398	43	27	4	128	81	117	.311	.348	May	.254	311	79	7	0	1	20	17	29	.293	.286
Grass	.276	1691	466	44	31	4	140	97	147	.314	.345	June	.288	281	81	11	5	0	26	15	22	.320	.363
Turf	.272	309	84	15	6	0	29	19	24	.313	.359	July	.286	308	88	8	7	1	31	13	26	.314	.354
First Pitch	.316	506	160	16	14	1	42	4	0	.321	.409	August	.265	359	95	9	9	2	35	23	28	.308	.357
Ahead on Count	.281	427	120	11	7	1	45	77	0	.389	.347	September/October	.301	479	144	21	14	0	41	38	39	.352	.403
Behind on Count	.210	582	122	12	5	1	43	0	118	.211	.253	Pre-All Star	.257	957	246	26	10	1	75	47	88	.291	.308
Two Strikes	.216	670	145	14	14	0	36	33	170	.253	.279	Post-All Star	.291	1043	304	33	27	3	94	69	83	.335	.384

Batter vs. Pitcher (career)

Hits Best Against	Avg	AB	H	2B	3B	HR	RBI	BB	SO	OBP	SLG	Hits Worst Against	Avg	AB	H	2B	3B	HR	RBI	BB	SO	OBP	SLG
Mike Boddicker	.500	16	8	0	2	0	6	0	1	.500	.750	Bob Welch	.071	14	1	0	0	0	0	2	1	.188	.071
Joe Grahe	.467	15	7	0	0	0	2	2	0	.529	.467	Jaime Navarro	.105	19	2	1	0	0	1	0	2	.100	.158
Luis Aquino	.462	13	6	2	2	0	2	1	0	.500	.923	Ben McDonald	.125	16	2	0	0	0	1	2	1	.222	.125
Rich DeLucia	.438	16	7	0	1	0	1	1	0	.471	.563	Roger Clemens	.147	34	5	0	0	0	0	0	6	.147	.147
Mark Gubicza	.375	8	3	0	0	0	0	4	1	.583	.375	Mike Flanagan	.154	13	2	0	0	0	1	0	2	.154	.154

Randy Johnson — Mariners
Pitches Left

	ERA	W	L	Sv	G	GS	IP	BB	SO	Avg	H	2B	3B	HR	RBI	OBP	SLG	CG	ShO	Sup	QS	#P/S	SB	CS	GB	FB	G/F
1992 Season	3.77	12	14	0	31	31	210.1	144	241	.206	154	33	2	13	90	.344	.307	6	2	4.32	19	121	42	16	192	212	0.91
Career (1988-1992)	3.95	49	48	0	130	129	818.0	519	818	.219	649	124	10	70	344	.340	.339	16	5	4.58	76	112	124	39	890	839	1.06

1992 Season

	ERA	W	L	Sv	G	GS	IP	H	HR	BB	SO		Avg	AB	H	2B	3B	HR	RBI	BB	SO	OBP	SLG
Home	2.76	8	6	0	17	17	117.1	72	4	68	146	vs. Left	.187	75	14	1	0	1	9	12	19	.303	.240
Away	5.03	4	8	0	14	14	93.0	82	9	76	95	vs. Right	.208	674	140	32	2	12	81	132	222	.348	.315
Day	2.79	2	0	0	5	5	38.2	27	0	24	53	Inning 1-6	.208	625	130	30	1	10	78	116	199	.341	.307
Night	3.98	10	14	0	26	26	171.2	127	13	120	188	Inning 7+	.194	124	24	3	1	3	12	28	42	.356	.306
Grass	5.49	3	7	0	12	12	77.0	70	8	68	79	None on	.204	397	81	18	1	4	4	80	132	.351	.285
Turf	2.77	9	7	0	19	19	133.1	84	5	76	162	Runners on	.207	352	73	15	1	9	86	64	109	.336	.332
April	1.53	3	0	0	4	4	29.1	21	3	10	30	Scoring Posn	.193	212	41	7	0	5	74	49	71	.351	.297
May	5.40	2	5	0	7	7	40.0	31	1	35	34	Close & Late	.181	83	15	2	1	2	10	19	34	.343	.301
June	5.73	0	2	0	2	2	11.0	7	2	13	11	None on/out	.221	190	42	9	1	3	3	30	62	.336	.326
July	4.28	2	4	0	6	6	40.0	39	4	33	43	vs. 1st Batr (relief)	.000	0	0	0	0	0	0	0	0	.000	.000
August	3.27	4	1	0	6	6	44.0	28	1	26	56	First Inning Pitched	.212	113	24	6	1	1	17	24	37	.366	.310
September/October	3.33	1	2	0	6	6	46.0	28	2	27	67	First 75 Pitches	.198	454	90	21	1	6	49	83	140	.333	.289
Starter	3.77	12	14	0	31	31	210.1	154	13	144	241	Pitch 76-90	.238	84	20	6	0	2	11	19	29	.381	.381
Reliever	0.00	0	0	0	0	0	0.0	0	0	0	0	Pitch 91-105	.191	89	17	2	0	2	15	16	32	.324	.281
0-3 Days Rest	13.50	0	1	0	1	1	2.0	3	0	3	2	Pitch 106+	.221	122	27	4	1	3	15	26	40	.372	.344
4 Days Rest	3.78	9	5	0	17	17	119.0	92	6	77	145	First Pitch	.267	75	20	1	0	0	7	1	0	.300	.280

1992 Season

	ERA	W	L	Sv	G	GS	IP	H	HR	BB	SO		Avg	AB	H	2B	3B	HR	RBI	BB	SO	OBP	SLG
5+ Days Rest	3.53	3	8	0	13	13	89.1	59	7	64	94	Ahead on Count	.125	393	49	16	1	4	25	0	210	.150	.201
Pre-All Star	4.04	5	9	0	15	15	93.2	72	9	71	86	Behind on Count	.338	142	48	11	1	5	33	67	0	.546	.535
Post-All Star	3.55	7	5	0	16	16	116.2	82	4	73	155	Two Strikes	.118	415	49	16	0	4	32	76	241	.268	.186

Career (1988-1992)

	ERA	W	L	Sv	G	GS	IP	H	HR	BB	SO		Avg	AB	H	2B	3B	HR	RBI	BB	SO	OBP	SLG
Home	3.45	26	21	0	64	64	412.1	299	27	248	421	vs. Left	.196	337	66	12	0	5	41	42	88	.268	.276
Away	4.45	23	27	0	66	65	405.2	350	43	271	397	vs. Right	.222	2621	583	112	10	65	303	477	730	.346	.347
Day	4.46	12	6	0	30	30	181.2	145	17	123	188	Inning 1-6	.221	2526	557	109	9	63	316	451	692	.342	.346
Night	3.80	37	42	0	100	99	636.1	504	53	396	630	Inning 7+	.213	432	92	15	1	7	28	68	126	.325	.301
Grass	4.31	21	18	0	50	50	319.2	263	34	215	315	None on	.212	1648	349	64	8	41	41	295	450	.339	.335
Turf	3.72	28	30	0	80	79	498.1	386	36	304	503	Runners on	.229	1310	300	60	2	29	303	224	368	.341	.344
April	4.06	7	6	0	17	16	99.2	84	15	59	86	Scoring Posn	.219	794	174	35	1	16	266	147	238	.337	.326
May	5.07	5	11	0	22	22	126.0	102	6	102	127	Close & Late	.201	239	48	7	1	4	17	42	78	.325	.289
June	3.34	10	3	0	17	17	105.0	71	8	80	100	None on/out	.237	748	177	32	4	19	19	137	202	.361	.366
July	3.37	8	11	0	23	23	157.2	127	14	100	154	vs. 1st Batr (relief)	1.000	1	1	0	0	0	0	0	0	1.000	1.000
August	3.61	12	7	0	23	23	157.0	117	13	81	160	First Inning Pitched	.213	442	94	25	2	7	50	77	130	.333	.326
September/October	4.27	7	10	0	28	28	172.2	148	14	97	191	First 75 Pitches	.219	1917	420	82	6	49	221	333	524	.339	.345
Starter	3.95	49	48	0	129	129	817.0	648	70	519	817	Pitch 76-90	.223	364	79	16	2	10	46	76	90	.361	.364
Reliever	0.00	0	0	0	1	0	1.0	1	0	0	1	Pitch 91-105	.203	330	67	13	1	6	40	47	96	.302	.303
0-3 Days Rest	13.50	0	1	0	1	1	2.0	3	0	3	2	Pitch 106+	.232	357	83	13	1	5	37	63	108	.354	.317
4 Days Rest	4.16	28	24	0	75	75	467.2	372	46	313	465	First Pitch	.331	329	109	17	0	12	61	3	0	.338	.492
5+ Days Rest	3.63	21	23	0	53	53	347.1	273	24	203	350	Ahead on Count	.153	1494	228	43	3	22	118	1	704	.164	.230
Pre-All Star	4.02	23	23	0	63	62	380.2	299	34	265	354	Behind on Count	.303	590	179	34	5	24	95	286	0	.529	.500
Post-All Star	3.89	26	25	0	67	67	437.1	350	36	254	464	Two Strikes	.137	1590	218	43	3	21	123	229	816	.253	.208

Pitcher vs. Batter (career)

Pitches Best Vs.	Avg	AB	H	2B	3B	HR	RBI	BB	SO	OBP	SLG	Pitches Worst Vs.	Avg	AB	H	2B	3B	HR	RBI	BB	SO	OBP	SLG
Tom Brunansky	.000	15	0	0	0	0	1	2	8	.111	.000	Rene Gonzales	.500	10	5	0	0	1	2	3	2	.706	.800
Craig Grebeck	.000	13	0	0	0	0	0	2	4	.235	.000	Jody Reed	.500	10	5	4	0	0	6	3	.688	.900
Charlie Hayes	.000	9	0	0	0	0	2	0	2	.167	.000	Travis Fryman	.455	11	5	0	0	2	5	1	4	.500	1.000
Steve Sax	.038	26	1	1	0	0	4	2	4	.107	.077	Frank Thomas	.400	15	6	2	0	1	3	8	5	.609	.733
Rafael Palmeiro	.059	17	1	0	0	0	0	2	5	.059	.059	Bill Pecota	.364	11	4	1	0	2	2	5	0	.563	1.000

Joel Johnston — Royals
Pitches Right (flyball pitcher)

	ERA	W	L	Sv	G	GS	IP	BB	SO	Avg	H	2B	3B	HR	RBI	OBP	SLG	GF	IR	IRS	Hld	SvOp	SB	CS	GB	FB	G/F
1992 Season	13.50	0	0	0	5	0	2.2	2	0	.273	3	0	0	2	3	.385	.818	1	4	1	0	0	0	4	6	0.67
Career (1991-1992)	1.80	1	0	0	18	0	25.0	11	21	.140	12	1	0	2	4	.237	.221	2	14	1	3	0	1	1	29	30	0.97

1992 Season

	ERA	W	L	Sv	G	GS	IP	H	HR	BB	SO		Avg	AB	H	2B	3B	HR	RBI	BB	SO	OBP	SLG
Home	0.00	0	0	0	2	0	0.0	2	1	1	0	vs. Left	.000	4	0	0	0	0	0	0	0	.000	.000
Away	3.38	0	0	0	3	0	2.2	1	1	1	0	vs. Right	.429	7	3	0	0	2	3	2	0	.556	1.286

Barry Jones — Mets
Pitches Right (groundball pitcher)

	ERA	W	L	Sv	G	GS	IP	BB	SO	Avg	H	2B	3B	HR	RBI	OBP	SLG	GF	IR	IRS	Hld	SvOp	SB	CS	GB	FB	G/F
1992 Season	5.68	7	6	1	61	0	69.2	35	30	.308	85	19	2	3	50	.386	.424	17	33	18	8	7	5	1	127	70	1.81
Last Five Years	3.39	28	24	19	264	0	345.0	147	186	.253	317	47	6	21	177	.330	.351	72	215	77	56	43	28	11	539	316	1.71

1992 Season

	ERA	W	L	Sv	G	GS	IP	H	HR	BB	SO		Avg	AB	H	2B	3B	HR	RBI	BB	SO	OBP	SLG
Home	4.97	5	4	1	31	0	38.0	47	1	17	19	vs. Left	.338	136	46	10	0	0	18	19	8	.418	.412
Away	6.54	2	2	0	30	0	31.2	38	2	18	11	vs. Right	.279	140	39	9	2	3	32	16	22	.354	.436
Day	3.86	2	0	0	12	0	16.1	12	2	5	7	Inning 1-6	.318	22	7	3	0	0	6	6	4	.464	.455
Night	6.24	5	6	1	49	0	53.1	73	1	30	23	Inning 7+	.307	254	78	16	2	3	44	29	26	.378	.421
Grass	7.67	2	1	1	25	0	29.1	38	2	17	13	None on	.252	131	33	9	0	1	1	15	11	.338	.344
Turf	4.24	5	5	0	36	0	40.1	47	1	18	17	Runners on	.359	145	52	10	2	2	49	20	19	.429	.497
April	3.57	1	1	0	12	0	17.2	17	1	7	5	Scoring Posn	.354	96	34	9	2	1	47	17	14	.440	.521
May	6.75	2	1	0	11	0	12.0	18	1	6	5	Close & Late	.309	123	38	6	1	2	19	14	8	.383	.423
June	2.13	1	1	0	10	0	12.2	9	1	4	3	None on/out	.222	54	12	2	0	0	13	4	4	.373	.259
July	6.75	1	3	0	11	0	12.0	21	0	7	6	vs. 1st Batr (relief)	.280	50	14	4	0	0	6	10	4	.393	.360
August	4.50	2	0	0	4	0	4.0	2	0	2	3	First Inning Pitched	.309	204	63	14	2	1	39	25	22	.382	.412
September/October	11.12	0	0	1	13	0	11.1	18	0	9	8	First 15 Pitches	.301	193	58	14	2	2	32	26	19	.383	.425
Starter	0.00	0	0	0	0	0	0.0	0	0	0	0	Pitch 16-30	.324	71	23	5	0	1	15	8	9	.395	.437
Reliever	5.68	7	6	1	61	0	69.2	85	3	35	30	Pitch 31-45	.333	12	4	0	0	0	3	1	2	.385	.333
0 Days rest	9.58	1	0	0	10	0	10.1	18	3	5	5	Pitch 46+	.000	0	0	0	0	0	0	0	0	.000	.000
1 or 2 Days rest	6.47	5	4	0	34	0	40.1	51	0	23	15	First Pitch	.315	54	17	2	0	1	10	6	0	.377	.407
3+ Days rest	1.89	2	1	1	17	0	19.0	16	0	9	10	Ahead on Count	.267	120	32	10	1	0	16	0	28	.273	.367
Pre-All Star	4.62	4	4	0	39	0	48.2	54	3	22	18	Behind on Count	.302	53	16	4	0	2	11	21	0	.507	.491
Post-All Star	8.14	3	2	1	22	0	21.0	31	0	13	12	Two Strikes	.260	104	27	8	1	0	14	8	30	.313	.356

Last Five Years

	ERA	W	L	Sv	G	GS	IP	H	HR	BB	SO
Home	3.46	17	10	8	141	0	176.2	171	7	70	99
Away	3.31	11	14	11	143	0	168.1	146	14	77	87
Day	2.61	5	4	8	76	0	89.2	77	8	31	48
Night	3.67	23	20	11	208	0	255.1	240	13	116	138
Grass	3.34	16	13	8	149	0	183.0	157	13	84	101
Turf	3.44	12	11	11	135	0	162.0	160	8	63	85
April	2.74	4	3	2	46	0	62.1	52	5	26	23
May	3.03	9	4	1	50	0	65.1	61	5	20	32
June	4.19	5	5	5	44	0	53.2	55	4	23	33
July	3.91	2	5	3	45	0	50.2	53	2	24	29
August	2.70	3	2	4	41	0	50.0	42	3	21	29
September/October	3.86	5	5	4	58	0	63.0	54	2	33	40
Starter	0.00	0	0	0	0	0	0.0	0	0	0	0
Reliever	3.39	28	24	19	284	0	345.0	317	21	147	186
0 Days rest	5.13	1	5	4	52	0	52.2	63	7	20	25
1 or 2 Days rest	3.39	19	16	8	166	0	215.0	190	11	92	112
3+ Days rest	2.21	8	3	7	66	0	77.1	64	3	35	49
Pre-All Star	3.53	19	14	9	158	0	201.1	192	15	81	102
Post-All Star	3.19	9	10	10	126	0	143.2	125	6	66	84

	Avg	AB	H	2B	3B	HR	RBI	BB	SO	OBP	SLG
vs. Left	.263	552	156	25	3	8	74	80	56	.370	.382
vs. Right	.230	700	161	22	3	13	103	67	130	.296	.326
Inning 1-6	.217	92	20	4	0	0	16	12	15	.299	.261
Inning 7+	.256	1160	297	43	6	21	161	135	171	.333	.358
None on	.229	637	146	22	1	9	9	65	97	.304	.309
Runners on	.278	615	171	25	5	12	168	82	89	.357	.393
Scoring Posn	.279	398	111	20	3	7	156	66	64	.367	.397
Close & Late	.272	673	183	23	4	11	98	78	96	.347	.367
None on/out	.237	278	66	10	1	6	6	30	39	.312	.345
vs. 1st Batr (relief)	.256	211	54	9	1	3	33	21	30	.324	.351
First Inning Pitched	.246	745	183	28	4	11	126	87	116	.322	.338
First 15 Pitches	.256	861	220	34	4	15	127	96	124	.328	.357
Pitch 16-30	.246	329	81	12	2	5	37	39	49	.325	.340
Pitch 31-45	.267	60	16	1	0	1	13	10	12	.380	.333
Pitch 46+	.000	2	0	0	0	0	0	2	1	.500	.000
First Pitch	.326	193	63	6	0	5	47	23	0	.390	.435
Ahead on Count	.220	527	116	21	3	3	56	0	154	.222	.288
Behind on Count	.264	292	77	11	0	8	37	75	0	.414	.384
Two Strikes	.178	511	91	14	1	5	49	49	186	.250	.239

Pitcher vs. Batter (career)

Pitches Best Vs.	Avg	AB	H	2B	3B	HR	RBI	BB	SO	OBP	SLG
Gary Carter	.182	11	2	0	0	1	4	0	2	.182	.182
Juan Samuel	.214	14	3	1	0	1	4	0	4	.214	.500
Andre Dawson	.231	13	3	1	0	1	3	0	3	.231	.538

Pitches Worst Vs.	Avg	AB	H	2B	3B	HR	RBI	BB	SO	OBP	SLG
Kurt Stillwell	.545	11	6	1	0	0	2	0	1	.545	.636
Vince Coleman	.500	10	5	1	0		3	1	1	.545	.800
Chris James	.500	10	5	1	1	0	2	1	1	.545	.800
Andres Galarraga	.400	15	6	3	0	1	5	0	2	.400	.800
Ryne Sandberg	.375	8	3	0	1	0	2	3	2	.571	.625

Calvin Jones — Mariners
Pitches Right (flyball pitcher)

	ERA	W	L	Sv	G	GS	IP	BB	SO	Avg	H	2B	3B	HR	RBI	OBP	SLG	GF	IR	IRS	Hld	SvOp	SB	CS	GB	FB	G/F
1992 Season	5.69	3	5	0	38	1	61.2	47	49	.226	50	9	1	8	30	.361	.385	14	25	4	3	2	6	3	63	73	0.86
Career (1991-1992)	4.33	5	7	2	65	1	108.0	76	91	.219	83	13	2	8	45	.351	.327	20	41	9	4	5	11	4	110	115	0.96

1992 Season

	ERA	W	L	Sv	G	GS	IP	H	HR	BB	SO
Home	4.22	2	2	0	20	0	32.0	24	4	20	23
Away	7.28	1	3	0	18	1	29.2	26	4	27	26
Starter	3.60	0	1	0	1	1	5.0	3	0	5	3
Reliever	5.88	3	4	0	37	0	56.2	47	8	42	46
0 Days rest	5.91	1	1	0	5	0	10.2	13	3	5	8
1 or 2 Days rest	7.61	1	1	0	16	0	23.2	20	1	19	12
3+ Days rest	4.03	1	2	0	16	0	22.1	14	4	18	17
Pre-All Star	6.48	2	2	0	21	1	33.1	30	5	27	30
Post-All Star	4.76	1	3	0	17	0	28.1	20	3	20	19

	Avg	AB	H	2B	3B	HR	RBI	BB	SO	OBP	SLG
vs. Left	.250	84	21	7	0	2	12	26	16	.420	.405
vs. Right	.212	137	29	2	1	6	18	21	33	.321	.372
Scoring Posn	.200	60	12	2	1	1	19	16	15	.366	.317
Close & Late	.268	41	11	0	1	1	8	11	7	.415	.390
None on/out	.184	49	9	1	0	1	1	12	14	.344	.265
First Pitch	.381	21	8	1	0	2	5	1	0	.435	.714
Behind on Count	.276	58	16	6	1	2	7	29	1	.517	.517
Ahead on Count	.165	115	19	0	0	4	13	0	45	.162	.270
Two Strikes	.158	101	16	1	0	4	12	17	48	.280	.287

Chris Jones — Astros
Bats Right (groundball hitter)

	Avg	G	AB	R	H	2B	3B	HR	RBI	BB	SO	HBP	GDP	SB	CS	OBP	SLG	IBB	SH	SF	#Pit	#P/PA	GB	FB	G/F
1992 Season	.190	54	63	7	12	2	1	1	4	7	21	0	1	3	0	.271	.302	0	3	0	269	3.84	20	14	1.43
Career (1991-1992)	.250	106	152	21	38	3	3	3	10	9	52	0	3	5	1	.290	.368	0	3	1	626	3.86	49	24	2.04

1992 Season

	Avg	AB	H	2B	3B	HR	RBI	BB	SO	OBP	SLG
vs. Left	.174	46	8	1	0	0	2	4	14	.240	.196
vs. Right	.235	17	4	1	1	1	2	3	7	.350	.588

	Avg	AB	H	2B	3B	HR	RBI	BB	SO	OBP	SLG
Scoring Posn	.200	15	3	0	0	0	2	3	5	.333	.200
Close & Late	.176	17	3	0	0	1	3	2	5	.263	.353

Doug Jones — Astros
Pitches Right (groundball pitcher)

	ERA	W	L	Sv	G	GS	IP	BB	SO	Avg	H	2B	3B	HR	RBI	OBP	SLG	GF	IR	IRS	Hld	SvOp	SB	CS	GB	FB	G/F
1992 Season	1.85	11	8	36	80	0	111.2	17	93	.235	96	14	3	5	37	.274	.320	70	37	11	0	42	5	4	160	80	2.00
Last Five Years	2.72	30	35	155	292	4	423.1	85	333	.246	394	71	10	22	175	.266	.344	163	234	78	0	189	12	7	599	382	1.57

1992 Season

	ERA	W	L	Sv	G	GS	IP	H	HR	BB	SO
Home	2.42	6	5	17	44	0	63.1	54	3	13	59
Away	1.12	5	3	19	36	0	48.1	42	2	4	34
Day	0.92	3	2	13	22	0	29.1	19	2	3	22
Night	2.19	8	6	23	58	0	82.1	77	3	14	71
Grass	0.89	3	3	12	22	0	30.1	28	1	3	23
Turf	2.21	8	5	24	58	0	81.1	68	4	14	70
April	1.62	1	1	6	11	0	16.2	17	1	2	21
May	3.38	2	2	6	15	0	18.2	17	1	3	14

	Avg	AB	H	2B	3B	HR	RBI	BB	SO	OBP	SLG
vs. Left	.253	217	55	11	1	3	20	12	41	.296	.355
vs. Right	.214	192	41	3	2	2	17	5	52	.249	.281
Inning 1-6	.000	0	0	0	0	0	0	0	0	.000	.000
Inning 7+	.235	409	96	14	3	5	37	17	93	.274	.320
None on	.288	215	62	10	1	2		6	44	.317	.372
Runners on	.175	194	34	4	2	3	35	11	49	.227	.263
Scoring Posn	.202	109	22	4	2	0	29	8	26	.263	.275
Close & Late	.239	322	77	12	3	5	31	15	72	.282	.342

1992 Season

	ERA	W	L	Sv	G	GS	IP	H	HR	BB	SO		Avg	AB	H	2B	3B	HR	RBI	BB	SO	OBP	SLG
June	1.10	1	2	5	14	0	16.1	15	0	4	13	None on/out	.247	93	23	4	0	0	0	3	17	.286	.290
July	2.21	4	2	4	12	0	20.1	14	1	4	14	vs. 1st Batr (relief)	.240	75	18	2	0	1	8	3	15	.288	.307
August	2.00	0	1	7	13	0	18.0	15	2	1	14	First Inning Pitched	.231	277	64	9	2	5	27	13	65	.276	.332
September/October	0.83	3	0	8	15	0	21.2	18	0	3	17	First 15 Pitches	.256	258	66	9	2	5	25	10	57	.294	.364
Starter	0.00	0	0	0	0	0	0.0	0	0	0	0	Pitch 16-30	.198	121	24	3	1	0	9	6	28	.236	.240
Reliever	1.85	11	8	36	80	0	111.2	96	5	17	93	Pitch 31-45	.207	29	6	2	0	0	3	1	8	.258	.276
0 Days rest	1.23	4	1	17	27	0	36.2	31	1	5	36	Pitch 46+	.000	1	0	0	0	0	0	0	0	.000	.000
1 or 2 Days rest	1.73	5	4	17	39	0	57.1	42	2	11	40	First Pitch	.475	40	19	1	0	1	4	5	0	.543	.575
3+ Days rest	3.57	2	3	2	14	0	17.2	23	2	1	17	Ahead on Count	.163	240	39	5	2	1	17	0	81	.169	.213
Pre-All Star	2.25	6	6	19	45	0	60.0	55	2	12	52	Behind on Count	.302	63	19	3	1	3	11	8	0	.380	.524
Post-All Star	1.39	5	2	17	35	0	51.2	41	3	5	41	Two Strikes	.158	222	35	9	1	0	14	4	93	.180	.207

Last Five Years

	ERA	W	L	Sv	G	GS	IP	H	HR	BB	SO		Avg	AB	H	2B	3B	HR	RBI	BB	SO	OBP	SLG
Home	3.26	18	21	75	156	2	220.2	208	10	46	172	vs. Left	.244	852	208	42	5	15	94	53	149	.288	.358
Away	2.13	12	14	80	136	2	202.2	186	12	39	161	vs. Right	.247	752	186	29	5	7	81	32	184	.284	.327
Day	2.10	6	8	49	80	0	107.1	85	4	20	83	Inning 1-6	.253	99	25	5	0	0	6	6	20	.292	.303
Night	2.93	24	27	106	212	4	316.0	309	18	65	250	Inning 7+	.245	1505	369	66	10	22	169	79	313	.286	.346
Grass	2.84	21	25	111	200	4	294.2	280	14	56	224	None on	.263	790	208	42	2	10	10	35	157	.298	.359
Turf	2.45	9	10	44	92	0	128.2	114	8	29	109	Runners on	.229	814	186	29	3	12	165	50	176	.275	.328
April	1.76	2	4	26	41	0	51.0	47	4	9	51	None on/out	.254	342	87	21	0	4	4	16	65	.292	.351
May	3.51	5	7	30	56	0	74.1	68	6	14	53	vs. 1st Batr (relief)	.254	264	67	12	0	4	29	15	44	.301	.443
June	2.14	5	6	25	50	0	63.0	57	2	12	48	First Inning Pitched	.250	1022	256	43	4	16	120	56	218	.293	.347
July	2.66	6	6	21	46	0	67.2	52	5	17	49	First 15 Pitches	.257	937	241	42	4	18	96	49	189	.296	.368
August	3.56	3	6	26	46	0	65.2	63	4	14	46	Pitch 16-30	.226	455	103	15	5	4	55	27	94	.267	.308
September/October	2.48	9	6	27	53	4	101.2	107	1	19	86	Pitch 31-45	.203	118	24	5	0	0	13	6	30	.254	.246
Starter	3.77	3	1	0	4	4	31.0	40	0	6	24	Pitch 46+	.277	94	26	9	1	0	11	3	20	.299	.394
Reliever	2.64	27	34	155	288	0	392.1	354	22	79	309	First Pitch	.372	199	74	10	1	5	36	18	0	.432	.508
0 Days rest	1.76	6	8	44	69	0	87.0	78	5	15	75	Ahead on Count	.185	914	169	34	5	9	76	0	295	.186	.263
1 or 2 Days rest	2.73	13	13	74	131	0	184.1	162	9	43	127	Behind on Count	.327	245	80	16	2	6	35	43	0	.428	.482
3+ Days rest	3.12	8	13	37	88	0	121.0	114	8	21	107	Two Strikes	.180	833	150	35	4	3	62	24	332	.205	.242
Pre-All Star	2.54	15	19	89	166	0	216.0	197	12	43	170												
Post-All Star	2.91	15	16	66	126	4	207.1	197	10	42	163												

Pitcher vs. Batter (since 1984)

Pitches Best Vs.	Avg	AB	H	2B	3B	HR	RBI	BB	SO	OBP	SLG	Pitches Worst Vs.	Avg	AB	H	2B	3B	HR	RBI	BB	SO	OBP	SLG
Fred McGriff	.000	11	0	0	0	0	0	1	3	.083	.000	Cal Ripken	.556	18	10	3	0	1	6	2	2	.600	.889
Ruben Sierra	.071	14	1	0	0	0	0	0	2	.071	.071	Gene Larkin	.556	9	5	0	0	0	3	2	0	.636	.556
Dan Pasqua	.077	13	1	0	0	0	1	0	5	.077	.077	Kent Hrbek	.500	14	7	2	0	2	5	1	1	.533	1.071
Paul Molitor	.100	20	2	0	0	0	0	0	3	.100	.100	Greg Vaughn	.500	12	6	4	0	1	3	0	1	.500	1.083
Danny Tartabull	.167	12	2	0	0	0	0	0	4	.167	.167	Mark McGwire	.467	15	7	1	0	1	5	2	3	.529	.733

Jimmy Jones — Astros

Pitches Right (groundball pitcher)

	ERA	W	L	Sv	G	GS	IP	BB	SO	Avg	H	2B	3B	HR	RBI	OBP	SLG	CG	ShO	Sup	QS	#P/S	SB	CS	GB	FB	G/F
1992 Season	4.07	10	6	0	25	23	139.1	39	69	.258	135	27	5	13	52	.313	.403	0	0	4.65	10	84	20	5	229	121	1.89
Last Five Years	4.47	28	31	0	108	87	551.2	173	289	.279	598	102	18	51	267	.333	.414	4	1	4.21	42	85	60	23	927	493	1.88

1992 Season

	ERA	W	L	Sv	G	GS	IP	H	HR	BB	SO		Avg	AB	H	2B	3B	HR	RBI	BB	SO	OBP	SLG
Home	3.33	5	2	0	11	9	54.0	45	1	21	29	vs. Left	.283	300	85	16	4	9	32	27	33	.343	.453
Away	4.54	5	4	0	14	14	85.1	90	12	18	40	vs. Right	.223	224	50	11	1	4	20	12	36	.272	.335
Starter	4.15	8	6	0	23	23	136.2	133	13	39	65	Scoring Posn	.232	112	26	7	1	2	35	17	15	.333	.366
Reliever	0.00	2	0	0	2	0	2.2	2	0	0	4	Close & Late	.243	37	9	0	1	0	1	0	7	.282	.297
0-3 Days Rest	0.00	0	0	0	0	0	0.0	0	0	0	0	None on/out	.300	140	42	9	1	4	4	8	16	.347	.464
4 Days Rest	5.43	5	3	0	13	13	69.2	78	11	23	34	First Pitch	.253	83	21	5	2	1	5	1	0	.259	.398
5+ Days Rest	2.82	3	3	0	10	10	67.0	55	2	16	31	Behind on Count	.240	125	30	4	0	6	18	22	0	.351	.416
Pre-All Star	4.39	4	3	0	12	12	69.2	67	6	20	37	Ahead on Count	.236	229	54	14	2	4	21	0	59	.247	.367
Post-All Star	3.75	6	3	0	13	11	69.2	68	7	19	32	Two Strikes	.199	206	41	11	2	4	14	16	69	.259	.330

Last Five Years

	ERA	W	L	Sv	G	GS	IP	H	HR	BB	SO		Avg	AB	H	2B	3B	HR	RBI	BB	SO	OBP	SLG
Home	3.67	15	14	0	58	46	301.2	297	20	96	161	vs. Left	.296	1194	354	57	14	27	134	110	151	.356	.436
Away	5.44	13	17	0	50	41	250.0	301	31	77	128	vs. Right	.256	953	244	45	4	24	133	63	138	.305	.387
Day	4.23	10	7	0	34	27	180.2	196	14	56	98	Inning 1-6	.274	1820	499	84	14	41	224	150	248	.330	.403
Night	4.58	18	24	0	74	60	371.0	402	37	117	191	Inning 7+	.303	327	99	18	4	10	43	23	41	.353	.474
Grass	5.03	12	17	0	61	44	293.1	345	35	91	134	None on	.275	1247	343	55	8	31	31	90	170	.327	.407
Turf	3.83	16	14	0	47	43	258.1	253	16	82	155	Runners on	.283	900	255	47	10	20	236	83	119	.342	.424
April	2.52	4	3	0	8	8	50.0	47	4	12	26	Scoring Posn	.302	493	149	29	6	10	201	59	65	.370	.434
May	3.22	6	5	0	17	17	114.2	102	8	33	65	Close & Late	.239	113	27	2	2	2	11	5	18	.283	.345
June	5.99	6	7	0	26	26	133.2	159	14	43	63	None on/out	.277	555	154	29	4	13	13	36	67	.325	.414
July	4.01	4	8	0	19	16	98.2	112	8	32	54	vs. 1st Batr (relief)	.368	19	7	1	0	1	5	1	1	.381	.579
August	4.46	5	5	0	22	14	101.0	110	13	35	55	First Inning Pitched	.313	419	131	20	3	8	70	56	55	.392	.432
September/October	6.04	3	3	0	16	6	53.2	68	4	18	26	First 75 Pitches	.279	1807	505	84	13	42	213	154	247	.336	.410

Last Five Years

	ERA	W	L	Sv	G	GS	IP	H	HR	BB	SO		Avg	AB	H	2B	3B	HR	RBI	BB	SO	OBP	SLG
Starter	4.38	25	30	0	87	87	503.1	533	45	151	265	Pitch 76-90	.261	211	55	14	3	3	37	11	23	.298	.398
Reliever	5.40	3	1	0	21	0	48.1	65	6	22	24	Pitch 91-105	.250	104	26	2	1	4	11	5	16	.304	.404
0-3 Days Rest	1.38	0	0	0	2	2	13.0	13	0	2	8	Pitch 106+	.480	25	12	2	1	2	6	3	3	.552	.880
4 Days Rest	4.74	14	15	0	45	45	252.2	266	32	82	131	First Pitch	.340	382	130	16	7	15	60	5	0	.347	.537
5+ Days Rest	4.17	11	15	0	40	40	237.2	254	13	67	126	Ahead on Count	.221	893	197	35	3	16	80	0	247	.226	.320
Pre-All Star	4.35	17	19	0	58	57	333.1	346	31	99	178	Behind on Count	.310	510	158	26	3	18	89	97	0	.419	.478
Post-All Star	4.66	11	12	0	50	30	218.1	252	20	74	111	Two Strikes	.211	831	175	36	4	14	74	71	289	.275	.314

Pitcher vs. Batter (career)

Pitches Best Vs.	Avg	AB	H	2B	3B	HR	RBI	BB	SO	OBP	SLG	Pitches Worst Vs.	Avg	AB	H	2B	3B	HR	RBI	BB	SO	OBP	SLG
Robby Thompson	.056	18	1	0	0	0	0	3	1	.190	.056	Hal Morris	.636	11	7	0	0	1	2	0	0	.636	.909
Benito Santiago	.083	12	1	0	0	0	2	1	3	.154	.083	Jay Bell	.615	13	8	1	0	2	4	1	1	.643	1.154
Mark Grace	.083	12	1	0	0	0	1	2	0	.294	.083	Will Clark	.444	18	8	2	1	2	7	4	2	.545	1.000
Tom Foley	.125	16	2	1	0	0	2	0	2	.118	.188	John Kruk	.444	9	4	1	0	1	2	2	1	.545	.889
Rafael Belliard	.143	14	2	0	0	0	0	0	4	.143	.143	Fred McGriff	.389	18	7	0	0	4	4	3	4	.476	1.056

Tim Jones — Cardinals
Bats Left

	Avg	G	AB	R	H	2B	3B	HR	RBI	BB	SO	HBP	GDP	SB	CS	OBP	SLG	IBB	SH	SF	#Pit	#P/PA	GB	FB	G/F
1992 Season	.200	67	145	9	29	4	0	0	3	11	29	0	1	5	2	.256	.228	1	2	0	541	3.47	49	38	1.29
Career (1988-1992)	.229	223	424	32	97	19	1	1	27	36	124	2	5	13	8	.290	.285	4	7	3	1595	3.43	154	124	1.24

1992 Season

	Avg	AB	H	2B	3B	HR	RBI	BB	SO	OBP	SLG		Avg	AB	H	2B	3B	HR	RBI	BB	SO	OBP	SLG
vs. Left	.229	35	8	2	0	0	1	2	7	.270	.286	Scoring Posn	.162	37	6	0	0	0	3	5	6	.262	.162
vs. Right	.191	110	21	2	0	0	2	9	22	.252	.209	Close & Late	.138	29	4	1	0	0	1	1	4	.167	.172
Home	.200	50	10	1	0	0	0	2	10	.231	.220	None on/out	.179	28	5	0	0	0	0	1	8	.207	.179
Away	.200	95	19	3	0	0	3	9	19	.269	.232	Batting #2	.276	29	8	0	0	0	0	3	3	.344	.276
First Pitch	.280	25	7	2	0	0	1	1	0	.308	.360	Batting #8	.212	99	21	4	0	0	2	8	21	.271	.253
Ahead on Count	.244	41	10	1	0	0	0	4	0	.311	.268	Other	.000	17	0	0	0	0	0	1	5	.000	.000
Behind on Count	.118	51	6	0	0	0	1	0	15	.118	.118	Pre-All Star	.200	120	24	3	0	0	2	6	23	.238	.225
Two Strikes	.074	54	4	0	0	0	1	6	29	.167	.074	Post-All Star	.200	25	5	1	0	0	1	5	6	.333	.240

Career (1988-1992)

	Avg	AB	H	2B	3B	HR	RBI	BB	SO	OBP	SLG		Avg	AB	H	2B	3B	HR	RBI	BB	SO	OBP	SLG
vs. Left	.214	84	18	5	0	0	9	8	14	.281	.274	Scoring Posn	.213	108	23	5	0	0	24	15	20	.307	.259
vs. Right	.232	340	79	14	1	1	18	28	59	.293	.288	Close & Late	.217	83	18	4	0	0	7	7	12	.278	.265
Groundball	.214	159	34	3	0	1	11	10	27	.257	.252	None on/out	.232	99	23	1	0	0	0	6	18	.283	.242
Flyball	.259	81	21	7	0	0	8	9	17	.341	.346	Batting #2	.286	70	20	1	0	0	6	7	12	.346	.300
Home	.201	179	36	7	0	1	10	15	29	.262	.257	Batting #8	.220	241	53	15	1	1	13	21	41	.283	.303
Away	.249	245	61	12	1	0	17	21	44	.311	.306	Other	.212	113	24	3	0	0	8	8	20	.270	.239
Day	.273	176	48	17	0	1	12	10	30	.307	.386	April	.189	90	17	3	0	0	8	8	10	.253	.222
Night	.196	248	49	2	1	0	15	26	43	.279	.214	May	.094	32	3	2	0	0	2	5	9	.237	.156
Grass	.206	141	29	6	1	0	5	12	27	.276	.262	June	.243	70	17	4	0	0	6	5	11	.289	.300
Turf	.240	283	68	13	0	1	22	24	46	.298	.297	July	.171	82	14	0	0	0	0	5	17	.218	.171
First Pitch	.293	82	24	4	0	0	6	3	0	.326	.341	August	.343	67	23	4	0	1	10	9	12	.421	.448
Ahead on Count	.319	113	36	7	1	1	9	19	0	.417	.425	September/October	.277	83	23	6	1	0	6	4	14	.315	.373
Behind on Count	.130	123	16	3	0	1	5	0	38	.136	.179	Pre-All Star	.191	225	43	9	0	0	11	21	37	.261	.231
Two Strikes	.118	152	18	5	0	0	5	13	73	.192	.151	Post-All Star	.271	199	54	10	1	1	16	15	36	.324	.347

Batter vs. Pitcher (career)

Hits Best Against	Avg	AB	H	2B	3B	HR	RBI	BB	SO	OBP	SLG	Hits Worst Against	Avg	AB	H	2B	3B	HR	RBI	BB	SO	OBP	SLG
Greg Maddux	.333	12	4	0	0	0	0	0	1	.333	.333	David Cone	.158	19	3	1	0	0	0	1	6	.200	.211
												Doug Drabek	.235	17	4	0	0	0	2	0	3	.235	.235

Brian Jordan — Cardinals
Bats Right (groundball hitter)

	Avg	G	AB	R	H	2B	3B	HR	RBI	BB	SO	HBP	GDP	SB	CS	OBP	SLG	IBB	SH	SF	#Pit	#P/PA	GB	FB	G/F
1992 Season	.207	55	193	17	40	9	4	5	22	10	48	1	6	7	2	.250	.373	1	0	0	721	3.53	77	44	1.75

1992 Season

	Avg	AB	H	2B	3B	HR	RBI	BB	SO	OBP	SLG		Avg	AB	H	2B	3B	HR	RBI	BB	SO	OBP	SLG
vs. Left	.219	64	14	2	0	4	10	6	14	.286	.438	Scoring Posn	.186	59	11	2	2	1	16	2	16	.226	.339
vs. Right	.202	129	26	7	4	1	12	4	34	.231	.341	Close & Late	.171	41	7	2	2	0	1	3	12	.244	.317
Home	.238	80	19	6	2	3	16	5	19	.291	.475	None on/out	.208	48	10	2	1	1	0	1	10	.208	.354
Away	.186	113	21	3	2	2	6	5	29	.220	.301	Batting #5	.184	136	25	7	3	2	17	6	30	.224	.324
First Pitch	.250	32	8	1	0	0	1	1	0	.273	.281	Batting #6	.344	32	11	2	1	3	5	2	10	.382	.750
Ahead on Count	.241	29	7	1	0	2	4	5	0	.371	.483	Other	.160	25	4	0	0	0	0	2	8	.222	.160
Behind on Count	.195	77	15	4	2	3	13	0	29	.195	.416	Pre-All Star	.207	193	40	9	4	5	22	10	48	.250	.373
Two Strikes	.172	99	17	5	3	2	10	5	48	.212	.343	Post-All Star	.000	0	0	0	0	0	0	0	0	.000	.000

Ricky Jordan — Phillies
Bats Right

	Avg	G	AB	R	H	2B	3B	HR	RBI	BB	SO	HBP	GDP	SB	CS	OBP	SLG	IBB	SH	SF	#Pit	#P/PA	GB	FB	G/F
1992 Season	.304	94	276	33	84	19	0	4	34	5	44	0	8	3	0	.313	.417	0	0	3	862	3.04	112	62	1.81
Career (1988-1992)	.281	500	1697	207	477	98	7	41	245	62	233	12	52	10	6	.307	.420	15	0	21	5550	3.10	676	474	1.43

1992 Season

	Avg	AB	H	2B	3B	HR	RBI	BB	SO	OBP	SLG		Avg	AB	H	2B	3B	HR	RBI	BB	SO	OBP	SLG
vs. Left	.371	132	49	11	0	3	21	2	18	.372	.523	Scoring Posn	.266	79	21	2	0	1	27	2	9	.274	.329
vs. Right	.243	144	35	8	0	1	13	3	26	.259	.319	Close & Late	.268	56	15	2	0	0	5	3	9	.305	.304
Home	.319	116	37	7	0	2	20	3	15	.331	.431	None on/out	.338	65	22	4	0	2	2	1	8	.348	.492
Away	.294	160	47	12	0	2	14	2	29	.301	.406	Batting #5	.312	109	34	8	0	3	18	2	13	.321	.468
First Pitch	.322	59	19	7	0	1	11	0	0	.311	.492	Batting #6	.299	77	23	5	0	1	5	0	13	.299	.403
Ahead on Count	.304	46	14	2	0	0	4	5	0	.365	.348	Other	.300	90	27	6	0	0	11	3	18	.316	.367
Behind on Count	.327	113	37	7	0	2	14	0	27	.325	.442	Pre-All Star	.241	133	32	7	0	2	15	3	27	.254	.338
Two Strikes	.229	109	25	4	0	1	9	0	44	.229	.294	Post-All Star	.364	143	52	12	0	2	19	2	17	.370	.490

Career (1988-1992)

	Avg	AB	H	2B	3B	HR	RBI	BB	SO	OBP	SLG		Avg	AB	H	2B	3B	HR	RBI	BB	SO	OBP	SLG
vs. Left	.318	658	209	48	3	19	98	37	72	.352	.486	Scoring Posn	.276	468	129	23	3	12	189	35	83	.321	.415
vs. Right	.258	1039	268	50	4	22	147	25	161	.278	.377	Close & Late	.272	301	82	14	2	6	48	18	50	.320	.392
Groundball	.283	607	172	38	2	7	80	25	85	.314	.387	None on/out	.304	405	123	18	1	13	13	11	43	.324	.449
Flyball	.291	385	112	25	3	12	68	11	61	.314	.465	Batting #4	.285	706	201	40	4	12	92	27	86	.313	.404
Home	.288	827	238	41	3	22	131	21	117	.306	.424	Batting #5	.298	439	131	30	2	18	81	18	48	.328	.499
Away	.275	870	239	57	4	19	114	41	116	.309	.415	Other	.263	552	145	28	1	11	72	17	99	.284	.377
Day	.294	513	151	36	2	15	92	18	64	.317	.460	April	.265	162	43	11	1	2	24	11 *	23	.311	.383
Night	.275	1184	326	62	5	26	153	44	169	.303	.402	May	.259	290	75	10	1	8	41	8	36	.279	.383
Grass	.267	464	133	28	2	13	63	14	61	.307	.440	June	.264	239	63	20	0	4	26	17	33	.314	.397
Turf	.279	1233	344	70	5	28	182	48	172	.308	.412	July	.260	288	75	11	1	7	43	8	49	.285	.378
First Pitch	.358	296	106	22	1	15	67	6	0	.374	.591	August	.293	341	100	24	2	12	63	7	41	.310	.481
Ahead on Count	.313	345	108	27	2	7	49	34	0	.370	.464	September/October	.321	377	121	22	2	8	45	11	51	.339	.454
Behind on Count	.277	705	195	43	3	14	96	0	157	.281	.406	Pre-All Star	.257	790	203	44	3	17	101	38	113	.291	.385
Two Strikes	.208	653	136	21	3	7	61	17	232	.228	.282	Post-All Star	.302	907	274	54	4	24	144	24	120	.322	.450

Batter vs. Pitcher (career)

Hits Best Against	Avg	AB	H	2B	3B	HR	RBI	BB	SO	OBP	SLG	Hits Worst Against	Avg	AB	H	2B	3B	HR	RBI	BB	SO	OBP	SLG
Charlie Leibrandt	.583	12	7	1	0	1	3	1	0	.615	.917	Doug Drabek	.059	17	1	1	0	0	1	0	8	.059	.118
Tom Browning	.500	18	9	1	0	4	5	0	0	.474	.722	Rob Dibble	.083	12	1	1	0	0	1	0	3	.083	.167
Ramon Martinez	.412	17	7	2	0	1	4	0	1	.412	.706	Cris Carpenter	.100	10	1	0	0	0	1	0	1	.182	.100
Jose DeLeon	.368	19	7	2	0	2	6	0	2	.368	.789	Ken Hill	.143	14	2	0	0	0	0	0	1	.143	.143
Steve Avery	.364	11	4	0	0	1	3	0	3	.364	.636	Kevin Gross	.154	13	2	1	0	0	0	0	5	.214	.154

Terry Jorgensen — Twins
Bats Right (groundball hitter)

	Avg	G	AB	R	H	2B	3B	HR	RBI	BB	SO	HBP	GDP	SB	CS	OBP	SLG	IBB	SH	SF	#Pit	#P/PA	GB	FB	G/F
1992 Season	.310	22	58	5	18	1	0	0	5	3	11	1	4	1	2	.349	.328	0	0	1	219	3.48	26	11	2.36
Career (1989-1992)	.272	32	81	6	22	2	0	0	7	7	16	1	5	1	2	.333	.296	0	0	1	321	3.57	38	15	2.53

1992 Season

	Avg	AB	H	2B	3B	HR	RBI	BB	SO	OBP	SLG		Avg	AB	H	2B	3B	HR	RBI	BB	SO	OBP	SLG
vs. Left	.296	27	8	1	0	0	2	1	4	.333	.333	Scoring Posn	.235	17	4	0	0	0	5	1	5	.263	.235
vs. Right	.323	31	10	0	0	0	3	2	7	.364	.323	Close & Late	.500	8	4	0	0	0	1	1	1	.556	.500

Felix Jose — Cardinals
Bats Both (groundball hitter)

	Avg	G	AB	R	H	2B	3B	HR	RBI	BB	SO	HBP	GDP	SB	CS	OBP	SLG	IBB	SH	SF	#Pit	#P/PA	GB	FB	G/F
1992 Season	.295	131	509	62	150	22	3	14	75	40	100	1	9	28	12	.347	.432	8	0	1	1956	3.55	213	111	1.92
Career (1988-1992)	.287	439	1566	190	449	81	10	33	210	118	308	8	32	61	31	.338	.414	16	2	7	5910	3.48	645	344	1.88

1992 Season

	Avg	AB	H	2B	3B	HR	RBI	BB	SO	OBP	SLG		Avg	AB	H	2B	3B	HR	RBI	BB	SO	OBP	SLG
vs. Left	.374	182	68	11	2	6	31	15	33	.419	.555	Scoring Posn	.261	153	40	6	1	1	56	18	36	.341	.333
vs. Right	.251	327	82	11	1	8	44	25	67	.306	.364	Close & Late	.319	113	36	4	1	4	20	10	28	.374	.478
Groundball	.304	184	56	7	1	3	25	16	34	.360	.402	None on/out	.383	133	51	10	0	3	3	8	21	.418	.526
Flyball	.296	98	29	5	1	5	23	7	20	.343	.520	Batting #3	.290	169	49	8	1	4	28	12	33	.335	.420
Home	.294	255	75	10	1	12	46	23	52	.354	.482	Batting #4	.288	302	87	12	2	8	41	27	61	.348	.421
Away	.295	254	75	12	2	2	29	17	48	.339	.382	Other	.368	38	14	2	0	2	6	1	6	.385	.579
Day	.285	130	37	5	1	2	21	9	26	.331	.385	April	.400	10	4	1	0	0	1	0	2	.400	.500
Night	.298	379	113	17	2	12	54	31	74	.352	.449	May	.346	104	36	4	2	4	25	13	20	.415	.538
Grass	.331	124	41	7	1	0	18	10	22	.381	.403	June	.276	105	29	6	0	3	16	7	20	.321	.419
Turf	.283	385	109	15	2	14	57	30	78	.336	.442	July	.256	78	20	2	0	1	3	7	19	.318	.321
First Pitch	.384	86	33	7	0	5	12	8	0	.432	.640	August	.305	105	32	5	0	3	12	5	26	.342	.438
Ahead on Count	.373	83	31	4	1	5	15	14	0	.464	.627	September/October	.271	107	29	4	1	3	18	8	13	.322	.411
Behind on Count	.273	172	47	9	1	3	30	0	55	.273	.390	Pre-All Star	.300	257	77	12	2	7	43	21	51	.351	.444
Two Strikes	.250	240	60	8	1	3	32	18	100	.302	.329	Post-All Star	.290	252	73	10	1	7	32	19	49	.342	.421

1992 By Position

Position	Avg	AB	H	2B	3B	HR	RBI	BB	SO	OBP	SLG	G	GS	Innings	PO	A	E	DP	Fld Pct	Rng Fctr	In Zone	Outs	Zone Rtg	MLB Zone
As rf	.294	504	148	22	3	14	74	39	98	.345	.433	127	124	1117.1	271	11	6	1	.979	2.27	309	258	.835	.814

Career (1988-1992)

	Avg	AB	H	2B	3B	HR	RBI	BB	SO	OBP	SLG		Avg	AB	H	2B	3B	HR	RBI	BB	SO	OBP	SLG
vs. Left	.323	570	184	36	5	10	83	46	111	.373	.456	Scoring Posn	.304	434	132	29	4	8	172	42	93	.366	.445
vs. Right	.266	996	265	45	5	23	127	72	197	.319	.391	Close & Late	.307	267	82	13	1	8	36	24	68	.365	.453
Groundball	.308	526	162	28	3	9	70	31	94	.349	.424	None on/out	.302	377	114	23	0	6	6	23	70	.343	.411
Flyball	.310	319	99	20	3	11	57	34	68	.377	.495	Batting #4	.277	343	95	13	2	8	47	34	70	.344	.397
Home	.277	781	216	36	7	20	117	64	152	.333	.417	Batting #5	.307	592	182	40	6	11	69	40	120	.351	.451
Away	.297	785	233	45	3	13	93	54	156	.344	.411	Other	.273	631	172	28	2	14	94	44	118	.324	.390
Day	.274	500	137	24	4	12	78	32	97	.318	.410	April	.314	153	48	13	2	4	24	14	21	.373	.503
Night	.293	1066	312	57	6	21	132	86	211	.348	.417	May	.303	264	80	12	2	6	44	30	56	.375	.432
Grass	.277	665	184	33	2	9	78	37	135	.318	.373	June	.274	266	73	17	1	3	34	14	50	.311	.380
Turf	.294	901	265	48	6	24	132	81	173	.353	.383	July	.271	266	72	12	0	6	27	20	62	.325	.383
First Pitch	.370	289	107	19	2	13	63	13	0	.399	.585	August	.296	301	89	14	0	3	28	17	64	.339	.372
Ahead on Count	.315	267	84	17	2	9	33	61	0	.441	.494	September/October	.275	316	87	13	5	11	53	23	55	.324	.453
Behind on Count	.238	563	139	31	3	5	55	1	192	.241	.326	Pre-All Star	.287	767	220	46	5	13	106	62	146	.341	.411
Two Strikes	.225	734	165	31	4	8	67	44	308	.270	.311	Post-All Star	.287	799	229	35	5	20	104	56	162	.336	.418

Batter vs. Pitcher (career)

Hits Best Against	Avg	AB	H	2B	3B	HR	RBI	BB	SO	OBP	SLG	Hits Worst Against	Avg	AB	H	2B	3B	HR	RBI	BB	SO	OBP	SLG
Chris Nabholz	.636	11	7	2	0	0	3	1	3	.667	.818	Greg Maddux	.000	16	0	0	0	0	0	1	7	.059	.000
Tommy Greene	.571	14	8	4	1	0	4	2	2	.556	1.000	Darryl Kile	.111	9	1	0	0	0	0	2	2	.385	.111
Danny Jackson	.500	12	6	5	0	0	4	0	1	.500	.917	Terry Mulholland	.167	24	4	0	0	0	2	1	4	.200	.167
Joe Boever	.500	8	4	1	0	1	2	3	0	.636	1.000	Doug Drabek	.172	29	5	1	0	0	3	1	5	.200	.207
Mark Gardner	.357	14	5	1	0	2	4	3	4	.471	.857	Randy Myers	.182	11	2	0	0	0	0	1	0	.182	.182

Wally Joyner — Royals   Bats Left (flyball hitter)

	Avg	G	AB	R	H	2B	3B	HR	RBI	BB	SO	HBP	GDP	SB	CS	OBP	SLG	IBB	SH	SF	#Pit	#P/PA	GB	FB	G/F
1992 Season	.269	149	572	66	154	36	2	9	66	55	50	4	19	11	5	.336	.386	4	0	2	2130	3.36	226	190	1.19
Last Five Years	.284	692	2623	339	746	146	9	67	367	249	269	17	71	26	10	.347	.424	33	4	26	10176	3.49	909	954	0.95

1992 Season

	Avg	AB	H	2B	3B	HR	RBI	BB	SO	OBP	SLG		Avg	AB	H	2B	3B	HR	RBI	BB	SO	OBP	SLG
vs. Left	.240	192	46	13	0	2	20	15	24	.307	.339	Scoring Posn	.284	141	40	13	0	3	52	18	11	.372	.440
vs. Right	.284	380	108	23	2	7	46	40	26	.352	.411	Close & Late	.238	105	25	4	0	3	12	9	8	.298	.362
Groundball	.295	146	43	5	0	1	19	7	8	.331	.349	None on/out	.234	128	30	7	1	3	3	7	7	.274	.375
Flyball	.270	196	53	12	2	3	20	21	23	.344	.398	Batting #3	.233	189	44	13	0	2	20	13	23	.284	.333
Home	.266	282	75	19	2	1	29	21	21	.324	.358	Batting #4	.292	144	42	12	0	4	21	15	8	.364	.458
Away	.272	290	79	17	0	8	37	34	29	.349	.414	Other	.285	239	68	11	2	3	25	27	19	.360	.385
Day	.248	141	35	6	0	3	17	19	15	.340	.355	April	.321	81	26	8	0	1	9	7	9	.375	.457
Night	.276	431	119	30	2	6	49	36	35	.335	.397	May	.328	67	22	5	0	3	8	2	6	.366	.537
Grass	.260	223	58	11	0	6	25	25	19	.336	.390	June	.229	105	24	8	0	1	16	7	10	.278	.333
Turf	.275	349	96	25	2	3	41	30	31	.337	.384	July	.236	110	26	8	0	1	11	12	14	.311	.336
First Pitch	.266	109	29	6	1	2	8	3	0	.286	.394	August	.280	107	30	1	1	2	14	12	5	.358	.364
Ahead on Count	.318	157	50	12	1	7	32	32	0	.435	.541	September/October	.255	102	26	6	1	1	8	15	6	.350	.363
Behind on Count	.229	188	43	12	1	1	21	0	38	.240	.319	Pre-All Star	.276	304	84	24	0	6	40	21	31	.327	.414
Two Strikes	.214	196	42	13	0	0	15	21	50	.299	.281	Post-All Star	.261	268	70	12	2	3	26	34	19	.347	.354

1992 By Position

Position	Avg	AB	H	2B	3B	HR	RBI	BB	SO	OBP	SLG	G	GS	Innings	PO	A	E	DP	Fld Pct	Rng Fctr	In Zone	Outs	Zone Rtg	MLB Zone
As 1b	.272	556	151	36	2	9	66	53	50	.338	.392	145	141	1262.1	1239	134	10	139	.993	---	272	251	.923	.843

Last Five Years

	Avg	AB	H	2B	3B	HR	RBI	BB	SO	OBP	SLG		Avg	AB	H	2B	3B	HR	RBI	BB	SO	OBP	SLG
vs. Left	.256	905	232	45	1	16	122	57	104	.305	.361	Scoring Posn	.298	667	199	40	2	20	295	103	68	.387	.454
vs. Right	.299	1718	514	101	8	51	245	192	155	.369	.456	Close & Late	.276	434	120	22	0	13	64	43	41	.340	.417
Groundball	.311	631	196	33	3	15	104	52	53	.366	.444	None on/out	.263	594	156	30	2	16	16	44	48	.313	.401
Flyball	.282	695	196	39	5	23	106	73	73	.351	.452	Batting #3	.280	1106	310	67	5	27	157	107	120	.343	.423
Home	.274	1261	345	68	4	30	169	121	117	.338	.405	Batting #4	.280	788	221	42	1	21	107	69	76	.345	.416
Away	.294	1362	401	78	5	37	198	128	142	.356	.441	Other	.295	729	215	37	3	19	103	73	63	.357	.432
Day	.279	617	172	32	2	21	92	78	68	.361	.439	April	.269	390	105	27	0	6	41	48	44	.350	.385
Night	.286	2006	574	114	7	46	275	171	191	.343	.419	May	.323	461	149	24	2	16	76	46	37	.386	.488
Grass	.278	1955	543	104	6	54	272	193	192	.342	.420	June	.277	501	139	28	2	7	68	36	54	.325	.383
Turf	.304	668	203	42	3	13	95	56	67	.362	.434	July	.285	459	131	30	1	12	77	37	53	.339	.434
First Pitch	.307	436	134	25	3	16	56	10	0	.323	.489	August	.272	426	116	19	3	19	65	45	35	.345	.465
Ahead on Count	.328	692	227	52	2	26	118	134	0	.436	.522	September/October	.275	386	106	18	1	7	40	37	36	.336	.381
Behind on Count	.248	832	206	38	1	14	100	4	154	.258	.346	Pre-All Star	.268	1540	444	91	5	32	216	140	158	.349	.416
Two Strikes	.227	1005	228	48	3	13	114	94	258	.296	.319	Post-All Star	.279	1083	302	55	4	35	151	109	101	.345	.434

Batter vs. Pitcher (career)

Hits Best Against	Avg	AB	H	2B	3B	HR	RBI	BB	SO	OBP	SLG	Hits Worst Against	Avg	AB	H	2B	3B	HR	RBI	BB	SO	OBP	SLG
Eric Plunk	.667	15	10	2	0	3	8	3	1	.722	1.400	Bud Black	.083	24	2	1	0	0	2	1	0	.115	.125
Dennis Lamp	.583	12	7	0	1	0	2	2	1	.643	.750	Jose DeLeon	.100	10	1	0	0	0	1	2	3	.231	.100
Eric Bell	.556	9	5	1	0	1	5	2	1	.692	1.000	Greg Hibbard	.158	19	3	0	0	0	0	0	0	.158	.158
Willie Banks	.500	10	5	2	0	0	4	1	2	.545	.700	Danny Jackson	.167	12	2	0	0	0	0	0	4	.167	.167
Mike Morgan	.417	12	5	2	0	1	4	0	1	.417	.833	John Dopson	.167	12	2	0	0	0	0	0	1	.167	.167

Dave Justice — Braves

Bats Left (flyball hitter)

	Avg	G	AB	R	H	2B	3B	HR	RBI	BB	SO	HBP	GDP	SB	CS	OBP	SLG	IBB	SH	SF	#Pit	#P/PA	GB	FB	G/F
1992 Season	.256	144	484	78	124	19	5	21	72	79	85	2	1	2	4	.359	.446	8	0	6	2219	3.89	150	162	0.93
Career (1989-1992)	.269	396	1370	228	369	70	8	71	240	211	267	6	8	23	19	.366	.488	22	1	12	6214	3.89	382	457	0.84

1992 Season

	Avg	AB	H	2B	3B	HR	RBI	BB	SO	OBP	SLG		Avg	AB	H	2B	3B	HR	RBI	BB	SO	OBP	SLG
vs. Left	.283	159	45	9	1	5	17	16	28	.352	.447	Scoring Posn	.230	126	29	6	2	7	50	41	21	.405	.476
vs. Right	.243	325	79	10	4	16	55	63	57	.362	.446	Close & Late	.247	77	19	5	0	3	8	8	20	.314	.429
Groundball	.298	198	59	11	2	8	33	33	31	.397	.495	None on/out	.187	123	23	4	2	4	15	27	281	.350	
Flyball	.220	127	28	4	3	2	14	22	26	.333	.346	Batting #4	.251	387	97	15	4	19	62	68	67	.359	.457
Home	.229	245	56	9	4	10	35	45	48	.346	.420	Batting #5	.286	91	26	4	1	2	10	10	16	.362	.418
Away	.285	239	68	10	1	11	37	34	37	.373	.473	Other	.167	6	1	0	0	0	0	1	2	.286	.167
Day	.257	140	36	5	2	3	20	28	23	.372	.386	April	.037	27	1	0	0	0	0	5	10	.188	.037
Night	.256	344	88	14	3	18	52	51	62	.353	.471	May	.232	99	23	3	0	4	11	17	18	.347	.384
Grass	.256	355	91	12	5	16	54	60	69	.363	.454	June	.291	86	25	4	1	4	19	15	13	.388	.500
Turf	.256	129	33	7	0	5	18	19	16	.349	.426	July	.278	90	25	5	1	1	7	12	11	.362	.389
First Pitch	.222	63	14	2	1	4	13	8	0	.301	.476	August	.286	98	28	4	2	4	13	13	16	.369	.490
Ahead on Count	.326	95	31	5	1	4	12	39	0	.519	.526	September/October	.262	84	22	3	1	8	22	17	17	.382	.607
Behind on Count	.250	168	42	12	1	4	20	0	49	.259	.405	Pre-All Star	.245	249	61	9	2	8	33	44	49	.358	.394
Two Strikes	.208	240	50	8	2	7	29	35	85	.309	.346	Post-All Star	.268	235	63	10	3	13	39	35	36	.360	.502

1992 By Position

Position	Avg	AB	H	2B	3B	HR	RBI	BB	SO	OBP	SLG	G	GS	Innings	PO	A	E	DP	Fld Pct	Rng Fctr	In Zone	Outs	Zone Rtg	MLB Zone
As rf	.258	481	124	19	5	21	72	77	85	.359	.449	140	134	1198.0	313	9	8	3	.976	2.42	351	306	.872	.814

Career (1989-1992)

	Avg	AB	H	2B	3B	HR	RBI	BB	SO	OBP	SLG		Avg	AB	H	2B	3B	HR	RBI	BB	SO	OBP	SLG
vs. Left	.301	455	137	23	2	22	88	48	75	.367	.505	Scoring Posn	.294	374	110	25	3	20	168	95	75	.429	.537
vs. Right	.254	915	232	47	6	49	152	163	192	.366	.479	Close & Late	.259	205	53	11	1	9	31	28	52	.346	.434
Groundball	.316	459	145	23	4	27	97	65	81	.400	.560	None on/out	.207	362	75	16	2	17	17	33	81	.275	.403
Flyball	.250	340	85	22	3	13	50	52	71	.348	.447	Batting #4	.266	880	234	42	7	49	168	147	164	.370	.497
Home	.270	682	184	42	6	41	126	109	143	.368	.529	Batting #5	.288	267	77	19	1	8	40	28	54	.357	.457
Away	.269	688	185	28	2	30	114	102	124	.365	.446	Other	.260	223	58	9	0	14	32	36	49	.363	.489
Day	.232	353	82	11	2	16	58	64	57	.348	.411	April	.177	96	17	4	0	2	10	12	27	.266	.281
Night	.282	1017	287	59	6	55	182	147	210	.373	.514	May	.296	270	80	18	0	11	49	36	49	.383	.485
Grass	.277	1001	277	54	6	55	177	150	205	.370	.511	June	.251	247	62	11	3	10	41	41	52	.357	.441
Turf	.249	369	92	16	2	16	63	61	62	.357	.423	July	.248	165	41	7	1	5	16	22	32	.337	.394
First Pitch	.331	169	56	7	2	14	46	17	0	.395	.645	August	.284	261	74	15	2	18	52	30	49	.357	.563
Ahead on Count	.362	290	105	21	1	25	57	105	0	.531	.700	September/October	.287	331	95	15	2	25	72	70	58	.408	.571
Behind on Count	.228	465	106	26	1	19	75	0	139	.229	.411	Pre-All Star	.261	666	174	36	4	24	104	98	141	.357	.435
Two Strikes	.186	663	123	22	3	17	89	88	267	.280	.280	Post-All Star	.277	704	195	34	4	47	136	113	126	.375	.537

Batter vs. Pitcher (career)

Hits Best Against	Avg	AB	H	2B	3B	HR	RBI	BB	SO	OBP	SLG	Hits Worst Against	Avg	AB	H	2B	3B	HR	RBI	BB	SO	OBP	SLG
Kevin Gross	.600	10	6	0	0	2	5	2	2	.571	1.200	Greg W. Harris	.091	11	1	0	0	0	0	0	2	.091	.091
Norm Charlton	.364	11	4	1	0	1	5	2	3	.462	.727	Danny Darwin	.100	10	1	0	0	0	0	2	5	.250	.100
John Burkett	.348	23	8	0	0	2	3	5	3	.464	.609	Mitch Williams	.100	10	1	0	0	0	0	1	4	.182	.100
Mike Morgan	.333	18	6	1	0	2	6	2	3	.381	.722	Jose DeLeon	.125	16	2	1	0	0	1	0	6	.125	.188
Danny Jackson	.333	15	5	1	0	2	3	3	3	.476	.800	Dwight Gooden	.167	12	2	0	0	0	1	1	4	.231	.167

Scott Kamieniecki — Yankees

Pitches Right

	ERA	W	L	Sv	G	GS	IP	BB	SO	Avg	H	2B	3B	HR	RBI	OBP	SLG	CG	ShO	Sup	QS	#P/S	SB	CS	GB	FB	G/F
1992 Season	4.36	6	14	0	28	28	188.0	74	88	.269	193	38	1	13	81	.340	.379	4	0	4.40	12	105	29	6	277	210	1.32
Career (1991-1992)	4.25	10	18	0	37	37	243.1	96	122	.266	247	50	4	21	104	.338	.397	4	0	4.40	19	104	33	8	351	278	1.26

1992 Season

	ERA	W	L	Sv	G	GS	IP	H	HR	BB	SO		Avg	AB	H	2B	3B	HR	RBI	BB	SO	OBP	SLG
Home	4.03	6	4	0	15	15	96.0	97	7	42	44	vs. Left	.279	337	94	17	1	5	35	35	43	.345	.380
Away	4.70	0	10	0	13	13	92.0	96	6	32	44	vs. Right	.261	380	99	21	0	8	46	39	45	.335	.379
Day	4.68	1	4	0	9	9	59.2	62	2	27	27	Inning 1-6	.254	595	151	29	1	10	62	64	78	.329	.356
Night	4.21	5	10	0	19	19	128.1	131	11	47	61	Inning 7+	.344	122	42	9	0	3	19	10	10	.394	.492
Grass	4.37	6	13	0	26	26	173.0	178	12	71	82	None on	.260	416	108	19	0	8	34	46	.320	.363
Turf	4.20	0	1	0	2	2	15.0	15	1	3	6	Runners on	.282	301	85	19	1	5	73	40	42	.365	.402
April	0.00	0	0	0	0	0	0.0	0	0	0	0	Scoring Posn	.282	181	51	11	1	3	67	29	29	.372	.403

233

1992 Season

	ERA	W	L	Sv	G	GS	IP	H	HR	BB	SO		Avg	AB	H	2B	3B	HR	RBI	BB	SO	OBP	SLG
May	3.40	1	2	0	6	6	42.1	39	0	18	16	Close & Late	.397	68	27	7	0	1	13	7	8	.453	.544
June	6.21	0	3	0	5	5	29.0	36	3	14	16	None on/out	.291	189	55	7	0	6	6	11	25	.337	.423
July	4.98	1	3	0	5	5	34.1	40	4	9	13	vs. 1st Batr (relief)	.000	0	0	0	0	0	0	0	0	.000	.000
August	3.95	2	3	0	6	6	41.0	36	4	16	18	First Inning Pitched	.252	107	27	3	0	4	17	17	15	.365	.393
September/October	3.92	2	3	0	6	6	41.1	42	2	17	25	First 75 Pitches	.249	485	121	23	1	8	50	52	61	.323	.351
Starter	4.36	6	14	0	28	28	188.0	193	13	74	88	Pitch 76-90	.276	98	27	5	0	1	7	10	14	.355	.357
Reliever	0.00	0	0	0	0	0	0.0	0	0	0	0	Pitch 91-105	.301	93	28	5	0	3	14	10	10	.369	.452
0-3 Days Rest	0.00	0	0	0	0	0	0.0	0	0	0	0	Pitch 106+	.415	41	17	5	0	1	10	2	3	.442	.610
4 Days Rest	5.06	2	5	0	14	14	89.0	96	10	41	52	First Pitch	.287	101	29	5	0	3	12	6	0	.342	.426
5+ Days Rest	3.73	4	9	0	14	14	99.0	97	3	33	36	Ahead on Count	.264	299	79	10	1	5	33	0	66	.269	.355
Pre-All Star	4.64	2	6	0	13	13	85.1	90	4	37	36	Behind on Count	.269	175	47	12	0	4	18	41	0	.404	.406
Post-All Star	4.12	4	8	0	15	15	102.2	103	9	37	52	Two Strikes	.240	312	75	12	1	5	33	27	88	.305	.333

Ron Karkovice — White Sox

Bats Right (flyball hitter)

	Avg	G	AB	R	H	2B	3B	HR	RBI	BB	SO	HBP	GDP	SB	CS	OBP	SLG	IBB	SH	SF	#Pit	#P/PA	GB	FB	G/F
1992 Season	.237	123	342	39	81	12	1	13	50	30	89	3	3	10	4	.302	.392	1	4	2	1361	3.61	97	101	0.96
Last Five Years	.238	363	969	125	235	48	3	30	125	78	269	8	7	16	6	.297	.383	3	30	6	3997	3.70	250	286	0.87

1992 Season

	Avg	AB	H	2B	3B	HR	RBI	BB	SO	OBP	SLG		Avg	AB	H	2B	3B	HR	RBI	BB	SO	OBP	SLG
vs. Left	.224	107	24	5	1	4	15	13	30	.314	.402	Scoring Posn	.267	90	24	3	1	2	34	14	24	.364	.389
vs. Right	.243	235	57	7	0	9	35	17	59	.297	.387	Close & Late	.204	54	11	1	0	1	4	7	16	.302	.278
Groundball	.200	90	18	2	0	2	8	10	19	.294	.289	None on/out	.247	81	20	2	0	4	4	3	20	.274	.420
Flyball	.241	108	26	5	0	4	14	9	31	.297	.398	Batting #7	.200	110	22	3	0	2	10	14	32	.296	.282
Home	.228	171	39	6	1	5	18	17	41	.305	.363	Batting #8	.293	150	44	8	1	8	31	7	36	.323	.520
Away	.246	171	42	6	0	8	32	13	48	.299	.421	Other	.183	82	15	1	0	3	9	9	21	.277	.305
Day	.211	76	16	3	0	3	11	3	30	.247	.368	April	.250	44	11	1	0	1	6	8	9	.370	.341
Night	.244	266	65	9	1	10	39	27	59	.318	.398	May	.167	72	12	2	0	1	5	6	25	.231	.236
Grass	.234	282	66	8	1	9	42	27	72	.306	.365	June	.239	46	11	1	0	3	6	6	15	.340	.457
Turf	.250	60	15	4	0	4	8	3	17	.286	.517	July	.191	47	9	2	0	1	5	3	5	.250	.298
First Pitch	.354	48	17	2	0	3	13	1	0	.373	.583	August	.222	45	10	1	0	1	8	3	9	.271	.311
Ahead on Count	.311	74	23	4	0	4	15	16	0	.440	.527	September/October	.318	88	28	5	1	6	20	4	26	.348	.602
Behind on Count	.164	122	20	2	1	3	12	0	45	.164	.282	Pre-All Star	.210	181	38	4	0	6	21	22	50	.300	.331
Two Strikes	.134	157	21	3	1	5	13	13	89	.205	.261	Post-All Star	.267	161	43	8	1	7	29	8	39	.306	.460

1992 By Position

Position	Avg	AB	H	2B	3B	HR	RBI	BB	SO	OBP	SLG	G	GS	Innings	PO	A	E	DP	Fld Pct	Rng Fctr	In Zone	Outs	Zone Rtg	MLB Zone
As c	.240	337	81	12	1	13	50	30	88	.306	.398	119	98	915.0	533	53	6	9	.990	---	---	---	---	---

Last Five Years

	Avg	AB	H	2B	3B	HR	RBI	BB	SO	OBP	SLG		Avg	AB	H	2B	3B	HR	RBI	BB	SO	OBP	SLG
vs. Left	.240	375	90	20	2	11	51	34	106	.303	.392	Scoring Posn	.245	253	62	9	1	7	92	36	81	.339	.372
vs. Right	.236	614	145	28	1	19	74	44	163	.293	.378	Close & Late	.257	167	43	6	0	2	9	13	46	.317	.329
Groundball	.221	271	60	13	0	5	19	21	74	.286	.325	None on/out	.267	247	66	18	0	7	7	10	59	.301	.425
Flyball	.198	273	54	10	0	8	32	18	84	.248	.322	Batting #7	.239	264	63	16	0	5	29	26	63	.314	.356
Home	.217	479	104	24	2	6	40	40	131	.281	.313	Batting #9	.198	283	56	9	0	7	29	19	76	.248	.304
Away	.257	510	131	24	1	24	85	38	138	.312	.449	Other	.262	442	116	23	3	18	67	33	130	.317	.450
Day	.244	369	90	23	1	11	54	23	116	.293	.401	April	.265	102	27	3	0	2	12	10	25	.333	.353
Night	.234	620	145	25	2	19	71	55	153	.299	.373	May	.197	188	37	5	0	4	22	17	49	.261	.287
Grass	.238	835	199	38	3	23	103	69	228	.299	.374	June	.219	155	34	6	0	6	13	11	44	.284	.374
Turf	.234	154	36	10	0	7	22	9	41	.283	.435	July	.251	179	45	16	0	5	19	11	41	.301	.425
First Pitch	.306	134	41	8	1	3	18	1	0	.324	.448	August	.264	178	47	10	2	6	30	15	52	.327	.444
Ahead on Count	.314	207	65	14	1	8	38	38	0	.423	.507	September/October	.241	187	45	8	1	7	29	14	58	.292	.406
Behind on Count	.192	370	71	11	1	10	35	0	140	.196	.308	Pre-All Star	.226	492	111	18	0	14	53	42	128	.290	.348
Two Strikes	.143	477	68	17	1	14	46	38	268	.208	.270	Post-All Star	.249	497	124	30	3	16	72	36	141	.304	.419

Batter vs. Pitcher (career)

Hits Best Against	Avg	AB	H	2B	3B	HR	RBI	BB	SO	OBP	SLG	Hits Worst Against	Avg	AB	H	2B	3B	HR	RBI	BB	SO	OBP	SLG
Chuck Finley	.364	11	4	0	0	0	1	0	5	.364	.364	Dave Stewart	.000	9	0	0	0	0	0	2	2	.182	.000
David West	.364	11	4	1	0	1	5	1	2	.417	.727	Greg Swindell	.077	13	1	0	0	0	1	1	7	.143	.077
												Mark Langston	.111	18	2	1	0	0	0	1	12	.238	.167
												Joe Grahe	.125	8	1	0	0	0	1	1	3	.364	.125
												Dave Stieb	.143	14	2	0	0	0	0	0	5	.143	.143

Eric Karros — Dodgers

Bats Right (flyball hitter)

	Avg	G	AB	R	H	2B	3B	HR	RBI	BB	SO	HBP	GDP	SB	CS	OBP	SLG	IBB	SH	SF	#Pit	#P/PA	GB	FB	G/F
1992 Season	.257	149	545	63	140	30	1	20	88	37	103	2	15	2	4	.304	.426	3	0	5	2157	3.66	174	177	0.98
Career (1991-1992)	.252	163	559	63	141	31	1	20	89	38	109	2	15	2	4	.300	.419	3	0	5	2214	3.67	174	183	0.95

1992 Season

	Avg	AB	H	2B	3B	HR	RBI	BB	SO	OBP	SLG		Avg	AB	H	2B	3B	HR	RBI	BB	SO	OBP	SLG
vs. Left	.277	213	59	10	0	8	32	16	26	.325	.437	Scoring Posn	.234	171	40	10	1	4	65	21	33	.313	.374
vs. Right	.244	332	81	20	1	12	56	21	77	.291	.419	Close & Late	.245	98	24	6	0	4	16	9	23	.308	.429
Groundball	.277	184	51	7	0	5	21	10	32	.316	.397	None on/out	.301	133	40	8	0	3	3	5	13	.326	.429
Flyball	.209	153	32	9	1	6	29	12	34	.265	.399	Batting #4	.246	333	82	21	0	11	59	28	64	.302	.408
Home	.259	251	65	14	1	6	35	23	45	.320	.394	Batting #5	.254	142	36	5	1	4	14	7	27	.287	.387
Away	.255	294	75	16	0	14	53	14	58	.289	.452	April	.286	35	10	2	0	2	6	2	5	.316	.514
Day	.264	174	46	9	0	6	25	7	35	.293	.420	May	.259	58	15	3	0	4	12	3	13	.290	.517
Night	.253	371	94	21	1	14	63	30	68	.309	.429	June	.274	106	29	5	0	3	9	6	20	.307	.406
Grass	.263	388	102	23	1	13	62	30	72	.316	.428	July	.244	119	29	5	1	6	20	4	18	.280	.454
Turf	.242	157	38	7	0	7	26	7	31	.273	.420	August	.226	106	24	8	0	3	21	11	22	.299	.387
First Pitch	.318	66	21	6	0	2	6	2	0	.338	.500	September/October	.273	121	33	7	0	2	20	11	25	.331	.380
Ahead on Count	.350	120	42	5	0	8	23	21	1	.451	.592	Post-All Star	.255	282	72	17	0	10	55	25	58	.317	.422
Behind on Count	.204	186	38	8	1	6	29	0	54	.205	.355												
Two Strikes	.181	243	44	7	0	7	25	14	102	.224	.296												

1992 By Position

Position	Avg	AB	H	2B	3B	HR	RBI	BB	SO	OBP	SLG	G	GS	Innings	PO	A	E	DP	Fld Pct	Rng Fctr	In Zone	Outs	Zone Rtg	MLB Zone
As 1b	.253	538	136	29	1	19	84	37	101	.301	.416	143	142	1201.1	1209	126	9	98	.993	---	298	246	.826	.843

Pat Kelly — Yankees

Bats Right (flyball hitter)

	Avg	G	AB	R	H	2B	3B	HR	RBI	BB	SO	HBP	GDP	SB	CS	OBP	SLG	IBB	SH	SF	#Pit	#P/PA	GB	FB	G/F
1992 Season	.226	106	318	38	72	22	2	7	27	25	72	10	6	8	5	.301	.374	1	6	3	1356	3.81	67	117	0.57
Career (1991-1992)	.234	202	616	73	144	34	6	10	50	40	124	15	11	20	6	.294	.357	1	8	5	2437	3.61	172	200	0.86

1992 Season

	Avg	AB	H	2B	3B	HR	RBI	BB	SO	OBP	SLG		Avg	AB	H	2B	3B	HR	RBI	BB	SO	OBP	SLG
vs. Left	.228	114	26	5	1	3	7	9	25	.288	.368	Scoring Posn	.194	62	12	2	0	1	17	5	21	.274	.274
vs. Right	.225	204	46	17	1	4	20	16	47	.307	.377	Close & Late	.180	50	9	5	0	0	5	4	13	.246	.280
Groundball	.169	83	14	5	0	0	5	4	15	.239	.229	None on/out	.222	72	16	3	0	1	1	8	15	.309	.306
Flyball	.307	88	27	12	2	2	11	7	21	.384	.557	Batting #1	.143	7	1	0	0	0	0	0	2	.143	.143
Home	.222	176	39	11	2	3	17	16	39	.298	.358	Batting #9	.229	310	71	22	2	7	27	25	70	.305	.381
Away	.232	142	33	11	0	4	10	9	33	.304	.394	Other	.000	1	0	0	0	0	0	0	0	.000	.000
Day	.230	100	23	7	1	3	13	10	24	.319	.410	April	.200	30	6	2	0	0	5	5	9	.333	.267
Night	.225	218	49	15	1	4	14	15	48	.292	.358	May	.273	66	18	6	1	2	8	5	20	.360	.485
Grass	.232	263	61	17	2	6	23	24	59	.318	.380	June	.100	30	3	0	0	1	1	1	9	.156	.200
Turf	.200	55	11	5	0	1	4	1	13	.211	.345	July	.194	72	14	3	1	1	5	4	15	.237	.306
First Pitch	.375	64	24	9	0	3	7	0	0	.403	.656	August	.294	68	20	5	0	3	11	6	9	.346	.500
Ahead on Count	.275	51	14	6	2	0	6	5	0	.339	.471	September/October	.212	52	11	6	0	0	2	4	10	.305	.327
Behind on Count	.212	99	21	6	1	2	6	0	31	.233	.354	Pre-All Star	.195	149	29	9	1	3	9	12	41	.281	.329
Two Strikes	.160	150	24	3	0	3	11	20	72	.277	.240	Post-All Star	.254	169	43	13	1	4	18	13	31	.317	.414

1992 By Position

Position	Avg	AB	H	2B	3B	HR	RBI	BB	SO	OBP	SLG	G	GS	Innings	PO	A	E	DP	Fld Pct	Rng Fctr	In Zone	Outs	Zone Rtg	MLB Zone
As 2b	.226	318	72	22	2	7	27	25	72	.301	.374	101	98	864.0	204	296	11	63	.978	5.21	328	286	.872	.892

Career (1991-1992)

	Avg	AB	H	2B	3B	HR	RBI	BB	SO	OBP	SLG		Avg	AB	H	2B	3B	HR	RBI	BB	SO	OBP	SLG
vs. Left	.244	213	52	10	1	4	14	13	38	.290	.357	Scoring Posn	.190	126	24	5	0	1	34	12	35	.277	.254
vs. Right	.228	403	92	24	5	6	36	27	86	.297	.357	Close & Late	.217	92	20	8	1	1	9	7	17	.282	.359
Groundball	.212	170	36	9	2	1	8		27	.269	.306	None on/out	.287	143	41	9	0	1	9	24		.333	.371
Flyball	.266	143	38	14	3	2	15	11	34	.342	.448	Batting #1	.143	7	1	0	0	0	0	0	2	.143	.143
Home	.236	326	77	17	4	6	29	26	65	.302	.368	Batting #9	.236	605	143	34	6	10	50	40	122	.298	.362
Away	.231	290	67	17	2	4	21	14	59	.286	.345	Other	.000	4	0	0	0	0	0	0	0	.000	.000
Day	.221	195	43	10	3	5	21	15	47	.294	.379	April	.200	30	6	2	0	0	0	5	9	.333	.267
Night	.240	421	101	24	3	5	29	25	77	.295	.347	May	.245	98	24	10	2	2	14	8	26	.333	.449
Grass	.236	516	122	29	4	9	44	37	104	.304	.360	June	.215	107	23	1	1	3	5	3	21	.257	.327
Turf	.220	100	22	5	2	1	6	3	20	.240	.340	July	.214	154	33	9	1	2	13	9	29	.261	.325
First Pitch	.293	116	34	10	0	4	9	0	0	.317	.483	August	.278	151	42	5	2	3	16	10	25	.323	.397
Ahead on Count	.318	110	35	9	3	1	12	8	0	.361	.482	September/October	.211	76	16	7	0	0	2	4	10	.286	.303
Behind on Count	.201	204	41	10	3	2	12	0	61	.218	.309	Pre-All Star	.224	281	63	16	3	5	20	19	62	.294	.356
Two Strikes	.164	268	44	6	3	4	22	32	124	.268	.254	Post-All Star	.242	335	81	18	3	5	30	21	62	.294	.358

Batter vs. Pitcher (career)

Hits Best Against	Avg	AB	H	2B	3B	HR	RBI	BB	SO	OBP	SLG	Hits Worst Against	Avg	AB	H	2B	3B	HR	RBI	BB	SO	OBP	SLG
												Bill Wegman	.083	12	1	0	0	0	0	0	0	.083	.083
												Todd Stottlemyre	.133	15	2	0	1	0	2	1	2	.188	.267
												Randy Johnson	.167	12	2	0	0	0	0	1	3	.333	.167

Batter vs. Pitcher (career)																				
Hits Best Against	Avg	AB	H	2B	3B	HR	RBI	BB	SO	OBP	SLG	Hits Worst Against	Avg	AB	H	2B	3B	HR	RBI	BB	SO	OBP	SLG
												Kevin Tapani	.182	11	2	0	0	0	0	0	1	.182	.182
												Jimmy Key	.231	13	3	2	0	0	0	0	2	.231	.385

Roberto Kelly — Yankees

Bats Right

	Avg	G	AB	R	H	2B	3B	HR	RBI	BB	SO	HBP	GDP	SB	CS	OBP	SLG	IBB	SH	SF	#Pit	#P/PA	GB	FB	G/F
1992 Season	.272	152	580	81	158	31	2	10	66	41	96	4	19	28	5	.322	.384	4	1	6	2210	3.50	227	160	1.42
Last Five Years	.280	615	2225	308	623	107	12	55	251	163	425	19	49	142	45	.332	.413	9	18	16	8878	3.66	793	608	1.30

1992 Season

	Avg	AB	H	2B	3B	HR	RBI	BB	SO	OBP	SLG		Avg	AB	H	2B	3B	HR	RBI	BB	SO	OBP	SLG
vs. Left	.277	184	51	9	0	4	21	20	28	.344	.391	Scoring Posn	.262	145	38	11	0	1	51	13	22	.319	.359
vs. Right	.270	396	107	22	2	6	45	21	68	.310	.381	Close & Late	.236	106	25	5	0	2	15	7	17	.287	.340
Groundball	.268	149	40	8	0	4	18	10	24	.313	.403	None on/out	.269	119	32	8	2	4	4	4	21	.293	.471
Flyball	.300	170	51	10	1	5	23	15	26	.360	.459	Batting #3	.274	354	97	20	2	8	49	23	60	.319	.410
Home	.257	296	76	16	1	6	37	21	52	.309	.378	Batting #5	.308	117	36	7	0	2	11	7	19	.352	.419
Away	.289	284	82	15	1	4	29	20	44	.336	.391	Other	.229	109	25	4	0	0	6	11	17	.298	.266
Day	.304	171	52	11	1	5	34	9	30	.335	.468	April	.353	85	30	6	1	1	14	5	14	.391	.482
Night	.259	409	106	20	1	5	32	32	66	.316	.350	May	.321	106	34	5	1	4	16	5	15	.357	.500
Grass	.269	498	134	27	2	9	56	37	79	.321	.386	June	.194	93	18	5	0	2	10	4	19	.232	.312
Turf	.293	82	24	4	0	1	10	4	17	.326	.378	July	.258	93	24	4	0	1	8	9	16	.317	.333
First Pitch	.303	99	30	5	1	1	13	4	0	.333	.404	August	.284	109	31	7	0	2	9	10	17	.347	.404
Ahead on Count	.333	120	40	12	0	3	21	20	0	.429	.508	September/October	.223	94	21	4	0	0	9	8	15	.282	.266
Behind on Count	.236	216	51	12	0	4	27	0	56	.243	.347	Pre-All Star	.281	324	91	18	2	7	44	17	56	.319	.414
Two Strikes	.217	249	54	10	0	5	21	17	96	.273	.317	Post-All Star	.262	256	67	13	0	3	22	24	40	.325	.348

1992 By Position

Position	Avg	AB	H	2B	3B	HR	RBI	BB	SO	OBP	SLG	G	GS	Innings	PO	A	E	DP	Fld Pct	Rng Fctr	In Zone	Outs	Zone Rtg	MLB Zone
As lf	.253	178	45	9	0	1	13	15	29	.311	.320	47	43	391.1	103	2	2	0	.981	2.41	118	101	.856	.809
As cf	.285	397	113	22	2	9	52	26	66	.331	.418	99	99	877.1	286	6	5	3	.983	3.00	314	274	.873	.824

Last Five Years

	Avg	AB	H	2B	3B	HR	RBI	BB	SO	OBP	SLG		Avg	AB	H	2B	3B	HR	RBI	BB	SO	OBP	SLG
vs. Left	.304	723	220	33	2	21	83	66	124	.363	.443	Scoring Posn	.269	506	136	28	2	9	185	46	93	.330	.385
vs. Right	.268	1502	403	74	10	34	168	97	301	.317	.399	Close & Late	.265	385	102	15	2	14	56	33	85	.326	.423
Groundball	.289	640	185	25	6	20	80	37	119	.330	.441	None on/out	.272	595	162	32	3	21	21	18	118	.314	.442
Flyball	.290	504	146	32	1	16	55	50	109	.358	.452	Batting #1	.275	585	161	29	3	19	55	35	120	.318	.432
Home	.293	1097	321	61	5	25	122	81	182	.344	.426	Batting #3	.291	506	147	30	2	13	76	42	89	.345	.435
Away	.268	1128	302	46	7	30	129	82	243	.321	.401	Other	.278	1134	315	48	7	23	120	86	216	.334	.393
Day	.297	656	195	37	3	16	88	50	122	.348	.436	April	.313	323	101	19	2	4	43	23	60	.359	.421
Night	.273	1569	428	70	9	39	163	113	303	.325	.403	May	.277	397	110	18	3	10	45	28	84	.326	.413
Grass	.279	1860	519	82	8	47	206	141	347	.333	.413	June	.254	386	98	13	3	11	35	18	84	.293	.389
Turf	.285	365	104	15	4	8	45	22	78	.327	.414	July	.300	317	95	17	1	8	44	24	58	.350	.435
First Pitch	.335	337	113	18	2	7	54	8	0	.351	.463	August	.292	394	115	22	1	11	35	34	76	.354	.437
Ahead on Count	.333	426	142	32	3	16	64	87	0	.449	.535	September/October	.255	408	104	18	2	11	49	36	63	.319	.390
Behind on Count	.244	831	203	37	6	18	78	0	257	.254	.366	Pre-All Star	.281	1231	346	58	8	27	139	77	253	.325	.407
Two Strikes	.222	1064	236	41	4	22	93	67	424	.272	.330	Post-All Star	.279	994	277	49	4	28	112	86	172	.341	.421

Batter vs. Pitcher (career)

Hits Best Against	Avg	AB	H	2B	3B	HR	RBI	BB	SO	OBP	SLG	Hits Worst Against	Avg	AB	H	2B	3B	HR	RBI	BB	SO	OBP	SLG
Curt Young	.600	10	6	1	0	1	1	1	2	.636	1.000	Tom Gordon	.000	13	0	0	0	0	1	0	6	.000	.000
Shawn Hillegas	.545	11	6	3	0	2	0	2	.545	.818		Jack McDowell	.000	9	0	0	0	0	0	2	5	.182	.000
Bill Gullickson	.455	11	5	1	0	2	7	1	3	.462	1.091	Chris Bosio	.077	13	1	0	0	0	0	0	4	.077	.077
Steve Olin	.364	11	4	0	0	2	6	0	3	.364	.909	John Dopson	.100	10	1	0	0	0	0	1	0	.182	.100
Greg Harris	.333	15	5	1	0	2	3	0	2	.333	.933	David Wells	.105	19	2	1	0	0	0	2	8	.190	.158

Jeff Kent — Mets

Bats Right (flyball hitter)

	Avg	G	AB	R	H	2B	3B	HR	RBI	BB	SO	HBP	GDP	SB	CS	OBP	SLG	IBB	SH	SF	#Pit	#P/PA	GB	FB	G/F
1992 Season	.239	102	305	52	73	21	2	11	50	27	76	7	5	2	3	.312	.430	0	0	4	1310	3.82	83	94	0.88

1992 Season

	Avg	AB	H	2B	3B	HR	RBI	BB	SO	OBP	SLG		Avg	AB	H	2B	3B	HR	RBI	BB	SO	OBP	SLG
vs. Left	.217	92	20	5	0	3	14	10	20	.291	.370	Scoring Posn	.256	90	23	7	2	5	42	7	21	.324	.544
vs. Right	.249	213	53	16	2	8	36	17	56	.321	.455	Close & Late	.313	48	15	5	0	4	12	1	14	.353	.667
Groundball	.226	93	21	5	1	3	13	4	23	.273	.430	None on/out	.319	72	23	7	0	2	7	19	.380	.500
Flyball	.225	80	18	5	1	1	12	5	24	.273	.350	Batting #7	.212	104	22	4	0	5	20	10	24	.294	.394
Home	.240	167	40	14	1	4	20	18	39	.317	.407	Batting #8	.220	59	13	3	0	1	8	6	18	.314	.322
Away	.239	138	33	7	1	7	30	9	37	.305	.457	Other	.268	142	38	14	2	5	22	11	34	.325	.500
Day	.170	88	15	7	0	2	6	6	23	.224	.318	April	.263	19	5	3	0	1	3	4	5	.400	.579
Night	.267	217	58	14	2	9	44	21	53	.347	.475	May	.300	10	3	2	0	0	1	2	2	.417	.500
Grass	.264	144	38	7	2	7	29	8	41	.318	.486	June	.262	61	16	4	1	2	9	8	14	.366	.459
Turf	.217	161	35	14	0	4	21	19	35	.306	.379	July	.185	65	12	3	0	2	14	5	16	.247	.323

236

1992 Season

	Avg	AB	H	2B	3B	HR	RBI	BB	SO	OBP	SLG		Avg	AB	H	2B	3B	HR	RBI	BB	SO	OBP	SLG
First Pitch	.333	39	13	3	1	1	6	0	0	.350	.538	August	.230	61	14	2	1	4	12	1	18	.262	.492
Ahead on Count	.306	49	15	6	1	2	13	13	0	.455	.592	September/October	.258	89	23	7	0	2	11	7	21	.320	.404
Behind on Count	.186	140	26	4	0	5	18	0	50	.200	.321	Pre-All Star	.244	127	31	10	1	3	15	15	30	.333	.409
Two Strikes	.185	168	31	12	0	7	23	14	76	.254	.381	Post-All Star	.236	178	42	11	1	8	35	12	46	.296	.444

1992 By Position

Position	Avg	AB	H	2B	3B	HR	RBI	BB	SO	OBP	SLG	G	GS	Innings	PO	A	E	DP	Fld Pct	Rng Fctr	In Zone	Outs	Zone Rtg	MLB Zone
As 2b	.229	144	33	10	2	4	20	10	34	.287	.410	51	39	361.0	85	121	4	19	.981	5.14	146	126	.863	.892
As 3b	.243	152	37	10	0	7	29	17	38	.333	.447	50	43	378.1	34	80	10	4	.919	2.71	103	81	.786	.841

Jimmy Key — Blue Jays   Pitches Left

	ERA	W	L	Sv	G	GS	IP	BB	SO	Avg	H	2B	3B	HR	RBI	OBP	SLG	CG	ShO	Sup	QS	#P/S	SB	CS	GB	FB	G/F
1992 Season	3.53	13	13	0	33	33	216.2	59	117	.248	205	45	1	24	81	.298	.391	4	2	5.36	21	103	14	9	308	259	1.19
Last Five Years	3.59	67	51	0	147	147	928.0	182	513	.260	934	192	14	87	353	.296	.394	13	7	4.98	86	96	39	20	1293	1109	1.17

1992 Season

	ERA	W	L	Sv	G	GS	IP	H	HR	BB	SO		Avg	AB	H	2B	3B	HR	RBI	BB	SO	OBP	SLG
Home	3.35	7	5	0	17	17	104.2	99	11	34	63	vs. Left	.176	131	23	4	0	2	8	6	19	.216	.252
Away	3.70	6	8	0	16	16	112.0	106	13	25	54	vs. Right	.261	697	182	41	1	22	73	53	98	.314	.418
Day	3.83	1	3	0	9	9	56.1	55	6	16	31	Inning 1-6	.245	706	173	39	1	19	75	51	104	.296	.384
Night	3.42	12	10	0	24	24	160.1	150	18	43	86	Inning 7+	.262	122	32	6	0	5	6	8	13	.313	.434
Grass	4.03	4	5	0	11	11	76.0	74	8	20	35	None on	.225	528	119	27	1	15	15	34	70	.276	.366
Turf	3.26	9	8	0	22	22	140.2	131	16	39	82	Runners on	.287	300	86	18	0	9	66	25	47	.336	.437
April	3.58	1	0	0	4	4	27.2	28	3	7	10	Scoring Posn	.265	155	41	10	0	6	56	22	27	.342	.445
May	2.88	2	3	0	6	6	40.2	36	6	10	14	Close & Late	.316	57	18	5	0	4	5	5	5	.371	.614
June	3.25	1	3	0	5	5	36.0	37	2	8	20	None on/out	.197	223	44	9	0	5	5	8	26	.225	.305
July	3.75	3	2	0	5	5	36.0	37	9	9	17	vs. 1st Batr (relief)	.000	0	0	0	0	0	0	0	0	.000	.000
August	6.25	1	4	0	6	6	31.2	34	4	12	21	First Inning Pitched	.276	127	35	7	0	3	14	10	26	.324	.402
September/October	2.22	5	1	0	7	7	44.2	33	3	13	35	First 75 Pitches	.250	580	145	32	1	13	58	37	88	.295	.376
Starter	3.53	13	13	0	33	33	216.2	205	24	59	117	Pitch 76-90	.225	111	25	5	0	6	16	9	14	.283	.432
Reliever	0.00	0	0	0	0	0	0.0	0	0	0	0	Pitch 91-105	.242	99	24	5	0	5	6	8	9	.299	.444
0-3 Days Rest	0.00	0	0	0	0	0	0.0	0	0	0	0	Pitch 106+	.289	38	11	3	0	0	1	5	6	.386	.368
4 Days Rest	3.91	7	8	0	19	19	119.2	120	16	32	68	First Pitch	.262	107	28	3	0	3	12	0	0	.270	.374
5+ Days Rest	3.06	6	5	0	14	14	97.0	85	8	27	49	Ahead on Count	.206	315	65	15	0	6	29	0	89	.204	.311
Pre-All Star	2.84	6	6	0	17	17	120.1	111	11	28	53	Behind on Count	.312	231	72	17	0	7	20	27	0	.382	.476
Post-All Star	4.39	7	7	0	16	16	96.1	94	13	31	64	Two Strikes	.228	347	79	19	1	11	36	32	117	.292	.383

Last Five Years

	ERA	W	L	Sv	G	GS	IP	H	HR	BB	SO		Avg	AB	H	2B	3B	HR	RBI	BB	SO	OBP	SLG
Home	3.82	32	27	0	78	78	478.2	502	44	100	269	vs. Left	.209	556	116	19	1	7	46	22	94	.243	.284
Away	3.34	35	24	0	69	69	449.1	432	43	82	244	vs. Right	.269	3036	818	173	13	80	307	160	419	.306	.414
Day	4.01	18	20	0	49	49	292.0	321	30	54	164	Inning 1-6	.260	3132	813	174	14	69	317	159	464	.296	.390
Night	3.40	49	31	0	98	98	636.0	613	57	128	349	Inning 7+	.263	460	121	18	0	18	36	23	49	.300	.420
Grass	3.54	27	20	0	55	55	358.1	350	35	72	192	None on	.247	2232	552	114	8	52	52	100	333	.284	.375
Turf	3.62	40	31	0	92	92	569.2	584	52	110	321	Runners on	.281	1360	382	78	6	35	301	82	180	.317	.424
April	3.30	11	4	0	21	21	133.2	128	11	21	76	Scoring Posn	.262	698	183	39	5	19	255	64	98	.314	.414
May	3.52	11	7	0	22	22	143.1	140	15	29	71	Close & Late	.279	208	58	9	0	6	16	11	23	.312	.409
June	3.54	6	9	0	20	20	129.2	143	10	22	67	None on/out	.240	960	230	46	4	25	25	32	132	.267	.374
July	3.70	9	13	0	26	26	172.2	181	18	31	77	vs. 1st Batr (relief)	.000	0	0	0	0	0	0	0	0	.000	.000
August	3.90	12	11	0	27	27	157.0	158	16	40	88	First Inning Pitched	.273	567	155	34	3	12	61	33	92	.312	.407
September/October	3.52	18	7	0	31	31	191.2	184	17	39	134	First 75 Pitches	.263	2699	710	151	13	57	259	123	383	.296	.392
Starter	3.59	67	51	0	147	147	928.0	934	87	162	513	Pitch 76-90	.222	454	101	20	1	13	47	31	75	.271	.357
Reliever	0.00	0	0	0	0	0	0.0	0	0	0	0	Pitch 91-105	.274	325	89	16	0	13	37	20	32	.318	.443
0-3 Days Rest	1.29	1	0	0	1	1	7.0	6	0	1	2	Pitch 106+	.298	114	34	5	0	4	10	8	13	.350	.447
4 Days Rest	3.65	38	33	0	91	91	575.0	585	54	107	308	First Pitch	.294	494	145	26	1	13	53	7	0	.303	.429
5+ Days Rest	3.54	28	18	0	55	55	346.0	343	33	74	203	Ahead on Count	.204	1499	306	65	4	24	129	0	420	.206	.301
Pre-All Star	3.25	33	23	0	71	71	467.1	464	40	80	239	Behind on Count	.319	882	281	60	7	24	89	97	0	.386	.484
Post-All Star	3.93	34	28	0	76	76	460.2	470	47	102	274	Two Strikes	.202	1572	318	60	4	33	131	78	513	.241	.309

Pitcher vs. Batter (career)

Pitches Best Vs.	Avg	AB	H	2B	3B	HR	RBI	BB	SO	OBP	SLG	Pitches Worst Vs.	Avg	AB	H	2B	3B	HR	RBI	BB	SO	OBP	SLG
Dante Bichette	.063	16	1	0	0	0	1	0	2	.059	.063	Carlos Baerga	.529	17	9	3	0	0	1	0	0	.529	.706
Darnell Coles	.077	26	2	0	0	0	1	2	2	.143	.077	Tony Pena	.476	21	10	2	0	2	6	0	0	.476	.857
Shawn Abner	.077	13	1	0	0	0	0	0	1	.143	.077	Edgar Martinez	.400	30	12	5	0	2	5	2	1	.438	.767
Ellis Burks	.080	25	2	1	0	0	1	1	3	.115	.120	Pat Tabler	.385	39	15	5	0	3	10	1	1	.400	.744
Eddie Murray	.083	24	2	0	0	0	1	1	4	.120	.063	Cecil Fielder	.357	28	10	1	0	4	9	2	6	.400	.621

John Kiely — Tigers

	ERA	W	L	Sv	G	GS	IP	BB	SO	Avg	H	2B	3B	HR	RBI	OBP	SLG	GF	IR	IRS	Hld	SvOp	SB	CS	GB	FB	G/F
1992 Season	2.13	4	2	0	39	0	55.0	28	18	.224	44	10	0	2	23	.317	.306	20	36	14	7	1	2	1	86	59	1.46
Career (1991-1992)	3.50	4	3	0	46	0	61.2	37	19	.253	57	14	0	2	32	.356	.342	23	44	18	7	1	2	1	95	70	1.36

1992 Season

	ERA	W	L	Sv	G	GS	IP	H	HR	BB	SO		Avg	AB	H	2B	3B	HR	RBI	BB	SO	OBP	SLG
Home	1.00	3	0	0	17	0	27.0	22	1	12	8	vs. Left	.179	84	15	2	0	0	7	13	7	.286	.202
Away	3.21	1	2	0	22	0	28.0	22	1	16	10	vs. Right	.259	112	29	8	0	2	16	15	11	.341	.384
Starter	0.00	0	0	0	0	0	0.0	0	0	0	0	Scoring Posn	.188	69	13	2	0	0	21	9	5	.272	.217
Reliever	2.13	4	2	0	39	0	55.0	44	2	28	18	Close & Late	.250	56	14	4	0	2	9	10	6	.358	.429
0 Days rest	1.10	1	0	0	10	0	16.1	14	0	4	8	None on/out	.268	41	11	2	0	1	1	6	4	.362	.390
1 or 2 Days rest	3.32	3	1	0	15	0	21.2	22	1	13	5	First Pitch	.192	26	5	1	0	0	3	0	0	.267	.231
3+ Days rest	1.59	0	1	0	14	0	17.0	8	1	11	5	Behind on Count	.184	49	9	3	0	1	5	13	0	.355	.306
Pre-All Star	2.25	2	0	0	9	0	16.0	14	0	5	4	Ahead on Count	.250	84	21	4	0	0	12	0	13	.244	.298
Post-All Star	2.08	2	2	0	30	0	39.0	30	2	23	14	Two Strikes	.232	82	19	4	0	0	11	12	18	.323	.280

Darryl Kile — Astros

	ERA	W	L	Sv	G	GS	IP	BB	SO	Avg	H	2B	3B	HR	RBI	OBP	SLG	CG	ShO	Sup	QS	#P/S	SB	CS	GB	FB	G/F
1992 Season	3.95	5	10	0	22	22	125.1	63	90	.261	124	26	6	8	49	.348	.391	1	0	3.23	11	90	6	3	151	149	1.01
Career (1991-1992)	3.81	12	21	0	59	44	279.0	147	190	.253	268	54	11	24	119	.346	.392	2	0	3.90	26	90	18	6	379	315	1.20

1992 Season

	ERA	W	L	Sv	G	GS	IP	H	HR	BB	SO		Avg	AB	H	2B	3B	HR	RBI	BB	SO	OBP	SLG
Home	3.53	3	5	0	11	11	63.2	61	1	36	51	vs. Left	.255	271	69	14	4	5	32	46	45	.361	.391
Away	4.38	2	5	0	11	11	61.2	63	7	27	39	vs. Right	.268	205	55	12	2	3	17	17	45	.329	.390
Starter	3.95	5	10	0	22	22	125.1	124	8	63	90	Scoring Posn	.204	137	28	5	1	2	37	23	28	.315	.299
Reliever	0.00	0	0	0	0	0	0.0	0	0	0	0	Close & Late	.273	22	6	1	1	0	1	2	4	.333	.409
0-3 Days Rest	0.00	0	0	0	0	0	0.0	0	0	0	0	None on/out	.299	117	35	11	3	3	3	18	29	.397	.521
4 Days Rest	4.55	2	7	0	11	11	57.1	61	4	37	44	First Pitch	.424	85	36	8	0	2	12	3	0	.433	.588
5+ Days Rest	3.44	3	3	0	11	11	68.0	63	4	26	46	Behind on Count	.256	125	32	8	4	2	12	36	0	.423	.432
Pre-All Star	4.13	2	6	0	12	12	65.1	64	5	41	46	Ahead on Count	.191	173	33	6	1	2	12	0	76	.194	.272
Post-All Star	3.75	3	4	0	10	10	60.0	60	3	22	44	Two Strikes	.182	187	34	5	0	2	13	24	90	.278	.241

Career (1991-1992)

	ERA	W	L	Sv	G	GS	IP	H	HR	BB	SO		Avg	AB	H	2B	3B	HR	RBI	BB	SO	OBP	SLG
Home	3.44	7	10	0	29	23	141.1	129	3	81	100	vs. Left	.259	614	159	34	7	12	68	102	109	.363	.396
Away	4.18	5	11	0	30	21	137.2	139	21	66	90	vs. Right	.244	447	109	20	4	12	51	45	81	.321	.387
Day	5.09	1	7	0	14	11	58.1	61	8	34	39	Inning 1-6	.242	923	223	45	6	20	96	124	170	.334	.368
Night	3.47	11	14	0	45	33	220.2	207	16	113	151	Inning 7+	.326	138	45	9	5	4	23	23	20	.422	.551
Grass	3.83	2	5	0	17	12	82.1	73	12	37	56	None on	.251	553	139	32	5	14	14	83	111	.352	.403
Turf	3.80	10	16	0	42	32	196.2	195	12	110	134	Runners on	.254	508	129	22	6	10	105	64	79	.339	.380
April	3.78	2	3	0	12	6	47.2	40	4	22	38	Scoring Posn	.213	319	68	12	2	7	90	52	60	.318	.329
May	5.09	0	3	0	11	5	35.1	45	4	28	15	Close & Late	.245	53	13	3	2	1	7	9	9	.349	.434
June	2.91	2	2	0	9	7	43.1	32	3	29	23	None on/out	.259	255	66	16	5	7	7	40	56	.361	.443
July	3.86	2	4	0	6	5	25.2	30	4	11	22	vs. 1st Batr (relief)	.200	10	2	0	1	0	0	5	2	.467	.400
August	4.58	2	5	0	10	10	55.0	61	5	26	37	First Inning Pitched	.239	218	52	11	2	4	28	42	41	.364	.384
September/October	3.13	4	4	0	11	11	72.0	60	4	31	55	First 75 Pitches	.254	856	217	41	7	19	96	116	154	.345	.384
Starter	3.50	12	19	0	44	44	254.1	236	19	128	182	Pitch 76-90	.270	115	31	10	3	5	17	16	25	.361	.539
Reliever	6.93	0	2	0	15	0	24.2	32	5	19	8	Pitch 91-105	.263	76	20	3	1	0	3	7	8	.329	.329
0-3 Days Rest	1.59	0	1	0	3	3	17.0	10	0	7	9	Pitch 106+	.000	14	0	0	0	0	3	8	3	.333	.000
4 Days Rest	3.65	6	10	0	21	21	120.2	112	12	71	87	First Pitch	.310	187	58	12	1	4	18	6	0	.342	.449
5+ Days Rest	3.63	6	8	0	20	20	116.2	114	7	50	86	Ahead on Count	.179	413	74	13	4	7	35	0	169	.182	.281
Pre-All Star	3.85	5	8	0	33	19	133.1	126	13	81	83	Behind on Count	.279	265	74	19	5	6	31	93	0	.463	.457
Post-All Star	3.77	7	13	0	26	25	145.2	142	11	66	107	Two Strikes	.179	431	77	12	2	6	33	48	190	.263	.258

Pitcher vs. Batter (career)

Pitches Best Vs.	Avg	AB	H	2B	3B	HR	RBI	BB	SO	OBP	SLG	Pitches Worst Vs.	Avg	AB	H	2B	3B	HR	RBI	BB	SO	OBP	SLG
Dave Hansen	.091	11	1	1	0	0	0	0	0	.091	.182	Willie McGee	.571	14	8	2	0	0	2	2	2	.625	.714
Howard Johnson	.100	10	1	1	0	0	1	0	4	.167	.200	Ozzie Smith	.500	12	6	0	1	0	2	1	0	.538	.667
Robby Thompson	.100	10	1	0	0	0	1	2	0	.308	.100	Eddie Murray	.500	12	6	2	0	1	4	4	3	.625	.917
Felix Jose	.111	9	1	0	0	0	0	2	2	.385	.111	Ray Lankford	.455	11	5	2	0	1	3	2	1	.538	.909
Tim Wallach	.154	13	2	1	0	0	0	0	1	.154	.231	Ryne Sandberg	.375	8	3	2	0	1	1	3	1	.500	1.000

Eric King — Tigers

	ERA	W	L	Sv	G	GS	IP	BB	SO	Avg	H	2B	3B	HR	RBI	OBP	SLG	CG	ShO	Sup	QS	#P/S	SB	CS	GB	FB	G/F
1992 Season	5.22	4	6	1	17	14	79.1	28	45	.285	90	12	2	12	45	.343	.449	0	0	5.45	6	79	8	3	124	88	1.41
Last Five Years	3.90	35	32	4	115	93	609.0	210	291	.256	595	88	15	47	249	.320	.367	5	4	4.80	52	91	41	20	941	663	1.42

1992 Season

	ERA	W	L	Sv	G	GS	IP	H	HR	BB	SO		Avg	AB	H	2B	3B	HR	RBI	BB	SO	OBP	SLG
Home	6.07	1	4	1	8	6	29.2	40	4	12	13	vs. Left	.291	141	41	6	0	7	23	15	16	.357	.482
Away	4.71	3	2	0	9	8	49.2	50	8	16	32	vs. Right	.280	175	49	6	2	5	22	13	29	.332	.423
Starter	6.01	4	6	0	14	14	67.1	85	12	26	33	Scoring Posn	.300	90	27	2	0	3	32	6	16	.337	.422

1992 Season

	ERA	W	L	Sv	G	GS	IP	H	HR	BB	SO		Avg	AB	H	2B	3B	HR	RBI	BB	SO	OBP	SLG
Reliever	0.75	0	0	1	3	0	12.0	5	0	2	12	Close & Late	.500	2	1	0	0	1	2	1	0	.667	2.000
0-3 Days Rest	9.00	0	1	0	1	1	6.0	9	2	5	2	None on/out	.228	79	18	3	1	5	5	7	10	.299	.481
4 Days Rest	7.18	1	2	0	6	6	26.1	40	7	5	15	First Pitch	.255	51	13	1	0	3	9	0	0	.255	.451
5+ Days Rest	4.63	3	3	0	7	7	35.0	36	3	16	16	Behind on Count	.390	77	30	4	0	4	13	10	0	.460	.597
Pre-All Star	7.51	2	4	0	9	9	38.1	60	9	11	18	Ahead on Count	.211	133	28	5	2	3	14	0	39	.215	.346
Post-All Star	3.07	2	2	1	8	5	41.0	30	3	17	27	Two Strikes	.191	131	25	4	2	2	15	18	45	.289	.298

Last Five Years

	ERA	W	L	Sv	G	GS	IP	H	HR	BB	SO		Avg	AB	H	2B	3B	HR	RBI	BB	SO	OBP	SLG
Home	4.19	16	22	4	60	48	307.0	321	21	121	142	vs. Left	.248	1151	286	35	12	31	133	120	139	.320	.381
Away	3.61	19	10	0	55	45	302.0	274	26	89	149	vs. Right	.263	1177	309	53	3	16	116	90	152	.321	.353
Day	4.65	10	9	1	37	29	182.0	198	12	61	74	Inning 1-6	.254	1992	506	72	12	39	212	167	245	.314	.361
Night	3.58	25	23	3	78	64	427.0	397	35	149	217	Inning 7+	.265	336	89	16	3	8	37	43	46	.353	.402
Grass	4.01	29	28	4	97	80	513.2	517	37	194	243	None on	.248	1347	334	45	10	30	30	119	172	.314	.363
Turf	3.30	6	4	0	18	13	95.1	78	10	16	48	Runners on	.266	981	261	43	5	17	219	91	119	.328	.372
April	4.27	5	8	0	17	17	99.0	108	7	23	55	Scoring Posn	.249	538	134	19	3	9	190	54	75	.314	.346
May	4.48	9	6	1	24	22	132.2	123	18	56	63	Close & Late	.269	119	32	7	3	2	14	19	11	.376	.429
June	3.87	5	4	0	15	9	74.1	77	4	34	35	None on/out	.244	598	146	19	7	17	17	62	79	.321	.385
July	4.48	0	5	1	15	11	70.1	78	5	18	36	vs. 1st Batr (relief)	.294	17	5	0	0	1	4	3	5	.400	.471
August	3.66	7	3	0	17	14	98.1	91	8	29	50	First Inning Pitched	.250	432	108	21	2	6	51	39	62	.310	.350
September/October	2.95	9	6	2	27	20	134.1	118	5	50	52	First 75 Pitches	.256	1865	478	68	11	33	194	152	248	.315	.358
Starter	3.99	34	32	0	93	93	559.0	552	46	188	253	Pitch 76-90	.261	249	65	9	2	8	26	24	22	.332	.410
Reliever	2.88	1	0	4	22	0	50.0	43	1	22	38	Pitch 91-105	.239	138	33	5	2	3	17	18	14	.331	.370
0-3 Days Rest	6.17	0	2	0	2	2	11.2	14	3	9	4	Pitch 106+	.250	76	19	6	0	3	12	16	7	.363	.447
4 Days Rest	4.01	13	16	0	38	38	233.2	224	20	87	100	First Pitch	.320	378	121	17	1	11	58	4	0	.322	.458
5+ Days Rest	3.90	21	14	0	53	53	313.2	314	23	92	149	Ahead on Count	.209	964	201	29	6	6	84	0	256	.218	.270
Pre-All Star	4.45	19	20	2	61	51	323.2	330	34	122	159	Behind on Count	.295	579	171	29	8	19	68	109	0	.405	.472
Post-All Star	3.28	16	12	2	54	42	285.1	265	13	88	132	Two Strikes	.175	939	164	26	5	6	64	97	290	.260	.232

Pitcher vs. Batter (career)

Pitches Best Vs.	Avg	AB	H	2B	3B	HR	RBI	BB	SO	OBP	SLG	Pitches Worst Vs.	Avg	AB	H	2B	3B	HR	RBI	BB	SO	OBP	SLG
Eddie Murray	.000	17	0	0	0	0	1	0	0	.000	.000	Dan Pasqua	.500	12	6	0	0	2	4	0	1	.500	1.000
Geno Petralli	.000	12	0	0	0	0	1	1	3	.077	.000	Matt Nokes	.474	19	9	1	0	3	9	1	0	.500	1.000
Brady Anderson	.063	16	1	0	1	0	2	1	4	.111	.188	Lou Whitaker	.357	14	5	0	1	2	6	0	0	.357	.929
Dave Henderson	.100	20	2	0	0	0	2	0	6	.100	.100	Jesse Barfield	.348	23	8	3	0	3	8	2	2	.400	.870
Chuck Knoblauch	.100	10	1	0	0	0	0	1	2	.182	.100	Sam Horn	.333	9	3	0	0	2	4	2	1	.455	1.000

Jeff King — Pirates   Bats Right (flyball hitter)

	Avg	G	AB	R	H	2B	3B	HR	RBI	BB	SO	HBP	GDP	SB	CS	OBP	SLG	IBB	SH	SF	#Pit	#P/PA	GB	FB	G/F
1992 Season	.231	130	480	56	111	21	2	14	65	27	56	2	8	4	6	.272	.371	3	8	5	1876	3.65	161	199	0.81
Career (1989-1992)	.230	365	1175	149	270	52	7	37	155	82	155	6	26	14	12	.280	.380	8	12	17	4611	3.60	407	445	0.91

1992 Season

	Avg	AB	H	2B	3B	HR	RBI	BB	SO	OBP	SLG		Avg	AB	H	2B	3B	HR	RBI	BB	SO	OBP	SLG
vs. Left	.236	216	51	12	2	6	32	13	18	.277	.394	Scoring Posn	.228	149	34	5	1	1	45	10	24	.277	.295
vs. Right	.227	264	60	9	0	8	33	14	38	.269	.352	Close & Late	.215	93	20	2	0	3	14	6	14	.263	.333
Groundball	.172	134	23	2	1	2	11	8	16	.224	.246	None on/out	.240	121	29	5	0	6	6	1	11	.246	.430
Flyball	.287	115	33	7	1	5	21	6	15	.320	.496	Batting #5	.219	169	37	5	0	3	28	11	27	.268	.302
Home	.239	247	59	12	0	6	37	14	26	.280	.360	Batting #6	.283	145	41	11	0	5	25	7	14	.312	.462
Away	.223	233	52	9	2	8	28	13	30	.264	.382	Other	.199	166	33	5	2	6	12	9	15	.243	.361
Day	.255	141	36	7	1	4	23	9	14	.294	.404	April	.180	50	9	0	2	0	2	5	4	.255	.260
Night	.221	339	75	14	1	10	42	18	42	.263	.357	May	.235	98	23	4	0	4	11	4	12	.262	.398
Grass	.252	135	34	8	1	4	19	7	18	.285	.415	June	.123	65	8	1	0	2	7	2	9	.162	.231
Turf	.223	345	77	13	1	10	46	20	38	.268	.354	July	.264	53	14	3	0	2	6	4	7	.310	.434
First Pitch	.154	52	8	2	0	2	10	2	0	.185	.308	August	.289	97	28	8	0	3	17	4	11	.314	.464
Ahead on Count	.268	97	26	5	0	5	19	15	0	.357	.474	September/October	.248	117	29	5	0	3	22	8	13	.297	.368
Behind on Count	.237	194	46	9	1	4	24	0	33	.242	.356	Pre-All Star	.187	219	41	5	2	6	20	11	26	.228	.311
Two Strikes	.193	207	40	6	2	3	15	10	56	.236	.285	Post-All Star	.268	261	70	16	0	8	45	16	30	.309	.421

1992 By Position

Position	Avg	AB	H	2B	3B	HR	RBI	BB	SO	OBP	SLG	G	GS	Innings	PO	A	E	DP	Fld Pct	Rng Fctr	In Zone	Outs	Zone Rtg	MLB Zone
As 1b	.185	124	23	3	1	2	7	5	17	.223	.274	32	30	266.1	270	21	2	27	.993	---	42	35	.833	.843
As 2b	.258	89	23	4	0	5	17	9	7	.320	.472	32	23	201.2	49	68	0	16	1.000	5.22	78	69	.885	.892
As 3b	.253	241	61	14	0	7	39	12	29	.288	.398	73	64	565.1	44	140	9	14	.953	2.93	180	157	.872	.841

Career (1989-1992)

	Avg	AB	H	2B	3B	HR	RBI	BB	SO	OBP	SLG		Avg	AB	H	2B	3B	HR	RBI	BB	SO	OBP	SLG
vs. Left	.244	590	144	33	6	16	80	51	61	.302	.402	Scoring Posn	.227	339	77	10	5	5	108	29	58	.283	.330
vs. Right	.215	585	126	19	1	21	75	31	94	.257	.359	Close & Late	.199	211	42	6	1	6	26	16	27	.259	.322
Groundball	.206	408	85	14	3	9	46	15	49	.241	.324	None on/out	.253	289	73	15	0	12	12	8	26	.273	.429
Flyball	.253	265	67	14	2	13	39	22	34	.308	.468	Batting #5	.216	232	50	7	0	6	39	14	32	.259	.323
Home	.237	608	144	28	3	21	87	41	74	.285	.396	Batting #6	.254	468	119	29	3	14	65	37	64	.305	.419

Career (1989-1992)

	Avg	AB	H	2B	3B	HR	RBI	BB	SO	OBP	SLG		Avg	AB	H	2B	3B	HR	RBI	BB	SO	OBP	SLG
Away	.222	567	126	24	4	16	68	41	81	.274	.363	Other	.213	475	101	16	4	17	51	31	59	.264	.371
Day	.246	345	85	14	1	11	49	26	47	.297	.388	April	.208	159	33	1	3	2	16	18	21	.291	.289
Night	.223	830	185	38	6	26	106	56	108	.272	.377	May	.228	162	37	8	0	6	17	8	19	.262	.389
Grass	.238	282	67	15	1	7	34	22	45	.289	.372	June	.186	167	31	5	2	4	19	12	22	.249	.311
Turf	.227	893	203	37	6	30	121	60	110	.277	.383	July	.261	142	37	9	0	5	19	13	16	.323	.430
First Pitch	.216	153	33	9	1	4	19	5	0	.250	.366	August	.250	256	64	15	1	11	40	12	37	.279	.445
Ahead on Count	.268	274	79	13	3	17	53	42	0	.377	.544	September/October	.235	289	68	14	1	9	44	19	40	.280	.384
Behind on Count	.222	432	96	19	1	10	52	0	82	.223	.340	Pre-All Star	.210	514	108	15	5	13	56	38	66	.267	.335
Two Strikes	.174	478	83	13	3	9	38	34	155	.233	.270	Post-All Star	.245	661	162	37	2	24	99	44	89	.290	.416

Batter vs. Pitcher (career)

Hits Best Against	Avg	AB	H	2B	3B	HR	RBI	BB	SO	OBP	SLG	Hits Worst Against	Avg	AB	H	2B	3B	HR	RBI	BB	SO	OBP	SLG
Danny Jackson	.500	12	6	0	1	0	1	0	0	.500	.667	Greg Maddux	.125	16	2	1	0	0	0	2	2	.222	.188
Ron Darling	.455	11	5	1	0	1	3	1	2	.500	.818	Dennis Martinez	.133	15	2	0	0	0	0	0	2	.133	.133
Steve Avery	.455	11	5	3	0	1	6	1	3	.462	1.000	Chris Nabholz	.133	15	2	0	0	0	1	1	2	.188	.133
Pete Schourek	.333	18	6	2	0	1	4	2	1	.400	.611	Jim Deshaies	.182	22	4	1	0	0	3	0	1	.167	.227
Steve Wilson	.333	15	5	1	0	2	4	2	2	.412	.800	Terry Mulholland	.214	28	6	2	0	0	1	1	1	.241	.286

Mike Kingery — Athletics
Bats Left

	Avg	G	AB	R	H	2B	3B	HR	RBI	BB	SO	HBP	GDP	SB	CS	OBP	SLG	IBB	SH	SF	#Pit	#P/PA	GB	FB	G/F
1992 Season	.107	12	28	3	3	0	0	0	1	1	3	0	1	0	0	.138	.107	0	0	0	100	3.45	10	9	1.11
Last Five Years	.232	296	544	75	126	18	3	3	48	54	80	2	7	11	3	.302	.292	2	6	3	2142	3.55	219	149	1.47

1992 Season

	Avg	AB	H	2B	3B	HR	RBI	BB	SO	OBP	SLG		Avg	AB	H	2B	3B	HR	RBI	BB	SO	OBP	SLG
vs. Left	.000	1	0	0	0	0	0	0	0	.000	.000	Scoring Posn	.143	7	1	0	0	0	1	1	0	.250	.143
vs. Right	.111	27	3	0	0	0	1	1	3	.143	.111	Close & Late	.143	7	1	0	0	0	0	0	0	.143	.143

Last Five Years

	Avg	AB	H	2B	3B	HR	RBI	BB	SO	OBP	SLG		Avg	AB	H	2B	3B	HR	RBI	BB	SO	OBP	SLG
vs. Left	.273	44	12	1	1	0	4	4	6	.347	.341	Scoring Posn	.268	142	38	5	1	0	44	17	20	.340	.317
vs. Right	.228	500	114	17	2	3	44	50	74	.298	.288	Close & Late	.236	106	25	1	1	0	15	15	16	.333	.264
Groundball	.243	148	36	6	1	0	11	12	19	.302	.297	None on/out	.304	112	34	4	1	3	3	11	13	.366	.438
Flyball	.195	113	22	3	0	0	9	14	21	.283	.221	Batting #2	.231	229	53	7	2	0	18	19	22	.292	.279
Home	.220	277	61	11	2	3	22	28	40	.295	.307	Batting #6	.214	70	15	2	0	0	4	7	9	.262	.243
Away	.243	267	65	7	1	0	26	26	40	.308	.277	Other	.237	245	58	9	1	3	26	28	49	.316	.318
Day	.282	177	50	5	1	1	20	16	14	.342	.339	April	.205	88	18	3	1	0	6	12	12	.304	.261
Night	.207	367	76	13	2	2	28	38	66	.283	.270	May	.188	48	9	2	0	0	4	9	13	.316	.229
Grass	.258	330	85	11	2	0	30	37	41	.332	.303	June	.216	111	24	2	1	1	15	12	7	.290	.279
Turf	.192	214	41	7	1	3	18	17	39	.253	.276	July	.225	71	16	2	1	0	8	11	14	.337	.282
First Pitch	.266	109	29	4	0	0	9	1	0	.273	.303	August	.250	116	29	6	0	2	10	5	20	.279	.353
Ahead on Count	.284	116	33	6	0	1	14	39	0	.456	.362	September/October	.273	110	30	3	0	0	5	5	14	.304	.300
Behind on Count	.202	173	35	6	1	1	18	0	48	.207	.266	Pre-All Star	.205	263	54	7	3	1	27	38	35	.306	.266
Two Strikes	.194	217	42	5	2	1	19	14	80	.246	.272	Post-All Star	.256	281	72	11	0	2	21	16	45	.298	.317

Batter vs. Pitcher (career)

Hits Best Against	Avg	AB	H	2B	3B	HR	RBI	BB	SO	OBP	SLG	Hits Worst Against	Avg	AB	H	2B	3B	HR	RBI	BB	SO	OBP	SLG
Kirk McCaskill	.444	18	8	3	0	1	4	1	0	.474	.778	Jack Armstrong	.000	12	0	0	0	0	0	1	1	.077	.000
Bob Welch	.364	11	4	1	0	0	1	0	2	.364	.455	Bret Saberhagen	.077	13	1	0	0	0	1	2	3	.200	.077
												Jose Rijo	.154	13	2	1	0	0	2	1	2	.200	.231
												Bert Blyleven	.161	31	5	0	0	0	0	2	6	.212	.161
												Andy Benes	.200	15	3	0	0	0	2	1	1	.250	.200

Bob Kipper — Twins
Pitches Left (flyball pitcher)

	ERA	W	L	Sv	G	GS	IP	BB	SO	Avg	H	2B	3B	HR	RBI	OBP	SLG	GF	IR	IRS	Hld	SvOp	SB	CS	GB	FB	G/F
1992 Season	4.42	3	3	0	25	0	38.2	14	22	.268	40	5	0	8	20	.343	.463	12	16	4	2	2	1	2	35	57	0.61
Last Five Years	3.64	15	17	11	220	1	309.1	121	192	.228	259	46	8	34	138	.304	.372	37	136	40	31	20	29	18	313	442	0.71

1992 Season

	ERA	W	L	Sv	G	GS	IP	H	HR	BB	SO		Avg	AB	H	2B	3B	HR	RBI	BB	SO	OBP	SLG
Home	5.55	1	2	0	14	0	24.1	27	6	9	14	vs. Left	.250	44	11	2	0	3	8	2	6	.313	.500
Away	2.51	2	1	0	11	0	14.1	13	2	5	8	vs. Right	.276	105	29	3	0	5	12	12	16	.356	.448
Starter	0.00	0	0	0	0	0	0.0	0	0	0	0	Scoring Posn	.216	37	8	2	0	1	12	4	7	.310	.351
Reliever	4.42	3	3	0	25	0	38.2	40	8	14	22	Close & Late	.235	51	12	0	0	2	5	5	9	.328	.353
0 Days rest	0.00	0	0	0	1	0	2.0	1	0	0	2	None on/out	.343	35	12	2	0	2	2	6	4	.439	.571
1 or 2 Days rest	8.49	1	3	0	11	0	11.2	17	4	6	6	First Pitch	.318	22	7	0	0	2	2	2	0	.423	.591
3+ Days rest	2.88	2	0	0	13	0	25.0	22	4	8	14	Behind on Count	.321	28	9	1	0	3	10	8	0	.472	.679
Pre-All Star	3.15	2	3	0	22	0	34.1	36	7	10	21	Ahead on Count	.209	67	14	3	0	0	4	0	17	.221	.254
Post-All Star	14.54	1	0	0	3	0	4.1	4	1	4	1	Two Strikes	.209	67	14	3	0	1	3	4	22	.264	.299

Last Five Years

	ERA	W	L	Sv	G	GS	IP	H	HR	BB	SO		Avg	AB	H	2B	3B	HR	RBI	BB	SO	OBP	SLG
Home	3.63	9	8	2	109	0	161.1	132	19	63	105	vs. Left	.238	382	91	13	3	9	49	32	71	.304	.359

Last Five Years

	ERA	W	L	Sv	G	GS	IP	H	HR	BB	SO
Away	3.65	6	9	9	111	1	148.0	127	15	58	87
Day	3.25	7	5	7	74	0	102.1	79	8	47	67
Night	3.83	8	12	4	146	1	207.0	180	26	74	125
Grass	3.63	4	2	4	65	1	91.2	73	11	36	55
Turf	3.64	11	15	7	155	0	217.2	186	23	85	137
April	4.62	2	3	0	27	1	37.0	35	3	15	28
May	4.39	2	2	1	43	1	55.1	51	7	25	36
June	3.27	5	5	3	48	0	74.1	66	11	25	47
July	3.08	5	1	1	41	0	61.1	38	4	26	32
August	3.30	1	5	2	26	0	46.1	41	5	18	22
September/October	3.60	0	1	4	33	0	35.0	28	4	12	27
Starter	47.25	0	1	0	1	1	1.1	4	2	3	1
Reliever	3.45	15	16	11	219	0	306.0	255	32	118	191
0 Days rest	4.28	1	3	3	34	0	40.0	33	2	14	21
1 or 2 Days rest	3.23	8	7	5	93	0	122.2	104	11	53	86
3+ Days rest	3.41	6	6	3	92	0	145.1	118	19	51	84
Pre-All Star	3.79	9	10	4	129	1	185.0	163	23	72	120
Post-All Star	3.40	6	7	7	91	0	124.1	96	11	49	72

	Avg	AB	H	2B	3B	HR	RBI	BB	SO	OBP	SLG
vs. Right	.222	756	168	33	5	25	89	89	121	.303	.378
Inning 1-6	.224	340	76	10	0	13	48	34	52	.296	.368
Inning 7+	.229	798	183	36	8	21	90	87	140	.307	.373
None on	.218	656	143	29	3	20	20	64	106	.293	.363
Runners on	.241	482	116	17	5	14	118	57	86	.317	.384
Scoring Posn	.245	273	67	9	3	9	104	44	48	.340	.399
Close & Late	.209	339	71	15	2	8	35	45	53	.309	.336
None on/out	.227	282	64	11	2	10	10	28	41	.304	.387
vs. 1st Batr (relief)	.200	200	40	6	2	4	21	14	31	.257	.310
First Inning Pitched	.227	664	151	24	6	20	96	65	108	.300	.372
First 15 Pitches	.227	626	142	25	5	17	83	58	95	.297	.364
Pitch 16-30	.229	336	77	10	2	14	39	42	56	.316	.396
Pitch 31-45	.223	130	29	8	1	1	12	15	33	.299	.323
Pitch 46+	.239	46	11	3	0	2	4	6	8	.321	.435
First Pitch	.329	173	57	8	2	7	31	12	0	.380	.520
Ahead on Count	.179	492	88	17	1	10	35	0	161	.181	.278
Behind on Count	.251	255	64	11	3	11	50	72	0	.414	.447
Two Strikes	.162	488	79	17	2	10	33	37	192	.222	.266

Pitcher vs. Batter (career)

Pitches Best Vs.	Avg	AB	H	2B	3B	HR	RBI	BB	SO	OBP	SLG
Andre Dawson	.000	14	0	0	0	0	1	2	3	.118	.000
Casey Candaele	.000	10	0	0	0	0	1	2	1	.167	.000
Kal Daniels	.059	17	1	0	0	0	1	0	5	.059	.059
Mitch Webster	.071	14	1	0	0	0	0	1	4	.133	.071
Jose Oquendo	.100	10	1	0	0	0	1	1	2	.182	.100

Pitches Worst Vs.	Avg	AB	H	2B	3B	HR	RBI	BB	SO	OBP	SLG
John Kruk	.526	19	10	3	1	0	4	1	2	.550	.789
Dale Murphy	.417	12	5	1	0	1	6	2	2	.467	.750
Randy Ready	.400	10	4	2	0	1	5	5	2	.600	.900
Mariano Duncan	.389	18	7	2	0	2	3	2	3	.450	.833
Ozzie Smith	.364	22	8	3	2	1	8	1	1	.375	.818

Wayne Kirby — Indians
Bats Left (groundball hitter)

	Avg	G	AB	R	H	2B	3B	HR	RBI	BB	SO	HBP	GDP	SB	CS	OBP	SLG	IBB	SH	SF	#Pit	#P/PA	GB	FB	G/F
1992 Season	.167	21	18	9	3	1	0	1	1	3	2	0	1	0	3	.286	.389	0	0	0	76	3.62	8	5	1.60
Career (1991-1992)	.197	42	61	13	12	3	0	1	6	5	8	0	3	1	5	.254	.295	0	1	1	232	3.46	26	17	1.53

1992 Season

	Avg	AB	H	2B	3B	HR	RBI	BB	SO	OBP	SLG
vs. Left	.000	2	0	0	0	0	0	0	1	.000	.000
vs. Right	.188	16	3	1	0	1	1	3	1	.316	.438

	Avg	AB	H	2B	3B	HR	RBI	BB	SO	OBP	SLG
Scoring Posn	.000	2	0	0	0	0	0	1	0	.333	.000
Close & Late	.111	9	1	0	0	1	1	2	1	.273	.444

Ryan Klesko — Braves
Bats Left

	Avg	G	AB	R	H	2B	3B	HR	RBI	BB	SO	HBP	GDP	SB	CS	OBP	SLG	IBB	SH	SF	#Pit	#P/PA	GB	FB	G/F
1992 Season	.000	13	14	0	0	0	0	0	1	0	5	1	0	0	0	0	.067	.000	0	0	0	50	3.33	4	4	1.00

1992 Season

	Avg	AB	H	2B	3B	HR	RBI	BB	SO	OBP	SLG
vs. Left	.000	1	0	0	0	0	0	0	1	.000	.000
vs. Right	.000	13	0	0	0	0	1	0	4	.071	.000

	Avg	AB	H	2B	3B	HR	RBI	BB	SO	OBP	SLG
Scoring Posn	.000	9	0	0	0	0	0	1	0	4	.000
Close & Late	.000	6	0	0	0	0	0	0	1	.143	.000

Chuck Knoblauch — Twins
Bats Right (groundball hitter)

	Avg	G	AB	R	H	2B	3B	HR	RBI	BB	SO	HBP	GDP	SB	CS	OBP	SLG	IBB	SH	SF	#Pit	#P/PA	GB	FB	G/F
1992 Season	.297	155	600	104	178	19	6	2	56	88	60	5	8	34	13	.384	.358	1	2	12	2618	3.71	250	172	1.45
Career (1991-1992)	.289	306	1165	182	337	43	12	3	106	147	100	9	16	59	18	.368	.355	1	3	17	4800	3.59	530	321	1.65

1992 Season

	Avg	AB	H	2B	3B	HR	RBI	BB	SO	OBP	SLG
vs. Left	.315	124	39	6	2	1	9	17	11	.401	.419
vs. Right	.292	476	139	13	4	1	47	71	49	.380	.342
Groundball	.331	157	52	4	2	1	15	14	15	.381	.401
Flyball	.276	170	47	5	0	1	15	35	22	.394	.324
Home	.287	289	83	5	2	0	23	49	23	.388	.318
Away	.305	311	95	14	4	2	33	39	37	.381	.395
Day	.319	185	59	9	2	0	17	28	17	.412	.389
Night	.287	415	119	10	4	2	39	60	43	.372	.345
Grass	.314	242	76	10	2	1	24	23	24	.371	.384
Turf	.285	358	102	9	4	1	32	65	36	.393	.341
First Pitch	.354	82	29	3	0	0	11	0	0	.345	.390
Ahead on Count	.364	121	44	4	1	1	17	59	0	.568	.438
Behind on Count	.254	205	52	2	3	0	16	1	35	.256	.293
Two Strikes	.243	251	61	7	4	0	16	29	60	.323	.303

	Avg	AB	H	2B	3B	HR	RBI	BB	SO	OBP	SLG
Scoring Posn	.262	145	38	2	4	0	52	24	20	.346	.331
Close & Late	.274	95	26	3	1	0	14	12	12	.360	.326
None on/out	.318	170	54	7	1	2	2	20	13	.399	.406
Batting #1	.299	264	79	10	5	1	19	34	28	.377	.386
Batting #2	.296	335	99	9	1	1	37	54	32	.391	.337
Other	.000	1	0	0	0	0	0	0	0	.000	.000
April	.288	80	23	0	0	1	8	8	8	.344	.325
May	.364	99	36	8	1	0	12	16	8	.449	.465
June	.253	95	24	3	1	0	11	22	7	.393	.305
July	.311	103	32	4	2	0	10	10	7	.362	.388
August	.304	115	35	3	1	0	4	8	18	.347	.348
September/October	.259	108	28	1	1	1	11	24	12	.400	.315
Pre-All Star	.303	317	96	13	2	1	35	51	25	.397	.366
Post-All Star	.290	283	82	6	4	1	21	37	35	.370	.350

1992 By Position

Position	Avg	AB	H	2B	3B	HR	RBI	BB	SO	OBP	SLG	G	GS	Innings	PO	A	E	DP	Fld Pct	Rng Fctr	In Zone	Outs	Zone Rtg	MLB Zone
As 2b	.296	595	176	19	6	2	56	88	60	.384	.358	154	150	1339.2	308	416	6	104	.992	4.86	452	423	.936	.892

Career (1991-1992)

	Avg	AB	H	2B	3B	HR	RBI	BB	SO	OBP	SLG		Avg	AB	H	2B	3B	HR	RBI	BB	SO	OBP	SLG
vs. Left	.283	272	77	14	3	1	15	31	21	.361	.368	Scoring Posn	.282	262	74	6	5	0	98	42	30	.363	.344
vs. Right	.291	893	260	29	9	2	91	116	79	.371	.351	Close & Late	.272	173	47	7	1	0	19	16	15	.335	.324
Groundball	.317	322	102	11	3	1	31	31	23	.373	.379	None on/out	.314	306	96	13	2	2	2	31	24	.386	.389
Flyball	.291	261	76	10	1	2	23	45	30	.390	.360	Batting #1	.275	349	96	12	6	1	23	40	42	.348	.352
Home	.307	576	177	17	7	1	49	79	41	.389	.366	Batting #2	.297	795	236	31	6	2	82	104	58	.378	.358
Away	.272	589	160	26	5	2	57	68	59	.346	.343	Other	.238	21	5	0	0	0	1	3	0	.333	.238
Day	.313	336	105	14	6	0	37	46	29	.395	.390	April	.310	155	48	3	2	1	17	16	16	.368	.374
Night	.280	829	232	29	6	3	69	101	71	.358	.340	May	.302	189	57	13	1	0	18	27	15	.386	.381
Grass	.280	454	127	19	2	1	41	47	38	.348	.337	June	.270	185	50	5	2	0	18	31	9	.378	.319
Turf	.295	711	210	24	10	2	65	100	62	.381	.366	July	.276	196	54	9	4	0	18	21	17	.339	.362
First Pitch	.326	184	60	9	1	0	21	0	0	.323	.386	August	.286	220	63	8	1	1	14	16	28	.336	.345
Ahead on Count	.346	257	89	13	4	2	34	99	0	.525	.451	September/October	.295	220	65	5	2	1	21	36	15	.400	.350
Behind on Count	.254	366	98	8	4	0	27	1	58	.254	.295	Pre-All Star	.292	593	173	25	5	1	58	81	45	.376	.356
Two Strikes	.252	444	112	14	5	0	33	48	100	.326	.306	Post-All Star	.287	572	164	18	7	2	48	66	55	.361	.353

Batter vs. Pitcher (career)

Hits Best Against	Avg	AB	H	2B	3B	HR	RBI	BB	SO	OBP	SLG	Hits Worst Against	Avg	AB	H	2B	3B	HR	RBI	BB	SO	OBP	SLG
Mike Mussina	.545	11	6	0	0	1	1	1	1	.583	.818	Juan Guzman	.000	13	0	0	0	0	1	4	4	.222	.000
Scott Sanderson	.500	14	7	1	0	0	3	0	1	.500	.571	Charles Nagy	.091	11	1	0	0	0	1	0	0	.083	.091
Bob Welch	.467	15	7	1	0	0	2	0	0	.529	.533	Eric King	.100	10	1	0	0	0	1	2	0	.182	.100
Bill Wegman	.462	13	6	1	1	0	0	1	0	.500	.692	Chris Bosio	.158	19	3	0	0	0	0	2	1	.238	.158
Joe Hesketh	.400	10	4	2	1	0	1	1	2	.455	.800	Nolan Ryan	.200	15	3	0	0	0	0	0	3	.200	.200

Randy Knorr — Blue Jays

Bats Right (flyball hitter)

	Avg	G	AB	R	H	2B	3B	HR	RBI	BB	SO	HBP	GDP	SB	CS	OBP	SLG	IBB	SH	SF	#Pit	#P/PA	GB	FB	G/F
1992 Season	.263	8	19	1	5	0	0	1	2	1	5	0	0	0	0	.300	.421	1	0	0	65	3.25	4	7	0.57
Career (1991-1992)	.250	11	20	1	5	0	0	1	2	2	6	0	0	0	0	.318	.400	1	0	0	75	3.41	4	7	0.57

1992 Season

	Avg	AB	H	2B	3B	HR	RBI	BB	SO	OBP	SLG		Avg	AB	H	2B	3B	HR	RBI	BB	SO	OBP	SLG
vs. Left	.429	7	3	0	0	1	2	1	0	.500	.857	Scoring Posn	.200	5	1	0	0	1	1	1	2	.333	.200
vs. Right	.167	12	2	0	0	0	0	0	5	.167	.167	Close & Late	.000	1	0	0	0	0	0	0	0	.000	.000

Kurt Knudsen — Tigers

Pitches Right (flyball pitcher)

	ERA	W	L	Sv	G	GS	IP	BB	SO	Avg	H	2B	3B	HR	RBI	OBP	SLG	GF	IR	IRS	Hld	SvOp	SB	CS	GB	FB	G/F
1992 Season	4.58	2	3	5	48	1	70.2	41	51	.264	70	13	1	9	43	.362	.423	14	42	13	8	7	6	5	50	104	0.48

1992 Season

	ERA	W	L	Sv	G	GS	IP	H	HR	BB	SO		Avg	AB	H	2B	3B	HR	RBI	BB	SO	OBP	SLG
Home	3.93	2	1	1	23	0	36.2	36	4	17	29	vs. Left	.266	109	29	5	0	4	17	16	7	.357	.422
Away	5.29	0	2	4	25	1	34.0	34	5	24	22	vs. Right	.263	156	41	8	1	5	26	25	44	.366	.423
Starter	22.50	0	1	0	1	1	2.0	4	0	4	1	Scoring Posn	.225	89	20	4	0	0	29	24	17	.388	.270
Reliever	4.06	2	2	5	47	0	68.2	66	9	37	50	Close & Late	.281	96	27	4	0	3	14	16	25	.381	.417
0 Days rest	4.05	0	0	1	7	0	13.1	13	3	6	9	None on/out	.327	55	18	3	0	4	4	10	13	.431	.600
1 or 2 Days rest	4.35	2	2	3	26	0	39.1	38	5	19	23	First Pitch	.346	26	9	1	0	2	5	7	0	.485	.615
3+ Days rest	3.38	0	0	1	14	0	16.0	15	1	12	18	Behind on Count	.317	63	20	3	1	5	13	14	0	.442	.635
Pre-All Star	2.72	2	0	2	25	0	36.1	31	6	19	19	Ahead on Count	.224	125	28	6	0	1	21	0	39	.227	.296
Post-All Star	6.55	0	3	3	23	1	34.1	39	3	22	32	Two Strikes	.224	134	30	7	0	1	21	20	51	.327	.299

Kevin Koslofski — Royals

Bats Left

	Avg	G	AB	R	H	2B	3B	HR	RBI	BB	SO	HBP	GDP	SB	CS	OBP	SLG	IBB	SH	SF	#Pit	#P/PA	GB	FB	G/F
1992 Season	.248	55	133	20	33	0	2	3	13	12	23	1	2	2	1	.313	.346	0	3	1	493	3.35	51	37	1.38

1992 Season

	Avg	AB	H	2B	3B	HR	RBI	BB	SO	OBP	SLG		Avg	AB	H	2B	3B	HR	RBI	BB	SO	OBP	SLG
vs. Left	.429	14	6	0	0	0	1	4	3	.556	.429	Scoring Posn	.200	35	7	0	0	0	10	2	7	.237	.200
vs. Right	.227	119	27	0	2	3	12	8	20	.279	.336	Close & Late	.227	22	5	0	1	1	2	4	5	.346	.455
Home	.195	82	16	0	1	1	8	7	17	.264	.256	None on/out	.310	29	9	0	0	2	2	5	4	.412	.517
Away	.333	51	17	0	1	2	5	5	6	.393	.490	Batting #7	.245	49	12	0	1	0	5	0	9	.245	.286
First Pitch	.296	27	8	0	0	0	3	0	0	.310	.296	Batting #8	.206	34	7	0	1	1	3	8	5	.357	.353
Ahead on Count	.323	31	10	0	1	2	5	4	0	.400	.581	Other	.280	50	14	0	0	2	5	4	9	.339	.400
Behind on Count	.213	47	10	0	1	0	2	0	16	.213	.255	Pre-All Star	.357	14	5	0	0	0	1	1	1	.400	.357
Two Strikes	.106	47	5	0	0	1	8	23	.236	.149		Post-All Star	.235	119	28	0	2	3	12	11	22	.303	.345

Randy Kramer — Mariners
Pitches Right

	ERA	W	L	Sv	G	GS	IP	BB	SO	Avg	H	2B	3B	HR	RBI	OBP	SLG	CG	ShO	Sup	QS	#P/S	SB	CS	GB	FB	G/F
1992 Season	7.71	0	1	0	4	4	16.1	7	6	.400	30	6	0	2	12	.458	.560	0	0	6.06	1	78	3	0	35	19	1.84
Career (1988-1992)	4.51	6	15	2	66	24	183.2	90	92	.259	179	27	7	19	92	.352	.400	1	1	3.92	5	77	32	9	288	204	1.41

1992 Season

	ERA	W	L	Sv	G	GS	IP	H	HR	BB	SO		Avg	AB	H	2B	3B	HR	RBI	BB	SO	OBP	SLG
Home	8.22	0	0	0	2	2	7.2	18	1	1	4	vs. Left	.341	44	15	4	0	1	5	4	3	.396	.500
Away	7.27	0	1	0	2	2	8.2	12	1	6	2	vs. Right	.484	31	15	2	0	1	7	3	3	.543	.645

Career (1988-1992)

	ERA	W	L	Sv	G	GS	IP	H	HR	BB	SO		Avg	AB	H	2B	3B	HR	RBI	BB	SO	OBP	SLG
Home	4.94	3	6	2	31	12	82.0	94	12	32	43	vs. Left	.266	361	96	16	5	10	51	59	41	.370	.421
Away	4.16	3	9	0	35	12	101.2	85	7	58	49	vs. Right	.251	331	83	11	2	9	41	31	51	.331	.378
Day	4.39	2	8	0	24	9	65.2	66	7	35	41	Inning 1-6	.275	506	139	22	5	16	72	69	65	.370	.433
Night	4.58	4	7	2	42	15	118.0	113	12	55	51	Inning 7+	.215	186	40	5	2	3	20	21	27	.302	.312
Grass	5.15	2	5	0	19	6	50.2	50	8	29	27	None on	.241	361	87	13	5	9	9	54	51	.351	.380
Turf	4.26	4	10	2	47	18	133.0	129	11	61	65	Runners on	.278	331	92	14	2	10	83	36	41	.353	.423
April	3.72	0	0	0	4	1	9.2	7	0	9	6	Scoring Posn	.260	204	53	8	2	7	76	28	24	.350	.422
May	2.77	1	1	1	15	3	39.0	30	5	12	18	Close & Late	.323	65	21	2	1	1	9	10	10	.416	.431
June	7.15	1	4	0	10	8	39.0	55	3	22	13	None on/out	.232	168	39	5	1	4	4	26	19	.348	.345
July	4.34	2	2	0	6	5	29.0	26	5	13	12	vs. 1st Batr (relief)	.200	35	7	0	0	1	3	4	7	.310	.286
August	3.10	1	2	0	9	2	20.1	16	0	10	10	First Inning Pitched	.264	227	60	6	3	5	35	25	37	.350	.383
September/October	4.63	1	6	1	22	5	46.2	45	6	24	33	First 75 Pitches	.262	641	168	25	7	19	86	81	85	.353	.412
Starter	5.45	4	12	0	24	24	112.1	121	14	61	56	Pitch 76-90	.192	26	5	1	0	0	4	7	4	.353	.231
Reliever	3.03	2	3	2	42	0	71.1	58	5	29	36	Pitch 91-105	.188	16	3	0	0	0	2	2	.316	.188
0-3 Days Rest	8.10	0	2	0	3	3	10.0	9	0	12	6	Pitch 106+	.333	9	3	1	0	0	2	0	1	.333	.444
4 Days Rest	6.75	1	3	0	7	7	29.1	36	4	20	12	First Pitch	.298	94	28	8	0	3	15	7	0	.389	.479
5+ Days Rest	4.56	3	7	0	14	14	73.0	76	10	29	38	Ahead on Count	.225	285	64	8	2	6	33	1	72	.231	.330
Pre-All Star	4.84	3	6	1	31	14	96.2	103	11	45	40	Behind on Count	.296	199	59	9	4	9	32	53	0	.443	.518
Post-All Star	4.14	3	9	1	35	10	87.0	76	8	45	32	Two Strikes	.204	280	57	6	2	5	24	30	92	.281	.293

Pitcher vs. Batter (career)

Pitches Best Vs.	Avg	AB	H	2B	3B	HR	RBI	BB	SO	OBP	SLG	Pitches Worst Vs.	Avg	AB	H	2B	3B	HR	RBI	BB	SO	OBP	SLG
Ryne Sandberg	.214	14	3	1	0	0	1	0	3	.214	.286	Gregg Jefferies	.455	11	5	0	0	1	2	0	0	.455	.727
												Mark Grace	.375	8	3	0	0	0	1	3	1	.545	.375

Chad Kreuter — Tigers
Bats Both

	Avg	G	AB	R	H	2B	3B	HR	RBI	BB	SO	HBP	GDP	SB	CS	OBP	SLG	IBB	SH	SF	#Pit	#P/PA	GB	FB	G/F
1992 Season	.253	67	190	22	48	9	0	2	16	20	38	0	8	0	1	.321	.332	1	3	2	838	3.95	70	48	1.46
Career (1988-1992)	.205	195	425	43	87	15	1	8	32	62	101	0	13	0	2	.303	.301	1	10	4	1979	4.03	138	121	1.14

1992 Season

	Avg	AB	H	2B	3B	HR	RBI	BB	SO	OBP	SLG		Avg	AB	H	2B	3B	HR	RBI	BB	SO	OBP	SLG
vs. Left	.182	66	12	4	0	1	7	10	12	.289	.288	Scoring Posn	.262	42	11	3	0	1	15	6	7	.340	.405
vs. Right	.290	124	36	5	0	1	9	10	26	.338	.355	Close & Late	.308	26	8	1	0	0	2	3	6	.367	.346
Home	.272	92	25	3	0	2	8	12	22	.349	.370	None on/out	.286	49	14	3	0	1	1	3	9	.327	.408
Away	.235	98	23	6	0	0	8	8	16	.292	.296	Batting #7	.361	36	13	2	0	1	2	5	4	.439	.500
First Pitch	.280	25	7	2	0	0	2	1	0	.308	.360	Batting #8	.205	112	23	6	0	0	7	8	27	.254	.259
Ahead on Count	.404	47	19	4	0	1	7	9	0	.491	.553	Other	.286	42	12	1	0	1	7	7	7	.388	.381
Behind on Count	.241	58	14	3	0	1	5	0	12	.237	.345	Pre-All Star	.217	106	23	5	0	2	7	8	18	.272	.321
Two Strikes	.170	88	15	2	0	1	6	10	38	.255	.227	Post-All Star	.298	84	25	4	0	0	9	12	20	.378	.345

Bill Krueger — Expos
Pitches Left

	ERA	W	L	Sv	G	GS	IP	BB	SO	Avg	H	2B	3B	HR	RBI	OBP	SLG	CG	ShO	Sup	QS	#P/S	SB	CS	GB	FB	G/F
1992 Season	4.53	10	8	0	36	29	178.2	53	99	.269	189	37	2	18	74	.323	.404	2	2	5.89	13	90	22	4	221	244	0.91
Last Five Years	4.04	30	26	3	136	77	578.2	202	327	.276	620	104	13	52	259	.336	.403	3	2	4.60	33	86	59	19	802	705	1.14

1992 Season

	ERA	W	L	Sv	G	GS	IP	H	HR	BB	SO		Avg	AB	H	2B	3B	HR	RBI	BB	SO	OBP	SLG
Home	4.80	2	4	0	14	10	65.2	69	9	25	42	vs. Left	.308	104	32	9	1	1	11	4	13	.345	.442
Away	4.38	8	4	0	22	19	113.0	120	9	28	57	vs. Right	.262	599	157	28	1	17	63	49	86	.320	.397
Day	4.50	1	1	0	8	5	30.0	43	3	6	14	Inning 1-6	.279	606	169	33	2	16	67	43	79	.330	.419
Night	4.54	9	7	0	28	24	148.2	146	15	47	85	Inning 7+	.206	97	20	4	0	2	7	10	20	.280	.309
Grass	4.45	6	3	0	17	15	87.0	88	8	20	47	None on	.251	434	109	23	0	10	10	20	61	.287	.373
Turf	4.61	4	5	0	19	14	91.2	101	10	33	52	Runners on	.297	269	80	14	2	8	64	33	38	.377	.454
April	0.84	4	0	0	4	4	32.0	18	1	4	16	Scoring Posn	.281	160	45	7	1	7	58	23	27	.373	.469
May	3.15	1	0	0	6	6	40.0	41	6	8	25	Close & Late	.189	53	10	1	0	1	4	6	11	.271	.264
June	3.49	3	2	0	6	6	38.2	39	4	11	19	None on/out	.243	189	46	5	0	6	6	7	28	.274	.365
July	6.20	1	0	0	5	5	24.2	28	2	12	12	vs. 1st Batr (relief)	.571	7	4	0	1	0	1	0	2	.571	.857
August	9.69	1	4	0	6	6	26.0	40	5	11	14	First Inning Pitched	.295	139	41	9	1	4	20	7	24	.342	.460
September/October	6.75	0	2	0	9	2	17.1	23	0	7	13	First 75 Pitches	.270	555	150	29	2	12	53	37	78	.320	.395
Starter	4.51	10	7	0	29	29	169.2	180	18	51	90	Pitch 76-90	.296	81	24	4	0	4	16	6	10	.345	.494
Reliever	5.00	0	1	0	7	0	9.0	9	0	2	9	Pitch 91-105	.244	45	11	3	0	2	5	9	7	.370	.444

	ERA	W	L	Sv	G	GS	IP	H	HR	BB	SO		Avg	AB	H	2B	3B	HR	RBI	BB	SO	OBP	SLG
0-3 Days Rest	1.50	1	0	0	1	1	6.0	5	1	0	1	Pitch 106+	.182	22	4	1	0	0	0	1	4	.217	.227
4 Days Rest	3.99	6	4	0	17	17	106.0	106	10	36	55	First Pitch	.345	113	39	6	0	3	11	0	0	.345	.478
5+ Days Rest	5.77	3	3	0	11	11	57.2	69	7	15	34	Ahead on Count	.185	259	48	8	1	5	18	0	88	.195	.282
Pre-All Star	3.19	9	2	0	18	18	118.2	108	13	29	64	Behind on Count	.315	203	64	15	1	5	25	27	0	.394	.473
Post-All Star	7.20	1	6	0	18	11	60.0	81	5	24	35	Two Strikes	.209	273	57	12	1	7	26	26	99	.285	.337

Last Five Years

	ERA	W	L	Sv	G	GS	IP	H	HR	BB	SO		Avg	AB	H	2B	3B	HR	RBI	BB	SO	OBP	SLG
Home	4.15	15	15	1	65	39	286.0	300	28	101	182	vs. Left	.273	432	118	21	3	4	46	28	71	.319	.363
Away	3.94	15	11	2	71	38	292.2	320	24	101	145	vs. Right	.277	1814	502	83	10	48	213	174	256	.340	.413
Day	4.26	4	6	0	31	14	105.2	116	10	37	52	Inning 1-6	.289	1852	535	89	13	43	234	167	253	.348	.421
Night	4.00	26	20	3	105	63	473.0	504	42	165	275	Inning 7+	.216	394	85	15	0	9	25	35	74	.279	.322
Grass	3.90	17	15	1	83	44	341.2	363	27	119	199	Runners on	.284	951	270	46	10	16	223	119	144	.359	.404
Turf	4.25	13	11	2	53	33	237.0	257	25	83	128	Scoring Posn	.263	547	144	23	6	11	200	84	94	.354	.388
April	1.86	5	0	0	12	4	48.1	40	1	10	28	Close & Late	.253	170	43	6	0	4	13	14	31	.308	.359
May	3.99	4	3	1	31	9	106.1	117	13	45	60	None on/out	.281	581	163	22	2	18	18	33	74	.325	.418
June	3.22	11	7	0	24	20	134.0	131	12	46	71	vs. 1st Batr (relief)	.353	51	18	1	2	1	14	7	8	.424	.510
July	3.24	6	3	0	25	17	119.1	118	11	43	70	First Inning Pitched	.300	513	154	25	3	10	91	52	90	.364	.419
August	6.37	2	9	2	19	14	82.0	102	8	29	51	First 75 Pitches	.279	1911	533	86	10	41	214	165	278	.337	.399
September/October	5.50	2	4	0	25	13	86.2	112	7	29	47	Pitch 76-90	.255	200	51	10	3	7	33	23	29	.329	.440
Starter	4.21	26	21	0	77	77	435.2	487	43	142	216	Pitch 91-105	.289	97	28	6	0	3	10	12	14	.367	.443
Reliever	3.52	4	5	3	59	0	143.0	133	9	60	111	Pitch 106+	.211	38	8	2	0	1	2	2	6	.250	.342
0-3 Days Rest	2.53	1	0	0	2	2	10.2	12	1	4	3	First Pitch	.337	395	133	22	1	10	49	6	0	.343	.473
4 Days Rest	3.95	18	10	0	45	45	262.1	276	25	86	121	Ahead on Count	.199	790	157	20	3	10	58	0	291	.206	.270
5+ Days Rest	4.76	7	11	0	30	30	162.2	199	17	52	92	Behind on Count	.319	636	203	42	7	21	90	108	0	.415	.506
Pre-All Star	3.56	21	11	1	75	39	325.2	324	30	115	182	Two Strikes	.207	870	180	28	2	13	77	88	327	.281	.289
Post-All Star	4.66	9	15	2	61	38	253.0	296	22	87	145												

Pitcher vs. Batter (since 1984)

Pitches Best Vs.	Avg	AB	H	2B	3B	HR	RBI	BB	SO	OBP	SLG	Pitches Worst Vs.	Avg	AB	H	2B	3B	HR	RBI	BB	SO	OBP	SLG
Junior Felix	.000	16	0	0	0	0	0	0	7	.000	.000	Mike Greenwell	.625	16	10	1	1	0	3	0	1	.625	.813
Mel Hall	.000	15	0	0	0	0	0	0	3	.000	.000	Shane Mack	.556	9	5	1	1	1	9	2	0	.636	1.222
Ellis Burks	.000	14	0	0	0	0	0	1	1	.067	.000	Willie Randolph	.524	21	11	2	1	1	7	3	2	.560	.857
Mike Gallego	.000	9	0	0	0	0	0	2	2	.182	.000	Jesse Barfield	.455	22	10	1	1	2	5	4	4	.538	.864
Brady Anderson	.000	8	0	0	0	0	0	3	1	.250	.000	Danny Tartabull	.455	11	5	0	0	3	9	2	2	.538	1.273

John Kruk — Phillies   Bats Left (groundball hitter)

	Avg	G	AB	R	H	2B	3B	HR	RBI	BB	SO	HBP	GDP	SB	CS	OBP	SLG	IBB	SH	SF	#Pit	#P/PA	GB	FB	G/F
1992 Season	.323	144	507	86	164	30	4	10	70	92	88	1	11	3	5	.423	.458	8	0	7	2377	3.92	224	92	2.43
Last Five Years	.292	670	2223	329	649	112	25	55	317	352	379	2	50	28	13	.385	.439	54	7	25	9759	3.75	916	497	1.84

1992 Season

	Avg	AB	H	2B	3B	HR	RBI	BB	SO	OBP	SLG		Avg	AB	H	2B	3B	HR	RBI	BB	SO	OBP	SLG
vs. Left	.314	210	66	9	1	1	18	37	42	.414	.381	Scoring Posn	.304	135	41	4	0	4	60	43	23	.454	.422
vs. Right	.330	297	98	21	3	9	52	55	46	.430	.512	Close & Late	.322	87	28	3	1	0	5	17	17	.429	.379
Groundball	.346	211	73	15	2	4	30	33	30	.433	.493	None on/out	.350	120	42	9	1	2		13	21	.414	.492
Flyball	.310	113	35	4	1	1	14	23	25	.420	.389	Batting #3	.257	113	29	7	1	3	17	25	20	.390	.416
Home	.306	248	76	11	1	7	37	46	39	.409	.444	Batting #4	.343	370	127	22	2	7	53	67	66	.439	.470
Away	.340	259	88	19	3	3	33	46	49	.437	.471	Other	.333	24	8	1	1	0	0	0	2	.333	.458
Day	.354	130	46	6	1	4	22	32	25	.479	.508	April	.407	81	33	3	1	0	16	11	12	.468	.469
Night	.313	377	118	24	3	6	48	60	63	.403	.440	May	.356	87	31	4	0	4	14	19	16	.472	.540
Grass	.321	134	43	8	1	3	17	29	29	.442	.463	June	.341	85	29	8	1	1	7	12	11	.418	.494
Turf	.324	373	121	22	3	7	53	63	59	.416	.456	July	.256	90	23	5	0	3	14	27	25	.420	.411
First Pitch	.339	59	20	4	2	1	9	5	0	.394	.525	August	.279	86	24	5	0	1	9	12	11	.366	.372
Ahead on Count	.402	132	53	12	0	2	20	50	0	.563	.538	September/October	.308	78	24	5	2	1	10	11	13	.393	.462
Behind on Count	.255	157	40	10	0	2	18	0	42	.250	.357	Pre-All Star	.346	298	103	16	2	8	43	57	54	.447	.493
Two Strikes	.252	230	58	9	2	3	18	38	88	.357	.348	Post-All Star	.292	209	61	14	2	2	27	35	34	.390	.407

1992 By Position

Position	Avg	AB	H	2B	3B	HR	RBI	BB	SO	OBP	SLG	G	GS	Innings	PO	A	E	DP	Fld Pct	Rng Fctr	In Zone	Outs	Zone Rtg	MLB Zone
As 1b	.334	389	130	27	4	9	58	66	66	.425	.494	121	106	958.0	980	58	7	78	.993	---	166	135	.813	.843
As rf	.294	102	30	3	0	1	12	20	20	.410	.353	47	29	225.2	47	0	1	0	.979	1.87	56	44	.786	.814

Last Five Years

	Avg	AB	H	2B	3B	HR	RBI	BB	SO	OBP	SLG		Avg	AB	H	2B	3B	HR	RBI	BB	SO	OBP	SLG
vs. Left	.272	728	198	32	6	10	93	87	140	.346	.374	Scoring Posn	.270	589	159	27	5	14	243	150	112	.405	.404
vs. Right	.302	1495	451	80	19	45	224	265	239	.404	.471	Close & Late	.286	370	106	13	4	7	48	75	70	.403	.400
Groundball	.298	815	243	37	7	11	111	128	131	.392	.423	None on/out	.312	555	173	31	3	13	13	60	87	.379	.449
Flyball	.301	479	144	20	6	13	75	77	95	.394	.449	Batting #4	.316	950	300	58	10	25	143	153	170	.408	.477
Home	.296	1118	331	59	11	31	183	188	174	.393	.452	Batting #5	.292	565	165	28	7	12	77	86	80	.384	.430
Away	.288	1105	318	53	14	24	134	164	205	.377	.426	Other	.260	708	184	26	8	18	97	113	129	.357	.395
Day	.287	585	168	30	7	16	81	97	109	.385	.444	April	.298	312	93	8	2	9	60	39	44	.372	.423

	Avg	AB	H	2B	3B	HR	RBI	BB	SO	OBP	SLG		Avg	AB	H	2B	3B	HR	RBI	BB	SO	OBP	SLG
Night	.294	1638	461	82	18	39	236	255	270	.386	.437	May	.293	352	103	20	4	9	50	65	68	.396	.449
Grass	.267	818	218	34	7	27	107	155	159	.382	.425	June	.269	418	121	22	7	8	57	61	58	.378	.433
Turf	.306	1407	431	78	16	28	210	197	220	.388	.447	July	.262	286	75	16	2	9	36	68	61	.401	.427
First Pitch	.327	321	105	20	8	10	54	19	1	.363	.533	August	.300	424	127	18	3	9	54	70	63	.396	.420
Ahead on Count	.375	555	208	44	3	22	110	178	0	.523	.584	September/October	.302	431	130	28	7	11	60	49	85	.371	.476
Behind on Count	.260	661	172	26	4	17	82	2	175	.259	.389	Pre-All Star	.287	1192	342	54	13	29	178	197	195	.384	.427
Two Strikes	.212	947	201	30	9	12	90	133	377	.307	.301	Post-All Star	.298	1031	307	58	12	26	139	155	184	.387	.453

Batter vs. Pitcher (career)

Hits Best Against	Avg	AB	H	2B	3B	HR	RBI	BB	SO	OBP	SLG	Hits Worst Against	Avg	AB	H	2B	3B	HR	RBI	BB	SO	OBP	SLG
Ted Power	.556	18	10	3	1	0	6	2	0	.600	.833	Lee Smith	.000	15	0	0	0	0	0	1	6	.063	.000
Bob Kipper	.526	19	10	3	1	0	4	1	2	.550	.789	Mark Portugal	.091	11	1	0	0	0	0	0	2	.091	.091
Roger Mason	.500	8	4	0	1	1	1	3	0	.636	1.125	Bob McClure	.100	10	1	1	0	0	0	1	2	.182	.200
Jimmy Jones	.444	9	4	1	0	1	2	2	1	.545	.889	Frank DiPino	.111	18	2	0	0	0	0	1	9	.111	.111
Wally Whitehurst	.444	9	4	1	0	1	3	0	1	.545	.889	Bobby Ojeda	.152	33	5	0	0	0	2	1	13	.171	.152

Jeff Kunkel — Cubs   Bats Right

	Avg	G	AB	R	H	2B	3B	HR	RBI	BB	SO	HBP	GDP	SB	CS	OBP	SLG	IBB	SH	SF	#Pit	#P/PA	GB	FB	G/F
1992 Season	.138	20	29	0	4	2	0	0	0	8	0	1	0	0		.138	.207	0	0	0	96	3.31	8	7	1.14
Last Five Years	.225	262	676	70	152	42	6	13	62	35	184	6	18	5	4	.269	.362	1	16	7	2539	3.54	209	160	1.31

1992 Season

	Avg	AB	H	2B	3B	HR	RBI	BB	SO	OBP	SLG		Avg	AB	H	2B	3B	HR	RBI	BB	SO	OBP	SLG
vs. Left	.045	22	1	1	0	0	0	0	7	.045	.091	Scoring Posn	.167	6	1	1	0	0	1	0	1	.167	.333
vs. Right	.429	7	3	1	0	0	1	0	1	.429	.571	Close & Late	.125	8	1	0	0	0	0	0	1	.125	.125

Last Five Years

	Avg	AB	H	2B	3B	HR	RBI	BB	SO	OBP	SLG		Avg	AB	H	2B	3B	HR	RBI	BB	SO	OBP	SLG
vs. Left	.267	356	95	28	5	7	41	16	93	.302	.433	Scoring Posn	.230	148	34	15	0	1	44	10	44	.281	.351
vs. Right	.178	320	57	14	1	6	21	19	91	.233	.284	Close & Late	.206	107	22	4	0	1	5	5	26	.241	.271
Groundball	.167	162	27	5	5	0	9	4	53	.192	.259	None on/out	.231	169	39	6	2	8	8	8	42	.274	.432
Flyball	.247	182	45	12	0	6	24	13	53	.299	.412	Batting #8	.200	210	42	12	2	2	12	8	53	.233	.305
Home	.215	335	72	20	3	11	36	20	89	.265	.391	Batting #9	.243	263	64	20	3	4	27	10	82	.275	.388
Away	.235	341	80	22	3	2	26	15	95	.272	.334	Other	.227	203	46	10	1	7	23	17	49	.296	.389
Day	.210	143	30	9	2	2	5	9	48	.271	.343	April	.154	52	8	2	1	0	4	2	19	.200	.231
Night	.229	533	122	33	4	11	57	26	136	.268	.368	May	.215	79	17	6	0	3	7	3	21	.253	.405
Grass	.226	575	130	34	5	13	56	33	156	.274	.370	June	.290	107	31	11	2	2	15	4	29	.315	.486
Turf	.218	101	22	8	1	0	6	2	28	.240	.317	July	.206	126	26	7	0	2	9	5	43	.237	.310
First Pitch	.259	116	30	10	1	3	13	0	0	.271	.440	August	.269	141	46	11	1	4	17	5	43	.294	.415
Ahead on Count	.346	81	28	10	1	5	18	11	0	.430	.679	September/October	.170	141	24	5	2	2	10	16	34	.267	.277
Behind on Count	.195	282	55	17	1	2	19	0	107	.201	.264	Pre-All Star	.229	292	67	22	3	5	28	10	85	.260	.377
Two Strikes	.163	350	57	13	2	2	20	23	183	.219	.229	Post-All Star	.221	384	85	20	3	8	34	25	99	.275	.352

Batter vs. Pitcher (career)

Hits Best Against	Avg	AB	H	2B	3B	HR	RBI	BB	SO	OBP	SLG	Hits Worst Against	Avg	AB	H	2B	3B	HR	RBI	BB	SO	OBP	SLG
Frank Viola	.357	14	5	1	0	0	2	0	4	.357	.429	Jim Abbott	.100	10	1	0	0	0	0	1	5	.182	.100
Chuck Finley	.353	17	6	1	1	0	1	0	5	.353	.529	Storm Davis	.118	17	2	0	0	1	1	0	3	.118	.294
Greg Hibbard	.333	12	4	1	1	0	2	0	3	.333	.583	Bud Black	.125	16	2	2	0	0	2	1	5	.176	.250
Frank Tanana	.316	19	6	0	0	1	1	0	3	.316	.474	Charlie Leibrandt	.154	13	2	0	0	0	2	0	1	.154	.154
Randy Johnson	.313	16	5	4	0	0	3	1	7	.353	.563	Scott Bankhead	.167	12	2	0	0	0	0	1	2	.231	.167

Steve Lake — Phillies   Bats Right

	Avg	G	AB	R	H	2B	3B	HR	RBI	BB	SO	HBP	GDP	SB	CS	OBP	SLG	IBB	SH	SF	#Pit	#P/PA	GB	FB	G/F
1992 Season	.245	20	53	3	13	2	0	1	2	1	8	0	1	0	0	.255	.340	0	0	1	142	2.58	22	14	1.57
Last Five Years	.246	201	500	33	123	16	2	5	37	21	81	3	12	0	0	.279	.316	6	5	2	1575	2.99	183	144	1.27

1992 Season

	Avg	AB	H	2B	3B	HR	RBI	BB	SO	OBP	SLG		Avg	AB	H	2B	3B	HR	RBI	BB	SO	OBP	SLG
vs. Left	.303	33	10	1	0	1	2	1	2	.314	.424	Scoring Posn	.111	9	1	0	0	0	1	0	2	.100	.111
vs. Right	.150	20	3	1	0	0	0	0	6	.150	.200	Close & Late	.273	11	3	0	0	0	0	0	3	.273	.273

Last Five Years

	Avg	AB	H	2B	3B	HR	RBI	BB	SO	OBP	SLG		Avg	AB	H	2B	3B	HR	RBI	BB	SO	OBP	SLG
vs. Left	.252	341	86	12	2	2	24	14	48	.284	.317	Scoring Posn	.239	113	27	2	0	0	28	12	27	.313	.257
vs. Right	.233	159	37	4	0	3	13	7	33	.269	.314	Close & Late	.235	85	20	4	0	0	2	6	14	.293	.282
Groundball	.232	177	41	8	1	2	15	7	19	.265	.322	None on/out	.292	120	35	3	1	3	3	5	23	.325	.408
Flyball	.257	136	35	1	0	2	9	5	30	.284	.309	Batting #7	.286	105	30	3	0	1	6	3	24	.303	.343
Home	.250	248	62	8	2	3	16	8	33	.278	.335	Batting #8	.236	352	83	11	2	4	29	17	48	.276	.313
Away	.242	252	61	8	0	2	21	13	48	.281	.298	Other	.233	43	10	2	0	0	2	1	9	.250	.279
Day	.249	193	48	3	1	2	13	11	35	.291	.306	April	.247	89	22	2	0	2	7	6	10	.295	.337
Night	.244	307	75	13	1	3	24	10	46	.272	.322	May	.234	107	25	2	0	1	4	4	17	.272	.280
Grass	.197	127	25	2	0	2	9	7	31	.239	.260	June	.250	124	31	5	0	1	10	2	18	.262	.315
Turf	.263	373	98	14	2	3	28	14	50	.293	.335	July	.213	80	17	2	1	1	8	6	17	.264	.300

Last Five Years

	Avg	AB	H	2B	3B	HR	RBI	BB	SO	OBP	SLG		Avg	AB	H	2B	3B	HR	RBI	BB	SO	OBP	SLG
First Pitch	.389	113	44	5	0	0	11	4	0	.407	.434	August	.250	48	12	1	0	0	3	3	8	.308	.271
Ahead on Count	.200	90	18	2	1	1	3	7	0	.263	.278	September/October	.308	52	16	4	1	0	5	0	11	.308	.423
Behind on Count	.201	199	40	8	1	3	15	0	56	.205	.296	Pre-All Star	.232	354	82	9	0	4	22	14	53	.264	.291
Two Strikes	.170	176	30	8	0	3	10	9	81	.219	.267	Post-All Star	.281	146	41	7	2	1	15	7	28	.316	.377

Batter vs. Pitcher (since 1984)

Hits Best Against	Avg	AB	H	2B	3B	HR	RBI	BB	SO	OBP	SLG	Hits Worst Against	Avg	AB	H	2B	3B	HR	RBI	BB	SO	OBP	SLG
Zane Smith	.429	21	9	0	0	0	3	2	0	.478	.429	Bobby Ojeda	.083	24	2	0	0	1	3	2	1	.148	.208
Danny Jackson	.385	13	5	1	0	0	1	1	1	.429	.462	Tom Browning	.095	21	2	0	0	0	0	1	4	.136	.095
Neal Heaton	.333	12	4	0	0	0	1	0	1	.308	.333	Tom Glavine	.125	16	2	2	0	0	1	1	3	.176	.250
Ron Darling	.308	13	4	0	0	0	3	0	3	.308	.308	Frank Viola	.182	11	2	0	0	0	0	0	1	.182	.182
												Jim Deshaies	.227	22	5	0	0	0	4	1	3	.261	.227

Tim Laker — Expos

Bats Right (groundball hitter)

	Avg	G	AB	R	H	2B	3B	HR	RBI	BB	SO	HBP	GDP	SB	CS	OBP	SLG	IBB	SH	SF	#Pit	#P/PA	GB	FB	G/F
1992 Season	.217	28	46	8	10	3	0	0	4	2	14	0	1	1	1	.250	.283	0	0	0	170	3.54	19	6	3.17

1992 Season

	Avg	AB	H	2B	3B	HR	RBI	BB	SO	OBP	SLG		Avg	AB	H	2B	3B	HR	RBI	BB	SO	OBP	SLG
vs. Left	.235	17	4	1	0	0	1	1	4	.278	.294	Scoring Posn	.111	9	1	0	0	0	4	1	2	.200	.111
vs. Right	.207	29	6	2	0	0	3	1	10	.233	.276	Close & Late	.222	9	2	0	0	0	2	1	2	.300	.222

Dennis Lamp — Pirates

Pitches Right (groundball pitcher)

	ERA	W	L	Sv	G	GS	IP	BB	SO	Avg	H	2B	3B	HR	RBI	OBP	SLG	GF	IR	IRS	Hld	SvOp	SB	CS	GB	FB	G/F
1992 Season	5.14	1	1	0	21	0	28.0	9	15	.292	33	3	1	3	14	.355	.416	2	14	7	3	1	2	2	50	30	1.67
Last Five Years	3.85	21	17	2	207	1	420.2	116	231	.269	435	74	11	28	227	.319	.380	19	257	100	25	7	58	12	732	396	1.85

1992 Season

	ERA	W	L	Sv	G	GS	IP	H	HR	BB	SO		Avg	AB	H	2B	3B	HR	RBI	BB	SO	OBP	SLG
Home	3.29	1	0	0	9	0	13.2	16	2	4	10	vs. Left	.280	50	14	1	0	2	7	7	4	.379	.420
Away	6.91	0	1	0	12	0	14.1	17	1	5	5	vs. Right	.302	63	19	2	1	1	7	2	11	.333	.413
Starter	0.00	0	0	0	0	0	0.0	0	0	0	0	Scoring Posn	.258	31	8	1	0	2	12	7	5	.395	.484
Reliever	5.14	1	1	0	21	0	28.0	33	3	9	15	Close & Late	.316	38	12	2	0	1	5	3	4	.381	.447
0 Days rest	8.10	0	1	0	6	0	6.2	8	1	3	2	None on/out	.200	25	5	0	0	0	0	1	2	.231	.200
1 or 2 Days rest	5.87	1	0	0	11	0	15.1	20	2	5	10	First Pitch	.350	20	7	2	0	2	7	4	0	.480	.750
3+ Days rest	0.00	0	0	0	4	0	6.0	5	0	1	3	Behind on Count	.190	21	4	0	0	1	4	1	0	.227	.333
Pre-All Star	5.14	1	1	0	21	0	28.0	33	3	9	15	Ahead on Count	.314	51	16	1	1	0	2	0	11	.314	.373
Post-All Star	0.00	0	0	0	0	0	0.0	0	0	0	0	Two Strikes	.282	39	11	0	0	0	1	4	15	.349	.282

Last Five Years

	ERA	W	L	Sv	G	GS	IP	H	HR	BB	SO		Avg	AB	H	2B	3B	HR	RBI	BB	SO	OBP	SLG
Home	4.13	14	6	2	106	1	226.2	247	16	64	116	vs. Left	.303	702	213	28	6	11	87	69	89	.367	.407
Away	3.53	7	11	0	101	0	194.0	188	12	52	115	vs. Right	.243	915	222	46	5	17	140	47	142	.282	.360
Day	4.55	5	8	2	74	0	154.1	166	8	41	82	Inning 1-6	.252	824	208	47	6	9	135	59	119	.303	.357
Night	3.45	16	9	0	133	1	266.1	269	20	75	149	Inning 7+	.286	793	227	27	5	19	92	57	112	.337	.405
Grass	3.99	18	15	2	174	1	365.0	375	25	103	203	None on	.248	850	211	39	6	15	15	45	131	.292	.361
Turf	2.91	3	2	0	33	0	55.2	60	3	13	28	Runners on	.292	767	224	35	5	13	212	71	100	.349	.402
April	2.97	2	1	0	22	0	39.1	36	2	12	22	Scoring Posn	.285	515	147	25	3	8	196	62	78	.356	.392
May	3.83	2	3	0	44	0	80.0	91	4	20	46	Close & Late	.290	283	82	11	1	7	34	25	36	.348	.410
June	3.84	2	4	0	34	0	72.2	74	7	25	40	None on/out	.245	363	89	17	2	5	5	21	48	.294	.344
July	4.41	7	1	0	36	0	85.2	83	5	20	37	vs. 1st Batr (relief)	.333	186	62	9	2	2	41	11	19	.366	.435
August	3.10	4	3	0	30	0	69.2	73	4	14	43	First Inning Pitched	.264	704	186	26	5	8	131	49	93	.311	.349
September/October	4.42	4	5	2	41	1	73.1	78	6	25	43	First 15 Pitches	.270	705	190	28	7	10	115	46	88	.313	.372
Starter	3.60	0	0	0	1	1	5.0	3	0	3	1	Pitch 16-30	.255	510	130	17	4	6	59	40	80	.316	.339
Reliever	3.85	21	17	2	206	0	415.2	432	28	113	230	Pitch 31-45	.278	273	76	20	0	8	29	20	42	.328	.440
0 Days rest	5.26	1	4	0	26	0	44.1	52	5	12	22	Pitch 46+	.302	129	39	9	0	4	24	10	21	.353	.465
1 or 2 Days rest	4.34	11	8	0	90	0	174.0	200	12	45	98	First Pitch	.303	238	72	13	1	7	50	20	0	.359	.454
3+ Days rest	3.10	9	5	2	90	0	197.1	180	11	56	110	Ahead on Count	.227	730	166	24	4	11	71	1	195	.232	.316
Pre-All Star	3.45	9	8	0	109	0	216.1	216	14	61	116	Behind on Count	.309	333	103	22	2	8	56	56	0	.407	.459
Post-All Star	4.27	12	9	2	98	0	204.1	219	14	55	115	Two Strikes	.216	684	148	22	4	8	69	40	231	.262	.295

Pitcher vs. Batter (since 1984)

Pitches Best Vs.	Avg	AB	H	2B	3B	HR	RBI	BB	SO	OBP	SLG	Pitches Worst Vs.	Avg	AB	H	2B	3B	HR	RBI	BB	SO	OBP	SLG
Mark McGwire	.000	15	0	0	0	0	0	1	3	.063	.000	Brett Butler	.700	10	7	1	0	0	2	2	0	.750	.800
Andy Allanson	.071	14	1	1	0	0	0	0	3	.071	.143	Dave Bergman	.600	10	6	1	0	0	2	2	0	.667	.700
Jose Canseco	.077	13	1	0	0	0	2	1	2	.143	.077	Wally Joyner	.583	12	7	0	1	0	0	2	1	.643	.750
Gary Pettis	.133	15	2	0	0	0	1	1	6	.188	.133	Junior Felix	.455	11	5	1	1	1	2	0	1	.455	1.000
Jesse Barfield	.154	13	2	0	0	0	2	0	4	.143	.154	Cecil Fielder	.364	11	4	1	0	2	2	1	2	.417	1.000

Tom Lampkin — Padres
Bats Left (groundball hitter)

	Avg	G	AB	R	H	2B	3B	HR	RBI	BB	SO	HBP	GDP	SB	CS	OBP	SLG	IBB	SH	SF	#Pit	#P/PA	GB	FB	G/F
1992 Season	.235	9	17	3	4	0	0	0	0	6	1	1	0	2	0	.458	.235	0	0	0	94	3.92	11	4	2.75
Career (1988-1992)	.204	77	142	11	29	3	2	1	7	14	13	1	2	3	2	.280	.275	1	0	0	560	3.57	69	35	1.97

1992 Season

	Avg	AB	H	2B	3B	HR	RBI	BB	SO	OBP	SLG		Avg	AB	H	2B	3B	HR	RBI	BB	SO	OBP	SLG
vs. Left	.000	2	0	0	0	0	0	0	0	.000	.000	Scoring Posn	.333	3	1	0	0	0	0	1	0	.500	.333
vs. Right	.267	15	4	0	0	0		6	1	.500	.267	Close & Late	.000	5	0	0	0	0	0	3	1	.444	.000

Les Lancaster — Tigers
Pitches Right

	ERA	W	L	Sv	G	GS	IP	BB	SO	Avg	H	2B	3B	HR	RBI	OBP	SLG	GF	IR	IRS	Hld	SvOp	SB	CS	GB	FB	G/F
1992 Season	6.33	3	4	0	41	1	86.2	51	35	.294	101	21	0	11	79	.386	.451	17	38	24	1	3	3	3	122	118	1.03
Last Five Years	3.97	29	24	22	246	21	510.0	189	294	.267	521	94	9	41	279	.331	.388	64	202	86	27	39	29	25	701	575	1.22

1992 Season

	ERA	W	L	Sv	G	GS	IP	H	HR	BB	SO		Avg	AB	H	2B	3B	HR	RBI	BB	SO	OBP	SLG
Home	5.47	1	2	0	22	1	54.1	55	4	31	17	vs. Left	.358	120	43	10	0	2	20	32	14	.490	.492
Away	7.79	2	2	0	19	0	32.1	46	7	20	18	vs. Right	.259	224	58	11	0	9	59	19	21	.321	.429
Starter	11.57	0	1	0	1	1	4.2	6	1	4	2	Scoring Posn	.322	115	37	7	0	6	68	22	13	.423	.539
Reliever	6.04	3	3	0	40	0	82.0	95	10	47	33	Close & Late	.372	43	16	2	0	2	15	7	6	.471	.558
0 Days rest	11.88	1	1	0	5	0	8.1	14	1	7	4	None on/out	.314	70	22	2	0	2	2	10	6	.400	.429
1 or 2 Days rest	6.19	1	2	0	17	0	36.1	41	4	28	16	First Pitch	.345	58	20	3	0	3	14	11	0	.443	.552
3+ Days rest	4.58	1	0	0	18	0	37.1	40	5	12	13	Behind on Count	.320	75	24	7	0	3	25	22	0	.465	.533
Pre-All Star	6.19	3	2	0	28	1	56.2	64	7	35	22	Ahead on Count	.278	144	40	6	0	3	26	0	29	.291	.382
Post-All Star	6.60	0	2	0	13	0	30.0	37	4	16	13	Two Strikes	.236	140	33	6	0	4	27	18	35	.333	.364

Last Five Years

	ERA	W	L	Sv	G	GS	IP	H	HR	BB	SO		Avg	AB	H	2B	3B	HR	RBI	BB	SO	OBP	SLG
Home	4.11	17	11	10	131	12	282.2	295	22	96	167	vs. Left	.274	945	259	52	3	13	100	124	134	.357	.377
Away	3.80	12	13	12	115	9	227.1	226	19	93	127	vs. Right	.261	1004	262	42	6	28	179	65	160	.305	.398
Day	4.08	17	13	14	129	13	264.2	274	23	93	179	Inning 1-6	.269	804	216	45	3	22	130	65	100	.321	.414
Night	3.85	12	11	8	117	8	245.1	247	18	96	115	Inning 7+	.266	1145	305	49	6	19	149	124	194	.338	.369
Grass	4.09	23	16	14	187	18	396.2	419	32	146	230	None on	.260	1054	274	50	5	20	20	83	169	.317	.374
Turf	3.56	6	8	8	59	3	111.1	102	9	43	64	Runners on	.276	895	247	44	4	21	259	106	125	.347	.404
April	5.66	3	4	1	37	0	62.0	65	7	32	28	Scoring Posn	.288	535	154	30	3	17	240	75	81	.364	.450
May	3.63	7	4	2	36	6	91.2	102	10	26	48	Close & Late	.292	521	152	18	2	11	79	60	89	.364	.397
June	3.19	6	3	5	45	6	104.1	99	4	49	59	None on/out	.258	457	118	17	3	8	33		70	.310	.361
July	5.07	8	5	4	45	7	108.1	119	9	34	61	vs. 1st Batr (relief)	.298	205	61	6	3	3	41	14	32	.339	.400
August	3.59	2	6	6	40	0	62.2	69	6	17	47	First Inning Pitched	.268	818	219	37	4	17	159	86	135	.332	.385
September/October	2.89	3	2	4	42	3	81.0	67	5	31	51	First 15 Pitches	.272	751	204	33	3	16	126	74	112	.333	.387
Starter	4.26	9	5	0	21	21	131.0	143	12	37	69	First Pitch 16-30	.260	511	133	25	2	10	64	48	97	.323	.376
Reliever	3.87	20	19	22	225	0	379.0	378	29	152	225	Pitch 31-45	.228	289	66	13	2	6	35	35	48	.309	.349
0 Days rest	3.88	6	7	4	50	0	65.0	69	4	26	54	Pitch 46+	.296	398	118	23	2	9	54	32	37	.355	.432
1 or 2 Days rest	4.52	12	9	15	114	0	197.1	215	16	90	122	First Pitch	.319	317	101	15	5	9	60	30	0	.374	.483
3+ Days rest	2.78	2	3	3	61	0	116.2	94	9	36	49	Ahead on Count	.200	847	169	29	2	9	79	1	243	.206	.270
Pre-All Star	4.26	18	14	10	136	14	295.2	307	25	123	157	Behind on Count	.361	391	141	23	1	12	76	82	0	.465	.517
Post-All Star	3.57	11	10	12	110	7	214.1	214	16	66	137	Two Strikes	.192	866	166	33	0	11	84	76	294	.260	.268

Pitcher vs. Batter (career)

Pitches Best Vs.	Avg	AB	H	2B	3B	HR	RBI	BB	SO	OBP	SLG	Pitches Worst Vs.	Avg	AB	H	2B	3B	HR	RBI	BB	SO	OBP	SLG
Alfredo Griffin	.000	7	0	0	0	0	0	4	1	.364	.000	Bobby Bonilla	.571	7	4	1	0	0	1	7	2	.733	.714
Jose Lind	.111	18	2	0	0	0	0	0	4	.111	.111	Thomas Howard	.545	11	6	4	0	1	3	0	2	.545	1.182
Steve Sax	.143	14	2	0	0	0	1	0	0	.143	.143	Chris James	.538	13	7	0	0	2	6	1	1	.571	1.000
Benito Santiago	.154	13	2	0	0	0	2	1	3	.214	.154	Darryl Strawberry	.429	21	9	1	1	2	4	4	4	.520	.857
Billy Hatcher	.167	12	2	0	0	0		0	2	.167	.167	Craig Biggio	.417	12	5	0	1	1	2	0	1	.385	.833

Bill Landrum — Expos
Pitches Right

	ERA	W	L	Sv	G	GS	IP	BB	SO	Avg	H	2B	3B	HR	RBI	OBP	SLG	GF	IR	IRS	Hld	SvOp	SB	CS	GB	FB	G/F
1992 Season	7.20	1	1	0	18	0	20.0	9	7	.325	27	4	1	3	12	.404	.506	6	3	1	2	0	4	1	37	21	1.76
Last Five Years	2.86	15	11	56	196	0	261.1	80	148	.253	251	27	9	14	110	.309	.341	90	127	40	10	67	27	8	392	271	1.45

1992 Season

	ERA	W	L	Sv	G	GS	IP	H	HR	BB	SO		Avg	AB	H	2B	3B	HR	RBI	BB	SO	OBP	SLG
Home	10.54	1	1	0	11	0	13.2	22	3	7	5	vs. Left	.341	44	15	3	0	3	8	3	5	.396	.614
Away	0.00	0	0	0	7	0	6.1	5	0	2	2	vs. Right	.308	39	12	1	1	0	4	6	2	.413	.385

Last Five Years

	ERA	W	L	Sv	G	GS	IP	H	HR	BB	SO		Avg	AB	H	2B	3B	HR	RBI	BB	SO	OBP	SLG
Home	3.02	8	6	27	99	0	128.0	119	4	37	70	vs. Left	.250	501	125	14	3	7	51	44	62	.310	.331
Away	2.70	7	5	29	97	0	133.1	132	10	43	78	vs. Right	.257	490	125	13	6	7	59	36	86	.308	.351
Day	4.01	3	5	12	56	0	76.1	74	5	25	49	Inning 1-6	.241	79	19	1	0	0	8	1	15	.295	.253
Night	2.38	12	6	44	140	0	185.0	177	9	55	99	Inning 7+	.254	912	232	26	9	14	102	79	133	.310	.349
Grass	3.09	6	2	16	54	0	75.2	67	9	18	43	None on	.259	525	136	13	5	8	8	26	77	.295	.349

Last Five Years

	ERA	W	L	Sv	G	GS	IP	H	HR	BB	SO		Avg	AB	H	2B	3B	HR	RBI	BB	SO	OBP	SLG
Turf	2.76	9	9	40	142	0	185.2	184	5	62	105	Runners on	.247	466	115	14	4	6	102	54	71	.323	.333
April	1.43	1	0	5	31	0	37.2	27	1	12	24	Scoring Posn	.253	288	73	12	3	1	91	46	42	.350	.326
May	2.63	3	2	11	41	0	54.2	51	3	12	27	Close & Late	.245	433	106	13	2	4	47	46	70	.315	.312
June	2.70	3	1	19	33	0	46.2	54	1	13	28	None on/out	.276	228	63	4	3	5	5	9	29	.307	.386
July	3.72	1	3	7	32	0	46.0	44	3	18	27	vs. 1st Batr (relief)	.282	181	51	4	3	4	16	11	19	.323	.403
August	2.86	2	4	8	33	0	44.0	40	3	14	28	First Inning Pitched	.244	676	165	14	6	8	76	48	106	.293	.318
September/October	3.90	5	1	6	26	0	32.1	35	3	11	14	First 15 Pitches	.245	645	158	16	6	8	62	40	99	.288	.326
Starter	0.00	0	0	0	0	0	0.0	0	0	0	0	Pitch 16-30	.276	268	74	9	1	4	34	29	36	.346	.362
Reliever	2.86	15	11	56	196	0	261.1	251	14	80	148	Pitch 31-45	.258	62	16	2	2	2	13	10	7	.370	.452
0 Days rest	2.88	2	1	17	37	0	40.2	38	0	17	19	Pitch 46+	.188	16	3	0	0	0	1	1	1	.235	.188
1 or 2 Days rest	2.55	6	8	28	92	0	130.2	127	9	39	75	First Pitch	.284	141	40	5	1	2	15	19	0	.377	.376
3+ Days rest	3.30	7	2	11	67	0	90.0	86	5	24	54	Ahead on Count	.193	441	85	10	1	5	42	0	137	.191	.254
Pre-All Star	2.26	8	4	38	113	0	151.1	142	7	43	87	Behind on Count	.318	233	74	7	3	3	31	37	0	.408	.412
Post-All Star	3.68	7	7	18	83	0	110.0	109	7	37	61	Two Strikes	.187	422	79	12	1	4	35	24	147	.229	.249

Pitcher vs. Batter (career)

Pitches Best Vs.	Avg	AB	H	2B	3B	HR	RBI	BB	SO	OBP	SLG	Pitches Worst Vs.	Avg	AB	H	2B	3B	HR	RBI	BB	SO	OBP	SLG
Tom Pagnozzi	.000	11	0	0	0	0	0	0	2	.000	.000	Dave Magadan	.714	7	5	0	0	0	0	4	0	.818	.714
Kevin Bass	.083	12	1	1	0	0	0	1	2	.154	.167	Billy Hatcher	.600	15	9	0	2	0	4	1	0	.625	.867
Gregg Jefferies	.083	12	1	1	0	0	0		3	.083	.167	Dave Martinez	.500	10	5	1	0	0	1	1	1	.545	.600
Ken Caminiti	.091	11	1	0	0	0	2	1	1	.167	.091	Kevin McReynolds	.467	15	7	1	0	0	4	0	1	.467	.533
Charlie Hayes	.091	11	1	0	0	0	0		2	.091	.091	Jerome Walton	.364	11	4	0	0	2	3	1	3	.417	.909

Mark Langston — Angels

Pitches Left

	ERA	W	L	Sv	G	GS	IP	BB	SO	Avg	H	2B	3B	HR	RBI	OBP	SLG	CG	ShO	Sup	QS	#P/S	SB	CS	GB	FB	G/F
1992 Season	3.66	13	14	0	32	32	229.0	74	174	.242	206	38	3	14	83	.305	.343	9	2	3.69	20	108	21	10	312	209	1.49
Last Five Years	3.40	73	64	0	168	168	1209.2	496	1022	.233	1031	190	23	105	445	.311	.358	38	11	4.03	111	114	92	72	1425	1296	1.10

1992 Season

	ERA	W	L	Sv	G	GS	IP	H	HR	BB	SO		Avg	AB	H	2B	3B	HR	RBI	BB	SO	OBP	SLG
Home	3.61	9	7	0	18	18	132.0	122	9	31	97	vs. Left	.173	110	19	4	1	2	12	9	21	.252	.282
Away	3.71	4	7	0	14	14	97.0	84	5	43	77	vs. Right	.252	742	187	34	2	12	71	65	153	.313	.352
Day	3.70	3	1	0	8	8	56.0	44	4	18	47	Inning 1-6	.250	675	169	32	2	9	69	57	136	.312	.344
Night	3.64	10	13	0	24	24	173.0	162	10	56	127	Inning 7+	.209	177	37	6	1	5	14	17	38	.278	.339
Grass	3.69	12	12	0	28	28	200.0	177	13	64	150	None on	.221	521	115	19	2	7	7	45	108	.288	.305
Turf	3.41	1	2	0	4	4	29.0	29	1	10	24	Runners on	.275	331	91	19	1	7	76	29	66	.332	.402
April	10.29	1	1	0	3	3	14.0	25	2	3	11	Scoring Posn	.282	170	48	11	0	2	64	20	40	.355	.382
May	2.53	4	1	0	6	6	46.1	34	4	15	32	Close & Late	.209	115	24	6	1	2	9	12	28	.283	.330
June	2.47	3	3	0	6	6	47.1	40	4	15	33	None on/out	.222	221	49	8	1	2	2	16	45	.283	.294
July	6.97	1	4	0	5	5	31.0	38	3	13	16	vs. 1st Batr (relief)	.000	0	0	0	0	0	0	0	0	.000	.000
August	2.90	3	2	0	6	6	40.1	30	1	16	31	First Inning Pitched	.276	127	35	4	0	3	18	17	24	.363	.378
September/October	2.52	1	3	0	6	6	50.0	39	0	12	51	First 75 Pitches	.245	588	144	24	1	8	57	48	116	.305	.330
Starter	3.66	13	14	0	32	32	229.0	206	14	74	174	Pitch 76-90	.279	104	29	8	0	3	14	11	23	.348	.442
Reliever	0.00	0	0	0	0	0	0.0	0	0	0	0	Pitch 91-105	.185	81	15	4	0	2	6	8	14	.267	.309
0-3 Days Rest	0.00	0	0	0	0	0	0.0	0	0	0	0	Pitch 106+	.228	79	18	2	2	1	6	7	21	.291	.342
4 Days Rest	2.85	10	9	0	21	21	161.1	125	8	48	119	Ahead on Count	.158	348	55	14	0	2	19	0	154	.165	.216
5+ Days Rest	5.59	3	5	0	11	11	67.2	81	6	26	55	Behind on Count	.331	245	81	9	2	6	34	37	1	.419	.457
Pre-All Star	4.02	8	7	0	17	17	116.1	113	10	39	79	Two Strikes	.138	355	49	15	1	3	21	35	173	.219	.211
Post-All Star	3.28	5	7	0	15	15	112.2	93	4	35	95												

Last Five Years

	ERA	W	L	Sv	G	GS	IP	H	HR	BB	SO		Avg	AB	H	2B	3B	HR	RBI	BB	SO	OBP	SLG
Home	3.70	37	32	0	86	86	627.2	549	64	239	539	vs. Left	.199	644	128	25	5	7	50	64	142	.276	.286
Away	3.08	36	32	0	82	82	582.0	482	41	257	483	vs. Right	.239	3780	903	165	18	98	395	432	880	.317	.370
Day	4.51	13	18	0	42	42	267.1	255	21	122	247	Inning 1-6	.231	3497	808	152	20	77	361	398	817	.311	.352
Night	3.08	60	46	0	126	126	942.1	776	84	374	775	Inning 7+	.241	927	223	38	3	28	84	98	205	.313	.379
Grass	3.40	46	43	0	112	112	794.0	670	68	324	653	None on	.228	2660	607	102	11	65	65	320	599	.313	.348
Turf	3.40	27	21	0	56	56	415.2	361	37	172	369	Runners on	.240	1764	424	88	12	40	380	176	423	.308	.372
April	4.29	8	9	0	23	23	153.0	151	17	57	142	Scoring Posn	.246	917	226	47	8	22	332	112	251	.323	.387
May	3.22	16	9	0	29	29	218.1	174	18	82	176	Close & Late	.235	490	115	23	1	13	51	51	112	.305	.365
June	3.07	12	12	0	27	27	199.1	180	19	83	173	None on/out	.227	1145	260	42	3	25	25	136	257	.311	.334
July	4.31	11	14	0	30	30	210.2	195	24	86	175	vs. 1st Batr (relief)	.000	0	0	0	0	0	0	0	0	.000	.000
August	3.88	12	10	0	29	29	197.1	170	18	96	143	First Inning Pitched	.237	574	136	24	1	15	67	83	136	.335	.361
September/October	2.03	14	10	0	30	30	231.0	161	9	92	213	First 75 Pitches	.226	2819	638	113	14	63	276	316	667	.306	.343
Starter	3.40	73	64	0	168	168	1209.2	1031	105	496	1022	Pitch 76-90	.268	557	149	32	3	16	69	64	117	.342	.422
Reliever	0.00	0	0	0	0	0	0.0	0	0	0	0	Pitch 91-105	.216	496	107	21	1	9	41	48	116	.268	.317
0-3 Days Rest	3.72	3	2	0	6	6	46.0	33	5	13	40	Pitch 106+	.248	552	137	24	5	17	59	68	122	.309	.402
4 Days Rest	3.36	43	30	0	106	106	776.1	657	70	334	659	First Pitch	.291	612	178	34	2	21	70	9	0	.302	.456
5+ Days Rest	3.44	27	20	0	56	56	387.1	341	30	149	323	Ahead on Count	.161	1974	318	63	7	19	129	0	849	.165	.229
Pre-All Star	3.64	40	34	0	89	89	633.1	563	60	258	538	Behind on Count	.337	1044	352	59	9	48	164	268	1	.471	.549
Post-All Star	3.14	33	30	0	79	79	576.1	468	45	238	484	Two Strikes	.147	2110	311	59	10	26	137	219	1021	.229	.222

Pitcher vs. Batter (career)																						
Pitches Best Vs.	Avg	AB	H	2B	3B	HR	RBI	BB	SO	OBP	SLG	Pitches Worst Vs.	Avg	AB	H	2B	3B	HR	RBI	BB	SO	OBP	SLG
Mel Hall	.000	11	0	0	0	0	0	0	4	.000	.000	Kevin McReynolds	.500	12	6	0	0	1	1	1	1	.538	.750
Scott Leius	.000	10	0	0	0	0	0	2	2	.167	.000	Bob Zupcic	.500	12	6	2	0	0	0	2	3	.571	.667
Keith Miller	.063	16	1	0	0	0	0	0	3	.063	.125	Kevin Mitchell	.467	15	7	2	0	1	4	0	2	.467	.800
Carlos Martinez	.077	13	1	0	0	0	0	0	3	.077	.077	Frank Thomas	.444	18	8	1	0	2	5	9	5	.630	.833
Jim Leyritz	.077	13	1	0	0	0	0	0	4	.077	.077	Danny Tartabull	.360	25	9	4	0	2	6	8	6	.515	.760

Ray Lankford — Cardinals   Bats Left

	Avg	G	AB	R	H	2B	3B	HR	RBI	BB	SO	HBP	GDP	SB	CS	OBP	SLG	IBB	SH	SF	#Pit	#P/PA	GB	FB	G/F
1992 Season	.293	153	598	87	175	40	6	20	86	72	147	5	6	42	24	.371	.480	6	2	5	2697	3.97	160	183	0.87
Career (1990-1992)	.274	343	1290	182	353	73	22	32	167	126	288	6	11	94	46	.339	.439	7	6	8	5569	3.89	410	364	1.13

1992 Season

	Avg	AB	H	2B	3B	HR	RBI	BB	SO	OBP	SLG		Avg	AB	H	2B	3B	HR	RBI	BB	SO	OBP	SLG
vs. Left	.255	216	55	11	2	4	32	27	61	.345	.380	Scoring Posn	.327	162	53	13	2	7	67	28	44	.421	.562
vs. Right	.314	382	120	29	4	16	54	45	86	.385	.537	Close & Late	.282	131	37	6	0	5	18	20	41	.381	.443
Groundball	.323	220	71	13	1	9	33	25	43	.395	.514	None on/out	.267	180	48	5	2	6	6	13	44	.316	.417
Flyball	.248	121	30	7	3	3	16	16	36	.340	.430	Batting #1	.288	236	68	10	3	5	19	30	55	.375	.419
Home	.309	314	97	18	3	13	54	35	70	.375	.510	Batting #3	.298	329	98	27	3	13	63	37	84	.367	.517
Away	.275	284	78	22	3	7	32	37	77	.366	.447	Other	.273	33	9	3	0	2	4	5	8	.368	.545
Day	.253	162	41	9	2	4	18	21	45	.342	.407	April	.270	89	24	2	1	2	4	14	20	.387	.382
Night	.307	436	134	31	4	16	68	51	102	.381	.507	May	.311	103	32	6	1	3	13	11	25	.377	.476
Grass	.291	151	44	13	2	3	17	20	39	.376	.464	June	.272	103	28	7	2	3	13	12	24	.345	.466
Turf	.293	447	131	27	4	17	69	52	108	.369	.485	July	.337	95	32	12	0	3	13	9	26	.394	.558
First Pitch	.379	58	22	5	2	3	12	6	0	.438	.690	August	.291	103	30	7	0	3	20	8	28	.342	.447
Ahead on Count	.339	124	42	8	2	5	22	36	0	.482	.556	September/October	.276	105	29	6	2	6	23	18	24	.381	.543
Behind on Count	.263	213	56	12	1	7	25	0	69	.269	.427	Pre-All Star	.287	328	94	20	4	9	35	41	77	.370	.454
Two Strikes	.209	301	63	16	1	7	30	30	147	.287	.339	Post-All Star	.300	270	81	20	2	11	51	31	70	.371	.511

1992 By Position

Position	Avg	AB	H	2B	3B	HR	RBI	BB	SO	OBP	SLG	G	GS	Innings	PO	A	E	DP	Fld Pct	Rng Fctr	In Zone	Zone Outs	Zone Rtg	MLB Zone
As cf	.293	597	175	40	6	20	86	72	146	.371	.481	153	151	1369.0	439	5	2	1	.996	2.92	515	424	823	824

Career (1990-1992)

	Avg	AB	H	2B	3B	HR	RBI	BB	SO	OBP	SLG		Avg	AB	H	2B	3B	HR	RBI	BB	SO	OBP	SLG
vs. Left	.252	481	121	25	10	4	59	47	121	.323	.370	Scoring Posn	.305	328	100	20	11	9	131	47	74	.389	.515
vs. Right	.287	809	232	48	12	28	108	79	167	.349	.480	Close & Late	.273	242	66	8	2	6	33	29	86	.355	.397
Groundball	.315	432	136	23	5	15	59	41	82	.377	.495	None on/out	.257	377	97	12	4	10	10	24	90	.302	.390
Flyball	.247	291	72	15	10	5	38	25	77	.308	.419	Batting #1	.269	557	150	26	10	13	60	53	130	.337	.422
Home	.273	640	175	31	14	19	93	65	132	.339	.455	Batting #3	.286	601	172	39	11	17	95	58	128	.348	.473
Away	.274	650	178	42	8	13	74	61	156	.339	.423	Other	.235	132	31	8	1	2	12	15	30	.311	.356
Day	.245	343	84	22	6	9	39	40	74	.325	.423	April	.264	144	38	3	3	2	7	18	26	.358	.368
Night	.284	947	269	51	16	23	128	86	214	.345	.445	May	.278	198	55	11	1	3	23	13	38	.322	.389
Grass	.290	334	97	25	5	6	45	31	76	.351	.449	June	.262	195	51	10	6	3	25	22	40	.336	.421
Turf	.268	956	256	48	17	26	122	95	212	.335	.435	July	.303	175	53	14	2	5	26	15	44	.354	.491
First Pitch	.348	135	47	10	5	4	23	7	0	.385	.585	August	.252	258	65	15	5	4	35	15	68	.293	.395
Ahead on Count	.339	274	93	19	7	13	57	65	0	.462	.602	September/October	.284	320	91	20	5	15	51	43	72	.369	.519
Behind on Count	.221	443	98	22	3	10	41	0	153	.224	.352	Pre-All Star	.266	594	158	29	10	10	62	57	120	.333	.399
Two Strikes	.201	647	130	28	6	9	54	54	288	.264	.304	Post-All Star	.280	696	195	44	12	22	105	69	168	.344	.473

Batter vs. Pitcher (career)

Hits Best Against	Avg	AB	H	2B	3B	HR	RBI	BB	SO	OBP	SLG	Hits Worst Against	Avg	AB	H	2B	3B	HR	RBI	BB	SO	OBP	SLG
Paul Assenmacher	.545	11	6	2	0	0	3	3	1	.643	.727	Bruce Ruffin	.111	9	1	0	0	0	0	2	2	.273	.111
Kevin Gross	.462	13	6	3	0	1	4	0	2	.462	.923	Randy Tomlin	.125	16	2	1	0	0	0	0	5	.125	.188
Darryl Kile	.455	11	5	2	0	1	3	2	1	.538	.909	Frank Castillo	.125	16	2	1	0	0	0	0	5	.125	.188
Tommy Greene	.389	18	7	2	1	2	5	1	2	.421	.944	Bobby Ojeda	.188	16	3	0	0	0	1	0	7	.188	.188
Ken Hill	.357	14	5	1	0	2	3	3	2	.471	.857	Zane Smith	.188	16	3	0	0	0	1	0	5	.235	.188

Carney Lansford — Athletics   Bats Right (groundball hitter)

	Avg	G	AB	R	H	2B	3B	HR	RBI	BB	SO	HBP	GDP	SB	CS	OBP	SLG	IBB	SH	SF	#Pit	#P/PA	GB	FB	G/F
1992 Season	.262	135	496	65	130	30	1	7	75	43	39	7	14	7	2	.325	.369	0	7	8	1871	3.38	206	166	1.24
Last Five Years	.266	572	2126	284	607	93	6	19	235	174	151	29	62	69	39	.345	.362	10	15	20	7426	3.16	942	621	1.52

1992 Season

	Avg	AB	H	2B	3B	HR	RBI	BB	SO	OBP	SLG		Avg	AB	H	2B	3B	HR	RBI	BB	SO	OBP	SLG
vs. Left	.280	132	37	12	0	1	17	11	8	.342	.394	Scoring Posn	.265	147	39	10	0	4	67	20	13	.337	.415
vs. Right	.255	364	93	18	1	6	58	32	31	.319	.360	Close & Late	.246	65	16	2	0	2	14	7	6	.329	.369
Groundball	.273	121	33	7	1	1	20	8	10	.313	.372	None on/out	.204	98	20	4	0	0	0	4	6	.243	.245
Flyball	.246	134	33	13	0	3	19	12	14	.318	.410	Batting #2	.271	280	76	13	1	6	44	21	23	.324	.389
Home	.234	218	51	13	1	4	33	19	22	.301	.358	Batting #6	.232	69	16	4	0	0	10	7	5	.308	.290
Away	.284	278	79	17	0	3	42	24	17	.344	.378	Other	.259	147	38	13	0	1	21	15	11	.335	.367
Day	.288	160	46	16	1	2	25	12	13	.339	.438	April	.364	77	28	9	0	0	11	9	4	.432	.481

1992 Season

	Avg	AB	H	2B	3B	HR	RBI	BB	SO	OBP	SLG		Avg	AB	H	2B	3B	HR	RBI	BB	SO	OBP	SLG
Night	.250	336	84	14	0	5	50	31	26	.318	.336	May	.217	92	20	3	0	0	12	5	8	.253	.250
Grass	.263	410	108	26	1	6	65	37	31	.328	.376	June	.239	88	21	4	1	1	9	6	8	.292	.341
Turf	.256	86	22	4	0	1	10	6	8	.309	.337	July	.262	84	22	5	0	1	9	6	6	.312	.357
First Pitch	.209	110	23	5	0	0	6	0	0	.235	.255	August	.284	74	21	7	0	5	23	7	4	.361	.581
Ahead on Count	.267	146	39	13	1	0	22	20	1	.349	.370	September/October	.222	81	18	2	0	0	11	10	9	.316	.247
Behind on Count	.267	131	35	7	0	2	19	0	19	.278	.366	Pre-All Star	.258	287	74	17	1	1	34	23	22	.313	.334
Two Strikes	.260	150	39	10	0	6	35	23	38	.362	.447	Post-All Star	.268	209	56	13	0	6	41	20	17	.340	.416

1992 By Position

Position	Avg	AB	H	2B	3B	HR	RBI	BB	SO	OBP	SLG	G	GS	Innings	PO	A	E	DP	Fld Pct	Rng Fctr	In Zone	Outs	Zone Rtg	MLB Zone
As 1b	.245	53	13	4	0	1	6	5	4	.333	.377	18	14	126.0	112	5	2	13	.983	---	24	18	.750	.843
As 3b	.265	437	116	25	1	6	69	38	33	.326	.368	119	112	963.1	86	159	9	8	.965	2.29	216	183	.847	.841

Last Five Years

	Avg	AB	H	2B	3B	HR	RBI	BB	SO	OBP	SLG		Avg	AB	H	2B	3B	HR	RBI	BB	SO	OBP	SLG
vs. Left	.297	562	167	30	3	3	52	61	33	.367	.377	Scoring Posn	.262	549	155	23	1	5	210	72	42	.360	.355
vs. Right	.281	1564	440	63	3	16	183	113	118	.337	.356	Close & Late	.234	303	71	10	0	2	30	33	22	.313	.287
Groundball	.286	567	162	24	1	4	70	46	43	.344	.353	None on/out	.295	488	144	25	3	6	6	28	28	.340	.395
Flyball	.265	514	136	29	3	4	46	44	48	.332	.356	Batting #1	.330	348	115	15	2	3	36	17	19	.368	.411
Home	.269	980	264	39	4	7	110	85	73	.334	.337	Batting #2	.304	993	302	38	2	12	127	75	68	.355	.383
Away	.299	1146	343	54	3	12	125	89	78	.354	.383	Other	.242	785	190	40	2	4	72	82	64	.322	.313
Day	.311	753	234	44	4	5	90	74	48	.374	.400	April	.325	345	112	29	2	4	43	24	14	.378	.455
Night	.272	1373	373	49	2	14	145	100	103	.328	.341	May	.351	404	142	21	1	2	47	34	25	.401	.423
Grass	.283	1815	514	78	4	17	213	144	127	.341	.359	June	.223	346	77	8	1	3	26	29	27	.290	277
Turf	.299	311	93	15	2	2	22	30	24	.368	.379	July	.251	338	85	9	0	3	32	26	27	.305	.305
First Pitch	.283	516	146	22	2	3	38	0	0	.294	.351	August	.300	373	112	16	1	7	55	28	25	.355	.405
Ahead on Count	.297	602	179	36	2	6	75	93	1	.387	.394	September/October	.247	320	79	10	1	0	32	33	33	.329	.284
Behind on Count	.255	580	148	25	0	4	67	1	71	.266	.319	Pre-All Star	.298	1229	366	60	4	10	124	97	78	.354	.378
Two Strikes	.245	592	145	20	2	8	76	76	150	.339	.326	Post-All Star	.269	897	241	33	2	9	111	77	73	.333	.340

Batter vs. Pitcher (since 1984)

Hits Best Against	Avg	AB	H	2B	3B	HR	RBI	BB	SO	OBP	SLG	Hits Worst Against	Avg	AB	H	2B	3B	HR	RBI	BB	SO	OBP	SLG
Neal Heaton	.647	17	11	0	0	0	1	0	0	.667	.647	Mike Henneman	.000	11	0	0	0	0	0	0	0	.000	.000
Scott Bankhead	.500	24	12	1	0	1	2	2	3	.538	.667	Edwin Nunez	.091	11	1	1	0	0	0	0	1	.091	.182
Alex Fernandez	.500	8	4	1	0	0	0	4	1	.667	.625	Kevin Brown	.133	15	2	0	0	0	1	0	2	.188	.133
Mark Williamson	.467	15	7	3	0	0	3	1	0	.500	.667	Jeff M. Robinson	.143	28	4	0	0	0	5	0	4	.138	.143
Mike Boddicker	.412	51	21	3	0	4	8	4	2	.455	.706	Tim Leary	.188	16	3	0	0	0	3	0	1	.167	.188

Barry Larkin — Reds

Bats Right (groundball hitter)

	Avg	G	AB	R	H	2B	3B	HR	RBI	BB	SO	HBP	GDP	SB	CS	OBP	SLG	IBB	SH	SF	#Pit	#P/PA	GB	FB	G/F
1992 Season	.304	140	533	76	162	32	6	12	78	63	58	4	13	15	4	.377	.454	8	2	7	2206	3.63	230	153	1.50
Last Five Years	.306	669	2524	387	772	130	25	55	306	228	218	24	48	119	27	.365	.443	20	24	26	10082	3.60	1121	741	1.51

1992 Season

	Avg	AB	H	2B	3B	HR	RBI	BB	SO	OBP	SLG		Avg	AB	H	2B	3B	HR	RBI	BB	SO	OBP	SLG
vs. Left	.355	200	71	20	4	6	29	33	18	.443	.585	Scoring Posn	.340	144	49	8	1	2	65	27	17	.430	.451
vs. Right	.273	333	91	12	2	6	49	30	40	.336	.375	Close & Late	.291	79	23	3	2	0	11	12	12	.380	.380
Groundball	.306	193	59	7	5	5	28	17	22	.357	.472	None on/out	.267	101	27	0	3	4	4	10	13	.339	.446
Flyball	.322	115	37	11	1	0	8	17	14	.410	.435	Batting #2	.286	63	18	2	1	0	4	5	9	.348	.349
Home	.307	254	78	14	2	8	53	34	29	.389	.472	Batting #3	.306	470	144	30	5	12	74	58	49	.381	.468
Away	.301	279	84	18	4	4	25	29	29	.366	.437	Other	.000	0	0	0	0	0	0	0	0	.000	.000
Day	.254	169	43	6	4	4	25	24	21	.345	.408	April	.179	39	7	0	1	1	5	6	6	.319	.308
Night	.327	364	119	26	2	8	53	39	37	.393	.475	May	.302	86	26	5	0	1	9	5	14	.341	.395
Grass	.247	154	38	8	2	2	12	13	17	.304	.364	June	.243	103	25	6	0	2	16	10	13	.307	.359
Turf	.327	379	124	24	4	10	66	50	41	.405	.491	July	.389	95	37	9	2	3	14	13	9	.464	.621
First Pitch	.329	70	23	1	2	1	13	9	0	.400	.443	August	.339	109	37	8	1	3	16	21	7	.443	.514
Ahead on Count	.346	130	45	9	2	5	23	44	0	.511	.562	September/October	.297	101	30	4	2	2	18	8	9	.339	.436
Behind on Count	.251	175	44	9	2	4	21	0	29	.249	.394	Pre-All Star	.287	268	77	18	3	4	37	28	35	.359	.422
Two Strikes	.250	232	58	12	2	4	24	10	58	.279	.371	Post-All Star	.321	265	85	14	3	8	41	35	23	.395	.487

1992 By Position

Position	Avg	AB	H	2B	3B	HR	RBI	BB	SO	OBP	SLG	G	GS	Innings	PO	A	E	DP	Fld Pct	Rng Fctr	In Zone	Outs	Zone Rtg	MLB Zone
As ss	.304	533	162	32	6	12	78	63	58	.377	.454	140	140	1207.2	232	405	11	69	.983	4.75	458	407	.889	.885

Last Five Years

	Avg	AB	H	2B	3B	HR	RBI	BB	SO	OBP	SLG		Avg	AB	H	2B	3B	HR	RBI	BB	SO	OBP	SLG
vs. Left	.330	804	265	54	12	25	108	112	50	.410	.520	Scoring Posn	.315	593	187	24	9	10	243	89	62	.392	.437
vs. Right	.295	1720	507	76	13	30	198	116	168	.343	.406	Close & Late	.304	404	123	16	6	4	52	42	46	.370	.403
Groundball	.299	909	272	46	11	12	102	71	81	.351	.414	None on/out	.288	650	187	29	6	16	16	43	53	.340	.425
Flyball	.291	525	153	26	6	14	67	55	49	.361	.444	Batting #2	.302	679	205	29	5	17	67	46	45	.353	.434
Home	.309	1241	383	64	11	38	186	122	111	.373	.488	Batting #3	.317	1353	429	72	16	24	192	140	125	.381	.447
Away	.303	1283	389	66	14	17	120	106	107	.358	.416	Other	.280	492	138	29	4	14	47	42	48	.340	.441

250

Last Five Years

	Avg	AB	H	2B	3B	HR	RBI	BB	SO	OBP	SLG		Avg	AB	H	2B	3B	HR	RBI	BB	SO	OBP	SLG
Day	.284	721	205	25	5	15	80	71	64	.352	.395	April	.286	346	99	10	4	9	42	25	33	.344	.416
Night	.314	1803	567	105	20	40	226	157	154	.371	.461	May	.328	403	132	18	6	5	50	32	37	.378	.439
Grass	.287	748	215	40	6	8	66	49	65	.334	.389	June	.314	525	165	25	1	18	76	48	50	.372	.469
Turf	.314	1776	557	90	19	47	240	179	153	.378	.465	July	.299	395	118	30	3	9	34	41	35	.370	.458
First Pitch	.335	260	87	11	3	4	34	13	0	.367	.446	August	.290	452	131	28	8	7	55	48	34	.359	.434
Ahead on Count	.338	701	237	40	7	24	101	158	0	.460	.518	September/October	.315	403	127	19	3	7	49	34	29	.366	.429
Behind on Count	.272	838	228	38	9	12	78	0	117	.279	.382	Pre-All Star	.307	1426	438	64	13	36	180	122	129	.366	.446
Two Strikes	.254	1012	257	36	9	17	105	49	215	.291	.358	Post-All Star	.304	1098	334	66	12	19	126	106	89	.365	.438

Batter vs. Pitcher (career)

Hits Best Against	Avg	AB	H	2B	3B	HR	RBI	BB	SO	OBP	SLG	Hits Worst Against	Avg	AB	H	2B	3B	HR	RBI	BB	SO	OBP	SLG
Zane Smith	.447	38	17	2	0	3	8	2	2	.463	.737	Marvin Freeman	.000	13	0	0	0	0	1	0	0	.000	.000
Jim Deshaies	.444	36	16	2	0	5	8	2	2	.474	.917	Mark Portugal	.071	14	1	0	0	0	0	0	2	.071	.071
Joe Magrane	.429	14	6	1	1	0	4	4	1	.556	.643	Jeff Brantley	.083	12	1	0	0	0	0	0	1	.083	.083
Ken Hill	.412	17	7	1	1	1	2	2	2	.474	.765	Bruce Ruffin	.143	21	3	0	0	0	0	2	3	.217	.143
Brian Barnes	.333	9	3	0	0	1	3	4	0	.538	.667	Tim Burke	.154	13	2	0	0	0	2	0	0	.154	.154

Gene Larkin — Twins

Bats Both

	Avg	G	AB	R	H	2B	3B	HR	RBI	BB	SO	HBP	GDP	SB	CS	OBP	SLG	IBB	SH	SF	#Pit	#P/PA	GB	FB	G/F
1992 Season	.246	115	337	38	83	18	1	6	42	28	43	4	7	7	2	.308	.359	6	0	4	1290	3.46	107	129	0.83
Last Five Years	.266	617	1944	235	518	113	9	27	219	222	231	34	48	22	12	.348	.376	25	14	21	7833	3.53	700	644	1.09

1992 Season

	Avg	AB	H	2B	3B	HR	RBI	BB	SO	OBP	SLG		Avg	AB	H	2B	3B	HR	RBI	BB	SO	OBP	SLG
vs. Left	.218	55	12	6	0	0	5	6	8	.295	.327	Scoring Posn	.284	95	27	5	0	1	32	11	15	.357	.368
vs. Right	.252	282	71	12	1	6	37	22	35	.311	.365	Close & Late	.302	63	19	7	0	0	10	8	12	.389	.413
Groundball	.305	95	29	5	1	1	12	5	14	.347	.411	None on/out	.213	80	17	7	0	0	0	4	7	.259	.300
Flyball	.191	89	17	5	0	2	7	11	10	.282	.315	Batting #6	.242	95	23	3	0	4	17	12	10	.327	.400
Home	.261	153	40	9	0	5	20	16	18	.326	.418	Batting #7	.245	159	39	7	1	2	15	12	16	.301	.340
Away	.234	184	43	9	1	1	22	12	25	.294	.310	Other	.253	83	21	8	0	0	10	4	17	.300	.349
Day	.253	95	24	6	1	3	12	10	8	.324	.432	April	.221	68	15	5	0	3	12	5	6	.270	.426
Night	.244	242	59	12	0	3	30	18	35	.302	.331	May	.351	37	13	1	0	1	9	7	8	.478	.459
Grass	.244	135	33	7	1	0	13	9	20	.306	.311	June	.250	60	15	2	0	0	5	4	8	.313	.283
Turf	.248	202	50	11	0	6	29	19	23	.310	.391	July	.213	47	10	1	0	1	2	5	4	.288	.298
First Pitch	.356	45	16	3	0	1	5	4	0	.408	.489	August	.235	51	12	5	1	0	3	6	7	.316	.373
Ahead on Count	.327	104	34	10	1	4	17	13	0	.398	.558	September/October	.243	74	18	4	0	1	11	1	10	.247	.338
Behind on Count	.178	118	21	3	0	2	13	0	24	.187	.254	Pre-All Star	.254	181	46	9	0	5	27	20	24	.338	.387
Two Strikes	.193	119	23	4	0	1	13	12	43	.271	.252	Post-All Star	.237	156	37	9	1	1	15	8	19	.271	.327

1992 By Position

Position	Avg	AB	H	2B	3B	HR	RBI	BB	SO	OBP	SLG	G	GS	Innings	PO	A	E	DP	Fld Pct	Rng Fctr	In Zone	Outs	Zone Rtg	MLB Zone
As Pinch Hitter	.333	24	8	3	0	0	5	2	3	.385	.458	26	0	---	---	---	---	---	---	---	---	---	---	---
As 1b	.222	180	40	10	0	4	25	14	22	.274	.344	55	48	431.2	456	29	4	50	.992	---	71	59	.831	.843
As rf	.283	120	34	5	1	2	12	10	16	.351	.392	43	34	286.0	53	5	1	1	.983	1.83	69	53	.768	.814

Last Five Years

	Avg	AB	H	2B	3B	HR	RBI	BB	SO	OBP	SLG		Avg	AB	H	2B	3B	HR	RBI	BB	SO	OBP	SLG
vs. Left	.296	568	168	43	4	4	67	61	56	.369	.407	Scoring Posn	.250	543	136	31	4	9	187	78	81	.347	.372
vs. Right	.254	1376	350	70	5	23	152	161	175	.340	.363	Close & Late	.264	318	84	18	1	2	38	37	45	.352	.346
Groundball	.268	530	142	30	4	3	59	59	53	.348	.357	None on/out	.281	441	124	27	3	3	3	45	48	.358	.376
Flyball	.256	442	113	29	3	11	61	58	45	.350	.410	Batting #6	.283	523	148	31	1	13	60	65	59	.370	.421
Home	.279	976	272	59	3	18	124	114	100	.358	.401	Batting #7	.263	567	149	27	1	5	52	57	66	.336	.340
Away	.254	968	246	54	6	9	95	108	131	.339	.350	Other	.259	854	221	55	7	9	107	100	106	.344	.371
Day	.292	606	177	42	5	7	56	83	57	.381	.413	April	.289	291	84	27	1	4	36	23	28	.351	.430
Night	.255	1338	341	71	4	20	163	139	174	.334	.359	May	.259	344	89	19	0	6	49	45	47	.356	.366
Grass	.257	738	190	42	5	8	74	84	102	.342	.360	June	.255	353	90	15	1	3	35	38	55	.336	.329
Turf	.272	1206	328	71	4	19	145	138	129	.352	.385	July	.282	284	80	11	3	2	21	40	33	.378	.363
First Pitch	.314	293	92	21	1	5	35	11	0	.341	.444	August	.279	323	90	17	3	6	39	39	32	.362	.406
Ahead on Count	.330	551	182	52	2	12	83	109	0	.437	.497	September/October	.244	349	85	24	1	6	39	37	36	.314	.370
Behind on Count	.211	617	130	23	0	3	48	2	121	.226	.263	Pre-All Star	.269	1095	295	67	3	14	129	122	143	.353	.374
Two Strikes	.190	690	131	16	3	6	60	97	230	.301	.248	Post-All Star	.263	849	223	46	6	13	90	100	88	.343	.377

Batter vs. Pitcher (career)

Hits Best Against	Avg	AB	H	2B	3B	HR	RBI	BB	SO	OBP	SLG	Hits Worst Against	Avg	AB	H	2B	3B	HR	RBI	BB	SO	OBP	SLG
Doug Jones	.556	9	5	0	0	0	3	2	0	.636	.556	Jeff Montgomery	.000	11	0	0	0	0	0	1	4	.083	.000
Bud Black	.529	17	9	1	0	1	2	1	1	.556	.765	Tom Henke	.000	8	0	0	0	0	0	3	1	273	.000
Tim Leary	.500	10	5	1	0	1	4	1	2	.545	.900	Greg Harris	.077	13	1	0	0	0	0	1	2	.143	.077
Bill Krueger	.400	10	4	2	0	0	1	2	0	.500	.600	Gene Nelson	.100	10	1	0	0	0	0	1	2	.182	.100
Melido Perez	.333	21	7	0	1	2	8	4	4	.423	.714	Ben McDonald	.100	10	1	0	0	0	0	1	3	.182	.100

Mike LaValliere — Pirates

Bats Left

	Avg	G	AB	R	H	2B	3B	HR	RBI	BB	SO	HBP	GDP	SB	CS	OBP	SLG	IBB	SH	SF	#Pit	#P/PA	GB	FB	G/F
1992 Season	.256	95	293	22	75	13	1	2	29	44	21	1	8	0	3	.350	.328	14	0	5	1161	3.38	123	95	1.29
Last Five Years	.273	487	1450	113	396	67	3	12	171	200	126	7	36	5	11	.361	.348	43	10	15	5806	3.47	576	474	1.22

1992 Season

	Avg	AB	H	2B	3B	HR	RBI	BB	SO	OBP	SLG		Avg	AB	H	2B	3B	HR	RBI	BB	SO	OBP	SLG
vs. Left	.161	31	5	0	1	0	5	5	5	.297	.226	Scoring Posn	.254	71	18	4	1	0	25	21	7	.408	.338
vs. Right	.267	262	70	13	0	2	24	39	16	.356	.340	Close & Late	.234	47	11	2	0	0	5	15	4	.419	.277
Groundball	.248	109	27	5	1	0	8	19	6	.354	.312	None on/out	.286	63	18	3	0	0	0	8	4	.366	.333
Flyball	.246	65	16	2	0	2	11	6	5	.311	.369	Batting #5	.286	14	4	0	0	1	4	3	1	.389	.500
Home	.259	135	35	2	1	1	16	26	12	.373	.311	Batting #7	.255	259	66	12	1	1	25	39	19	.350	.320
Away	.253	158	40	11	0	1	13	18	9	.328	.342	Other	.250	20	5	1	0	0	0	2	1	.318	.300
Day	.299	87	26	4	1	1	12	8	7	.354	.402	April	.308	39	12	2	1	0	4	5	4	.378	.410
Night	.238	206	49	9	0	1	17	36	14	.348	.296	May	.220	41	9	1	0	0	1	11	2	.385	.244
Grass	.300	70	21	6	0	1	6	10	5	.388	.429	June	.196	56	11	3	0	1	9	8	5	.284	.304
Turf	.242	223	54	7	1	1	23	34	16	.338	.296	July	.286	56	16	2	0	0	1	5	4	.344	.321
First Pitch	.281	57	16	3	1	0	6	12	0	.406	.368	August	.370	46	17	4	0	1	10	6	3	.434	.522
Ahead on Count	.264	72	19	3	0	0	5	23	0	.438	.306	September/October	.182	55	10	1	0	0	4	9	3	.308	.200
Behind on Count	.181	83	15	2	0	0	8	0	12	.179	.205	Pre-All Star	.236	157	37	6	1	1	14	26	13	.337	.306
Two Strikes	.196	102	20	3	0	1	13	10	21	.267	.255	Post-All Star	.279	136	38	7	0	1	15	18	8	.365	.353

1992 By Position

Position	Avg	AB	H	2B	3B	HR	RBI	BB	SO	OBP	SLG	G	GS	Innings	PO	A	E	DP	Fld Pct	Rng Fctr	In Zone	Outs	Zone Rtg	MLB Zone
As c	.257	292	75	13	1	2	29	43	20	.349	.329	92	87	767.0	421	62	3	7	.994	---	---	---	---	---

Last Five Years

	Avg	AB	H	2B	3B	HR	RBI	BB	SO	OBP	SLG		Avg	AB	H	2B	3B	HR	RBI	BB	SO	OBP	SLG
vs. Left	.240	229	55	8	2	2	35	31	41	.340	.319	Scoring Posn	.285	379	108	26	3	6	163	88	35	.409	.417
vs. Right	.279	1221	341	59	1	10	136	169	85	.365	.354	Close & Late	.238	210	50	14	0	1	31	44	28	.372	.319
Groundball	.264	518	137	22	2	3	58	70	44	.352	.332	None on/out	.278	370	103	22	0	0	0	42	28	.357	.338
Flyball	.272	302	82	14	1	5	39	47	28	.368	.374	Batting #6	.255	110	28	3	0	1	6	12	9	.328	.309
Home	.295	701	207	30	2	6	89	106	58	.387	.369	Batting #7	.274	1272	348	62	3	10	154	180	110	.363	.351
Away	.252	749	189	37	1	6	82	94	68	.335	.328	Other	.294	68	20	2	0	1	11	8	7	.359	.368
Day	.289	436	126	20	1	3	56	56	40	.369	.360	April	.282	206	58	9	1	1	34	28	10	.366	.350
Night	.266	1014	270	47	2	9	115	144	86	.357	.343	May	.278	187	52	6	1	1	20	37	15	.390	.337
Grass	.254	382	97	18	0	5	39	45	33	.335	.340	June	.228	206	47	11	0	2	19	30	14	.324	.311
Turf	.280	1068	299	49	3	7	132	155	93	.370	.351	July	.297	279	83	13	0	2	29	34	27	.380	.366
First Pitch	.275	269	74	13	2	2	27	19	0	.325	.361	August	.278	281	78	15	0	4	36	36	34	.357	.374
Ahead on Count	.307	365	112	20	0	4	46	122	0	.479	.395	September/October	.268	291	78	13	1	2	33	35	26	.348	.340
Behind on Count	.233	416	97	14	0	2	41	2	71	.238	.281	Pre-All Star	.274	694	190	31	2	5	83	109	49	.370	.346
Two Strikes	.239	515	123	15	1	2	58	51	126	.307	.283	Post-All Star	.272	756	206	36	1	7	88	91	77	.352	.351

Batter vs. Pitcher (career)

Hits Best Against	Avg	AB	H	2B	3B	HR	RBI	BB	SO	OBP	SLG	Hits Worst Against	Avg	AB	H	2B	3B	HR	RBI	BB	SO	OBP	SLG
John Smoltz	.550	20	11	2	0	1	3	5	0	.640	.800	Bob Welch	.083	12	1	0	0	0	1	1	0	.154	.083
Omar Olivares	.545	11	6	0	0	0	1	2	0	.615	.545	Frank DiPino	.111	18	2	1	0	0	2	0	4	.111	.167
Frank Castillo	.500	16	8	1	0	0	1	2	0	.556	.563	Bob Tewksbury	.138	29	4	1	0	0	1	1	1	.167	.172
Kelly Downs	.478	23	11	3	0	0	3	5	1	.571	.609	Danny Cox	.154	13	2	0	0	0	1	1	2	.214	.154
Jack Armstrong	.444	9	4	0	0	0	0	3	0	.583	.444	Pete Harnisch	.182	11	2	0	0	0	0	1	1	.250	.182

Terry Leach — White Sox

Pitches Right (groundball pitcher)

	ERA	W	L	Sv	G	GS	IP	BB	SO	Avg	H	2B	3B	HR	RBI	OBP	SLG	GF	IR	IRS	Hld	SvOp	SB	CS	GB	FB	G/F
1992 Season	1.95	6	5	0	51	0	73.2	20	22	.215	57	9	3	2	23	.279	.294	21	35	11	6	0	7	3	112	76	1.47
Last Five Years	3.12	21	20	5	248	3	409.2	119	187	.265	415	79	9	17	191	.319	.360	72	203	67	18	12	48	11	673	411	1.54

1992 Season

	ERA	W	L	Sv	G	GS	IP	H	HR	BB	SO		Avg	AB	H	2B	3B	HR	RBI	BB	SO	OBP	SLG
Home	0.84	3	0	0	23	0	32.0	17	0	5	13	vs. Left	.263	99	26	3	1	0	6	11	3	.333	.313
Away	2.81	3	5	0	28	0	41.2	40	2	15	9	vs. Right	.187	166	31	6	2	2	17	9	19	.246	.283
Starter	0.00	0	0	0	0	0	0.0	0	0	0	0	Scoring Posn	.200	65	13	1	1	1	20	10	4	.303	.292
Reliever	1.95	6	5	0	51	0	73.2	57	2	20	22	Close & Late	.272	114	31	3	3	1	9	8	8	.325	.377
0 Days rest	1.69	1	0	0	6	0	5.1	2	0	3	3	None on/out	.162	68	11	2	0	0	0	1	10	.186	.191
1 or 2 Days rest	2.04	3	4	0	26	0	35.1	27	0	9	10	First Pitch	.298	47	14	1	1	0	5	4	0	.353	.362
3+ Days rest	1.91	2	1	0	19	0	33.0	28	2	8	9	Behind on Count	.321	56	18	5	0	1	8	11	0	.443	.464
Pre-All Star	1.88	1	3	0	27	0	38.1	32	1	11	10	Ahead on Count	.139	122	17	3	2	1	8	0	20	.153	.221
Post-All Star	2.04	5	2	0	24	0	35.1	25	1	9	12	Two Strikes	.140	93	13	2	1	1	6	5	22	.192	.215

Last Five Years

	ERA	W	L	Sv	G	GS	IP	H	HR	BB	SO		Avg	AB	H	2B	3B	HR	RBI	BB	SO	OBP	SLG
Home	2.68	7	1	4	117	1	201.1	193	6	43	99	vs. Left	.301	664	200	42	5	6	79	64	44	.362	.407
Away	3.54	14	19	1	131	2	208.1	222	11	76	88	vs. Right	.239	901	215	37	4	11	112	55	143	.286	.325
Day	3.22	3	9	1	75	1	120.1	129	7	30	58	Inning 1-6	.284	525	149	33	2	8	92	38	58	.330	.400
Night	3.08	18	11	4	173	2	289.1	286	10	89	129	Inning 7+	.256	1040	266	46	7	9	99	81	129	.313	.339
Grass	3.00	13	16	4	133	2	215.2	217	9	59	100	None on	.251	849	213	44	4	10	10	52	105	.298	.347

Last Five Years

	ERA	W	L	Sv	G	GS	IP	H	HR	BB	SO		Avg	AB	H	2B	3B	HR	RBI	BB	SO	OBP	SLG
Turf	3.25	8	4	1	115	1	194.0	198	8	60	87	Runners on	.262	716	202	35	5	7	181	67	82	.342	.374
April	2.94	1	1	0	29	0	49.0	43	1	9	20	Scoring Posn	.263	475	125	24	4	5	168	55	62	.335	.362
May	2.55	3	0	1	46	0	67.0	53	3	15	33	Close & Late	.296	361	107	18	4	2	43	34	39	.362	.385
June	3.86	2	5	1	44	0	74.2	87	1	24	25	None on/out	.227	366	83	12	1	5	5	21	53	.274	.306
July	2.71	5	6	2	40	2	76.1	78	6	27	33	vs. 1st Batr (relief)	.231	216	50	5	1	4	34	10	36	.277	.319
August	2.15	5	3	0	41	0	79.2	72	5	12	38	First Inning Pitched	.265	785	208	33	5	8	117	63	102	.321	.350
September/October	4.71	5	5	1	48	1	63.0	82	1	32	38	First 15 Pitches	.266	854	227	39	5	7	109	61	100	.318	.348
Starter	7.71	1	2	0	3	3	14.0	23	1	5	10	Pitch 16-30	.262	450	118	25	2	7	45	35	53	.315	.373
Reliever	2.96	20	18	5	245	0	395.2	392	16	114	177	Pitch 31-45	.211	166	35	11	1	1	12	14	23	.275	.307
0 Days rest	2.52	3	3	1	35	0	53.2	62	3	17	27	Pitch 46+	.368	95	35	4	1	2	25	9	11	.421	.495
1 or 2 Days rest	3.40	6	10	1	105	0	156.1	155	6	47	70	First Pitch	.314	303	95	19	2	5	38	27	0	.366	.439
3+ Days rest	2.71	11	5	3	105	0	185.2	175	7	50	80	Ahead on Count	.222	680	151	26	3	7	75	1	167	.225	.300
Pre-All Star	3.07	7	9	2	132	1	220.0	210	7	59	95	Behind on Count	.294	344	101	19	3	2	48	50	0	.386	.384
Post-All Star	3.18	14	11	3	116	2	189.2	205	10	60	92	Two Strikes	.221	587	130	23	2	7	54	40	187	.271	.303

Pitcher vs. Batter (since 1984)

Pitches Best Vs.	Avg	AB	H	2B	3B	HR	RBI	BB	SO	OBP	SLG	Pitches Worst Vs.	Avg	AB	H	2B	3B	HR	RBI	BB	SO	OBP	SLG
Glenn Davis	.000	10	0	0	0	0	1	3	1	.231	.000	Don Mattingly	.636	11	7	0	1	0	2	0	0	.636	.818
Luis Rivera	.091	11	1	0	0	0	0	0	0	.091	.091	Felix Fermin	.636	11	7	3	0	0	1	0	0	.636	.909
Bob Melvin	.100	10	1	0	0	0	2	1	2	.182	.100	Dave Martinez	.455	11	5	2	0	1	2	0	2	.455	.909
Andres Galarraga	.133	15	2	0	0	0	0	2	2	.235	.133	Ruben Sierra	.400	10	4	1	0	1	5	2	0	.462	.800
Rafael Ramirez	.143	14	2	0	0	0	2	0	1	.143	.143	Randy Milligan	.400	10	4	1	0	2	4	1	1	.455	1.100

Tim Leary — Mariners
Pitches Right (groundball pitcher)

	ERA	W	L	Sv	G	GS	IP	BB	SO	Avg	H	2B	3B	HR	RBI	OBP	SLG	CG	ShO	Sup	QS	#P/S	SB	CS	GB	FB	G/F
1992 Season	5.36	8	10	0	26	23	141.0	87	46	.256	131	26	2	12	71	.367	.386	3	0	4.85	7	93	27	5	228	159	1.43
Last Five Years	4.19	46	64	0	153	137	905.1	346	570	.260	889	156	19	80	378	.331	.387	21	7	3.77	66	96	96	32	1373	909	1.51

1992 Season

	ERA	W	L	Sv	G	GS	IP	H	HR	BB	SO		Avg	AB	H	2B	3B	HR	RBI	BB	SO	OBP	SLG
Home	5.37	3	5	0	11	10	57.0	52	3	44	19	vs. Left	.234	244	57	14	2	7	35	39	24	.336	.393
Away	5.36	5	5	0	15	13	84.0	79	9	43	27	vs. Right	.277	267	74	12	0	5	36	48	22	.395	.378
Starter	5.12	8	10	0	23	23	137.0	124	11	82	45	Scoring Posn	.292	137	40	12	0	4	59	26	11	.386	.467
Reliever	13.50	0	0	0	3	0	4.0	7	1	5	1	Close & Late	.214	42	9	2	0	0	6	9	5	.358	.262
0-3 Days Rest	6.75	0	0	0	1	1	4.0	5	0	3	2	None on/out	.286	126	36	7	1	4	4	25	9	.412	.452
4 Days Rest	5.74	3	6	0	12	12	64.1	65	6	48	18	First Pitch	.299	97	29	8	1	2	20	4	0	.343	.464
5+ Days Rest	4.46	5	4	0	10	10	68.2	54	5	31	25	Behind on Count	.299	144	43	6	0	5	23	48	0	.469	.444
Pre-All Star	5.23	5	6	0	15	15	93.0	77	8	52	33	Ahead on Count	.205	166	34	9	0	2	15	0	38	.216	.295
Post-All Star	5.63	3	4	0	11	8	48.0	54	4	35	13	Two Strikes	.186	172	32	7	0	5	21	35	46	.319	.314

Last Five Years

	ERA	W	L	Sv	G	GS	IP	H	HR	BB	SO		Avg	AB	H	2B	3B	HR	RBI	BB	SO	OBP	SLG
Home	4.01	20	32	0	73	66	440.1	434	37	175	295	vs. Left	.267	1745	466	84	15	42	199	192	267	.340	.405
Away	4.35	26	32	0	80	71	465.0	455	43	171	275	vs. Right	.252	1678	423	72	4	38	179	154	303	.321	.396
Day	5.25	11	18	0	45	41	245.1	261	20	108	168	Inning 1-6	.256	2870	735	126	18	66	324	288	478	.327	.382
Night	3.79	35	46	0	108	96	660.0	628	60	238	402	Inning 7+	.278	553	154	30	1	14	54	58	92	.352	.412
Grass	4.15	29	45	0	105	92	611.0	607	58	241	398	None on	.253	2024	512	87	10	49	49	177	347	.317	.378
Turf	4.25	17	19	0	48	45	294.1	282	22	105	172	Runners on	.269	1399	377	69	9	31	329	169	223	.349	.398
April	3.44	9	5	0	20	20	133.1	113	12	37	94	Scoring Posn	.253	780	197	36	8	19	292	133	147	.357	.392
May	3.58	8	15	0	28	27	183.1	170	15	74	122	Close & Late	.245	282	69	10	1	4	26	36	50	.334	.330
June	4.66	7	12	0	28	27	174.0	178	19	57	82	None on/out	.259	885	229	38	3	26	26	85	135	.330	.397
July	5.25	7	10	0	25	19	121.2	144	5	51	81	vs. 1st Batr (relief)	.357	14	5	0	0	1	2	2	4	.438	.571
August	3.97	10	9	0	28	21	149.2	138	12	64	100	First Inning Pitched	.286	500	143	26	5	11	73	61	95	.364	.424
September/October	4.40	5	13	0	24	23	143.1	146	17	63	91	First 75 Pitches	.258	2630	678	113	17	55	272	239	438	.322	.376
Starter	4.06	45	61	0	137	137	875.1	851	76	328	553	Pitch 76-90	.280	386	108	20	2	16	62	58	63	.373	.466
Reliever	7.80	1	3	0	16	0	30.0	38	4	18	17	Pitch 91-105	.262	248	65	16	0	7	32	28	40	.343	.411
0-3 Days Rest	3.15	3	3	0	8	8	54.1	49	3	14	42	Pitch 106+	.239	159	38	7	0	2	12	21	29	.341	.321
4 Days Rest	4.28	23	38	0	80	80	496.1	492	40	206	316	First Pitch	.317	584	185	30	4	16	82	19	0	.348	.464
5+ Days Rest	3.88	19	20	0	49	49	324.2	310	33	108	195	Ahead on Count	.195	1422	277	50	4	19	102	0	502	.200	.276
Pre-All Star	4.18	25	38	0	85	83	534.0	524	48	193	322	Behind on Count	.327	820	268	49	4	30	114	174	0	.444	.506
Post-All Star	4.19	21	26	0	68	54	371.1	365	32	153	248	Two Strikes	.171	1394	238	41	6	20	115	153	570	.254	.252

Pitcher vs. Batter (since 1984)

Pitches Best Vs.	Avg	AB	H	2B	3B	HR	RBI	BB	SO	OBP	SLG	Pitches Worst Vs.	Avg	AB	H	2B	3B	HR	RBI	BB	SO	OBP	SLG
Milt Cuyler	.000	12	0	0	0	0	0	0	2	.000	.000	Luis Rivera	.700	10	7	2	0	1	3	1	0	.727	1.200
Gary Gaetti	.056	18	1	0	0	0	1	1	2	.105	.056	Joe Carter	.588	17	10	2	0	4	7	0	2	.526	1.412
Spike Owen	.059	17	1	0	0	0	1	1	1	.111	.059	Cory Snyder	.583	12	7	0	0	2	8	0	2	.583	1.083
Ken Oberkfell	.067	15	1	0	0	0	0	0	2	.067	.067	Rance Mulliniks	.500	14	7	4	0	1	3	3	2	.588	1.000
Kirk Gibson	.071	14	1	0	0	0	0	1	3	.133	.071	Steve Buechele	.462	13	6	1	1	2	6	2	1	.533	1.154

Manuel Lee — Blue Jays   Bats Both (groundball hitter)

	Avg	G	AB	R	H	2B	3B	HR	RBI	BB	SO	HBP	GDP	SB	CS	OBP	SLG	IBB	SH	SF	#Pit	#P/PA	GB	FB	G/F
1992 Season	.263	128	396	49	104	10	1	3	39	50	73	0	8	6	2	.343	.316	0	8	3	1724	3.84	166	81	2.05
Last Five Years	.257	598	1913	200	492	65	13	14	181	146	394	2	48	23	10	.308	.327	2	24	15	7771	3.74	620	378	2.17

1992 Season

	Avg	AB	H	2B	3B	HR	RBI	BB	SO	OBP	SLG		Avg	AB	H	2B	3B	HR	RBI	BB	SO	OBP	SLG
vs. Left	.212	118	25	4	0	0	12	15	17	.299	.246	Scoring Posn	.330	94	31	4	0	1	37	9	17	.377	.404
vs. Right	.284	278	79	6	1	3	27	35	56	.362	.345	Close & Late	.210	62	13	0	0	0	3	9	12	.306	.210
Groundball	.263	118	31	3	0	0	9	13	24	.336	.288	None on/out	.258	93	24	0	0	0	0	14	16	.355	.280
Flyball	.243	111	27	2	1	0	10	16	21	.336	.279	Total	.263	396	104	10	1	3	39	50	73	.343	.316
Home	.223	184	41	4	0	1	18	27	36	.321	.261	Batting #9	.263	396	104	10	1	3	39	50	73	.343	.316
Away	.297	212	63	6	1	2	21	23	37	.363	.363	Other	.000	0	0	0	0	0	0	0	0	.000	.000
Day	.228	114	26	1	0	0	7	15	20	.318	.237	April	.246	65	16	3	0	0	7	7	15	.315	.292
Night	.277	282	78	9	1	3	32	35	53	.353	.348	May	.250	80	20	1	0	3	7	8	15	.318	.375
Grass	.317	161	51	5	1	1	15	16	27	.374	.379	June	.256	82	21	4	1	0	13	14	13	.365	.329
Turf	.226	235	53	5	0	2	24	34	46	.322	.272	July	.234	77	18	0	0	0	7	10	10	.318	.234
First Pitch	.396	48	19	2	0	1	8	0	0	.396	.500	August	.295	78	23	2	0	0	2	6	17	.341	.321
Ahead on Count	.282	85	24	2	0	0	10	35	0	.484	.306	September/October	.429	14	6	0	0	0	3	5	3	.579	.429
Behind on Count	.276	134	37	3	1	1	13	0	41	.272	.336	Pre-All Star	.245	257	63	8	1	3	28	32	49	.328	.319
Two Strikes	.212	179	38	5	1	2	14	15	73	.272	.285	Post-All Star	.295	139	41	2	0	0	11	18	24	.371	.309

1992 By Position

Position	Avg	AB	H	2B	3B	HR	RBI	BB	SO	OBP	SLG	G	GS	Innings	PO	A	E	DP	Fld Pct	Rng Fctr	In Zone	Outs	Zone Rtg	MLB Zone
As ss	.263	396	104	10	1	3	39	50	73	.343	.316	128	126	1079.1	186	330	7	68	.987	4.30	387	365	.943	.885

Last Five Years

	Avg	AB	H	2B	3B	HR	RBI	BB	SO	OBP	SLG		Avg	AB	H	2B	3B	HR	RBI	BB	SO	OBP	SLG
vs. Left	.273	710	194	33	5	9	80	48	122	.318	.372	Scoring Posn	.277	473	131	20	4	3	165	28	104	.309	.355
vs. Right	.248	1203	298	32	8	5	101	98	272	.302	.300	Close & Late	.228	338	77	5	1	1	29	36	73	.302	.257
Groundball	.236	512	121	14	4	1	48	39	107	.288	.285	None on/out	.253	463	117	17	2	4	4	38	100	.309	.324
Flyball	.257	460	118	14	5	4	36	42	105	.316	.335	Batting #8	.244	610	149	19	4	7	56	37	139	.286	.323
Home	.255	909	232	33	8	6	82	79	182	.313	.328	Batting #9	.266	1087	289	36	6	6	103	93	208	.322	.327
Away	.259	1004	260	32	5	8	99	67	212	.304	.325	Other	.250	216	54	10	3	1	22	16	47	.300	.338
Day	.245	591	145	16	4	7	54	41	116	.293	.321	April	.253	289	73	12	1	0	24	30	63	.321	.301
Night	.262	1322	347	49	9	7	127	105	278	.315	.329	May	.271	207	56	3	3	8	24	14	43	.318	.430
Grass	.270	786	212	23	5	6	81	51	157	.312	.335	June	.279	380	106	15	3	2	40	23	75	.319	.350
Turf	.248	1127	280	42	8	8	100	95	237	.305	.321	July	.228	372	85	10	1	1	34	28	79	.280	.269
First Pitch	.336	253	85	15	0	3	41	1	0	.337	.431	August	.251	403	101	17	3	2	25	29	79	.293	.318
Ahead on Count	.311	354	110	14	4	2	39	94	0	.445	.390	September/October	.271	262	71	13	2	0	22	26	55	.334	.336
Behind on Count	.206	709	146	16	3	4	49	0	244	.207	.254	Pre-All Star	.263	1002	264	34	8	10	95	78	203	.316	.343
Two Strikes	.179	943	169	20	8	6	55	50	391	.221	.236	Post-All Star	.250	911	228	31	5	4	86	68	191	.300	.308

Batter vs. Pitcher (career)

Hits Best Against	Avg	AB	H	2B	3B	HR	RBI	BB	SO	OBP	SLG	Hits Worst Against	Avg	AB	H	2B	3B	HR	RBI	BB	SO	OBP	SLG
Tom Candiotti	.500	12	6	0	1	0	3	0	1	.462	.667	Luis Aquino	.000	14	0	0	0	0	1	1	3	.067	.000
Dave Righetti	.471	17	8	0	0	0	4	1	2	.500	.471	Bill Gullickson	.000	13	0	0	0	0	0	2	1	.133	.000
Chuck Finley	.450	20	9	1	0	0	3	3	2	.522	.500	Rick Honeycutt	.000	11	0	0	0	0	0	2	2	.154	.000
Roger Clemens	.421	19	8	1	0	0	0	2	5	.476	.474	Charles Nagy	.067	15	1	0	0	0	0	2	5	.176	.067
Frank Viola	.412	17	7	3	1	0	5	0	3	.412	.706	Mark Guthrie	.071	14	1	0	0	0	0	1	4	.133	.071

Craig Lefferts — Orioles   Pitches Left

	ERA	W	L	Sv	G	GS	IP	BB	SO	Avg	H	2B	3B	HR	RBI	OBP	SLG	CG	ShO	Sup	QS	#P/S	SB	CS	GB	FB	G/F
1992 Season	3.76	14	12	0	32	32	196.1	41	104	.282	214	33	4	19	80	.316	.411	1	0	4.45	19	85	20	10	274	212	1.29
Last Five Years	3.25	27	35	77	276	32	543.1	122	341	.256	523	79	13	52	230	.296	.383	1	0	3.79	19	85	46	25	674	601	1.12

1992 Season

	ERA	W	L	Sv	G	GS	IP	H	HR	BB	SO		Avg	AB	H	2B	3B	HR	RBI	BB	SO	OBP	SLG
Home	3.67	7	6	0	16	16	95.2	103	9	20	48	vs. Left	.244	123	30	5	1	2	13	3	25	.258	.350
Away	3.84	7	6	0	16	16	100.2	111	10	21	56	vs. Right	.289	636	184	28	3	17	67	38	79	.327	.423
Day	3.08	4	3	0	10	10	64.1	65	6	8	40	Inning 1-6	.277	664	184	29	4	15	70	35	99	.311	.401
Night	4.09	10	9	0	22	22	132.0	149	13	33	64	Inning 7+	.316	95	30	4	0	4	10	6	5	.353	.484
Grass	3.80	10	9	0	24	24	144.1	156	13	31	77	None on	.287	456	131	17	1	12	12	20	56	.317	.408
Turf	3.63	4	3	0	8	8	52.0	58	6	10	27	Runners on	.274	303	83	16	3	7	68	21	48	.315	.416
April	5.09	2	2	0	4	4	17.2	23	3	5	10	Scoring Posn	.278	158	44	8	2	2	54	11	32	.314	.392
May	3.52	4	1	0	6	6	38.1	44	4	9	22	Close & Late	.288	52	15	1	0	1	3	0	3	.283	.365
June	2.62	3	2	0	5	5	34.1	32	2	5	18	None on/out	.310	210	65	6	0	8	8	7	25	.332	.452
July	3.16	3	1	0	6	6	37.0	40	2	7	18	vs. 1st Batr (relief)	.000	0	0	0	0	0	0	0	0	.000	.000
August	4.75	1	3	0	6	6	36.0	41	5	9	13	First Inning Pitched	.303	122	37	4	1	6	19	10	21	.356	.500
September/October	4.09	1	3	0	5	5	33.0	34	3	6	23	First 75 Pitches	.275	625	172	28	3	15	67	30	93	.306	.402
Starter	3.76	14	12	0	32	32	196.1	214	19	41	104	Pitch 76-90	.333	87	29	3	1	2	7	6	4	.372	.460
Reliever	0.00	0	0	0	0	0	0.0	0	0	0	0	Pitch 91-105	.297	37	11	1	0	2	4	5	4	.381	.486
0-3 Days Rest	0.00	0	0	0	0	0	0.0	0	0	0	0	Pitch 106+	.200	10	2	1	0	0	2	0	3	.200	.300
4 Days Rest	4.31	5	7	0	16	16	94.0	115	7	24	49	First Pitch	.388	134	52	8	0	5	22	2	0	.391	.567
5+ Days Rest	3.25	9	5	0	16	16	102.1	99	12	17	55	Ahead on Count	.236	330	78	12	2	5	27	0	90	.236	.330

1992 Season

	ERA	W	L	Sv	G	GS	IP	H	HR	BB	SO		Avg	AB	H	2B	3B	HR	RBI	BB	SO	OBP	SLG
Pre-All Star	3.54	10	6	0	18	18	109.1	123	11	22	60	Behind on Count	.294	160	47	7	1	6	19	25	0	.389	.463
Post-All Star	4.03	4	6	0	14	14	87.0	91	8	19	44	Two Strikes	.203	291	59	8	1	3	20	13	104	.236	.268

Last Five Years

	ERA	W	L	Sv	G	GS	IP	H	HR	BB	SO		Avg	AB	H	2B	3B	HR	RBI	BB	SO	OBP	SLG
Home	3.05	13	18	35	136	16	268.1	255	25	53	172	vs. Left	.233	454	106	10	5	8	49	21	96	.269	.330
Away	3.44	14	17	42	140	16	275.0	268	27	69	169	vs. Right	.262	1591	417	69	8	44	181	101	245	.304	.398
Day	3.06	10	14	24	95	10	185.1	162	18	37	124	Inning 1-6	.260	724	203	32	4	17	87	37	107	.313	.406
Night	3.34	17	21	53	181	16	358.0	361	34	85	217	Inning 7+	.242	1321	320	47	9	35	143	85	234	.287	.371
Grass	3.30	20	28	56	203	24	401.1	389	39	91	256	None on	.268	1146	307	50	4	30	30	55	186	.303	.397
Turf	3.11	7	7	21	73	8	142.0	134	13	31	85	Runners on	.240	989	216	29	9	22	200	67	155	.299	.366
April	2.34	5	4	10	38	4	65.1	54	5	13	45	Scoring Posn	.229	512	117	13	6	11	166	49	98	.289	.342
May	3.08	5	7	21	49	6	111.0	101	11	30	68	Close & Late	.230	729	168	18	2	18	86	49	113	.279	.335
June	3.67	8	8	14	49	5	100.2	93	9	19	52	None on/out	.277	502	139	17	1	12	12	19	76	.306	.386
July	3.39	4	5	10	44	6	87.2	86	7	21	62	vs. 1st Batr (relief)	.248	226	56	6	2	3	27	12	42	.281	.332
August	3.90	2	6	12	53	6	94.2	108	12	22	42	First Inning Pitched	.240	928	223	36	8	23	128	63	176	.287	.371
September/October	2.79	3	5	10	43	5	84.0	81	8	17	71	First 75 Pitches	.252	1911	481	74	12	48	217	111	330	.292	.378
Starter	3.76	14	12	0	32	32	196.1	214	19	41	104	Pitch 76-90	.333	87	29	3	1	2	7	6	4	.372	.460
Reliever	2.96	13	23	77	244	0	347.0	309	33	81	237	Pitch 91-105	.297	37	11	1	0	2	4	5	4	.361	.486
0-3 Days Rest	0.00	0	0	0	0	0	0.0	0	0	0	0	Pitch 106+	.200	10	2	1	0	0	2	0	3	.200	.300
4 Days Rest	4.31	5	7	0	16	16	94.0	115	7	24	49	First Pitch	.332	328	109	17	4	11	55	16	0	.361	.509
5+ Days Rest	3.25	9	5	0	16	16	102.1	99	12	17	55	Ahead on Count	.202	974	197	29	5	16	83	1	304	.203	.292
Pre-All Star	3.23	19	22	46	149	18	309.0	289	26	70	181	Behind on Count	.291	374	109	17	2	12	44	64	0	.393	.444
Post-All Star	3.26	8	13	31	127	14	234.1	234	24	52	160	Two Strikes	.181	877	159	29	4	9	60	40	341	.216	.254

Pitcher vs. Batter (since 1984)

Pitches Best Vs.	Avg	AB	H	2B	3B	HR	RBI	BB	SO	OBP	SLG	Pitches Worst Vs.	Avg	AB	H	2B	3B	HR	RBI	BB	SO	OBP	SLG
Dave Anderson	.071	14	1	0	0	0	0	1	4	.133	.071	Tim Raines	.556	18	10	3	1	1	4	3	1	.619	1.000
Wally Backman	.083	12	1	0	0	0	0	1	4	.154	.083	Brett Butler	.545	11	6	0	0	1	1	1	1	.583	.818
Bobby Bonilla	.087	23	2	0	0	0	3	0	4	.083	.087	Mark Grace	.500	10	5	2	0	0	1	3	0	.615	.700
Don Slaught	.091	11	1	0	0	0	0	0	1	.091	.091	Jack Clark	.455	11	5	1	0	4	9	4	2	.600	1.636
Roberto Alomar	.091	11	1	0	0	0	0		3	.091	.091	Mike Sharperson	.400	10	4	0	0	2	5	2	1	.500	1.000

Charlie Leibrandt — Braves

Pitches Left

	ERA	W	L	Sv	G	GS	IP	BB	SO	Avg	H	2B	3B	HR	RBI	OBP	SLG	CG	ShO	Sup	QS	#P/S	SB	CS	GB	FB	G/F
1992 Season	3.36	15	7	0	32	31	193.0	42	104	.258	191	34	4	9	66	.301	.351	5	2	4.29	18	92	28	16	258	193	1.34
Last Five Years	3.60	57	54	0	160	153	989.0	249	506	.265	1007	186	22	69	392	.311	.380	21	8	4.51	90	96	114	52	1420	1124	1.26

1992 Season

	ERA	W	L	Sv	G	GS	IP	H	HR	BB	SO		Avg	AB	H	2B	3B	HR	RBI	BB	SO	OBP	SLG
Home	3.76	9	4	0	18	18	110.0	114	5	21	55	vs. Left	.228	171	39	2	1	1	13	9	23	.276	.269
Away	2.82	6	3	0	14	13	83.0	77	4	21	49	vs. Right	.267	570	152	32	3	8	53	33	81	.308	.375
Day	4.86	3	3	0	8	8	46.1	49	4	17	26	Inning 1-6	.264	611	161	29	3	7	57	37	96	.308	.355
Night	2.88	12	4	0	24	23	146.2	142	5	25	78	Inning 7+	.231	130	30	5	1	2	9	5	8	.263	.331
Grass	3.32	11	5	0	23	23	141.0	144	5	29	69	None on	.266	458	122	18	2	4	4	14	56	.293	.341
Turf	3.46	4	2	0	9	8	52.0	47	4	13	35	Runners on	.244	283	69	16	2	5	62	28	48	.312	.367
April	3.05	2	1	0	4	4	20.2	21	0	8	14	Scoring Posn	.240	154	37	9	0	1	49	22	30	.328	.318
May	5.70	2	1	0	6	5	30.0	36	1	5	12	Close & Late	.222	45	10	3	0	0	2	4	4	.286	.289
June	3.14	2	1	0	5	5	28.2	31	3	8	11	None on/out	.264	197	52	9	2	2	2	5	19	.286	.360
July	1.67	2	2	0	5	5	37.2	26	1	9	18	vs. 1st Batr (relief)	.000	1	0	0	0	0	0	0	0	.000	.000
August	2.92	3	1	0	5	5	37.0	29	4	3	23	First Inning Pitched	.333	129	43	7	0	0	13	7	17	.370	.388
September/October	3.92	4	2	0	7	7	39.0	48	0	9	26	First 75 Pitches	.268	557	149	28	3	6	54	30	83	.306	.361
Starter	3.39	15	7	0	31	31	191.0	191	9	42	103	Pitch 76-90	.197	76	15	2	1	1	4	6	12	.265	.289
Reliever	0.00	0	0	0	1	0	2.0	0	0	0	1	Pitch 91-105	.266	64	17	2	0	1	4	3	4	.309	.344
0-3 Days Rest	0.00	0	0	0	1	1	5.0	3	0	5	5	Pitch 106+	.227	44	10	2	0	1	4	3	5	.277	.341
4 Days Rest	4.70	5	6	0	17	17	95.2	117	3	25	47	First Pitch	.300	110	33	6	1	1	11	3	0	.316	.400
5+ Days Rest	2.19	9	1	0	13	13	90.1	71	6	17	51	Ahead on Count	.209	316	66	11	2	1	15	0	85	.220	.266
Pre-All Star	3.64	7	3	0	17	16	94.0	97	4	26	40	Behind on Count	.314	156	49	10	0	2	20	18	0	.383	.417
Post-All Star	3.09	8	4	0	15	15	99.0	94	5	16	64	Two Strikes	.179	318	57	8	1	1	17	21	104	.238	.220

Last Five Years

	ERA	W	L	Sv	G	GS	IP	H	HR	BB	SO		Avg	AB	H	2B	3B	HR	RBI	BB	SO	OBP	SLG
Home	3.47	32	23	0	75	71	476.2	506	28	109	214	vs. Left	.262	740	194	36	4	8	75	39	85	.303	.354
Away	3.72	25	31	0	85	82	512.1	501	41	140	292	vs. Right	.266	3061	813	150	18	61	317	210	421	.313	.386
Day	3.85	12	20	0	49	46	285.1	298	23	82	163	Inning 1-6	.269	3177	854	164	20	59	354	211	437	.315	.389
Night	3.50	45	34	0	111	107	703.2	709	46	167	343	Inning 7+	.245	624	153	22	2	10	38	38	69	.291	.335
Grass	3.51	35	38	0	98	96	619.2	603	46	151	329	None on	.261	2306	602	104	13	38	38	117	298	.300	.367
Turf	3.75	22	16	0	62	57	369.1	404	23	98	177	Runners on	.271	1495	405	82	9	31	354	132	208	.328	.400
April	3.28	7	10	0	21	21	134.1	129	7	49	68	Scoring Posn	.263	851	224	45	5	16	302	97	126	.333	.384
May	4.64	6	9	0	24	23	139.2	164	11	30	63	Close & Late	.223	309	69	10	0	3	18	25	34	.284	.265
June	2.84	11	8	0	27	27	190.1	177	11	39	76	None on/out	.255	998	254	45	4	19	19	43	117	.288	.365
July	4.67	8	11	0	27	27	163.2	184	16	51	96	vs. 1st Batr (relief)	.429	7	3	0	0	0	0	0	2	.429	.429
August	3.51	13	7	0	27	26	166.2	167	15	30	95	First Inning Pitched	.286	622	178	42	1	9	79	61	90	.353	.400
September/October	3.01	12	9	0	34	29	194.1	186	9	50	108	First 75 Pitches	.272	2799	761	154	18	52	314	184	378	.318	.395

Last Five Years

	ERA	W	L	Sv	G	GS	IP	H	HR	BB	SO		Avg	AB	H	2B	3B	HR	RBI	BB	SO	OBP	SLG
Starter	3.63	57	54	0	153	153	976.0	997	69	246	494	Pitch 76-90	.233	467	109	14	2	7	29	22	60	.270	.317
Reliever	1.38	0	0	0	7	0	13.0	10	0	3	12	Pitch 91-105	.259	332	86	12	1	4	21	22	46	.309	.337
0-3 Days Rest	3.75	4	6	0	16	16	93.2	97	5	24	53	Pitch 106+	.251	203	51	6	1	6	28	21	22	.323	.379
4 Days Rest	3.65	34	32	0	90	90	571.2	594	39	144	277	First Pitch	.295	597	176	33	5	9	67	9	0	.304	.412
5+ Days Rest	3.56	19	16	0	47	47	310.2	306	25	78	164	Ahead on Count	.213	1589	338	63	13	18	110	1	405	.219	.303
Pre-All Star	3.59	27	29	0	80	79	514.0	529	34	131	225	Behind on Count	.309	834	258	48	3	22	119	131	0	.401	.453
Post-All Star	3.62	30	25	0	80	74	475.0	478	33	118	281	Two Strikes	.205	1581	324	59	10	18	104	108	506	.259	.289

Pitcher vs. Batter (since 1984)

Pitches Best Vs.	Avg	AB	H	2B	3B	HR	RBI	BB	SO	OBP	SLG	Pitches Worst Vs.	Avg	AB	H	2B	3B	HR	RBI	BB	SO	OBP	SLG
Chris James	.000	12	0	0	0	0	0	1	2	.077	.000	Ricky Jordan	.583	12	7	1	0	1	3	1	0	.615	.917
Jerald Clark	.000	11	0	0	0	0	0	0	1	.000	.000	Ryne Sandberg	.500	16	8	1	0	2	3	3	1	.579	.938
Jose Vizcaino	.083	12	1	1	0	0	0	0	1	.083	.167	Larry Walker	.500	14	7	2	1	1	4	1	1	.500	1.000
Barry Bonds	.133	15	2	0	0	0	1	0	5	.133	.133	Kirk Gibson	.500	12	6	2	0	1	3	0	1	.500	.917
Reggie Sanders	.133	15	2	0	0	0	0	0	3	.133	.133	Mike Stanley	.500	12	6	0	0	2	7	0	0	.500	1.000

Al Leiter — Blue Jays   Pitches Left (flyball pitcher)

	ERA	W	L	Sv	G	GS	IP	BB	SO	Avg	H	2B	3B	HR	RBI	OBP	SLG	GF	IR	IRS	Hld	SvOp	SB	CS	GB	FB	G/F
1992 Season	9.00	0	0	0	1	0	1.0	2	0	.200	1	0	0	0	0	.429	.200	0	0	0	0	0	0	0	4	1	4.00
Last Five Years	4.70	5	6	0	27	19	99.2	65	92	.232	86	19	0	9	42	.356	.356	3	2	0	0	0	9	7	97	118	0.82

1992 Season

	ERA	W	L	Sv	G	GS	IP	H	HR	BB	SO		Avg	AB	H	2B	3B	HR	RBI	BB	SO	OBP	SLG
Home	9.00	0	0	0	1	0	1.0	1	0	2	0	vs. Left	.000	0	0	0	0	0	0	1	0	1.000	.000
Away	0.00	0	0	0	0	0	0.0	0	0	0	0	vs. Right	.200	5	1	0	0	0	0	1	0	.333	.200

Mark Leiter — Tigers   Pitches Right (flyball pitcher)

	ERA	W	L	Sv	G	GS	IP	BB	SO	Avg	H	2B	3B	HR	RBI	OBP	SLG	GF	IR	IRS	Hld	SvOp	SB	CS	GB	FB	G/F
1992 Season	4.18	8	5	0	35	14	112.0	43	75	.277	116	19	6	9	47	.342	.415	7	16	2	3	0	7	9	125	127	0.98
Career (1990-1992)	4.45	18	13	1	81	32	273.0	102	199	.265	274	45	11	30	132	.333	.416	16	57	17	5	2	16	16	301	324	0.93

1992 Season

	ERA	W	L	Sv	G	GS	IP	H	HR	BB	SO		Avg	AB	H	2B	3B	HR	RBI	BB	SO	OBP	SLG
Home	4.28	4	3	0	20	8	61.0	66	6	29	47	vs. Left	.312	189	59	9	5	4	26	25	24	.384	.476
Away	4.06	4	2	0	15	6	51.0	50	3	14	28	vs. Right	.248	230	57	10	1	5	21	18	51	.307	.365
Starter	4.94	5	3	0	14	14	74.2	91	7	30	50	Scoring Posn	.276	98	27	3	1	0	34	17	19	.363	.327
Reliever	2.65	3	2	0	21	0	37.1	25	2	13	25	Close & Late	.143	49	7	2	0	1	5		5	.218	.245
0 Days rest	0.00	0	0	0	0	0	0.0	0	0	0	0	None on/out	.277	101	28	2	0	2	2	14	16	.371	.356
1 or 2 Days rest	2.12	1	0	0	11	0	17.0	8	1	4	15	First Pitch	.294	51	15	1	1	0	3	5	0	.362	.353
3+ Days rest	3.10	2	2	0	10	0	20.1	17	1	9	10	Behind on Count	.429	77	33	5	2	6	19	18	1	.520	.779
Pre-All Star	4.89	5	4	0	23	12	81.0	90	7	36	61	Ahead on Count	.209	201	42	8	2	2	13	0	66	.212	.299
Post-All Star	2.32	3	1	0	12	2	31.0	26	2	7	14	Two Strikes	.216	218	47	9	2	1	17	20	74	.281	.289

Career (1990-1992)

	ERA	W	L	Sv	G	GS	IP	H	HR	BB	SO		Avg	AB	H	2B	3B	HR	RBI	BB	SO	OBP	SLG
Home	4.44	9	6	1	45	18	156.0	156	17	65	123	vs. Left	.276	471	130	22	7	15	61	57	68	.353	.448
Away	4.46	9	7	0	36	14	117.0	118	13	37	76	vs. Right	.255	564	144	23	4	15	71	45	131	.316	.390
Day	4.91	6	4	1	23	9	77.0	83	10	24	66	Inning 1-6	.266	766	204	31	8	23	95	75	154	.335	.418
Night	4.27	12	9	0	58	23	196.0	191	20	78	133	Inning 7+	.260	269	70	14	3	7	37	27	45	.326	.413
Grass	4.35	17	11	1	71	29	248.0	251	27	88	186	None on	.253	594	150	30	8	17	17	56	124	.323	.416
Turf	5.40	1	2	0	10	3	25.0	23	3	14	13	Runners on	.281	441	124	15	3	13	115	46	75	.345	.417
April	5.17	3	2	0	11	0	15.2	12	1	8	15	Scoring Posn	.295	244	72	9	2	4	94	34	41	.368	.398
May	2.70	2	1	0	19	4	53.1	44	4	32	42	Close & Late	.247	97	24	4	1	2	13	7	11	.299	.371
June	7.56	2	2	1	10	6	33.1	47	5	17	27	None on/out	.244	250	61	9	1	6	6	31	50	.335	.360
July	4.74	3	2	0	14	8	57.0	59	5	9	33	vs. 1st Batr (relief)	.184	38	7	2	0	0	10	8	7	.333	.237
August	3.75	5	0	0	8	5	36.0	39	5	8	26	First Inning Pitched	.227	269	61	9	3	8	43	31	56	.318	.372
September/October	4.29	3	6	0	19	9	77.2	73	6	22	56	First 15 Pitches	.212	231	49	10	1	5	31	23	41	.295	.329
Starter	4.52	13	9	0	32	32	185.0	202	21	59	131	Pitch 16-30	.254	193	49	4	2	7	19	21	51	.338	.404
Reliever	4.30	5	4	1	49	0	88.0	72	9	43	68	Pitch 31-45	.253	162	41	5	1	3	25	17	35	.315	.352
0 Days rest	4.26	0	1	0	5	0	6.1	6	1	5	5	Pitch 46+	.301	449	135	26	7	15	57	41	72	.357	.490
1 or 2 Days rest	2.50	3	1	1	24	0	39.2	27	3	19	30	First Pitch	.326	138	45	6	1	4	20	8	0	.367	.471
3+ Days rest	6.00	2	2	0	20	0	42.0	39	5	19	30	Ahead on Count	.207	484	100	15	4	6	41	0	170	.216	.291
Pre-All Star	4.54	7	5	1	45	12	117.0	118	10	61	93	Behind on Count	.362	188	68	10	4	12	34	43	1	.472	.649
Post-All Star	4.38	11	8	0	36	20	156.0	156	20	41	106	Two Strikes	.199	522	104	17	5	6	44	51	198	.272	.285

Pitcher vs. Batter (career)

Pitches Best Vs.	Avg	AB	H	2B	3B	HR	RBI	BB	SO	OBP	SLG	Pitches Worst Vs.	Avg	AB	H	2B	3B	HR	RBI	BB	SO	OBP	SLG
Harold Baines	.071	14	1	0	0	0	2	1	2	.133	.071	Rafael Palmeiro	.538	13	7	2	0	2	5	3	0	.625	1.154
Ruben Sierra	.083	12	1	1	0	0	2	1	2	.143	.167	Gary Gaetti	.462	13	6	2	0	1	1	0	1	.462	.846
Leo Gomez	.100	10	1	0	0	0	0	1	5	.182	.100	Paul Molitor	.455	11	5	1	0	0	1	0	2	.455	.545
Juan Gonzalez	.143	14	2	0	0	0	3	1	3	.200	.143	Greg Vaughn	.417	12	5	0	0	1	6	0	4	.417	.667
Mike Devereaux	.167	12	2	0	0	0	0	0	5	.167	.167	Chito Martinez	.364	11	4	0	2	2	6	1	2	.417	1.273

Scott Leius — Twins

Bats Right (groundball hitter)

	Avg	G	AB	R	H	2B	3B	HR	RBI	BB	SO	HBP	GDP	SB	CS	OBP	SLG	IBB	SH	SF	#Pit	#P/PA	GB	FB	G/F
1992 Season	.249	129	409	50	102	18	2	2	35	34	61	1	10	6	5	.309	.318	0	5	0	1632	3.68	175	101	1.73
Career (1990-1992)	.261	252	633	89	165	26	4	8	59	66	98	1	16	11	10	.331	.352	1	11	1	2582	3.68	267	157	1.70

1992 Season

	Avg	AB	H	2B	3B	HR	RBI	BB	SO	OBP	SLG		Avg	AB	H	2B	3B	HR	RBI	BB	SO	OBP	SLG
vs. Left	.314	118	37	5	0	0	10	11	13	.372	.356	Scoring Posn	.238	126	30	5	1	0	33	9	22	.289	.294
vs. Right	.223	291	65	13	2	2	25	23	48	.283	.302	Close & Late	.224	67	15	4	0	0	6	3	9	.257	.284
Groundball	.236	106	25	4	0	0	10	5	17	.277	.274	None on/out	.264	106	28	8	1	1	1	5	19	.304	.387
Flyball	.218	110	24	2	1	1	11	14	18	.306	.282	Batting #7	.270	89	24	5	1	0	10	4	13	.301	.348
Home	.258	221	57	6	2	2	24	21	31	.325	.330	Batting #8	.249	257	64	10	1	2	22	21	41	.308	.319
Away	.239	188	45	12	0	0	11	13	30	.289	.303	Other	.222	63	14	3	0	0	3	9	7	.319	.270
Day	.222	126	28	5	1	1	11	11	12	.285	.302	April	.279	61	17	2	1	1	10	3	6	.313	.393
Night	.261	283	74	13	1	1	24	23	49	.319	.325	May	.258	66	17	2	1	0	5	4	10	.300	.318
Grass	.234	141	33	8	0	0	8	9	21	.280	.291	June	.275	102	28	6	0	1	7	5	15	.308	.363
Turf	.257	268	69	10	2	2	27	25	40	.323	.332	July	.275	69	19	4	0	0	8	6	5	.333	.333
First Pitch	.383	47	18	3	1	0	8	0	0	.383	.489	August	.229	35	8	3	0	0	3	9	8	.386	.314
Ahead on Count	.312	109	34	3	1	0	9	18	0	.409	.358	September/October	.171	76	13	1	0	0	2	7	17	.250	.184
Behind on Count	.207	135	28	7	0	1	10	0	32	.213	.281	Pre-All Star	.275	265	73	12	2	2	24	17	34	.319	.358
Two Strikes	.186	172	32	7	0	2	12	16	61	.255	.262	Post-All Star	.201	144	29	6	0	0	11	17	27	.290	.243

1992 By Position

Position	Avg	AB	H	2B	3B	HR	RBI	BB	SO	OBP	SLG	G	GS	Innings	PO	A	E	DP	Fld Pct	Rng Fctr	In Zone	Outs	Zone Rtg	MLB Zone
As 3b	.248	399	99	17	2	2	34	33	59	.307	.316	125	117	1025.1	58	257	15	12	.955	2.76	311	263	.846	.841
As ss	.143	7	1	1	0	0	0	1	2	.250	.286	10	0	21.2	5	4	0	1	1.000	3.74	8	8	1.000	.885

Mark Lemke — Braves

Bats Both

	Avg	G	AB	R	H	2B	3B	HR	RBI	BB	SO	HBP	GDP	SB	CS	OBP	SLG	IBB	SH	SF	#Pit	#P/PA	GB	FB	G/F
1992 Season	.227	155	427	38	97	7	4	6	26	50	39	0	9	0	3	.307	.304	11	12	2	1568	3.27	165	137	1.20
Career (1988-1992)	.226	423	1048	108	237	37	7	10	82	109	100	0	26	1	9	.297	.303	16	24	8	3787	3.25	410	341	1.20

1992 Season

	Avg	AB	H	2B	3B	HR	RBI	BB	SO	OBP	SLG		Avg	AB	H	2B	3B	HR	RBI	BB	SO	OBP	SLG
vs. Left	.228	145	33	1	1	5	14	13	11	.289	.352	Scoring Posn	.210	105	22	3	2	0	19	18	12	.320	.276
vs. Right	.227	282	64	6	3	1	12	37	28	.316	.280	Close & Late	.203	69	14	2	1	1	7	13	7	.325	.304
Groundball	.214	173	37	3	1	0	4	22	22	.303	.243	None on/out	.208	101	21	1	1	3	3	9	3	.273	.327
Flyball	.268	112	30	3	2	3	12	13	8	.344	.411	Batting #7	.228	158	36	5	1	2	9	13	6	.287	.310
Home	.225	222	50	5	0	4	13	25	20	.302	.302	Batting #8	.198	217	43	1	2	3	13	28	27	.287	.263
Away	.229	205	47	2	4	2	13	25	19	.312	.307	Other	.346	52	18	1	1	1	4	9	6	.443	.462
Day	.286	119	34	3	1	1	9	12	13	.346	.353	April	.222	45	10	1	0	0	2	3	4	.271	.244
Night	.205	308	63	4	3	5	17	38	26	.292	.286	May	.215	93	20	3	1	1	2	2	7	.232	.301
Grass	.234	321	75	5	2	4	17	40	31	.318	.299	June	.250	76	19	0	1	1	3	10	7	.337	.316
Turf	.208	106	22	2	2	2	9	10	8	.274	.321	July	.180	50	9	2	1	0	6	9	3	.300	.260
First Pitch	.327	104	34	0	1	3	11	10	0	.383	.433	August	.310	87	27	1	0	3	7	11	6	.388	.425
Ahead on Count	.192	99	19	4	1	1	6	28	0	.370	.283	September/October	.158	76	12	0	1	1	6	15	12	.293	.224
Behind on Count	.212	118	25	5	1	1	7	0	22	.210	.297	Pre-All Star	.224	197	46	4	2	2	20	22	21	.306	.289
Two Strikes	.169	136	23	3	0	1	5	13	39	.240	.213	Post-All Star	.232	190	44	3	1	4	17	31	20	.336	.321

1992 By Position

Position	Avg	AB	H	2B	3B	HR	RBI	BB	SO	OBP	SLG	G	GS	Innings	PO	A	E	DP	Fld Pct	Rng Fctr	In Zone	Outs	Zone Rtg	MLB Zone
As Pinch Hitter	.000	10	0	0	0	0	0	1	3	.091	.000	12	0	---	---	---	---	---	---	---	---	---	---	---
As 2b	.238	403	96	7	4	6	26	49	34	.319	.320	145	114	1065.0	236	324	9	57	.984	4.73	376	343	.912	.892
As 3b	.071	14	1	0	0	0	0	0	2	.071	.071	13	1	32.2	0	10	0	0	1.000	2.76	10	9	.900	.841

Career (1988-1992)

	Avg	AB	H	2B	3B	HR	RBI	BB	SO	OBP	SLG		Avg	AB	H	2B	3B	HR	RBI	BB	SO	OBP	SLG
vs. Left	.246	411	101	19	3	7	45	36	28	.304	.358	Scoring Posn	.243	263	64	11	4	1	71	35	23	.324	.327
vs. Right	.214	637	136	18	4	3	37	73	72	.293	.268	Close & Late	.234	197	46	4	2	1	20	22	21	.306	.289
Groundball	.227	348	79	11	2	2	24	39	41	.303	.287	None on/out	.219	251	55	9	2	5	5	20	23	.277	.331
Flyball	.259	278	72	13	2	5	27	29	25	.328	.374	Batting #7	.222	261	58	13	2	2	15	22	13	.281	.310
Home	.236	533	126	24	1	7	45	47	47	.303	.325	Batting #8	.218	372	81	7	2	4	24	40	45	.292	.280
Away	.216	515	111	13	6	3	37	57	53	.291	.282	Other	.236	415	98	17	3	4	43	47	42	.312	.320
Day	.275	269	74	13	1	1	22	25	24	.331	.342	April	.213	94	20	5	0	0	7	7	13	.265	.266
Night	.209	779	163	24	6	9	60	84	76	.285	.290	May	.212	165	35	6	1	1	8	19	14	.289	.279
Grass	.240	772	185	28	5	8	64	83	71	.312	.320	June	.240	104	25	2	2	1	6	13	10	.325	.327
Turf	.188	276	52	9	2	2	18	26	29	.255	.257	July	.213	127	27	4	1	0	17	17	9	.303	.283
First Pitch	.235	230	54	5	1	3	20	12	0	.270	.304	August	.280	200	56	4	0	4	16	18	22	.338	.360
Ahead on Count	.262	279	73	20	2	4	32	68	0	.404	.391	September/October	.207	358	74	16	3	3	28	35	32	.276	.293
Behind on Count	.197	304	60	10	3	2	22	0	64	.195	.270	Pre-All Star	.219	397	87	13	4	2	26	44	38	.294	.287
Two Strikes	.165	333	55	8	0	2	18	27	100	.225	.207	Post-All Star	.230	651	150	24	3	8	56	65	62	.299	.313

Batter vs. Pitcher (career)																							
Hits Best Against	Avg	AB	H	2B	3B	HR	RBI	BB	SO	OBP	SLG	Hits Worst Against	Avg	AB	H	2B	3B	HR	RBI	BB	SO	OBP	SLG
Pete Harnisch	.417	12	5	0	0	0	2	0	1	.417	.417	Danny Jackson	.000	11	0	0	0	0	0	2	0	.154	.000
Jose Rijo	.364	11	4	2	0	0	0	0	1	.364	.545	Bob Tewksbury	.077	13	1	1	0	0	0	1	1	.143	.154
												John Burkett	.091	11	1	0	0	0	0	1	1	.167	.091
												Dennis Rasmussen	.100	10	1	0	0	0	0	1	1	.182	.100
												Doug Drabek	.100	10	1	0	0	0	0	1	1	.182	.100

Patrick Lennon — Mariners
Bats Right (flyball hitter)

	Avg	G	AB	R	H	2B	3B	HR	RBI	BB	SO	HBP	GDP	SB	CS	OBP	SLG	IBB	SH	SF	#Pit	#P/PA	GB	FB	G/F
1992 Season	.000	1	2	0	0	0	0	0	0	0	0	0	0	0	0	.000	.000	0	0	0	8	4.00	1	1	1.00
Career (1991-1992)	.100	10	10	2	1	1	0	0	0	3	0	0	0	0	0	.308	.200	0	0	0	54	4.15	4	5	0.80

1992 Season

	Avg	AB	H	2B	3B	HR	RBI	BB	SO	OBP	SLG		Avg	AB	H	2B	3B	HR	RBI	BB	SO	OBP	SLG
vs. Left	.000	0	0	0	0	0	0	0	0	.000	.000	Scoring Posn	.000	0	0	0	0	0	0	0	0	.000	.000
vs. Right	.000	2	0	0	0	0	0	0	0	.000	.000	Close & Late	.000	0	0	0	0	0	0	0	0	.000	.000

Danilo Leon — Rangers
Pitches Right

	ERA	W	L	Sv	G	GS	IP	BB	SO	Avg	H	2B	3B	HR	RBI	OBP	SLG	GF	IR	IRS	Hld	SvOp	SB	CS	GB	FB	G/F
1992 Season	5.89	1	1	0	15	0	18.1	10	15	.254	18	2	1	5	13	.369	.521	3	9	3	0	0	1	1	27	21	1.29

1992 Season

	ERA	W	L	Sv	G	GS	IP	H	HR	BB	SO		Avg	AB	H	2B	3B	HR	RBI	BB	SO	OBP	SLG
Home	4.76	0	1	0	7	0	11.1	11	2	7	7	vs. Left	.280	25	7	1	0	1	5	3	5	.379	.440
Away	7.71	1	0	0	8	0	7.0	7	3	3	8	vs. Right	.239	46	11	1	1	4	8	7	10	.364	.565

Mark Leonard — Giants
Bats Left

	Avg	G	AB	R	H	2B	3B	HR	RBI	BB	SO	HBP	GDP	SB	CS	OBP	SLG	IBB	SH	SF	#Pit	#P/PA	GB	FB	G/F
1992 Season	.234	55	128	13	30	7	0	4	16	16	31	3	3	0	1	.331	.383	0	0	1	586	3.96	41	41	1.00
Career (1990-1992)	.234	130	274	30	64	15	1	7	32	31	64	4	6	0	2	.317	.372	1	1	3	1231	3.95	83	83	1.00

1992 Season

	Avg	AB	H	2B	3B	HR	RBI	BB	SO	OBP	SLG		Avg	AB	H	2B	3B	HR	RBI	BB	SO	OBP	SLG
vs. Left	.158	19	3	0	0	0	0	2	6	.238	.158	Scoring Posn	.182	33	6	2	0	1	9	2	10	.263	.333
vs. Right	.248	109	27	7	0	4	16	14	25	.346	.422	Close & Late	.231	26	6	2	0	1	3	3	11	.355	.423
Home	.208	53	11	2	0	3	10	6	13	.288	.415	None on/out	.235	34	8	2	0	0	0	6	9	.366	.294
Away	.253	75	19	5	0	1	6	10	18	.360	.360	Batting #4	.256	86	22	6	0	2	10	8	18	.333	.395
First Pitch	.385	13	5	3	0	0	3	0	0	.385	.615	Batting #6	.167	12	2	0	0	0	0	2	4	.286	.167
Ahead on Count	.243	37	9	1	0	2	5	6	0	.349	.432	Other	.200	30	6	1	0	2	6	6	9	.342	.433
Behind on Count	.143	42	6	0	0	2	6	0	16	.178	.286	Pre-All Star	.273	11	3	2	0	1	5	1	4	.308	.727
Two Strikes	.164	55	9	3	0	3	10	31		.319	.218	Post-All Star	.231	117	27	5	0	3	11	15	27	.333	.350

Jesse Levis — Indians
Bats Left (groundball hitter)

	Avg	G	AB	R	H	2B	3B	HR	RBI	BB	SO	HBP	GDP	SB	CS	OBP	SLG	IBB	SH	SF	#Pit	#P/PA	GB	FB	G/F
1992 Season	.279	28	43	2	12	4	0	1	3	0	5	0	1	0	0	.279	.442	0	0	0	140	3.26	19	10	1.90

1992 Season

	Avg	AB	H	2B	3B	HR	RBI	BB	SO	OBP	SLG		Avg	AB	H	2B	3B	HR	RBI	BB	SO	OBP	SLG
vs. Left	1.000	2	2	1	0	0	1	0	0	1.000	1.500	Scoring Posn	.222	9	2	1	0	0	2	0	2	.222	.333
vs. Right	.244	41	10	3	0	1	2	0	5	.244	.390	Close & Late	.167	12	2	1	0	0	0	0	2	.167	.250

Darren Lewis — Giants
Bats Right (groundball hitter)

	Avg	G	AB	R	H	2B	3B	HR	RBI	BB	SO	HBP	GDP	SB	CS	OBP	SLG	IBB	SH	SF	#Pit	#P/PA	GB	FB	G/F
1992 Season	.231	100	320	38	74	8	1	1	18	29	46	1	3	28	8	.295	.272	0	10	2	1360	3.86	132	72	1.83
Career (1990-1992)	.237	197	577	83	137	13	4	2	34	72	80	4	6	43	15	.325	.284	0	20	2	2572	3.93	250	131	1.91

1992 Season

	Avg	AB	H	2B	3B	HR	RBI	BB	SO	OBP	SLG		Avg	AB	H	2B	3B	HR	RBI	BB	SO	OBP	SLG
vs. Left	.216	125	27	3	0	1	5	12	16	.285	.264	Scoring Posn	.271	59	16	1	0	0	17	3	9	.297	.288
vs. Right	.241	195	47	5	1	0	13	17	30	.302	.277	Close & Late	.222	54	12	2	0	0	2	4	9	.276	.259
Groundball	.203	153	31	5	0	0	9	14	16	.268	.235	None on/out	.223	130	29	1	1	1	1	15	18	.303	.269
Flyball	.246	61	15	1	0	1	6	6	15	.324	.311	Batting #1	.220	255	56	4	1	1	14	25	37	.287	.255
Home	.176	142	25	2	0	1	8	13	18	.248	.211	Batting #2	.292	48	14	3	0	0	3	6	3	.333	.354
Away	.275	178	49	6	1	0	10	16	28	.333	.320	Other	.235	17	4	1	0	0	2	1	3	.316	.294
Day	.208	130	27	1	0	0	9	11	19	.270	.215	April	.319	91	29	2	1	0	6	12	14	.398	.363
Night	.247	190	47	7	1	1	9	18	27	.313	.311	May	.172	87	15	0	0	0	4	6	14	.229	.172
Grass	.206	214	44	5	0	1	11	22	27	.282	.243	June	.176	51	9	2	0	1	4	5	8	.250	.275
Turf	.283	106	30	3	1	0	7	7	19	.325	.330	July	.091	11	1	0	0	0	0	1	1	.167	.091
First Pitch	.116	43	5	0	0	0	2	0	0	.114	.116	August	.125	8	1	0	0	0	0	0	1	.125	.125

1992 Season

	Avg	AB	H	2B	3B	HR	RBI	BB	SO	OBP	SLG
Ahead on Count	.220	59	13	2	0	1	3	14	0	.370	.305
Behind on Count	.237	114	27	2	0	0	8	0	25	.237	.254
Two Strikes	.204	152	31	4	0	0	8	15	46	.280	.230

	Avg	AB	H	2B	3B	HR	RBI	BB	SO	OBP	SLG
September/October	.264	72	19	4	0	0	4	5	8	.312	.319
Pre-All Star	.225	240	54	4	1	1	14	24	37	.296	.263
Post-All Star	.250	80	20	4	0	0	4	5	9	.294	.300

1992 By Position

Position	Avg	AB	H	2B	3B	HR	RBI	BB	SO	OBP	SLG	G	GS	Innings	PO	A	E	DP	Fld Pct	Rng Fctr	In Zone	Outs	Zone Rtg	MLB Zone
As cf	.232	314	73	8	1	1	17	29	44	.298	.274	94	77	720.1	224	3	0	2	1.000	2.84	261	217	.831	.824

Career (1990-1992)

	Avg	AB	H	2B	3B	HR	RBI	BB	SO	OBP	SLG
vs. Left	.245	208	51	7	1	2	11	26	25	.332	.317
vs. Right	.233	369	86	6	3	0	23	46	55	.321	.266
Groundball	.225	218	49	5	0	0	14	25	21	.303	.248
Flyball	.245	106	26	2	0	1	11	18	26	.350	.292
Home	.199	281	56	4	0	1	14	36	34	.296	.224
Away	.274	296	81	9	4	1	20	36	46	.353	.341
Day	.232	233	54	2	0	0	14	29	30	.319	.240
Night	.241	344	83	11	4	2	20	43	50	.329	.314
Grass	.214	406	87	8	1	2	21	54	52	.310	.254
Turf	.292	171	50	5	3	0	13	18	26	.361	.357
First Pitch	.211	71	15	1	0	0	5	0	0	.208	.225
Ahead on Count	.258	132	34	5	1	1	8	36	0	.420	.333
Behind on Count	.209	187	39	3	0	1	14	0	39	.217	.241
Two Strikes	.204	260	53	5	0	0	11	36	80	.308	.230

	Avg	AB	H	2B	3B	HR	RBI	BB	SO	OBP	SLG
Scoring Posn	.233	120	28	2	0	0	31	15	20	.319	.250
Close & Late	.256	90	23	3	1	0	8	12	17	.350	.311
None on/out	.239	222	53	2	3	2	2	34	34	.340	.302
Batting #1	.233	472	110	9	4	2	28	59	67	.320	.282
Batting #2	.278	54	15	3	0	0	2	4	6	.328	.333
Other	.235	51	12	1	0	0	4	9	7	.371	.255
April	.319	91	29	2	1	0	6	12	14	.398	.363
May	.172	87	15	0	0	0	4	6	14	.229	.172
June	.176	51	9	2	0	1	4	5	8	.250	.275
July	.301	73	22	4	1	0	5	12	11	.407	.384
August	.256	117	30	1	2	1	8	13	13	.336	.325
September/October	.203	158	32	4	0	0	7	24	20	.311	.228
Pre-All Star	.225	240	54	4	1	1	14	24	37	.296	.263
Post-All Star	.246	337	83	9	3	1	20	48	43	.345	.300

Batter vs. Pitcher (career)

Hits Best Against	Avg	AB	H	2B	3B	HR	RBI	BB	SO	OBP	SLG
Tom Browning	.462	13	6	1	0	0	1	0	2	.462	.538

Hits Worst Against	Avg	AB	H	2B	3B	HR	RBI	BB	SO	OBP	SLG
Greg Maddux	.125	8	1	0	0	0	1	3	0	.364	.125
Steve Avery	.200	15	3	0	0	0	1	1	2	.250	.200

Mark Lewis — Indians

Bats Right

	Avg	G	AB	R	H	2B	3B	HR	RBI	BB	SO	HBP	GDP	SB	CS	OBP	SLG	IBB	SH	SF	#Pit	#P/PA	GB	FB	G/F
1992 Season	.264	122	413	44	109	21	0	5	30	25	69	3	12	4	5	.308	.351	1	1	4	1584	3.56	124	130	0.95
Career (1991-1992)	.264	206	727	73	192	36	1	5	60	40	114	3	24	6	7	.302	.337	1	3	9	2739	3.52	233	228	1.02

1992 Season

	Avg	AB	H	2B	3B	HR	RBI	BB	SO	OBP	SLG
vs. Left	.289	97	28	10	0	2	10	8	13	.343	.454
vs. Right	.256	316	81	11	0	3	20	17	56	.297	.320
Groundball	.295	88	26	6	0	0	8	7	17	.351	.364
Flyball	.214	126	27	5	0	2	5	9	22	.272	.302
Home	.277	195	54	13	0	2	17	13	28	.321	.374
Away	.252	218	55	8	0	3	13	12	41	.296	.330
Day	.264	110	29	6	0	0	5	9	17	.311	.318
Night	.264	303	80	15	0	5	25	16	52	.307	.363
Grass	.261	352	92	18	0	5	26	20	57	.301	.355
Turf	.279	61	17	3	0	0	4	5	12	.348	.328
First Pitch	.245	53	13	3	0	0	2	1	0	.268	.302
Ahead on Count	.305	95	29	6	0	2	11	16	0	.407	.432
Behind on Count	.231	147	34	4	0	2	8	0	42	.230	.299
Two Strikes	.192	177	34	6	0	2	6	8	69	.226	.260

	Avg	AB	H	2B	3B	HR	RBI	BB	SO	OBP	SLG
Scoring Posn	.193	83	16	4	0	0	22	9	18	.260	.241
Close & Late	.200	75	15	2	0	0	3	6	17	.277	.227
None on/out	.277	101	28	6	0	2	2	7	17	.330	.396
Batting #2	.266	109	29	7	0	2	7	7	21	.314	.385
Batting #8	.262	191	50	8	0	1	9	7	26	.288	.319
Other	.265	113	30	6	0	2	14	11	22	.333	.372
April	.289	76	22	3	0	1	4	7	12	.341	.368
May	.286	77	22	5	0	2	13	5	13	.333	.429
June	.215	79	17	3	0	0	4	1	12	.225	.253
July	.194	62	12	2	0	1	2	4	12	.254	.274
August	.337	86	29	7	0	1	5	7	15	.394	.453
September/October	.212	33	7	1	0	0	2	2	1	.229	.242
Pre-All Star	.258	264	68	13	0	3	22	15	45	.297	.341
Post-All Star	.275	149	41	8	0	2	8	10	24	.327	.369

1992 By Position

Position	Avg	AB	H	2B	3B	HR	RBI	BB	SO	OBP	SLG	G	GS	Innings	PO	A	E	DP	Fld Pct	Rng Fctr	In Zone	Outs	Zone Rtg	MLB Zone
As ss	.266	410	109	21	0	5	30	25	69	.310	.354	121	113	1017.1	184	333	25	72	.954	4.57	421	366	.869	.885

Career (1991-1992)

	Avg	AB	H	2B	3B	HR	RBI	BB	SO	OBP	SLG
vs. Left	.283	184	52	13	0	2	17	13	25	.325	.366
vs. Right	.258	543	140	23	1	3	43	27	89	.293	.320
Groundball	.251	183	46	8	1	0	12	8	25	.284	.306
Flyball	.237	194	46	8	0	2	12	13	33	.288	.309
Home	.277	354	98	19	1	2	32	20	47	.312	.353
Away	.252	373	94	17	0	3	28	20	67	.291	.322
Day	.308	195	60	12	0	0	20	13	27	.343	.369
Night	.248	532	132	24	1	5	40	27	87	.286	.325
Grass	.267	629	168	32	1	5	53	35	99	.304	.345
Turf	.245	98	24	4	0	0	7	5	15	.290	.286
First Pitch	.258	97	25	6	0	0	1	1	0	.267	.320
Ahead on Count	.329	173	57	11	0	2	26	23	0	.405	.428
Behind on Count	.217	258	56	5	0	2	16	0	74	.215	.260
Two Strikes	.191	298	57	10	1	2	10	16	114	.231	.252

	Avg	AB	H	2B	3B	HR	RBI	BB	SO	OBP	SLG
Scoring Posn	.255	157	40	8	0	0	52	12	28	.292	.306
Close & Late	.199	141	28	5	0	0	11	11	30	.266	.234
None on/out	.269	145	39	9	1	2	2	11	21	.325	.386
Batting #2	.287	272	78	19	0	2	23	14	45	.322	.379
Batting #8	.265	196	52	8	0	1	9	7	27	.291	.321
Other	.239	259	62	9	1	2	26	19	42	.289	.305
April	.311	90	28	6	0	1	6	8	14	.360	.411
May	.326	187	61	10	0	2	26	11	28	.361	.412
June	.178	169	30	5	0	0	10	5	21	.220	.207
July	.176	102	18	2	1	1	3	5	20	.220	.245
August	.337	86	29	7	0	1	5	7	15	.394	.453
September/October	.280	93	26	6	0	0	10	4	16	.303	.344
Pre-All Star	.263	498	131	23	1	3	44	26	75	.297	.331
Post-All Star	.266	229	61	13	0	2	16	14	39	.312	.349

Batter vs. Pitcher (career)

Hits Best Against	Avg	AB	H	2B	3B	HR	RBI	BB	SO	OBP	SLG	Hits Worst Against	Avg	AB	H	2B	3B	HR	RBI	BB	SO	OBP	SLG
Mike Moore	.636	11	7	3	0	0	3	0	1	.636	.909	Greg Hibbard	.091	11	1	1	0	0	0	0	1	.091	.182
Randy Johnson	.333	6	2	0	0	0	1	2	1	.545	.333	Jaime Navarro	.118	17	2	1	0	0	0	0	1	.118	.176
Jack Morris	.308	13	4	1	0	0	2	1	1	.333	.385	Chuck Finley	.150	20	3	0	0	0	0	3	3	.261	.150
												Dave Stewart	.182	11	2	0	0	0	0	1	5	.250	.182
												Kevin Appier	.182	11	2	0	0	0	0	0	2	.182	.182

Richie Lewis — Orioles   Pitches Right

	ERA	W	L	Sv	G	GS	IP	BB	SO	Avg	H	2B	3B	HR	RBI	OBP	SLG	CG	ShO	Sup	QS	#P/S	SB	CS	GB	FB	G/F
1992 Season	10.80	1	1	0	2	2	6.2	7	4	.406	13	3	0	1	8	.500	.594	0	0	9.45	0	73	3	0	10	10	1.00

1992 Season

	ERA	W	L	Sv	G	GS	IP	H	HR	BB	SO		Avg	AB	H	2B	3B	HR	RBI	BB	SO	OBP	SLG
Home	19.29	0	1	0	1	1	2.1	8	0	1	1	vs. Left	.385	13	5	1	0	0	3	3	0	.500	.462
Away	6.23	1	0	0	1	1	4.1	5	1	6	3	vs. Right	.421	19	8	2	0	1	5	4	4	.500	.684

Scott Lewis — Angels   Pitches Right (flyball pitcher)

	ERA	W	L	Sv	G	GS	IP	BB	SO	Avg	H	2B	3B	HR	RBI	OBP	SLG	GF	IR	IRS	Hld	SvOp	SB	CS	GB	FB	G/F
1992 Season	3.99	4	0	0	21	2		14	18	.255	36	2	0	3	9	.325	.333	7	14	2	5	0	2	3	51	55	0.93
Career (1990-1992)	4.93	8	6	0	39	15	115.0	37	64	.279	127	21	0	14	55	.337	.418	7	23	5	5	0	6		152	161	0.94

1992 Season

	ERA	W	L	Sv	G	GS	IP	H	HR	BB	SO		Avg	AB	H	2B	3B	HR	RBI	BB	SO	OBP	SLG
Home	3.09	3	0	0	13	1	23.1	25	2	7	11	vs. Left	.211	57	12	1	0	0	1	10	5	.328	.228
Away	5.40	1	0	0	8	1	15.0	11	1	7	7	vs. Right	.286	84	24	1	0	3	8	4	13	.323	.405
Starter	3.00	1	0	0	2	2	12.0	8	2	5	3	Scoring Posn	.125	24	3	0	0	0	6	3	5	.226	.125
Reliever	4.44	3	0	0	19	0	26.1	28	1	9	15	Close & Late	.250	44	11	1	0	0	1	2	5	.298	.273
0 Days rest	0.00	0	0	0	2	0	2.1	1	0	0	2	None on/out	.286	42	12	1	0	3	3	1	4	.318	.524
1 or 2 Days rest	2.51	3	0	0	9	0	14.1	16	0	3	7	First Pitch	.263	19	5	0	0	0	1	1	0	.300	.263
3+ Days rest	8.38	0	0	0	8	0	9.2	11	1	6	6	Behind on Count	.297	37	11	0	0	1	4	4	0	.341	.378
Pre-All Star	5.94	1	0	0	6	2	16.2	15	3	9	6	Ahead on Count	.185	54	10	2	0	1	2	0	11	.214	.278
Post-All Star	2.49	3	0	0	15	0	21.2	21	0	5	12	Two Strikes	.172	58	10	1	0	1	2	9	18	.294	.241

Jim Leyritz — Yankees   Bats Right

	Avg	G	AB	R	H	2B	3B	HR	RBI	BB	SO	HBP	GDP	SB	CS	OBP	SLG	IBB	SH	SF	#Pit	#P/PA	GB	FB	G/F
1992 Season	.257	63	144	17	37	6	0	7	26	14	22	6	2	0	3	.341	.444	1	0	3	664	3.98	47	53	0.89
Career (1990-1992)	.246	187	524	53	129	22	1	12	55	54	88	13	13	2	5	.329	.361	2	2	8	2310	3.88	202	147	1.37

1992 Season

	Avg	AB	H	2B	3B	HR	RBI	BB	SO	OBP	SLG		Avg	AB	H	2B	3B	HR	RBI	BB	SO	OBP	SLG
vs. Left	.245	102	25	5	0	5	20	10	14	.339	.441	Scoring Posn	.219	32	7	2	0	1	18	5	7	.317	.375
vs. Right	.286	42	12	1	0	2	6	4	8	.347	.452	Close & Late	.235	17	4	1	0	1	6	1	2	.391	.471
Home	.246	69	17	3	0	3	10	8	12	.354	.420	None on/out	.333	39	13	2	0	1		3	3	.395	.462
Away	.267	75	20	3	0	4	16	6	10	.329	.467	Batting #5	.238	42	10	3	0	2	9	3	8	.306	.452
First Pitch	.429	7	3	1	0	0	2	1	0	.556	.571	Batting #6	.270	74	20	3	0	4	11	7	11	.353	.473
Ahead on Count	.447	38	17	0	0	6	13	8	0	.531	.921	Other	.250	28	7	0	0	1	6	4	3	.364	.357
Behind on Count	.203	59	12	3	0	2	13	0	11	.222	.356	Pre-All Star	.263	80	21	3	0	5	16	13	10	.378	.488
Two Strikes	.151	73	11	3	0	1	10	5	22	.232	.233	Post-All Star	.250	64	16	3	0	2	10	1	12	.290	.391

Career (1990-1992)

	Avg	AB	H	2B	3B	HR	RBI	BB	SO	OBP	SLG		Avg	AB	H	2B	3B	HR	RBI	BB	SO	OBP	SLG
vs. Left	.264	242	64	14	1	7	29	30	38	.361	.417	Scoring Posn	.207	111	23	4	0	2	40	18	19	.313	.297
vs. Right	.230	282	65	8	0	5	26	24	50	.302	.312	Close & Late	.258	97	25	5	0	1	12	6	12	.330	.340
Groundball	.283	145	41	4	1	6	22	16	24	.364	.448	None on/out	.303	132	40	6	0	3		9	15	.361	.417
Flyball	.243	107	26	4	0	3	14	16	25	.352	.364	Batting #6	.188	170	32	5	0	4	15	16	25	.272	.288
Home	.253	257	65	14	1	4	25	30	43	.345	.362	Batting #7	.320	150	48	6	1	6	23	14	23	.387	.493
Away	.240	267	64	8	0	8	30	24	45	.314	.360	Other	.240	204	49	11	0	2	17	24	40	.335	.324
Day	.253	178	45	7	1	4	15	22	32	.346	.371	April	.150	20	3	0	0	1	2	8	5	.393	.300
Night	.243	346	84	15	0	8	40	32	56	.321	.355	May	.222	54	12	3	0	2	6	6	7	.300	.389
Grass	.238	421	100	17	1	8	41	44	77	.322	.340	June	.317	101	32	4	0	4	14	7	12	.360	.475
Turf	.282	103	29	5	0	4	14	10	11	.359	.447	July	.192	125	24	2	0	1	5	18	24	.322	.232
First Pitch	.457	35	16	4	0	2	1		0	.486	.571	August	.254	114	29	6	1	1	12	7	21	.317	.351
Ahead on Count	.350	123	43	4	0	9	23	28	0	.465	.602	September/October	.264	110	29	7	0	3	16	8	19	.322	.409
Behind on Count	.188	207	39	8	1	2	21	0	50	.213	.266	Pre-All Star	.250	220	55	7	0	7	24	29	26	.343	.377
Two Strikes	.126	247	31	6	0	2	24	23	87	.222	.174	Post-All Star	.243	304	74	15	1	5	31	25	60	.320	.349

Batter vs. Pitcher (career)

Hits Best Against	Avg	AB	H	2B	3B	HR	RBI	BB	SO	OBP	SLG	Hits Worst Against	Avg	AB	H	2B	3B	HR	RBI	BB	SO	OBP	SLG
												Frank Tanana	.077	13	1	0	0	0	0	0	1	.077	.077
												Mark Langston	.077	13	1	0	0	0	0	0	4	.077	.077
												Jack Morris	.125	8	1	0	0	1	2	3	1	.364	.500
												Randy Johnson	.200	5	1	0	0	0	0		4	.692	.200

Derek Lilliquist — Indians

Pitches Left (flyball pitcher)

	ERA	W	L	Sv	G	GS	IP	BB	SO	Avg	H	2B	3B	HR	RBI	OBP	SLG	GF	IR	IRS	Hld	SvOp	SB	CS	GB	FB	G/F
1992 Season	1.75	5	3	6	71	0	61.2	18	47	.187	39	10	0	5	18	.253	.306	22	54	12	15	11	4	2	43	93	0.46
Career (1989-1992)	4.23	18	26	6	137	50	363.2	98	196	.282	402	77	3	40	162	.329	.425	26	61	14	16	12	22	12	436	506	0.86

1992 Season

	ERA	W	L	Sv	G	GS	IP	H	HR	BB	SO		Avg	AB	H	2B	3B	HR	RBI	BB	SO	OBP	SLG
Home	2.25	2	2	5	38	0	32.0	16	3	9	24	vs. Left	.200	90	18	4	0	1	7	5	24	.245	.278
Away	1.21	3	1	1	33	0	29.2	23	2	9	23	vs. Right	.176	119	21	6	0	4	11	13	23	.259	.328
Day	2.66	2	1	3	25	0	20.1	12	2	9	18	Inning 1-6	.000	1	0	0	0	0	0	0	0	.000	.000
Night	1.31	3	2	3	46	0	41.1	27	3	9	29	Inning 7+	.188	208	39	10	0	5	18	18	47	.254	.308
Grass	2.03	3	3	6	60	0	53.1	32	5	12	39	None on	.153	118	18	5	0	3	3	8	28	.219	.271
Turf	0.00	2	0	0	11	0	8.1	7	0	6	8	Runners on	.231	91	21	5	0	2	15	10	19	.295	.352
April	0.93	0	0	1	10	0	9.2	3	0	4	4	Scoring Posn	.169	59	10	4	0	1	13	10	14	.274	.288
May	3.18	2	2	0	13	0	11.1	6	1	6	11	Close & Late	.231	130	30	5	0	3	13	11	29	.290	.338
June	1.04	1	0	0	11	0	8.2	3	1	2	4	None on/out	.106	47	5	2	0	0	6	6	10	.208	.149
July	1.00	1	0	2	10	0	9.0	7	1	3	11	vs. 1st Batr (relief)	.237	59	14	4	0	2	12	6	11	.294	.407
August	0.84	1	0	2	13	0	10.2	6	0	3	8	First Inning Pitched	.183	164	30	7	0	4	17	17	31	.258	.299
September/October	2.92	0	1	1	14	0	12.1	14	2	0	9	First 15 Pitches	.206	160	33	8	0	4	17	15	28	.276	.331
Starter	0.00	0	0	0	0	0	0.0	0	0	0	0	Pitch 16-30	.095	42	4	2	0	0	0	3	17	.156	.143
Reliever	1.75	5	3	6	71	0	61.2	39	5	18	47	Pitch 31-45	.286	7	2	0	0	1	1	0	2	.286	.714
0 Days rest	3.60	1	2	2	21	0	15.0	13	2	7	10	Pitch 46+	.000	0	0	0	0	0	0	0	0	.000	.000
1 or 2 Days rest	1.15	3	1	4	33	0	31.1	19	2	8	24	First Pitch	.385	26	10	1	0	1	2	5	0	.485	.538
3+ Days rest	1.17	1	0	0	17	0	15.1	7	1	3	13	Ahead on Count	.140	107	15	7	0	1	9	0	41	.144	.234
Pre-All Star	1.71	3	2	1	36	0	31.2	12	2	12	21	Behind on Count	.243	37	9	1	0	2	3	6	0	.349	.432
Post-All Star	1.80	2	1	5	35	0	30.0	27	3	6	26	Two Strikes	.088	102	9	4	0	0	7	7	47	.150	.127

Career (1989-1992)

	ERA	W	L	Sv	G	GS	IP	H	HR	BB	SO		Avg	AB	H	2B	3B	HR	RBI	BB	SO	OBP	SLG
Home	3.78	9	14	5	73	25	192.2	205	21	45	109	vs. Left	.268	302	81	15	1	8	34	18	68	.314	.404
Away	4.74	9	12	1	64	25	171.0	197	19	53	87	vs. Right	.286	1122	321	62	2	32	128	80	128	.333	.430
Day	5.09	7	8	3	47	16	109.2	128	14	34	63	Inning 1-6	.293	1066	312	57	3	30	128	65	130	.334	.436
Night	3.86	11	18	3	90	34	254.0	274	26	64	133	Inning 7+	.251	358	90	20	0	10	34	33	85	.316	.391
Grass	4.33	12	22	6	111	38	284.2	311	32	71	156	None on	.263	835	220	46	3	24	24	47	125	.307	.412
Turf	3.87	6	4	0	26	12	79.0	91	8	27	40	Runners on	.309	589	182	31	0	16	138	51	71	.358	.443
April	4.91	1	6	1	18	8	51.1	60	8	15	30	Scoring Posn	.284	335	95	20	0	9	117	40	47	.351	.424
May	3.30	6	7	0	25	12	87.1	78	8	23	39	Close & Late	.258	194	50	9	0	4	18	19	40	.321	.366
June	5.91	3	3	0	21	8	45.2	63	4	12	23	None on/out	.243	358	87	17	1	11	11	25	56	.298	.388
July	5.01	2	2	2	21	6	46.2	59	9	16	27	vs. 1st Batr (relief)	.236	72	17	4	0	2	13	9	12	.310	.375
August	3.95	3	2	2	24	6	54.2	64	4	19	26	First Inning Pitched	.251	422	106	20	0	14	46	40	59	.314	.398
September/October	3.56	3	6	1	28	10	78.0	78	7	13	51	First 15 Pitches	.286	405	116	22	0	14	44	33	49	.339	.444
Starter	4.64	13	22	0	50	50	275.2	330	31	66	133	Pitch 16-30	.256	293	75	17	1	5	24	14	57	.292	.372
Reliever	2.97	5	4	6	87	0	88.0	72	9	32	63	Pitch 31-45	.242	215	67	16	0	5	26	14	28	.352	.456
0 Days rest	4.15	1	2	2	22	0	17.1	17	3	8	10	Pitch 46+	.282	511	144	22	2	16	68	37	62	.332	.427
1 or 2 Days rest	1.67	3	1	4	37	0	37.2	25	4	10	28	First Pitch	.371	251	93	14	0	4	30	13	0	.401	.474
3+ Days rest	3.82	1	1	0	28	0	33.0	30	2	14	25	Ahead on Count	.206	608	125	27	1	11	47	0	175	.210	.308
Pre-All Star	4.37	10	16	1	68	29	191.2	211	22	52	97	Behind on Count	.362	323	117	25	2	12	51	49	1	.444	.563
Post-All Star	4.08	8	10	5	69	21	172.0	191	18	46	99	Two Strikes	.176	550	97	16	1	10	39	36	195	.226	.264

Pitcher vs. Batter (career)

Pitches Best Vs.	Avg	AB	H	2B	3B	HR	RBI	BB	SO	OBP	SLG	Pitches Worst Vs.	Avg	AB	H	2B	3B	HR	RBI	BB	SO	OBP	SLG
Kevin McReynolds	.067	15	1	0	0	0	1	2	2	.176	.067	Todd Benzinger	.688	16	11	0	0	0	1	1	1	.706	.688
Jose Lind	.091	11	1	0	0	0	0	0	1	.091	.091	Willie McGee	.538	13	7	0	1	1	2	1	0	.571	.923
Vince Coleman	.143	14	2	0	0	1	1	2	3	.250	.357	Will Clark	.526	19	10	3	0	2	3	1	2	.550	1.000
Gerald Young	.167	12	2	1	0	0	1	1	1	.231	.250	Howard Johnson	.417	12	5	1	0	2	3	0	0	.417	1.000
Kevin Mitchell	.214	14	3	0	0	0	0	2	0	.313	.214	Glenn Davis	.417	12	5	0	0	2	6	1	1	.462	.917

Jose Lind — Pirates

Bats Right (groundball hitter)

	Avg	G	AB	R	H	2B	3B	HR	RBI	BB	SO	HBP	GDP	SB	CS	OBP	SLG	IBB	SH	SF	#Pit	#P/PA	GB	FB	G/F
1992 Season	.235	135	468	38	110	14	1	0	39	26	29	1	14	3	1	.275	.269	12	7	4	1686	3.38	228	137	1.66
Last Five Years	.251	744	2673	271	671	103	19	8	238	172	276	17	48	35	10	.295	.313	48	41	25	10024	3.49	1247	708	1.76

1992 Season

	Avg	AB	H	2B	3B	HR	RBI	BB	SO	OBP	SLG		Avg	AB	H	2B	3B	HR	RBI	BB	SO	OBP	SLG
vs. Left	.237	177	42	6	1	0	14	11	16	.277	.282	Scoring Posn	.257	136	35	5	0	0	38	17	9	.331	.294
vs. Right	.234	291	68	8	0	0	25	15	13	.273	.261	Close & Late	.289	90	26	5	0	0	9	4	5	.326	.344
Groundball	.224	170	38	4	0	0	11	12	6	.279	.247	None on/out	.245	106	26	4	0	0	0	2	4	.259	.283
Flyball	.260	104	27	4	0	0	9	3	13	.275	.298	Batting #6	.000	3	0	0	0	0	0	0	1	.000	.000
Home	.253	229	58	7	1	0	24	16	14	.298	.293	Batting #8	.237	464	110	14	1	0	39	26	28	.277	.272
Away	.218	239	52	7	0	0	15	10	15	.251	.247	Other	.000	1	0	0	0	0	0	0	0	.000	.000
Day	.158	114	18	2	1	0	5	10	8	.226	.193	April	.161	56	9	0	1	0	4	2	0	.186	.196
Night	.260	354	92	12	0	0	34	16	21	.291	.294	May	.297	74	22	2	0	0	13	0	6	.289	.324
Grass	.211	114	24	2	0	0	6	5	8	.244	.228	June	.269	93	25	5	0	0	7	9	8	.333	.323

261

1992 Season

	Avg	AB	H	2B	3B	HR	RBI	BB	SO	OBP	SLG		Avg	AB	H	2B	3B	HR	RBI	BB	SO	OBP	SLG
Turf	.243	354	86	12	1	0	33	21	21	.284	.282	July	.159	88	14	3	0	0	2	4	7	.196	.193
First Pitch	.324	68	22	3	0	0	9	11	0	.413	.368	August	.255	94	24	3	0	0	7	7	5	.307	.287
Ahead on Count	.325	123	40	5	0	0	10	9	0	.368	.366	September/October	.254	63	16	1	0	0	6	4	3	.304	.270
Behind on Count	.190	158	30	4	1	0	8	0	20	.193	.228	Pre-All Star	.233	262	61	7	1	0	24	15	19	.271	.267
Two Strikes	.155	181	28	2	1	0	11	7	29	.189	.177	Post-All Star	.238	206	49	7	0	0	15	11	10	.279	.272

1992 By Position

Position	Avg	AB	H	2B	3B	HR	RBI	BB	SO	OBP	SLG	G	GS	Innings	PO	A	E	DP	Fld Pct	Rng Fctr	In Zone	Outs	Zone Rtg	MLB Zone
As 2b	.236	467	110	14	1	0	39	26	29	.275	.270	134	131	1190.2	311	425	6	79	.992	5.56	481	412	.857	.892

Last Five Years

	Avg	AB	H	2B	3B	HR	RBI	BB	SO	OBP	SLG		Avg	AB	H	2B	3B	HR	RBI	BB	SO	OBP	SLG
vs. Left	.248	969	240	6		4	80		106	.301	.313	Scoring Posn	.263	681	179	27	9	1	218	79	72	.331	.333
vs. Right	.253	1704	431	64	13	4	158	92	170	.292	.313	Close & Late	.265	486	129	17	2	1	38	29	53	.305	.315
Groundball	.246	987	243	31	8	2	83	64	102	.293	.300	None on/out	.243	526	128	26	2	3		22	50	.274	.317
Flyball	.250	564	141	24	4	3	53	36	70	.292	.323	Batting #2	.247	1042	257	39	7	4	87	71	121	.294	.309
Home	.257	1345	345	54	11	6	142	90	137	.300	.326	Batting #8	.254	1461	371	61	10	4	135	92	133	.296	.318
Away	.245	1328	326	49	8	2	96	82	139	.290	.299	Other	.253	170	43	3	2	0	16	9	22	.293	.294
Day	.241	718	173	25	8	1	67	52	95	.292	.302	April	.229	376	86	11	1	2	28	24	34	.272	.279
Night	.255	1955	498	78	7	7	171	120	181	.296	.317	May	.278	442	123	22	4	1	57	23	41	.314	.353
Grass	.230	699	161	18	1	1	43	37	72	.271	.263	June	.261	475	124	20	2	3	47	36	51	.311	.331
Turf	.258	1974	510	85	18	7	195	135	204	.304	.330	July	.240	455	109	16	4	2	29	24	44	.279	.305
First Pitch	.306	321	99	16	3	0	42	22	0	.348	.377	August	.212	491	104	18	3	0	33	36	59	.263	.261
Ahead on Count	.307	714	219	31	7	6	75	97	0	.388	.395	September/October	.288	434	125	16	5	0	44	29	47	.333	.348
Behind on Count	.223	951	212	32	6	1	82	4	168	.228	.272	Pre-All Star	.254	1443	367	57	8	7	141	92	136	.298	.319
Two Strikes	.192	1075	206	26	5	1	68	36	275	.218	.272	Post-All Star	.247	1230	304	46	11	1	97	80	140	.292	.305

Batter vs. Pitcher (career)

Hits Best Against	Avg	AB	H	2B	3B	HR	RBI	BB	SO	OBP	SLG	Hits Worst Against	Avg	AB	H	2B	3B	HR	RBI	BB	SO	OBP	SLG
Don Carman	.500	22	11	2	1	1	4	2	2	.542	.818	Bud Black	.000	14	0	0	0	0	0	0	1	.000	.000
Shawn Boskie	.500	12	6	1	0	0	1	0	0	.500	.583	Tommy Greene	.000	13	0	0	0	0	1	1	1	.067	.000
Joe Boever	.444	18	8	1	0	2	3	1	0	.524	.556	John Franco	.083	12	1	0	0	0	0	0	1	.083	.083
Chris Hammond	.429	14	6	1	0	2	3	0		.529	.500	Mike Maddux	.091	11	1	0	0	0	0	0	0	.091	.091
Dennis Rasmussen	.412	17	7	2	0	0	3	2	1	.474	.529	Derek Lilliquist	.091	11	1	0	0	0	0	0	1	.091	.091

Jim Lindeman — Phillies   Bats Right (groundball hitter)

	Avg	G	AB	R	H	2B	3B	HR	RBI	BB	SO	HBP	GDP	SB	CS	OBP	SLG	IBB	SH	SF	#Pit	#P/PA	GB	FB	G/F
1992 Season	.256	29	39	6	10	1	0	1	6	3	11	0	1	0	0	.310	.359	0	0	0	150	3.57	15	7	2.14
Last Five Years	.248	196	254	35	63	9	0	5	35	23	65	0	5	0	1	.308	.343	1	4	2	1099	3.94	91	57	1.60

1992 Season

	Avg	AB	H	2B	3B	HR	RBI	BB	SO	OBP	SLG		Avg	AB	H	2B	3B	HR	RBI	BB	SO	OBP	SLG
vs. Left	.167	24	4	1	0	1	2	2	6	.231	.333	Scoring Posn	.385	13	5	0	0	1	6	1	3	.429	.615
vs. Right	.400	15	6	0	0	0	4	1	5	.438	.400	Close & Late	.308	13	4	0	0	1	4	3	4	.438	.615

Doug Linton — Blue Jays   Pitches Right (flyball pitcher)

	ERA	W	L	Sv	G	GS	IP	BB	SO	Avg	H	2B	3B	HR	RBI	OBP	SLG	GF	IR	IRS	Hld	SvOp	SB	CS	GB	FB	G/F
1992 Season	8.63	1	3	0	8	3	24.0	17	16	.323	31	5	0	5	19	.417	.531	2	5	1	0	0	0	2	29	31	0.94

1992 Season

	ERA	W	L	Sv	G	GS	IP	H	HR	BB	SO		Avg	AB	H	2B	3B	HR	RBI	BB	SO	OBP	SLG
Home	7.71	1	0	0	3	1	9.1	10	1	4	4	vs. Left	.324	37	12	1	0	2	6	9	5	.447	.514
Away	9.20	0	3	0	5	2	14.2	21	4	13	12	vs. Right	.322	59	19	4	0	3	13	8	11	.397	.542

Pat Listach — Brewers   Bats Both (groundball hitter)

	Avg	G	AB	R	H	2B	3B	HR	RBI	BB	SO	HBP	GDP	SB	CS	OBP	SLG	IBB	SH	SF	#Pit	#P/PA	GB	FB	G/F
1992 Season	.290	149	579	93	168	19	6	1	47	55	124	1	3	54	18	.352	.349	0	12	2	2597	4.08	208	98	2.12

1992 Season

	Avg	AB	H	2B	3B	HR	RBI	BB	SO	OBP	SLG		Avg	AB	H	2B	3B	HR	RBI	BB	SO	OBP	SLG
vs. Left	.345	148	51	7	3	1	18	8	25	.382	.453	Scoring Posn	.262	145	38	5	1	0	41	15	38	.331	.310
vs. Right	.271	431	117	12	3	0	29	47	99	.342	.313	Close & Late	.348	89	31	5	1	0	12	9	17	.404	.427
Groundball	.266	139	37	1	1	0	14	6	32	.295	.288	None on/out	.286	196	56	4	3	1	1	23	35	.361	.352
Flyball	.283	159	45	5	1	1	16	17	31	.356	.346	Batting #1	.291	443	129	16	4	1	38	40	96	.351	.352
Home	.251	267	67	9	1	0	26	22	53	.308	.292	Batting #9	.286	70	20	1	1	0	5	9	18	.358	.329
Away	.324	312	101	10	5	1	21	33	71	.388	.397	Other	.288	66	19	2	1	0	4	6	10	.347	.348
Day	.299	177	53	7	0	0	17	23	37	.380	.339	April	.357	28	10	1	1	0	1	3	3	.419	.464
Night	.286	402	115	12	6	1	30	32	87	.333	.353	May	.305	105	32	2	1	0	7	11	17	.371	.343
Grass	.290	483	140	17	2	1	37	41	97	.345	.340	June	.240	100	24	1	1	0	9	5	28	.271	.270
Turf	.292	96	28	2	4	0	10	14	27	.382	.396	July	.321	106	34	5	3	0	11	17	27	.415	.425
First Pitch	.481	81	39	7	0	0	9	0	0	.481	.568	August	.310	116	36	5	0	0	10	6	19	.350	.353

1992 Season

	Avg	AB	H	2B	3B	HR	RBI	BB	SO	OBP	SLG		Avg	AB	H	2B	3B	HR	RBI	BB	SO	OBP	SLG
Ahead on Count	.324	111	36	2	2	0	15	34	0	.483	.378	September/October	.258	124	32	5	0	1	9	13	30	.328	.323
Behind on Count	.172	163	28	4	2	1	11	0	60	.171	.239	Pre-All Star	.293	276	81	7	5	0	21	28	62	.356	.355
Two Strikes	.222	302	67	8	4	1	16	21	124	.272	.285	Post-All Star	.287	303	87	12	1	1	26	27	62	.347	.343

1992 By Position

Position	Avg	AB	H	2B	3B	HR	RBI	BB	SO	OBP	SLG	G	GS	Innings	PO	A	E	DP	Fld Pct	Rng Fctr	In Zone	Outs	Zone Rtg	MLB Zone
As ss	.291	577	168	19	6	1	47	55	124	.353	.350	148	145	1279.0	238	451	24	89	.966	4.85	531	475	.895	.885

Greg Litton — Giants
Bats Right (groundball hitter)

	Avg	G	AB	R	H	2B	3B	HR	RBI	BB	SO	HBP	GDP	SB	CS	OBP	SLG	IBB	SH	SF	#Pit	#P/PA	GB	FB	G/F
1992 Season	.229	68	140	9	32	5	0	4	15	11	33	0	2	0	1	.285	.350	0	3	0	596	3.95	50	38	1.32
Career (1989-1992)	.230	291	614	51	141	26	5	10	71	40	132	3	12	1	5	.279	.337	0	12	3	2420	3.67	242	155	1.56

1992 Season

	Avg	AB	H	2B	3B	HR	RBI	BB	SO	OBP	SLG		Avg	AB	H	2B	3B	HR	RBI	BB	SO	OBP	SLG
vs. Left	.255	47	12	2	0	3	12	3	8	.300	.489	Scoring Posn	.222	36	8	1	0	1	10	5	12	.317	.333
vs. Right	.215	93	20	3	0	1	3	8	25	.277	.280	Close & Late	.355	31	11	1	0	2	5	3	5	.412	.581
Home	.244	45	11	3	0	2	4	7	10	.346	.444	None on/out	.281	32	9	1	0	1	1	1	7	.303	.406
Away	.221	95	21	2	0	2	11	4	23	.253	.305	Batting #6	.119	42	5	0	0	0	0	7	12	.245	.119
First Pitch	.357	14	5	0	0	0	0	0	0	.357	.357	Batting #7	.324	34	11	4	0	1	5	4	5	.395	.529
Ahead on Count	.269	26	7	1	0	2	3	4	0	.367	.538	Other	.250	64	16	1	0	3	10	0	16	.250	.406
Behind on Count	.169	65	11	0	0	1	2	0	20	.169	.215	Pre-All Star	.190	79	15	3	0	2	6	9	20	.273	.304
Two Strikes	.187	75	14	2	0	2	10	7	33	.256	.293	Post-All Star	.279	61	17	2	0	2	9	2	13	.302	.410

Career (1989-1992)

	Avg	AB	H	2B	3B	HR	RBI	BB	SO	OBP	SLG		Avg	AB	H	2B	3B	HR	RBI	BB	SO	OBP	SLG
vs. Left	.260	331	86	18	4	8	42	15	58	.292	.411	Scoring Posn	.236	174	41	10	1	2	59	10	41	.280	.339
vs. Right	.194	283	55	8	1	2	29	25	74	.264	.251	Close & Late	.271	144	39	8	1	3	23	8	32	.303	.403
Groundball	.233	236	55	13	1	3	26	16	52	.287	.335	None on/out	.313	131	41	5	2	4	4	8	21	.353	.473
Flyball	.220	168	37	6	2	3	15	5	36	.241	.333	Batting #2	.248	133	33	7	0	2	10	6	26	.279	.346
Home	.276	268	74	16	5	5	35	19	58	.328	.429	Batting #6	.176	205	36	7	2	2	15	17	45	.238	.259
Away	.194	346	67	10	0	5	36	21	74	.241	.266	Other	.261	276	72	12	3	6	46	17	59	.310	.391
Day	.266	229	61	11	1	5	30	16	48	.317	.389	April	.150	20	3	1	0	0	2	6	6	.227	.200
Night	.208	385	80	15	4	5	41	24	84	.256	.306	May	.205	122	25	5	0	3	10	9	36	.271	.320
Grass	.242	417	101	18	5	6	49	31	92	.298	.353	June	.245	147	36	6	3	2	19	12	24	.300	.367
Turf	.203	197	40	8	0	4	22	9	40	.237	.305	July	.233	103	24	1	1	2	12	1	17	.248	.320
First Pitch	.318	88	28	3	1	1	13	0	0	.318	.409	August	.211	128	27	6	0	2	10	12	31	.279	.305
Ahead on Count	.227	119	27	4	0	4	15	18	0	.326	.361	September/October	.277	94	26	7	1	1	18	4	18	.300	.404
Behind on Count	.186	237	44	7	2	3	19	0	73	.185	.270	Pre-All Star	.226	328	74	13	3	5	33	24	73	.284	.329
Two Strikes	.175	291	51	12	4	4	28	22	132	.232	.285	Post-All Star	.234	286	67	13	2	5	38	16	59	.273	.346

Batter vs. Pitcher (career)

Hits Best Against	Avg	AB	H	2B	3B	HR	RBI	BB	SO	OBP	SLG	Hits Worst Against	Avg	AB	H	2B	3B	HR	RBI	BB	SO	OBP	SLG
Dennis Cook	.615	13	8	1	0	1	2	0	0	.615	.923	Zane Smith	.091	11	1	0	0	0	1	0	1	.091	.091
Charlie Leibrandt	.545	11	6	1	0	0	1	0	1	.545	.636	Bruce Hurst	.143	14	2	0	0	0	1	2	.200	.143	
Norm Charlton	.417	12	5	2	0	0	0	0	2	.417	.583	Tom Glavine	.143	14	2	0	0	1	1	3	.200	.357	
Frank Viola	.333	12	4	0	0	0	2	4	.429	.500	John Smoltz	.200	10	2	0	0	2	1	2	.273	.200		
Greg Maddux	.333	9	3	1	0	0	2	2	5	.455	.444	Terry Mulholland	.217	23	5	1	0	0	1	4	.217	.261

Scott Livingstone — Tigers
Bats Left

	Avg	G	AB	R	H	2B	3B	HR	RBI	BB	SO	HBP	GDP	SB	CS	OBP	SLG	IBB	SH	SF	#Pit	#P/PA	GB	FB	G/F
1992 Season	.282	117	354	43	100	21	0	4	46	21	36	0	8	1	3	.319	.376	1	3	4	1267	3.34	138	102	1.35
Career (1991-1992)	.285	161	481	62	137	26	0	6	57	31	61	0	8	3	4	.325	.376	1	4	5	1725	3.34	184	129	1.43

1992 Season

	Avg	AB	H	2B	3B	HR	RBI	BB	SO	OBP	SLG		Avg	AB	H	2B	3B	HR	RBI	BB	SO	OBP	SLG
vs. Left	.289	45	13	2	0	1	7	4	8	.340	.400	Scoring Posn	.269	93	25	3	0	2	43	6	13	.301	.366
vs. Right	.282	309	87	19	0	3	39	17	28	.316	.372	Close & Late	.222	45	10	2	0	1	8	4	3	.280	.333
Groundball	.219	73	16	1	0	1	10	2	6	.240	.274	None on/out	.337	95	32	7	0	2	5	7	.370	.474	
Flyball	.263	114	30	5	0	2	17	11	13	.325	.360	Batting #7	.310	116	36	13	0	1	15	5	10	.333	.448
Home	.229	175	40	8	0	2	26	12	23	.274	.309	Batting #8	.286	161	46	7	0	1	23	10	13	.326	.335
Away	.335	179	60	13	0	2	20	9	13	.365	.441	Other	.234	77	18	3	0	2	8	6	13	.286	.351
Day	.283	120	34	8	0	1	17	8	14	.323	.375	April	.286	14	4	0	0	1	1	3	.333	.286	
Night	.282	234	66	13	0	3	29	13	22	.317	.376	May	.229	35	8	1	0	0	0	7	.229	.257	
Grass	.272	298	81	18	0	4	44	19	33	.312	.372	June	.354	65	23	5	0	0	8	9	8	.427	.431
Turf	.339	56	19	3	0	0	2	2	3	.362	.393	July	.222	63	14	2	0	0	7	2	2	.242	.254
First Pitch	.244	82	20	2	0	0	9	1	0	.247	.268	August	.248	101	25	6	0	0	15	3	11	.267	.307
Ahead on Count	.366	71	26	6	0	2	14	14	0	.471	.535	September/October	.342	76	26	7	0	4	15	6	5	.386	.592
Behind on Count	.283	106	30	6	0	3	16	0	19	.280	.425	Pre-All Star	.279	147	41	6	0	1	15	11	20	.327	.320
Two Strikes	.233	133	31	4	0	2	18	7	36	.268	.308	Post-All Star	.285	207	59	15	0	4	31	10	16	.314	.415

263

Position	Avg	AB	H	2B	3B	HR	RBI	BB	SO	OBP	SLG	G	GS	Innings	PO	A	E	DP	Fld Pct	Rng Fctr	In Zone	Outs	Zone Rtg	MLB Zone
As Pinch Hitter	.231	13	3	3	0	0	1	1	0	.267	.462	16	0	---	---	---	---	---	---	---	---	---	---	---
As 3b	.284	341	97	18	0	4	45	20	36	.321	.372	112	90	841.1	67	189	10	15	.962	2.74	236	202	.856	.841

Kenny Lofton — Indians   Bats Left (groundball hitter)

	Avg	G	AB	R	H	2B	3B	HR	RBI	BB	SO	HBP	GDP	SB	CS	OBP	SLG	IBB	SH	SF	#Pit	#P/PA	GB	FB	G/F
1992 Season	.285	148	576	96	164	15	8	5	42	68	54	2	7	66	12	.362	.365	3	4	1	2324	3.59	243	116	2.09
Career (1991-1992)	.275	168	650	105	179	16	8	5	42	73	73	2	7	68	13	.350	.348	3	4	1	2611	3.60	269	127	2.12

1992 Season

	Avg	AB	H	2B	3B	HR	RBI	BB	SO	OBP	SLG		Avg	AB	H	2B	3B	HR	RBI	BB	SO	OBP	SLG
vs. Left	.369	122	45	6	1	0	12	21	15	.466	.434	Scoring Posn	.325	114	37	1	3	2	37	10	11	.376	.439
vs. Right	.262	454	119	9	7	5	30	47	39	.331	.346	Close & Late	.225	102	23	1	0	1	5	15	9	.331	.265
Groundball	.267	135	36	5	0	1	7	22	8	.369	.326	None on/out	.254	224	57	5	2	2	2	33	25	.353	.321
Flyball	.288	170	49	6	3	2	9	28	25	.392	.394	Batting #1	.281	551	155	15	8	4	36	66	52	.360	.359
Home	.292	277	81	7	4	3	22	36	23	.375	.379	Batting #9	.391	23	9	0	0	1	6	1	1	.417	.522
Away	.278	299	83	8	4	2	20	32	31	.349	.351	Other	.000	2	0	0	0	0	0	1	1	.333	.000
Day	.292	185	54	5	2	1	10	32	14	.402	.357	April	.215	65	14	1	0	0	3	9	5	.320	.231
Night	.281	391	110	10	6	4	32	36	40	.341	.368	May	.303	109	33	2	1	1	11	9	7	.356	.367
Grass	.286	490	140	13	8	5	40	60	46	.365	.376	June	.247	97	24	2	2	0	4	9	5	.311	.309
Turf	.279	86	24	2	0	0	2	8	8	.340	.302	July	.245	94	23	3	1	2	6	9	8	.317	.362
First Pitch	.343	108	37	2	0	1	13	3	0	.360	.389	August	.340	94	32	4	4	2	10	16	12	.436	.532
Ahead on Count	.345	119	41	5	3	2	10	38	0	.503	.487	September/October	.325	117	38	3	0	0	8	16	17	.403	.350
Behind on Count	.215	149	32	2	2	1	8	0	24	.225	.275	Pre-All Star	.261	307	80	7	4	2	20	29	21	.326	.329
Two Strikes	.228	232	53	6	4	1	15	27	54	.313	.302	Post-All Star	.312	269	84	8	4	3	22	39	33	.400	.405

1992 By Position

Position	Avg	AB	H	2B	3B	HR	RBI	BB	SO	OBP	SLG	G	GS	Innings	PO	A	E	DP	Fld Pct	Rng Fctr	In Zone	Outs	Zone Rtg	MLB Zone
As cf	.286	574	164	15	8	5	42	67	53	.362	.366	143	140	1256.1	419	14	8	4	.982	3.10	470	411	.874	.824

Javier Lopez — Braves   Bats Right

	Avg	G	AB	R	H	2B	3B	HR	RBI	BB	SO	HBP	GDP	SB	CS	OBP	SLG	IBB	SH	SF	#Pit	#P/PA	GB	FB	G/F
1992 Season	.375	9	16	3	6	2	0	0	2	0	1	0	0	0	0	.375	.500	0	0	0	34	2.13	5	5	1.00

1992 Season

	Avg	AB	H	2B	3B	HR	RBI	BB	SO	OBP	SLG		Avg	AB	H	2B	3B	HR	RBI	BB	SO	OBP	SLG
vs. Left	.333	6	2	1	0	0	0	0	0	.333	.500	Scoring Posn	.333	3	1	0	0	0	1	0	0	.333	.333
vs. Right	.400	10	4	1	0	0	2	0	1	.400	.500	Close & Late	.200	5	1	0	0	0	1	0	0	.200	.200

Steve Lyons — Red Sox   Bats Left (flyball hitter)

	Avg	G	AB	R	H	2B	3B	HR	RBI	BB	SO	HBP	GDP	SB	CS	OBP	SLG	IBB	SH	SF	#Pit	#P/PA	GB	FB	G/F
1992 Season	.200	48	55	5	11	0	2	0	4	3	8	0	2	1	3	.241	.273	0	1	0	214	3.69	16	16	1.00
Last Five Years	.252	514	1328	152	334	65	10	12	127	91	211	3	13	22	14	.298	.343	7	35	12	5142	3.59	389	429	0.91

1992 Season

	Avg	AB	H	2B	3B	HR	RBI	BB	SO	OBP	SLG		Avg	AB	H	2B	3B	HR	RBI	BB	SO	OBP	SLG
vs. Left	.333	6	2	0	0	0	1	0	1	.333	.333	Scoring Posn	.286	14	4	0	1	0	4	1	2	.333	.429
vs. Right	.184	49	9	0	2	0	3	3	7	.231	.265	Close & Late	.235	17	4	0	0	0	1	2	1	.316	.235

Last Five Years

	Avg	AB	H	2B	3B	HR	RBI	BB	SO	OBP	SLG		Avg	AB	H	2B	3B	HR	RBI	BB	SO	OBP	SLG
vs. Left	.228	276	63	6	2	4	31	17	60	.269	.308	Scoring Posn	.257	339	87	18	4	3	111	25	54	.298	.360
vs. Right	.258	1052	271	59	8	8	96	74	151	.306	.352	Close & Late	.252	266	67	13	0	2	25	19	43	.300	.323
Groundball	.280	353	99	18	2	3	31	22	53	.323	.368	None on/out	.230	278	64	14	3	0	0	21	46	.284	.302
Flyball	.214	337	72	10	4	4	27	21	57	.263	.303	Batting #2	.259	613	159	34	6	4	51	35	90	.298	.354
Home	.229	645	148	27	7	3	51	40	90	.275	.307	Batting #7	.251	239	60	12	3	3	35	16	34	.298	.364
Away	.272	683	186	38	3	9	76	51	121	.320	.376	Other	.242	476	115	19	1	5	41	40	87	.299	.317
Day	.256	394	101	17	4	4	41	23	68	.297	.350	April	.183	120	22	2	1	1	9	10	17	.246	.242
Night	.249	934	233	48	6	8	86	68	143	.299	.339	May	.257	183	47	9	0	4	21	22	33	.335	.372
Grass	.252	1113	281	54	10	9	108	74	170	.298	.343	June	.296	240	71	12	1	2	17	19	32	.344	.379
Turf	.247	215	53	11	0	3	19	17	41	.300	.340	July	.238	273	65	15	4	3	26	12	49	.274	.355
First Pitch	.336	229	77	18	3	4	24	4	0	.346	.443	August	.231	247	57	11	2	0	23	13	44	.267	.291
Ahead on Count	.280	257	72	16	2	5	28	44	0	.383	.416	September/October	.272	265	72	16	2	2	31	15	36	.309	.370
Behind on Count	.208	466	97	18	3	3	48	0	131	.210	.279	Pre-All Star	.252	627	158	25	3	7	52	58	98	.314	.335
Two Strikes	.193	592	114	14	3	3	52	42	211	.245	.242	Post-All Star	.251	701	176	40	7	5	75	33	113	.284	.350

Batter vs. Pitcher (career)

Hits Best Against	Avg	AB	H	2B	3B	HR	RBI	BB	SO	OBP	SLG	Hits Worst Against	Avg	AB	H	2B	3B	HR	RBI	BB	SO	OBP	SLG
Jaime Navarro	.467	15	7	0	0	0	1	1	1	.471	.467	Dave Stieb	.040	25	1	1	0	0	0	1	7	.077	.080
Terry Leach	.444	9	4	2	0	0	2	2	0	.545	.667	Dave Stewart	.043	23	1	1	0	0	0	2	5	.120	.087
Rod Nichols	.444	9	4	0	1	0	2	2	0	.545	.667	Frank Viola	.083	12	1	1	0	0	0	0	5	.063	.167

Batter vs. Pitcher (career)

Hits Best Against	Avg	AB	H	2B	3B	HR	RBI	BB	SO	OBP	SLG	Hits Worst Against	Avg	AB	H	2B	3B	HR	RBI	BB	SO	OBP	SLG
Erik Hanson	.417	12	5	3	0	0	1	1	2	.429	.667	Chuck Finley	.083	12	1	0	0	0	0	0	5	.063	.083
Juan Berenguer	.364	11	4	1	0	0	0	2	0	.462	.455	Rick Aguilera	.100	10	1	0	0	0	0	1	3	.182	.100

Kevin Maas — Yankees

Bats Left (flyball hitter)

	Avg	G	AB	R	H	2B	3B	HR	RBI	BB	SO	HBP	GDP	SB	CS	OBP	SLG	IBB	SH	SF	#Pit	#P/PA	GB	FB	G/F
1992 Season	.248	98	286	35	71	12	0	11	35	25	63	0	1	3	1	.305	.406	4	0	4	1260	4.00	74	107	0.69
Career (1990-1992)	.236	325	1040	146	245	35	1	55	139	151	267	7	7	9	4	.334	.430	17	0	9	4900	4.06	241	394	0.61

1992 Season

	Avg	AB	H	2B	3B	HR	RBI	BB	SO	OBP	SLG		Avg	AB	H	2B	3B	HR	RBI	BB	SO	OBP	SLG
vs. Left	.185	54	10	0	0	1	4	2	19	.214	.241	Scoring Posn	.183	60	11	1	0	2	22	12	15	.303	.300
vs. Right	.263	232	61	12	0	10	31	23	44	.324	.444	Close & Late	.197	66	13	2	0	2	7	7	20	.274	.318
Groundball	.333	84	28	1	0	2	11	4	15	.360	.417	None on/out	.200	80	16	1	0	2	2	7	18	.264	.288
Flyball	.192	78	15	4	0	3	10	7	20	.253	.359	Batting #6	.231	117	27	6	0	3	13	7	21	.266	.359
Home	.211	128	27	4	0	7	15	11	28	.270	.406	Batting #7	.295	78	23	5	0	4	8	6	16	.345	.513
Away	.278	158	44	8	0	4	20	14	35	.333	.405	Other	.231	91	21	1	0	4	14	12	26	.320	.374
Day	.165	79	13	2	0	4	11	5	15	.207	.342	April	.344	32	11	1	0	2	7	7	5	.462	.563
Night	.280	207	58	10	0	7	24	20	48	.342	.430	May	.267	60	16	3	0	4	8	5	11	.323	.517
Grass	.238	240	57	8	0	9	27	23	53	.300	.383	June	.232	82	19	4	0	4	10	6	20	.281	.427
Turf	.304	46	14	4	0	2	8	2	10	.333	.522	July	.167	54	9	3	0	1	4	7	14	.262	.278
First Pitch	.206	34	7	2	0	1	5	2	0	.250	.353	August	.270	37	10	1	0	2	0	8	.256	.297
Ahead on Count	.246	69	17	4	0	1	7	14	0	.369	.348	September/October	.286	21	6	0	0	0	4	0	5	.273	.286
Behind on Count	.224	98	22	5	0	2	7	0	30	.222	.337	Pre-All Star	.249	197	49	9	0	10	27	19	44	.313	.447
Two Strikes	.248	149	37	6	0	7	19	10	63	.290	.430	Post-All Star	.247	89	22	3	0	1	8	6	19	.286	.315

1992 By Position

Position	Avg	AB	H	2B	3B	HR	RBI	BB	SO	OBP	SLG	G	GS	Innings	PO	A	E	DP	Fld Pct	Rng Fctr	In Zone	Outs	Zone Rtg	MLB Zone
As Designated Hitter	.238	214	51	8	0	7	26	21	46	.301	.374	62	54	---	---	---	---	---	---	---	---	---	---	---
As Pinch Hitter	.368	19	7	1	0	1	3	2	5	.429	.579	25	0	---	---	---	---	---	---	---	---	---	---	---
As 1b	.233	60	14	3	0	3	6	3	14	.270	.433	22	15	140.2	142	4	2	10	.986	---	23	20	.870	.843

Career (1990-1992)

	Avg	AB	H	2B	3B	HR	RBI	BB	SO	OBP	SLG		Avg	AB	H	2B	3B	HR	RBI	BB	SO	OBP	SLG
vs. Left	.202	302	61	8	0	13	43	42	98	.304	.358	Scoring Posn	.187	241	45	6	0	8	80	59	64	.343	.311
vs. Right	.249	738	184	27	1	42	96	109	169	.346	.459	Close & Late	.223	193	43	5	0	11	30	33	62	.338	.420
Groundball	.243	301	73	6	0	13	40	36	72	.324	.392	None on/out	.242	256	62	7	1	14	14	32	58	.326	.441
Flyball	.234	239	56	8	1	12	29	34	66	.325	.427	Batting #4	.264	268	76	11	1	16	36	52	66	.405	.511
Home	.214	499	107	18	0	27	67	74	121	.318	.413	Batting #7	.241	257	62	9	0	16	40	29	68	.322	.463
Away	.255	541	138	17	1	28	72	77	146	.349	.445	Other	.208	515	107	15	0	23	63	70	133	.301	.371
Day	.236	297	70	10	0	17	50	49	63	.342	.441	April	.274	84	23	1	1	4	15	30	17	.465	.452
Night	.236	743	175	25	1	38	89	102	204	.331	.425	May	.288	160	46	7	0	11	19	23	39	.380	.538
Grass	.231	872	201	30	0	45	116	130	225	.332	.420	June	.223	188	42	9	0	8	25	18	40	.290	.399
Turf	.262	168	44	5	1	10	23	21	42	.342	.482	July	.192	203	39	7	0	10	23	30	59	.298	.374
First Pitch	.263	114	30	3	0	6	15	4	0	.300	.447	August	.226	217	49	7	0	12	31	23	58	.303	.426
Ahead on Count	.310	242	75	11	0	22	50	73	0	.464	.626	September/October	.245	188	46	4	0	10	26	27	54	.341	.426
Behind on Count	.207	329	68	7	0	14	35	1	114	.211	.356	Pre-All Star	.252	496	125	21	1	26	67	82	114	.358	.456
Two Strikes	.194	532	103	15	1	22	60	65	267	.284	.350	Post-All Star	.221	544	120	14	0	29	72	69	153	.311	.406

Batter vs. Pitcher (career)

Hits Best Against	Avg	AB	H	2B	3B	HR	RBI	BB	SO	OBP	SLG	Hits Worst Against	Avg	AB	H	2B	3B	HR	RBI	BB	SO	OBP	SLG
Jose Mesa	.615	13	8	1	0	1	2	0	1	.615	.923	Kevin Tapani	.091	22	2	0	1	3	0	6	.091	.227
Kirk McCaskill	.421	19	8	2	0	1	2	0	0	.421	.684	Alex Fernandez	.091	11	1	0	0	1	2	2	.231	.091
Todd Stottlemyre	.333	21	7	1	0	1	2	2	3	.391	.524	Jim Abbott	.100	10	1	1	0	0	1	1	7	.182	.200
Kevin Brown	.313	16	5	0	0	1	3	0	4	.294	.500	Jack McDowell	.167	12	2	0	0	0	0	2	3	.286	.167
Greg Swindell	.308	13	4	0	0	2	3	0	3	.308	.769	Roger Clemens	.211	19	4	0	0	0	0	0	7	.250	.211

Bob MacDonald — Blue Jays

Pitches Left (flyball pitcher)

	ERA	W	L	Sv	G	GS	IP	BB	SO	Avg	H	2B	3B	HR	RBI	OBP	SLG	GF	IR	IRS	Hld	SvOp	SB	CS	GB	FB	G/F
1992 Season	4.37	1	0	0	27	0	47.1	16	26	.270	50	12	2	4	23	.330	.422	9	13	4	9	0	4	0	47	65	0.72
Career (1990-1992)	3.48	4	3	0	76	0	103.1	43	50	.257	101	19	2	9	58	.330	.384	20	65	24	7	4	9	4	127	139	0.91

1992 Season

	ERA	W	L	Sv	G	GS	IP	H	HR	BB	SO		Avg	AB	H	2B	3B	HR	RBI	BB	SO	OBP	SLG
Home	5.40	0	0	0	13	0	23.1	35	3	7	12	vs. Left	.143	63	9	2	0	0	4	1	14	.156	.175
Away	3.38	1	0	0	14	0	24.0	15	1	9	14	vs. Right	.336	122	41	10	2	4	19	15	12	.410	.549
Starter	0.00	0	0	0	0	0	0.0	0	0	0	0	Scoring Posn	.357	42	15	3	0	1	18	8	7	.451	.500
Reliever	4.37	1	0	0	27	0	47.1	50	4	16	26	Close & Late	.115	26	3	0	0	1	1	3	4	.207	.231
0 Days rest	2.16	1	0	0	4	0	8.1	5	0	2	3	None on/out	.174	46	8	1	0	3	3	2	3	.208	.391
1 or 2 Days rest	0.00	0	0	0	6	0	7.0	3	0	5	4	First Pitch	.231	26	6	2	0	3	5	3	0	.310	.654
3+ Days rest	5.91	0	0	0	17	0	32.0	42	4	9	19	Behind on Count	.345	55	19	5	0	0	7	4	0	.383	.436
Pre-All Star	4.19	1	0	0	21	0	38.2	37	4	15	21	Ahead on Count	.260	73	19	4	2	0	5	0	22	.270	.370

1992 Season																					
	ERA	W	L	Sv	G	GS	IP	H	HR	BB	SO		Avg	AB	H	2B	3B	HR	RBI	BB	SO	OBP	SLG
Post-All Star	5.19	0	0	0	6	0	8.2	13	0	1	5	Two Strikes	.225	71	16	3	1	0	5	9	26	.313	.296

Mike Macfarlane — Royals

Bats Right

	Avg	G	AB	R	H	2B	3B	HR	RBI	BB	SO	HBP	GDP	SB	CS	OBP	SLG	IBB	SH	SF	#Pit	#P/PA	GB	FB	G/F
1992 Season	.234	129	402	51	94	28	3	17	48	30	89	15	8	1	5	.310	.445	2	1	2	1551	3.45	123	126	0.98
Last Five Years	.251	476	1437	160	361	91	9	42	192	100	274	31	34	3	5	.311	.415	6	4	15	5366	3.39	469	459	1.02

1992 Season

	Avg	AB	H	2B	3B	HR	RBI	BB	SO	OBP	SLG		Avg	AB	H	2B	3B	HR	RBI	BB	SO	OBP	SLG
vs. Left	.261	138	36	10	1	7	18	10	28	.331	.500	Scoring Posn	.126	95	12	4	1	2	25	10	19	.254	.253
vs. Right	.220	264	58	18	2	10	30	20	61	.298	.417	Close & Late	.243	74	18	3	2	4	11	9	16	.349	.500
Groundball	.200	95	19	3	1	4	11	10	16	.330	.379	None on/out	.252	111	28	10	1	5	5	6	27	.314	.495
Flyball	.226	155	35	12	1	9	23	12	39	.292	.490	Batting #6	.218	101	22	14	0	0	9	9	23	.298	.356
Home	.239	184	44	16	1	7	21	13	35	.319	.451	Batting #7	.287	108	31	6	1	6	13	5	29	.330	.528
Away	.229	218	50	12	2	10	27	17	54	.302	.440	Other	.212	193	41	8	2	11	26	16	37	.305	.446
Day	.212	85	18	5	0	4	7	8	22	.309	.412	April	.171	41	7	3	0	1	4	8	13	.352	.317
Night	.240	317	76	23	3	13	41	22	67	.310	.454	May	.218	78	17	6	0	4	12	6	20	.299	.449
Grass	.244	164	40	8	2	8	25	11	36	.313	.463	June	.247	77	19	6	1	1	4	2	17	.266	.390
Turf	.227	238	54	20	1	9	23	19	53	.307	.433	July	.176	51	9	3	0	0	4	4	13	.263	.235
First Pitch	.278	72	20	6	0	4	7	2	0	.321	.528	August	.284	67	19	4	0	7	11	6	15	.360	.657
Ahead on Count	.345	84	29	10	1	4	14	10	0	.439	.631	September/October	.261	88	23	6	2	4	13	4	11	.320	.511
Behind on Count	.176	153	27	7	1	4	15	0	53	.208	.314	Pre-All Star	.216	222	48	16	1	6	23	17	56	.294	.378
Two Strikes	.135	170	23	8	1	3	18	18	89	.234	.247	Post-All Star	.256	180	46	12	2	11	25	13	33	.328	.528

1992 By Position

Position	Avg	AB	H	2B	3B	HR	RBI	BB	SO	OBP	SLG	G	GS	Innings	PO	A	E	DP	Fld Pct	Rng Fctr	In Zone	Outs	Zone Rtg	MLB Zone
As Designated Hitter	.255	51	13	2	0	4	6	3	17	.296	.529	13	13	---	---	---	---	---	---	---	---	---	---	---
As Pinch Hitter	.250	16	4	1	1	0	3	1	3	.368	.438	19	0	---	---	---	---	---	---	---	---	---	---	---
As c	.230	335	77	25	2	13	39	26	69	.309	.433	104	97	845.0	527	43	4	7	.993	---	---	---	---	---

Last Five Years

	Avg	AB	H	2B	3B	HR	RBI	BB	SO	OBP	SLG		Avg	AB	H	2B	3B	HR	RBI	BB	SO	OBP	SLG
vs. Left	.254	544	138	36	5	15	57	30	101	.303	.421	Scoring Posn	.236	369	87	20	2	8	140	38	67	.316	.366
vs. Right	.250	893	223	55	4	27	135	70	173	.316	.411	Close & Late	.233	253	59	12	4	7	32	23	59	.314	.395
Groundball	.263	376	99	23	4	9	56	22	60	.320	.418	None on/out	.229	375	86	21	3	15	15	19	74	.279	.421
Flyball	.232	414	96	25	2	19	61	29	91	.291	.440	Batting #7	.257	362	93	23	1	11	49	20	82	.299	.417
Home	.262	669	175	47	6	16	87	45	107	.322	.422	Batting #8	.253	384	97	22	3	5	49	33	62	.325	.365
Away	.242	768	186	44	3	26	105	55	167	.301	.409	Other	.247	691	171	46	5	26	94	47	130	.309	.441
Day	.262	325	85	20	1	11	43	29	69	.332	.431	April	.296	179	53	21	1	1	18	17	38	.371	.441
Night	.248	1112	276	71	8	31	149	71	205	.304	.410	May	.227	321	73	19	2	11	42	26	66	.299	.402
Grass	.248	597	148	33	3	20	91	44	122	.308	.414	June	.246	329	81	17	3	5	37	14	55	.279	.362
Turf	.254	840	213	58	6	22	101	56	152	.313	.415	July	.277	235	65	17	0	10	43	18	44	.336	.477
First Pitch	.281	274	77	24	1	9	37	2	0	.293	.474	August	.250	168	42	6	0	11	33	12	37	.305	.482
Ahead on Count	.326	301	98	25	4	14	61	53	0	.434	.575	September/October	.229	205	47	11	3	4	13	14	34	.301	.371
Behind on Count	.208	505	105	21	2	9	54	1	162	.228	.311	Pre-All Star	.253	926	234	64	6	19	109	65	177	.311	.396
Two Strikes	.170	578	98	22	2	7	43	42	274	.259	.251	Post-All Star	.249	511	127	27	3	23	83	35	97	.310	.448

Batter vs. Pitcher (career)

Hits Best Against	Avg	AB	H	2B	3B	HR	RBI	BB	SO	OBP	SLG	Hits Worst Against	Avg	AB	H	2B	3B	HR	RBI	BB	SO	OBP	SLG
Mark Williamson	.700	10	7	1	0	1	4	1	0	.727	1.100	Dave Stewart	.000	11	0	0	0	0	0	1	2	.083	.000
Jim Abbott	.476	21	10	3	1	1	4	1	3	.500	.857	Randy Johnson	.056	18	1	1	0	0	1	3	11	.182	.111
Mark Langston	.348	23	8	1	0	1	2	2	6	.400	.522	Mike Jeffcoat	.083	12	1	1	0	0	3	0	3	.083	.167
Bob Welch	.333	12	4	0	0	1	2	1	0	.357	.583	Greg Swindell	.143	21	3	1	0	0	1	0	5	.143	.143
Greg Hibbard	.333	9	3	0	0	2	3	2	0	.455	1.000	Roger Clemens	.174	23	4	0	0	0	0	0	8	.174	.174

Shane Mack — Twins

Bats Right (groundball hitter)

	Avg	G	AB	R	H	2B	3B	HR	RBI	BB	SO	HBP	GDP	SB	CS	OBP	SLG	IBB	SH	SF	#Pit	#P/PA	GB	FB	G/F
1992 Season	.315	156	600	101	189	31	6	16	75	64	106	15	9	26	14	.394	.467	1	11	2	2401	3.53	272	119	2.29
Last Five Years	.310	480	1474	243	457	71	18	42	205	141	275	29	29	57	28	.380	.468	3	22	8	5776	3.50	634	321	1.98

1992 Season

	Avg	AB	H	2B	3B	HR	RBI	BB	SO	OBP	SLG		Avg	AB	H	2B	3B	HR	RBI	BB	SO	OBP	SLG
vs. Left	.297	128	38	10	3	4	24	11	21	.357	.516	Scoring Posn	.298	141	42	5	2	3	56	21	21	.402	.426
vs. Right	.320	472	151	21	3	12	51	53	85	.403	.453	Close & Late	.277	94	26	4	0	0	6	10	19	.352	.319
Groundball	.335	158	53	6	2	3	22	12	33	.391	.456	None on/out	.337	190	64	14	1	7	7	19	35	.411	.532
Flyball	.301	166	50	7	3	5	21	21	23	.393	.470	Batting #1	.299	365	109	18	3	10	42	34	66	.369	.447
Home	.304	286	87	14	5	10	41	36	53	.390	.493	Batting #2	.387	106	41	5	2	3	15	14	20	.463	.557
Away	.325	314	102	17	1	6	34	28	53	.397	.443	Other	.302	129	39	8	1	3	18	16	20	.401	.450
Day	.306	186	57	6	3	7	23	25	19	.396	.484	April	.308	78	24	3	2	2	9	5	16	.372	.474
Night	.319	414	132	25	3	9	52	39	87	.392	.459	May	.330	106	35	4	0	5	18	11	19	.403	.509
Grass	.333	237	79	15	0	6	26	22	42	.408	.473	June	.261	115	30	10	1	2	12	11	19	.336	.417

1992 Season

	Avg	AB	H	2B	3B	HR	RBI	BB	SO	OBP	SLG		Avg	AB	H	2B	3B	HR	RBI	BB	SO	OBP	SLG
Turf	.303	363	110	16	6	10	49	42	64	.384	.463	July	.372	94	35	4	2	3	17	15	17	.455	.553
First Pitch	.381	97	37	4	0	4	16	1	0	.412	.546	August	.358	106	38	6	0	1	8	10	18	.430	.443
Ahead on Count	.355	124	44	9	4	4	18	33	0	.497	.589	September/October	.267	101	27	4	1	3	11	12	17	.368	.416
Behind on Count	.275	218	60	12	0	5	21	0	66	.295	.399	Pre-All Star	.288	333	96	18	3	10	45	34	63	.366	.450
Two Strikes	.223	251	56	9	2	4	20	30	106	.315	.323	Post-All Star	.348	267	93	13	3	6	30	30	43	.427	.487

1992 By Position

Position	Avg	AB	H	2B	3B	HR	RBI	BB	SO	OBP	SLG	G	GS	Innings	PO	A	E	DP	Fld Pct	Rng Fctr	In Zone	Outs	Zone Rtg	MLB Zone
As If	.310	564	175	28	6	15	68	59	103	.388	.461	150	142	1265.0	306	7	4	1	.987	2.23	350	284	.811	.809

Last Five Years

	Avg	AB	H	2B	3B	HR	RBI	BB	SO	OBP	SLG		Avg	AB	H	2B	3B	HR	RBI	BB	SO	OBP	SLG
vs. Left	.328	466	153	33	8	18	85	48	71	.398	.549	Scoring Posn	.300	350	105	17	3	9	154	47	70	.389	.443
vs. Right	.302	1008	304	38	10	24	120	93	204	.371	.431	Close & Late	.275	222	61	7	1	3	27	19	48	.331	.356
Groundball	.309	411	127	15	6	9	58	35	87	.371	.440	None on/out	.332	401	133	22	5	13	13	30	68	.390	.509
Flyball	.299	314	94	19	3	11	42	34	58	.374	.484	Batting #1	.302	453	137	19	6	12	54	40	85	.369	.450
Home	.317	690	219	37	15	19	102	70	131	.388	.497	Batting #7	.288	250	72	11	3	9	41	18	49	.342	.464
Away	.304	784	238	34	3	23	103	71	144	.372	.443	Other	.322	771	248	41	9	21	110	83	141	.397	.480
Day	.324	460	149	25	6	14	70	53	65	.403	.496	April	.267	131	35	7	3	4	14	10	26	.342	.458
Night	.304	1014	308	46	12	28	135	88	210	.368	.456	May	.312	250	78	8	2	7	37	27	38	.389	.444
Grass	.303	833	192	29	1	19	83	61	117	.375	.442	June	.263	266	70	15	1	9	39	27	51	.337	.425
Turf	.315	841	265	42	17	23	122	80	158	.383	.488	July	.338	272	92	12	6	8	37	33	53	.410	.515
First Pitch	.410	268	110	16	3	14	53	2	0	.427	.649	August	.317	271	86	15	4	7	37	22	55	.379	.480
Ahead on Count	.382	301	115	23	9	14	55	70	0	.500	.658	September/October	.338	284	96	14	2	7	41	22	52	.400	.475
Behind on Count	.264	512	135	21	3	10	57	0	169	.280	.375	Pre-All Star	.269	720	194	33	6	21	99	73	132	.346	.419
Two Strikes	.182	614	112	18	4	7	56	68	275	.273	.259	Post-All Star	.349	754	263	38	12	21	106	68	143	.411	.515

Batter vs. Pitcher (career)

Hits Best Against	Avg	AB	H	2B	3B	HR	RBI	BB	SO	OBP	SLG	Hits Worst Against	Avg	AB	H	2B	3B	HR	RBI	BB	SO	OBP	SLG
Scott Sanderson	.700	10	7	0	0	3	6	1	0	.727	1.600	Tim Leary	.077	13	1	0	0	0	0	3	6	.250	.077
Joe Hesketh	.571	14	8	1	0	2	5	1	1	.600	1.071	Jim Abbott	.111	18	2	1	0	0	1	3	3	.238	.167
Bill Krueger	.556	9	5	1	1	1	9	2	0	.636	1.222	Greg Hibbard	.133	15	2	1	0	0	2	1	2	.188	.200
Bill Gullickson	.500	14	7	1	1	1	2	0	2	.500	.929	Greg Swindell	.167	12	2	0	0	0	0	1	2	.231	.167
Chuck Finley	.464	28	13	5	1	1	1	5	5	.545	.821	Alex Fernandez	.182	11	2	0	0	0	1	0	5	.182	.182

Greg Maddux — Cubs

Pitches Right (groundball pitcher)

	ERA	W	L	Sv	G	GS	IP	BB	SO	Avg	H	2B	3B	HR	RBI	OBP	SLG	CG	ShO	Sup	QS	#P/S	SB	CS	GB	FB	G/F
1992 Season	2.18	20	11	0	35	35	268.0	70	199	.210	201	36	5	7	64	.272	.279	9	4	3.96	30	106	26	13	446	171	2.61
Last Five Years	3.01	87	57	0	176	176	1255.1	370	816	.241	1127	182	24	62	421	.300	.329	40	12	4.24	120	100	95	41	2173	898	2.42

1992 Season

	ERA	W	L	Sv	G	GS	IP	H	HR	BB	SO		Avg	AB	H	2B	3B	HR	RBI	BB	SO	OBP	SLG
Home	1.91	12	4	0	17	17	137.0	92	4	36	110	vs. Left	.233	566	132	23	4	6	41	51	118	.304	.320
Away	2.47	8	7	0	18	18	131.0	109	3	34	89	vs. Right	.176	393	69	13	1	1	23	19	81	.226	.221
Day	2.12	8	5	0	14	14	106.0	79	2	27	85	Inning 1-6	.205	750	154	30	4	5	52	48	159	.264	.276
Night	2.22	12	6	0	21	21	162.0	122	5	43	114	Inning 7+	.225	209	47	6	1	2	12	22	40	.300	.292
Grass	1.98	15	8	0	25	25	195.2	140	5	49	157	None on	.197	609	120	17	1	5	5	31	126	.243	.253
Turf	2.74	5	3	0	10	10	72.1	61	2	21	42	Runners on	.231	350	81	19	4	2	59	39	73	.320	.326
April	2.79	3	1	0	4	4	29.0	23	0	7	18	Scoring Posn	.204	211	43	9	3	0	50	30	43	.316	.275
May	2.49	1	4	0	6	6	43.1	31	1	14	36	Close & Late	.210	124	26	3	0	0	6	18	24	.313	.234
June	2.45	5	2	0	7	7	55.0	33	1	16	40	None on/out	.198	253	50	5	1	2	2	18	51	.262	.249
July	1.13	4	1	0	5	5	40.0	29	1	11	26	vs. 1st Batr (relief)	.000	0	0	0	0	0	0	0	0	.000	.000
August	1.91	3	2	0	7	7	56.2	41	2	13	37	First Inning Pitched	.208	125	26	3	1	1	8	11	28	.291	.272
September/October	2.45	4	1	0	6	6	44.0	44	2	9	42	First 75 Pitches	.216	667	144	24	4	5	45	44	136	.275	.286
Starter	2.18	20	11	0	35	35	268.0	201	7	70	199	Pitch 76-90	.138	138	19	6	0	0	5	8	30	.190	.181
Reliever	0.00	0	0	0	0	0	0.0	0	0	0	0	Pitch 91-105	.264	87	23	2	0	1	10	11	18	.350	.322
0-3 Days Rest	4.38	0	1	0	2	2	12.1	14	0	3	5	Pitch 106+	.224	67	15	4	1	1	4	7	15	.307	.358
4 Days Rest	1.90	16	8	0	27	27	212.2	149	6	58	163	First Pitch	.267	135	36	7	1	2	12	5	0	.313	.378
5+ Days Rest	2.93	4	2	0	6	6	43.0	38	1	9	31	Ahead on Count	.144	450	65	6	2	0	18	0	163	.159	.167
Pre-All Star	2.40	10	8	0	19	19	142.1	98	2	38	106	Behind on Count	.307	199	61	14	1	3	19	39	0	.421	.432
Post-All Star	1.93	10	3	0	16	16	125.2	103	5	32	93	Two Strikes	.129	428	55	7	3	1	25	26	199	.187	.166

Last Five Years

	ERA	W	L	Sv	G	GS	IP	H	HR	BB	SO		Avg	AB	H	2B	3B	HR	RBI	BB	SO	OBP	SLG
Home	3.11	45	26	0	86	86	626.0	569	32	190	411	vs. Left	.259	2707	700	109	18	37	264	264	440	.327	.353
Away	2.92	42	31	0	90	90	629.1	558	30	180	405	vs. Right	.216	1977	427	73	6	25	157	106	376	.263	.297
Day	3.27	44	31	0	91	91	637.2	609	34	205	417	Inning 1-6	.237	3749	888	157	20	49	345	290	668	.296	.329
Night	2.74	43	26	0	85	85	617.2	518	28	155	399	Inning 7+	.256	935	239	25	4	13	76	80	148	.316	.333
Grass	3.11	63	42	0	125	125	888.0	795	47	277	580	None on	.226	2814	636	95	9	33	33	197	523	.282	.301
Turf	2.77	24	15	0	51	51	367.1	332	15	93	237	Runners on	.263	1870	491	87	15	29	388	173	293	.328	.372
April	2.92	13	7	0	22	22	154.0	134	6	45	85	Scoring Posn	.247	1051	260	41	11	11	332	133	187	.317	.339
May	2.85	12	13	0	29	29	214.2	172	9	58	142	Close & Late	.243	498	121	10	3	3	40	52	85	.333	.293

Last Five Years

	ERA	W	L	Sv	G	GS	IP	H	HR	BB	SO
June	3.13	13	11	0	31	31	212.2	174	12	76	148
July	3.23	16	5	0	29	29	208.2	197	10	63	130
August	2.84	16	9	0	32	32	234.1	216	11	77	148
September/October	3.08	17	12	0	33	33	231.0	234	14	51	153
Starter	3.01	87	57	0	176	176	1255.1	1127	62	370	816
Reliever	0.00	0	0	0	0	0	0.0	0	0	0	0
0-3 Days Rest	2.98	10	5	0	19	19	139.0	127	6	33	88
4 Days Rest	3.01	57	42	0	120	120	847.0	761	42	254	579
5+ Days Rest	3.04	20	10	0	37	37	269.1	239	14	83	149
Pre-All Star	3.02	43	32	0	91	91	642.2	542	30	198	418
Post-All Star	3.00	44	25	0	85	85	612.2	585	32	172	398

	Avg	AB	H	2B	3B	HR	RBI	BB	SO	OBP	SLG
None on/out	.240	1223	294	40	5	18	88	88	210	.296	.325
vs. 1st Batr (relief)	.000	0	0	0	0	0	0	0	0	.000	.000
First Inning Pitched	.240	659	158	28	4	5	56	67	136	.314	.317
First 75 Pitches	.238	3368	801	138	19	41	281	257	596	.296	.327
Pitch 76-90	.231	624	144	20	1	9	59	42	112	.284	.309
Pitch 91-105	.263	414	109	14	1	7	54	39	62	.326	.353
Pitch 106+	.263	278	73	10	3	5	27	32	46	.347	.374
First Pitch	.285	801	228	40	5	16	100	35	0	.318	.407
Ahead on Count	.175	2032	356	41	9	13	117	1	667	.183	.223
Behind on Count	.321	1041	334	65	4	20	127	201	0	.432	.449
Two Strikes	.154	1887	291	37	11	8	100	133	815	.214	.198

Pitcher vs. Batter (career)

Pitches Best Vs.	Avg	AB	H	2B	3B	HR	RBI	BB	SO	OBP	SLG
Felix Jose	.000	16	0	0	0	0	0	1	7	.059	.000
Bob Melvin	.000	11	0	0	0	0	0	1	4	.083	.000
Dale Murphy	.059	34	2	0	0	0	0	1	12	.086	.059
Charlie Hayes	.087	23	2	0	0	0	0	0	3	.087	.087
Keith Miller	.091	11	1	0	0	0	0	0	1	.091	.091

Pitches Worst Vs.	Avg	AB	H	2B	3B	HR	RBI	BB	SO	OBP	SLG
Kal Daniels	.471	17	8	1	0	2	8	2	2	.526	.882
Gary Carter	.429	14	6	3	0	1	5	0	1	.429	.857
Luis Gonzalez	.409	22	9	2	0	3	9	2	3	.458	.909
Dion James	.333	12	4	1	1	1	5	2	2	.429	.833
Jack Clark	.316	19	6	3	0	2	6	5	5	.458	.789

Mike Maddux — Padres

Pitches Right (groundball pitcher)

	ERA	W	L	Sv	G	GS	IP	BB	SO	Avg	H	2B	3B	HR	RBI	OBP	SLG	GF	IR	IRS	Hld	SvOp	SB	CS	GB	FB	G/F
1992 Season	2.37	2	2	5	50	1	79.2	24	60	.236	71	7	2	2	26	.290	.292	14	26	11	8	9	15	3	133	54	2.46
Last Five Years	3.40	14	11	11	166	19	331.1	103	213	.255	316	54	5	18	130	.315	.351	44	106	34	20	17	35	23	573	223	2.57

1992 Season

	ERA	W	L	Sv	G	GS	IP	H	HR	BB	SO
Home	1.87	2	0	2	26	0	33.2	28	0	11	27
Away	2.74	0	2	3	24	1	46.0	43	2	13	33
Starter	1.80	0	1	0	1	1	5.0	2	0	2	6
Reliever	2.41	2	1	5	49	0	74.2	69	2	22	54
0 Days rest	7.20	0	0	0	4	0	5.0	8	0	1	2
1 or 2 Days rest	2.20	1	1	3	29	0	45.0	37	2	17	35
3+ Days rest	1.82	1	0	2	16	0	24.2	24	0	4	17
Pre-All Star	1.82	1	0	4	29	0	39.2	31	1	13	28
Post-All Star	2.93	2	1	1	21	1	40.0	40	1	11	32

	Avg	AB	H	2B	3B	HR	RBI	BB	SO	OBP	SLG
vs. Left	.235	162	38	4	1	1	12	15	31	.294	.290
vs. Right	.237	139	33	3	1	1	14	9	29	.284	.295
Scoring Posn	.220	82	18	4	1	0	23	14	16	.323	.293
Close & Late	.267	101	27	3	0	1	16	13	17	.348	.327
None on/out	.282	71	20	2	0	1	1	6	8	.338	.352
First Pitch	.304	56	17	1	0	0	3	2	0	.328	.321
Behind on Count	.259	54	14	2	1	2	12	11	0	.379	.444
Ahead on Count	.204	137	28	2	1	0	7	0	51	.203	.234
Two Strikes	.132	114	15	1	1	0	6	11	60	.205	.158

Last Five Years

	ERA	W	L	Sv	G	GS	IP	H	HR	BB	SO
Home	3.25	10	3	3	66	9	163.1	147	5	47	111
Away	3.54	4	8	8	80	10	168.0	169	13	56	102
Day	4.12	4	2	2	48	7	107.0	110	8	31	65
Night	3.05	10	9	9	118	12	224.1	206	10	72	148
Grass	3.20	9	6	10	104	8	196.2	182	12	63	120
Turf	3.68	5	5	1	62	11	134.2	136	6	40	93
April	3.30	4	1	2	24	1	46.1	45	1	12	36
May	3.39	0	2	0	40	3	71.2	70	3	22	42
June	3.52	2	2	4	27	5	53.2	55	6	14	31
July	3.40	2	1	1	23	5	47.2	51	2	13	26
August	5.14	3	3	1	23	4	56.0	63	5	23	41
September/October	1.61	3	2	3	29	1	56.0	34	1	19	37
Starter	4.64	4	7	0	19	19	95.0	110	9	30	59
Reliever	2.89	10	4	11	147	0	236.1	206	9	73	154
0 Days rest	2.18	1	1	2	21	0	18.0	13	0	10	13
1 or 2 Days rest	2.56	4	1	5	73	0	105.1	78	5	23	72
3+ Days rest	3.49	5	2	4	53	0	98.0	96	4	31	69
Pre-All Star	3.36	6	5	7	100	10	182.0	179	10	54	117
Post-All Star	3.44	8	6	4	66	9	149.1	137	8	49	96

	Avg	AB	H	2B	3B	HR	RBI	BB	SO	OBP	SLG
vs. Left	.267	633	169	28	3	7	67	58	103	.330	.354
vs. Right	.243	605	147	26	2	11	63	45	110	.299	.347
Inning 1-6	.263	638	168	38	2	11	80	49	113	.320	.381
Inning 7+	.247	600	148	16	3	7	50	54	100	.309	.318
None on	.254	700	178	29	3	10	10	42	125	.299	.347
Runners on	.257	538	138	25	2	8	120	61	88	.333	.355
Scoring Posn	.236	331	78	18	1	4	106	53	58	.338	.332
Close & Late	.243	247	60	7	0	2	26	27	45	.317	.296
None on/out	.262	308	87	16	2	8	8	24	47	.338	.425
vs. 1st Batr (relief)	.200	130	26	2	1	2	16	13	24	.271	.277
First Inning Pitched	.251	553	139	23	3	7	70	44	94	.310	.342
First 15 Pitches	.266	561	149	23	4	10	63	34	90	.307	.374
Pitch 16-30	.224	313	70	14	1	3	30	35	57	.307	.304
Pitch 31-45	.230	152	35	2	0	3	12	11	30	.267	.303
Pitch 45+	.292	212	62	15	0	2	25	23	36	.364	.392
First Pitch	.306	219	67	12	0	4	20	8	0	.333	.416
Ahead on Count	.211	525	111	19	1	4	40	0	186	.221	.274
Behind on Count	.301	269	81	13	4	9	47	52	0	.407	.480
Two Strikes	.162	520	84	15	1	3	33	4	213	.233	.212

Pitcher vs. Batter (career)

Pitches Best Vs.	Avg	AB	H	2B	3B	HR	RBI	BB	SO	OBP	SLG
Jay Bell	.077	13	1	0	0	0	0	0	0	.077	.077
Tony Gwynn	.063	12	1	1	0	0	1	1	0	.154	.167
Andy Van Slyke	.063	12	1	0	0	0	0	1	5	.154	.063
Jose Lind	.091	11	1	0	0	0	1	0	0	.091	.091
Matt D. Williams	.182	11	2	0	0	0	1	1	2	.250	.182

Pitches Worst Vs.	Avg	AB	H	2B	3B	HR	RBI	BB	SO	OBP	SLG
Kevin Bass	.600	10	6	1	0	2	2	2	1	.667	.900
Sid Bream	.529	17	9	1	1	0	3	4	3	.619	.706
Mark Grace	.474	19	9	1	0	1	5	2	2	.524	.684
Robby Thompson	.467	15	7	1	1	2	5	0	2	.467	1.067
Billy Doran	.400	15	6	2	0	1	2	4	2	.526	.733

Dave Magadan — Mets

Bats Left (groundball hitter)

	Avg	G	AB	R	H	2B	3B	HR	RBI	BB	SO	HBP	GDP	SB	CS	OBP	SLG	IBB	SH	SF	#Pit	#P/PA	GB	FB	G/F
1992 Season	.283	99	321	33	91	9	1	3	28	56	44	0	6	1	0	.390	.346	3	2	0	1544	4.10	135	70	1.93
Last Five Years	.288	606	1878	251	541	97	10	18	227	322	225	7	31	5	3	.390	.379	20	15	24	8933	4.00	724	443	1.63

1992 Season

	Avg	AB	H	2B	3B	HR	RBI	BB	SO	OBP	SLG		Avg	AB	H	2B	3B	HR	RBI	BB	SO	OBP	SLG
vs. Left	.308	120	37	3	0	0	7	16	22	.390	.333	Scoring Posn	.290	69	20	0	0	2	26	23	12	.467	.377
vs. Right	.269	201	54	6	1	3	21	40	22	.390	.353	Close & Late	.298	47	14	0	0	0	6	16	6	.476	.426
Groundball	.210	124	26	3	0	1	7	29	19	.359	.258	None on/out	.273	77	21	1	0	1	1	12	14	.371	.325
Flyball	.263	57	15	0	0	0	6	10	6	.373	.263	Batting #2	.304	112	34	6	1	2	12	21	5	.414	.429
Home	.314	153	48	5	1	2	13	30	16	.426	.399	Batting #3	.250	80	20	0	0	1	7	10	16	.333	.288
Away	.256	168	43	4	0	1	15	26	28	.356	.298	Other	.287	129	37	3	0	0	9	25	23	.403	.310
Day	.245	106	26	2	1	1	8	23	18	.380	.311	April	.317	63	20	4	0	0	5	5	13	.368	.381
Night	.302	215	65	7	0	2	20	33	26	.395	.363	May	.300	90	27	2	1	1	7	16	11	.406	.378
Grass	.302	222	67	5	1	2	17	38	28	.404	.360	June	.237	59	14	1	0	0	6	17	7	.408	.254
Turf	.242	99	24	4	0	1	11	18	16	.359	.313	July	.309	81	25	2	0	2	9	15	10	.417	.407
First Pitch	.294	34	10	3	0	0	1	2	0	.333	.382	August	.179	28	5	0	0	0	1	3	3	.258	.179
Ahead on Count	.392	79	31	3	1	2	11	34	0	.575	.532	September/October	.000	0	0	0	0	0	0	0	0	.000	.000
Behind on Count	.279	86	24	1	0	1	7	0	17	.279	.326	Pre-All Star	.295	254	75	7	1	1	21	43	38	.397	.343
Two Strikes	.230	148	34	3	0	1	12	20	44	.321	.270	Post-All Star	.239	67	16	2	0	2	7	13	6	.363	.358

1992 By Position

Position	Avg	AB	H	2B	3B	HR	RBI	BB	SO	OBP	SLG	G	GS	Innings	PO	A	E	DP	Fld Pct	Rng Fctr	In Zone	Outs	Zone Rtg	MLB Zone
As 3b	.288	312	90	9	1	2	25	53	41	.392	.343	89	89	755.0	41	135	11	10	.941	2.10	168	140	.833	.841

Last Five Years

	Avg	AB	H	2B	3B	HR	RBI	BB	SO	OBP	SLG		Avg	AB	H	2B	3B	HR	RBI	BB	SO	OBP	SLG
vs. Left	.267	617	165	20	2	2	67	83	79	.356	.316	Scoring Posn	.318	466	148	25	1	7	202	96	56	.419	.421
vs. Right	.298	1261	376	77	8	16	160	239	146	.406	.410	Close & Late	.266	312	83	6	1	5	39	58	45	.368	.346
Groundball	.267	641	171	30	3	5	71	137	78	.391	.346	None on/out	.268	399	107	16	1	6	6	65	46	.373	.358
Flyball	.273	370	101	24	1	2	50	57	40	.371	.359	Batting #2	.302	835	252	51	6	11	107	146	78	.402	.417
Home	.286	916	262	39	5	10	116	163	109	.390	.372	Batting #3	.273	443	121	20	2	5	56	70	60	.380	.361
Away	.290	962	279	58	5	8	111	159	116	.390	.386	Other	.280	600	168	26	2	2	64	97	87	.381	.340
Day	.269	635	171	34	4	6	70	116	78	.378	.373	April	.268	198	53	9	1	0	17	37	35	.378	.323
Night	.298	1243	370	63	6	10	157	206	147	.396	.382	May	.291	296	86	9	2	4	29	40	42	.374	.375
Grass	.286	1312	375	67	6	13	158	217	161	.384	.368	June	.313	406	127	23	3	7	57	80	38	.425	.439
Turf	.293	566	166	40	4	5	69	105	64	.404	.405	July	.290	427	124	23	1	5	54	69	38	.386	.384
First Pitch	.354	212	75	19	0	3	24	8	0	.377	.486	August	.268	336	90	15	0	3	37	56	40	.372	.313
Ahead on Count	.348	451	157	29	4	8	74	177	0	.528	.483	September/October	.284	215	61	18	3	2	33	40	32	.390	.423
Behind on Count	.238	546	130	18	3	5	55	2	101	.242	.310	Pre-All Star	.298	1028	306	44	6	12	115	179	129	.401	.387
Two Strikes	.243	842	205	28	5	6	80	129	225	.343	.310	Post-All Star	.276	850	235	53	4	6	112	143	96	.377	.369

Batter vs. Pitcher (career)

Hits Best Against	Avg	AB	H	2B	3B	HR	RBI	BB	SO	OBP	SLG	Hits Worst Against	Avg	AB	H	2B	3B	HR	RBI	BB	SO	OBP	SLG
Bill Landrum	.714	7	5	0	0	0	0	4	0	.818	.714	Jose Rijo	.063	16	1	0	0	0	1	3	5	.211	.063
Neal Heaton	.600	10	6	1	0	0	3	1	0	.538	.700	Bud Black	.077	13	1	0	0	0	0	1	0	.143	.077
Tim Belcher	.529	17	9	2	0	0	3	2	3	.579	.647	Steve Wilson	.091	11	1	0	0	0	0	1	0	.091	.091
Roger McDowell	.444	9	4	1	0	1	5	2	5	.500	.889	Randy Tomlin	.100	20	2	0	0	0	0	4	1	.250	.100
Pete Harnisch	.400	15	6	3	0	0	2	2	1	.471	.600	Jim Gott	.100	10	1	0	0	0	0	2	1	.250	.100

Mike Magnante — Royals

Pitches Left

	ERA	W	L	Sv	G	GS	IP	BB	SO	Avg	H	2B	3B	HR	RBI	OBP	SLG	GF	IR	IRS	Hld	SvOp	SB	CS	GB	FB	G/F
1992 Season	4.94	4	9	0	44	12	89.1	35	31	.325	115	17	2	5	51	.382	.427	11	18	4	4	3	9	3	134	118	1.14
Career (1991-1992)	3.99	4	10	0	82	12	144.1	58	73	.301	170	32	3	8	75	.364	.411	21	54	14	6	3	10	5	214	173	1.24

1992 Season

	ERA	W	L	Sv	G	GS	IP	H	HR	BB	SO		Avg	AB	H	2B	3B	HR	RBI	BB	SO	OBP	SLG
Home	4.22	2	4	0	23	5	49.0	55	1	12	18	vs. Left	.375	72	27	2	1	1	9	8	7	.438	.472
Away	5.80	2	5	0	21	7	40.1	60	4	23	13	vs. Right	.312	282	88	15	1	4	42	27	24	.368	.415
Starter	5.43	3	5	0	12	12	54.2	77	4	20	15	Scoring Posn	.323	96	31	5	1	3	47	17	8	.410	.490
Reliever	4.15	1	4	0	32	0	34.2	38	1	15	16	Close & Late	.391	69	27	4	1	1	10	6	3	.434	.522
0 Days rest	6.75	0	1	0	6	0	6.2	9	1	1	1	None on/out	.322	87	28	5	0	1	1	4	10	.352	.414
1 or 2 Days rest	5.51	1	2	0	15	0	16.1	22	0	8	8	First Pitch	.429	56	24	4	0	2	13	3	0	.450	.607
3+ Days rest	0.77	0	0	0	11	0	11.2	7	0	6	7	Behind on Count	.356	87	31	6	1	1	10	21	0	.473	.483
Pre-All Star	5.31	3	6	0	19	12	62.2	89	4	25	22	Ahead on Count	.281	146	41	5	1	1	21	0	25	.283	.349
Post-All Star	4.05	1	3	0	25	0	26.2	26	1	10	9	Two Strikes	.237	135	32	2	1	2	19	11	31	.287	.311

Joe Magrane — Cardinals
Pitches Left (groundball pitcher)

	ERA	W	L	Sv	G	GS	IP	BB	SO	Avg	H	2B	3B	HR	RBI	OBP	SLG	CG	ShO	Sup	QS	#P/S	SB	CS	GB	FB	G/F
1992 Season	4.02	1	2	0	5	5	31.1	15	20	.279	34	3	2	2	12	.364	.385	0	0	2.01	3	110	2	1	49	33	1.48
Last Five Years	2.99	34	37	0	94	93	634.2	197	347	.248	590	107	24	23	191	.308	.342	16	8	3.46	70	97	66	36	1088	557	1.95

1992 Season

	ERA	W	L	Sv	G	GS	IP	H	HR	BB	SO		Avg	AB	H	2B	3B	HR	RBI	BB	SO	OBP	SLG
Home	2.57	0	0	0	1	1	7.0	7	0	3	3	vs. Left	.133	15	2	0	0	0	2	3	3	.278	.133
Away	4.44	1	2	0	4	4	24.1	27	2	12	17	vs. Right	.299	107	32	3	2	2	10	12	17	.377	.421

Last Five Years

	ERA	W	L	Sv	G	GS	IP	H	HR	BB	SO		Avg	AB	H	2B	3B	HR	RBI	BB	SO	OBP	SLG
Home	3.19	14	21	0	49	48	330.0	314	12	95	165	vs. Left	.233	407	95	16	4	3	39	43	76	.311	.314
Away	2.78	20	16	0	45	45	304.2	276	11	102	182	vs. Right	.251	1971	495	91	20	20	152	154	271	.308	.348
Day	3.85	12	7	0	29	28	173.0	184	9	54	112	Inning 1-6	.246	1942	477	92	19	18	153	165	291	.307	.340
Night	2.67	22	30	0	65	65	461.2	406	14	143	235	Inning 7+	.259	436	113	15	5	5	38	32	56	.315	.351
Grass	2.84	7	6	0	19	19	120.1	109	3	37	86	None on	.252	1418	357	72	10	15	15	98	206	.306	.348
Turf	3.03	27	31	0	75	74	514.1	481	20	160	261	Runners on	.243	960	233	35	14	8	176	99	141	.312	.333
April	5.96	2	6	0	12	12	61.2	76	2	21	35	Scoring Posn	.221	561	124	18	7	2	152	75	91	.307	.289
May	2.68	3	5	0	11	10	74.0	65	2	20	35	Close & Late	.279	215	60	7	4	3	23	13	28	.325	.391
June	3.06	7	7	0	16	16	114.0	102	2	38	68	None on/out	.245	620	152	26	4	6	6	42	94	.296	.329
July	2.41	7	5	0	17	17	119.2	107	2	34	70	vs. 1st Batr (relief)	1.000	1	1	0	0	0	0	0	0	1.000	1.000
August	2.22	9	7	0	17	17	133.2	96	9	34	66	First Inning Pitched	.268	362	97	14	6	4	32	30	52	.328	.373
September/October	3.01	6	7	0	21	21	131.2	144	6	50	73	First 75 Pitches	.249	1746	434	86	19	16	142	145	265	.308	.347
Starter	2.97	34	37	0	93	93	633.2	588	23	196	346	Pitch 76-90	.245	319	78	12	0	2	18	28	35	.313	.301
Reliever	18.00	0	0	0	1	0	1.0	2	0	1	1	Pitch 91-105	.244	205	50	7	4	3	18	12	27	.285	.361
0-3 Days Rest	2.50	3	4	0	8	8	54.0	47	1	14	28	Pitch 105+	.259	108	28	2	1	2	13	12	20	.339	.352
4 Days Rest	3.31	20	26	0	57	57	391.2	374	17	129	211	First Pitch	.266	418	111	17	4	6	35	16	0	.294	.368
5+ Days Rest	2.39	11	7	0	28	28	188.0	167	5	53	107	Ahead on Count	.201	941	189	35	6	5	65	0	300	.208	.267
Pre-All Star	3.48	14	21	0	45	44	292.0	281	7	94	159	Behind on Count	.307	599	184	33	11	5	56	99	0	.404	.424
Post-All Star	2.57	20	16	0	49	49	342.2	309	16	103	188	Two Strikes	.193	928	179	31	4	7	60	82	346	.262	.258

Pitcher vs. Batter (career)

Pitches Best Vs.	Avg	AB	H	2B	3B	HR	RBI	BB	SO	OBP	SLG	Pitches Worst Vs.	Avg	AB	H	2B	3B	HR	RBI	BB	SO	OBP	SLG
Joe Oliver	.083	12	1	0	0	0	0	2	2	.063	.063	Juan Samuel	.471	17	8	1	0	1	2	1	2	.500	.706
Lenny Dykstra	.087	23	2	0	0	0	1	1	1	.125	.087	Rex Hudler	.429	14	6	3	0	2	6	1	1	.438	1.071
Junior Ortiz	.091	11	1	0	0	0	0	0	0	.091	.091	Barry Larkin	.429	14	6	1	1	0	4	4	1	.556	.643
Billy Hatcher	.100	30	3	0	0	0	0	1	4	.129	.100	Gary Redus	.409	22	9	4	2	0	4	1	3	.417	.773
Bip Roberts	.100	10	1	0	0	0	0	1	2	.182	.100	Ron Gant	.364	11	4	1	0	2	2	0	0	.364	1.000

Pat Mahomes — Twins
Pitches Right (flyball pitcher)

	ERA	W	L	Sv	G	GS	IP	BB	SO	Avg	H	2B	3B	HR	RBI	OBP	SLG	CG	ShO	Sup	QS	#P/S	SB	CS	GB	FB	G/F
1992 Season	5.04	3	4	0	14	13	69.2	37	44	.279	73	19	4	5	39	.364	.439	0	0	4.91	4	92	9	8	71	90	0.79

1992 Season

	ERA	W	L	Sv	G	GS	IP	H	HR	BB	SO		Avg	AB	H	2B	3B	HR	RBI	BB	SO	OBP	SLG
Home	7.02	1	2	0	7	7	33.1	41	3	18	26	vs. Left	.281	135	38	8	2	3	20	17	17	.355	.437
Away	3.22	2	2	0	7	6	36.1	32	2	19	18	vs. Right	.276	127	35	11	2	2	19	20	27	.374	.441
Starter	5.11	3	4	0	13	13	68.2	72	5	37	44	Scoring Posn	.267	75	20	4	2	3	34	10	16	.341	.493
Reliever	0.00	0	0	0	1	0	1.0	1	0	0	0	Close & Late	.167	6	1	0	0	0	2	0	0	.375	.167
0-3 Days Rest	1.29	1	0	0	1	1	7.0	4	0	3	5	None on/out	.317	63	20	4	1	0	0	10	7	.411	.413
4 Days Rest	5.21	1	0	0	4	4	19.0	19	1	13	14	First Pitch	.405	37	15	4	2	2	12	0	0	.405	.784
5+ Days Rest	5.70	1	4	0	8	8	42.2	49	4	21	25	Behind on Count	.373	51	19	5	0	1	6	26	0	.584	.529
Pre-All Star	5.23	3	2	0	9	8	41.1	43	3	25	28	Ahead on Count	.221	122	27	5	1	1	15	0	38	.216	.303
Post-All Star	4.76	0	2	0	5	5	28.1	30	2	12	16	Two Strikes	.185	135	25	8	1	0	13	11	44	.245	.259

Mike Maksudian — Blue Jays
Bats Left (flyball hitter)

	Avg	G	AB	R	H	2B	3B	HR	RBI	BB	SO	HBP	GDP	SB	CS	OBP	SLG	IBB	SH	SF	#Pit	#P/PA	GB	FB	G/F
1992 Season	.000	3	3	0	0	0	0	0	0	0	0	0	0	0	0	.000	.000	0	0	0	16	5.33	1	2	0.50

1992 Season

	Avg	AB	H	2B	3B	HR	RBI	BB	SO	OBP	SLG		Avg	AB	H	2B	3B	HR	RBI	BB	SO	OBP	SLG
vs. Left	.000	0	0	0	0	0	0	0	0	.000	.000	Scoring Posn	.000	0	0	0	0	0	0	0	0	.000	.000
vs. Right	.000	3	0	0	0	0	0	0	0	.000	.000	Close & Late	.000	2	0	0	0	0	0	0	0	.000	.000

Candy Maldonado — Blue Jays
Bats Right

	Avg	G	AB	R	H	2B	3B	HR	RBI	BB	SO	HBP	GDP	SB	CS	OBP	SLG	IBB	SH	SF	#Pit	#P/PA	GB	FB	G/F
1992 Season	.272	137	489	64	133	25	4	20	66	59	112	7	13	2	2	.357	.462	3	2	3	2147	3.85	145	143	1.01
Last Five Years	.257	649	2211	269	568	118	7	75	318	218	480	28	55	19	13	.328	.418	16	6	22	9195	3.71	717	665	1.08

1992 Season

	Avg	AB	H	2B	3B	HR	RBI	BB	SO	OBP	SLG		Avg	AB	H	2B	3B	HR	RBI	BB	SO	OBP	SLG
vs. Left	.291	117	34	4	1	4	16	22	26	.400	.444	Scoring Posn	.252	115	29	6	2	2	33	25	30	.386	.391
vs. Right	.266	372	99	21	3	16	50	37	86	.342	.468	Close & Late	.284	67	19	1	0	2	9	9	20	.377	.388
Groundball	.277	141	39	6	1	5	18	19	32	.368	.440	None on/out	.235	132	31	4	0	4	5	34		.268	.356
Flyball	.300	120	36	6	0	6	16	20	34	.410	.500	Batting #6	.277	264	73	15	3	12	40	36	60	.373	.492
Home	.251	219	55	10	3	8	32	27	50	.343	.434	Batting #7	.261	138	36	8	1	3	16	13	38	.327	.399
Away	.289	270	78	15	1	12	34	32	62	.368	.485	Other	.276	87	24	2	0	5	10	10	14	.351	.471
Day	.219	151	33	6	2	3	14	10	43	.274	.344	April	.167	78	13	3	0	0	6	8	15	.250	.205
Night	.296	338	100	19	2	17	52	49	69	.391	.515	May	.341	44	15	5	0	1	5	6	12	.420	.523
Grass	.288	212	61	8	1	11	27	27	46	.374	.491	June	.275	80	22	7	1	4	14	5	24	.322	.538
Turf	.260	277	72	17	3	9	39	32	66	.343	.440	July	.352	88	31	1	1	5	13	13	12	.441	.557
First Pitch	.391	64	25	6	0	1	10	2	0	.418	.531	August	.267	105	28	5	1	8	18	9	26	.328	.562
Ahead on Count	.379	124	47	7	2	9	24	25	0	.480	.685	September/October	.255	94	24	4	1	2	10	18	23	.391	.383
Behind on Count	.258	151	39	6	2	6	17	0	53	.280	.444	Pre-All Star	.251	235	59	15	2	6	31	21	58	.318	.409
Two Strikes	.167	215	36	7	1	6	20	32	112	.281	.293	Post-All Star	.291	254	74	10	2	14	35	38	54	.391	.512

1992 By Position

Position	Avg	AB	H	2B	3B	HR	RBI	BB	SO	OBP	SLG	G	GS	Innings	PO	A	E	DP	Fld Pct	Rng Fctr	In Zone	Outs	Zone Rtg	MLB Zone
As If	.279	466	130	24	4	20	66	55	106	.359	.476	129	128	1123.0	257	13	6	2	.978	2.16	318	254	.799	.809

Last Five Years

	Avg	AB	H	2B	3B	HR	RBI	BB	SO	OBP	SLG		Avg	AB	H	2B	3B	HR	RBI	BB	SO	OBP	SLG
vs. Left	.272	698	190	33	1	20	95	86	121	.353	.408	Scoring Posn	.249	595	148	36	3	15	224	97	139	.350	.395
vs. Right	.250	1513	378	85	6	55	223	132	359	.317	.423	Close & Late	.219	351	77	11	0	7	36	34	94	.290	.311
Groundball	.264	749	198	42	1	22	105	70	164	.335	.411	None on/out	.254	567	144	25	1	19	19	37	122	.305	.402
Flyball	.265	514	136	26	2	15	62	56	119	.336	.411	Batting #4	.264	918	242	49	3	29	140	73	198	.321	.418
Home	.242	1046	253	46	3	33	144	90	243	.306	.386	Batting #6	.256	558	143	30	3	23	80	68	124	.347	.444
Away	.270	1165	315	72	4	42	174	128	237	.348	.447	Other	.249	735	183	39	1	23	98	77	158	.323	.399
Day	.243	732	178	31	3	27	110	69	161	.311	.404	April	.237	312	74	17	0	7	41	33	58	.314	.359
Night	.264	1479	390	87	4	48	208	149	319	.337	.425	May	.261	299	78	17	0	12	45	24	59	.320	.438
Grass	.258	1502	387	79	2	50	212	138	313	.323	.413	June	.257	338	87	24	1	13	59	35	80	.331	.450
Turf	.255	709	181	39	5	25	106	80	167	.339	.430	July	.279	426	119	21	2	11	50	39	81	.342	.415
First Pitch	.367	343	126	23	1	7	55	8	0	.383	.501	August	.249	429	107	20	1	19	63	35	99	.308	.434
Ahead on Count	.340	536	182	35	3	26	104	106	0	.449	.562	September/October	.253	407	103	19	3	13	60	52	103	.350	.410
Behind on Count	.189	721	136	21	2	21	78	0	247	.204	.311	Pre-All Star	.247	1083	268	65	2	33	155	100	226	.315	.403
Two Strikes	.155	981	152	37	2	22	96	101	479	.239	.264	Post-All Star	.266	1128	300	53	5	42	163	118	254	.341	.434

Batter vs. Pitcher (since 1984)

Hits Best Against	Avg	AB	H	2B	3B	HR	RBI	BB	SO	OBP	SLG	Hits Worst Against	Avg	AB	H	2B	3B	HR	RBI	BB	SO	OBP	SLG
Frank DiPino	.615	13	8	0	0	1	5	1	2	.643	.846	Kevin Tapani	.000	11	0	0	0	0	0	1	5	.083	.000
Mike Jackson	.455	11	5	1	0	2	6	0	3	.455	1.091	Tim Burke	.077	13	1	0	0	0	0	3	.077	.077
Chuck Finley	.444	18	8	2	0	2	6	2	3	.500	.889	Eric Plunk	.083	12	1	0	0	0	2	4	.214	.083
Lance McCullers	.429	14	6	3	0	1	7	3	0	.500	.857	Sid Fernandez	.120	25	3	0	0	1	1	5	.154	.120
Jesse Orosco	.333	9	3	0	0	2	4	1	2	.364	1.000	Jeff Robinson	.154	13	2	0	0	0	2	0	4	.154	.154

Rob Mallicoat — Astros
Pitches Left

	ERA	W	L	Sv	G	GS	IP	BB	SO	Avg	H	2B	3B	HR	RBI	OBP	SLG	GF	IR	IRS	Hld	SvOp	SB	CS	GB	FB	G/F
1992 Season	7.23	0	0	0	23	0	23.2	19	20	.283	26	6	2	2	22	.427	.457	6	18	4	1	0	3	1	32	27	1.19
Last Five Years	5.55	0	2	1	47	0	47.0	32	38	.271	48	11	2	4	38	.397	.424	10	41	11	12	1	4	2	54	49	1.31

1992 Season

	ERA	W	L	Sv	G	GS	IP	H	HR	BB	SO		Avg	AB	H	2B	3B	HR	RBI	BB	SO	OBP	SLG
Home	8.71	0	0	0	9	0	10.1	10	1	6	10	vs. Left	.353	34	12	3	1	1	11	4	9	.436	.588
Away	6.08	0	0	0	14	0	13.1	16	1	13	10	vs. Right	.241	58	14	3	1	1	11	15	11	.423	.379
Starter	0.00	0	0	0	0	0	0.0	0	0	0	0	Scoring Posn	.283	46	13	1	1	1	20	8	11	.404	.413
Reliever	7.23	0	0	0	23	0	23.2	26	2	19	20	Close & Late	.190	21	4	0	1	0	2	1	5	.292	.286
0 Days rest	6.75	0	0	0	5	0	6.2	8	0	5	6	None on/out	.250	16	4	3	0	0	5	2	.455	.438
1 or 2 Days rest	4.76	0	0	0	11	0	11.1	10	0	11	11	First Pitch	.263	19	5	1	1	1	6	2	0	.391	.579
3+ Days rest	12.71	0	0	0	7	0	5.2	8	2	3	3	Behind on Count	.588	17	10	2	1	1	10	10	0	.724	1.000
Pre-All Star	5.96	0	0	0	21	0	22.2	23	2	17	19	Ahead on Count	.190	42	8	2	0	0	6	0	18	.227	.238
Post-All Star	36.00	0	0	0	2	0	1.0	3	0	2	1	Two Strikes	.140	43	6	3	0	0	4	7	20	.288	.209

Barry Manuel — Rangers
Pitches Right (flyball pitcher)

	ERA	W	L	Sv	G	GS	IP	BB	SO	Avg	H	2B	3B	HR	RBI	OBP	SLG	GF	IR	IRS	Hld	SvOp	SB	CS	GB	FB	G/F
1992 Season	4.76	1	0	0	3	0	5.2	1	9	.261	6	1	0	2	6	.320	.565	0	3	3	0	0	2	0	2	8	0.25
Career (1991-1992)	2.08	2	0	0	11	0	21.2	7	14	.181	13	2	0	2	10	.253	.292	5	9	5	0	0	2	0	19	29	0.66

1992 Season

	ERA	W	L	Sv	G	GS	IP	H	HR	BB	SO		Avg	AB	H	2B	3B	HR	RBI	BB	SO	OBP	SLG
Home	4.15	1	0	0	2	0	4.1	4	1	1	5	vs. Left	.167	6	1	0	0	0	0	0	2	.167	.167
Away	6.75	0	0	0	1	0	1.1	2	1	0	4	vs. Right	.294	17	5	1	0	2	6	1	7	.368	.706

Kirt Manwaring — Giants
Bats Right (groundball hitter)

	Avg	G	AB	R	H	2B	3B	HR	RBI	BB	SO	HBP	GDP	SB	CS	OBP	SLG	IBB	SH	SF	#Pit	#P/PA	GB	FB	G/F
1992 Season	.244	109	349	24	85	10	5	4	26	29	42	5	12	2	1	.311	.335	0	6	0	1363	3.56	150	88	1.70
Last Five Years	.231	309	856	66	198	30	8	5	79	51	116	15	20	5	4	.285	.303	1	21	4	3228	3.49	370	217	1.71

1992 Season

	Avg	AB	H	2B	3B	HR	RBI	BB	SO	OBP	SLG		Avg	AB	H	2B	3B	HR	RBI	BB	SO	OBP	SLG
vs. Left	.305	131	40	4	3	0	6	10	12	.355	.382	Scoring Posn	.214	84	18	5	2	0	22	8	7	.283	.321
vs. Right	.206	218	45	6	2	4	20	19	30	.285	.307	Close & Late	.243	70	17	2	1	2	6	7	10	.321	.386
Groundball	.234	154	36	5	3	0	14	13	0	.306	.305	None on/out	.253	75	19	0	1	3	3	11	13	.364	.400
Flyball	.190	58	11	2	0	0	6	7	18	.299	.224	Batting #7	.224	277	62	8	4	4	19	19	30	.281	.325
Home	.232	168	39	8	3	1	15	10	16	.275	.333	Batting #8	.357	42	15	0	0	3	6	10	.449	.357
Away	.254	181	46	2	2	3	11	19	26	.341	.337	Other	.267	30	8	2	1	0	4	4	2	.371	.400
Day	.266	154	41	6	1	4	18	10	12	.319	.396	April	.264	53	14	0	0	0	5	3	5	.304	.264
Night	.226	195	44	4	4	0	8	19	30	.304	.287	May	.273	55	15	3	2	0	5	11	3	.412	.400
Grass	.252	258	65	8	3	3	21	16	30	.298	.341	June	.270	74	20	1	2	1	6	6	11	.325	.378
Turf	.220	91	20	2	2	1	5	13	12	.343	.319	July	.185	54	10	1	0	0	3	2	11	.214	.204
First Pitch	.310	58	18	2	1	1	4	0	0	.322	.431	August	.219	64	14	3	1	2	5	5	7	.275	.391
Ahead on Count	.250	64	16	1	3	0	7	14	0	.385	.359	September/October	.245	49	12	2	0	1	2	2	5	.315	.347
Behind on Count	.274	124	34	2	1	3	14	0	19	.286	.379	Pre-All Star	.259	220	57	5	4	1	18	21	24	.329	.332
Two Strikes	.186	140	26	3	0	2	8	15	42	.274	.250	Post-All Star	.217	129	28	5	1	3	8	8	18	.279	.341

1992 By Position

Position	Avg	AB	H	2B	3B	HR	RBI	BB	SO	OBP	SLG	G	GS	Innings	PO	A	E	DP	Fld Pct	Rng Fctr	In Zone	Outs	Zone Rtg	MLB Zone
As c	.242	347	84	10	5	4	25	29	42	.310	.334	108	98	874.0	563	68	4	12	.994	---	---	---	---	---

Last Five Years

	Avg	AB	H	2B	3B	HR	RBI	BB	SO	OBP	SLG		Avg	AB	H	2B	3B	HR	RBI	BB	SO	OBP	SLG
vs. Left	.260	373	97	12	5	0	26	22	45	.306	.319	Scoring Posn	.248	206	51	9	3	0	71	17	24	.303	.320
vs. Right	.209	483	101	18	3	5	53	29	71	.269	.290	Close & Late	.231	134	31	2	1	2	14	12	18	.299	.306
Groundball	.222	325	72	11	5	1	25	20	37	.281	.295	None on/out	.230	196	45	6	1	3	3	15	25	.301	.316
Flyball	.212	189	40	5	1	0	23	13	42	.275	.249	Batting #7	.221	643	142	24	6	5	62	37	72	.271	.300
Home	.236	416	98	18	4	1	44	16	51	.272	.305	Batting #8	.281	135	38	4	0	0	10	8	31	.336	.311
Away	.227	440	100	12	4	4	35	35	65	.297	.300	Other	.231	78	18	2	2	0	7	6	13	.310	.308
Day	.242	359	87	11	3	4	41	15	42	.286	.323	April	.253	91	23	1	1	0	7	5	10	.306	.286
Night	.223	497	111	19	5	1	38	36	74	.284	.288	May	.270	89	24	4	2	0	9	12	10	.369	.360
Grass	.245	642	157	23	5	4	63	28	84	.286	.315	June	.266	173	46	5	2	1	15	10	26	.310	.335
Turf	.192	214	41	7	3	1	16	23	32	.284	.256	July	.203	133	27	3	2	0	13	7	19	.248	.256
First Pitch	.266	143	38	7	1	1	12	1	0	.286	.350	August	.224	201	45	10	1	2	22	11	29	.272	.313
Ahead on Count	.219	155	34	3	4	1	17	26	0	.339	.310	September/October	.195	169	33	7	0	2	13	6	22	.246	.272
Behind on Count	.254	323	82	9	3	3	33	0	64	.267	.328	Pre-All Star	.253	399	101	11	5	1	33	28	52	.310	.313
Two Strikes	.191	351	67	9	2	2	30	24	115	.254	.245	Post-All Star	.212	457	97	19	3	4	46	23	64	.263	.293

Batter vs. Pitcher (career)

Hits Best Against	Avg	AB	H	2B	3B	HR	RBI	BB	SO	OBP	SLG	Hits Worst Against	Avg	AB	H	2B	3B	HR	RBI	BB	SO	OBP	SLG
Charlie Leibrandt	.526	19	10	2	0	0	2	0	1	.526	.632	Zane Smith	.000	13	0	0	0	0	0	0	1	.000	.000
Dennis Rasmussen	.364	11	4	1	0	0	0	0	0	.364	.455	Doug Drabek	.000	11	0	0	0	0	0	1	3	.083	.000
Ramon Martinez	.364	11	4	0	0	0	1	0	0	.364	.364	Mike Morgan	.050	20	1	0	0	0	0	1	5	.095	.050
Bruce Hurst	.357	14	5	1	0	0	0	0	1	.357	.429	Orel Hershiser	.083	12	1	0	0	0	0	0	1	.083	.083
Danny Jackson	.304	23	7	0	0	0	2	3	2	.385	.304	Randy Myers	.100	10	1	0	0	0	0	1	1	.182	.100

Tom Marsh — Phillies
Bats Right

	Avg	G	AB	R	H	2B	3B	HR	RBI	BB	SO	HBP	GDP	SB	CS	OBP	SLG	IBB	SH	SF	#Pit	#P/PA	GB	FB	G/F
1992 Season	.200	42	125	7	25	3	2	2	16	2	23	1	2	0	1	.215	.304	0	2	2	429	3.30	44	41	1.07

1992 Season

	Avg	AB	H	2B	3B	HR	RBI	BB	SO	OBP	SLG		Avg	AB	H	2B	3B	HR	RBI	BB	SO	OBP	SLG
vs. Left	.182	66	12	1	1	1	6	1	14	.203	.273	Scoring Posn	.243	37	9	1	1	1	15	0	5	.231	.405
vs. Right	.220	59	13	2	1	1	10	1	9	.230	.339	Close & Late	.267	15	4	1	0	0	1	0	4	.250	.333
Home	.177	62	11	1	2	1	10	1	13	.203	.306	None on/out	.172	29	5	1	0	1	1	1	9	.200	.310
Away	.222	63	14	2	0	1	6	1	10	.227	.302	Batting #8	.000	12	0	0	0	0	0	0	5	.000	.000
First Pitch	.435	23	10	1	1	1	5	0	0	.435	.696	Batting #7	.219	105	23	3	2	2	16	2	17	.236	.343
Ahead on Count	.148	27	4	0	0	1	6	1	0	.172	.259	Other	.250	8	2	0	0	0	0	0	1	.250	.250

	Avg	AB	H	2B	3B	HR	RBI	BB	SO	OBP	SLG		Avg	AB	H	2B	3B	HR	RBI	BB	SO	OBP	SLG
Behind on Count	.143	49	7	1	0	0	6	0	16	.157	.163	Pre-All Star	.257	35	9	1	0	1	2	2	1	.308	.371
Two Strikes	.105	57	6	1	1	0	5	1	23	.133	.158	Post-All Star	.178	90	16	2	2	1	14	0	22	.176	.278

Al Martin — Pirates   Bats Left (groundball hitter)

	Avg	G	AB	R	H	2B	3B	HR	RBI	BB	SO	HBP	GDP	SB	CS	OBP	SLG	IBB	SH	SF	#Pit	#P/PA	GB	FB	G/F
1992 Season	.167	12	12	1	2	0	1	0	2	0	5	0	0	0	0	.154	.333	0	0	1	50	3.85	5	2	2.50

1992 Season

	Avg	AB	H	2B	3B	HR	RBI	BB	SO	OBP	SLG		Avg	AB	H	2B	3B	HR	RBI	BB	SO	OBP	SLG
vs. Left	.000	2	0	0	0	0	0	0	1	.000	.000	Scoring Posn	.167	6	1	0	0	0	2	0	3	.143	.167
vs. Right	.200	10	2	0	1	0	2	0	4	.182	.400	Close & Late	.000	5	0	0	0	0	0	0	3	.000	.000

Carlos Martinez — Indians   Bats Right

	Avg	G	AB	R	H	2B	3B	HR	RBI	BB	SO	HBP	GDP	SB	CS	OBP	SLG	IBB	SH	SF	#Pit	#P/PA	GB	FB	G/F
1992 Season	.263	69	228	23	60	9	1	5	35	7	21	1	5	1	2	.283	.377	0	1	4	822	3.43	87	81	1.07
Career (1988-1992)	.265	359	1162	112	308	52	6	19	121	48	173	4	38	9	9	.294	.369	6	9	10	4141	3.38	444	335	1.33

1992 Season

	Avg	AB	H	2B	3B	HR	RBI	BB	SO	OBP	SLG		Avg	AB	H	2B	3B	HR	RBI	BB	SO	OBP	SLG
vs. Left	.260	96	25	5	1	1	14	4	9	.287	.365	Scoring Posn	.250	64	16	2	1	2	32	1	7	.257	.406
vs. Right	.265	132	35	4	0	4	21	3	12	.281	.386	Close & Late	.238	42	10	3	0	1	10	1	5	.244	.381
Home	.303	99	30	3	1	2	18	3	10	.320	.414	None on/out	.259	54	14	2	0	1	1	1	6	.273	.352
Away	.233	129	30	6	0	3	17	4	11	.255	.349	Batting #5	.279	122	34	6	1	2	15	4	14	.299	.393
First Pitch	.194	31	6	0	1	0	7	0	0	.194	.258	Batting #6	.203	69	14	1	0	3	12	2	3	.233	.348
Ahead on Count	.294	51	15	2	0	0	6	6	0	.362	.333	Other	.324	37	12	2	0	0	8	1	4	.325	.378
Behind on Count	.289	83	24	3	0	3	10	0	12	.294	.434	Pre-All Star	.262	65	17	4	0	1	5	3	7	.294	.369
Two Strikes	.247	93	23	4	0	3	12	1	21	.260	.387	Post-All Star	.264	163	43	5	1	4	30	4	14	.279	.380

Career (1988-1992)

	Avg	AB	H	2B	3B	HR	RBI	BB	SO	OBP	SLG		Avg	AB	H	2B	3B	HR	RBI	BB	SO	OBP	SLG
vs. Left	.266	481	128	19	3	9	50	19	67	.291	.374	Scoring Posn	.259	290	75	14	3	3	103	17	48	.292	.359
vs. Right	.264	681	180	33	3	10	71	29	106	.296	.366	Close & Late	.224	174	39	12	0	2	25	9	34	.259	.328
Groundball	.254	268	68	12	0	3	26	12	39	.284	.332	None on/out	.278	263	73	13	1	7	7	5	35	.296	.414
Flyball	.230	282	65	10	2	1	22	12	40	.259	.291	Batting #5	.253	296	75	14	1	4	30	14	39	.265	.348
Home	.274	576	158	24	4	9	67	26	87	.305	.377	Batting #6	.249	465	116	17	5	9	53	14	63	.271	.366
Away	.256	586	150	28	2	10	54	22	86	.284	.362	Other	.292	401	117	21	0	6	38	20	71	.327	.389
Day	.227	326	74	9	0	11	42	11	59	.253	.356	April	.230	61	14	2	1	2	10	2	9	.254	.393
Night	.280	836	234	43	6	8	79	37	114	.310	.374	May	.197	142	28	7	1	2	17	6	23	.235	.303
Grass	.275	965	265	45	6	17	112	43	135	.304	.387	June	.277	130	36	6	0	1	10	8	21	.319	.346
Turf	.218	197	43	7	0	2	9	5	38	.248	.284	July	.294	187	55	8	2	5	16	9	25	.325	.439
First Pitch	.285	200	57	11	1	3	30	1	0	.287	.395	August	.301	269	81	11	1	3	26	12	44	.330	.383
Ahead on Count	.311	212	66	8	1	3	16	27	0	.391	.401	September/October	.252	373	94	18	1	6	42	11	51	.272	.354
Behind on Count	.234	465	109	16	2	9	39	2	113	.239	.335	Pre-All Star	.234	359	84	16	2	5	39	18	55	.272	.331
Two Strikes	.189	518	98	17	2	5	39	18	173	.217	.259	Post-All Star	.279	803	224	36	4	14	82	30	118	.304	.386

Batter vs. Pitcher (career)

Hits Best Against	Avg	AB	H	2B	3B	HR	RBI	BB	SO	OBP	SLG	Hits Worst Against	Avg	AB	H	2B	3B	HR	RBI	BB	SO	OBP	SLG
Bob Milacki	.500	18	9	5	0	1	4	0	2	.500	.944	Mark Langston	.077	13	1	0	0	0	0	0	3	.077	.077
Joe Hesketh	.455	11	5	1	0	0	0	0	2	.455	.545	Jack McDowell	.063	12	1	0	0	0	1	0	1	.063	.063
Greg Hibbard	.417	12	5	1	0	0	3	0	0	.417	.500	Mark Williamson	.091	11	1	0	0	0	1	0	0	.091	.091
Jimmy Key	.391	23	9	1	0	1	1	0	3	.391	.565	Dave Stieb	.182	11	2	0	0	0	0	0	3	.182	.182
Jack Morris	.320	25	8	1	0	1	4	0	2	.320	.480	Bud Black	.182	11	2	0	0	0	0	0	3	.182	.182

Chito Martinez — Orioles   Bats Left

	Avg	G	AB	R	H	2B	3B	HR	RBI	BB	SO	HBP	GDP	SB	CS	OBP	SLG	IBB	SH	SF	#Pit	#P/PA	GB	FB	G/F
1992 Season	.268	83	198	26	53	10	1	5	25	31	47	2	9	0	1	.366	.404	4	0	4	912	3.88	59	64	0.92
Career (1991-1992)	.268	150	414	58	111	22	2	18	58	42	98	2	10	1	2	.335	.461	4	0	5	1808	3.90	127	125	1.02

1992 Season

	Avg	AB	H	2B	3B	HR	RBI	BB	SO	OBP	SLG		Avg	AB	H	2B	3B	HR	RBI	BB	SO	OBP	SLG
vs. Left	.308	39	12	2	0	2	9	3	13	.364	.513	Scoring Posn	.244	45	11	2	0	2	20	12	12	.377	.422
vs. Right	.258	159	41	8	1	3	16	28	34	.366	.377	Close & Late	.257	35	9	1	0	0	2	7	7	.395	.286
Home	.310	100	31	7	0	2	14	19	25	.415	.440	None on/out	.240	50	12	3	0	2	2	8	12	.367	.420
Away	.224	98	22	3	1	3	11	12	22	.313	.367	Batting #6	.280	93	26	6	1	1	6	10	24	.352	.398
First Pitch	.360	25	9	1	0	0	3	3	0	.414	.400	Batting #7	.238	42	10	1	0	2	9	7	13	.333	.405
Ahead on Count	.360	50	18	6	1	3	10	17	0	.515	.700	Other	.270	63	17	3	0	2	10	14	10	.405	.413
Behind on Count	.254	63	16	1	0	2	10	0	21	.254	.365	Pre-All Star	.207	92	19	3	1	4	17	16	19	.324	.391
Two Strikes	.129	93	12	1	0	2	8	11	47	.231	.204	Post-All Star	.321	106	34	7	0	1	8	15	28	.403	.415

Dave Martinez — Reds
Bats Left

	Avg	G	AB	R	H	2B	3B	HR	RBI	BB	SO	HBP	GDP	SB	CS	OBP	SLG	IBB	SH	SF	#Pit	#P/PA	GB	FB	G/F
1992 Season	.254	135	393	47	100	20	5	3	31	42	54	0	6	12	8	.323	.354	4	6	4	1697	3.87	152	118	1.29
Last Five Years	.271	641	1988	246	539	80	28	30	185	151	307	6	21	87	39	.322	.385	19	23	15	8169	3.78	716	569	1.26

1992 Season

	Avg	AB	H	2B	3B	HR	RBI	BB	SO	OBP	SLG		Avg	AB	H	2B	3B	HR	RBI	BB	SO	OBP	SLG
vs. Left	.271	59	16	5	0	0	8	7	15	.348	.356	Scoring Posn	.207	111	23	5	2	1	28	19	19	.313	.315
vs. Right	.251	334	84	15	5	3	23	35	39	.319	.353	Close & Late	.058	52	3	2	0	0	2	7	14	.169	.096
Groundball	.229	153	35	3	1	0	6	19	23	.310	.261	None on/out	.276	76	21	4	2	0	0	9	10	.353	.382
Flyball	.226	84	19	4	1	2	9	10	11	.309	.369	Batting #2	.226	234	53	9	3	1	16	21	32	.288	.303
Home	.291	196	57	11	3	3	20	21	20	.355	.423	Batting #7	.304	46	14	2	1	0	1	6	3	.333	.391
Away	.218	197	43	9	2	0	11	21	34	.292	.284	Other	.292	113	33	9	1	2	14	19	16	.388	.442
Day	.244	131	32	7	2	3	13	17	19	.331	.397	April	.275	51	14	3	0	0	4	7	6	.362	.333
Night	.260	262	68	13	3	0	18	25	35	.320	.332	May	.219	64	14	1	1	0	5	9	9	.315	.266
Grass	.254	114	29	6	1	0	5	15	23	.338	.325	June	.284	67	19	4	2	0	7	3	12	.306	.403
Turf	.254	279	71	14	4	3	26	27	31	.317	.366	July	.250	84	21	2	1	1	2	6	10	.300	.333
First Pitch	.333	45	15	4	1	1	7	3	0	.360	.533	August	.220	50	11	2	0	0	4	9	7	.333	.260
Ahead on Count	.274	117	32	8	1	2	9	21	0	.381	.410	September/October	.273	77	21	8	1	2	9	8	10	.337	.481
Behind on Count	.220	127	28	2	1	1	6	0	36	.220	.276	Pre-All Star	.249	221	55	10	3	1	18	22	35	.314	.335
Two Strikes	.183	175	32	7	2	0	9	18	54	.258	.246	Post-All Star	.262	172	45	10	2	2	13	20	19	.335	.378

1992 By Position

Position	Avg	AB	H	2B	3B	HR	RBI	BB	SO	OBP	SLG	G	GS	Innings	PO	A	E	DP	Fld Pct	Rng Fctr	In Zone	Outs	Zone Rtg	MLB Zone
As Pinch Hitter	.000	12	0	0	0	0	2	1	2	.071	.000	15	0	---	---	---	---	---	---	---	---	---	---	---
As 1b	.274	62	17	4	0	0	6	12	7	.387	.339	21	17	161.1	156	11	4	22	.977	---	26	22	.846	.843
As cf	.272	298	81	15	5	3	22	27	41	.330	.386	105	76	718.2	212	5	2	1	.991	2.72	248	207	.835	.824

Last Five Years

	Avg	AB	H	2B	3B	HR	RBI	BB	SO	OBP	SLG		Avg	AB	H	2B	3B	HR	RBI	BB	SO	OBP	SLG
vs. Left	.229	306	70	12	2	3	33	29	81	.301	.310	Scoring Posn	.258	462	119	22	7	5	149	55	83	.335	.368
vs. Right	.279	1686	470	68	26	27	152	122	226	.326	.398	Close & Late	.187	337	63	11	4	0	31	28	75	.251	.243
Groundball	.267	688	184	29	8	4	51	60	106	.324	.350	None on/out	.266	541	144	18	6	7	7	34	74	.311	.360
Flyball	.261	421	110	18	8	8	46	43	66	.328	.399	Batting #1	.271	535	145	22	7	9	52	42	95	.321	.389
Home	.264	951	251	35	11	14	84	72	132	.315	.368	Batting #2	.261	783	204	29	11	9	65	51	94	.307	.360
Away	.278	1041	289	45	17	16	101	79	175	.324	.400	Other	.283	674	191	29	10	12	68	58	118	.341	.409
Day	.260	666	173	26	7	16	67	63	126	.325	.392	April	.233	249	58	9	2	2	26	18	33	.289	.309
Night	.277	1326	367	54	21	14	118	88	181	.321	.381	May	.254	291	74	10	5	2	34	30	56	.320	.344
Grass	.279	663	185	26	11	11	66	56	120	.335	.401	June	.283	385	109	17	7	9	45	23	62	.320	.434
Turf	.267	1329	355	54	17	19	119	95	187	.316	.376	July	.289	357	103	12	2	7	17	24	51	.336	.392
First Pitch	.329	228	75	13	5	2	24	6	0	.342	.456	August	.278	370	103	16	5	4	34	28	55	.331	.381
Ahead on Count	.316	582	184	32	9	15	65	86	0	.404	.479	September/October	.274	340	93	16	7	6	29	28	50	.329	.415
Behind on Count	.261	658	172	23	7	11	53	2	162	.267	.368	Pre-All Star	.265	1057	280	46	14	16	114	81	177	.316	.380
Two Strikes	.208	888	185	25	9	10	64	52	304	.252	.291	Post-All Star	.278	931	259	34	14	14	71	70	130	.335	.390

Batter vs. Pitcher (career)

Hits Best Against	Avg	AB	H	2B	3B	HR	RBI	BB	SO	OBP	SLG	Hits Worst Against	Avg	AB	H	2B	3B	HR	RBI	BB	SO	OBP	SLG
Mike Jackson	.571	7	4	0	0	0	3	1	.636	.571	Paul Assenmacher	.067	15	1	0	0	0	1	1	7	.125	.067
Mike Maddux	.545	11	6	0	0	0	0	3	1	.643	.545	Alejandro Pena	.077	13	1	0	0	0	0	0	5	.077	.077
Mike Dunne	.500	16	8	0	2	0	0	1	1	.529	.750	Shawn Boskie	.087	23	2	0	0	0	0	3	3	.192	.087
Bill Landrum	.500	10	5	1	0	0	1	1	1	.545	.600	Nolan Ryan	.133	15	2	0	0	0	0	2	5	.235	.133
Terry Leach	.455	11	5	2	0	1	2	0	2	.455	.909	Pete Harnisch	.158	19	3	1	0	0	0	1	1	.200	.158

Dennis Martinez — Expos
Pitches Right (groundball pitcher)

	ERA	W	L	Sv	G	GS	IP	BB	SO	Avg	H	2B	3B	HR	RBI	OBP	SLG	CG	ShO	Sup	QS	#P/S	SB	CS	GB	FB	G/F
1992 Season	2.47	16	11	0	32	32	226.1	60	147	.211	172	26	0	12	64	.271	.287	6	0	4.02	25	102	22	17	342	195	1.75
Last Five Years	2.74	71	53	0	163	162	1141.2	275	688	.233	992	164	32	79	355	.283	.342	36	11	4.12	112	101	106	50	1751	1123	1.56

1992 Season

	ERA	W	L	Sv	G	GS	IP	H	HR	BB	SO		Avg	AB	H	2B	3B	HR	RBI	BB	SO	OBP	SLG
Home	2.09	8	4	0	16	16	116.0	73	5	28	74	vs. Left	.211	503	106	15	0	8	39	34	94	.261	.288
Away	2.85	8	7	0	16	16	110.1	99	7	32	73	vs. Right	.212	311	66	11	0	4	25	26	53	.288	.286
Day	4.25	2	5	0	9	9	55.0	56	4	21	41	Inning 1-6	.214	663	142	24	0	7	51	51	126	.272	.282
Night	1.89	14	6	0	23	23	171.1	116	8	39	106	Inning 7+	.199	151	30	2	0	5	13	9	21	.267	.311
Grass	3.29	4	4	0	8	8	52.0	55	3	17	33	None on	.206	530	109	18	0	8	8	34	92	.259	.285
Turf	2.22	12	7	0	24	24	174.1	117	9	43	114	Runners on	.222	284	63	8	0	4	56	26	55	.294	.292
April	2.65	1	4	0	5	5	34.0	20	1	12	20	Scoring Posn	.224	165	37	3	0	2	50	15	34	.289	.279
May	1.83	4	0	0	5	5	34.1	25	1	8	19	Close & Late	.173	81	14	2	0	3	8	6	14	.264	.309
June	3.51	3	2	0	6	6	41.0	34	3	16	26	None on/out	.220	223	49	8	0	4	4	15	35	.275	.309
July	3.76	2	4	0	6	6	38.1	41	5	11	27	vs. 1st Batr (relief)	.000	0	0	0	0	0	0	0	0	.000	.000
August	1.42	4	0	0	5	5	38.0	24	1	7	25	First Inning Pitched	.151	106	16	1	0	1	4	13	27	.250	.189
September/October	1.55	2	1	0	5	5	40.2	28	1	6	27	First 75 Pitches	.214	576	123	20	0	6	40	47	114	.276	.280
Starter	2.47	16	11	0	32	32	226.1	172	12	60	147	Pitch 76-90	.230	113	26	4	0	4	12	6	15	.270	.372
Reliever	0.00	0	0	0	0	0	0.0	0	0	0	0	Pitch 91-105	.165	79	13	1	0	5	6	13	.241	.177

274

1992 Season

	ERA	W	L	Sv	G	GS	IP	H	HR	BB	SO		Avg	AB	H	2B	3B	HR	RBI	BB	SO	OBP	SLG
0-3 Days Rest	12.27	0	1	0	1	1	3.2	5	1	4	3	Pitch 106+	.217	46	10	1	0	2	7	1	5	.265	.370
4 Days Rest	2.64	8	7	0	17	17	119.1	100	7	33	78	First Pitch	.325	126	41	5	0	2	12	2	0	.344	.413
5+ Days Rest	1.92	8	3	0	14	14	103.1	67	4	23	66	Ahead on Count	.180	384	69	11	0	5	21	0	125	.194	.247
Pre-All Star	2.88	9	8	0	19	19	125.0	104	7	40	77	Behind on Count	.209	148	31	7	0	4	19	28	0	.330	.338
Post-All Star	1.95	7	3	0	13	13	101.1	68	5	20	70	Two Strikes	.160	376	60	10	0	4	23	30	147	.229	.218

Last Five Years

	ERA	W	L	Sv	G	GS	IP	H	HR	BB	SO		Avg	AB	H	2B	3B	HR	RBI	BB	SO	OBP	SLG
Home	2.63	34	26	0	77	76	560.1	469	43	122	331	vs. Left	.236	2467	583	90	17	41	198	186	396	.289	.336
Away	2.85	37	27	0	86	86	581.1	523	36	153	357	vs. Right	.227	1798	409	74	15	38	157	89	292	.274	.349
Day	3.47	17	20	0	48	48	316.2	308	32	77	200	Inning 1-6	.234	3464	811	138	28	55	287	230	570	.285	.338
Night	2.47	54	33	0	115	114	825.0	684	47	198	488	Inning 7+	.226	801	181	26	4	24	68	45	118	.275	.358
Grass	2.93	18	15	0	41	41	276.0	271	19	71	180	None on	.235	2680	630	110	18	49	49	132	416	.275	.344
Turf	2.68	53	38	0	122	121	865.2	721	60	204	508	Runners on	.228	1585	362	54	14	30	306	143	272	.296	.337
April	2.43	10	10	0	26	26	181.2	143	11	52	107	Close & Late	.218	445	97	14	3	14	42	23	60	.268	.357
May	2.66	12	9	0	28	28	192.2	185	15	42	115	None on/out	.238	1146	273	41	9	25	25	52	160	.274	.355
June	2.48	15	6	0	30	30	217.1	180	12	64	122	vs. 1st Batr (relief)	.000	1	0	0	0	0	0	0	0	.000	.000
July	3.09	15	6	0	28	28	195.1	187	12	44	115	First Inning Pitched	.248	608	151	28	4	10	58	54	106	.312	.357
August	2.67	14	11	0	29	28	209.0	173	18	36	138	First 75 Pitches	.233	3066	715	121	24	50	233	195	510	.282	.337
September/October	3.27	5	11	0	22	22	145.2	124	11	37	91	Pitch 76-90	.231	550	127	19	5	12	56	35	72	.283	.349
Starter	2.74	71	52	0	162	162	1139.2	991	78	275	686	Pitch 91-105	.225	395	89	16	3	7	36	27	61	.282	.334
Reliever	4.50	0	1	0	1	0	2.0	1	1	0	2	Pitch 106+	.240	254	61	8	0	10	30	18	45	.300	.390
0-3 Days Rest	4.04	2	3	0	6	6	35.2	36	2	9	31	First Pitch	.296	679	201	41	3	18	79	14	0	.317	.445
4 Days Rest	2.82	48	37	0	108	108	760.2	683	55	183	452	Ahead on Count	.193	1955	377	62	12	27	122	0	592	.199	.278
5+ Days Rest	2.44	21	12	0	48	48	343.1	272	21	83	203	Behind on Count	.250	869	217	38	6	23	89	138	0	.352	.387
Pre-All Star	2.65	43	28	0	93	93	649.1	578	43	170	376	Two Strikes	.183	1872	343	47	17	27	118	123	688	.237	.270
Post-All Star	2.87	28	25	0	70	69	492.1	414	36	105	312												

Pitcher vs. Batter (since 1984)

Pitches Best Vs.	Avg	AB	H	2B	3B	HR	RBI	BB	SO	OBP	SLG	Pitches Worst Vs.	Avg	AB	H	2B	3B	HR	RBI	BB	SO	OBP	SLG
Rich Gedman	.000	15	0	0	0	0		1	2	.063	.000	Kent Hrbek	.545	11	6	2	0	1	3	1	0	.583	1.000
Alvin Davis	.000	13	0	0	0	0		2	2	.133	.000	Don Slaught	.538	13	7	2	1	0	2	1	0	.571	.846
Mickey Morandini	.056	18	1	0	0	0		1	2	.105	.056	Glenn Davis	.481	27	13	0	0	6	12	3	2	.516	1.148
Curt Wilkerson	.059	17	1	0	0	0		0	7	.059	.059	George Brett	.455	11	5	2	0	1	4	1	0	.500	.909
Gary Carter	.071	28	2	0	0	0		0	2	.071	.071	Kevin Mitchell	.320	25	8	0	0	5	7	2	3	.370	.920

Domingo Martinez — Blue Jays
Bats Right (groundball hitter)

	Avg	G	AB	R	H	2B	3B	HR	RBI	BB	SO	HBP	GDP	SB	CS	OBP	SLG	IBB	SH	SF	#Pit	#P/PA	GB	FB	G/F
1992 Season	.625	7	8	2	5	0	0	1	3	0	1	0	0	0	0	.625	1.000	0	0	0	22	2.75	2	1	2.00

1992 Season

	Avg	AB	H	2B	3B	HR	RBI	BB	SO	OBP	SLG		Avg	AB	H	2B	3B	HR	RBI	BB	SO	OBP	SLG
vs. Left	.667	6	4	0	0	1	3	0	0	.667	1.167	Scoring Posn	.333	3	1	0	0	0	1	0	1	.333	.333
vs. Right	.500	2	1	0	0	0	0	0	1	.500	.500	Close & Late	.000	0	0	0	0	0	0	0	0	.000	.000

Edgar Martinez — Mariners
Bats Right

	Avg	G	AB	R	H	2B	3B	HR	RBI	BB	SO	HBP	GDP	SB	CS	OBP	SLG	IBB	SH	SF	#Pit	#P/PA	GB	FB	G/F
1992 Season	.343	135	528	100	181	46	3	18	73	54	61	4	15	14	4	.404	.544	2	1	5	2386	4.04	199	145	1.37
Last Five Years	.309	508	1762	289	545	117	6	45	199	233	228	20	50	17	12	.393	.459	15	7	16	8239	4.06	652	514	1.27

1992 Season

	Avg	AB	H	2B	3B	HR	RBI	BB	SO	OBP	SLG		Avg	AB	H	2B	3B	HR	RBI	BB	SO	OBP	SLG
vs. Left	.376	141	53	16	0	4	17	18	14	.444	.574	Scoring Posn	.308	133	41	10	1	8	62	12	14	.358	.579
vs. Right	.331	387	128	30	3	14	56	36	47	.390	.532	Close & Late	.390	82	32	9	0	2	10	8	8	.440	.573
Groundball	.321	137	44	9	0	5	19	19	12	.396	.496	None on/out	.418	98	41	9	0	4	8	8		.467	.633
Flyball	.340	150	51	18	3	2	17	14	22	.398	.540	Batting #2	.349	384	134	38	1	12	49	44	41	.416	.547
Home	.313	268	84	27	1	11	39	27	37	.377	.545	Batting #3	.313	96	30	6	2	5	17	7	15	.362	.573
Away	.373	260	97	19	2	7	34	27	24	.432	.542	Other	.354	48	17	2	0	1	7	3	5	.392	.458
Day	.388	139	54	13	2	6	20	13	12	.439	.640	April	.224	67	15	7	0	1	8	11	8	.342	.373
Night	.326	389	127	33	1	12	53	41	49	.392	.509	May	.340	103	35	7	3	5	15	9	15	.395	.612
Grass	.403	206	83	18	2	4	30	25	18	.466	.568	June	.352	108	38	10	0	6	17	8	14	.402	.611
Turf	.304	322	98	28	1	14	43	29	43	.363	.528	July	.388	98	38	6	0	3	12	12	11	.455	.541
First Pitch	.405	37	15	2	0	2	6	1	0	.436	.622	August	.395	114	45	16	0	3	19	9	10	.433	.614
Ahead on Count	.422	173	73	17	1	6	20	29	0	.498	.636	September/October	.263	38	10	0	0	0	2	5	3	.341	.263
Behind on Count	.336	143	48	12	2	3	16	0	21	.340	.510	Pre-All Star	.328	314	103	26	3	14	47	33	39	.395	.564
Two Strikes	.279	226	63	20	0	8	31	25	61	.353	.473	Post-All Star	.364	214	78	20	0	4	26	21	22	.417	.514

1992 By Position

Position	Avg	AB	H	2B	3B	HR	RBI	BB	SO	OBP	SLG	G	GS	Innings	PO	A	E	DP	Fld Pct	Rng Fctr	In Zone	Outs	Zone Rtg	MLB Zone
As Designated Hitter	.392	120	47	9	0	4	17	10	9	.435	.567	28	28	---	---	---	---	---	---	---	---	---	---	---
As 3b	.335	397	133	37	3	14	56	44	49	.403	.549	103	102	869.2	72	208	17	23	.943	2.90	287	240	.836	.841

Last Five Years

	Avg	AB	H	2B	3B	HR	RBI	BB	SO	OBP	SLG		Avg	AB	H	2B	3B	HR	RBI	BB	SO	OBP	SLG
vs. Left	.336	530	178	42	1	13	65	73	55	.416	.492	Scoring Posn	.267	405	106	18	1	13	152	74	45	.378	.412
vs. Right	.298	1232	367	75	5	32	134	160	173	.383	.445	Close & Late	.335	266	89	19	0	7	41	51	40	.446	.485
Groundball	.313	453	142	29	0	11	57	61	58	.399	.450	None on/out	.336	437	147	38	2	14	14	46	55	.403	.529
Flyball	.284	402	114	30	4	9	43	50	59	.363	.445	Batting #1	.300	273	82	24	1	9	25	44	34	.401	.495
Home	.304	849	258	63	3	22	95	119	114	.392	.463	Batting #2	.332	485	161	40	1	13	58	59	53	.406	.499
Away	.314	913	287	54	3	23	104	114	114	.394	.456	Other	.301	1004	302	53	4	23	116	130	141	.384	.430
Day	.300	453	136	30	4	13	57	55	51	.375	.470	April	.289	239	69	15	0	5	27	38	29	.306	.414
Night	.312	1309	409	87	2	32	142	178	177	.399	.455	May	.319	326	104	13	5	13	42	44	44	.402	.509
Grass	.318	682	217	39	3	17	78	90	83	.401	.459	June	.304	329	100	23	0	8	33	37	54	.379	.447
Turf	.304	1080	328	78	3	28	121	143	145	.388	.459	July	.317	306	97	17	1	9	36	38	41	.397	.467
First Pitch	.352	128	45	10	0	3	13	5	0	.384	.500	August	.313	300	94	30	0	8	35	39	28	.394	.493
Ahead on Count	.363	476	173	34	2	16	56	125	0	.494	.544	September/October	.309	262	81	19	0	2	26	37	32	.389	.405
Behind on Count	.299	559	167	33	3	11	56	1	101	.308	.426	Pre-All Star	.300	993	296	54	5	28	115	130	139	.385	.449
Two Strikes	.257	805	207	47	2	17	84	100	228	.343	.384	Post-All Star	.321	769	247	63	1	17	84	103	89	.403	.472

Batter vs. Pitcher (career)

Hits Best Against	Avg	AB	H	2B	3B	HR	RBI	BB	SO	OBP	SLG	Hits Worst Against	Avg	AB	H	2B	3B	HR	RBI	BB	SO	OBP	SLG
Greg Cadaret	.778	9	7	4	0	0	1	2	0	.818	1.222	Jose Mesa	.000	10	0	0	0	0	0	0	2	.167	.000
Rick Sutcliffe	.538	13	7	3	1	0	1	1	2	.533	.923	Nolan Ryan	.053	19	1	0	0	0	2	1	10	.100	.053
Greg Swindell	.500	14	7	0	1	1	1	1	1	.533	.857	Tom Candiotti	.083	12	1	0	0	0	0	1	5	.154	.083
Mark Gubicza	.500	12	6	2	0	1	3	1	1	.538	.917	Bud Black	.091	11	1	0	0	0	0	1	3	.167	.091
Joe Hesketh	.455	11	5	3	0	1	1	3	2	.571	.727	Dave Stieb	.100	10	1	0	0	0	1	2	3	.250	.100

Pedro Martinez — Dodgers   Pitches Right

	ERA	W	L	Sv	G	GS	IP	BB	SO	Avg	H	2B	3B	HR	RBI	OBP	SLG	CG	ShO	Sup	QS	#P/S	SB	CS	GB	FB	G/F
1992 Season	2.25	0	1	0	2	1	8.0	1	8	.200	6	3	0	0	2	.226	.300	0	0	1.13	1	89	0	0	9	8	1.13

1992 Season

	ERA	W	L	Sv	G	GS	IP	H	HR	BB	SO		Avg	AB	H	2B	3B	HR	RBI	BB	SO	OBP	SLG
Home	0.00	0	0	0	1	0	2.0	2	0	1	1	vs. Left	.200	15	3	2	0	0	2	1	2	.250	.333
Away	3.00	0	1	0	1	1	6.0	4	0	0	7	vs. Right	.200	15	3	1	0	0	0	0	6	.200	.267

Ramon Martinez — Dodgers   Pitches Right (flyball pitcher)

	ERA	W	L	Sv	G	GS	IP	BB	SO	Avg	H	2B	3B	HR	RBI	OBP	SLG	CG	ShO	Sup	QS	#P/S	SB	CS	GB	FB	G/F
1992 Season	4.00	8	11	0	25	25	150.2	69	101	.245	141	30	2	11	68	.331	.362	5	1	3.52	14	100	19	7	203	177	1.15
Career (1988-1992)	3.32	52	37	0	115	112	739.2	268	586	.228	628	116	12	62	273	.300	.346	21	10	4.71	70	107	64	42	836	867	0.96

1992 Season

	ERA	W	L	Sv	G	GS	IP	H	HR	BB	SO		Avg	AB	H	2B	3B	HR	RBI	BB	SO	OBP	SLG
Home	4.29	4	7	0	15	15	92.1	90	10	42	61	vs. Left	.256	316	81	19	2	9	40	54	47	.367	.415
Away	3.55	4	4	0	10	10	58.1	51	1	27	40	vs. Right	.232	259	60	11	0	2	28	15	54	.282	.297
Day	3.18	3	3	0	7	7	39.2	38	4	16	21	Inning 1-6	.234	500	117	23	2	10	59	58	87	.318	.348
Night	4.30	5	8	0	18	18	111.0	103	7	53	80	Inning 7+	.320	75	24	7	0	1	9	11	14	.414	.453
Grass	3.57	7	7	0	19	19	121.0	104	10	52	74	None on	.237	321	76	17	2	6	6	35	54	.316	.358
Turf	5.76	1	4	0	6	6	29.2	37	1	17	27	Runners on	.256	254	65	13	0	5	62	34	47	.349	.366
April	3.64	0	1	0	5	5	29.2	27	1	15	13	Scoring Posn	.271	155	42	8	0	4	56	21	30	.363	.400
May	3.06	3	0	0	5	5	35.1	34	2	18	31	Close & Late	.231	52	12	4	0	0	5	5	9	.298	.308
June	4.33	1	4	0	5	5	27.0	31	2	13	14	None on/out	.253	146	37	4	1	5	5	17	25	.331	.397
July	4.30	2	3	0	5	5	29.1	26	2	13	23	vs. 1st Batr (relief)	.000	0	0	0	0	0	0	0	0	.000	.000
August	4.91	2	3	0	5	5	29.1	23	4	10	20	First Inning Pitched	.229	96	22	4	1	1	11	10	13	.308	.323
September/October	0.00	0	0	0	0	0	0.0	0	0	0	0	First 75 Pitches	.249	426	106	20	2	8	54	44	69	.324	.362
Starter	4.00	8	11	0	25	25	150.2	141	11	69	101	Pitch 76-90	.226	62	14	3	0	2	5	11	13	.342	.371
Reliever	0.00	0	0	0	0	0	0.0	0	0	0	0	Pitch 91-105	.208	53	11	4	0	1	7	7	12	.300	.340
0-3 Days Rest	0.00	1	0	0	1	1	8.0	3	0	4	8	Pitch 106+	.294	34	10	3	0	0	2	7	7	.429	.382
4 Days Rest	5.23	1	7	0	11	11	63.2	63	7	31	41	First Pitch	.295	78	23	2	0	2	11	3	0	.329	.397
5+ Days Rest	3.42	6	4	0	13	13	79.0	75	4	34	52	Ahead on Count	.183	246	45	10	0	2	21	0	88	.190	.248
Pre-All Star	3.51	5	6	0	17	17	105.0	104	7	52	69	Behind on Count	.321	134	43	12	2	5	22	45	0	.497	.552
Post-All Star	5.12	3	5	0	8	8	45.2	37	4	17	32	Two Strikes	.170	259	44	8	0	4	27	21	101	.238	.247

Career (1988-1992)

	ERA	W	L	Sv	G	GS	IP	H	HR	BB	SO		Avg	AB	H	2B	3B	HR	RBI	BB	SO	OBP	SLG
Home	3.22	28	19	0	61	59	402.1	319	35	161	347	vs. Left	.242	1539	372	73	7	35	157	196	299	.330	.366
Away	3.44	24	18	0	54	53	337.1	309	27	107	239	vs. Right	.211	1215	256	43	5	27	116	72	287	.260	.321
Day	3.05	16	10	0	33	32	209.1	172	19	78	160	Inning 1-6	.228	2288	522	98	12	53	240	221	488	.300	.351
Night	3.43	36	27	0	82	80	530.1	456	43	190	426	Inning 7+	.227	466	106	18	0	9	33	47	98	.300	.324
Grass	3.18	41	27	0	88	85	576.2	472	49	207	456	None on	.217	1652	359	74	7	38	38	159	372	.291	.340
Turf	3.81	11	10	0	27	27	163.0	156	13	61	130	Runners on	.244	1102	269	42	5	24	235	109	214	.315	.357
April	2.70	5	2	0	13	13	86.2	68	5	25	62	Scoring Posn	.234	628	147	24	2	13	201	68	134	.311	.341
May	3.59	11	4	0	17	17	110.1	104	9	43	100	Close & Late	.192	255	49	10	0	3	14	23	53	.262	.267
June	2.47	8	5	0	17	17	120.0	102	6	42	105	None on/out	.235	715	168	29	4	23	23	69	150	.308	.383
July	2.99	11	6	0	19	19	126.1	103	11	40	93	vs. 1st Batr (relief)	.000	3	0	0	0	0	0	0	0	.000	.000

Career (1988-1992)

	ERA	W	L	Sv	G	GS	IP	H	HR	BB	SO		Avg	AB	H	2B	3B	HR	RBI	BB	SO	OBP	SLG
August	4.11	8	13	0	26	26	164.1	149	19	60	119	First Inning Pitched	.220	432	95	16	4	12	50	49	79	.305	.359
September/October	3.61	9	7	0	23	20	132.0	102	12	58	107	First 75 Pitches	.226	1677	425	82	10	44	196	170	408	.295	.351
Starter	3.35	52	37	0	112	112	733.2	627	62	265	584	Pitch 76-90	.246	345	85	13	2	5	29	35	63	.319	.339
Reliever	0.00	0	0	0	3	0	6.0	1	0	3	2	Pitch 91-105	.216	268	58	11	0	6	25	28	57	.290	.325
0-3 Days Rest	3.44	2	1	0	3	3	18.1	14	2	10	20	Pitch 106+	.227	264	60	10	0	7	23	35	58	.322	.345
4 Days Rest	3.58	26	21	0	60	60	392.0	351	38	146	331	First Pitch	.289	336	97	15	2	13	49	11	0	.319	.461
5+ Days Rest	3.06	24	15	0	49	49	323.1	262	22	109	233	Ahead on Count	.172	1291	222	35	2	18	88	0	500	.179	.244
Pre-All Star	2.98	27	13	0	52	52	347.0	306	25	120	289	Behind on Count	.318	560	178	38	5	25	85	148	0	.459	.538
Post-All Star	3.62	25	24	0	63	60	392.2	322	37	148	297	Two Strikes	.164	1375	226	42	5	21	105	109	586	.230	.248

Pitcher vs. Batter (career)

Pitches Best Vs.	Avg	AB	H	2B	3B	HR	RBI	BB	SO	OBP	SLG	Pitches Worst Vs.	Avg	AB	H	2B	3B	HR	RBI	BB	SO	OBP	SLG
Lonnie Smith	.000	12	0	0	0	0	1	0	6	.000	.000	Mackey Sasser	.438	16	7	2	0	1	1	0	1	.438	.750
Spike Owen	.000	10	0	0	0	0	1	2	4	.167	.000	Delino DeShields	.429	21	9	2	0	1	2	4	2	.520	.667
Darrin Jackson	.059	17	1	0	0	0	1	0	2	.059	.059	Andy Van Slyke	.353	17	6	2	0	1	3	6	2	.522	.647
Rafael Belliard	.077	13	1	0	0	0	0	1	2	.250	.077	Howard Johnson	.333	24	8	5	0	2	5	5	3	.448	.792
Darryl Strawberry	.083	12	1	0	0	0	1	0	4	.083	.083	Chris Sabo	.333	21	7	2	0	3	7	1	5	.364	.857

Tino Martinez — Mariners
Bats Left

	Avg	G	AB	R	H	2B	3B	HR	RBI	BB	SO	HBP	GDP	SB	CS	OBP	SLG	IBB	SH	SF	#Pit	#P/PA	GB	FB	G/F
1992 Season	.257	136	460	53	118	19	2	16	66	42	77	2	24	2	1	.316	.411	9	1	8	1913	3.74	161	142	1.13
Career (1990-1992)	.244	196	640	68	156	25	2	20	80	62	110	2	26	2	1	.308	.383	9	1	11	2703	3.78	231	203	1.14

1992 Season

	Avg	AB	H	2B	3B	HR	RBI	BB	SO	OBP	SLG		Avg	AB	H	2B	3B	HR	RBI	BB	SO	OBP	SLG
vs. Left	.228	101	23	4	0	3	19	5	23	.261	.356	Scoring Posn	.274	117	32	6	2	3	52	19	18	.359	.436
vs. Right	.265	359	95	15	2	13	47	37	54	.332	.426	Close & Late	.278	90	25	5	0	2	13	8	21	.343	.400
Groundball	.214	112	24	2	0	2	14	16	20	.321	.286	None on/out	.277	112	31	7	0	4	4	4	18	.308	.446
Flyball	.271	140	38	5	0	4	17	9	22	.307	.393	Batting #5	.348	89	31	1	0	6	16	11	14	.417	.562
Home	.267	232	62	12	0	10	40	22	34	.326	.448	Batting #7	.236	178	42	10	1	7	26	14	25	.290	.421
Away	.246	228	56	7	2	6	26	20	43	.307	.373	Other	.233	193	45	8	1	3	24	17	38	.292	.332
Day	.262	130	34	4	1	3	16	11	29	.313	.377	April	.290	62	18	2	1	3	9	3	9	.323	.500
Night	.255	330	84	15	1	13	50	31	48	.318	.424	May	.278	79	22	7	0	1	10	8	12	.344	.405
Grass	.275	178	49	7	1	6	21	14	33	.328	.427	June	.241	87	21	2	1	3	17	5	10	.280	.391
Turf	.245	282	69	12	1	10	45	28	44	.309	.401	July	.154	65	10	1	0	1	4	4	18	.243	.215
First Pitch	.350	40	14	0	0	3	4	8	0	.480	.575	August	.281	96	27	3	0	4	14	7	18	.324	.438
Ahead on Count	.347	95	33	6	0	5	22	25	1	.464	.568	September/October	.282	71	20	4	0	4	12	11	14	.376	.507
Behind on Count	.241	174	42	8	2	6	32	0	48	.240	.414	Pre-All Star	.255	259	66	11	2	7	37	18	36	.301	.394
Two Strikes	.178	214	38	11	1	6	28	10	76	.212	.322	Post-All Star	.259	201	52	8	0	9	29	24	41	.335	.433

1992 By Position

Position	Avg	AB	H	2B	3B	HR	RBI	BB	SO	OBP	SLG	G	GS	Innings	PO	A	E	DP	Fld Pct	Rng Fctr	In Zone	Zone Outs	Zone Rtg	MLB Zone
As Designated Hitter	.250	168	42	13	0	7	25	13	23	.299	.452	47	47	---	---	---	---	---	---	---	---	---	---	---
As Pinch Hitter	.091	11	1	0	0	0	0	0	4	.091	.091	12	0	---	---	---	---	---	---	---	---	---	---	---
As 1b	.267	281	75	6	2	9	41	29	50	.334	.399	78	74	663.2	678	58	4	63	.995	---	128	112	.875	.843

John Marzano — Red Sox
Bats Right (groundball hitter)

	Avg	G	AB	R	H	2B	3B	HR	RBI	BB	SO	HBP	GDP	SB	CS	OBP	SLG	IBB	SH	SF	#Pit	#P/PA	GB	FB	G/F
1992 Season	.080	19	50	4	4	2	1	0	1	2	12	1	0	0	0	.132	.160	0	1	0	190	3.58	20	14	1.43
Last Five Years	.224	117	294	30	66	18	1	1	20	9	43	2	7	0	1	.249	.303	0	5	4	990	3.20	126	83	1.52

1992 Season

	Avg	AB	H	2B	3B	HR	RBI	BB	SO	OBP	SLG		Avg	AB	H	2B	3B	HR	RBI	BB	SO	OBP	SLG
vs. Left	.100	10	1	1	0	0	0	0	2	.100	.200	Scoring Posn	.083	12	1	0	0	0	0	1	5	.154	.083
vs. Right	.075	40	3	1	1	0	1	2	10	.140	.150	Close & Late	.111	9	1	0	0	0	0	2	1	.273	.111

Roger Mason — Pirates
Pitches Right (flyball pitcher)

	ERA	W	L	Sv	G	GS	IP	BB	SO	Avg	H	2B	3B	HR	RBI	OBP	SLG	GF	IR	IRS	Hld	SvOp	SB	CS	GB	FB	G/F
1992 Season	4.09	5	7	8	65	0	88.0	33	56	.246	80	14	3	11	41	.320	.409	26	44	9	11	10	4	5	101	123	0.82
Last Five Years	4.01	8	9	11	91	0	119.0	41	80	.236	103	17	4	13	51	.306	.383	32	65	10	14	13	4	7	145	149	0.97

1992 Season

	ERA	W	L	Sv	G	GS	IP	H	HR	BB	SO		Avg	AB	H	2B	3B	HR	RBI	BB	SO	OBP	SLG
Home	3.60	2	1	4	28	0	45.0	39	4	12	26	vs. Left	.216	162	35	9	2	2	10	22	26	.306	.333
Away	4.60	3	6	4	37	0	43.0	41	7	21	30	vs. Right	.276	163	45	5	1	9	31	11	30	.333	.485
Day	2.70	3	2	0	18	0	26.2	19	3	13	13	Inning 1-6	.250	72	18	0	0	4	12	4	11	.304	.417
Night	4.70	2	5	8	47	0	61.1	61	8	20	43	Inning 7+	.245	253	62	14	3	7	29	29	45	.324	.407
Grass	3.42	1	1	2	19	0	23.2	20	1	11	11	None on	.272	180	49	11	2	5	5	15	27	.342	.439
Turf	4.34	4	6	6	46	0	64.1	60	10	22	45	Runners on	.214	145	31	3	1	6	36	18	29	.293	.372
April	2.45	1	1	3	8	0	11.0	10	1	9	5	Scoring Posn	.229	83	19	2	1	4	32	16	18	.340	.422

1992 Season

	ERA	W	L	Sv	G	GS	IP	H	HR	BB	SO		Avg	AB	H	2B	3B	HR	RBI	BB	SO	OBP	SLG
May	3.68	0	2	1	14	0	22.0	17	2	7	11	Close & Late	.272	180	49	10	3	7	26	21	34	.346	.478
June	3.68	1	0	2	12	0	14.2	18	1	3	11	None on/out	.244	78	19	3	1	2	2	6	10	.298	.385
July	5.23	0	3	0	9	0	10.1	8	3	6	5	vs. 1st Batr (relief)	.153	59	9	2	1	0	6	4	12	.215	.220
August	5.28	2	0	1	8	0	15.1	15	3	2	9	First Inning Pitched	.213	197	42	9	1	5	18	23	34	.302	.345
September/October	4.30	1	1	1	14	0	14.2	12	1	6	15	First 15 Pitches	.215	191	41	10	1	6	19	20	32	.296	.372
Starter	0.00	0	0	0	0	0	0.0	0	0	0	0	Pitch 16-30	.226	93	21	1	1	3	11	9	18	.294	.355
Reliever	4.09	5	7	8	65	0	88.0	80	11	33	56	Pitch 31-45	.476	21	10	2	1	1	7	4	5	.519	.810
0 Days rest	6.48	1	4	3	14	0	16.2	19	4	6	11	Pitch 46+	.400	20	8	1	0	1	4	0	1	.429	.600
1 or 2 Days rest	3.54	4	1	3	32	0	40.2	35	4	17	25	First Pitch	.314	51	16	2	0	5	16	7	0	.383	.647
3+ Days rest	3.52	0	2	2	19	0	30.2	26	3	10	20	Ahead on Count	.247	154	38	8	2	2	13	0	45	.263	.364
Pre-All Star	3.29	2	4	6	37	0	52.0	48	4	21	30	Behind on Count	.233	60	14	2	0	3	5	15	0	.387	.417
Post-All Star	5.25	3	3	2	28	0	36.0	32	7	12	26	Two Strikes	.182	154	28	6	2	1	10	11	56	.246	.266

Greg Mathews — Phillies   Pitches Left

	ERA	W	L	Sv	G	GS	IP	BB	SO	Avg	H	2B	3B	HR	RBI	OBP	SLG	CG	ShO	Sup	QS	#P/S	SB	CS	GB	FB	G/F
1992 Season	5.16	2	3	0	14	7	52.1	24	27	.270	54	13	0	7	25	.350	.440	0	0	3.61	3	86	3	3	74	63	1.17
Last Five Years	4.84	6	14	0	38	30	171.0	87	76	.263	168	40	7	13	75	.353	.409	1	0	3.63	11	80	26	13	262	178	1.47

1992 Season

	ERA	W	L	Sv	G	GS	IP	H	HR	BB	SO		Avg	AB	H	2B	3B	HR	RBI	BB	SO	OBP	SLG
Home	2.92	0	1	0	7	3	24.2	17	3	10	12	vs. Left	.313	48	15	4	0	2	9	6	9	.400	.521
Away	7.16	2	2	0	7	4	27.2	37	4	14	15	vs. Right	.257	152	39	9	0	5	16	18	18	.333	.414
Starter	5.01	1	3	0	7	7	41.1	43	7	17	16	Scoring Posn	.239	46	11	3	0	2	15	5	10	.321	.435
Reliever	5.73	1	0	0	7	0	11.0	11	0	7	11	Close & Late	.167	12	2	0	0	0	0	3	2	.333	.167
0-3 Days Rest	8.03	1	1	0	2	2	12.1	17	2	3	5	None on/out	.216	51	11	5	0	1	1	4	7	.273	.373
4 Days Rest	4.50	0	4	4	22.0	23	4	11	7	First Pitch	.286	28	8	2	0	2	6	1	0	.300	.571
5+ Days Rest	1.29	0	0	0	1	1	7.0	3	1	3	4	Behind on Count	.333	69	23	7	0	2	8	16	0	.465	.522
Pre-All Star	0.00	0	0	0	0	0	0.0	0	0	0	0	Ahead on Count	.187	75	14	2	0	6	6	0	25	.187	.293
Post-All Star	5.16	2	3	0	14	7	52.1	54	7	24	27	Two Strikes	.197	71	14	2	0	2	6	7	27	.269	.310

Terry Mathews — Rangers   Pitches Right (flyball pitcher)

	ERA	W	L	Sv	G	GS	IP	BB	SO	Avg	H	2B	3B	HR	RBI	OBP	SLG	GF	IR	IRS	Hld	SvOp	SB	CS	GB	FB	G/F
1992 Season	5.95	2	4	0	40	0	42.1	31	26	.294	48	13	0	4	28	.404	.448	11	31	14	6	4	0	4	43	58	0.74
Career (1991-1992)	4.61	6	4	1	74	2	99.2	49	77	.270	102	32	1	9	50	.354	.431	19	52	21	8	7	8	7	107	120	0.89

1992 Season

	ERA	W	L	Sv	G	GS	IP	H	HR	BB	SO		Avg	AB	H	2B	3B	HR	RBI	BB	SO	OBP	SLG
Home	5.59	0	2	0	19	0	19.1	24	3	10	14	vs. Left	.328	61	20	3	0	2	10	9	9	.414	.475
Away	6.26	2	2	0	21	0	23.0	24	1	21	12	vs. Right	.275	102	28	10	0	2	18	22	17	.398	.431
Starter	0.00	0	0	0	0	0	0.0	0	0	0	0	Scoring Posn	.328	58	19	3	0	2	25	9	8	.400	.483
Reliever	5.95	2	4	0	40	0	42.1	48	4	31	26	Close & Late	.393	56	22	5	0	3	11	13	12	.507	.643
0 Days rest	7.27	0	2	0	10	0	8.2	12	2	10	3	None on/out	.314	35	11	4	0	1	1	6	9	.415	.514
1 or 2 Days rest	6.29	2	2	0	19	0	24.1	26	2	16	20	First Pitch	.143	14	2	0	0	0	2	1	0	.188	.143
3+ Days rest	3.86	0	0	0	11	0	9.1	10	0	5	3	Behind on Count	.406	32	13	5	0	3	10	15	0	.596	.844
Pre-All Star	5.85	1	3	0	29	0	32.1	37	4	25	23	Ahead on Count	.271	96	26	5	0	1	11	0	24	.273	.354
Post-All Star	6.30	1	1	0	11	0	10.0	11	0	6	3	Two Strikes	.272	81	22	5	0	0	9	15	26	.388	.333

Don Mattingly — Yankees   Bats Left

	Avg	G	AB	R	H	2B	3B	HR	RBI	BB	SO	HBP	GDP	SB	CS	OBP	SLG	IBB	SH	SF	#Pit	#P/PA	GB	FB	G/F
1992 Season	.288	157	640	89	184	40	0	14	86	39	43	1	11	3	0	.327	.416	7	0	6	2238	3.26	223	245	0.91
Last Five Years	.291	713	2851	366	831	165	2	69	397	205	164	12	73	10	0	.338	.423	63	0	36	10066	3.24	1036	1027	1.01

1992 Season

	Avg	AB	H	2B	3B	HR	RBI	BB	SO	OBP	SLG		Avg	AB	H	2B	3B	HR	RBI	BB	SO	OBP	SLG
vs. Left	.284	204	58	17	0	2	32	10	18	.318	.397	Scoring Posn	.313	160	50	13	0	4	69	16	11	.363	.469
vs. Right	.289	436	126	23	0	12	54	29	25	.330	.424	Close & Late	.263	114	30	6	0	5	19	9	7	.317	.447
Groundball	.253	178	45	11	0	2	21	8	11	.283	.348	None on/out	.261	134	35	9	0	3	3	4	7	.288	.396
Flyball	.311	180	56	15	0	4	17	17	9	.369	.461	Batting #2	.245	237	58	17	0	7	30	20	17	.304	.405
Home	.317	303	96	22	0	6	42	27	14	.371	.449	Batting #3	.312	266	83	14	0	4	37	15	15	.349	.410
Away	.261	337	88	18	0	8	44	12	29	.284	.386	Other	.314	137	43	9	0	3	19	4	11	.324	.445
Day	.299	204	61	12	0	5	29	18	14	.356	.431	April	.232	82	19	4	0	2	9	5	4	.276	.354
Night	.282	436	123	28	0	9	57	21	29	.312	.408	May	.264	110	29	11	0	4	17	11	10	.331	.473
Grass	.300	543	163	35	0	13	73	34	37	.340	.436	June	.310	113	35	7	0	3	15	7	7	.347	.451
Turf	.216	97	21	5	0	1	13	5	6	.250	.299	July	.330	103	34	5	0	1	12	5	5	.355	.408
First Pitch	.394	71	28	4	0	2	17	6	0	.425	.535	August	.280	107	30	7	0	1	13	3	8	.298	.374
Ahead on Count	.341	208	71	15	0	5	30	21	0	.398	.486	September/October	.296	125	37	6	0	3	20	8	9	.338	.416
Behind on Count	.248	230	57	10	0	6	28	0	26	.250	.370	Pre-All Star	.279	348	97	25	0	9	45	24	24	.324	.428
Two Strikes	.181	193	35	11	0	1	11	12	43	.229	.254	Post-All Star	.298	292	87	15	0	5	41	15	19	.330	.401

278

Position	Avg	AB	H	2B	3B	HR	RBI	BB	SO	OBP	SLG	G	GS	Innings	PO	A	E	DP	Fld Pct	Rng Fctr	In Zone	Outs	Zone Rtg	MLB Zone
As Designated Hitter	.297	64	19	4	0	3	11	4	5	.338	.500	15	15	---	---	---	---	---	---	---	---	---	---	---
As 1b	.287	574	165	36	0	11	75	35	38	.326	.408	143	138	1223.2	1212	115	4	133	.997	---	274	237	865	843

Last Five Years

	Avg	AB	H	2B	3B	HR	RBI	BB	SO	OBP	SLG		Avg	AB	H	2B	3B	HR	RBI	BB	SO	OBP	SLG
vs. Left	.291	1014	295	68	1	18	164	62	71	.331	.413	Scoring Posn	.306	735	225	49	0	17	315	102	48	.377	.442
vs. Right	.292	1837	536	97	1	51	233	143	93	.341	.429	Close & Late	.271	443	120	26	0	17	74	49	32	.347	.445
Groundball	.292	763	223	45	0	17	106	63	45	.342	.418	None on/out	.264	561	148	35	1	14	14	21	24	.294	.405
Flyball	.306	671	205	52	1	16	96	54	38	.354	.458	Batting #2	.286	524	150	31	0	12	63	39	28	.336	.414
Home	.304	1365	415	81	0	47	216	109	75	.354	.467	Batting #3	.292	2144	626	122	2	54	312	159	118	.340	.426
Away	.280	1486	416	84	2	22	181	96	89	.323	.384	Other	.301	183	55	12	0	3	22	7	18	.320	.415
Day	.309	878	271	59	0	18	128	87	46	.369	.437	April	.259	382	99	22	0	5	37	45	25	.336	.356
Night	.284	1973	560	106	2	51	269	118	118	.323	.417	May	.306	503	154	35	0	16	86	39	34	.358	.471
Grass	.294	2387	702	135	0	65	342	180	140	.342	.432	June	.294	506	149	22	1	14	67	31	22	.333	.425
Turf	.278	464	129	30	2	4	55	25	24	.317	.377	July	.300	486	146	31	0	9	62	24	22	.332	.420
First Pitch	.348	273	95	20	0	7	56	29	0	.407	.496	August	.284	451	128	30	1	9	69	26	29	.322	.415
Ahead on Count	.321	931	299	56	2	24	141	115	0	.395	.463	September/October	.296	523	155	25	0	16	76	40	32	.343	.436
Behind on Count	.269	1046	281	53	0	25	132	2	98	.270	.391	Pre-All Star	.291	1542	449	88	1	37	209	123	88	.342	.422
Two Strikes	.225	853	192	35	0	15	76	45	164	.264	.319	Post-All Star	.292	1309	382	77	1	32	188	82	76	.332	.426

Batter vs. Pitcher (since 1984)

Hits Best Against	Avg	AB	H	2B	3B	HR	RBI	BB	SO	OBP	SLG	Hits Worst Against	Avg	AB	H	2B	3B	HR	RBI	BB	SO	OBP	SLG
Terry Leach	.636	11	7	0	1	0	2	0	0	.636	.818	Rick Aguilera	.067	15	1	0	0	0	1	1	2	.125	.067
Bill Gullickson	.533	15	8	2	0	1	5	1	0	.563	.867	Joe Hesketh	.071	14	1	0	0	0	3	1	2	.118	.071
Shawn Hillegas	.444	9	4	0	0	2	4	1	0	.455	1.111	Bobby Thigpen	.077	13	1	0	0	0	1	1	0	.143	.077
Steve Farr	.400	15	6	1	0	2	4	2	0	.471	.867	Kevin Tapani	.091	22	2	0	0	0	1	0	1	.130	.091
Edwin Nunez	.353	17	6	0	0	3	6	3	3	.450	.882	Gregg Olson	.091	11	1	0	0	0	0	2	1	.231	.091

Rob Maurer — Rangers — Bats Left

	Avg	G	AB	R	H	2B	3B	HR	RBI	BB	SO	HBP	GDP	SB	CS	OBP	SLG	IBB	SH	SF	#Pit	#P/PA	GB	FB	G/F
1992 Season	.222	8	9	1	2	0	0	0	1	1	2	0	0	0	0	.300	.222	0	0	0	43	4.30	2	4	0.50
Career (1991-1992)	.120	21	25	1	3	1	0	0	3	3	8	1	0	0	0	.241	.160	0	0	0	116	4.00	9	7	1.29

1992 Season

	Avg	AB	H	2B	3B	HR	RBI	BB	SO	OBP	SLG		Avg	AB	H	2B	3B	HR	RBI	BB	SO	OBP	SLG
vs. Left	.000	1	0	0	0	0	0	0	0	.000	.000	Scoring Posn	1.000	1	1	0	0	0	1	0	0	1.000	1.000
vs. Right	.250	8	2	0	0	0	1	1	2	.333	.250	Close & Late	.333	3	1	0	0	0	1	1	1	.500	.333

Derrick May — Cubs — Bats Left

	Avg	G	AB	R	H	2B	3B	HR	RBI	BB	SO	HBP	GDP	SB	CS	OBP	SLG	IBB	SH	SF	#Pit	#P/PA	GB	FB	G/F
1992 Season	.274	124	351	33	96	11	0	8	45	14	40	3	9	5	3	.306	.373	4	2	1	1103	2.99	141	94	1.50
Career (1990-1992)	.267	156	434	45	116	16	0	10	59	18	48	3	11	6	3	.300	.373	4	2	1	1367	2.99	166	121	1.37

1992 Season

	Avg	AB	H	2B	3B	HR	RBI	BB	SO	OBP	SLG		Avg	AB	H	2B	3B	HR	RBI	BB	SO	OBP	SLG
vs. Left	.250	76	19	2	0	2	9	3	13	.288	.355	Scoring Posn	.283	92	26	4	0	4	38	5	12	.330	.457
vs. Right	.280	275	77	9	0	6	36	11	27	.313	.378	Close & Late	.250	64	16	1	0	3	9	3	9	.290	.406
Groundball	.292	137	40	4	0	2	14	7	15	.331	.365	None on/out	.231	78	18	2	0	1	1	4	5	.268	.295
Flyball	.273	77	21	1	0	2	8	2	8	.296	.364	Batting #5	.275	131	36	6	0	3	23	4	16	.301	.389
Home	.292	202	59	8	0	3	28	10	19	.327	.376	Batting #6	.290	183	53	4	0	4	19	7	11	.321	.377
Away	.248	149	37	3	0	5	17	4	21	.277	.369	Other	.189	37	7	1	0	1	3	3	7	.250	.297
Day	.244	201	49	5	0	3	24	12	25	.288	.313	April	.091	11	1	0	0	0	1	2	1	.231	.091
Night	.313	150	47	6	0	5	21	2	15	.331	.453	May	.228	57	13	2	0	2		3	8	.267	.263
Grass	.292	260	76	10	0	4	34	14	26	.332	.377	June	.314	70	22	2	0	3	14	2	7	.333	.471
Turf	.220	91	20	1	0	4	11	0	14	.228	.363	July	.143	28	4	0	0	1	2	2	4	.194	.250
First Pitch	.374	91	34	4	0	5	18	3	0	.394	.582	August	.313	80	25	4	0	1	10	4	10	.368	.400
Ahead on Count	.305	82	25	2	0	1	9	2	0	.318	.366	September/October	.295	105	31	3	0	3	16	1	10	.302	.410
Behind on Count	.230	126	29	2	0	1	9	0	24	.270	.270	Pre-All Star	.243	152	37	4	0	3	18	8	17	.280	.329
Two Strikes	.191	115	22	4	0	2	15	9	40	.250	.278	Post-All Star	.296	199	59	7	0	5	27	6	23	.327	.407

1992 By Position

Position	Avg	AB	H	2B	3B	HR	RBI	BB	SO	OBP	SLG	G	GS	Innings	PO	A	E	DP	Fld Pct	Rng Fctr	In Zone	Outs	Zone Rtg	MLB Zone
As Pinch Hitter	.286	21	6	0	0	1	1	2	7	.348	.429	25	0	---	---	---	---	---	---	---	---	---	---	---
As lf	.269	283	76	9	0	7	37	10	33	.300	.375	98	72	667.2	134	3	5	0	.965	1.85	160	134	.838	.809
As rf	.298	47	14	2	0	0	7	2	0	.327	.340	14	13	112.0	19	0	0	0	1.000	1.53	26	19	.731	.814

Brent Mayne — Royals
Bats Left (groundball hitter)

	Avg	G	AB	R	H	2B	3B	HR	RBI	BB	SO	HBP	GDP	SB	CS	OBP	SLG	IBB	SH	SF	#Pit	#P/PA	GB	FB	G/F
1992 Season	.225	82	213	16	48	10	0	0	18	11	26	0	5	0	4	.260	.272	0	2	3	862	3.80	102	51	2.00
Career (1990-1992)	.239	172	457	40	109	18	0	3	50	37	71	0	11	2	9	.292	.298	4	4	6	1878	3.76	200	103	1.94

1992 Season

	Avg	AB	H	2B	3B	HR	RBI	BB	SO	OBP	SLG		Avg	AB	H	2B	3B	HR	RBI	BB	SO	OBP	SLG
vs. Left	.136	22	3	0	0	0	1	2	3	.208	.136	Scoring Posn	.192	52	10	3	0	0	17	4	7	.237	.250
vs. Right	.236	191	45	10	0	0	17	9	23	.266	.288	Close & Late	.304	46	14	1	0	0	3	4	8	.360	.326
Home	.231	117	27	7	0	0	9	6	12	.264	.291	None on/out	.300	40	12	1	0	0	3	1	.349	.325
Away	.219	96	21	3	0	0	9	5	14	.255	.250	Batting #6	.206	68	14	5	0	0	10	7	8	.276	.279
First Pitch	.333	24	8	2	0	0	5	0	0	.308	.417	Batting #7	.238	84	20	4	0	0	5	2	12	.256	.286
Ahead on Count	.275	51	14	5	0	0	5	5	0	.333	.373	Other	.230	61	14	1	0	0	3	2	6	.246	.246
Behind on Count	.145	76	11	2	0	0	3	0	16	.145	.171	Pre-All Star	.247	89	22	4	0	0	5	4	8	.274	.292
Two Strikes	.151	93	14	1	0	0	6	6	26	.202	.151	Post-All Star	.210	124	26	6	0	0	13	7	18	.250	.258

Matt Maysey — Expos
Pitches Right (flyball pitcher)

	ERA	W	L	Sv	G	GS	IP	BB	SO	Avg	H	2B	3B	HR	RBI	OBP	SLG	GF	IR	IRS	Hld	SvOp	SB	CS	GB	FB	G/F
1992 Season	3.86	0	0	0	2	0	2.1	0	1	.364	4	0	0	1	2	.417	.636	1	2	1	0	0	0	1	2	4	0.50

1992 Season

	ERA	W	L	Sv	G	GS	IP	H	HR	BB	SO		Avg	AB	H	2B	3B	HR	RBI	BB	SO	OBP	SLG
Home	0.00	0	0	0	0	0	0.0	0	0	0	0	vs. Left	.429	7	3	0	0	0	1	0	0	.429	.429
Away	3.86	0	0	0	2	0	2.1	4	1	0	1	vs. Right	.250	4	1	0	0	1	1	0	1	.400	1.000

Kirk McCaskill — White Sox
Pitches Right

	ERA	W	L	Sv	G	GS	IP	BB	SO	Avg	H	2B	3B	HR	RBI	OBP	SLG	CG	ShO	Sup	QS	#P/S	SB	CS	GB	FB	G/F
1992 Season	4.18	12	13	0	34	34	209.0	95	109	.242	193	31	8	11	99	.325	.343	0	0	4.74	15	153	12	9	319	211	1.51
Last Five Years	3.75	57	59	0	148	148	919.1	353	463	.258	904	139	27	64	381	.327	.368	13	7	4.22	79	98	33	38	1400	973	1.44

1992 Season

	ERA	W	L	Sv	G	GS	IP	H	HR	BB	SO		Avg	AB	H	2B	3B	HR	RBI	BB	SO	OBP	SLG
Home	3.54	6	7	0	17	17	109.1	99	7	48	61	vs. Left	.280	379	106	16	4	6	50	47	43	.358	.391
Away	4.88	6	6	0	17	17	99.2	94	4	47	48	vs. Right	.209	417	87	15	4	5	49	48	66	.295	.300
Day	2.92	3	2	0	8	8	52.1	42	2	17	24	Inning 1-6	.241	719	173	26	7	10	93	85	99	.322	.338
Night	4.60	9	11	0	26	26	156.2	151	9	78	85	Inning 7+	.260	77	20	5	1	1	6	10	10	.356	.390
Grass	4.32	11	10	0	28	28	173.0	161	11	79	89	None on	.213	445	95	14	2	4	55	61	.306	.281
Turf	3.50	1	3	0	6	6	36.0	32	0	16	20	Runners on	.279	351	98	17	6	7	95	40	48	.350	.422
April	6.85	1	3	0	4	4	22.1	25	3	16	10	Scoring Posn	.298	171	51	10	5	3	83	26	27	.383	.468
May	2.30	2	1	0	6	6	43.0	33	1	12	18	Close & Late	.255	51	13	5	1	1	6	6	6	.350	.451
June	3.21	2	2	0	5	5	33.2	25	2	12	20	None on/out	.200	195	39	7	1	0	0	24	26	.294	.246
July	7.63	1	2	0	6	6	30.2	36	3	20	10	vs. 1st Batr (relief)	.000	0	0	0	0	0	0	0	0	.000	.000
August	2.39	3	2	0	6	6	37.2	29	1	13	27	First Inning Pitched	.252	123	31	5	0	1	11	20	14	.349	.317
September/October	4.54	3	3	0	7	7	41.2	45	1	22	24	First 75 Pitches	.216	560	121	18	4	4	44	67	77	.301	.284
Starter	4.18	12	13	0	34	34	209.0	193	11	95	109	Pitch 76-90	.376	117	44	8	1	4	33	14	14	.440	.564
Reliever	0.00	0	0	0	0	0	0.0	0	0	0	0	Pitch 91-105	.181	83	15	0	2	3	16	6	15	.233	.337
0-3 Days Rest	0.00	0	0	0	0	0	0.0	0	0	0	0	Pitch 106+	.361	36	13	5	1	0	6	8	3	.500	.556
4 Days Rest	4.11	7	7	0	22	22	135.2	127	5	59	71	First Pitch	.273	99	27	5	1	2	22	3	0	.295	.404
5+ Days Rest	4.30	5	6	0	12	12	73.1	66	6	36	38	Ahead on Count	.213	347	74	14	4	4	32	0	88	.222	.311
Pre-All Star	4.15	6	7	0	18	18	115.0	102	8	52	57	Behind on Count	.274	190	52	9	3	1	30	47	0	.418	.368
Post-All Star	4.21	6	6	0	16	16	94.0	91	3	43	52	Two Strikes	.198	364	72	11	3	6	29	45	109	.294	.294

Last Five Years

	ERA	W	L	Sv	G	GS	IP	H	HR	BB	SO		Avg	AB	H	2B	3B	HR	RBI	BB	SO	OBP	SLG
Home	3.48	32	29	0	75	75	478.2	454	38	163	259	vs. Left	.272	1751	477	64	17	36	195	160	190	.333	.390
Away	4.04	25	30	0	73	73	440.2	450	26	190	204	vs. Right	.244	1747	427	75	10	28	186	193	273	.321	.347
Day	3.02	15	7	0	32	32	202.2	184	8	68	123	Inning 1-6	.260	3062	796	119	25	57	339	313	410	.329	.371
Night	3.96	42	52	0	116	116	716.2	720	56	285	340	Inning 7+	.248	436	108	20	2	7	42	40	53	.311	.351
Grass	3.61	49	50	0	126	126	786.1	759	55	301	399	None on	.248	1995	495	80	13	37	37	208	267	.322	.357
Turf	4.60	8	9	0	22	22	133.0	145	9	52	64	Runners on	.272	1503	409	59	14	27	344	145	196	.333	.384
April	3.03	10	9	0	21	21	136.2	116	10	65	62	Scoring Posn	.270	789	213	35	11	14	307	98	118	.344	.395
May	3.15	9	7	0	27	27	168.1	175	10	54	88	Close & Late	.238	261	62	11	2	5	27	25	32	.308	.352
June	3.86	11	12	0	26	26	158.2	155	16	60	99	None on/out	.242	885	214	35	5	14	14	92	111	.317	.340
July	4.41	9	11	0	28	28	171.1	169	9	73	68	vs. 1st Batr (relief)	.000	0	0	0	0	0	0	0	0	.000	.000
August	3.95	12	11	0	26	26	157.1	164	9	53	73	First Inning Pitched	.262	554	145	22	3	8	59	58	69	.330	.356
September/October	4.04	6	9	0	20	20	127.0	125	10	48	73	First 75 Pitches	.254	2580	656	96	19	40	243	248	337	.320	.353
Starter	3.75	57	59	0	148	148	919.1	904	64	353	463	Pitch 76-90	.299	448	134	20	4	17	80	50	56	.368	.475
Reliever	0.00	0	0	0	0	0	0.0	0	0	0	0	Pitch 91-105	.220	318	70	11	2	6	40	33	49	.292	.342
0-3 Days Rest	7.46	1	2	0	5	5	25.1	35	2	12	8	Pitch 106+	.289	152	44	12	2	1	18	22	21	.386	.414
4 Days Rest	3.97	31	30	0	81	81	506.0	486	34	185	265	First Pitch	.285	516	147	22	6	10	70	6	0	.295	.409
5+ Days Rest	3.22	25	27	0	62	62	388.0	383	28	156	192	Ahead on Count	.205	1423	292	42	6	17	126	1	365	.210	.279
Pre-All Star	3.52	34	32	0	83	83	519.0	510	41	203	269	Behind on Count	.309	857	265	46	7	22	104	185	0	.430	.456
Post-All Star	4.05	23	27	0	65	65	400.1	394	23	150	194	Two Strikes	.205	1476	302	43	8	20	134	162	463	.286	.265

Pitcher vs. Batter (career)

Pitches Best Vs.	Avg	AB	H	2B	3B	HR	RBI	BB	SO	OBP	SLG	Pitches Worst Vs.	Avg	AB	H	2B	3B	HR	RBI	BB	SO	OBP	SLG
Mike Stanley	.000	11	0	0	0	0	0	1	5	.083	.000	Glenn Braggs	.556	9	5	1	0	0	1	2	1	.636	.667
Tony Pena	.053	19	1	0	0	0	1	1	4	.100	.053	Junior Felix	.556	9	5	0	0	1	2	2	0	.636	.889
John Olerud	.056	18	1	0	0	0	2	1	3	.100	.056	Kirk Gibson	.526	19	10	2	0	4	6	7	4	.654	1.263
Jerry Browne	.083	24	2	0	0	0	3	3	4	.185	.083	Mike Devereaux	.409	22	9	3	0	2	4	2	1	.458	.818
Robin Ventura	.091	11	1	0	0	0	0	1	2	.167	.091	Lance Parrish	.400	15	6	1	0	3	4	0	4	.400	1.067

Lloyd McClendon — Pirates
Bats Right (flyball hitter)

	Avg	G	AB	R	H	2B	3B	HR	RBI	BB	SO	HBP	GDP	SB	CS	OBP	SLG	IBB	SH	SF	#Pit	#P/PA	GB	FB	G/F
1992 Season	.253	84	190	26	48	8	1	3	20	28	24	2	5	1	3	.350	.353	0	1	3	843	3.78	60	73	0.82
Last Five Years	.253	386	859	112	217	34	2	27	110	112	122	7	18	14	8	.339	.391	6	3	13	3769	3.80	293	319	0.92

1992 Season

	Avg	AB	H	2B	3B	HR	RBI	BB	SO	OBP	SLG		Avg	AB	H	2B	3B	HR	RBI	BB	SO	OBP	SLG
vs. Left	.259	166	43	8	1	2	17	24	18	.351	.355	Scoring Posn	.259	58	15	0	0	1	17	10	8	.352	.310
vs. Right	.208	24	5	0	0	1	3	4	6	.345	.333	Close & Late	.195	41	8	0	0	0	3	0	6	.205	.195
Home	.236	89	21	3	1	3	16	16	11	.355	.393	None on/out	.279	43	12	2	0	2	2	6	10	.380	.465
Away	.267	101	27	5	0	0	4	12	13	.345	.317	Batting #4	.239	134	32	5	1	2	10	21	17	.340	.336
First Pitch	.333	27	9	0	0	1	4	0	0	.333	.444	Batting #6	.214	28	6	2	0	1	4	3	2	.313	.393
Ahead on Count	.328	58	19	7	1	0	7	12	0	.431	.483	Other	.357	28	10	1	0	0	6	4	5	.429	.393
Behind on Count	.236	55	13	2	0	2	5	0	13	.246	.382	Pre-All Star	.284	102	29	5	0	1	12	17	14	.380	.363
Two Strikes	.213	75	16	1	0	1	7	16	24	.355	.267	Post-All Star	.216	88	19	3	1	2	8	11	10	.314	.341

Last Five Years

	Avg	AB	H	2B	3B	HR	RBI	BB	SO	OBP	SLG		Avg	AB	H	2B	3B	HR	RBI	BB	SO	OBP	SLG
vs. Left	.275	560	154	25	1	17	74	74	73	.358	.414	Scoring Posn	.229	245	56	7	0	6	81	37	35	.320	.331
vs. Right	.211	299	63	9	1	10	36	38	49	.303	.348	Close & Late	.207	184	38	1	0	1	14	18	35	.282	.228
Groundball	.259	282	73	8	0	8	37	42	40	.356	.372	None on/out	.253	194	49	9	0	9	9	23	36	.335	.438
Flyball	.196	189	37	11	0	7	26	21	27	.274	.365	Batting #5	.235	268	63	12	0	6	30	33	38	.316	.347
Home	.245	412	101	16	1	14	58	50	62	.329	.391	Batting #6	.298	191	57	8	1	10	31	24	23	.379	.508
Away	.260	447	116	18	1	13	52	62	60	.348	.391	Other	.243	400	97	14	1	11	49	55	61	.335	.365
Day	.273	352	96	16	0	16	52	43	55	.353	.455	April	.286	77	22	5	0	3	15	10	13	.367	.468
Night	.239	507	121	18	2	11	58	69	67	.329	.347	May	.240	171	41	4	0	5	21	26	26	.347	.351
Grass	.274	424	116	18	1	18	63	50	58	.347	.448	June	.270	211	57	7	0	5	26	23	28	.336	.374
Turf	.232	435	101	16	1	9	47	62	64	.331	.336	July	.229	118	27	4	1	7	17	20	17	.345	.458
First Pitch	.339	115	39	6	0	5	18	3	0	.350	.522	August	.248	133	33	8	1	4	15	14	21	.322	.414
Ahead on Count	.312	234	73	16	2	8	35	64	0	.452	.500	September/October	.248	149	37	6	0	3	16	17	17	.329	.349
Behind on Count	.214	257	55	7	0	6	20	0	65	.218	.311	Pre-All Star	.250	496	124	16	0	16	65	65	74	.335	.379
Two Strikes	.197	366	72	8	0	10	39	43	122	.262	.301	Post-All Star	.256	363	93	18	2	11	45	47	48	.345	.408

Batter vs. Pitcher (career)

Hits Best Against	Avg	AB	H	2B	3B	HR	RBI	BB	SO	OBP	SLG	Hits Worst Against	Avg	AB	H	2B	3B	HR	RBI	BB	SO	OBP	SLG
Dennis Rasmussen	.478	23	11	3	0	2	5	3	1	.538	.870	Trevor Wilson	.000	10	0	0	0	0	0	4	1	.286	.000
Bud Black	.462	13	6	1	0	0	0	6	2	.632	.538	John Smiley	.167	18	3	0	0	0	0	1	4	.211	.167
Danny Jackson	.462	13	6	2	0	0	2	5	0	.579	.615	Tom Browning	.167	12	2	0	0	0	3	1	1	.231	.417
Craig Lefferts	.429	14	6	0	0	1	3	3	2	.529	.643	Bruce Hurst	.222	9	2	0	0	0	3	1	0	.273	.222
Tom Glavine	.407	27	11	0	0	2	7	6	4	.515	.630	John Franco	.222	9	2	0	0	0	1	2	2	.364	.222

Bob McClure — Cardinals
Pitches Left (flyball pitcher)

	ERA	W	L	Sv	G	GS	IP	BB	SO	Avg	H	2B	3B	HR	RBI	OBP	SLG	GF	IR	IRS	Hld	SvOp	SB	CS	GB	FB	G/F
1992 Season	3.17	2	2	0	71	0	54.0	25	24	.261	52	13	0	6	29	.345	.417	16	67	15	14	0	1	2	58	83	0.70
Last Five Years	3.53	13	7	6	208	0	176.0	64	105	.260	170	34	3	16	90	.327	.395	28	226	50	35	11	9	4	201	237	0.85

1992 Season

	ERA	W	L	Sv	G	GS	IP	H	HR	BB	SO		Avg	AB	H	2B	3B	HR	RBI	BB	SO	OBP	SLG
Home	2.22	1	0	0	34	0	28.1	27	1	16	12	vs. Left	.198	91	18	7	0	4	13	10	18	.272	.407
Away	4.21	1	2	0	37	0	25.2	25	5	9	12	vs. Right	.315	108	34	6	0	2	16	15	6	.405	.426
Day	2.87	0	1	0	23	0	15.2	14	2	5	7	Inning 1-6	.300	20	6	1	0	0	2	3	1	.391	.350
Night	3.29	2	1	0	48	0	38.1	38	4	20	17	Inning 7+	.257	179	46	12	0	6	27	22	23	.340	.425
Grass	5.06	0	1	0	17	0	10.2	9	3	3	4	None on	.294	102	30	8	0	4	4	5	12	.327	.490
Turf	2.70	2	1	0	54	0	43.1	43	3	22	20	Runners on	.227	97	22	5	0	2	25	20	12	.361	.340
April	5.63	0	0	0	11	0	8.0	9	1	7	6	Scoring Posn	.217	69	15	5	0	1	23	12	10	.337	.333
May	2.16	1	0	0	9	0	8.1	8	0	6	5	Close & Late	.247	73	18	6	0	1	10	8	10	.313	.370
June	3.12	0	2	0	12	0	8.2	8	1	6	3	None on/out	.222	45	10	1	0	3	3	5	3	.300	.444
July	1.54	0	0	0	15	0	11.2	10	0	3	4	vs. 1st Batr (relief)	.180	61	11	2	0	4	9	8	7	.271	.410
August	2.35	1	0	0	11	0	7.2	9	2	6	3	First Inning Pitched	.250	164	41	13	0	4	26	20	19	.332	.402
September/October	4.66	0	0	0	13	0	9.2	8	2	4	2	First 15 Pitches	.261	157	41	13	0	4	25	18	17	.337	.420
Starter	0.00	0	0	0	0	0	0.0	0	0	0	0	Pitch 16-30	.241	29	7	0	0	2	3	5	4	.353	.448
Reliever	3.17	2	2	0	71	0	54.0	52	6	25	24	Pitch 31-45	.444	9	4	0	0	0	1	2	3	.500	.444
0 Days rest	2.11	0	1	0	24	0	21.1	15	2	7	11	Pitch 46+	.000	4	0	0	0	0	0	0	0	.200	.000
1 or 2 Days rest	4.26	1	0	0	32	0	25.1	34	3	12	6	First Pitch	.375	24	9	1	0	1	7	5	0	.500	.542
3+ Days rest	2.45	1	1	0	15	0	7.1	3	1	6	7	Ahead on Count	.250	96	24	5	0	3	11	0	17	.253	.396

1992 Season

	ERA	W	L	Sv	G	GS	IP	H	HR	BB	SO		Avg	AB	H	2B	3B	HR	RBI	BB	SO	OBP	SLG
Pre-All Star	3.41	1	2	0	38	0	29.0	29	2	14	14	Behind on Count	.262	42	11	5	0	1	7	7	0	.367	.452
Post-All Star	2.88	1	0	0	33	0	25.0	23	4	11	10	Two Strikes	.226	93	21	6	0	2	6	13	24	.315	.355

Last Five Years

	ERA	W	L	Sv	G	GS	IP	H	HR	BB	SO		Avg	AB	H	2B	3B	HR	RBI	BB	SO	OBP	SLG
Home	3.36	8	3	2	104	0	88.1	92	5	36	46	vs. Left	.210	261	59	11	2	6	39	32	56	.286	.327
Away	3.70	5	4	4	104	0	87.2	78	11	28	59	vs. Right	.298	372	111	23	1	10	51	32	49	.359	.446
Day	2.60	4	2	2	68	0	55.1	56	5	16	35	Inning 1-6	.316	57	18	5	1	1	9	7	6	.373	.491
Night	3.95	9	5	4	140	0	120.2	114	11	48	70	Inning 7+	.255	596	152	29	2	15	81	57	99	.322	.386
Grass	3.87	7	2	4	99	0	83.2	81	10	29	53	None on	.282	330	93	22	1	9	9	17	45	.319	.436
Turf	3.22	6	5	2	109	0	92.1	81	6	35	52	Runners on	.238	323	77	12	2	7	81	47	60	.334	.353
April	3.38	1	1	0	23	0	18.2	18	2	5	11	Scoring Posn	.230	209	48	10	1	3	71	34	32	.331	.330
May	6.04	3	1	1	27	0	25.1	28	5	13	14	Close & Late	.238	223	53	9	2	2	27	27	37	.315	.323
June	3.66	0	3	4	37	0	32.0	32	2	11	18	None on/out	.253	146	37	8	1	4	4	10	14	.301	.404
July	3.09	1	1	0	33	0	23.1	24	1	7	13	vs. 1st Batr (relief)	.206	160	33	4	1	5	23	20	20	.294	.338
August	1.83	4	0	0	45	0	39.1	32	4	9	24	First Inning Pitched	.258	458	118	25	2	10	72	49	69	.329	.386
September/October	3.86	4	1	1	43	0	37.1	36	2	19	25	First 15 Pitches	.267	490	131	30	3	11	71	48	69	.333	.408
Starter	0.00	0	0	0	0	0	0.0	0	0	0	0	Pitch 16-30	.213	122	26	3	0	5	16	12	29	.286	.361
Reliever	3.53	13	7	6	208	0	176.0	170	16	64	105	Pitch 31-45	.387	31	12	1	0	0	3	3	6	.429	.419
0 Days rest	3.57	1	3	0	48	0	40.1	36	3	15	18	Pitch 46+	.100	10	1	0	0	0	0	1	1	.250	.100
1 or 2 Days rest	3.63	4	1	3	78	0	62.0	72	5	22	29	First Pitch	.330	91	30	4	1	2	17	8	0	.392	.462
3+ Days rest	3.42	8	3	3	82	0	73.2	62	8	27	58	Ahead on Count	.228	294	67	15	2	4	29	0	81	.231	.333
Pre-All Star	4.71	4	5	5	97	0	80.1	86	9	31	44	Behind on Count	.293	140	41	7	0	6	24	27	0	.404	.471
Post-All Star	2.54	9	2	1	111	0	95.2	84	7	33	61	Two Strikes	.201	298	60	16	2	3	24	29	105	.269	.299

Pitcher vs. Batter (since 1984)

Pitches Best Vs.	Avg	AB	H	2B	3B	HR	RBI	BB	SO	OBP	SLG	Pitches Worst Vs.	Avg	AB	H	2B	3B	HR	RBI	BB	SO	OBP	SLG
John Kruk	.100	10	1	1	0	0	0	1	2	.182	.200	Don Mattingly	.467	15	7	1	0	0	2	2	2	.529	.533
Eddie Murray	.143	14	2	0	0	0	0	1	1	.200	.200	George Brett	.455	11	5	1	0	0	2	0	0	.455	.545
Brett Butler	.154	13	2	0	0	0	1	1	5	.200	.154	Tim Teufel	.444	9	4	0	0	1	4	4	2	.615	.778
Ozzie Guillen	.167	12	2	0	0	0	2	0	0	.167	.167	Darryl Strawberry	.381	21	8	1	2	2	6	2	6	.417	.905
Andy Van Slyke	.182	22	4	1	1	0	3	0	3	.174	.318	Vince Coleman	.364	11	4	2	1	0	4	0	0	.364	.727

Rodney McCray — Mets   **Bats Both (groundball hitter)**

	Avg	G	AB	R	H	2B	3B	HR	RBI	BB	SO	HBP	GDP	SB	CS	OBP	SLG	IBB	SH	SF	#Pit	#P/PA	GB	FB	G/F
1992 Season	1.000	18	1	3	1	0	0	0	1	0	0	0	0	2	0	1.000	1.000	0	0	0	3	3.00	0	0	0.00
Career (1990-1992)	.214	67	14	13	3	0	0	0	1	1	6	0	0	9	1	.267	.214	0	0	0	59	3.93	5	2	2.50

1992 Season

	Avg	AB	H	2B	3B	HR	RBI	BB	SO	OBP	SLG		Avg	AB	H	2B	3B	HR	RBI	BB	SO	OBP	SLG
vs. Left	.000	0	0	0	0	0	0	0	0	.000	.000	Scoring Posn	1.000	1	1	0	0	0	1	0	0	1.000	1.000
vs. Right	1.000	1	1	0	0	0	1	0	0	1.000	1.000	Close & Late	1.000	1	1	0	0	0	1	0	0	1.000	1.000

Lance McCullers — Rangers   **Pitches Right (flyball pitcher)**

	ERA	W	L	Sv	G	GS	IP	BB	SO	Avg	H	2B	3B	HR	RBI	OBP	SLG	GF	IR	IRS	Hld	SvOp	SB	CS	GB	FB	G/F
1992 Season	5.40	1	0	0	5	0	5.0	8	3	.067	1	0	0	0	2	.391	.067	1	6	3	0	0	1	0	5	7	0.71
Last Five Years	3.41	10	9	13	137	1	232.0	119	197	.220	186	41	6	21	117	.315	.357	15	178	63	15	22	20	6	228	298	0.77

1992 Season

	ERA	W	L	Sv	G	GS	IP	H	HR	BB	SO		Avg	AB	H	2B	3B	HR	RBI	BB	SO	OBP	SLG
Home	10.13	0	0	0	3	0	2.2	1	0	7	2	vs. Left	.125	8	1	0	0	0	0	2	0	.300	.125
Away	0.00	1	0	0	2	0	2.1	0	0	1	1	vs. Right	.000	7	0	0	0	0	0	2	3	.462	.000

Last Five Years

	ERA	W	L	Sv	G	GS	IP	H	HR	BB	SO		Avg	AB	H	2B	3B	HR	RBI	BB	SO	OBP	SLG
Home	3.24	5	3	9	73	2	141.2	101	13	68	128	vs. Left	.198	384	76	18	0	4	32	65	77	.313	.276
Away	3.69	5	6	4	64	0	90.1	85	8	51	69	vs. Right	.238	462	110	23	6	17	85	54	120	.316	.424
Day	4.28	4	5	7	50	2	94.2	84	9	50	94	Inning 1-6	.267	161	43	8	0	6	39	25	31	.367	.429
Night	2.82	6	4	6	87	0	137.1	102	12	69	103	Inning 7+	.209	685	143	33	6	15	78	94	166	.302	.340
Grass	3.27	8	7	13	111	2	195.2	149	15	98	168	None on	.204	457	93	26	5	6	6	57	102	.293	.322
Turf	4.21	2	2	0	26	0	36.1	37	6	21	29	Runners on	.239	389	93	15	1	15	111	62	95	.338	.398
April	3.18	0	2	3	21	0	28.1	22	4	12	31	Scoring Posn	.236	246	58	4	0	11	101	49	59	.354	.386
May	3.40	3	2	1	33	0	45.0	41	5	28	36	Close & Late	.220	227	50	10	2	5	28	38	63	.332	.348
June	4.55	3	2	3	27	0	55.1	50	4	31	39	None on/out	.216	194	42	8	3	2	2	22	37	.300	.320
July	3.38	1	3	2	18	2	37.1	20	4	19	31	vs. 1st Batr (relief)	.228	114	26	5	0	4	23	16	23	.321	.377
August	1.75	3	0	2	18	0	36.0	26	2	17	36	First Inning Pitched	.241	439	106	21	3	10	76	63	105	.334	.371
September/October	3.60	0	0	2	18	0	30.0	27	2	12	24	First 15 Pitches	.258	388	100	24	3	10	66	53	83	.344	.412
Starter	8.59	0	1	0	2	2	7.1	9	1	8	7	Pitch 16-30	.190	263	50	7	3	6	32	39	75	.294	.308
Reliever	3.24	10	8	13	135	0	224.2	177	20	111	190	Pitch 31-45	.197	127	25	7	0	3	12	20	25	.307	.299
0 Days rest	5.00	0	2	1	15	0	18.0	24	2	15	18	Pitch 46+	.162	68	11	3	0	3	7	7	14	.240	.338
1 or 2 Days rest	2.78	5	4	7	72	0	120.0	89	9	63	106	First Pitch	.319	116	37	7	1	6	26	16	3	.397	.552
3+ Days rest	3.53	5	2	5	48	0	86.2	64	9	33	66	Ahead on Count	.155	407	63	11	2	5	35	0	172	.157	.229

Last Five Years

	ERA	W	L	Sv	G	GS	IP	H	HR	BB	SO		Avg	AB	H	2B	3B	HR	RBI	BB	SO	OBP	SLG
Pre-All Star	3.86	7	8	7	88	2	149.1	125	15	84	123	Behind on Count	.259	189	49	16	2	8	38	55	0	.421	.492
Post-All Star	2.61	3	1	6	49	0	82.2	61	6	35	74	Two Strikes	.133	405	54	8	2	6	33	48	193	.227	.207

Pitcher vs. Batter (career)

Pitches Best Vs.	Avg	AB	H	2B	3B	HR	RBI	BB	SO	OBP	SLG	Pitches Worst Vs.	Avg	AB	H	2B	3B	HR	RBI	BB	SO	OBP	SLG
Eric Davis	.000	9	0	0	0	0	0	2	4	.182	.000	Candy Maldonado	.429	14	6	3	0	1	7	3	0	.500	.857
Glenn Davis	.050	20	1	0	0	0	1	2	6	.136	.050	Jose Uribe	.400	10	4	0	0	1	1	2	2	.500	.700
Gerald Perry	.083	12	1	0	0	0	1	2	2	.214	.083	Hubie Brooks	.364	11	4	0	0	2	2	1	1	.417	.909
Mitch Webster	.091	11	1	0	0	0	1	2	0	.214	.091	Dale Murphy	.333	21	7	1	0	2	2	3	7	.417	.667
Dion James	.100	10	1	0	0	0	0	2	3	.250	.100	Gary Carter	.308	13	4	0	0	2	4	0	5	.308	.769

Ben McDonald — Orioles

Pitches Right

	ERA	W	L	Sv	G	GS	IP	BB	SO	Avg	H	2B	3B	HR	RBI	OBP	SLG	CG	ShO	Sup	QS	#P/S	SB	CS	GB	FB	G/F
1992 Season	4.24	13	13	0	35	35	227.0	74	158	.247	213	44	5	32	100	.311	.421	4	2	4.64	19	103	20	8	289	270	1.07
Career (1989-1992)	4.02	28	26	0	83	71	479.1	156	311	.241	435	81	8	59	201	.303	.393	8	4	4.49	38	102	45	13	618	566	1.09

1992 Season

	ERA	W	L	Sv	G	GS	IP	H	HR	BB	SO		Avg	AB	H	2B	3B	HR	RBI	BB	SO	OBP	SLG
Home	4.90	5	8	0	18	18	117.2	113	21	39	73	vs. Left	.235	405	95	20	2	14	41	44	74	.311	.398
Away	3.54	8	5	0	17	17	109.1	100	11	35	85	vs. Right	.258	458	118	24	3	18	59	30	84	.311	.441
Day	4.79	3	5	0	11	11	67.2	66	7	32	53	Inning 1-6	.231	723	167	33	5	24	78	65	136	.299	.390
Night	4.01	10	8	0	24	24	159.1	147	25	42	105	Inning 7+	.329	140	46	11	0	8	22	9	22	.375	.579
Grass	4.02	12	11	0	32	32	210.1	186	27	72	141	None on	.232	552	128	28	2	21	21	43	98	.296	.404
Turf	7.02	1	2	0	3	3	16.2	27	5	2	17	Runners on	.273	311	85	16	3	11	79	31	60	.337	.450
April	3.47	2	0	0	4	4	23.1	18	3	12	19	Scoring Posn	.285	179	51	9	2	7	66	20	35	.350	.475
May	4.32	4	2	0	6	6	41.2	37	8	8	31	Close & Late	.276	58	16	5	0	3	10	5	9	.338	.517
June	6.08	1	3	0	6	6	37.0	38	8	9	26	None on/out	.236	242	57	15	1	11	11	12	44	.280	.442
July	3.98	3	2	0	6	6	43.0	39	6	14	29	vs. 1st Batr (relief)	.000	0	0	0	0	0	0	0	0	.000	.000
August	4.58	2	3	0	6	6	37.1	45	5	13	21	First Inning Pitched	.148	122	18	2	0	5	8	14	21	.241	.287
September/October	3.02	1	3	0	7	7	44.2	36	2	18	32	First 75 Pitches	.234	594	139	27	5	21	60	50	116	.300	.402
Starter	4.24	13	13	0	35	35	227.0	213	32	74	158	Pitch 76-90	.242	120	29	4	0	4	12	9	19	.290	.375
Reliever	0.00	0	0	0	0	0	0.0	0	0	0	0	Pitch 91-105	.337	89	30	10	0	4	20	7	9	.388	.584
0-3 Days Rest	0.00	0	0	0	0	0	0.0	0	0	0	0	Pitch 106+	.250	60	15	3	0	3	8	8	14	.343	.450
4 Days Rest	5.03	9	10	0	27	27	168.1	173	30	57	117	First Pitch	.331	124	41	12	1	5	22	5	0	.364	.565
5+ Days Rest	1.99	4	3	0	8	8	58.2	40	2	17	41	Ahead on Count	.180	328	59	11	3	4	16	0	130	.192	.268
Pre-All Star	5.00	8	6	0	19	19	120.2	115	23	37	84	Behind on Count	.331	248	82	14	1	20	43	27	0	.392	.637
Post-All Star	3.39	5	7	0	16	16	106.1	98	9	37	74	Two Strikes	.153	365	56	14	3	5	23	42	158	.245	.249

Career (1989-1992)

	ERA	W	L	Sv	G	GS	IP	H	HR	BB	SO		Avg	AB	H	2B	3B	HR	RBI	BB	SO	OBP	SLG
Home	4.01	11	15	0	44	37	269.1	253	35	72	168	vs. Left	.216	890	192	34	3	24	81	90	163	.287	.342
Away	4.03	17	11	0	39	34	210.0	182	24	84	143	vs. Right	.266	913	243	47	5	35	120	66	148	.319	.444
Day	5.15	5	7	0	22	18	110.0	110	13	48	79	Inning 1-6	.239	1478	353	64	8	43	163	135	265	.303	.380
Night	3.68	23	19	0	61	53	369.1	325	46	108	232	Inning 7+	.252	325	82	17	0	16	38	21	46	.301	.452
Grass	3.91	23	24	0	74	63	430.0	382	50	142	273	None on	.224	1142	256	48	4	36	36	91	202	.285	.368
Turf	4.93	5	2	0	9	8	49.1	53	9	14	38	Runners on	.271	661	179	33	4	23	165	65	109	.332	.437
April	5.58	2	1	0	6	6	30.2	33	4	16	23	Scoring Posn	.263	358	94	18	3	12	135	44	68	.333	.430
May	4.75	6	4	0	11	11	66.1	55	11	20	46	Close & Late	.223	166	37	9	0	9	24	13	25	.282	.440
June	6.08	1	3	0	6	6	37.0	38	8	9	26	None on/out	.217	488	106	25	1	16	16	33	87	.271	.379
July	3.47	8	4	0	21	15	114.0	103	14	30	79	vs. 1st Batr (relief)	.182	11	2	1	0	0	0	1	1	.250	.273
August	4.18	5	9	0	17	17	112.0	116	12	40	60	First Inning Pitched	.205	293	60	9	2	9	31	30	49	.260	.341
September/October	2.94	6	5	0	22	16	119.1	90	10	41	77	First 75 Pitches	.239	1262	301	54	8	37	132	112	232	.302	.382
Starter	4.01	27	26	0	71	71	462.1	419	57	151	303	Pitch 76-90	.238	239	57	8	0	5	23	14	34	.277	.335
Reliever	4.24	1	0	0	12	0	17.0	16	2	5	8	Pitch 91-105	.254	177	45	14	0	9	29	18	19	.325	.486
0-3 Days Rest	4.98	2	2	0	4	4	21.2	19	2	8	12	Pitch 106+	.256	125	32	5	0	8	17	12	26	.324	.488
4 Days Rest	4.39	15	19	0	48	48	309.1	294	45	107	199	First Pitch	.310	258	80	16	1	11	44	6	0	.330	.508
5+ Days Rest	2.95	10	5	0	19	19	131.1	106	10	36	92	Ahead on Count	.188	723	136	23	5	14	45	0	258	.193	.292
Pre-All Star	5.16	11	9	0	30	28	169.1	157	29	58	115	Behind on Count	.303	482	146	27	2	27	75	77	1	.394	.535
Post-All Star	3.40	17	17	0	53	43	310.0	278	30	98	196	Two Strikes	.171	774	132	27	4	15	51	73	310	.244	.274

Pitcher vs. Batter (career)

Pitches Best Vs.	Avg	AB	H	2B	3B	HR	RBI	BB	SO	OBP	SLG	Pitches Worst Vs.	Avg	AB	H	2B	3B	HR	RBI	BB	SO	OBP	SLG
Dan Pasqua	.000	8	0	0	0	0	0	3	4	.273	.000	Steve Sax	.545	11	6	1	1	1	3	0	0	.500	1.091
Lou Whitaker	.063	16	1	0	0	0	0	1	0	.118	.063	Tino Martinez	.545	11	6	2	0	1	1	0	3	.545	1.000
Lance Parrish	.071	14	1	0	0	0	1	1	5	.133	.071	Rickey Henderson	.500	16	8	2	0	2	3	5	1	.619	1.000
Terry Steinbach	.083	12	1	0	0	0	0	0	2	.083	.083	Harold Baines	.462	13	6	1	0	2	5	2	1	.533	1.000
Ruben Sierra	.091	11	1	0	0	0	0	1	1	.167	.091	Jay Buhner	.455	11	5	0	0	2	4	1	1	.500	1.000

Jack McDowell — White Sox
Pitches Right

	ERA	W	L	Sv	G	GS	IP	BB	SO	Avg	H	2B	3B	HR	RBI	OBP	SLG	CG	ShO	Sup	QS	#P/S	SB	CS	GB	FB	G/F
1992 Season	3.18	20	10	0	34	34	260.2	75	178	.251	247	45	9	21	90	.307	.379	13	1	5.46	22	117	29	16	291	289	1.01
Last Five Years	3.54	56	39	0	128	128	878.0	302	618	.242	795	149	23	72	325	.308	.367	33	4	4.95	80	106	90	40	1034	989	1.05

1992 Season

	ERA	W	L	Sv	G	GS	IP	H	HR	BB	SO
Home	2.77	9	5	0	15	15	120.1	103	9	35	83
Away	3.53	11	5	0	19	19	140.1	144	12	40	95
Day	3.35	6	3	0	11	11	86.0	82	9	29	58
Night	3.09	14	7	0	23	23	174.2	165	12	46	120
Grass	3.30	18	9	0	28	28	215.2	199	20	63	148
Turf	2.60	2	1	0	6	6	45.0	48	1	12	30
April	3.00	5	0	0	5	5	39.0	31	6	4	24
May	5.08	2	3	0	5	5	33.2	35	5	7	25
June	3.14	4	0	0	6	6	43.0	44	4	16	26
July	3.07	3	2	0	5	5	41.0	39	0	12	29
August	2.25	4	2	0	6	6	48.0	44	5	18	33
September/October	3.05	2	3	0	7	7	56.0	54	1	18	41
Starter	3.18	20	10	0	34	34	260.2	247	21	75	178
Reliever	0.00	0	0	0	0	0	0.0	0	0	0	0
0-3 Days Rest	0.00	0	0	0	0	0	0.0	0	0	0	0
4 Days Rest	2.69	12	5	0	21	21	167.1	159	9	54	111
5+ Days Rest	4.05	8	5	0	13	13	93.1	88	12	21	67
Pre-All Star	3.50	12	4	0	18	18	133.2	125	15	33	87
Post-All Star	2.83	8	6	0	16	16	127.0	122	6	42	91

	Avg	AB	H	2B	3B	HR	RBI	BB	SO	OBP	SLG
vs. Left	.263	486	128	20	6	13	46	44	85	.328	.409
vs. Right	.239	497	119	25	3	8	44	31	93	.287	.350
Inning 1-6	.252	753	190	40	7	19	73	60	135	.311	.400
Inning 7+	.248	230	57	5	2	2	17	15	43	.294	.313
None on	.262	596	156	27	6	12	12	40	117	.313	.388
Runners on	.235	387	91	18	3	9	78	35	61	.299	.367
Scoring Posn	.221	208	46	11	2	6	67	27	39	.311	.380
Close & Late	.218	101	22	2	1	0	7	8	26	.270	.257
None on/out	.263	262	69	9	4	7	7	14	49	.301	.408
vs. 1st Batr (relief)	.000	0	0	0	0	0	0	0	0	.000	.000
First Inning Pitched	.271	133	36	8	2	5	18	9	23	.315	.474
First 75 Pitches	.250	609	152	31	5	18	62	45	109	.305	.406
Pitch 76-90	.274	124	34	9	3	1	10	9	16	.321	.419
Pitch 91-105	.264	121	32	4	1	1	8	12	24	.333	.339
Pitch 106+	.225	129	29	1	0	1	10	9	29	.279	.256
First Pitch	.323	133	43	5	2	6	23	8	0	.371	.526
Ahead on Count	.228	470	107	17	5	10	39	0	151	.231	.349
Behind on Count	.271	207	56	15	2	4	17	28	0	.359	.420
Two Strikes	.195	451	88	13	4	10	31	39	178	.258	.308

Last Five Years

	ERA	W	L	Sv	G	GS	IP	H	HR	BB	SO
Home	3.28	30	18	0	69	69	474.0	412	35	165	340
Away	3.83	26	21	0	59	59	404.0	383	37	137	278
Day	3.57	17	11	0	38	38	267.0	229	24	95	181
Night	3.52	39	28	0	90	90	611.0	566	48	207	437
Grass	3.52	50	33	0	112	112	766.2	682	63	270	556
Turf	3.64	6	6	0	16	16	111.1	113	9	32	62
April	4.03	11	4	0	19	19	118.1	97	16	37	88
May	4.93	4	10	0	20	20	126.0	137	17	49	96
June	2.57	13	3	0	23	23	164.1	130	9	60	109
July	3.40	9	6	0	21	21	153.2	142	9	43	106
August	3.06	12	8	0	25	25	178.1	155	12	62	114
September/October	3.74	7	8	0	20	20	137.1	134	9	51	105
Starter	3.54	56	39	0	128	128	878.0	795	72	302	618
Reliever	0.00	0	0	0	0	0	0.0	0	0	0	0
0-3 Days Rest	2.35	2	0	0	3	3	23.0	18	1	3	8
4 Days Rest	3.17	39	22	0	84	84	589.2	527	42	210	417
5+ Days Rest	4.44	15	17	0	41	41	265.1	250	29	89	193
Pre-All Star	3.63	31	18	0	68	68	455.2	402	45	157	325
Post-All Star	3.43	25	21	0	60	60	422.1	393	27	145	293

	Avg	AB	H	2B	3B	HR	RBI	BB	SO	OBP	SLG
vs. Left	.249	1690	420	72	13	37	159	161	267	.316	.372
vs. Right	.235	1598	375	77	10	35	166	141	331	.301	.361
Inning 1-6	.242	2646	641	119	20	63	274	247	500	.310	.374
Inning 7+	.240	642	154	30	3	9	51	55	118	.302	.338
None on	.237	2004	474	82	17	38	38	174	387	.301	.351
Runners on	.250	1284	321	67	6	34	287	128	231	.319	.391
Scoring Posn	.236	708	167	38	3	20	236	93	148	.322	.383
Close & Late	.228	311	71	16	2	4	25	27	70	.292	.331
None on/out	.231	873	202	39	7	17	17	64	171	.287	.351
vs. 1st Batr (relief)	.000	0	0	0	0	0	0	0	0	.000	.000
First Inning Pitched	.261	498	130	24	5	14	63	39	95	.319	.414
First 75 Pitches	.243	2226	542	103	14	53	234	201	419	.309	.374
Pitch 76-90	.231	412	95	17	4	6	26	32	70	.290	.335
Pitch 91-105	.266	346	92	22	4	9	45	40	63	.344	.431
Pitch 106+	.217	304	66	7	1	4	20	29	66	.287	.266
First Pitch	.270	474	128	21	2	15	56	11	0	.291	.418
Ahead on Count	.204	1575	321	55	10	23	121	0	533	.208	.295
Behind on Count	.308	678	209	47	8	23	94	159	0	.440	.503
Two Strikes	.179	1544	276	50	10	21	106	132	618	.245	.265

Pitcher vs. Batter (career)

Pitches Best Vs.	Avg	AB	H	2B	3B	HR	RBI	BB	SO	OBP	SLG
Willie Wilson	.000	13	0	0	0	0	0	0	4	.000	.000
Kurt Stilwell	.000	10	0	0	0	0	0	2	1	.154	.000
Walt Weiss	.048	21	1	0	0	0	1	0	4	.048	.048
Billy Ripken	.077	13	1	0	0	0	1	0	2	.077	.077
Carlos Martinez	.083	12	1	0	0	0	1	0	1	.083	.083

Pitches Worst Vs.	Avg	AB	H	2B	3B	HR	RBI	BB	SO	OBP	SLG
Roberto Alomar	.615	13	8	0	0	1	2	2	2	.667	.846
Gary Sheffield	.545	11	6	0	0	2	2	0	0	.615	.727
Joe Orsulak	.458	24	11	2	0	2	5	1	1	.480	.792
Rickey Henderson	.440	25	11	2	1	3	6	3		.531	.720
Fred McGriff	.400	10	4	1	1	1	1	3		.455	1.000

Roger McDowell — Dodgers
Pitches Right (groundball pitcher)

	ERA	W	L	Sv	G	GS	IP	BB	SO	Avg	H	2B	3B	HR	RBI	OBP	SLG	GF	IR	IRS	Hld	SvOp	SB	CS	GB	FB	G/F
1992 Season	4.09	6	10	14	65	0	83.2	42	50	.306	103	10	2	3	45	.381	.374	39	42	10	5	22	3	2	178	52	3.42
Last Five Years	3.06	30	40	85	339	0	452.1	194	232	.265	454	62	11	13	213	.340	.336	133	246	78	25	113	37	11	940	268	3.51

1992 Season

	ERA	W	L	Sv	G	GS	IP	H	HR	BB	SO
Home	2.92	2	2	8	28	0	37.0	41	0	12	27
Away	5.01	4	8	6	37	0	46.2	62	3	30	23
Day	4.55	3	3	3	20	0	29.2	38	2	14	18
Night	3.83	3	7	11	45	0	54.0	65	1	28	32
Grass	4.01	5	8	13	50	0	67.1	83	3	30	38
Turf	4.41	1	2	1	15	0	16.1	20	0	12	12
April	1.59	3	2	2	9	0	11.1	7	0	6	9
May	3.52	0	3	5	12	0	15.1	18	1	5	11
June	3.86	1	1	3	11	0	9.1	10	0	7	4
July	4.26	0	1	2	12	0	12.2	15	1	4	14

	Avg	AB	H	2B	3B	HR	RBI	BB	SO	OBP	SLG
vs. Left	.318	154	49	5	1	3	29	30	20	.428	.422
vs. Right	.295	183	54	5	1	0	16	12	30	.337	.333
Inning 1-6	.250	16	4	0	1	0	0	3	2	.368	.375
Inning 7+	.308	321	99	10	1	3	45	39	48	.382	.374
None on	.312	154	48	4	1	0	0	12	22	.365	.351
Runners on	.301	183	55	6	1	3	45	30	28	.394	.393
Scoring Posn	.266	128	34	4	1	2	41	28	21	.390	.359
Close & Late	.279	215	60	6	1	2	32	24	28	.350	.344
None on/out	.329	76	25	2	1	0	0	5	12	.370	.382
vs. 1st Batr (relief)	.311	61	19	3	1	0	6	4	11	.354	.393

1992 Season

	ERA	W	L	Sv	G	GS	IP	H	HR	BB	SO		Avg	AB	H	2B	3B	HR	RBI	BB	SO	OBP	SLG
August	6.89	1	1	0	9	0	15.2	28	1	7	5	First Inning Pitched	.284	225	64	7	2	2	31	26	37	.356	.360
September/October	3.72	1	2	2	12	0	19.1	25	0	13	7	First 15 Pitches	.296	216	64	7	2	1	22	25	32	.368	.361
Starter	0.00	0	0	0	0	0	0.0	0	0	0	0	Pitch 16-30	.302	96	29	3	0	2	19	14	14	.393	.396
Reliever	4.09	6	10	14	65	0	83.2	103	3	42	50	Pitch 31-45	.412	17	7	0	0	0	3	1	2	.421	.412
0 Days rest	3.54	2	3	3	18	0	20.1	31	1	5	10	Pitch 46+	.375	8	3	0	0	0	1	2	2	.500	.375
1 or 2 Days rest	4.30	2	5	4	26	0	37.2	41	2	27	19	First Pitch	.297	64	19	3	1	0	8	12	0	.408	.375
3+ Days rest	4.21	2	2	7	21	0	25.2	31	0	10	21	Ahead on Count	.293	150	44	4	1	1	15	0	41	.291	.353
Pre-All Star	2.55	4	6	11	37	0	42.1	39	1	19	33	Behind on Count	.397	68	27	2	0	2	16	12	0	.481	.515
Post-All Star	5.66	2	4	3	28	0	41.1	64	2	23	17	Two Strikes	.248	125	31	2	0	1	13	18	50	.340	.288

Last Five Years

	ERA	W	L	Sv	G	GS	IP	H	HR	BB	SO		Avg	AB	H	2B	3B	HR	RBI	BB	SO	OBP	SLG
Home	2.97	16	17	36	152	0	199.2	203	5	70	109	vs. Left	.288	872	251	30	9	10	128	138	95	.385	.377
Away	3.13	14	23	49	187	0	252.2	251	8	124	123	vs. Right	.241	843	203	32	2	3	85	56	137	.291	.294
Day	3.07	8	12	23	107	0	143.2	146	6	64	75	Inning 1-6	.295	44	13	1	2	0	8	8	4	.407	.409
Night	3.06	22	28	62	232	0	306.2	308	7	130	157	Inning 7+	.264	1671	441	61	9	13	205	186	226	.338	.335
Grass	2.64	15	20	45	176	0	242.0	243	8	95	125	None on	.266	834	222	31	8	7	7	67	107	.322	.348
Turf	3.55	15	20	40	163	0	210.1	211	5	99	107	Runners on	.263	881	232	31	3	6	206	127	125	.356	.326
April	2.58	10	2	12	41	0	59.1	41	2	25	25	Scoring Posn	.248	585	145	18	3	5	200	109	91	.364	.315
May	3.16	2	8	19	58	0	77.0	80	2	28	39	Close & Late	.288	923	266	35	5	8	133	116	116	.368	.363
June	4.24	2	10	9	57	0	76.1	90	1	48	40	None on/out	.264	375	99	18	3	0	0	31	56	.322	.328
July	2.17	2	4	13	51	0	66.1	59	2	29	39	vs. 1st Batr (relief)	.265	283	75	15	2	0	23	23	44	.318	.332
August	3.33	8	7	11	69	0	92.0	93	5	33	50	First Inning Pitched	.266	1059	282	35	8	8	141	119	147	.340	.337
September/October	2.66	6	9	21	63	0	81.1	91	1	31	39	First 15 Pitches	.267	1088	291	37	9	6	118	113	134	.336	.335
Starter	0.00	0	0	0	0	0	0.0	0	0	0	0	Pitch 16-30	.249	514	128	22	2	7	80	65	78	.340	.340
Reliever	3.06	30	40	85	339	0	452.1	454	13	194	232	Pitch 31-45	.302	96	29	3	0	0	14	12	17	.373	.333
0 Days rest	4.39	7	17	26	92	0	108.2	120	4	49	46	Pitch 46+	.353	17	6	0	0	0	1	4	3	.476	.353
1 or 2 Days rest	2.56	17	17	38	165	0	225.0	231	7	99	124	First Pitch	.271	306	83	14	1	2	40	46	0	.373	.343
3+ Days rest	2.81	6	6	21	82	0	118.2	103	2	46	62	Ahead on Count	.236	764	180	28	5	3	76	1	201	.236	.297
Pre-All Star	3.13	16	21	43	172	0	239.0	232	5	112	119	Behind on Count	.312	346	108	12	2	7	67	80	0	.443	.419
Post-All Star	3.00	14	19	42	167	0	213.1	222	8	82	113	Two Strikes	.216	690	149	21	3	2	63	65	232	.282	.264

Pitcher vs. Batter (career)

Pitches Best Vs.	Avg	AB	H	2B	3B	HR	RBI	BB	SO	OBP	SLG	Pitches Worst Vs.	Avg	AB	H	2B	3B	HR	RBI	BB	SO	OBP	SLG
Gerald Young	.000	12	0	0	0	0	0	2	2	.143	.000	Eddie Murray	.600	10	6	2	0	0	2	2	0	.667	.800
Gerald Perry	.063	16	1	0	0	0	0	2	3	.167	.125	Andy Van Slyke	.478	23	11	2	0	2	4	2	3	.520	.826
Dwight Smith	.083	12	1	0	0	0	0	2	1	.214	.083	Dave Magadan	.444	9	4	1	0	1	5	2	3	.500	.889
Craig Biggio	.133	15	2	0	0	0	0	1	2	.188	.133	Terry Pendleton	.375	32	12	2	0	4	12	6	4	.474	.813
Andres Galarraga	.150	20	3	0	0	0	0	4	4	.150	.150	Steve Finley	.375	8	3	0	2	0	1	2	0	.455	.875

Chuck McElroy — Cubs

Pitches Left

	ERA	W	L	Sv	G	GS	IP	BB	SO	Avg	H	2B	3B	HR	RBI	OBP	SLG	GF	IR	IRS	Hld	SvOp	SB	CS	GB	FB	G/F
1992 Season	3.55	4	7	6	72	0	83.2	51	83	.237	73	19	3	5	42	.341	.367	30	51	15	3	11	4	3	80	91	0.88
Career (1989-1992)	2.97	10	10	9	170	0	209.1	122	199	.239	182	40	4	13	98	.339	.353	50	125	42	13	17	19	13	226	210	1.08

1992 Season

	ERA	W	L	Sv	G	GS	IP	H	HR	BB	SO		Avg	AB	H	2B	3B	HR	RBI	BB	SO	OBP	SLG
Home	3.64	3	4	1	37	0	42.0	36	3	20	43	vs. Left	.275	102	28	7	1	2	16	12	30	.345	.422
Away	3.46	1	3	5	35	0	41.2	37	2	31	40	vs. Right	.218	206	45	12	2	3	26	39	53	.339	.340
Day	3.59	3	2	5	40	0	47.2	39	4	25	52	Inning 1-6	.138	29	4	1	1	0	4	9	7	.342	.241
Night	3.50	1	5	1	32	0	36.0	34	1	26	31	Inning 7+	.247	279	69	18	2	5	38	42	76	.340	.380
Grass	3.36	3	4	4	51	0	59.0	49	4	29	56	None on	.245	159	39	11	2	4	4	16	44	.314	.415
Turf	4.01	1	3	2	21	0	24.2	24	1	22	27	Runners on	.228	149	34	8	1	1	38	35	39	.365	.315
April	0.82	1	0	3	10	0	11.0	4	0	8	12	Scoring Posn	.250	96	24	7	1	1	37	27	27	.398	.375
May	4.60	1	3	2	14	0	15.2	16	0	9	17	Close & Late	.253	166	42	13	2	1	21	31	49	.365	.373
June	0.96	1	1	0	6	0	9.1	7	1	5	9	None on/out	.239	71	17	5	1	0	0	6	22	.299	.338
July	3.50	0	2	0	15	0	18.0	14	1	9	14	vs. 1st Batr (relief)	.286	63	18	9	1	0	10	8	20	.361	.460
August	3.95	1	0	1	11	0	13.2	15	2	6	10	First Inning Pitched	.243	218	53	15	3	3	31	37	63	.346	.381
September/October	5.63	0	1	0	16	0	16.0	17	1	14	21	First 15 Pitches	.231	195	45	12	3	3	23	34	53	.338	.369
Starter	0.00	0	0	0	0	0	0.0	0	0	0	0	Pitch 16-30	.260	96	25	6	0	1	14	16	25	.366	.354
Reliever	3.55	4	7	6	72	0	83.2	73	5	51	83	Pitch 31-45	.125	16	2	0	0	1	3	1	5	.176	.313
0 Days rest	3.66	0	2	1	20	0	19.2	15	1	13	21	Pitch 46+	1.000	1	1	1	0	0	2	0	0	1.000	2.000
1 or 2 Days rest	3.91	4	4	3	36	0	46.0	42	2	27	43	First Pitch	.283	46	13	3	2	1	9	10	1	.390	.435
3+ Days rest	2.50	0	1	2	16	0	18.0	16	2	11	19	Ahead on Count	.226	155	35	9	1	2	20	0	68	.226	.335
Pre-All Star	2.58	3	4	5	38	0	45.1	31	1	25	47	Behind on Count	.264	53	14	3	0	2	7	19	1	.446	.434
Post-All Star	4.70	1	3	1	34	0	38.1	42	4	26	36	Two Strikes	.211	171	36	11	1	1	24	22	81	.301	.304

Career (1989-1992)

	ERA	W	L	Sv	G	GS	IP	H	HR	BB	SO		Avg	AB	H	2B	3B	HR	RBI	BB	SO	OBP	SLG
Home	3.03	6	6	4	90	0	115.2	106	5	58	112	vs. Left	.229	253	58	14	1	5	35	35	76	.317	.352
Away	2.88	4	4	5	80	0	93.2	76	8	64	87	vs. Right	.244	509	124	26	3	8	63	87	123	.350	.354
Day	2.18	7	2	7	83	0	111.1	79	4	50	105	Inning 1-6	.208	154	32	2	1	2	26	29	39	.330	.273
Night	3.86	3	8	2	87	0	98.0	103	9	72	94	Inning 7+	.247	608	150	38	3	11	72	93	160	.342	.373

Career (1989-1992)

	ERA	W	L	Sv	G	GS	IP	H	HR	BB	SO
Grass	2.29	8	5	7	106	0	145.2	111	8	72	132
Turf	4.52	2	5	2	64	0	63.2	71	5	50	67
April	2.59	1	0	3	25	0	24.1	15	0	14	32
May	2.97	2	3	3	25	0	33.1	26	1	19	27
June	1.45	4	1	0	19	0	31.0	25	4	20	28
July	2.88	1	3	1	26	0	34.1	29	4	15	29
August	2.65	1	1	2	26	0	34.0	29	2	18	31
September/October	4.30	1	2	0	49	0	52.1	58	2	36	52
Starter	0.00	0	0	0	0	0	0.0	0	0	0	0
Reliever	2.97	10	10	9	170	0	209.1	182	13	122	199
0 Days rest	2.74	2	3	2	45	0	46.0	38	3	26	45
1 or 2 Days rest	2.67	7	6	4	83	0	106.0	90	5	60	100
3+ Days rest	3.74	1	3	0	42	0	55.1	54	5	36	54
Pre-All Star	2.38	8	4	6	81	0	102.0	74	5	56	97
Post-All Star	3.52	2	6	3	89	0	107.1	108	8	66	102

	Avg	AB	H	2B	3B	HR	RBI	BB	SO	OBP	SLG
None on	.244	386	94	24	2	8	8	55	98	.338	.378
Runners on	.234	376	88	16	2	5	90	67	101	.341	.327
Scoring posn	.243	226	55	11	2	4	85	50	63	.365	.363
Close & Late	.250	324	81	22	3	4	39	59	90	.361	.373
None on/out	.241	174	42	12	1	1	1	24	45	.333	.339
vs. 1st Batr (relief)	.299	144	43	13	1	1	26	19	38	.371	.424
First Inning Pitched	.251	518	130	30	4	7	71	75	133	.341	.365
First 15 Pitches	.262	466	122	30	4	7	62	67	107	.349	.388
Pitch 16-30	.211	228	48	9	0	3	24	44	71	.336	.289
Pitch 31-45	.204	54	11	0	0	3	10	6	19	.279	.370
Pitch 46+	.071	14	1	1	0	0	2	5	2	.316	.143
First Pitch	.318	107	34	10	2	2	18	19	1	.405	.505
Ahead on Count	.218	376	82	17	2	5	38	0	165	.216	.314
Behind on Count	.250	140	35	8	0	4	21	52	1	.446	.393
Two Strikes	.195	406	79	18	2	5	42	51	197	.283	.286

Pitcher vs. Batter (career)

Pitches Best Vs.	Avg	AB	H	2B	3B	HR	RBI	BB	SO	OBP	SLG
Ozzie Smith	.000	9	0	0	0	0	0	2	2	.182	.000
Barry Bonds	.071	14	1	1	0	0	1	1	3	.125	.143
Andy Van Slyke	.167	12	2	1	0	0	0	3	4	.333	.250
Delino DeShields	.200	10	2	0	0	0	1	1	4	.250	.200
Ray Lankford	.222	9	2	0	0	0	0	5	6	.500	.222

Pitches Worst Vs.	Avg	AB	H	2B	3B	HR	RBI	BB	SO	OBP	SLG
Brett Butler	.500	6	3	1	0	0	1	6	2	.750	.667
Larry Walker	.400	10	4	1	0	0	3	2	3	.500	.500

Willie McGee — Giants   Bats Both (groundball hitter)

	Avg	G	AB	R	H	2B	3B	HR	RBI	BB	SO	HBP	GDP	SB	CS	OBP	SLG	IBB	SH	SF	#Pit	#P/PA	GB	FB	G/F
1992 Season	.297	138	474	56	141	20	2	1	36	29	88	1	7	13	4	.339	.354	3	5	1	1816	3.60	242	67	3.61
Last Five Years	.301	618	2346	318	706	119	20	14	223	153	384	6	43	110	34	.344	.387	17	15	9	9068	3.61	1230	339	3.63

1992 Season

	Avg	AB	H	2B	3B	HR	RBI	BB	SO	OBP	SLG
vs. Left	.283	159	45	6	2	1	12	4	36	.305	.365
vs. Right	.305	315	96	14	0	0	24	25	52	.355	.349
Groundball	.370	192	71	11	2	0	18	12	33	.408	.448
Flyball	.310	87	27	2	0	0	6	5	11	.348	.333
Home	.317	224	71	13	1	0	14	16	30	.361	.384
Away	.280	250	70	7	1	1	22	13	58	.318	.328
Day	.357	182	65	9	2	0	17	15	27	.404	.429
Night	.260	292	76	11	0	1	19	14	61	.296	.308
Grass	.302	328	99	17	1	0	26	23	52	.347	.360
Turf	.288	146	42	3	1	1	10	6	36	.320	.342
First Pitch	.349	83	29	5	0	0	7	2	0	.365	.410
Ahead on Count	.421	76	32	9	0	0	8	13	0	.506	.539
Behind on Count	.235	170	40	5	2	0	8	0	50	.238	.288
Two Strikes	.208	216	45	1	2	1	15	14	88	.245	.259

	Avg	AB	H	2B	3B	HR	RBI	BB	SO	OBP	SLG
Scoring Posn	.337	101	34	3	0	0	29	11	13	.398	.366
Close & Late	.274	95	26	4	0	0	11	3	16	.296	.316
None on/out	.259	135	35	3	0	0		7	32	.301	.281
Batting #1	.315	130	41	4	0	0	10	5	23	.346	.346
Batting #2	.273	260	71	13	0	0	15	13	51	.307	.323
Other	.345	84	29	3	2	1	11	11	14	.421	.464
April	.276	76	21	3	0	0	5	9	12	.349	.316
May	.294	85	25	5	1	0	10	2	18	.310	.376
June	.341	88	30	1	0	0	2	4	16	.370	.352
July	.253	83	21	6	0	1	4	4	22	.295	.361
August	.322	90	29	4	0	0	11	4	13	.351	.367
September/October	.288	52	15	1	1	0	4	6	7	.362	.346
Pre-All Star	.309	275	85	13	1	0	17	17	52	.348	.364
Post-All Star	.281	199	56	7	1	1	19	12	36	.325	.342

1992 By Position

Position	Avg	AB	H	2B	3B	HR	RBI	BB	SO	OBP	SLG	G	GS	Innings	PO	A	E	DP	Fld Pct	Rng Fctr	In Zone	Zone Outs	Zone Rtg	MLB Zone
As Pinch Hitter	.524	21	11	3	1	0	7	2	4	.565	.762	23	0	---	---	---	---	---	---	---	---	---	---
As cf	.265	113	30	5	0	0	10	5	21	.303	.310	31	27	248.1	66	2	0	1	1.000	2.46	76	64	.842	.824
As rf	.294	340	100	12	1	1	19	22	63	.336	.344	90	84	721.0	164	9	6	1	.966	2.16	180	156	.867	.814

Last Five Years

	Avg	AB	H	2B	3B	HR	RBI	BB	SO	OBP	SLG
vs. Left	.296	812	240	37	8	7	83	36	152	.326	.387
vs. Right	.304	1534	466	82	12	7	140	117	232	.353	.387
Groundball	.316	833	263	36	12	7	92	53	133	.357	.413
Flyball	.289	471	136	20	4	3	36	31	80	.333	.367
Home	.299	1163	348	59	9	5	119	74	164	.340	.378
Away	.303	1183	358	60	11	9	104	79	220	.348	.395
Day	.334	778	260	42	9	4	85	49	116	.373	.427
Night	.284	1568	446	77	11	10	138	104	268	.330	.367
Grass	.299	1115	333	51	9	6	98	75	187	.343	.377
Turf	.303	1231	373	68	11	8	125	78	197	.345	.396
First Pitch	.399	391	156	35	1	5	54	5	0	.407	.532
Ahead on Count	.347	403	140	35	5	4	50	83	0	.455	.489
Behind on Count	.266	869	231	32	9	4	73	1	225	.268	.337
Two Strikes	.224	1063	238	24	7	3	71	57	383	.266	.268

	Avg	AB	H	2B	3B	HR	RBI	BB	SO	OBP	SLG
Scoring Posn	.302	590	178	33	6	0	190	64	106	.367	.378
Close & Late	.307	433	133	18	1	3	45	23	77	.341	.374
None on/out	.279	552	154	23	3	5	5	29	96	.317	.359
Batting #2	.296	928	275	53	8	7	82	65	154	.343	.393
Batting #3	.332	805	267	39	7	6	96	46	126	.366	.420
Other	.268	613	164	27	5	1	45	42	104	.318	.333
April	.310	316	98	17	4	3	32	23	57	.356	.418
May	.282	504	142	26	4	3	43	27	73	.317	.367
June	.340	415	141	20	3	2	38	39	63	.394	.417
July	.297	317	94	18	0	3	30	16	60	.333	.382
August	.280	429	120	21	4	3	48	25	68	.323	.368
September/October	.304	365	111	17	5	0	32	23	63	.345	.378
Pre-All Star	.309	1327	410	71	11	8	117	95	214	.354	.397
Post-All Star	.290	1019	296	48	9	6	106	58	170	.331	.373

Batter vs. Pitcher (since 1984)

Hits Best Against	Avg	AB	H	2B	3B	HR	RBI	BB	SO	OBP	SLG
Darryl Kile	.571	14	8	2	0	0	2	2	2	.625	.714

Hits Worst Against	Avg	AB	H	2B	3B	HR	RBI	BB	SO	OBP	SLG
Danny Jackson	.071	14	1	0	0	0	0	1	2	.133	.214

Batter vs. Pitcher (since 1984)

Hits Best Against	Avg	AB	H	2B	3B	HR	RBI	BB	SO	OBP	SLG	Hits Worst Against	Avg	AB	H	2B	3B	HR	RBI	BB	SO	OBP	SLG
Derek Lilliquist	.538	13	7	0	1	1	2	1	0	.571	.923	Jim Acker	.083	12	1	0	0	1	0	0	3	.083	.167
Ted Power	.462	13	6	2	1	0	5	0	2	.462	.769	Kelly Downs	.083	12	1	0	0	0	1	0	2	.083	.083
Bobby Ojeda	.375	40	15	6	1	3	9	1	5	.390	.800	Steve Avery	.091	11	1	0	0	0	0	1	2	.167	.091
Mark Davis	.353	17	6	1	0	2	6	2	6	.421	.765	Norm Charlton	.143	14	2	0	0	0	0	0	6	.143	.143

Russ McGinnis — Rangers

Bats Right (flyball hitter)

	Avg	G	AB	R	H	2B	3B	HR	RBI	BB	SO	HBP	GDP	SB	CS	OBP	SLG	IBB	SH	SF	#Pit	#P/PA	GB	FB	G/F
1992 Season	.242	14	33	2	8	4	0	0	4	3	7	0	1	0	0	.306	.364	0	0	0	131	3.64	9	13	0.69

1992 Season

	Avg	AB	H	2B	3B	HR	RBI	BB	SO	OBP	SLG		Avg	AB	H	2B	3B	HR	RBI	BB	SO	OBP	SLG
vs. Left	.240	25	6	2	0	0	2	2	5	.296	.320	Scoring Posn	.200	10	2	1	0	0	2	0	4	.200	.300
vs. Right	.250	8	2	2	0	0	2	1	2	.333	.500	Close & Late	.000	1	0	0	0	0	0	1	0	.500	.000

Fred McGriff — Padres

Bats Left

	Avg	G	AB	R	H	2B	3B	HR	RBI	BB	SO	HBP	GDP	SB	CS	OBP	SLG	IBB	SH	SF	#Pit	#P/PA	GB	FB	G/F
1992 Season	.286	152	531	79	152	30	4	35	104	96	108	1	14	8	6	.394	.556	23	0	4	2335	3.69	187	136	1.38
Last Five Years	.283	773	2703	452	765	132	13	171	472	493	632	13	64	30	15	.393	.531	76	2	24	12426	3.84	881	742	1.19

1992 Season

	Avg	AB	H	2B	3B	HR	RBI	BB	SO	OBP	SLG		Avg	AB	H	2B	3B	HR	RBI	BB	SO	OBP	SLG
vs. Left	.283	205	58	10	3	13	50	28	49	.369	.551	Scoring Posn	.298	131	39	12	3	7	63	49	27	.478	.595
vs. Right	.288	326	94	20	1	22	54	68	59	.409	.558	Close & Late	.321	81	26	8	0	2	13	15	19	.418	.494
Groundball	.297	212	63	13	1	11	33	39	42	.402	.524	None on/out	.310	158	49	8	0	11	11	14	27	.366	.570
Flyball	.308	107	33	7	0	6	19	17	25	.400	.542	Batting #4	.287	530	152	30	4	35	104	96	108	.395	.557
Home	.304	273	83	17	2	21	56	47	51	.406	.612	Batting #5	.000	1	0	0	0	0	0	0	0	.000	.000
Away	.267	258	69	13	2	14	48	49	57	.381	.496	Other	.000	0	0	0	0	0	0	0	0	.000	.000
Day	.267	146	39	10	0	9	28	27	30	.382	.521	April	.271	85	23	3	1	6	21	15	17	.376	.541
Night	.294	385	113	20	4	26	76	69	78	.399	.569	May	.392	97	38	8	1	6	16	16	18	.478	.680
Grass	.283	385	109	24	2	26	74	70	72	.392	.558	June	.276	58	16	5	0	2	11	16	12	.434	.466
Turf	.295	146	43	6	2	9	30	26	36	.399	.548	July	.258	93	24	2	1	7	16	14	16	.352	.527
First Pitch	.313	80	25	4	1	8	18	20	0	.455	.688	August	.225	89	20	2	0	10	21	14	20	.330	.584
Ahead on Count	.385	135	52	8	1	15	42	41	0	.525	.793	September/October	.284	109	31	10	1	4	19	21	25	.397	.505
Behind on Count	.267	150	40	6	1	7	28	0	50	.263	.460	Pre-All Star	.316	282	89	16	2	18	55	55	52	.426	.578
Two Strikes	.204	235	48	13	2	7	24	37	108	.309	.366	Post-All Star	.253	249	63	14	2	17	49	41	56	.356	.530

1992 By Position

Position	Avg	AB	H	2B	3B	HR	RBI	BB	SO	OBP	SLG	G	GS	Innings	PO	A	E	DP	Fld Pct	Rng Fctr	In Zone	Outs	Zone Rtg	MLB Zone
As 1b	.287	530	152	30	4	35	104	96	108	.395	.557	151	151	1334.2	1219	104	12	95	.991	---	235	197	.838	.843

Last Five Years

	Avg	AB	H	2B	3B	HR	RBI	BB	SO	OBP	SLG		Avg	AB	H	2B	3B	HR	RBI	BB	SO	OBP	SLG
vs. Left	.261	980	256	34	7	45	167	134	267	.350	.448	Scoring Posn	.262	667	175	30	4	32	277	196	177	.422	.463
vs. Right	.295	1723	509	98	6	126	305	359	365	.416	.579	Close & Late	.271	413	112	28	2	14	53	83	111	.392	.450
Groundball	.301	778	234	47	3	43	129	155	169	.414	.535	None on/out	.296	713	211	38	5	42	42	98	149	.383	.540
Flyball	.255	599	153	31	2	41	103	104	156	.363	.519	Batting #4	.279	1360	380	63	5	78	242	268	305	.396	.505
Home	.280	1299	364	63	5	89	235	259	278	.400	.542	Batting #5	.263	1027	291	51	7	72	173	177	234	.389	.557
Away	.286	1404	401	69	8	82	237	234	354	.386	.521	Other	.297	316	94	18	1	21	57	48	93	.394	.560
Day	.269	815	219	45	3	45	133	140	178	.376	.497	April	.301	359	108	14	2	23	61	79	96	.429	.543
Night	.289	1868	546	87	10	126	339	353	454	.400	.546	May	.301	465	140	32	2	28	82	73	105	.398	.559
Grass	.285	1447	412	74	5	87	246	263	351	.393	.523	June	.259	428	111	22	1	26	79	84	99	.381	.498
Turf	.281	1256	353	58	8	84	226	230	281	.393	.541	July	.282	450	127	17	1	36	84	72	108	.380	.564
First Pitch	.368	391	144	23	2	41	97	50	0	.437	.752	August	.275	480	132	20	6	37	88	91	124	.388	.573
Ahead on Count	.399	684	273	35	6	67	182	185	0	.527	.762	September/October	.282	521	147	27	1	37	78	94	98	.390	.459
Behind on Count	.235	756	178	35	3	28	97	2	289	.242	.401	Pre-All Star	.264	1400	397	71	5	87	244	260	331	.397	.528
Two Strikes	.173	1247	216	51	5	39	127	245	630	.307	.316	Post-All Star	.282	1303	368	61	8	84	228	233	301	.389	.535

Batter vs. Pitcher (career)

Hits Best Against	Avg	AB	H	2B	3B	HR	RBI	BB	SO	OBP	SLG	Hits Worst Against	Avg	AB	H	2B	3B	HR	RBI	BB	SO	OBP	SLG
Trevor Wilson	.700	10	7	0	0	2	6	4	0	.813	1.300	Randy Tomlin	.000	19	0	0	0	0	1	3	6	.130	.000
Chris Nabholz	.625	8	5	0	1	2	4	4	0	.750	1.625	Mike Henneman	.000	16	0	0	0	0	1	1	4	.059	.000
Terry Mulholland	.500	22	11	0	1	3	8	2	3	.542	1.000	Rick Honeycutt	.000	12	0	0	0	0	1	0	5	.000	.000
Mark Gubicza	.500	20	10	3	0	4	4	3	3	.565	1.250	Doug Jones	.000	11	0	0	0	0	1	1	3	.063	.000
Jeff M. Robinson	.467	15	7	0	3	3	7	3	6	.556	1.067	Dave Schmidt	.091	11	1	0	0	0	1	1	4	.167	.091

Mark McGwire — Athletics

Bats Right (flyball hitter)

	Avg	G	AB	R	H	2B	3B	HR	RBI	BB	SO	HBP	GDP	SB	CS	OBP	SLG	IBB	SH	SF	#Pit	#P/PA	GB	FB	G/F
1992 Season	.268	139	467	87	125	22	0	42	104	90	105	5	10	0	1	.385	.585	12	0	9	2065	3.62	84	214	0.39
Last Five Years	.239	747	2513	397	601	99	1	168	481	452	548	22	74	5	4	.355	.480	33	3	38	11165	3.69	576	1053	0.55

1992 Season

	Avg	AB	H	2B	3B	HR	RBI	BB	SO	OBP	SLG		Avg	AB	H	2B	3B	HR	RBI	BB	SO	OBP	SLG
vs. Left	.330	97	32	4	0	14	27	22	14	.447	.804	Scoring Posn	.280	107	30	9	0	7	61	29	20	.415	.561
vs. Right	.251	370	93	18	0	28	77	68	91	.368	.527	Close & Late	.237	59	14	1	0	5	14	14	14	.373	.508
Groundball	.295	112	33	4	0	10	27	23	26	.412	.598	None on/out	.312	138	43	7	0	17	17	20	23	.399	.732
Flyball	.270	122	33	7	0	13	31	25	31	.399	.648	Batting #4	.262	225	59	11	0	21	50	37	48	.365	.591
Home	.252	218	55	8	0	24	52	52	51	.398	.619	Batting #5	.275	240	66	11	0	21	54	53	56	.406	.583
Away	.281	249	70	14	0	18	52	38	54	.373	.554	Other	.000	2	0	0	0	0	0	0	1	.000	.000
Day	.289	180	52	10	0	20	46	40	40	.416	.678	April	.333	75	25	5	0	10	17	20	12	.480	.800
Night	.254	287	73	12	0	22	58	50	65	.365	.526	May	.237	93	22	6	0	8	23	19	27	.360	.559
Grass	.255	377	96	15	0	34	85	76	96	.379	.565	June	.277	94	26	0	0	8	24	18	25	.389	.532
Turf	.322	90	29	7	0	8	19	14	9	.411	.667	July	.256	86	22	7	0	6	17	12	18	.359	.547
First Pitch	.375	96	36	6	0	13	35	7	0	.415	.844	August	.254	63	16	1	0	6	12	12	15	.364	.556
Ahead on Count	.245	110	27	5	0	10	17	48	0	.475	.564	September/October	.250	56	14	3	0	4	11	9	8	.348	.518
Behind on Count	.191	115	22	5	0	8	21	0	40	.190	.443	Pre-All Star	.262	302	79	13	0	28	69	60	73	.383	.583
Two Strikes	.156	186	29	8	0	8	31	35	105	.291	.328	Post-All Star	.279	165	46	9	0	14	35	30	32	.389	.588

1992 By Position

Position	Avg	AB	H	2B	3B	HR	RBI	BB	SO	OBP	SLG	G	GS	Innings	PO	A	E	DP	Fld Pct	Rng Fctr	In Zone	Outs	Zone Rtg	MLB Zone
As 1b	.268	466	125	22	0	42	104	90	105	.386	.586	139	136	1181.2	1119	70	6	119	.995	---	217	193	.889	.843

Last Five Years

	Avg	AB	H	2B	3B	HR	RBI	BB	SO	OBP	SLG		Avg	AB	H	2B	3B	HR	RBI	BB	SO	OBP	SLG
vs. Left	.250	641	160	29	1	47	140	124	110	.367	.518	Scoring Posn	.277	625	173	25	1	42	312	146	147	.399	.522
vs. Right	.236	1872	441	70	0	121	341	328	438	.351	.467	Close & Late	.249	350	87	7	0	25	86	75	84	.382	.483
Groundball	.250	707	177	27	0	38	117	130	128	.369	.450	None on/out	.240	622	149	29	0	47	47	101	119	.351	.513
Flyball	.221	583	129	22	1	42	111	106	163	.342	.479	Batting #4	.248	1212	301	48	1	91	258	198	242	.352	.515
Home	.228	1208	275	49	0	77	227	230	272	.352	.459	Batting #5	.231	743	172	25	0	41	116	153	184	.365	.431
Away	.250	1305	326	50	1	91	254	222	276	.358	.499	Other	.229	558	128	26	0	36	107	101	122	.350	.470
Day	.259	954	247	43	0	76	209	159	199	.366	.543	April	.274	332	91	16	0	28	69	63	63	.395	.575
Night	.227	1559	354	56	1	92	272	293	349	.349	.441	May	.227	454	103	21	0	28	87	96	97	.359	.458
Grass	.237	2091	496	79	1	144	409	386	469	.356	.483	June	.226	443	100	10	1	31	87	76	114	.337	.463
Turf	.249	422	105	20	0	24	72	66	79	.353	.467	July	.228	473	108	20	0	24	78	61	97	.320	.423
First Pitch	.331	459	152	22	0	47	125	12	0	.348	.686	August	.241	431	104	11	0	37	87	84	94	.363	.483
Ahead on Count	.285	575	164	31	1	46	131	240	0	.497	.583	September/October	.250	380	95	21	0	26	73	72	83	.371	.511
Behind on Count	.195	708	138	27	0	36	123	1	229	.197	.386	Pre-All Star	.237	1392	330	54	1	96	275	258	307	.355	.484
Two Strikes	.143	1066	152	30	0	36	126	189	548	.271	.272	Post-All Star	.242	1121	271	45	0	72	206	194	241	.356	.475

Batter vs. Pitcher (career)

Hits Best Against	Avg	AB	H	2B	3B	HR	RBI	BB	SO	OBP	SLG	Hits Worst Against	Avg	AB	H	2B	3B	HR	RBI	BB	SO	OBP	SLG
John Smiley	.500	10	5	2	0	2	2	3	2	.615	1.300	Dennis Lamp	.000	15	0	0	0	0	0	1	3	.063	.000
Mark Williamson	.444	18	8	2	0	3	7	4	4	.545	1.056	Juan Guzman	.000	8	0	0	0	0	0	2	3	.333	.000
Scott Erickson	.444	18	8	2	0	3	7	3	3	.524	1.056	Roger Clemens	.036	28	1	1	0	0	0	3	10	.129	.071
Gregg Olson	.444	9	4	0	0	1	4	3	3	.583	.778	Greg Hibbard	.063	16	1	0	0	0	1	2	2	.158	.063
Mike Gardiner	.333	9	3	0	0	3	7	3	3	.462	1.333	Jeff Russell	.077	13	1	0	0	0	0	1	3	.143	.077

Tim McIntosh — Brewers

Bats Right (flyball hitter)

	Avg	G	AB	R	H	2B	3B	HR	RBI	BB	SO	HBP	GDP	SB	CS	OBP	SLG	IBB	SH	SF	#Pit	#P/PA	GB	FB	G/F
1992 Season	.182	35	77	7	14	3	0	0	6	3	9	2	1	1	3	.229	.221	0	1	1	282	3.40	23	33	0.70
Career (1990-1992)	.204	47	93	10	19	4	0	2	8	3	15	2	1	1	3	.242	.312	0	1	1	333	3.36	25	39	0.64

1992 Season

	Avg	AB	H	2B	3B	HR	RBI	BB	SO	OBP	SLG		Avg	AB	H	2B	3B	HR	RBI	BB	SO	OBP	SLG
vs. Left	.161	31	5	1	0	0	4	2	2	.229	.194	Scoring Posn	.158	19	3	1	0	0	6	1	2	.190	.211
vs. Right	.196	46	9	2	0	0	2	1	7	.229	.239	Close & Late	.154	13	2	0	0	0	0	1	3	.214	.154

Jeff McKnight — Mets

Bats Both

	Avg	G	AB	R	H	2B	3B	HR	RBI	BB	SO	HBP	GDP	SB	CS	OBP	SLG	IBB	SH	SF	#Pit	#P/PA	GB	FB	G/F
1992 Season	.271	31	85	10	23	3	1	2	13	2	8	0	2	0	1	.287	.400	0	0	0	301	3.46	33	30	1.10
Career (1989-1992)	.225	82	213	25	48	6	1	3	19	11	33	1	5	1	1	.267	.305	0	3	0	857	3.81	74	70	1.06

1992 Season

	Avg	AB	H	2B	3B	HR	RBI	BB	SO	OBP	SLG		Avg	AB	H	2B	3B	HR	RBI	BB	SO	OBP	SLG
vs. Left	.385	26	10	1	0	0	5	1	1	.407	.423	Scoring Posn	.217	23	5	2	0	0	9	0	1	.217	.304
vs. Right	.220	59	13	2	1	2	8	1	7	.233	.390	Close & Late	.286	28	8	1	0	0	1	0	3	.286	.321

Mark McLemore — Orioles
Bats Both (groundball hitter)

	Avg	G	AB	R	H	2B	3B	HR	RBI	BB	SO	HBP	GDP	SB	CS	OBP	SLG	IBB	SH	SF	#Pit	#P/PA	GB	FB	G/F
1992 Season	.246	101	228	40	56	7	2	0	27	21	26	0	6	11	5	.308	.294	1	6	1	916	3.66	99	49	2.02
Last Five Years	.226	259	685	102	155	24	5	2	61	63	101	1	16	31	14	.290	.285	1	15	5	2744	3.64	270	165	1.64

1992 Season

	Avg	AB	H	2B	3B	HR	RBI	BB	SO	OBP	SLG		Avg	AB	H	2B	3B	HR	RBI	BB	SO	OBP	SLG
vs. Left	.276	58	16	2	0	0	10	5	9	.333	.310	Scoring Posn	.307	75	23	4	1	0	26	8	8	.369	.387
vs. Right	.235	170	40	5	2	0	17	16	17	.299	.288	Close & Late	.231	52	12	1	0	0	6	5	8	.298	.250
Home	.198	111	22	4	1	0	11	8	12	.250	.252	None on/out	.250	40	10	1	0	0	6	4	.348	.275
Away	.291	117	34	3	1	0	16	13	14	.362	.333	Batting #8	.290	69	20	3	1	0	6	5	10	.338	.362
First Pitch	.220	41	9	0	0	0	2	1	0	.238	.220	Batting #9	.259	85	22	2	1	0	12	9	6	.326	.306
Ahead on Count	.345	58	20	1	2	0	14	12	0	.451	.431	Other	.189	74	14	2	0	0	9	7	10	.259	.216
Behind on Count	.167	60	10	0	1	0	6	0	13	.164	.200	Pre-All Star	.247	154	38	6	0	0	21	18	20	.324	.286
Two Strikes	.213	89	19	5	0	0	8	8	26	.278	.270	Post-All Star	.243	74	18	1	2	0	6	3	6	.273	.311

Last Five Years

	Avg	AB	H	2B	3B	HR	RBI	BB	SO	OBP	SLG		Avg	AB	H	2B	3B	HR	RBI	BB	SO	OBP	SLG
vs. Left	.240	208	50	8	1	0	23	15	35	.291	.288	Scoring Posn	.243	185	45	6	2	0	57	17	29	.300	.297
vs. Right	.220	477	105	16	4	2	38	48	66	.290	.283	None on/out	.218	142	31	2	0	0	14	13	25	.282	.232
Groundball	.240	175	42	7	1	0	16	18	23	.308	.291	None on/out	.208	168	35	8	2	0	0	21	27	.300	.280
Flyball	.210	181	38	11	0	1	16	16	32	.274	.287	Batting #1	.190	163	31	5	2	1	8	17	24	.265	.264
Home	.205	322	66	9	3	1	25	31	47	.273	.261	Batting #2	.250	196	49	8	1	1	25	18	27	.313	.316
Away	.245	363	89	15	2	1	36	32	54	.306	.306	Other	.230	326	75	11	2	0	28	28	50	.289	.289
Day	.248	214	53	8	4	0	26	19	34	.305	.322	April	.215	256	55	8	3	1	24	20	47	.295	.281
Night	.217	471	102	16	1	2	35	44	67	.284	.268	May	.226	168	38	7	0	0	15	18	15	.296	.268
Grass	.223	528	118	18	4	2	46	49	75	.289	.284	June	.225	40	9	1	0	0	5	3	7	.279	.250
Turf	.236	157	37	6	1	0	15	14	26	.295	.287	July	.350	40	14	2	2	0	7	4	6	.409	.500
First Pitch	.258	120	31	7	0	1	10	1	0	.262	.342	August	.244	41	10	2	0	1	3	1	2	.262	.366
Ahead on Count	.268	168	45	6	3	1	28	32	0	.379	.357	September/October	.207	140	29	4	0	0	7	9	24	.252	.236
Behind on Count	.200	200	40	3	2	1	11	0	50	.202	.250	Pre-All Star	.226	492	111	18	3	1	46	51	74	.298	.260
Two Strikes	.165	267	44	5	0	0	14	30	101	.249	.184	Post-All Star	.228	193	44	6	2	1	15	12	27	.271	.295

Batter vs. Pitcher (career)

Hits Best Against	Avg	AB	H	2B	3B	HR	RBI	BB	SO	OBP	SLG	Hits Worst Against	Avg	AB	H	2B	3B	HR	RBI	BB	SO	OBP	SLG
Mark Langston	.400	25	10	0	0	1	4	2	5	.444	.520	Mark Gubicza	.083	12	1	0	0	0	1	0	1	.083	.063
Jack McDowell	.333	15	5	0	0	0	0	1	1	.375	.333	Mark Williamson	.091	11	1	0	0	0	0	1	1	.167	.091
Dave Stieb	.333	12	4	0	0	3	2	0	.400	.333	Jeff Russell	.100	10	1	0	0	0	1	0	.308	.100
												Jack Morris	.143	14	2	0	0	0	1	2	2	.250	.143
												Mike Boddicker	.188	16	3	0	0	0	0	1	1	.235	.188

Jim McNamara — Giants
Bats Left (groundball hitter)

	Avg	G	AB	R	H	2B	3B	HR	RBI	BB	SO	HBP	GDP	SB	CS	OBP	SLG	IBB	SH	SF	#Pit	#P/PA	GB	FB	G/F
1992 Season	.216	30	74	6	16	1	0	1	9	6	25	1	0	0	0	.275	.270	2	2	0	287	3.59	20	12	1.67

1992 Season

	Avg	AB	H	2B	3B	HR	RBI	BB	SO	OBP	SLG		Avg	AB	H	2B	3B	HR	RBI	BB	SO	OBP	SLG
vs. Left	.167	6	1	0	0	0	0	0	2	.167	.167	Scoring Posn	.333	21	7	0	0	0	6	5	8	.462	.333
vs. Right	.221	68	15	1	0	1	9	6	23	.284	.279	Close & Late	.300	10	3	0	0	0	1	3	.364	.300

Brian McRae — Royals
Bats Both (groundball hitter)

	Avg	G	AB	R	H	2B	3B	HR	RBI	BB	SO	HBP	GDP	SB	CS	OBP	SLG	IBB	SH	SF	#Pit	#P/PA	GB	FB	G/F
1992 Season	.223	149	533	63	119	23	5	4	52	42	88	6	10	18	5	.285	.308	1	7	4	2182	3.73	224	111	2.02
Career (1990-1992)	.249	347	1330	170	331	59	17	14	139	75	216	8	27	42	19	.291	.350	2	13	11	5171	3.63	535	307	1.74

1992 Season

	Avg	AB	H	2B	3B	HR	RBI	BB	SO	OBP	SLG		Avg	AB	H	2B	3B	HR	RBI	BB	SO	OBP	SLG
vs. Left	.233	163	38	8	2	3	20	10	27	.282	.362	Scoring Posn	.237	131	31	2	3	2	44	10	27	.288	.344
vs. Right	.219	370	81	15	3	1	32	32	61	.287	.284	Close & Late	.210	100	21	4	2	0	13	10	17	.281	.290
Groundball	.230	135	31	9	0	0	13	4	20	.257	.296	None on/out	.231	143	33	8	1	0	0	4	17	.267	.301
Flyball	.220	200	44	8	2	2	18	14	31	.279	.310	Batting #2	.175	126	22	6	0	1	11	12	24	.245	.246
Home	.245	257	63	12	4	2	34	19	46	.301	.346	Batting #8	.259	212	55	11	2	2	21	17	32	.319	.358
Away	.203	276	56	11	1	2	18	23	42	.271	.272	Other	.215	195	42	6	3	1	20	13	32	.276	.292
Day	.164	128	21	1	1	1	10	9	21	.223	.211	April	.177	79	14	3	1	1	6	6	9	.235	.278
Night	.242	405	98	22	4	3	42	33	67	.305	.338	May	.206	102	21	5	1	0	11	11	20	.281	.275
Grass	.198	207	41	6	1	0	13	16	32	.258	.237	June	.275	91	25	5	1	1	12	7	14	.323	.385
Turf	.239	326	78	17	4	4	39	26	56	.303	.353	July	.230	100	23	2	1	0	7	9	11	.313	.270
First Pitch	.323	93	30	8	0	0	10	1	0	.326	.409	August	.212	66	14	2	0	1	7	6	12	.274	.288
Ahead on Count	.243	115	28	2	2	2	14	19	0	.348	.348	September/October	.232	95	22	6	1	1	9	3	22	.275	.347
Behind on Count	.236	165	39	8	2	1	17	0	42	.259	.327	Pre-All Star	.227	309	70	15	3	2	30	27	46	.289	.314
Two Strikes	.137	241	33	8	2	1	12	22	88	.223	.199	Post-All Star	.219	224	49	8	2	2	22	15	42	.280	.299

289

1992 By Position

Position	Avg	AB	H	2B	3B	HR	RBI	BB	SO	OBP	SLG	G	GS	Innings	PO	A	E	DP	Fld Pct	Rng Fctr	In Zone	Outs	Zone Rtg	MLB Zone
As cf	.222	528	117	23	5	4	52	42	87	.284	.307	148	143	1283.1	421	8	3	2	.993	3.01	484	406	.839	.824

Career (1990-1992)

	Avg	AB	H	2B	3B	HR	RBI	BB	SO	OBP	SLG		Avg	AB	H	2B	3B	HR	RBI	BB	SO	OBP	SLG
vs. Left	.282	439	124	25	4	6	52	22	50	.318	.399	Scoring Posn	.260	304	79	8	5	5	116	21	58	.302	.368
vs. Right	.232	891	207	34	13	8	87	53	166	.277	.327	Close & Late	.248	218	54	8	4	1	24	18	32	.303	.335
Groundball	.246	362	89	22	5	1	28	11	56	.269	.343	None on/out	.269	417	112	27	5	1	1	15	61	.299	.365
Flyball	.228	372	85	18	4	4	39	18	60	.270	.331	Batting #1	.239	574	137	17	8	6	54	29	90	.280	.328
Home	.264	656	173	34	12	6	78	42	111	.309	.380	Batting #2	.244	353	86	19	3	4	33	19	57	.280	.348
Away	.234	674	158	25	5	8	61	33	105	.272	.322	Other	.268	403	106	23	6	4	52	27	69	.315	.385
Day	.202	331	67	10	5	6	38	17	58	.241	.317	April	.164	128	21	4	1	2	14	6	20	.199	.258
Night	.264	999	264	49	12	8	101	58	158	.307	.361	May	.244	205	50	9	3	3	26	21	33	.313	.361
Grass	.239	506	121	16	4	4	44	22	78	.271	.310	June	.275	211	58	9	3	1	21	11	35	.308	.360
Turf	.255	824	210	43	13	10	95	53	138	.302	.375	July	.266	214	57	8	2	2	22	14	29	.319	.350
First Pitch	.273	209	57	14	1	1	23	1	0	.271	.364	August	.263	251	66	11	4	2	24	12	34	.299	.363
Ahead on Count	.269	280	81	12	6	6	34	39	0	.375	.439	September/October	.246	321	79	18	4	4	32	11	65	.276	.364
Behind on Count	.257	455	117	19	7	3	45	0	113	.267	.349	Pre-All Star	.243	614	149	26	8	6	65	41	98	.289	.340
Two Strikes	.186	601	112	19	6	2	37	35	248	.237	.248	Post-All Star	.254	716	182	33	9	8	74	34	118	.292	.359

Batter vs. Pitcher (career)

Hits Best Against	Avg	AB	H	2B	3B	HR	RBI	BB	SO	OBP	SLG	Hits Worst Against	Avg	AB	H	2B	3B	HR	RBI	BB	SO	OBP	SLG
Kevin Tapani	.563	16	9	1	0	1	4	0	4	.611	.813	Ron Darling	.000	12	0	0	0	0	0	0	4	.000	.000
Scott Scudder	.556	9	5	0	1	0	2	3	0	.667	.778	Scott Sanderson	.077	13	1	0	0	0	1	0	2	.077	.077
Greg Hibbard	.471	17	8	1	0	0	1	0	0	.471	.529	Jose Guzman	.077	13	1	0	0	0	0	0	2	.200	.077
David Wells	.462	13	6	2	0	0	0	0	0	.462	.615	Matt Young	.091	11	1	0	0	0	0	0	3	.091	.091
Chuck Finley	.333	27	9	1	0	2	8	4	3	.419	.593	Frank Viola	.111	9	1	0	0	0	3	0	0	.273	.111

Kevin McReynolds — Royals   Bats Right (flyball hitter)

	Avg	G	AB	R	H	2B	3B	HR	RBI	BB	SO	HBP	GDP	SB	CS	OBP	SLG	IBB	SH	SF	#Pit	#P/PA	GB	FB	G/F
1992 Season	.247	109	373	45	92	25	0	13	49	67	48	0	6	7	1	.357	.418	3	0	5	1859	4.18	100	162	0.62
Last Five Years	.268	694	2513	341	674	135	7	102	369	271	265	8	36	58	16	.338	.449	34	2	29	10216	3.62	734	1047	0.70

1992 Season

	Avg	AB	H	2B	3B	HR	RBI	BB	SO	OBP	SLG		Avg	AB	H	2B	3B	HR	RBI	BB	SO	OBP	SLG
vs. Left	.345	113	39	11	0	5	22	26	13	.461	.575	Scoring Posn	.224	85	19	2	0	1	29	21	15	.360	.282
vs. Right	.204	260	53	14	0	8	27	41	35	.309	.350	Close & Late	.236	72	17	5	0	4	8	13	12	.353	.472
Groundball	.275	91	25	7	0	2	8	17	7	.389	.418	None on/out	.195	87	17	7	0	3	3	15	12	.314	.379
Flyball	.204	137	28	9	0	4	12	26	20	.329	.358	Batting #4	.245	220	54	17	0	4	28	36	31	.349	.377
Home	.253	186	47	15	0	4	17	34	22	.363	.398	Batting #6	.229	109	25	6	0	6	14	22	13	.351	.450
Away	.241	187	45	10	0	9	32	33	26	.351	.439	Other	.295	44	13	2	0	3	7	9	4	.415	.545
Day	.232	82	19	2	0	4	11	15	17	.351	.402	April	.169	71	12	1	0	3	5	7	9	.244	.310
Night	.251	291	73	23	0	9	38	52	31	.359	.423	May	.267	86	23	8	0	4	14	23	6	.414	.500
Grass	.248	141	35	5	0	8	24	26	19	.361	.454	June	.280	93	26	7	0	1	13	12	16	.358	.387
Turf	.246	232	57	20	0	5	25	41	29	.355	.397	July	.242	91	22	6	0	5	15	22	13	.383	.473
First Pitch	.088	34	3	1	0	1	4	3	0	.162	.206	August	.000	6	0	0	0	0	0	1	1	.143	.000
Ahead on Count	.363	102	37	11	0	3	18	35	0	.518	.559	September/October	.346	26	9	3	0	0	2	2	3	.393	.462
Behind on Count	.184	103	19	5	0	5	12	0	21	.181	.379	Pre-All Star	.257	292	75	18	0	12	42	53	35	.367	.442
Two Strikes	.198	177	35	10	0	4	18	29	48	.306	.322	Post-All Star	.210	81	17	7	0	1	7	14	13	.323	.333

1992 By Position

Position	Avg	AB	H	2B	3B	HR	RBI	BB	SO	OBP	SLG	G	GS	Innings	PO	A	E	DP	Fld Pct	Rng Fctr	In Zone	Outs	Zone Rtg	MLB Zone
As lf	.260	319	83	24	0	12	47	62	41	.376	.448	94	92	818.0	184	4	2	0	.989	2.07	220	178	.809	.809
As rf	.191	47	9	1	0	1	2	4	5	.255	.277	12	12	109.2	19	0	1	0	.950	1.56	29	18	.621	.814

Last Five Years

	Avg	AB	H	2B	3B	HR	RBI	BB	SO	OBP	SLG		Avg	AB	H	2B	3B	HR	RBI	BB	SO	OBP	SLG
vs. Left	.275	870	239	49	5	37	116	113	85	.357	.470	Scoring Posn	.290	663	192	33	2	27	282	112	82	.380	.468
vs. Right	.265	1643	435	86	2	65	273	158	200	.328	.438	Close & Late	.287	443	127	22	0	24	79	46	57	.354	.499
Groundball	.266	841	224	39	4	21	124	85	87	.332	.397	None on/out	.247	632	156	33	2	25	25	59	67	.313	.424
Flyball	.257	560	149	30	1	28	79	67	77	.332	.457	Batting #4	.262	821	215	47	2	25	114	101	107	.342	.415
Home	.259	1219	316	61	2	47	174	127	123	.327	.428	Batting #5	.272	1286	350	64	5	57	206	122	134	.334	.463
Away	.277	1294	358	74	5	55	215	144	162	.342	.469	Other	.268	406	109	24	0	20	69	48	44	.342	.475
Day	.275	789	217	42	2	36	122	78	106	.342	.470	April	.246	313	77	11	0	11	39	30	33	.310	.387
Night	.265	1724	457	93	5	66	267	193	179	.336	.440	May	.267	449	120	26	1	14	61	59	41	.351	.423
Grass	.264	1655	437	81	3	75	255	159	180	.327	.453	June	.287	467	134	30	1	18	80	60	54	.368	.471
Turf	.276	858	237	54	4	27	134	112	105	.358	.443	July	.270	488	132	36	1	17	78	64	62	.351	.453
First Pitch	.300	327	98	16	1	18	49	12	0	.327	.520	August	.249	398	99	10	3	21	62	27	47	.293	.447
Ahead on Count	.332	590	196	39	3	32	116	150	0	.461	.571	September/October	.281	398	112	22	1	21	69	31	48	.335	.500
Behind on Count	.243	889	216	50	1	23	128	4	158	.244	.379	Pre-All Star	.271	1391	377	81	2	50	213	174	145	.350	.440
Two Strikes	.226	1038	235	53	2	30	138	96	264	.290	.322	Post-All Star	.265	1122	297	54	5	52	176	97	140	.322	.461

Batter vs. Pitcher (since 1984)

Hits Best Against	Avg	AB	H	2B	3B	HR	RBI	BB	SO	OBP	SLG	Hits Worst Against	Avg	AB	H	2B	3B	HR	RBI	BB	SO	OBP	SLG
Paul Assenmacher	.474	19	9	3	0	1	6	2	3	.524	.789	Derek Lilliquist	.067	15	1	0	0	0	1	2	2	.176	.067
Dave Smith	.438	16	7	1	0	3	9	1	2	.471	1.063	Dennis Cook	.071	14	1	0	0	0	1	2	3	.188	.071
Bruce Ruffin	.429	35	15	4	0	3	11	6	3	.512	.800	John Burkett	.083	12	1	0	0	0	0	0	0	.083	.083
Jeff Parrett	.375	24	9	1	1	3	8	4	2	.464	.875	Jose Rijo	.087	23	2	1	0	0	1	0	4	.083	.130
Jesse Orosco	.333	12	4	0	0	2	2	4	2	.500	.833	Danny Jackson	.091	22	2	0	0	0	1	2	5	.167	.091

Rusty Meacham — Royals   Pitches Right

	ERA	W	L	Sv	G	GS	IP	BB	SO	Avg	H	2B	3B	HR	RBI	OBP	SLG	GF	IR	IRS	Hld	SvOp	SB	CS	GB	FB	G/F
1992 Season	2.74	10	4	2	64	0	101.2	21	64	.233	88	15	3	5	47	.269	.328	20	55	17	15	6	0	1	156	111	1.41
Career (1991-1992)	3.27	12	5	2	74	4	129.1	32	78	.252	123	9	3	9	63	.292	.366	21	59	18	16	6	1	1	191	142	1.35

1992 Season

	ERA	W	L	Sv	G	GS	IP	H	HR	BB	SO		Avg	AB	H	2B	3B	HR	RBI	BB	SO	OBP	SLG
Home	3.81	6	0	1	34	0	54.1	53	4	7	29	vs. Left	.188	144	27	3	1	1	15	12	23	.247	.243
Away	1.52	4	4	1	30	0	47.1	35	1	14	35	vs. Right	.261	234	61	12	2	4	32	9	41	.283	.380
Day	2.16	1	0	0	10	0	16.2	13	0	6	14	Inning 1-6	.254	59	15	3	1	1	13	5	7	.294	.390
Night	2.86	9	4	2	54	0	85.0	75	5	15	50	Inning 7+	.229	319	73	12	2	4	34	16	57	.264	.317
Grass	1.85	3	4	1	24	0	39.0	29	1	13	31	None on	.205	205	42	7	2	2		9	34	.238	.288
Turf	3.30	7	0	1	40	0	62.2	59	4	8	33	Runners on	.266	173	46	8	1	3	45	12	30	.303	.376
April	1.23	0	0	0	5	0	7.1	6	1	2	3	Scoring Posn	.220	109	24	3	1	1	40	10	20	.266	.294
May	0.00	3	0	0	13	0	21.2	11	0	2	15	Close & Late	.237	194	46	7	0	3	16	9	36	.273	.320
June	2.41	1	1	0	13	0	18.2	13	1	2	9	None on/out	.181	83	15	2	1	0	0	5	10	.227	.229
July	3.79	1	2	2	12	0	19.0	22	1	4	11	vs. 1st Batr (relief)	.250	56	14	4	0	1	8	4	7	.281	.375
August	2.29	3	1	0	11	0	19.2	21	2	7	13	First Inning Pitched	.212	212	45	9	2	3	31	12	38	.246	.316
September/October	7.04	0	0	0	10	0	15.1	15	0	4	13	First 15 Pitches	.224	210	47	7	2	3	25	9	36	.248	.319
Starter	0.00	0	0	0	0	0	0.0	0	0	0	0	Pitch 16-30	.230	113	26	6	1	1	12	10	20	.296	.327
Reliever	2.74	10	4	2	64	0	101.2	88	5	21	64	Pitch 31-45	.245	49	12	2	0	0	8	2	8	.269	.286
0 Days rest	2.61	1	1	0	14	0	20.2	19	0	6	13	Pitch 46+	.500	6	3	0	0	1	2	0	0	.500	1.000
1 or 2 Days rest	2.66	4	3	2	32	0	50.2	41	4	11	38	First Pitch	.222	54	12	2	0	0	4	5	0	.279	.259
3+ Days rest	2.97	5	0	0	18	0	30.1	28	1	4	13	Ahead on Count	.220	164	36	3	2	2	19	0	55	.219	.299
Pre-All Star	1.79	4	2	1	35	0	55.1	42	2	10	31	Behind on Count	.250	96	24	6	1	2	17	7	0	.295	.396
Post-All Star	3.88	6	2	1	29	0	46.1	46	3	11	33	Two Strikes	.218	156	34	6	1	1	17	9	64	.257	.288

Jose Melendez — Padres   Pitches Right (flyball pitcher)

	ERA	W	L	Sv	G	GS	IP	BB	SO	Avg	H	2B	3B	HR	RBI	OBP	SLG	GF	IR	IRS	Hld	SvOp	SB	CS	GB	FB	G/F
1992 Season	2.92	6	7	0	56	3	89.1	20	82	.249	82	9	0	9	42	.295	.359	18	38	16	4	2	3	4	84	101	0.83
Career (1990-1992)	3.35	14	12	3	90	12	188.1	47	149	.238	167	26	1	22	81	.287	.372	29	47	19	6	6	5	10	186	240	0.78

1992 Season

	ERA	W	L	Sv	G	GS	IP	H	HR	BB	SO		Avg	AB	H	2B	3B	HR	RBI	BB	SO	OBP	SLG
Home	3.51	2	4	0	28	2	51.1	55	8	11	49	vs. Left	.281	160	45	4	0	6	22	15	34	.341	.419
Away	2.13	4	3	0	28	1	38.0	27	1	9	33	vs. Right	.219	169	37	5	0	3	20	5	48	.249	.302
Starter	8.59	0	3	0	3	3	14.2	20	5	2	12	Scoring Posn	.316	76	24	2	0	0	30	10	19	.385	.342
Reliever	1.81	6	4	0	53	0	74.2	62	4	18	70	Close & Late	.215	107	23	3	0	0	8	10	29	.286	.243
0 Days rest	2.60	2	1	0	10	0	17.1	16	2	5	20	None on/out	.247	81	20	3	0	3	3	3	24	.291	.395
1 or 2 Days rest	1.95	1	3	0	29	0	37.0	28	2	8	29	First Pitch	.390	41	16	1	0	2	8	7	0	.490	.561
3+ Days rest	0.89	3	0	0	14	0	20.1	18	0	5	21	Behind on Count	.238	42	10	0	0	0	3	6	1	.327	.238
Pre-All Star	3.09	5	6	0	36	3	64.0	51	8	13	59	Ahead on Count	.211	199	42	8	0	4	20	0	76	.216	.312
Post-All Star	2.49	1	1	0	20	0	25.1	31	1	7	23	Two Strikes	.198	182	36	7	0	4	19	7	81	.232	.302

Bob Melvin — Royals   Bats Right (groundball hitter)

	Avg	G	AB	R	H	2B	3B	HR	RBI	BB	SO	HBP	GDP	SB	CS	OBP	SLG	IBB	SH	SF	#Pit	#P/PA	GB	FB	G/F
1992 Season	.314	32	70	5	22	5	0	0	6	5	13	0	3	0	0	.351	.386	0	0	2	276	3.58	29	14	2.07
Last Five Years	.246	381	1150	91	283	52	3	15	125	55	211	0	31	1	7	278	.336	6	12	12	4129	3.39	452	285	1.59

1992 Season

	Avg	AB	H	2B	3B	HR	RBI	BB	SO	OBP	SLG		Avg	AB	H	2B	3B	HR	RBI	BB	SO	OBP	SLG
vs. Left	.360	50	18	4	0	0	5	5	7	.411	.440	Scoring Posn	.211	19	4	1	0	0	6	2	4	.261	.263
vs. Right	.200	20	4	1	0	0	1	0	6	.190	.250	Close & Late	.059	17	1	0	0	0	1	1	6	.105	.059

Last Five Years

	Avg	AB	H	2B	3B	HR	RBI	BB	SO	OBP	SLG		Avg	AB	H	2B	3B	HR	RBI	BB	SO	OBP	SLG
vs. Left	.291	516	150	34	1	7	58	36	89	.333	.401	Scoring Posn	.264	311	82	11	3	5	107	17	59	.291	.367
vs. Right	.210	634	133	18	2	8	67	19	142	.231	.282	Close & Late	.209	191	40	3	1	2	18	12	37	.252	.267
Groundball	.235	298	70	8	1	4	33	10	19	.278	.309	None on/out	.215	297	64	14	0	3		13	59	.248	.293
Flyball	.237	299	71	13	0	3	30	14	61	.269	.311	Batting #7	.247	385	95	22	2	7	45	21	64	.285	.369
Home	.226	563	127	19	2	7	60	24	118	.254	.304	Batting #8	.243	424	103	17	1	5	43	18	89	.270	.323
Away	.266	587	156	33	1	8	65	31	93	.300	.366	Other	.249	341	85	13	0	3	37	16	58	.273	.314
Day	.261	375	98	25	2	8	48	15	56	.287	.403	April	.224	152	34	8	0	4	14	5	41	.247	.355
Night	.239	775	185	27	1	7	77	40	155	.273	.303	May	.251	223	56	9	0	3	26	13	27	.291	.332

Last Five Years

	Avg	AB	H	2B	3B	HR	RBI	BB	SO	OBP	SLG		Avg	AB	H	2B	3B	HR	RBI	BB	SO	OBP	SLG
Grass	.230	907	209	34	3	13	103	44	171	.263	.318	June	.280	168	47	8	0	1	22	9	38	.315	.345
Turf	.305	243	74	18	0	2	22	11	40	.332	.403	July	.232	190	44	8	2	2	26	8	37	.259	.326
First Pitch	.307	176	54	8	2	1	26	4	0	.317	.392	August	.267	221	59	9	1	4	24	13	36	.304	.371
Ahead on Count	.298	255	76	15	1	7	41	23	0	.354	.447	September/October	.219	196	43	10	0	1	13	7	34	.243	.286
Behind on Count	.200	420	84	16	0	3	30	0	138	.198	.260	Pre-All Star	.253	598	151	29	0	9	74	31	116	.287	.346
Two Strikes	.182	488	89	22	0	1	34	28	210	.225	.234	Post-All Star	.239	552	132	23	3	6	51	24	95	.268	.324

Batter vs. Pitcher (career)

Hits Best Against	Avg	AB	H	2B	3B	HR	RBI	BB	SO	OBP	SLG	Hits Worst Against	Avg	AB	H	2B	3B	HR	RBI	BB	SO	OBP	SLG
Bill Gullickson	.500	10	5	1	0	0	0	1	2	.545	.600	Greg Maddux	.000	11	0	0	0	0	0	1	4	.083	.000
Bobby Ojeda	.455	11	5	0	1	1	3	1	1	.462	.909	Kevin Gross	.000	10	0	0	0	0	0	1	4	.091	.000
Greg Mathews	.455	11	5	1	0	0	2	1	0	.500	.545	Bud Black	.083	12	1	0	0	0	0	1	3	.083	.083
Jim Deshaies	.444	9	4	2	0	0	1	1	0	.455	.667	Terry Leach	.100	10	1	0	0	0	2	1	2	.182	.100
Scott Sanderson	.400	15	6	1	0	1	5	1	1	.438	.667	Tim Leary	.133	15	2	0	0	0	0	1	3	.133	.133

Tony Menendez — Reds   Pitches Right (flyball pitcher)

	ERA	W	L	Sv	G	GS	IP	BB	SO	Avg	H	2B	3B	HR	RBI	OBP	SLG	GF	IR	IRS	Hld	SvOp	SB	CS	GB	FB	G/F
1992 Season	1.93	1	0	0	3	0	4.2	0	5	.067	1	0	0	0	1	.067	.267	1	0	0	0	0	0	0	2	7	0.29

1992 Season

	ERA	W	L	Sv	G	GS	IP	H	HR	BB	SO		Avg	AB	H	2B	3B	HR	RBI	BB	SO	OBP	SLG
Home	3.38	0	0	0	1	0	2.2	1	1	0	1	vs. Left	.000	4	0	0	0	0	0	0	1	.000	.000
Away	0.00	1	0	0	2	0	2.0	0	0	0	4	vs. Right	.091	11	1	0	0	1	1	0	4	.091	.364

Orlando Merced — Pirates   Bats Both (groundball hitter)

	Avg	G	AB	R	H	2B	3B	HR	RBI	BB	SO	HBP	GDP	SB	CS	OBP	SLG	IBB	SH	SF	#Pit	#P/PA	GB	FB	G/F
1992 Season	.247	134	405	50	100	28	5	6	60	52	63	2	6	5	4	.332	.385	8	1	5	1726	3.72	160	122	1.31
Career (1990-1992)	.260	279	840	136	218	46	7	16	110	117	153	3	13	13	8	.350	.388	12	2	6	3833	3.97	343	218	1.57

1992 Season

	Avg	AB	H	2B	3B	HR	RBI	BB	SO	OBP	SLG		Avg	AB	H	2B	3B	HR	RBI	BB	SO	OBP	SLG
vs. Left	.190	84	16	3	0	0	7	14	11	.306	.226	Scoring Posn	.289	121	35	8	2	2	53	22	11	.389	.438
vs. Right	.262	321	84	25	5	6	53	38	52	.339	.427	Close & Late	.233	86	20	9	0	1	14	11	16	.320	.372
Groundball	.258	155	40	10	2	2	21	10	12	.356	.387	None on/out	.263	99	26	8	3	1	1	8	21	.318	.434
Flyball	.255	98	25	8	1	3	17	10	12	.327	.449	Batting #1	.276	87	24	8	2	0	11	15	14	.379	.414
Home	.251	199	50	15	2	4	25	29	27	.345	.407	Batting #5	.211	171	36	8	0	2	23	23	26	.302	.292
Away	.243	206	50	13	3	2	35	23	36	.319	.364	Other	.272	147	40	12	3	4	26	14	23	.340	.476
Day	.296	115	34	8	1	1	21	16	14	.377	.409	April	.195	41	8	1	0	0	5	11	7	.370	.220
Night	.228	290	66	20	4	5	39	36	49	.313	.376	May	.264	72	19	9	1	0	7	10	12	.349	.417
Grass	.213	108	23	7	0	0	12	12	22	.293	.278	June	.250	76	19	5	2	3	13	5	9	.296	.487
Turf	.259	297	77	21	5	6	48	40	41	.346	.424	July	.222	72	16	4	0	2	10	4	10	.260	.361
First Pitch	.404	47	19	8	0	0	8	5	0	.453	.574	August	.210	62	13	2	1	0	11	11	15	.320	.274
Ahead on Count	.333	105	35	11	2	3	27	27	0	.467	.562	September/October	.305	82	25	7	1	1	14	11	10	.394	.402
Behind on Count	.197	122	24	3	3	2	20	0	35	.200	.320	Pre-All Star	.249	217	54	17	3	5	30	27	33	.332	.424
Two Strikes	.160	169	27	7	1	2	18	21	63	.251	.249	Post-All Star	.245	188	46	11	2	1	30	25	30	.332	.340

1992 By Position

Position	Avg	AB	H	2B	3B	HR	RBI	BB	SO	OBP	SLG	G	GS	Innings	PO	A	E	DP	Fld Pct	Rng Fctr	In Zone	Outs	Zone Rtg	MLB Zone
As Pinch Hitter	.400	25	10	4	1	0	11	6	2	.516	.640	31	0	---	---	---	---	---	---	---	---	---	---	---
As 1b	.245	335	82	22	4	6	47	40	53	.325	.388	114	87	834.1	882	73	5	73	.995	---	178	152	.854	.843
As rf	.178	45	8	2	0	0	2	6	8	.275	.222	17	11	112.2	23	3	0	1	1.000	2.08	34	24	.706	.814

Career (1990-1992)

	Avg	AB	H	2B	3B	HR	RBI	BB	SO	OBP	SLG		Avg	AB	H	2B	3B	HR	RBI	BB	SO	OBP	SLG
vs. Left	.193	145	28	6	1	0	13	17	26	.262	.248	Scoring Posn	.302	222	67	15	3	8	99	32	39	.383	.505
vs. Right	.273	695	190	40	6	16	97	100	127	.364	.417	Close & Late	.232	155	36	13	0	4	26	27	35	.344	.394
Groundball	.239	301	72	16	2	2	28	45	68	.338	.326	None on/out	.245	277	68	16	4	1	1	38	49	.337	.343
Flyball	.235	196	46	9	1	6	26	31	35	.343	.383	Batting #1	.275	461	127	25	4	9	56	75	90	.377	.406
Home	.253	403	102	25	3	9	47	65	73	.356	.397	Batting #5	.205	176	36	8	0	2	23	23	27	.294	.284
Away	.265	437	116	21	4	7	63	52	80	.344	.380	Other	.271	203	55	13	3	5	31	19	36	.336	.438
Day	.297	236	70	14	3	5	46	36	40	.388	.445	April	.238	63	15	1	1	0	8	17	12	.402	.286
Night	.245	604	148	32	4	11	64	81	113	.334	.366	May	.312	141	44	11	3	4	19	20	26	.399	.518
Grass	.266	222	59	10	1	3	29	20	42	.325	.360	June	.205	146	30	7	2	3	15	13	26	.269	.342
Turf	.257	618	159	36	6	13	81	97	111	.358	.398	July	.269	167	45	7	1	4	22	20	30	.346	.395
First Pitch	.368	76	28	10	1	0	14	8	0	.424	.526	August	.247	154	38	8	1	1	22	23	32	.341	.331
Ahead on Count	.355	200	71	17	3	5	39	62	0	.504	.545	September/October	.272	169	46	8	1	4	24	24	27	.366	.402
Behind on Count	.202	257	52	6	3	4	28	1	78	.210	.296	Pre-All Star	.266	417	111	27	5	11	56	54	77	.351	.434
Two Strikes	.171	398	68	14	1	7	35	47	153	.260	.264	Post-All Star	.253	423	107	19	2	5	54	63	76	.349	.343

Batter vs. Pitcher (career)

Hits Best Against	Avg	AB	H	2B	3B	HR	RBI	BB	SO	OBP	SLG	Hits Worst Against	Avg	AB	H	2B	3B	HR	RBI	BB	SO	OBP	SLG
Mark Portugal	.600	10	6	1	1	1	3	1	0	.636	1.200	John Burkett	.056	18	1	0	0	0	1	1	4	.105	.056

Batter vs. Pitcher (career)																					
Hits Best Against	Avg	AB	H	2B	3B	HR	RBI	BB	SO	OBP	SLG	Hits Worst Against	Avg	AB	H	2B	3B	HR	RBI	BB	SO	OBP	SLG
Jimmy Jones	.462	13	6	2	0	1	1	2	2	.533	.846	Kevin Gross	.100	10	1	0	0	0	1	1	1	.182	.100
Jose Rijo	.455	11	5	2	0	0	1	1	2	.500	.636	David Cone	.125	16	2	0	0	1	1	1	5	.176	.125
Bob Tewksbury	.391	23	9	2	1	1	3	0	3	.391	.696	Mark Clark	.182	11	2	1	0	0	3	0	1	.167	.273
John Smoltz	.375	16	6	1	0	1	1	2	2	.444	.625	Greg Maddux	.200	20	4	1	0	0	0	1	5	.304	.250

Henry Mercedes — Athletics

Bats Right

	Avg	G	AB	R	H	2B	3B	HR	RBI	BB	SO	HBP	GDP	SB	CS	OBP	SLG	IBB	SH	SF	#Pit	#P/PA	GB	FB	G/F
1992 Season	.800	9	5	1	4	0	1	0	1	0	1	0	0	0	0	.800	1.200	0	0	0	19	3.80	2	2	1.00

1992 Season

	Avg	AB	H	2B	3B	HR	RBI	BB	SO	OBP	SLG		Avg	AB	H	2B	3B	HR	RBI	BB	SO	OBP	SLG
vs. Left	1.000	2	2	0	0	0	0	0	0	1.000	1.000	Scoring Posn	.000	0	0	0	0	0	0	0	0	.000	.000
vs. Right	.667	3	2	0	1	0	1	0	1	.667	1.333	Close & Late	1.000	1	1	0	1	0	1	0	0	1.000	3.000

Luis Mercedes — Orioles

Bats Right (groundball hitter)

	Avg	G	AB	R	H	2B	3B	HR	RBI	BB	SO	HBP	GDP	SB	CS	OBP	SLG	IBB	SH	SF	#Pit	#P/PA	GB	FB	G/F
1992 Season	.140	23	50	7	7	2	0	0	4	8	9	1	2	0	1	.267	.180	0	2	1	243	4.05	26	9	2.89
Career (1991-1992)	.173	42	104	17	18	4	0	0	6	12	18	1	3	0	1	.263	.212	0	3	1	480	4.07	49	16	3.06

1992 Season

	Avg	AB	H	2B	3B	HR	RBI	BB	SO	OBP	SLG		Avg	AB	H	2B	3B	HR	RBI	BB	SO	OBP	SLG
vs. Left	.167	36	6	2	0	0	4	5	4	.279	.222	Scoring Posn	.167	12	2	0	0	0	4	2	3	.267	.167
vs. Right	.071	14	1	0	0	0	3	5	.235	.071		Close & Late	.125	8	1	0	0	0	0	0	2	.125	.125

Kent Mercker — Braves

Pitches Left

	ERA	W	L	Sv	G	GS	IP	BB	SO	Avg	H	2B	3B	HR	RBI	OBP	SLG	GF	IR	IRS	Hld	SvOp	SB	CS	GB	FB	G/F
1992 Season	3.42	3	2	6	53	0	68.1	35	49	.207	51	10	0	4	32	.312	.297	18	22	9	6	9	12	2	77	75	1.03
Career (1989-1992)	3.24	12	12	19	141	5	194.1	100	154	.221	158	28	3	15	84	.320	.332	74	50	21	9	27	28	6	233	212	1.10

1992 Season

	ERA	W	L	Sv	G	GS	IP	H	HR	BB	SO		Avg	AB	H	2B	3B	HR	RBI	BB	SO	OBP	SLG
Home	4.35	2	1	4	30	0	41.1	31	3	21	30	vs. Left	.260	73	19	4	0	1	11	9	18	.337	.356
Away	2.00	1	1	2	23	0	27.0	20	1	14	19	vs. Right	.185	173	32	6	0	3	21	26	31	.302	.272
Starter	0.00	0	0	0	0	0	0.0	0	0	0	0	Scoring Posn	.324	71	23	4	0	3	31	14	13	.437	.507
Reliever	3.42	3	2	6	53	0	68.1	51	4	35	49	Close & Late	.202	99	20	4	0	0	9	14	19	.298	.242
0 Days rest	2.61	1	0	4	9	0	10.1	6	0	4	12	None on/out	.183	60	11	2	0	0	5	12	.269	.217
1 or 2 Days rest	1.57	1	0	2	25	0	34.1	23	0	14	20	First Pitch	.273	33	9	2	0	0	4	1	0	.294	.333
3+ Days rest	6.46	1	2	0	19	0	23.2	22	4	17	17	Behind on Count	.327	49	16	3	0	2	12	16	0	.492	.510
Pre-All Star	2.08	3	0	3	29	0	43.1	30	3	19	36	Ahead on Count	.124	113	14	3	0	1	6	0	40	.145	.177
Post-All Star	5.76	0	2	3	24	0	25.0	21	1	16	13	Two Strikes	.145	131	19	3	0	2	11	18	49	.261	.214

Career (1989-1992)

	ERA	W	L	Sv	G	GS	IP	H	HR	BB	SO		Avg	AB	H	2B	3B	HR	RBI	BB	SO	OBP	SLG
Home	3.48	9	4	14	74	1	101.0	85	7	50	77	vs. Left	.231	195	45	7	0	3	19	31	50	.333	.313
Away	2.99	3	8	5	67	4	93.1	73	8	50	77	vs. Right	.218	519	113	21	3	12	65	69	104	.315	.339
Day	2.47	4	5	3	34	1	43.2	39	2	20	36	Inning 1-6	.195	164	32	7	1	3	21	25	42	.307	.305
Night	3.46	8	7	16	107	4	150.2	119	13	80	118	Inning 7+	.229	550	126	21	2	12	63	75	112	.324	.340
Grass	3.53	11	10	15	104	3	142.2	126	12	76	103	None on	.199	392	78	17	3	7	7	56	86	.304	.311
Turf	2.44	1	2	4	37	2	51.2	32	3	24	51	Runners on	.248	322	80	11	0	8	77	44	68	.340	.357
April	3.44	0	1	1	12	0	18.1	10	3	10	13	Scoring Posn	.276	196	54	9	0	6	72	34	43	.382	.413
May	2.08	3	1	2	21	0	30.1	25	3	9	28	Close & Late	.223	318	71	9	1	8	36	47	68	.324	.333
June	1.23	3	1	3	22	0	22.0	15	0	12	24	None on/out	.164	165	27	7	2	1	1	26	36	.285	.248
July	1.94	5	2	6	33	0	46.1	36	3	25	32	vs. 1st Batr (relief)	.195	113	22	5	1	2	15	21	29	.324	.310
August	4.78	0	3	4	26	0	32.0	30	3	12	28	First Inning Pitched	.202	455	92	16	2	8	51	58	105	.296	.299
September/October	5.16	1	4	3	27	5	45.1	42	3	32	29	First 15 Pitches	.202	382	77	14	1	8	35	49	86	.296	.306
Starter	3.74	1	0	0	5	5	21.2	15	0	14	20	Pitch 16-30	.218	206	45	7	1	4	27	30	45	.325	.320
Reliever	3.18	11	12	19	136	0	172.2	143	15	86	134	Pitch 31-45	.352	71	25	4	1	1	15	12	13	.435	.479
0 Days rest	2.56	3	5	8	29	0	31.2	25	4	17	30	Pitch 46+	.200	55	11	3	0	2	7	9	10	.313	.364
1 or 2 Days rest	2.24	4	3	10	60	0	84.1	60	5	39	60	First Pitch	.282	78	22	6	0	2	12	4	0	.317	.436
3+ Days rest	4.92	4	4	1	47	0	56.2	58	6	30	44	Ahead on Count	.164	360	59	12	2	4	25	0	135	.177	.242
Pre-All Star	1.92	8	3	7	65	0	84.1	61	7	36	76	Behind on Count	.268	138	37	6	0	3	23	48	0	.455	.377
Post-All Star	4.25	4	9	12	76	5	110.0	97	8	64	78	Two Strikes	.167	390	65	9	2	9	34	48	154	.264	.269

Pitcher vs. Batter (career)																					
Pitches Best Vs.	Avg	AB	H	2B	3B	HR	RBI	BB	SO	OBP	SLG	Pitches Worst Vs.	Avg	AB	H	2B	3B	HR	RBI	BB	SO	OBP	SLG
Barry Bonds	.091	11	1	0	0	0	0	0	4	.091	.091												

293

Matt Merullo — White Sox — Bats Left (flyball hitter)

	Avg	G	AB	R	H	2B	3B	HR	RBI	BB	SO	HBP	GDP	SB	CS	OBP	SLG	IBB	SH	SF	#Pit	#P/PA	GB	FB	G/F
1992 Season	.180	24	50	3	9	1	1	0	3	1	8	1	0	0	0	.208	.240	0	0	1	175	3.30	16	17	0.94
Career (1989-1992)	.218	135	271	16	59	3	1	6	32	16	40	1	3	0	1	.259	.303	1	3	6	958	3.26	80	100	0.80

1992 Season

	Avg	AB	H	2B	3B	HR	RBI	BB	SO	OBP	SLG		Avg	AB	H	2B	3B	HR	RBI	BB	SO	OBP	SLG
vs. Left	.333	3	1	0	0	0	0	0	0	.333	.333	Scoring Posn	.200	15	3	0	0	0	3	1	3	.278	.200
vs. Right	.170	47	8	1	1	0	3	1	8	.200	.234	Close & Late	.100	10	1	0	0	0	0	1	0	.250	.100

Jose Mesa — Indians — Pitches Right (flyball pitcher)

	ERA	W	L	Sv	G	GS	IP	BB	SO	Avg	H	2B	3B	HR	RBI	OBP	SLG	CG	ShO	Sup	QS	#P/S	SB	CS	GB	FB	G/F
1992 Season	4.59	7	12	0	28	27	160.2	70	62	.273	169	33	1	14	69	.348	.397	1	1	4.54	13	95	14	8	205	226	0.91
Last Five Years	5.00	16	25	0	58	57	331.0	159	150	.279	279	75	3	27	152	.359	.405	3	2	4.84	25	94	27	14	431	444	0.97

1992 Season

	ERA	W	L	Sv	G	GS	IP	H	HR	BB	SO		Avg	AB	H	2B	3B	HR	RBI	BB	SO	OBP	SLG
Home	4.40	2	5	0	14	13	77.2	84	6	32	26	vs. Left	.305	328	100	19	0	8	33	29	23	.363	.436
Away	4.77	5	7	0	14	14	83.0	85	8	38	36	vs. Right	.237	291	69	14	1	6	36	41	39	.332	.354
Day	5.99	1	8	0	13	13	73.2	87	12	27	28	Inning 1-6	.268	553	148	28	1	12	64	61	56	.342	.387
Night	3.41	6	4	0	15	14	87.0	82	2	43	34	Inning 7+	.318	66	21	5	0	2	5	9	6	.400	.485
Grass	4.98	4	9	0	22	21	123.0	130	11	60	44	None on	.247	360	89	19	1	9	9	42	34	.328	.381
Turf	3.35	3	3	0	6	6	37.2	39	3	10	18	Runners on	.309	259	80	14	0	5	60	28	28	.376	.421
April	3.26	1	2	0	3	3	19.1	23	3	3	9	Scoring Posn	.298	151	45	10	0	3	55	16	16	.358	.424
May	6.75	1	3	0	5	5	24.0	29	5	15	8	Close & Late	.297	37	11	2	0	1	3	3	5	.350	.432
June	5.32	1	3	0	4	4	22.0	23	1	5	5	None on/out	.263	167	44	13	0	3		11	17	.313	.395
July	1.96	1	1	0	4	3	23.0	20	1	9	9	vs. 1st Batr (relief)	.000	1	0	0	0	0	0	0	0	.000	.000
August	4.38	1	1	0	6	6	37.0	36	2	20	15	First Inning Pitched	.230	100	23	6	0	2	12	14	12	.325	.350
September/October	5.35	2	2	0	6	6	35.1	38	2	16	16	First 75 Pitches	.264	469	124	25	1	10	48	56	47	.345	.386
Starter	4.60	7	12	0	27	27	158.1	167	14	66	62	Pitch 76-90	.300	80	24	5	0	2	16	5	8	.337	.438
Reliever	3.86	0	0	0	1	0	2.1	2	0	4	0	Pitch 91-105	.275	40	11	1	0	1	2	8	5	.396	.375
0-3 Days Rest	0.00	0	0	0	0	0	0.0	0	0	0	0	Pitch 106+	.333	30	10	2	0	1	3	1	2	.355	.500
4 Days Rest	4.06	3	4	0	12	12	75.1	76	5	29	27	First Pitch	.220	91	20	5	1	4	12	1	0	.242	.429
5+ Days Rest	5.10	4	8	0	15	15	83.0	91	9	37	35	Ahead on Count	.241	261	63	8	0	3	19	0	52	.243	.307
Pre-All Star	5.19	3	8	0	13	12	67.2	77	9	27	22	Behind on Count	.326	138	45	12	0	4	21	40	0	.470	.500
Post-All Star	4.16	4	4	0	15	15	93.0	92	5	43	40	Two Strikes	.238	261	62	9	0	6	22	29	62	.315	.341

Last Five Years

	ERA	W	L	Sv	G	GS	IP	H	HR	BB	SO		Avg	AB	H	2B	3B	HR	RBI	BB	SO	OBP	SLG
Home	4.85	6	14	0	30	29	163.1	169	12	81	72	vs. Left	.292	677	198	37	0	12	71	79	61	.366	.400
Away	5.15	10	11	0	28	28	167.2	188	15	78	78	vs. Right	.263	604	159	36	3	15	81	80	89	.351	.411
Day	5.43	3	10	0	19	19	109.1	125	13	43	52	Inning 1-6	.278	1155	321	67	3	25	142	141	139	.357	.406
Night	4.79	13	15	0	39	38	221.2	232	14	116	98	Inning 7+	.286	126	36	8	0	2	10	18	11	.375	.397
Grass	5.07	11	21	0	47	46	264.2	282	21	133	122	None on	.254	729	185	38	2	14	14	93	79	.341	.369
Turf	4.75	5	4	0	11	11	66.1	75	6	26	28	Runners on	.312	552	172	37	1	13	138	66	71	.382	.453
April	3.30	2	5	0	7	7	43.2	45	4	14	26	Scoring Posn	.316	310	98	22	1	8	123	41	38	.386	.471
May	5.27	4	5	0	12	12	68.1	77	8	37	23	Close & Late	.250	60	15	3	0	1	3	9	6	.348	.350
June	8.34	1	6	0	9	9	41.0	58	4	16	13	None on/out	.277	339	94	19	0	8	8	32	33	.341	.404
July	1.96	1	1	0	4	3	23.0	20	1	9	9	vs. 1st Batr (relief)	.000	1	0	0	0	0	0	0	0	.000	.000
August	5.08	2	2	0	9	9	56.2	52	7	27	29	First Inning Pitched	.256	215	55	16	0	3	32	34	29	.357	.372
September/October	4.85	6	6	0	17	17	98.1	105	3	56	50	First 75 Pitches	.276	960	265	55	3	22	114	118	114	.357	.408
Starter	5.01	16	25	0	57	57	326.2	355	27	155	150	Pitch 76-90	.284	162	46	12	0	3	25	19	19	.355	.414
Reliever	3.86	0	0	0	1	0	2.1	2	0	4	0	Pitch 91-105	.272	92	25	4	0	1	7	19	12	.396	.348
0-3 Days Rest	0.00	0	0	0	0	0	0.0	0	0	0	0	Pitch 106+	.313	67	21	4	0	1	6	3	5	.343	.418
4 Days Rest	4.97	9	12	0	30	30	177.1	187	13	87	73	First Pitch	.297	192	57	12	2	7	30	4	0	.312	.490
5+ Days Rest	5.06	7	13	0	27	27	151.1	168	14	68	77	Ahead on Count	.250	537	134	28	0	9	53	1	126	.256	.352
Pre-All Star	5.50	7	16	0	29	28	155.1	182	16	71	62	Behind on Count	.327	284	93	24	1	6	44	89	0	.483	.482
Post-All Star	4.56	9	9	0	29	29	175.2	175	11	88	88	Two Strikes	.230	540	124	21	0	12	50	66	150	.315	.335

Pitcher vs. Batter (career)

Pitches Best Vs.	Avg	AB	H	2B	3B	HR	RBI	BB	SO	OBP	SLG	Pitches Worst Vs.	Avg	AB	H	2B	3B	HR	RBI	BB	SO	OBP	SLG
Matt Nokes	.000	15	0	0	0	0	0	2	2	.118	.000	Greg Briley	.636	11	7	2	0	0	0	0	0	.636	.818
Edgar Martinez	.000	10	0	0	0	0	0	0	2	.167	.000	Gregg Jefferies	.615	13	8	2	0	1	1	0	0	.615	1.000
Rafael Palmeiro	.000	9	0	0	0	0	2	3	1	.214	.000	Kevin Maas	.615	13	8	1	0	1	2	0	1	.615	.923
Tim Raines	.091	11	1	0	0	0	0	0	0	.091	.091	Rickey Henderson	.600	5	3	0	0	0	0	6	0	.818	.600
John Olerud	.100	10	1	0	0	0	0	0	0	.182	.100	Kevin Reimer	.364	11	4	0	0	3	5	1	2	.500	1.182

Hensley Meulens — Yankees
Bats Right (groundball hitter)

	Avg	G	AB	R	H	2B	3B	HR	RBI	BB	SO	HBP	GDP	SB	CS	OBP	SLG	IBB	SH	SF	#Pit	#P/PA	GB	FB	G/F
1992 Season	.600	2	5	1	3	0	0	1	1	1	0	0	1	0	0	.667	1.200	0	0	0	22	3.67	2	3	0.67
Career (1989-1992)	.228	129	404	52	92	15	1	10	41	30	130	7	13	4	1	.291	.344	1	1	2	1698	3.83	141	81	1.74

1992 Season

	Avg	AB	H	2B	3B	HR	RBI	BB	SO	OBP	SLG		Avg	AB	H	2B	3B	HR	RBI	BB	SO	OBP	SLG
vs. Left	.000	0	0	0	0	0	0	0	0	.000	.000	Scoring Posn	.000	0	0	0	0	0	0	0	0	.000	.000
vs. Right	.600	5	3	0	0	1	1	1	0	.667	1.200	Close & Late	.000	0	0	0	0	0	0	0	0	.000	.000

Career (1989-1992)

	Avg	AB	H	2B	3B	HR	RBI	BB	SO	OBP	SLG		Avg	AB	H	2B	3B	HR	RBI	BB	SO	OBP	SLG
vs. Left	.243	214	52	9	1	6	24	14	64	.300	.379	Scoring Posn	.234	94	22	3	1	2	31	6	27	.295	.351
vs. Right	.211	190	40	6	0	4	17	16	66	.281	.305	Close & Late	.212	52	11	2	0	0	4	2	17	.268	.250
Groundball	.165	91	15	4	0	1	3	6	34	.240	.242	None on/out	.211	114	24	2	0	3	3	8	38	.268	.307
Flyball	.239	92	22	3	0	4	18	9	29	.304	.402	Batting #5	.177	96	17	1	1	2	12	6	36	.223	.271
Home	.239	234	56	11	0	7	23	15	73	.292	.376	Batting #6	.270	174	47	10	0	6	19	11	48	.335	.431
Away	.212	170	36	4	1	3	18	15	57	.289	.300	Other	.209	134	28	4	0	2	10	13	46	.282	.284
Day	.238	130	31	4	1	0	11	10	33	.296	.285	April	.205	44	9	0	1	0	4	3	16	.255	.250
Night	.223	274	61	11	0	10	30	20	97	.289	.372	May	.220	59	13	2	0	3	6	3	23	.258	.407
Grass	.216	356	77	12	1	8	35	26	111	.281	.323	June	.282	39	11	1	0	0	6	1	12	.300	.308
Turf	.313	48	15	3	0	2	6	4	19	.365	.500	July	.191	47	9	1	0	2	3	3	18	.255	.340
First Pitch	.302	53	16	4	0	2	1	0		.339	.377	August	.205	78	16	1	0	0	9	6	22	.264	.218
Ahead on Count	.379	66	25	1	0	5	13	16	0	.506	.621	September/October	.248	137	34	10	0	5	13	14	39	.340	.431
Behind on Count	.154	149	23	7	0	4	16	0	69	.166	.282	Pre-All Star	.225	151	34	3	1	3	16	7	53	.259	.318
Two Strikes	.143	230	33	6	0	4	17	13	130	.198	.222	Post-All Star	.229	253	58	12	0	7	25	23	77	.309	.360

Batter vs. Pitcher (career)

Hits Best Against	Avg	AB	H	2B	3B	HR	RBI	BB	SO	OBP	SLG	Hits Worst Against	Avg	AB	H	2B	3B	HR	RBI	BB	SO	OBP	SLG
Greg Swindell	.400	10	4	2	0	1	1	1	2	.455	.900	Mark Langston	.091	11	1	0	0	1	1	1	5	.167	.364
Jimmy Key	.364	11	4	1	0	1	2	0	4	.364	.727												
Frank Tanana	.308	13	4	0	0	2	1	4		.333	.308												

Bob Milacki — Orioles
Pitches Right

	ERA	W	L	Sv	G	GS	IP	BB	SO	Avg	H	2B	3B	HR	RBI	OBP	SLG	CG	ShO	Sup	QS	#P/S	SB	CS	GB	FB	G/F
1992 Season	5.84	6	8	1	23	20	115.2	44	51	.297	140	31	4	16	71	.357	.481	0	0	4.98	7	85	11	1	170	156	1.09
Career (1988-1992)	4.19	37	37	1	121	109	703.0	255	350	.260	700	137	10	73	314	.324	.400	8	5	4.24	55	93	63	16	992	833	1.19

1992 Season

	ERA	W	L	Sv	G	GS	IP	H	HR	BB	SO		Avg	AB	H	2B	3B	HR	RBI	BB	SO	OBP	SLG
Home	6.00	4	4	0	12	10	60.0	76	10	17	33	vs. Left	.261	211	55	14	2	6	24	22	25	.329	.431
Away	5.66	2	4	1	11	10	55.2	64	6	27	18	vs. Right	.326	261	85	17	2	10	47	22	26	.380	.521
Starter	5.92	6	8	0	20	20	106.1	130	16	41	49	Scoring Posn	.285	130	37	10	0	3	52	10	10	.333	.431
Reliever	4.82	0	0	1	3	0	9.1	10	0	3	2	Close & Late	.333	18	6	1	0	3	4	1	2	.368	.889
0-3 Days Rest	0.00	0	0	0	0	0	0.0	0	0	0	0	None on/out	.270	115	31	8	1	2	2	9	14	.323	.409
4 Days Rest	6.75	2	4	0	11	11	53.1	73	7	28	25	First Pitch	.329	73	24	3	0	3	13	1	0	.338	.493
5+ Days Rest	5.09	4	4	0	9	9	53.0	57	9	13	24	Behind on Count	.366	142	52	13	1	5	21	19	0	.442	.577
Pre-All Star	6.34	5	7	0	18	18	92.1	119	16	36	45	Ahead on Count	.256	168	43	7	2	6	26	0	40	.257	.429
Post-All Star	3.86	1	1	1	5	2	23.1	21	0	8	6	Two Strikes	.239	163	39	4	3	6	23	24	51	.337	.411

Career (1988-1992)

	ERA	W	L	Sv	G	GS	IP	H	HR	BB	SO		Avg	AB	H	2B	3B	HR	RBI	BB	SO	OBP	SLG
Home	4.50	17	18	0	59	53	340.0	359	38	116	182	vs. Left	.254	1346	342	67	6	28	132	137	181	.322	.375
Away	3.89	20	19	1	62	56	363.0	341	35	139	168	vs. Right	.267	1342	358	70	4	45	182	118	169	.326	.425
Day	3.78	9	7	1	29	25	164.1	141	17	61	84	Inning 1-6	.265	2280	604	122	9	62	283	210	302	.326	.408
Night	4.31	28	30	0	92	84	538.2	559	56	194	266	Inning 7+	.235	408	96	15	1	11	31	45	48	.312	.358
Grass	4.11	31	33	1	103	92	599.2	590	64	228	298	None on	.254	1589	404	83	6	42	42	161	222	.324	.393
Turf	4.62	6	4	0	18	17	103.1	110	9	29	52	Runners on	.269	1099	296	54	4	31	272	94	128	.322	.410
April	3.83	4	3	0	16	15	94.0	79	8	44	37	Scoring Posn	.280	575	161	30	2	14	225	60	67	.339	.412
May	5.12	5	10	0	23	19	117.2	144	14	56	50	Close & Late	.205	205	42	8	0	8	12	29	24	.303	.361
June	4.54	8	6	0	24	24	146.2	160	17	46	84	None on/out	.256	703	180	34	3	22	22	69	92	.324	.400
July	5.59	3	10	0	19	18	96.2	105	16	36	47	vs. 1st Batr (relief)	.500	12	6	2	0	0	7	0	0	.500	.667
August	3.46	6	4	0	12	12	88.1	76	11	17	50	First Inning Pitched	.274	482	132	24	2	13	89	57	62	.350	.413
September/October	2.93	11	4	1	27	21	159.2	136	7	56	82	First 75 Pitches	.264	2061	544	105	7	54	256	183	261	.323	.400
Starter	4.21	36	37	0	109	109	665.0	662	70	241	336	Pitch 76-90	.256	293	75	19	1	9	22	29	38	.322	.420
Reliever	3.79	1	0	1	12	0	38.0	38	3	14	14	Pitch 91-105	.235	196	46	8	0	4	20	21	29	.309	.337
0-3 Days Rest	3.57	8	3	0	13	13	80.2	67	7	34	35	Pitch 106+	.254	138	35	5	2	6	16	22	22	.358	.449
4 Days Rest	4.26	16	25	0	63	63	382.0	397	43	141	202	First Pitch	.275	426	117	26	1	8	47	8	0	.287	.397
5+ Days Rest	4.36	12	9	0	33	33	202.1	198	20	66	99	Ahead on Count	.211	1067	225	40	3	22	109	0	283	.212	.316
Pre-All Star	4.84	18	23	0	69	63	383.1	421	44	157	186	Behind on Count	.332	683	227	44	5	28	108	135	0	.439	.534
Post-All Star	3.41	19	14	1	52	46	319.2	279	29	98	164	Two Strikes	.198	1057	209	39	4	19	86	112	350	.275	.296

Pitcher vs. Batter (career)

Pitches Best Vs.	Avg	AB	H	2B	3B	HR	RBI	BB	SO	OBP	SLG	Pitches Worst Vs.	Avg	AB	H	2B	3B	HR	RBI	BB	SO	OBP	SLG
Sandy Alomar Jr	.000	13	0	0	0	0	0	0	1	.000	.000	Ken Griffey Jr	.667	9	6	1	0	0	3	2	0	.727	.778
Alan Trammell	.067	30	2	0	0	0	0	5	5	.200	.067	Rafael Palmeiro	.571	14	8	2	0	1	4	4	0	.667	.929

Pitcher vs. Batter (career)

Pitches Best Vs.	Avg	AB	H	2B	3B	HR	RBI	BB	SO	OBP	SLG	Pitches Worst Vs.	Avg	AB	H	2B	3B	HR	RBI	BB	SO	OBP	SLG
Mike Gallego	.071	14	1	0	0	0	0	0	1	.071	.071	Carlos Martinez	.500	18	9	5	0	1	4	0	2	.500	.944
Greg Briley	.091	11	1	1	0	0	0	0	4	.091	.182	Rob Deer	.500	14	7	2	1	1	4	2	2	.563	1.000
Scott Fletcher	.100	10	1	0	0	0	1	1	0	.167	.100	Pete Incaviglia	.462	13	6	3	0	3	8	2	3	.533	1.385

Sam Militello — Yankees
Pitches Right (flyball pitcher)

	ERA	W	L	Sv	G	GS	IP	BB	SO	Avg	H	2B	3B	HR	RBI	OBP	SLG	CG	ShO	Sup	QS	#P/S	SB	CS	GB	FB	G/F
1992 Season	3.45	3	3	0	9	9	60.0	32	42	195	43	13	0	6	20	.302	.335	0	0	4.05	6	104	7	0	56	88	0.64

1992 Season

	ERA	W	L	Sv	G	GS	IP	H	HR	BB	SO		Avg	AB	H	2B	3B	HR	RBI	BB	SO	OBP	SLG
Home	2.50	2	1	0	6	6	39.2	21	3	22	31	vs. Left	.262	107	28	7	0	5	13	15	12	.352	.467
Away	5.31	1	2	0	3	3	20.1	22	3	10	11	vs. Right	.132	114	15	6	0	1	7	17	30	.256	.211
Starter	3.45	3	3	0	9	9	60.0	43	6	32	42	Scoring Posn	.190	58	11	3	0	1	13	9	12	.299	.293
Reliever	0.00	0	0	0	0	0	0.0	0	0	0	0	Close & Late	.208	24	5	0	0	2	3	1	1	.240	.458
0-3 Days Rest	0.00	0	0	0	0	0	0.0	0	0	0	0	None on/out	.118	51	6	3	0	0	0	9	10	.262	.176
4 Days Rest	4.42	1	1	0	3	3	18.1	18	0	13	18	First Pitch	.118	34	4	1	0	1	2	1	0	.143	.235
5+ Days Rest	3.02	2	2	0	6	6	41.2	25	6	19	24	Behind on Count	.245	49	12	4	0	1	7	24	0	.493	.388
Pre-All Star	0.00	0	0	0	0	0	0.0	0	0	0	0	Ahead on Count	.194	93	18	6	0	1	6	0	34	.211	.290
Post-All Star	3.45	3	3	0	9	9	60.0	43	6	32	42	Two Strikes	.153	98	15	5	0	2	9	7	42	.210	.265

Keith Miller — Royals
Bats Right

	Avg	G	AB	R	H	2B	3B	HR	RBI	BB	SO	HBP	GDP	SB	CS	OBP	SLG	IBB	SH	SF	#Pit	#P/PA	GB	FB	G/F
1992 Season	.284	106	416	57	118	24	4	4	38	31	46	14	1	16	6	.352	.389	0	1	2	1634	3.53	147	127	1.16
Last Five Years	.266	389	1137	164	303	62	6	11	85	88	173	22	9	52	18	.330	.361	1	9	5	4534	3.62	403	312	1.29

1992 Season

	Avg	AB	H	2B	3B	HR	RBI	BB	SO	OBP	SLG		Avg	AB	H	2B	3B	HR	RBI	BB	SO	OBP	SLG
vs. Left	.267	120	32	9	2	0	10	12	15	.333	.375	Scoring Posn	.341	88	30	6	1	0	32	6	11	.412	.432
vs. Right	.291	296	86	15	2	4	28	19	31	.360	.395	Close & Late	.300	70	21	2	0	1	7	6	16	.359	.371
Groundball	.290	93	27	6	1	0	8	8	11	.377	.376	None on/out	.235	136	32	6	2	1	1	10	10	.302	.331
Flyball	.255	149	38	8	1	1	13	10	20	.329	.342	Batting #1	.294	286	84	18	4	3	28	23	32	.362	.416
Home	.301	183	55	8	2	1	17	18	12	.384	.383	Batting #2	.258	97	25	4	0	1	9	4	9	.305	.330
Away	.270	233	63	16	2	3	21	13	34	.325	.395	Other	.273	33	9	2	0	0	1	4	5	.400	.333
Day	.167	108	18	3	0	0	5	7	18	.231	.194	April	.297	74	22	7	0	1	2	6	11	.366	.432
Night	.325	308	100	21	4	4	33	24	28	.393	.458	May	.314	51	16	4	0	1	8	5	5	.386	.431
Grass	.259	185	48	11	0	2	15	8	26	.305	.351	June	.270	100	27	5	2	1	13	9	14	.357	.390
Turf	.303	231	70	13	4	2	23	23	20	.387	.420	July	.378	45	17	4	0	0	4	1	4	.404	.467
First Pitch	.397	68	27	5	2	0	7	0	0	.446	.529	August	.189	37	7	2	0	1	4	3	3	.302	.324
Ahead on Count	.320	97	31	9	1	3	13	17	0	.419	.526	September/October	.266	109	29	2	2	0	7	7	9	.319	.321
Behind on Count	.236	127	30	5	1	0	10	0	27	.242	.291	Pre-All Star	.304	270	82	20	2	3	27	21	34	.372	.426
Two Strikes	.219	169	37	7	1	0	11	14	46	.294	.272	Post-All Star	.247	146	36	4	2	1	11	10	12	.315	.322

1992 By Position

Position	Avg	AB	H	2B	3B	HR	RBI	BB	SO	OBP	SLG	G	GS	Innings	PO	A	E	DP	Fld Pct	Rng Fctr	In Zone	Outs	Zone Rtg	MLB Zone
As 2b	.290	362	105	22	4	4	37	26	39	.356	.406	93	88	786.1	189	250	13	60	.971	5.02	279	247	.885	.892
As lf	.250	48	12	2	0	0	1	5	7	.345	.292	16	14	117.0	41	0	2	0	.953	3.15	47	41	.872	.809

Last Five Years

	Avg	AB	H	2B	3B	HR	RBI	BB	SO	OBP	SLG		Avg	AB	H	2B	3B	HR	RBI	BB	SO	OBP	SLG
vs. Left	.259	505	131	32	2	3	31	41	86	.316	.349	Scoring Posn	.290	224	65	14	1	0	69	19	37	.359	.362
vs. Right	.272	632	172	30	4	8	54	47	87	.340	.370	Close & Late	.276	181	50	6	0	2	13	21	38	.353	.343
Groundball	.256	332	85	14	2	0	21	28	47	.324	.310	None on/out	.234	394	92	16	2	5	5	35	55	.306	.322
Flyball	.267	311	83	16	1	3	25	17	46	.322	.354	Batting #1	.274	664	182	38	4	6	60	53	97	.338	.370
Home	.269	550	148	27	3	5	42	54	72	.345	.356	Batting #2	.280	350	98	21	2	5	21	23	51	.332	.394
Away	.264	587	155	35	3	6	43	34	101	.315	.365	Other	.187	123	23	3	0	0	4	12	25	.279	.211
Day	.241	374	90	26	1	3	26	26	55	.299	.340	April	.273	143	39	14	0	2	5	16	22	.354	.413
Night	.279	763	213	36	5	8	59	62	118	.345	.371	May	.298	114	34	6	0	2	10	6	18	.339	.404
Grass	.250	644	161	33	1	7	45	52	107	.312	.337	June	.273	187	51	9	3	1	19	15	29	.338	.369
Turf	.288	493	142	29	5	4	40	36	66	.353	.391	July	.299	157	47	9	0	1	12	3	22	.329	.376
First Pitch	.363	190	69	17	3	1	21	0	0	.386	.500	August	.205	190	39	7	0	2	15	14	37	.278	.274
Ahead on Count	.316	250	79	20	2	4	28	55	0	.441	.460	September/October	.269	346	93	17	3	3	24	34	45	.341	.361
Behind on Count	.210	367	77	16	1	1	18	0	95	.215	.267	Pre-All Star	.287	527	151	34	3	6	42	38	79	.344	.397
Two Strikes	.201	493	99	16	1	4	22	32	173	.258	.262	Post-All Star	.249	610	152	28	3	5	43	50	94	.318	.330

Batter vs. Pitcher (career)

Hits Best Against	Avg	AB	H	2B	3B	HR	RBI	BB	SO	OBP	SLG	Hits Worst Against	Avg	AB	H	2B	3B	HR	RBI	BB	SO	OBP	SLG
Bruce Ruffin	.500	16	8	4	1	0	1	4	3	.600	.875	Mark Langston	.063	16	1	1	0	0	0	0	3	.063	.125
Don Carman	.400	10	4	0	0	0	1	1	1	.455	.400	Paul Assenmacher	.091	11	1	0	0	0	0	1	8	.167	.091
Melido Perez	.364	11	4	0	0	0	2	0	2	.462	.545	Greg Maddux	.091	11	1	0	0	0	0	0	1	.091	.091
Mike Mussina	.364	11	4	1	0	0	0	0	1	.462	.455	Rheal Cormier	.143	14	2	1	0	0	0	0	3	.143	.214
Bryn Smith	.333	12	4	1	0	1	2	1	2	.385	.667	Bruce Hurst	.182	11	2	0	0	0	0	0	4	.182	.182

296

Paul Miller — Pirates

Pitches Right

	ERA	W	L	Sv	G	GS	IP	BB	SO	Avg	H	2B	3B	HR	RBI	OBP	SLG	GF	IR	IRS	Hld	SvOp	SB	CS	GB	FB	G/F
1992 Season	2.38	1	0	0	6	0	11.1	1	5	.256	11	5	0	0	6	.267	.372	1	10	3	0	0	0	1	16	16	1.00
Career (1991-1992)	3.31	1	0	0	7	1	16.1	4	7	.246	15	7	0	0	6	.288	.361	1	10	3	0	0	0	1	25	21	1.19

1992 Season

	ERA	W	L	Sv	G	GS	IP	H	HR	BB	SO		Avg	AB	H	2B	3B	HR	RBI	BB	SO	OBP	SLG
Home	3.00	1	0	0	4	0	9.0	10	0	1	1	vs. Left	.300	20	6	2	0	0	2	0	2	.300	.400
Away	0.00	0	0	0	2	0	2.1	1	0	0	4	vs. Right	.217	23	5	3	0	0	4	1	3	.240	.348

Joe Millette — Phillies

Bats Right (groundball hitter)

	Avg	G	AB	R	H	2B	3B	HR	RBI	BB	SO	HBP	GDP	SB	CS	OBP	SLG	IBB	SH	SF	#Pit	#P/PA	GB	FB	G/F
1992 Season	.205	33	78	5	16	0	0	0	2	5	10	2	8	1	0	.271	.205	2	2	0	.252	2.96	33	21	1.57

1992 Season

	Avg	AB	H	2B	3B	HR	RBI	BB	SO	OBP	SLG		Avg	AB	H	2B	3B	HR	RBI	BB	SO	OBP	SLG
vs. Left	.120	25	3	0	0	0	1	2	2	.185	.120	Scoring Posn	.100	20	2	0	0	0	2	3	5	.250	.100
vs. Right	.245	53	13	0	0	0	1	3	8	.310	.245	Close & Late	.400	5	2	0	0	0	0	1	1	.500	.400

Randy Milligan — Orioles

Bats Right

	Avg	G	AB	R	H	2B	3B	HR	RBI	BB	SO	HBP	GDP	SB	CS	OBP	SLG	IBB	SH	SF	#Pit	#P/PA	GB	FB	G/F
1992 Season	.240	137	462	71	111	21	1	11	53	106	81	4	15	0	1	.383	.361	0	0	5	2346	4.07	169	139	1.22
Last Five Years	.257	551	1754	258	450	86	9	62	236	372	356	12	63	16	16	.388	.422	9	0	13	8996	4.18	584	520	1.12

1992 Season

	Avg	AB	H	2B	3B	HR	RBI	BB	SO	OBP	SLG		Avg	AB	H	2B	3B	HR	RBI	BB	SO	OBP	SLG
vs. Left	.280	107	30	6	0	3	14	35	22	.462	.421	Scoring Posn	.218	119	26	5	0	3	42	22	22	.333	.336
vs. Right	.228	355	81	15	1	8	39	71	59	.356	.344	Close & Late	.200	75	15	5	0	2	8	12	14	.307	.347
Groundball	.218	119	26	4	1	0	10	24	23	.356	.269	None on/out	.225	111	25	4	1	4	4	31	18	.399	.387
Flyball	.262	122	32	7	0	3	16	36	29	.431	.393	Batting #2	.216	88	19	4	1	3	11	17	21	.346	.386
Home	.193	233	45	5	1	7	26	61	38	.361	.313	Batting #5	.232	254	59	10	0	4	23	53	39	.364	.319
Away	.288	229	66	16	0	4	27	45	43	.406	.410	Other	.275	120	33	7	0	4	19	36	21	.446	.433
Day	.271	140	38	7	0	1	16	25	14	.387	.343	April	.213	47	10	2	0	2	9	6	10	.315	.383
Night	.227	322	73	14	1	10	37	81	67	.381	.370	May	.306	72	22	7	0	1	9	22	9	.474	.444
Grass	.228	391	89	13	1	11	45	92	64	.377	.350	June	.247	89	22	2	0	4	11	17	14	.374	.404
Turf	.310	71	22	8	0	0	8	14	17	.416	.423	July	.222	90	20	2	0	1	8	21	17	.363	.278
First Pitch	.269	67	18	2	0	2	7	0	0	.275	.388	August	.288	80	23	4	0	2	10	23	12	.443	.413
Ahead on Count	.260	100	26	8	0	3	11	57	0	.522	.430	September/October	.167	84	14	4	1	1	6	17	19	.304	.274
Behind on Count	.200	135	27	5	0	3	9	0	32	.204	.304	Pre-All Star	.253	245	62	13	0	7	32	58	38	.401	.392
Two Strikes	.200	225	45	4	1	5	28	49	81	.349	.293	Post-All Star	.226	217	49	8	1	4	21	48	43	.363	.327

1992 By Position

Position	Avg	AB	H	2B	3B	HR	RBI	BB	SO	OBP	SLG		G	GS	Innings	PO	A	E	DP	Fld Pct	Rng Fctr	In Zone	Outs	Zone Rtg	MLB Zone
As 1b	.240	442	106	21	1	11	52	100	75	.381	.367		129	129	1061.0	1009	75	7	109	.994	---	201	167	831	843

Last Five Years

	Avg	AB	H	2B	3B	HR	RBI	BB	SO	OBP	SLG		Avg	AB	H	2B	3B	HR	RBI	BB	SO	OBP	SLG
vs. Left	.252	572	144	31	3	24	81	136	114	.396	.442	Scoring Posn	.258	449	116	20	1	14	173	104	101	.394	.401
vs. Right	.259	1182	306	55	6	38	155	236	242	.383	.412	Close & Late	.255	286	73	16	1	10	42	66	56	.396	.423
Groundball	.252	484	122	26	2	10	71	92	88	.375	.376	None on/out	.251	394	99	19	2	17	17	92	79	.394	.439
Flyball	.276	362	100	19	2	20	51	100	76	.433	.506	Batting #5	.249	863	215	42	4	29	113	182	162	.379	.408
Home	.242	856	207	37	4	33	113	213	162	.394	.410	Batting #6	.261	283	74	17	2	9	33	52	67	.384	.431
Away	.271	898	243	49	5	29	123	159	194	.382	.433	Other	.265	608	161	27	3	24	90	138	127	.401	.438
Day	.279	452	126	24	2	15	66	95	84	.404	.440	April	.217	217	47	8	0	6	26	41	55	.342	.336
Night	.249	1302	324	62	7	47	170	277	272	.382	.416	May	.257	338	87	25	3	8	41	85	79	.411	.420
Grass	.253	1432	363	63	5	52	190	307	282	.386	.416	June	.311	344	107	18	0	23	70	74	58	.435	.564
Turf	.270	322	87	23	2	10	46	65	74	.393	.447	July	.237	338	80	10	2	15	48	74	58	.373	.411
First Pitch	.306	206	63	12	1	10	33	6	0	.324	.519	August	.261	261	68	12	2	4	30	59	50	.397	.368
Ahead on Count	.308	364	112	24	3	18	64	201	0	.551	.538	September/October	.238	256	61	13	2	6	21	39	56	.339	.375
Behind on Count	.222	510	113	20	3	14	59	1	135	.230	.355	Pre-All Star	.264	1002	265	54	3	41	148	229	207	.403	.447
Two Strikes	.203	927	188	31	4	20	95	164	356	.328	.310	Post-All Star	.246	752	185	32	6	21	88	143	149	.367	.388

Batter vs. Pitcher (career)

Hits Best Against	Avg	AB	H	2B	3B	HR	RBI	BB	SO	OBP	SLG	Hits Worst Against	Avg	AB	H	2B	3B	HR	RBI	BB	SO	OBP	SLG
Mark Gubicza	.417	12	5	1	1	2	7	1	4	.462	1.167	Nolan Ryan	.000	13	0	0	0	0	0	2	8	.133	.000
Terry Leach	.400	10	4	1	0	2	4	1	1	.455	1.100	Bud Black	.000	12	0	0	0	0	0	2	4	.143	.000
Joe Slusarski	.400	10	4	0	0	1	2	4	1	.571	.700	Walt Terrell	.000	8	0	0	0	0	1	2	3	.182	.000
Frank Viola	.375	8	3	0	0	1	5	4	1	.583	.750	Jack Morris	.053	19	1	1	0	0	0	0	6	.053	.105
Melido Perez	.333	12	4	0	0	2	2	1	3	.385	.833	Rod Nichols	.118	17	2	1	0	0	0	0	3	.118	.118

Alan Mills — Orioles
Pitches Right

	ERA	W	L	Sv	G	GS	IP	BB	SO	Avg	H	2B	3B	HR	RBI	OBP	SLG	GF	IR	IRS	Hld	SvOp	SB	CS	GB	FB	G/F
1992 Season	2.61	10	4	2	35	3	103.1	54	60	.215	78	16	2	5	37	.315	.312	12	32	9	2	3	12	4	132	114	1.16
Career (1990-1992)	3.18	12	10	2	77	5	161.1	95	95	.242	142	28	4	10	71	.346	.355	33	63	20	5	5	19	5	214	181	1.18

1992 Season

	ERA	W	L	Sv	G	GS	IP	H	HR	BB	SO		Avg	AB	H	2B	3B	HR	RBI	BB	SO	OBP	SLG
Home	2.54	5	2	2	18	0	49.2	36	1	25	29	vs. Left	.244	168	41	10	1	2	17	24	15	.337	.351
Away	2.68	5	2	0	17	3	53.2	42	4	29	31	vs. Right	.191	194	37	6	1	3	20	30	45	.297	.278
Starter	5.40	1	1	0	3	3	13.1	17	2	7	6	Scoring Posn	.193	109	21	3	2	2	32	22	29	.316	.312
Reliever	2.20	9	3	2	32	0	90.0	61	3	47	54	Close & Late	.183	104	19	5	1	0	7	17	20	.303	.250
0 Days rest	0.00	0	0	1	1	0	1.1	2	0	0	1	None on/out	.261	88	23	5	0	1	1	8	9	.330	.352
1 or 2 Days rest	2.03	3	0	1	12	0	31.0	17	2	21	20	First Pitch	.319	47	15	3	0	1	9	7	0	.407	.447
3+ Days rest	2.34	6	3	0	19	0	57.2	42	1	26	33	Behind on Count	.255	98	25	7	1	3	15	25	0	.397	.439
Pre-All Star	1.36	7	1	1	19	0	53.0	34	2	25	30	Ahead on Count	.200	145	29	6	1	0	10	0	46	.204	.255
Post-All Star	3.93	3	3	1	16	3	50.1	44	3	29	30	Two Strikes	.141	149	21	5	1	1	9	22	60	.253	.208

Blas Minor — Pirates
Pitches Right (groundball pitcher)

	ERA	W	L	Sv	G	GS	IP	BB	SO	Avg	H	2B	3B	HR	RBI	OBP	SLG	GF	IR	IRS	Hld	SvOp	SB	CS	GB	FB	G/F
1992 Season	4.50	0	0	0	1	0	2.0	0	0	.333	3	1	1	0	0	.333	.667	0	0	0	0	0	0	0	4	2	2.00

1992 Season

	ERA	W	L	Sv	G	GS	IP	H	HR	BB	SO		Avg	AB	H	2B	3B	HR	RBI	BB	SO	OBP	SLG
Home	0.00	0	0	0	0	0	0.0	0	0	0	0	vs. Left	.500	2	1	0	0	0	0	0	0	.500	.500
Away	4.50	0	0	0	1	0	2.0	3	0	0	0	vs. Right	.286	7	2	1	1	0	0	0	0	.286	.714

Kevin Mitchell — Mariners
Bats Right (flyball hitter)

	Avg	G	AB	R	H	2B	3B	HR	RBI	BB	SO	HBP	GDP	SB	CS	OBP	SLG	IBB	SH	SF	#Pit	#P/PA	GB	FB	G/F
1992 Season	.286	99	360	48	103	24	0	9	67	35	46	3	4	0	2	.351	.428	4	0	4	1393	3.47	125	136	0.92
Last Five Years	.276	654	2303	350	635	120	16	137	434	271	390	18	34	14	21	.353	.520	60	1	27	9145	3.49	682	872	0.78

1992 Season

	Avg	AB	H	2B	3B	HR	RBI	BB	SO	OBP	SLG		Avg	AB	H	2B	3B	HR	RBI	BB	SO	OBP	SLG
vs. Left	.380	92	35	5	0	5	27	11	11	.438	.598	Scoring Posn	.292	113	33	9	0	3	54	12	14	.349	.451
vs. Right	.254	268	68	19	0	4	40	24	35	.320	.369	Close & Late	.293	58	17	2	0	0	5	4	7	.339	.328
Groundball	.351	97	34	9	0	2	26	12	11	.423	.505	None on/out	.194	98	19	5	0	3	3	9	14	.269	.337
Flyball	.279	104	29	4	0	3	16	6	15	.324	.404	Batting #4	.282	351	99	22	0	9	63	34	46	.347	.422
Home	.319	207	66	17	0	5	41	17	25	.368	.473	Batting #5	.250	4	1	1	0	0	0	1	0	.400	.500
Away	.242	153	37	7	0	4	26	18	21	.328	.366	Other	.600	5	3	1	0	0	4	0	0	.600	.800
Day	.313	96	30	6	0	5	22	7	16	.358	.531	April	.261	69	18	4	0	0	3		8	.289	.319
Night	.277	264	73	18	0	4	45	28	30	.348	.390	May	.191	89	17	3	0	2	11	12	18	.287	.292
Grass	.250	120	30	5	0	4	25	15	18	.341	.392	June	.330	94	31	9	0	3	12	6	2	.376	.521
Turf	.304	240	73	19	0	5	42	20	28	.356	.446	July	.286	77	22	7	0	3	24	10	17	.368	.494
First Pitch	.309	68	21	6	0	2	13	2	0	.342	.485	August	.484	31	15	1	0	1	11	4	1	.541	.613
Ahead on Count	.357	84	30	5	0	2	22	20	0	.472	.488	September/October	.000	0	0	0	0	0	0	0	0	.000	.000
Behind on Count	.243	103	25	6	0	4	25	0	17	.245	.417	Pre-All Star	.259	270	70	17	0	5	36	26	34	.326	.378
Two Strikes	.259	139	36	11	0	2	20	13	46	.320	.381	Post-All Star	.367	90	33	7	0	4	31	9	12	.426	.500

1992 By Position

Position	Avg	AB	H	2B	3B	HR	RBI	BB	SO	OBP	SLG	G	GS	Innings	PO	A	E	DP	Fld Pct	Rng Fctr	In Zone	Outs	Zone Rtg	MLB Zone
As Designated Hitter	.304	102	31	6	0	4	27	11	22	.374	.480	26	26	---	---	---	---	---	---	---	---	---	---	---
As lf	.273	253	69	17	0	5	36	24	24	.337	.399	69	67	570.2	130	4	0	0	1.000	2.11	171	125	.731	.809

Last Five Years

	Avg	AB	H	2B	3B	HR	RBI	BB	SO	OBP	SLG		Avg	AB	H	2B	3B	HR	RBI	BB	SO	OBP	SLG
vs. Left	.286	707	202	38	2	46	141	109	94	.379	.540	Scoring Posn	.264	659	174	34	3	28	278	125	110	.373	.452
vs. Right	.271	1596	433	82	14	91	293	162	296	.341	.511	Close & Late	.262	363	95	14	0	21	53	50	77	.351	.474
Groundball	.295	765	226	46	7	46	154	71	120	.358	.554	None on/out	.272	563	153	27	5	41	41	99	93	.334	.556
Flyball	.259	556	144	29	4	33	99	75	98	.347	.504	Batting #4	.279	2044	570	110	14	126	392	246	346	.357	.531
Home	.281	1146	322	65	11	61	221	132	180	.354	.517	Batting #5	.247	85	21	1	0	6	18	6	12	.290	.471
Away	.271	1157	313	55	5	76	213	139	210	.352	.524	Other	.253	174	44	9	2	5	24	19	32	.332	.414
Day	.280	860	241	51	6	47	147	116	151	.366	.517	April	.274	380	104	22	3	20	71	41	67	.340	.505
Night	.273	1443	394	69	10	90	287	155	239	.345	.522	May	.257	436	112	22	6	26	70	58	69	.346	.514
Grass	.275	1562	430	76	14	93	298	175	275	.349	.520	June	.307	361	111	23	1	24	73	41	37	.378	.576
Turf	.277	741	205	44	2	44	136	96	115	.360	.520	July	.280	404	113	19	0	30	97	47	80	.357	.550
First Pitch	.313	409	128	27	1	33	95	32	0	.365	.626	August	.293	440	129	21	5	23	85	52	83	.370	.520
Ahead on Count	.386	533	206	34	10	48	141	126	0	.504	.758	September/October	.234	282	66	13	1	14	38	32	54	.316	.436
Behind on Count	.241	739	178	29	1	41	142	3	190	.245	.449	Pre-All Star	.279	1285	359	70	10	80	242	151	195	.355	.536
Two Strikes	.184	940	173	36	3	27	116	98	387	.260	.315	Post-All Star	.271	1018	276	50	6	57	192	120	195	.350	.500

Batter vs. Pitcher (career)

Hits Best Against	Avg	AB	H	2B	3B	HR	RBI	BB	SO	OBP	SLG	Hits Worst Against	Avg	AB	H	2B	3B	HR	RBI	BB	SO	OBP	SLG
Joe Hesketh	.600	15	9	2	0	1	3	2	2	.647	.933	Jim Gott	.000	10	0	0	0	0	0	1	2	.091	.000

Batter vs. Pitcher (career)

Hits Best Against	Avg	AB	H	2B	3B	HR	RBI	BB	SO	OBP	SLG	Hits Worst Against	Avg	AB	H	2B	3B	HR	RBI	BB	SO	OBP	SLG
Rick Honeycutt	.538	13	7	2	0	2	3	0	0	.538	1.154	Mike Morgan	.077	13	1	0	0	0	0	2	3	.200	.077
Tim Crews	.444	18	8	1	0	3	7	1	2	.474	1.000	Paul Assenmacher	.111	9	1	0	0	0	0	3	3	.333	.111
Mark Grant	.421	19	8	2	0	3	6	2	4	.476	1.000	Kevin Gross	.156	32	5	1	1	0	6	3	8	.222	.250
Bruce Hurst	.333	21	7	1	0	5	8	5	2	.462	1.095	Roger McDowell	.214	14	3	0	0	0	0	0	3	.214	.214

Dave Mlicki — Indians
Pitches Right (flyball pitcher)

	ERA	W	L	Sv	G	GS	IP	BB	SO	Avg	H	2B	3B	HR	RBI	OBP	SLG	CG	ShO	Sup	QS	#P/S	SB	CS	GB	FB	G/F
1992 Season	4.98	0	2	0	4	4	21.2	16	16	.280	23	3	1	3	8	.404	.451	0	0	5.40	2	99	7	1	20	26	0.77

1992 Season

	ERA	W	L	Sv	G	GS	IP	H	HR	BB	SO		Avg	AB	H	2B	3B	HR	RBI	BB	SO	OBP	SLG
Home	7.59	0	2	0	2	2	10.2	15	3	7	8	vs. Left	.304	46	14	2	1	1	4	8	8	.418	.457
Away	2.45	0	0	0	2	2	11.0	8	0	9	8	vs. Right	.250	36	9	1	0	2	4	8	8	.386	.444

Dennis Moeller — Royals
Pitches Left (flyball pitcher)

	ERA	W	L	Sv	G	GS	IP	BB	SO	Avg	H	2B	3B	HR	RBI	OBP	SLG	CG	ShO	Sup	QS	#P/S	SB	CS	GB	FB	G/F
1992 Season	7.00	0	3	0	5	4	18.0	11	6	.333	24	4	0	5	15	.407	.597	0	0	3.00	0	75	2	0	25	27	0.93

1992 Season

	ERA	W	L	Sv	G	GS	IP	H	HR	BB	SO		Avg	AB	H	2B	3B	HR	RBI	BB	SO	OBP	SLG
Home	0.00	0	0	0	2	1	6.0	5	0	3	2	vs. Left	.500	6	3	0	0	1	4	1	0	.500	1.000
Away	10.50	0	3	0	3	3	12.0	19	5	8	4	vs. Right	.318	66	21	4	0	4	11	10	6	.397	.561

Paul Molitor — Brewers
Bats Right

	Avg	G	AB	R	H	2B	3B	HR	RBI	BB	SO	HBP	GDP	SB	CS	OBP	SLG	IBB	SH	SF	#Pit	#P/PA	GB	FB	G/F
1992 Season	.320	158	609	89	195	36	7	12	89	73	66	3	12	31	6	.389	.461	12	4	11	2495	3.58	175	1.33
Last Five Years	.313	728	2916	485	914	164	36	65	325	322	300	16	51	136	38	.382	.461	44	13	26	11604	3.54	1130	839	1.35

1992 Season

	Avg	AB	H	2B	3B	HR	RBI	BB	SO	OBP	SLG		Avg	AB	H	2B	3B	HR	RBI	BB	SO	OBP	SLG
vs. Left	.424	132	56	11	1	6	32	14	11	.464	.659	Scoring Posn	.323	164	53	8	2	3	75	32	21	.416	.451
vs. Right	.291	477	139	25	6	6	57	59	55	.369	.407	Close & Late	.322	87	28	4	0	1	12	14	11	.417	.402
Groundball	.345	145	50	10	3	1	22	20	15	.423	.476	None on/out	.317	142	45	12	2	0	0	12	13	.370	.430
Flyball	.288	170	49	13	1	3	26	22	19	.360	.429	Batting #1	.316	133	42	7	1	2	15	17	17	.383	.429
Home	.304	286	87	13	4	4	36	43	34	.390	.420	Batting #3	.323	474	153	29	6	10	74	56	49	.393	.473
Away	.334	323	108	23	3	8	53	30	32	.389	.498	Other	.000	2	0	0	0	0	0	0	0	.000	.000
Day	.310	200	62	10	1	5	35	23	24	.376	.445	April	.260	77	20	3	0	1	12	6	9	.302	.338
Night	.325	409	133	26	6	7	54	50	42	.396	.469	May	.357	98	35	6	2	5	13	14	15	.439	.612
Grass	.310	507	157	27	5	10	68	64	52	.383	.442	June	.337	98	33	7	0	4	15	13	6	.409	.531
Turf	.373	102	38	9	2	2	21	9	14	.422	.559	July	.288	104	30	3	2	1	15	14	15	.375	.385
First Pitch	.367	90	33	8	1	4	17	10	0	.423	.611	August	.330	109	36	5	2	1	21	12	13	.390	.440
Ahead on Count	.337	175	59	11	0	4	31	38	0	.447	.469	September/October	.333	123	41	12	1	0	13	14	8	.399	.447
Behind on Count	.350	183	64	11	2	5	35	0	34	.351	.514	Pre-All Star	.319	313	100	19	2	10	46	40	37	.393	.489
Two Strikes	.265	226	60	9	3	1	20	26	66	.341	.345	Post-All Star	.321	296	95	17	5	2	43	33	29	.386	.432

1992 By Position

Position	Avg	AB	H	2B	3B	HR	RBI	BB	SO	OBP	SLG	G	GS	Innings	PO	A	E	DP	Fld Pct	Rng Fctr	In Zone	Outs	Zone Rtg	MLB Zone
As Designated Hitter	.298	413	123	20	3	9	57	56	53	.378	.426	108	108	---	---	---	---	---	---	---	---	---	---	---
As 1b	.371	194	72	16	4	3	32	17	13	.419	.541	48	48	425.2	461	26	2	45	.996	---	84	72	.857	.843

Last Five Years

	Avg	AB	H	2B	3B	HR	RBI	BB	SO	OBP	SLG		Avg	AB	H	2B	3B	HR	RBI	BB	SO	OBP	SLG
vs. Left	.327	771	252	48	8	24	91	95	63	.398	.503	Scoring Posn	.328	603	198	33	5	12	253	113	69	.425	.459
vs. Right	.309	2145	662	116	28	41	234	227	237	.376	.446	Close & Late	.292	373	109	16	1	8	49	62	40	.393	.405
Groundball	.322	732	236	33	10	13	86	91	76	.400	.448	None on/out	.307	1068	328	62	18	26	26	84	105	.361	.472
Flyball	.322	676	218	45	6	21	94	72	72	.384	.500	Batting #1	.308	2238	690	117	30	50	223	251	232	.379	.454
Home	.307	1398	429	75	16	32	160	171	141	.381	.452	Batting #3	.332	671	223	46	6	15	102	71	67	.393	.486
Away	.319	1518	485	89	20	33	165	151	159	.383	.470	Other	.143	7	1	1	0	0	0	0	1	.143	.286
Day	.331	880	291	57	4	21	105	106	92	.402	.476	April	.310	300	93	16	0	8	31	29	28	.371	.443
Night	.306	2036	623	107	32	44	220	216	208	.373	.455	May	.308	548	169	31	7	13	52	57	56	.373	.462
Grass	.307	2414	740	129	28	54	261	285	243	.380	.450	June	.329	468	154	30	6	12	58	60	49	.406	.496
Turf	.347	502	174	35	8	11	64	37	57	.391	.514	July	.305	442	135	18	8	7	44	46	52	.373	.430
First Pitch	.340	491	167	31	4	17	61	25	0	.371	.523	August	.312	596	186	34	7	15	78	66	61	.380	.468
Ahead on Count	.336	750	252	46	8	19	92	178	0	.461	.495	September/October	.315	562	177	35	8	10	62	64	54	.384	.459
Behind on Count	.303	910	276	48	10	20	101	3	143	.310	.444	Pre-All Star	.315	1464	461	87	15	37	157	159	147	.382	.471
Two Strikes	.251	1105	277	46	12	15	95	113	299	.322	.355	Post-All Star	.312	1452	453	77	21	28	168	163	153	.381	.452

Batter vs. Pitcher (since 1984)

Hits Best Against	Avg	AB	H	2B	3B	HR	RBI	BB	SO	OBP	SLG	Hits Worst Against	Avg	AB	H	2B	3B	HR	RBI	BB	SO	OBP	SLG
Mike Campbell	.600	10	6	1	0	0	0	2	1	.667	.700	Mike Jackson	.000	12	0	0	0	0	0	1	4	.077	.000
Eric Plunk	.583	12	7	1	0	1	4	4	1	.688	.917	Luis Aquino	.071	14	1	0	0	0	0	0	3	.071	.071

Batter vs. Pitcher (since 1984)																				
Hits Best Against	Avg	AB	H	2B	3B	HR	RBI	BB	SO	OBP	SLG	Hits Worst Against	Avg	AB	H	2B	3B	HR	RBI	BB	SO	OBP	SLG
Brian Fisher	.538	13	7	4	0	0	3	2	1	.600	.846	John Habyan	.083	12	1	0	0	0	0	1	4	.154	.083
Mike Henneman	.385	13	5	0	0	2	7	0	2	.357	1.000	Doug Jones	.100	20	2	0	0	0	0	0	3	.100	.100
Scott Aldred	.333	9	3	1	0	2	3	2	1	.417	1.111	Mark Guthrie	.143	14	2	0	0	0	1	0	3	.143	.143

Rich Monteleone — Yankees — Pitches Right

	ERA	W	L	Sv	G	GS	IP	BB	SO	Avg	H	2B	3B	HR	RBI	OBP	SLG	GF	IR	IRS	Hld	SvOp	SB	CS	GB	FB	G/F
1992 Season	3.30	7	3	0	47	0	92.2	27	62	.235	82	13	4	7	41	.289	.355	15	23	14	7	2	3	5	108	126	0.86
Last Five Years	3.39	12	7	0	105	0	191.0	62	134	.241	175	34	5	15	94	.300	.363	27	75	32	8	4	6	9	244	229	1.07

1992 Season

	ERA	W	L	Sv	G	GS	IP	H	HR	BB	SO		Avg	AB	H	2B	3B	HR	RBI	BB	SO	OBP	SLG
Home	3.67	4	3	0	30	0	54.0	49	6	13	36	vs. Left	.226	146	33	8	2	1	11	10	17	.276	.329
Away	2.79	3	0	0	17	0	38.2	33	1	14	26	vs. Right	.241	203	49	5	2	6	30	17	45	.299	.374
Starter	0.00	0	0	0	0	0	0.0	0	0	0	0	Scoring Posn	.342	76	26	4	1	1	33	12	12	.427	.461
Reliever	3.30	7	3	0	47	0	92.2	82	7	27	62	Close & Late	.218	142	31	5	0	4	13	10	25	.270	.338
0 Days rest	0.00	0	0	0	3	0	6.0	4	0	1	6	None on/out	.170	88	15	0	0	3	3	4	16	.207	.273
1 or 2 Days rest	2.78	2	1	0	18	0	32.1	27	2	9	23	First Pitch	.356	45	16	1	1	1	7	3	0	.396	.489
3+ Days rest	3.98	5	2	0	26	0	54.1	51	5	17	33	Behind on Count	.311	74	23	7	0	2	12	12	0	.407	.486
Pre-All Star	2.36	5	1	0	26	0	53.1	42	2	15	41	Ahead on Count	.194	165	32	3	2	3	17	0	48	.193	.291
Post-All Star	4.58	2	2	0	21	0	39.1	40	5	12	21	Two Strikes	.165	158	26	2	1	4	18	12	62	.224	.266

Jeff Montgomery — Royals — Pitches Right

	ERA	W	L	Sv	G	GS	IP	BB	SO	Avg	H	2B	3B	HR	RBI	OBP	SLG	GF	IR	IRS	Hld	SvOp	SB	CS	GB	FB	G/F
1992 Season	2.18	1	6	39	65	0	82.2	27	69	.205	61	7	0	5	29	.277	.279	62	20	7	0	46	5	2	104	79	1.32
Last Five Years	2.39	25	20	115	313	0	421.2	144	381	.221	361	61	4	26	167	.291	.316	176	167	64	30	146	34	13	538	399	1.35

1992 Season

	ERA	W	L	Sv	G	GS	IP	H	HR	BB	SO		Avg	AB	H	2B	3B	HR	RBI	BB	SO	OBP	SLG
Home	1.85	1	4	24	36	0	48.2	44	4	8	44	vs. Left	.205	146	30	4	0	2	11	16	36	.293	.274
Away	2.65	0	2	15	29	0	34.0	17	1	19	25	vs. Right	.205	151	31	3	0	3	18	11	33	.261	.285
Day	3.44	0	3	7	14	0	18.1	13	1	7	18	Inning 1-6	.000	0	0	0	0	0	0	0	0	.000	.000
Night	1.82	1	3	32	51	0	64.1	48	4	20	51	Inning 7+	.205	297	61	7	0	5	29	27	69	.277	.279
Grass	3.08	0	2	11	22	0	26.1	15	1	16	20	None on	.207	164	34	5	0	3	3	17	42	.286	.293
Turf	1.76	1	4	28	43	0	56.1	46	4	11	49	Runners on	.203	133	27	2	0	2	26	10	27	.265	.263
April	2.45	0	2	2	9	0	11.0	10	0	3	8	Scoring Posn	.191	68	13	1	0	1	23	7	12	.260	.250
May	2.84	0	2	6	11	0	12.2	10	1	5	11	Close & Late	.244	209	51	5	0	4	24	21	48	.313	.325
June	0.00	0	0	11	12	0	14.1	7	0	5	11	None on/out	.174	69	12	2	0	1	1	9	21	.269	.246
July	2.40	1	1	6	10	0	15.0	10	2	6	10	vs. 1st Batr (relief)	.143	56	8	2	0	1	5	7	16	.231	.232
August	3.55	0	1	7	13	0	12.2	7	2	8	12	First Inning Pitched	.199	221	44	6	0	5	25	22	50	.272	.294
September/October	2.12	0	0	7	10	0	17.0	17	0	4	19	First 15 Pitches	.215	200	43	6	0	5	21	18	43	.281	.320
Starter	0.00	0	0	0	0	0	0.0	0	0	0	0	Pitch 16-30	.186	86	16	1	0	0	5	8	23	.271	.198
Reliever	2.18	1	6	39	65	0	82.2	61	5	27	69	Pitch 31-45	.222	9	2	0	0	0	2	1	3	.300	.222
0 Days rest	1.37	1	1	14	18	0	19.2	14	2	6	14	Pitch 46+	.000	2	0	0	0	0	1	0	0	.000	.000
1 or 2 Days rest	3.15	0	5	13	25	0	34.1	25	2	12	24	First Pitch	.214	42	9	1	0	1	9	1	0	.261	.310
3+ Days rest	1.57	0	0	12	22	0	28.2	22	1	9	31	Ahead on Count	.158	158	25	4	0	1	11	0	60	.164	.203
Pre-All Star	1.60	1	5	21	36	0	45.0	31	1	13	33	Behind on Count	.250	48	12	2	0	2	3	17	0	.439	.417
Post-All Star	2.87	1	1	18	29	0	37.2	30	4	14	36	Two Strikes	.153	157	24	3	0	1	10	9	69	.199	.191

Last Five Years

	ERA	W	L	Sv	G	GS	IP	H	HR	BB	SO		Avg	AB	H	2B	3B	HR	RBI	BB	SO	OBP	SLG
Home	2.06	19	11	63	169	0	231.0	196	14	56	219	vs. Left	.238	745	177	33	2	14	84	77	137	.312	.344
Away	2.78	6	9	52	144	0	190.2	149	12	88	162	vs. Right	.206	814	168	28	2	12	83	67	244	.273	.290
Day	2.85	6	7	26	78	0	110.1	87	9	41	105	Inning 1-6	.185	81	15	5	0	2	15	13	17	.309	.321
Night	2.23	19	13	89	235	0	311.1	258	17	103	276	Inning 7+	.223	1478	330	56	4	24	152	131	364	.290	.315
Grass	2.61	6	8	38	104	0	145.0	108	8	67	119	None on	.227	819	186	39	3	13	13	72	194	.295	.330
Turf	2.28	19	12	77	209	0	276.2	237	18	77	262	Runners on	.215	740	159	22	1	13	154	72	167	.287	.300
April	2.47	4	5	7	35	0	47.1	43	2	10	42	Scoring Posn	.201	452	91	13	1	7	137	55	120	.288	.281
May	2.54	7	4	14	44	0	67.1	48	4	19	65	Close & Late	.241	851	205	36	3	14	112	74	193	.303	.340
June	3.17	0	3	22	56	0	76.2	72	7	24	70	None on/out	.207	352	73	15	0	7	7	33	88	.281	.310
July	1.65	5	3	24	60	0	92.2	69	4	36	80	vs. 1st Batr (relief)	.229	279	64	13	0	5	33	25	70	.301	.330
August	2.09	7	2	26	59	0	69.0	46	5	28	70	First Inning Pitched	.225	1081	243	44	3	20	135	100	255	.294	.327
September/October	2.62	2	3	22	59	0	68.2	67	4	27	54	First 15 Pitches	.239	964	230	45	4	20	116	81	212	.302	.356
Starter	0.00	0	0	0	0	0	0.0	0	0	0	0	Pitch 16-30	.182	428	78	12	0	1	26	49	131	.271	.217
Reliever	2.39	25	20	115	313	0	421.2	345	26	144	381	Pitch 31-45	.231	134	31	3	0	4	21	11	33	.295	.343
0 Days rest	1.89	6	3	45	75	0	90.2	66	5	34	81	Pitch 46+	.182	33	6	1	0	1	4	3	5	.250	.303
1 or 2 Days rest	3.31	11	15	45	152	0	204.0	194	16	73	189	First Pitch	.286	210	60	13	1	4	34	12	0	.335	.414
3+ Days rest	1.28	8	2	25	86	0	127.0	85	5	37	111	Ahead on Count	.165	835	138	17	2	11	72	1	332	.172	.230
Pre-All Star	2.64	14	13	47	156	0	222.0	187	15	62	210	Behind on Count	.300	253	76	19	1	6	35	81	0	.470	.455
Post-All Star	2.12	11	7	68	157	0	199.2	158	11	82	171	Two Strikes	.139	821	114	13	0	8	49	50	381	.192	.184

Pitcher vs. Batter (career)

Pitches Best Vs.	Avg	AB	H	2B	3B	HR	RBI	BB	SO	OBP	SLG	Pitches Worst Vs.	Avg	AB	H	2B	3B	HR	RBI	BB	SO	OBP	SLG
Chili Davis	.000	12	0	0	0	0	4	4	4	.250	.000	Joe Orsulak	.462	13	6	2	0	0	2	1	0	.500	.615
Gene Larkin	.000	11	0	0	0	0	1	1	4	.083	.000	Kent Hrbek	.417	12	5	1	0	1	4	1	0	.462	.750
Darryl Hamilton	.000	11	0	0	0	0	1	1	0	.083	.000	Cal Ripken	.417	12	5	2	0	0	0	3	1	.533	.583
Franklin Stubbs	.000	10	0	0	0	0	1	1	3	.091	.000	Scott Bradley	.400	10	4	1	0	1	4	1	1	.455	.800
Brook Jacoby	.083	12	1	0	0	0	1	4	.154	.083	Don Mattingly	.385	13	5	2	0	1	3	1	0	.429	.769

Mike Moore — Athletics　　　　　　　　　　　　Pitches Right

	ERA	W	L	Sv	G	GS	IP	BB	SO	Avg	H	2B	3B	HR	RBI	OBP	SLG	CG	ShO	Sup	QS	#P/S	SB	CS	GB	FB	G/F
1992 Season	4.12	17	12	0	36	36	223.0	103	117	.269	229	43	4	20	102	.349	.399	2	0	4.96	19	104	19	13	355	235	1.51
Last Five Years	3.59	75	61	1	174	169	1102.2	438	697	.243	185	16	83	423	.317	.356	23	7	4.29	100	104	70	51	1574	1104	1.43

1992 Season

	ERA	W	L	Sv	G	GS	IP	H	HR	BB	SO		Avg	AB	H	2B	3B	HR	RBI	BB	SO	OBP	SLG
Home	3.55	7	4	0	17	17	104.0	112	12	42	48	vs. Left	.261	445	116	20	1	8	51	41	48	.326	.364
Away	4.61	10	8	0	19	19	119.0	117	8	61	69	vs. Right	.278	407	113	23	3	12	51	62	69	.373	.437
Day	3.54	9	7	0	18	18	122.0	108	13	47	63	Inning 1-6	.273	743	203	40	3	17	94	93	108	.355	.404
Night	4.81	8	5	0	18	18	101.0	121	7	56	54	Inning 7+	.239	109	26	3	1	3	8	10	9	.306	.367
Grass	4.28	13	11	0	30	30	185.0	199	17	88	99	None on	.281	488	137	25	3	16	16	50	65	.355	.443
Turf	3.32	4	1	0	6	6	38.0	30	3	15	18	Runners on	.253	364	92	18	1	4	86	53	52	.342	.341
April	1.51	4	0	0	5	5	35.2	31	0	13	19	Scoring Posn	.269	201	54	11	1	3	80	42	29	.383	.378
May	6.31	2	3	0	6	6	35.2	45	4	24	23	Close & Late	.238	63	15	2	0	2	6	5	6	.300	.365
June	6.75	1	4	0	6	6	32.0	39	6	22	15	None on/out	.238	223	53	14	2	7	7	20	37	.306	.413
July	4.91	3	2	0	6	6	33.0	34	7	12	17	vs. 1st Batr (relief)	.000	0	0	0	0	0	0	0	0	.000	.000
August	2.79	3	1	0	6	6	42.0	38	1	15	23	First Inning Pitched	.258	132	34	11	0	2	18	17	16	.336	.386
September/October	3.22	4	2	0	7	7	44.2	42	2	17	20	First 75 Pitches	.265	586	155	33	2	12	68	75	90	.348	.389
Starter	4.12	17	12	0	36	36	223.0	229	20	103	117	Pitch 76-90	.309	110	34	5	0	4	20	13	8	.392	.464
Reliever	0.00	0	0	0	0	0	0.0	0	0	0	0	Pitch 91-105	.188	85	16	1	0	4	9	9	13	.265	.341
0-3 Days Rest	1.65	3	1	0	4	4	27.1	20	1	12	12	Pitch 106+	.338	71	24	4	2	0	5	6	6	.392	.451
4 Days Rest	5.24	9	10	0	25	25	147.2	168	15	75	82	First Pitch	.288	104	30	4	1	2	14	5	0	.321	.404
5+ Days Rest	2.06	5	1	0	7	7	48.0	41	4	16	23	Ahead on Count	.242	360	87	12	1	7	29	1	100	.253	.339
Pre-All Star	4.42	10	7	0	20	20	124.1	129	13	63	71	Behind on Count	.293	198	58	12	2	8	37	56	0	.446	.495
Post-All Star	3.74	7	5	0	16	16	98.2	100	7	40	46	Two Strikes	.243	378	92	22	1	3	24	42	117	.323	.331

Last Five Years

	ERA	W	L	Sv	G	GS	IP	H	HR	BB	SO		Avg	AB	H	2B	3B	HR	RBI	BB	SO	OBP	SLG
Home	3.11	41	25	1	90	86	569.1	483	39	219	337	vs. Left	.240	2162	519	101	6	32	215	230	330	.313	.337
Away	4.10	34	36	0	84	83	533.1	515	44	219	360	vs. Right	.246	1948	479	84	10	51	208	206	367	.321	.378
Day	3.73	33	23	0	66	66	429.1	364	35	172	264	Inning 1-6	.246	3497	862	156	15	70	383	388	597	.322	.360
Night	3.50	42	38	1	108	103	673.1	614	48	266	433	Inning 7+	.222	613	136	29	1	13	40	50	100	.283	.336
Grass	3.55	60	47	0	130	130	843.2	770	65	341	523	None on	.238	2477	590	104	8	55	55	226	452	.306	.353
Turf	3.72	15	14	1	44	39	259.0	228	18	97	174	Runners on	.250	1633	408	81	8	28	368	212	245	.332	.361
April	3.48	13	4	0	23	23	150.0	131	9	67	84	Scoring Posn	.257	901	232	49	6	17	329	143	138	.351	.382
May	4.35	12	14	0	30	29	184.0	176	19	87	99	Close & Late	.243	305	74	18	0	7	26	25	47	.304	.370
June	3.69	9	15	1	33	29	192.2	177	17	79	109	None on/out	.224	1063	243	41	6	22	22	98	208	.292	.334
July	4.02	12	10	0	28	29	172.1	166	14	68	119	vs. 1st Batr (relief)	.200	5	1	0	0	0	0	0	2	.200	.200
August	2.98	13	9	0	29	29	202.2	180	13	57	160	First Inning Pitched	.256	641	164	36	2	14	86	78	110	.334	.384
September/October	3.13	16	9	0	31	31	201.0	168	11	80	126	First 75 Pitches	.244	2863	699	134	13	54	296	308	491	.318	.357
Starter	3.59	74	61	0	169	169	1097.1	992	82	437	694	Pitch 76-90	.261	517	135	24	1	16	77	60	73	.339	.404
Reliever	3.38	1	0	1	5	0	5.1	6	1	1	3	Pitch 91-105	.202	391	79	6	0	9	27	41	79	.280	.286
0-3 Days Rest	3.37	11	6	0	21	21	136.1	113	9	59	72	Pitch 106+	.251	339	85	21	2	4	23	29	54	.312	.360
4 Days Rest	3.65	48	41	0	115	115	750.1	691	52	289	516	First Pitch	.297	539	160	30	3	13	76	9	0	.306	.436
5+ Days Rest	3.55	15	14	0	33	33	210.2	188	21	89	106	Ahead on Count	.197	1716	338	51	6	29	117	1	566	.203	.284
Pre-All Star	3.76	41	34	0	96	91	594.1	536	53	254	347	Behind on Count	.290	964	280	61	5	26	140	227	0	.423	.445
Post-All Star	3.40	34	27	0	78	78	508.1	462	30	184	350	Two Strikes	.190	1813	344	60	7	25	114	202	696	.274	.272

Pitcher vs. Batter (since 1984)

Pitches Best Vs.	Avg	AB	H	2B	3B	HR	RBI	BB	SO	OBP	SLG	Pitches Worst Vs.	Avg	AB	H	2B	3B	HR	RBI	BB	SO	OBP	SLG
Dante Bichette	.000	9	0	0	0	0	0	2	2	.182	.000	Mark Lewis	.636	11	7	3	0	0	3	0	1	.636	.909
Juan Gonzalez	.050	20	1	1	0	0	0	0	6	.050	.100	Sammy Sosa	.462	13	6	2	1	1	3	1	1	.500	1.000
Ivan Rodriguez	.077	13	1	1	0	0	0	0	1	.077	.154	Darnell Coles	.444	9	4	0	1	3	9	2	0	.545	1.667
Willie Randolph	.095	21	2	0	0	0	1	3	.136	.095	Rob Deer	.415	41	17	2	0	6	13	8	8	.500	.902
John Moses	.095	21	2	0	0	0	0	2	.095	.095	Greg Vaughn	.364	11	4	1	1	1	7	2	3	.429	.909

Mickey Morandini — Phillies　　　　　　　　Bats Left (groundball hitter)

	Avg	G	AB	R	H	2B	3B	HR	RBI	BB	SO	HBP	GDP	SB	CS	OBP	SLG	IBB	SH	SF	#Pit	#P/PA	GB	FB	G/F
1992 Season	.265	127	422	47	112	8	8	3	30	25	64	0	4	8	3	.305	.344	2	6	2	1686	3.76	184	90	2.04
Career (1990-1992)	.257	250	826	94	212	23	12	5	53	60	126	2	12	24	5	.307	.332	2	14	4	3379	3.79	352	175	2.01

1992 Season

	Avg	AB	H	2B	3B	HR	RBI	BB	SO	OBP	SLG		Avg	AB	H	2B	3B	HR	RBI	BB	SO	OBP	SLG
vs. Left	.198	121	24	1	1	1	8	7	19	.240	.248	Scoring Posn	.238	101	24	1	3	1	25	14	23	.325	.337

1992 Season

	Avg	AB	H	2B	3B	HR	RBI	BB	SO	OBP	SLG		Avg	AB	H	2B	3B	HR	RBI	BB	SO	OBP	SLG
vs. Right	.292	301	88	7	7	2	22	18	45	.331	.382	Close & Late	.284	74	21	1	0	0	5	6	11	.333	.297
Groundball	.324	179	58	4	5	2	15	8	23	.353	.436	None on/out	.235	102	24	2	1	1	1	3	11	.257	.304
Flyball	.155	84	13	0	0	1	7	8	18	.226	.190	Batting #2	.285	158	45	1	3	1	8	6	12	.309	.348
Home	.272	202	55	5	4	2	16	12	36	.313	.366	Batting #8	.281	128	36	4	3	1	10	7	26	.316	.383
Away	.259	220	57	3	4	1	14	13	28	.298	.323	Other	.228	136	31	3	2	1	12	12	26	.291	.301
Day	.307	114	35	4	2	0	6	9	11	.358	.377	April	.364	66	24	1	2	1	5	4	11	.400	.485
Night	.250	308	77	4	6	3	24	16	53	.285	.331	May	.222	54	12	1	0	1	6	6	16	.300	.296
Grass	.322	118	38	2	2	1	12	7	17	.354	.398	June	.138	58	8	3	2	0	2	7	7	.227	.259
Turf	.243	304	74	6	6	2	18	18	47	.286	.322	July	.308	78	24	2	2	0	7	3	16	.333	.385
First Pitch	.226	62	14	1	1	0	1	1	0	.238	.274	August	.217	46	10	1	1	0	2	2	5	.250	.283
Ahead on Count	.337	86	29	1	1	2	11	14	0	.430	.442	September/October	.283	120	34	0	1	1	8	3	9	.298	.325
Behind on Count	.262	149	39	4	3	1	13	0	35	.260	.349	Pre-All Star	.267	217	58	6	4	2	15	17	43	.319	.359
Two Strikes	.230	196	45	5	5	0	10	10	64	.267	.306	Post-All Star	.263	205	54	2	4	1	15	8	21	.290	.327

1992 By Position

Position	Avg	AB	H	2B	3B	HR	RBI	BB	SO	OBP	SLG	G	GS	Innings	PO	A	E	DP	Fld Pct	Rng Fctr	In Zone	Outs	Zone Rtg	MLB Zone
As 2b	.254	410	104	7	8	3	30	23	63	.292	.332	124	106	944.1	236	332	5	64	.991	5.41	366	325	.888	.892

Career (1990-1992)

	Avg	AB	H	2B	3B	HR	RBI	BB	SO	OBP	SLG		Avg	AB	H	2B	3B	HR	RBI	BB	SO	OBP	SLG
vs. Left	.189	201	38	2	1	1	11	11	35	.230	.224	Scoring Posn	.247	178	44	1	4	2	46	19	37	.313	.331
vs. Right	.278	625	174	21	11	4	42	49	93	.331	.366	Close & Late	.284	141	40	5	1	0	7	13	19	.346	.333
Groundball	.284	324	92	8	7	2	21	22	43	.331	.370	None on/out	.276	210	58	7	1	1	1	5	29	.327	.333
Flyball	.218	170	37	3	1	1	10	15	35	.280	.265	Batting #2	.265	358	95	7	4	2	24	28	43	.319	.324
Home	.260	415	108	10	7	4	29	29	67	.309	.347	Batting #8	.266	199	53	8	3	2	13	10	42	.300	.367
Away	.253	411	104	13	5	1	24	31	61	.306	.316	Other	.238	269	64	8	5	1	16	22	43	.297	.316
Day	.274	208	57	8	3	0	11	14	28	.318	.341	April	.346	81	28	1	2	1	5	5	15	.384	.444
Night	.251	618	155	15	9	5	42	46	100	.303	.328	May	.250	100	25	2	0	1	9	10	20	.324	.300
Grass	.313	217	68	9	3	1	21	14	29	.352	.396	June	.201	149	30	6	2	1	14	16	22	.275	.289
Turf	.236	609	144	14	9	4	32	46	99	.291	.309	July	.273	139	38	6	3	0	10	8	20	.311	.360
First Pitch	.225	120	27	1	1	0	4	1	0	.231	.250	August	.232	99	23	2	2	0	2	7	12	.290	.293
Ahead on Count	.319	166	53	4	2	3	19	35	0	.436	.422	September/October	.264	258	68	6	3	2	13	14	39	.300	.333
Behind on Count	.248	282	70	11	6	2	21	0	71	.246	.351	Pre-All Star	.260	393	102	11	4	3	30	33	67	.317	.331
Two Strikes	.213	380	81	14	7	1	19	24	128	.261	.295	Post-All Star	.254	433	110	12	8	2	23	27	61	.298	.333

Batter vs. Pitcher (career)

Hits Best Against	Avg	AB	H	2B	3B	HR	RBI	BB	SO	OBP	SLG	Hits Worst Against	Avg	AB	H	2B	3B	HR	RBI	BB	SO	OBP	SLG
Greg Maddux	.433	30	13	0	2	0	1	2	4	.469	.567	Dennis Martinez	.056	18	1	0	0	0	0	1	2	.105	.056
Mike Bielecki	.417	12	5	2	0	0	2	1	1	.462	.583	Omar Olivares	.077	13	1	0	0	0	0	1	1	.143	.077
Dwight Gooden	.375	24	9	1	0	0	2	3	4	.444	.417	Mike Morgan	.125	24	3	1	0	0	0	2	1	.192	.167
Anthony Young	.333	12	4	0	1	0	0	1	2	.333	.500	Bob Tewksbury	.133	15	2	0	0	0	0	1	1	.133	.133
Bryn Smith	.333	9	3	1	0	0	1	2	0	.455	.556	Tim Belcher	.143	14	2	0	0	0	0	1	6	.143	.143

Mike Morgan — Cubs

Pitches Right (groundball pitcher)

	ERA	W	L	Sv	G	GS	IP	BB	SO	Avg	H	2B	3B	HR	RBI	OBP	SLG	CG	ShO	Sup	QS	#P/S	SB	CS	GB	FB	G/F
1992 Season	2.55	16	8	0	34	34	240.0	79	123	.234	203	39	3	14	70	.298	.334	6	1	4.13	27	101	6	9	400	162	2.47
Last Five Years	3.11	50	50	2	163	129	911.1	256	470	.241	816	133	19	57	316	.296	.343	19	6	3.65	89	93	56	35	1659	679	2.44

1992 Season

	ERA	W	L	Sv	G	GS	IP	H	HR	BB	SO		Avg	AB	H	2B	3B	HR	RBI	BB	SO	OBP	SLG
Home	1.38	9	2	0	17	17	130.1	100	3	40	62	vs. Left	.248	491	122	22	3	8	35	57	57	.328	.354
Away	3.94	7	6	0	17	17	109.2	103	11	39	61	vs. Right	.215	377	81	17	0	6	35	22	66	.257	.308
Day	2.02	12	3	0	22	22	164.2	130	7	56	76	Inning 1-6	.237	718	170	32	2	12	64	71	106	.306	.337
Night	3.70	4	5	0	12	12	75.1	73	7	23	47	Inning 7+	.220	150	33	7	1	2	6	8	17	.263	.320
Grass	1.85	13	3	0	23	23	170.1	141	9	50	81	None on	.231	532	123	28	1	4	4	41	72	.289	.310
Turf	4.26	3	5	0	11	11	69.2	62	5	29	42	Runners on	.238	336	80	11	2	10	66	38	51	.313	.372
April	5.63	0	2	0	4	4	24.0	23	1	14	16	Scoring Posn	.224	174	39	6	0	3	47	32	39	.340	.310
May	2.32	5	0	0	6	6	42.2	34	2	15	25	Close & Late	.228	57	13	4	1	0	3	4	8	.274	.333
June	1.93	2	0	0	5	5	37.1	31	2	12	17	None on/out	.214	224	48	11	0	0	0	21	27	.285	.263
July	1.18	2	2	0	6	6	38.0	31	1	11	25	vs. 1st Batr (relief)	.000	0	0	0	0	0	0	0	0	.000	.000
August	2.11	4	2	0	6	6	47.0	51	3	15	22	First Inning Pitched	.174	115	20	5	0	0	8	12	25	.258	.217
September/October	3.18	3	2	0	7	7	51.0	33	5	12	18	First 75 Pitches	.227	616	140	27	2	9	45	61	92	.298	.321
Starter	2.55	16	8	0	34	34	240.0	203	14	79	123	Pitch 76-90	.268	127	34	8	0	3	14	10	13	.317	.402
Reliever	0.00	0	0	0	0	0	0.0	0	0	0	0	Pitch 91-105	.173	81	14	3	0	0	6	4	14	.212	.210
0-3 Days Rest	0.00	1	0	0	1	1	7.0	5	0	1	3	Pitch 106+	.341	44	15	1	1	2	5	4	4	.400	.545
4 Days Rest	2.34	10	5	0	24	24	173.1	138	10	53	84	First Pitch	.219	151	33	8	0	5	17	6	0	.252	.371
5+ Days Rest	3.47	5	3	0	9	9	59.2	60	4	25	36	Ahead on Count	.186	328	61	11	1	1	17	0	100	.190	.235
Pre-All Star	2.66	7	3	0	18	18	122.0	104	6	45	72	Behind on Count	.274	219	60	12	1	5	22	42	0	.388	.406
Post-All Star	2.44	9	5	0	16	16	118.0	99	8	34	51	Two Strikes	.183	349	64	13	2	2	20	31	123	.251	.249

Last Five Years

	ERA	W	L	Sv	G	GS	IP	H	HR	BB	SO		Avg	AB	H	2B	3B	HR	RBI	BB	SO	OBP	SLG
Home	2.62	24	21	2	80	64	485.0	409	34	122	242	vs. Left	.258	1871	483	85	9	35	177	169	242	.320	.369
Away	3.67	26	29	0	83	65	426.1	407	23	134	228	vs. Right	.221	1508	333	48	10	22	139	87	228	.265	.310
Day	2.43	24	13	2	53	45	329.0	279	15	96	168	Inning 1-6	.243	2716	659	111	13	47	271	215	390	.299	.345
Night	3.49	26	37	0	110	84	582.1	537	42	160	302	Inning 7+	.237	663	157	22	6	10	45	41	80	.283	.333
Grass	2.78	38	30	2	117	91	680.0	588	44	174	337	None on	.228	2119	484	75	11	33	33	124	305	.273	.321
Turf	4.09	12	20	0	46	38	231.1	228	13	82	133	Runners on	.263	1260	332	58	8	24	283	132	165	.333	.379
April	3.06	7	10	0	23	20	141.0	112	9	32	61	Scoring Posn	.248	698	173	35	5	10	244	105	121	.342	.355
May	2.90	13	6	1	32	25	174.0	148	11	53	115	Close & Late	.245	302	74	11	4	4	25	23	33	.301	.348
June	2.67	8	9	0	24	22	162.0	147	9	32	73	None on/out	.226	895	202	32	4	12	12	53	119	.272	.311
July	3.54	7	10	1	29	22	145.0	139	5	57	73	vs. 1st Batr (relief)	.167	30	5	3	0	0	6	3	1	.242	.267
August	3.01	9	6	0	30	20	152.2	150	7	46	72	First Inning Pitched	.240	574	138	28	1	5	67	48	68	.300	.319
September/October	3.62	9	6	0	25	20	136.2	120	16	36	76	First 75 Pitches	.239	2597	620	104	13	39	241	196	371	.294	.334
Starter	3.18	47	50	0	129	129	854.2	782	57	241	443	Pitch 76-90	.238	416	99	15	2	10	38	29	54	.286	.356
Reliever	2.06	3	0	2	34	0	56.2	34	0	15	27	Pitch 91-105	.261	261	68	10	2	4	27	20	33	.314	.360
0-3 Days Rest	2.95	2	3	0	6	6	36.2	35	2	7	15	Pitch 106+	.276	105	29	4	2	4	10	11	12	.347	.467
4 Days Rest	2.90	29	27	0	79	79	533.0	476	38	145	262	First Pitch	.270	597	161	31	2	16	69	22	0	.298	.409
5+ Days Rest	3.73	16	20	0	44	44	285.0	271	17	89	166	Behind on Count	.297	827	246	32	3	20	95	144	0	.400	.416
Pre-All Star	2.85	29	28	2	88	75	526.2	462	31	131	277	Two Strikes	.179	1301	233	40	11	10	83	88	469	.233	.250
Post-All Star	3.46	21	22	0	75	54	384.2	354	26	125	193												

Pitcher vs. Batter (since 1984)

Pitches Best Vs.	Avg	AB	H	2B	3B	HR	RBI	BB	SO	OBP	SLG	Pitches Worst Vs.	Avg	AB	H	2B	3B	HR	RBI	BB	SO	OBP	SLG
Von Hayes	.000	11	0	0	0	0	0	0	2	.000	.000	Danny Tartabull	.727	11	8	0	0	1	4	1	0	.750	1.000
Gerald Young	.000	11	0	0	0	0	1	0	1	.000	.000	Randy Bush	.478	23	11	2	0	2	8	3	1	.538	.826
Greg Olson	.000	11	0	0	0	0	0	0	3	.000	.000	Dave Hollins	.400	20	8	3	0	2	5	6	4	.538	.850
Kirt Manwaring	.050	20	1	0	0	0	0	1	3	.095	.050	Rickey Henderson	.400	10	4	0	0	2	2	1	2	.455	1.000
Cal Ripken	.091	22	2	0	0	0	0	0	4	.091	.091	Dan Pasqua	.385	13	5	0	0	2	2	2	4	.467	.846

Hal Morris — Reds

Bats Left (groundball hitter)

	Avg	G	AB	R	H	2B	3B	HR	RBI	BB	SO	HBP	GDP	SB	CS	OBP	SLG	IBB	SH	SF	#Pit	#P/PA	GB	FB	G/F
1992 Season	.271	115	395	41	107	21	3	6	53	45	53	2	12	6	6	.347	.385	8	2	2	1703	3.84	159	108	1.47
Career (1988-1992)	.304	388	1220	166	371	76	7	27	152	113	159	4	30	25	13	.362	.444	19	10	11	4948	3.67	500	312	1.60

1992 Season

	Avg	AB	H	2B	3B	HR	RBI	BB	SO	OBP	SLG		Avg	AB	H	2B	3B	HR	RBI	BB	SO	OBP	SLG
vs. Left	.252	139	35	5	0	1	11	13	30	.325	.309	Scoring Posn	.300	110	33	9	0	2	48	19	14	.397	.436
vs. Right	.281	256	72	16	3	5	42	32	23	.359	.426	Close & Late	.290	62	18	5	3	1	5	5	11	.353	.516
Groundball	.265	151	40	8	0	3	19	12	16	.317	.377	None on/out	.205	83	17	2	2	0	0	8	13	.275	.277
Flyball	.212	85	18	4	0	3	17	10	15	.299	.365	Batting #2	.250	92	23	3	0	1	6	7	11	.314	.315
Home	.273	198	54	12	1	3	29	16	27	.333	.389	Batting #5	.282	117	33	8	1	2	15	15	17	.361	.419
Away	.269	197	53	9	2	3	24	29	26	.360	.381	Other	.274	186	51	10	2	3	32	23	25	.354	.398
Day	.259	135	35	8	2	3	21	19	15	.353	.415	April	.265	34	9	1	1	0	2	3	5	.342	.353
Night	.277	260	72	13	1	3	32	26	38	.344	.369	May	.324	37	12	3	1	0	9	8	3	.435	.459
Grass	.208	96	20	4	1	1	9	13	14	.297	.302	June	.345	87	30	5	1	2	20	11	10	.418	.494
Turf	.291	299	87	17	2	5	44	32	39	.363	.411	July	.252	103	26	5	0	2	8	12	16	.328	.359
First Pitch	.333	57	19	4	2	1	10	6	0	.394	.526	August	.250	56	14	4	0	2	8	4	9	.300	.429
Ahead on Count	.343	99	34	8	0	4	17	19	0	.449	.545	September/October	.205	78	16	3	0	0	6	7	10	.279	.244
Behind on Count	.235	115	27	5	1	1	16	0	23	.235	.322	Pre-All Star	.320	200	64	11	3	2	34	31	22	.410	.435
Two Strikes	.215	177	38	6	0	1	20	21	53	.302	.266	Post-All Star	.221	195	43	10	0	4	19	14	31	.276	.333

1992 By Position

Position	Avg	AB	H	2B	3B	HR	RBI	BB	SO	OBP	SLG	G	GS	Innings	PO	A	E	DP	Fld Pct	Rng Fctr	In Zone	Outs	Zone Rtg	MLB Zone
As 1b	.271	387	105	20	3	6	53	44	48	.347	.385	109	109	908.2	840	84	1	66	.999	---	158	138	.873	.843

Career (1988-1992)

	Avg	AB	H	2B	3B	HR	RBI	BB	SO	OBP	SLG		Avg	AB	H	2B	3B	HR	RBI	BB	SO	OBP	SLG
vs. Left	.239	326	78	13	1	2	28	26	72	.298	.304	Scoring Posn	.304	319	97	20	1	4	120	49	47	.385	.411
vs. Right	.328	894	293	63	6	25	124	87	87	.385	.496	Close & Late	.274	201	55	12	3	2	12	14	37	.327	.393
Groundball	.308	402	124	27	1	7	53	31	44	.358	.433	None on/out	.315	270	85	17	3	5	5	15	34	.351	.456
Flyball	.286	301	86	21	1	10	36	27	43	.343	.462	Batting #2	.303	271	82	18	1	6	26	29	40	.369	.443
Home	.303	604	183	44	3	15	84	50	77	.356	.460	Batting #5	.320	337	108	26	1	10	46	28	34	.370	.493
Away	.305	616	188	32	4	12	68	63	82	.368	.429	Other	.296	612	181	32	5	11	80	56	85	.354	.418
Day	.291	399	116	30	2	11	55	39	45	.353	.459	April	.307	101	31	8	1	2	12	4	14	.336	.465
Night	.311	821	255	46	5	16	97	74	114	.367	.437	May	.311	151	47	10	2	2	26	16	17	.376	.444
Grass	.286	367	105	21	3	6	41	36	55	.349	.409	June	.321	184	59	12	1	3	30	17	26	.377	.446
Turf	.312	853	266	55	4	21	111	77	104	.368	.460	July	.338	260	88	15	2	8	32	29	31	.399	.504
First Pitch	.354	195	69	17	2	6	32	11	0	.388	.554	August	.277	235	65	15	0	7	23	14	31	.316	.430
Ahead on Count	.377	318	120	27	0	12	54	54	0	.465	.575	September/October	.280	289	81	16	1	5	29	33	40	.355	.399
Behind on Count	.249	370	92	15	2	6	43	1	78	.247	.349	Pre-All Star	.325	511	166	34	4	10	80	50	63	.384	.466
Two Strikes	.220	500	110	16	3	5	43	45	159	.285	.294	Post-All Star	.289	709	205	42	3	17	72	63	96	.346	.429

Batter vs. Pitcher (career)

Hits Best Against	Avg	AB	H	2B	3B	HR	RBI	BB	SO	OBP	SLG	Hits Worst Against	Avg	AB	H	2B	3B	HR	RBI	BB	SO	OBP	SLG
Jimmy Jones	.636	11	7	0	0	1	2	0	0	.636	.909	Bob Tewksbury	.111	18	2	1	0	1	4	0	1	.111	.333
Greg Maddux	.529	17	9	2	0	0	2	1	1	.556	.647	Bruce Hurst	.133	15	2	1	0	0	2	0	2	.133	.200
Kevin Gross	.444	9	4	0	0	0	1	2	0	.545	.444	Greg W. Harris	.133	15	2	0	0	1	1	0	4	.133	.333
John Burkett	.381	21	8	1	0	2	4	2	1	.435	.714	Pete Harnisch	.136	22	3	0	0	1	4	3	4	.240	.273
Bob Walk	.364	11	4	0	0	0	1	1	1	.417	.545	Ken Hill	.231	13	3	0	0	0	1	0	2	.231	.231

Jack Morris — Blue Jays
Pitches Right

	ERA	W	L	Sv	G	GS	IP	BB	SO	Avg	H	2B	3B	HR	RBI	OBP	SLG	CG	ShO	Sup	QS	#P/S	SB	CS	GB	FB	G/F
1992 Season	4.04	21	6	0	34	34	240.2	80	132	.246	222	41	3	18	107	.312	.358	6	1	5.98	19	104	22	16	346	255	1.36
Last Five Years	4.11	75	63	0	163	163	1142.1	411	740	.252	1093	187	21	105	520	.318	.377	47	8	4.91	88	105	148	44	1550	1216	1.27

1992 Season

	ERA	W	L	Sv	G	GS	IP	H	HR	BB	SO		Avg	AB	H	2B	3B	HR	RBI	BB	SO	OBP	SLG
Home	3.09	11	2	0	17	17	128.0	98	7	43	63	vs. Left	.263	460	121	22	3	10	57	42	61	.322	.389
Away	5.11	10	4	0	17	17	112.2	124	11	37	69	vs. Right	.229	442	101	19	0	8	50	38	71	.302	.326
Day	4.18	7	3	0	13	13	92.2	83	8	30	48	Inning 1-6	.250	741	185	31	3	13	87	72	107	.321	.352
Night	3.95	14	3	0	21	21	148.0	139	10	50	84	Inning 7+	.230	161	37	10	0	5	20	8	25	.271	.385
Grass	5.27	8	4	0	13	13	85.1	93	8	30	51	None on	.221	539	119	18	2	10	10	52	84	.294	.317
Turf	3.36	13	2	0	21	21	155.1	129	10	50	81	Runners on	.284	363	103	23	1	8	97	28	48	.339	.419
April	3.69	3	1	0	5	5	39.0	31	6	13	24	Scoring Posn	.260	200	52	14	1	2	77	22	33	.332	.370
May	4.99	2	2	0	6	6	39.2	38	5	21	15	Close & Late	.208	106	22	7	0	2	12	5	14	.250	.330
June	4.11	4	0	0	5	5	35.0	35	3	14	15	None on/out	.210	229	48	9	1	6	6	21	40	.279	.336
July	5.45	3	1	0	5	5	33.0	35	1	6	20	vs. 1st Batr (relief)	.000	0	0	0	0	0	0	0	0	.000	.000
August	3.07	5	1	0	6	6	41.0	38	1	15	28	First Inning Pitched	.314	140	44	10	0	4	25	13	17	.378	.471
September/October	3.40	4	1	0	7	7	53.0	45	2	11	30	First 75 Pitches	.262	625	164	27	2	12	74	64	92	.333	.370
Starter	4.04	21	6	0	34	34	240.2	222	18	80	132	Pitch 76-90	.193	109	21	4	0	2	13	10	17	.270	.284
Reliever	0.00	0	0	0	0	0	0.0	0	0	0	0	Pitch 91-105	.204	108	22	6	1	1	12	5	11	.250	.306
0-3 Days Rest	0.00	1	0	0	1	1	6.0	3	0	1	2	Pitch 106+	.250	60	15	4	0	3	8	1	12	.274	.467
4 Days Rest	4.40	11	3	0	19	19	135.0	123	12	46	75	First Pitch	.291	148	43	8	0	4	18	2	0	.309	.426
5+ Days Rest	3.79	9	3	0	14	14	99.2	96	6	33	55	Ahead on Count	.205	405	83	13	0	5	39	0	115	.211	.274
Pre-All Star	4.41	10	3	0	18	18	126.2	116	14	52	58	Behind on Count	.289	194	56	12	1	7	34	50	0	.436	.469
Post-All Star	3.63	11	3	0	16	16	114.0	106	4	28	74	Two Strikes	.184	374	69	11	0	5	37	28	132	.245	.254

Last Five Years

	ERA	W	L	Sv	G	GS	IP	H	HR	BB	SO		Avg	AB	H	2B	3B	HR	RBI	BB	SO	OBP	SLG
Home	3.91	42	25	0	80	80	566.0	536	49	192	360	vs. Left	.266	2176	579	91	14	52	271	241	337	.332	.392
Away	4.31	33	38	0	83	83	576.1	557	56	219	380	vs. Right	.237	2165	514	96	7	53	248	170	403	.298	.362
Day	3.77	31	20	0	57	57	396.0	383	37	142	253	Inning 1-6	.258	3486	898	148	19	88	441	343	588	.326	.387
Night	4.29	44	43	0	106	106	746.1	710	68	269	487	Inning 7+	.228	855	195	39	2	17	78	68	152	.285	.338
Grass	4.14	45	52	0	112	112	777.0	753	75	289	526	None on	.241	2551	616	106	13	59	59	230	447	.307	.363
Turf	4.06	30	11	0	51	51	365.1	340	30	122	214	Runners on	.266	1790	477	81	8	46	460	181	293	.333	.398
April	4.80	9	14	0	26	26	174.1	194	14	77	137	Scoring Posn	.271	1029	279	51	4	29	403	132	203	.349	.413
May	4.67	9	14	0	28	28	194.2	187	26	85	116	Close & Late	.238	483	115	18	1	9	51	34	81	.289	.335
June	4.17	17	4	0	23	23	149.0	154	16	54	63	None on/out	.253	1114	282	48	7	34	34	97	182	.315	.404
July	4.51	8	11	0	23	23	155.2	148	16	40	105	vs. 1st Batr (relief)	.000	0	0	0	0	0	0	0	0	.000	.000
August	3.86	15	10	0	30	30	216.2	195	13	75	132	First Inning Pitched	.266	639	170	26	4	12	86	61	103	.332	.376
September/October	3.14	17	10	0	33	33	252.0	215	20	80	167	First 75 Pitches	.255	2961	756	124	15	79	354	284	499	.322	.387
Starter	4.11	75	63	0	163	163	1142.1	1093	105	411	740	Pitch 76-90	.270	534	144	27	1	13	80	61	90	.347	.397
Reliever	0.00	0	0	0	0	0	0.0	0	0	0	0	Pitch 91-105	.229	484	111	21	5	5	49	40	79	.288	.324
0-3 Days Rest	3.36	6	0	0	8	8	56.1	48	2	24	39	Pitch 106+	.227	362	82	15	0	8	37	26	72	.279	.334
4 Days Rest	4.13	49	46	0	110	110	776.1	747	75	283	516	First Pitch	.310	703	218	41	3	25	113	13	0	.326	.484
5+ Days Rest	4.21	20	17	0	45	45	309.2	298	28	104	185	Ahead on Count	.197	1905	376	61	3	25	177	0	639	.200	.272
Pre-All Star	4.60	38	34	0	83	83	557.2	568	62	225	361	Behind on Count	.315	974	307	53	9	38	149	231	0	.447	.505
Post-All Star	3.65	37	29	0	80	80	584.2	525	43	186	379	Two Strikes	.182	1819	331	56	5	25	158	166	740	.252	.259

Pitcher vs. Batter (since 1984)

Pitches Best Vs.	Avg	AB	H	2B	3B	HR	RBI	BB	SO	OBP	SLG	Pitches Worst Vs.	Avg	AB	H	2B	3B	HR	RBI	BB	SO	OBP	SLG
Paul Sorrento	.000	15	0	0	0	0	0	2	5	.118	.000	Darnell Coles	.600	10	6	1	0	0	1	1	2	.636	.700
Randy Milligan	.053	19	1	1	0	0	0	6	0	.053	.105	Henry Cotto	.500	16	8	2	0	1	1	0	2	.500	.813
Walt Weiss	.071	14	1	0	0	0	1	2	3	.176	.071	Franklin Stubbs	.444	9	4	0	0	1	3	3	1	.538	.778
Rene Gonzales	.091	11	1	0	0	0	1	0	4	.091	.091	Cecil Fielder	.375	16	6	1	0	3	7	1	3	.412	1.000
Steve Sax	.100	20	2	0	0	0	0	0	1	.100	.100	Ken Griffey Jr.	.333	21	7	2	0	3	7	3	3	.400	.857

John Morris — Angels
Bats Left

	Avg	G	AB	R	H	2B	3B	HR	RBI	BB	SO	HBP	GDP	SB	CS	OBP	SLG	IBB	SH	SF	#Pit	#P/PA	GB	FB	G/F
1992 Season	.193	43	57	4	11	1	0	1	3	4	11	1	0	1	0	.258	.263	1	1	0	235	3.79	28	8	3.50
Last Five Years	.224	262	357	30	80	9	3	4	26	24	71	2	5	4	0	.277	.300	5	4	0	1424	3.72	127	100	1.27

1992 Season

	Avg	AB	H	2B	3B	HR	RBI	BB	SO	OBP	SLG		Avg	AB	H	2B	3B	HR	RBI	BB	SO	OBP	SLG
vs. Left	.250	4	1	0	0	0	0	0	0	.250	.250	Scoring Posn	.200	10	2	0	0	0	2	2	1	.333	.200

1992 Season

	Avg	AB	H	2B	3B	HR	RBI	BB	SO	OBP	SLG		Avg	AB	H	2B	3B	HR	RBI	BB	SO	OBP	SLG
vs. Right	.189	53	10	1	0	1	3	4	11	.259	.264	Close & Late	.278	18	5	0	0	0	1	2	2	.350	.278

Last Five Years

	Avg	AB	H	2B	3B	HR	RBI	BB	SO	OBP	SLG		Avg	AB	H	2B	3B	HR	RBI	BB	SO	OBP	SLG
vs. Left	.229	35	8	1	0	0	1	1	9	.270	.257	Scoring Posn	.233	73	17	4	1	0	21	7	16	.309	.315
vs. Right	.224	322	72	8	3	4	25	23	62	.277	.304	Close & Late	.250	96	24	2	2	1	10	5	23	.294	.344
Groundball	.248	125	31	2	1	1	12	14	21	.324	.304	None on/out	.292	96	28	2	1	2	2	7	19	.340	.396
Flyball	.227	75	17	0	1	1	3	3	21	.256	.293	Batting #8	.222	72	16	0	1	0	4	8	17	.300	.250
Home	.222	167	37	5	2	3	18	11	33	.278	.329	Batting #9	.211	95	20	2	0	1	8	8	21	.272	.263
Away	.226	190	43	4	1	1	8	13	38	.276	.274	Other	.232	190	44	7	2	3	14	8	33	.270	.337
Day	.228	136	31	1	2	2	10	12	27	.295	.309	April	.347	49	17	4	1	1	9	5	11	.407	.531
Night	.222	221	49	8	1	2	16	12	44	.265	.294	May	.211	71	15	0	1	0	3	4	14	.253	.239
Grass	.212	118	25	1	1	1	2	8	25	.268	.263	June	.162	74	12	1	0	0	2	8	14	.244	.176
Turf	.230	239	55	8	2	3	24	16	46	.281	.318	July	.193	57	11	1	0	1	2	5	12	.270	.263
First Pitch	.452	31	14	1	0	0	8	5	0	.541	.484	August	.194	36	7	0	0	0	2	1	8	.216	.194
Ahead on Count	.257	70	18	0	1	1	8	11	0	.358	.329	September/October	.257	70	18	3	1	2	8	1	12	.278	.414
Behind on Count	.179	145	26	5	0	1	2	0	41	.185	.234	Pre-All Star	.230	226	52	6	2	2	16	21	45	.298	.301
Two Strikes	.145	165	24	5	1	2	6	8	71	.190	.224	Post-All Star	.214	131	28	3	1	2	10	3	26	.237	.298

Batter vs. Pitcher (career)

Hits Best Against	Avg	AB	H	2B	3B	HR	RBI	BB	SO	OBP	SLG	Hits Worst Against	Avg	AB	H	2B	3B	HR	RBI	BB	SO	OBP	SLG
David Cone	.435	23	10	3	1	1	6	0	2	.435	.783												
Kevin Gross	.417	12	5	1	0	1	3	2	1	.500	.750												
Bryn Smith	.375	16	6	1	0	0	3	0	1	.353	.438												

John Moses — Mariners

Bats Both (groundball hitter)

	Avg	G	AB	R	H	2B	3B	HR	RBI	BB	SO	HBP	GDP	SB	CS	OBP	SLG	IBB	SH	SF	#Pit	#P/PA	GB	FB	G/F
1992 Season	.136	21	22	3	3	1	0	0	1	5	4	0	0	0	0	.296	.182	0	2	0	97	3.59	8	6	1.33
Last Five Years	.264	363	663	100	175	27	7	4	59	60	74	5	13	31	16	.327	.344	4	7	5	2437	3.32	272	177	1.54

1992 Season

	Avg	AB	H	2B	3B	HR	RBI	BB	SO	OBP	SLG		Avg	AB	H	2B	3B	HR	RBI	BB	SO	OBP	SLG
vs. Left	.000	3	0	0	0	0	0	0	0	.000	.000	Scoring Posn	.200	5	1	0	0	0	1	2	1	.429	.200
vs. Right	.158	19	3	1	0	0	1	5	4	.333	.211	Close & Late	.167	6	1	0	0	0	0	1	2	.286	.167

Last Five Years

	Avg	AB	H	2B	3B	HR	RBI	BB	SO	OBP	SLG		Avg	AB	H	2B	3B	HR	RBI	BB	SO	OBP	SLG
vs. Left	.283	99	28	1	1	0	12	9	9	.339	.313	Scoring Posn	.241	145	35	4	3	0	51	20	20	.331	.310
vs. Right	.261	564	147	26	6	4	47	51	65	.325	.349	Close & Late	.250	132	33	4	1	1	15	8	19	.301	.318
Groundball	.219	178	39	2	1	1	13	12	18	.280	.258	None on/out	.271	188	51	7	3	0	0	8	17	.301	.340
Flyball	.273	139	38	11	1	2	16	17	19	.350	.410	Batting #2	.251	175	44	9	1	2	10	13	17	.311	.349
Home	.264	276	73	16	6	0	35	28	33	.334	.366	Batting #8	.221	140	31	4	1	1	18	14	18	.287	.286
Away	.264	387	102	11	1	4	24	32	41	.322	.328	Other	.287	348	100	14	5	1	31	33	39	.352	.365
Day	.269	249	67	15	2	0	28	19	23	.322	.345	April	.269	52	14	3	1	0	4	10	3	.391	.365
Night	.261	414	108	12	5	4	31	41	51	.330	.343	May	.285	123	35	2	2	1	12	12	13	.350	.358
Grass	.243	317	77	7	0	4	21	29	35	.308	.303	June	.297	128	38	5	2	1	15	9	13	.345	.391
Turf	.283	346	98	20	7	0	38	31	39	.346	.382	July	.236	127	30	4	1	1	9	8	13	.279	.307
First Pitch	.301	136	41	7	3	0	8	0	0	.301	.397	August	.244	156	38	11	0	1	17	12	22	.304	.333
Ahead on Count	.331	172	57	7	1	3	26	40	0	.456	.436	September/October	.260	77	20	2	1	0	2	9	10	.337	.312
Behind on Count	.242	194	47	10	0	0	20	1	47	.249	.294	Pre-All Star	.284	352	100	10	5	2	33	32	35	.346	.358
Two Strikes	.196	235	46	8	2	1	12	17	74	.257	.260	Post-All Star	.241	311	75	17	2	2	26	28	39	.306	.328

Batter vs. Pitcher (since 1984)

Hits Best Against	Avg	AB	H	2B	3B	HR	RBI	BB	SO	OBP	SLG	Hits Worst Against	Avg	AB	H	2B	3B	HR	RBI	BB	SO	OBP	SLG
Tim Leary	.500	10	5	0	0	0	1	1	2	.545	.500	Dave Stieb	.077	13	1	0	0	0	1	2	3	.200	.077
Bill Swift	.471	17	8	1	0	0	3	2	2	.526	.529	Chris Bosio	.091	11	1	0	0	0	0	1	4	.167	.091
Walt Terrell	.455	11	5	0	0	1	1	2	2	.538	.727	Mike Moore	.095	21	2	0	0	0	0	0	2	.095	.095
Bob Welch	.438	16	7	2	1	0	2	2	2	.500	.688	Mark Eichhorn	.100	10	1	0	0	0	0	0	4	.182	.100
Dave Stewart	.429	21	9	1	0	0	1	2	4	.478	.476	Eric Plunk	.154	13	2	0	0	0	0	0	3	.154	.154

Terry Mulholland — Phillies

Pitches Left

	ERA	W	L	Sv	G	GS	IP	BB	SO	Avg	H	2B	3B	HR	RBI	OBP	SLG	CG	ShO	Sup	QS	#P/S	SB	CS	GB	FB	G/F
1992 Season	3.81	13	11	0	32	32	229.0	46	125	.261	227	43	3	14	91	.298	.365	12	2	4.99	17	100	2	5	342	249	1.37
Last Five Years	3.80	44	42	0	133	116	803.0	180	426	.265	817	163	16	55	334	.306	.382	30	8	4.34	65	95	17	17	1204	877	1.37

1992 Season

	ERA	W	L	Sv	G	GS	IP	H	HR	BB	SO		Avg	AB	H	2B	3B	HR	RBI	BB	SO	OBP	SLG
Home	3.63	9	6	0	20	20	146.1	145	9	31	78	vs. Left	.211	161	34	7	1	4	18	11	25	.263	.342
Away	4.14	4	5	0	12	12	82.2	82	5	15	47	vs. Right	.272	710	193	36	2	10	73	35	100	.306	.370
Day	4.29	3	5	0	9	9	65.0	66	8	13	44	Inning 1-6	.261	689	180	35	2	11	76	40	107	.302	.366
Night	3.62	10	6	0	23	23	164.0	161	6	33	81	Inning 7+	.258	182	47	8	1	3	15	6	18	.282	.363
Grass	5.93	1	2	0	4	4	27.1	30	4	6	22	None on	.258	535	138	26	1	8	8	18	70	.283	.355
Turf	3.53	12	9	0	28	28	201.2	197	10	40	103	Runners on	.265	336	89	17	2	6	83	28	55	.319	.381

1992 Season

	ERA	W	L	Sv	G	GS	IP	H	HR	BB	SO		Avg	AB	H	2B	3B	HR	RBI	BB	SO	OBP	SLG
April	7.28	0	3	0	5	5	29.2	34	3	13	24	Scoring Posn	.345	171	59	10	2	3	74	15	28	.387	.480
May	2.16	5	1	0	6	6	50.0	49	2	9	23	Close & Late	.280	93	26	6	1	1	10	2	11	.295	.398
June	2.79	3	0	0	5	5	38.2	28	2	7	19	None on/out	.263	228	60	10	0	4	4	9	29	.294	.360
July	2.47	3	3	0	6	6	51.0	44	5	2	28	vs. 1st Batr (relief)	.000	0	0	0	0	0	0	0	0	.000	.000
August	5.76	1	1	0	5	5	29.2	40	1	8	11	First Inning Pitched	.248	121	30	4	0	4	14	7	19	.287	.380
September/October	4.80	1	3	0	5	5	30.0	32	1	7	20	First 75 Pitches	.261	620	162	32	1	9	66	34	96	.300	.360
Starter	3.81	13	11	0	32	32	229.0	227	14	46	125	Pitch 76-90	.243	111	27	3	2	2	9	5	16	.276	.360
Reliever	0.00	0	0	0	0	0	0.0	0	0	0	0	Pitch 91-105	.279	86	24	4	0	2	10	3	11	.303	.395
0-3 Days Rest	6.00	0	0	0	1	1	6.0	6	0	1	2	Pitch 106+	.259	54	14	4	0	1	6	4	2	.310	.389
4 Days Rest	3.49	9	8	0	22	22	154.2	145	9	26	90	First Pitch	.317	126	40	8	1	3	14	3	0	.328	.468
5+ Days Rest	4.35	4	3	0	9	9	68.1	76	5	19	33	Ahead on Count	.222	409	91	20	0	5	41	0	113	.225	.308
Pre-All Star	3.52	9	5	0	18	18	135.1	126	10	30	75	Behind on Count	.269	208	56	8	1	2	22	26	0	.352	.346
Post-All Star	4.23	4	6	0	14	14	93.2	101	4	16	50	Two Strikes	.215	362	78	19	0	5	36	17	125	.254	.309

Last Five Years

	ERA	W	L	Sv	G	GS	IP	H	HR	BB	SO		Avg	AB	H	2B	3B	HR	RBI	BB	SO	OBP	SLG
Home	3.18	27	16	0	68	59	438.2	407	26	97	229	vs. Left	.239	523	125	20	3	12	60	26	79	.275	.358
Away	4.55	17	26	0	65	57	364.1	410	29	83	197	vs. Right	.270	2561	692	143	13	43	274	154	347	.312	.387
Day	4.32	12	18	0	43	35	243.2	261	22	55	149	Inning 1-6	.264	2504	662	130	9	42	277	159	362	.308	.374
Night	3.57	32	24	0	90	81	559.1	556	33	125	277	Inning 7+	.267	580	155	33	7	13	57	21	64	.295	.416
Grass	4.66	11	18	0	42	33	218.1	257	21	50	125	None on	.259	1833	474	94	11	30	30	86	248	.294	.371
Turf	3.48	33	24	0	91	83	584.2	560	34	130	301	Runners on	.274	1251	343	69	5	25	304	94	178	.322	.397
April	4.88	3	5	0	14	14	83.0	91	5	27	39	Scoring Posn	.295	679	200	42	4	15	273	60	93	.343	.434
May	3.18	11	4	0	23	16	130.1	128	10	29	58	Close & Late	.271	299	81	20	5	7	32	7	39	.294	.441
June	5.57	4	8	0	20	16	95.1	109	8	30	52	None on/out	.278	805	224	44	5	15	15	39	102	.316	.401
July	2.62	10	10	0	29	26	203.0	190	14	28	106	vs. 1st Batr (relief)	.417	12	5	3	0	0	5	0	2	.385	.667
August	4.01	9	7	0	25	22	150.1	164	10	36	93	First Inning Pitched	.265	495	141	27	3	11	83	43	71	.341	.418
September/October	4.02	7	8	0	22	22	141.0	135	8	30	78	First 75 Pitches	.264	2312	610	118	8	35	251	146	338	.307	.367
Starter	3.74	44	42	0	116	116	780.0	786	53	172	415	Pitch 76-90	.256	386	99	24	4	9	39	16	46	.290	.409
Reliever	5.87	0	0	0	17	0	23.0	31	2	8	11	Pitch 91-105	.290	262	76	15	4	7	30	10	31	.318	.458
0-3 Days Rest	4.97	2	3	0	8	8	50.2	57	4	14	20	Pitch 106+	.258	124	32	6	0	4	14	6	11	.303	.403
4 Days Rest	3.72	28	26	0	72	72	485.2	482	34	95	278	First Pitch	.306	513	157	39	3	14	73	11	0	.319	.476
5+ Days Rest	3.51	14	13	0	36	36	243.2	247	15	63	117	Ahead on Count	.230	1411	324	67	7	14	120	1	380	.234	.317
Pre-All Star	3.88	22	19	0	66	53	373.2	376	26	98	189	Behind on Count	.291	683	199	28	4	19	97	104	0	.383	.428
Post-All Star	3.73	22	23	0	67	63	429.1	441	29	82	237	Two Strikes	.211	1293	273	28	6	10	91	64	426	.251	.268

Pitcher vs. Batter (career)

Pitches Best Vs.	Avg	AB	H	2B	3B	HR	RBI	BB	SO	OBP	SLG	Pitches Worst Vs.	Avg	AB	H	2B	3B	HR	RBI	BB	SO	OBP	SLG
Geronimo Pena	.000	9	0	0	0	0	1	1	2	.091	.000	Bernard Gilkey	.526	19	10	1	2	0	2	1	0	.550	.789
Will Clark	.071	28	2	1	0	1	4	0	7	.071	.214	Fred McGriff	.500	22	11	0	1	3	8	2	3	.542	1.000
Darrin Jackson	.087	23	2	0	1	0	3	1	5	.125	.174	Tom Pagnozzi	.478	23	11	2	0	1	6	0	3	.458	.696
Todd Benzinger	.118	17	2	0	0	0	1	1	2	.167	.118	Ryne Sandberg	.333	45	15	1	1	6	14	3	7	.367	.800
Doug Dascenzo	.158	19	3	0	0	0	0	0	1	.158	.158	Barry Bonds	.321	28	9	2	0	5	9	2	2	.367	.929

Rance Mulliniks — Blue Jays
Bats Left (groundball hitter)

	Avg	G	AB	R	H	2B	3B	HR	RBI	BB	SO	HBP	GDP	SB	CS	OBP	SLG	IBB	SH	SF	#Pit	#P/PA	GB	FB	G/F
1992 Season	.500	3	2	1	1	0	0	0	0	1	0	0	0	0	0	.667	.500	0	0	0	12	4.00	1	0	0.00
Last Five Years	.269	379	949	113	255	48	4	19	117	157	160	0	33	3	1	.370	.388	13	2	9	4195	3.76	422	209	2.02

1992 Season

	Avg	AB	H	2B	3B	HR	RBI	BB	SO	OBP	SLG		Avg	AB	H	2B	3B	HR	RBI	BB	SO	OBP	SLG
vs. Left	1.000	1	1	0	0	0	0	0	0	1.000	1.000	Scoring Posn	.000	1	0	0	0	0	0	0	0	.000	.000
vs. Right	.000	1	0	0	0	0	0	1	0	.500	.000	Close & Late	.000	1	0	0	0	0	0	0	0	.000	.000

Last Five Years

	Avg	AB	H	2B	3B	HR	RBI	BB	SO	OBP	SLG		Avg	AB	H	2B	3B	HR	RBI	BB	SO	OBP	SLG
vs. Left	.235	51	12	3	0	1	6	10	12	.361	.353	Scoring Posn	.271	247	67	12	0	4	92	69	42	.418	.368
vs. Right	.271	898	243	45	4	18	111	147	148	.370	.390	Close & Late	.277	155	43	7	0	3	20	31	27	.394	.381
Groundball	.274	263	72	16	1	6	39	54	38	.395	.411	None on/out	.255	212	54	10	2	4	30	33	33	.347	.377
Flyball	.246	211	52	11	2	5	26	41	39	.365	.389	Batting #3	.309	259	80	17	1	10	47	55	40	.425	.498
Home	.272	448	122	28	2	10	66	69	81	.366	.411	Batting #7	.276	181	50	8	0	2	22	17	34	.338	.354
Away	.265	501	133	20	2	9	51	88	79	.373	.367	Other	.246	509	125	23	3	7	46	85	86	.351	.344
Day	.270	282	76	20	1	4	29	48	46	.372	.390	April	.224	116	26	3	1	1	9	16	16	.316	.293
Night	.268	667	179	28	3	15	88	109	114	.368	.387	May	.291	151	44	6	0	7	21	21	28	.378	.470
Grass	.285	386	110	15	2	8	45	68	60	.368	.396	June	.293	208	61	14	3	1	23	37	27	.395	.404
Turf	.258	563	145	33	2	11	72	89	100	.356	.382	July	.268	164	44	7	0	4	18	25	22	.365	.384
First Pitch	.336	137	46	8	1	2	22	7	0	.363	.453	August	.245	184	45	9	0	4	20	34	39	.362	.359
Ahead on Count	.326	239	78	19	2	7	40	80	0	.491	.510	September/October	.278	126	35	9	0	2	26	24	28	.381	.397
Behind on Count	.216	287	62	12	1	5	28	0	76	.215	.317	Pre-All Star	.273	532	145	24	4	11	59	82	78	.367	.395
Two Strikes	.200	406	81	17	1	7	36	66	160	.309	.298	Post-All Star	.264	417	110	24	0	8	58	75	82	.372	.379

Batter vs. Pitcher (since 1984)																			
Hits Best Against	Avg	AB	H	2B	3B	HR	RBI	BB	SO	OBP	SLG	Hits Worst Against	Avg	AB	H	2B	3B	HR	RBI	BB	SO	OBP	SLG

Hits Best Against	Avg	AB	H	2B	3B	HR	RBI	BB	SO	OBP	SLG
Charles Nagy	.538	13	7	2	0	0	4	1	0	.571	.692
Tim Leary	.500	14	7	4	0	1	3	3	2	.588	1.000
Greg Harris	.364	11	4	1	1	1	1	4	2	.533	.909
Bob Welch	.333	12	4	0	0	1	4	1	2	.385	.583
Bill Wegman	.313	16	5	0	0	1	3	1	1	.421	.500

Hits Worst Against	Avg	AB	H	2B	3B	HR	RBI	BB	SO	OBP	SLG
Dave Stewart	.040	25	1	0	0	0	0	3	7	.143	.040
Steve Farr	.111	9	1	0	0	0	1	2	3	.273	.111
Kirk McCaskill	.147	34	5	2	0	0	1	2	7	.194	.206
Bert Blyleven	.156	32	5	1	0	0	2	3	8	.229	.188
Chris Bosio	.200	30	6	1	0	0	1	1	5	.226	.233

Mike Munoz — Tigers
Pitches Left (groundball pitcher)

	ERA	W	L	Sv	G	GS	IP	BB	SO	Avg	H	2B	3B	HR	RBI	OBP	SLG	GF	IR	IRS	Hld	SvOp	SB	CS	GB	FB	G/F
1992 Season	3.00	1	2	2	65	0	48.0	25	23	.246	44	6	1	3	18	.335	.341	15	55	11	15	3	3	1	91	35	2.60
Career (1989-1992)	4.52	1	3	2	82	0	65.2	35	31	.275	68	9	1	4	36	.360	.367	22	66	16	17	4	3	3	126	47	2.68

1992 Season

	ERA	W	L	Sv	G	GS	IP	H	HR	BB	SO		Avg	AB	H	2B	3B	HR	RBI	BB	SO	OBP	SLG
Home	3.68	0	2	0	29	0	22.0	24	2	11	13	vs. Left	.192	73	14	2	0	0	4	7	10	.259	.219
Away	2.42	1	0	2	36	0	26.0	20	1	14	10	vs. Right	.283	106	30	4	1	3	14	18	13	.384	.425
Day	3.77	1	0	0	22	0	14.1	12	1	10	6	Inning 1-6	.200	20	4	0	0	0	1	6	1	.370	.200
Night	2.67	0	2	2	43	0	33.2	32	2	15	17	Inning 7+	.252	159	40	6	1	3	17	19	22	.330	.358
Grass	3.00	0	2	2	50	0	36.0	32	3	19	19	None on	.322	87	28	4	1	3	3	9	11	.385	.494
Turf	3.00	1	0	0	15	0	12.0	12	0	6	4	Runners on	.174	92	16	2	0	0	15	16	12	.291	.196
April	2.45	0	0	0	8	0	7.1	8	1	5	5	Scoring Posn	.161	56	9	2	0	0	15	14	9	.319	.196
May	4.26	0	0	0	12	0	12.2	14	0	7	5	Close & Late	.218	55	12	2	0	2	9	7	8	.302	.364
June	6.00	1	1	0	10	0	6.0	5	2	6	5	None on/out	.318	44	14	3	0	2	2	4	7	.375	.523
July	1.50	0	1	0	14	0	6.0	5	0	2	2	vs. 1st Batr (relief)	.286	56	16	4	0	1	8	7	9	.359	.411
August	3.24	0	0	1	9	0	8.1	7	0	1	2	First Inning Pitched	.232	142	33	4	1	3	15	21	21	.327	.338
September/October	0.00	0	0	1	12	0	7.2	5	0	4	4	First 15 Pitches	.237	135	32	4	1	3	14	17	19	.318	.348
Starter	0.00	0	0	0	0	0	0.0	0	0	0	0	Pitch 16-30	.303	33	10	2	0	0	3	6	4	.410	.364
Reliever	3.00	1	2	2	65	0	48.0	44	3	25	23	Pitch 31-45	.222	9	2	0	0	0	1	2	0	.364	.222
0 Days rest	3.00	0	1	1	27	0	21.0	18	1	10	11	Pitch 46+	.000	2	0	0	0	0	0	0	0	.000	.000
1 or 2 Days rest	2.70	0	0	0	16	0	10.0	11	0	8	4	First Pitch	.350	20	7	0	0	0	0	4	0	.458	.350
3+ Days rest	3.18	1	1	1	22	0	17.0	15	2	7	3	Ahead on Count	.176	68	12	3	0	2	9	0	20	.171	.309
Pre-All Star	3.60	1	1	0	38	0	30.0	31	3	20	17	Behind on Count	.264	53	14	2	1	0	3	14	0	.418	.340
Post-All Star	2.00	0	1	2	27	0	18.0	13	0	5	6	Two Strikes	.153	72	11	3	0	2	10	7	23	.222	.278

Pedro Munoz — Twins
Bats Right (groundball hitter)

	Avg	G	AB	R	H	2B	3B	HR	RBI	BB	SO	HBP	GDP	SB	CS	OBP	SLG	IBB	SH	SF	#Pit	#P/PA	GB	FB	G/F
1992 Season	.270	127	418	44	113	16	3	12	71	17	90	1	18	4	5	.298	.409	1	0	3	1597	3.64	174	95	1.83
Career (1990-1992)	.273	200	641	72	175	27	5	19	102	28	137	2	23	10	5	.302	.420	1	2	7	2477	3.65	263	143	1.84

1992 Season

	Avg	AB	H	2B	3B	HR	RBI	BB	SO	OBP	SLG		Avg	AB	H	2B	3B	HR	RBI	BB	SO	OBP	SLG
vs. Left	.295	122	36	6	1	3	21	6	23	.326	.434	Scoring Posn	.322	121	39	8	1	6	62	7	21	.356	.554
vs. Right	.260	296	77	10	2	9	50	11	67	.287	.399	Close & Late	.321	53	17	3	0	2	8	3	16	.351	.491
Groundball	.237	93	22	6	1	1	14	6	21	.283	.355	None on/out	.259	108	28	4	0	3	3	5	26	.292	.380
Flyball	.299	117	35	4	1	5	19	5	30	.325	.479	Batting #5	.283	145	41	5	2	3	28	7	24	.314	.407
Home	.275	193	53	10	1	8	36	10	39	.314	.461	Batting #7	.275	160	44	5	1	4	21	5	34	.293	.394
Away	.267	225	60	6	2	4	35	7	51	.285	.364	Other	.248	113	28	6	0	5	22	5	32	.286	.434
Day	.209	134	28	2	0	7	27	5	36	.241	.381	April	.319	69	22	3	0	3	13	3	13	.347	.493
Night	.299	284	85	14	3	5	44	12	54	.326	.423	May	.229	70	16	2	0	2	12	3	17	.257	.343
Grass	.246	179	44	5	1	3	30	6	38	.266	.335	June	.333	63	21	5	0	3	16	3	10	.364	.556
Turf	.289	239	69	11	2	9	41	11	52	.323	.464	July	.246	69	17	2	0	2	9	2	11	.268	.362
First Pitch	.297	74	22	3	0	4	14	0	0	.293	.500	August	.241	54	13	2	1	1	6	1	15	.250	.370
Ahead on Count	.400	80	32	4	0	2	16	12	0	.468	.525	September/October	.258	93	24	2	2	1	15	5	24	.300	.355
Behind on Count	.236	127	30	3	1	0	16	0	43	.242	.276	Pre-All Star	.289	232	67	10	0	10	46	10	46	.317	.461
Two Strikes	.190	195	37	5	2	3	25	5	90	.210	.282	Post-All Star	.247	186	46	6	3	2	25	7	44	.276	.344

1992 By Position

Position	Avg	AB	H	2B	3B	HR	RBI	BB	SO	OBP	SLG	G	GS	Innings	PO	A	E	DP	Fld Pct	Rng Fctr	In Zone	Outs	Zone Rtg	MLB Zone
As rf	.277	393	109	16	2	12	68	17	83	.307	.420	117	110	920.1	214	8	3	3	.987	2.17	238	209	.878	.814

Dale Murphy — Phillies
Bats Right

	Avg	G	AB	R	H	2B	3B	HR	RBI	BB	SO	HBP	GDP	SB	CS	OBP	SLG	IBB	SH	SF	#Pit	#P/PA	GB	FB	G/F
1992 Season	.161	18	62	5	10	1	0	2	7	1	13	0	3	0	0	.175	.274	0	0	0	210	3.33	26	14	1.86
Last Five Years	.236	635	2335	268	550	108	6	88	332	249	503	5	84	16	10	.308	.400	43	0	20	9111	3.49	860	665	1.29

1992 Season

	Avg	AB	H	2B	3B	HR	RBI	BB	SO	OBP	SLG		Avg	AB	H	2B	3B	HR	RBI	BB	SO	OBP	SLG
vs. Left	.194	31	6	1	0	1	3	1	7	.219	.323	Scoring Posn	.267	15	4	0	0	0	4	0	4	.267	.267
vs. Right	.129	31	4	0	0	1	4	0	6	.129	.226	Close & Late	.000	13	0	0	0	0	0	0	6	.000	.000

Last Five Years

	Avg	AB	H	2B	3B	HR	RBI	BB	SO	OBP	SLG
vs. Left	.274	755	207	40	2	34	113	122	129	.373	.468
vs. Right	.217	1580	343	68	4	54	219	127	374	.275	.368
Groundball	.229	840	192	38	4	19	97	89	182	.300	.351
Flyball	.253	517	131	29	0	24	79	55	101	.323	.449
Home	.253	1164	294	60	3	43	184	134	240	.326	.420
Away	.219	1171	256	48	3	45	148	115	263	.288	.380
Day	.225	550	124	27	2	14	66	51	121	.289	.358
Night	.239	1785	426	81	4	74	266	198	382	.314	.413
Grass	.236	1333	317	52	4	57	200	145	295	.311	.411
Turf	.233	1002	233	56	2	31	132	104	208	.304	.385
First Pitch	.320	438	140	32	1	20	83	8	0	.330	.534
Ahead on Count	.303	489	148	25	3	29	77	129	0	.446	.544
Behind on Count	.173	779	135	30	1	23	84	8	292	.182	.303
Two Strikes	.143	1006	144	28	0	18	87	85	503	.209	.225

	Avg	AB	H	2B	3B	HR	RBI	BB	SO	OBP	SLG
Scoring Posn	.262	614	161	25	2	28	248	116	148	.371	.446
Close & Late	.204	416	85	16	1	12	55	47	107	.283	.334
None on/out	.225	608	137	27	3	20	20	35	128	.267	.378
Batting #4	.235	1418	333	63	5	53	198	144	325	.304	.398
Batting #5	.240	588	141	32	1	23	94	67	115	.316	.415
Other	.231	329	76	13	0	12	40	38	63	.311	.380
April	.243	325	79	10	0	13	50	32	78	.310	.394
May	.236	423	100	25	2	13	41	50	81	.316	.397
June	.231	396	92	18	2	16	66	36	92	.295	.407
July	.233	377	88	17	1	19	57	49	81	.321	.435
August	.212	411	87	18	0	17	61	36	91	.275	.380
September/October	.259	401	104	20	1	10	57	46	80	.333	.389
Pre-All Star	.234	1256	294	55	4	46	172	137	283	.309	.394
Post-All Star	.237	1079	256	53	2	42	160	112	220	.307	.407

Batter vs. Pitcher (since 1984)

Hits Best Against	Avg	AB	H	2B	3B	HR	RBI	BB	SO	OBP	SLG
Bobby Ojeda	.500	26	13	5	1	1	3	9	2	.629	.885
Bob Tewksbury	.500	14	7	2	0	1	3	0	1	.500	.857
Brian Fisher	.500	12	6	1	1	2	5	3	3	.600	1.250
Mark Davis	.393	28	11	0	0	4	10	6	4	.486	.821
Ron Robinson	.375	24	9	1	0	5	7	2	8	.423	1.042

Hits Worst Against	Avg	AB	H	2B	3B	HR	RBI	BB	SO	OBP	SLG
Rob Murphy	.000	13	0	0	0	0	0	1	3	.071	.000
Ken Hill	.000	12	0	0	0	0	1	1	3	.077	.000
Greg Maddux	.059	34	2	0	0	0	0	1	12	.066	.059
Greg Mathews	.059	17	1	0	0	0	0	2	2	.158	.059
Jeff Robinson	.097	31	3	1	0	0	2	1	10	.125	.129

Rob Murphy — Astros — Pitches Left

	ERA	W	L	Sv	G	GS	IP	BB	SO	Avg	H	2B	3B	HR	RBI	OBP	SLG	GF	IR	IRS	Hld	SvOp	SB	CS	GB	FB	G/F
1992 Season	4.04	3	1	0	59	0	55.2	21	42	.260	56	8	3	2	34	.322	.353	6	37	9	9	2	4	1	86	49	1.76
Last Five Years	3.65	8	21	23	334	0	350.1	151	311	.265	354	66	10	26	189	.339	.388	52	305	80	61	38	30	12	447	356	1.26

1992 Season

	ERA	W	L	Sv	G	GS	IP	H	HR	BB	SO
Home	3.69	1	1	0	29	0	31.2	26	0	11	21
Away	4.50	2	0	0	30	0	24.0	30	2	10	21
Starter	0.00	0	0	0	0	0	0.0	0	0	0	0
Reliever	4.04	3	1	0	59	0	55.2	56	2	21	42
0 Days rest	5.14	1	1	0	16	0	14.0	16	0	7	14
1 or 2 Days rest	4.24	1	0	0	24	0	23.1	21	1	9	15
3+ Days rest	2.95	1	0	0	19	0	18.1	19	1	5	13
Pre-All Star	3.18	2	1	0	28	0	28.1	26	0	16	18
Post-All Star	4.94	1	0	0	31	0	27.1	30	2	5	24

	Avg	AB	H	2B	3B	HR	RBI	BB	SO	OBP	SLG
vs. Left	.256	86	22	2	0	0	12	11	17	.337	.279
vs. Right	.264	129	34	6	3	2	22	10	25	.312	.403
Scoring Posn	.324	68	22	1	1	1	31	9	11	.388	.412
Close & Late	.292	65	19	2	2	2	13	11	17	.390	.477
None on/out	.269	52	14	3	1	1		5	10	.333	.423
First Pitch	.356	45	16	3	0	1	10	3	0	.380	.489
Behind on Count	.353	51	18	2	2	1	10	11	0	.468	.529
Ahead on Count	.193	88	17	2	1	0	13	0	36	.191	.239
Two Strikes	.143	84	12	1	0	0	11	7	42	.207	.179

Last Five Years

	ERA	W	L	Sv	G	GS	IP	H	HR	BB	SO
Home	3.13	3	8	8	164	0	181.1	167	10	70	163
Away	4.21	5	13	15	170	0	169.0	187	16	81	148
Day	3.28	5	7	9	116	0	123.1	125	8	54	118
Night	3.85	3	14	14	218	0	227.0	229	18	97	193
Grass	4.01	6	12	15	184	0	195.1	213	22	83	197
Turf	3.19	2	9	8	150	0	155.0	141	4	68	114
April	3.15	0	4	1	46	0	60.0	60	4	31	52
May	3.79	0	4	3	52	0	57.0	60	6	28	44
June	2.60	1	3	5	67	0	65.2	55	4	21	66
July	3.26	2	6	6	57	0	58.0	61	2	18	55
August	5.56	4	5	5	50	0	56.2	66	6	36	48
September/October	3.74	1	3	2	53	0	53.0	52	4	17	46
Starter	0.00	0	0	0	0	0	0.0	0	0	0	0
Reliever	3.65	8	21	23	334	0	350.1	354	26	151	311
0 Days rest	2.50	2	4	11	100	0	106.0	102	6	43	105
1 or 2 Days rest	4.32	3	11	11	150	0	150.0	149	13	64	134
3+ Days rest	3.90	3	6	1	84	0	92.1	103	7	44	72
Pre-All Star	3.17	3	13	11	186	0	201.1	195	14	86	178
Post-All Star	4.29	5	8	12	148	0	149.0	159	12	65	133

	Avg	AB	H	2B	3B	HR	RBI	BB	SO	OBP	SLG
vs. Left	.235	439	103	19	1	4	48	35	92	.293	.310
vs. Right	.280	895	251	47	9	22	141	116	219	.361	.427
Inning 1-6	.218	119	26	5	2	1	24	9	25	.275	.319
Inning 7+	.270	1215	328	61	8	25	165	142	286	.346	.395
None on	.252	652	164	35	2	14	14	67	144	.322	.376
Runners on	.279	682	190	31	8	12	175	84	167	.355	.400
Scoring Posn	.277	444	123	14	4	9	159	63	116	.363	.387
Close & Late	.264	455	129	17	2	9	69	63	108	.368	.389
None on/out	.259	293	76	18	1	8	8	31	68	.330	.410
vs. 1st Batr (relief)	.261	303	79	14	0	6	43	20	68	.304	.366
First Inning Pitched	.266	981	261	50	7	21	157	91	228	.328	.396
First 15 Pitches	.260	880	229	43	8	19	118	84	196	.325	.392
Pitch 16-30	.266	369	98	18	1	6	53	54	92	.357	.369
Pitch 31-45	.329	70	23	5	0	1	13	12	18	.427	.443
Pitch 46+	.267	15	4	0	1	0	5	1	5	.313	.400
First Pitch	.305	203	62	12	3	6	31	19	0	.363	.483
Ahead on Count	.218	648	141	28	4	6	76	0	261	.218	.301
Behind on Count	.350	260	91	15	3	10	52	66	0	.483	.546
Two Strikes	.186	656	122	21	3	6	68	66	311	.259	.255

Pitcher vs. Batter (career)

Pitches Best Vs.	Avg	AB	H	2B	3B	HR	RBI	BB	SO	OBP	SLG
Dale Murphy	.000	13	0	0	0	0	0	1	3	.071	.000
Andy Van Slyke	.000	10	0	0	0	0	0	1	4	.091	.000
Billy Doran	.077	13	1	0	0	0	2	3	0	.250	.077
Brett Butler	.083	12	1	0	0	0	2	3	4	.267	.083
Darryl Strawberry	.091	11	1	0	0	0	1	0	7	.083	.091

Pitches Worst Vs.	Avg	AB	H	2B	3B	HR	RBI	BB	SO	OBP	SLG
Barry Bonds	.417	12	5	2	0	1	2	2	3	.500	.833
Kevin Bass	.364	11	4	2	0	1	1	0	3	.364	.818
Don Mattingly	.364	11	4	0	0	1	4	0	1	.364	.636
Chili Davis	.308	13	4	2	0	0	2	3	5	.438	.462
Candy Maldonado	.308	13	4	1	1	0	3	0	4	.308	.538

Eddie Murray — Mets
Bats Both

	Avg	G	AB	R	H	2B	3B	HR	RBI	BB	SO	HBP	GDP	SB	CS	OBP	SLG	IBB	SH	SF	#Pit	#P/PA	GB	FB	G/F
1992 Season	.261	156	551	64	144	37	2	16	93	66	74	0	14	4	2	.336	.423	8	0	8	2318	3.71	207	182	1.14
Last Five Years	.275	785	2882	370	796	138	9	109	456	365	375	3	82	34	14	.355	.444	78	0	30	11790	3.59	1039	954	1.08

1992 Season

	Avg	AB	H	2B	3B	HR	RBI	BB	SO	OBP	SLG		Avg	AB	H	2B	3B	HR	RBI	BB	SO	OBP	SLG
vs. Left	.238	202	48	16	1	3	35	16	16	.286	.371	Scoring Posn	.270	141	38	18	0	4	76	33	24	.390	.482
vs. Right	.275	349	96	21	1	13	58	50	58	.364	.453	Close & Late	.209	91	19	8	0	1	19	16	14	.318	.330
Groundball	.268	239	64	16	0	5	38	23	30	.327	.397	None on/out	.265	155	41	8	1	5	5	9	18	.305	.426
Flyball	.202	99	20	5	2	4	18	18	14	.317	.414	Batting #4	.257	389	100	23	1	13	62	44	52	.327	.422
Home	.226	266	60	16	2	7	43	30	39	.303	.380	Batting #5	.281	135	38	14	0	2	24	17	19	.359	.430
Away	.295	285	84	21	0	9	50	36	35	.366	.463	Other	.222	27	6	0	1	1	7	5	3	.344	.407
Day	.316	155	49	10	0	7	24	17	21	.379	.516	April	.269	78	21	8	0	1	19	11	11	.360	.410
Night	.240	396	95	27	2	9	69	49	53	.319	.386	May	.264	91	24	3	0	4	12	13	16	.346	.429
Grass	.256	387	99	24	2	14	62	42	53	.326	.437	June	.227	97	22	5	1	3	20	11	16	.295	.392
Turf	.274	164	45	13	0	2	31	24	21	.358	.390	July	.264	91	24	9	0	1	12	4	9	.295	.396
First Pitch	.295	105	31	9	1	4	16	6	0	.333	.514	August	.245	94	23	4	0	4	11	9	9	.311	.415
Ahead on Count	.357	115	41	12	0	4	28	34	0	.493	.565	September/October	.300	100	30	8	1	3	19	18	13	.403	.490
Behind on Count	.250	156	39	8	1	3	23	0	27	.244	.372	Pre-All Star	.262	309	81	22	1	9	59	39	46	.338	.427
Two Strikes	.178	236	42	13	0	3	30	28	74	.263	.271	Post-All Star	.260	242	63	15	1	7	34	27	28	.333	.417

1992 By Position

Position	Avg	AB	H	2B	3B	HR	RBI	BB	SO	OBP	SLG	G	GS	Innings	PO	A	E	DP	Fld Pct	Rng Fctr	In Zone	Outs	Zone Rtg	MLB Zone
As 1b	.261	548	143	37	2	16	91	66	72	.336	.423	154	152	1308.1	1278	94	12	111	.991	---	251	205	.817	.843

Last Five Years

	Avg	AB	H	2B	3B	HR	RBI	BB	SO	OBP	SLG		Avg	AB	H	2B	3B	HR	RBI	BB	SO	OBP	SLG
vs. Left	.241	1084	261	53	2	28	156	111	128	.308	.371	Scoring Posn	.270	723	195	45	2	34	340	175	103	.399	.479
vs. Right	.298	1798	535	85	7	81	300	254	247	.382	.488	Close & Late	.246	463	114	20	2	12	68	79	78	.353	.376
Groundball	.281	928	261	49	1	26	137	124	110	.362	.420	None on/out	.264	773	204	29	3	23	23	46	98	.306	.398
Flyball	.270	656	177	29	4	29	109	90	86	.355	.459	Batting #3	.217	249	54	6	1	9	31	31	39	.301	.357
Home	.275	1408	387	58	6	48	215	195	203	.362	.427	Batting #4	.281	2383	669	116	8	91	377	303	305	.359	.451
Away	.277	1474	409	80	3	61	241	170	172	.348	.460	Other	.292	250	73	16	0	9	48	31	31	.369	.464
Day	.282	777	219	35	1	35	123	91	98	.355	.465	April	.265	392	104	27	0	12	61	46	47	.339	.426
Night	.274	2105	577	103	8	74	333	274	277	.355	.436	May	.276	450	124	21	1	14	89	65	63	.363	.420
Grass	.282	2149	606	94	6	91	346	264	281	.363	.458	June	.238	488	116	24	2	17	81	71	73	.331	.400
Turf	.259	733	190	44	3	18	110	81	94	.332	.432	July	.259	491	127	22	0	21	74	55	74	.332	.432
First Pitch	.323	501	162	31	5	22	83	41	0	.371	.537	August	.297	532	158	18	4	22	83	63	58	.371	.470
Ahead on Count	.328	670	220	40	2	35	135	176	0	.466	.551	September/October	.316	529	167	26	2	23	88	65	60	.387	.503
Behind on Count	.245	942	231	30	1	29	125	7	192	.250	.372	Pre-All Star	.260	1490	388	81	4	49	237	205	202	.347	.417
Two Strikes	.210	1197	251	42	1	26	144	144	374	.285	.312	Post-All Star	.293	1392	408	57	6	60	219	160	173	.364	.472

Batter vs. Pitcher (since 1984)

Hits Best Against	Avg	AB	H	2B	3B	HR	RBI	BB	SO	OBP	SLG	Hits Worst Against	Avg	AB	H	2B	3B	HR	RBI	BB	SO	OBP	SLG
Roger McDowell	.600	10	6	2	0	0	2	2	0	.667	.800	Eric King	.000	17	0	0	0	0	1	0	0	.000	.000
Joe Boever	.556	9	5	1	0	1	6	3	0	.667	1.000	Curt Schilling	.000	11	0	0	0	0	0	2	4	.154	.000
Darryl Kile	.500	12	6	2	0	1	4	4	3	.625	.917	Jimmy Key	.083	24	2	0	0	0	1	1	4	.120	.083
Mark Grant	.500	8	4	0	0	2	6	3	0	.636	1.250	Al Osuna	.083	12	1	0	0	0	3	1	3	.133	.083
Bert Blyleven	.432	37	16	1	0	6	8	4	4	.488	.946	Mike Stanton	.091	11	1	0	0	0	0	0	1	.091	.091

Mike Mussina — Orioles
Pitches Right (flyball pitcher)

	ERA	W	L	Sv	G	GS	IP	BB	SO	Avg	H	2B	3B	HR	RBI	OBP	SLG	CG	ShO	Sup	QS	#P/S	SB	CS	GB	FB	G/F
1992 Season	2.54	18	5	0	32	32	241.0	48	130	.239	212	39	5	16	65	.278	.348	8	4	4.78	24	106	9	9	270	313	0.86
Career (1991-1992)	2.63	22	10	0	44	44	326.2	69	182	.239	289	53	6	23	94	.280	.350	10	4	4.55	33	107	13	13	365	429	0.85

1992 Season

	ERA	W	L	Sv	G	GS	IP	H	HR	BB	SO		Avg	AB	H	2B	3B	HR	RBI	BB	SO	OBP	SLG
Home	2.65	7	3	0	15	15	115.2	100	9	19	66	vs. Left	.220	422	93	18	2	1	17	29	64	.269	.280
Away	2.44	11	2	0	17	17	125.1	112	7	29	64	vs. Right	.255	466	119	21	3	15	48	19	66	.286	.410
Day	3.33	3	2	0	8	8	51.1	54	4	13	23	Inning 1-6	.244	692	169	31	5	12	51	39	104	.285	.355
Night	2.33	15	3	0	24	24	189.2	158	12	35	107	Inning 7+	.219	196	43	8	0	4	14	9	26	.251	.321
Grass	2.25	15	4	0	26	26	196.1	161	10	38	116	None on	.251	558	140	28	2	8	8	33	82	.294	.351
Turf	3.83	3	1	0	6	6	44.2	51	6	10	14	Runners on	.218	330	72	11	3	8	57	15	48	.250	.342
April	2.37	3	0	0	4	4	30.1	27	2	8	10	Scoring Posn	.175	154	27	6	2	1	39	11	19	.227	.260
May	3.03	2	1	0	4	4	29.2	24	1	4	14	Close & Late	.256	82	21	4	0	1	7	5	9	.292	.341
June	2.01	3	2	0	6	6	44.2	33	3	8	24	None on/out	.247	243	60	11	1	3	3	11	40	.280	.337
July	3.05	2	1	0	6	6	41.1	44	4	6	23	vs. 1st Batr (relief)	.000	0	0	0	0	0	0	0	0	.000	.000
August	3.56	3	1	0	6	6	43.0	44	5	11	27	First Inning Pitched	.200	110	22	4	0	2	6	7	16	.248	.291
September/October	1.56	5	0	0	6	6	52.0	40	1	11	32	First 75 Pitches	.253	604	153	28	4	12	45	36	90	.296	.373
Starter	2.54	18	5	0	32	32	241.0	212	16	48	130	Pitch 76-90	.200	110	22	4	1	0	8	3	21	.217	.255
Reliever	0.00	0	0	0	0	0	0.0	0	0	0	0	Pitch 91-105	.268	97	26	3	0	2	6	4	10	.294	.361
0-3 Days Rest	4.50	0	1	0	1	1	8.0	10	2	1	5	Pitch 106+	.143	77	11	4	0	0	5	5	9	.195	.273
4 Days Rest	2.86	11	4	0	23	23	173.1	153	13	34	90	First Pitch	.267	131	35	8	1	3	7	1	0	.284	.412

							1992 Season														
	ERA	W	L	Sv	G	GS	IP	H	HR	BB	SO		Avg	AB	H	2B	3B	HR	RBI	BB	SO	OBP	SLG
5+ Days Rest	1.36	7	0	0	8	8	59.2	49	1	13	35	Ahead on Count	.218	441	96	12	2	5	28	0	116	.217	.288
Pre-All Star	2.40	9	3	0	16	16	120.0	104	7	22	51	Behind on Count	.282	177	50	9	2	6	18	1	0	.342	.458
Post-All Star	2.68	9	2	0	16	16	121.0	108	9	26	79	Two Strikes	.197	401	79	11	1	5	17	30	130	.253	.267

Jeff Mutis — Indians
Pitches Left

	ERA	W	L	Sv	G	GS	IP	BB	SO	Avg	H	2B	3B	HR	RBI	OBP	SLG	CG	ShO	Sup	QS	#P/S	SB	CS	GB	FB	G/F
1992 Season	9.53	0	2	0	3	2	11.1	6	8	.429	24	3	2	4	12	.469	.768	0	0	3.18	0	78	0	0	18	19	0.95
Career (1991-1992)	10.65	0	5	0	6	5	23.2	13	14	.412	47	8	4	5	23	.462	.684	0	0	3.80	0	80	0	0	44	31	1.42

							1992 Season											
	ERA	W	L	Sv	G	GS	IP	H	HR	BB	SO		Avg	AB	H	2B	3B	HR	RBI	BB	SO	OBP	SLG
Home	7.71	0	1	0	2	1	9.1	16	3	5	5	vs. Left	.500	12	6	1	1	3	0	1	.500	1.000
Away	18.00	0	1	0	1	1	2.0	8	1	1	3	vs. Right	.409	44	18	2	1	3	9	6	7	.462	.705

Greg Myers — Angels
Bats Left

	Avg	G	AB	R	H	2B	3B	HR	RBI	BB	SO	HBP	GDP	SB	CS	OBP	SLG	IBB	SH	SF	#Pit	#P/PA	GB	FB	G/F
1992 Season	.231	30	78	4	18	7	0	1	13	5	11	0	1	0	0	.271	.359	0	1	2	285	3.35	26	25	1.04
Last Five Years	.239	241	681	62	163	38	1	14	72	50	98	0	28	0	2	.288	.360	4	2	9	2450	3.31	261	200	1.30

							1992 Season											
	Avg	AB	H	2B	3B	HR	RBI	BB	SO	OBP	SLG		Avg	AB	H	2B	3B	HR	RBI	BB	SO	OBP	SLG
vs. Left	.000	5	0	0	0	0	0	0	1	.000	.000	Scoring Posn	.273	22	6	2	0	1	12	1	1	.280	.500
vs. Right	.247	73	18	7	0	1	13	5	10	.288	.384	Close & Late	.273	11	3	1	0	0	3	2	2	.429	.364

							Last Five Years											
	Avg	AB	H	2B	3B	HR	RBI	BB	SO	OBP	SLG		Avg	AB	H	2B	3B	HR	RBI	BB	SO	OBP	SLG
vs. Left	.167	66	11	1	0	1	5	5	13	.219	.227	Scoring Posn	.203	187	38	8	1	6	62	17	28	.258	.353
vs. Right	.247	615	152	37	1	13	67	45	85	.295	.374	Close & Late	.300	100	30	9	0	1	9	7	14	.346	.420
Groundball	.215	209	45	15	1	2	25	14	28	.260	.325	None on/out	.315	130	41	15	0	5	5	7	15	.350	.546
Flyball	.278	144	40	6	0	6	16	9	25	.320	.444	Batting #7	.252	318	80	19	1	7	32	26	43	.304	.384
Home	.254	323	82	20	0	8	39	31	48	.315	.390	Batting #8	.221	195	43	9	0	6	26	16	28	.277	.359
Away	.226	358	81	18	1	6	33	19	50	.262	.332	Other	.238	168	40	10	0	1	14	8	27	.270	.315
Day	.230	183	42	9	0	4	23	13	29	.278	.344	April	.268	97	26	4	0	3	14	10	9	.327	.402
Night	.243	498	121	29	1	10	49	37	69	.292	.365	May	.262	84	22	9	0	1	9	11	11	.344	.405
Grass	.212	250	53	9	1	5	20	15	39	.254	.316	June	.255	153	39	8	0	4	16	8	20	.292	.386
Turf	.255	431	110	29	0	9	52	35	59	.307	.385	July	.192	151	29	10	1	1	17	5	27	.216	.291
First Pitch	.320	172	55	14	0	3	22	3	0	.326	.453	August	.281	96	27	4	0	3	6	3	18	.303	.417
Ahead on Count	.265	155	41	9	0	5	18	29	0	.376	.419	September/October	.200	100	20	3	0	2	10	12	13	.286	.290
Behind on Count	.206	212	44	10	0	3	15	0	54	.297	.297	Pre-All Star	.255	380	97	25	0	8	40	31	43	.308	.384
Two Strikes	.169	249	42	9	1	3	18	14	98	.224	.249	Post-All Star	.219	301	66	13	1	6	32	19	55	.262	.329

							Batter vs. Pitcher (career)										
Hits Best Against	Avg	AB	H	2B	3B	HR	RBI	BB	SO	OBP	SLG	Hits Worst Against	Avg	AB	H	2B	3B	HR	RBI	BB	SO	OBP	SLG
Kevin Tapani	.545	11	6	1	0	0	0	1	.545	.636	Nolan Ryan	.100	20	2	0	0	1	1	2	9	.182	.250
Kevin Appier	.400	15	6	0	0	0	3	1	1	.412	.400	Roger Clemens	.125	16	2	0	0	0	0	0	3	.125	.125
Jack McDowell	.357	14	5	0	0	1	1	0	1	.357	.571	Bob Welch	.133	15	2	1	0	0	0	2	2	.235	.200
												Tom Gordon	.167	12	2	0	0	0	1	0	2	.167	.167
												Dave Stewart	.200	10	2	0	0	0	0	1	4	.273	.200

Randy Myers — Padres
Pitches Left (flyball pitcher)

	ERA	W	L	Sv	G	GS	IP	BB	SO	Avg	H	2B	3B	HR	RBI	OBP	SLG	GF	IR	IRS	Hld	SvOp	SB	CS	GB	FB	G/F
1992 Season	4.29	3	6	38	66	0	79.2	34	66	.279	84	16	0	7	53	.349	.402	57	40	16	0	46	2	3	83	77	1.08
Last Five Years	2.90	27	32	125	310	12	450.2	209	429	.225	366	54	10	30	190	.313	.326	134	256	53	13	151	15	21	450	481	0.94

							1992 Season											
	ERA	W	L	Sv	G	GS	IP	H	HR	BB	SO		Avg	AB	H	2B	3B	HR	RBI	BB	SO	OBP	SLG
Home	4.58	2	3	20	35	0	39.1	46	4	14	31	vs. Left	.270	63	17	6	0	0	9	13	20	.390	.365
Away	4.02	1	3	18	31	0	40.1	38	3	20	35	vs. Right	.282	238	67	10	0	7	44	21	46	.337	.412
Day	3.77	3	1	11	21	0	28.2	32	2	12	22	Inning 1-6	.000	0	0	0	0	0	0	0	0	.000	.000
Night	4.59	0	5	27	45	0	51.0	52	5	22	44	Inning 7+	.279	301	84	16	0	7	53	34	66	.349	.402
Grass	3.49	3	3	27	49	0	59.1	56	5	21	45	None on	.294	136	40	6	0	4	4	12	28	.351	.426
Turf	6.64	0	3	11	17	0	20.1	28	2	13	21	Runners on	.267	165	44	10	0	3	49	22	38	.347	.382
April	5.02	1	1	5	9	0	14.1	18	1	5	14	Scoring Posn	.257	101	26	5	0	0	40	15	19	.344	.307
May	6.17	1	0	8	11	0	11.2	13	0	6	11	Close & Late	.275	244	67	11	0	6	46	28	55	.343	.393
June	7.20	1	0	8	8	0	10.0	14	3	5	8	None on/out	.333	60	20	3	0	2	2	5	14	.385	.483
July	1.50	0	1	7	12	0	12.0	9	1	9	12	vs. 1st Batr (relief)	.276	58	16	5	0	1	7	8	17	.364	.414
August	2.31	0	1	9	12	0	11.2	9	1	2	11	First Inning Pitched	.275	229	63	14	0	6	48	26	46	.346	.415
September/October	4.05	0	2	9	14	0	20.0	21	1	7	14	First 15 Pitches	.298	191	57	13	0	6	36	18	37	.354	.461
Starter	0.00	0	0	0	0	0	0.0	0	0	0	0	Pitch 16-30	.253	87	22	2	0	0	14	13	17	.350	.276
Reliever	4.29	3	6	38	66	0	79.2	84	7	34	66	Pitch 31-45	.222	18	4	1	0	1	3	3	9	.333	.444
0 Days rest	5.27	2	1	11	16	0	13.2	16	1	5	9	Pitch 46+	.200	5	1	0	0	0	0	0	5	.200	.200

1992 Season

	ERA	W	L	Sv	G	GS	IP	H	HR	BB	SO		Avg	AB	H	2B	3B	HR	RBI	BB	SO	OBP	SLG
1 or 2 Days rest	3.21	1	4	17	30	0	42.0	39	3	17	43	First Pitch	.375	32	12	2	0	2	12	3	0	.417	.625
3+ Days rest	5.63	0	1	10	20	0	24.0	29	3	12	14	Ahead on Count	.209	163	34	6	0	0	15	0	56	.211	.245
Pre-All Star	5.66	2	3	15	34	0	41.1	51	5	20	43	Behind on Count	.383	60	23	5	0	2	15	14	0	.493	.567
Post-All Star	2.82	1	3	23	32	0	38.1	33	2	14	28	Two Strikes	.210	167	35	7	0	2	16	17	66	.283	.287

Last Five Years

	ERA	W	L	Sv	G	GS	IP	H	HR	BB	SO		Avg	AB	H	2B	3B	HR	RBI	BB	SO	OBP	SLG
Home	2.64	17	11	71	170	5	242.0	185	13	110	218	vs. Left	.226	380	86	15	3	7	45	63	134	.333	.337
Away	3.19	10	21	54	140	7	208.2	181	17	99	211	vs. Right	.225	1245	280	39	7	23	145	146	295	.307	.323
Day	3.00	6	6	33	97	2	126.0	107	9	55	125	Inning 1-6	.236	237	56	6	2	4	28	36	55	.333	.329
Night	2.86	21	26	92	213	10	324.2	259	21	154	304	Inning 7+	.223	1388	310	48	8	26	162	173	374	.310	.326
Grass	2.76	16	13	74	169	5	228.2	175	17	92	218	None on	.230	820	189	25	4	19	19	94	222	.311	.340
Turf	3.04	11	19	51	141	7	222.0	191	13	117	211	Runners on	.220	805	177	29	6	11	171	115	207	.315	.312
April	3.06	4	3	21	41	0	50.0	48	1	23	58	Scoring Posn	.206	491	101	16	4	6	153	77	136	.308	.291
May	2.50	8	2	21	56	0	68.1	50	3	26	73	Close & Late	.220	900	198	28	4	19	112	117	248	.308	.323
June	2.67	8	7	14	60	0	64.1	67	8	40	78	None on/out	.251	362	91	15	3	11	11	35	96	.319	.401
July	2.79	0	6	22	49	2	71.0	51	6	35	59	vs. 1st Batr (relief)	.205	268	55	11	3	6	26	24	84	.270	.336
August	2.85	1	9	26	52	5	85.1	76	6	41	67	First Inning Pitched	.223	1010	225	43	8	16	136	126	270	.309	.329
September/October	3.44	6	5	21	52	5	91.2	74	6	44	94	First 15 Pitches	.223	851	190	34	7	15	89	94	223	.301	.333
Starter	3.45	2	6	0	12	12	70.1	62	5	43	55	Pitch 16-30	.224	451	101	11	1	5	56	69	124	.326	.286
Reliever	2.79	25	26	125	298	0	380.1	304	25	166	374	Pitch 31-45	.229	153	35	5	0	6	29	19	47	.310	.379
0 Days rest	1.91	10	7	37	71	0	89.2	63	5	33	81	Pitch 46+	.235	170	40	4	2	4	16	27	35	.340	.353
1 or 2 Days rest	2.77	8	13	54	139	0	185.1	148	10	83	198	First Pitch	.337	172	58	7	5	4	42	18	0	.399	.506
3+ Days rest	3.59	7	6	34	88	0	105.1	93	10	50	95	Ahead on Count	.173	845	146	22	1	8	55	0	353	.176	.230
Pre-All Star	2.58	20	13	63	172	0	220.0	174	13	95	224	Behind on Count	.325	280	91	13	2	9	52	85	0	.477	.482
Post-All Star	3.20	7	19	62	138	12	230.2	192	17	114	205	Two Strikes	.157	927	146	27	2	8	61	104	429	.244	.217

Pitcher vs. Batter (career)

Pitches Best Vs.	Avg	AB	H	2B	3B	HR	RBI	BB	SO	OBP	SLG	Pitches Worst Vs.	Avg	AB	H	2B	3B	HR	RBI	BB	SO	OBP	SLG
Craig Biggio	.071	14	1	0	0	0	0	0	3	.071	.071	Sid Bream	.500	8	4	2	0	1	4	2	2	.500	1.125
Hubie Brooks	.077	13	1	0	0	0	0	0	5	.077	.077	Jeff Bagwell	.455	11	5	3	0	2	5	0	3	.455	1.273
Mark Carreon	.091	11	1	0	0	0	0	0	4	.091	.091	Mark Grace	.429	14	6	0	2	1	6	1	3	.467	.929
Kirt Manwaring	.100	10	1	0	0	0	0	1	2	.182	.100	Jay Bell	.400	10	4	1	1	1	6	3	3	.538	1.000
Todd Zeile	.100	10	1	0	0	0	0	1	4	.182	.100	Kevin Bass	.385	13	5	0	0	2	3	2	2	.467	.846

Chris Nabholz — Expos
Pitches Left

	ERA	W	L	Sv	G	GS	IP	BB	SO	Avg	H	2B	3B	HR	RBI	OBP	SLG	CG	ShO	Sup	QS	#P/S	SB	CS	GB	FB	G/F
1992 Season	3.32	11	12	0	32	32	195.0	74	130	.244	176	29	7	11	63	.317	.349	1	1	4.29	17	88	23	6	307	160	1.92
Career (1990-1992)	3.35	25	21	0	67	67	418.2	163	282	.230	353	72	12	22	133	.306	.336	3	2	4.39	37	91	45	20	587	407	1.44

1992 Season

	ERA	W	L	Sv	G	GS	IP	H	HR	BB	SO		Avg	AB	H	2B	3B	HR	RBI	BB	SO	OBP	SLG
Home	3.09	5	7	0	15	15	99.0	79	5	31	59	vs. Left	.267	131	35	2	1	3	14	12	33	.336	.366
Away	3.56	6	5	0	17	17	96.0	97	6	43	71	vs. Right	.239	591	141	27	6	8	49	62	97	.313	.345
Day	1.96	6	1	0	9	9	59.2	41	2	19	39	Inning 1-6	.241	651	157	27	7	10	61	66	123	.313	.350
Night	3.92	5	11	0	23	23	135.1	135	9	55	91	Inning 7+	.268	71	19	2	0	1	2	8	7	.350	.338
Grass	4.22	2	4	0	8	8	49.0	51	2	16	32	None on	.242	417	101	18	5	6	6	43	69	.320	.353
Turf	3.02	9	8	0	24	24	146.0	125	9	58	98	Runners on	.246	305	75	11	2	5	57	31	61	.312	.344
April	3.62	1	2	0	5	5	27.1	26	1	14	20	Scoring Posn	.259	158	41	9	1	1	47	21	37	.339	.348
May	4.65	2	2	0	5	5	31.0	24	2	13	21	Close & Late	.282	39	11	1	0	1	2	4	4	.364	.385
June	3.26	2	2	0	5	5	30.1	27	0	15	31	None on/out	.255	192	49	6	2	4	4	20	36	.329	.370
July	3.58	1	1	0	5	5	32.2	33	3	11	17	vs. 1st Batr (relief)	.000	0	0	0	0	0	0	0	0	.000	.000
August	2.18	3	2	0	6	6	41.1	33	4	13	20	First Inning Pitched	.209	110	23	2	1	1	11	10	20	.282	.273
September/October	3.06	2	3	0	6	6	32.1	33	1	8	21	First 75 Pitches	.242	592	143	24	5	9	53	55	108	.308	.345
Starter	3.32	11	12	0	32	32	195.0	176	11	74	130	Pitch 76-90	.228	92	21	5	2	1	9	13	14	.324	.359
Reliever	0.00	0	0	0	0	0	0.0	0	0	0	0	Pitch 91-105	.343	35	12	0	0	1	1	5	8	.439	.429
0-3 Days Rest	0.00	0	0	0	0	0	0.0	0	0	0	0	Pitch 106+	.000	3	0	0	0	0	0	1	0	.250	.000
4 Days Rest	2.93	7	7	0	19	19	119.2	106	5	43	74	First Pitch	.211	109	23	2	1	1	9	2	0	.223	.275
5+ Days Rest	3.94	4	5	0	13	13	75.1	70	6	31	56	Ahead on Count	.189	301	57	8	0	2	14	0	114	.197	.236
Pre-All Star	3.90	5	6	0	17	17	101.2	89	4	48	78	Behind on Count	.343	172	59	13	5	5	25	47	0	.480	.564
Post-All Star	2.70	6	6	0	15	15	93.1	87	7	26	52	Two Strikes	.177	282	50	8	1	2	18	25	130	.252	.234

Career (1990-1992)

	ERA	W	L	Sv	G	GS	IP	H	HR	BB	SO		Avg	AB	H	2B	3B	HR	RBI	BB	SO	OBP	SLG
Home	3.12	11	14	0	32	32	213.2	160	12	80	138	vs. Left	.230	269	62	9	3	6	25	31	71	.316	.353
Away	3.60	14	7	0	35	35	205.0	193	10	83	144	vs. Right	.230	1264	291	63	9	16	108	132	211	.304	.332
Day	3.00	9	4	0	18	18	120.0	83	4	46	75	Inning 1-6	.230	1376	316	66	12	21	126	139	263	.302	.341
Night	3.50	16	17	0	49	49	298.2	270	18	117	207	Inning 7+	.236	157	37	6	0	1	7	24	19	.341	.293
Grass	4.48	5	6	0	15	15	92.1	89	5	36	62	None on	.228	908	207	39	9	15	15	101	169	.310	.340
Turf	3.03	20	15	0	52	52	326.1	264	17	127	220	Runners on	.234	625	146	33	3	7	118	62	113	.300	.330
April	4.08	1	5	0	9	9	53.0	49	3	26	31	Scoring Posn	.242	322	78	20	1	1	101	41	64	.323	.320
May	4.07	4	2	0	9	9	55.1	40	2	24	43	Close & Late	.207	92	19	2	0	1	4	15	9	.324	.261
June	3.81	2	3	0	10	10	56.2	57	0	25	49	None on/out	.238	407	97	18	5	9	9	44	78	.316	.373

Career (1990-1992)

	ERA	W	L	Sv	G	GS	IP	H	HR	BB	SO		Avg	AB	H	2B	3B	HR	RBI	BB	SO	OBP	SLG
July	3.58	1	1	0	5	5	32.2	33	3	11	17	vs. 1st Batr (relief)	.000	0	0	0	0	0	0	0	0	.000	.000
August	3.10	6	5	0	15	15	98.2	74	7	34	56	First Inning Pitched	.213	235	50	9	1	3	27	24	42	.288	.298
September/October	2.65	11	5	0	19	19	122.1	100	6	43	86	First 75 Pitches	.231	1225	283	59	8	16	110	117	233	.299	.331
Starter	3.35	25	21	0	67	67	418.2	353	22	163	282	Pitch 76-90	.219	201	44	9	4	4	17	27	32	.314	.363
Reliever	0.00	0	0	0	0	0	0.0	0	0	0	0	Pitch 91-105	.279	86	24	4	0	2	6	17	14	.404	.395
0-3 Days Rest	0.00	0	0	0	0	0	0.0	0	0	0	0	Pitch 106+	.095	21	2	0	0	0	0	2	3	.174	.095
4 Days Rest	3.42	14	14	0	39	39	247.2	215	12	97	161	First Pitch	.257	230	59	13	2	3	23	7	0	.276	.370
5+ Days Rest	3.26	11	7	0	28	28	171.0	138	10	66	121	Ahead on Count	.183	652	119	20	1	5	38	0	249	.190	.239
Pre-All Star	3.99	7	10	0	30	30	178.0	158	7	81	129	Behind on Count	.297	370	110	27	8	10	46	102	0	.446	.495
Post-All Star	2.88	18	11	0	37	37	240.2	195	15	82	153	Two Strikes	.160	624	100	21	2	3	40	54	262	.233	.215

Pitcher vs. Batter (career)

Pitches Best Vs.	Avg	AB	H	2B	3B	HR	RBI	BB	SO	OBP	SLG	Pitches Worst Vs.	Avg	AB	H	2B	3B	HR	RBI	BB	SO	OBP	SLG
Ken Caminiti	.000	13	0	0	0	0	0	0	1	.000	.000	Felix Jose	.636	11	7	2	0	0	3	1	3	.667	.818
Tony Fernandez	.000	12	0	0	0	0	1	1	0	.077	.000	Fred McGriff	.625	8	5	0	1	2	4	4	0	.750	1.625
Will Clark	.000	12	0	0	0	0	0	1	0	.077	.000	Jeff Bagwell	.583	12	7	2	0	0	1	1	2	.615	.750
Benito Santiago	.091	11	1	0	0	0	1	0	2	.091	.091	Chris Sabo	.538	13	7	3	1	2	5	2	0	.600	1.385
Howard Johnson	.100	10	1	0	0	0	1	1	3	.167	.100	Rex Hudler	.429	14	6	2	0	2	2	2	2	.500	1.000

Tim Naehring — Red Sox   Bats Right

	Avg	G	AB	R	H	2B	3B	HR	RBI	BB	SO	HBP	GDP	SB	CS	OBP	SLG	IBB	SH	SF	#Pit	#P/PA	GB	FB	G/F
1992 Season	.231	72	186	12	43	8	0	3	14	18	31	3	1	0	0	.308	.323	0	6	1	808	3.88	63	59	1.07
Career (1990-1992)	.221	116	326	23	72	15	0	5	29	32	61	3	3	0	0	.296	.313	1	10	1	1399	3.86	119	93	1.28

1992 Season

	Avg	AB	H	2B	3B	HR	RBI	BB	SO	OBP	SLG		Avg	AB	H	2B	3B	HR	RBI	BB	SO	OBP	SLG
vs. Left	.235	68	16	3	0	2	9	3	12	.284	.368	Scoring Posn	.297	37	11	3	0	1	12	6	2	.386	.459
vs. Right	.229	118	27	5	0	1	5	15	19	.321	.297	Close & Late	.244	41	10	1	0	2	4	3	10	.295	.415
Home	.229	83	19	3	0	0	4	12	13	.326	.265	None on/out	.185	54	10	1	0	1	1	4	14	.267	.259
Away	.233	103	24	5	0	3	10	6	18	.292	.369	Batting #7	.186	70	13	2	0	0	4	2	13	.208	.214
First Pitch	.174	23	4	0	0	0	2	0	0	.167	.174	Batting #8	.234	47	11	2	0	0	4	7	8	.345	.277
Ahead on Count	.233	43	10	1	0	1	1	8	0	.353	.326	Other	.275	69	19	4	0	3	6	9	10	.370	.464
Behind on Count	.182	55	10	1	0	0	5	0	17	.211	.200	Pre-All Star	.217	115	25	3	0	2	7	9	20	.291	.296
Two Strikes	.213	80	17	1	0	2	9	10	31	.323	.350	Post-All Star	.254	71	18	5	0	1	7	9	11	.333	.366

Charles Nagy — Indians   Pitches Right (groundball pitcher)

	ERA	W	L	Sv	G	GS	IP	BB	SO	Avg	H	2B	3B	HR	RBI	OBP	SLG	CG	ShO	Sup	QS	#P/S	SB	CS	GB	FB	G/F
1992 Season	2.96	17	10	0	33	33	252.0	57	169	.260	245	41	4	11	79	.300	.346	10	3	4.36	24	109	12	15	433	178	2.43
Career (1990-1992)	3.71	29	29	0	75	74	509.0	144	304	.271	531	95	12	33	197	.321	.383	16	4	4.03	47	102	37	24	867	427	2.03

1992 Season

	ERA	W	L	Sv	G	GS	IP	H	HR	BB	SO		Avg	AB	H	2B	3B	HR	RBI	BB	SO	OBP	SLG
Home	2.34	8	4	0	17	17	134.1	126	5	29	95	vs. Left	.250	424	106	15	2	5	38	27	68	.292	.330
Away	3.67	9	6	0	16	16	117.2	119	6	28	74	vs. Right	.267	520	139	26	2	6	41	30	101	.308	.360
Day	3.29	4	4	0	11	11	82.0	88	4	21	62	Inning 1-6	.252	726	183	31	4	9	66	52	140	.301	.343
Night	2.81	13	6	0	22	22	170.0	157	7	36	107	Inning 7+	.284	218	62	10	0	2	13	5	29	.300	.358
Grass	2.64	15	7	0	27	27	208.1	194	9	45	140	None on	.269	566	152	31	3	8	8	31	107	.308	.376
Turf	4.53	2	3	0	6	6	43.2	51	2	12	29	Runners on	.246	378	93	10	1	3	71	26	62	.290	.302
April	1.63	3	1	0	5	5	38.2	32	0	8	27	Scoring Posn	.271	207	56	6	1	2	68	16	46	.313	.338
May	3.38	3	2	0	6	6	45.1	51	2	11	27	Close & Late	.320	100	32	5	0	1	4	4	12	.349	.400
June	1.99	3	1	0	5	5	40.2	38	1	4	22	None on/out	.254	252	64	14	1	3	3	14	51	.293	.353
July	2.95	2	2	0	5	5	36.2	39	1	11	22	vs. 1st Batr (relief)	.000	0	0	0	0	0	0	0	0	.000	.000
August	4.34	2	4	0	6	6	47.2	48	3	13	40	First Inning Pitched	.198	116	23	8	1	0	6	12	25	.273	.284
September/October	3.14	4	0	0	6	6	43.0	37	4	10	31	First 75 Pitches	.247	623	154	29	3	7	50	47	122	.299	.337
Starter	2.96	17	10	0	33	33	252.0	245	11	57	169	Pitch 76-90	.271	129	35	3	1	3	16	4	22	.289	.380
Reliever	0.00	0	0	0	0	0	0.0	0	0	0	0	Pitch 91-105	.273	121	33	3	0	1	9	1	15	.274	.322
0-3 Days Rest	0.00	0	0	0	0	0	0.0	0	0	0	0	Pitch 106+	.324	71	23	6	0	0	4	5	10	.372	.408
4 Days Rest	3.89	6	7	0	16	16	118.0	144	4	27	85	First Pitch	.340	150	51	5	3	3	24	1	0	.338	.473
5+ Days Rest	2.15	11	3	0	17	17	134.0	101	7	30	84	Ahead on Count	.193	414	80	15	0	1	23	0	149	.192	.237
Pre-All Star	2.40	11	4	0	18	18	138.2	133	4	26	81	Behind on Count	.320	231	74	13	0	4	19	35	0	.410	.429
Post-All Star	3.65	6	6	0	15	15	113.1	112	7	31	88	Two Strikes	.178	400	71	14	1	0	20	21	169	.217	.218

Career (1990-1992)

	ERA	W	L	Sv	G	GS	IP	H	HR	BB	SO		Avg	AB	H	2B	3B	HR	RBI	BB	SO	OBP	SLG
Home	3.18	16	12	0	37	36	266.0	265	13	68	171	vs. Left	.276	990	273	44	8	15	101	76	148	.326	.382
Away	4.30	13	17	0	38	38	243.0	266	20	76	133	vs. Right	.267	966	258	51	4	18	96	68	156	.317	.384
Day	4.09	8	12	0	25	25	167.1	183	15	48	117	Inning 1-6	.270	1589	429	79	12	28	171	130	257	.326	.388
Night	3.53	21	17	0	50	49	341.2	348	18	96	187	Inning 7+	.278	367	102	16	0	5	26	14	47	.302	.362
Grass	3.46	27	20	0	61	60	418.2	425	26	108	246	None on	.275	1140	314	63	9	17	17	77	193	.322	.391
Turf	4.88	2	9	0	14	14	90.1	106	7	36	58	Runners on	.266	816	217	32	3	16	180	67	111	.321	.371
April	1.60	4	2	0	9	9	67.1	51	1	18	44	Scoring Posn	.266	463	123	17	2	10	162	44	83	.324	.376

Career (1990-1992)

	ERA	W	L	Sv	G	GS	IP	H	HR	BB	SO		Avg	AB	H	2B	3B	HR	RBI	BB	SO	OBP	SLG
May	4.67	3	6	0	12	12	79.0	90	6	26	42	Close & Late	.278	180	50	7	0	1	7	10	24	.316	.333
June	2.96	5	6	0	12	12	82.0	91	2	20	49	vs. 1st Batr (relief)	.000	0	0	0	0	0	0	1	0	1.000	.000
July	2.93	5	5	0	12	12	83.0	85	3	25	35	None on/out	.264	508	134	27	4	6	6	34	90	.310	.368
August	5.34	4	5	0	13	13	86.0	101	9	27	63	First Inning Pitched	.268	295	85	21	3	4	43	35	48	.364	.420
September/October	4.19	8	5	0	17	16	111.2	113	12	26	71	First 75 Pitches	.271	1358	368	70	11	25	144	112	217	.327	.394
Starter	3.69	29	29	0	74	74	507.1	528	32	143	302	Pitch 76-90	.277	256	71	10	1	6	33	14	38	.313	.395
Reliever	10.80	0	0	0	1	0	1.2	3	1	1	2	Pitch 91-105	.258	213	55	9	0	1	13	8	32	.263	.315
0-3 Days Rest	0.00	0	0	0	0	0	0.0	0	0	0	0	Pitch 106+	.287	129	37	6	0	1	7	10	17	.338	.357
4 Days Rest	4.33	8	17	0	35	35	230.2	279	16	69	144	First Pitch	.308	279	86	11	4	6	41	8	0	.327	.441
5+ Days Rest	3.16	21	12	0	39	39	276.2	249	16	74	158	Ahead on Count	.204	837	171	29	2	9	57	0	269	.207	.276
Pre-All Star	3.03	15	15	0	37	37	258.1	257	11	70	144	Behind on Count	.354	511	181	35	5	10	61	82	0	.439	.501
Post-All Star	4.42	14	14	0	38	37	250.2	274	22	74	160	Two Strikes	.189	804	152	29	3	8	47	54	304	.242	.262

Pitcher vs. Batter (career)

Pitches Best Vs.	Avg	AB	H	2B	3B	HR	RBI	BB	SO	OBP	SLG	Pitches Worst Vs.	Avg	AB	H	2B	3B	HR	RBI	BB	SO	OBP	SLG
Jose Canseco	.000	12	0	0	0	0	0	0	2	.143	.000	Luis Polonia	.556	18	10	0	1	0	3	3	0	.619	.667
Rickey Henderson	.000	9	0	0	0	0	2	2	1	.182	.000	Rance Mulliniks	.538	13	7	2	0	0	4	1	0	.571	.692
Kent Hrbek	.067	15	1	0	0	0	0	2	4	.176	.067	Ken Griffey Jr	.412	17	7	2	1	2	5	3	4	.500	1.000
Pete O'Brien	.071	14	1	0	0	0	1	0	1	.071	.071	Kelly Gruber	.400	20	8	3	0	2	6	2	2	.455	.850
Chuck Knoblauch	.091	11	1	0	0	0	1	0	0	.083	.091	Mickey Tettleton	.313	16	5	0	0	3	4	3	.421	.875

Bob Natal — Expos
Bats Right (groundball hitter)

	Avg	G	AB	R	H	2B	3B	HR	RBI	BB	SO	HBP	GDP	SB	CS	OBP	SLG	IBB	SH	SF	#Pit	#P/PA	GB	FB	G/F
1992 Season	.000	5	6	0	0	0	0	0	0	1	1	0	1	0	0	.143	.000	0	0	0	24	3.43	4	1	4.00

1992 Season

	Avg	AB	H	2B	3B	HR	RBI	BB	SO	OBP	SLG		Avg	AB	H	2B	3B	HR	RBI	BB	SO	OBP	SLG
vs. Left	.000	4	0	0	0	0	0	1	1	.200	.000	Scoring Posn	.000	1	0	0	0	0	0	0	0	.000	.000
vs. Right	.000	2	0	0	0	0	0	0	0	.000	.000	Close & Late	.000	1	0	0	0	0	0	0	0	.000	.000

Jaime Navarro — Brewers
Pitches Right

	ERA	W	L	Sv	G	GS	IP	BB	SO	Avg	H	2B	3B	HR	RBI	OBP	SLG	CG	ShO	Sup	QS	#P/S	SB	CS	GB	FB	G/F
1992 Season	3.33	17	11	0	34	34	246.0	64	100	.246	224	42	6	14	79	.295	.351	5	3	4.65	23	102	17	11	362	279	1.30
Career (1989-1992)	3.71	47	38	1	119	107	739.0	210	345	.265	756	122	16	49	286	.317	.371	19	5	4.65	60	99	63	27	1150	830	1.39

1992 Season

	ERA	W	L	Sv	G	GS	IP	H	HR	BB	SO		Avg	AB	H	2B	3B	HR	RBI	BB	SO	OBP	SLG
Home	3.29	9	4	0	15	15	109.1	104	6	26	49	vs. Left	.257	435	112	25	3	6	41	32	46	.304	.370
Away	3.36	8	7	0	19	19	136.2	120	8	38	51	vs. Right	.235	477	112	17	3	8	38	32	54	.288	.333
Day	3.25	6	3	0	10	10	72.0	67	1	25	26	Inning 1-6	.246	716	176	33	3	11	66	53	79	.299	.346
Night	3.36	11	8	0	24	24	174.0	157	13	39	74	Inning 7+	.245	196	48	9	3	3	13	11	21	.281	.367
Grass	3.18	14	7	0	27	27	195.0	180	8	55	82	None on	.236	589	139	26	4	11	11	36	68	.282	.350
Turf	3.88	3	4	0	7	7	51.0	44	6	9	18	Runners on	.263	323	85	16	2	3	68	28	32	.318	.353
April	4.50	1	2	0	4	4	28.0	29	0	9	6	Scoring Posn	.250	180	45	8	2	2	65	20	18	.312	.350
May	3.95	3	2	0	6	6	43.1	45	4	8	16	Close & Late	.265	102	27	4	2	1	7	6	9	.300	.373
June	3.77	4	2	0	6	6	45.1	41	6	14	16	None on/out	.240	250	60	11	1	5	5	12	26	.278	.352
July	1.60	3	0	0	5	5	39.1	18	0	10	15	vs. 1st Batr (relief)	.000	0	0	0	0	0	0	0	0	.000	.000
August	2.35	3	3	0	6	6	46.0	39	3	7	22	First Inning Pitched	.244	123	30	5	0	1	10	13	17	.312	.309
September/October	4.09	3	2	0	7	7	44.0	52	1	16	25	First 75 Pitches	.238	643	153	30	3	8	52	49	71	.292	.331
Starter	3.33	17	11	0	34	34	246.0	224	14	64	100	Pitch 76-90	.233	120	28	5	1	4	15	6	14	.273	.392
Reliever	0.00	0	0	0	0	0	0.0	0	0	0	0	Pitch 91-105	.265	98	26	2	1	2	5	7	12	.318	.367
0-3 Days Rest	0.00	0	0	0	0	0	0.0	0	0	0	0	Pitch 106+	.333	51	17	5	1	0	7	2	3	.345	.471
4 Days Rest	3.25	15	6	0	26	26	185.1	175	9	50	74	First Pitch	.299	137	41	9	1	2	17	4	0	.310	.423
5+ Days Rest	3.56	2	5	0	8	8	60.2	49	5	14	26	Ahead on Count	.189	392	74	9	1	2	21	0	88	.195	.232
Pre-All Star	3.95	9	6	0	18	18	130.0	127	10	37	42	Behind on Count	.327	217	71	16	3	7	25	29	0	.404	.525
Post-All Star	2.64	8	5	0	16	16	116.0	97	4	27	58	Two Strikes	.170	358	61	9	1	1	15	31	100	.240	.209

Career (1989-1992)

	ERA	W	L	Sv	G	GS	IP	H	HR	BB	SO		Avg	AB	H	2B	3B	HR	RBI	BB	SO	OBP	SLG
Home	3.46	28	15	1	58	51	362.0	361	20	103	175	vs. Left	.273	1430	391	60	6	25	145	116	161	.325	.376
Away	3.96	19	23	0	61	56	377.0	395	29	107	170	vs. Right	.257	1420	365	62	10	24	141	94	184	.308	.365
Day	3.42	16	12	0	40	32	226.0	227	11	70	111	Inning 1-6	.258	2282	589	95	12	35	225	175	277	.312	.356
Night	3.84	31	26	1	79	75	513.0	529	36	140	234	Inning 7+	.294	568	167	27	4	14	61	35	68	.334	.430
Grass	3.46	38	28	1	97	86	606.1	602	35	180	276	None on	.258	1690	436	71	11	30	30	115	212	.309	.366
Turf	4.88	9	10	0	22	21	132.2	154	14	30	69	Runners on	.276	1160	320	51	5	19	256	95	133	.328	.378
April	5.21	2	2	0	12	12	65.2	86	3	24	27	Scoring Posn	.262	641	168	27	3	9	225	64	78	.321	.356
May	4.07	8	5	0	16	16	106.1	118	10	19	48	Close & Late	.286	259	74	11	3	6	29	16	28	.323	.421
June	3.81	8	5	0	16	16	111.0	110	10	41	51	None on/out	.243	738	179	28	3	14	14	48	92	.293	.346
July	2.80	5	7	1	24	15	125.1	112	3	37	60	vs. 1st Batr (relief)	.000	11	0	0	0	0	0	0	5	.000	.000
August	4.23	12	11	0	25	22	146.2	146	11	38	76	First Inning Pitched	.237	427	101	13	3	3	36	43	51	.304	.302

Career (1989-1992)

	ERA	W	L	Sv	G	GS	IP	H	HR	BB	SO		Avg	AB	H	2B	3B	HR	RBI	BB	SO	OBP	SLG
September/October	3.12	12	8	0	26	26	182.0	184	12	51	63	First 75 Pitches	.253	2074	525	79	12	31	184	155	255	.306	.348
Starter	3.80	46	38	0	107	107	713.2	737	48	206	328	Pitch 76-90	.288	361	104	22	2	8	50	22	48	.330	.427
Reliever	1.42	1	0	1	12	0	25.1	19	1	4	17	Pitch 91-105	.275	258	71	10	1	2	17	19	28	.332	.345
0-3 Days Rest	2.89	2	2	0	5	5	37.1	34	1	6	19	Pitch 106+	.357	157	56	11	1	8	35	14	14	.398	.592
4 Days Rest	3.90	36	22	0	70	70	471.0	490	34	130	214	First Pitch	.346	422	146	24	3	7	54	10	0	.362	.467
5+ Days Rest	3.73	8	14	0	32	32	205.1	213	13	70	95	Ahead on Count	.199	1216	242	32	5	11	84	1	301	.204	.261
Pre-All Star	4.22	19	15	0	51	49	321.2	354	25	98	139	Behind on Count	.340	683	232	40	7	19	94	100	0	.419	.502
Post-All Star	3.32	28	23	1	68	58	417.1	402	24	112	206	Two Strikes	.188	1146	215	32	3	13	79	99	345	.254	.255

Pitcher vs. Batter (career)

Pitches Best Vs.	Avg	AB	H	2B	3B	HR	RBI	BB	SO	OBP	SLG	Pitches Worst Vs.	Avg	AB	H	2B	3B	HR	RBI	BB	SO	OBP	SLG
Dean Palmer	.000	11	0	0	0	0	0	3	1	.214	.000	Danny Tartabull	.643	14	9	1	0	3	6	2	3	.688	1.357
Tim Raines	.067	15	1	0	0	0	0	0	1	.067	.067	Julio Franco	.563	16	9	1	0	0	3	1	1	.588	.625
Ellis Burks	.083	12	1	0	0	0	1	0	1	.083	.083	Dan Gladden	.533	15	8	2	0	0	2	0	1	.533	.667
Gary DiSarcina	.091	11	1	0	0	0	1	0	0	.091	.091	Kevin Seitzer	.500	8	4	1	0	0	1	4	0	.667	.625
Kelly Gruber	.100	20	2	0	0	0	2	1	1	.143	.100	Luis Rivera	.462	13	6	0	0	1	4	1	0	.500	.692

Denny Neagle — Pirates   Pitches Left (flyball pitcher)

	ERA	W	L	Sv	G	GS	IP	BB	SO	Avg	H	2B	3B	HR	RBI	OBP	SLG	GF	IR	IRS	Hld	SvOp	SB	CS	GB	FB	G/F
1992 Season	4.48	4	6	2	55	6	86.1	43	77	.247	81	17	1	9	39	.335	.387	8	26	4	5	4	14	3	93	97	0.96
Career (1991-1992)	4.40	4	7	2	62	9	106.1	50	91	.264	109	25	2	12	46	.344	.421	10	26	4	5	4	16	4	118	123	0.96

1992 Season

	ERA	W	L	Sv	G	GS	IP	H	HR	BB	SO		Avg	AB	H	2B	3B	HR	RBI	BB	SO	OBP	SLG
Home	6.05	1	5	0	27	3	38.2	47	6	21	39	vs. Left	.228	92	21	5	0	2	13	15	27	.343	.348
Away	3.21	3	1	2	28	3	47.2	34	3	22	38	vs. Right	.254	236	60	12	1	7	26	28	50	.332	.403
Starter	5.40	1	3	0	6	6	26.2	31	3	8	17	Scoring Posn	.309	81	25	7	0	4	34	22	25	.443	.543
Reliever	4.07	3	3	2	49	0	59.2	50	6	35	60	Close & Late	.194	103	20	1	0	3	5	12	33	.284	.291
0 Days rest	3.86	1	0	0	4	0	4.2	3	0	4	3	None on/out	.235	85	20	5	1	2	2	8	14	.316	.388
1 or 2 Days rest	4.85	1	2	2	30	0	39.0	32	6	22	42	First Pitch	.257	35	9	1	0	3	10	6	0	.372	.543
3+ Days rest	2.25	1	1	0	15	0	16.0	15	0	9	15	Behind on Count	.362	58	21	5	0	3	13	16	0	.493	.603
Pre-All Star	4.61	3	4	1	28	6	56.2	53	6	26	50	Ahead on Count	.190	168	32	6	1	2	7	0	67	.195	.274
Post-All Star	4.25	1	2	1	27	0	29.2	28	3	17	27	Two Strikes	.169	178	30	6	0	3	10	21	77	.260	.253

Troy Neel — Athletics   Bats Left

	Avg	G	AB	R	H	2B	3B	HR	RBI	BB	SO	HBP	GDP	SB	CS	OBP	SLG	IBB	SH	SF	#Pit	#P/PA	GB	FB	G/F
1992 Season	.264	24	53	8	14	3	0	3	9	5	15	1	1	1	0	1	.339	.491	0	0	0	250	4.24	16	16	1.00

1992 Season

	Avg	AB	H	2B	3B	HR	RBI	BB	SO	OBP	SLG		Avg	AB	H	2B	3B	HR	RBI	BB	SO	OBP	SLG
vs. Left	.400	5	2	0	0	1	2	0	1	.400	1.000	Scoring Posn	.200	10	2	2	0	0	3	0	2	.200	.400
vs. Right	.250	48	12	3	0	2	7	5	14	.333	.438	Close & Late	.000	4	0	0	0	0	0	0	2	.000	.000

Gene Nelson — Athletics   Pitches Right

	ERA	W	L	Sv	G	GS	IP	BB	SO	Avg	H	2B	3B	HR	RBI	OBP	SLG	GF	IR	IRS	Hld	SvOp	SB	CS	GB	FB	G/F
1992 Season	6.45	3	1	0	28	2	51.2	22	23	.335	68	8	3	5	40	.391	.478	8	26	7	2	1	4	3	68	68	1.00
Last Five Years	3.78	19	20	11	227	3	366.2	130	221	.246	336	47	13	36	186	.312	.378	36	245	79	48	24	21	7	471	442	1.07

1992 Season

	ERA	W	L	Sv	G	GS	IP	H	HR	BB	SO		Avg	AB	H	2B	3B	HR	RBI	BB	SO	OBP	SLG
Home	5.67	2	1	0	14	1	27.0	29	5	8	14	vs. Left	.333	93	31	3	3	0	14	15	10	.411	.430
Away	7.30	1	0	0	14	1	24.2	39	0	14	9	vs. Right	.336	110	37	5	0	5	26	7	13	.373	.518
Starter	3.12	1	0	0	2	2	8.2	12	0	4	6	Scoring Posn	.323	62	20	2	2	2	34	10	8	.390	.516
Reliever	7.12	2	1	0	26	0	43.0	56	5	18	17	Close & Late	.267	15	4	0	1	1	3	3	2	.368	.600
0 Days rest	5.40	0	0	0	1	0	1.2	2	0	0	1	None on/out	.409	44	18	4	0	1	1	5	8	.469	.568
1 or 2 Days rest	7.41	0	1	0	11	0	17.0	19	3	4	6	First Pitch	.357	28	10	0	1	1	8	4	0	.438	.536
3+ Days rest	7.03	2	0	0	14	0	24.1	35	2	14	10	Behind on Count	.393	56	22	2	0	1	9	8	0	.448	.482
Pre-All Star	6.63	1	1	0	24	1	38.0	52	4	14	17	Ahead on Count	.272	81	22	3	0	2	0	0	21	.265	.383
Post-All Star	5.93	2	0	0	4	1	13.2	16	1	8	6	Two Strikes	.253	79	20	3	1	2	14	10	23	.330	.392

Last Five Years

	ERA	W	L	Sv	G	GS	IP	H	HR	BB	SO		Avg	AB	H	2B	3B	HR	RBI	BB	SO	OBP	SLG
Home	3.86	11	10	4	103	1	179.1	148	20	65	121	vs. Left	.270	560	151	18	9	12	69	69	72	.345	.398
Away	3.70	8	10	7	124	2	187.1	188	16	65	100	vs. Right	.229	808	185	29	4	24	117	61	149	.287	.364
Day	3.90	6	8	6	83	1	150.0	131	13	54	96	Inning 1-6	.275	408	112	12	5	13	82	45	64	.340	.424
Night	3.70	13	12	5	144	2	216.2	205	23	76	125	Inning 7+	.233	960	224	35	8	23	104	85	157	.299	.358
Grass	3.52	18	17	9	188	2	312.0	271	29	108	196	None on	.248	751	186	30	6	20	20	58	131	.307	.383
Turf	5.27	1	3	2	39	1	54.2	65	7	22	25	Runners on	.243	617	150	17	7	16	166	72	90	.317	.371
April	4.04	4	4	2	25	1	42.1	40	3	16	26	Scoring Posn	.249	361	90	8	6	10	147	56	57	.339	.368
May	3.12	2	2	3	32	0	52.0	39	4	17	31	Close & Late	.241	373	90	12	4	12	52	39	54	.318	.391
June	5.31	4	5	1	46	0	78.0	83	9	33	48	None on/out	.254	323	82	13	2	6	6	24	56	.309	.362

Last Five Years

	ERA	W	L	Sv	G	GS	IP	H	HR	BB	SO		Avg	AB	H	2B	3B	HR	RBI	BB	SO	OBP	SLG
July	4.92	3	3	2	41	2	78.2	90	12	32	43	vs. 1st Batr (relief)	.177	203	36	4	0	5	32	11	40	.221	.271
August	1.96	3	4	1	41	0	59.2	42	3	16	33	First Inning Pitched	.241	729	176	23	5	18	120	61	119	.300	.361
September/October	2.41	3	2	2	42	0	56.0	42	5	16	40	First 15 Pitches	.237	761	180	24	7	18	105	52	116	.287	.357
Starter	5.11	1	1	0	3	3	12.1	18	2	5	7	Pitch 16-30	.243	354	86	15	5	5	46	49	68	.333	.356
Reliever	3.73	18	19	11	224	0	354.1	318	34	125	214	Pitch 31-45	.306	157	48	6	1	13	28	16	20	.374	.605
0 Days rest	4.23	4	4	1	30	0	38.1	36	2	19	13	Pitch 46+	.229	96	22	2	0	0	7	13	17	.318	.250
1 or 2 Days rest	3.70	7	7	6	95	0	150.2	136	15	45	94	First Pitch	.280	225	63	10	3	10	43	10	0	.304	.484
3+ Days rest	3.65	7	8	4	99	0	165.1	146	17	61	107	Ahead on Count	.195	589	115	14	3	11	60	0	192	.199	.285
Pre-All Star	4.36	10	12	7	115	2	196.1	199	19	73	122	Behind on Count	.294	323	95	15	3	7	53	75	0	.423	.424
Post-All Star	3.10	9	8	4	112	0	168.1	137	17	57	99	Two Strikes	.193	570	110	13	4	13	56	44	221	.252	.298

Pitcher vs. Batter (since 1984)

Pitches Best Vs.	Avg	AB	H	2B	3B	HR	RBI	BB	SO	OBP	SLG	Pitches Worst Vs.	Avg	AB	H	2B	3B	HR	RBI	BB	SO	OBP	SLG
Cecil Fielder	.050	20	1	0	0	0	0	1	5	.095	.050	Randy Bush	.545	11	6	1	0	1	3	1	2	.583	.909
Tom Brunansky	.063	16	1	0	0	0	1	1	4	.118	.063	Don Mattingly	.455	22	10	4	0	1	2	1	1	.478	.773
Don Slaught	.077	13	1	0	0	0	0	0	2	.077	.077	Greg Vaughn	.364	11	4	0	0	2	5	0	2	.364	.909
Billy Ripken	.091	11	1	1	0	0	0	0	1	.091	.182	George Brett	.350	20	7	0	0	4	5	1	0	.381	.950
Gene Larkin	.100	10	1	0	0	0	0	1	2	.182	.100	Rich Gedman	.333	12	4	1	0	2	3	0	1	.333	.917

Jeff Nelson — Mariners

Pitches Right

	ERA	W	L	Sv	G	GS	IP	BB	SO	Avg	H	2B	3B	HR	RBI	OBP	SLG	GF	IR	IRS	Hld	SvOp	SB	CS	GB	FB	G/F
1992 Season	3.44	1	7	6	66	0	81.0	44	46	.245	71	10	3	7	40	.353	.372	27	63	18	6	14	4	3	110	92	1.20

1992 Season

	ERA	W	L	Sv	G	GS	IP	H	HR	BB	SO		Avg	AB	H	2B	3B	HR	RBI	BB	SO	OBP	SLG
Home	3.46	1	2	5	30	0	41.2	34	2	14	23	vs. Left	.287	108	31	4	1	2	10	25	18	.418	.398
Away	3.43	0	5	1	36	0	39.1	37	5	30	23	vs. Right	.220	182	40	6	2	5	30	19	28	.311	.357
Day	2.48	1	2	2	26	0	36.1	26	2	13	18	Inning 1-6	.300	40	12	0	0	0	6	4	4	.391	.300
Night	4.23	0	5	4	40	0	44.2	45	5	31	28	Inning 7+	.236	250	59	10	3	7	34	40	42	.347	.384
Grass	4.06	0	4	1	27	0	31.0	32	5	26	15	None on	.257	136	35	4	2	5	5	13	23	.344	.426
Turf	3.06	1	3	5	39	0	50.0	39	2	18	31	Runners on	.234	154	36	6	1	2	35	31	23	.360	.325
April	3.24	0	1	0	6	0	8.1	6	0	4	3	Scoring Posn	.214	103	22	2	1	1	33	26	16	.364	.282
May	4.91	0	1	0	13	0	11.0	12	1	3	6	Close & Late	.244	127	31	4	1	3	22	25	21	.372	.362
June	4.02	0	1	0	12	0	15.2	17	2	10	8	None on/out	.300	60	18	3	2	0	0	5	9	.373	.417
July	3.86	0	1	1	9	0	14.0	15	2	6	8	vs. 1st Batr (relief)	.254	59	15	3	1	1	12	6	9	.323	.390
August	0.53	1	0	3	12	0	17.0	6	0	7	11	First Inning Pitched	.261	203	53	8	2	5	33	31	35	.357	.394
September/October	4.80	0	3	2	14	0	15.0	15	2	14	10	First 15 Pitches	.272	202	55	8	3	5	30	20	32	.335	.416
Starter	0.00	0	0	0	0	0	0.0	0	0	0	0	First 15 Pitches	.176	68	12	1	0	1	8	23	10	.412	.235
Reliever	3.44	1	7	6	66	0	81.0	71	7	44	46	Pitch 31-45	.222	18	4	1	0	1	2	1	4	.300	.444
0 Days rest	4.63	0	3	0	13	0	11.2	16	1	8	6	Pitch 46+	.000	2	0	0	0	0	0	0	0	.000	.000
1 or 2 Days rest	2.29	0	2	5	39	0	51.0	35	4	27	29	First Pitch	.255	47	12	2	2	1	3	8	0	.397	.447
3+ Days rest	5.89	1	2	1	14	0	18.1	20	2	9	11	Ahead on Count	.187	123	23	2	0	4	12	0	39	.200	.301
Pre-All Star	4.17	0	4	0	35	0	41.0	41	4	19	21	Behind on Count	.347	75	26	4	0	1	16	20	0	.480	.440
Post-All Star	2.70	1	3	6	31	0	40.0	30	3	25	25	Two Strikes	.179	117	21	2	1	4	12	16	46	.284	.316

Al Newman — Rangers

Bats Both (groundball hitter)

	Avg	G	AB	R	H	2B	3B	HR	RBI	BB	SO	HBP	GDP	SB	CS	OBP	SLG	IBB	SH	SF	#Pit	#P/PA	GB	FB	G/F
1992 Season	.220	116	246	25	54	5	0	0	12	34	26	1	5	9	6	.317	.240	0	8	0	1040	3.70	116	58	2.00
Last Five Years	.231	624	1586	190	366	49	2	0	118	178	161	6	25	63	32	.309	.264	0	37	9	6200	3.49	758	378	2.01

1992 Season

	Avg	AB	H	2B	3B	HR	RBI	BB	SO	OBP	SLG		Avg	AB	H	2B	3B	HR	RBI	BB	SO	OBP	SLG
vs. Left	.268	56	15	1	0	0	3	14	9	.423	.286	Scoring Posn	.216	51	11	2	0	0	12	7	4	.310	.255
vs. Right	.205	190	39	4	0	0	9	20	17	.281	.226	Close & Late	.233	30	7	0	0	0	1	5	5	.343	.233
Home	.202	114	23	3	0	0	3	15	12	.300	.228	None on/out	.257	74	19	1	0	0	0	15	10	.382	.270
Away	.235	132	31	2	0	0	9	19	14	.331	.250	Batting #8	.160	50	8	1	0	0	1	8	8	.276	.180
First Pitch	.310	42	13	0	0	0	5	0	0	.310	.310	Batting #9	.250	136	34	1	0	0	8	19	12	.346	.257
Ahead on Count	.222	54	12	1	0	0	4	20	0	.432	.241	Other	.200	60	12	3	0	0	3	7	6	.284	.250
Behind on Count	.157	70	11	1	0	0	1	0	16	.169	.171	Pre-All Star	.212	151	32	4	0	0	10	17	14	.296	.238
Two Strikes	.147	95	14	2	0	0	3	14	26	.257	.168	Post-All Star	.232	95	22	1	0	0	2	17	12	.348	.242

Last Five Years

	Avg	AB	H	2B	3B	HR	RBI	BB	SO	OBP	SLG		Avg	AB	H	2B	3B	HR	RBI	BB	SO	OBP	SLG
vs. Left	.241	477	115	23	0	0	40	57	61	.324	.289	Scoring Posn	.222	405	90	16	0	0	114	34	35	.278	.262
vs. Right	.226	1109	251	26	2	0	78	121	100	.303	.253	Close & Late	.238	239	57	8	0	0	17	28	27	.322	.272
Groundball	.211	412	87	7	0	0	31	47	35	.294	.228	None on/out	.217	446	97	9	1	0	0	63	49	.314	.242
Flyball	.193	347	67	10	1	0	26	44	41	.285	.228	Batting #1	.243	424	103	15	1	0	29	47	38	.317	.283
Home	.235	782	184	24	1	0	55	99	67	.322	.269	Batting #9	.234	666	156	15	1	0	51	71	73	.310	.260
Away	.226	804	182	25	1	0	63	79	94	.296	.260	Other	.216	496	107	19	0	0	38	60	50	.301	.254
Day	.249	510	127	16	0	0	44	52	52	.317	.280	April	.214	140	30	7	0	0	11	12	17	.276	.264
Night	.222	1076	239	33	2	0	74	126	109	.305	.257	May	.238	261	62	5	0	0	17	37	25	.330	.257

Last Five Years

	Avg	AB	H	2B	3B	HR	RBI	BB	SO	OBP	SLG		Avg	AB	H	2B	3B	HR	RBI	BB	SO	OBP	SLG
Grass	.234	722	169	26	1	0	51	74	92	.307	.273	June	.230	265	61	10	0	0	26	24	22	.296	.268
Turf	.228	864	197	23	1	0	67	104	69	.311	.257	July	.237	274	65	12	1	0	20	27	23	.307	.288
First Pitch	.297	343	102	13	1	0	33	0	0	.294	.341	August	.272	316	86	10	1	0	22	35	30	.345	.310
Ahead on Count	.260	392	102	13	1	0	34	104	0	.414	.298	September/October	.188	330	62	5	0	0	22	43	44	.285	.203
Behind on Count	.179	403	72	12	0	0	26	0	90	.189	.258	Pre-All Star	.226	743	168	24	0	0	57	80	69	.301	.258
Two Strikes	.155	555	86	12	0	0	38	74	160	.258	.177	Post-All Star	.235	843	198	25	2	0	61	98	92	.316	.269

Batter vs. Pitcher (career)

Hits Best Against	Avg	AB	H	2B	3B	HR	RBI	BB	SO	OBP	SLG	Hits Worst Against	Avg	AB	H	2B	3B	HR	RBI	BB	SO	OBP	SLG
Curt Young	.563	16	9	2	0	0	3	1	2	.588	.688	Kevin Appier	.000	13	0	0	0	0	0	1	1	.071	.000
Erik Hanson	.438	16	7	2	0	0	3	1	2	.471	.563	Melido Perez	.000	10	0	0	0	0	0	2	1	.167	.000
Walt Terrell	.429	7	3	0	0	0	2	4	0	.636	.429	Bill Swift	.067	15	1	0	0	0	2	0	1	.067	.067
Bob Milacki	.409	22	9	2	1	0	2	0	1	.409	.591	John Candelaria	.083	12	1	0	0	0	1	0	1	.083	.083
Greg Cadaret	.333	15	5	2	0	0	2	6	1	.524	.467	Storm Davis	.083	12	1	0	0	0	0	0	0	.083	.083

Warren Newson — White Sox
Bats Left (groundball hitter)

	Avg	G	AB	R	H	2B	3B	HR	RBI	BB	SO	HBP	GDP	SB	CS	OBP	SLG	IBB	SH	SF	#Pit	#P/PA	GB	FB	G/F
1992 Season	.221	63	136	19	30	3	0	1	11	37	38	0	4	3	0	.387	.265	2	0	0	701	4.05	51	24	2.13
Career (1991-1992)	.257	134	268	39	69	8	0	5	36	65	72	0	8	5	2	.402	.343	3	0	1	1376	4.13	102	43	2.37

1992 Season

	Avg	AB	H	2B	3B	HR	RBI	BB	SO	OBP	SLG		Avg	AB	H	2B	3B	HR	RBI	BB	SO	OBP	SLG
vs. Left	.250	4	1	0	0	0	0	3	2	.571	.250	Scoring Posn	.161	31	5	2	0	0	10	13	13	.409	.226
vs. Right	.220	132	29	3	0	1	11	34	36	.380	.265	Close & Late	.200	25	5	0	0	0	3	6	10	.355	.200
Home	.188	64	12	1	0	1	6	21	14	.388	.250	None on/out	.256	39	10	0	0	0	0	12	7	.431	.256
Away	.250	72	18	2	0	0	5	16	24	.386	.278	Batting #5	.231	65	15	2	0	1	6	15	17	.375	.308
First Pitch	.238	21	5	2	0	0	4	1	0	.273	.333	Batting #6	.148	27	4	0	0	0	2	6	13	.303	.148
Ahead on Count	.448	29	13	0	0	0	3	7	0	.556	.448	Other	.250	44	11	1	0	0	3	16	8	.450	.273
Behind on Count	.186	43	8	0	0	1	3	0	19	.186	.256	Pre-All Star	.245	94	23	2	0	1	9	23	28	.393	.298
Two Strikes	.097	62	6	0	0	0	3	29	38	.385	.097	Post-All Star	.167	42	7	1	0	0	2	14	10	.375	.190

Rod Nichols — Indians
Pitches Right (flyball pitcher)

	ERA	W	L	Sv	G	GS	IP	BB	SO	Avg	H	2B	3B	HR	RBI	OBP	SLG	GF	IR	IRS	Hld	SvOp	SB	CS	GB	FB	G/F
1992 Season	4.53	4	3	0	30	9	105.1	31	56	.273	114	16	5	13	58	.323	.429	5	20	10	1	0	6	2	144	139	1.04
Career (1988-1992)	4.39	11	30	1	91	48	399.2	114	208	.278	437	64	13	38	204	.330	.408	9	42	23	2	2	41	17	512	532	0.96

1992 Season

	ERA	W	L	Sv	G	GS	IP	H	HR	BB	SO		Avg	AB	H	2B	3B	HR	RBI	BB	SO	OBP	SLG
Home	5.88	2	3	0	17	5	56.2	68	10	17	30	vs. Left	.292	171	50	8	3	7	29	12	21	.335	.497
Away	2.96	2	0	0	13	4	48.2	46	3	14	26	vs. Right	.260	246	64	8	2	6	29	19	35	.315	.382
Starter	4.24	2	1	0	9	9	57.1	57	7	12	34	Scoring Posn	.269	108	29	4	2	2	40	5	15	.288	.398
Reliever	4.88	2	2	0	21	0	48.0	57	6	19	22	Close & Late	.306	49	15	3	1	2	5	2	3	.333	.531
0 Days rest	13.50	0	0	0	2	0	2.0	4	1	1	3	None on/out	.287	101	29	4	1	1	1	9	13	.345	.376
1 or 2 Days rest	5.70	1	2	0	12	0	23.2	32	4	9	11	First Pitch	.315	54	17	2	0	3	10	1	0	.339	.519
3+ Days rest	3.22	1	0	0	7	0	22.1	21	1	9	8	Behind on Count	.311	103	32	3	3	5	21	18	0	.403	.544
Pre-All Star	4.46	1	2	0	16	0	34.1	38	4	12	19	Ahead on Count	.249	173	43	6	1	2	11	0	49	.250	.329
Post-All Star	4.56	3	1	0	14	9	71.0	76	9	19	37	Two Strikes	.215	181	39	5	2	2	14	12	56	.267	.298

Career (1988-1992)

	ERA	W	L	Sv	G	GS	IP	H	HR	BB	SO		Avg	AB	H	2B	3B	HR	RBI	BB	SO	OBP	SLG
Home	4.36	5	16	0	48	27	221.0	242	18	65	114	vs. Left	.298	739	220	35	6	17	100	58	86	.351	.430
Away	4.43	6	14	1	43	21	178.2	195	20	49	94	vs. Right	.261	832	217	29	7	21	104	56	122	.311	.388
Day	5.23	1	9	0	23	12	96.1	110	13	22	61	Inning 1-6	.282	1229	346	54	11	28	169	97	164	.337	.412
Night	4.12	10	21	1	68	36	303.1	327	25	92	147	Inning 7+	.266	342	91	10	2	10	35	17	44	.303	.395
Grass	4.36	11	25	1	80	43	355.2	386	34	101	184	None on	.277	884	245	37	5	20	20	58	120	.329	.398
Turf	4.50	0	5	0	11	5	44.0	51	4	13	24	Runners on	.279	687	192	27	8	18	184	56	88	.331	.421
April	6.38	0	2	0	12	0	24.0	34	4	8	14	Scoring Posn	.279	377	105	17	5	7	151	33	52	.331	.406
May	2.98	1	4	0	11	4	45.1	42	2	13	25	Close & Late	.238	185	44	5	1	6	19	9	23	.276	.373
June	4.50	0	3	1	6	4	32.0	34	4	8	17	None on/out	.289	402	116	21	2	5	5	20	54	.330	.388
July	3.99	3	6	0	12	11	67.2	71	7	14	36	vs. 1st Batr (relief)	.410	39	16	2	1	1	16	3	3	.465	.590
August	4.94	4	8	0	24	16	122.0	140	12	37	56	First Inning Pitched	.290	359	104	12	3	11	71	32	60	.348	.432
September/October	4.14	3	7	0	26	13	106.2	116	9	34	60	First 15 Pitches	.299	294	88	9	2	7	48	23	43	.349	.415
Starter	4.53	9	23	0	48	48	288.1	318	28	81	154	Pitch 16-30	.226	314	71	12	2	8	38	16	46	.271	.354
Reliever	4.04	2	7	1	43	0	111.1	119	10	33	54	Pitch 31-45	.323	251	81	12	3	4	28	24	34	.386	.442
0 Days rest	6.23	0	0	0	3	0	4.1	4	1	1	4	Pitch 46+	.277	712	197	31	6	19	90	51	85	.328	.417
1 or 2 Days rest	4.40	1	2	0	15	0	30.2	36	4	9	14	First Pitch	.364	231	84	10	2	14	48	2	0	.378	.606
3+ Days rest	3.77	1	5	1	25	0	76.1	79	5	23	36	Ahead on Count	.228	688	157	24	6	8	61	0	180	.234	.315
Pre-All Star	4.21	1	10	1	30	9	107.0	116	10	32	58	Behind on Count	.314	363	114	15	4	9	52	65	0	.411	.452
Post-All Star	4.46	10	20	0	61	39	292.2	321	28	82	150	Two Strikes	.219	685	150	25	5	8	60	47	208	.273	.305

Pitcher vs. Batter (career)

Pitches Best Vs.	Avg	AB	H	2B	3B	HR	RBI	BB	SO	OBP	SLG	Pitches Worst Vs.	Avg	AB	H	2B	3B	HR	RBI	BB	SO	OBP	SLG
Brady Anderson	.000	11	0	0	0	0	0	0	4	.000	.000	Dave Winfield	.714	7	5	1	0	0	4	4	2	.818	.857
George Bell	.083	12	1	1	0	0	2	0	0	.188	.167	Jamie Quirk	.545	11	6	0	0	1	4	0	0	.545	.818
George Brett	.111	9	1	0	0	0	1	2	0	.273	.111	Pete O'Brien	.500	12	6	1	0	0	4	3	1	.600	.583
Randy Milligan	.118	17	2	0	0	0	0	0	3	.118	.118	Steve Lyons	.444	9	4	0	1	0	2	2	0	.545	.667
Brian Harper	.182	11	2	0	0	0	0	0	0	.182	.182	Cal Ripken	.368	19	7	0	0	3	4	0	4	.368	.842

Dave Nied — Braves
Pitches Right (flyball pitcher)

	ERA	W	L	Sv	G	GS	IP	BB	SO	Avg	H	2B	3B	HR	RBI	OBP	SLG	GF	IR	IRS	Hld	SvOp	SB	CS	GB	FB	G/F
1992 Season	1.17	3	0	0	6	2	23.0	5	19	.130	10	5	0	0	3	.183	.195	0	3	0	0	0	2	0	21	23	0.91

1992 Season

	ERA	W	L	Sv	G	GS	IP	H	HR	BB	SO		Avg	AB	H	2B	3B	HR	RBI	BB	SO	OBP	SLG
Home	1.64	1	0	0	3	1	11.0	4	0	1	13	vs. Left	.190	42	8	4	0	0	3	4	5	.261	.286
Away	0.75	2	0	0	3	1	12.0	6	0	4	6	vs. Right	.057	35	2	1	0	0	0	1	14	.083	.086

Jerry Nielsen — Yankees
Pitches Left

	ERA	W	L	Sv	G	GS	IP	BB	SO	Avg	H	2B	3B	HR	RBI	OBP	SLG	GF	IR	IRS	Hld	SvOp	SB	CS	GB	FB	G/F
1992 Season	4.58	1	0	0	20	0	19.2	18	12	.243	17	2	1	1	6	.393	.343	12	8	2	0	0	2	2	27	24	1.13

1992 Season

	ERA	W	L	Sv	G	GS	IP	H	HR	BB	SO		Avg	AB	H	2B	3B	HR	RBI	BB	SO	OBP	SLG
Home	2.70	1	0	0	9	0	10.0	6	0	8	6	vs. Left	.273	22	6	1	0	1	3	6	4	.414	.455
Away	6.52	0	0	0	11	0	9.2	11	1	10	6	vs. Right	.229	48	11	1	1	0	3	12	8	.383	.292
Starter	0.00	0	0	0	0	0	0.0	0	0	0	0	Scoring Posn	.143	21	3	1	0	0	5	5	5	.296	.190
Reliever	4.58	1	0	0	20	0	19.2	17	1	18	12	Close & Late	.294	17	5	0	0	0	1	3	4	.400	.294
0 Days rest	0.00	1	0	0	3	0	2.1	0	0	1	1	None on/out	.200	15	3	0	0	0	0	3	2	.333	.200
1 or 2 Days rest	0.00	0	0	0	5	0	3.1	0	0	1	4	First Pitch	.154	13	2	0	0	0	1	2	0	.267	.154
3+ Days rest	6.43	0	0	0	12	0	14.0	17	1	16	7	Behind on Count	.294	17	5	0	0	1	3	6	0	.458	.471
Pre-All Star	0.00	0	0	0	1	0	3.0	2	0	2	1	Ahead on Count	.250	32	8	2	0	0	2	0	10	.250	.313
Post-All Star	5.40	1	0	0	19	0	16.2	15	1	16	11	Two Strikes	.185	27	5	1	1	0	1	10	12	.405	.296

Melvin Nieves — Braves
Bats Both

	Avg	G	AB	R	H	2B	3B	HR	RBI	BB	SO	HBP	GDP	SB	CS	OBP	SLG	IBB	SH	SF	#Pit	#P/PA	GB	FB	G/F
1992 Season	.211	12	19	0	4	1	0	0	1	2	7	0	0	0	0	.286	.263	0	0	0	89	4.24	6	4	1.50

1992 Season

	Avg	AB	H	2B	3B	HR	RBI	BB	SO	OBP	SLG		Avg	AB	H	2B	3B	HR	RBI	BB	SO	OBP	SLG
vs. Left	.200	5	1	0	0	0	0	1	3	.333	.200	Scoring Posn	.250	4	1	0	0	0	1	0	2	.250	.250
vs. Right	.214	14	3	1	0	0	1	1	4	.267	.286	Close & Late	.200	5	1	0	0	0	0	2	2	.429	.200

Dave Nilsson — Brewers
Bats Left (flyball hitter)

	Avg	G	AB	R	H	2B	3B	HR	RBI	BB	SO	HBP	GDP	SB	CS	OBP	SLG	IBB	SH	SF	#Pit	#P/PA	GB	FB	G/F
1992 Season	.232	51	164	15	38	8	0	4	25	17	18	0	1	2	2	.304	.354	1	2	0	674	3.72	48	66	0.73

1992 Season

	Avg	AB	H	2B	3B	HR	RBI	BB	SO	OBP	SLG		Avg	AB	H	2B	3B	HR	RBI	BB	SO	OBP	SLG
vs. Left	.222	27	6	2	0	0	7	2	3	.276	.296	Scoring Posn	.238	63	15	6	0	1	21	8	6	.324	.381
vs. Right	.234	137	32	6	0	4	18	15	15	.309	.365	Close & Late	.160	25	4	0	0	0	2	2	2	.222	.160
Home	.236	55	13	1	0	1	4	12	7	.373	.309	None on/out	.154	39	6	1	0	1	1	3	4	.214	.256
Away	.229	109	25	7	0	3	21	5	11	.263	.376	Batting #7	.200	50	10	0	0	2	5	3	4	.245	.320
First Pitch	.292	24	7	2	0	0	4	0	0	.292	.375	Batting #8	.265	98	26	7	0	2	16	11	9	.339	.398
Ahead on Count	.238	42	10	2	0	1	9	12	0	.407	.357	Other	.125	16	2	1	0	0	4	3	5	.263	.188
Behind on Count	.146	48	7	1	0	1	5	0	8	.146	.229	Pre-All Star	.200	100	20	3	0	3	15	5	12	.238	.320
Two Strikes	.171	70	12	3	0	2	8	5	18	.227	.300	Post-All Star	.281	64	18	5	0	1	10	12	6	.395	.406

Otis Nixon — Braves
Bats Both (groundball hitter)

	Avg	G	AB	R	H	2B	3B	HR	RBI	BB	SO	HBP	GDP	SB	CS	OBP	SLG	IBB	SH	SF	#Pit	#P/PA	GB	FB	G/F
1992 Season	.294	120	456	79	134	14	2	2	22	39	54	0	4	41	18	.348	.346	0	5	2	1685	3.39	215	72	2.99
Last Five Years	.268	579	1617	294	433	45	9	3	104	175	205	2	15	246	77	.339	.312	4	21	8	6220	3.45	675	331	2.04

1992 Season

	Avg	AB	H	2B	3B	HR	RBI	BB	SO	OBP	SLG		Avg	AB	H	2B	3B	HR	RBI	BB	SO	OBP	SLG
vs. Left	.343	178	61	8	1	2	16	11	15	.379	.433	Scoring Posn	.244	86	21	2	0	1	20	5	8	.280	.302
vs. Right	.263	278	73	6	1	0	6	28	39	.329	.291	Close & Late	.288	73	21	2	0	0	9	9	9	.366	.315
Groundball	.296	162	48	6	0	0	4	18	19	.365	.333	None on/out	.310	200	62	11	1	0	0	15	29	.358	.375
Flyball	.256	125	32	3	0	0	7	11	17	.316	.280	Batting #1	.290	445	129	14	2	2	22	38	53	.344	.344
Home	.299	221	66	5	0	1	11	24	27	.366	.335	Batting #9	.400	5	2	0	0	0	0	1	1	.500	.400
Away	.289	235	68	9	2	1	11	15	27	.331	.357	Other	.500	6	3	0	0	0	0	0	0	.500	.500

1992 Season

	Avg	AB	H	2B	3B	HR	RBI	BB	SO	OBP	SLG		Avg	AB	H	2B	3B	HR	RBI	BB	SO	OBP	SLG
Day	.343	134	46	4	1	1	8	11	13	.393	.410	April	.375	16	6	1	0	0	1	2	2	.444	.438
Night	.273	322	88	.10	1	1	14	28	41	.330	.320	May	.373	75	28	2	0	0	2	5	3	.413	.400
Grass	.290	328	95	11	0	2	19	32	40	.351	.341	June	.295	61	18	1	0	2	8	6	7	.353	.410
Turf	.305	128	39	3	2	0	3	7	14	.341	.359	July	.301	73	22	5	0	0	2	5	8	.346	.370
First Pitch	.282	85	24	0	2	0	4	0	0	.279	.329	August	.295	112	33	5	2	0	7	11	13	.358	.375
Ahead on Count	.328	116	38	4	0	0	3	22	0	.432	.362	September/October	.227	119	27	0	0	0	2	10	21	.285	.227
Behind on Count	.283	120	34	3	0	1	8	1	28	.289	.333	Pre-All Star	.339	174	59	6	0	2	11	17	16	.396	.408
Two Strikes	.205	156	32	3	0	1	5	17	54	.283	.244	Post-All Star	.266	282	75	8	2	0	11	22	38	.318	.309

1992 By Position

Position	Avg	AB	H	2B	3B	HR	RBI	BB	SO	OBP	SLG	G	GS	Innings	PO	A	E	DP	Fld Pct	Rng Fctr	In Zone	Outs	Zone Rtg	MLB Zone
As Pinch Hitter	.444	9	4	0	0	0	2	1	1	.500	.444	10	0	---	---	---	---	---	---	---	---	---	---	---
As cf	.297	380	113	12	2	2	19	30	46	.347	.355	102		826.0	291	6	2	2	.993	3.24	325	282	.868	.824
As rf	.254	63	16	1	0	0	1	7	7	.329	.270	16	15	125.0	38	0	1	0	.974	2.74	41	38	.927	.814

Last Five Years

	Avg	AB	H	2B	3B	HR	RBI	BB	SO	OBP	SLG		Avg	AB	H	2B	3B	HR	RBI	BB	SO	OBP	SLG
vs. Left	.273	667	182	23	5	3	50	65	68	.338	.336	Scoring Posn	.262	324	85	13	2	1	97	29	40	.318	.324
vs. Right	.264	950	251	22	4	0	54	110	137	.339	.296	Close & Late	.308	302	93	10	2	0	25	32	47	.374	.354
Groundball	.271	582	158	14	2	0	35	67	63	.346	.302	None on/out	.284	652	185	21	3	0	0	78	66	.361	.325
Flyball	.229	396	91	12	2	0	30	53	65	.319	.269	Batting #1	.265	1333	353	37	6	2	76	146	160	.336	.306
Home	.273	813	222	24	5	1	53	99	102	.352	.319	Batting #2	.269	119	32	2	2	1	16	10	15	.326	.345
Away	.262	804	211	21	4	2	51	76	103	.325	.306	Other	.291	165	48	6	1	0	12	19	30	.371	.339
Day	.297	454	135	16	6	1	42	31	58	.342	.366	April	.245	94	23	3	1	0	10	12	10	.330	.298
Night	.256	1163	298	29	3	2	62	144	147	.337	.291	May	.341	208	71	7	1	0	11	24	22	.406	.385
Grass	.292	785	229	26	0	3	54	81	102	.356	.336	June	.263	304	80	6	2	2	25	36	34	.344	.316
Turf	.245	832	204	19	9	0	50	94	103	.322	.290	July	.277	372	103	16	1	0	18	37	43	.341	.325
First Pitch	.303	314	95	6	2	0	21	3	0	.307	.334	August	.240	329	79	8	2	1	24	32	52	.307	.286
Ahead on Count	.284	395	112	10	2	0	22	107	0	.435	.319	September/October	.248	310	77	5	2	0	16	34	44	.320	.277
Behind on Count	.244	464	113	11	2	1	27	1	117	.245	.282	Pre-All Star	.261	730	205	21	5	2	50	85	79	.356	.332
Two Strikes	.202	594	120	17	3	2	30	65	204	.280	.251	Post-All Star	.257	887	228	24	4	1	54	90	126	.324	.297

Batter vs. Pitcher (since 1984)

Hits Best Against	Avg	AB	H	2B	3B	HR	RBI	BB	SO	OBP	SLG	Hits Worst Against	Avg	AB	H	2B	3B	HR	RBI	BB	SO	OBP	SLG
Ken Hill	.600	15	9	1	0	0	0	4	1	.684	.667	Don Carman	.000	14	0	0	0	0	0	1	1	.067	.000
Mike Bielecki	.545	11	6	0	1	0	2	1	3	.583	.727	Tom Browning	.067	15	1	0	0	0	0	3	2	.152	.067
Zane Smith	.500	14	7	1	0	0	0	2	0	.563	.571	Doug Drabek	.083	24	2	0	0	0	0	2	3	.154	.083
Danny Cox	.444	9	4	1	0	0	0	3	1	.583	.556	Danny Darwin	.091	11	1	0	0	0	0	0	3	.091	.091
Dennis Rasmussen	.333	9	3	0	0	1	3	2	0	.455	.667	Jack Morris	.100	10	1	0	0	0	0	1	1	.182	.100

Junior Noboa — Mets

Bats Right (groundball hitter)

	Avg	G	AB	R	H	2B	3B	HR	RBI	BB	SO	HBP	GDP	SB	CS	OBP	SLG	IBB	SH	SF	#Pit	#P/PA	GB	FB	G/F
1992 Season	.149	46	47	7	7	0	0	0	3	3	8	1	2	0	0	.212	.149	0	0	1	158	3.04	19	15	1.27
Last Five Years	.231	236	360	34	83	10	2	1	20	12	34	2	7	6	4	.256	.278	3	3	5	1167	3.08	166	102	1.63

1992 Season

	Avg	AB	H	2B	3B	HR	RBI	BB	SO	OBP	SLG		Avg	AB	H	2B	3B	HR	RBI	BB	SO	OBP	SLG
vs. Left	.240	25	6	0	0	0	3	2	4	.310	.240	Scoring Posn	.111	9	1	0	0	0	3	1	3	.250	.111
vs. Right	.045	22	1	0	0	0	0	1	4	.087	.045	Close & Late	.143	14	2	0	0	0	2	2	4	.235	.143

Last Five Years

	Avg	AB	H	2B	3B	HR	RBI	BB	SO	OBP	SLG		Avg	AB	H	2B	3B	HR	RBI	BB	SO	OBP	SLG
vs. Left	.257	245	63	7	1	1	13	10	23	.285	.306	Scoring Posn	.200	80	16	2	0	0	16	6	9	.258	.225
vs. Right	.174	115	20	3	1	0	7	2	11	.193	.217	Close & Late	.231	104	24	3	1	1	9	5	18	.263	.308
Groundball	.262	130	34	4	1	0	9	6	10	.295	.308	None on/out	.260	96	25	1	1	0	0	2	10	.276	.292
Flyball	.122	74	9	0	0	0	2	5	10	.183	.122	Batting #7	.281	89	25	2	2	0	4	3	10	.298	.348
Home	.241	174	42	6	0	0	7	4	17	.260	.276	Batting #9	.204	98	20	1	0	0	3	1	12	.220	.214
Away	.220	186	41	4	2	1	13	8	17	.253	.280	Other	.220	173	38	7	0	1	13	8	12	.254	.277
Day	.196	148	29	3	0	1	10	3	11	.208	.236	April	.273	55	15	2	0	0	2	4	4	.333	.309
Night	.255	212	54	7	2	0	10	9	23	.289	.307	May	.171	82	14	1	0	1	1	1	9	.181	.220
Grass	.213	127	27	3	2	1	9	4	7	.231	.291	June	.188	80	15	1	2	0	4	3	5	.212	.250
Turf	.240	233	56	7	0	0	11	8	27	.269	.291	July	.302	63	19	4	0	0	9	2	6	.313	.365
First Pitch	.297	74	22	2	0	0	4	1	0	.303	.324	August	.238	21	5	1	0	0	1	0	3	.238	.286
Ahead on Count	.222	81	18	3	0	0	8	7	0	.278	.259	September/October	.254	59	15	1	0	0	3	2	7	.286	.271
Behind on Count	.227	119	27	3	2	1	4	0	25	.238	.311	Pre-All Star	.207	241	50	7	2	1	12	9	21	.235	.266
Two Strikes	.145	117	17	1	1	0	2	1	34	.158	.171	Post-All Star	.277	119	33	3	0	0	8	3	13	.298	.303

Batter vs. Pitcher (career)

Hits Best Against	Avg	AB	H	2B	3B	HR	RBI	BB	SO	OBP	SLG	Hits Worst Against	Avg	AB	H	2B	3B	HR	RBI	BB	SO	OBP	SLG
John Smiley	.545	11	6	2	0	0	1	0	2	.545	.727	Frank Viola	.188	16	3	1	0	0	0	1	0	.235	.250
												Tom Glavine	.200	15	3	0	0	0	0	1	1	.250	.200

Matt Nokes — Yankees
Bats Left (flyball hitter)

	Avg	G	AB	R	H	2B	3B	HR	RBI	BB	SO	HBP	GDP	SB	CS	OBP	SLG	IBB	SH	SF	#Pit	#P/PA	GB	FB	G/F
1992 Season	.224	121	384	42	86	9	1	22	59	37	62	3	14	0	1	.293	.424	11	0	6	1413	3.29	107	159	0.67
Last Five Years	.249	601	1841	195	458	66	2	82	268	137	253	17	49	6	6	.304	.420	26	7	18	6818	3.39	585	691	0.85

1992 Season

	Avg	AB	H	2B	3B	HR	RBI	BB	SO	OBP	SLG		Avg	AB	H	2B	3B	HR	RBI	BB	SO	OBP	SLG
vs. Left	.197	71	14	4	0	5	15	8	18	.275	.465	Scoring Posn	.189	90	17	2	0	6	37	15	21	.288	.411
vs. Right	.230	313	72	5	1	17	44	29	44	.297	.415	Close & Late	.194	72	14	1	0	6	11	10	15	.310	.458
Groundball	.222	108	24	2	0	5	17	9	23	.288	.380	None on/out	.254	71	18	4	0	2	2	6	8	.321	.394
Flyball	.174	115	20	4	1	4	15	13	17	.254	.330	Batting #6	.242	128	31	2	0	6	17	15	14	.324	.398
Home	.266	177	47	4	0	18	41	20	26	.347	.593	Batting #7	.203	177	36	5	1	8	23	17	37	.274	.379
Away	.188	207	39	5	1	4	18	17	36	.246	.280	Other	.241	79	19	2	0	8	19	5	11	.282	.570
Day	.264	121	32	3	0	9	22	10	13	.326	.512	April	.228	57	13	1	0	3	3	5	9	.290	.404
Night	.205	263	54	6	1	13	37	27	49	.278	.384	May	.233	73	17	1	0	4	14	9	11	.310	.411
Grass	.221	326	72	7	1	21	52	35	55	.299	.442	June	.164	73	12	1	0	2	7	7	15	.244	.260
Turf	.241	58	14	2	0	1	7	2	7	.258	.328	July	.218	55	12	1	0	4	11	5	9	.286	.455
First Pitch	.284	74	21	3	0	5	14	11	0	.375	.527	August	.217	60	13	0	0	6	15	4	9	.262	.517
Ahead on Count	.273	99	27	2	0	8	20	14	0	.353	.535	September/October	.288	66	19	5	1	3	9	7	9	.365	.530
Behind on Count	.188	128	24	5	0	3	12	0	37	.200	.297	Pre-All Star	.206	228	47	3	0	12	30	22	42	.275	.377
Two Strikes	.139	144	20	3	0	5	15	12	62	.214	.264	Post-All Star	.250	156	39	6	1	10	29	15	20	.320	.494

1992 By Position

Position	Avg	AB	H	2B	3B	HR	RBI	BB	SO	OBP	SLG	G	GS	Innings	PO	A	E	DP	Fld Pct	Rng Fctr	In Zone	Outs	Zone Rtg	MLB Zone
As Pinch Hitter	.308	13	4	0	0	1	2	1	4	.400	.538	16	0	---	---	---	---	---	---	---	---	---	---	---
As c	.221	371	82	9	1	21	57	36	58	.289	.420	111	101	903.0	552	47	4	6	.993	---	---	---	---	---

Last Five Years

	Avg	AB	H	2B	3B	HR	RBI	BB	SO	OBP	SLG		Avg	AB	H	2B	3B	HR	RBI	BB	SO	OBP	SLG
vs. Left	.238	277	66	10	0	16	53	16	53	.287	.448	Scoring Posn	.256	465	119	16	0	20	179	56	70	.332	.419
vs. Right	.251	1564	392	56	2	66	215	121	200	.307	.416	Close & Late	.247	296	73	7	0	15	51	31	50	.321	.422
Groundball	.237	518	123	20	0	16	67	36	69	.290	.369	None on/out	.261	422	110	18	0	21	21	27	57	.311	.453
Flyball	.235	408	96	16	1	25	75	40	66	.309	.463	Batting #5	.240	463	111	19	0	22	68	29	61	.285	.423
Home	.259	857	222	24	0	51	153	66	120	.314	.466	Batting #6	.258	581	150	18	1	25	78	40	71	.310	.422
Away	.240	984	236	42	2	31	115	71	133	.296	.381	Other	.247	797	197	29	1	35	122	68	121	.311	.418
Day	.263	632	166	18	0	40	115	45	76	.313	.481	April	.269	279	75	11	0	15	41	21	37	.320	.470
Night	.242	1209	292	48	2	42	153	92	177	.299	.389	May	.242	326	79	9	1	16	50	20	49	.291	.423
Grass	.245	1533	376	48	1	72	230	116	211	.301	.419	June	.232	315	73	11	0	12	45	17	46	.272	.381
Turf	.266	308	82	18	1	10	38	21	42	.320	.429	July	.241	266	64	7	0	15	49	28	42	.319	.436
First Pitch	.281	363	102	15	0	18	61	18	0	.318	.471	August	.261	322	84	10	0	16	46	30	36	.321	.441
Ahead on Count	.289	454	131	13	0	28	74	69	0	.380	.502	September/October	.249	333	83	18	1	8	37	23	43	.303	.381
Behind on Count	.232	594	138	28	0	23	81	0	137	.242	.396	Pre-All Star	.247	1007	249	32	1	50	158	68	150	.297	.430
Two Strikes	.185	699	129	24	0	20	80	44	253	.237	.305	Post-All Star	.251	834	209	34	1	32	110	69	103	.312	.409

Batter vs. Pitcher (career)

Hits Best Against	Avg	AB	H	2B	3B	HR	RBI	BB	SO	OBP	SLG	Hits Worst Against	Avg	AB	H	2B	3B	HR	RBI	BB	SO	OBP	SLG
Eric King	.474	19	9	1	0	3	9	1	0	.500	1.000	Jose Mesa	.000	15	0	0	0	0	0	2	2	.118	.000
Jeff Russell	.455	11	5	0	0	1	3	1	1	.500	.727	Charles Nagy	.067	15	1	1	0	0	0	1	5	.125	.133
Scott Bankhead	.417	12	5	1	0	2	7	0	2	.417	1.000	Eric Plunk	.083	12	1	0	0	0	0	2	3	.214	.083
Ben McDonald	.385	13	5	1	0	2	3	2	2	.529	.923	Juan Guzman	.083	12	1	0	0	0	0	2	.083	.083
Tom Gordon	.364	11	4	0	0	2	6	1	1	.385	.909	Tom Henke	.091	11	1	0	0	0	0	1	4	.167	.091

Edwin Nunez — Rangers
Pitches Right

	ERA	W	L	Sv	G	GS	IP	BB	SO	Avg	H	2B	3B	HR	RBI	OBP	SLG	GF	IR	IRS	Hld	SvOp	SB	CS	GB	FB	G/F
1992 Season	4.85	1	3	3	49	0	59.1	22	49	.268	63	13	3	6	40	.331	.426	16	37	13	5	4	1	2	50	85	0.59
Last Five Years	4.36	11	13	18	165	3	262.1	125	207	.268	271	60	6	27	157	.347	.419	49	163	47	13	23	22	8	310	308	1.01

1992 Season

	ERA	W	L	Sv	G	GS	IP	H	HR	BB	SO		Avg	AB	H	2B	3B	HR	RBI	BB	SO	OBP	SLG
Home	5.40	0	2	1	22	0	25.0	30	3	8	20	vs. Left	.230	87	20	6	2	3	17	10	20	.303	.448
Away	4.46	1	1	2	27	0	34.1	33	3	14	29	vs. Right	.291	148	43	7	1	3	23	12	29	.348	.412
Starter	0.00	0	0	0	0	0	0.0	0	0	0	0	Scoring Posn	.338	68	23	5	2	2	33	5	12	.372	.559
Reliever	4.85	1	3	3	49	0	59.1	63	6	22	49	Close & Late	.287	87	25	7	0	3	16	9	17	.343	.471
0 Days rest	5.52	0	1	2	10	0	14.2	15	4	2	13	None on/out	.288	52	15	1	0	2	2	7	13	.373	.423
1 or 2 Days rest	2.00	1	1	0	23	0	27.0	22	0	9	24	First Pitch	.310	29	9	0	0	2	6	0	0	.310	.517
3+ Days rest	8.66	0	1	1	16	0	17.2	26	2	11	12	Behind on Count	.346	52	18	3	1	2	14	12	0	.455	.558
Pre-All Star	5.04	1	2	1	23	0	30.1	35	4	11	23	Ahead on Count	.177	113	20	4	1	2	10	0	43	.190	.283
Post-All Star	4.66	0	1	2	26	0	29.0	28	2	11	26	Two Strikes	.208	120	25	7	2	1	11	10	49	.280	.325

Last Five Years

	ERA	W	L	Sv	G	GS	IP	H	HR	BB	SO		Avg	AB	H	2B	3B	HR	RBI	BB	SO	OBP	SLG
Home	4.64	5	7	8	80	2	135.2	150	17	65	112	vs. Left	.265	430	114	24	3	14	76	65	92	.357	.433
Away	4.05	6	6	10	85	1	126.2	121	10	60	95	vs. Right	.270	582	157	36	3	13	81	60	115	.340	.409
Day	4.58	4	3	3	38	1	57.0	64	5	25	47	Inning 1-6	.281	302	85	26	0	6	49	41	65	.368	.427
Night	4.30	7	10	15	127	2	205.1	207	22	100	160	Inning 7+	.262	710	186	34	6	21	108	84	142	.339	.415

319

Last Five Years

	ERA	W	L	Sv	G	GS	IP	H	HR	BB	SO
Grass	4.19	9	9	16	131	0	206.1	203	19	103	166
Turf	4.98	2	4	2	34	3	56.0	68	6	22	41
April	4.79	2	2	2	26	0	41.1	45	4	18	36
May	2.73	2	2	2	20	1	29.2	27	3	15	17
June	4.30	1	4	2	24	2	52.1	52	4	25	43
July	3.02	3	2	2	29	0	41.2	36	1	21	29
August	3.45	1	1	8	40	0	62.2	55	9	24	50
September/October	6.57	2	2	2	26	0	34.2	56	6	22	32
Starter	7.11	0	3	0	3	3	12.2	19	2	4	9
Reliever	4.22	11	10	18	162	0	249.2	252	25	121	198
0 Days rest	3.30	0	1	5	20	0	30.0	24	5	11	24
1 or 2 Days rest	2.74	8	6	8	72	0	105.0	85	6	54	77
3+ Days rest	5.81	3	3	5	70	0	114.2	143	14	56	97
Pre-All Star	4.05	7	8	6	80	3	137.2	138	11	63	105
Post-All Star	4.69	4	5	12	85	0	124.2	133	16	62	102

	Avg	AB	H	2B	3B	HR	RBI	BB	SO	OBP	SLG
None on	.259	514	133	30	2	16	16	54	112	.332	.418
Runners on	.277	498	138	30	4	11	141	71	95	.363	.420
Scoring Posn	.285	312	89	15	4	8	131	55	66	.383	.436
Close & Late	.266	271	72	16	0	10	49	45	49	.364	.435
None on/out	.253	225	57	10	1	6	6	25	49	.333	.387
vs. 1st Batr (relief)	.254	122	31	5	0	6	24	26	28	.377	.443
First Inning Pitched	.261	498	130	23	3	14	88	63	98	.341	.404
First 15 Pitches	.265	498	132	25	3	15	72	59	102	.337	.418
Pitch 16-30	.266	335	89	19	3	10	56	37	68	.346	.430
Pitch 31-45	.271	129	35	12	0	2	22	21	26	.370	.411
Pitch 46+	.300	50	15	4	0	0	7	8	11	.400	.380
Ahead on Count	.205	493	101	18	3	10	52	0	184	.210	.314
Behind on Count	.322	205	66	22	2	7	48	66	0	.475	.551
Two Strikes	.199	483	96	20	3	8	48	41	207	.267	.302

Pitcher vs. Batter (since 1984)

Pitches Best Vs.	Avg	AB	H	2B	3B	HR	RBI	BB	SO	OBP	SLG
Kent Hrbek	.067	15	1	0	0	0	1	3	3	.222	.067
Carney Lansford	.091	11	1	1	0	0	0	0	1	.091	.182
Dan Gladden	.167	12	2	0	0	0	2	1	3	.214	.167
Willie Wilson	.182	11	2	1	0	0	1	1	1	.250	.273
Wally Joyner	.222	9	2	0	0	0	1	1	1	.273	.222

Pitches Worst Vs.	Avg	AB	H	2B	3B	HR	RBI	BB	SO	OBP	SLG
Harold Baines	.545	11	6	2	0	2	7	1	2	.583	1.273
George Brett	.455	11	5	1	0	2	5	1	1	.500	1.091
Mickey Tettleton	.417	12	5	0	0	2	9	2	3	.500	.917
Jesse Barfield	.389	18	7	0	0	3	6	2	5	.450	.889
Devon White	.385	13	5	0	0	2	5	3	4	.500	.846

Charlie O'Brien — Mets
Bats Right (flyball hitter)

	Avg	G	AB	R	H	2B	3B	HR	RBI	BB	SO	HBP	GDP	SB	CS	OBP	SLG	IBB	SH	SF	#Pit	#P/PA	GB	FB	G/F
1992 Season	.212	68	156	15	33	12	0	2	13	16	18	1	4	0	1	.289	.327	1	4	0	671	3.88	60	57	1.05
Last Five Years	.204	313	843	82	172	44	2	12	91	80	104	17	27	0	4	.285	.304	6	26	4	3640	3.86	279	311	0.90

1992 Season

	Avg	AB	H	2B	3B	HR	RBI	BB	SO	OBP	SLG
vs. Left	.247	89	22	6	0	1	6	9	9	.316	.348
vs. Right	.164	67	11	6	0	1	7	7	9	.253	.299
Home	.212	66	14	4	0	1	4	11	11	.325	.348
Away	.211	90	19	8	0	1	9	5	17	.260	.333
First Pitch	.269	26	7	3	0	0	3	0	0	.269	.385
Ahead on Count	.242	33	8	3	0	1	5	8	0	.405	.424
Behind on Count	.178	45	8	5	0	1	5	0	10	.196	.356
Two Strikes	.171	70	12	4	0	1	2	8	18	.256	.271

	Avg	AB	H	2B	3B	HR	RBI	BB	SO	OBP	SLG
Scoring Posn	.118	34	4	2	0	1	11	5	7	.231	.265
Close & Late	.316	19	6	2	0	0	4	3	3	.409	.421
None on/out	.212	33	7	4	0	1	1	4	5	.297	.424
Batting #7	.209	86	18	5	0	1	7	5	11	.253	.302
Batting #8	.232	56	13	6	0	1	6	7	5	.328	.393
Other	.143	14	2	1	0	0	0	4	2	.333	.214
Pre-All Star	.211	90	19	9	0	1	8	12	11	.304	.344
Post-All Star	.212	66	14	3	0	1	5	4	7	.268	.303

Last Five Years

	Avg	AB	H	2B	3B	HR	RBI	BB	SO	OBP	SLG
vs. Left	.201	406	82	24	1	6	32	32	43	.268	.309
vs. Right	.207	435	90	20	1	6	59	48	61	.300	.299
Groundball	.219	224	49	10	0	1	24	29	26	.317	.277
Flyball	.215	177	38	17	1	2	24	16	22	.282	.356
Home	.204	367	75	15	2	8	41	42	36	.293	.322
Away	.204	476	97	29	0	4	50	38	68	.279	.290
Day	.209	296	62	16	0	3	27	28	39	.293	.294
Night	.201	547	110	28	2	9	64	52	65	.280	.309
Grass	.214	607	130	33	2	10	75	62	70	.298	.325
Turf	.178	236	42	11	0	2	16	18	34	.251	.250
First Pitch	.211	128	27	10	1	1	13	1	0	.241	.328
Ahead on Count	.271	170	46	12	1	3	28	54	0	.456	.406
Behind on Count	.156	295	46	14	0	4	24	1	57	.177	.244
Two Strikes	.160	399	64	15	0	5	30	23	104	.216	.315

	Avg	AB	H	2B	3B	HR	RBI	BB	SO	OBP	SLG
Scoring Posn	.233	189	44	11	2	5	79	28	27	.335	.392
Close & Late	.248	101	25	7	0	0	8	7	14	.303	.317
None on/out	.178	197	35	10	0	4		19	25	.260	.269
Batting #7	.220	186	41	10	0	3	24	13	23	.286	.323
Batting #8	.205	487	100	27	2	4	49	54	60	.294	.294
Other	.182	170	31	7	0	5	18	13	21	.257	.312
April	.196	102	20	8	0	0	10	15	13	.322	.275
May	.198	106	21	4	1	2	12	7	16	.259	.311
June	.180	100	18	5	1	1	8	11	9	.261	.280
July	.218	165	36	8	0	3	22	11	22	.278	.321
August	.230	183	42	10	0	4	20	17	25	.312	.350
September/October	.187	187	35	9	0	2	19	19	19	.270	.267
Pre-All Star	.194	361	70	21	2	3	34	34	44	.274	.288
Post-All Star	.212	482	102	23	0	9	57	46	60	.293	.315

Batter vs. Pitcher (career)

Hits Best Against	Avg	AB	H	2B	3B	HR	RBI	BB	SO	OBP	SLG
Rheal Cormier	.400	10	4	1	0	0	0	1	1	.455	.500

Hits Worst Against	Avg	AB	H	2B	3B	HR	RBI	BB	SO	OBP	SLG
Randy Tomlin	.125	16	2	0	0	0	0	0	1	.125	.125
Randy Johnson	.167	12	2	0	0	0	2	2	1	.286	.167
Floyd Bannister	.182	11	2	0	0	1	2	0	1	.182	.455
Terry Mulholland	.182	11	2	0	0	0	1	1	2	.250	.182
Bruce Hurst	.200	15	3	1	0	0	0	1	0	.250	.267

Pete O'Brien — Mariners

Bats Left

	Avg	G	AB	R	H	2B	3B	HR	RBI	BB	SO	HBP	GDP	SB	CS	OBP	SLG	IBB	SH	SF	#Pit	#P/PA	GB	FB	G/F
1992 Season	.222	134	396	40	88	15	1	14	52	40	27	0	8	2	1	.289	.371	8	1	7	1549	3.50	139	168	0.83
Last Five Years	.248	705	2423	262	602	110	6	64	293	263	242	5	56	6	7	.324	.378	42	8	33	9776	3.56	815	849	1.08

1992 Season

	Avg	AB	H	2B	3B	HR	RBI	BB	SO	OBP	SLG		Avg	AB	H	2B	3B	HR	RBI	BB	SO	OBP	SLG
vs. Left	.214	56	12	2	1	1	8	7	6	.288	.339	Scoring Posn	.259	85	22	5	0	4	39	18	8	.364	.459
vs. Right	.224	340	76	13	0	13	44	33	21	.289	.376	Close & Late	.303	76	23	3	0	5	18	12	5	.380	.539
Groundball	.184	114	21	4	0	2	10	10	12	.250	.272	None on/out	.212	99	21	0	6	6	7	3	.264	.414
Flyball	.256	117	30	4	0	6	19	9	4	.305	.444	Batting #5	.220	232	51	8	0	9	26	28	20	.302	.371
Home	.218	188	41	9	1	6	27	19	12	.286	.372	Batting #6	.240	75	18	5	0	1	11	6	1	.293	.347
Away	.226	208	47	6	0	8	25	21	15	.292	.370	Other	.213	89	19	2	1	4	15	6	6	.253	.393
Day	.198	106	21	4	0	1	7	8	9	.250	.264	April	.235	68	16	2	0	6	12	2	4	.254	.529
Night	.231	290	67	11	1	13	45	32	18	.303	.410	May	.196	92	18	4	1	5	15	7	7	.250	.424
Grass	.210	162	34	4	0	6	17	16	11	.276	.346	June	.244	78	19	3	0	1	6	12	5	.344	.321
Turf	.231	234	54	11	1	8	35	24	16	.298	.389	July	.183	60	11	1	0	2	7	9	6	.286	.300
First Pitch	.204	49	10	0	0	3	7	6	0	.281	.388	August	.150	40	6	1	0	0	6	4	4	.217	.175
Ahead on Count	.267	131	35	8	1	6	23	21	0	.361	.481	September/October	.310	58	18	4	0	0	6	6	1	.364	.379
Behind on Count	.213	108	23	2	0	4	15	0	16	.211	.343	Pre-All Star	.223	269	60	10	1	14	38	24	18	.285	.424
Two Strikes	.171	123	21	2	0	5	16	14	27	.254	.309	Post-All Star	.220	127	28	5	0	0	14	16	9	.297	.260

1992 By Position

Position	Avg	AB	H	2B	3B	HR	RBI	BB	SO	OBP	SLG	G	GS	Innings	PO	A	E	DP	Fld Pct	Rng Fctr	In Zone	Outs	Zone Rtg	MLB Zone
As Designated Hitter	.220	118	26	5	0	4	13	14	9	.299	.364	35	32	---	---	---	---	---	---	---	---	---	---	---
As Pinch Hitter	.174	23	4	2	0	0	5	0	3	.160	.261	26	0	---	---	---	---	---	---	---	---	---	---	---
As 1b	.225	258	58	8	1	10	34	26	15	.293	.380	81	68	625.1	623	54	3	73	.996	---	121	95	785	843

Last Five Years

	Avg	AB	H	2B	3B	HR	RBI	BB	SO	OBP	SLG		Avg	AB	H	2B	3B	HR	RBI	BB	SO	OBP	SLG
vs. Left	.245	695	170	30	2	13	88	65	91	.309	.350	Scoring Posn	.245	621	152	31	1	16	230	119	71	.351	.375
vs. Right	.250	1728	432	80	4	51	205	218	151	.330	.389	Close & Late	.231	416	96	18	1	14	59	56	47	.320	.380
Groundball	.232	573	133	24	1	14	55	70	50	.315	.351	None on/out	.278	612	170	31	2	20	20	55	52	.338	.433
Flyball	.259	626	162	31	0	24	91	75	68	.335	.423	Batting #4	.256	582	149	27	1	16	85	68	61	.329	.388
Home	.260	1177	306	59	6	32	164	146	110	.338	.402	Batting #5	.264	1038	274	45	4	31	120	131	104	.344	.405
Away	.238	1246	296	51	0	32	129	137	132	.311	.356	Other	.223	803	179	38	1	17	88	84	77	.295	.336
Day	.260	624	162	30	1	20	74	72	58	.334	.407	April	.298	373	111	19	0	16	49	35	28	.355	.477
Night	.245	1799	440	80	5	44	219	211	184	.321	.368	May	.210	404	85	13	3	18	60	44	43	.284	.391
Grass	.257	1441	371	54	2	35	167	181	150	.338	.371	June	.251	394	99	22	0	5	38	58	41	.351	.345
Turf	.235	982	231	56	4	29	126	102	92	.305	.389	July	.256	450	115	25	2	7	50	50	34	.325	.367
First Pitch	.283	336	95	17	0	6	46	21	0	.322	.387	August	.245	404	99	15	0	8	49	42	48	.313	.342
Ahead on Count	.272	729	198	42	4	24	98	148	0	.392	.439	September/October	.234	398	93	16	1	10	47	54	48	.320	.354
Behind on Count	.226	727	164	28	2	16	91	5	124	.231	.336	Pre-All Star	.250	1319	330	61	4	42	162	154	123	.327	.398
Two Strikes	.198	857	170	18	2	23	79	107	242	.266	.305	Post-All Star	.246	1104	272	49	2	22	131	129	119	.321	.354

Batter vs. Pitcher (since 1984)

Hits Best Against	Avg	AB	H	2B	3B	HR	RBI	BB	SO	OBP	SLG	Hits Worst Against	Avg	AB	H	2B	3B	HR	RBI	BB	SO	OBP	SLG
Jim Acker	.538	13	7	2	0	0	1	1	1	.571	.692	Kenny Rogers	.067	15	1	0	0	0	2	2	3	.167	.067
Dave Righetti	.533	15	8	2	0	0	3	4	1	.600	.667	Gregg Olson	.071	14	1	0	0	0	1	0	3	.071	.071
Bobby Witt	.474	19	9	2	0	1	6	3	0	.545	.737	Charles Nagy	.071	14	1	0	0	0	1	0	1	.071	.071
Jeff M. Robinson	.429	14	6	1	0	1	4	2	0	.471	.714	Greg Hibbard	.083	12	1	0	0	0	0	0	1	.083	.083
Eric Plunk	.375	8	3	0	0	1	2	8	2	.668	.750	Dennis Rasmussen	.118	17	2	0	0	0	1	0	4	.118	.118

Paul O'Neill — Reds

Bats Left

	Avg	G	AB	R	H	2B	3B	HR	RBI	BB	SO	HBP	GDP	SB	CS	OBP	SLG	IBB	SH	SF	#Pit	#P/PA	GB	FB	G/F
1992 Season	.246	148	496	59	122	19	1	14	66	77	85	2	11	6	3	.346	.373	15	3	6	2097	3.61	196	136	1.44
Last Five Years	.259	707	2444	296	634	132	6	89	382	287	424	9	45	59	32	.337	.428	55	7	21	9860	3.57	865	741	1.17

1992 Season

	Avg	AB	H	2B	3B	HR	RBI	BB	SO	OBP	SLG		Avg	AB	H	2B	3B	HR	RBI	BB	SO	OBP	SLG
vs. Left	.225	173	39	6	0	2	26	14	46	.279	.295	Scoring Posn	.220	141	31	5	0	0	47	42	18	.386	.255
vs. Right	.257	323	83	13	1	12	40	63	39	.379	.415	Close & Late	.222	81	18	3	0	3	13	15	21	.337	.370
Groundball	.268	168	45	3	0	6	27	33	21	.387	.393	None on/out	.263	118	31	1	1	7	7	13	21	.341	.466
Flyball	.221	113	25	6	1	3	14	15	20	.308	.372	Batting #4	.262	256	67	8	1	9	37	40	35	.362	.406
Home	.237	245	58	10	1	6	33	43	39	.354	.359	Batting #7	.174	86	15	3	0	0	9	11	17	.263	.209
Away	.255	251	64	9	0	8	33	34	46	.338	.386	Other	.260	154	40	8	0	5	20	26	33	.365	.409
Day	.257	175	45	6	0	4	24	30	32	.359	.360	April	.338	74	25	5	0	3	6	16	13	.456	.527
Night	.240	321	77	13	1	10	42	47	53	.339	.380	May	.250	80	20	3	0	3	20	14	16	.368	.400
Grass	.281	146	41	5	0	5	20	17	27	.352	.418	June	.192	73	14	2	1	3	11	9	14	.286	.370
Turf	.231	350	81	14	1	9	46	60	58	.344	.354	July	.238	80	19	3	0	1	9	14	14	.344	.313
First Pitch	.357	84	30	6	0	2	11	14	0	.447	.500	August	.247	81	20	4	0	1	11	16	14	.360	.333
Ahead on Count	.342	114	39	4	0	7	21	38	0	.503	.561	September/October	.222	108	24	2	0	3	9	8	14	.276	.324
Behind on Count	.149	148	22	6	1	2	16	0	47	.148	.243	Pre-All Star	.260	258	67	11	1	9	41	47	50	.374	.415
Two Strikes	.132	212	28	3	0	3	21	28	85	.233	.208	Post-All Star	.231	238	55	8	0	5	25	30	35	.314	.326

1992 By Position

Position	Avg	AB	H	2B	3B	HR	RBI	BB	SO	OBP	SLG	G	GS	Innings	PO	A	E	DP	Fld Pct	Rng Fctr	In Zone	Outs	Zone Rtg	MLB Zone
As Pinch Hitter	.333	9	3	0	0	0	4	0	0	.333	.333	10	0	---	---	---	---	---	---	---	---	---	---	---
As rf	.244	487	119	19	1	14	62	77	85	.346	.374	143	134	1209.2	291	12	1	2	.997	2.25	327	275	.841	.814

Last Five Years

	Avg	AB	H	2B	3B	HR	RBI	BB	SO	OBP	SLG		Avg	AB	H	2B	3B	HR	RBI	BB	SO	OBP	SLG
vs. Left	.217	723	157	37	2	13	102	54	197	.272	.328	Scoring Posn	.259	687	178	38	2	22	281	144	117	.380	.418
vs. Right	.277	1721	477	95	4	76	280	233	227	.363	.469	Close & Late	.230	400	92	20	1	10	52	63	83	.337	.360
Groundball	.282	840	237	47	2	24	131	105	113	.363	.429	None on/out	.246	590	145	29	1	29	29	48	99	.306	.446
Flyball	.235	548	129	26	2	29	95	71	116	.322	.449	Batting #4	.261	755	212	37	1	34	126	97	112	.363	.468
Home	.274	1222	335	68	2	59	205	139	199	.349	.478	Batting #5	.240	816	196	40	4	26	122	94	138	.317	.395
Away	.245	1222	299	64	4	30	177	148	225	.325	.377	Other	.259	873	226	55	1	29	134	96	174	.333	.424
Day	.253	755	191	43	2	26	113	84	134	.324	.419	April	.284	334	95	20	0	12	50	40	60	.361	.452
Night	.262	1689	443	89	4	63	269	203	290	.342	.432	May	.257	428	110	22	0	16	77	50	78	.338	.421
Grass	.268	730	196	37	4	22	106	86	134	.344	.421	June	.275	448	123	25	1	25	83	57	63	.359	.502
Turf	.256	1714	438	95	2	67	276	201	290	.334	.431	July	.242	380	92	17	1	10	45	43	69	.319	.371
First Pitch	.342	418	143	34	3	17	80	33	0	.387	.560	August	.267	359	96	24	0	13	53	52	67	.355	.443
Ahead on Count	.336	586	197	42	4	36	131	124	0	.451	.592	September/October	.238	495	118	24	4	13	74	45	67	.298	.362
Behind on Count	.187	766	143	29	1	14	82	2	222	.190	.282	Pre-All Star	.266	1326	353	71	1	56	225	163	227	.348	.447
Two Strikes	.160	1041	167	39	2	20	107	115	424	.245	.259	Post-All Star	.252	1116	281	61	5	33	157	124	197	.324	.404

Batter vs. Pitcher (career)

Hits Best Against	Avg	AB	H	2B	3B	HR	RBI	BB	SO	OBP	SLG	Hits Worst Against	Avg	AB	H	2B	3B	HR	RBI	BB	SO	OBP	SLG
Jay Howell	.727	11	8	2	1	2	10	2	1	.769	1.636	Jeff Parrett	.000	15	0	0	0	0	0	1	6	.063	.000
Shawn Boskie	.600	10	6	1	0	2	2	2	1	.667	1.300	Bob Patterson	.000	11	0	0	0	0	0	0	3	.000	.000
Frank DiPino	.500	10	5	2	1	0	4	2	3	.583	.900	Tom Glavine	.050	20	1	0	0	0	0	0	1	.050	.050
Mike Harkey	.500	10	5	0	0	2	4	3	0	.615	1.100	Paul Assenmacher	.071	14	1	0	0	0	0	1	7	.133	.071
Jeff Brantley	.364	11	4	0	0	2	6	6	1	.588	.909	Alejandro Pena	.083	12	1	0	0	0	0	0	3	.083	.083

Ken Oberkfell — Angels   Bats Left

	Avg	G	AB	R	H	2B	3B	HR	RBI	BB	SO	HBP	GDP	SB	CS	OBP	SLG	IBB	SH	SF	#Pit	#P/PA	GB	FB	G/F
1992 Season	.264	41	91	6	24	1	0	0	10	8	5	0	2	0	1	.317	.275	2	0	2	364	3.60	41	24	1.71
Last Five Years	.257	408	943	91	242	39	6	6	95	84	74	5	17	5	8	.316	.330	14	9	14	3783	3.62	408	296	1.38

1992 Season

	Avg	AB	H	2B	3B	HR	RBI	BB	SO	OBP	SLG		Avg	AB	H	2B	3B	HR	RBI	BB	SO	OBP	SLG
vs. Left	.083	12	1	0	0	0	0	0	0	.083	.083	Scoring Posn	.269	26	7	0	0	0	10	5	2	.364	.269
vs. Right	.291	79	23	1	0	0	10	8	5	.348	.304	Close & Late	.211	19	4	0	0	0	4	6	0	.370	.211
Home	.235	51	12	0	0	0	7	5	3	.293	.235	None on/out	.267	15	4	0	0	0	0	2	1	.353	.267
Away	.300	40	12	1	0	0	3	3	2	.349	.325	Batting #2	.276	29	8	0	0	0	2	1	2	.300	.276
First Pitch	.364	11	4	0	0	0	1	2	0	.462	.364	Batting #6	.226	31	7	0	0	0	5	2	2	.273	.226
Ahead on Count	.250	20	5	0	0	0	3	7	0	.429	.250	Other	.290	31	9	1	0	0	3	5	1	.368	.323
Behind on Count	.214	28	6	0	0	0	3	0	3	.207	.214	Pre-All Star	.222	9	2	0	0	0	1	0	1	.222	.222
Two Strikes	.171	35	6	0	0	0	2	0	5	.167	.171	Post-All Star	.268	82	22	1	0	0	9	8	4	.326	.280

Last Five Years

	Avg	AB	H	2B	3B	HR	RBI	BB	SO	OBP	SLG		Avg	AB	H	2B	3B	HR	RBI	BB	SO	OBP	SLG
vs. Left	.203	153	31	5	2	0	16	9	15	.240	.261	Scoring Posn	.239	226	54	8	4	3	85	41	25	.338	.350
vs. Right	.267	790	211	34	4	6	79	75	59	.331	.343	Close & Late	.226	212	48	8	1	0	23	22	19	.297	.274
Groundball	.256	316	81	11	1	2	32	28	19	.318	.316	None on/out	.257	206	53	8	1	1	1	12	19	.301	.320
Flyball	.239	201	48	8	0	0	17	23	19	.322	.279	Batting #2	.279	398	111	20	2	3	40	25	29	.323	.362
Home	.259	425	110	13	3	2	52	43	33	.322	.318	Batting #6	.253	146	37	7	1	1	21	10	13	.313	.336
Away	.255	518	132	26	3	4	43	41	41	.312	.340	Other	.236	399	94	12	3	2	34	46	35	.311	.296
Day	.245	310	76	12	0	1	33	23	25	.293	.294	April	.198	111	22	3	1	1	8	16	12	.300	.270
Night	.262	633	166	27	6	5	62	61	49	.328	.348	May	.244	172	42	7	1	2	26	18	12	.306	.331
Grass	.272	574	156	24	3	4	64	40	43	.317	.345	June	.246	175	43	11	0	2	23	12	18	.291	.343
Turf	.233	369	86	15	3	2	31	44	31	.316	.306	July	.326	178	58	8	1	1	11	12	11	.373	.399
First Pitch	.254	134	34	4	1	1	11	5	0	.279	.321	August	.264	178	47	10	3	0	18	16	7	.323	.354
Ahead on Count	.275	218	60	9	2	1	23	51	0	.402	.349	September/October	.233	129	30	0	0	0	9	10	14	.294	.233
Behind on Count	.240	321	77	10	1	1	26	0	39	.245	.287	Pre-All Star	.248	528	131	24	2	6	63	51	46	.311	.335
Two Strikes	.239	377	90	14	3	3	36	33	74	.323	.323	Post-All Star	.267	415	111	15	4	0	32	33	28	.323	.323

Batter vs. Pitcher (since 1984)

Hits Best Against	Avg	AB	H	2B	3B	HR	RBI	BB	SO	OBP	SLG	Hits Worst Against	Avg	AB	H	2B	3B	HR	RBI	BB	SO	OBP	SLG
Tim Burke	.500	12	6	0	0	0	0	2	0	.571	.500	Jeff Parrett	.000	11	0	0	0	0	0	3	2	.214	.000
Greg Maddux	.458	24	11	1	0	0	5	2	0	.500	.500	Tim Leary	.067	15	1	0	0	0	0	0	2	.067	.067
David Cone	.412	17	7	1	0	0	2	3	1	.500	.471	Frank DiPino	.067	15	1	0	0	0	3	1	2	.118	.067
Bob Walk	.379	29	11	4	1	0	4	3	2	.438	.586	Dave Smith	.095	21	2	1	0	0	3	1	1	.136	.143
Bill Gullickson	.343	35	12	3	0	1	5	6	2	.439	.514	John Franco	.118	17	2	0	0	0	0	1	1	.167	.118

Jose Offerman — Dodgers

Bats Both (groundball hitter)

	Avg	G	AB	R	H	2B	3B	HR	RBI	BB	SO	HBP	GDP	SB	CS	OBP	SLG	IBB	SH	SF	#Pit	#P/PA	GB	FB	G/F
1992 Season	.260	149	534	67	139	20	8	1	30	57	98	0	6	23	16	.331	.333	4	5	2	2259	3.81	209	104	2.01
Career (1990-1992)	.241	230	705	84	170	22	8	2	40	86	144	1	11	27	18	.324	.304	7	7	2	3021	3.80	272	127	2.14

1992 Season

	Avg	AB	H	2B	3B	HR	RBI	BB	SO	OBP	SLG
vs. Left	.269	201	54	8	1	1	7	20	27	.332	.333
vs. Right	.255	333	85	12	7	0	23	37	71	.330	.333
Groundball	.327	168	55	10	1	1	16	19	28	.394	.417
Flyball	.232	151	35	2	3	0	5	16	34	.304	.285
Home	.272	283	77	14	5	1	20	33	44	.348	.367
Away	.247	251	62	6	3	0	10	24	54	.310	.295
Day	.270	159	43	5	3	0	5	13	27	.326	.340
Night	.256	375	96	15	5	1	25	44	71	.333	.331
Grass	.254	410	104	14	5	1	26	43	68	.323	.320
Turf	.282	124	35	6	3	0	4	14	30	.355	.379
First Pitch	.297	74	22	1	4	0	7	3	0	.321	.419
Ahead on Count	.349	109	38	7	1	0	8	21	0	.450	.431
Behind on Count	.233	176	41	4	2	0	6	0	53	.233	.278
Two Strikes	.183	257	47	6	0	0	10	33	97	.276	.206

	Avg	AB	H	2B	3B	HR	RBI	BB	SO	OBP	SLG
Scoring Posn	.276	98	27	3	2	0	26	18	18	.381	.347
Close & Late	.257	105	27	1	1	0	6	4	21	.284	.286
None on/out	.267	180	48	5	3	0	0	19	28	.337	.328
Batting #1	.265	268	71	11	3	1	15	28	50	.332	.340
Batting #8	.258	264	68	9	5	0	15	28	47	.329	.330
Other	.000	2	0	0	0	0	0	1	1	.333	.000
April	.216	74	16	3	2	0	4	7	14	.284	.311
May	.281	64	18	1	1	0	4	9	12	.370	.328
June	.286	91	26	3	2	0	5	9	15	.350	.363
July	.243	115	28	5	1	0	3	11	27	.310	.304
August	.309	97	30	4	2	1	8	12	15	.385	.423
September/October	.226	93	21	4	0	0	6	9	15	.288	.269
Pre-All Star	.254	279	71	10	5	0	16	31	50	.329	.326
Post-All Star	.267	255	68	10	3	1	14	26	48	.332	.341

1992 By Position

Position	Avg	AB	H	2B	3B	HR	RBI	BB	SO	OBP	SLG	G	GS	Innings	PO	A	E	DP	Fld Pct	Rng Fctr	In Zone	Outs	Zone Rtg	MLB Zone
As ss	.261	533	139	20	8	1	30	57	98	.331	.334	149	146	1290.0	208	398	42	75	.935	4.23	511	432	.845	.885

Bobby Ojeda — Dodgers

Pitches Left (groundball pitcher)

	ERA	W	L	Sv	G	GS	IP	BB	SO	Avg	H	2B	3B	HR	RBI	OBP	SLG	CG	ShO	Sup	QS	#P/S	SB	CS	GB	FB	G/F
1992 Season	3.63	6	9	0	29	29	166.1	81	94	.268	169	29	6	8	76	.349	.371	2	1	3.90	14	93	20	15	228	170	1.34
Last Five Years	3.33	48	48	0	158	132	856.0	302	504	.251	810	155	21	55	331	.315	.364	14	9	3.80	80	93	59		1255	802	1.56

1992 Season

	ERA	W	L	Sv	G	GS	IP	H	HR	BB	SO
Home	2.40	4	2	0	13	13	82.2	81	2	36	44
Away	4.84	2	7	0	16	16	83.2	88	6	45	50
Day	3.19	2	4	0	11	11	67.2	69	2	26	40
Night	3.92	4	5	0	18	18	98.2	100	6	55	54
Grass	3.22	4	6	0	21	21	123.0	124	6	59	66
Turf	4.78	2	3	0	8	8	43.1	45	2	22	28
April	4.01	1	2	0	4	4	24.2	29	3	15	15
May	2.60	2	1	0	4	4	27.2	19	0	18	12
June	4.23	1	1	0	6	6	27.2	29	3	15	22
July	2.48	1	1	0	5	5	32.2	34	1	10	15
August	3.41	1	1	0	5	5	29.0	26	0	13	19
September/October	5.47	0	3	0	5	5	24.2	32	1	10	11
Starter	3.63	6	9	0	29	29	166.1	169	8	81	94
Reliever	0.00	0	0	0	0	0	0.0	0	0	0	0
0-3 Days Rest	0.00	0	0	0	0	0	0.0	0	0	0	0
4 Days Rest	2.87	3	4	0	14	14	84.2	90	5	33	48
5+ Days Rest	4.41	3	5	0	15	15	81.2	79	3	48	46
Pre-All Star	3.01	5	4	0	16	16	95.2	91	6	52	60
Post-All Star	4.46	1	5	0	13	13	70.2	78	2	29	34

	Avg	AB	H	2B	3B	HR	RBI	BB	SO	OBP	SLG
vs. Left	.216	116	25	4	0	1	12	13	27	.290	.276
vs. Right	.280	515	144	25	6	7	64	68	67	.362	.392
Inning 1-6	.265	574	152	27	6	7	73	72	86	.344	.369
Inning 7+	.298	57	17	2	0	1	3	9	8	.394	.386
None on	.257	362	93	14	3	7	7	35	54	.324	.370
Runners on	.283	269	76	15	3	1	69	46	40	.379	.372
Scoring Posn	.271	166	45	10	3	1	67	38	29	.393	.386
Close & Late	.368	19	7	0	0	1	2	5	3	.500	.526
None on/out	.199	161	32	6	1	5	5	16	25	.271	.342
vs. 1st Batr (relief)	.000	0	0	0	0	0	0	0	0	.000	.000
First Inning Pitched	.232	112	26	7	1	1	15	11	17	.296	.339
First 75 Pitches	.251	499	125	23	5	7	56	55	73	.322	.359
Pitch 76-90	.366	71	26	4	1	0	14	13	9	.464	.451
Pitch 91-105	.300	30	9	1	0	0	5	8	7	.447	.333
Pitch 106+	.290	31	9	1	0	1	1	5	5	.389	.419
First Pitch	.303	99	30	6	0	0	14	5	0	.327	.364
Ahead on Count	.217	226	49	11	2	4	19	0	68	.215	.336
Behind on Count	.320	169	54	9	2	3	30	45	0	.460	.450
Two Strikes	.187	251	47	10	2	3	18	31	94	.276	.279

Last Five Years

	ERA	W	L	Sv	G	GS	IP	H	HR	BB	SO
Home	2.99	26	21	0	77	63	439.2	416	22	141	267
Away	3.70	22	27	0	81	69	416.1	394	33	161	237
Day	3.45	15	18	0	53	45	281.2	270	17	89	149
Night	3.28	33	30	0	105	87	574.1	540	38	213	355
Grass	3.23	34	33	0	112	93	617.2	588	41	204	371
Turf	3.59	14	15	0	46	39	238.1	222	14	98	133
April	4.41	4	9	0	22	17	102.0	120	9	39	60
May	2.71	10	10	0	27	24	172.2	125	12	63	98
June	3.38	11	6	0	26	26	165.1	168	12	58	100
July	3.75	6	10	0	26	23	139.1	142	8	74	94
August	2.93	10	5	0	33	22	147.2	131	3	56	84
September/October	3.28	7	8	0	24	20	129.0	124	11	37	88
Starter	3.40	45	47	0	132	132	806.2	771	54	262	478
Reliever	2.19	3	1	0	26	0	49.1	39	1	20	26
0-3 Days Rest	4.24	2	4	0	6	6	34.0	37	4	14	15
4 Days Rest	3.34	20	21	0	62	62	379.2	386	29	125	240
5+ Days Rest	3.39	23	22	0	64	64	393.0	348	21	143	223
Pre-All Star	3.46	27	27	0	82	74	476.1	460	36	172	283

	Avg	AB	H	2B	3B	HR	RBI	BB	SO	OBP	SLG
vs. Left	.212	651	138	24	5	10	52	52	151	.274	.310
vs. Right	.261	2571	672	131	16	45	279	250	353	.325	.377
Inning 1-6	.249	2692	670	125	18	46	291	248	429	.311	.360
Inning 7+	.264	530	140	30	3	9	40	54	75	.333	.368
None on	.252	1911	481	92	14	41	41	152	304	.310	.379
Runners on	.251	1311	329	63	7	14	290	150	200	.323	.342
Scoring Posn	.249	759	189	30	5	6	258	115	132	.336	.325
Close & Late	.251	231	58	11	2	2	18	28	35	.333	.342
None on/out	.239	841	201	41	7	23	23	69	117	.301	.386
vs. 1st Batr (relief)	.333	24	8	3	0	0	0	2	3	.385	.458
First Inning Pitched	.260	600	156	40	4	6	76	53	100	.319	.370
First 75 Pitches	.249	2514	626	123	14	44	262	216	396	.308	.362
Pitch 76-90	.255	499	90	16	4	4	33	44	48	.338	.357
Pitch 91-105	.252	214	54	12	1	3	20	27	38	.337	.360
Pitch 106+	.284	141	40	4	2	4	16	15	22	.350	.426
First Pitch	.281	499	140	30	1	5	58	19	0	.307	.375
Ahead on Count	.184	1252	230	40	6	20	93	0	402	.186	.273
Behind on Count	.326	818	267	51	9	20	111	160	0	.434	.484

Last Five Years

	ERA	W	L	Sv	G	GS	IP	H	HR	BB	SO		Avg	AB	H	2B	3B	HR	RBI	BB	SO	OBP	SLG
Post-All Star	3.18	21	21	0	76	58	379.2	350	19	130	221	Two Strikes	.161	1279	206	40	8	22	85	123	504	.235	.256

Pitcher vs. Batter (since 1984)

Pitches Best Vs.	Avg	AB	H	2B	3B	HR	RBI	BB	SO	OBP	SLG	Pitches Worst Vs.	Avg	AB	H	2B	3B	HR	RBI	BB	SO	OBP	SLG
Darren Daulton	.000	11	0	0	0	0	0	0	5	.000	.000	Ken Caminiti	.611	18	11	2	0	1	4	4	1	.682	.889
Brian Downing	.000	10	0	0	0	0	1	3	0	.214	.000	Dale Murphy	.500	26	13	5	1	1	3	9	2	.629	.885
Mike Fitzgerald	.050	20	1	0	0	0	0	3	4	.174	.050	Bob Melvin	.455	11	5	0	1	1	3	1	1	.462	.909
Joe Oliver	.071	28	2	1	0	0	3	1	7	.103	.107	Dave Winfield	.444	9	4	1	1	0	1	2	0	.545	.778
John Cangelosi	.091	11	1	0	0	0	0	0	2	.091	.091	Reggie Sanders	.429	14	6	2	0	1		1	2	.467	.786

John Olerud — Blue Jays — Bats Left (groundball hitter)

	Avg	G	AB	R	H	2B	3B	HR	RBI	BB	SO	HBP	GDP	SB	CS	OBP	SLG	IBB	SH	SF	#Pit	#P/PA	GB	FB	G/F
1992 Season	.284	138	458	68	130	28	0	16	66	70	61	1	15	1	0	.375	.508	11	1	7	1918	3.58	187	123	1.52
Career (1989-1992)	.269	394	1278	177	344	73	2	47	182	195	221	8	32	1	4	.364	.440	26	5	21	5764	3.84	499	329	1.52

1992 Season

	Avg	AB	H	2B	3B	HR	RBI	BB	SO	OBP	SLG		Avg	AB	H	2B	3B	HR	RBI	BB	SO	OBP	SLG
vs. Left	.258	97	25	4	0	3	15	22	16	.393	.392	Scoring Posn	.217	120	26	7	0	3	48	22	19	.327	.350
vs. Right	.291	361	105	24	0	13	51	48	45	.370	.465	Close & Late	.361	72	26	6	0	3	14	9	7	.427	.569
Groundball	.279	147	41	8	0	3	19	15	17	.343	.395	None on/out	.364	88	32	12	0	4	4	10	9	.429	.636
Flyball	.315	124	39	9	0	7	25	17	21	.386	.556	Batting #5	.320	284	91	18	0	11	40	43	36	.404	.500
Home	.264	231	61	16	0	4	28	39	30	.368	.385	Batting #6	.220	159	35	8	0	3	20	26	21	.330	.327
Away	.304	227	69	12	0	12	38	31	31	.383	.515	Other	.267	15	4	2	0	2	6	1	4	.313	.800
Day	.321	134	43	10	0	4	20	22	17	.411	.485	April	.254	67	17	4	0	1	5	17	8	.400	.358
Night	.269	324	87	18	0	12	46	48	44	.360	.435	May	.206	68	14	3	0	2	8	8	13	.299	.338
Grass	.311	164	51	10	0	11	30	28	21	.408	.573	June	.318	88	28	6	0	5	18	10	9	.376	.557
Turf	.269	294	79	18	0	5	36	42	40	.356	.381	July	.378	74	28	6	0	2	8	10	8	.452	.541
First Pitch	.299	77	23	3	0	2	7	11	0	.393	.416	August	.303	66	20	3	0	3	14	11	6	.392	.485
Ahead on Count	.309	110	34	9	0	7	22	38	0	.480	.582	September/October	.242	95	23	6	0	3	13	14	17	.336	.400
Behind on Count	.262	145	38	8	0	4	23	0	35	.255	.400	Pre-All Star	.275	258	71	16	0	9	35	40	33	.370	.442
Two Strikes	.223	184	41	8	0	2	16	22	61	.301	.381	Post-All Star	.295	200	59	12	0	7	31	30	28	.382	.460

1992 By Position

Position	Avg	AB	H	2B	3B	HR	RBI	BB	SO	OBP	SLG	G	GS	Innings	PO	A	E	DP	Fld Pct	Rng Fctr	In Zone	Zone Outs	Zone Rtg	MLB Zone
As Pinch Hitter	.400	10	4	2	0	0	6	0	1	.400	.600	11	0	---	---	---	---	---	---	---	---	---	---	---
As 1b	.282	447	126	26	0	16	60	70	60	.375	.447	133	125	1095.2	1057	81	7	73	.994	---	218	197	.904	.843

Career (1989-1992)

	Avg	AB	H	2B	3B	HR	RBI	BB	SO	OBP	SLG		Avg	AB	H	2B	3B	HR	RBI	BB	SO	OBP	SLG
vs. Left	.268	254	68	12	1	9	46	54	54	.395	.429	Scoring Posn	.244	324	79	18	0	8	120	75	64	.373	.373
vs. Right	.270	1024	276	61	1	38	136	141	167	.356	.442	Close & Late	.307	231	71	18	0	8	42	33	45	.390	.489
Groundball	.279	394	110	30	0	10	57	61	61	.376	.431	None on/out	.319	270	86	25	1	14	14	41	47	.410	.574
Flyball	.282	266	75	15	1	14	44	43	59	.377	.504	Batting #5	.292	489	143	30	0	19	66	76	74	.385	.470
Home	.270	651	176	40	2	22	93	104	109	.371	.439	Batting #6	.254	480	122	21	2	18	71	73	86	.351	.419
Away	.268	627	168	33	0	25	89	91	112	.357	.440	Other	.256	309	79	22	0	10	45	46	61	.352	.424
Day	.261	372	97	21	0	12	58	64	70	.368	.414	April	.256	176	45	10	0	6	19	35	24	.380	.415
Night	.273	906	247	52	2	35	124	131	151	.362	.450	May	.199	216	43	8	1	6	24	35	48	.311	.319
Grass	.282	472	133	30	0	21	73	77	83	.379	.479	June	.309	233	72	14	1	12	44	26	40	.372	.532
Turf	.262	806	211	43	2	26	109	118	138	.356	.417	July	.336	220	74	14	0	9	23	23	32	.405	.523
First Pitch	.324	185	60	11	0	8	29	19	0	.389	.614	August	.250	212	53	14	0	8	39	33	32	.345	.429
Ahead on Count	.332	295	98	24	1	19	64	102	0	.496	.614	September/October	.258	221	57	15	0	8	33	43	45	.375	.407
Behind on Count	.224	388	87	20	1	11	50	2	119	.229	.366	Pre-All Star	.260	695	181	34	2	29	97	105	122	.357	.440
Two Strikes	.212	589	125	24	1	10	52	72	298	.298	.307	Post-All Star	.280	583	163	39	0	18	85	90	99	.373	.439

Batter vs. Pitcher (career)

Hits Best Against	Avg	AB	H	2B	3B	HR	RBI	BB	SO	OBP	SLG	Hits Worst Against	Avg	AB	H	2B	3B	HR	RBI	BB	SO	OBP	SLG
Kevin Brown	.478	23	11	4	0	1	6	3	4	.538	.783	Kirk McCaskill	.056	18	1	0	0	0	2	1	3	.100	.056
Jaime Navarro	.429	14	6	3	0	0	2	1	0	.467	.643	Tom Gordon	.056	18	1	0	0	1		1	3	.105	.222
Tim Leary	.385	13	5	4	0	0	3	4	3	.529	.692	Jose Mesa	.100	10	1	0	0	0	1		2	.182	.100
Erik Hanson	.350	20	7	1	0	1	5	1	5	.364	.550	Scott Sanderson	.105	19	2	0	0	0	2	1	7	.143	.105
Dave Stewart	.308	13	4	0	0		3	0	6	.308	.538	Nolan Ryan	.118	17	2	0	0	0	1		4	.167	.176

Steve Olin — Indians — Pitches Right (groundball pitcher)

	ERA	W	L	Sv	G	GS	IP	BB	SO	Avg	H	2B	3B	HR	RBI	OBP	SLG	GF	IR	IRS	Hld	SvOp	SB	CS	GB	FB	G/F
1992 Season	2.34	8	5	29	72	0	88.1	27	47	.249	80	8	1	8	32	.314	.355	62	49	11	0	36	2	4	143	73	1.96
Career (1989-1992)	3.10	16	19	48	195	1	273.0	90	173	.263	272	37	4	14	127	.327	.347	110	158	49	5	62	18	10	514	176	2.92

1992 Season

	ERA	W	L	Sv	G	GS	IP	H	HR	BB	SO		Avg	AB	H	2B	3B	HR	RBI	BB	SO	OBP	SLG
Home	4.37	4	3	13	37	0	45.1	53	8	16	27	vs. Left	.324	145	47	6	1	1	12	13	19	.385	.400
Away	0.21	4	2	16	35	0	43.0	27	0	11	20	vs. Right	.188	176	33	2	0	7	20	14	28	.254	.318
Day	3.56	3	1	10	26	0	30.1	29	5	8	17	Inning 1-6	.000	0	0	0	0	0	0	0	0	.000	.000

1992 Season

	ERA	W	L	Sv	G	GS	IP	H	HR	BB	SO		Avg	AB	H	2B	3B	HR	RBI	BB	SO	OBP	SLG
Night	1.71	5	4	19	46	0	58.0	51	3	19	30	Inning 7+	.249	321	80	8	1	8	32	27	47	.314	.355
Grass	2.67	8	4	23	62	0	77.2	73	8	22	40	None on	.263	167	44	5	1	3	3	11	27	.317	.359
Turf	0.00	0	1	6	10	0	10.2	7	0	5	7	Runners on	.234	154	36	3	0	5	29	16	20	.310	.351
April	2.53	0	1	3	10	0	10.2	8	1	4	6	Scoring Posn	.184	87	16	1	0	1	20	10	15	.277	.230
May	3.86	0	2	7	13	0	11.2	12	1	5	6	Close & Late	.246	211	52	4	0	6	25	21	30	.324	.351
June	1.46	2	0	4	9	0	12.1	9	1	5	6	None on/out	.231	65	15	3	0	0	0	3	11	.275	.277
July	1.42	3	0	4	14	0	19.0	19	1	2	9	vs. 1st Batr (relief)	.234	64	15	2	0	1	5	4	12	.296	.313
August	4.38	1	1	5	11	0	12.1	11	3	4	8	First Inning Pitched	.221	222	49	4	1	5	24	20	33	.291	.315
September/October	1.61	2	1	6	15	0	22.1	21	1	7	12	First 15 Pitches	.249	213	53	4	1	4	21	20	30	.319	.333
Starter	0.00	0	0	0	0	0	0.0	0	0	0	0	Pitch 16-30	.253	83	21	2	0	3	8	4	14	.287	.386
Reliever	2.34	8	5	29	72	0	88.1	80	8	27	47	Pitch 31-45	.286	21	6	2	0	1	3	3	3	.400	.524
0 Days rest	1.69	2	3	8	22	0	26.2	28	1	7	17	Pitch 46+	.000	4	0	0	0	0	0	0	0	.000	.000
1 or 2 Days rest	2.15	4	1	15	33	0	37.2	29	4	12	15	First Pitch	.286	49	14	1	0	2	8	5	0	.364	.429
3+ Days rest	3.38	2	1	6	17	0	24.0	23	3	8	15	Ahead on Count	.181	149	27	3	0	1	7	0	41	.191	.221
Pre-All Star	2.20	3	3	15	39	0	45.0	40	3	16	22	Behind on Count	.299	67	20	2	0	2	9	13	0	.420	.418
Post-All Star	2.49	5	2	14	33	0	43.1	40	5	11	25	Two Strikes	.174	132	23	4	0	1	5	9	47	.234	.227

Career (1989-1992)

	ERA	W	L	Sv	G	GS	IP	H	HR	BB	SO		Avg	AB	H	2B	3B	HR	RBI	BB	SO	OBP	SLG
Home	4.44	5	6	20	90	1	121.2	136	10	50	78	vs. Left	.319	439	140	21	3	4	48	45	52	.386	.408
Away	2.02	11	13	28	105	0	151.1	136	4	40	95	vs. Right	.221	597	132	16	1	10	79	45	121	.283	.302
Day	4.06	5	5	14	67	0	86.0	101	10	30	67	Inning 1-6	.300	200	60	9	1	2	37	18	31	.362	.385
Night	2.65	11	14	34	128	1	187.0	171	4	60	106	Inning 7+	.254	836	212	28	3	12	90	72	142	.318	.337
Grass	3.15	15	14	40	168	1	240.0	236	13	77	154	None on	.256	519	133	18	3	4	4	35	100	.309	.326
Turf	2.73	1	5	8	27	0	33.0	36	1	13	19	Runners on	.269	517	139	19	1	10	123	55	73	.344	.368
April	2.59	2	3	3	23	0	31.1	28	1	8	20	Scoring Posn	.268	314	84	11	0	3	103	43	51	.361	.331
May	5.24	1	5	7	29	0	34.1	38	1	11	17	Close & Late	.249	426	106	10	1	8	49	49	70	.331	.333
June	3.24	2	0	4	13	0	16.2	17	2	7	9	None on/out	.233	219	51	10	1	0	0	13	45	.285	.288
July	2.23	3	0	8	31	0	48.1	46	2	10	31	vs. 1st Batr (relief)	.253	174	44	4	0	2	24	15	30	.321	.310
August	3.38	3	7	11	42	0	64.0	67	5	21	46	First Inning Pitched	.244	624	152	23	1	9	93	51	103	.305	.327
September/October	2.64	5	4	15	57	1	78.1	76	3	33	50	First 15 Pitches	.253	588	149	21	1	7	81	45	94	.310	.328
Starter	2.57	1	0	0	1	1	7.0	6	0	1	3	Pitch 16-30	.279	283	79	13	1	5	29	31	46	.354	.385
Reliever	3.11	15	19	48	194	0	266.0	266	14	89	170	Pitch 31-45	.250	96	24	3	1	1	9	12	18	.342	.333
0 Days rest	2.83	6	11	12	50	0	70.0	80	4	24	54	Pitch 46+	.290	69	20	0	1	1	8	2	13	.329	.362
1 or 2 Days rest	2.75	5	4	27	89	0	114.2	105	7	40	67	First Pitch	.308	146	45	7	0	2	21	13	0	.380	.397
3+ Days rest	3.87	4	3	9	55	0	81.1	81	3	25	49	Ahead on Count	.205	493	101	17	3	4	40	0	151	.214	.276
Pre-All Star	3.50	6	8	15	72	0	92.2	94	4	28	50	Behind on Count	.347	216	75	10	0	4	42	45	1	.460	.449
Post-All Star	2.89	10	11	33	123	1	180.1	178	10	62	123	Two Strikes	.197	467	92	13	3	4	40	32	172	.254	.263

Pitcher vs. Batter (career)

Pitches Best Vs.	Avg	AB	H	2B	3B	HR	RBI	BB	SO	OBP	SLG	Pitches Worst Vs.	Avg	AB	H	2B	3B	HR	RBI	BB	SO	OBP	SLG
Terry Steinbach	.077	13	1	0	0	0	0	1	4	.143	.077	Paul Molitor	.500	10	5	1	0	0	1	1	1	.545	.600
Lance Parrish	.091	11	1	0	0	0	3	0	2	.091	.091	Travis Fryman	.455	11	5	0	0	0	0	0	3	.455	.455
Mike Devereaux	.100	10	1	0	0	0	0	1	1	.182	.100	Ruben Sierra	.417	12	5	1	0	1	4	0	0	.417	.750
Mark McGwire	.111	9	1	0	0	0	0	3	3	.333	.111	Wade Boggs	.364	11	4	0	0	2	4	2	1	.462	.909
												Roberto Kelly	.364	11	4	0	0	2	6	0	3	.364	.909

Omar Olivares — Cardinals   Pitches Right (groundball pitcher)

	ERA	W	L	Sv	G	GS	IP	BB	SO	Avg	H	2B	3B	HR	RBI	OBP	SLG	CG	ShO	Sup	QS	#P/S	SB	CS	GB	FB	G/F
1992 Season	3.84	9	9	0	32	30	197.0	63	124	.257	189	35	3	20	74	.316	.394	1	0	3.88	18	97	11	13	313	186	1.68
Career (1990-1992)	3.68	21	17	0	69	60	413.2	141	235	.250	382	64	8	35	152	.317	.372	0		3.96	37	98	23	27	629	390	1.61

1992 Season

	ERA	W	L	Sv	G	GS	IP	H	HR	BB	SO		Avg	AB	H	2B	3B	HR	RBI	BB	SO	OBP	SLG
Home	3.96	5	6	0	19	18	120.1	113	12	36	77	vs. Left	.285	428	122	28	2	13	47	40	65	.345	.451
Away	3.64	4	3	0	13	12	76.2	76	8	27	47	vs. Right	.218	308	67	7	1	7	27	23	59	.275	.315
Day	4.91	0	3	0	9	8	55.0	56	7	23	36	Inning 1-6	.250	613	153	27	3	18	62	50	102	.308	.392
Night	3.42	9	6	0	23	22	142.0	133	13	40	88	Inning 7+	.293	123	36	8	0	2	12	13	22	.358	.407
Grass	3.92	3	2	0	8	7	43.2	42	4	19	29	None on	.264	450	119	19	2	10	10	36	72	.323	.382
Turf	3.82	6	7	0	24	23	153.1	147	16	44	95	Runners on	.245	286	70	16	1	10	64	27	52	.305	.413
April	3.65	2	2	0	5	5	37.0	33	2	9	20	Scoring Posn	.199	151	30	6	0	5	48	17	25	.273	.338
May	7.20	0	1	0	4	4	20.0	23	6	7	12	Close & Late	.287	87	25	6	0	2	10	8	16	.344	.425
June	1.95	2	0	0	4	4	27.2	17	2	13	14	None on/out	.307	202	62	12	0	5	5	10	21	.343	.441
July	3.41	2	3	0	6	5	34.1	34	5	8	17	vs. 1st Batr (relief)	1.000	2	2	0	0	0	0	0	0	1.000	1.000
August	3.43	2	2	0	6	6	39.1	41	2	16	27	First Inning Pitched	.259	116	30	6	0	4	16	13	17	.336	.414
September/October	4.42	1	1	0	7	6	38.2	41	3	10	34	First 75 Pitches	.241	547	132	23	1	16	52	40	98	.295	.375
Starter	3.85	9	9	0	30	30	194.0	186	20	61	121	Pitch 76-90	.284	102	29	6	2	2	12	13	11	.365	.441
Reliever	3.00	0	0	0	2	0	3.0	3	0	2	3	Pitch 91-105	.375	64	24	5	0	1	8	7	11	.431	.500
0-3 Days Rest	4.66	1	0	0	3	3	19.1	18	3	6	16	Pitch 106+	.174	23	4	1	0	1	2	3	4	.269	.348
4 Days Rest	3.13	4	4	0	14	14	92.0	85	8	36	51	First Pitch	.313	115	36	3	1	1	12	4	0	.328	.383
5+ Days Rest	4.46	4	5	0	13	13	82.2	83	9	19	54	Ahead on Count	.210	314	66	10	1	9	30	0	102	.216	.334
Pre-All Star	3.83	5	4	0	16	15	98.2	86	11	32	51	Behind on Count	.312	173	54	15	0	6	18	32	0	.420	.503

1992 Season

	ERA	W	L	Sv	G	GS	IP	H	HR	BB	SO		Avg	AB	H	2B	3B	HR	RBI	BB	SO	OBP	SLG
Post-All Star	3.84	4	5	0	16	15	98.1	103	9	31	73	Two Strikes	.194	309	60	11	2	5	18	27	124	.265	.291

Career (1990-1992)

	ERA	W	L	Sv	G	GS	IP	H	HR	BB	SO		Avg	AB	H	2B	3B	HR	RBI	BB	SO	OBP	SLG
Home	3.59	12	11	1	38	33	230.1	210	19	71	131	vs. Left	.256	861	220	39	5	18	85	95	124	.331	.375
Away	3.78	9	6	0	31	27	183.1	172	16	70	104	vs. Right	.244	665	162	25	3	17	67	46	111	.297	.367
Day	4.96	2	5	0	16	15	98.0	103	15	38	61	Inning 1-6	.248	1276	316	49	6	30	131	112	196	.312	.366
Night	3.26	19	12	1	53	45	315.2	279	20	103	174	Inning 7+	.264	250	66	15	2	5	21	29	39	.342	.400
Grass	4.82	4	3	0	16	15	93.1	97	11	39	52	None on	.250	931	233	35	5	20	20	83	147	.318	.363
Turf	3.34	6	4	1	53	45	320.1	285	24	102	183	Runners on	.250	595	149	29	3	15	132	58	88	.315	.385
April	3.89	2	2	1	8	5	44.0	39	2	12	25	Scoring Posn	.232	314	73	13	1	6	101	37	43	.307	.338
May	7.20	0	1	0	5	5	25.0	28	7	9	14	Close & Late	.252	163	41	9	1	3	11	20	26	.335	.374
June	3.84	3	1	0	10	10	63.1	51	5	30	24	None on/out	.267	415	111	21	2	8	8	25	53	.311	.366
July	4.01	4	5	0	11	9	58.1	57	8	21	34	vs. 1st Batr (relief)	.333	9	3	0	0	0	1	0	1	.333	.333
August	2.62	6	4	0	15	15	103.0	97	5	32	56	First Inning Pitched	.247	251	62	11	2	7	36	27	39	.322	.390
September/October	3.53	6	4	0	20	16	120.0	110	8	37	82	First 75 Pitches	.240	1147	275	43	5	25	109	96	183	.303	.351
Starter	3.72	21	17	0	60	60	392.1	365	35	133	223	Pitch 76-90	.273	205	56	10	3	5	22	24	23	.349	.424
Reliever	2.95	0	0	1	9	0	21.1	17	0	8	12	Pitch 91-105	.298	121	36	8	0	3	15	15	18	.372	.438
0-3 Days Rest	5.18	1	0	0	4	4	24.1	26	4	9	16	Pitch 106+	.283	53	15	3	0	2	6	6	11	.356	.453
4 Days Rest	3.25	11	8	0	28	28	188.1	165	12	73	110	First Pitch	.301	236	71	11	1	4	26	5	0	.316	.407
5+ Days Rest	4.01	9	9	0	28	28	179.2	174	19	51	97	Ahead on Count	.211	650	137	17	4	16	63	0	196	.218	.323
Pre-All Star	4.25	7	5	1	28	23	154.2	136	15	58	76	Behind on Count	.291	381	111	26	0	9	41	75	0	.406	.430
Post-All Star	3.34	14	12	0	41	37	259.0	246	20	83	159	Two Strikes	.182	632	115	17	5	9	39	61	235	.260	.267

Pitcher vs. Batter (career)

Pitches Best Vs.	Avg	AB	H	2B	3B	HR	RBI	BB	SO	OBP	SLG	Pitches Worst Vs.	Avg	AB	H	2B	3B	HR	RBI	BB	SO	OBP	SLG
Tony Gwynn	.000	10	0	0	0	0	0	1	0	.091	.000	Ron Gant	.600	10	6	2	0	2	3	3	1	.692	1.400
John VanderWal	.071	14	1	0	0	0	0	0	2	.071	.071	Terry Pendleton	.538	13	7	1	0	1	1	1	2	.571	.846
Mickey Morandini	.077	13	1	0	0	0	0	1	1	.143	.077	Dwight Smith	.500	14	7	3	1	1	6	1	3	.533	1.071
Tom Foley	.083	12	1	0	0	0	0	0	1	.063	.083	Andre Dawson	.429	14	6	0	0	2	7	0	1	.500	.857
Tim Wallach	.091	22	2	0	0	0	0	1	3	.130	.091	Daryl Boston	.421	19	8	1	1	1	3	2	1	.455	.737

Joe Oliver — Reds

Bats Right (flyball hitter)

	Avg	G	AB	R	H	2B	3B	HR	RBI	BB	SO	HBP	GDP	SB	CS	OBP	SLG	IBB	SH	SF	#Pit	#P/PA	GB	FB	G/F
1992 Season	.270	143	485	42	131	25	1	10	57	35	75	1	12	2	3	.316	.388	19	6	7	1780	3.37	168	156	1.08
Career (1989-1992)	.247	407	1269	110	314	67	1	32	173	96	231	4	35	3	4	.300	.377	40	16	10	4685	3.40	411	416	0.99

1992 Season

	Avg	AB	H	2B	3B	HR	RBI	BB	SO	OBP	SLG		Avg	AB	H	2B	3B	HR	RBI	BB	SO	OBP	SLG
vs. Left	.307	176	54	11	0	4	24	16	22	.359	.438	Scoring Posn	.172	122	21	2	0	4	45	25	25	.303	.287
vs. Right	.249	309	77	14	1	6	33	19	53	.291	.359	Close & Late	.253	79	20	4	0	0	5	8	14	.311	.304
Groundball	.312	186	58	9	1	5	27	8	22	.337	.452	None on/out	.319	113	36	11	0	2	2	3	18	.336	.469
Flyball	.183	104	19	5	0	1	8	12	24	.258	.260	Batting #7	.316	133	42	14	1	2	20	7	16	.345	.481
Home	.278	245	68	16	0	7	36	17	37	.320	.429	Batting #8	.224	246	55	7	0	6	26	23	45	.288	.325
Away	.263	240	63	9	1	3	21	18	38	.313	.346	Other	.321	106	34	4	0	2	11	5	14	.348	.415
Day	.259	143	37	9	0	1	17	12	23	.314	.343	April	.224	58	13	3	1	1	9	6	7	.297	.362
Night	.275	342	94	16	1	9	40	23	52	.317	.406	May	.200	70	14	3	0	1	4	10	17	.309	.286
Grass	.262	141	37	5	1	2	14	5	21	.286	.355	June	.240	75	18	2	0	3	8	4	10	.275	.387
Turf	.273	344	94	20	0	8	43	30	54	.328	.401	July	.329	85	28	7	0	1	9	7	8	.372	.447
First Pitch	.228	79	18	3	0	1	10	17	0	.357	.304	August	.289	97	28	5	0	3	18	4	20	.314	.433
Ahead on Count	.400	85	34	4	1	5	20	12	0	.465	.647	September/October	.300	100	30	5	0	1	9	4	13	.318	.380
Behind on Count	.220	186	41	7	0	3	11	0	50	.219	.306	Pre-All Star	.238	240	57	12	1	5	28	23	38	.303	.358
Two Strikes	.171	205	35	7	0	2	13	6	75	.192	.234	Post-All Star	.302	245	74	13	0	5	29	12	37	.330	.416

1992 By Position

Position	Avg	AB	H	2B	3B	HR	RBI	BB	SO	OBP	SLG	G	GS	Innings	PO	A	E	DP	Fld Pct	Rng Fctr	In Zone	Outs	Zone Rtg	MLB Zone
As c	.268	482	129	25	1	10	55	35	75	.314	.386	141	137	1199.2	924	63	8	10	.992	---	---	---	---	---

Career (1989-1992)

	Avg	AB	H	2B	3B	HR	RBI	BB	SO	OBP	SLG		Avg	AB	H	2B	3B	HR	RBI	BB	SO	OBP	SLG
vs. Left	.287	565	162	34	0	18	92	53	97	.346	.442	Scoring Posn	.236	330	78	21	0	12	140	52	65	.335	.409
vs. Right	.216	704	152	33	1	14	81	43	134	.263	.325	Close & Late	.256	207	53	11	0	2	17	19	35	.317	.338
Groundball	.259	479	124	24	1	10	60	26	76	.297	.376	None on/out	.241	303	73	17	0	8	8	11	60	.270	.376
Flyball	.179	268	48	11	0	8	30	30	68	.258	.310	Batting #7	.268	340	91	23	1	6	50	15	52	.298	.394
Home	.245	641	157	39	0	18	92	48	116	.297	.390	Batting #8	.226	690	156	31	0	22	97	71	140	.296	.367
Away	.250	628	157	28	1	14	81	48	115	.303	.365	Other	.280	239	67	13	0	4	26	10	39	.310	.385
Day	.289	318	92	21	0	5	45	25	57	.340	.403	April	.218	142	31	8	1	1	12	16	26	.297	.310
Night	.233	951	222	46	1	27	128	71	174	.287	.369	May	.226	177	40	7	0	6	20	22	34	.318	.367
Grass	.250	368	92	19	1	10	55	18	71	.284	.389	June	.235	183	43	8	0	4	20	17	34	.299	.344
Turf	.246	901	222	48	0	22	118	78	160	.307	.373	July	.259	239	62	14	0	5	33	17	40	.304	.381
First Pitch	.276	246	68	14	0	7	43	22	0	.337	.419	August	.261	268	70	14	0	11	52	13	54	.293	.437
Ahead on Count	.321	212	68	15	1	10	40	34	0	.411	.542	September/October	.262	260	68	16	0	5	36	11	43	.293	.381

Career (1989-1992)

	Avg	AB	H	2B	3B	HR	RBI	BB	SO	OBP	SLG		Avg	AB	H	2B	3B	HR	RBI	BB	SO	OBP	SLG
Behind on Count	.214	448	96	17	0	8	48	1	134	.216	.306	Pre-All Star	.238	579	138	30	1	13	67	58	105	.306	.361
Two Strikes	.165	558	92	19	0	5	40	25	231	.200	.226	Post-All Star	.255	690	176	37	0	19	106	38	126	.293	.391

Batter vs. Pitcher (career)

Hits Best Against	Avg	AB	H	2B	3B	HR	RBI	BB	SO	OBP	SLG	Hits Worst Against	Avg	AB	H	2B	3B	HR	RBI	BB	SO	OBP	SLG
Bob Tewksbury	.385	13	5	1	0	0	0	0	0	.385	.462	Bobby Ojeda	.071	28	2	1	0	0	3	1	7	.103	.107
Terry Mulholland	.368	19	7	2	0	0	4	2	2	.429	.474	Pete Harnisch	.077	13	1	0	0	0	0	0	3	.077	.077
Zane Smith	.367	30	11	1	0	3	3	0	4	.367	.700	Joe Magrane	.083	12	1	0	0	0	0	0	2	.083	.083
Bud Black	.357	14	5	1	0	2	5	1	3	.400	.857	John Burkett	.083	12	1	0	0	0	0	0	0	.083	.083
Charlie Leibrandt	.304	23	7	1	0	2	5	2	0	.360	.609	Joe Boever	.091	11	1	0	0	0	0	1	3	.167	.091

Francisco Oliveras — Giants

Pitches Right (flyball pitcher)

	ERA	W	L	Sv	G	GS	IP	BB	SO	Avg	H	2B	3B	HR	RBI	OBP	SLG	GF	IR	IRS	Hld	SvOp	SB	CS	GB	FB	G/F
1992 Season	3.63	0	3	0	16	7	44.2	10	17	.250	41	10	0	11	21	.294	.512	3	10	3	0	0	0	3	50	70	0.71
Career (1989-1992)	3.71	11	15	5	116	18	235.0	68	130	.253	221	33	4	36	111	.307	.423	29	68	18	12	6	16	15	244	353	0.69

1992 Season

	ERA	W	L	Sv	G	GS	IP	H	HR	BB	SO		Avg	AB	H	2B	3B	HR	RBI	BB	SO	OBP	SLG
Home	5.16	0	2	0	6	5	22.2	23	8	4	8	vs. Left	.255	94	24	7	0	7	14	7	9	.307	.553
Away	2.05	0	1	0	10	2	22.0	18	3	6	9	vs. Right	.243	70	17	3	0	4	7	3	8	.276	.457

Career (1989-1992)

	ERA	W	L	Sv	G	GS	IP	H	HR	BB	SO		Avg	AB	H	2B	3B	HR	RBI	BB	SO	OBP	SLG
Home	4.49	7	8	5	61	10	120.1	123	19	37	59	vs. Left	.256	465	119	21	4	21	64	46	60	.322	.454
Away	2.90	4	7	0	55	8	114.2	98	17	31	71	vs. Right	.249	410	102	12	0	15	47	22	70	.290	.388
Day	4.76	3	8	4	43	8	85.0	83	19	26	53	Inning 1-6	.265	517	137	24	1	23	66	37	66	.316	.449
Night	3.12	8	7	1	73	10	150.0	138	17	42	77	Inning 7+	.235	358	84	9	3	13	45	31	64	.295	.385
Grass	3.47	9	10	5	83	12	160.2	144	24	47	90	None on	.257	526	135	24	4	22	22	37	79	.308	.443
Turf	4.24	2	5	0	33	6	74.1	77	12	21	40	Runners on	.246	349	86	9	0	14	89	31	51	.306	.393
April	3.38	0	0	0	2	0	5.1	4	1	2	5	Scoring Posn	.260	200	52	5	0	6	71	24	32	.326	.375
May	2.42	3	3	1	18	3	48.1	43	6	7	20	Close & Late	.241	162	39	3	1	6	17	17	31	.313	.383
June	4.00	3	4	2	27	7	63.0	61	6	25	32	None on/out	.263	224	59	10	1	11	11	14	34	.313	.464
July	4.74	1	1	0	16	3	24.2	25	6	3	14	vs. 1st Batr (relief)	.218	87	19	1	1	1	9	7	15	.268	.287
August	4.37	1	5	0	29	5	59.2	62	14	15	38	First Inning Pitched	.214	373	80	7	2	11	53	39	57	.287	.332
September/October	3.16	3	2	2	24	0	34.0	26	3	16	21	First 15 Pitches	.226	358	81	9	1	11	42	30	54	.285	.349
Starter	4.81	3	8	18	18	18	86.0	92	18	22	39	Pitch 16-30	.257	218	56	4	2	11	29	18	29	.318	.445
Reliever	3.08	8	7	5	98	0	149.0	129	18	46	91	Pitch 31-45	.268	123	33	9	1	6	19	10	23	.323	.504
0 Days rest	0.57	0	0	0	11	0	15.2	7	0	1	6	Pitch 46+	.290	176	51	11	0	8	21	10	24	.328	.489
1 or 2 Days rest	2.76	6	4	5	54	0	78.1	62	6	30	53	First Pitch	.270	122	33	3	1	6	18	11	0	.331	.459
3+ Days rest	4.25	2	3	0	33	0	55.0	60	12	15	32	Ahead on Count	.214	374	80	8	1	10	38	0	105	.220	.321
Pre-All Star	3.67	6	8	3	53	12	127.2	121	18	34	64	Behind on Count	.287	188	54	10	1	14	31	31	0	.385	.574
Post-All Star	3.77	5	7	2	63	6	107.1	100	18	34	66	Two Strikes	.216	399	86	13	2	13	41	26	130	.266	.356

Greg Olson — Braves

Bats Right

	Avg	G	AB	R	H	2B	3B	HR	RBI	BB	SO	HBP	GDP	SB	CS	OBP	SLG	IBB	SH	SF	#Pit	#P/PA	GB	FB	G/F
1992 Season	.238	95	302	27	72	14	2	3	27	34	31	1	8	2	1	.316	.328	4	1	2	1206	3.56	129	91	1.42
Career (1989-1992)	.247	331	1013	109	250	51	3	16	107	108	130	6	29	4	3	.321	.350	11	4	7	3986	3.51	420	291	1.44

1992 Season

	Avg	AB	H	2B	3B	HR	RBI	BB	SO	OBP	SLG		Avg	AB	H	2B	3B	HR	RBI	BB	SO	OBP	SLG
vs. Left	.256	117	30	5	2	1	10	6	7	.288	.359	Scoring Posn	.188	80	15	2	0	0	20	14	11	.302	.213
vs. Right	.227	185	42	9	0	2	17	28	24	.332	.308	Close & Late	.216	51	11	3	0	3	8	10	5	.339	.451
Groundball	.216	102	22	4	0	2	12	10	15	.281	.314	None on/out	.234	77	18	4	0	0	0	6	5	.289	.286
Flyball	.310	87	27	6	1	1	9	11	7	.394	.437	Batting #6	.236	89	21	4	1	1	11	6	7	.278	.337
Home	.237	135	32	6	0	0	11	19	11	.327	.281	Batting #7	.234	197	46	10	1	1	14	25	22	.323	.310
Away	.240	167	40	8	2	3	16	15	20	.306	.365	Other	.313	16	5	0	0	1	2	3	2	.421	.500
Day	.318	85	27	3	1	2	13	6	12	.363	.447	April	.233	43	10	3	0	0	2	7	8	.340	.302
Night	.207	217	45	11	1	1	14	28	19	.298	.281	May	.264	53	14	2	0	1	7	4	5	.316	.358
Grass	.246	203	50	9	1	1	17	25	21	.326	.315	June	.246	57	14	3	0	1	3	6	5	.317	.351
Turf	.222	99	22	5	1	2	10	9	10	.294	.354	July	.222	45	10	2	2	1	4	8	5	.340	.422
First Pitch	.216	37	8	2	1	0	1	3	0	.275	.324	August	.231	65	15	3	0	0	8	7	6	.307	.277
Ahead on Count	.280	107	30	6	1	2	15	18	0	.381	.411	September/October	.231	39	9	1	0	0	3	2	2	.268	.256
Behind on Count	.270	74	20	5	0	1	12	0	15	.276	.378	Pre-All Star	.256	168	43	9	1	3	14	21	19	.339	.375
Two Strikes	.168	107	18	4	0	1	7	13	31	.256	.234	Post-All Star	.216	134	29	5	1	0	13	13	12	.287	.269

1992 By Position

Position	Avg	AB	H	2B	3B	HR	RBI	BB	SO	OBP	SLG	G	GS	Innings	PO	A	E	DP	Fld Pct	Rng Fctr	In Zone	Outs	Zone Rtg	MLB Zone
As c	.239	301	72	14	2	3	27	33	31	.315	.329	94	85	754.2	522	43	1	9	.998	---	---	---	---	---

Career (1989-1992)

	Avg	AB	H	2B	3B	HR	RBI	BB	SO	OBP	SLG		Avg	AB	H	2B	3B	HR	RBI	BB	SO	OBP	SLG
vs. Left	.288	371	107	22	3	8	52	31	45	.341	.429	Scoring Posn	.235	247	58	9	0	4	80	46	39	.347	.320

Career (1989-1992)

	Avg	AB	H	2B	3B	HR	RBI	BB	SO	OBP	SLG		Avg	AB	H	2B	3B	HR	RBI	BB	SO	OBP	SLG
vs. Right	.223	642	143	29	0	8	55	77	85	.310	.305	Close & Late	.205	176	36	8	0	3	20	23	26	.298	.301
Groundball	.220	318	70	11	0	7	38	31	46	.289	.321	None on/out	.240	263	63	14	0	4	4	26	26	.310	.338
Flyball	.281	267	75	19	1	6	30	34	33	.367	.427	Batting #7	.240	542	130	31	1	6	53	62	70	.320	.334
Home	.273	490	134	23	1	10	63	46	49	.331	.386	Batting #8	.254	284	72	10	1	7	33	28	41	.323	.370
Away	.222	523	116	28	2	6	44	62	81	.311	.317	Other	.257	187	48	10	1	3	21	18	19	.321	.369
Day	.273	264	72	13	1	4	27	25	37	.338	.375	April	.316	76	24	6	0	0	4	10	14	.395	.395
Night	.238	749	178	38	2	12	80	83	93	.315	.342	May	.255	165	42	4	0	6	25	15	23	.326	.388
Grass	.250	727	182	35	2	12	76	75	87	.319	.354	June	.263	209	55	10	0	5	22	22	18	.335	.383
Turf	.238	286	68	16	1	4	31	33	43	.325	.343	July	.223	188	42	8	2	3	18	23	25	.307	.335
First Pitch	.320	153	49	10	1	0	14	6	0	.348	.399	August	.280	189	53	13	1	2	26	19	25	.344	.392
Ahead on Count	.272	305	83	17	2	7	41	61	0	.392	.410	September/October	.183	186	34	10	0	2	12	19	25	.261	.237
Behind on Count	.211	298	63	13	0	4	31	1	69	.216	.295	Pre-All Star	.272	503	137	22	1	12	55	55	63	.348	.392
Two Strikes	.150	366	55	12	0	6	27	38	130	.232	.232	Post-All Star	.222	510	113	29	2	4	52	53	67	.295	.310

Batter vs. Pitcher (career)

Hits Best Against	Avg	AB	H	2B	3B	HR	RBI	BB	SO	OBP	SLG	Hits Worst Against	Avg	AB	H	2B	3B	HR	RBI	BB	SO	OBP	SLG
Mark Gardner	.556	9	5	0	0	0	3	2	2	.636	.556	Mike Morgan	.000	11	0	0	0	0	0	0	3	.000	.000
Jack Armstrong	.455	11	5	2	0	0	2	0	1	.455	.636	Tim Crews	.077	13	1	0	0	0	0	1	2	.143	.077
Tom Browning	.350	20	7	2	0	0	0	1	2	.381	.450	Andy Benes	.130	23	3	0	0	0	0	2	4	.200	.130
Bud Black	.333	15	5	1	1	0	0	2	1	.412	.533	Kevin Gross	.167	12	2	1	0	0	0	2	4	.286	.250
Mitch Williams	.333	6	2	1	0	0	2	4	1	.545	.500	John Burkett	.200	20	4	0	0	0	0	2	4	.273	.200

Gregg Olson — Orioles

Pitches Right

	ERA	W	L	Sv	G	GS	IP	BB	SO	Avg	H	2B	3B	HR	RBI	OBP	SLG	GF	IR	IRS	Hld	SvOp	SB	CS	GB	FB	G/F
1992 Season	2.05	1	5	36	60	0	61.1	24	58	.211	46	4	1	3	17	.287	.280	56	31	5	0	44	10	0	84	43	1.95
Career (1988-1992)	2.36	17	19	131	270	0	305.1	140	303	.219	244	33	3	9	103	.308	.279	176	148	38	3	159	52	4	370	273	1.36

1992 Season

	ERA	W	L	Sv	G	GS	IP	H	HR	BB	SO		Avg	AB	H	2B	3B	HR	RBI	BB	SO	OBP	SLG
Home	1.38	1	1	17	31	0	32.2	20	2	12	28	vs. Left	.195	113	22	4	0	0	8	9	30	.252	.230
Away	2.83	0	4	19	29	0	28.2	26	1	12	30	vs. Right	.229	105	24	0	1	3	9	15	28	.322	.333
Day	2.86	0	3	10	21	0	22.0	23	1	9	26	Inning 1-6	.000	0	0	0	0	0	0	0	0	.000	.000
Night	1.60	1	2	26	39	0	39.1	23	2	15	32	Inning 7+	.211	218	46	4	1	3	17	24	58	.287	.280
Grass	1.33	1	2	31	50	0	54.0	32	2	21	51	None on	.232	112	26	3	1	2	2	13	29	.312	.330
Turf	7.36	0	3	5	10	0	7.1	14	1	3	7	Runners on	.189	106	20	1	0	1	15	11	29	.261	.226
April	2.35	0	1	3	7	0	7.2	8	1	4	9	Scoring Posn	.175	63	11	1	0	0	13	7	18	.250	.190
May	1.15	0	1	9	13	0	15.2	14	1	5	13	Close & Late	.228	162	37	4	1	3	17	19	41	.306	.321
June	1.86	1	0	8	9	0	9.2	3	1	4	11	None on/out	.222	45	10	2	1	0	0	6	10	.314	.311
July	6.75	0	2	4	8	0	5.1	8	0	4	5	vs. 1st Batr (relief)	.245	53	13	2	1	1	3	6	15	.322	.377
August	2.19	0	1	7	13	0	12.1	10	0	2	9	First Inning Pitched	.225	191	43	4	1	2	16	22	46	.302	.288
September/October	0.84	0	0	5	10	0	10.2	3	0	5	11	First 15 Pitches	.222	167	37	3	1	2	12	19	40	.298	.287
Starter	0.00	0	0	0	0	0	0.0	0	0	0	0	Pitch 16-30	.167	48	8	1	0	1	5	5	16	.245	.250
Reliever	2.05	1	5	36	60	0	61.1	46	2	24	58	Pitch 31-45	.333	3	1	0	0	0	0	0	2	.333	.333
0 Days rest	1.35	0	1	11	14	0	13.1	11	0	7	13	Pitch 46+	.000	0	0	0	0	0	0	0	0	.000	.000
1 or 2 Days rest	2.96	1	3	14	26	0	27.1	19	2	9	27	First Pitch	.333	30	10	0	0	0	1	0	0	.333	.333
3+ Days rest	1.31	0	1	11	20	0	20.2	16	1	8	18	Ahead on Count	.108	102	11	2	0	4	0	51	.108	.127
Pre-All Star	2.06	1	3	21	33	0	35.0	30	3	15	36	Behind on Count	.349	43	15	1	1	2	8	11	0	.473	.558
Post-All Star	2.05	0	2	15	27	0	26.1	16	0	9	22	Two Strikes	.106	104	11	1	0	1	4	13	58	.205	.144

Career (1988-1992)

	ERA	W	L	Sv	G	GS	IP	H	HR	BB	SO		Avg	AB	H	2B	3B	HR	RBI	BB	SO	OBP	SLG
Home	1.94	12	2	55	135	0	148.2	102	5	74	158	vs. Left	.187	556	104	12	0	2	42	71	146	.282	.219
Away	2.76	5	17	76	135	0	156.2	142	4	66	145	vs. Right	.251	557	140	21	3	7	61	69	157	.334	.338
Day	3.83	1	10	38	73	0	84.2	82	6	35	78	Inning 1-6	.313	16	5	2	0	0	4	2	2	.389	.438
Night	1.79	16	9	93	197	0	220.2	162	3	105	225	Inning 7+	.218	1097	239	31	3	9	99	138	301	.301	.301
Grass	1.94	14	10	113	222	0	250.0	172	7	113	252	None on	.230	544	125	21	2	6	6	52	146	.301	.309
Turf	4.23	3	9	18	48	0	55.1	72	2	27	51	Runners on	.209	569	119	12	1	3	97	88	157	.314	.250
April	1.87	3	1	11	31	0	43.1	33	2	17	33	Scoring Posn	.198	363	72	7	1	1	92	69	109	.323	.231
May	1.40	2	2	22	45	0	57.2	39	2	26	64	Close & Late	.230	673	155	18	3	7	78	94	183	.325	.297
June	2.77	4	4	29	45	0	48.2	34	2	18	54	None on/out	.194	232	45	5	2	4	4	24	57	.275	.284
July	3.19	1	6	24	46	0	48.0	49	0	29	53	vs. 1st Batr (relief)	.210	243	51	6	1	3	21	23	59	.281	.280
August	3.11	2	2	22	46	0	46.1	42	2	21	37	First Inning Pitched	.232	896	208	25	2	6	90	103	239	.313	.285
September/October	2.05	5	4	23	57	0	61.1	47	1	29	62	First 15 Pitches	.237	769	182	24	2	6	65	75	202	.306	.296
Starter	0.00	0	0	0	0	0	0.0	0	0	0	0	Pitch 16-30	.174	270	47	7	0	2	30	49	81	.303	.222
Reliever	2.36	17	19	131	270	0	305.1	244	9	140	303	Pitch 31-45	.212	66	14	2	1	1	7	13	19	.342	.318
0 Days rest	2.57	4	5	40	62	0	66.2	60	1	27	64	Pitch 46+	.125	8	1	0	0	0	0	3	1	.333	.125
1 or 2 Days rest	2.30	9	9	62	127	0	140.2	107	6	74	140	First Pitch	.271	140	38	2	0	1	16	13	0	.335	.307
3+ Days rest	2.30	4	5	29	81	0	98.0	77	2	39	99	Ahead on Count	.152	538	82	14	2	3	32	1	261	.160	.203
Pre-All Star	2.10	9	9	69	135	0	162.2	121	6	69	166	Behind on Count	.324	225	73	12	1	3	28	60	0	.462	.427
Post-All Star	2.65	8	10	62	135	0	142.2	123	3	71	137	Two Strikes	.146	575	84	12	2	4	40	64	303	.235	.195

Pitcher vs. Batter (career)

Pitches Best Vs.	Avg	AB	H	2B	3B	HR	RBI	BB	SO	OBP	SLG	Pitches Worst Vs.	Avg	AB	H	2B	3B	HR	RBI	BB	SO	OBP	SLG
Ruben Sierra	.000	10	0	0	0	0	0	1	3	.091	.000	Mark McGwire	.444	9	4	0	0	1	4	3	3	.583	.778
Ellis Burks	.000	10	0	0	0	0	0	1	3	.091	.000	Danny Tartabull	.417	12	5	0	0	0	2	4	.500	.417
Pete O'Brien	.071	14	1	0	0	0	1	0	3	.071	.071												
Don Mattingly	.091	11	1	0	0	0	0	2	1	.231	.091												
Steve Sax	.154	13	2	0	0	0	0	0	0	.154	.154												

Jose Oquendo — Cardinals
Bats Both

	Avg	G	AB	R	H	2B	3B	HR	RBI	BB	SO	HBP	GDP	SB	CS	OBP	SLG	IBB	SH	SF	#Pit	#P/PA	GB	FB	G/F
1992 Season	.257	14	35	3	9	3	1	0	3	5	3	0	0	0	0	.350	.400	1	0	0	134	3.35	12	12	1.00
Last Five Years	.267	508	1877	173	502	69	18	10	160	277	196	1	32	9	14	.359	.339	36	28	19	7831	3.60	694	604	1.15

1992 Season

	Avg	AB	H	2B	3B	HR	RBI	BB	SO	OBP	SLG		Avg	AB	H	2B	3B	HR	RBI	BB	SO	OBP	SLG
vs. Left	.167	12	2	1	0	0	1	3	2	.333	.250	Scoring Posn	.250	8	2	1	0	0	3	2	0	.400	.375
vs. Right	.304	23	7	2	1	0	2	2	1	.360	.478	Close & Late	.333	6	2	2	0	0	1	2	0	.500	.667

Last Five Years

	Avg	AB	H	2B	3B	HR	RBI	BB	SO	OBP	SLG		Avg	AB	H	2B	3B	HR	RBI	BB	SO	OBP	SLG
vs. Left	.255	709	181	31	6	9	67	95	73	.341	.354	Scoring Posn	.263	456	120	16	7	3	151	93	58	.375	.349
vs. Right	.275	1168	321	38	12	1	93	182	123	.369	.330	Close & Late	.281	345	97	14	1	3	26	58	47	.383	.354
Groundball	.285	674	192	20	13	2	60	103	64	.377	.362	None on/out	.259	456	118	21	3	2	61	48	.346	.331
Flyball	.253	439	111	24	4	6	42	58	46	.338	.358	Batting #7	.287	522	150	18	4	6	44	78	50	.376	.372
Home	.274	931	255	30	10	5	82	133	87	.363	.344	Batting #8	.265	720	191	27	9	2	61	127	70	.374	.336
Away	.261	946	247	39	8	5	78	144	109	.355	.335	Other	.254	635	161	24	5	2	55	72	76	.326	.317
Day	.242	563	136	17	5	2	60	80	60	.332	.300	April	.243	226	55	8	4	0	20	39	29	.352	.314
Night	.279	1314	366	52	13	8	100	197	136	.370	.356	May	.225	285	64	6	1	2	12	37	30	.312	.274
Grass	.274	489	134	14	3	1	39	73	63	.364	.321	June	.274	365	100	12	3	2	34	54	31	.363	.340
Turf	.265	1388	368	55	15	9	121	204	133	.357	.346	July	.310	342	106	16	6	1	27	47	38	.392	.401
First Pitch	.297	374	111	20	2	3	33	14	0	.321	.385	August	.289	377	109	21	0	4	44	49	35	.368	.377
Ahead on Count	.310	462	143	14	6	2	50	139	0	.462	.379	September/October	.241	282	68	6	4	1	23	51	33	.353	.301
Behind on Count	.289	484	140	17	5	3	45	13	91	.291	.364	Pre-All Star	.262	976	256	32	12	4	79	145	102	.355	.332
Two Strikes	.223	740	165	22	7	3	52	109	196	.322	.284	Post-All Star	.273	901	246	37	6	6	81	132	94	.363	.347

Batter vs. Pitcher (since 1984)

Hits Best Against	Avg	AB	H	2B	3B	HR	RBI	BB	SO	OBP	SLG	Hits Worst Against	Avg	AB	H	2B	3B	HR	RBI	BB	SO	OBP	SLG
John Burkett	.462	13	6	0	0	0	0	2	1	.533	.462	Dwight Gooden	.077	26	2	0	0	0	0	1	3	.111	.077
Norm Charlton	.417	12	5	1	0	1	3	3	0	.533	.750	Mark Gardner	.091	11	1	0	0	0	1	2	2	.214	.091
Tom Browning	.400	25	10	4	0	2	3	4	0	.483	.800	Bob Kipper	.100	10	1	0	0	0	1	1	2	.182	.100
Frank Viola	.389	18	7	0	1	1	3	5	1	.500	.667	Kelly Downs	.100	10	1	0	0	0	1	2	2	.250	.100
Jose Rijo	.333	9	3	1	1	0	2	2	2	.455	.667	Don Carman	.154	26	4	0	0	0	1	3	2	.241	.154

Jesse Orosco — Brewers
Pitches Left (flyball pitcher)

	ERA	W	L	Sv	G	GS	IP	BB	SO	Avg	H	2B	3B	HR	RBI	OBP	SLG	GF	IR	IRS	Hld	SvOp	SB	CS	GB	FB	G/F
1992 Season	3.23	3	1	1	59	0	39.0	13	40	.232	33	4	0	5	24	.297	.366	14	64	14	11	2	3	4	43	42	1.02
Last Five Years	3.05	16	11	15	285	0	280.1	122	253	.231	238	40	5	29	142	.312	.364	62	312	82	42	27	23	13	298	314	0.95

1992 Season

	ERA	W	L	Sv	G	GS	IP	H	HR	BB	SO		Avg	AB	H	2B	3B	HR	RBI	BB	SO	OBP	SLG
Home	3.52	3	1	0	33	0	23.0	18	3	7	23	vs. Left	.273	55	15	2	0	2	10	5	16	.328	.418
Away	2.81	0	0	1	26	0	16.0	15	2	6	17	vs. Right	.207	87	18	2	0	3	14	8	24	.278	.333
Starter	0.00	0	0	0	0	0	0.0	0	0	0	0	Scoring Posn	.279	43	12	1	0	2	19	4	16	.340	.442
Reliever	3.23	3	1	1	59	0	39.0	33	5	13	40	Close & Late	.192	52	10	0	0	1	6	6	14	.283	.250
0 Days rest	0.90	1	0	1	20	0	10.0	6	0	1	11	None on/out	.200	35	7	3	0	1	1	3	10	.263	.371
1 or 2 Days rest	2.45	1	0	0	14	0	11.0	6	2	6	10	First Pitch	.267	15	4	2	0	1	6	0	0	.267	.600
3+ Days rest	5.00	1	0	0	25	0	18.0	21	3	6	19	Behind on Count	.385	26	10	0	0	3	6	8	0	.529	.731
Pre-All Star	3.38	2	1	1	33	0	21.1	17	2	9	24	Ahead on Count	.194	72	14	2	0	0	6	0	36	.200	.222
Post-All Star	3.06	1	0	0	26	0	17.2	16	3	4	16	Two Strikes	.162	74	12	2	0	1	9	5	40	.210	.230

Last Five Years

	ERA	W	L	Sv	G	GS	IP	H	HR	BB	SO		Avg	AB	H	2B	3B	HR	RBI	BB	SO	OBP	SLG
Home	2.49	10	6	5	140	0	148.0	114	14	50	134	vs. Left	.222	333	74	14	0	6	45	39	90	.301	.318
Away	3.67	6	5	10	145	0	132.1	124	15	72	119	vs. Right	.235	698	164	26	5	23	97	83	163	.317	.385
Day	3.38	6	4	8	85	0	77.1	60	13	32	64	Inning 1-6	.354	65	23	4	1	3	22	7	14	.411	.585
Night	2.93	10	7	7	200	0	203.0	178	16	90	189	Inning 7+	.223	966	215	36	4	26	120	115	239	.305	.349
Grass	2.94	13	9	13	229	0	232.2	185	26	95	210	None on	.247	515	127	21	4	17	17	57	122	.325	.402
Turf	3.59	3	2	2	56	0	47.2	53	3	27	43	Runners on	.215	516	111	19	1	12	125	65	131	.299	.326
April	1.57	0	2	4	32	0	23.0	12	1	18	15	Scoring Posn	.215	325	70	11	1	5	109	51	90	.316	.302
May	3.78	6	2	4	53	0	52.1	46	5	19	46	Close & Late	.207	382	79	13	0	8	47	52	102	.302	.304
June	3.76	1	2	1	49	0	52.2	44	4	18	55	None on/out	.271	225	61	8	2	10	10	25	48	.349	.458
July	2.65	2	2	1	56	0	54.1	52	4	28	45	vs. 1st Batr (relief)	.223	247	55	7	0	6	41	27	63	.299	.324
August	3.27	2	2	3	51	0	52.1	48	9	17	46	First Inning Pitched	.221	760	168	27	4	18	117	97	179	.309	.338
September/October	2.36	5	1	2	44	0	45.2	36	6	22	46	First 15 Pitches	.217	706	153	24	3	18	99	84	165	.300	.336

329

Last Five Years

	ERA	W	L	Sv	G	GS	IP	H	HR	BB	SO		Avg	AB	H	2B	3B	HR	RBI	BB	SO	OBP	SLG
Starter	0.00	0	0	0	0	0	0.0	0	0	0	0	Pitch 16-30	.256	258	66	10	2	9	33	31	73	.333	.415
Reliever	3.05	16	11	15	285	0	280.1	238	29	122	253	Pitch 31-45	.291	55	16	6	0	2	9	7	14	.381	.509
0 Days rest	2.26	6	2	4	73	0	59.2	54	7	22	62	Pitch 46+	.250	12	3	0	0	0	1	0	1	.231	.250
1 or 2 Days rest	3.73	6	6	9	117	0	128.0	111	14	55	111	First Pitch	.315	149	47	9	2	7	30	16	0	.375	.544
3+ Days rest	2.62	4	3	2	95	0	92.2	73	8	45	80	Ahead on Count	.167	514	86	10	1	8	50	0	219	.168	.237
Pre-All Star	3.36	7	8	9	151	0	150.0	122	13	64	137	Behind on Count	.332	193	64	10	2	10	35	58	0	.490	.560
Post-All Star	2.69	9	3	6	134	0	130.1	116	16	58	116	Two Strikes	.145	516	75	15	1	6	47	47	253	.215	.213

Pitcher vs. Batter (since 1984)

Pitches Best Vs.	Avg	AB	H	2B	3B	HR	RBI	BB	SO	OBP	SLG	Pitches Worst Vs.	Avg	AB	H	2B	3B	HR	RBI	BB	SO	OBP	SLG
Steve Sax	.000	13	0	0	0	0	0	2	0	.133	.000	Andre Dawson	.600	10	6	1	0	1	3	1	1	.636	1.000
Chili Davis	.000	11	0	0	0	0	0	4	6	.267	.000	Jack Clark	.375	8	3	2	0	0	0	4	1	.583	.625
Terry Pendleton	.063	16	1	0	0	0	0	4	4	.250	.063	Ruben Sierra	.357	14	5	2	0	1	4	0	0	.357	.714
Bobby Bonilla	.182	11	2	0	0	0	0	1	0	.250	.182	Kevin McReynolds	.333	12	4	0	0	2	2	4	2	.500	.833
Rafael Palmeiro	.182	11	2	0	0	0	4	1	1	.250	.182	Candy Maldonado	.333	9	3	1	0	0	2	4	1	.364	1.000

Joe Orsulak — Orioles

Bats Left

	Avg	G	AB	R	H	2B	3B	HR	RBI	BB	SO	HBP	GDP	SB	CS	OBP	SLG	IBB	SH	SF	#Pit	#P/PA	GB	FB	G/F
1992 Season	.289	117	391	45	113	18	3	4	39	28	34	4	3	5	4	.342	.381	5	4	1	1357	3.20	164	109	1.50
Last Five Years	.281	632	2059	258	579	97	15	35	221	166	192	14	35	31	25	.337	.394	23	23	14	7723	3.43	815	600	1.36

1992 Season

	Avg	AB	H	2B	3B	HR	RBI	BB	SO	OBP	SLG		Avg	AB	H	2B	3B	HR	RBI	BB	SO	OBP	SLG
vs. Left	.250	80	20	5	1	0	11	4	10	.307	.338	Scoring Posn	.306	85	26	5	0	2	36	13	13	.406	.435
vs. Right	.299	311	93	13	2	4	28	24	24	.351	.392	Close & Late	.323	65	21	2	1	1	3	5	5	.380	.431
Groundball	.243	115	28	2	2	0	8	7	10	.293	.296	None on/out	.232	99	23	4	1	1	1	5	5	.276	.323
Flyball	.327	107	35	7	1	3	17	8	8	.385	.495	Batting #2	.259	54	14	2	1	0	5	1	8	.273	.333
Home	.278	180	50	5	2	2	18	18	13	.347	.361	Batting #6	.295	227	67	13	1	3	22	15	19	.340	.401
Away	.299	211	63	13	1	2	21	10	21	.338	.398	Other	.291	110	32	3	1	1	12	12	7	.376	.364
Day	.293	116	34	9	1	0	6	8	14	.349	.388	April	.220	50	11	3	0	0	4	0	9	.220	.280
Night	.287	275	79	9	2	4	33	20	20	.339	.378	May	.213	47	10	0	1	0	5	7	5	.333	.255
Grass	.294	326	96	14	2	4	32	27	25	.355	.387	June	.361	72	26	2	1	1	11	4	10	.395	.458
Turf	.262	65	17	4	1	0	7	1	9	.273	.354	July	.370	100	37	10	1	1	8	10	4	.427	.520
First Pitch	.329	76	25	5	0	1	4	5	0	.378	.434	August	.273	44	12	1	0	0	5	5	2	.360	.295
Ahead on Count	.315	89	28	6	0	1	7	18	0	.430	.416	September/October	.218	78	17	2	0	2	6	2	4	.247	.321
Behind on Count	.260	127	33	4	1	1	14	0	15	.271	.331	Pre-All Star	.290	214	62	8	3	2	23	14	28	.338	.383
Two Strikes	.201	134	27	1	2	2	13	5	34	.241	.284	Post-All Star	.288	177	51	10	0	2	16	14	6	.347	.379

1992 By Position

Position	Avg	AB	H	2B	3B	HR	RBI	BB	SO	OBP	SLG	G	GS	Innings	PO	A	E	DP	Fld Pct	Rng Fctr	In Zone	Outs	Zone Rtg	MLB Zone
As lf	.277	47	13	1	0	1	7	3	4	.314	.362	14	10	105.0	25	1	1	0	.963	2.23	33	25	.758	.809
As rf	.295	336	99	16	3	3	32	25	28	.351	.387	98	88	812.1	203	8	3	1	.986	2.34	242	197	.814	.814

Last Five Years

	Avg	AB	H	2B	3B	HR	RBI	BB	SO	OBP	SLG		Avg	AB	H	2B	3B	HR	RBI	BB	SO	OBP	SLG
vs. Left	.234	368	86	13	2	0	32	27	41	.294	.280	Scoring Posn	.274	467	128	23	4	9	183	70	51	.367	.398
vs. Right	.292	1691	493	84	13	35	189	139	151	.346	.419	Close & Late	.257	331	85	14	3	5	31	39	33	.339	.363
Groundball	.271	582	158	26	3	6	68	59	49	.338	.357	None on/out	.290	527	153	33	3	10	10	34	40	.337	.421
Flyball	.280	446	125	26	2	10	52	36	42	.338	.415	Batting #2	.267	517	138	20	4	8	56	35	57	.313	.368
Home	.277	985	273	42	7	17	109	85	91	.336	.386	Batting #6	.286	371	106	19	1	10	48	33	41	.346	.423
Away	.285	1074	306	55	8	18	112	81	101	.338	.401	Other	.286	1171	335	58	10	17	117	98	94	.344	.396
Day	.254	516	131	25	3	9	45	44	53	.316	.366	April	.255	271	69	14	1	3	23	17	34	.303	.347
Night	.290	1543	448	72	12	26	176	122	139	.344	.403	May	.294	286	84	14	3	6	41	31	28	.368	.427
Grass	.280	1739	487	80	9	31	179	147	156	.338	.390	June	.267	423	113	16	3	3	44	31	36	.319	.340
Turf	.288	320	92	17	6	4	42	19	36	.331	.416	July	.307	407	125	23	5	6	39	25	30	.342	.432
First Pitch	.301	342	103	18	2	6	29	10	0	.324	.418	August	.305	383	117	22	3	9	49	38	39	.369	.449
Ahead on Count	.340	483	164	31	4	14	78	99	0	.449	.507	September/October	.246	289	71	8	0	8	25	24	25	.311	.356
Behind on Count	.264	694	183	33	5	9	68	0	120	.268	.365	Pre-All Star	.278	1127	313	52	10	16	121	84	107	.330	.384
Two Strikes	.209	776	162	24	6	7	62	49	192	.259	.282	Post-All Star	.285	932	266	45	5	19	100	82	85	.345	.406

Batter vs. Pitcher (since 1984)

Hits Best Against	Avg	AB	H	2B	3B	HR	RBI	BB	SO	OBP	SLG	Hits Worst Against	Avg	AB	H	2B	3B	HR	RBI	BB	SO	OBP	SLG
Rick Sutcliffe	.500	22	11	3	1	0	1	2	3	.542	.727	Ron Robinson	.000	13	0	0	0	0	0	1	2	.071	.000
Alex Fernandez	.467	15	7	1	2	0	2	0	0	.467	.800	Jeff M. Robinson	.000	12	0	0	0	0	0	1	1	.077	.000
Jack McDowell	.458	24	11	2	0	2	5	1	1	.480	.792	Greg Swindell	.091	11	1	0	0	0	0	0	1	.091	.091
Bill Gullickson	.417	24	10	5	0	1	4	2	1	.462	.750	Kevin Appier	.167	18	3	0	0	0	0	1	1	.211	.167
Kevin Brown	.400	20	8	3	0	1	7	4	1	.500	.700	Jeff Reardon	.167	12	2	0	0	0	0	0	0	.167	.167

Junior Ortiz — Indians
Bats Right (groundball hitter)

	Avg	G	AB	R	H	2B	3B	HR	RBI	BB	SO	HBP	GDP	SB	CS	OBP	SLG	IBB	SH	SF	#Pit	#P/PA	GB	FB	G/F
1992 Season	.250	86	244	20	61	7	0	0	24	12	23	4	7	1	3	.296	.279	0	2	0	913	3.51	129	49	2.63
Last Five Years	.256	358	896	71	229	31	3	3	93	68	80	11	32	4	14	.314	.307	4	9	6	3402	3.47	465	201	2.31

1992 Season

	Avg	AB	H	2B	3B	HR	RBI	BB	SO	OBP	SLG		Avg	AB	H	2B	3B	HR	RBI	BB	SO	OBP	SLG
vs. Left	.277	65	18	2	0	0	6	6	3	.338	.308	Scoring Posn	.299	67	20	3	0	0	24	5	8	.347	.343
vs. Right	.240	179	43	5	0	0	18	6	20	.280	.268	Close & Late	.229	35	8	1	0	0	2	1	4	.270	.257
Home	.296	115	34	2	0	0	12	9	12	.362	.313	None on/out	.169	59	10	2	0	0	0	2	5	.210	.203
Away	.209	129	27	5	0	0	12	3	11	.233	.248	Batting #8	.269	52	14	1	0	0	7	6	4	.356	.288
First Pitch	.286	42	12	2	0	0	5	0	0	.286	.333	Batting #9	.250	180	45	6	0	0	16	6	19	.286	.283
Ahead on Count	.316	57	18	1	0	0	5	9	0	.418	.333	Other	.167	12	2	0	0	0	0	1	0	.167	.167
Behind on Count	.214	84	18	3	0	0	7	0	13	.250	.250	Pre-All Star	.227	97	22	3	0	0	11	7	8	.292	.258
Two Strikes	.215	107	23	3	0	0	8	3	23	.250	.243	Post-All Star	.265	147	39	4	0	0	13	5	15	.299	.293

Last Five Years

	Avg	AB	H	2B	3B	HR	RBI	BB	SO	OBP	SLG		Avg	AB	H	2B	3B	HR	RBI	BB	SO	OBP	SLG
vs. Left	.265	328	87	11	2	2	36	30	28	.332	.329	Scoring Posn	.269	245	66	9	0	1	88	25	28	.335	.318
vs. Right	.250	568	142	20	1	1	57	38	52	.303	.294	Close & Late	.241	141	34	6	0	0	10	6	15	.280	.284
Groundball	.224	286	64	10	1	0	24	23	39	.294	.266	None on/out	.222	216	48	7	1	1		15	16	.279	.278
Flyball	.260	196	51	6	0	2	15	16	17	.321	.321	Batting #7	.243	280	68	9	2	3	38	24	28	.309	.321
Home	.301	449	135	16	2	1	65	44	37	.369	.352	Batting #8	.264	333	88	12	1	0	29	32	28	.335	.306
Away	.210	447	94	15	1	2	28	24	43	.255	.262	Other	.258	283	73	10	0	0	26	12	28	.293	.293
Day	.252	326	82	12	2	1	32	22	33	.310	.310	April	.229	109	25	0		2	16	16	7	.320	.284
Night	.258	570	147	19	1	2	61	46	47	.316	.305	May	.254	201	51	13	0	0	19	13	16	.307	.318
Grass	.259	394	102	11	0	1	29	24	40	.310	.294	June	.306	147	45	5	2	0	16	10	12	.356	.367
Turf	.253	502	127	20	3	2	64	44	40	.317	.317	July	.290	169	49	7	1	1	23	7	20	.324	.361
First Pitch	.256	168	43	8	1	0	15	4	0	.276	.315	August	.197	127	25	2	0	0	9	14	11	.287	.213
Ahead on Count	.310	197	61	8	0	3	28	35	0	.414	.396	September/October	.238	143	34	4	0	0	10	8	14	.288	.266
Behind on Count	.225	307	69	6	1	2	30	0	42	.241	.270	Pre-All Star	.259	494	128	19	2	2	54	44	39	.325	.318
Two Strikes	.218	371	81	12	1	0	27	29	80	.285	.256	Post-All Star	.251	402	101	12	1	1	39	24	41	.299	.294

Batter vs. Pitcher (since 1984)

Hits Best Against	Avg	AB	H	2B	3B	HR	RBI	BB	SO	OBP	SLG	Hits Worst Against	Avg	AB	H	2B	3B	HR	RBI	BB	SO	OBP	SLG
Zane Smith	.563	16	9	2	0	0	1	1	1	.588	.688	Orel Hershiser	.000	11	0	0	0	0	1	0	0	.000	.000
Bill Gullickson	.417	12	5	2	0	0	1	1	1	.462	.583	Joe Magrane	.091	11	1	0	0	0	0	0	0	.091	.091
Mark Langston	.308	13	4	0	0	0	2	1	2	.357	.308	Chuck Finley	.133	15	2	0	0	0	0	1	0	.188	.133
												Sid Fernandez	.143	21	3	0	0	0	0	1	5	.182	.143
												Jim Deshaies	.154	13	2	0	0	0	0	1	1	.214	.154

John Orton — Angels
Bats Right

	Avg	G	AB	R	H	2B	3B	HR	RBI	BB	SO	HBP	GDP	SB	CS	OBP	SLG	IBB	SH	SF	#Pit	#P/PA	GB	FB	G/F
1992 Season	.219	43	114	11	25	3	0	2	12	7	32	2	1	1	1	.276	.298	0	2	0	481	3.91	30	37	0.81
Career (1989-1992)	.203	119	306	30	62	13	0	3	25	24	51	4	5	1	3	.269	.275	0	9	0	1328	3.98	92	77	1.19

1992 Season

	Avg	AB	H	2B	3B	HR	RBI	BB	SO	OBP	SLG		Avg	AB	H	2B	3B	HR	RBI	BB	SO	OBP	SLG
vs. Left	.120	25	3	1	0	1	5	2	11	.241	.280	Scoring Posn	.240	25	6	1	0	1	11	2	7	.321	.400
vs. Right	.247	89	22	2	0	1	7	5	21	.287	.303	Close & Late	.111	9	1	0	0	0	0	2	1	.273	.111
Home	.225	71	16	1	0	1	6	5	18	.276	.282	None on/out	.233	30	7	1	0	1	1	0	8	.233	.367
Away	.209	43	9	2	0	1	6	2	14	.277	.326	Batting #8	.196	46	9	0	0	0	3	3	11	.245	.196
First Pitch	.273	22	6	1	0	0	4	0	0	.273	.318	Batting #9	.246	65	16	3	0	2	10	3	20	.300	.385
Ahead on Count	.350	20	7	0	0	1	3	2	0	.409	.500	Other	.000	3	0	0	0	0	0	1	1	.250	.000
Behind on Count	.094	32	3	1	0	0	1	0	15	.147	.125	Pre-All Star	.174	46	8	0	0	0	2	4	12	.240	.174
Two Strikes	.133	60	8	1	0	0	2	5	32	.212	.150	Post-All Star	.250	68	17	3	0	2	10	3	20	.301	.382

Donovan Osborne — Cardinals
Pitches Left

	ERA	W	L	Sv	G	GS	IP	BB	SO	Avg	H	2B	3B	HR	RBI	OBP	SLG	CG	ShO	Sup	QS	#P/S	SB	CS	GB	FB	G/F
1992 Season	3.77	11	9	0	34	29	179.0	38	104	.275	193	39	5	14	76	.312	.404	0	0	3.62	16	87	15	3	257	215	1.20

1992 Season

	ERA	W	L	Sv	G	GS	IP	H	HR	BB	SO		Avg	AB	H	2B	3B	HR	RBI	BB	SO	OBP	SLG
Home	3.42	5	3	0	16	12	79.0	84	4	17	49	vs. Left	.318	151	48	13	0	3	23	8	23	.348	.464
Away	4.05	6	6	0	18	17	100.0	109	10	21	55	vs. Right	.263	552	145	26	5	11	53	30	81	.302	.388
Day	4.47	2	3	0	12	10	56.1	66	7	12	39	Inning 1-6	.278	612	170	32	5	13	71	34	91	.316	.410
Night	3.45	9	6	0	22	19	122.2	127	7	26	65	Inning 7+	.253	91	23	7	0	1	5	4	13	.284	.363
Grass	3.91	4	3	0	9	9	53.0	57	5	9	27	None on	.249	422	105	22	2	10	10	16	68	.278	.382
Turf	3.71	7	6	0	25	20	126.0	136	9	29	77	Runners on	.313	281	88	17	3	4	66	22	36	.360	.438
April	1.71	2	0	0	4	4	21.0	17	1	5	9	Scoring Posn	.298	171	51	8	2	2	57	13	28	.340	.404
May	2.84	3	2	0	6	6	44.1	39	4	6	26	Close & Late	.234	64	15	5	0	1	4	2	10	.258	.359
June	3.86	0	2	0	5	5	30.1	32	4	8	16	None on/out	.261	184	48	14	0	5	5	11	23	.306	.418
July	7.20	2	2	0	7	5	25.0	37	3	7	19	vs. 1st Batr (relief)	.200	5	1	1	0	0	0	0	0	.200	.400
August	3.47	2	1	0	6	3	23.1	22	2	3	20	First Inning Pitched	.263	137	36	7	1	2	20	9	25	.308	.372

1992 Season

	ERA	W	L	Sv	G	GS	IP	H	HR	BB	SO
September/October	3.86	2	2	0	6	6	35.0	46	0	9	14
Starter	3.78	10	8	0	29	29	169.0	183	14	37	98
Reliever	3.60	1	1	0	5	0	10.0	10	0	1	6
0-3 Days Rest	3.27	1	0	0	2	2	11.0	10	1	5	7
4 Days Rest	3.62	7	4	0	15	15	92.0	100	9	16	61
5+ Days Rest	4.09	2	4	0	12	12	66.0	73	4	16	30
Pre-All Star	3.19	7	5	0	18	18	110.0	106	10	23	60
Post-All Star	4.70	4	4	0	16	11	69.0	87	4	15	44

	Avg	AB	H	2B	3B	HR	RBI	BB	SO	OBP	SLG
First 75 Pitches	.278	569	158	31	4	12	64	31	88	.315	.409
Pitch 76-90	.295	88	26	5	1	2	10	4	11	.326	.443
Pitch 91-105	.211	38	8	3	0	0	2	3	4	.268	.289
Pitch 106+	.125	8	1	0	0	0	0	0	1	.125	.125
First Pitch	.355	110	39	6	1	1	7	1	0	.354	.455
Ahead on Count	.249	301	75	17	0	3	29	0	80	.252	.336
Behind on Count	.288	160	46	11	2	6	24	21	0	.370	.494
Two Strikes	.211	304	64	10	1	4	27	16	104	.251	.289

Al Osuna — Astros   Pitches Left (flyball pitcher)

	ERA	W	L	Sv	G	GS	IP	BB	SO	Avg	H	2B	3B	HR	RBI	OBP	SLG	GF	IR	IRS	Hld	SvOp	SB	CS	GB	FB	G/F
1992 Season	4.23	6	3	0	66	0	61.2	38	37	.236	52	7	0	8	26	.343	.377	17	40	6	2	4	1	0	49	101	0.49
Career (1990-1992)	3.84	15	9	12	149	0	154.2	90	111	.220	121	23	2	14	68	.330	.345	51	100	26	17	24	6	2	161	215	0.75

1992 Season

	ERA	W	L	Sv	G	GS	IP	H	HR	BB	SO
Home	1.97	5	1	0	37	0	32.0	22	2	13	18
Away	6.67	1	2	0	29	0	29.2	30	6	25	19
Day	4.15	0	1	0	22	0	26.0	22	6	12	15
Night	4.29	6	2	0	44	0	35.2	30	2	26	22
Grass	6.32	1	0	0	14	0	15.2	16	4	9	14
Turf	3.52	5	3	0	52	0	46.0	36	4	29	23
April	0.00	2	0	0	9	0	9.2	5	0	7	7
May	6.00	1	3	0	13	0	12.0	10	3	10	4
June	4.82	1	0	0	9	0	9.1	9	0	4	8
July	4.00	1	0	0	15	0	9.0	9	2	3	3
August	3.38	0	0	0	11	0	10.2	9	0	6	5
September/October	6.55	1	0	0	9	0	11.0	10	3	8	10
Starter	0.00	0	0	0	0	0	0.0	0	0	0	0
Reliever	4.23	6	3	0	66	0	61.2	52	8	38	37
0 Days rest	5.65	3	2	0	17	0	14.1	10	3	10	6
1 or 2 Days rest	3.38	2	1	0	32	0	26.2	22	2	18	21
3+ Days rest	4.35	1	0	0	17	0	20.2	20	3	10	10
Pre-All Star	3.75	5	3	0	39	0	36.0	29	4	23	20
Post-All Star	4.91	1	0	0	27	0	25.2	23	4	15	17

	Avg	AB	H	2B	3B	HR	RBI	BB	SO	OBP	SLG
vs. Left	.247	73	18	4	0	2	8	12	16	.349	.384
vs. Right	.231	147	34	3	0	6	18	26	21	.341	.374
Inning 1-6	.189	37	7	0	0	4	7	3	11	.250	.514
Inning 7+	.246	183	45	7	0	4	19	35	26	.360	.350
None on	.272	103	28	2	0	6	6	20	14	.395	.466
Runners on	.205	117	24	5	0	2	20	18	23	.298	.299
Scoring Posn	.206	63	13	2	0	2	19	15	15	.333	.333
Close & Late	.250	76	19	3	0	4	11	17	9	.375	.447
None on/out	.260	50	13	0	0	2	2	14	7	.422	.380
vs. 1st Batr (relief)	.245	53	13	1	0	3	5	10	11	.359	.434
First Inning Pitched	.231	173	40	6	0	5	18	26	29	.325	.353
First 15 Pitches	.209	153	32	4	0	5	14	22	27	.302	.333
Pitch 16-30	.276	58	16	3	0	0	4	15	9	.432	.328
Pitch 31-45	.444	9	4	0	0	3	8	1	1	.417	1.444
Pitch 46+	.000	0	0	0	0	0	0	0	0	.000	.000
First Pitch	.258	31	8	2	0	1	4	0	0	.333	.419
Ahead on Count	.186	97	18	5	0	1	7	0	31	.182	.268
Behind on Count	.333	48	16	0	0	2	4	16	0	.492	.458
Two Strikes	.170	94	16	4	0	2	10	18	37	.296	.277

Career (1990-1992)

	ERA	W	L	Sv	G	GS	IP	H	HR	BB	SO
Home	3.71	10	4	5	80	0	77.2	59	7	38	53
Away	3.97	5	5	7	69	0	77.0	62	7	52	58
Day	2.86	1	1	3	41	0	50.1	36	7	20	36
Night	4.31	14	8	9	108	0	104.1	85	7	70	75
Grass	4.08	4	0	5	37	0	39.2	32	5	21	34
Turf	3.76	11	9	7	112	0	115.0	89	9	69	77
April	0.48	3	0	0	19	0	18.2	12	0	10	10
May	4.74	1	5	4	24	0	24.2	17	4	16	17
June	3.52	4	0	1	22	0	23.0	23	0	13	16
July	2.39	3	1	2	26	0	26.1	17	3	17	20
August	3.51	1	2	2	24	0	25.2	22	0	13	16
September/October	6.44	3	1	3	34	0	36.1	30	7	21	32
Starter	0.00	0	0	0	0	0	0.0	0	0	0	0
Reliever	3.84	15	9	12	149	0	154.2	121	14	90	111
0 Days rest	3.63	6	4	4	41	0	39.2	28	4	24	21
1 or 2 Days rest	4.19	7	4	5	70	0	68.2	56	7	41	58
3+ Days rest	3.50	2	1	3	38	0	46.1	37	3	25	32
Pre-All Star	3.15	9	5	5	75	0	74.1	59	5	42	49
Post-All Star	4.48	6	4	7	74	0	80.1	62	9	48	62

	Avg	AB	H	2B	3B	HR	RBI	BB	SO	OBP	SLG
vs. Left	.237	198	47	7	0	5	29	25	44	.328	.348
vs. Right	.210	352	74	16	2	9	39	65	67	.332	.344
Inning 1-6	.188	48	9	0	0	4	7	3	14	.235	.438
Inning 7+	.223	502	112	23	2	10	61	87	97	.338	.337
None on	.204	285	58	9	1	10	10	47	60	.322	.347
Runners on	.238	265	63	14	1	4	58	43	51	.338	.343
Scoring Posn	.238	147	35	5	1	4	56	35	33	.365	.367
Close & Late	.223	296	66	14	1	9	45	56	52	.345	.368
None on/out	.205	127	26	3	1	3	3	25	27	.340	.315
vs. 1st Batr (relief)	.244	123	30	5	1	4	12	19	19	.347	.398
First Inning Pitched	.231	403	93	20	2	8	50	56	71	.323	.345
First 15 Pitches	.226	368	83	17	1	8	42	48	67	.312	.342
Pitch 16-30	.194	144	28	5	0	1	9	33	34	.354	.250
Pitch 31-45	.206	34	7	1	1	3	12	9	10	.356	.559
Pitch 46+	.750	4	3	0	0	2	5	0	0	.800	2.250
First Pitch	.296	71	21	6	0	4	13	8	0	.369	.549
Ahead on Count	.155	245	38	7	1	2	20	0	84	.155	.216
Behind on Count	.324	108	35	5	1	2	14	44	0	.523	.444
Two Strikes	.134	262	35	8	1	2	25	38	111	.239	.195

Pitcher vs. Batter (career)

Pitches Best Vs.	Avg	AB	H	2B	3B	HR	RBI	BB	SO	OBP	SLG	Pitches Worst Vs.	Avg	AB	H	2B	3B	HR	RBI	BB	SO	OBP	SLG
Brett Butler	.000	7	0	0	0	0		4	3	.364	.000												
Eddie Murray	.083	12	1	0	0	0	3	1	3	.133	.083												
Paul O'Neill	.100	10	1	1	0	0		2	5	.250	.200												
Bobby Bonilla	.125	8	1	0	0	1	2	2	0	.273	.500												

Dave Otto — Indians

Pitches Left (groundball pitcher)

	ERA	W	L	Sv	G	GS	IP	BB	SO	Avg	H	2B	3B	HR	RBI	OBP	SLG	CG	ShO	Sup	QS	#P/S	SB	CS	GB	FB	G/F
1992 Season	7.06	5	9	0	18	16	80.1	33	32	.333	110	17	0	12	57	.395	.494	0	0	3.59	5	78	11	2	147	83	1.77
Last Five Years	5.24	7	17	0	42	33	199.1	71	92	.302	236	34	4	19	107	.362	.426	1	0	3.88	15	84	18	7	359	181	1.96

1992 Season

	ERA	W	L	Sv	G	GS	IP	H	HR	BB	SO		Avg	AB	H	2B	3B	HR	RBI	BB	SO	OBP	SLG
Home	6.63	3	2	0	8	7	36.2	48	8	14	18	vs. Left	.352	54	19	4	0	1	7	5	3	.407	.481
Away	7.42	2	7	0	10	9	43.2	62	4	19	14	vs. Right	.330	276	91	13	0	11	50	28	29	.392	.496
Starter	6.64	5	9	0	16	16	78.2	105	11	31	32	Scoring Posn	.371	89	33	6	0	6	48	9	6	.424	.640
Reliever	27.00	0	0	0	2	0	1.2	5	1	2	0	Close & Late	.500	8	4	0	0	2	4	1	0	.556	1.250
0-3 Days Rest	0.00	0	0	0	0	0	0.0	0	0	0	0	None on/out	.326	89	29	6	0	2	2	6	9	.368	.461
4 Days Rest	11.05	0	7	0	9	9	36.2	65	8	19	13	First Pitch	.321	53	17	3	0	1	7	0	0	.333	.434
5+ Days Rest	2.79	5	2	0	7	7	42.0	40	3	12	19	Behind on Count	.388	103	40	6	0	6	24	12	0	.448	.621
Pre-All Star	6.38	4	7	0	13	13	67.2	85	8	26	31	Ahead on Count	.236	106	25	3	0	2	16	0	31	.236	.321
Post-All Star	10.66	1	2	0	5	3	12.2	25	4	7	1	Two Strikes	.275	109	30	7	0	2	18	21	32	.392	.394

Spike Owen — Expos

Bats Both

	Avg	G	AB	R	H	2B	3B	HR	RBI	BB	SO	HBP	GDP	SB	CS	OBP	SLG	IBB	SH	SF	#Pit	#P/PA	GB	FB	G/F
1992 Season	.269	122	386	52	104	16	3	7	40	50	30	0	10	9	4	.348	.381	3	4	6	1736	3.93	157	129	1.22
Last Five Years	.247	641	1957	238	484	93	21	26	160	265	222	6	45	22	19	.336	.356	51	23	19	8620	3.84	766	632	1.21

1992 Season

	Avg	AB	H	2B	3B	HR	RBI	BB	SO	OBP	SLG		Avg	AB	H	2B	3B	HR	RBI	BB	SO	OBP	SLG
vs. Left	.286	161	46	10	2	4	23	16	11	.346	.447	Scoring Posn	.319	91	29	4	0	0	28	16	6	.398	.363
vs. Right	.258	225	58	6	1	3	17	34	19	.350	.333	Close & Late	.368	57	21	4	0	0	8	13	2	.479	.439
Groundball	.262	130	34	5	1	0	16	20	14	.351	.315	None on/out	.205	88	18	4	0	2	2	15	3	.320	.318
Flyball	.280	93	26	5	0	5	11	15	4	.376	.495	Batting #2	.319	91	29	4	1	0	9	9	5	.373	.385
Home	.243	173	42	9	0	3	19	23	11	.323	.347	Batting #8	.260	177	46	7	1	5	19	25	13	.348	.395
Away	.291	213	62	7	3	4	21	27	19	.369	.408	Other	.246	118	29	5	1	2	12	16	12	.331	.356
Day	.236	123	29	3	1	4	14	18	13	.329	.374	April	.246	69	17	4	1	1	9	7	8	.308	.377
Night	.285	263	75	13	2	3	26	32	17	.358	.384	May	.239	67	16	2	0	4	8	7	5	.311	.448
Grass	.269	104	28	1	0	3	11	17	8	.369	.365	June	.294	68	20	5	1	1	8	10	3	.380	.441
Turf	.270	282	76	15	3	4	29	33	22	.341	.387	July	.227	44	10	0	0	1	7	5	5	.327	.227
First Pitch	.241	29	7	1	0	1	2	2	0	.290	.379	August	.394	66	26	5	1	0	10	8	5	.453	.500
Ahead on Count	.308	117	36	6	1	3	17	31	0	.447	.453	September/October	.208	72	15	0	0	1	4	4	4	.310	.250
Behind on Count	.258	120	31	4	1	2	8	0	18	.256	.358	Pre-All Star	.254	240	61	11	2	6	26	30	21	.332	.392
Two Strikes	.218	165	36	3	2	0	10	18	30	.292	.261	Post-All Star	.295	146	43	5	1	1	14	20	9	.375	.363

1992 By Position

Position	Avg	AB	H	2B	3B	HR	RBI	BB	SO	OBP	SLG	G	GS	Innings	PO	A	E	DP	Fld Pct	Rng Fctr	In Zone	Outs	Zone Rtg	MLB Zone
As ss	.270	381	103	16	3	7	40	49	30	.349	.383	116	112	972.0	188	300	9	45	.982	4.52	374	323	.864	.885

Last Five Years

	Avg	AB	H	2B	3B	HR	RBI	BB	SO	OBP	SLG		Avg	AB	H	2B	3B	HR	RBI	BB	SO	OBP	SLG
vs. Left	.281	790	222	57	7	14	74	79	90	.345	.424	Scoring Posn	.232	444	103	19	4	2	121	107	57	.371	.306
vs. Right	.225	1167	262	36	14	12	86	186	132	.330	.310	Close & Late	.271	358	97	14	3	8	39	49	51	.354	.394
Groundball	.231	636	147	29	7	3	58	97	65	.331	.313	None on/out	.237	468	111	21	8	6	62	42	39	.329	.355
Flyball	.226	508	115	23	4	13	38	67	67	.317	.364	Batting #2	.294	310	91	20	3	3	26	27	39	.346	.406
Home	.245	854	209	43	6	13	76	122	92	.337	.355	Batting #8	.238	1293	306	56	16	17	109	197	144	.338	.346
Away	.249	1103	275	50	15	13	84	143	130	.335	.357	Other	.240	354	85	17	2	6	25	41	39	.320	.350
Day	.260	605	157	33	10	12	55	77	77	.343	.407	April	.259	297	77	18	6	5	32	34	30	.331	.411
Night	.242	1352	327	60	11	14	105	188	145	.333	.334	May	.219	333	73	11	0	9	32	60	39	.338	.333
Grass	.235	707	166	29	6	9	55	95	87	.325	.331	June	.241	398	96	27	3	6	30	66	38	.348	.369
Turf	.254	1250	318	64	15	17	105	170	135	.342	.370	July	.244	246	60	9	3	2	13	38	31	.348	.329
First Pitch	.269	186	50	11	1	5	19	31	0	.373	.419	August	.276	322	89	15	4	2	32	38	45	.351	.366
Ahead on Count	.330	515	170	36	9	8	56	150	0	.481	.482	September/October	.247	361	89	13	5	2	21	29	39	.301	.327
Behind on Count	.217	591	128	22	4	5	37	7	122	.227	.293	Pre-All Star	.243	1160	282	61	11	22	102	179	126	.344	.372
Two Strikes	.202	860	174	32	8	7	57	20	222	.263	.283	Post-All Star	.253	797	202	32	10	4	58	86	96	.324	.334

Batter vs. Pitcher (since 1984)

Hits Best Against	Avg	AB	H	2B	3B	HR	RBI	BB	SO	OBP	SLG	Hits Worst Against	Avg	AB	H	2B	3B	HR	RBI	BB	SO	OBP	SLG
Juan Agosto	.545	11	6	2	1	1	3	0	0	.545	1.182	Mike Bielecki	.000	22	0	0	0	0	0	1	5	.043	.000
Dave Schmidt	.529	17	9	1	1	1	6	0	1	.529	.882	Orel Hershiser	.000	13	0	0	0	0	0	2	4	.133	.000
Tom Browning	.500	24	12	4	1	1	2	1	1	.520	.875	Ramon Martinez	.000	10	0	0	0	0	1	2	4	.167	.000
Greg Swindell	.500	12	6	1	0	0	1	1	0	.538	.583	Tom Candiotti	.034	29	1	0	0	0	0	2	2	.097	.034
Danny Darwin	.474	19	9	3	0	0	3	3	2	.522	.632	Tim Leary	.059	17	1	1	0	0	0	1	1	.111	.059

Mike Pagliarulo — Twins
Bats Left

	Avg	G	AB	R	H	2B	3B	HR	RBI	BB	SO	HBP	GDP	SB	CS	OBP	SLG	IBB	SH	SF	#Pit	#P/PA	GB	FB	G/F
1992 Season	.200	42	105	10	21	4	0	0	9	1	17	1	1	1	0	.213	.238	0	0	1	330	3.06	44	34	1.29
Last Five Years	.234	540	1683	154	393	84	3	35	180	135	324	12	32	7	6	.293	.349	19	6	13	6645	3.61	583	500	1.17

1992 Season

	Avg	AB	H	2B	3B	HR	RBI	BB	SO	OBP	SLG		Avg	AB	H	2B	3B	HR	RBI	BB	SO	OBP	SLG
vs. Left	.167	6	1	0	0	0	0	0	2	.167	.167	Scoring Posn	.231	26	6	1	0	0	9	1	4	.250	.269
vs. Right	.202	99	20	4	0	0	9	1	15	.216	.242	Close & Late	.143	14	2	0	0	0	0	0	2	.143	.143
Home	.217	46	10	2	0	0	5	1	8	.229	.261	None on/out	.222	27	6	2	0	0	0	0	5	.250	.296
Away	.186	59	11	2	0	0	4	0	9	.200	.220	Batting #8	.169	71	12	1	0	0	5	0	12	.178	.183
First Pitch	.263	19	5	2	0	0	2	0	0	.263	.368	Batting #9	.250	24	6	2	0	0	3	1	4	.280	.333
Ahead on Count	.333	24	8	2	0	0	6	1	0	.360	.417	Other	.300	10	3	1	0	0	1	0	1	.300	.400
Behind on Count	.211	38	8	0	0	0	1	0	8	.231	.211	Pre-All Star	.118	17	2	0	0	0	1	0	1	.118	.118
Two Strikes	.128	39	5	0	0	0	1	0	17	.125	.128	Post-All Star	.216	88	19	4	0	0	8	1	16	.231	.261

Last Five Years

	Avg	AB	H	2B	3B	HR	RBI	BB	SO	OBP	SLG		Avg	AB	H	2B	3B	HR	RBI	BB	SO	OBP	SLG
vs. Left	.206	286	59	10	1	9	39	27	73	.281	.343	Scoring Posn	.233	430	100	18	1	9	138	50	89	.308	.342
vs. Right	.239	1397	334	74	2	26	141	108	251	.295	.351	Close & Late	.237	262	62	15	1	2	16	27	58	.307	.324
Groundball	.230	505	116	26	0	10	50	35	103	.281	.341	None on/out	.210	395	83	16	1	8	8	27	86	.264	.316
Flyball	.226	412	93	26	1	10	44	30	92	.283	.367	Batting #6	.224	517	116	27	0	11	47	41	104	.283	.340
Home	.234	790	185	35	2	18	98	66	168	.297	.352	Batting #7	.220	528	116	22	1	14	60	46	101	.285	.345
Away	.233	893	208	49	1	17	82	69	156	.289	.347	Other	.252	638	161	35	2	10	73	48	119	.307	.361
Day	.230	500	115	26	1	13	49	42	97	.296	.364	April	.184	201	37	6	1	6	29	16	45	.250	.313
Night	.235	1183	278	58	2	22	131	93	227	.292	.343	May	.259	301	78	22	0	7	35	30	51	.326	.402
Grass	.221	1125	249	51	3	26	117	97	222	.287	.341	June	.227	304	69	16	1	5	28	21	56	.280	.336
Turf	.258	558	144	33	0	9	63	38	102	.306	.366	July	.276	246	68	15	1	2	23	26	48	.350	.370
First Pitch	.311	286	89	22	1	8	43	6	0	.327	.479	August	.218	349	76	12	0	5	30	21	72	.261	.295
Ahead on Count	.296	363	108	22	0	10	46	66	0	.409	.444	September/October	.230	282	65	13	0	10	35	21	52	.289	.383
Behind on Count	.201	582	117	23	2	10	44	0	180	.206	.299	Pre-All Star	.233	889	207	51	2	19	99	77	170	.297	.359
Two Strikes	.163	755	123	30	2	8	51	60	324	.224	.240	Post-All Star	.234	794	186	33	1	16	81	58	154	.288	.339

Batter vs. Pitcher (career)

Hits Best Against	Avg	AB	H	2B	3B	HR	RBI	BB	SO	OBP	SLG	Hits Worst Against	Avg	AB	H	2B	3B	HR	RBI	BB	SO	OBP	SLG
Floyd Bannister	.600	10	6	1	0	2	6	1	0	.583	1.300	Curt Young	.063	16	1	0	0	0	0	1	4	.118	.063
Jeff Russell	.500	10	5	0	0	2	9	2	2	.583	1.100	Bert Blyleven	.065	31	2	0	0	0	1	2	5	.121	.065
Jay Howell	.385	13	5	2	0	0	3	1	3	.429	.538	Jose Rijo	.100	10	1	0	0	0	0	1	1	.182	.100
Eric King	.368	19	7	3	0	1	5	2	2	.429	.684	Jimmy Key	.111	18	2	0	0	0	0	1	7	.158	.111
Mike Henneman	.308	13	4	2	0	1	2	0	4	.308	.692	Dave Schmidt	.118	17	2	0	0	0	2	0	3	.118	.118

Tom Pagnozzi — Cardinals
Bats Right

	Avg	G	AB	R	H	2B	3B	HR	RBI	BB	SO	HBP	GDP	SB	CS	OBP	SLG	IBB	SH	SF	#Pit	#P/PA	GB	FB	G/F
1992 Season	.249	139	485	33	121	26	3	7	44	28	64	1	15	2	5	.290	.359	9	6	3	1666	3.22	176	142	1.24
Last Five Years	.257	481	1439	111	370	76	8	11	142	95	215	7	37	12	19	.304	.344	19	14	12	5233	3.37	525	401	1.31

1992 Season

	Avg	AB	H	2B	3B	HR	RBI	BB	SO	OBP	SLG		Avg	AB	H	2B	3B	HR	RBI	BB	SO	OBP	SLG
vs. Left	.244	176	43	9	1	5	15	11	28	.287	.392	Scoring Posn	.242	128	31	8	1	1	32	16	24	.324	.344
vs. Right	.252	309	78	17	2	2	29	17	36	.292	.340	Close & Late	.198	111	22	4	0	2	7	7	19	.252	.288
Groundball	.250	204	51	12	1	3	17	14	17	.301	.363	None on/out	.174	109	19	3	1	1	1	6	20	.217	.248
Flyball	.200	85	17	4	0	1	7	5	20	.239	.282	Batting #7	.263	243	64	16	1	4	26	12	31	.297	.387
Home	.247	223	55	9	2	3	18	13	32	.291	.345	Batting #8	.237	236	56	10	2	3	18	14	33	.281	.335
Away	.252	262	66	17	1	4	26	15	32	.289	.370	Other	.167	6	1	0	0	0	0	2	0	.375	.167
Day	.260	123	32	9	1	1	15	9	11	.308	.374	April	.301	73	22	5	1	0	8	2	9	.320	.397
Night	.246	362	89	17	2	6	29	19	53	.284	.354	May	.289	90	26	5	1	1	7	6	13	.333	.400
Grass	.313	128	40	13	1	1	13	7	12	.343	.453	June	.293	75	22	5	0	2	10	8	7	.357	.440
Turf	.227	357	81	13	2	6	31	21	52	.271	.325	July	.226	84	19	4	1	3	9	4	13	.261	.405
First Pitch	.253	79	20	4	2	1	5	9	0	.330	.392	August	.174	86	15	5	0	0	5	5	13	.217	.233
Ahead on Count	.365	104	38	9	1	4	20	12	0	.424	.587	September/October	.221	77	17	2	0	1	5	3	9	.256	.286
Behind on Count	.202	188	38	8	0	2	14	0	41	.205	.277	Pre-All Star	.282	273	77	16	3	4	28	16	33	.321	.407
Two Strikes	.193	187	36	7	0	1	7	8	64	.230	.246	Post-All Star	.208	212	44	10	0	3	16	12	31	.251	.297

1992 By Position

Position	Avg	AB	H	2B	3B	HR	RBI	BB	SO	OBP	SLG		G	GS	Innings	PO	A	E	DP	Fld Pct	Rng Fctr	In Zone	Outs	Zone Rtg	MLB Zone
As c	.251	482	121	26	3	7	44	27	63	.290	.361		138	131	1189.0	688	53	1	10	.999	---	---	---	---	---

Last Five Years

	Avg	AB	H	2B	3B	HR	RBI	BB	SO	OBP	SLG		Avg	AB	H	2B	3B	HR	RBI	BB	SO	OBP	SLG
vs. Left	.250	604	151	31	3	8	60	47	102	.303	.351	Scoring Posn	.252	385	97	22	3	2	121	39	75	.315	.340
vs. Right	.262	835	219	45	5	3	82	48	113	.305	.339	Close & Late	.201	294	59	9	0	2	22	17	56	.250	.252
Groundball	.236	537	127	27	1	4	44	40	69	.291	.313	None on/out	.222	343	76	14	2	2	2	22	49	.270	.292
Flyball	.237	300	71	15	2	1	24	25	58	.296	.310	Batting #7	.255	811	207	46	6	6	86	51	117	.300	.349
Home	.249	666	166	30	4	7	59	54	97	.310	.338	Batting #8	.268	503	135	24	2	5	42	38	71	.322	.354
Away	.264	773	204	46	4	4	83	41	118	.299	.349	Other	.224	125	28	6	0	0	14	6	27	.256	.272

Last Five Years

	Avg	AB	H	2B	3B	HR	RBI	BB	SO	OBP	SLG		Avg	AB	H	2B	3B	HR	RBI	BB	SO	OBP	SLG
Day	.261	452	118	27	3	4	60	35	58	.312	.361	April	.259	158	41	6	1	0	12	6	21	.263	.310
Night	.255	987	252	49	5	7	82	60	157	.300	.336	May	.274	237	65	13	2	2	27	20	32	.336	.371
Grass	.274	368	101	26	3	1	46	18	55	.308	.370	June	.236	250	59	13	1	4	27	15	39	.279	.344
Turf	.251	1071	269	50	5	10	96	77	160	.303	.335	July	.256	223	57	9	3	3	28	20	34	.318	.363
First Pitch	.283	258	73	16	4	1	26	17	0	.330	.388	August	.221	261	62	19	1	0	19	17	47	.262	.295
Ahead on Count	.343	277	95	18	2	5	38	45	0	.431	.477	September/October	.297	290	86	16	0	2	29	17	42	.340	.372
Behind on Count	.226	509	116	23	1	4	45	0	136	.230	.301	Pre-All Star	.262	715	187	35	5	7	75	42	102	.304	.354
Two Strikes	.184	587	108	23	0	3	43	32	215	.230	.239	Post-All Star	.253	724	183	41	3	4	67	53	113	.304	.334

Batter vs. Pitcher (career)

Hits Best Against	Avg	AB	H	2B	3B	HR	RBI	BB	SO	OBP	SLG	Hits Worst Against	Avg	AB	H	2B	3B	HR	RBI	BB	SO	OBP	SLG
Dwight Gooden	.565	23	13	2	0	0	4	0	1	.565	.652	John Franco	.000	12	0	0	0	0	0	2	5	.143	.000
Terry Mulholland	.478	23	11	2	0	1	8	0	3	.458	.696	Bill Landrum	.000	11	0	0	0	0	0	0	2	.000	.000
Tom Browning	.455	11	5	2	0	0	0	2	1	.538	.636	Norm Charlton	.000	10	0	0	0	0	0	1	2	.091	.000
John Smiley	.368	19	7	3	0	1	3	2	5	.429	.684	Zane Smith	.067	23	2	0	0	0	1	2	4	.160	.067
Jose Rijo	.364	11	4	2	0	1	2	1	5	.417	.818	Tom Glavine	.091	11	1	0	1	0	0	0	2	.091	.182

Vince Palacios — Pirates
Pitches Right (flyball pitcher)

	ERA	W	L	Sv	G	GS	IP	BB	SO	Avg	H	2B	3B	HR	RBI	OBP	SLG	GF	IR	IRS	Hld	SvOp	SB	CS	GB	FB	G/F
1992 Season	4.25	3	2	0	20	8	53.0	27	33	.280	56	10	1	1	23	.364	.355	4	5	1	0	0	2	4	61	69	0.88
Last Five Years	3.98	10	7	6	70	18	174.0	82	120	.243	157	24	4	16	78	.328	.367	16	26	10	6	8	9	10	176	231	0.76

1992 Season

	ERA	W	L	Sv	G	GS	IP	H	HR	BB	SO		Avg	AB	H	2B	3B	HR	RBI	BB	SO	OBP	SLG
Home	5.27	1	1	0	10	4	27.1	32	0	15	18	vs. Left	.328	122	40	6	1	0	10	16	14	.406	.393
Away	3.16	2	1	0	10	4	25.2	24	1	12	15	vs. Right	.205	78	16	4	0	1	13	11	19	.300	.295
Starter	4.54	1	2	0	8	8	35.2	39	1	14	18	Scoring Posn	.322	59	19	3	0	1	22	11	14	.423	.424
Reliever	3.63	2	0	0	12	0	17.1	17	0	13	15	Close & Late	.286	7	2	1	0	0	0	1	1	.375	.429
0 Days rest	0.00	0	0	0	1	0	2.0	0	0	2	1	None on/out	.298	47	14	3	0	0	0	8	7	.400	.362
1 or 2 Days rest	2.79	2	0	0	7	0	9.2	8	0	7	7	First Pitch	.276	29	8	0	0	0	4	0	0	.276	.276
3+ Days rest	6.35	0	0	0	4	0	5.2	9	0	4	7	Behind on Count	.400	40	16	3	0	0	6	16	0	.571	.475
Pre-All Star	4.25	3	2	0	20	8	53.0	56	1	27	33	Ahead on Count	.205	88	18	4	0	1	8	0	30	.205	.284
Post-All Star	0.00	0	0	0	0	0	0.0	0	0	0	0	Two Strikes	.182	88	16	2	0	1	6	11	33	.273	.239

Donn Pall — White Sox
Pitches Right (groundball pitcher)

	ERA	W	L	Sv	G	GS	IP	BB	SO	Avg	H	2B	3B	HR	RBI	OBP	SLG	GF	IR	IRS	Hld	SvOp	SB	CS	GB	FB	G/F
1992 Season	4.93	5	2	1	39	0	73.0	27	27	.272	79	13	0	9	43	.335	.410	12	16	4	2	2	10	1	117	83	1.41
Career (1988-1992)	3.49	19	16	9	216	0	335.2	98	180	.260	330	55	5	33	167	.320	.389	30	183	66	36	16	28	9	573	302	1.90

1992 Season

	ERA	W	L	Sv	G	GS	IP	H	HR	BB	SO		Avg	AB	H	2B	3B	HR	RBI	BB	SO	OBP	SLG
Home	5.26	4	0	1	20	0	39.1	45	5	13	15	vs. Left	.291	103	30	2	0	2	13	13	12	.373	.369
Away	4.54	1	2	0	19	0	33.2	34	4	14	12	vs. Right	.262	187	49	11	0	7	30	14	15	.314	.403
Starter	0.00	0	0	0	0	0	0.0	0	0	0	0	Scoring Posn	.293	75	22	3	0	4	35	15	9	.404	.493
Reliever	4.93	5	2	1	39	0	73.0	79	9	27	27	Close & Late	.269	78	21	4	0	0	6	13	7	.370	.321
0 Days rest	10.80	1	0	0	3	0	5.0	12	2	1	0	None on/out	.217	69	15	3	0	1	2	6	2	.250	.304
1 or 2 Days rest	5.19	2	1	0	11	0	17.1	22	1	9	8	First Pitch	.314	51	16	3	0	0	7	5	0	.383	.373
3+ Days rest	4.26	2	1	1	25	0	50.2	45	6	17	19	Behind on Count	.262	61	16	1	0	2	9	13	0	.387	.377
Pre-All Star	5.21	3	2	0	24	0	38.0	44	6	17	17	Ahead on Count	.242	120	29	4	0	6	24	0	21	.242	.425
Post-All Star	4.63	2	0	1	15	0	35.0	35	3	10	10	Two Strikes	.220	109	24	4	0	4	15	7	27	.280	.367

Career (1988-1992)

	ERA	W	L	Sv	G	GS	IP	H	HR	BB	SO		Avg	AB	H	2B	3B	HR	RBI	BB	SO	OBP	SLG
Home	3.80	10	5	5	109	0	170.2	171	15	46	101	vs. Left	.262	530	139	22	4	9	60	46	82	.323	.370
Away	3.16	9	11	4	107	0	165.0	159	18	52	79	vs. Right	.258	739	191	33	1	24	107	52	98	.317	.403
Day	3.06	6	4	3	64	0	111.2	98	13	30	45	Inning 1-6	.233	356	83	16	1	7	64	27	61	.293	.343
Night	3.70	13	12	6	152	0	224.0	232	20	68	135	Inning 7+	.271	913	247	39	4	26	103	71	119	.330	.407
Grass	3.61	18	12	8	184	0	282.0	282	28	87	158	Runners on	.259	656	170	27	4	18	149	55	81	.324	.383
Turf	2.85	1	4	1	32	0	53.2	48	5	11	22	Scoring Posn	.259	363	94	14	1	10	133	47	56	.340	.386
April	2.16	1	0	2	32	0	50.0	44	3	10	33	Close & Late	.259	406	105	13	3	10	38	45	52	.338	.379
May	3.38	4	4	0	39	0	48.0	44	2	16	29	None on/out	.271	284	77	11	2	9	9	17	38	.324	.419
June	3.26	2	2	1	36	0	47.0	44	6	15	16	vs. 1st Batr (relief)	.212	193	41	2	3	3	27	12	29	.269	.306
July	4.19	6	3	4	33	0	58.0	56	4	20	28	First 15 Pitches	.264	689	182	27	5	16	122	59	97	.329	.398
August	3.54	4	6	1	42	0	76.1	81	8	20	44	Pitch 16-30	.249	397	99	15	0	10	43	33	70	.312	.363
September/October	4.15	2	1	1	34	0	56.1	61	10	17	30	Pitch 31-45	.253	150	38	9	0	6	16	15	18	.323	.433
Starter	0.00	0	0	0	0	0	0.0	0	0	0	0	Pitch 46+	.172	29	5	3	0	0	1	2	2	.226	.276
Reliever	3.49	19	16	9	216	0	335.2	330	33	98	180	First Pitch	.317	221	70	11	1	3	30	18	0	.382	.416
0 Days rest	5.33	2	1	0	22	0	25.1	29	3	9	12	Ahead on Count	.207	545	113	20	0	16	75	0	158	.218	.332
1 or 2 Days rest	3.26	10	10	3	103	0	154.2	165	15	46	92	Behind on Count	.320	266	85	14	1	10	40	44	0	.419	.492
3+ Days rest	3.41	7	5	6	91	0	155.2	137	14	43	76												
Pre-All Star	3.09	8	6	4	119	0	163.0	147	12	49	86												

Career (1988-1992)

	ERA	W	L	Sv	G	GS	IP	H	HR	BB	SO		Avg	AB	H	2B	3B	HR	RBI	BB	SO	OBP	SLG
Post-All Star	3.86	11	10	5	97	0	172.2	183	21	49	94	Two Strikes	176	522	92	18	2	13	51	35	180	231	293

Pitcher vs. Batter (career)

Pitches Best Vs.	Avg	AB	H	2B	3B	HR	RBI	BB	SO	OBP	SLG	Pitches Worst Vs.	Avg	AB	H	2B	3B	HR	RBI	BB	SO	OBP	SLG
Kirby Puckett	.000	9	0	0	0	0	1	1	1	.250	.000	Jody Reed	.500	10	5	0	0	0	1	2	0	.583	.500
Kevin Seitzer	.083	12	1	1	0	0	0	1	0	.154	.167	Mark McGwire	.417	12	5	1	0	1	2	2	1	.500	.750
Gary Gaetti	.091	11	1	0	0	0	0	0	1	.091	.091	Rickey Henderson	.400	10	4	1	0	0	3	1	0	.455	.500
Terry Steinbach	.100	10	1	0	0	0	0	1	2	.182	.100	Rob Deer	.385	13	5	0	0	3	3	1	0	.385	1.077
Tony Phillips	.125	16	2	0	0	0	0	2	2	.222	.125	Wade Boggs	.364	11	4	0	0	0	1	4	2	.533	.364

Rafael Palmeiro — Rangers
Bats Left

	Avg	G	AB	R	H	2B	3B	HR	RBI	BB	SO	HBP	GDP	SB	CS	OBP	SLG	IBB	SH	SF	#Pit	#P/PA	GB	FB	G/F
1992 Season	.268	159	608	84	163	27	4	22	85	72	83	10	10	2	3	.352	.434	8	5	6	2646	3.80	192	213	0.90
Last Five Years	.299	780	2976	422	889	175	22	78	379	261	296	28	82	25	14	.361	.451	33	13	29	11792	3.56	1089	951	1.15

1992 Season

	Avg	AB	H	2B	3B	HR	RBI	BB	SO	OBP	SLG		Avg	AB	H	2B	3B	HR	RBI	BB	SO	OBP	SLG
vs. Left	.281	178	50	7	3	5	27	20	27	.365	.438	Scoring Posn	.270	148	40	7	1	4	60	30	21	.390	.412
vs. Right	.263	430	113	20	1	17	58	52	56	.347	.433	Close & Late	.196	97	19	2	1	3	11	9	15	.273	.330
Groundball	.245	155	38	6	1	6	19	13	22	.316	.413	None on/out	.260	123	32	6	1	4	4	10	15	.326	.423
Flyball	.345	165	57	10	2	9	37	23	18	.427	.594	Batting #2	.282	181	51	9	1	8	22	20	23	.355	.475
Home	.263	297	78	11	3	8	33	39	38	.354	.401	Batting #3	.276	322	89	15	3	12	53	38	44	.364	.453
Away	.273	311	85	16	1	14	52	33	45	.350	.466	Other	.219	105	23	3	0	2	10	14	16	.311	.305
Day	.267	116	31	4	0	3	20	14	14	.346	.379	April	.235	85	20	5	1	3	13	9	15	.333	.424
Night	.268	492	132	23	4	19	65	58	69	.353	.447	May	.305	105	32	5	1	3	14	17	8	.408	.457
Grass	.267	510	136	20	4	19	72	59	61	.347	.433	June	.218	101	22	5	0	2	12	12	18	.304	.327
Turf	.276	98	27	7	0	3	13	13	22	.379	.439	July	.303	109	33	3	2	4	17	6	12	.336	.477
First Pitch	.343	67	23	3	0	3	11	6	0	.408	.522	August	.230	113	26	2	0	3	10	13	19	.318	.327
Ahead on Count	.285	144	41	7	1	6	19	38	0	.432	.472	September/October	.316	95	30	7	0	7	19	15	11	.411	.611
Behind on Count	.273	220	60	10	1	9	34	0	50	.292	.450	Pre-All Star	.276	337	93	17	4	8	44	42	46	.364	.421
Two Strikes	.216	269	58	13	2	9	37	28	83	.298	.379	Post-All Star	.258	271	70	10	0	14	41	30	37	.337	.450

1992 By Position

Position	Avg	AB	H	2B	3B	HR	RBI	BB	SO	OBP	SLG	G	GS	Innings	PO	A	E	DP	Fld Pct	Rng Fctr	In Zone	Outs	Zone Rtg	MLB Zone
As 1b	.269	603	162	27	4	21	82	70	83	.352	.431	156	154	1382.2	1251	142	7	130	.995	---	311	263	.846	.843

Last Five Years

	Avg	AB	H	2B	3B	HR	RBI	BB	SO	OBP	SLG		Avg	AB	H	2B	3B	HR	RBI	BB	SO	OBP	SLG
vs. Left	.296	889	263	43	9	23	124	62	94	.345	.442	Scoring Posn	.273	721	197	41	6	10	270	122	86	.372	.388
vs. Right	.300	2087	626	132	13	55	255	219	202	.368	.455	Close & Late	.260	485	126	24	4	14	55	39	54	.315	.412
Groundball	.292	863	252	45	7	21	96	73	92	.352	.433	None on/out	.291	588	171	33	4	18	18	37	53	.338	.452
Flyball	.321	672	216	41	9	19	101	74	56	.390	.494	Batting #2	.289	1002	290	53	9	32	109	83	115	.349	.456
Home	.295	1443	425	77	15	41	185	157	149	.366	.454	Batting #3	.297	1363	405	80	10	33	199	129	130	.360	.443
Away	.303	1533	464	98	7	37	194	124	147	.357	.448	Other	.318	611	194	42	3	13	71	69	51	.384	.460
Day	.301	814	245	53	5	20	114	68	72	.355	.452	April	.299	384	115	29	3	12	59	39	41	.367	.484
Night	.298	2162	644	122	17	58	265	213	224	.364	.451	May	.335	535	179	36	3	12	65	45	46	.387	.480
Grass	.298	2433	724	124	21	71	327	236	242	.362	.453	June	.283	544	154	31	1	11	61	40	54	.338	.404
Turf	.304	543	165	51	1	7	52	45	54	.361	.440	July	.297	495	147	17	5	18	65	40	46	.352	.461
First Pitch	.336	402	135	29	4	9	53	16	0	.364	.495	August	.276	539	149	28	6	10	61	54	61	.343	.406
Ahead on Count	.330	792	261	58	6	30	113	169	0	.444	.532	September/October	.303	479	145	34	4	15	68	63	48	.384	.484
Behind on Count	.273	1000	273	49	6	26	126	0	170	.280	.412	Pre-All Star	.304	1630	496	101	11	40	205	140	157	.362	.453
Two Strikes	.253	1153	292	60	8	23	133	85	296	.309	.379	Post-All Star	.292	1346	393	74	11	38	174	141	139	.360	.448

Batter vs. Pitcher (career)

Hits Best Against	Avg	AB	H	2B	3B	HR	RBI	BB	SO	OBP	SLG	Hits Worst Against	Avg	AB	H	2B	3B	HR	RBI	BB	SO	OBP	SLG
Mike Jackson	.778	9	7	1	0	2	3	2	1	.818	1.556	Jose Mesa	.000	9	0	0	0	0	2	3	1	.214	.000
Bob Milacki	.571	14	8	2	0	1	4	4	0	.667	.929	Randy Johnson	.059	17	1	0	0	0	0	0	2	.059	.059
Mark Leiter	.538	13	7	2	0	2	5	3	0	.625	1.154	Mike Flanagan	.071	14	1	0	0	0	1	1	1	.133	.071
Kevin Gross	.429	14	6	2	1	1	5	3	0	.529	.929	Mike Mussina	.071	14	1	0	0	0	0	0	2	.071	.071
Todd Stottlemyre	.400	20	8	0	2	2	5	6	1	.538	.900	Rick Honeycutt	.105	19	2	0	0	0	0	0	2	.190	.105

Dean Palmer — Rangers
Bats Right (flyball hitter)

	Avg	G	AB	R	H	2B	3B	HR	RBI	BB	SO	HBP	GDP	SB	CS	OBP	SLG	IBB	SH	SF	#Pit	#P/PA	GB	FB	G/F
1992 Season	.229	152	541	74	124	25	0	26	72	62	154	4	8	10	4	.311	.420	2	2	4	2474	4.05	127	173	0.73
Career (1989-1992)	.213	249	828	112	176	36	2	41	110	94	264	7	12	10	6	.297	.409	2	3	5	3824	4.09	185	265	0.70

1992 Season

	Avg	AB	H	2B	3B	HR	RBI	BB	SO	OBP	SLG		Avg	AB	H	2B	3B	HR	RBI	BB	SO	OBP	SLG
vs. Left	.252	143	36	7	0	8	20	18	41	.333	.469	Scoring Posn	.185	124	23	3	0	3	37	14	36	.266	.282
vs. Right	.221	398	88	18	0	18	52	44	113	.303	.402	Close & Late	.221	95	21	4	0	5	11	14	23	.321	.421
Groundball	.285	130	37	6	0	10	25	16	30	.367	.562	None on/out	.304	115	35	11	0	4	4	16	22	.394	.504
Flyball	.224	147	33	11	0	8	22	21	46	.325	.463	Batting #2	.270	196	53	10	0	11	36	29	47	.365	.490

336

1992 Season

	Avg	AB	H	2B	3B	HR	RBI	BB	SO	OBP	SLG		Avg	AB	H	2B	3B	HR	RBI	BB	SO	OBP	SLG
Home	.242	264	64	12	0	11	34	35	76	.337	.413	Batting #6	.221	181	40	10	0	7	18	21	57	.302	.392
Away	.217	277	60	13	0	15	38	27	78	.286	.426	Other	.189	164	31	5	0	8	18	12	50	.251	.366
Day	.204	113	23	5	0	4	11	9	33	.268	.354	April	.250	76	19	2	0	5	13	14	26	.363	.474
Night	.236	428	101	20	0	22	61	53	121	.322	.437	May	.218	101	22	10	0	3	12	3	34	.252	.406
Grass	.217	447	97	18	0	18	51	53	128	.303	.378	June	.277	94	26	5	0	4	19	14	23	.369	.457
Turf	.287	94	27	7	0	8	21	9	26	.349	.617	July	.211	90	19	2	0	5	11	16	21	.330	.400
First Pitch	.327	49	16	1	0	6	12	2	0	.353	.714	August	.218	78	17	3	0	5	7	5	20	.274	.449
Ahead on Count	.327	101	33	9	0	6	19	32	0	.489	.594	September/October	.206	102	21	3	0	4	10	10	30	.277	.353
Behind on Count	.210	186	39	9	0	7	23	0	72	.218	.371	Pre-All Star	.253	312	79	17	0	16	53	39	98	.338	.462
Two Strikes	.126	293	37	6	0	7	24	29	154	.206	.218	Post-All Star	.197	229	45	8	0	10	19	23	56	.273	.362

1992 By Position

Position	Avg	AB	H	2B	3B	HR	RBI	BB	SO	OBP	SLG	G	GS	Innings	PO	A	E	DP	Fld Pct	Rng Fctr	In Zone	Outs	Zone Rtg	MLB Zone
As 3b	.227	537	122	25	0	25	70	60	153	.307	.413	150	143	1272.0	124	253	22	24	.945	2.67	349	278	.797	.841

Career (1989-1992)

	Avg	AB	H	2B	3B	HR	RBI	BB	SO	OBP	SLG		Avg	AB	H	2B	3B	HR	RBI	BB	SO	OBP	SLG
vs. Left	.247	235	58	12	0	17	36	29	76	.328	.515	Scoring Posn	.196	184	36	4	0	9	63	23	60	.288	.364
vs. Right	.199	593	118	24	2	24	74	65	186	.284	.368	Close & Late	.238	143	34	6	1	10	23	19	45	.325	.503
Groundball	.241	199	48	7	2	13	33	25	56	.333	.492	None on/out	.252	202	51	15	0	9	9	25		.341	.460
Flyball	.212	212	45	14	0	12	35	27	73	.304	.448	Batting #6	.210	252	53	12	1	10	27	32	85	.299	.385
Home	.208	389	81	16	1	17	46	54	127	.313	.386	Batting #7	.183	219	40	7	1	12	27	18	76	.247	.388
Away	.216	439	95	20	1	24	64	40	137	.262	.431	Other	.232	357	83	17	0	19	56	44	103	.324	.440
Day	.215	181	39	10	1	7	22	15	60	.281	.396	April	.250	76	19	2	0	5	13	14	26	.363	.474
Night	.212	647	137	26	1	34	88	79	204	.301	.413	May	.218	101	22	10	0	3	12	3	34	.252	.406
Grass	.201	693	139	28	1	30	80	84	220	.291	.374	June	.283	113	32	5	0	6	27	16	28	.371	.487
Turf	.274	135	37	8	1	11	30	10	44	.324	.593	July	.215	163	35	4	1	9	19	22	43	.316	.417
First Pitch	.359	64	23	5	1	6	12	2	0	.388	.750	August	.203	158	32	6	1	7	13	13	50	.267	.386
Ahead on Count	.279	147	41	9	0	8	23	49	0	.463	.503	September/October	.166	217	36	9	0	11	26	26	83	.257	.359
Behind on Count	.177	294	52	12	0	12	35	0	134	.185	.340	Pre-All Star	.251	350	88	17	0	19	64	43	108	.337	.463
Two Strikes	.121	470	57	12	0	12	39	44	264	.198	.270	Post-All Star	.184	478	88	19	2	22	46	51	156	.266	.370

Batter vs. Pitcher (career)

Hits Best Against	Avg	AB	H	2B	3B	HR	RBI	BB	SO	OBP	SLG	Hits Worst Against	Avg	AB	H	2B	3B	HR	RBI	BB	SO	OBP	SLG
Dave Fleming	.500	14	7	2	0	1	2	0	0	.500	.000	Dave Stewart	.000	12	0	0	0	0	0	3	5	.200	.000
Bill Wegman	.400	10	4	2	0	1	1	1	3	.455	.900	Jaime Navarro	.000	11	0	0	0	0	0	3	1	.214	.000
Chuck Finley	.400	10	4	2	0	1	1	1	2	.455	.900	Mark Langston	.067	15	1	0	0	0	0	2	7	.176	.067
Jim Abbott	.333	12	4	0	0	1	1	2	3	.429	.583	Mike Mussina	.077	13	1	0	0	0	0	0	4	.077	.077
David Wells	.308	13	4	2	0	0	0	1	3	.357	.462	John Smiley	.091	11	1	0	0	0	0	0	3	.091	.091

Mark Parent — Orioles

Bats Right

	Avg	G	AB	R	H	2B	3B	HR	RBI	BB	SO	HBP	GDP	SB	CS	OBP	SLG	IBB	SH	SF	#Pit	#P/PA	GB	FB	G/F
1992 Season	.235	17	34	4	8	1	0	2	4	3	7	1	0	0	0	.316	.441	0	2	0	157	4.13	10	11	0.91
Last Five Years	.207	178	483	38	100	19	0	18	56	33	94	1	8	2	0	.257	.358	5	6	5	1798	3.44	165	154	1.07

1992 Season

	Avg	AB	H	2B	3B	HR	RBI	BB	SO	OBP	SLG		Avg	AB	H	2B	3B	HR	RBI	BB	SO	OBP	SLG
vs. Left	.111	9	1	0	0	1	1	2	2	.273	.444	Scoring Posn	.125	8	1	0	0	0	2	1	3	.222	.125
vs. Right	.280	25	7	1	0	1	3	1	5	.333	.440	Close & Late	.250	4	1	0	0	0	0	0	2	.250	.250

Last Five Years

	Avg	AB	H	2B	3B	HR	RBI	BB	SO	OBP	SLG		Avg	AB	H	2B	3B	HR	RBI	BB	SO	OBP	SLG
vs. Left	.242	198	48	9	0	8	19	21	36	.314	.409	Scoring Posn	.178	118	21	5	0	3	38	13	28	.250	.297
vs. Right	.182	285	52	10	0	10	37	12	58	.215	.323	Close & Late	.213	75	16	3	0	1	2	9	16	.298	.293
Groundball	.160	175	28	5	0	4	14	9	30	.202	.257	None on/out	.286	112	32	6	0	8	8	4	17	.310	.571
Flyball	.212	113	24	6	0	4	10	9	25	.270	.372	Batting #7	.189	196	37	9	0	5	18	9	40	.222	.311
Home	.231	199	46	8	0	11	28	11	42	.268	.437	Batting #8	.224	210	47	6	0	8	28	16	34	.275	.367
Away	.190	264	54	11	0	7	28	22	52	.249	.303	Other	.206	77	16	4	0	5	10	8	20	.291	.455
Day	.194	252	49	9	0	8	29	13	47	.236	.325	April	.256	39	10	1	0	2	4	2	9	.293	.436
Night	.221	231	51	10	0	10	27	20	47	.278	.394	May	.169	65	11	3	0	1	10	3	14	.200	.262
Grass	.222	347	77	13	0	15	43	22	70	.265	.389	June	.179	106	19	3	0	3	5	9	21	.243	.292
Turf	.169	136	23	6	0	3	13	11	24	.235	.279	July	.177	113	20	5	0	2	6	7	16	.223	.274
First Pitch	.258	89	23	2	0	5	9	4	0	.290	.449	August	.263	80	21	4	0	3	17	6	15	.318	.425
Ahead on Count	.317	104	33	7	0	6	19	14	0	.385	.558	September/October	.238	80	19	3	0	1	7	14	19	.287	.538
Behind on Count	.143	168	24	4	0	3	13	0	46	.143	.220	Pre-All Star	.180	244	44	7	0	7	21	18	53	.235	.295
Two Strikes	.112	196	22	4	0	3	12	13	93	.171	.179	Post-All Star	.234	239	56	12	0	11	35	15	41	.279	.423

Batter vs. Pitcher (career)

Hits Best Against	Avg	AB	H	2B	3B	HR	RBI	BB	SO	OBP	SLG	Hits Worst Against	Avg	AB	H	2B	3B	HR	RBI	BB	SO	OBP	SLG
Jim Deshaies	.357	14	5	1	0	1	2	0	2	.357	.643	Tom Glavine	.050	20	1	0	0	0	0	0	2	.050	.050
												Tom Browning	.154	13	2	1	0	0	2	0	3	.154	.231
												Joe Magrane	.200	10	2	1	0	0	0	2	0	.333	.300

Clay Parker — Mariners
Pitches Right (groundball pitcher)

	ERA	W	L	Sv	G	GS	IP	BB	SO	Avg	H	2B	3B	HR	RBI	OBP	SLG	CG	ShO	Sup	QS	#P/S	SB	CS	GB	FB	G/F
1992 Season	7.56	0	2	0	8	6	33.1	11	20	.338	47	12	0	6	26	.390	.554	0	0	4.05	1	78	3	1	44	47	0.94
Last Five Years	4.22	7	10	0	59	26	226.1	74	113	.268	234	40	5	29	110	.326	.424	2	0	4.06	10	87	13	6	397	231	1.72

1992 Season

	ERA	W	L	Sv	G	GS	IP	H	HR	BB	SO		Avg	AB	H	2B	3B	HR	RBI	BB	SO	OBP	SLG
Home	5.06	0	0	0	5	3	21.1	29	2	6	13	vs. Left	.279	68	19	6	0	2	11	4	9	.311	.456
Away	12.00	0	2	0	3	3	12.0	18	4	5	7	vs. Right	.394	71	28	6	0	4	15	7	11	.463	.648

Last Five Years

	ERA	W	L	Sv	G	GS	IP	H	HR	BB	SO		Avg	AB	H	2B	3B	HR	RBI	BB	SO	OBP	SLG
Home	3.91	2	4	0	30	13	117.1	115	16	48	57	vs. Left	.262	381	100	19	2	7	49	37	47	.324	.378
Away	4.54	5	6	0	29	13	109.0	119	13	26	56	vs. Right	.272	493	134	21	3	22	61	37	66	.328	.460
Day	4.82	3	2	0	17	9	71.0	71	9	22	42	Inning 1-6	.276	720	199	38	4	22	96	64	86	.337	.432
Night	3.94	4	8	0	42	17	155.1	163	20	52	71	Inning 7+	.227	154	35	2	1	7	14	10	27	.274	.390
Grass	4.26	5	9	0	49	20	179.2	184	25	66	83	None on	.252	524	132	24	3	22	22	38	75	.306	.435
Turf	4.05	2	1	0	10	6	46.2	50	4	8	30	Runners on	.291	350	102	16	2	7	88	36	38	.354	.409
April	5.79	0	1	0	6	1	18.2	22	5	7	18	Scoring Posn	.273	220	60	12	0	3	77	29	27	.350	.368
May	4.13	3	1	0	8	8	52.1	48	6	10	38	Close & Late	.206	34	7	0	0	1	1	1	2	.229	.294
June	6.75	0	2	0	4	4	18.2	23	5	7	5	None out	.266	231	66	12	0	12	12	14	27	.332	.494
July	4.89	1	0	0	13	6	53.1	62	9	26	26	vs. 1st Batr (relief)	.222	27	6	1	0	1	8	4	3	.323	.370
August	3.09	2	3	0	15	4	46.2	51	1	13	17	First Inning Pitched	.240	200	48	8	0	3	31	24	20	.323	.325
September/October	2.70	1	3	0	13	3	36.2	28	3	11	9	First 75 Pitches	.267	753	201	35	5	21	93	70	98	.331	.410
Starter	4.94	5	9	0	26	26	147.2	165	22	43	74	Pitch 76-90	.280	75	21	5	0	5	11	2	11	.299	.547
Reliever	2.86	2	1	0	33	0	78.2	69	7	31	39	Pitch 91-105	.265	34	9	0	0	2	4	2	1	.306	.441
0-3 Days Rest	0.00	0	0	0	0	0	0.0	0	0	0	0	Pitch 106+	.250	12	3	0	0	1	2	0	3	.250	.500
4 Days Rest	5.63	2	6	0	15	15	78.1	99	10	27	39	First Pitch	.303	142	43	6	0	4	21	6	0	.329	.430
5+ Days Rest	4.15	3	3	0	11	11	69.1	66	12	16	35	Ahead on Count	.215	344	74	11	0	10	35	0	89	.221	.334
Pre-All Star	4.53	4	4	0	21	15	103.1	106	17	29	69	Behind on Count	.272	224	61	12	3	8	29	36	0	.374	.460
Post-All Star	3.95	3	6	0	38	11	123.0	128	12	45	44	Two Strikes	.198	343	68	7	1	10	33	32	113	.268	.312

Pitcher vs. Batter (career)

Pitches Best Vs.	Avg	AB	H	2B	3B	HR	RBI	BB	SO	OBP	SLG	Pitches Worst Vs.	Avg	AB	H	2B	3B	HR	RBI	BB	SO	OBP	SLG
Robin Yount	.091	11	1	0	0	0	1	2	1	.231	.091	Paul Molitor	.462	13	6	0	1	1	2	0	0	.462	.846
Rickey Henderson	.100	10	1	0	0	1	1	1	0	.182	.400	Alan Trammell	.444	9	4	0	0	1	2	0	0	.545	.444
Dave Henderson	.182	11	2	0	0	1	1	0	2	.182	.455	Carney Lansford	.438	16	7	3	0	0	1	0	0	.438	.625
												Jody Reed	.400	15	6	0	0	1	3	0	3	.400	.600
												Mike Greenwell	.400	10	4	2	0	0	1	0	0	.500	.600

Derek Parks — Twins
Bats Right

	Avg	G	AB	R	H	2B	3B	HR	RBI	BB	SO	HBP	GDP	SB	CS	OBP	SLG	IBB	SH	SF	#Pit	#P/PA	GB	FB	G/F
1992 Season	.333	7	6	1	2	0	0	0	0	1	1	0	0	0	0	.500	.333	0	0	0	26	3.25	2	2	1.00

1992 Season

	Avg	AB	H	2B	3B	HR	RBI	BB	SO	OBP	SLG		Avg	AB	H	2B	3B	HR	RBI	BB	SO	OBP	SLG
vs. Left	.400	5	2	0	0	0	0	1	0	.500	.400	Scoring Posn	.000	1	0	0	0	0	0	1	0	.500	.000
vs. Right	.000	1	0	0	0	0	0	0	1	.500	.000	Close & Late	.000	0	0	0	0	0	0	0	0	.000	.000

Jeff Parrett — Athletics
Pitches Right (flyball pitcher)

	ERA	W	L	Sv	G	GS	IP	BB	SO	Avg	H	2B	3B	HR	RBI	OBP	SLG	GF	IR	IRS	Hld	SvOp	SB	CS	GB	FB	G/F
1992 Season	3.02	9	1	0	66	0	98.1	42	78	.226	81	17	2	7	47	.308	.344	14	65	21	19	1	14	4	88	131	0.67
Last Five Years	3.51	39	23	15	264	5	425.2	198	338	.248	387	77	13	34	211	.331	.380	42	196	75	38	32	37	20	476	481	0.99

1992 Season

	ERA	W	L	Sv	G	GS	IP	H	HR	BB	SO		Avg	AB	H	2B	3B	HR	RBI	BB	SO	OBP	SLG
Home	3.29	4	0	0	37	0	52.0	47	3	23	41	vs. Left	.278	144	40	6	1	2	24	23	29	.376	.375
Away	2.72	5	1	0	29	0	46.1	34	4	19	37	vs. Right	.192	214	41	11	1	5	23	19	49	.258	.322
Day	3.74	3	0	0	25	0	33.2	36	2	17	25	Inning 1-6	.232	112	26	7	0	0	18	13	23	.307	.295
Night	2.64	6	1	0	41	0	64.2	45	5	25	53	Inning 7+	.224	246	55	10	2	7	29	29	55	.308	.366
Grass	3.11	7	0	0	59	0	81.0	66	7	36	66	None on	.217	184	40	9	0	5	5	16	38	.284	.348
Turf	2.60	2	1	0	7	0	17.1	15	0	6	12	Runners on	.236	174	41	8	2	2	42	26	40	.332	.339
April	2.12	3	0	0	9	0	17.0	9	0	7	15	Scoring Posn	.264	110	29	6	1	1	37	18	22	.361	.364
May	4.08	1	0	0	11	0	17.2	9	3	9	18	Close & Late	.214	145	31	5	1	2	13	15	32	.292	.303
June	2.66	1	0	0	11	0	20.1	23	1	6	12	None on/out	.226	84	19	4	0	3	6	14	20	.278	.381
July	2.12	2	1	0	12	0	17.0	13	0	6	14	vs. 1st Batr (relief)	.145	55	8	1	0	1	6	7	14	.246	.218
August	4.70	2	0	0	13	0	15.1	14	3	10	12	First Inning Pitched	.214	210	45	4	1	6	34	26	46	.299	.329
September/October	2.45	0	0	0	10	0	11.0	13	0	4	7	First 15 Pitches	.223	197	44	6	1	6	32	21	39	.300	.355
Starter	0.00	0	0	0	0	0	0.0	0	0	0	0	Pitch 16-30	.203	118	24	5	1	1	12	14	31	.286	.288
Reliever	3.02	9	1	0	66	0	98.1	81	7	42	78	Pitch 31-45	.286	28	8	3	0	0	2	5	6	.394	.393
0 Days rest	4.26	2	0	0	12	0	12.2	12	0	8	12	Pitch 46+	.333	15	5	3	0	0	1	2	2	.412	.533
1 or 2 Days rest	3.44	5	1	0	36	0	55.0	45	7	23	47	First Pitch	.240	50	12	4	2	0	9	2	0	.283	.400
3+ Days rest	1.76	2	0	0	18	0	30.2	24	0	11	19	Ahead on Count	.191	162	31	6	0	4	18	0	64	.189	.302
Pre-All Star	2.97	5	0	0	35	0	60.2	47	4	25	49	Behind on Count	.256	78	20	5	0	1	8	25	0	.442	.359

1992 Season

	ERA	W	L	Sv	G	GS	IP	H	HR	BB	SO		Avg	AB	H	2B	3B	HR	RBI	BB	SO	OBP	SLG
Post-All Star	3.11	4	1	0	31	0	37.2	34	3	17	29	Two Strikes	.148	169	25	3	0	3	13	15	78	.215	.219

Last Five Years

	ERA	W	L	Sv	G	GS	IP	H	HR	BB	SO		Avg	AB	H	2B	3B	HR	RBI	BB	SO	OBP	SLG
Home	3.60	19	10	9	143	3	222.2	197	17	108	164	vs. Left	.253	740	187	33	9	9	101	119	146	.354	.358
Away	3.41	20	13	6	141	2	203.0	190	17	90	174	vs. Right	.244	819	200	44	4	25	110	79	192	.309	.399
Day	3.99	12	7	3	86	3	124.0	126	11	64	97	Inning 1-6	.250	296	74	18	3	4	47	37	61	.326	.372
Night	3.31	27	16	12	198	2	301.2	259	23	134	241	Inning 7+	.248	1263	313	59	10	30	164	161	277	.332	.382
Grass	3.76	15	8	3	140	0	186.2	184	16	84	152	None on	.252	824	208	45	4	21	21	88	179	.326	.393
Turf	3.31	24	15	12	144	5	239.0	203	18	114	186	Runners on	.244	735	179	32	9	13	190	110	159	.336	.365
April	2.80	6	3	2	50	0	74.0	66	5	29	57	Scoring Posn	.255	466	119	23	6	6	167	89	101	.364	.369
May	4.50	5	4	2	50	0	68.0	58	7	40	50	Close & Late	.253	616	156	22	6	13	87	87	145	.343	.372
June	3.87	7	5	5	56	0	83.2	80	6	36	60	None on/out	.270	370	100	17	3	12	12	38	75	.340	.430
July	2.76	12	6	3	40	5	78.1	64	5	35	63	vs. 1st Batr (relief)	.266	237	63	11	2	5	32	31	51	.349	.392
August	2.94	6	1	2	44	0	67.1	55	7	30	62	First Inning Pitched	.234	913	214	37	6	20	146	125	195	.324	.354
September/October	4.47	3	4	1	44	0	54.1	64	4	28	46	First 15 Pitches	.246	844	208	37	7	19	118	101	165	.325	.374
Starter	4.44	1	3	0	5	5	26.1	28	2	13	19	Pitch 16-30	.229	494	113	21	4	12	59	65	125	.317	.360
Reliever	3.45	38	20	15	279	0	399.1	359	32	185	319	Pitch 31-45	.273	139	38	10	1	2	15	19	35	.361	.403
0 Days rest	3.09	11	7	4	66	0	84.1	79	5	43	82	Pitch 46+	.341	82	28	9	1	1	19	13	13	.427	.512
1 or 2 Days rest	3.95	19	9	9	145	0	212.0	197	20	101	165	First Pitch	.291	206	60	11	3	6	31	30	0	.378	.461
3+ Days rest	2.71	8	4	2	68	0	103.0	83	7	41	72	Ahead on Count	.207	765	158	29	5	14	98	1	299	.208	.312
Pre-All Star	3.51	22	13	11	171	2	256.1	232	19	121	193	Behind on Count	.307	313	96	24	2	9	48	92	0	.461	.482
Post-All Star	3.51	17	10	4	113	3	169.1	155	15	77	145	Two Strikes	.184	777	143	24	3	11	87	74	338	.256	.265

Pitcher vs. Batter (career)

Pitches Best Vs.	Avg	AB	H	2B	3B	HR	RBI	BB	SO	OBP	SLG	Pitches Worst Vs.	Avg	AB	H	2B	3B	HR	RBI	BB	SO	OBP	SLG
Paul O'Neill	.000	15	0	0	0	0	0	1	6	.063	.000	Tim Raines	.538	13	7	1	1	0	6	0	2	.538	.769
Ken Oberkfell	.000	11	0	0	0	0	0	3	2	.214	.000	Glenn Davis	.455	11	5	2	0	2	4	4	3	.600	1.182
Howard Johnson	.077	13	1	0	1	0	0	1	4	.143	.231	Darryl Strawberry	.417	12	5	1	0	1	1	2	1	.500	.750
John Cangelosi	.083	12	1	0	0	0	0	1	1	.154	.083	Kevin McReynolds	.375	24	9	1	1	3	8	4	2	.464	.875
Ozzie Smith	.143	14	2	0	0	0	3	2	0	.250	.143	Kevin Mitchell	.364	11	4	2	0	1	3	2	1	.462	.818

Lance Parrish — Mariners Bats Right

	Avg	G	AB	R	H	2B	3B	HR	RBI	BB	SO	HBP	GDP	SB	CS	OBP	SLG	IBB	SH	SF	#Pit	#P/PA	GB	FB	G/F
1992 Season	.233	93	275	26	64	13	1	12	32	24	70	1	7	1	1	.294	.418	3	1	3	1181	3.90	76	95	0.80
Last Five Years	.235	592	2004	210	471	68	4	87	263	194	491	15	48	4	5	.305	.403	22	2	17	8423	3.78	632	606	1.04

1992 Season

	Avg	AB	H	2B	3B	HR	RBI	BB	SO	OBP	SLG		Avg	AB	H	2B	3B	HR	RBI	BB	SO	OBP	SLG
vs. Left	.232	95	22	7	0	4	10	12	18	.315	.432	Scoring Posn	.194	72	14	1	0	3	21	9	18	.274	.333
vs. Right	.233	180	42	6	1	8	22	12	52	.282	.411	Close & Late	.145	62	9	1	0	1	4	4	25	.194	.210
Groundball	.273	66	18	2	1	1	4	6	12	.338	.379	None on/out	.178	73	13	2	0	2	2	3	22	.211	.288
Flyball	.205	88	18	7	0	2	8	6	24	.253	.352	Batting #4	.155	58	9	5	0	1	4	7	18	.242	.293
Home	.230	135	31	6	0	7	19	10	31	.277	.430	Batting #7	.250	104	26	4	1	5	15	10	26	.310	.452
Away	.236	140	33	7	1	5	13	14	39	.310	.407	Other	.257	113	29	4	0	6	13	7	26	.306	.451
Day	.228	101	23	5	0	4	14	7	22	.275	.396	April	.269	52	14	1	0	4	10	4	15	.316	.519
Night	.236	174	41	8	1	8	18	17	48	.304	.431	May	.150	20	3	1	0	0	1	1	6	.190	.200
Grass	.209	148	31	4	1	3	16	13	39	.276	.311	June	.167	12	2	0	0	0	0	0	1	.167	.167
Turf	.260	127	33	9	0	9	16	11	31	.314	.543	July	.295	61	18	2	1	5	13	7	11	.368	.607
First Pitch	.375	24	9	3	0	2	4	2	0	.423	.750	August	.225	71	16	4	0	3	5	6	15	.291	.408
Ahead on Count	.367	79	29	5	0	6	18	8	0	.411	.658	September/October	.186	59	11	5	0	0	3	6	22	.258	.271
Behind on Count	.175	103	18	4	0	2	9	0	36	.183	.272	Pre-All Star	.234	111	26	3	0	5	14	6	24	.271	.396
Two Strikes	.106	132	14	2	0	2	4	14	70	.197	.167	Post-All Star	.232	164	38	10	1	7	18	18	46	.308	.433

1992 By Position

Position	Avg	AB	H	2B	3B	HR	RBI	BB	SO	OBP	SLG	G	GS	Innings	PO	A	E	DP	Fld Pct	Rng Fctr	In Zone	Zone Outs	Zone Rtg	MLB Zone
As Designated Hitter	.161	56	9	5	0	1	2	6	15	.242	.304	16	14	---	---	---	---	---	---	---	---	---	---	---
As Pinch Hitter	.000	11	0	0	0	0	0	0	5	.000	.000	12	0	---	---	---	---	---	---	---	---	---	---	---
As c	.263	171	45	6	1	9	24	13	43	.314	.468	56	44	416.0	290	20	4	6	.987	---	---	---	---	---
As 1b	.256	39	10	2	0	2	6	5	7	.341	.462	16	14	95.0	92	4	2	9	.980	---	15	10	.667	.843

Last Five Years

	Avg	AB	H	2B	3B	HR	RBI	BB	SO	OBP	SLG		Avg	AB	H	2B	3B	HR	RBI	BB	SO	OBP	SLG
vs. Left	.250	600	150	17	2	25	76	70	113	.326	.410	Scoring Posn	.229	507	116	17	1	18	164	75	128	.322	.373
vs. Right	.229	1404	321	51	2	62	187	124	378	.295	.400	Close & Late	.185	362	67	6	1	10	34	41	115	.267	.290
Groundball	.243	552	134	16	1	23	74	58	136	.319	.404	None on/out	.222	464	103	12	0	26	26	30	110	.275	.416
Flyball	.244	464	113	20	1	24	68	42	122	.307	.446	Batting #6	.216	578	125	20	1	24	73	58	164	.293	.379
Home	.244	1014	247	36	2	49	141	87	228	.303	.428	Batting #7	.252	636	160	15	2	32	85	59	150	.316	.432
Away	.226	990	224	32	2	38	122	107	263	.307	.378	Other	.235	790	186	33	1	31	105	77	177	.305	.397
Day	.234	435	102	13	1	22	70	41	107	.300	.421	April	.240	304	73	14	2	14	45	36	78	.328	.438
Night	.235	1569	369	55	3	65	193	153	384	.306	.398	May	.262	340	89	14	0	18	60	33	69	.327	.462
Grass	.238	1366	325	41	2	57	181	128	341	.307	.396	June	.239	297	71	9	0	13	39	31	61	.313	.401

Last Five Years

	Avg	AB	H	2B	3B	HR	RBI	BB	SO	OBP	SLG
Turf	.229	638	146	27	2	30	82	66	150	.300	.418
First Pitch	.291	265	77	12	0	13	44	9	0	.319	.483
Ahead on Count	.333	466	155	26	1	26	94	75	0	.419	.560
Behind on Count	.186	683	127	16	0	26	72	0	251	.194	.324
Two Strikes	.157	967	152	18	2	30	79	102	491	.240	.359

	Avg	AB	H	2B	3B	HR	RBI	BB	SO	OBP	SLG
July	.261	329	86	10	1	18	55	35	76	.333	.462
August	.196	372	73	8	0	14	34	30	111	.263	.331
September/October	.218	362	79	13	1	10	30	29	96	.273	.343
Pre-All Star	.250	1054	264	40	2	53	163	114	226	.327	.443
Post-All Star	.218	950	207	28	2	34	100	80	265	.280	.359

Batter vs. Pitcher (since 1984)

Hits Best Against	Avg	AB	H	2B	3B	HR	RBI	BB	SO	OBP	SLG
Greg Hibbard	.500	18	9	0	0	2	3	2	1	.550	.833
Tom Browning	.455	11	5	1	0	1	3	1	1	.500	.818
Jose Rijo	.444	9	4	0	0	1	1	2	1	.545	.778
Kirk McCaskill	.400	15	6	1	0	3	4	0	4	.400	1.067
Bruce Hurst	.385	13	5	0	0	3	7	3	4	.500	1.077

Hits Worst Against	Avg	AB	H	2B	3B	HR	RBI	BB	SO	OBP	SLG
Dennis Eckersley	.000	12	0	0	0	0	0	0	5	.000	.000
Todd Worrell	.000	11	0	0	0	0	0	2	4	.154	.000
David Wells	.063	16	1	0	0	0	0	1	7	.118	.063
Ben McDonald	.071	14	1	0	0	0	0	1	5	.133	.071
Steve Olin	.091	11	1	0	0	0	3	0	2	.091	.091

Dan Pasqua — White Sox   Bats Left (flyball hitter)

	Avg	G	AB	R	H	2B	3B	HR	RBI	BB	SO	HBP	GDP	SB	CS	OBP	SLG	IBB	SH	SF	#Pit	#P/PA	GB	FB	G/F
1992 Season	.211	93	265	26	56	16	1	6	33	36	57	1	4	0	1	.305	.347	1	1	3	1235	4.05	73	88	0.83
Last Five Years	.245	541	1675	214	410	90	12	68	254	206	367	10	27	3	6	.328	.435	18	5	15	7284	3.82	475	563	0.84

1992 Season

	Avg	AB	H	2B	3B	HR	RBI	BB	SO	OBP	SLG
vs. Left	.111	18	2	0	0	0	2	2	4	.200	.111
vs. Right	.219	247	54	16	1	6	31	34	53	.312	.364
Groundball	.078	64	5	1	0	0	3	9	17	.187	.094
Flyball	.247	77	19	3	0	4	13	15	14	.366	.442
Home	.188	128	24	5	0	2	11	17	27	.284	.273
Away	.234	137	32	11	1	4	22	19	30	.325	.416
Day	.294	51	15	4	1	2	14	11	11	.413	.529
Night	.192	214	41	12	0	4	19	25	46	.277	.304
Grass	.204	225	46	13	1	5	26	34	49	.308	.338
Turf	.250	40	10	3	0	1	7	2	8	.286	.400
First Pitch	.294	34	10	1	1	3	9	1	0	.314	.647
Ahead on Count	.268	71	19	7	0	0	5	16	0	.398	.366
Behind on Count	.186	86	16	5	0	1	9	0	25	.195	.279
Two Strikes	.136	125	17	5	0	3	15	20	57	.257	.248

	Avg	AB	H	2B	3B	HR	RBI	BB	SO	OBP	SLG
Scoring Posn	.203	69	14	4	0	2	26	7	17	.266	.348
Close & Late	.176	34	6	1	1	1	3	2	4	.222	.353
None on/out	.167	60	10	4	0	1	1	7	11	.254	.283
Batting #5	.235	34	8	3	1	2	6	7	6	.366	.559
Batting #6	.211	223	47	13	0	4	27	27	48	.295	.323
Other	.125	8	1	0	0	0	0	2	3	.300	.125
April	.289	45	13	3	1	2	8	5	14	.360	.533
May	.107	56	6	4	0	0	3	9	15	.227	.179
June	.357	14	5	3	0	0	3	1	1	.400	.571
July	.154	26	4	1	0	1	2	6	4	.313	.308
August	.226	62	14	3	0	0	5	6	9	.300	.274
September/October	.226	62	14	2	0	3	12	9	14	.319	.403
Pre-All Star	.199	136	27	11	1	3	16	19	33	.295	.360
Post-All Star	.225	129	29	5	0	3	17	17	24	.315	.333

1992 By Position

Position	Avg	AB	H	2B	3B	HR	RBI	BB	SO	OBP	SLG	G	GS	Innings	PO	A	E	DP	Fld Pct	Rng Fctr	In Zone	Outs	Zone Rtg	MLB Zone
As rf	.197	244	48	13	1	4	28	34	53	.294	.307	81	80	622.0	152	4	6	0	.963	2.26	182	153	.841	.814

Last Five Years

	Avg	AB	H	2B	3B	HR	RBI	BB	SO	OBP	SLG
vs. Left	.188	255	48	9	1	6	31	24	64	.267	.302
vs. Right	.255	1420	362	81	11	62	223	182	303	.339	.458
Groundball	.254	456	116	28	1	11	58	53	87	.332	.393
Flyball	.232	414	96	16	6	24	75	51	93	.318	.473
Home	.258	807	208	41	9	32	115	108	176	.345	.450
Away	.233	868	202	49	3	36	139	98	191	.313	.421
Day	.312	413	129	26	5	23	88	59	89	.398	.567
Night	.223	1262	281	64	7	45	166	147	278	.305	.391
Grass	.241	1420	342	75	11	55	206	185	312	.329	.425
Turf	.267	255	68	15	1	13	48	21	55	.323	.486
First Pitch	.321	221	71	17	1	10	39	3	0	.330	.543
Ahead on Count	.328	396	130	22	3	22	73	109	0	.473	.566
Behind on Count	.204	554	113	27	2	18	66	5	179	.214	.357
Two Strikes	.153	778	119	33	6	15	78	90	367	.241	.269

	Avg	AB	H	2B	3B	HR	RBI	BB	SO	OBP	SLG
Scoring Posn	.242	455	110	27	6	12	175	76	117	.344	.407
Close & Late	.230	287	66	11	3	12	44	32	65	.312	.415
None on/out	.240	417	100	27	3	20	20	37	89	.306	.463
Batting #4	.259	648	168	41	6	31	110	80	135	.343	.485
Batting #6	.224	447	100	24	0	12	53	48	98	.299	.358
Other	.245	580	142	25	6	25	91	78	134	.334	.438
April	.252	151	38	6	1	6	24	18	46	.327	.424
May	.231	273	63	17	2	9	33	41	58	.329	.407
June	.278	295	82	18	3	16	56	31	57	.351	.522
July	.263	377	99	20	2	17	67	43	82	.339	.462
August	.196	317	62	17	0	8	29	37	69	.286	.325
September/October	.252	262	66	12	4	12	45	36	55	.340	.466
Pre-All Star	.257	848	218	50	6	38	132	102	194	.336	.465
Post-All Star	.232	827	192	40	6	30	122	104	173	.321	.404

Batter vs. Pitcher (career)

Hits Best Against	Avg	AB	H	2B	3B	HR	RBI	BB	SO	OBP	SLG
Eric King	.500	12	6	0	0	2	4	0	1	.500	1.000
Luis Aquino	.400	15	6	1	0	2	3	1	2	.438	.867
Scott Erickson	.400	15	6	1	0	3	5	0	3	.400	1.067
Greg Harris	.400	10	4	2	1	0	1	2	2	.500	.800
Mike Morgan	.385	13	5	0	0	2	2	2	4	.467	.846

Hits Worst Against	Avg	AB	H	2B	3B	HR	RBI	BB	SO	OBP	SLG
Mike Mussina	.000	14	0	0	0	0	0	0	3	.000	.000
Jose Guzman	.000	10	0	0	0	0	0	2	2	.167	.000
Curt Young	.077	13	1	0	0	0	2	0	2	.077	.077
Doug Jones	.077	13	1	0	0	0	1	0	5	.077	.077
Mike Campbell	.077	13	1	0	0	0	0	1	2	.143	.077

Bob Patterson — Pirates

Pitches Left (flyball pitcher)

	ERA	W	L	Sv	G	GS	IP	BB	SO	Avg	H	2B	3B	HR	RBI	OBP	SLG	GF	IR	IRS	Hld	SvOp	SB	CS	GB	FB	G/F
1992 Season	2.92	6	3	9	60	0	64.2	23	43	.246	59	12	2	7	30	.309	.400	26	36	13	10	13	1	3	63	95	0.66
Last Five Years	3.36	22	14	17	181	9	251.2	67	190	.251	237	41	5	26	116	.301	.388	64	116	37	31	25	8	14	265	322	0.82

1992 Season

	ERA	W	L	Sv	G	GS	IP	H	HR	BB	SO		Avg	AB	H	2B	3B	HR	RBI	BB	SO	OBP	SLG
Home	3.47	4	2	6	29	0	36.1	30	5	14	25	vs. Left	.256	78	20	3	1	1	10	9	15	.330	.359
Away	2.22	2	1	3	31	0	28.1	29	2	9	18	vs. Right	.241	162	39	9	1	6	20	14	28	.299	.420
Day	4.91	2	1	1	17	0	14.2	19	3	5	11	Inning 1-6	.188	16	3	1	0	0	4	2	4	.263	.250
Night	2.34	4	2	8	43	0	50.0	40	4	18	32	Inning 7+	.250	224	56	11	2	7	26	21	39	.313	.411
Grass	0.87	0	0	2	15	0	10.1	13	0	5	9	None on	.250	136	34	9	1	2	2	9	22	.297	.375
Turf	3.31	6	3	7	45	0	54.1	46	7	18	34	Runners on	.240	104	25	3	1	5	28	14	21	.325	.433
April	0.00	1	0	0	5	0	6.0	3	0	0	3	Scoring Posn	.255	55	14	2	1	5	28	10	11	.358	.600
May	4.38	1	0	1	10	0	12.1	17	2	4	7	Close & Late	.269	130	35	8	1	6	22	13	24	.333	.485
June	1.54	2	0	3	13	0	11.2	8	0	5	6	None on/out	.328	58	19	4	0	2	2	4	10	.371	.500
July	3.14	1	1	3	11	0	14.1	11	2	3	13	vs. 1st Batr (relief)	.309	55	17	4	1	4	14	3	10	.333	.636
August	0.75	0	1	1	11	0	12.0	11	0	6	7	First Inning Pitched	.261	176	46	6	2	7	28	18	31	.327	.438
September/October	7.56	1	1	1	10	0	8.1	9	3	5	7	First 15 Pitches	.265	166	44	7	1	7	26	13	29	.315	.446
Starter	0.00	0	0	0	0	0	0.0	0	0	0	0	Pitch 16-30	.200	60	12	3	1	0	4	10	9	.314	.283
Reliever	2.92	6	3	9	60	0	64.2	59	7	23	43	Pitch 31-45	.250	12	3	2	0	0	0	0	3	.250	.417
0 Days rest	2.19	3	1	2	12	0	12.1	10	1	6	6	Pitch 46+	.000	2	0	0	0	0	0	0	2	.000	.000
1 or 2 Days rest	4.50	2	1	3	28	0	28.0	28	4	11	19	First Pitch	.367	49	18	6	0	4	11	5	0	.418	.735
3+ Days rest	1.48	1	1	4	20	0	24.1	21	2	6	18	Ahead on Count	.224	116	26	3	1	2	9	0	35	.224	.319
Pre-All Star	3.09	5	1	4	33	0	35.0	33	3	11	23	Behind on Count	.176	34	6	3	0	1	4	10	0	.364	.353
Post-All Star	2.73	1	2	5	27	0	29.2	26	4	12	20	Two Strikes	.188	112	21	3	1	2	10	8	43	.242	.286

Last Five Years

	ERA	W	L	Sv	G	GS	IP	H	HR	BB	SO		Avg	AB	H	2B	3B	HR	RBI	BB	SO	OBP	SLG
Home	3.63	12	7	9	85	6	136.1	123	17	37	109	vs. Left	.204	289	59	10	2	3	27	21	75	.259	.284
Away	3.04	10	7	8	96	3	115.1	114	9	30	81	vs. Right	.272	654	178	31	3	23	89	46	115	.319	.434
Day	4.62	5	5	5	54	2	60.1	58	9	16	39	Inning 1-6	.247	292	72	10	1	6	34	17	53	.287	.349
Night	2.96	17	9	11	127	7	191.1	179	17	51	151	Inning 7+	.253	651	165	31	4	20	82	50	137	.307	.406
Grass	2.30	5	1	5	52	2	70.1	69	4	17	56	None on	.243	543	132	30	3	12	12	35	110	.293	.376
Turf	3.77	17	13	12	129	7	181.1	168	22	50	134	Runners on	.263	400	105	11	2	14	104	32	80	.311	.405
April	2.52	4	0	0	22	0	25.0	18	2	6	18	Scoring Posn	.282	216	61	7	1	12	97	26	40	.348	.491
May	4.66	2	1	2	28	1	38.2	45	6	9	36	Close & Late	.254	307	78	15	1	11	45	28	71	.317	.417
June	2.62	3	2	4	28	4	44.2	40	4	11	22	None on/out	.275	236	65	13	0	7	7	15	47	.324	.419
July	2.66	4	1	5	33	0	47.0	38	3	10	41	vs. 1st Batr (relief)	.280	157	44	6	1	5	21	10	33	.322	.427
August	3.28	2	4	2	30	1	35.2	37	4	15	26	First Inning Pitched	.261	559	146	18	3	15	86	40	125	.311	.385
September/October	4.01	7	6	4	40	3	60.2	59	7	16	47	First 15 Pitches	.255	525	134	19	1	14	68	34	110	.302	.375
Starter	4.33	3	4	0	9	9	43.2	44	5	12	28	Pitch 16-30	.240	262	63	12	4	8	34	25	54	.304	.408
Reliever	3.16	19	10	17	172	0	206.0	193	21	55	162	Pitch 31-45	.197	71	14	5	0	1	6	4	13	.237	.310
0 Days rest	3.05	6	3	4	30	0	38.1	28	3	12	32	Pitch 46+	.306	85	26	5	0	3	8	4	13	.337	.471
1 or 2 Days rest	3.79	7	4	6	83	0	90.1	89	12	26	71	First Pitch	.297	165	49	12	0	6	24	15	0	.350	.479
3+ Days rest	2.50	6	3	7	59	0	79.1	76	6	17	59	Ahead on Count	.201	468	94	13	1	9	39	0	169	.205	.291
Pre-All Star	3.30	11	4	7	90	5	122.2	112	13	29	92	Behind on Count	.322	149	48	11	1	7	23	27	0	.421	.550
Post-All Star	3.42	11	10	10	91	4	129.0	125	13	38	98	Two Strikes	.168	447	75	13	1	8	37	25	190	.215	.255

Pitcher vs. Batter (career)

Pitches Best Vs.	Avg	AB	H	2B	3B	HR	RBI	BB	SO	OBP	SLG	Pitches Worst Vs.	Avg	AB	H	2B	3B	HR	RBI	BB	SO	OBP	SLG
Paul O'Neill	.000	11	0	0	0	0	0	0	3	.000	.000	Casey Candaele	.563	12	7	2	0	0	1	0	0	.583	.750
Darren Daulton	.077	13	1	0	0	0	1	1	2	.143	.077	Tim Teufel	.444	18	8	2	0	1	6	3	3	.524	.722
Eddie Murray	.143	14	2	0	0	0	1	0	3	.133	.143	Kevin McReynolds	.389	18	7	1	0	2	5	0	2	.389	.778
Kal Daniels	.182	11	2	0	0	0	0	0	2	.182	.182	Dickie Thon	.364	11	4	0	0	1	1	1	3	.417	.636
Gary Carter	.214	14	3	0	0	0	2	0	2	.188	.214	Todd Zeile	.333	12	4	2	0	1	4	0	2	.333	.750

John Patterson — Giants

Bats Both (groundball hitter)

	Avg	G	AB	R	H	2B	3B	HR	RBI	BB	SO	HBP	GDP	SB	CS	OBP	SLG	IBB	SH	SF	#Pit	#P/PA	GB	FB	G/F
1992 Season	.184	32	103	10	19	1	1	0	4	5	24	1	2	5	1	.229	.214	0	0	0	404	3.71	40	24	1.67

1992 Season

	Avg	AB	H	2B	3B	HR	RBI	BB	SO	OBP	SLG		Avg	AB	H	2B	3B	HR	RBI	BB	SO	OBP	SLG
vs. Left	.240	25	6	1	0	0	1	1	6	.269	.280	Scoring Posn	.263	19	5	0	0	0	3	0	6	.263	.263
vs. Right	.167	78	13	0	1	0	3	4	18	.217	.192	Close & Late	.167	24	4	0	0	0	0	0	7	.167	.167
Home	.188	48	9	1	1	0	2	2	9	.240	.250	None on/out	.237	38	9	1	0	0	1	7		.256	.263
Away	.182	55	10	0	0	0	2	3	15	.237	.182	Batting #1	.158	38	6	0	0	0	1	2	8	.200	.158
First Pitch	.154	13	2	0	1	0	1	0		.214	.308	Batting #2	.200	50	10	1	1	0	3	1	10	.231	.260
Ahead on Count	.238	21	5	1	0	0	1	4	0	.360	.286	Other	.200	15	3	0	0	0	0	2	6	.294	.200
Behind on Count	.100	40	4	0	0	0	1	0	17	.100	.100	Pre-All Star	.207	29	6	1	0	0	1	1	8	.258	.241
Two Strikes	.148	54	8	0	0	0	1	1	24	.164	.148	Post-All Star	.176	74	13	0	1	0	3	4	16	.218	.203

341

Ken Patterson — Cubs
Pitches Left (flyball pitcher)

	ERA	W	L	Sv	G	GS	IP	BB	SO	Avg	H	2B	3B	HR	RBI	OBP	SLG	GF	IR	IRS	Hld	SvOp	SB	CS	GB	FB	G/F
1992 Season	3.89	2	3	0	32	1	41.2	27	23	.268	41	9	2	7	25	.373	.490	4	23	7	2	2	2	3	52	53	0.98
Career (1988-1992)	3.73	13	7	4	177	4	258.0	131	146	.248	236	39	9	31	144	.338	.406	32	175	52	10	8	18	11	289	352	0.82

1992 Season

	ERA	W	L	Sv	G	GS	IP	H	HR	BB	SO		Avg	AB	H	2B	3B	HR	RBI	BB	SO	OBP	SLG
Home	3.38	0	1	0	13	1	16.0	18	2	12	17	vs. Left	.266	64	17	3	1	0	4	9	11	.365	.344
Away	4.21	2	2	0	19	0	25.2	23	5	15	6	vs. Right	.270	89	24	6	1	7	21	18	12	.378	.596
Starter	9.00	0	0	0	1	1	3.0	5	1	2	2	Scoring Posn	.214	42	9	2	0	1	16	13	7	.383	.333
Reliever	3.49	2	3	0	31	0	38.2	36	6	25	21	Close & Late	.286	21	6	1	0	1	3	5	3	.423	.476
0 Days rest	2.89	0	0	0	6	0	9.1	6	1	8	9	None on/out	.263	38	10	4	1	1	1	4	7	.333	.500
1 or 2 Days rest	4.70	0	2	0	7	0	7.2	10	1	6	4	First Pitch	.381	21	8	3	0	2	6	5	0	.500	.810
3+ Days rest	3.32	2	1	0	18	0	21.2	20	4	11	8	Behind on Count	.227	44	10	3	0	2	6	12	0	.373	.432
Pre-All Star	3.57	0	1	0	15	0	17.2	18	4	12	15	Ahead on Count	.264	53	14	1	0	2	7	0	17	.264	.396
Post-All Star	4.13	2	2	0	17	1	24.0	23	1	15	8	Two Strikes	.193	57	11	0	0	2	6	10	23	.324	.298

Career (1988-1992)

	ERA	W	L	Sv	G	GS	IP	H	HR	BB	SO		Avg	AB	H	2B	3B	HR	RBI	BB	SO	OBP	SLG
Home	3.77	5	4	3	86	2	126.2	117	17	60	78	vs. Left	.258	283	73	8	3	5	44	40	45	.347	.360
Away	3.70	8	3	1	91	2	131.1	119	14	71	68	vs. Right	.244	668	163	31	6	26	100	91	101	.335	.425
Day	2.89	5	1	1	52	3	74.2	58	8	40	52	Inning 1-6	.255	428	109	19	5	16	79	60	62	.343	.435
Night	4.07	8	6	3	125	1	183.1	176	23	91	94	Inning 7+	.243	523	127	20	4	15	65	71	84	.334	.382
Grass	3.56	12	6	3	142	3	209.2	185	26	105	127	None on	.270	496	134	25	5	16	64	78		.356	.438
Turf	4.47	1	1	1	35	1	48.1	51	1	26	19	Runners on	.224	455	102	14	4	15	128	67	68	.320	.371
April	5.05	1	0	0	27	0	35.2	38	9	18	17	Scoring Posn	.241	278	67	10	3	9	114	52	43	.349	.396
May	3.17	3	1	0	29	0	48.1	34	5	30	32	Close & Late	.276	105	29	5	1	4	19	21	18	.391	.457
June	4.17	2	1	1	22	1	41.0	38	5	22	21	None on/out	.270	230	62	14	2	7	7	19	38	.328	.439
July	2.33	4	1	1	27	0	38.2	30	2	16	27	vs. 1st Batr (relief)	.309	139	43	8	1	6	41	27	21	.415	.511
August	4.02	3	2	0	36	0	47.0	47	5	22	28	First Inning Pitched	.265	528	140	24	9	23	113	80	62	.358	.475
September/October	3.80	0	2	2	36	3	47.1	49	5	23	21	First 15 Pitches	.264	477	126	20	7	19	86	65	61	.351	.455
Starter	7.63	0	0	0	4	4	15.1	23	4	8	10	Pitch 16-30	.213	244	52	12	2	5	29	37	44	.312	.340
Reliever	3.49	13	6	4	173	0	242.2	213	27	123	136	Pitch 31-45	.244	123	30	5	0	1	9	17	23	.343	.309
0 Days rest	4.85	1	1	0	32	0	42.2	43	10	22	35	Pitch 46+	.262	107	28	2	0	6	20	12	18	.336	.449
1 or 2 Days rest	3.18	4	2	2	58	0	70.2	62	3	39	34	First Pitch	.294	143	42	9	0	4	27	7	0	.323	.441
3+ Days rest	3.20	8	3	2	83	0	129.1	106	14	62	67	Ahead on Count	.226	394	89	11	1	15	59	0	119	.228	.373
Pre-All Star	4.02	7	3	1	87	1	136.2	122	20	75	79	Behind on Count	.253	217	55	12	3	6	32	64	0	.417	.419
Post-All Star	3.41	6	4	3	90	3	121.1	114	11	56	67	Two Strikes	.208	413	86	11	3	15	59	60	146	.310	.356

Pitcher vs. Batter (career)

Pitches Best Vs.	Avg	AB	H	2B	3B	HR	RBI	BB	SO	OBP	SLG	Pitches Worst Vs.	Avg	AB	H	2B	3B	HR	RBI	BB	SO	OBP	SLG
Jody Reed	.200	10	2	0	0	0	1	1	1	.273	.200	Mike Greenwell	.333	15	5	0	0	0	1	1	0	.375	.333
												Alvin Davis	.333	6	2	0	0	0	3	4	0	.545	.333

Roger Pavlik — Rangers
Pitches Right (flyball pitcher)

	ERA	W	L	Sv	G	GS	IP	BB	SO	Avg	H	2B	3B	HR	RBI	OBP	SLG	CG	ShO	Sup	QS	#P/S	SB	CS	GB	FB	G/F
1992 Season	4.21	4	4	0	13	12	62.0	34	45	.280	66	7	4	3	23	.375	.381	1	0	3.92	7	88	3	8	70	72	0.97

1992 Season

	ERA	W	L	Sv	G	GS	IP	H	HR	BB	SO		Avg	AB	H	2B	3B	HR	RBI	BB	SO	OBP	SLG
Home	6.95	2	2	0	6	5	22.0	31	2	13	18	vs. Left	.271	133	36	4	2	1	16	18	26	.353	.353
Away	2.70	2	2	0	7	7	40.0	35	1	21	27	vs. Right	.291	103	30	3	2	2	7	16	19	.402	.417
Starter	4.28	4	4	0	12	12	61.0	66	3	33	44	Scoring Posn	.308	52	16	0	0	1	18	7	11	.387	.365
Reliever	0.00	0	0	0	1	0	1.0	0	0	0	1	Close & Late	.313	16	5	2	0	0	1	5	3	.476	.438
0-3 Days Rest	0.00	0	0	0	0	0	0.0	0	0	0	0	None on/out	.328	58	19	2	1	0	0	13	7	.451	.397
4 Days Rest	3.58	2	2	0	6	6	37.2	40	1	17	26	First Pitch	.382	34	13	2	0	3	0	0	0	.382	.441
5+ Days Rest	5.40	2	2	0	6	6	23.1	26	2	16	18	Behind on Count	.324	68	22	1	1	2	9	19	0	.472	.456
Pre-All Star	4.66	0	0	0	3	3	9.2	9	0	12	7	Ahead on Count	.179	84	15	2	1	1	4	0	35	.195	.262
Post-All Star	4.13	4	4	0	10	9	52.1	57	3	22	38	Two Strikes	.177	96	17	2	2	1	8	15	45	.298	.271

Bill Pecota — Mets
Bats Right

	Avg	G	AB	R	H	2B	3B	HR	RBI	BB	SO	HBP	GDP	SB	CS	OBP	SLG	IBB	SH	SF	#Pit	#P/PA	GB	FB	G/F
1992 Season	.227	117	269	28	61	13	0	2	26	25	40	1	6	9	3	.293	.297	3	5	2	1100	3.70	112	68	1.65
Last Five Years	.246	484	1168	170	287	58	9	17	111	124	167	7	28	45	17	.321	.354	10	26	3	4937	3.79	455	336	1.35

1992 Season

	Avg	AB	H	2B	3B	HR	RBI	BB	SO	OBP	SLG		Avg	AB	H	2B	3B	HR	RBI	BB	SO	OBP	SLG
vs. Left	.234	107	25	6	0	2	13	9	12	.291	.346	Scoring Posn	.185	54	10	3	0	0	21	13	6	.333	.241
vs. Right	.222	162	36	7	0	0	13	16	28	.294	.265	Close & Late	.286	49	14	3	0	0	4	7	6	.379	.347
Groundball	.204	113	23	2	0	0	8	9	18	.260	.221	None on/out	.167	72	12	2	0	0	0	1	7	.178	.194
Flyball	.236	55	13	5	0	0	4	5	10	.306	.327	Batting #6	.255	94	24	6	0	0	9	8	15	.311	.319
Home	.272	125	34	10	0	1	17	13	20	.336	.376	Batting #8	.224	49	11	0	0	1	5	7	8	.333	.286
Away	.188	144	27	3	0	1	9	12	20	.255	.229	Other	.206	126	26	7	0	1	12	10	17	.263	.286
Day	.221	95	21	2	0	0	6	13	14	.321	.242	April	.188	32	6	1	0	0	4	2	2	.235	.219

1992 Season

	Avg	AB	H	2B	3B	HR	RBI	BB	SO	OBP	SLG		Avg	AB	H	2B	3B	HR	RBI	BB	SO	OBP	SLG
Night	.230	174	40	11	0	2	20	12	26	.277	.328	May	.176	34	6	2	0	0	5	3	6	.263	.235
Grass	.254	173	44	11	0	2	25	19	28	.325	.353	June	.280	50	14	3	0	0	4	7	10	.368	.340
Turf	.177	96	17	2	0	0	1	6	12	.233	.198	July	.238	63	15	3	0	0	3	6	12	.304	.286
First Pitch	.241	29	7	1	0	0	6	2	0	.290	.276	August	.250	48	12	2	0	2	7	4	4	.302	.417
Ahead on Count	.261	69	18	6	0	2	8	17	0	.407	.435	September/October	.190	42	8	2	0	0	3	3	6	.239	.238
Behind on Count	.247	93	23	4	0	1	9	0	21	.250	.323	Pre-All Star	.217	152	33	8	0	0	15	15	25	.292	.270
Two Strikes	.162	117	19	3	0	0	10	6	40	.208	.188	Post-All Star	.239	117	28	5	0	2	11	10	15	.295	.333

1992 By Position

Position	Avg	AB	H	2B	3B	HR	RBI	BB	SO	OBP	SLG	G	GS	Innings	PO	A	E	DP	Fld Pct	Rng Fctr	In Zone	Outs	Zone Rtg	MLB Zone
As Pinch Hitter	.300	20	6	2	0	1	6	1	1	.333	.550	21	0	---	---	---	---	---	---	---	---	---	---	---
As 2b	.193	88	17	3	0	0	5	10	16	.280	.227	38	14	230.2	46	95	4	16	.972	5.50	103	92	.893	.892
As 3b	.274	84	23	5	0	0	10	8	13	.337	.333	48	21	228.1	12	51	5	6	.926	2.48	65	57	.877	.841
As ss	.195	77	15	3	0	1	5	6	10	.250	.273	39	20	202.0	34	71	3	11	.972	4.68	79	70	.886	.885

Last Five Years

	Avg	AB	H	2B	3B	HR	RBI	BB	SO	OBP	SLG		Avg	AB	H	2B	3B	HR	RBI	BB	SO	OBP	SLG
vs. Left	.276	431	119	29	2	6	39	48	50	.351	.394	Scoring Posn	.239	272	65	10	2	3	85	57	37	.371	.324
vs. Right	.228	737	168	29	7	11	72	76	117	.304	.331	Close & Late	.235	187	44	9	0	0	13	22	29	.321	.283
Groundball	.245	383	94	18	0	7	44	43	54	.322	.347	None on/out	.247	255	63	16	0	4	4	17	37	.299	.357
Flyball	.239	280	67	16	4	5	21	25	51	.305	.379	Batting #2	.241	245	59	13	3	2	15	30	40	.326	.343
Home	.255	530	135	28	5	8	60	61	72	.336	.372	Batting #6	.283	290	82	14	2	3	34	29	40	.351	.376
Away	.238	638	152	30	4	9	51	63	95	.309	.340	Other	.231	633	146	31	4	12	62	65	87	.305	.349
Day	.264	356	94	15	2	5	32	45	59	.348	.360	April	.185	65	12	2	1	0	5	8	8	.274	.246
Night	.238	812	193	43	7	12	79	79	108	.309	.352	May	.212	132	28	6	0	3	20	10	17	.273	.326
Grass	.254	520	132	29	3	9	57	54	85	.324	.373	June	.336	131	44	9	0	2	14	13	23	.396	.450
Turf	.239	648	155	29	6	8	54	70	82	.319	.340	July	.243	292	71	13	3	4	24	25	53	.309	.349
First Pitch	.283	92	26	4	0	1	14	5	0	.327	.359	August	.236	267	63	15	3	6	26	28	28	.309	.382
Ahead on Count	.290	314	91	23	4	12	38	77	0	.430	.503	September/October	.246	281	69	13	2	2	22	40	38	.343	.327
Behind on Count	.229	432	99	18	2	7	38	3	86	.239	.329	Pre-All Star	.256	399	102	22	1	5	44	36	60	.319	.353
Two Strikes	.185	498	92	19	3	1	40	42	167	.250	.241	Post-All Star	.241	769	185	36	8	12	67	86	107	.322	.355

Batter vs. Pitcher (career)

Hits Best Against	Avg	AB	H	2B	3B	HR	RBI	BB	SO	OBP	SLG	Hits Worst Against	Avg	AB	H	2B	3B	HR	RBI	BB	SO	OBP	SLG
David Wells	.462	13	6	3	0	0	1	0	1	.462	.462	Jack Morris	.091	11	1	0	0	0	0	1	1	.167	.091
Matt Young	.417	12	5	2	0	0	0	1	2	.462	.583	Jose DeLeon	.091	11	1	1	0	0	0	0	3	.091	.182
Randy Johnson	.364	11	4	1	0	2	2	5	0	.563	1.000	Roger Clemens	.091	11	1	1	0	0	0	1	4	.167	.182
Greg Swindell	.304	23	7	2	0	0	2	3	2	.385	.391	Tom Bolton	.091	11	1	0	0	0	1	0	2	.091	.091
												Tom Candiotti	.154	13	2	0	0	0	1	1	6	.214	.154

Jorge Pedre — Cubs — Bats Right (flyball hitter)

	Avg	G	AB	R	H	2B	3B	HR	RBI	BB	SO	HBP	GDP	SB	CS	OBP	SLG	IBB	SH	SF	#Pit	#P/PA	GB	FB	G/F
1992 Season	.000	4	4	0	0	0	0	0	0	0	1	0	0	0	0	.000	.000	0	0	0	8	2.00	1	1	1.00
Career (1991-1992)	.217	14	23	2	5	1	1	0	3	3	6	0	0	0	0	.308	.348	0	0	0	97	3.73	5	7	0.71

1992 Season

	Avg	AB	H	2B	3B	HR	RBI	BB	SO	OBP	SLG		Avg	AB	H	2B	3B	HR	RBI	BB	SO	OBP	SLG
vs. Left	.000	1	0	0	0	0	0	0	0	.000	.000	Scoring Posn	.000	1	0	0	0	0	0	0	1	.000	.000
vs. Right	.000	3	0	0	0	0	0	0	1	.000	.000	Close & Late	.000	0	0	0	0	0	0	0	0	.000	.000

Julio Peguero — Dodgers — Bats Both (flyball hitter)

	Avg	G	AB	R	H	2B	3B	HR	RBI	BB	SO	HBP	GDP	SB	CS	OBP	SLG	IBB	SH	SF	#Pit	#P/PA	GB	FB	G/F
1992 Season	.222	14	9	3	2	0	0	0	0	3	3	0	0	0	0	.417	.222	0	1	0	50	4.17	2	3	0.67

1992 Season

	Avg	AB	H	2B	3B	HR	RBI	BB	SO	OBP	SLG		Avg	AB	H	2B	3B	HR	RBI	BB	SO	OBP	SLG
vs. Left	.143	7	1	0	0	0	0	0	2	.143	.143	Scoring Posn	.000	2	0	0	0	0	0	0	1	.333	.000
vs. Right	.500	2	1	0	0	0	0	3	1	.800	.500	Close & Late	.000	1	0	0	0	0	0	0	0	.000	.000

Dan Peltier — Rangers — Bats Left

	Avg	G	AB	R	H	2B	3B	HR	RBI	BB	SO	HBP	GDP	SB	CS	OBP	SLG	IBB	SH	SF	#Pit	#P/PA	GB	FB	G/F
1992 Season	.167	12	24	1	4	0	0	0	2	0	3	0	0	0	0	.167	.167	0	0	0	80	3.33	10	9	1.11

1992 Season

	Avg	AB	H	2B	3B	HR	RBI	BB	SO	OBP	SLG		Avg	AB	H	2B	3B	HR	RBI	BB	SO	OBP	SLG
vs. Left	.000	1	0	0	0	0	0	0	1	.000	.000	Scoring Posn	.143	7	1	0	0	0	2	0	0	.143	.143
vs. Right	.174	23	4	0	0	0	2	0	2	.174	.174	Close & Late	.000	6	0	0	0	0	0	0	2	.000	.000

Alejandro Pena — Braves — Pitches Right (flyball pitcher)

	ERA	W	L	Sv	G	GS	IP	BB	SO	Avg	H	2B	3B	HR	RBI	OBP	SLG	GF	IR	IRS	Hld	SvOp	SB	CS	GB	FB	G/F
1992 Season	4.07	1	6	15	41	0	42.0	13	34	.255	40	5	0	7	21	.310	.420	31	13	3	4	18	5	1	46	56	0.82
Last Five Years	2.57	22	20	52	265	0	370.2	102	330	.234	322	43	4	27	134	.286	.330	99	132	37	25	66	37	12	388	453	0.86

1992 Season

	ERA	W	L	Sv	G	GS	IP	H	HR	BB	SO
Home	4.42	0	2	5	19	0	18.1	17	4	4	13
Away	3.80	1	4	10	22	0	23.2	23	3	9	21
Starter	0.00	0	0	0	0	0	0.0	0	0	0	0
Reliever	4.07	1	6	15	41	0	42.0	40	7	13	34
0 Days rest	2.00	0	0	4	8	0	9.0	8	0	3	7
1 or 2 Days rest	5.40	1	4	7	19	0	20.0	24	5	7	13
3+ Days rest	3.46	0	2	4	14	0	13.0	8	2	3	14
Pre-All Star	4.56	0	4	7	23	0	25.2	27	6	7	19
Post-All Star	3.31	1	2	8	18	0	16.1	13	1	6	15

	Avg	AB	H	2B	3B	HR	RBI	BB	SO	OBP	SLG
vs. Left	.205	78	16	3	0	5	11	6	19	.262	.436
vs. Right	.304	79	24	2	0	2	10	7	15	.356	.405
Scoring Posn	.286	35	10	1	0	1	13	9	7	.422	.400
Close & Late	.267	105	28	4	0	4	16	13	23	.345	.419
None on/out	.154	39	6	0	0	3	3	2	8	.195	.385
First Pitch	.381	21	8	0	0	1	3	4	0	.480	.524
Behind on Count	.481	27	13	2	0	4	9	9	0	.611	1.000
Ahead on Count	.127	79	10	1	0	1	4	0	30	.127	.177
Two Strikes	.120	83	10	2	0	1	3	0	34	.119	.181

Last Five Years

	ERA	W	L	Sv	G	GS	IP	H	HR	BB	SO
Home	2.80	8	7	20	127	0	167.0	149	15	51	146
Away	2.39	14	13	32	138	0	203.2	173	12	51	184
Day	2.59	6	6	19	80	0	114.2	94	5	32	83
Night	2.57	16	14	33	185	0	256.0	226	22	70	247
Grass	2.68	16	13	36	188	0	258.2	227	21	72	218
Turf	2.33	6	7	16	77	0	112.0	95	6	30	112
April	2.72	2	1	9	34	0	49.2	43	5	11	40
May	4.34	4	7	3	44	0	56.0	62	11	26	43
June	3.02	4	3	4	45	0	62.2	59	2	18	51
July	1.84	5	5	13	48	0	68.1	48	2	24	58
August	3.14	2	5	6	45	0	66.0	76	6	15	64
September/October	0.79	5	2	17	49	0	68.0	34	1	8	66
Starter	0.00	0	0	0	0	0	0.0	0	0	0	0
Reliever	2.57	22	20	52	265	0	370.2	322	27	102	330
0 Days rest	2.34	5	5	18	56	0	77.0	65	5	25	71
1 or 2 Days rest	2.68	8	8	26	115	0	161.0	150	12	41	137
3+ Days rest	2.58	9	7	8	94	0	132.2	107	10	36	122
Pre-All Star	2.99	12	11	20	138	0	189.1	172	18	60	156
Post-All Star	2.13	10	9	32	127	0	181.1	150	9	42	174

	Avg	AB	H	2B	3B	HR	RBI	BB	SO	OBP	SLG
vs. Left	.229	678	155	18	2	13	58	63	170	.292	.319
vs. Right	.240	697	167	25	2	14	76	39	160	.280	.341
Inning 1-6	.202	114	23	2	0	1	10	7	28	.246	.246
Inning 7+	.237	1261	299	41	4	26	124	95	302	.290	.338
None on	.221	813	180	21	2	20	50	50	189	.268	.326
Runners on	.253	562	142	22	2	7	114	52	141	.311	.336
Scoring Posn	.258	325	84	14	2	4	106	45	94	.337	.351
Close & Late	.225	641	144	21	2	14	76	55	152	.286	.329
None on/out	.189	339	64	8	0	9	9	20	74	.236	.292
vs. 1st Batr (relief)	.204	245	50	8	0	6	22	16	51	.250	.310
First Inning Pitched	.231	878	203	29	2	19	103	70	190	.286	.334
First 15 Pitches	.221	780	172	23	0	18	68	59	164	.274	.319
Pitch 16-30	.263	471	124	19	3	6	49	30	117	.308	.355
Pitch 31-45	.218	101	22	1	1	3	16	12	39	.296	.337
Pitch 46+	.174	23	4	0	0	0	1	1	10	.208	.174
First Pitch	.319	207	66	11	0	10	31	15	1	.363	.517
Ahead on Count	.172	733	126	11	1	4	44	1	297	.174	.206
Behind on Count	.362	199	72	10	1	12	41	54	0	.492	.603
Two Strikes	.154	727	112	10	2	3	36	32	329	.190	.186

Pitcher vs. Batter (since 1984)

Pitches Best Vs.	Avg	AB	H	2B	3B	HR	RBI	BB	SO	OBP	SLG	Pitches Worst Vs.	Avg	AB	H	2B	3B	HR	RBI	BB	SO	OBP	SLG
Gary Redus	.000	11	0	0	0	0	0	1	0	.077	.000	Robby Thompson	.500	12	6	2	0	0	2	1	0	.538	.667
Ron Gant	.000	11	0	0	0	0	0	0	3	.000	.000	Billy Hatcher	.474	19	9	4	0	1	5	1	0	.474	.842
Dave Martinez	.077	13	1	0	0	0	0	0	3	.077	.077	Ken Caminiti	.429	14	6	1	1	1	1	1	2	.467	.857
Paul O'Neill	.083	12	1	0	0	0	0	0	3	.083	.083	Ryne Sandberg	.343	35	12	3	0	3	8	2	2	.378	.686
Kevin Bass	.111	18	2	0	0	0	1	4		.158	.111	Will Clark	.333	15	5	1	0	2	3	3	7	.444	.800

Geronimo Pena — Cardinals — Bats Both

	Avg	G	AB	R	H	2B	3B	HR	RBI	BB	SO	HBP	GDP	SB	CS	OBP	SLG	IBB	SH	SF	#Pit	#P/PA	GB	FB	G/F
1992 Season	.305	62	203	31	62	12	1	7	31	24	37	5	1	13	8	.386	.478	0	0	4	854	3.62	61	64	0.95
Career (1990-1992)	.273	184	433	74	118	22	4	12	50	46	96	11	1	29	14	.351	.425	1	1	8	1838	3.69	140	126	1.11

1992 Season

	Avg	AB	H	2B	3B	HR	RBI	BB	SO	OBP	SLG
vs. Left	.328	67	22	3	0	3	10	9	10	.425	.507
vs. Right	.294	136	40	9	1	4	21	15	27	.365	.463
Home	.291	103	30	4	1	4	12	13	17	.375	.466
Away	.320	100	32	8	0	3	19	11	20	.397	.490
First Pitch	.303	33	10	1	0	3	5	0	0	.303	.606
Ahead on Count	.404	52	21	5	1	1	10	12	0	.500	.596
Behind on Count	.347	72	25	0	0	3	13	0	21	.355	.542
Two Strikes	.222	90	20	0	0	3	11	12	37	.324	.344

	Avg	AB	H	2B	3B	HR	RBI	BB	SO	OBP	SLG
Scoring Posn	.292	48	14	2	1	0	20	3	11	.345	.375
Close & Late	.295	44	13	2	0	0	2	4	8	.367	.341
None on/out	.344	64	22	2	0	4	4	9		.425	.563
Batting #1	.289	97	28	4	1	2	8	11	17	.378	.412
Batting #7	.338	68	23	4	0	4	18	10	14	.407	.574
Other	.289	38	11	4	0	1	5	3	6	.364	.474
Pre-All Star	.295	95	28	7	0	3	12	10		.376	.463
Post-All Star	.315	108	34	5	1	4	19	14	21	.394	.491

Jim Pena — Giants — Pitches Left (flyball pitcher)

	ERA	W	L	Sv	G	GS	IP	BB	SO	Avg	H	2B	3B	HR	RBI	OBP	SLG	GF	IR	IRS	Hld	SvOp	SB	CS	GB	FB	G/F
1992 Season	3.48	1	1	0	25	2	44.0	20	32	.282	49	13	1	4	19	.357	.437	4	14	4	1	0	1	0	46	67	0.69

1992 Season

	ERA	W	L	Sv	G	GS	IP	H	HR	BB	SO
Home	2.84	1	0	0	13	2	25.1	26	2	6	23
Away	4.34	0	1	0	12	0	18.2	23	2	14	9
Starter	4.35	1	0	0	2	2	10.1	10	1	4	9
Reliever	3.21	0	1	0	23	0	33.2	39	3	16	23
0 Days rest	2.25	0	0	0	2	0	4.0	4	0	1	3

	Avg	AB	H	2B	3B	HR	RBI	BB	SO	OBP	SLG
vs. Left	.296	54	16	2	0	2	8	5	12	.356	.444
vs. Right	.275	120	33	11	1	2	11	15	20	.358	.433
Scoring Posn	.196	56	11	2	0	1	14	9	14	.303	.286
Close & Late	.167	24	4	1	0	0	0	8	4	.375	.208
None on/out	.243	37	9	4	0	0		7	5	.364	.351

1992 Season

	ERA	W	L	Sv	G	GS	IP	H	HR	BB	SO		Avg	AB	H	2B	3B	HR	RBI	BB	SO	OBP	SLG
1 or 2 Days rest	3.00	0	0	0	13	0	15.0	20	2	6	14	First Pitch	.250	24	6	3	0	0	2	5	0	.387	.375
3+ Days rest	3.68	0	1	0	8	0	14.2	15	1	9	6	Behind on Count	.297	37	11	5	0	0	3	10	0	.447	.432
Pre-All Star	4.26	1	0	0	2	1	6.1	5	1	1	4	Ahead on Count	.262	84	22	5	1	1	7	0	30	.262	.381
Post-All Star	3.35	0	1	0	23	1	37.2	44	3	19	28	Two Strikes	.247	85	21	5	1	1	7	5	32	.289	.365

Tony Pena — Red Sox

Bats Right (groundball hitter)

	Avg	G	AB	R	H	2B	3B	HR	RBI	BB	SO	HBP	GDP	SB	CS	OBP	SLG	IBB	SH	SF	#Pit	#P/PA	GB	FB	G/F
1992 Season	.241	133	410	39	99	21	1	1	38	24	61	1	11	3	2	.284	.305	0	13	2	1609	3.68	196	75	2.61
Last Five Years	.252	707	2294	237	578	103	7	27	230	172	68	9	68	30	16	.305	.338	34	24	13	8442	3.39	1075	538	2.00

1992 Season

	Avg	AB	H	2B	3B	HR	RBI	BB	SO	OBP	SLG		Avg	AB	H	2B	3B	HR	RBI	BB	SO	OBP	SLG
vs. Left	.252	111	28	6	0	1	11	2	14	.270	.333	Scoring Posn	.243	111	27	5	0	0	34	7	17	.283	.288
vs. Right	.237	299	71	15	1	0	27	22	47	.289	.294	Close & Late	.304	79	24	4	0	1	6	8	11	.375	.392
Groundball	.242	95	23	4	0	0	9	6	8	.287	.284	None on/out	.224	98	22	5	0	0	0	4	11	.262	.276
Flyball	.206	107	22	6	0	0	11	7	26	.250	.262	Batting #8	.248	258	64	15	1	0	28	17	44	.293	.314
Home	.276	203	56	16	1	1	20	12	30	.316	.379	Batting #9	.244	123	30	5	0	1	10	7	14	.288	.309
Away	.208	207	43	5	0	0	18	12	31	.252	.232	Other	.172	29	5	1	0	0	0	0	3	.172	.207
Day	.297	118	35	7	0	0	15	10	17	.352	.356	April	.236	55	13	4	0	1	6	2	10	.263	.364
Night	.219	292	64	14	1	1	23	14	44	.256	.284	May	.195	77	15	3	0	0	4	4	15	.244	.234
Grass	.255	349	89	20	1	1	35	20	50	.294	.327	June	.268	71	19	2	0	0	8	4	11	.303	.296
Turf	.164	61	10	1	0	0	3	4	11	.227	.180	July	.227	66	15	4	0	0	3	6	4	.292	.288
First Pitch	.321	78	25	7	0	0	11	0	0	.316	.410	August	.279	68	19	4	0	0	11	4	14	.315	.338
Ahead on Count	.321	84	27	2	1	1	11	12	0	.406	.405	September/October	.247	73	18	4	1	0	6	4	7	.286	.329
Behind on Count	.172	128	22	6	0	0	8	0	37	.178	.219	Pre-All Star	.238	235	56	11	0	1	18	10	38	.271	.298
Two Strikes	.181	177	32	8	0	0	9	12	61	.236	.226	Post-All Star	.246	175	43	10	1	0	20	14	23	.300	.314

1992 By Position

Position	Avg	AB	H	2B	3B	HR	RBI	BB	SO	OBP	SLG	G	GS	Innings	PO	A	E	DP	Fld Pct	Rng Fctr	In Zone	Outs	Zone Rtg	MLB Zone
As c	.240	409	98	21	1	1	38	24	61	.282	.303	132	122	1084.0	786	55	6	11	.993	---	---	---	---	---

Last Five Years

	Avg	AB	H	2B	3B	HR	RBI	BB	SO	OBP	SLG		Avg	AB	H	2B	3B	HR	RBI	BB	SO	OBP	SLG
vs. Left	.294	708	208	34	1	17	84	54	62	.345	.417	Scoring Posn	.251	617	155	24	1	4	194	66	68	.319	.313
vs. Right	.233	1586	370	69	6	10	146	118	216	.287	.303	Close & Late	.241	431	104	14	3	5	40	33	59	.295	.323
Groundball	.250	731	183	33	2	4	67	48	80	.299	.317	None on/out	.244	525	126	27	2	10	10	46	62	.307	.360
Flyball	.266	530	141	28	1	7	52	49	78	.326	.362	Batting #7	.247	316	78	16	2	1	30	22	43	.295	.320
Home	.253	1136	267	55	3	13	108	95	144	.312	.341	Batting #8	.256	1414	362	65	4	16	139	119	170	.315	.342
Away	.251	1158	291	48	4	14	122	77	134	.299	.336	Other	.245	564	138	22	1	10	61	31	65	.284	.340
Day	.264	643	170	36	3	5	77	52	83	.321	.353	April	.265	336	89	18	0	7	30	8	42	.281	.381
Night	.247	1651	408	67	4	22	153	120	195	.299	.333	May	.249	437	109	18	1	8	41	27	52	.300	.350
Grass	.249	1397	348	67	6	11	155	116	187	.308	.329	June	.264	387	102	14	5	2	50	30	48	.314	.341
Turf	.256	897	230	36	1	16	75	56	91	.301	.352	July	.216	389	84	17	0	4	30	35	45	.283	.290
First Pitch	.321	439	141	25	2	9	64	18	0	.346	.449	August	.245	368	90	12	0	3	40	36	51	.311	.302
Ahead on Count	.324	485	157	25	2	9	64	85	0	.422	.439	September/October	.276	377	104	24	1	3	39	36	40	.338	.369
Behind on Count	.205	772	158	27	3	6	58	1	171	.212	.271	Pre-All Star	.254	1285	327	55	6	17	130	78	156	.299	.346
Two Strikes	.188	926	174	35	0	4	57	57	278	.239	.239	Post-All Star	.249	1009	251	48	1	10	100	94	122	.313	.328

Batter vs. Pitcher (since 1984)

Hits Best Against	Avg	AB	H	2B	3B	HR	RBI	BB	SO	OBP	SLG	Hits Worst Against	Avg	AB	H	2B	3B	HR	RBI	BB	SO	OBP	SLG
Don Carman	.500	22	11	2	0	1	5	3	2	.560	.727	Duane Ward	.000	11	0	0	0	0	1	2	1	.154	.000
Jimmy Key	.476	21	10	2	0	2	6	0	0	.476	.857	Bob Walk	.053	19	1	1	0	0	1	1	1	.100	.105
Greg Hibbard	.462	13	6	0	0	1	3	1	1	.500	.692	Kirk McCaskill	.053	19	1	0	0	0	1	1	4	.100	.053
Dennis Rasmussen	.400	10	4	2	0	0	2	3	1	.538	.600	Chris Bosio	.077	13	1	0	0	0	1	0	2	.077	.077
Alejandro Pena	.368	19	7	2	0	0	1	5	1	.500	.474	Jose Guzman	.083	12	1	0	0	0	0	0	1	.083	.083

Terry Pendleton — Braves

Bats Both

	Avg	G	AB	R	H	2B	3B	HR	RBI	BB	SO	HBP	GDP	SB	CS	OBP	SLG	IBB	SH	SF	#Pit	#P/PA	GB	FB	G/F
1992 Season	.311	160	640	98	199	39	1	21	105	37	67	0	16	5	2	.345	.473	8	5	7	2341	3.42	266	172	1.55
Last Five Years	.280	706	2677	365	750	141	18	68	376	175	327	4	69	34	17	.322	.422	31	18	25	9769	3.39	1075	777	1.38

1992 Season

	Avg	AB	H	2B	3B	HR	RBI	BB	SO	OBP	SLG		Avg	AB	H	2B	3B	HR	RBI	BB	SO	OBP	SLG
vs. Left	.357	207	74	11	0	8	41	13	13	.390	.527	Scoring Posn	.391	161	63	10	1	8	86	20	21	.441	.615
vs. Right	.289	433	125	28	1	13	64	24	54	.323	.448	Close & Late	.286	91	26	2	0	5	14	7	9	.330	.473
Groundball	.352	264	93	15	1	8	44	15	27	.383	.508	None on/out	.347	118	41	6	0	3	3	6	6	.364	.475
Flyball	.267	165	44	15	0	6	28	8	22	.297	.467	Batting #2	.313	224	70	12	1	14	38	11	23	.340	.563
Home	.307	306	94	19	1	13	56	22	36	.353	.503	Batting #3	.309	411	127	27	0	7	65	26	44	.348	.426
Away	.314	334	105	20	0	8	49	15	31	.338	.446	Other	.400	5	2	0	0	0	2	0	0	.333	.400
Day	.328	183	60	9	0	8	33	7	23	.345	.508	April	.306	85	26	9	0	1	15	2	7	.315	.447
Night	.304	457	139	30	1	13	72	30	44	.345	.460	May	.314	118	37	5	0	8	21	8	17	.354	.559

1992 Season

	Avg	AB	H	2B	3B	HR	RBI	BB	SO	OBP	SLG		Avg	AB	H	2B	3B	HR	RBI	BB	SO	OBP	SLG
Grass	.325	471	153	30	1	19	83	29	51	.361	.514	June	.314	105	33	3	1	3	14	2	10	.321	.448
Turf	.272	169	46	9	0	2	22	8	16	.300	.361	July	.252	103	26	3	0	2	9	3	14	.274	.340
First Pitch	.358	109	39	7	0	5	23	7	0	.393	.560	August	.348	112	39	8	0	4	27	10	8	.398	.527
Ahead on Count	.338	142	48	10	0	9	30	19	0	.414	.599	September/October	.325	117	38	11	0	3	19	12	11	.385	.496
Behind on Count	.294	231	68	16	1	3	26	0	35	.292	.411	Pre-All Star	.296	351	104	19	1	13	51	13	39	.317	.467
Two Strikes	.263	266	70	13	1	5	30	11	67	.290	.376	Post-All Star	.329	289	95	20	0	8	54	24	28	.378	.481

1992 By Position

Position	Avg	AB	H	2B	3B	HR	RBI	BB	SO	OBP	SLG	G	GS	Innings	PO	A	E	DP	Fld Pct	Rng Fctr	In Zone	Outs	Zone Rtg	MLB Zone
As 3b	.312	638	199	39	1	21	105	37	67	.346	.475	158	158	1389.0	133	322	19	28	.960	2.95	424	360	.849	.841

Last Five Years

	Avg	AB	H	2B	3B	HR	RBI	BB	SO	OBP	SLG		Avg	AB	H	2B	3B	HR	RBI	BB	SO	OBP	SLG
vs. Left	.295	908	268	56	5	19	133	50	63	.330	.431	Scoring Posn	.304	739	225	47	6	21	310	71	103	.356	.470
vs. Right	.272	1769	482	85	13	49	243	125	264	.319	.418	Close & Late	.255	432	110	19	2	8	51	37	63	.312	.363
Groundball	.310	957	297	51	7	22	137	62	109	.351	.447	None on/out	.315	552	174	34	5	12	12	22	51	.341	.460
Flyball	.246	633	156	37	2	20	81	43	86	.293	.406	Batting #3	.299	1028	307	58	6	25	155	66	121	.339	.440
Home	.290	1344	390	80	12	43	210	95	156	.335	.464	Batting #5	.247	810	200	40	3	17	111	47	114	.288	.367
Away	.270	1333	360	61	6	25	166	80	171	.309	.381	Other	.290	839	243	43	9	26	110	62	92	.335	.455
Day	.299	780	233	34	2	27	117	52	99	.342	.451	April	.251	351	88	24	0	4	48	32	38	.308	.353
Night	.273	1897	517	107	16	41	259	123	228	.315	.411	May	.304	441	134	23	3	15	67	36	49	.353	.472
Grass	.303	1272	386	70	6	41	190	82	147	.343	.465	June	.282	415	117	19	4	11	62	25	57	.320	.427
Turf	.259	1405	364	71	12	27	186	93	180	.304	.384	July	.263	498	131	23	3	12	67	16	64	.285	.394
First Pitch	.336	470	158	32	3	13	73	18	0	.358	.500	August	.262	557	146	27	2	14	74	33	70	.304	.393
Ahead on Count	.322	580	187	36	4	26	88	91	0	.412	.533	September/October	.323	415	134	25	6	12	58	33	49	.373	.499
Behind on Count	.240	990	238	48	5	12	121	0	195	.239	.335	Pre-All Star	.277	1369	379	73	8	35	192	98	164	.322	.419
Two Strikes	.234	1087	254	46	5	19	134	54	326	.269	.338	Post-All Star	.284	1308	371	68	10	33	184	77	163	.323	.427

Batter vs. Pitcher (career)

Hits Best Against	Avg	AB	H	2B	3B	HR	RBI	BB	SO	OBP	SLG	Hits Worst Against	Avg	AB	H	2B	3B	HR	RBI	BB	SO	OBP	SLG
Shawn Boskie	.545	11	6	4	0	1	1	1	1	.583	1.182	Ken Hill	.000	14	0	0	0	0	0	0	2	.000	.000
Jose DeLeon	.542	24	13	3	2	0	3	3	2	.593	.833	Jesse Orosco	.063	16	1	0	0	0	0	4	4	.250	.063
Omar Olivares	.538	13	7	1	0	1	1	1	2	.571	.846	Lee Smith	.071	14	1	1	0	0	0	2	5	.188	.143
Norm Charlton	.500	18	9	1	1	1	6	1	1	.526	.833	Juan Agosto	.083	12	1	0	0	0	0	1	0	.154	.083
Mark Portugal	.500	10	5	2	0	0	3	3	2	.615	.700	Pat Combs	.091	11	1	0	0	0	0	0	1	.091	.091

William Pennyfeather — Pirates   Bats Right

	Avg	G	AB	R	H	2B	3B	HR	RBI	BB	SO	HBP	GDP	SB	CS	OBP	SLG	IBB	SH	SF	#Pit	#P/PA	GB	FB	G/F
1992 Season	.222	15	9	2	2	0	0	0	0	0	0	0	1	0	1	.222	.222	0	1	0	23	2.56	4	3	1.33

1992 Season

	Avg	AB	H	2B	3B	HR	RBI	BB	SO	OBP	SLG		Avg	AB	H	2B	3B	HR	RBI	BB	SO	OBP	SLG
vs. Left	.000	4	0	0	0	0	0	0	0	.000	.000	Scoring Posn	.333	3	1	0	0	0	0	0	0	.333	.333
vs. Right	.400	5	2	0	0	0	0	0	0	.400	.400	Close & Late	1.000	1	1	0	0	0	0	0	0	1.000	1.000

Melido Perez — Yankees   Pitches Right

	ERA	W	L	Sv	G	GS	IP	BB	SO	Avg	H	2B	3B	HR	RBI	OBP	SLG	CG	ShO	Sup	QS	#P/S	SB	CS	GB	FB	G/F
1992 Season	2.87	13	16	0	33	33	247.2	93	218	.235	212	33	3	16	88	.308	.332	10	1	4.07	23	112	18	18	300	245	1.22
Last Five Years	3.86	57	61	1	180	139	960.2	393	786	.243	873	140	30	94	399	.318	.376	18	5	4.43	78	100	75	57	1129	1047	1.06

1992 Season

	ERA	W	L	Sv	G	GS	IP	H	HR	BB	SO		Avg	AB	H	2B	3B	HR	RBI	BB	SO	OBP	SLG
Home	3.01	5	6	0	13	13	98.2	79	7	42	94	vs. Left	.247	430	106	16	1	8	37	50	99	.324	.344
Away	2.78	8	10	0	20	20	149.0	133	9	51	124	vs. Right	.225	471	106	17	2	8	51	43	119	.293	.321
Day	3.18	3	6	0	10	10	70.2	64	7	33	62	Inning 1-6	.232	707	164	23	3	14	72	75	154	.308	.332
Night	2.75	10	10	0	23	23	177.0	148	9	60	156	Inning 7+	.247	194	48	10	0	2	16	18	44	.330	.330
Grass	2.94	12	10	0	26	26	196.0	166	13	74	173	None on	.244	542	132	24	1	10	10	48	136	.307	.347
Turf	2.61	1	6	0	7	7	51.2	46	3	19	45	Runners on	.223	359	80	9	2	6	78	45	82	.308	.309
April	2.36	1	2	0	4	4	26.2	20	1	16	26	Scoring Posn	.210	200	42	3	0	3	67	30	55	.305	.270
May	2.82	3	2	0	6	6	44.2	40	3	19	36	Close & Late	.264	87	23	7	0	1	10	10	21	.337	.379
June	3.51	3	2	0	6	6	41.0	37	3	21	34	None on/out	.270	230	62	10	1	4	4	24	50	.339	.374
July	3.29	2	3	0	5	5	38.1	34	3	16	36	vs. 1st Batr (relief)	.000	0	0	0	0	0	0	0	0	.000	.000
August	2.39	2	4	0	6	6	49.0	38	3	11	42	First Inning Pitched	.287	122	35	2	2	3	15	15	27	.355	.410
September/October	2.81	2	3	0	6	6	48.0	43	3	10	44	First 75 Pitches	.241	593	143	16	3	12	58	60	140	.314	.339
Starter	2.87	13	16	0	33	33	247.2	212	16	93	218	Pitch 76-90	.263	118	31	9	0	3	17	14	27	.341	.415
Reliever	0.00	0	0	0	0	0	0.0	0	0	0	0	Pitch 91-105	.155	103	16	4	0	1	5	8	25	.214	.223
0-3 Days Rest	0.00	0	0	0	0	0	0.0	0	0	0	0	Pitch 106+	.253	87	22	4	0	0	8	11	26	.330	.299
4 Days Rest	2.78	9	10	0	21	21	158.2	131	9	59	136	First Pitch	.290	145	42	6	0	1	9	3	0	.305	.352
5+ Days Rest	3.03	4	6	0	12	12	89.0	81	7	34	82	Ahead on Count	.160	399	64	9	2	5	30	0	189	.164	.231
Pre-All Star	3.11	8	7	0	18	18	127.1	111	8	62	109	Behind on Count	.337	202	68	12	1	6	29	55	0	.471	.495
Post-All Star	2.62	5	9	0	15	15	120.1	101	8	31	109	Two Strikes	.145	421	61	7	1	5	29	35	218	.214	.202

Last Five Years

	ERA	W	L	Sv	G	GS	IP	H	HR	BB	SO		Avg	AB	H	2B	3B	HR	RBI	BB	SO	OBP	SLG
Home	4.02	22	23	0	80	58	412.1	385	42	165	328	vs. Left	.242	1799	435	72	21	44	196	204	385	.318	.379
Away	3.74	35	38	1	100	81	548.1	488	52	228	458	vs. Right	.245	1789	438	66	9	50	203	189	401	.318	.377
Day	4.00	18	14	0	47	43	268.0	253	28	126	213	Inning 1-6	.242	2863	692	111	24	74	335	323	624	.318	.375
Night	3.81	39	47	1	133	96	692.2	620	66	267	573	Inning 7+	.250	725	181	29	6	20	64	70	162	.317	.389
Grass	3.83	48	47	1	147	112	786.1	706	73	322	638	None on	.241	2111	508	82	13	62	230	230	471	.317	.380
Turf	3.98	9	14	0	33	27	174.1	167	21	71	148	Runners on	.247	1477	365	58	17	32	337	163	315	.319	.374
April	4.06	5	7	0	19	19	108.2	98	10	51	98	Scoring Posn	.244	816	199	28	6	18	289	99	194	.319	.359
May	4.11	12	11	0	29	28	177.1	158	19	87	145	Close & Late	.246	345	85	15	2	9	35	35	78	.317	.380
June	4.13	10	13	0	34	25	167.2	160	17	68	118	None on/out	.257	923	237	36	8	25	25	101	188	.332	.394
July	3.35	14	6	0	28	19	153.0	132	17	58	107	vs. 1st Batr (relief)	.371	35	13	3	0	1	9	2	8	.395	.543
August	4.19	5	13	0	34	24	171.2	171	18	60	148	First Inning Pitched	.272	666	181	27	6	10	96	83	152	.351	.375
September/October	3.36	11	11	1	36	24	182.1	154	13	69	170	First 75 Pitches	.245	2603	637	94	20	65	282	284	575	.320	.371
Starter	4.03	50	58	0	139	139	871.2	801	88	369	701	Pitch 76-90	.243	440	107	19	3	14	55	43	88	.307	.395
Reliever	2.22	7	3	1	41	0	89.0	72	6	24	85	Pitch 91-105	.226	328	74	17	4	10	32	34	74	.301	.393
0-3 Days Rest	6.86	0	4	0	4	4	21.0	21	1	13	11	Pitch 106+	.253	217	55	10	3	5	30	32	49	.347	.396
4 Days Rest	3.91	27	34	0	78	78	483.2	453	48	208	389	First Pitch	.342	514	176	29	8	13	84	5	0	.346	.506
5+ Days Rest	4.02	23	20	0	57	57	367.0	327	39	148	301	Ahead on Count	.179	1577	282	40	11	18	127	0	677	.181	.252
Pre-All Star	4.03	32	33	0	91	78	499.2	459	50	220	390	Behind on Count	.292	832	243	44	9	37	115	226	0	.440	.500
Post-All Star	3.67	25	26	1	89	61	461.0	414	44	173	395	Two Strikes	.170	1672	285	38	9	27	127	162	786	.245	.252

Pitcher vs. Batter (career)

Pitches Best Vs.	Avg	AB	H	2B	3B	HR	RBI	BB	SO	OBP	SLG	Pitches Worst Vs.	Avg	AB	H	2B	3B	HR	RBI	BB	SO	OBP	SLG
Travis Fryman	.000	16	0	0	0	0	0	0	6	.000	.000	Kirby Puckett	.488	41	20	1	0	2	8	2	4	.512	.659
Al Newman	.000	10	0	0	0	0	0	2	1	.167	.000	Dave Henderson	.368	19	7	1	1	1	8	3	4	.455	.684
Greg Vaughn	.000	10	0	0	0	0	0	2	3	.167	.000	Fred McGriff	.368	19	7	0	1	4	7	2	2	.429	1.105
Felix Fermin	.077	13	1	0	0	0	1	0	0	.071	.077	Ellis Burks	.333	18	6	1	0	2	2	4	2	.455	.722
Scott Leius	.077	13	1	0	1	0	0	3	0	4	.077	.154	Randy Milligan	.333	12	4	0	0	2	2	2	1	.385	.833

Mike Perez — Cardinals — Pitches Right

	ERA	W	L	Sv	G	GS	IP	BB	SO	Avg	H	2B	3B	HR	RBI	OBP	SLG	GF	IR	IRS	Hld	SvOp	SB	CS	GB	FB	G/F
1992 Season	1.84	9	3	0	77	0	93.0	32	46	.210	70	6	2	4	26	.278	.276	22	45	10	9	3	5	2	129	107	1.21
Career (1990-1992)	2.62	10	5	1	104	0	123.2	42	58	.225	101	15	3	5	40	.291	.305	31	60	15	13	5	9	3	170	147	1.16

1992 Season

	ERA	W	L	Sv	G	GS	IP	H	HR	BB	SO		Avg	AB	H	2B	3B	HR	RBI	BB	SO	OBP	SLG
Home	0.96	5	1	0	36	0	47.0	30	0	14	20	vs. Left	.244	156	38	3	0	2	17	20	20	.328	.301
Away	2.74	4	2	0	41	0	46.0	40	4	18	26	vs. Right	.181	177	32	3	2	2	9	12	26	.232	.254
Day	3.09	2	0	0	23	0	32.0	24	3	10	20	Inning 1-6	.174	69	12	1	0	0	5	4	11	.211	.188
Night	1.18	7	3	0	54	0	61.0	46	1	22	26	Inning 7+	.220	264	58	5	2	4	21	28	35	.296	.299
Grass	2.11	4	1	0	19	0	21.1	19	1	10	14	None on	.201	209	42	4	2	3	12	31		.244	.282
Turf	1.76	5	2	0	58	0	71.2	51	3	22	32	Runners on	.226	124	28	2	0	1	23	20	15	.329	.266
April	1.40	2	0	0	10	0	19.1	14	0	5	11	Scoring Posn	.192	73	14	0	0	1	22	17	7	.337	.233
May	0.75	2	0	0	12	0	12.0	11	0	3	8	Close & Late	.226	159	36	5	1	2	13	22	20	.322	.308
June	2.25	1	1	0	16	0	16.0	11	1	6	10	None on/out	.209	86	18	1	0	2	2	3	5	.236	.291
July	1.23	1	1	0	11	0	14.2	13	0	5	6	vs. 1st Batr (relief)	.205	73	15	1	0	1	6	3	6	.237	.260
August	2.40	1	1	0	12	0	15.0	11	3	10	4	First Inning Pitched	.198	227	45	5	1	3	23	19	30	.259	.269
September/October	2.81	2	0	0	16	0	16.0	10	0	3	7	First 15 Pitches	.188	229	43	4	1	3	20	17	29	.240	.253
Starter	0.00	0	0	0	0	0	0.0	0	0	0	0	Pitch 16-30	.264	87	23	2	1	1	6	12	14	.360	.345
Reliever	1.84	9	3	0	77	0	93.0	70	4	32	46	Pitch 31-45	.235	17	4	0	0	0	0	3	3	.350	.235
0 Days rest	2.20	3	2	0	25	0	28.2	22	0	8	10	Pitch 46+	.000	0	0	0	0	0	0	0	0	.000	.000
1 or 2 Days rest	1.69	3	1	0	36	0	42.2	29	3	12	24	First Pitch	.238	42	10	1	0	1	5	5	0	.306	.333
3+ Days rest	1.66	3	0	0	16	0	21.2	19	1	12	12	Ahead on Count	.180	161	29	4	0	2	7	0	38	.185	.242
Pre-All Star	1.59	6	1	0	42	0	51.0	41	1	17	32	Behind on Count	.227	66	15	1	1	0	8	16	0	.369	.273
Post-All Star	2.14	3	2	0	35	0	42.0	29	3	15	14	Two Strikes	.149	148	22	2	0	0	6	11	46	.213	.162

Tony Perezchica — Indians — Bats Right (flyball hitter)

	Avg	G	AB	R	H	2B	3B	HR	RBI	BB	SO	HBP	GDP	SB	CS	OBP	SLG	IBB	SH	SF	#Pit	#P/PA	GB	FB	G/F
1992 Season	.100	18	20	2	2	1	0	0	1	2	6	0	0	0	0	.182	.150	0	2	0	92	4.18	3	8	0.38
Career (1988-1992)	.228	69	101	10	23	7	1	0	5	10	26	0	0	2	1	.295	.317	0	2	1	384	3.43	26	31	0.90

1992 Season

	Avg	AB	H	2B	3B	HR	RBI	BB	SO	OBP	SLG		Avg	AB	H	2B	3B	HR	RBI	BB	SO	OBP	SLG
vs. Left	.083	12	1	1	0	0	1	1	4	.154	.167	Scoring Posn	.250	4	1	1	0	0	1	1	1	.400	.500
vs. Right	.125	8	1	0	0	0	1	2		.222	.125	Close & Late	.500	4	2	1	0	0	1	0		.500	.750

Gerald Perry — Cardinals — Bats Left (groundball hitter)

	Avg	G	AB	R	H	2B	3B	HR	RBI	BB	SO	HBP	GDP	SB	CS	OBP	SLG	IBB	SH	SF	#Pit	#P/PA	GB	FB	G/F
1992 Season	.238	87	143	13	34	8	0	1	18	15	23	1	3	3	6	.311	.315	4	0	2	577	3.58	55	44	1.25
Last Five Years	.265	542	1663	184	441	78	7	27	206	144	190	8	42	74	38	.323	.369	23	1	22	6264	3.41	742	464	1.60

1992 Season

	Avg	AB	H	2B	3B	HR	RBI	BB	SO	OBP	SLG		Avg	AB	H	2B	3B	HR	RBI	BB	SO	OBP	SLG
vs. Left	.200	25	5	0	0	0	2	4	2	.310	.200	Scoring Posn	.220	41	9	3	0	0	14	8	9	.346	.293
vs. Right	.246	118	29	8	0	1	16	11	21	.311	.339	Close & Late	.230	61	14	3	0	1	9	5	12	.284	.328
Home	.260	73	19	4	0	1	10	7	14	.329	.356	None on/out	.222	27	6	2	0	0	1	0		.250	.296
Away	.214	70	15	4	0	0	8	8	9	.291	.271	Batting #4	.208	48	10	2	0	0	0	5	7	.283	.250
First Pitch	.435	23	10	3	0	1	6	4	0	.500	.696	Batting #9	.231	39	9	1	0	1	10	5	6	.311	.333
Ahead on Count	.222	36	8	1	0	0	4	7	0	.349	.250	Other	.268	56	15	5	0	0	8	5	10	.333	.357
Behind on Count	.190	42	8	2	0	0	2	0	9	.205	.238	Pre-All Star	.240	104	25	7	0	0	12	10	12	.310	.308
Two Strikes	.158	57	9	2	0	0	3	5	23	.222	.193	Post-All Star	.231	39	9	1	0	1	6	5	11	.311	.333

Last Five Years

	Avg	AB	H	2B	3B	HR	RBI	BB	SO	OBP	SLG		Avg	AB	H	2B	3B	HR	RBI	BB	SO	OBP	SLG
vs. Left	.260	578	150	20	2	9	66	29	73	.295	.348	Scoring Posn	.261	441	124	31	4	4	168	71	55	.368	.397
vs. Right	.268	1085	291	58	5	18	140	115	117	.337	.381	Close & Late	.226	336	76	11	3	7	46	37	44	.305	.339
Groundball	.246	561	138	29	3	3	58	47	52	.303	.324	None on/out	.236	347	82	13	0	7	1	14	25	.270	.334
Flyball	.289	398	115	17	3	10	56	29	58	.334	.422	Batting #3	.274	898	246	41	3	13	102	73	94	.329	.370
Home	.278	863	240	47	5	11	109	71	98	.332	.382	Batting #5	.292	312	91	19	2	5	42	24	38	.339	.413
Away	.251	800	201	31	2	16	97	73	92	.313	.355	Other	.230	453	104	18	2	9	62	47	58	.300	.338
Day	.294	422	124	15	3	10	57	37	49	.348	.415	April	.271	247	67	10	1	6	36	39	22	.370	.393
Night	.255	1241	317	63	4	17	149	107	141	.314	.354	May	.262	370	97	21	1	5	48	30	43	.317	.365
Grass	.274	888	243	44	2	14	113	77	96	.330	.375	June	.289	270	78	10	2	4	34	15	30	.326	.385
Turf	.255	775	198	34	5	13	93	67	94	.314	.363	July	.270	326	88	16	0	8	33	27	44	.323	.393
First Pitch	.306	307	94	19	3	6	46	9	0	.322	.446	August	.296	247	73	9	3	1	38	18	24	.338	.368
Ahead on Count	.250	432	108	20	3	11	60	77	1	.341	.387	September/October	.187	203	38	12	0	3	17	15	27	.248	.291
Behind on Count	.250	524	131	19	1	5	43	2	103	.257	.319	Pre-All Star	.270	976	264	44	4	18	131	93	105	.333	.379
Two Strikes	.219	636	139	24	1	4	57	50	189	.277	.278	Post-All Star	.258	687	177	34	3	9	75	51	85	.308	.355

Batter vs. Pitcher (since 1984)

Hits Best Against	Avg	AB	H	2B	3B	HR	RBI	BB	SO	OBP	SLG	Hits Worst Against	Avg	AB	H	2B	3B	HR	RBI	BB	SO	OBP	SLG
Danny Cox	.550	20	11	2	0	0	2	2	1	.591	.650	Steve Avery	.000	11	0	0	0	0	0	2	1	.154	.000
Dennis Rasmussen	.438	16	7	0	1	2	5	1	2	.444	.938	Dave Stewart	.000	10	0	0	0	0	0	1	2	.091	.000
Tom Browning	.429	21	9	2	0	1	2	0	2	.429	.667	Roger McDowell	.063	16	1	1	0	0	0	2	3	.167	.125
Brian Fisher	.385	13	5	0	0	2	5	1	1	.429	.846	Bobby Ojeda	.091	11	1	0	0	0	0	1	1	.167	.091
Nolan Ryan	.364	22	8	1	0	1	5	8	4	.533	.545	Goose Gossage	.100	10	1	0	0	0	2	1	1	.091	.100

Geno Petralli — Rangers — Bats Left

	Avg	G	AB	R	H	2B	3B	HR	RBI	BB	SO	HBP	GDP	SB	CS	OBP	SLG	IBB	SH	SF	#Pit	#P/PA	GB	FB	G/F
1992 Season	.198	94	192	11	38	12	0	1	18	20	34	0	8	0	0	.274	.276	2	1	0	825	3.89	69	48	1.44
Last Five Years	.264	513	1251	113	330	54	4	14	118	149	184	7	41	2	4	.343	.347	12	11	10	5335	3.76	421	371	1.13

1992 Season

	Avg	AB	H	2B	3B	HR	RBI	BB	SO	OBP	SLG		Avg	AB	H	2B	3B	HR	RBI	BB	SO	OBP	SLG
vs. Left	.136	22	3	0	0	0	0		8	.136	.136	Scoring Posn	.261	46	12	3	0	1	18	9	9	.382	.391
vs. Right	.206	170	35	12	0	1	18	20	26	.289	.294	Close & Late	.180	50	9	1	0	1	5	8	12	.293	.260
Home	.220	100	22	6	0	0	9	7	12	.271	.280	None on/out	.229	35	8	2	0	0	0	3	7	.289	.286
Away	.174	92	16	6	0	1	9	13	22	.276	.272	Batting #6	.132	38	5	0	0	0	2	3	5	.195	.132
First Pitch	.333	18	6	3	0	0	2	0	0	.400	.500	Batting #7	.188	80	15	7	0	0	7	8	12	.261	.275
Ahead on Count	.246	57	14	4	0	1	9	9	0	.348	.368	Other	.243	74	18	5	0	1	9	9	17	.325	.351
Behind on Count	.169	65	11	3	0	0	4	0	21	.169	.215	Pre-All Star	.197	117	23	9	0	1	8	11	21	.266	.299
Two Strikes	.143	91	13	5	0	0	5	9	34	.220	.198	Post-All Star	.200	75	15	3	0	0	10	9	13	.286	.240

Last Five Years

	Avg	AB	H	2B	3B	HR	RBI	BB	SO	OBP	SLG		Avg	AB	H	2B	3B	HR	RBI	BB	SO	OBP	SLG
vs. Left	.183	104	19	1	0	0	8	15	23	.279	.192	Scoring Posn	.245	298	73	15	3	4	104	52	47	.349	.356
vs. Right	.271	1147	311	53	4	14	110	134	161	.349	.361	Close & Late	.237	224	53	9	0	2	12	35	41	.338	.304
Groundball	.332	337	112	16	1	3	37	40	31	.402	.412	None on/out	.268	291	78	14	0	4	4	35	45	.351	.357
Flyball	.237	325	77	14	0	4	27	47	59	.338	.317	Batting #6	.275	357	98	13	1	6	27	35	49	.346	.367
Home	.245	612	150	23	2	2	46	75	97	.331	.299	Batting #7	.257	443	114	21	0	2	31	56	61	.340	.318
Away	.282	639	180	31	2	12	72	74	87	.355	.393	Other	.262	451	118	20	3	6	60	58	74	.344	.359
Day	.268	272	73	15	0	3	26	29	34	.338	.357	April	.258	194	50	8	1	2	13	20	30	.326	.340
Night	.263	979	257	39	4	11	92	120	150	.344	.344	May	.245	245	60	10	1	2	27	30	27	.329	.318
Grass	.259	1052	272	43	4	12	99	124	153	.338	.341	June	.240	192	46	10	1	4	20	24	33	.333	.365
Turf	.291	199	58	11	0	2	19	25	31	.370	.377	July	.287	150	43	4	0	2	10	22	29	.374	.353
First Pitch	.303	218	66	14	1	1	23	3	0	.310	.390	August	.320	247	79	13	0	3	35	20	38	.368	.409
Ahead on Count	.337	332	112	20	2	7	45	69	0	.449	.473	September/October	.233	223	52	9	1	1	13	19	27	.335	.322
Behind on Count	.221	357	79	11	0	2	19	2	95	.233	.269	Pre-All Star	.255	686	175	30	3	9	62	80	101	.335	.347
Two Strikes	.179	535	96	13	0	3	27	73	184	.284	.221	Post-All Star	.274	565	155	24	1	5	56	69	83	.352	.347

Batter vs. Pitcher (since 1984)

Hits Best Against	Avg	AB	H	2B	3B	HR	RBI	BB	SO	OBP	SLG	Hits Worst Against	Avg	AB	H	2B	3B	HR	RBI	BB	SO	OBP	SLG
Dennis Lamp	.500	14	7	0	0	1	3	0	2	.500	.714	Eric King	.000	12	0	0	0	0	1	1	3	.077	.000
Dave Stieb	.476	21	10	2	0	0	1	5	1	.577	.571	Mark Gubicza	.053	19	1	0	0	0	1	2	6	.136	.053
Mike Boddicker	.444	36	16	4	0	2	3	4	5	.500	.722	Bobby Thigpen	.063	16	1	0	0	0	1	0	5	.063	.063
Juan Berenguer	.385	13	5	1	0	1	2	2	1	.467	.692	Dave Stewart	.095	21	2	1	0	0	1	2	4	.167	.143
Eric Plunk	.357	14	5	2	0	0	6	1	2	.400	.714	Bert Blyleven	.143	21	3	1	0	0	2	3	3	.250	.190

Gary Pettis — Tigers — Bats Both (groundball hitter)

	Avg	G	AB	R	H	2B	3B	HR	RBI	BB	SO	HBP	GDP	SB	CS	OBP	SLG	IBB	SH	SF	#Pit	#P/PA	GB	FB	G/F
1992 Season	.201	78	159	27	32	5	3	1	12	29	45	0	3	14	4	.323	.289	0	3	1	742	3.93	49	37	1.32
Last Five Years	.229	599	1766	272	404	50	26	8	116	271	445	5	31	168	57	.332	.300	0	34	5	8255	4.03	663	337	1.97

1992 Season

	Avg	AB	H	2B	3B	HR	RBI	BB	SO	OBP	SLG		Avg	AB	H	2B	3B	HR	RBI	BB	SO	OBP	SLG
vs. Left	.302	43	13	3	3	0	6	10	12	.434	.512	Scoring Posn	.212	33	7	0	1	0	9	10	9	.386	.273
vs. Right	.164	116	19	2	0	1	6	19	33	.279	.207	Close & Late	.158	19	3	1	0	0		3	8	.273	.211
Home	.250	60	15	0	1	1	6	15	21	.400	.333	None on/out	.189	37	7	2	0	0		8	12	.333	.243
Away	.172	99	17	5	2	0	6	14	24	.272	.263	Batting #8	.200	15	3	0	0	0	0		4	.200	.200
First Pitch	.233	30	7	1	0	0	1	0	0	.233	.267	Batting #9	.210	138	29	5	3	1	12	29	38	.345	.312
Ahead on Count	.333	27	9	3	3	0	6	8	0	.472	.667	Other	.000	6	0	0	0	0	0	0	3	.000	.000
Behind on Count	.164	55	9	1	0	1	5	0	22	.161	.236	Pre-All Star	.200	30	6	1	0	0	0	2	11	.250	.233
Two Strikes	.118	76	9	1	0	0	3	21	45	.309	.132	Post-All Star	.202	129	26	4	3	1	12	27	34	.338	.302

Last Five Years

	Avg	AB	H	2B	3B	HR	RBI	BB	SO	OBP	SLG		Avg	AB	H	2B	3B	HR	RBI	BB	SO	OBP	SLG
vs. Left	.231	592	137	18	10	0	39	84	119	.326	.296	Scoring Posn	.229	371	85	8	6	1	97	55	97	.328	.291
vs. Right	.227	1174	267	32	16	8	77	187	326	.326	.302	Close & Late	.228	276	63	6	3	1	19	38	80	.324	.283
Groundball	.248	484	120	13	6	1	30	65	118	.338	.306	None on/out	.207	642	133	19	10	2	2	105	183	.320	.277
Flyball	.225	426	96	13	4	3	30	73	106	.339	.296	Batting #1	.229	1229	282	33	18	5	78	183	290	.330	.298
Home	.237	862	204	20	17	5	61	145	211	.348	.317	Batting #9	.236	437	103	16	7	3	32	73	118	.346	.325
Away	.221	904	200	30	9	3	55	126	234	.317	.284	Other	.190	100	19	1	1	0	6	15	39	.296	.292
Day	.248	460	114	18	4	3	36	71	104	.349	.324	April	.211	194	41	6	1	0	12	34	45	.335	.253
Night	.222	1306	290	32	22	5	80	200	341	.326	.292	May	.231	308	71	11	2	3	18	38	74	.314	.308
Grass	.231	1479	342	39	23	6	95	240	363	.340	.301	June	.240	329	79	8	7	3	29	53	83	.346	.334
Turf	.216	287	62	11	3	2	21	31	82	.292	.296	July	.220	286	63	8	6	1	20	36	64	.310	.301
First Pitch	.305	236	72	6	4	1	24	0	0	.304	.377	August	.227	383	87	11	7	1	21	64	112	.337	.300
Ahead on Count	.304	306	93	15	9	3	41	118	0	.494	.441	September/October	.237	266	63	6	3	0	16	46	67	.349	.262
Behind on Count	.191	561	107	17	6	4	31	0	215	.195	.264	Pre-All Star	.234	894	209	29	12	6	63	134	207	.336	.313
Two Strikes	.164	917	150	14	7	1	30	153	445	.284	.197	Post-All Star	.224	872	195	21	14	2	53	137	238	.329	.287

Batter vs. Pitcher (since 1984)

Hits Best Against	Avg	AB	H	2B	3B	HR	RBI	BB	SO	OBP	SLG	Hits Worst Against	Avg	AB	H	2B	3B	HR	RBI	BB	SO	OBP	SLG
David Wells	.429	14	6	0	1	0	1	1	3	.467	.571	Lee Guetterman	.000	11	0	0	0	0	0	0	2	.000	.000
Gene Nelson	.385	13	5	1	0	0	2	2	2	.467	.462	Juan Berenguer	.067	15	1	0	0	0	3	1	10	.125	.067
Dennis Rasmussen	.364	11	4	2	0	0	4	3	2	.500	.545	Mark Williamson	.077	13	1	0	0	0	1	1	7	.143	.077
Scott Bailes	.364	11	4	2	1	0	1	1	0	.417	.727	Alex Fernandez	.091	11	1	0	0	0	0	1	3	.167	.091
Jose Guzman	.357	14	5	2	0	0	0	2	4	.438	.500	Bert Blyleven	.122	41	5	0	0	0	2	1	14	.143	.122

Tony Phillips — Tigers — Bats Both

	Avg	G	AB	R	H	2B	3B	HR	RBI	BB	SO	HBP	GDP	SB	CS	OBP	SLG	IBB	SH	SF	#Pit	#P/PA	GB	FB	G/F
1992 Season	.276	159	606	114	167	32	3	10	64	114	93	1	13	12	10	.387	.388	2	5	7	2898	3.98	255	155	1.65
Last Five Years	.263	679	2406	378	632	106	22	41	255	386	389	12	54	44	34	.364	.376	9	23	23	11269	3.99	923	633	1.46

1992 Season

	Avg	AB	H	2B	3B	HR	RBI	BB	SO	OBP	SLG		Avg	AB	H	2B	3B	HR	RBI	BB	SO	OBP	SLG
vs. Left	.270	174	47	9	1	5	23	37	21	.401	.420	Scoring Posn	.306	124	38	11	0	3	55	28	15	.415	.468
vs. Right	.278	432	120	23	2	5	41	77	72	.382	.375	Close & Late	.271	85	23	4	1	2	15	14	18	.380	.412
Groundball	.286	140	40	4	2	4	17	23	20	.382	.429	None on/out	.295	241	71	12	2	5	5	37	41	.388	.423
Flyball	.219	192	42	8	0	3	14	41	34	.355	.307	Batting #1	.276	550	152	31	3	9	59	92	79	.377	.393
Home	.273	289	79	12	1	3	31	64	42	.398	.353	Batting #6	.229	35	8	0	0	1	3	15	11	.460	.314
Away	.278	317	88	20	2	7	33	50	51	.377	.420	Other	.333	21	7	1	0	0	2	7	3	.500	.381
Day	.255	200	51	9	1	4	19	34	36	.361	.370	April	.237	59	14	1	0	0	3	12	14	.444	.254
Night	.286	406	116	23	2	6	45	80	57	.400	.397	May	.250	100	25	5	2	5	23	20	13	.366	.490
Grass	.269	517	139	25	2	7	45	98	81	.382	.366	June	.233	103	24	6	0	2	10	24	18	.375	.350
Turf	.315	89	28	7	1	3	19	16	12	.419	.517	July	.342	111	38	6	0	3	9	15	16	.421	.477
First Pitch	.256	78	20	3	2	1	9	1	0	.262	.385	August	.281	114	32	7	1	0	10	15	17	.362	.360
Ahead on Count	.395	167	66	13	0	8	30	58	0	.546	.617	September/October	.286	119	34	7	0	0	9	18	15	.379	.345
Behind on Count	.220	173	38	9	0	2	15	0	40	.220	.306	Pre-All Star	.258	310	80	15	2	7	36	74	48	.397	.387
Two Strikes	.199	272	54	9	1	1	15	55	93	.332	.250	Post-All Star	.294	296	87	17	1	3	28	40	45	.376	.389

1992 By Position

Position	Avg	AB	H	2B	3B	HR	RBI	BB	SO	OBP	SLG	G	GS	Innings	PO	A	E	DP	Fld Pct	Rng Fctr	In Zone	Outs	Zone Rtg	MLB Zone
As Designated Hitter	.209	115	24	1	0	4	17	27	29	.349	.322	34	34	---	---	---	---	---	---	---	---	---	---	---
As 2b	.268	194	52	11	1	4	21	42	23	.397	.397	57	50	437.1	110	167	4	40	.986	5.70	166	156	.940	.892
As 3b	.289	45	13	4	0	0	4	11	6	.429	.378	20	12	104.0	11	24	1	4	.972	3.03	37	24	.649	.841
As lf	.192	52	10	1	0	0	5	5	9	.254	.212	14	14	111.0	42	0	2	0	.955	3.41	47	40	.851	.809
As cf	.243	70	17	6	0	0	4	14	8	.376	.329	24	19	169.0	48	1	0	0	1.000	2.61	58	48	.828	.824
As rf	.402	127	51	9	2	2	13	15	16	.465	.551	35	29	259.2	90	2	4	0	.958	3.19	104	90	.865	.814

Last Five Years

	Avg	AB	H	2B	3B	HR	RBI	BB	SO	OBP	SLG		Avg	AB	H	2B	3B	HR	RBI	BB	SO	OBP	SLG
vs. Left	.281	740	208	37	10	18	82	136	95	.395	.431	Scoring Posn	.280	518	145	24	9	7	200	89	76	.375	.402
vs. Right	.255	1666	424	69	12	23	173	250	294	.351	.352	Close & Late	.234	354	83	18	3	7	39	61	69	.350	.362
Groundball	.264	663	175	25	2	11	69	102	88	.363	.357	None on/out	.258	826	213	34	4	15	15	128	139	.359	.363
Flyball	.264	602	159	30	6	12	61	98	105	.365	.394	Batting #1	.268	1594	427	79	14	27	168	254	251	.369	.386
Home	.265	1187	315	43	7	20	130	207	192	.374	.364	Batting #2	.284	271	77	11	2	6	28	49	40	.393	.406
Away	.260	1219	317	63	15	21	125	179	197	.355	.388	Other	.237	541	128	16	6	8	59	83	98	.337	.333
Day	.257	820	211	29	4	13	78	119	135	.351	.350	April	.256	359	92	13	4	4	30	60	65	.363	.348
Night	.265	1586	421	77	18	28	177	267	254	.371	.390	May	.253	387	98	16	5	9	57	71	59	.370	.390
Grass	.259	2020	524	80	17	31	204	331	333	.363	.362	June	.247	360	89	17	3	8	41	68	62	.366	.378
Turf	.280	366	108	26	5	10	51	55	56	.369	.451	July	.267	420	112	22	4	7	41	63	66	.362	.388
First Pitch	.318	324	103	13	6	10	42	6	0	.329	.488	August	.269	405	109	16	3	7	40	56	64	.355	.375
Ahead on Count	.339	604	205	39	4	18	97	205	0	.502	.507	September/October	.278	475	132	22	3	6	46	68	73	.369	.375
Behind on Count	.226	713	161	27	4	13	60	0	178	.230	.330	Pre-All Star	.259	1246	323	57	14	21	132	218	207	.370	.378
Two Strikes	.196	1119	219	35	7	9	75	174	389	.306	.264	Post-All Star	.266	1160	309	49	8	20	123	168	182	.358	.374

Batter vs. Pitcher (since 1984)

Hits Best Against	Avg	AB	H	2B	3B	HR	RBI	BB	SO	OBP	SLG	Hits Worst Against	Avg	AB	H	2B	3B	HR	RBI	BB	SO	OBP	SLG
Jose Mesa	.462	13	6	1	0	0	1	3	1	.563	.538	Juan Guzman	.000	12	0	0	0	0	0	1	5	.077	.000
Mike Flanagan	.429	21	9	2	0	0	2	5	0	.538	.524	Mike Mussina	.067	15	1	0	0	0	0	1	3	.125	.067
Eric King	.417	24	10	3	0	0	2	4	5	.500	.542	Mark Guthrie	.077	13	1	0	0	0	1	3	4	.235	.077
David West	.364	11	4	1	0	1	3	0	1	.364	.727	John Habyan	.091	11	1	0	0	0	0	1	1	.091	.091
Storm Davis	.333	21	7	1	0	2	7	4	3	.440	.667	David Wells	.100	20	2	1	0	0	1	1	5	.143	.150

Mike Piazza — Dodgers   Bats Right (groundball hitter)

	Avg	G	AB	R	H	2B	3B	HR	RBI	BB	SO	HBP	GDP	SB	CS	OBP	SLG	IBB	SH	SF	#Pit	#P/PA	GB	FB	G/F
1992 Season	.232	21	69	5	16	3	0	1	7	4	12	1	1	1	0	0	.284	.319	0	0	0	259	3.50	29	12	2.42

1992 Season

	Avg	AB	H	2B	3B	HR	RBI	BB	SO	OBP	SLG		Avg	AB	H	2B	3B	HR	RBI	BB	SO	OBP	SLG
vs. Left	.267	30	8	2	0	0	4	2	5	.313	.333	Scoring Posn	.200	20	4	0	0	1	7	2	2	.273	.350
vs. Right	.205	39	8	1	0	1	3	2	7	.262	.308	Close & Late	.214	14	3	1	0	0	2	1	1	.313	.286

Hipolito Pichardo — Royals   Pitches Right (groundball pitcher)

	ERA	W	L	Sv	G	GS	IP	BB	SO	Avg	H	2B	3B	HR	RBI	OBP	SLG	CG	ShO	Sup	QS	#P/S	SB	CS	GB	FB	G/F
1992 Season	3.95	9	6	0	31	24	143.2	49	59	.267	148	31	2	9	55	.327	.379	1	1	5.70	12	82	11	3	241	154	1.56

1992 Season

	ERA	W	L	Sv	G	GS	IP	H	HR	BB	SO		Avg	AB	H	2B	3B	HR	RBI	BB	SO	OBP	SLG
Home	3.94	5	2	0	16	12	75.1	75	4	16	30	vs. Left	.287	244	70	18	1	3	25	23	21	.346	.406
Away	3.95	4	4	0	15	12	68.1	73	5	33	29	vs. Right	.252	310	78	13	1	6	30	26	38	.313	.358
Starter	3.87	9	5	0	24	24	130.1	134	8	45	54	Scoring Posn	.286	140	40	7	0	3	45	11	16	.327	.400
Reliever	4.72	0	1	0	7	0	13.1	14	1	4	5	Close & Late	.333	9	3	0	0	0	0	1	0	.400	.333
0-3 Days Rest	0.00	1	0	0	1	1	5.0	3	0	0	2	None on/out	.284	134	38	10	1	1	1	18	17	.377	.396
4 Days Rest	3.97	5	2	0	14	14	81.2	88	7	28	33	First Pitch	.353	85	30	6	0	3	12	1	0	.352	.529
5+ Days Rest	4.12	3	3	0	9	9	43.2	43	1	17	19	Behind on Count	.328	131	43	11	1	4	19	25	0	.433	.519
Pre-All Star	3.60	3	4	0	17	10	70.0	71	4	24	30	Ahead on Count	.184	223	41	6	1	2	14	0	46	.189	.247
Post-All Star	4.28	6	2	0	14	14	73.2	77	5	25	29	Two Strikes	.203	222	45	8	1	1	12	23	59	.285	.261

Eddie Pierce — Royals   Pitches Left (flyball pitcher)

	ERA	W	L	Sv	G	GS	IP	BB	SO	Avg	H	2B	3B	HR	RBI	OBP	SLG	CG	ShO	Sup	QS	#P/S	SB	CS	GB	FB	G/F
1992 Season	3.38	0	0	0	2	1	5.1	4	3	.429	9	0	0	1	2	.500	.571	0	0	6.75	0	75	0	1	6	7	0.86

1992 Season

	ERA	W	L	Sv	G	GS	IP	H	HR	BB	SO		Avg	AB	H	2B	3B	HR	RBI	BB	SO	OBP	SLG
Home	4.50	0	0	0	1	1	4.0	8	1	3	3	vs. Left	.250	4	1	0	0	0	0	0	1	.250	.250
Away	0.00	0	0	0	1	0	1.1	1	0	1	0	vs. Right	.471	17	8	0	0	1	2	4	2	.545	.647

Phil Plantier — Red Sox
Bats Left (flyball hitter)

	Avg	G	AB	R	H	2B	3B	HR	RBI	BB	SO	HBP	GDP	SB	CS	OBP	SLG	IBB	SH	SF	#Pit	#P/PA	GB	FB	G/F
1992 Season	.246	108	349	46	86	19	0	7	30	44	83	2	8	2	3	.332	.361	8	2	2	1555	3.92	91	112	0.81
Career (1990-1992)	.268	175	512	74	137	27	1	18	68	71	127	4	12	3	3	.358	.430	10	2	5	2361	4.02	131	157	0.83

1992 Season

	Avg	AB	H	2B	3B	HR	RBI	BB	SO	OBP	SLG
vs. Left	.155	71	11	1	0	0	1	7	22	.238	.169
vs. Right	.270	278	75	18	0	7	29	37	61	.356	.410
Groundball	.225	89	20	1	0	1	4	8	27	.300	.270
Flyball	.300	90	27	6	0	4	12	6	12	.344	.500
Home	.269	201	54	10	0	5	23	22	44	.342	.393
Away	.216	148	32	9	0	2	7	22	39	.320	.318
Day	.232	138	32	3	0	4	13	19	32	.327	.341
Night	.256	211	54	16	0	3	17	25	51	.336	.374
Grass	.240	300	72	14	0	6	27	40	72	.332	.347
Turf	.286	49	14	5	0	1	3	4	11	.333	.391
First Pitch	.350	20	7	3	0	1	4	6	0	.481	.650
Ahead on Count	.385	91	35	8	0	3	10	24	0	.513	.571
Behind on Count	.220	141	31	8	0	2	12	0	48	.224	.319
Two Strikes	.143	182	26	6	0	1	10	14	83	.192	.207

	Avg	AB	H	2B	3B	HR	RBI	BB	SO	OBP	SLG
Scoring Posn	.167	90	15	5	0	1	21	23	22	.330	.256
Close & Late	.254	71	18	3	0	1	6	12	26	.369	.338
None on/out	.247	73	18	5	0	2	2	7	17	.313	.397
Batting #3	.290	93	27	5	0	1	7	10	23	.365	.376
Batting #5	.211	114	24	10	0	3	14	16	26	.305	.377
Other	.246	142	35	4	0	3	9	18	34	.333	.338
April	.239	67	16	5	0	1	9	8	18	.309	.358
May	.176	74	13	7	0	0	2	12	17	.287	.270
June	.250	60	15	2	0	4	12	8	15	.333	.483
July	.322	87	28	3	0	1	5	6	18	.372	.391
August	.200	35	7	0	0	0	0	5	9	.300	.200
September/October	.269	26	7	2	0	1	2	5	6	.387	.462
Pre-All Star	.238	239	57	15	0	6	26	30	57	.326	.377
Post-All Star	.264	110	29	4	0	1	4	14	26	.347	.327

1992 By Position

Position	Avg	AB	H	2B	3B	HR	RBI	BB	SO	OBP	SLG	G	GS	Innings	PO	A	E	DP	Fld Pct	Rng Fctr	In Zone	Outs	Zone Rtg	MLB Zone
As Designated Hitter	.296	81	24	3	0	1	5	8	17	.356	.370	23	22	---	---	---	---	---	---	---	---	---	---	---
As Pinch Hitter	.333	12	4	0	0	1	2	1	4	.385	.583	14	0	---	---	---	---	---	---	---	---	---	---	---
As lf	.286	42	12	1	0	1	4	3	9	.326	.381	13	11	95.0	18	0	2	0	.900	1.71	28	20	.714	.809
As rf	.219	215	47	15	0	5	21	32	53	.325	.358	63	60	529.2	128	6	2	1	.985	2.28	156	123	.788	.814

Dan Plesac — Brewers
Pitches Left (flyball pitcher)

	ERA	W	L	Sv	G	GS	IP	BB	SO	Avg	H	2B	3B	HR	RBI	OBP	SLG	GF	IR	IRS	Hld	SvOp	SB	CS	GB	FB	G/F
1992 Season	2.96	5	4	1	44	4	79.0	35	54	.229	64	17	0	5	38	.317	.343	13	28	12	1	3	2	3	84	99	0.85
Last Five Years	3.41	14	24	96	257	14	354.0	134	264	.241	316	64	5	30	192	.312	.367	90	222	75	4	124	18	12	386	422	0.91

1992 Season

	ERA	W	L	Sv	G	GS	IP	H	HR	BB	SO
Home	2.48	2	2	0	18	1	29.0	28	1	7	21
Away	3.24	3	2	1	26	3	50.0	36	4	28	33
Starter	5.14	1	1	0	4	4	21.0	18	2	11	18
Reliever	2.17	4	3	1	40	0	58.0	46	3	24	36
0 Days rest	1.35	1	0	0	5	0	6.2	5	1	4	4
1 or 2 Days rest	1.62	0	1	1	13	0	16.2	13	0	4	4
3+ Days rest	2.60	3	2	0	22	0	34.2	28	2	15	20
Pre-All Star	3.78	3	2	0	21	4	50.0	41	3	24	35
Post-All Star	1.55	2	2	1	23	0	29.0	23	2	11	19

	Avg	AB	H	2B	3B	HR	RBI	BB	SO	OBP	SLG
vs. Left	.254	67	17	4	0	2	11	8	18	.342	.403
vs. Right	.221	213	47	13	0	3	27	27	36	.309	.324
Scoring Posn	.289	90	26	7	0	4	36	11	19	.358	.500
Close & Late	.275	51	14	0	0	1	7	8	7	.383	.333
None on/out	.238	63	15	4	0	0	0	9	12	.333	.302
First Pitch	.308	39	12	4	0	0	4	4	0	.386	.410
Behind on Count	.345	55	19	3	0	2	15	17	0	.486	.509
Ahead on Count	.159	126	20	5	0	2	14	0	42	.169	.246
Two Strikes	.164	140	23	6	0	3	15	14	54	.248	.271

Last Five Years

	ERA	W	L	Sv	G	GS	IP	H	HR	BB	SO
Home	3.80	6	10	47	123	6	168.1	152	13	62	145
Away	3.05	8	14	49	134	8	185.2	164	17	72	139
Day	2.95	4	7	27	79	3	110.0	98	4	40	102
Night	3.61	10	17	69	178	11	244.0	218	26	94	182
Grass	3.66	13	20	76	212	12	292.2	267	26	114	248
Turf	2.20	1	4	20	45	2	61.1	49	4	20	36
April	2.85	3	4	10	35	4	47.1	40	4	14	46
May	4.01	2	3	22	40	3	60.2	54	6	20	60
June	3.86	1	4	21	55	0	58.1	57	6	25	35
July	2.49	3	4	20	50	0	61.1	54	3	23	46
August	2.63	3	4	13	40	3	61.2	40	7	21	48
September/October	4.45	2	5	10	37	4	64.2	71	4	31	49
Starter	4.83	3	4	0	14	14	69.0	70	7	32	51
Reliever	3.06	11	20	96	243	0	285.0	246	23	102	233
0 Days rest	4.06	2	4	17	37	0	37.2	37	4	17	26
1 or 2 Days rest	2.73	4	8	52	114	0	132.0	111	10	42	111
3+ Days rest	3.12	5	8	27	92	0	115.1	98	9	43	96
Pre-All Star	3.25	6	11	65	149	4	191.1	166	16	67	157
Post-All Star	3.60	8	13	31	108	10	162.2	148	14	67	127

	Avg	AB	H	2B	3B	HR	RBI	BB	SO	OBP	SLG
vs. Left	.235	281	66	11	3	7	54	24	69	.298	.370
vs. Right	.243	1028	250	53	2	23	138	110	215	.309	.366
Inning 1-6	.252	349	88	23	2	10	52	42	63	.331	.415
Inning 7+	.238	960	228	41	3	20	140	92	221	.306	.349
None on	.235	637	150	25	2	17	73	145	371	.361	.361
Runners on	.247	672	166	39	3	13	175	61	139	.308	.372
Scoring Posn	.273	396	108	26	3	9	162	45	81	.340	.422
Close & Late	.278	431	120	21	2	13	96	47	85	.352	.427
None on/out	.265	275	73	10	1	8	32	54	348	.348	.396
vs. 1st Batr (relief)	.240	221	53	10	1	5	33	17	49	.302	.362
First Inning Pitched	.243	815	198	45	3	19	137	77	171	.309	.345
Pitch 1-15	.244	746	182	37	3	19	107	68	153	.310	.378
Pitch 16-30	.214	299	64	15	0	5	42	37	72	.301	.314
Pitch 31-45	.211	114	24	3	1	1	15	14	22	.295	.281
Pitch 46+	.307	150	46	9	1	5	28	15	37	.360	.480
First Pitch	.290	200	58	12	0	6	36	11	0	.335	.440
Ahead on Count	.186	639	119	27	1	8	75	0	249	.191	.269
Behind on Count	.322	227	73	10	1	11	50	82	0	.492	.520
Two Strikes	.194	660	128	29	3	13	80	41	284	.242	.305

Pitcher vs. Batter (career)

Pitches Best Vs.	Avg	AB	H	2B	3B	HR	RBI	BB	SO	OBP	SLG
Rob Deer	.000	11	0	0	0	0	0	0	5	.000	.000
Kent Hrbek	.000	8	0	0	0	0	0	1	1	.091	.000
Pete Incaviglia	.063	16	1	0	0	0	2	1	1	.118	.063
Brook Jacoby	.071	14	1	0	0	0	1	0	4	.067	.071

Pitches Worst Vs.	Avg	AB	H	2B	3B	HR	RBI	BB	SO	OBP	SLG
Brian Harper	.545	11	6	0	0	3	8	1	0	.583	1.364
Julio Franco	.455	11	5	0	0	1	2	1		.538	.727
Lou Whitaker	.444	9	4	0	0	1	3	2		.500	.778
Jesse Barfield	.444	9	4	1	0	1	3	3	2	.583	.889

Pitcher vs. Batter (career)

Pitches Best Vs.	Avg	AB	H	2B	3B	HR	RBI	BB	SO	OBP	SLG	Pitches Worst Vs.	Avg	AB	H	2B	3B	HR	RBI	BB	SO	OBP	SLG
Roberto Alomar	.077	13	1	0	0	0	1	1	2	.143	.077	Alvin Davis	.417	12	5	0	1	1	4	2	1	.500	.833

Eric Plunk — Indians
Pitches Right (flyball pitcher)

	ERA	W	L	Sv	G	GS	IP	BB	SO	Avg	H	2B	3B	HR	RBI	OBP	SLG	GF	IR	IRS	Hld	SvOp	SB	CS	GB	FB	G/F
1992 Season	3.64	9	6	4	58	0	71.2	38	50	.229	61	9	0	5	31	.324	.320	20	44	11	7	8	3	2	81	81	1.00
Last Five Years	3.57	32	22	10	247	15	438.1	246	384	.240	391	55	13	45	218	.339	.372	42	207	77	24	21	54	23	462	516	0.90

1992 Season

	ERA	W	L	Sv	G	GS	IP	H	HR	BB	SO		Avg	AB	H	2B	3B	HR	RBI	BB	SO	OBP	SLG
Home	4.10	6	3	2	27	0	37.1	32	3	21	27	vs. Left	.237	118	28	6	0	1	9	10	18	.297	.314
Away	3.15	3	3	2	31	0	34.1	29	2	17	23	vs. Right	.223	148	33	3	0	4	22	28	32	.343	.324
Starter	0.00	0	0	0	0	0	0.0	0	0	0	0	Scoring Posn	.233	73	17	3	0	2	26	14	11	.348	.356
Reliever	3.64	9	6	4	58	0	71.2	61	5	38	50	Close & Late	.200	165	33	4	0	5	17	23	31	.295	.315
0 Days rest	2.87	2	1	3	12	0	15.2	13	0	7	7	None on/out	.232	69	16	1	0	2	7	12	.303	.333
1 or 2 Days rest	4.05	3	3	1	33	0	40.0	35	4	23	31	First Pitch	.421	38	16	2	0	4	12	1	0	.436	.789
3+ Days rest	3.38	4	2	0	13	0	16.0	13	1	8	12	Behind on Count	.304	46	14	0	0	7	22	0	.522	.370
Pre-All Star	3.91	1	0	2	23	0	23.0	18	0	11	19	Ahead on Count	.136	125	17	1	0	1	5	0	44	.135	.168
Post-All Star	3.51	8	6	2	35	0	48.2	43	5	27	31	Two Strikes	.145	145	21	3	0	1	8	15	50	.225	.186

Last Five Years

	ERA	W	L	Sv	G	GS	IP	H	HR	BB	SO		Avg	AB	H	2B	3B	HR	RBI	BB	SO	OBP	SLG
Home	3.84	20	8	5	111	9	211.0	197	23	119	176	vs. Left	.251	721	181	23	10	19	76	115	168	.352	.390
Away	3.33	12	14	5	136	6	227.1	194	22	127	208	vs. Right	.231	910	210	32	3	26	142	131	216	.328	.358
Day	2.82	15	6	3	83	3	137.1	114	6	89	120	Inning 1-6	.255	701	179	32	6	22	110	105	158	.351	.412
Night	3.92	17	16	7	164	12	301.0	277	39	157	264	Inning 7+	.228	930	212	23	7	23	108	141	226	.330	.342
Grass	3.61	28	19	9	210	13	384.0	341	40	214	335	None on	.246	874	215	27	10	24	24	119	190	.338	.382
Turf	3.31	4	3	1	37	2	54.1	50	5	32	49	Runners on	.232	757	176	28	3	21	194	127	194	.340	.361
April	3.83	4	2	1	30	0	40.0	43	7	29	35	Scoring Posn	.231	485	112	21	2	10	168	97	127	.355	.344
May	4.02	2	3	2	44	0	65.0	53	3	36	55	Close & Late	.231	390	90	8	2	13	52	60	78	.333	.362
June	2.31	4	1	1	43	0	58.1	45	2	29	52	None on/out	.233	386	90	13	4	10	10	51	84	.324	.365
July	3.25	6	2	2	39	0	63.2	62	4	37	53	vs. 1st Batr (relief)	.237	177	42	6	0	6	35	26	43	.332	.373
August	3.81	6	5	3	46	6	99.1	86	16	60	92	First Inning Pitched	.228	701	160	23	7	16	113	117	179	.336	.350
September/October	3.86	10	9	1	45	9	112.0	102	13	55	97	First 15 Pitches	.227	665	151	20	8	16	99	94	152	.323	.353
Starter	4.34	4	6	0	15	15	87.0	83	13	50	69	Pitch 16-30	.216	425	92	14	0	9	44	65	126	.319	.313
Reliever	3.38	28	16	10	232	0	351.1	308	32	196	315	Pitch 31-45	.281	217	61	10	3	6	35	42	47	.397	.438
0 Days rest	4.07	6	4	3	38	0	55.1	48	7	27	44	Pitch 46+	.269	324	87	11	2	14	40	45	59	.357	.444
1 or 2 Days rest	3.33	13	7	6	110	0	156.2	141	16	94	143	First Pitch	.338	207	70	12	3	10	51	9	0	.362	.570
3+ Days rest	3.17	9	5	1	84	0	139.1	119	9	75	128	Ahead on Count	.168	757	127	14	6	6	51	0	314	.170	.226
Pre-All Star	3.38	14	6	5	128	0	176.0	147	13	101	148	Behind on Count	.328	317	104	13	2	17	63	119	0	.508	.543
Post-All Star	3.71	18	16	5	119	15	262.1	244	32	145	236	Two Strikes	.159	856	136	19	7	8	54	118	384	.263	.225

Pitcher vs. Batter (career)

Pitches Best Vs.	Avg	AB	H	2B	3B	HR	RBI	BB	SO	OBP	SLG	Pitches Worst Vs.	Avg	AB	H	2B	3B	HR	RBI	BB	SO	OBP	SLG
Cory Snyder	.000	11	0	0	0	0	0	1	4	.083	.000	Wally Joyner	.667	15	10	2	0	3	8	3	1	.722	1.400
Danny Tartabull	.053	19	1	1	0	0	2	3	4	.182	.105	Paul Molitor	.583	12	7	1	0	1	4	1	1	.688	.917
Dave Henderson	.083	12	1	0	0	0	0	1	1	.154	.083	Kirk Gibson	.500	10	5	0	0	3	5	3	3	.615	1.400
Candy Maldonado	.083	12	1	0	0	0	2	2	4	.214	.083	Carlton Fisk	.462	13	6	0	0	2	6	2	2	.533	.923
Ozzie Guillen	.091	11	1	0	0	0	1	1	0	.154	.091	Pete O'Brien	.375	8	3	0	0	1	2	8	2	.688	.750

Luis Polonia — Angels
Bats Left (groundball hitter)

	Avg	G	AB	R	H	2B	3B	HR	RBI	BB	SO	HBP	GDP	SB	CS	OBP	SLG	IBB	SH	SF	#Pit	#P/PA	GB	FB	G/F
1992 Season	.286	149	577	83	165	17	4	0	35	45	64	1	17	51	21	.337	.329	6	8	4	2117	3.38	261	104	2.51
Last Five Years	.301	628	2305	348	693	80	31	9	193	168	265	5	53	166	75	.347	.374	12	17	17	8738	3.50	1053	463	2.27

1992 Season

	Avg	AB	H	2B	3B	HR	RBI	BB	SO	OBP	SLG		Avg	AB	H	2B	3B	HR	RBI	BB	SO	OBP	SLG
vs. Left	.227	132	30	3	0	0	5	9	25	.280	.250	Scoring Posn	.303	99	30	4	1	0	35	11	10	.360	.364
vs. Right	.303	445	135	14	4	0	30	36	39	.353	.353	Close & Late	.287	87	25	4	0	0	8	2	11	.311	.333
Groundball	.248	141	35	3	0	0	9	11	13	.301	.270	None on/out	.269	238	64	9	1	0	0	19	33	.323	.315
Flyball	.268	168	45	5	2	0	8	14	24	.321	.321	Batting #1	.286	569	163	17	4	0	35	45	61	.338	.330
Home	.286	266	76	11	3	0	19	22	32	.340	.350	Batting #9	.400	5	2	0	0	0	0	0	2	.400	.400
Away	.286	311	89	6	1	0	16	23	32	.333	.312	Other	.000	3	0	0	0	0	0	0	1	.000	.000
Day	.281	167	47	8	1	0	9	12	25	.330	.341	April	.275	69	19	1	0	0	6	12	1	.378	.290
Night	.288	410	118	9	3	0	26	33	39	.339	.324	May	.287	101	29	2	2	0	9	6	11	.324	.347
Grass	.285	478	136	16	4	0	29	39	49	.337	.335	June	.306	111	34	3	1	0	6	7	16	.345	.351
Turf	.293	99	29	1	0	0	6	6	15	.333	.303	July	.370	92	34	6	0	0	6	6	11	.408	.435
First Pitch	.276	98	27	2	0	0	8	6	0	.314	.296	August	.250	116	29	2	1	0	5	11	10	.318	.284
Ahead on Count	.368	114	42	7	0	0	8	25	0	.479	.430	September/October	.227	88	20	3	0	0	3	3	15	.253	.261
Behind on Count	.274	226	62	3	3	0	10	0	43	.275	.314	Pre-All Star	.290	317	92	7	3	0	21	27	34	.343	.331
Two Strikes	.253	225	57	4	2	0	13	14	64	.298	.289	Post-All Star	.281	260	73	10	1	0	14	18	30	.329	.327

1992 By Position

Position	Avg	AB	H	2B	3B	HR	RBI	BB	SO	OBP	SLG	G	GS	Innings	PO	A	E	DP	Fld Pct	Rng Fctr	In Zone	Outs	Zone Rtg	MLB Zone
As Designated Hitter	.314	188	59	8	2	0	12	12	20	.356	.378	47	46	---	---	---	---	---	---	---	---	---	---	---
As lf	.273	385	105	9	2	0	23	33	42	.328	.306	99	96	841.0	191	8	4	2	.980	2.13	233	185	794	.809

Last Five Years

	Avg	AB	H	2B	3B	HR	RBI	BB	SO	OBP	SLG		Avg	AB	H	2B	3B	HR	RBI	BB	SO	OBP	SLG
vs. Left	.250	440	110	13	4	0	33	27	73	.294	.298	Scoring Posn	.312	493	154	16	7	3	177	39	60	.352	.391
vs. Right	.313	1865	583	67	27	9	160	141	192	.359	.392	Close & Late	.290	334	97	12	1	2	24	17	46	.324	.350
Groundball	.289	612	177	20	4	3	60	43	67	.335	.350	None on/out	.294	840	247	34	12	3	3	73	109	.351	.374
Flyball	.307	541	166	22	9	3	45	47	76	.359	.397	Batting #1	.301	1953	588	68	27	7	157	150	217	.350	.374
Home	.311	1127	351	39	15	5	100	88	129	.362	.386	Batting #2	.322	233	75	10	3	1	29	12	31	.355	.403
Away	.290	1178	342	41	16	4	93	80	136	.332	.362	Other	.252	119	30	2	1	1	7	6	17	.286	.311
Day	.320	700	224	33	11	2	60	53	83	.369	.407	April	.268	226	65	5	3	0	23	23	15	.352	.336
Night	.292	1605	469	47	20	7	133	115	182	.338	.360	May	.295	359	106	10	9	1	28	20	39	.331	.382
Grass	.296	1939	574	64	27	9	162	145	212	.344	.371	June	.300	403	121	12	3	1	38	28	46	.343	.352
Turf	.325	366	119	16	4	0	31	23	53	.362	.391	July	.307	433	133	16	5	4	31	27	56	.349	.395
First Pitch	.311	357	111	13	2	1	37	8	0	.324	.367	August	.296	456	135	16	6	3	47	37	49	.347	.377
Ahead on Count	.365	427	156	18	3	0	35	100	0	.483	.422	September/October	.311	428	133	21	5	0	26	33	60	.360	.383
Behind on Count	.270	860	232	20	15	4	64	2	169	.274	.342	Pre-All Star	.293	1134	332	31	16	3	99	83	123	.340	.356
Two Strikes	.267	1003	268	27	15	6	83	59	265	.308	.342	Post-All Star	.308	1171	361	49	15	6	94	85	142	.354	.391

Batter vs. Pitcher (career)

Hits Best Against	Avg	AB	H	2B	3B	HR	RBI	BB	SO	OBP	SLG	Hits Worst Against	Avg	AB	H	2B	3B	HR	RBI	BB	SO	OBP	SLG
Mike Henneman	.600	10	6	0	0	0	2	1	0	.636	.600	Kenny Rogers	.000	14	0	0	0	0	0	1	3	.067	.000
Charles Nagy	.556	18	10	0	1	0	3	3	0	.619	.667	Frank Viola	.083	12	1	0	0	0	0	0	5	.083	.083
Scott Kamieniecki	.556	9	5	1	0	0	2	2	0	.636	.667	Greg Hibbard	.091	11	1	0	0	0	1	1	2	.167	.091
Jose DeLeon	.538	13	7	0	1	0	1	1	0	.571	.692	Charlie Hough	.115	26	3	0	0	0	1	1	2	.148	.115
Kevin Appier	.500	22	11	3	1	0	4	2	0	.542	.727	Danny Darwin	.167	12	2	0	0	0	0	0	2	.167	.167

Jim Poole — Orioles   Pitches Left

	ERA	W	L	Sv	G	GS	IP	BB	SO	Avg	H	2B	3B	HR	RBI	OBP	SLG	GF	IR	IRS	Hld	SvOp	SB	CS	GB	FB	G/F
1992 Season	0.00	0	0	0	6	0	3.1	1	3	.231	3	0	0	0	4	.286	.231	1	7	3	0	1	2	1	6	3	2.00
Career (1990-1992)	2.57	3	2	1	51	0	56.0	21	47	.196	39	6	0	4	26	.269	.286	10	53	15	6	2	2	2	74	50	1.48

1992 Season

	ERA	W	L	Sv	G	GS	IP	H	HR	BB	SO		Avg	AB	H	2B	3B	HR	RBI	BB	SO	OBP	SLG
Home	0.00	0	0	0	4	0	2.2	0	0	1	2	vs. Left	.286	7	2	0	0	0	2	0	2	.286	.286
Away	0.00	0	0	0	2	0	0.2	3	0	0	1	vs. Right	.167	6	1	0	0	0	2	1	1	.286	.167

Mark Portugal — Astros   Pitches Right

	ERA	W	L	Sv	G	GS	IP	BB	SO	Avg	H	2B	3B	HR	RBI	OBP	SLG	CG	ShO	Sup	QS	#P/S	SB	CS	GB	FB	G/F
1992 Season	2.66	6	3	0	18	16	101.1	41	62	.213	76	13	4	7	27	.295	.331	1	1	3.38	11	89	7	6	147	99	1.48
Last Five Years	3.63	37	29	4	128	90	632.0	221	435	.245	577	98	9	65	253	.311	.378	5	2	4.10	58	92	49	32	890	644	1.38

1992 Season

	ERA	W	L	Sv	G	GS	IP	H	HR	BB	SO		Avg	AB	H	2B	3B	HR	RBI	BB	SO	OBP	SLG
Home	1.86	4	0	0	10	9	58.0	41	3	23	37	vs. Left	.244	205	50	10	3	5	19	26	40	.328	.395
Away	3.74	2	3	0	8	7	43.1	35	4	18	25	vs. Right	.171	152	26	3	1	2	8	15	22	.250	.243
Starter	2.51	5	3	0	16	16	100.1	75	7	39	61	Scoring Posn	.269	78	21	1	1	1	21	8	12	.341	.346
Reliever	18.00	1	0	0	2	0	1.0	1	0	2	1	Close & Late	.194	31	6	1	0	2	2	4	6	.286	.419
0-3 Days Rest	3.46	1	0	0	2	2	13.0	11	1	2	10	None on/out	.248	101	25	3	2	6	6	11	15	.321	.495
4 Days Rest	3.24	2	3	0	9	9	50.0	40	3	23	30	First Pitch	.197	61	12	1	1	2	7	1	0	.210	.344
5+ Days Rest	1.21	2	0	0	5	5	37.1	24	3	14	21	Behind on Count	.274	95	26	5	1	3	11	18	0	.395	.442
Pre-All Star	2.60	5	3	0	15	15	93.1	71	6	39	56	Ahead on Count	.132	152	20	2	0	2	5	0	54	.132	.184
Post-All Star	3.38	1	0	0	3	1	8.0	5	1	2	6	Two Strikes	.141	142	20	4	0	1	4	22	62	.256	.190

Last Five Years

	ERA	W	L	Sv	G	GS	IP	H	HR	BB	SO		Avg	AB	H	2B	3B	HR	RBI	BB	SO	OBP	SLG
Home	2.67	22	10	2	66	42	320.2	278	25	101	230	vs. Left	.239	1331	318	52	8	36	143	139	272	.311	.371
Away	4.63	15	19	2	62	48	311.1	299	40	120	205	vs. Right	.254	1021	259	46	1	29	110	82	163	.310	.386
Day	4.29	13	12	4	44	28	211.2	209	26	79	137	Inning 1-6	.242	1927	467	78	9	51	210	184	366	.309	.372
Night	3.30	24	17	0	84	62	420.1	368	39	142	298	Inning 7+	.259	425	110	20	0	14	43	37	69	.318	.405
Grass	5.10	10	15	2	46	32	213.2	224	28	83	143	None on	.249	1398	348	60	6	39	39	125	262	.312	.384
Turf	2.88	27	14	2	82	58	418.1	353	37	138	292	Runners on	.240	954	229	38	3	26	214	96	173	.306	.368
April	3.86	5	5	1	14	12	74.2	75	4	24	50	Scoring Posn	.255	530	135	21	2	15	184	62	102	.326	.387
May	4.27	5	4	0	21	16	109.2	105	17	41	73	Close & Late	.272	206	56	8	0	6	19	22	34	.341	.398
June	3.46	3	7	0	22	15	119.2	99	13	32	76	None on/out	.264	614	162	24	5	24	24	64	104	.336	.436
July	3.25	7	3	2	23	15	97.0	90	12	36	72	vs. 1st Batr (relief)	.242	33	8	2	0	1	7	4	7	.342	.394
August	3.02	7	2	0	18	14	101.1	95	6	35	81	First Inning Pitched	.275	466	128	23	3	11	72	51	86	.345	.408
September/October	3.89	10	8	1	30	18	129.2	113	13	53	83	Pitch First 75 Pitches	.247	1854	458	79	8	48	201	182	352	.315	.376
Starter	3.45	33	24	0	90	90	560.1	501	53	194	395	Pitch 76-90	.212	273	58	9	1	8	21	18	44	.262	.341
Reliever	5.02	4	5	4	38	0	71.2	76	12	27	40	Pitch 91-105	.255	165	42	8	0	5	17	19	29	.332	.394

Last Five Years

	ERA	W	L	Sv	G	GS	IP	H	HR	BB	SO		Avg	AB	H	2B	3B	HR	RBI	BB	SO	OBP	SLG
0-3 Days Rest	2.08	3	0	0	6	6	39.0	33	2	11	34	Pitch 106+	.317	60	19	2	0	4	14	2	10	.349	.550
4 Days Rest	3.41	17	14	0	54	54	340.0	298	33	112	235	First Pitch	.311	367	114	24	2	8	48	5	0	.321	.452
5+ Days Rest	3.82	13	10	0	30	30	181.1	170	18	71	126	Ahead on Count	.175	1021	179	27	0	15	68	0	366	.175	.246
Pre-All Star	3.82	16	17	1	64	49	336.2	309	40	111	221	Behind on Count	.303	568	172	27	3	26	82	130	0	.433	.498
Post-All Star	3.41	21	12	3	64	41	295.1	268	25	110	214	Two Strikes	.160	1005	161	26	0	16	74	86	435	.227	.234

Pitcher vs. Batter (career)

Pitches Best Vs.	Avg	AB	H	2B	3B	HR	RBI	BB	SO	OBP	SLG	Pitches Worst Vs.	Avg	AB	H	2B	3B	HR	RBI	BB	SO	OBP	SLG
Jose Uribe	.067	15	1	0	0	0	0	2	6	.176	.067	Orlando Merced	.600	10	6	1	1	1	3	1	0	.636	1.200
Barry Larkin	.071	14	1	0	0	0	0	2	2	.071	.071	Terry Pendleton	.500	10	5	2	0	0	3	3	2	.615	.700
Matt D. Williams	.081	37	3	0	0	0	0	1	12	.105	.081	Rickey Henderson	.500	8	4	1	0	1	0	3	2	.545	1.000
Kevin Elster	.083	12	1	0	0	0	1	0	1	.077	.083	Jeff Blauser	.462	13	6	0	0	3	5	1	2	.500	1.154
John Kruk	.091	11	1	0	0	0	0	0	2	.091	.091	Darryl Strawberry	.421	19	8	1	0	3	6	3	7	.500	.947

Dennis Powell — Mariners

Pitches Left

	ERA	W	L	Sv	G	GS	IP	BB	SO	Avg	H	2B	3B	HR	RBI	OBP	SLG	GF	IR	IRS	Hld	SvOp	SB	CS	GB	FB	G/F
1992 Season	4.58	4	2	0	49	0	57.0	29	35	.238	49	13	0	5	25	.340	.374	11	50	6	6	0	3	3	76	60	1.27
Last Five Years	5.80	7	11	2	115	10	163.0	82	100	.296	191	36	6	13	103	.380	.431	13	108	24	17	2	13	5	246	172	1.43

1992 Season

	ERA	W	L	Sv	G	GS	IP	H	HR	BB	SO		Avg	AB	H	2B	3B	HR	RBI	BB	SO	OBP	SLG
Home	3.00	1	1	0	23	0	27.0	22	2	14	16	vs. Left	.250	68	17	4	0	2	13	6	14	.311	.397
Away	6.00	3	1	0	26	0	30.0	27	3	15	19	vs. Right	.232	138	32	9	0	3	12	23	21	.354	.362
Starter	0.00	0	0	0	0	0	0.0	0	0	0	0	Scoring Posn	.206	63	13	1	0	2	21	7	12	.296	.317
Reliever	4.58	4	2	0	49	0	57.0	49	5	29	35	Close & Late	.241	58	14	6	0	2	6	8	12	.343	.448
0 Days rest	9.95	1	1	0	8	0	6.1	9	0	4	3	None on/out	.224	49	11	4	0	1	1	6	8	.321	.367
1 or 2 Days rest	5.03	0	0	0	21	0	19.2	18	3	13	12	First Pitch	.296	27	8	2	0	1	3	2	0	.367	.481
3+ Days rest	3.19	3	1	0	20	0	31.0	22	2	12	20	Behind on Count	.407	54	22	7	0	2	13	18	0	.562	.648
Pre-All Star	5.59	2	1	0	35	0	37.0	33	3	24	21	Ahead on Count	.149	87	13	3	0	1	8	0	29	.159	.218
Post-All Star	2.70	2	1	0	14	0	20.0	16	2	5	14	Two Strikes	.069	87	6	1	0	0	4	9	35	.165	.080

Last Five Years

	ERA	W	L	Sv	G	GS	IP	H	HR	BB	SO		Avg	AB	H	2B	3B	HR	RBI	BB	SO	OBP	SLG
Home	5.29	3	4	1	58	4	78.1	87	7	44	53	vs. Left	.277	206	57	11	2	7	45	15	42	.333	.451
Away	6.27	4	7	1	57	6	84.2	104	6	38	47	vs. Right	.305	439	134	25	4	6	58	67	58	.400	.421
Day	4.89	3	3	1	37	5	70.0	69	2	30	38	Inning 1-6	.296	331	98	21	2	4	64	40	52	.373	.408
Night	6.48	4	8	1	78	5	93.0	122	11	52	62	Inning 7+	.296	314	93	15	4	9	39	42	48	.387	.455
Grass	5.97	2	7	1	45	7	78.1	89	3	37	42	None on	.301	309	93	15	2	8	8	42	52	.388	.440
Turf	5.63	5	4	1	70	3	84.2	102	10	45	58	Runners on	.292	336	98	21	4	5	95	40	48	.372	.423
April	3.20	0	0	0	17	0	19.2	13	1	12	9	Scoring Posn	.286	203	58	9	1	3	85	28	37	.374	.384
May	5.44	4	5	1	36	1	46.1	51	1	24	32	Close & Late	.305	118	36	8	1	3	11	14	22	.388	.466
June	6.57	1	2	0	24	3	38.1	50	4	21	26	None on/out	.305	151	46	9	1	2	2	18	18	.382	.417
July	5.48	0	1	1	17	2	21.1	23	3	10	9	vs. 1st Batr (relief)	.239	88	21	2	1	3	14	11	19	.343	.386
August	9.00	1	3	0	11	4	26.0	46	2	12	14	First Inning Pitched	.270	319	86	18	1	7	51	45	55	.365	.398
September/October	2.38	1	0	0	10	0	11.1	8	2	3	10	First 15 Pitches	.287	282	81	16	1	7	38	39	45	.383	.426
Starter	7.47	0	6	0	10	10	47.0	71	1	21	26	Pitch 16-30	.305	151	46	7	2	4	24	23	24	.397	.457
Reliever	5.12	7	5	2	105	0	116.0	120	12	61	74	Pitch 31-45	.286	98	28	4	2	1	20	11	15	.351	.398
0 Days rest	4.91	3	1	1	18	0	18.1	20	0	12	10	Pitch 46+	.316	114	36	9	1	1	21	9	16	.371	.439
1 or 2 Days rest	5.27	0	0	0	46	0	42.2	48	5	22	26	First Pitch	.392	97	38	6	2	1	16	2	0	.402	.526
3+ Days rest	5.07	4	3	1	41	0	55.0	52	7	27	38	Ahead on Count	.238	282	67	10	2	4	41	0	86	.244	.330
Pre-All Star	5.32	5	7	1	86	6	118.1	130	7	64	73	Behind on Count	.361	155	56	14	1	6	34	47	0	.515	.581
Post-All Star	7.05	2	4	1	29	4	44.2	61	6	18	27	Two Strikes	.169	267	45	5	3	3	30	33	100	.263	.243

Pitcher vs. Batter (career)

Pitches Best Vs.	Avg	AB	H	2B	3B	HR	RBI	BB	SO	OBP	SLG	Pitches Worst Vs.	Avg	AB	H	2B	3B	HR	RBI	BB	SO	OBP	SLG
												Don Mattingly	.400	20	8	2	0	1	5	1	0	.409	.650

Ted Power — Indians

Pitches Right

	ERA	W	L	Sv	G	GS	IP	BB	SO	Avg	H	2B	3B	HR	RBI	OBP	SLG	GF	IR	IRS	Hld	SvOp	SB	CS	GB	FB	G/F
1992 Season	2.54	3	3	6	64	0	99.1	35	51	.248	88	14	0	7	51	.316	.346	16	84	25	14	11	8	3	127	110	1.15
Last Five Years	3.92	22	23	16	221	29	434.0	142	244	.268	442	85	10	33	205	.325	.391	63	159	43	26	22	41	17	571	533	1.07

1992 Season

	ERA	W	L	Sv	G	GS	IP	H	HR	BB	SO		Avg	AB	H	2B	3B	HR	RBI	BB	SO	OBP	SLG
Home	1.64	2	1	3	32	0	55.0	44	3	20	33	vs. Left	.226	133	30	7	0	1	9	13	25	.302	.301
Away	3.65	1	2	3	32	0	44.1	44	4	15	18	vs. Right	.261	222	58	7	0	6	42	22	26	.324	.374
Day	2.29	0	2	2	24	0	39.1	32	2	17	24	Inning 1-6	.195	77	15	0	0	4	18	8	14	.281	.351
Night	2.70	3	1	4	40	0	60.0	56	5	18	27	Inning 7+	.263	278	73	14	0	3	33	27	37	.326	.345
Grass	2.55	3	3	4	52	0	88.1	76	7	34	48	None on	.291	158	46	10	0	2	2	12	19	.349	.392
Turf	2.45	0	0	2	12	0	11.0	12	0	1	3	Runners on	.213	197	42	4	0	5	49	23	32	.291	.310
April	1.06	1	0	2	10	0	17.0	9	0	11	10	Scoring Posn	.202	114	23	1	0	3	43	21	19	.313	.289
May	0.00	0	0	1	7	0	8.0	7	0	1	0	Close & Late	.238	151	36	5	0	2	20	14	18	.308	.311

1992 Season

	ERA	W	L	Sv	G	GS	IP	H	HR	BB	SO		Avg	AB	H	2B	3B	HR	RBI	BB	SO	OBP	SLG
June	5.84	0	2	0	11	0	12.1	18	0	5	12	None on/out	.338	74	25	5	0	0	0	4	9	.380	.405
July	2.70	0	0	1	11	0	20.0	17	2	5	13	vs. 1st Batr (relief)	.208	53	11	1	0	0	9	3	11	.274	.226
August	2.53	0	1	1	13	0	21.1	22	1	4	11	First Inning Pitched	.229	192	44	3	0	5	39	19	34	.301	.323
September/October	2.61	2	0	1	12	0	20.2	15	4	9	5	First 15 Pitches	.234	192	45	6	0	5	35	14	33	.291	.344
Starter	0.00	0	0	0	0	0	0.0	0	0	0	0	Pitch 16-30	.287	108	31	5	0	0	7	16	11	.378	.333
Reliever	2.54	3	3	6	64	0	99.1	88	7	35	51	Pitch 31-45	.220	50	11	2	0	2	8	5	7	.286	.380
0 Days rest	2.18	0	1	2	16	0	20.2	25	1	4	12	Pitch 46+	.200	5	1	1	0	0	1	0	0	.167	.400
1 or 2 Days rest	2.68	2	1	2	30	0	50.1	40	4	15	25	First Pitch	.224	49	11	2	0	1	4	7	0	.321	.327
3+ Days rest	2.54	1	1	2	18	0	28.1	23	2	16	14	Ahead on Count	.234	175	41	4	0	6	28	0	45	.242	.360
Pre-All Star	2.40	1	2	4	32	0	48.2	43	1	20	29	Behind on Count	.299	67	20	5	0	0	14	18	1	.442	.373
Post-All Star	2.66	2	1	2	32	0	50.2	45	6	15	22	Two Strikes	.199	161	32	1	0	6	29	10	50	.256	.317

Last Five Years

	ERA	W	L	Sv	G	GS	IP	H	HR	BB	SO		Avg	AB	H	2B	3B	HR	RBI	BB	SO	OBP	SLG
Home	3.31	14	7	10	117	13	226.1	220	13	75	129	vs. Left	.273	765	209	43	5	15	84	83	110	.346	.401
Away	4.59	8	16	6	104	16	205.2	222	20	67	115	vs. Right	.263	887	233	42	5	18	121	59	134	.308	.382
Day	4.15	5	7	5	69	6	112.2	114	9	42	74	Inning 1-6	.271	805	218	50	6	19	113	65	114	.327	.419
Night	3.84	17	16	11	152	23	321.1	328	24	100	170	Inning 7+	.264	847	224	35	4	14	92	77	130	.324	.365
Grass	4.06	8	11	5	96	9	190.2	186	21	69	109	None on	.266	890	237	51	6	13	13	59	128	.316	.381
Turf	3.81	14	12	11	125	20	243.1	256	12	73	135	Runners on	.269	762	205	34	4	20	192	83	116	.336	.403
April	1.93	4	1	3	28	0	42.0	27	1	18	22	Scoring Posn	.269	449	121	20	2	12	169	64	72	.349	.403
May	4.85	4	4	4	36	4	55.2	67	5	22	31	Close & Late	.255	377	96	14	3	5	44	33	54	.316	.347
June	3.63	4	3	0	34	6	72.0	83	3	20	51	None on/out	.290	397	115	26	2	4	4	23	53	.333	.395
July	5.53	5	5	4	37	8	84.2	92	9	26	51	vs. 1st Batr (relief)	.235	162	38	5	0	2	17	11	32	.269	.302
August	2.53	5	3	5	41	7	99.2	86	6	27	51	First Inning Pitched	.248	656	163	24	3	12	96	61	115	.312	.349
September/October	4.61	6	5	3	45	4	80.0	87	9	27	42	First 15 Pitches	.256	659	169	31	4	12	84	57	111	.319	.370
Starter	5.11	8	12	0	29	29	151.1	178	13	44	78	Pitch 16-30	.277	419	116	18	1	8	48	36	67	.333	.382
Reliever	3.28	14	11	16	192	0	282.2	264	20	98	166	Pitch 31-45	.268	224	60	15	3	7	36	21	32	.328	.455
0 Days rest	3.21	2	2	3	40	0	47.2	52	4	12	24	Pitch 46+	.277	350	97	21	2	6	37	28	34	.327	.400
1 or 2 Days rest	3.43	6	6	7	89	0	126.0	108	11	44	74	First Pitch	.321	234	75	18	3	7	37	22	0	.378	.513
3+ Days rest	3.14	8	3	6	63	0	109.0	104	5	42	68	Ahead on Count	.220	812	179	33	2	14	83	0	209	.225	.318
Pre-All Star	3.93	9	11	8	108	13	199.1	217	14	67	122	Behind on Count	.315	314	99	18	3	5	45	62	1	.427	.439
Post-All Star	3.91	13	12	8	113	16	234.2	225	19	75	122	Two Strikes	.212	775	164	31	3	12	80	58	243	.269	.305

Pitcher vs. Batter (since 1984)

Pitches Best Vs.	Avg	AB	H	2B	3B	HR	RBI	BB	SO	OBP	SLG	Pitches Worst Vs.	Avg	AB	H	2B	3B	HR	RBI	BB	SO	OBP	SLG
Benito Santiago	.063	16	1	0	0	0	0	0	3	.063	.063	John Kruk	.556	18	10	3	1	0	6	2	0	.600	.833
Kevin Elster	.063	12	1	1	0	0	0	1	2	.154	.167	Dan Gladden	.545	11	6	2	0	1	5	3	0	.643	1.000
Charlie Hayes	.100	10	1	0	0	0	1	0	4	.091	.100	Dion James	.500	12	6	2	0	0	3	3	1	.600	.667
Hubie Brooks	.143	28	4	0	0	0	1	1	4	.172	.143	Will Clark	.467	15	7	1	0	2	5	3	1	.556	.933
Sid Bream	.167	18	3	0	0	0	2	0	1	.167	.167	Gregg Jefferies	.417	12	5	1	0	2	4	1	0	.462	1.000

Todd Pratt — Phillies
Bats Right (groundball hitter)

	Avg	G	AB	R	H	2B	3B	HR	RBI	BB	SO	HBP	GDP	SB	CS	OBP	SLG	IBB	SH	SF	#Pit	#P/PA	GB	FB	G/F
1992 Season	.283	16	46	6	13	1	0	2	10	4	12	0	2	0	0	.340	.435	0	0	0	193	3.86	15	9	1.67

1992 Season

	Avg	AB	H	2B	3B	HR	RBI	BB	SO	OBP	SLG		Avg	AB	H	2B	3B	HR	RBI	BB	SO	OBP	SLG
vs. Left	.303	33	10	1	0	1	8	3	7	.361	.424	Scoring Posn	.375	16	6	0	0	1	9	0	2	.375	.563
vs. Right	.231	13	3	0	0	1	2	1	5	.286	.462	Close & Late	.333	6	2	0	0	1	3	0	1	.333	.833

Tom Prince — Pirates
Bats Right

	Avg	G	AB	R	H	2B	3B	HR	RBI	BB	SO	HBP	GDP	SB	CS	OBP	SLG	IBB	SH	SF	#Pit	#P/PA	GB	FB	G/F
1992 Season	.091	27	44	1	4	2	0	0	5	6	9	0	2	1	1	.192	.136	0	0	2	174	3.35	18	14	1.29
Last Five Years	.159	107	214	10	34	11	0	1	18	24	41	1	11	2	3	.244	.224	1	2	3	847	3.50	82	68	1.21

1992 Season

	Avg	AB	H	2B	3B	HR	RBI	BB	SO	OBP	SLG		Avg	AB	H	2B	3B	HR	RBI	BB	SO	OBP	SLG
vs. Left	.095	21	2	1	0	0	2	5	5	.259	.143	Scoring Posn	.125	16	2	2	0	0	5	1	3	.158	.250
vs. Right	.087	23	2	1	0	0	3	1	4	.120	.130	Close & Late	.125	8	1	0	0	0	1	0	1	.111	.125

Kirby Puckett — Twins
Bats Right (groundball hitter)

	Avg	G	AB	R	H	2B	3B	HR	RBI	BB	SO	HBP	GDP	SB	CS	OBP	SLG	IBB	SH	SF	#Pit	#P/PA	GB	FB	G/F
1992 Season	.329	160	639	104	210	38	4	19	110	44	97	6	17	17	7	.374	.490	13	1	6	2214	3.19	271	151	1.79
Last Five Years	.329	775	3093	462	1018	194	22	79	485	196	390	18	97	50	27	.369	.483	41	10	30	10207	3.06	1374	740	1.86

1992 Season

	Avg	AB	H	2B	3B	HR	RBI	BB	SO	OBP	SLG		Avg	AB	H	2B	3B	HR	RBI	BB	SO	OBP	SLG
vs. Left	.328	125	41	7	0	3	22	12	23	.381	.456	Scoring Posn	.346	188	65	14	0	6	87	26	35	.419	.516
vs. Right	.329	514	169	31	4	16	88	32	74	.372	.498	Close & Late	.317	104	33	8	0	1	14	10	15	.376	.423
Groundball	.335	155	52	8	1	2	21	11	18	.382	.439	None on/out	.358	123	44	7	0	4	4	5	18	.392	.512

1992 Season

	Avg	AB	H	2B	3B	HR	RBI	BB	SO	OBP	SLG		Avg	AB	H	2B	3B	HR	RBI	BB	SO	OBP	SLG
Flyball	.310	174	54	10	2	8	34	12	38	.354	.529	Batting #3	.334	548	183	33	4	17	87	35	77	.375	.502
Home	.348	325	113	17	4	9	54	22	53	.392	.508	Batting #4	.292	89	26	5	0	2	23	8	19	.360	.416
Away	.309	314	97	21	0	10	56	22	44	.356	.471	Other	.500	2	1	0	0	0	0	1	1	.667	.500
Day	.305	200	61	10	3	5	35	20	29	.379	.460	April	.307	88	27	7	2	2	12	3	7	.326	.500
Night	.339	439	149	28	1	14	75	24	68	.372	.503	May	.374	107	40	5	1	7	25	3	11	.387	.636
Grass	.307	238	73	16	0	8	39	15	35	.350	.475	June	.336	119	40	8	1	5	24	7	11	.375	.546
Turf	.342	401	137	22	4	11	71	29	62	.388	.499	July	.291	103	30	4	0	0	11	8	16	.348	.330
First Pitch	.440	166	73	12	1	7	45	13	0	.484	.651	August	.324	111	36	5	0	4	20	9	28	.390	.477
Ahead on Count	.383	115	44	10	1	3	20	20	0	.467	.565	September/October	.333	111	37	9	0	1	18	14	24	.405	.441
Behind on Count	.251	215	54	14	2	2	24	0	60	.256	.363	Pre-All Star	.334	359	120	22	4	14	65	16	36	.361	.535
Two Strikes	.226	239	54	10	1	3	23	12	97	.260	.314	Post-All Star	.321	280	90	16	0	5	45	28	61	.389	.432

1992 By Position

Position	Avg	AB	H	2B	3B	HR	RBI	BB	SO	OBP	SLG	G	GS	Innings	PO	A	E	DP	Fld Pct	Rng Fctr	In Zone	Outs	Zone Rtg	MLB Zone
As cf	.331	601	199	36	4	19	104	39	88	.375	.499	149	147	1274.2	394	9	3	3	.993	2.85	459	382	832	824

Last Five Years

	Avg	AB	H	2B	3B	HR	RBI	BB	SO	OBP	SLG		Avg	AB	H	2B	3B	HR	RBI	BB	SO	OBP	SLG
vs. Left	.344	799	275	52	7	23	114	62	96	.390	.513	Scoring Posn	.338	845	286	55	6	20	379	92	128	.395	.489
vs. Right	.324	2294	743	142	15	56	371	134	294	.362	.472	Close & Late	.314	452	142	29	3	11	71	37	69	.367	.465
Groundball	.318	811	258	45	7	12	115	59	98	.366	.435	None on/out	.337	564	190	39	2	18	18	29	70	.374	.509
Flyball	.306	686	210	45	5	26	108	46	111	.349	.500	Batting #3	.329	2886	950	183	22	74	444	181	354	.369	.485
Home	.363	1577	573	111	16	42	257	96	205	.399	.534	Batting #4	.323	201	65	11	0	5	41	13	35	.365	.453
Away	.294	1516	445	83	6	37	228	100	185	.338	.429	Other	.500	6	3	0	0	0	0	2	1	.625	.500
Day	.322	923	297	62	9	27	141	74	122	.374	.496	April	.309	411	127	30	5	11	54	29	51	.354	.487
Night	.332	2170	721	132	13	52	344	122	268	.367	.477	May	.360	550	198	39	6	22	100	30	50	.392	.573
Grass	.300	1158	347	62	5	32	182	78	144	.344	.445	June	.316	545	172	31	4	16	94	32	68	.356	.475
Turf	.347	1935	671	132	17	47	303	118	246	.384	.505	July	.344	518	178	30	5	10	81	36	68	.385	.479
First Pitch	.383	791	303	55	4	27	147	21	0	.401	.565	August	.314	525	165	29	0	13	73	28	83	.351	.444
Ahead on Count	.384	628	241	54	7	12	109	106	0	.472	.549	September/October	.327	544	178	35	2	7	83	41	70	.373	.438
Behind on Count	.291	1036	301	56	8	22	139	3	235	.295	.424	Pre-All Star	.329	1674	551	113	16	51	265	105	194	.369	.507
Two Strikes	.233	1048	244	42	6	18	112	58	389	.271	.336	Post-All Star	.329	1419	467	81	6	28	220	91	196	.369	.454

Batter vs. Pitcher (career)

Hits Best Against	Avg	AB	H	2B	3B	HR	RBI	BB	SO	OBP	SLG	Hits Worst Against	Avg	AB	H	2B	3B	HR	RBI	BB	SO	OBP	SLG
Mike Birkbeck	.750	12	9	3	1	0	5	0	1	.750	1.167	Todd Frohwirth	.000	13	0	0	0	0	0	0	4	.000	.000
Scott Bailes	.600	10	6	3	0	0	5	1	1	.636	.900	Donn Pall	.000	9	0	0	0	0	1	1	1	.250	.000
Jose DeLeon	.538	13	7	1	0	2	3	0	2	.538	1.077	Dennis Eckersley	.063	16	1	0	0	0	0	0	4	.059	.063
Mike Jeffcoat	.500	12	6	1	2	1	5	0	2	.500	1.167	Rick Sutcliffe	.071	14	1	0	0	0	1	1	1	.133	.071
Jeff Johnson	.444	9	4	1	0	1	3	2	1	.545	.889	Danny Darwin	.143	28	4	0	0	0	2	0	6	.138	.143

Tim Pugh — Reds
Pitches Right

	ERA	W	L	Sv	G	GS	IP	BB	SO	Avg	H	2B	3B	HR	RBI	OBP	SLG	CG	ShO	Sup	QS	#P/S	SB	CS	GB	FB	G/F
1992 Season	2.58	4	2	0	7	7	45.1	13	18	.276	47	11	2	2	12	.330	.400	0	0	2.78	5	90	1	1	67	51	1.31

1992 Season

	ERA	W	L	Sv	G	GS	IP	H	HR	BB	SO		Avg	AB	H	2B	3B	HR	RBI	BB	SO	OBP	SLG
Home	3.68	2	2	0	5	5	29.1	38	2	10	11	vs. Left	.279	86	24	5	2	0	3	12	8	.367	.384
Away	0.56	2	0	0	2	2	16.0	9	0	3	7	vs. Right	.274	84	23	6	0	2	9	1	10	.287	.417

Harvey Pulliam — Royals
Bats Right

	Avg	G	AB	R	H	2B	3B	HR	RBI	BB	SO	HBP	GDP	SB	CS	OBP	SLG	IBB	SH	SF	#Pit	#P/PA	GB	FB	G/F
1992 Season	.200	4	5	2	1	1	0	0	0	1	3	0	0	0	0	.333	.400	0	0	0	29	4.83	0	2	0.00
Career (1991-1992)	.263	22	38	6	10	2	0	3	4	12	0	0	1	0		.333	.553	1	1	0	172	4.10	11	11	1.00

1992 Season

	Avg	AB	H	2B	3B	HR	RBI	BB	SO	OBP	SLG		Avg	AB	H	2B	3B	HR	RBI	BB	SO	OBP	SLG
vs. Left	.250	4	1	1	0	0	0	1	2	.400	.500	Scoring Posn	.000	1	0	0	0	0	0	0	1	.000	.000
vs. Right	.000	1	0	0	0	0	0	0	1	.000	.000	Close & Late	.000	0	0	0	0	0	0	1	0	1.000	.000

Paul Quantrill — Red Sox
Pitches Right

	ERA	W	L	Sv	G	GS	IP	BB	SO	Avg	H	2B	3B	HR	RBI	OBP	SLG	GF	IR	IRS	Hld	SvOp	SB	CS	GB	FB	G/F
1992 Season	2.19	2	3	1	27	0	49.1	15	24	.288	55	6	1	1	13	.340	.346	10	17	7	3	5	3	2	74	50	1.48

1992 Season

	ERA	W	L	Sv	G	GS	IP	H	HR	BB	SO		Avg	AB	H	2B	3B	HR	RBI	BB	SO	OBP	SLG
Home	2.48	1	1	1	16	0	32.2	41	1	6	13	vs. Left	.260	73	19	3	1	0	5	7	11	.333	.329
Away	1.62	1	2	0	11	0	16.2	14	0	9	11	vs. Right	.305	118	36	3	1	1	8	8	13	.344	.356
Starter	0.00	0	0	0	0	0	0.0	0	0	0	0	Scoring Posn	.246	57	14	2	0	0	12	9	7	.338	.281
Reliever	2.19	2	3	1	27	0	49.1	55	1	15	24	Close & Late	.348	69	24	1	0	1	7	6	12	.397	.406
0 Days rest	3.18	0	0	0	3	0	5.2	6	0	0	4	None on/out	.273	44	12	1	1	0	0	3	10	.333	.341

1992 Season

	ERA	W	L	Sv	G	GS	IP	H	HR	BB	SO		Avg	AB	H	2B	3B	HR	RBI	BB	SO	OBP	SLG
1 or 2 Days rest	2.17	1	3	1	15	0	29.0	30	1	12	13	First Pitch	.414	29	12	0	1	0	1	5	0	.500	.483
3+ Days rest	1.84	1	0	0	9	0	14.2	19	0	3	7	Behind on Count	.293	41	12	1	0	1	2	6	0	.383	.390
Pre-All Star	0.00	0	0	0	0	0	0.0	0	0	0	0	Ahead on Count	.241	87	21	2	0	0	5	0	22	.250	.264
Post-All Star	2.19	2	3	1	27	0	49.1	55	1	15	24	Two Strikes	.232	82	19	3	0	0	8	4	24	.270	.268

Tom Quinlan — Blue Jays
Bats Right (groundball hitter)

	Avg	G	AB	R	H	2B	3B	HR	RBI	BB	SO	HBP	GDP	SB	CS	OBP	SLG	IBB	SH	SF	#Pit	#P/PA	GB	FB	G/F
1992 Season	.067	13	15	2	1	1	0	0	2	2	9	0	0	0	0	.176	.133	0	0	0	75	4.41	4	2	2.00
Career (1990-1992)	.118	14	17	2	2	1	0	0	2	2	10	1	0	0	0	.250	.176	0	0	0	86	4.30	4	2	2.00

1992 Season

	Avg	AB	H	2B	3B	HR	RBI	BB	SO	OBP	SLG		Avg	AB	H	2B	3B	HR	RBI	BB	SO	OBP	SLG
vs. Left	.000	4	0	0	0	0	0	2	3	.333	.000	Scoring Posn	.333	3	1	1	0	0	2	0	2	.333	.667
vs. Right	.091	11	1	1	0	0	2	0	6	.091	.182	Close & Late	1.000	1	1	0	0	0	2	0	0	1.000	2.000

Luis Quinones — Twins
Bats Both (flyball hitter)

	Avg	G	AB	R	H	2B	3B	HR	RBI	BB	SO	HBP	GDP	SB	CS	OBP	SLG	IBB	SH	SF	#Pit	#P/PA	GB	FB	G/F
1992 Season	.200	3	5	0	1	0	0	0	1	0	0	0	0	0	0	.167	.200	0	0	1	20	3.33	2	3	0.67
Last Five Years	.236	303	754	72	178	27	7	19	83	61	117	6	8	5	7	.295	.366	7	12	9	2983	3.59	222	300	0.74

1992 Season

	Avg	AB	H	2B	3B	HR	RBI	BB	SO	OBP	SLG		Avg	AB	H	2B	3B	HR	RBI	BB	SO	OBP	SLG
vs. Left	.000	0	0	0	0	0	0	0	0	.000	.000	Scoring Posn	.000	0	0	0	0	0	1	0	0	.000	.000
vs. Right	.200	5	1	0	0	0	1	0	0	.167	.200	Close & Late	.500	2	1	0	0	0	1	0	0	.333	.500

Last Five Years

	Avg	AB	H	2B	3B	HR	RBI	BB	SO	OBP	SLG		Avg	AB	H	2B	3B	HR	RBI	BB	SO	OBP	SLG
vs. Left	.233	287	67	10	2	13	41	25	47	.298	.418	Scoring Posn	.266	188	50	9	4	3	63	19	37	.326	.404
vs. Right	.238	467	111	17	5	6	42	36	70	.294	.334	Close & Late	.231	169	39	7	1	3	13	11	29	.275	.337
Groundball	.215	251	54	9	1	3	21	22	44	.282	.295	None on/out	.185	178	33	5	1	5	5	9	27	.229	.309
Flyball	.182	198	36	4	1	7	25	14	34	.241	.318	Batting #2	.267	221	59	7	4	6	23	15	30	.317	.416
Home	.241	345	83	14	4	8	35	28	51	.303	.374	Batting #6	.201	144	29	3	1	2	13	10	23	.256	.278
Away	.232	409	95	13	3	11	48	33	66	.288	.359	Other	.231	389	90	17	2	11	47	36	64	.297	.370
Day	.240	263	63	3	2	7	26	13	50	.276	.346	April	.259	27	7	0	0	1	5	2	4	.300	.370
Night	.234	491	115	24	5	12	57	48	67	.305	.377	May	.185	108	20	2	1	1	6	5	13	.217	.250
Grass	.229	258	59	7	2	9	32	20	41	.279	.376	June	.261	92	24	8	0	2	9	8	16	.320	.413
Turf	.240	496	119	20	5	10	51	41	76	.303	.361	July	.203	118	24	2	0	3	8	15	20	.294	.297
First Pitch	.293	99	29	3	3	3	21	3	0	.306	.475	August	.292	161	47	8	3	4	21	14	27	.360	.453
Ahead on Count	.263	190	50	7	3	9	24	30	0	.368	.474	September/October	.226	248	56	7	3	8	34	17	37	.277	.375
Behind on Count	.219	219	48	7	0	6	19	0	56	.228	.333	Pre-All Star	.219	269	59	11	1	7	25	20	37	.273	.346
Two Strikes	.181	309	56	7	1	4	18	24	117	.241	.249	Post-All Star	.245	485	119	16	6	12	58	41	80	.307	.377

Batter vs. Pitcher (since 1984)

Hits Best Against	Avg	AB	H	2B	3B	HR	RBI	BB	SO	OBP	SLG	Hits Worst Against	Avg	AB	H	2B	3B	HR	RBI	BB	SO	OBP	SLG
Bryn Smith	.385	13	5	0	2	0	2	1	2	.400	.692	Jim Deshaies	.053	19	1	0	0	0	0	1	4	.100	.053
Bobby Ojeda	.333	12	4	0	0	1	1	1	3	.385	.583	Don Robinson	.077	13	1	0	0	0	0	0	1	.077	.077
Tim Belcher	.313	16	5	0	0	1	1	0	1	.313	.500	Ron Darling	.154	13	2	0	0	0	0	2	3	.267	.154
Greg Maddux	.306	13	4	0	0	0	0	1	4	.357	.306	Joe Magrane	.167	12	2	0	0	0	0	0	2	.167	.167
												Kevin Gross	.182	11	2	0	0	0	0	1	3	.182	.182

Jamie Quirk — Athletics
Bats Left

	Avg	G	AB	R	H	2B	3B	HR	RBI	BB	SO	HBP	GDP	SB	CS	OBP	SLG	IBB	SH	SF	#Pit	#P/PA	GB	FB	G/F
1992 Season	.220	78	177	13	39	7	1	2	11	16	28	3	4	0	0	.294	.305	3	5	1	704	3.57	60	60	1.00
Last Five Years	.240	341	782	69	188	25	3	15	89	86	151	7	18	1	10	.318	.338	7	18	8	3234	3.66	269	225	1.20

1992 Season

	Avg	AB	H	2B	3B	HR	RBI	BB	SO	OBP	SLG		Avg	AB	H	2B	3B	HR	RBI	BB	SO	OBP	SLG
vs. Left	.238	21	5	1	0	0	1	0	5	.238	.286	Scoring Posn	.174	46	8	2	0	0	9	7	11	.291	.217
vs. Right	.218	156	34	6	1	2	10	16	23	.301	.308	Close & Late	.304	23	7	1	0	0	2	3	4	.393	.348
Home	.205	83	17	4	1	2	9	9	12	.295	.349	None on/out	.222	36	8	1	1	1	1	0	4	.222	.389
Away	.234	94	22	3	0	0	2	7	16	.294	.266	Batting #6	.195	87	17	3	0	1	4	8	12	.271	.264
First Pitch	.162	37	6	1	0	1	3	2	0	.220	.270	Batting #7	.192	52	10	2	1	1	3	7	11	.288	.327
Ahead on Count	.323	31	10	0	0	1	3	7	0	.462	.419	Other	.316	38	12	2	0	0	4	1	5	.357	.368
Behind on Count	.106	47	5	1	0	1	0	1	14	.125	.128	Pre-All Star	.238	105	25	3	0	1	5	9	13	.308	.295
Two Strikes	.210	81	17	4	0	0	5	7	28	.281	.259	Post-All Star	.194	72	14	4	1	1	6	7	15	.275	.319

Last Five Years

	Avg	AB	H	2B	3B	HR	RBI	BB	SO	OBP	SLG		Avg	AB	H	2B	3B	HR	RBI	BB	SO	OBP	SLG
vs. Left	.341	88	30	5	0	0	18	7	18	.381	.398	Scoring Posn	.271	199	54	8	0	0	67	33	40	.365	.312
vs. Right	.228	694	158	20	3	15	71	79	133	.310	.330	Close & Late	.256	125	32	5	0	1	16	20	30	.361	.320
Groundball	.262	214	56	6	0	1	22	25	33	.343	.304	None on/out	.253	186	47	5	2	6	6	15	30	.308	.398
Flyball	.189	180	34	3	1	6	16	19	35	.271	.317	Batting #7	.245	241	59	5	2	3	29	23	58	.310	.320

357

Last Five Years

	Avg	AB	H	2B	3B	HR	RBI	BB	SO	OBP	SLG		Avg	AB	H	2B	3B	HR	RBI	BB	SO	OBP	SLG
Home	.244	373	91	15	3	5	43	46	79	.329	.340	Batting #8	.250	180	45	7	1	5	26	24	39	.337	.383
Away	.237	409	97	10	0	10	46	40	72	.306	.335	Other	.233	361	84	13	0	7	34	39	54	.314	.327
Day	.246	285	70	9	3	7	31	24	62	.310	.372	April	.195	128	25	2	1	2	9	9	29	.252	.273
Night	.237	497	118	16	0	8	58	62	89	.323	.318	May	.267	101	27	2	1	1	10	14	14	.357	.337
Grass	.217	568	123	17	2	9	60	58	111	.294	.301	June	.236	106	25	6	0	2	10	10	17	.303	.349
Turf	.304	214	65	8	1	6	29	28	40	.382	.435	July	.215	144	31	2	0	3	17	11	31	.274	.292
First Pitch	.320	153	49	8	2	4	33	3	0	.333	.477	August	.248	129	32	8	0	3	17	16	20	.333	.380
Ahead on Count	.312	157	49	4	0	5	23	36	0	.446	.433	September/October	.276	174	48	5	1	4	26	26	40	.374	.385
Behind on Count	.160	257	41	5	0	2	16	1	84	.167	.202	Pre-All Star	.233	378	88	10	2	7	35	37	65	.304	.325
Two Strikes	.165	351	58	6	0	5	23	45	151	.262	.225	Post-All Star	.248	404	100	15	1	8	54	49	86	.331	.349

Batter vs. Pitcher (since 1984)

Hits Best Against	Avg	AB	H	2B	3B	HR	RBI	BB	SO	OBP	SLG	Hits Worst Against	Avg	AB	H	2B	3B	HR	RBI	BB	SO	OBP	SLG
Rod Nichols	.545	11	6	0	0	1	4	0	0	.545	.818	Nolan Ryan	.000	10	0	0	0	0	0	2	2	.167	.000
Tom Gordon	.429	14	6	1	0	0	0	1	1	.467	.500	Mike Morgan	.067	15	1	0	0	0	0	2	3	.176	.067
Jeff Russell	.385	13	5	1	0	0	3	1	1	.429	.462	Tom Candiotti	.077	13	1	0	0	0	0	2	0	.200	.077
Jose Rijo	.333	12	4	0	0	2	4	1	3	.385	.833	Mike Boddicker	.091	11	1	0	0	0	0	1	1	.167	.091
Bill Swift	.333	12	4	2	0	0	3	1	1	.385	.500	Jack McDowell	.091	11	1	0	0	0	0	0	3	.091	.091

Mike Raczka — Athletics

Pitches Left

	ERA	W	L	Sv	G	GS	IP	BB	SO	Avg	H	2B	3B	HR	RBI	OBP	SLG	GF	IR	IRS	Hld	SvOp	SB	CS	GB	FB	G/F
1992 Season	8.53	0	0	0	8	0	6.1	5	2	308	8	2	1	0	11	.394	.462	1	15	6	2	0	0	0	10	10	1.00

1992 Season

	ERA	W	L	Sv	G	GS	IP	H	HR	BB	SO		Avg	AB	H	2B	3B	HR	RBI	BB	SO	OBP	SLG
Home	9.00	0	0	0	4	0	2.0	4	0	1	2	vs. Left	.273	11	3	1	0	0	6	4	1	.438	.364
Away	8.31	0	0	0	4	0	4.1	4	0	4	0	vs. Right	.333	15	5	1	1	0	5	1	1	.353	.533

Scott Radinsky — White Sox

Pitches Left

	ERA	W	L	Sv	G	GS	IP	BB	SO	Avg	H	2B	3B	HR	RBI	OBP	SLG	GF	IR	IRS	Hld	SvOp	SB	CS	GB	FB	G/F
1992 Season	2.73	3	7	15	68	0	59.1	34	48	.243	54	11	2	3	34	.347	.351	33	65	22	16	23	1	3	70	56	1.25
Career (1990-1992)	3.05	14	13	27	197	0	183.0	93	143	.228	154	26	3	8	85	.323	.312	70	187	52	41	43	4	3	227	178	1.26

1992 Season

	ERA	W	L	Sv	G	GS	IP	H	HR	BB	SO		Avg	AB	H	2B	3B	HR	RBI	BB	SO	OBP	SLG
Home	1.17	3	2	9	31	0	30.2	28	1	12	30	vs. Left	.182	66	12	1	1	2	8	8	24	.280	.318
Away	4.40	0	5	6	37	0	28.2	26	2	22	18	vs. Right	.269	156	42	10	1	1	26	26	24	.375	.365
Day	2.70	1	2	3	18	0	20.0	23	0	14	15	Inning 1-6	.000	0	0	0	0	0	0	0	0	.000	.000
Night	2.75	2	5	12	50	0	39.1	31	3	20	33	Inning 7+	.243	222	54	11	2	3	34	34	48	.347	.351
Grass	1.44	3	3	15	57	0	50.0	39	1	25	44	None on	.213	89	19	2	0	1	1	16	23	.346	.270
Turf	9.64	0	4	0	11	0	9.1	15	2	9	4	Runners on	.263	133	35	9	2	2	33	18	25	.349	.406
April	1.29	0	1	1	8	0	7.0	5	0	2	7	Scoring Posn	.234	77	18	5	2	1	27	12	19	.333	.390
May	1.35	2	0	0	14	0	13.1	8	0	10	15	Close & Late	.231	160	37	8	0	3	21	25	32	.340	.338
June	6.00	0	4	2	11	0	9.0	6	2	6	5	None on/out	.167	42	7	1	0	0	6	6	15	.286	.190
July	3.48	0	1	5	14	0	10.1	10	1	7	13	vs. 1st Batr (relief)	.288	59	17	4	0	1	16	7	18	.358	.407
August	0.00	1	0	6	9	0	9.1	9	0	3	4	First Inning Pitched	.257	191	49	10	2	3	33	26	41	.347	.377
September/October	4.35	0	1	1	12	0	10.1	16	0	6	4	First 15 Pitches	.264	163	43	9	2	3	27	22	34	.353	.399
Starter	0.00	0	0	0	0	0	0.0	0	0	0	0	Pitch 16-30	.167	54	9	2	0	0	7	11	12	.318	.204
Reliever	2.73	3	7	15	68	0	59.1	54	3	34	48	Pitch 31-45	.400	5	2	0	0	0	0	1	2	.500	.400
0 Days rest	1.62	1	3	5	23	0	16.2	13	0	11	13	Pitch 46+	.000	0	0	0	0	0	0	0	0	.000	.000
1 or 2 Days rest	3.80	2	2	7	27	0	21.1	22	2	10	17	First Pitch	.276	29	8	3	0	0	3	5	0	.382	.379
3+ Days rest	2.53	0	2	3	18	0	21.1	19	1	13	18	Ahead on Count	.162	111	18	2	0	0	12	0	40	.168	.180
Pre-All Star	2.45	2	5	4	39	0	33.0	19	2	22	31	Behind on Count	.364	44	16	4	1	3	12	15	0	.525	.705
Post-All Star	3.08	1	2	11	29	0	26.1	35	1	12	17	Two Strikes	.150	113	17	2	1	1	12	14	48	.254	.186

Career (1990-1992)

	ERA	W	L	Sv	G	GS	IP	H	HR	BB	SO		Avg	AB	H	2B	3B	HR	RBI	BB	SO	OBP	SLG
Home	2.20	6	5	18	99	0	98.1	74	3	36	84	vs. Left	.189	206	39	4	2	5	27	17	62	.254	.301
Away	4.04	8	8	9	98	0	84.2	80	5	57	59	vs. Right	.246	468	115	22	1	3	58	76	81	.352	.316
Day	3.59	5	5	6	58	0	57.2	59	1	31	41	Inning 1-6	.207	29	6	1	0	0	9	6	8	.342	.241
Night	2.80	9	8	21	139	0	125.1	95	7	62	102	Inning 7+	.229	645	148	25	3	8	76	87	135	.323	.315
Grass	2.58	11	9	25	164	0	153.1	120	4	74	127	None on	.247	304	75	10	1	5	5	35	60	.330	.336
Turf	5.46	3	4	2	33	0	29.2	34	4	19	16	Runners on	.214	370	79	16	2	3	80	58	83	.318	.292
April	1.40	2	2	1	24	0	19.1	15	0	8	18	Scoring Posn	.188	234	44	8	2	1	70	43	61	.309	.252
May	2.29	6	1	2	37	0	39.1	24	1	19	37	Close & Late	.210	391	82	16	1	5	41	54	79	.309	.294
June	2.81	1	4	6	34	0	32.0	21	4	15	22	None on/out	.250	140	35	7	0	3	3	18	27	.344	.364
July	4.41	2	3	5	40	0	34.2	37	3	20	35	vs. 1st Batr (relief)	.243	169	41	8	0	2	31	22	46	.330	.325
August	1.78	2	1	9	29	0	30.1	27	0	12	18	First Inning Pitched	.230	538	124	20	2	7	74	68	124	.318	.314
September/October	5.27	1	2	4	33	0	27.1	30	0	19	13	First 15 Pitches	.232	491	114	20	2	6	60	58	103	.315	.318
Starter	0.00	0	0	0	0	0	0.0	0	0	0	0	Pitch 16-30	.213	164	35	5	1	2	21	30	37	.338	.293
Reliever	3.05	14	13	27	197	0	183.0	154	8	93	143	Pitch 31-45	.263	19	5	1	0	0	4	5	3	.400	.316

Career (1990-1992)

	ERA	W	L	Sv	G	GS	IP	H	HR	BB	SO		Avg	AB	H	2B	3B	HR	RBI	BB	SO	OBP	SLG
0 Days rest	2.72	4	5	10	61	0	49.2	35	2	29	36	Pitch 46+	.000	0	0	0	0	0	0	0	0	.000	.000
1 or 2 Days rest	2.40	8	5	14	84	0	78.2	62	3	38	65	First Pitch	.270	100	27	10	0	0	16	8	0	.327	.370
3+ Days rest	4.28	2	3	3	52	0	54.2	57	3	26	42	Ahead on Count	.156	352	55	5	0	2	26	0	127	.162	.188
Pre-All Star	2.39	9	8	10	109	0	101.2	67	6	51	88	Behind on Count	.321	112	36	8	1	4	27	49	0	.518	.518
Post-All Star	3.87	5	5	17	88	0	81.1	87	3	42	55	Two Strikes	.160	343	55	1	1	3	30	36	143	.246	.207

Pitcher vs. Batter (career)

Pitches Best Vs.	Avg	AB	H	2B	3B	HR	RBI	BB	SO	OBP	SLG	Pitches Worst Vs.	Avg	AB	H	2B	3B	HR	RBI	BB	SO	OBP	SLG
George Brett	.000	10	0	0	0	0	0	0	1	.167	.000												
Mel Hall	.154	13	2	1	0	0	0	0	2	.154	.231												

Tim Raines — White Sox

Bats Both

	Avg	G	AB	R	H	2B	3B	HR	RBI	BB	SO	HBP	GDP	SB	CS	OBP	SLG	IBB	SH	SF	#Pit	#P/PA	GB	FB	G/F
1992 Season	.294	144	551	102	162	22	9	7	54	81	48	0	5	45	6	.380	.405	4	4	8	2340	3.66	197	172	1.15
Last Five Years	.281	683	2563	411	720	101	33	42	274	380	251	13	37	219	53	.373	.395	53	13	26	10797	3.62	1054	732	1.44

1992 Season

	Avg	AB	H	2B	3B	HR	RBI	BB	SO	OBP	SLG		Avg	AB	H	2B	3B	HR	RBI	BB	SO	OBP	SLG
vs. Left	.252	135	34	3	2	0	11	25	10	.369	.304	Scoring Posn	.361	108	39	4	4	1	45	29	9	.469	.500
vs. Right	.308	416	128	19	7	7	43	56	38	.383	.438	Close & Late	.287	87	25	3	1	3	11	20	9	.417	.448
Groundball	.282	149	42	6	2	1	11	24	14	.377	.369	None on/out	.303	178	54	8	2	3	3	23	15	.383	.421
Flyball	.331	145	48	5	3	5	18	26	8	.430	.510	Batting #1	.255	345	88	12	5	2	24	53	34	.350	.336
Home	.319	263	84	13	4	4	24	41	20	.405	.445	Batting #2	.355	200	71	9	4	5	28	26	14	.424	.515
Away	.271	288	78	9	5	3	30	40	28	.356	.368	Other	.500	6	3	1	0	0	2	2	0	.625	.667
Day	.233	116	27	3	3	1	11	26	13	.366	.336	April	.269	67	18	3	1	0	6	7	4	.333	.343
Night	.310	435	135	19	6	6	43	55	35	.384	.423	May	.287	101	29	7	2	2	7	18	13	.392	.455
Grass	.302	473	143	21	7	6	44	72	41	.389	.414	June	.196	92	18	2	0	0	7	15	11	.303	.217
Turf	.244	78	19	1	2	1	10	9	7	.322	.346	July	.321	106	34	4	2	0	12	14	7	.397	.396
First Pitch	.273	77	21	2	1	1	7	3	0	.293	.364	August	.296	98	29	4	1	0	7	16	9	.388	.357
Ahead on Count	.369	195	72	10	3	5	20	45	0	.480	.528	September/October	.391	87	34	2	3	5	15	11	4	.455	.655
Behind on Count	.226	155	35	3	0	0	11	0	29	.222	.245	Pre-All Star	.252	305	77	12	5	2	23	48	32	.350	.344
Two Strikes	.208	192	40	8	2	1	15	33	48	.324	.286	Post-All Star	.346	246	85	10	4	5	31	33	16	.417	.480

1992 By Position

Position	Avg	AB	H	2B	3B	HR	RBI	BB	SO	OBP	SLG	G	GS	Innings	PO	A	E	DP	Fld Pct	Rng Fctr	In Zone	Zone Outs	Zone Rtg	MLB Zone
As Designated Hitter	.212	52	11	3	2	0	2	10	5	.333	.346	14	14	---	---	---	---	---	---	---	---	---	---	---
As lf	.299	495	148	18	7	7	50	69	43	.380	.406	129	125	1118.1	312	12	2	0	.994	2.61	352	300	.852	.809

Last Five Years

	Avg	AB	H	2B	3B	HR	RBI	BB	SO	OBP	SLG		Avg	AB	H	2B	3B	HR	RBI	BB	SO	OBP	SLG
vs. Left	.275	781	215	20	6	12	84	99	67	.356	.362	Scoring Posn	.323	530	171	25	11	8	223	167	49	.468	.457
vs. Right	.283	1782	505	81	27	30	190	281	184	.380	.410	Close & Late	.296	476	141	15	4	10	67	88	46	.404	.408
Groundball	.278	906	252	44	10	11	89	128	90	.367	.385	None on/out	.267	887	237	35	11	14	14	90	95	.339	.379
Flyball	.296	564	167	17	7	11	61	99	48	.400	.410	Batting #1	.270	1527	413	61	23	17	138	230	148	.366	.374
Home	.285	1209	345	52	13	22	128	173	113	.374	.404	Batting #3	.291	413	120	13	4	8	54	64	41	.383	.400
Away	.277	1354	375	49	20	20	146	207	138	.372	.387	Other	.300	623	187	27	6	17	82	86	52	.383	.445
Day	.255	693	177	24	9	16	76	125	82	.367	.385	April	.251	367	92	12	7	3	47	53	31	.341	.346
Night	.290	1870	543	77	24	26	198	255	169	.375	.399	May	.309	501	155	22	11	11	50	95	57	.421	.463
Grass	.264	1396	397	47	17	19	129	213	142	.379	.383	June	.261	402	105	22	4	3	47	63	38	.359	.358
Turf	.277	1167	323	54	16	23	145	167	109	.366	.410	July	.266	376	100	9	3	6	43	47	38	.351	.354
First Pitch	.288	427	123	15	5	6	38	23	0	.322	.389	August	.285	515	147	24	4	11	50	75	60	.372	.412
Ahead on Count	.318	826	263	39	11	19	108	184	0	.437	.461	September/October	.301	402	121	12	4	8	36	47	27	.375	.410
Behind on Count	.270	688	186	27	6	12	69	0	117	.274	.379	Pre-All Star	.276	1357	374	57	24	18	154	223	133	.377	.383
Two Strikes	.229	903	207	32	10	9	80	150	251	.345	.317	Post-All Star	.287	1206	346	44	9	24	120	157	118	.369	.398

Batter vs. Pitcher (since 1984)

Hits Best Against	Avg	AB	H	2B	3B	HR	RBI	BB	SO	OBP	SLG	Hits Worst Against	Avg	AB	H	2B	3B	HR	RBI	BB	SO	OBP	SLG
Ken Hill	.714	14	10	3	1	0	4	7	1	.810	1.071	Jack Armstrong	.063	16	1	0	0	0	1	1	2	.118	.063
Dave Stewart	.556	18	10	0	2	1	3	3	0	.619	.944	Jaime Navarro	.067	15	1	0	0	0	0	0	1	.067	.067
Craig Lefferts	.556	18	10	3	1	1	4	3	0	.619	1.000	Luis Aquino	.091	11	1	0	0	0	0	2	1	.214	.091
Jeff Parrett	.538	13	7	1	1	0	6	0	2	.538	.769	Jose Mesa	.091	11	1	0	0	0	0	0	0	.091	.091
Frank DiPino	.417	12	5	1	0	1	4	3	0	.533	.750	Jim Deshaies	.111	18	2	0	0	0	0	1	2	.105	.111

Rafael Ramirez — Astros

Bats Right

	Avg	G	AB	R	H	2B	3B	HR	RBI	BB	SO	HBP	GDP	SB	CS	OBP	SLG	IBB	SH	SF	#Pit	#P/PA	GB	FB	G/F
1992 Season	.250	73	176	17	44	6	0	1	13	7	24	1	5	0	0	.283	.301	1	1	0	600	3.26	64	55	1.16
Last Five Years	.257	612	1957	175	503	85	10	16	183	91	186	5	41	19	11	.290	.335	20	21	12	6863	3.32	775	573	1.35

1992 Season

	Avg	AB	H	2B	3B	HR	RBI	BB	SO	OBP	SLG		Avg	AB	H	2B	3B	HR	RBI	BB	SO	OBP	SLG
vs. Left	.329	82	27	5	0	1	6	3	14	.353	.427	Scoring Posn	.238	42	10	0	0	0	9	3	6	.289	.238
vs. Right	.181	94	17	1	0	0	7	4	10	.222	.191	Close & Late	.204	49	10	2	0	1	3	2	11	.235	.306

1992 Season

	Avg	AB	H	2B	3B	HR	RBI	BB	SO	OBP	SLG		Avg	AB	H	2B	3B	HR	RBI	BB	SO	OBP	SLG
Home	.225	89	20	3	0	0	5	5	14	.266	.258	None on/out	.300	50	15	3	0	0	0	2	10	.327	.360
Away	.276	87	24	3	0	1	8	2	10	.300	.345	Batting #7	.255	47	12	2	0	0	6	1	4	.271	.298
First Pitch	.346	26	9	2	0	0	1	1	0	.370	.423	Batting #8	.232	82	19	4	0	1	5	5	12	.284	.317
Ahead on Count	.345	29	10	2	0	0	1	2	0	.387	.414	Other	.277	47	13	0	0	0	2	1	8	.292	.277
Behind on Count	.227	75	17	0	0	0	5	0	17	.237	.227	Pre-All Star	.243	136	33	6	0	1	12	6	19	.280	.309
Two Strikes	.154	65	10	0	0	0	3	4	24	.203	.154	Post-All Star	.275	40	11	0	0	0	1	1	5	.293	.275

Last Five Years

	Avg	AB	H	2B	3B	HR	RBI	BB	SO	OBP	SLG		Avg	AB	H	2B	3B	HR	RBI	BB	SO	OBP	SLG
vs. Left	.280	733	205	37	5	7	74	40	84	.315	.372	Scoring Posn	.268	493	132	19	3	4	154	44	64	.322	.343
vs. Right	.243	1224	298	48	5	9	109	51	151	.275	.313	Close & Late	.239	415	99	18	0	3	42	29	65	.288	.304
Groundball	.258	689	178	33	3	5	66	26	73	.288	.337	None on/out	.258	446	115	19	1	3	3	19	57	.290	.325
Flyball	.263	460	121	20	2	6	41	23	64	.299	.354	Batting #7	.268	597	160	25	4	5	54	22	71	.295	.348
Home	.251	928	233	40	6	6	93	53	115	.291	.327	Batting #8	.230	538	124	21	0	5	51	31	57	.274	.297
Away	.262	1029	270	45	4	10	90	38	120	.289	.343	Other	.266	822	219	39	6	6	78	38	107	.297	.350
Day	.271	554	150	26	6	6	60	24	63	.304	.372	April	.246	285	70	8	3	3	18	11	40	.273	.326
Night	.252	1403	353	59	4	10	123	67	172	.285	.321	May	.242	347	84	14	2	3	32	14	33	.276	.320
Grass	.263	600	158	24	1	6	54	22	68	.288	.334	June	.269	386	104	15	2	1	40	20	45	.307	.326
Turf	.254	1357	345	61	9	10	129	69	167	.291	.335	July	.255	294	75	20	1	2	28	10	36	.276	.350
First Pitch	.305	262	80	14	2	5	31	5	0	.320	.431	August	.268	343	92	16	1	4	38	23	40	.312	.358
Ahead on Count	.301	448	135	28	3	6	51	47	0	.364	.417	September/October	.258	302	78	12	1	3	27	13	41	.289	.334
Behind on Count	.232	798	185	25	5	2	50	3	156	.236	.283	Pre-All Star	.261	1113	290	47	7	7	102	50	130	.294	.334
Two Strikes	.190	764	145	16	3	2	44	28	234	.220	.226	Post-All Star	.252	844	213	38	3	9	81	41	105	.285	.336

Batter vs. Pitcher (since 1984)

Hits Best Against	Avg	AB	H	2B	3B	HR	RBI	BB	SO	OBP	SLG	Hits Worst Against	Avg	AB	H	2B	3B	HR	RBI	BB	SO	OBP	SLG
Jim Gott	.529	17	9	2	0	0	1	0	5	.529	.647	David Cone	.067	15	1	0	0	0	0	1	1	.125	.067
Larry Andersen	.500	14	7	0	0	0	2	0	3	.500	.500	Mark Grant	.083	12	1	0	0	0	2	0	1	.077	.083
Terry Mulholland	.455	22	10	2	0	0	4	3	1	.520	.545	Pete Smith	.091	11	1	0	0	0	0	0	0	.091	.091
Jim Deshaies	.375	16	6	1	0	1	2	1	3	.412	.625	Jose Rijo	.105	19	2	0	0	0	1	1	2	.150	.105
Lee Smith	.364	11	4	0	1	0	2	1	2	.417	.909	Greg Harris	.133	15	2	0	0	0	0	0	3	.133	.133

Fernando Ramsey — Cubs   Bats Right (groundball hitter)

	Avg	G	AB	R	H	2B	3B	HR	RBI	BB	SO	HBP	GDP	SB	CS	OBP	SLG	IBB	SH	SF	#Pit	#P/PA	GB	FB	G/F
1992 Season	.120	18	25	0	3	0	0	0	2	0	6	0	0	0	0	.120	.120	0	0	0	92	3.68	7	4	1.75

1992 Season

	Avg	AB	H	2B	3B	HR	RBI	BB	SO	OBP	SLG		Avg	AB	H	2B	3B	HR	RBI	BB	SO	OBP	SLG
vs. Left	.063	16	1	0	0	0	2	0	5	.063	.063	Scoring Posn	.200	5	1	0	0	0	2	0	1	.200	.200
vs. Right	.222	9	2	0	0	0	0	0	1	.222	.222	Close & Late	.000	1	0	0	0	0	0	0	1	.000	.000

Willie Randolph — Mets   Bats Right (groundball hitter)

	Avg	G	AB	R	H	2B	3B	HR	RBI	BB	SO	HBP	GDP	SB	CS	OBP	SLG	IBB	SH	SF	#Pit	#P/PA	GB	FB	G/F
1992 Season	.252	90	286	29	72	11	1	2	15	40	34	4	6	1	3	.352	.318	1	6	0	1252	3.79	132	59	2.24
Last Five Years	.273	588	2058	246	562	76	8	8	169	286	196	12	53	27	16	.363	.329	9	31	14	8777	3.70	914	523	1.75

1992 Season

	Avg	AB	H	2B	3B	HR	RBI	BB	SO	OBP	SLG		Avg	AB	H	2B	3B	HR	RBI	BB	SO	OBP	SLG
vs. Left	.276	105	29	2	1	2	8	21	5	.397	.371	Scoring Posn	.172	58	10	2	0	0	11	13	10	.351	.207
vs. Right	.238	181	43	9	0	0	7	19	29	.324	.287	Close & Late	.302	43	13	2	0	1	2	9	9	.444	.419
Groundball	.265	113	30	5	1	0	4	16	13	.362	.327	None on/out	.238	80	19	2	0	1	1	7	7	.299	.300
Flyball	.246	57	14	3	0	1	4	8	9	.358	.351	Batting #1	.234	94	22	2	0	0	4	15	12	.339	.255
Home	.255	153	39	8	1	2	6	20	24	.349	.359	Batting #2	.254	142	36	6	1	2	9	17	12	.346	.352
Away	.248	133	33	3	0	0	9	20	10	.355	.271	Other	.280	50	14	3	0	0	2	8	10	.390	.340
Day	.231	65	15	1	0	1	2	9	7	.333	.292	April	.265	68	18	4	0	1	5	14	10	.390	.368
Night	.258	221	57	10	1	1	13	31	27	.357	.326	May	.230	87	20	2	0	0	5	8	7	.295	.253
Grass	.263	217	57	10	1	2	10	26	27	.347	.346	June	.243	74	18	4	1	1	3	7	11	.333	.365
Turf	.217	69	15	1	0	0	5	14	7	.365	.232	July	.306	36	11	0	0	0	2	4	3	.375	.306
First Pitch	.195	41	8	3	0	0	1	0	0	.195	.268	August	.278	18	5	1	0	0	0	6	2	.480	.333
Ahead on Count	.256	82	21	5	1	1	6	25	0	.435	.378	September/October	.000	3	0	0	0	0	0	1	1	.250	.000
Behind on Count	.259	81	21	2	0	0	6	0	13	.268	.284	Pre-All Star	.249	241	60	10	1	2	13	32	29	.344	.324
Two Strikes	.235	115	27	3	0	1	5	15	34	.333	.287	Post-All Star	.267	45	12	1	0	0	2	8	5	.389	.289

1992 By Position

Position	Avg	AB	H	2B	3B	HR	RBI	BB	SO	OBP	SLG	G	GS	Innings	PO	A	E	DP	Fld Pct	Rng Fctr	In Zone	Zone Outs	Zone Rtg	MLB Zone
As Pinch Hitter	.143	7	1	0	0	0	0	2	1	.500	.143	13	0	---	---	---	---	---	---	---	---	---	---	---
As 2b	.254	279	71	11	1	2	15	36	32	.346	.323	79	74	651.2	151	194	8	53	.977	4.76	228	205	899	892

Last Five Years

	Avg	AB	H	2B	3B	HR	RBI	BB	SO	OBP	SLG		Avg	AB	H	2B	3B	HR	RBI	BB	SO	OBP	SLG
vs. Left	.300	683	205	27	4	4	63	105	45	.393	.369	Scoring Posn	.277	458	127	16	5	3	157	109	47	.410	.354
vs. Right	.260	1375	357	49	4	4	106	181	151	.348	.310	Close & Late	.255	333	85	13	1	3	27	47	37	.351	.327

Last Five Years

	Avg	AB	H	2B	3B	HR	RBI	BB	SO	OBP	SLG
Groundball	.271	704	191	24	4	1	51	94	63	.356	.321
Flyball	.271	421	114	18	2	4	33	59	39	.364	.352
Home	.278	1009	280	39	4	4	78	134	104	.364	.336
Away	.269	1049	282	37	4	4	91	152	92	.362	.323
Day	.273	593	162	20	1	4	50	90	48	.368	.331
Night	.273	1465	400	56	7	4	119	196	148	.361	.329
Grass	.277	1626	450	59	8	5	135	225	154	.365	.332
Turf	.259	432	112	17	0	3	34	61	42	.355	.319
First Pitch	.265	317	84	16	1	1	22	1	0	.270	.331
Ahead on Count	.306	577	178	30	6	4	57	181	0	.473	.402
Behind on Count	.258	574	148	17	2	1	49	1	111	.260	.300
Two Strikes	.245	807	198	17	0	3	60	103	196	.332	.278

	Avg	AB	H	2B	3B	HR	RBI	BB	SO	OBP	SLG
None on/out	.247	473	117	16	0	1	1	51	38	.321	.288
Batting #1	.223	283	63	5	0	0	13	43	26	.326	.240
Batting #2	.284	1255	357	52	4	8	115	181	110	.376	.351
Other	.273	520	142	19	4	0	41	62	60	.351	.325
April	.234	316	74	8	0	2	17	46	39	.333	.278
May	.260	420	109	15	1	2	33	57	31	.349	.314
June	.297	337	100	15	2	1	35	40	34	.376	.362
July	.269	290	78	15	1	0	22	49	27	.374	.328
August	.293	314	92	13	2	2	32	38	27	.367	.366
September/October	.286	381	109	10	2	1	30	56	38	.379	.331
Pre-All Star	.266	1186	315	43	4	5	95	163	115	.356	.321
Post-All Star	.283	872	247	33	4	3	74	123	81	.372	.341

Batter vs. Pitcher (since 1984)

Hits Best Against	Avg	AB	H	2B	3B	HR	RBI	BB	SO	OBP	SLG
Ben McDonald	.556	9	5	0	0	0	1	3	0	.636	.556
Tom Browning	.533	15	8	1	0	1	3	3	0	.611	.800
Greg Harris	.524	21	11	3	0	0	2	3	2	.583	.667
Bill Krueger	.524	21	11	2	1	1	7	3	2	.560	.857
John Smoltz	.375	8	3	1	0	0	1	4	0	.583	.500

Hits Worst Against	Avg	AB	H	2B	3B	HR	RBI	BB	SO	OBP	SLG
Mitch Williams	.000	8	0	0	0	0	0	3	0	.273	.000
Jose DeLeon	.071	14	1	0	0	0	0	1	0	.133	.071
Doug Drabek	.091	11	1	0	0	0	0	0	2	.091	.091
Mike Moore	.095	21	2	0	0	0	0	1	3	.136	.095
Sid Fernandez	.133	15	2	0	0	0	1	0	1	.133	.133

Pat Rapp — Giants

Pitches Right (groundball pitcher)

	ERA	W	L	Sv	G	GS	IP	BB	SO	Avg	H	2B	3B	HR	RBI	OBP	SLG	CG	ShO	Sup	QS	#P/S	SB	CS	GB	FB	G/F
1992 Season	7.20	0	2	0	3	2	10.0	6	3	.235	8	3	1	0	7	.366	.382	0	0	0.90	0	62	4	1	17	8	2.13

1992 Season

	ERA	W	L	Sv	G	GS	IP	H	HR	BB	SO		Avg	AB	H	2B	3B	HR	RBI	BB	SO	OBP	SLG
Home	0.00	0	0	0	1	0	2.0	1	0	1	0	vs. Left	.316	19	6	1	1	0	5	4	2	.435	.474
Away	9.00	0	2	0	2	2	8.0	7	0	5	3	vs. Right	.133	15	2	2	0	0	2	2	1	.278	.267

Dennis Rasmussen — Royals

Pitches Left

	ERA	W	L	Sv	G	GS	IP	BB	SO	Avg	H	2B	3B	HR	RBI	OBP	SLG	CG	ShO	Sup	QS	#P/S	SB	CS	GB	FB	G/F
1992 Season	2.53	4	1	0	8	6	42.2	8	12	.218	32	6	0	2	9	.261	.299	1	1	2.95	4	91	2	7	57	55	1.04
Last Five Years	3.90	47	49	0	128	126	765.1	249	372	.269	793	125	16	77	321	.327	.401	13	4	4.57	69	91	68	48	1052	929	1.13

1992 Season

	ERA	W	L	Sv	G	GS	IP	H	HR	BB	SO		Avg	AB	H	2B	3B	HR	RBI	BB	SO	OBP	SLG
Home	3.16	2	1	0	4	4	25.2	22	1	6	8	vs. Left	.200	20	4	0	0	0	0	1	1	.273	.200
Away	1.59	2	0	0	4	2	17.0	10	1	2	4	vs. Right	.220	127	28	6	0	2	9	7	11	.259	.315

Last Five Years

	ERA	W	L	Sv	G	GS	IP	H	HR	BB	SO		Avg	AB	H	2B	3B	HR	RBI	BB	SO	OBP	SLG
Home	3.62	23	23	0	57	57	351.0	350	40	108	183	vs. Left	.273	488	133	15	6	14	65	36	71	.325	.414
Away	4.15	24	26	0	71	69	414.1	443	37	141	189	vs. Right	.269	2455	660	110	10	63	256	213	301	.327	.399
Day	4.28	12	16	0	38	38	208.1	239	27	78	87	Inning 1-6	.271		690	111	15	67	290	212	323	.327	.405
Night	3.76	35	33	0	90	88	557.0	554	50	171	285	Inning 7+	.261	395	103	14	1	10	31	37	49	.326	.377
Grass	4.03	32	38	0	89	88	531.2	559	61	167	258	None on	.262	1754	460	81	11	43	43	137	221	.319	.395
Turf	3.62	15	11	0	39	38	233.2	234	16	82	114	Runners on	.280	1189	333	44	5	34	278	112	151	.338	.411
April	5.75	3	7	0	13	13	67.1	87	10	25	26	Scoring Posn	.266	623	166	27	4	14	231	81	100	.342	.390
May	3.22	7	5	0	20	20	120.0	116	14	40	63	Close & Late	.270	163	44	5	0	4	16	22	26	.357	.374
June	3.28	9	5	0	22	20	134.1	138	15	38	66	None on/out	.275	772	212	42	6	20	20	58	81	.329	.422
July	5.18	4	14	0	23	23	132.0	155	9	57	62	vs. 1st Batr (relief)	.500	2	1	0	0	1	1	0	0	.500	2.000
August	3.38	9	10	0	23	23	141.0	124	9	50	70	First Inning Pitched	.335	480	161	25	1	18	84	51	53	.399	.504
September/October	3.59	15	8	0	27	27	170.2	173	20	39	85	First 75 Pitches	.269	2247	605	100	14	61	250	184	282	.325	.408
Starter	3.87	47	49	0	126	126	764.1	790	76	249	372	Pitch 76-90	.276	352	97	12	1	9	39	31	47	.333	.392
Reliever	27.00	0	0	0	2	0	1.0	3	1	0	0	Pitch 91-105	.253	221	56	9	1	4	21	24	33	.325	.357
0-3 Days Rest	4.12	2	0	0	3	3	19.2	19	2	7	5	Pitch 106+	.285	123	35	4	0	3	11	10	10	.343	.390
4 Days Rest	4.00	22	31	0	67	67	394.0	410	46	130	191	First Pitch	.315	489	154	24	3	16	54	15	0	.335	.474
5+ Days Rest	3.72	23	18	0	56	56	350.2	361	28	112	176	Ahead on Count	.228	1173	267	49	4	11	83	0	303	.230	.304
Pre-All Star	4.06	20	21	0	63	61	361.0	389	44	120	175	Behind on Count	.310	746	231	30	6	41	134	148	0	.423	.531
Post-All Star	3.76	27	28	0	65	65	404.1	404	33	129	197	Two Strikes	.211	1182	249	52	5	13	89	84	372	.266	.296

Pitcher vs. Batter (since 1984)

Pitches Best Vs.	Avg	AB	H	2B	3B	HR	RBI	BB	SO	OBP	SLG
Mike Fitzgerald	.083	12	1	0	0	0	2	1	3	.154	.083
Vince Coleman	.083	12	1	0	0	0	0	0	5	.083	.083
Lance Parrish	.087	23	2	0	0	0	0	2	7	.160	.087
Luis Salazar	.087	23	2	0	0	0	0	1	2	.125	.087
Pete O'Brien	.118	17	2	0	0	0	1	0	4	.118	.118

Pitches Worst Vs.	Avg	AB	H	2B	3B	HR	RBI	BB	SO	OBP	SLG
Pedro Guerrero	.733	15	11	2	0	0	4	0	0	.733	.867
Matt D. Williams	.600	20	12	2	0	3	11	2	3	.583	1.150
Andres Galarraga	.500	10	5	1	0	2	4	2	1	.583	1.200
Ivan Calderon	.400	15	6	0	0	3	6	2	3	.471	1.000
Ruben Sierra	.375	8	3	0	1	1	2	3	1	.500	1.000

Randy Ready — Athletics   Bats Right (flyball hitter)

	Avg	G	AB	R	H	2B	3B	HR	RBI	BB	SO	HBP	GDP	SB	CS	OBP	SLG	IBB	SH	SF	#Pit	#P/PA	GB	FB	G/F
1992 Season	.200	61	125	17	25	2	0	3	17	25	23	0	1	1	0	.329	.288	1	2	2	680	4.47	42	40	1.05
Last Five Years	.251	452	1132	155	264	50	6	20	128	182	158	7	16	16	8	.354	.359	5	11	16	5500	4.11	379	402	0.94

1992 Season

	Avg	AB	H	2B	3B	HR	RBI	BB	SO	OBP	SLG		Avg	AB	H	2B	3B	HR	RBI	BB	SO	OBP	SLG
vs. Left	.271	59	16	0	0	3	13	11	12	.375	.424	Scoring Posn	.206	34	7	2	0	1	14	11	6	.383	.353
vs. Right	.136	66	9	2	0	4	14	11	11	.288	.167	Close & Late	.381	21	8	1	0	1	6	5	3	.500	.571
Home	.151	73	11	1	0	1	8	17	16	.304	.205	None on/out	.200	25	5	0	0	0	4	4	.310	.200
Away	.269	52	14	1	0	2	9	8	7	.367	.404	Batting #6	.231	26	6	0	0	1	1	5	4	.355	.346
First Pitch	.600	5	3	0	0	0	1	1	0	.667	.600	Batting #7	.071	28	2	1	0	0	1	4	7	.188	.107
Ahead on Count	.259	27	7	1	0	1	7	10	0	.459	.407	Other	.239	71	17	1	0	2	15	16	12	.371	.338
Behind on Count	.125	40	5	0	0	1	2	0	13	.122	.200	Pre-All Star	.195	41	8	0	0	2	5	11	5	.358	.341
Two Strikes	.129	70	9	0	0	1	6	14	23	.271	.171	Post-All Star	.202	84	17	2	0	1	12	14	18	.313	.262

Last Five Years

	Avg	AB	H	2B	3B	HR	RBI	BB	SO	OBP	SLG		Avg	AB	H	2B	3B	HR	RBI	BB	SO	OBP	SLG
vs. Left	.271	631	171	33	5	15	83	109	81	.375	.410	Scoring Posn	.252	302	76	12	2	2	99	65	48	.371	.325
vs. Right	.226	501	113	17	1	5	45	73	77	.326	.293	Close & Late	.272	235	64	8	0	4	31	46	38	.394	.357
Groundball	.268	441	118	20	2	7	52	67	58	.362	.370	None on/out	.248	238	59	14	1	5	5	27	26	.335	.378
Flyball	.196	235	46	13	0	3	18	37	37	.308	.289	Batting #2	.261	348	91	18	3	3	43	54	41	.360	.356
Home	.247	559	138	22	3	8	60	103	77	.363	.340	Batting #5	.304	168	51	6	2	6	26	22	23	.381	.470
Away	.255	573	146	28	3	12	68	79	81	.344	.377	Other	.231	616	142	26	1	11	59	106	94	.343	.330
Day	.304	336	102	15	1	7	42	69	47	.419	.417	April	.260	169	44	4	0	3	18	27	20	.362	.337
Night	.229	796	182	35	5	13	86	113	111	.325	.334	May	.290	169	49	9	2	3	23	35	21	.413	.420
Grass	.239	531	127	19	3	8	54	83	78	.340	.366	June	.251	191	48	13	0	3	16	21	34	.333	.366
Turf	.261	601	157	31	3	12	74	99	80	.366	.383	July	.263	179	47	8	2	5	29	29	30	.366	.413
First Pitch	.397	58	23	3	1	0	10	2	1	.431	.483	August	.191	194	37	3	2	2	16	34	26	.305	.258
Ahead on Count	.228	268	61	9	2	5	33	99	0	.433	.332	September/October	.257	230	59	13	0	4	24	36	27	.352	.365
Behind on Count	.266	406	108	15	1	8	40	1	81	.269	.367	Pre-All Star	.273	571	156	29	4	11	67	90	82	.374	.389
Two Strikes	.219	535	117	17	2	6	47	81	157	.321	.292	Post-All Star	.228	561	128	21	4	9	61	92	76	.334	.326

Batter vs. Pitcher (since 1984)

Hits Best Against	Avg	AB	H	2B	3B	HR	RBI	BB	SO	OBP	SLG	Hits Worst Against	Avg	AB	H	2B	3B	HR	RBI	BB	SO	OBP	SLG
Dwight Gooden	.500	12	6	1	1	0	0	1	2	.538	.750	Orel Hershiser	.000	11	0	0	0	0	0	1	1	.083	.000
Bryn Smith	.450	20	9	2	0	1	1	0	2	.450	.700	Don Robinson	.111	9	1	1	0	0	1	0	2	.182	.222
Jim Deshaies	.429	14	6	2	0	1	7	6	1	.571	.786	Dennis Martinez	.154	13	2	0	0	0	1	0	4	.143	.154
Bob Kipper	.400	10	4	2	0	1	5	5	2	.600	.900	Alejandro Pena	.200	10	2	0	0	0	1	1	2	.273	.200
Tom Glavine	.353	34	12	2	1	1	4	6	2	.450	.559	Mark Langston	.231	13	3	0	0	0	0	0	3	.231	.231

Jeff Reardon — Braves   Pitches Right (flyball pitcher)

	ERA	W	L	Sv	G	GS	IP	BB	SO	Avg	H	2B	3B	HR	RBI	OBP	SLG	GF	IR	IRS	Hld	SvOp	SB	CS	GB	FB	G/F
1992 Season	3.41	5	2	30	60	0	58.0	9	39	.291	67	11	1	6	37	.321	.426	50	30	15	0	40	4	0	53	88	0.60
Last Five Years	3.23	18	17	164	292	0	314.2	71	218	.246	296	60	3	34	165	.291	.386	138	204	73	1	209	24	3	279	499	0.56

1992 Season

	ERA	W	L	Sv	G	GS	IP	H	HR	BB	SO		Avg	AB	H	2B	3B	HR	RBI	BB	SO	OBP	SLG
Home	3.60	3	1	19	37	0	35.0	41	4	3	22	vs. Left	.306	108	33	5	1	5	15	5	12	.342	.509
Away	3.13	2	1	11	23	0	23.0	26	2	6	17	vs. Right	.279	122	34	6	0	1	22	4	27	.302	.352
Day	2.70	2	0	8	20	0	20.0	20	1	3	8	Inning 1-6	.000	0	0	0	0	0	0	0	0	.000	.000
Night	3.79	3	2	22	40	0	38.0	47	5	6	31	Inning 7+	.291	230	67	11	1	6	37	9	39	.321	.426
Grass	3.35	5	2	28	54	0	53.2	60	6	8	37	None on	.268	123	33	5	1	4	4	3	18	.297	.423
Turf	4.15	0	0	2	6	0	4.1	7	0	1	2	Runners on	.318	107	34	6	0	2	33	6	21	.348	.430
April	1.13	0	0	4	7	0	8.0	7	1	1	4	Scoring Posn	.344	61	21	3	0	2	32	5	13	.382	.492
May	3.00	1	0	8	10	0	9.0	8	1	1	7	Close & Late	.281	167	47	7	1	5	33	6	32	.311	.425
June	7.50	0	0	3	7	0	6.0	12	0	1	6	None on/out	.229	48	11	1	0	1	1	2	7	.275	.313
July	2.25	1	0	7	12	0	12.0	12	2	2	7	vs. 1st Batr (relief)	.268	56	15	1	0	0	8	3	7	.300	.286
August	6.97	0	2	6	12	0	10.1	15	2	3	9	First Inning Pitched	.299	204	61	10	0	4	35	7	36	.319	.407
September/October	1.42	3	0	2	12	0	12.2	13	0	1	6	First 15 Pitches	.317	189	60	10	1	5	31	6	27	.337	.460
Starter	0.00	0	0	0	0	0	0.0	0	0	0	0	Pitch 16-30	.175	40	7	1	0	1	6	3	12	.261	.275
Reliever	3.41	5	2	30	60	0	58.0	67	6	9	39	Pitch 31-45	.000	1	0	0	0	0	0	0	0	.000	.000
0 Days rest	5.84	2	1	10	16	0	12.1	20	1	2	5	Pitch 46+	.000	0	0	0	0	0	0	0	0	.000	.000
1 or 2 Days rest	2.74	2	0	14	23	0	23.0	26	3	3	20	First Pitch	.270	37	10	0	1	2	6	0	0	.282	.486
3+ Days rest	2.78	1	1	6	21	0	22.2	21	2	4	14	Ahead on Count	.271	118	32	7	0	3	22	0	36	.271	.407
Pre-All Star	3.14	2	0	18	29	0	28.2	32	3	3	22	Behind on Count	.310	42	13	2	0	1	4	5	0	.383	.429
Post-All Star	3.68	3	2	12	31	0	29.1	35	3	6	17	Two Strikes	.252	103	26	4	0	2	17	4	39	.278	.350

Last Five Years

	ERA	W	L	Sv	G	GS	IP	H	HR	BB	SO		Avg	AB	H	2B	3B	HR	RBI	BB	SO	OBP	SLG
Home	3.25	14	10	92	162	0	171.2	153	20	37	116	vs. Left	.256	605	155	26	2	20	75	44	82	.309	.408
Away	3.21	4	7	72	130	0	143.0	143	14	34	102	vs. Right	.237	596	141	32	1	14	90	27	136	.273	.364
Day	4.06	3	6	41	88	0	88.2	93	11	16	49	Inning 1-6	.000	0	0	0	0	0	0	0	0	.000	.000
Night	2.91	15	11	123	204	0	226.0	203	23	55	169	Inning 7+	.246	1201	296	60	3	34	165	71	218	.291	.386
Grass	3.06	13	8	100	189	0	199.0	185	24	46	147	None on	.232	643	149	30	3	20	20	29	122	.269	.381

Last Five Years

	ERA	W	L	Sv	G	GS	IP	H	HR	BB	SO
Turf	3.50	5	9	64	103	0	115.2	111	10	25	71
April	1.77	1	2	21	41	0	45.2	31	4	15	26
May	4.02	1	4	30	53	0	56.0	49	7	7	34
June	3.40	4	2	30	51	0	55.2	49	6	12	41
July	3.52	2	2	26	49	0	53.2	53	7	13	40
August	4.44	3	5	33	49	0	52.2	64	6	12	44
September/October	1.94	7	2	24	49	0	51.0	50	4	12	31
Starter	0.00	0	0	0	0	0	0.0	0	0	0	0
Reliever	3.23	18	17	164	292	0	314.2	296	34	71	218
0 Days rest	3.52	9	9	56	91	0	92.0	91	8	23	50
1 or 2 Days rest	2.87	7	4	71	107	0	119.1	111	14	23	87
3+ Days rest	3.40	2	4	37	94	0	103.1	94	12	25	81
Pre-All Star	3.41	7	9	90	162	0	176.2	155	19	39	120
Post-All Star	3.00	11	8	74	130	0	138.0	141	15	32	98

	Avg	AB	H	2B	3B	HR	RBI	BB	SO	OBP	SLG
Runners on	.263	558	147	30	0	14	145	42	96	.315	.392
Scoring Posn	.261	360	94	21	0	12	137	38	65	.327	.419
None on/out	.181	248	45	14	1	5	5	13	47	.228	.306
vs. 1st Batr (relief)	.219	270	59	14	1	4	34	15	47	.259	.322
First Inning Pitched	.252	1008	254	52	2	28	145	53	188	.290	.385
First 15 Pitches	.258	910	235	49	3	24	120	46	148	.295	.398
Pitch 16-30	.208	265	55	11	0	9	40	24	65	.283	.351
Pitch 31-45	.231	26	6	0	0	1	5	1	5	.259	.346
Pitch 46+	.000	0	0	0	0	0	0	0	0	.000	.000
First Pitch	.277	177	49	15	1	5	23	11	0	.328	.458
Ahead on Count	.201	613	123	19	1	16	62	1	195	.204	.313
Behind on Count	.319	207	66	14	0	7	45	37	0	.423	.488
Two Strikes	.196	581	114	18	1	15	61	22	218	.227	.308

Pitcher vs. Batter (since 1984)

Pitches Best Vs.	Avg	AB	H	2B	3B	HR	RBI	BB	SO	OBP	SLG	Pitches Worst Vs.	Avg	AB	H	2B	3B	HR	RBI	BB	SO	OBP	SLG
Jay Buhner	.000	10	0	0	0	0	0	1	2	.091	.000	Kelly Gruber	.500	12	6	2	0	1	2	2	1	.571	.917
Ryne Sandberg	.071	14	1	0	0	0	2	0	4	.071	.071	Dan Pasqua	.429	7	3	1	0	0	1	4	1	.636	.571
Pete Incaviglia	.077	13	1	1	0	0	2	0	6	.077	.154	Jack Clark	.400	10	4	1	0	1	1	4	3	.571	.800
Ozzie Guillen	.100	10	1	0	0	0	1	1	1	.167	.100	Danny Tartabull	.375	8	3	0	1	1	4	3	3	.545	1.000
Cory Snyder	.154	13	2	0	0	0	0	0	6	.154	.154	Carlton Fisk	.333	15	5	2	0	2	5	0	5	.333	.867

Jeff Reboulet — Twins
Bats Right (groundball hitter)

	Avg	G	AB	R	H	2B	3B	HR	RBI	BB	SO	HBP	GDP	SB	CS	OBP	SLG	IBB	SH	SF	#Pit	#P/PA	GB	FB	G/F
1992 Season	.190	73	137	15	26	7	1	1	16	23	26	1	0	3	2	.311	.277	0	7	0	689	4.28	52	31	1.68

1992 Season

	Avg	AB	H	2B	3B	HR	RBI	BB	SO	OBP	SLG		Avg	AB	H	2B	3B	HR	RBI	BB	SO	OBP	SLG
vs. Left	.222	27	6	1	0	0	2	5	6	.364	.259	Scoring Posn	.344	32	11	3	1	0	14	8	5	.475	.500
vs. Right	.182	110	20	6	1	1	14	18	20	.297	.282	Close & Late	.333	15	5	2	0	0	3	5	2	.500	.467
Home	.273	55	15	3	1	1	11	12	9	.412	.418	None on/out	.125	32	4	1	0	1	1	5	6	.243	.250
Away	.134	82	11	4	0	0	5	11	17	.237	.183	Batting #2	.167	30	5	1	0	1	6	3	5	.242	.300
First Pitch	.154	13	2	0	1	0	2	0	0	.154	.308	Batting #9	.196	102	20	6	1	0	10	18	19	.322	.275
Ahead on Count	.214	14	3	1	0	0	3	11	0	.560	.286	Other	.200	5	1	0	0	0	0	2	2	.429	.200
Behind on Count	.264	53	14	4	0	0	7	0	13	.278	.340	Pre-All Star	.208	48	10	3	1	0	9	9	9	.345	.313
Two Strikes	.153	85	13	5	0	0	7	12	26	.258	.212	Post-All Star	.180	89	16	4	0	1	7	14	17	.291	.258

Gary Redus — Pirates
Bats Right (flyball hitter)

	Avg	G	AB	R	H	2B	3B	HR	RBI	BB	SO	HBP	GDP	SB	CS	OBP	SLG	IBB	SH	SF	#Pit	#P/PA	GB	FB	G/F
1992 Season	.256	76	176	26	45	7	3	3	12	17	25	0	1	11	4	.321	.381	0	0	0	725	3.76	65	63	1.03
Last Five Years	.257	475	1267	199	325	64	19	30	130	166	224	9	13	95	22	.342	.408	6	3	20	5629	3.85	394	455	0.87

1992 Season

	Avg	AB	H	2B	3B	HR	RBI	BB	SO	OBP	SLG		Avg	AB	H	2B	3B	HR	RBI	BB	SO	OBP	SLG
vs. Left	.258	151	39	5	3	2	10	16	22	.329	.371	Scoring Posn	.300	30	9	0	0	1	10	4	5	.382	.400
vs. Right	.240	25	6	2	0	1	2	1	3	.269	.440	Close & Late	.400	25	10	1	1	1	4	4	1	.483	.640
Home	.284	88	25	6	1	1	8	8	10	.344	.409	None on/out	.216	88	19	4	2	2	2	4	15	.250	.375
Away	.227	88	20	1	2	2	4	9	15	.299	.352	Batting #1	.242	157	38	7	3	2	9	10	23	.287	.363
First Pitch	.158	19	3	0	0	0	1	0	0	.158	.158	Batting #9	.333	12	4	0	0	1	3	6	1	.556	.583
Ahead on Count	.370	54	20	3	2	2	7	9	0	.460	.611	Other	.429	7	3	0	0	0	0	1	1	.500	.429
Behind on Count	.264	53	14	2	1	1	2	0	14	.264	.396	Pre-All Star	.208	72	15	2	2	1	4	10	8	.305	.333
Two Strikes	.147	68	10	4	0	1	4	8	25	.237	.250	Post-All Star	.288	104	30	5	1	2	8	7	17	.333	.413

Last Five Years

	Avg	AB	H	2B	3B	HR	RBI	BB	SO	OBP	SLG		Avg	AB	H	2B	3B	HR	RBI	BB	SO	OBP	SLG
vs. Left	.260	788	205	42	15	20	78	100	131	.340	.428	Scoring Posn	.222	248	55	3	4	10	103	45	54	.328	.387
vs. Right	.251	479	120	22	4	10	52	66	93	.345	.376	Close & Late	.287	237	68	13	2	7	27	33	50	.375	.447
Groundball	.297	407	121	29	6	9	47	50	58	.374	.464	None on/out	.272	464	126	26	7	13	13	52	70	.347	.442
Flyball	.230	344	79	11	5	11	40	44	71	.311	.387	Batting #1	.257	785	202	43	9	18	73	88	133	.331	.404
Home	.262	645	169	40	10	12	69	92	110	.354	.411	Batting #6	.275	178	49	8	2	5	20	27	30	.375	.427
Away	.251	622	156	24	9	18	61	74	114	.330	.405	Other	.243	304	74	13	8	7	37	51	61	.350	.408
Day	.246	345	85	15	5	7	38	55	61	.347	.380	April	.260	131	34	5	4	1	9	20	16	.368	.382
Night	.260	922	240	49	14	23	92	111	163	.340	.419	May	.215	186	40	7	3	2	15	18	32	.284	.317
Grass	.254	493	125	16	8	11	50	60	98	.329	.385	June	.280	250	70	17	1	6	29	33	42	.360	.428
Turf	.258	774	200	48	11	19	80	106	126	.350	.422	July	.263	255	67	11	5	7	30	32	51	.344	.427
First Pitch	.312	138	43	11	1	5	24	5	0	.338	.514	August	.251	203	51	7	2	8	23	29	40	.346	.424
Ahead on Count	.376	335	126	18	9	16	62	85	0	.496	.627	September/October	.260	242	63	17	4	6	24	34	43	.348	.438
Behind on Count	.220	368	81	14	6	5	26	0	95	.225	.332	Pre-All Star	.257	665	171	35	11	11	65	79	112	.336	.392
Two Strikes	.170	559	95	28	2	7	28	75	224	.272	.265	Post-All Star	.256	602	154	29	8	19	65	87	112	.349	.425

Batter vs. Pitcher (since 1984)

Hits Best Against	Avg	AB	H	2B	3B	HR	RBI	BB	SO	OBP	SLG	Hits Worst Against	Avg	AB	H	2B	3B	HR	RBI	BB	SO	OBP	SLG
Randy Myers	.429	7	3	1	0	0	1	5	2	.667	.571	Danny Jackson	.000	18	0	0	0	0	1	4	2	.182	.000
Joe Magrane	.409	22	9	4	2	0	4	1	3	.417	.773	Greg Swindell	.000	16	0	0	0	0	0	2	3	.111	.000
Chris Hammond	.368	19	7	2	2	0	2	4	2	.478	.684	Danny Cox	.000	14	0	0	0	0	0	0	2	.000	.000
Scott Sanderson	.364	11	4	2	1	0	2	1	3	.417	.727	Alejandro Pena	.000	12	0	0	0	0	0	1	0	.077	.000
Mike Boddicker	.357	14	5	2	1	1	3	0	4	.333	.857	Dwight Gooden	.067	15	1	0	0	0	1	1	5	.118	.133

Darren Reed — Twins   Bats Right (flyball hitter)

	Avg	G	AB	R	H	2B	3B	HR	RBI	BB	SO	HBP	GDP	SB	CS	OBP	SLG	IBB	SH	SF	#Pit	#P/PA	GB	FB	G/F
1992 Season	.175	56	114	12	20	4	0	5	14	8	34	1	3	0	0	.232	.342	2	0	2	473	3.78	26	42	0.62
Career (1990-1992)	.183	82	153	17	28	8	1	6	16	11	45	1	3	1	0	.240	.366	2	0	2	661	3.96	35	53	0.66

1992 Season

	Avg	AB	H	2B	3B	HR	RBI	BB	SO	OBP	SLG		Avg	AB	H	2B	3B	HR	RBI	BB	SO	OBP	SLG
vs. Left	.167	66	11	3	0	3	6	4	21	.208	.348	Scoring Posn	.185	27	5	0	0	2	11	4	9	.273	.407
vs. Right	.188	48	9	1	0	2	8	4	13	.264	.333	Close & Late	.154	26	4	1	0	0	2	0	10	.179	.192
Home	.189	53	10	3	0	1	5	1	12	.200	.302	None on/out	.261	23	6	1	0	2		1	4	.292	.565
Away	.164	61	10	1	0	4	9	7	22	.257	.377	Batting #7	.267	30	8	2	0	1	6	1	7	.273	.433
First Pitch	.188	16	3	0	0	1	2	0		.278	.375	Batting #8	.174	23	4	0	0	2	4	4	6	.296	.435
Ahead on Count	.381	21	8	3	0	2	3	4	0	.480	.810	Other	.131	61	8	2	0	2	4	3	21	.185	.262
Behind on Count	.109	46	5	0	0	1	5	0	15	.125	.174	Pre-All Star	.132	38	5	1	0	2	3	4	11	.233	.316
Two Strikes	.066	61	4	1	0	1	4	2	34	.106	.131	Post-All Star	.197	76	15	3	0	3	11	4	23	.232	.355

Jeff Reed — Reds   Bats Left (groundball hitter)

	Avg	G	AB	R	H	2B	3B	HR	RBI	BB	SO	HBP	GDP	SB	CS	OBP	SLG	IBB	SH	SF	#Pit	#P/PA	GB	FB	G/F
1992 Season	.160	15	25	2	4	0	0	0	2	1	4	0	1	0	0	.192	.160	1	0	0	93	3.58	11	6	1.83
Last Five Years	.239	372	1022	70	244	43	5	10	88	110	155	3	22	1	1	.312	.320	15	10	11	4334	3.78	412	260	1.58

1992 Season

	Avg	AB	H	2B	3B	HR	RBI	BB	SO	OBP	SLG		Avg	AB	H	2B	3B	HR	RBI	BB	SO	OBP	SLG
vs. Left	.000	4	0	0	0	0	0	0	0	.000	.000	Scoring Posn	.167	6	1	0	0	0	2	1	1	.286	.167
vs. Right	.190	21	4	0	0	0	2	1	4	.227	.190	Close & Late	.000	7	0	0	0	0	0	0	1	.000	.000

Last Five Years

	Avg	AB	H	2B	3B	HR	RBI	BB	SO	OBP	SLG		Avg	AB	H	2B	3B	HR	RBI	BB	SO	OBP	SLG
vs. Left	.202	119	24	6	0	2	15	18	27	.315	.303	Scoring Posn	.232	237	55	4	3	2	73	46	48	.346	.300
vs. Right	.244	903	220	37	5	8	73	92	128	.311	.322	Close & Late	.176	153	27	4	1	0	8	19	23	.263	.216
Groundball	.231	363	84	13	1	3	31	43	38	.312	.296	None on/out	.228	267	61	11	2	1	1	22	31	.287	.296
Flyball	.229	214	49	10	0	4	24	21	52	.296	.332	Batting #7	.242	615	149	29	0	5	51	62	102	.310	.314
Home	.233	463	108	23	3	5	40	51	79	.308	.326	Batting #8	.229	266	61	9	3	5	27	24	30	.293	.342
Away	.243	559	136	20	2	5	48	59	76	.315	.313	Other	.241	141	34	5	2	0	10	24	23	.349	.305
Day	.269	361	97	13	3	4	40	49	50	.353	.355	April	.265	151	40	6	1	2	15	19	23	.343	.358
Night	.222	661	147	30	2	6	48	61	105	.288	.301	May	.240	179	43	5	1	2	16	13	33	.296	.313
Grass	.238	361	86	11	0	3	23	39	53	.314	.294	June	.202	163	33	7	0	1	15	17	20	.276	.264
Turf	.239	661	158	32	5	7	65	71	102	.310	.334	July	.279	122	34	8	1	1	12	15	20	.360	.385
First Pitch	.314	140	44	10	0	2	16	8	0	.349	.429	August	.247	174	43	5	0	2	16	17	23	.309	.310
Ahead on Count	.291	275	80	14	1	2	26	60	0	.418	.371	September/October	.219	233	51	12	2	2	14	29	36	.303	.313
Behind on Count	.207	319	66	11	3	3	24	1	88	.213	.288	Pre-All Star	.230	518	119	19	3	5	46	52	83	.301	.307
Two Strikes	.179	459	82	11	3	3	30	37	154	.240	.235	Post-All Star	.248	504	125	24	2	5	42	58	72	.322	.333

Batter vs. Pitcher (career)

Hits Best Against	Avg	AB	H	2B	3B	HR	RBI	BB	SO	OBP	SLG	Hits Worst Against	Avg	AB	H	2B	3B	HR	RBI	BB	SO	OBP	SLG
Andy Benes	.438	16	7	0	0	1	5	2	1	.474	.625	Mike Dunne	.091	11	1	0	0	0	0	0	0	.091	.091
Ken Hill	.400	10	4	0	0	0	2	1	0	.500	.400	David Cone	.095	21	2	0	0	0	2	3	7	.208	.095
Tim Leary	.385	13	5	2	0	0	1	1	4	.429	.538	John Smoltz	.133	15	2	0	0	0	1	2	1	.235	.133
Danny Darwin	.333	15	5	3	1	0	2	2	1	.412	.667	Bob Walk	.154	13	2	0	0	0	1	1	1	.214	.154
Greg Maddux	.324	34	11	0	0	1	7	4	1	.395	.412	Mike Morgan	.154	13	2	0	0	0	0	0	1	.154	.154

Jody Reed — Red Sox   Bats Right

	Avg	G	AB	R	H	2B	3B	HR	RBI	BB	SO	HBP	GDP	SB	CS	OBP	SLG	IBB	SH	SF	#Pit	#P/PA	GB	FB	G/F
1992 Season	.247	143	550	64	136	27	1	3	40	62	44	0	17	7	8	.321	.316	2	10	4	2288	3.71	218	168	1.30
Last Five Years	.279	706	2628	357	734	179	6	17	219	315	227	16	68	22	25	.358	.371	9	56	17	11452	3.85	994	819	1.21

1992 Season

	Avg	AB	H	2B	3B	HR	RBI	BB	SO	OBP	SLG		Avg	AB	H	2B	3B	HR	RBI	BB	SO	OBP	SLG
vs. Left	.260	154	40	12	1	1	7	21	14	.345	.370	Scoring Posn	.238	101	24	3	0	0	36	23	9	.367	.267
vs. Right	.242	396	96	15	0	2	33	41	30	.312	.295	Close & Late	.196	107	21	5	0	0	7	11	11	.267	.243
Groundball	.220	123	27	3	1	1	10	13	16	.294	.285	None on/out	.266	158	42	8	0	1	1	15	11	.329	.335
Flyball	.256	160	41	8	0	2	12	19	14	.331	.344	Batting #1	.236	191	45	10	0	1	10	17	17	.294	.304
Home	.276	279	77	17	0	2	22	39	21	.366	.358	Batting #2	.250	200	50	12	1	1	16	22	12	.323	.335
Away	.218	271	59	10	1	1	18	23	23	.276	.273	Other	.258	159	41	5	0	1	14	23	15	.352	.308
Day	.255	192	49	9	0	1	14	23	13	.330	.318	April	.253	75	19	4	0	1	6	12	2	.352	.347

1992 Season

	Avg	AB	H	2B	3B	HR	RBI	BB	SO	OBP	SLG		Avg	AB	H	2B	3B	HR	RBI	BB	SO	OBP	SLG
Night	.243	358	87	18	1	2	26	39	31	.317	.316	May	.333	114	38	11	1	0	7	11	9	.392	.447
Grass	.246	479	118	24	1	3	35	53	37	.319	.319	June	.189	106	20	3	0	0	8	8	7	.241	.217
Turf	.254	71	18	3	0	0	5	9	7	.338	.296	July	.253	83	21	4	0	1	8	11	11	.337	.337
First Pitch	.244	45	11	1	0	0	4	2	0	.271	.267	August	.223	103	23	5	0	1	7	13	12	.310	.301
Ahead on Count	.265	166	44	8	0	2	14	39	0	.401	.349	September/October	.217	69	15	0	0	0	4	7	3	.289	.217
Behind on Count	.243	177	43	9	1	0	10	0	21	.242	.305	Pre-All Star	.263	339	89	21	1	2	25	34	21	.326	.348
Two Strikes	.196	209	41	9	0	1	8	21	44	.270	.254	Post-All Star	.223	211	47	6	0	1	15	28	23	.314	.265

1992 By Position

Position	Avg	AB	H	2B	3B	HR	RBI	BB	SO	OBP	SLG	G	GS	Innings	PO	A	E	DP	Fld Pct	Rng Fctr	In Zone	Outs	Zone Rtg	MLB Zone
As 2b	.247	550	136	27	1	3	40	62	44	.321	.316	142	141	1256.0	304	471	14	113	.982	5.55	509	461	.906	.892

Last Five Years

	Avg	AB	H	2B	3B	HR	RBI	BB	SO	OBP	SLG		Avg	AB	H	2B	3B	HR	RBI	BB	SO	OBP	SLG
vs. Left	.279	727	203	53	2	2	52	89	58	.356	.366	Scoring Posn	.266	580	154	36	1	1	191	106	54	.377	.336
vs. Right	.279	1901	531	126	4	15	167	226	169	.359	.373	Close & Late	.262	401	105	20	0	1	42	56	40	.353	.319
Groundball	.280	682	191	40	2	3	66	75	68	.356	.358	None on/out	.275	677	186	48	1	3	3	72	52	.346	.362
Flyball	.293	608	178	40	2	7	46	86	50	.379	.400	Batting #1	.269	817	220	49	2	4	54	92	75	.345	.349
Home	.286	1360	389	107	2	11	128	138	101	.367	.392	Batting #2	.284	1181	335	91	2	7	106	137	102	.359	.382
Away	.272	1268	345	72	4	6	91	146	101	.348	.349	Other	.264	630	179	39	2	6	59	86	50	.373	.381
Day	.282	849	239	59	1	4	75	109	68	.363	.367	April	.224	286	64	12	0	3	22	37	27	.314	.297
Night	.278	1779	495	120	5	13	144	206	159	.355	.373	May	.305	452	138	36	3	1	37	45	41	.368	.405
Grass	.281	2276	639	158	4	17	202	279	191	.360	.376	June	.246	415	102	32	0	2	32	47	38	.321	.337
Turf	.270	352	95	21	2	0	17	36	36	.344	.341	July	.307	475	146	40	0	4	45	57	43	.379	.417
First Pitch	.305	223	68	21	0	4	21	3	0	.320	.453	August	.278	496	138	30	1	4	38	54	40	.351	.367
Ahead on Count	.315	721	227	70	1	8	83	197	0	.457	.448	September/October	.290	504	146	29	2	3	45	75	38	.389	.373
Behind on Count	.278	859	239	49	3	0	59	0	108	.282	.342	Pre-All Star	.271	1306	354	93	3	7	106	143	118	.342	.363
Two Strikes	.235	1098	258	52	2	2	54	111	227	.309	.291	Post-All Star	.287	1322	380	86	3	10	113	172	109	.373	.380

Batter vs. Pitcher (career)

Hits Best Against	Avg	AB	H	2B	3B	HR	RBI	BB	SO	OBP	SLG	Hits Worst Against	Avg	AB	H	2B	3B	HR	RBI	BB	SO	OBP	SLG
Tom Henke	.556	9	5	1	0	0	1	2	0	.636	.667	Steve Farr	.091	11	1	0	0	0	0	1	1	.167	.091
Rod Nichols	.545	11	6	0	0	0	0	1	0	.583	.545	Scott Bailes	.091	11	1	1	0	0	2	1	4	.167	.182
Randy Johnson	.500	10	5	4	0	0	0	6	3	.688	.900	Duane Ward	.111	18	2	1	0	0	1	0	2	.111	.167
Scott Sanderson	.464	28	13	6	0	2	3	2	1	.500	.786	Tom Candiotti	.150	20	3	1	0	0	0	0	4	.150	.200
Curt Young	.462	13	6	2	0	2	0	3	0	.563	.615	Mike Flanagan	.154	13	2	0	0	0	0	0	2	.154	.154

Rick Reed — Royals   Pitches Right

	ERA	W	L	Sv	G	GS	IP	BB	SO	Avg	H	2B	3B	HR	RBI	OBP	SLG	CG	ShO	Sup	QS	#P/S	SB	CS	GB	FB	G/F
1992 Season	3.68	3	7	0	19	18	100.1	20	49	.271	105	21	2	10	38	.312	.413	1		3.50	6	74	6	3	144	114	1.26
Career (1988-1992)	4.40	7	14	0	50	36	225.0	46	118	.279	247	49	4	23	105	.317	.421	2	2	4.16	13	77	23	4	304	290	1.05

1992 Season

	ERA	W	L	Sv	G	GS	IP	H	HR	BB	SO		Avg	AB	H	2B	3B	HR	RBI	BB	SO	OBP	SLG
Home	4.53	1	2	0	10	9	43.2	54	3	7	18	vs. Left	.201	169	34	11	1	5	18	9	27	.236	.367
Away	3.02	2	5	0	9	9	56.2	51	7	13	31	vs. Right	.326	218	71	10	1	5	20	11	22	.370	.450
Starter	3.94	2	7	0	18	18	93.2	100	10	19	47	Scoring Posn	.238	84	20	4	0	0	22	7	13	.289	.286
Reliever	0.00	1	0	0	1	0	6.2	5	0	1	2	Close & Late	.667	6	4	1	0	1	3	1	0	.714	1.333
0-3 Days Rest	0.00	0	0	0	0	0	0.0	0	0	0	0	None on/out	.286	105	30	4	1	3	3	2	9	.312	.429
4 Days Rest	3.64	1	3	0	9	9	47.0	51	3	10	30	First Pitch	.355	62	22	3	0	2	11	3	0	.400	.500
5+ Days Rest	4.24	1	4	0	9	9	46.2	49	7	9	17	Behind on Count	.305	82	25	5	2	1	10	9	0	.376	.451
Pre-All Star	4.15	2	4	0	6	5	34.2	38	5	8	14	Ahead on Count	.232	181	42	8	0	4	10	0	45	.231	.343
Post-All Star	3.43	1	3	0	13	13	65.2	67	5	12	35	Two Strikes	.200	160	32	7	0	5	10	8	49	.237	.338

Steve Reed — Giants   Pitches Right (groundball pitcher)

	ERA	W	L	Sv	G	GS	IP	BB	SO	Avg	H	2B	3B	HR	RBI	OBP	SLG	GF	IR	IRS	Hld	SvOp	SB	CS	GB	FB	G/F
1992 Season	2.30	1	0	0	18	0	15.2	3	11	.220	11	4	0	2	12	.270	.390	2	22	8	1	0	1	0	31	10	3.10

1992 Season

	ERA	W	L	Sv	G	GS	IP	H	HR	BB	SO		Avg	AB	H	2B	3B	HR	RBI	BB	SO	OBP	SLG
Home	2.35	0	0	0	6	0	7.2	5	0	2	7	vs. Left	.273	22	6	3	0	0	5	1	3	.304	.409
Away	2.25	1	0	0	12	0	8.0	6	2	1	4	vs. Right	.189	37	7	1	0	2	7	2	8	.250	.378

Kevin Reimer — Rangers   Bats Left (flyball hitter)

	Avg	G	AB	R	H	2B	3B	HR	RBI	BB	SO	HBP	GDP	SB	CS	OBP	SLG	IBB	SH	SF	#Pit	#P/PA	GB	FB	G/F
1992 Season	.267	148	494	56	132	32	2	16	58	42	103	10	10	2	4	.336	.437	5	0	1	2113	3.86	134	161	0.83
Career (1988-1992)	.262	363	1018	109	267	63	3	39	144	85	225	18	24	2	8	.328	.445	11	0	8	4227	3.74	302	312	0.97

1992 Season

	Avg	AB	H	2B	3B	HR	RBI	BB	SO	OBP	SLG		Avg	AB	H	2B	3B	HR	RBI	BB	SO	OBP	SLG
vs. Left	.247	89	22	4	0	2	8	12	29	.356	.360	Scoring Posn	.211	123	26	2	1	1	35	17	32	.333	.268

1992 Season

	Avg	AB	H	2B	3B	HR	RBI	BB	SO	OBP	SLG		Avg	AB	H	2B	3B	HR	RBI	BB	SO	OBP	SLG
vs. Right	.272	405	110	28	2	14	50	30	74	.332	.454	Close & Late	.289	83	24	9	0	3	11	11	24	.368	.506
Groundball	.288	125	36	9	0	5	15	7	23	.341	.480	None on/out	.248	121	30	7	1	5	5	7	22	.305	.446
Flyball	.256	129	33	9	0	5	15	13	27	.336	.442	Batting #5	.220	223	49	10	1	4	18	17	55	.281	.327
Home	.285	239	68	13	2	10	34	20	53	.356	.481	Batting #6	.310	168	52	12	0	6	21	12	26	.371	.488
Away	.251	255	64	19	0	6	24	22	50	.318	.396	Other	.301	103	31	10	1	6	19	13	22	.395	.592
Day	.262	103	27	9	0	6	14	8	26	.321	.524	April	.321	78	25	9	0	2	12	7	10	.376	.513
Night	.269	391	105	23	2	10	44	34	77	.340	.414	May	.269	108	29	7	0	3	12	3	25	.292	.417
Grass	.262	409	107	23	2	14	48	37	81	.336	.430	June	.277	83	23	4	1	4	16	9	13	.362	.494
Turf	.294	85	25	9	0	2	10	5	22	.341	.471	July	.299	67	20	6	0	2	3	8	15	.397	.478
First Pitch	.316	76	24	6	2	3	6	5	0	.373	.566	August	.273	88	24	4	1	5	13	7	20	.354	.511
Ahead on Count	.373	118	44	7	0	6	17	17	0	.456	.585	September/October	.157	70	11	2	0	0	2	8	20	.244	.186
Behind on Count	.225	151	34	7	0	5	21	0	45	.245	.371	Pre-All Star	.291	299	87	21	1	10	42	21	55	.345	.468
Two Strikes	.183	246	45	12	0	7	25	20	103	.258	.317	Post-All Star	.231	195	45	11	1	6	16	21	48	.324	.390

1992 By Position

Position	Avg	AB	H	2B	3B	HR	RBI	BB	SO	OBP	SLG	G	GS	Innings	PO	A	E	DP	Fld Pct	Rng Fctr	In Zone	Outs	Zone Rtg	MLB Zone
As Designated Hitter	.212	113	24	7	0	3	8	6	28	.276	.354	32	28	---	---	---	---	---	---	---	---	---	---	---
As Pinch Hitter	.333	15	5	2	0	0	4	3	6	.444	.467	20	0	---	---	---	---	---	---	---	---	---	---	---
As 1f	.282	369	104	23	2	13	46	33	71	.350	.461	110	100	840.2	197	7	11	1	.949	2.18	250	192	768	809

Career (1988-1992)

	Avg	AB	H	2B	3B	HR	RBI	BB	SO	OBP	SLG		Avg	AB	H	2B	3B	HR	RBI	BB	SO	OBP	SLG
vs. Left	.233	133	31	5	0	3	12	14	41	.322	.338	Scoring Posn	.242	273	66	13	2	10	101	36	79	.336	.414
vs. Right	.267	885	236	58	3	36	132	71	184	.329	.461	Close & Late	.306	180	55	14	1	6	24	21	42	.380	.494
Groundball	.308	276	85	19	1	11	40	18	57	.359	.504	None on/out	.271	221	60	16	1	11	11	14	44	.329	.502
Flyball	.236	258	61	15	0	14	43	23	62	.306	.457	Batting #5	.228	447	102	22	1	14	52	32	106	.287	.376
Home	.275	477	131	35	2	23	84	40	121	.342	.480	Batting #6	.291	302	88	18	0	13	43	23	57	.351	.480
Away	.251	541	136	28	1	16	60	45	104	.315	.396	Other	.286	269	77	23	2	12	49	30	62	.367	.520
Day	.276	210	58	14	0	10	30	18	46	.342	.486	April	.299	117	35	11	0	4	18	9	22	.352	.496
Night	.259	808	209	49	3	29	114	67	179	.324	.434	May	.281	167	47	13	0	3	21	9	35	.320	.413
Grass	.262	836	219	50	3	35	129	71	189	.329	.455	June	.260	169	44	7	1	6	28	15	30	.328	.420
Turf	.264	182	48	13	0	4	15	14	36	.323	.401	July	.290	155	45	16	0	5	17	15	37	.368	.490
First Pitch	.367	177	65	9	2	12	29	10	0	.404	.644	August	.264	216	57	9	1	14	38	17	51	.335	.509
Ahead on Count	.335	218	73	16	0	13	34	31	0	.421	.587	September/October	.201	194	39	7	1	7	22	20	50	.280	.356
Behind on Count	.200	320	64	15	1	12	52	0	113	.224	.366	Pre-All Star	.263	519	147	37	1	15	74	38	102	.338	.445
Two Strikes	.170	487	83	23	0	10	54	44	225	.252	.279	Post-All Star	.240	499	120	26	2	24	70	47	123	.317	.445

Batter vs. Pitcher (career)

Hits Best Against	Avg	AB	H	2B	3B	HR	RBI	BB	SO	OBP	SLG	Hits Worst Against	Avg	AB	H	2B	3B	HR	RBI	BB	SO	OBP	SLG
Tom Gordon	.444	9	4	2	0	1	2	2	4	.545	1.000	Jack McDowell	.053	19	1	0	1	0	1	1	5	.182	.158
Walt Terrell	.385	13	5	1	0	1	3	0	1	.385	.692	Chris Bosio	.087	23	2	1	0	0	0	1	8	.125	.130
Bill Wegman	.364	11	4	1	0	1	2	0	2	.364	.727	Erik Hanson	.091	11	1	0	0	0	0	1	5	.167	.091
Jose Mesa	.364	11	4	0	0	3	5	1	2	.500	1.182	Charlie Hough	.100	10	1	1	0	0	0	1	0	.182	.200
Kevin Appier	.308	13	4	2	0	2	6	3	2	.412	.923	Todd Stottlemyre	.100	10	1	0	0	0	0	0	2	.182	.100

Todd Revenig — Athletics   Pitches Right

	ERA	W	L	Sv	G	GS	IP	BB	SO	Avg	H	2B	3B	HR	RBI	OBP	SLG	GF	IR	IRS	Hld	SvOp	SB	CS	GB	FB	G/F
1992 Season	0.00	0	0	0	2	0	2.0	0	1	.286	2	1	0	0	0	.286	.429	2	0	0	0	0	0	0	2	2	1.00

1992 Season

	ERA	W	L	Sv	G	GS	IP	H	HR	BB	SO		Avg	AB	H	2B	3B	HR	RBI	BB	SO	OBP	SLG
Home	0.00	0	0	0	1	0	1.0	1	0	0	0	vs. Left	.333	3	1	1	0	0	0	0	1	.333	.667
Away	0.00	0	0	0	1	0	1.0	1	0	0	1	vs. Right	.250	4	1	0	0	0	0	0	0	.250	.250

Harold Reynolds — Mariners   Bats Both

	Avg	G	AB	R	H	2B	3B	HR	RBI	BB	SO	HBP	GDP	SB	CS	OBP	SLG	IBB	SH	SF	#Pit	#P/PA	GB	FB	G/F
1992 Season	.247	140	458	55	113	23	3	3	33	45	41	3	12	15	12	.316	.330	1	11	4	1873	3.67	178	131	1.36
Last Five Years	.268	772	2942	398	788	143	34	15	229	304	252	16	45	134	83	.337	.355	8	43	21	11984	3.65	1168	858	1.36

1992 Season

	Avg	AB	H	2B	3B	HR	RBI	BB	SO	OBP	SLG		Avg	AB	H	2B	3B	HR	RBI	BB	SO	OBP	SLG
vs. Left	.250	116	29	6	0	0	12	17	4	.348	.302	Scoring Posn	.280	107	30	11	0	1	30	9	8	.325	.411
vs. Right	.246	342	84	17	3	3	21	28	37	.304	.339	Close & Late	.167	84	14	1	0	1	7	7	16	.228	.214
Groundball	.173	110	19	6	0	2	8	15	15	.278	.282	None on/out	.221	136	30	6	2	0	0	11	14	.284	.294
Flyball	.221	140	31	3	1	0	5	9	11	.268	.257	Batting #1	.228	136	31	3	1	1	6	16	12	.307	.287
Home	.262	237	62	15	3	2	17	20	20	.326	.376	Batting #9	.272	202	55	14	1	1	16	20	14	.338	.366
Away	.231	221	51	8	0	1	16	25	21	.305	.281	Other	.225	120	27	6	1	1	11	9	15	.288	.317
Day	.256	129	33	6	1	1	12	14	11	.331	.341	April	.269	78	21	3	1	1	6	7	5	.329	.372
Night	.243	329	80	17	2	2	21	31	30	.310	.325	May	.223	94	21	5	1	0	6	13	8	.312	.298
Grass	.246	183	45	6	0	1	14	22	15	.324	.295	June	.245	98	24	4	1	1	7	8	13	.312	.337
Turf	.247	275	68	17	3	2	19	23	26	.310	.353	July	.236	89	21	4	0	1	6	7	7	.289	.315

1992 Season

	Avg	AB	H	2B	3B	HR	RBI	BB	SO	OBP	SLG		Avg	AB	H	2B	3B	HR	RBI	BB	SO	OBP	SLG
First Pitch	.295	61	18	4	2	0	7	0	0	.317	.426	August	.298	57	17	5	0	0	6	8	4	.394	.386
Ahead on Count	.273	132	36	10	0	3	15	35	0	.423	.417	September/October	.214	42	9	2	0	0	2	2	4	.250	.262
Behind on Count	.185	135	25	7	0	2	7	0	27	.188	.281	Pre-All Star	.239	306	73	13	3	3	24	31	28	.309	.330
Two Strikes	.193	176	34	3	0	0	7	10	41	.233	.210	Post-All Star	.263	152	40	10	0	0	9	14	13	.329	.329

1992 By Position

Position	Avg	AB	H	2B	3B	HR	RBI	BB	SO	OBP	SLG	G	GS	Innings	PO	A	E	DP	Fld Pct	Rng Fctr	In Zone	Outs	Zone Rtg	MLB Zone
As Pinch Hitter	.182	11	2	0	0	0	1	0	3	.167	.182	12	0	---	---	---	---	---	---	---	---	---	---	---
As 2b	.249	446	111	23	3	3	32	45	38	.320	.334	134	123	1107.1	301	361	12	89	.982	5.38	400	342	.855	.892

Last Five Years

	Avg	AB	H	2B	3B	HR	RBI	BB	SO	OBP	SLG		Avg	AB	H	2B	3B	HR	RBI	BB	SO	OBP	SLG
vs. Left	.290	852	247	47	4	4	75	74	49	.345	.369	Scoring Posn	.298	607	181	40	4	5	206	67	53	.359	.402
vs. Right	.259	2090	541	96	30	11	154	230	203	.335	.349	Close & Late	.283	449	127	20	2	4	59	45	62	.346	.363
Groundball	.270	727	196	42	4	4	47	80	72	.347	.355	None on/out	.248	975	242	46	14	1	1	111	87	.329	.327
Flyball	.246	659	162	22	12	3	40	75	49	.323	.329	Batting #1	.268	1808	485	81	19	7	138	195	139	.340	.346
Home	.281	1445	406	74	20	7	114	157	111	.353	.374	Batting #2	.261	739	193	40	9	5	58	79	83	.336	.360
Away	.255	1497	382	69	14	8	115	147	141	.322	.336	Other	.278	395	110	22	6	3	33	30	30	.328	.387
Day	.258	740	191	31	9	3	58	81	73	.335	.336	April	.253	430	109	15	9	3	44	28	28	.299	.351
Night	.271	2202	597	112	25	12	171	223	179	.338	.361	May	.292	517	151	31	8	1	44	55	47	.355	.381
Grass	.252	1169	295	51	11	6	97	113	105	.319	.329	June	.253	479	121	21	5	2	29	60	41	.340	.330
Turf	.278	1773	483	92	23	9	132	191	147	.350	.371	July	.268	512	137	17	4	3	41	57	40	.341	.334
First Pitch	.296	345	102	18	5	3	37	1	0	.302	.403	August	.268	514	138	33	4	0	30	55	46	.344	.348
Ahead on Count	.299	899	269	58	13	10	80	191	0	.420	.426	September/October	.269	490	132	26	6	6	41	49	50	.337	.364
Behind on Count	.227	878	199	38	4	4	58	2	147	.235	.293	Pre-All Star	.267	1587	423	73	22	7	132	159	125	.333	.353
Two Strikes	.214	1069	233	33	9	2	66	110	252	.288	.266	Post-All Star	.269	1355	365	70	12	8	97	145	127	.343	.356

Batter vs. Pitcher (since 1984)

Hits Best Against	Avg	AB	H	2B	3B	HR	RBI	BB	SO	OBP	SLG	Hits Worst Against	Avg	AB	H	2B	3B	HR	RBI	BB	SO	OBP	SLG
Mike Henneman	.615	13	8	2	1	1	5	2	1	.667	1.154	Jeff M. Robinson	.048	21	1	0	0	0	1	6	2	.250	.048
Chris Bosio	.524	21	11	2	0	0	1	0	1	.524	.619	Danny Darwin	.071	14	1	1	0	0	1	0	0	.071	.143
Steve Farr	.450	20	9	2	1	0	0	2	2	.500	.650	Tom Gordon	.080	25	2	0	0	0	0	5	4	.233	.080
Greg Cadaret	.412	17	7	1	0	1	5	1	1	.444	.647	Bobby Thigpen	.091	11	1	0	0	0	0	2	1	.231	.091
Luis Aquino	.400	15	6	1	0	0	3	1	0	.438	.667	Eric King	.129	31	4	0	0	0	1	2	5	.182	.129

Shane Reynolds — Astros

Pitches Right (groundball pitcher)

	ERA	W	L	Sv	G	GS	IP	BB	SO	Avg	H	2B	3B	HR	RBI	OBP	SLG	CG	ShO	Sup	QS	#P/S	SB	CS	GB	FB	G/F
1992 Season	7.11	1	3	0	8	5	25.1	6	10	.385	42	11	3	2	19	.414	.596	0	0	2.84	0	72	6	1	43	27	1.59

1992 Season

	ERA	W	L	Sv	G	GS	IP	H	HR	BB	SO		Avg	AB	H	2B	3B	HR	RBI	BB	SO	OBP	SLG
Home	12.15	0	1	0	2	2	6.2	14	2	3	3	vs. Left	.413	63	26	8	2	1	13	5	6	.449	.651
Away	5.30	1	2	0	6	3	18.2	28	0	3	7	vs. Right	.348	46	16	3	1	1	6	1	4	.362	.522

Armando Reynoso — Braves

Pitches Right

	ERA	W	L	Sv	G	GS	IP	BB	SO	Avg	H	2B	3B	HR	RBI	OBP	SLG	GF	IR	IRS	Hld	SvOp	SB	CS	GB	FB	G/F
1992 Season	4.70	1	0	1	3	1	7.2	2	2	.393	11	4	0	2	6	.452	.750	1	2	2	0	1	0	1	8	13	0.62
Career (1991-1992)	5.81	3	1	1	9	5	31.0	12	12	.322	37	8	3	6	22	.405	.600	2	2	2	0	1	1	2	45	33	1.36

1992 Season

	ERA	W	L	Sv	G	GS	IP	H	HR	BB	SO		Avg	AB	H	2B	3B	HR	RBI	BB	SO	OBP	SLG
Home	0.00	0	0	1	2	0	2.2	3	0	0	1	vs. Left	.615	13	8	3	0	2	3	1	0	.667	1.308
Away	7.20	1	0	0	1	1	5.0	8	2	2	1	vs. Right	.200	15	3	1	0	0	3	1	2	.250	.267

Arthur Rhodes — Orioles

Pitches Left

	ERA	W	L	Sv	G	GS	IP	BB	SO	Avg	H	2B	3B	HR	RBI	OBP	SLG	CG	ShO	Sup	QS	#P/S	SB	CS	GB	FB	G/F
1992 Season	3.63	7	5	0	15	15	94.1	38	77	.250	87	20	4	6	30	.325	.382	2	1	4.67	10	103	4	4	107	108	0.99
Career (1991-1992)	4.83	7	8	0	23	23	130.1	61	100	.271	134	26	5	10	58	.349	.408	2	1	4.90	12	97	11	6	155	155	1.00

1992 Season

	ERA	W	L	Sv	G	GS	IP	H	HR	BB	SO		Avg	AB	H	2B	3B	HR	RBI	BB	SO	OBP	SLG
Home	4.81	4	4	0	10	10	58.0	59	4	26	47	vs. Left	.250	40	10	0	0	0	2	6	9	.348	.250
Away	1.73	3	1	0	5	5	36.1	28	2	12	30	vs. Right	.250	308	77	20	4	6	28	32	68	.322	.399
Starter	3.63	7	5	0	15	15	94.1	87	6	38	77	Scoring Posn	.217	83	18	4	0	1	23	11	22	.305	.301
Reliever	0.00	0	0	0	0	0	0.0	0	0	0	0	Close & Late	.500	16	8	1	1	0	5	0	1	.500	.688
0-3 Days Rest	0.00	0	0	0	0	0	0.0	0	0	0	0	None on/out	.253	95	24	3	2	2	2	9	24	.317	.389
4 Days Rest	3.34	5	3	0	9	9	59.1	60	6	20	49	First Pitch	.395	38	15	4	0	1	5	0	0	.395	.579
5+ Days Rest	4.11	2	2	0	6	6	35.0	27	0	18	28	Behind on Count	.324	68	22	6	2	2	6	31	0	.535	.559
Pre-All Star	2.35	1	0	0	1	1	7.2	6	0	2	4	Ahead on Count	.182	176	32	7	1	1	13	0	68	.185	.245
Post-All Star	3.74	6	5	0	14	14	86.2	81	6	36	73	Two Strikes	.170	188	32	7	2	1	14	7	77	.203	.245

Karl Rhodes — Astros
Bats Left

	Avg	G	AB	R	H	2B	3B	HR	RBI	BB	SO	HBP	GDP	SB	CS	OBP	SLG	IBB	SH	SF	#Pit	#P/PA	GB	FB	G/F
1992 Season	.000	5	4	0	0	0	0	0	0	0	2	0	0	0	0	.000	.000	0	0	0	20	5.00	1	1	1.00
Career (1990-1992)	.221	87	226	19	50	9	2	2	15	27	40	1	4	6	3	.305	.305	6	1	2	982	3.84	88	59	1.49

1992 Season

	Avg	AB	H	2B	3B	HR	RBI	BB	SO	OBP	SLG		Avg	AB	H	2B	3B	HR	RBI	BB	SO	OBP	SLG
vs. Left	.000	0	0	0	0	0	0	0	0	.000	.000	Scoring Posn	.000	0	0	0	0	0	0	0	0	.000	.000
vs. Right	.000	4	0	0	0	0	0	2	.000	.000		Close & Late	.000	1	0	0	0	0	0	0	1	.000	.000

Dave Righetti — Giants
Pitches Left

	ERA	W	L	Sv	G	GS	IP	BB	SO	Avg	H	2B	3B	HR	RBI	OBP	SLG	GF	IR	IRS	Hld	SvOp	SB	CS	GB	FB	G/F
1992 Season	5.06	2	7	3	54	4	78.1	36	47	.269	79	13	3	4	31	.344	.374	23	17	5	2	5	7	4	106	95	1.12
Last Five Years	3.74	12	25	113	263	4	359.0	153	262	.256	350	56	9	24	167	.332	.363	119	190	48	12	141	24	9	478	404	1.18

1992 Season

	ERA	W	L	Sv	G	GS	IP	H	HR	BB	SO		Avg	AB	H	2B	3B	HR	RBI	BB	SO	OBP	SLG
Home	2.82	1	3	3	27	2	44.2	38	0	16	25	vs. Left	.236	89	21	5	2	0	9	13	17	.330	.337
Away	8.02	1	4	0	27	2	33.2	41	4	20	22	vs. Right	.283	205	58	8	1	4	22	23	30	.351	.390
Starter	8.68	0	2	0	4	4	18.2	20	2	9	5	Scoring Posn	.224	76	17	3	1	1	24	15	14	.337	.329
Reliever	3.92	2	5	3	50	0	59.2	59	2	27	42	Close & Late	.296	98	29	4	0	1	6	16	23	.391	.367
0 Days rest	7.36	0	0	0	3	0	3.2	8	0	2	3	None on/out	.243	74	18	4	0	0	0	7	15	.309	.297
1 or 2 Days rest	6.19	0	4	2	28	0	32.0	38	1	9	20	First Pitch	.360	50	18	4	0	2	8	4	0	.407	.560
3+ Days rest	0.38	2	1	1	19	0	24.0	13	1	16	19	Behind on Count	.323	65	21	3	1	2	9	22	0	.478	.492
Pre-All Star	5.83	1	6	3	28	4	46.1	47	3	28	28	Ahead on Count	.233	133	31	5	2	0	11	0	43	.231	.301
Post-All Star	3.94	1	1	0	26	0	32.0	32	1	8	19	Two Strikes	.185	124	23	2	2	0	10	10	47	.244	.234

Last Five Years

	ERA	W	L	Sv	G	GS	IP	H	HR	BB	SO		Avg	AB	H	2B	3B	HR	RBI	BB	SO	OBP	SLG
Home	3.06	7	10	59	147	2	188.0	169	6	66	147	vs. Left	.241	349	84	12	4	5	45	33	71	.307	.341
Away	4.47	5	15	54	136	2	171.0	181	18	87	115	vs. Right	.262	1016	266	44	5	19	122	120	191	.341	.371
Day	4.14	7	10	31	92	1	113.0	107	9	52	82	Inning 1-6	.250	88	22	5	1	2	13	10	9	.323	.398
Night	3.55	5	15	82	191	3	246.0	243	15	101	180	Inning 7+	.257	1277	328	51	8	22	154	143	253	.333	.361
Grass	3.75	10	21	87	226	3	288.1	284	19	118	210	None on	.241	690	166	27	5	13	13	70	129	.316	.351
Turf	3.69	2	4	26	57	1	70.2	66	5	35	52	Runners on	.273	675	184	29	4	11	154	83	133	.349	.376
April	4.27	3	3	14	39	0	46.1	53	4	22	40	Scoring Posn	.247	417	103	18	2	5	135	60	80	.337	.336
May	3.46	1	3	16	44	0	54.2	56	2	23	39	Close & Late	.239	666	159	20	3	14	79	81	143	.324	.341
June	4.75	5	4	25	51	4	77.2	74	7	41	38	None on/out	.205	298	61	16	1	5	5	30	64	.284	.315
July	2.67	0	4	17	47	0	54.0	47	4	24	39	vs. 1st Batr (relief)	.204	250	51	10	0	6	19	24	58	.278	.316
August	3.74	2	6	19	54	0	67.1	62	4	21	52	First Inning Pitched	.244	964	235	35	5	15	117	112	193	.324	.337
September/October	3.20	1	5	22	48	0	59.0	58	3	22	54	First 15 Pitches	.240	836	201	31	5	14	77	82	159	.311	.340
Starter	8.68	0	2	0	4	4	18.2	20	2	9	5	Pitch 16-30	.287	369	106	16	2	7	64	54	76	.377	.398
Reliever	3.46	12	23	113	279	0	340.1	330	22	144	257	Pitch 31-45	.267	116	31	7	0	1	17	10	20	.323	.353
0 Days rest	3.57	1	5	29	48	0	53.0	57	4	17	45	Pitch 46+	.273	44	12	2	2	2	7	7	7	.333	.545
1 or 2 Days rest	3.91	5	14	57	132	0	163.1	163	7	63	110	First Pitch	.316	196	62	13	0	6	36	14	0	.362	.474
3+ Days rest	2.83	6	4	27	99	0	124.0	110	11	64	102	Ahead on Count	.220	642	141	18	7	9	60	1	225	.224	.312
Pre-All Star	4.10	9	11	58	146	4	193.0	199	13	95	127	Behind on Count	.311	286	89	14	1	5	43	89	0	.472	.420
Post-All Star	3.31	3	14	55	137	0	166.0	151	11	58	135	Two Strikes	.184	642	118	14	6	7	50	49	262	.244	.257

Pitcher vs. Batter (since 1984)

Pitches Best Vs.	Avg	AB	H	2B	3B	HR	RBI	BB	SO	OBP	SLG	Pitches Worst Vs.	Avg	AB	H	2B	3B	HR	RBI	BB	SO	OBP	SLG
Don Slaught	.000	13	0	0	0	0	0	1	6	.071	.000	Lou Whitaker	.583	12	7	1	0	1	3	4	1	.688	.917
Darnell Coles	.000	12	0	0	0	0	0	2	4	.143	.000	Pete O'Brien	.533	15	8	2	0	0	3	4	1	.600	.667
Dave Henderson	.000	10	0	0	0	0	1	0	0	.000	.000	Rick Dempsey	.462	13	6	2	0	1	2	2	2	.533	.846
Ivan Calderon	.133	15	2	0	0	0	0	1	6	.188	.133	George Bell	.400	25	10	3	1	3	10	0	3	.400	.960
Kelly Gruber	.154	13	2	0	0	0	1	2	1	.267	.154	Pete Incaviglia	.400	10	4	2	0	2	6	3	3	.538	1.200

Jose Rijo — Reds
Pitches Right (groundball pitcher)

	ERA	W	L	Sv	G	GS	IP	BB	SO	Avg	H	2B	3B	HR	RBI	OBP	SLG	CG	ShO	Sup	QS	#P/S	SB	CS	GB	FB	G/F
1992 Season	2.56	15	10	0	33	33	211.0	44	171	.238	185	26	4	15	61	.281	.340	2	0	4.31	23	94	17	12	312	156	2.00
Last Five Years	2.58	64	38	0	160	130	885.1	288	741	.224	722	132	17	46	256	.288	.318	13	3	4.66	89	98	61	37	1179	764	1.54

1992 Season

	ERA	W	L	Sv	G	GS	IP	H	HR	BB	SO		Avg	AB	H	2B	3B	HR	RBI	BB	SO	OBP	SLG
Home	2.74	6	4	0	14	14	88.2	79	9	17	77	vs. Left	.266	429	114	20	3	6	33	32	89	.317	.368
Away	2.43	9	6	0	19	19	122.1	106	6	27	94	vs. Right	.205	347	71	6	1	9	28	12	82	.234	.305
Day	2.43	7	5	0	17	17	103.2	86	9	21	92	Inning 1-6	.238	698	166	25	4	10	53	41	150	.282	.328
Night	2.68	8	5	0	16	16	107.1	99	6	23	79	Inning 7+	.244	78	19	1	0	5	8	3	21	.268	.449
Grass	2.53	5	3	0	10	10	64.0	58	5	11	44	None on	.256	473	121	15	1	12	12	24	93	.293	.368
Turf	2.57	10	7	0	23	23	147.0	127	10	33	127	Runners on	.211	303	64	11	3	3	49	20	78	.261	.297
April	4.30	3	3	0	3	3	23.0	26	2	4	20	Scoring Posn	.203	158	32	5	1	0	38	16	47	.278	.247
May	3.10	1	1	0	6	6	29.0	28	2	7	24	Close & Late	.258	62	16	0	0	5	8	1	17	.266	.500
June	3.19	3	2	0	5	5	31.0	33	4	3	41	None on/out	.262	210	55	8	0	9	11	36	.302	.429
July	2.37	4	1	0	6	6	38.0	34	3	13	25	vs. 1st Batr (relief)	.000	0	0	0	0	0	0	0	0	.000	.000

1992 Season

	ERA	W	L	Sv	G	GS	IP	H	HR	BB	SO		Avg	AB	H	2B	3B	HR	RBI	BB	SO	OBP	SLG
August	2.41	2	2	0	6	6	41.0	30	4	4	34	First Inning Pitched	.243	115	28	5	0	0	4	10	17	.310	.287
September/October	1.29	5	1	0	7	7	49.0	34	0	13	27	First 75 Pitches	.244	607	148	22	3	10	42	35	124	.288	.339
Starter	2.56	15	10	0	33	33	211.0	185	15	44	171	Pitch 76-90	.206	97	20	4	0	1	12	6	24	.243	.278
Reliever	0.00	0	0	0	0	0	0.0	0	0	0	0	Pitch 91-105	.250	56	14	0	1	4	6	2	18	.276	.500
0-3 Days Rest	0.00	0	0	0	0	0	0.0	0	0	0	0	Pitch 106+	.188	16	3	0	0	0	1	1	5	.235	.188
4 Days Rest	2.19	11	7	0	24	24	156.1	133	8	34	120	Ahead on Count	.182	336	61	8	0	2	11	0	139	.188	.223
5+ Days Rest	3.62	4	3	0	9	9	54.2	52	7	10	51	Behind on Count	.329	164	54	5	2	10	23	23	0	.412	.567
Pre-All Star	3.18	6	6	0	17	17	102.0	103	10	20	100	Two Strikes	.154	356	55	8	0	1	12	20	171	.204	.185
Post-All Star	1.98	9	4	0	16	16	109.0	82	5	24	71												

Last Five Years

	ERA	W	L	Sv	G	GS	IP	H	HR	BB	SO		Avg	AB	H	2B	3B	HR	RBI	BB	SO	OBP	SLG
Home	2.80	31	17	0	78	64	431.1	341	25	154	385	vs. Left	.247	1822	450	81	12	29	155	212	399	.325	.352
Away	2.38	33	21	0	82	66	454.0	381	21	134	356	vs. Right	.194	1400	272	51	5	17	101	76	342	.238	.274
Day	2.26	18	12	0	56	42	282.1	218	14	82	254	Inning 1-6	.225	2699	606	114	13	35	218	236	622	.287	.315
Night	2.73	46	26	0	104	88	603.0	504	32	206	487	Inning 7+	.222	523	116	18	4	11	38	52	119	.294	.335
Grass	2.41	19	14	0	48	41	280.0	244	14	80	222	None on	.222	1997	444	87	10	37		149	442	.278	.331
Turf	2.66	45	24	0	112	89	605.1	478	32	208	519	Runners on	.227	1225	278	45	7	9	219	139	299	.304	.297
April	2.83	6	6	0	27	15	111.1	97	3	43	89	Scoring Posn	.222	707	157	26	3	2	194	100	200	.313	.276
May	2.93	12	3	0	37	23	163.0	140	13	60	139	Close & Late	.228	267	61	9	1	8	21	25	60	.298	.360
June	3.43	12	10	0	31	27	178.1	151	13	51	160	None on/out	.220	849	187	33	5	24		66	174	.280	.356
July	2.15	10	5	0	19	19	121.1	101	6	41	119	vs. 1st Batr (relief)	.120	25	3	0	0	0	2	4	6	.241	.120
August	2.60	9	9	0	21	21	138.2	109	9	44	119	First Inning Pitched	.248	573	142	30	3	4	56	69	120	.332	.332
September/October	1.51	15	5	0	25	25	172.2	124	2	49	137	First 75 Pitches	.228	2425	553	102	13	34	194	216	544	.293	.323
Starter	2.60	58	37	0	130	130	836.1	689	44	260	702	Pitch 76-90	.215	385	83	17	0	3	33	34	90	.275	.283
Reliever	2.20	6	1	0	30	0	49.0	33	2	28	39	Pitch 91-105	.200	245	49	5	2	6	16	21	62	.263	.310
0-3 Days Rest	1.89	8	6	0	17	17	119.0	84	7	35	111	Pitch 106+	.222	167	37	8	2	3	13	17	45	.293	.347
4 Days Rest	2.48	35	21	0	78	78	518.0	433	26	159	424	First Pitch	.307	446	137	26	6	5	52	11	0	.326	.426
5+ Days Rest	3.34	15	10	0	35	35	199.1	172	11	66	167	Ahead on Count	.166	1539	256	41	6	13	84	1	620	.169	.226
Pre-All Star	2.98	33	21	0	101	71	493.0	416	32	172	422	Behind on Count	.327	611	200	40	5	24	84	148	0	.456	.527
Post-All Star	2.09	31	17	0	59	59	392.1	306	14	116	319	Two Strikes	.146	1573	230	41	5	13	75	126	741	.212	.203

Pitcher vs. Batter (career)

Pitches Best Vs.	Avg	AB	H	2B	3B	HR	RBI	BB	SO	OBP	SLG	Pitches Worst Vs.	Avg	AB	H	2B	3B	HR	RBI	BB	SO	OBP	SLG
Andujar Cedeno	.000	14	0	0	0	0	0	0	6	.000	.000	George Brett	.500	12	6	1	0	2	7	5	2	.647	1.083
Tom Foley	.000	13	0	0	0	0	1	0	3	.000	.000	Joe Girardi	.455	11	5	1	0	1	2	1	1	.500	.818
Doug Dascenzo	.000	13	0	0	0	0	0	1	3	.071	.000	Lance Parrish	.444	9	4	0	0	1	1	2	1	.545	.778
Jerald Clark	.053	19	1	0	0	0	0	1	8	.100	.053	Cory Snyder	.400	15	6	1	0	3	7	1	5	.412	1.067
Alan Trammell	.091	11	1	0	0	0	0	0	0	.091	.091	Alvin Davis	.350	20	7	0	0	3	7	4	5	.458	.800

Ernest Riles — Astros

Bats Left

	Avg	G	AB	R	H	2B	3B	HR	RBI	BB	SO	HBP	GDP	SB	CS	OBP	SLG	IBB	SH	SF	#Pit	#P/PA	GB	FB	G/F
1992 Season	.262	39	61	5	16	1	0	1	4	2	11	0	0	1	0	.281	.328	0	0	1	254	3.97	22	21	1.05
Last Five Years	.250	481	1113	133	278	37	10	25	134	104	188	3	25	7	12	.312	.368	11	8	14	4743	3.64	441	316	1.40

1992 Season

	Avg	AB	H	2B	3B	HR	RBI	BB	SO	OBP	SLG		Avg	AB	H	2B	3B	HR	RBI	BB	SO	OBP	SLG
vs. Left	.000	6	0	0	0	0	0	0	1	.000	.000	Scoring Posn	.231	13	3	0	0	0	3	2	4	.313	.231
vs. Right	.291	55	16	1	0	1	4	2	10	.310	.364	Close & Late	.250	20	5	0	0	1	2	0	3	.250	.400

Last Five Years

	Avg	AB	H	2B	3B	HR	RBI	BB	SO	OBP	SLG		Avg	AB	H	2B	3B	HR	RBI	BB	SO	OBP	SLG
vs. Left	.196	112	22	2	1	2	10	9	27	.256	.286	Scoring Posn	.263	278	73	11	2	10	114	43	54	.352	.424
vs. Right	.256	1001	256	35	9	23	124	95	161	.318	.378	Close & Late	.266	188	50	5	4	6	28	25	36	.349	.431
Groundball	.251	387	97	14	1	9	52	42	56	.322	.362	None on/out	.229	275	63	6	3	6	6	19	44	.279	.338
Flyball	.262	252	66	10	2	7	24	22	44	.325	.401	Batting #5	.274	215	59	11	2	4	27	24	31	.344	.400
Home	.261	533	139	22	6	19	69	61	88	.338	.432	Batting #6	.276	239	66	8	3	8	31	27	41	.344	.435
Away	.240	580	139	15	4	6	65	43	100	.288	.310	Other	.232	659	153	18	5	13	76	53	116	.289	.334
Day	.242	418	101	16	5	3	37	36	80	.302	.325	April	.261	153	40	3	1	4	10	18	28	.337	.373
Night	.255	695	177	21	5	22	97	68	108	.318	.394	May	.262	229	60	9	5	5	32	23	35	.329	.410
Grass	.255	846	216	28	8	23	99	84	132	.322	.399	June	.274	186	51	13	1	2	26	16	37	.330	.387
Turf	.232	267	62	9	2	2	35	20	56	.279	.303	July	.185	184	34	4	0	4	19	15	29	.244	.272
First Pitch	.281	114	32	0	0	4	18	5	0	.314	.386	August	.250	148	37	4	0	5	26	12	26	.301	.378
Ahead on Count	.293	239	70	13	3	10	51	51	0	.407	.498	September/October	.263	213	56	4	3	5	19	20	33	.325	.360
Behind on Count	.225	378	85	10	4	4	39	0	101	.226	.304	Pre-All Star	.263	623	164	25	7	12	72	65	109	.332	.384
Two Strikes	.200	535	107	13	5	6	35	44	188	.261	.277	Post-All Star	.233	490	114	12	3	13	62	39	79	.286	.349

Batter vs. Pitcher (career)

Hits Best Against	Avg	AB	H	2B	3B	HR	RBI	BB	SO	OBP	SLG	Hits Worst Against	Avg	AB	H	2B	3B	HR	RBI	BB	SO	OBP	SLG
Scott Bailes	.500	10	5	0	0	1	4	1	1	.545	.800	Mark Portugal	.053	19	1	0	0	0	0	4	5	.217	.053
Bill Gullickson	.467	15	7	0	0	2	2	1	3	.500	.867	Ramon Martinez	.077	13	1	0	0	0	0	2	2	.200	.077
John Smoltz	.440	25	11	2	0	1	1	1	1	.462	.640	Mark Langston	.091	11	1	1	0	0	0	1	3	.167	.182
Mark Gubicza	.400	20	8	1	0	0	3	1	3	.429	.450	Kirk McCaskill	.136	22	3	0	0	0	3	2	6	.208	.136

Batter vs. Pitcher (career)

Hits Best Against	Avg	AB	H	2B	3B	HR	RBI	BB	SO	OBP	SLG	Hits Worst Against	Avg	AB	H	2B	3B	HR	RBI	BB	SO	OBP	SLG
Tim Leary	.400	10	4	0	1	0	2	1	0	.455	.600	Charlie Leibrandt	.182	11	2	0	0	0	1	0	1	.182	.182

Billy Ripken — Orioles
Bats Right (groundball hitter)

	Avg	G	AB	R	H	2B	3B	HR	RBI	BB	SO	HBP	GDP	SB	CS	OBP	SLG	IBB	SH	SF	#Pit	#P/PA	GB	FB	G/F
1992 Season	.230	111	330	35	76	15	0	4	36	18	26	3	10	2	3	.275	.312	1	10	2	1189	3.37	146	96	1.52
Last Five Years	.236	609	1853	190	438	83	5	11	148	116	216	12	57	16	10	.284	.304	3	63	13	7005	3.51	830	467	1.78

1992 Season

	Avg	AB	H	2B	3B	HR	RBI	BB	SO	OBP	SLG		Avg	AB	H	2B	3B	HR	RBI	BB	SO	OBP	SLG
vs. Left	.229	109	25	7	0	0	9	7	5	.280	.294	Scoring Posn	.264	87	23	3	0	1	30	7	8	.327	.333
vs. Right	.231	221	51	8	0	4	27	11	21	.272	.321	Close & Late	.208	24	5	2	0	1	5	3	3	.296	.417
Groundball	.210	81	17	3	0	1	10	4	9	.256	.284	None on/out	.169	77	13	3	0	0	0	2	8	.190	.208
Flyball	.300	80	24	5	0	2	10	5	5	.345	.438	Batting #8	.215	130	28	6	0	2	17	10	11	.270	.308
Home	.255	149	38	5	0	3	22	13	9	.325	.349	Batting #9	.241	195	47	8	0	2	19	8	15	.280	.313
Away	.210	181	38	10	0	1	14	5	17	.230	.282	Other	.200	5	1	0	0	0	0	0	0	.200	.400
Day	.217	92	20	7	0	2	10	5	7	.258	.359	April	.182	44	8	4	0	0	5	1	7	.200	.273
Night	.235	238	56	8	0	2	26	13	19	.281	.294	May	.244	41	10	0	0	1	6	2	2	.311	.317
Grass	.218	271	59	12	0	4	28	17	19	.270	.306	June	.196	56	11	4	0	1	4	3	3	.246	.321
Turf	.288	59	17	3	0	0	8	1	7	.300	.339	July	.286	56	16	3	0	2	6	1	3	.298	.446
First Pitch	.309	68	21	5	0	1	12	1	0	.329	.426	August	.234	77	18	3	0	0	13	7	9	.294	.273
Ahead on Count	.254	67	17	2	0	2	11	14	0	.373	.373	September/October	.232	56	13	1	0	0	2	4	2	.283	.250
Behind on Count	.204	103	21	3	0	1	6	0	14	.204	.262	Pre-All Star	.234	154	36	9	0	3	18	7	12	.279	.351
Two Strikes	.144	125	18	6	0	1	9	3	26	.171	.216	Post-All Star	.227	176	40	6	0	1	18	11	14	.271	.278

1992 By Position

Position	Avg	AB	H	2B	3B	HR	RBI	BB	SO	OBP	SLG	G	GS	Innings	PO	A	E	DP	Fld Pct	Rng Fctr	In Zone	Outs	Zone Rtg	MLB Zone
As 2b	.230	330	76	15	0	4	36	18	26	.275	.312	108	108	893.2	218	317	4	65	.993	5.39	354	316	.893	.892

Last Five Years

	Avg	AB	H	2B	3B	HR	RBI	BB	SO	OBP	SLG		Avg	AB	H	2B	3B	HR	RBI	BB	SO	OBP	SLG
vs. Left	.259	637	165	32	1	2	46	47	67	.310	.322	Scoring Posn	.258	423	109	15	0	2	131	24	51	.295	.307
vs. Right	.225	1216	273	51	4	9	102	69	149	.270	.295	Close & Late	.261	218	57	7	1	1	17	19	26	.324	.317
Groundball	.214	467	100	16	0	3	36	28	64	.264	.268	None on/out	.230	431	99	21	2	3	3	25	51	.280	.309
Flyball	.251	419	105	25	1	5	35	27	42	.298	.351	Batting #2	.218	367	80	16	0	2	29	20	54	.264	.278
Home	.241	901	217	41	3	5	76	65	100	.295	.310	Batting #9	.237	1244	295	53	5	7	96	81	146	.286	.305
Away	.232	952	221	42	2	6	72	51	116	.273	.299	Other	.260	242	63	14	0	2	23	15	16	.305	.343
Day	.222	446	99	21	0	4	35	31	49	.273	.296	April	.194	252	49	11	0	1	17	15	33	.242	.250
Night	.241	1407	339	62	5	7	113	85	167	.287	.307	May	.236	322	76	14	1	2	29	23	34	.289	.304
Grass	.234	1588	371	72	3	9	122	97	182	.280	.300	June	.231	373	86	20	1	3	28	17	44	.270	.314
Turf	.253	265	67	11	2	2	26	19	34	.308	.332	July	.258	318	82	14	2	2	22	23	27	.306	.333
First Pitch	.299	328	98	15	0	3	27	2	0	.304	.372	August	.248	298	74	10	0	0	28	22	42	.300	.282
Ahead on Count	.272	375	102	25	3	5	41	79	0	.399	.395	September/October	.245	290	71	14	1	3	24	16	36	.291	.331
Behind on Count	.206	630	130	19	3	1	42	0	145	.209	.262	Pre-All Star	.233	1052	245	49	3	7	82	67	117	.282	.305
Two Strikes	.177	776	137	26	1	3	52	34	216	.214	.224	Post-All Star	.241	801	193	34	2	4	66	49	99	.287	.303

Batter vs. Pitcher (career)

Hits Best Against	Avg	AB	H	2B	3B	HR	RBI	BB	SO	OBP	SLG	Hits Worst Against	Avg	AB	H	2B	3B	HR	RBI	BB	SO	OBP	SLG
Bill Wegman	.647	17	11	0	0	1	5	1	1	.632	.824	Walt Terrell	.000	19	0	0	0	0	2	4	.095	.000
Storm Davis	.462	13	6	1	1	0	0	1	0	.500	.692	Dave Stewart	.071	14	1	1	0	0	1	0	3	.071	.143
Charlie Leibrandt	.429	14	6	1	0	0	1	1	3	.467	.500	Jack McDowell	.077	13	1	0	0	0	1	0	2	.077	.077
David Wells	.400	15	6	2	0	1	1	3	0	.500	.733	Jim Abbott	.091	11	1	0	0	0	0	0	2	.091	.091
Scott Bankhead	.333	12	4	0	0	1	3	0	1	.333	.583	Jeff Johnson	.100	10	1	0	0	0	1	0	1	.250	.100

Cal Ripken — Orioles
Bats Right

	Avg	G	AB	R	H	2B	3B	HR	RBI	BB	SO	HBP	GDP	SB	CS	OBP	SLG	IBB	SH	SF	#Pit	#P/PA	GB	FB	G/F
1992 Season	.251	162	637	73	160	29	1	14	72	64	50	7	13	4	3	.323	.366	14	0	7	2366	3.31	262	215	1.22
Last Five Years	.270	806	3106	417	838	158	11	113	444	358	303	22	76	18	9	.345	.437	59	1	39	12828	3.64	1257	1014	1.24

1992 Season

	Avg	AB	H	2B	3B	HR	RBI	BB	SO	OBP	SLG		Avg	AB	H	2B	3B	HR	RBI	BB	SO	OBP	SLG
vs. Left	.230	165	38	6	1	2	13	14	8	.297	.315	Scoring Posn	.276	145	40	5	0	4	57	30	13	.395	.393
vs. Right	.258	472	122	23	0	12	59	50	42	.332	.383	Close & Late	.247	77	19	3	0	0	9	15	5	.372	.286
Groundball	.237	173	41	6	0	1	13	14	17	.293	.289	None on/out	.258	132	34	7	1	0	0	12	6	.329	.326
Flyball	.241	170	41	7	1	7	28	17	12	.313	.418	Batting #3	.254	516	131	23	1	12	63	55	39	.330	.372
Home	.237	312	74	17	1	5	23	31	30	.310	.346	Batting #5	.264	91	24	5	0	2	8	7	8	.316	.385
Away	.265	325	86	12	0	9	49	33	20	.335	.385	Other	.167	30	5	1	0	0	1	2	3	.219	.200
Day	.268	198	53	7	0	5	25	14	11	.323	.379	April	.250	76	19	6	1	1	11	12	6	.359	.395
Night	.244	439	107	22	1	9	47	50	39	.323	.360	May	.264	106	28	4	0	5	11	13	8	.347	.443
Grass	.253	541	137	24	1	13	59	52	41	.321	.373	June	.327	113	37	4	0	4	16	10	9	.387	.469
Turf	.240	96	23	5	0	1	13	12	9	.336	.323	July	.178	107	19	4	0	0	10	14	7	.286	.215
First Pitch	.240	100	24	4	0	2	10	12	0	.336	.340	August	.218	110	24	4	0	0	11	8	12	.267	.255

1992 Season

	Avg	AB	H	2B	3B	HR	RBI	BB	SO	OBP	SLG		Avg	AB	H	2B	3B	HR	RBI	BB	SO	OBP	SLG
Ahead on Count	.290	193	56	16	0	6	34	33	0	.390	.466	September/October	.264	125	33	7	0	4	13	7	8	.303	.416
Behind on Count	.259	205	53	6	0	5	23	0	20	.265	.361	Pre-All Star	.262	340	89	14	1	10	40	41	26	.347	.397
Two Strikes	.204	201	41	3	1	3	14	22	50	.286	.274	Post-All Star	.239	297	71	15	0	4	32	23	24	.294	.330

1992 By Position

Position	Avg	AB	H	2B	3B	HR	RBI	BB	SO	OBP	SLG	G	GS	Innings	PO	A	E	DP	Fld Pct	Rng Fctr	In Zone	Zone Outs	Zone Rtg	MLB Zone
As ss	.251	637	160	29	1	14	72	64	50	.323	.366	162	162	1440.0	287	445	12	117	.984	4.57	487	456	.936	.885

Last Five Years

	Avg	AB	H	2B	3B	HR	RBI	BB	SO	OBP	SLG		Avg	AB	H	2B	3B	HR	RBI	BB	SO	OBP	SLG
vs. Left	.278	896	249	49	4	37	115	117	85	.359	.465	Scoring Posn	.261	758	198	38	4	24	311	158	86	.377	.417
vs. Right	.266	2212	589	109	7	76	329	241	218	.340	.425	Close & Late	.275	444	122	26	2	14	60	66	47	.368	.437
Groundball	.270	821	222	40	2	13	93	91	86	.342	.371	None on/out	.269	610	164	21	1	27	27	48	45	.328	.449
Flyball	.261	706	184	41	3	31	114	78	77	.332	.459	Batting #3	.269	2574	693	125	10	99	374	300	256	.346	.441
Home	.249	1524	360	72	4	53	214	177	164	.327	.406	Batting #4	.239	230	55	18	0	4	25	25	18	.317	.370
Away	.289	1584	458	86	7	60	230	181	139	.363	.466	Other	.296	304	90	15	1	10	45	33	29	.365	.451
Day	.278	809	225	31	1	36	112	90	86	.352	.452	April	.277	397	110	23	3	14	66	59	40	.377	.456
Night	.267	2299	613	127	10	77	332	268	217	.343	.431	May	.272	503	137	22	1	24	68	72	42	.363	.463
Grass	.265	2631	698	123	9	98	367	298	266	.340	.431	June	.309	547	169	30	2	17	77	62	48	.381	.464
Turf	.294	477	140	35	2	15	77	60	37	.373	.470	July	.250	521	130	24	0	19	75	59	47	.328	.405
First Pitch	.321	365	117	24	0	20	53	29	0	.374	.551	August	.268	556	149	30	3	19	86	52	66	.327	.435
Ahead on Count	.289	809	234	42	1	49	154	179	0	.414	.525	September/October	.245	584	143	29	2	20	72	54	60	.306	.404
Behind on Count	.257	1037	266	40	4	34	143	4	143	.263	.401	Pre-All Star	.282	1623	457	81	6	62	233	211	146	.367	.453
Two Strikes	.220	1214	267	51	7	20	133	136	303	.300	.323	Post-All Star	.257	1485	381	77	5	51	211	147	157	.322	.418

Batter vs. Pitcher (since 1984)

Hits Best Against	Avg	AB	H	2B	3B	HR	RBI	BB	SO	OBP	SLG	Hits Worst Against	Avg	AB	H	2B	3B	HR	RBI	BB	SO	OBP	SLG
Doug Jones	.556	18	10	3	0	1	6	2	2	.600	.889	Tom Filer	.000	12	0	0	0	0	0	2	3	.133	.000
Scott Aldred	.545	11	6	0	1	2	4	1	1	.583	1.273	Jose DeLeon	.000	10	0	0	0	0	0	3	4	.231	.000
Chuck Crim	.529	17	9	1	0	1	6	1	1	.556	.765	Terry Mathews	.000	8	0	0	0	0	1	0	2	.182	.000
David Wells	.421	19	8	2	0	3	6	1	2	.500	1.000	Mike Morgan	.091	22	2	0	0	0	0	1	4	.091	.091
Rich DeLucia	.357	14	5	2	0	2	3	0	0	.357	.929	Jay Howell	.143	14	2	1	0	0	1	0	2	.143	.143

Bill Risley — Expos
Pitches Right (flyball pitcher)

	ERA	W	L	Sv	G	GS	IP	BB	SO	Avg	H	2B	3B	HR	RBI	OBP	SLG	CG	ShO	Sup	QS	#P/S	SB	CS	GB	FB	G/F
1992 Season	1.80	1	0	0	1	1	5.0	1	2	.235	4	1	0	0	1	.278	.294	0	0	3.60	0	73	2	0	3	6	0.50

1992 Season

	ERA	W	L	Sv	G	GS	IP	H	HR	BB	SO		Avg	AB	H	2B	3B	HR	RBI	BB	SO	OBP	SLG
Home	0.00	0	0	0	0	0	0.0	0	0	0	0	vs. Left	.214	14	3	0	0	0	1	1	1	.267	.214
Away	1.80	1	0	0	1	1	5.0	4	0	1	2	vs. Right	.333	3	1	1	0	0	0	0	1	.333	.667

Wally Ritchie — Phillies
Pitches Left

	ERA	W	L	Sv	G	GS	IP	BB	SO	Avg	H	2B	3B	HR	RBI	OBP	SLG	GF	IR	IRS	Hld	SvOp	SB	CS	GB	FB	G/F
1992 Season	3.00	2	1	1	40	0	39.0	17	19	.288	44	10	2	3	26	.359	.438	13	38	16	3	2	3	0	57	48	1.19
Last Five Years	2.81	3	3	1	98	0	115.1	51	53	.247	107	23	4	8	62	.326	.374	26	105	32	11	5	14	1	155	154	1.01

1992 Season

	ERA	W	L	Sv	G	GS	IP	H	HR	BB	SO		Avg	AB	H	2B	3B	HR	RBI	BB	SO	OBP	SLG
Home	2.29	1	0	0	23	0	19.2	22	1	7	14	vs. Left	.220	59	13	2	1	1	12	4	11	.270	.339
Away	3.72	1	1	1	17	0	19.1	22	2	10	5	vs. Right	.330	94	31	8	1	2	14	13	8	.411	.500
Starter	0.00	0	0	0	0	0	0.0	0	0	0	0	Scoring Posn	.271	59	16	6	1	0	23	12	10	.394	.407
Reliever	3.00	2	1	1	40	0	39.0	44	3	17	19	Close & Late	.341	41	14	6	0	1	11	7	5	.438	.561
0 Days rest	1.93	1	0	0	8	0	4.2	5	0	2	0	None on/out	.406	32	13	2	0	2	2	2	2	.441	.656
1 or 2 Days rest	2.20	1	0	0	17	0	16.1	15	1	6	9	First Pitch	.308	26	8	1	0	0	2	3	0	.379	.346
3+ Days rest	4.00	0	1	1	15	0	18.0	24	2	9	10	Behind on Count	.333	30	10	2	0	1	8	5	0	.429	.500
Pre-All Star	2.78	1	1	1	36	0	35.2	40	3	14	17	Ahead on Count	.253	75	19	5	2	2	12	0	17	.253	.453
Post-All Star	5.40	1	0	0	4	0	3.1	4	0	3	2	Two Strikes	.224	67	15	4	2	1	10	9	19	.316	.388

Kevin Ritz — Tigers
Pitches Right (groundball pitcher)

	ERA	W	L	Sv	G	GS	IP	BB	SO	Avg	H	2B	3B	HR	RBI	OBP	SLG	GF	IR	IRS	Hld	SvOp	SB	CS	GB	FB	G/F
1992 Season	5.60	2	5	0	23	11	80.1	44	57	.278	88	14	0	4	42	.368	.361	4	8	2	0	0	11	5	120	67	1.79
Career (1989-1992)	5.85	6	18	0	50	32	177.0	124	125	.280	194	32	3	7	98	.388	.365	7	11	4	0	1	22	10	273	162	1.69

1992 Season

	ERA	W	L	Sv	G	GS	IP	H	HR	BB	SO		Avg	AB	H	2B	3B	HR	RBI	BB	SO	OBP	SLG
Home	4.75	1	1	0	15	6	55.0	54	4	27	40	vs. Left	.295	129	38	8	0	2	20	23	30	.404	.403
Away	7.46	1	4	0	8	5	25.1	34	0	17	17	vs. Right	.267	187	50	6	0	2	22	21	27	.341	.332
Starter	5.77	2	5	0	11	11	53.0	58	4	30	30	Scoring Posn	.301	83	25	7	0	1	38	18	14	.415	.422
Reliever	5.27	0	0	0	12	0	27.1	30	0	14	27	Close & Late	.167	6	1	0	0	1	1	3	0	.444	.667
0 Days rest	0.00	0	0	0	0	0	0.0	0	0	0	0	None on/out	.269	78	21	1	0	2	2	7	10	.329	.359

	ERA	W	L	Sv	G	GS	IP	H	HR	BB	SO		Avg	AB	H	2B	3B	HR	RBI	BB	SO	OBP	SLG
1 or 2 Days rest	5.23	0	0	0	5	0	10.1	12	0	6	12	First Pitch	.194	36	7	3	0	0	3	1	0	.237	.278
3+ Days rest	5.29	0	0	0	7	0	17.0	18	0	8	15	Behind on Count	.393	89	35	6	0	3	16	26	0	.517	.562
Pre-All Star	5.68	2	3	0	20	8	65.0	75	4	33	45	Ahead on Count	.224	125	28	3	0	0	12	0	48	.236	.248
Post-All Star	5.28	0	2	0	3	3	15.1	13	0	11	12	Two Strikes	.211	142	30	4	0	1	19	17	57	.302	.261

Ben Rivera — Phillies

Pitches Right

	ERA	W	L	Sv	G	GS	IP	BB	SO	Avg	H	2B	3B	HR	RBI	OBP	SLG	CG	ShO	Sup	QS	#P/S	SB	CS	GB	FB	G/F
1992 Season	3.07	7	4	0	28	14	117.1	45	77	.230	99	18	5	9	42	.307	.357	4	1	5.91	9	97	15	4	159	126	1.26

1992 Season

	ERA	W	L	Sv	G	GS	IP	H	HR	BB	SO		Avg	AB	H	2B	3B	HR	RBI	BB	SO	OBP	SLG
Home	2.01	5	0	0	12	6	53.2	39	1	23	35	vs. Left	.236	250	59	12	3	4	24	27	32	.317	.356
Away	3.96	2	4	0	16	8	63.2	60	8	22	42	vs. Right	.221	181	40	6	2	5	18	18	45	.294	.359
Starter	2.95	7	3	0	14	14	91.2	68	8	29	60	Scoring Posn	.236	106	25	4	0	2	32	16	20	.341	.330
Reliever	3.51	0	1	0	14	0	25.2	31	1	16	17	Close & Late	.231	26	6	1	1	1	3	4	3	.355	.462
0-3 Days Rest	0.00	0	0	0	0	0	0.0	0	0	0	0	None on/out	.252	111	28	4	2	3	3	9	21	.314	.405
4 Days Rest	3.62	4	2	0	6	6	37.1	29	3	12	24	First Pitch	.269	67	18	3	1	1	6	1	0	.275	.388
5+ Days Rest	2.48	3	1	0	8	8	54.1	39	5	17	36	Behind on Count	.307	88	27	5	1	2	8	26	0	.465	.455
Pre-All Star	3.66	0	1	0	16	2	32.0	37	2	22	23	Ahead on Count	.179	195	35	3		4	20	0	54	.191	.297
Post-All Star	2.85	7	3	0	12	12	85.1	62	7	23	54	Two Strikes	.172	209	36	6	3	5	22	18	77	.247	.301

Luis Rivera — Red Sox

Bats Right

	Avg	G	AB	R	H	2B	3B	HR	RBI	BB	SO	HBP	GDP	SB	CS	OBP	SLG	IBB	SH	SF	#Pit	#P/PA	GB	FB	G/F
1992 Season	.215	102	288	17	62	11	1	0	29	26	56	3	5	4	3	.287	.260	0	5	0	1105	3.49	88	89	0.99
Last Five Years	.237	565	1742	189	413	87	8	24	173	130	329	9	41	17	17	.292	.338	5	36	9	6724	3.56	546	523	1.04

1992 Season

	Avg	AB	H	2B	3B	HR	RBI	BB	SO	OBP	SLG		Avg	AB	H	2B	3B	HR	RBI	BB	SO	OBP	SLG
vs. Left	.179	78	14	3	0	0	7	10	16	.273	.218	Scoring Posn	.264	87	23	2	1	0	28	8	20	.326	.310
vs. Right	.229	210	48	8	1	0	22	16	40	.293	.276	Close & Late	.132	53	7	2	1	0	3	7	12	.233	.208
Groundball	.169	65	11	2	0	0	7	2	9	.194	.200	None on/out	.186	70	13	4	0	0	0	8	10	.278	.243
Flyball	.247	73	18	5	0	0	9	7	22	.321	.315	Batting #8	.231	108	25	2	0	0	13	9	20	.291	.250
Home	.173	127	22	5	0	0	14	9	24	.245	.213	Batting #9	.207	111	23	5	0	0	7	10	20	.273	.252
Away	.248	161	40	6	1	0	15	17	32	.320	.298	Other	.203	69	14	4	1	0	9	7	16	.304	.290
Day	.269	93	25	4	0	0	11	9	16	.333	.312	April	.342	38	13	2	0	0	2	4	11	.405	.395
Night	.190	195	37	7	1	0	18	17	40	.265	.236	May	.203	69	14	1	0	0	8	11	10	.313	.217
Grass	.206	228	47	7	1	0	23	20	45	.279	.246	June	.239	88	21	6	0	0	11	8	18	.323	.307
Turf	.250	60	15	4	0	0	6	6	11	.318	.317	July	.121	58	7	1	0	0	3	2	9	.150	.138
First Pitch	.188	48	9	0	1	0	4	0	0	.204	.229	August	.227	22	5	1	1	0	5	1	5	.261	.364
Ahead on Count	.260	73	19	2	0	0	11	14	0	.379	.288	September/October	.154	13	2	0	0	0	0	0	3	.154	.154
Behind on Count	.194	93	18	2	0	0	8	0	38	.202	.215	Pre-All Star	.230	222	51	9	0	0	22	24	44	.313	.270
Two Strikes	.170	112	19	6	0	0	10	12	56	.256	.223	Post-All Star	.167	66	11	2	1	0	7	2	12	.191	.227

1992 By Position

Position	Avg	AB	H	2B	3B	HR	RBI	BB	SO	OBP	SLG	G	GS	Innings	PO	A	E	DP	Fld Pct	Rng Fctr	In Zone	Outs	Zone Rtg	MLB Zone
As ss	.219	279	61	11	0	0	27	26	52	.292	.258	93	85	732.0	118	285	14	56	.966	4.95	332	301	907	885

Last Five Years

	Avg	AB	H	2B	3B	HR	RBI	BB	SO	OBP	SLG		Avg	AB	H	2B	3B	HR	RBI	BB	SO	OBP	SLG
vs. Left	.233	558	130	32	3	10	64	39	113	.285	.355	Scoring Posn	.228	486	111	22	4	5	144	51	96	.298	.321
vs. Right	.239	1184	283	55	5	14	109	91	216	.296	.329	None on/out	.191	288	55	12	3	3	21	21	64	.244	.285
Groundball	.259	518	134	26	3	9	66	27	75	.298	.373	Batting #8	.218	431	94	21	0	3	3	31	87	.275	.288
Flyball	.206	403	83	19	1	5	33	28	110	.256	.295	Batting #9	.241	548	132	23	3	5	53	39	100	.292	.321
Home	.243	860	209	48	2	14	69	62	153	.297	.352	Other	.205	366	75	23	1	7	41	26	82	.261	.331
Away	.231	882	204	39	6	10	74	68	176	.287	.323	April	.226	124	28	4	0	1	8	8	26	.273	.282
Day	.249	534	133	32	0	12	62	48	89	.311	.376	May	.269	283	76	14	2	5	35	31	46	.340	.385
Night	.232	1208	280	55	8	12	111	82	240	.284	.320	June	.234	384	90	18	0	5	35	27	69	.290	.320
Grass	.239	1220	291	58	6	20	134	106	241	.303	.340	July	.228	355	81	23	4	5	33	25	67	.279	.328
Turf	.234	522	122	29	5	4	39	24	88	.265	.331	August	.245	298	73	12	1	6	34	21	55	.298	.352
First Pitch	.236	305	72	16	1	7	29	1	0	.241	.364	September/October	.218	298	65	16	1	2	18	18	66	.264	.299
Ahead on Count	.280	400	112	27	2	10	60	57	0	.367	.433	Pre-All Star	.246	920	226	44	3	12	92	78	162	.307	.339
Behind on Count	.241	602	145	24	3	6	54	1	186	.249	.321	Post-All Star	.227	822	187	43	5	12	81	52	167	.275	.336
Two Strikes	.189	723	137	25	3	5	59	71	328	.266	.253												

Batter vs. Pitcher (career)

Hits Best Against	Avg	AB	H	2B	3B	HR	RBI	BB	SO	OBP	SLG	Hits Worst Against	Avg	AB	H	2B	3B	HR	RBI	BB	SO	OBP	SLG
Tim Leary	.700	10	7	2	0	1	3	1	0	.727	1.200	Sid Fernandez	.000	12	0	0	0	0	0	2	3	.143	.000
Kenny Rogers	.500	12	6	3	1	0	3	0	2	.500	.917	Kevin Tapani	.000	11	0	0	0	0	0	0	3	.000	.000
Jaime Navarro	.462	13	6	0	0	1	4	1	0	.500	.692	Nolan Ryan	.000	10	0	0	0	0	0	1	4	.000	.000
Alex Fernandez	.438	16	7	0	0	1	1	1	3	.471	.625	Terry Leach	.091	11	1	0	0	0	0	0	0	.091	.091
Melido Perez	.375	16	6	2	0	0	1	3	2	.474	.500	Luis Aquino	.100	20	2	1	0	0	0	0	2	.100	.150

Bip Roberts — Reds

Bats Both (groundball hitter)

	Avg	G	AB	R	H	2B	3B	HR	RBI	BB	SO	HBP	GDP	SB	CS	OBP	SLG	IBB	SH	SF	#Pit	#P/PA	GB	FB	G/F
1992 Season	.323	147	532	92	172	34	6	4	45	62	54	2	7	44	16	.393	.432	4	1	4	2155	3.59	254	110	2.31
Last Five Years	.305	535	1850	344	565	98	20	19	146	204	237	13	24	137	52	.376	.411	5	19	13	7772	3.74	833	375	2.22

1992 Season

	Avg	AB	H	2B	3B	HR	RBI	BB	SO	OBP	SLG		Avg	AB	H	2B	3B	HR	RBI	BB	SO	OBP	SLG
vs. Left	.292	185	54	7	0	3	15	17	20	.350	.378	Scoring Posn	.337	98	33	10	3	1	40	15	9	.415	.531
vs. Right	.340	347	118	27	6	1	30	45	34	.416	.461	Close & Late	.310	84	26	5	1	1	9	7	12	.363	.429
Groundball	.341	208	71	16	3	0	17	20	12	.396	.447	None on/out	.341	252	86	13	3	2	2	23	30	.396	.440
Flyball	.318	110	35	6	0	1	7	15	16	.402	.400	Batting #1	.325	505	164	34	5	4	41	60	47	.396	.436
Home	.353	252	89	22	3	3	23	36	24	.432	.500	Batting #2	.308	13	4	0	0	0	0	2	3	.400	.308
Away	.296	280	83	12	3	1	22	26	30	.357	.371	Other	.286	14	4	0	1	0	4	0	4	.286	.429
Day	.344	163	56	13	1	1	13	23	21	.426	.454	April	.277	83	23	4	2	0	6	12	8	.371	.373
Night	.314	369	116	21	5	3	32	39	33	.379	.423	May	.305	95	29	5	0	0	7	13	10	.385	.358
Grass	.312	173	54	6	3	1	16	15	19	.367	.399	June	.323	99	32	8	0	0	7	7	12	.364	.404
Turf	.329	359	118	28	3	3	29	47	35	.405	.448	July	.267	75	20	4	0	1	8	13	11	.375	.360
First Pitch	.354	113	40	7	3	1	11	5	1	.378	.496	August	.310	87	27	6	1	1	6	7	7	.358	.437
Ahead on Count	.389	108	42	13	2	2	17	40	0	.550	.602	September/October	.441	93	41	7	3	2	11	10	6	.500	.645
Behind on Count	.299	164	49	10	0	1	7	0	30	.299	.378	Pre-All Star	.290	307	89	17	2	0	23	40	38	.370	.358
Two Strikes	.269	216	58	8	0	1	6	17	53	.323	.319	Post-All Star	.369	225	83	17	4	4	22	22	16	.426	.533

1992 By Position

Position	Avg	AB	H	2B	3B	HR	RBI	BB	SO	OBP	SLG	G	GS	Innings	PO	A	E	DP	Fld Pct	Rng Fctr	In Zone	Outs	Zone Rtg	MLB Zone
As Pinch Hitter	.333	12	4	1	0	4	0	4		.333	.500	12	0	---	---	---	---	---	---	---	---	---	---	---
As 2b	.266	128	34	6	0	0	5	9	11	.309	.313	42	31	277.2	51	83	1	7	.993	4.34	101	84	.832	.892
As 3b	.250	120	30	4	2	0	5	17	13	.343	.317	36	29	271.2	20	68	5	6	.946	2.92	87	72	.828	.841
As lf	.391	233	91	21	3	4	26	35	22	.472	.558	69	62	496.1	115	1	1	0	.991	2.10	126	112	.889	.809
As cf	.333	39	13	3	0	0	5	1	4	.350	.410	16	11	70.1	23	0	0	0	1.000	2.94	30	23	.767	.824

Last Five Years

	Avg	AB	H	2B	3B	HR	RBI	BB	SO	OBP	SLG		Avg	AB	H	2B	3B	HR	RBI	BB	SO	OBP	SLG
vs. Left	.291	643	187	32	5	10	52	53	78	.349	.403	Scoring Posn	.304	335	102	26	5	7	124	36	43	.364	.475
vs. Right	.313	1207	378	66	15	9	94	151	159	.390	.415	Close & Late	.287	296	85	9	3	3	30	33	47	.362	.368
Groundball	.322	677	218	37	8	6	56	68	78	.383	.427	None on/out	.306	816	250	40	9	7	7	90	112	.379	.403
Flyball	.314	408	128	20	4	5	30	49	61	.390	.419	Batting #1	.306	1716	525	95	17	17	134	185	215	.375	.411
Home	.307	928	285	47	10	12	72	89	115	.371	.418	Batting #2	.321	56	18	1	2	1	4	10	8	.424	.464
Away	.304	922	280	51	10	7	74	115	122	.381	.403	Other	.282	78	22	2	1	1	8	9	14	.356	.372
Day	.319	539	172	26	5	8	43	70	83	.402	.430	April	.261	238	62	9	5	2	17	26	27	.336	.366
Night	.300	1311	393	72	15	11	103	134	154	.365	.403	May	.307	316	97	17	5	2	25	41	44	.388	.411
Grass	.290	1151	334	44	13	12	85	109	148	.355	.382	June	.295	332	98	19	4	1	24	29	52	.360	.386
Turf	.330	699	231	54	7	7	61	95	89	.410	.458	July	.287	286	82	12	1	2	26	37	37	.367	.357
First Pitch	.380	287	109	19	4	5	33	5	1	.386	.526	August	.317	331	105	22	2	7	24	31	44	.373	.394
Ahead on Count	.367	327	120	28	5	4	40	142	0	.557	.520	September/October	.349	347	121	19	3	5	30	40	33	.418	.454
Behind on Count	.264	644	170	27	3	5	37	0	146	.269	.339	Pre-All Star	.284	974	277	46	15	5	71	112	137	.362	.378
Two Strikes	.242	826	200	30	9	7	40	56	236	.295	.326	Post-All Star	.329	876	288	52	5	14	75	92	100	.392	.447

Batter vs. Pitcher (career)

Hits Best Against	Avg	AB	H	2B	3B	HR	RBI	BB	SO	OBP	SLG	Hits Worst Against	Avg	AB	H	2B	3B	HR	RBI	BB	SO	OBP	SLG
Greg Maddux	.476	21	10	3	0	0	3	7	3	.607	.619	Rick Honeycutt	.000	11	0	0	0	0	0	1	2	.083	.000
Ken Hill	.467	15	7	1	1	0	1	2	2	.529	.667	Tim Belcher	.067	15	1	0	0	0	0	2	1	.176	.067
Jose DeLeon	.444	9	4	0	0	1	3	1	1	.538	.778	Scott Scudder	.083	12	1	0	0	0	1	0	2	.083	.083
Ron Darling	.429	14	6	2	0	0	1	3	2	.500	.571	Joe Magrane	.100	10	1	0	0	0	0	1	2	.182	.100
Andy Benes	.417	12	5	2	0	0	3	1	1	.533	.583	Bobby Ojeda	.125	16	2	0	0	0	2	2	1	.222	.125

Don Robinson — Phillies

Pitches Right (flyball pitcher)

	ERA	W	L	Sv	G	GS	IP	BB	SO	Avg	H	2B	3B	HR	RBI	OBP	SLG	CG	ShO	Sup	QS	#P/S	SB	CS	GB	FB	G/F
1992 Season	5.10	2	4	0	11	11	60.0	7	26	.291	68	13	1	7	34	.306	.444	0	0	4.05	5	73	11	0	70	90	0.78
Last Five Years	3.74	39	36	7	156	103	712.2	184	400	.258	700	137	19	70	310	.304	.399	12	3	3.90	61	84	74	31	883	954	0.93

1992 Season

	ERA	W	L	Sv	G	GS	IP	H	HR	BB	SO		Avg	AB	H	2B	3B	HR	RBI	BB	SO	OBP	SLG
Home	2.45	2	0	0	3	3	18.1	13	0	2	9	vs. Left	.313	128	40	6	1	2	19	1	11	.311	.422
Away	6.26	0	4	0	8	8	41.2	55	7	5	17	vs. Right	.264	106	28	7	0	5	15	6	15	.302	.472
Starter	5.10	2	4	0	11	11	60.0	68	7	7	26	Scoring Posn	.218	55	12	3	0	1	25	1	7	.222	.327
Reliever	0.00	0	0	0	0	0	0.0	0	0	0	0	Close & Late	.333	6	2	0	0	0	1	0	1	.333	.333
0-3 Days Rest	7.50	0	1	0	1	1	6.0	10	1	0	3	None on/out	.453	64	29	8	1	2	2	3	6	.478	.703
4 Days Rest	6.29	0	2	0	5	5	24.1	32	6	3	12	First Pitch	.372	43	16	5	0	3	7	0	0	.372	.698
5+ Days Rest	3.64	2	1	0	5	5	29.2	26	0	4	11	Behind on Count	.345	55	19	3	0	2	10	4	0	.377	.509
Pre-All Star	5.10	2	4	0	11	11	60.0	68	7	7	26	Ahead on Count	.186	97	18	1	0	2	12	0	22	.188	.258
Post-All Star	0.00	0	0	0	0	0	0.0	0	0	0	0	Two Strikes	.198	86	17	2	0	2	12	3	26	.220	.291

Last Five Years

	ERA	W	L	Sv	G	GS	IP	H	HR	BB	SO		Avg	AB	H	2B	3B	HR	RBI	BB	SO	OBP	SLG
Home	2.87	22	7	3	67	43	326.1	300	32	76	200	vs. Left	.265	1506	399	77	11	38	168	122	201	.319	.406
Away	4.47	17	29	4	89	60	386.1	400	36	108	200	vs. Right	.248	1212	301	60	8	32	142	62	199	.264	.390
Day	3.33	14	10	4	64	38	278.0	268	25	80	170	Inning 1-6	.261	2162	564	110	15	59	263	143	312	.305	.407
Night	4.00	25	26	3	92	65	434.2	432	45	104	230	Inning 7+	.245	556	136	27	4	11	47	41	88	.297	.367
Grass	3.26	29	21	6	105	69	486.1	466	46	112	277	None on	.252	1681	423	87	16	41	41	91	244	.292	.396
Turf	4.77	10	15	1	51	34	226.1	234	24	72	123	Runners on	.267	1037	277	50	3	29	269	93	156	.322	.405
April	3.00	3	3	2	25	9	69.0	78	7	20	41	Scoring Posn	.277	606	168	32	2	17	233	73	104	.344	.421
May	3.41	6	6	1	28	15	113.1	109	13	39	72	Close & Late	.243	247	60	12	3	2	17	22	38	.300	.340
June	3.87	9	5	3	32	20	130.1	127	14	34	65	None on/out	.268	714	191	41	7	21	21	41	99	.308	.433
July	4.00	8	6	0	24	23	150.2	149	11	39	96	vs. 1st Batr (relief)	.348	46	16	5	1	2	10	5	11	.415	.630
August	3.77	7	10	0	24	20	141.0	118	16	32	80	First Inning Pitched	.308	591	182	38	10	22	118	50	67	.360	.518
September/October	3.99	6	6	1	23	16	108.1	119	9	20	46	First 75 Pitches	.259	2268	587	119	17	62	268	150	346	.303	.408
Starter	3.86	37	33	0	103	103	625.2	614	62	155	334	Pitch 76-90	.263	285	75	12	2	5	29	20	30	.314	.372
Reliever	2.90	2	3	7	53	0	87.0	86	8	29	66	Pitch 91-105	.211	128	27	5	0	5	8	8	19	.257	.297
0-3 Days Rest	4.20	6	7	0	21	21	122.0	126	9	29	69	Pitch 106+	.297	37	11	1	0	1	4	6	5	.395	.405
4 Days Rest	3.87	21	16	0	55	55	332.2	321	39	86	195	First Pitch	.320	485	155	30	3	22	71	17	0	.340	.530
5+ Days Rest	3.58	10	10	0	27	27	171.0	167	14	40	70	Ahead on Count	.191	1255	240	42	7	18	99	3	363	.195	.279
Pre-All Star	3.80	20	18	6	94	53	367.0	373	42	103	210	Behind on Count	.323	554	179	32	4	20	85	91	0	.415	.504
Post-All Star	3.67	19	18	1	62	50	345.2	327	36	81	190	Two Strikes	.174	1126	196	39	6	17	90	73	400	.226	.265

Pitcher vs. Batter (since 1984)

Pitches Best Vs.	Avg	AB	H	2B	3B	HR	RBI	BB	SO	OBP	SLG	Pitches Worst Vs.	Avg	AB	H	2B	3B	HR	RBI	BB	SO	OBP	SLG
Todd Zeile	.050	20	1	0	0	0	0	0	2	.050	.050	Jeff Treadway	.500	16	8	2	0	1	6	1	2	.529	.813
Tony Pena	.077	13	1	0	0	0	0	1	1	.143	.077	Tim Teufel	.455	11	5	3	0	1	2	1	1	.462	1.000
Luis Quinones	.077	13	1	0	0	0	0	1	1	.077	.077	Darryl Strawberry	.433	30	13	3	0	2	6	7	4	.541	.733
Alfredo Griffin	.095	21	2	0	0	0	2	1	1	.136	.095	Ray Lankford	.429	14	6	2	1	0	2	2	2	.500	.714
Wally Backman	.100	20	2	0	0	0	0	1	5	.143	.100	Mike Scioscia	.406	32	13	4	0	4	10	6	1	.487	.906

Jeff Robinson — Cubs
Pitches Right (groundball pitcher)

	ERA	W	L	Sv	G	GS	IP	BB	SO	Avg	H	2B	3B	HR	RBI	OBP	SLG	GF	IR	IRS	Hld	SvOp	SB	CS	GB	FB	G/F
1992 Season	3.00	4	3	1	49	5	78.0	40	76	.263	76	15	3	5	30	.354	.388	12	24	7	4	9	8		113	70	1.61
Last Five Years	3.82	25	30	17	267	28	489.2	201	328	.261	488	89	14	42	235	.333	.391	40	230	64	29	32	57	22	805	447	1.80

1992 Season

	ERA	W	L	Sv	G	GS	IP	H	HR	BB	SO		Avg	AB	H	2B	3B	HR	RBI	BB	SO	OBP	SLG
Home	3.25	1	2	1	25	1	36.0	42	3	14	20	vs. Left	.290	155	45	8	1	2	16	14	25	.351	.394
Away	2.79	3	1	0	24	4	42.0	34	2	26	26	vs. Right	.231	134	31	7	2	3	14	26	21	.358	.381
Starter	4.22	1	1	0	5	5	21.1	21	1	13	9	Scoring Posn	.195	82	16	6	0	0	21	20	16	.346	.268
Reliever	2.54	3	2	1	44	0	56.2	55	4	27	37	Close & Late	.264	106	28	4	1	2	14	10	19	.328	.377
0 Days rest	4.70	0	1	0	8	0	7.2	10	2	7	4	None on/out	.222	72	16	3	1	2	2	8	10	.300	.375
1 or 2 Days rest	1.26	1	0	1	19	0	28.2	19	1	12	20	First Pitch	.256	39	10	3	1	0	7	6	0	.383	.385
3+ Days rest	3.54	2	1	0	17	0	20.1	26	1	8	13	Behind on Count	.390	77	30	7	1	1	6	25	0	.539	.545
Pre-All Star	2.32	1	0	0	22	0	31.0	36	2	16	21	Ahead on Count	.197	122	24	3	1	2	11	0	38	.197	.287
Post-All Star	3.45	3	3	1	27	5	47.0	40	3	24	25	Two Strikes	.172	134	23	3	0	2	11	9	46	.224	.239

Last Five Years

	ERA	W	L	Sv	G	GS	IP	H	HR	BB	SO		Avg	AB	H	2B	3B	HR	RBI	BB	SO	OBP	SLG
Home	3.42	7	16	7	139	10	234.0	225	21	90	171	vs. Left	.259	935	242	39	7	17	110	76	140	.313	.370
Away	4.19	18	14	10	128	18	255.2	263	21	111	157	vs. Right	.264	933	246	50	7	25	125	125	188	.352	.413
Day	3.93	9	9	6	86	11	165.0	174	16	65	116	Inning 1-6	.259	758	196	36	5	14	85	73	119	.324	.375
Night	3.77	16	21	11	181	17	324.2	314	26	136	212	Inning 7+	.263	1110	292	53	9	28	150	128	209	.339	.403
Grass	3.36	11	13	5	145	12	246.1	233	22	100	171	None on	.267	1030	275	54	11	22	22	79	176	.322	.405
Turf	4.29	14	17	12	122	16	243.1	255	20	101	157	Runners on	.254	838	213	35	3	20	213	122	152	.346	.375
April	3.05	4	3	9	38	0	65.0	62	4	24	40	Scoring Posn	.237	557	132	24	3	11	191	103	109	.349	.350
May	3.39	1	6	3	52	0	69.0	66	4	25	54	Close & Late	.247	535	132	24	3	9	72	63	106	.326	.353
June	5.82	6	6	2	53	2	82.0	97	10	47	65	None on/out	.254	449	114	27	3	11	11	30	78	.302	.401
July	2.84	6	4	2	37	9	92.0	87	8	36	56	vs. 1st Batr (relief)	.244	217	53	7	2	6	31	17	41	.301	.378
August	4.10	4	0	4	43	11	105.1	112	9	34	53	First Inning Pitched	.241	864	208	35	5	16	116	103	157	.321	.348
September/October	3.54	4	7	1	44	6	76.1	73	7	35	60	First 15 Pitches	.255	826	211	35	7	17	96	97	140	.334	.377
Starter	3.55	8	9	0	28	28	149.2	155	16	80	80	Pitch 16-30	.249	518	129	28	4	10	61	53	102	.318	.376
Reliever	3.94	17	21	17	239	0	340.0	333	31	145	248	Pitch 31-45	.257	230	59	10	2	6	29	21	42	.320	.396
0 Days rest	3.41	2	5	4	44	0	58.0	55	7	26	38	Pitch 46+	.303	294	89	16	1	9	49	30	44	.366	.456
1 or 2 Days rest	3.82	11	9	10	124	0	179.0	167	13	74	128	First Pitch	.294	296	87	20	2	9	53	19	0	.334	.466
3+ Days rest	4.46	4	7	3	71	0	103.0	111	11	45	82	Ahead on Count	.197	778	153	25	3	8	57	0	283	.197	.267
Pre-All Star	3.94	13	16	15	158	4	251.0	243	23	110	189	Behind on Count	.327	474	155	24	5	15	79	123	0	.466	.494
Post-All Star	3.70	12	14	2	109	24	238.2	245	19	91	139	Two Strikes	.176	763	134	24	6	17	90	63	328	.236	.239

Pitcher vs. Batter (career)

Pitches Best Vs.	Avg	AB	H	2B	3B	HR	RBI	BB	SO	OBP	SLG	Pitches Worst Vs.	Avg	AB	H	2B	3B	HR	RBI	BB	SO	OBP	SLG
Wally Backman	.077	13	1	0	0	0	1	0	1	.071	.077	Denny Walling	.625	16	10	3	0	1	5	1	0	.647	1.000
Franklin Stubbs	.077	13	1	0	0	0	0	0	6	.077	.077	Lonnie Smith	.500	10	5	3	0	0	4	3	2	.571	.800
Kurt Stillwell	.077	13	1	0	0	0	0	0	0	.077	.077	Tony Gwynn	.483	29	14	2	2	0	3	2	0	.516	.690
Dale Murphy	.097	31	3	1	0	0	2	1	10	.125	.129	Gary Carter	.476	21	10	0	1	3	5	0	3	.476	1.000

Jeff M. Robinson — Pirates

Pitches Right (flyball pitcher)

	ERA	W	L	Sv	G	GS	IP	BB	SO	Avg	H	2B	3B	HR	RBI	OBP	SLG	GF	IR	IRS	Hld	SvOp	SB	CS	GB	FB	G/F
1992 Season	5.16	7	5	0	24	11	82.0	36	32	.265	83	15	1	8	42	.339	.396	2	16	9	0	2	7	5	108	121	0.89
Last Five Years	4.66	38	34	0	112	96	581.1	293	327	.247	540	106	10	72	271	.338	.404	2	19	11	0	2	35	28	742	748	0.99

1992 Season

	ERA	W	L	Sv	G	GS	IP	H	HR	BB	SO		Avg	AB	H	2B	3B	HR	RBI	BB	SO	OBP	SLG
Home	4.93	2	4	0	13	6	45.2	45	5	24	18	vs. Left	.258	151	39	3	1	5	20	18	11	.335	.391
Away	5.45	5	1	0	11	5	36.1	38	3	12	14	vs. Right	.272	162	44	12	0	3	22	18	21	.342	.401
Starter	4.76	3	2	0	11	11	56.2	61	3	19	22	Scoring Posn	.220	82	18	2	0	4	33	13	10	.313	.390
Reliever	6.04	4	3	0	13	0	25.1	22	5	17	10	Close & Late	.179	28	5	1	0	2	8	4	5	.265	.429
0 Days rest	0.00	0	0	0	0	0	0.0	0	0	0	0	None on/out	.263	76	20	4	0	1	8	11	.333	.355
1 or 2 Days rest	8.04	1	2	0	9	0	15.2	18	4	13	4	First Pitch	.314	51	16	3	0	2	8	1	0	.321	.490
3+ Days rest	2.79	3	1	0	4	0	9.2	4	1	4	6	Behind on Count	.296	81	24	3	0	2	5	21	0	.441	.407
Pre-All Star	4.75	7	5	0	23	10	77.2	76	7	36	31	Ahead on Count	.207	111	23	4	1	2	17	0	30	.202	.315
Post-All Star	12.46	0	0	0	1	1	4.1	7	1	0	1	Two Strikes	.225	120	27	6	1	3	17	14	32	.301	.367

Last Five Years

	ERA	W	L	Sv	G	GS	IP	H	HR	BB	SO		Avg	AB	H	2B	3B	HR	RBI	BB	SO	OBP	SLG
Home	3.81	24	15	0	60	53	345.1	292	34	164	199	vs. Left	.257	1076	277	53	6	41	129	157	149	.353	.432
Away	5.91	14	19	0	52	43	236.0	248	38	129	128	vs. Right	.237	1109	263	53	4	31	142	136	178	.324	.376
Day	4.68	10	10	0	33	30	173.0	160	23	86	113	Inning 1-6	.250	1862	466	91	7	63	236	268	282	.347	.408
Night	4.65	28	24	0	79	66	408.1	380	49	207	214	Inning 7+	.229	323	74	15	3	9	35	25	45	.283	.378
Grass	4.41	31	24	0	87	72	447.1	403	51	228	262	None on	.240	1290	310	58	5	44	44	167	196	.332	.395
Turf	5.51	7	10	0	25	24	134.0	137	21	65	65	Runners on	.257	895	230	48	5	28	227	126	131	.346	.416
April	4.83	6	9	0	21	20	117.1	124	12	49	63	Scoring Posn	.249	489	122	24	2	17	187	82	83	.351	.411
May	4.90	11	5	0	28	16	112.0	109	16	58	77	Close & Late	.210	138	29	7	1	3	15	12	22	.270	.341
June	3.46	8	6	0	24	21	135.1	119	15	68	77	None on/out	.232	582	135	23	2	23	23	59	85	.306	.397
July	4.78	7	8	0	20	20	111.0	91	11	57	57	vs. 1st Batr (relief)	.333	12	4	1	0	0	3	2	0	.375	.417
August	5.58	5	5	0	17	17	98.1	90	15	56	48	First Inning Pitched	.269	401	108	19	2	19	78	81	61	.394	.469
September/October	6.14	1	1	0	2	2	7.1	7	1	5	5	First 15 Pitches	.275	331	91	16	1	19	53	55	37	.380	.502
Starter	4.60	34	31	0	96	96	547.1	508	66	273	312	Pitch 16-30	.227	331	75	13	2	10	38	59	67	.351	.369
Reliever	5.56	4	3	0	16	0	34.0	32	6	20	15	Pitch 31-45	.228	320	73	14	1	7	28	53	44	.341	.344
0 Days rest	0.00	0	0	0	0	0	0.0	0	0	0	0	Pitch 46+	.250	1203	301	63	6	36	152	126	179	.321	.402
1 or 2 Days rest	6.04	1	2	0	11	0	22.1	24	5	15	9	First Pitch	.324	333	108	20	1	20	57	7	0	.336	.571
3+ Days rest	4.63	3	1	0	5	0	11.2	8	1	5	6	Ahead on Count	.190	856	163	28	3	16	72	0	269	.197	.286
Pre-All Star	4.33	28	21	0	80	64	403.2	380	49	193	239	Behind on Count	.280	571	160	28	5	24	84	166	0	.443	.473
Post-All Star	5.42	10	13	0	32	32	177.2	160	23	100	88	Two Strikes	.187	899	168	36	3	19	78	119	327	.287	.297

Pitcher vs. Batter (career)

Pitches Best Vs.	Avg	AB	H	2B	3B	HR	RBI	BB	SO	OBP	SLG	Pitches Worst Vs.	Avg	AB	H	2B	3B	HR	RBI	BB	SO	OBP	SLG
Joe Orsulak	.000	12	0	0	0	0	0	1	1	.077	.000	Tony Fernandez	.500	18	9	3	0	1	3	3	1	.571	.833
Felix Fermin	.000	9	0	0	0	0	0	2	0	.182	.000	Brian Downing	.500	8	4	0	0	1	1	5	1	.692	.875
Ivan Calderon	.077	13	1	0	0	0	0	2	3	.200	.077	Fred McGriff	.467	15	7	0	0	3	7	3	6	.556	1.067
Al Newman	.091	11	1	0	0	0	1	0	1	.083	.091	Chili Davis	.429	21	9	1	0	3	6	5	4	.538	.905
Dick Schofield	.095	21	2	1	0	0	0	0	5	.095	.143	Kent Hrbek	.423	26	11	2	0	5	9	6	4	.531	1.077

Ron Robinson — Brewers

Pitches Right

	ERA	W	L	Sv	G	GS	IP	BB	SO	Avg	H	2B	3B	HR	RBI	OBP	SLG	CG	ShO	Sup	QS	#P/S	SB	CS	GB	FB	G/F
1992 Season	5.86	1	4	0	8	8	35.1	14	12	.331	51	12	1	3	24	.392	.481	0	0	5.86	1	79	3	1	51	53	0.96
Last Five Years	3.73	23	22	0	69	67	381.1	122	157	.281	419	74	9	23	163	.337	.388	7	2	5.00	28	90	31	23	541	486	1.11

1992 Season

	ERA	W	L	Sv	G	GS	IP	H	HR	BB	SO		Avg	AB	H	2B	3B	HR	RBI	BB	SO	OBP	SLG
Home	5.68	0	1	0	3	3	12.2	21	0	6	2	vs. Left	.347	75	26	8	1	2	11	9	5	.417	.560
Away	5.96	1	3	0	5	5	22.2	30	3	8	10	vs. Right	.316	79	25	4	0	1	13	5	7	.368	.405

Last Five Years

	ERA	W	L	Sv	G	GS	IP	H	HR	BB	SO		Avg	AB	H	2B	3B	HR	RBI	BB	SO	OBP	SLG
Home	3.39	10	8	0	28	26	159.1	172	8	45	60	vs. Left	.290	797	231	40	7	13	77	75	60	.353	.407
Away	3.97	13	14	0	41	41	222.0	247	15	77	97	vs. Right	.270	695	188	34	2	10	86	47	97	.320	.368
Day	5.46	3	7	0	18	17	89.0	121	10	32	41	Inning 1-6	.287	1345	386	69	9	20	152	112	141	.344	.396
Night	3.20	20	15	0	51	50	292.1	298	13	90	116	Inning 7+	.223	148	33	5	0	3	11	10	16	.272	.318
Grass	3.85	13	14	0	38	38	215.0	245	10	65	82	None on	.269	843	227	40	6	18	18	69	97	.330	.395
Turf	3.57	10	8	0	31	29	166.1	174	13	57	75	Runners on	.295	650	192	34	3	5	145	53	60	.347	.380
April	4.35	1	4	0	6	5	31.0	29	0	13	12	Scoring Posn	.284	366	104	20	3	3	135	34	32	.338	.380
May	4.10	3	3	0	12	12	63.2	72	8	22	34	Close & Late	.298	57	17	3	0	2	9	9	8	.394	.456
June	4.11	3	6	0	14	14	70.0	89	3	28	26	None on/out	.268	377	101	21	3	7	7	26	42	.319	.395
July	4.50	3	3	0	10	9	48.0	64	3	12	22	vs. 1st Batr (relief)	.000	2	0	0	0	0	0	0	0	.000	.000
August	2.94	7	1	0	13	13	85.2	85	6	25	31	First Inning Pitched	.317	281	89	23	2	4	44	30	25	.384	.427

Last Five Years

	ERA	W	L	Sv	G	GS	IP	H	HR	BB	SO
September/October	3.25	6	5	0	14	14	83.0	80	3	22	32
Starter	3.75	23	21	0	67	67	374.2	415	23	119	155
Reliever	2.70	0	1	0	2	0	6.2	4	0	3	2
0-3 Days Rest	7.50	0	0	0	1	1	6.0	5	1	5	1
4 Days Rest	3.03	14	10	0	37	37	226.0	244	13	62	94
5+ Days Rest	4.73	9	11	0	29	29	142.2	166	9	52	60
Pre-All Star	4.22	8	14	0	34	33	175.0	206	12	65	77
Post-All Star	3.32	15	8	0	35	34	206.1	213	11	57	80

	Avg	AB	H	2B	3B	HR	RBI	BB	SO	OBP	SLG
First 75 Pitches	.264	1162	330	57	5	15	131	95	123	.342	.380
Pitch 76-90	.269	166	48	10	4	3	14	15	19	.346	.452
Pitch 91-105	.280	107	30	5	0	4	12	10	10	.336	.439
Pitch 106+	.190	58	11	2	0	1	6	2	5	.217	.276
First Pitch	.315	213	67	6	1	3	23	6	0	.332	.394
Ahead on Count	.269	569	153	23	6	6	52	0	116	.276	.373
Behind on Count	.286	381	109	29	2	6	46	64	0	.391	.420
Two Strikes	.234	595	139	20	6	9	55	52	157	.299	.333

Pitcher vs. Batter (career)

Pitches Best Vs.	Avg	AB	H	2B	3B	HR	RBI	BB	SO	OBP	SLG
Andres Galarraga	.000	15	0	0	0	0	0	1	6	.063	.000
Joe Orsulak	.000	13	0	0	0	0	0	1	2	.071	.000
Mike Fitzgerald	.000	11	0	0	0	0	0	2	2	.154	.000
Cal Ripken	.111	9	1	0	0	0	1	1	1	.182	.111
Benito Santiago	.133	15	2	0	0	0	0	0	5	.133	.133

Pitches Worst Vs.	Avg	AB	H	2B	3B	HR	RBI	BB	SO	OBP	SLG
Will Clark	.632	19	12	2	1	1	5	3	0	.682	1.000
Herm Winningham	.455	11	5	1	1	0	2	2	0	.538	.727
Howard Johnson	.417	12	5	2	0	1	3	1	2	.462	.833
Dale Murphy	.375	24	9	1	0	5	7	2	8	.423	1.042
Barry Bonds	.364	11	4	1	0	2	2	0	0	.364	1.000

Henry Rodriguez — Dodgers — Bats Left (flyball hitter)

	Avg	G	AB	R	H	2B	3B	HR	RBI	BB	SO	HBP	GDP	SB	CS	OBP	SLG	IBB	SH	SF	#Pit	#P/PA	GB	FB	G/F
1992 Season	.219	53	146	11	32	7	0	3	14	8	30	0	2	0	0	.258	.329	0	1	1	558	3.60	40	50	0.80

1992 Season

	Avg	AB	H	2B	3B	HR	RBI	BB	SO	OBP	SLG
vs. Left	.400	15	6	0	0	0	1	1	5	.438	.400
vs. Right	.198	131	26	7	0	3	13	7	25	.237	.321
Home	.253	83	21	3	0	2	9	5	17	.292	.361
Away	.175	63	11	4	0	1	5	3	13	.212	.286
First Pitch	.296	27	8	0	0	1	2	0	0	.296	.407
Ahead on Count	.290	31	9	5	0	2	7	1	0	.313	.645
Behind on Count	.172	58	10	1	0	1	4	0	18	.172	.241
Two Strikes	.123	65	8	1	0	0	3	7	30	.205	.138

	Avg	AB	H	2B	3B	HR	RBI	BB	SO	OBP	SLG
Scoring Posn	.163	43	7	2	0	0	8	2	15	.196	.209
Close & Late	.185	27	5	2	0	0	2	1	6	.214	.259
None on/out	.100	40	4	0	0	0	0	3	10	.163	.100
Batting #5	.194	98	19	4	0	3	10	6	17	.240	.327
Batting #6	.176	17	3	0	0	0	2	0	5	.167	.176
Other	.323	31	10	3	0	0	2	2	8	.364	.419
Pre-All Star	.000	2	0	0	0	0	0	0	0	.000	.000
Post-All Star	.222	144	32	7	0	3	14	8	30	.261	.333

Ivan Rodriguez — Rangers — Bats Right (groundball hitter)

	Avg	G	AB	R	H	2B	3B	HR	RBI	BB	SO	HBP	GDP	SB	CS	OBP	SLG	IBB	SH	SF	#Pit	#P/PA	GB	FB	G/F
1992 Season	.260	123	420	39	109	16	1	8	37	24	73	1	15	0	0	.300	.360	2	7	2	1565	3.50	169	103	1.64
Career (1991-1992)	.261	211	700	63	183	32	1	11	64	29	115	1	25	0	1	.291	.357	2	9	3	2525	3.44	290	171	1.70

1992 Season

	Avg	AB	H	2B	3B	HR	RBI	BB	SO	OBP	SLG
vs. Left	.276	105	29	4	0	2	9	7	14	.319	.371
vs. Right	.254	315	80	12	1	6	28	17	59	.293	.356
Groundball	.187	91	17	2	0	2	12	3	11	.219	.275
Flyball	.271	118	32	7	1	3	8	10	27	.326	.424
Home	.237	211	50	5	1	4	19	10	45	.270	.327
Away	.282	209	59	11	0	4	18	14	28	.329	.392
Day	.277	83	23	3	0	2	9	5	11	.318	.386
Night	.255	337	86	13	1	6	28	19	62	.295	.353
Grass	.246	334	82	11	1	6	27	16	61	.279	.338
Turf	.314	86	27	5	0	2	10	8	12	.375	.442
First Pitch	.422	64	27	4	0	2	8	1	0	.439	.578
Ahead on Count	.275	80	22	4	1	2	8	9	0	.348	.425
Behind on Count	.234	175	41	6	0	3	15	0	46	.233	.320
Two Strikes	.163	184	30	3	0	2	14	14	73	.220	.212

	Avg	AB	H	2B	3B	HR	RBI	BB	SO	OBP	SLG
Scoring Posn	.235	102	24	2	0	2	28	10	22	.298	.314
Close & Late	.317	82	26	1	0	1	9	6	12	.360	.366
None on/out	.318	88	28	4	0	2	2	7	10	.375	.432
Batting #7	.257	226	58	9	1	4	21	15	40	.302	.358
Batting #8	.324	74	24	2	0	2	6	2	11	.342	.432
Other	.225	120	27	5	0	2	10	7	22	.271	.317
April	.314	70	22	5	0	1	8	3	9	.347	.429
May	.253	83	21	0	0	4	13	5	19	.292	.398
June	.263	19	5	1	0	2	4	3	3	.364	.632
July	.243	74	18	2	1	1	4	5	15	.291	.338
August	.255	94	24	5	0	0	6	4	13	.286	.309
September/October	.238	80	19	3	0	0	2	4	14	.274	.275
Pre-All Star	.278	209	58	7	1	8	28	14	38	.323	.435
Post-All Star	.242	211	51	9	0	0	9	10	35	.276	.284

1992 By Position

Position	Avg	AB	H	2B	3B	HR	RBI	BB	SO	OBP	SLG	G	GS	Innings	PO	A	E	DP	Fld Pct	Rng Fctr	In Zone	Outs	Zone Rtg	MLB Zone
As Pinch Hitter	.111	9	1	0	0	0	0	1	1	.200	.111	10	0	---	---	---	---	---	---	---	---	---	---	---
As c	.263	411	108	16	1	8	37	23	72	.302	.365	116	112	982.2	764	84	15	10	.983	---	---	---	---	---

Rich Rodriguez — Padres
Pitches Left (groundball pitcher)

	ERA	W	L	Sv	G	GS	IP	BB	SO	Avg	H	2B	3B	HR	RBI	OBP	SLG	GF	IR	IRS	Hld		SB	CS	GB	FB	G/F
1992 Season	2.37	6	3	0	61	1	91.0	29	64	.229	77	14	1	4	33	.289	.313	15	43	13	5	1	6	5	124	76	1.63
Career (1990-1992)	2.80	10	5	1	157	2	218.2	89	126	.244	195	35	2	14	89	.319	.345	49	112	30	16	4	16	11	319	178	1.79

1992 Season

	ERA	W	L	Sv	G	GS	IP	H	HR	BB	SO		Avg	AB	H	2B	3B	HR	RBI	BB	SO	OBP	SLG
Home	1.93	4	1	0	33	0	51.1	46	2	13	31	vs. Left	.233	103	24	4	0	2	12	11	21	.304	.330
Away	2.95	2	2	0	28	1	39.2	31	2	16	33	vs. Right	.227	233	53	10	1	2	21	18	43	.282	.305
Day	2.48	0	1	0	18	0	29.0	21	0	13	26	Inning 1-6	.234	154	36	8	1	4	17	10	35	.279	.377
Night	2.32	6	2	0	43	1	62.0	56	4	16	38	Inning 7+	.225	182	41	6	0	0	16	19	29	.297	.258
Grass	2.03	4	1	0	44	0	66.2	56	2	17	44	None on	.215	186	40	8	1	2	2	18	43	.284	.301
Turf	3.33	2	2	0	17	1	24.1	21	2	12	20	Runners on	.247	150	37	6	0	2	31	11	21	.294	.327
April	2.29	1	1	0	10	0	19.2	18	1	7	8	Scoring Posn	.220	91	20	4	0	1	28	9	15	.284	.297
May	1.08	2	0	0	9	0	16.2	11	1	5	11	Close & Late	.216	51	11	1	0	0	3	9	6	.333	.235
June	3.46	0	1	0	7	1	13.0	14	0	7	11	None on/out	.169	77	13	2	1	1	8	15	.247	.260
July	1.88	2	0	0	9	0	14.1	9	0	3	10	vs. 1st Batr (relief)	.218	55	12	3	1	0	8	4	10	.267	.309
August	4.26	1	0	0	9	0	12.2	14	1	3	7	First Inning Pitched	.210	186	39	5	1	1	19	16	35	.270	.263
September/October	1.84	0	1	0	17	0	14.2	11	1	4	17	First 15 Pitches	.226	195	44	7	1	1	17	15	35	.278	.287
Starter	4.50	1	0	1	1	1	4.0	5	0	3	5	Pitch 16-30	.226	84	19	3	0	3	10	10	19	.309	.369
Reliever	2.28	6	2	0	60	0	87.0	72	4	26	59	Pitch 31-45	.211	38	8	3	0	0	3	2	7	.250	.289
0 Days rest	3.12	2	0	0	13	0	17.1	11	1	6	11	Pitch 46+	.316	19	6	1	0	0	3	2	3	.381	.368
1 or 2 Days rest	2.23	3	2	0	28	0	40.1	37	2	13	28	Ahead on Count	.170	171	29	4	0	0	8	0	56	.169	.193
3+ Days rest	1.84	1	0	0	19	0	29.1	24	1	7	20	Behind on Count	.319	69	22	5	0	3	14	16	0	.442	.522
Pre-All Star	2.15	4	2	0	30	1	58.2	49	2	20	37	Two Strikes	.188	170	32	4	0	0	9	9	64	.229	.212
Post-All Star	2.78	2	1	0	31	0	32.1	28	2	9	27												

Career (1990-1992)

	ERA	W	L	Sv	G	GS	IP	H	HR	BB	SO		Avg	AB	H	2B	3B	HR	RBI	BB	SO	OBP	SLG
Home	2.93	6	2	0	84	0	116.2	110	6	51	73	vs. Left	.231	264	61	9	0	5	32	34	46	.318	.322
Away	2.65	4	3	1	73	2	102.0	85	8	38	53	vs. Right	.250	535	134	26	2	9	57	55	80	.319	.357
Day	2.89	3	2	0	42	0	62.1	57	4	28	46	Inning 1-6	.229	266	61	14	2	6	31	19	44	.282	.365
Night	2.76	7	3	1	115	2	156.1	138	10	61	80	Inning 7+	.251	533	134	21	0	8	58	70	82	.336	.336
Grass	2.91	6	2	1	113	1	161.0	144	9	64	94	None on	.245	420	103	16	1	10	10	43	77	.317	.360
Turf	2.50	4	3	0	44	1	57.2	51	5	25	32	Runners on	.243	379	92	19	1	4	79	46	49	.321	.330
April	2.94	1	1	0	19	0	33.2	34	1	17	13	Scoring Posn	.236	229	54	13	1	2	73	41	29	.345	.328
May	1.07	4	1	0	21	1	33.2	21	2	13	16	Close & Late	.209	196	41	4	0	4	19	33	29	.322	.291
June	5.26	0	1	0	20	1	25.2	27	3	17	15	None on/out	.243	189	46	4	1	5	13	36	.292	.354
July	2.56	2	0	0	32	0	45.2	39	0	17	29	vs. 1st Batr (relief)	.255	141	36	7	1	2	20	12	18	.312	.362
August	3.09	2	0	0	31	0	35.0	32	3	10	22	First Inning Pitched	.230	473	109	21	2	3	59	60	75	.315	.302
September/October	2.60	1	2	1	34	0	45.0	42	3	15	31	First 15 Pitches	.235	472	111	20	2	5	46	54	71	.313	.318
Starter	3.00	0	1	0	2	2	9.0	7	1	4	6	Pitch 16-30	.258	221	57	10	0	8	33	29	38	.343	.412
Reliever	2.79	10	4	1	155	0	209.2	188	13	85	120	Pitch 31-45	.257	74	19	4	0	1	7	3	14	.286	.351
0 Days rest	3.35	3	1	0	38	0	51.0	36	4	20	28	Pitch 46+	.250	32	8	1	0	0	3	3	5	.314	.281
1 or 2 Days rest	2.95	3	3	0	71	0	91.2	96	6	38	52	First Pitch	.269	108	29	9	1	2	16	13	0	.341	.426
3+ Days rest	2.15	4	1	0	46	0	67.0	56	3	27	40	Ahead on Count	.171	350	60	8	0	2	23	0	109	.173	.211
Pre-All Star	2.75	6	3	0	71	2	111.1	97	8	56	55	Behind on Count	.325	197	64	11	1	9	37	50	0	.458	.528
Post-All Star	2.85	4	2	1	86	0	107.1	98	6	33	71	Two Strikes	.175	349	61	7	0	3	22	25	126	.230	.221

Pitcher vs. Batter (career)

Pitches Best Vs.	Avg	AB	H	2B	3B	HR	RBI	BB	SO	OBP	SLG	Pitches Worst Vs.	Avg	AB	H	2B	3B	HR	RBI	BB	SO	OBP	SLG
Larry Walker	.182	11	2	0	0	0	2	1	2	.250	.182	Craig Biggio	.500	10	5	3	0	0	2	2	0	.583	.800
Will Clark	.200	10	2	0	0	0	3	1	2	.273	.200	Barry Bonds	.375	8	3	1	0	1	1	3	0	.545	.875
Delino DeShields	.222	9	2	2	0	0	0	2	1	.364	.444	Jeff Blauser	.364	11	4	3	0	0	1	2	0	.462	.636
												Ken Caminiti	.333	12	4	0	0	1	2	1	3	.385	.583
												Brett Butler	.333	9	3	0	0	0	0	3	0	.500	.333

Kenny Rogers — Rangers
Pitches Left

	ERA	W	L	Sv	G	GS	IP	BB	SO	Avg	H	2B	3B	HR	RBI	OBP	SLG	GF	IR	IRS	Hld	SvOp	SB	CS	GB	FB	G/F
1992 Season	3.09	3	6	6	81	0	78.2	26	70	.261	80	17	1	7	50	.318	.392	38	66	29	16	10	2	3	84	97	0.87
Career (1989-1992)	3.78	26	26	28	286	12	359.2	171	280	.259	354	73	7	29	199	.343	.386	104	242	77	49	44	12	13	454	397	1.14

1992 Season

	ERA	W	L	Sv	G	GS	IP	H	HR	BB	SO		Avg	AB	H	2B	3B	HR	RBI	BB	SO	OBP	SLG
Home	3.53	1	4	2	42	0	43.1	46	4	17	38	vs. Left	.261	92	24	5	0	1	12	3	21	.284	.348
Away	2.55	2	2	4	39	0	35.1	34	3	9	32	vs. Right	.262	214	56	12	1	6	38	23	49	.332	.411
Day	3.32	1	2	0	18	0	19.0	21	1	9	20	Inning 1-6	.250	4	1	1	0	0	1	0	0	.250	.500
Night	3.02	2	5	4	63	0	59.2	59	6	17	50	Inning 7+	.262	302	79	16	1	7	49	26	70	.319	.391
Grass	3.15	3	5	5	70	0	68.2	70	6	24	60	None on	.240	146	35	9	0	2	2	9	34	.284	.342
Turf	2.70	0	1	1	11	0	10.0	10	1	2	10	Runners on	.281	160	45	8	1	5	48	17	36	.348	.438
April	2.45	0	0	2	10	0	11.0	13	1	1	10	Scoring Posn	.309	94	29	5	1	5	48	15	18	.400	.543
May	4.00	0	2	1	14	0	18.0	18	3	8	18	Close & Late	.289	180	52	14	1	4	36	17	43	.350	.444
June	1.59	1	1	2	13	0	11.1	9	1	3	7	None on/out	.281	64	18	4	0	0	3	13	.313	.344
July	4.91	0	1	0	13	0	11.0	16	2	4	6	vs. 1st Batr (relief)	.241	79	19	2	0	0	8	2	21	.259	.266

377

1992 Season

	ERA	W	L	Sv	G	GS	IP	H	HR	BB	SO		Avg	AB	H	2B	3B	HR	RBI	BB	SO	OBP	SLG
August	2.25	1	1	0	15	0	12.0	12	0	4	11	First Inning Pitched	.251	243	61	11	1	6	42	20	61	.307	.379
September/October	2.93	1	1	1	16	0	15.1	12	0	6	18	First 15 Pitches	.265	219	58	13	1	6	40	17	52	.316	.416
Starter	0.00	0	0	0	0	0	0.0	0	0	0	0	Pitch 16-30	.231	78	18	3	0	0	6	9	16	.310	.269
Reliever	3.09	3	6	6	81	0	78.2	80	7	26	70	Pitch 31-45	.444	9	4	1	0	1	4	0	2	.444	.889
0 Days rest	3.00	3	1	2	24	0	21.0	20	1	8	20	Pitch 46+	.000	0	0	0	0	0	0	0	0	.000	.000
1 or 2 Days rest	3.38	0	5	4	45	0	45.1	44	4	14	45	First Pitch	.333	39	13	4	0	1	11	8	0	.438	.513
3+ Days rest	2.19	0	0	0	12	0	12.1	16	2	4	5	Ahead on Count	.235	136	32	9	1	3	20	0	52	.235	.382
Pre-All Star	3.52	1	4	5	42	0	46.0	49	7	15	40	Behind on Count	.317	63	20	1	0	3	14	8	0	.394	.476
Post-All Star	2.48	2	2	1	39	0	32.2	31	0	11	30	Two Strikes	.208	154	32	9	1	2	17	10	70	.256	.318

Career (1989-1992)

	ERA	W	L	Sv	G	GS	IP	H	HR	BB	SO		Avg	AB	H	2B	3B	HR	RBI	BB	SO	OBP	SLG
Home	3.56	19	13	14	153	4	189.2	185	11	92	145	vs. Left	.221	367	81	19	1	5	49	38	81	.304	.319
Away	4.02	7	13	14	133	8	170.0	169	18	79	135	vs. Right	.272	1002	273	54	6	24	150	133	199	.357	.410
Day	4.13	3	5	7	48	3	61.0	67	7	32	49	Inning 1-6	.317	287	91	18	3	7	47	43	42	.408	.474
Night	3.71	23	21	21	238	9	298.2	287	22	139	231	Inning 7+	.243	1082	263	55	4	22	152	128	238	.325	.362
Grass	3.73	23	21	26	239	9	302.0	291	24	146	241	None on	.256	649	166	33	4	13	67	133		.328	.379
Turf	4.06	3	5	2	47	3	57.2	63	5	25	39	Runners on	.261	720	188	40	3	16	186	104	147	.355	.392
April	5.70	2	4	2	30	4	42.2	54	5	20	31	Scoring Posn	.267	449	120	25	2	14	180	81	97	.378	.425
May	4.20	6	3	1	49	5	83.2	88	8	46	60	Close & Late	.247	575	142	35	2	11	82	70	123	.330	.372
June	4.63	1	6	8	48	1	58.1	67	7	29	43	None on/out	.242	281	68	12	1	2	2	29	52	.315	.313
July	3.23	4	3	8	51	0	53.0	45	5	21	55	vs. 1st Batr (relief)	.248	238	59	9	1	2	33	25	58	.320	.319
August	2.87	5	4	3	57	0	59.2	50	2	26	46	First Inning Pitched	.243	841	204	41	5	17	139	108	190	.331	.364
September/October	2.45	8	6	6	51	2	62.1	50	2	29	45	First 15 Pitches	.255	734	187	34	3	15	102	94	153	.341	.371
Starter	6.17	5	6	0	12	12	58.1	81	7	36	30	Pitch 16-30	.224	362	81	17	2	4	48	45	84	.313	.315
Reliever	3.32	21	20	28	274	0	301.1	273	22	135	250	Pitch 31-45	.280	118	33	8	1	5	25	18	19	.375	.492
0 Days rest	2.65	9	6	10	88	0	91.2	80	2	33	72	Pitch 46+	.342	155	53	14	1	5	24	14	24	.398	.542
1 or 2 Days rest	3.93	9	12	12	129	0	146.2	139	12	68	127	First Pitch	.329	173	57	12	0	6	38	26	0	.412	.503
3+ Days rest	2.86	3	2	6	57	0	63.0	54	8	34	51	Ahead on Count	.196	613	120	27	4	7	65	0	228	.204	.287
Pre-All Star	4.67	11	15	13	142	10	198.2	227	23	103	144	Behind on Count	.351	319	112	16	3	12	64	82	0	.480	.533
Post-All Star	2.68	15	11	15	144	2	161.0	127	6	68	136	Two Strikes	.177	655	116	28	4	8	58	63	260	.254	.269

Pitcher vs. Batter (career)

Pitches Best Vs.	Avg	AB	H	2B	3B	HR	RBI	BB	SO	OBP	SLG	Pitches Worst Vs.	Avg	AB	H	2B	3B	HR	RBI	BB	SO	OBP	SLG
Luis Polonia	.000	14	0	0	0	0	0	1	3	.067	.000	Luis Rivera	.500	12	6	3	1	0	3	0	2	.500	.917
Pete O'Brien	.067	15	1	0	0	0	2	2	3	.167	.067	Edgar Martinez	.500	10	5	1	0	0	3	4	1	.643	.600
Mike Greenwell	.067	15	1	1	0	0	0	2	3	.067	.133	Robin Yount	.500	8	4	1	0	0	2	3	1	.636	.625
Ozzie Guillen	.071	14	1	0	0	0	2	0	0	.071	.071	Pat Tabler	.375	8	3	0	0	1	3	3	0	.545	.750
Lou Whitaker	.100	10	1	0	0	0	0	1	6	.182	.100	Pat Borders	.375	8	3	1	0	0	1	4	0	.583	.500

Kevin Rogers — Giants   Pitches Left (flyball pitcher)

	ERA	W	L	Sv	G	GS	IP	BB	SO	Avg	H	2B	3B	HR	RBI	OBP	SLG	CG	ShO	Sup	QS	#P/S	SB	CS	GB	FB	G/F
1992 Season	4.24	0	2	0	6	6	34.0	13	26	.280	37	2	0	4	14	.349	.386	0	0	3.18	4	92	1	2	39	45	0.87

1992 Season

	ERA	W	L	Sv	G	GS	IP	H	HR	BB	SO		Avg	AB	H	2B	3B	HR	RBI	BB	SO	OBP	SLG
Home	4.76	0	1	0	3	3	17.0	21	2	7	14	vs. Left	.280	25	7	0	0	0	3	0	4	.280	.280
Away	3.71	0	1	0	3	3	17.0	16	2	6	12	vs. Right	.280	107	30	2	0	4	11	13	22	.364	.411

Dave Rohde — Indians   Bats Both

	Avg	G	AB	R	H	2B	3B	HR	RBI	BB	SO	HBP	GDP	SB	CS	OBP	SLG	IBB	SH	SF	#Pit	#P/PA	GB	FB	G/F
1992 Season	.000	5	7	0	0	0	0	0	0	2	3	0	0	0	0	.222	.000	1	0	0	39	4.33	1	3	0.33
Career (1990-1992)	.158	93	146	11	23	4	0	0	5	16	31	5	4	0	0	.262	.185	3	6	1	631	3.76	54	41	1.32

1992 Season

	Avg	AB	H	2B	3B	HR	RBI	BB	SO	OBP	SLG		Avg	AB	H	2B	3B	HR	RBI	BB	SO	OBP	SLG
vs. Left	.000	3	0	0	0	0	0	0	3	.000	.000	Scoring Posn	.000	3	0	0	0	0	0	1	1	.250	.000
vs. Right	.000	4	0	0	0	0	0	2	0	.333	.000	Close & Late	.000	4	0	0	0	0	0	2	1	.333	.000

Mel Rojas — Expos

	ERA	W	L	Sv	G	GS	IP	BB	SO	Avg	H	2B	3B	HR	RBI	OBP	SLG	GF	IR	IRS	Hld	SvOp	SB	CS	GB	FB	G/F
1992 Season	1.43	7	1	10	68	0	100.2	34	70	.199	71	15	2	2	22	.271	.269	26	58	10	13	11	12	3	133	104	1.28
Career (1990-1992)	2.48	13	5	17	128	0	188.2	71	133	.214	147	31	5	11	62	.291	.322	44	94	19	21	22	21	6	244	209	1.17

1992 Season

	ERA	W	L	Sv	G	GS	IP	H	HR	BB	SO		Avg	AB	H	2B	3B	HR	RBI	BB	SO	OBP	SLG
Home	1.72	5	0	3	38	0	52.1	39	1	14	39	vs. Left	.196	199	39	7	0	1	11	20	40	.268	.246
Away	1.12	2	1	7	30	0	48.1	32	1	20	31	vs. Right	.203	158	32	8	2	1	11	14	30	.274	.297
Day	0.68	3	0	2	19	0	26.1	14	0	5	18	Inning 1-6	.154	39	6	2	0	0	1	3	6	.233	.205
Night	1.70	4	1	8	49	0	74.1	57	2	29	52	Inning 7+	.204	318	65	13	2	2	21	31	64	.276	.277
Grass	1.80	1	0	6	15	0	20.0	14	0	9	12	None on	.253	182	46	12	2	2	2	14	38	.306	.374
Turf	1.34	6	1	4	53	0	80.2	57	2	25	58	Runners on	.143	175	25	3	0	0	20	20	32	.236	.160
April	2.25	0	1	0	4	0	8.0	9	0	6	4	Scoring Posn	.122	115	14	1	0	0	19	20	23	.254	.130
May	0.51	1	0	1	13	0	17.2	10	0	7	14	Close & Late	.238	151	36	2	1	0	14	18	30	.318	.265
June	1.59	0	0	2	13	0	17.0	13	1	4	10	None on/out	.272	81	22	4	2	0	0	5	18	.314	.370
July	0.90	2	0	4	12	0	20.0	15	0	3	13	vs. 1st Batr (relief)	.213	61	13	2	1	0	4	4	19	.265	.279
August	1.31	2	0	2	13	0	20.2	12	1	3	13	First Inning Pitched	.185	211	39	8	2	0	17	20	45	.260	.242
September/October	2.60	2	0	1	13	0	17.1	12	0	11	16	First 15 Pitches	.183	213	39	7	2	0	14	17	45	.245	.235
Starter	0.00	0	0	0	0	0	0.0	0	0	0	0	Pitch 16-30	.213	108	23	6	0	0	4	15	19	.315	.269
Reliever	1.43	7	1	10	68	0	100.2	71	2	34	70	Pitch 31-45	.273	33	9	2	0	2	4	2	6	.314	.515
0 Days rest	0.64	4	0	4	18	0	28.1	19	1	7	20	Pitch 46+	.000	3	0	0	0	0	0	0	0	.000	.000
1 or 2 Days rest	1.70	2	1	4	35	0	53.0	35	1	19	35	Ahead on Count	.136	177	24	5	0	1	9	0	63	.144	.181
3+ Days rest	1.86	1	0	2	15	0	19.1	17	0	8	15	Behind on Count	.360	75	27	7	2	0	7	11	0	.437	.507
Pre-All Star	1.07	2	1	6	35	0	50.1	37	1	19	33	Two Strikes	.117	171	20	3	0	1	7	17	70	.205	.152
Post-All Star	1.79	5	0	4	33	0	50.1	34	1	15	37												

Career (1990-1992)

	ERA	W	L	Sv	G	GS	IP	H	HR	BB	SO		Avg	AB	H	2B	3B	HR	RBI	BB	SO	OBP	SLG
Home	2.81	6	2	6	61	0	83.1	68	5	25	60	vs. Left	.211	380	80	17	3	6	36	46	69	.297	.318
Away	2.22	7	3	11	67	0	105.1	79	6	46	73	vs. Right	.219	306	67	14	2	5	26	23	64	.284	.327
Day	2.32	6	0	3	35	0	50.1	37	5	13	32	Inning 1-6	.256	164	42	10	1	7	23	15	32	.328	.457
Night	2.54	7	5	14	93	0	138.1	110	6	58	101	Inning 7+	.201	522	105	21	4	4	39	56	108	.280	.280
Grass	2.85	4	2	8	32	0	47.1	36	2	21	32	None on	.271	343	93	23	3	6	6	30	69	.332	.408
Turf	2.36	9	3	9	96	0	141.1	111	9	50	101	Runners on	.157	343	54	8	2	5	56	41	64	.253	.236
April	4.20	0	1	0	9	0	15.0	19	1	9	7	Scoring Posn	.157	217	34	5	2	2	49	35	45	.278	.226
May	0.51	1	0	1	13	0	17.2	10	0	7	14	Close & Late	.213	268	57	5	2	2	25	34	52	.303	.269
June	1.59	0	0	2	13	0	17.0	13	1	4	10	None on/out	.301	153	46	11	3	2	2	16	31	.367	.451
July	1.69	2	2	4	17	0	26.2	23	0	4	20	vs. 1st Batr (relief)	.223	112	25	4	1	2	8	10	26	.297	.330
August	2.61	4	2	4	39	0	58.2	39	5	23	46	First Inning Pitched	.196	414	81	19	4	5	46	41	90	.274	.297
September/October	3.19	6	0	6	37	0	53.2	43	4	24	36	First 15 Pitches	.197	395	78	17	2	4	34	37	83	.271	.281
Starter	0.00	0	0	0	0	0	0.0	0	0	0	0	Pitch 16-30	.213	202	43	9	3	2	17	29	38	.315	.317
Reliever	2.48	13	5	17	128	0	188.2	147	11	71	133	Pitch 31-45	.268	71	19	5	0	2	5	5	10	.316	.423
0 Days rest	1.55	6	1	4	31	0	46.1	31	5	20	36	Pitch 46+	.389	18	7	0	0	3	6	0	2	.368	.889
1 or 2 Days rest	2.80	4	3	8	63	0	96.1	76	2	34	67	First Pitch	.284	88	25	6	0	4	9	10	0	.357	.489
3+ Days rest	2.74	3	1	5	34	0	46.0	40	4	17	30	Ahead on Count	.154	332	51	10	0	3	22	0	117	.163	.211
Pre-All Star	1.73	2	1	6	40	0	57.1	47	2	22	36	Behind on Count	.293	150	44	9	3	4	23	33	0	.414	.473
Post-All Star	2.81	11	4	11	88	0	131.1	100	9	49	97	Two Strikes	.138	320	44	7	1	2	16	28	133	.216	.191

Pitcher vs. Batter (career)

Pitches Best Vs.	Avg	AB	H	2B	3B	HR	RBI	BB	SO	OBP	SLG	Pitches Worst Vs.	Avg	AB	H	2B	3B	HR	RBI	BB	SO	OBP	SLG
												Barry Bonds	.500	10	5	1	0	1	2	1	1	.545	.900
												Bobby Bonilla	.400	10	4	1	0	1	1	1	3	.455	.800

Bobby Rose — Angels

	Avg	G	AB	R	H	2B	3B	HR	RBI	BB	SO	HBP	GDP	SB	CS	OBP	SLG	IBB	SH	SF	#Pit	#P/PA	GB	FB	G/F
1992 Season	.214	30	84	10	18	5	0	2	10	8	9	2	2	1	1	.295	.345	1	1	1	357	3.76	31	35	0.89
Career (1989-1992)	.245	73	200	24	49	11	3	5	23	15	33	3	5	1	1	.305	.405	1	3	2	780	3.55	72	72	1.00

1992 Season

	Avg	AB	H	2B	3B	HR	RBI	BB	SO	OBP	SLG		Avg	AB	H	2B	3B	HR	RBI	BB	SO	OBP	SLG
vs. Left	.167	24	4	0	0	1	2	4	2	.286	.292	Scoring Posn	.200	20	4	2	0	0	5	3	3	.292	.300
vs. Right	.233	60	14	5	0	1	8	4	7	.299	.367	Close & Late	.250	16	4	0	0	1	3	0	5	.250	.438

Wayne Rosenthal — Rangers

Pitches Right (flyball pitcher)

	ERA	W	L	Sv	G	GS	IP	BB	SO	Avg	H	2B	3B	HR	RBI	OBP	SLG	GF	IR	IRS	Hld	SvOp	SB	CS	GB	FB	G/F
1992 Season	7.71	0	0	0	6	0	4.2	2	1	.333	7	1	0	1	1	.391	.524	2	4	0	0	0	1	0	9	6	1.50
Career (1991-1992)	5.40	1	4	1	42	0	75.0	38	62	.262	79	17	2	10	48	.344	.432	10	38	16	2	2	7	1	96	97	0.99

1992 Season

	ERA	W	L	Sv	G	GS	IP	H	HR	BB	SO		Avg	AB	H	2B	3B	HR	RBI	BB	SO	OBP	SLG
Home	9.00	0	0	0	2	0	2.0	4	1	0	1	vs. Left	.286	7	2	0	0	0	0	0	0	.286	.286
Away	6.75	0	0	0	4	0	2.2	3	0	2	0	vs. Right	.357	14	5	1	0	1	1	2	1	.438	.643

Rico Rossy — Royals

Bats Right

	Avg	G	AB	R	H	2B	3B	HR	RBI	BB	SO	HBP	GDP	SB	CS	OBP	SLG	IBB	SH	SF	#Pit	#P/PA	GB	FB	G/F
1992 Season	.215	59	149	21	32	8	1	1	12	20	20	1	6	0	3	.310	.302	1	7	1	660	3.86	59	47	1.26

1992 Season

	Avg	AB	H	2B	3B	HR	RBI	BB	SO	OBP	SLG		Avg	AB	H	2B	3B	HR	RBI	BB	SO	OBP	SLG
vs. Left	.200	50	10	5	0	0	6	9	5	.317	.300	Scoring Posn	.257	35	9	4	0	0	10	6	5	.357	.371
vs. Right	.222	99	22	3	1	1	6	11	15	.306	.303	Close & Late	.176	17	3	2	0	0	4	2		.364	.294
Home	.236	55	13	3	1	0	5	7	11	.323	.327	None on/out	.167	30	5	0	0	1	6	5		.324	.267
Away	.202	94	19	5	0	1	7	13	9	.303	.287	Batting #8	.250	4	1	0	0	0	2	0	0	.250	.250
First Pitch	.304	23	7	0	0	1	4	0	0	.304	.435	Batting #9	.215	144	31	8	1	1	10	20	20	.313	.306
Ahead on Count	.294	34	10	3	0	0	5	13	0	.479	.382	Other	.000	1	0	0	0	0	0	0	0	.000	.000
Behind on Count	.186	43	8	2	1	0	2	0	12	.205	.279	Pre-All Star	.206	136	28	7	1	1	9	19	18	.306	.294
Two Strikes	.117	60	7	1	0	0	0	7	20	.209	.133	Post-All Star	.308	13	4	1	0	0	3	1	2	.357	.385

Rich Rowland — Tigers

Bats Right

	Avg	G	AB	R	H	2B	3B	HR	RBI	BB	SO	HBP	GDP	SB	CS	OBP	SLG	IBB	SH	SF	#Pit	#P/PA	GB	FB	G/F
1992 Season	.214	6	14	2	3	0	0	0	0	3	3	0	1	0	0	.353	.214	0	0	0	69	4.06	3	5	0.60
Career (1990-1992)	.189	17	37	5	7	1	0	0	0	6	9	0	2	0	0	.295	.216	1	0	1	175	3.98	12	9	1.33

1992 Season

	Avg	AB	H	2B	3B	HR	RBI	BB	SO	OBP	SLG		Avg	AB	H	2B	3B	HR	RBI	BB	SO	OBP	SLG
vs. Left	.250	8	2	0	0	0	0	2	1	.400	.250	Scoring Posn	.500	2	1	0	0	0	0	1	0	.667	.500
vs. Right	.167	6	1	0	0	0		1	2	.286	.167	Close & Late	.500	2	1	0	0	0	0	0	0	.500	.500

Stan Royer — Cardinals

Bats Right

	Avg	G	AB	R	H	2B	3B	HR	RBI	BB	SO	HBP	GDP	SB	CS	OBP	SLG	IBB	SH	SF	#Pit	#P/PA	GB	FB	G/F
1992 Season	.323	13	31	6	10	2	0	2	9	1	4	0	0	0	0	.333	.581	0	0	1	109	3.30	12	10	1.20
Career (1991-1992)	.308	22	52	7	16	3	0	2	10	2	6	0	0	0	0	.327	.481	0	0	1	171	3.11	21	16	1.31

1992 Season

	Avg	AB	H	2B	3B	HR	RBI	BB	SO	OBP	SLG		Avg	AB	H	2B	3B	HR	RBI	BB	SO	OBP	SLG
vs. Left	.500	8	4	1	0	0	3	0	1	.444	.625	Scoring Posn	.333	9	3	0	0	0	4	1	1	.364	.333
vs. Right	.261	23	6	1	0	2	6	1	3	.292	.565	Close & Late	.333	9	3	0	0	1	3	0	1	.333	.667

Bruce Ruffin — Brewers

Pitches Left (groundball pitcher)

	ERA	W	L	Sv	G	GS	IP	BB	SO	Avg	H	2B	3B	HR	RBI	OBP	SLG	GF	IR	IRS	Hld	SvOp	SB	CS	GB	FB	G/F
1992 Season	6.67	1	6	0	25	6	58.0	41	45	.293	66	11	2	7	44	.398	.453	6	18	11	1	2	5	3	84	65	1.29
Last Five Years	4.76	23	46	3	167	84	596.0	283	361	.287	672	143	15	44	312	.363	.418	9	58	29	14	7	33	24	1010	520	1.94

1992 Season

	ERA	W	L	Sv	G	GS	IP	H	HR	BB	SO		Avg	AB	H	2B	3B	HR	RBI	BB	SO	OBP	SLG
Home	7.88	1	3	0	11	2	16.0	20	1	11	14	vs. Left	.221	68	15	2	0	1	11	14	12	.354	.294
Away	6.21	0	3	0	14	4	42.0	46	6	30	31	vs. Right	.325	157	51	9	2	6	33	27	33	.417	.522
Starter	9.86	0	4	0	6	6	21.0	31	3	16	18	Scoring Posn	.333	60	20	6	0	3	37	18	11	.469	.583
Reliever	4.86	1	2	0	19	0	37.0	35	4	25	27	Close & Late	.281	32	9	3	0	0	2	4	6	.361	.375
0 Days rest	7.04	0	1	0	3	0	7.2	9	1	4	5	None on/out	.255	51	13	3	0	2	2	8	9	.356	.431
1 or 2 Days rest	8.10	0	1	0	4	0	6.2	12	1	6	5	First Pitch	.636	22	14	1	0	2	15	3	0	.654	.955
3+ Days rest	3.18	1	0	0	12	0	22.2	14	2	15	17	Behind on Count	.306	62	19	6	1	2	10	19	0	.463	.532
Pre-All Star	6.65	1	3	0	21	3	43.1	50	5	33	31	Ahead on Count	.253	95	24	4	0	2	13	0	35	.253	.358
Post-All Star	6.75	0	3	0	4	3	14.2	16	2	8	14	Two Strikes	.204	93	19	3	0	3	11	19	45	.339	.333

Last Five Years

	ERA	W	L	Sv	G	GS	IP	H	HR	BB	SO		Avg	AB	H	2B	3B	HR	RBI	BB	SO	OBP	SLG
Home	4.49	16	25	2	91	48	327.0	359	25	152	201	vs. Left	.267	483	129	27	2	3	72	77	83	.367	.350
Away	5.09	7	21	1	76	36	269.0	313	19	131	160	vs. Right	.293	1855	543	116	13	41	240	206	278	.362	.436
Day	5.36	5	11	2	48	22	166.1	190	13	79	94	Inning 1-6	.295	1869	552	116	14	40	267	207	287	.364	.437
Night	4.52	18	35	1	119	62	429.2	482	31	204	267	Inning 7+	.256	469	120	27	1	4	45	76	74	.361	.343
Grass	6.05	6	15	0	56	21	165.0	196	18	91	106	None on	.277	1244	344	77	6	25	25	138	203	.350	.408
Turf	4.26	17	31	3	111	63	431.0	476	26	192	255	Runners on	.300	1094	328	66	9	19	267	145	158	.378	.429
April	5.48	4	6	0	16	10	64.0	83	5	25	29	Scoring Posn	.314	611	192	44	5	13	261	104	82	.406	.466
May	4.36	4	7	0	20	12	86.1	92	6	40	41	Close & Late	.287	164	47	13	0	1	17	29	23	.397	.384

Last Five Years

	ERA	W	L	Sv	G	GS	IP	H	HR	BB	SO		Avg	AB	H	2B	3B	HR	RBI	BB	SO	OBP	SLG
June	4.57	4	5	1	31	15	120.0	132	6	45	69	None on/out	.294	562	165	39	4	10	10	71	90	.376	.431
July	4.26	7	10	2	34	21	133.0	142	12	70	85	vs. 1st Batr (relief)	.317	60	19	3	0	0	9	15	14	.469	.367
August	5.98	1	12	0	38	15	105.1	125	9	63	71	First Inning Pitched	.305	613	187	36	3	11	122	93	116	.395	.427
September/October	4.12	3	6	0	28	11	87.1	98	6	40	66	First 15 Pitches	.290	527	153	30	2	10	71	78	100	.382	.412
Starter	4.75	19	40	0	84	84	456.2	530	36	194	262	Pitch 16-30	.285	456	130	29	4	8	79	64	75	.372	.419
Reliever	4.78	4	6	3	83	0	139.1	142	8	89	99	Pitch 31-45	.275	382	105	24	4	6	42	43	66	.347	.406
0 Days rest	4.11	1	2	0	22	0	35.0	39	1	21	21	Pitch 46+	.292	973	284	60	5	20	120	98	120	.354	.405
1 or 2 Days rest	5.75	2	4	3	33	0	51.2	61	4	34	37	First Pitch	.373	391	146	33	3	8	82	16	1	.393	.535
3+ Days rest	4.27	1	0	0	26	0	52.2	42	3	34	41	Ahead on Count	.232	1011	235	49	4	13	103	0	318	.232	.327
Pre-All Star	4.61	15	23	1	79	46	324.1	370	20	140	181	Behind on Count	.311	547	170	37	4	10	63	186	0	.486	.448
Post-All Star	4.94	8	23	2	88	38	271.2	302	24	143	180	Two Strikes	.227	946	215	42	4	18	92	81	359	.288	.337

Pitcher vs. Batter (career)

Pitches Best Vs.	Avg	AB	H	2B	3B	HR	RBI	BB	SO	OBP	SLG	Pitches Worst Vs.	Avg	AB	H	2B	3B	HR	RBI	BB	SO	OBP	SLG
Dave Anderson	.000	8	0	0	0	0	0	3	1	.273	.000	Jack Clark	.556	9	5	0	0	1	4	6	3	.688	.889
Ray Lankford	.111	9	1	0	0	0	0	2	2	.273	.111	Keith Miller	.500	16	8	4	1	0	1	4	3	.600	.875
Barry Larkin	.143	21	3	0	0	0	0	2	3	.217	.143	Mariano Duncan	.500	14	7	1	1	1	8	1	3	.533	.929
Ken Oberkfell	.160	25	4	0	0	0	1	2	1	.222	.160	Joe Girardi	.500	12	6	2	0	1	4	1	2	.538	.917
Jose Uribe	.188	16	3	0	0	0	0	2	0	.188	.188	Matt D. Williams	.333	12	4	0	0	3	5	2	2	.429	1.083

Scott Ruskin — Reds   Pitches Left

	ERA	W	L	Sv	G	GS	IP	BB	SO	Avg	H	2B	3B	HR	RBI	OBP	SLG	GF	IR	IRS	Hld	SvOp	SB	CS	GB	FB	G/F
1992 Season	5.03	4	3	0	57	0	53.2	20	43	.275	56	10	0	6	36	.339	.412	19	37	15	5	3	5	3	63	61	1.03
Career (1990-1992)	3.88	11	9	8	188	0	192.2	88	146	.258	188	36	3	14	90	.341	.373	55	119	33	27	22	32	8	258	206	1.25

1992 Season

	ERA	W	L	Sv	G	GS	IP	H	HR	BB	SO		Avg	AB	H	2B	3B	HR	RBI	BB	SO	OBP	SLG
Home	4.10	2	2	0	29	0	26.1	26	4	11	23	vs. Left	.250	68	17	4	0	1	14	9	23	.333	.353
Away	5.93	2	1	0	28	0	27.1	30	2	9	20	vs. Right	.287	136	39	6	0	5	22	11	20	.342	.441
Starter	0.00	0	0	0	0	0	0.0	0	0	0	0	Scoring Posn	.350	60	21	4	0	3	31	8	7	.423	.567
Reliever	5.03	4	3	0	57	0	53.2	56	6	20	43	Close & Late	.299	77	23	4	0	3	17	8	18	.360	.468
0 Days rest	2.65	1	1	0	18	0	17.0	14	0	5	12	None on/out	.265	49	13	4	0	0	0	5	14	.333	.347
1 or 2 Days rest	5.59	2	1	0	21	0	19.1	21	3	8	19	First Pitch	.241	29	7	1	0	1	4	3	0	.313	.379
3+ Days rest	6.75	1	1	0	18	0	17.1	21	3	7	12	Behind on Count	.231	26	6	1	0	0	1	5	1	.344	.269
Pre-All Star	5.97	3	1	0	31	0	28.2	34	2	10	28	Ahead on Count	.257	105	27	4	0	3	19	0	37	.262	.381
Post-All Star	3.96	1	2	0	26	0	25.0	22	4	10	15	Two Strikes	.245	106	26	3	0	3	23	12	41	.325	.358

Career (1990-1992)

	ERA	W	L	Sv	G	GS	IP	H	HR	BB	SO		Avg	AB	H	2B	3B	HR	RBI	BB	SO	OBP	SLG
Home	2.26	7	4	7	87	0	95.2	85	5	40	71	vs. Left	.271	273	74	12	1	4	37	32	67	.346	.366
Away	5.47	4	5	4	101	0	97.0	103	9	48	75	vs. Right	.249	457	114	24	2	10	53	56	79	.337	.376
Day	3.44	2	3	2	55	0	65.1	51	4	22	52	Inning 1-6	.243	115	28	5	0	2	16	14	17	.326	.339
Night	4.10	9	6	6	133	0	127.1	137	10	66	94	Inning 7+	.260	615	160	31	3	12	74	74	129	.343	.379
Grass	4.07	3	0	3	56	0	55.1	55	3	19	42	None on	.235	391	92	18	2	4	4	41	83	.311	.322
Turf	3.80	8	9	5	132	0	137.1	133	11	69	104	Runners on	.283	339	96	18	1	10	86	47	63	.373	.431
April	2.70	1	1	0	27	0	26.2	24	0	11	22	Scoring Posn	.250	208	52	11	1	5	73	39	42	.370	.385
May	4.94	1	1	4	27	0	31.0	33	3	15	24	Close & Late	.286	332	95	19	0	7	45	39	68	.363	.407
June	3.26	4	2	3	35	0	30.1	25	1	12	18	None on/out	.253	182	46	7	2	3	3	18	41	.320	.363
July	3.00	3	0	1	31	0	33.0	30	2	15	27	vs. 1st Batr (relief)	.244	168	41	8	1	3	20	17	40	.312	.357
August	4.71	0	2	0	33	0	36.1	42	3	15	24	First Inning Pitched	.254	544	138	24	3	8	65	60	115	.332	.353
September/October	4.33	2	3	0	35	0	35.1	34	5	20	31	First 15 Pitches	.255	513	131	22	2	9	56	54	107	.328	.359
Starter	0.00	0	0	0	0	0	0.0	0	0	0	0	Pitch 16-30	.259	174	45	9	1	3	22	28	36	.366	.374
Reliever	3.88	11	9	8	188	0	192.2	188	14	88	146	Pitch 31-45	.300	40	12	5	0	2	12	5	2	.391	.575
0 Days rest	3.28	3	4	2	46	0	49.1	44	0	19	31	Pitch 46+	.000	3	0	0	0	0	0	1	1	.250	.000
1 or 2 Days rest	3.70	6	3	4	92	0	87.2	92	8	48	79	First Pitch	.272	92	25	4	1	2	11	7	0	.323	.402
3+ Days rest	4.69	2	2	2	50	0	55.2	52	6	21	36	Ahead on Count	.203	359	73	10	1	6	37	0	128	.211	.287
Pre-All Star	3.54	7	4	7	96	0	96.2	92	5	40	74	Behind on Count	.338	148	50	11	1	4	20	47	1	.497	.507
Post-All Star	4.22	4	5	1	90	0	96.0	96	9	48	72	Two Strikes	.182	362	66	12	1	6	43	33	144	.255	.271

Pitcher vs. Batter (career)

Pitches Best Vs.	Avg	AB	H	2B	3B	HR	RBI	BB	SO	OBP	SLG	Pitches Worst Vs.	Avg	AB	H	2B	3B	HR	RBI	BB	SO	OBP	SLG
Brett Butler	.182	11	2	2	0	0	0	1	3	.250	.364	Von Hayes	.545	11	6	1	0	1	2	1	3	.583	.909
Tony Gwynn	.200	15	3	0	0	0	0	0	0	.200	.200	John Kruk	.500	8	4	1	0	0	1	3	0	.636	.625
Robby Thompson	.200	10	2	1	0	0	0	1	3	.273	.300	Barry Bonds	.462	13	6	0	0	1	2	2	2	.533	.692
												Bobby Bonilla	.333	12	4	3	0	1	2	2	1	.429	.833
												Kal Daniels	.308	13	4	1	0	0	3	1	5	.357	.385

Jeff Russell — Athletics

	ERA	W	L	Sv	G	GS	IP	BB	SO	Avg	H	2B	3B	HR	RBI	OBP	SLG	GF	IR	IRS	Hld	SvOp	SB	CS	GB	FB	G/F
1992 Season	1.63	4	3	30	59	0	66.1	25	48	.224	55	10	1	3	22	.298	.309	46	43	12	1	39	1	3	76	81	0.94
Last Five Years	3.10	27	25	108	259	24	432.1	157	281	.236	377	59	2	34	206	.307	.339	124	257	92	3	135	35	11	615	439	1.40

1992 Season

	ERA	W	L	Sv	G	GS	IP	H	HR	BB	SO		Avg	AB	H	2B	3B	HR	RBI	BB	SO	OBP	SLG
Home	0.94	2	1	16	31	0	38.1	23	2	10	26	vs. Left	.245	110	27	7	1	1	8	14	17	.339	.355
Away	2.57	2	2	14	28	0	28.0	32	1	15	22	vs. Right	.206	136	28	3	0	2	14	11	31	.264	.272
Starter	0.00	0	0	0	0	0	0.0	0	0	0	0	Scoring Posn	.188	80	15	2	1	1	19	10	15	.272	.275
Reliever	1.63	4	3	30	59	0	66.1	55	3	25	48	Close & Late	.230	191	44	7	1	2	19	19	37	.300	.309
0 Days rest	3.48	0	2	4	10	0	10.1	17	2	1	8	None on/out	.217	46	10	2	0	1	1	4	6	.294	.326
1 or 2 Days rest	1.19	2	1	18	32	0	37.2	29	0	17	26	First Pitch	.265	34	9	2	1	1	4	2	0	.316	.471
3+ Days rest	1.47	2	0	8	17	0	18.1	9	1	7	14	Behind on Count	.239	46	11	3	0	0	5	12	0	.390	.304
Pre-All Star	1.90	2	3	21	37	0	42.2	37	1	18	33	Ahead on Count	.188	117	22	4	0	1	10	0	39	.188	.248
Post-All Star	1.14	2	0	9	22	0	23.2	18	2	7	15	Two Strikes	.198	121	24	3	0	2	8	11	48	.265	.273

Last Five Years

	ERA	W	L	Sv	G	GS	IP	H	HR	BB	SO		Avg	AB	H	2B	3B	HR	RBI	BB	SO	OBP	SLG
Home	2.94	12	13	64	137	14	239.0	191	20	70	153	vs. Left	.255	777	198	26	1	14	104	92	118	.336	.347
Away	3.31	15	12	44	122	10	193.1	186	14	87	128	vs. Right	.218	821	179	31	1	20	102	65	163	.279	.331
Day	3.36	10	9	20	64	4	99.0	91	9	44	72	Inning 1-6	.260	551	143	19	0	13	65	51	67	.326	.365
Night	3.02	17	16	88	195	20	333.1	286	25	113	209	Inning 7+	.223	1047	234	40	2	21	141	106	214	.298	.326
Grass	2.90	20	19	96	222	20	369.0	306	27	129	245	None on	.209	838	175	27	0	13	13	77	153	.281	.288
Turf	4.26	7	6	12	37	4	63.1	71	7	28	36	Runners on	.266	760	202	32	2	21	193	80	128	.335	.396
April	1.58	4	2	20	42	0	51.1	35	3	15	39	Scoring Posn	.247	478	118	19	2	7	160	58	89	.325	.339
May	3.19	7	6	23	60	3	84.2	81	7	29	49	Close & Late	.231	635	147	27	2	14	102	69	120	.308	.346
June	3.24	4	3	17	35	5	75.0	59	6	31	54	None on/out	.196	342	67	10	0	4	4	30	54	.265	.260
July	2.94	4	5	15	36	5	70.1	65	5	26	47	vs. 1st Batr (relief)	.254	209	53	9	0	7	41	21	42	.318	.397
August	3.87	2	6	16	41	6	76.2	68	7	23	47	First Inning Pitched	.238	840	200	31	2	20	134	77	167	.302	.351
September/October	3.27	6	3	17	45	5	74.1	69	6	33	45	First 15 Pitches	.232	759	176	28	2	22	112	69	155	.297	.361
Starter	3.68	9	9	0	24	24	174.0	170	13	60	83	Pitch 16-30	.237	334	79	13	0	5	45	30	53	.303	.320
Reliever	2.58	18	16	108	235	0	258.1	207	21	97	198	Pitch 31-45	.218	119	26	3	0	0	13	22	23	.350	.244
0 Days rest	2.64	6	4	31	58	0	58.0	53	6	21	53	Pitch 46+	.249	386	96	15	0	7	36	36	50	.316	.342
1 or 2 Days rest	2.66	6	10	53	110	0	125.0	104	9	54	90	First Pitch	.267	251	67	11	1	6	37	10	0	.294	.390
3+ Days rest	2.39	6	2	24	67	0	75.1	50	6	22	55	Ahead on Count	.190	725	138	22	0	10	77	0	233	.196	.262
Pre-All Star	2.82	18	13	66	150	10	239.1	207	18	88	160	Behind on Count	.293	352	103	16	1	10	62	81	0	.421	.429
Post-All Star	3.45	9	12	42	109	14	193.0	170	16	69	121	Two Strikes	.161	706	114	15	0	6	53	66	281	.238	.208

Pitcher vs. Batter (since 1984)

Pitches Best Vs.	Avg	AB	H	2B	3B	HR	RBI	BB	SO	OBP	SLG	Pitches Worst Vs.	Avg	AB	H	2B	3B	HR	RBI	BB	SO	OBP	SLG
Gary Gaetti	.053	19	1	0	0	0	1	0	5	.050	.053	Mike Greenwell	.615	13	8	1	0	2	11	2	2	.667	1.154
Joe Carter	.067	15	1	0	0	0	1	0	4	.063	.067	Dave Winfield	.538	13	7	3	0	0	5	2	4	.600	.769
Brook Jacoby	.071	14	1	0	0	0	0	2	1	.188	.071	Mike Pagliarulo	.500	10	5	0	2	9	2	2		.583	1.100
Mark McGwire	.077	13	1	0	0	0	0	1	3	.143	.077	Ellis Burks	.450	20	9	2	0	2	6	2	3	.500	.850
Dan Gladden	.133	30	4	0	0	0	2	0	8	.129	.133	George Brett	.400	15	6	0	0	3	9	5	2	.524	1.000

John Russell — Rangers

	Avg	G	AB	R	H	2B	3B	HR	RBI	BB	SO	HBP	GDP	SB	CS	OBP	SLG	IBB	SH	SF	#Pit	#P/PA	GB	FB	G/F
1992 Season	.100	7	10	1	1	0	0	0	2	1	4	1	0	0	0	.231	.100	0	0	1	57	4.38	4	2	2.00
Last Five Years	.214	193	373	39	80	7	0	6	24	24	120	3	9	1	0	.266	.282	3	1	3	1470	3.65	108	100	1.08

1992 Season

	Avg	AB	H	2B	3B	HR	RBI	BB	SO	OBP	SLG		Avg	AB	H	2B	3B	HR	RBI	BB	SO	OBP	SLG
vs. Left	.200	5	1	0	0	0	1	0	1	.333	.200	Scoring Posn	.250	4	1	0	0	0	2	1	1	.429	.250
vs. Right	.000	5	0	0	0	0	0	1	3	.143	.000	Close & Late	.000	2	0	0	0	0	0	0	0	.000	.000

Last Five Years

	Avg	AB	H	2B	3B	HR	RBI	BB	SO	OBP	SLG		Avg	AB	H	2B	3B	HR	RBI	BB	SO	OBP	SLG
vs. Left	.208	207	43	4	0	3	11	11	65	.251	.271	Scoring Posn	.188	85	16	2	0	0	16	8	26	.265	.212
vs. Right	.223	166	37	3	0	3	13	13	55	.283	.295	Close & Late	.173	81	14	2	0	0	5	4	31	.212	.198
Groundball	.229	109	25	3	0	1	8	7	33	.280	.284	None on/out	.161	87	14	1	0	3	3	4	26	.198	.276
Flyball	.242	99	24	2	0	3	7	8	31	.303	.354	Batting #7	.234	94	22	3	0	3	6	2	23	.265	.362
Home	.189	169	32	3	0	2	9	9	52	.235	.243	Batting #8	.189	127	24	2	0	2	11	9	37	.245	.252
Away	.235	204	48	4	0	4	15	15	68	.291	.314	Other	.224	152	34	2	0	1	7	13	60	.283	.257
Day	.158	95	15	2	0	1	4	7	35	.223	.211	April	.161	31	5	0	0	0	0	0	11	.161	.161
Night	.234	278	65	5	0	5	20	17	85	.280	.306	May	.200	25	5	0	0	0	0	0	7	.200	.200
Grass	.194	253	49	3	0	3	15	15	61	.239	.241	June	.213	80	17	2	0	2	6	6	23	.270	.313
Turf	.258	120	31	4	0	3	9	9	39	.321	.367	July	.213	80	17	2	0	1	6	2	30	.241	.275
First Pitch	.386	57	22	1	0	1	2	1	0	.397	.456	August	.241	87	21	2	0	1	7	10	23	.316	.299
Ahead on Count	.352	54	19	2	0	1	8	14	1	.471	.444	September/October	.214	70	15	1	0	2	5	6	26	.266	.314
Behind on Count	.163	141	23	1	0	2	9	0	69	.174	.213	Pre-All Star	.214	154	33	2	0	3	7	7	47	.250	.286
Two Strikes	.115	200	23	2	0	2	8	7	119	.157	.155	Post-All Star	.215	219	47	5	0	3	17	17	73	.276	.279

Batter vs. Pitcher (career)

Hits Best Against	Avg	AB	H	2B	3B	HR	RBI	BB	SO	OBP	SLG	Hits Worst Against	Avg	AB	H	2B	3B	HR	RBI	BB	SO	OBP	SLG
Joe Hesketh	.357	14	5	3	0	0	2	0	2	.357	.571	Sid Fernandez	.000	14	0	0	0	0	0	6	8	.300	.000
Randy Johnson	.313	16	5	1	0	0	2	0	4	.389	.375	Rick Sutcliffe	.059	17	1	0	0	1	2	1	7	.111	.235
Zane Smith	.308	13	4	2	0	0	3	1	4	.357	.462	Bobby Ojeda	.100	10	1	0	0	0	1	1	3	.182	.100
												Mike Bielecki	.111	9	1	0	0	0	0	3	4	.333	.111
												Bob Walk	.143	14	2	0	0	0	0	0	5	.143	.143

Ken Ryan — Red Sox

Pitches Right (groundball pitcher)

	ERA	W	L	Sv	G	GS	IP	BB	SO	Avg	H	2B	3B	HR	RBI	OBP	SLG	GF	IR	IRS	Hld	SvOp	SB	CS	GB	FB	G/F
1992 Season	6.43	0	0	1	7	0	7.0	5	5	.174	4	0	0	2	5	.310	.435	6	7	4	0	1	0	0	13	5	2.60

1992 Season

	ERA	W	L	Sv	G	GS	IP	H	HR	BB	SO		Avg	AB	H	2B	3B	HR	RBI	BB	SO	OBP	SLG
Home	0.00	0	0	1	4	0	3.2	1	0	1	2	vs. Left	.000	7	0	0	0	0	0	2	2	.222	.000
Away	13.50	0	0	0	3	0	3.1	3	2	4	3	vs. Right	.250	16	4	0	0	2	5	3	3	.350	.625

Nolan Ryan — Rangers

Pitches Right (flyball pitcher)

	ERA	W	L	Sv	G	GS	IP	BB	SO	Avg	H	2B	3B	HR	RBI	OBP	SLG	CG	ShO	Sup	QS	#P/S	SB	CS	GB	FB	G/F
1992 Season	3.72	5	9	0	27	27	157.1	69	157	.238	138	27	3	9	60	.328	.341	2	0	4.12	18	100	26	12	145	190	0.76
Last Five Years	3.35	58	45	0	149	149	993.2	400	1121	.202	725	136	24	74	356	.287	.315	19	7	4.45	93	110	157	42	951	1047	0.91

1992 Season

	ERA	W	L	Sv	G	GS	IP	H	HR	BB	SO		Avg	AB	H	2B	3B	HR	RBI	BB	SO	OBP	SLG
Home	3.40	3	6	0	15	15	92.2	73	5	39	99	vs. Left	.245	294	72	14	3	5	30	43	69	.339	.364
Away	4.18	2	3	0	12	12	64.2	65	4	30	58	vs. Right	.231	286	66	13	0	4	30	26	88	.316	.318
Day	2.17	2	0	0	5	5	29.0	26	1	12	25	Inning 1-6	.237	518	123	24	2	8	54	66	146	.332	.338
Night	4.07	3	9	0	22	22	128.1	112	8	57	132	Inning 7+	.242	62	15	3	1	1	6	3	11	.288	.371
Grass	3.96	5	9	0	24	24	141.0	124	8	64	141	None on	.230	330	76	15	3	5	5	37	94	.319	.339
Turf	1.65	0	0	0	3	3	16.1	14	1	5	16	Runners on	.248	250	62	12	0	4	55	32	63	.339	.344
April	10.80	0	1	0	2	2	6.2	10	0	6	7	Scoring Posn	.225	151	34	8	0	3	51	19	44	.322	.338
May	3.21	0	0	0	5	5	28.0	21	1	8	33	Close & Late	.294	34	10	2	1	0	4	1	4	.314	.412
June	3.46	1	2	0	5	5	26.0	26	1	15	26	None on/out	.220	150	33	5	3	3	3	14	40	.304	.353
July	1.96	4	0	0	5	5	36.2	23	2	13	34	vs. 1st Batr (relief)	.000	0	0	0	0	0	0	0	0	.000	.000
August	7.16	0	5	0	6	6	32.2	36	5	22	37	First Inning Pitched	.211	95	20	3	2	3	13	18	33	.348	.379
September/October	0.99	0	1	0	4	4	27.1	22	0	5	20	First 75 Pitches	.229	407	93	17	2	8	39	45	113	.317	.339
Starter	3.72	5	9	0	27	27	157.1	138	9	69	157	Pitch 76-90	.297	74	22	5	0	0	7	8	20	.353	.365
Reliever	0.00	0	0	0	0	0	0.0	0	0	0	0	Pitch 91-105	.250	52	13	2	1	0	6	11	15	.381	.327
0-3 Days Rest	4.50	0	0	0	1	1	6.0	5	0	2	9	Pitch 106+	.213	47	10	3	0	1	8	5	9	.321	.340
4 Days Rest	3.63	2	5	0	14	14	79.1	69	6	37	75	First Pitch	.283	60	17	5	0	0	8	0	0	.328	.367
5+ Days Rest	3.75	3	4	0	12	12	72.0	64	3	30	73	Ahead on Count	.158	291	46	7	1	3	16	0	132	.167	.220
Pre-All Star	3.76	3	3	0	14	14	76.2	67	4	32	87	Behind on Count	.380	121	46	13	0	5	28	29	0	.497	.612
Post-All Star	3.68	2	6	0	13	13	80.2	71	5	37	70	Two Strikes	.150	314	47	7	2	3	18	40	157	.249	.213

Last Five Years

	ERA	W	L	Sv	G	GS	IP	H	HR	BB	SO		Avg	AB	H	2B	3B	HR	RBI	BB	SO	OBP	SLG
Home	3.29	37	25	0	88	88	599.0	413	51	230	691	vs. Left	.205	1885	387	63	18	34	169	228	525	.291	.312
Away	3.44	21	20	0	61	61	394.2	312	23	170	430	vs. Right	.198	1703	338	73	6	40	187	172	596	.283	.319
Day	2.63	12	5	0	28	28	192.0	136	5	87	214	Inning 1-6	.201	2986	601	108	21	62	309	355	936	.291	.314
Night	3.53	46	40	0	121	121	801.2	589	69	313	907	Inning 7+	.206	602	124	28	3	12	47	45	185	.266	.322
Grass	3.45	44	36	0	111	111	739.0	531	62	304	853	None on	.184	2237	412	82	18	49	49	239	773	.269	.303
Turf	3.07	14	9	0	38	38	254.2	194	12	96	268	Runners on	.232	1351	313	54	6	25	307	161	348	.315	.336
April	3.10	11	5	0	20	20	136.1	89	8	55	171	Scoring Posn	.210	847	178	28	2	16	271	119	242	.309	.305
May	4.64	6	7	0	24	24	143.2	113	14	65	156	Close & Late	.191	299	57	12	2	4	24	26	100	.258	.284
June	3.24	9	9	0	26	26	169.1	126	18	65	187	None on/out	.192	954	183	39	6	21	21	89	309	.268	.311
July	3.01	17	4	0	27	27	188.1	134	13	82	210	vs. 1st Batr (relief)	.000	0	0	0	0	0	0	0	0	.000	.000
August	4.00	6	16	0	26	26	171.0	143	14	69	190	First Inning Pitched	.223	548	122	21	11	11	74	60	173	.320	.361
September/October	2.38	9	4	0	26	26	185.0	120	7	64	207	First 75 Pitches	.197	2349	463	78	19	54	236	249	722	.280	.315
Starter	3.35	58	45	0	149	149	993.2	725	74	400	1121	Pitch 76-90	.230	430	99	25	1	7	39	62	140	.329	.342
Reliever	0.00	0	0	0	0	0	0.0	0	0	0	0	Pitch 91-105	.198	389	77	12	3	5	39	46	134	.286	.283
0-3 Days Rest	3.74	2	1	0	7	7	45.2	42	2	17	50	Pitch 106+	.205	420	86	21	1	8	42	43	125	.282	.317
4 Days Rest	3.52	25	26	0	72	72	475.2	365	42	185	512	First Pitch	.331	396	131	25	5	14	64	5	0	.345	.525
5+ Days Rest	3.14	31	18	0	70	70	472.1	318	30	198	559	Ahead on Count	.143	1888	270	51	4	22	114	1	924	.149	.209
Pre-All Star	3.48	32	22	0	79	79	517.0	374	45	209	597	Behind on Count	.291	649	189	46	10	22	110	183	1	.450	.495
Post-All Star	3.21	26	23	0	70	70	476.2	351	29	191	524	Two Strikes	.125	2060	258	48	6	21	119	211	1119	.210	.183

Pitcher vs. Batter (since 1984)

Pitches Best Vs.	Avg	AB	H	2B	3B	HR	RBI	BB	SO	OBP	SLG	Pitches Worst Vs.	Avg	AB	H	2B	3B	HR	RBI	BB	SO	OBP	SLG
Sammy Sosa	.000	16	0	0	0	0	0	2	8	.111	.000	Rick Cerone	.467	15	7	2	0	2	4	1	1	.500	1.000
Rob Deer	.000	14	0	0	0	0	0	0	10	.000	.000	Albert Belle	.417	12	5	1	0	1	5	2	5	.500	.750
Randy Milligan	.000	13	0	0	0	0	0	2	8	.133	.000	Harold Baines	.368	19	7	1	0	4	6	1	4	.400	1.053
Jesse Barfield	.000	12	0	0	0	0	0	0	10	.000	.000	Joe Carter	.357	14	5	3	1	1	4	2	4	.438	.929
Luis Rivera	.000	10	0	0	0	0	0	1	4	.000	.000	Will Clark	.333	36	12	2	0	6	11	3	12	.385	.889

383

Bret Saberhagen — Mets
Pitches Right

	ERA	W	L	Sv	G	GS	IP	BB	SO	Avg	H	2B	3B	HR	RBI	OBP	SLG	CG	ShO	Sup	QS	#P/S	SB	CS	GB	FB	G/F
1992 Season	3.50	3	5	0	17	15	97.2	27	81	.233	84	14	4	6	36	.292	.344	1	1	2.95	7	91	6	5	115	94	1.22
Last Five Years	3.09	58	44	0	136	133	952.0	202	668	.245	875	153	35	58	322	.287	.356	34	7	4.26	91	105	33	31	1253	1066	1.18

1992 Season

	ERA	W	L	Sv	G	GS	IP	H	HR	BB	SO		Avg	AB	H	2B	3B	HR	RBI	BB	SO	OBP	SLG
Home	2.41	1	2	0	9	9	59.2	42	3	15	49	vs. Left	.226	212	48	10	3	3	22	20	48	.292	.344
Away	5.21	2	3	0	8	6	38.0	42	3	12	32	vs. Right	.243	148	36	4	1	3	14	7	33	.291	.345
Starter	3.29	3	4	0	15	15	93.0	76	4	25	79	Scoring Posn	.200	65	13	4	2	1	26	12	14	.313	.369
Reliever	7.71	0	1	0	2	0	4.2	8	2	2	2	Close & Late	.254	59	15	2	0	2	4	2	8	.279	.390
0-3 Days Rest	0.00	0	0	0	0	0	0.0	0	0	0	0	None on/out	.194	93	18	0	0	1	1	8	23	.257	.226
4 Days Rest	2.34	1	2	0	9	9	61.2	45	3	12	47	First Pitch	.259	58	15	3	0	1	3	1	0	.271	.362
5+ Days Rest	5.17	2	2	0	6	6	31.1	31	1	13	32	Behind on Count	.292	65	19	3	0	3	10	11	0	.390	.477
Pre-All Star	3.81	3	2	0	8	8	52.0	44	3	13	54	Ahead on Count	.161	180	29	4	4	0	15	0	74	.165	.228
Post-All Star	3.15	0	3	0	9	7	45.2	40	3	14	27	Two Strikes	.148	169	25	4	2	1	9	15	81	.220	.213

Last Five Years

	ERA	W	L	Sv	G	GS	IP	H	HR	BB	SO		Avg	AB	H	2B	3B	HR	RBI	BB	SO	OBP	SLG
Home	2.96	28	20	0	68	68	489.1	444	22	92	345	vs. Left	.226	1842	417	65	20	31	157	134	387	.277	.334
Away	3.23	30	24	0	68	65	462.2	431	36	110	323	vs. Right	.264	1735	458	88	15	27	165	68	281	.297	.379
Day	3.60	10	16	0	40	39	272.1	252	26	65	216	Inning 1-6	.243	2643	690	125	27	41	267	172	549	.287	.349
Night	2.89	48	28	0	96	94	679.2	623	32	137	452	Inning 7+	.252	734	185	28	8	17	55	30	119	.284	.381
Grass	2.67	22	18	0	55	54	388.0	331	26	86	279	None on	.237	2217	525	91	20	38	38	106	427	.276	.347
Turf	3.38	36	26	0	81	79	564.0	544	32	116	389	Runners on	.257	1360	350	62	15	20	284	96	241	.304	.369
April	3.86	8	11	0	27	26	175.0	181	14	35	119	Scoring Posn	.250	732	183	36	9	13	252	64	135	.305	.377
May	2.52	16	8	0	27	27	207.0	171	9	42	140	Close & Late	.229	397	91	14	5	11	38	17	73	.268	.373
June	2.92	7	5	0	17	17	123.1	116	5	28	84	None on/out	.238	934	222	41	11	15	15	51	176	.281	.353
July	4.95	5	8	0	19	19	116.1	135	9	37	81	vs. 1st Batr (relief)	.000	3	0	0	0	0	0	0	0	.000	.000
August	1.83	12	4	0	19	19	147.1	119	7	21	101	First Inning Pitched	.256	520	133	27	6	7	58	43	107	.316	.371
September/October	2.95	10	10	0	27	25	183.0	153	14	39	143	First 75 Pitches	.245	2407	590	105	22	34	218	151	458	.292	.349
Starter	3.05	58	42	0	133	133	945.0	864	55	198	664	Pitch 76-90	.210	495	104	25	3	8	41	20	95	.242	.321
Reliever	9.00	0	2	0	3	0	7.0	11	3	4	4	Pitch 91-105	.271	402	109	14	4	7	33	20	72	.304	.378
0-3 Days Rest	1.92	6	4	0	11	11	89.0	67	3	16	63	Pitch 106+	.264	273	72	9	6	9	30	11	43	.300	.440
4 Days Rest	2.84	39	23	0	79	79	573.2	510	30	112	397	First Pitch	.298	521	155	37	4	14	60	12	0	.312	.464
5+ Days Rest	3.83	13	15	0	43	43	282.1	287	22	70	204	Ahead on Count	.201	1758	353	53	16	16	103	0	589	.204	.276
Pre-All Star	3.17	32	23	0	76	75	537.0	508	29	113	374	Behind on Count	.295	685	202	34	6	20	94	85	0	.372	.450
Post-All Star	2.99	26	21	0	60	58	415.0	367	29	89	294	Two Strikes	.188	1703	320	50	13	18	106	105	668	.237	.264

Pitcher vs. Batter (career)

Pitches Best Vs.	Avg	AB	H	2B	3B	HR	RBI	BB	SO	OBP	SLG	Pitches Worst Vs.	Avg	AB	H	2B	3B	HR	RBI	BB	SO	OBP	SLG
Dave Valle	.000	9	0	0	0	0	0	2	2	.182	.000	Sam Horn	.421	19	8	1	0	4	9	0	7	.421	1.105
Glenallen Hill	.063	16	1	0	0	0	0	0	7	.063	.063	Fred McGriff	.414	29	12	2	1	2	4	3	8	.469	.759
Mike Kingery	.077	13	1	0	0	0	1	2	3	.200	.077	Albert Belle	.385	13	5	2	0	1	4	0	3	.385	.769
Mike Devereaux	.077	13	1	0	0	0	1	0	3	.077	.077	George Bell	.372	43	16	4	0	5	13	1	1	.378	.814
Steve Finley	.091	11	1	1	0	0	0	1	0	.091	.182	Darryl Hamilton	.364	11	4	1	0	1	4	5	1	.417	.727

Chris Sabo — Reds
Bats Right (flyball hitter)

	Avg	G	AB	R	H	2B	3B	HR	RBI	BB	SO	HBP	GDP	SB	CS	OBP	SLG	IBB	SH	SF	#Pit	#P/PA	GB	FB	G/F
1992 Season	.244	96	344	42	84	19	3	12	43	30	54	1	12	4	5	.302	.422	1	1	6	1330	3.49	104	140	0.74
Career (1988-1992)	.273	618	2335	342	637	153	11	80	275	189	276	18	47	108	44	.330	.451	14	16	18	9003	3.52	745	900	0.83

1992 Season

	Avg	AB	H	2B	3B	HR	RBI	BB	SO	OBP	SLG		Avg	AB	H	2B	3B	HR	RBI	BB	SO	OBP	SLG
vs. Left	.247	146	36	8	1	6	21	14	23	.311	.438	Scoring Posn	.215	107	23	2	0	4	33	14	16	.291	.346
vs. Right	.242	198	48	11	2	6	22	16	31	.295	.409	Close & Late	.262	42	11	0	0	0	4	7	7	.353	.262
Groundball	.231	117	27	6	1	6	20	5	16	.258	.453	None on/out	.277	94	26	9	0	6	6	6	14	.327	.564
Flyball	.167	78	13	3	0	0	2	12	18	.278	.205	Batting #4	.253	154	39	7	1	6	23	16	20	.324	.429
Home	.236	148	35	11	0	8	22	11	27	.282	.473	Batting #5	.278	72	20	6	1	4	11	5	13	.321	.556
Away	.250	196	49	8	3	4	21	19	27	.317	.383	Other	.212	118	25	6	1	2	9	9	21	.262	.331
Day	.273	110	30	9	0	3	12	12	16	.341	.436	April	.154	26	4	0	0	0	3	2	.241	.154
Night	.231	234	54	10	3	9	31	18	38	.282	.415	May	.261	92	24	7	2	2	10	9	14	.324	.446
Grass	.211	114	24	5	1	1	8	10	16	.272	.298	June	.276	87	24	5	1	5	16	6	15	.319	.529
Turf	.261	230	60	14	2	11	35	20	38	.316	.483	July	.236	55	13	1	0	1	5	4	9	.279	.309
First Pitch	.333	63	21	3	3	2	5	2	1	.353	.571	August	.236	55	13	6	0	3	7	4	7	.283	.509
Ahead on Count	.372	78	29	10	0	3	10	19	0	.495	.615	September/October	.207	29	6	0	0	1	5	4	7	.314	.310
Behind on Count	.250	112	28	3	0	5	18	0	27	.248	.411	Pre-All Star	.256	246	63	13	3	8	31	20	37	.307	.431
Two Strikes	.135	133	18	5	0	2	13	9	53	.189	.218	Post-All Star	.214	98	21	6	0	4	12	10	17	.288	.398

1992 By Position

Position	Avg	AB	H	2B	3B	HR	RBI	BB	SO	OBP	SLG	G	GS	Innings	PO	A	E	DP	Fld Pct	Rng Fctr	In Zone	Outs	Zone Rtg	MLB Zone
As 3b	.246	342	84	19	3	12	43	30	54	.303	.424	94	94	790.0	60	158	9	12	.960	2.48	195	156	.800	.841

Career (1988-1992)

	Avg	AB	H	2B	3B	HR	RBI	BB	SO	OBP	SLG		Avg	AB	H	2B	3B	HR	RBI	BB	SO	OBP	SLG
vs. Left	.308	793	244	56	4	33	102	78	80	.373	.513	Scoring Posn	.261	568	148	34	1	20	201	72	75	.342	.430
vs. Right	.255	1542	393	97	7	47	173	111	196	.307	.418	Close & Late	.251	359	90	15	1	12	42	37	48	.323	.398
Groundball	.290	871	253	59	2	26	109	57	86	.337	.452	None on/out	.284	626	178	39	2	29	29	56	61	.346	.492
Flyball	.242	455	110	29	2	16	49	51	64	.320	.420	Batting #1	.283	587	166	36	2	23	65	62	68	.355	.468
Home	.287	1139	327	84	5	49	147	100	124	.347	.499	Batting #2	.267	420	112	30	2	8	29	24	50	.308	.405
Away	.259	1196	310	69	6	31	128	89	152	.313	.405	Other	.270	1328	359	87	7	49	161	103	158	.325	.457
Day	.237	655	155	42	3	19	67	63	81	.307	.397	April	.261	329	86	23	0	11	26	31	34	.328	.432
Night	.267	1680	482	111	8	61	208	126	195	.339	.471	May	.264	469	124	28	2	17	59	41	60	.324	.441
Grass	.258	714	184	41	2	20	77	50	89	.310	.405	June	.318	491	156	40	7	21	70	47	64	.381	.556
Turf	.279	1621	453	112	9	60	198	139	187	.338	.471	July	.230	339	78	18	1	9	36	26	38	.289	.369
First Pitch	.333	360	120	30	3	15	47	6	1	.346	.558	August	.283	381	108	25	1	13	36	18	39	.320	.457
Ahead on Count	.345	608	210	49	3	26	78	100	0	.436	.564	September/October	.261	326	85	19	0	9	44	26	41	.317	.402
Behind on Count	.252	781	197	41	2	26	92	1	149	.259	.410	Pre-All Star	.281	1411	396	97	10	51	170	124	171	.340	.472
Two Strikes	.190	883	168	41	2	19	79	75	274	.256	.306	Post-All Star	.261	924	241	56	1	29	105	65	105	.313	.418

Batter vs. Pitcher (career)

Hits Best Against	Avg	AB	H	2B	3B	HR	RBI	BB	SO	OBP	SLG	Hits Worst Against	Avg	AB	H	2B	3B	HR	RBI	BB	SO	OBP	SLG
Frank Viola	.545	11	6	1	0	1	2	4	2	.667	.909	Sid Fernandez	.042	24	1	1	0	0	0	2	6	.115	.083
Kelly Downs	.545	11	6	3	0	1	3	1	0	.583	1.091	Pete Harnisch	.083	12	1	0	0	0	0	2	5	.214	.083
Chris Nabholz	.538	13	7	3	1	2	5	2	0	.600	1.385	David Cone	.118	17	2	1	0	0	0	2	8	.211	.176
Tim Burke	.444	9	4	0	0	1	4	1	1	.455	.778	Larry Andersen	.143	14	2	0	0	0	1	1	4	.200	.143
Ramon Martinez	.333	21	7	2	0	3	7	1	5	.364	.857	Don Carman	.167	12	2	0	0	0	0	0	0	.167	.167

Luis Salazar — Cubs
Bats Right

	Avg	G	AB	R	H	2B	3B	HR	RBI	BB	SO	HBP	GDP	SB	CS	OBP	SLG	IBB	SH	SF	#Pit	#P/PA	GB	FB	G/F
1992 Season	.208	98	255	20	53	7	2	5	25	11	34	0	10	1	1	.237	.310	2	3	4	1013	3.75	80	97	0.82
Last Five Years	.257	567	1776	193	457	60	9	52	206	81	265	9	41	11	9	.292	.389	11	22	8	7063	3.77	605	579	1.04

1992 Season

	Avg	AB	H	2B	3B	HR	RBI	BB	SO	OBP	SLG		Avg	AB	H	2B	3B	HR	RBI	BB	SO	OBP	SLG
vs. Left	.250	156	39	6	2	4	18	6	16	.273	.391	Scoring Posn	.226	62	14	1	2	0	18	5	11	.268	.306
vs. Right	.141	99	14	1	0	1	7	5	18	.181	.182	Close & Late	.140	43	6	1	0	0	4	5	7	.220	.163
Home	.235	119	28	4	2	3	16	7	15	.271	.378	None on/out	.189	53	10	1	0	1	1	2	4	.218	.264
Away	.184	136	25	3	0	2	9	4	19	.206	.250	Batting #5	.316	38	12	1	2	2	9	2	3	.350	.605
First Pitch	.280	25	7	1	0	1	6	2	0	.310	.440	Batting #6	.169	148	25	5	0	1	10	7	20	.203	.223
Ahead on Count	.194	36	7	1	0	2	3	5	0	.286	.389	Other	.232	69	16	1	0	2	6	2	11	.250	.333
Behind on Count	.191	110	21	3	0	1	5	0	19	.191	.245	Pre-All Star	.203	153	31	5	0	2	14	9	25	.244	.275
Two Strikes	.188	133	25	4	0	1	6	4	34	.212	.241	Post-All Star	.216	102	22	2	2	3	11	2	9	.226	.363

Last Five Years

	Avg	AB	H	2B	3B	HR	RBI	BB	SO	OBP	SLG		Avg	AB	H	2B	3B	HR	RBI	BB	SO	OBP	SLG
vs. Left	.267	804	231	36	6	33	124	36	90	.319	.470	Scoring Posn	.261	445	116	15	3	12	153	33	73	.312	.389
vs. Right	.233	972	226	24	3	19	82	45	175	.270	.322	Close & Late	.295	312	92	9	2	8	48	23	44	.343	.413
Groundball	.269	525	141	17	3	10	59	32	80	.308	.370	None on/out	.280	404	113	15	2	15	15	10	49	.299	.438
Flyball	.243	470	114	21	1	15	47	23	72	.279	.387	Batting #6	.255	754	192	29	4	21	81	34	99	.288	.387
Home	.263	889	234	35	6	29	100	41	133	.298	.414	Batting #7	.285	242	69	5	1	11	33	12	36	.323	.450
Away	.251	887	223	25	3	23	106	40	132	.286	.364	Other	.251	780	196	26	4	20	92	35	130	.286	.372
Day	.248	767	190	30	4	22	90	27	115	.276	.383	April	.251	183	46	6	0	4	15	7	27	.279	.350
Night	.265	1009	267	30	5	30	116	54	150	.304	.393	May	.246	317	78	8	0	11	34	20	53	.292	.375
Grass	.260	1344	349	47	9	44	165	62	187	.294	.406	June	.306	320	98	12	2	9	46	20	47	.347	.441
Turf	.250	432	108	13	0	8	41	19	78	.286	.336	July	.255	286	73	10	2	12	31	9	40	.264	.430
First Pitch	.354	147	52	7	1	6	18	3	0	.368	.537	August	.240	304	73	10	1	9	36	8	41	.263	.368
Ahead on Count	.325	332	108	19	1	15	63	55	0	.421	.524	September/October	.243	366	89	14	4	7	44	17	57	.279	.361
Behind on Count	.219	770	169	19	3	17	78	1	161	.223	.318	Pre-All Star	.264	916	242	29	2	29	109	52	145	.305	.395
Two Strikes	.199	920	183	20	3	16	66	19	265	.219	.279	Post-All Star	.250	860	215	31	7	23	97	29	120	.278	.383

Batter vs. Pitcher (since 1984)

Hits Best Against	Avg	AB	H	2B	3B	HR	RBI	BB	SO	OBP	SLG	Hits Worst Against	Avg	AB	H	2B	3B	HR	RBI	BB	SO	OBP	SLG
Curt Young	.500	12	6	1	0	2	5	0	0	.500	1.083	Bob Welch	.000	11	0	0	0	0	0	0	2	.000	.000
Pat Combs	.500	12	6	1	0	0	2	0	1	.500	.583	Brian Barnes	.056	18	1	0	0	0	0	0	2	.056	.056
Bill Sampen	.400	10	4	0	0	1	2	1	2	.455	.700	Joe Boever	.083	12	1	0	0	0	1	0	3	.077	.083
Bud Black	.391	23	9	1	1	3	8	1	4	.417	.913	Steve Avery	.083	12	1	0	0	0	0	0	2	.083	.083
Zane Smith	.333	15	5	0	0	2	3	2	2	.412	.733	Dennis Rasmussen	.087	23	2	0	0	0	0	0	2	.125	.087

Tim Salmon — Angels
Bats Right

	Avg	G	AB	R	H	2B	3B	HR	RBI	BB	SO	HBP	GDP	SB	CS	OBP	SLG	IBB	SH	SF	#Pit	#P/PA	GB	FB	G/F
1992 Season	.177	23	79	8	14	1	0	2	6	11	23	1	1	1	1	.283	.266	1	0	1	386	4.20	25	18	1.39

1992 Season

	Avg	AB	H	2B	3B	HR	RBI	BB	SO	OBP	SLG		Avg	AB	H	2B	3B	HR	RBI	BB	SO	OBP	SLG
vs. Left	.231	13	3	0	0	1	2	3	4	.375	.462	Scoring Posn	.190	21	4	0	0	0	4	9	8	.419	.190
vs. Right	.167	66	11	1	0	1	4	8	19	.263	.227	Close & Late	.105	19	2	0	0	1	2	3	5	.227	.263

Bill Sampen — Royals

	ERA	W	L	Sv	G	GS	IP	BB	SO	Avg	H	2B	3B	HR	RBI	OBP	SLG	GF	IR	IRS	Hld	SvOp	SB	CS	GB	FB	G/F
1992 Season	3.25	1	6	0	52	2	83.0	32	37	.274	83	10	2	4	42	.348	.360	13	42	13	6	1	15	2	131	75	1.75
Career (1990-1992)	3.42	22	18	2	154	14	265.2	111	158	.271	273	44	3	24	131	.346	.393	47	91	30	12	4	46	13	374	300	1.25

1992 Season

	ERA	W	L	Sv	G	GS	IP	H	HR	BB	SO		Avg	AB	H	2B	3B	HR	RBI	BB	SO	OBP	SLG
Home	2.92	0	1	0	25	0	37.0	35	2	20	22	vs. Left	.305	141	43	6	1	3	22	23	13	.401	.426
Away	3.52	1	5	0	27	2	46.0	48	2	12	15	vs. Right	.247	162	40	4	1	1	20	9	24	.297	.302
Starter	6.75	0	2	0	2	2	8.0	9	0	3	3	Scoring Posn	.273	88	24	5	1	3	41	15	9	.374	.455
Reliever	2.88	1	4	0	50	0	75.0	74	4	29	34	Close & Late	.359	78	28	3	1	1	13	8	8	.416	.462
0 Days rest	3.66	1	1	0	12	0	19.2	26	2	7	8	None on/out	.278	72	20	3	1	1	1	3	9	.325	.389
1 or 2 Days rest	3.00	0	2	0	17	0	24.0	21	1	6	11	First Pitch	.313	48	15	3	0	1	9	6	0	.389	.438
3+ Days rest	2.30	0	1	0	21	0	31.1	27	1	16	15	Behind on Count	.389	54	21	2	0	1	6	15	0	.521	.481
Pre-All Star	3.31	0	3	0	33	1	51.2	51	4	23	21	Ahead on Count	.179	134	24	3	2	0	12	0	31	.188	.231
Post-All Star	3.16	1	3	0	19	1	31.1	32	0	9	16	Two Strikes	.209	115	24	2	2	2	21	11	37	.283	.313

Career (1990-1992)

	ERA	W	L	Sv	G	GS	IP	H	HR	BB	SO		Avg	AB	H	2B	3B	HR	RBI	BB	SO	OBP	SLG
Home	3.05	11	7	0	73	5	118.0	123	9	51	83	vs. Left	.270	496	134	22	2	11	66	71	62	.358	.389
Away	3.72	11	11	2	81	9	147.2	150	15	60	75	vs. Right	.273	510	139	22	1	13	65	40	96	.333	.396
Day	3.48	9	4	0	55	6	93.0	100	10	24	40	Inning 1-6	.248	451	112	18	1	13	55	41	69	.317	.379
Night	3.39	13	14	2	99	8	172.2	173	14	87	118	Inning 7+	.290	555	161	26	2	11	76	70	89	.369	.404
Grass	3.48	8	5	1	48	5	85.1	90	11	27	49	None on	.275	524	144	23	1	15	55	59	97	.354	.408
Turf	3.39	14	13	1	106	9	180.1	183	13	84	109	Runners on	.268	482	129	21	2	9	116	52	61	.336	.376
April	3.21	1	2	0	20	4	42.0	34	6	23	20	Scoring Posn	.252	301	76	14	2	7	110	44	44	.344	.382
May	3.52	4	1	0	30	2	46.0	48	5	16	35	Close & Late	.295	292	86	10	2	5	39	39	48	.376	.394
June	3.42	5	3	1	32	1	50.0	52	4	24	33	None on/out	.265	239	68	12	1	6	6	20	39	.347	.418
July	4.02	2	2	0	22	1	31.1	41	1	17	17	vs. 1st Batr (relief)	.308	130	40	6	0	5	28	10	22	.357	.469
August	3.34	4	5	1	22	0	32.1	30	4	11	18	First Inning Pitched	.271	495	134	26	0	14	77	62	82	.353	.408
September/October	3.23	5	5	0	28	6	64.0	68	4	20	35	First 15 Pitches	.273	477	130	22	0	13	58	48	66	.342	.400
Starter	3.88	4	5	0	14	14	62.2	63	8	29	35	Pitch 16-30	.269	283	76	13	2	5	40	33	51	.345	.382
Reliever	3.28	18	13	2	140	0	203.0	210	16	82	123	Pitch 31-45	.296	135	40	6	0	3	16	14	24	.364	.407
0 Days rest	3.79	4	4	1	28	0	40.1	53	4	16	19	Pitch 46+	.243	111	27	3	1	3	16	16	17	.344	.360
1 or 2 Days rest	3.93	7	7	0	64	0	84.2	88	7	37	56	First Pitch	.291	165	48	10	0	2	25	16	0	.361	.388
3+ Days rest	2.31	7	2	1	48	0	78.0	69	5	29	48	Ahead on Count	.212	457	97	15	2	9	39	0	141	.217	.313
Pre-All Star	3.31	12	6	1	90	7	149.2	148	16	63	93	Behind on Count	.378	201	76	12	1	7	41	52	0	.502	.552
Post-All Star	3.57	10	12	1	64	7	116.0	125	8	48	65	Two Strikes	.202	430	87	12	2	10	45	43	158	.277	.309

Pitcher vs. Batter (career)

Pitches Best Vs.	Avg	AB	H	2B	3B	HR	RBI	BB	SO	OBP	SLG	Pitches Worst Vs.	Avg	AB	H	2B	3B	HR	RBI	BB	SO	OBP	SLG
Andre Dawson	.091	11	1	0	0	0	0	1	2	.167	.091	Sid Bream	.500	10	5	0	0	1	3	0	2	.455	.800
Howard Johnson	.125	8	1	0	0	0	2	4	2	.417	.250	Barry Bonds	.429	7	3	0	0	2	4	1	1	.636	1.286
Ozzie Smith	.167	12	2	1	0	0	1	1	0	.214	.250	Luis Salazar	.400	10	4	0	0	1	2	1	2	.455	.700
Jose Lind	.167	12	2	0	0	0	1	2	5	.286	.167	Ryne Sandberg	.333	15	5	0	0	2	3	2	4	.412	.733
Terry Pendleton	.200	10	2	0	0	0	1	1	1	.273	.200	Ron Gant	.333	9	3	0	0	1	1	2	2	.455	.667

Juan Samuel — Royals

	Avg	G	AB	R	H	2B	3B	HR	RBI	BB	SO	HBP	GDP	SB	CS	OBP	SLG	IBB	SH	SF	#Pit	#P/PA	GB	FB	G/F
1992 Season	.272	76	224	22	61	8	4	0	23	14	49	2	2	8	3	.318	.344	4	4	2	861	3.56	90	48	1.88
Last Five Years	.251	666	2471	295	619	102	24	48	248	195	579	33	33	144	53	.312	.369	21	21	17	10229	3.77	883	586	1.51

1992 Season

	Avg	AB	H	2B	3B	HR	RBI	BB	SO	OBP	SLG		Avg	AB	H	2B	3B	HR	RBI	BB	SO	OBP	SLG
vs. Left	.288	104	30	5	2	0	9	8	19	.345	.375	Scoring Posn	.246	57	14	1	1	0	23	9	17	.348	.298
vs. Right	.258	120	31	3	2	0	14	6	30	.295	.317	Close & Late	.400	40	16	3	0	0	5	1	10	.415	.475
Home	.295	105	31	3	2	0	15	6	21	.339	.362	None on/out	.322	59	19	1	1	0	0	0	8	.333	.373
Away	.252	119	30	5	2	0	8	8	28	.300	.328	Batting #5	.326	43	14	1	2	0	3	3	11	.383	.442
First Pitch	.382	34	13	2	0	0	6	4	0	.447	.441	Batting #6	.259	112	29	5	2	0	12	8	29	.309	.339
Ahead on Count	.392	51	20	3	1	0	2	6	0	.456	.490	Other	.261	69	18	2	0	0	8	3	9	.292	.290
Behind on Count	.195	82	16	2	0	0	6	0	29	.202	.220	Pre-All Star	.269	108	29	2	1	0	15	7	21	.314	.306
Two Strikes	.155	103	16	1	2	0	10	4	49	.200	.204	Post-All Star	.276	116	32	6	3	0	8	7	28	.323	.379

Last Five Years

	Avg	AB	H	2B	3B	HR	RBI	BB	SO	OBP	SLG		Avg	AB	H	2B	3B	HR	RBI	BB	SO	OBP	SLG
vs. Left	.264	899	237	43	9	25	99	76	194	.326	.415	Scoring Posn	.243	588	143	20	8	8	189	68	156	.326	.345
vs. Right	.243	1572	382	59	15	23	149	119	385	.304	.344	Close & Late	.272	386	105	19	6	7	53	35	95	.336	.407
Groundball	.253	823	208	29	9	15	85	69	196	.318	.365	None on/out	.244	661	161	25	6	17	57	136	310	.310	.377
Flyball	.232	547	127	29	5	7	47	38	135	.287	.342	Batting #1	.234	704	165	32	8	13	59	50	159	.292	.358
Home	.256	1213	310	57	13	22	134	102	270	.322	.378	Batting #2	.274	647	177	27	4	11	66	53	146	.336	.379
Away	.246	1258	309	45	11	26	114	93	309	.302	.361	Other	.247	1120	277	43	12	24	123	92	274	.310	.371
Day	.256	657	168	28	6	8	48	51	149	.314	.353	April	.249	342	85	14	5	6	36	28	80	.309	.371
Night	.249	1814	451	74	18	40	200	144	430	.311	.375	May	.262	404	106	15	2	11	38	31	102	.319	.391

Last Five Years

	Avg	AB	H	2B	3B	HR	RBI	BB	SO	OBP	SLG		Avg	AB	H	2B	3B	HR	RBI	BB	SO	OBP	SLG
Grass	.247	1371	339	47	11	25	131	109	330	.306	.352	June	.254	425	106	12	3	10	50	40	106	.318	.367
Turf	.255	1100	280	55	13	23	117	86	249	.319	.391	July	.263	434	114	21	3	10	47	26	79	.316	.394
First Pitch	.353	303	107	19	6	10	50	10	1	.379	.554	August	.210	434	91	13	6	2	32	41	118	.285	.281
Ahead on Count	.376	465	175	27	4	21	75	102	0	.494	.587	September/October	.266	432	115	27	5	9	45	29	94	.326	.414
Behind on Count	.212	943	200	38	4	15	75	0	318	.219	.309	Pre-All Star	.257	1305	335	46	11	30	141	103	311	.314	.378
Two Strikes	.162	1274	206	29	9	11	75	77	578	.215	.224	Post-All Star	.244	1166	284	56	13	18	107	92	268	.309	.360

Batter vs. Pitcher (since 1984)

Hits Best Against	Avg	AB	H	2B	3B	HR	RBI	BB	SO	OBP	SLG	Hits Worst Against	Avg	AB	H	2B	3B	HR	RBI	BB	SO	OBP	SLG
Bud Black	.500	16	8	1	0	3	2	0		.556	.938	Mark Langston	.063	16	1	0	0	0	1	3	5	.211	.063
Mike Bielecki	.474	19	9	2	0	2	8	2	2	.478	.895	Craig Lefferts	.091	22	2	1	0	0	1	3	3	.200	.136
Jim Gott	.455	11	5	1	0	1	3	0	2	.455	.818	Steve Avery	.120	25	3	1	0	0	2	0	6	.120	.160
Todd Worrell	.375	16	6	3	1	1	7	0	2	.375	.875	Roger McDowell	.125	24	3	0	0	0	3	3	3	.214	.125
John Dopson	.333	12	4	0	2	1	3	0	1	.333	.917	Danny Darwin	.133	15	2	0	0	0	1		3	.176	.133

Rey Sanchez — Cubs
Bats Right (groundball hitter)

	Avg	G	AB	R	H	2B	3B	HR	RBI	BB	SO	HBP	GDP	SB	CS	OBP	SLG	IBB	SH	SF	#Pit	#P/PA	GB	FB	G/F
1992 Season	.251	74	255	24	64	14	3	1	19	10	17	3	7	2	1	.285	.341	1	5	2	797	2.95	120	55	2.18
Career (1991-1992)	.252	87	278	25	70	14	3	1	21	14	20	3	7	2	1	.293	.335	1	5	2	893	3.01	126	61	2.07

1992 Season

	Avg	AB	H	2B	3B	HR	RBI	BB	SO	OBP	SLG		Avg	AB	H	2B	3B	HR	RBI	BB	SO	OBP	SLG
vs. Left	.283	106	30	8	2	0	8	7	4	.327	.396	Scoring Posn	.250	48	12	3	1	0	16	3	3	.296	.354
vs. Right	.228	149	34	6	1	1	11	3	13	.255	.302	Close & Late	.185	54	10	1	0	0	3	2	2	.237	.204
Home	.300	130	39	9	1	1	11	5	11	.328	.408	None on/out	.272	81	22	4	0	1		2	4	.306	.358
Away	.200	125	25	5	2	0	8	5	6	.241	.272	Batting #1	.187	75	14	2	0	1	3	3	7	.238	.253
First Pitch	.279	61	17	4	2	0	6	0	0	.286	.410	Batting #8	.284	169	48	12	3	0	16	7	9	.313	.391
Ahead on Count	.366	71	26	4	1	1	6	7	0	.423	.493	Other	.182	11	2	0	0	0	0	0	1	.182	.182
Behind on Count	.162	68	11	2	0	0	4	0	12	.186	.191	Pre-All Star	.245	106	26	4	3	0	10	3	6	.270	.340
Two Strikes	.164	67	11	4	0	0	4	3	17	.197	.224	Post-All Star	.255	149	38	10	0	1	9	7	11	.296	.342

Ryne Sandberg — Cubs
Bats Right

	Avg	G	AB	R	H	2B	3B	HR	RBI	BB	SO	HBP	GDP	SB	CS	OBP	SLG	IBB	SH	SF	#Pit	#P/PA	GB	FB	G/F
1992 Season	.304	158	612	100	186	32	8	26	87	68	73	1	13	17	6	.371	.510	4	0	6	2644	3.85	241	185	1.30
Last Five Years	.291	783	3036	501	883	142	26	141	432	318	422	9	53	104	36	.357	.494	27	3	31	12462	3.67	1166	918	1.27

1992 Season

	Avg	AB	H	2B	3B	HR	RBI	BB	SO	OBP	SLG		Avg	AB	H	2B	3B	HR	RBI	BB	SO	OBP	SLG
vs. Left	.340	206	70	13	4	4	24	23	19	.403	.500	Scoring Posn	.296	125	37	5	2	7	54	19	17	.373	.536
vs. Right	.286	406	116	19	4	22	63	45	54	.355	.515	Close & Late	.312	109	34	3	0	4	15	11	18	.377	.450
Groundball	.303	251	76	12	5	7	29	26	27	.367	.474	None on/out	.320	122	39	8	1	5	5	5	15	.394	.525
Flyball	.327	150	49	10	1	7	21	17	18	.393	.547	Batting #2	.319	304	97	14	5	16	41	36	32	.390	.556
Home	.307	300	92	19	6	16	46	41	35	.386	.570	Batting #3	.322	202	65	14	3	6	31	18	27	.372	.510
Away	.301	312	94	13	2	10	41	27	38	.357	.452	Other	.226	106	24	4	0	4	15	14	17	.317	.377
Day	.328	314	103	17	3	17	52	38	37	.397	.564	April	.250	64	16	3	1	2	11	8	5	.333	.422
Night	.279	298	83	15	5	9	35	30	36	.343	.453	May	.284	109	31	5	0	5	15	13	17	.361	.468
Grass	.300	423	127	23	7	20	62	49	50	.370	.530	June	.294	109	32	8	2	3	18	10	13	.344	.486
Turf	.312	189	59	9	1	6	25	19	23	.374	.466	July	.316	95	30	4	2	3	9	13	10	.398	.495
First Pitch	.400	20	8	1	0	2	3	5	0	.520	.750	August	.288	118	34	6	2	3	11	12	8	.351	.449
Ahead on Count	.387	150	58	12	4	9	28	36	0	.505	.700	September/October	.368	117	43	6	1	10	23	12	20	.426	.692
Behind on Count	.253	237	60	11	2	9	33	0	43	.251	.430	Pre-All Star	.279	323	90	19	4	11	47	41	42	.357	.464
Two Strikes	.237	266	63	9	0	12	36	27	73	.305	.406	Post-All Star	.332	289	96	13	4	15	40	27	31	.388	.561

1992 By Position

Position	Avg	AB	H	2B	3B	HR	RBI	BB	SO	OBP	SLG	G	GS	Innings	PO	A	E	DP	Fld Pct	Rng Fctr	In Zone	Outs	Zone Rtg	MLB Zone
As 2b	.304	611	186	32	8	26	87	68	72	.372	.511	157	157	1379.1	283	539	8	93	.990	5.36	573	542	.946	.892

Last Five Years

	Avg	AB	H	2B	3B	HR	RBI	BB	SO	OBP	SLG		Avg	AB	H	2B	3B	HR	RBI	BB	SO	OBP	SLG
vs. Left	.312	965	301	61	8	36	120	130	116	.392	.504	Scoring Posn	.289	641	185	24	10	29	265	111	93	.379	.493
vs. Right	.281	2071	582	81	18	105	312	188	306	.339	.490	Close & Late	.278	507	141	15	4	19	72	61	91	.354	.436
Groundball	.301	1093	329	51	8	47	150	99	138	.359	.491	None on/out	.260	621	174	29	6	39	39	64	89	.348	.535
Flyball	.280	729	204	33	7	35	100	81	89	.350	.488	Batting #2	.295	1836	542	87	16	97	253	175	248	.354	.519
Home	.310	1511	468	73	19	82	254	165	203	.376	.546	Batting #3	.293	782	229	40	5	31	125	93	112	.368	.476
Away	.272	1525	415	69	7	59	178	153	219	.337	.443	Other	.258	418	112	15	5	13	54	50	62	.345	.421
Day	.308	1638	505	78	14	81	246	168	213	.371	.521	April	.233	407	95	16	2	9	40	32	52	.268	.349
Night	.270	1398	378	64	12	60	186	150	209	.340	.462	May	.322	525	169	30	4	25	75	48	67	.379	.537
Grass	.298	2149	641	99	23	106	333	220	291	.361	.514	June	.302	523	158	25	6	32	89	62	67	.376	.556
Turf	.273	887	242	43	3	35	99	98	131	.345	.446	July	.266	473	126	18	4	14	55	57	61	.345	.410
First Pitch	.374	230	86	14	1	19	38	13	0	.411	.691	August	.286	549	157	22	6	29	77	62	90	.355	.506
Ahead on Count	.343	796	273	56	8	50	138	166	0	.453	.622	September/October	.318	559	178	31	4	32	96	57	85	.378	.560

Last Five Years

	Avg	AB	H	2B	3B	HR	RBI	BB	SO	OBP	SLG
Behind on Count	.248	1107	275	38	8	43	142	2	239	.251	.414
Two Strikes	.220	1278	261	36	7	43	138	128	422	.290	.360

	Avg	AB	H	2B	3B	HR	RBI	BB	SO	OBP	SLG
Pre-All Star	.289	1608	464	77	13	69	223	164	208	.354	.481
Post-All Star	.293	1428	419	65	13	72	209	154	214	.360	.508

Batter vs. Pitcher (since 1984)

Hits Best Against	Avg	AB	H	2B	3B	HR	RBI	BB	SO	OBP	SLG
Randy Tomlin	.560	25	14	2	2	1	5	2	0	.593	.920
Charlie Leibrandt	.500	16	8	1	0	2	3	3	1	.579	.938
Wally Whitehurst	.450	20	9	1	2	2	5	1	3	.476	1.000
Don Carman	.444	18	8	1	1	2	5	4	3	.545	.944
Darryl Kile	.375	8	3	2	0	1	4	3	1	.500	1.000

Hits Worst Against	Avg	AB	H	2B	3B	HR	RBI	BB	SO	OBP	SLG
Mark Langston	.000	8	0	0	0	0	0	3	3	.273	.000
Jeff Reardon	.071	14	1	0	0	0	2	0	4	.071	.071
Larry Andersen	.091	33	3	0	0	0	3	0	8	.068	.091
Brian Fisher	.118	17	2	0	0	0	0	1	3	.167	.118
Ramon Martinez	.125	24	3	0	0	1	1	0	4	.125	.250

Deion Sanders — Braves
Bats Left

	Avg	G	AB	R	H	2B	3B	HR	RBI	BB	SO	HBP	GDP	SB	CS	OBP	SLG	IBB	SH	SF	#Pit	#P/PA	GB	FB	G/F
1992 Season	.304	97	303	54	92	6	14	8	28	18	52	2	5	26	9	.346	.495	0	1	1	1064	3.28	111	80	1.39
Career (1989-1992)	.245	222	593	101	145	11	18	17	57	46	110	3	8	46	14	.301	.410	1	2	2	2204	3.42	226	158	1.43

1992 Season

	Avg	AB	H	2B	3B	HR	RBI	BB	SO	OBP	SLG
vs. Left	.271	48	13	1	4	2	5	2	12	.300	.583
vs. Right	.310	255	79	5	10	6	23	16	40	.354	.478
Groundball	.291	141	41	1	6	5	15	6	21	.322	.489
Flyball	.415	65	27	2	4	3	4	5	10	.465	.708
Home	.261	138	36	2	4	5	14	13	27	.329	.442
Away	.339	165	56	4	10	3	14	5	25	.360	.539
Day	.300	80	24	1	3	2	7	6	17	.345	.463
Night	.305	223	68	5	11	6	21	12	35	.346	.507
Grass	.282	213	60	3	9	7	19	17	38	.336	.479
Turf	.356	90	32	3	5	1	9	1	14	.370	.533
First Pitch	.359	64	23	0	4	2	7	0	0	.359	.578
Ahead on Count	.360	75	27	3	3	2	12	6	0	.410	.560
Behind on Count	.241	108	26	3	4	4	7	0	35	.248	.454
Two Strikes	.179	106	19	1	2	3	6	12	52	.269	.311

	Avg	AB	H	2B	3B	HR	RBI	BB	SO	OBP	SLG
Scoring Posn	.266	64	17	1	5	0	19	7	11	.333	.438
Close & Late	.295	44	13	3	3	3	8	5	9	.392	.705
None on/out	.345	119	41	2	3	5	5	5	21	.371	.538
Batting #1	.306	229	70	4	12	7	21	11	39	.336	.520
Batting #2	.293	58	17	2	2	0	6	5	10	.359	.397
Other	.313	16	5	0	0	1	1	2	3	.421	.500
April	.329	82	27	4	6	2	4	7	12	.382	.598
May	.344	61	21	0	3	0	5	3	9	.375	.443
June	.354	48	17	0	2	4	7	5	10	.415	.688
July	.220	41	9	0	2	2	6	1	9	.250	.463
August	.262	61	16	2	1	0	6	1	10	.286	.328
September/October	.200	10	2	0	0	0	0	1	2	.273	.200
Pre-All Star	.317	221	70	4	12	8	20	16	38	.361	.552
Post-All Star	.268	82	22	2	2	0	8	2	14	.302	.341

1992 By Position

Position	Avg	AB	H	2B	3B	HR	RBI	BB	SO	OBP	SLG	G	GS	Innings	PO	A	E	DP	Fld Pct	Rng Fctr	In Zone	Outs	Zone Rtg	MLB Zone
As Pinch Hitter	.357	14	5	0	0	1	1	1	1	.438	.571	16	0	---	---	---	---	---	---	---	---	---	---	---
As lf	.279	43	12	2	1	0	4	1	7	.311	.372	12	9	87.2	25	0	0	0	1.000	2.57	30	24	.800	.809
As cf	.303	221	67	3	12	5	21	15	39	.346	.493	60	55	477.1	137	2	2	0	.986	2.62	155	134	.865	.824

Career (1989-1992)

	Avg	AB	H	2B	3B	HR	RBI	BB	SO	OBP	SLG
vs. Left	.208	96	20	2	5	2	7	6	29	.255	.396
vs. Right	.252	497	125	9	13	15	50	40	81	.310	.412
Groundball	.266	222	59	4	6	7	24	17	35	.320	.432
Flyball	.303	152	46	4	6	8	17	13	3	.361	.566
Home	.229	275	63	2	6	8	29	28	56	.305	.367
Away	.258	318	82	9	12	9	28	18	54	.298	.447
Day	.233	163	38	3	4	4	10	14	28	.292	.374
Night	.249	430	107	8	14	13	47	32	82	.305	.423
Grass	.232	422	98	4	12	13	39	40	81	.300	.391
Turf	.275	171	47	7	6	4	18	6	29	.303	.456
First Pitch	.278	108	30	3	3	0	10	1	0	.284	.435
Ahead on Count	.298	141	42	7	4	3	17	20	0	.387	.468
Behind on Count	.198	202	40	3	6	9	22	0	63	.205	.406
Two Strikes	.162	228	37	2	4	6	18	25	110	.247	.285

	Avg	AB	H	2B	3B	HR	RBI	BB	SO	OBP	SLG
Scoring Posn	.270	137	37	2	5	3	41	22	27	.366	.423
Close & Late	.212	85	18	3	4	3	10	12	16	.323	.447
None on/out	.264	212	56	3	5	7	7	9	33	.297	.425
Batting #1	.270	378	102	5	16	12	35	27	64	.319	.463
Batting #2	.222	99	22	3	2	2	11	9	20	.294	.354
Other	.181	116	21	3	0	3	11	10	26	.250	.284
April	.269	145	39	4	8	4	11	15	25	.338	.490
May	.269	108	29	1	4	1	9	8	18	.319	.380
June	.221	131	29	1	2	5	12	13	23	.292	.374
July	.211	123	26	1	3	6	15	8	29	.267	.415
August	.262	61	16	2	1	0	6	1	10	.286	.328
September/October	.240	25	6	2	0	1	4	1	5	.269	.440
Pre-All Star	.242	426	103	6	15	12	36	38	76	.303	.411
Post-All Star	.251	167	42	5	3	5	21	8	34	.296	.407

Batter vs. Pitcher (career)

Hits Best Against	Avg	AB	H	2B	3B	HR	RBI	BB	SO	OBP	SLG
David Cone	.600	10	6	0	0	1	1	1	1	.636	.900
Tim Belcher	.474	19	9	1	2	1	1	2	2	.524	.895
Orel Hershiser	.375	16	6	0	1	1	1	1	2	.412	.688
Andy Benes	.364	11	4	0	1	0	0	0	1	.364	.545
Pete Harnisch	.333	15	5	1	0	1	2	2		.412	.533

Hits Worst Against	Avg	AB	H	2B	3B	HR	RBI	BB	SO	OBP	SLG
Dennis Martinez	.133	15	2	0	0	0	2	0	4	.133	.133
Doug Drabek	.154	13	2	1	0	0	1	0	2	.154	.231
Mike Morgan	.182	11	2	0	0	1	2	0	0	.182	.455
Ramon Martinez	.214	14	3	1	0	0	2	1	0	.267	.286

Reggie Sanders — Reds
Bats Right

	Avg	G	AB	R	H	2B	3B	HR	RBI	BB	SO	HBP	GDP	SB	CS	OBP	SLG	IBB	SH	SF	#Pit	#P/PA	GB	FB	G/F
1992 Season	.270	116	385	62	104	26	6	12	36	48	98	4	6	16	7	.356	.462	2	0	1	1685	3.85	108	104	1.04
Career (1991-1992)	.264	125	425	68	112	26	6	13	39	48	107	4	7	17	8	.343	.445	2	0	1	1825	3.82	120	119	1.01

1992 Season

	Avg	AB	H	2B	3B	HR	RBI	BB	SO	OBP	SLG
vs. Left	.314	175	55	15	4	7	18	19	30	.391	.566

	Avg	AB	H	2B	3B	HR	RBI	BB	SO	OBP	SLG
Scoring Posn	.184	98	18	3	1	0	19	11	38	.277	.235

1992 Season

	Avg	AB	H	2B	3B	HR	RBI	BB	SO	OBP	SLG		Avg	AB	H	2B	3B	HR	RBI	BB	SO	OBP	SLG
vs. Right	.233	210	49	11	2	5	18	29	68	.328	.376	Close & Late	.308	65	20	5	0	2	8	9	21	.392	.477
Groundball	.281	128	36	9	2	2	12	15	38	.354	.430	None on/out	.250	88	22	5	0	2	2	14	23	.353	.375
Flyball	.173	75	13	2	0	1	4	22	25	.380	.240	Batting #1	.282	71	20	4	1	3	8	13	13	.393	.493
Home	.244	205	50	14	3	6	22	32	51	.353	.429	Batting #2	.229	105	24	9	1	4	7	14	28	.336	.448
Away	.300	180	54	12	3	6	14	16	47	.360	.500	Other	.287	209	60	13	4	5	21	21	57	.353	.459
Day	.252	119	30	10	1	2	12	20	35	.362	.403	April	.315	73	23	4	2	2	6	6	16	.367	.507
Night	.278	266	74	16	5	10	24	28	63	.354	.489	May	.316	38	12	4	0	0	7	6	9	.413	.421
Grass	.271	118	32	6	2	3	7	8	24	.323	.432	June	.235	81	19	5	1	2	8	6	21	.287	.395
Turf	.270	267	72	20	4	9	29	40	74	.370	.476	July	.321	28	9	3	2	0	0	2	9	.367	.571
First Pitch	.279	61	17	2	1	4	7	2	1	.302	.541	August	.253	91	23	5	1	6	8	16	23	.376	.527
Ahead on Count	.391	69	27	5	0	3	10	22	0	.543	.594	September/October	.243	74	18	5	0	2	7	12	20	.356	.392
Behind on Count	.254	126	32	10	1	3	11	0	44	.271	.421	Pre-All Star	.283	219	62	16	4	4	21	20	55	.344	.447
Two Strikes	.169	195	33	11	3	0	8	24	97	.266	.256	Post-All Star	.253	166	42	10	2	8	15	28	43	.371	.482

1992 By Position

Position	Avg	AB	H	2B	3B	HR	RBI	BB	SO	OBP	SLG	G	GS	Innings	PO	A	E	DP	Fld Pct	Rng Fctr	In Zone	Outs	Zone Rtg	MLB Zone
As Pinch Hitter	.273	11	3	1	0	1	2	0	4	.273	.636	11	0	---	---	---	---	---	---	---	---	---	---	---
As lf	.213	108	23	6	3	2	9	15	33	.317	.380	53	26	275.2	57	3	0	1	1.000	1.96	60	52	.867	.809
As cf	.293	266	78	19	3	9	25	33	61	.375	.489	77	70	600.2	205	8	6	3	.973	3.19	241	205	.851	.824

Scott Sanderson — Yankees

Pitches Right (flyball pitcher)

	ERA	W	L	Sv	G	GS	IP	BB	SO	Avg	H	2B	3B	HR	RBI	OBP	SLG	CG	ShO	Sup	QS	#P/S	SB	CS	GB	FB	G/F
1992 Season	4.93	12	11	0	33	33	193.1	64	104	.286	220	35	9	28	104	.340	.464	2	1	6.24	17	95	18	8	237	277	0.86
Last Five Years	4.16	57	43	0	149	124	769.1	193	454	.265	793	150	24	94	358	.310	.426	8	4	5.31	56	90	64	25	908	1094	0.83

1992 Season

	ERA	W	L	Sv	G	GS	IP	H	HR	BB	SO		Avg	AB	H	2B	3B	HR	RBI	BB	SO	OBP	SLG
Home	5.47	5	6	0	17	17	97.0	117	20	32	51	vs. Left	.300	367	110	14	4	13	50	38	40	.362	.466
Away	4.39	7	5	0	16	16	96.1	103	8	32	53	vs. Right	.274	402	110	21	5	15	54	26	64	.319	.463
Day	6.07	4	2	0	11	11	59.1	76	10	21	39	Inning 1-6	.286	707	202	32	9	27	101	55	98	.335	.471
Night	4.43	8	9	0	22	22	134.0	144	18	43	65	Inning 7+	.290	62	18	3	0	1		3	6	.389	.387
Grass	5.03	11	11	0	30	30	175.1	203	27	55	98	None on	.306	431	132	20	7	16	16	29	55	.351	.497
Turf	4.00	1	0	0	3	3	18.0	17	1	9	6	Runners on	.260	338	88	15	2	12	88	35	49	.326	.423
April	5.34	2	1	0	5	5	28.2	36	7	10	15	Scoring Posn	.309	162	50	10	1	5	72	22	24	.376	.475
May	4.66	2	1	0	6	6	36.2	45	7	12	23	Close & Late	.294	17	5	1	0	0	1	4	3	.455	.353
June	3.65	3	3	0	6	6	37.0	33	4	14	22	None on/out	.323	195	63	12	4	7	7	15	24	.371	.533
July	6.99	1	3	0	5	5	28.1	42	3	8	13	vs. 1st Batr (relief)	.000	0	0	0	0	0	0	0	0	.000	.000
August	2.79	3	0	0	6	6	38.2	29	3	13	19	First Inning Pitched	.266	128	34	3	2	3	18	11	24	.324	.391
September/October	7.88	1	3	0	5	5	24.0	35	4	7	12	First 75 Pitches	.271	583	158	22	7	19	78	44	85	.321	.431
Starter	4.93	12	11	0	33	33	193.1	220	28	64	104	Pitch 76-90	.333	108	36	5	2	7	15	5	9	.362	.611
Reliever	0.00	0	0	0	0	0	0.0	0	0	0	0	Pitch 91-105	.352	54	19	5	0	2	8	7	6	.426	.556
0-3 Days Rest	0.00	0	0	0	0	0	0.0	0	0	0	0	Pitch 106+	.292	24	7	3	0	0	3	8	4	.469	.417
4 Days Rest	4.95	7	7	0	22	22	132.2	154	20	43	73	First Pitch	.345	116	40	5	4	5	16	4	0	.369	.586
5+ Days Rest	4.90	5	4	0	11	11	60.2	66	8	21	31	Ahead on Count	.224	362	81	12	3	8	41	0	91	.226	.340
Pre-All Star	4.60	8	6	0	19	19	115.1	134	21	37	67	Behind on Count	.368	171	63	11	1	8	31	30	0	.454	.585
Post-All Star	5.42	4	5	0	14	14	78.0	86	7	27	37	Two Strikes	.205	342	70	11	2	8	38	30	104	.268	.319

Last Five Years

	ERA	W	L	Sv	G	GS	IP	H	HR	BB	SO		Avg	AB	H	2B	3B	HR	RBI	BB	SO	OBP	SLG
Home	4.38	24	24	0	72	57	364.0	387	55	93	209	vs. Left	.270	1576	425	72	14	49	195	116	216	.319	.426
Away	3.97	33	19	0	77	67	405.1	406	39	100	245	vs. Right	.260	1413	368	78	10	45	163	77	238	.300	.425
Day	4.22	16	18	0	59	43	288.0	289	35	81	184	Inning 1-6	.267	2655	709	136	20	85	332	169	405	.311	.429
Night	4.13	41	25	0	90	81	481.1	504	59	112	270	Inning 7+	.251	334	84	14	4	9	26	24	49	.301	.398
Grass	4.26	46	38	0	120	103	633.1	671	82	157	374	None on	.262	1813	475	90	14	54	54	99	271	.303	.416
Turf	3.71	11	5	0	29	21	136.0	122	12	36	80	Runners on	.270	1176	318	60	10	40	304	94	183	.320	.440
April	5.02	7	5	0	18	18	98.2	112	19	26	50	Scoring Posn	.277	622	172	34	5	17	245	68	106	.337	.429
May	3.27	13	4	0	21	21	129.1	128	10	28	81	Close & Late	.237	135	32	4	2	2	9	14	20	.311	.341
June	3.56	11	9	0	23	23	144.0	143	13	39	78	None on/out	.283	789	223	40	9	20	20	37	107	.317	.432
July	5.19	7	9	0	23	23	137.0	156	21	24	78	vs. 1st Batr (relief)	.304	23	7	2	0	0	4	2	5	.360	.391
August	3.70	10	6	0	30	20	143.1	129	19	45	102	First Inning Pitched	.279	580	162	25	5	15	82	42	108	.327	.417
September/October	4.54	9	10	0	34	19	117.0	125	12	31	65	First 75 Pitches	.268	2377	637	115	18	74	290	144	369	.310	.425
Starter	4.17	55	39	0	124	124	727.1	750	89	181	426	Pitch 76-90	.275	334	92	17	4	16	48	22	39	.320	.494
Reliever	4.07	2	4	0	25	0	42.0	43	5	12	28	Pitch 91-105	.221	195	43	10	1	3	14	16	30	.280	.326
0-3 Days Rest	3.31	3	1	0	6	6	32.2	31	3	9	12	Pitch 106+	.253	83	21	8	1	1	6	11	16	.340	.410
4 Days Rest	4.28	36	29	0	83	83	500.2	523	67	133	306	First Pitch	.315	428	135	26	7	19	70	12	0	.335	.542
5+ Days Rest	4.04	16	9	0	35	35	194.0	196	19	39	108	Ahead on Count	.217	1435	311	51	7	26	158	0	401	.219	.316
Pre-All Star	4.03	34	20	0	69	69	415.1	440	51	100	233	Behind on Count	.334	628	210	49	7	28	92	96	0	.418	.568
Post-All Star	4.32	23	23	0	80	55	354.0	353	43	93	221	Two Strikes	.200	1378	275	49	6	25	128	85	454	.247	.298

Pitcher vs. Batter (since 1984)

Pitches Best Vs.	Avg	AB	H	2B	3B	HR	RBI	BB	SO	OBP	SLG	Pitches Worst Vs.	Avg	AB	H	2B	3B	HR	RBI	BB	SO	OBP	SLG
Greg Briley	.000	20	0	0	0	0	0	0	3	.000	.000	Shane Mack	.700	10	7	0	0	3	6	1	0	.727	1.600

Pitcher vs. Batter (since 1984)

Pitches Best Vs.	Avg	AB	H	2B	3B	HR	RBI	BB	SO	OBP	SLG	Pitches Worst Vs.	Avg	AB	H	2B	3B	HR	RBI	BB	SO	OBP	SLG
Herm Winningham	.000	11	0	0	0	0	0	0	2	.000	.000	Scott Fletcher	.550	20	11	1	0	2	7	0	1	.550	.900
Lance Parrish	.048	21	1	1	0	0	2	2	7	.125	.095	Julio Franco	.500	14	7	0	0	2	4	3	0	.588	.929
Brian McRae	.077	13	1	0	0	0	1	0	2	.077	.077	Joe Carter	.467	15	7	1	1	1	8	1	1	.471	.867
Omar Vizquel	.105	19	2	0	0	0	1	0	1	.105	.105	Robin Yount	.333	9	3	0	1	1	4	5	0	.571	.889

Benito Santiago — Padres
Bats Right

	Avg	G	AB	R	H	2B	3B	HR	RBI	BB	SO	HBP	GDP	SB	CS	OBP	SLG	IBB	SH	SF	#Pit	#P/PA	GB	FB	G/F
1992 Season	.251	106	386	37	97	21	0	10	42	21	52	0	14	2	5	.287	.383	1	0	4	1411	3.43	134	122	1.10
Last Five Years	.254	626	2264	238	576	89	13	64	290	121	392	9	66	41	33	.292	.390	16	9	25	8050	3.33	734	715	1.03

1992 Season

	Avg	AB	H	2B	3B	HR	RBI	BB	SO	OBP	SLG		Avg	AB	H	2B	3B	HR	RBI	BB	SO	OBP	SLG
vs. Left	.292	130	38	7	0	7	17	7	17	.326	.508	Scoring Posn	.262	103	27	2	0	1	30	5	14	.286	.311
vs. Right	.230	256	59	14	0	3	25	14	35	.267	.320	Close & Late	.258	66	17	5	0	3	8	6	12	.315	.470
Groundball	.257	175	45	8	0	3	22	6	18	.280	.354	None on/out	.228	92	21	8	0	3	3	6	17	.276	.413
Flyball	.296	81	24	6	0	4	10	5	17	.330	.519	Batting #5	.252	250	63	14	0	5	31	15	37	.291	.368
Home	.308	195	60	10	0	8	30	7	28	.328	.482	Batting #6	.246	122	30	7	0	5	11	5	11	.273	.426
Away	.194	191	37	11	0	2	12	14	24	.246	.283	Other	.286	14	4	0	0	0	1	4	.333	.286
Day	.209	86	18	3	0	2	8	3	12	.233	.314	April	.239	88	21	3	0	1	8	3	9	.264	.307
Night	.263	300	79	18	0	8	34	18	40	.302	.403	May	.274	95	26	7	0	3	16	6	12	.311	.442
Grass	.287	272	78	13	0	9	37	16	37	.324	.434	June	.000	0	0	0	0	0	0	0	0	.000	.000
Turf	.167	114	19	8	0	1	5	5	15	.198	.263	July	.298	57	17	3	0	0	7	5	5	.349	.351
First Pitch	.344	61	21	5	0	2	11	1	0	.344	.525	August	.222	90	20	5	0	5	7	1	11	.231	.444
Ahead on Count	.265	98	26	4	0	4	14	9	0	.324	.429	September/October	.232	56	13	3	0	1	4	6	15	.302	.339
Behind on Count	.228	136	31	2	0	1	10	0	31	.228	.265	Pre-All Star	.250	192	48	10	0	4	24	9	23	.281	.365
Two Strikes	.209	153	32	10	0	2	8	11	52	.262	.314	Post-All Star	.253	194	49	11	0	6	18	12	29	.293	.402

1992 By Position

Position	Avg	AB	H	2B	3B	HR	RBI	BB	SO	OBP	SLG	G	GS	Innings	PO	A	E	DP	Fld Pct	Rng Fctr	In Zone	Outs	Zone Rtg	MLB Zone
As c	.251	382	96	21	0	10	42	21	51	.287	.385	103	98	885.1	584	53	12	6	.982	---	---	---	---	---

Last Five Years

	Avg	AB	H	2B	3B	HR	RBI	BB	SO	OBP	SLG		Avg	AB	H	2B	3B	HR	RBI	BB	SO	OBP	SLG
vs. Left	.269	707	190	29	4	23	93	44	125	.310	.419	Scoring Posn	.237	621	147	18	4	19	223	40	127	.275	.370
vs. Right	.248	1557	386	60	9	41	197	77	267	.283	.377	Close & Late	.294	419	123	16	3	13	52	26	72	.335	.439
Groundball	.260	855	222	30	6	18	110	40	124	.293	.372	None on/out	.255	517	132	19	2	13	13	29	92	.297	.375
Flyball	.246	509	125	18	2	20	67	21	118	.273	.407	Batting #5	.245	854	209	31	2	21	124	43	151	.279	.359
Home	.262	1144	300	42	8	30	143	55	196	.295	.392	Batting #6	.261	911	238	38	7	27	107	52	155	.298	.407
Away	.246	1120	276	47	5	34	147	66	196	.288	.388	Other	.259	499	129	20	4	16	59	26	86	.301	.411
Day	.284	486	138	16	3	18	70	31	88	.330	.440	April	.276	387	107	14	1	12	52	11	55	.298	.411
Night	.246	1778	438	73	10	46	220	90	304	.281	.376	May	.226	451	102	18	2	9	54	19	75	.255	.335
Grass	.267	1684	449	63	11	57	237	86	296	.302	.419	June	.280	296	83	11	2	7	36	19	63	.323	.402
Turf	.219	580	127	26	2	7	53	35	96	.264	.307	July	.276	275	76	15	2	6	27	20	44	.327	.411
First Pitch	.324	460	149	26	0	17	84	11	0	.333	.491	August	.245	421	103	13	5	14	45	25	73	.288	.399
Ahead on Count	.304	457	139	22	3	18	69	50	1	.369	.484	September/October	.242	434	105	18	1	16	76	27	82	.285	.399
Behind on Count	.224	772	173	22	5	19	87	0	228	.229	.339	Pre-All Star	.257	1216	312	45	5	31	145	50	206	.285	.378
Two Strikes	.165	919	152	27	5	15	77	55	390	.216	.255	Post-All Star	.252	1048	264	44	8	33	145	71	184	.299	.404

Batter vs. Pitcher (career)

Hits Best Against	Avg	AB	H	2B	3B	HR	RBI	BB	SO	OBP	SLG	Hits Worst Against	Avg	AB	H	2B	3B	HR	RBI	BB	SO	OBP	SLG
Paul Assenmacher	.444	9	4	1	0	0	2	2	2	.545	.556	Ted Power	.063	16	1	0	0	0	1	0	3	.063	.063
Zane Smith	.429	28	12	3	0	5	10	2	3	.467	1.071	Pete Harnisch	.067	15	1	1	0	0	0	0	4	.067	.133
Trevor Wilson	.417	12	5	2	1	0	5	0	2	.417	.750	Larry Andersen	.077	13	1	0	0	0	2	1	3	.143	.077
Rick Sutcliffe	.385	13	5	1	0	1	2	2	2	.467	.692	Chris Nabholz	.091	11	1	0	0	0	1	0	2	.091	.091
Don Robinson	.344	32	11	1	1	3	6	2	5	.382	.719	Dave Smith	.100	10	1	0	0	0	5	0	1	.083	.100

Nelson Santovenia — White Sox
Bats Right

	Avg	G	AB	R	H	2B	3B	HR	RBI	BB	SO	HBP	GDP	SB	CS	OBP	SLG	IBB	SH	SF	#Pit	#P/PA	GB	FB	G/F
1992 Season	.333	2	3	1	1	0	0	1	2	0	0	0	0	0	0	.333	1.333	0	0	0	9	3.00	1	2	0.50
Last Five Years	.234	291	875	77	205	42	4	22	116	58	163	6	25	4	7	.281	.367	7	6	17	3334	3.49	291	287	1.01

1992 Season

	Avg	AB	H	2B	3B	HR	RBI	BB	SO	OBP	SLG		Avg	AB	H	2B	3B	HR	RBI	BB	SO	OBP	SLG
vs. Left	.000	0	0	0	0	0	0	0	0	.000	.000	Scoring Posn	.000	0	0	0	0	0	0	0	0	.000	.000
vs. Right	.333	3	1	0	0	1	2	0	0	.333	1.333	Close & Late	.000	0	0	0	0	0	0	0	0	.000	.000

Last Five Years

	Avg	AB	H	2B	3B	HR	RBI	BB	SO	OBP	SLG		Avg	AB	H	2B	3B	HR	RBI	BB	SO	OBP	SLG
vs. Left	.252	294	74	13	2	8	40	23	41	.305	.391	Scoring Posn	.246	236	58	10	2	5	90	24	49	.299	.369
vs. Right	.225	581	131	29	2	14	76	35	122	.269	.355	Close & Late	.259	193	50	14	2	4	29	15	37	.311	.415
Groundball	.266	346	92	21	2	6	53	22	48	.309	.390	None on/out	.151	192	29	6	0	5	5	10	41	.197	.260
Flyball	.180	211	38	7	1	5	21	13	52	.237	.294	Batting #6	.235	170	40	9	0	3	21	12	39	.285	.341

Last Five Years

	Avg	AB	H	2B	3B	HR	RBI	BB	SO	OBP	SLG		Avg	AB	H	2B	3B	HR	RBI	BB	SO	OBP	SLG
Home	.278	410	114	25	2	15	72	30	64	.324	.459	Batting #7	.229	597	137	26	3	15	76	40	107	.278	.358
Away	.196	465	91	17	2	7	44	28	99	.243	.286	Other	.259	108	26	7	1	4	19	6	17	.293	.454
Day	.229	205	47	9	1	5	20	14	43	.278	.356	April	.219	128	28	5	0	3	15	9	19	.275	.328
Night	.236	670	158	33	3	17	96	44	120	.282	.370	May	.276	123	34	8	0	2	14	14	25	.348	.390
Grass	.198	207	41	6	0	3	17	13	49	.244	.271	June	.245	139	34	8	0	5	23	8	34	.269	.410
Turf	.246	668	164	36	4	19	99	45	114	.293	.397	July	.234	141	33	6	2	5	24	9	21	.277	.411
First Pitch	.306	133	41	8	1	3	25	4	0	.329	.436	August	.227	132	30	9	0	2	11	7	27	.262	.341
Ahead on Count	.296	199	59	15	0	11	33	34	0	.397	.538	September/October	.217	212	46	6	2	5	29	11	37	.254	.335
Behind on Count	.202	342	69	18	2	7	36	0	100	.203	.327	Pre-All Star	.240	442	106	23	1	11	62	34	87	.295	.371
Two Strikes	.155	381	59	11	2	4	34	18	161	.192	.226	Post-All Star	.229	433	99	19	3	11	54	24	76	.267	.363

Batter vs. Pitcher (career)

Hits Best Against	Avg	AB	H	2B	3B	HR	RBI	BB	SO	OBP	SLG	Hits Worst Against	Avg	AB	H	2B	3B	HR	RBI	BB	SO	OBP	SLG
Joe Magrane	.429	14	6	1	0	0	5	2	1	.500	.500	Tim Belcher	.077	13	1	1	0	0	2	1	2	.143	.154
Zane Smith	.364	11	4	0	0	0	0	0	0	.364	.364	Jose DeLeon	.100	20	2	0	0	0	2	1	10	.143	.100
Bobby Ojeda	.333	12	4	2	0	0	1	0	2	.333	.500	David Cone	.167	12	2	0	0	0	0	0	4	.167	.167
Tom Glavine	.308	13	4	1	0	1	4	1	2	.333	.615	Greg Maddux	.200	15	3	0	0	0	1	0	4	.188	.200
												Pat Combs	.200	15	3	1	0	0	2	1	1	.222	.267

Mackey Sasser — Mets   Bats Left

	Avg	G	AB	R	H	2B	3B	HR	RBI	BB	SO	HBP	GDP	SB	CS	OBP	SLG	IBB	SH	SF	#Pit	#P/PA	GB	FB	G/F
1992 Season	.241	92	141	7	34	6	0	2	18	3	10	0	4	0	0	.248	.326	0	0	5	426	2.86	62	51	1.22
Last Five Years	.283	420	944	82	267	58	5	15	133	40	72	0	24	0	3	.309	.403	19	2	14	2814	2.81	338	316	1.07

1992 Season

	Avg	AB	H	2B	3B	HR	RBI	BB	SO	OBP	SLG		Avg	AB	H	2B	3B	HR	RBI	BB	SO	OBP	SLG
vs. Left	.222	18	4	0	0	0	2	0	1	.211	.222	Scoring Posn	.200	45	9	3	0	0	15	2	2	.212	.267
vs. Right	.244	123	30	6	0	2	16	3	9	.254	.341	Close & Late	.093	43	4	1	0	0	5	1	6	.109	.116
Home	.253	75	19	4	0	1	11	2	2	.263	.347	None on/out	.296	27	8	1	0	1	1	0	0	.296	.444
Away	.227	66	15	2	0	1	7	1	8	.232	.303	Batting #6	.325	40	13	2	0	1	2	1	4	.341	.450
First Pitch	.343	35	12	1	0	0	4	0	0	.333	.377	Batting #9	.128	39	5	2	0	0	3	1	4	.150	.179
Ahead on Count	.167	36	6	2	0	1	5	1	0	.179	.306	Other	.258	62	16	2	0	1	13	1	2	.250	.339
Behind on Count	.182	44	8	1	0	0	2	0	7	.182	.205	Pre-All Star	.243	74	18	4	0	0	7	2	7	.260	.297
Two Strikes	.256	43	11	2	0	1	6	2	10	.277	.372	Post-All Star	.239	67	16	2	0	2	11	1	3	.236	.358

Last Five Years

	Avg	AB	H	2B	3B	HR	RBI	BB	SO	OBP	SLG		Avg	AB	H	2B	3B	HR	RBI	BB	SO	OBP	SLG
vs. Left	.201	134	27	8	0	1	12	6	23	.232	.284	Scoring Posn	.293	263	77	11	3	7	118	25	25	.340	.460
vs. Right	.296	810	240	50	5	14	121	34	49	.322	.422	Close & Late	.216	213	46	11	3	3	27	8	23	.239	.319
Groundball	.311	325	101	20	1	5	54	12	20	.331	.425	None on/out	.295	217	64	16	1	3	3	2	12	.305	.419
Flyball	.271	210	57	14	2	4	32	2	15	.279	.414	Batting #7	.305	383	117	31	2	6	58	19	23	.337	.444
Home	.277	477	132	32	3	8	74	22	38	.305	.407	Batting #8	.245	208	51	11	1	3	26	10	18	.279	.351
Away	.289	467	135	26	2	7	59	18	34	.314	.398	Other	.280	353	99	16	2	6	49	11	31	.296	.388
Day	.316	345	109	24	4	6	54	13	30	.337	.461	April	.197	66	13	2	0	0	4	4	5	.239	.227
Night	.264	599	158	34	1	9	79	27	42	.293	.369	May	.316	114	36	7	1	5	17	7	8	.352	.526
Grass	.290	670	194	40	4	11	99	24	52	.312	.410	June	.309	188	58	13	1	1	28	13	11	.351	.404
Turf	.266	274	73	18	1	4	34	16	20	.303	.383	July	.323	201	65	17	2	5	43	2	15	.325	.502
First Pitch	.331	269	89	27	2	3	43	4	0	.336	.480	August	.238	206	49	10	1	2	16	7	21	.261	.325
Ahead on Count	.319	216	69	15	2	3	35	15	0	.361	.449	September/October	.272	169	46	9	0	2	25	7	12	.298	.361
Behind on Count	.249	281	70	11	1	6	39	1	46	.253	.359	Pre-All Star	.289	436	126	27	4	7	61	24	33	.324	.417
Two Strikes	.218	262	57	8	0	5	29	8	72	.243	.305	Post-All Star	.278	508	141	31	1	8	72	16	39	.296	.390

Batter vs. Pitcher (career)

Hits Best Against	Avg	AB	H	2B	3B	HR	RBI	BB	SO	OBP	SLG	Hits Worst Against	Avg	AB	H	2B	3B	HR	RBI	BB	SO	OBP	SLG
Mark Portugal	.444	18	8	1	1	1	5	1	2	.474	.778	Pete Smith	.182	11	2	0	0	0	1	0	0	.167	.182
Ramon Martinez	.438	16	7	2	0	1	1	0	1	.438	.750	Mark Gardner	.182	11	2	0	0	1	4	1	1	.231	.455
Bob Tewksbury	.385	13	5	1	0	0	1	0	1	.385	.462	Lee Smith	.200	15	3	1	1	0	3	0	2	.200	.400
Doug Drabek	.333	18	6	1	0	1	4	2	0	.381	.556	John Smoltz	.211	19	4	1	0	0	5	0	2	.200	.263
Jose DeLeon	.333	15	5	1	0	1	5	0	0	.333	.600	Greg Maddux	.214	28	6	1	0	0	1	0	3	.241	.250

Rich Sauveur — Royals   Pitches Left (groundball pitcher)

	ERA	W	L	Sv	G	GS	IP	BB	SO	Avg	H	2B	3B	HR	RBI	OBP	SLG	GF	IR	IRS	Hld	SvOp	SB	CS	GB	FB	G/F
1992 Season	4.40	0	1	0	8	0	14.1	8	7	.273	15	1	0	1	5	.385	.345	0	0	5	0	0	0		26	6	4.33
Last Five Years	5.66	0	1	0	18	0	20.2	12	14	.305	25	3	1	3	13	.406	.476	2	15	3	4	2	0	0	32	10	3.20

1992 Season

	ERA	W	L	Sv	G	GS	IP	H	HR	BB	SO		Avg	AB	H	2B	3B	HR	RBI	BB	SO	OBP	SLG
Home	1.13	0	0	0	4	0	8.0	6	1	3	4	vs. Left	.200	15	3	0	0	0	3	1	3	.333	.200
Away	8.53	0	0	0	4	0	6.1	9	0	5	3	vs. Right	.300	40	12	1	0	1	2	7	4	.404	.400

Steve Sax — White Sox
Bats Right (groundball hitter)

	Avg	G	AB	R	H	2B	3B	HR	RBI	BB	SO	HBP	GDP	SB	CS	OBP	SLG	IBB	SH	SF	#Pit	#P/PA	GB	FB	G/F
1992 Season	.236	143	567	74	134	26	4	4	47	43	42	2	15	30	12	.290	.317	4	12	6	2177	3.52	312	118	2.64
Last Five Years	.280	774	3117	387	872	133	15	28	265	230	221	11	74	189	61	.329	.359	17	36	25	11925	3.52	1716	614	2.79

1992 Season

	Avg	AB	H	2B	3B	HR	RBI	BB	SO	OBP	SLG		Avg	AB	H	2B	3B	HR	RBI	BB	SO	OBP	SLG
vs. Left	.229	157	36	8	0	1	7	11	7	.278	.299	Scoring Posn	.205	122	25	3	3	2	44	14	9	.285	.328
vs. Right	.239	410	98	18	4	3	40	32	35	.294	.324	Close & Late	.202	89	18	3	1	0	7	8	10	.273	.258
Groundball	.239	155	37	6	0	1	12	9	12	.287	.297	None on/out	.196	163	32	8	0	1	1	10	13	.243	.264
Flyball	.216	153	33	7	2	1	16	15	13	.284	.307	Batting #1	.248	234	58	14	0	2	14	14	19	.289	.333
Home	.226	292	66	14	4	1	21	25	20	.287	.312	Batting #2	.229	205	47	6	3	0	18	18	16	.293	.288
Away	.247	275	68	12	0	3	26	18	22	.293	.324	Other	.227	128	29	6	1	2	15	11	7	.286	.336
Day	.258	128	33	6	3	0	11	10	4	.314	.352	April	.269	67	18	3	0	0	5	7	5	.338	.313
Night	.230	439	101	20	1	4	36	33	38	.282	.308	May	.209	91	19	2	2	0	10	10	6	.282	.275
Grass	.236	479	113	23	4	2	33	39	35	.293	.313	June	.207	92	19	2	0	1	9	7	5	.263	.261
Turf	.239	88	21	3	0	2	14	4	7	.272	.341	July	.253	99	25	7	2	1	9	8	8	.312	.394
First Pitch	.298	57	17	3	1	1	7	4	0	.339	.439	August	.219	105	23	8	0	1	6	6	12	.259	.324
Ahead on Count	.293	174	51	13	1	2	19	29	0	.392	.414	September/October	.265	113	30	4	0	1	8	5	6	.297	.327
Behind on Count	.186	199	37	5	1	1	14	0	18	.187	.236	Pre-All Star	.229	288	66	10	2	2	28	28	19	.295	.299
Two Strikes	.204	186	38	6	2	1	15	11	42	.251	.274	Post-All Star	.244	279	68	16	2	2	19	15	23	.284	.337

1992 By Position

Position	Avg	AB	H	2B	3B	HR	RBI	BB	SO	OBP	SLG	G	GS	Innings	PO	A	E	DP	Fld Pct	Rng Fctr	In Zone	Outs	Zone Rtg	MLB Zone
As 2b	.237	566	134	26	4	4	47	43	42	.290	.318	141	141	1251.1	305	391	20	73	.972	5.01	458	397	867	892

Last Five Years

	Avg	AB	H	2B	3B	HR	RBI	BB	SO	OBP	SLG		Avg	AB	H	2B	3B	HR	RBI	BB	SO	OBP	SLG
vs. Left	.304	951	289	53	2	11	72	84	44	.359	.399	Scoring Posn	.281	679	191	19	7	8	235	73	53	.343	.365
vs. Right	.269	2166	583	80	13	17	193	146	177	.316	.342	Close & Late	.287	470	135	17	3	3	52	41	35	.341	.355
Groundball	.268	945	253	33	3	7	89	70	78	.318	.331	None on/out	.260	983	256	39	5	11	11	56	63	.302	.340
Flyball	.282	666	188	31	7	5	57	58	43	.340	.372	Batting #1	.286	1565	477	69	7	17	137	114	119	.332	.367
Home	.282	1548	436	72	9	14	140	123	104	.334	.367	Batting #2	.275	1293	356	56	7	9	107	102	94	.328	.350
Away	.278	1569	436	61	6	14	125	107	117	.324	.351	Other	.245	159	39	8	1	2	21	14	8	.307	.346
Day	.287	915	263	43	8	6	90	71	52	.338	.372	April	.270	385	104	9	1	4	43	31	27	.322	.330
Night	.277	2202	609	90	7	22	175	159	169	.325	.354	May	.265	514	136	22	4	5	42	54	30	.333	.352
Grass	.279	2560	713	113	12	23	209	193	176	.328	.359	June	.311	533	166	20	2	3	45	39	38	.359	.373
Turf	.285	557	159	20	3	5	56	37	45	.333	.359	July	.290	534	155	29	4	8	52	34	41	.333	.404
First Pitch	.329	340	112	14	4	6	40	8	0	.348	.447	August	.261	579	151	25	2	1	41	42	51	.311	.316
Ahead on Count	.325	757	246	48	5	11	78	142	0	.428	.445	September/October	.280	572	160	28	2	7	42	30	34	.316	.372
Behind on Count	.249	1117	278	35	5	8	86	0	127	.255	.311	Pre-All Star	.282	1611	455	59	8	16	143	136	109	.337	.359
Two Strikes	.231	1190	275	37	4	6	74	73	221	.276	.284	Post-All Star	.277	1506	417	74	7	12	122	94	112	.320	.359

Batter vs. Pitcher (since 1984)

Hits Best Against	Avg	AB	H	2B	3B	HR	RBI	BB	SO	OBP	SLG	Hits Worst Against	Avg	AB	H	2B	3B	HR	RBI	BB	SO	OBP	SLG
Todd Worrell	.600	10	6	2	1	0	1	1	0	.636	1.000	Jesse Orosco	.000	13	0	0	0	0	0	2	0	.133	.000
Ben McDonald	.545	11	6	1	1	1	3	0	0	.500	1.091	Randy Johnson	.038	26	1	1	0	0	0	2	4	.107	.077
Mike Flanagan	.500	16	8	1	0	2	4	1	0	.529	.938	John Dopson	.087	23	2	0	0	0	0	3	1	.192	.087
Neal Heaton	.471	17	8	4	0	0	1	2	1	.526	.706	Jack Morris	.100	20	2	0	0	0	0	0	1	.100	.100
Mike Henneman	.417	12	5	1	0	1	3	2	2	.438	.750	Bob Walk	.105	19	2	0	0	0	0	0	2	.105	.105

Bob Scanlan — Cubs
Pitches Right (groundball pitcher)

	ERA	W	L	Sv	G	GS	IP	BB	SO	Avg	H	2B	3B	HR	RBI	OBP	SLG	GF	IR	IRS	Hld	SvOp	SB	CS	GB	FB	G/F
1992 Season	2.89	3	6	14	69	0	87.1	30	42	.235	76	1	4	33		.301	.319	41	41	12	7	18	6	3	150	68	2.21
Career (1991-1992)	3.45	10	14	15	109	13	198.1	70	86	.254	190	32	6	9	88	.318	.349	57	56	17	9	20	11	10	360	158	2.28

1992 Season

	ERA	W	L	Sv	G	GS	IP	H	HR	BB	SO		Avg	AB	H	2B	3B	HR	RBI	BB	SO	OBP	SLG
Home	2.66	2	2	3	30	0	40.2	37	3	10	20	vs. Left	.231	160	37	7	1	3	22	20	20	.319	.344
Away	3.09	1	4	11	39	0	46.2	39	1	20	22	vs. Right	.239	163	39	6	0	1	11	10	22	.282	.294
Day	3.00	1	2	6	35	0	42.0	38	2	16	20	Inning 1-6	.182	11	2	0	0	0	2	1	2	.231	.182
Night	2.78	2	4	8	34	0	45.1	38	2	14	22	Inning 7+	.237	312	74	13	1	4	31	29	40	.303	.324
Grass	2.16	2	2	8	46	0	58.1	48	3	17	28	None on	.250	168	42	8	1	2	2	16	23	.315	.345
Turf	4.34	1	4	6	23	0	29.0	28	1	13	14	Runners on	.219	155	34	5	0	2	31	14	19	.285	.290
April	1.74	0	1	0	10	0	10.1	7	1	2	4	Scoring Posn	.208	101	21	4	0	0	27	13	15	.293	.248
May	1.80	1	0	1	11	0	15.0	10	0	9	12	Close & Late	.249	197	49	8	0	2	21	16	24	.307	.320
June	3.60	1	3	2	12	0	15.0	15	0	6	4	None on/out	.253	75	19	3	1	0	0	3	10	.282	.320
July	1.10	1	1	3	12	0	16.1	6	1	2	10	vs. 1st Batr (relief)	.231	65	15	3	0	0	2	3	9	.261	.277
August	0.66	0	0	6	11	0	13.2	6	0	5	5	First Inning Pitched	.235	230	54	11	0	2	26	21	30	.296	.309
September/October	7.41	0	1	2	13	0	17.0	30	2	6	7	First 15 Pitches	.228	219	50	10	0	2	22	18	25	.285	.301
Starter	0.00	0	0	0	0	0	0.0	0	0	0	0	Pitch 16-30	.247	85	21	2	1	1	7	10	14	.333	.329
Reliever	2.89	3	6	14	69	0	87.1	76	4	30	42	Pitch 31-45	.294	17	5	1	0	1	4	2	3	.368	.529
0 Days rest	2.39	0	1	6	22	0	26.1	21	1	5	11	Pitch 46+	.000	2	0	0	0	0	0	0	0	.000	.000
1 or 2 Days rest	4.07	2	5	5	31	0	42.0	45	3	21	26	First Pitch	.218	55	12	2	0	0	7	5	0	.290	.255

	ERA	W	L	Sv	G	GS	IP	H	HR	BB	SO		Avg	AB	H	2B	3B	HR	RBI	BB	SO	OBP	SLG
												1992 Season											
3+ Days rest	0.95	1	0	3	16	0	19.0	10	0	4	5	Ahead on Count	.228	136	31	5	1	2	14	0	39	.228	.324
Pre-All Star	2.25	2	5	3	40	0	52.0	38	2	18	27	Behind on Count	.253	75	19	4	0	2	8	13	0	.364	.387
Post-All Star	3.82	1	1	11	29	0	35.1	38	2	12	15	Two Strikes	.213	127	27	3	1	1	14	12	42	.279	.276

Steve Scarsone — Orioles
Bats Right (flyball hitter)

	Avg	G	AB	R	H	2B	3B	HR	RBI	BB	SO	HBP	GDP	SB	CS	OBP	SLG	IBB	SH	SF	#Pit	#P/PA	GB	FB	G/F
1992 Season	.167	18	30	3	5	0	0	0	0	2	12	0	0	0	0	.219	.167	0	1	0	117	3.66	5	7	0.71

											1992 Season									
	Avg	AB	H	2B	3B	HR	RBI	BB	SO	OBP	SLG		Avg	AB	H	2B	3B	HR	RBI	BB	SO	OBP	SLG
vs. Left	.125	16	2	0	0	0	0	0	9	.125	.125	Scoring Posn	.111	9	1	0	0	0	0	1	4	.200	.111
vs. Right	.214	14	3	0	0	0	2	3	.313	.214	Close & Late	.125	8	1	0	0	0	0	0	4	.125	.125

Jeff Schaefer — Mariners
Bats Right

	Avg	G	AB	R	H	2B	3B	HR	RBI	BB	SO	HBP	GDP	SB	CS	OBP	SLG	IBB	SH	SF	#Pit	#P/PA	GB	FB	G/F
1992 Season	.114	65	70	5	8	2	0	1	3	2	10	0	2	0	1	.139	.186	0	6	0	250	3.47	24	22	1.09
Career (1989-1992)	.205	219	351	37	72	12	1	2	20	10	48	2	10	8	4	.231	.262	0	15	1	1209	3.32	127	101	1.26

											1992 Season									
	Avg	AB	H	2B	3B	HR	RBI	BB	SO	OBP	SLG		Avg	AB	H	2B	3B	HR	RBI	BB	SO	OBP	SLG
vs. Left	.154	26	4	1	0	0	0	1	5	.185	.192	Scoring Posn	.059	17	1	1	0	0	1	0	4	.059	.118
vs. Right	.091	44	4	1	0	1	3	1	5	.111	.182	Close & Late	.000	7	0	0	0	0	0	0	1	.000	.000

											Career (1989-1992)									
	Avg	AB	H	2B	3B	HR	RBI	BB	SO	OBP	SLG		Avg	AB	H	2B	3B	HR	RBI	BB	SO	OBP	SLG
vs. Left	.250	156	39	7	0	1	6	6	22	.276	.314	Scoring Posn	.163	80	13	3	1	0	17	2	18	.190	.225
vs. Right	.169	195	33	5	1	1	14	4	26	.194	.221	None on/out	.181	83	15	3	0	1	1	2	8	.200	.253
Groundball	.262	107	28	1	1	2	9	3	10	.286	.346	Batting #8	.207	92	19	4	0	0	5	5	15	.263	.250
Flyball	.207	82	17	4	0	0	2	1	16	.217	.256	Batting #9	.213	202	43	7	0	2	10	5	24	.231	.277
Home	.181	155	28	5	1	0	11	4	23	.211	.226	Other	.175	57	10	1	1	0	5	0	9	.175	.228
Away	.224	196	44	7	0	2	9	6	25	.246	.291	April	.211	57	12	2	0	1	3	2	5	.237	.298
Day	.221	95	21	7	1	0	5	7	12	.282	.316	May	.111	36	4	1	0	0	1	2	8	.158	.139
Night	.199	256	51	5	0	2	15	3	36	.211	.242	June	.250	72	18	3	1	1	6	1	7	.257	.361
Grass	.198	162	32	6	0	2	7	5	21	.220	.272	July	.123	65	8	1	0	0	3	0	12	.123	.138
Turf	.212	189	40	6	1	0	13	5	27	.240	.254	August	.325	40	13	3	0	0	2	0	4	.325	.400
First Pitch	.297	74	22	7	0	0	5	0	0	.297	.392	September/October	.210	81	17	2	0	0	5	5	12	.273	.235
Ahead on Count	.203	69	14	3	1	0	6	5	0	.267	.275	Pre-All Star	.192	198	38	7	1	2	10	5	25	.211	.268
Behind on Count	.211	123	26	1	0	1	8	0	33	.216	.244	Post-All Star	.222	153	34	5	0	0	10	5	23	.256	.255
Two Strikes	.157	134	21	1	0	1	4	5	48	.191	.164												

											Batter vs. Pitcher (career)									
Hits Best Against	Avg	AB	H	2B	3B	HR	RBI	BB	SO	OBP	SLG	Hits Worst Against	Avg	AB	H	2B	3B	HR	RBI	BB	SO	OBP	SLG
Greg Hibbard	.364	11	4	1	0	1	1	0	2	.364	.727												

Rich Scheid — Astros
Pitches Left

	ERA	W	L	Sv	G	GS	IP	BB	SO	Avg	H	2B	3B	HR	RBI	OBP	SLG	GF	IR	IRS	Hld	SvOp	SB	CS	GB	FB	G/F
1992 Season	6.00	0	1	0	7	1	12.0	6	8	.280	14	3	0	2	7	.357	.460	3	0	0	0	0	2	0	18	16	1.13

										1992 Season									
	ERA	W	L	Sv	G	GS	IP	H	HR	BB	SO		Avg	AB	H	2B	3B	HR	RBI	BB	SO	OBP	SLG
Home	4.15	0	0	0	3	0	4.1	4	1	1	3	vs. Left	.200	10	2	0	0	0	0	2	2	.333	.200
Away	7.04	0	1	0	4	1	7.2	10	1	5	5	vs. Right	.300	40	12	3	0	2	7	4	6	.364	.525

Curt Schilling — Phillies
Pitches Right

	ERA	W	L	Sv	G	GS	IP	BB	SO	Avg	H	2B	3B	HR	RBI	OBP	SLG	CG	ShO	Sup	QS	#P/S	SB	CS	GB	FB	G/F
1992 Season	2.35	14	11	2	42	26	226.1	59	147	.201	165	30	4	11	61	.254	.288	10	4	3.42	22	108	7	7	282	253	1.11
Career (1988-1992)	3.05	18	22	13	142	31	371.1	130	260	.229	314	60	9	19	143	.293	.327	10	4	3.18	23	101	14	12	463	410	1.13

											1992 Season									
	ERA	W	L	Sv	G	GS	IP	H	HR	BB	SO		Avg	AB	H	2B	3B	HR	RBI	BB	SO	OBP	SLG
Home	2.21	8	6	0	21	15	130.1	87	8	33	84	vs. Left	.197	456	90	15	3	7	30	39	77	.259	.289
Away	2.53	6	5	2	21	11	96.0	78	3	26	63	vs. Right	.207	363	75	15	1	4	31	20	70	.247	.287
Day	3.14	1	4	2	11	7	57.1	52	1	13	40	Inning 1-6	.209	589	123	19	3	8	47	46	101	.265	.292
Night	2.08	13	7	0	31	19	169.0	113	10	46	107	Inning 7+	.183	230	42	11	1	3	14	13	46	.224	.278
Grass	3.00	4	3	2	14	5	48.0	41	2	17	37	None on	.205	521	107	20	2	6	6	34	92	.254	.286
Turf	2.17	10	8	0	28	21	178.1	124	9	42	110	Runners on	.195	298	58	10	2	5	55	25	55	.253	.292
April	2.76	2	1	1	11	0	16.1	10	1	8	17	Scoring Posn	.176	148	26	4	0	1	42	20	34	.266	.223
May	2.78	1	3	0	8	3	32.1	23	2	10	26	Close & Late	.216	102	22	6	1	3	10	7	22	.261	.382
June	2.30	3	2	0	6	6	43.0	33	1	11	28	None on/out	.191	220	42	3	2	5	5	13	37	.236	.291
July	2.03	3	1	0	5	5	40.0	31	1	5	26	vs. 1st Batr (relief)	.200	15	3	0	0	1	1	0	5	.250	.400

1992 Season

	ERA	W	L	Sv	G	GS	IP	H	HR	BB	SO		Avg	AB	H	2B	3B	HR	RBI	BB	SO	OBP	SLG
August	3.02	2	3	0	6	6	44.2	38	5	14	25	First Inning Pitched	.221	149	33	3	0	3	18	15	35	.293	.302
September/October	1.62	3	2	0	6	6	50.0	30	1	11	25	First 75 Pitches	.208	577	120	19	2	10	49	47	109	.266	.300
Starter	2.27	12	9	0	26	26	198.0	147	8	48	118	Pitch 76-90	.194	108	21	4	0	0	2	7	19	.243	.231
Reliever	2.86	2	2	2	16	0	28.1	18	3	11	29	Pitch 91-105	.213	80	17	4	2	1	8	2	11	.229	.350
0-3 Days Rest	0.00	0	0	0	0	0	0.0	0	0	0	0	Pitch 106+	.130	54	7	3	0	0	2	3	8	.175	.185
4 Days Rest	2.46	7	6	0	17	17	128.0	99	6	24	85	First Pitch	.245	110	27	9	1	1	8	3	0	.261	.373
5+ Days Rest	1.93	5	3	0	9	9	70.0	48	2	24	33	Ahead on Count	.169	409	69	14	2	1	18	0	133	.168	.220
Pre-All Star	2.75	6	6	2	27	11	104.2	80	5	30	80	Behind on Count	.272	147	40	4	1	3	18	31	0	.398	.374
Post-All Star	2.00	8	5	0	15	15	121.2	85	6	29	67	Two Strikes	.158	387	61	12	1	5	19	25	147	.208	.233

Career (1988-1992)

	ERA	W	L	Sv	G	GS	IP	H	HR	BB	SO		Avg	AB	H	2B	3B	HR	RBI	BB	SO	OBP	SLG
Home	3.05	12	12	5	76	18	221.2	186	13	80	152	vs. Left	.228	715	163	30	6	11	63	77	128	.300	.333
Away	3.07	6	10	8	66	13	149.2	128	6	50	108	vs. Right	.229	658	151	30	3	8	80	53	132	.296	.321
Day	3.70	1	7	4	32	8	87.2	82	3	29	67	Inning 1-6	.232	712	165	27	5	13	76	65	119	.294	.338
Night	2.86	17	15	9	110	23	283.2	232	16	101	193	Inning 7+	.225	661	149	33	4	6	67	65	141	.292	.315
Grass	3.84	5	8	6	66	9	126.2	119	9	55	88	None on	.220	795	175	33	3	10	10	64	142	.279	.307
Turf	2.65	13	14	7	76	22	244.2	195	10	75	172	Runners on	.240	578	139	27	6	9	133	66	118	.312	.355
April	3.18	2	2	4	19	0	28.1	21	2	13	29	Scoring Posn	.236	322	76	17	3	3	114	50	80	.326	.335
May	3.43	2	4	3	20	3	44.2	43	2	17	41	Close & Late	.247	288	71	12	4	5	40	31	64	.317	.368
June	2.82	5	4	1	15	6	54.1	44	1	15	41	None on/out	.224	343	77	9	2	5	5	27	55	.281	.306
July	2.29	4	1	1	15	5	55.0	47	1	7	36	vs. 1st Batr (relief)	.309	97	30	7	0	2	11	11	20	.382	.443
August	2.41	2	3	1	30	6	82.0	66	6	40	53	First Inning Pitched	.251	475	119	24	2	6	68	54	100	.323	.347
September/October	3.87	3	8	3	43	11	107.0	93	7	38	60	First 75 Pitches	.237	1121	266	48	7	18	129	114	222	.305	.341
Starter	2.93	12	13	0	31	31	215.0	175	12	59	125	Pitch 76-90	.209	110	23	5	0	0	4	9	19	.269	.255
Reliever	3.22	6	9	13	111	0	156.1	139	7	71	135	Pitch 91-105	.205	83	17	4	2	1	8	3	11	.230	.337
0-3 Days Rest	0.00	0	0	0	0	0	0.0	0	0	0	0	Pitch 106+	.136	59	8	3	0	0	2	4	8	.190	.186
4 Days Rest	2.94	7	8	0	19	19	131.2	108	6	27	86	First Pitch	.276	181	50	12	1	2	15	11	0	.313	.387
5+ Days Rest	2.92	5	5	0	12	12	83.1	67	6	32	39	Ahead on Count	.178	667	119	26	3	1	43	0	231	.178	.231
Pre-All Star	3.12	9	11	8	59	11	144.1	123	6	46	123	Behind on Count	.314	264	83	10	3	7	46	71	0	.457	.455
Post-All Star	3.01	9	11	5	83	20	227.0	191	13	84	137	Two Strikes	.170	654	111	29	1	7	45	48	260	.226	.249

Pitcher vs. Batter (career)

Pitches Best Vs.	Avg	AB	H	2B	3B	HR	RBI	BB	SO	OBP	SLG	Pitches Worst Vs.	Avg	AB	H	2B	3B	HR	RBI	BB	SO	OBP	SLG
Darrin Fletcher	.000	14	0	0	0	0	1	0	2	.000	.000	Marquis Grissom	.688	16	11	2	0	1	5	0	1	.688	1.000
Eddie Murray	.000	11	0	0	0	0	0	2	4	.154	.000	Tony Fernandez	.500	10	5	2	1	0	2	2	3	.583	.900
Craig Biggio	.000	10	0	0	0	0	0	1	2	.091	.000	Tim Wallach	.400	15	6	1	0	0	2	0	1	.400	.467
Kevin Bass	.154	13	2	0	0	0	1	1	2	.214	.154	Delino DeShields	.400	15	6	0	0	2	6	1	2	.438	.600
Jeff Blauser	.182	11	2	0	0	0	0	2	1	.182	.182	Ray Lankford	.333	15	5	1	0	2	1	1	1	.375	.600

Dave Schmidt — Mariners   Pitches Right

	ERA	W	L	Sv	G	GS	IP	BB	SO	Avg	H	2B	3B	HR	RBI	OBP	SLG	GF	IR	IRS	Hld	SvOp	SB	CS	GB	FB	G/F
1992 Season	18.90	0	0	0	3	0	3.1	3	1	.438	7	1	0	1	7	.526	.688	0	1	0	0	0	0	0	6	3	2.00
Last Five Years	4.82	21	22	15	120	35	342.0	92	139	.294	399	60	7	44	181	.339	.446	21	86	24	5	20	30	13	542	416	1.30

1992 Season

	ERA	W	L	Sv	G	GS	IP	H	HR	BB	SO		Avg	AB	H	2B	3B	HR	RBI	BB	SO	OBP	SLG
Home	15.43	0	0	0	2	0	2.1	3	0	2	1	vs. Left	.333	6	2	1	0	1	5	1	0	.429	1.000
Away	27.00	0	0	0	1	0	1.0	4	1	1	0	vs. Right	.500	10	5	0	0	0	2	1	1	.583	.500

Last Five Years

	ERA	W	L	Sv	G	GS	IP	H	HR	BB	SO		Avg	AB	H	2B	3B	HR	RBI	BB	SO	OBP	SLG
Home	5.22	8	8	8	56	15	150.0	183	17	45	77	vs. Left	.298	689	205	31	4	24	96	38	74	.332	.459
Away	4.50	13	14	7	64	20	192.0	216	17	47	62	vs. Right	.291	666	194	29	3	20	85	54	65	.347	.434
Day	5.71	4	3	3	23	6	63.0	76	8	19	27	Inning 1-6	.301	881	265	44	3	29	126	57	87	.341	.456
Night	4.61	17	19	12	97	29	279.0	323	26	73	112	Inning 7+	.263	474	134	16	4	15	55	35	52	.335	.428
Grass	4.86	18	17	4	83	29	263.0	305	27	72	103	None on	.298	765	228	36	4	27	27	41	71	.335	.461
Turf	4.67	3	5	11	37	6	79.0	94	7	20	36	Runners on	.290	590	171	24	3	17	154	51	68	.344	.427
April	5.81	1	4	1	13	6	52.2	65	7	17	23	Scoring Posn	.307	348	107	15	3	13	142	38	43	.368	.480
May	4.18	6	2	0	29	5	71.0	66	6	18	38	Close & Late	.278	237	66	6	2	4	24	19	27	.333	.371
June	4.26	6	4	9	27	6	67.2	79	11	17	17	None on/out	.323	337	109	15	1	15	15	21	35	.367	.507
July	5.91	1	8	5	28	6	70.0	97	8	21	25	vs. 1st Batr (relief)	.259	81	21	2	0	3	11	4	12	.294	.395
August	3.02	6	1	0	14	8	56.2	55	7	11	22	First Inning Pitched	.311	457	142	16	3	18	84	33	56	.355	.477
September/October	7.13	1	3	0	9	4	24.0	35	5	8	14	First 15 Pitches	.295	461	136	17	2	19	66	30	51	.336	.464
Starter	4.94	14	15	0	35	35	191.1	227	25	45	68	Pitch 16-30	.297	310	92	14	3	8	41	19	41	.340	.439
Reliever	4.66	7	7	15	85	0	150.2	172	19	47	71	Pitch 31-45	.263	217	57	6	1	5	19	9	17	.291	.369
0 Days rest	3.65	0	0	7	10	0	12.1	13	1	3	8	Pitch 46+	.311	367	114	23	1	12	55	34	30	.369	.477
1 or 2 Days rest	4.16	4	2	7	40	0	62.2	72	7	17	25	First Pitch	.336	238	80	16	1	10	39	7	0	.352	.538
3+ Days rest	5.23	3	5	1	35	0	75.2	87	11	27	38	Ahead on Count	.254	559	142	23	5	17	67	0	119	.260	.404
Pre-All Star	4.35	14	11	14	79	19	217.0	235	24	57	89	Behind on Count	.326	328	107	14	1	9	48	47	0	.406	.457
Post-All Star	5.62	7	11	1	41	16	125.0	164	20	35	50	Two Strikes	.221	507	112	17	3	9	45	37	139	.278	.320

Pitcher vs. Batter (since 1984)

Pitches Best Vs.	Avg	AB	H	2B	3B	HR	RBI	BB	SO	OBP	SLG	Pitches Worst Vs.	Avg	AB	H	2B	3B	HR	RBI	BB	SO	OBP	SLG
Steve Buechele	.000	15	0	0	0	0	0	2	4	.118	.000	Spike Owen	.529	17	9	1	1	1	6	0	1	.529	.882
Rich Gedman	.056	18	1	0	0	0	1	2	6	.143	.056	Mike Greenwell	.500	16	8	0	0	3	6	1	0	.529	1.063
Greg Gagne	.077	13	1	0	0	1	0	2	.071	.077		Jose Canseco	.455	11	5	0	0	2	4	0	2	.455	1.000
Ivan Calderon	.091	11	1	0	0	1	0	4	.091	.091		Cory Snyder	.429	14	6	2	0	2	2	2	1	.500	1.000
Mike Pagliarulo	.118	17	2	0	0	2	0	3	.118	.118		Kent Hrbek	.364	22	8	1	0	3	5	1	2	.391	.818

Dick Schofield — Mets
Bats Right

	Avg	G	AB	R	H	2B	3B	HR	RBI	BB	SO	HBP	GDP	SB	CS	OBP	SLG	IBB	SH	SF	#Pit	#P/PA	GB	FB	G/F
1992 Season	.206	143	423	52	87	18	2	4	36	61	82	5	11	11	4	.311	.286	4	10	3	1879	3.82	123	140	0.88
Last Five Years	.230	622	1989	240	457	57	14	15	145	231	181	22	26	51	20	.315	.295	9	52	9	8537	3.79	678	628	1.08

1992 Season

	Avg	AB	H	2B	3B	HR	RBI	BB	SO	OBP	SLG		Avg	AB	H	2B	3B	HR	RBI	BB	SO	OBP	SLG
vs. Left	.200	145	29	6	2	2	17	23	28	.316	.310	Scoring Posn	.210	100	21	4	1	1	29	26	19	.374	.300
vs. Right	.209	278	58	12	0	2	19	38	54	.308	.273	Close & Late	.198	81	16	3	0	1	7	6	17	.258	.272
Groundball	.196	184	36	4	0	1	10	15	35	.267	.234	None on/out	.234	94	22	4	0	1	1	12	20	.321	.309
Flyball	.181	72	13	5	0	2	8	15	21	.315	.333	Batting #2	.225	138	31	7	1	1	7	19	26	.333	.312
Home	.216	204	44	7	1	3	18	33	37	.326	.304	Batting #8	.190	205	39	9	1	3	23	27	44	.282	.288
Away	.196	219	43	11	1	1	18	28	45	.296	.269	Other	.213	80	17	2	0	0	6	15	12	.344	.238
Day	.213	122	26	4	0	2	15	18	24	.326	.295	April	.277	47	13	5	0	0	1	9	12	.414	.383
Night	.203	301	61	14	2	2	21	43	58	.305	.282	May	.202	94	19	2	0	2	9	14	14	.306	.287
Grass	.224	308	69	12	2	3	26	42	55	.322	.305	June	.180	89	16	3	0	0	3	12	13	.277	.213
Turf	.157	115	18	6	0	1	10	19	27	.283	.235	July	.193	57	11	3	0	1	8	6	14	.281	.298
First Pitch	.237	59	14	3	0	1	5	3	0	.270	.339	August	.213	75	16	2	1	0	7	10	16	.314	.267
Ahead on Count	.325	83	27	6	0	1	16	31	0	.513	.434	September/October	.197	61	12	3	1	1	8	10	13	.306	.328
Behind on Count	.175	154	27	5	0	2	13	0	43	.185	.247	Pre-All Star	.199	251	50	10	0	2	13	38	46	.310	.263
Two Strikes	.121	198	24	5	0	1	6	27	82	.236	.162	Post-All Star	.215	172	37	8	2	2	23	23	36	.313	.320

1992 By Position

Position	Avg	AB	H	2B	3B	HR	RBI	BB	SO	OBP	SLG	G	GS	Innings	PO	A	E	DP	Fld Pct	Rng Fctr	In Zone	Zone Outs	Zone Rtg	MLB Zone
As ss	.206	423	87	18	2	4	36	61	82	.311	.286	142	131	1153.2	207	391	7	79	.988	4.67	444	415	935	885

Last Five Years

	Avg	AB	H	2B	3B	HR	RBI	BB	SO	OBP	SLG		Avg	AB	H	2B	3B	HR	RBI	BB	SO	OBP	SLG
vs. Left	.227	656	149	20	5	8	46	85	90	.322	.309	Scoring Posn	.239	440	105	14	4	4	129	80	73	.358	.316
vs. Right	.231	1333	308	37	9	7	99	146	226	.312	.288	Close & Late	.239	326	78	7	3	1	24	42	65	.330	.288
Groundball	.257	540	139	16	3	3	57	55	75	.323	.315	None on/out	.232	565	131	14	4	4	4	47	83	.298	.292
Flyball	.178	456	81	14	3	5	30	48	88	.262	.254	Batting #8	.211	322	68	14	3	3	29	39	61	.294	.301
Home	.225	990	223	25	7	8	81	108	147	.306	.289	Batting #9	.222	919	204	20	6	4	72	103	150	.304	.270
Away	.234	999	234	32	7	7	64	123	169	.324	.301	Other	.247	748	185	23	5	8	44	89	105	.338	.324
Day	.226	499	113	14	3	4	49	60	68	.317	.291	April	.263	198	52	10	1	1	13	24	35	.350	.338
Night	.231	1490	344	43	11	11	96	171	248	.315	.297	May	.232	298	69	9	3	3	26	27	41	.302	.312
Grass	.235	1628	382	45	13	13	125	177	246	.316	.302	June	.215	409	88	10	1	2	26	52	62	.306	.259
Turf	.208	361	75	12	1	2	20	54	70	.314	.263	July	.216	384	83	8	3	7	31	39	66	.295	.307
First Pitch	.256	242	62	6	1	2	18	4	0	.271	.314	August	.258	360	93	10	1	1	27	49	53	.354	.300
Ahead on Count	.310	461	143	17	5	5	50	129	0	.463	.401	September/October	.212	340	72	10	5	1	22	40	58	.299	.279
Behind on Count	.205	657	135	17	2	6	46	0	162	.216	.265	Pre-All Star	.226	1028	232	32	7	7	68	117	166	.310	.291
Two Strikes	.168	857	144	22	5	4	39	98	316	.261	.219	Post-All Star	.234	961	225	25	7	8	77	114	150	.321	.300

Batter vs. Pitcher (since 1984)

Hits Best Against	Avg	AB	H	2B	3B	HR	RBI	BB	SO	OBP	SLG	Hits Worst Against	Avg	AB	H	2B	3B	HR	RBI	BB	SO	OBP	SLG
Bill Krueger	.462	13	6	2	1	0	4	3	2	.563	.769	Mark Gubicza	.000	27	0	0	0	0	0	1	5	.036	.000
Bill Swift	.421	19	8	1	0	1	7	1	2	.450	.632	Scott Bailes	.000	18	0	0	0	0	0	0	2	.000	.000
Mike Henneman	.417	12	5	1	0	0	3	1	2	.462	.500	Nolan Ryan	.000	13	0	0	0	0	0	3	9	.188	.000
Charlie Leibrandt	.366	41	15	2	2	0	1	5	3	.458	.512	Tom Henke	.000	11	0	0	0	0	0	1	4	.083	.000
Matt Young	.357	14	5	1	0	1	2	4	0	.500	.643	Mitch Williams	.000	10	0	0	0	0	0	2	3	.167	.000

Mike Schooler — Mariners
Pitches Right

	ERA	W	L	Sv	G	GS	IP	BB	SO	Avg	H	2B	3B	HR	RBI	OBP	SLG	GF	IR	IRS	Hld	SvOp	SB	CS	GB	FB	G/F
1992 Season	4.70	2	7	13	53	0	51.2	24	33	.275	55	6	1	7	45	.351	.420	36	40	17	3	18	8	1	68	60	1.13
Career (1988-1992)	3.30	12	29	98	243	0	267.1	93	232	.248	253	34	6	20	142	.311	.352	104	140	56	7	123	29	5	349	263	1.33

1992 Season

	ERA	W	L	Sv	G	GS	IP	H	HR	BB	SO		Avg	AB	H	2B	3B	HR	RBI	BB	SO	OBP	SLG
Home	4.55	1	4	6	29	0	27.2	27	3	9	17	vs. Left	.278	79	22	4	1	3	19	15	10	.394	.468
Away	4.88	1	3	7	24	0	24.0	28	4	15	16	vs. Right	.273	121	33	2	0	4	26	9	23	.321	.388
Starter	0.00	0	0	0	0	0	0.0	0	0	0	0	Scoring Posn	.406	64	26	3	0	6	44	9	7	.461	.734
Reliever	4.70	2	7	13	53	0	51.2	55	7	24	33	Close & Late	.327	110	36	3	1	6	34	16	16	.406	.536
0 Days rest	7.59	1	3	5	11	0	10.2	12	2	5	4	None on/out	.195	41	8	2	1	0	0	4	10	.267	.293
1 or 2 Days rest	3.96	0	3	6	26	0	25.0	23	3	13	17	First Pitch	.129	31	4	0	0	2	6	0	0	.270	.129
3+ Days rest	3.94	1	1	2	16	0	16.0	20	2	6	12	Behind on Count	.512	41	21	1	0	2	16	9	0	.596	.683

395

1992 Season

	ERA	W	L	Sv	G	GS	IP	H	HR	BB	SO		Avg	AB	H	2B	3B	HR	RBI	BB	SO	OBP	SLG
Pre-All Star	4.84	1	5	13	37	0	35.1	34	5	17	22	Ahead on Count	.211	95	20	4	0	4	22	0	31	.206	.379
Post-All Star	4.41	1	2	0	16	0	16.1	21	2	7	11	Two Strikes	.167	90	15	2	0	2	11	9	33	.240	.256

Career (1988-1992)

	ERA	W	L	Sv	G	GS	IP	H	HR	BB	SO		Avg	AB	H	2B	3B	HR	RBI	BB	SO	OBP	SLG
Home	3.16	7	14	54	130	0	142.1	132	7	39	125	vs. Left	.254	489	124	21	5	10	78	62	99	.336	.378
Away	3.46	5	15	44	113	0	125.0	121	13	54	107	vs. Right	.242	532	129	13	1	10	64	31	133	.286	.327
Day	3.18	3	7	23	65	0	76.1	90	8	23	52	Inning 1-6	.412	17	7	1	0	1	8	2	3	.450	.647
Night	3.35	9	22	75	178	0	191.0	163	12	70	180	Inning 7+	.245	1004	246	33	6	19	134	91	229	.308	.347
Grass	3.11	5	11	34	90	0	104.1	99	11	42	87	None on	.214	514	110	14	4	8	8	44	124	.279	.304
Turf	3.42	7	18	64	153	0	163.0	154	9	51	145	Runners on	.282	507	143	20	2	12	134	49	108	.343	.400
April	3.33	0	1	12	23	0	27.0	26	2	13	23	Scoring Posn	.303	314	95	13	1	10	128	36	65	.366	.446
May	2.51	1	2	24	42	0	43.0	36	4	13	30	Close & Late	.273	539	147	19	2	16	94	54	130	.337	.404
June	2.72	2	6	16	44	0	46.1	41	1	19	41	None on/out	.228	215	49	8	2	2	2	14	50	.275	.312
July	3.06	2	3	18	40	0	50.0	41	4	13	50	vs. 1st Batr (relief)	.211	227	48	8	2	5	27	8	55	.239	.330
August	3.74	3	11	13	50	0	55.1	66	8	12	46	First Inning Pitched	.240	807	194	26	4	13	114	68	185	.300	.331
September/October	4.34	4	6	15	44	0	45.2	43	1	23	42	First 15 Pitches	.244	710	173	25	4	11	87	60	165	.304	.337
Starter	0.00	0	0	0	0	0	0.0	0	0	0	0	Pitch 16-30	.246	244	60	6	1	4	40	27	53	.320	.328
Reliever	3.30	12	29	98	243	0	267.1	253	20	93	232	Pitch 31-45	.286	63	18	3	1	3	10	6	13	.343	.508
0 Days rest	4.14	3	9	31	60	0	63.0	66	7	21	56	Pitch 46+	.500	4	2	0	0	2	5	0	1	.500	2.000
1 or 2 Days rest	3.10	3	13	41	106	0	116.0	105	8	39	97	First Pitch	.313	147	46	6	1	1	19	16	0	.378	.388
3+ Days rest	2.95	6	7	26	77	0	88.1	82	5	33	79	Ahead on Count	.180	528	95	18	3	12	68	0	214	.181	.294
Pre-All Star	2.88	4	10	59	121	0	131.1	119	8	49	109	Behind on Count	.356	174	62	6	0	4	35	44	0	.491	.460
Post-All Star	3.71	8	19	39	122	0	136.0	134	12	44	123	Two Strikes	.156	508	79	11	4	7	45	33	232	.208	.234

Pitcher vs. Batter (career)

Pitches Best Vs.	Avg	AB	H	2B	3B	HR	RBI	BB	SO	OBP	SLG	Pitches Worst Vs.	Avg	AB	H	2B	3B	HR	RBI	BB	SO	OBP	SLG
Dan Gladden	.182	11	2	0	0	0	0	0	6	.306	.182	Terry Steinbach	.500	12	6	1	0	0	3	0	2	.462	.583
Al Newman	.200	10	2	0	0	1	4	0	.429	.200	Lou Whitaker	.455	11	5	0	0	1	4	2	1	.538	.727
												Ruben Sierra	.455	11	5	1	0	0	3	1	1	.500	.545
												Randy Bush	.385	13	5	0	0	2	7	1	2	.429	.846
												Kirby Puckett	.308	13	4	1	0	0	1	0	3	.308	.385

Pete Schourek — Mets
Pitches Left (flyball pitcher)

	ERA	W	L	Sv	G	GS	IP	BB	SO	Avg	H	2B	3B	HR	RBI	OBP	SLG	CG	ShO	Sup	QS	#P/S	SB	CS	GB	FB	G/F
1992 Season	3.64	6	8	0	22	21	136.0	44	60	.261	137	28	5	9	52	.319	.385	0	0	3.18	11	94	15	5	186	172	1.08
Career (1991-1992)	3.89	11	12	2	57	29	222.1	87	127	.256	219	42	11	16	104	.325	.387	1	1	3.52	16	94	27	5	268	291	0.92

1992 Season

	ERA	W	L	Sv	G	GS	IP	H	HR	BB	SO		Avg	AB	H	2B	3B	HR	RBI	BB	SO	OBP	SLG
Home	2.89	5	3	0	14	13	90.1	83	6	29	36	vs. Left	.258	120	31	4	1	2	8	16	14	.341	.358
Away	5.12	1	5	0	8	8	45.2	54	3	15	24	vs. Right	.262	404	106	24	4	7	44	28	46	.312	.394
Starter	3.78	5	8	0	21	21	131.0	133	9	44	57	Scoring Posn	.283	127	36	5	1	1	42	20	18	.371	.362
Reliever	0.00	1	0	0	1	0	5.0	4	0	0	3	Close & Late	.204	49	10	3	0	2	4	5	4	.273	.388
0-3 Days Rest	18.00	0	1	0	1	1	3.0	6	0	3	2	None on/out	.219	137	30	6	0	5	5	6	21	.262	.372
4 Days Rest	4.11	4	3	0	12	12	76.2	80	6	26	34	First Pitch	.264	87	23	6	2	1	3	5	0	.304	.414
5+ Days Rest	2.45	1	4	0	8	8	51.1	47	3	15	21	Behind on Count	.270	148	40	10	0	2	16	25	0	.376	.378
Pre-All Star	2.85	1	3	0	8	8	47.1	47	0	17	21	Ahead on Count	.244	197	48	7	2	2	16	0	53	.250	.330
Post-All Star	4.06	5	5	0	14	13	88.2	90	9	27	39	Two Strikes	.230	196	45	8	2	2	22	14	60	.285	.321

Mike Scioscia — Dodgers
Bats Left

	Avg	G	AB	R	H	2B	3B	HR	RBI	BB	SO	HBP	GDP	SB	CS	OBP	SLG	IBB	SH	SF	#Pit	#P/PA	GB	FB	G/F
1992 Season	.221	117	348	19	77	6	3	3	24	32	31	1	8	3	2	.286	.282	4	5	3	1372	3.57	160	102	1.57
Last Five Years	.252	634	1944	173	490	81	5	36	209	224	154	10	42	11	11	.330	.354	47	21	15	7863	3.59	803	614	1.31

1992 Season

	Avg	AB	H	2B	3B	HR	RBI	BB	SO	OBP	SLG		Avg	AB	H	2B	3B	HR	RBI	BB	SO	OBP	SLG
vs. Left	.235	81	19	1	2	1	10	8	6	.297	.333	Scoring Posn	.197	76	15	0	1	0	19	12	7	.297	.224
vs. Right	.217	267	58	5	1	2	14	24	25	.283	.266	Close & Late	.265	68	18	1	0	1	5	6	6	.324	.324
Groundball	.265	132	35	1	1	0	6	9	9	.312	.288	None on/out	.202	84	17	1	1	0	0	6	7	.256	.238
Flyball	.158	95	15	0	1	1	9	13	13	.264	.211	Batting #6	.248	121	30	4	1	0	5	7	6	.289	.298
Home	.247	178	44	3	3	1	17	13	16	.297	.315	Batting #7	.207	188	39	2	2	3	18	21	22	.283	.287
Away	.194	170	33	3	0	2	7	19	15	.275	.247	Other	.205	39	8	0	0	0	1	4	3	.295	.205
Day	.174	92	16	1	0	1	4	15	11	.290	.217	April	.206	63	13	2	0	1	7	9	7	.297	.286
Night	.238	256	61	5	3	2	20	17	20	.285	.305	May	.143	56	8	0	0	1	3	3	3	.186	.196
Grass	.233	257	60	3	3	3	23	24	24	.298	.304	June	.245	53	13	2	1	0	3	7	6	.333	.321
Turf	.187	91	17	3	0	0	1	8	7	.253	.220	July	.273	66	18	1	1	0	4	5	6	.319	.318
First Pitch	.280	50	14	1	0	0	3	4	0	.333	.300	August	.278	54	15	0	0	0	2	5	6	.339	.278
Ahead on Count	.261	92	24	2	1	1	9	20	1	.389	.337	September/October	.179	56	10	1	1	0	5	3	3	.233	.286
Behind on Count	.160	106	17	1	1	0	4	0	16	.165	.189	Pre-All Star	.218	206	45	5	2	2	17	20	18	.284	.291

1992 Season

	Avg	AB	H	2B	3B	HR	RBI	BB	SO	OBP	SLG		Avg	AB	H	2B	3B	HR	RBI	BB	SO	OBP	SLG
Two Strikes	.151	126	19	3	1	1	7	8	30	.206	.214	Post-All Star	.225	142	32	1	1	1	7	12	13	.290	.268

1992 By Position

Position	Avg	AB	H	2B	3B	HR	RBI	BB	SO	OBP	SLG	G	GS	Innings	PO	A	E	DP	Fld Pct	Rng Fctr	In Zone	Outs	Zone Rtg	MLB Zone
As Pinch Hitter	.154	13	2	0	0	0	0	0	4	.214	.154	14	0	---	---	---	---	---	---	---	---	---	---	---
As c	.224	335	75	6	3	3	24	32	27	.289	.287	108	99	864.2	642	74	9	9	.988	---	---	---	---	---

Last Five Years

	Avg	AB	H	2B	3B	HR	RBI	BB	SO	OBP	SLG		Avg	AB	H	2B	3B	HR	RBI	BB	SO	OBP	SLG
vs. Left	.225	484	109	9	2	9	57	44	44	.291	.308	Scoring Posn	.249	470	117	21	4	165	85	40	.358	.326		
vs. Right	.261	1460	381	72	3	27	152	180	110	.343	.370	Close & Late	.262	340	89	12	0	5	23	51	36	.360	.341
Groundball	.266	691	184	30	2	9	86	80	45	.343	.355	None on/out	.235	480	113	20	2	12	12	53	37	.314	.360
Flyball	.242	396	96	11	2	14	50	50	38	.331	.386	Batting #6	.263	813	214	40	2	19	97	100	53	.345	.387
Home	.262	957	251	39	3	14	112	108	75	.336	.353	Batting #7	.230	640	147	21	3	12	61	78	65	.312	.328
Away	.242	987	239	42	2	22	97	116	79	.324	.356	Other	.263	491	129	20	0	5	51	46	36	.330	.334
Day	.265	573	152	26	1	11	58	71	42	.350	.372	April	.293	314	92	19	1	9	39	35	21	.362	.408
Night	.247	1371	338	55	4	25	151	153	112	.322	.347	May	.224	344	77	9	0	9	35	44	28	.316	.328
Grass	.260	1412	367	58	5	21	154	158	113	.333	.353	June	.242	343	83	13	1	4	34	34	31	.311	.321
Turf	.231	532	123	23	0	15	55	66	41	.323	.359	July	.264	292	77	18	1	2	32	41	22	.352	.353
First Pitch	.272	235	64	10	0	3	26	17	0	.329	.353	August	.251	343	86	8	0	5	32	39	36	.329	.318
Ahead on Count	.287	527	151	27	1	17	71	139	1	.435	.438	September/October	.244	308	75	14	2	11	37	31	16	.316	.409
Behind on Count	.232	633	147	21	1	13	72	5	81	.240	.330	Pre-All Star	.259	1097	284	51	3	18	121	125	86	.334	.360
Two Strikes	.220	738	162	30	1	9	67	46	152	.266	.299	Post-All Star	.243	847	206	30	2	18	88	99	68	.325	.347

Batter vs. Pitcher (since 1984)

Hits Best Against	Avg	AB	H	2B	3B	HR	RBI	BB	SO	OBP	SLG	Hits Worst Against	Avg	AB	H	2B	3B	HR	RBI	BB	SO	OBP	SLG
Kelly Downs	.439	41	18	3	0	0	3	8	2	.531	.512	Larry Andersen	.000	17	0	0	0	0	0	1	1	.056	.000
Don Carman	.417	12	5	0	0	2	3	0	0	.417	.917	Steve Avery	.000	11	0	0	0	0	1	1	1	.077	.000
Don Robinson	.406	32	13	4	0	4	10	6	1	.487	.906	Juan Agosto	.056	18	1	0	0	0	0	0	2	.056	.056
Lance McCullers	.400	10	4	2	0	0	0	1	0	.455	.600	John Franco	.071	14	1	0	0	0	0	1	2	.133	.071
Lee Smith	.357	14	5	0	0	1	3	5	1	.500	.571	Rick Aguilera	.083	12	1	1	0	0	0	1	1	.154	.167

Gary Scott — Cubs

Bats Right (flyball hitter)

	Avg	G	AB	R	H	2B	3B	HR	RBI	BB	SO	HBP	GDP	SB	CS	OBP	SLG	IBB	SH	SF	#Pit	#P/PA	GB	FB	G/F
1992 Season	.156	36	96	8	15	2	0	2	11	5	14	0	3	0	1	.198	.240	1	1	0	357	3.53	35	28	1.25
Career (1991-1992)	.160	67	175	16	28	5	0	3	16	18	28	3	5	0	2	.250	.240	5	2	0	721	3.68	53	60	0.88

1992 Season

	Avg	AB	H	2B	3B	HR	RBI	BB	SO	OBP	SLG		Avg	AB	H	2B	3B	HR	RBI	BB	SO	OBP	SLG
vs. Left	.167	30	5	2	0	1	6	1	4	.194	.333	Scoring Posn	.222	27	6	0	0	2	10	3	5	.300	.444
vs. Right	.152	66	10	0	0	1	5	4	10	.200	.197	Close & Late	.200	15	3	1	0	1	2	1	3	.250	.467
Home	.151	53	8	1	0	1	7	2	8	.182	.226	None on/out	.217	23	5	1	0	0	0	0	2	.217	.261
Away	.163	43	7	1	0	1	4	3	6	.217	.256	Batting #7	.125	8	1	0	0	0	1	0	1	.125	.125
First Pitch	.211	19	4	1	0	0	1	0	0	.211	.263	Batting #8	.135	74	10	2	0	1	8	5	10	.190	.203
Ahead on Count	.143	21	3	1	0	0	1	3	0	.250	.190	Other	.286	14	4	0	0	1	2	0	3	.286	.500
Behind on Count	.130	23	3	1	0	0	1	0	9	.130	.174	Pre-All Star	.144	90	13	2	0	1	9	5	13	.189	.200
Two Strikes	.114	35	4	0	0	2	7	2	14	.162	.286	Post-All Star	.333	6	2	0	0	1	2	0	1	.333	.833

Tim Scott — Padres

Pitches Right (groundball pitcher)

	ERA	W	L	Sv	G	GS	IP	BB	SO	Avg	H	2B	3B	HR	RBI	OBP	SLG	GF	IR	IRS	Hld	SvOp	SB	CS	GB	FB	G/F
1992 Season	5.26	4	1	0	34	0	37.2	21	30	.267	39	5	3	4	20	.361	.425	16	8	2	4	1	6	1	59	34	1.74
Career (1991-1992)	5.35	4	1	0	36	0	38.2	21	31	.272	41	6	3	4	21	.362	.430	16	10	2	4	1	6	2	60	34	1.76

1992 Season

	ERA	W	L	Sv	G	GS	IP	H	HR	BB	SO		Avg	AB	H	2B	3B	HR	RBI	BB	SO	OBP	SLG
Home	5.23	4	1	0	17	0	20.2	19	3	9	19	vs. Left	.270	63	17	2	2	3	12	17	16	.420	.508
Away	5.29	0	0	0	17	0	17.0	20	1	12	11	vs. Right	.265	83	22	3	1	1	8	4	14	.307	.361
Starter	0.00	0	0	0	0	0	0.0	0	0	0	0	Scoring Posn	.281	32	9	3	1	0	12	8	9	.429	.438
Reliever	5.26	4	1	0	34	0	37.2	39	4	21	30	Close & Late	.245	53	13	2	1	0	5	12	13	.388	.321
0 Days rest	0.00	0	0	0	2	0	2.0	1	0	1	1	None on/out	.175	40	7	1	0	1	1	2	9	.214	.275
1 or 2 Days rest	7.71	3	0	0	15	0	14.0	22	2	7	11	First Pitch	.333	12	4	0	0	0	0	5	0	.529	.333
3+ Days rest	4.15	1	1	0	17	0	21.2	16	2	13	18	Behind on Count	.160	25	4	1	0	1	5	9	0	.400	.320
Pre-All Star	4.97	2	1	0	10	0	12.2	9	1	8	10	Ahead on Count	.272	81	22	3	3	1	8	0	24	.268	.420
Post-All Star	5.40	2	0	0	24	0	25.0	30	3	13	20	Two Strikes	.259	81	21	3	1	2	8	7	30	.315	.395

397

Scott Scudder — Indians

Pitches Right

	ERA	W	L	Sv	G	GS	IP	BB	SO	Avg	H	2B	3B	HR	RBI	OBP	SLG	CG	ShO	Sup	QS	#P/S	SB	CS	GB	FB	G/F
1992 Season	5.28	6	10	0	23	22	109.0	55	66	.303	134	23	2	10	57	.380	.432	0	0	4.21	12	89	14	7	159	119	1.34
Career (1989-1992)	4.76	21	33	1	94	63	382.1	202	225	.265	390	72	10	42	185	.356	.413	0	0	4.07	32	88	51	18	500	458	1.09

1992 Season

	ERA	W	L	Sv	G	GS	IP	H	HR	BB	SO		Avg	AB	H	2B	3B	HR	RBI	BB	SO	OBP	SLG
Home	5.06	2	5	0	11	10	53.1	77	3	22	33	vs. Left	.299	251	75	11	1	5	36	31	30	.376	.410
Away	5.50	4	5	0	12	12	55.2	57	7	33	33	vs. Right	.309	191	59	12	1	5	21	24	36	.384	.461
Starter	4.83	6	10	0	22	22	108.0	128	9	54	65	Scoring Posn	.294	119	35	3	1	3	45	18	16	.376	.412
Reliever	54.00	0	0	0	1	0	1.0	6	1	1	1	Close & Late	.484	31	15	3	1	0	4	5	3	.556	.645
0-3 Days Rest	1.50	1	1	0	2	2	12.0	5	1	3	6	None on/out	.250	112	28	5	0	1	1	9	19	.306	.321
4 Days Rest	5.93	4	5	0	11	11	54.2	74	7	28	35	First Pitch	.294	51	15	2	0	2	10	0	0	.288	.451
5+ Days Rest	4.35	1	4	0	9	9	41.1	49	1	23	24	Behind on Count	.358	123	44	9	1	4	25	26	0	.461	.545
Pre-All Star	4.94	6	8	0	18	17	93.0	110	10	46	57	Ahead on Count	.228	171	39	2	0	2	11	0	59	.237	.275
Post-All Star	7.31	0	2	0	5	5	16.0	24	0	9	9	Two Strikes	.241	195	47	6	0	4	15	29	66	.345	.333

Career (1989-1992)

	ERA	W	L	Sv	G	GS	IP	H	HR	BB	SO		Avg	AB	H	2B	3B	HR	RBI	BB	SO	OBP	SLG
Home	5.18	10	17	0	50	31	193.0	214	24	94	120	vs. Left	.268	821	220	42	8	16	96	115	107	.360	.397
Away	4.33	11	16	1	44	32	189.1	176	18	108	105	vs. Right	.262	650	170	30	2	26	89	87	118	.352	.434
Day	4.90	8	11	0	34	21	141.1	140	14	78	75	Inning 1-6	.250	1243	311	59	8	36	157	178	197	.347	.397
Night	4.67	13	22	1	60	42	241.0	250	28	124	150	Inning 7+	.346	228	79	13	2	6	28	26	28	.411	.500
Grass	4.74	11	15	1	39	32	178.1	189	18	90	107	None on	.263	820	216	40	6	21	102	131		.350	.404
Turf	4.76	10	18	0	55	31	204.0	201	24	104	118	Runners on	.267	651	174	32	4	21	164	100	94	.364	.425
April	4.97	1	3	1	9	3	29.0	33	4	9	16	Scoring Posn	.249	373	93	16	3	8	133	76	62	.371	.373
May	3.46	4	5	0	18	9	67.2	64	5	39	33	Close & Late	.323	124	40	7	1	2	14	18	14	.406	.444
June	4.65	6	4	0	13	13	69.2	73	6	38	44	None on/out	.238	374	89	13	2	5	38	57		.313	.324
July	5.98	2	7	0	17	11	61.2	73	9	28	45	vs. 1st Batr (relief)	.310	29	9	2	0	2	5	2	4	.355	.586
August	3.93	4	4	0	15	11	71.0	62	10	35	36	First Inning Pitched	.319	361	115	20	4	17	74	61	56	.421	.537
September/October	5.62	4	10	0	22	16	83.1	85	8	53	51	First 75 Pitches	.258	1169	302	57	9	34	150	164	184	.353	.410
Starter	4.90	19	30	0	63	63	323.1	330	35	178	192	Pitch 76-90	.309	139	43	8	0	6	25	25	14	.416	.496
Reliever	3.97	2	3	1	31	0	59.0	60	7	24	33	Pitch 91-105	.202	109	22	3	0	1	1	6	19	.243	.257
0-3 Days Rest	2.59	3	2	0	5	5	31.1	23	7	7	22	Pitch 106+	.426	54	23	4	1	1	9	7	8	.476	.593
4 Days Rest	5.09	12	17	0	36	36	187.1	190	20	115	107	First Pitch	.294	201	59	11	1	9	42	15	0	.344	.493
5+ Days Rest	5.25	4	11	0	22	22	104.2	117	8	56	63	Ahead on Count	.209	607	127	17	1	9	44	0	191	.216	.285
Pre-All Star	4.93	12	16	1	45	30	180.2	197	18	98	104	Behind on Count	.329	368	121	23	4	14	58	110	0	.481	.527
Post-All Star	4.60	9	17	0	49	33	201.2	193	24	104	121	Two Strikes	.213	653	139	22	2	17	60	77	225	.301	.331

Pitcher vs. Batter (career)

Pitches Best Vs.	Avg	AB	H	2B	3B	HR	RBI	BB	SO	OBP	SLG	Pitches Worst Vs.	Avg	AB	H	2B	3B	HR	RBI	BB	SO	OBP	SLG
Darryl Strawberry	.000	9	0	0	0	0	1	3	2	.231	.000	Howard Johnson	.833	6	5	3	0	2	6	4	0	.818	2.333
Tommy Gregg	.077	13	1	0	0	0	1	1	3	.143	.077	Brian McRae	.556	9	5	0	1	0	2	3	0	.667	.778
Alfredo Griffin	.083	12	1	0	0	0	1	1	0	.143	.083	Will Clark	.444	18	8	3	0	0	2	4	1	.545	.611
Bip Roberts	.083	12	1	0	0	0	1	0	2	.063	.083	Willie McGee	.364	11	4	2	0	0	0	2	0	.462	.545
Lenny Harris	.100	10	1	0	0	0	0	2	1	.250	.100	Dale Murphy	.313	16	5	1	0	2	3	0	3	.313	.750

Steve Searcy — Dodgers

Pitches Left (groundball pitcher)

	ERA	W	L	Sv	G	GS	IP	BB	SO	Avg	H	2B	3B	HR	RBI	OBP	SLG	GF	IR	IRS	Hld	SvOp	SB	CS	GB	FB	G/F
1992 Season	6.10	0	0	0	10	0	10.1	8	5	.325	13	2	1	0	10	.429	.425	3	8	2	0	0	0	1	17	9	1.89
Career (1988-1992)	5.68	6	13	0	70	21	187.0	119	140	.283	205	35	5	25	122	.379	.449	13	33	11	3	1	16	9	312	158	1.97

1992 Season

	ERA	W	L	Sv	G	GS	IP	H	HR	BB	SO		Avg	AB	H	2B	3B	HR	RBI	BB	SO	OBP	SLG
Home	6.23	0	0	0	5	0	4.1	5	0	5	5	vs. Left	.231	13	3	0	1	0	3	1	2	.286	.385
Away	6.00	0	0	0	5	0	6.0	8	0	3	0	vs. Right	.370	27	10	2	0	0	7	7	3	.486	.444

Career (1988-1992)

	ERA	W	L	Sv	G	GS	IP	H	HR	BB	SO		Avg	AB	H	2B	3B	HR	RBI	BB	SO	OBP	SLG
Home	5.10	4	4	0	33	9	90.0	93	12	52	63	vs. Left	.263	152	40	4	2	3	22	23	23	.354	.375
Away	6.22	2	9	0	37	12	97.0	112	13	67	77	vs. Right	.288	572	165	31	3	22	100	96	117	.386	.469
Day	3.87	3	2	0	28	8	79.0	80	7	48	63	Inning 1-6	.270	540	146	26	4	19	94	95	112	.385	.439
Night	7.00	3	11	0	42	13	106.0	125	18	71	87	Inning 7+	.321	184	59	9	1	6	28	24	28	.392	.478
Grass	5.56	2	12	0	44	18	137.2	147	23	86	104	None on	.249	382	95	15	3	11	66	82		.359	.390
Turf	6.02	4	1	0	26	3	49.1	58	2	33	36	Runners on	.322	342	110	20	2	14	111	53	58	.400	.515
April	7.06	1	1	0	9	4	21.2	24	1	20	12	Scoring Posn	.271	199	54	11	1	7	94	37	34	.367	.442
May	8.53	0	1	0	11	1	19.0	31	5	9	14	Close & Late	.383	47	18	2	0	2	7	6	5	.444	.553
June	7.56	0	0	0	5	0	8.1	8	0	7	10	None on/out	.230	178	41	7	2	2	19	39		.305	.326
July	6.84	2	3	0	9	4	26.1	33	7	15	27	vs. 1st Batr (relief)	.326	43	14	3	1	1	7	4	10	.375	.512
August	4.99	1	5	0	16	5	52.1	57	8	31	32	First Inning Pitched	.275	240	66	12	2	6	42	34	51	.357	.417
September/October	4.10	2	3	0	20	7	59.1	52	4	37	45	First 75 Pitches	.296	203	60	12	2	5	29	25	41	.365	.448
Starter	5.21	4	10	0	21	21	103.2	109	15	66	84	Pitch 16-30	.228	167	38	5	1	5	23	29	37	.338	.359
Reliever	6.26	2	3	0	49	0	83.1	96	10	53	56	Pitch 31-45	.286	105	30	4	2	3	17	17	17	.382	.448
0 Days rest	8.62	0	0	0	5	0	15.2	20	2	13	8	Pitch 46+	.309	249	77	14	0	12	53	48	45	.415	.510
1 or 2 Days rest	6.20	0	3	0	14	0	24.2	26	3	11	12	First Pitch	.375	112	42	8	2	6	23	2	0	.383	.643

Career (1988-1992)

	ERA	W	L	Sv	G	GS	IP	H	HR	BB	SO		Avg	AB	H	2B	3B	HR	RBI	BB	SO	OBP	SLG
3+ Days rest	5.44	2	0	0	30	0	43.0	50	5	29	36	Ahead on Count	.215	311	67	11	1	8	34	1	125	.215	.334
Pre-All Star	7.81	1	2	0	27	5	53.0	67	8	40	38	Behind on Count	.351	191	67	12	1	7	43	74	0	.526	.534
Post-All Star	4.84	5	11	0	43	16	134.0	138	17	79	102	Two Strikes	.171	304	52	7	1	8	33	42	140	.267	.280

Pitcher vs. Batter (career)

Pitches Best Vs.	Avg	AB	H	2B	3B	HR	RBI	BB	SO	OBP	SLG	Pitches Worst Vs.	Avg	AB	H	2B	3B	HR	RBI	BB	SO	OBP	SLG
Mike Greenwell	.100	10	1	1	0	0	2	1	0	.182	.200												
Roberto Kelly	.167	12	2	1	0	0	0	2	6	.286	.250												
Steve Sax	.182	11	2	1	0	0	1	4	1	.400	.273												

David Segui — Orioles   Bats Both (groundball hitter)

	Avg	G	AB	R	H	2B	3B	HR	RBI	BB	SO	HBP	GDP	SB	CS	OBP	SLG	IBB	SH	SF	#Pit	#P/PA	GB	FB	G/F
1992 Season	.233	115	189	21	44	9	0	1	17	20	23	0	4	1	0	.306	.296	3	2	0	753	3.60	77	54	1.43
Career (1990-1992)	.254	241	524	50	133	23	0	5	54	43	57	1	23	2	1	.311	.326	7	6	1	1967	3.46	227	131	1.73

1992 Season

	Avg	AB	H	2B	3B	HR	RBI	BB	SO	OBP	SLG		Avg	AB	H	2B	3B	HR	RBI	BB	SO	OBP	SLG
vs. Left	.205	78	16	3	0	0	9	7	14	.271	.244	Scoring Posn	.220	59	13	1	0	0	15	8	8	.313	.237
vs. Right	.252	111	28	6	0	1	8	13	9	.331	.333	Close & Late	.273	33	9	1	0	0	1	7	4	.400	.303
Home	.213	75	16	2	0	1	11	8	12	.289	.280	None on/out	.308	39	12	1	0	1	1	3	5	.357	.410
Away	.246	114	28	7	0	0	6	12	11	.317	.307	Batting #7	.160	50	8	2	0	0	1	7	10	.263	.200
First Pitch	.320	25	8	0	0	1	6	3	0	.393	.440	Batting #8	.284	81	23	6	0	1	12	10	7	.363	.395
Ahead on Count	.319	47	15	2	0	0	3	6	0	.396	.362	Other	.224	58	13	1	0	0	4	3	6	.262	.241
Behind on Count	.195	77	15	7	0	0	5	0	15	.195	.286	Pre-All Star	.236	123	29	6	0	1	11	13	12	.309	.309
Two Strikes	.143	77	11	5	0	0	6	11	23	.250	.208	Post-All Star	.227	66	15	3	0	0	6	7	11	.301	.273

Career (1990-1992)

	Avg	AB	H	2B	3B	HR	RBI	BB	SO	OBP	SLG		Avg	AB	H	2B	3B	HR	RBI	BB	SO	OBP	SLG
vs. Left	.273	216	59	11	0	2	27	12	27	.311	.352	Scoring Posn	.264	140	37	5	0	2	49	15	17	.333	.343
vs. Right	.240	308	74	12	0	3	27	31	30	.311	.308	Close & Late	.258	97	25	2	0	3	13	13	12	.345	.371
Groundball	.252	151	38	4	0	1	13	13	22	.311	.298	None on/out	.297	118	35	6	0	1	1	8	10	.341	.373
Flyball	.313	96	30	5	0	2	8	8	8	.371	.427	Batting #7	.211	142	30	7	0	2	12	12	22	.271	.303
Home	.238	260	62	8	0	3	31	20	34	.292	.304	Batting #8	.295	166	49	13	0	3	29	16	18	.355	.428
Away	.269	264	71	15	0	2	23	23	23	.330	.348	Other	.250	216	54	3	0	0	13	15	17	.302	.264
Day	.248	149	37	6	0	0	10	17	16	.325	.289	April	.222	45	10	3	0	0	4	5	3	.300	.289
Night	.256	375	96	17	0	5	44	26	41	.305	.341	May	.216	116	25	7	0	1	13	8	11	.272	.302
Grass	.255	432	110	18	0	3	43	39	49	.317	.317	June	.270	100	27	4	0	1	10	8	10	.321	.340
Turf	.250	92	23	5	0	2	11	4	8	.281	.370	July	.258	62	16	3	0	1	6	3	7	.292	.355
First Pitch	.309	68	21	4	0	2	16	5	0	.356	.456	August	.274	73	20	0	0	0	8	6	8	.329	.274
Ahead on Count	.352	128	45	8	0	1	14	20	0	.439	.438	September/October	.273	128	35	6	0	2	13	13	18	.340	.367
Behind on Count	.199	196	39	9	0	1	11	0	41	.199	.260	Pre-All Star	.241	278	67	15	0	3	32	21	28	.296	.327
Two Strikes	.186	204	38	8	0	1	13	16	57	.249	.240	Post-All Star	.268	246	66	8	0	2	22	22	29	.326	.325

Batter vs. Pitcher (career)

Hits Best Against	Avg	AB	H	2B	3B	HR	RBI	BB	SO	OBP	SLG	Hits Worst Against	Avg	AB	H	2B	3B	HR	RBI	BB	SO	OBP	SLG
Jack Morris	.400	20	8	1	0	0	1	2	1	.455	.450	Jimmy Key	.143	14	2	1	0	0	0	0	4	.143	.214
Chuck Finley	.333	9	3	2	0	0	0	4	3	.538	.556	Greg Harris	.182	11	2	1	0	0	3	2	4	.308	.273
												Frank Tanana	.200	10	2	1	0	0	1	1	3	.273	.300
												Bill Krueger	.231	13	3	0	0	0	0	1	2	.286	.231

Kevin Seitzer — Brewers   Bats Right (groundball hitter)

	Avg	G	AB	R	H	2B	3B	HR	RBI	BB	SO	HBP	GDP	SB	CS	OBP	SLG	IBB	SH	SF	#Pit	#P/PA	GB	FB	G/F
1992 Season	.270	148	540	74	146	35	1	5	71	57	44	2	16	13	11	.337	.367	4	7	9	2286	3.76	234	154	1.52
Last Five Years	.281	700	2552	361	717	126	16	21	242	327	271	17	62	51	33	.364	.368	20	19	22	11063	3.79	1136	679	1.67

1992 Season

	Avg	AB	H	2B	3B	HR	RBI	BB	SO	OBP	SLG		Avg	AB	H	2B	3B	HR	RBI	BB	SO	OBP	SLG
vs. Left	.313	128	40	10	1	2	17	21	9	.404	.453	Scoring Posn	.287	150	43	12	0	0	64	24	14	.370	.367
vs. Right	.257	412	106	25	0	3	54	36	35	.315	.340	Close & Late	.349	86	30	6	0	1	16	12	7	.416	.453
Groundball	.313	128	40	8	0	0	11	12	5	.371	.375	None on/out	.276	123	34	6	1	2	2	13	9	.350	.390
Flyball	.309	152	47	14	1	4	31	16	9	.368	.493	Batting #2	.254	264	67	14	1	3	40	30	26	.326	.348
Home	.236	259	61	10	1	2	32	30	20	.315	.305	Batting #7	.284	169	48	13	0	2	19	22	11	.361	.396
Away	.302	281	85	25	0	3	39	27	24	.358	.423	Other	.290	107	31	8	0	0	12	5	7	.327	.364
Day	.261	176	46	14	0	0	22	21	12	.343	.341	April	.266	64	17	4	0	1	9	7	3	.333	.375
Night	.275	364	100	21	1	5	49	36	32	.334	.379	May	.339	109	37	11	0	1	12	8	10	.385	.468
Grass	.252	464	117	26	1	5	55	44	39	.314	.345	June	.284	95	27	4	1	0	13	9	6	.336	.347
Turf	.382	76	29	9	0	0	16	13	5	.472	.500	July	.205	88	18	4	0	2	14	12	10	.298	.318
First Pitch	.259	58	15	5	0	1	4	4	0	.306	.397	August	.224	76	17	5	0	0	8	11	8	.322	.289
Ahead on Count	.333	147	49	18	0	1	30	24	0	.420	.476	September/October	.278	108	30	7	0	1	15	10	7	.339	.370
Behind on Count	.228	167	38	5	0	2	17	0	22	.234	.293	Pre-All Star	.281	299	84	20	1	2	39	26	23	.334	.375
Two Strikes	.241	216	52	6	0	2	23	29	44	.327	.296	Post-All Star	.257	241	62	15	0	3	32	31	21	.341	.357

399

1992 By Position

Position	Avg	AB	H	2B	3B	HR	RBI	BB	SO	OBP	SLG	G	GS	Innings	PO	A	E	DP	Fld Pct	Rng Fctr	In Zone	Outs	Zone Rtg	MLB Zone
As 3b	.269	535	144	35	1	5	70	56	44	.336	.366	146	146	1265.0	99	271	12	18	.969	2.63	353	290	.822	.841

Last Five Years

	Avg	AB	H	2B	3B	HR	RBI	BB	SO	OBP	SLG		Avg	AB	H	2B	3B	HR	RBI	BB	SO	OBP	SLG
vs. Left	.300	731	219	46	8	11	78	111	71	.392	.430	Scoring Posn	.280	599	168	36	5	0	207	124	64	.397	.357
vs. Right	.273	1821	498	80	8	10	164	216	200	.352	.343	Close & Late	.280	389	109	20	1	2	46	50	51	.360	.352
Groundball	.292	644	188	28	4	3	51	76	66	.366	.362	None on/out	.259	648	168	33	4	5	5	58	71	.329	.346
Flyball	.280	657	184	38	4	7	78	84	72	.360	.382	Batting #1	.273	616	168	32	7	5	38	72	65	.352	.372
Home	.294	1255	369	65	9	13	128	160	123	.375	.391	Batting #2	.276	1139	314	48	4	10	120	168	135	.368	.351
Away	.268	1297	348	61	7	8	114	167	148	.353	.345	Other	.295	797	235	46	5	6	84	87	71	.366	.388
Day	.270	681	184	40	2	2	67	99	75	.367	.344	April	.268	377	101	19	1	3	45	33	37	.329	.347
Night	.285	1871	533	86	14	19	175	228	196	.362	.376	May	.310	410	127	24	1	5	40	52	47	.392	.410
Grass	.253	1251	317	51	7	8	110	150	129	.334	.325	June	.300	493	148	23	5	5	45	61	36	.376	.398
Turf	.307	1301	400	75	9	13	132	177	142	.392	.409	July	.268	455	122	19	4	4	40	63	57	.357	.354
First Pitch	.341	302	103	20	1	4	38	11	0	.368	.454	August	.251	383	96	19	2	0	35	55	45	.344	.311
Ahead on Count	.322	693	223	51	5	4	80	179	0	.460	.427	September/October	.283	434	123	22	3	4	37	63	49	.376	.376
Behind on Count	.252	799	201	22	6	6	56	1	145	.256	.317	Pre-All Star	.291	1428	415	70	9	15	148	167	141	.367	.384
Two Strikes	.216	1057	228	28	5	5	77	132	271	.304	.266	Post-All Star	.269	1124	302	56	7	6	94	160	130	.360	.347

Batter vs. Pitcher (career)

Hits Best Against	Avg	AB	H	2B	3B	HR	RBI	BB	SO	OBP	SLG	Hits Worst Against	Avg	AB	H	2B	3B	HR	RBI	BB	SO	OBP	SLG
Erik Hanson	.600	15	9	2	0	0	2	6	2	.714	.733	Scott Erickson	.000	12	0	0	0	0	1	0	0	.000	.000
Kevin Ritz	.500	10	5	2	0	0	2	2	1	.538	.700	Scott Bankhead	.000	11	0	0	0	0	2	2	1	.154	.000
Jaime Navarro	.500	8	4	1	0	0	1	4	0	.667	.625	Jack McDowell	.045	22	1	0	0	0	2	3	3	.207	.045
Greg Cadaret	.444	18	8	2	0	1	3	2	0	.500	.722	Scott Kamieniecki	.077	13	1	0	0	0	0	1	0	.143	.077
Juan Berenguer	.429	7	3	1	0	0	1	4	1	.583	.571	Dave Schmidt	.158	19	3	0	0	0	0	0	2	.158	.158

Frank Seminara — Padres
Pitches Right (groundball pitcher)

	ERA	W	L	Sv	G	GS	IP	BB	SO	Avg	H	2B	3B	HR	RBI	OBP	SLG	CG	ShO	Sup	QS	#P/S	SB	CS	GB	FB	G/F
1992 Season	3.68	9	4	0	19	18	100.1	46	61	.258	98	12	3	5	38	.341	.345	0	0	5.56	10	88	10	6	154	81	1.90

1992 Season

	ERA	W	L	Sv	G	GS	IP	H	HR	BB	SO		Avg	AB	H	2B	3B	HR	RBI	BB	SO	OBP	SLG
Home	3.04	6	1	0	10	10	56.1	53	1	33	37	vs. Left	.294	204	60	7	2	4	25	32	24	.390	.407
Away	4.50	3	3	0	9	8	44.0	45	4	13	24	vs. Right	.216	176	38	5	1	1	13	14	37	.282	.273
Starter	3.59	9	4	0	18	18	100.1	96	5	45	61	Scoring Posn	.256	86	22	2	2	1	29	16	16	.365	.360
Reliever	0.00	0	0	0	1	0	0.0	2	0	1	0	Close & Late	.333	9	3	0	0	0	1	1	.400	.333
0-3 Days Rest	0.00	0	0	0	0	0	0.0	0	0	0	0	None on/out	.240	96	23	3	1	1	1	11	11	.330	.323
4 Days Rest	3.51	6	1	0	10	10	56.1	54	2	32	35	First Pitch	.333	63	21	4	1	1	5	2	0	.373	.476
5+ Days Rest	3.68	3	3	0	8	8	44.0	42	3	13	26	Behind on Count	.274	84	23	2	1	2	13	29	0	.460	.393
Pre-All Star	3.97	4	2	0	8	8	45.1	42	2	25	24	Ahead on Count	.214	168	36	3	0	1	11	0	52	.216	.250
Post-All Star	3.44	5	2	0	11	10	55.0	56	3	21	37	Two Strikes	.212	170	36	3	1	1	12	15	61	.280	.259

Scott Servais — Astros
Bats Right

	Avg	G	AB	R	H	2B	3B	HR	RBI	BB	SO	HBP	GDP	SB	CS	OBP	SLG	IBB	SH	SF	#Pit	#P/PA	GB	FB	G/F
1992 Season	.239	77	205	12	49	9	0	0	15	11	25	5	7	0	0	.294	.283	2	6	0	762	3.45	82	61	1.34
Career (1991-1992)	.227	93	242	12	55	12	0	0	21	14	33	5	7	0	0	.286	.277	2	7	0	906	3.46	93	73	1.27

1992 Season

	Avg	AB	H	2B	3B	HR	RBI	BB	SO	OBP	SLG		Avg	AB	H	2B	3B	HR	RBI	BB	SO	OBP	SLG
vs. Left	.248	145	36	8	0	0	15	8	14	.297	.303	Scoring Posn	.185	54	10	2	0	0	15	4	7	.267	.222
vs. Right	.217	60	13	1	0	0	3	11	.288	.233	Close & Late	.163	43	7	3	0	0	1	3	6	.234	.233
Home	.242	95	23	3	0	0	6	5	15	.287	.274	None on/out	.265	49	13	5	0	0	0	0	6	.265	.367
Away	.236	110	26	6	0	0	9	6	10	.300	.291	Batting #7	.220	150	33	7	0	0	9	5	18	.259	.267
First Pitch	.297	37	11	3	0	0	2	1	0	.316	.378	Batting #8	.294	51	15	2	0	0	6	6	6	.390	.333
Ahead on Count	.245	49	12	3	0	0	4	2	0	.275	.306	Other	.250	4	1	0	0	0	0	0	1	.250	.250
Behind on Count	.154	65	10	1	0	0	4	0	17	.203	.169	Pre-All Star	.200	120	24	5	0	0	7	5	17	.262	.242
Two Strikes	.139	79	11	2	0	0	6	8	25	.236	.165	Post-All Star	.294	85	25	4	0	0	8	6	8	.341	.341

Scott Service — Expos
Pitches Right (groundball pitcher)

	ERA	W	L	Sv	G	GS	IP	BB	SO	Avg	H	2B	3B	HR	RBI	OBP	SLG	GF	IR	IRS	Hld	SvOp	SB	CS	GB	FB	G/F
1992 Season	14.14	0	0	0	5	0	7.0	5	11	.417	15	1	1	1	11	.488	.583	0	4	2	1	0	2	0	13	4	3.25
Career (1988-1992)	8.76	0	0	0	10	0	12.1	6	17	.386	22	2	1	1	12	.453	.509	0	7	3	1	0	2	1	21	6	3.50

1992 Season

	ERA	W	L	Sv	G	GS	IP	H	HR	BB	SO		Avg	AB	H	2B	3B	HR	RBI	BB	SO	OBP	SLG
Home	21.00	0	0	0	3	0	3.0	9	1	3	5	vs. Left	.467	15	7	0	1	0	4	3	2	.556	.600
Away	9.00	0	0	0	2	0	4.0	6	0	2	6	vs. Right	.381	21	8	1	0	1	7	2	9	.435	.571

400

Mike Sharperson — Dodgers
Bats Right

	Avg	G	AB	R	H	2B	3B	HR	RBI	BB	SO	HBP	GDP	SB	CS	OBP	SLG	IBB	SH	SF	#Pit	#P/PA	GB	FB	G/F
1992 Season	.300	128	317	48	95	21	0	3	36	47	33	0	9	2	2	.387	.394	0	5	3	1464	3.99	116	97	1.20
Last Five Years	.291	435	977	124	284	50	4	8	101	123	115	3	18	18	13	.369	.375	8	26	8	4210	3.79	378	260	1.45

1992 Season

	Avg	AB	H	2B	3B	HR	RBI	BB	SO	OBP	SLG		Avg	AB	H	2B	3B	HR	RBI	BB	SO	OBP	SLG
vs. Left	.312	199	62	13	0	3	22	27	15	.390	.422	Scoring Posn	.256	90	23	8	0	0	30	23	12	.397	.344
vs. Right	.280	118	33	8	0	0	14	20	18	.381	.347	Close & Late	.267	75	20	6	0	1	12	13	13	.367	.387
Groundball	.320	97	31	8	0	0	11	16	9	.416	.402	None on/out	.372	43	16	3	0	0	0	5	5	.438	.442
Flyball	.215	93	20	5	0	0	4	10	9	.291	.269	Batting #2	.354	195	69	16	0	2	27	30	17	.436	.467
Home	.314	159	50	11	0	2	19	18	18	.382	.421	Batting #3	.205	83	17	4	0	1	8	6	10	.256	.289
Away	.285	158	45	10	0	1	17	29	15	.392	.367	Other	.231	39	9	1	0	0	1	11	6	.400	.256
Day	.340	94	32	5	0	3	11	18	12	.442	.489	April	.325	40	13	1	0	0	3	8	5	.429	.350
Night	.283	223	63	16	0	0	25	29	21	.362	.354	May	.405	37	15	4	0	0	6	9	2	.522	.514
Grass	.304	250	76	19	0	2	32	35	29	.387	.404	June	.313	80	25	8	0	1	12	12	5	.398	.450
Turf	.284	67	19	2	0	1	4	12	4	.388	.358	July	.244	86	21	4	0	2	13	11	13	.327	.360
First Pitch	.375	32	12	2	0	1	3	1	0	.394	.531	August	.308	26	8	2	0	0	0	5	4	.419	.385
Ahead on Count	.324	68	22	4	0	1	12	29	0	.510	.426	September/October	.271	48	13	2	0	0	2	2	4	.300	.313
Behind on Count	.340	106	36	5	0	1	16	0	14	.333	.415	Pre-All Star	.328	201	66	15	0	2	27	35	19	.424	.433
Two Strikes	.275	153	42	11	0	1	14	17	33	.347	.366	Post-All Star	.250	116	29	6	0	1	9	12	14	.318	.328

1992 By Position

Position	Avg	AB	H	2B	3B	HR	RBI	BB	SO	OBP	SLG	G	GS	Innings	PO	A	E	DP	Fld Pct	Rng Fctr	In Zone	Outs	Zone Rtg	MLB Zone
As Pinch Hitter	.211	38	8	3	0	0	2	9	4	.362	.289	48	0	---	---	---	---	---	---	---	---	---	---	---
As 2b	.318	129	41	9	0	2	18	21	12	.408	.434	63	33	331.2	104	134	5	26	.979	6.46	156	131	.840	.892
As 3b	.311	148	46	9	0	1	16	17	17	.380	.392	60	39	335.0	15	85	8	5	.926	2.69	100	79	.790	.841

Last Five Years

	Avg	AB	H	2B	3B	HR	RBI	BB	SO	OBP	SLG		Avg	AB	H	2B	3B	HR	RBI	BB	SO	OBP	SLG
vs. Left	.313	600	188	33	3	6	61	74	67	.387	.408	Scoring Posn	.254	256	65	9	1	0	85	46	37	.364	.297
vs. Right	.255	377	96	17	1	2	40	49	48	.340	.321	Close & Late	.261	199	52	11	2	2	28	28	32	.351	.367
Groundball	.336	298	100	18	0	0	30	42	28	.417	.396	Batting #2	.293	215	63	10	1	0	0	12	22	.345	.349
Flyball	.251	243	61	10	2	0	14	23	27	.313	.309	Batting #7	.323	390	126	26	2	2	43	50	43	.397	.415
Home	.302	486	147	22	1	4	50	55	60	.372	.377	Other	.325	160	52	7	0	4	19	20	19	.399	.444
Away	.279	491	137	28	3	4	51	68	55	.366	.373		.248	427	106	17	2	2	39	53	53	.332	.311
Day	.310	290	90	17	0	5	39	38	35	.387	.421	April	.265	98	26	4	0	0	9	12	8	.348	.306
Night	.282	687	194	33	4	3	62	85	80	.361	.355	May	.339	109	37	7	0	0	11	17	13	.425	.404
Grass	.303	766	232	42	1	6	80	93	94	.378	.384	June	.330	185	61	11	1	2	28	25	19	.406	.432
Turf	.246	211	52	8	3	2	21	30	21	.337	.341	July	.295	176	52	9	1	2	20	24	23	.378	.392
First Pitch	.321	140	45	10	1	1	14	2	1	.333	.429	August	.259	170	44	6	1	2	10	24	25	.347	.341
Ahead on Count	.338	219	74	12	0	5	34	64	0	.479	.461	September/October	.268	239	64	13	1	2	23	21	27	.331	.356
Behind on Count	.274	317	87	12	0	2	31	0	59	.272	.331	Pre-All Star	.314	459	144	25	1	3	55	63	50	.395	.392
Two Strikes	.239	440	105	18	2	2	34	51	114	.318	.302	Post-All Star	.270	518	140	25	3	5	46	60	65	.346	.359

Batter vs. Pitcher (career)

Hits Best Against	Avg	AB	H	2B	3B	HR	RBI	BB	SO	OBP	SLG	Hits Worst Against	Avg	AB	H	2B	3B	HR	RBI	BB	SO	OBP	SLG
Butch Henry	.667	9	6	0	0	0	0	2	0	.727	.667	Jim Deshaies	.105	19	2	1	0	0	0	1	1	.105	.105
Danny Jackson	.464	28	13	2	0	0	4	2	0	.500	.536	Chris Hammond	.111	9	1	0	0	0	0	2	1	.273	.111
Pat Combs	.444	9	4	1	0	0	2	2	2	.545	.556	David Cone	.167	12	2	2	0	0	1	0	4	.167	.333
Craig Lefferts	.400	10	4	0	0	2	5	2	1	.500	1.000	Bud Black	.190	21	4	0	0	0	1	1	1	.227	.190
Randy Myers	.375	16	6	2	0	3	5	4	.500	.750	Dennis Rasmussen	.222	18	4	0	0	0	1	0	1	.222	.222

Jeff Shaw — Indians
Pitches Right

	ERA	W	L	Sv	G	GS	IP	BB	SO	Avg	H	2B	3B	HR	RBI	OBP	SLG	CG	ShO	Sup	QS	#P/S	SB	CS	GB	FB	G/F
1992 Season	8.22	0	1	0	2	1	7.2	4	3	.259	7	0	0	2	7	.355	.481	0	0	3.52	0	81	1	0	7	12	0.58
Career (1990-1992)	4.90	3	10	1	43	11	128.2	51	59	.300	152	26	2	19	76	.364	.471	0	0	3.99	2	76	6	4	203	152	1.34

1992 Season

	ERA	W	L	Sv	G	GS	IP	H	HR	BB	SO		Avg	AB	H	2B	3B	HR	RBI	BB	SO	OBP	SLG
Home	8.22	0	1	0	2	1	7.2	7	2	4	3	vs. Left	.364	11	4	0	0	1	5	2	0	.462	.636
Away	0.00	0	0	0	0	0	0.0	0	0	0	0	vs. Right	.188	16	3	0	0	1	2	2	3	.278	.375

Gary Sheffield — Padres
Bats Right (flyball hitter)

	Avg	G	AB	R	H	2B	3B	HR	RBI	BB	SO	HBP	GDP	SB	CS	OBP	SLG	IBB	SH	SF	#Pit	#P/PA	GB	FB	G/F
1992 Season	.330	146	557	87	184	34	3	33	100	48	40	6	19	5	6	.385	.580	5	0	7	1966	3.18	186	192	0.97
Career (1988-1992)	.283	440	1667	225	471	95	6	54	233	145	136	16	42	48	28	.341	.444	7	9	25	6033	3.26	570	611	0.93

1992 Season

	Avg	AB	H	2B	3B	HR	RBI	BB	SO	OBP	SLG		Avg	AB	H	2B	3B	HR	RBI	BB	SO	OBP	SLG
vs. Left	.365	189	69	9	2	13	38	18	13	.420	.640	Scoring Posn	.339	127	43	4	1	11	71	18	10	.409	.646
vs. Right	.313	368	115	25	1	20	62	30	27	.367	.549	Close & Late	.410	78	32	3	1	4	15	8	5	.467	.628
Groundball	.320	228	73	15	0	11	37	20	14	.380	.531	None on/out	.358	95	34	9	1	6	6	4	6	.390	.663

1992 Season

	Avg	AB	H	2B	3B	HR	RBI	BB	SO	OBP	SLG		Avg	AB	H	2B	3B	HR	RBI	BB	SO	OBP	SLG
Flyball	.301	113	34	5	0	5	19	10	15	.359	.478	Batting #3	.322	537	173	32	3	31	93	46	39	.378	.566
Home	.365	288	105	19	2	23	58	30	18	.426	.684	Batting #4	.556	18	10	2	0	2	6	2	1	.600	1.000
Away	.294	269	79	15	1	10	42	18	22	.340	.468	Other	.500	2	1	0	0	0	1	0	0	.500	.500
Day	.325	163	53	10	2	8	21	16	10	.386	.558	April	.333	84	28	6	1	3	15	16	9	.431	.536
Night	.332	394	131	24	1	25	79	32	30	.385	.589	May	.324	105	34	3	0	7	23	6	7	.357	.552
Grass	.346	402	139	27	3	30	77	40	29	.408	.652	June	.298	94	28	5	0	5	17	7	5	.359	.511
Turf	.290	155	45	7	0	3	23	8	11	.323	.394	July	.352	91	32	10	1	4	11	5	2	.390	.615
First Pitch	.387	124	48	9	2	9	18	5	0	.424	.710	August	.361	97	35	6	0	10	26	6	10	.390	.732
Ahead on Count	.358	123	44	7	0	9	32	29	0	.474	.634	September/October	.314	86	27	4	1	4	8	8	7	.385	.523
Behind on Count	.293	181	53	11	0	8	28	0	21	.296	.486	Pre-All Star	.325	323	105	17	2	18	62	31	23	.385	.557
Two Strikes	.247	178	44	10	1	7	28	14	40	.301	.433	Post-All Star	.338	234	79	17	1	15	38	17	17	.385	.611

1992 By Position

Position	Avg	AB	H	2B	3B	HR	RBI	BB	SO	OBP	SLG	G	GS	Innings	PO	A	E	DP	Fld Pct	Rng Fctr	In Zone	Outs	Zone Rtg	MLB Zone
As 3b	.330	555	183	34	3	33	99	48	40	.385	.580	144	144	1247.2	99	299	16	25	.961	2.87	.386	.326	.845	.841

Career (1988-1992)

	Avg	AB	H	2B	3B	HR	RBI	BB	SO	OBP	SLG		Avg	AB	H	2B	3B	HR	RBI	BB	SO	OBP	SLG
vs. Left	.298	503	150	31	4	20	76	49	39	.358	.495	Scoring Posn	.290	407	118	21	3	13	173	50	40	.355	.452
vs. Right	.276	1164	321	64	2	34	157	96	97	.334	.422	Close & Late	.347	236	82	10	2	8	39	26	16	.412	.508
Groundball	.290	527	153	31	0	15	72	48	40	.354	.435	None on/out	.271	306	83	17	1	9	9	21	20	.322	.422
Flyball	.263	369	97	17	1	11	45	30	35	.318	.404	Batting #2	.293	304	89	21	1	7	37	20	27	.333	.438
Home	.296	831	246	53	4	31	108	84	74	.362	.481	Batting #3	.285	1054	300	55	5	38	159	99	83	.348	.454
Away	.269	836	225	42	2	23	125	61	62	.320	.407	Other	.265	309	82	19	0	9	37	26	26	.324	.414
Day	.261	541	141	28	3	14	62	44	45	.313	.401	April	.280	289	81	22	2	7	38	34	24	.356	.443
Night	.293	1126	330	67	3	40	171	101	91	.354	.464	May	.306	301	92	14	1	10	44	24	27	.358	.458
Grass	.290	1330	386	80	6	49	180	124	114	.353	.470	June	.262	317	83	20	0	8	50	25	33	.314	.401
Turf	.252	337	85	15	0	5	53	21	22	.295	.341	July	.296	297	88	22	2	7	37	20	9	.349	.455
First Pitch	.327	339	111	26	3	13	49	5	0	.337	.537	August	.289	201	58	8	0	12	38	18	20	.342	.507
Ahead on Count	.301	355	107	19	1	15	67	88	0	.438	.487	September/October	.263	262	69	9	1	10	26	24	23	.329	.420
Behind on Count	.254	566	144	25	0	14	63	1	78	.262	.373	Pre-All Star	.286	1018	291	63	5	29	152	89	89	.343	.443
Two Strikes	.221	565	125	20	2	11	59	50	136	.288	.322	Post-All Star	.277	649	180	32	1	25	81	56	47	.338	.445

Batter vs. Pitcher (career)

Hits Best Against	Avg	AB	H	2B	3B	HR	RBI	BB	SO	OBP	SLG	Hits Worst Against	Avg	AB	H	2B	3B	HR	RBI	BB	SO	OBP	SLG
Jack McDowell	.545	11	6	2	0	0	2	2	0	.615	.727	Bob Tewksbury	.000	12	0	0	0	0	0	0	2	.000	.000
Roger Clemens	.533	15	8	1	0	0	2	1	1	.563	.600	Bill Swift	.067	15	1	0	0	0	2	0	0	.067	.067
Frank Castillo	.455	11	5	2	1	0	1	0	1	.417	.818	Greg Hibbard	.083	12	1	0	0	0	1	0	2	.154	.083
Greg Harris	.444	9	4	1	0	1	3	2	0	.545	.889	Bobby Witt	.091	11	1	0	0	0	1	2	0	.231	.091
Bud Black	.412	17	7	1	0	2	3	1	2	.421	.824	Dave Stieb	.118	17	2	0	0	0	0	0	2	.118	.118

Keith Shepherd — Phillies
Pitches Right

	ERA	W	L	Sv	G	GS	IP	BB	SO	Avg	H	2B	3B	HR	RBI	OBP	SLG	GF	IR	IRS	Hld	SvOp	SB	CS	GB	FB	G/F
1992 Season	3.27	1	1	2	12	0	22.0	6	10	.247	19	6	0	0	11	.291	.325	6	6	4	0	6	3	3	27	24	1.13

1992 Season

	ERA	W	L	Sv	G	GS	IP	H	HR	BB	SO		Avg	AB	H	2B	3B	HR	RBI	BB	SO	OBP	SLG
Home	2.61	1	0	1	5	0	10.1	10	0	3	5	vs. Left	.261	46	12	3	0	0	7	4	4	.308	.326
Away	3.86	0	1	1	7	0	11.2	9	0	3	5	vs. Right	.226	31	7	3	0	0	4	2	6	.265	.323

Steve Shifflett — Royals
Pitches Right (groundball pitcher)

	ERA	W	L	Sv	G	GS	IP	BB	SO	Avg	H	2B	3B	HR	RBI	OBP	SLG	GF	IR	IRS	Hld	SvOp	SB	CS	GB	FB	G/F
1992 Season	2.60	1	4	0	34	0	52.0	17	25	.279	55	8	1	6	21	.341	.421	15	14	7	1	2	3	1	101	42	2.40

1992 Season

	ERA	W	L	Sv	G	GS	IP	H	HR	BB	SO		Avg	AB	H	2B	3B	HR	RBI	BB	SO	OBP	SLG
Home	2.30	0	2	0	17	0	27.1	27	2	8	15	vs. Left	.272	81	22	3	0	5	12	8	9	.337	.494
Away	2.92	1	2	0	17	0	24.2	28	4	9	10	vs. Right	.284	116	33	5	1	1	9	9	16	.344	.371
Starter	0.00	0	0	0	0	0	0.0	0	0	0	0	Scoring Posn	.220	50	11	3	1	0	13	9	7	.355	.320
Reliever	2.60	1	4	0	34	0	52.0	55	6	17	25	Close & Late	.286	63	18	1	1	1	6	8	5	.378	.381
0 Days rest	4.15	0	1	0	6	0	8.2	11	1	3	4	None on/out	.408	49	20	1	0	2	2	4	6	.453	.551
1 or 2 Days rest	2.43	1	2	0	21	0	33.1	34	4	11	17	First Pitch	.214	28	6	0	0	0	4	6	0	.343	.214
3+ Days rest	1.80	0	1	0	7	0	10.0	10	1	3	4	Behind on Count	.341	41	14	2	1	2	7	8	0	.460	.585
Pre-All Star	0.00	1	0	0	5	0	6.2	5	0	1	3	Ahead on Count	.235	98	23	5	0	1	4	0	23	.242	.316
Post-All Star	2.98	0	4	0	29	0	45.1	50	6	16	22	Two Strikes	.227	88	20	3	0	1	4	3	25	.261	.295

Craig Shipley — Padres
Bats Right

	Avg	G	AB	R	H	2B	3B	HR	RBI	BB	SO	HBP	GDP	SB	CS	OBP	SLG	IBB	SH	SF	#Pit	#P/PA	GB	FB	G/F
1992 Season	.248	52	105	7	26	6	0	0	7	2	21	0	2	1	1	.262	.305	1	1	0	357	3.34	39	24	1.63
Last Five Years	.256	93	203	16	52	9	0	1	13	4	36	1	3	1	2	.274	.315	1	2	0	673	3.24	69	56	1.23

1992 Season

	Avg	AB	H	2B	3B	HR	RBI	BB	SO	OBP	SLG		Avg	AB	H	2B	3B	HR	RBI	BB	SO	OBP	SLG
vs. Left	.294	34	10	1	0	0	0	1	6	.314	.324	Scoring Posn	.308	26	8	3	0	0	7	1	3	.333	.423
vs. Right	.225	71	16	5	0	0	7	1	15	.236	.296	Close & Late	.258	31	8	2	0	0	4	0	8	.258	.323
Home	.250	52	13	2	0	0	5	2	11	.278	.288	None on/out	.259	27	7	1	0	0	0	0	6	.259	.296
Away	.245	53	13	4	0	0	2	0	10	.245	.321	Batting #1	.174	23	4	1	0	0	1	0	2	.174	.217
First Pitch	.417	24	10	1	0	0	2	1	0	.440	.458	Batting #8	.275	40	11	3	0	0	3	1	10	.293	.350
Ahead on Count	.167	18	3	1	0	0	0	0	0	.167	.222	Other	.262	42	11	2	0	0	3	1	9	.279	.310
Behind on Count	.136	44	6	1	0	0	2	0	15	.136	.159	Pre-All Star	.211	57	12	1	0	0	3	1	12	.224	.228
Two Strikes	.130	46	6	2	0	0	3	1	21	.149	.174	Post-All Star	.292	48	14	5	0	0	4	1	9	.306	.396

Terry Shumpert — Royals
Bats Right (flyball hitter)

	Avg	G	AB	R	H	2B	3B	HR	RBI	BB	SO	HBP	GDP	SB	CS	OBP	SLG	IBB	SH	SF	#Pit	#P/PA	GB	FB	G/F
1992 Season	.149	36	94	6	14	5	1	1	11	3	17	0	2	2	2	.175	.255	0	2	0	324	3.34	24	45	0.53
Career (1990-1992)	.215	212	554	58	119	27	6	6	53	35	109	6	16	22	16	.267	.318	0	12	5	2162	3.60	161	196	0.82

1992 Season

	Avg	AB	H	2B	3B	HR	RBI	BB	SO	OBP	SLG		Avg	AB	H	2B	3B	HR	RBI	BB	SO	OBP	SLG
vs. Left	.207	29	6	3	0	1	6	1	4	.233	.414	Scoring Posn	.240	25	6	3	1	1	11	1	7	.269	.560
vs. Right	.123	65	8	2	1	0	5	2	13	.149	.185	Close & Late	.182	11	2	0	0	1	3	1	1	.250	.455

Career (1990-1992)

	Avg	AB	H	2B	3B	HR	RBI	BB	SO	OBP	SLG		Avg	AB	H	2B	3B	HR	RBI	BB	SO	OBP	SLG
vs. Left	.232	194	45	12	0	3	21	10	32	.282	.340	Scoring Posn	.266	143	38	8	2	1	45	11	35	.321	.371
vs. Right	.206	360	74	15	6	3	32	25	77	.258	.306	Close & Late	.284	74	21	4	3	1	7	6	11	.333	.459
Groundball	.172	157	27	5	3	0	13	11	36	.234	.242	None on/out	.213	136	29	6	2	2	12	29	.291	.331	
Flyball	.230	148	34	7	1	4	11	10	31	.281	.372	Batting #8	.219	96	21	3	0	1	5	9	17	.299	.281
Home	.207	270	56	12	5	1	23	15	49	.258	.300	Batting #9	.221	439	97	23	6	5	48	25	86	.266	.335
Away	.222	264	63	15	1	5	30	20	60	.275	.335	Other	.053	19	1	1	0	0	0	1	6	.100	.105
Day	.162	142	23	4	3	1	10	11	38	.227	.254	April	.169	83	14	3	1	0	7	4	23	.205	.229
Night	.233	412	96	23	3	5	43	24	71	.280	.340	May	.261	176	46	12	3	1	19	6	27	.285	.381
Grass	.220	227	50	11	0	5	26	19	47	.280	.335	June	.164	73	12	1	0	3	8	7	14	.235	.301
Turf	.211	327	69	16	6	1	27	16	62	.257	.306	July	.244	82	20	3	1	1	9	6	10	.303	.341
First Pitch	.267	90	24	6	3	0	4	0	0	.283	.400	August	.260	77	20	5	1	0	5	11	19	.360	.351
Ahead on Count	.279	86	24	9	1	4	17	20	0	.407	.547	September/October	.111	63	7	3	0	1	5	1	16	.164	.206
Behind on Count	.182	214	39	6	0	1	21	0	65	.195	.224	Pre-All Star	.222	352	78	17	4	5	37	19	65	.260	.335
Two Strikes	.169	267	45	8	2	2	23	15	109	.211	.247	Post-All Star	.203	202	41	10	2	1	16	16	44	.278	.287

Batter vs. Pitcher (career)

Hits Best Against	Avg	AB	H	2B	3B	HR	RBI	BB	SO	OBP	SLG	Hits Worst Against	Avg	AB	H	2B	3B	HR	RBI	BB	SO	OBP	SLG
												Chuck Finley	.000	14	0	0	0	0	0	0	1	.000	.000
												Bill Gullickson	.182	11	2	0	0	0	2	0	2	.167	.182
												Kevin Brown	.214	14	3	0	0	0	0	0	3	.214	.214

Ruben Sierra — Athletics
Bats Both

	Avg	G	AB	R	H	2B	3B	HR	RBI	BB	SO	HBP	GDP	SB	CS	OBP	SLG	IBB	SH	SF	#Pit	#P/PA	GB	FB	G/F
1992 Season	.278	151	601	83	167	34	7	17	87	45	68	0	11	14	4	.323	.443	12	0	10	2300	3.51	205	222	0.92
Last Five Years	.285	789	3119	441	890	182	30	110	509	237	418	4	65	65	14	.332	.469	45	0	45	11912	3.50	1148	1000	1.15

1992 Season

	Avg	AB	H	2B	3B	HR	RBI	BB	SO	OBP	SLG		Avg	AB	H	2B	3B	HR	RBI	BB	SO	OBP	SLG
vs. Left	.339	171	58	10	3	5	33	14	13	.385	.520	Scoring Posn	.282	156	44	8	1	5	63	24	18	.358	.442
vs. Right	.253	430	109	24	4	12	54	31	55	.299	.412	Close & Late	.216	97	21	2	1	2	14	8	16	.271	.320
Groundball	.276	152	42	7	1	1	17	5	17	.294	.355	None on/out	.268	142	38	10	2	2	2	9	12	.311	.408
Flyball	.272	162	44	13	4	6	23	18	21	.341	.512	Batting #3	.255	204	52	7	1	6	31	20	18	.316	.387
Home	.241	294	71	15	2	10	40	20	37	.285	.408	Batting #4	.289	394	114	27	6	11	56	25	50	.327	.472
Away	.313	307	96	19	5	7	47	25	31	.359	.476	Other	.333	3	1	0	0	0	0	0	0	.333	.333
Day	.267	131	35	7	1	4	22	11	11	.319	.427	April	.307	88	27	7	1	2	13	7	13	.354	.477
Night	.281	470	132	27	6	13	65	34	57	.324	.447	May	.282	117	33	4	1	6	22	6	9	.312	.487
Grass	.261	506	132	25	3	13	69	34	56	.303	.399	June	.341	91	31	8	2	2	15	5	13	.367	.538
Turf	.368	95	35	9	4	4	18	11	12	.426	.674	July	.231	104	24	7	1	1	8	7	13	.279	.346
First Pitch	.304	56	17	2	1	5	16	12	0	.414	.643	August	.240	100	24	4	1	3	12	6	11	.275	.390
Ahead on Count	.355	183	65	15	2	7	27	21	0	.411	.574	September/October	.277	101	28	4	1	3	17	14	9	.359	.426
Behind on Count	.252	206	52	10	2	4	28	0	29	.251	.379	Pre-All Star	.306	340	104	20	5	11	55	20	43	.340	.491
Two Strikes	.189	222	42	5	2	4	25	12	68	.229	.284	Post-All Star	.241	261	63	14	2	6	32	25	25	.302	.379

403

1992 By Position

Position	Avg	AB	H	2B	3B	HR	RBI	BB	SO	OBP	SLG	G	GS	Innings	PO	A	E	DP	Fld Pct	Rng Fctr	In Zone	Outs	Zone Rtg	MLB Zone
As rf	.276	580	160	32	7	16	81	44	66	.322	.438	144	144	1269.1	284	6	7	0	.976	2.06	311	275	.884	.814

Last Five Years

	Avg	AB	H	2B	3B	HR	RBI	BB	SO	OBP	SLG		Avg	AB	H	2B	3B	HR	RBI	BB	SO	OBP	SLG
vs. Left	.325	973	316	71	9	33	171	68	93	.365	.518	Scoring Posn	.304	838	255	47	9	33	383	97	115	.359	.500
vs. Right	.267	2146	574	111	21	77	338	169	325	.318	.446	Close & Late	.267	487	130	21	3	16	76	51	67	.333	.421
Groundball	.311	821	255	50	4	25	141	53	104	.350	.473	None on/out	.282	719	203	46	10	27	27	47	89	.329	.487
Flyball	.280	775	217	45	11	25	103	76	100	.340	.463	Batting #3	.273	1030	281	57	5	33	159	76	139	.320	.434
Home	.286	1531	438	89	16	68	266	110	224	.330	.498	Batting #4	.291	2031	591	124	25	74	342	159	267	.338	.486
Away	.285	1588	452	93	14	42	243	127	194	.334	.440	Other	.310	58	18	1	0	3	8	2	12	.333	.483
Day	.281	608	171	38	1	21	105	53	69	.335	.451	April	.279	383	107	28	3	16	66	33	62	.333	.493
Night	.286	2511	719	144	29	89	404	184	349	.331	.473	May	.302	526	159	26	8	17	84	37	70	.348	.471
Grass	.279	2599	725	147	21	96	429	195	349	.326	.462	June	.318	553	176	41	10	20	100	46	72	.369	.537
Turf	.317	520	165	35	9	14	80	42	69	.365	.500	July	.242	509	123	24	3	18	75	30	72	.280	.407
First Pitch	.298	382	114	13	9	21	89	18	0	.321	.545	August	.275	568	156	32	5	18	81	37	79	.313	.444
Ahead on Count	.348	891	310	62	4	40	174	124	0	.422	.561	September/October	.291	580	169	31	3	21	103	54	63	.346	.464
Behind on Count	.258	999	258	62	7	26	150	2	220	.259	.412	Pre-All Star	.296	1622	480	99	20	60	272	127	222	.345	.493
Two Strikes	.197	1184	233	49	8	26	123	78	417	.246	.319	Post-All Star	.274	1497	410	83	10	50	237	110	196	.318	.443

Batter vs. Pitcher (career)

Hits Best Against	Avg	AB	H	2B	3B	HR	RBI	BB	SO	OBP	SLG	Hits Worst Against	Avg	AB	H	2B	3B	HR	RBI	BB	SO	OBP	SLG
Bud Black	.667	21	14	4	0	2	7	1	0	.682	1.143	Gregg Olson	.000	10	0	0	0	0	0	1	3	.091	.000
Steve Farr	.500	18	9	1	0	1	3	2	6	.550	.722	Jeff Shaw	.000	10	0	0	0	0	0	1	1	.091	.000
Mike Mussina	.417	12	5	2	0	1	2	1	0	.462	.833	Pete Harnisch	.067	15	1	0	0	0	1	1	3	.118	.067
Dennis Rasmussen	.375	8	3	0	1	1	2	3	1	.500	1.000	Doug Jones	.071	14	1	0	0	0	0	0	2	.071	.071
Brian Fisher	.333	6	2	0	0	1	1	5	0	.636	.833	Ben McDonald	.091	11	1	0	0	0	0	1	1	.167	.091

Dave Silvestri — Yankees   Bats Right (flyball hitter)

	Avg	G	AB	R	H	2B	3B	HR	RBI	BB	SO	HBP	GDP	SB	CS	OBP	SLG	IBB	SH	SF	#Pit	#P/PA	GB	FB	G/F
1992 Season	.308	7	13	3	4	0	2	0	1	0	3	0	1	0	1	.308	.615	0	0	0	42	3.23	4	5	0.80

1992 Season

	Avg	AB	H	2B	3B	HR	RBI	BB	SO	OBP	SLG		Avg	AB	H	2B	3B	HR	RBI	BB	SO	OBP	SLG
vs. Left	.286	7	2	0	1	0	1	0	1	.286	.571	Scoring Posn	.000	1	0	0	0	0	0	0	1	.000	.000
vs. Right	.333	6	2	0	1	0	0	0	2	.333	.667	Close & Late	.500	2	1	0	1	0	1	0	0	.500	1.500

Mike Simms — Astros   Bats Right

	Avg	G	AB	R	H	2B	3B	HR	RBI	BB	SO	HBP	GDP	SB	CS	OBP	SLG	IBB	SH	SF	#Pit	#P/PA	GB	FB	G/F
1992 Season	.250	15	24	1	6	1	0	1	3	2	9	1	1	0	0	.333	.417	0	0	0	109	4.04	8	5	1.60
Career (1990-1992)	.219	76	160	22	35	7	0	5	21	20	51	1	4	1	0	.306	.356	0	0	2	726	3.97	50	43	1.16

1992 Season

	Avg	AB	H	2B	3B	HR	RBI	BB	SO	OBP	SLG		Avg	AB	H	2B	3B	HR	RBI	BB	SO	OBP	SLG
vs. Left	.286	14	4	1	0	1	2	1	4	.375	.571	Scoring Posn	.143	7	1	0	0	0	2	1	2	.250	.143
vs. Right	.200	10	2	0	0	0	1	1	5	.273	.200	Close & Late	.250	8	2	0	0	1	0	3	.250	.250

Doug Simons — Expos   Pitches Left

	ERA	W	L	Sv	G	GS	IP	BB	SO	Avg	H	2B	3B	HR	RBI	OBP	SLG	GF	IR	IRS	Hld	SvOp	SB	CS	GB	FB	G/F
1992 Season	23.63	0	0	0	7	0	5.1	2	6	.500	15	3	0	3	11	.529	.900	2	1	1	0	0	0	0	8	9	0.89
Career (1991-1992)	6.68	2	3	1	49	0	66.0	21	44	.276	70	16	1	8	45	.332	.441	13	18	7	3	1	5	4	97	75	1.29

1992 Season

	ERA	W	L	Sv	G	GS	IP	H	HR	BB	SO		Avg	AB	H	2B	3B	HR	RBI	BB	SO	OBP	SLG
Home	23.63	0	0	0	6	0	5.1	15	3	1	6	vs. Left	.444	9	4	0	0	1	3	1	3	.545	.778
Away	0.00	0	0	0	1	0	0.0	0	0	1	0	vs. Right	.524	21	11	3	0	2	8	1	3	.522	.952

Matt Sinatro — Mariners   Bats Right (groundball hitter)

	Avg	G	AB	R	H	2B	3B	HR	RBI	BB	SO	HBP	GDP	SB	CS	OBP	SLG	IBB	SH	SF	#Pit	#P/PA	GB	FB	G/F
1992 Season	.107	18	28	0	3	0	0	0	0	0	5	0	1	0	0	.107	.107	0	0	0	105	3.75	9	12	0.75
Last Five Years	.217	76	120	6	26	3	0	0	11	6	20	2	1	7	1	.258	.242	0	3	1	455	3.55	46	30	1.53

1992 Season

	Avg	AB	H	2B	3B	HR	RBI	BB	SO	OBP	SLG		Avg	AB	H	2B	3B	HR	RBI	BB	SO	OBP	SLG
vs. Left	.286	7	2	0	0	0	0	0	0	.286	.286	Scoring Posn	.000	4	0	0	0	0	0	0	1	.000	.000
vs. Right	.048	21	1	0	0	0	0	0	5	.048	.048	Close & Late	.000	2	0	0	0	0	0	0	0	.000	.000

404

Don Slaught — Pirates
Bats Right

	Avg	G	AB	R	H	2B	3B	HR	RBI	BB	SO	HBP	GDP	SB	CS	OBP	SLG	IBB	SH	SF	#Pit	#P/PA	GB	FB	G/F
1992 Season	.345	87	255	26	88	17	3	4	37	17	23	2	6	2	2	.384	.482	5	6	5	907	3.25	85	86	0.99
Last Five Years	.291	462	1377	139	401	96	11	23	176	119	193	16	33	5	4	.350	.426	14	21	19	5142	3.36	454	453	1.00

1992 Season

	Avg	AB	H	2B	3B	HR	RBI	BB	SO	OBP	SLG		Avg	AB	H	2B	3B	HR	RBI	BB	SO	OBP	SLG
vs. Left	.322	174	56	9	1	3	21	11	13	.362	.437	Scoring Posn	.296	71	21	3	0	0	27	8	7	.353	.338
vs. Right	.395	81	32	8	2	1	16	6	10	.429	.580	Close & Late	.308	52	16	1	1	0	9	3	7	.356	.365
Home	.336	131	44	11	3	2	21	11	14	.379	.511	None on/out	.265	68	18	4	1	3	2	4		.296	.485
Away	.355	124	44	6	0	2	16	6	9	.388	.452	Batting #7	.358	190	68	16	3	3	27	14	19	.400	.521
First Pitch	.400	55	22	4	0	0	5	5	0	.443	.473	Batting #8	.375	24	9	0	0	0	2	0	0	.375	.375
Ahead on Count	.433	60	26	4	1	2	12	7	0	.485	.633	Other	.268	41	11	1	0	1	8	3	4	.311	.366
Behind on Count	.314	86	27	3	1	0	12	0	17	.326	.372	Pre-All Star	.367	128	47	7	2	1	14	8	13	.399	.477
Two Strikes	.250	92	23	3	1	2	12	5	23	.294	.370	Post-All Star	.323	127	41	10	1	3	23	9	10	.369	.488

Last Five Years

	Avg	AB	H	2B	3B	HR	RBI	BB	SO	OBP	SLG		Avg	AB	H	2B	3B	HR	RBI	BB	SO	OBP	SLG
vs. Left	.293	710	208	52	6	10	81	71	101	.357	.425	Scoring Posn	.283	361	102	25	1	0	141	45	55	.352	.357
vs. Right	.289	667	193	46	5	13	95	48	92	.342	.432	Close & Late	.282	248	70	14	3	4	41	23	45	.356	.411
Groundball	.300	403	121	32	2	3	54	32	61	.359	.412	None on/out	.320	344	110	30	3	10	10	25	33	.378	.512
Flyball	.277	303	84	21	3	8	37	29	47	.343	.439	Batting #6	.303	274	83	24	2	3	33	15	41	.337	.438
Home	.296	703	208	60	7	13	96	63	98	.353	.457	Batting #7	.285	762	217	51	5	11	91	80	102	.357	.408
Away	.286	674	193	38	4	10	80	56	95	.347	.399	Other	.296	341	101	23	4	9	52	34	50	.345	.466
Day	.261	360	101	24	3	7	51	40	54	.350	.422	April	.347	202	70	17	3	7	37	13	33	.382	.564
Night	.295	1017	300	74	8	16	125	79	139	.350	.431	May	.323	254	82	20	5	4	38	29	26	.397	.488
Grass	.291	731	213	52	2	18	96	51	110	.340	.442	June	.322	230	74	16	0	2	23	15	35	.364	.417
Turf	.291	646	188	46	9	5	80	68	83	.361	.413	July	.210	195	41	11	0	2	20	25	35	.284	.297
First Pitch	.379	301	114	31	1	8	44	9	0	.399	.568	August	.257	268	69	18	1	5	32	21	35	.315	.388
Ahead on Count	.363	326	119	25	4	8	53	50	0	.445	.537	September/October	.285	228	65	16	2	3	26	21	29	.354	.412
Behind on Count	.217	420	91	21	1	4	41	0	118	.224	.300	Pre-All Star	.316	751	237	56	8	14	104	64	110	.370	.467
Two Strikes	.174	501	87	21	3	4	40	58	192	.260	.251	Post-All Star	.262	626	164	42	3	9	72	55	83	.327	.382

Batter vs. Pitcher (since 1984)

Hits Best Against	Avg	AB	H	2B	3B	HR	RBI	BB	SO	OBP	SLG	Hits Worst Against	Avg	AB	H	2B	3B	HR	RBI	BB	SO	OBP	SLG
Matt Young	.600	15	9	3	0	0	2	1	1	.625	.600	Dave Stewart	.000	19	0	0	0	0	2	2	5	.091	.000
Jim Deshaies	.583	12	7	3	0	0	3	3	1	.625	.833	Dave Righetti	.000	13	0	0	0	0	0	1	6	.071	.000
Dennis Martinez	.538	13	7	2	1	0	2	1	0	.571	.846	Mike Henneman	.000	10	0	0	0	0	0	1	3	.091	.000
Bill Krueger	.500	12	6	1	0	0	4	1	1	.538	.583	Bert Blyleven	.056	36	2	0	0	1	0	0	9	.056	.056
Chris Bosio	.417	12	5	1	0	1	2	0	2	.417	.750	Gene Nelson	.077	13	1	0	0	0	0	0	2	.077	.077

Heathcliff Slocumb — Cubs
Pitches Right (groundball pitcher)

	ERA	W	L	Sv	G	GS	IP	BB	SO	Avg	H	2B	3B	HR	RBI	OBP	SLG	GF	IR	IRS	Hld	SvOp	SB	CS	GB	FB	G/F
1992 Season	6.50	0	3	1	30	0	36.0	21	27	.351	52	3	0	3	29	.430	.432	11	22	6	1	1	4	4	55	27	2.04
Career (1991-1992)	4.56	2	4	2	82	0	98.2	51	61	.279	105	13	1	6	59	.364	.366	32	62	19	7	4	16	5	160	85	1.88

1992 Season

	ERA	W	L	Sv	G	GS	IP	H	HR	BB	SO		Avg	AB	H	2B	3B	HR	RBI	BB	SO	OBP	SLG
Home	4.58	0	2	1	11	0	19.2	23	0	11	16	vs. Left	.413	75	31	0	0	3	17	13	14	.506	.533
Away	8.82	0	1	0	19	0	16.1	29	3	10	11	vs. Right	.288	73	21	3	0	0	12	8	13	.349	.329
Starter	0.00	0	0	0	0	0	0.0	0	0	0	0	Scoring Posn	.396	53	21	1	0	2	28	8	7	.460	.528
Reliever	6.50	0	3	1	30	0	36.0	52	3	21	27	Close & Late	.419	31	13	0	0	1	6	6	4	.513	.516
0 Days rest	15.19	0	0	0	7	0	5.1	15	1	3	3	None on/out	.265	34	9	0	0	0	0	2	7	.324	.265
1 or 2 Days rest	5.02	0	2	1	13	0	14.1	15	2	11	4	First Pitch	.353	17	6	0	0	0	3	3	0	.429	.353
3+ Days rest	4.96	0	1	0	10	0	16.1	22	0	7	20	Behind on Count	.353	34	12	1	0	0	8	12	0	.511	.382
Pre-All Star	5.91	0	1	1	11	0	10.2	12	1	10	7	Ahead on Count	.380	71	27	2	0	2	14	0	20	.389	.493
Post-All Star	6.75	0	2	0	19	0	25.1	40	2	11	20	Two Strikes	.246	65	16	0	0	2	11	6	27	.310	.338

Joe Slusarski — Athletics
Pitches Right

	ERA	W	L	Sv	G	GS	IP	BB	SO	Avg	H	2B	3B	HR	RBI	OBP	SLG	CG	ShO	Sup	QS	#P/S	SB	CS	GB	FB	G/F
1992 Season	5.45	5	5	0	15	14	76.0	27	38	.284	85	17	3	15	40	.350	.512	0	0	5.21	3	83	6	4	103	100	1.03
Career (1991-1992)	5.34	10	12	0	35	33	185.1	79	98	.284	206	34	6	29	93	.358	.467	1	0	5.20	10	86	11	9	254	220	1.15

1992 Season

	ERA	W	L	Sv	G	GS	IP	H	HR	BB	SO		Avg	AB	H	2B	3B	HR	RBI	BB	SO	OBP	SLG
Home	4.96	3	4	0	10	9	52.2	60	11	17	32	vs. Left	.269	134	36	8	3	6	18	12	18	.324	.507
Away	6.56	2	1	0	5	5	23.1	25	4	10	6	vs. Right	.297	165	49	9	0	9	22	15	20	.370	.515
Starter	5.75	5	5	0	14	14	72.0	82	15	26	35	Scoring Posn	.321	56	18	4	1	3	25	7	10	.368	.589
Reliever	0.00	0	0	0	1	0	4.0	3	0	1	3	Close & Late	.000	4	0	0	0	0	0	0	1	.000	.000
0-3 Days Rest	4.91	0	0	0	1	1	3.2	7	0	2	4	None on/out	.272	81	22	4	2	5	5	4	10	.337	.556
4 Days Rest	5.56	2	3	0	8	8	43.2	46	9	15	22	First Pitch	.426	47	20	4	0	4	12	0	0	.417	.766
5+ Days Rest	6.20	3	2	0	5	5	24.2	29	6	9	9	Behind on Count	.271	70	19	5	1	4	8	15	0	.398	.543
Pre-All Star	5.58	5	4	0	14	13	71.0	81	14	25	33	Ahead on Count	.214	117	25	5	0	4	10	0	31	.236	.359
Post-All Star	3.60	0	1	0	1	1	5.0	4	1	2	5	Two Strikes	.232	112	26	4	1	4	8	12	38	.313	.393

405

John Smiley — Twins

	ERA	W	L	Sv	G	GS	IP	BB	SO	Avg	H	2B	3B	HR	RBI	OBP	SLG	CG	ShO	Sup	QS	#P/S	SB	CS	GB	FB	G/F
1992 Season	3.21	16	9	0	34	34	241.0	65	163	.231	205	51	4	17	84	.286	.356	5	2	4.44	22	104	25	16	290	283	1.02
Last Five Years	3.32	70	46	0	155	151	1008.1	240	630	.243	919	161	21	86	370	.289	.370	22	5	4.19	95	93	110	52	1247	1246	1.00

1992 Season

	ERA	W	L	Sv	G	GS	IP	H	HR	BB	SO		Avg	AB	H	2B	3B	HR	RBI	BB	SO	OBP	SLG
Home	2.83	10	4	0	19	19	136.2	117	8	40	94	vs. Left	.259	139	36	8	2	1	12	12	16	.316	.367
Away	3.71	6	5	0	15	15	104.1	88	9	25	69	vs. Right	.226	747	169	43	2	16	72	53	147	.280	.353
Day	4.22	5	4	0	11	11	74.2	75	6	19	47	Inning 1-6	.231	715	165	40	3	15	80	57	139	.290	.358
Night	2.76	11	5	0	23	23	166.1	130	11	46	116	Inning 7+	.234	171	40	11	1	2	4	8	24	.268	.345
Grass	3.20	5	4	0	12	12	84.1	66	8	23	56	None on	.236	552	130	37	3	11	11	38	105	.288	.373
Turf	3.22	11	5	0	22	22	156.2	139	9	42	107	Runners on	.225	334	75	14	1	6	73	27	58	.282	.326
April	6.84	2	0	0	5	5	25.0	24	3	17	13	Scoring Posn	.269	193	52	11	1	3	66	14	29	.315	.383
May	3.79	4	1	0	5	5	35.2	36	4	11	24	Close & Late	.185	81	15	4	0	1	1	6	14	.241	.272
June	1.34	4	0	0	6	6	47.0	34	4	8	35	None on/out	.255	239	61	21	1	5	5	15	38	.305	.414
July	3.25	2	2	0	5	5	36.0	26	3	11	28	vs. 1st Batr (relief)	.000	0	0	0	0	0	0	0	0	.000	.000
August	2.91	4	1	0	7	7	52.2	48	3	11	38	First Inning Pitched	.186	118	22	3	1	3	12	15	31	.284	.305
September/October	3.02	2	3	0	6	6	44.2	37	0	7	28	First 75 Pitches	.228	610	139	34	2	13	60	51	115	.290	.354
Starter	3.21	16	9	0	34	34	241.0	205	17	65	163	Pitch 76-90	.252	119	30	7	1	1	14	7	22	.292	.353
Reliever	0.00	0	0	0	0	0	0.0	0	0	0	0	Pitch 91-105	.204	93	19	3	0	2	6	5	18	.245	.301
0-3 Days Rest	0.00	0	0	0	0	0	0.0	0	0	0	0	Pitch 106+	.266	64	17	7	1	1	4	2	8	.288	.453
4 Days Rest	2.59	14	5	0	24	24	177.0	142	12	41	119	First Pitch	.315	124	39	6	0	2	13	0	0	.315	.411
5+ Days Rest	4.92	2	4	0	10	10	64.0	63	5	24	44	Ahead on Count	.169	439	74	20	2	3	27	0	138	.175	.244
Pre-All Star	3.48	9	4	0	18	18	121.2	105	12	41	80	Behind on Count	.325	166	54	13	2	7	24	38	0	.449	.554
Post-All Star	2.94	7	5	0	16	16	119.1	100	5	24	83	Two Strikes	.146	412	60	15	1	5	22	27	163	.205	.223

Last Five Years

	ERA	W	L	Sv	G	GS	IP	H	HR	BB	SO		Avg	AB	H	2B	3B	HR	RBI	BB	SO	OBP	SLG
Home	3.08	36	23	0	75	73	496.2	439	40	135	311	vs. Left	.230	592	136	22	8	10	57	43	91	.282	.345
Away	3.55	34	23	0	80	78	511.2	480	46	105	319	vs. Right	.245	3190	783	159	13	76	313	197	539	.290	.375
Day	3.56	26	15	0	51	50	318.1	322	23	62	179	Inning 1-6	.241	3173	765	150	19	69	325	205	554	.288	.366
Night	3.21	44	31	0	104	101	690.0	597	63	178	451	Inning 7+	.253	609	154	31	2	17	45	35	76	.293	.394
Grass	3.36	22	17	0	47	47	310.2	272	33	73	187	None on	.237	2354	558	117	11	51	51	148	407	.286	.361
Turf	3.30	48	29	0	108	104	697.2	647	53	167	443	Runners on	.253	1428	361	64	10	35	319	92	223	.295	.385
April	3.49	9	7	0	23	22	142.0	122	9	40	80	Scoring Posn	.271	797	216	39	6	19	271	64	126	.318	.407
May	3.48	14	6	0	24	24	160.1	158	13	36	101	Close & Late	.208	327	68	13	1	8	20	23	53	.260	.327
June	2.58	12	4	0	22	22	153.2	126	14	29	118	None on/out	.247	1012	250	58	6	23	23	58	161	.292	.384
July	3.36	9	13	0	28	28	193.0	157	20	65	129	vs. 1st Batr (relief)	.250	4	1	1	0	0	1	0	0	.250	.500
August	3.25	13	7	0	29	28	185.1	189	14	39	107	First Inning Pitched	.244	574	140	24	5	16	72	48	102	.301	.387
September/October	3.72	13	9	0	29	27	174.0	167	16	31	95	First 75 Pitches	.240	2917	700	136	18	63	282	184	501	.286	.364
Starter	3.33	69	46	0	151	151	1002.0	912	86	237	626	Pitch 76-90	.261	467	122	25	1	12	53	27	68	.302	.396
Reliever	1.42	1	0	0	4	0	6.1	7	0	3	2	Pitch 91-105	.223	269	60	11	0	7	22	20	44	.277	.342
0-3 Days Rest	5.11	0	1	0	2	2	12.1	15	0	4	10	Pitch 106+	.287	129	37	9	2	4	13	9	17	.333	.481
4 Days Rest	3.13	44	26	0	90	90	608.2	541	56	139	384	First Pitch	.319	637	203	34	3	21	87	7	0	.326	.480
5+ Days Rest	3.59	25	19	0	59	59	381.0	356	30	94	234	Ahead on Count	.194	1891	367	71	12	20	129	0	563	.198	.276
Pre-All Star	3.15	38	21	0	78	77	520.1	457	40	124	342	Behind on Count	.312	667	208	48	3	28	85	138	0	.428	.519
Post-All Star	3.50	32	25	0	77	74	488.0	462	46	116	288	Two Strikes	.163	1692	276	54	8	17	95	95	630	.211	.235

Pitcher vs. Batter (career)

Pitches Best Vs.	Avg	AB	H	2B	3B	HR	RBI	BB	SO	OBP	SLG	Pitches Worst Vs.	Avg	AB	H	2B	3B	HR	RBI	BB	SO	OBP	SLG
Jack Clark	.000	9	0	0	0	0	0	2	4	.182	.000	Junior Noboa	.545	11	6	2	0	0	1	0	2	.545	.727
Lance Blankenship	.000	9	0	0	0	0	0	0	0	.182	.000	Mark McGwire	.500	10	5	2	0	2	2	3	2	.615	1.300
Joey Cora	.000	8	0	0	0	0	0	2	1	.333	.000	Andre Dawson	.447	38	17	1	1	4	9	0	4	.447	.842
George Brett	.091	11	1	0	0	0	0	0	1	.091	.091	Matt D. Williams	.429	21	9	0	0	4	11	1	4	.455	1.000
Dean Palmer	.091	11	1	0	0	0	0		3	.091	.091	Glenn Davis	.333	24	8	0	0	4	9	3	3	.379	.833

Bryn Smith — Cardinals

	ERA	W	L	Sv	G	GS	IP	BB	SO	Avg	H	2B	3B	HR	RBI	OBP	SLG	GF	IR	IRS	Hld	SvOp	SB	CS	GB	FB	G/F
1992 Season	4.64	4	2	0	13	1	21.1	5	9	.247	20	2	0	3	10	.315	.383	3	0	0	3	0	4	0	38	21	1.81
Last Five Years	3.45	47	40	0	135	121	775.0	166	432	.248	724	113	24	61	302	.293	.366	3	1	0	4	0	101	26	1174	766	1.53

1992 Season

	ERA	W	L	Sv	G	GS	IP	H	HR	BB	SO		Avg	AB	H	2B	3B	HR	RBI	BB	SO	OBP	SLG
Home	5.11	2	0	0	7	1	12.1	12	1	4	7	vs. Left	.270	37	10	2	0	0	2	3	3	.341	.324
Away	4.00	2	2	0	6	0	9.0	8	2	1	2	vs. Right	.227	44	10	0	0	3	8	2	6	.292	.432

Last Five Years

	ERA	W	L	Sv	G	GS	IP	H	HR	BB	SO		Avg	AB	H	2B	3B	HR	RBI	BB	SO	OBP	SLG
Home	3.15	25	15	0	70	63	416.2	376	28	102	241	vs. Left	.260	1637	426	70	16	22	169	97	194	.305	.363
Away	3.79	22	25	0	65	58	358.1	348	33	64	191	vs. Right	.232	1282	298	43	8	39	133	69	238	.278	.370
Day	3.70	14	14	0	43	38	245.2	224	21	55	144	Inning 1-6	.247	2555	631	101	20	51	276	150	383	.293	.382
Night	3.33	33	26	0	92	83	529.1	500	40	111	288	Inning 7+	.255	364	93	12	4	10	26	16	49	.294	.393

Last Five Years

	ERA	W	L	Sv	G	GS	IP	H	HR	BB	SO
Grass	4.01	10	18	0	37	34	213.1	215	25	36	117
Turf	3.24	37	22	0	98	87	561.2	509	36	130	315
April	3.30	7	4	0	17	17	106.1	97	10	23	50
May	3.62	10	8	0	24	24	156.2	151	12	29	88
June	3.71	7	6	0	21	20	126.0	123	10	27	69
July	2.85	8	7	0	22	22	139.0	112	10	31	90
August	3.94	5	7	0	18	17	107.1	108	9	20	55
September/October	3.35	10	8	0	33	21	139.2	133	10	36	80
Starter	3.44	43	38	0	121	121	754.0	703	58	163	422
Reliever	3.86	4	2	0	14	0	21.0	21	3	3	10
0 Days rest	0.00	1	0	0	2	0	1.2	0	0	1	0
1 or 2 Days rest	4.26	2	2	0	8	0	12.2	15	2	1	5
3+ Days rest	4.05	1	0	0	4	0	6.2	6	1	1	5
Pre-All Star	3.31	27	19	0	69	68	438.0	399	35	87	235
Post-All Star	3.63	20	21	0	66	53	337.0	325	26	79	197

	Avg	AB	H	2B	3B	HR	RBI	BB	SO	OBP	SLG
None on	.239	1817	435	56	14	34	34	95	264	.282	.342
Runners on	.262	1102	289	57	10	27	268	71	168	.310	.406
Scoring Posn	.254	633	161	31	10	18	239	56	116	.313	.420
Close & Late	.323	155	50	6	1	5	13	6	20	.352	.471
None on/out	.249	782	195	23	8	19	19	32	103	.283	.372
vs. 1st Batr (relief)	.154	13	2	0	0	0	0	0	0	.214	.154
First Inning Pitched	.278	518	144	19	7	14	76	41	65	.336	.423
First 15 Pitches	.282	479	135	17	5	12	47	32	49	.333	.413
Pitch 16-30	.211	526	111	12	3	8	43	28	96	.256	.291
Pitch 31-45	.246	512	126	27	5	13	54	27	79	.288	.395
Pitch 46+	.251	1402	352	57	11	28	158	79	208	.294	.367
First Pitch	.336	530	178	21	4	11	75	9	0	.346	.453
Ahead on Count	.192	1346	258	33	7	18	93	0	371	.201	.267
Behind on Count	.317	575	182	40	7	22	95	90	0	.407	.525
Two Strikes	.163	1197	195	21	5	19	72	67	430	.216	.236

Pitcher vs. Batter (since 1984)

Pitches Best Vs.	Avg	AB	H	2B	3B	HR	RBI	BB	SO	OBP	SLG
Tim Teufel	.000	10	0	0	0	0	0	2	4	.167	.000
Gregg Jefferies	.059	17	1	0	0	0	0	0	1	.059	.059
Larry Walker	.067	15	1	0	0	0	1	0	1	.067	.067
Luis Gonzalez	.083	12	1	0	0	0	1	0	3	.083	.083
Casey Candaele	.091	11	1	0	0	0	0	1	1	.167	.091

Pitches Worst Vs.	Avg	AB	H	2B	3B	HR	RBI	BB	SO	OBP	SLG
Daryl Boston	.700	10	7	1	1	0	3	3	0	.769	1.000
Randy Ready	.450	20	9	2	0	1		0	2	.450	.700
Andy Van Slyke	.432	37	16	4	0	1	6	5	3	.500	.622
Chili Davis	.429	14	6	1	0	2	3	1	2	.467	.929
Franklin Stubbs	.400	20	8	3	0		4	3	4	.478	1.150

Dan Smith — Rangers   Pitches Left

	ERA	W	L	Sv	G	GS	IP	BB	SO	Avg	H	2B	3B	HR	RBI	OBP	SLG	CG	ShO	Sup	QS	#P/S	SB	CS	GB	FB	G/F
1992 Season	5.02	0	3	0	4	2	14.1	8	5	.321	18	7	0	1	8	.400	.500	0	0	2.51	0	92	1	2	25	17	1.47

1992 Season

	ERA	W	L	Sv	G	GS	IP	H	HR	BB	SO		Avg	AB	H	2B	3B	HR	RBI	BB	SO	OBP	SLG
Home	4.82	0	2	0	2	1	9.1	11	0	5	3	vs. Left	.143	7	1	1	0	0	0	0	2	.143	.286
Away	5.40	0	1	0	2	1	5.0	7	1	3	2	vs. Right	.347	49	17	6	0	1	8	8	3	.431	.531

Dave Smith — Cubs   Pitches Right (groundball pitcher)

	ERA	W	L	Sv	G	GS	IP	BB	SO	Avg	H	2B	3B	HR	RBI	OBP	SLG	GF	IR	IRS	Hld	SvOp	SB	CS	GB	FB	G/F
1992 Season	2.51	0	0	0	11	0	14.1	4	3	.273	15	1	1	0	6	.317	.327	4	8	3	1	0	2	0	23	19	1.21
Last Five Years	3.07	13	21	92	198	0	223.0	81	138	.250	208	26	12	12	104	.317	.353	74	115	42	4	112	16	10	331	219	1.51

1992 Season

	ERA	W	L	Sv	G	GS	IP	H	HR	BB	SO		Avg	AB	H	2B	3B	HR	RBI	BB	SO	OBP	SLG
Home	1.35	0	0	0	6	0	6.2	7	0	0	2	vs. Left	.333	27	9	1	1	0	5	3	1	.400	.444
Away	3.52	0	0	0	5	0	7.2	8	0	4	1	vs. Right	.214	28	6	0	0	0	1	1	2	.233	.214

Last Five Years

	ERA	W	L	Sv	G	GS	IP	H	HR	BB	SO		Avg	AB	H	2B	3B	HR	RBI	BB	SO	OBP	SLG
Home	3.22	9	11	52	104	0	114.2	105	7	33	81	vs. Left	.284	429	122	16	6	6	59	43	57	.352	.392
Away	2.91	4	10	40	94	0	106.1	103	5	48	57	vs. Right	.213	403	86	10	6	6	45	38	81	.281	.313
Day	4.07	3	8	30	71	0	77.1	74	7	31	43	Inning 1-6	.091	11	1	0	0	0	1	2	0	.214	.091
Night	2.53	10	13	62	127	0	145.2	134	5	50	95	Inning 7+	.252	821	207	26	12	12	103	79	138	.319	.357
Grass	3.46	2	10	29	73	0	83.1	84	7	30	50	None on	.243	419	102	14	3	3	38	74		.309	.313
Turf	2.84	11	11	63	125	0	139.2	124	5	51	88	Runners on	.257	413	106	12	9	9	101	43	64	.325	.395
April	3.30	1	6	20	40	0	43.2	42	2	19	32	Scoring Posn	.254	264	67	6	5	7	89	40	40	.347	.394
May	2.41	2	2	21	36	0	41.0	27	1	12	21	Close & Late	.247	457	113	15	9	9	66	55	86	.329	.379
June	3.14	1	3	19	41	0	43.0	49	2	15	31	None on/out	.290	186	54	3	1	2	16	26		.350	.349
July	3.55	1	3	12	30	0	33.0	31	5	11	22	vs. 1st Batr (relief)	.277	184	51	2	2	5	18	13	27	.323	.391
August	2.67	4	4	10	25	0	30.1	27	0	14	11	First Inning Pitched	.244	672	164	21	10	12	89	67	111	.313	.359
September/October	3.38	2	2	10	26	0	32.0	32	2	10	21	First 15 Pitches	.248	589	146	16	8	12	68	58	96	.315	.363
Starter	0.00	0	0	0	0	0	0.0	0	0	0	0	Pitch 16-30	.248	214	53	9	3	0	30	21	34	.318	.318
Reliever	3.07	13	21	92	198	0	223.0	208	12	81	138	Pitch 31-45	.321	28	9	1	1	0	6	2	7	.367	.429
0 Days rest	2.43	3	4		43	0	40.2	38	5	3	20	Pitch 46+	.000	1	0	0	0	0	0	0	0	.000	.000
1 or 2 Days rest	3.66	5	7	36	70	0	76.1	68	6	28	60	First Pitch	.295	105	31	5	0	1	13	21	0	.417	.371
3+ Days rest	2.89	5	8	32	85	0	106.0	102	3	33	50	Ahead on Count	.210	400	84	8	7	1	28	1	113	.213	.273
Pre-All Star	2.91	6	13	64	126	0	139.0	125	6	51	88	Behind on Count	.301	163	49	6	1	6	31	33	0	.416	.460
Post-All Star	3.32	7	8	28	72	0	84.0	83	6	30	50	Two Strikes	.176	387	68	6	8	4	35	26	138	.228	.264

Pitcher vs. Batter (since 1984)

Pitches Best Vs.	Avg	AB	H	2B	3B	HR	RBI	BB	SO	OBP	SLG
Von Hayes	.000	13	0	0	0	0	0	0	3	.000	.000
Andre Dawson	.000	10	0	0	0	0	0	1	1	.091	.000
Pedro Guerrero	.000	10	0	0	0	0	0	3	1	.231	.000
Ken Oberkfell	.095	21	2	1	0	0	3	1	1	.136	.143
Benito Santiago	.100	10	1	0	0	0	5	0	1	.083	.100

Pitches Worst Vs.	Avg	AB	H	2B	3B	HR	RBI	BB	SO	OBP	SLG
Tony Gwynn	.583	12	7	0	0	0	0	1	0	.615	.583
Milt Thompson	.455	11	5	1	0	0		2	1	.538	.545
Kevin McReynolds	.438	16	7	1	0	3	9	1	2	.471	1.063
Will Clark	.375	8	3	1	1	0	4	2	1	.455	.750
Tim Wallach	.313	16	5	1	0	1	3	0	5	.313	.563

Dwight Smith — Cubs
Bats Left (groundball hitter)

	Avg	G	AB	R	H	2B	3B	HR	RBI	BB	SO	HBP	GDP	SB	CS	OBP	SLG	IBB	SH	SF	#Pit	#P/PA	GB	FB	G/F
1992 Season	.276	109	217	28	60	10	3	3	24	13	40	1	1	9	8	.318	.392	0	0	2	858	3.68	82	47	1.74
Career (1989-1992)	.280	425	1017	130	265	51	11	21	124	83	169	6	13	31	21	.337	.414	4	5	5	4075	3.67	418	238	1.76

1992 Season

	Avg	AB	H	2B	3B	HR	RBI	BB	SO	OBP	SLG		Avg	AB	H	2B	3B	HR	RBI	BB	SO	OBP	SLG
vs. Left	.200	20	4	0	0	1	4	0	5	.200	.350	Scoring Posn	.347	49	17	1	0	0	17	2	11	.358	.367
vs. Right	.284	197	56	10	3	2	20	13	35	.329	.396	Close & Late	.250	64	16	3	0	1	4	4	13	.304	.344
Home	.290	100	29	3	1	3	13	7	15	.339	.430	None on/out	.233	60	14	3	0	3	3	2	5	.258	.433
Away	.265	117	31	7	2	0	11	6	25	.298	.359	Batting #1	.323	62	20	2	1	1	9	3	7	.343	.435
First Pitch	.368	38	14	3	1	1	4	0	0	.368	.579	Batting #9	.243	37	9	3	0	1	3	2	7	.282	.405
Ahead on Count	.291	55	16	4	0	0	6	6	0	.355	.364	Other	.263	118	31	5	2	1	12	8	26	.315	.364
Behind on Count	.281	64	18	1	1	1	6	0	25	.281	.375	Pre-All Star	.248	101	25	4	1	2	7	4	20	.276	.366
Two Strikes	.220	100	22	3	0	1	11	7	40	.269	.280	Post-All Star	.302	116	35	6	2	1	17	9	20	.352	.414

Career (1989-1992)

	Avg	AB	H	2B	3B	HR	RBI	BB	SO	OBP	SLG		Avg	AB	H	2B	3B	HR	RBI	BB	SO	OBP	SLG
vs. Left	.211	90	19	2	1	3	12	6	26	.265	.356	Scoring Posn	.305	256	78	15	1	4	95	26	54	.367	.418
vs. Right	.287	927	266	49	10	18	112	77	143	.344	.420	Close & Late	.244	209	51	10	2	4	22	12	36	.289	.368
Groundball	.296	412	122	21	5	8	58	22	69	.334	.430	None on/out	.232	246	57	15	2	7	7	17	39	.284	.394
Flyball	.289	225	65	11	5	4	27	25	39	.364	.436	Batting #3	.285	207	59	6	2	7	25	22	35	.357	.435
Home	.296	483	143	24	4	13	69	41	73	.353	.443	Batting #5	.291	220	64	13	1	7	29	17	30	.346	.455
Away	.266	534	142	27	7	8	55	42	96	.322	.388	Other	.275	590	162	32	8	7	70	44	104	.326	.392
Day	.292	545	159	26	7	11	70	45	82	.348	.426	April	.211	90	19	5	1	1	7	10	15	.297	.322
Night	.267	472	126	25	4	10	54	38	87	.324	.400	May	.311	183	57	11	3	3	19	11	29	.354	.454
Grass	.297	687	204	32	6	16	80	52	106	.348	.431	June	.286	213	61	12	1	6	26	20	37	.347	.437
Turf	.245	330	81	19	5	5	44	31	63	.314	.379	July	.278	144	40	11	1	4	17	9	21	.325	.451
First Pitch	.333	180	60	10	2	2	14	1	0	.337	.444	August	.241	174	42	5	1	4	26	7	39	.269	.351
Ahead on Count	.319	279	89	22	2	9	46	38	0	.400	.509	September/October	.310	213	66	7	4	3	29	26	28	.387	.423
Behind on Count	.230	269	62	8	4	4	27	0	84	.242	.335	Pre-All Star	.288	538	155	31	5	11	55	45	85	.345	.426
Two Strikes	.205	430	88	16	5	4	43	42	169	.277	.293	Post-All Star	.271	479	130	20	6	10	69	38	84	.327	.401

Batter vs. Pitcher (career)

Hits Best Against	Avg	AB	H	2B	3B	HR	RBI	BB	SO	OBP	SLG	Hits Worst Against	Avg	AB	H	2B	3B	HR	RBI	BB	SO	OBP	SLG
Walt Terrell	.579	19	11	2	0	1	2	1	1	.600	.842	John Smoltz	.000	15	0	0	0	0	0	0	2	.000	.000
Omar Olivares	.500	14	7	3	1	1	6	1	3	.533	1.071	Roger McDowell	.083	12	1	0	0	0	0	0	0	.214	.083
David Cone	.462	13	6	1	1	3	2	1	1	.533	.923	Mike Morgan	.125	16	2	0	0	0	0	1	4	.176	.125
Cris Carpenter	.455	11	5	3	0	0	1	1	2	.500	.727	Tim Belcher	.143	14	2	1	0	0	0	2	2	.250	.214
Mark Gardner	.429	14	6	1	1	1	3	2	2	.471	.857	John Burkett	.214	14	3	0	0	0	0	0	2	.214	.214

Lee Smith — Cardinals
Pitches Right (flyball pitcher)

	ERA	W	L	Sv	G	GS	IP	BB	SO	Avg	H	2B	3B	HR	RBI	OBP	SLG	GF	IR	IRS	Hld	SvOp	SB	CS	GB	FB	G/F
1992 Season	3.12	4	9	43	70	0	75.0	26	60	.221	62	8	4	4	31	.286	.320	55	13	4	0	51	12	1	77	93	0.83
Last Five Years	2.76	25	23	175	329	0	385.1	138	406	.227	328	49	10	25	160	.293	.327	169	188	52	6	208	51	13	376	438	0.86

1992 Season

	ERA	W	L	Sv	G	GS	IP	H	HR	BB	SO		Avg	AB	H	2B	3B	HR	RBI	BB	SO	OBP	SLG
Home	3.25	3	8	18	40	0	44.1	40	1	17	44	vs. Left	.220	164	36	5	4	2	19	20	38	.303	.335
Away	2.93	1	1	25	30	0	30.2	22	3	9	16	vs. Right	.222	117	26	3	0	2	12	6	22	.260	.299
Day	3.72	2	3	11	18	0	19.1	19	1	10	14	Inning 1-6	.000	0	0	0	0	0	0	0	0	.000	.000
Night	2.91	2	6	32	52	0	55.2	43	3	16	46	Inning 7+	.221	281	62	8	4	4	31	26	60	.286	.320
Grass	2.70	1	0	13	16	0	16.2	10	2	4	5	None on	.194	165	32	2	3	2	2	11	31	.244	.279
Turf	3.24	3	9	30	54	0	58.1	52	2	22	55	Runners on	.259	116	30	6	1	2	29	15	29	.341	.379
April	2.38	0	1	7	9	0	11.1	7	1	1	7	Scoring Posn	.257	74	19	3	1	1	24	12	22	.356	.365
May	3.72	1	1	7	11	0	9.2	9	1	4	13	Close & Late	.204	240	49	6	1	2	24	23	55	.274	.263
June	4.50	1	1	3	9	0	12.0	14	1	6	11	None on/out	.230	74	17	1	2	1	1	1	11	.240	.338
July	0.82	1	1	7	10	0	11.0	6	0	2	14	vs. 1st Batr (relief)	.200	70	14	0	1	2		0	10	.200	.271
August	2.87	0	2	12	15	0	15.2	12	0	5	14	First Inning Pitched	.217	249	54	7	3	3	26	23	53	.282	.305
September/October	4.11	1	4	7	16	0	15.1	14	1	8	9	First 15 Pitches	.213	207	44	5	4	3	16	14	38	.261	.319
Starter	0.00	0	0	0	0	0	0.0	0	0	0	0	Pitch 16-30	.250	64	16	1	0	1	12	10	19	.351	.313
Reliever	3.12	4	9	43	70	0	75.0	62	4	26	60	Pitch 31-45	.125	8	1	1	0	0	0	2	2	.300	.250
0 Days rest	2.96	0	5	14	26	0	27.1	24	0	15	24	Pitch 46+	.500	2	1	1	0	0	1	0	1	.500	1.000
1 or 2 Days rest	2.00	3	1	20	26	0	27.0	16	2	5	24	First Pitch	.265	34	9	1	0	0	3	2	0	.306	.294
3+ Days rest	4.79	1	3	9	18	0	20.2	22	2	6	12	Ahead on Count	.188	154	29	4	1	3	16	0	54	.188	.286
Pre-All Star	3.03	2	3	23	35	0	38.2	33	3	12	33	Behind on Count	.275	40	11	1	1	1	5	9	0	.400	.425
Post-All Star	3.22	2	6	20	35	0	36.1	29	1	14	27	Two Strikes	.167	150	25	3	3	3	16	15	60	.242	.287

Last Five Years

	ERA	W	L	Sv	G	GS	IP	H	HR	BB	SO		Avg	AB	H	2B	3B	HR	RBI	BB	SO	OBP	SLG
Home	2.72	21	14	87	183	0	222.0	191	12	74	246	vs. Left	.231	792	183	27	6	16	96	93	228	.311	.341
Away	2.81	4	9	88	146	0	163.1	137	13	64	160	vs. Right	.222	653	145	22	4	9	64	45	178	.271	.309
Day	2.90	10	8	57	113	0	136.1	113	10	55	165	Inning 1-6	.000	0	0	0	0	0	0	0	0	.000	.000

Last Five Years

	ERA	W	L	Sv	G	GS	IP	H	HR	BB	SO		Avg	AB	H	2B	3B	HR	RBI	BB	SO	OBP	SLG
Night	2.67	15	15	118	216	0	249.0	215	15	83	241	Inning 7+	.227	1445	328	49	10	25	160	138	406	.293	.327
Grass	2.58	14	5	82	162	0	195.1	144	12	84	227	None on	.211	750	158	23	8	9	9	63	203	.273	.299
Turf	2.94	11	18	93	167	0	190.0	184	13	54	179	Runners on	.245	695	170	26	2	16	151	75	203	.315	.357
April	2.44	7	4	25	44	0	55.1	43	3	22	62	Scoring Posn	.227	440	100	17	2	9	132	58	137	.312	.336
May	4.03	5	4	20	50	0	51.1	50	3	16	53	Close & Late	.231	914	211	32	5	16	109	86	252	.296	.329
June	3.22	2	3	25	56	0	72.2	67	5	29	76	None on/out	.208	322	67	8	3	5	5	24	80	.265	.298
July	2.40	8	2	33	55	0	71.1	60	7	20	74	vs. 1st Batr (relief)	.223	309	69	10	1	5	28	19	70	.267	.311
August	2.25	1	4	35	60	0	64.0	51	3	19	65	First Inning Pitched	.232	1145	266	41	9	20	138	109	323	.297	.336
September/October	2.42	2	6	37	64	0	70.2	57	4	32	76	First 15 Pitches	.235	948	223	38	8	16	89	76	237	.291	.343
Starter	0.00	0	0	0	0	0	0.0	0	0	0	0	Pitch 16-30	.216	398	86	6	2	8	58	52	138	.304	.302
Reliever	2.76	25	23	175	329	0	385.1	328	25	138	406	Pitch 31-45	.198	91	18	4	0	1	12	10	27	.277	.275
0 Days rest	2.05	3	8	55	89	0	101.0	83	4	41	111	Pitch 46+	.125	8	1	1	0	0	1	0	4	.125	.250
1 or 2 Days rest	2.79	11	5	86	149	0	177.1	146	14	53	178	First Pitch	.280	164	46	6	1	5	29	20	0	.357	.421
3+ Days rest	3.36	11	10	34	91	0	107.0	99	7	44	117	Ahead on Count	.181	785	142	16	5	10	65	0	328	.181	.252
Pre-All Star	3.10	17	13	84	172	0	206.0	179	14	79	212	Behind on Count	.308	198	61	7	2	5	30	56	0	.455	.439
Post-All Star	2.36	8	10	91	157	0	179.1	149	11	59	194	Two Strikes	.168	835	140	18	6	10	66	61	406	.224	.240

Pitcher vs. Batter (since 1984)

Pitches Best Vs.	Avg	AB	H	2B	3B	HR	RBI	BB	SO	OBP	SLG	Pitches Worst Vs.	Avg	AB	H	2B	3B	HR	RBI	BB	SO	OBP	SLG
John Kruk	.000	15	0	0	0	0	0	1	6	.063	.000	Jack Clark	.500	14	7	0	2	1	7	4	0	.611	1.000
Herm Winningham	.077	13	1	0	0	0	0	1	7	.077	.154	Mariano Duncan	.500	14	7	0	2	0	3	0	1	.500	.786
Dickie Thon	.091	11	1	0	0	0	0	0	1	.091	.091	Vince Coleman	.500	8	4	0	0	0	0	3	2	.636	.500
Gary Carter	.105	19	2	0	0	0	0	0	6	.105	.105	Rafael Ramirez	.364	11	4	3	0	1	2	1	2	.417	.909
Kevin Bass	.111	18	2	0	0	0	0	0	4	.111	.111	Tim Wallach	.333	21	7	2	0	2	2	3	3	.417	.714

Lonnie Smith — Braves   Bats Right (flyball hitter)

	Avg	G	AB	R	H	2B	3B	HR	RBI	BB	SO	HBP	GDP	SB	CS	OBP	SLG	IBB	SH	SF	#Pit	#P/PA	GB	FB	G/F
1992 Season	.247	84	158	23	39	8	2	6	33	17	37	3	1	4	0	.324	.437	1	0	4	691	3.80	44	53	0.83
Last Five Years	.291	518	1573	256	457	91	16	46	207	211	290	29	14	52	29	.380	.456	10	4	20	6898	3.76	459	517	0.89

1992 Season

	Avg	AB	H	2B	3B	HR	RBI	BB	SO	OBP	SLG		Avg	AB	H	2B	3B	HR	RBI	BB	SO	OBP	SLG
vs. Left	.277	65	18	4	1	3	14	7	13	.347	.508	Scoring Posn	.319	47	15	1	1	4	29	8	13	.390	.638
vs. Right	.226	93	21	4	1	3	19	10	24	.308	.387	Close & Late	.167	42	7	2	0	2	8	7	8	.288	.357
Home	.239	71	17	3	1	3	13	10	13	.333	.437	None on/out	.211	38	8	1	0	2	2	4	5	.302	.395
Away	.253	87	22	5	1	3	20	7	20	.316	.437	Batting #4	.370	46	17	3	1	3	17	4	6	.423	.674
First Pitch	.250	24	6	0	0	1	3	1	0	.333	.375	Batting #9	.176	34	6	1	0	2	5	6	8	.317	.382
Ahead on Count	.267	30	8	2	0	1	7	7	0	.395	.433	Other	.205	78	16	4	1	1	11	7	23	.270	.321
Behind on Count	.245	49	12	2	0	2	11	0	18	.250	.408	Pre-All Star	.204	54	11	1	0	1	7	6	15	.274	.278
Two Strikes	.187	75	14	3	2	2	12	9	37	.271	.360	Post-All Star	.269	104	28	7	2	5	26	11	22	.350	.519

Last Five Years

	Avg	AB	H	2B	3B	HR	RBI	BB	SO	OBP	SLG		Avg	AB	H	2B	3B	HR	RBI	BB	SO	OBP	SLG
vs. Left	.303	621	188	43	8	19	78	81	102	.388	.490	Scoring Posn	.314	350	110	15	3	9	152	65	70	.413	.451
vs. Right	.283	952	269	48	8	27	129	130	188	.376	.435	Close & Late	.243	259	63	12	2	7	24	39	59	.359	.386
Groundball	.306	536	164	32	7	13	72	73	105	.394	.465	None on/out	.273	472	129	22	6	13	13	49	83	.352	.428
Flyball	.251	371	93	20	3	15	49	55	71	.353	.442	Batting #1	.326	558	182	33	8	16	57	74	79	.412	.500
Home	.308	780	240	49	8	23	112	100	145	.389	.479	Batting #3	.282	472	133	27	4	13	74	68	101	.377	.439
Away	.274	793	217	42	8	23	95	111	145	.372	.434	Other	.262	543	142	31	4	17	76	69	110	.351	.427
Day	.301	379	114	20	3	16	44	59	78	.399	.496	April	.259	170	44	7	2	4	19	27	38	.369	.394
Night	.287	1194	343	71	13	30	163	152	212	.374	.444	May	.269	193	52	14	2	5	27	34	41	.386	.440
Grass	.296	1170	346	66	11	38	159	160	216	.385	.468	June	.308	214	66	10	4	9	27	22	28	.379	.519
Turf	.275	403	111	25	5	8	48	51	74	.368	.422	July	.324	272	88	13	4	10	41	48	52	.430	.511
First Pitch	.382	296	113	26	5	11	40	6	0	.408	.615	August	.301	335	101	28	1	6	44	30	53	.364	.445
Ahead on Count	.328	348	114	24	2	18	59	102	0	.474	.563	September/October	.272	389	106	19	3	12	49	50	78	.361	.429
Behind on Count	.244	446	109	19	4	11	67	2	118	.267	.379	Pre-All Star	.285	653	186	36	8	22	81	95	124	.383	.466
Two Strikes	.205	683	140	28	8	5	61	96	289	.319	.291	Post-All Star	.295	920	271	55	8	24	126	116	166	.378	.450

Batter vs. Pitcher (since 1984)

Hits Best Against	Avg	AB	H	2B	3B	HR	RBI	BB	SO	OBP	SLG	Hits Worst Against	Avg	AB	H	2B	3B	HR	RBI	BB	SO	OBP	SLG
Bob Walk	.714	14	10	2	0	2	7	0	0	.714	1.286	Ramon Martinez	.000	12	0	0	0	0	1	0	6	.000	.000
Ken Hill	.545	11	6	3	0	0	2	3	0	.643	.818	Greg Swindell	.000	9	0	0	0	0	0	0	1	.182	.000
Mitch Williams	.500	4	2	1	1	0	3	7	1	.818	1.250	Larry Andersen	.091	11	1	0	0	0	0	1	3	.167	.091
Norm Charlton	.412	17	7	1	1	2	3	2	4	.474	.941	Neal Heaton	.111	18	2	0	0	0	1	2	2	.200	.111
Dennis Cook	.412	17	7	1	0	3	6	0	1	.412	1.000	Jose DeLeon	.133	30	4	0	0	0	1	5	12	.257	.133

Ozzie Smith — Cardinals — Bats Both (groundball hitter)

	Avg	G	AB	R	H	2B	3B	HR	RBI	BB	SO	HBP	GDP	SB	CS	OBP	SLG	IBB	SH	SF	#Pit	#P/PA	GB	FB	G/F
1992 Season	.295	132	518	73	153	20	2	0	31	59	34	0	11	43	9	.367	.342	4	12	1	2171	3.76	273	109	2.50
Last Five Years	.275	733	2748	392	757	128	15	9	232	332	183	6	45	196	40	.352	.343	15	48	22	11290	3.63	1341	704	1.90

1992 Season

	Avg	AB	H	2B	3B	HR	RBI	BB	SO	OBP	SLG		Avg	AB	H	2B	3B	HR	RBI	BB	SO	OBP	SLG
vs. Left	.272	202	55	10	1	0	13	21	14	.339	.332	Scoring Posn	.245	110	27	2	0	0	29	24	9	.378	.264
vs. Right	.310	316	98	10	1	0	18	38	20	.384	.348	Close & Late	.265	113	30	2	0	0	11	15	7	.349	.283
Groundball	.313	195	61	6	0	0	11	14	8	.359	.344	None on/out	.348	92	32	9	1	0	0	10	6	.412	.467
Flyball	.333	87	29	3	0	0	5	14	8	.426	.368	Batting #2	.297	511	152	20	2	0	31	59	34	.370	.344
Home	.335	278	93	10	1	0	18	29	15	.396	.378	Batting #8	.000	4	0	0	0	0	0	0	0	.000	.000
Away	.250	240	60	10	1	0	13	30	19	.333	.300	Other	.333	3	1	0	0	0	0	0	0	.333	.333
Day	.313	112	35	3	0	0	4	10	5	.369	.339	April	.267	60	16	1	0	0	5	9	4	.362	.283
Night	.291	406	118	17	2	0	27	49	29	.366	.342	May	.298	104	31	5	1	0	8	12	4	.371	.365
Grass	.234	124	29	5	0	0	5	15	9	.317	.274	June	.298	57	17	0	0	0	6	2	2	.322	.298
Turf	.315	394	124	15	2	0	26	44	25	.383	.363	July	.326	92	30	3	0	0	2	14	11	.415	.359
First Pitch	.205	73	15	4	0	0	1	4	0	.247	.260	August	.260	100	26	4	1	0	2	11	6	.333	.320
Ahead on Count	.320	153	49	8	2	0	15	35	0	.447	.399	September/October	.314	105	33	7	0	0	8	11	7	.376	.381
Behind on Count	.289	159	46	4	0	0	9	0	15	.288	.314	Pre-All Star	.303	267	81	7	1	0	20	29	14	.372	.337
Two Strikes	.303	208	63	6	0	0	12	21	34	.367	.332	Post-All Star	.287	251	72	13	1	0	11	30	20	.362	.347

1992 By Position

Position	Avg	AB	H	2B	3B	HR	RBI	BB	SO	OBP	SLG	G	GS	Innings	PO	A	E	DP	Fld Pct	Rng Fctr	In Zone	Outs	Zone Rtg	MLB Zone
As ss	.295	518	153	20	2	0	31	59	34	.367	.342	132	128	1156.1	231	418	10	82	.985	5.05	485	447	.922	.885

Last Five Years

	Avg	AB	H	2B	3B	HR	RBI	BB	SO	OBP	SLG		Avg	AB	H	2B	3B	HR	RBI	BB	SO	OBP	SLG
vs. Left	.274	1100	301	68	6	7	92	130	76	.349	.365	Scoring Posn	.261	667	174	29	2	2	207	114	40	.360	.319
vs. Right	.277	1648	456	60	9	2	140	202	107	.354	.328	Close & Late	.259	460	119	15	4	2	54	65	31	.348	.322
Groundball	.273	997	272	41	5	2	78	103	53	.338	.330	None on/out	.259	521	135	27	5	1	1	68	32	.347	.336
Flyball	.274	598	164	32	4	4	43	78	47	.360	.361	Batting #2	.278	2349	652	104	12	9	193	289	155	.356	.344
Home	.291	1410	410	65	9	5	130	180	92	.370	.360	Batting #3	.269	145	39	7	3	0	14	16	8	.340	.359
Away	.259	1338	347	63	6	4	102	152	91	.334	.324	Other	.260	254	66	17	0	0	25	27	20	.326	.327
Day	.289	778	225	38	5	3	59	76	41	.354	.362	April	.275	320	88	10	0	1	31	47	20	.362	.316
Night	.270	1970	532	90	10	6	173	256	142	.352	.335	May	.286	518	148	22	3	1	41	52	31	.354	.346
Grass	.249	706	176	33	4	0	45	64	54	.311	.307	June	.271	439	119	22	3	1	54	65	30	.363	.342
Turf	.285	2042	581	95	11	9	187	268	129	.366	.355	July	.300	446	134	21	1	1	32	55	36	.375	.359
First Pitch	.294	377	111	27	0	1	36	6	0	.303	.374	August	.254	512	130	20	5	3	36	61	37	.332	.330
Ahead on Count	.315	809	255	52	9	4	94	198	0	.448	.417	September/October	.269	513	138	33	3	2	36	52	29	.335	.357
Behind on Count	.247	791	195	28	3	3	65	1	78	.248	.301	Pre-All Star	.283	1433	406	62	7	3	139	182	93	.363	.343
Two Strikes	.227	1017	231	22	1	1	58	121	183	.308	.254	Post-All Star	.267	1315	351	66	8	6	93	150	90	.340	.343

Batter vs. Pitcher (since 1984)

Hits Best Against	Avg	AB	H	2B	3B	HR	RBI	BB	SO	OBP	SLG	Hits Worst Against	Avg	AB	H	2B	3B	HR	RBI	BB	SO	OBP	SLG
Frank Castillo	.700	10	7	1	0	0	0	4	0	.786	.800	Walt Terrell	.000	13	0	0	0	0	0	0	0	.000	.000
Tim Crews	.545	11	6	2	0	1	4	0	1	.545	1.000	Chuck McElroy	.000	9	0	0	0	0	0	2	2	.182	.000
Tim Belcher	.542	24	13	1	0	0	1	3	1	.593	.583	Greg W. Harris	.083	12	1	1	0	0	2	1	1	.154	.167
Darryl Kile	.500	12	6	0	1	0	2	1	0	.538	.667	Mark Portugal	.133	15	2	0	0	0	0	1	1	.188	.133
Bob Kipper	.364	22	8	3	2	1	8	1	1	.375	.818	Jim Gott	.154	13	2	0	0	0	0	1	1	.143	.154

Pete Smith — Braves — Pitches Right

	ERA	W	L	Sv	G	GS	IP	BB	SO	Avg	H	2B	3B	HR	RBI	OBP	SLG	CG	ShO	Sup	QS	#P/S	SB	CS	GB	FB	G/F
1992 Season	2.05	7	0	0	12	11	79.0	28	43	.217	63	11	2	3	16	.285	.300	2	1	4.44	8	103	8	2	92	90	1.02
Last Five Years	4.01	25	38	0	99	93	541.1	219	367	.251	515	91	11	47	223	.322	.375	11	4	3.77	51	90	73	30	700	659	1.06

1992 Season

	ERA	W	L	Sv	G	GS	IP	H	HR	BB	SO		Avg	AB	H	2B	3B	HR	RBI	BB	SO	OBP	SLG
Home	2.28	3	0	0	5	4	27.2	27	1	10	17	vs. Left	.253	178	45	9	2	1	10	22	21	.333	.343
Away	1.93	4	0	0	7	7	51.1	36	2	18	26	vs. Right	.161	112	18	2	0	2	6	6	22	.203	.232
Starter	2.10	7	0	0	11	11	77.0	61	3	28	42	Scoring Posn	.131	61	8	2	0	0	11	7	7	.217	.164
Reliever	0.00	0	0	0	1	0	2.0	2	0	0	1	Close & Late	.167	30	5	0	0	0	0	4	5	.265	.167
0-3 Days Rest	0.00	0	0	0	0	0	0.0	0	0	0	0	None on/out	.269	78	21	5	1	1		4	13	.305	.397
4 Days Rest	1.13	3	0	0	5	5	39.2	21	0	14	21	First Pitch	.250	44	11	2	1	1	3	2	0	.283	.409
5+ Days Rest	3.13	4	0	0	6	6	37.1	40	3	14	21	Behind on Count	.242	62	15	1	0	0	3	18	0	.407	.258
Pre-All Star	0.00	0	0	0	1	0	2.0	2	0	0	1	Ahead on Count	.196	138	27	5	1	2	9	0	42	.196	.290
Post-All Star	2.10	7	0	0	11	11	77.0	61	3	28	42	Two Strikes	.187	134	25	5	0	1	7	8	43	.232	.246

Last Five Years

	ERA	W	L	Sv	G	GS	IP	H	HR	BB	SO		Avg	AB	H	2B	3B	HR	RBI	BB	SO	OBP	SLG
Home	4.28	14	21	0	52	50	288.0	291	30	126	188	vs. Left	.275	1182	325	60	7	23	128	150	169	.354	.396
Away	3.69	11	17	0	47	43	253.1	224	17	93	179	vs. Right	.219	866	190	31	4	24	95	69	198	.276	.348
Day	3.26	8	11	0	29	27	171.0	146	17	65	119	Inning 1-6	.251	1830	460	77	11	46	210	193	335	.321	.381
Night	4.35	17	27	0	70	66	370.1	369	30	154	248	Inning 7+	.252	218	55	14	0	1	13	26	32	.329	.330
Grass	3.73	22	29	0	78	74	436.2	401	41	177	311	None on	.243	1246	303	53	3	28	122		237	.311	.358

	ERA	W	L	Sv	G	GS	IP	H	HR	BB	SO		Avg	AB	H	2B	3B	HR	RBI	BB	SO	OBP	SLG
Turf	5.16	3	9	0	21	19	104.2	114	6	42	56	Runners on	.264	602	212	38	8	19	195	97	130	.338	.403
April	3.24	3	5	0	13	13	80.2	74	6	28	72	Scoring Posn	.256	477	122	22	6	9	167	68	88	.338	.384
May	5.43	3	11	0	19	19	107.2	113	12	49	74	Close & Late	.248	137	34	7	0	1	12	12	19	.305	.321
June	5.46	4	7	0	20	19	89.0	95	9	44	58	None on/out	.238	541	129	28	2	14	14	44	98	.296	.375
July	5.00	1	8	0	14	13	66.2	72	11	34	42	vs. 1st Batr (relief)	.333	6	2	1	0	0	2	0	1	.333	.500
August	2.70	10	4	0	16	16	106.2	90	5	30	64	First Inning Pitched	.266	379	101	18	4	5	54	45	75	.340	.375
September/October	2.38	4	3	0	17	13	90.2	71	4	34	57	First 75 Pitches	.249	1595	397	67	10	36	178	166	302	.318	.371
Starter	4.07	25	38	0	93	93	532.1	510	47	217	361	First Pitch	.352	293	103	24	1	13	51	8	0	.366	.573
Reliever	0.00	0	0	0	6	0	9.0	5	0	2	6	Ahead on Count	.204	983	201	30	4	15	82	0	317	.203	.289
0-3 Days Rest	2.40	0	2	0	2	2	15.0	14	1	4	7	Behind on Count	.295	427	126	23	4	11	56	132	1	.459	.445
4 Days Rest	3.67	15	20	0	48	48	282.0	254	21	108	214	Two Strikes	.189	951	180	29	1	14	74	78	363	.249	.266
5+ Days Rest	4.67	10	16	0	43	43	235.1	242	25	105	140												
Pre-All Star	4.86	11	27	0	57	56	301.2	311	30	134	221												
Post-All Star	2.93	14	11	0	42	37	239.2	204	17	85	146												

Pitcher vs. Batter (career)

Pitches Best Vs.	Avg	AB	H	2B	3B	HR	RBI	BB	SO	OBP	SLG	Pitches Worst Vs.	Avg	AB	H	2B	3B	HR	RBI	BB	SO	OBP	SLG
Milt Thompson	.000	12	0	0	0	0	0	2	1	.143	.000	Paul O'Neill	.524	21	11	3	0	0	3	2	3	.565	.667
Vince Coleman	.071	14	1	0	0	0	0	2	2	.188	.071	Bobby Bonilla	.467	15	7	1	0	3	6	3	3	.526	1.133
Rafael Ramirez	.091	11	1	0	0	0	0	0	0	.091	.091	Will Clark	.407	27	11	0	0	3	5	4	4	.484	.741
Kevin Elster	.091	11	1	1	0	0	0	0	7	.091	.182	Andre Dawson	.368	19	7	2	0	4	8	0	1	.350	1.105
Pedro Guerrero	.118	17	2	0	0	0	0	3	1	.111	.118	Darryl Strawberry	.333	12	4	0	0	3	4	4	3	.500	1.083

Zane Smith — Pirates

Pitches Left (groundball pitcher)

	ERA	W	L	Sv	G	GS	IP	BB	SO	Avg	H	2B	3B	HR	RBI	OBP	SLG	CG	ShO	Sup	QS	#P/S	SB	CS	GB	FB	G/F
1992 Season	3.06	8	8	0	23	22	141.0	19	56	.261	138	23	4	8	50	.287	.365	4	3	3.70	14	85	9	4	279	124	2.25
Last Five Years	3.24	42	50	2	162	127	871.2	194	458	.262	868	126	20	53	340	.304	.361	17	8	3.76	81	92	80	28	1647	701	2.35

1992 Season

	ERA	W	L	Sv	G	GS	IP	H	HR	BB	SO		Avg	AB	H	2B	3B	HR	RBI	BB	SO	OBP	SLG
Home	3.25	4	4	0	10	10	63.2	69	3	10	32	vs. Left	.215	93	20	1	1	2	9	2	17	.232	.312
Away	2.91	4	4	0	13	12	77.1	69	5	9	24	vs. Right	.271	436	118	22	3	6	41	17	39	.298	.376
Starter	3.11	8	8	0	22	22	139.0	138	8	18	56	Scoring Posn	.333	105	35	8	2	4	45	6	11	.362	.562
Reliever	0.00	0	0	0	1	0	2.0	0	0	0	1	Close & Late	.246	69	17	3	0	1	4	3	6	.278	.333
0-3 Days Rest	1.00	1	0	0	1		9.0	5	1	0	6	None on/out	.271	140	38	10	0	1	1	6	19	.301	.364
4 Days Rest	2.95	4	4	0	12	12	85.1	84	6	14	31	First Pitch	.250	96	24	5	1	0	7	3	0	.273	.323
5+ Days Rest	3.83	3	4	0	9	9	44.2	49	1	4	19	Behind on Count	.296	108	32	3	0	4	18	10	0	.353	.435
Pre-All Star	2.96	8	7	0	19	19	130.2	125	8	18	52	Ahead on Count	.211	209	44	4	2	3	13	0	51	.216	.292
Post-All Star	4.35	0	1	0	4	3	10.1	13	0	1	4	Two Strikes	.200	210	42	5	2	2	12	6	56	.224	.271

Last Five Years

	ERA	W	L	Sv	G	GS	IP	H	HR	BB	SO		Avg	AB	H	2B	3B	HR	RBI	BB	SO	OBP	SLG
Home	2.78	27	20	1	80	64	463.2	454	26	92	266	vs. Left	.204	579	118	10	4	5	54	34	129	.248	.261
Away	3.77	15	30	1	82	63	408.0	414	27	102	192	vs. Right	.275	2728	750	116	16	48	286	160	329	.316	.382
Day	3.18	10	14	0	40	30	204.0	204	13	53	92	Inning 1-6	.262	2644	693	105	18	41	283	158	363	.305	.362
Night	3.26	32	36	2	122	97	667.2	664	40	141	366	Inning 7+	.264	663	175	21	2	12	57	36	95	.302	.356
Grass	3.72	8	25	0	55	45	299.2	306	18	80	139	None on	.253	2008	509	75	12	28		99	281	.290	.345
Turf	2.99	34	25	2	107	82	572.0	562	35	114	319	Runners on	.276	1299	359	51	8	25	312	95	177	.325	.386
April	2.95	9	9	0	23	23	149.2	143	8	27	75	Scoring Posn	.300	730	219	35	5	19	290	64	100	.353	.440
May	3.97	8	10	0	27	26	170.0	170	8	41	89	Close & Late	.252	393	99	12	0	6	38	22	60	.293	.328
June	3.63	4	16	0	27	27	168.2	173	12	50	82	None on/out	.271	868	235	40	4	14	14	39	122	.304	.374
July	3.49	8	8	1	27	18	126.1	126	9	41	61	vs. 1st Batr (relief)	.226	31	7	2	0	1	3	3	8	.294	.387
August	3.17	6	4	1	30	18	136.1	134	9	20	72	First Inning Pitched	.260	549	143	29	5	6	61	40	86	.313	.364
September/October	1.86	7	3	0	28	15	120.2	95	7	15	79	First 75 Pitches	.259	2574	667	103	18	40	258	151	360	.302	.360
Starter	3.31	42	49	0	127	127	818.2	823	51	173	420	Pitch 76-90	.275	393	108	13	2	8	44	27	57	.319	.364
Reliever	2.21	0	1	2	35	0	53.0	45	2	21	38	Pitch 91-105	.264	246	65	7	0	4	26	13	31	.301	.341
0-3 Days Rest	3.66	4	3	0	11	11	64.0	65	6	11	44	Pitch 106+	.298	94	28	3	0	3	12	3	10	.320	.426
4 Days Rest	2.89	30	25	0	71	71	492.0	463	31	100	232	First Pitch	.308	529	163	25	4	9	68	17	0	.331	.422
5+ Days Rest	4.01	8	21	0	45	45	262.2	295	14	62	144	Ahead on Count	.201	1365	274	31	7	13	91	1	405	.204	.262
Pre-All Star	3.40	27	37	1	87	84	550.1	569	30	132	271	Behind on Count	.331	779	258	37	6	19	116	102	0	.406	.467
Post-All Star	2.97	15	13	1	75	43	321.1	299	23	62	187	Two Strikes	.207	1321	273	34	7	16	100	74	455	.251	.279

Pitcher vs. Batter (career)

Pitches Best Vs.	Avg	AB	H	2B	3B	HR	RBI	BB	SO	OBP	SLG	Pitches Worst Vs.	Avg	AB	H	2B	3B	HR	RBI	BB	SO	OBP	SLG
Kirt Manwaring	.000	13	0	0	0	0	0	0	0	.000	.000	Junior Ortiz	.563	16	9	2	0	0	1	1	1	.588	.688
Tom Pagnozzi	.087	23	2	0	0	0	1	2	4	.160	.087	Terry Pendleton	.491	53	26	5	0	2	15	1	3	.500	.698
Jerome Walton	.091	11	1	0	0	0	0	0	3	.091	.091	Barry Larkin	.447	38	17	2	0	3	8	2	2	.463	.737
Greg Litton	.091	11	1	0	0	0	1	0	1	.091	.091	Benito Santiago	.429	28	12	3	0	5	10	2	3	.467	1.071
Andy Van Slyke	.100	20	2	0	0	0	0		8	.100	.100	Chris James	.400	15	6	1	0	2	4	1	2	.438	.867

John Smoltz — Braves

	ERA	W	L	Sv	G	GS	IP	BB	SO	Avg	H	2B	3B	HR	RBI	OBP	SLG	CG	ShO	Sup	QS	#P/S	SB	CS	GB	FB	G/F
1992 Season	2.85	15	12	0	35	35	246.2	80	215	.224	206	39	5	17	72	.287	.332	9	3	4.27	23	107	11	7	299	250	1.20
Career (1988-1992)	3.50	57	54	0	146	146	979.2	352	738	.234	852	153	22	78	362	.301	.352	25	5	4.31	88	103	76	36	1172	1144	1.02

1992 Season

	ERA	W	L	Sv	G	GS	IP	H	HR	BB	SO		Avg	AB	H	2B	3B	HR	RBI	BB	SO	OBP	SLG
Home	2.87	5	6	0	15	15	103.1	81	12	33	87	vs. Left	.246	544	134	17	3	9	38	49	103	.309	.338
Away	2.83	10	6	0	20	20	143.1	125	5	47	128	vs. Right	.191	377	72	22	2	8	34	31	112	.254	.324
Day	2.36	7	4	0	12	12	87.2	68	6	29	85	Inning 1-6	.233	731	170	30	5	13	63	67	174	.298	.341
Night	3.11	8	8	0	23	23	159.0	138	11	51	130	Inning 7+	.189	190	36	9	0	4	9	13	41	.244	.300
Grass	2.65	11	8	0	25	25	179.2	140	15	60	144	None on	.226	552	125	29	4	10	10	41	123	.284	.348
Turf	3.36	4	4	0	10	10	67.0	66	2	20	71	Runners on	.220	369	81	10	1	7	62	39	92	.292	.309
April	3.24	2	2	0	5	5	33.1	29	1	14	33	Scoring Posn	.191	199	38	3	1	5	54	26	58	.281	.291
May	3.33	3	2	0	6	6	46.0	39	1	20	44	Close & Late	.182	110	20	6	0	3	5	6	24	.224	.318
June	2.96	4	1	0	6	6	45.2	34	3	11	34	None on/out	.210	233	49	8	3	2	2	20	52	.276	.296
July	0.94	3	1	0	5	5	38.1	30	3	9	32	vs. 1st Batr (relief)	.000	0	0	0	0	0	0	0	0	.000	.000
August	3.43	2	3	0	6	6	42.0	35	6	12	33	First Inning Pitched	.230	135	31	3	0	5	13	12	37	.291	.363
September/October	3.05	1	3	0	7	7	41.1	39	3	14	39	First 75 Pitches	.235	600	141	24	4	11	51	57	148	.302	.343
Starter	2.85	15	12	0	35	35	246.2	206	17	80	215	Pitch 76-90	.219	114	25	5	1	2	10	6	23	.264	.333
Reliever	0.00	0	0	0	0	0	0.0	0	0	0	0	Pitch 91-105	.178	107	19	5	0	2	5	8	18	.233	.280
0-3 Days Rest	4.00	1	0	0	1	1	9.0	6	0	4	5	Pitch 106+	.210	100	21	5	0	2	6	9	26	.275	.320
4 Days Rest	2.97	9	10	0	27	27	181.2	161	14	66	155	First Pitch	.300	130	39	7	2	2	13	5	0	.329	.431
5+ Days Rest	2.25	5	2	0	7	7	56.0	39	3	10	55	Ahead on Count	.150	440	66	10	2	3	22	0	179	.153	.202
Pre-All Star	3.04	10	6	0	19	19	139.0	112	8	51	123	Behind on Count	.296	179	53	13	1	5	16	44	0	.433	.464
Post-All Star	2.59	5	6	0	16	16	107.2	94	9	29	92	Two Strikes	.161	446	72	11	1	6	22	31	215	.220	.231

Career (1988-1992)

	ERA	W	L	Sv	G	GS	IP	H	HR	BB	SO		Avg	AB	H	2B	3B	HR	RBI	BB	SO	OBP	SLG
Home	3.36	30	25	0	72	72	496.0	422	49	158	374	vs. Left	.258	2150	555	94	18	39	209	242	351	.333	.373
Away	3.64	27	29	0	74	74	481.2	430	29	194	364	vs. Right	.199	1494	297	59	4	39	153	110	387	.254	.322
Day	2.94	16	11	0	33	33	242.0	187	19	68	183	Inning 1-6	.238	3016	719	125	19	63	311	300	623	.307	.355
Night	3.68	41	43	0	113	113	737.2	665	59	284	555	Inning 7+	.212	628	133	28	3	15	51	52	115	.272	.338
Grass	3.54	42	37	0	107	107	725.0	624	69	249	528	None on	.228	2180	497	93	11	44	44	193	450	.293	.341
Turf	3.39	15	17	0	39	39	254.2	228	9	103	210	Runners on	.242	1464	355	60	11	34	318	159	288	.313	.368
April	4.03	6	9	0	19	19	116.0	110	9	48	89	Scoring Posn	.231	796	184	29	10	18	271	122	190	.326	.361
May	3.07	11	8	0	23	23	170.0	132	9	57	135	Close & Late	.208	308	64	15	1	7	29	22	64	.261	.331
June	4.13	8	10	0	23	23	152.2	150	11	52	127	None on/out	.234	947	222	35	6	16	16	81	189	.298	.335
July	3.10	12	7	0	25	25	177.1	131	18	56	117	vs. 1st Batr (relief)	.000	0	0	0	0	0	0	0	0	.000	.000
August	3.57	13	12	0	30	30	199.1	174	17	78	156	First Inning Pitched	.239	545	130	18	3	11	65	66	122	.321	.343
September/October	3.34	7	8	0	26	26	164.1	155	14	61	114	First 75 Pitches	.240	2515	604	103	15	47	249	249	533	.308	.349
Starter	3.50	57	54	0	146	146	979.2	852	78	352	738	Pitch 76-90	.246	463	114	21	5	17	54	39	79	.306	.423
Reliever	0.00	0	0	0	0	0	0.0	0	0	0	0	Pitch 91-105	.174	384	67	15	1	7	27	33	73	.241	.273
0-3 Days Rest	5.08	3	4	0	9	9	56.2	53	5	25	32	Pitch 106+	.238	282	67	14	1	7	32	31	53	.313	.369
4 Days Rest	3.36	40	34	0	96	96	659.2	582	57	230	494	First Pitch	.310	525	163	26	4	20	74	14	0	.332	.490
5+ Days Rest	3.52	14	16	0	41	41	263.1	217	16	97	212	Ahead on Count	.171	1616	276	46	6	18	126	0	605	.172	.240
Pre-All Star	3.63	29	29	0	72	72	485.2	425	33	181	380	Behind on Count	.302	838	253	57	5	26	86	180	0	.423	.475
Post-All Star	3.37	28	25	0	74	74	494.0	427	45	171	358	Two Strikes	.153	1638	251	38	7	20	119	157	738	.229	.222

Pitcher vs. Batter (career)

Pitches Best Vs.	Avg	AB	H	2B	3B	HR	RBI	BB	SO	OBP	SLG	Pitches Worst Vs.	Avg	AB	H	2B	3B	HR	RBI	BB	SO	OBP	SLG
Dwight Smith	.000	15	0	0	0	0	0	0	2	.000	.000	Eric Davis	.556	18	10	2	0	4	6	2	2	.600	1.333
Jerald Clark	.000	11	0	0	0	0	0	0	4	.000	.000	Mike LaValliere	.550	20	11	2	0	1	3	5	0	.640	.800
Luis Alicea	.000	7	0	0	0	0	0	1	1	.273	.000	Tony Gwynn	.465	43	20	2	2	9	1	1		.477	.744
Jay Bell	.077	26	2	0	0	0	1	1	6	.111	.077	Franklin Stubbs	.462	13	6	2	0	2	3	4	3	.588	1.077
Derrick May	.091	11	1	0	0	0	0	0	1	.091	.091	Kevin Mitchell	.321	28	9	4	0	3	9	4	4	.406	.786

J.T. Snow — Yankees

	Avg	G	AB	R	H	2B	3B	HR	RBI	BB	SO	HBP	GDP	SB	CS	OBP	SLG	IBB	SH	SF	#Pit	#P/PA	GB	FB	G/F
1992 Season	.143	7	14	1	2	1	0	0	2	5	5	0	0	0	0	.368	.214	1	0	0	76	4.00	2	3	0.67

1992 Season

	Avg	AB	H	2B	3B	HR	RBI	BB	SO	OBP	SLG		Avg	AB	H	2B	3B	HR	RBI	BB	SO	OBP	SLG
vs. Left	.000	3	0	0	0	0	0	0	1	.000	.000	Scoring Posn	.167	6	1	0	0	0	2	1	2	.286	.167
vs. Right	.182	11	2	1	0	0	2	5	4	.438	.273	Close & Late	.000	3	0	0	0	0	0	0	1	.250	.000

Cory Snyder — Giants

	Avg	G	AB	R	H	2B	3B	HR	RBI	BB	SO	HBP	GDP	SB	CS	OBP	SLG	IBB	SH	SF	#Pit	#P/PA	GB	FB	G/F
1992 Season	.269	124	390	48	105	22	2	14	57	23	96	2	10	4	4	.311	.444	2	2	3	1472	3.52	123	121	1.02
Last Five Years	.241	592	1994	228	480	94	9	75	263	118	509	7	50	16	14	.283	.410	14	7	18	7453	3.49	590	618	0.95

1992 Season

	Avg	AB	H	2B	3B	HR	RBI	BB	SO	OBP	SLG		Avg	AB	H	2B	3B	HR	RBI	BB	SO	OBP	SLG
vs. Left	.294	170	50	12	0	6	20	9	31	.331	.471	Scoring Posn	.254	118	30	8	0	2	41	11	38	.316	.373

1992 Season

	Avg	AB	H	2B	3B	HR	RBI	BB	SO	OBP	SLG		Avg	AB	H	2B	3B	HR	RBI	BB	SO	OBP	SLG
vs. Right	.250	220	55	10	2	8	37	14	65	.295	.423	Close & Late	.228	79	18	4	2	2	10	5	22	.271	.405
Groundball	.270	185	50	11	1	8	29	12	46	.313	.470	None on/out	.277	94	26	6	0	7	7	6	21	.320	.564
Flyball	.243	74	18	3	1	2	6	3	19	.273	.392	Batting #4	.271	221	60	13	0	9	38	13	53	.318	.452
Home	.299	184	55	14	0	8	34	12	40	.342	.505	Batting #5	.295	105	31	7	2	2	12	4	25	.318	.457
Away	.243	206	50	8	2	6	23	11	56	.283	.388	Other	.219	64	14	2	0	3	7	6	18	.278	.391
Day	.289	152	44	10	0	7	33	13	36	.347	.493	April	.200	25	5	1	0	0	2	1	8	.231	.240
Night	.256	238	61	12	2	7	24	10	60	.287	.412	May	.217	46	10	2	0	3	7	4	10	.280	.457
Grass	.278	291	81	15	1	11	43	19	70	.322	.450	June	.372	94	35	9	1	5	24	2	24	.388	.649
Turf	.242	99	24	7	1	3	14	4	26	.279	.424	July	.250	92	23	3	0	3	11	5	18	.289	.380
First Pitch	.356	73	26	4	1	4	13	2	0	.382	.603	August	.222	72	16	3	1	1	5	7	21	.296	.333
Ahead on Count	.368	57	21	4	0	4	9	15	0	.500	.649	September/October	.262	61	16	4	0	2	8	4	15	.303	.426
Behind on Count	.158	146	23	3	0	2	12	0	57	.161	.219	Pre-All Star	.294	201	59	14	1	9	37	10	48	.329	.507
Two Strikes	.181	188	34	5	0	5	21	6	96	.210	.287	Post-All Star	.243	189	46	8	1	5	20	13	48	.293	.376

1992 By Position

Position	Avg	AB	H	2B	3B	HR	RBI	BB	SO	OBP	SLG	G	GS	Innings	PO	A	E	DP	Fld Pct	Rng Fctr	In Zone	Outs	Zone Rtg	MLB Zone
As Pinch Hitter	.133	15	2	0	0	0	0	3	6	.278	.133	19	0	---	---	---	---	---	---	---	---	---	---	---
As 1b	.322	90	29	5	0	6	17	4	20	.358	.578	27	18	196.0	170	18	2	14	.989	---	31	22	.710	.843
As 3b	.255	47	12	5	0	1	11	4	12	.302	.426	14	13	112.0	7	22	2	2	.935	2.33	32	24	.750	.841
As lf	.267	60	16	5	0	4	12	3	15	.302	.550	22	15	134.0	33	0	0	0	1.000	2.22	35	32	.914	.809
As cf	.400	35	14	3	0	0	3	2	10	.432	.486	13	9	73.2	21	1	0	0	1.000	2.69	28	21	.750	.824
As rf	.223	139	31	4	1	3	14	7	32	.264	.331	48	36	332.1	67	6	1	1	.986	1.98	83	65	.783	.814

Last Five Years

	Avg	AB	H	2B	3B	HR	RBI	BB	SO	OBP	SLG		Avg	AB	H	2B	3B	HR	RBI	BB	SO	OBP	SLG
vs. Left	.255	697	178	36	1	32	97	51	169	.307	.448	Scoring Posn	.232	514	119	23	1	14	175	46	152	.289	.362
vs. Right	.233	1297	302	58	8	43	166	67	340	.270	.389	Close & Late	.212	372	79	17	3	13	38	20	104	.252	.379
Groundball	.249	602	150	28	3	17	93	34	134	.298	.390	None on/out	.223	498	111	21	2	23	23	21	55	.254	.412
Flyball	.237	459	109	20	2	21	60	25	127	.276	.427	Batting #4	.235	541	127	20	0	18	74	31	134	.280	.377
Home	.236	967	228	51	2	30	118	60	240	.281	.386	Batting #5	.250	544	136	29	4	21	71	28	139	.285	.434
Away	.245	1027	252	43	7	45	145	58	269	.285	.432	Other	.239	909	217	42	5	36	118	59	236	.284	.415
Day	.229	620	142	27	1	22	86	34	163	.270	.382	April	.270	293	79	15	0	12	50	22	77	.321	.444
Night	.246	1374	338	67	8	53	177	84	346	.289	.422	May	.202	376	76	16	1	12	42	21	100	.248	.346
Grass	.245	1663	408	78	8	62	220	95	405	.284	.414	June	.284	416	118	27	3	26	75	15	94	.307	.550
Turf	.218	331	72	16	1	13	43	23	104	.269	.390	July	.243	342	83	14	2	6	34	19	89	.281	.348
First Pitch	.331	357	118	21	2	16	63	2	0	.337	.535	August	.213	319	68	12	3	10	35	19	84	.258	.364
Ahead on Count	.363	317	115	20	2	24	71	60	0	.461	.666	September/October	.226	248	56	10	0	9	27	22	65	.287	.375
Behind on Count	.162	776	126	22	4	24	73	0	304	.163	.294	Pre-All Star	.249	1213	302	61	4	52	181	68	297	.289	.434
Two Strikes	.152	969	147	29	3	22	77	49	507	.193	.256	Post-All Star	.228	781	178	33	5	23	82	50	212	.274	.371

Batter vs. Pitcher (career)

Hits Best Against	Avg	AB	H	2B	3B	HR	RBI	BB	SO	OBP	SLG	Hits Worst Against	Avg	AB	H	2B	3B	HR	RBI	BB	SO	OBP	SLG
Tim Leary	.583	12	7	0	0	2	8	0	2	.583	1.083	Eric Plunk	.000	11	0	0	0	0	0	1	4	.083	.000
Mark Williamson	.455	11	5	0	1	2	4	0	2	.455	1.182	Mike Jackson	.000	10	0	0	0	0	0	2	5	.167	.000
Dave Schmidt	.429	14	6	2	0	2	2	2	1	.500	1.000	Walt Terrell	.059	17	1	0	0	0	0	1	2	.111	.059
Jose Rijo	.400	15	6	1	0	3	7	1	5	.412	1.067	Chuck Crim	.063	16	1	0	0	0	0	0	5	.063	.063
Floyd Bannister	.385	13	5	0	0	2	3	2	1	.467	.846	Todd Stottlemyre	.063	16	1	0	0	0	0	1	5	.111	.063

Luis Sojo — Angels   Bats Right

	Avg	G	AB	R	H	2B	3B	HR	RBI	BB	SO	HBP	GDP	SB	CS	OBP	SLG	IBB	SH	SF	#Pit	#P/PA	GB	FB	G/F
1992 Season	.272	106	368	37	100	12	3	7	43	14	24	1	14	7	11	.299	.378	0	7	1	1294	3.37	148	118	1.25
Career (1990-1992)	.261	252	812	89	212	29	4	11	72	33	55	6	27	12	14	.295	.347	0	26	1	2878	3.38	322	261	1.23

1992 Season

	Avg	AB	H	2B	3B	HR	RBI	BB	SO	OBP	SLG		Avg	AB	H	2B	3B	HR	RBI	BB	SO	OBP	SLG
vs. Left	.221	95	21	2	0	0	6	5	10	.260	.242	Scoring Posn	.356	90	32	4	2	2	38	4	6	.385	.511
vs. Right	.289	273	79	10	3	7	37	9	14	.313	.425	Close & Late	.328	64	21	1	1	2	10	1	5	.348	.469
Groundball	.280	100	28	4	0	2	16	3	5	.298	.380	None on/out	.265	68	18	4	0	1	1	3	5	.296	.368
Flyball	.225	111	25	7	2	2	10	4	9	.252	.378	Batting #2	.262	263	69	11	3	5	30	9	20	.289	.384
Home	.269	186	50	6	0	2	25	7	8	.294	.333	Batting #7	.250	60	15	1	0	0	4	2	3	.270	.267
Away	.275	182	50	6	3	5	18	7	16	.305	.423	Other	.356	45	16	0	0	2	9	3	1	.396	.489
Day	.302	106	32	5	1	4	17	4	6	.324	.481	April	.000	0	0	0	0	0	0	0	0	.000	.000
Night	.260	262	68	7	2	3	26	10	18	.289	.336	May	.500	6	3	0	0	0	0	0	0	.500	.500
Grass	.283	304	86	10	3	6	37	12	16	.311	.395	June	.269	52	14	1	0	2	7	1	2	.283	.404
Turf	.219	64	14	2	0	1	6	2	8	.242	.297	July	.315	108	34	6	0	3	14	0	7	.321	.454
First Pitch	.243	37	9	1	1	1	6	0	0	.263	.405	August	.271	107	29	2	3	1	11	4	8	.297	.374
Ahead on Count	.322	90	29	5	1	3	14	13	0	.408	.500	September/October	.211	95	20	3	0	1	11	9	7	.276	.274
Behind on Count	.224	143	32	2	1	2	16	0	19	.222	.294	Pre-All Star	.313	99	31	4	0	4	11	1	5	.320	.475
Two Strikes	.226	137	31	3	0	1	12	1	24	.232	.270	Post-All Star	.257	269	69	8	3	3	32	13	19	.292	.342

1992 By Position

Position	Avg	AB	H	2B	3B	HR	RBI	BB	SO	OBP	SLG	G	GS	Innings	PO	A	E	DP	Fld Pct	Rng Fctr	In Zone	Outs	Zone Rtg	MLB Zone
As 2b	.266	335	89	12	2	7	40	11	24	.291	.376	96	85	761.0	188	267	7	73	.985	5.38	255	243	.953	.892

Career (1990-1992)

	Avg	AB	H	2B	3B	HR	RBI	BB	SO	OBP	SLG		Avg	AB	H	2B	3B	HR	RBI	BB	SO	OBP	SLG
vs. Left	.257	245	63	11	1	0	13	13	19	.295	.310	Scoring Posn	.284	218	62	11	2	3	63	9	12	.314	.394
vs. Right	.263	567	149	18	3	11	59	20	36	.295	.363	Close & Late	.315	124	39	2	1	2	12	7	7	.361	.395
Groundball	.239	218	52	7	0	4	25	4	11	.254	.326	None on/out	.251	167	42	9	0	1	1	13	11	.313	.323
Flyball	.260	196	51	11	2	3	19	6	16	.282	.383	Batting #2	.246	386	95	16	4	8	42	14	28	.276	.370
Home	.252	377	95	12	0	3	33	19	19	.289	.308	Batting #8	.263	190	50	11	0	2	17	7	13	.300	.353
Away	.269	435	117	17	4	8	39	14	36	.300	.382	Other	.284	236	67	2	0	1	13	12	14	.320	.305
Day	.284	194	55	10	1	5	22	9	13	.317	.423	April	.241	54	13	1	1	0	3	1	3	.268	.296
Night	.254	618	157	19	3	6	50	24	42	.287	.324	May	.226	62	14	4	0	0	3	2	4	.250	.290
Grass	.266	654	174	22	3	8	56	29	41	.302	.346	June	.263	99	26	4	0	2	11	3	4	.298	.364
Turf	.241	158	38	7	1	3	16	4	14	.264	.354	July	.301	206	62	9	0	3	20	4	16	.318	.388
First Pitch	.302	96	29	4	1	1	13	0	0	.323	.396	August	.253	217	55	6	3	5	21	10	16	.286	.378
Ahead on Count	.320	181	58	10	1	5	20	26	0	.406	.470	September/October	.241	174	42	5	0	1	14	13	12	.300	.287
Behind on Count	.204	318	65	6	1	3	24	0	43	.211	.258	Pre-All Star	.259	270	70	12	1	4	22	6	19	.283	.356
Two Strikes	.179	301	54	6	0	2	14	7	55	.203	.219	Post-All Star	.262	542	142	17	3	7	50	27	36	.300	.343

Batter vs. Pitcher (career)

Hits Best Against	Avg	AB	H	2B	3B	HR	RBI	BB	SO	OBP	SLG	Hits Worst Against	Avg	AB	H	2B	3B	HR	RBI	BB	SO	OBP	SLG
Scott Sanderson	.462	13	6	3	0	0	1	0	0	.462	.692	Greg Hibbard	.091	11	1	0	0	0	1	0	1	.091	.091
Greg Swindell	.400	15	6	2	0	0	2	0	2	.400	.533	Kevin Tapani	.143	14	2	0	0	0	0	0	0	.143	.143
Ben McDonald	.385	13	5	0	0	0	0	0	0	.385	.385	Frank Tanana	.154	13	2	1	0	0	0	0	0	.154	.231
Charlie Hough	.375	16	6	1	0	0	1	0	1	.375	.438	Randy Johnson	.176	17	3	1	0	0	1	1	4	.222	.235
												Chris Bosio	.182	11	2	0	0	0	0	0	3	.182	.182

Paul Sorrento — Indians

Bats Left

	Avg	G	AB	R	H	2B	3B	HR	RBI	BB	SO	HBP	GDP	SB	CS	OBP	SLG	IBB	SH	SF	#Pit	#P/PA	GB	FB	G/F
1992 Season	.269	140	458	52	123	24	1	18	60	51	89	1	13	0	3	.341	.443	7	1	3	1928	3.76	164	116	1.41
Career (1989-1992)	.255	221	647	71	165	30	2	27	87	72	135	2	19	1	4	.329	.433	10	1	5	2701	3.72	224	177	1.27

1992 Season

	Avg	AB	H	2B	3B	HR	RBI	BB	SO	OBP	SLG		Avg	AB	H	2B	3B	HR	RBI	BB	SO	OBP	SLG
vs. Left	.156	45	7	1	0	0	4	6	16	.250	.178	Scoring Posn	.217	115	25	6	1	4	43	14	18	.295	.391
vs. Right	.281	413	116	23	1	18	56	45	73	.351	.472	Close & Late	.247	89	22	7	0	4	14	12	21	.333	.461
Groundball	.288	104	30	7	1	2	13	13	13	.433	.433	None on/out	.324	108	35	6	0	6	6	11	18	.392	.546
Flyball	.266	143	38	4	0	6	16	13	34	.323	.420	Batting #5	.271	321	87	20	1	11	35	33	55	.338	.442
Home	.288	226	65	13	1	11	31	27	43	.362	.500	Batting #6	.247	93	23	4	0	5	16	15	25	.352	.452
Away	.250	232	58	11	0	7	29	24	46	.320	.388	Other	.295	44	13	0	0	2	9	3	9	.340	.432
Day	.289	159	46	4	0	9	22	13	27	.341	.484	April	.214	84	18	1	0	1	7	6	20	.272	.262
Night	.258	299	77	20	1	9	38	38	62	.341	.421	May	.217	69	15	1	0	5	15	10	20	.316	.449
Grass	.281	385	108	21	1	17	53	43	74	.352	.473	June	.367	60	22	3	0	2	6	6	5	.424	.517
Turf	.205	73	15	3	0	1	7	8	15	.284	.288	July	.367	79	29	7	0	4	9	9	12	.432	.608
First Pitch	.203	64	13	1	1	4	10	7	0	.278	.438	August	.273	77	21	5	0	4	12	8	13	.337	.494
Ahead on Count	.325	123	40	7	0	5	18	20	0	.417	.504	September/October	.202	89	18	7	1	2	11	12	19	.294	.371
Behind on Count	.270	126	34	5	0	5	17	0	37	.273	.429	Pre-All Star	.271	240	65	7	0	10	32	25	50	.341	.425
Two Strikes	.184	201	37	10	0	4	12	25	89	.273	.294	Post-All Star	.266	218	58	17	1	8	28	26	39	.341	.463

1992 By Position

Position	Avg	AB	H	2B	3B	HR	RBI	BB	SO	OBP	SLG	G	GS	Innings	PO	A	E	DP	Fld Pct	Rng Fctr	In Zone	Outs	Zone Rtg	MLB Zone
As Designated Hitter	.282	39	11	2	0	3	3	4	6	.349	.564	11	11	---	---	---	---	---	---	---	---	---	---	---
As Pinch Hitter	.143	14	2	0	0	1	3	0	6	.143	.357	14	0	---	---	---	---	---	---	---	---	---	---	---
As 1b	.272	405	110	22	1	14	54	47	77	.346	.435	121	113	1016.2	997	75	8	109	.993	---	207	170	.821	.843

Sammy Sosa — Cubs

Bats Right

	Avg	G	AB	R	H	2B	3B	HR	RBI	BB	SO	HBP	GDP	SB	CS	OBP	SLG	IBB	SH	SF	#Pit	#P/PA	GB	FB	G/F
1992 Season	.260	67	262	41	68	7	2	8	25	19	63	4	4	15	7	.317	.393	1	4	2	1068	3.79	73	71	1.03
Career (1989-1992)	.234	394	1293	179	303	51	13	37	141	77	358	14	25	67	34	.282	.380	9	16	11	5185	3.72	413	318	1.30

1992 Season

	Avg	AB	H	2B	3B	HR	RBI	BB	SO	OBP	SLG		Avg	AB	H	2B	3B	HR	RBI	BB	SO	OBP	SLG
vs. Left	.280	75	21	3	0	0	5	8	19	.353	.320	Scoring Posn	.229	48	11	2	0	2	16	4	14	.291	.396
vs. Right	.251	187	47	4	2	8	20	11	44	.302	.422	Close & Late	.216	51	11	1	1	1	4	5	11	.298	.333
Home	.267	116	31	6	1	4	10	12	28	.344	.440	None on/out	.263	76	20	3	1	2	2	6	17	.325	.408
Away	.253	146	37	1	1	4	15	7	35	.295	.356	Batting #1	.274	113	31	4	0	4	15	8	28	.323	.416
First Pitch	.395	43	17	2	0	5	11	1	0	.400	.791	Batting #2	.209	91	19	3	1	0	2	7	20	.287	.264
Ahead on Count	.282	39	11	1	2	1	7	7	0	.404	.487	Other	.310	58	18	0	1	4	8	4	15	.355	.552
Behind on Count	.241	83	20	0	0	1	3	0	30	.259	.277	Pre-All Star	.238	223	53	6	2	5	16	17	52	.301	.350
Two Strikes	.150	133	20	3	0	1	5	11	63	.224	.195	Post-All Star	.385	39	15	1	0	3	9	2	11	.415	.641

Career (1989-1992)

	Avg	AB	H	2B	3B	HR	RBI	BB	SO	OBP	SLG		Avg	AB	H	2B	3B	HR	RBI	BB	SO	OBP	SLG
vs. Left	.268	514	138	27	3	19	62	43	136	.324	.444	Scoring Posn	.235	306	72	15	4	11	104	23	86	.288	.418
vs. Right	.212	779	165	24	10	18	79	34	222	.254	.338	Close & Late	.219	228	50	9	2	4	13	17	59	.279	.329
Groundball	.257	378	97	17	4	12	46	22	93	.306	.418	None on/out	.219	384	84	12	4	9	9	22	104	.270	.341
Flyball	.229	328	75	11	4	10	29	20	99	.277	.378	Batting #1	.269	417	112	21	5	14	54	25	104	.309	.444
Home	.244	594	145	28	9	18	61	45	168	.302	.412	Batting #6	.242	227	55	10	2	8	33	14	69	.293	.410
Away	.226	699	158	23	4	19	80	32	190	.266	.352	Other	.210	649	136	20	6	15	54	38	185	.262	.328
Day	.214	379	81	19	3	10	39	21	111	.267	.359	April	.241	191	46	6	3	5	18	15	51	.300	.382
Night	.243	914	222	32	10	27	102	56	247	.289	.388	May	.235	298	70	8	1	8	24	15	88	.276	.349
Grass	.228	1056	241	42	12	29	106	67	295	.279	.373	June	.247	263	65	10	6	9	30	10	68	.281	.433
Turf	.262	237	62	9	1	8	35	10	63	.296	.409	July	.209	172	36	13	2	4	22	6	48	.236	.378
First Pitch	.369	203	75	12	2	14	43	4	0	.374	.655	August	.246	167	41	5	0	5	22	15	43	.311	.365
Ahead on Count	.318	195	62	13	3	7	34	27	0	.403	.523	September/October	.223	202	45	9	1	6	25	16	60	.291	.366
Behind on Count	.173	468	81	9	2	5	22	1	195	.186	.233	Pre-All Star	.239	817	195	30	10	23	77	41	222	.279	.384
Two Strikes	.148	668	99	17	6	7	36	41	358	.204	.223	Post-All Star	.227	476	108	21	3	14	64	36	136	.287	.372

Batter vs. Pitcher (career)

Hits Best Against	Avg	AB	H	2B	3B	HR	RBI	BB	SO	OBP	SLG	Hits Worst Against	Avg	AB	H	2B	3B	HR	RBI	BB	SO	OBP	SLG
David West	.545	11	6	2	1	2	2	2	2	.615	1.182	Nolan Ryan	.000	16	0	0	0	0	0	2	8	.111	.000
Mike Moore	.462	13	6	2	1	1	3	1	1	.500	1.000	Roger Clemens	.077	13	1	0	0	1	1	0	6	.077	.308
Scott Sanderson	.417	12	5	0	1	0	2	0	5	.385	.583	Mike Boddicker	.100	10	1	0	0	0	2	2	1	.250	.100
Jim Abbott	.368	19	7	3	0	0	1	3	2	.455	.526	Bud Black	.143	21	3	0	0	0	1	1	6	.174	.143
Jaime Navarro	.364	11	4	1	1	0	3	1	3	.417	.636	Tom Candiotti	.167	12	2	1	0	0	0	0	5	.167	.250

Bill Spiers — Brewers
Bats Left (groundball hitter)

	Avg	G	AB	R	H	2B	3B	HR	RBI	BB	SO	HBP	GDP	SB	CS	OBP	SLG	IBB	SH	SF	#Pit	#P/PA	GB	FB	G/F
1992 Season	.313	12	16	2	5	2	0	0	2	1	4	0	0	1	1	.353	.438	0	1	0	69	4.06	2	6	0.33
Career (1989-1992)	.262	371	1138	161	298	39	12	14	125	72	167	4	23	36	17	.306	.354	1	21	9	4248	3.47	460	290	1.59

1992 Season

	Avg	AB	H	2B	3B	HR	RBI	BB	SO	OBP	SLG		Avg	AB	H	2B	3B	HR	RBI	BB	SO	OBP	SLG
vs. Left	.000	3	0	0	0	0	1	0	1	.000	.000	Scoring Posn	.333	3	1	1	0	0	2	1	1	.500	.667
vs. Right	.385	13	5	2	0	0	1	1	3	.429	.538	Close & Late	.500	2	1	1	0	0	1	0	1	.500	1.000

Career (1989-1992)

	Avg	AB	H	2B	3B	HR	RBI	BB	SO	OBP	SLG		Avg	AB	H	2B	3B	HR	RBI	BB	SO	OBP	SLG
vs. Left	.236	271	64	6	2	3	29	19	49	.289	.306	Scoring Posn	.286	280	80	14	6	5	113	24	46	.332	.432
vs. Right	.270	867	234	33	10	11	96	53	118	.311	.369	Close & Late	.289	194	56	5	3	1	24	14	31	.335	.361
Groundball	.275	349	96	13	6	5	57	29	52	.330	.390	None on/out	.217	313	68	13	2	2	12	40	.248	.291
Flyball	.291	203	59	7	2	5	17	15	32	.338	.419	Batting #8	.178	73	13	1	1	1	7	6	11	.238	.260
Home	.285	541	154	22	6	4	64	37	83	.330	.370	Batting #9	.267	900	240	33	8	9	102	58	127	.311	.351
Away	.241	597	144	17	6	10	61	35	84	.284	.340	Other	.273	165	45	5	3	4	16	8	29	.306	.412
Day	.251	351	88	17	3	5	40	23	63	.296	.359	April	.241	83	20	1	0	4	15	9	13	.312	.398
Night	.267	787	210	22	9	9	85	49	104	.310	.352	May	.214	145	31	8	0	0	9	11	26	.274	.269
Grass	.273	976	266	34	12	12	112	60	146	.315	.369	June	.270	178	48	9	2	1	15	14	25	.326	.360
Turf	.198	162	32	5	0	2	13	12	21	.250	.265	July	.265	200	53	4	1	3	24	8	33	.286	.340
First Pitch	.295	207	61	7	1	4	25	1	0	.302	.396	August	.254	244	62	7	3	1	32	20	30	.311	.320
Ahead on Count	.340	244	83	12	2	2	28	50	0	.448	.430	September/October	.292	288	84	10	6	5	30	10	40	.317	.420
Behind on Count	.214	379	81	8	1	3	34	0	95	.216	.264	Pre-All Star	.251	447	112	20	2	6	47	36	69	.307	.345
Two Strikes	.205	468	96	13	6	6	53	21	166	.240	.297	Post-All Star	.269	691	186	19	10	8	78	36	98	.305	.360

Batter vs. Pitcher (career)

Hits Best Against	Avg	AB	H	2B	3B	HR	RBI	BB	SO	OBP	SLG	Hits Worst Against	Avg	AB	H	2B	3B	HR	RBI	BB	SO	OBP	SLG
Bob Welch	.417	12	5	1	0	0	0	0	3	.417	.500	Bert Blyleven	.083	12	1	0	0	0	0	0	5	.083	.083
Jack McDowell	.400	15	6	0	1	0	0	0	2	.400	.533	Tom Candiotti	.100	20	2	0	0	0	3	1	5	.136	.100
Roger Clemens	.357	14	5	1	1	1	1	0	4	.357	.786	Erik Hanson	.100	20	2	0	0	0	0	0	5	.100	.100
Doug Jones	.357	14	5	0	1	0	2	1	1	.400	.500	Bill Swift	.111	9	1	0	0	0	0	2	1	.273	.111
Bobby Witt	.350	20	7	1	0	1	2	0	4	.350	.550	Jack Morris	.133	15	2	0	0	0	1	0	2	.133	.133

Ed Sprague — Blue Jays
Bats Right (flyball hitter)

	Avg	G	AB	R	H	2B	3B	HR	RBI	BB	SO	HBP	GDP	SB	CS	OBP	SLG	IBB	SH	SF	#Pit	#P/PA	GB	FB	G/F
1992 Season	.234	22	47	6	11	2	0	1	7	3	7	0	0	0	0	.280	.340	0	0	0	172	3.44	13	14	0.93
Career (1991-1992)	.266	83	207	23	55	9	0	5	27	22	50	3	2	0	3	.343	.382	2	0	1	815	3.50	57	61	0.93

1992 Season

	Avg	AB	H	2B	3B	HR	RBI	BB	SO	OBP	SLG		Avg	AB	H	2B	3B	HR	RBI	BB	SO	OBP	SLG
vs. Left	.400	10	4	1	0	0	3	1	0	.455	.500	Scoring Posn	.286	14	4	1	0	1	7	2	1	.375	.571
vs. Right	.189	37	7	1	0	1	4	2	7	.231	.297	Close & Late	.250	8	2	0	0	1	3	0	1	.250	.625

Russ Springer — Yankees
Pitches Right (flyball pitcher)

	ERA	W	L	Sv	G	GS	IP	BB	SO	Avg	H	2B	3B	HR	RBI	OBP	SLG	GF	IR	IRS	Hld	SvOp	SB	CS	GB	FB	G/F
1992 Season	6.19	0	0	0	14	0	16.0	10	12	.281	18	4	1	0	13	.387	.375	5	11	5	2	0	3	0	18	25	0.72

1992 Season

	ERA	W	L	Sv	G	GS	IP	H	HR	BB	SO		Avg	AB	H	2B	3B	HR	RBI	BB	SO	OBP	SLG
Home	8.31	0	0	0	7	0	8.2	11	0	4	5	vs. Left	.320	25	8	0	1	0	5	4	7	.433	.400
Away	3.68	0	0	0	7	0	7.1	7	0	6	7	vs. Right	.256	39	10	4	0	0	8	6	5	.356	.359

Steve Springer — Mets
Bats Right (flyball hitter)

	Avg	G	AB	R	H	2B	3B	HR	RBI	BB	SO	HBP	GDP	SB	CS	OBP	SLG	IBB	SH	SF	#Pit	#P/PA	GB	FB	G/F
1992 Season	.400	4	5	0	2	1	0	0	0	0	1	0	0	0	0	.400	.600	0	0	0	17	3.40	2	1	2.00
Career (1990-1992)	.235	8	17	1	4	1	0	0	1	0	7	0	0	0	0	.222	.294	0	0	1	64	3.56	2	5	0.40

1992 Season

	Avg	AB	H	2B	3B	HR	RBI	BB	SO	OBP	SLG		Avg	AB	H	2B	3B	HR	RBI	BB	SO	OBP	SLG
vs. Left	.400	5	2	1	0	0	0	0	1	.400	.600	Scoring Posn	.000	1	0	0	0	0	0	0	0	.000	.000
vs. Right	.000	0	0	0	0	0	0	0	0	.000	.000	Close & Late	.333	3	1	0	0	0	0	0	1	.333	.333

Randy St. Claire — Braves
Pitches Right (groundball pitcher)

	ERA	W	L	Sv	G	GS	IP	BB	SO	Avg	H	2B	3B	HR	RBI	OBP	SLG	GF	IR	IRS	Hld	SvOp	SB	CS	GB	FB	G/F
1992 Season	5.87	0	0	0	10	0	15.1	8	7	.283	17	5	0	1	9	.368	.417	1	8	2	0	0	0	0	30	11	2.73
Last Five Years	4.64	2	0	1	59	0	87.1	37	65	.268	91	18	0	14	50	.339	.444	6	67	23	1	1	5	3	133	80	1.66

1992 Season

	ERA	W	L	Sv	G	GS	IP	H	HR	BB	SO		Avg	AB	H	2B	3B	HR	RBI	BB	SO	OBP	SLG
Home	5.54	0	0	0	8	0	13.0	14	1	7	6	vs. Left	.231	26	6	2	0	0	2	5	4	.355	.308
Away	7.71	0	0	0	2	0	2.1	3	0	1	1	vs. Right	.324	34	11	3	0	1	7	3	3	.378	.500

Matt Stairs — Expos
Bats Left (groundball hitter)

	Avg	G	AB	R	H	2B	3B	HR	RBI	BB	SO	HBP	GDP	SB	CS	OBP	SLG	IBB	SH	SF	#Pit	#P/PA	GB	FB	G/F
1992 Season	.167	13	30	2	5	2	0	0	5	7	7	0	0	0	0	.316	.233	0	0	1	142	3.74	13	7	1.86

1992 Season

	Avg	AB	H	2B	3B	HR	RBI	BB	SO	OBP	SLG		Avg	AB	H	2B	3B	HR	RBI	BB	SO	OBP	SLG
vs. Left	.000	2	0	0	0	0	0	2	0	.500	.000	Scoring Posn	.429	7	3	1	0	0	5	2	2	.500	.571
vs. Right	.179	28	5	2	0	0	5	5	7	.294	.250	Close & Late	.333	3	1	1	0	0	0	1	2	.500	.667

Andy Stankiewicz — Yankees
Bats Right

	Avg	G	AB	R	H	2B	3B	HR	RBI	BB	SO	HBP	GDP	SB	CS	OBP	SLG	IBB	SH	SF	#Pit	#P/PA	GB	FB	G/F
1992 Season	.268	116	400	52	107	22	2	2	25	38	42	5	13	9	5	.338	.348	0	7	1	1603	3.61	153	116	1.32

1992 Season

	Avg	AB	H	2B	3B	HR	RBI	BB	SO	OBP	SLG		Avg	AB	H	2B	3B	HR	RBI	BB	SO	OBP	SLG
vs. Left	.272	136	37	5	1	0	11	10	11	.336	.324	Scoring Posn	.304	69	21	4	1	0	21	8	11	.372	.391
vs. Right	.265	264	70	17	1	2	15	28	31	.339	.360	Close & Late	.254	71	18	5	0	0	6	6	7	.329	.324
Groundball	.257	113	29	6	1	0	7	6	15	.300	.327	None on/out	.257	140	36	5	0	1	1	15	18	.333	.314
Flyball	.283	113	32	9	0	0	8	10	9	.344	.363	Batting #1	.274	259	71	15	1	2	17	23	34	.337	.363
Home	.295	207	61	13	1	2	15	19	18	.354	.396	Batting #8	.247	77	19	3	1	0	5	9	3	.341	.312
Away	.238	193	46	9	1	0	10	19	24	.321	.295	Other	.266	64	17	4	0	0	3	6	5	.338	.328
Day	.295	132	39	9	0	1	6	10	13	.350	.386	April	.308	39	12	2	0	1	4	8	7	.438	.436
Night	.254	268	68	13	2	1	19	28	29	.332	.328	May	.353	34	12	5	0	0	4	1	0	.371	.500
Grass	.257	350	90	17	2	2	23	33	41	.327	.334	June	.295	105	31	7	1	1	7	12	15	.375	.410
Turf	.340	50	17	5	0	0	2	5	1	.411	.440	July	.188	101	19	2	0	0	3	7	13	.241	.208
First Pitch	.317	60	19	3	0	1	3	0	0	.311	.417	August	.290	62	18	3	0	0	3	4	4	.343	.339
Ahead on Count	.277	112	31	6	1	1	11	24	0	.404	.375	September/October	.254	59	15	3	1	0	4	7	3	.333	.339
Behind on Count	.231	108	25	2	0	0	3	0	23	.259	.250	Pre-All Star	.290	224	65	15	1	2	16	26	27	.370	.393
Two Strikes	.197	152	30	5	1	0	7	14	42	.278	.243	Post-All Star	.239	176	42	7	1	0	9	12	15	.295	.290

1992 By Position

Position	Avg	AB	H	2B	3B	HR	RBI	BB	SO	OBP	SLG	G	GS	Innings	PO	A	E	DP	Fld Pct	Rng Fctr	In Zone	Outs	Zone Rtg	MLB Zone
As 2b	.315	92	29	7	0	1	7	10	7	.388	.424	34	25	238.0	52	89	1	20	.993	5.33	99	89	.899	.892
As ss	.256	305	78	15	2	1	18	28	34	.325	.328	81	78	696.0	132	252	11	54	.972	4.97	281	264	.940	.885

Mike Stanley — Yankees
Bats Right

	Avg	G	AB	R	H	2B	3B	HR	RBI	BB	SO	HBP	GDP	SB	CS	OBP	SLG	IBB	SH	SF	#Pit	#P/PA	GB	FB	G/F
1992 Season	.249	68	173	24	43	7	0	8	27	33	45	1	6	0	0	.372	.428	0	0	0	807	3.90	45	50	0.90
Last Five Years	.243	427	914	100	222	39	3	17	109	146	205	5	23	2	0	.348	.348	3	13	7	4266	3.98	285	264	1.08

1992 Season

	Avg	AB	H	2B	3B	HR	RBI	BB	SO	OBP	SLG		Avg	AB	H	2B	3B	HR	RBI	BB	SO	OBP	SLG
vs. Left	.241	112	27	4	0	5	16	22	26	.366	.411	Scoring Posn	.190	42	8	0	0	2	18	13	12	.382	.333
vs. Right	.262	61	16	3	0	3	11	11	19	.384	.459	Close & Late	.231	26	6	2	0	1	4	5	6	.355	.423
Home	.264	91	24	5	0	5	18	18	26	.391	.484	None on/out	.186	43	8	0	0	2	2	7	12	.314	.326
Away	.232	82	19	2	0	3	9	15	19	.351	.366	Batting #7	.230	74	17	3	0	3	13	9	23	.321	.392
First Pitch	.192	26	5	0	0	0	3	0	0	.192	.192	Batting #8	.292	48	14	3	0	3	8	8	8	.393	.542
Ahead on Count	.385	39	15	2	0	3	10	18	0	.579	.667	Other	.235	51	12	1	0	2	6	16	14	.418	.373
Behind on Count	.161	56	9	3	0	2	6	0	23	.175	.321	Pre-All Star	.222	72	16	2	0	3	11	13	18	.349	.375
Two Strikes	.133	75	10	2	0	3	6	15	45	.286	.280	Post-All Star	.267	101	27	5	0	5	16	20	27	.388	.465

Last Five Years

	Avg	AB	H	2B	3B	HR	RBI	BB	SO	OBP	SLG		Avg	AB	H	2B	3B	HR	RBI	BB	SO	OBP	SLG
vs. Left	.258	543	140	23	3	13	65	95	114	.368	.383	Scoring Posn	.249	233	58	11	0	3	85	44	55	.361	.335
vs. Right	.221	371	82	16	0	4	44	51	91	.319	.296	Close & Late	.212	146	31	6	0	4	22	28	37	.339	.336
Groundball	.233	210	49	4	2	2	26	29	40	.326	.300	None on/out	.245	229	56	8	0	7	33	48	347	.371
Flyball	.210	229	48	15	0	6	28	48	66	.349	.354	Batting #7	.249	414	103	16	1	8	48	60	107	.344	.350
Home	.273	472	129	23	2	9	69	71	101	.369	.388	Batting #8	.265	200	53	12	0	5	29	26	33	.349	.400
Away	.210	442	93	16	1	8	40	75	104	.326	.305	Other	.220	300	66	11	2	4	32	60	65	.352	.310
Day	.209	196	41	5	2	6	26	40	48	.346	.347	April	.220	100	22	2	0	1	10	20	24	.352	.270
Night	.252	718	181	34	1	11	83	106	157	.349	.348	May	.203	172	35	6	1	6	23	27	37	.308	.355
Grass	.248	767	190	33	3	15	95	119	173	.350	.357	June	.205	185	38	7	0	1	17	25	47	.299	.259
Turf	.218	147	32	6	0	2	14	27	32	.339	.299	July	.301	133	40	7	1	4	18	10	25	.350	.459
First Pitch	.250	136	34	6	1	1	19	1	0	.259	.331	August	.314	121	38	10	0	0	11	24	27	.428	.397
Ahead on Count	.347	176	61	11	0	7	40	75	0	.535	.528	September/October	.241	203	49	7	1	5	30	40	45	.372	.360
Behind on Count	.195	287	56	13	0	2	22	0	99	.205	.261	Pre-All Star	.221	497	110	18	2	9	60	74	111	.321	.320
Two Strikes	.156	448	70	10	1	5	26	68	205	.271	.217	Post-All Star	.269	417	112	21	1	8	49	72	94	.379	.381

Batter vs. Pitcher (career)

Hits Best Against	Avg	AB	H	2B	3B	HR	RBI	BB	SO	OBP	SLG	Hits Worst Against	Avg	AB	H	2B	3B	HR	RBI	BB	SO	OBP	SLG
Charlie Leibrandt	.500	12	6	0	0	2	7	0	0	.500	1.000	Kirk McCaskill	.000	11	0	0	0	0	0	1	5	.083	.000
Chuck Finley	.455	33	15	4	0	1	8	5	5	.526	.667	Mark Langston	.115	26	3	0	0	0	1	5	10	.258	.115
Matt Young	.333	12	4	0	1	0	3	2	5	.429	.500	Bret Saberhagen	.154	13	2	0	0	0	1	1	2	.214	.154
Dave Stewart	.308	13	4	0	0	0	2	3	2	.412	.308	Scott Bailes	.167	12	2	1	0	0	0	0	1	.167	.250
Bill Krueger	.308	13	4	2	0	0	1	3	1	.438	.462	John Candelaria	.182	11	2	0	0	0	1	1	2	.250	.182

Mike Stanton — Braves
Pitches Left

	ERA	W	L	Sv	G	GS	IP	BB	SO	Avg	H	2B	3B	HR	RBI	OBP	SLG	GF	IR	IRS	Hld	SvOp	SB	CS	GB	FB	G/F
1992 Season	4.10	5	4	8	65	0	63.2	20	44	.247	59	11	0	6	27	.308	.368	23	40	10	15	11	1	2	72	77	0.94
Career (1989-1992)	3.75	10	13	24	166	0	172.2	53	132	.240	154	22	4	13	84	.301	.347	47	122	34	32	32	13	3	214	183	1.17

1992 Season

	ERA	W	L	Sv	G	GS	IP	H	HR	BB	SO		Avg	AB	H	2B	3B	HR	RBI	BB	SO	OBP	SLG
Home	3.00	2	1	3	29	0	30.0	26	1	8	21	vs. Left	.237	76	18	3	0	4	9	12	24	.344	.434
Away	5.08	3	3	5	36	0	33.2	33	5	12	23	vs. Right	.252	163	41	8	0	2	18	8	20	.289	.337
Day	5.87	0	1	1	17	0	15.1	16	2	6	11	Inning 1-6	.000	11	0	0	0	0	0	0	3	.000	.000
Night	3.54	5	3	7	48	0	48.1	43	4	14	33	Inning 7+	.259	228	59	11	0	6	27	20	41	.321	.386
Grass	3.15	4	3	6	45	0	45.2	38	2	14	27	None on	.277	130	36	4	0	4	4	9	24	.333	.400
Turf	6.50	1	1	2	20	0	18.0	21	4	6	17	Runners on	.211	109	23	7	0	2	23	11	20	.279	.330
April	4.26	0	1	1	7	0	6.1	3	0	2	1	Scoring Posn	.213	61	13	3	0	1	21	5	15	.265	.311
May	8.10	0	1	2	11	0	10.0	12	4	3	8	Close & Late	.245	139	34	6	0	4	18	11	22	.303	.374
June	8.31	1	2	2	10	0	8.2	11	2	4	9	None on/out	.310	58	18	2	0	2	2	4	12	.365	.448
July	2.84	1	0	0	7	0	6.1	1	0	4	3	vs. 1st Batr (relief)	.233	60	14	2	0	0	5	4	17	.292	.267
August	3.29	0	0	2	14	0	13.2	11	0	6	12	First Inning Pitched	.260	192	50	11	0	4	24	17	39	.324	.380
September/October	0.96	3	0	1	16	0	18.2	21	0	1	11	First 15 Pitches	.267	180	48	10	0	4	16	14	32	.327	.389
Starter	0.00	0	0	0	0	0	0.0	0	0	0	0	Pitch 16-30	.208	53	11	1	0	2	11	6	10	.279	.340
Reliever	4.10	5	4	8	65	0	63.2	59	6	20	44	Pitch 31-45	.000	6	0	0	0	0	0	0	2	.000	.000
0 Days rest	5.00	2	2	3	21	0	18.0	18	2	10	15	Pitch 46+	.000	0	0	0	0	0	0	0	0	.000	.000
1 or 2 Days rest	4.34	2	1	3	29	0	29.0	30	3	7	17	First Pitch	.279	43	12	2	0	0	5	2	0	.326	.326
3+ Days rest	2.70	1	1	2	15	0	16.2	11	1	3	12	Ahead on Count	.229	109	25	4	0	2	10	0	39	.225	.321
Pre-All Star	6.10	2	4	5	33	0	31.0	27	6	10	21	Behind on Count	.286	42	12	3	0	2	7	8	0	.400	.500
Post-All Star	2.20	3	0	3	32	0	32.2	32	0	10	23	Two Strikes	.230	113	26	4	0	3	9	10	44	.290	.345

Career (1989-1992)

	ERA	W	L	Sv	G	GS	IP	H	HR	BB	SO		Avg	AB	H	2B	3B	HR	RBI	BB	SO	OBP	SLG
Home	3.44	3	4	11	78	0	89.0	80	5	19	61	vs. Left	.214	201	43	4	1	5	20	23	58	.300	.318
Away	4.09	7	9	13	88	0	83.2	74	8	34	71	vs. Right	.251	442	111	18	3	8	64	30	74	.301	.360
Day	4.57	1	2	4	44	0	41.1	32	5	16	37	Inning 1-6	.088	34	3	0	0	0	1	2	9	.139	.088
Night	3.49	9	11	20	122	0	131.1	122	8	37	95	Inning 7+	.248	609	151	22	4	13	83	51	123	.309	.361
Grass	3.68	6	10	18	119	0	127.1	111	8	36	86	None on	.246	342	84	12	0	7	7	18	68	.289	.342

Career (1989-1992)

	ERA	W	L	Sv	G	GS	IP	H	HR	BB	SO		Avg	AB	H	2B	3B	HR	RBI	BB	SO	OBP	SLG
Turf	3.97	4	3	6	47	0	45.1	43	5	17	46	Runners on	.233	301	70	10	4	6	77	35	64	.313	.352
April	7.06	0	4	3	24	0	21.2	26	1	11	16	Scoring Posn	.241	195	47	5	3	4	71	22	46	.318	.359
May	7.45	1	1	3	21	0	19.1	20	8	4	12	Close & Late	.235	375	88	14	4	5	49	31	72	.298	.333
June	5.14	3	3	2	24	0	21.0	20	2	6	16	None on/out	.278	151	42	7	0	3	3	7	32	.314	.384
July	2.18	1	1	1	18	0	20.2	8	1	10	12	vs. 1st Batr (relief)	.209	153	32	5	1	0	16	12	36	.271	.255
August	1.98	0	0	7	31	0	36.1	25	1	11	26	First Inning Pitched	.234	491	115	16	3	10	69	42	108	.299	.340
September/October	2.35	5	4	8	48	0	53.2	55	0	11	50	First 15 Pitches	.238	463	110	16	3	8	54	37	91	.300	.337
Starter	0.00	0	0	0	0	0	0.0	0	0	0	0	Pitch 16-30	.250	152	38	6	1	5	27	13	33	.305	.401
Reliever	3.75	10	13	24	166	0	172.2	154	13	53	132	Pitch 31-45	.240	25	6	0	0	0	3	3	7	.321	.240
0 Days rest	4.34	4	5	6	51	0	47.2	47	3	20	41	Pitch 46+	.000	3	0	0	0	0	0	0	1	.000	.000
1 or 2 Days rest	3.39	5	7	13	79	0	79.2	71	4	23	56	First Pitch	.279	104	29	4	1	1	14	9	0	.348	.365
3+ Days rest	3.77	1	1	5	36	0	45.1	36	6	10	35	Ahead on Count	.197	299	59	6	1	5	28	0	114	.196	.274
Pre-All Star	5.86	5	8	8	77	0	70.2	67	11	23	50	Behind on Count	.302	129	39	8	2	5	26	28	0	.427	.512
Post-All Star	2.29	5	5	16	89	0	102.0	87	2	30	82	Two Strikes	.189	312	59	7	1	6	29	16	132	.228	.276

Pitcher vs. Batter (career)

Pitches Best Vs.	Avg	AB	H	2B	3B	HR	RBI	BB	SO	OBP	SLG	Pitches Worst Vs.	Avg	AB	H	2B	3B	HR	RBI	BB	SO	OBP	SLG
Eddie Murray	.091	11	1	0	0	0	0	0	1	.091	.091	Hal Morris	.375	8	3	0	0	0	0	3	2	.615	.375
Fred McGriff	.167	12	2	0	0	1	1	0	3	.167	.417												
Craig Biggio	.200	10	2	0	0	0	1	1	2	.273	.200												
Mark Grace	.222	9	2	0	0	0	0	3	1	.417	.222												

Terry Steinbach — Athletics
Bats Right

	Avg	G	AB	R	H	2B	3B	HR	RBI	BB	SO	HBP	GDP	SB	CS	OBP	SLG	IBB	SH	SF	#Pit	#P/PA	GB	FB	G/F
1992 Season	.279	128	438	48	122	20	1	12	53	45	58	1	20	2	3	.345	.411	3	0	3	1747	3.59	152	137	1.11
Last Five Years	.269	605	2078	209	559	98	6	43	270	149	307	20	73	8	8	.321	.384	12	10	23	8015	3.53	774	618	1.25

1992 Season

	Avg	AB	H	2B	3B	HR	RBI	BB	SO	OBP	SLG		Avg	AB	H	2B	3B	HR	RBI	BB	SO	OBP	SLG
vs. Left	.300	110	33	5	0	5	18	11	15	.361	.482	Scoring Posn	.340	97	33	5	1	3	42	16	11	.422	.505
vs. Right	.271	328	89	15	1	7	35	34	43	.340	.387	Close & Late	.180	50	9	0	0	0	5	6	7	.268	.180
Groundball	.276	116	32	4	0	3	12	9	17	.328	.388	None on/out	.192	99	19	2	0	2	2	10	18	.273	.273
Flyball	.262	130	34	7	0	6	13	9	19	.312	.454	Batting #5	.290	186	54	5	1	7	25	17	23	.348	.441
Home	.229	214	49	7	1	3	19	22	26	.301	.313	Batting #6	.271	218	59	12	0	5	27	24	30	.343	.394
Away	.326	224	73	13	0	9	34	23	32	.386	.504	Other	.265	34	9	3	0	0	1	4	5	.342	.353
Day	.253	154	39	8	0	2	14	12	24	.305	.344	April	.250	24	6	2	0	1	2	4	4	.345	.458
Night	.292	284	83	12	1	10	39	33	34	.366	.447	May	.241	79	19	2	0	2	5	7	17	.302	.342
Grass	.251	367	92	14	1	8	37	40	46	.323	.360	June	.313	80	25	1	1	4	14	10	3	.396	.500
Turf	.423	71	30	6	0	4	16	5	12	.462	.676	July	.353	85	30	9	0	2	15	6	12	.396	.529
First Pitch	.267	75	20	1	0	2	10	2	0	.278	.360	August	.234	94	22	2	0	3	11	10	13	.305	.351
Ahead on Count	.375	96	36	9	1	3	16	26	0	.504	.583	September/October	.263	76	20	4	0	0	6	8	9	.329	.316
Behind on Count	.245	147	36	7	0	4	15	0	41	.245	.374	Pre-All Star	.280	218	61	7	1	8	23	24	31	.352	.431
Two Strikes	.245	192	47	8	0	5	21	17	58	.306	.365	Post-All Star	.277	220	61	13	0	4	30	21	27	.337	.391

1992 By Position

Position	Avg	AB	H	2B	3B	HR	RBI	BB	SO	OBP	SLG	G	GS	Innings	PO	A	E	DP	Fld Pct	Rng Fctr	In Zone	Outs	Zone Rtg	MLB Zone
As c	.282	419	118	20	1	12	52	44	53	.349	.420	124	116	998.2	579	70	10	6	.985	---	---	---	---	

Last Five Years

	Avg	AB	H	2B	3B	HR	RBI	BB	SO	OBP	SLG		Avg	AB	H	2B	3B	HR	RBI	BB	SO	OBP	SLG
vs. Left	.287	631	181	31	1	16	84	47	75	.336	.415	Scoring Posn	.288	517	149	25	2	12	225	50	76	.344	.414
vs. Right	.261	1447	378	67	5	27	186	102	232	.314	.370	Close & Late	.226	319	72	8	0	2	36	24	53	.288	.270
Groundball	.270	618	167	26	2	10	81	33	89	.312	.367	None on/out	.244	475	116	18	2	8	8	39	65	.306	.341
Flyball	.256	469	120	17	2	13	59	39	74	.312	.384	Batting #5	.301	828	249	38	4	19	116	50	120	.340	.425
Home	.266	1006	268	42	2	18	127	74	134	.318	.366	Batting #6	.261	606	158	28	1	15	85	46	96	.317	.384
Away	.271	1072	291	56	4	25	143	75	173	.324	.401	Other	.236	644	152	32	1	9	69	53	91	.301	.331
Day	.274	776	213	43	2	17	109	51	120	.319	.401	April	.258	264	68	16	0	4	31	24	47	.329	.364
Night	.266	1302	346	55	4	26	161	98	187	.321	.374	May	.269	327	88	13	1	9	37	21	49	.315	.398
Grass	.267	1731	463	78	3	35	223	132	241	.321	.377	June	.287	380	109	15	3	11	47	21	53	.329	.429
Turf	.277	347	96	20	3	8	47	17	66	.319	.421	July	.315	333	105	23	1	6	54	19	41	.353	.444
First Pitch	.297	333	99	16	1	6	59	3	0	.304	.405	August	.236	394	93	18	0	6	46	32	57	.294	.327
Ahead on Count	.313	521	163	32	2	14	77	84	0	.408	.463	September/October	.253	380	96	13	1	7	55	32	60	.311	.347
Behind on Count	.240	692	166	29	1	10	78	1	183	.246	.328	Pre-All Star	.276	1087	300	50	4	27	130	74	164	.327	.404
Two Strikes	.211	861	182	35	3	15	91	57	306	.265	.311	Post-All Star	.261	991	259	48	2	16	140	75	143	.313	.362

Batter vs. Pitcher (career)

Hits Best Against	Avg	AB	H	2B	3B	HR	RBI	BB	SO	OBP	SLG	Hits Worst Against	Avg	AB	H	2B	3B	HR	RBI	BB	SO	OBP	SLG
Jeff M. Robinson	.500	16	8	1	1	1	6	1	2	.529	.875	Dave Stieb	.063	16	1	0	0	0	0	0	2	.063	.063
Danny Darwin	.500	10	5	0	0	3	4	1	2	.545	1.400	Steve Olin	.077	13	1	0	0	0	0	1	4	.143	.077
Kevin Tapani	.429	14	6	3	0	1	3	1	2	.467	.857	Ben McDonald	.083	12	1	0	0	0	0	0	2	.083	.083
Chuck Finley	.400	30	12	3	0	2	9	1	3	.419	.700	Bobby Witt	.133	15	2	0	0	0	1	0	5	.133	.133
Tom Gordon	.333	12	4	0	0	1	3	3	5	.467	.583	Kevin Brown	.136	22	3	0	0	0	4	0	4	.130	.136

Ray Stephens — Rangers
Bats Right (groundball hitter)

	Avg	G	AB	R	H	2B	3B	HR	RBI	BB	SO	HBP	GDP	SB	CS	OBP	SLG	IBB	SH	SF	#Pit	#P/PA	GB	FB	G/F
1992 Season	.154	8	13	0	2	0	0	0	0	0	5	0	0	0	0	.154	.154	0	1	0	46	3.54	4	2	2.00
Career (1990-1992)	.171	19	35	2	6	1	0	1	1	1	11	0	2	0	0	.194	.286	0	1	0	121	3.36	13	7	1.86

1992 Season

	Avg	AB	H	2B	3B	HR	RBI	BB	SO	OBP	SLG		Avg	AB	H	2B	3B	HR	RBI	BB	SO	OBP	SLG
vs. Left	.182	11	2	0	0	0	0	0	5	.182	.182	Scoring Posn	.000	3	0	0	0	0	0	0	2	.000	.000
vs. Right	.000	2	0	0	0	0	0	0	0	.000	.000	Close & Late	.000	1	0	0	0	0	0	0	1	.000	.000

Phil Stephenson — Padres
Bats Left

	Avg	G	AB	R	H	2B	3B	HR	RBI	BB	SO	HBP	GDP	SB	CS	OBP	SLG	IBB	SH	SF	#Pit	#P/PA	GB	FB	G/F
1992 Season	.155	53	71	5	11	2	1	0	8	10	11	0	0	0	0	.259	.211	0	3	0	335	4.14	31	21	1.48
Career (1989-1992)	.201	194	298	35	60	11	2	6	29	47	62	0	2	3	1	.309	.312	1	5	1	1444	4.17	111	82	1.35

1992 Season

	Avg	AB	H	2B	3B	HR	RBI	BB	SO	OBP	SLG		Avg	AB	H	2B	3B	HR	RBI	BB	SO	OBP	SLG
vs. Left	.400	5	2	0	0	0	0	0	2	.400	.400	Scoring Posn	.240	25	6	1	0	0	7	3	3	.321	.280
vs. Right	.136	66	9	2	1	0	8	10	9	.250	.197	Close & Late	.045	22	1	0	0	0	0	2	5	.125	.045

Lee Stevens — Angels
Bats Left

	Avg	G	AB	R	H	2B	3B	HR	RBI	BB	SO	HBP	GDP	SB	CS	OBP	SLG	IBB	SH	SF	#Pit	#P/PA	GB	FB	G/F
1992 Season	.221	106	312	25	69	19	0	7	37	26	64	1	4	1	4	.288	.349	6	1	2	1209	3.51	127	85	1.49
Career (1990-1992)	.225	191	618	61	139	36	0	14	78	57	151	1	12	3	7	.289	.351	11	4	6	2487	3.65	202	183	1.10

1992 Season

	Avg	AB	H	2B	3B	HR	RBI	BB	SO	OBP	SLG		Avg	AB	H	2B	3B	HR	RBI	BB	SO	OBP	SLG
vs. Left	.159	44	7	2	0	0	5	4	9	.245	.205	Scoring Posn	.250	72	18	5	0	2	29	13	13	.356	.403
vs. Right	.231	268	62	17	0	7	32	25	55	.295	.373	Close & Late	.255	51	13	4	0	0	3	5	12	.321	.333
Groundball	.273	77	21	5	0	1	6	7	17	.333	.377	None on/out	.244	82	20	4	0	3	3	6	21	.295	.402
Flyball	.215	93	20	6	0	3	16	9	20	.288	.376	Batting #5	.268	164	44	13	0	6	23	17	30	.337	.457
Home	.183	169	31	11	0	2	21	9	40	.223	.284	Batting #6	.167	66	11	6	0	0	4	5	13	.225	.258
Away	.266	143	38	8	0	5	16	20	24	.358	.427	Other	.171	82	14	0	0	1	10	7	21	.239	.207
Day	.256	90	23	3	0	3	11	8	19	.316	.389	April	.196	46	9	2	0	2	2	5	10	.275	.370
Night	.207	222	46	16	0	4	26	21	45	.276	.333	May	.208	53	11	2	0	1	4	5	13	.276	.302
Grass	.218	275	60	17	0	7	34	25	57	.282	.356	June	.197	71	14	5	0	2	11	5	12	.260	.352
Turf	.243	37	9	2	0	0	3	4	7	.326	.297	July	.162	37	6	0	0	1	3	2	6	.200	.243
First Pitch	.193	57	11	2	0	2	3	5	0	.270	.333	August	.357	42	15	7	0	0	8	5	8	.417	.524
Ahead on Count	.266	64	17	4	0	3	12	12	0	.382	.469	September/October	.222	63	14	3	0	1	9	7	15	.300	.317
Behind on Count	.252	107	27	6	0	2	13	0	38	.252	.364	Pre-All Star	.199	191	38	9	0	6	18	16	38	.264	.340
Two Strikes	.165	139	23	7	0	0	10	12	64	.229	.216	Post-All Star	.256	121	31	10	0	1	19	13	26	.324	.364

1992 By Position

Position	Avg	AB	H	2B	3B	HR	RBI	BB	SO	OBP	SLG		G	GS	Innings	PO	A	E	DP	Fld Pct	Rng Fctr	In Zone	Outs	Zone Rtg	MLB Zone
As Pinch Hitter	.250	12	3	1	0	0	2	2	4	.357	.333		16	0	---	---	---	---	---	---	---	---	---	---	---
As 1b	.221	294	65	18	0	7	34	26	59	.285	.354		91	85	738.0	764	49	4	87	.995	---	126	109	.865	.843

Career (1990-1992)

	Avg	AB	H	2B	3B	HR	RBI	BB	SO	OBP	SLG		Avg	AB	H	2B	3B	HR	RBI	BB	SO	OBP	SLG
vs. Left	.200	115	23	4	0	1	19	9	31	.262	.261	Scoring Posn	.240	154	37	7	0	6	64	21	39	.320	.403
vs. Right	.231	503	116	32	0	13	59	48	120	.295	.372	Close & Late	.213	94	20	5	0	1	8	11	29	.295	.298
Groundball	.243	148	36	7	0	2	16	15	41	.309	.331	None on/out	.247	162	40	10	0	5	5	9	46	.287	.401
Flyball	.240	171	41	12	0	5	24	17	47	.311	.398	Batting #5	.236	356	84	24	0	10	47	35	94	.303	.388
Home	.227	335	76	20	0	6	49	24	84	.275	.340	Batting #6	.231	130	30	10	0	3	16	12	25	.294	.377
Away	.223	283	63	16	0	8	29	33	67	.304	.364	Other	.189	132	25	2	0	1	15	10	32	.247	.227
Day	.193	166	32	9	0	3	16	10	49	.237	.277	April	.196	46	9	2	0	2	2	5	10	.275	.370
Night	.237	452	107	31	0	11	62	47	102	.307	.378	May	.208	53	11	2	0	1	4	5	13	.276	.302
Grass	.225	542	122	31	0	13	71	50	133	.288	.354	June	.197	71	14	5	0	2	11	5	12	.260	.352
Turf	.224	76	17	5	0	1	7	7	18	.294	.329	July	.204	93	19	4	0	3	11	6	22	.250	.344
First Pitch	.277	112	31	8	0	3	11	7	0	.320	.429	August	.269	145	39	8	0	0	16	16	37	.337	.386
Ahead on Count	.248	125	31	8	0	6	25	24	0	.367	.456	September/October	.224	210	47	15	0	3	29	20	57	.288	.338
Behind on Count	.201	209	42	9	0	5	25	0	88	.200	.316	Pre-All Star	.199	191	38	9	0	6	18	16	38	.264	.340
Two Strikes	.163	289	47	13	0	3	23	23	142	.222	.239	Post-All Star	.237	427	101	27	0	8	60	41	113	.300	.356

Batter vs. Pitcher (career)

Hits Best Against	Avg	AB	H	2B	3B	HR	RBI	BB	SO	OBP	SLG	Hits Worst Against	Avg	AB	H	2B	3B	HR	RBI	BB	SO	OBP	SLG
Scott Sanderson	.462	13	6	1	0	0	1	1	4	.500	.538	Greg Hibbard	.000	11	0	0	0	0	2	1	2	.083	.000
Mike Moore	.455	11	5	1	0	2	1	1	1	.500	.545	Kevin Tapani	.091	11	1	0	0	0	2	3	3	.231	.091
Kevin Brown	.333	12	4	1	0	1	1	3		.385	.417	Nolan Ryan	.167	12	2	0	0	0	1	6		.231	.167
												Melido Perez	.167	12	2	1	0	0	2	0	2	.167	.250
												Roger Clemens	.182	11	2	0	0	0	0	2	4	.308	.182

Dave Stewart — Athletics
Pitches Right (flyball pitcher)

	ERA	W	L	Sv	G	GS	IP	BB	SO	Avg	H	2B	3B	HR	RBI	OBP	SLG	CG	ShO	Sup	QS	#P/S	SB	CS	GB	FB	G/F
1992 Season	3.66	12	10	0	31	31	199.1	79	130	.237	175	28	6	25	83	.315	.393	2	0	4.61	17	102	15	10	200	286	0.70
Last Five Years	3.53	87	53	0	175	175	1225.2	446	787	.249	1146	209	28	102	485	.316	.372	37	7	5.17	106	109	77	41	1454	1529	0.95

1992 Season

	ERA	W	L	Sv	G	GS	IP	H	HR	BB	SO
Home	3.73	4	5	0	15	15	101.1	82	14	38	76
Away	3.58	8	5	0	16	16	98.0	93	11	41	54
Day	4.18	4	4	0	9	9	64.2	52	8	25	42
Night	3.41	8	6	0	22	22	134.2	123	17	54	88
Grass	3.87	10	8	0	25	25	160.2	130	21	69	112
Turf	2.79	2	2	0	6	6	38.2	45	4	10	18
April	3.86	1	2	0	5	5	37.1	32	4	15	17
May	4.65	2	3	0	6	6	40.2	30	9	24	36
June	3.24	4	0	0	6	6	33.1	32	5	11	20
July	5.23	0	0	0	2	2	10.1	19	0	1	7
August	3.18	3	3	0	6	6	39.2	29	3	16	20
September/October	2.84	2	2	0	6	6	38.0	33	4	12	30
Starter	3.66	12	10	0	31	31	199.1	175	25	79	130
Reliever	0.00	0	0	0	0	0	0.0	0	0	0	0
0-3 Days Rest	0.00	0	0	0	0	0	0.0	0	0	0	0
4 Days Rest	4.06	8	8	0	22	22	139.2	124	18	62	90
5+ Days Rest	2.72	4	2	0	9	9	59.2	51	7	17	40
Pre-All Star	3.96	7	5	0	17	17	111.1	94	18	50	73
Post-All Star	3.27	5	5	0	14	14	88.0	81	7	29	57

	Avg	AB	H	2B	3B	HR	RBI	BB	SO	OBP	SLG
vs. Left	.262	340	89	17	1	11	39	47	51	.351	.415
vs. Right	.217	397	86	11	5	14	44	32	79	.282	.375
Inning 1-6	.229	632	145	24	6	19	72	64	116	.305	.377
Inning 7+	.286	105	30	4	0	6	11	15	14	.374	.495
None on	.216	454	98	14	3	16	16	51	85	.303	.366
Runners on	.272	283	77	14	3	9	67	28	45	.333	.438
Scoring Posn	.255	149	38	8	1	6	57	18	29	.328	.443
Close & Late	.304	69	21	2	0	4	8	11	7	.395	.507
None on/out	.245	196	48	6	1	7	7	22	39	.327	.393
vs. 1st Batr (relief)	.000	0	0	0	0	0	0	0	0	.000	.000
First Inning Pitched	.239	117	28	3	1	4	17	12	20	.326	.385
First 75 Pitches	.235	515	121	19	6	15	58	54	97	.313	.383
Pitch 76-90	.234	107	25	5	0	6	14	8	14	.282	.449
Pitch 91-105	.275	69	19	2	0	3	6	9	17	.367	.435
Pitch 106+	.217	46	10	2	0	1	5	8	2	.327	.326
First Pitch	.393	107	42	9	1	2	15	1	0	.407	.551
Ahead on Count	.164	354	58	7	2	9	26	0	113	.169	.271
Behind on Count	.275	153	42	6	2	8	24	42	0	.429	.497
Two Strikes	.174	351	61	8	3	10	29	36	130	.251	.299

Last Five Years

	ERA	W	L	Sv	G	GS	IP	H	HR	BB	SO
Home	3.05	43	21	0	86	86	622.1	539	45	202	407
Away	4.03	44	32	0	89	89	603.1	607	57	244	380
Day	3.24	37	16	0	63	63	455.0	411	33	143	292
Night	3.70	50	37	0	112	112	770.2	735	69	303	495
Grass	3.40	71	41	0	144	144	1019.0	927	84	365	665
Turf	4.18	16	12	0	31	31	206.2	219	18	81	122
April	3.44	19	4	0	27	27	193.2	176	12	73	97
May	3.52	12	10	0	28	28	192.0	181	19	80	111
June	4.39	13	11	0	30	30	203.0	191	18	79	132
July	3.48	12	9	0	28	28	199.1	194	21	59	137
August	3.35	15	11	0	31	31	222.2	200	20	79	147
September/October	3.06	16	8	0	31	31	215.0	204	12	76	163
Starter	3.53	87	53	0	175	175	1225.2	1146	102	446	787
Reliever	0.00	0	0	0	0	0	0.0	0	0	0	0
0-3 Days Rest	2.81	10	7	0	18	18	134.2	123	9	38	74
4 Days Rest	3.87	60	39	0	129	129	869.2	852	75	347	579
5+ Days Rest	2.50	17	7	0	26	26	201.1	171	18	61	134
Pre-All Star	3.73	49	28	0	94	94	651.0	605	57	249	375
Post-All Star	3.30	38	25	0	81	81	574.2	541	45	197	412

	Avg	AB	H	2B	3B	HR	RBI	BB	SO	OBP	SLG
vs. Left	.250	2348	587	107	12	48	262	250	351	.320	.367
vs. Right	.247	2262	559	102	16	54	223	196	436	.312	.378
Inning 1-6	.249	3771	940	175	24	82	422	363	649	.316	.374
Inning 7+	.246	839	206	34	4	20	63	83	138	.314	.367
None on	.245	2706	663	117	15	60	60	248	460	.313	.366
Runners on	.254	1904	483	92	13	42	425	198	327	.320	.382
Scoring Posn	.232	1067	248	50	9	21	369	128	183	.307	.355
Close & Late	.256	347	89	14	1	7	30	43	55	.336	.363
None on/out	.251	1203	302	56	6	32	32	107	206	.316	.387
vs. 1st Batr (relief)	.000	0	0	0	0	0	0	0	0	.000	.000
First Inning Pitched	.273	666	182	33	4	12	81	80	109	.353	.389
First 75 Pitches	.244	3053	744	146	17	59	301	289	542	.311	.361
Pitch 76-90	.275	608	167	31	8	17	82	54	90	.331	.436
Pitch 91-105	.241	522	126	11	2	17	62	47	93	.306	.368
Pitch 106+	.255	427	109	21	1	9	40	56	62	.340	.372
First Pitch	.329	686	226	46	6	17	88	5	0	.341	.488
Ahead on Count	.200	2155	430	75	9	30	182	0	680	.232	.264
Behind on Count	.290	972	282	46	11	32	139	242	0	.430	.459
Two Strikes	.189	2109	398	71	10	31	155	199	787	.259	.276

Pitcher vs. Batter (since 1984)

Pitches Best Vs.	Avg	AB	H	2B	3B	HR	RBI	BB	SO	OBP	SLG
Don Slaught	.000	19	0	0	0	0	2	2	5	.091	.000
Mike Macfarlane	.000	11	0	0	0	0	0	1	2	.083	.000
Travis Fryman	.000	11	0	0	0	0	0	1	5	.083	.000
Gerald Perry	.000	10	0	0	0	0	0	1	2	.091	.000
Gary DiSarcina	.000	9	0	0	0	0	0	1	1	.250	.000

Pitches Worst Vs.	Avg	AB	H	2B	3B	HR	RBI	BB	SO	OBP	SLG
Tim Raines	.556	18	10	0	2	1	3	3	0	.619	.944
Gregg Jefferies	.556	9	5	1	0	1	1	2	1	.636	1.000
Edgar Martinez	.500	18	9	3	0	0	1	6	1	.625	.667
Danny Tartabull	.417	36	15	1	0	5	9	8	10	.523	.861
Greg Vaughn	.333	24	8	2	0	5	14	7	5	.484	1.042

Dave Stieb — Blue Jays
Pitches Right

	ERA	W	L	Sv	G	GS	IP	BB	SO	Avg	H	2B	3B	HR	RBI	OBP	SLG	CG	ShO	Sup	QS	#P/S	SB	CS	GB	FB	G/F
1992 Season	5.04	4	6	0	21	14	96.1	43	45	.275	98	21	2	9	58	.355	.420	1	0	3.27	5	86	3	6	141	111	1.27
Last Five Years	3.35	59	31	0	128	120	778.2	285	447	.228	714	114	14	51	279	.306	.332	15	8	4.60	73	95	45	39	1113	792	1.41

1992 Season

	ERA	W	L	Sv	G	GS	IP	H	HR	BB	SO
Home	5.53	2	4	0	12	9	57.0	61	5	23	27
Away	4.35	2	2	0	9	5	39.1	37	4	20	18
Starter	5.70	3	6	0	14	14	79.0	83	9	37	38
Reliever	2.08	1	0	0	7	0	17.1	15	0	6	7
0-3 Days Rest	5.00	0	0	0	2	2	9.0	11	0	6	4
4 Days Rest	4.03	1	3	0	4	4	29.0	23	4	12	12
5+ Days Rest	7.02	2	3	0	8	8	41.0	49	5	19	22
Pre-All Star	5.35	3	6	0	15	12	79.0	79	9	33	37
Post-All Star	3.63	1	0	0	6	2	17.1	19	0	10	8

	Avg	AB	H	2B	3B	HR	RBI	BB	SO	OBP	SLG
vs. Left	.279	172	48	12	0	4	34	20	20	.354	.419
vs. Right	.270	185	50	9	2	5	24	23	25	.355	.422
Scoring Posn	.322	90	29	8	1	2	48	12	8	.383	.500
Close & Late	.227	22	5	0	0	2	6	4	3	.346	.500
None on/out	.267	90	24	4	1	3	3	10	8	.347	.433
First Pitch	.263	57	15	3	0	1	4	2	0	.288	.368
Behind on Count	.432	88	38	6	0	5	25	24	0	.549	.670
Ahead on Count	.221	136	30	7	2	2	18	0	38	.241	.346
Two Strikes	.158	133	21	5	2	2	12	17	45	.266	.271

Last Five Years

	ERA	W	L	Sv	G	GS	IP	H	HR	BB	SO		Avg	AB	H	2B	3B	HR	RBI	BB	SO	OBP	SLG
Home	3.50	31	20	0	66	63	399.0	336	26	144	245	vs. Left	.244	1483	362	57	5	29	158	153	185	.318	.348
Away	3.20	26	11	0	62	57	379.2	312	23	141	202	vs. Right	.211	1362	288	57	9	22	121	132	262	.294	.315
Day	4.22	17	14	0	44	41	256.0	232	20	100	142	Inning 1-6	.233	2431	567	103	10	46	250	248	384	.311	.341
Night	2.93	42	17	0	84	79	522.2	418	31	185	305	Inning 7+	.200	414	83	11	4	5	29	37	63	.280	.283
Grass	3.01	24	7	0	50	46	311.1	242	16	118	172	None on	.212	1690	358	60	10	34	34	188	283	.302	.320
Turf	3.58	35	24	0	78	74	467.1	408	35	167	275	Runners on	.253	1155	292	54	4	17	245	97	164	.313	.351
April	4.03	8	8	0	20	20	120.2	117	10	42	69	Scoring Posn	.257	637	164	31	3	11	226	59	90	.318	.367
May	3.20	15	7	0	28	28	188.2	153	10	61	97	Close & Late	.198	182	36	6	2	2	12	14	27	.281	.286
June	5.10	11	5	0	21	21	109.1	115	12	59	62	None on/out	.211	726	153	22	5	16	16	85	104	.305	.321
July	2.51	7	5	0	21	15	114.2	87	6	42	57	vs. 1st Batr (relief)	.167	6	1	0	0	0	0	2	0	.375	.167
August	3.51	9	5	0	20	18	120.2	91	8	45	82	First Inning Pitched	.236	467	110	19	2	7	53	53	75	.316	.330
September/October	2.02	9	1	0	18	18	124.2	87	5	36	80	First 75 Pitches	.226	2131	482	91	8	40	213	221	334	.306	.333
Starter	3.39	58	31	0	120	120	756.1	633	51	275	438	Pitch 76-90	.261	360	94	14	4	7	34	33	62	.330	.381
Reliever	2.01	1	0	0	8	0	22.1	17	0	10	9	Pitch 91-105	.212	250	53	6	2	2	23	26	31	.294	.276
0-3 Days Rest	9.00	0	1	0	3	3	11.0	16	1	7	5	Pitch 106+	.202	104	21	3	0	2	9	5	20	.259	.288
4 Days Rest	3.56	32	20	0	67	67	419.1	339	34	156	257	First Pitch	.247	397	98	14	4	6	40	3	0	.261	.348
5+ Days Rest	2.98	26	10	0	50	50	326.0	278	16	112	176	Ahead on Count	.188	1229	231	40	3	14	89	0	378	.200	.260
Pre-All Star	3.68	36	22	0	77	74	462.2	413	33	175	254	Behind on Count	.295	657	194	37	4	21	99	165	0	.440	.460
Post-All Star	2.88	23	9	0	51	46	316.0	237	18	110	193	Two Strikes	.164	1227	201	36	3	18	87	117	446	.248	.242

Pitcher vs. Batter (since 1984)

Pitches Best Vs.	Avg	AB	H	2B	3B	HR	RBI	BB	SO	OBP	SLG	Pitches Worst Vs.	Avg	AB	H	2B	3B	HR	RBI	BB	SO	OBP	SLG
Brady Anderson	.000	15	0	0	0	0	0	3	6	.167	.000	Geno Petralli	.476	21	10	2	0	1		5	1	.577	.571
Carlos Baerga	.000	9	0	0	0	0	0	2	0	.182	.000	Gene Larkin	.385	13	5	1	0	1	1	0	3	.385	.692
Steve Lyons	.040	25	1	1	0	0	0	1	7	.077	.080	Wally Joyner	.375	40	15	3	0	4	8	4	3	.432	.750
Rob Deer	.043	23	1	0	0	0	0	3	10	.154	.043	Jose Canseco	.364	33	12	8	0	2	9	3	9	.405	.788
Terry Steinbach	.063	16	1	0	0	0	0	0	2	.063	.063	Franklin Stubbs	.333	9	3	1	0	1	1	1	1	.500	.778

Kurt Stillwell — Padres
Bats Both

	Avg	G	AB	R	H	2B	3B	HR	RBI	BB	SO	HBP	GDP	SB	CS	OBP	SLG	IBB	SH	SF	#Pit	#P/PA	GB	FB	G/F
1992 Season	.227	114	379	35	86	15	3	2	24	26	58	1	6	4	1	.274	.298	9	4	6	1430	3.47	162	96	1.69
Last Five Years	.251	638	2192	254	550	115	20	28	233	187	314	12	35	22	18	.310	.360	17	24	23	8694	3.60	798	707	1.13

1992 Season

	Avg	AB	H	2B	3B	HR	RBI	BB	SO	OBP	SLG		Avg	AB	H	2B	3B	HR	RBI	BB	SO	OBP	SLG
vs. Left	.250	112	28	1	2	1	8	7	19	.289	.321	Scoring Posn	.184	87	16	1	0	0	20	12	15	.267	.195
vs. Right	.217	267	58	14	1	1	16	19	39	.268	.288	Close & Late	.225	71	16	3	1	0	3	6	13	.282	.296
Groundball	.293	147	43	6	2	2	13	9	19	.335	.401	None on/out	.257	105	27	9	1	1	1	5	20	.297	.390
Flyball	.210	81	17	4	1	0	5	5	13	.247	.284	Batting #2	.152	33	5	2	0	0	1	3	3	.243	.212
Home	.220	191	42	6	1	1	14	16	32	.274	.277	Batting #8	.240	288	69	11	2	2	19	18	49	.281	.313
Away	.234	188	44	9	2	1	10	10	26	.275	.319	Other	.207	58	12	2	1	0	4	5	6	.262	.276
Day	.244	119	29	5	2	1	9	11	12	.299	.345	April	.298	57	17	4	1	0	3	1	12	.305	.404
Night	.219	260	57	10	1	1	15	15	46	.263	.277	May	.281	64	18	6	0	0	4	5	12	.324	.375
Grass	.217	277	60	10	1	1	19	22	42	.270	.271	June	.167	78	13	0	0	0	5	8	15	.241	.167
Turf	.255	102	26	5	2	1	5	4	16	.287	.373	July	.208	77	16	3	2	2	7	5	5	.256	.377
First Pitch	.277	47	13	2	0	0	4	8	0	.375	.319	August	.245	49	12	1	0	0	3	2	6	.264	.265
Ahead on Count	.286	105	30	7	1	1	9	12	0	.353	.400	September/October	.185	54	10	1	0	0	2	5	8	.267	.204
Behind on Count	.144	125	18	3	0	1	5	0	36	.150	.192	Pre-All Star	.227	233	53	11	1	0	15	16	40	.273	.283
Two Strikes	.122	148	18	3	1	0	5	6	58	.155	.155	Post-All Star	.226	146	33	4	2	2	9	10	18	.277	.322

1992 By Position

Position	Avg	AB	H	2B	3B	HR	RBI	BB	SO	OBP	SLG	G	GS	Innings	PO	A	E	DP	Fld Pct	Rng Fctr	In Zone	Outs	Zone Rtg	MLB Zone
As 2b	.227	374	85	15	3	2	24	26	57	.275	.299	111	109	938.1	251	265	16	63	.970	4.95	319	274	.859	.892

Last Five Years

	Avg	AB	H	2B	3B	HR	RBI	BB	SO	OBP	SLG		Avg	AB	H	2B	3B	HR	RBI	BB	SO	OBP	SLG
vs. Left	.241	593	143	25	8	5	67	53	81	.305	.336	Scoring Posn	.267	529	141	27	10	7	196	63	77	.335	.395
vs. Right	.255	1599	407	90	12	23	166	134	233	.312	.369	Close & Late	.225	356	80	11	2	1	18	44	62	.311	.275
Groundball	.263	624	164	29	5	7	60	52	74	.319	.359	None on/out	.234	512	120	34	5	7	7	50	81	.305	.361
Flyball	.224	523	117	24	8	9	49	47	92	.286	.352	Batting #2	.249	571	142	38	4	4	61	61	77	.324	.350
Home	.247	1094	270	57	13	11	127	97	156	.307	.353	Batting #8	.249	502	125	21	2	6	43	39	82	.301	.335
Away	.255	1098	280	58	7	17	106	90	158	.314	.367	Other	.253	1119	283	56	14	18	129	87	155	.307	.376
Day	.270	582	157	40	4	9	66	55	77	.330	.399	April	.292	305	89	20	4	4	32	21	52	.338	.423
Night	.244	1610	393	75	16	19	167	132	237	.303	.346	May	.264	440	116	20	3	7	49	52	67	.339	.370
Grass	.240	962	236	48	4	9	78	64	141	.300	.325	June	.247	454	112	26	4	4	44	38	62	.306	.348
Turf	.260	1210	314	67	16	19	155	103	173	.319	.388	July	.209	316	66	15	3	6	34	20	38	.256	.332
First Pitch	.327	278	91	17	3	8	46	12	0	.359	.496	August	.262	344	90	14	6	4	40	28	54	.316	.372
Ahead on Count	.306	568	174	41	6	9	77	106	0	.412	.447	September/October	.231	333	77	20	0	3	34	28	41	.296	.318
Behind on Count	.207	753	156	27	5	8	54	0	189	.211	.288	Pre-All Star	.258	1331	344	74	12	15	141	120	189	.320	.366
Two Strikes	.171	912	156	33	8	6	67	66	314	.228	.245	Post-All Star	.239	861	206	41	8	13	92	67	125	.296	.351

Batter vs. Pitcher (career)

Hits Best Against	Avg	AB	H	2B	3B	HR	RBI	BB	SO	OBP	SLG	Hits Worst Against	Avg	AB	H	2B	3B	HR	RBI	BB	SO	OBP	SLG
Barry Jones	.545	11	6	1	0	0	2	0	1	.545	.636	Bud Black	.000	12	0	0	0	0	0	0	5	.000	.000
Lance McCullers	.455	11	5	0	0	0	0	2	1	.538	.455	Jack McDowell	.000	10	0	0	0	0	0	2	1	.154	.000
Mike Flanagan	.400	10	4	1	1	0	2	1	0	.455	.700	Jeff Robinson	.077	13	1	0	0	0	0	0	1	.077	.077
Orel Hershiser	.368	19	7	2	1	0	2	2	1	.429	.579	Kevin Tapani	.091	11	1	0	0	0	1	1	0	.167	.091
Mark Williamson	.333	12	4	0	1	1	2	1	1	.385	.750	Roger Clemens	.129	31	4	1	0	0	0	8		.129	.161

Todd Stottlemyre — Blue Jays
Pitches Right

	ERA	W	L	Sv	G	GS	IP	BB	SO	Avg	H	2B	3B	HR	RBI	OBP	SLG	CG	ShO	Sup	QS	#P/S	SB	CS	GB	FB	G/F
1992 Season	4.50	12	11	0	28	27	174.0	63	98	.262	175	31	0	20	88	.329	.398	6	2	5.90	13	100	17	3	242	210	1.15
Career (1988-1992)	4.32	51	51	0	150	128	821.2	297	459	.263	829	141	18	85	377	.331	.401	11	2	4.94	63	95	95	29	1120	1000	1.12

1992 Season

	ERA	W	L	Sv	G	GS	IP	H	HR	BB	SO		Avg	AB	H	2B	3B	HR	RBI	BB	SO	OBP	SLG
Home	4.79	7	5	0	13	12	82.2	87	10	26	50	vs. Left	.282	284	80	14	0	6	34	32	21	.355	.394
Away	4.24	5	6	0	15	15	91.1	88	10	37	48	vs. Right	.247	385	95	17	0	14	54	31	77	.310	.400
Day	5.31	3	3	0	8	7	39.0	41	7	20	22	Inning 1-6	.265	570	151	27	0	19	79	56	78	.335	.412
Night	4.27	9	8	0	20	20	135.0	134	13	43	76	Inning 7+	.242	99	24	4	0	1	9	7	20	.292	.313
Grass	3.43	5	4	0	12	12	76.0	63	8	28	43	None on	.239	394	94	19	0	10	10	29	52	.297	.363
Turf	5.33	7	7	0	16	15	98.0	112	12	35	55	Runners on	.295	275	81	12	0	10	78	34	46	.371	.447
April	4.50	3	1	0	5	5	36.0	33	3	16	21	Scoring Posn	.311	151	47	7	0	6	67	21	29	.388	.477
May	5.28	1	3	0	5	5	30.2	31	5	14	17	Close & Late	.209	43	9	1	0	1	4	3	12	.261	.302
June	6.75	1	2	0	4	4	21.1	31	4	10	9	None on/out	.265	170	45	6	0	4	4	14	14	.324	.371
July	3.00	1	1	0	3	3	18.0	17	0	9	10	vs. 1st Batr (relief)	.000	1	0	0	0	0	0	0	0	.000	.000
August	3.76	3	2	0	6	6	38.1	32	3	11	23	First Inning Pitched	.240	104	25	5	0	6	18	8	16	.303	.462
September/October	3.94	3	2	0	5	4	29.2	31	5	3	18	First 75 Pitches	.265	479	127	24	0	15	64	44	67	.330	.409
Starter	4.53	11	11	0	27	27	173.0	175	20	63	97	Pitch 76-90	.250	80	20	3	0	2	6	10	10	.337	.363
Reliever	0.00	1	0	0	1	0	1.0	0	0	0	0	Pitch 91-105	.268	82	22	4	0	3	16	6	10	.333	.427
0-3 Days Rest	0.00	0	0	0	0	0	0.0	0	0	0	0	Pitch 106+	.214	28	6	0	0	2	3	11		.290	.214
4 Days Rest	4.84	6	7	0	15	15	96.2	93	13	32	61	First Pitch	.337	101	34	2	0	5	19	4	0	.376	.505
5+ Days Rest	4.13	5	4	0	12	12	76.1	82	7	31	36	Ahead on Count	.179	279	50	11	0	7	30	0	83	.194	.294
Pre-All Star	5.32	5	6	0	14	14	88.0	95	12	40	47	Behind on Count	.323	161	52	12	0	6	26	32	0	.429	.509
Post-All Star	3.66	7	5	0	14	13	86.0	80	8	23	51	Two Strikes	.186	274	51	11	0	4	24	27	98	.265	.270

Career (1988-1992)

	ERA	W	L	Sv	G	GS	IP	H	HR	BB	SO		Avg	AB	H	2B	3B	HR	RBI	BB	SO	OBP	SLG
Home	4.42	28	23	0	72	63	419.1	436	47	138	230	vs. Left	.292	1519	443	72	10	39	176	151	155	.358	.429
Away	4.21	23	28	0	78	65	402.1	393	38	159	229	vs. Right	.237	1628	386	69	8	46	201	146	304	.306	.374
Day	5.21	11	20	0	47	41	242.0	267	30	98	135	Inning 1-6	.262	2718	713	117	17	79	344	265	401	.332	.405
Night	3.94	40	31	0	103	87	579.2	562	55	199	324	Inning 7+	.270	429	116	24	1	6	33	32	58	.326	.373
Grass	3.77	18	19	0	56	48	303.1	281	32	111	178	None on	.262	1819	476	88	9	42	42	154	261	.327	.389
Turf	4.64	33	32	0	94	80	518.1	548	53	186	281	Runners on	.266	1328	353	53	9	43	335	143	198	.337	.416
April	4.83	8	8	0	27	19	119.1	118	10	63	75	Scoring Posn	.266	728	194	38	3	20	274	99	108	.350	.409
May	4.71	6	12	0	25	21	137.2	133	15	50	88	Close & Late	.263	194	51	9	1	2	16	16	38	.322	.351
June	3.34	11	6	0	23	20	148.1	150	17	40	60	None on/out	.293	813	238	35	4	24	24	61	101	.347	.434
July	5.18	6	8	0	23	22	116.1	133	11	54	71	vs. 1st Batr (relief)	.176	17	3	0	0	0	1	4	0	.333	.176
August	3.80	9	8	0	23	23	149.1	143	14	43	81	First Inning Pitched	.258	535	138	21	1	22	86	63	88	.340	.424
September/October	4.36	11	9	0	29	23	150.2	152	18	47	80	First 75 Pitches	.260	2392	622	103	13	63	288	235	355	.330	.393
Starter	4.30	48	49	0	128	128	783.2	789	85	272	444	Pitch 76-90	.266	399	106	19	3	12	53	35	50	.331	.419
Reliever	4.74	3	2	0	22	0	38.0	40	0	25	15	Pitch 91-105	.290	279	81	16	2	10	30	23	34	.348	.470
0-3 Days Rest	3.45	0	1	0	5	5	31.1	28	4	10	15	Pitch 106+	.260	77	20	3	0	0	6	4	20	.301	.299
4 Days Rest	4.40	32	28	0	73	73	445.2	442	54	151	262	First Pitch	.315	447	141	18	2	16	77	15	0	.352	.472
5+ Days Rest	4.23	16	20	0	50	50	306.2	319	27	111	167	Ahead on Count	.211	1409	298	43	9	24	104	0	388	.220	.306
Pre-All Star	4.36	27	29	0	82	67	440.0	453	47	170	249	Behind on Count	.317	703	223	49	4	31	123	155	0	.437	.531
Post-All Star	4.27	24	22	0	68	61	381.2	376	38	127	210	Two Strikes	.193	1326	256	46	5	19	94	126	459	.269	.278

Pitcher vs. Batter (career)

Pitches Best Vs.	Avg	AB	H	2B	3B	HR	RBI	BB	SO	OBP	SLG	Pitches Worst Vs.	Avg	AB	H	2B	3B	HR	RBI	BB	SO	OBP	SLG
Joe Carter	.000	11	0	0	0	0	0	0	2	.000	.000	Dion James	.636	11	7	1	0	0	1	4	0	.733	.727
Jeff Huson	.000	9	0	0	0	0	0	2	1	.182	.000	George Brett	.571	21	12	2	2	0	1	2	1	.609	.857
Cory Snyder	.063	16	1	0	0	0	1	1	5	.111	.063	Rafael Palmeiro	.400	20	8	0	0	2	5	6	1	.538	.900
Dante Bichette	.091	11	1	0	0	0	0	0	2	.091	.091	Jose Canseco	.375	24	9	0	0	7	14	3	6	.444	1.250
Gary DiSarcina	.091	11	1	0	0	0	0	0	0	.091	.091	Rickey Henderson	.364	11	4	0	0	2	2	7	2	.611	.909

Doug Strange — Cubs
Bats Both

	Avg	G	AB	R	H	2B	3B	HR	RBI	BB	SO	HBP	GDP	SB	CS	OBP	SLG	IBB	SH	SF	#Pit	#P/PA	GB	FB	G/F
1992 Season	.160	52	94	7	15	1	0	1	5	10	15	0	2	1	0	.240	.202	2	2	0	363	3.49	32	31	1.03
Career (1989-1992)	.204	119	299	23	61	6	1	2	20	27	52	2	8	5	3	.274	.251	2	5	1	1160	3.53	116	82	1.41

1992 Season

	Avg	AB	H	2B	3B	HR	RBI	BB	SO	OBP	SLG		Avg	AB	H	2B	3B	HR	RBI	BB	SO	OBP	SLG
vs. Left	.158	19	3	0	0	0	1	4	4	.304	.158	Scoring Posn	.211	19	4	0	0	0	4	5	2	.375	.211

1992 Season

	Avg	AB	H	2B	3B	HR	RBI	BB	SO	OBP	SLG		Avg	AB	H	2B	3B	HR	RBI	BB	SO	OBP	SLG
vs. Right	.160	75	12	1	0	1	4	6	11	.222	.213	Close & Late	.087	23	2	0	0	0	0	3	2	.192	.087
Home	.135	52	7	1	0	0	4	6	6	.224	.154	None on/out	.231	26	6	0	0	1	1	3	4	.310	.346
Away	.190	42	8	0	0	1	1	4	9	.261	.262	Batting #8	.167	54	9	1	0	1	5	5	6	.237	.241
First Pitch	.150	20	3	0	0	0	1	2	0	.227	.150	Batting #9	.250	12	3	0	0	0	0	2	0	.357	.250
Ahead on Count	.313	16	5	1	0	0	2	6	0	.500	.375	Other	.107	28	3	0	0	0	0	3	9	.194	.107
Behind on Count	.172	29	5	0	0	0	3	0	7	.172	.172	Pre-All Star	.173	75	13	1	0	1	5	9	10	.262	.227
Two Strikes	.073	41	3	0	0	1	2	2	15	.116	.146	Post-All Star	.105	19	2	0	0	0	0	1	5	.150	.105

Darryl Strawberry — Dodgers
Bats Left (flyball hitter)

	Avg	G	AB	R	H	2B	3B	HR	RBI	BB	SO	HBP	GDP	SB	CS	OBP	SLG	IBB	SH	SF	#Pit	#P/PA	GB	FB	G/F
1992 Season	.237	43	156	20	37	8	0	5	25	19	34	1	2	3	1	.322	.385	4	0	1	667	3.77	48	53	0.91
Last Five Years	.258	621	2222	368	574	101	9	138	410	310	501	12	25	68	35	.349	.498	57	0	23	9870	3.84	659	671	0.98

1992 Season

	Avg	AB	H	2B	3B	HR	RBI	BB	SO	OBP	SLG		Avg	AB	H	2B	3B	HR	RBI	BB	SO	OBP	SLG
vs. Left	.242	66	16	1	0	2	10	7	15	.324	.348	Scoring Posn	.306	49	15	2	0	4	22	12	10	.435	.592
vs. Right	.233	90	21	7	0	3	15	12	19	.320	.411	Close & Late	.200	25	5	0	0	2	5	4	6	.333	.440
Home	.278	72	20	4	0	3	13	9	13	.366	.458	None on/out	.143	42	6	3	0	0	0	4	10	.217	.214
Away	.202	84	17	4	0	2	12	10	21	.284	.321	Batting #3	.194	31	6	2	0	1	4	1	8	.219	.355
First Pitch	.333	15	5	0	0	1	5	4	0	.500	.533	Batting #4	.238	122	29	6	0	4	21	18	26	.338	.385
Ahead on Count	.395	38	15	4	0	3	11	9	0	.500	.737	Other	.667	3	2	0	0	0	0	0	0	.667	.667
Behind on Count	.145	55	8	4	0	0	4	0	14	.145	.218	Pre-All Star	.242	124	30	7	0	5	21	14	28	.324	.419
Two Strikes	.173	75	13	3	0	1	9	6	34	.235	.253	Post-All Star	.219	32	7	1	0	0	4	5	6	.316	.250

Last Five Years

	Avg	AB	H	2B	3B	HR	RBI	BB	SO	OBP	SLG		Avg	AB	H	2B	3B	HR	RBI	BB	SO	OBP	SLG
vs. Left	.249	905	225	37	2	51	167	98	220	.320	.463	Scoring Posn	.258	640	165	21	3	37	264	132	150	.376	.473
vs. Right	.265	1317	349	64	7	87	243	212	281	.368	.522	Close & Late	.208	365	76	12	0	16	55	59	101	.321	.373
Groundball	.269	726	195	34	3	46	142	106	155	.364	.514	None on/out	.252	535	135	25	2	33	33	58	117	.328	.492
Flyball	.250	472	118	25	0	40	100	60	136	.333	.557	Batting #3	.258	361	93	18	3	19	63	48	88	.343	.482
Home	.269	1074	289	47	7	77	230	153	235	.360	.541	Batting #4	.256	1741	445	78	5	114	326	246	392	.348	.503
Away	.248	1148	285	54	2	61	180	157	266	.339	.458	Other	.300	120	36	5	1	5	21	16	21	.379	.483
Day	.264	708	187	34	5	38	129	102	152	.358	.487	April	.288	358	103	22	2	18	52	59	81	.391	.511
Night	.256	1514	387	67	4	100	281	208	349	.345	.503	May	.222	379	84	15	1	23	64	49	103	.311	.449
Grass	.255	1605	410	74	8	102	298	219	357	.345	.502	June	.283	269	76	9	2	23	63	53	43	.401	.587
Turf	.266	617	164	27	1	36	112	91	144	.358	.488	July	.256	407	104	18	2	28	77	48	95	.335	.516
First Pitch	.296	267	79	13	4	23	70	19	0	.341	.633	August	.244	410	100	19	1	21	75	56	88	.333	.449
Ahead on Count	.370	525	194	33	1	51	144	151	0	.508	.728	September/October	.268	399	107	18	1	25	79	45	91	.340	.506
Behind on Count	.224	695	156	26	2	35	99	2	231	.227	.419	Pre-All Star	.265	1129	299	54	6	72	204	174	253	.364	.515
Two Strikes	.174	1091	190	36	2	37	115	108	501	.251	.313	Post-All Star	.252	1093	275	47	3	66	206	136	248	.333	.481

Batter vs. Pitcher (since 1984)

Hits Best Against	Avg	AB	H	2B	3B	HR	RBI	BB	SO	OBP	SLG	Hits Worst Against	Avg	AB	H	2B	3B	HR	RBI	BB	SO	OBP	SLG
Brian Fisher	.500	10	5	1	0	2	5	2	3	.583	1.200	Trevor Wilson	.000	16	0	0	0	0	1	2	5	.111	.000
Bill Gullickson	.433	30	13	3	0	4	10	6	5	.500	.933	Mitch Williams	.000	12	0	0	0	0	0	2	7	.143	.000
Mark Portugal	.421	19	8	1	0	3	6	3	7	.500	.947	Rob Dibble	.000	10	0	0	0	0	0	2	6	.167	.000
Bob Walk	.400	20	8	1	0	4	11	4	4	.480	1.050	Ramon Martinez	.083	12	1	0	0	0	1	0	4	.083	.083
Pete Smith	.333	12	4	0	0	3	4	4	3	.500	1.083	Bob Murphy	.091	11	1	0	0	0	0	1	7	.083	.091

Franklin Stubbs — Brewers
Bats Left (flyball hitter)

	Avg	G	AB	R	H	2B	3B	HR	RBI	BB	SO	HBP	GDP	SB	CS	OBP	SLG	IBB	SH	SF	#Pit	#P/PA	GB	FB	G/F
1992 Season	.229	92	288	37	66	11	1	9	42	27	68	1	2	11	8	.297	.368	3	5	1	1221	3.85	82	92	0.89
Last Five Years	.238	525	1443	185	344	69	5	55	200	149	341	6	17	57	23	.310	.407	14	9	13	6084	3.78	411	452	0.91

1992 Season

	Avg	AB	H	2B	3B	HR	RBI	BB	SO	OBP	SLG		Avg	AB	H	2B	3B	HR	RBI	BB	SO	OBP	SLG
vs. Left	.256	43	11	1	1	1	10	0	12	.256	.395	Scoring Posn	.286	77	22	4	1	2	32	15	14	.398	.442
vs. Right	.224	245	55	10	0	8	32	27	56	.303	.363	Close & Late	.200	65	13	2	0	3	12	4	16	.246	.369
Groundball	.267	60	16	2	0	1	6	4	9	.313	.350	None on/out	.191	68	13	1	0	3	3	2	16	.214	.338
Flyball	.176	85	15	2	0	3	11	28	.268	.306	Batting #4	.203	59	12	3	0	1	7	5	15	.266	.305
Home	.198	101	20	1	0	3	12	9	25	.268	.297	Batting #6	.206	126	26	5	1	5	16	7	29	.254	.381
Away	.246	187	46	10	1	6	30	18	43	.312	.406	Other	.272	103	28	3	0	3	19	15	24	.361	.388
Day	.256	90	23	3	0	4	15	12	17	.350	.422	April	.250	60	15	3	1	1	10	4	15	.297	.383
Night	.217	198	43	8	1	5	27	15	51	.271	.343	May	.162	74	12	2	0	5	12	13	17	.295	.392
Grass	.224	228	51	6	0	9	33	22	56	.294	.368	June	.250	44	11	2	0	0	6	5	7	.327	.295
Turf	.250	60	15	5	1	0	9	5	12	.308	.367	July	.233	43	10	1	0	2	6	6	15	.233	.395
First Pitch	.381	42	16	0	0	3	10	3	0	.422	.595	August	.250	36	9	3	0	0	6	3	7	.308	.333
Ahead on Count	.304	46	14	3	0	2	7	13	0	.458	.500	September/October	.290	31	9	0	0	1	2	2	7	.324	.387
Behind on Count	.206	102	21	5	1	1	17	0	33	.212	.304	Pre-All Star	.218	206	45	8	1	8	33	22	46	.297	.383
Two Strikes	.109	147	16	5	0	4	14	11	68	.171	.224	Post-All Star	.256	82	21	3	0	1	9	5	22	.295	.329

423

1992 By Position

Position	Avg	AB	H	2B	3B	HR	RBI	BB	SO	OBP	SLG	G	GS	Innings	PO	A	E	DP	Fld Pct	Rng Fctr	In Zone	Outs	Zone Rtg	MLB Zone
As Designated Hitter	.278	54	15	1	0	1	9	5	12	.333	.352	16	13	---	---	---	---	---	---	---	---	---	---	---
As Pinch Hitter	.300	10	3	1	0	0	2	3	1	.462	.400	14	0	---	---	---	---	---	---	---	---	---	---	---
As 1b	.219	224	49	9	1	8	31	20	55	.286	.375	68	59	550.0	525	63	8	44	.987	---	135	116	.859	.843

Last Five Years

	Avg	AB	H	2B	3B	HR	RBI	BB	SO	OBP	SLG		Avg	AB	H	2B	3B	HR	RBI	BB	SO	OBP	SLG
vs. Left	.242	330	80	19	2	11	48	13	79	.272	.412	Scoring Posn	.223	376	84	15	1	19	148	62	99	.328	.420
vs. Right	.237	1113	264	50	3	44	152	136	262	.320	.406	Close & Late	.241	291	70	11	0	12	40	25	74	.303	.409
Groundball	.256	450	115	19	4	20	64	32	93	.304	.449	None on/out	.273	333	91	16	1	16	16	18	71	.313	.471
Flyball	.240	275	66	14	0	13	46	27	77	.306	.433	Batting #4	.232	336	78	20	0	9	43	33	75	.300	.372
Home	.236	703	166	35	1	24	96	75	166	.311	.391	Batting #6	.225	346	78	18	3	13	41	27	78	.261	.408
Away	.241	740	178	34	4	31	104	74	175	.309	.423	Other	.247	761	188	31	2	33	116	89	188	.325	.423
Day	.245	428	105	18	0	20	68	49	103	.326	.428	April	.246	175	43	10	1	5	20	15	41	.307	.400
Night	.235	1015	239	51	5	35	132	100	238	.303	.399	May	.207	242	50	10	1	9	32	35	58	.309	.368
Grass	.221	917	203	34	0	34	119	101	219	.299	.370	June	.233	258	60	13	0	11	35	23	63	.294	.411
Turf	.268	526	141	35	5	21	81	48	122	.329	.473	July	.232	306	71	10	2	13	47	22	82	.283	.405
First Pitch	.390	210	82	10	0	16	46	5	1	.398	.667	August	.271	262	71	17	0	10	42	34	55	.351	.450
Ahead on Count	.262	271	71	19	1	11	42	76	0	.424	.461	September/October	.245	200	49	9	1	7	24	20	42	.317	.405
Behind on Count	.195	522	102	24	3	13	56	1	186	.198	.328	Pre-All Star	.222	778	173	36	2	30	104	78	193	.294	.389
Two Strikes	.159	711	113	26	1	19	68	61	338	.225	.278	Post-All Star	.257	665	171	33	3	25	96	71	148	.328	.429

Batter vs. Pitcher (career)

Hits Best Against	Avg	AB	H	2B	3B	HR	RBI	BB	SO	OBP	SLG	Hits Worst Against	Avg	AB	H	2B	3B	HR	RBI	BB	SO	OBP	SLG
Greg Maddux	.500	24	12	2	1	0	2	2	2	.538	.667	Alex Fernandez	.000	11	0	0	0	0	0	0	7	.000	.000
John Smoltz	.462	13	6	2	0	2	3	4	3	.588	1.077	Jeff Montgomery	.000	10	0	0	0	0	0	1	3	.091	.000
Jack Morris	.444	9	4	0	0	1	3	3	1	.538	.778	Rick Aguilera	.056	18	1	0	0	0	0	0	5	.056	.056
Bryn Smith	.400	20	8	3	0	4	9	3	4	.478	1.150	Jeff Robinson	.077	13	1	0	0	0	0	0	6	.077	.077
Dave Stieb	.333	9	3	1	0	1	1	1	1	.500	.778	Dave Stewart	.083	12	1	0	0	0	0	0	3	.083	.083

William Suero — Brewers   Bats Right (flyball hitter)

	Avg	G	AB	R	H	2B	3B	HR	RBI	BB	SO	HBP	GDP	SB	CS	OBP	SLG	IBB	SH	SF	#Pit	#P/PA	GB	FB	G/F
1992 Season	.188	18	16	4	3	1	0	0	0	2	1			2	1	.316	.250	0	0	0	63	3.32	6	7	0.86

1992 Season

	Avg	AB	H	2B	3B	HR	RBI	BB	SO	OBP	SLG		Avg	AB	H	2B	3B	HR	RBI	BB	SO	OBP	SLG
vs. Left	.273	11	3	1	0	0	0	2	1	.385	.364	Scoring Posn	.000	3	0	0	0	0	0	1	1	.250	.000
vs. Right	.000	5	0	0	0	0	0	0	0	.167	.000	Close & Late	.000	2	0	0	0	0	0	0	1	.333	.000

B.J. Surhoff — Brewers   Bats Left (groundball hitter)

	Avg	G	AB	R	H	2B	3B	HR	RBI	BB	SO	HBP	GDP	SB	CS	OBP	SLG	IBB	SH	SF	#Pit	#P/PA	GB	FB	G/F
1992 Season	.252	139	480	63	121	19	1	4	62	46	41	2	8	14	8	.314	.321	8	5	10	1883	3.50	218	124	1.76
Last Five Years	.263	682	2388	264	627	97	13	25	282	169	189	9	57	72	41	.309	.345	25	39	39	8697	3.34	1057	662	1.60

1992 Season

	Avg	AB	H	2B	3B	HR	RBI	BB	SO	OBP	SLG		Avg	AB	H	2B	3B	HR	RBI	BB	SO	OBP	SLG
vs. Left	.270	126	34	3	1	2	20	11	17	.329	.357	Scoring Posn	.299	134	40	7	0	2	57	18	7	.366	.396
vs. Right	.246	354	87	16	0	2	42	35	24	.309	.308	Close & Late	.247	93	23	2	0	2	13	7	14	.297	.333
Groundball	.299	117	35	8	0	0	17	8	7	.341	.368	None on/out	.239	117	28	5	0	0	11	12		.305	.282
Flyball	.252	131	33	4	1	1	14	19	14	.346	.321	Batting #6	.266	79	21	2	0	0	9	14	5	.375	.291
Home	.280	243	68	8	0	3	29	27	20	.349	.350	Batting #8	.247	190	47	4	0	2	23	17	20	.310	.300
Away	.224	237	53	11	1	1	33	19	21	.278	.291	Other	.251	211	53	13	1	2	30	15	16	.293	.351
Day	.265	147	39	5	0	0	20	16	11	.343	.299	April	.136	66	9	0	0	1	10	4	5	.181	.182
Night	.246	333	82	14	1	4	42	30	30	.301	.330	May	.215	65	14	2	0	1	12	2	5	.235	.292
Grass	.261	403	105	15	1	4	46	40	32	.326	.333	June	.326	95	31	6	0	1	13	7	5	.371	.421
Turf	.208	77	16	4	0	0	16	6	9	.253	.260	July	.279	86	24	4	0	1	6	9	4	.340	.360
First Pitch	.313	67	21	3	0	0	7	6	0	.368	.358	August	.244	78	19	2	0	0	9	12	13	.348	.269
Ahead on Count	.257	136	35	7	0	4	29	18	0	.333	.397	September/October	.267	90	24	5	1	0	12	12	9	.346	.344
Behind on Count	.255	133	39	7	0	0	20	0	18	.255	.306	Pre-All Star	.234	265	62	10	0	3	37	17	17	.277	.306
Two Strikes	.216	171	37	4	0	0	15	24	41	.313	.240	Post-All Star	.274	215	59	9	1	1	25	29	24	.357	.340

1992 By Position

Position	Avg	AB	H	2B	3B	HR	RBI	BB	SO	OBP	SLG	G	GS	Innings	PO	A	E	DP	Fld Pct	Rng Fctr	In Zone	Outs	Zone Rtg	MLB Zone
As c	.236	368	87	10	0	3	48	31	32	.294	.288	109	103	926.0	546	59	6	7	.990	---	---	---	---	---
As 1b	.269	52	14	2	0	1	6	9	6	.359	.365	17	17	129.0	143	13	0	18	1.000	---	33	30	.909	.843

Last Five Years

	Avg	AB	H	2B	3B	HR	RBI	BB	SO	OBP	SLG		Avg	AB	H	2B	3B	HR	RBI	BB	SO	OBP	SLG
vs. Left	.266	531	141	18	3	8	71	33	57	.309	.356	Scoring Posn	.284	610	173	28	7	8	253	61	49	.335	.392
vs. Right	.262	1857	486	79	10	17	211	136	132	.309	.342	Close & Late	.246	395	97	15	1	5	49	30	44	.296	.327
Groundball	.291	595	173	32	3	4	93	47	36	.340	.375	None on/out	.235	536	126	20	0	6	6	31	38	.277	.306
Flyball	.292	552	161	25	6	6	58	46	52	.347	.391	Batting #7	.259	621	161	31	4	6	74	47	48	.310	.351

Last Five Years

	Avg	AB	H	2B	3B	HR	RBI	BB	SO	OBP	SLG		Avg	AB	H	2B	3B	HR	RBI	BB	SO	OBP	SLG
Home	.264	1171	309	45	6	15	142	103	92	.323	.351	Batting #8	.239	461	110	12	0	3	46	42	39	.303	.284
Away	.261	1217	318	52	7	10	140	66	97	.295	.340	Other	.273	1306	356	54	9	16	162	80	102	.311	.364
Day	.265	702	186	28	2	6	79	52	58	.315	.336	April	.190	295	56	6	1	5	37	20	31	.236	.268
Night	.262	1686	441	69	11	19	203	117	131	.307	.349	May	.261	376	98	14	1	5	43	27	27	.306	.343
Grass	.265	2036	540	83	11	24	236	148	165	.313	.352	June	.260	443	124	22	2	4	44	22	33	.313	.366
Turf	.247	352	87	14	2	1	46	21	33	.283	.307	July	.269	402	108	15	1	2	43	24	25	.309	.326
First Pitch	.315	330	104	11	3	4	59	8	0	.325	.403	August	.273	417	114	21	3	3	48	32	40	.326	.360
Ahead on Count	.268	719	193	33	4	15	101	97	0	.351	.388	September/October	.279	455	127	19	5	6	67	44	33	.339	.382
Behind on Count	.241	822	198	32	3	3	83	4	102	.246	.296	Pre-All Star	.254	1246	317	49	4	14	134	81	99	.297	.334
Two Strikes	.224	787	176	25	2	3	59	59	189	.280	.272	Post-All Star	.271	1142	310	48	9	11	148	88	90	.322	.358

Batter vs. Pitcher (career)

Hits Best Against	Avg	AB	H	2B	3B	HR	RBI	BB	SO	OBP	SLG	Hits Worst Against	Avg	AB	H	2B	3B	HR	RBI	BB	SO	OBP	SLG
Jim Abbott	.583	12	7	0	0	0	2	1	0	.615	.583	Floyd Bannister	.000	10	0	0	0	0	1	0	0	.000	.000
Jeff M. Robinson	.462	13	6	1	1	0	2	2	0	.533	.692	Bud Black	.000	10	0	0	0	0	1	0	0	.000	.000
Juan Berenguer	.444	9	4	2	0	0	3	3	1	.583	.667	Nolan Ryan	.059	17	1	0	0	0	0	1	3	.111	.059
Scott Sanderson	.429	14	6	2	0	1	3	0	1	.400	.786	Bill Gullickson	.077	13	1	0	0	0	1	1	0	.133	.077
Mike Henneman	.400	10	4	2	0	1	1	1	1	.455	.800	Greg Swindell	.077	13	1	0	0	0	1	0	1	.077	.077

Rick Sutcliffe — Orioles Pitches Right

	ERA	W	L	Sv	G	GS	IP	BB	SO	Avg	H	2B	3B	HR	RBI	OBP	SLG	CG	ShO	Sup	QS	#P/S	SB	CS	GB	FB	G/F
1992 Season	4.47	16	15	0	36	36	237.1	74	109	.273	251	37	7	20	99	.328	.393	5	2	4.21	18	105	22	5	308	341	0.90
Last Five Years	4.06	51	47	0	127	125	810.1	270	465	.262	806	139	19	62	324	.321	.381	22	5	4.34	66	99	97	28	1132	908	1.25

1992 Season

	ERA	W	L	Sv	G	GS	IP	H	HR	BB	SO		Avg	AB	H	2B	3B	HR	RBI	BB	SO	OBP	SLG
Home	4.17	9	8	0	20	20	131.2	117	12	45	63	vs. Left	.265	431	114	19	4	13	49	37	44	.320	.418
Away	4.85	7	7	0	16	16	105.2	134	8	29	46	vs. Right	.280	489	137	18	3	7	50	37	65	.335	.372
Day	3.69	3	6	0	11	11	70.2	80	1	26	35	Inning 1-6	.269	756	203	29	7	16	83	63	86	.326	.389
Night	4.81	13	9	0	25	25	166.2	171	19	48	74	Inning 7+	.293	164	48	8	0	4	16	11	23	.339	.415
Grass	4.69	12	12	0	29	29	188.0	188	19	61	85	None on	.287	516	148	24	3	10	10	42	65	.346	.403
Turf	3.65	4	3	0	7	7	49.1	63	1	13	24	Runners on	.255	404	103	13	4	10	89	32	44	.305	.381
April	2.65	3	2	0	5	5	37.1	34	0	7	21	Scoring Posn	.251	207	52	5	1	8	81	21	29	.311	.401
May	6.33	4	2	0	7	7	42.2	52	8	12	17	Close & Late	.248	101	25	3	0	2	8	7	18	.291	.337
June	3.21	3	2	0	6	6	42.0	43	1	12	15	None on/out	.321	234	75	11	1	3	3	21	22	.384	.415
July	5.85	0	5	0	6	6	40.0	49	3	16	23	vs. 1st Batr (relief)	.000	0	0	0	0	0	0	0	0	.000	.000
August	1.60	4	0	0	6	6	45.0	39	1	17	19	First Inning Pitched	.268	142	38	6	2	3	21	14	18	.331	.401
September/October	8.31	2	4	0	6	6	30.1	34	7	10	14	First 75 Pitches	.266	610	162	23	5	10	59	51	77	.324	.369
Starter	4.47	16	15	0	36	36	237.1	251	20	74	109	Pitch 76-90	.241	116	28	3	1	4	14	8	10	.295	.388
Reliever	0.00	0	0	0	0	0	0.0	0	0	0	0	Pitch 91-105	.286	119	34	3	1	3	15	8	13	.326	.403
0-3 Days Rest	11.72	1	3	0	4	4	17.2	28	4	7	10	Pitch 106+	.360	75	27	8	0	3	11	7	9	.412	.587
4 Days Rest	4.38	12	11	0	27	27	181.0	190	12	57	78	First Pitch	.290	107	31	3	1	2	19	3	0	.305	.393
5+ Days Rest	1.63	3	1	0	5	5	38.2	33	4	10	21	Ahead on Count	.247	324	80	8	3	6	24	0	87	.252	.346
Pre-All Star	4.00	10	8	0	20	20	139.1	147	9	35	62	Behind on Count	.291	296	86	19	0	6	31	35	0	.364	.416
Post-All Star	5.14	6	7	0	16	16	98.0	104	11	39	47	Two Strikes	.228	355	81	9	3	7	27	36	109	.306	.330

Last Five Years

	ERA	W	L	Sv	G	GS	IP	H	HR	BB	SO		Avg	AB	H	2B	3B	HR	RBI	BB	SO	OBP	SLG
Home	4.08	22	22	0	63	61	399.2	382	34	132	247	vs. Left	.263	1659	436	80	12	35	180	169	222	.327	.389
Away	4.05	29	25	0	64	64	410.2	424	28	138	218	vs. Right	.262	1413	370	59	7	27	144	101	243	.313	.371
Day	3.82	21	26	0	64	62	410.0	410	29	135	260	Inning 1-6	.259	2552	662	118	18	52	279	230	390	.319	.381
Night	4.32	30	21	0	63	63	400.1	396	33	135	205	Inning 7+	.277	520	144	21	1	10	45	40	75	.328	.379
Grass	4.46	30	35	0	89	87	556.2	567	53	187	326	None on	.261	1833	479	83	10	40	40	132	268	.313	.383
Turf	3.19	21	12	0	38	38	253.2	239	9	83	139	Runners on	.264	1239	327	56	9	22	284	138	197	.331	.377
April	3.78	9	8	0	19	19	138.0	132	10	36	87	Scoring Posn	.246	704	173	25	6	15	254	106	137	.334	.362
May	5.66	9	7	0	22	21	125.2	134	16	47	61	Close & Late	.259	239	62	10	0	4	22	18	36	.310	.351
June	3.38	9	5	0	15	15	101.1	103	3	29	56	None on/out	.277	819	227	40	4	19	19	50	95	.321	.405
July	3.90	4	13	0	19	18	127.0	128	8	44	79	vs. 1st Batr (relief)	1.000	2	2	0	0	0	1	0	0	1.000	1.000
August	2.58	11	5	0	26	26	174.1	147	9	62	98	First Inning Pitched	.275	491	135	22	6	9	70	44	75	.330	.399
September/October	5.38	9	9	0	26	26	144.0	162	16	52	84	First 75 Pitches	.259	2189	566	102	14	42	220	169	349	.316	.376
Starter	4.06	51	47	0	125	125	808.1	803	62	270	464	Pitch 76-90	.260	369	96	18	2	8	47	38	43	.330	.385
Reliever	4.50	0	0	0	2	0	2.0	3	0	0	1	Pitch 91-105	.286	301	86	7	2	7	36	23	44	.330	.392
0-3 Days Rest	6.53	3	6	0	11	11	62.0	69	8	23	36	Pitch 106+	.272	213	58	12	1	5	21	20	29	.335	.408
4 Days Rest	3.85	31	31	0	83	83	563.0	551	41	169	312	First Pitch	.305	446	136	24	3	7	56	14	0	.321	.419
5+ Days Rest	3.88	17	10	0	31	31	183.1	183	13	78	116	Ahead on Count	.218	1240	270	43	8	12	92	0	401	.218	.294
Pre-All Star	4.22	29	24	0	63	61	407.1	414	30	122	229	Behind on Count	.296	834	247	49	4	24	109	139	0	.395	.451
Post-All Star	3.91	22	23	0	64	64	403.0	392	32	148	236	Two Strikes	.204	1265	258	41	7	17	99	117	464	.272	.288

Pitcher vs. Batter (since 1984)

Pitches Best Vs.	Avg	AB	H	2B	3B	HR	RBI	BB	SO	OBP	SLG	Pitches Worst Vs.	Avg	AB	H	2B	3B	HR	RBI	BB	SO	OBP	SLG
Mariano Duncan	.000	14	0	0	0	0	0	0	4	.000	.000	Rickey Henderson	.667	6	4	0	0	1	3	5	2	.818	1.167
Gary Redus	.071	14	1	0	0	0	1	3	2	.222	.071	Edgar Martinez	.538	13	7	3	1	0	1	1	2	.533	.923

Pitcher vs. Batter (since 1984)

Pitches Best Vs.	Avg	AB	H	2B	3B	HR	RBI	BB	SO	OBP	SLG	Pitches Worst Vs.	Avg	AB	H	2B	3B	HR	RBI	BB	SO	OBP	SLG
Kirby Puckett	.071	14	1	0	0	0	0	1	1	.133	.071	Von Hayes	.443	61	27	9	1	5	13	9	8	.514	.869
Benny Distefano	.077	13	1	0	0	0	2	1	3	.143	.077	Don Mattingly	.385	13	5	0	0	2	7	2	0	.438	.846
Tony Phillips	.091	11	1	0	0	0	0	2	3	.231	.091	Larry Walker	.375	8	3	1	0	1	1	5	0	.615	.875

Dale Sveum — White Sox

Bats Both (flyball hitter)

	Avg	G	AB	R	H	2B	3B	HR	RBI	BB	SO	HBP	GDP	SB	CS	OBP	SLG	IBB	SH	SF	#Pit	#P/PA	GB	FB	G/F
1992 Season	.197	94	249	28	49	13	0	4	28	28	68	0	6	1	1	.273	.297	4	2	5	1121	3.98	80	77	1.04
Last Five Years	.227	361	1099	117	249	53	5	18	134	93	298	4	22	4	6	.286	.333	4	10	14	4778	3.95	312	324	0.96

1992 Season

	Avg	AB	H	2B	3B	HR	RBI	BB	SO	OBP	SLG		Avg	AB	H	2B	3B	HR	RBI	BB	SO	OBP	SLG
vs. Left	.203	69	14	5	0	0	5	15	24	.345	.275	Scoring Posn	.206	68	14	5	0	1	24	7	20	.263	.324
vs. Right	.194	180	35	8	0	4	23	13	44	.242	.306	Close & Late	.263	57	15	2	0	1	6	6	20	.333	.351
Home	.160	119	19	5	0	1	13	16	30	.255	.227	None on/out	.208	53	11	4	0	1	1	9	12	.323	.340
Away	.231	130	30	8	0	3	15	12	38	.290	.362	Batting #7	.233	43	10	2	0	2	7	2	7	.267	.419
First Pitch	.500	26	13	4	0	0	6	4	0	.548	.654	Batting #9	.213	122	26	9	0	2	12	10	35	.267	.336
Ahead on Count	.282	39	11	1	0	2	8	13	0	.453	.462	Other	.155	84	13	2	0	0	9	16	26	.284	.179
Behind on Count	.146	89	13	4	0	1	7	0	33	.144	.225	Pre-All Star	.179	134	24	4	0	2	16	16	39	.263	.254
Two Strikes	.087	138	12	5	0	1	9	11	68	.152	.145	Post-All Star	.217	115	25	9	0	2	12	12	29	.285	.348

Last Five Years

	Avg	AB	H	2B	3B	HR	RBI	BB	SO	OBP	SLG		Avg	AB	H	2B	3B	HR	RBI	BB	SO	OBP	SLG
vs. Left	.233	412	96	19	5	7	44	38	116	.299	.354	Scoring Posn	.263	289	76	18	3	5	115	25	81	.312	.398
vs. Right	.223	687	153	34	0	11	90	55	182	.278	.320	Close & Late	.276	210	58	11	3	2	26	14	59	.319	.386
Groundball	.293	263	77	21	1	3	34	29	47	.359	.414	None on/out	.211	246	52	17	1	5	5	26	64	.292	.350
Flyball	.201	274	55	7	2	5	31	23	95	.259	.296	Batting #8	.244	234	57	7	2	4	21	28	62	.325	.342
Home	.231	576	133	28	4	7	68	55	143	.296	.330	Batting #9	.238	491	117	31	2	5	61	43	135	.299	.340
Away	.222	523	116	25	1	11	66	38	155	.275	.337	Other	.201	374	75	15	1	9	52	22	101	.243	.318
Day	.227	362	82	18	2	8	45	26	110	.277	.354	April	.203	123	25	1	1	3	14	8	39	.259	.301
Night	.227	737	167	35	3	10	89	67	188	.290	.323	May	.247	227	56	10	3	6	36	26	65	.324	.396
Grass	.245	882	216	41	4	17	113	68	231	.298	.358	June	.181	199	36	8	0	3	21	20	66	.252	.266
Turf	.152	217	33	12	1	1	21	25	67	.239	.230	July	.213	197	42	12	1	3	17	10	51	.252	.330
First Pitch	.333	129	43	9	2	1	23	4	0	.356	.457	August	.246	167	41	8	0	1	21	10	34	.287	.311
Ahead on Count	.327	199	65	13	1	3	34	45	0	.448	.447	September/October	.263	186	49	14	0	2	25	19	43	.325	.371
Behind on Count	.180	394	71	18	1	7	41	0	147	.182	.284	Pre-All Star	.215	636	137	23	4	14	80	56	191	.279	.330
Two Strikes	.134	581	78	21	1	9	48	44	298	.195	.220	Post-All Star	.242	463	112	30	1	4	54	37	107	.295	.337

Batter vs. Pitcher (career)

Hits Best Against	Avg	AB	H	2B	3B	HR	RBI	BB	SO	OBP	SLG	Hits Worst Against	Avg	AB	H	2B	3B	HR	RBI	BB	SO	OBP	SLG
Mark Eichhorn	.462	13	6	1	0	0	5	0	1	.462	.538	Bud Black	.000	12	0	0	0	0	0	2	4	.143	.000
Greg Cadaret	.364	11	4	2	0	0	2	2	6	.462	.545	Roger Clemens	.083	24	2	1	0	0	0	2	12	.154	.125
Scott Bailes	.353	17	6	1	0	1	4	3	5	.450	.588	John Candelaria	.091	11	1	0	0	0	0	2	3	.231	.091
Floyd Bannister	.333	18	6	2	1	0	1	1	1	.368	.556	Jose Guzman	.125	24	3	1	0	0	2	0	8	.125	.167
Doug Jones	.333	12	4	2	0	0	1	2	2	.429	.500	Gene Nelson	.182	11	2	0	0	0	0	0	2	.167	.182

Russ Swan — Mariners

Pitches Left (groundball pitcher)

	ERA	W	L	Sv	G	GS	IP	BB	SO	Avg	H	2B	3B	HR	RBI	OBP	SLG	GF	IR	IRS	Hld	SvOp	SB	CS	GB	FB	G/F
1992 Season	4.74	3	10	9	55	9	104.1	45	45	.262	104	22	4	8	59	.338	.398	26	44	11	7	11	5	2	205	86	2.38
Career (1989-1992)	4.26	11	18	11	133	20	239.0	99	96	.268	244	49	6	23	128	.338	.410	37	108	25	20	16	17	4	478	194	2.46

1992 Season

	ERA	W	L	Sv	G	GS	IP	H	HR	BB	SO		Avg	AB	H	2B	3B	HR	RBI	BB	SO	OBP	SLG
Home	6.44	1	6	4	26	4	43.1	60	5	15	20	vs. Left	.198	81	16	2	0	0	6	8	15	.275	.222
Away	3.54	2	4	5	29	5	61.0	44	3	30	25	vs. Right	.278	316	88	20	4	8	53	37	30	.354	.443
Starter	6.14	2	5	0	9	9	51.1	50	4	22	21	Scoring Posn	.261	115	30	8	2	2	47	15	16	.338	.417
Reliever	3.40	1	5	9	46	0	53.0	54	4	23	24	Close & Late	.239	142	34	5	0	4	18	13	19	.299	.359
0 Days rest	0.63	0	2	0	11	0	14.1	6	0	6	6	None on/out	.250	92	23	1	1	2	2	9	6	.317	.348
1 or 2 Days rest	3.04	0	2	5	19	0	23.2	23	3	8	11	First Pitch	.258	66	17	5	0	1	13	5	0	.315	.379
3+ Days rest	6.60	0	3	2	16	0	15.0	25	1	9	7	Behind on Count	.330	94	31	6	2	4	15	23	0	.458	.564
Pre-All Star	4.69	3	5	5	32	9	78.2	72	4	32	31	Ahead on Count	.226	164	37	5	2	1	21	0	36	.232	.299
Post-All Star	4.91	0	5	4	23	0	25.2	32	4	13	14	Two Strikes	.221	154	34	7	1	1	16	17	45	.305	.299

Career (1989-1992)

	ERA	W	L	Sv	G	GS	IP	H	HR	BB	SO		Avg	AB	H	2B	3B	HR	RBI	BB	SO	OBP	SLG
Home	5.58	3	9	4	62	8	101.2	132	16	37	50	vs. Left	.200	240	48	4	0	1	22	20	30	.260	.229
Away	3.28	8	9	7	71	12	137.1	112	7	62	46	vs. Right	.292	672	196	45	6	22	106	79	66	.365	.475
Day	3.08	4	5	2	37	5	73.0	56	8	26	34	Inning 1-6	.260	450	117	29	5	12	74	53	46	.337	.427
Night	4.77	7	13	9	96	15	166.0	188	15	73	62	Inning 7+	.275	462	127	20	1	11	54	46	50	.339	.394
Grass	2.92	7	7	7	56	9	111.0	86	9	49	39	None on	.265	487	129	24	4	11	11	50	46	.333	.386
Turf	5.41	4	11	4	77	11	128.0	158	14	50	57	Runners on	.271	425	115	25	5	12	117	49	50	.344	.438
April	3.66	2	4	2	14	6	46.2	38	1	16	17	Scoring Posn	.265	268	71	13	3	7	101	33	37	.338	.414
May	6.00	1	3	0	19	4	39.0	51	5	21	18	Close & Late	.240	271	65	10	0	7	30	23	32	.297	.354

Career (1989-1992)

	ERA	W	L	Sv	G	GS	IP	H	HR	BB	SO
June	3.02	3	1	2	28	4	50.2	50	4	15	21
July	3.15	2	4	6	24	1	34.1	30	5	10	15
August	7.62	0	4	1	18	2	28.1	39	7	17	11
September/October	3.38	3	2	0	30	3	40.0	36	1	20	14
Starter	5.27	4	11	0	20	20	100.2	100	11	44	38
Reliever	3.51	7	7	11	113	0	138.1	144	12	55	58
0 Days rest	1.39	2	1	2	26	0	32.1	22	0	17	14
1 or 2 Days rest	3.57	4	3	6	51	0	63.0	65	7	19	30
3+ Days rest	5.02	1	3	3	36	0	43.0	57	5	19	14
Pre-All Star	3.95	7	10	7	74	15	152.2	152	12	56	60
Post-All Star	4.80	4	8	4	59	5	86.1	92	11	43	36

	Avg	AB	H	2B	3B	HR	RBI	BB	SO	OBP	SLG
None on/out	.268	220	59	6	1	6	6	20	19	.329	.386
vs. 1st Batr (relief)	.304	102	31	5	0	2	21	4	11	.318	.412
First Inning Pitched	.272	416	113	18	2	7	57	37	49	.329	.375
First 15 Pitches	.278	403	112	19	2	8	50	32	38	.329	.395
Pitch 16-30	.255	216	55	10	0	4	28	30	27	.344	.356
Pitch 31-45	.260	100	26	6	1	3	18	17	12	.367	.430
Pitch 46+	.264	193	51	14	3	8	32	20	19	.335	.492
First Pitch	.267	146	39	8	1	2	22	10	0	.314	.377
Ahead on Count	.227	352	80	14	3	5	48	1	78	.231	.327
Behind on Count	.314	226	71	11	2	11	33	51	0	.437	.527
Two Strikes	.219	338	74	17	2	5	42	37	96	.298	.325

Pitcher vs. Batter (career)

Pitches Best Vs.	Avg	AB	H	2B	3B	HR	RBI	BB	SO	OBP	SLG
Lou Whitaker	.000	11	0	0	0	0	1	2	1	.154	.000
Mike Greenwell	.091	11	1	0	0	0	1	1	3	.154	.091
Don Mattingly	.100	10	1	0	0	0	1	2	2	.250	.100
Danny Tartabull	.182	11	2	0	0	1	2	2	2	.308	.455

Pitches Worst Vs.	Avg	AB	H	2B	3B	HR	RBI	BB	SO	OBP	SLG
Ruben Sierra	.417	12	5	1	0	0	1	0	1	.417	.500
Alan Trammell	.357	14	5	2	0	2	0	0		.333	.500
Dan Gladden	.333	12	4	1	1	0	3	1	0	.385	.583
Tony Phillips	.313	16	5	1	0	1	3	2	1	.389	.563
Rafael Palmeiro	.308	13	4	0	0	0	2	0	2	.353	.308

Bill Swift — Giants   Pitches Right (groundball pitcher)

	ERA	W	L	Sv	G	GS	IP	BB	SO	Avg	H	2B	3B	HR	RBI	OBP	SLG	CG	ShO	Sup	QS	#P/S	SB	CS	GB	FB	G/F
1992 Season	2.08	10	4	1	30	22	164.2	43	77	.239	144	19	4	6	40	.292	.314	3	2	4.04	17	91	5	4	314	120	2.62
Last Five Years	3.21	32	25	25	231	70	687.2	193	259	.265	692	104	10	30	272	.320	.348	9	3	4.14	40	86	15	15	1498	428	3.50

1992 Season

	ERA	W	L	Sv	G	GS	IP	H	HR	BB	SO
Home	2.55	4	3	1	16	12	84.2	75	5	25	38
Away	1.58	6	1	0	14	10	80.0	69	1	18	39
Day	1.79	7	1	1	14	10	80.2	64	3	18	34
Night	2.36	3	3	0	16	12	84.0	80	3	25	43
Grass	2.21	7	4	1	23	17	126.0	112	5	37	62
Turf	1.63	3	0	0	7	5	38.2	32	1	6	15
April	1.55	4	0	0	5	5	40.2	34	1	9	17
May	3.60	2	0	0	4	4	25.0	22	1	9	12
June	2.45	0	0	0	2	2	11.0	10	0	2	3
July	2.25	2	2	0	6	6	36.0	34	3	11	12
August	1.69	1	1	0	5	5	32.0	28	1	9	18
September/October	1.35	1	1	1	8	0	20.0	16	0	3	15
Starter	2.18	9	3	0	22	22	144.2	128	6	40	62
Reliever	1.35	1	1	1	8	0	20.0	16	0	3	15
0-3 Days Rest	0.00	0	0	0	0	0	0.0	0	0	0	0
4 Days Rest	1.91	7	3	0	14	14	94.1	81	5	25	42
5+ Days Rest	2.68	2	0	0	8	8	50.1	47	1	15	20
Pre-All Star	2.53	7	1	0	14	14	92.1	83	4	27	35
Post-All Star	1.49	3	3	1	16	8	72.1	61	2	16	42

	Avg	AB	H	2B	3B	HR	RBI	BB	SO	OBP	SLG
vs. Left	.264	383	101	16	3	5	31	38	36	.332	.360
vs. Right	.196	219	43	3	1	1	9	5	41	.218	.233
Inning 1-6	.229	463	106	15	3	4	30	41	56	.293	.300
Inning 7+	.273	139	38	4	1	2	10	2	21	.289	.360
None on	.249	361	90	12	1	2	2	27	47	.307	.305
Runners on	.224	241	54	7	3	4	38	16	30	.270	.328
Scoring Posn	.167	114	19	3	3	2	31	12	16	.242	.298
Close & Late	.232	69	16	1	0	2	6	1	13	.254	.333
None on/out	.253	158	40	3	0	2	2	10	15	.302	.310
vs. 1st Batr (relief)	.125	8	1	0	0	0	0	0	2	.125	.125
First Inning Pitched	.287	115	33	5	1	2	14	10	18	.341	.400
First 75 Pitches	.234	475	111	16	3	5	33	39	56	.295	.312
Pitch 76-90	.239	71	17	2	0	0	2	4	12	.280	.268
Pitch 91-105	.344	32	11	0	1	0	0	0	5	.344	.406
Pitch 106+	.208	24	5	1	0	1	5	0	4	.208	.375
First Pitch	.255	106	27	4	2	2	12	3	0	.275	.387
Ahead on Count	.201	229	46	6	1	1	9	0	67	.206	.249
Behind on Count	.284	148	42	6	0	1	9	22	0	.376	.345
Two Strikes	.191	230	44	5	1	3	8	18	77	.254	.248

Last Five Years

	ERA	W	L	Sv	G	GS	IP	H	HR	BB	SO
Home	3.01	16	12	10	113	35	346.2	339	18	98	120
Away	3.40	16	13	15	118	35	341.0	353	12	95	139
Day	2.72	15	8	6	69	23	225.1	218	10	56	76
Night	3.45	17	17	19	162	47	462.1	474	20	137	183
Grass	3.22	14	11	14	99	34	310.0	311	13	95	141
Turf	3.19	18	14	11	132	36	377.2	361	17	98	118
April	2.58	5	0	1	21	8	80.1	88	2	21	33
May	3.42	10	4	5	42	15	139.2	135	6	40	63
June	4.00	4	5	1	35	13	110.1	121	8	32	31
July	3.41	7	8	4	36	17	134.2	138	7	39	47
August	2.85	1	5	4	40	14	116.2	117	5	36	37
September/October	2.72	5	3	10	57	3	106.0	93	2	25	48
Starter	3.72	22	19	0	70	70	427.2	451	24	129	144
Reliever	2.35	10	6	25	161	0	260.0	241	6	64	115
0-3 Days Rest	3.91	1	1	0	4	4	23.0	23	1	7	6
4 Days Rest	3.50	13	11	0	39	39	236.1	254	17	76	89
5+ Days Rest	4.01	8	7	0	27	27	168.1	174	6	46	49
Pre-All Star	3.57	21	12	7	110	42	373.0	392	19	109	139
Post-All Star	2.77	11	13	18	121	28	314.2	300	11	60	120

	Avg	AB	H	2B	3B	HR	RBI	BB	SO	OBP	SLG
vs. Left	.285	1287	367	60	4	18	137	108	95	.342	.380
vs. Right	.246	1320	325	44	6	12	135	85	164	.298	.316
Inning 1-6	.275	1707	469	77	6	19	199	139	155	.333	.360
Inning 7+	.248	900	223	27	4	11	73	54	104	.294	.323
None on	.258	1425	367	51	3	13	13	101	157	.313	.325
Runners on	.275	1182	325	53	7	17	259	92	102	.328	.375
Scoring Posn	.245	654	160	26	4	7	224	75	66	.324	.325
Close & Late	.252	437	110	11	0	7	41	32	55	.307	.325
None on/out	.264	644	170	21	1	4	4	29	70	.300	.318
vs. 1st Batr (relief)	.205	146	30	6	1	0	15	8	17	.250	.260
First Inning Pitched	.259	788	204	33	4	4	111	67	94	.319	.324
First 75 Pitches	.264	2284	602	89	7	22	240	171	223	.318	.338
Pitch 76-90	.275	193	53	9	2	5	19	14	24	.329	.420
Pitch 91-105	.292	89	26	4	1	1	6	6	8	.344	.393
Pitch 106+	.268	41	11	2	0	2	7	2	4	.302	.463
First Pitch	.285	499	142	16	2	6	57	13	0	.302	.361
Ahead on Count	.221	950	210	38	4	6	78	0	229	.227	.249
Behind on Count	.301	695	209	29	2	14	84	105	0	.397	.409
Two Strikes	.208	856	178	28	5	8	66	74	259	.275	.280

Pitcher vs. Batter (career)

Pitches Best Vs.	Avg	AB	H	2B	3B	HR	RBI	BB	SO	OBP	SLG
Jack Clark	.000	14	0	0	0	0	0	0	5	.000	.000
Steve Buechele	.063	16	1	0	0	0	1	1	6	.118	.063

Pitches Worst Vs.	Avg	AB	H	2B	3B	HR	RBI	BB	SO	OBP	SLG
Dave Henderson	.615	13	8	1	0	0	2	1	0	.600	.692
Rich Gedman	.600	15	9	2	0	0	2	2	1	.647	.733

Pitcher vs. Batter (career)

Pitches Best Vs.	Avg	AB	H	2B	3B	HR	RBI	BB	SO	OBP	SLG	Pitches Worst Vs.	Avg	AB	H	2B	3B	HR	RBI	BB	SO	OBP	SLG
Al Newman	.067	15	1	0	0	0	2	0	1	.067	.067	Kent Hrbek	.500	26	13	3	0	1	5	5	1	.561	.731
Gary Sheffield	.067	15	1	0	0	0	2	0	0	.067	.067	Ruben Sierra	.455	22	10	1	0	2	7	0	1	.455	.773
Brook Jacoby	.118	17	2	0	0	0	5	0	0	.111	.118	Harold Baines	.452	31	14	3	0	2	7	3	0	.486	.742

Greg Swindell — Reds
Pitches Left (flyball pitcher)

	ERA	W	L	Sv	G	GS	IP	BB	SO	Avg	H	2B	3B	HR	RBI	OBP	SLG	CG	ShO	Sup	QS	#P/S	SB	CS	GB	FB	G/F
1992 Season	2.70	12	8	0	31	30	213.2	41	138	.260	210	37	3	14	63	.295	.365	5	3	4.93	21	101	17	9	254	287	0.89
Last Five Years	3.43	64	53	0	159	158	1092.2	215	751	.262	1100	187	27	96	409	.297	.389	32	9	4.31	95	99	61	52	1288	1367	0.94

1992 Season

	ERA	W	L	Sv	G	GS	IP	H	HR	BB	SO		Avg	AB	H	2B	3B	HR	RBI	BB	SO	OBP	SLG
Home	2.31	7	2	0	15	15	109.0	107	6	23	68	vs. Left	.242	165	40	9	1	2	11	9	29	.284	.345
Away	3.10	5	6	0	16	15	104.2	103	8	18	70	vs. Right	.264	643	170	28	2	12	52	32	109	.298	.370
Day	4.23	1	1	0	5	4	27.2	33	2	2	21	Inning 1-6	.250	651	163	31	2	11	54	34	111	.288	.355
Night	2.47	11	7	0	26	26	186.0	177	12	39	117	Inning 7+	.299	157	47	6	1	3	9	7	27	.325	.408
Grass	4.38	2	4	0	8	8	49.1	60	6	12	32	None on	.279	506	141	27	3	10	10	24	87	.314	.403
Turf	2.19	10	4	0	23	22	164.1	150	8	29	106	Runners on	.228	302	69	10	0	4	53	17	51	.264	.301
April	4.78	1	1	0	4	4	26.1	29	3	6	18	Scoring Posn	.266	154	41	5	0	2	47	12	27	.306	.338
May	1.77	3	1	0	6	6	45.2	41	3	8	31	Close & Late	.292	65	19	0	1	3	7	4	12	.329	.462
June	3.32	3	0	0	6	6	40.2	46	5	9	26	None on/out	.261	218	57	12	2	7	7	9	41	.297	.431
July	2.13	2	2	0	5	5	38.0	36	0	8	18	vs. 1st Batr (relief)	.000	1	0	0	0	0	0	0	0	.000	.000
August	1.66	3	2	0	5	5	38.0	35	2	5	26	First Inning Pitched	.219	114	25	4	1	3	9	8	18	.268	.351
September/October	3.60	0	2	0	5	4	25.0	23	1	5	19	First 75 Pitches	.245	571	140	26	2	8	43	31	100	.285	.340
Starter	2.71	12	8	0	30	30	212.2	210	14	41	136	Pitch 76-90	.308	117	36	6	0	5	12	4	19	.325	.487
Reliever	0.00	0	0	0	1	0	1.0	0	0	0	2	Pitch 91-105	.258	89	23	3	1	1	3	5	16	.280	.348
0-3 Days Rest	2.45	0	1	0	2	2	11.0	13	1	2	9	Pitch 106+	.355	31	11	2	0	0	5	3	3	.400	.419
4 Days Rest	3.18	6	4	0	16	16	113.1	116	10	23	72	First Pitch	.298	124	37	6	0	5	15	3	0	.313	.468
5+ Days Rest	2.14	6	3	0	12	12	88.1	81	3	16	55	Ahead on Count	.207	416	86	14	2	3	26	0	121	.208	.272
Pre-All Star	2.94	8	2	0	18	18	128.2	126	11	24	85	Behind on Count	.346	136	47	9	1	3	12	18	0	.419	.493
Post-All Star	2.33	4	6	0	13	12	85.0	84	3	17	53	Two Strikes	.182	379	69	11	1	4	25	20	138	.223	.248

Last Five Years

	ERA	W	L	Sv	G	GS	IP	H	HR	BB	SO		Avg	AB	H	2B	3B	HR	RBI	BB	SO	OBP	SLG
Home	3.10	36	24	0	82	82	583.0	556	44	111	391	vs. Left	.263	712	187	33	3	11	65	36	118	.298	.364
Away	3.80	28	29	0	77	76	509.2	544	52	104	360	vs. Right	.262	3480	913	154	24	85	344	179	633	.297	.394
Day	3.08	16	13	0	38	37	269.0	275	24	43	186	Inning 1-6	.258	3378	872	148	21	81	350	179	620	.295	.386
Night	3.54	48	40	0	121	121	823.2	825	72	172	565	Inning 7+	.280	814	228	39	6	15	59	36	131	.309	.398
Grass	3.48	49	39	0	119	119	816.1	823	74	158	575	None on	.255	2622	668	115	18	60	60	119	495	.289	.361
Turf	3.26	15	14	0	40	39	276.1	277	22	57	176	Runners on	.275	1570	432	72	9	36	349	96	256	.311	.401
April	3.27	10	6	0	23	23	159.2	153	11	32	113	Scoring Posn	.270	829	224	34	6	14	288	70	150	.316	.376
May	2.74	13	7	0	28	28	204.0	178	16	37	126	Close & Late	.270	411	111	19	2	8	32	24	70	.310	.384
June	3.89	10	8	0	29	29	199.0	232	26	42	136	None on/out	.259	1139	295	58	13	36	36	38	216	.287	.428
July	2.96	13	10	0	27	27	191.2	171	15	37	142	vs. 1st Batr (relief)	.000	1	0	0	0	0	0	0	0	.000	.000
August	3.58	11	12	0	24	24	163.1	181	9	33	115	First Inning Pitched	.253	601	152	25	5	17	73	37	116	.296	.396
September/October	4.22	7	10	0	28	27	175.0	185	19	34	119	First 75 Pitches	.251	2968	751	121	19	66	279	168	558	.291	.371
Starter	3.43	64	53	0	158	158	1091.2	1100	96	215	749	Pitch 76-90	.301	571	172	35	3	18	70	18	86	.320	.468
Reliever	0.00	0	0	0	1	0	1.0	0	0	0	2	Pitch 91-105	.260	400	104	12	2	7	27	20	70	.292	.353
0-3 Days Rest	2.45	0	1	0	2	2	11.0	13	1	2	9	Pitch 106+	.313	233	73	19	3	5	33	9	37	.336	.485
4 Days Rest	3.49	41	30	0	99	99	677.2	684	69	142	460	First Pitch	.321	707	227	37	6	20	92	7	0	.325	.475
5+ Days Rest	3.35	23	22	0	57	57	403.0	403	26	71	280	Ahead on Count	.209	2055	430	70	13	23	139	0	668	.210	.290
Pre-All Star	3.30	38	23	0	89	89	624.2	617	56	124	422	Behind on Count	.309	777	240	44	5	37	117	102	0	.387	.521
Post-All Star	3.60	26	30	0	70	69	468.0	483	40	91	329	Two Strikes	.188	1876	352	65	7	21	115	106	751	.232	.263

Pitcher vs. Batter (career)

Pitches Best Vs.	Avg	AB	H	2B	3B	HR	RBI	BB	SO	OBP	SLG	Pitches Worst Vs.	Avg	AB	H	2B	3B	HR	RBI	BB	SO	OBP	SLG
Gary Redus	.000	16	0	0	0	0	0	2	3	.111	.000	Edgar Martinez	.500	14	7	0	1	1	1	1	1	.533	.857
Lonnie Smith	.000	9	0	0	0	0	0	0	1	.182	.000	Frank Thomas	.500	10	5	1	0	1	4	1	2	.545	.900
Donnie Hill	.071	14	1	0	0	0	0	3	.071	.071	Carlton Fisk	.478	23	11	1	0	4	9	1	3	.500	1.043
B.J. Surhoff	.077	13	1	0	0	0	1	0	1	.077	.077	Jack Clark	.444	18	8	1	0	2	5	2	3	.500	.833
Joe Orsulak	.091	11	1	0	0	0	0	0	1	.091	.091	Hensley Meulens	.400	10	4	2	0	1	1	2	1	.455	.900

Pat Tabler — Blue Jays
Bats Right (groundball hitter)

	Avg	G	AB	R	H	2B	3B	HR	RBI	BB	SO	HBP	GDP	SB	CS	OBP	SLG	IBB	SH	SF	#Pit	#P/PA	GB	FB	G/F
1992 Season	.252	67	135	11	34	5	0	0	16	11	14	0	6	0	0	.306	.289	0	0	1	525	3.57	52	38	1.37
Last Five Years	.262	476	1392	138	365	58	6	7	174	146	174	8	40	3	5	.332	.328	8	5	16	5508	3.53	585	368	1.51

1992 Season

	Avg	AB	H	2B	3B	HR	RBI	BB	SO	OBP	SLG		Avg	AB	H	2B	3B	HR	RBI	BB	SO	OBP	SLG
vs. Left	.284	67	19	2	0	0	12	8	4	.355	.313	Scoring Posn	.297	37	11	1	0	0	16	6	3	.386	.324
vs. Right	.221	68	15	3	0	0	4	3	10	.254	.265	Close & Late	.231	13	3	0	0	0	1	2	1	.333	.231
Home	.196	51	10	2	0	0	4	7	6	.293	.235	None on/out	.231	26	6	1	0	0	0	0	1	.231	.269

1992 Season

	Avg	AB	H	2B	3B	HR	RBI	BB	SO	OBP	SLG		Avg	AB	H	2B	3B	HR	RBI	BB	SO	OBP	SLG
Away	.286	84	24	3	0	0	12	4	8	.315	.321	Batting #6	.222	81	18	2	0	0	9	7	4	.281	.247
First Pitch	.250	20	5	1	0	0	2	0	0	.250	.300	Batting #7	.263	19	5	1	0	0	1	3	4	.364	.316
Ahead on Count	.270	37	10	2	0	0	7	7	0	.378	.324	Other	.314	35	11	2	0	0	6	1	6	.333	.371
Behind on Count	.243	37	9	1	0	0	2	0	7	.243	.270	Pre-All Star	.224	67	15	1	0	0	8	7	7	.293	.239
Two Strikes	.196	56	11	1	0	0	5	4	14	.250	.214	Post-All Star	.279	68	19	4	0	0	8	4	7	.319	.338

Last Five Years

	Avg	AB	H	2B	3B	HR	RBI	BB	SO	OBP	SLG		Avg	AB	H	2B	3B	HR	RBI	BB	SO	OBP	SLG
vs. Left	.291	618	180	27	3	4	89	70	50	.360	.364	Scoring Posn	.281	417	117	17	3	6	165	60	55	.368	.379
vs. Right	.239	774	185	31	3	3	85	76	124	.310	.298	Close & Late	.240	225	54	8	0	2	34	26	34	.315	.302
Groundball	.227	365	83	6	2	2	47	48	41	.317	.271	None on/out	.223	310	69	16	1	0	0	32	38	.297	.281
Flyball	.231	342	79	19	1	0	33	27	43	.290	.292	Batting #5	.279	391	109	14	3	2	46	36	34	.337	.345
Home	.256	653	167	31	4	4	77	72	77	.329	.334	Batting #6	.258	264	68	14	2	0	36	29	26	.330	.326
Away	.268	739	198	27	2	3	97	74	97	.335	.322	Other	.255	737	188	30	1	5	92	81	114	.331	.319
Day	.267	382	102	13	1	1	58	43	49	.340	.314	April	.254	201	51	6	1	1	23	31	22	.353	.308
Night	.260	1010	263	45	5	6	116	103	125	.329	.333	May	.227	242	55	5	0	1	26	22	41	.294	.260
Grass	.276	641	177	19	2	4	88	71	84	.349	.331	June	.237	245	58	11	1	0	26	27	33	.310	.290
Turf	.250	751	188	39	4	3	86	75	90	.317	.325	July	.322	245	79	13	2	2	33	22	25	.379	.416
First Pitch	.340	212	72	3	1	0	30	5	0	.353	.363	August	.279	258	72	19	1	0	33	30	23	.350	.360
Ahead on Count	.303	356	108	18	1	4	63	90	0	.443	.393	September/October	.249	201	50	4	1	3	33	14	30	.303	.323
Behind on Count	.216	458	99	16	3	1	47	0	106	.213	.271	Pre-All Star	.251	766	192	24	4	2	82	89	108	.328	.300
Two Strikes	.189	541	102	23	1	2	39	51	174	.259	.246	Post-All Star	.276	626	173	34	2	5	92	57	66	.338	.361

Batter vs. Pitcher (since 1984)

Hits Best Against	Avg	AB	H	2B	3B	HR	RBI	BB	SO	OBP	SLG	Hits Worst Against	Avg	AB	H	2B	3B	HR	RBI	BB	SO	OBP	SLG
Greg Harris	.474	19	9	1	0	1	6	1	3	.500	.684	Jim Abbott	.000	13	0	0	0	0	2	2	3	.133	.000
Dennis Rasmussen	.444	9	4	2	0	0	1	2	0	.545	.667	Dennis Eckersley	.077	13	1	0	0	0	0	1	4	.143	.077
Chuck Finley	.429	28	12	0	0	1	8	8	4	.541	.536	Tom Candiotti	.077	13	1	0	0	0	0	0	0	.077	.077
Jimmy Key	.385	39	15	5	0	3	10	1	1	.400	.744	Randy Johnson	.100	20	2	0	0	0	3	3	1	.208	.100
Kenny Rogers	.375	8	3	0	0	1	3	3	0	.545	.750	Danny Darwin	.167	12	2	0	0	0	0	0	4	.167	.167

Jeff Tackett — Orioles   Bats Right

	Avg	G	AB	R	H	2B	3B	HR	RBI	BB	SO	HBP	GDP	SB	CS	OBP	SLG	IBB	SH	SF	#Pit	#P/PA	GB	FB	G/F
1992 Season	.240	65	179	21	43	8	1	5	24	17	28	2	11	0	0	.307	.380	1	6	4	788	3.90	77	52	1.48
Career (1991-1992)	.235	71	187	22	44	8	1	5	24	19	30	2	11	0	0	.307	.369	1	7	4	833	3.93	81	54	1.50

1992 Season

	Avg	AB	H	2B	3B	HR	RBI	BB	SO	OBP	SLG		Avg	AB	H	2B	3B	HR	RBI	BB	SO	OBP	SLG
vs. Left	.288	52	15	1	0	4	7	6	5	.373	.538	Scoring Posn	.220	50	11	2	0	1	19	5	10	.271	.320
vs. Right	.220	127	28	7	1	1	17	11	23	.280	.315	Close & Late	.238	21	5	0	0	1	5	4	1	.346	.381
Home	.253	87	22	5	1	4	16	4	11	.284	.471	None on/out	.277	47	13	3	0	2	2	5	7	.358	.468
Away	.228	92	21	3	0	1	8	13	17	.327	.293	Batting #8	.000	2	0	0	0	0	2	2	0	.400	.000
First Pitch	.240	25	6	1	0	0	2	0	0	.259	.280	Batting #9	.244	168	41	8	1	5	21	15	27	.309	.393
Ahead on Count	.238	42	10	1	0	0	5	11	0	.389	.262	Other	.222	9	2	0	0	0	1	0	1	.222	.222
Behind on Count	.140	57	8	2	1	1	7	0	16	.153	.263	Pre-All Star	.259	85	22	4	1	5	15	9	9	.330	.506
Two Strikes	.202	84	17	3	1	5	12	6	28	.261	.440	Post-All Star	.223	94	21	4	0	9	8	19	.286	.266

Frank Tanana — Tigers   Pitches Left

	ERA	W	L	Sv	G	GS	IP	BB	SO	Avg	H	2B	3B	HR	RBI	OBP	SLG	CG	ShO	Sup	QS	#F/S	SB	CS	GB	FB	G/F
1992 Season	4.39	13	11	0	32	31	186.2	90	91	.267	188	34	2	22	88	.351	.415	3	0	4.29	18	100	21	11	246	232	1.06
Last Five Years	4.20	59	56	1	164	158	1007.0	372	586	.268	1035	174	14	119	463	.334	.413	15	3	4.54	87	102	78	57	1284	1190	1.08

1992 Season

	ERA	W	L	Sv	G	GS	IP	H	HR	BB	SO		Avg	AB	H	2B	3B	HR	RBI	BB	SO	OBP	SLG
Home	4.98	7	5	0	14	14	77.2	84	12	37	41	vs. Left	.225	102	23	5	0	2	10	8	15	.282	.333
Away	3.96	6	6	0	18	17	109.0	104	10	53	50	vs. Right	.274	602	165	29	2	20	78	82	76	.362	.429
Day	4.28	4	4	0	11	11	69.1	65	6	38	30	Inning 1-6	.262	611	160	29	0	16	75	72	86	.341	.388
Night	4.45	9	7	0	21	20	117.1	123	16	52	61	Inning 7+	.301	93	28	5	2	6	13	18	5	.414	.591
Grass	4.55	12	11	0	30	29	172.0	176	20	84	85	None on	.269	401	108	19	0	15	15	51	43	.359	.429
Turf	2.45	1	0	0	2	2	14.2	12	2	6	6	Runners on	.264	303	80	15	2	7	73	39	48	.342	.396
April	9.20	0	2	0	4	4	14.2	22	2	13	8	Scoring Posn	.224	156	35	5	0	3	60	27	29	.325	.314
May	4.18	3	2	0	6	5	32.1	32	4	17	15	Close & Late	.217	46	10	3	1	2	4	11	3	.368	.457
June	3.96	4	1	0	6	6	36.1	35	5	17	20	None on/out	.244	180	44	8	0	8	8	22	18	.333	.422
July	2.65	2	1	0	5	5	34.0	26	3	17	14	vs. 1st Batr (relief)	.000	1	0	0	0	0	0	0	0	.000	.000
August	4.00	2	2	0	6	6	36.0	39	4	13	17	First Inning Pitched	.296	125	37	7	0	2	21	17	25	.378	.400
September/October	5.13	2	3	0	5	5	33.1	34	4	13	17	First 75 Pitches	.267	501	134	24	0	13	60	60	75	.347	.393
Starter	4.44	12	11	0	31	31	184.2	186	22	88	90	Pitch 76-90	.319	91	29	7	0	1	12	12	7	.400	.429
Reliever	0.00	1	0	0	1	0	2.0	2	0	2	1	Pitch 91-105	.250	72	18	2	1	5	12	8	6	.325	.514
0-3 Days Rest	0.00	0	0	0	0	0	0.0	0	0	0	0	Pitch 106+	.175	40	7	1	1	3	4	10	3	.340	.475
4 Days Rest	4.75	9	7	0	21	21	119.1	126	16	57	65	First Pitch	.329	79	26	5	0	2	6	4	0	.360	.468
5+ Days Rest	3.86	3	4	0	10	10	65.1	60	6	31	25	Ahead on Count	.199	287	57	10	1	5	28	0	73	.207	.293

429

1992 Season

	ERA	W	L	Sv	G	GS	IP	H	HR	BB	SO		Avg	AB	H	2B	3B	HR	RBI	BB	SO	OBP	SLG
Pre-All Star	4.70	8	5	0	18	17	95.2	100	12	52	50	Behind on Count	.349	175	61	8	0	11	33	46	0	.480	.583
Post-All Star	4.05	5	6	0	14	14	91.0	88	10	38	41	Two Strikes	.201	313	63	11	1	5	29	40	91	.296	.291

Last Five Years

	ERA	W	L	Sv	G	GS	IP	H	HR	BB	SO		Avg	AB	H	2B	3B	HR	RBI	BB	SO	OBP	SLG
Home	4.45	29	27	0	85	84	524.1	533	63	201	329	vs. Left	.241	611	147	23	1	12	64	45	94	.295	.340
Away	3.93	30	29	1	79	74	482.2	502	56	171	257	vs. Right	.274	3244	888	151	13	107	399	327	492	.342	.427
Day	4.02	21	24	1	57	56	367.0	374	41	133	198	Inning 1-6	.267	3273	875	142	11	97	394	299	509	.330	.406
Night	4.30	38	32	0	107	102	640.0	661	78	239	388	Inning 7+	.275	582	160	32	3	22	69	73	77	.359	.454
Grass	4.29	55	50	1	148	143	900.0	931	111	331	537	None on	.269	2295	617	108	7	73	73	179	334	.328	.417
Turf	3.45	4	6	0	16	15	107.0	104	8	41	49	Runners on	.268	1560	418	66	7	46	390	193	252	.344	.408
April	4.70	10	8	0	23	23	145.2	167	16	49	75	Scoring Posn	.263	815	214	32	4	22	327	139	142	.359	.393
May	5.08	11	10	0	29	28	170.0	180	27	71	88	Close & Late	.245	265	65	14	2	8	27	44	32	.356	.404
June	3.53	13	9	0	28	28	186.1	183	23	68	131	None on/out	.268	1022	274	49	4	35	35	68	152	.316	.427
July	3.95	6	8	0	25	24	145.2	146	8	57	79	vs. 1st Batr (relief)	.500	4	2	1	0	0	4	1	0	.667	.750
August	4.38	11	8	1	28	24	156.0	168	22	58	81	First Inning Pitched	.302	633	191	28	4	21	109	73	113	.372	.458
September/October	3.76	8	13	0	31	31	203.1	191	23	69	132	First 75 Pitches	.274	2707	742	120	10	83	327	250	420	.337	.418
Starter	4.18	58	56	0	158	158	994.1	1018	118	361	577	Pitch 76-90	.257	475	122	22	0	13	59	50	66	.330	.385
Reliever	5.68	1	0	1	6	0	12.2	17	1	11	9	Pitch 91-105	.263	388	102	14	3	11	42	31	56	.318	.399
0-3 Days Rest	11.57	0	0	0	1	1	2.1	7	2	0	2	Pitch 106+	.242	285	69	18	1	12	35	41	44	.344	.439
4 Days Rest	4.32	40	39	0	106	106	656.1	681	82	239	399	First Pitch	.314	477	150	23	1	14	57	16	0	.339	.455
5+ Days Rest	3.86	18	17	0	51	51	335.2	330	34	122	176	Ahead on Count	.198	1668	331	50	4	32	127	0	477	.203	.291
Pre-All Star	4.29	37	30	0	89	88	556.0	584	69	209	323	Behind on Count	.351	931	327	53	6	48	168	196	0	.462	.576
Post-All Star	4.09	22	26	1	75	70	451.0	451	50	163	263	Two Strikes	.193	1725	333	51	6	33	138	158	586	.263	.287

Pitcher vs. Batter (since 1984)

Pitches Best Vs.	Avg	AB	H	2B	3B	HR	RBI	BB	SO	OBP	SLG	Pitches Worst Vs.	Avg	AB	H	2B	3B	HR	RBI	BB	SO	OBP	SLG
Rene Gonzales	.063	16	1	0	0	0	0	2	4	.167	.063	George Brett	.410	39	16	5	0	4	9	3	5	.452	.846
Mike Huff	.077	13	1	0	0	0	0	1	2	.143	.077	Junior Felix	.400	15	6	3	0	1	3	2		.500	.800
Jim Leyritz	.077	13	1	0	0	0	0	0	1	.077	.077	Mike Blowers	.385	13	5	0	0	2	2	1	3	.429	.846
Cory Snyder	.086	35	3	1	0	0	1	3	11	.158	.114	Mickey Tettleton	.375	24	9	2	0	3	5	5	7	.467	.833
Stan Javier	.095	21	2	1	0	0	4	0	4	.095	.143	Rickey Henderson	.352	71	25	5	0	10	15	11	5	.439	.845

Kevin Tapani — Twins

Pitches Right

	ERA	W	L	Sv	G	GS	IP	BB	SO	Avg	H	2B	3B	HR	RBI	OBP	SLG	CG	ShO	Sup	QS	#P/S	SB	CS	GB	FB	G/F
1992 Season	3.97	16	11	0	34	34	220.0	48	138	.269	226	53	5	17	94	.309	.405	4	1	6.05	19	99	26	11	309	239	1.29
Career (1989-1992)	3.62	46	30	0	104	101	663.1	129	397	.258	654	136	18	55	248	.294	.392	9	3	5.44	59	94	58	23	936	733	1.28

1992 Season

	ERA	W	L	Sv	G	GS	IP	H	HR	BB	SO		Avg	AB	H	2B	3B	HR	RBI	BB	SO	OBP	SLG
Home	3.48	11	4	0	19	19	126.2	135	6	24	83	vs. Left	.279	434	121	31	4	12	56	24	78	.313	.452
Away	4.63	5	7	0	15	15	93.1	91	11	24	55	vs. Right	.259	405	105	22	1	5	38	24	60	.304	.356
Day	3.99	6	1	0	9	9	58.2	64	4	8	43	Inning 1-6	.279	728	203	49	4	15	87	37	122	.313	.419
Night	3.96	10	10	0	25	25	161.1	162	13	40	95	Inning 7+	.207	111	23	4	1	2	7	11	16	.285	.315
Grass	4.25	5	5	0	11	11	72.0	68	9	17	41	None on	.265	514	136	30	2	13	13	32	89	.311	.407
Turf	3.83	11	6	0	23	23	148.0	158	8	31	97	Runners on	.277	325	90	23	3	4	81	16	49	.305	.403
April	4.81	1	2	0	4	4	24.1	28	1	7	14	Scoring Posn	.283	191	54	12	3	2	71	12	34	.315	.408
May	5.35	4	2	0	6	6	35.1	43	6	7	28	Close & Late	.200	65	13	3	1	2	6	8	8	.288	.369
June	3.02	3	1	0	6	6	41.2	39	2	5	26	None on/out	.239	222	53	12	1	6	6	11	33	.278	.383
July	2.95	4	1	0	6	6	39.2	37	3	9	21	vs. 1st Batr (relief)	.000	0	0	0	0	0	0	0	0	.000	.000
August	4.15	2	3	0	6	6	43.1	42	5	11	28	First Inning Pitched	.210	119	25	4	0	3	9	5	27	.244	.319
September/October	4.04	2	2	0	6	6	35.2	37	0	9	21	First 75 Pitches	.266	617	164	44	2	11	64	34	108	.304	.397
Starter	3.97	16	11	0	34	34	220.0	226	17	48	138	Pitch 76-90	.346	107	37	6	3	5	20	4	13	.374	.598
Reliever	0.00	0	0	0	0	0	0.0	0	0	0	0	Pitch 91-105	.239	71	17	2	0	1	8	6	13	.291	.310
0-3 Days Rest	0.00	0	0	0	0	0	0.0	0	0	0	0	Pitch 106+	.182	44	8	1	0	0	2	4	4	.250	.205
4 Days Rest	4.09	10	10	0	25	25	162.2	163	13	39	95	First Pitch	.326	129	42	15	2	3	16	1	0	.326	.543
5+ Days Rest	3.61	6	1	0	9	9	57.1	63	4	9	43	Ahead on Count	.230	392	90	18	1	5	44	0	116	.234	.319
Pre-All Star	3.84	10	5	0	18	18	117.1	120	9	23	73	Behind on Count	.296	152	45	8	0	5	16	23	0	.385	.447
Post-All Star	4.12	6	6	0	16	16	102.2	106	8	25	65	Two Strikes	.238	399	95	17	2	7	43	24	138	.285	.343

Career (1989-1992)

	ERA	W	L	Sv	G	GS	IP	H	HR	BB	SO		Avg	AB	H	2B	3B	HR	RBI	BB	SO	OBP	SLG
Home	3.32	30	13	0	53	52	352.0	356	20	72	220	vs. Left	.264	1361	359	79	15	28	138	69	211	.298	.406
Away	3.96	16	17	0	51	49	311.1	298	35	57	177	vs. Right	.252	1170	295	57	3	27	110	60	186	.290	.375
Day	3.24	13	5	0	27	25	169.1	159	16	31	109	Inning 1-6	.260	2146	558	122	15	47	221	108	337	.295	.397
Night	3.75	33	25	0	77	76	494.0	495	39	98	288	Inning 7+	.249	385	96	14	3	8	27	21	60	.292	.364
Grass	3.89	14	11	0	37	35	220.0	212	25	39	125	None on	.252	1599	403	86	11	40	40	79	268	.289	.395
Turf	3.49	32	19	0	67	66	443.1	442	30	90	272	Runners on	.269	932	251	50	7	15	208	50	129	.302	.386
April	3.18	5	4	0	12	12	76.1	74	3	16	52	Scoring Posn	.265	533	141	25	5	7	179	34	82	.299	.370
May	4.90	8	9	0	18	18	112.0	131	16	24	81	Close & Late	.253	190	48	8	2	4	19	15	30	.306	.379
June	3.09	8	4	0	17	17	119.1	108	8	12	69	None on/out	.246	682	168	40	9	20	20	26	108	.276	.419
July	2.96	10	1	0	21	18	121.2	117	7	22	57	vs. 1st Batr (relief)	.000	2	0	0	0	0	0	1	1	.333	.000
August	3.53	7	4	0	14	14	99.1	84	11	25	51	First Inning Pitched	.229	362	83	13	4	6	31	20	69	.267	.337

Career (1989-1992)

	ERA	W	L	Sv	G	GS	IP	H	HR	BB	SO		Avg	AB	H	2B	3B	HR	RBI	BB	SO	OBP	SLG
September/October	3.94	8	8	0	22	22	134.2	140	10	30	87	First 75 Pitches	.257	1936	497	112	12	42	187	96	299	.291	.392
Starter	3.62	46	30	0	101	101	656.0	649	54	125	395	Pitch 76-90	.275	306	84	11	5	10	35	13	44	.310	.441
Reliever	3.68	0	0	0	3	0	7.1	5	1	4	2	Pitch 91-105	.263	213	56	8	1	3	20	13	42	.303	.352
0-3 Days Rest	4.58	0	1	0	3	3	17.2	21	1	3	14	Pitch 106+	.224	76	17	5	0	0	6	7	12	.286	.289
4 Days Rest	3.55	29	20	0	66	66	438.1	416	33	87	255	First Pitch	.312	436	136	38	5	13	54	2	0	.314	.511
5+ Days Rest	3.69	17	9	0	32	32	200.0	212	20	35	126	Ahead on Count	.210	1176	247	46	6	16	100	0	342	.213	.300
Pre-All Star	3.63	24	17	0	55	53	355.0	357	30	65	219	Behind on Count	.329	490	161	34	1	17	55	71	0	.412	.506
Post-All Star	3.62	22	13	0	49	48	308.1	297	25	64	178	Two Strikes	.206	1119	230	40	8	16	89	56	397	.245	.298

Pitcher vs. Batter (career)

Pitches Best Vs.	Avg	AB	H	2B	3B	HR	RBI	BB	SO	OBP	SLG	Pitches Worst Vs.	Avg	AB	H	2B	3B	HR	RBI	BB	SO	OBP	SLG
Candy Maldonado	.000	11	0	0	0	0	0	1	5	.083	.000	Brian McRae	.563	16	9	1	0	1	4	0	4	.611	.813
Luis Rivera	.000	11	0	0	0	0	0	0	3	.000	.000	Brady Anderson	.545	11	6	0	0	1	4	1	2	.583	.818
Jeff Huson	.056	18	1	1	0	0	1	0	2	.056	.111	George Bell	.500	18	9	3	0	1	6	0	1	.474	.833
Scott Bradley	.059	17	1	0	0	0	0	0	0	.059	.059	Terry Steinbach	.429	14	6	3	0	1	3	1	2	.467	.857
Jesse Barfield	.083	12	1	0	0	0	0	0	0	.083	.083	Mickey Tettleton	.385	13	5	2	0	2	5	1	2	.429	1.000

Danny Tartabull — Yankees   Bats Right

	Avg	G	AB	R	H	2B	3B	HR	RBI	BB	SO	HBP	GDP	SB	CS	OBP	SLG	IBB	SH	SF	#Pit	#P/PA	GB	FB	G/F
1992 Season	.266	123	421	72	112	19	0	25	85	103	115	0	7	2	2	.409	.489	14	0	2	2178	4.14	150	97	1.55
Last Five Years	.280	622	2166	325	606	133	6	115	409	349	571	10	47	21	13	.379	.506	26	0	18	10152	3.99	684	589	1.16

1992 Season

	Avg	AB	H	2B	3B	HR	RBI	BB	SO	OBP	SLG		Avg	AB	H	2B	3B	HR	RBI	BB	SO	OBP	SLG
vs. Left	.286	119	34	6	0	11	35	50	29	.494	.613	Scoring Posn	.297	118	35	7	0	12	67	42	30	.475	.661
vs. Right	.258	302	78	13	0	14	50	53	86	.368	.440	Close & Late	.262	84	22	5	0	4	15	18	18	.392	.464
Groundball	.230	113	26	3	0	3	12	21	31	.351	.336	None on/out	.202	114	23	5	0	3	3	20	34	.321	.325
Flyball	.230	122	28	4	0	11	24	35	36	.401	.533	Batting #4	.272	224	61	10	0	13	44	53	50	.412	.491
Home	.289	204	59	10	0	11	48	51	55	.428	.500	Batting #5	.251	171	43	6	0	11	35	42	61	.395	.480
Away	.244	217	53	9	0	14	37	52	60	.390	.479	Other	.308	26	8	3	0	1	6	8	4	.471	.538
Day	.203	133	27	3	0	4	18	26	42	.329	.316	April	.308	39	12	3	0	1	10	9	14	.438	.462
Night	.295	288	85	16	0	21	67	77	73	.444	.569	May	.260	73	19	2	0	3	11	17	23	.396	.411
Grass	.279	369	103	18	0	22	76	94	103	.424	.507	June	.216	74	16	3	0	2	10	25	22	.414	.338
Turf	.173	52	9	1	0	3	9	9	12	.295	.365	July	.217	69	15	3	0	8	16	18	20	.375	.609
First Pitch	.348	46	16	4	0	3	10	13	0	.492	.630	August	.290	62	18	2	0	5	16	16	15	.436	.565
Ahead on Count	.363	102	37	5	0	11	32	42	0	.549	.735	September/October	.308	104	32	6	0	6	22	18	21	.410	.538
Behind on Count	.218	124	27	5	0	3	20	0	52	.214	.331	Pre-All Star	.251	223	56	10	0	12	43	60	71	.407	.457
Two Strikes	.177	226	40	6	0	10	39	48	115	.319	.336	Post-All Star	.283	198	56	9	0	13	42	43	44	.411	.525

1992 By Position

Position	Avg	AB	H	2B	3B	HR	RBI	BB	SO	OBP	SLG	G	GS	Innings	PO	A	E	DP	Fld Pct	Rng Fctr	In Zone	Outs	Zone Rtg	MLB Zone
As Designated Hitter	.270	185	50	9	0	7	33	38	51	.395	.432	53	51	---	---	---	---	---	---	---	---	---	---	---
As rf	.263	232	61	10	0	18	52	63	64	.418	.539	68	67	599.1	135	3	3	1	.979	2.07	158	133	.842	.814

Last Five Years

	Avg	AB	H	2B	3B	HR	RBI	BB	SO	OBP	SLG		Avg	AB	H	2B	3B	HR	RBI	BB	SO	OBP	SLG
vs. Left	.300	640	192	41	1	40	123	150	148	.431	.555	Scoring Posn	.287	624	179	46	3	32	292	143	171	.415	.524
vs. Right	.271	1526	414	92	5	75	286	199	423	.356	.486	Close & Late	.288	365	105	26	2	18	69	55	90	.381	.518
Groundball	.267	547	146	33	0	17	83	77	131	.357	.420	None on/out	.264	557	147	37	2	25	25	71	153	.348	.472
Flyball	.284	566	161	37	2	37	111	97	162	.390	.553	Batting #4	.294	1405	413	93	4	77	273	222	344	.390	.530
Home	.285	1035	295	58	5	53	187	177	258	.388	.504	Batting #5	.227	374	85	18	2	17	70	66	115	.341	.422
Away	.275	1131	311	75	1	62	222	172	313	.372	.508	Other	.279	387	108	22	0	21	66	61	112	.378	.499
Day	.272	574	156	35	1	26	105	89	157	.370	.472	April	.307	274	84	23	1	8	50	39	69	.391	.485
Night	.283	1592	450	98	5	89	304	260	414	.383	.518	May	.245	380	93	16	1	19	58	56	103	.345	.442
Grass	.280	1052	295	68	5	59	216	182	292	.386	.515	June	.290	369	107	19	0	23	69	59	94	.386	.528
Turf	.279	1114	311	65	5	56	193	167	279	.373	.497	July	.269	323	87	22	1	22	69	49	95	.367	.548
First Pitch	.393	272	107	23	3	23	65	18	0	.437	.754	August	.291	419	122	27	2	21	80	76	110	.397	.516
Ahead on Count	.368	476	175	42	1	35	118	157	0	.519	.681	September/October	.282	401	113	26	1	22	83	70	100	.389	.516
Behind on Count	.217	667	145	23	1	22	92	0	257	.217	.354	Pre-All Star	.272	1156	314	66	2	63	207	171	313	.366	.496
Two Strikes	.187	1106	207	36	2	43	156	171	570	.296	.340	Post-All Star	.289	1010	292	67	4	52	202	178	258	.395	.518

Batter vs. Pitcher (career)

Hits Best Against	Avg	AB	H	2B	3B	HR	RBI	BB	SO	OBP	SLG	Hits Worst Against	Avg	AB	H	2B	3B	HR	RBI	BB	SO	OBP	SLG
Mike Morgan	.727	11	8	0	0	1	4	1	0	.750	1.000	Juan Berenguer	.000	12	0	0	0	0	0	4	8	.250	.000
Jaime Navarro	.643	14	9	1	0	3	6	2	3	.688	1.357	Eric Plunk	.053	19	1	1	0	0	2	3	4	.182	.105
Mark Guthrie	.545	11	6	0	0	2	5	6	2	.706	1.091	Tom Henke	.071	14	1	1	0	0	0	2	6	.188	.143
Scott Bailes	.500	18	9	1	0	3	7	2	0	.550	1.056	Mike Henneman	.077	13	1	0	0	0	0	3	4	.250	.077
Bill Krueger	.455	11	5	0	0	3	9	2	2	.538	1.273	Kevin Tapani	.091	11	1	0	0	0	1	1	4	.167	.091

Jimmy Tatum — Brewers
Bats Right

	Avg	G	AB	R	H	2B	3B	HR	RBI	BB	SO	HBP	GDP	SB	CS	OBP	SLG	IBB	SH	SF	#Pit	#P/PA	GB	FB	G/F
1992 Season	.125	5	8	0	1	0	0	0	0	1	2	0	0	0	0	.222	.125	0	0	0	32	3.56	3	2	1.50

1992 Season

	Avg	AB	H	2B	3B	HR	RBI	BB	SO	OBP	SLG		Avg	AB	H	2B	3B	HR	RBI	BB	SO	OBP	SLG
vs. Left	.250	4	1	0	0	0	0	0	1	.250	.250	Scoring Posn	.000	3	0	0	0	0	0	0	1	2	.250	.000
vs. Right	.000	4	0	0	0	0	0	1	1	.200	.000	Close & Late	.000	0	0	0	0	0	0	0	0	.000	.000

Eddie Taubensee — Astros
Bats Left

	Avg	G	AB	R	H	2B	3B	HR	RBI	BB	SO	HBP	GDP	SB	CS	OBP	SLG	IBB	SH	SF	#Pit	#P/PA	GB	FB	G/F
1992 Season	.222	104	297	23	66	15	0	5	28	31	78	2	4	2	1	.299	.323	3	0	1	1184	3.58	85	77	1.10
Career (1991-1992)	.226	130	363	28	82	17	1	5	36	36	94	2	5	2	1	.297	.320	4	0	1	1447	3.58	105	98	1.07

1992 Season

	Avg	AB	H	2B	3B	HR	RBI	BB	SO	OBP	SLG		Avg	AB	H	2B	3B	HR	RBI	BB	SO	OBP	SLG
vs. Left	.234	47	11	3	0	2	5	6	12	.291	.426	Scoring Posn	.192	73	14	2	0	0	18	14	22	.326	.219
vs. Right	.220	250	55	12	0	3	23	25	66	.292	.304	Close & Late	.170	53	9	1	0	1	7	4	14	.228	.245
Groundball	.218	133	29	6	0	2	13	13	40	.286	.308	None on/out	.258	62	16	4	0	1	1	7	17	.333	.371
Flyball	.211	71	15	4	0	3	8	8	16	.291	.394	Batting #7	.210	167	35	7	0	1	11	12	43	.267	.269
Home	.242	157	38	10	0	2	12	18	39	.324	.344	Batting #8	.232	125	29	8	0	4	16	18	33	.331	.392
Away	.200	140	28	5	0	3	16	13	39	.271	.300	Other	.400	5	2	0	0	0	1	1	2	.500	.400
Day	.217	69	15	4	0	2	9	8	20	.295	.362	April	.213	47	10	2	0	0	2	6	17	.302	.255
Night	.224	228	51	11	0	3	19	23	58	.300	.311	May	.150	60	9	3	0	0	4	6	10	.224	.200
Grass	.191	89	17	2	0	2	10	8	27	.265	.281	June	.087	23	2	1	0	0	4	3	9	.192	.130
Turf	.236	208	49	13	0	3	18	23	51	.313	.341	July	.412	34	14	3	0	1	4	1	5	.429	.588
First Pitch	.354	48	17	4	0	1	9	3	0	.392	.500	August	.205	73	15	4	0	4	10	5	22	.275	.425
Ahead on Count	.302	63	19	7	0	2	9	10	0	.400	.508	September/October	.267	60	16	2	0	0	4	10	15	.371	.300
Behind on Count	.149	114	17	3	0	1	3	0	39	.155	.202	Pre-All Star	.173	133	23	6	0	0	11	16	36	.260	.218
Two Strikes	.141	135	19	2	0	1	5	18	78	.247	.178	Post-All Star	.262	164	43	9	0	5	17	15	42	.331	.409

1992 By Position

Position	Avg	AB	H	2B	3B	HR	RBI	BB	SO	OBP	SLG	G	GS	Innings	PO	A	E	DP	Fld Pct	Rng Fctr	In Zone	Zone Outs	Zone Rtg	MLB Zone
As c	.225	293	66	15	0	5	28	30	75	.301	.328	103	88	804.1	557	66	5	6	.992	---	---	---	---	---

Scott Taylor — Red Sox
Pitches Left (flyball pitcher)

	ERA	W	L	Sv	G	GS	IP	BB	SO	Avg	H	2B	3B	HR	RBI	OBP	SLG	GF	IR	IRS	Hld	SvOp	SB	CS	GB	FB	G/F
1992 Season	4.91	1	1	0	4	1	14.2	4	7	.245	13	2	2	4	12	.298	.585	1	7	4	0	0	0	1	19	23	0.83

1992 Season

	ERA	W	L	Sv	G	GS	IP	H	HR	BB	SO		Avg	AB	H	2B	3B	HR	RBI	BB	SO	OBP	SLG
Home	4.61	1	1	0	3	1	13.2	11	3	4	6	vs. Left	.286	14	4	0	1	1	3	1	2	.333	.643
Away	9.00	0	0	0	1	0	1.0	2	1	0	1	vs. Right	.231	39	9	2	1	3	9	3	5	.286	.564

Walt Terrell — Tigers
Pitches Right (groundball pitcher)

	ERA	W	L	Sv	G	GS	IP	BB	SO	Avg	H	2B	3B	HR	RBI	OBP	SLG	GF	IR	IRS	Hld	SvOp	SB	CS	GB	FB	G/F
1992 Season	5.20	7	10	0	36	14	136.2	48	61	.298	163	27	2	14	84	.354	.431	7	16	6	2	1	7	3	230	133	1.73
Last Five Years	4.55	45	69	0	161	136	926.0	312	382	.287	1039	178	28	93	448	.345	.429	8	18	8	3	1	39	26	1555	914	1.70

1992 Season

	ERA	W	L	Sv	G	GS	IP	H	HR	BB	SO		Avg	AB	H	2B	3B	HR	RBI	BB	SO	OBP	SLG
Home	4.76	4	3	0	17	6	62.1	68	9	22	32	vs. Left	.285	235	67	15	0	3	29	20	20	.342	.387
Away	5.57	3	7	0	19	8	74.1	95	5	26	29	vs. Right	.308	312	96	12	2	11	55	28	41	.362	.465
Starter	6.63	3	6	0	14	14	77.1	103	8	31	37	Scoring Posn	.344	131	45	6	0	2	64	24	16	.429	.435
Reliever	3.34	4	4	0	22	0	59.1	60	6	17	24	Close & Late	.282	71	20	3	0	3	6	4	10	.338	.451
0 Days rest	0.00	0	0	0	1	0	1.0	1	0	0	1	None on/out	.214	131	28	6	1	2	2	12	15	.285	.321
1 or 2 Days rest	0.96	2	1	0	7	0	18.2	16	2	5	11	First Pitch	.277	83	23	3	0	3	11	8	0	.337	.422
3+ Days rest	4.54	2	3	0	14	0	39.2	43	4	12	12	Behind on Count	.365	156	57	12	1	4	31	26	0	.454	.532
Pre-All Star	4.54	3	8	0	23	6	79.1	82	9	31	34	Ahead on Count	.252	202	51	7	0	3	25	0	47	.256	.332
Post-All Star	6.12	4	2	0	13	8	57.1	81	5	17	27	Two Strikes	.243	210	51	8	0	6	30	14	61	.293	.367

Last Five Years

	ERA	W	L	Sv	G	GS	IP	H	HR	BB	SO		Avg	AB	H	2B	3B	HR	RBI	BB	SO	OBP	SLG
Home	4.54	26	28	0	75	61	420.0	468	56	128	169	vs. Left	.296	1866	552	98	11	49	239	178	158	.356	.439
Away	4.55	19	41	0	86	75	506.0	571	37	184	213	vs. Right	.278	1750	487	80	17	44	209	134	224	.333	.419
Day	4.36	12	26	0	49	39	276.2	303	30	85	124	Inning 1-6	.290	2966	859	147	26	67	384	268	306	.349	.424
Night	4.63	33	43	0	112	97	649.1	736	63	227	258	Inning 7+	.277	650	180	31	2	26	64	44	76	.326	.451
Grass	4.32	38	52	0	126	106	735.1	813	74	242	307	None on	.275	2082	573	104	21	56	56	162	237	.331	.426
Turf	5.43	7	17	0	35	30	190.2	226	19	70	75	Runners on	.304	1534	466	74	7	37	392	150	145	.363	.434
April	3.86	3	8	0	18	18	114.1	120	11	30	55	Scoring Posn	.308	832	256	41	4	23	346	114	93	.385	.450
May	4.82	7	14	0	30	24	155.0	178	10	60	64	Close & Late	.289	332	96	19	0	15	42	23	43	.340	.482
June	4.94	4	16	0	31	23	165.2	185	25	54	67	None on/out	.268	920	247	52	7	18	18	71	93	.325	.399

Last Five Years

	ERA	W	L	Sv	G	GS	IP	H	HR	BB	SO		Avg	AB	H	2B	3B	HR	RBI	BB	SO	OBP	SLG
July	4.88	9	8	0	24	18	118.0	142	10	43	51	vs. 1st Batr (relief)	.333	21	7	1	1	0	3	3	0	.440	.476
August	4.88	11	10	0	29	25	180.2	212	22	67	74	First Inning Pitched	.273	520	142	24	4	13	66	49	59	.336	.410
September/October	3.88	11	13	0	29	28	192.1	202	15	58	71	First 15 Pitches	.268	579	155	24	5	15	54	50	62	.327	.404
Starter	4.62	40	65	0	136	136	861.0	972	87	292	358	Pitch 16-30	.287	575	165	28	5	11	55	49	68	.342	.410
Reliever	3.60	5	4	0	25	0	65.0	67	6	20	24	Pitch 31-45	.301	572	172	31	7	11	82	40	52	.345	.437
0 Days rest	0.00	1	0	0	2	0	4.0	3	0	2	1	Pitch 46+	.289	1890	547	95	11	56	257	173	200	.351	.440
1 or 2 Days rest	1.86	2	1	0	8	0	19.1	17	2	6	11	First Pitch	.306	595	182	24	5	15	75	25	0	.334	.439
3+ Days rest	4.75	2	3	0	15	0	41.2	47	4	12	12	Ahead on Count	.230	1355	312	56	11	21	123	0	310	.235	.334
Pre-All Star	4.72	16	43	0	88	71	472.2	530	50	163	205	Behind on Count	.338	996	337	59	8	42	168	153	0	.426	.540
Post-All Star	4.37	29	26	0	73	65	453.1	509	43	149	177	Two Strikes	.204	1282	261	49	7	20	125	134	382	.282	.300

Pitcher vs. Batter (since 1984)

Pitches Best Vs.	Avg	AB	H	2B	3B	HR	RBI	BB	SO	OBP	SLG	Pitches Worst Vs.	Avg	AB	H	2B	3B	HR	RBI	BB	SO	OBP	SLG
Billy Ripken	.000	19	0	0	0	0	0	2	4	.095	.000	Dwight Smith	.579	19	11	2	0	1	2	1	1	.600	.842
Ozzie Smith	.000	13	0	0	0	0	0	0	0	.000	.000	Carlos Baerga	.526	19	10	2	0	1	6	3	0	.591	.789
Don Slaught	.000	11	0	0	0	0	0	2	0	.154	.000	Paul Molitor	.477	44	21	3	2	2	4	6	6	.540	.773
Randy Milligan	.000	8	0	0	0	0	1	2	3	.182	.000	Charlie Hayes	.444	9	4	0	1	1	1	2	1	.545	1.000
Cory Snyder	.059	17	1	0	0	0	1		2	.111	.059	Todd Benzinger	.353	17	6	1	0	4	9	1	4	.368	1.118

Mickey Tettleton — Tigers

Bats Both (flyball hitter)

	Avg	G	AB	R	H	2B	3B	HR	RBI	BB	SO	HBP	GDP	SB	CS	OBP	SLG	IBB	SH	SF	#Pit	#P/PA	GB	FB	G/F
1992 Season	.238	157	525	82	125	25	0	32	83	122	137	1	5	0	6	.379	.469	18	0	6	2761	4.22	128	184	0.70
Last Five Years	.248	649	2164	338	536	95	7	115	325	430	615	11	41	8	16	.372	.457	36	2	19	10987	4.19	601	630	0.95

1992 Season

	Avg	AB	H	2B	3B	HR	RBI	BB	SO	OBP	SLG		Avg	AB	H	2B	3B	HR	RBI	BB	SO	OBP	SLG
vs. Left	.274	135	37	8	0	8	23	22	28	.373	.511	Scoring Posn	.218	133	29	7	0	10	58	44	34	.399	.496
vs. Right	.226	390	88	17	0	24	60	100	109	.381	.454	Close & Late	.257	74	19	2	0	5	8	17	20	.396	.486
Groundball	.271	118	32	6	0	10	22	28	27	.405	.576	None on/out	.257	136	35	8	0	9	9	25	31	.377	.515
Flyball	.206	170	35	6	0	9	33	40	54	.355	.400	Batting #4	.222	9	2	0	0	0	0	5	1	.500	.222
Home	.271	255	69	16	0	18	41	60	72	.408	.545	Batting #5	.238	512	122	25	0	32	82	117	135	.378	.475
Away	.207	270	56	9	0	14	42	62	65	.352	.396	Other	.250	4	1	0	0	0	0	1	0	.200	.250
Day	.250	160	40	6	0	11	29	58	45	.443	.494	April	.268	71	19	4	0	7	15	16	17	.402	.620
Night	.233	365	85	19	0	21	54	64	92	.346	.458	May	.200	95	19	3	0	3	10	12	19	.287	.326
Grass	.242	447	108	19	0	29	73	108	125	.386	.479	June	.284	102	29	6	0	8	24	18	33	.392	.578
Turf	.218	78	17	6	0	3	10	14	12	.337	.410	July	.247	89	22	4	0	4	9	24	26	.400	.427
First Pitch	.370	27	10	3	0	1	5	18	0	.609	.593	August	.179	84	15	4	0	4	8	25	17	.364	.369
Ahead on Count	.301	146	44	7	0	14	30	53	0	.480	.637	September/October	.250	84	21	4	0	6	17	27	25	.430	.512
Behind on Count	.216	153	33	9	0	8	19	0	59	.214	.431	Pre-All Star	.250	308	77	15	0	19	52	57	80	.365	.484
Two Strikes	.157	268	42	6	0	9	26	51	137	.293	.280	Post-All Star	.221	217	48	10	0	13	31	65	57	.397	.447

1992 By Position

Position	Avg	AB	H	2B	3B	HR	RBI	BB	SO	OBP	SLG	G	GS	Innings	PO	A	E	DP	Fld Pct	Rng Fctr	In Zone	Outs	Zone Rtg	MLB Zone
As Designated Hitter	.295	139	41	5	0	9	25	37	35	.443	.525	40	40	...	---	---	---	---	---	---	---	---	---	---
As c	.219	375	82	20	0	22	56	85	99	.361	.448	113	110	943.0	475	47	2	10	.996	---	---	---	---	---

Last Five Years

	Avg	AB	H	2B	3B	HR	RBI	BB	SO	OBP	SLG		Avg	AB	H	2B	3B	HR	RBI	BB	SO	OBP	SLG
vs. Left	.251	658	165	34	0	41	110	98	192	.346	.489	Scoring Posn	.214	533	114	19	0	30	216	171	165	.398	.418
vs. Right	.246	1506	371	61	7	74	215	332	423	.383	.444	Close & Late	.235	366	86	10	0	20	53	58	119	.343	.426
Groundball	.281	597	168	28	1	35	88	111	144	.394	.506	None on/out	.251	578	145	27	4	27	27	85	155	.350	.452
Flyball	.212	514	109	19	1	36	81	101	166	.340	.463	Batting #4	.240	549	132	26	4	26	73	130	171	.385	.444
Home	.271	1045	283	49	7	63	174	221	292	.396	.512	Batting #5	.254	1234	313	53	3	71	193	248	337	.378	.474
Away	.226	1119	253	46	0	52	151	209	323	.349	.407	Other	.239	381	91	16	0	18	59	52	107	.333	.423
Day	.252	615	155	28	2	29	78	126	191	.378	.446	April	.223	247	55	13	0	14	39	47	81	.345	.445
Night	.246	1549	381	67	5	86	247	304	424	.370	.462	May	.260	385	100	13	1	23	64	58	92	.358	.478
Grass	.254	1808	459	78	7	105	295	368	513	.379	.479	June	.270	430	116	20	4	29	86	95	123	.400	.537
Turf	.216	356	77	17	0	10	30	62	102	.336	.348	July	.248	407	101	18	1	18	50	79	122	.369	.430
First Pitch	.314	172	54	10	2	12	30	28	0	.410	.605	August	.229	336	77	13	1	12	34	79	82	.376	.381
Ahead on Count	.350	589	206	43	2	52	143	205	0	.513	.694	September/October	.242	359	87	18	0	19	52	72	115	.372	.451
Behind on Count	.223	622	139	27	2	23	76	1	234	.224	.384	Pre-All Star	.252	1195	301	52	5	71	204	225	334	.370	.482
Two Strikes	.163	1110	181	21	3	37	101	194	614	.289	.287	Post-All Star	.243	969	235	43	2	44	121	205	281	.376	.427

Batter vs. Pitcher (career)

Hits Best Against	Avg	AB	H	2B	3B	HR	RBI	BB	SO	OBP	SLG	Hits Worst Against	Avg	AB	H	2B	3B	HR	RBI	BB	SO	OBP	SLG
Greg Hibbard	.500	16	8	3	0	2	4	1	3	.529	1.063	Erik Hanson	.000	13	0	0	0	0	0	3	8	.188	.000
Joe Hesketh	.462	13	6	2	0	2	3	2	3	.533	1.077	Floyd Bannister	.000	11	0	0	0	0	0	1	3	.077	.000
Edwin Nunez	.417	12	5	0	0	2	9	2	3	.500	.917	John Dopson	.000	10	0	0	0	0	0	1	2	.091	.000
Kevin Tapani	.385	13	5	2	0	2	5	1	2	.429	1.000	Todd Burns	.000	10	0	0	0	0	0	1	5	.091	.000
Mark Eichhorn	.364	11	4	0	0	4	5	2	5	.429	1.455	Dennis Eckersley	.077	13	1	0	0	0	0	2	4	.077	.077

Tim Teufel — Padres
Bats Right

	Avg	G	AB	R	H	2B	3B	HR	RBI	BB	SO	HBP	GDP	SB	CS	OBP	SLG	IBB	SH	SF	#Pit	#P/PA	GB	FB	G/F
1992 Season	.224	101	246	23	55	10	0	6	25	31	45	1	7	2	1	.312	.337	3	0	1	1134	4.06	87	72	1.21
Last Five Years	.233	471	1254	154	292	64	2	34	139	158	246	4	30	12	8	.318	.368	10	7	10	5700	4.00	409	337	1.21

1992 Season

	Avg	AB	H	2B	3B	HR	RBI	BB	SO	OBP	SLG		Avg	AB	H	2B	3B	HR	RBI	BB	SO	OBP	SLG
vs. Left	.239	92	22	6	0	4	14	12	13	.333	.435	Scoring Posn	.237	59	14	4	0	1	17	9	9	.333	.356
vs. Right	.214	154	33	4	0	2	11	19	32	.299	.279	Close & Late	.182	55	10	1	0	1	4	13	9	.338	.255
Home	.257	109	28	6	0	2	14	16	14	.357	.367	None on/out	.262	65	17	1	0	2	2	6	7	.333	.369
Away	.197	137	27	4	0	4	11	15	31	.275	.314	Batting #6	.250	40	10	2	0	1	5	8	8	.367	.375
First Pitch	.259	27	7	0	0	1	2	3	0	.333	.370	Batting #8	.280	93	26	2	0	3	9	13	14	.374	.398
Ahead on Count	.294	68	20	4	0	4	11	10	0	.380	.529	Other	.168	113	19	6	0	2	11	10	23	.236	.274
Behind on Count	.197	71	14	2	0	1	5	0	21	.208	.268	Pre-All Star	.259	139	36	8	0	4	18	16	23	.338	.403
Two Strikes	.161	118	19	5	0	0	7	18	45	.277	.203	Post-All Star	.178	107	19	2	0	2	7	15	22	.279	.252

Last Five Years

	Avg	AB	H	2B	3B	HR	RBI	BB	SO	OBP	SLG		Avg	AB	H	2B	3B	HR	RBI	BB	SO	OBP	SLG
vs. Left	.256	630	161	39	1	20	80	87	99	.345	.416	Scoring Posn	.201	323	65	16	0	10	101	52	72	.304	.344
vs. Right	.210	624	131	25	1	14	59	71	147	.291	.321	Close & Late	.219	251	55	12	0	6	25	37	46	.316	.339
Groundball	.212	444	94	19	1	9	35	60	88	.305	.320	None on/out	.248	290	72	11	0	10	10	29	49	.319	.390
Flyball	.285	302	86	19	0	14	49	39	55	.365	.487	Batting #2	.250	276	69	16	0	5	32	33	43	.330	.362
Home	.229	572	131	26	0	14	64	75	100	.319	.348	Batting #7	.230	252	58	14	1	9	28	42	58	.340	.401
Away	.236	682	161	38	2	20	75	83	146	.318	.386	Other	.227	726	165	34	1	20	79	83	145	.306	.360
Day	.254	422	107	28	0	15	58	37	82	.315	.427	April	.209	153	32	5	1	0	11	24	17	.322	.255
Night	.222	832	185	36	2	19	81	121	164	.320	.339	May	.253	182	46	7	0	6	21	26	43	.343	.390
Grass	.223	862	192	38	0	19	92	111	168	.311	.333	June	.291	189	55	8	0	3	29	25	32	.372	.381
Turf	.255	392	100	26	2	15	47	47	78	.335	.446	July	.211	209	44	9	0	4	13	25	42	.297	.311
First Pitch	.243	107	26	7	0	3	11	6	0	.293	.393	August	.227	220	50	12	0	10	36	28	47	.310	.418
Ahead on Count	.313	319	100	22	1	18	54	77	0	.441	.558	September/October	.216	301	65	23	1	11	29	30	65	.288	.409
Behind on Count	.197	411	81	20	0	8	40	1	133	.200	.304	Pre-All Star	.253	593	150	24	1	12	68	86	107	.348	.358
Two Strikes	.175	612	107	20	1	9	42	74	264	.255	.255	Post-All Star	.215	661	142	40	1	22	71	72	139	.291	.378

Batter vs. Pitcher (since 1984)

Hits Best Against	Avg	AB	H	2B	3B	HR	RBI	BB	SO	OBP	SLG	Hits Worst Against	Avg	AB	H	2B	3B	HR	RBI	BB	SO	OBP	SLG
Tim Burke	.500	10	5	1	0	1	3	0	1	.455	.900	Floyd Bannister	.000	11	0	0	0	0	0	3	1	.214	.000
Don Robinson	.455	11	5	3	0	1	2	1	1	.462	1.000	Bryn Smith	.000	10	0	0	0	0	0	2	4	.167	.000
Bob McClure	.444	9	4	0	0	1	4	4	2	.615	.778	Roger Clemens	.000	10	0	0	0	0	1	1	3	.083	.000
Tom Browning	.429	42	18	3	0	4	6	5	5	.489	.786	Greg Mathews	.056	18	1	0	0	0	0	2	3	.150	.056
Bob Walk	.400	10	4	0	0	1	4	4	2	.571	.700	Bud Black	.063	16	1	0	0	0	1	2	3	.158	.063

Bob Tewksbury — Cardinals
Pitches Right (groundball pitcher)

	ERA	W	L	Sv	IP	BB	SO	Avg	H	2B	3B	HR	RBI	OBP	SLG	CG	ShO	Sup	QS	#P/S	SB	CS	GB	FB	G/F
1992 Season	2.16	16	5	0	233.0	20	91	.248	217	39	4	15	58	.265	.353	5	0	4.09	27	89	7	4	394	223	1.77
Last Five Years	2.91	38	26	1	602.2	85	234	.263	605	123	15	38	211	.290	.379	12	3	4.44	59	84	27	19	996	635	1.57

1992 Season

	ERA	W	L	Sv	G	GS	IP	H	HR	BB	SO		Avg	AB	H	2B	3B	HR	RBI	BB	SO	OBP	SLG
Home	1.52	10	2	0	17	16	124.1	99	8	8	49	vs. Left	.242	517	125	19	2	10	36	7	57	.250	.344
Away	2.90	6	3	0	16	16	108.2	118	7	12	42	vs. Right	.256	359	92	20	2	5	22	13	34	.286	.365
Day	3.18	2	0	0	5	5	34.0	31	2	4	12	Inning 1-6	.255	717	183	34	3	13	54	17	74	.273	.365
Night	1.99	14	5	0	28	27	199.0	186	13	16	79	Inning 7+	.214	159	34	5	1	2	4	3	17	.228	.296
Grass	2.52	3	2	0	10	10	71.1	72	6	6	30	None on	.261	567	148	28	4	11	11	14	60	.281	.383
Turf	2.00	13	3	0	23	22	161.2	145	9	14	61	Runners on	.223	309	69	11	0	4	47	6	31	.235	.298
April	1.61	2	0	0	5	4	28.0	26	1	1	11	Scoring Posn	.198	162	32	4	0	3	42	5	13	.213	.278
May	1.88	4	1	0	6	6	48.0	39	4	5	18	Close & Late	.210	81	17	3	0	2	3	2	10	.229	.321
June	2.23	3	1	0	6	6	44.1	47	3	3	15	None on/out	.199	231	46	10	2	2	2	7	22	.226	.286
July	2.04	1	2	0	5	5	35.1	36	2	5	17	vs. 1st Batr (relief)	.000	0	0	0	0	0	0	0	0	.000	.000
August	2.18	4	1	0	6	6	45.1	38	1	2	17	First Inning Pitched	.311	135	42	6	1	2	17	5	18	.329	.415
September/October	3.09	2	0	0	5	5	32.0	31	4	4	13	First 75 Pitches	.256	722	185	35	3	15	56	16	72	.273	.375
Starter	2.18	15	5	0	32	32	231.0	216	15	20	89	Pitch 76-90	.200	105	21	2	0	0	1	4	16	.229	.219
Reliever	0.00	1	0	0	1	0	2.0	1	0	0	2	Pitch 91-105	.214	42	9	2	1	0	1	0	3	.214	.310
0-3 Days Rest	0.89	1	0	0	3	3	20.1	28	0	1	6	Pitch 106+	.286	7	2	0	0	0	0	0	0	.286	.286
4 Days Rest	1.78	8	3	0	16	16	121.2	99	7	9	53	First Pitch	.293	181	53	9	0	0	8	0	0	.297	.343
5+ Days Rest	3.03	6	2	0	13	13	89.0	89	8	10	30	Ahead on Count	.186	371	69	10	2	8	22	0	81	.189	.288
Pre-All Star	1.87	9	3	0	19	18	134.2	127	8	9	51	Behind on Count	.291	182	53	11	1	5	11	13	0	.335	.445
Post-All Star	2.56	7	2	0	14	14	98.1	90	7	11	40	Two Strikes	.173	307	53	8	1	7	15	7	91	.190	.274

Last Five Years

	ERA	W	L	Sv	G	GS	IP	H	HR	BB	SO		Avg	AB	H	2B	3B	HR	RBI	BB	SO	OBP	SLG
Home	2.63	20	10	0	49	42	304.0	272	17	39	117	vs. Left	.265	1319	350	70	6	20	120	59	119	.294	.373
Away	3.19	18	16	1	50	45	298.2	333	21	46	117	vs. Right	.260	981	255	53	9	18	91	26	115	.285	.387
Day	3.22	11	9	0	28	25	170.2	169	10	34	63	Inning 1-6	.269	1902	510	99	12	31	194	67	199	.294	.382
Night	2.79	27	17	1	71	62	432.0	436	28	51	171	Inning 7+	.236	398	94	24	3	7	17	18	45	.272	.364
Grass	2.94	9	9	0	27	24	171.1	185	14	23	72	None on	.262	1441	378	82	10	24	24	44	155	.288	.383

Last Five Years

	ERA	W	L	Sv	G	GS	IP	H	HR	BB	SO		Avg	AB	H	2B	3B	HR	RBI	BB	SO	OBP	SLG
Turf	2.90	29	17	1	72	63	431.1	420	24	62	162	Runners on	.264	659	227	41	5	14	187	41	79	.292	.373
April	3.06	4	1	1	15	8	64.1	66	2	12	30	Scoring Posn	.264	488	129	25	2	12	174	32	42	.297	.396
May	2.87	5	2	0	13	11	75.1	77	5	12	24	Close & Late	.211	152	32	6	1	4	7	9	18	.255	.342
June	2.14	9	3	0	15	15	109.1	102	7	13	40	None on/out	.242	608	147	33	5	8	8	20	70	.272	.352
July	2.20	4	8	0	15	15	98.1	100	6	15	45	vs. 1st Batr (relief)	.364	11	4	0	0	0	1	0	2	.333	.364
August	2.87	9	4	0	17	17	119.1	116	3	10	37	First Inning Pitched	.333	400	133	28	3	6	64	17	44	.351	.463
September/October	4.04	7	8	0	24	21	136.0	144	15	23	58	First 75 Pitches	.263	1960	516	101	12	37	187	69	194	.289	.384
Starter	2.82	37	26	0	87	87	581.1	577	37	80	223	Pitch 76-90	.258	252	65	17	1	1	20	12	35	.294	.345
Reliever	5.48	1	0	1	12	0	21.1	28	1	5	11	Pitch 91-105	.266	79	21	5	2	0	3	3	5	.293	.380
0-3 Days Rest	1.38	3	0	0	6	6	39.0	41	2	4	9	Pitch 106+	.333	9	3	0	0	0	1	1	0	.364	.333
4 Days Rest	2.56	20	17	0	46	46	316.1	298	17	38	131	First Pitch	.317	461	146	32	1	5	48	7	0	.326	.423
5+ Days Rest	3.42	14	9	0	35	35	226.0	238	18	38	83	Ahead on Count	.208	1000	208	35	8	14	72	1	218	.215	.301
Pre-All Star	2.52	19	9	1	48	39	281.2	275	16	40	107	Behind on Count	.321	492	158	37	4	13	46	50	0	.379	.492
Post-All Star	3.25	19	17	0	51	48	321.0	330	22	45	127	Two Strikes	.185	813	150	25	5	12	53	27	234	.213	.272

Pitcher vs. Batter (career)

Pitches Best Vs.	Avg	AB	H	2B	3B	HR	RBI	BB	SO	OBP	SLG	Pitches Worst Vs.	Avg	AB	H	2B	3B	HR	RBI	BB	SO	OBP	SLG
Andres Galarraga	.000	13	0	0	0	0	0	0	2	.000	.000	Dale Murphy	.500	14	7	2	0	1	3	0	1	.500	.857
Gary Sheffield	.000	12	0	0	0	0	0	0	2	.000	.000	Jeff Treadway	.500	10	5	0	0	0	2	2	0	.583	.500
Todd Benzinger	.000	10	0	0	0	0	0	1	1	.091	.000	Joe Carter	.455	11	5	0	0	2	3	1	0	.500	1.000
Joe Girardi	.063	16	1	0	0	0	0	0	1	.167	.063	Ryne Sandberg	.406	32	13	3	1	4	9	1	1	.412	.938
Mickey Morandini	.133	15	2	0	0	0	0	0	1	.133	.133	Orlando Merced	.391	23	9	2	1	1	3	0	3	.391	.696

Bobby Thigpen — White Sox   Pitches Right

	ERA	W	L	Sv	G	GS	IP	BB	SO	Avg	H	2B	3B	HR	RBI	OBP	SLG	GF	IR	IRS	Hld	SvOp	SB	CS	GB	FB	G/F
1992 Season	4.75	1	3	22	55	0	55.0	33	45	.275	58	9	0	4	35	.375	.374	40	39	12	3	29	3	0	59	64	0.92
Last Five Years	3.30	19	28	177	328	0	382.1	176	271	.240	339	42	5	35	195	.326	.351	171	248	72	4	219	23	6	457	419	1.09

1992 Season

	ERA	W	L	Sv	G	GS	IP	H	HR	BB	SO		Avg	AB	H	2B	3B	HR	RBI	BB	SO	OBP	SLG
Home	3.77	1	2	9	26	0	28.2	33	1	12	28	vs. Left	.338	80	27	2	0	1	12	15	10	.429	.400
Away	5.81	0	1	13	29	0	26.1	25	3	21	17	vs. Right	.237	131	31	7	0	3	23	18	35	.340	.359
Starter	0.00	0	0	0	0	0	0.0	0	0	0	0	Scoring Posn	.264	72	19	5	0	1	31	13	12	.367	.375
Reliever	4.75	1	3	22	55	0	55.0	58	4	33	45	Close & Late	.252	143	36	7	0	2	26	22	34	.351	.343
0 Days rest	0.93	0	0	9	11	0	9.2	6	0	4	7	None on/out	.256	39	10	1	0	1	1	9	10	.396	.359
1 or 2 Days rest	4.68	1	2	10	23	0	25.0	27	1	19	22	First Pitch	.259	27	7	0	0	0	2	5	0	.364	.259
3+ Days rest	6.64	0	1	3	21	0	20.1	25	3	10	16	Behind on Count	.414	29	12	1	0	1	7	14	0	.605	.552
Pre-All Star	3.25	1	2	19	35	0	36.0	32	2	20	34	Ahead on Count	.238	105	25	4	0	3	15	0	37	.257	.362
Post-All Star	7.58	0	1	3	20	0	19.0	26	2	13	11	Two Strikes	.221	113	25	6	0	3	15	14	45	.318	.354

Last Five Years

	ERA	W	L	Sv	G	GS	IP	H	HR	BB	SO		Avg	AB	H	2B	3B	HR	RBI	BB	SO	OBP	SLG
Home	3.32	15	13	81	170	0	203.1	201	14	89	144	vs. Left	.258	664	171	15	4	16	98	100	102	.349	.364
Away	3.27	4	15	96	158	0	179.0	138	21	87	127	vs. Right	.225	748	168	27	1	19	97	76	169	.304	.340
Day	3.04	3	9	56	97	0	109.2	101	6	55	79	Inning 1-6	.000	0	0	0	0	0	0	0	0	.000	.000
Night	3.40	16	19	121	231	0	272.2	238	29	121	192	Inning 7+	.240	1412	339	42	5	35	195	176	271	.326	.351
Grass	3.21	17	22	154	292	0	339.2	299	30	159	244	None on	.247	644	159	21	3	14	14	86	131	.338	.354
Turf	4.01	2	6	23	36	0	42.2	40	5	17	27	Runners on	.234	768	180	21	2	21	181	90	140	.315	.349
April	2.83	1	2	23	46	0	57.1	46	6	28	36	Scoring Posn	.235	442	104	15	2	12	160	59	84	.323	.360
May	4.83	5	10	29	63	0	69.0	67	12	38	54	Close & Late	.241	822	198	28	3	21	130	116	176	.335	.359
June	2.29	5	2	36	57	0	63.0	50	5	29	46	None on/out	.215	274	59	6	0	6	6	47	54	.332	.303
July	3.09	7	4	31	60	0	75.2	63	5	31	51	vs. 1st Batr (relief)	.194	283	55	8	0	10	36	32	54	.282	.329
August	3.17	1	6	29	53	0	65.1	66	4	23	51	First Inning Pitched	.237	1075	255	30	4	31	154	115	195	.314	.359
September/October	3.46	0	4	29	49	0	52.0	48	3	27	33	First 15 Pitches	.237	933	221	26	3	32	126	94	163	.309	.374
Starter	0.00	0	0	0	0	0	0.0	0	0	0	0	Pitch 16-30	.250	388	97	13	2	3	51	72	92	.366	.317
Reliever	3.30	19	28	177	328	0	382.1	339	35	176	271	Pitch 31-45	.238	80	19	3	0	0	17	10	14	.323	.275
0 Days rest	2.56	5	7	65	88	0	95.0	75	7	44	72	Pitch 46+	.182	11	2	0	0	0	1	0	2	.182	.182
1 or 2 Days rest	3.25	11	15	78	148	0	185.2	157	17	94	139	First Pitch	.237	211	50	3	1	6	29	15	0	.287	.346
3+ Days rest	4.07	3	6	34	92	0	101.2	107	11	38	60	Ahead on Count	.208	686	143	22	3	15	69	0	228	.216	.315
Pre-All Star	3.26	15	15	97	187	0	221.0	192	25	107	160	Behind on Count	.336	256	86	6	0	13	59	101	0	.521	.512
Post-All Star	3.35	4	13	80	141	0	161.1	147	10	69	111	Two Strikes	.188	682	128	22	2	11	59	59	271	.257	.274

Pitcher vs. Batter (career)

Pitches Best Vs.	Avg	AB	H	2B	3B	HR	RBI	BB	SO	OBP	SLG	Pitches Worst Vs.	Avg	AB	H	2B	3B	HR	RBI	BB	SO	OBP	SLG
Jim Gantner	.000	11	0	0	0	0	0	1	1	.083	.000	Randy Bush	.667	9	6	2	0	1	6	3	0	.750	1.222
Tony Fernandez	.000	10	0	0	0	0	0	1	1	.091	.000	Julio Franco	.636	11	7	2	0	1	1	0	1	.636	1.091
Geno Petralli	.063	16	1	0	0	0	1	0	5	.063	.063	Mel Hall	.500	14	7	0	0	2	3	0	0	.500	.929
Don Mattingly	.077	13	1	0	0	0	1	1	0	.143	.077	Dave Winfield	.462	13	6	0	0	2	3	0	1	.462	.923
Joe Carter	.077	13	1	1	0	0	1	0	5	.077	.154	Rickey Henderson	.400	10	4	1	0	1	4	4	1	.571	.800

Frank Thomas — White Sox — Bats Right (flyball hitter)

	Avg	G	AB	R	H	2B	3B	HR	RBI	BB	SO	HBP	GDP	SB	CS	OBP	SLG	IBB	SH	SF	#Pit	#P/PA	GB	FB	G/F
1992 Season	.323	160	573	108	185	46	2	24	115	122	88	5	19	6	3	.439	.536	6	0	11	2840	3.99	178	192	0.93
Career (1990-1992)	.322	378	1323	251	426	88	7	63	255	304	254	8	44	7	6	.447	.542	19	0	16	6930	4.20	395	417	0.95

1992 Season

	Avg	AB	H	2B	3B	HR	RBI	BB	SO	OBP	SLG		Avg	AB	H	2B	3B	HR	RBI	BB	SO	OBP	SLG
vs. Left	.357	140	50	15	1	8	26	28	20	.456	.650	Scoring Posn	.310	174	54	13	0	5	84	45	30	.430	.471
vs. Right	.312	433	135	31	1	16	89	94	68	.433	.499	Close & Late	.296	108	32	7	1	4	23	13	18	.379	.491
Groundball	.425	153	65	14	1	10	39	36	18	.526	.725	None on/out	.333	114	38	11	0	6	6	20	14	.441	.588
Flyball	.314	156	49	13	0	7	31	36	30	.439	.532	Batting #3	.344	401	138	35	1	17	85	79	52	.450	.564
Home	.305	292	89	23	2	10	54	64	45	.430	.500	Batting #4	.275	171	47	11	1	7	30	43	36	.416	.474
Away	.342	281	96	23	0	14	61	58	43	.448	.573	Other	.000	1	0	0	0	0	0	0	0	.000	.000
Day	.298	151	45	12	1	7	34	29	19	.404	.530	April	.210	62	13	4	1	1	7	19	17	.398	.355
Night	.332	422	140	34	1	17	81	93	69	.451	.538	May	.337	95	32	7	0	6	22	23	17	.458	.600
Grass	.325	483	157	37	2	22	101	109	74	.448	.547	June	.310	100	31	6	1	4	21	23	13	.437	.510
Turf	.311	90	28	9	0	2	14	13	14	.389	.478	July	.354	99	35	7	0	5	18	20	9	.459	.576
First Pitch	.373	75	28	10	0	3	16	6	0	.422	.627	August	.367	98	36	5	0	6	22	20	10	.475	.602
Ahead on Count	.371	170	63	14	1	11	44	64	0	.534	.659	September/October	.319	119	38	17	0	2	25	17	22	.400	.513
Behind on Count	.308	143	44	10	1	5	28	0	33	.315	.497	Pre-All Star	.306	294	90	19	2	13	57	74	49	.442	.517
Two Strikes	.231	242	56	12	1	4	31	52	88	.365	.339	Post-All Star	.341	279	95	27	0	11	58	48	39	.435	.556

1992 By Position

Position	Avg	AB	H	2B	3B	HR	RBI	BB	SO	OBP	SLG	G	GS	Innings	PO	A	E	DP	Fld Pct	Rng Fctr	In Zone	Outs	Zone Rtg	MLB Zone
As 1b	.326	565	184	45	2	24	114	121	86	.442	.540	158	157	1406.0	1428	90	13	113	.992	---	268	212	.791	.843

Career (1990-1992)

	Avg	AB	H	2B	3B	HR	RBI	BB	SO	OBP	SLG		Avg	AB	H	2B	3B	HR	RBI	BB	SO	OBP	SLG
vs. Left	.375	381	143	30	2	24	73	91	64	.492	.654	Scoring Posn	.329	374	123	24	3	13	183	101	77	.458	.553
vs. Right	.300	942	283	58	5	39	182	213	190	.429	.497	Close & Late	.303	231	70	14	2	9	52	47	53	.422	.498
Groundball	.352	381	134	23	2	15	71	90	61	.470	.541	None on/out	.307	254	78	23	1	15	15	53	51	.430	.583
Flyball	.324	296	96	29	3	16	59	71	74	.455	.505	Batting #3	.332	852	283	60	2	44	169	189	145	.453	.562
Home	.337	632	213	43	5	36	128	166	129	.474	.592	Batting #4	.292	342	100	20	3	13	60	85	76	.430	.482
Away	.308	691	213	45	2	27	127	138	125	.421	.496	Other	.333	129	43	8	2	6	26	30	33	.456	.566
Day	.316	342	108	24	1	19	69	79	62	.440	.558	April	.262	126	33	7	2	4	20	30	28	.405	.444
Night	.324	981	318	64	6	44	186	225	192	.449	.536	May	.330	182	60	12	0	11	46	53	36	.475	.577
Grass	.333	1094	364	74	7	56	223	264	211	.461	.567	June	.295	207	61	12	1	9	41	46	42	.424	.493
Turf	.271	229	62	14	0	7	32	40	43	.376	.424	July	.338	198	67	12	0	12	33	45	27	.459	.581
First Pitch	.435	131	57	14	0	6	29	14	0	.493	.735	August	.350	297	104	20	4	16	62	65	46	.466	.606
Ahead on Count	.402	366	147	26	3	30	98	157	0	.575	.735	September/October	.323	313	101	25	0	11	53	65	75	.437	.508
Behind on Count	.312	346	108	23	3	13	65	0	92	.314	.509	Pre-All Star	.304	575	175	35	3	27	115	146	113	.443	.517
Two Strikes	.220	644	142	31	4	17	83	133	254	.352	.360	Post-All Star	.336	748	251	53	4	36	140	158	141	.450	.561

Batter vs. Pitcher (career)

Hits Best Against	Avg	AB	H	2B	3B	HR	RBI	BB	SO	OBP	SLG	Hits Worst Against	Avg	AB	H	2B	3B	HR	RBI	BB	SO	OBP	SLG
Mike Gardiner	.643	14	9	1	0	2	5	2	1	.688	1.143	Nolan Ryan	.000	12	0	0	0	0	0	2	11	.143	.000
Mike Mussina	.625	16	10	3	0	3	5	2	1	.667	1.375	Greg Harris	.077	13	1	0	0	0	1	2	4	.188	.077
Luis Aquino	.545	11	6	1	0	3	6	2	0	.615	1.455	Bill Krueger	.167	12	2	1	0	0	0	2	1	.286	.250
Erik Hanson	.533	15	8	1	0	1	2	6	3	.667	.800	Frank Viola	.182	11	2	0	0	0	0	0	2	.182	.182
Matt Young	.444	9	4	0	0	2	4	6	2	.667	1.111	Charles Nagy	.214	14	3	0	0	0	1	2	3	.313	.214

Jim Thome — Indians — Bats Left (groundball hitter)

	Avg	G	AB	R	H	2B	3B	HR	RBI	BB	SO	HBP	GDP	SB	CS	OBP	SLG	IBB	SH	SF	#Pit	#P/PA	GB	FB	G/F
1992 Season	.205	40	117	8	24	3	1	2	12	10	34	2	2	3	2	0	.275	.299	2	0	2	509	3.89	41	27	1.52
Career (1991-1992)	.228	67	215	15	49	7	3	3	21	15	50	3	7	3	1	.285	.330	3	0	2	868	3.69	83	53	1.57

1992 Season

	Avg	AB	H	2B	3B	HR	RBI	BB	SO	OBP	SLG		Avg	AB	H	2B	3B	HR	RBI	BB	SO	OBP	SLG
vs. Left	.214	14	3	0	0	0	0	0	8	.214	.214	Scoring Posn	.182	33	6	1	1	0	10	4	11	.275	.273
vs. Right	.204	103	21	3	1	2	12	10	26	.282	.311	Close & Late	.087	23	2	1	0	0	1	1	7	.125	.130
Home	.222	81	18	2	1	1	9	7	23	.297	.309	None on/out	.200	25	5	0	0	0	0	1	5	.231	.200
Away	.167	36	6	1	0	1	3	3	11	.225	.278	Batting #7	.162	37	6	1	1	0	4	2	6	.205	.243
First Pitch	.182	11	2	0	0	0	1	2	0	.333	.182	Batting #8	.225	80	18	2	0	2	8	8	28	.304	.325
Ahead on Count	.313	32	10	2	0	2	6	4	0	.378	.563	Other	.000	0	0	0	0	0	0	0	0	.000	.000
Behind on Count	.122	41	5	0	0	1	3	0	18	.122	.195	Pre-All Star	.231	52	12	2	0	1	4	4	17	.298	.327
Two Strikes	.129	62	8	1	0		3	5	34	.194	.161	Post-All Star	.185	65	12	1	1	1	8	6	17	.257	.277

Milt Thompson — Cardinals
Bats Left (groundball hitter)

	Avg	G	AB	R	H	2B	3B	HR	RBI	BB	SO	HBP	GDP	SB	CS	OBP	SLG	IBB	SH	SF	#Pit	#P/PA	GB	FB	G/F
1992 Season	.293	109	208	31	61	9	1	4	17	16	39	2	3	18	6	.350	.404	3	0	0	782	3.46	108	29	3.72
Last Five Years	.277	636	1875	241	519	83	23	22	182	165	302	12	31	103	37	.338	.381	26	5	7	7232	3.51	924	320	2.89

1992 Season

	Avg	AB	H	2B	3B	HR	RBI	BB	SO	OBP	SLG		Avg	AB	H	2B	3B	HR	RBI	BB	SO	OBP	SLG
vs. Left	.318	22	7	3	0	0	0	2	5	.375	.455	Scoring Posn	.250	40	10	0	1	0	13	6	11	.350	.300
vs. Right	.290	186	54	6	1	4	17	14	34	.347	.398	Close & Late	.304	69	21	7	0	1	4	7	12	.368	.449
Home	.276	105	29	4	1	1	9	7	23	.327	.362	None on/out	.367	60	22	4	0	2	2	3	7	.397	.533
Away	.311	103	32	5	0	3	8	9	16	.372	.447	Batting #6	.293	58	17	3	1	2	8	1	9	.328	.483
First Pitch	.419	43	18	2	0	2	6	1	0	.432	.605	Batting #9	.263	57	15	3	0	1	3	9	12	.364	.368
Ahead on Count	.292	48	14	3	0	1	2	6	1	.382	.417	Other	.312	93	29	3	0	1	6	6	18	.354	.376
Behind on Count	.234	64	15	1	1	1	7	0	22	.234	.328	Pre-All Star	.312	138	43	5	1	4	12	7	28	.354	.449
Two Strikes	.186	86	16	1	0	0	5	9	38	.271	.198	Post-All Star	.257	70	18	4	0	0	5	9	11	.342	.314

Last Five Years

	Avg	AB	H	2B	3B	HR	RBI	BB	SO	OBP	SLG		Avg	AB	H	2B	3B	HR	RBI	BB	SO	OBP	SLG
vs. Left	.240	446	107	25	5	2	41	23	102	.283	.332	Scoring Posn	.268	436	117	17	8	4	152	67	91	.365	.372
vs. Right	.288	1429	412	58	18	20	141	142	200	.355	.396	Close & Late	.294	364	107	23	4	4	40	42	72	.364	.412
Groundball	.317	652	207	29	8	4	73	57	93	.375	.405	None on/out	.277	447	124	24	2	7	7	34	59	.331	.387
Flyball	.233	424	99	17	3	5	35	32	81	.292	.323	Batting #2	.300	347	104	14	2	1	36	44	55	.366	.360
Home	.273	929	254	40	16	11	106	82	133	.334	.386	Batting #6	.267	341	91	15	5	8	34	33	53	.334	.411
Away	.280	946	265	43	7	11	76	83	169	.342	.375	Other	.273	1187	324	54	16	13	112	98	194	.331	.378
Day	.270	603	163	34	7	6	63	49	98	.331	.380	April	.293	259	76	13	2	2	25	29	43	.369	.382
Night	.280	1272	356	49	16	16	119	116	204	.341	.381	May	.244	266	65	7	4	6	21	32	44	.332	.368
Grass	.280	521	146	27	6	5	38	50	87	.349	.384	June	.301	365	110	18	9	4	47	31	52	.353	.433
Turf	.275	1354	373	56	17	17	144	115	215	.334	.380	July	.251	338	85	8	5	2	26	29	56	.315	.322
First Pitch	.364	313	114	18	0	5	40	9	0	.382	.470	August	.303	346	105	18	2	5	37	28	58	.359	.410
Ahead on Count	.306	454	140	24	9	6	55	79	1	.414	.441	September/October	.259	301	78	19	1	3	26	16	49	.299	.359
Behind on Count	.221	592	131	15	7	7	50	3	168	.229	.306	Pre-All Star	.275	1001	275	41	15	14	97	101	155	.345	.388
Two Strikes	.189	762	144	18	5	3	50	70	301	.261	.238	Post-All Star	.279	874	244	42	8	8	85	64	147	.330	.373

Batter vs. Pitcher (career)

Hits Best Against	Avg	AB	H	2B	3B	HR	RBI	BB	SO	OBP	SLG	Hits Worst Against	Avg	AB	H	2B	3B	HR	RBI	BB	SO	OBP	SLG
Dave Smith	.455	11	5	1	0	0	0	2	1	.538	.545	Pete Smith	.000	12	0	0	0	0	0	2	1	.143	.000
Neal Heaton	.429	14	6	3	0	0	1	0	0	.429	.643	Paul Assenmacher	.063	16	1	1	0	0	1	1	2	.118	.125
John Burkett	.429	14	6	1	0	1	3	1	1	.467	.714	Tom Browning	.071	14	1	0	0	0	0	1	3	.133	.071
Jeff Parrett	.417	12	5	1	1	0	5	2	4	.500	.667	Dennis Martinez	.121	33	4	2	0	0	0	1	8	.147	.182
Bill Gullickson	.409	22	9	3	1	1	2	1	0	.435	.773	Tommy Greene	.133	15	2	1	0	0	0	0	0	.133	.200

Robby Thompson — Giants
Bats Right

	Avg	G	AB	R	H	2B	3B	HR	RBI	BB	SO	HBP	GDP	SB	CS	OBP	SLG	IBB	SH	SF	#Pit	#P/PA	GB	FB	G/F
1992 Season	.260	128	443	54	115	25	1	14	49	43	75	8	8	5	9	.333	.415	1	7	4	1925	3.87	172	132	1.30
Last Five Years	.254	702	2457	352	624	121	26	68	251	231	510	37	35	59	27	.326	.407	4	49	13	10483	3.83	789	754	1.03

1992 Season

	Avg	AB	H	2B	3B	HR	RBI	BB	SO	OBP	SLG		Avg	AB	H	2B	3B	HR	RBI	BB	SO	OBP	SLG
vs. Left	.280	164	46	14	1	1	11	20	22	.357	.396	Scoring Posn	.205	88	18	3	0	4	35	14	13	.308	.375
vs. Right	.247	279	69	11	0	13	38	23	53	.319	.427	Close & Late	.163	86	14	2	0	2	10	4	13	.223	.256
Groundball	.240	200	48	8	1	5	16	12	33	.292	.365	None on/out	.270	100	27	8	1	5	5	6	17	.336	.520
Flyball	.274	73	20	3	0	3	8	7	12	.341	.438	Batting #2	.251	167	42	12	0	4	12	17	20	.326	.395
Home	.271	236	64	14	1	8	27	22	38	.342	.441	Batting #6	.255	220	56	10	1	8	28	20	47	.329	.418
Away	.246	207	51	11	0	6	22	21	37	.323	.386	Other	.304	56	17	3	0	2	9	6	8	.371	.464
Day	.300	170	51	13	1	6	21	20	32	.379	.494	April	.353	68	24	5	0	3	11	10	7	.432	.559
Night	.234	273	64	12	0	8	28	23	43	.304	.366	May	.318	22	7	1	0	0	0	1	4	.348	.364
Grass	.267	356	95	22	1	12	42	31	58	.332	.435	June	.136	81	11	4	0	1	5	11	19	.271	.222
Turf	.230	87	20	3	0	2	7	12	17	.337	.333	July	.250	96	24	4	0	4	12	9	13	.324	.417
First Pitch	.256	39	10	3	0	1	6	1	0	.310	.410	August	.257	101	26	6	1	4	14	6	14	.303	.455
Ahead on Count	.339	118	40	10	1	8	23	27	0	.450	.644	September/October	.307	75	23	5	0	2	7	6	6	.358	.453
Behind on Count	.242	161	39	6	0	3	14	0	40	.261	.335	Pre-All Star	.253	217	55	11	0	7	26	27	35	.348	.401
Two Strikes	.185	200	37	6	0	3	12	15	75	.262	.260	Post-All Star	.265	226	60	14	1	7	23	16	40	.318	.429

1992 By Position

Position	Avg	AB	H	2B	3B	HR	RBI	BB	SO	OBP	SLG	G	GS	Innings	PO	A	E	DP	Fld Pct	Rng Fctr	In Zone	Outs	Zone Rtg	MLB Zone
As 2b	.262	435	114	24	1	14	47	43	74	.337	.418	120	120	1051.0	298	381	15	99	.978	5.81	421	373	.886	.892

Last Five Years

	Avg	AB	H	2B	3B	HR	RBI	BB	SO	OBP	SLG		Avg	AB	H	2B	3B	HR	RBI	BB	SO	OBP	SLG
vs. Left	.293	830	243	61	12	22	88	89	150	.364	.475	Scoring Posn	.217	534	116	23	4	15	168	68	132	.307	.360
vs. Right	.234	1627	381	60	14	46	163	142	360	.306	.373	Close & Late	.243	424	103	19	3	9	52	33	88	.307	.366
Groundball	.244	890	217	39	9	17	81	74	168	.313	.365	None on/out	.263	514	135	28	5	15	15	42	107	.330	.424
Flyball	.226	539	122	27	4	18	55	43	126	.292	.391	Batting #2	.245	1333	326	68	16	32	132	115	267	.313	.392
Home	.271	1225	332	68	15	37	142	129	252	.348	.442	Batting #6	.266	504	134	22	4	19	54	54	104	.347	.438
Away	.237	1232	292	53	11	31	109	102	258	.304	.373	Other	.265	620	164	31	6	17	65	62	119	.337	.416

Last Five Years

	Avg	AB	H	2B	3B	HR	RBI	BB	SO	OBP	SLG		Avg	AB	H	2B	3B	HR	RBI	BB	SO	OBP	SLG
Day	.261	966	252	52	14	28	109	99	202	.336	.431	April	.263	380	100	18	5	8	33	40	76	.336	.400
Night	.249	1491	372	69	12	40	142	132	308	.318	.392	May	.290	389	113	22	5	12	40	36	72	.357	.465
Grass	.261	1830	477	93	21	52	197	182	375	.334	.420	June	.239	402	96	19	6	11	47	49	90	.337	.398
Turf	.234	627	147	28	5	16	54	49	135	.301	.372	July	.249	442	110	22	2	14	45	32	89	.311	.403
First Pitch	.339	289	98	22	3	6	39	2	0	.363	.498	August	.260	466	121	24	5	13	46	38	95	.321	.416
Ahead on Count	.341	548	187	33	11	30	93	117	0	.456	.606	September/October	.222	378	84	16	3	10	40	36	88	.295	.362
Behind on Count	.228	871	199	44	8	13	64	0	275	.239	.342	Pre-All Star	.263	1310	344	65	16	37	141	142	259	.343	.421
Two Strikes	.164	1162	191	42	7	18	63	109	509	.243	.259	Post-All Star	.244	1147	280	56	10	31	110	89	251	.305	.391

Batter vs. Pitcher (career)

Hits Best Against	Avg	AB	H	2B	3B	HR	RBI	BB	SO	OBP	SLG	Hits Worst Against	Avg	AB	H	2B	3B	HR	RBI	BB	SO	OBP	SLG
Paul Assenmacher	.545	11	6	2	0	0	3	0	1	.545	.727	Jimmy Jones	.056	18	1	0	0	0	0	3	3	.190	.056
Alejandro Pena	.500	12	6	2	0	0	2	1	0	.538	.667	Todd Worrell	.077	13	1	0	0	0	0	0	3	.077	.077
Jim Acker	.500	8	4	1	0	2	5	3	0	.636	1.375	Norm Charlton	.091	11	1	0	0	0	1	0	4	.091	.091
Mike Maddux	.467	15	7	1	1	2	5	0	2	.467	1.067	Ken Hill	.091	11	1	0	0	0	0	0	1	.091	.091
Tom Glavine	.441	34	15	7	1	1	3	3	5	.486	.794	Tim Burke	.118	17	2	0	0	0	0	0	5	.118	.118

Ryan Thompson — Mets   Bats Right (flyball hitter)

	Avg	G	AB	R	H	2B	3B	HR	RBI	BB	SO	HBP	GDP	SB	CS	OBP	SLG	IBB	SH	SF	#Pit	#P/PA	GB	FB	G/F
1992 Season	.222	30	108	15	24	7	1	3	10	8	24	0	2	2	2	.274	.389	0	0	1	404	3.45	34	38	0.89

1992 Season

	Avg	AB	H	2B	3B	HR	RBI	BB	SO	OBP	SLG		Avg	AB	H	2B	3B	HR	RBI	BB	SO	OBP	SLG
vs. Left	.216	37	8	4	0	0	0	6	4	.326	.324	Scoring Posn	.160	25	4	0	0	1	7	4	8	.267	.280
vs. Right	.225	71	16	3	1	3	10	2	20	.243	.423	Close & Late	.238	21	5	1	0	1	2	4	5	.360	.429
Home	.267	45	12	2	0	3	8	6	10	.353	.511	None on/out	.211	38	8	3	1	1	1	2	4	.250	.421
Away	.190	63	12	5	1	0	2	2	14	.212	.302	Batting #1	.206	63	13	5	1	0	3	4	12	.254	.317
First Pitch	.188	16	3	1	1	0	0	0	0	.188	.375	Batting #2	.200	25	5	1	0	0	1	1	6	.222	.240
Ahead on Count	.375	24	9	4	0	1	3	4	0	.464	.667	Other	.300	20	6	1	0	3	6	3	6	.391	.800
Behind on Count	.250	52	13	3	0	0	3	0	15	.250	.308	Pre-All Star	.000	0	0	0	0	0	0	0	0	.000	.000
Two Strikes	.163	49	8	1	0	2	6	4	24	.222	.306	Post-All Star	.222	108	24	7	1	3	10	8	24	.274	.389

Dickie Thon — Rangers   Bats Right

	Avg	G	AB	R	H	2B	3B	HR	RBI	BB	SO	HBP	GDP	SB	CS	OBP	SLG	IBB	SH	SF	#Pit	#P/PA	GB	FB	G/F
1992 Season	.247	95	275	30	68	15	3	4	37	20	40	0	2	12	2	.293	.367	1	3	5	914	3.05	101	88	1.15
Last Five Years	.258	621	2059	209	531	83	17	37	207	148	331	4	35	60	19	.307	.369	23	9	16	7082	3.18	782	588	1.33

1992 Season

	Avg	AB	H	2B	3B	HR	RBI	BB	SO	OBP	SLG		Avg	AB	H	2B	3B	HR	RBI	BB	SO	OBP	SLG
vs. Left	.293	99	29	7	2	3	17	11	13	.360	.495	Scoring Posn	.288	73	21	7	0	0	28	8	15	.337	.384
vs. Right	.222	176	39	8	1	1	20	9	27	.254	.295	Close & Late	.292	48	14	1	1	0	5	3	6	.327	.354
Groundball	.191	68	13	5	0	0	6	5	13	.243	.265	None on/out	.232	69	16	2	0	2	2	4	12	.274	.348
Flyball	.273	77	21	5	1	2	12	6	9	.321	.442	Batting #7	.306	49	15	4	1	1	10	5	8	.370	.490
Home	.261	142	37	9	3	2	18	11	24	.306	.408	Batting #8	.228	123	28	7	1	1	14	7	18	.261	.325
Away	.233	133	31	6	0	2	19	9	16	.280	.323	Other	.243	103	25	4	1	2	13	8	14	.295	.359
Day	.232	56	13	1	0	1	6	2	6	.259	.304	April	.258	66	17	5	0	0	7	7	8	.333	.333
Night	.251	219	55	14	3	3	31	18	34	.302	.384	May	.222	72	16	1	1	2	13	3	9	.247	.347
Grass	.235	234	55	10	3	3	29	17	36	.281	.342	June	.240	75	18	5	0	2	9	8	10	.310	.387
Turf	.317	41	13	5	0	1	8	3	4	.364	.512	July	.288	52	15	3	2	0	7	1	9	.296	.423
First Pitch	.324	71	23	3	2	2	13	1	0	.320	.507	August	.143	7	1	1	0	0	0	1	3	.222	.286
Ahead on Count	.271	59	16	5	0	2	9	14	0	.411	.458	September/October	.333	3	1	0	0	0	0	0	1	.333	.333
Behind on Count	.138	94	13	4	0	0	8	0	28	.135	.181	Pre-All Star	.250	244	61	14	3	4	35	19	31	.300	.381
Two Strikes	.188	96	18	5	0	0	9	5	40	.223	.240	Post-All Star	.226	31	7	1	0	0	2	1	9	.242	.258

1992 By Position

Position	Avg	AB	H	2B	3B	HR	RBI	BB	SO	OBP	SLG	G	GS	Innings	PO	A	E	DP	Fld Pct	Rng Fctr	In Zone	Outs	Zone Rtg	MLB Zone
As Pinch Hitter	.375	8	3	1	0	0	1	1	1	.444	.500	11	0	---	---	---	---	---	---	---	---	---	---	---
As ss	.243	267	65	14	3	4	36	19	39	.289	.363	87	75	678.2	117	225	15	38	.958	4.54	268	229	.854	.885

Last Five Years

	Avg	AB	H	2B	3B	HR	RBI	BB	SO	OBP	SLG		Avg	AB	H	2B	3B	HR	RBI	BB	SO	OBP	SLG
vs. Left	.274	821	225	36	10	17	85	76	116	.334	.404	Scoring Posn	.270	489	132	27	1	8	160	52	82	.330	.378
vs. Right	.247	1238	306	47	7	20	122	72	215	.288	.345	Close & Late	.261	375	98	10	3	6	32	27	61	.309	.352
Groundball	.251	736	185	26	1	11	67	57	116	.305	.334	None on/out	.264	546	144	16	5	10	10	29	88	.304	.366
Flyball	.271	458	124	29	6	12	55	36	71	.325	.439	Batting #7	.252	652	164	29	4	12	68	39	115	.294	.363
Home	.257	986	253	33	8	17	108	74	170	.307	.358	Batting #8	.256	554	142	20	3	12	59	50	82	.315	.368
Away	.259	1073	278	50	9	20	99	74	161	.307	.378	Other	.264	853	225	34	10	13	80	59	134	.311	.373
Day	.239	574	137	27	2	8	44	39	91	.286	.334	April	.226	274	62	10	1	1	20	26	42	.292	.281
Night	.265	1485	394	56	15	29	163	110	240	.315	.382	May	.255	388	99	12	4	6	47	30	68	.307	.353
Grass	.253	833	211	37	6	9	71	73	145	.312	.345	June	.242	364	88	12	3	9	36	34	61	.305	.365
Turf	.261	1226	320	46	11	28	136	75	186	.303	.385	July	.279	326	91	14	4	5	33	13	53	.308	.393

Last Five Years

	Avg	AB	H	2B	3B	HR	RBI	BB	SO	OBP	SLG		Avg	AB	H	2B	3B	HR	RBI	BB	SO	OBP	SLG
First Pitch	.305	426	130	22	4	17	68	9	0	.315	.495	August	.259	351	91	21	2	6	39	25	56	.307	.382
Ahead on Count	.311	437	136	20	4	9	50	81	0	.415	.437	September/October	.281	356	100	14	3	10	32	20	51	.319	.421
Behind on Count	.196	759	149	25	3	5	52	2	235	.200	.257	Pre-All Star	.241	1118	269	41	10	16	114	93	191	.297	.338
Two Strikes	.184	784	144	24	5	4	50	48	331	.232	.242	Post-All Star	.278	941	262	42	7	21	93	55	140	.318	.405

Batter vs. Pitcher (since 1984)

Hits Best Against	Avg	AB	H	2B	3B	HR	RBI	BB	SO	OBP	SLG	Hits Worst Against	Avg	AB	H	2B	3B	HR	RBI	BB	SO	OBP	SLG
Jeff Robinson	.444	9	4	1	0	2	8	3	2	.583	1.222	Mark Langston	.067	15	1	1	0	0	0	1	7	.125	.133
Mark Davis	.400	10	4	0	1	2	4	3	2	.538	1.200	Lee Smith	.091	11	1	0	0	0	0	0	1	.091	.091
Scott Sanderson	.400	10	4	0	0	1	2	1	0	.417	.700	Norm Charlton	.100	10	1	0	0	0	0	1	3	.182	.100
Neal Heaton	.389	18	7	1	0	2	8	1	2	.421	.778	Randy Tomlin	.100	10	1	0	0	0	0	1	1	.182	.100
Jim Deshaies	.357	28	10	2	2	1	2	2	6	.400	.679	Brian Barnes	.125	16	2	0	0	0	0	0	4	.125	.125

Gary Thurman — Royals

Bats Right (groundball hitter)

	Avg	G	AB	R	H	2B	3B	HR	RBI	BB	SO	HBP	GDP	SB	CS	OBP	SLG	IBB	SH	SF	#Pit	#P/PA	GB	FB	G/F
1992 Season	.245	88	200	25	49	6	3	0	20	9	34	1	3	9	6	.281	.305	0	6	0	766	3.65	86	40	2.15
Last Five Years	.238	297	597	84	142	21	4	2	43	41	134	2	9	46	13	.288	.296	0	12	2	2401	3.74	236	115	2.05

1992 Season

	Avg	AB	H	2B	3B	HR	RBI	BB	SO	OBP	SLG		Avg	AB	H	2B	3B	HR	RBI	BB	SO	OBP	SLG
vs. Left	.244	123	30	5	3	0	15	5	19	.273	.333	Scoring Posn	.321	53	17	2	1	0	19	3	10	.357	.396
vs. Right	.247	77	19	1	0	0	5	4	15	.293	.260	Close & Late	.192	26	5	0	1	0	0	2	6	.276	.269
Home	.223	94	21	3	0	0	7	5	16	.270	.255	None on/out	.214	56	12	2	1	0	0	4	9	.267	.286
Away	.264	106	28	3	3	0	13	4	18	.291	.349	Batting #1	.291	55	16	0	0	0	4	4	9	.339	.291
First Pitch	.333	36	12	3	1	0	5	0	0	.333	.472	Batting #8	.298	57	17	3	1	0	10	1	8	.310	.386
Ahead on Count	.319	47	15	1	1	0	4	4	0	.373	.383	Other	.182	88	16	3	2	0	6	4	17	.226	.261
Behind on Count	.224	58	13	1	1	0	4	0	15	.224	.276	Pre-All Star	.243	103	25	3	3	0	11	4	18	.271	.330
Two Strikes	.157	89	14	1	1	0	11	5	34	.211	.191	Post-All Star	.247	97	24	3	0	0	9	5	16	.291	.278

Last Five Years

	Avg	AB	H	2B	3B	HR	RBI	BB	SO	OBP	SLG		Avg	AB	H	2B	3B	HR	RBI	BB	SO	OBP	SLG
vs. Left	.248	359	89	16	4	1	30	22	69	.291	.323	Scoring Posn	.252	151	38	4	1	0	39	14	37	.311	.291
vs. Right	.223	238	53	5	0	1	13	19	65	.284	.256	Close & Late	.244	86	21	2	1	0	7	7	27	.305	.291
Groundball	.286	161	46	4	2	1	16	9	31	.326	.354	None on/out	.226	190	43	8	1	2	2	14	39	.279	.311
Flyball	.241	158	38	7	1	0	6	14	36	.305	.316	Batting #1	.277	256	71	10	0	2	15	20	51	.332	.340
Home	.214	281	60	11	1	1	18	20	57	.270	.270	Batting #9	.194	93	18	1	2	0	3	10	26	.272	.247
Away	.259	316	82	10	3	1	25	21	77	.305	.320	Other	.214	248	53	10	2	0	25	11	57	.248	.270
Day	.230	165	38	4	1	0	13	14	42	.293	.267	April	.212	52	11	1	1	0	3	4	12	.268	.269
Night	.241	432	104	17	3	2	30	27	92	.286	.306	May	.265	98	26	5	1	1	13	10	23	.333	.367
Grass	.249	229	57	6	2	0	21	13	58	.288	.293	June	.170	100	17	2	1	0	4	2	20	.186	.210
Turf	.231	368	85	15	2	2	22	28	76	.288	.299	July	.286	91	26	5	1	1	4	8	22	.350	.396
First Pitch	.326	95	31	7	1	1	8	0	0	.326	.453	August	.263	80	21	2	0	0	11	5	15	.307	.288
Ahead on Count	.324	105	34	4	2	1	13	15	0	.405	.429	September/October	.233	176	41	6	0	0	8	12	42	.282	.267
Behind on Count	.184	207	38	4	1	0	9	0	66	.183	.213	Pre-All Star	.229	284	65	10	3	2	22	18	64	.277	.306
Two Strikes	.168	297	50	6	1	0	15	26	134	.240	.195	Post-All Star	.246	313	77	11	1	0	21	23	70	.298	.288

Batter vs. Pitcher (career)

Hits Best Against	Avg	AB	H	2B	3B	HR	RBI	BB	SO	OBP	SLG	Hits Worst Against	Avg	AB	H	2B	3B	HR	RBI	BB	SO	OBP	SLG
Dave Otto	.556	9	5	1	0	0	3	2	3	.636	.667	Curt Young	.067	15	1	0	0	0	1	1	5	.125	.067
Jimmy Key	.357	14	5	1	0	0	2	0	1	.357	.429	Jim Abbott	.100	20	2	0	0	0	0	2	3	.182	.100
Greg Swindell	.333	12	4	1	0	0	0	0	3	.333	.417	Mark Langston	.160	25	4	0	0	0	0	2	7	.222	.160
												Dave Fleming	.182	11	2	0	0	0	1	0	1	.182	.182
												Kevin Brown	.231	13	3	0	0	0	0	0	3	.231	.231

Mike Timlin — Blue Jays

Pitches Right (groundball pitcher)

	ERA	W	L	Sv	G	GS	IP	BB	SO	Avg	H	2B	3B	HR	RBI	OBP	SLG	GF	IR	IRS	Hld	SvOp	SB	CS	GB	FB	G/F
1992 Season	4.12	0	2	1	26	0	43.2	20	35	.271	45	6	0	0	29	.351	.307	14	23	8	1	1	4	3	70	27	2.59
Career (1991-1992)	3.43	11	8	4	89	3	152.0	70	120	.244	139	12	1	6	81	.327	.300	31	67	28	10	9	15	8	271	88	3.08

1992 Season

	ERA	W	L	Sv	G	GS	IP	H	HR	BB	SO		Avg	AB	H	2B	3B	HR	RBI	BB	SO	OBP	SLG
Home	5.84	0	2	1	14	0	24.2	26	0	15	21	vs. Left	.311	74	23	5	0	0	17	12	11	.407	.378
Away	1.89	0	0	0	12	0	19.0	19	0	5	14	vs. Right	.239	92	22	1	0	0	12	8	24	.304	.250
Starter	0.00	0	0	0	0	0	0.0	0	0	0	0	Scoring Posn	.262	61	16	2	0	0	29	15	14	.410	.295
Reliever	4.12	0	2	1	26	0	43.2	45	0	20	35	Close & Late	.304	23	7	1	0	0	4	6	5	.433	.348
0 Days rest	4.50	0	0	0	2	0	4.0	4	0	0	2	None on/out	.257	35	9	2	0	0	0	3	5	.316	.314
1 or 2 Days rest	3.63	0	2	0	10	0	17.1	17	0	12	9	First Pitch	.381	21	8	0	0	0	0	3	0	.458	.381
3+ Days rest	4.43	0	0	1	14	0	22.1	24	0	8	24	Behind on Count	.324	34	11	0	0	0	4	7	0	.439	.324
Pre-All Star	1.98	0	1	0	8	0	13.2	12	0	8	14	Ahead on Count	.241	87	21	4	0	0	17	0	32	.247	.287
Post-All Star	5.10	0	1	1	18	0	30.0	33	0	12	21	Two Strikes	.215	79	17	3	0	0	15	10	35	.308	.253

Career (1991-1992)

	ERA	W	L	Sv	G	GS	IP	H	HR	BB	SO		Avg	AB	H	2B	3B	HR	RBI	BB	SO	OBP	SLG
Home	3.35	7	4	2	47	2	86.0	85	2	39	62	vs. Left	.300	243	73	7	1	3	39	39	38	.396	.374
Away	3.55	4	4	2	42	1	66.0	54	4	31	58	vs. Right	.202	327	66	5	0	3	42	31	82	.272	.245
Day	2.18	4	3	1	33	1	53.2	37	2	27	37	Inning 1-6	.283	226	64	3	0	2	43	30	46	.369	.323
Night	4.12	7	5	3	56	2	98.1	102	4	43	83	Inning 7+	.218	344	75	9	1	4	38	40	74	.299	.285
Grass	3.76	2	4	2	32	1	55.0	43	4	27	54	None on	.198	308	61	6	0	2	2	29	67	.267	.237
Turf	3.25	9	4	2	57	2	97.0	96	2	43	66	Runners on	.298	262	78	6	1	4	79	41	53	.393	.374
April	3.12	3	0	0	9	0	17.1	11	3	5	13	Scoring Posn	.278	176	49	5	0	2	74	37	42	.404	.341
May	5.06	1	2	2	13	0	16.0	16	1	13	12	Close & Late	.243	181	44	4	0	3	24	26	37	.337	.315
June	2.38	2	3	0	14	3	34.0	34	0	15	24	None on/out	.181	127	23	3	0	0	0	12	28	.252	.205
July	3.82	3	3	1	18	0	33.0	27	1	15	27	vs. 1st Batr (relief)	.243	74	18	2	0	0	12	11	12	.341	.270
August	4.10	0	0	0	12	0	26.1	25	1	10	23	First Inning Pitched	.271	310	84	7	0	4	55	40	56	.355	.332
September/October	2.84	2	0	1	23	0	25.1	26	0	12	21	First 15 Pitches	.268	280	75	8	1	2	41	29	42	.338	.325
Starter	1.84	1	1	0	3	3	14.2	14	0	7	10	Pitch 16-30	.216	171	37	2	0	2	23	26	46	.320	.263
Reliever	3.60	10	7	4	86	0	137.1	125	6	63	110	Pitch 31-45	.237	76	18	2	0	2	14	10	19	.326	.342
0 Days rest	2.35	3	0	0	15	0	23.0	17	0	9	15	Pitch 46+	.209	43	9	0	0	0	3	5	13	.292	.209
1 or 2 Days rest	3.23	5	6	2	40	0	69.2	60	4	30	52	Ahead on Count	.233	296	69	6	1	1	42	0	101	.237	.270
3+ Days rest	4.84	2	1	2	31	0	44.2	48	2	24	43	Behind on Count	.294	109	32	2	0	0	13	34	0	.458	.312
Pre-All Star	2.87	7	5	2	41	3	78.1	65	4	36	59	Two Strikes	.203	276	56	4	1	3	38	23	120	.266	.257
Post-All Star	4.03	4	3	2	48	0	73.2	74	2	34	61												

Ron Tingley — Angels

Bats Right

	Avg	G	AB	R	H	2B	3B	HR	RBI	BB	SO	HBP	GDP	SB	CS	OBP	SLG	IBB	SH	SF	#Pit	#P/PA	GB	FB	G/F
1992 Season	.197	71	127	15	25	2	1	3	8	13	35	2	4	0	1	.282	.299	0	5	0	561	3.95	44	32	1.38
Last Five Years	.195	134	272	27	53	9	1	5	23	25	78	3	7	1	2	.270	.290	0	9	0	1234	4.11	90	68	1.32

1992 Season

	Avg	AB	H	2B	3B	HR	RBI	BB	SO	OBP	SLG		Avg	AB	H	2B	3B	HR	RBI	BB	SO	OBP	SLG
vs. Left	.200	35	7	1	0	1	1	2	12	.263	.314	Scoring Posn	.120	25	3	0	0	0	3	1	7	.185	.120
vs. Right	.196	92	18	1	1	2	7	11	23	.288	.293	Close & Late	.182	22	4	0	1	0	1	0	7	.182	.273
Home	.273	55	15	1	1	2	7	6	12	.355	.436	None on/out	.268	41	11	1	0	0	0	2	9	.302	.293
Away	.139	72	10	1	0	1	1	7	23	.225	.194	Batting #8	.165	97	16	2	1	3	7	7	27	.236	.299
First Pitch	.250	12	3	0	0	0	0	0	0	.250	.250	Batting #9	.389	18	7	0	0	0	1	4	4	.500	.389
Ahead on Count	.387	31	12	2	0	2	3	5	0	.472	.645	Other	.167	12	2	0	0	0	0	2	4	.286	.167
Behind on Count	.167	42	7	0	1	1	3	0	17	.205	.286	Pre-All Star	.180	61	11	2	0	3	4	3	13	.219	.361
Two Strikes	.095	63	6	0	1	0	3	8	35	.208	.127	Post-All Star	.212	66	14	0	1	0	4	10	22	.333	.242

Randy Tomlin — Pirates

Pitches Left (groundball pitcher)

	ERA	W	L	Sv	G	GS	IP	BB	SO	Avg	H	2B	3B	HR	RBI	OBP	SLG	CG	ShO	Sup	QS	#P/S	SB	CS	GB	FB	G/F
1992 Season	3.41	14	9	0	35	33	208.2	42	90	.282	226	45	7	11	75	.320	.397	1	1	3.97	20	90	21	8	350	201	1.74
Career (1990-1992)	3.10	26	20	0	78	72	461.1	108	236	.262	260	90	14	25	158	.308	.372	7	3	4.12	46	91	40	26	751	453	1.66

1992 Season

	ERA	W	L	Sv	G	GS	IP	H	HR	BB	SO		Avg	AB	H	2B	3B	HR	RBI	BB	SO	OBP	SLG
Home	2.37	7	3	0	16	16	110.0	111	4	13	56	vs. Left	.250	148	37	5	0	2	9	11	26	.304	.324
Away	4.56	7	6	0	19	17	98.2	115	7	29	34	vs. Right	.289	653	189	40	7	9	66	31	64	.324	.413
Day	4.03	3	5	0	13	12	76.0	85	6	21	34	Inning 1-6	.278	688	191	40	7	7	61	36	71	.317	.387
Night	3.05	11	4	0	22	21	132.2	141	5	21	56	Inning 7+	.310	113	35	5	0	4	14	6	19	.342	.460
Grass	4.50	4	4	0	11	10	58.0	67	3	17	16	None on	.285	471	134	25	4	6	6	22	55	.321	.393
Turf	2.99	10	5	0	24	23	150.2	159	8	25	74	Runners on	.279	330	92	20	3	5	69	20	35	.319	.403
April	1.67	4	0	0	4	4	27.0	19	1	10	10	Scoring Posn	.268	194	52	11	2	3	58	17	21	.323	.392
May	7.33	1	3	0	6	6	23.1	42	2	10	8	Close & Late	.229	70	16	3	0	1	5	5	16	.280	.314
June	2.22	5	1	0	6	6	44.2	42	4	5	22	None on/out	.330	212	70	13	1	4	4	8	20	.363	.458
July	5.45	0	3	0	6	5	33.0	45	1	6	11	vs. 1st Batr (relief)	.500	2	1	0	0	0	1	0	0	.500	.500
August	2.68	1	1	0	6	6	43.2	42	2	6	19	First Inning Pitched	.248	125	31	7	2	1	11	7	11	.289	.360
September/October	2.68	1	1	0	7	6	37.0	38	1	5	20	First 75 Pitches	.285	643	183	37	6	7	55	32	66	.319	.393
Starter	3.44	14	9	0	33	33	206.2	224	11	42	89	Pitch 76-90	.318	88	28	6	1	2	13	5	13	.375	.477
Reliever	0.00	0	0	0	2	0	2.0	2	0	0	1	Pitch 91-105	.137	51	7	0	0	2	4	3	8	.182	.255
0-3 Days Rest	0.00	0	0	0	0	0	0.0	0	0	0	0	Pitch 106+	.421	19	8	2	0	0	3	2	3	.476	.526
4 Days Rest	3.39	10	4	0	22	22	143.1	156	8	29	61	First Pitch	.320	125	40	6	1	1	11	3	0	.346	.408
5+ Days Rest	3.55	4	5	0	11	11	63.1	68	3	13	28	Ahead on Count	.232	336	78	15	3	5	26	0	76	.238	.339
Pre-All Star	3.47	10	5	0	19	18	109.0	119	8	26	48	Behind on Count	.298	181	54	16	2	3	23	28	0	.387	.459
Post-All Star	3.34	4	4	0	16	15	99.2	107	3	16	42	Two Strikes	.214	332	71	13	1	4	24	11	90	.243	.295

Career (1990-1992)

	ERA	W	L	Sv	G	GS	IP	H	HR	BB	SO		Avg	AB	H	2B	3B	HR	RBI	BB	SO	OBP	SLG
Home	2.67	14	10	0	40	38	253.0	237	12	42	146	vs. Left	.220	327	72	10	0	5	24	25	67	.283	.297
Away	3.63	12	10	0	38	34	208.1	221	13	66	90	vs. Right	.271	1423	386	80	14	20	134	83	169	.313	.389
Day	3.71	4	10	0	26	22	145.2	158	10	35	69	Inning 1-6	.258	1505	389	79	14	18	136	90	200	.303	.365
Night	2.82	22	10	0	52	50	315.2	300	15	73	167	Inning 7+	.282	245	69	11	0	7	22	18	36	.335	.412
Grass	3.41	6	5	0	20	17	108.1	109	8	32	38	None on	.259	1025	265	51	6	15	15	68	134	.309	.364
Turf	3.01	20	15	0	58	55	353.0	349	17	76	198	Runners on	.266	725	193	39	8	10	143	40	102	.306	.383

440

Career (1990-1992)

	ERA	W	L	Sv	G	GS	IP	H	HR	BB	SO		Avg	AB	H	2B	3B	HR	RBI	BB	SO	OBP	SLG
April	2.11	6	0	0	7	7	47.0	35	4	15	15	Scoring Posn	.271	391	106	22	4	4	121	35	54	.329	.379
May	5.18	2	4	0	11	9	41.2	60	2	17	20	Close & Late	.270	137	37	9	0	4	11	10	24	.329	.423
June	2.62	5	3	0	11	10	68.2	62	4	14	40	None on/out	.280	454	127	22	2	7	7	31	51	.333	.383
July	3.25	3	3	0	10	9	63.2	68	3	17	28	vs. 1st Batr (relief)	.200	5	1	0	0	0	1	1	1	.333	.200
August	3.05	6	4	0	18	18	121.0	107	7	21	65	First Inning Pitched	.254	287	73	17	2	5	32	24	31	.313	.380
September/October	3.02	4	6	0	21	19	119.1	126	5	24	68	First 75 Pitches	.251	1376	346	73	9	16	108	78	183	.294	.352
Starter	3.16	26	20	0	72	72	453.1	454	25	106	230	Pitch 76-90	.348	210	73	10	4	5	36	18	30	.405	.505
Reliever	0.00	0	0	0	6	0	8.0	4	0	2	6	Pitch 91-105	.209	110	23	4	1	3	8	8	17	.267	.345
0-3 Days Rest	3.38	1	2	0	3	3	16.0	21	1	5	11	Pitch 106+	.296	54	16	3	0	1	6	4	6	.356	.407
4 Days Rest	3.36	15	11	0	45	45	284.1	291	18	60	141	First Pitch	.332	244	81	19	1	1	29	7	0	.355	.430
5+ Days Rest	2.76	10	7	0	24	24	153.0	142	6	41	78	Ahead on Count	.229	765	175	29	6	11	63	0	198	.234	.325
Pre-All Star	3.25	13	8	0	33	29	177.0	181	13	50	84	Behind on Count	.265	400	106	27	3	7	39	67	0	.369	.400
Post-All Star	3.01	13	12	0	45	43	284.1	277	12	58	152	Two Strikes	.194	738	143	24	2	11	48	34	236	.234	.276

Pitcher vs. Batter (career)

Pitches Best Vs.	Avg	AB	H	2B	3B	HR	RBI	BB	SO	OBP	SLG	Pitches Worst Vs.	Avg	AB	H	2B	3B	HR	RBI	BB	SO	OBP	SLG
Fred McGriff	.000	19	0	0	0	0	1	3	6	.130	.000	Charlie Hayes	.600	10	6	1	0	0	1	1	1	.636	.700
Darrin Jackson	.000	11	0	0	0	0	0	1	2	.083	.000	Ryne Sandberg	.560	25	14	2	2	1	5	2	0	.593	.920
Vince Coleman	.050	20	1	0	0	0	0	0	3	.050	.050	Tony Gwynn	.450	20	9	1	0	1	3	0	0	.450	.650
Andres Galarraga	.083	12	1	0	0	0	0	0	4	.083	.083	Kevin Ward	.417	12	5	0	0	2	2	1	4	.462	.917
Charlie O'Brien	.125	16	2	0	0	0	0	0	1	.125	.125	Jerald Clark	.385	13	5	1	0	1	2	0	0	.385	.692

Alan Trammell — Tigers
Bats Right

	Avg	G	AB	R	H	2B	3B	HR	RBI	BB	SO	HBP	GDP	SB	CS	OBP	SLG	IBB	SH	SF	#Pit	#P/PA	GB	FB	G/F
1992 Season	.275	29	102	11	28	7	1	1	11	15	4	1	6	2	2	.370	.392	0	1	1	433	3.64	40	29	1.38
Last Five Years	.279	525	1951	266	545	108	6	44	267	211	189	13	47	42	20	.350	.409	17	12	20	7830	3.57	672	658	1.02

1992 Season

	Avg	AB	H	2B	3B	HR	RBI	BB	SO	OBP	SLG		Avg	AB	H	2B	3B	HR	RBI	BB	SO	OBP	SLG
vs. Left	.357	28	10	4	0	0	6	3	0	.406	.500	Scoring Posn	.455	22	10	3	0	0	10	4	0	.519	.591
vs. Right	.243	74	18	3	1	1	5	12	4	.356	.351	Close & Late	.143	14	2	0	0	0	1	1	1	.200	.143
Home	.229	48	11	3	1	0	3	8	1	.339	.333	None on/out	.385	13	5	1	1	0	0	1	1	.429	.615
Away	.315	54	17	4	0	1	8	7	3	.397	.444	Total	.275	102	28	7	1	1	11	15	4	.370	.392
First Pitch	.250	12	3	0	0	1	0	0	0	.250	.250	Batting #3	.275	102	28	7	1	1	11	15	4	.370	.392
Ahead on Count	.351	37	13	4	1	1	7	11	0	.500	.595	Other	.000	0	0	0	0	0	0	0	0	.000	.000
Behind on Count	.233	30	7	3	0	0	1	0	3	.233	.333	Pre-All Star	.275	102	28	7	1	1	11	15	4	.370	.392
Two Strikes	.192	26	5	2	0	0	2	4	4	.300	.269	Post-All Star	.000	0	0	0	0	0	0	0	0	.000	.000

Last Five Years

	Avg	AB	H	2B	3B	HR	RBI	BB	SO	OBP	SLG		Avg	AB	H	2B	3B	HR	RBI	BB	SO	OBP	SLG
vs. Left	.291	615	179	41	1	17	84	65	44	.357	.444	Scoring Posn	.313	502	157	32	1	12	222	73	47	.389	.452
vs. Right	.274	1336	366	67	5	27	183	146	145	.347	.392	Close & Late	.297	293	87	16	0	7	47	40	35	.387	.423
Groundball	.289	540	156	31	1	11	75	48	49	.347	.411	None on/out	.258	384	99	15	1	11	11	26	34	.305	.388
Flyball	.278	446	124	26	2	10	68	55	45	.356	.413	Batting #3	.288	871	251	55	1	25	136	96	81	.359	.440
Home	.285	988	282	55	4	24	162	110	76	.358	.422	Batting #4	.281	604	170	26	2	14	70	63	62	.348	.401
Away	.273	963	263	53	2	20	105	101	113	.343	.395	Other	.261	476	124	27	3	5	61	52	46	.337	.351
Day	.286	654	187	37	3	14	83	71	65	.359	.416	April	.276	380	105	25	2	8	48	44	38	.356	.416
Night	.276	1297	358	71	3	30	184	140	124	.346	.405	May	.295	413	122	21	1	7	51	54	38	.374	.402
Grass	.279	1666	464	93	5	39	238	180	160	.349	.411	June	.279	315	88	9	0	10	47	31	34	.344	.403
Turf	.284	285	81	15	1	5	29	31	29	.356	.396	July	.268	257	69	16	2	4	24	32	23	.352	.393
First Pitch	.308	224	69	7	0	4	31	1	0	.306	.393	August	.287	341	98	24	1	10	57	25	26	.332	.452
Ahead on Count	.334	548	183	45	2	22	105	139	0	.467	.544	September/October	.257	245	63	13	0	5	40	25	30	.333	.371
Behind on Count	.276	692	191	38	1	14	86	2	104	.282	.395	Pre-All Star	.281	1162	326	57	3	25	149	137	117	.357	.399
Two Strikes	.234	723	169	36	2	15	83	60	188	.296	.354	Post-All Star	.278	789	219	51	3	19	118	74	72	.341	.422

Batter vs. Pitcher (since 1984)

Hits Best Against	Avg	AB	H	2B	3B	HR	RBI	BB	SO	OBP	SLG	Hits Worst Against	Avg	AB	H	2B	3B	HR	RBI	BB	SO	OBP	SLG
Bobby Thigpen	.600	10	6	0	0	0	3	3	0	.692	.600	Luis Aquino	.059	17	1	0	0	0	0	1	0	.111	.059
Greg Harris	.458	24	11	4	0	1	6	4	2	.536	.750	Bob Milacki	.067	30	2	0	0	0	0	5	5	.200	.067
Tom Gordon	.455	11	5	0	0	2	3	3	1	.571	1.000	Bobby Ojeda	.067	15	1	0	0	0	0	3	3	.222	.067
Jim Acker	.400	10	4	1	0	1	2	1	1	.455	.800	Scott Sanderson	.071	14	1	0	0	0	0	1	0	.133	.143
Dennis Rasmussen	.385	26	10	2	1	2	4	3	3	.448	.769	Jose Rijo	.091	11	1	0	0	0	0	0	0	.091	.091

Jeff Treadway — Braves
Bats Left

	Avg	G	AB	R	H	2B	3B	HR	RBI	BB	SO	HBP	GDP	SB	CS	OBP	SLG	IBB	SH	SF	#Pit	#P/PA	GB	FB	G/F
1992 Season	.222	61	126	5	28	6	1	0	5	9	16	0	3	1	2	.274	.286	4	1	0	459	3.40	40	45	0.89
Last Five Years	.278	532	1680	190	467	80	12	24	159	114	145	8	34	11	10	.324	.383	16	18	18	5930	3.26	594	568	1.05

1992 Season

	Avg	AB	H	2B	3B	HR	RBI	BB	SO	OBP	SLG		Avg	AB	H	2B	3B	HR	RBI	BB	SO	OBP	SLG
vs. Left	.100	10	1	0	0	0	0	2	2	.250	.100	Scoring Posn	.160	25	4	0	1	0	5	4	3	.276	.240
vs. Right	.233	116	27	6	1	0	5	7	14	.276	.302	Close & Late	.056	18	1	0	0	0	0	1	3	.105	.056

1992 Season

	Avg	AB	H	2B	3B	HR	RBI	BB	SO	OBP	SLG		Avg	AB	H	2B	3B	HR	RBI	BB	SO	OBP	SLG
Home	.234	64	15	3	1	0	3	3	7	.269	.313	None on/out	.192	26	5	1	0	0	0	1	3	.222	.231
Away	.210	62	13	3	0	0	2	6	9	.279	.258	Batting #2	.206	68	14	2	1	0	4	3	11	.239	.265
First Pitch	.278	18	5	0	0	0	0	4	0	.409	.278	Batting #8	.133	15	2	0	0	0	0	3	2	.278	.133
Ahead on Count	.231	26	6	1	0	0	1	3	0	.310	.269	Other	.279	43	12	4	0	0	1	3	3	.326	.372
Behind on Count	.224	49	11	2	0	0	2	0	9	.224	.265	Pre-All Star	.154	26	4	2	0	0	1	1	6	.185	.231
Two Strikes	.211	57	12	3	1	0	3	2	16	.237	.298	Post-All Star	.240	100	24	4	1	0	4	8	10	.296	.300

Last Five Years

	Avg	AB	H	2B	3B	HR	RBI	BB	SO	OBP	SLG		Avg	AB	H	2B	3B	HR	RBI	BB	SO	OBP	SLG
vs. Left	.247	288	71	7	1	4	33	21	34	.299	.319	Scoring Posn	.294	354	104	16	3	5	128	45	29	.359	.398
vs. Right	.284	1392	396	73	11	20	126	93	111	.329	.396	Close & Late	.260	269	70	9	4	3	34	17	29	.302	.357
Groundball	.276	608	168	25	5	5	44	34	48	.314	.359	None on/out	.271	388	105	18	3	7	7	14	33	.300	.387
Flyball	.282	397	112	22	2	7	39	32	39	.335	.401	Batting #2	.286	962	275	44	5	18	107	60	74	.327	.398
Home	.277	813	225	39	5	10	76	63	59	.331	.374	Batting #8	.240	275	66	11	4	1	12	24	31	.302	.320
Away	.279	867	242	41	7	14	83	51	86	.316	.391	Other	.284	443	126	25	3	5	40	30	40	.331	.388
Day	.263	457	120	24	2	4	40	31	54	.310	.350	April	.264	220	58	9	3	4	23	11	13	.296	.386
Night	.284	1223	347	56	10	20	119	83	91	.329	.395	May	.337	276	93	13	3	4	30	23	14	.388	.449
Grass	.269	1062	286	44	6	12	90	73	99	.317	.356	June	.284	345	98	21	1	5	28	21	46	.327	.394
Turf	.293	618	181	36	6	12	69	41	46	.335	.429	July	.248	303	75	11	2	6	31	22	29	.298	.356
First Pitch	.330	351	116	17	5	6	41	8	0	.342	.459	August	.277	325	90	13	1	4	21	18	24	.313	.360
Ahead on Count	.316	418	132	24	2	8	40	77	0	.420	.444	September/October	.251	211	53	13	2	1	26	19	19	.312	.346
Behind on Count	.232	543	126	16	3	3	43	0	87	.239	.289	Pre-All Star	.284	950	270	44	7	16	90	62	90	.328	.396
Two Strikes	.211	596	126	24	4	7	52	22	145	.244	.300	Post-All Star	.270	730	197	36	5	8	69	52	55	.317	.366

Batter vs. Pitcher (career)

Hits Best Against	Avg	AB	H	2B	3B	HR	RBI	BB	SO	OBP	SLG	Hits Worst Against	Avg	AB	H	2B	3B	HR	RBI	BB	SO	OBP	SLG
Don Robinson	.500	16	8	2	0	1	6	1	2	.529	.813	Bill Gullickson	.167	12	2	0	0	0	1	0	0	.167	.167
Wally Whitehurst	.500	12	6	3	0	0	1	0	0	.500	.750	Jimmy Jones	.176	17	3	0	0	0	1	0	2	.176	.176
Bob Tewksbury	.500	10	5	0	0	0	2	2	0	.583	.500	Mark Grant	.182	11	2	0	0	0	1	1	1	.231	.182
Orel Hershiser	.350	20	7	2	0	1	2	3	0	.435	.600	Paul Assenmacher	.182	11	2	0	0	0	2	0	1	.182	.182
Doug Drabek	.344	32	11	3	0	2	7	3	2	.400	.625	Greg Maddux	.188	32	6	0	0	0	1	1	1	.212	.188

Ricky Trlicek — Blue Jays
Pitches Right (groundball pitcher)

	ERA	W	L	Sv	G	GS	IP	BB	SO	Avg	H	2B	3B	HR	RBI	OBP	SLG	GF	IR	IRS	Hld	SvOp	SB	CS	GB	FB	G/F
1992 Season	10.80	0	0	0	2	0	1.2	2	1	.286	4	0	0	0	2	.444	.286	0	2	1	0	0	0	0	2	1	2.00

1992 Season

	ERA	W	L	Sv	G	GS	IP	H	HR	BB	SO		Avg	AB	H	2B	3B	HR	RBI	BB	SO	OBP	SLG
Home	0.00	0	0	0	1	0	1.0	0	0	0	0	vs. Left	.000	2	0	0	0	0	0	1	1	.333	.000
Away	27.00	0	0	0	1	0	0.2	2	0	2	1	vs. Right	.400	5	2	0	0	0	2	1	0	.500	.400

Mike Trombley — Twins
Pitches Right

	ERA	W	L	Sv	G	GS	IP	BB	SO	Avg	H	2B	3B	HR	RBI	OBP	SLG	CG	ShO	Sup	QS	#P/S	SB	CS	GB	FB	G/F
1992 Season	3.30	3	2	0	10	7	46.1	17	38	.247	43	12	0	5	18	.318	.402	0	0	3.50	2	85	2	3	59	48	1.23

1992 Season

	ERA	W	L	Sv	G	GS	IP	H	HR	BB	SO		Avg	AB	H	2B	3B	HR	RBI	BB	SO	OBP	SLG
Home	3.50	1	0	0	4	2	18.0	15	3	5	17	vs. Left	.278	79	22	7	0	2	10	10	17	.360	.443
Away	3.18	2	2	0	6	5	28.1	28	2	12	21	vs. Right	.221	95	21	5	0	3	8	7	21	.282	.368

Scooter Tucker — Astros
Bats Right (flyball hitter)

	Avg	G	AB	R	H	2B	3B	HR	RBI	BB	SO	HBP	GDP	SB	CS	OBP	SLG	IBB	SH	SF	#Pit	#P/PA	GB	FB	G/F
1992 Season	.120	20	50	5	6	1	0	0	3	3	13	2	2	1	1	.200	.140	0	1	0	223	4.05	16	18	0.89

1992 Season

	Avg	AB	H	2B	3B	HR	RBI	BB	SO	OBP	SLG		Avg	AB	H	2B	3B	HR	RBI	BB	SO	OBP	SLG
vs. Left	.105	19	2	0	0	0	2	2	5	.227	.105	Scoring Posn	.083	12	1	0	0	0	2	1	4	.214	.083
vs. Right	.129	31	4	1	0	0	1	1	8	.182	.161	Close & Late	.167	6	1	0	0	0	0	0	2	.167	.167

Shane Turner — Mariners
Bats Left (groundball hitter)

	Avg	G	AB	R	H	2B	3B	HR	RBI	BB	SO	HBP	GDP	SB	CS	OBP	SLG	IBB	SH	SF	#Pit	#P/PA	GB	FB	G/F
1992 Season	.270	34	74	8	20	5	0	0	5	9	15	0	4	2	1	.341	.338	0	2	2	343	4.04	27	11	2.45
Career (1988-1992)	.236	56	110	9	26	5	0	0	6	14	24	0	5	2	1	.317	.282	0	2	2	482	3.83	46	19	2.42

1992 Season

	Avg	AB	H	2B	3B	HR	RBI	BB	SO	OBP	SLG		Avg	AB	H	2B	3B	HR	RBI	BB	SO	OBP	SLG
vs. Left	.000	0	0	0	0	0	0	0	0	.000	.000	Scoring Posn	.308	13	4	2	0	0	5	1	5	.313	.462
vs. Right	.270	74	20	5	0	0	5	9	15	.341	.338	Close & Late	.250	16	4	1	0	0	2	3	5	.333	.313

Jose Uribe — Giants

Bats Both

	Avg	G	AB	R	H	2B	3B	HR	RBI	BB	SO	HBP	GDP	SB	CS	OBP	SLG	IBB	SH	SF	#Pit	#P/PA	GB	FB	G/F
1992 Season	.241	66	162	24	39	9	1	2	13	14	25	0	3	2	2	.299	.346	3	4	1	636	3.59	59	53	1.11
Last Five Years	.238	586	1754	163	417	47	24	8	114	133	250	0	23	30	31	.290	.306	44	19	7	6234	3.29	674	550	1.23

1992 Season

	Avg	AB	H	2B	3B	HR	RBI	BB	SO	OBP	SLG		Avg	AB	H	2B	3B	HR	RBI	BB	SO	OBP	SLG
vs. Left	.302	53	16	4	1	1	6	3	9	.333	.472	Scoring Posn	.355	31	11	3	0	0	11	6	5	.447	.452
vs. Right	.211	109	23	5	0	1	7	11	16	.283	.284	Close & Late	.256	39	10	3	0	0	2	3	8	.310	.333
Home	.275	69	19	6	0	0	6	4	9	.311	.362	None on/out	.196	46	9	1	1	1	1	5	9	.275	.326
Away	.215	93	20	3	1	2	7	10	16	.291	.333	Batting #8	.247	150	37	8	1	2	11	13	22	.305	.353
First Pitch	.235	34	8	0	0	1	3	3	0	.297	.324	Batting #9	.125	8	1	0	0	0	1	0	2	.125	.125
Ahead on Count	.250	32	8	2	1	1	2	5	0	.342	.469	Other	.250	4	1	1	0	0	1	1	1	.400	.500
Behind on Count	.140	50	7	2	0	0	1	0	15	.140	.180	Pre-All Star	.257	101	26	8	1	1	10	6	16	.296	.386
Two Strikes	.191	68	13	2	0	0	4	6	25	.257	.221	Post-All Star	.213	61	13	1	0	1	3	8	9	.304	.279

Last Five Years

	Avg	AB	H	2B	3B	HR	RBI	BB	SO	OBP	SLG		Avg	AB	H	2B	3B	HR	RBI	BB	SO	OBP	SLG
vs. Left	.268	557	149	18	6	3	43	43	63	.317	.338	Scoring Posn	.243	395	96	10	7	2	101	65	59	.345	.319
vs. Right	.224	1197	268	29	18	5	71	90	187	.278	.291	Close & Late	.229	266	61	7	2	1	13	28	43	.303	.282
Groundball	.281	644	181	24	7	5	53	44	83	.327	.363	None on/out	.241	444	107	13	4	3	21	64	275	.309	
Flyball	.222	396	88	10	8	2	22	31	66	.277	.303	Batting #7	.213	47	10	1	1	0	5	7	6	.315	.277
Home	.242	819	198	25	9	1	46	63	122	.295	.298	Batting #8	.240	1680	403	44	23	8	107	124	234	.291	.308
Away	.234	935	219	22	15	7	68	70	128	.287	.312	Other	.148	27	4	2	0	0	2	2	10	.207	.222
Day	.229	738	169	23	9	4	37	46	106	.274	.301	April	.229	240	55	4	4	0	15	18	41	.282	.279
Night	.244	1016	248	24	15	4	77	87	144	.302	.309	May	.265	339	90	9	4	5	22	31	50	.326	.360
Grass	.236	1229	290	33	13	2	82	99	180	.291	.289	June	.251	303	76	9	7	1	23	17	35	.289	.337
Turf	.242	525	127	14	11	6	32	34	70	.288	.345	July	.227	322	73	11	4	0	17	19	40	.269	.286
First Pitch	.268	310	83	9	1	2	22	16	0	.303	.323	August	.226	319	72	10	4	1	25	29	49	.289	.292
Ahead on Count	.306	435	133	11	9	3	31	61	0	.390	.393	September/October	.221	231	51	4	1	1	12	19	35	.279	.260
Behind on Count	.204	598	122	14	11	1	33	5	148	.210	.269	Pre-All Star	.253	989	250	27	18	6	67	72	137	.302	.335
Two Strikes	.163	676	110	7	10	2	31	37	248	.205	.212	Post-All Star	.218	765	167	20	6	2	47	61	113	.275	.268

Batter vs. Pitcher (career)

Hits Best Against	Avg	AB	H	2B	3B	HR	RBI	BB	SO	OBP	SLG	Hits Worst Against	Avg	AB	H	2B	3B	HR	RBI	BB	SO	OBP	SLG
Danny Jackson	.462	26	12	0	0	0	0	2	0	.500	.462	Tim Crews	.000	12	0	0	0	0	0	0	3	.000	.000
Jose DeLeon	.455	22	10	0	2	0	2	4	3	.538	.636	Joe Boever	.000	11	0	0	0	0	0	0	2	.000	.000
Tim Burke	.429	14	6	2	0	1	4	1	0	.467	.786	Mark Portugal	.067	15	1	0	0	0	0	2	6	.176	.067
Ron Robinson	.400	15	6	0	1	0	2	2	0	.471	.533	Doug Drabek	.095	21	2	0	0	0	1	1	4	.136	.095
Lance McCullers	.400	10	4	0	0	1	2	2	2	.500	.700	Tim Belcher	.095	21	2	0	0	0	0	0	4	.095	.095

Sergio Valdez — Expos

Pitches Right

	ERA	W	L	Sv	G	GS	IP	BB	SO	Avg	H	2B	3B	HR	RBI	OBP	SLG	GF	IR	IRS	Hld	SvOp	SB	CS	GB	FB	G/F
1992 Season	2.41	0	2	0	27	0	37.1	12	32	.185	25	5	1	2	15	.252	.281	9	18	9	0	0	9	1	54	31	1.74
Last Five Years	4.64	8	10	0	82	14	194.0	72	135	.251	186	41	2	27	104	.316	.421	17	52	17	1	1	18	6	276	212	1.30

1992 Season

	ERA	W	L	Sv	G	GS	IP	H	HR	BB	SO		Avg	AB	H	2B	3B	HR	RBI	BB	SO	OBP	SLG
Home	4.50	0	0	0	12	0	14.0	12	1	3	8	vs. Left	.225	71	16	1	1	1	8	8	14	.304	.310
Away	1.16	0	2	0	15	0	23.1	13	1	9	24	vs. Right	.141	64	9	4	0	1	7	4	18	.191	.250
Starter	0.00	0	0	0	0	0	0.0	0	0	0	0	Scoring Posn	.238	42	10	3	0	0	13	4	8	.304	.310
Reliever	2.41	0	2	0	27	0	37.1	25	2	12	32	Close & Late	.167	24	4	0	0	0	1	2	5	.231	.167
0 Days rest	1.93	0	1	0	6	0	9.1	6	1	3	10	None on/out	.161	31	5	0	0	2	2	4	6	.257	.355
1 or 2 Days rest	1.32	0	1	0	10	0	13.2	10	0	4	8	First Pitch	.294	17	5	4	0	0	6	0	0	.294	.529
3+ Days rest	3.77	0	0	0	11	0	14.1	9	1	5	14	Behind on Count	.296	27	8	0	0	1	2	4	0	.387	.407
Pre-All Star	0.00	0	1	0	7	0	9.0	5	0	5	8	Ahead on Count	.130	69	9	0	1	1	4	0	29	.130	.203
Post-All Star	3.18	0	1	0	20	0	28.1	20	2	7	24	Two Strikes	.092	65	6	1	1	0	2	8	32	.192	.138

Last Five Years

	ERA	W	L	Sv	G	GS	IP	H	HR	BB	SO		Avg	AB	H	2B	3B	HR	RBI	BB	SO	OBP	SLG
Home	4.00	4	3	0	40	5	96.2	87	12	26	62	vs. Left	.222	352	78	13	2	10	41	45	57	.308	.355
Away	5.27	4	7	0	42	9	97.1	99	15	46	73	vs. Right	.278	389	108	28	0	17	63	27	78	.323	.481
Day	5.93	2	4	0	23	5	44.0	50	9	13	33	Inning 1-6	.265	461	122	30	0	15	72	43	83	.325	.427
Night	4.26	6	6	0	59	9	150.0	136	18	59	102	Inning 7+	.229	280	64	11	2	12	32	29	52	.301	.411
Grass	5.09	6	9	0	50	11	139.2	140	23	50	100	None on	.237	426	101	20	1	18	18	40	83	.304	.415
Turf	3.48	2	1	0	32	3	54.1	46	4	22	35	Runners on	.270	315	85	21	1	9	86	32	52	.331	.429
April	6.75	0	0	0	6	0	5.1	6	0	3	3	Scoring Posn	.243	177	43	13	0	3	70	26	35	.330	.367
May	5.10	2	1	0	9	2	30.0	33	4	10	20	Close & Late	.282	85	24	3	0	2	11	9	18	.351	.388
June	5.87	1	3	0	14	2	38.1	35	8	15	28	None on/out	.238	185	44	8	0	9	9	15	29	.299	.427
July	6.75	0	4	0	15	2	22.2	22	6	13	19	vs. 1st Batr (relief)	.150	60	9	1	0	3	9	7	10	.235	.317
August	2.55	1	0	0	16	2	35.1	32	3	12	22	First Inning Pitched	.221	269	64	19	1	8	49	34	64	.302	.388
September/October	3.90	4	2	0	22	6	62.1	58	6	19	24	First 15 Pitches	.222	257	57	15	0	11	41	27	55	.295	.409
Starter	5.63	5	6	0	14	14	76.2	91	13	30	41	Pitch 16-30	.218	188	41	7	1	2	13	20	40	.293	.298
Reliever	3.99	3	4	0	68	0	117.1	95	14	42	94	Pitch 31-45	.276	98	27	4	0	6	24	14	17	.363	.500
0 Days rest	5.68	0	1	0	9	0	12.2	12	1	5	11	Pitch 46+	.308	198	61	15	1	8	26	11	23	.341	.515

Last Five Years																					
	ERA	W	L	Sv	G	GS	IP	H	HR	BB	SO		Avg	AB	H	2B	3B	HR	RBI	BB	SO	OBP	SLG
1 or 2 Days rest	3.48	1	2	0	27	0	41.1	31	5	19	30	First Pitch	.311	148	46	16	0	5	30	4	0	.327	.520
3+ Days rest	3.96	2	1	0	32	0	63.1	52	8	18	53	Ahead on Count	.182	308	56	11	2	7	22	0	117	.179	.299
Pre-All Star	5.46	3	6	0	36	5	85.2	84	17	31	61	Behind on Count	.335	170	57	8	0	9	29	32	0	.438	.541
Post-All Star	3.99	5	4	0	46	9	108.1	102	10	41	74	Two Strikes	.125	303	38	6	2	4	19	36	135	.215	.198

Pitcher vs. Batter (career)																					
Pitches Best Vs.	Avg	AB	H	2B	3B	HR	RBI	BB	SO	OBP	SLG	Pitches Worst Vs.	Avg	AB	H	2B	3B	HR	RBI	BB	SO	OBP	SLG
Steve Finley	.222	9	2	0	0	0	2	1	1	.364	.222												

John Valentin — Red Sox   Bats Right

	Avg	G	AB	R	H	2B	3B	HR	RBI	BB	SO	HBP	GDP	SB	CS	OBP	SLG	IBB	SH	SF	#Pit	#P/PA	GB	FB	G/F
1992 Season	.276	58	185	21	51	13	0	5	25	20	17	2	5	1	0	.351	.427	0	4	1	741	3.56	66	57	1.16

1992 Season

	Avg	AB	H	2B	3B	HR	RBI	BB	SO	OBP	SLG		Avg	AB	H	2B	3B	HR	RBI	BB	SO	OBP	SLG
vs. Left	.212	33	7	3	0	1	3	8	2	.381	.394	Scoring Posn	.268	56	15	3	0	1	21	10	6	.382	.375
vs. Right	.289	152	44	10	0	4	22	12	15	.343	.434	Close & Late	.212	33	7	1	0	1	3	3	4	.278	.333
Home	.247	89	22	6	0	1	9	10	8	.327	.348	None on/out	.304	46	14	2	0	1	1	1	3	.333	.413
Away	.302	96	29	7	0	4	16	10	9	.374	.500	Batting #7	.231	26	6	2	0	0	2	3	2	.310	.308
First Pitch	.303	33	10	4	0	2	6	0	0	.303	.606	Batting #9	.286	126	36	8	0	2	15	14	13	.359	.397
Ahead on Count	.357	42	15	8	0	1	7	13	0	.500	.619	Other	.273	33	9	3	0	3	8	3	2	.351	.636
Behind on Count	.232	69	16	2	0	1	8	0	12	.254	.304	Pre-All Star	.000	0	0	0	0	0	0	0	0	.000	.000
Two Strikes	.214	70	15	0	0	0	5	7	17	.304	.214	Post-All Star	.276	185	51	13	0	5	25	20	17	.351	.427

Jose Valentin — Brewers   Bats Both

	Avg	G	AB	R	H	2B	3B	HR	RBI	BB	SO	HBP	GDP	SB	CS	OBP	SLG	IBB	SH	SF	#Pit	#P/PA	GB	FB	G/F
1992 Season	.000	4	3	1	0	0	0	0	1	0	0	0	0	0	0	.000	.000	0	0	1	9	2.25	2	2	1.00

1992 Season

	Avg	AB	H	2B	3B	HR	RBI	BB	SO	OBP	SLG		Avg	AB	H	2B	3B	HR	RBI	BB	SO	OBP	SLG
vs. Left	.000	0	0	0	0	0	0	0	0	.000	.000	Scoring Posn	.000	1	0	0	0	0	1	0	0	.000	.000
vs. Right	.000	3	0	0	0	1	0	0	0	.000	.000	Close & Late	.000	1	0	0	0	0	0	0	0	.000	.000

Julio Valera — Angels   Pitches Right

	ERA	W	L	Sv	G	GS	IP	BB	SO	Avg	H	2B	3B	HR	RBI	OBP	SLG	CG	ShO	Sup	QS	#P/S	SB	CS	GB	FB	G/F
1992 Season	3.73	8	11	0	30	28	188.0	64	113	.262	188	38	3	15	69	.323	.386	4	2	3.88	14	103	14	4	245	234	1.05
Career (1990-1992)	3.90	9	12	0	35	31	203.0	75	120	.267	209	43	3	16	79	.332	.391	4	2	4.03	15	100	15	6	272	253	1.08

1992 Season

	ERA	W	L	Sv	G	GS	IP	H	HR	BB	SO		Avg	AB	H	2B	3B	HR	RBI	BB	SO	OBP	SLG
Home	2.34	6	3	0	13	13	96.0	84	4	21	53	vs. Left	.292	336	98	18	1	4	26	27	33	.343	.387
Away	5.18	2	8	0	17	15	92.0	104	11	43	60	vs. Right	.236	382	90	20	2	11	43	37	80	.306	.385
Day	2.98	3	3	0	9	9	60.1	57	4	23	35	Inning 1-6	.262	603	158	29	2	13	58	57	97	.327	.381
Night	4.09	5	8	0	21	19	127.2	131	11	41	78	Inning 7+	.261	115	30	9	1	2	11	7	16	.301	.409
Grass	2.99	8	7	0	25	24	165.2	156	9	50	100	None on	.278	414	115	28	1	10	10	30	67	.330	.423
Turf	9.27	0	4	0	5	4	22.1	32	6	14	13	Runners on	.240	304	73	10	2	5	59	34	46	.315	.336
April	3.46	1	1	0	3	1	13.0	10	1	3	11	Scoring Posn	.229	170	39	5	0	1	45	27	23	.332	.276
May	2.94	1	2	0	5	5	33.2	26	0	14	21	Close & Late	.298	47	14	4	1	0	5	2	8	.327	.426
June	4.08	2	4	0	6	6	39.2	37	3	12	21	None on/out	.319	185	59	13	0	4	4	16	29	.376	.454
July	3.86	1	1	0	6	6	39.2	48	6	10	25	vs. 1st Batr (relief)	.000	2	0	0	0	0	0	0	0	.000	.000
August	4.50	1	1	0	5	5	30.0	32	3	15	14	First Inning Pitched	.308	120	37	7	0	4	11	10	16	.362	.467
September/October	3.38	2	2	0	5	5	32.0	35	2	10	21	First 75 Pitches	.249	510	127	23	2	10	42	42	81	.308	.361
Starter	3.76	7	11	0	28	28	182.0	184	14	63	110	Pitch 76-90	.309	94	29	7	0	2	11	14	12	.398	.447
Reliever	3.00	1	0	0	2	0	6.0	4	1	1	3	Pitch 91-105	.243	74	18	5	0	2	11	6	15	.300	.392
0-3 Days Rest	1.80	0	0	0	1	1	5.0	6	0	2	0	Pitch 106+	.350	40	14	3	1	1	5	2	5	.372	.550
4 Days Rest	4.06	4	6	0	16	16	102.0	112	11	35	61	First Pitch	.320	103	33	7	0	4	13	5	0	.355	.505
5+ Days Rest	3.48	3	5	0	11	11	75.0	66	3	26	49	Ahead on Count	.206	296	61	11	1	4	20	0	90	.209	.291
Pre-All Star	3.59	5	8	0	16	14	100.1	86	7	33	68	Behind on Count	.337	169	57	11	2	5	20	32	0	.443	.515
Post-All Star	3.90	3	3	0	14	14	87.2	102	8	31	45	Two Strikes	.175	314	55	10	1	3	22	27	113	.242	.242

Dave Valle — Mariners   Bats Right (groundball hitter)

	Avg	G	AB	R	H	2B	3B	HR	RBI	BB	SO	HBP	GDP	SB	CS	OBP	SLG	IBB	SH	SF	#Pit	#P/PA	GB	FB	G/F
1992 Season	.240	124	367	39	88	16	1	9	30	27	58	8	7	0	0	.305	.362	1	7	1	1492	3.70	139	109	1.28
Last Five Years	.224	549	1605	175	359	64	7	41	179	153	225	39	63	1	5	.305	.349	3	21	9	6629	3.67	701	458	1.53

1992 Season

	Avg	AB	H	2B	3B	HR	RBI	BB	SO	OBP	SLG		Avg	AB	H	2B	3B	HR	RBI	BB	SO	OBP	SLG
vs. Left	.283	120	34	4	0	4	11	11	16	.348	.417	Scoring Posn	.195	87	17	5	0	0	20	5	16	.245	.253
vs. Right	.219	247	54	12	1	5	19	16	42	.284	.336	Close & Late	.213	47	10	0	0	0	3	4	10	.302	.213
Groundball	.398	88	35	8	0	4	11	5	12	.438	.625	None on/out	.217	106	23	7	0	3	3	6	13	.284	.368

444

1992 Season

	Avg	AB	H	2B	3B	HR	RBI	BB	SO	OBP	SLG		Avg	AB	H	2B	3B	HR	RBI	BB	SO	OBP	SLG
Flyball	.206	102	21	2	1	4	9	10	17	.296	.363	Batting #7	.212	104	22	5	0	4	13	8	13	.278	.375
Home	.247	198	49	14	0	7	19	12	33	.307	.424	Batting #8	.252	246	62	10	1	5	17	19	43	.321	.362
Away	.231	169	39	2	1	2	11	15	25	.303	.290	Other	.235	17	4	1	0	0	0	0	2	.235	.294
Day	.202	94	19	1	0	3	6	3	16	.235	.309	April	.273	55	15	1	0	1	4	4	16	.328	.345
Night	.253	273	69	15	1	6	24	24	42	.328	.381	May	.286	35	10	4	0	1	4	1	4	.324	.486
Grass	.207	135	28	2	1	1	9	14	24	.289	.259	June	.241	87	21	5	0	4	9	7	11	.313	.437
Turf	.259	232	60	14	0	8	21	13	34	.315	.422	July	.169	65	11	0	1	1	2	3	9	.206	.246
First Pitch	.379	29	11	5	0	2	7	1	0	.455	.759	August	.300	70	21	5	0	1	9	11	12	.402	.414
Ahead on Count	.327	113	37	3	1	6	16	11	0	.387	.531	September/October	.182	55	10	1	0	1	2	1	6	.237	.255
Behind on Count	.229	140	32	3	0	4	10	0	36	.248	.336	Pre-All Star	.251	203	51	10	1	6	17	14	36	.311	.399
Two Strikes	.160	156	25	6	0	0	1	15	58	.247	.199	Post-All Star	.226	164	37	6	0	3	13	13	22	.298	.317

1992 By Position

Position	Avg	AB	H	2B	3B	HR	RBI	BB	SO	OBP	SLG	G	GS	Innings	PO	A	E	DP	Fld Pct	Rng Fctr	In Zone	Zone Outs	Zone Rtg	MLB Zone
As c	.236	364	86	16	1	9	29	27	57	.303	.360	122	116	972.1	608	61	7	10	.990	---	---	---	---	---

Last Five Years

	Avg	AB	H	2B	3B	HR	RBI	BB	SO	OBP	SLG		Avg	AB	H	2B	3B	HR	RBI	BB	SO	OBP	SLG
vs. Left	.245	567	139	19	1	20	63	56	64	.322	.388	Scoring Posn	.230	422	97	23	3	7	136	34	62	.301	.348
vs. Right	.212	1038	220	45	6	21	116	97	161	.296	.328	Close & Late	.211	266	56	9	3	4	26	22	45	.293	.312
Groundball	.275	429	118	19	1	10	54	35	61	.341	.394	None on/out	.205	386	79	15	2	11	11	33	51	.289	.339
Flyball	.206	408	84	16	4	13	47	47	55	.297	.360	Batting #7	.221	367	81	15	0	15	47	33	45	.295	.384
Home	.221	810	179	42	4	14	82	76	111	.301	.335	Batting #8	.232	866	201	36	4	15	86	91	134	.320	.335
Away	.226	795	180	22	3	27	97	77	114	.309	.364	Other	.207	372	77	13	3	11	46	29	46	.280	.347
Day	.217	391	85	12	1	11	37	34	54	.293	.338	April	.226	305	69	8	1	11	39	26	51	.298	.367
Night	.226	1214	274	52	6	30	142	119	171	.309	.353	May	.233	245	57	13	3	5	27	29	30	.321	.371
Grass	.222	618	137	15	3	22	81	59	101	.301	.362	June	.214	215	46	7	0	7	18	15	32	.284	.344
Turf	.225	987	222	49	4	19	98	94	124	.306	.340	July	.201	269	54	11	2	6	32	15	32	.259	.323
First Pitch	.258	163	42	11	0	8	28	1	0	.295	.472	August	.227	242	55	9	0	6	21	32	39	.324	.339
Ahead on Count	.302	427	129	21	3	17	60	94	0	.434	.485	September/October	.237	329	78	16	1	6	42	36	41	.334	.347
Behind on Count	.213	587	125	17	3	11	54	1	125	.234	.308	Pre-All Star	.224	857	192	32	6	25	98	75	127	.297	.363
Two Strikes	.160	689	110	22	3	10	55	57	225	.236	.244	Post-All Star	.223	748	167	32	1	16	81	78	98	.314	.333

Batter vs. Pitcher (career)

Hits Best Against	Avg	AB	H	2B	3B	HR	RBI	BB	SO	OBP	SLG	Hits Worst Against	Avg	AB	H	2B	3B	HR	RBI	BB	SO	OBP	SLG
Mark Guthrie	.462	13	6	0	0	1	4	0	2	.462	.692	Tom Gordon	.000	10	0	0	0	0	0	2	6	.167	.000
Mark Eichhorn	.455	11	5	2	0	0	3	1	0	.500	.636	Bret Saberhagen	.000	9	0	0	0	0	0	2	2	.182	.000
Charles Nagy	.417	12	5	2	0	1	1	0	1	.417	.833	Scott Erickson	.000	6	0	0	0	0	1	4	2	.500	.000
John Candelaria	.400	10	4	2	0	1	3	1	0	.455	.900	Jeff Russell	.154	13	2	0	0	0	3	0	0	.154	.154
Nolan Ryan	.333	12	4	2	0	1	2	2	5	.400	.750	Greg Harris	.167	12	2	0	0	0	1	1	0	.231	.167

Andy Van Slyke — Pirates   Bats Left

	Avg	G	AB	R	H	2B	3B	HR	RBI	BB	SO	HBP	GDP	SB	CS	OBP	SLG	IBB	SH	SF	#Pit	#P/PA	GB	FB	G/F
1992 Season	.324	154	614	103	199	45	12	14	89	58	99	4	9	12	3	.381	.505	4	0	9	2662	3.89	198	195	1.02
Last Five Years	.282	712	2661	422	751	136	49	82	402	299	499	13	41	82	23	.353	.463	12	5	41	11529	3.83	878	831	1.06

1992 Season

	Avg	AB	H	2B	3B	HR	RBI	BB	SO	OBP	SLG		Avg	AB	H	2B	3B	HR	RBI	BB	SO	OBP	SLG
vs. Left	.297	269	80	22	4	4	41	18	46	.341	.454	Scoring Posn	.338	145	49	12	4	3	64	17	21	.390	.538
vs. Right	.345	345	119	23	8	10	48	40	53	.411	.545	Close & Late	.315	111	35	8	0	1	13	15	21	.389	.414
Groundball	.279	190	53	13	1	2	23	28	35	.376	.389	None on/out	.358	120	43	14	0	3	3	8	27	.408	.550
Flyball	.331	157	52	14	4	5	24	14	31	.379	.567	Batting #1	.000	0	0	0	0	0	0	1	0	1.000	.000
Home	.321	315	101	24	6	6	40	22	44	.360	.492	Batting #3	.324	614	199	45	12	14	89	57	99	.380	.505
Away	.328	299	98	21	6	8	49	36	55	.402	.518	Other	.000	0	0	0	0	0	0	0	0	.000	.000
Day	.335	176	59	14	4	3	22	15	28	.383	.511	April	.284	67	19	4	1	0	12	16	17	.422	.373
Night	.320	438	140	31	8	11	67	43	71	.380	.502	May	.415	94	39	11	2	1	17	12	13	.486	.606
Grass	.333	153	51	11	1	6	23	21	25	.416	.536	June	.301	103	31	5	2	2	11	8	19	.345	.447
Turf	.321	461	148	34	11	8	66	37	74	.369	.495	July	.333	102	34	7	3	4	17	11	11	.391	.578
First Pitch	.398	83	33	7	2	3	23	3	0	.419	.639	August	.315	108	34	6	2	4	18	8	18	.367	.519
Ahead on Count	.349	149	52	12	2	5	17	33	0	.464	.557	September/October	.300	140	42	12	2	3	14	3	21	.310	.479
Behind on Count	.267	195	52	10	3	3	25	0	48	.266	.492	Pre-All Star	.340	312	106	26	6	4	49	39	55	.411	.500
Two Strikes	.251	283	71	17	5	4	31	21	99	.301	.389	Post-All Star	.308	302	93	19	6	10	40	19	44	.349	.510

1992 By Position

Position	Avg	AB	H	2B	3B	HR	RBI	BB	SO	OBP	SLG	G	GS	Innings	PO	A	E	DP	Fld Pct	Rng Fctr	In Zone	Zone Outs	Zone Rtg	MLB Zone
As cf	.324	614	199	45	12	14	89	58	99	.381	.505	154	153	1373.2	421	11	5	3	.989	2.83	507	406	.801	.824

Last Five Years

	Avg	AB	H	2B	3B	HR	RBI	BB	SO	OBP	SLG		Avg	AB	H	2B	3B	HR	RBI	BB	SO	OBP	SLG
vs. Left	.242	1008	244	48	17	17	136	104	207	.312	.374	Scoring Posn	.283	692	196	35	21	10	274	105	135	.362	.438
vs. Right	.307	1653	507	88	32	65	266	195	292	.377	.517	Close & Late	.266	470	125	19	8	11	60	46	114	.325	.411
Groundball	.284	938	266	47	16	28	139	123	174	.365	.457	None on/out	.259	498	129	32	2	12	12	56	100	.340	.404

445

Last Five Years

	Avg	AB	H	2B	3B	HR	RBI	BB	SO	OBP	SLG
Flyball	.250	572	143	28	15	19	96	72	119	.330	.451
Home	.272	1295	352	66	26	41	196	150	231	.345	.458
Away	.292	1366	399	70	23	41	205	149	268	.360	.467
Day	.293	788	231	43	13	30	125	75	156	.350	.495
Night	.278	1873	520	93	36	52	277	224	343	.354	.449
Grass	.303	706	214	28	11	27	104	79	130	.371	.489
Turf	.275	1955	537	108	38	55	298	220	369	.346	.453
First Pitch	.355	397	141	22	8	16	85	6	0	.363	.572
Ahead on Count	.346	586	203	40	12	30	117	168	0	.487	.609
Behind on Count	.250	899	225	36	15	24	117	0	245	.249	.404
Two Strikes	.202	1252	253	46	21	24	131	119	499	.266	.330

	Avg	AB	H	2B	3B	HR	RBI	BB	SO	OBP	SLG
Batting #3	.286	2521	720	132	48	79	383	279	472	.355	.470
Batting #6	.177	62	11	2	1	1	9	10	13	.288	.290
Other	.256	78	20	2	0	2	10	10	14	.341	.359
April	.259	309	80	13	6	11	53	44	61	.345	.447
May	.319	439	140	20	9	10	67	60	75	.400	.474
June	.275	473	130	23	12	9	64	46	96	.338	.431
July	.268	452	121	21	11	17	68	55	77	.344	.476
August	.285	467	133	22	5	21	79	44	89	.347	.488
September/October	.282	521	147	37	6	14	71	50	99	.341	.457
Pre-All Star	.290	1395	404	66	29	39	215	168	265	.363	.462
Post-All Star	.274	1266	347	70	20	43	187	131	234	.341	.453

Batter vs. Pitcher (since 1984)

Hits Best Against	Avg	AB	H	2B	3B	HR	RBI	BB	SO	OBP	SLG
Ben Rivera	.700	10	7	0	1	1	2	1	0	.727	1.200
Frank Castillo	.526	19	10	0	1	2	5	1	3	.550	.947
Shawn Boskie	.462	13	6	0	1	2	3	1	2	.467	1.077
Steve Wilson	.444	18	8	1	1	2	5	4	2	.545	.944
Jimmy Jones	.429	28	12	1	2	3	10	2	2	.452	.929

Hits Worst Against	Avg	AB	H	2B	3B	HR	RBI	BB	SO	OBP	SLG
Rob Murphy	.000	10	0	0	0	0	0	1	4	.091	.000
Mike Maddux	.083	12	1	0	0	0	1	1	5	.154	.083
Zane Smith	.100	20	2	0	0	0	0	0	8	.100	.100
Neal Heaton	.167	12	2	0	0	0	0	0	3	.167	.167
Tom Candiotti	.167	12	2	0	0	0	1	0	1	.154	.167

John VanderWal — Expos   Bats Left

	Avg	G	AB	R	H	2B	3B	HR	RBI	BB	SO	HBP	GDP	SB	CS	OBP	SLG	IBB	SH	SF	#Pit	#P/PA	GB	FB	G/F
1992 Season	.239	105	213	21	51	8	2	4	20	24	36	0	2	3	0	.316	.352	2	0	0	823	3.47	79	59	1.34
Career (1991-1992)	.234	126	274	25	64	12	3	5	28	25	54	0	4	3	0	.297	.354	2	0	1	1064	3.55	102	74	1.38

1992 Season

	Avg	AB	H	2B	3B	HR	RBI	BB	SO	OBP	SLG
vs. Left	.241	29	7	0	0	0	1	2	6	.290	.241
vs. Right	.239	184	44	8	2	4	19	22	30	.320	.370
Home	.242	99	24	5	0	2	11	12	17	.324	.354
Away	.237	114	27	3	2	2	9	12	19	.310	.351
First Pitch	.250	40	10	1	0	2	5	2	0	.286	.425
Ahead on Count	.234	47	11	1	1	1	5	15	0	.419	.362
Behind on Count	.288	73	21	2	0	2	7	0	24	.288	.397
Two Strikes	.189	90	17	2	1	0	7	7	36	.247	.233

	Avg	AB	H	2B	3B	HR	RBI	BB	SO	OBP	SLG
Scoring Posn	.217	60	13	4	0	0	13	10	14	.329	.283
Close & Late	.130	46	6	1	1	0	4	12	10	.310	.196
None on/out	.214	42	9	1	0	3	3	4	5	.283	.452
Batting #3	.337	83	28	5	0	2	8	8	12	.396	.470
Batting #4	.156	32	5	1	1	0	3	1	0	.182	.250
Other	.184	98	18	2	1	2	9	15	24	.292	.286
Pre-All Star	.272	125	34	5	0	3	13	17	25	.359	.384
Post-All Star	.193	88	17	3	2	1	7	7	11	.253	.307

Gary Varsho — Pirates   Bats Left

	Avg	G	AB	R	H	2B	3B	HR	RBI	BB	SO	HBP	GDP	SB	CS	OBP	SLG	IBB	SH	SF	#Pit	#P/PA	GB	FB	G/F
1992 Season	.222	103	162	22	36	6	3	4	22	10	32	0	2	5	2	.266	.370	1	0	1	588	3.40	60	48	1.25
Career (1988-1992)	.242	355	557	71	135	28	7	8	57	35	91	2	5	24	4	.288	.361	5	1	3	2034	3.41	205	162	1.27

1992 Season

	Avg	AB	H	2B	3B	HR	RBI	BB	SO	OBP	SLG
vs. Left	.231	13	3	1	0	1	3	0	3	.231	.538
vs. Right	.221	149	33	5	3	3	19	10	29	.269	.356
Home	.224	85	19	3	3	3	15	4	16	.256	.435
Away	.221	77	17	3	0	1	7	6	16	.277	.299
First Pitch	.250	32	8	0	0	2	6	1	0	.273	.438
Ahead on Count	.257	35	9	2	2	0	3	4	0	.333	.429
Behind on Count	.148	54	8	2	0	1	6	0	19	.148	.241
Two Strikes	.200	70	14	4	1	1	9	5	32	.253	.329

	Avg	AB	H	2B	3B	HR	RBI	BB	SO	OBP	SLG
Scoring Posn	.250	48	12	2	0	2	18	3	7	.288	.417
Close & Late	.125	48	6	1	1	0	2	5	12	.204	.188
None on/out	.146	48	7	3	1	1	1	6	11	.241	.313
Batting #1	.188	64	12	4	1	2	9	3	12	.224	.375
Batting #9	.306	36	11	1	1	1	5	5	6	.381	.472
Other	.210	62	13	1	1	1	8	2	14	.234	.306
Pre-All Star	.225	102	23	3	3	2	11	5	18	.262	.373
Post-All Star	.217	60	13	3	0	2	11	5	14	.273	.367

Career (1988-1992)

	Avg	AB	H	2B	3B	HR	RBI	BB	SO	OBP	SLG
vs. Left	.152	33	5	2	0	1	4	0	8	.176	.303
vs. Right	.248	524	130	26	7	7	53	35	83	.295	.365
Groundball	.235	217	51	11	3	2	18	15	28	.288	.341
Flyball	.241	137	33	7	2	3	14	5	28	.268	.387
Home	.237	287	68	14	5	4	30	15	38	.279	.362
Away	.248	270	67	14	2	4	27	20	53	.298	.359
Day	.269	242	70	19	3	5	36	11	26	.318	.455
Night	.206	315	65	9	4	3	21	24	65	.266	.289
Grass	.260	246	64	14	2	3	21	16	36	.304	.370
Turf	.228	311	71	14	5	5	36	19	55	.275	.354
First Pitch	.274	106	29	6	0	3	15	4	0	.297	.415
Ahead on Count	.307	137	42	10	4	1	16	17	0	.387	.460
Behind on Count	.169	178	30	8	1	1	12	0	49	.172	.242
Two Strikes	.174	218	38	7	2	1	14	13	91	.223	.239

	Avg	AB	H	2B	3B	HR	RBI	BB	SO	OBP	SLG
Scoring Posn	.237	131	31	9	0	4	44	15	28	.313	.397
Close & Late	.216	171	37	12	1	0	11	10	31	.262	.298
None on/out	.245	163	40	9	2	1	1	7	26	.261	.344
Batting #6	.232	99	23	4	2	2	11	10	15	.300	.374
Batting #9	.273	154	42	9	1	2	15	9	29	.311	.383
Other	.230	304	70	15	4	4	31	16	47	.272	.345
April	.273	55	15	4	2	1	8	5	11	.344	.473
May	.219	96	21	4	2	0	7	5	18	.257	.302
June	.215	93	20	4	1	1	5	8	14	.277	.312
July	.254	134	34	7	2	3	19	10	15	.303	.403
August	.239	67	16	3	0	0	6	2	16	.261	.264
September/October	.259	112	29	6	0	3	12	5	17	.292	.393
Pre-All Star	.249	293	73	16	7	4	30	20	48	.298	.392
Post-All Star	.235	264	62	12	0	4	27	15	43	.277	.326

Batter vs. Pitcher (career)

Hits Best Against	Avg	AB	H	2B	3B	HR	RBI	BB	SO	OBP	SLG
David Cone	.471	17	8	3	0	0	3	0	2	.471	.647

Hits Worst Against	Avg	AB	H	2B	3B	HR	RBI	BB	SO	OBP	SLG
John Smoltz	.056	18	1	0	0	0	0	4	4	.227	.056

Batter vs. Pitcher (career)

Hits Best Against	Avg	AB	H	2B	3B	HR	RBI	BB	SO	OBP	SLG	Hits Worst Against	Avg	AB	H	2B	3B	HR	RBI	BB	SO	OBP	SLG
Andy Benes	.455	11	5	2	0	0	2	0	2	.455	.636	Mark Gardner	.167	12	2	0	0	0	0	0	1	.167	.167
Mike Morgan	.417	12	5	1	1	0	3	0	1	.417	.667	Tommy Greene	.182	11	2	0	0	1	2	0	4	.182	.455
Bill Sampen	.364	11	4	1	0	0	1	0	1	.364	.455	Dennis Martinez	.190	21	4	1	0	0	2	1	1	.227	.238
Jimmy Jones	.333	12	4	0	0	0	0	1	2	.385	.333	Jose Rijo	.200	10	2	1	0	0	0	1	1	.273	.300

Jim Vatcher — Padres
Bats Right (groundball hitter)

	Avg	G	AB	R	H	2B	3B	HR	RBI	BB	SO	HBP	GDP	SB	CS	OBP	SLG	IBB	SH	SF	#Pit	#P/PA	GB	FB	G/F
1992 Season	.250	13	16	1	4	1	0	0	2	3	6	0	0	0	0	.368	.313	0	1	0	74	3.89	6	2	3.00
Career (1990-1992)	.248	87	109	11	27	3	1	1	11	12	27	0	0	1	1	.322	.321	0	1	0	476	3.93	48	15	3.20

1992 Season

	Avg	AB	H	2B	3B	HR	RBI	BB	SO	OBP	SLG		Avg	AB	H	2B	3B	HR	RBI	BB	SO	OBP	SLG
vs. Left	.000	2	0	0	0	0	0	1	1	.333	.000	Scoring Posn	.250	4	1	0	0	0	2	1	1	.400	.250
vs. Right	.286	14	4	1	0	0	2	2	5	.375	.357	Close & Late	.333	3	1	0	0	0	0	0	2	.333	.333

Greg Vaughn — Brewers
Bats Right (flyball hitter)

	Avg	G	AB	R	H	2B	3B	HR	RBI	BB	SO	HBP	GDP	SB	CS	OBP	SLG	IBB	SH	SF	#Pit	#P/PA	GB	FB	G/F
1992 Season	.228	141	501	77	114	18	2	23	78	60	123	5	8	15	15	.313	.409	1	2	5	2205	3.86	127	172	0.74
Career (1989-1992)	.234	444	1538	227	360	71	9	72	260	168	362	7	24	28	22	.309	.432	4	11	20	6568	3.79	417	528	0.79

1992 Season

	Avg	AB	H	2B	3B	HR	RBI	BB	SO	OBP	SLG		Avg	AB	H	2B	3B	HR	RBI	BB	SO	OBP	SLG
vs. Left	.248	105	26	4	1	6	23	21	19	.370	.476	Scoring Posn	.250	144	36	2	0	8	58	24	43	.358	.431
vs. Right	.222	396	88	14	1	17	55	39	104	.297	.391	Close & Late	.210	81	17	1	0	2	6	13	19	.319	.296
Groundball	.235	115	27	3	1	2	15	12	31	.305	.330	None on/out	.239	142	34	8	2	7	7	12	26	.321	.472
Flyball	.230	152	35	5	0	10	26	15	41	.300	.461	Batting #4	.208	293	61	11	1	11	39	31	77	.284	.365
Home	.234	244	57	8	1	11	42	35	58	.330	.410	Batting #6	.236	72	17	3	0	4	13	11	16	.352	.444
Away	.222	257	57	10	1	12	36	25	65	.297	.409	Other	.265	136	36	4	1	8	26	18	30	.355	.485
Day	.216	148	32	3	1	8	21	23	37	.320	.412	April	.267	60	16	3	1	4	10	9	13	.357	.550
Night	.232	353	82	15	1	15	57	37	86	.311	.408	May	.157	102	16	3	0	5	15	14	26	.259	.333
Grass	.231	429	99	14	2	20	69	52	108	.315	.413	June	.154	52	8	1	0	1	9	5	12	.237	.231
Turf	.208	72	15	4	0	3	9	8	15	.305	.389	July	.253	99	25	5	1	3	10	4	29	.288	.414
First Pitch	.309	81	25	4	0	6	16	1	0	.321	.580	August	.213	89	19	1	0	4	11	12	22	.308	.360
Ahead on Count	.256	117	30	5	0	7	31	32	0	.405	.479	September/October	.303	99	30	5	0	6	23	16	21	.407	.535
Behind on Count	.240	146	35	3	1	10	22	0	51	.250	.479	Pre-All Star	.204	260	53	9	1	11	38	30	62	.289	.373
Two Strikes	.161	236	38	7	1	5	18	27	123	.253	.263	Post-All Star	.253	241	61	9	1	12	40	30	61	.339	.448

1992 By Position

Position	Avg	AB	H	2B	3B	HR	RBI	BB	SO	OBP	SLG	G	GS	Innings	PO	A	E	DP	Fld Pct	Rng Fctr	In Zone	Outs	Zone Rtg	MLB Zone
As lf	.228	470	107	17	2	21	70	60	118	.319	.406	131	130	1147.0	288	6	3	0	.990	2.31	311	275	.884	.809

Career (1989-1992)

	Avg	AB	H	2B	3B	HR	RBI	BB	SO	OBP	SLG		Avg	AB	H	2B	3B	HR	RBI	BB	SO	OBP	SLG
vs. Left	.223	408	91	20	3	15	62	56	88	.312	.397	Scoring Posn	.281	417	117	23	1	23	192	61	113	.361	.506
vs. Right	.238	1130	269	51	6	57	198	112	274	.307	.445	Close & Late	.205	234	48	5	0	9	35	29	55	.292	.342
Groundball	.246	435	107	22	5	12	68	36	94	.300	.402	None on/out	.218	408	89	18	3	21	21	40	79	.290	.431
Flyball	.208	346	72	11	1	22	58	38	99	.285	.436	Batting #4	.210	420	88	15	1	17	61	41	109	.277	.371
Home	.231	743	172	37	3	37	133	92	170	.314	.439	Batting #5	.251	466	117	24	3	24	92	52	109	.325	.470
Away	.236	795	188	34	6	35	127	76	192	.303	.426	Other	.238	652	155	32	5	31	107	75	144	.317	.445
Day	.220	423	93	15	3	20	74	58	101	.311	.411	April	.270	159	43	12	1	10	32	21	37	.355	.547
Night	.239	1115	267	56	6	52	186	110	261	.308	.440	May	.200	230	46	11	1	11	37	32	55	.297	.400
Grass	.240	1331	319	62	7	67	235	146	307	.313	.448	June	.222	221	49	11	2	9	43	20	48	.290	.412
Turf	.198	207	41	9	2	5	25	22	55	.280	.333	July	.215	274	59	10	3	11	37	21	80	.271	.394
First Pitch	.291	254	74	10	2	17	59	3	0	.294	.547	August	.224	268	60	7	1	11	35	31	62	.301	.381
Ahead on Count	.283	346	98	23	4	22	83	85	0	.417	.564	September/October	.267	386	103	20	1	20	76	43	80	.339	.479
Behind on Count	.208	486	101	15	3	26	73	0	167	.213	.412	Pre-All Star	.227	701	159	38	5	32	120	79	166	.307	.432
Two Strikes	.160	724	116	25	2	20	74	79	362	.245	.283	Post-All Star	.240	837	201	33	4	40	140	89	196	.310	.432

Batter vs. Pitcher (career)

Hits Best Against	Avg	AB	H	2B	3B	HR	RBI	BB	SO	OBP	SLG	Hits Worst Against	Avg	AB	H	2B	3B	HR	RBI	BB	SO	OBP	SLG
Doug Jones	.500	12	6	4	0	1	3	0	1	.500	1.083	Chuck Finley	.000	14	0	0	0	0	0	0	7	.000	.000
Kevin Appier	.500	10	5	1	1	0	1	1	3	.615	.800	Mark Guthrie	.000	11	0	0	0	0	0	1	3	.083	.000
Joe Slusarski	.500	6	3	2	0	1	4	3	2	.727	1.333	Melido Perez	.000	10	0	0	0	0	0	2	3	.167	.000
Mike Moore	.364	11	4	1	1	1	2	3	1	.500	.909	Roger Clemens	.056	18	1	0	0	0	0	0	10	.056	.056
Dave Stewart	.333	24	8	2	0	5	14	7	5	.484	1.042	Joe Grahe	.091	11	1	0	0	0	2	0	2	.091	.091

447

Mo Vaughn — Red Sox *Bats Left*

	Avg	G	AB	R	H	2B	3B	HR	RBI	BB	SO	HBP	GDP	SB	CS	OBP	SLG	IBB	SH	SF	#Pit	#P/PA	GB	FB	G/F
1992 Season	.234	113	355	42	83	16	2	13	57	47	67	3	8	3	3	.326	.400	7	0	3	1565	3.84	129	108	1.19
Career (1991-1992)	.244	187	574	63	140	28	2	17	89	73	110	5	15	5	4	.331	.389	9	0	7	2471	3.75	206	165	1.25

1992 Season

	Avg	AB	H	2B	3B	HR	RBI	BB	SO	OBP	SLG		Avg	AB	H	2B	3B	HR	RBI	BB	SO	OBP	SLG
vs. Left	.190	79	15	3	0	5	14	10	17	.281	.418	Scoring Posn	.220	100	22	7	0	4	44	19	29	.336	.410
vs. Right	.246	276	68	13	2	8	43	37	50	.339	.395	Close & Late	.257	70	18	0	1	1	8	9	15	.350	.329
Groundball	.250	76	19	2	0	3	11	11	11	.352	.395	None on/out	.188	80	15	5	0	3	12	10		.301	.363
Flyball	.208	106	22	2	0	6	16	8	20	.263	.396	Batting #5	.247	162	40	11	1	4	21	14	20	.315	.401
Home	.262	202	53	11	2	8	37	24	38	.343	.455	Batting #7	.253	91	23	3	0	7	25	21	25	.386	.516
Away	.196	153	30	5	0	5	20	23	29	.303	.327	Other	.196	102	20	2	1	2	11	12	22	.284	.294
Day	.238	122	29	5	0	5	19	28	23	.384	.402	April	.204	49	10	1	0	2	7	12	15	.355	.347
Night	.232	233	54	11	2	8	38	19	44	.292	.399	May	.125	16	2	0	0	0	4	8	7	.417	.125
Grass	.240	321	77	15	2	11	51	42	56	.332	.402	June	.321	28	9	2	0	1	3	4	1	.406	.500
Turf	.176	34	6	1	0	2	6	5	11	.275	.382	July	.225	80	18	3	1	3	13	11	14	.312	.400
First Pitch	.273	44	12	3	0	2	7	7	0	.385	.477	August	.250	92	23	3	0	4	14	7	13	.310	.413
Ahead on Count	.284	88	25	7	1	3	19	19	0	.404	.489	September/October	.233	90	21	7	1	3	16	5	17	.289	.433
Behind on Count	.190	116	22	6	1	3	13	0	37	.202	.336	Pre-All Star	.194	129	25	3	1	5	20	30	33	.342	.349
Two Strikes	.168	167	28	4	0	7	23	21	67	.268	.317	Post-All Star	.257	226	58	13	1	8	37	17	34	.316	.429

1992 By Position

Position	Avg	AB	H	2B	3B	HR	RBI	BB	SO	OBP	SLG	G	GS	Innings	PO	A	E	DP	Fld Pct	Rng Fctr	In Zone	Outs	Zone Rtg	MLB Zone
As Designated Hitter	.200	70	14	3	0	2	9	2	11	.233	.329	20	16	---	---	---	---	---	---	---	---	---	---	---
As Pinch Hitter	.308	13	4	0	0	1	3	1	1	.357	.538	14	0	---	---	---	---	---	---	---	---	---	---	---
As 1b	.239	276	66	13	2	10	46	44	55	.345	.409	85	82	720.1	740	54	15	75	.981	---	125	105	.840	.843

Randy Velarde — Yankees *Bats Right (groundball hitter)*

	Avg	G	AB	R	H	2B	3B	HR	RBI	BB	SO	HBP	GDP	SB	CS	OBP	SLG	IBB	SH	SF	#Pit	#P/PA	GB	FB	G/F
1992 Season	.272	121	412	57	112	24	1	7	46	38	78	2	13	7	2	.333	.386	1	4	5	1720	3.76	167	100	1.67
Last Five Years	.249	377	1040	127	259	51	6	20	103	91	212	9	28	11	10	.313	.367	1	14	6	4261	3.72	425	251	1.69

1992 Season

	Avg	AB	H	2B	3B	HR	RBI	BB	SO	OBP	SLG		Avg	AB	H	2B	3B	HR	RBI	BB	SO	OBP	SLG
vs. Left	.307	140	43	10	0	4	22	15	23	.376	.464	Scoring Posn	.286	91	26	6	0	3	40	13	18	.358	.451
vs. Right	.254	272	69	14	1	3	24	23	55	.310	.346	Close & Late	.263	76	20	3	0	2	8	6	13	.317	.382
Groundball	.230	113	26	7	0	1	10	15	19	.321	.319	None on/out	.300	100	30	7	1	1	1	5	18	.340	.420
Flyball	.283	120	34	7	0	3	21	6	24	.310	.417	Batting #2	.278	133	37	10	1	2	14	16	21	.355	.414
Home	.278	198	55	8	0	2	24	20	33	.345	.348	Batting #6	.267	135	36	5	0	2	19	14	31	.331	.348
Away	.266	214	57	16	1	5	22	18	45	.321	.421	Other	.271	144	39	9	0	3	13	8	26	.312	.396
Day	.318	132	42	7	0	4	14	12	18	.370	.462	April	.211	71	15	4	0	1	6	3	14	.250	.310
Night	.250	280	70	17	1	3	32	26	60	.315	.350	May	.259	54	14	3	0	0	3	3	12	.298	.315
Grass	.260	334	87	12	0	6	36	30	60	.322	.350	June	.238	21	5	0	0	1	4	2	5	.304	.381
Turf	.321	78	25	12	1	1	10	8	18	.379	.538	July	.396	53	21	8	1	2	6	3	7	.429	.698
First Pitch	.302	43	13	2	1	0	6	1	0	.319	.395	August	.280	107	30	3	0	1	13	15	17	.363	.336
Ahead on Count	.355	110	39	9	0	1	12	17	0	.441	.464	September/October	.255	106	27	6	0	2	14	12	23	.331	.368
Behind on Count	.218	133	29	8	0	1	9	0	42	.216	.301	Pre-All Star	.223	157	35	8	0	2	13	9	32	.268	.312
Two Strikes	.190	179	34	5	0	3	19	20	78	.267	.291	Post-All Star	.302	255	77	16	1	5	33	29	46	.370	.431

1992 By Position

Position	Avg	AB	H	2B	3B	HR	RBI	BB	SO	OBP	SLG	G	GS	Innings	PO	A	E	DP	Fld Pct	Rng Fctr	In Zone	Outs	Zone Rtg	MLB Zone
As 3b	.341	91	31	4	0	4	15	11	15	.408	.516	26	23	219.2	14	35	5	7	.907	2.01	54	46	.852	.841
As ss	.238	252	60	15	1	1	21	23	50	.302	.317	75	68	606.1	129	212	9	42	.974	5.06	258	239	.926	.885
As lf	.333	42	14	4	0	1	5	1	9	.349	.500	14	11	93.0	22	1	0	0	1.000	2.23	29	21	.724	.809

Last Five Years

	Avg	AB	H	2B	3B	HR	RBI	BB	SO	OBP	SLG		Avg	AB	H	2B	3B	HR	RBI	BB	SO	OBP	SLG
vs. Left	.276	340	94	19	2	6	33	32	66	.344	.397	Scoring Posn	.254	232	59	15	0	7	84	26	51	.327	.409
vs. Right	.236	700	165	32	4	14	70	59	146	.298	.353	Close & Late	.232	168	39	8	1	3	10	14	34	.291	.345
Groundball	.247	291	72	14	1	3	23	24	42	.312	.333	None on/out	.288	267	77	16	3	4	4	16	55	.333	.416
Flyball	.263	270	71	12	1	10	39	28	60	.336	.426	Batting #7	.264	201	53	8	1	6	15	22	41	.335	.403
Home	.263	501	132	25	2	6	57	46	90	.333	.357	Batting #8	.246	248	61	7	4	7	24	17	52	.307	.391
Away	.236	539	127	26	4	14	46	45	122	.295	.377	Other	.245	591	145	36	1	7	64	52	119	.308	.345
Day	.275	327	90	14	1	5	23	24	55	.332	.370	April	.192	99	19	5	0	1	6	6	23	.250	.273
Night	.237	713	169	37	5	15	80	67	157	.305	.366	May	.221	136	30	5	1	0	7	11	36	.293	.272
Grass	.253	879	222	36	3	19	91	77	170	.317	.365	June	.238	101	24	2	1	4	10	7	15	.287	.396
Turf	.230	161	37	15	3	1	12	14	42	.294	.379	July	.270	152	41	14	2	3	11	15	30	.339	.447
First Pitch	.313	131	41	10	3	0	12	1	0	.328	.435	August	.270	259	70	12	2	5	35	27	48	.339	.390
Ahead on Count	.323	248	80	17	1	6	30	45	0	.429	.472	September/October	.256	293	75	13	0	7	34	25	60	.316	.372
Behind on Count	.189	360	68	14	1	3	24	0	120	.195	.258	Pre-All Star	.211	365	77	13	2	5	24	29	81	.279	.299
Two Strikes	.158	463	73	14	0	7	33	45	212	.235	.233	Post-All Star	.270	675	182	38	4	15	79	62	131	.332	.404

Batter vs. Pitcher (career)

Hits Best Against	Avg	AB	H	2B	3B	HR	RBI	BB	SO	OBP	SLG	Hits Worst Against	Avg	AB	H	2B	3B	HR	RBI	BB	SO	OBP	SLG
Joe Hesketh	.500	10	5	2	0	0	0	1	0	.545	.700	Jack Morris	.063	16	1	0	0	1	1	1	4	.118	.250
Mike Boddicker	.417	12	5	1	0	0	3	0	5	.417	.500	Greg Hibbard	.063	16	1	1	0	0	2	0	2	.063	.125
Jimmy Key	.400	15	6	2	0	0	0	0	2	.400	.533	Kirk McCaskill	.091	11	1	1	0	0	0	0	1	.091	.182
Ben McDonald	.400	10	4	0	0	0	1	1	1	.455	.400	Erik Hanson	.091	11	1	0	0	0	0	0	3	.091	.091
Randy Johnson	.364	11	4	2	0	0	4	1	4	.417	.545	Todd Stottlemyre	.100	10	1	1	0	0	0	1	2	.182	.200

Guillermo Velasquez — Padres
Bats Left

	Avg	G	AB	R	H	2B	3B	HR	RBI	BB	SO	HBP	GDP	SB	CS	OBP	SLG	IBB	SH	SF	#Pit	#P/PA	GB	FB	G/F
1992 Season	.304	15	23	1	7	0	0	1	5	1	7	0	0	0	0	.333	.435	0	0	0	80	3.33	5	4	1.25

1992 Season

	Avg	AB	H	2B	3B	HR	RBI	BB	SO	OBP	SLG		Avg	AB	H	2B	3B	HR	RBI	BB	SO	OBP	SLG
vs. Left	.167	6	1	0	0	0	0	0	1	.167	.167	Scoring Posn	.250	8	2	0	0	0	3	0	3	.250	.250
vs. Right	.353	17	6	0	0	1	5	1	6	.389	.529	Close & Late	.182	11	2	0	0	0	2	0	4	.182	.182

Robin Ventura — White Sox
Bats Left

	Avg	G	AB	R	H	2B	3B	HR	RBI	BB	SO	HBP	GDP	SB	CS	OBP	SLG	IBB	SH	SF	#Pit	#P/PA	GB	FB	G/F
1992 Season	.282	157	592	85	167	38	1	16	93	93	71	0	16	2	4	.375	.431	9	1	8	2664	3.84	207	192	1.08
Career (1989-1992)	.271	480	1736	230	470	83	3	44	254	236	197	6	44	5	12	.356	.398	14	23	21	7704	3.85	693	521	1.33

1992 Season

	Avg	AB	H	2B	3B	HR	RBI	BB	SO	OBP	SLG		Avg	AB	H	2B	3B	HR	RBI	BB	SO	OBP	SLG
vs. Left	.258	182	47	12	1	2	28	26	34	.348	.368	Scoring Posn	.324	148	48	10	0	3	69	38	20	.443	.453
vs. Right	.293	410	120	26	0	14	65	67	37	.387	.459	Close & Late	.260	100	26	7	0	2	12	14	14	.345	.390
Groundball	.311	161	50	15	1	3	26	23	16	.392	.472	None on/out	.200	130	26	6	1	3	3	15	15	.283	.331
Flyball	.263	175	46	13	0	1	21	18	22	.328	.354	Batting #3	.263	186	49	13	0	3	26	37	21	.377	.382
Home	.295	285	84	19	1	7	50	49	30	.392	.442	Batting #5	.274	248	68	17	0	7	49	40	29	.371	.427
Away	.270	307	83	19	0	9	43	44	41	.359	.420	Other	.316	158	50	8	1	6	18	16	21	.379	.494
Day	.373	150	56	14	0	7	28	24	23	.452	.607	April	.275	69	19	6	0	1	11	15	5	.400	.406
Night	.251	442	111	24	1	9	65	69	48	.349	.371	May	.287	101	29	7	0	2	15	18	14	.382	.416
Grass	.281	499	140	32	1	14	84	78	62	.373	.433	June	.354	99	35	6	1	4	14	16	14	.443	.556
Turf	.290	93	27	6	0	2	9	15	9	.385	.419	July	.185	108	20	3	0	2	8	7	14	.231	.269
First Pitch	.236	72	17	5	0	1	13	7	0	.300	.347	August	.333	102	34	8	0	3	23	12	10	.400	.500
Ahead on Count	.366	194	71	17	0	9	45	58	0	.506	.593	September/October	.265	113	30	8	0	4	22	25	14	.399	.442
Behind on Count	.303	152	46	9	0	5	22	0	29	.299	.461	Pre-All Star	.298	319	95	20	1	8	42	51	40	.389	.442
Two Strikes	.235	230	54	12	1	3	25	28	71	.313	.335	Post-All Star	.264	273	72	18	0	8	51	42	31	.358	.418

1992 By Position

Position	Avg	AB	H	2B	3B	HR	RBI	BB	SO	OBP	SLG	G	GS	Innings	PO	A	E	DP	Fld Pct	Rng Fctr	In Zone	Outs	Zone Rtg	MLB Zone
As 3b	.283	591	167	38	1	16	93	92	70	.375	.431	157	157	1395.1	141	371	23	27	.957	3.30	441	387	.878	.841

Career (1989-1992)

	Avg	AB	H	2B	3B	HR	RBI	BB	SO	OBP	SLG		Avg	AB	H	2B	3B	HR	RBI	BB	SO	OBP	SLG
vs. Left	.249	535	133	20	2	7	60	81	90	.347	.333	Scoring Posn	.316	433	137	22	0	11	196	80	53	.407	.443
vs. Right	.281	1201	337	63	1	37	194	155	107	.361	.427	Close & Late	.260	292	76	13	1	6	42	32	36	.331	.373
Groundball	.275	488	134	30	1	10	76	63	38	.354	.402	None on/out	.222	351	78	14	1	8	8	36	38	.296	.336
Flyball	.264	425	112	30	0	9	59	47	51	.336	.398	Batting #2	.292	881	257	37	2	28	136	104	100	.366	.434
Home	.284	850	241	37	2	25	136	117	94	.369	.420	Batting #3	.255	306	78	16	0	5	36	52	34	.358	.356
Away	.258	866	229	46	1	19	118	119	103	.344	.377	Other	.246	549	135	30	1	11	82	80	63	.340	.364
Day	.297	448	133	25	1	12	60	61	61	.377	.438	April	.265	170	45	10	1	4	23	34	20	.388	.406
Night	.262	1288	337	58	2	32	194	175	136	.349	.384	May	.230	274	63	9	0	4	27	36	37	.317	.307
Grass	.272	1483	403	71	3	41	229	196	171	.355	.407	June	.321	302	97	16	1	6	39	40	35	.399	.440
Turf	.265	253	67	12	0	3	25	40	26	.360	.348	July	.270	330	89	14	0	15	52	27	30	.325	.448
First Pitch	.258	178	46	9	0	3	25	9	0	.296	.360	August	.272	283	77	14	1	8	55	36	29	.349	.413
Ahead on Count	.344	546	188	36	2	22	112	140	0	.474	.538	September/October	.263	377	99	20	0	7	58	63	46	.366	.371
Behind on Count	.241	536	129	25	1	11	75	0	92	.242	.353	Pre-All Star	.273	853	233	38	2	18	100	119	103	.361	.386
Two Strikes	.215	683	147	22	1	12	77	85	197	.301	.303	Post-All Star	.268	883	237	45	1	26	154	117	94	.351	.410

Batter vs. Pitcher (career)

Hits Best Against	Avg	AB	H	2B	3B	HR	RBI	BB	SO	OBP	SLG	Hits Worst Against	Avg	AB	H	2B	3B	HR	RBI	BB	SO	OBP	SLG
Dave Fleming	.545	11	6	3	0	0	3	1	0	.583	.818	Tom Gordon	.000	12	0	0	0	0	0	2	4	.143	.000
Scott Sanderson	.467	15	7	1	0	1	6	3	1	.556	.733	Kirk McCaskill	.091	11	1	0	0	0	0	1	2	.167	.091
Bill Gullickson	.429	14	6	1	1	1	2	0	1	.429	.857	Jaime Navarro	.100	20	2	1	0	0	4	1	1	.143	.150
Greg Harris	.400	10	4	1	0	1	2	1	0	.455	.800	Jose Guzman	.100	10	1	0	0	0	1	1	1	.182	.100
Mike Magnante	.400	10	4	0	0	1	2	2	0	.500	.700	Frank Viola	.111	9	1	0	0	0	1	1	3	.182	.111

Hector Villanueva — Cubs — Bats Right

	Avg	G	AB	R	H	2B	3B	HR	RBI	BB	SO	HBP	GDP	SB	CS	OBP	SLG	IBB	SH	SF	#Pit	#P/PA	GB	FB	G/F
1992 Season	.152	51	112	9	17	6	0	2	13	11	24	0	4	0	0	.228	.259	2	0	0	465	3.78	38	34	1.12
Career (1990-1992)	.242	174	418	46	101	20	2	22	63	36	81	2	10	1	0	.304	.457	5	0	1	1709	3.74	135	128	1.05

1992 Season

	Avg	AB	H	2B	3B	HR	RBI	BB	SO	OBP	SLG		Avg	AB	H	2B	3B	HR	RBI	BB	SO	OBP	SLG
vs. Left	.152	46	7	2	0	0	5	5	11	.235	.196	Scoring Posn	.242	33	8	3	0	2	13	6	4	.359	.515
vs. Right	.152	66	10	4	0	2	8	6	13	.222	.303	Close & Late	.214	28	6	0	0	1	4	3	7	.290	.321
Home	.164	61	10	4	0	2	11	5	14	.227	.328	None on/out	.125	24	3	1	0	0	0	1	8	.160	.167
Away	.137	51	7	2	0	0	2	6	10	.228	.176	Batting #6	.132	38	5	2	0	0	3	6	6	.250	.184
First Pitch	.063	16	1	1	0	0	0	1	0	.118	.125	Batting #7	.191	47	9	2	0	2	7	4	7	.255	.362
Ahead on Count	.238	21	5	1	0	1	6	6	0	.407	.429												
Behind on Count	.143	42	6	2	0	1	5	0	15	.143	.262	Pre-All Star	.162	99	16	5	0	2	12	9	19	.231	.273
Two Strikes	.113	62	7	2	0	1	5	4	24	.167	.194	Post-All Star	.077	13	1	1	0	0	1	2	5	.200	.154

Career (1990-1992)

	Avg	AB	H	2B	3B	HR	RBI	BB	SO	OBP	SLG		Avg	AB	H	2B	3B	HR	RBI	BB	SO	OBP	SLG
vs. Left	.244	209	51	9	2	12	35	25	41	.325	.478	Scoring Posn	.240	104	25	4	0	7	39	11	19	.322	.481
vs. Right	.239	209	50	11	0	10	28	11	40	.283	.435	Close & Late	.228	92	21	2	1	3	12	4	26	.260	.370
Groundball	.284	116	33	10	1	6	21	11	20	.357	.543	None on/out	.196	92	18	9	1	1	1	8	24	.260	.348
Flyball	.245	106	26	4	0	7	16	8	23	.296	.481	Batting #6	.235	196	46	10	1	10	28	14	39	.284	.449
Home	.265	215	57	8	1	15	43	18	42	.326	.521	Batting #7	.269	104	28	4	0	7	16	11	16	.350	.510
Away	.217	203	44	12	1	7	20	18	39	.281	.389	Other	.229	118	27	6	1	5	19	11	26	.295	.424
Day	.270	200	54	7	1	13	34	19	36	.338	.510	April	.200	45	9	3	0	2	12	4	10	.265	.400
Night	.216	218	47	13	1	9	29	17	45	.272	.408	May	.165	79	13	2	0	3	6	7	16	.230	.304
Grass	.264	296	78	13	1	18	50	24	60	.322	.497	June	.227	110	25	4	1	7	17	10	14	.303	.473
Turf	.189	122	23	7	1	4	13	12	21	.261	.361	July	.360	50	18	2	0	2	6	3	12	.396	.520
First Pitch	.203	64	13	2	0	5	8	1	0	.215	.469	August	.280	25	7	2	1	2	7	1	6	.308	.680
Ahead on Count	.290	93	27	5	1	5	20	19	0	.411	.527	September/October	.266	109	29	7	0	6	15	11	23	.333	.495
Behind on Count	.203	138	28	6	1	4	13	1	45	.220	.348	Pre-All Star	.227	260	59	10	1	14	39	22	46	.291	.435
Two Strikes	.180	200	36	7	0	8	23	14	81	.240	.335	Post-All Star	.266	158	42	10	1	8	24	14	35	.326	.494

Batter vs. Pitcher (career)

Hits Best Against	Avg	AB	H	2B	3B	HR	RBI	BB	SO	OBP	SLG	Hits Worst Against	Avg	AB	H	2B	3B	HR	RBI	BB	SO	OBP	SLG
Randy Tomlin	.364	11	4	1	0	0	1	1	0	.417	.455	Terry Mulholland	.167	12	2	1	0	0	3	2	3	.286	.250
Dennis Rasmussen	.333	15	5	1	0	2	4	1	0	.375	.800	Zane Smith	.182	11	2	0	0	1	2	0	0	.182	.455

Frank Viola — Red Sox — Pitches Left

	ERA	W	L	Sv	G	GS	IP	BB	SO	Avg	H	2B	3B	HR	RBI	OBP	SLG	CG	ShO	Sup	QS	#P/S	SB	CS	GB	FB	G/F
1992 Season	3.44	13	12	0	35	35	238.0	89	121	.242	214	40	0	13	88	.313	.331	6	1	3.63	23	108	12	5	390	202	1.93
Last Five Years	3.26	83	63	0	176	176	1235.1	331	839	.253	1182	197	17	95	436	.303	.363	32	8	4.44	114	105	66	55	1704	1280	1.33

1992 Season

	ERA	W	L	Sv	G	GS	IP	H	HR	BB	SO		Avg	AB	H	2B	3B	HR	RBI	BB	SO	OBP	SLG
Home	4.08	8	7	0	18	18	117.0	121	7	44	65	vs. Left	.211	109	23	6	0	1	11	10	9	.281	.294
Away	2.83	5	5	0	17	17	121.0	93	6	45	56	vs. Right	.246	777	191	34	0	12	77	79	112	.317	.336
Day	3.24	6	5	0	12	12	83.1	68	3	32	38	Inning 1-6	.248	730	181	36	0	11	80	74	106	.319	.342
Night	3.55	7	7	0	23	23	154.2	146	10	57	83	Inning 7+	.212	156	33	4	0	2	8	15	15	.283	.276
Grass	3.36	10	10	0	29	29	201.0	183	11	73	104	None on	.242	517	125	20	0	6	6	45	77	.307	.315
Turf	3.89	3	2	0	6	6	37.0	31	2	16	17	Runners on	.241	369	89	20	0	7	82	44	44	.319	.352
April	3.06	2	2	0	5	5	32.1	27	1	11	19	Scoring Posn	.249	193	48	13	0	4	73	32	24	.346	.378
May	2.86	3	1	0	5	5	34.2	32	3	8	20	Close & Late	.190	121	23	2	0	2	8	9	13	.244	.256
June	4.28	2	2	0	6	6	40.0	38	4	14	21	None on/out	.232	233	54	11	0	2	2	16	32	.281	.305
July	2.32	2	1	0	6	6	42.2	40	1	17	16	vs. 1st Batr (relief)	.000	0	0	0	0	0	0	0	0	.000	.000
August	4.25	2	5	0	7	7	48.2	44	3	20	24	First Inning Pitched	.228	123	28	7	0	2	13	12	24	.293	.333
September/October	3.63	2	1	0	6	6	39.2	33	1	19	21	First 75 Pitches	.257	583	150	30	0	9	67	57	88	.325	.355
Starter	3.44	13	12	0	35	35	238.0	214	13	89	121	Pitch 76-90	.206	107	22	4	0	2	7	9	11	.274	.299
Reliever	0.00	0	0	0	0	0	0.0	0	0	0	0	Pitch 91-105	.191	94	18	3	0	0	6	13	12	.287	.223
0-3 Days Rest	4.50	2	1	0	4	4	24.0	21	1	11	15	Pitch 106+	.235	102	24	3	0	2	8	10	10	.307	.324
4 Days Rest	3.49	7	8	0	22	22	152.1	137	9	55	73	First Pitch	.304	138	42	9	0	4	23	3	0	.322	.457
5+ Days Rest	2.92	4	3	0	9	9	61.2	56	3	23	33	Ahead on Count	.158	336	53	9	0	3	20	0	92	.166	.211
Pre-All Star	3.12	8	5	0	19	19	129.2	113	9	41	67	Behind on Count	.292	195	57	8	0	5	21	43	0	.417	.410
Post-All Star	3.82	5	7	0	16	16	108.1	101	4	48	54	Two Strikes	.190	395	75	17	0	3	29	43	121	.271	.256

Last Five Years

	ERA	W	L	Sv	G	GS	IP	H	HR	BB	SO		Avg	AB	H	2B	3B	HR	RBI	BB	SO	OBP	SLG
Home	3.27	48	31	0	88	88	625.1	601	47	156	439	vs. Left	.243	820	199	45	3	14	74	52	144	.292	.356
Away	3.26	35	32	0	88	88	610.0	581	48	175	400	vs. Right	.255	3857	983	152	14	81	362	279	695	.305	.365
Day	2.97	34	23	0	63	63	442.1	412	35	99	308	Inning 1-6	.258	3841	990	170	16	77	392	272	714	.307	.370
Night	3.43	49	40	0	113	113	793.0	770	60	232	531	Inning 7+	.230	836	192	27	1	18	44	59	125	.281	.329
Grass	3.43	51	43	0	112	112	769.1	764	62	204	514	None on	.254	2786	707	115	12	57	57	188	481	.303	.365
Turf	2.99	32	20	0	64	64	466.0	418	33	127	325	Runners on	.251	1891	475	82	5	38	379	143	358	.303	.360
April	3.07	11	7	0	24	24	164.0	152	15	41	124	Scoring Posn	.244	1016	248	45	2	21	327	98	211	.305	.354
May	2.92	18	8	0	28	28	203.1	198	14	37	149	Close & Late	.220	449	99	5	1	10	27	34	56	.276	.303

Last Five Years

	ERA	W	L	Sv	G	GS	IP	H	HR	BB	SO		Avg	AB	H	2B	3B	HR	RBI	BB	SO	OBP	SLG
June	3.04	15	8	0	30	30	216.1	212	13	60	129	None on/out	.247	1219	301	54	6	23	23	81	190	.294	.358
July	2.70	14	10	0	29	29	207.0	167	20	68	126	vs. 1st Batr (relief)	.000	0	0	0	0	0	0	0	0	.000	.000
August	3.99	12	20	0	33	33	228.0	230	17	64	164	First Inning Pitched	.211	544	115	17	2	5	33	38	118	.262	.278
September/October	3.74	13	10	0	32	32	216.2	223	16	61	147	First 75 Pitches	.255	3213	819	139	13	54	287	212	616	.301	.357
Starter	3.26	83	63	0	176	176	1235.1	1182	95	331	839	Pitch 76-90	.266	628	167	29	3	17	75	49	90	.322	.403
Reliever	0.00	0	0	0	0	0	0.0	0	0	0	0	Pitch 91-105	.229	471	108	17	1	13	43	37	80	.284	.352
0-3 Days Rest	2.99	8	5	0	15	15	102.1	92	5	28	75	Pitch 106+	.241	365	88	12	0	11	31	33	53	.304	.364
4 Days Rest	3.36	55	45	0	121	121	860.2	835	70	222	575	First Pitch	.349	734	256	45	3	24	105	10	0	.357	.516
5+ Days Rest	3.07	20	13	0	40	40	272.1	255	20	81	189	Ahead on Count	.187	2089	390	62	3	26	124	0	698	.189	.257
Pre-All Star	2.81	52	24	0	93	93	672.2	625	47	162	450	Behind on Count	.317	958	304	41	9	30	113	179	0	.424	.473
Post-All Star	3.81	31	39	0	83	83	562.2	557	48	169	389	Two Strikes	.172	2126	366	64	1	22	130	142	839	.225	.234

Pitcher vs. Batter (since 1984)

Pitches Best Vs.	Avg	AB	H	2B	3B	HR	RBI	BB	SO	OBP	SLG	Pitches Worst Vs.	Avg	AB	H	2B	3B	HR	RBI	BB	SO	OBP	SLG
Steve Lyons	.083	12	1	1	0	0	1	0	5	.083	.167	Chris Sabo	.545	11	6	1	0	1	2	4	2	.667	.909
Jose Gonzalez	.083	12	1	0	0	0	0	1	4	.154	.083	Dale Murphy	.429	21	9	2	0	2	2	1	4	.455	.810
Luis Polonia	.083	12	1	0	0	0	0	0	5	.083	.083	Danny Tartabull	.417	24	10	3	0	2	10	4	7	.500	.792
Larry Walker	.083	12	1	1	0	0	0	0	5	.083	.167	Ryne Sandberg	.375	24	9	1	0	3	5	7	6	.500	.792
Brian McRae	.111	9	1	0	0	0	3	0	0	.273	.111	Randy Milligan	.375	8	3	0	0	1	5	1	1	.583	.750

Joe Vitko — Mets   Pitches Right

	ERA	W	L	Sv	G	GS	IP	BB	SO	Avg	H	2B	3B	HR	RBI	OBP	SLG	GF	IR	IRS	Hld	SvOp	SB	CS	GB	FB	G/F
1992 Season	13.50	0	1	0	3	1	4.2	1	6	.444	12	2	0	1	9	.448	.630	1	0	0	0	0	0	1	9	6	1.50

1992 Season

	ERA	W	L	Sv	G	GS	IP	H	HR	BB	SO		Avg	AB	H	2B	3B	HR	RBI	BB	SO	OBP	SLG
Home	13.50	0	1	0	3	1	4.2	12	1	1	6	vs. Left	.500	12	6	1	0	0	6	1	2	.500	.583
Away	0.00	0	0	0	0	0	0.0	0	0	0	0	vs. Right	.400	15	6	1	0	1	3	0	4	.400	.667

Jose Vizcaino — Cubs   Bats Both (groundball hitter)

	Avg	G	AB	R	H	2B	3B	HR	RBI	BB	SO	HBP	GDP	SB	CS	OBP	SLG	IBB	SH	SF	#Pit	#P/PA	GB	FB	G/F
1992 Season	.225	86	285	25	64	10	4	1	17	14	35	0	4	3	0	.260	.298	2	5	1	960	3.20	113	69	1.64
Career (1989-1992)	.240	223	491	37	118	16	5	1	29	23	62	0	6	6	2	.273	.299	3	8	3	1661	3.21	219	96	2.28

1992 Season

	Avg	AB	H	2B	3B	HR	RBI	BB	SO	OBP	SLG		Avg	AB	H	2B	3B	HR	RBI	BB	SO	OBP	SLG
vs. Left	.216	88	19	3	3	0	5	3	7	.242	.318	Scoring Posn	.268	56	15	0	0	0	14	5	6	.323	.268
vs. Right	.228	197	45	7	1	1	12	11	28	.268	.289	Close & Late	.250	52	13	3	0	0	7	4	6	.298	.308
Groundball	.218	119	26	4	1	0	3	4	17	.244	.269	None on/out	.188	101	19	5	1	1	1	7	17	.241	.287
Flyball	.250	56	14	3	1	0	4	3	8	.283	.339	Batting #1	.205	166	34	9	0	0	6	6	25	.233	.259
Home	.230	126	29	4	1	0	3	7	18	.269	.278	Batting #2	.304	56	17	1	3	0	6	1	3	.310	.429
Away	.220	159	35	6	3	1	14	7	17	.253	.314	Other	.206	63	13	0	1	1	5	7	7	.286	.286
Day	.250	152	38	7	3	0	8	5	22	.272	.336	April	.091	22	2	0	0	0	1	0	2	.087	.091
Night	.195	133	26	3	1	1	9	9	13	.246	.256	May	.179	56	10	0	2	0	1	4	5	.233	.250
Grass	.236	220	52	6	3	1	12	12	26	.275	.305	June	.248	113	28	7	0	0	6	5	15	.280	.310
Turf	.185	65	12	4	1	0	5	2	9	.209	.277	July	.156	45	7	3	0	0	0	3	7	.208	.222
First Pitch	.266	64	17	0	1	0	5	2	2	.288	.297	August	.347	49	17	0	2	1	9	2	6	.373	.490
Ahead on Count	.283	60	17	2	0	0	7	9	0	.371	.317	September/October	.000	0	0	0	0	0	0	0	0	.000	.000
Behind on Count	.179	84	15	4	3	1	2	0	20	.179	.333	Pre-All Star	.203	231	47	10	2	0	8	11	28	.239	.264
Two Strikes	.196	102	20	7	1	1	3	3	33	.219	.314	Post-All Star	.315	54	17	0	2	1	9	3	7	.351	.444

1992 By Position

Position	Avg	AB	H	2B	3B	HR	RBI	BB	SO	OBP	SLG	G	GS	Innings	PO	A	E	DP	Fld Pct	Rng Fctr	In Zone	Outs	Zone Rtg	MLB Zone
As 3b	.208	106	22	5	0	1	5	6	16	.250	.283	29	26	226.2	18	51	2	6	.972	2.74	69	60	.870	.841
As ss	.229	170	39	5	4	0	11	7	17	.258	.306	50	41	386.2	73	143	7	29	.969	5.03	169	155	.917	.885

Omar Vizquel — Mariners   Bats Both (groundball hitter)

	Avg	G	AB	R	H	2B	3B	HR	RBI	BB	SO	HBP	GDP	SB	CS	OBP	SLG	IBB	SH	SF	#Pit	#P/PA	GB	FB	G/F
1992 Season	.294	136	483	49	142	20	4	0	21	32	38	2	14	15	13	.340	.352	0	9	1	1918	3.70	197	139	1.42
Career (1989-1992)	.250	502	1551	155	388	46	13	4	100	123	137	3	35	27	20	.305	.304	0	40	8	6033	3.58	671	411	1.63

1992 Season

	Avg	AB	H	2B	3B	HR	RBI	BB	SO	OBP	SLG		Avg	AB	H	2B	3B	HR	RBI	BB	SO	OBP	SLG
vs. Left	.229	105	24	4	0	0	5	8	4	.283	.267	Scoring Posn	.307	101	31	2	1	0	20	5	7	.343	.347
vs. Right	.312	378	118	16	4	0	16	24	34	.356	.376	Close & Late	.287	87	25	2	2	0	4	4	7	.319	.356
Groundball	.269	119	32	2	0	0	7	11	8	.336	.286	None on/out	.282	163	46	6	2	0	0	11	18	.328	.344
Flyball	.354	130	46	6	1	0	6	8	4	.391	.415	Batting #1	.323	266	86	11	3	0	13	16	25	.366	.387
Home	.286	241	69	11	3	0	12	17	23	.337	.357	Batting #9	.273	110	30	5	1	0	5	9	7	.325	.336
Away	.302	242	73	9	1	0	9	15	15	.342	.347	Other	.243	107	26	4	0	0	3	7	6	.289	.280
Day	.276	134	37	7	1	0	11	12	16	.342	.343	April	.190	21	4	0	0	0	1	0	2	.190	.190

1992 Season

	Avg	AB	H	2B	3B	HR	RBI	BB	SO	OBP	SLG
Night	.301	349	105	13	3	0	10	20	22	.339	.355
Grass	.305	187	57	7	0	0	9	9	12	.337	.342
Turf	.287	296	85	13	4	0	12	23	26	.342	.358
First Pitch	.328	67	22	5	0	0	4	0	0	.338	.403
Ahead on Count	.329	85	28	5	0	0	5	20	0	.453	.388
Behind on Count	.272	184	50	5	3	0	6	0	24	.276	.332
Two Strikes	.228	215	49	5	2	0	7	12	38	.269	.270

	Avg	AB	H	2B	3B	HR	RBI	BB	SO	OBP	SLG
May	.300	50	15	1	1	0	3	3	2	.333	.360
June	.325	80	26	6	0	0	1	9	6	.393	.400
July	.351	114	40	8	1	0	8	6	8	.388	.439
August	.287	108	31	1	1	0	4	7	9	.330	.315
September/October	.236	110	26	4	1	0	4	7	11	.288	.291
Pre-All Star	.318	201	64	10	2	0	8	15	13	.367	.388
Post-All Star	.277	282	78	10	2	0	13	17	25	.320	.326

1992 By Position

Position	Avg	AB	H	2B	3B	HR	RBI	BB	SO	OBP	SLG	G	GS	Innings	PO	A	E	DP	Fld Pct	Rng Fctr	In Zone	Outs	Zone Rtg	MLB Zone
As ss	.297	478	142	20	4	0	21	32	36	.343	.356	136	128	1152.0	224	403	7	93	.989	4.90	486	436	.897	.885

Career (1989-1992)

	Avg	AB	H	2B	3B	HR	RBI	BB	SO	OBP	SLG
vs. Left	.221	375	83	14	0	2	30	22	23	.264	.275
vs. Right	.259	1176	305	32	13	2	70	101	114	.318	.314
Groundball	.237	409	97	8	3	1	20	35	38	.300	.279
Flyball	.262	324	85	11	2	1	26	28	19	.321	.318
Home	.255	750	191	30	9	2	54	55	82	.306	.327
Away	.246	801	197	16	4	2	46	68	55	.304	.283
Day	.261	422	110	13	2	1	32	37	34	.321	.308
Night	.246	1129	278	33	11	3	68	86	103	.299	.303
Grass	.250	611	153	12	2	1	34	46	38	.302	.282
Turf	.250	940	235	34	11	3	66	77	99	.307	.319
First Pitch	.274	215	59	9	3	1	17	0	0	.274	.358
Ahead on Count	.297	337	100	13	3	2	28	74	0	.420	.377
Behind on Count	.236	564	133	15	6	0	36	0	88	.237	.284
Two Strikes	.190	615	117	16	5	1	31	49	137	.250	.237

	Avg	AB	H	2B	3B	HR	RBI	BB	SO	OBP	SLG
Scoring Posn	.251	370	93	11	3	1	93	29	29	.301	.305
Close & Late	.246	256	63	10	4	0	8	16	19	.290	.316
None on/out	.264	409	106	13	5	2	2	37	44	.325	.335
Batting #8	.229	353	81	12	3	1	29	27	33	.282	.289
Batting #9	.240	906	217	21	7	3	57	79	78	.300	.288
Other	.308	292	90	13	3	0	14	17	26	.350	.373
April	.168	119	20	1	1	0	5	10	6	.233	.193
May	.258	182	47	4	5	0	17	12	15	.299	.335
June	.273	238	65	12	0	0	11	27	22	.346	.324
July	.301	326	98	14	2	3	26	20	23	.342	.383
August	.222	333	74	5	2	1	19	23	37	.273	.258
September/October	.238	353	84	10	3	0	22	31	34	.301	.283
Pre-All Star	.257	635	163	23	8	1	40	56	49	.316	.323
Post-All Star	.246	916	225	23	5	3	60	87	88	.297	.291

Batter vs. Pitcher (career)

Hits Best Against	Avg	AB	H	2B	3B	HR	RBI	BB	SO	OBP	SLG
Juan Guzman	.556	9	5	0	0	0		3	0	.667	.556
Shawn Hillegas	.467	15	7	1	0	0	0	2	1	.529	.533
Storm Davis	.462	13	6	0	1	0	2	2	1	.533	.615
Ben McDonald	.400	10	4	0	1	0	3	3	1	.467	.600
Mike Gardiner	.400	10	4	0	1	0	2	1	0	.455	.600

Hits Worst Against	Avg	AB	H	2B	3B	HR	RBI	BB	SO	OBP	SLG
Bobby Witt	.000	9	0	0	0	0	0	4	3	.308	.000
Mike Moore	.067	15	1	0	0	0	0	2	0	.263	.067
Scott Sanderson	.105	19	2	0	0	0	1	0	1	.105	.105
Bob Welch	.111	18	2	0	0	0	1	3	2	.227	.111
Roger Clemens	.160	25	4	0	0	0	1	0	1	.160	.160

Paul Wagner — Pirates — Pitches Right

	ERA	W	L	Sv	G	GS	IP	BB	SO	Avg	H	2B	3B	HR	RBI	OBP	SLG	GF	IR	IRS	Hld	SvOp	SB	CS	GB	FB	G/F
1992 Season	0.69	2	0	0	6	1	13.0	5	5	.191	9	3	0	0	1	.269	.255	1	2	0	0	0	0	1	19	17	1.12

1992 Season

	ERA	W	L	Sv	G	GS	IP	H	HR	BB	SO		Avg	AB	H	2B	3B	HR	RBI	BB	SO	OBP	SLG
Home	0.00	0	0	0	2	0	2.2	3	0	1	1	vs. Left	.263	19	5	1	0	0	1	4	2	.391	.316
Away	0.87	2	0	0	4	1	10.1	6	0	4	4	vs. Right	.143	28	4	2	0	0	0	1	3	.172	.214

Tim Wakefield — Pirates — Pitches Right

	ERA	W	L	Sv	G	GS	IP	BB	SO	Avg	H	2B	3B	HR	RBI	OBP	SLG	CG	ShO	Sup	QS	#P/S	SB	CS	GB	FB	G/F
1992 Season	2.15	8	1	0	13	13	92.0	35	51	.232	76	12	2	3	25	.305	.309	4	1	4.30	10	100	4	9	114	105	1.09

1992 Season

	ERA	W	L	Sv	G	GS	IP	H	HR	BB	SO		Avg	AB	H	2B	3B	HR	RBI	BB	SO	OBP	SLG
Home	2.09	5	0	0	6	6	43.0	42	1	19	26	vs. Left	.213	202	43	6	1	1	12	25	35	.297	.267
Away	2.20	3	1	0	7	7	49.0	34	2	16	25	vs. Right	.264	125	33	6	1	2	13	10	16	.319	.376
Starter	2.15	8	1	0	13	13	92.0	76	3	35	51	Scoring Posn	.184	76	14	4	2	1	22	13	17	.298	.329
Reliever	0.00	0	0	0	0	0	0.0	0	0	0	0	Close & Late	.207	58	12	3	0	0	4	2	6	.233	.259
0-3 Days Rest	0.00	0	0	0	0	0	0.0	0	0	0	0	None on/out	.259	85	22	2	0	0		9	12	.330	.282
4 Days Rest	2.53	4	1	0	8	8	53.1	46	2	22	28	First Pitch	.302	53	16	3	1	0	3		0	.302	.396
5+ Days Rest	1.63	4	0	0	5	5	38.2	30	1	13	23	Behind on Count	.284	67	19	2	0	3	12	24	0	.463	.448
Pre-All Star	0.00	0	0	0	0	0	0.0	0	0	0	0	Ahead on Count	.199	161	32	4	1	0	8	0	47	.199	.236
Post-All Star	2.15	8	1	0	13	13	92.0	76	3	35	51	Two Strikes	.174	149	26	5	1	0	9	11	51	.230	.221

Bob Walk — Pirates — Pitches Right (groundball pitcher)

	ERA	W	L	Sv	G	GS	IP	BB	SO	Avg	H	2B	3B	HR	RBI	OBP	SLG	CG	ShO	Sup	QS	#P/S	SB	CS	GB	FB	G/F
1992 Season	3.20	10	6	2	36	19	135.0	43	60	.258	132	26	3	10	50	.322	.379	1	0	5.47	10	86	19	5	234	119	1.97
Last Five Years	3.52	51	33	3	152	125	788.1	244	354	.253	763	151	16	58	300	.312	.372	5	2	4.92	64	88	75	30	1297	823	1.58

1992 Season

	ERA	W	L	Sv	G	GS	IP	H	HR	BB	SO		Avg	AB	H	2B	3B	HR	RBI	BB	SO	OBP	SLG
Home	2.82	8	3	1	20	12	76.2	71	5	24	40	vs. Left	.289	287	83	17	2	6	33	30	21	.359	.425
Away	3.70	2	3	1	16	7	58.1	61	5	19	20	vs. Right	.218	225	49	9	1	4	17	13	39	.273	.320

1992 Season

	ERA	W	L	Sv	G	GS	IP	H	HR	BB	SO		Avg	AB	H	2B	3B	HR	RBI	BB	SO	OBP	SLG
Starter	3.38	6	6	0	19	19	109.1	102	9	38	49	Scoring Posn	.289	128	37	11	0	2	41	20	21	.387	.422
Reliever	2.45	4	0	2	17	0	25.2	30	1	5	11	Close & Late	.348	66	23	4	0	1	9	4	3	.403	.455
0-3 Days Rest	1.29	1	0	0	1	1	7.0	6	1	1	2	None on/out	.277	137	38	4	1	4	4	6	11	.308	.409
4 Days Rest	3.16	2	2	0	9	9	51.1	46	3	21	23	First Pitch	.389	54	21	5	0	1	9	5	0	.433	.537
5+ Days Rest	3.88	3	4	0	9	9	51.0	50	5	16	24	Behind on Count	.308	143	44	12	0	6	24	23	0	.407	.517
Pre-All Star	3.98	2	3	1	16	8	52.0	57	2	19	33	Ahead on Count	.191	199	38	4	2	0	7	0	44	.199	.231
Post-All Star	2.71	8	3	1	20	11	83.0	75	8	24	27	Two Strikes	.204	201	41	5	2	2	9	15	60	.266	.279

Last Five Years

	ERA	W	L	Sv	G	GS	IP	H	HR	BB	SO		Avg	AB	H	2B	3B	HR	RBI	BB	SO	OBP	SLG
Home	3.27	28	16	1	75	64	399.0	385	22	117	194	vs. Left	.270	1686	456	89	12	31	166	157	167	.335	.393
Away	3.77	23	17	2	77	62	389.1	378	36	127	170	vs. Right	.232	1325	307	62	4	27	134	87	197	.283	.346
Day	3.59	15	7	2	43	33	215.1	205	16	68	104	Inning 1-6	.251	2593	650	129	15	50	268	212	329	.310	.370
Night	3.49	36	26	1	109	93	573.0	558	42	176	260	Inning 7+	.270	418	113	22	1	8	32	32	35	.328	.385
Grass	3.51	13	8	1	39	33	202.1	195	19	73	77	None on	.247	1801	444	90	9	30	30	131	206	.303	.356
Turf	3.52	38	25	2	113	93	586.0	568	39	171	287	Runners on	.264	1210	319	61	7	28	270	113	158	.326	.395
April	3.15	8	7	0	21	20	120.0	113	8	43	60	Scoring Posn	.258	718	185	40	6	15	233	84	104	.334	.393
May	3.37	8	5	0	23	21	130.2	119	5	41	62	Close & Late	.249	205	51	12	0	2	14	15	18	.309	.337
June	3.71	10	3	1	24	20	123.2	116	14	42	64	None on/out	.241	791	191	34	4	15	15	49	87	.287	.351
July	3.82	8	8	0	28	23	139.0	147	10	40	55	vs. 1st Batr (relief)	.500	24	12	0	0	1	3	1	3	.538	.625
August	3.27	8	6	2	24	16	121.0	114	9	37	43	First Inning Pitched	.289	584	169	28	4	12	79	58	57	.356	.413
September/October	3.68	9	4	0	32	26	154.0	154	12	41	80	First 75 Pitches	.255	2416	617	118	13	44	236	181	316	.310	.370
Starter	3.61	45	33	0	126	126	748.1	716	56	235	347	Pitch 76-90	.257	342	88	23	3	6	44	31	24	.324	.395
Reliever	1.80	6	0	3	26	0	40.0	47	2	9	14	Pitch 91-105	.217	184	40	7	0	6	11	20	20	.298	.353
0-3 Days Rest	5.59	4	1	0	7	7	38.2	45	4	16	13	Pitch 106+	.261	69	18	3	0	2	9	12	4	.370	.391
4 Days Rest	4.16	20	20	0	66	66	393.2	412	32	130	175	First Pitch	.283	403	114	19	2	6	44	12	0	.303	.385
5+ Days Rest	2.68	21	12	0	53	53	316.0	259	20	89	159	Ahead on Count	.208	1199	249	46	6	15	89	0	309	.214	.294
Pre-All Star	3.37	29	17	1	78	66	416.2	396	28	132	196	Behind on Count	.316	807	255	55	6	23	109	144	0	.419	.485
Post-All Star	3.68	22	16	2	74	60	371.2	367	30	112	168	Two Strikes	.198	1139	226	46	5	18	89	88	354	.260	.295

Pitcher vs. Batter (since 1984)

Pitches Best Vs.	Avg	AB	H	2B	3B	HR	RBI	BB	SO	OBP	SLG	Pitches Worst Vs.	Avg	AB	H	2B	3B	HR	RBI	BB	SO	OBP	SLG
Matt D. Williams	.000	12	0	0	0	0	1	1	5	.071	.000	Lonnie Smith	.714	14	10	2	0	2	7	0	0	.714	1.286
Tony Pena	.053	19	1	1	0	0	0	1	1	.100	.105	Daryl Boston	.545	11	6	1	0	2	9	3	0	.643	1.182
Casey Candaele	.083	12	1	0	0	0	0	1	0	.154	.083	Bret Barberie	.500	10	5	2	0	0	1	2	0	.643	.700
Doug Dascenzo	.083	12	1	1	0	0	0	0	0	.083	.167	Darryl Strawberry	.400	20	8	1	0	4	11	4	4	.480	1.050
Steve Sax	.105	19	2	0	0	0	0	0	2	.105	.105	Tim Teufel	.400	10	4	0	0	1	4	4	2	.571	.700

Chico Walker — Mets
Bats Both (groundball hitter)

	Avg	G	AB	R	H	2B	3B	HR	RBI	BB	SO	HBP	GDP	SB	CS	OBP	SLG	IBB	SH	SF	#Pit	#P/PA	GB	FB	G/F
1992 Season	.289	126	253	26	73	12	1	4	38	27	50	0	8	15	1	.351	.391	3	0	5	1058	3.71	103	58	1.78
Last Five Years	.257	283	705	85	181	23	2	10	74	66	122	0	13	30	7	.317	.338	5	3	8	2866	3.68	275	175	1.57

1992 Season

	Avg	AB	H	2B	3B	HR	RBI	BB	SO	OBP	SLG		Avg	AB	H	2B	3B	HR	RBI	BB	SO	OBP	SLG
vs. Left	.322	90	29	4	0	0	13	4	13	.340	.367	Scoring Posn	.286	70	20	3	1	2	36	15	14	.389	.443
vs. Right	.270	163	44	8	1	4	25	23	37	.356	.405	Close & Late	.243	74	18	3	0	0	13	11	13	.337	.284
Home	.317	104	33	5	0	0	18	14	26	.388	.365	None on/out	.220	59	13	1	0	1	1	6	14	.292	.288
Away	.268	149	40	7	1	4	20	13	24	.323	.409	Batting #3	.280	75	21	3	1	0	12	9	21	.349	.347
First Pitch	.452	42	19	4	0	1	10	1	0	.465	.619	Batting #9	.167	42	7	2	0	0	8	7	8	.280	.214
Ahead on Count	.316	38	12	2	0	3	11	13	0	.481	.605	Other	.331	136	45	7	0	4	18	11	21	.376	.471
Behind on Count	.282	85	24	5	0	1	8	0	26	.276	.376	Pre-All Star	.250	108	27	4	0	3	17	9	18	.303	.370
Two Strikes	.189	122	23	4	0	0	10	13	50	.259	.221	Post-All Star	.317	145	46	8	1	1	21	18	32	.386	.407

Last Five Years

	Avg	AB	H	2B	3B	HR	RBI	BB	SO	OBP	SLG		Avg	AB	H	2B	3B	HR	RBI	BB	SO	OBP	SLG
vs. Left	.263	224	59	7	1	3	26	13	33	.339	.344	Scoring Posn	.268	168	45	5	1	4	65	33	36	.373	.381
vs. Right	.254	481	122	16	1	7	48	53	89	.326	.335	Close & Late	.265	189	50	7	0	1	24	25	36	.347	.317
Groundball	.284	229	65	7	0	4	27	11	31	.310	.367	None on/out	.207	213	44	5	0	2	2	17	34	.265	.258
Flyball	.237	177	42	6	0	3	13	27	39	.335	.322	Batting #1	.248	306	76	7	1	5	24	24	45	.300	.327
Home	.280	339	95	11	1	4	38	34	58	.341	.354	Batting #9	.242	91	22	3	0	1	14	13	18	.333	.308
Away	.235	366	86	12	1	6	36	32	64	.294	.322	Other	.269	308	83	13	1	4	36	29	59	.328	.357
Day	.265	302	80	7	1	4	22	26	45	.319	.334	April	.121	33	4	0	0	0	1	3	4	.194	.121
Night	.251	403	101	16	1	6	52	40	77	.315	.340	May	.279	111	31	0	0	2	10	12	21	.344	.333
Grass	.267	524	140	13	2	7	59	49	90	.326	.340	June	.200	120	24	6	0	1	12	9	24	.256	.275
Turf	.227	181	41	10	0	3	15	17	32	.290	.331	July	.326	129	42	6	1	2	15	11	18	.433	.434
First Pitch	.357	115	41	8	0	5	24	3	0	.373	.557	August	.266	158	42	4	1	2	16	14	19	.324	.357
Ahead on Count	.319	138	44	6	0	4	21	26	0	.424	.449	September/October	.247	154	38	7	0	3	20	17	36	.316	.351
Behind on Count	.196	225	44	8	0	1	15	0	65	.193	.244	Pre-All Star	.238	311	74	9	0	5	30	28	59	.299	.315
Two Strikes	.173	318	55	5	1	1	17	37	122	.256	.204	Post-All Star	.272	394	107	14	2	5	44	38	63	.331	.355

Batter vs. Pitcher (since 1984)

Hits Best Against	Avg	AB	H	2B	3B	HR	RBI	BB	SO	OBP	SLG
Dennis Martinez	.500	16	8	0	0	1	2	0	1	.500	.688
Pete Harnisch	.375	8	3	0	0	0	3	1		.545	.375
Ken Hill	.364	11	4	0	0	0	0	1	2	.417	.364
Bruce Hurst	.316	19	6	1	0	0	0	0	1	.316	.368
Mark Gardner	.313	16	5	1	0	2	4	0	5	.294	.750

Hits Worst Against	Avg	AB	H	2B	3B	HR	RBI	BB	SO	OBP	SLG
Andy Benes	.000	12	0	0	0	0	0	0	3	.000	.000
Dwight Gooden	.063	16	1	0	0	0	0	1	1	.118	.063
Brian Barnes	.071	14	1	0	0	0	0	1	3	.133	.071
Tom Browning	.077	13	1	0	0	0	0	0	1	.077	.077
Mitch Williams	.111	9	1	0	0	0	1	1	3	.182	.111

Larry Walker — Expos
Bats Left (groundball hitter)

	Avg	G	AB	R	H	2B	3B	HR	RBI	BB	SO	HBP	GDP	SB	CS	OBP	SLG	IBB	SH	SF	#Pit	#P/PA	GB	FB	G/F
1992 Season	.301	143	528	85	159	31	4	23	93	41	97	6	9	18	6	.353	.506	10	0	8	1838	3.15	205	147	1.39
Career (1989-1992)	.276	433	1481	207	409	79	9	58	212	137	324	17	24	54	23	.341	.459	17	7	14	5655	3.43	567	362	1.57

1992 Season

	Avg	AB	H	2B	3B	HR	RBI	BB	SO	OBP	SLG
vs. Left	.316	209	66	8	2	10	42	10	38	.354	.517
vs. Right	.292	319	93	23	2	13	51	31	59	.353	.498
Groundball	.317	202	64	10	1	6	33	11	31	.356	.465
Flyball	.270	115	31	7	1	7	25	11	27	.333	.530
Home	.284	257	73	12	3	13	43	23	47	.349	.506
Away	.317	271	86	19	1	10	50	18	50	.357	.506
Day	.243	169	41	8	2	6	27	10	40	.290	.420
Night	.329	359	118	23	2	17	66	31	57	.383	.546
Grass	.319	163	52	11	1	8	30	9	34	.356	.546
Turf	.293	365	107	20	3	15	63	32	63	.352	.488
First Pitch	.398	128	51	11	0	10	38	10	0	.444	.719
Ahead on Count	.398	88	35	4	1	4	10	16	0	.486	.602
Behind on Count	.264	174	46	11	1	6	25	0	54	.274	.443
Two Strikes	.175	200	35	6	1	4	24	15	97	.237	.275

	Avg	AB	H	2B	3B	HR	RBI	BB	SO	OBP	SLG
Scoring Posn	.310	158	49	10	0	6	68	24	28	.387	.487
Close & Late	.281	89	25	2	0	4	15	13	17	.369	.438
None on/out	.307	140	43	7	2	10	10	8	27	.353	.600
Batting #4	.305	512	156	31	4	22	90	40	93	.358	.510
Batting #5	.182	11	2	0	0	1	1	1	2	.250	.455
Other	.200	5	1	0	0	0	2	0	2	.167	.200
April	.258	89	23	5	0	5	15	7	19	.327	.483
May	.293	75	22	4	1	4	15	9	15	.365	.533
June	.300	60	18	2	0	5	14	5	11	.338	.583
July	.296	98	29	3	1	4	15	4	21	.320	.469
August	.333	96	32	7	1	2	14	7	14	.377	.490
September/October	.318	110	35	10	1	3	20	9	17	.382	.509
Pre-All Star	.278	284	79	14	2	16	53	24	59	.333	.511
Post-All Star	.328	244	80	17	2	7	40	17	38	.377	.500

1992 By Position

Position	Avg	AB	H	2B	3B	HR	RBI	BB	SO	OBP	SLG	G	GS	Innings	PO	A	E	DP	Fld Pct	Rng Fctr	In Zone	Outs	Zone Rtg	MLB Zone
As rf	.301	525	158	31	4	23	91	41	97	.354	.507	139	137	1216.2	269	16	2	2	.993	2.11	310	260	.839	.814

Career (1989-1992)

	Avg	AB	H	2B	3B	HR	RBI	BB	SO	OBP	SLG
vs. Left	.278	489	136	23	2	20	85	31	108	.330	.456
vs. Right	.275	992	273	56	7	38	127	106	216	.347	.461
Groundball	.275	512	141	27	2	16	70	45	96	.339	.430
Flyball	.254	331	84	15	3	17	51	32	91	.326	.471
Home	.267	677	181	34	5	27	98	63	152	.337	.452
Away	.284	804	228	45	4	31	114	74	172	.345	.465
Day	.232	423	98	18	5	16	64	45	108	.311	.411
Night	.294	1058	311	61	4	42	148	92	216	.354	.478
Grass	.298	429	128	19	3	23	73	46	95	.367	.517
Turf	.267	1052	281	60	6	35	139	91	229	.331	.435
First Pitch	.356	295	105	19	0	18	66	12	0	.394	.603
Ahead on Count	.416	281	117	18	3	19	57	49	0	.497	.705
Behind on Count	.208	525	109	21	3	15	59	1	186	.216	.345
Two Strikes	.174	638	111	24	3	13	49	72	324	.261	.282

	Avg	AB	H	2B	3B	HR	RBI	BB	SO	OBP	SLG
Scoring Posn	.264	398	105	21	1	12	145	62	89	.356	.412
Close & Late	.268	284	76	13	2	10	35	36	65	.353	.433
None on/out	.304	375	114	22	4	19	19	25	81	.351	.536
Batting #4	.300	527	158	31	4	23	93	41	98	.354	.505
Batting #5	.272	486	132	28	1	12	52	41	108	.333	.407
Other	.254	468	119	20	4	23	67	55	118	.336	.462
April	.234	197	46	13	1	6	23	20	50	.311	.401
May	.268	231	62	10	2	10	29	26	50	.340	.459
June	.270	211	57	11	0	12	36	26	49	.350	.493
July	.245	216	53	5	2	10	33	9	58	.278	.426
August	.327	294	96	21	1	11	42	24	49	.385	.517
September/October	.286	332	95	19	3	9	49	32	68	.357	.443
Pre-All Star	.255	729	186	37	4	32	100	77	174	.328	.449
Post-All Star	.297	752	223	42	5	26	112	60	150	.355	.469

Batter vs. Pitcher (career)

Hits Best Against	Avg	AB	H	2B	3B	HR	RBI	BB	SO	OBP	SLG
Greg W. Harris	.643	14	9	1	0	3	5	2	1	.688	1.357
Charlie Leibrandt	.500	14	7	2	1	1	4	1	1	.500	1.000
Jack Armstrong	.417	12	5	1	0	1	4	1	1	.462	.750
John Burkett	.412	17	7	0	0	3	7	0	1	.412	.941
Rick Sutcliffe	.375	8	3	1	0	1	1	5	0	.615	.875

Hits Worst Against	Avg	AB	H	2B	3B	HR	RBI	BB	SO	OBP	SLG
Bryn Smith	.067	15	1	0	0	0	1	0	1	.067	.067
Frank Viola	.083	12	1	1	0	0	0	0	5	.083	.167
Paul Assenmacher	.111	18	2	0	0	0	2	2	5	.200	.111
Terry Mulholland	.143	14	2	0	0	0	1	1	2	.200	.143
Zane Smith	.154	13	2	0	0	0	2	0	1	.154	.154

Mike Walker — Mariners
Pitches Right (flyball pitcher)

	ERA	W	L	Sv	G	GS	IP	BB	SO	Avg	H	2B	3B	HR	RBI	OBP	SLG	CG	ShO	Sup	QS	#P/S	SB	CS	GB	FB	G/F
1992 Season	7.36	0	3	0	5	3	14.2	9	5	.333	21	4	0	4	14	.411	.587	0	0	1.23	0	72	3	0	20	24	0.83

1992 Season

	ERA	W	L	Sv	G	GS	IP	H	HR	BB	SO		Avg	AB	H	2B	3B	HR	RBI	BB	SO	OBP	SLG
Home	8.64	0	1	0	2	2	8.1	10	3	5	2	vs. Left	.308	26	8	1	0	0	3	5	2	.419	.346
Away	5.68	0	2	0	3	1	6.1	11	1	4	3	vs. Right	.351	37	13	3	0	4	11	4	3	.405	.757

454

Tim Wallach — Expos
Bats Right (flyball hitter)

	Avg	G	AB	R	H	2B	3B	HR	RBI	BB	SO	HBP	GDP	SB	CS	OBP	SLG	IBB	SH	SF	#Pit	#P/PA	GB	FB	G/F
1992 Season	.223	150	537	53	120	29	1	9	59	50	90	8	10	2	2	.296	.331	2	0	7	2239	3.72	187	176	1.06
Last Five Years	.257	775	2905	310	746	162	12	68	376	238	439	21	74	15	28	.314	.391	38	0	32	11352	3.55	968	991	0.98

1992 Season

	Avg	AB	H	2B	3B	HR	RBI	BB	SO	OBP	SLG		Avg	AB	H	2B	3B	HR	RBI	BB	SO	OBP	SLG
vs. Left	.263	198	52	11	1	7	29	17	25	.329	.434	Scoring Posn	.227	132	30	6	1	2	45	17	27	.314	.333
vs. Right	.201	339	68	18	0	2	30	33	65	.276	.271	Close & Late	.224	98	22	8	0	2	10	7	14	.280	.367
Groundball	.220	209	46	9	0	2	24	21	38	.301	.292	None on/out	.233	150	35	13	0	1	1	13	20	.299	.340
Flyball	.270	126	34	9	0	3	15	11	15	.340	.413	Batting #5	.210	267	56	13	1	4	28	28	40	.289	.311
Home	.263	262	69	19	0	5	41	24	47	.333	.393	Batting #6	.220	177	39	11	0	3	20	14	30	.284	.333
Away	.185	275	51	10	1	4	18	26	43	.259	.273	Other	.269	93	25	5	0	2	11	8	20	.340	.387
Day	.220	159	35	11	0	3	16	15	32	.302	.346	April	.224	85	19	7	0	1	8	12	16	.327	.341
Night	.225	378	85	18	1	6	43	35	58	.293	.325	May	.216	74	16	6	0	2	7	5	10	.289	.378
Grass	.185	146	27	5	1	3	11	14	24	.265	.295	June	.291	103	30	5	0	0	13	6	12	.336	.340
Turf	.238	391	93	24	0	6	48	36	66	.307	.345	July	.180	100	18	4	0	1	8	12	15	.265	.250
First Pitch	.227	75	17	5	0	1	4	2	0	.259	.333	August	.222	90	20	3	1	2	8	7	21	.283	.344
Ahead on Count	.274	124	34	9	0	1	15	24	0	.387	.371	September/October	.200	85	17	4	0	3	15	8	16	.271	.353
Behind on Count	.198	182	36	8	0	4	20	0	48	.214	.308	Pre-All Star	.232	311	72	19	0	4	31	32	46	.313	.331
Two Strikes	.176	245	43	6	1	6	28	24	90	.261	.282	Post-All Star	.212	226	48	10	1	5	28	18	44	.272	.332

1992 By Position

Position	Avg	AB	H	2B	3B	HR	RBI	BB	SO	OBP	SLG	G	GS	Innings	PO	A	E	DP	Fld Pct	Rng Fctr	In Zone	Outs	Zone Rtg	MLB Zone
As 1b	.236	237	56	14	0	5	24	28	41	.325	.359	71	65	594.2	630	61	6	42	.991	---	142	122	.859	.843
As 3b	.215	297	64	15	1	4	35	22	47	.274	.313	85	80	700.2	56	184	9	17	.964	3.08	230	199	.865	.841

Last Five Years

	Avg	AB	H	2B	3B	HR	RBI	BB	SO	OBP	SLG		Avg	AB	H	2B	3B	HR	RBI	BB	SO	OBP	SLG
vs. Left	.264	919	243	51	5	30	117	87	111	.329	.429	Scoring Posn	.265	774	205	41	6	17	293	113	133	.355	.399
vs. Right	.253	1986	503	111	7	38	259	151	328	.308	.374	Close & Late	.245	576	141	31	1	11	68	63	88	.322	.359
Groundball	.280	1117	313	64	4	28	165	85	161	.331	.420	None on/out	.269	784	211	58	1	17	17	43	101	.308	.411
Flyball	.238	652	155	37	0	19	80	66	101	.311	.382	Batting #4	.257	1178	303	53	6	24	144	85	175	.310	.374
Home	.267	1371	366	86	7	28	182	127	205	.331	.401	Batting #5	.255	1246	318	77	6	35	170	101	180	.311	.411
Away	.248	1534	380	76	5	40	194	111	234	.299	.382	Other	.260	481	125	32	0	9	62	52	84	.333	.383
Day	.267	829	221	45	3	24	115	68	140	.323	.415	April	.260	400	104	27	0	8	35	30	59	.314	.388
Night	.253	2076	525	117	9	44	261	170	299	.311	.382	May	.256	488	125	30	4	15	67	39	75	.316	.426
Grass	.250	793	198	35	2	22	104	52	125	.297	.382	June	.275	528	145	33	3	9	75	54	72	.345	.400
Turf	.259	2112	548	127	10	46	272	186	314	.321	.394	July	.255	478	122	27	2	15	70	48	75	.321	.414
First Pitch	.306	471	144	33	0	17	64	18	0	.335	.484	August	.259	521	135	22	2	10	57	34	80	.304	.367
Ahead on Count	.314	641	201	50	5	14	103	111	0	.410	.473	September/October	.235	490	115	23	1	12	73	33	78	.285	.353
Behind on Count	.215	991	213	43	6	17	119	3	247	.223	.322	Pre-All Star	.261	1591	416	100	7	38	199	143	237	.326	.405
Two Strikes	.183	1276	234	49	4	21	124	96	439	.246	.277	Post-All Star	.251	1314	330	62	5	30	177	95	202	.301	.374

Batter vs. Pitcher (since 1984)

Hits Best Against	Avg	AB	H	2B	3B	HR	RBI	BB	SO	OBP	SLG	Hits Worst Against	Avg	AB	H	2B	3B	HR	RBI	BB	SO	OBP	SLG
Mark Grant	.474	19	9	2	0	2	4	1	4	.500	.895	Wally Whitehurst	.000	12	0	0	0	0	1	0	3	.000	.000
Bruce Ruffin	.444	27	12	3	1	2	8	1	2	.464	.852	Mark Davis	.000	11	0	0	0	0	0	1	5	.083	.000
Tom Glavine	.386	44	17	4	1	5	11	5	2	.449	.864	Frank DiPino	.077	13	1	0	0	0	0	2	5	.200	.077
Brian Fisher	.368	19	7	0	0	4	6	2	1	.429	1.000	Omar Olivares	.091	22	2	0	0	0	0	1	3	.130	.091
Jim Acker	.357	14	5	1	0	2	3	0	5	.357	.857	Tim Leary	.118	17	2	0	0	0	0	0	4	.118	.118

Denny Walling — Astros
Bats Left (groundball hitter)

	Avg	G	AB	R	H	2B	3B	HR	RBI	BB	SO	HBP	GDP	SB	CS	OBP	SLG	IBB	SH	SF	#Pit	#P/PA	GB	FB	G/F
1992 Season	.333	3	3	1	1	0	0	0	0	0	0	0	0	0	0	.333	.333	0	0	0	8	2.67	1	1	1.00
Last Five Years	.232	258	487	40	113	26	2	3	53	42	60	2	12	2	0	.295	.312	5	2	1	1802	3.39	209	139	1.50

1992 Season

	Avg	AB	H	2B	3B	HR	RBI	BB	SO	OBP	SLG		Avg	AB	H	2B	3B	HR	RBI	BB	SO	OBP	SLG
vs. Left	.000	0	0	0	0	0	0	0	0	.000	.000	Scoring Posn	.000	0	0	0	0	0	0	0	0	.000	.000
vs. Right	.333	3	1	0	0	0	0	0	0	.333	.333	Close & Late	.000	1	0	0	0	0	0	0	0	.000	.000

Last Five Years

	Avg	AB	H	2B	3B	HR	RBI	BB	SO	OBP	SLG		Avg	AB	H	2B	3B	HR	RBI	BB	SO	OBP	SLG
vs. Left	.167	36	6	2	0	0	3	4	6	.250	.222	Scoring Posn	.246	142	35	9	1	0	46	17	25	.329	.324
vs. Right	.237	451	107	24	2	3	50	38	54	.299	.319	Close & Late	.258	124	32	5	0	0	16	11	17	.316	.298
Groundball	.217	180	39	7	0	0	19	17	24	.284	.256	None on/out	.212	113	24	8	0	0	0	3	7	.233	.283
Flyball	.208	77	16	6	1	1	9	14	11	.330	.351	Batting #5	.247	97	24	5	0	0	5	9	11	.311	.299
Home	.241	228	55	15	1	1	25	22	24	.313	.326	Batting #6	.247	85	21	2	1	0	13	7	7	.309	.294
Away	.224	259	58	11	1	2	28	20	36	.279	.297	Other	.223	305	68	19	1	3	35	26	42	.286	.321
Day	.296	162	48	10	0	1	16	12	14	.343	.377	April	.232	82	19	4	2	0	10	4	11	.273	.329
Night	.200	325	65	16	2	2	37	30	46	.272	.280	May	.233	103	24	6	0	0	16	11	10	.307	.291
Grass	.224	147	33	8	1	1	16	13	22	.294	.313	June	.200	110	22	4	0	1	10	11	14	.279	.264
Turf	.235	340	80	18	1	2	37	29	38	.295	.312	July	.226	31	7	3	0	0	4	3	7	.294	.323
First Pitch	.241	79	19	8	0	1	9	2	0	.259	.380	August	.269	67	18	5	0	2	9	9	9	.355	.433

Last Five Years

	Avg	AB	H	2B	3B	HR	RBI	BB	SO	OBP	SLG		Avg	AB	H	2B	3B	HR	RBI	BB	SO	OBP	SLG
Ahead on Count	.270	141	38	6	1	0	18	27	0	.385	.326	September/October	.245	94	23	4	0	0	4	4	9	.276	.287
Behind on Count	.209	148	31	8	0	1	12	0	26	.220	.284	Pre-All Star	.224	303	68	15	2	1	38	26	37	.289	.297
Two Strikes	.197	173	34	9	0	2	19	10	60	.249	.283	Post-All Star	.245	184	45	11	0	2	15	16	23	.305	.337

Batter vs. Pitcher (since 1984)

Hits Best Against	Avg	AB	H	2B	3B	HR	RBI	BB	SO	OBP	SLG	Hits Worst Against	Avg	AB	H	2B	3B	HR	RBI	BB	SO	OBP	SLG
Jeff Robinson	.625	16	10	3	0	1	5	1	0	.647	1.000	Goose Gossage	.000	10	0	0	0	0	0	1	0	.091	.000
Roger McDowell	.545	11	6	0	0	0	5	3	1	.643	.545	Dennis Martinez	.071	14	1	0	1	0	0	2	1	.188	.214
Rick Sutcliffe	.500	18	9	2	0	0	3	3	1	.571	.611	Mark Davis	.091	11	1	0	0	0	0	0	3	.091	.091
Mark Grant	.500	10	5	1	1	0	1	1	0	.545	.800	David Cone	.125	16	2	1	0	0	0	1	4	.176	.188
Scott Sanderson	.471	17	8	2	0	1	3	0	2	.471	.765	Mike Bielecki	.167	12	2	0	0	0	0	0	2	.231	.167

Dan Walters — Padres
Bats Right (groundball hitter)

	Avg	G	AB	R	H	2B	3B	HR	RBI	BB	SO	HBP	GDP	SB	CS	OBP	SLG	IBB	SH	SF	#Pit	#P/PA	GB	FB	G/F
1992 Season	.251	57	179	14	45	11	1	4	22	10	28	2	3	1	0	.295	.391	0	1	2	644	3.34	74	48	1.54

1992 Season

	Avg	AB	H	2B	3B	HR	RBI	BB	SO	OBP	SLG		Avg	AB	H	2B	3B	HR	RBI	BB	SO	OBP	SLG
vs. Left	.262	61	16	4	0	1	8	1	9	.270	.377	Scoring Posn	.204	49	10	2	0	0	16	3	11	.241	.245
vs. Right	.246	118	29	7	1	3	14	9	19	.308	.398	Close & Late	.208	24	5	2	1	1	6	6	4	.375	.500
Home	.267	90	24	7	1	3	12	6	10	.316	.467	None on/out	.273	33	9	2	0	3	3	0	2	.273	.606
Away	.236	89	21	4	0	1	10	4	18	.274	.315	Batting #6	.244	78	19	5	0	1	8	6	12	.310	.346
First Pitch	.321	28	9	3	0	0	7	0	0	.355	.429	Batting #7	.269	78	21	5	1	3	12	2	11	.288	.474
Ahead on Count	.256	43	11	2	0	1	4	3	0	.304	.372	Other	.217	23	5	1	0	0	2	2	5	.269	.261
Behind on Count	.208	72	15	4	0	1	7	0	20	.208	.306	Pre-All Star	.276	116	32	6	1	3	17	7	16	.320	.422
Two Strikes	.174	69	12	3	1	0	6	7	28	.250	.246	Post-All Star	.206	63	13	5	0	1	5	3	12	.250	.333

Bruce Walton — Athletics
Pitches Right

	ERA	W	L	Sv	G	GS	IP	BB	SO	Avg	H	2B	3B	HR	RBI	OBP	SLG	GF	IR	IRS	Hld	SvOp	SB	CS	GB	FB	G/F
1992 Season	9.90	0	0	0	7	0	10.0	3	7	.378	17	4	0	1	10	.408	.533	2	4	0	2	0	0	0	11	12	0.92
Career (1991-1992)	7.83	1	0	0	19	0	23.0	9	17	.301	28	6	0	4	19	.362	.495	7	14	3	3	1	2	0	30	28	1.07

1992 Season

	ERA	W	L	Sv	G	GS	IP	H	HR	BB	SO		Avg	AB	H	2B	3B	HR	RBI	BB	SO	OBP	SLG
Home	0.00	0	0	0	1	0	1.0	0	0	0	2	vs. Left	.375	16	6	1	0	0	2	1	1	.412	.438
Away	11.00	0	0	0	6	0	9.0	17	4	3	5	vs. Right	.379	29	11	3	0	1	8	2	6	.406	.586

Jerome Walton — Cubs
Bats Right (groundball hitter)

	Avg	G	AB	R	H	2B	3B	HR	RBI	BB	SO	HBP	GDP	SB	CS	OBP	SLG	IBB	SH	SF	#Pit	#P/PA	GB	FB	G/F
1992 Season	.127	30	55	7	7	0	1	0	1	9	13	2	1	1	2	.273	.164	0	3	0	242	3.67	18	12	1.50
Career (1989-1992)	.258	370	1192	176	308	52	7	12	85	105	215	15	18	46	19	.324	.344	2	9	10	4730	3.58	471	247	1.91

1992 Season

	Avg	AB	H	2B	3B	HR	RBI	BB	SO	OBP	SLG		Avg	AB	H	2B	3B	HR	RBI	BB	SO	OBP	SLG
vs. Left	.149	47	7	0	1	0	1	7	10	.273	.191	Scoring Posn	.000	10	0	0	0	0	1	1	5	.167	.000
vs. Right	.000	8	0	0	0	0	0	2	3	.273	.000	Close & Late	.000	7	0	0	0	0	0	1	2	.300	.000

Career (1989-1992)

	Avg	AB	H	2B	3B	HR	RBI	BB	SO	OBP	SLG		Avg	AB	H	2B	3B	HR	RBI	BB	SO	OBP	SLG
vs. Left	.256	449	115	18	4	3	38	46	77	.329	.334	Scoring Posn	.256	227	58	9	3	0	72	25	51	.325	.322
vs. Right	.260	743	193	34	3	9	47	59	138	.320	.350	Close & Late	.210	186	39	5	2	1	18	18	41	.286	.274
Groundball	.228	451	103	18	1	2	31	31	88	.282	.286	None on/out	.284	510	145	28	2	11	11	41	83	.344	.412
Flyball	.229	262	60	7	2	5	15	36	44	.330	.328	Batting #1	.262	1075	282	45	6	10	75	91	192	.325	.343
Home	.277	571	158	21	5	8	39	50	88	.336	.373	Batting #7	.182	33	6	1	1	0	1	2	5	.229	.273
Away	.242	621	150	31	2	4	46	55	127	.313	.317	Other	.238	84	20	6	0	2	9	12	18	.337	.381
Day	.281	602	169	25	5	5	50	54	96	.343	.364	April	.256	207	53	11	1	3	13	16	37	.322	.362
Night	.236	590	139	27	2	7	35	51	119	.304	.324	May	.247	178	44	9	2	0	8	17	31	.313	.320
Grass	.273	791	216	33	5	9	48	72	130	.340	.362	June	.260	223	58	11	0	2	14	26	43	.345	.336
Turf	.229	401	92	19	2	3	37	33	85	.292	.309	July	.287	143	41	10	0	2	16	5	26	.316	.399
First Pitch	.298	178	53	9	0	3	9	1	0	.324	.399	August	.277	235	65	5	2	3	22	23	36	.346	.353
Ahead on Count	.329	277	91	14	2	4	27	68	0	.457	.437	September/October	.228	206	47	6	2	2	12	18	42	.290	.306
Behind on Count	.231	411	95	18	1	3	27	0	123	.235	.302	Pre-All Star	.260	662	172	37	3	6	43	60	122	.327	.352
Two Strikes	.180	528	95	18	4	2	26	35	215	.234	.241	Post-All Star	.257	530	136	15	4	6	42	45	93	.319	.334

Batter vs. Pitcher (career)

Hits Best Against	Avg	AB	H	2B	3B	HR	RBI	BB	SO	OBP	SLG	Hits Worst Against	Avg	AB	H	2B	3B	HR	RBI	BB	SO	OBP	SLG
Bruce Hurst	.500	12	6	0	0	0	2	2	1	.571	.500	Bud Black	.091	11	1	0	0	0	0	2	1	.231	.091
Dennis Rasmussen	.474	19	9	2	0	0	0	1	2	.500	.579	Zane Smith	.091	11	1	0	0	0	0	0	3	.091	.091
John Smiley	.400	20	8	0	0	2	4	0	5	.400	.700	Walt Terrell	.111	18	2	0	0	0	0	0	1	.111	.111
Dennis Martinez	.364	11	4	2	0	1	1	0	3	.364	.818	Jose Rijo	.167	18	3	1	0	0	0	1	2	.211	.222
Bill Landrum	.364	11	4	0	0	2	3	1	3	.417	.909	Mike Morgan	.231	13	3	1	0	0	0	0	0	.231	.231

Duane Ward — Blue Jays
Pitches Right (groundball pitcher)

	ERA	W	L	Sv	G	GS	IP	BB	SO	Avg	H	2B	3B	HR	RBI	OBP	SLG	GF	IR	IRS	Hld	SvOp	SB	CS	GB	FB	G/F
1992 Season	1.95	7	4	12	79	0	101.1	39	103	.207	76	10	2	5	32	.282	.286	35	30	9	25	16	14	4	127	85	1.49
Last Five Years	3.09	29	31	76	363	0	562.2	232	560	.223	223	60	11	26	220	.303	.301	120	228	70	68	106	58	22	775	400	1.94

1992 Season

	ERA	W	L	Sv	G	GS	IP	H	HR	BB	SO		Avg	AB	H	2B	3B	HR	RBI	BB	SO	OBP	SLG
Home	1.57	6	1	6	40	0	51.2	37	3	21	56	vs. Left	.197	183	36	6	1	5	20	25	61	.289	.322
Away	2.36	1	3	6	39	0	49.2	39	2	18	47	vs. Right	.217	184	40	4	1	0	12	14	42	.275	.250
Day	2.06	3	2	8	27	0	35.0	26	1	19	39	Inning 1-6	.000	0	0	0	0	0	0	0	0	.000	.000
Night	1.90	4	2	4	52	0	66.1	50	4	20	64	Inning 7+	.207	367	76	10	2	5	32	39	103	.282	.286
Grass	2.88	0	3	6	32	0	40.2	35	2	16	36	None on	.230	191	44	5	0	2	2	20	59	.303	.288
Turf	1.34	7	1	6	47	0	60.2	41	3	23	67	Runners on	.182	176	32	5	2	3	30	19	44	.260	.284
April	4.22	1	1	4	11	0	10.2	10	1	6	10	Scoring Posn	.178	101	18	2	2	3	29	12	24	.263	.327
May	2.60	1	1	2	12	0	17.1	17	0	10	14	Close & Late	.199	231	46	8	0	4	21	25	62	.278	.286
June	2.12	1	2	2	11	0	17.0	9	1	6	17	None on/out	.183	82	15	1	0	1	1	10	25	.272	.232
July	1.37	2	0	1	14	0	19.2	18	1	7	23	vs. 1st Batr (relief)	.236	72	17	2	0	1	5	6	21	.291	.306
August	1.72	1	0	1	13	0	15.2	13	1	2	16	First Inning Pitched	.223	278	62	9	2	5	29	27	73	.288	.324
September/October	0.86	1	0	2	18	0	21.0	9	1	8	23	First 15 Pitches	.232	237	55	7	1	5	22	17	58	.280	.333
Starter	0.00	0	0	0	0	0	0.0	0	0	0	0	Pitch 16-30	.170	106	18	3	1	0	7	18	35	.294	.217
Reliever	1.95	7	4	12	79	0	101.1	76	5	39	103	Pitch 31-45	.130	23	3	0	0	0	3	4	10	.259	.130
0 Days rest	2.59	2	2	4	20	0	24.1	16	2	11	25	Pitch 46+	.000	1	0	0	0	0	0	0	0	.000	.000
1 or 2 Days rest	1.74	4	1	7	47	0	62.0	51	3	19	60	First Pitch	.426	47	20	4	0	2	10	3	0	.451	.638
3+ Days rest	1.80	1	1	1	12	0	15.0	9	0	9	18	Ahead on Count	.144	208	30	2	1	2	12	0	93	.147	.192
Pre-All Star	2.50	5	4	8	40	0	54.0	42	3	25	53	Behind on Count	.204	54	11	3	0	0	2	17	0	.394	.259
Post-All Star	1.33	2	0	4	39	0	47.1	34	2	14	50	Two Strikes	.130	207	27	2	2	1	11	19	103	.202	.174

Last Five Years

	ERA	W	L	Sv	G	GS	IP	H	HR	BB	SO		Avg	AB	H	2B	3B	HR	RBI	BB	SO	OBP	SLG
Home	2.79	18	16	41	186	0	293.2	222	12	110	299	vs. Left	.228	907	207	32	4	18	104	142	265	.331	.332
Away	3.41	11	15	35	177	0	269.0	230	14	122	261	vs. Right	.218	1124	245	28	7	8	116	90	295	.279	.277
Day	2.96	14	10	26	117	0	182.1	132	8	80	197	Inning 1-6	.248	125	31	4	0	3	24	21	27	.351	.352
Night	3.15	15	21	50	246	0	380.1	320	18	152	363	Inning 7+	.221	1906	421	56	11	23	196	211	533	.300	.298
Grass	3.60	9	12	23	135	0	202.2	173	12	96	196	None on	.214	1101	236	38	4	11	11	108	286	.286	.286
Turf	2.80	20	19	53	228	0	360.0	279	14	136	364	Runners on	.232	930	216	22	7	15	209	124	232	.322	.319
April	2.89	2	5	14	51	0	65.1	56	2	29	72	Scoring Posn	.232	583	135	10	4	13	198	88	154	.328	.329
May	2.76	3	7	13	62	0	91.1	77	1	55	83	Close & Late	.224	965	216	33	5	13	118	116	269	.307	.309
June	3.46	9	5	11	63	0	112.0	86	5	47	104	None on/out	.206	465	96	15	2	3	3	55	136	.290	.267
July	3.02	5	5	13	56	0	98.1	91	7	28	101	vs. 1st Batr (relief)	.216	324	70	6	0	3	30	30	100	.286	.262
August	3.36	7	5	10	60	0	96.1	83	4	29	90	First Inning Pitched	.219	1217	266	30	6	13	163	135	328	.297	.300
September/October	2.90	3	4	15	71	0	99.1	59	7	44	110	First 15 Pitches	.216	1069	231	25	5	15	105	102	277	.286	.291
Starter	0.00	0	0	0	0	0	0.0	0	0	0	0	Pitch 16-30	.226	633	143	20	3	7	79	90	187	.322	.300
Reliever	3.09	29	31	76	363	0	562.2	452	36	232	560	Pitch 31-45	.249	257	64	14	3	3	31	3	78	.332	.362
0 Days rest	2.91	9	7	16	64	0	89.2	63	4	32	93	Pitch 46+	.194	72	14	1	0	1	5	7	18	.275	.250
1 or 2 Days rest	3.20	17	18	50	236	0	371.0	314	17	161	357	First Pitch	.344	224	77	12	2	5	37	28	0	.413	.482
3+ Days rest	2.82	3	6	10	63	0	102.0	75	5	39	110	Ahead on Count	.158	1126	178	19	6	13	85	0	505	.160	.220
Pre-All Star	2.81	17	17	44	197	0	304.1	239	10	140	301	Behind on Count	.311	325	101	13	2	4	46	106	0	.477	.400
Post-All Star	3.41	12	14	32	166	0	258.1	213	16	92	259	Two Strikes	.155	1139	177	21	6	11	87	97	560	.223	.213

Pitcher vs. Batter (career)

Pitches Best Vs.	Avg	AB	H	2B	3B	HR	RBI	BB	SO	OBP	SLG	Pitches Worst Vs.	Avg	AB	H	2B	3B	HR	RBI	BB	SO	OBP	SLG
Jose Canseco	.000	17	0	0	0	0	1	0	10	.000	.000	Mike Greenwell	.500	16	8	2	0	0	0	2	1	.556	.625
Tony Pena	.000	11	0	0	0	0	1	2	1	.154	.000	Rickey Henderson	.478	23	11	1	1	0	3	3	3	.538	.609
Steve Buechele	.000	10	0	0	0	0	0	2	6	.167	.000	Alan Trammell	.455	11	5	2	0	0	0	3	1	.571	.636
Dave Henderson	.100	20	2	0	0	0	2	0	5	.100	.100	Ken Griffey Jr	.417	12	5	1	0	1	1	2	1	.500	.750
Jody Reed	.111	18	2	1	0	0	0	2	.111	.167	Tom Brunansky	.400	10	4	0	0	1	5	2	0	.500	.700

Kevin Ward — Padres
Bats Right

	Avg	G	AB	R	H	2B	3B	HR	RBI	BB	SO	HBP	GDP	SB	CS	OBP	SLG	IBB	SH	SF	#Pit	#P/PA	GB	FB	G/F
1992 Season	.197	81	147	12	29	5	0	3	12	14	38	2	8	2	3	.274	.293	0	1	1	656	4.00	42	41	1.02
Career (1991-1992)	.217	125	254	25	55	12	2	5	20	23	65	3	11	3	7	.288	.339	0	2	1	1104	3.93	72	72	1.00

1992 Season

	Avg	AB	H	2B	3B	HR	RBI	BB	SO	OBP	SLG		Avg	AB	H	2B	3B	HR	RBI	BB	SO	OBP	SLG
vs. Left	.253	87	22	2	0	3	9	9	27	.320	.379	Scoring Posn	.133	30	4	4	0	0	7	2	8	.182	.267
vs. Right	.117	60	7	3	0	0	3	5	11	.209	.167	Close & Late	.103	29	3	1	0	1	4	3	9	.182	.241
Home	.224	67	15	3	0	0	3	8	13	.307	.269	None on/out	.212	33	7	0	0	1	1	1	10	.235	.303
Away	.175	80	14	2	0	3	9	6	25	.247	.313	Batting #6	.200	30	6	1	0	0	2	3	7	.273	.233
First Pitch	.333	18	6	1	0	1	4	0	0	.368	.556	Batting #9	.148	27	4	0	0	1	3	2	6	.200	.259
Ahead on Count	.240	25	6	2	0	1	2	7	0	.406	.440	Other	.211	90	19	4	0	2	7	9	25	.297	.322
Behind on Count	.163	43	7	3	0	0	2	0	16	.182	.233	Pre-All Star	.193	83	16	2	0	2	7	10	18	.292	.289
Two Strikes	.160	75	12	1	0	1	5	7	38	.238	.213	Post-All Star	.203	64	13	3	0	1	5	4	20	.250	.297

457

Turner Ward — Blue Jays
Bats Both

	Avg	G	AB	R	H	2B	3B	HR	RBI	BB	SO	HBP	GDP	SB	CS	OBP	SLG	IBB	SH	SF	#Pit	#P/PA	GB	FB	G/F
1992 Season	.345	18	29	7	10	3	0	1	3	4	4	0	1	0	1	.424	.552	0	0	0	132	4.00	7	9	0.78
Career (1990-1992)	.282	80	188	29	53	12	1	2	20	18	30	0	4	3	1	.345	.388	0	4	0	788	3.83	63	51	1.24

1992 Season

	Avg	AB	H	2B	3B	HR	RBI	BB	SO	OBP	SLG		Avg	AB	H	2B	3B	HR	RBI	BB	SO	OBP	SLG
vs. Left	.625	8	5	2	0	0	2	1	0	.667	.875	Scoring Posn	.222	9	2	1	0	0	2	2	2	.364	.333
vs. Right	.238	21	5	1	0	1	1	3	4	.333	.429	Close & Late	.000	7	0	0	0	0	0	0	2	.000	.000

Gary Wayne — Twins
Pitches Left (flyball pitcher)

	ERA	W	L	Sv	G	GS	IP	BB	SO	Avg	H	2B	3B	HR	RBI	OBP	SLG	GF	IR	IRS	Hld	SvOp	SB	CS	GB	FB	G/F
1992 Season	2.63	3	3	0	41	0	48.0	19	29	.260	46	11	3	2	23	.337	.390	13	34	10	9	3	5	0	54	62	0.87
Career (1989-1992)	3.44	8	8	3	147	0	170.0	72	105	.238	150	38	4	12	91	.318	.368	27	127	36	26	9	12	3	203	221	0.92

1992 Season

	ERA	W	L	Sv	G	GS	IP	H	HR	BB	SO		Avg	AB	H	2B	3B	HR	RBI	BB	SO	OBP	SLG
Home	2.70	1	2	0	19	0	26.2	22	0	10	19	vs. Left	.250	48	12	4	0	1	8	3	13	.302	.396
Away	2.53	2	1	0	22	0	21.1	24	2	9	10	vs. Right	.264	129	34	7	3	1	15	16	16	.349	.388
Starter	0.00	0	0	0	0	0	0.0	0	0	0	0	Scoring Posn	.286	49	14	2	2	1	21	7	12	.356	.469
Reliever	2.63	3	3	0	41	0	48.0	46	2	19	29	Close & Late	.253	95	24	7	1	1	10	12	20	.345	.379
0 Days rest	3.86	1	1	0	4	0	4.2	5	0	1	4	None on/out	.295	44	13	7	0	0	3	8	.367	.455
1 or 2 Days rest	3.13	1	1	0	19	0	23.0	27	2	9	10	First Pitch	.324	34	11	4	1	1	5	5	0	.410	.588
3+ Days rest	1.77	1	1	0	18	0	20.1	14	0	9	15	Behind on Count	.326	43	14	2	1	0	7	7	0	.420	.419
Pre-All Star	2.53	1	2	0	29	0	32.0	34	1	14	19	Ahead on Count	.184	76	14	3	1	0	7	0	24	.207	.250
Post-All Star	2.81	2	1	0	12	0	16.0	12	1	5	10	Two Strikes	.157	70	11	4	1	0	7	7	29	.244	.243

Career (1989-1992)

	ERA	W	L	Sv	G	GS	IP	H	HR	BB	SO		Avg	AB	H	2B	3B	HR	RBI	BB	SO	OBP	SLG
Home	3.48	5	2	2	76	0	88.0	72	6	42	59	vs. Left	.207	188	39	10	0	5	34	17	41	.278	.340
Away	3.40	3	6	1	71	0	82.0	78	6	30	46	vs. Right	.251	442	111	28	4	7	57	55	64	.335	.380
Day	4.66	1	3	0	42	0	46.1	53	5	18	25	Inning 1-6	.226	84	19	4	0	2	18	13	17	.333	.345
Night	2.98	7	5	3	105	0	123.2	97	7	54	80	Inning 7+	.240	546	131	34	4	10	73	59	88	.316	.372
Grass	3.36	2	4	0	57	0	64.1	57	5	27	40	None on	.237	321	76	23	1	4	4	34	52	.318	.352
Turf	3.49	6	4	3	90	0	105.2	93	7	45	65	Runners on	.239	309	74	15	3	8	87	38	53	.319	.385
April	4.05	0	1	0	24	0	26.2	26	3	18	21	Scoring Posn	.266	192	51	11	2	7	84	28	38	.349	.453
May	2.04	1	0	0	28	0	39.2	28	2	11	18	Close & Late	.196	199	39	8	1	1	16	25	39	.294	.261
June	5.03	3	1	0	29	0	34.0	38	2	18	23	None on/out	.252	147	37	15	1	2	2	16	22	.333	.408
July	3.79	0	2	0	17	0	19.0	16	1	6	12	vs. 1st Batr (relief)	.208	130	27	6	0	4	26	12	29	.274	.346
August	2.70	1	2	1	15	0	16.2	13	2	6	8	First Inning Pitched	.222	397	88	24	4	5	67	50	65	.309	.340
September/October	3.18	3	2	2	34	0	34.0	29	2	13	23	First 15 Pitches	.217	374	81	19	3	6	56	40	62	.294	.332
Starter	0.00	0	0	0	0	0	0.0	0	0	0	0	Pitch 16-30	.246	171	42	12	1	4	24	25	32	.343	.398
Reliever	3.44	8	8	3	147	0	170.0	150	12	72	105	Pitch 31-45	.288	59	17	4	0	1	7	7	10	.364	.407
0 Days rest	5.63	1	4	1	31	0	32.0	38	3	16	21	Pitch 45+	.385	26	10	3	0	1	4	0	1	.407	.615
1 or 2 Days rest	3.25	4	2	1	66	0	80.1	68	6	33	44	First Pitch	.333	87	29	8	1	2	14	7	0	.383	.517
3+ Days rest	2.50	3	2	1	50	0	57.2	44	1	23	40	Ahead on Count	.184	288	53	12	2	3	32	0	91	.197	.271
Pre-All Star	3.70	4	3	0	90	0	107.0	101	7	50	66	Behind on Count	.277	159	44	11	1	3	27	39	0	.417	.415
Post-All Star	3.00	4	5	3	57	0	63.0	49	5	22	39	Two Strikes	.167	287	48	13	2	3	28	26	105	.241	.258

Pitcher vs. Batter (career)

Pitches Best Vs.	Avg	AB	H	2B	3B	HR	RBI	BB	SO	OBP	SLG	Pitches Worst Vs.	Avg	AB	H	2B	3B	HR	RBI	BB	SO	OBP	SLG
Wally Joyner	.200	10	2	1	0	0	3	0	0	.182	.300												

Dave Weathers — Blue Jays
Pitches Right (groundball pitcher)

	ERA	W	L	Sv	G	GS	IP	BB	SO	Avg	H	2B	3B	HR	RBI	OBP	SLG	GF	IR	IRS	Hld	SvOp	SB	CS	GB	FB	G/F
1992 Season	8.10	0	0	0	2	0	3.1	2	3	.385	5	0	0	1	3	.467	.615	2	1	0	0	0	0	5	0	0.00
Career (1991-1992)	5.50	1	0	0	17	0	18.0	19	16	.286	20	4	0	2	13	.446	.429	4	20	8	1	0	4	1	24	13	1.85

1992 Season

	ERA	W	L	Sv	G	GS	IP	H	HR	BB	SO		Avg	AB	H	2B	3B	HR	RBI	BB	SO	OBP	SLG
Home	0.00	0	0	0	0	0	0.0	0	0	0	0	vs. Left	.500	6	3	0	0	1	0	2	.500	.500
Away	8.10	0	0	0	2	0	3.1	5	1	2	3	vs. Right	.286	7	2	0	0	1	2	1	.444	.714

Lenny Webster — Twins
Bats Right (groundball hitter)

	Avg	G	AB	R	H	2B	3B	HR	RBI	BB	SO	HBP	GDP	SB	CS	OBP	SLG	IBB	SH	SF	#Pit	#P/PA	GB	FB	G/F
1992 Season	.280	53	118	10	33	10	1	1	13	9	11	0	3	0	2	.331	.407	0	2	0	447	3.52	58	31	1.87
Career (1989-1992)	.287	87	178	21	51	14	1	4	22	19	24	0	5	0	2	.354	.444	0	2	1	702	3.55	79	48	1.65

1992 Season

	Avg	AB	H	2B	3B	HR	RBI	BB	SO	OBP	SLG		Avg	AB	H	2B	3B	HR	RBI	BB	SO	OBP	SLG
vs. Left	.321	28	9	4	0	1	7	4	4	.406	.571	Scoring Posn	.219	32	7	4	0	0	11	1	3	.242	.344
vs. Right	.267	90	24	6	1	0	6	5	7	.305	.356	Close & Late	.353	17	6	1	0	0	2	1	2	.389	.412
Home	.288	66	19	5	1	1	7	4	6	.329	.439	None on/out	.250	32	8	2	0	0	0	2	4	.294	.313

458

1992 Season

	Avg	AB	H	2B	3B	HR	RBI	BB	SO	OBP	SLG		Avg	AB	H	2B	3B	HR	RBI	BB	SO	OBP	SLG
Away	.269	52	14	5	0	0	6	5	5	.333	.365	Batting #7	.368	19	7	4	0	0	2	1	1	.400	.579
First Pitch	.200	15	3	0	0	0	0	0	0	.200	.200	Batting #8	.256	82	21	4	0	1	7	8	7	.322	.341
Ahead on Count	.326	43	14	6	1	0	9	6	0	.396	.512	Other	.294	17	5	2	1	0	4	0	3	.294	.529
Behind on Count	.242	33	8	4	0	0	7	0	8	.242	.364	Pre-All Star	.206	68	14	3	1	0	5	5	6	.260	.279
Two Strikes	.250	40	10	3	0	1	4	4	11	.318	.400	Post-All Star	.380	50	19	7	0	1	8	4	5	.426	.580

Mitch Webster — Dodgers   Bats Both (flyball hitter)

	Avg	G	AB	R	H	2B	3B	HR	RBI	BB	SO	HBP	GDP	SB	CS	OBP	SLG	IBB	SH	SF	#Pit	#P/PA	GB	FB	G/F
1992 Season	.267	135	262	33	70	12	5	6	35	27	49	2	1	11	5	.334	.420	3	8	5	1069	3.61	68	104	0.65
Last Five Years	.252	619	1697	223	426	68	28	29	167	153	313	14	17	71	30	.316	.377	12	29	17	6574	3.49	466	600	0.78

1992 Season

	Avg	AB	H	2B	3B	HR	RBI	BB	SO	OBP	SLG		Avg	AB	H	2B	3B	HR	RBI	BB	SO	OBP	SLG
vs. Left	.292	130	38	8	1	3	17	15	18	.361	.438	Scoring Posn	.214	70	15	4	1	1	28	10	15	.302	.343
vs. Right	.242	132	32	4	4	3	18	12	31	.309	.402	Close & Late	.318	66	21	1	2	1	9	13	13	.432	.439
Groundball	.260	77	20	4	3	1	8	5	13	.313	.429	None on/out	.267	60	16	4	2	0	0	4	9	.323	.400
Flyball	.264	91	24	4	2	3	13	8	19	.317	.451	Batting #3	.283	60	17	2	1	1	11	6	12	.348	.400
Home	.216	125	27	5	1	1	13	16	16	.308	.296	Batting #5	.215	65	14	4	1	1	6	6	11	.278	.354
Away	.314	137	43	7	4	5	22	11	33	.360	.533	Other	.285	137	39	6	3	4	18	15	26	.355	.460
Day	.321	81	26	8	0	2	14	6	18	.367	.494	April	.333	9	3	0	0	0	4	2	3	.385	.333
Night	.243	181	44	4	5	4	21	21	31	.320	.387	May	.217	46	10	1	3	2	5	4	17	.275	.500
Grass	.245	188	46	6	3	3	26	20	32	.316	.356	June	.261	46	12	1	0	1	8	9	6	.393	.348
Turf	.324	74	24	6	2	3	9	7	17	.383	.581	July	.296	54	16	3	1	0	5	2	6	.321	.389
First Pitch	.360	50	18	3	0	2	11	2	0	.370	.540	August	.246	57	14	4	0	1	5	5	9	.302	.368
Ahead on Count	.355	62	22	3	3	1	8	16	0	.481	.548	September/October	.300	50	15	3	1	2	8	5	8	.368	.520
Behind on Count	.233	86	20	5	1	1	4	0	29	.233	.349												
Two Strikes	.110	109	12	2	2	2	7	9	49	.176	.220												

1992 By Position

Position	Avg	AB	H	2B	3B	HR	RBI	BB	SO	OBP	SLG	G	GS	Innings	PO	A	E	DP	Fld Pct	Rng Fctr	In Zone	Outs	Zone Rtg	MLB Zone
As Pinch Hitter	.362	47	17	0	0	2	12	5	10	.418	.489	56	0	---	---	---	---	---	---	---	---	---	---	---
As lf	.241	79	19	4	1	3	12	6	13	.299	.430	36	19	198.2	46	0	0	0	1.000	2.08	54	45	.833	.809
As rf	.263	118	31	7	3	8	24	13	24	.333	.398	56	30	300.2	65	0	2	0	.970	1.95	68	64	.941	.814

Last Five Years

	Avg	AB	H	2B	3B	HR	RBI	BB	SO	OBP	SLG		Avg	AB	H	2B	3B	HR	RBI	BB	SO	OBP	SLG
vs. Left	.272	655	178	29	7	14	70	49	93	.324	.402	Scoring Posn	.253	396	100	15	5	9	136	53	81	.333	.384
vs. Right	.240	1042	250	39	21	15	97	104	220	.312	.361	Close & Late	.239	347	83	9	7	7	43	50	82	.337	.366
Groundball	.275	579	159	28	11	10	61	43	108	.328	.413	None on/out	.290	428	124	26	10	5	5	31	75	.348	.432
Flyball	.232	409	95	15	7	11	51	38	79	.300	.384	Batting #1	.245	306	75	7	6	6	30	17	61	.290	.366
Home	.250	827	207	28	11	13	88	86	140	.324	.358	Batting #2	.253	592	150	25	8	13	56	56	83	.319	.389
Away	.254	870	221	40	17	16	79	67	173	.308	.394	Other	.254	799	203	36	14	10	81	80	169	.324	.372
Day	.255	659	168	28	11	9	64	58	138	.316	.372	April	.286	234	67	10	4	3	24	26	42	.355	.402
Night	.250	1038	259	40	17	20	103	95	175	.316	.380	May	.214	323	69	5	7	5	23	28	65	.281	.319
Grass	.237	1115	264	35	18	19	111	85	208	.316	.352	June	.231	324	75	10	4	5	28	34	63	.310	.333
Turf	.282	582	164	33	10	10	56	68	105	.360	.424	July	.299	308	92	16	6	4	30	20	45	.344	.429
First Pitch	.314	357	112	16	8	9	43	7	0	.324	.479	August	.232	272	63	13	2	8	34	20	57	.285	.382
Ahead on Count	.319	379	121	23	9	5	55	72	0	.428	.467	September/October	.263	236	62	14	5	4	28	25	41	.335	.415
Behind on Count	.210	537	113	14	9	4	28	1	173	.220	.292	Pre-All Star	.244	984	240	29	17	15	89	94	184	.313	.354
Two Strikes	.143	694	99	16	7	9	37	70	312	.224	.225	Post-All Star	.264	713	188	39	11	14	78	59	129	.321	.408

Batter vs. Pitcher (since 1984)

Hits Best Against	Avg	AB	H	2B	3B	HR	RBI	BB	SO	OBP	SLG	Hits Worst Against	Avg	AB	H	2B	3B	HR	RBI	BB	SO	OBP	SLG
Bruce Ruffin	.556	18	10	2	1	0	0	2	0	.600	.778	Tim Burke	.000	10	0	0	0	0	0	1	3	.091	.000
Zane Smith	.462	26	12	4	1	0	2	2	1	.500	.692	Tim Belcher	.059	17	1	0	0	0	0	1	5	.111	.059
Mike Dunne	.444	27	12	0	1	3	6	2	4	.483	.852	Bob Kipper	.071	14	1	0	0	0	0	1	3	.133	.071
Danny Darwin	.435	23	10	3	1	0	1	2	5	.480	.652	Randy Johnson	.071	14	1	0	0	0	1	2	2	.188	.071
Ron Darling	.350	40	14			2	4	6	10	.426	.625	Pete Harnisch	.091	11	1	0	0	0	0	0	3	.091	.091

Eric Wedge — Red Sox   Bats Right (flyball hitter)

	Avg	G	AB	R	H	2B	3B	HR	RBI	BB	SO	HBP	GDP	SB	CS	OBP	SLG	IBB	SH	SF	#Pit	#P/PA	GB	FB	G/F
1992 Season	.250	27	68	11	17	2	0	5	11	13	18	1	0	0	0	.370	.500	0	0	0	328	4.05	14	22	0.64

1992 Season

	Avg	AB	H	2B	3B	HR	RBI	BB	SO	OBP	SLG		Avg	AB	H	2B	3B	HR	RBI	BB	SO	OBP	SLG
vs. Left	.306	36	11	1	0	4	8	5	8	.390	.667	Scoring Posn	.353	17	6	1	0	1	5	7	5	.542	.588
vs. Right	.188	32	6	1	0	1	3	8	10	.350	.313	Close & Late	.188	16	3	0	0	1		2	4	.278	.188

Bill Wegman — Brewers

Pitches Right

	ERA	W	L	Sv	G	GS	IP	BB	SO	Avg	H	2B	3B	HR	RBI	OBP	SLG	CG	ShO	Sup	QS	#P/S	SB	CS	GB	FB	G/F
1992 Season	3.20	13	14	0	35	35	261.2	55	127	.250	251	50	2	28	93	.294	.387	7	0	4.85	21	110	18	6	427	255	1.67
Last Five Years	3.66	45	42	0	114	107	734.2	172	347	.260	740	140	10	80	300	.304	.400	19	4	4.57	58	98	45	20	1100	846	1.30

1992 Season

	ERA	W	L	Sv	G	GS	IP	H	HR	BB	SO		Avg	AB	H	2B	3B	HR	RBI	BB	SO	OBP	SLG
Home	2.26	9	5	0	19	19	143.2	127	14	33	59	vs. Left	.209	469	98	20	0	7	30	25	30	.247	.296
Away	4.35	4	9	0	16	16	118.0	124	14	22	68	vs. Right	.286	535	153	30	2	21	63	30	97	.334	.467
Day	3.46	4	5	0	11	11	78.0	80	13	22	37	Inning 1-6	.246	780	192	36	2	23	74	45	97	.291	.386
Night	3.09	9	9	0	24	24	183.2	171	15	33	90	Inning 7+	.263	224	59	14	0	5	19	10	30	.303	.393
Grass	2.93	12	12	0	31	31	233.1	220	25	48	110	None on	.247	632	156	28	2	19	19	26	91	.281	.388
Turf	5.40	1	2	0	4	4	28.1	31	3	7	17	Runners on	.255	372	95	22	0	9	74	29	36	.315	.387
April	2.38	2	1	0	5	5	41.2	34	1	13	14	Scoring Posn	.255	204	52	10	0	5	62	23	20	.333	.377
May	2.77	3	3	0	6	6	48.2	46	9	5	25	Close & Late	.281	128	36	11	0	3	15	8	16	.336	.438
June	4.50	2	1	0	5	5	32.0	31	5	11	19	None on/out	.234	273	64	10	2	11	11	8	35	.261	.407
July	3.78	2	3	0	7	7	52.1	60	8	7	21	vs. 1st Batr (relief)	.000	0	0	0	0	0	0	0	0	.000	.000
August	3.24	2	4	0	6	6	41.2	43	3	8	25	First Inning Pitched	.221	131	29	2	0	4	12	11	19	.282	.328
September/October	2.78	2	2	0	6	6	45.1	37	2	11	23	First 75 Pitches	.244	656	160	28	1	18	61	37	84	.287	.372
Starter	3.20	13	14	0	35	35	261.2	251	28	55	127	Pitch 76-90	.253	146	37	10	1	7	11	7	15	.297	.479
Reliever	0.00	0	0	0	0	0	0.0	0	0	0	0	Pitch 91-105	.239	113	27	7	0	1	14	5	16	.281	.327
0-3 Days Rest	0.00	0	0	0	0	0	0.0	0	0	0	0	Pitch 106+	.303	89	27	5	0	2	7	6	12	.354	.427
4 Days Rest	3.03	9	12	0	27	27	204.2	187	20	36	98	First Pitch	.274	157	43	4	0	7	15	3	0	.288	.433
5+ Days Rest	3.79	4	2	0	8	8	57.0	64	8	19	29	Ahead on Count	.241	424	102	20	1	9	38	0	103	.249	.356
Pre-All Star	3.28	8	7	0	19	19	145.1	143	20	31	67	Behind on Count	.270	215	58	16	0	4	19	28	0	.358	.400
Post-All Star	3.09	5	7	0	16	16	116.1	108	8	24	60	Two Strikes	.204	431	88	20	1	9	35	24	127	.253	.318

Last Five Years

	ERA	W	L	Sv	G	GS	IP	H	HR	BB	SO		Avg	AB	H	2B	3B	HR	RBI	BB	SO	OBP	SLG
Home	3.19	25	17	0	59	55	389.2	385	36	91	177	vs. Left	.245	1426	350	63	4	31	140	87	114	.287	.360
Away	4.20	20	25	0	55	52	345.0	355	44	81	170	vs. Right	.274	1425	390	77	6	49	160	85	233	.321	.439
Day	4.01	13	14	0	38	35	226.2	254	32	60	98	Inning 1-6	.259	2305	597	109	9	66	250	148	275	.305	.400
Night	3.51	32	28	0	76	72	508.0	486	48	112	249	Inning 7+	.262	546	143	31	1	14	50	24	72	.299	.399
Grass	3.44	40	35	0	98	93	648.2	640	68	154	301	None on	.252	1782	449	89	7	52	52	87	230	.291	.397
Turf	5.34	5	7	0	16	14	86.0	100	12	18	46	Runners on	.272	1069	291	51	3	28	248	85	117	.324	.404
April	3.11	5	7	0	16	15	110.0	100	5	31	41	Scoring Posn	.275	579	159	22	2	14	209	55	62	.331	.392
May	4.94	9	11	0	27	22	138.1	160	24	34	67	Close & Late	.265	249	66	15	0	9	32	15	41	.316	.434
June	3.67	6	4	0	16	16	95.2	93	10	26	46	None on/out	.248	769	191	29	4	31	31	29	86	.279	.417
July	3.37	9	7	0	18	18	130.2	133	16	25	62	vs. 1st Batr (relief)	.286	7	2	1	0	0	1	0	0	.266	.429
August	4.34	6	8	0	18	17	114.0	130	13	25	52	First Inning Pitched	.266	436	116	19	2	11	61	39	62	.325	.394
September/October	2.59	10	5	0	19	19	146.0	124	12	31	79	First 75 Pitches	.252	2060	520	91	6	58	220	135	251	.299	.387
Starter	3.62	45	41	0	107	107	717.2	716	77	169	336	Pitch 76-90	.288	372	107	24	2	15	35	12	41	.316	.484
Reliever	5.29	0	1	0	7	0	17.0	24	3	3	11	Pitch 91-105	.256	254	65	18	2	3	29	13	33	.299	.378
0-3 Days Rest	3.14	1	1	0	2	2	14.1	18	2	3	8	Pitch 106+	.291	165	48	7	0	4	16	12	22	.343	.406
4 Days Rest	3.81	29	27	0	70	70	476.2	479	55	103	217	First Pitch	.279	462	129	20	2	16	52	8	0	.288	.435
5+ Days Rest	3.26	15	13	0	35	35	226.2	219	20	63	111	Ahead on Count	.229	1191	273	47	4	25	112	0	297	.236	.338
Pre-All Star	3.95	24	24	0	65	59	389.1	405	47	96	176	Behind on Count	.308	660	203	51	2	22	81	89	0	.390	.491
Post-All Star	3.34	21	18	0	49	48	345.1	335	33	76	171	Two Strikes	.206	1143	236	42	4	27	101	75	347	.261	.321

Pitcher vs. Batter (career)

Pitcher Best Vs.	Avg	AB	H	2B	3B	HR	RBI	BB	SO	OBP	SLG	Pitches Worst Vs.	Avg	AB	H	2B	3B	HR	RBI	BB	SO	OBP	SLG
Brett Butler	.056	18	1	0	0	0	1	0	0	.056	.111	Billy Ripken	.647	17	11	0	0	1	5	1	1	.632	.824
Steve Buechele	.059	17	1	0	0	2	1	2	.111	.059		Mike Greenwell	.529	17	9	2	0	1	4	5	0	.636	.824
Alex Cole	.077	13	1	0	0	0	1	2	1	.200	.077	Sam Horn	.500	16	8	2	0	2	4	2	0	.556	1.000
Pat Kelly	.083	12	1	0	0	0	0	0	0	.083	.083	Darnell Coles	.455	11	5	2	0	1	3	3	3	.571	.909
Alvin Davis	.107	28	3	0	0	0	3	1	1	.138	.107	Joe Carter	.415	41	17	4	2	5	10	2	4	.442	.976

John Wehner — Pirates

Bats Right (groundball hitter)

	Avg	G	AB	R	H	2B	3B	HR	RBI	BB	SO	HBP	GDP	SB	CS	OBP	SLG	IBB	SH	SF	#Pit	#P/PA	GB	FB	G/F
1992 Season	.179	55	123	11	22	6	0	0	4	12	22	0	4	3	0	.252	.228	2	2	0	483	3.58	48	36	1.33
Career (1991-1992)	.253	92	229	26	58	13	0	0	11	19	39	0	6	5	0	.310	.310	2	2	0	898	3.62	100	56	1.79

1992 Season

	Avg	AB	H	2B	3B	HR	RBI	BB	SO	OBP	SLG		Avg	AB	H	2B	3B	HR	RBI	BB	SO	OBP	SLG
vs. Left	.179	56	10	3	0	0	3	5	9	.246	.232	Scoring Posn	.125	32	4	1	0	0	3	4	11	.222	.156
vs. Right	.179	67	12	3	0	0	1	7	13	.257	.224	Close & Late	.148	27	4	1	0	0	1	2	8	.207	.185
Home	.195	41	8	2	0	0	2	3	7	.250	.244	None on/out	.121	33	4	2	0	0	0	2	5	.171	.182
Away	.171	82	14	4	0	0	2	9	15	.253	.220	Batting #7	.107	28	3	2	0	0	1	3	5	.194	.179
First Pitch	.194	31	6	2	0	0	2	0	0	.242	.258	Batting #8	.208	24	5	1	0	0	1	3	4	.296	.250
Ahead on Count	.200	25	5	1	0	0	1	2	0	.259	.240	Other	.197	71	14	3	0	0	2	6	13	.260	.239
Behind on Count	.167	30	5	1	0	0	2	0	10	.167	.200	Pre-All Star	.200	45	9	4	0	0	1	6	6	.294	.289
Two Strikes	.120	50	6	2	0	0	1	8	22	.241	.160	Post-All Star	.167	78	13	2	0	0	3	6	16	.226	.192

Walt Weiss — Athletics
Bats Both (groundball hitter)

	Avg	G	AB	R	H	2B	3B	HR	RBI	BB	SO	HBP	GDP	SB	CS	OBP	SLG	IBB	SH	SF	#Pit	#P/PA	GB	FB	G/F
1992 Season	.212	103	316	36	67	5	2	0	21	43	39	1	10	6	3	.305	.241	1	11	4	1418	3.90	132	93	1.42
Last Five Years	.242	512	1582	175	383	56	7	8	129	157	201	15	35	31	11	.313	.302	7	31	17	6562	3.71	668	417	1.60

1992 Season

	Avg	AB	H	2B	3B	HR	RBI	BB	SO	OBP	SLG		Avg	AB	H	2B	3B	HR	RBI	BB	SO	OBP	SLG
vs. Left	.135	74	10	0	1	0	2	5	3	.190	.162	Scoring Posn	.138	87	12	2	0	0	20	13	10	.240	.161
vs. Right	.236	242	57	5	1	0	19	38	36	.337	.264	Close & Late	.225	40	9	0	0	0	3	11	2	.377	.225
Groundball	.203	74	15	3	0	0	6	9	10	.289	.243	None on/out	.221	77	17	0	1	0	0	9	7	.302	.247
Flyball	.265	102	27	2	1	0	10	13	10	.350	.304	Batting #8	.192	120	23	2	0	0	7	14	18	.279	.208
Home	.174	144	25	3	1	0	8	21	18	.280	.208	Batting #9	.235	170	40	3	2	0	14	23	17	.321	.276
Away	.244	172	42	2	1	0	13	22	21	.327	.267	Other	.154	26	4	0	0	0	0	6	4	.313	.154
Day	.203	118	24	2	2	0	7	16	14	.301	.254	April	.000	0	0	0	0	0	0	0	0	.000	.000
Night	.217	198	43	3	0	0	14	27	25	.307	.232	May	.000	0	0	0	0	0	0	0	0	.000	.000
Grass	.211	265	56	5	1	0	16	36	33	.306	.238	June	.232	82	19	1	0	0	6	9	6	.304	.244
Turf	.216	51	11	0	1	0	5	7	6	.300	.255	July	.244	82	20	1	1	0	5	12	11	.330	.280
First Pitch	.225	40	9	1	1	0	7	1	0	.250	.300	August	.222	81	18	1	1	0	6	13	12	.330	.259
Ahead on Count	.284	88	25	1	0	0	4	22	0	.427	.295	September/October	.141	71	10	2	0	0	4	9	10	.247	.169
Behind on Count	.144	97	14	3	1	0	3	0	26	.144	.196	Pre-All Star	.263	118	31	2	1	0	9	15	6	.341	.297
Two Strikes	.178	135	24	2	0	0	7	20	39	.282	.193	Post-All Star	.182	198	36	3	1	0	12	28	33	.284	.207

1992 By Position

Position	Avg	AB	H	2B	3B	HR	RBI	BB	SO	OBP	SLG	G	GS	Innings	PO	A	E	DP	Fld Pct	Rng Fctr	In Zone	Outs	Zone Rtg	MLB Zone
As ss	.213	315	67	5	2	0	21	42	39	.304	.241	103	96	859.2	144	269	19	56	.956	4.32	336	264	.845	.885

Last Five Years

	Avg	AB	H	2B	3B	HR	RBI	BB	SO	OBP	SLG		Avg	AB	H	2B	3B	HR	RBI	BB	SO	OBP	SLG
vs. Left	.212	378	80	13	2	0	26	22	30	.254	.257	Scoring Posn	.209	398	83	9	3	2	117	49	52	.289	.261
vs. Right	.252	1204	303	43	5	8	103	135	171	.331	.316	Close & Late	.235	230	54	6	2	0	20	26	31	.310	.278
Groundball	.222	442	98	16	1	1	43	32	63	.279	.269	None on/out	.245	379	93	18	1	0	0	32	48	.314	.298
Flyball	.276	392	108	15	3	6	42	52	45	.362	.375	Batting #8	.238	762	181	27	3	2	62	73	105	.307	.289
Home	.216	788	170	23	2	3	51	74	116	.288	.261	Batting #9	.244	724	177	26	4	6	62	71	85	.315	.316
Away	.268	794	213	33	5	5	78	83	85	.339	.341	Other	.260	96	25	3	0	0	5	13	11	.355	.292
Day	.233	634	148	20	2	4	50	64	88	.308	.290	April	.243	218	53	11	0	4	21	16	20	.293	.349
Night	.248	948	235	36	5	4	79	93	113	.317	.309	May	.238	281	67	10	0	1	21	31	33	.315	.285
Grass	.242	1333	323	47	6	7	101	131	172	.315	.302	June	.261	272	71	9	2	1	20	22	32	.322	.320
Turf	.241	249	60	9	1	1	28	26	29	.307	.297	July	.226	261	59	7	2	1	24	26	30	.296	.280
First Pitch	.312	247	77	11	3	3	34	1	0	.314	.417	August	.258	287	74	11	3	1	21	28	44	.326	.328
Ahead on Count	.275	443	122	20	1	2	34	70	0	.371	.339	September/October	.224	263	59	8	0	0	22	34	42	.322	.255
Behind on Count	.214	449	96	16	1	0	29	1	114	.220	.254	Pre-All Star	.244	872	213	31	4	7	76	81	95	.310	.313
Two Strikes	.191	640	122	18	1	3	40	81	201	.289	.236	Post-All Star	.239	710	170	25	3	1	53	76	106	.318	.287

Batter vs. Pitcher (career)

Hits Best Against	Avg	AB	H	2B	3B	HR	RBI	BB	SO	OBP	SLG	Hits Worst Against	Avg	AB	H	2B	3B	HR	RBI	BB	SO	OBP	SLG
Tim Leary	.583	12	7	1	0	0	0	4	1	.688	.667	Jack McDowell	.048	21	1	0	0	0	1	0	4	.048	.048
Scott Bankhead	.545	11	6	1	1	1	4	1	0	.583	1.091	Greg Swindell	.067	15	1	0	1	0	2	0	4	.067	.200
Charles Nagy	.462	13	6	2	0	0	2	0	1	.462	.615	Jack Morris	.071	14	1	0	0	0	1	2	3	.176	.071
Mark Williamson	.444	9	4	1	0	1	3	2	1	.545	.889	Bill Krueger	.091	11	1	0	0	0	1	1	0	.167	.091
Bert Blyleven	.381	21	8	4	0	0	4	4	4	.480	.571	David Wells	.091	11	1	0	0	0	0	2	1	.167	.091

Bob Welch — Athletics
Pitches Right

	ERA	W	L	Sv	G	GS	IP	BB	SO	Avg	H	2B	3B	HR	RBI	OBP	SLG	CG	ShO	Sup	QS	#P/S	SB	CS	GB	FB	G/F
1992 Season	3.27	11	7	0	20	20	123.2	43	47	.247	114	11	1	13	40	.312	.360	0	0	5.31	10	88	8	5	159	168	0.95
Last Five Years	3.51	84	43	0	159	159	1036.0	370	570	.250	976	169	22	99	395	.319	.381	14	5	5.02	93	99	68	46	1376	1231	1.12

1992 Season

	ERA	W	L	Sv	G	GS	IP	H	HR	BB	SO		Avg	AB	H	2B	3B	HR	RBI	BB	SO	OBP	SLG
Home	2.94	4	3	0	9	9	52.0	45	5	15	20	vs. Left	.266	241	64	6	1	6	18	22	20	.325	.373
Away	3.52	7	4	0	11	11	71.2	69	8	28	27	vs. Right	.227	220	50	5	0	7	22	21	27	.299	.345
Starter	3.27	11	7	0	20	20	123.2	114	13	43	47	Scoring Posn	.276	87	24	0	0	3	29	8	14	.327	.379
Reliever	0.00	0	0	0	0	0	0.0	0	0	0	0	Close & Late	.136	22	3	0	0	0	1	1	1	.174	.136
0-3 Days Rest	0.00	0	0	0	0	0	0.0	0	0	0	0	None on/out	.258	120	31	2	0	5	5	13	9	.336	.400
4 Days Rest	2.03	9	0	0	10	10	66.2	58	5	23	27	First Pitch	.242	91	22	3	0	3	10	0	0	.239	.374
5+ Days Rest	4.74	2	7	0	10	10	57.0	56	8	20	20	Behind on Count	.306	108	33	3	1	5	13	23	0	.427	.491
Pre-All Star	2.70	7	4	0	11	11	73.1	65	10	22	27	Ahead on Count	.247	182	45	4	0	3	12	0	33	.254	.319
Post-All Star	4.11	4	3	0	9	9	50.1	49	3	21	20	Two Strikes	.189	169	32	3	0	3	13	20	47	.280	.260

Last Five Years

	ERA	W	L	Sv	G	GS	IP	H	HR	BB	SO		Avg	AB	H	2B	3B	HR	RBI	BB	SO	OBP	SLG
Home	2.74	49	18	0	80	80	549.0	476	34	161	328	vs. Left	.250	2020	504	87	16	41	191	217	267	.323	.369
Away	4.38	35	25	0	79	79	487.0	500	65	209	242	vs. Right	.251	1877	472	82	6	58	204	153	303	.314	.394
Day	2.82	39	13	0	61	61	412.0	353	33	147	242	Inning 1-6	.252	3301	832	149	19	83	353	326	494	.322	.384
Night	3.97	45	30	0	98	98	624.0	623	66	223	328	Inning 7+	.242	596	144	20	3	16	42	44	76	.300	.366
Grass	3.19	72	32	0	130	130	858.0	780	76	294	486	None on	.254	2370	603	112	14	60	60	193	304	.315	.389

Last Five Years

	ERA	W	L	Sv	G	GS	IP	H	HR	BB	SO		Avg	AB	H	2B	3B	HR	RBI	BB	SO	OBP	SLG
Turf	5.06	12	11	0	29	29	178.0	196	23	76	84	Runners on	.244	1527	373	57	8	39	335	177	266	.325	.369
April	2.66	12	6	0	21	21	145.1	117	10	45	75	Scoring Posn	.269	826	222	34	6	22	291	121	173	.359	.404
May	3.31	15	8	0	29	29	203.2	182	23	75	99	Close & Late	.223	296	66	8	1	5	22	23	48	.286	.307
June	3.21	17	5	0	25	25	165.1	154	14	57	79	None on/out	.246	1042	256	52	3	28	28	75	125	.299	.382
July	3.91	11	7	0	27	27	168.0	178	20	57	109	vs. 1st Batr (relief)	.000	0	0	0	0	0	0	0	0	.000	.000
August	3.66	18	7	0	27	27	182.0	182	16	61	114	First Inning Pitched	.241	590	142	25	2	14	60	52	96	.305	.361
September/October	4.19	11	10	0	30	30	171.2	163	16	75	94	First 75 Pitches	.256	2828	723	129	14	69	288	253	419	.320	.384
Starter	3.51	84	43	0	159	159	1036.0	976	99	370	570	Pitch 76-90	.214	471	101	19	3	11	38	63	60	.312	.338
Reliever	0.00	0	0	0	0	0	0.0	0	0	0	0	Pitch 91-105	.235	353	83	10	3	9	36	31	66	.300	.357
0-3 Days Rest	3.79	9	3	0	14	14	90.1	96	13	21	49	Pitch 106+	.282	245	69	11	2	10	33	23	25	.347	.465
4 Days Rest	3.40	57	26	0	105	105	690.2	634	62	250	366	First Pitch	.303	608	184	27	4	30	85	10	0	.320	.508
5+ Days Rest	3.71	18	14	0	40	40	255.0	246	24	99	155	Ahead on Count	.212	1732	368	61	8	22	125	0	457	.219	.295
Pre-All Star	3.24	48	21	0	84	84	566.2	517	59	189	281	Behind on Count	.300	794	238	43	7	34	126	198	0	.440	.500
Post-All Star	3.84	36	22	0	75	75	469.1	459	40	181	289	Two Strikes	.188	1696	318	57	5	24	124	162	570	.262	.269

Pitcher vs. Batter (since 1984)

Pitches Best Vs.	Avg	AB	H	2B	3B	HR	RBI	BB	SO	OBP	SLG	Pitches Worst Vs.	Avg	AB	H	2B	3B	HR	RBI	BB	SO	OBP	SLG
Joey Cora	.000	12	0	0	0	0	0	2	2	.143	.000	Carlos Baerga	.474	19	9	3	0	1	3	0	1	.474	.789
Luis Salazar	.000	11	0	0	0	0	0	0	2	.000	.000	Glenn Davis	.455	33	15	3	0	2	7	3	3	.500	.727
Jesse Barfield	.000	11	0	0	0	0	0	2	3	.154	.000	Kelly Gruber	.412	17	7	2	0	1	2	4	2	.500	.706
Rene Gonzales	.000	11	0	0	0	0	0	0	3	.000	.000	Jay Buhner	.385	13	5	1	0	2	6	1	4	.400	.923
Pete Incaviglia	.056	18	1	0	0	0	0	1	7	.105	.056	Harold Baines	.381	21	8	4	0	1	1	5	3	.500	.714

David Wells — Blue Jays · Pitches Left (flyball pitcher)

	ERA	W	L	Sv	G	GS	IP	BB	SO	Avg	H	2B	3B	HR	RBI	OBP	SLG	GF	IR	IRS	Hld	SvOp	SB	CS	GB	FB	G/F
1992 Season	5.40	7	9	2	41	14	120.0	36	62	.289	138	35	2	16	76	.346	.471	14	22	6	3	4	14	6	154	168	0.92
Last Five Years	3.78	43	34	12	219	67	658.0	189	417	.250	622	135	15	71	277	.305	.402	25	147	40	26	24	49	34	814	833	0.98

1992 Season

	ERA	W	L	Sv	G	GS	IP	H	HR	BB	SO		Avg	AB	H	2B	3B	HR	RBI	BB	SO	OBP	SLG
Home	3.60	4	3	1	22	5	60.0	61	8	12	30	vs. Left	.293	92	27	5	0	3	16	4	13	.363	.446
Away	7.20	3	6	1	19	9	60.0	77	8	24	32	vs. Right	.288	386	111	30	2	13	60	32	49	.342	.477
Starter	6.39	6	7	0	14	14	76.0	90	12	23	34	Scoring Posn	.345	119	41	12	2	2	58	19	17	.438	.529
Reliever	3.68	1	2	2	27	0	44.0	48	4	13	28	Close & Late	.313	67	21	2	0	1	7	4	12	.356	.388
0 Days rest	0.00	0	0	1	2	0	5.0	4	0	0	3	None on/out	.286	119	34	10	0	3		5	19	.320	.445
1 or 2 Days rest	4.85	0	1	1	16	0	26.0	33	3	7	20	First Pitch	.300	70	21	7	0	1	8	4	0	.338	.443
3+ Days rest	2.77	1	1	0	9	0	13.0	11	1	6	5	Behind on Count	.412	131	54	12	0	10	33	19	0	.490	.733
Pre-All Star	3.29	4	4	2	26	6	68.1	69	7	18	37	Ahead on Count	.209	187	39	8	2	4	23	0	55	.228	.337
Post-All Star	8.19	3	5	0	15	8	51.2	69	9	18	25	Two Strikes	.192	203	39	12	2	2	22	13	62	.245	.300

Last Five Years

	ERA	W	L	Sv	G	GS	IP	H	HR	BB	SO		Avg	AB	H	2B	3B	HR	RBI	BB	SO	OBP	SLG
Home	3.49	19	15	6	107	28	309.1	287	41	86	195	vs. Left	.249	477	119	27	3	9	53	32	61	.310	.375
Away	4.03	24	19	6	112	39	348.2	335	30	103	222	vs. Right	.250	2010	503	108	12	62	224	157	356	.304	.408
Day	4.76	10	11	2	68	17	175.2	174	19	59	97	Inning 1-6	.251	1566	393	94	10	42	176	110	230	.302	.404
Night	3.41	33	23	10	151	50	482.1	448	52	130	320	Inning 7+	.249	921	229	41	5	29	101	79	187	.309	.398
Grass	4.41	19	16	5	89	32	275.1	275	25	88	187	None on/out	.247	1471	364	76	5	39	39	105	263	.300	.385
Turf	3.32	24	18	7	130	35	382.2	347	46	101	230	Runners on	.254	1016	258	59	10	32	238	84	154	.311	.426
April	4.32	5	7	3	37	6	85.1	75	10	27	58	Scoring Posn	.252	555	140	37	6	12	188	72	90	.336	.405
May	2.22	9	3	4	51	8	109.2	81	9	35	88	Close & Late	.268	471	126	20	3	15	52	41	92	.327	.418
June	3.55	8	6	4	40	12	129.1	126	14	42	98	None on/out	.243	625	152	27	2	16	16	49	113	.299	.370
July	3.12	11	4	0	27	17	130.0	111	17	28	65	vs. 1st Batr (relief)	.246	138	34	8	1	4	21	11	29	.305	.406
August	6.56	5	10	0	25	16	105.2	137	15	40	50	First Inning Pitched	.241	723	174	44	4	17	88	56	143	.295	.383
September/October	3.21	5	4	1	39	8	98.0	92	10	17	58	First 15 Pitches	.243	655	159	41	2	16	70	48	119	.295	.385
Starter	3.97	30	22	0	67	67	423.2	411	46	110	227	Pitch 16-30	.266	493	131	21	6	19	51	39	99	.322	.448
Reliever	3.42	13	12	12	152	0	234.1	211	25	79	190	Pitch 31-45	.236	386	91	22	1	10	46	37	66	.305	.376
0 Days rest	2.75	3	0	5	28	0	36.0	28	3	12	28	Pitch 46+	.253	953	241	51	6	26	110	65	133	.303	.401
1 or 2 Days rest	3.61	5	8	6	77	0	124.2	120	16	42	110	First Pitch	.301	326	98	17	3	16	44	17	0	.337	.518
3+ Days rest	3.42	5	4	1	47	0	73.2	63	6	25	52	Ahead on Count	.187	1105	207	46	4	14	86	1	366	.193	.274
Pre-All Star	3.37	24	19	11	140	32	376.1	333	38	116	269	Behind on Count	.321	635	204	41	5	32	105	90	0	.404	.553
Post-All Star	4.31	19	15	1	79	35	281.2	289	33	73	148	Two Strikes	.178	1098	195	53	6	12	83	80	417	.236	.270

Pitcher vs. Batter (career)

Pitches Best Vs.	Avg	AB	H	2B	3B	HR	RBI	BB	SO	OBP	SLG	Pitches Worst Vs.	Avg	AB	H	2B	3B	HR	RBI	BB	SO	OBP	SLG
Jay Buhner	.000	11	0	0	0	0	0	1	2	.083	.000	Jack Clark	.500	10	5	1	0	2	4	1	1	.545	1.200
Brook Jacoby	.053	19	1	0	0	0	0	2	7	.143	.053	Tom Brunansky	.467	15	7	2	0	2	4	0	1	.467	1.000
Lance Parrish	.063	16	1	0	0	0	0	1	7	.118	.063	Ken Griffey Jr	.444	18	8	2	0	2	4	0	4	.500	.889
Brian Harper	.083	12	1	0	0	0	1	0	1	.077	.083	Cal Ripken	.421	19	8	2	0	3	6	1	2	.500	1.000
Jim Eisenreich	.091	11	1	0	0	0	0	0	0	.091	.091	Cecil Fielder	.385	13	5	0	0	2	5	5	2	.556	.846

David West — Twins
Pitches Left (flyball pitcher)

	ERA	W	L	Sv	G	GS	IP	BB	SO	Avg	H	2B	3B	HR	RBI	OBP	SLG	GF	IR	IRS	Hld	SvOp	SB	CS	GB	FB	G/F
1992 Season	6.99	1	3	0	9	3	28.1	20	19	.276	32	5	0	3	20	.381	.397	1	2	1	0	0	2	0	38	40	0.95
Career (1988-1992)	5.45	16	20	0	76	50	315.2	162	216	.262	319	73	7	46	186	.350	.447	1	11	5	2	1	11	8	351	418	0.84

1992 Season

	ERA	W	L	Sv	G	GS	IP	H	HR	BB	SO		Avg	AB	H	2B	3B	HR	RBI	BB	SO	OBP	SLG
Home	7.94	0	2	0	4	2	11.1	15	1	7	14	vs. Left	.238	21	5	1	0	0	2	4	4	.360	.286
Away	6.35	1	1	0	5	1	17.0	17	2	13	5	vs. Right	.284	95	27	4	0	3	18	16	15	.386	.421

Career (1988-1992)

	ERA	W	L	Sv	G	GS	IP	H	HR	BB	SO		Avg	AB	H	2B	3B	HR	RBI	BB	SO	OBP	SLG
Home	6.93	6	12	0	36	25	140.1	146	23	75	117	vs. Left	.236	195	46	7	3	3	22	28	38	.333	.349
Away	4.26	10	8	0	40	25	175.1	173	23	87	99	vs. Right	.267	1021	273	66	4	43	164	134	178	.353	.466
Day	5.58	4	5	0	22	14	79.0	76	12	46	58	Inning 1-6	.261	1049	274	63	5	43	165	145	180	.352	.454
Night	5.40	12	15	0	54	36	236.2	243	34	116	158	Inning 7+	.269	167	45	10	2	3	21	17	28	.341	.407
Grass	5.85	5	8	0	32	21	124.2	143	23	70	75	None on	.236	704	166	41	5	19	19	93	121	.327	.389
Turf	5.18	11	12	0	44	29	191.0	176	23	92	141	Runners on	.299	512	153	32	2	27	167	69	95	.382	.527
April	3.52	1	3	0	4	4	23.0	20	5	11	12	Scoring Posn	.290	297	86	22	2	11	132	41	58	.370	.488
May	6.56	1	0	0	5	5	23.1	21	5	16	12	Close & Late	.313	48	15	1	1	1	6	4	8	.365	.438
June	3.67	1	3	0	11	6	41.2	41	2	15	35	None on/out	.239	318	76	16	2	13	13	31	50	.309	.425
July	6.30	4	5	0	17	13	74.1	83	12	40	54	vs. 1st Batr (relief)	.266	14	4	1	0	1	3	3	1	.412	.571
August	5.87	7	6	0	24	15	107.1	105	19	53	64	First Inning Pitched	.280	243	68	13	3	12	46	44	47	.392	.506
September/October	5.09	2	3	0	15	7	46.0	49	3	27	39	First 15 Pitches	.261	222	58	10	2	10	29	32	38	.358	.459
Starter	5.32	15	20	0	50	50	262.1	268	40	129	175	Pitch 16-30	.239	209	50	13	1	10	36	41	46	.366	.455
Reliever	6.08	1	0	0	26	0	53.1	51	6	33	41	Pitch 31-45	.281	210	59	11	0	8	30	26	39	.358	.448
0 Days rest	0.00	0	0	0	0	0	0.0	0	0	0	0	Pitch 46+	.264	575	152	39	4	18	91	63	93	.338	.440
1 or 2 Days rest	6.60	0	0	0	7	0	15.0	20	2	11	13	First Pitch	.302	169	51	16	2	9	43	4	0	.330	.580
3+ Days rest	5.87	1	0	0	19	0	38.1	31	4	22	28	Ahead on Count	.221	565	125	27	4	17	65	0	177	.223	.373
Pre-All Star	4.30	5	7	0	25	19	115.0	103	16	53	79	Behind on Count	.336	265	89	19	0	13	50	89	0	.499	.555
Post-All Star	6.10	11	13	0	51	31	200.2	216	30		137	Two Strikes	.196	567	111	25	4	14	56	68	216	.283	.328

Pitcher vs. Batter (career)

Pitches Best Vs.	Avg	AB	H	2B	3B	HR	RBI	BB	SO	OBP	SLG	Pitches Worst Vs.	Avg	AB	H	2B	3B	HR	RBI	BB	SO	OBP	SLG
Manuel Lee	.091	11	1	0	0	0	0	3	4	.286	.091	Sammy Sosa	.545	11	6	2	1	1	2	2	2	.615	1.182
Harold Reynolds	.154	13	2	0	0	0	0	2	0	.267	.154	Ken Griffey Jr	.400	15	6	1	0	2	3	1	3	.438	.867
Kelly Gruber	.154	13	2	0	0	0	0	1	4	.214	.154	Tony Phillips	.364	11	4	1	0	1	1	0	1	.364	.727
Pat Borders	.176	17	3	2	0	0	1	0	2	.176	.294	Ron Karkovice	.364	11	4	1	0	1	5	1	2	.417	.727
Devon White	.188	16	3	0	0	0	1	0	5	.188	.188	Ruben Sierra	.364	11	4	0	0	2	3	1		.500	.545

Mickey Weston — Phillies
Pitches Right (groundball pitcher)

	ERA	W	L	Sv	G	GS	IP	BB	SO	Avg	H	2B	3B	HR	RBI	OBP	SLG	CG	ShO	Sup	QS	#P/S	SB	CS	GB	FB	G/F
1992 Season	12.27	0	1	0	1	1	3.2	1	0	.412	7	2	0	1	5	.474	.706	0	0	2.45	0	69	1	0	9	4	2.25
Career (1989-1992)	7.03	1	2	1	19	3	39.2	10	17	.331	54	7	1	8	33	.377	.534	0	0	4.76	0	63	1	0	69	45	1.53

1992 Season

	ERA	W	L	Sv	G	GS	IP	H	HR	BB	SO		Avg	AB	H	2B	3B	HR	RBI	BB	SO	OBP	SLG
Home	0.00	0	0	0	0	0	0.0	0	0	0	0	vs. Left	.444	9	4	1	0	0	2	0	0	.444	.556
Away	12.27	0	1	0	1	1	3.2	7	1	1	0	vs. Right	.375	8	3	1	0	1	3	1	0	.500	.875

John Wetteland — Expos
Pitches Right (flyball pitcher)

	ERA	W	L	Sv	G	GS	IP	BB	SO	Avg	H	2B	3B	HR	RBI	OBP	SLG	GF	IR	IRS	Hld	SvOp	SB	CS	GB	FB	G/F
1992 Season	2.92	4	4	37	67	0	83.1	36	99	.213	64	8	1	6	31	.304	.306	58	37	8	0	46	14	3	80	84	0.95
Career (1989-1992)	3.52	12	16	38	126	17	238.0	90	240	.223	194	30	2	20	109	.301	.331	68	60	19	1	48	30	9	243	256	0.95

1992 Season

	ERA	W	L	Sv	G	GS	IP	H	HR	BB	SO		Avg	AB	H	2B	3B	HR	RBI	BB	SO	OBP	SLG
Home	3.83	2	3	21	38	0	44.2	35	4	15	50	vs. Left	.200	175	35	5	1	3	17	21	66	.288	.291
Away	1.86	2	1	16	29	0	38.2	29	4	21	49	vs. Right	.230	126	29	3	0	3	14	15	33	.326	.325
Day	3.41	1	1	10	22	0	29.0	26	4	11	36	Inning 1-6	.000	0	0	0	0	0	0	0	0	.000	.000
Night	2.65	3	3	27	45	0	54.1	38	2	25	63	Inning 7+	.213	301	64	8	1	6	31	36	99	.304	.306
Grass	1.37	2	0	7	13	0	19.2	14	2	8	21	None on	.217	143	31	3	1	3	3	17	45	.300	.315
Turf	3.39	2	4	30	54	0	63.2	50	4	28	78	Runners on	.209	158	33	5	0	3	28	19	54	.308	.297
April	4.50	0	1	3	8	0	8.0	9	0	4	10	Scoring Posn	.238	101	24	3	0	3	27	15	30	.339	.356
May	5.93	0	1	5	11	0	13.2	13	3	5	19	Close & Late	.227	207	47	4	1	6	26	25	70	.315	.343
June	4.50	0	0	4	9	0	10.0	7	0	2	9	None on/out	.254	67	17	2	1	2	2	3	19	.286	.403
July	0.57	2	0	10	12	0	15.2	10	0	4	15	vs. 1st Batr (relief)	.238	63	15	3	0	1	4	4	19	.284	.333
August	2.93	1	1	7	13	0	15.1	12	2	12	19	First Inning Pitched	.222	230	51	7	1	4	27	28	68	.313	.313
September/October	1.31	1	1	8	14	0	20.2	13	1	9	27	First 15 Pitches	.222	180	40	6	0	2	14	23	45	.316	.289
Starter	0.00	0	0	0	0	0	0.0	0	0	0	0	Pitch 16-30	.208	101	21	2	1	4	17	10	45	.292	.366
Reliever	2.92	4	4	37	67	0	83.1	64	6	36	99	Pitch 31-45	.150	20	3	0	0	0	0	3	9	.261	.150
0 Days rest	2.08	0	2	13	19	0	26.0	21	1	9	38	Pitch 46+	.000	0	0	0	0	0	0	0	0	.000	.000
1 or 2 Days rest	3.73	4	2	11	27	0	31.1	26	2	18	36	First Pitch	.300	40	12	1	0	2	2	0	0	.349	.325
3+ Days rest	2.77	0	0	13	21	0	26.0	17	3	9	25	Ahead on Count	.119	159	19	4	0	1	7	0	82	.135	.164

1992 Season

	ERA	W	L	Sv	G	GS	IP	H	HR	BB	SO		Avg	AB	H	2B	3B	HR	RBI	BB	SO	OBP	SLG
Pre-All Star	3.92	2	2	16	34	0	41.1	35	3	14	48	Behind on Count	.366	41	15	2	0	2	12	18	0	.559	.561
Post-All Star	1.93	2	2	21	33	0	42.0	29	3	22	51	Two Strikes	.144	181	26	3	1	4	13	16	99	.224	.238

Career (1989-1992)

	ERA	W	L	Sv	G	GS	IP	H	HR	BB	SO		Avg	AB	H	2B	3B	HR	RBI	BB	SO	OBP	SLG
Home	3.67	8	8	22	66	7	110.1	92	10	36	110	vs. Left	.222	472	105	14	2	9	53	49	132	.301	.318
Away	3.38	4	8	16	60	10	127.2	102	10	54	130	vs. Right	.224	398	89	16	0	11	56	41	108	.300	.347
Day	4.96	3	6	10	43	7	81.2	81	11	32	84	Inning 1-6	.234	393	92	18	0	10	59	39	101	.308	.356
Night	2.76	9	10	28	83	10	156.1	113	9	58	156	Inning 7+	.214	477	102	12	2	10	50	51	139	.295	.310
Grass	3.35	9	10	8	57	13	134.1	112	10	47	118	None on	.214	471	101	12	2	11	50	133	.294	.318
Turf	3.73	3	6	30	69	4	103.2	82	10	43	122	Runners on	.233	399	93	18	0	9	98	40	107	.309	.346
April	7.88	1	3	3	14	1	16.0	24	3	5	17	Scoring Posn	.264	242	64	13	0	8	92	34	61	.353	.417
May	6.18	0	2	5	17	3	27.2	30	6	13	33	Close & Late	.245	290	71	8	2	8	39	33	87	.325	.369
June	2.53	2	1	5	25	2	46.1	30	1	14	46	None on/out	.250	212	53	7	2	8	8	22	59	.321	.415
July	2.09	3	3	10	21	2	38.2	28	0	13	36	vs. 1st Batr (relief)	.276	98	27	5	1	3	14	10	28	.339	.439
August	3.05	3	4	7	18	4	44.1	32	3	22	43	First Inning Pitched	.214	429	92	14	2	9	55	46	117	.295	.319
September/October	3.18	3	3	8	31	5	65.0	50	7	23	65	First 15 Pitches	.225	356	80	11	1	7	37	40	81	.307	.320
Starter	5.49	2	9	0	17	17	82.0	79	10	31	74	Pitch 16-30	.187	230	43	5	1	6	27	18	85	.256	.296
Reliever	2.48	10	7	38	109	0	156.0	115	10	59	166	Pitch 31-45	.195	113	22	4	0	0	3	10	35	.266	.230
0 Days rest	1.94	2	3	13	27	0	41.2	32	2	14	53	Pitch 46+	.287	171	49	0	0	7	42	22	39	.369	.468
1 or 2 Days rest	3.36	6	4	12	47	0	61.2	48	5	28	65	First Pitch	.319	94	30	2	0	2	7	7	0	.379	.404
3+ Days rest	1.88	2	0	13	35	0	52.2	35	3	17	48	Ahead on Count	.155	459	71	9	0	5	36	1	201	.164	.207
Pre-All Star	4.17	6	8	17	66	6	108.0	99	10	39	115	Behind on Count	.346	159	55	14	0	9	44	46	0	.493	.604
Post-All Star	2.98	6	8	21	60	11	130.0	95	10	51	125	Two Strikes	.159	491	78	7	2	8	41	36	240	.221	.230

Pitcher vs. Batter (career)

Pitches Best Vs.	Avg	AB	H	2B	3B	HR	RBI	BB	SO	OBP	SLG	Pitches Worst Vs.	Avg	AB	H	2B	3B	HR	RBI	BB	SO	OBP	SLG
Will Clark	.154	13	2	0	0	1	1	0	3	.154	.385	Craig Biggio	.556	9	5	0	0	2	5	2	3	.636	1.222
Mike Pagliarulo	.182	11	2	0	0	0	0	0	2	.182	.182	Benito Santiago	.417	12	5	0	0	1	1	1	4	.462	.417
Robby Thompson	.200	10	2	0	0	0	0	1	5	.273	.200	Kevin Bass	.400	10	4	0	1	0	0	1	1	.455	.600
Bip Roberts	.222	18	4	0	0	0	3	1	3	.263	.222	Billy Doran	.400	10	4	0	0	1	5	2	1	.500	.700
												Matt D. Williams	.364	11	4	1	0	1	4	1	3	.417	.727

Lou Whitaker — Tigers

Bats Left (flyball hitter)

	Avg	G	AB	R	H	2B	3B	HR	RBI	BB	SO	HBP	GDP	SB	CS	OBP	SLG	IBB	SH	SF	#Pit	#P/PA	GB	FB	G/F
1992 Season	.278	130	453	77	126	26	0	19	71	81	46	1	9	6	4	.386	.461	5	5	4	2080	3.86	130	174	0.75
Last Five Years	.264	663	2307	377	608	113	7	100	349	400	282	6	37	26	11	.370	.449	29	15	28	10482	3.82	712	847	0.84

1992 Season

	Avg	AB	H	2B	3B	HR	RBI	BB	SO	OBP	SLG		Avg	AB	H	2B	3B	HR	RBI	BB	SO	OBP	SLG
vs. Left	.355	62	22	6	0	2	15	15	11	.481	.548	Scoring Posn	.369	111	41	7	0	6	55	20	7	.452	.595
vs. Right	.266	391	104	20	0	17	56	66	35	.370	.448	Close & Late	.269	67	18	3	0	3	11	13	13	.388	.448
Groundball	.221	86	19	6	0	2	11	13	8	.327	.360	None on/out	.288	80	23	6	0	1	1	13	6	.387	.400
Flyball	.290	145	42	10	0	8	21	29	8	.406	.524	Batting #2	.281	442	124	26	0	18	68	78	44	.387	.462
Home	.320	228	73	19	0	11	37	50	26	.442	.548	Batting #7	.167	6	1	0	0	1	1	1	2	.286	.667
Away	.236	225	53	7	0	8	34	31	20	.326	.373	Other	.200	5	1	0	0	0	2	2	0	.429	.200
Day	.282	149	42	10	0	4	19	30	13	.406	.430	April	.192	52	10	1	0	2	3	13	6	.348	.327
Night	.276	304	84	16	0	15	52	51	33	.376	.477	May	.266	79	21	6	0	4	11	13	10	.376	.494
Grass	.278	385	107	23	0	18	61	77	36	.396	.478	June	.354	79	28	8	0	3	11	16	6	.463	.570
Turf	.279	68	19	3	0	1	10	4	10	.324	.368	July	.317	63	20	4	0	1	9	12	2	.421	.429
First Pitch	.310	58	18	4	0	1	7	5	0	.359	.431	August	.274	84	23	1	0	6	21	15	9	.376	.500
Ahead on Count	.323	127	41	10	0	8	26	44	0	.494	.591	September/October	.250	96	24	6	0	3	16	12	13	.333	.406
Behind on Count	.234	137	32	6	0	2	21	0	16	.237	.321	Pre-All Star	.294	235	69	17	0	10	29	51	23	.420	.494
Two Strikes	.239	184	44	6	0	8	26	32	46	.352	.402	Post-All Star	.261	218	57	9	0	9	42	30	23	.347	.427

1992 By Position

Position	Avg	AB	H	2B	3B	HR	RBI	BB	SO	OBP	SLG	G	GS	Innings	PO	A	E	DP	Fld Pct	Rng Fctr	In Zone	Outs	Zone Rtg	MLB Zone
As Designated Hitter	.350	20	7	2	0	1	7	8	2	.536	.600	10	5	---	---	---	---	---	---	---	---	---	---	---
As Pinch Hitter	.000	8	0	0	0	0	1	4	2	.333	.000	12	0	---	---	---	---	---	---	---	---	---	---	---
As 2b	.278	428	119	24	0	18	63	71	43	.379	.460	119	112	978.1	258	312	9	70	.984	5.24	360	312	867	892

Last Five Years

	Avg	AB	H	2B	3B	HR	RBI	BB	SO	OBP	SLG		Avg	AB	H	2B	3B	HR	RBI	BB	SO	OBP	SLG
vs. Left	.222	499	111	19	3	11	62	85	85	.338	.339	Scoring Posn	.291	557	162	28	1	27	240	117	71	.398	.490
vs. Right	.275	1808	497	94	4	89	287	315	197	.379	.479	Close & Late	.229	353	81	13	0	15	54	72	53	.358	.394
Groundball	.281	631	177	37	4	21	102	101	57	.378	.452	None on/out	.259	499	129	23	1	12	12	65	52	.344	.381
Flyball	.251	510	128	26	0	25	71	111	72	.381	.449	Batting #2	.278	1215	338	64	4	51	189	215	130	.384	.463
Home	.275	1094	301	56	3	59	182	221	136	.395	.494	Batting #3	.239	698	167	27	1	36	110	124	91	.352	.436
Away	.253	1213	307	57	4	41	167	179	146	.346	.408	Other	.261	394	103	22	2	13	50	61	61	.357	.426
Day	.263	722	190	40	1	30	110	132	81	.374	.446	April	.239	293	70	10	1	15	42	67	32	.377	.433
Night	.264	1585	418	73	6	70	239	268	201	.368	.450	May	.253	427	108	16	2	19	60	70	61	.358	.433
Grass	.264	1938	511	88	7	89	299	355	233	.375	.454	June	.266	433	115	24	2	16	56	75	57	.370	.441

464

Last Five Years

	Avg	AB	H	2B	3B	HR	RBI	BB	SO	OBP	SLG		Avg	AB	H	2B	3B	HR	RBI	BB	SO	OBP	SLG
Turf	.263	369	97	25	0	11	50	45	49	.342	.420	July	.304	381	116	23	2	14	56	53	37	.386	.486
First Pitch	.283	332	94	22	1	15	58	14	0	.306	.491	August	.278	421	117	19	0	25	85	85	55	.396	.501
Ahead on Count	.310	583	181	32	2	35	116	235	0	.505	.552	September/October	.233	352	82	21	0	11	50	50	40	.328	.386
Behind on Count	.242	677	164	35	5	23	99	2	118	.245	.411	Pre-All Star	.260	1281	333	55	7	56	180	233	161	.372	.445
Two Strikes	.226	984	222	37	2	37	117	144	281	.325	.380	Post-All Star	.268	1026	275	58	0	44	169	167	121	.368	.453

Batter vs. Pitcher (since 1984)

Hits Best Against	Avg	AB	H	2B	3B	HR	RBI	BB	SO	OBP	SLG	Hits Worst Against	Avg	AB	H	2B	3B	HR	RBI	BB	SO	OBP	SLG
Juan Berenguer	.625	8	5	0	0	2	5	6	1	.786	1.375	Russ Swan	.000	11	0	0	0	0	1	2	1	.154	.000
Dave Righetti	.583	12	7	1	0	1	3	4	1	.688	.917	Rick Aguilera	.000	10	0	0	0	0	0	1	1	.091	.000
Neal Heaton	.545	11	6	2	0	0	1	1	2	.583	.727	Mike Mussina	.056	18	1	1	0	0	1	0	3	.053	.111
Jim Acker	.375	8	3	0	0	1	1	3	1	.545	.750	Ben McDonald	.063	16	1	0	0	0	0	1	0	.118	.063
Eric King	.357	14	5	0	1	2	6	0	0	.357	.929	Tom Henke	.074	27	2	0	0	0	0	1	6	.107	.074

Devon White — Blue Jays   Bats Both

	Avg	G	AB	R	H	2B	3B	HR	RBI	BB	SO	HBP	GDP	SB	CS	OBP	SLG	IBB	SH	SF	#Pit	#P/PA	GB	FB	G/F
1992 Season	.248	153	641	98	159	26	7	17	60	47	133	5	8	37	4	.303	.390	0	0	3	2699	3.88	243	155	1.57
Last Five Years	.252	712	2817	427	710	123	35	68	271	200	597	19	37	132	44	.304	.393	10	27	15	11668	3.82	1040	703	1.48

1992 Season

	Avg	AB	H	2B	3B	HR	RBI	BB	SO	OBP	SLG		Avg	AB	H	2B	3B	HR	RBI	BB	SO	OBP	SLG
vs. Left	.212	179	38	5	0	5	19	13	41	.272	.324	Scoring Posn	.228	136	31	7	2	2	39	11	31	.285	.353
vs. Right	.262	462	121	21	7	12	41	34	92	.315	.416	Close & Late	.222	90	20	3	2	3	11	11	18	.314	.400
Groundball	.248	202	50	8	1	3	17	14	40	.298	.342	None on/out	.245	233	57	7	2	7	7	14	49	.287	.382
Flyball	.263	179	47	8	4	5	16	11	42	.309	.436	Batting #1	.248	640	159	26	7	17	60	47	132	.304	.391
Home	.265	306	81	17	4	7	34	24	64	.321	.415	Batting #7	.000	1	0	0	0	0	0	0	1	.000	.000
Away	.233	335	78	9	3	10	26	23	69	.286	.367	Other	.000	0	0	0	0	0	0	0	0	.000	.000
Day	.259	193	50	10	2	2	13	12	46	.308	.363	April	.237	93	22	4	0	2	10	6	23	.297	.344
Night	.243	448	109	16	5	15	47	35	87	.301	.402	May	.232	112	26	4	1	2	7	11	22	.306	.339
Grass	.220	255	56	7	3	8	21	17	52	.274	.365	June	.262	107	28	2	3	5	13	8	17	.316	.477
Turf	.267	386	103	19	4	9	39	30	81	.322	.407	July	.206	107	22	5	1	1	12	7	22	.250	.299
First Pitch	.277	83	23	6	3	3	18	0	0	.274	.530	August	.223	103	23	3	1	4	6	2	23	.245	.388
Ahead on Count	.303	119	36	6	1	8	17	22	0	.411	.571	September/October	.319	119	38	8	1	3	12	13	26	.386	.479
Behind on Count	.242	248	60	7	2	7	20	0	78	.253	.371	Pre-All Star	.242	356	86	14	5	10	39	27	71	.301	.393
Two Strikes	.196	342	67	8	1	4	17	25	133	.257	.260	Post-All Star	.256	285	73	12	2	7	21	20	62	.306	.386

1992 By Position

Position	Avg	AB	H	2B	3B	HR	RBI	BB	SO	OBP	SLG	G	GS	Innings	PO	A	E	DP	Fld Pct	Rng Fctr	In Zone	Outs	Zone Rtg	MLB Zone
As cf	.249	638	159	26	7	17	60	46	133	.303	.392	152	151	1307.0	443	8	7	2	.985	3.11	465	424	912	824

Last Five Years

	Avg	AB	H	2B	3B	HR	RBI	BB	SO	OBP	SLG		Avg	AB	H	2B	3B	HR	RBI	BB	SO	OBP	SLG
vs. Left	.252	872	220	40	7	24	81	62	161	.304	.397	Scoring Posn	.216	625	135	25	6	10	191	63	151	.285	.323
vs. Right	.252	1945	490	83	28	44	190	138	436	.305	.391	Close & Late	.247	446	110	16	4	7	41	47	110	.321	.348
Groundball	.269	756	203	39	6	15	83	48	154	.314	.396	None on/out	.288	914	263	45	11	29	29	46	181	.325	.456
Flyball	.242	662	160	35	10	15	61	48	134	.295	.393	Batting #1	.260	1734	451	86	18	44	155	121	364	.312	.407
Home	.255	1379	352	70	21	33	140	99	293	.308	.408	Batting #3	.248	520	129	18	10	11	51	30	115	.292	.385
Away	.249	1438	358	53	14	35	131	101	304	.301	.378	Other	.231	563	130	19	7	13	65	49	118	.295	.359
Day	.274	775	212	44	9	13	62	50	182	.322	.404	April	.262	412	108	26	5	8	50	27	82	.315	.408
Night	.244	2042	498	79	26	55	209	150	415	.298	.389	May	.249	438	109	21	8	10	44	44	82	.320	.402
Grass	.242	1772	428	70	16	43	164	122	384	.292	.372	June	.251	471	118	17	7	12	40	30	105	.298	.393
Turf	.270	1045	282	53	19	25	107	78	213	.325	.429	July	.257	486	125	16	5	10	46	31	101	.302	.372
First Pitch	.306	337	103	24	6	11	47	1	0	.309	.510	August	.247	542	134	22	7	20	54	38	113	.298	.424
Ahead on Count	.349	565	197	40	10	35	94	103	0	.445	.641	September/October	.248	468	116	21	3	8	37	30	114	.296	.357
Behind on Count	.225	1033	232	33	7	20	80	1	341	.235	.328	Pre-All Star	.250	1490	373	71	23	35	155	109	310	.305	.399
Two Strikes	.171	1458	249	35	14	9	75	89	595	.223	.233	Post-All Star	.254	1327	337	52	12	33	116	91	287	.303	.386

Batter vs. Pitcher (career)

Hits Best Against	Avg	AB	H	2B	3B	HR	RBI	BB	SO	OBP	SLG	Hits Worst Against	Avg	AB	H	2B	3B	HR	RBI	BB	SO	OBP	SLG
Jeff Johnson	.455	11	5	1	0	1	3	1	2	.462	.818	Juan Berenguer	.000	11	0	0	0	0	0	0	3	.000	.000
Bud Black	.450	20	9	1	1	1	2	0	3	.429	.750	Mike Flanagan	.071	14	1	1	0	0	1	0	1	.071	.143
Shawn Hillegas	.417	12	5	2	1	0	2	1	0	.462	.750	Mike Mussina	.091	11	1	0	0	0	0	0	1	.091	.091
Bill Gullickson	.389	18	7	1	1	2	4	1	1	.400	.889	Bret Saberhagen	.114	35	4	2	0	0	0	0	9	.114	.171
Edwin Nunez	.385	13	5	0	0	2	5	3	4	.500	.846	Jeff M. Robinson	.150	20	3	0	0	0	0	0	4	.150	.150

Wally Whitehurst — Mets — Pitches Right (groundball pitcher)

	ERA	W	L	Sv	G	GS	IP	BB	SO	Avg	H	2B	3B	HR	RBI	OBP	SLG	GF	IR	IRS	Hld	SvOp	SB	CS	GB	FB	G/F
1992 Season	3.62	3	9	0	44	11	97.0	33	70	.264	99	25	4	4	50	.328	.384	7	34	13	4	3	9	3	155	82	1.89
Career (1989-1992)	3.83	11	22	3	127	32	310.0	72	212	.267	321	59	10	23	145	.311	.390	29	70	25		6	23	14	535	249	2.15

1992 Season

	ERA	W	L	Sv	G	GS	IP	H	HR	BB	SO		Avg	AB	H	2B	3B	HR	RBI	BB	SO	OBP	SLG
Home	3.17	3	4	0	22	5	54.0	51	2	12	36	vs. Left	.260	204	53	14	1	3	28	18	41	.323	.382
Away	4.19	0	5	0	22	6	43.0	48	2	21	34	vs. Right	.269	171	46	11	3	1	22	15	29	.333	.386
Starter	3.91	1	5	0	11	11	50.2	56	2	11	36	Scoring Posn	.254	122	31	6	1	2	42	16	23	.343	.369
Reliever	3.30	2	4	0	33	0	46.1	43	2	22	34	Close & Late	.329	76	25	4	0	1	15	10	14	.416	.421
0 Days rest	0.00	0	0	0	1	0	1.0	0	0	0	0	None on/out	.322	87	28	4	3	1	1	7	13	.372	.471
1 or 2 Days rest	5.47	1	3	0	18	0	24.2	29	2	10	16	First Pitch	.355	62	22	5	0	0	10	4	0	.391	.435
3+ Days rest	0.87	1	1	0	14	0	20.2	14	0	12	18	Ahead on Count	.381	84	32	8	4	0	16	21	0	.505	.571
Pre-All Star	2.92	1	4	0	28	3	52.1	53	2	17	39	Behind on Count	.201	159	32	9	0	3	18	0	54	.211	.314
Post-All Star	4.43	2	5	0	16	8	44.2	46	2	16	31	Two Strikes	.149	181	27	8	0	3	17	8	70	.194	.243

Career (1989-1992)

	ERA	W	L	Sv	G	GS	IP	H	HR	BB	SO		Avg	AB	H	2B	3B	HR	RBI	BB	SO	OBP	SLG
Home	3.42	6	11	1	63	14	150.0	144	8	35	104	vs. Left	.269	625	168	35	5	11	67	42	120	.316	.394
Away	4.22	5	11	2	64	18	160.0	177	15	37	108	vs. Right	.265	577	153	24	5	12	78	30	92	.305	.386
Day	4.96	1	8	1	44	10	90.2	111	11	21	63	Inning 1-6	.272	821	223	44	10	15	95	49	140	.314	.404
Night	3.36	10	14	2	83	22	219.1	210	12	51	149	Inning 7+	.257	381	98	15	0	8	50	23	72	.306	.360
Grass	3.72	8	16	3	86	24	222.1	226	17	49	160	None on	.259	688	178	32	5	11	11	32	114	.296	.368
Turf	4.11	3	6	0	41	8	87.2	95	6	23	52	Runners on	.278	514	143	27	5	12	134	40	98	.331	.420
April	3.47	1	3	0	17	3	36.1	34	2	5	15	Scoring Posn	.271	310	84	11	4	6	111	31	67	.336	.390
May	2.51	2	1	2	23	3	46.2	42	2	11	44	Close & Late	.286	168	48	9	0	2	23	10	23	.335	.375
June	3.21	2	3	0	19	6	56.0	58	6	16	37	None on/out	.272	302	82	16	4	6	6	13	34	.304	.411
July	4.50	2	6	0	18	8	64.0	64	6	11	40	vs. 1st Batr (relief)	.256	86	22	4	0	1	14	7	9	.316	.337
August	4.82	1	5	0	18	7	46.2	56	2	13	27	First Inning Pitched	.257	459	118	22	3	7	62	32	85	.310	.364
September/October	4.18	3	4	1	32	5	60.1	67	5	16	49	First 15 Pitches	.271	439	119	22	3	7	56	23	71	.314	.383
Starter	4.48	6	17	0	32	32	160.2	186	12	34	103	Pitch 16-30	.248	306	76	16	2	8	35	22	67	.303	.392
Reliever	3.13	5	5	3	95	0	149.1	135	11	38	109	Pitch 31-45	.290	162	47	4	1	3	22	13	32	.337	.383
0 Days rest	2.19	0	0	0	8	0	12.1	10	0	1	8	Pitch 46+	.268	295	79	17	4	5	32	14	42	.300	.403
1 or 2 Days rest	3.63	3	4	1	42	0	62.0	60	6	15	42	First Pitch	.313	211	66	14	1	4	35	8	0	.339	.445
3+ Days rest	2.88	2	1	2	45	0	75.0	65	5	22	59	Ahead on Count	.182	501	91	18	0	7	36	0	180	.188	.259
Pre-All Star	2.97	7	8	2	62	14	157.1	148	11	34	111	Behind on Count	.382	285	109	20	8	7	47	43	0	.464	.582
Post-All Star	4.72	4	14	1	65	18	152.2	173	12	38	101	Two Strikes	.178	528	94	16	1	8	44	21	212	.213	.258

Pitcher vs. Batter (career)

Pitches Best Vs.	Avg	AB	H	2B	3B	HR	RBI	BB	SO	OBP	SLG	Pitches Worst Vs.	Avg	AB	H	2B	3B	HR	RBI	BB	SO	OBP	SLG
Tim Wallach	.000	12	0	0	0	0	1	0	3	.000	.000	Jeff Treadway	.500	12	6	3	0	0	1	0	0	.500	.750
Andres Galarraga	.083	12	1	0	0	0	0	0	2	.214	.083	Ryne Sandberg	.450	20	9	1	2	2	5	1	3	.476	1.000
Delino DeShields	.091	11	1	0	1	0	1	0	3	.091	.273	John Kruk	.444	9	4	1	0	1	3	0	1	.545	.889
Dave Martinez	.182	11	2	1	0	0	1	0	1	.182	.273	Andre Dawson	.400	15	6	1	0	2	6	1	1	.412	.867
Todd Zeile	.214	14	3	0	0	0	1	1	2	.267	.214	Dave Justice	.333	12	4	0	0	0	2	1	3	.385	.583

Mark Whiten — Indians — Bats Both (groundball hitter)

	Avg	G	AB	R	H	2B	3B	HR	RBI	BB	SO	HBP	GDP	SB	CS	OBP	SLG	IBB	SH	SF	#Pit	#P/PA	GB	FB	G/F
1992 Season	.254	148	508	73	129	19	4	9	43	72	102	2	12	16	12	.347	.360	10	3	3	2214	3.78	203	112	1.81
Career (1990-1992)	.251	297	1003	131	252	38	12	20	95	109	201	5	26	22	15	.325	.373	12	3	9	4108	3.65	376	247	1.52

1992 Season

	Avg	AB	H	2B	3B	HR	RBI	BB	SO	OBP	SLG		Avg	AB	H	2B	3B	HR	RBI	BB	SO	OBP	SLG
vs. Left	.283	127	36	7	0	3	8	23	21	.401	.409	Scoring Posn	.214	112	24	2	0	3	33	30	22	.372	.313
vs. Right	.244	381	93	12	4	6	35	49	81	.328	.344	Close & Late	.242	91	22	3	0	3	10	19	20	.373	.374
Groundball	.224	125	28	4	2	2	7	16	33	.312	.336	None on/out	.241	137	33	5	2	1	1	12	31	.311	.328
Flyball	.285	137	39	3	0	4	21	26	17	.399	.394	Batting #6	.254	173	44	3	2	2	9	20	32	.335	.329
Home	.269	260	70	11	3	6	25	32	55	.350	.404	Batting #7	.267	146	39	6	1	3	18	18	22	.348	.384
Away	.238	248	59	8	1	3	18	40	47	.344	.315	Other	.243	189	46	10	1	4	16	34	48	.357	.370
Day	.283	159	45	8	1	2	10	20	33	.365	.384	April	.279	86	24	0	1	3	12	7	21	.333	.407
Night	.241	349	84	11	3	7	33	52	69	.339	.350	May	.297	91	27	7	1	2	8	18	24	.411	.462
Grass	.252	424	107	17	3	8	37	59	86	.344	.363	June	.208	53	11	2	1	0	2	8	12	.311	.283
Turf	.262	84	22	2	1	1	6	13	16	.360	.345	July	.212	85	18	5	0	2	9	11	12	.309	.341
First Pitch	.226	84	19	1	0	1	3	8	0	.293	.274	August	.283	92	26	4	1	2	8	13	18	.368	.413
Ahead on Count	.354	130	46	5	1	3	17	29	1	.469	.477	September/October	.228	101	23	1	0	0	4	15	15	.328	.238
Behind on Count	.223	148	33	9	2	3	13	0	51	.233	.372	Pre-All Star	.272	268	73	12	3	7	30	38	62	.362	.418
Two Strikes	.175	229	40	7	3	2	11	37	101	.290	.258	Post-All Star	.233	240	56	7	1	2	13	34	40	.330	.296

1992 By Position

Position	Avg	AB	H	2B	3B	HR	RBI	BB	SO	OBP	SLG	G	GS	Innings	PO	A	E	DP	Fld Pct	Rng Fctr	In Zone	Outs	Zone Rtg	MLB Zone
As rf	.255	499	127	18	4	9	43	71	100	.348	.361	144	142	1278.1	321	14	7	2	.980	2.36	358	303	.846	.814

Career (1990-1992)

	Avg	AB	H	2B	3B	HR	RBI	BB	SO	OBP	SLG		Avg	AB	H	2B	3B	HR	RBI	BB	SO	OBP	SLG
vs. Left	.277	274	76	15	3	6	22	35	56	.361	.420	Scoring Posn	.217	226	49	8	1	3	68	42	52	.329	.301
vs. Right	.241	729	176	23	9	14	73	74	145	.311	.355	Close & Late	.227	185	42	6	1	5	19	25	36	.321	.351
Groundball	.220	287	63	11	5	5	26	28	66	.289	.345	None on/out	.272	261	71	11	3	7	7	18	50	.326	.418
Flyball	.282	220	62	5	1	9	33	36	30	.385	.436	Batting #5	.237	291	69	18	4	3	21	33	68	.316	.357
Home	.259	486	126	20	8	11	44	50	101	.331	.401	Batting #6	.269	309	83	9	5	6	30	28	58	.333	.388
Away	.244	517	126	18	4	9	51	59	100	.320	.346	Other	.248	403	100	11	3	11	44	48	75	.325	.372
Day	.249	289	72	12	3	3	22	29	65	.317	.343	April	.291	141	41	2	2	4	26	11	34	.335	.418
Night	.252	714	180	26	9	17	73	80	136	.328	.385	May	.256	156	40	9	3	2	12	22	38	.352	.391
Grass	.257	754	194	30	8	15	72	85	144	.332	.378	June	.196	97	19	4	1	1	4	12	22	.284	.289
Turf	.233	249	58	8	4	5	23	24	57	.303	.357	July	.243	239	58	10	3	6	23	19	41	.307	.385
First Pitch	.303	165	50	5	0	4	12	10	0	.343	.406	August	.259	216	56	12	2	6	22	26	39	.336	.417
Ahead on Count	.317	252	80	9	4	5	30	47	1	.422	.444	September/October	.247	154	38	1	1	1	8	19	27	.326	.286
Behind on Count	.199	322	64	15	5	5	33	0	113	.209	.323	Pre-All Star	.263	457	120	19	6	11	54	51	101	.336	.403
Two Strikes	.169	445	75	16	4	6	31	31	200	.261	.263	Post-All Star	.242	546	132	19	6	9	41	58	100	.316	.348

Batter vs. Pitcher (career)

Hits Best Against	Avg	AB	H	2B	3B	HR	RBI	BB	SO	OBP	SLG	Hits Worst Against	Avg	AB	H	2B	3B	HR	RBI	BB	SO	OBP	SLG
Chuck Finley	.500	16	8	3	1	0	1	2	3	.556	.813	Matt Young	.077	13	1	1	0	0	1	2	3	.200	.154
Todd Stottlemyre	.400	10	4	2	0	0	1	1	0	.455	.600	Nolan Ryan	.100	10	1	0	0	0	1	1	2	.167	.100
Jack McDowell	.381	21	8	2	1	0	1	3	2	.458	.571	Mike Moore	.143	14	2	0	0	0	0	0	3	.143	.143
Kevin Brown	.333	18	6	1	0	2	6	4	4	.455	.722	Jaime Navarro	.143	14	2	0	0	0	2	0	3	.143	.143
Chris Bosio	.333	9	3	0	0	1	3	1	2	.364	.667	Bob Welch	.154	13	2	0	0	0	0	0	3	.154	.154

Matt Whiteside — Rangers   Pitches Right

	ERA	W	L	Sv	G	GS	IP	BB	SO	Avg	H	2B	3B	HR	RBI	OBP	SLG	GF	IR	IRS	Hld	SvOp	SB	CS	GB	FB	G/F
1992 Season	1.93	1	1	4	20	0	28.0	11	13	.245	26	6	0	1	10	.314	.330	8	18	2	0	4	1	0	40	35	1.14

1992 Season

	ERA	W	L	Sv	G	GS	IP	H	HR	BB	SO		Avg	AB	H	2B	3B	HR	RBI	BB	SO	OBP	SLG
Home	1.10	1	0	0	11	0	16.1	14	0	5	9	vs. Left	.294	51	15	3	0	1	6	5	2	.357	.412
Away	3.09	0	1	4	9	0	11.2	12	1	6	4	vs. Right	.200	55	11	3	0	0	4	6	11	.274	.255
Starter	0.00	0	0	0	0	0	0.0	0	0	0	0	Scoring Posn	.182	33	6	0	0	0	8	8	2	.333	.182
Reliever	1.93	1	1	4	20	0	28.0	26	1	11	13	Close & Late	.195	41	8	1	0	0	2	4	8	.267	.220
0 Days rest	0.00	0	1	1	3	0	5.0	2	0	3	3	None on/out	.167	24	4	1	0	0	0	0	5	.167	.208
1 or 2 Days rest	2.63	1	0	2	10	0	13.2	15	1	5	7	First Pitch	.222	18	4	0	0	1	5	1	0	.263	.389
3+ Days rest	1.93	0	0	1	7	0	9.1	9	0	3	3	Behind on Count	.393	28	11	4	0	0	0	6	0	.500	.536
Pre-All Star	0.00	0	0	0	0	0	0.0	0	0	0	0	Ahead on Count	.109	46	5	0	0	0	4	0	12	.106	.109
Post-All Star	1.93	1	1	4	20	0	28.0	26	1	11	13	Two Strikes	.119	42	5	2	0	0	2	4	13	.196	.167

Kevin Wickander — Indians   Pitches Left (flyball pitcher)

	ERA	W	L	Sv	G	GS	IP	BB	SO	Avg	H	2B	3B	HR	RBI	OBP	SLG	GF	IR	IRS	Hld	SvOp	SB	CS	GB	FB	G/F
1992 Season	3.07	2	0	1	44	0	41.0	28	38	.260	39	5	1	1	14	.386	.327	10	38	9	7	3	3	0	43	40	1.08
Career (1989-1992)	3.21	2	1	1	56	0	56.0	34	48	.282	59	8	2	1	21	.389	.354	13	53	15	8	4	3	1	56	60	0.93

1992 Season

	ERA	W	L	Sv	G	GS	IP	H	HR	BB	SO		Avg	AB	H	2B	3B	HR	RBI	BB	SO	OBP	SLG
Home	1.47	1	0	0	16	0	18.1	13	0	12	14	vs. Left	.278	54	15	1	1	0	6	15	19	.431	.333
Away	4.37	1	0	1	28	0	22.2	26	1	16	24	vs. Right	.250	96	24	4	0	1	8	13	19	.357	.323
Starter	0.00	0	0	0	0	0	0.0	0	0	0	0	Scoring Posn	.185	54	10	1	0	0	12	12	16	.324	.204
Reliever	3.07	2	0	1	44	0	41.0	39	1	28	38	Close & Late	.295	44	13	2	1	0	6	10	13	.441	.386
0 Days rest	0.00	0	0	0	5	0	2.1	4	0	1	4	None on/out	.314	35	11	2	1	0	0	3	10	.385	.429
1 or 2 Days rest	4.15	1	0	0	22	0	17.1	15	1	12	14	First Pitch	.333	12	4	1	0	0	0	2	0	.529	.417
3+ Days rest	2.53	1	0	1	17	0	21.1	20	0	15	20	Behind on Count	.281	32	9	3	0	0	5	17	0	.520	.375
Pre-All Star	3.71	0	0	1	22	0	26.2	28	1	18	26	Ahead on Count	.274	73	20	1	0	1	6	0	29	.284	.329
Post-All Star	1.88	2	0	0	22	0	14.1	11	0	10	12	Two Strikes	.231	78	18	1	1	0	5	9	38	.318	.269

Bob Wickman — Yankees   Pitches Right (groundball pitcher)

	ERA	W	L	Sv	G	GS	IP	BB	SO	Avg	H	2B	3B	HR	RBI	OBP	SLG	CG	ShO	Sup	QS	#P/S	SB	CS	GB	FB	G/F
1992 Season	4.11	6	1	0	8	8	50.1	20	21	.273	51	9	3	2	23	.344	.385	0	0	6.97	5	98	8	1	98	37	2.65

1992 Season

	ERA	W	L	Sv	G	GS	IP	H	HR	BB	SO		Avg	AB	H	2B	3B	HR	RBI	BB	SO	OBP	SLG
Home	5.09	2	1	0	4	4	23.0	25	1	6	8	vs. Left	.281	89	25	4	3	1	13	10	8	.347	.427
Away	3.29	4	0	0	4	4	27.1	26	1	14	13	vs. Right	.265	96	26	5	0	1	10	10	13	.342	.347
Starter	4.11	6	1	0	8	8	50.1	51	2	20	21	Scoring Posn	.222	54	12	4	2	0	20	2	3	.237	.370
Reliever	0.00	0	0	0	0	0	0.0	0	0	0	0	Close & Late	.385	13	5	1	0	0	3	3	0	.500	.462
0-3 Days Rest	0.00	0	0	0	0	0	0.0	0	0	0	0	None on/out	.244	45	11	1	0	0	0	6	7	.346	.267
4 Days Rest	4.95	2	1	0	3	3	20.0	19	1	13	11	First Pitch	.379	29	11	0	0	0	1	0	0	.387	.379
5+ Days Rest	3.56	4	0	0	5	5	30.1	32	1	7	10	Behind on Count	.273	55	15	3	0	2	6	12	0	.403	.436
Pre-All Star	0.00	0	0	0	0	0	0.0	0	0	0	0	Ahead on Count	.286	63	18	4	3	0	9	0	16	.297	.444

1992 Season

	ERA	W	L	Sv	G	GS	IP	H	HR	BB	SO		Avg	AB	H	2B	3B	HR	RBI	BB	SO	OBP	SLG
Post-All Star	4.11	6	1	0	8	8	50.1	51	2	20	21	Two Strikes	.211	71	15	4	2	0	9	8	21	.288	.324

Curt Wilkerson — Royals
Bats Both (groundball hitter)

	Avg	G	AB	R	H	2B	3B	HR	RBI	BB	SO	HBP	GDP	SB	CS	OBP	SLG	IBB	SH	SF	#Pit	#P/PA	GB	FB	G/F
1992 Season	.250	111	296	27	74	10	1	2	29	18	47	1	4	18	7	.292	.311	3	7	4	972	3.05	112	76	1.47
Last Five Years	.247	467	1171	127	289	40	10	5	101	74	199	3	20	35	16	.291	.311	8	14	11	4079	3.24	462	302	1.53

1992 Season

	Avg	AB	H	2B	3B	HR	RBI	BB	SO	OBP	SLG		Avg	AB	H	2B	3B	HR	RBI	BB	SO	OBP	SLG
vs. Left	.294	68	20	2	0	1	7	6	10	.351	.368	Scoring Posn	.246	69	17	1	1	1	28	7	12	.309	.333
vs. Right	.237	228	54	8	1	1	22	12	37	.273	.294	Close & Late	.241	54	13	1	0	0	4	4	9	.300	.259
Groundball	.239	67	16	1	0	0	4	3	8	.271	.254	None on/out	.215	79	17	2	0	1	1	2	13	.235	.278
Flyball	.271	96	26	5	1	2	16	8	15	.324	.406	Batting #8	.272	114	31	2	1	1	15	6	19	.301	.333
Home	.269	160	43	4	1	2	19	13	20	.326	.344	Batting #9	.216	88	19	2	0	1	8	3	15	.239	.273
Away	.228	136	31	6	0	0	10	5	27	.250	.272	Other	.255	94	24	6	0	0	6	9	13	.327	.319
Day	.270	89	24	4	0	0	9	5	17	.305	.315	April	.045	22	1	0	0	0	1	0	5	.043	.045
Night	.242	207	50	6	1	2	20	13	30	.286	.309	May	.255	51	13	1	1	1	10	4	5	.298	.373
Grass	.264	110	29	6	0	0	7	4	23	.282	.318	June	.277	47	13	2	0	0	1	4	9	.333	.319
Turf	.242	186	45	4	1	2	22	14	24	.297	.306	July	.262	65	17	1	0	1	6	3	10	.290	.323
First Pitch	.289	76	22	2	0	0	9	3	0	.313	.316	August	.340	53	18	3	0	0	7	4	9	.386	.396
Ahead on Count	.228	57	13	3	1	1	7	9	0	.338	.368	September/October	.207	58	12	3	0	0	4	3	9	.258	.259
Behind on Count	.248	113	28	6	1	0	12	0	35	.250	.319	Pre-All Star	.228	149	34	3	1	2	15	10	24	.272	.302
Two Strikes	.179	106	19	1	0	1	5	7	47	.228	.217	Post-All Star	.272	147	40	7	0	0	14	8	23	.312	.320

1992 By Position

Position	Avg	AB	H	2B	3B	HR	RBI	BB	SO	OBP	SLG	G	GS	Innings	PO	A	E	DP	Fld Pct	Rng Fctr	In Zone	Outs	Zone Rtg	MLB Zone
As 2b	.296	115	34	5	0	1	15	7	18	.336	.365	70	39	295.2	70	106	2	29	.989	5.36	110	103	.936	.892
As ss	.228	162	37	5	1	1	13	8	23	.262	.290	69	46	449.1	73	143	7	27	.969	4.33	174	153	.879	.885

Last Five Years

	Avg	AB	H	2B	3B	HR	RBI	BB	SO	OBP	SLG		Avg	AB	H	2B	3B	HR	RBI	BB	SO	OBP	SLG
vs. Left	.244	262	64	9	1	2	23	18	41	.291	.309	Scoring Posn	.226	301	68	6	5	2	94	30	54	.291	.299
vs. Right	.248	909	225	31	9	3	78	56	158	.291	.311	Close & Late	.271	229	62	9	2	2	23	16	39	.320	.354
Groundball	.257	346	89	9	1	0	26	23	44	.304	.289	None on/out	.255	278	71	12	1	3	3	8	45	.276	.338
Flyball	.236	331	78	12	3	3	38	22	64	.281	.317	Batting #8	.239	259	62	10	1	1	32	18	55	.285	.297
Home	.267	570	152	22	7	5	62	36	91	.311	.356	Batting #9	.285	435	124	12	7	2	35	26	63	.328	.359
Away	.228	601	137	18	3	0	39	38	108	.272	.268	Other	.216	477	103	18	2	2	34	28	81	.260	.275
Day	.240	421	101	15	4	1	32	20	82	.271	.302	April	.212	99	21	4	1	1	7	5	17	.245	.303
Night	.251	750	188	25	6	4	69	54	117	.301	.316	May	.279	240	67	9	4	1	24	10	40	.308	.363
Grass	.272	669	182	26	6	1	57	38	115	.310	.333	June	.241	237	57	8	3	0	20	20	38	.300	.300
Turf	.213	502	107	14	4	4	44	36	84	.265	.281	July	.260	200	52	5	0	1	18	11	29	.293	.300
First Pitch	.287	251	72	12	1	1	25	3	0	.295	.355	August	.245	192	47	5	2	0	15	14	37	.297	.292
Ahead on Count	.297	239	71	10	4	1	26	42	0	.401	.385	September/October	.222	203	45	9	0	2	17	14	38	.274	.296
Behind on Count	.216	417	90	17	5	1	33	0	126	.216	.288	Pre-All Star	.250	649	162	22	8	3	56	38	109	.290	.322
Two Strikes	.168	452	76	8	2	2	19	25	199	.211	.206	Post-All Star	.243	522	127	18	2	2	45	36	90	.291	.297

Batter vs. Pitcher (since 1984)

Hits Best Against	Avg	AB	H	2B	3B	HR	RBI	BB	SO	OBP	SLG	Hits Worst Against	Avg	AB	H	2B	3B	HR	RBI	BB	SO	OBP	SLG
Jack McDowell	.500	8	4	0	0	0	0	3	0	.636	.500	Doug Drabek	.000	11	0	0	0	0	0	0	4	.000	.000
Bill Krueger	.462	13	6	1	0	0	1	3	1	.563	.538	Danny Darwin	.000	10	0	0	0	0	1	1	1	.083	.000
Ron Darling	.455	11	5	1	0	0	0	0	3	.455	.545	Dennis Martinez	.059	17	1	0	0	0	0	0	7	.059	.059
Juan Berenguer	.417	12	5	0	0	0	0	1	1	.462	.417	Matt Young	.083	12	1	0	0	0	2	0	2	.083	.083
Kirk McCaskill	.391	23	9	2	1	0	1	2	3	.440	.565	Bert Blyleven	.125	32	4	0	0	0	0	0	4	.125	.125

Rick Wilkins — Cubs
Bats Left (flyball hitter)

	Avg	G	AB	R	H	2B	3B	HR	RBI	BB	SO	HBP	GDP	SB	CS	OBP	SLG	IBB	SH	SF	#Pit	#P/PA	GB	FB	G/F
1992 Season	.270	83	244	20	66	9	1	8	22	28	53	0	6	0	2	.344	.414	7	1	1	1018	3.73	57	79	0.72
Career (1991-1992)	.248	169	447	41	111	18	1	14	44	47	109	6	8	3	5	.327	.387	9	8	1	1914	3.82	117	133	0.88

1992 Season

	Avg	AB	H	2B	3B	HR	RBI	BB	SO	OBP	SLG		Avg	AB	H	2B	3B	HR	RBI	BB	SO	OBP	SLG
vs. Left	.280	50	14	3	0	0	1	5	10	.345	.340	Scoring Posn	.245	53	13	1	1	2	16	15	9	.406	.415
vs. Right	.268	194	52	6	1	8	21	23	43	.344	.433	Close & Late	.224	49	11	0	0	2	4	8	11	.333	.347
Home	.264	129	34	3	0	3	9	18	26	.354	.357	None on/out	.302	53	16	3	0	0	0	3	14	.339	.358
Away	.278	115	32	6	1	5	13	10	27	.333	.478	Batting #6	.235	68	16	1	0	1	3	0	13	.235	.294
First Pitch	.351	37	13	1	0	2	4	7	0	.455	.541	Batting #7	.288	146	42	8	1	6	18	21	34	.375	.479
Ahead on Count	.417	48	20	3	0	1	5	13	0	.541	.542	Other	.267	30	8	0	0	1	1	7	6	.405	.367
Behind on Count	.194	93	18	1	1	5	11	0	35	.194	.387	Pre-All Star	.318	66	21	3	0	2	8	3	10	.343	.455
Two Strikes	.185	119	22	4	1	2	9	11	53	.252	.286	Post-All Star	.253	178	45	6	1	6	14	25	43	.345	.399

Jerry Willard — Expos
Bats Left (flyball hitter)

	Avg	G	AB	R	H	2B	3B	HR	RBI	BB	SO	HBP	GDP	SB	CS	OBP	SLG	IBB	SH	SF	#Pit	#P/PA	GB	FB	G/F
1992 Season	.229	47	48	2	11	1	0	2	8	2	10	0	5	0	0	.260	.375	1	0	0	204	4.08	13	19	0.68
Last Five Years	.215	67	65	3	14	1	0	3	12	4	17	0	5	0	0	.261	.369	1	0	0	269	4.19	16	24	0.67

1992 Season

	Avg	AB	H	2B	3B	HR	RBI	BB	SO	OBP	SLG		Avg	AB	H	2B	3B	HR	RBI	BB	SO	OBP	SLG
vs. Left	.000	0	0	0	0	0	0	0	0	.000	.000	Scoring Posn	.313	16	5	0	0	1	6	1	6	.353	.500
vs. Right	.229	48	11	1	0	2	8	2	10	.260	.375	Close & Late	.286	21	6	1	0	1	5	2	7	.348	.476

Bernie Williams — Yankees
Bats Both (groundball hitter)

	Avg	G	AB	R	H	2B	3B	HR	RBI	BB	SO	HBP	GDP	SB	CS	OBP	SLG	IBB	SH	SF	#Pit	#P/PA	GB	FB	G/F
1992 Season	.280	62	261	39	73	14	2	5	26	29	36	1	5	7	6	.354	.406	1	2	0	1029	3.54	105	72	1.46
Career (1991-1992)	.256	147	561	82	149	33	6	8	60	77	93	2	9	17	11	.344	.375	1	4	3	2478	3.74	232	152	1.53

1992 Season

	Avg	AB	H	2B	3B	HR	RBI	BB	SO	OBP	SLG		Avg	AB	H	2B	3B	HR	RBI	BB	SO	OBP	SLG
vs. Left	.298	84	25	6	1	1	9	10	11	.379	.429	Scoring Posn	.231	65	15	2	1	1	20	7	10	.306	.338
vs. Right	.271	177	48	8	1	4	17	19	25	.342	.395	Close & Late	.196	46	9	2	1	0	5	4	11	.260	.283
Home	.291	134	39	8	1	3	13	17	20	.375	.433	None on/out	.262	103	27	4	0	1	1	10	17	.327	.330
Away	.268	127	34	6	1	2	13	12	16	.331	.378	Batting #1	.277	260	72	14	2	5	26	29	36	.352	.404
First Pitch	.350	40	14	4	0	0	4	1	0	.381	.450	Batting #2	1.000	1	1	0	0	0	0	0	0	1.000	1.000
Ahead on Count	.329	76	25	7	0	2	7	18	0	.457	.500	Other	.000	0	0	0	0	0	0	0	0	.000	.000
Behind on Count	.260	73	19	3	1	1	7	0	20	.260	.370	Pre-All Star	.200	5	1	0	0	0	0	0	2	.200	.200
Two Strikes	.219	96	21	2	1	2	7	10	36	.292	.323	Post-All Star	.281	256	72	14	2	5	26	29	34	.357	.410

Career (1991-1992)

	Avg	AB	H	2B	3B	HR	RBI	BB	SO	OBP	SLG		Avg	AB	H	2B	3B	HR	RBI	BB	SO	OBP	SLG
vs. Left	.245	188	46	12	1	3	22	27	22	.339	.367	Scoring Posn	.288	132	38	8	2	1	49	16	22	.358	.402
vs. Right	.252	393	103	21	5	5	38	50	71	.346	.379	Close & Late	.208	101	21	5	1	0	13	11	24	.292	.277
Groundball	.275	171	47	10	1	2	17	24	27	.367	.380	None on/out	.246	207	51	8	1	2	2	30	32	.342	.324
Flyball	.258	128	33	7	1	3	17	14	20	.333	.398	Batting #1	.251	470	118	28	4	6	46	62	82	.341	.366
Home	.276	293	81	18	3	4	32	40	42	.364	.399	Batting #9	.327	52	17	3	1	0	7	6	2	.383	.423
Away	.236	268	68	15	3	4	28	37	51	.323	.351	Other	.237	59	14	2	1	2	7	9	9	.333	.407
Day	.302	189	57	14	2	1	29	19	34	.368	.413	April	.200	5	1	0	0	0	0	0	2	.200	.200
Night	.235	392	92	19	4	7	31	58	59	.333	.357	May	.000	0	0	0	0	0	0	0	0	.000	.000
Grass	.258	497	128	26	6	7	54	65	73	.344	.376	June	.000	0	0	0	0	0	0	0	0	.000	.000
Turf	.250	84	21	7	0	1	6	12	20	.344	.369	July	.254	71	18	4	1	2	11	15	14	.386	.423
First Pitch	.280	82	23	6	0	0	6	1	0	.298	.354	August	.244	250	61	16	1	5	26	36	41	.341	.376
Ahead on Count	.324	148	48	13	1	4	20	48	0	.487	.507	September/October	.271	255	69	13	4	1	23	26	36	.336	.365
Behind on Count	.243	189	46	10	3	3	20	0	49	.247	.376	Pre-All Star	.250	8	2	0	0	0	2	0	2	.222	.250
Two Strikes	.199	251	50	11	3	2	20	28	93	.279	.291	Post-All Star	.257	573	147	33	6	8	58	77	91	.346	.377

Batter vs. Pitcher (career)

Hits Best Against	Avg	AB	H	2B	3B	HR	RBI	BB	SO	OBP	SLG	Hits Worst Against	Avg	AB	H	2B	3B	HR	RBI	BB	SO	OBP	SLG
Frank Tanana	.333	12	4	0	1	0	1	0	0	.333	.500	Roger Clemens	.091	11	1	1	0	0	1	1	2	.167	.182
												Jack Morris	.111	9	1	0	0	0	0	2	1	.273	.111
												Jose Guzman	.143	7	1	1	0	0	0	4	1	.455	.286
												Kevin Tapani	.200	10	2	1	0	0	0	0	4	.273	.300

Brian Williams — Astros
Pitches Right

	ERA	W	L	Sv	G	GS	IP	BB	SO	Avg	H	2B	3B	HR	RBI	OBP	SLG	CG	ShO	Sup	QS	#P/S	SB	CS	GB	FB	G/F
1992 Season	3.92	7	6	0	16	16	96.1	42	54	.255	92	16	2	10	42	.330	.393	0	0	4.20	11	92	7	3	131	110	1.19
Career (1991-1992)	3.90	7	7	0	18	18	108.1	46	58	.254	103	16	2	12	47	.330	.393	0	0	3.90	12	91	8	5	152	119	1.28

1992 Season

	ERA	W	L	Sv	G	GS	IP	H	HR	BB	SO		Avg	AB	H	2B	3B	HR	RBI	BB	SO	OBP	SLG
Home	4.10	3	3	0	7	7	41.2	43	3	23	24	vs. Left	.269	223	60	8	2	5	26	27	29	.345	.390
Away	3.79	4	3	0	9	9	54.2	49	7	19	30	vs. Right	.232	138	32	8	0	5	16	15	25	.305	.399
Starter	3.92	7	6	0	16	16	96.1	92	10	42	54	Scoring Posn	.198	101	20	3	0	2	30	11	17	.270	.287
Reliever	0.00	0	0	0	0	0	0.0	0	0	0	0	Close & Late	.286	21	6	1	0	0	1	1	1	.318	.333
0-3 Days Rest	0.00	0	0	0	0	0	0.0	0	0	0	0	None on/out	.277	94	26	4	0	1	1	7	15	.327	.351
4 Days Rest	5.08	4	4	0	9	9	51.1	51	9	27	34	First Pitch	.288	52	15	3	0	0	5	0	0	.283	.346
5+ Days Rest	2.60	3	2	0	7	7	45.0	41	1	15	20	Behind on Count	.329	85	28	3	1	5	11	29	0	.500	.565
Pre-All Star	1.57	3	0	0	4	4	28.2	18	1	9	11	Ahead on Count	.194	170	33	8	1	2	17	0	50	.192	.288
Post-All Star	4.92	4	6	0	12	12	67.2	74	9	33	43	Two Strikes	.196	153	30	5	1	4	18	13	54	.257	.320

Gerald Williams — Yankees
Bats Right (flyball hitter)

	Avg	G	AB	R	H	2B	3B	HR	RBI	BB	SO	HBP	GDP	SB	CS	OBP	SLG	IBB	SH	SF	#Pit	#P/PA	GB	FB	G/F
1992 Season	.296	15	27	7	8	2	0	3	6	3	0	0	2	0		.296	.704	0	0	0	77	2.85	10	11	0.91

1992 Season

	Avg	AB	H	2B	3B	HR	RBI	BB	SO	OBP	SLG		Avg	AB	H	2B	3B	HR	RBI	BB	SO	OBP	SLG
vs. Left	.357	14	5	1	0	2	4	0	2	.357	.857	Scoring Posn	.375	8	3	1	0	1	4	0	1	.375	.875
vs. Right	.231	13	3	1	0	1	2	0	1	.231	.538	Close & Late	.250	4	1	0	0	0	0	0	0	.250	.250

Matt D. Williams — Giants
Bats Right (flyball hitter)

	Avg	G	AB	R	H	2B	3B	HR	RBI	BB	SO	HBP	GDP	SB	CS	OBP	SLG	IBB	SH	SF	#Pit	#P/PA	GB	FB	G/F
1992 Season	.227	146	529	58	120	13	5	20	66	39	109	6	15	7	7	.286	.384	11	0	2	1987	3.45	174	172	1.01
Last Five Years	.247	598	2183	265	540	88	14	113	355	127	488	23	51	20	19	.294	.456	27	6	17	7942	3.38	675	718	0.94

1992 Season

	Avg	AB	H	2B	3B	HR	RBI	BB	SO	OBP	SLG		Avg	AB	H	2B	3B	HR	RBI	BB	SO	OBP	SLG
vs. Left	.226	164	37	2	2	10	21	13	30	.279	.445	Scoring Posn	.208	149	31	4	2	8	49	17	42	.298	.423
vs. Right	.227	365	83	11	3	10	45	26	79	.290	.356	Close & Late	.187	107	20	1	1	2	13	12	25	.281	.271
Groundball	.229	253	58	5	0	8	30	16	52	.279	.344	None on/out	.254	138	35	4	1	7	7	11	20	.313	.449
Flyball	.268	82	22	2	1	2	9	7	14	.341	.390	Batting #4	.176	85	15	3	3	2	15	3	19	.211	.353
Home	.230	269	62	5	5	9	29	17	51	.283	.387	Batting #5	.243	371	90	8	2	16	44	26	81	.300	.404
Away	.223	260	58	8	0	11	37	22	58	.290	.381	Other	.205	73	15	2	0	2	7	10	9	.301	.315
Day	.207	213	44	5	2	8	24	14	43	.264	.362	April	.173	81	14	2	1	5	16	3	16	.221	.407
Night	.241	316	76	8	3	12	42	25	66	.301	.399	May	.264	87	23	2	1	6	18	15	22	.369	.517
Grass	.210	390	82	8	5	12	40	25	83	.264	.349	June	.193	88	17	1	1	0	2	1	19	.202	.227
Turf	.273	139	38	5	0	8	26	14	26	.346	.482	July	.256	78	20	2	1	2	7	10	18	.352	.385
First Pitch	.295	78	23	5	0	4	14	9	0	.375	.513	August	.186	97	18	1	1	3	9	3	19	.210	.309
Ahead on Count	.344	96	33	1	2	7	19	14	0	.429	.594	September/October	.286	98	28	5	0	4	14	7	15	.346	.459
Behind on Count	.216	208	45	6	3	7	22	0	60	.231	.375	Pre-All Star	.221	289	64	5	4	12	40	21	67	.282	.391
Two Strikes	.135	245	33	4	3	5	21	16	109	.193	.237	Post-All Star	.233	240	56	8	1	8	26	18	42	.292	.375

1992 By Position

Position	Avg	AB	H	2B	3B	HR	RBI	BB	SO	OBP	SLG	G	GS	Innings	PO	A	E	DP	Fld Pct	Rng Fctr	In Zone	Outs	Zone Rtg	MLB Zone
As 3b	.227	524	119	13	5	20	65	39	108	.287	.385	144	140	1247.2	104	287	23	32	.944	2.82	339	303	.894	.841

Last Five Years

	Avg	AB	H	2B	3B	HR	RBI	BB	SO	OBP	SLG		Avg	AB	H	2B	3B	HR	RBI	BB	SO	OBP	SLG
vs. Left	.257	678	174	26	2	43	120	49	133	.307	.491	Scoring Posn	.241	573	138	21	3	29	235	58	142	.311	.440
vs. Right	.243	1505	366	62	12	70	235	78	355	.287	.440	Close & Late	.206	360	74	15	1	10	42	25	85	.269	.336
Groundball	.250	773	193	22	3	31	115	43	163	.294	.419	None on/out	.256	539	138	19	6	32	32	30	102	.301	.492
Flyball	.222	468	104	20	5	24	64	29	106	.279	.440	Batting #4	.239	335	80	15	3	16	70	17	73	.283	.445
Home	.254	1102	280	45	10	63	187	59	237	.296	.485	Batting #5	.254	1381	351	52	10	76	223	79	305	.299	.471
Away	.241	1081	260	43	4	50	168	68	251	.291	.426	Other	.233	467	109	21	1	21	62	31	110	.284	.418
Day	.263	871	229	40	6	55	165	44	183	.301	.512	April	.225	289	65	8	2	12	51	14	62	.266	.391
Night	.237	1312	311	48	8	58	190	83	305	.289	.418	May	.234	304	71	10	2	15	44	22	64	.287	.428
Grass	.255	1648	421	72	10	85	270	83	356	.295	.466	June	.260	323	84	15	1	15	58	14	73	.292	.452
Turf	.222	535	119	16	4	28	85	44	132	.289	.424	July	.279	298	83	11	4	17	50	22	72	.338	.513
First Pitch	.310	378	117	27	1	19	82	15	0	.342	.537	August	.233	480	112	21	4	28	66	24	109	.274	.469
Ahead on Count	.346	407	141	20	4	41	114	51	0	.418	.717	September/October	.256	489	125	23	1	26	86	31	108	.306	.466
Behind on Count	.205	857	176	27	7	31	92	0	295	.211	.362	Pre-All Star	.246	1006	247	35	7	46	168	54	223	.268	.431
Two Strikes	.160	962	154	25	6	30	91	52	488	.206	.292	Post-All Star	.249	1177	293	53	7	67	187	73	265	.298	.477

Batter vs. Pitcher (career)

Hits Best Against	Avg	AB	H	2B	3B	HR	RBI	BB	SO	OBP	SLG	Hits Worst Against	Avg	AB	H	2B	3B	HR	RBI	BB	SO	OBP	SLG
Dennis Rasmussen	.600	20	12	2	0	3	11	2	3	.583	1.150	Greg W. Harris	.000	14	0	0	0	0	0	0	0	.000	.000
Mike Harkey	.545	11	6	0	0	2	4	0	1	.545	1.091	Bob Walk	.000	12	0	0	0	0	0	1	5	.071	.000
Danny Cox	.455	11	5	1	0	3	5	1	0	.500	1.364	Rob Dibble	.071	14	1	0	0	0	0	0	9	.071	.071
John Smiley	.429	21	9	0	0	4	11	1	4	.455	1.000	Mark Portugal	.081	37	3	0	0	0	0	1	12	.105	.081
Bruce Ruffin	.333	12	4	0	0	3	9	2	2	.429	1.083	Sid Fernandez	.091	22	2	1	0	0	0	0	9	.091	.136

Mike Williams — Phillies
Pitches Right

	ERA	W	L	Sv	G	GS	IP	BB	SO	Avg	H	2B	3B	HR	RBI	OBP	SLG	CG	ShO	Sup	QS	#P/S	SB	CS	GB	FB	G/F
1992 Season	5.34	1	1	0	5	5	28.2	7	5	.259	29	9	1	3	16	.300	.438	1	0	7.53	1	79	1	1	42	41	1.02

1992 Season

	ERA	W	L	Sv	G	GS	IP	H	HR	BB	SO		Avg	AB	H	2B	3B	HR	RBI	BB	SO	OBP	SLG
Home	7.36	0	1	0	3	3	14.2	17	2	6	3	vs. Left	.247	73	18	7	1	2	13	5	3	.291	.452
Away	3.21	1	0	0	2	2	14.0	12	1	1	2	vs. Right	.282	39	11	2	0	1	3	2	2	.317	.410

Mitch Williams — Phillies — Pitches Left (flyball pitcher)

	ERA	W	L	Sv	G	GS	IP	BB	SO	Avg	H	2B	3B	HR	RBI	OBP	SLG	GF	IR	IRS	Hld	SvOp	SB	CS	GB	FB	G/F
1992 Season	3.78	5	8	29	66	0	81.0	64	74	.240	69	16	3	4	38	.386	.359	56	12	4	0	36	8	9	68	97	0.70
Last Five Years	3.39	24	32	129	337	2	385.1	275	341	.220	304	69	9	22	189	.357	.331	155	299	88	9	168	34	14	346	478	0.72

1992 Season

	ERA	W	L	Sv	G	GS	IP	H	HR	BB	SO		Avg	AB	H	2B	3B	HR	RBI	BB	SO	OBP	SLG
Home	4.29	3	5	16	35	0	42.0	37	1	35	43	vs. Left	.265	49	13	1	0	0	7	8	9	.379	.286
Away	3.23	2	3	13	31	0	39.0	32	3	29	31	vs. Right	.235	238	56	15	3	4	31	56	65	.387	.374
Day	3.10	2	0	6	16	0	20.1	18	1	16	21	Inning 1-6	.000	0	0	0	0	0	0	0	0	.000	.000
Night	4.01	3	8	23	50	0	60.2	51	3	48	53	Inning 7+	.240	287	69	16	3	4	38	64	74	.386	.359
Grass	3.72	2	2	7	16	0	19.1	19	3	16	14	None on	.256	129	33	7	0	2	2	33	33	.422	.357
Turf	3.79	3	6	22	50	0	61.2	50	1	48	60	Runners on	.228	158	36	9	3	2	36	31	41	.356	.361
April	4.91	2	0	3	9	0	11.0	12	0	7	5	Scoring Posn	.243	107	26	5	3	2	35	20	25	.364	.402
May	1.20	0	1	5	12	0	15.0	7	0	15	15	Close & Late	.250	212	53	13	1	3	29	47	49	.388	.363
June	1.98	0	1	9	12	0	13.2	8	1	13	13	None on/out	.250	64	16	3	0	1	1	15	19	.400	.344
July	8.18	1	1	2	8	0	11.0	15	2	9	13	vs. 1st Batr (relief)	.286	49	14	2	0	1	3	16	14	.470	.388
August	5.14	0	3	3	12	0	14.0	15	0	5	14	First Inning Pitched	.226	217	49	12	2	2	29	55	55	.389	.327
September/October	2.76	2	2	7	13	0	16.1	12	1	15	14	First 15 Pitches	.242	161	39	10	1	2	15	40	38	.400	.354
Starter	0.00	0	0	0	0	0	0.0	0	0	0	0	Pitch 16-30	.242	91	22	6	1	1	20	21	26	.393	.363
Reliever	3.78	5	8	29	66	0	81.0	69	4	64	74	Pitch 31-45	.207	29	6	0	0	1	2	3	8	.281	.310
0 Days rest	5.00	1	4	9	15	0	18.0	19	1	13	17	Pitch 46+	.333	6	2	0	1	0	1	0	2	.333	.667
1 or 2 Days rest	3.69	1	3	16	32	0	39.0	31	1	35	32	First Pitch	.310	29	9	2	0	0	3	2	0	.355	.379
3+ Days rest	3.00	1	1	4	19	0	24.0	19	2	16	25	Ahead on Count	.225	142	32	11	2	2	20	0	54	.236	.373
Pre-All Star	2.47	2	2	17	36	0	43.2	29	2	38	37	Behind on Count	.255	47	12	2	0	2	8	32	0	.568	.426
Post-All Star	5.30	3	6	12	30	0	37.1	40	2	26	37	Two Strikes	.201	169	34	7	2	2	20	30	74	.320	.302

Last Five Years

	ERA	W	L	Sv	G	GS	IP	H	HR	BB	SO		Avg	AB	H	2B	3B	HR	RBI	BB	SO	OBP	SLG
Home	3.80	17	13	62	173	1	194.0	170	10	152	180	vs. Left	.223	319	71	16	2	2	48	58	89	.355	.304
Away	2.96	7	19	67	164	1	191.1	134	12	123	161	vs. Right	.220	1061	233	53	7	20	141	217	252	.358	.339
Day	3.21	7	9	45	126	0	134.2	115	11	96	109	Inning 1-6	.325	40	13	4	3	1	11	7	4	.426	.650
Night	3.48	17	23	84	211	2	250.2	189	11	179	232	Inning 7+	.217	1340	291	65	6	21	178	268	337	.355	.322
Grass	3.97	9	18	60	180	1	199.1	172	18	144	161	None on	.230	592	136	29	0	9	9	124	121	.375	.324
Turf	2.76	15	14	69	157	1	186.0	132	4	131	180	Runners on	.213	788	168	40	9	13	180	151	220	.343	.336
April	2.34	2	5	26	52	0	57.2	43	2	39	50	Scoring Posn	.209	508	106	20	6	10	164	101	142	.341	.331
May	3.55	1	5	21	58	0	66.0	47	6	57	68	Close & Late	.206	780	161	38	4	12	112	162	205	.346	.312
June	2.73	3	4	22	54	0	62.2	43	5	42	50	None on/out	.196	275	54	7	0	5	5	53	59	.336	.276
July	3.46	1	4	21	46	0	52.0	45	3	33	42	vs. 1st Batr (relief)	.225	267	60	10	1	3	26	60	64	.367	.303
August	3.22	12	5	18	66	0	78.1	63	1	53	65	First Inning Pitched	.210	1023	215	51	6	15	154	216	254	.355	.316
September/October	4.85	5	9	21	61	2	68.2	63	5	51	57	First 15 Pitches	.226	787	178	42	5	13	100	169	181	.372	.342
Starter	9.95	0	1	0	2	2	6.1	11	0	4	2	Pitch 16-30	.211	440	93	23	1	7	72	79	116	.338	.316
Reliever	3.28	24	31	129	335	0	379.0	293	22	271	339	Pitch 31-45	.203	118	24	3	2	2	12	21	35	.319	.314
0 Days rest	3.47	3	13	45	93	0	98.2	80	9	77	92	Pitch 46+	.257	35	9	1	1	0	5	6	9	.366	.343
1 or 2 Days rest	3.42	18	11	57	157	0	184.1	140	9	140	166	First Pitch	.289	142	41	4	3	3	27	18	0	.380	.423
3+ Days rest	2.81	3	7	27	85	0	96.0	73	4	54	81	Ahead on Count	.200	691	138	42	3	10	74	0	261	.206	.313
Pre-All Star	2.72	6	14	73	176	0	201.2	140	14	148	190	Behind on Count	.263	247	65	11	2	7	51	132	0	.528	.409
Post-All Star	4.12	18	18	56	161	2	183.2	164	8	127	151	Two Strikes	.192	782	150	42	3	9	80	123	341	.306	.288

Pitcher vs. Batter (career)

Pitches Best Vs.	Avg	AB	H	2B	3B	HR	RBI	BB	SO	OBP	SLG	Pitches Worst Vs.	Avg	AB	H	2B	3B	HR	RBI	BB	SO	OBP	SLG
Darryl Strawberry	.000	12	0	0	0	0	0	2	7	.143	.000	Ken Caminiti	.500	10	5	0	0	1	3	3	2	.615	.800
Marquis Grissom	.000	11	0	0	0	0	0	2	1	.154	.000	Lonnie Smith	.500	4	2	1	1	0	3	7	1	.818	1.250
Dick Schofield	.000	10	0	0	0	0	0	2	3	.167	.000	Kevin Bass	.455	11	5	2	0	2	5	0	3	.455	1.182
Mark Grace	.083	12	1	0	0	0	0	0	2	.083	.083	Brett Butler	.429	7	3	0	0	0	2	7	1	.714	.429
Rex Hudler	.091	11	1	0	0	0	0	0	3	.091	.091	Greg Olson	.333	6	2	1	0	0	2	4	1	.545	.500

Reggie Williams — Angels — Bats Both (groundball hitter)

	Avg	G	AB	R	H	2B	3B	HR	RBI	BB	SO	HBP	GDP	SB	CS	OBP	SLG	IBB	SH	SF	#Pit	#P/PA	GB	FB	G/F
1992 Season	.231	14	26	5	6	1	1	0	2	1	10	0	0	0	2	.259	.346	0	0	0	93	3.44	8	3	2.67

1992 Season

	Avg	AB	H	2B	3B	HR	RBI	BB	SO	OBP	SLG		Avg	AB	H	2B	3B	HR	RBI	BB	SO	OBP	SLG
vs. Left	.250	8	2	1	0	0	2	1	3	.333	.375	Scoring Posn	.250	8	2	1	0	0	2	1	4	.333	.375
vs. Right	.222	18	4	0	1	0	0	7	.222	.333	Close & Late	.000	1	0	0	0	0	0	0	1	.000	.000

Mark Williamson — Orioles — Pitches Right

	ERA	W	L	Sv	G	GS	IP	BB	SO	Avg	H	2B	3B	HR	RBI	OBP	SLG	GF	IR	IRS	Hld	SvOp	SB	CS	GB	FB	G/F
1992 Season	0.96	0	0	1	12	0	18.2	10	14	.239	16	1	1	1	13	.338	.328	5	22	13	0	1	2	1	19	18	1.06
Last Five Years	3.56	28	20	17	228	10	409.1	143	251	.257	398	77	8	36	235	.319	.387	41	291	109	33	31	23	14	566	446	1.27

1992 Season

	ERA	W	L	Sv	G	GS	IP	H	HR	BB	SO		Avg	AB	H	2B	3B	HR	RBI	BB	SO	OBP	SLG
Home	0.00	0	0	0	5	0	8.1	7	0	4	3	vs. Left	.188	32	6	0	0	0	5	3	7	.257	.188

471

1992 Season

	ERA	W	L	Sv	G	GS	IP	H	HR	BB	SO		Avg	AB	H	2B	3B	HR	RBI	BB	SO	OBP	SLG
Away	1.74	0	0	1	7	0	10.1	9	1	6	11	vs. Right	.286	35	10	1	1	1	8	7	7	.405	.457

Last Five Years

	ERA	W	L	Sv	G	GS	IP	H	HR	BB	SO		Avg	AB	H	2B	3B	HR	RBI	BB	SO	OBP	SLG
Home	2.43	17	10	7	115	5	222.1	181	17	64	131	vs. Left	.249	692	172	27	5	15	89	60	108	.306	.367
Away	4.91	11	10	10	113	5	187.0	217	19	79	120	vs. Right	.264	855	226	50	3	21	146	83	143	.329	.404
Day	5.05	9	8	8	68	4	132.0	140	18	49	83	Inning 1-6	.281	474	133	30	2	15	98	43	82	.340	.447
Night	2.86	19	12	9	160	6	277.1	258	18	94	168	Inning 7+	.247	1073	265	47	6	21	137	100	169	.309	.361
Grass	3.44	26	14	14	201	9	355.2	337	29	121	221	None on	.232	824	191	37	4	16	16	56	121	.282	.345
Turf	4.36	2	6	3	27	1	53.2	61	7	22	30	Runners on	.286	723	207	40	4	20	219	87	130	.357	.436
April	3.43	2	1	5	31	2	57.2	58	3	22	37	Scoring Posn	.285	438	125	23	3	11	193	68	89	.371	.427
May	4.34	5	7	1	44	5	95.1	86	13	27	53	Close & Late	.265	505	134	26	5	11	81	61	66	.343	.402
June	3.31	6	2	4	46	0	84.1	83	4	29	48	None on/out	.244	353	86	21	2	6	6	18	54	.280	.365
July	3.61	6	4	1	32	0	52.1	55	4	19	30	vs. 1st Batr (relief)	.284	190	54	9	2	3	44	17	29	.336	.400
August	3.43	5	2	1	32	0	42.0	48	4	17	34	First Inning Pitched	.274	748	205	38	6	22	161	74	119	.337	.429
September/October	3.01	4	4	5	43	3	77.2	68	8	29	49	First 15 Pitches	.281	697	196	38	6	23	137	72	99	.346	.452
Starter	4.04	1	6	0	10	10	69.0	64	10	13	36	Pitch 16-30	.236	423	100	21	1	3	49	38	81	.298	.312
Reliever	3.46	27	14	17	218	0	340.1	334	26	130	215	Pitch 31-45	.229	205	47	6	0	4	21	19	46	.296	.317
0 Days rest	4.19	10	6	5	54	0	77.1	78	5	40	41	Pitch 46+	.248	222	55	12	1	6	28	14	25	.290	.392
1 or 2 Days rest	3.18	11	6	9	107	0	175.1	162	15	52	108	First Pitch	.302	248	75	18	0	7	49	16	0	.338	.460
3+ Days rest	3.39	6	2	3	57	0	87.2	94	6	38	66	Ahead on Count	.204	653	133	25	3	7	71	0	213	.206	.283
Pre-All Star	3.64	14	10	11	131	7	254.2	240	20	80	148	Behind on Count	.300	367	110	19	3	13	67	71	0	.409	.474
Post-All Star	3.43	14	10	6	97	3	154.2	158	16	63	103	Two Strikes	.186	671	125	23	5	9	66	55	251	.250	.276

Pitcher vs. Batter (career)

Pitches Best Vs.	Avg	AB	H	2B	3B	HR	RBI	BB	SO	OBP	SLG	Pitches Worst Vs.	Avg	AB	H	2B	3B	HR	RBI	BB	SO	OBP	SLG
Gary Pettis	.077	13	1	0	0	0	1	1	7	.143	.077	Mike Macfarlane	.700	10	7	1	0	1	4	1	0	.727	1.100
Mark McLemore	.091	11	1	0	0	0	0	1	1	.167	.091	Alvin Davis	.462	13	6	0	0	2	3	1	1	.500	.923
Carlos Martinez	.091	11	1	0	0	0	1	0	0	.091	.091	Cory Snyder	.455	11	5	0	1	2	4	0	2	.455	1.182
Joe Carter	.095	21	2	0	0	1	1		6	.136	.095	Mark McGwire	.444	18	8	2	0	3	7	4	4	.545	1.056
Ozzie Guillen	.133	15	2	0	0	0	3	0	2	.133	.133	Walt Weiss	.444	9	4	1	0	1	3	2	1	.545	.889

Carl Willis — Twins

Pitches Right (groundball pitcher)

	ERA	W	L	Sv	G	GS	IP	BB	SO	Avg	H	2B	3B	HR	RBI	OBP	SLG	GF	IR	IRS	Hld	SvOp	SB	CS	GB	FB	G/F
1992 Season	2.72	7	3	1	59	0	79.1	11	45	.246	73	12	3	4	37	.270	.347	21	50	21	10	3	2	1	130	66	1.97
Last Five Years	3.04	15	6	3	105	0	180.1	37	104	.247	166	28	5	11	78	.284	.353	30	84	31	16	6	8	5	271	169	1.60

1992 Season

	ERA	W	L	Sv	G	GS	IP	H	HR	BB	SO		Avg	AB	H	2B	3B	HR	RBI	BB	SO	OBP	SLG
Home	2.93	4	2	1	29	0	43.0	36	3	5	18	vs. Left	.231	108	25	1	2	2	10	5	15	.265	.333
Away	2.48	3	1	0	30	0	36.1	37	1	6	27	vs. Right	.254	189	48	11	1	2	27	6	30	.273	.354
Starter	0.00	0	0	0	0	0	0.0	0	0	0	0	Scoring Posn	.250	80	20	3	0	0	29	3	10	.267	.288
Reliever	2.72	7	3	1	59	0	79.1	73	4	11	45	Close & Late	.238	101	24	4	0	1	10	7	11	.284	.307
0 Days rest	1.69	3	0	0	6	0	5.1	8	0	0	3	None on/out	.268	71	19	4	2	1	1	3	11	.297	.423
1 or 2 Days rest	2.38	2	1	0	35	0	45.1	40	2	7	27	First Pitch	.320	50	16	2	1	0	5	1	0	.333	.400
3+ Days rest	3.45	2	2	1	18	0	28.2	25	2	4	15	Behind on Count	.288	59	17	2	1	2	9	4	0	.333	.458
Pre-All Star	4.02	3	2	1	33	0	40.1	40	3	9	24	Ahead on Count	.191	141	27	6	1	1	17	0	43	.189	.270
Post-All Star	1.38	4	1	0	26	0	39.0	33	1	2	21	Two Strikes	.171	140	24	6	1	1	12	6	45	.204	.250

Craig Wilson — Cardinals

Bats Right (groundball hitter)

	Avg	G	AB	R	H	2B	3B	HR	RBI	BB	SO	HBP	GDP	SB	CS	OBP	SLG	IBB	SH	SF	#Pit	#P/PA	GB	FB	G/F
1992 Season	.311	61	106	6	33	6	0	0	13	10	18	0	4	1	2	.368	.368	2	2	1	410	3.50	51	21	2.43
Career (1989-1992)	.249	182	313	25	78	10	0	0	34	25	44	0	1	3	4	.300	.281	4	2	5	1146	3.34	137	83	1.65

1992 Season

	Avg	AB	H	2B	3B	HR	RBI	BB	SO	OBP	SLG		Avg	AB	H	2B	3B	HR	RBI	BB	SO	OBP	SLG
vs. Left	.288	52	15	2	0	0	6	6	10	.356	.327	Scoring Posn	.308	39	12	3	0	0	12	6	11	.391	.385
vs. Right	.333	54	18	4	0	0	7	4	8	.379	.407	Close & Late	.357	42	15	2	0	0	2	5	8	.426	.405
Home	.274	62	17	4	0	0	5	6	8	.338	.339	None on/out	.250	24	6	0	0	0	0	2	1	.308	.250
Away	.364	44	16	2	0	0	8	4	10	.408	.409	Batting #6	.276	29	8	2	0	0	2	1	4	.300	.345
First Pitch	.444	18	8	1	0	0	5	1	0	.474	.500	Batting #7	.348	46	16	3	0	0	4	2	7	.375	.413
Ahead on Count	.400	30	12	2	0	0	3	5	0	.486	.467	Other	.290	31	9	1	0	0	7	7	7	.410	.323
Behind on Count	.235	34	8	1	0	0	0	1	11	.257	.265	Pre-All Star	.311	74	23	5	0	0	9	7	15	.366	.378
Two Strikes	.190	42	8	2	0	0	4	4	18	.255	.238	Post-All Star	.313	32	10	1	0	0	4	3	3	.371	.344

Dan Wilson — Reds
Bats Right (groundball hitter)

	Avg	G	AB	R	H	2B	3B	HR	RBI	BB	SO	HBP	GDP	SB	CS	OBP	SLG	IBB	SH	SF	#Pit	#P/PA	GB	FB	G/F
1992 Season	.360	12	25	2	9	1	0	0	3	3	8	0	2	0	0	.429	.400	0	0	0	125	4.46	9	1	9.00

1992 Season

	Avg	AB	H	2B	3B	HR	RBI	BB	SO	OBP	SLG		Avg	AB	H	2B	3B	HR	RBI	BB	SO	OBP	SLG
vs. Left	.417	12	5	1	0	0	3	0	4	.417	.500	Scoring Posn	.250	8	2	1	0	0	3	0	2	.250	.375
vs. Right	.308	13	4	0	0	0	3		4	.438	.308	Close & Late	.429	7	3	1	0	0	2	1	2	.500	.571

Steve Wilson — Dodgers
Pitches Left (flyball pitcher)

	ERA	W	L	Sv	G	GS	IP	BB	SO	Avg	H	2B	3B	HR	RBI	OBP	SLG	GF	IR	IRS	Hld	SvOp	SB	CS	GB	FB	G/F
1992 Season	4.18	2	5	0	60	0	66.2	29	54	.282	74	13	3	6	39	.351	.424	18	48	11	6	4	4	1	86	77	1.12
Career (1988-1992)	4.39	12	18	5	180	23	319.2	116	229	.260	260	53	15	31	163	.323	.404	28	150	29	29	11	17	15	363	399	0.91

1992 Season

	ERA	W	L	Sv	G	GS	IP	H	HR	BB	SO		Avg	AB	H	2B	3B	HR	RBI	BB	SO	OBP	SLG
Home	4.25	2	2	0	26	0	29.2	34	3	11	29	vs. Left	.255	98	25	2	2	2	15	10	25	.318	.378
Away	4.14	0	3	0	34	0	37.0	40	3	18	25	vs. Right	.299	164	49	11	1	4	24	19	29	.371	.451
Day	3.86	0	2	0	18	0	16.1	21	0	5	16	Inning 1-6	.226	93	21	4	1	2	14	11	20	.302	.355
Night	4.29	2	3	0	42	0	50.1	53	6	24	38	Inning 7+	.314	169	53	9	2	4	25	18	34	.379	.462
Grass	3.89	2	3	0	38	0	41.2	49	4	14	36	None on	.311	119	37	7	1	2	2	13	19	.379	.437
Turf	4.68	0	2	0	22	0	25.0	25	2	15	18	Runners on	.259	143	37	6	2	4	37	16	35	.329	.413
April	2.53	0	2	0	11	0	10.2	14	0	6	11	Scoring Posn	.228	92	21	4	1	1	29	13	27	.318	.326
May	2.84	1	1	0	11	0	6.1	6	0	3	8	Close & Late	.415	53	22	3	1	1	13	8	4	.492	.566
June	4.50	1	1	0	10	0	16.0	17	1	7	13	None on/out	.204	54	11	3	0	0	5	5	9	.271	.259
July	4.85	0	1	0	10	0	13.0	13	2	6	9	vs. 1st Batr (relief)	.176	51	9	2	1	0	8	5	11	.250	.255
August	7.20	0	0	0	7	0	10.0	14	3	3	7	First Inning Pitched	.299	164	49	7	2	1	23	16	32	.359	.384
September/October	2.53	0	0	0	11	0	10.2	10	0	4	6	First 15 Pitches	.320	153	49	9	2	1	21	16	27	.382	.425
Starter	0.00	0	0	0	0	0	0.0	0	0	0	0	Pitch 16-30	.254	63	16	3	1	2	10	10	15	.356	.429
Reliever	4.18	2	5	0	60	0	66.2	74	6	29	54	Pitch 31-45	.206	34	7	0	0	3	7	2	11	.243	.471
0 Days rest	4.41	1	1	0	15	0	16.1	17	1	7	7	Pitch 46+	.167	12	2	1	0	0	1	1	1	.231	.250
1 or 2 Days rest	3.38	1	2	0	27	0	26.2	24	1	12	23	First Pitch	.207	29	6	1	0	0	5	7	0	.351	.241
3+ Days rest	4.94	0	2	0	18	0	23.2	33	4	10	24	Ahead on Count	.295	132	39	7	2	1	11	0	47	.301	.402
Pre-All Star	3.38	2	4	0	36	0	40.0	41	1	19	39	Behind on Count	.288	52	15	2	0	4	16	13	0	.424	.558
Post-All Star	5.40	0	1	0	24	0	26.2	33	5	10	15	Two Strikes	.265	132	35	8	1	2	11	9	54	.315	.386

Career (1988-1992)

	ERA	W	L	Sv	G	GS	IP	H	HR	BB	SO		Avg	AB	H	2B	3B	HR	RBI	BB	SO	OBP	SLG
Home	5.06	7	10	4	84	15	153.0	166	20	59	119	vs. Left	.244	360	88	12	6	6	51	34	80	.309	.361
Away	3.78	5	8	1	96	8	166.2	152	11	57	110	vs. Right	.267	863	230	41	9	25	112	82	149	.329	.422
Day	4.84	7	10	2	84	15	150.2	158	17	57	121	Inning 1-6	.249	730	182	31	9	21	101	67	131	.311	.403
Night	3.99	5	8	3	96	8	169.0	160	14	59	108	Inning 7+	.276	493	136	22	6	10	62	49	98	.341	.406
Grass	4.45	10	12	5	123	18	222.1	229	25	78	163	None on	.259	673	174	26	5	19	19	59	126	.319	.397
Turf	4.25	2	6	0	57	5	97.1	89	6	38	66	Runners on	.262	550	144	27	10	12	144	57	103	.328	.413
April	4.74	1	5	1	22	4	38.0	48	2	15	22	Scoring Posn	.267	329	88	17	7	3	117	39	67	.338	.389
May	4.99	2	2	0	24	1	30.2	31	5	14	23	Close & Late	.310	168	52	8	2	2	26	20	30	.383	.417
June	3.38	4	2	1	31	4	72.0	62	6	24	44	None on/out	.256	305	78	14	1	5	5	19	53	.299	.357
July	3.81	1	2	1	31	3	52.0	53	5	17	42	vs. 1st Batr (relief)	.184	136	25	5	2	0	20	14	32	.256	.250
August	4.79	3	3	0	30	3	56.1	58	7	16	45	First Inning Pitched	.233	515	120	20	4	8	72	62	104	.314	.334
September/October	5.09	1	4	2	42	8	70.2	66	6	30	53	First 15 Pitches	.237	468	111	20	4	8	61	57	91	.320	.348
Starter	5.50	5	9	0	23	23	113.0	127	16	36	75	Pitch 16-30	.302	275	83	12	2	8	37	28	52	.365	.447
Reliever	3.79	7	9	5	157	0	206.2	191	15	80	154	Pitch 31-45	.232	177	41	9	3	6	25	10	40	.272	.418
0 Days rest	3.83	2	1	3	37	0	44.2	39	4	15	25	Pitch 46+	.274	303	83	12	6	9	40	21	46	.320	.442
1 or 2 Days rest	3.39	3	4	1	67	0	82.1	74	2	31	67	First Pitch	.306	147	45	10	2	4	25	19	0	.381	.483
3+ Days rest	4.18	2	4	1	53	0	79.2	78	9	34	62	Ahead on Count	.217	572	124	19	7	10	55	0	195	.220	.327
Pre-All Star	3.94	7	9	3	88	9	157.2	150	9	60	105	Behind on Count	.300	260	78	12	3	9	54	53	0	.413	.473
Post-All Star	4.83	5	9	2	92	14	162.0	163	16	56	124	Two Strikes	.206	602	124	21	8	15	58	43	229	.260	.342

Pitcher vs. Batter (career)

Pitches Best Vs.	Avg	AB	H	2B	3B	HR	RBI	BB	SO	OBP	SLG	Pitches Worst Vs.	Avg	AB	H	2B	3B	HR	RBI	BB	SO	OBP	SLG
Charlie Hayes	.071	14	1	0	0	1	2	1	2	.133	.286	Willie McGee	.500	10	5	0	0	0	2	1	4	.545	.500
Dave Magadan	.091	11	1	0	0	0	1	0	1	.091	.091	Andy Van Slyke	.444	18	8	1	1	2	5	4	2	.545	.944
Gregg Jefferies	.143	14	2	0	1	0	1	2	1	.250	.286	Jay Bell	.417	12	5	0	1	0	1	3	2	.533	.583
Jose Oquendo	.167	12	2	1	0	0	0	0	3	.167	.250	Pedro Guerrero	.333	15	5	4	0	1	5	3	2	.444	.800
Gary Redus	.182	11	2	0	0	0	1	1	0	.250	.182	Jeff King	.333	15	5	1	0	1	4	2	2	.412	.800

Trevor Wilson — Giants
Pitches Left (groundball pitcher)

	ERA	W	L	Sv	G	GS	IP	BB	SO	Avg	H	2B	3B	HR	RBI	OBP	SLG	CG	ShO	Sup	QS	#P/S	SB	CS	GB	FB	G/F
1992 Season	4.21	8	14	0	26	26	154.0	64	88	.265	152	25	4	18	72	.342	.416	1	1	2.81	12	92	6	7	215	174	1.24
Career (1988-1992)	3.92	31	37	0	115	80	527.2	222	330	.241	465	80	11	45	216	.322	.363	6	4	3.84	41	92	18	28	786	494	1.59

1992 Season

	ERA	W	L	Sv	G	GS	IP	H	HR	BB	SO		Avg	AB	H	2B	3B	HR	RBI	BB	SO	OBP	SLG
Home	4.17	4	9	0	14	14	86.1	87	11	30	45	vs. Left	.261	134	35	4	0	3	16	15	30	.351	.358

1992 Season

	ERA	W	L	Sv	G	GS	IP	H	HR	BB	SO
Away	4.26	4	5	0	12	12	67.2	65	7	34	43
Day	3.57	4	6	0	11	11	68.0	60	6	19	41
Night	4.71	4	8	0	15	15	86.0	92	12	45	47
Grass	4.40	5	13	0	20	20	120.2	125	15	41	63
Turf	3.51	3	1	0	6	6	33.1	27	3	23	25
April	3.38	1	1	0	3	3	18.2	21	3	5	10
May	4.91	3	3	0	6	6	33.0	29	3	20	21
June	4.63	1	4	0	6	6	35.0	33	6	17	19
July	3.41	1	3	0	5	5	31.2	31	3	11	24
August	4.29	2	3	0	6	6	35.2	38	3	11	14
September/October	0.00	0	0	0	0	0	0.0	0	0	0	0
Starter	4.21	8	14	0	26	26	154.0	152	18	64	88
Reliever	0.00	0	0	0	0	0	0.0	0	0	0	0
0-3 Days Rest	11.37	0	2	0	2	2	6.1	10	2	4	7
4 Days Rest	4.27	4	8	0	14	14	84.1	81	10	32	48
5+ Days Rest	3.41	4	4	0	10	10	63.1	61	6	28	33
Pre-All Star	4.19	6	9	0	17	17	101.0	94	13	45	61
Post-All Star	4.25	2	5	0	9	9	53.0	58	5	19	27

	Avg	AB	H	2B	3B	HR	RBI	BB	SO	OBP	SLG
vs. Right	.266	440	117	21	4	15	56	49	58	.339	.434
Inning 1-6	.268	523	140	23	4	18	69	61	75	.346	.430
Inning 7+	.235	51	12	2	0	0	3	3	13	.298	.275
None on	.265	313	83	15	2	7	7	42	53	.356	.393
Runners on	.264	261	69	10	2	11	65	22	35	.324	.444
Scoring Posn	.260	131	34	5	0	6	51	17	19	.344	.435
Close & Late	.208	24	5	2	0	0	0	0	7	.240	.292
None on/out	.264	148	39	6	2	3	3	16	27	.339	.392
vs. 1st Batr (relief)	.000	0	0	0	0	0	0	0	0	.000	.000
First Inning Pitched	.268	97	26	3	0	2	10	13	14	.348	.361
First 75 Pitches	.272	448	122	20	4	15	58	51	65	.348	.435
Pitch 76-90	.230	74	17	3	0	3	11	5	11	.284	.392
Pitch 91-105	.286	42	12	1	0	0	3	6	8	.380	.310
Pitch 106+	.100	10	1	1	0	0	0	2	4	.308	.200
Ahead on Count	.237	274	65	11	4	7	24	0	74	.239	.383
Behind on Count	.321	134	43	5	0	4	14	34	0	.456	.448
Two Strikes	.198	247	49	8	2	5	18	29	88	.284	.308

Career (1988-1992)

	ERA	W	L	Sv	G	GS	IP	H	HR	BB	SO
Home	3.35	18	19	0	57	46	309.0	257	24	123	181
Away	4.73	13	18	0	58	34	218.2	208	21	99	149
Day	3.51	17	11	0	45	35	223.1	200	21	81	150
Night	4.23	14	26	0	70	45	304.1	265	24	141	180
Grass	3.71	24	28	0	87	60	409.2	357	35	156	244
Turf	4.65	7	9	0	28	20	118.0	108	10	66	86
April	4.83	1	3	0	12	3	31.2	34	4	16	22
May	3.92	4	5	0	15	10	64.1	51	5	30	41
June	3.45	8	7	0	23	18	117.1	100	11	49	68
July	4.21	7	10	0	24	21	126.0	111	12	59	81
August	4.11	6	7	0	18	16	100.2	94	7	37	63
September/October	3.59	5	5	0	23	12	87.2	75	6	31	55
Starter	3.86	29	32	0	80	80	471.0	421	39	192	291
Reliever	4.45	2	5	0	35	0	56.2	44	6	30	39
0-3 Days Rest	3.57	7	5	0	15	15	85.2	76	6	25	52
4 Days Rest	4.20	15	19	0	45	45	259.0	232	23	114	168
5+ Days Rest	3.35	7	8	0	20	20	126.1	113	10	53	71
Pre-All Star	3.67	17	18	0	57	38	257.1	218	23	114	159
Post-All Star	4.16	14	19	0	58	42	270.1	247	22	108	171

	Avg	AB	H	2B	3B	HR	RBI	BB	SO	OBP	SLG
vs. Left	.213	395	84	10	2	5	43	45	87	.301	.286
vs. Right	.248	1537	381	70	9	40	173	177	243	.337	.383
Inning 1-6	.250	1618	405	70	11	41	196	191	266	.331	.383
Inning 7+	.191	314	60	10	0	4	20	31	64	.273	.261
None on	.225	1112	250	43	3	21	21	141	198	.316	.326
Runners on	.262	820	215	37	8	24	195	81	132	.330	.415
Scoring Posn	.283	428	121	21	4	16	172	59	69	.367	.463
Close & Late	.206	155	32	8	0	1	7	16	34	.289	.277
None on/out	.227	485	110	16	2	6	6	67	80	.324	.305
vs. 1st Batr (relief)	.258	31	8	1	0	1	3	4	6	.343	.387
First Inning Pitched	.241	403	97	15	1	12	58	56	61	.333	.372
First 75 Pitches	.246	1538	379	67	10	39	182	185	256	.329	.379
Pitch 76-90	.237	207	49	8	1	6	24	16	33	.295	.372
Pitch 91-105	.221	140	31	4	0	0	6	12	28	.286	.250
Pitch 106+	.128	47	6	1	0	0	0	4	9	.293	.149
First Pitch	.300	260	78	13	1	8	42	6	0	.324	.450
Ahead on Count	.187	893	167	28	8	14	82	0	272	.192	.283
Behind on Count	.307	427	131	19	1	16	56	135	0	.473	.468
Two Strikes	.170	859	146	22	6	11	69	81	330	.245	.248

Pitcher vs. Batter (career)

Pitches Best Vs.	Avg	AB	H	2B	3B	HR	RBI	BB	SO	OBP	SLG
Darryl Strawberry	.000	16	0	0	0	0	1	2	5	.111	.000
Lloyd McClendon	.000	10	0	0	0	0	0	4	1	.286	.000
Delino DeShields	.067	15	1	0	0	0	0	2	4	.176	.067
Roberto Alomar	.091	11	1	0	0	0	0	0	1	.091	.091
Eric Anthony	.091	11	1	0	0	0	0	0	4	.091	.091

Pitches Worst Vs.	Avg	AB	H	2B	3B	HR	RBI	BB	SO	OBP	SLG
Fred McGriff	.700	10	7	0	0	2	6	4	0	.813	1.300
Mariano Duncan	.435	23	10	2	1	1	5	0	1	.435	.739
Andre Dawson	.417	24	10	1	2	1	6	0	1	.417	.750
Marquis Grissom	.353	17	6	1	0	2	3	2	1	.421	.765
George Bell	.333	9	3	1	0	2	4	2	0	.417	1.111

Willie Wilson — Athletics

Bats Both (groundball hitter)

	Avg	G	AB	R	H	2B	3B	HR	RBI	BB	SO	HBP	GDP	SB	CS	OBP	SLG	IBB	SH	SF	#Pit	#P/PA	GB	FB	G/F
1992 Season	.270	132	396	38	107	15	5	0	37	35	65	1	11	28	8	.329	.333	2	2	3	1568	3.60	176	77	2.29
Last Five Years	.263	619	1971	264	518	76	30	6	187	132	349	10	40	131	32	.310	.341	5	20	18	7858	3.69	816	458	1.78

1992 Season

	Avg	AB	H	2B	3B	HR	RBI	BB	SO	OBP	SLG
vs. Left	.248	121	30	7	0	0	14	13	30	.316	.306
vs. Right	.280	275	77	8	5	0	23	22	35	.334	.345
Groundball	.306	98	30	4	0	0	10	4	12	.333	.347
Flyball	.294	102	30	6	2	0	11	11	21	.365	.392
Home	.271	199	.54	6	2	0	13	21	33	.339	.322
Away	.269	197	53	9	3	0	24	14	32	.318	.345
Day	.221	136	30	3	1	0	12	14	22	.291	.257
Night	.296	260	77	12	4	0	25	21	43	.349	.373
Grass	.268	313	84	10	3	0	22	27	51	.327	.319
Turf	.277	83	23	5	2	0	15	8	14	.337	.386
First Pitch	.333	72	24	0	0	0	7	2	0	.351	.333
Ahead on Count	.370	73	27	4	0	0	6	17	0	.484	.425
Behind on Count	.212	132	28	3	2	0	8	0	40	.211	.265
Two Strikes	.201	179	36	7	2	0	16	17	65	.269	.263

	Avg	AB	H	2B	3B	HR	RBI	BB	SO	OBP	SLG
Scoring Posn	.237	97	23	7	1	0	34	9	17	.300	.330
Close & Late	.286	63	18	1	1	0	5	6	17	.348	.333
None on/out	.228	79	18	2	1	0	0	8	15	.299	.278
Batting #6	.243	136	33	3	1	0	10	12	26	.307	.279
Batting #7	.314	194	61	8	4	0	23	19	29	.372	.397
Other	.197	66	13	4	0	0	4	4	10	.243	.258
April	.315	73	23	6	1	0	14	5	8	.350	.425
May	.203	74	15	2	1	0	3	11	14	.306	.257
June	.279	61	17	3	0	0	7	11	10	.389	.328
July	.272	81	22	1	1	0	7	4	13	.302	.309
August	.316	38	12	0	1	0	3	1	9	.350	.368
September/October	.261	69	18	3	1	0	3	3	11	.292	.333
Pre-All Star	.259	243	63	11	2	0	26	28	40	.333	.321
Post-All Star	.288	153	44	4	3	0	11	7	25	.321	.353

1992 By Position

Position	Avg	AB	H	2B	3B	HR	RBI	BB	SO	OBP	SLG	G	GS	Innings	PO	A	E	DP	Fld Pct	Rng Fctr	In Zone	Outs	Zone Rtg	MLB Zone
As Pinch Hitter	.300	10	3	0	0	0	0	2	2	.417	.300	12	0	---	---	---	---	---	---	---	---	---	---	---
As cf	.269	376	101	15	4	0	37	32	60	.325	.330	118	98	903.0	351	2	7	1	.981	3.52	403	345	.856	.824

Last Five Years

	Avg	AB	H	2B	3B	HR	RBI	BB	SO	OBP	SLG		Avg	AB	H	2B	3B	HR	RBI	BB	SO	OBP	SLG
vs. Left	.261	632	165	33	9	1	62	36	133	.299	.347	Scoring Posn	.272	456	124	21	8	1	172	35	84	.318	.360
vs. Right	.264	1339	353	43	21	5	125	96	216	.315	.338	Close & Late	.246	301	74	10	2	2	36	25	55	.305	.312
Groundball	.247	466	115	15	4	1	41	26	71	.284	.303	None on/out	.240	559	134	17	10	2	2	41	103	.295	.317
Flyball	.284	525	149	27	4	1	44	33	106	.327	.356	Batting #1	.262	762	200	26	14	3	56	44	124	.302	.345
Home	.282	991	279	38	16	2	91	68	163	.327	.358	Batting #7	.294	398	117	19	6	0	44	40	61	.356	.372
Away	.244	980	239	38	14	4	96	64	186	.293	.323	Other	.248	811	201	31	10	3	87	46	164	.294	.322
Day	.265	536	142	24	10	2	51	42	98	.318	.358	April	.274	332	91	17	8	1	41	27	47	.330	.383
Night	.262	1435	376	52	20	4	136	90	251	.307	.334	May	.234	350	82	12	2	2	33	24	63	.280	.297
Grass	.245	1018	249	38	11	3	95	73	185	.297	.312	June	.263	300	79	10	4	0	21	24	58	.319	.323
Turf	.262	953	269	38	19	3	92	59	164	.324	.371	July	.282	372	105	11	4	1	51	26	68	.331	.341
First Pitch	.292	291	85	11	6	0	31	3	0	.300	.371	August	.273	311	85	14	7	2	24	11	52	.299	.383
Ahead on Count	.339	404	137	24	5	3	42	75	0	.439	.446	September/October	.248	306	76	12	5	0	17	20	61	.296	.320
Behind on Count	.221	701	155	20	5	2	55	0	198	.227	.272	Pre-All Star	.254	1105	281	41	15	3	109	85	198	.308	.327
Two Strikes	.194	932	181	22	12	3	74	54	349	.240	.253	Post-All Star	.274	866	237	35	15	3	78	47	151	.312	.359

Batter vs. Pitcher (since 1984)

Hits Best Against	Avg	AB	H	2B	3B	HR	RBI	BB	SO	OBP	SLG	Hits Worst Against	Avg	AB	H	2B	3B	HR	RBI	BB	SO	OBP	SLG
Bobby Ojeda	.545	11	6	0	0	0	2	1	3	.583	.545	Jack McDowell	.000	13	0	0	0	0	0	0	4	.000	.000
Juan Berenguer	.524	21	11	1	0	1	6	2	0	.565	.714	Chris Bosio	.045	22	1	0	0	0	2	0	6	.043	.045
Neal Heaton	.522	23	12	1	1	0	3	3	0	.577	.652	Jim Abbott	.091	11	1	0	0	0	3	0	2	.083	.091
Tom Gordon	.500	10	5	1	0	0	1	2	2	.583	.600	Mike Morgan	.120	25	3	0	0	0	0	0	2	.120	.120
Rich DeLucia	.455	11	5	2	0	0	4	1	0	.500	.636	Greg Swindell	.158	19	3	0	0	0	0	0	8	.158	.158

Dave Winfield — Blue Jays

Bats Right (groundball hitter)

	Avg	G	AB	R	H	2B	3B	HR	RBI	BB	SO	HBP	GDP	SB	CS	OBP	SLG	IBB	SH	SF	#Pit	#P/PA	GB	FB	G/F
1992 Season	.290	156	583	92	169	33	3	26	108	82	89	1	10	2	3	.377	.491	10	1	3	2526	3.78	231	163	1.42
Last Five Years	.286	587	2185	333	625	118	11	100	379	259	367	4	68	18	10	.361	.487	27	4	17	9331	3.78	878	573	1.53

1992 Season

	Avg	AB	H	2B	3B	HR	RBI	BB	SO	OBP	SLG		Avg	AB	H	2B	3B	HR	RBI	BB	SO	OBP	SLG
vs. Left	.301	146	44	7	1	8	28	24	21	.395	.527	Scoring Posn	.303	165	50	11	1	9	82	35	25	.419	.545
vs. Right	.286	437	125	26	2	18	80	58	68	.370	.478	Close & Late	.243	70	17	2	0	4	12	17	14	.386	.443
Groundball	.337	172	58	7	1	9	26	28	28	.430	.547	None on/out	.267	176	47	9	1	6	6	14	26	.325	.432
Flyball	.261	165	43	11	2	6	28	23	22	.353	.461	Total	.290	583	169	33	3	26	108	82	89	.377	.491
Home	.302	268	81	10	2	13	47	47	37	.403	.500	Batting #4	.290	583	169	33	3	26	108	82	89	.377	.491
Away	.279	315	88	23	1	13	61	35	52	.353	.483	Other	.000	0	0	0	0	0	0	0	0	.000	.000
Day	.286	175	50	10	1	8	27	22	29	.365	.491	April	.375	88	33	3	0	4	12	9	16	.424	.545
Night	.292	408	119	23	2	18	81	60	60	.382	.490	May	.223	94	21	5	1	5	15	15	11	.330	.457
Grass	.271	240	65	17	0	11	46	26	44	.345	.479	June	.316	98	31	9	0	4	17	17	12	.417	.531
Turf	.303	343	104	16	3	15	62	56	45	.398	.499	July	.239	92	22	7	1	3	11	11	14	.327	.435
First Pitch	.408	49	20	5	2	3	15	8	0	.491	.776	August	.303	109	33	6	1	7	32	12	19	.372	.569
Ahead on Count	.381	160	61	13	1	10	38	40	0	.502	.663	September/October	.284	102	29	3	0	2	11	18	17	.388	.402
Behind on Count	.220	200	44	8	0	5	24	0	48	.223	.335	Pre-All Star	.303	314	95	19	1	14	47	44	46	.386	.503
Two Strikes	.210	252	53	7	0	8	31	35	89	.307	.333	Post-All Star	.275	269	74	14	2	12	61	38	43	.366	.476

1992 By Position

Position	Avg	AB	H	2B	3B	HR	RBI	BB	SO	OBP	SLG	G	GS	Innings	PO	A	E	DP	Fld Pct	Rng Fctr	In Zone	Outs	Zone Rtg	MLB Zone
As Designated Hitter	.278	490	136	27	1	23	91	67	81	.364	.478	130	130	---	---	---	---	---	---	---	---	---	---	---
As rf	.355	93	33	6	2	3	17	15	8	.444	.559	26	26	217.1	52	1	0	0	1.000	2.19	60	51	.850	.814

Last Five Years

	Avg	AB	H	2B	3B	HR	RBI	BB	SO	OBP	SLG		Avg	AB	H	2B	3B	HR	RBI	BB	SO	OBP	SLG
vs. Left	.308	634	195	36	5	35	123	95	87	.396	.546	Scoring Posn	.294	581	171	34	4	25	272	106	85	.394	.496
vs. Right	.277	1551	430	82	6	65	256	164	280	.346	.464	Close & Late	.274	318	87	13	1	14	46	40	66	.353	.453
Groundball	.310	561	174	27	4	24	88	77	97	.392	.501	None on/out	.268	568	152	31	2	20	20	59	93	.341	.435
Flyball	.278	547	152	34	3	26	111	59	85	.346	.494	Batting #4	.277	1328	368	69	6	54	232	171	231	.358	.460
Home	.285	1051	300	47	4	51	166	133	173	.363	.483	Batting #5	.324	364	118	18	1	26	68	42	51	.394	.500
Away	.287	1134	325	71	7	49	213	126	194	.358	.491	Other	.282	493	139	31	4	20	79	46	85	.343	.483
Day	.278	594	165	28	2	23	98	74	105	.355	.448	April	.321	274	88	14	1	16	60	27	49	.377	.555
Night	.289	1591	460	90	9	77	281	185	262	.363	.502	May	.272	357	97	18	3	17	53	40	54	.344	.482
Grass	.273	1581	431	85	6	65	239	182	276	.347	.457	June	.303	376	114	29	3	20	68	50	57	.385	.556
Turf	.321	604	194	33	5	35	140	77	91	.396	.566	July	.272	375	102	18	2	15	52	40	56	.344	.451
First Pitch	.376	189	71	15	3	14	53	13	0	.417	.709	August	.282	387	109	22	1	17	67	45	77	.357	.475
Ahead on Count	.371	544	202	42	3	37	113	148	0	.504	.664	September/October	.276	416	115	17	1	15	79	57	74	.361	.430
Behind on Count	.234	762	178	24	2	19	97	0	201	.233	.345	Pre-All Star	.296	1121	332	65	8	57	192	130	183	.368	.521
Two Strikes	.211	988	208	38	3	31	120	96	367	.279	.349	Post-All Star	.275	1064	293	53	3	43	187	129	184	.354	.452

Batter vs. Pitcher (since 1984)

Hits Best Against	Avg	AB	H	2B	3B	HR	RBI	BB	SO	OBP	SLG	Hits Worst Against	Avg	AB	H	2B	3B	HR	RBI	BB	SO	OBP	SLG
Lee Guetterman	.900	10	9	0	1	1	4	1	0	.909	1.400	Ron Darling	.083	12	1	0	0	0	0	1	2	.154	.083
Rod Nichols	.714	7	5	1	0	0	4	4	2	.818	.857	Mike Henneman	.091	11	1	0	0	0	0	0	4	.091	.091
John Habyan	.600	10	6	3	0	0	3	2	1	.667	.900	Jose Mesa	.125	16	2	0	0	0	0	1	2	.176	.125
Ben McDonald	.438	16	7	3	0	2	4	1	1	.471	1.000	Nolan Ryan	.143	14	2	0	0	0	3	0	6	.125	.143
Matt Young	.423	26	11	2	0	4	14	6	2	.531	.962	Storm Davis	.158	19	3	0	0	0	2	0	2	.150	.158

Herm Winningham — Red Sox   Bats Left (groundball hitter)

	Avg	G	AB	R	H	2B	3B	HR	RBI	BB	SO	HBP	GDP	SB	CS	OBP	SLG	IBB	SH	SF	#Pit	#P/PA	GB	FB	G/F
1992 Season	.235	105	234	27	55	8	1	1	14	10	53	0	3	6	5	.266	.291	0	0	0	851	3.49	91	43	2.12
Last Five Years	.240	502	1017	120	244	36	14	8	69	76	219	0	12	42	26	.292	.326	4	10	3	3841	3.50	394	222	1.77

1992 Season

	Avg	AB	H	2B	3B	HR	RBI	BB	SO	OBP	SLG		Avg	AB	H	2B	3B	HR	RBI	BB	SO	OBP	SLG
vs. Left	.143	21	3	1	0	0	1	0	7	.143	.190	Scoring Posn	.234	47	11	0	0	1	14	4	9	.294	.298
vs. Right	.244	213	52	7	1	1	13	10	46	.278	.300	Close & Late	.190	58	11	0	0	0	4	3	23	.230	.190
Home	.240	125	30	6	1	1	10	6	22	.275	.328	None on/out	.271	59	16	2	0	0	0		13	.271	.305
Away	.229	109	25	2	0	0	4	4	31	.257	.248	Batting #2	.208	48	10	3	0	1	4	4	12	.269	.333
First Pitch	.143	42	6	1	0	0	1	0	0	.143	.167	Batting #7	.192	52	10	1	0	0	1	2	12	.222	.212
Ahead on Count	.412	51	21	4	1	0	3	5	0	.464	.529	Other	.261	134	35	4	1	0	9	4	29	.283	.306
Behind on Count	.274	73	20	3	1	0	3	0	23	.274	.342	Pre-All Star	.222	117	26	4	1	0	6	3	26	.242	.274
Two Strikes	.204	103	21	2	0	1	8	5	53	.241	.252	Post-All Star	.248	117	29	4	0	1	8	7	27	.290	.308

Last Five Years

	Avg	AB	H	2B	3B	HR	RBI	BB	SO	OBP	SLG		Avg	AB	H	2B	3B	HR	RBI	BB	SO	OBP	SLG
vs. Left	.190	137	26	4	2	2	13	3	34	.204	.292	Scoring Posn	.243	214	52	4	3	1	56	23	56	.313	.304
vs. Right	.248	880	218	32	12	6	56	73	185	.305	.332	Close & Late	.276	217	60	7	6	2	22	12	53	.313	.392
Groundball	.209	354	74	9	3	2	22	26	77	.263	.268	None on/out	.240	283	68	11	3	2	2	23	54	.297	.322
Flyball	.230	257	59	11	5	3	15	14	61	.267	.346	Batting #1	.253	277	70	16	7	1	18	23	52	.309	.372
Home	.240	520	125	19	6	3	32	39	107	.293	.317	Batting #2	.208	240	50	8	2	1	20	23	48	.277	.271
Away	.239	497	119	17	8	5	37	37	112	.291	.336	Other	.248	500	124	12	5	6	31	30	119	.290	.328
Day	.254	339	86	9	5	2	19	28	73	.311	.327	April	.274	95	26	2	1	2	8	9	20	.333	.379
Night	.233	678	158	27	9	6	50	48	146	.283	.326	May	.241	191	46	8	3	0	8	13	38	.289	.314
Grass	.244	401	98	16	2	5	32	35	85	.305	.332	June	.241	145	35	5	1	2	12	10	35	.288	.331
Turf	.237	616	146	20	12	3	37	41	134	.283	.323	July	.162	130	21	1	1	2	6	10	33	.221	.231
First Pitch	.247	198	49	6	4	1	14	2	0	.252	.333	August	.297	209	62	9	6	0	15	14	40	.339	.397
Ahead on Count	.366	223	82	15	4	3	16	42	0	.468	.511	September/October	.219	247	54	11	2	2	20	20	53	.277	.304
Behind on Count	.219	320	70	7	4	2	20	1	115	.221	.284	Pre-All Star	.234	471	110	15	5	4	29	33	102	.283	.312
Two Strikes	.155	431	67	7	3	2	24	31	219	.212	.200	Post-All Star	.245	546	134	21	9	4	40	43	117	.300	.339

Batter vs. Pitcher (career)

Hits Best Against	Avg	AB	H	2B	3B	HR	RBI	BB	SO	OBP	SLG	Hits Worst Against	Avg	AB	H	2B	3B	HR	RBI	BB	SO	OBP	SLG
Jim Gott	.500	12	6	0	0	0	1	2	4	.571	.500	Scott Sanderson	.000	11	0	0	0	0	0	0	2	.000	.000
Ron Robinson	.455	11	5	1	1	0	2	2	0	.538	.727	Danny Darwin	.063	16	1	0	0	0	1	2	1	.167	.063
Bill Gullickson	.375	16	6	0	0	1	3	0	2	.375	.563	Dennis Martinez	.071	14	1	1	0	0	0	0	4	.071	.143
Jesse Orosco	.364	11	4	0	0	0	0	3		.364	.364	Lee Smith	.077	13	1	1	0	0	0	0	7	.077	.154
Kevin Appier	.364	11	4	0	0	0	0	2		.364	.545	Terry Leach	.188	16	3	0	0	0	0	0	0	.188	.188

Bobby Witt — Athletics   Pitches Right

	ERA	W	L	Sv	G	GS	IP	BB	SO	Avg	H	2B	3B	HR	RBI	OBP	SLG	CG	ShO	Sup	QS	#P/S	SB	CS	GB	FB	G/F
1992 Season	4.29	10	14	0	31	31	193.0	114	125	.256	183	28	3	16	79	.356	.371	0	0	4.24	15	101	22	10	285	201	1.42
Last Five Years	4.35	50	54	0	134	132	872.1	513	742	.242	780	120	17	59	383	.344	.344	26	5	4.45	63	110	121	33	1096	894	1.23

1992 Season

	ERA	W	L	Sv	G	GS	IP	H	HR	BB	SO		Avg	AB	H	2B	3B	HR	RBI	BB	SO	OBP	SLG
Home	3.76	7	8	0	19	19	124.1	113	8	67	82	vs. Left	.243	292	71	11	3	4	38	63	52	.373	.342
Away	5.24	3	6	0	12	12	68.2	70	8	47	43	vs. Right	.265	423	112	17	0	12	41	51	73	.342	.390
Day	4.23	3	2	0	7	7	38.1	38	2	24	22	Inning 1-6	.257	627	161	27	3	14	72	104	110	.358	.376
Night	4.31	7	12	0	24	24	154.2	145	14	90	103	Inning 7+	.250	88	22	1	0	2	7	10	15	.333	.330
Grass	4.02	10	11	0	28	28	177.0	162	14	100	122	None on	.270	404	109	18	1	12	12	58	64	.361	.408
Turf	7.31	0	3	0	3	3	16.0	21	2	14	13	Runners on	.238	311	74	10	2	4	67	56	61	.348	.322
April	3.12	2	2	0	4	4	26.0	27	3	11	20	Scoring Posn	.218	165	36	5	1	2	59	39	39	.353	.297
May	3.40	3	2	0	6	6	42.1	33	4	22	30	Close & Late	.237	59	14	1	0	2	5	10	8	.357	.356
June	3.92	3	3	0	6	6	41.1	30	2	26	21	None on/out	.283	184	52	11	1	5	5	24	25	.365	.435
July	6.04	1	1	0	4	4	22.1	24	3	9	13	vs. 1st Batr (relief)	.000	0	0	0	0	0	0	0	0	.000	.000
August	6.75	0	5	0	5	5	29.1	38	2	27	16	First Inning Pitched	.268	112	30	5	0	0	3	14	21	.375	.393
September/October	3.41	1	1	0	6	6	31.2	31	2	19	25	First 75 Pitches	.261	510	133	23	2	11	57	86	89	.362	.378
Starter	4.29	10	14	0	31	31	193.0	183	16	114	125	Pitch 76-90	.186	102	19	2	0	2	8	9	23	.252	.265
Reliever	0.00	0	0	0	0	0	0.0	0	0	0	0	Pitch 91-105	.303	76	23	3	1	2	7	12	7	.404	.447
0-3 Days Rest	0.00	0	0	0	0	0	0.0	0	0	0	0	Pitch 106+	.296	27	8	0	0	1	7	7	6	.441	.407
4 Days Rest	4.12	8	6	0	17	17	107.0	99	5	71	84	First Pitch	.291	103	30	2	1	2	13	1	0	.294	.388
5+ Days Rest	4.50	2	8	0	14	14	86.0	84	11	43	41	Ahead on Count	.203	305	62	9	1	5	20	0	100	.205	.289

1992 Season

	ERA	W	L	Sv	G	GS	IP	H	HR	BB	SO		Avg	AB	H	2B	3B	HR	RBI	BB	SO	OBP	SLG
Pre-All Star	3.79	8	7	0	17	17	111.2	95	10	62	72	Behind on Count	.342	190	65	11	1	6	33	60	0	.492	.505
Post-All Star	4.98	2	7	0	14	14	81.1	88	6	52	53	Two Strikes	.162	296	48	11	1	4	20	53	125	.290	.247

Last Five Years

	ERA	W	L	Sv	G	GS	IP	H	HR	BB	SO		Avg	AB	H	2B	3B	HR	RBI	BB	SO	OBP	SLG
Home	4.11	23	28	0	65	64	420.0	387	25	231	336	vs. Left	.236	1533	362	53	13	25	187	276	346	.350	.337
Away	4.58	27	26	0	69	68	452.1	393	34	262	406	vs. Right	.246	1696	418	67	4	34	196	237	396	.339	.351
Day	4.13	7	12	0	26	25	172.1	156	8	113	151	Inning 1-6	.248	2694	667	112	12	51	343	431	628	.349	.355
Night	4.41	43	42	0	108	107	700.0	624	51	400	591	Inning 7+	.211	535	113	8	5	8	40	82	114	.317	.290
Grass	4.40	42	47	0	115	114	744.0	667	50	439	629	None on	.232	1804	418	61	6	39	39	282	420	.337	.337
Turf	4.07	8	7	0	19	18	128.1	113	9	74	113	Runners on	.254	1425	362	59	11	20	344	231	322	.353	.353
April	4.76	6	11	0	21	20	126.2	120	13	88	102	Scoring Posn	.256	810	207	37	5	11	312	148	201	.360	.354
May	5.29	8	12	0	23	23	151.1	145	11	97	125	Close & Late	.206	252	52	4	3	4	22	46	59	.333	.294
June	4.57	6	8	0	17	17	104.1	103	5	62	78	None on/out	.241	814	196	32	3	19	19	118	174	.338	.357
July	2.78	13	3	0	20	20	149.0	107	11	71	133	vs. 1st Batr (relief)	.000	2	0	0	0	0	1	0	0	.000	.000
August	5.03	8	13	0	28	28	180.2	160	11	108	152	First Inning Pitched	.254	503	128	28	1	5	75	95	116	.369	.344
September/October	3.70	9	7	0	25	24	160.1	145	8	87	152	First 75 Pitches	.248	2115	524	86	10	37	257	339	498	.350	.350
Starter	4.40	50	54	0	132	132	863.1	776	59	507	732	Pitch 76-90	.237	413	98	15	1	8	54	58	79	.329	.337
Reliever	0.00	0	0	0	2	0	9.0	4	0	6	10	Pitch 91-105	.218	330	72	10	3	9	27	49	86	.321	.348
0-3 Days Rest	5.01	2	1	0	4	4	23.1	22	2	15	22	Pitch 106+	.232	371	86	9	3	5	45	67	79	.349	.313
4 Days Rest	4.21	24	21	0	59	59	398.0	350	25	230	344	First Pitch	.318	449	143	22	3	9	70	7	0	.329	.441
5+ Days Rest	4.54	24	32	0	69	69	442.0	404	32	262	366	Ahead on Count	.166	1487	247	38	4	16	130	0	591	.166	.229
Pre-All Star	4.68	23	32	0	67	66	422.2	397	32	271	342	Behind on Count	.337	716	241	37	7	26	123	298	0	.526	.517
Post-All Star	4.04	27	22	0	67	66	449.2	383	27	242	400	Two Strikes	.149	1527	228	41	3	14	124	208	742	.252	.208

Pitcher vs. Batter (career)

Pitches Best Vs.	Avg	AB	H	2B	3B	HR	RBI	BB	SO	OBP	SLG	Pitches Worst Vs.	Avg	AB	H	2B	3B	HR	RBI	BB	SO	OBP	SLG
Sam Horn	.000	10	0	0	0	0	1	2	7	.154	.000	Felix Fermin	.611	18	11	2	0	0	5	4	0	.682	.722
Andy Allanson	.071	14	1	0	0	0	1	0	4	.071	.071	Pete O'Brien	.474	19	9	2	0	1	6	3	0	.545	.737
Pedro Munoz	.083	12	1	0	0	0	1	0	7	.083	.083	Paul Sorrento	.444	9	4	1	0	1	1	3	3	.583	.889
Mike Devereaux	.091	11	1	0	0	0	0	0	1	.091	.091	Brook Jacoby	.323	31	10	2	1	2	7	10	6	.476	.645
Terry Steinbach	.133	15	2	0	0	0	1	0	5	.133	.133	Cecil Fielder	.313	16	5	1	0	3	7	3	6	.400	.938

Mark Wohlers — Braves   Pitches Right (groundball pitcher)

	ERA	W	L	Sv	G	GS	IP	BB	SO	Avg	H	2B	3B	HR	RBI	OBP	SLG	GF	IR	IRS	Hld	SvOp	SB	CS	GB	FB	G/F
1992 Season	2.55	1	2	4	32	0	35.1	14	17	.235	28	3	0	0	8	.319	.261	16	2	2	6	3	1		49	29	1.69
Career (1991-1992)	2.78	4	3	6	49	0	55.0	27	30	.237	45	8	1	1	19	.338	.305	20	22	6	4	10	8	1	77	47	1.64

1992 Season

	ERA	W	L	Sv	G	GS	IP	H	HR	BB	SO		Avg	AB	H	2B	3B	HR	RBI	BB	SO	OBP	SLG
Home	3.38	0	1	2	14	0	16.0	14	0	9	6	vs. Left	.231	65	15	1	0	0	2	11	12	.342	.246
Away	1.86	1	1	2	18	0	19.1	14	0	5	11	vs. Right	.241	54	13	2	0	0	6	3	5	.288	.278
Starter	0.00	0	0	0	0	0	0.0	0	0	0	0	Scoring Posn	.167	30	5	1	0	0	8	6	4	.316	.200
Reliever	2.55	1	2	4	32	0	35.1	28	0	14	17	Close & Late	.290	62	18	2	0	0	4	8	9	.380	.323
0 Days rest	1.50	1	0	1	5	0	6.0	6	0	0	6	None on/out	.346	26	9	0	0	0	0	4	3	.433	.346
1 or 2 Days rest	2.95	0	1	2	17	0	21.1	16	0	11	8	First Pitch	.412	17	7	0	0	0	2	4	0	.500	.412
3+ Days rest	2.25	0	1	1	10	0	8.0	6	0	3	3	Behind on Count	.292	24	7	1	0	0	1	5	0	.414	.333
Pre-All Star	5.63	0	1	3	11	0	8.0	8	0	5	4	Ahead on Count	.179	56	10	1	0	0	5	0	13	.193	.196
Post-All Star	1.65	1	1	1	21	0	27.1	20	0	9	13	Two Strikes	.193	57	11	1	0	0	5	5	17	.270	.211

Ted Wood — Giants   Bats Left

	Avg	G	AB	R	H	2B	3B	HR	RBI	BB	SO	HBP	GDP	SB	CS	OBP	SLG	IBB	SH	SF	#Pit	#P/PA	GB	FB	G/F
1992 Season	.207	24	58	5	12	2	0	1	3	6	15	1	4	0	0	.292	.293	0	2	0	276	4.25	21	16	1.31
Career (1991-1992)	.181	34	83	5	15	2	0	1	4	8	26	1	4	0	0	.261	.241	0	3	0	391	4.25	27	22	1.23

1992 Season

	Avg	AB	H	2B	3B	HR	RBI	BB	SO	OBP	SLG		Avg	AB	H	2B	3B	HR	RBI	BB	SO	OBP	SLG
vs. Left	.385	13	5	0	0	0	0	0	2	.429	.385	Scoring Posn	.100	10	1	0	0	0	2	5	4	.400	.100
vs. Right	.156	45	7	2	0	1	3	6	13	.255	.267	Close & Late	.000	12	0	0	0	0	0	3	4	.200	.000

Kerry Woodson — Mariners   Pitches Right

	ERA	W	L	Sv	G	GS	IP	BB	SO	Avg	H	2B	3B	HR	RBI	OBP	SLG	GF	IR	IRS	Hld	SvOp	SB	CS	GB	FB	G/F
1992 Season	3.29	0	1	0	8	1	13.2	11	6	.245	12	2	0	0	9	.403	.286	0	11	4	1	0	0	0	18	12	1.50

1992 Season

	ERA	W	L	Sv	G	GS	IP	H	HR	BB	SO		Avg	AB	H	2B	3B	HR	RBI	BB	SO	OBP	SLG
Home	3.18	0	1	0	5	1	11.1	9	0	9	6	vs. Left	.368	19	7	1	0	0	5	5	2	.500	.421
Away	3.86	0	0	0	3	0	2.1	3	0	2	0	vs. Right	.167	30	5	1	0	0	4	6	4	.342	.200

Tracy Woodson — Cardinals

Bats Right

	Avg	G	AB	R	H	2B	3B	HR	RBI	BB	SO	HBP	GDP	SB	CS	OBP	SLG	IBB	SH	SF	#Pit	#P/PA	GB	FB	G/F
1992 Season	.307	31	114	9	35	8	0	1	22	3	10	1	1	0	0	.331	.404	0	1	0	363	3.08	56	27	2.07
Last Five Years	.266	100	293	24	78	12	1	4	37	10	43	2	7	1	2	.293	.355	1	1	2	1033	3.36	115	86	1.34

1992 Season

	Avg	AB	H	2B	3B	HR	RBI	BB	SO	OBP	SLG		Avg	AB	H	2B	3B	HR	RBI	BB	SO	OBP	SLG
vs. Left	.372	43	16	4	0	1	11	1	4	.386	.535	Scoring Posn	.405	37	15	5	0	1	22	1	7	.436	.622
vs. Right	.268	71	19	4	0	0	11	2	6	.297	.324	Close & Late	.292	24	7	1	0	0	2	2	2	.370	.333
Home	.262	42	11	1	0	0	6	2	4	.311	.286	None on/out	.171	35	6	1	0	0	0	0	0	.171	.200
Away	.333	72	24	7	0	1	16	1	6	.342	.472	Batting #5	.292	24	7	1	0	0	3	1	0	.320	.333
First Pitch	.208	24	5	0	0	0	4	0	0	.208	.208	Batting #6	.321	81	26	6	0	1	18	2	8	.345	.432
Ahead on Count	.452	31	14	2	0	1	6	3	0	.500	.613	Other	.222	9	2	1	0	0	1	0	2	.222	.333
Behind on Count	.289	38	11	3	0	1	10	0	7	.289	.447	Pre-All Star	.000	0	0	0	0	0	0	0	0	.000	.000
Two Strikes	.176	34	6	1	0	0	3	0	10	.176	.206	Post-All Star	.307	114	35	8	0	1	22	3	10	.331	.404

Todd Worrell — Cardinals

Pitches Right (flyball pitcher)

	ERA	W	L	Sv	G	GS	IP	BB	SO	Avg	H	2B	3B	HR	RBI	OBP	SLG	GF	IR	IRS	Hld	SvOp	SB	CS	GB	FB	G/F
1992 Season	2.11	5	3	3	67	0	64.0	25	64	.198	45	7	0	4	12	.281	.282	14	8	2	25	7	13	0	56	70	0.80
Last Five Years	2.71	13	17	55	182	0	205.2	85	183	.211	156	37	2	15	77	.292	.327	14	154	43	29	71	31	3	215	240	0.90

1992 Season

	ERA	W	L	Sv	G	GS	IP	H	HR	BB	SO		Avg	AB	H	2B	3B	HR	RBI	BB	SO	OBP	SLG
Home	0.76	1	0	2	37	0	35.1	15	0	14	37	vs. Left	.174	121	21	2	0	3	8	12	38	.254	.264
Away	3.77	4	3	1	30	0	28.2	30	4	11	27	vs. Right	.226	106	24	5	0	1	4	13	26	.311	.302
Day	1.59	1	0	1	20	0	17.0	10	1	4	20	Inning 1-6	.000	0	0	0	0	0	0	0	0	.000	.000
Night	2.30	4	3	2	47	0	47.0	35	3	21	44	Inning 7+	.198	227	45	7	0	4	12	25	64	.281	.282
Grass	3.07	1	1	0	15	0	14.2	12	1	6	8	None on	.209	134	28	5	0	2	2	15	41	.293	.291
Turf	1.82	4	2	3	52	0	49.1	33	3	19	56	Runners on	.183	93	17	2	0	2	10	10	23	.262	.269
April	0.00	1	0	0	10	0	11.0	2	0	5	12	Scoring Posn	.129	62	8	1	0	1	8	6	17	.206	.194
May	5.06	1	1	0	12	0	10.2	11	1	4	13	Close & Late	.189	169	32	6	0	3	10	15	46	.259	.278
June	11.12	1	2	0	7	0	5.2	11	2	4	6	None on/out	.241	58	14	1	0	1	1	6	14	.313	.310
July	0.96	0	0	1	11	0	9.1	9	0	3	4	vs. 1st Batr (relief)	.206	63	13	1	0	2	2	4	14	.254	.317
August	0.00	2	0	0	13	0	12.2	8	0	2	15	First Inning Pitched	.199	216	43	7	0	4	12	22	60	.276	.287
September/October	0.61	0	0	2	14	0	14.2	4	1	7	14	First 15 Pitches	.217	175	38	6	0	4	10	19	43	.297	.320
Starter	0.00	0	0	0	0	0	0.0	0	0	0	0	Pitch 16-30	.143	49	7	1	0	0	2	6	19	.236	.163
Reliever	2.11	5	3	3	67	0	64.0	45	4	25	64	Pitch 31-45	.000	3	0	0	0	0	0	0	2	.000	.000
0 Days rest	0.61	2	0	1	18	0	14.2	10	1	3	11	Pitch 46+	.000	0	0	0	0	0	0	0	0	.000	.000
1 or 2 Days rest	2.32	2	1	0	30	0	31.0	20	1	13	34	First Pitch	.200	30	6	0	0	2	4	5	0	.314	.400
3+ Days rest	2.95	1	2	2	19	0	18.1	15	2	9	19	Ahead on Count	.179	112	20	4	0	0	4	0	50	.186	.214
Pre-All Star	3.77	3	3	0	33	0	31.0	27	3	13	33	Behind on Count	.171	35	6	1	0	2	3	10	0	.356	.371
Post-All Star	0.55	2	0	3	34	0	33.0	18	1	12	31	Two Strikes	.183	131	24	6	0	0	3	10	64	.246	.229

Last Five Years

	ERA	W	L	Sv	G	GS	IP	H	HR	BB	SO		Avg	AB	H	2B	3B	HR	RBI	BB	SO	OBP	SLG
Home	2.20	7	10	29	97	0	110.2	71	4	46	100	vs. Left	.207	352	73	18	2	11	43	46	98	.298	.364
Away	3.32	6	7	26	85	0	95.0	85	11	39	83	vs. Right	.214	387	83	19	0	4	34	39	85	.287	.295
Day	2.90	6	3	16	59	0	59.0	48	8	20	56	Inning 1-6	.000	0	0	0	0	0	0	0	0	.000	.000
Night	2.64	7	14	39	123	0	146.2	108	7	65	127	Inning 7+	.211	739	156	37	2	15	77	85	183	.292	.327
Grass	3.31	2	3	14	44	0	51.2	46	7	20	40	None on	.204	401	82	24	1	6	6	35	104	.270	.314
Turf	2.51	11	14	41	138	0	154.0	110	8	65	143	Runners on	.219	338	74	13	1	9	71	50	79	.316	.343
April	2.17	3	3	9	31	0	37.1	21	5	13	31	Scoring Posn	.188	239	45	9	1	6	64	43	63	.308	.310
May	2.50	3	1	11	31	0	39.2	31	3	13	35	Close & Late	.202	416	84	21	2	9	51	54	104	.294	.327
June	3.13	3	5	6	27	0	31.2	31	2	19	27	None on/out	.229	166	38	7	1	5	5	14	34	.289	.373
July	4.06	1	5	10	32	0	31.0	27	3	11	33	vs. 1st Batr (relief)	.226	168	38	6	0	6	18	11	32	.272	.369
August	3.29	4	3	12	38	0	38.1	28	1	19	34	First Inning Pitched	.219	566	124	29	1	14	65	66	146	.299	.348
September/October	0.96	1	0	7	23	0	27.2	16	1	10	23	First 15 Pitches	.226	513	116	30	0	13	49	56	117	.302	.361
Starter	0.00	0	0	0	0	0	0.0	0	0	0	0	Pitch 16-30	.187	198	37	7	2	2	23	27	56	.285	.273
Reliever	2.71	13	17	55	182	0	205.2	156	15	85	183	Pitch 31-45	.107	28	3	0	0	0	5	2	10	.161	.107
0 Days rest	1.12	4	3	21	52	0	48.1	40	3	15	43	Pitch 46+	.000	0	0	0	0	0	0	0	0	.000	.000
1 or 2 Days rest	3.54	4	11	23	80	0	96.2	75	7	43	87	First Pitch	.267	116	31	8	0	3	14	28	0	.410	.414
3+ Days rest	2.67	5	3	11	50	0	60.2	41	5	27	53	Ahead on Count	.152	387	59	14	2	4	30	1	154	.157	.230
Pre-All Star	2.83	8	10	27	98	0	117.2	94	12	47	103	Behind on Count	.307	101	31	6	0	6	15	28	0	.457	.545
Post-All Star	2.56	5	7	28	84	0	88.0	62	3	38	80	Two Strikes	.144	381	55	13	2	4	30	27	183	.203	.220

Pitcher vs. Batter (career)

Pitches Best Vs.	Avg	AB	H	2B	3B	HR	RBI	BB	SO	OBP	SLG	Pitches Worst Vs.	Avg	AB	H	2B	3B	HR	RBI	BB	SO	OBP	SLG
Eric Davis	.000	12	0	0	0	0	0	3	2	.200	.000	Steve Sax	.600	10	6	2	1	0	1	1	0	.636	1.000
Lance Parrish	.000	11	0	0	0	0	0	2	4	.154	.000	Will Clark	.600	10	6	2	0	1	3	3	2	.692	1.100
Robby Thompson	.077	13	1	0	0	0	0	0	3	.077	.077	Howard Johnson	.556	9	5	0	0	4	8	6	1	.733	1.889
Kevin Bass	.091	11	1	0	0	0	1	0	1	.091	.091	Andres Galarraga	.421	19	8	3	1	0	3	1	4	.450	.684
Shawon Dunston	.133	15	2	0	0	0	2	0	4	.133	.133	Juan Samuel	.375	16	6	3	1	1	7	0	2	.375	.875

Craig Worthington — Indians — Bats Right

	Avg	G	AB	R	H	2B	3B	HR	RBI	BB	SO	HBP	GDP	SB	CS	OBP	SLG	IBB	SH	SF	#Pit	#P/PA	GB	FB	G/F
1992 Season	.167	9	24	0	4	0	0	0	2	2	4	0	0	0	1	.231	.167	0	0	0	109	4.19	5	10	0.50
Career (1988-1992)	.231	344	1129	119	261	45	0	29	132	147	252	8	28	3	6	.323	.348	4	11	4	5332	4.14	404	291	1.39

1992 Season

	Avg	AB	H	2B	3B	HR	RBI	BB	SO	OBP	SLG		Avg	AB	H	2B	3B	HR	RBI	BB	SO	OBP	SLG
vs. Left	.188	16	3	0	0	0	2	1	2	.235	.188	Scoring Posn	.300	10	3	0	0	0	2	1	2	.364	.300
vs. Right	.125	8	1	0	0	0	1	1	2	.222	.125	Close & Late	.000	3	0	0	0	0	0	0	1	.000	.000

Career (1988-1992)

	Avg	AB	H	2B	3B	HR	RBI	BB	SO	OBP	SLG		Avg	AB	H	2B	3B	HR	RBI	BB	SO	OBP	SLG
vs. Left	.247	360	89	15	0	7	38	61	65	.358	.347	Scoring Posn	.248	298	74	9	0	1	95	40	64	.341	.289
vs. Right	.224	769	172	30	0	22	94	86	187	.306	.349	Close & Late	.217	180	39	10	0	6	17	25	44	.319	.372
Groundball	.261	314	82	19	0	5	37	38	65	.342	.369	None on/out	.221	253	56	14	0	9	9	32	56	.314	.383
Flyball	.185	216	40	7	0	5	19	27	57	.282	.287	Batting #7	.232	341	79	10	0	11	42	48	82	.334	.358
Home	.240	562	135	18	0	16	67	78	121	.336	.358	Batting #8	.239	461	110	21	0	12	58	58	95	.325	.362
Away	.222	567	126	27	0	13	65	69	131	.309	.339	Other	.220	327	72	14	0	6	32	41	75	.308	.339
Day	.218	289	63	12	0	6	32	46	56	.327	.322	April	.211	218	46	10	0	5	26	29	54	.305	.326
Night	.236	840	198	33	0	23	100	101	196	.321	.357	May	.202	247	50	8	0	5	28	28	54	.289	.296
Grass	.230	934	215	36	0	22	100	125	204	.325	.339	June	.265	162	43	8	0	5	22	20	27	.346	.407
Turf	.236	195	46	9	0	7	32	22	48	.313	.390	July	.229	157	36	3	0	6	27	29		.349	.363
First Pitch	.293	99	29	1	0	9	22	1	0	.307	.576	August	.238	130	31	7	0	4	15	22	31	.353	.385
Ahead on Count	.291	254	74	10	0	9	43	72	0	.447	.437	September/October	.256	215	55	9	0	4	14	21	57	.324	.353
Behind on Count	.186	377	70	14	0	5	35	0	133	.192	.263	Pre-All Star	.225	676	152	27	0	17	85	85	143	.315	.340
Two Strikes	.174	619	108	23	0	5	44	73	252	.267	.236	Post-All Star	.241	453	109	18	0	12	47	62	109	.335	.360

Batter vs. Pitcher (career)

Hits Best Against	Avg	AB	H	2B	3B	HR	RBI	BB	SO	OBP	SLG	Hits Worst Against	Avg	AB	H	2B	3B	HR	RBI	BB	SO	OBP	SLG
Mike Moore	.333	18	6	1	0	1	1	4	4	.455	.556	Eric King	.071	14	1	1	0	0	1	3	4	.235	.143
Kevin Brown	.333	12	4	1	0	0	0	1	3	.385	.417	Mike Boddicker	.100	10	1	1	0	0	1	1	3	.182	.200
Curt Young	.333	9	3	0	0	0	0	3	0	.500	.333	Bud Black	.100	10	1	0	0	0	0	2	1	.250	.100
												Jimmy Key	.154	13	2	1	0	0	1	0	2	.154	.231
												Bret Saberhagen	.182	11	2	0	0	0	1	0	2	.182	.182

Rick Wrona — Reds — Bats Right (groundball hitter)

	Avg	G	AB	R	H	2B	3B	HR	RBI	BB	SO	HBP	GDP	SB	CS	OBP	SLG	IBB	SH	SF	#Pit	#P/PA	GB	FB	G/F
1992 Season	.174	11	23	0	4	0	0	0	0	0	3	0	2	0	0	.174	.174	0	0	0	65	2.83	11	6	1.83
Career (1988-1992)	.233	69	150	14	35	2	1	2	14	4	36	1	3	1	0	.255	.300	2	1	2	514	3.27	62	28	2.21

1992 Season

	Avg	AB	H	2B	3B	HR	RBI	BB	SO	OBP	SLG		Avg	AB	H	2B	3B	HR	RBI	BB	SO	OBP	SLG
vs. Left	.000	6	0	0	0	0	0	0	2	.000	.000	Scoring Posn	.000	9	0	0	0	0	0	0	1	.000	.000
vs. Right	.235	17	4	0	0	0	0	0	1	.235	.235	Close & Late	.000	4	0	0	0	0	0	0	0	.000	.000

Eric Yelding — White Sox — Bats Right (groundball hitter)

	Avg	G	AB	R	H	2B	3B	HR	RBI	BB	SO	HBP	GDP	SB	CS	OBP	SLG	IBB	SH	SF	#Pit	#P/PA	GB	FB	G/F
1992 Season	.250	9	8	1	2	0	0	0	0	0	3	0	0	0	0	.250	.250	0	0	0	25	3.13	1	2	0.50
Career (1989-1992)	.249	299	885	108	220	22	6	2	57	59	155	1	18	86	39	.294	.294	4	9	8	3445	3.61	340	209	1.63

1992 Season

	Avg	AB	H	2B	3B	HR	RBI	BB	SO	OBP	SLG		Avg	AB	H	2B	3B	HR	RBI	BB	SO	OBP	SLG
vs. Left	.250	4	1	0	0	0	0	0	1	.250	.250	Scoring Posn	.000	0	0	0	0	0	0	0	0	.000	.000
vs. Right	.250	4	1	0	0	0	0	0	2	.250	.250	Close & Late	.167	6	1	0	0	0	0	0	3	.167	.167

Career (1989-1992)

	Avg	AB	H	2B	3B	HR	RBI	BB	SO	OBP	SLG		Avg	AB	H	2B	3B	HR	RBI	BB	SO	OBP	SLG
vs. Left	.278	378	105	10	4	0	25	27	55	.322	.325	Scoring Posn	.251	187	47	4	2	0	52	11	23	.282	.294
vs. Right	.227	507	115	12	2	2	32	32	100	.273	.270	Close & Late	.270	152	41	2	0	0	12	13	29	.329	.283
Groundball	.254	299	76	10	0	0	7	16	45	.292	.288	None on/out	.239	331	79	6	1	1	1	26	60	.296	.272
Flyball	.217	161	35	1	2	0	17	12	32	.266	.248	Batting #1	.247	632	156	16	5	1	34	43	113	.294	.293
Home	.240	425	102	4	4	0	24	32	74	.290	.268	Batting #8	.310	84	26	3	0	1	8	6	12	.352	.381
Away	.257	460	118	18	2	2	33	27	81	.297	.317	Other	.225	169	38	3	1	0	15	10	30	.264	.254
Day	.262	248	65	7	2	1	18	20	43	.320	.319	April	.220	109	24	3	2	0	6	3	19	.237	.284
Night	.243	637	155	15	4	1	39	39	112	.284	.264	May	.292	192	56	5	1	1	16	9	32	.323	.344
Grass	.273	267	73	11	1	0	20	22	44	.328	.322	June	.234	171	40	3	1	0	12	19	27	.309	.263
Turf	.238	618	147	11	5	2	37	37	111	.279	.282	July	.281	167	47	4	1	0	12	10	29	.317	.317
First Pitch	.291	141	41	5	2	2	22	2	0	.295	.397	August	.175	126	22	3	0	0	5	7	20	.221	.198
Ahead on Count	.225	169	38	3	1	0	9	28	0	.333	.254	September/October	.258	120	31	4	1	0	6	11	28	.321	.333
Behind on Count	.265	339	90	8	2	0	15	0	111	.265	.301	Pre-All Star	.253	521	132	11	4	1	35	33	86	.296	.296
Two Strikes	.205	435	89	12	1	0	14	29	154	.254	.237	Post-All Star	.242	364	88	11	2	1	22	26	69	.290	.291

Batter vs. Pitcher (career)

Hits Best Against	Avg	AB	H	2B	3B	HR	RBI	BB	SO	OBP	SLG	Hits Worst Against	Avg	AB	H	2B	3B	HR	RBI	BB	SO	OBP	SLG
Frank Viola	.600	15	9	0	0	0	1	2	2	.647	.600	Trevor Wilson	.077	13	1	0	0	0	0	3	4	.250	.077

Batter vs. Pitcher (career)

Hits Best Against	Avg	AB	H	2B	3B	HR	RBI	BB	SO	OBP	SLG	Hits Worst Against	Avg	AB	H	2B	3B	HR	RBI	BB	SO	OBP	SLG
Steve Avery	.500	10	5	3	0	0	2	3	1	.615	.800	Greg Maddux	.115	26	3	1	0	0	0	1	6	.148	.154
Pat Combs	.385	13	5	0	0	0	1	2	1	.438	.385	Mark Gardner	.154	13	2	0	0	0	0	0	4	.154	.154
Mike Bielecki	.375	16	6	2	0	0	0	0	3	.375	.500	Bruce Hurst	.182	11	2	0	0	0	0	0	2	.182	.182
Doug Drabek	.364	11	4	1	0	0	0	3		.364	.455	Shawn Boskie	.200	10	2	0	0	0	1	1	1	.273	.200

Anthony Young — Mets
Pitches Right (groundball pitcher)

	ERA	W	L	Sv	G	GS	IP	BB	SO	Avg	H	2B	3B	HR	RBI	OBP	SLG	GF	IR	IRS	Hld	SvOp	SB	CS	GB	FB	G/F
1992 Season	4.17	2	14	15	52	13	121.0	31	64	.285	134	23	9	8	58	.328	.423	26	17	4	2	20	10	6	210	118	1.78
Career (1991-1992)	3.86	4	19	15	62	21	170.1	43	84	.277	182	31	10	12	77	.321	.409	28	19	4	2	20	13	7	305	164	1.86

1992 Season

	ERA	W	L	Sv	G	GS	IP	H	HR	BB	SO		Avg	AB	H	2B	3B	HR	RBI	BB	SO	OBP	SLG
Home	3.96	0	7	8	25	6	52.1	66	3	17	28	vs. Left	.324	259	84	13	7	3	34	18	31	.366	.463
Away	4.33	2	7	7	27	7	68.2	68	5	14	36	vs. Right	.237	211	50	10	2	5	24	13	33	.282	.374
Starter	4.81	1	7	0	13	13	73.0	95	5	16	45	Scoring Posn	.330	109	36	6	1	5	49	9	12	.369	.541
Reliever	3.19	1	7	15	39	0	48.0	39	3	15	19	Close & Late	.248	121	30	2	2	3	17	11	13	.311	.372
0 Days rest	4.70		2	5	10	0	7.2	7	0	4	2	None on/out	.258	120	31	6	2	1	1	7	18	.299	.367
1 or 2 Days rest	1.93	0	3	6	17	0	23.1	17	1	5	13	First Pitch	.368	76	28	3	3	2	19	4	0	.395	.566
3+ Days rest	4.24	1	2	4	12	0	17.0	15	2	6	4	Behind on Count	.365	96	35	8	3	1	9	17	0	.456	.542
Pre-All Star	4.59	2	9	3	22	13	86.1	100	5	21	50	Ahead on Count	.216	218	47	8	1	4	20	0	55	.219	.317
Post-All Star	3.12	0	5	12	30	0	34.2	30	3	10	14	Two Strikes	.204	196	40	7	2	4	14	10	64	.243	.321

Curt Young — Yankees
Pitches Left

	ERA	W	L	Sv	G	GS	IP	BB	SO	Avg	H	2B	3B	HR	RBI	OBP	SLG	GF	IR	IRS	Hld	SvOp	SB	CS	GB	FB	G/F
1992 Season	3.99	4	2	0	23	7	67.2	17	20	.296	80	20	1	2	31	.339	.400	5	6	3	0	2	5	2	101	90	1.12
Last Five Years	4.32	33	27	0	141	75	527.2	201	227	.274	557	98	5	60	230	.341	.417	11	35	12	7	2	47	30	735	680	1.08

1992 Season

	ERA	W	L	Sv	G	GS	IP	H	HR	BB	SO		Avg	AB	H	2B	3B	HR	RBI	BB	SO	OBP	SLG
Home	4.87	3	1	0	14	5	40.2	55	2	10	9	vs. Left	.392	51	20	4	0	0	13	1	7	.396	.471
Away	2.67	1	1	0	9	2	27.0	25	0	7	11	vs. Right	.274	219	60	16	1	2	18	16	13	.326	.384
Starter	3.89	4	1	0	7	7	39.1	49	2	10	11	Scoring Posn	.299	67	20	2	0	1	27	6	6	.351	.373
Reliever	4.13	0	1	0	16	0	28.1	31	0	7	9	Close & Late	.250	12	3	1	0	0	1	0	1	.286	.333
0 Days rest	0.00	0	0	0	1	0	1.0	0	0	0	1	None on/out	.194	62	12	4	0	0	0	7	3	.275	.258
1 or 2 Days rest	2.70	0	1	0	6	0	13.1	14	0	2	4	First Pitch	.417	36	15	4	0	0	6	2	0	.475	.528
3+ Days rest	5.79	0	0	0	9	0	14.0	17	0	5	4	Behind on Count	.373	75	28	8	1	2	11	10	0	.447	.587
Pre-All Star	5.04	1	2	0	11	3	30.1	37	1	9	8	Ahead on Count	.248	105	26	6	0	0	11	0	18	.243	.305
Post-All Star	3.13	3	0	0	12	4	37.1	40	1	8	12	Two Strikes	.248	101	25	5	0	0	10	5	20	.278	.297

Last Five Years

	ERA	W	L	Sv	G	GS	IP	H	HR	BB	SO		Avg	AB	H	2B	3B	HR	RBI	BB	SO	OBP	SLG
Home	4.08	14	13	0	74	40	276.0	293	35	104	128	vs. Left	.259	433	112	17	1	6	51	25	53	.305	.344
Away	4.58	19	14	0	67	35	251.2	264	35	97	99	vs. Right	.278	1602	445	81	6	54	179	176	174	.350	.437
Day	4.13	15	7	0	59	31	215.2	220	24	87	96	Inning 1-6	.280	1723	483	84	6	50	207	171	198	.347	.423
Night	4.44	18	20	0	82	44	312.0	337	36	114	131	Inning 7+	.237	312	74	14	1	10	23	30	29	.309	.385
Grass	3.82	26	20	0	114	60	435.1	427	43	167	188	None on/out	.267	1208	322	63	4	40	40	111	145	.331	.425
Turf	6.63	7	7	0	27	15	92.1	130	17	34	39	Runners on	.284	827	235	35	3	20	190	90	82	.356	.406
April	6.38	2	5	0	20	9	82.2	87	13	28	28	Scoring Posn	.270	444	120	13	2	13	168	61	50	.358	.396
May	3.70	9	5	0	28	15	112.0	110	15	44	44	Close & Late	.220	118	26	5	0	4	9	18	10	.329	.364
June	5.18	2	8	0	18	12	73.0	74	7	37	33	None on/out	.232	531	123	23	1	15	15	45	64	.293	.363
July	5.07	7	5	0	25	15	92.1	103	13	29	45	vs. 1st Batr (relief)	.217	60	13	4	0	0	3	6	7	.288	.283
August	2.32	6	1	0	18	11	77.2	74	6	23	31	First Inning Pitched	.275	509	140	27	1	14	73	52	57	.347	.415
September/October	3.86	7	3	0	32	13	105.0	109	6	40	46	First 15 Pitches	.291	453	132	25	1	11	44	38	50	.351	.424
Starter	4.22	29	25	0	75	75	416.0	440	51	155	185	Pitch 16-30	.255	392	100	23	1	14	50	47	46	.338	.426
Reliever	4.67	4	2	0	66	0	111.2	117	9	46	42	Pitch 31-45	.287	334	96	15	0	11	49	28	38	.348	.431
0 Days rest	0.00	1	0	0	3	0	4.0	2	0	1	5	Pitch 46+	.268	856	229	35	5	24	87	88	93	.335	.404
1 or 2 Days rest	2.40	1	1	0	21	0	41.1	38	0	10	13	First Pitch	.322	255	82	13	0	9	31	6	0	.349	.478
3+ Days rest	6.38	2	1	0	42	0	66.1	77	9	35	24	Ahead on Count	.213	813	173	29	3	10	68	0	192	.213	.293
Pre-All Star	4.91	15	20	0	75	41	280.2	307	42	117	114	Behind on Count	.334	545	182	37	3	27	87	116	0	.451	.561
Post-All Star	3.64	18	7	0	66	34	247.0	250	18	84	113	Two Strikes	.216	812	175	31	1	18	79	79	227	.285	.323

Pitcher vs. Batter (since 1984)

Pitches Best Vs.	Avg	AB	H	2B	3B	HR	RBI	BB	SO	OBP	SLG	Pitches Worst Vs.	Avg	AB	H	2B	3B	HR	RBI	BB	SO	OBP	SLG
Mike Pagliarulo	.063	16	1	0	0	0	0	1	4	.118	.063	Dante Bichette	.625	8	5	0	0	2	3	4	1	.750	1.375
Gary Thurman	.067	15	1	0	0	0	1	1	5	.125	.067	Roberto Kelly	.600	10	6	1	0	1	1	1	2	.636	1.000
Carlton Fisk	.069	29	2	0	0	0	1	1	4	.097	.069	Luis Salazar	.500	12	6	1	0	2	5	0	0	.500	1.083
Dan Pasqua	.077	13	1	0	0	0	2	0	2	.077	.077	Jay Buhner	.455	11	5	1	0	1	4	5	1	.588	.818
Brady Anderson	.083	12	1	0	0	0	0	0	1	.083	.083	Jack Clark	.385	13	5	3	0	2	2	2	1	.467	1.077

Eric Young — Dodgers

	Avg	G	AB	R	H	2B	3B	HR	RBI	BB	SO	HBP	GDP	SB	CS	OBP	SLG	IBB	SH	SF	#Pit	#P/PA	GB	FB	G/F
1992 Season	.258	49	132	9	34	1	0	1	11	8	9	0	3	6	1	.300	.288	0	4	0	502	3.59	54	33	1.64

1992 Season

	Avg	AB	H	2B	3B	HR	RBI	BB	SO	OBP	SLG		Avg	AB	H	2B	3B	HR	RBI	BB	SO	OBP	SLG
vs. Left	.273	66	18	0	0	1	6	3	4	.304	.318	Scoring Posn	.341	41	14	0	0	0	9	3	3	.386	.341
vs. Right	.242	66	16	1	0	0	5	5	5	.296	.258	Close & Late	.409	22	9	0	0	0	2	2	1	.458	.409
Home	.250	56	14	0	0	0	6	3	4	.288	.250	None on/out	.143	28	4	0	0	0	0	2	1	.200	.143
Away	.263	76	20	1	0	1	5	5	5	.309	.316	Batting #1	.269	26	7	0	0	0	2	0	1	.269	.269
First Pitch	.316	19	6	0	0	1	3	0	0	.316	.474	Batting #3	.181	72	13	0	0	0	4	7	6	.253	.181
Ahead on Count	.286	35	10	1	0	0	3	0	0	.342	.314	Other	.412	34	14	1	0	1	5	1	2	.429	.529
Behind on Count	.238	42	10	1	0	0	4	0	5	.238	.262	Pre-All Star	.000	0	0	0	0	0	0	0	0	.000	.000
Two Strikes	.255	47	12	0	0	0	4	5	9	.327	.255	Post-All Star	.258	132	34	1	0	1	11	8	9	.300	.288

Gerald Young — Astros

	Avg	G	AB	R	H	2B	3B	HR	RBI	BB	SO	HBP	GDP	SB	CS	OBP	SLG	IBB	SH	SF	#Pit	#P/PA	GB	FB	G/F
1992 Season	.184	74	76	14	14	1	1	0	4	10	11	0	2	6	2	.279	.224	0	4	0	367	4.27	33	21	1.57
Last Five Years	.232	534	1481	205	344	46	15	2	94	194	177	5	25	127	62	.321	.288	5	20	13	6262	3.70	631	423	1.49

1992 Season

	Avg	AB	H	2B	3B	HR	RBI	BB	SO	OBP	SLG		Avg	AB	H	2B	3B	HR	RBI	BB	SO	OBP	SLG
vs. Left	.171	35	6	0	0	0	4	6	5	.293	.171	Scoring Posn	.250	16	4	0	0	0	4	5	3	.429	.250
vs. Right	.195	41	8	1	1	0	0	4	6	.267	.268	Close & Late	.192	26	5	1	1	0	1	4	4	.300	.308

Last Five Years

	Avg	AB	H	2B	3B	HR	RBI	BB	SO	OBP	SLG		Avg	AB	H	2B	3B	HR	RBI	BB	SO	OBP	SLG
vs. Left	.243	511	124	17	4	2	34	62	64	.326	.303	Scoring Posn	.280	293	82	17	4	0	92	58	35	.391	.365
vs. Right	.227	970	220	29	11	0	60	132	113	.318	.279	Close & Late	.240	300	72	11	4	0	27	34	43	.314	.303
Groundball	.214	537	115	12	6	1	33	66	60	.300	.264	None on/out	.225	556	125	15	8	2	67	68	68	.308	.291
Flyball	.240	358	86	15	2	0	22	55	42	.340	.293	Batting #1	.233	1011	236	37	12	2	61	121	113	.316	.300
Home	.234	757	177	22	8	1	48	90	82	.315	.288	Batting #2	.241	224	54	4	1	0	17	28	32	.319	.268
Away	.231	724	167	24	7	1	46	104	95	.327	.287	Other	.220	246	54	5	2	0	16	45	32	.339	.256
Day	.236	402	95	11	6	0	32	61	51	.338	.294	April	.220	241	53	9	1	1	8	21	29	.284	.278
Night	.231	1079	249	35	9	2	62	133	126	.314	.285	May	.236	263	62	7	3	0	19	43	29	.341	.285
Grass	.239	414	99	14	3	0	31	63	61	.338	.287	June	.232	228	53	10	1	1	18	32	27	.325	.298
Turf	.230	1067	245	32	12	2	63	131	116	.314	.288	July	.221	217	48	7	5	0	19	37	34	.333	.300
First Pitch	.243	243	59	11	3	0	17	3	0	.249	.313	August	.262	248	65	5	3	0	14	26	24	.332	.306
Ahead on Count	.243	400	97	9	2	2	28	113	0	.407	.290	September/October	.222	284	63	8	2	0	16	35	34	.308	.264
Behind on Count	.205	404	83	11	3	1	23	0	97	.206	.255	Pre-All Star	.232	806	187	28	7	2	53	110	97	.323	.292
Two Strikes	.191	585	112	13	6	0	22	78	177	.287	.234	Post-All Star	.233	675	157	18	8	0	41	84	80	.318	.283

Batter vs. Pitcher (career)

Hits Best Against	Avg	AB	H	2B	3B	HR	RBI	BB	SO	OBP	SLG	Hits Worst Against	Avg	AB	H	2B	3B	HR	RBI	BB	SO	OBP	SLG
Ramon Martinez	.462	13	6	0	0	0	1	1	1	.500	.462	Roger McDowell	.000	12	0	0	0	0	0	2	2	.143	.000
Joe Boever	.444	9	4	0	1	0	3	3	0	.583	.667	Mike Morgan	.000	11	0	0	0	0	1	0	1	.000	.000
Pete Smith	.409	22	9	1	0	0	1	3	0	.480	.455	John Smiley	.056	18	1	0	0	0	0	0	4	.227	.056
Mike Bielecki	.375	16	6	1	0	0	1	1	2	.412	.438	Greg W. Harris	.071	14	1	0	0	0	0	0	1	.071	.071
Rick Sutcliffe	.348	23	8	1	0	0	2	3	1	.407	.391	Ron Darling	.083	12	1	0	0	0	0	1	3	.154	.083

Kevin Young — Pirates

	Avg	G	AB	R	H	2B	3B	HR	RBI	BB	SO	HBP	GDP	SB	CS	OBP	SLG	IBB	SH	SF	#Pit	#P/PA	GB	FB	G/F
1992 Season	.571	10	7	2	4	0	0	0	4	2	0	0	0	1	0	.667	.571	0	0	0	43	4.78	3	2	1.50

1992 Season

	Avg	AB	H	2B	3B	HR	RBI	BB	SO	OBP	SLG		Avg	AB	H	2B	3B	HR	RBI	BB	SO	OBP	SLG
vs. Left	.000	1	0	0	0	0	0	1	0	.500	.000	Scoring Posn	1.000	3	3	0	0	0	4	1	0	1.000	1.000
vs. Right	.667	6	4	0	0	0	4	1	0	.714	.667	Close & Late	.000	1	0	0	0	0	0	0	0	.000	.000

Matt Young — Red Sox

	ERA	W	L	Sv	G	GS	IP	BB	SO	Avg	H	2B	3B	HR	RBI	OBP	SLG	GF	IR	IRS	Hld	SvOp	SB	CS	GB	FB	G/F
1992 Season	4.58	0	4	0	28	8	70.2	42	57	.257	69	14	4	27	43	.360	.379	4	24	8	1	0	10	3	120	45	2.67
Last Five Years	4.33	12	33	0	107	61	422.0	233	329	.251	401	55	6	28	190	.348	.345	5	110	35	5	1	46	20	707	294	2.40

1992 Season

	ERA	W	L	Sv	G	GS	IP	H	HR	BB	SO		Avg	AB	H	2B	3B	HR	RBI	BB	SO	OBP	SLG
Home	5.23	0	2	0	9	4	31.0	37	4	14	27	vs. Left	.269	52	14	3	0	1	10	11	15	.409	.385
Away	4.08	0	2	0	19	4	39.2	32	3	28	30	vs. Right	.253	217	55	9	0	6	33	31	42	.347	.378
Starter	6.42	0	4	0	8	8	33.2	38	5	22	21	Scoring Posn	.302	86	26	6	0	2	36	15	17	.406	.442
Reliever	2.92	0	0	0	20	0	37.0	31	2	20	36	Close & Late	.118	17	2	0	0	1	2	5	2	.211	.118
0 Days rest	0.00	0	0	0	0	0	0.0	0	0	0	0	None on/out	.281	64	18	1	0	3	3	11	12	.387	.438
1 or 2 Days rest	3.72	0	0	0	6	0	9.2	6	1	5	6	First Pitch	.476	42	20	2	0	1	10	2	0	.511	.595
3+ Days rest	2.63	0	0	0	14	0	27.1	25	1	15	30	Behind on Count	.303	66	20	3	0	3	10	28	0	.511	.485

1992 Season

	ERA	W	L	Sv	G	GS	IP	H	HR	BB	SO		Avg	AB	H	2B	3B	HR	RBI	BB	SO	OBP	SLG
Pre-All Star	5.20	0	2	0	14	5	36.1	39	3	24	24	Ahead on Count	.145	110	16	5	0	2	15	0	48	.150	.245
Post-All Star	3.93	0	2	0	14	3	34.1	30	4	18	33	Two Strikes	.161	124	20	4	0	3	22	12	57	.241	.266

Last Five Years

	ERA	W	L	Sv	G	GS	IP	H	HR	BB	SO		Avg	AB	H	2B	3B	HR	RBI	BB	SO	OBP	SLG
Home	3.87	7	18	0	50	33	228.0	211	17	123	178	vs. Left	.216	250	54	8	0	2	31	34	62	.317	.272
Away	4.87	5	15	0	57	28	194.0	190	11	110	151	vs. Right	.257	1348	347	47	6	26	159	199	267	.353	.359
Day	4.03	7	11	0	39	20	145.0	137	9	76	119	Inning 1-6	.252	1325	334	43	4	22	164	189	264	.347	.340
Night	4.48	5	22	0	68	41	277.0	264	19	157	210	Inning 7+	.245	273	67	12	2	6	26	44	65	.351	.370
Grass	5.56	6	23	0	71	35	228.1	247	16	141	189	None on	.248	864	214	27	3	16	16	123	186	.343	.341
Turf	2.88	6	10	0	36	26	193.2	154	12	92	140	Runners on	.255	734	187	28	3	12	174	110	143	.353	.350
April	3.84	6	8	0	11	11	63.1	47	3	43	37	Scoring Posn	.260	438	114	17	1	9	163	72	94	.364	.365
May	5.20	4	4	0	16	14	72.2	81	5	40	60	Close & Late	.313	128	40	10	0	4	13	19	26	.405	.484
June	3.86	1	4	0	16	8	60.2	57	4	31	48	None on/out	.242	389	94	14	0	7	7	65	79	.352	.332
July	3.75	4	6	0	17	8	62.1	46	5	40	43	vs. 1st Batr (relief)	.297	37	11	2	0	1	11	7	9	.391	.432
August	3.53	1	5	0	21	10	89.1	84	6	30	70	First Inning Pitched	.257	373	96	12	2	6	63	50	94	.345	.349
September/October	5.74	2	8	0	26	10	73.2	86	5	49	71	First 15 Pitches	.257	303	78	9	1	6	36	40	72	.345	.353
Starter	4.30	11	30	0	61	61	360.1	343	24	193	270	Pitch 16-30	.251	287	72	10	3	6	36	39	66	.343	.369
Reliever	4.52	1	3	0	46	0	61.2	58	4	40	59	Pitch 31-45	.230	256	59	7	1	3	32	29	48	.310	.301
0 Days rest	0.00	0	0	0	2	0	0.2	2	0	0	2	Pitch 46+	.255	752	192	29	1	13	86	125	143	.363	.348
1 or 2 Days rest	4.87	1	0	0	17	0	20.1	21	2	16	14	First Pitch	.338	225	76	11	1	3	27	7	0	.369	.436
3+ Days rest	4.43	0	3	0	27	0	40.2	35	2	24	43	Ahead on Count	.180	671	121	22	1	8	66	0	283	.184	.252
Pre-All Star	4.57	6	17	0	47	36	214.2	203	13	126	160	Behind on Count	.311	402	125	13	2	11	55	136	0	.483	.435
Post-All Star	4.08	6	16	0	60	25	207.1	198	15	107	169	Two Strikes	.179	703	126	17	0	8	69	88	329	.273	.238

Pitcher vs. Batter (since 1984)

Pitches Best Vs.	Avg	AB	H	2B	3B	HR	RBI	BB	SO	OBP	SLG	Pitches Worst Vs.	Avg	AB	H	2B	3B	HR	RBI	BB	SO	OBP	SLG
Ozzie Guillen	.000	17	0	0	0	0	0	0	5	.000	.000	Don Slaught	.600	15	9	3	0	0	2	1	1	.625	.800
Curt Wilkerson	.083	12	1	0	0	0	2	0	2	.063	.083	Jose Canseco	.500	8	4	2	0	0	5	3	3	.692	.750
Wade Boggs	.091	22	2	0	0	0	3	1	5	.130	.091	Frank Thomas	.444	9	4	0	0	2	4	6	2	.667	1.111
Brian McRae	.091	11	1	0	0	0	0	0	3	.091	.091	Dave Winfield	.423	26	11	2	0	4	14	6	2	.531	.962
Glenallen Hill	.100	10	1	0	0	0	0	1	2	.182	.100	Cecil Fielder	.308	13	4	0	0	3	10	4	4	.471	1.000

Pete Young — Expos

Pitches Right (groundball pitcher)

	ERA	W	L	Sv	G	GS	IP	BB	SO	Avg	H	2B	3B	HR	RBI	OBP	SLG	GF	IR	IRS	Hld	SvOpp	SB	CS	GB	FB	G/F
1992 Season	3.98	0	0	0	13	0	20.1	9	11	.247	18	5	2	0	14	.329	.370	6	13	5	0	0	2	1	29	19	1.53

1992 Season

	ERA	W	L	Sv	G	GS	IP	H	HR	BB	SO		Avg	AB	H	2B	3B	HR	RBI	BB	SO	OBP	SLG
Home	4.82	0	0	0	7	0	9.1	8	0	4	3	vs. Left	.343	35	12	3	2	0	11	8	5	.444	.543
Away	3.27	0	0	0	6	0	11.0	10	0	5	8	vs. Right	.158	38	6	2	0	0	3	1	6	.200	.211

Robin Yount — Brewers

Bats Right

	Avg	G	AB	R	H	2B	3B	HR	RBI	BB	SO	HBP	GDP	SB	CS	OBP	SLG	IBB	SH	SF	#Pit	#P/PA	GB	FB	G/F
1992 Season	.264	150	557	71	147	40	3	8	77	53	81	3	9	15	6	.325	.390	9	4	12	2220	3.55	185	183	1.01
Last Five Years	.280	760	2682	428	808	153	32	69	425	311	383	22	59	77	25	.351	.427	42	14	40	11630	3.57	1021	950	1.07

1992 Season

	Avg	AB	H	2B	3B	HR	RBI	BB	SO	OBP	SLG		Avg	AB	H	2B	3B	HR	RBI	BB	SO	OBP	SLG
vs. Left	.280	125	35	10	1	2	18	16	24	.359	.424	Scoring Posn	.287	157	45	12	2	1	62	23	25	.358	.408
vs. Right	.259	432	112	30	2	6	59	37	57	.315	.380	Close & Late	.257	74	19	4	0	1	8	15	7	.366	.351
Groundball	.263	133	35	9	0	1	19	12	20	.313	.353	None on/out	.282	124	35	6	0	2	10	10	16	.341	.379
Flyball	.292	161	47	10	3	2	25	17	22	.352	.429	Batting #4	.324	102	33	8	1	3	22	11	8	.379	.510
Home	.268	269	72	17	2	3	35	25	35	.327	.379	Batting #5	.247	340	84	25	2	4	39	35	53	.315	.368
Away	.260	288	75	23	1	5	42	28	46	.323	.399	Other	.261	115	30	7	0	1	16	7	20	.304	.348
Day	.319	160	51	13	2	3	27	13	18	.359	.481	April	.234	64	15	3	0	0	5	6	14	.306	.281
Night	.242	397	96	27	1	5	50	40	63	.311	.353	May	.252	103	26	9	0	3	16	10	15	.322	.427
Grass	.262	465	122	30	2	7	68	42	67	.323	.381	June	.344	90	31	8	0	2	12	11	10	.408	.500
Turf	.272	92	25	10	1	1	9	11	14	.350	.435	July	.192	99	19	7	0	0	7	5	15	.231	.263
First Pitch	.301	83	25	7	0	0	18	9	0	.365	.386	August	.241	87	21	5	2	0	14	10	16	.313	.345
Ahead on Count	.336	125	42	13	0	4	23	23	0	.429	.536	September/October	.307	114	35	8	1	3	23	11	11	.359	.474
Behind on Count	.234	192	45	15	3	2	21	0	34	.230	.375	Pre-All Star	.276	304	84	25	0	5	37	28	43	.337	.408
Two Strikes	.194	227	44	12	2	2	18	22	81	.266	.291	Post-All Star	.249	253	63	15	3	3	40	25	38	.310	.368

1992 By Position

Position	Avg	AB	H	2B	3B	HR	RBI	BB	SO	OBP	SLG	G	GS	Innings	PO	A	E	DP	Fld Pct	Rng Fctr	In Zone	Outs	Zone Rtg	MLB Zone
As Designated Hitter	.342	38	13	4	0	0	4	9	6	.458	.447	11	11	---	---	---	---	---	---	---	---	---	---	---
As cf	.259	518	134	36	3	8	73	44	74	.314	.386	139	138	1196.0	371	6	2	0	.995	2.84	441	362	821	824

Last Five Years

	Avg	AB	H	2B	3B	HR	RBI	BB	SO	OBP	SLG		Avg	AB	H	2B	3B	HR	RBI	BB	SO	OBP	SLG
vs. Left	.288	760	219	42	7	22	107	109	100	.375	.449	Scoring Posn	.306	798	244	43	13	20	347	116	115	.381	.467

Last Five Years

	Avg	AB	H	2B	3B	HR	RBI	BB	SO	OBP	SLG		Avg	AB	H	2B	3B	HR	RBI	BB	SO	OBP	SLG
vs. Right	.278	2122	589	111	25	47	318	202	283	.341	.420	Close & Late	.261	399	112	19	5	7	66	48	63	.358	.406
Groundball	.262	738	208	36	5	11	109	74	94	.346	.389	None on/out	.273	623	170	32	5	17	17	39	76	.322	.422
Flyball	.288	666	192	34	9	17	100	70	104	.353	.443	Batting #3	.277	1133	314	51	16	19	169	127	147	.349	.401
Home	.269	1412	380	69	17	40	217	156	182	.342	.427	Batting #4	.302	758	229	43	8	21	126	86	103	.373	.463
Away	.291	1470	428	84	15	29	208	155	201	.359	.428	Other	.267	991	265	59	8	29	130	98	133	.335	.431
Day	.285	902	257	47	7	28	140	97	117	.352	.446	April	.273	373	102	16	5	12	49	38	49	.347	.440
Night	.278	1960	551	106	25	41	285	214	266	.350	.419	May	.273	527	144	27	3	15	75	56	62	.346	.421
Grass	.279	2430	677	122	28	63	367	268	326	.350	.430	June	.284	507	144	27	7	10	74	61	68	.357	.424
Turf	.290	452	131	31	4	6	58	43	57	.351	.416	July	.288	430	124	29	8	9	55	46	58	.359	.456
First Pitch	.320	422	135	29	3	10	85	19	0	.345	.474	August	.273	527	144	24	7	8	79	54	76	.338	.391
Ahead on Count	.359	711	255	49	12	29	154	158	0	.470	.584	September/October	.290	518	150	30	2	15	93	56	70	.356	.442
Behind on Count	.250	996	249	45	9	16	108	8	179	.259	.361	Pre-All Star	.277	1568	435	81	18	39	216	171	193	.350	.427
Two Strikes	.217	1154	250	41	10	19	116	123	383	.297	.319	Post-All Star	.284	1314	373	72	14	30	209	140	190	.351	.428

Batter vs. Pitcher (since 1984)

Hits Best Against	Avg	AB	H	2B	3B	HR	RBI	BB	SO	OBP	SLG	Hits Worst Against	Avg	AB	H	2B	3B	HR	RBI	BB	SO	OBP	SLG
Scott Bankhead	.545	11	6	2	0	0	0	1	1	.583	.727	Clay Parker	.091	11	1	0	0	0	1	2	1	.231	.091
Mike Flanagan	.543	35	19	4	1	2	8	3	0	.579	.886	Mike Gardiner	.091	11	1	0	0	0	1	2	3	.231	.091
Shawn Hillegas	.429	14	6	1	0	2	4	0	1	.429	.929	Bobby Ojeda	.100	10	1	0	0	0	0	1	2	.182	.100
Bud Black	.387	31	12	4	1	2	8	7	3	.500	.774	Kevin Appier	.143	14	2	0	0	0	1	0	0	.133	.143
Scott Sanderson	.333	9	3	0	1	1	4	5	0	.571	.889	Jeff Montgomery	.154	13	2	0	0	0	2	0	5	.154	.154

Todd Zeile — Cardinals

Bats Right

	Avg	G	AB	R	H	2B	3B	HR	RBI	BB	SO	HBP	GDP	SB	CS	OBP	SLG	IBB	SH	SF	#Pit	#P/PA	GB	FB	G/F
1992 Season	.257	126	439	51	113	18	4	7	48	68	70	0	11	7	10	.352	.364	4	0	7	2044	3.98	155	137	1.13
Career (1989-1992)	.261	453	1581	196	413	82	11	34	194	206	255	7	38	26	25	.345	.392	11	1	20	7231	3.99	600	470	1.28

1992 Season

	Avg	AB	H	2B	3B	HR	RBI	BB	SO	OBP	SLG		Avg	AB	H	2B	3B	HR	RBI	BB	SO	OBP	SLG
vs. Left	.278	133	37	5	1	1	15	26	16	.394	.353	Scoring Posn	.214	131	28	6	0	1	39	28	26	.337	.282
vs. Right	.248	306	76	13	3	6	33	42	54	.333	.369	Close & Late	.212	99	21	1	2	0	5	12	20	.295	.263
Groundball	.247	178	44	6	1	2	24	35	29	.366	.326	None on/out	.286	98	28	1	1	3	3	14	14	.375	.408
Flyball	.202	89	18	2	1	2	8	11	14	.287	.315	Batting #3	.272	81	22	5	1	3	13	13	15	.357	.469
Home	.230	226	52	7	2	4	27	38	34	.337	.332	Batting #5	.256	164	42	7	0	3	18	27	21	.359	.354
Away	.286	213	61	11	2	3	21	30	36	.368	.399	Other	.253	194	49	6	3	1	17	28	34	.344	.330
Day	.225	120	27	2	1	3	10	20	21	.333	.333	April	.257	74	19	3	1	3	11	13	11	.356	.446
Night	.270	319	86	16	3	4	38	48	49	.360	.376	May	.182	88	16	4	0	0	7	15	19	.295	.227
Grass	.298	124	37	6	2	3	12	17	19	.375	.452	June	.291	86	25	5	2	1	8	10	9	.361	.430
Turf	.241	315	76	12	2	4	36	51	51	.343	.330	July	.297	91	27	3	0	1	10	15	14	.396	.363
First Pitch	.302	53	16	3	1	2	7	4	0	.351	.509	August	.133	15	2	0	0	0	0	0	4	.133	.133
Ahead on Count	.304	92	28	3	0	0	10	36	0	.492	.337	September/October	.282	85	24	3	1	2	12	15	13	.386	.412
Behind on Count	.291	148	43	6	2	2	14	0	31	.289	.399	Pre-All Star	.264	288	76	15	3	5	30	43	44	.353	.389
Two Strikes	.192	213	41	9	2	2	13	29	70	.286	.282	Post-All Star	.245	151	37	3	1	2	18	25	26	.350	.318

1992 By Position

Position	Avg	AB	H	2B	3B	HR	RBI	BB	SO	OBP	SLG	G	GS	Innings	PO	A	E	DP	Fld Pct	Rng Fctr	In Zone	Outs	Zone Rtg	MLB Zone
As 3b	.259	436	113	18	4	7	48	67	70	.353	.367	124	120	1079.0	81	235	13	19	.960	2.64	302	259	.858	.841

Career (1989-1992)

	Avg	AB	H	2B	3B	HR	RBI	BB	SO	OBP	SLG		Avg	AB	H	2B	3B	HR	RBI	BB	SO	OBP	SLG
vs. Left	.285	562	166	33	3	12	75	78	87	.370	.414	Scoring Posn	.234	440	103	26	1	4	145	88	83	.352	.325
vs. Right	.247	999	247	49	8	22	119	128	168	.330	.378	Close & Late	.234	308	72	10	3	2	19	41	59	.325	.305
Groundball	.245	535	131	29	5	9	67	74	81	.337	.368	None on/out	.287	401	115	18	1	15	15	46	62	.362	.449
Flyball	.240	345	83	15	2	9	48	39	57	.312	.373	Batting #5	.239	394	94	18	1	7	47	51	53	.327	.343
Home	.264	777	205	40	4	19	109	108	112	.354	.404	Batting #6	.279	391	109	22	3	9	44	43	72	.352	.419
Away	.259	804	208	42	5	15	85	98	143	.337	.379	Other	.264	796	210	42	7	18	103	112	130	.351	.402
Day	.278	410	114	24	2	12	54	58	70	.362	.434	April	.276	203	56	10	3	6	31	27	33	.357	.443
Night	.255	1171	299	58	9	22	140	148	185	.339	.377	May	.234	256	60	15	1	3	27	36	53	.327	.336
Grass	.255	416	106	26	2	6	36	46	81	.327	.370	June	.254	280	71	14	3	6	28	33	36	.332	.389
Turf	.264	1165	307	56	9	28	158	160	174	.351	.399	July	.262	263	69	10	1	8	31	32	39	.341	.399
First Pitch	.329	149	49	8	1	6	21	7	0	.354	.517	August	.293	249	73	7	2	5	30	18	36	.368	.398
Ahead on Count	.316	399	126	24	3	9	55	116	0	.464	.459	September/October	.255	330	84	26	1	6	47	60	58	.368	.394
Behind on Count	.243	502	122	17	5	7	62	0	122	.244	.339	Pre-All Star	.260	832	216	44	7	17	96	105	135	.341	.391
Two Strikes	.190	738	140	26	5	11	66	83	255	.275	.283	Post-All Star	.263	749	197	38	4	17	98	101	120	.350	.393

Batter vs. Pitcher (career)

Hits Best Against	Avg	AB	H	2B	3B	HR	RBI	BB	SO	OBP	SLG	Hits Worst Against	Avg	AB	H	2B	3B	HR	RBI	BB	SO	OBP	SLG
Roger McDowell	.462	13	6	4	0	0	4	0	4	.462	.769	Jose Rijo	.000	11	0	0	0	0	0	3	2	.214	.000
Bruce Ruffin	.444	18	8	1	0	1	4	2	2	.500	.667	Don Robinson	.050	20	1	0	0	0	0	0	2	.050	.050
Pete Harnisch	.429	14	6	1	0	1	5	1	0	.467	.714	Tom Browning	.063	16	1	0	0	1	1	0	1	.059	.063
John Franco	.417	12	5	0	0	1	1	1	3	.462	.667	Randy Myers	.100	10	1	0	0	0	1	1	4	.182	.100
Tim Burke	.364	11	4	0	1	1	2	1	3	.462	.818	Bobby Ojeda	.111	18	2	0	0	0	2	1	4	.158	.111

Eddie Zosky — Blue Jays
Bats Right

	Avg	G	AB	R	H	2B	3B	HR	RBI	BB	SO	HBP	GDP	SB	CS	OBP	SLG	IBB	SH	SF	#Pit	#P/PA	GB	FB	G/F
1992 Season	.286	8	7	1	2	0	1	0	1	0	2	0	0	0	0	.250	.571	0	0	1	21	2.63	1	2	0.50
Career (1991-1992)	.176	26	34	3	6	1	2	0	3	0	10	0	1	0	1	.171	.324	0	1	1	119	3.40	9	9	1.00

1992 Season

	Avg	AB	H	2B	3B	HR	RBI	BB	SO	OBP	SLG		Avg	AB	H	2B	3B	HR	RBI	BB	SO	OBP	SLG
vs. Left	.500	2	1	0	0	0	1	0	1	.333	.500	Scoring Posn	.000	2	0	0	0	0	1	0	1	.000	.000
vs. Right	.200	5	1	0	1	0	0	0	1	.200	.600	Close & Late	.000	1	0	0	0	0	0	0	1	.000	.000

Bob Zupcic — Red Sox
Bats Right (flyball hitter)

	Avg	G	AB	R	H	2B	3B	HR	RBI	BB	SO	HBP	GDP	SB	CS	OBP	SLG	IBB	SH	SF	#Pit	#P/PA	GB	FB	G/F
1992 Season	.276	124	392	46	108	19	1	3	43	25	60	4	6	2	2	.322	.352	1	7	4	1506	3.54	115	142	0.81
Career (1991-1992)	.269	142	417	49	112	19	1	4	46	26	66	4	6	2	2	.315	.348	1	8	4	1600	3.55	123	150	0.82

1992 Season

	Avg	AB	H	2B	3B	HR	RBI	BB	SO	OBP	SLG		Avg	AB	H	2B	3B	HR	RBI	BB	SO	OBP	SLG
vs. Left	.293	133	39	8	1	0	15	13	14	.356	.368	Scoring Posn	.295	95	28	3	1	2	40	6	18	.324	.411
vs. Right	.266	259	69	11	0	3	28	12	46	.304	.344	Close & Late	.324	68	22	4	0	2	16	7	8	.395	.471
Groundball	.295	105	31	7	0	1	12	7	13	.351	.390	None on/out	.218	78	17	3	0	1	1	5	12	.274	.295
Flyball	.241	108	26	5	0	2	11	7	22	.282	.343	Batting #3	.211	95	20	3	0	0	9	5	15	.262	.242
Home	.265	189	50	11	1	3	25	10	32	.310	.381	Batting #6	.358	81	29	6	1	0	12	4	14	.379	.457
Away	.286	203	58	8	0	0	18	15	28	.333	.325	Other	.273	216	59	10	0	3	22	16	31	.328	.361
Day	.286	133	38	8	1	1	14	8	28	.338	.383	April	.400	5	2	1	0	0	1	0	1	.400	.600
Night	.270	259	70	11	0	2	29	17	32	.314	.336	May	.326	46	15	5	0	0	3	4	6	.392	.435
Grass	.280	332	93	17	1	3	40	22	53	.328	.364	June	.300	50	15	3	0	1	7	1	9	.302	.420
Turf	.250	60	15	2	0	0	3	3	7	.292	.283	July	.300	80	24	4	0	2	10	7	10	.352	.425
First Pitch	.300	50	15	2	0	1	4	1	0	.308	.400	August	.220	109	24	3	0	0	11	7	18	.286	.248
Ahead on Count	.316	95	30	3	1	1	13	9	1	.381	.400	September/October	.275	102	28	3	1	0	11	6	16	.312	.324
Behind on Count	.235	149	35	4	1	0	9	0	38	.237	.275	Pre-All Star	.328	137	45	11	0	3	19	11	20	.377	.474
Two Strikes	.193	161	31	8	0	1	16	15	59	.264	.261	Post-All Star	.247	255	63	8	1	0	24	14	40	.292	.286

1992 By Position

Position	Avg	AB	H	2B	3B	HR	RBI	BB	SO	OBP	SLG	G	GS	Innings	PO	A	E	DP	Fld Pct	Rng Fctr	In Zone	Outs	Zone Rtg	MLB Zone
As Pinch Hitter	.200	10	2	0	0	0	1	1	1	.273	.200	11	0	---	---	---	---	---	---	---	---	---	---	---
As lf	.300	90	27	6	0	2	11	3	15	.333	.433	32	23	216.1	39	4	1	1	.977	1.79	56	38	.679	.809
As cf	.280	246	69	11	1	1	27	15	39	.323	.346	68	65	575.1	172	6	5	1	.973	2.78	209	176	.842	.824
As rf	.200	45	9	2	0	0	3	6	5	.294	.244	22	12	121.1	29	1	0	1	1.000	2.23	33	29	.879	.814

Leader Boards

Well, now that you have looked at every number of every stat split of every player, you might want to know how everybody ranks. The following pages list out the leaders in 36 batting and 24 pitching categories, sorted by batting average and/or ERA.

There are a couple of things you may wish to keep in mind. First of all, the listing of #9 hitters is of American Leaguers only. Don't go looking for Tom Glavine or Dwight Gooden here.

Second, "Clutch" is defined as a) the game is in the seventh inning or later and b) the batting team is either leading by one run, tied or has the potential tying run on base, at bat or on deck.

The minimum cutoffs that were used varied for each category, depending on the frequency that the particular event occurred. Thus, the cutoff was higher for "Vs. RHP" than for "Vs. LHP", since there are more right-handed pitchers then left-handers. However, all the minimums were high enough to exclude people like Gerald Alexander and his 0.00 home ERA (1.0 innings) from these lists.

1992 Batting Leaders

Overall

Player, Team	AB	H	AVG
E MARTINEZ, Sea	528	181	.343
G Sheffield, SD	557	184	.330
K Puckett, Min	639	210	.329
A Van Slyke, Pit	614	199	.324
J Kruk, Phi	507	164	.323
B Roberts, Cin	532	172	.323
F Thomas, ChA	573	185	.323
P Molitor, Mil	609	195	.320
T Gwynn, SD	520	165	.317
S Mack, Min	600	189	.315

LHP

Player, Team	AB	H	AVG
P MOLITOR, Mil	132	56	.424
E Martinez, Sea	141	53	.376
C Baerga, Cle	168	63	.375
F Jose, StL	182	68	.374
G Sheffield, SD	189	69	.365
K Griffey Jr, Sea	173	62	.358
T Pendleton, Atl	207	74	.357
F Thomas, ChA	140	50	.357
B Larkin, Cin	200	71	.355
B Gilkey, StL	176	62	.352

RHP

Player, Team	AB	H	AVG
A VAN SLYKE, Pit	345	119	.345
B Roberts, Cin	347	118	.340
E Martinez, Sea	387	128	.331
J Kruk, Phi	297	98	.330
K Puckett, Min	514	169	.329
M Grace, ChN	378	122	.323
S Mack, Min	472	151	.320
B Butler, LA	330	105	.318
B Harper, Min	393	124	.316
R Lankford, StL	382	120	.314

Home

Player, Team	AB	H	AVG
G SHEFFIELD, SD	288	105	.365
R Alomar, Tor	268	95	.354
B Roberts, Cin	252	89	.353
C Baerga, Cle	329	116	.353
K Puckett, Min	325	113	.348
B Bonds, Pit	210	71	.338
W Clark, SF	270	91	.337
M Alou, Mon	143	48	.336
O Smith, StL	278	93	.335
K Caminiti, Hou	246	81	.329

Away

Player, Team	AB	H	AVG
E MARTINEZ, Sea	260	97	.373
F Thomas, ChA	281	96	.342
J Kruk, Phi	259	88	.340
D Sanders, Atl	165	56	.339
S Livingstone, Det	179	60	.335
P Molitor, Mil	323	108	.334
M Grace, ChN	318	105	.330
A Van Slyke, Pit	299	98	.328
T Gwynn, SD	291	95	.326
T Steinbach, Oak	224	73	.326

Groundball Pitchers

Player, Team	AB	H	AVG
F THOMAS, ChA	153	65	.425
W McGee, SF	192	71	.370
T Gwynn, SD	203	73	.360
K Griffey Jr, Sea	154	55	.357
T Pendleton, Atl	264	93	.352
J Kruk, Phi	211	73	.346
P Molitor, Mil	145	50	.345
M Grace, ChN	232	80	.345
B Roberts, Cin	208	71	.341
D Winfield, Tor	172	58	.337

Grass

Player, Team	AB	H	AVG
E MARTINEZ, Sea	206	83	.403
G Sheffield, SD	402	139	.346
A Van Slyke, Pit	153	51	.333
S Mack, Min	237	79	.333
J Bagwell, Hou	172	56	.326
F Thomas, ChA	483	157	.325
T Pendleton, Atl	471	153	.325
C Baerga, Cle	557	180	.323
D DeShields, Mon	146	47	.322
J Kruk, Phi	134	43	.321

Turf

Player, Team	AB	H	AVG
T GWYNN, SD	148	57	.385
M Grace, ChN	185	65	.351
K Puckett, Min	401	137	.342
R Alomar, Tor	333	113	.339
B Roberts, Cin	359	118	.329
B Larkin, Cin	379	124	.327
B Bonds, Pit	326	106	.325
J Kruk, Phi	373	121	.324
A Van Slyke, Pit	461	148	.321
O Smith, StL	394	124	.315

Flyball Pitchers

Player, Team	AB	H	AVG
D HAMILTON, Mil	130	45	.346
R Palmeiro, Tex	165	57	.345
E Martinez, Sea	150	51	.340
B Butler, LA	159	54	.340
A Van Slyke, Pit	157	52	.331
T Raines, ChA	145	48	.331
R Sandberg, ChN	150	49	.327
G Jefferies, KC	215	70	.326
F Thomas, ChA	156	49	.314
D Mattingly, NYA	180	56	.311

Day

Player, Team	AB	H	AVG
E MARTINEZ, Sea	139	54	.388
R Ventura, ChA	150	56	.373
W McGee, SF	182	65	.357
K Griffey Jr, Sea	152	54	.355
J Kruk, Phi	130	46	.354
M Duncan, Phi	151	52	.344
B Roberts, Cin	163	56	.344
D Bichette, Mil	149	50	.336
A Van Slyke, Pit	176	59	.335
B Harper, Min	141	47	.333

Night

Player, Team	AB	H	AVG
D SLAUGHT, Pit	194	67	.345
K Puckett, Min	439	149	.339
T Gwynn, SD	359	120	.334
G Sheffield, SD	394	131	.332
F Thomas, ChA	422	140	.332
D Hamilton, Mil	325	107	.329
L Walker, Mon	359	118	.329
B Larkin, Cin	364	119	.327
E Martinez, Sea	389	127	.326
P Molitor, Mil	409	133	.325

Scoring Position

Player, Team	AB	H	AVG
T PENDLETON, Atl	161	63	.391
L Whitaker, Det	111	41	.369
T Raines, ChA	108	39	.361
L Sojo, Cal	90	32	.356
R Alomar, Tor	147	52	.354
K Puckett, Min	188	65	.346
K Miller, KC	88	30	.341
B Larkin, Cin	144	49	.340
T Steinbach, Oak	97	33	.340
G Sheffield, SD	127	43	.339

1992 Batting Leaders

April

Player, Team	AB	H	AVG
J KRUK, Phi	81	33	.407
R Alomar, Tor	89	34	.382
D Winfield, Tor	88	33	.375
C Lansford, Oak	77	28	.364
G Bell, ChA	73	26	.356
M Bordick, Oak	76	27	.355
R Thompson, SF	68	24	.353
R Kelly, NYA	85	30	.353
T Gwynn, SD	98	34	.347
W Clark, SF	81	28	.346

May

Player, Team	AB	H	AVG
A VAN SLYKE, Pit	94	39	.415
F McGriff, SD	97	38	.392
T Gwynn, SD	90	35	.389
K Puckett, Min	107	40	.374
C Knoblauch, Min	99	36	.364
P Molitor, Mil	98	35	.357
J Kruk, Phi	87	31	.356
F Jose, StL	104	36	.346
K Griffey Jr, Sea	100	34	.340
E Martinez, Sea	103	35	.340

June

Player, Team	AB	H	AVG
M GRACE, ChN	94	38	.404
R Ventura, ChA	99	35	.354
E Martinez, Sea	108	38	.352
K Caminiti, Hou	109	38	.349
M Devereaux, Bal	119	41	.345
R Yount, Mil	90	31	.344
P Molitor, Mil	98	33	.337
K Puckett, Min	119	40	.336
J Carter, Tor	106	35	.330
D DeShields, Mon	100	33	.330

July

Player, Team	AB	H	AVG
B BUTLER, LA	95	42	.442
B Larkin, Cin	95	37	.389
E Martinez, Sea	98	38	.388
D DeShields, Mon	117	44	.376
S Mack, Min	94	35	.372
J Orsulak, Bal	100	37	.370
L Polonia, Cal	92	34	.370
F Thomas, ChA	99	35	.354
C Maldonado, Tor	88	31	.352
L Johnson, ChA	108	38	.352

August

Player, Team	AB	H	AVG
E MARTINEZ, Sea	114	45	.395
F Thomas, ChA	98	36	.367
G Sheffield, SD	97	35	.361
S Mack, Min	106	38	.358
T Pendleton, Atl	112	39	.348
K Lofton, Cle	94	32	.340
B Larkin, Cin	109	37	.339
T Gwynn, SD	99	33	.333
L Walker, Mon	96	32	.333
R Ventura, ChA	102	34	.333

September-October

Player, Team	AB	H	AVG
B ROBERTS, Cin	93	41	.441
B Bonds, Pit	102	40	.392
J Bagwell, Hou	113	43	.381
R Sandberg, ChN	117	43	.368
S Finley, Hou	118	42	.356
C Baerga, Cle	130	45	.346
P Molitor, Mil	123	41	.333
K Puckett, Min	111	37	.333
G Pena, StL	89	29	.326
T Pendleton, Atl	117	38	.325

1st Pitch

Player, Team	AB	H	AVG
K PUCKETT, Min	166	73	.440
L Walker, Mon	128	51	.398
G Sheffield, SD	124	48	.387
S Mack, Min	97	37	.381
M McGwire, Oak	96	36	.375
B Bonilla, NYN	103	38	.369
K Griffey Jr, Sea	109	40	.367
P Molitor, Mil	90	33	.367
T Pendleton, Atl	109	39	.358
P O'Neill, Cin	84	30	.357

Ahead in Count

Player, Team	AB	H	AVG
E MARTINEZ, Sea	173	73	.422
J Kruk, Phi	132	53	.402
T Phillips, Det	167	66	.395
R Sandberg, ChN	150	58	.387
B Butler, LA	109	42	.385
F McGriff, SD	135	52	.385
D Winfield, Tor	160	61	.381
C Maldonado, Tor	124	47	.379
T Fryman, Det	155	58	.374
C Baerga, Cle	164	61	.372

Behind in Count

Player, Team	AB	H	AVG
P MOLITOR, Mil	227	71	.313
T Gwynn, SD	224	70	.313
G Jefferies, KC	222	67	.302
O Smith, StL	198	58	.293
B Harper, Min	226	66	.292
B Larkin, Cin	230	67	.291
C Baerga, Cle	324	94	.290
G Davis, Bal	173	50	.289
B Roberts, Cin	222	64	.288
T Pendleton, Atl	284	81	.285

Two Strikes

Player, Team	AB	H	AVG
B HARPER, Min	170	49	.288
O Smith, StL	157	44	.280
B Roberts, Cin	175	49	.280
B Larkin, Cin	185	51	.276
P Molitor, Mil	175	48	.274
T Pendleton, Atl	222	60	.270
A Dawson, ChN	201	52	.259
C Baerga, Cle	232	59	.254
R Alomar, Tor	178	45	.253
E Martinez, Sea	167	42	.251

Full Count

Player, Team	AB	H	AVG
W McGEE, SF	31	13	.419
W Weiss, Oak	37	15	.405
L Dykstra, Phi	36	14	.389
K Maas, NYA	37	14	.378
J Kent, NYN	32	12	.375
O Smith, StL	51	19	.373
M Sharperson, LA	36	13	.361
A Stankiewicz, NYA	36	13	.361
G Brett, KC	39	14	.359
D Jackson, SD	39	14	.359

Close & Late

Player, Team	AB	H	AVG
R ALOMAR, Tor	79	34	.430
G Sheffield, SD	78	32	.410
E Martinez, Sea	82	32	.390
D Hamilton, Mil	69	25	.362
J Olerud, Tor	72	26	.361
T Gwynn, SD	75	27	.360
J Bagwell, Hou	99	35	.354
C Fielder, Det	83	29	.349
K Seitzer, Mil	86	30	.349
P Listach, Mil	89	31	.348

1992 Batting Leaders

Batting #1

Player, Team	AB	H	AVG
B ROBERTS, Cin	**505**	**164**	**.325**
O Vizquel, Sea	266	86	.323
P Molitor, Mil	133	42	.316
G Jefferies, KC	145	45	.310
D DeShields, Mon	343	106	.309
D Sanders, Atl	229	70	.306
L Dykstra, Phi	345	104	.301
C Knoblauch, Min	264	79	.299
S Mack, Min	365	109	.299
M Grissom, Mon	320	95	.297

Batting #2

Player, Team	AB	H	AVG
B BUTLER, LA	**224**	**81**	**.362**
T Raines, ChA	200	71	.355
M Sharperson, LA	195	69	.354
E Martinez, Sea	384	134	.349
R Sandberg, ChN	304	97	.319
T Gwynn, SD	519	165	.318
R Ventura, ChA	151	48	.318
T Pendleton, Atl	224	70	.313
J Browne, Oak	158	49	.310
R Alomar, Tor	552	171	.310

Batting #3

Player, Team	AB	H	AVG
F THOMAS, ChA	**401**	**138**	**.344**
K Puckett, Min	548	183	.334
A Van Slyke, Pit	614	199	.324
P Molitor, Mil	474	153	.323
G Sheffield, SD	537	173	.322
R Sandberg, ChN	202	65	.322
D Mattingly, NYA	266	83	.312
C Baerga, Cle	657	205	.312
T Pendleton, Atl	411	127	.309
B Larkin, Cin	470	144	.306

Batting #4

Player, Team	AB	H	AVG
J KRUK, Phi	**370**	**127**	**.343**
B Bonds, Pit	339	111	.327
L Walker, Mon	512	156	.305
J Bagwell, Hou	264	79	.299
W Joyner, KC	144	42	.292
D Winfield, Tor	583	169	.290
R Sierra, Oak	394	114	.289
F Jose, StL	302	87	.288
F McGriff, SD	530	152	.287
K Mitchell, Sea	351	99	.282

Batting #5

Player, Team	AB	H	AVG
J OLERUD, Tor	**284**	**91**	**.320**
T Steinbach, Oak	186	54	.290
C Davis, Min	142	41	.289
P Munoz, Min	145	41	.283
E Murray, NYN	135	38	.281
B Harper, Min	221	62	.281
S Buechele, ChN	160	44	.275
M McGwire, Oak	240	66	.275
R Ventura, ChA	248	68	.274
B Bonds, Pit	132	36	.273

Batting #6

Player, Team	AB	H	AVG
B HARPER, Min	**271**	**91**	**.336**
K Reimer, Tex	168	52	.310
J Orsulak, Bal	227	67	.295
D May, ChN	183	53	.290
R Gonzales, Cal	159	45	.283
J King, Pit	145	41	.283
C Maldonado, Tor	264	73	.277
T Steinbach, Oak	218	59	.271
D Gladden, Det	148	40	.270
R Velarde, NYA	135	36	.267

Batting #7

Player, Team	AB	H	AVG
D SLAUGHT, Pit	**190**	**68**	**.358**
G Gaetti, Cal	103	34	.330
J Oliver, Cin	133	42	.316
W Wilson, Oak	194	61	.314
S Livingstone, Det	116	36	.310
D Hansen, LA	113	33	.292
R Wilkins, ChN	146	42	.288
M Macfarlane, KC	108	31	.287
K Seitzer, Mil	169	48	.284
C Hernandez, LA	131	37	.282

Batting #8

Player, Team	AB	H	AVG
C HOILES, Bal	**111**	**36**	**.324**
L Alicea, StL	87	27	.310
M Bordick, Oak	374	112	.299
R Karkovice, ChA	150	44	.293
S Livingstone, Det	161	46	.286
R Sanchez, ChN	169	48	.284
M Morandini, Phi	128	36	.281
B Jacoby, Cle	93	26	.280
T Teufel, SD	93	26	.280
C Hayes, NYA	363	100	.275

Batting #9

Player, Team	AB	H	AVG
S ALOMAR JR, Cle	**161**	**46**	**.286**
J Valentin, Bos	126	36	.286
S Fletcher, Mil	307	85	.277
O Vizquel, Sea	110	30	.273
H Reynolds, Sea	202	55	.272
L Blankenship, Oak	203	54	.266
M Lee, Tor	396	104	.263
M Gallego, NYA	115	30	.261
C Grebeck, ChA	162	42	.259
J Ortiz, Cle	180	45	.250

None on/out

Player, Team	AB	H	AVG
E MARTINEZ, Sea	**98**	**41**	**.418**
F Jose, StL	133	51	.383
K Bass, NYN	109	41	.376
A Van Slyke, Pit	120	43	.358
T Gwynn, SD	95	34	.358
G Sheffield, SD	95	34	.358
K Puckett, Min	123	44	.358
R Alomar, Tor	117	41	.350
J Kruk, Phi	120	42	.350
O Smith, StL	92	32	.348

Pre-All Star

Player, Team	AB	H	AVG
J KRUK, Phi	**298**	**103**	**.346**
A Van Slyke, Pit	312	106	.340
O Nixon, Atl	174	59	.339
K Puckett, Min	359	120	.334
B Zupcic, Bos	137	45	.328
M Sharperson, LA	201	66	.328
E Martinez, Sea	314	103	.328
G Sheffield, SD	323	105	.325
R Alomar, Tor	300	97	.323
C Baerga, Cle	350	113	.323

Post-All Star

Player, Team	AB	H	AVG
B ROBERTS, Cin	**225**	**83**	**.369**
E Martinez, Sea	214	78	.364
B Butler, LA	239	84	.351
S Mack, Min	267	93	.348
T Raines, ChA	246	85	.346
F Thomas, ChA	279	95	.341
G Sheffield, SD	234	79	.338
R Sandberg, ChN	289	96	.332
K Griffey Jr, Sea	288	95	.330
T Pendleton, Atl	289	95	.329

5-Year Batting Leaders

Overall

Player	AB	H	AVG
K PUCKETT	3093	1018	.329
W Boggs	2884	920	.319
T Gwynn	2748	876	.319
P Molitor	2916	914	.313
J Franco	2439	757	.310
E Martinez	1762	545	.309
B Harper	1973	606	.307
B Larkin	2524	772	.306
B Roberts	1850	565	.305
W Clark	2841	859	.302

LHP

Player	AB	H	AVG
K PUCKETT	799	275	.344
E Martinez	530	178	.336
J Franco	667	220	.330
B Larkin	804	265	.330
P Molitor	771	252	.327
M Duncan	658	215	.327
R Sierra	973	316	.325
F Jose	570	184	.323
D Henderson	619	197	.318
R Jordan	658	209	.318

RHP

Player	AB	H	AVG
W BOGGS	1949	651	.334
T Gwynn	1700	558	.328
H Morris	894	293	.328
K Puckett	2294	743	.324
B Roberts	1207	378	.313
M Greenwell	1675	524	.313
L Polonia	1865	583	.313
W Clark	1754	543	.310
M Grace	1839	568	.309
P Molitor	2145	662	.309

Home

Player	AB	H	AVG
K PUCKETT	1577	573	.363
W Boggs	1397	492	.352
J Franco	1214	416	.343
F Thomas	632	213	.337
C Baerga	778	248	.319
S Mack	690	219	.317
T Gwynn	1309	409	.312
M Greenwell	1235	385	.312
L Polonia	1127	351	.311
B Harper	951	296	.311

Away

Player	AB	H	AVG
T GWYNN	1439	467	.325
P Molitor	1518	485	.319
E Martinez	913	287	.314
F Thomas	691	213	.308
H Morris	616	188	.305
B Roberts	922	280	.304
S Mack	784	238	.304
B Harper	1022	310	.303
B Larkin	1283	389	.303
R Palmeiro	1533	464	.303

Groundball Pitchers

Player	AB	H	AVG
T GWYNN	995	337	.339
K Griffey Jr	562	184	.327
P Molitor	732	236	.322
B Roberts	677	218	.322
W Boggs	742	237	.319
K Puckett	811	258	.318
M Thompson	652	207	.317
W McGee	833	263	.316
H Baines	673	211	.314
W Joyner	631	196	.311

Grass

Player	AB	H	AVG
F THOMAS	1094	364	.333
W Boggs	2420	779	.322
J Franco	2027	648	.320
E Martinez	682	217	.318
T Gwynn	1994	617	.309
W Clark	2079	641	.308
M Greenwell	2120	651	.307
P Molitor	2414	740	.307
B Butler	2187	670	.306
T Pendleton	1272	386	.303

Turf

Player	AB	H	AVG
K PUCKETT	1935	671	.347
T Gwynn	754	259	.344
B Roberts	699	231	.330
D Winfield	604	194	.321
S Mack	841	265	.315
B Harper	1208	379	.314
B Larkin	1776	557	.314
R Alomar	1191	372	.312
H Morris	853	266	.312
K Seitzer	1301	400	.307

Flyball Pitchers

Player	AB	H	AVG
P MOLITOR	676	218	.322
R Palmeiro	672	216	.321
K Puckett	686	210	.306
W Boggs	720	220	.306
D Mattingly	671	205	.306
J Franco	587	179	.305
G Brett	723	217	.300
R Henderson	552	165	.299
W Clark	646	193	.299
B Butler	681	203	.298

Day

Player	AB	H	AVG
W McGEE	778	260	.334
P Molitor	880	291	.331
K Puckett	923	297	.322
L Polonia	700	224	.320
K Griffey Jr	570	182	.319
B Roberts	539	172	.319
M Greenwell	819	258	.315
W Boggs	970	305	.314
G Brett	685	215	.314
H Baines	719	224	.312

Night

Player	AB	H	AVG
K PUCKETT	2170	721	.332
T Gwynn	1934	633	.327
F Thomas	981	318	.324
W Boggs	1914	615	.321
J Franco	1940	613	.316
B Larkin	1803	567	.314
E Martinez	1309	409	.312
H Morris	821	255	.311
P Molitor	2036	623	.306
B Butler	1904	580	.305

Scoring Position

Player	AB	H	AVG
T GWYNN	617	209	.339
K Puckett	845	286	.338
W Clark	752	249	.331
F Thomas	374	123	.329
P Molitor	603	198	.328
W Boggs	576	188	.326
P Guerrero	622	203	.326
T Raines	530	171	.323
J Franco	566	181	.320
K Griffey Jr	562	179	.319

5-Year Batting Leaders

April

Player	AB	H	AVG
T GWYNN	**434**	**141**	**.325**
C Lansford	345	112	.325
W Clark	415	134	.323
D Winfield	274	88	.321
B Butler	433	139	.321
K Griffey Jr	310	98	.316
L Dykstra	270	85	.315
R Kelly	323	101	.313
W McGee	316	98	.310
P Molitor	300	93	.310

May

Player	AB	H	AVG
K PUCKETT	**550**	**198**	**.360**
C Lansford	404	142	.351
J Franco	426	143	.336
R Palmeiro	535	179	.335
T Gwynn	457	152	.333
B Larkin	403	132	.328
W Joyner	461	149	.323
R Sandberg	525	169	.322
A Van Slyke	439	140	.319
W Boggs	457	144	.315

June

Player	AB	H	AVG
W McGEE	**415**	**141**	**.340**
P Molitor	468	154	.329
W Clark	443	145	.327
M Greenwell	500	163	.326
T Gwynn	537	173	.322
L Dykstra	383	123	.321
R Sierra	553	176	.318
C Sabo	491	156	.318
M Grace	426	135	.317
K Puckett	545	172	.316

July

Player	AB	H	AVG
W BOGGS	**492**	**172**	**.350**
K Puckett	518	178	.344
K Griffey Jr	364	121	.332
H Baines	394	129	.327
B Butler	502	164	.327
M Hall	387	126	.326
B Bonds	428	138	.322
G Brett	531	171	.322
J Franco	399	128	.321
R Henderson	404	128	.317

August

Player	AB	H	AVG
T GWYNN	**525**	**178**	**.339**
M Greenwell	390	126	.323
M Grace	567	181	.319
W Boggs	565	180	.319
K Griffey Jr	369	116	.314
K Puckett	525	165	.314
P Molitor	596	186	.312
J Franco	389	121	.311
W Clark	518	160	.309
B Butler	515	158	.307

September-October

Player	AB	H	AVG
K PUCKETT	**544**	**178**	**.327**
T Pendleton	415	134	.323
R Sandberg	559	178	.318
W Boggs	489	155	.317
R Alomar	516	163	.316
E Murray	529	167	.316
B Larkin	403	127	.315
P Molitor	562	177	.315
J Franco	399	125	.313
L Polonia	428	133	.311

1st Pitch

Player	AB	H	AVG
W McGEE	**391**	**156**	**.399**
K Puckett	791	303	.383
F McGriff	391	144	.368
H Baines	511	186	.364
A Van Slyke	397	141	.355
B Bonilla	568	200	.352
J Carter	386	134	.347
T Fernandez	545	187	.343
W Clark	485	166	.342
P O'Neill	418	143	.342

Ahead in Count

Player	AB	H	AVG
W CLARK	**586**	**238**	**.406**
F McGriff	684	273	.399
K Mitchell	533	206	.386
K Puckett	628	241	.384
W Boggs	800	307	.384
J Franco	647	243	.376
J Kruk	555	208	.375
J Canseco	499	186	.373
D Winfield	544	202	.371
D Strawberry	525	194	.370

Behind in Count

Player	AB	H	AVG
T GWYNN	**1125**	**340**	**.302**
B Larkin	1079	300	.278
P Molitor	1146	318	.277
L Polonia	1135	310	.273
C Baerga	730	198	.271
B Harper	873	236	.270
E Martinez	766	207	.270
K Puckett	1221	327	.268
R Palmeiro	1226	327	.267
B Roberts	869	226	.260

2 Strikes

Player	AB	H	AVG
T GWYNN	**902**	**251**	**.278**
L Polonia	1003	268	.267
B Harper	684	179	.262
W Boggs	1362	354	.260
E Martinez	805	207	.257
B Larkin	1012	257	.254
R Palmeiro	1153	292	.253
P Molitor	1105	277	.251
J Franco	1092	272	.249
R Henderson	1252	311	.248

Full Count

Player	AB	H	AVG
W BOGGS	**353**	**116**	**.329**
T Gwynn	163	50	.307
E Martinez	200	61	.305
J Franco	219	66	.301
D Mattingly	123	37	.301
L Walker	101	30	.297
R Palmeiro	233	69	.296
K Bass	159	47	.296
G Perry	116	34	.293
L Polonia	151	44	.291

Close & Late

Player	AB	H	AVG
E MARTINEZ	**266**	**89**	**.335**
T Gwynn	458	152	.332
J Franco	382	124	.325
L Dykstra	341	110	.323
K Hrbek	326	103	.316
K Puckett	452	142	.314
B Harper	309	96	.311
J Browne	322	100	.311
M Grace	466	144	.309
T Fernandez	441	136	.308

5-Year Batting Leaders

Batting #1

Player	AB	H	AVG
L SMITH	**558**	**182**	**.326**
W Boggs	1844	590	.320
P Molitor	2238	690	.308
B Roberts	1716	525	.306
B Larkin	679	205	.302
L Polonia	1953	588	.301
R Henderson	2433	710	.292
B Butler	2715	790	.291
A Cole	823	238	.289
S Sax	1665	477	.286

Batting #2

Player	AB	H	AVG
T GWYNN	**696**	**220**	**.316**
C Lansford	993	302	.304
D Magadan	835	252	.302
C Knoblauch	795	236	.297
W McGee	928	275	.296
R Sandberg	1836	542	.295
R Yount	534	156	.292
R Ventura	881	257	.292
J Gantner	611	177	.290
R Palmeiro	1002	290	.289

Batting #3

Player	AB	H	AVG
P MOLITOR	**671**	**223**	**.332**
F Thomas	852	283	.332
W McGee	805	267	.332
K Puckett	2886	950	.329
T Gwynn	1933	621	.321
B Larkin	1353	429	.317
W Boggs	1030	326	.317
K Griffey Jr	1413	436	.309
W Clark	2818	856	.304
T Pendleton	1028	307	.299

Batting #4

Player	AB	H	AVG
J KRUK	**950**	**300**	**.316**
M Greenwell	1056	327	.310
R Yount	758	229	.302
D Tartabull	1405	413	.294
R Sierra	2031	591	.291
K Hrbek	1581	453	.287
R Jordan	706	201	.285
A Dawson	1791	506	.283
P Guerrero	1594	450	.282
B Bonilla	2464	694	.282

Batting #5

Player	AB	H	AVG
M GREENWELL	**892**	**280**	**.314**
F Jose	592	182	.307
J Franco	758	232	.306
B Harper	635	192	.302
T Steinbach	828	249	.301
C Davis	905	269	.297
B Bonds	1224	360	.294
J Kruk	565	165	.292
C Fisk	614	178	.290
F McGriff	1027	291	.283

Batting #6

Player	AB	H	AVG
B HARPER	**768**	**237**	**.309**
G Larkin	523	148	.283
G Braggs	552	147	.266
B Jacoby	1014	268	.264
M Scioscia	813	214	.263
S Bream	696	183	.263
B Santiago	911	238	.261
T Steinbach	606	158	.261
M Nokes	581	150	.258
C Maldonado	558	143	.256

Batting #7

Player	AB	H	AVG
M SASSER	**383**	**117**	**.305**
R Cerone	390	116	.297
W Wilson	398	117	.294
J Oquendo	522	150	.287
D Slaught	762	217	.285
L Johnson	492	136	.276
J Barfield	383	105	.274
M LaValliere	1272	348	.274
P Borders	457	124	.271
R Ramirez	597	160	.268

Batting #8

Player	AB	H	AVG
M BORDICK	**382**	**113**	**.296**
O Guillen	493	138	.280
C Hayes	484	133	.275
S Dunston	687	185	.269
T Pagnozzi	503	135	.268
J Girardi	617	164	.266
J Oquendo	720	191	.265
C Hoiles	416	110	.264
S Leius	367	97	.264
J Gantner	511	134	.262

Batting #9

Player	AB	H	AVG
R KELLY	**378**	**125**	**.331**
H Reynolds	368	106	.288
S Fletcher	412	115	.279
O Guillen	1257	343	.273
B Spiers	900	240	.267
M Lee	1087	289	.266
J Gantner	415	106	.255
G Gagne	1310	334	.255
J Huson	348	88	.253
M Cuyler	641	162	.253

None on/out

Player	AB	H	AVG
K PUCKETT	**564**	**190**	**.337**
E Martinez	437	147	.336
S Mack	401	133	.332
W Boggs	977	312	.319
T Pendleton	552	174	.315
B Harper	435	136	.313
J Kruk	555	173	.312
P Molitor	1068	328	.307
J Gantner	495	152	.307
B Roberts	816	250	.306

Pre-All Star

Player	AB	H	AVG
K PUCKETT	**1674**	**551**	**.329**
T Gwynn	1579	516	.327
W Boggs	1497	473	.316
D Slaught	751	237	.316
B Harper	962	303	.315
P Molitor	1464	461	.315
W McGee	1327	410	.309
B Larkin	1426	438	.307
L Dykstra	1106	338	.306
J Franco	1375	420	.305

Post-All Star

Player	AB	H	AVG
S MACK	**754**	**263**	**.349**
F Thomas	748	251	.336
K Puckett	1419	467	.329
B Roberts	876	288	.329
W Boggs	1387	447	.322
E Martinez	769	247	.321
J Franco	1064	337	.317
P Molitor	1452	453	.312
G Brett	1390	429	.309
L Polonia	1171	361	.308

1992 Pitching Leaders

Overall

Pitcher, Team	IP	ER	ERA
B SWIFT, SF	**164.2**	**38**	**2.08**
B Tewksbury, StL	233.0	56	2.16
G Maddux, ChN	268.0	65	2.18
C Schilling, Phi	226.1	59	2.35
R Clemens, Bos	246.2	66	2.41
K Appier, KC	208.1	57	2.46
D Martinez, Mon	226.1	62	2.47
M Mussina, Bal	241.0	68	2.54
M Morgan, ChN	240.0	68	2.55
J Rijo, Cin	211.0	60	2.56

Home

Pitcher, Team	IP	ER	ERA
C ELDRED, Mil	**59.0**	**5**	**0.76**
J Boever, Hou	61.1	9	1.32
M Morgan, ChN	130.1	20	1.38
B Tewksbury, StL	124.1	21	1.52
D Ward, Tor	51.2	9	1.57
T Power, Cle	55.0	10	1.64
M Rojas, Mon	52.1	10	1.72
X Hernandez, Hou	59.0	12	1.83
T Frohwirth, Bal	58.2	12	1.84
M Portugal, Hou	58.0	12	1.86

Away

Pitcher, Team	IP	ER	ERA
B SWIFT, SF	**80.0**	**14**	**1.58**
R Clemens, Bos	118.1	25	1.90
P Smith, Atl	51.1	11	1.93
D Cone, Tor	127.1	32	2.26
J Abbott, Cal	116.0	30	2.33
K Hill, Mon	123.2	32	2.33
K Appier, KC	104.1	27	2.33
J Guzman, Tor	96.2	26	2.42
X Hernandez, Hou	52.0	14	2.42
J Rijo, Cin	122.1	33	2.43

April

Pitcher, Team	IP	ER	ERA
B KRUEGER, Mon	**32.0**	**3**	**0.84**
K Appier, KC	35.1	5	1.27
R Clemens, Bos	39.0	6	1.38
K Hill, Mon	38.0	6	1.42
M Moore, Oak	35.2	6	1.51
R Johnson, Sea	29.1	5	1.53
B Swift, SF	40.2	7	1.55
B Tewksbury, StL	28.0	5	1.61
C Nagy, Cle	38.2	7	1.63
R Tomlin, Pit	27.0	5	1.67

May

Pitcher, Team	IP	ER	ERA
K GROSS, LA	**32.2**	**6**	**1.65**
R Clemens, Bos	51.0	10	1.76
G Swindell, Cin	45.2	9	1.77
D Martinez, Mon	34.1	7	1.83
D Fleming, Sea	43.1	9	1.87
B Tewksbury, StL	48.0	10	1.88
S Fernandez, NYN	33.1	7	1.89
J Guzman, Tor	37.0	8	1.95
F Castillo, ChN	31.1	7	2.01
B Gullickson, Det	43.0	10	2.09

June

Pitcher, Team	IP	ER	ERA
J SMILEY, Min	**47.0**	**7**	**1.34**
B Hurst, SD	46.2	10	1.93
M Morgan, ChN	37.1	8	1.93
O Olivares, StL	27.2	6	1.95
C Nagy, Cle	40.2	9	1.99
M Mussina, Bal	44.2	10	2.01
S Avery, Atl	35.1	8	2.04
T Candiotti, LA	42.2	10	2.11
T Burns, Tex	25.1	6	2.13
R Tomlin, Pit	44.2	11	2.22

July

Pitcher, Team	IP	ER	ERA
J SMOLTZ, Atl	**38.1**	**4**	**0.94**
G Maddux, ChN	40.0	5	1.13
M Morgan, ChN	38.0	5	1.18
T Gordon, KC	27.1	4	1.32
T Glavine, Atl	38.0	6	1.42
K Appier, KC	46.1	8	1.55
B Black, SF	45.1	8	1.59
J Navarro, Mil	39.1	7	1.60
F Seminara, SD	33.0	6	1.64
C Leibrandt, Atl	37.2	7	1.67

August

Pitcher, Team	IP	ER	ERA
C ELDRED, Mil	**29.2**	**2**	**0.61**
D Martinez, Mon	38.0	6	1.42
R Sutcliffe, Bal	45.0	8	1.60
J Bullinger, ChN	27.2	5	1.63
B Walk, Pit	32.2	6	1.65
G Swindell, Cin	38.0	7	1.66
B Swift, SF	32.0	6	1.69
R Clemens, Bos	47.1	10	1.90
G Maddux, ChN	56.2	12	1.91
R Cormier, StL	42.1	9	1.91

September-October

Pitcher, Team	IP	ER	ERA
N RYAN, Tex	**27.1**	**3**	**0.99**
J Brantley, SF	26.2	3	1.01
J Rijo, Cin	49.0	7	1.29
D Rasmussen, KC	37.2	6	1.43
D Martinez, Mon	40.2	7	1.55
D Cone, Tor	46.1	8	1.55
M Mussina, Bal	52.0	9	1.56
S Fernandez, NYN	39.1	7	1.60
C Schilling, Phi	50.0	9	1.62
P Smith, Atl	41.2	8	1.73

Grass

Pitcher, Team	IP	ER	ERA
J RUSSELL, Oak	**59.0**	**7**	**1.07**
T Leach, ChA	63.1	9	1.28
G Olson, Bal	54.0	8	1.33
S Radinsky, ChA	50.0	8	1.44
R Hernandez, ChA	64.0	11	1.55
R Beck, SF	65.0	12	1.66
C Eldred, Mil	86.1	16	1.67
J Austin, Mil	54.2	11	1.81
M Morgan, ChN	170.1	35	1.85
G Maddux, ChN	195.2	43	1.98

Turf

Pitcher, Team	IP	ER	ERA
D WARD, Tor	**60.2**	**9**	**1.34**
M Rojas, Mon	80.2	12	1.34
J Boever, Hou	83.1	14	1.51
J Montgomery, KC	56.1	11	1.76
M Perez, StL	71.2	14	1.76
S Belinda, Pit	52.1	11	1.89
X Hernandez, Hou	80.1	17	1.90
B Tewksbury, StL	161.2	36	2.00
T Wakefield, Pit	57.0	13	2.05
C Schilling, Phi	178.1	43	2.17

1st Batter

Player, Team	AB	H	AVG
D POWELL, Sea	**40**	**4**	**.100**
B Hickerson, SF	53	6	.113
D Neagle, Pit	45	6	.133
J Austin, Mil	37	5	.135
P Assenmacher, ChN	63	9	.143
J Montgomery, KC	56	8	.143
J Parrett, Oak	55	8	.145
K Mercker, Atl	46	7	.152
R Mason, Pit	59	9	.153
A Pena, Atl	38	6	.158

1992 Pitching Leaders

Overall

Player, Team	AB	H	AVG
C SCHILLING, Phi	819	165	.201
R Johnson, Sea	749	154	.206
J Guzman, Tor	652	135	.207
G Maddux, ChN	959	201	.210
S Fernandez, NYN	771	162	.210
D Martinez, Mon	814	172	.211
K Appier, KC	771	167	.217
D Cone, Tor	916	201	.219
J Smoltz, Atl	921	206	.224
R Clemens, Bos	907	203	.224

LHB

Player, Team	AB	H	AVG
R BECK, SF	180	32	.178
R Dibble, Cin	128	23	.180
J Brantley, SF	193	35	.181
R Meacham, KC	144	27	.188
S Fernandez, NYN	149	28	.188
C Eldred, Mil	154	29	.188
S Belinda, Pit	135	26	.193
M Rojas, Mon	199	39	.196
D Ward, Tor	183	36	.197
C Schilling, Phi	456	90	.197

RHB

Player, Team	AB	H	AVG
G MADDUX, ChN	393	69	.176
T Belcher, Cin	331	59	.178
K Mercker, Atl	173	32	.185
D Drabek, Pit	397	75	.189
X Hernandez, Hou	195	37	.190
A Mills, Bal	194	37	.191
J Smoltz, Atl	377	72	.191
J Parrett, Oak	214	41	.192
B Swift, SF	219	43	.196
K Gross, LA	347	69	.199

None on/out

Player, Team	AB	H	AVG
C SCHILLING, Phi	220	42	.191
J Key, Tor	223	44	.197
G Maddux, ChN	253	50	.198
B Ojeda, LA	161	32	.199
B Tewksbury, StL	231	46	.199
K McCaskill, ChA	195	39	.200
C Hough, ChA	177	36	.203
J Morris, Tor	229	48	.210
J Smoltz, Atl	233	49	.210
S Fernandez, NYN	217	46	.212

None on

Player, Team	AB	H	AVG
K MERCKER, Atl	138	23	.167
R Hernandez, ChA	142	24	.169
D Henry, Cin	167	29	.174
J Brantley, SF	180	34	.189
W Blair, Hou	180	34	.189
R Monteleone, NYA	222	42	.189
J Bullinger, ChN	176	34	.193
L Smith, StL	165	32	.194
R Beck, SF	190	37	.195
X Hernandez, Hou	224	44	.196

Runners on

Player, Team	AB	H	AVG
M ROJAS, Mon	175	25	.143
D Jones, Hou	194	34	.175
D Ward, Tor	176	32	.182
K Appier, KC	329	60	.182
R Beck, SF	137	25	.182
D Cone, Tor	409	79	.193
C Schilling, Phi	298	58	.195
A Mills, Bal	167	33	.198
J Gott, LA	160	32	.200
T Candiotti, LA	289	58	.201

1st Pitch

Player, Team	AB	H	AVG
K DOWNS, Oak	93	16	.172
C Nabholz, Mon	109	23	.211
M Morgan, ChN	151	33	.219
T Glavine, Atl	135	32	.237
B Gullickson, Det	142	34	.239
G Hibbard, ChA	112	27	.241
S Avery, Atl	147	36	.245
C Schilling, Phi	110	27	.245
Z Smith, Pit	96	24	.250
B Swift, SF	106	27	.255

2 Strikes

Player, Team	AB	H	AVG
R DIBBLE, Cin	161	16	.099
B Barnes, Mon	156	16	.103
M Rojas, Mon	171	20	.117
R Johnson, Sea	415	49	.118
J Brantley, SF	183	22	.120
K Hill, Mon	356	43	.121
X Hernandez, Hou	172	21	.122
D Henry, Cin	164	21	.128
G Maddux, ChN	428	55	.129
D Ward, Tor	207	27	.130

Scoring Position

Player, Team	AB	H	AVG
M ROJAS, Mon	115	14	.122
M Guthrie, Min	83	13	.157
X Hernandez, Hou	106	17	.160
B Swift, SF	114	19	.167
K Appier, KC	180	30	.167
M Mussina, Bal	154	27	.175
C Schilling, Phi	148	26	.176
K Downs, Oak	136	24	.176
D Drabek, Pit	192	34	.177
D Ward, Tor	101	18	.178

Ahead in Count

Player, Team	AB	H	AVG
J WETTELAND, Mon	159	19	.119
R Dibble, Cin	154	19	.123
R Johnson, Sea	393	49	.125
M Portugal, Hou	152	20	.132
M Rojas, Mon	177	24	.136
D Cone, Tor	447	62	.139
B Barnes, Mon	164	23	.140
D Ward, Tor	208	30	.144
G Maddux, ChN	450	65	.144
X Hernandez, Hou	180	26	.144

Behind in Count

Player, Team	AB	H	AVG
D MARTINEZ, Mon	148	31	.209
C Hough, ChA	163	41	.252
D Kile, Hou	125	32	.256
R Bones, Mil	148	38	.257
S Erickson, Min	243	64	.263
S Kamieniecki, NYA	175	47	.269
C Bosio, Mil	212	57	.269
B Gullickson, Det	234	63	.269
T Mulholland, Phi	208	56	.269
B Wegman, Mil	215	58	.270

Close & Late

Player, Team	AB	H	AVG
K APPIER, KC	91	10	.110
R Darling, Oak	44	6	.136
S Howe, NYA	64	9	.141
M Leiter, Det	49	7	.143
M Fetters, Mil	89	13	.146
D Henry, Cin	73	11	.151
D Eckersley, Oak	227	39	.172
D Martinez, Mon	81	14	.173
S Foster, Cin	46	8	.174
J Austin, Mil	51	9	.176

5-Year Pitching Leaders

Overall

Pitcher	IP	ER	ERA
J RIJO	**885.1**	**254**	**2.58**
R Clemens	1263.2	368	2.62
D Martinez	1141.2	348	2.74
O Hershiser	871.2	274	2.83
D Drabek	1186.1	381	2.89
S Fernandez	844.1	280	2.98
D Cone	1145.0	382	3.00
G Maddux	1255.1	420	3.01
B Saberhagen	952.0	327	3.09
M Morgan	911.1	315	3.11

Home

Pitcher	IP	ER	ERA
S FARR	**210.1**	**46**	**1.97**
J Montgomery	231.0	53	2.06
T Burns	210.1	53	2.27
S Fernandez	451.0	115	2.29
R Dibble	201.2	52	2.32
GW Harris	260.1	68	2.35
M Williamson	222.1	60	2.43
D Drabek	601.0	170	2.55
M Morgan	485.0	141	2.62
D Martinez	560.1	164	2.63

Away

Pitcher	IP	ER	ERA
D JONES	**202.2**	**48**	**2.13**
J Rijo	454.0	120	2.38
A Pena	203.2	54	2.39
R Dibble	207.1	55	2.39
R Clemens	653.1	180	2.48
J Magrane	304.2	94	2.78
D Martinez	581.1	184	2.85
S Erickson	230.1	73	2.85
A Benes	357.1	114	2.87
N Charlton	261.2	84	2.89

April

Pitcher	IP	ER	ERA
R CLEMENS	**203.1**	**39**	**1.73**
C Bosio	178.0	44	2.22
D Martinez	181.2	49	2.43
C Finley	135.0	38	2.53
B Welch	145.1	43	2.66
O Hershiser	135.0	42	2.80
J Rijo	111.1	35	2.83
D Gooden	165.2	53	2.88
G Maddux	154.0	50	2.92
Z Smith	149.2	49	2.95

May

Pitcher	IP	ER	ERA
D WELLS	**109.2**	**27**	**2.22**
B Saberhagen	207.0	58	2.52
D Cone	177.2	50	2.53
S Fernandez	125.2	37	2.65
D Martinez	192.2	57	2.66
R Clemens	237.0	71	2.70
B Black	176.2	53	2.70
B Ojeda	172.2	52	2.71
G Swindell	204.0	62	2.74
B Blyleven	139.0	44	2.85

June

Pitcher	IP	ER	ERA
B TEWKSBURY	**109.1**	**26**	**2.14**
R Martinez	120.0	33	2.47
D Martinez	217.1	60	2.48
J McDowell	164.1	47	2.57
J Smiley	153.2	44	2.58
O Hershiser	163.1	47	2.59
M Morgan	162.0	48	2.67
K Brown	175.2	53	2.72
C Leibrandt	190.1	60	2.84
S Bankhead	101.0	32	2.85

July

Pitcher	IP	ER	ERA
D JACKSON	**126.0**	**28**	**2.00**
M Gardner	123.2	28	2.04
J Rijo	121.1	29	2.15
L Aquino	119.2	29	2.18
J Magrane	119.2	32	2.41
D Stieb	114.2	32	2.51
S Fernandez	151.0	43	2.56
J Abbott	136.0	39	2.58
D Gooden	132.1	38	2.58
R Clemens	217.0	63	2.61

August

Pitcher	IP	ER	ERA
B SABERHAGEN	**147.1**	**30**	**1.83**
J Magrane	133.2	33	2.22
D Drabek	219.2	59	2.42
T Gordon	128.1	35	2.45
R Sutcliffe	174.1	50	2.58
J Rijo	138.2	40	2.60
N Charlton	117.1	34	2.61
O Olivares	103.0	30	2.62
D Martinez	209.0	62	2.67
GW Harris	107.1	32	2.68

September-October

Pitcher	IP	ER	ERA
J RIJO	**172.2**	**29**	**1.51**
O Hershiser	162.0	28	1.56
M Mussina	100.2	18	1.61
Z Smith	120.2	25	1.86
D Stieb	124.2	28	2.02
M Langston	231.0	52	2.03
GW Harris	155.1	37	2.14
T Belcher	161.0	41	2.29
S Erickson	133.1	35	2.36
N Ryan	185.0	49	2.38

Grass

Pitcher	IP	ER	ERA
D ECKERSLEY	**302.2**	**63**	**1.87**
G Olson	250.0	54	1.94
J Howell	230.2	52	2.03
GW Harris	379.1	97	2.30
M Mussina	277.2	72	2.33
J Rijo	280.0	75	2.41
R McDowell	242.0	71	2.64
B Saberhagen	388.0	115	2.67
A Pena	258.2	77	2.68
B Harvey	265.0	79	2.68

Turf

Pitcher	IP	ER	ERA
R DIBBLE	**279.2**	**68**	**2.19**
J Montgomery	276.2	70	2.28
D Drabek	888.2	236	2.39
C Schilling	244.2	72	2.65
J Rijo	605.1	179	2.66
D Martinez	865.2	258	2.68
G Maddux	367.1	113	2.77
T Candiotti	239.1	74	2.78
D Ward	360.0	112	2.80
D Darwin	363.2	116	2.87

vs 1st Batter

Player	AB	H	AVG
S BELINDA	**156**	**27**	**.173**
G Nelson	203	36	.177
J Fassero	107	19	.178
S Wilson	136	25	.184
M Davis	198	37	.187
R Honeycutt	250	47	.188
D Eckersley	302	58	.192
B Thigpen	283	55	.194
K Mercker	113	22	.195
D Carman	102	20	.196

5-Year Pitching Leaders

Overall

Player	AB	H	AVG
S FERNANDEZ	3043	612	.201
N Ryan	3588	725	.202
R Johnson	2958	649	.219
D Ward	2031	452	.223
D Cone	4226	943	.223
J Rijo	3222	722	.224
R Clemens	4662	1047	.225
R Martinez	2754	628	.228
D Stieb	2845	650	.228
GW Harris	1923	440	.229

LHB

Player	AB	H	AVG
B HARVEY	571	99	.173
G Olson	556	104	.187
R Dibble	739	141	.191
M Langston	644	128	.199
Z Smith	579	118	.204
Juan Guzman	561	115	.205
N Ryan	1885	387	.205
J Howell	621	129	.208
T Henke	621	130	.209
B Ojeda	651	138	.212

RHB

Player	AB	H	AVG
J BERENGUER	893	173	.194
J Rijo	1400	272	.194
J DeLeon	1525	298	.195
S Fernandez	2539	502	.198
N Ryan	1703	338	.198
J Smoltz	1494	297	.199
GW Harris	781	156	.200
M Jackson	913	183	.200
D Cone	1826	375	.205
J Montgomery	814	168	.206

None on/out

Player	AB	H	AVG
N RYAN	954	183	.192
S Fernandez	839	174	.207
D Stieb	726	153	.211
J Rijo	849	187	.220
T Belcher	981	218	.222
J DeLeon	893	200	.224
E Hanson	758	170	.224
M Moore	1083	243	.224
R Clemens	1234	278	.225
C Hough	1011	228	.226

None on

Player	AB	H	AVG
N RYAN	2237	412	.184
R Dibble	769	144	.187
D Eckersley	784	151	.193
S Fernandez	1977	385	.195
Juan Guzman	668	133	.199
J Russell	838	175	.209
J Howell	639	134	.210
L Smith	750	158	.211
R Johnson	1648	349	.212
D Stieb	1690	358	.212

Runners on

Player	AB	H	AVG
B HARVEY	537	98	.182
T Henke	524	106	.202
R Dibble	680	138	.203
G Olson	569	119	.209
S Fernandez	1066	227	.213
M Williams	788	168	.213
S Farr	659	141	.214
J Montgomery	740	159	.215
J Orosco	516	111	.215
R Myers	805	177	.220

1st Pitch

Player	AB	H	AVG
D STIEB	397	98	.247
GW Harris	345	88	.255
J Magrane	418	111	.266
K Downs	402	107	.266
B Gullickson	427	115	.269
M Morgan	597	161	.270
J McDowell	474	128	.270
O Hershiser	574	157	.274
B Milacki	426	117	.275
B Wegman	462	129	.279

Two Strikes

Player	AB	H	AVG
R DIBBLE	881	100	.114
D Eckersley	788	98	.124
N Ryan	2060	258	.125
Juan Guzman	619	79	.128
B Harvey	645	86	.133
S Fernandez	1666	224	.134
R Johnson	1590	218	.137
J Montgomery	821	114	.139
N Charlton	800	115	.144
T Gordon	1214	176	.145

Scoring Position

Player	AB	H	AVG
B HARVEY	342	54	.158
R Dibble	496	91	.183
S Farr	400	79	.198
G Olson	363	72	.198
D Cone	992	199	.201
J Montgomery	452	91	.201
S Fernandez	556	113	.203
R Myers	491	101	.206
M Williams	508	106	.209
J Brantley	430	90	.209

Ahead in Count

Player	AB	H	AVG
R DIBBLE	878	121	.138
N Ryan	1888	270	.143
B Harvey	637	94	.148
D Eckersley	842	127	.151
S Fernandez	1616	245	.152
R Johnson	1494	228	.153
M Jackson	793	123	.155
D Ward	1126	178	.158
GW Harris	857	136	.159
M Langston	1974	318	.161

Behind in Count

Player	AB	H	AVG
D MARTINEZ	869	217	.250
J Deshaies	723	190	.263
S Fernandez	551	151	.274
T Belcher	653	181	.277
D Drabek	965	269	.279
JM Robinson	571	160	.280
P Harnisch	500	142	.284
S Erickson	578	165	.285
D Stewart	972	282	.290
M Moore	964	280	.290

Close & Late

Player	AB	H	AVG
D ECKERSLEY	753	132	.175
K Appier	232	43	.185
N Ryan	299	57	.191
R Martinez	255	49	.192
R Clemens	560	109	.195
G Wayne	199	39	.196
D Stieb	182	36	.198
J Grahe	187	37	.198
B Harvey	626	124	.198
GW Harris	499	99	.198

About STATS, Inc.

It all starts with the system. The STATS scoring method, which includes pitch-by-pitch information and the direction, distance, and velocity of each ball hit into play, yields an immense amount of information. Sure, we have all the statistics you're used to seeing, but where other statistical sources stop, STATS is just getting started.

Then, there's the network. Our information is timely because our game reporters send their information by computer as soon as the game is over. Statistics are checked, rechecked, updated, and are available daily.

Analysis comes next. STATS constantly searches for new ways to use this wealth of information to open windows into the workings of baseball. Accurate numbers, intelligent computer programming, and a large dose of imagination all help coax the most valuable information from its elusive cover.

Finally, distribution!

For 13 years now, STATS has served over a dozen Major League teams. The box scores that STATS provides to *The Associated Press* and *USA Today* have revolutionized what baseball fans expect from a box score. *Baseball Weekly* is chock full of STATS handiwork, while ESPN's nightly baseball coverage is supported by a full-time STATS statistician. We provide statistics for *Earl Weaver Baseball, Tony LaRussa Baseball, Rotisserie Baseball* and many other baseball games and fantasy leagues all over the country.

For the baseball fan, STATS publishes monthly and year-end reports on each Major League team. We offer a host of year-end statistical breakdowns on paper or disk that cover hitting, pitching, catching, baserunning, fielding, and more. STATS even produces custom reports on request.

Computer users with modems can access the STATS computer for information with STATS On-Line. If you own a computer with a modem, there is no other source with the scope of baseball information that STATS can offer.

STATS and Bill James enjoy an on-going affiliation that has produced the book you are now holding. We also administer Bill James Fantasy Baseball (BJFB), the ultimate baseball game, designed by Bill James himself, which allows you to manage your own team and compete with other team owners around the country. Whether you play BJFB or another fantasy game, our new STATSfax report can show you what your players did the previous night as soon as you can get to the fax machine in the morning. STATS also offers a head-to-head fantasy football game STATS Fantasy Football. BJFB The Winter Game is a brand new, totally unique, historically based fantasy baseball game for those who can't wait for spring.

Always innovative, STATS has other exciting future projects underway for sports fans nationwide. It is the purpose of STATS to make the best possible sports information available to all interests: fans, player, teams, and media. For more information write to:

STATS, Inc.
7366 North Lincoln Ave.
Lincolnwood, IL 60646-1708

... or call us at 1-708-676-3322. We can send you a STATS brochure, a free information kit on Bill James Fantasy Baseball, the BJFB Winter Game or STATS Fantasy Football, and/or information on STATS On-Line or STATSfax.

To maintain our information, STATS hires people around the country to cover games using the STATS scoring method. If you are interested in applying for a part-time reporter's position, please write or call STATS.

For the story behind the numbers, check out STATS' other publications: The STATS 1993 Baseball Scoreboard: The first edition of this book in 1990 took the nation's baseball fans by storm. This all new 1993 edition, available in book stores or directly from STATS, is back with the same great writing, great graphics and stats you won't find anywhere else. The STATS 1993 Major League Handbook and the STATS 1993 Minor League Handbook will add to your 1993 reference library, especially important for the coming expansion. STATS continues a tradition with The Scouting Report:1993, available in book stores in the Spring of 1993. You'll find scouting reports on over 700 players, including team prospect reports, backed by statistical findings you can only get from STATS, Inc.

Turn to the last pages in this book to find a handy order form and additional information about the fine products from STATS.

Glossary

There are quite a few abbreviations in the book, most of which you are probably familiar with. But for the sake of completeness, here is a rundown of all the abbreviations, plus descriptions of many of the categories for the stat splits and some of the formulas used.

For Hitters:

Avg=batting average, G=games played, AB=at-bats, R=runs scored, H=hits, 2B=doubles, 3B=triples, HR=home runs, RBI=runs batted in, BB=walks, SO=strikeouts, HBP=times hit by pitch, GDP=times grounded into double play, SB=stolen bases, CS=caught stealing, OBP=on base percentage, SLG=slugging percentage, IBB=intentional walks received, SH=sacrifice hits, SF=sacrifice flies, #Pit=number of pitches offered to the hitter, #P/PA=average number of pitches per plate appearance, GB=number of fair ground balls hit (hits, outs and errors), FB=number of fly balls hit (excludes line drives), G/F=ratio of grounders to fly balls.

For Fielders:

G=number of games the player appeared at that position, GS=number of starts the player made, Innings=number of innings played at that position, PO=putouts, A=assists, E=errors, DP=double plays turned, Fld.Pct=fielding percentage, Rng.Fctr=Range Factor, In Zone=balls hit in the player's area, Outs=number of outs resulting from a ball hit to a player, Zone Rtg=Zone Rating (see below), MLB Zone=major league average zone rating for that position.

For Pitchers:

ERA=earned run average, W=wins, L=losses, Sv=saves, G=games pitched, GS=games started, IP=innings pitched, BB=walks issued, SO=strikeouts, Avg.=opposition batting average against the pitcher, H=hits allowed, 2B=doubles allowed, 3B=triples allowed, HR=homers allowed, RBI=RBI's allowed, OBP=on base percentage against the pitcher, SLG=slugging percentage against the pitcher, CG=complete games, ShO=shutouts, Sup=run support per nine innings, GF=games finished, IR=inherited runners, IRS=inherited runners who scored, QS=quality starts, Hld=holds, SvOp=save opportunities, SB=stolen bases against the pitcher, CS=times runners were caught stealing while the pitcher was on the mound, GB=groundballs hit against the pitcher (hits, outs and errors), FB=fly balls hit against the pitcher (excludes line drives), G/F=ratio of grounders to flies.

Formulas and Definitions

OBP = (H + BB + HBP) / (AB + BB + HBP + SF)

SLG = Total Bases / At Bats

Fld.Pct. = (PO + A) / (PO + A + E)

Rng.Fctr. = (PO + A) * 9 / defensive innings played, or the average number of plays a fielder makes over a nine-inning game.

Zone Rating = The Zone Rating measures all the balls hit in the area where a fielder can reasonably be expected to record an out, then counts the percentage of outs actually made. Thus, a zone rating of .904, like John Olerud had last year, means that he got 197 outs on the 218 balls hit into his general area last year, or 90.4%.

GF = games in which the pitcher was the last reliever in the game.

Hold = A pitcher gets a hold when he enters the game in a save situation, records at least one out, and leaves the game while still in a save situation. A player cannot get a hold and a save in the same game.

Player Breakdowns

There are three styles of player breakdowns in this book. The first is for all the Regulars, the second is for Subs and the final type is for the "Cup-of-Coffee" players. We defined Regulars as being any batters with 300 or more plate appearances last season or pitchers with either 150+ innings or 60 appearances. Subs are hitters with between 100 and 299 plate appearances or pitchers who threw between 50 and 149.2 innings last year or appeared in between 20 and 59 games. The "COC" players are everyone else who appeared in a game in 1992. What this means is that the Regulars have stat splits in every category, the Subs have splits in most categories and the Coffees have just a few breakdowns. We figured that you wouldn't be interested in paying an additional $15 for an 800-page book just to see a breakdown of Ryan Klesko's one HBP or Troy Afenir's six hits.

The multi-year section (career or five-year) is shown for any hitter whose career exceeds his 1992 playing time by 300+ appearances or for any pitcher whose career exceeds his 1992 playing time by 150 innings or 60 games.

Starting pitchers have slightly different formats than relief pitchers. In the top section, starters have stats for CG, ShO, Sup, QS and #P/S. For relievers, defined as pitchers with more games relieved than started, we show GF, IR, IRS, Hld and SvOp. In the stat breakdowns, starters have statistics based on longer rest between starts and higher pitch levels per outing.

Breakdown Categories

Most of the categories are fairly straight forward, but below is some information that could make a few of them a little less ambiguous.

The 1992 season refers to his total stats for last year, even if he got traded midway though the year. So David Cone's line is for both the Mets and the Jays. The next line is either the pitcher's performance since 1988 or his career if he broke in since 1988.

GROUNDBALL and FLYBALL are a player's stats against pitchers that induce mostly grounders or flies, respectively. Performances against pitchers that induce approximately the same number of grounders or flies (neutral pitchers) are not counted here.

DAY/NIGHT splits are different between the leagues. Night games in the National League are those that start after 5:00 p.m., while night games in the AL begin after 6:00 p.m. GRASS is grass and TURF is artificial turf.

For hitters, FIRST PITCH refers to the first pitch of a given at bat. AHEAD ON COUNT includes 1-0, 2-0, 3-0, 2-1, and 3-1. BEHIND ON COUNT includes 0-1, 0-2, 1-2, and 2-2. For pitchers, it's opposite.

SCORING POSITION is having at least one runner at either second or third base. CLOSE AND LATE occurs when a) the game is in the seventh inning or later and b) the batting team is either leading by one run, tied, or has the potential tying run on base, at bat or on deck. NONE ON/OUT is when there are no outs and the bases are empty (generally leadoff situations).

INNING 1-6 and INNING 7+ refer to the actual innings in which a pitcher worked. NONE ON/RUNNERS ON is the status of the baserunners.

VS. 1ST BATR (RELIEF) is what happened to the first batter a reliever faced. FIRST INNING PITCHED is the result of the pitcher's work until he recorded three outs.

The NUMBER OF PITCHES section shows the results of balls put into play while his pitch count was in that range.

All of the above is the same for the multi-year (shaded) data as well.

In the PITCHER/BATTER MATCHUPS, the following conditions must be met before a player is added to the list: a) There must be at least 10 plate appearances between the batter and the pitcher; b) Batters must have a .300 average against a pitcher to be listed, and pitchers must limit hitters to under .250 to be listed. Thus, not all hitters will have five pitchers that qualify, and not all pitchers will have five batters that qualify.

— Allan Spear

Two More Hits from
Bill James and STATS, Inc.

Bill James/STATS 1993
Major League Handbook

Available November 1, 1992!

- Exclusive Bill James' Projections for 1993

- The Earliest You Can Get Complete Career Stats of Every Active Major Leaguer

- Lefty/Righty Stats — Every 1992 Player

- Unique Leader Boards, complete fielding and team stats.

"I find the Handbook is a complete and comprehensive tool . . . my coaches and I refer to [it] constantly to help us in our game preparation."
Jeff Torborg, New York Mets manager

Bill James/STATS 1993
Minor League Handbook

Available November 1, 1992!

- Bill James' Major League Equivalencies for every AAA and AA player.

- Official career year-by-year statistical data for all 1992 AAA and AA players.

- 1992 stats for all A and Rookie League players.

- Minor League Leader Boards, Team Stats and more.

"STATS has been very helpful over the years in assisting me to evaluate players and in making trades."
Larry Himes, Chicago Cubs, executive vice president, baseball operations

To order, use the STATS order form on the last page of this book.

Bill James
FANTASY
BASEBALL

If You Like Fantasy Baseball, You'll Love Bill James Fantasy Baseball...

"Hi, This is Bill James. A few years ago I designed a set of rules for a new fantasy baseball league, which has been updated with the benefits of experience and the input of a few thousand owners.

The idea of a fantasy league, of course, is that it forges a link between you and your ballplayers; YOU win or lose based on how the players that you picked have performed. My goal was to develop a fantasy league based on the simplest and yet most realistic principles possible — a league in which the values are as nearly as possible what they ought to be, without being distorted by artificial category values or rankings, but which at the same time are so simple that you can keep track of how you've done just by checking the boxscores. There are a lot of different rules around for fantasy leagues, but none of them before this provided exactly what I was looking for. Here's what we want:

1)We want it to be realistic. We don't want the rules to make Randy Johnson the MVP because of his strikeouts. We don't want Kenny Lofton to be worth more than Dave Hollins because he steals lots of bases. We want good ballplayers to be good ballplayers.

2) We prefer it simple. We want you to be able to look up your players in the morning paper, and know how you've done.

3) We want you to have to develop a real team. We don't want somebody to win by stacking up starting pitchers and leadoff men. We don't want somebody to corner the market on home run hitters.

I made up the rules and I'll be playing the game with you. STATS, Inc. is running the leagues. They'll run the draft, man the computers, keep the rosters straight and provide you with weekly updates. Of course you can make trades, pick up free agents and move players on and off the inactive list; that's not my department, but there are rules for that, too. It all starts with a draft..."

- Draft Your Own Team and Play vs. Other Owners! Play by Mail or With a Computer On-Line!

- Manage Your Roster All Season With Daily Transactions! Live Fantasy Phone Lines Every Day of the Baseball Season!

- Realistic Team and Individual Player Totals That Even Take Fielding Into Account!

- The Best Weekly Reports in the Business!

- Play Against Bill James' Own Drafted Teams!

- Get Discounted Prices by Forming Your Own Private League of 11 or 12 Owners! (Call or write for more information)

- Money-Back Guarantee! Play one month, and if not satisfied, we'll return your franchise fee!

All This, All Summer Long — For Less Than An Average of $5 per week.

Reserve your BJFB team now! Sign up with the STATS Order Form on the next page, or send for additional Free Information.

STATS Order Form

Product (date available)	Quantity	Your Price	Total
Bill James Fantasy Baseball Franchise		$25 deposit	
Bill James/STATS 1993 Major League Handbook (11/92)		$17.95	
Bill James/STATS 1993 Minor League Handbook (11/92)		17.95	
STATS 1993 Player Profiles (11/92)		17.95	
STATS 1993 Baseball Scoreboard (2/93)		15.00	
The Scouting Report: 1993 (2/93)		16.00	
Discounts on previous editions while supplies last:			
Bill James/STATS 1992 Major League Handbook		9.95	
Bill James/STATS 1991 Major League Handbook		9.95	
Bill James/STATS 1990 Major League Handbook		9.95	
Bill James/STATS 1992 Minor League Handbook		9.95	
STATS 1992 Baseball Scoreboard		9.95	
STATS 1991 Baseball Scoreboard		9.95	
The STATS Baseball Scoreboard (1990)		7.95	
The Scouting Report: 1992		9.95	
U.S. – For First Class Mailing – add $2.50 per book		2.50	
Canada – all orders – add $3.50 per book		3.50	
Order 2 or more books – subtract $1 per book		−1.00	–
Subtotal			
Illinois Residents Include 7% Sales Tax			
Total			

☐ Yes, I can't wait! Sign me up to play Bill James Fantasy Baseball in 1993. Enclosed is my deposit of $25.00 on the franchise fee of $89.00. A processing fee of $1.00 per player is charged during the season for roster moves.

Team Nickname:_____ _____ (example: San Francisco Crab)

Would you like to play in a league with a team drafted by Bill James? Yes No (circle one)

Would you like to receive information on playing BJFB on-line by computer? Yes No (circle one)

Please Rush Me These Free Informational Brochures:

☐ **Bill James Fantasy Baseball Info Kit**

☐ **STATS Year-End Reports Brochure**

☐ **STATSfax Brochure (sent via fax)**

☐ **STATS On-Line Brochure**

☐ **STATS Fantasy Football Info Kit**

☐ **STATS Reporter Brochure**

☐ **STATS Pro-Line Brochure**

Please Print:

Name_____ Phone_____

Address_____ Fax_____

City_____ State_____ Zip_____

Method of Payment (U.S. Funds only):

☐ Check (no Canadian checks)   ☐ Money Order   ☐ Visa   ☐ MasterCard

Credit Card Information:

Cardholder Name_____

Visa/MC #_____ Exp. Date_____

Signature_____

Return this form (don't tear your book; copy this page) to:

STATS, Inc.
7366 N. Lincoln Ave.
Lincolnwood, IL
60646-1708

For faster credit card service: call 1-800-63-STATS to place your order, or fax this page to 1-708-676-0821.